D1001613

TECHNICAL COLLEGE OF THE LOWCOUNTRY
LEARNING RESOURCES CENTER
POST OFFICE BOX 1288
BEAUFORT, SOUTH CAROLINA 29901-1288

TECHNICAL COLLEGE OF THE LOWCOUNTRY
LEARNING RESOURCES CENTER
POST OFFICE BOX 1288
BEAUFORT, SOUTH CAROLINA 29901-1288

CQ's
Politics in America
2006
THE 109TH CONGRESS

By Congressional Quarterly's Staff
Jackie Koszczuk and H. Amy Stern, Editors

Congressional Profiles
Contact Information
District Data
Key Votes

TECHNICAL COLLEGE OF THE LOWCOUNTRY
LEARNING RESOURCES CENTER
POST OFFICE BOX 1288
BEAUFORT, SOUTH CAROLINA 29901-1288

Robert W. Merry, President and Publisher
David Rapp, Editor and Senior Vice President
Keith A. White, General Manager and Senior Vice President
John A. Jenkins, General Manager and Senior Vice President, CQ Press

Published by Congressional Quarterly Inc.
Paul C. Tash, Chairman
Andrew P. Corty, Vice Chairman
Nelson Poynter (1903–1978), Founder

CQ Press
1255 22nd Street N.W., Suite 400
Washington, DC 20037
202-729-1900; toll-free, 1-866-427-7737
www.cqpress.com

Copyright © 2005 by CQ Press, a division of Congressional Quarterly Inc.

All rights reserved. No part of this publication may be reproduced or transmitted in any form or by any means, electronic or mechanical, including photocopy, recording or any information storage and retrieval system, without permission in writing from the publisher.

The paper used in this publication exceeds the requirements of the American National Standard for Information Sciences — Permanence of Paper for Printed Library Materials, ANSI Z39.48-1992.

Printed and bound in the United States of America

09 08 07 06 05 5 4 3 2 1

ISBN 1-933116-1-2 (cloth)   ISBN 1-933116-09-9 (paper)

ISSN 1064-6809

The Library of Congress catalogued an earlier edition of this title as follows:

Congressional Quarterly's Politics in America: 1994, the 103rd Congress / by CQ's political staff: Phil Duncan, Editor

p.   cm.

Includes index.

1. United States. Congress — Biography. 2. United States. Congress — Committees. 3. United States. Congress — Election districts — Handbooks, manuals, etc. I. Duncan, Phil. II. Congressional Quarterly Inc. III. Title: Politics in America.
JK1010.C67 1993   328.73'073'45'0202

EDITORS
Jackie Koszczuk, H. Amy Stern

DEPUTY EDITORS
Peter H. King, Christine C. Lawrence, Brian Nutting

MANAGING EDITOR
Kimberly Hallock

SENIOR EDITORS
Martha Angle, Gregory L. Giroux, Susan Shipp, Katrina Van Duyn

CONTRIBUTING EDITORS
Bob Benenson, Nell Benton, Laura Cavender,
Lara Hearnburg Johnson, Peter Roybal

CONTRIBUTING WRITERS
Rebecca Adams, Jonathan Allen, Jill Barshay, Sandy Bergo,
Adriel Bettelheim, Jonathan Broder, Mary Agnes Carey, John Cochran,
Susan Crabtree, John Cranford, Julie Hirschfeld Davis, John M. Donnelly,
Philip D. Duncan, Jon Frandsen, Peter E. Harrell, David Hosansky,
Martin Kady II, Chuck McCutcheon, David Miller, Jennifer Mock, David Nather,
Alan K. Ota, Daniel J. Parks, Keith Perine, Jeff Plungis, Isaiah J. Poole,
Charles Pope, Elaine Povich, Daphne Retter, Jonathan Riehl,
Joseph J. Schatz, Kate Schuler, Tim Starks, Seth Stern, Allison Stevens,
Andrew Taylor, Michael Teitelbaum, Alex Wayne, Stephanie C. Weintraub

RESEARCHERS
Liza Ackerman, James Bayot, Arwen Bicknell, Geoffrey Bosworth,
Alecia Burke, Charlene Carter, Loren Duggan, Andrew Freedman,
Jacob Freedman, Jeff Friedman, Seth Goldman, Shweta Govindarajan,
Liriel Higa, Benton Ives-Halperin, Marian Jarlenski, Toni Johnson,
Rachel Kapochunas, Jonathan M. Katz, Emi Kolawole, Daniel Link,
Sarah Molenkamp, Laurie Notch, Veronika Oleksyn, Gayle S. Putrich,
Neil Ripley, Katie Rooney, Heather M. Rothman, Joe Warminsky

PHOTOGRAPHY
Scott J. Ferrell

COPY EDITORS
Pat Joy, Chris Kapler, Melinda W. Nahmias, Jessica Scheuer,
Kathleen Silvassy, Mike Slevin, Charlie Southwell, Chris Wright

PRESIDENTIAL VOTE CALCULATION
Gregory L. Giroux

DISTRICT MAPS
SpatiaLogic Mapping (Lafayette, Calif.), Kimberly Hallock

ONLINE EDITION
Poya Golriz, Jerry Orvedahl,
Mary Grace Palumbo

ACQUISITIONS EDITOR
Doug Goldenberg-Hart

Politics in America 2006

THE 109TH CONGRESS

Politics in America

THE 13TH EDITION

Since the last edition of this book was published two years ago, Republicans have celebrated their 10th anniversary as a majority in the House of Representatives. They solidified their power in Washington with the elections of 2004, taking firm control of both the House and the Senate while President George W. Bush won re-election to a second term.

In other words, Washington, for the next two years at least, is an unmistakably GOP town. The "Republican Revolution" of 1994 has become ingrained and institutionalized. House Speaker J. Dennis Hastert and Senate Majority Leader Bill Frist wield as much influence as any leader of recent memory, by virtue of strengthened GOP numbers in each chamber.

Or so it seemed at the outset of the 109th Congress, which convened in January 2005 with Republicans holding a 231-202 majority in the House (with one vacancy and one independent who votes Democratic) and a 55-44 majority in the Senate (with one independent). In fact, the political forces that were expected to foreshadow the 2006 midterm elections were already at play as this book went to press. Individual senators and representatives were beginning to question the party orthodoxy on issues ranging from Social Security "reform" to judicial nominations to ethics practices. House Majority Leader Tom DeLay — a hero to many House Republicans for his ability to galvanize grass-roots support and raise mountains of cash — discovered that his growing power and his outsize personality (nickname: "The Hammer") had become a lightning rod for criticism from all corners of the nation.

So, far from consolidating their power and ramming through a full agenda of Republican initiatives, Bush and his GOP allies in Congress were immediately forced to pick their fights to avoid being put on the defensive. Democrats, having learned to live with being in the minority, were exploiting the limited parliamentary devices available to them.

What better reason, then, to make a thorough study of the 435 representatives and 100 senators who engage in this ongoing dance of power and influence in the nation's capital? This 13th edition of Congressional Quarterly's "Politics in America" gives you that one-stop shop for learning what makes each member of Congress tick; what local, state and national forces shape their behavior; and what ideologies and political interests determine their aspirations.

The men and women who make up the U.S. Congress cover the gamut of race, creed, ideology and psychology.

Congressional Quarterly, which has been the "bible" on Congress since 1945, sets out every two years to compile the definitive insider's guide to the people who constitute the world's greatest democratic institution. The book is organized so that each member's "chapter" provides a full political profile, statistical information on votes and positions and a demographic description of the state or district the member represents.

We evaluate every member by his or her own standards. We do not try to decide where a politician ought to stand on a controversial issue; our interest has been to assess how they go about expressing their views and how effective they are at achieving their self-proclaimed goals.

The 125 reporters, editors and researchers at CQ cover Congress and its members on a weekly, daily and even hourly basis, through the pages of the CQ Weekly and CQ Today, and our online news service, CQ.com.

Under the direction of editors Jackie Koszczuk and H. Amy Stern, they have produced the most objective, authoritative and interesting volume of political analysis available on this fascinating collection of people.

David Rapp
Editor and Senior Vice President
Congressional Quarterly Inc.

A Revolution Becomes Regular Order

Ten years after the revolution, Republicans in Congress are looking increasingly like the Democrats of yore. They use the rules and parliamentary sleights of hand to control the floor, they keep minority dissent to a whimper and they command the resources of K Street. An increasing amount of their time is spent on coast-to-coast incumbent preservation efforts. Where have we seen this before?

In keeping with the past, the minority party yowls about the suppression of debate and every so often stages a protest. That is a cue for the GOP chairman of the House Ways and Means Committee, Bill Thomas of California, to call in the Capitol police, as he did when disgruntled committee Democrats defied him in 2003. Thomas later apologized for heavy-handedness, but conceded none of his considerable power to the Democrats.

A number of institutional reforms ushered in with the Republican takeover of 1995 have been quietly escorted back out through the kitchen door. Term limits for the Speaker are gone, as are some of the rules changes once deemed crucial for warding off the corrosive effects of a long stay in power. The filibuster, so useful a few years ago for the minority GOP to block President Clinton's agenda, was by 2005 under attack by Senate Majority Leader Bill Frist as too handy a tool for minority Democrats to block President Bush's judicial nominees.

On an individual level, too, the more Congress changes, the more it stays the same. A decade ago, many of the GOP newcomers had no experience in government and pledged to stay only long enough to clean up the Democrats' mess. Over time, most of those promises were retracted, as insurgents evolved into legislators and started to think that Washington was not such a bad place after all. Today, the weakest advocacy group in town is the formerly fearsome U.S. Term Limits.

With every election since 1994, new arrivals are increasingly apt to have cut their teeth in state capitols. There are 10 former governors in Congress today; more than half of the House members served in state and local government. Their political seasoning makes them less prone to think of the normal give-and-take of legislating as a sellout of principle.

Republicans today are more pragmatic than their philosophical forebears of the 104th Congress. They are more likely to write a bill that they know can get 218 votes than a manifesto with a catchy title. How else to explain a Republican Congress enacting the biggest expansion of Medicare in a generation? Nothing in the "Contract With America" prepared the GOP vanguard for dealing with elderly voters demanding a big-government solution to the high costs of prescription drugs. Speaker J. Dennis Hastert even took a page from predecessor Jim Wright's playbook to pass the bill, holding open the vote for several hours until he got the number of "yea" votes he needed. The conservatives who supplied those votes did not want to vote to make the federal government bigger, but they also did not want their party to lose a benchmark vote.

The GOP-controlled Congress these days seems to like federalism a little more and states' rights a little less. Congress' intervention in the spring of 2005 in the case of brain-damaged Terri Schiavo might be called a big-government solution to one family's disagreement about when life ends. And is there a school teacher in America who thinks the federal government is less involved in the classroom now than it was before Bush's signature No Child Left Behind initiative was enacted in early 2002?

In one significant way, the GOP Congress of today differs from the Dem-

The GOP insurgents who pledged to stay only long enough to clean up the Democrats' mess have evolved into legislators who think Washington is not such a bad place after all.

About the Editors

Jackie Koszczuk has covered Congress since 1989, when Jim Wright was the House Speaker and George Mitchell was the Senate Majority Leader. She has been both an editor and senior writer for CQ's Weekly Report. She also covered Capitol Hill for the Knight Ridder Washington Bureau and for the Fort Worth Star-Telegram. Born in Chicago, Koszczuk has a bachelor's degree in communications from Southern Illinois University. She lives in Bethesda, Md., with her husband, Joe Sobczyk, also a journalist, and their two children, Nicholas and Eleanor. This is her second edition of Politics in America.

H. Amy Stern came to Congressional Quarterly in 1981 as an editorial assistant for the CQ Weekly magazine. Since then, she has worked as an environmental reporter and an editor on the CQ Daily Monitor, as a managing editor of the New Media Department, and as a recruiter for the CQ News Division. Born in Trenton, N.J., she earned a bachelor's degree in American government from the University of Virginia and has studied at the Alliance Française in Paris. She owes her editing ability to her mother, Marcia Stern, who corrected her grammar as a teenager and whose wisdom continues to inspire her. This is her fourth edition of Politics in America.

ocratic model of yesterday, at least in the House. In their heyday, Democrats put power in the hands of era-defining committee chairmen such as Dan Rostenkowski at Ways and Means and John Dingell at Energy and Commerce. Republicans have adopted a corporate model that centralizes power at the level of a chairman (Hastert) and a CEO (Majority Leader Tom DeLay). The committees have gotten weaker in the process.

Long-serving House Republicans, such as Connecticut's Chris Shays and New Jersey's Chris Smith, were denied chairmanships not because of any leadership deficiencies, but because they had bucked the party hierarchy a few too many times. House Judiciary Chairman James Sensenbrenner Jr. of Wisconsin, a crafty politician with cordial relations with Democrats, is capable of writing bipartisan bills, but they are often rewritten in the red-carpeted Speaker's suite on the second floor of the Capitol.

Senators generally enjoy more autonomy, but they, too, feel the pressure to conform. Moderate Republican Arlen Specter of Pennsylvania was unable to ascend to Judiciary chairman until he pledged to support all of Bush's judicial nominees even if they opposed legalized abortion.

For their part, Democrats are beginning to suffer from minority-think, reminiscent of the Bob Michel Republicans of a decade ago. Rep. David Obey of Wisconsin saw it happening when he tried to get fellow Democrats to withhold their support for appropriations bills they thought short-changed education programs. His colleagues demurred out of concern the majority would retaliate by holding up hometown spending projects.

The new status quo isn't likely to change short of a dramatic political shift. The GOP has a 231-202 edge in the House (with one independent voting Democratic and one vacancy) and a 55-44 advantage in the Senate (with one independent voting Democratic). Democrats would need no less than a six-seat gain to win a Senate majority, yet more Democrats than Republicans will be defending seats in 2006.

As with the Democrats in the mid-1990s, Republicans in the mid-2000s are dogged by annual budget deficits that they in part helped create. There are still tens of millions of Americans without health insurance and the military is spread thin. The GOP Congress has had scarcely more success than the Democrats in reaching a consensus on how to solve those problems.

In small ways, Congress is changing. With each election, it gets a little more female and gains a little more color. In the 109th Congress, the House had six more women and four more minority members than before; the number of women in the Senate held constant at 14 and the minority count grew by two. But by and large, the typical member continued to look like he did a decade ago: a white male in his 50s.

Congress continues to lose some of its stars to retirement, like Rep. Henry Hyde of Illinois, the single most influential voice against legalized abortion. But a few newcomers show potential to captivate and inspire. Illinois Democrat Barack Obama's first term portends some great C-SPAN moments from the Senate floor. As always, some of Capitol Hill's most erudite and persuasive members came from the humblest backgrounds. The father of new Senate Minority Leader Harry Reid was a miner and his mother took in laundry to make ends meet in tiny Searchlight, Nev.

When voters select the 110th Congress in 2006, the lessons of the past decade suggest it won't matter fundamentally if they keep Republicans in charge or switch back to Democrats. The institution itself is sturdier than the people who comprise it. It tends to resist the radical, outlast the revolutionary and move only incrementally toward change — just as the people who concocted it more than two centuries ago intended.

Jackie Koszczuk, April 2005

Narrow Republican Wins in Kerry Districts

These five Republicans won by fewer than 10 percentage points in 2004 in House districts whose voters preferred John Kerry for president:

Member	Percentage Point Victory Margin
Jim Gerlach, Pa. (6)	2.0
Dave Reichert, Wash. (8)	4.8
Christopher Shays, Conn. (4)	4.9
Rob Simmons, Conn. (2)	8.4
Heather A. Wilson, N.M. (1)	8.9

Narrow Republican Wins in Bush Districts

These eight Republicans won by fewer than 10 percentage points in 2004 in House districts whose voters preferred George W. Bush for president:

Member	Percentage Point Victory Margin
Mike Sodrel, Ind. (9)	0.5
Marilyn Musgrave, Colo. (4)	6.3
Mark Kennedy, Minn. (6)	8.0
John Hostettler, Ind. (8)	8.9
Chris Chocola, Ind. (2)	9.6
Charles H. Taylor, N.C. (11)	9.8
John R. "Randy" Kuhl Jr., N.Y. (29)	9.9
Charles Boustany Jr., La. (7)	9.9

Narrow Democratic Wins in Bush Districts

These six Democrats won by fewer than 10 percentage points in 2004 in House districts whose voters preferred George W. Bush for president:

Member	Percentage Point Victory Margin
Charlie Melancon, La. (3)	0.5
Melissa Bean, Ill. (8)	3.4
Chet Edwards, Tex. (17)	3.8
John Salazar, Colo. (3)	4.0
Stephanie Herseth, S.D. (AL)	7.4
Darlene Hooley, Ore. (5)	8.5

Narrow Democratic Wins in Kerry Districts

These four Democrats won by fewer than 10 percentage points in 2004 in House districts whose voters preferred John Kerry for president:

Member	Percentage Point Victory Margin
Brian Higgins, N.Y. (27)	1.3
John Barrow, Ga. (12)	3.6
Jim Costa, Calif. (20)	6.8
Russ Carnahan, Mo. (3)	7.7

Table of Contents

www.cqpress.com

www.cqpress.com

Explanation of Statistics

State Profiles

State profile pages contain information on governors, compositions of state legislatures and information about major cities. Information on state legislatures reflects their status as of April 2005. Details about the makeup of the state legislatures, salaries of members, the legislative schedule, registered voters and state term limits were obtained from state officials.

POPULATION AND URBAN STATISTICS

Demographic information for each state and congressional district was obtained from the Census Bureau and the Bureau of Economic Analysis, both within the Department of Commerce.

Violent crime rates are from 2000. The poverty rate is from 1999. The numbers of federal workers and military personnel are from 2001.

DISTRICT STATISTICS

The tables include the popular vote for the major candidates for president in 2004 in each congressional district. The totals have been calculated to reflect the results within the House district lines in effect for the 2004 election (for the 109th Congress). Gregory L. Giroux of Congressional Quarterly calculated the election results for 38 states. Calculations by state election officials were used for five states — Connecticut, Maine, Minnesota, Nebraska and Virginia. The remaining seven states have only one House seat.

Demographic information relates to current district lines, including districts in Maine and Pennsylvania and Texas that did not take effect until the 2004 election. The figures for racial composition, Hispanic origin, median household income, types of employment, age, education, urban vs. rural residence and size of each congressional district are from the Census Bureau. The racial composition figures reflect census respondents who described themselves as of one race. The white population figure is for non-Hispanic whites. The median household income figure is for 1999. The occupational breakdown combines figures from the Census Bureau's management, professional and relations occupations category and its sales and office occupations category to comprise the white-collar category we have presented. The blue-collar category includes three Census Bureau categories: farming, fishing and forestry; construction, extraction and maintenance; and production, transportation and material moving occupations. The college education table shows the percentage of people, age 25 and older, who have completed at least a bachelor's degree. The district's area is presented in square miles of land area.

Member Profiles

Committees

Standing and select committee assignments as of April 2005 are listed for Senate and House members, as are assignments to major joint committees. Full committee and subcommittee chairmanships are noted.

A complete roster of committee and subcommittee assignments is in the back of the book.

Career and Political Highlights

The member's principal occupations before becoming a full-time public official are given, with the most recent occupation listed first. Often, the political offices listed were part-time jobs and the member continued working at his or her "career" job. Where available, the member's college major is given. Political highlights listed include elected positions in government, high party

Presidential Vote by District

CQ determined the 2004 presidential vote in each House district by acquiring and recalculating vote returns from state and county election offices in the 43 states that have more than one House district. In five of those states — Connecticut, Maine, Minnesota, Nebraska and Virginia — CQ used the presidential vote by district calculations produced by state election officials. Seven states — Alaska, Delaware, Montana, North Dakota, South Dakota, Vermont and Wyoming — have only one House district.

Key to Party Abbreviations

21ST	21st Century
AC	American Constitution
AF	America First
AFE	Anti Federalist
AKI	Alaskan Independence
AMH	American Heritage
AMI	American Independent
C	Conservative
CA	Constitutional American
CC	Concerned Citizens
CFC	Conscience for Congress
CITFIRST	Citizens First
CMO	Cool Moose
CNSTP	Constitution
CONSTL	Constitutional
COPP	Concerns of People
D	Democratic
DCSTATE	D.C. Statehood
EF	Earth Federation
FDM	Freedom
FE	Free Energy
GI	Green Independent
GR	Grassroots
GREEN	Green
HHD	Honesty, Humanity, Duty
HUM	Human Rights
I	Independent
IA	Independent American
ICM	Independent Citizens Movement
INDC	Independence
IP	Independent Party
L	Liberal
LAWR	LaRouche Was Right
LIBERT	Libertarian
LMN	Legal Marijuana Now
LMP	Legalize Marijuana
LTI	Lower Tax Independent

continued on next page

posts, posts requiring legislative confirmation and unsuccessful candidacies for public office. Dates given cover years of service, not election dates.

Elections

General election returns for 2002 and 2004 are listed for House members, with primary results for 2004 as well. For senators and governors, their most recent election results are listed in detail. Returns do not include candidates who received less than 1 percent of the vote. Because percentages have been rounded and some minor candidates have been excluded, election results do not always add up to 100 percent.

Earlier election victories are noted for members of the House and Senate, with the member's percentage of the vote given. If no percentage is given for a year, the member either did not run or lost the election.

For special elections and primaries where a candidate would have won outright if he or she had received a majority of the votes, two election tallies are given, one for the initial election and one for the subsequent runoff.

PRIMARY ELECTIONS

Louisiana holds its primary on Election Day. It is an open primary, with candidates from all parties on the ballot. Any candidate who receives more than half the votes, or who is unopposed, is elected. If no candidate receives an outright majority, the top two vote-getters, regardless of party, advance to a runoff election later.

Key Votes

Profiles of members who served in the 108th Congress are accompanied by a selection of key votes in 2003 and 2004, as chosen by CQ's editors. These captions give the bill number, a brief description of the matter being voted upon, a breakdown of the vote, the date of the vote, and President Bush's position on that particular vote, if he unambiguously took one beforehand.

Senate Key Votes

2004

Pass $318.9 billion, six-year highway and mass transit bill: Passage of the bill (S 1072) that would authorize $318 billion in federal aid for highways, highway safety programs and transit programs over six years. The total funding would include $255 billion for highways, $56.5 billion for transit and $6 billion for safety programs. The bill would ensure that states receive a 95 percent return on their Highway Trust Fund contributions by 2009. A "nay" was a vote in support of the president's position. Passed 76-21: R 34-17; D 41-4 (ND 35-2, SD 6-2); I 1-0. Feb. 12, 2004.

Extend assault weapons ban for 10 years: Feinstein, D-Calif., amendment to S 1805 that would provide for a 10-year reauthorization of the assault weapons ban set to expire in September 2004. Adopted 52-47: R 10-41; D 41-6 (ND 34-4, SD 7-2); I 1-0. March 2, 2004.

Restore pay-as-you-go rules for new tax cuts and entitlement spending: Feingold, D-Wis., amendment to S Con Res 95 that would restore pay-as-you-go (PAYGO) rules, which would create a 60-vote point of order against any direct spending or revenue legislation that would increase the on-budget deficit or cause an on-budget deficit. Tax cuts and new entitlement spending would have to be offset with revenue increases or spending cuts. Adopted 51-48: R 4-47; D 46-1 (ND 38-0, SD 8-1); I 1-0. March 10, 2004.

Criminalize harm to a fetus in an attack on the mother: Passage of the bill (HR 1997) that would make it a criminal offense to injure or kill a fetus

Key to Party Abbreviations

continued from previous page

LU	Liberty Union
MML	Make Marijuana Legal
MNTAX	Minnesota Taxpayers
MOD	Republican Moderate
MOUNT	Mountain
MRF	Marijuana Reform
NEB	Nebraska
NJC	New Jersey Conservative
NJI	New Jersey Independents
NL	Natural Law
NNT	No New Taxes
NON	Non-Partisan
NP	New Progressive
PAC	Politicians Are Crooks
PACIFIC	Pacific
PAT	Patriot
PCH	The People's Champion
PFP	Peace and Freedom
PLC	Pro Life Conservative
PLP	Pro Life
POPDEM	Popular Democratic
PPD	Popular Democratic
PRI	Puerto Rican Independence
PRO	Progressive
R	Republican
REF	Reform
RJF	Restore Justice Freedom
RTL	Right to Life
S	Socialist
SSS	Save Social Security
SW	Socialist Workers
TAX	Taxpayers
TLC	Term Limits Candidate
UC	United Citizens
USP	U.S. Pacifist
USTAX	U.S. Taxpayers
VG	Vermont Grassroots
WFM	Working Families
WG	Wisconsin Greens
X	Not applicable

Key Votes

CQ editors selected key votes from roll-call votes taken during the 108th Congress. The following symbols are used:

Y   voted for (yea)
N   voted against (nay)
paired for
+   announced for
X   paired against
−   announced against
P   voted "present"
C   voted "present" to avoid possible conflict of interest
?   did not vote or otherwise make a position known
I   ineligible
S   Speaker exercised his discretion to not vote

during the commission of a violent crime. The measure would establish criminal penalties, equal to those that would apply if the pregnant woman were injured or killed, for those who harm a fetus, regardless of the perpetrator's knowledge of the pregnancy or intent to harm the fetus. The bill states that its provisions should not be interpreted to apply to consensual abortion or to a woman's actions with respect to her pregnancy. The death penalty could not be imposed under this bill. A "yea" was a vote in support of the president's position. Passed (thus cleared for the president) 61-38: R 48-2; D 13-35 (ND 9-30, SD 4-5); I 0-1. March 25, 2004.

Increase mandatory child care funding to states by $6 billion over five years: Snowe, R-Maine, amendment to HR 4 that would increase mandatory child care funding by $6 billion over the next five years. The spending would be offset by extending expiring Customs user fees. A "nay" was a vote in support of the president's position. Adopted 78-20: R 31-19; D 46-1 (ND 38-0, SD 8-1); I 1-0. March 30, 2004.

Amend the Constitution to prohibit same-sex marriage: Motion to invoke cloture (thus limiting debate) on the motion to proceed to the joint resolution (S J Res 40) to propose a constitutional amendment that would define marriage as consisting only of the union of a man and a woman. It would provide that the U.S. Constitution or any state's constitution could not be construed to require that marriage or any other constructs of marriage be conferred to any other union. Three-fifths of the total Senate (60) is required to invoke cloture. A "yea" was a vote in support of the president's position. Motion rejected 48-50: R 45-6; D 3-43 (ND 2-36, SD 1-7); I 0-1. July 14, 2004.

Approve $146 billion multi-year extension of previously enacted middle-class tax breaks: Adoption of the conference report on the bill (HR 1308) that would extend the $1,000 per child tax credit through 2009, the upper limit for the current 10 percent bracket through 2010 and tax breaks for married couples through 2008. It also would provide a one-year extension of current income exemptions from the alternative minimum tax and extend the expiring research and development tax credit through 2005. A "yea" was a vote in support of the president's position. Adopted (thus cleared for the president) 92-3: R 49-2; D 42-1 (ND 35-0, SD 7-1); I 1-0. Sept. 23, 2004.

Reorganize U.S. intelligence agencies as proposed by Sept. 11 commission: Passage of the bill (S 2845) that would reorganize 15 U.S. intelligence agencies and create a national intelligence director with the power to freely transfer money among the CIA, National Security Agency and other defense and civilian agencies. It also would create a counterterrorism center with operational planning capabilities and a Privacy and Civil Liberties Oversight Board to investigate use of intelligence powers and act as a watchdog for civil liberties concerns. The bill, as amended, would require the Homeland Security secretary to develop and implement a comprehensive national transportation security plan and exempt certain "joint military programs" from the authority of the new director. Passed 96-2: R 51-0; D 44-2 (ND 37-1, SD 7-1); I 1-0. Oct. 6, 2004.

Cut corporate taxes $137 billion over 10 years: Adoption of the conference report on the bill (HR 4520) that would repeal an export provision in the U.S. tax code that has been ruled an unfair subsidy by the World Trade Organization, and would provide for $137 billion in new tax cuts for corporations over 10 years. It also includes a $10 billion buyout of tobacco farmers. The cost of the tax breaks would be offset by curbs on tax-avoidance practices. Adopted (thus cleared for the president) 69-17: R 43-3; D 25-14 (ND 20-14, SD 5-0); I 1-0. Oct. 11, 2004.

2003

Delay Bush changes to Clean Air Act: Edwards, D-N.C., amendment to H J Res 2 that would authorize a National Academy of Sciences study of new rules regarding the New Source Review (NSR) section of the Clean Air Act and would delay implementation of those rules for six months. NSR requires utilities to install better pollution controls when an expansion or modernization results in the release of increased pollution from a coal-burning plant. A "nay" was a vote in support of the president's position. Rejected 46-50: R 6-45; D 39-5 (ND 36-0, SD 3-5); I 1-0. Jan. 22, 2003.

Allow confirmation vote on Miguel A. Estrada to the U.S. Court of Appeals for the D.C. Circuit: Motion to invoke cloture (thus limiting debate) on the motion to proceed to a vote on the nomination of Miguel A. Estrada of Virginia to be a judge for the U.S. Circuit Court of Appeals for the District of Columbia. Three-fifths of the total Senate (60) is required to invoke cloture. A "yea" was a vote in support of the president's position. Motion rejected 55-44: R 51-0; D 4-43 (ND 1-38, SD 3-5); I 0-1. March 6, 2003.

Block a Bush proposal opening Alaska's Arctic National Wildlife Refuge to oil drilling: Boxer, D-Calif., amendment to S Con Res 23 that would strike language in the resolution that could give procedural protection to legislation authorizing oil drilling in part of the Arctic National Wildlife Refuge (ANWR) in Alaska. A "nay" was a vote in support of the president's position. Adopted 52-48: R 8-43; D 43-5 (ND 37-2, SD 6-3); I 1-0. March 19, 2003.

Limit size of Bush's proposed tax cut to $350 billion through fiscal 2013: Breaux, D-La., amendment to S Con Res 23 that would reduce tax cuts protected by reconciliation instructions to $350 billion and create a $396 billion Social Security reserve account for use in implementing future legislation to strengthen Social Security. A "nay" was a vote in support of the president's position. Adopted 51-48: R 3-48; D 47-0 (ND 39-0, SD 8-0); I 1-0. March 25, 2003.

Overhaul Medicare and create prescription drug benefit: Passage of the bill (S 1) that would authorize $400 billion over 10 years to create a prescription drug benefit for Medicare recipients beginning in 2006. Seniors would be allowed to remain within the traditional fee-for-service program or switch to a MedicareAdvantage program that includes prescription drug coverage. Drug coverage would be provided by private insurers that would engage in competitive bidding to be awarded two-year regional contracts by the Center for Medicare Choices under the Department of Health and Human Services. If a region had fewer than two qualified bidders, a federal "fallback" drug coverage plan would be put in place for one year, after which competitive bidding would resume. Enrolled seniors would pay a $275 deductible and an average monthly premium of $35. Annual drug costs beyond the deductible and up to $4,500 would be split equally between the beneficiary and the insurer, after which benefits would stop until the beneficiary's out-of-pocket drug costs reached $3,700, when the insurer would be required to pick up 90 percent of drug costs. Beneficiaries with incomes below 160 percent of the poverty level would be eligible for additional assistance. Passed 76-21: R 40-10; D 35-11 (ND 29-8, SD 6-3); I 1-0. June 27, 2003.

Block Bush rule scaling back overtime pay for some white-collar federal workers: Harkin, D-Iowa, amendment to the Specter, R-Pa., substitute amendment to HR 2660. The Harkin amendment would prohibit funds in the bill from being used to promulgate or implement any regulation that would take away eligibility for overtime for any worker. A "nay" was a vote in support of the president's position. Adopted 54-45: R 6-44; D 47-1 (ND 39-0, SD 8-1); I 1-0. Sept. 10, 2003.

Key Votes

CQ editors selected key votes from roll-call votes taken during the 108th Congress. The following symbols are used:

Y	voted for (yea)
N	voted against (nay)
#	paired for
+	announced for
X	paired against
−	announced against
P	voted "present"
C	voted "present" to avoid possible conflict of interest
?	did not vote or otherwise make a position known
I	ineligible
S	Speaker exercised his discretion to not vote

Split $20 billion in Iraq aid into half-grant, half-loan: Bayh, D-Ind., amendment to S 1689 that would provide a total of $10.3 billion as a grant to rebuild Iraq, including $5.1 billion for security and $5.2 billion for reconstruction costs. It would structure the remaining $10 billion as a loan that would be converted to a grant if 90 percent of all bilateral debt incurred by the former Iraqi regime of Saddam Hussein has been forgiven by other countries. It would require the Coalition Provisional Authority to ensure that the money is spent for the purposes stated. The president would be required to notify Congress if any single obligation in Iraq amounts to $250 million or more. It also would express the sense of the Congress that each country that is owed bilateral debt by Iraq should forgive such debt and provide reconstruction aid beginning at the Madrid Donor Conference on Oct. 23, 2003. A "nay" was a vote in support of the president's position. Adopted 51-47: R 8-43; D 42-4 (ND 34-3, SD 8-1); I 1-0. Oct. 16, 2003.

Ban "partial birth" abortion except to save a woman's life: Adoption of the conference report on the bill (S 3) that would ban a medical procedure opponents refer to as "partial-birth" abortion. The procedure would only be allowed when it is necessary to save a woman's life. Those who unlawfully performed the procedure would face fines and up to two years in prison. A "yea" was a vote in support of the president's position. Adopted (thus cleared for the president) 64-34: R 47-3; D 17-30 (ND 11-28, SD 6-2); I 0-1. Oct. 21, 2003.

Stop proposal allowing travel to Cuba: Stevens, R-Alaska, motion to table (kill) the Dorgan, D-N.D., amendment to HR 2989 that would prohibit any funds in the bill from being used to enforce a ban on U.S. citizens traveling to Cuba. Subsequently, the amendment was adopted by voice vote. A "yea" was a vote in support of the president's position. Motion rejected 36-59: R 30-19; D 6-39 (ND 4-33, SD 2-6); I 0-1. Oct. 23, 2003.

Allow final vote on energy policy overhaul: Motion to invoke cloture (thus limiting debate) on the conference report on the bill (HR 6) that would implement a comprehensive national policy for energy conservation, research and development. It would authorize $25.7 billion in tax breaks over 10 years, including $11.9 billion to encourage oil and gas production, $2.5 billion for "clean coal" programs, $2.2 billion in incentives for alternative motor vehicles, and $1.8 billion for the electric power industry and other businesses. It would authorize $18 billion in loan guarantees for a natural gas pipeline from Alaska. Ethanol producers would be required to double their output. Makers of the gasoline additive MTBE would be protected from liability, but would have to cease production of the additive by 2015. The bill would also impose reliability standards for electricity transmission networks and ease restrictions on utility ownership and mergers. Three-fifths of the total Senate (60) is required to invoke cloture. A "yea" was a vote in support of the president's position. Motion rejected 57-40: R 44-7; D 13-32 (ND 8-30, SD 5-2); I 0-1. Nov. 21, 2003.

House Key Votes

2004

Extend federal unemployment benefits by 13 weeks: Miller, D-Calif., amendment to HR 3030 that would authorize such sums as necessary under the Community Service Block Grants (CSBG) program for a six-month federal program to provide an additional 13 weeks of unemployment benefits for people who have exhausted their state jobless benefits. Adopted 227-179: R 39-179; D 187-0 (ND 132-0, SD 55-0); I 1-0. Feb. 4, 2004.

Pass $283.2 billion, six-year federal highway and mass transit bill: Passage of the bill (HR 3550) that would authorize $283.2 billion for federal-aid highway, mass transit, safety and research programs from fiscal 2004 to 2009. The funding total includes $217 billion in guaranteed spending for highways, $51.5 billion for mass transit and other public transportation programs, and $11.1 billion for members' projects. It also would freeze funding in fiscal 2006 and beyond unless legislation is enacted that would ensure that states get back at least 95 percent of the dollars their motorists send to the Highway Trust Fund by fiscal 2009. A "nay" was a vote in support of the president's position. Passed 357-65: R 162-59; D 194-6 (ND 144-1, SD 50-5); I 1-0. April 2, 2004.

Approve $146 billion multi-year extension of previously enacted middle-class tax breaks: Adoption of the conference report on the bill (HR 1308) that would extend the $1,000 per child tax credit through 2009, the upper limit for the current 10 percent bracket through 2010 and tax breaks for married couples through 2008. It also would provide a one-year extension of current income exemptions from the alternative minimum tax and extend the expiring research and development tax credit through 2005. A "yea" vote was a vote in support of the president's position. Adopted (thus sent to the Senate) 339-65: R 213-0; D 125-65 (ND 83-57, SD 42-8); I 1-0. Sept. 23, 2004.

Amend the Constitution to prohibit same-sex marriage: Passage of a joint resolution (H J Res 106) to propose a constitutional amendment that would define marriage as consisting only of the union of a man and a woman. The U.S. Constitution or any state's constitution could not be construed to require that marriage or any other constructs of marriage be conferred to any other union. A two-thirds majority vote of those present and voting (276 in this case) is required to pass a joint resolution proposing an amendment to the Constitution. A "yea" was a vote in support of the president's position. Rejected 227-186: R 191-27; D 36-158 (ND 7-135, SD 29-23); I 0-1. Sept. 30, 2004.

Cut corporate taxes $137 billion over 10 years: Adoption of the conference report on the bill (HR 4520) that would repeal an export provision in the U.S. tax code that has been ruled an unfair subsidy by the World Trade Organization, and would provide for $137 billion in new tax cuts for corporations over 10 years. It also includes a $10 billion buyout of tobacco farmers. The cost of the tax breaks would be offset by curbs on tax-avoidance practices. Adopted (thus sent to the Senate) 280-141: R 207-16; D 73-124 (ND 25-118, SD 48-6); I 0-1. Oct. 7, 2004.

Reorganize U.S. intelligence agencies as proposed by Sept. 11 commission: Adoption of the conference report on the bill (S 2845) that would reorganize 15 U.S. intelligence agencies and create a new director of national intelligence to oversee all U.S. intelligence activities and determine the intelligence budget. The director would be allowed to move no more than 5 percent of an agency's budget. The National Counterterrorism Center would serve as the primary organization for analyzing and integrating all U.S. intelligence pertaining to terrorism and counterterrorism. The measure would authorize approximately 10,000 additional border patrol agents over five years, and new programs and pilot projects to upgrade airport and airplane security. The FBI would be allowed to conduct surveillance and wiretaps on suspected terrorists who have no ties to any foreign country or entity. A "yea" was a vote in support of the president's position. Adopted (thus sent to the Senate) 336-75: R 152-67; D 183-8 (ND 133-7, SD 50-1); I 1-0. Dec. 7, 2004.

Key Votes

CQ editors selected key votes from roll-call votes taken during the 108th Congress. The following symbols are used:

Y   voted for (yea)
N   voted against (nay)
paired for
+   announced for
X   paired against
−   announced against
P   voted "present"
C   voted "present" to avoid possible conflict of interest
?   did not vote or otherwise make a position known
I   ineligible
S   Speaker exercised his discretion to not vote

2003

Cut taxes by $330 billion through fiscal 2013: Adoption of the conference report on the bill (HR 2) that would provide $350 billion in tax breaks over 11 years. It would provide $20 billion in state aid that consists of $10 billion for Medicaid and $10 billion to be used at states' discretion. The agreement includes a new top tax rate of 15 percent on capital gains and dividends through 2007 (5 percent for lower-income taxpayers in 2007 and no tax in 2008). Income tax cuts enacted in 2001 and scheduled to take effect in 2006 would be accelerated. The child tax credit would increase to $1,000 through 2004. The standard deduction for married couples would be double that for a single filer through 2004. Tax breaks for businesses would include increasing the deduction that small businesses could take on investments to $100,000 through 2005. A "yea" was a vote in support of the president's position. Adopted (thus sent to the Senate) 231-200: R 224-1; D 7-198 (ND 1-147, SD 6-51); I 0-1. May 23, 2003.

Block Bush rule scaling back overtime pay for some white-collar federal workers: Obey, D-Wis., amendment to HR 2660 that would block the use of funds for the Labor Department to implement a March 31 proposal that would make it easier for employers to reclassify some workers as "executive, administrative or professional employees," exempt from overtime pay. A "nay" was a vote in support of the president's position. Rejected 210-213: R 14-210; D 195-3 (ND 141-1, SD 54-2); I 1-0. July 10, 2003.

Do not allow use of search warrants without first notifying subjects: Otter, R-Idaho, amendment to HR 2799 that would bar the use of funds to implement a provision of the 2001 anti-terrorism act that allows the government to delay giving notice that a search warrant has been obtained, thereby facilitating so-called sneak-and-peak searches. Adopted 309-118: R 113-114; D 195-4 (ND 143-2, SD 52-2); I 1-0. July 22, 2003.

Allow importation of prescription drugs: Passage of the bill (HR 2427) that would require the Food and Drug Administration to establish a program that would allow the importation of FDA-approved prescription drugs from FDA-approved facilities in the European Union, Australia, Canada, Iceland, Israel, Japan, Lichtenstein, New Zealand, Norway, Switzerland and South Africa. A "nay" was a vote in support of the president's position. Passed 243-186: R 87-141; D 155-45 (ND 114-31, SD 41-14); I 1-0. July 25, 2003.

Create private school voucher program in Washington, D.C.: Thomas M. Davis III, R-Va., amendment to HR 2765 that would authorize a school voucher program in the District of Columbia. Students would be eligible for up to $7,500 in funds to attend a private elementary or high school in the District. Eligible students would have to be residents of the District and their family income could not exceed 185 percent of the federal poverty level. It would authorize $10 million for the program for fiscal 2004 and such sums as may be necessary for each of the four succeeding fiscal years. Adopted 205-203: R 201-14; D 4-188 (ND 1-136, SD 3-52); I 0-1. Sept. 5, 2003.

Ban "partial birth" abortion except to save a woman's life: Adoption of the conference report on the bill (S 3) that would ban a medical procedure opponents refer to as "partial-birth" abortion. The procedure would be allowed only when it is necessary to save a woman's life. Those who unlawfully performed the procedure would face fines and up to two years in prison. A "yea" was a vote in support of the president's position. Adopted (thus sent to the Senate) 281-142: R 218-4; D 63-137 (ND 32-111, SD 31-26); I 0-1. Oct. 2, 2003.

Split $18.6 billion in Iraq aid into half-grant, half-loan: Obey, D-Wis., amendment to HR 3289 that would require half of all reconstruction aid to Iraq to be in the form of loans. A "nay" was a vote in support of the president's position. Rejected 200-226: R 18-208; D 181-18 (ND 129-15, SD 52-3); I 1-0. Oct. 16, 2003.

Overhaul Medicare and create prescription drug benefit: Adoption of the conference report on the bill (HR 1) that would create a prescription drug benefit for Medicare recipients. Beginning in 2006, prescription coverage would be available through private insurers to seniors paying a monthly premium estimated at $35 in 2006. Those enrolled in the plan would cover the first $250 of annual drug costs themselves and 25 percent of all drug costs up to $2,250. Benefits would then stop until out-of-pocket drug costs exceeded $3,600, after which a beneficiary would cover 5 percent of all costs. Low-income seniors would be eligible for discounts on premiums, deductibles and co-payments. If no private plans bid in a region, the government would offer a fallback prescription drug plan. In 2004 and 2005, beneficiaries would be able to use drug discount cards to reduce prices by up to 25 percent. Medicare payments to managed care plans would increase by $14.2 billion over 10 years. A pilot project would begin in 2010 in which Medicare would compete with private insurers to provide coverage for hospital and doctor costs in six metropolitan areas for six years. Drugs from Canada would be eligible for importation only if the Health and Human Services Department determines there is no safety risk and the move would save consumers money. Beginning in 2007, Part B premiums would increase for some higher-income recipients. Certain individuals under 65 years of age, as well as Medicare recipients, would be able to establish health-savings accounts to pay for health care services not covered by their insurance policy. A "yea" was a vote in support of the president's position. Adopted (thus sent to the Senate) 220-215: R 204-25; D 16-189 (ND 5-143, SD 11-46); I 0-1. Nov. 22, 2003.

Voting Studies

Each year, Congressional Quarterly studies the frequency with which each member of Congress supports or opposes a given position. For example, a score of 25 percent under the support column in the presidential support study would indicate that the member supported the president 25 percent of the time on the votes that were used in the study. An explanation of each of the voting studies follows.

PARTY UNITY

Party unity votes are defined as votes in the Senate and House that split the parties, a majority of voting Democrats opposing a majority of voting Republicans. Votes on which the parties agree, or on which either party divides evenly, are excluded. Party unity scores represent the percentage of party unity votes on which a member voted "yea" or "nay" in agreement with a majority of the member's party. Opposition-to-party scores represent the percentage of party unity votes on which a member voted "yea" or "nay" in disagreement with a majority of the member's party. The score is based only on votes cast; failure to vote did not alter a member's score. All votes have equal statistical weight in the analysis.

PRESIDENTIAL SUPPORT

CQ tries to determine what the president personally, as distinct from other administration officials, does and does not want in the way of legislative action. This is done by analyzing his messages to Congress, news conference remarks and other public statements and documents.

Occasionally, important measures are so extensively amended that it is impossible to characterize final passage as a victory or a defeat for the president. These votes have been excluded from the study. Votes on motions to

Congress by its Numbers

A new Congress is elected in each even-numbered year and convenes at the beginning of each odd-numbered year. As a shorthand, this book frequently refers to the actions of a particular Congress by its number. The sequence began with the 1st Congress, which was elected in 1788.

	Elected:	Met in:
98th Congress	1982	1983 and 1984
99th Congress	1984	1985 and 1986
100th Congress	1986	1987 and 1988
101st Congress	1988	1989 and 1990
102nd Congress	1990	1991 and 1992
103rd Congress	1992	1993 and 1994
104th Congress	1994	1995 and 1996
105th Congress	1996	1997 and 1998
106th Congress	1998	1999 and 2000
107th Congress	2000	2001 and 2002
108th Congress	2002	2003 and 2004
109th Congress	2004	2005 and 2006

recommit, to reconsider or to table (kill) often are key tests that govern the outcome. Such votes are included in the presidential support tabulations.

The score is based only on votes cast; failure to vote did not lower a member's score. All votes have equal statistical weight in the analysis.

Interest Group Ratings

Ratings for members of Congress by four advocacy groups are chosen to represent liberal, conservative, business and labor viewpoints. Following is a description of each group in the order they appear.

AMERICAN FEDERATION OF LABOR-CONGRESS OF INDUSTRIAL ORGANIZATIONS (AFL-CIO)

The AFL-CIO was formed when the American Federation of Labor and the Congress of Industrial Organizations merged in 1955. With affiliates claiming more than 13 million members, the AFL-CIO accounts for about three-fourths of national union membership. For senators, the ratings are based on 12 votes in 1995, seven votes in 1996, seven votes in 1997, eight votes in 1998, nine votes in 1999, eight votes in 2000, 16 votes in 2001, 13 votes in 2002, 13 votes in 2003 and 12 votes in 2004. For members of the House, the ratings are based on 10 votes in 2000, 12 votes in 2001, nine votes in 2002, 16 votes in 2003 and 15 votes in 2004. (www.aflcio.org)

AMERICANS FOR DEMOCRATIC ACTION (ADA)

Americans for Democratic Action was founded in 1947 by a group of liberal Democrats that included Minnesota Sen. Hubert H. Humphrey and Eleanor Roosevelt. The ADA ratings are based on 20 votes each year in each chamber of Congress. (www.adaction.org)

CHAMBER OF COMMERCE OF THE UNITED STATES (CCUS)

The Chamber of Commerce of the United States represents local, regional and state chambers as well as trade and professional organizations. It was founded in 1912 to be "a voice for organized business." For senators, the ratings are based on 18 votes in 1998, 17 in 1999, 15 in 2000, 14 in 2001, 20 in 2002, 23 in 2003 and 17 in 2004. For members of the House, the ratings are based on 21 votes in 2000, 22 in 2001, 20 in 2002, 30 in 2003 and 21 in 2004. (www.uschamber.org)

AMERICAN CONSERVATIVE UNION (ACU)

The American Conservative Union was founded in 1964 "to mobilize resources of responsible conservative thought across the country and further the general cause of conservatism." The organization intends to provide education in political activity, "prejudice in the press," foreign and military policy, domestic economic policy, the arts, professions and sciences. For senators, the ratings are based on 22 votes in 1995, 20 in 1996, 24 in 1997, 25 in 1998, 25 in 1999, 25 in 2000, 24 in 2001, 20 votes in 2002, 19 in 2003 and 25 in 2004. For members of the House, the ratings are based on 25 votes each year, except for 24 votes in 2003. (www.conservative.org)

District Descriptions

In most states, congressional district lines were redrawn in 2001 or 2002 to reflect reapportionment and changes in population patterns revealed in the 2000 census. Maine and Texas districts were redrawn in 2003, while a second set of Pennsylvania district lines drawn in 2002 was not effective until the 2004 election.

The description briefly sets forth the economic, sociological, demographic and political forces that are the keys to elections and which influence the legislative agenda of the district's member of Congress. Some city population figures are from the Census Bureau; other data come from Congressional Staff Directories, compiled in partnership with Capitol Technology Group.

ALABAMA

Gov. Bob Riley (R)

First elected: 2002
Length of term: 4 years
Term expires: 1/07
Salary: $101,433
Phone: (334) 242-7100

Hometown: Ashland
Born: Oct. 3, 1944; Ashland, Ala.
Religion: Baptist
Family: Wife, Patsy Riley; four children (one deceased)
Education: U. of Alabama, B.A. 1965 (business administration)
Career: Auto dealer; trucking company executive; farmer
Political highlights: Ashland City Council, 1972-76; candidate for mayor of Ashland, 1976; U.S. House, 1997-2003

Election results:
2002 GENERAL

Bob Riley (R)	672,225	49.2%
Donald Siegelman (D)	669,105	49.0%
John Sophocleus (LIBERT)	23,272	1.7%

Lt. Gov. Lucy Baxley (D)

First elected: 2002
Length of term: 4 years
Term expires: 1/07
Salary: $48,620
Phone: (334) 242-7900

STATE LEGISLATURE

Legislature: Annually, limit of 30 legislative days within 105 calendar days

House: 105 members, 4-year terms
2005 breakdown: 62D, 41R, 2 vacancies; 91 men, 12 women
Salary: $10/day; $50 for each 3-day week; $2,280/month expenses
Phone: (334) 242-7600

Senate: 35 senators, 4-year terms
2005 breakdown: 25D, 10R; 32 men, 3 women
Salary: $10/day; $50 for each 3-day week; $2,280/month expenses
Phone: (334) 242-7800

STATE TERM LIMITS

Governor: 2 consecutive terms
House: No
Senate: No

URBAN STATISTICS

CITY	POPULATION
Birmingham	242,820
Montgomery	201,568
Mobile	198,915
Huntsville	158,216
Tuscaloosa	77,906

REGISTERED VOTERS

Voters do not register by party.

POPULATION

2004 population (est.)	4,530,182
2000 population	4,447,100
1990 population	4,040,587
Percent change (1990-2000)	+10.1%
Rank among states (2004)	23

Median age	35.8
Born in state	73.4%
Foreign born	2%
Violent crime rate	486/100,000
Poverty level	16.1%
Federal workers	50,081
Military	38,706

REDISTRICTING

Alabama retained its seven House seats in reapportionment. The state legislature drew a new map, which the governor signed on Jan. 31, 2002.

MISCELLANEOUS

Web: www.alabama.gov
Capital: Montgomery
STATE ELECTION OFFICIAL
(334) 242-7210
DEMOCRATIC HEADQUARTERS
(334) 262-2221
REPUBLICAN HEADQUARTERS
(205) 212-5900

District Statistics

DIST.	2004 VOTE FOR PRESIDENT BUSH	KERRY	WHITE	BLACK	ASIAN	HISP	MEDIAN INCOME	WHITE COLLAR	BLUE COLLAR	SERVICE INDUSTRY	OVER 64	UNDER 18	COLLEGE EDUCATION	RURAL	SQ. MILES
1	64%	35%	68%	28%	1%	1%	$34,739	55%	31%	15%	13%	27%	19%	36%	6,317
2	66	33	67	29	1	2	$32,460	55	31	14	13	26	18	50	10,502
3	58	41	65	32	1	1	$30,806	52	34	14	13	25	17	47	7,834
4	71	28	90	5	0	3	$31,344	46	42	12	15	24	11	73	8,372
5	60	39	78	17	1	2	$38,054	57	30	13	12	25	24	41	4,486
6	78	22	89	8	1	2	$46,946	68	22	10	12	24	30	38	4,564
7	35	64	36	62	1	1	$26,672	53	29	17	13	26	15	28	8,669
STATE	62	37	70	26	1	2	$34,135	55	31	13	13	25	19	45	50,744
U.S.	50.7	48.3	69	12	4	13	$41,994	60	25	15	12	26	24	21	3,537,438

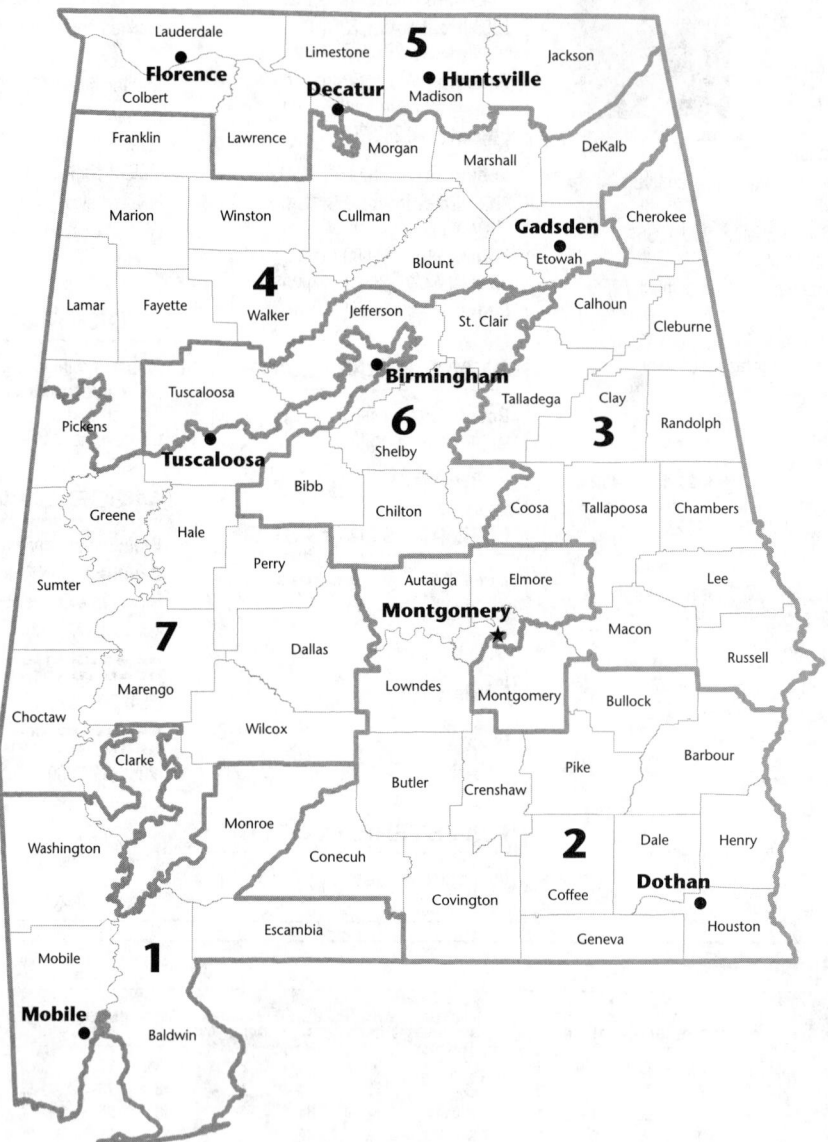

Sen. Richard C. Shelby (R)

Elected 1986; 4th term

CAPITOL OFFICE
224-5744
senator@shelby.senate.gov
shelby.senate.gov
110 Hart 20510-0103; fax 224-3416

COMMITTEES
Appropriations
  (Commerce, Justice & Science - chairman)
Banking, Housing & Urban Affairs - chairman
Special Aging

HOMETOWN
Tuscaloosa

BORN
May 6, 1934, Birmingham, Ala.

RELIGION
Presbyterian

FAMILY
Wife, Annette Nevin Shelby; two children

EDUCATION
U. of Alabama, A.B. 1957, LL.B. 1963

CAREER
Lawyer; city prosecutor

POLITICAL HIGHLIGHTS
Ala. Senate, 1971-79 (served as a Democrat);
U.S. House, 1979-87 (served as a Democrat)

ELECTION RESULTS

2004 GENERAL

Richard C. Shelby (R)	1,242,200	67.6%
Wayne Sowell (D)	595,018	32.4%

2004 PRIMARY

Richard C. Shelby (R)	unopposed

PREVIOUS WINNING PERCENTAGES *
1998 (63%); 1992 (65%); 1986 (50%); 1984 House
Election (97%); 1982 House Election (97%); 1980
House Election (73%); 1978 House Election (94%)
* Elected as a Democrat 1978-92

After a quarter-century in Congress, the genial Shelby is a prodigious fundraiser and provider for his home state. On national issues, he is a Republican anomaly who occasionally behaves like the Democrat he once was. One of Congress' first party switchers in the mid-1990s, his departures from the Republican mainstream come most notably on consumer protection matters, where he has a strong populist bent on questions of privacy, predatory lending and stock market regulation.

Among his colleagues, he is seen as one of the most amiable and least excitable senators. But Shelby is unafraid to pick a fight with the big boys on the block. As chairman of the Banking, Housing and Urban Affairs Committee, he says his role is to serve the public's interest, rather than corporate America's interests, attracting heated opposition from business groups.

He took the helm of the Banking panel at the outset of the 108th Congress, after term limits forced him to give up the more high-profile vice chairmanship of the Intelligence Committee, a job he had at a sensitive moment in history — Sept. 11, 2001, the day New York and Washington, D.C. were attacked by terrorists. Shelby was one of Capitol Hill's harshest critics of perceived failures on the part of the intelligence community to detect evidence of the plot. He called 9-11 "an intelligence failure of unprecedented magnitude," and singled out the Central Intelligence Agency for relying too much on technological tools and not enough on the work of agents in the field. He was given to lengthy and thoughtful critiques of the intelligence agency's shortcomings, and regularly called for CIA Director George J. Tenet's resignation.

Shelby pushed for greater sharing of intelligence information among federal agencies as part of the law that created the Department of Homeland Security. When he left the panel, it was none too soon for his legion of critics in the spy agencies who had been the targets of his verbal lashings.

Fallout from that period in his career continued into the 109th Congress, with an ongoing Ethics Committee investigation of allegations that Shelby leaked secret government information to the media. The information, which infuriated top Bush administration officials when made public, was the National Security Agency's interception of two messages on the eve of the attacks that were not translated until Sept. 12. The Arabic-language messages said, "The match is about to begin" and "Tomorrow is zero hour." Shelby denied that he knowingly compromised classified information.

He has been equally feisty on the Banking panel. In 2004, he unveiled a bill to create a new agency to regulate Fannie Mae, Freddie Mac and the Federal Home Loan banks, stripping power from the Department of Housing and Urban Development (HUD), which currently oversees the mortgage giants. The government-chartered Fannie Mae, the nation's largest provider of U.S. mortgage financing, and its allies in the housing industry strongly opposed the regulatory legislation, and it failed to pass.

Shelby's pet issue is consumer privacy, which he feels passionately about. His immersion in the subject dates to the 106th Congress, when he learned that some states were providing information from driver's licenses to marketing firms without motorists' knowledge. He often takes pro-consumer positions out of step with the Republican Party. Shelby was a co-founder of the Congressional Privacy Caucus in 1999 and that year won enactment of a law requiring states to obtain permission before sharing personal data, such as Social Security numbers and driver's license information.

Shelby sometimes does take some pro-business stands more in line with the mainstream GOP. He favors doing away with a raft of what he calls unnecessary regulations of banks, credit unions and thrifts, saying that there have been "a lot of laws put on the books in the last 50 years that make no sense today." He advocates a limited role for the federal government in economic affairs, except when the actions of malefactors endanger the free-market system. His vision for government is that it should "try first to do no harm, except where people are doing harm to the marketplace. We have to root those people out."

No matter what his record has been on the national scene, it has been Shelby's ability to deliver federal money to Alabama that has fueled his popularity back home. As a senior member of the Appropriations Committee and chairman of the Commerce, Justice and Science Subcommittee, he looks out for federal installations in the state.

Shelby has been of special service to the city of Huntsville, seeking to leverage his subcommittee chairmanship to protect the booming space and defense economy there. Huntsville is home to NASA's Marshall Space Flight Center and to the Army's Redstone Arsenal. The Army was so thankful for Shelby's help securing a new 200,000-square-foot, $33 million scientific and technical center, it named the facility the Richard C. Shelby Center for Missile Intelligence.

When it comes to inserting home-state earmarks in spending bills, Shelby has "made a kind of art form out of it," former Rep. Jack Edwards, an Alabama Republican, told the Mobile Register. Shelby got the Appropriations seat after he switched parties following the Republican takeover of Congress in 1994. Although the switch struck many as opportunistic, he said he made the move because of what he saw as the demise of the pro-defense, conservative wing of the Democratic Party. "I grew up a Southern Democrat," Shelby said, adding that like him, many Democrats simply inherited their party label. Southern Democrats came about "because of the Civil War, not because of ideology."

Shelby spent most of the 1960s as a municipal prosecutor in Tuscaloosa, and as a legislator, he sometimes cites his law enforcement background. He entered electoral politics by serving eight years in the state Senate, where he often was at odds with Gov. George C. Wallace. Although Shelby initially was interested in running for lieutenant governor in 1978, more than a dozen other Democrats had the same idea. Then, one of his former law partners, Democrat Walter Flowers, gave up his House seat that year to run for the Senate, and Shelby was easily persuaded to change course and run for Congress.

For eight years, Shelby operated largely behind the scenes in the House, working to bring federal projects to his district. But he also became an increasingly reliable ally for Republicans. Ironically, his election to the Senate as a Democrat in 1986 was a 1 percentage point victory over one-term incumbent Jeremiah Denton, who had been the first Republican elected to statewide office in Alabama since Reconstruction.

Shelby has had less trouble running for re-election to the Senate since then, thanks to the inability of either party to recruit top-tier opponents against him and the senator's considerable skill at raising money. In addition to accepting contributions from the usual range of pro-GOP business interests, he also has collected from a constituency not usually inclined to give to a Republican — trial lawyers. During one six-month blitz in 2002 and 2003, Shelby raised more than $4 million at a time when no serious opponent loomed on the horizon. He rationalizes this by saying, "You wait until you need it and then it's too late."

KEY VOTES

2004

Yes   Pass $318.9 billion, six-year highway and mass transit bill

No   Extend assault weapons ban for 10 years

No   Restore pay-as-you-go rules for new tax cuts and entitlement spending

Yes   Criminalize harm to a fetus in an attack on the mother

Yes   Increase mandatory child care funding to states by $6 billion over five years

Yes   Amend the Constitution to prohibit same-sex marriage

Yes   Approve $146 billion multi-year extension of previously enacted middle-class tax breaks

Yes   Reorganize U.S. intelligence agencies as proposed by Sept. 11 commission

Yes   Cut corporate taxes $137 billion over 10 years

2003

No   Delay Bush changes to Clean Air Act

Yes   Allow confirmation vote on Miguel A. Estrada to the U.S. Court of Appeals for the D.C. Circuit

No   Block a Bush proposal opening Alaska's Arctic National Wildlife Refuge to oil drilling

No   Limit size of Bush's proposed tax cut to $350 billion through fiscal 2013

Yes   Overhaul Medicare and create prescription drug benefit

No   Block Bush rule scaling back overtime pay for some white-collar federal workers

No   Split $20 billion in Iraq aid into half-grant, half-loan

Yes   Ban "partial birth" abortion except to save a woman's life

Yes   Stop proposal allowing travel to Cuba

Yes   Allow final vote on energy policy overhaul

CQ VOTE STUDIES

	PARTY UNITY		PRESIDENTIAL SUPPORT	
	Support	Oppose	Support	Oppose
2004	94%	6%	86%	14%
2003	96%	4%	95%	5%
2002	80%	20%	87%	13%
2001	88%	12%	97%	3%
2000	97%	3%	45%	55%
1999	89%	11%	38%	62%
1998	91%	9%	34%	66%
1997	93%	7%	57%	43%
1996	94%	6%	33%	67%
1995	90%	10%	30%	70%

INTEREST GROUPS

	AFL-CIO	ADA	CCUS	ACU
2004	25%	20%	88%	84%
2003	15%	10%	82%	90%
2002	38%	10%	85%	80%
2001	19%	5%	93%	100%
2000	0%	0%	93%	100%
1999	22%	10%	71%	84%
1998	0%	5%	78%	92%
1997	14%	5%	90%	92%
1996	0%	5%	77%	90%
1995	0%	5%	89%	91%

Sen. Jeff Sessions (R)

CAPITOL OFFICE
224-4124
senator@sessions.senate.gov
sessions.senate.gov
335 Russell 20510-0104; fax 224-3149

COMMITTEES
Armed Services
   (Strategic Forces - chairman)
Budget
Health, Education, Labor & Pensions
Judiciary
   (Administrative Oversight & the Courts -
   chairman)
Joint Economic

HOMETOWN
Mobile

BORN
Dec. 24, 1946, Hybart, Ala.

RELIGION
Methodist

FAMILY
Wife, Mary Blackshear Sessions; three children

EDUCATION
Huntingdon College, B.A. 1969 (history); U. of
Alabama, J.D. 1973

MILITARY SERVICE
Army Reserve, 1973-86

CAREER
Lawyer; teacher

POLITICAL HIGHLIGHTS
Assistant U.S. attorney, 1975-77; U.S. attorney,
1981-93; Ala. attorney general, 1995-97

ELECTION RESULTS

2002 GENERAL

Jeff Sessions (R)	792,561	58.6%
Susan Parker (D)	538,878	39.8%
Jeff Allen (LIBERT)	20,234	1.5%

2002 PRIMARY

Jeff Sessions (R)	unopposed

PREVIOUS WINNING PERCENTAGES
1996 (52%)

Elected 1996; 2nd term

A former Alabama attorney general, Sessions shares the deep fiscal and social conservatism of many of his Republican colleagues from the South and West. The second-term senator places himself in the center of a new generation of southern GOP senators focused not just on the rural concerns of their populist Democratic predecessors but on traditional values and economic policy.

He traces the transformation back to the election of Thad Cochran of Mississippi in 1978. "Southern Republican senators represent heartland middle-class values. They don't want the government to run the lives of people or take care of everything," he said.

He uses his seat as chairman of the Senate Republican Steering Committee, a group of 30 mostly conservative GOP senators, to promote spending controls, smaller government and tax cuts. In 2005, he helped lead a push to pare entitlement spending in order to allow more funding for the military and other discretionary programs. Sessions also called for legislation to enforce a cap on spending on the new Medicare prescription drug benefit enacted in 2003, after criticizing the administration for underestimating the program's cost. "First, we've got to stay within our budget and not cheat or manipulate the numbers," he said. "Second, we've got to look at cutting some mandatory spending."

Although he has been critical of some of President Bush's spending priorities, Sessions usually lines up with his party leadership on key legislation. In 2004, he voted with the majority of his party 97 percent of the time.

The Senate's role in confirming judges is the issue most closely associated with Sessions since he came to Congress in 1997. At the start of the 109th Congress, Sessions, who serves as chairman of the Judiciary Committee's Administrative Oversight and the Courts Subcommittee, threatened to push for a change in Senate rules to curb filibusters if Democrats blocked judicial nominations in 2005. "It is the Democrats' policies that are threatening collegiality and are contrary to the history of the Senate since its founding," Sessions argued.

He and other conservatives briefly held up the choice of moderate Republican Arlen Specter of Pennsylvania to be Judiciary chairman, after he expressed doubts about the political viability of judicial candidates with socially conservative views. But Sessions helped resolve the dispute by extracting a vow from Specter to move nominations.

Sessions then promoted the renomination of William Pryor, a former Alabama attorney general, to a permanent seat on the 11th Circuit Court of Appeals. Bush had used a recess appointment in the 108th to put Pryor on the 11th Circuit bench through the end of 2005. Sessions stressed that Pryor had the "strong support of the entire spectrum of Alabama political leaders."

Sessions has a unique perspective on judicial confirmations. In 1986, he was only the second federal judicial nominee in 48 years whose nomination was killed by the Judiciary Committee. President Reagan had nominated Sessions, then chief prosecutor for the Southern District of Alabama. But critics accused him of "gross insensitivity" on racial issues. According to sworn statements by Justice Department lawyers, Sessions called the NAACP and the American Civil Liberties Union "communist-inspired" and said they tried to "force civil rights down the throats of people." Sessions said his words were misrepresented.

After voting 8-10 against his confirmation, the panel refused, 9-9, to send the nomination to the floor for a vote. (The no votes included the man Sessions replaced in the Senate, Democrat Howell Heflin.) On Judiciary, Sessions now serves with several lawmakers who prevented him from becoming a federal judge, including Specter and Democrats Joseph R. Biden Jr. of Delaware, Edward M. Kennedy of Massachusetts and top-ranking member Patrick J. Leahy of Vermont.

On other Judiciary issues, Sessions strongly supports an overhaul of bankruptcy law, which is important to the financial services industry based in Alabama. In the 108th, he opposed additional funding for DNA testing on the grounds that it provided support for defense lawyers in death-penalty cases.

Sessions also sits on Armed Services, where he is chairman of the Strategic Forces Subcommittee. He often lines up with committee Chairman John W. Warner of Virginia and keeps an eye out for military installations in his state, including Maxwell Air Force Base near Montgomery. In 2005, Session took the lead on a proposal to increase from $12,400 to $100,000 the benefit paid to survivors of soldiers killed in combat, after winning passage of a 2004 provision directing the Pentagon to study the issue.

An advocate for a missile defense system, Sessions has pushed for more development of space-based devices, which could be a boon to his state's aerospace industry near Huntsville. "We're going to be looking as time goes by to space-based systems that may be even more effective and may be even less expensive," Sessions said in 2004.

Sessions and his wife both taught school long ago, and he lists education as a top priority. On the Health, Education, Labor and Pensions Committee, he helped win passage in the 108th of a new law that gave schools greater leeway in dealing with disruptive students with disabilities.

Sessions made headlines in his home state just before the Republican National Convention in 2004 when he was one of three white delegates to step aside, allowing state GOP officials to name three black replacements.

A history buff, Sessions takes pride in his middle name — Beauregard, from the Confederate commander who was the "hero of Fort Sumter" at the start of the Civil War, Gen. P.G.T. Beauregard. Sessions grew up in the tiny towns of Hybart and Camden, southwest of Montgomery. His father owned a general store and then a farm equipment dealership. Sessions worked around the stores and had what he describes as an idyllic childhood.

A student of political science and history, he joined the Young Republicans and served as student body president at Huntingdon College in Alabama. After earning his law degree, Sessions was a lawyer for a firm in Russellville, Ala., becoming assistant U.S. attorney in 1975. He was named U.S. attorney for the Southern District of Alabama in 1981 and eventually won the notice of the Reagan White House.

After the Senate turned back his nomination, Sessions returned to his work as a federal prosecutor. In 1994, he ran for state attorney general, and with a corruption scandal raging in Montgomery, he rode to victory on a vow to clean up the ethics mess. Two years later, Sessions was on the move again, lured into the Senate race by Heflin's retirement after 18 years in Washington. Six other Republicans joined Sessions in the party primary, and he emerged the winner in a runoff.

In the general election, Sessions faced Roger Bedford, chairman of the state Senate Judiciary Committee. Sessions appealed to Alabama's conservative Christian activists with his advocacy of a constitutional amendment permitting school prayer. In the end, he prevailed over Bedford with 52 percent of the vote, giving Alabama two Republican senators for the first time since Reconstruction. In 2002, he cruised past Democrat Susan Parker, the state auditor, by 19 percentage points.

KEY VOTES

2004

No Pass $318.9 billion, six-year highway and mass transit bill

No Extend assault weapons ban for 10 years

No Restore pay-as-you-go rules for new tax cuts and entitlement spending

Yes Criminalize harm to a fetus in an attack on the mother

No Increase mandatory child care funding to states by $6 billion over five years

Yes Amend the Constitution to prohibit same-sex marriage

Yes Approve $146 billion multi-year extension of previously enacted middle-class tax breaks

Yes Reorganize U.S. intelligence agencies as proposed by Sept. 11 commission

Yes Cut corporate taxes $137 billion over 10 years

2003

No Delay Bush changes to Clean Air Act

Yes Allow confirmation vote on Miguel A. Estrada to the U.S. Court of Appeals for the D.C. Circuit

No Block a Bush proposal opening Alaska's Arctic National Wildlife Refuge to oil drilling

No Limit size of Bush's proposed tax cut to $350 billion through fiscal 2013

Yes Overhaul Medicare and create prescription drug benefit

No Block Bush rule scaling back overtime pay for some white-collar federal workers

No Split $20 billion in Iraq aid into half-grant, half-loan

Yes Ban "partial birth" abortion except to save a woman's life

Yes Stop proposal allowing travel to Cuba

Yes Allow final vote on energy policy overhaul

CQ VOTE STUDIES

	PARTY UNITY		PRESIDENTIAL SUPPORT	
	Support	Oppose	Support	Oppose
2004	97%	3%	96%	4%
2003	98%	2%	99%	1%
2002	87%	13%	88%	12%
2001	95%	5%	97%	3%
2000	97%	3%	42%	58%
1999	94%	6%	24%	76%
1998	98%	2%	28%	72%
1997	99%	1%	56%	44%

INTEREST GROUPS

	AFL-CIO	ADA	CCUS	ACU
2004	8%	10%	88%	96%
2003	0%	0%	100%	75%
2002	25%	10%	84%	90%
2001	20%	5%	86%	96%
2000	0%	0%	86%	100%
1999	11%	0%	88%	100%
1998	0%	0%	89%	100%
1997	0%	0%	70%	100%

Rep. Jo Bonner (R)

CAPITOL OFFICE
225-4931
bonner.house.gov
315 Cannon 20515-0101; fax 225-0562

COMMITTEES
Agriculture
Budget
Science

HOMETOWN
Mobile

BORN
Nov. 19, 1959, Selma, Ala.

RELIGION
Episcopalian

FAMILY
Wife, Janee Bonner; two children

EDUCATION
U. of Alabama, B.A. 1982 (journalism), attended 1998 (law)

CAREER
Congressional chief of staff; congressional aide; campaign aide

POLITICAL HIGHLIGHTS
No previous office

ELECTION RESULTS

2004 GENERAL

Jo Bonner (R)	161,067	63.1%
Judy McCain Belk (D)	93,938	36.8%

2004 PRIMARY

Jo Bonner (R)	unopposed

2002 GENERAL

Jo Bonner (R)	108,102	60.5%
Judy McCain Belk (D)	67,507	37.8%
Richard M. Coffee (LIBERT)	2,957	1.7%

Elected 2002; 2nd term

A scion of an old Southern family, Bonner came to Congress not with soaring hopes of rewriting national policy but with the aim of perpetuating a tradition in his Alabama district of sending federal dollars back home. He comes from a long line of accommodating lawmakers. Bonner got the seat from Republican Sonny Callahan, an Appropriations chairman on energy and water projects, who endorsed Bonner as he was stepping down in 2002. Bonner had been Callahan's longtime chief of staff. Before Callahan, the seat belonged for 20 years to Republican Jack Edwards, another appropriator who, upon his retirement, endorsed Callahan as his successor.

Bonner makes no secret of his desire for a seat on the spending panel, a plum assignment viewed almost as an entitlement by voters in the Mobile-based district. But he has been handicapped by his lack of seniority and, ironically, his political good health. Seats on Appropriations are often used by leaders to shore up vulnerable House members, which Bonner is not.

He makes no apologies for angling for as much federal largess for his district as he can get. True to the legacies of Callahan and Edwards, more than two-thirds of his press pronouncements in the 108th Congress touted spending he helped send home. "I love politics and I love people," Bonner said. "Government service is a people-driven job if you're in it for the right reason."

Bonner's family is among the most prominent in southern Alabama. His grandfather was a banker in Wilcox County and his great-uncles a doctor, a lawyer and the local newspaper publisher. Bonner, whose given name is Josiah Robins Bonner Jr., is named for his father, also Josiah, a Georgetown-trained attorney who was a county judge, a powerful local post.

The district is anchored by Mobile, an old Confederate port city that exudes charm and Southern gentility and hosts an annual Mardi Gras celebration that predates its more famous New Orleans sister. North of the city are dense pine forests where timber harvesting is a mainstay. To the north are also Mayberry-style towns, which have produced a remarkable number of great Southern writers. Monroeville was the home of both Truman Capote and Harper Lee, whose classic novel "To Kill a Mockingbird" is set there. Bonner's father used to take his sister to visit the Lees, to demonstrate to her that women could have interesting careers.

Like many Southern politicians, Bonner began his career as a Democrat but switched to the Republican Party in the 1990s without a wholesale change in his conservative political philosophy. Bonner favors lower taxes and less government involvement with business. He was a ready supporter of President Bush's tax bill in 2003, though he says he worries about a growing federal deficit and wants future tax cuts to be matched by cuts in spending. Bonner calls himself a "team player," and he voted with his president and his party over 95 percent of the time in the 108th Congress.

At one time, Bonner thought he'd be a journalist, not a member of Congress. As a kid in Camden, which he calls a "storybook hometown," Bonner launched a community newspaper, borrowing a press from the local newspaper editor, whose son was a playmate. In high school, Bonner was a broadcast announcer at basketball games and president of the student council.

Like Selma and Montgomery a few miles to the north, Camden boiled with racial strife during the 1960s, with blacks boycotting white-owned businesses. Bonner's parents took him out of the integrating Wilcox County public schools to attend the newly formed Ft. Dale Academy, which was mostly white.

After getting a degree in print journalism from the University of Alabama, Bonner's expanding interest in politics led him to join the 1982 gubernatorial campaign of Democrat George McMillan, who was challenging Democratic incumbent George Wallace. To young professionals like Bonner, McMillan represented a "new chapter" for Alabama after the race-tinged politics of Wallace and the state's history of violence during the civil rights movement.

McMillan lost to Wallace, but Bonner in the meantime had met Callahan, who was then a candidate for lieutenant governor. Callahan also lost at the state level, but two years later, won a race for the House seat and hired Bonner to be his press secretary. Bonner spent the next 17 years working for Callahan, eventually being named his chief of staff.

Callahan quietly encouraged his trusted aide to run for the seat himself when the congressman was ready to retire. In the meantime, in 1997, Bonner moved from Washington to the district, a rarity for a chief of staff, most of whom work on Capitol Hill. He paid close attention to constituent service. He joined both the local Rotary Club and the board of the local Junior League. By the time Callahan announced he was stepping down in 2002, Bonner was well-known in the district and well situated to run.

His toughest competition came from Tom Young, a Mobile native and a fellow Republican who, like Bonner, was a career congressional aide. Young was chief of staff for Republican Sen. Richard C. Shelby of Alabama. Despite their similarities, Bonner managed to portray Young as a Washington insider not in touch with voters. It became one of the most expensive and hotly contested races of the season. Bonner got the most votes in a seven-way June primary but fell short of a majority, forcing a runoff. He went on to get 62 percent to Young's 38 percent. In the general election, Bonner easily defeated Democratic businesswoman Judy McCain Belk in the GOP-dominated district.

Setting up shop was relatively easy for Bonner. He kept all but two of Callahan's staff, whom he had helped hire through the years. He also took over from his former boss a weekly cable talk show called "The Gulf Coast Congressional Report," which airs Sunday mornings right after "Face the Nation" on Mobile's CBS affiliate station. Bonner produces the show for a fee at the House recording studio, and although his guests typically are friendly Republicans, he has gotten good reviews in the press as a smooth, telegenic interviewer.

In 2004, Belk challenged him in a rematch. Bonner won decisively with 63 percent of the vote.

KEY VOTES

2004

No Extend federal unemployment benefits by 13 weeks

Yes Pass $283.2 billion, six-year federal highway and mass transit bill

? Approve $146 billion multi-year extension of previously enacted middle-class tax breaks

Yes Amend the Constitution to prohibit same-sex marriage

Yes Cut corporate taxes $137 billion over 10 years

Yes Reorganize U.S. intelligence agencies as proposed by Sept. 11 commission

2003

Yes Cut taxes by $330 billion through fiscal 2013

No Block Bush rule scaling back overtime pay for some white-collar federal workers

Yes Do not allow use of search warrants without first notifying subjects

No Allow importation of prescription drugs

Yes Create private school voucher program in Washington, D.C.

Yes Ban "partial birth" abortion except to save a woman's life

No Split $18.6 billion in Iraq aid into half-grant, half-loan

Yes Overhaul Medicare and create prescription drug benefit

CQ VOTE STUDIES

	PARTY UNITY		PRESIDENTIAL SUPPORT	
	Support	Oppose	Support	Oppose
2004	97%	3%	92%	8%
2003	97%	3%	98%	2%

INTEREST GROUPS

	AFL-CIO	ADA	CCUS	ACU
2004	15%	0%	100%	95%
2003	7%	5%	97%	88%

ALABAMA 1
Southwest – Mobile

Crop fields and pine forests merge with Alabama's shoreline to form the 1st. Although the city of Mobile is the anchor of the state's only Gulf Coast district, a symbiotic relationship between the industrial and rural areas balances the district's economy.

Forestry feeds the district's timber mills and shipping companies, though a deep recession in the Southeast Asian market in the mid- to late-1990s forced cutbacks in the local timber industry. Mobile's State Docks, one of the nation's largest commercial shipping centers, supports a shipbuilding industry that has stagnated in recent years. Ship repair and other services have kept the ports busy, and South Alabama still relies on its rich soil for the staple products — trees, cotton and soybeans — that have given the region strength for decades.

But the overall contraction of timber, ship-related industries and a once-thriving textile industry forced the district to diversify. Tourism, based around the Gulf Coast, has been the most immediate remedy. Retail outlets spur employment and chemical and aerospace companies help broaden the district's economy.

The shift to Republican voting seen in much of the South took root early in Alabama's 1st. Republicans have held the House seat since 1965, and the district overwhelmingly favored GOP presidential candidates in the 1990s, 2000 and 2004. But the 1st's voters do not always follow the GOP line. Democrats long have had a foothold in rural parts of the district, while Mobile residents lean Republican. Local elections can become battles over issues such as farm subsidies and trade.

MAJOR INDUSTRY
Commercial shipping, timber, textiles

CITIES
Mobile, 198,915; Prichard, 28,633; Daphne, 16,581; Tillmans Corner, 15,685

NOTABLE
Gulf Shores' National Shrimp Festival, which was cancelled in 2004 due to hurricane damage, draws more than 200,000 visitors each October; Mobile annually hosts America's Junior Miss competition and college football's Senior Bowl.

Rep. Terry Everett (R)

Elected 1992; 7th term

CAPITOL OFFICE
225-2901
www.house.gov/everett
2312 Rayburn 20515-0102; fax 225-8913

COMMITTEES
Agriculture
Armed Services
  (Strategic Forces - chairman)
Veterans' Affairs
Select Intelligence

HOMETOWN
Rehobeth

BORN
Feb. 15, 1937, Dothan, Ala.

RELIGION
Baptist

FAMILY
Wife, Barbara Everett

EDUCATION
Dale County H.S., graduated 1955

MILITARY SERVICE
Air Force, 1955-59

CAREER
Newspaper executive; construction company owner; farm owner; real estate developer; newspaper reporter

POLITICAL HIGHLIGHTS
No previous office

ELECTION RESULTS

2004 GENERAL

Terry Everett (R)	177,086	71.4%
Charles "Chuck" James (D)	70,562	28.5%

2004 PRIMARY

Terry Everett (R)	unopposed

2002 GENERAL

Terry Everett (R)	129,233	68.8%
Charles Woods (D)	55,495	29.5%
Floyd Shackelford (LIBERT)	2,948	1.6%

PREVIOUS WINNING PERCENTAGES
2000 (68%); 1998 (69%); 1996 (63%); 1994 (74%); 1992 (49%)

Everett was 55 years old when he gained his House seat, which was his first elected office. Now, 13 years later, he is a major player on a number of House committees. He is also a self-made millionaire who started out as a farm reporter for southeastern Alabama's Dothan Eagle and later built a chain of newspapers. He has owned a homebuilding company and served as chairman of the board of a local bank.

The district's farm and military interests and Everett's own experience in farming and the Air Force have made him a good match for his long roster of committee assignments: Agriculture, Armed Services, Veterans' Affairs and Intelligence. An Air Force intelligence analyst in the 1950s, Everett won a seat on the Intelligence panel in 2002, as the war on terrorism took center stage in Congress.

When lawmakers cleared a broad intelligence reform measure at the end of the 108th Congress, Everett complained that the measure fell short in terrorism prevention. He said the compromise bill dropped important House-passed provisions, including making it harder for refugees to obtain U.S. asylum, allowing expedited deportation of illegal aliens without judicial review, and preventing states from giving driver's licenses to illegal aliens. "I agreed that passage of an intelligence reform bill which adds to America's security should be a congressional priority," Everett said in a news release. "However, ramming such a large and far-reaching piece of legislation through Congress at breakneck speed for the sake of having a bill is unwise." He voted against the bill's final version.

Everett had sought the chairmanship of the Agriculture Committee early in the 108th but lost out to Virginian Robert W. Goodlatte. Instead, he was given the chairmanship of the Armed Services panel's Strategic Forces Subcommittee, which has jurisdiction over missile defense, military space activities and Department of Energy defense programs.

On Armed Services, Everett looks out for his district's numerous defense contractors and its two major military bases, Maxwell Air Force Base and Fort Rucker, where Army and Air Force helicopter crews train. As Strategic Forces chairman, he worked to trim money from the Missile Defense Agency while increasing the focus on shorter-range antimissile systems. He helped lead efforts in the 108th to preserve funding for the nuclear bunker buster program, which explored the feasibility of building a weapon that could penetrate deeply buried structures.

Everett has had a seat on Veterans' Affairs since he arrived in Washington in 1993. From 1997 through 2000, he chaired the panel's Oversight and Investigations Subcommittee, and he aggressively investigated reported problems within the Department of Veterans Affairs (VA). His probes of favoritism in burial policies, delays in payment of disability claims, complaints about substandard medical care, and the department's problem-riddled computer modernization program put Everett in the news nationally.

Early in the 109th Congress, he introduced legislation to increase military combat death benefits for current servicemen and also retroactively for soldiers who have lost their lives in combat in Afghanistan and Iraq. His bill seeks to raise the military death benefit from $12,000 to $100,000. Our military deserve "the peace of mind that if they should lose their lives in combat their families will receive adequate death benefits," he said.

Everett's seniority and committee assignments have allowed him to serve his region vigorously, most notably in helping to revamp the government's peanut subsidy program and save it from extinction. During the rewrite of the farm bill in 2002, he argued that maintaining government help for peanut growers was vital to national security — a view that played well back home but earned him some tart criticism elsewhere. Despite rising budget deficits in the 108th, he won funds for peanut research and for his district's National Peanut Festival.

Southeastern Alabama is among the nation's leading peanut producers since the boll weevil wiped out most of the cotton crop a century ago. As chairman of the Agriculture Subcommittee on Specialty Crops, Everett led the effort that ended the Depression-era peanut program, which had kept prices high by effectively limiting who may grow peanuts to those who held a government quota. Instead, peanuts were placed under the same system that is used for other major crops such as corn and grains.

A solid conservative vote on social issues, Everett cosponsored a measure in the 108th that would have allowed Congress, by a two-thirds vote, to override the Supreme Court if the justices ruled that a particular law passed by Congress was unconstitutional.

In a rare departure from his customary focus on military and agriculture issues, Everett in 2004 proposed requiring public companies to give shareholders two months' notice before granting large raises for top executives.

Everett's parents died when he was a youth in Midland City, just north of Dothan, and he was largely responsible for his younger siblings when he returned from a four-year hitch in the Air Force. He became a wealthy man when he sold most of his small weekly and daily newspapers in the late 1980s. He also was a homebuilder for a while and served as chairman of the board of a savings and loan in his birthplace of Dothan.

He was virtually unknown in political circles in 1992 when Republican Bill Dickinson decided to retire after 14 terms. An insurgent within his own party, Everett claimed the GOP nomination by defeating a state senator who was the choice of the party establishment.

In the fall campaign against state Treasurer George C. Wallace Jr., son of the former governor, Everett proved to have a winning combination of message and means. He spent hundreds of thousands of dollars of his own money blanketing the district in billboards and radio and TV ads blaring: "Send a message, not a politician."

Everett won with a bare plurality of 49 percent of the vote that year, but has had no trouble winning re-election since. His victories in both 2002 and 2004 were with more than two-thirds of the vote.

KEY VOTES

2004

No	Extend federal unemployment benefits by 13 weeks
Yes	Pass $283.2 billion, six-year federal highway and mass transit bill
Yes	Approve $146 billion multi-year extension of previously enacted middle-class tax breaks
Yes	Amend the Constitution to prohibit same-sex marriage
Yes	Cut corporate taxes $137 billion over 10 years
No	Reorganize U.S. intelligence agencies as proposed by Sept. 11 commission

2003

Yes	Cut taxes by $330 billion through fiscal 2013
No	Block Bush rule scaling back overtime pay for some white-collar federal workers
Yes	Do not allow use of search warrants without first notifying subjects
Yes	Allow importation of prescription drugs
Yes	Create private school voucher program in Washington, D.C.
Yes	Ban "partial birth" abortion except to save a woman's life
No	Split $18.6 billion in Iraq aid into half-grant, half-loan
Yes	Overhaul Medicare and create prescription drug benefit

CQ VOTE STUDIES

	PARTY UNITY		PRESIDENTIAL SUPPORT	
	Support	Oppose	Support	Oppose
2004	93%	7%	76%	24%
2003	97%	3%	89%	11%
2002	99%	1%	85%	15%
2001	97%	3%	93%	7%
2000	97%	3%	14%	86%

INTEREST GROUPS

	AFL-CIO	ADA	CCUS	ACU
2004	13%	0%	100%	92%
2003	13%	10%	90%	84%
2002	0%	0%	84%	100%
2001	8%	5%	87%	100%
2000	0%	0%	78%	90%

ALABAMA 2
Southeast — part of Montgomery, Dothan

Besides Dothan and part of the state capital, Montgomery, the 2nd consists of scattered small towns. The district is probably best known for its peanut farms, but poultry, cotton and tree farming also are important. The local economy has suffered in recent years from hurricanes, floods and droughts. Farther south, around Dothan, technology and auto parts plants have replaced textile mills that moved overseas.

Defense and state government provide steady employment. Maxwell Air Force Base and its Gunter Annex are responsible for most of the Air Force's computer systems. A Hyundai plant scheduled to open in 2005 in the neighboring 3rd District is expected to employ about 2,000 people.

Tourism also contributes to the economy, particularly in Montgomery, though many historic sites of the Civil Rights movement are in the 3rd. The Robert Trent Jones Golf Trail, large antebellum homes in Eufaula and fishing at Lake Eufaula attract visitors to the area.

Redistricting following the 2000 census shuffled the population of

Montgomery: The 2nd now shares the city with the 3rd, and the 7th was completely removed from the city. A large military retiree population underscores a conservative constituency that usually votes Republican. On the local level, the 2nd has been known to send Democrats to the state legislature.

MAJOR INDUSTRY
Agriculture, defense, manufacturing

MILITARY BASES
Fort Rucker (Army), 5,607 military, 7,367 civilian (2003); Maxwell Air Force Base, 4,018 military, 3,652 civilian (2005)

CITIES
Montgomery (pt.), 127,986; Dothan, 57,737; Prattville, 24,303; Enterprise, 21,178; Ozark, 15,119; Troy, 13,935; Eufaula, 13,908

NOTABLE
Dothan hosts a national peanut festival annually; The Hank Williams Sr. museum is in Georgiana; The Boll Weevil Monument in Enterprise is a tribute to the insect, whose destruction of the cotton crop persuaded farmers to switch to peanuts.

Rep. Mike D. Rogers (R)

Elected 2002; 2nd term

CAPITOL OFFICE
225-3261
www.house.gov/mike-rogers
514 Cannon 20515-0103; fax 226-8485

COMMITTEES
Agriculture
Armed Services
Homeland Security
(Management, Integration & Oversight -
chairman)

HOMETOWN
Anniston

BORN
July 16, 1958, Hammond, Ind.

RELIGION
Baptist

FAMILY
Wife, Donna Elizabeth "Beth" Rogers; three
children

EDUCATION
Jacksonville State U., B.A. 1981 (political science
& psychology), M.P.A. 1985; Birmingham School of
Law, J.D. 1991

CAREER
Lawyer; laid-off worker assistance program
director; psychiatric counselor

POLITICAL HIGHLIGHTS
Calhoun County Commission, 1987-91; candidate
for Ala. House, 1990; Ala. House, 1995-2002
(minority leader, 1998-2000)

ELECTION RESULTS

2004 GENERAL

Mike D. Rogers (R)	150,411	61.2%
Bill Fuller (D)	95,240	38.8%

2004 PRIMARY

Mike D. Rogers (R)	unopposed

2002 GENERAL

Mike D. Rogers (R)	91,169	50.3%
Joe Turnham (D)	87,351	48.2%
George Crispin (LIBERT)	2,565	1.4%

With ambitions of getting into the leadership one day, Rogers is a reliable vote for the Bush White House and a dutiful foot soldier for GOP Speaker J. Dennis Hastert. He strays only on a few issues important to his rural east Alabama district, which has struggled economically. The son of a textile worker and a defender of that diminished industry in his state, he opposes free trade with China. Rogers also departs from President Bush on one of Bush's premier second-term agenda items: the creation of personal accounts within Social Security, which Rogers opposes.

Rogers' loyalty to his party comes at some personal peril. The district, though culturally conservative, has a significant number of Democratic voters. That makes Rogers a ready target at election time. Though Democrats failed to unseat him during his first re-election bid in 2004, they continue to try to portray him as a yes-man for Majority Leader Tom DeLay. When Rogers voted in favor of changing a party rule to allow DeLay to keep his job even if he were indicted as part of a campaign finance scandal unfolding in Texas, Democrats singled out Rogers for criticism along with a handful of other Republicans from competitive districts. Rogers called the probe a political vendetta by the attorney general in Texas, DeLay's home state.

Rogers voted with his party 96 percent of the time in the 108th Congress on crucial votes. And despite making him a political target, that kind of dependability has its rewards.

He was one of the few freshmen who succeeded in getting a bill through the House, thanks in no small part to GOP leaders making room for it on the legislative calendar in early 2004. His bill, popular in his military-heavy district, withholds federal funds from colleges and universities that fail to give ROTC recruiters the same access to students as civilian employers. It targets schools that Rogers said discriminate against the military, such as the University of California at Los Angeles. Gay rights supporters said the legislation promotes intolerance on campuses by advancing the "don't ask, don't tell" policy toward homosexuals.

Rogers' primary focus is defense and the work he does on the Armed Services Committee. His district is home to many military families, including a large share with sons and daughters serving in Iraq. It includes the shuttered Fort McClellan, which survived several rounds of review before being closed in 1999 and is now the target of redevelopment efforts. The Anniston Army Depot employs several hundred of his constituents, and Rogers has tried to inoculate Anniston against the threat of closure. He helped secure $24 million for building Army ground combat vehicles there. And he worked to get $55 million in homeland security funds for domestic security training at the old McClellan base, which will increase its training of law enforcement personnel to 50,000 a year, from 10,000 a year.

A fiscal conservative who typically votes for any type of tax cut, Rogers' major departures from the party line are on Social Security and trade. Allowing some Social Security funds to be invested privately could jeopardize the overall stability of the fund, he says. On trade, he says China has violated trade rules and he wants tariffs against Chinese-made clothing. He opposed the Morocco Free Trade Agreement in 2004, saying the country has become a conduit for the many Chinese manufacturers there.

Rogers is a fervent social conservative and the sponsor of an amendment to the Constitution allowing prayer in public schools, which he calls "restoring religious freedom." He opposes abortion except in cases of rape, incest and a threat to the life of the woman and also opposes human cloning. He is outspoken in the movement for more restrictions on content in broadcast programming, cosponsoring a bill in the 108th Congress hiking penalties for violations of federal standards of decency.

The one bump for him his first term came on a local issue that aroused passions in the district. Rogers supported moving ahead with the burning of chemical agents and munitions at a new federal incinerator at the Anniston Depot, though school officials said they had not adequately prepared their buildings for an accidental release of air toxins. GOP Sen. Richard C. Shelby of Alabama came out in favor of a delay. Ultimately, all sides agreed to a timetable to begin destroying more than 2,000 tons of chemicals being stored in aging, leaky igloos.

Rogers nonetheless withstood the first big test of incumbency by handily winning re-election in 2004, dramatically improving on the margin he had gotten when he won the seat two years earlier. Democrats had an impressive candidate in Bill Fuller, a veteran state legislator who chaired the Alabama House Ways and Means Committee. The district is a third African-American as a result of Democrat-engineered remapping after the 2000 census, and two of the state's leading black political groups endorsed Fuller.

But Rogers raised more than $2 million, with the help of DeLay and other leaders, who put him on their list of 10 most vulnerable members. He beat Fuller, capturing 61 percent of the vote. Two years earlier, Rogers also got a big helping hand from top Republicans, including Bush who stumped for him in Auburn. His competition then was Joe Turnham, a businessman aided by national party organizations that saw an opportunity to claim a seat left open when Republican Bob Riley ran successfully for governor. Rogers won by a slim 2 percentage points.

Rogers traces his ancestry back five generations in east Alabama, where his mother worked in a textile factory for 33 years. After getting a degree from Birmingham School of Law, he returned to Anniston, population 2,400, to start his own law practice. At age 28, he was the first Republican elected to the Calhoun County Commission, long dominated by conservative Democrats. He was elected to the Alabama House in 1994, where he focused on health care and wrote a bill forcing every insurance plan to cover payments to doctors not in their networks. He eventually became House minority leader.

In Congress, Rogers often has to deal with the confusion caused by the presence of another House lawmaker named Mike Rogers. That Rogers is a Michigan Republican.

KEY VOTES

2004

No	Extend federal unemployment benefits by 13 weeks
Yes	Pass $283.2 billion, six-year federal highway and mass transit bill
Yes	Approve $146 billion multi-year extension of previously enacted middle-class tax breaks
Yes	Amend the Constitution to prohibit same-sex marriage
Yes	Cut corporate taxes $137 billion over 10 years
Yes	Reorganize U.S. intelligence agencies as proposed by Sept. 11 commission

2003

Yes	Cut taxes by $330 billion through fiscal 2013
No	Block Bush rule scaling back overtime pay for some white-collar federal workers
Yes	Do not allow use of search warrants without first notifying subjects
No	Allow importation of prescription drugs
?	Create private school voucher program in Washington, D.C.
Yes	Ban "partial birth" abortion except to save a woman's life
No	Split $18.6 billion in Iraq aid into half-grant, half-loan
Yes	Overhaul Medicare and create prescription drug benefit

CQ VOTE STUDIES

	PARTY UNITY		PRESIDENTIAL SUPPORT	
	Support	Oppose	Support	Oppose
2004	95%	5%	76%	24%
2003	97%	3%	94%	6%

INTEREST GROUPS

	AFL-CIO	ADA	CCUS	ACU
2004	13%	10%	100%	88%
2003	7%	5%	97%	88%

ALABAMA 3

East — part of Montgomery, Auburn, Anniston

With agriculture, industry, universities and part of the capital city of Montgomery, the 3rd can claim to be a microcosm of the state. Revised during redistricting following the 2000 census to decrease its Republican strength, the 3rd has many longtime socially conservative Democrats who now favor GOP presidential candidates, as well as blacks, who make up one-third of the population, and small pockets of university liberals who support Democrats on all levels.

Anniston, the Calhoun County seat, relies heavily on the federal government. The Army left Fort McClellan in 1999, but the Justice Department turned the base into a training facility for first responders to chemical, biological and nuclear terrorist attacks. There is a Honda plant in Lincoln, and Hyundai's first U.S. facility was scheduled to open in 2005 south of Montgomery.

Auburn University is one of the state's largest employers and a leading agricultural research center. A chemical weapons incinerator at the Anniston Army Depot has raised environmental concerns, but has so far operated without incident.

Redistricting removed all or part of four counties on the old 3rd's western edge, while adding many Montgomery attractions with its portion of the city, including the state Capitol, the first White House of the Confederacy and the Dexter Avenue Baptist Church, where the 1955 bus boycott was launched.

MAJOR INDUSTRY
Higher education, agriculture, textiles

MILITARY BASES
Anniston Army Depot, 5 military, 5,800 civilian (2005)

CITIES
Montgomery (pt.), 73,582; Auburn, 42,987; Phenix City, 28,265; Anniston, 24,276; Opelika, 23,498

NOTABLE
Tuskegee University, founded in 1881 through the efforts of Booker T. Washington, was one of the nation's first black colleges and was the first historically black college to be recognized as a National Historic Landmark; Talladega Superspeedway and the International Motorsports Hall of Fame and Museum are north of Talladega.

Rep. Robert B. Aderholt (R)

Elected 1996; 5th term

CAPITOL OFFICE
225-4876
aderholt.house.gov
1433 Longworth 20515-0104; fax 225-5587

COMMITTEES
Appropriations

HOMETOWN
Haleyville

BORN
July 22, 1965, Haleyville, Ala.

RELIGION
Congregationalist Baptist

FAMILY
Wife, Caroline Aderholt; two children

EDUCATION
Birmingham Southern U., B.A. 1987 (history &
political science); Samford U., J.D. 1990

CAREER
Lawyer; gubernatorial aide

POLITICAL HIGHLIGHTS
Republican nominee for Ala. House, 1990;
Haleyville municipal judge, 1992-96

ELECTION RESULTS

2004 GENERAL

Robert B. Aderholt (R)	191,110	74.7%
Carl Cole (D)	64,278	25.1%

2004 PRIMARY

Robert B. Aderholt (R)	unopposed

2002 GENERAL

Robert B. Aderholt (R)	139,705	86.7%
Tony H. McLendon (LIBERT)	20,858	13.0%

PREVIOUS WINNING PERCENTAGES
2000 (61%); 1998 (56%); 1996 (50%)

The son of a judge who also was a Baptist pastor, Aderholt's own judicious and strait-laced demeanor was nurtured not only in his home but also all around it. Northern Alabama has long been one of the most religiously conservative areas of the nation.

Aderholt (ADD-er-holt) is best known for his efforts to bring religious values into the public sphere. His vigorous advocacy of traditional values in a congenial and soft-spoken manner is the hallmark of his legislative career. His most publicized cause in Washington has been to permit public displays of the Ten Commandments, a mission he embraced soon after he arrived in 1997, when a federal judge, citing the First Amendment, ordered a judge in Aderholt's district to remove a copy of the commandments from his courtroom wall.

In 2003 when another federal judge ordered the removal of a stone display of the Ten Commandments from Montgomery's state judicial complex, Aderholt said it was a "scene one would expect to see in the former Soviet Union, not the United States of America."

Aderholt's promotion of the Ten Commandments is his attempt to counter what he sees as the unnecessary exclusion of religion from public life. The House in 1997 adopted his resolution endorsing the public display of the commandments. Aderholt, however, has since changed his tack by seeking legislation leaving it up to each state to decide whether to allow displays of the commandments in public offices and courtrooms. Aderholt argues that the First and Tenth Amendments have been misinterpreted over the past 40 years by activist judges infringing upon religious rights by denying the freedom of expression of faith. "Discrimination against religion under the guise of separation of church and state needs to end," he says.

Aderholt is also an unstinting conservative on other social policy issues. He favors constitutional amendments to outlaw all abortions except to save the life of the woman, and to allow prayer on public property and in public schools. He also opposes human cloning and embryonic stem cell research.

As a member of the U.S. Helsinki Commission monitoring human rights in Europe and the former Soviet Union, Aderholt has extended his campaign for freedom of religious expression overseas, particularly in Georgia and Turkmenistan.

Ever since GOP leaders awarded him a prized appointment to the Appropriations Committee in 1997, Aderholt has quietly steered federal dollars toward northern Alabama. He assiduously attends to the economic needs of his constituents, who often are as economically strapped as they are socially conservative.

He has waged more combative — though unsuccessful — efforts to protect the regionally important steel and textile industries that have been clobbered by foreign competition. After a Gulf States Steel plant in Gadsden closed in 2000, eliminating 1,700 jobs, Aderholt backed legislation to provide loan guarantees for steel companies hurt by foreign imports, part of an effort to attract a buyer to reopen the plant.

The next year, when VF Corp., manufacturer of Lee and Wrangler jeans, closed four factories in and around the 4th District, Aderholt voted against granting the president fast-track authority to negotiate trade deals. Seven months later, he voted for the final version of the bill, reversing course after

House leaders promised to fight against lifting tariffs on socks made in the Caribbean — an issue of parochial importance because of the important role that area textile mills play in the local economy.

In an effort to show the damage that the import of foreign socks was doing to his district's economy, Aderholt requested in 2004 that appropriators include in the spending bill for the Commerce Department a requirement that the Census Bureau report on national sock production. Textile companies want the data so they can prove their contention that cheap Chinese imports are hurting the U.S. sock business.

Aderholt wants to see the government tax and spend less, but he still works to get a share of federal money for his district. He has been particularly energetic in funding the continued construction of an interstate-grade highway from Birmingham to Memphis.

Aderholt in 2003 sought a provision in NASA's spending bill to provide $1 million for an environmental research site at the Little River Canyon Field School in Fort Payne. This home-state provision, and others like it, drew criticism from other lawmakers and taxpayer groups. They said the number of earmarks in the NASA spending bill for local projects would divert valuable resources from the space agency at a time when it needed to invest in safety improvements for the manned space program.

Aderholt grew up with politics. When he was 5, he wrote a campaign letter touting his father, a judge, in a local election, and he recalls meeting Bob Dole when he was about 11. A month after his law school graduation, Aderholt was nominated for a state House seat, but he lost the general election. Appointed to a municipal court judgeship in 1992, he went to work for Republican Gov. Fob James Jr. in 1995.

When Rep. Tom Bevill retired in 1996 after 15 terms, Aderholt says that he was encouraged to try for the seat because he felt it shared demographic and political characteristics with the neighboring 1st District of Mississippi, a longtime Democratic bastion that Roger Wicker had won for the Republican Party two years before. In the GOP primary, Aderholt took 49 percent against four rivals and got the nomination when the second-place finisher declined to demand a runoff.

Democrats put up a strong candidate in former state Sen. Robert T. "Bob" Wilson Jr., who was nearly as conservative as Aderholt on social issues. Republican presidential candidate Bob Dole carried the 4th District by 5 percentage points over Bill Clinton that year, while Aderholt prevailed by 2 points. In subsequent elections, Aderholt has strengthened his hold on the district, winning with 75 percent of the vote in 2004.

KEY VOTES

2004
No Extend federal unemployment benefits by 13 weeks
Yes Pass $283.2 billion, six-year federal highway and mass transit bill
Yes Approve $146 billion multi-year extension of previously enacted middle-class tax breaks
Yes Amend the Constitution to prohibit same-sex marriage
Yes Cut corporate taxes $137 billion over 10 years
No Reorganize U.S. intelligence agencies as proposed by Sept. 11 commission

2003
Yes Cut taxes by $330 billion through fiscal 2013
No Block Bush rule scaling back overtime pay for some white-collar federal workers
No Do not allow use of search warrants without first notifying subjects
Yes Allow importation of prescription drugs
Yes Create private school voucher program in Washington, D.C.
Yes Ban "partial birth" abortion except to save a woman's life
No Split $18.6 billion in Iraq aid into half-grant, half-loan
Yes Overhaul Medicare and create prescription drug benefit

CQ VOTE STUDIES

	PARTY UNITY		PRESIDENTIAL SUPPORT	
	Support	Oppose	Support	Oppose
2004	93%	7%	85%	15%
2003	96%	4%	92%	8%
2002	96%	4%	82%	18%
2001	96%	4%	85%	15%
2000	91%	9%	20%	80%

INTEREST GROUPS

	AFL-CIO	ADA	CCUS	ACU
2004	7%	0%	100%	92%
2003	20%	10%	89%	83%
2002	11%	0%	90%	92%
2001	17%	10%	87%	91%
2000	30%	15%	71%	88%

ALABAMA 4
North central — Gadsden, part of Decatur

Encompassing mountains, foothills, flatlands and large waterways, the 4th stretches the width of the state, bordering Georgia and Mississippi. A small black population and the absence of a major city distinguish it from the rest of Alabama.

One of the state's poorest districts, the 4th has suffered through textile companies moving overseas and a decline in coal mining, with some relief from an underlying agricultural economy. Rubber and steel plants in Gadsden, the district's only sizable city, have closed or downsized as a result of strikes and foreign competition.

Efforts by local officials to attract new, moderate-size businesses may be helped by "Corridor X," a half-finished interstate that will connect Birmingham to Memphis, Tenn. Many residents work in surrounding metropolitan areas — such as Huntsville in the 5th, and Birmingham, which is split between the 6th and 7th districts. Mobile home manufacturing plants fuel Marshall County's economy. Cullman County's agricultural industry includes everything from cotton and soybeans to chickens and cattle. DeKalb County, a mountainous region in the northeastern part of the state, includes some of the region's natural sights and tourist destinations.

The rural 4th's population is socially conservative, especially on gun control and religious issues. The district originally adhered to Democratic populism, but has voted Republican on recent presidential ballots. In 1996, voters sent a Republican to Congress for just the second time since Reconstruction, and have re-elected him since.

MAJOR INDUSTRY
Agriculture, manufacturing, mining

CITIES
Gadsden, 38,978; Albertville, 17,247; Jasper, 14,052; Cullman, 13,995

NOTABLE
Fort Payne and surrounding DeKalb County, billed as the Sock Capital of the World, have more than 150 mills that employ more than 6,000 workers; Winston County briefly became the "free state of Winston" when Alabama seceded from the union; The world's longest yard sale, which starts in Gadsden and ends 450 miles later in Covington, Ky., attracts 400,000 bargain shoppers for one weekend in August; Albertville calls itself the Fire Hydrant Capital of the World.

Rep. Robert E. 'Bud' Cramer (D)

Elected 1990; 8th term

CAPITOL OFFICE
225-4801
budmail@mail.house.gov
cramer.house.gov
2368 Rayburn 20515-0105; fax 225-4392

COMMITTEES
Appropriations
Select Intelligence

HOMETOWN
Huntsville

BORN
Aug. 22, 1947, Huntsville, Ala.

RELIGION
Methodist

FAMILY
Widowed; one child

EDUCATION
U. of Alabama, B.A. 1969 (English), J.D. 1972

MILITARY SERVICE
Army, 1972; Army Reserve, 1976-78

CAREER
Lawyer

POLITICAL HIGHLIGHTS
Madison County district attorney, 1981-91

ELECTION RESULTS

2004 GENERAL

Robert E. "Bud" Cramer (D)	200,999	73.0%
Gerald "Gerry" Wallace (R)	74,145	26.9%

2004 PRIMARY

Robert E. "Bud" Cramer (D)	37,573	89.5%
Michael Williams (D)	4,393	10.5%

2002 GENERAL

Robert E. "Bud" Cramer (D)	143,029	73.3%
Stephen P. Engel (R)	48,226	24.7%
Alan F. Barksdale (LIBERT)	3,772	1.9%

PREVIOUS WINNING PERCENTAGES
2000 (89%); 1998 (70%); 1996 (56%); 1994 (50%);
1992 (66%); 1990 (67%)

Cramer, whose official biography on his House Web site makes no mention of his party, voted less often with the Democrats in the 108th Congress than any other Democrat. On votes that pit one party against the other, Cramer sided with Republicans 39 percent of the time.

Cramer's voting record since 1995 has consistently marked him as one of the most conservative House Democrats: He has sided with his party on key votes only slightly more than half the time. But his support of conservative causes is a necessity for political survival in the 5th District; Jimmy Carter was the last Democratic presidential candidate to carry Alabama's northernmost district.

After a surge of Republican voting nearly ousted him in 1994, Cramer — never a liberal — reacted by further distancing himself from Democratic Party stances, and he redoubled his work on district needs. But this was not a new role for him. Since his first term, Cramer has taken the socially as well as fiscally conservative stand on many issues, opposing gun control proposals, for instance, and supporting a constitutional amendment to mandate federal balanced budgets.

In the 108th Congress, Cramer was one of just seven House Democrats who voted for the 2003 tax cut bill, and one of only 16 to vote for a GOP bill to cap malpractice awards. He was the chief Democratic cosponsor of legislation to permanently repeal the estate tax. He also broke party lines to support measures to outlaw gay marriage, renew the welfare law and limit class action lawsuits.

Nevertheless, his party loyalty in the 108th was the highest it had been since the Democratic-controlled 103rd Congress (1993-94). Then, he backed his party's leadership and President Clinton more than three-fourths of the time.

An approachable and pragmatic man, Cramer is a founding member of the "Blue Dogs," the coalition of conservative House Democrats, and he was co-chairman of its political action committee during the 2002 election cycle. The Blue Dogs have been more concerned about erasing budget deficits than either their more liberal Democratic colleagues or the GOP majority on Capitol Hill; they annually offer an alternative budget plan to that end. In the 108th, Cramer voted for the Blue Dog budget and against the GOP-drafted measure.

Cramer joined with Democrats in the 108th on a bill to permit reimportation of prescription drugs, and he voted with his party to oppose vouchers for District of Columbia schools and to fight a GOP bill that aimed to privatize many federal jobs.

Nevertheless, Cramer is often the target of entreaties from Republicans to switch parties. Early in 2002, shortly after it was reported that the GOP was dangling an assignment to the Intelligence Committee as an inducement, Democrats arranged for Cramer to get a seat on the panel.

Economic development is one of Cramer's priorities. He says he likes to "knock on the doors of businesses" to tout North Alabama as an attractive place to do business. In 2004, Cramer announced that Toyota would undertake a major expansion of its engine manufacturing plant in north Huntsville — a plant that he was instrumental in attracting to the area back in 2001. Also in 2004, Cramer was involved in discussions with U.S. Gypsum Co. that led to an expansion of its plant in Bridgeport. In the 1990s, he helped persuade McDonnell-Douglas (since merged with Boeing Corp.) to build a $450 million rocket booster plant in Decatur.

Cramer in 2001 got the Commerce Department to reverse its plans to close a weather station in his tornado-prone district, arguing that doing so would put thousands of lives at risk because the nearest radar would be too far away to provide timely warnings. A state-of-the-art station was opened in Huntsville in 2003, along with a science research complex. In 2004, Cramer's father (also nicknamed Bud), who worked at the old Huntsville weather facility in the 1940s, looked on proudly as the complex was named in honor of his son.

Cramer serves on the Appropriations subcommittees that fund the departments of Housing and Veterans Affairs and many independent agencies, as well as NASA. His fiscal conservatism is tempered by his support for NASA and the Pentagon, both of which have a major presence in the 5th District. Huntsville is home to NASA's Marshall Space Flight Center and the Army's Redstone Arsenal.

Although conservative on social issues, Cramer supports abortion rights in general. As his late wife battled cancer (she died in 1987), she needed an abortion to prolong her life. He does, however, favor a ban on a procedure its opponents call "partial birth" abortion.

For a decade before coming to Congress, Cramer was the district attorney in Huntsville, where he founded the Children's Advocacy Center to shelter and counsel abused children. (In Congress, he was responsible for legislation in 1992 to provide federal assistance to a growing national network of centers modeled on the Huntsville program.) Cramer has been able to ensure funding for the centers from his seat on the Appropriations Committee.

His work on behalf of children, coupled with programs his office instituted to prosecute bad-check cases and spousal abuse, earned Cramer a reputation as a champion of the victim; he was honored by President Reagan in a 1987 White House ceremony.

When Democrat Ronnie G. Flippo left the district open in 1990 to run for governor, Cramer won his seat with two-thirds of the vote. But in the GOP landslide four years later — which swept out a cadre of other white Southern Democrats in the House — Cramer won by just 1,770 votes over well-funded and well-connected Wayne Parker, son-in-law of Texas GOP Rep. Bill Archer, later the Ways and Means Committee chairman.

Since then, Cramer has won by comfortable margins. In a district minimally changed by redistricting before the 2002 election, he took 73 percent of the vote in both 2002 and 2004.

KEY VOTES

2004

Yes Extend federal unemployment benefits by 13 weeks

Yes Pass $283.2 billion, six-year federal highway and mass transit bill

Yes Approve $146 billion multi-year extension of previously enacted middle-class tax breaks

Yes Amend the Constitution to prohibit same-sex marriage

Yes Cut corporate taxes $137 billion over 10 years

Yes Reorganize U.S. intelligence agencies as proposed by Sept. 11 commission

2003

Yes Cut taxes by $330 billion through fiscal 2013

? Block Bush rule scaling back overtime pay for some white-collar federal workers

Yes Do not allow use of search warrants without first notifying subjects

Yes Allow importation of prescription drugs

No Create private school voucher program in Washington, D.C.

Yes Ban "partial birth" abortion except to save a woman's life

No Split $18.6 billion in Iraq aid into half-grant, half-loan

Yes Overhaul Medicare and create prescription drug benefit

CQ VOTE STUDIES

	PARTY UNITY		PRESIDENTIAL SUPPORT	
	Support	Oppose	Support	Oppose
2004	61%	39%	64%	36%
2003	62%	38%	73%	27%
2002	61%	39%	62%	38%
2001	50%	50%	67%	33%
2000	66%	34%	49%	51%

INTEREST GROUPS

	AFL-CIO	ADA	CCUS	ACU
2004	60%	75%	86%	50%
2003	58%	45%	89%	52%
2002	44%	45%	80%	56%
2001	50%	45%	82%	65%
2000	40%	35%	80%	40%

ALABAMA 5
North — Huntsville

A large section of the Tennessee River winds through the 5th, a strip of land across the northern tier of Alabama that borders Georgia, Mississippi and Tennessee.

Reliant on agriculture before World War II, the district now owes its economic well-being to the federal government. Huntsville is best known for hosting the NASA Marshall Space Flight Center, but defense has contributed more to its economy.

Redstone Arsenal benefited from base closures in the 1990s, incorporating Army aviation duties into its missile command center and increasing its personnel. Redstone has attracted several high-tech plants, and Cummings Research Park in Huntsville, with more than 200 tenants and a workforce of 24,000, boasts that it is the second-largest research park in the United States.

Tennessee Valley Authority facilities line the river's shores throughout the 5th. Boeing has a satellite rocket booster plant in Decatur, which aids the

local economy, but the company laid off 100 workers in January 2005 due to an ethics suspension from the Air Force. The rocket program now employs about 550 workers. Toyota's first V-8 engine plant outside of Japan began operating in 2003 and has since expanded.

Voters in the 5th have never sent a Republican to Congress, but GOP presidential candidates have enjoyed an edge recently. George W. Bush won 54 percent of the vote here in 2000 and then 60 percent in 2004. The district generally claims a socially conservative constituency.

MAJOR INDUSTRY
Defense, government, technology

MILITARY BASES
Redstone Arsenal (Army), 2,024 military, 14,023 civilian (2003)

CITIES
Huntsville, 158,216; Decatur (pt.), 44,655; Florence, 36,264; Madison, 29,329; Athens, 18,967

NOTABLE
"Muscle Shoals Sound" originated at Fame Recording Studios, where Aretha Franklin, Otis Redding and Wilson Pickett recorded hit songs; Helen Keller was born in Tuscumbia.

Rep. Spencer Bachus (R)

Elected 1992; 7th term

CAPITOL OFFICE
225-4921
bachus.house.gov
442 Cannon 20515-0106; fax 225-2082

COMMITTEES
Financial Services
(Financial Institutions & Consumer Credit - chairman)
Judiciary
Transportation & Infrastructure

HOMETOWN
Vestavia Hills

BORN
Dec. 28, 1947, Birmingham, Ala.

RELIGION
Baptist

FAMILY
Wife, Linda Bachus; five children

EDUCATION
Auburn U., B.A. 1969; U. of Alabama, J.D. 1972

MILITARY SERVICE
Ala. National Guard, 1969-71

CAREER
Lawyer; sawmill owner

POLITICAL HIGHLIGHTS
Ala. Senate, 1983; Ala. House, 1983-87; Ala. Board of Education, 1987-91; candidate for Ala. attorney general, 1990; Ala. Republican Party chairman, 1991-92

ELECTION RESULTS

2004 GENERAL

Spencer Bachus (R)	264,819	98.8%
write-ins	3,224	1.2%

2004 PRIMARY

Spencer Bachus (R)	45,448	86.7%
Phillip Jauregui (R)	7,000	13.4%

2002 GENERAL

Spencer Bachus (R)	178,171	89.8%
J. Holden McAllister (LIBERT)	19,639	9.9%

PREVIOUS WINNING PERCENTAGES
2000 (88%); 1998 (72%); 1996 (71%); 1994 (79%); 1992 (52%)

A steadfast conservative with strong religious views, Bachus casts a dependable Republican vote on issues such as tax cuts, gay marriage and abortion. "The ACLU voted me as the worst Alabama congressman four years in a row," Bachus (BACK-us) told The Birmingham News in 2004. "I'm proud of it."

A devout Baptist, Bachus' religious beliefs have led to his active support of Third World debt relief. He maintains that Americans have a moral obligation to help the less fortunate in poor countries. His interest in aiding the world's poorest nations was sparked by a meeting he attended at a Birmingham church where he heard a presentation on the Bread for the World relief organization. "We have so much and these countries have so little," he told The Washington Post. "We're all members of the human race, you know."

In the 107th and 108th Congresses, Bachus sought to impose economic sanctions on Sudan in hopes of halting what he characterized as genocide against Christians in southern Sudan. Renewing his effort to cut off the Sudanese government from oil revenues, he sponsored legislation in 2004 to prevent foreign oil companies from raising capital through American financial markets if they continue to do business in Sudan. "This doesn't require one soldier to be sent into Sudan," Bachus told The Birmingham News. "It simply makes it harder for them to finance the genocide." The Bush administration has said it prefers to negotiate with oil companies and opposes the legislation.

Now in his seventh term, Bachus is moving up the House ranks. In the 109th Congress, he was selected for a seat on the GOP Steering Committee, which makes committee assignments.

As chairman of the Financial Services Subcommittee on Financial Institutions and Consumer Credit, Bachus sponsored a measure, which became law in 2003, to block states from imposing tougher financial privacy rules than those required by the federal government. The bill also renewed expiring provisions intended to establish a single federal standard on the sharing of credit-related information. Bachus worked hard to develop strong bipartisan support for the measure, and it passed the House by a 392-30 vote. Democrats were coaxed into supporting the bill after provisions were added to give consumers more tools to combat identity theft and access to free information about their credit reports.

Bachus wrote legislation in 2003 to substantially increase federal deposit insurance coverage levels. He acknowledged that his bill gave the Federal Reserve and the Treasury "a lot of heartburn." The measure was reintroduced in the 108th and approved by the Financial Services Committee.

Also in the 107th, he supported an amendment by liberal Democrat Maxine Waters of California that encouraged banks to offer basic "lifeline" accounts to make banking more accessible to poor people. The House passed the bill overwhelmingly in 2002, but the Senate never took it up. Bachus reintroduced the measure in the 108th.

Bachus, who also sits on the Transportation and Judiciary committees, keeps his constituents happy by paying attention to local needs. He has worked hard to gain a new national veterans center in Birmingham, to set aside 30,000 more acres for a wildlife refuge along a stretch of the Cahaba River, and to provide federal funds for local highway construction. He was able to get $25 million in 2004 appropriations for the Corridor X project — an upgrade of U.S. 78, the highway between Birmingham and Memphis. "This funding will be instrumental in creating thousands of new jobs throughout the entire Birmingham Metro Area," Bachus said when announcing the funding.

He took on another issue important to Alabama in 2004 when he initiated a Judiciary Committee hearing on how the National Collegiate Athletic Association investigates rules violations. The Washington Post reported that Bachus criticized NCAA officials for an enforcement process that is closed to the public, and one in which penalties are determined by a panel that is composed mostly of faculty from NCAA member schools. "Student-athletes are victimized by this system," he said during the hearing. Two Alabama schools — the University of Alabama and Auburn University — had been placed on probation by the NCAA within the past three years. But Bachus told The Washington Post he wanted to discuss the NCAA's process, not the particulars of the Alabama or Auburn cases.

In 2002, he was an early proponent of making permanent the temporary $1.35 trillion package of tax cuts enacted the year before. The tax law contained measures, akin to those proposed by Bachus, to double the adoption tax credit and to eliminate federal taxes on state-sponsored college tuition savings plans. In the 108th Congress, he sponsored a bill to curb Internet gambling and supported a measure targeting online child pornographers.

His conservative views on social policy issues influence his committee work. During a 2004 debate in the Judiciary Committee on a bill to toughen penalties for the promotion of animal fighting, Bachus condemned the committee for having "chosen to protect the rights of a chicken but not those of a child that is three months away from being born."

Bachus, who once owned a sawmill and was a practicing criminal trial lawyer for two decades, began his career in elective office in 1983. He served in the state legislature, on the state board of education and as chairman of the Alabama GOP.

In his first House election bid, Bachus benefited handsomely from the post-1990 census remapping of Alabama's congressional districts, which eviscerated the district held for five terms by Democratic Rep. Ben Erdreich and transformed it into a solidly Republican bastion. Bachus won with 52 percent of the vote in 1992 and has been re-elected with at least 70 percent since.

In redistricting for the 2002 election, Bachus' district became even more securely Republican. He faced no opposition in 2004.

KEY VOTES

2004

No Extend federal unemployment benefits by 13 weeks

Yes Pass $283.2 billion, six-year federal highway and mass transit bill

Yes Approve $146 billion multi-year extension of previously enacted middle-class tax breaks

Yes Amend the Constitution to prohibit same-sex marriage

Yes Cut corporate taxes $137 billion over 10 years

No Reorganize U.S. intelligence agencies as proposed by Sept. 11 commission

2003

Yes Cut taxes by $330 billion through fiscal 2013

No Block Bush rule scaling back overtime pay for some white-collar federal workers

Yes Do not allow use of search warrants without first notifying subjects

No Allow importation of prescription drugs

Yes Create private school voucher program in Washington, D.C.

Yes Ban "partial birth" abortion except to save a woman's life

No Split $18.6 billion in Iraq aid into half-grant, half-loan

Yes Overhaul Medicare and create prescription drug benefit

CQ VOTE STUDIES

	PARTY UNITY		PRESIDENTIAL SUPPORT	
	Support	Oppose	Support	Oppose
2004	95%	5%	88%	12%
2003	96%	4%	98%	2%
2002	98%	2%	89%	11%
2001	96%	4%	97%	3%
2000	89%	11%	24%	76%

INTEREST GROUPS

	AFL-CIO	ADA	CCUS	ACU
2004	13%	5%	100%	96%
2003	13%	10%	96%	88%
2002	11%	0%	100%	100%
2001	8%	0%	95%	96%
2000	10%	5%	85%	88%

ALABAMA 6
Central — suburban Birmingham and Tuscaloosa

Alabama's most prosperous district, the 6th is a combination of the whiter and wealthier portions of Birmingham and Tuscaloosa and their suburbs. Rural life still dots the district, but fields and forests are steadily turning into shopping malls.

Birmingham's success beginning in the 1980s started with a shift from steel to white-collar business. Banks and medical facilities have made the city a hub for the deep South. Though most of Birmingham's population is in the neighboring 7th, commuters from suburbs in the 6th enjoy the bulk of the city's wealth. Jefferson County's well-to-do, almost exclusively white bedroom communities such as Homewood, Mountain Brook and Hoover are home to people who work in Birmingham's business district.

The 6th takes in a small portion of Tuscaloosa, a medium-size city that is starting to feel the effects of Birmingham's expansion. A nearby Mercedes-Benz plant (in the 7th District) joins the city's chemical and rubber manufacturers and adds to the district's employment base. But the area's signature undoubtedly is University of Alabama football, which attracts fanatics statewide to watch the "Crimson Tide." The campus falls just outside of the 6th's borders.

The Republican 6th moved further into the GOP column after redistricting following the 2000 census. GOP-leaning areas in Bibb, Chilton, Coosa and St. Clair counties were added from the 3rd District, where Democrats hoped to gain an advantage. More Birmingham- and Tuscaloosa-area voters were shifted from the 6th into the overwhelmingly Democratic, black-majority 7th. The contrast between the 6th and 7th can lead to conflict, particularly when funds for infrastructure are at stake. Universities in Birmingham and Tuscaloosa account for the 6th's few Democratic votes.

MAJOR INDUSTRY
Banking, manufacturing, higher education

CITIES
Hoover, 62,742; Birmingham (pt.), 26,723; Vestavia Hills, 24,476; Alabaster, 22,619; Mountain Brook, 20,604

NOTABLE
A 55-foot cast-iron statue in Birmingham of Vulcan, the Roman god of fire and metalworking, is one of the world's largest iron figures.

Rep. Artur Davis (D)

Elected 2002; 2nd term

Davis is a new style of African-American leader who believes in an activist federal government yet is generally more conservative on cultural issues than his civil rights-era predecessors. He is a product of his times: the 30-something Alabamian was not yet born when John F. Kennedy was president; Ronald Reagan was setting the political agenda during Davis' formative years.

Arriving in Congress in 2003, Davis (his first name is pronounced ar-TOUR) joined both the liberal Congressional Black Caucus and the politically moderate New Democrats. He thinks the government should do more to lift people out of poverty — his district is the fifth-poorest in the country — but he supports a constitutional amendment to ban gay marriage. "We lose our ability as Southern Democrats to reach voters because they see us as so out of touch on cultural issues, they tune us out on economic issues," Davis says.

Even though he was only in his first term, Davis chalked up some successes on legislation with a national reach. He also consolidated his power back home, winning over the black political establishment that had backed his competitor in his first House race. After just one year on the job, The Birmingham News called him "a political player to be reckoned with."

In 2004, Davis was a chief sponsor of a measure to help people trying to buy their first homes. Congress approved the provision in the agriculture appropriations bill, reducing the required amount of upfront money from buyers taking part in the government's single-family guaranteed loan program. With the change, borrowers could finance loan fees along with the rest of the loan rather than paying for them at closing time.

Davis also worked with Charles B. Rangel of New York, the top-ranking Democrat on the Ways and Means Committee and the most influential African-American in the House, on expanding the child tax credit for poor families, though it is rare for a freshman to take such a prominent role in tax legislation. While their efforts failed to expand President Bush's $1,000 per child tax credit to all families who pay little or no taxes, they won a modified version of the proposal that made it possible for 6.5 million low-income families to get a refundable credit.

Davis voted against the final version of the president's tax cut bill in 2003, the only member of the Alabama delegation to do so, and was highly critical of the way the benefits were distributed. "This administration has a genuine indifference to people in this country who are struggling to make it," he told The Birmingham News. "It's paying for tax cuts on the backs of the people who can least afford to bear that burden."

Davis sits on the Budget and Financial Services committees. As a junior member of Budget, he engineered a change in the funding formula for black colleges that earned him kudos at home and nationally. Davis discovered that Bush's 2004 budget would have cut funding for 1890 land-grant schools, which are predominately black, while keeping the level the same for 1862 land-grant colleges, which are predominately white. Two of the country's 17 black schools are in Alabama. Casting it as an issue of racial fairness, he won approval of an amendment on the House floor that reversed the proposed cuts for black colleges. Red-faced House majority Republicans called the discrepancy an oversight.

Davis votes most often with House liberals, but they can't always rely on him on hot-button issues. He was one of 63 Democrats in 2003 to vote for

CAPITOL OFFICE
225-2665
www.house.gov/arturdavis
208 Cannon 20515-0107; fax 226-9567

COMMITTEES
Budget
Financial Services

HOMETOWN
Birmingham

BORN
Oct. 9, 1967, Montgomery, Ala.

RELIGION
Lutheran

FAMILY
Single

EDUCATION
Harvard U., A.B. 1990 (government), J.D. 1993

CAREER
Lawyer

POLITICAL HIGHLIGHTS
Assistant U.S. attorney, 1994-98; sought Democratic nomination for U.S. House, 2000

ELECTION RESULTS

2004 GENERAL
Artur Davis (D)	183,408	75.0%
Steve F. Cameron (R)	61,019	24.9%

2004 PRIMARY
Artur Davis (D)	58,193	87.8%
Albert Turner (D)	8,061	12.2%

2002 GENERAL
Artur Davis (D)	153,735	92.4%
Lauren Orth McCay (LIBERT)	12,100	7.3%

a conservative-backed ban on "partial birth" abortion, a controversial procedure for ending pregnancies. And he supported the ban on human cloning, one of only 42 Democrats to do so. Davis also voted for a bill insulating the gun industry from liability when guns are used in crimes.

Davis' personal history is one of the House's remarkable bootstraps stories. He grew up in the hard-pressed west end of Montgomery near downtown. His parents divorced when he was young, and Davis, an only child, was raised by his grandmother and his mother, an elementary school teacher. As a boy, Davis was a voracious reader, loved history and excelled in school. He was admitted to Harvard, where he graduated magna cum laude in 1990, and went on to get his law degree. Davis worked his way through and borrowed money to pay tuition. He's still paying back more than $15,000 in student loans.

After graduation, Davis probably would have been welcomed by a dozen corporate law firms. But by that time, he had already decided on a life in politics. He went home to Montgomery, working as an assistant U.S. attorney from 1994 to 1998 until he launched his first bid for the House in 2000. He lost that race.

But two years later, voters in the 7th District had grown weary of their controversial congressman, Rep. Earl F. Hilliard, who after five terms had accrued little influence in the House and was further weakened by ethics scandals and by his decision to visit terrorist-friendly Libya.

Two locally prominent black political groups — the Alabama Democratic Conference and the Alabama New South Coalition — backed Hilliard anyway and were cool to Davis for taking on an African-American incumbent. But Davis had support from the mayors of Selma and Birmingham; he raised more than $1.5 million, helped in large part by pro-Israel groups who felt Hilliard had been too pro-Palestinian.

Hilliard fell short of the majority he needed in the three-candidate primary to avoid a runoff. Davis, who finished second, blew past Hilliard to win the runoff with 56 percent. In the heavily Democratic district and with no Republican challenger, Davis' general-election win was a foregone conclusion.

Davis moved quickly to consolidate power. By the time of his first re-election campaign, he had opened five offices across the district and hired eight times as many staff as his predecessor. He also launched a private-public initiative aimed at bringing new businesses to the district. Davis won solid endorsements from the two black political groups that had opposed him in 2002. The Birmingham News concluded a year into his first term that "7th District voters traded up. Way up." He won with 75 percent of the vote.

KEY VOTES

2004

Yes Extend federal unemployment benefits by 13 weeks

Yes Pass $283.2 billion, six-year federal highway and mass transit bill

Yes Approve $146 billion multi-year extension of previously enacted middle-class tax breaks

Yes Amend the Constitution to prohibit same-sex marriage

Yes Cut corporate taxes $137 billion over 10 years

? Reorganize U.S. intelligence agencies as proposed by Sept. 11 commission

2003

No Cut taxes by $330 billion through fiscal 2013

Yes Block Bush rule scaling back overtime pay for some white-collar federal workers

Yes Do not allow use of search warrants without first notifying subjects

Yes Allow importation of prescription drugs

No Create private school voucher program in Washington, D.C.

Yes Ban "partial birth" abortion except to save a woman's life

Yes Split $18.6 billion in Iraq aid into half-grant, half-loan

No Overhaul Medicare and create prescription drug benefit

CQ VOTE STUDIES

	PARTY UNITY		PRESIDENTIAL SUPPORT	
	Support	Oppose	Support	Oppose
2004	87%	13%	44%	56%
2003	86%	14%	40%	60%

INTEREST GROUPS

	AFL-CIO	ADA	CCUS	ACU
2004	73%	75%	71%	24%
2003	87%	90%	50%	28%

ALABAMA 7

West central — parts of Birmingham and Tuscaloosa

The 7th combines large portions of Birmingham and Tuscaloosa with poor, rural communities in west-central Alabama. In contrast to its white, well-to-do neighbor, the Republican 6th District, the 7th's residents tend to be lower- to middle-class blacks who vote overwhelmingly Democratic. The 7th lost its portion of Montgomery to the 3rd during redistricting following the 2000 census, while it gained parts of Jefferson and Tuscaloosa counties.

The 7th's part of Birmingham, the densely populated downtown area, has lagged behind the rest of the city. Still, there are signs of revitalization, such as the restoration of old buildings into high-rent apartments.

Several steel plants and communications firms have kept district unemployment down. Near Tuscaloosa, a Mercedes-Benz plant in Vance now tops an industrial sector that complements small- to medium-size businesses. One of the district's best-known employers is the

University of Alabama in Tuscaloosa.

The Black Belt, named for the traditionally rich soil in rural Alabama, accounts for the rest of the district. This poverty-filled area has not known prosperity since before the Civil War, when cotton plantation owners made fortunes from slave labor.

Power struggles between the region's aging black political machine and a new generation of black leaders have made for interesting primaries here in recent years, but general elections are easier to predict. The 7th was the only Alabama district won by the Democratic presidential nominee in 2000, and voters here repeated the feat in 2004.

MAJOR INDUSTRY
Agriculture, higher education, manufacturing

CITIES
Birmingham (pt.), 216,097; Tuscaloosa (pt.), 68,928; Bessemer (pt.), 27,599

NOTABLE
Edmund Pettus Bridge in Selma was the site of "Bloody Sunday," when Alabama state troopers beat and gassed peaceful civil rights marchers — the marchers were co-led by current Georgia Democratic Rep. John Lewis — on their way from Selma to Montgomery in 1965.

Gov. Frank H. Murkowski (R)

First elected: 2002
Length of term: 4 years
Term expires: 12/06
Salary: $85,776
Phone: (907) 465-3500

Hometown: Fairbanks
Born: March 28, 1933; Seattle, Wash.
Religion: Roman Catholic
Family: Wife, Nancy Gore; six children
Education: U. of Santa Clara, attended 1951-53; Seattle U., B.A. 1955 (economics)
Military Service: Coast Guard, 1955-56
Career: Banker
Political highlights: Alaska commissioner of economic development, 1966-70; Republican nominee for U.S. House, 1970; U.S. Senate, 1981-2002

Election results:

2002 GENERAL

Frank H. Murkowski (R)	129,279	55.9%
Fran Ulmer (D)	94,216	40.7%
Diane E. Benson (GREEN)	2,926	1.3%

Lt. Gov. Loren Leman (R)

First elected: 2002
Length of term: 4 years
Term expires: 12/06
Salary: $80,040
Phone: (907) 465-3520

STATE LEGISLATURE

Legislature: January-May, limit of 120 calendar days

House: 40 members, 2-year terms
2005 breakdown: 26R, 14D; 32 men, 8 women
Salary: $24,012
Phone: (907) 465-3725

Senate: 20 members, 4-year terms
2005 breakdown: 12R, 8D; 17 men, 3 women
Salary: $24,012
Phone: (907) 465-3701

STATE TERM LIMITS

Governor: 2 consecutive terms
House: No
Senate: No

URBAN STATISTICS

CITY	POPULATION
Anchorage	260,283
Juneau	30,711
Fairbanks	30,224
Sitka	8,835
Ketchikan	7,922

REGISTERED VOTERS

Unaffiliated	38%
Republican	25%
Others	22%
Democrat	15%

POPULATION

2004 population (est.)	655,435
2000 population	626,932
1990 population	550,043
Percent change (1990-2000)	+14%
Rank among states (2004)	47
Median age	32.4
Born in state	38.1%
Foreign born	5.9%
Violent crime rate	567/100,000
Poverty level	9.4%
Federal workers	16,363
Military	22,786

REDISTRICTING

Alaska retained its one House seat in reapportionment.

MISCELLANEOUS

Web: www.state.ak.us
Capital: Juneau
STATE ELECTION OFFICIAL
(907) 465-4611
DEMOCRATIC HEADQUARTERS
(907) 258-3050
REPUBLICAN HEADQUARTERS
(907) 276-4467

District Statistics

DIST.	2004 VOTE FOR PRESIDENT BUSH	KERRY	WHITE	BLACK	ASIAN	HISP	MEDIAN INCOME	WHITE COLLAR	BLUE COLLAR	SERVICE INDUSTRY	OVER 64	UNDER 18	COLLEGE EDUCATION	RURAL	SQ. MILES
AL	61%	36%	68%	3%	4%	4%	$51,571	61%	24%	16%	6%	30%	25%	34%	571,951
STATE	61	36	68	3	4	4	$51,571	61	24	16	6	30	25	34	571,951
U.S.	50.7	48.3	69	12	4	13	$41,994	60	25	15	12	26	24	21	3,537,438

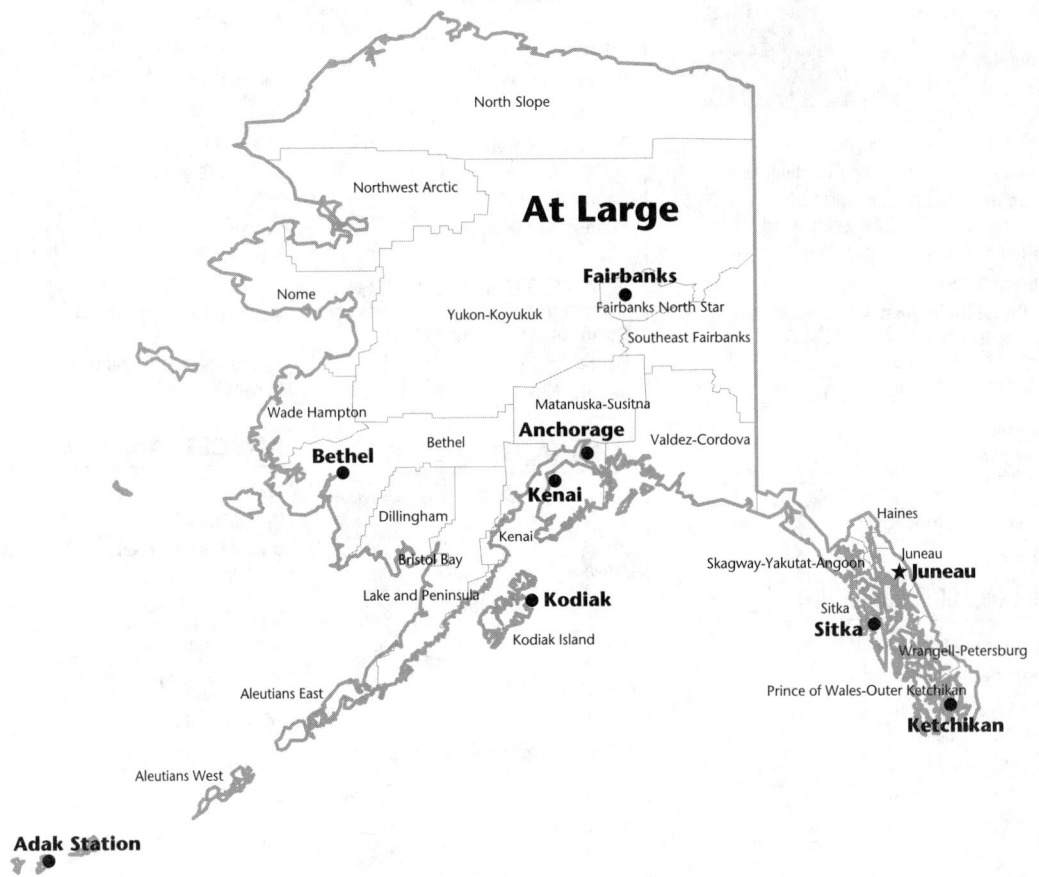

North Slope

Northwest Arctic

At Large

Nome

Fairbanks

Yukon-Koyukuk

Fairbanks North Star

Southeast Fairbanks

Matanuska-Susitna

Wade Hampton

Anchorage

Valdez-Cordova

Bethel

Bethel

Haines

Kenai

Dillingham

Kenai

Skagway-Yakutat-Angoon

Juneau

Juneau

Bristol Bay

Lake and Peninsula

Kodiak

Sitka

Sitka

Aleutians East

Kodiak Island

Wrangell-Petersburg

Prince of Wales-Outer Ketchikan

Ketchikan

Aleutians West

Adak Station

Sen. Ted Stevens (R)

Elected 1970; 6th full term
Appointed December 1968

In his fourth decade in the Senate, Stevens is a tough and unabashedly old school veteran making a transition to a new role, as chairman of the Commerce, Science and Transportation Committee. It is a relatively big change for Stevens, who was used to being a singular power on the Appropriations Committee as the longtime chairman there.

Stevens has another role in the Senate by virtue of his longevity. As the most-senior member of the majority party in the Senate, he is the chamber's president pro tempore. The job day-to-day is mostly symbolic — the Republican leader controls the legislative agenda on the floor — but it places Stevens constitutionally third in line of presidential succession, after the vice president and the Speaker of the House.

He has been best known as the appropriations chief, a job he held from 1997 to 2005 except for the 18-month interlude when Democrats controlled the chamber. That gave him a lot of influence with fellow senators, who relied on him for home-state project funds, all of which flowed through his committee. He had to give up the gavel at the start of the 109th Congress under GOP rules that limit committee chairmanships to six years.

But he is hardly out of the thick of things. As chairman of the Commerce panel, he has purview over the regulation of U.S. businesses and industry, and transportation policy. After taking over in early 2005, he immediately proposed a controversial reorganization of the panel's subcommittees that allowed him to assert more control over telecommunications policy. It also left his frequent rival on spending and policy issues, Republican John McCain of Arizona, without a subcommittee chairmanship even though McCain had preceded Stevens as committee chairman.

Stevens differs from McCain stylistically. The Alaskan is close to the Commerce panel's senior Democrat, Daniel K. Inouye of Hawaii, and he and Inouye like to work out their differences on bills behind the scenes, before committee debate begins. Committee meetings under McCain were more freewheeling and unpredictable.

Stevens kept his defense spending subcommittee chairmanship in the 109th Congress, leaving him some authority over federal purse strings.

As Appropriations chairman, he routinely butted heads with conservatives, who have more sway over writing the annual federal budget than they do in producing the bills to put that budget into practice. Stevens was just as likely to battle with Republican lawmakers as he was with Democrats. While he lost battles along the way, he often got his way in the end.

But his final years as the top appropriator were frustrating for him. He struggled to control an increasingly rocky and partisan process, and he only slowly adapted to the reality of a Republican president determined to compel a Republican Congress to hold down spending.

In late 2004, Stevens tried to use a series of time-tested budgetary gimmicks to wring more spending out of a tight domestic budget. The old tricks would no longer work. President Bush and House conservatives balked, and Stevens relented, agreeing to finish the spending bills under budget. The year before, GOP leaders compelled Stevens to overturn bipartisan agreements he'd made with Robert C. Byrd of West Virginia, the panel's like-minded top Democrat; Stevens grumbled that Bush was using veto threats as a "club" to get his way.

Still, Stevens has had little trouble tending to what often appears to be his top priority — bringing home federal funding to Alaska. His attentiveness to

CAPITOL OFFICE
224-3004
stevens.senate.gov
522 Hart 20510-0201; fax 224-2354

COMMITTEES
Appropriations
  (Defense - chairman)
Commerce, Science & Transportation - chairman
Homeland Security & Governmental Affairs
Rules & Administration
Joint Library - chairman

HOMETOWN
Girdwood

BORN
Nov. 18, 1923, Indianapolis, Ind.

RELIGION
Episcopalian

FAMILY
Wife, Catherine Stevens; six children

EDUCATION
U. of California, Los Angeles, B.A. 1947 (political science); Harvard U., LL.B. 1950

MILITARY SERVICE
Army Air Corps, 1943-46

CAREER
Lawyer

POLITICAL HIGHLIGHTS
U.S. attorney, 1953-56; Republican nominee for U.S. Senate, 1962; Alaska House, 1965-68 (majority leader and Speaker pro tempore, 1967-68); sought Republican nomination for U.S. Senate, 1968

ELECTION RESULTS

2002 GENERAL

Ted Stevens (R)	179,438	78.2%
Frank Vondersaar (D)	24,133	10.5%
Jim Sykes (GREEN)	16,608	7.2%
Jim Dore (AKI)	6,724	2.9%
Leonard Karpinski (LIBERT)	2,354	1.0%

2002 PRIMARY

Ted Stevens (R)	64,315	88.9%
Mike Aubrey (R)	7,997	11.1%

PREVIOUS WINNING PERCENTAGES
1996 (77%); 1990 (66%); 1984 (71%); 1978 (76%); 1972 (77%); 1970 Special Election (60%)

the state's needs is legendary, and his hand is felt in virtually every remote region of Alaska. The catchall spending package in 2004 included $67 million for the Denali Commission, a program that Stevens created in 1998 to distribute grants for rural health clinics, energy projects and clothes-washing centers in communities without running water. In 2000, a grateful state legislature named the Anchorage International Airport for Stevens.

On other fronts, Stevens is known as an ardent promoter of timber cutting and oil drilling in wilderness areas that environmentalists want to preserve. He was a major force behind a White House initiative in 2003 to open parts of the Arctic National Wildlife Refuge in Alaska to oil drilling. When Senate Democrats succeeded in killing the plan, a livid Stevens announced, "People who vote against this today are voting against me, and I will not forget it."

Stevens' reputation at home and nationally suffered in 2003 after a front-page story in the Los Angeles Times said he had become a millionaire through investments with businessmen who had gotten government contracts and other favors with his help. In one instance, the Times reported, Stevens helped save a $450 million housing contract for an Alaska businessman who had made the senator a partner in other real estate investments. Stevens denied wrongdoing, saying his actions were aimed at helping his state. But he eventually sold off his real estate interests, saying that his investment partners were coming under too much scrutiny.

Stevens is one of the Senate's curmudgeons. He once described himself as "a mean, miserable SOB." Often when dealing with thorny issues, he dons a necktie with images of cartoon tough guys like the Incredible Hulk and the Tasmanian Devil. As the ties suggest, his bark is worse than his bite. His temper explosions are usually short-lived, and offense is rarely taken. Stevens watchers say they have seen him throw a fit and then exit the room with a wink. "I believe in using my emotions, not losing my emotions," he says.

His dream of being at the top of the GOP leadership has been frustrated over the years. In 1984, after eight years as Republican whip, he ran a strong race for Senate majority leader, losing to Bob Dole of Kansas by three votes.

Stevens remains a throwback to the clubby pragmatism that once permeated the Senate. Still, old-timers like Stevens and Byrd have experienced strains in their relationships as the chamber has become more partisan in recent years. In particular, Byrd's adamant opposition to the war in Iraq has grated on Stevens, an ardent supporter of the Bush administration's policies in Iraq.

With his typical concern for the Senate as an institution, in 1999 Stevens helped broker a bipartisan agreement on how to conduct the impeachment trial of President Clinton in a way that avoided the partisanship that marked the House proceedings and outraged much of the public.

As a young man, Stevens flew C-46 transports throughout China during World War II and earned the Distinguished Flying Cross. After the war, he got a law degree and worked as a federal prosecutor for three years. He began his pursuit of a Senate seat not long after Alaska became a state in 1959. He got the party's nomination in 1962 but took just 41 percent of the vote against Democrat Ernest J. Gruening that fall.

Stevens won election to the Alaska House, including a stint as majority leader. He tried again for the Senate in 1968 but was defeated in the GOP primary. Later that year, Democratic Sen. E.L. Bartlett died, and Stevens was appointed to the seat by GOP Gov. Walter J. Hickel. In the 1970 contest to serve the final two years of Bartlett's term, Stevens defeated liberal Democrat Wendell P. Kay with 60 percent of the vote.

He has cruised to re-election since. In 1978, he won during a time of great personal hardship. A plane crash took the life of his first wife, and Stevens, who was with her, suffered serious injuries.

KEY VOTES

2004

Yes Pass $318.9 billion, six-year highway and mass transit bill
No Extend assault weapons ban for 10 years
No Restore pay-as-you-go rules for new tax cuts and entitlement spending
Yes Criminalize harm to a fetus in an attack on the mother
Yes Increase mandatory child care funding to states by $6 billion over five years
Yes Amend the Constitution to prohibit same-sex marriage
Yes Approve $146 billion multi-year extension of previously enacted middle-class tax breaks
Yes Reorganize U.S. intelligence agencies as proposed by Sept. 11 commission
Yes Cut corporate taxes $137 billion over 10 years

2003

No Delay Bush changes to Clean Air Act
Yes Allow confirmation vote on Miguel A. Estrada to the U.S. Court of Appeals for the D.C. Circuit
No Block a Bush proposal opening Alaska's Arctic National Wildlife Refuge to oil drilling
No Limit size of Bush's proposed tax cut to $350 billion through fiscal 2013
Yes Overhaul Medicare and create prescription drug benefit
Yes Block Bush rule scaling back overtime pay for some white-collar federal workers
No Split $20 billion in Iraq aid into half-grant, half-loan
Yes Ban "partial birth" abortion except to save a woman's life
Yes Stop proposal allowing travel to Cuba
Yes Allow final vote on energy policy overhaul

CQ VOTE STUDIES

	PARTY UNITY		PRESIDENTIAL SUPPORT	
	Support	Oppose	Support	Oppose
2004	97%	3%	92%	8%
2003	95%	5%	96%	4%
2002	89%	11%	95%	5%
2001	88%	12%	97%	3%
2000	92%	8%	56%	44%
1999	90%	10%	36%	64%
1998	82%	18%	54%	46%
1997	79%	21%	71%	29%
1996	90%	10%	45%	55%
1995	89%	11%	32%	68%

INTEREST GROUPS

	AFL-CIO	ADA	CCUS	ACU
2004	8%	20%	100%	92%
2003	15%	10%	91%	70%
2002	23%	10%	100%	83%
2001	25%	20%	86%	92%
2000	0%	5%	100%	92%
1999	33%	10%	88%	84%
1998	25%	20%	94%	56%
1997	14%	30%	80%	58%
1996	29%	20%	85%	80%
1995	8%	5%	94%	73%

Sen. Lisa Murkowski (R)

Elected 2004; 1st term
Appointed December 2002

CAPITOL OFFICE
224-6665
murkowski.senate.gov
709 Hart 20510-0202; fax 224-5301

COMMITTEES
Energy & Natural Resources
 (Water & Power - chairwoman)
Environment & Public Works
Foreign Relations
 (East Asian & Pacific Affairs - chairwoman)
Indian Affairs

HOMETOWN
Anchorage

BORN
May 22, 1957, Ketchikan, Alaska

RELIGION
Roman Catholic

FAMILY
Husband, Verne Martell; two children

EDUCATION
Willamette U., attended 1975-77; Georgetown U.,
B.A. 1980 (economics); Willamette U., J.D. 1985

CAREER
Lawyer; state legislative aide

POLITICAL HIGHLIGHTS
Anchorage district attorney, 1987-89; Alaska
House, 1999-2002

ELECTION RESULTS

2004 GENERAL

Lisa Murkowski (R)	149,773	48.6%
Tony Knowles (D)	140,424	45.6%
Marc J. Millican (NON)	8,885	2.9%
Jerry Sanders (AKI)	3,785	1.2%

2004 PRIMARY

Lisa Murkowski (R)	45,710	58.1%
Mike Miller (R)	29,313	37.3%
Wev Shea (R)	2,857	3.6%

Murkowski began the 109th Congress in a much stronger position politically after winning her seat in her own right in the 2004 election. That lifted the cloud over her appointment to the Senate two years earlier by her father, outgoing Sen. Frank H. Murkowski, which many Alaskans thought smacked of nepotism. The elder Murkowski, also a Republican, vacated the seat to run successfully for governor, and after claiming to have examined a long list of qualified replacements, chose his daughter to fill out the rest of his term.

By election time, the built-in advantages of incumbency were, for Murkowski, nearly erased by resentment back home, made worse by her father's growing unpopularity as governor. But she used her opportunities skillfully in her two years as an appointive senator, chalking up several legislative victories in the 108th Congress. As a result, she was able to beat back a serious threat by Tony Knowles, a former two-term governor and the state's most powerful Democrat. The race was one of the closest of the midterm elections. Though her winning margin was small — just 3 percentage points — it went a long way toward casting off her father's shadow. "There were many people that did not like the way I came into this office, and I have not asked them to like it," she told The New York Times shortly before the election. "I have asked them to judge me on my performance."

Her biggest legislative win came just a few weeks before the election, when President Bush signed a military construction spending bill that included federal loan guarantees for a 3,500-mile natural gas pipeline to carry Alaska's abundant natural gas to the Midwest. Under the bill, the government covers 80 percent of the pipeline's costs, up to $18 billion, should builders default on the project, considered vital to the state's economic future and a potential source of thousands of jobs. Murkowski got help from fellow Alaska Republican Ted Stevens, with whom she once interned. Stevens chaired the Appropriations Committee, is the Senate's senior Republican and is a popular figure at home. He calls Murkowski "a hell of a lot better senator than her dad ever was."

In late 2004, the Alaska delegation scored one of its biggest parochial legislative victories of recent years, thanks to Murkowski. The House passed her bill to transfer 89 million acres from the federal government to the state of Alaska and native Alaskans. The measure had already passed the Senate and was supported by the Bush administration.

Murkowski stepped out front in the national debate over whether to allow oil exploration in the Arctic National Wildlife Refuge, which Alaskans overwhelmingly support. She was a lead negotiator with environmental groups and Democrats who opposed drilling and who ultimately prevailed in the 108th. Murkowski also is a promoter of a proposed repeal of Clinton-era rules restricting logging in Alaska's 17-million-acre Tongass National Forest.

Already, Murkowski is responsible for an extraordinary number of Senate "firsts." She is its first native-born Alaskan, and she is the first daughter of a senator to serve in the Senate. She is also the only senator to be appointed by a parent, though offspring have followed their parents to the Senate via the ballot box before. Murkowski has broken ground at home, too. She is the first female senator from Alaska, and the first woman to be elected statewide in Alaska, admitted to the union in 1959. She brought the roster of women in the 109th Congress to 14, the most in history.

In contrast to her conservative father, Lisa Murkowski is a moderate. She generally supports abortion rights and joined eight other Senate Republicans in 2003 in voting to affirm support of the landmark Supreme Court case *Roe v. Wade*, which legalized abortion. But she backs some restrictions, voting in 2003 to ban a procedure its opponents call "partial birth" abortion.

Murkowski is also emerging as a labor supporter in the GOP. She voted against the Bush White House in the debate over whether to restrict overtime pay for some classes of workers. She also backed Democratic proposals to extend unemployment benefits by 26 weeks and cosponsored a Republican bill to give workers looking for jobs an extra 13 weeks of pay. Alaska's unemployment rate hovered at more than 7 percent in recent years, 2 percentage points above the national average.

She also bucked the president in voting to convert part of a $20 billion grant for reconstruction in Iraq to loans that the country would ultimately have to repay when its economy recovers from the war. Bush wanted all of the aid to be in grant form.

Among her colleagues in the Senate, Murkowski is known as more personable and approachable than her father. She has many of his same committee assignments though, including a seat on the Energy and Natural Resources panel, where her father served as chairman before his departure.

The second of six children, Murkowski grew up in Ketchikan in the Alaskan panhandle and attended high school in Fairbanks. In her senior year, she interned for Stevens, then went to Georgetown University in Washington, D.C., graduating with a degree in economics. After getting a law degree from Willamette University in Oregon, she spent two years in the Anchorage district attorney's office before opening a solo law practice. Married with two sons, one of her early elective offices was as president of the Government Hill Elementary School PTA.

Murkowski says that her parents stressed civic duty, although her father, originally a banker, did not run for the Senate until she was out of college. Growing up a Murkowski, she says, meant "knowing that you were a part of a family that was involved in shaping the state of Alaska."

She ran successfully for the state house in 1998, was re-elected twice and chosen by her peers late in 2002 as majority leader (a post she never actually took, because she was appointed to the Senate). When the state suffered a funding shortfall, she joined a bipartisan coalition that advocated raising taxes and was instrumental in the passage of a boost in the state's alcohol tax to a dime a drink — at the time the highest rate in the nation. She also supported public funding for abortions.

When Sen. Frank Murkowski was elected governor in November 2002, he announced that he had considered more than two dozen candidates to fill out the remainder of his term but that his daughter was the best choice, a decision that did not fly with most Alaskans. Facing election in 2004, the younger Murkowski looked vulnerable. Her challenger Knowles was a former two-term governor, a former mayor of Anchorage, a Vietnam veteran, and a onetime oil rig worker who could relate to everyday Alaskans.

Murkowski did the best she could to distance herself politically from her father, especially since by then he was coming under criticism for supporting a tax increase and for attempting to use federal homeland security funds for a jet to carry him around the state. Her campaign buttons and lawn signs advertised "Lisa" prominently with "Murkowski" in much smaller type. Under the banner "Team Alaska," she played up her working relationships with Stevens and GOP Rep. Don Young, Alaska's sole House member, who chairs the Transportation and Infrastructure Committee. Both men are known for fiercely protecting parochial projects in a state where federal spending is a top concern. Alaska gets more federal funding per capita — roughly $11,700 — than any other state.

KEY VOTES

2004

Yes Pass $318.9 billion, six-year highway and mass transit bill
No Extend assault weapons ban for 10 years
No Restore pay-as-you-go rules for new tax cuts and entitlement spending
Yes Criminalize harm to a fetus in an attack on the mother
Yes Increase mandatory child care funding to states by $6 billion over five years
Yes Amend the Constitution to prohibit same-sex marriage
Yes Approve $146 billion multi-year extension of previously enacted middle-class tax breaks
Yes Reorganize U.S. intelligence agencies as proposed by Sept. 11 commission
Yes Cut corporate taxes $137 billion over 10 years

2003

No Delay Bush changes to Clean Air Act
Yes Allow confirmation vote on Miguel A. Estrada to the U.S. Court of Appeals for the D.C. Circuit
No Block a Bush proposal opening Alaska's Arctic National Wildlife Refuge to oil drilling
No Limit size of Bush's proposed tax cut to $350 billion through fiscal 2013
Yes Overhaul Medicare and create prescription drug benefit
Yes Block Bush rule scaling back overtime pay for some white-collar federal workers
Yes Split $20 billion in Iraq aid into half-grant, half-loan
Yes Ban "partial birth" abortion except to save a woman's life
Yes Stop proposal allowing travel to Cuba
Yes Allow final vote on energy policy overhaul

CQ VOTE STUDIES

	PARTY UNITY		PRESIDENTIAL SUPPORT	
	Support	Oppose	Support	Oppose
2004	92%	8%	87%	13%
2003	94%	6%	93%	7%

INTEREST GROUPS

	AFL-CIO	ADA	CCUS	ACU
2004	50%	35%	94%	74%
2003	15%	20%	86%	70%

Rep. Don Young (R)

Elected March 1973; 16th full term

As the lone representative of America's largest state, Young brings the characteristics of a frontiersman to the House — rugged individualism, certainty of opinion, an outsize personality and little patience for those who want to fence him in. He rarely backs down from a fight.

Young is the chairman of the Transportation and Infrastructure Committee, and the 109th Congress will be his last at its helm: GOP term limits say he must step aside as chairman after six years. Young is determined to leave his legacy on the transportation issues of the nation, despite his failure to get a highway reauthorization bill through the 108th Congress. His control over the large federal purse that the transportation bill distributes to every state makes him a powerful force.

Yet his power has been diminished somewhat in the 109th Congress by the GOP leadership's decision to place control of the Transportation Security Administration under the new Homeland Security Committee. Young also serves on that panel, however, giving him some input.

Young may find that his public spats over the highway and public transit bill in 2004 could hamper his efforts to reach agreement on a bill in the 109th. In the 108th, he initially proposed a $375 billion, six-year authorization that also would have increased the 18.4-cents-per-gallon federal tax on gasoline. But the White House wanted a $256 billion bill with no tax increase. Young criticized the president's proposal and staged a symbolic committee vote in favor of his original $375 billion bill. Without a significant spending increase, Young said, "we will be what we call a nation of potholes, and it is hard to arrive at a future if you are going to be driving through potholes."

Under pressure from the House leadership, Young reluctantly scaled back his bill but found enough room in the less expensive measure to authorize $11 billion for "high priority" projects requested by his colleagues. The bill included 2,838 such projects that cost about $8.6 billion. No. 1 on the list was a $4 million road project in Alaska's Matanuska-Susitna Borough. The bill died at the end of the 108th Congress, after House-Senate negotiators could not agree on how to distribute the funds among the states.

Young had named the bill "The Transportation Equity Act: A Legacy For Users" — or TEA-LU, for his wife, Lula. In his first statement of the 109th Congress, Young attributed his political achievements to "my lovely wife Lu, who is a very integral part of my career and has been by my side now for over 40 years."

In the 108th, Young also engaged in another public intraparty fight, when he went head-to-head with chairman of the House Appropriations Committee, C.W. Bill Young of Florida, over the spending panel's lack of funds for certain transportation programs. In 2004, the two lawmakers could not agree on what items in the Transportation-Treasury spending measure should be protected, so they instead took turns eliminating provisions important to each other. Most of the money was put back during House-Senate negotiations on the legislation.

In his first term as Transportation chairman, Young was a central player in moving several major laws enacted in late 2001 and in 2002 in response to the Sept. 11, 2001, terrorist attacks. Principal among them was the aviation security law that federalized airport screeners and mandated the inspection of all checked baggage.

For the six years before he took over the Transportation gavel, Young

CAPITOL OFFICE
225-5765
donyoung.house.gov
2111 Rayburn 20515-0201; fax 225-0425

COMMITTEES
Homeland Security
Resources
Transportation & Infrastructure - chairman

HOMETOWN
Fort Yukon

BORN
June 9, 1933, Meridian, Calif.

RELIGION
Episcopalian

FAMILY
Wife, Lula Young; two children

EDUCATION
Yuba Junior College, A.A. 1952; California State U., Chico, B.A. 1958

MILITARY SERVICE
Army, 1955-57

CAREER
Elementary school teacher; riverboat captain

POLITICAL HIGHLIGHTS
Fort Yukon City Council, 1960-64; mayor of Fort Yukon, 1964-68; Alaska House, 1967-70; Alaska Senate, 1971-73; Republican nominee for U.S. House, 1972

ELECTION RESULTS

2004 GENERAL

Don Young (R)	213,216	71.1%
Thomas M. Higgins (D)	67,074	22.4%
Timothy A. Feller (GREEN)	11,434	3.8%
Alvin A. Anders (LIBERT)	7,157	2.4%

2004 PRIMARY

Don Young (R)	unopposed

2002 GENERAL

Don Young (R)	169,685	74.5%
Clifford Mark Greene (D)	39,357	17.3%
Russell deForest (GREEN)	14,435	6.3%

PREVIOUS WINNING PERCENTAGES
2000 (70%); 1998 (63%); 1996 (59%); 1994 (57%); 1992 (47%); 1990 (52%); 1988 (63%); 1986 (56%); 1984 (55%); 1982 (71%); 1980 (74%); 1978 (55%); 1976 (71%); 1974 (54%); 1973 Special Election (51%)

chaired the Resources Committee, which has jurisdiction over public lands and the environment. Like many Western Republicans, Young is an eager ally of energy, mining and timber interests and a vigorous advocate of the rights of private property holders. His zeal for loosening the government's grip on federal lands puts him squarely at odds with environmentalists, who deride him as a blatant exploiter of the nation's most precious resources. Young, in turn, has likened environmentalists to communists.

Young also plays a critical role in the debate on drilling for oil in Alaska's Arctic National Wildlife Refuge. He is adamant that it is a good thing and says he has no worries about the environmental risks. "It is right for my people in the state of Alaska," he declared on the House floor in 2001. "It is the best thing we have going, and how dare members talk about something when they have never been there. Shame on them."

Along with Alaska's two senators, Young has disputed the conclusion of leading scientists that human activity is causing the rapid depletion of the ozone that leads to the melting of Arctic glaciers. He called the report ammunition for fearmongers. "I don't believe it is our fault. That's an opinion," Young told the Anchorage Daily News. "It's as sound as any scientist's."

Young is a determined guardian of the economic interests of his state. In late 2004, Young offered a list of the special appropriations he has "helped to secure" for Alaska, including $200 million for a bridge over Knik Arm north of Anchorage and at least $137 million for a bridge to Gravina Island west of Ketchikan. He also was the leading force behind a $1 million federal grant to Alaska Christian College, a Bible college for Alaskan natives. It has 37 students.

Born in California, Young moved to Alaska to teach, then became a licensed riverboat captain and a member of the Dog Mushers Association. The only election he has ever lost was his first, in 1972. His opponent, freshman Democrat Nick Begich, disappeared without a trace along with House Majority Leader Hale Boggs during an October airplane flight from Anchorage to Juneau. Begich still beat Young by almost 12,000 votes.

When Begich's seat was declared vacant a few weeks later, Young edged out Emil Notti, the former state Democratic chairman, in a 1973 special election. Young weathered a vigorous challenge in the post-Watergate election of 1974, then enjoyed relatively comfortable re-election margins until 1990. That year and in 1992, he barely survived challenges from John E. Devens, the former Democratic mayor of Valdez. Young conceded in advertisements that he was "abrasive" and "arrogant" but a worthy fighter for Alaska's interests. He has not been seriously challenged since.

KEY VOTES

2004

No   Extend federal unemployment benefits by 13 weeks

Yes   Pass $283.2 billion, six-year federal highway and mass transit bill

Yes   Approve $146 billion multi-year extension of previously enacted middle-class tax breaks

Yes   Amend the Constitution to prohibit same-sex marriage

Yes   Cut corporate taxes $137 billion over 10 years

?   Reorganize U.S. intelligence agencies as proposed by Sept. 11 commission

2003

Yes   Cut taxes by $330 billion through fiscal 2013

No   Block Bush rule scaling back overtime pay for some white-collar federal workers

Yes   Do not allow use of search warrants without first notifying subjects

No   Allow importation of prescription drugs

?   Create private school voucher program in Washington, D.C.

Yes   Ban "partial birth" abortion except to save a woman's life

No   Split $18.6 billion in Iraq aid into half-grant, half-loan

Yes   Overhaul Medicare and create prescription drug benefit

CQ VOTE STUDIES

	PARTY UNITY		PRESIDENTIAL SUPPORT	
	Support	Oppose	Support	Oppose
2004	92%	8%	87%	13%
2003	96%	4%	92%	8%
2002	94%	6%	86%	14%
2001	98%	2%	86%	14%
2000	86%	14%	21%	79%

INTEREST GROUPS

	AFL-CIO	ADA	CCUS	ACU
2004	17%	0%	100%	95%
2003	21%	5%	93%	79%
2002	13%	10%	90%	86%
2001	13%	5%	89%	91%
2000	22%	10%	78%	73%

ALASKA
At large

Alaska's remoteness belies its dependence on Washington, D.C. The state's proximity to Russia and the Far East makes it a military stronghold, and its economic boosters, such as oil, minerals and timber, lie mostly on federally owned land.

A never-ending battle for control over the local economy has made voters hostile to Washington and led them to vote overwhelmingly Republican in national elections. Alaska has not elected a Democrat to Congress since 1974. Its congressional delegation vigorously opposed a Clinton administration rule banning road building and most logging in the Tongass National Forest, and the lawmakers have been the most outspoken advocates of opening land to oil and gas exploration.

State and local government is Alaska's largest employer. The state continues to build a privatized economy through tourism — a booming industry that is rebounding from the nation's post-Sept. 11 economic downturn — but most Alaskans view oil exploration as the best way to independence and heavily favor drilling in the Arctic National Wildlife

Refuge. The state was able to scrap its sales and income taxes and provide residents with annual royalties when it struck black gold near Prudhoe Bay in the 1970s.

Alaska's partisan vote is majority Republican, but voters in a few cities, the panhandle and the sparsely populated tundra vote more Democratic. Third parties proliferate in this cold, conservative frontier state, where most voters register as either independent or nonpartisan.

MAJOR INDUSTRY
Oil, defense, government, tourism, fishing, timber, mining

MILITARY BASES
Elmendorf Air Force Base, 6,781 military, 1,500 civilian (2004); Fort Wainwright (Army), 4,490 military, 878 civilian ; Eielson Air Force Base, 2,877 military, 1,020 civilian; Fort Richardson (Army), 2,272 military, 1,116 civilian; Clear Air Force Station, 96 military, 122 civilian; Fort Greely (Army), 200 military, 170 civilian (2003)

CITIES
Anchorage, 260,283; Juneau, 30,711; Fairbanks, 30,224

NOTABLE
Mt. McKinley is the highest point in North America, at 20,320 feet.

Gov. Janet Napolitano (D)

First elected: 2002
Length of term: 4 years
Term expires: 1/07
Salary: $95,000
Phone: (602) 542-4331

Hometown: Phoenix
Born: Nov. 29, 1957; Manhattan, N.Y.
Religion: Methodist
Family: Single
Education: U. of Santa Clara, B.S. 1979 (political science); U. of Virginia, J.D. 1983
Career: Lawyer
Political highlights: U.S. attorney, 1993-97; Ariz. attorney general, 1999-2003

Election results:

2002 GENERAL

Janet Napolitano (D)	566,284	46.2%
Matt Salmon (R)	554,465	45.2%
Richard Mahoney (I)	84,947	6.9%
Barry Hess (LIBERT)	20,356	1.7%

Secretary of State Jan Brewer (R)

(no lieutenant governor)
First elected: 2002
Length of term: 4 years
Term expires: 1/07
Salary: $70,000
Phone: (602) 542-4285

STATE LEGISLATURE

Legislature: 100 days January-April

House: 60 members, 2-year terms
2005 breakdown: 38R, 22D; 40 men, 20 women
Salary: $24,000
Phone: (602) 926-4221

Senate: 30 members, 2-year terms
2005 breakdown: 18R, 12D; 20 men, 10 women
Salary: $24,000
Phone: (602) 926-3559

STATE TERM LIMITS

Governor: 2 consecutive terms
House: 4 consecutive terms
Senate: 4 consecutive terms

URBAN STATISTICS

CITY	POPULATION
Phoenix	1,321,045
Tucson	486,699
Mesa	396,375
Glendale	218,812
Scottsdale	202,705

REGISTERED VOTERS

Republican	35%
Democrat	40%
Others	25%

POPULATION

2004 population (est.)	5,743,834
2000 population	5,130,632
1990 population	3,665,228
Percent change (1990-2000)	+40%
Rank among states (2004)	18

Median age	34.2
Born in state	34.7%
Foreign born	12.8%
Violent crime rate	532/100,000
Poverty level	13.9%
Federal workers	46,967
Military	33,485

REDISTRICTING

Arizona gained two House seats in reapportionment. The Arizona Independent Redistricting Commission adopted a new, eight-district map on Oct. 12, 2001.

MISCELLANEOUS

Web: www.az.gov
Capital: Phoenix
STATE ELECTION OFFICIAL
(602) 542-8683
DEMOCRATIC HEADQUARTERS
(602) 298-4200
REPUBLICAN HEADQUARTERS
(602) 957-7770

District Statistics

DIST.	2004 VOTE FOR PRESIDENT BUSH	KERRY	WHITE	BLACK	ASIAN	HISP	MEDIAN INCOME	WHITE COLLAR	BLUE COLLAR	SERVICE INDUSTRY	OVER 64	UNDER 18	COLLEGE EDUCATION	RURAL	SQ. MILES
1	54%	45%	58%	1%	1%	16%	$32,979	53%	27%	20%	14%	28%	18%	45%	58,608
2	61	38	78	2	2	14	$42,432	60	23	17	20	24	19	11	20,220
3	58	41	79	2	2	14	$48,108	68	18	14	10	25	30	4	598
4	38	62	29	7	1	58	$30,624	44	36	20	7	33	10	0	199
5	54	45	77	3	3	13	$51,780	73	14	13	10	23	40	3	1,406
6	64	35	77	2	2	17	$47,976	63	23	14	14	28	24	3	724
7	43	57	39	3	1	51	$30,828	51	29	20	11	30	13	16	22,873
8	53	46	74	3	2	18	$40,656	67	17	16	17	23	31	13	9,007
STATE	55	44	64	3	2	25	$40,558	61	23	16	13	27	24	12	113,635
U.S.	50.7	48.3	69	12	4	13	$41,994	60	25	15	12	26	24	21	3,537,438

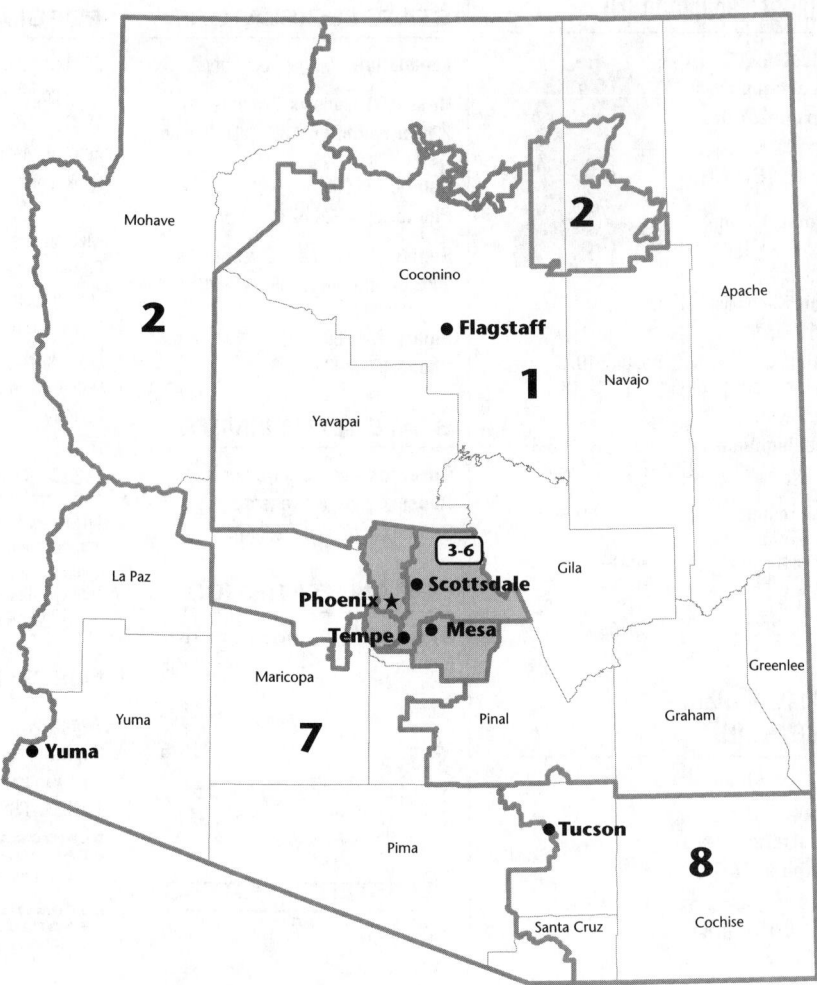

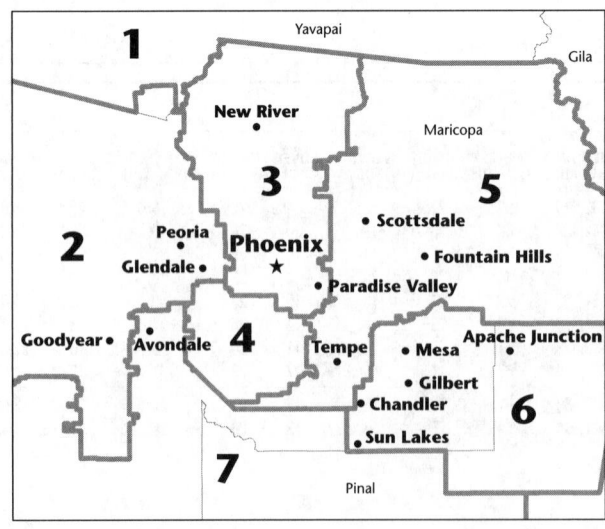

Sen. John McCain (R)

Elected 1986; 4th term

As he mulls whether to make a final run for president in 2008, McCain occupies a unique place in American politics. A conservative attacked by some in his party but adored by many Democrats and independent voters, he commands a vast amount of media coverage — mostly positive — for almost everything he says and does.

With a national profile of his own, he does not readily fall in line with the Bush White House. He is immensely effective in taking the lead in the Senate on issues for President Bush when he agrees with him. When he doesn't, he can be a noisy and worrisome obstacle. Bush ignores McCain's views from the Hill at his peril.

McCain's independence stems in part from the respectable race he gave Bush for the Republican nomination in 2000. It is also a result of life experience. He survived five years as a prisoner during the Vietnam War — his upper body is slightly crooked from the physical abuse he endured — and as a consequence, he is not intimidated by political combat.

He has skillfully burnished his image as an unvarnished, aggressive reformer who always shoots straight. "I've had many people come up to me and say, 'I'm a Democrat from San Francisco and I don't agree with you on many issues, but I'll support you because I think you're honest,' " he told the San Francisco Chronicle.

Since running for president, and since the enactment in 2002 of the campaign finance overhaul law that bears his name, McCain increasingly has positioned himself near the center, and frequently to the left, of the national party on defining domestic issues, including health care, the environment and the economy. And despite what appeared to be a rapprochement with Bush during the president's 2004 re-election bid, McCain has shown no tendency to shy away from disagreements with the president.

During the campaign, he helped Bush with public appearances in his behalf and by repeatedly backing him on the war in Iraq. Yet within weeks of Bush's victory, McCain renewed his opposition to the president's policy on global warming and urged action against greenhouse gases. He traveled to Europe to urge a harder line against Russian President Vladimir V. Putin. Returning home, he sharply criticized steroid use in baseball in stronger terms than the administration used. McCain caused an uproar when he said he had "no confidence" in Defense Secretary Donald H. Rumsfeld, citing "very strong differences of opinion" on the number of U.S. troops required in Iraq.

McCain's voting pattern bears out his independence. In the 108th Congress, he voted with most Senate Republicans against most Democrats 84 percent of the time, and he backed Bush 91 percent of the time. Only the four most moderate GOP senators had lower presidential support scores. "I've always had this streak, but I would argue that the presidential campaign did make me more of a populist," McCain said in 2002.

His repositioning, especially when it is at the expense of the party's agenda in the closely divided Senate, has brought grumbled accusations from GOP colleagues that McCain is a grandstander. His boosters say he has a broader goal, which is to stoke a rebirth of dormant progressivism in the party and attract the pivotal portion of the electorate that remains dissatisfied with both major political parties.

Nowhere has McCain strayed more publicly, or with more success, than on the campaign finance bill, the legislative high point of his two decades in

CAPITOL OFFICE
224-2235
john_mccain@mccain.senate.gov
mccain.senate.gov
241 Russell 20510-0303; fax 228-2862

COMMITTEES
Armed Services
  (Airland - chairman)
Commerce, Science & Transportation
Indian Affairs - chairman

HOMETOWN
Phoenix

BORN
Aug. 29, 1936, Panama Canal Zone, Panama

RELIGION
Episcopalian

FAMILY
Wife, Cindy McCain; seven children

EDUCATION
U.S. Naval Academy, B.S. 1958; National War College, attended 1973-74

MILITARY SERVICE
Navy, 1958-81

CAREER
Navy officer; Senate Navy liaison; beer distributor

POLITICAL HIGHLIGHTS
U.S. House, 1983-87; sought Republican nomination for president, 2000

ELECTION RESULTS

2004 GENERAL

John McCain (R)	1,505,372	76.7%
Stuart Starky (D)	404,507	20.6%
Ernest Hancock (LIBERT)	51,798	2.6%

2004 PRIMARY

John McCain (R)	unopposed

PREVIOUS WINNING PERCENTAGES
1998 (69%); 1992 (56%); 1986 (61%); 1984 House Election (78%); 1982 House Election (66%)

Congress. After a seven-year battle against Republican filibusters and other delaying tactics, McCain and Wisconsin Democrat Russell D. Feingold won enactment of their bill that banned unlimited corporate and labor donations to political parties and restricted issue advertisements. Bush signed the measure, hoping to get McCain off his back and out of the limelight.

In the 109th Congress, GOP-mandated term limits forced McCain to relinquish the chairmanship of the Commerce, Science and Transportation Committee, where he had used the panel's broad jurisdiction to oversee U.S. industry, especially in transportation and telecommunications. He settled for the chairmanship of Indian Affairs, a traditionally obscure panel that will get more notice with him at the helm. He began by taking up an inquiry into how a lobbyist and a GOP public relations consultant convinced Indian tribes to pay them more than $80 million for lobbying on casino gambling.

McCain is in line to eventually take over the Armed Services Committee. He is the Airland Subcommittee chairman, with an interest in aggressive oversight of the defense industry. For several years, McCain has battled the Air Force and defense giant Boeing Co. over a deal to lease aerial refueling tankers for at least $23 billion. With McCain's help, the agreement became one of the biggest procurement scandals in the Pentagon's history, prompting the resignations of top Boeing and Air Force officials.

McCain's maverick streak does not perturb his colleagues as much as his attitude does. In a chamber where members of the club are expected to treat each other with deference, McCain comes off as too eager to use sharp elbows, too quick to discard customary courtesies and too self-righteous. He angers GOP leaders and individual senators by attempting to eliminate spending projects that he labels "pork." Even some who share his disdain for directing funds to lawmakers' pet projects have criticized him. In his 2004 book "The Wastrels of Defense," former Republican Senate aide Winslow Wheeler complained that McCain makes a show of objecting to all the money being wasted but doesn't follow up to solve the problem.

McCain is the son of an admiral, who also was the son of an admiral, the first father-and-son pair to achieve that status in U.S. Navy history. McCain was sent off to Annapolis with great family expectations but didn't prove to be admiral material. He finished fifth from the bottom in the class of 1958. But he was a good Navy flyer and, it turned out, a good patriot. Nine years after graduation, his plane was shot down and he was captured by the North Vietnamese. Both arms and a leg broken, McCain was dragged from the crash and thrown, without benefit of medical treatment, into a cell. He spent the next five and a half years enduring torture and solitary confinement, an experience recounted in his best-selling memoir, "Faith of My Fathers," and also the subject of a 2005 movie on the A&E cable network.

After a stint as the Navy's Senate liaison, McCain ran for Congress in 1982, winning the seat of retiring House Minority Leader John J. Rhodes. After two House terms, McCain drew 61 percent of the vote to succeed retiring GOP Sen. Barry Goldwater in 1986. During his first Senate term, McCain was one of five senators accused of interceding with federal regulators on behalf of wealthy savings and loan operator Charles H. Keating Jr. A protracted Ethics Committee investigation ended with McCain receiving a mild rebuke in 1991, marking the low point of his Senate career.

The black mark led to a decline in voter support; in his 1992 race, he won with only 56 percent. But he rebounded in 1998, with 69 percent of the vote. Two years later, 5 million people, including a majority of New Hampshire's first-in-the-nation voters, chose McCain over Bush in the GOP primaries. Bush ultimately overtook McCain in South Carolina. In 2004, McCain was easily returned to the Senate, winning 77 percent of the vote.

KEY VOTES

2004

No Pass $318.9 billion, six-year highway and mass transit bill

No Extend assault weapons ban for 10 years

Yes Restore pay-as-you-go rules for new tax cuts and entitlement spending

Yes Criminalize harm to a fetus in an attack on the mother

Yes Increase mandatory child care funding to states by $6 billion over five years

No Amend the Constitution to prohibit same-sex marriage

Yes Approve $146 billion multi-year extension of previously enacted middle-class tax breaks

Yes Reorganize U.S. intelligence agencies as proposed by Sept. 11 commission

?   Cut corporate taxes $137 billion over 10 years

2003

Yes Delay Bush changes to Clean Air Act

Yes Allow confirmation vote on Miguel A. Estrada to the U.S. Court of Appeals for the D.C. Circuit

Yes Block a Bush proposal opening Alaska's Arctic National Wildlife Refuge to oil drilling

No Limit size of Bush's proposed tax cut to $350 billion through fiscal 2013

No Overhaul Medicare and create prescription drug benefit

No Block Bush rule scaling back overtime pay for some white-collar federal workers

No Split $20 billion in Iraq aid into half-grant, half-loan

Yes Ban "partial birth" abortion except to save a woman's life

Yes Stop proposal allowing travel to Cuba

No Allow final vote on energy policy overhaul

CQ VOTE STUDIES

	PARTY UNITY		PRESIDENTIAL SUPPORT	
	Support	Oppose	Support	Oppose
2004	79%	21%	92%	8%
2003	86%	14%	91%	9%
2002	80%	20%	90%	10%
2001	67%	33%	91%	9%
2000	83%	17%	38%	62%
1999	90%	10%	38%	62%
1998	84%	16%	49%	51%
1997	84%	16%	70%	30%
1996	95%	5%	32%	68%
1995	90%	10%	36%	64%

INTEREST GROUPS

	AFL-CIO	ADA	CCUS	ACU
2004	33%	35%	67%	72%
2003	15%	35%	61%	75%
2002	33%	20%	79%	78%
2001	27%	40%	50%	68%
2000	14%	5%	75%	81%
1999	0%	5%	75%	77%
1998	29%	20%	76%	68%
1997	14%	5%	100%	80%
1996	0%	0%	100%	95%
1995	8%	0%	100%	91%

Sen. Jon Kyl (R)

CAPITOL OFFICE
224-4521
info@kyl.senate.gov
kyl.senate.gov
730 Hart 20510-0304; fax 224-2207

COMMITTEES
Finance
(Taxation & IRS Oversight - chairman)
Judiciary
(Terrorism, Technology & Homeland Security - chairman)

HOMETOWN
Phoenix

BORN
April 25, 1942, Oakland, Neb.

RELIGION
Presbyterian

FAMILY
Wife, Caryll Kyl; two children

EDUCATION
U. of Arizona, B.A. 1964 (political science), LL.B. 1966

CAREER
Lawyer

POLITICAL HIGHLIGHTS
U.S. House, 1987-95

ELECTION RESULTS

2000 GENERAL

Jon Kyl (R)	1,108,196	79.3%
William Toel (I)	109,230	7.8%
Vance Hansen (GREEN)	108,926	7.8%
Barry Hess (LIBERT)	70,724	5.1%

2000 PRIMARY

Jon Kyl (R)	unopposed

PREVIOUS WINNING PERCENTAGES
1994 (54%); 1992 House Election (59%); 1990 House Election (61%); 1988 House Election (87%); 1986 House Election (65%)

Elected 1994; 2nd term

Kyl is the chairman of the Republican Policy Committee, the No. 4 spot in the Senate GOP hierarchy, where his main job is to help shape the party's message and agenda. This is a good role for him as Kyl is patient and willing to spend years pursuing his unambiguously conservative goals.

As part of the Senate leadership in the 109th Congress, Kyl is likely to play a prominent role in the partisan battle over President Bush's judicial nominees. Kyl has said that Democratic filibusters of judicial nominees "demean the process," and "are a violation of the comity between the Senate and the president."

Hardworking and trusted by his Republican colleagues, Kyl has a reputation as one of the clearest voices among the Senate's ultra-conservatives. He pushes an agenda aimed at increasing national defense budgets while reducing the influence of the federal government. His voting record makes him one of the most reliable votes for Bush and the GOP leadership. In 2004, he backed the president 100 percent of the time and sided with his party 98 percent of the time when it squared off against the Democrats.

He is one of his party's pre-eminent advocates for the creation of a national missile defense system and for a robust national security posture overall. As a member of the Intelligence Committee in the 107th Congress, he also had an interest in anti-terrorism long before the attacks of Sept. 11, 2001. A month before the attacks, he had visited Pakistan, which would be a crucial U.S. ally for the campaign in Afghanistan.

As chairman of the Judiciary Subcommittee on Technology, Terrorism and Homeland Security, Kyl has led the effort to rewrite wiretapping laws and other statutes to make it easier for law enforcement officials to track and capture terrorists. Ideas he long advocated — such as allowing investigators to use "roving wiretaps" to follow suspects using multiple cell phones — were included in the anti-terrorism law enacted soon after the 2001 attacks.

Kyl is also willing to join forces with Democrats if the partnership can help him achieve his legislative goals. He cosponsored a measure with liberal Democrat Charles E. Schumer of New York to expand the FBI's authority for surveillance of non-citizens suspected of planning terrorist attacks. The bill, which passed the Senate, was aimed at "lone wolf" terrorists operating independently of any foreign government. When it stalled in the House, a frustrated Kyl said that in the event of a terrorist attack, "people are going to say, 'How come we couldn't get that?' and I'm going to say, because — and I'll name names — of these people that are slowing the process down."

For years, Kyl struggled, along with California Democrat Dianne Feinstein, to win passage of a constitutional amendment to guarantee certain rights to crime victims, such as the right to be heard at public release, plea sentencing and other proceedings. In 2004, they decided to abandon the amendment in favor of a stand-alone victims' rights bill, which passed the Senate but stalled in the House.

Kyl led Senate opposition in 2004 to criminal justice legislation to give federal inmates access to DNA testing, as well as to improve the quality of legal representation for state and federal inmates. One of his objections was that the legislation would make it too easy for federal inmates to secure post-conviction DNA tests and win new trials. House Republicans overcame Kyl's opposition to the criminal justice measure by folding in his victims' rights bill.

National security is the one policy sphere in which Kyl consistently has taken a leading role. Since his time in the House, where he was a member of the Armed Services panel, he has been a strong advocate of a national missile defense system. He strongly supported Bush's decision in 2002 to withdraw from the 1972 Anti-Ballistic Missile Treaty, which banned nationwide antimissile defense. Kyl pushed to include $7.4 billion for missile defenses in that year's defense spending law — a major victory for the administration on the most politically contentious military issue of the past two decades.

Kyl favors unilateral steps over negotiated agreements to neutralize emerging military threats; as a general proposition, he contends, the United States should rely on its own military means to guarantee its national security rather than on diplomatic agreements. He called the U.S. invasion of Iraq "one of the most ambitious and important missions in world history."

Kyl picked up a seat on the Finance Committee in the 107th Congress. There he promised to make supply-side tax relief one of his top priorities. He favored inserting a new round of tax cuts in the fiscal 2006 budget resolution in order to protect the cuts from Senate filibusters. Kyl also wants to speed up and broaden reductions in the estate tax. For the 109th, he has switched his subcommittee chairmanship from Health Care to Taxation and IRS Oversight.

His refusal to go along with what he sees as excessive federal spending sometimes has led Kyl to cast the only no vote on an appropriations bill. He decried the nine-bill omnibus appropriations measure cleared at the end of the 108th Congress as "a lousy way to legislate" — but said that the omnibus measure was necessary because of Democrats' "obstructionist tactics" on spending bills.

Before leaving the Energy Committee at the end of the 108th Congress, Kyl scored a major legislative victory when Bush signed legislation to settle several claims and disputes over Indian tribal water rights, including the disputed allocation of water from the Gila River among native Indian tribes, farmers and cities.

Kyl is usually seen racing through the Capitol — often to and from the offices of other top leaders. He is not one to take a casual stroll.

Raised in a political family, Kyl was active in Republican Party affairs long before his first House run in 1986. His father, John H. Kyl, represented Iowa for 11 years in the 1960s and 1970s, and helped prepare the younger Kyl for a life in politics by coaching him in public speaking.

A business-oriented lawyer and former president of the Phoenix Chamber of Commerce, the younger Kyl was able to garner strong support from the business community to win a primary over John Conlon, a former House member trying for a comeback. Kyl then easily won the general election in the traditionally Republican 4th District, from which GOP Rep. Eldon Rudd was retiring after a decade.

Kyl won three easy re-elections to the House and launched a Senate bid in 1994 even before incumbent Democrat Dennis DeConcini announced his retirement. He breezed through to the GOP nomination while first-term Rep. Sam Coppersmith struggled through a three-way battle to secure the Democratic nomination. Voters in Arizona were in a mood to hear the themes Kyl had always stressed — too much government, too much taxation and too much regulation. He prevailed over Coppersmith by 14 percentage points. Six years later, the Democrats did not even field a candidate.

KEY VOTES

2004

No Pass $318.9 billion, six-year highway and mass transit bill

No Extend assault weapons ban for 10 years

No Restore pay-as-you-go rules for new tax cuts and entitlement spending

Yes Criminalize harm to a fetus in an attack on the mother

No Increase mandatory child care funding to states by $6 billion over five years

Yes Amend the Constitution to prohibit same-sex marriage

Yes Approve $146 billion multi-year extension of previously enacted middle-class tax breaks

Yes Reorganize U.S. intelligence agencies as proposed by Sept. 11 commission

Yes Cut corporate taxes $137 billion over 10 years

2003

No Delay Bush changes to Clean Air Act

Yes Allow confirmation vote on Miguel A. Estrada to the U.S. Court of Appeals for the D.C. Circuit

No Block a Bush proposal opening Alaska's Arctic National Wildlife Refuge to oil drilling

No Limit size of Bush's proposed tax cut to $350 billion through fiscal 2013

Yes Overhaul Medicare and create prescription drug benefit

No Block Bush rule scaling back overtime pay for some white-collar federal workers

No Split $20 billion in Iraq aid into half-grant, half-loan

Yes Ban "partial birth" abortion except to save a woman's life

Yes Stop proposal allowing travel to Cuba

Yes Allow final vote on energy policy overhaul

CQ VOTE STUDIES

	PARTY UNITY		PRESIDENTIAL SUPPORT	
	Support	Oppose	Support	Oppose
2004	98%	2%	100%	0%
2003	99%	1%	99%	1%
2002	96%	4%	96%	4%
2001	98%	2%	99%	1%
2000	99%	1%	41%	59%
1999	97%	3%	34%	66%
1998	96%	4%	33%	67%
1997	99%	1%	57%	43%
1996	98%	2%	23%	77%
1995	98%	2%	21%	79%

INTEREST GROUPS

	AFL-CIO	ADA	CCUS	ACU
2004	0%	5%	88%	100%
2003	0%	10%	96%	90%
2002	15%	0%	90%	100%
2001	6%	5%	100%	100%
2000	0%	0%	85%	100%
1999	0%	0%	82%	100%
1998	0%	0%	76%	96%
1997	0%	0%	70%	96%
1996	0%	5%	100%	100%
1995	0%	0%	100%	100%

Rep. Rick Renzi (R)

Elected 2002; 2nd term

CAPITOL OFFICE
225-2315
www.house.gov/renzi
418 Cannon 20515-0301; fax 226-9739

COMMITTEES
Financial Services
Resources
Select Intelligence

HOMETOWN
Flagstaff

BORN
June 11, 1958, Fort Monmouth, N.J.

RELIGION
Roman Catholic

FAMILY
Wife, Roberta Renzi; 12 children

EDUCATION
Northern Arizona U., B.S. 1980 (criminal justice);
Catholic U. of America, J.D. 2002

CAREER
Insurance company owner; Defense Department
counter-intelligence contractor; real estate agent

POLITICAL HIGHLIGHTS
No previous office

ELECTION RESULTS

2004 GENERAL

Rick Renzi (R)	148,315	58.5%
Paul Babbitt (D)	91,776	36.2%
John Crockett (LIBERT)	13,260	5.2%

2004 PRIMARY

Rick Renzi (R)	unopposed

2002 GENERAL

Rick Renzi (R)	85,967	49.2%
George Cordova (D)	79,730	45.6%
Edwin Porr (LIBERT)	8,990	5.2%

Renzi is one of the GOP's most aggressive newcomers. He sponsored more bills than any other Republican freshman in the 108th Congress, and even managed to get a few of them passed and signed into law. As a conservative, he also made surprising inroads with a key constituency that typically doesn't vote for Republicans — American Indians. They make up more than 20 percent of the voters in Renzi's sprawling, sparsely populated district covering the eastern half of Arizona, and helped Renzi coast to re-election in 2004 despite the best efforts of national Democrats to defeat him.

As a lawmaker and in his private life, the 40-something Renzi seems tireless. He and his wife, Roberta, have the distinction of having more children than any other congressional family — a total of 12 ranging in age from 4 years to 22 years old. Renzi jokes that any outing involving his kids is "very loud, like a rock concert." During his first major re-election test in 2004, his opponent tried to make an issue of the fact that most of the Renzi children live and go to school in a Virginia suburb close to Washington, D.C. rather than in Arizona. But voters apparently were satisfied with Renzi's explanation that he needs to be close to his children to be an involved parent.

Renzi is not afraid to buck the House GOP leadership on occasion, though he tends to fall in line at crucial moments. In 2003, he first supported a Democratic measure to give a one-time $1,500 bonus to soldiers in Iraq and Afghanistan but then switched his vote at the request of Republican leaders, who suspected that Democrats were using the bill to convince the public that the war in Iraq was underfunded.

Renzi also fought GOP leaders on the issue of increasing money for veterans, organizing a group of 20 freshmen in 2004 to hold out their votes on the Republicans' proposed budget to get their point across. But the leadership ultimately got sufficient votes to approve both the budget and the appropriations bill without the big boost in funding for veterans Renzi and his group had demanded.

At the start of the 109th Congress, he left the Veterans panel to take a choice seat on the Intelligence Committee, which gives him a role in the battle against terrorism.

Renzi's self-pronounced conservatism on fiscal issues is also shaded by a liberal's appetite for spending for his district. Renzi boasts of securing hundreds of millions of dollars in federal projects, grants and loan guarantees for the folks back home, prompting the National Taxpayers Union to rate him last among Arizona Republicans for holding the line on spending. But the flip side for Renzi is the newfound appreciation for him among Indian tribes, which typically vote Democratic and are important in a district that has 30,000 more Democrats than Republicans.

Among the bills he got signed into law was one boosting federal support for home loans to American Indians. It raised from 80 percent to 95 percent the portion of a loan guaranteed by the federal government in the case of default, making the loans less risky and therefore more attractive to lenders. The bill passed after Renzi brought fellow members of the Financial Services panel's Housing Subcommittee to his district to tour dilapidated houses on Indian reservations. Renzi also voted against a GOP budget resolution in 2004 because he said it did not adequately fund Native American programs.

In the final weeks of his re-election campaign, he got the support of the Tribal Council of the Navajo Nation, the country's largest tribe. Two years earlier, American Indian voters supported Renzi's rival, Democrat George

Cordova, a businessman.

A devout Roman Catholic, Renzi also identifies with the Republicans who worry about deteriorating cultural values in American society. Like many like-minded conservatives, he blames activist judges for imposing ideas out of sync with local mores. He sponsored a bill, which passed the House in 2004, to remove Arizona from the Ninth Circuit Court of Appeals and break up the circuit into three smaller units. He said the court had grown hopelessly out of touch with Western state voters on issues such as grazing on federal land and the use of the phrase "under God" in the Pledge of Allegiance.

The low point in Renzi's first term came with newspaper reports that he pushed to exempt a military installation from water restrictions, changes that, if enacted, could deplete one of the last undammed rivers in the Southwest, the San Pedro, an oasis for migratory birds. Renzi's father, retired Maj. Gen. Eugene Renzi, is senior executive vice president of Man-Tech, a defense contractor that does at least $1 billion in business with the base, Fort Huachuca, according to news accounts.

Renzi grew up as one of five children in Sierra Vista, Ariz., a town of about 40,000, 70 miles southeast of Tucson. He went to Northern Arizona University in Flagstaff on an athletic scholarship, was elected captain of the football team and led the Lumberjacks to the Big Sky Conference championship. He graduated with a degree in criminal justice and soon afterward married and started a family. Renzi prospered in business for several years after that, moving to Virginia and founding an insurance brokerage. He bought a vineyard and ranch in southern Arizona in Sonoita with an eight-bedroom house, where his older sons live.

His decision to run for the House seat was his first venture in electoral politics, but he had prepared for it in recent years. He took time out from his business pursuits to get a law degree from Catholic University and interned for Arizona Republican Sen. Jon Kyl while in school.

In 2002, he launched his first campaign for public office by running for Arizona's 1st District, which was drawn to favor Democrats. Renzi lucked out when the best Democratic challengers, Apache County Attorney Steve Udall and former Clinton aide Fred DuVal were defeated by the relatively unknown Cordova, who had run unsuccessfully for the state House. Two years later, Democrats fielded a much stronger and better financed candidate in Paul Babbitt, the brother of Bruce Babbitt, former Arizona governor and interior secretary under President Clinton. The contest was one of a handful of closely contested House races in 2004. Renzi prevailed, with 59 percent of the vote.

KEY VOTES

2004

No Extend federal unemployment benefits by 13 weeks

Yes Pass $283.2 billion, six-year federal highway and mass transit bill

Yes Approve $146 billion multi-year extension of previously enacted middle-class tax breaks

Yes Amend the Constitution to prohibit same-sex marriage

Yes Cut corporate taxes $137 billion over 10 years

Yes Reorganize U.S. intelligence agencies as proposed by Sept. 11 commission

2003

Yes Cut taxes by $330 billion through fiscal 2013

No Block Bush rule scaling back overtime pay for some white-collar federal workers

No Do not allow use of search warrants without first notifying subjects

Yes Allow importation of prescription drugs

Yes Create private school voucher program in Washington, D.C.

Yes Ban "partial birth" abortion except to save a woman's life

No Split $18.6 billion in Iraq aid into half-grant, half-loan

Yes Overhaul Medicare and create prescription drug benefit

CQ VOTE STUDIES

	PARTY UNITY		PRESIDENTIAL SUPPORT	
	Support	Oppose	Support	Oppose
2004	92%	8%	82%	18%
2003	91%	9%	93%	7%

INTEREST GROUPS

	AFL-CIO	ADA	CCUS	ACU
2004	20%	10%	95%	88%
2003	20%	10%	90%	84%

ARIZONA 1

North and east — Flagstaff, Prescott, Navajo reservation

A mix of rural conservatives, artistic liberals and dependably Democratic Navajo voters makes the immense 1st appear ripe for unpredictable elections, but that does not mean the residents have nothing in common.

Tired of being represented by politicians in Phoenix and Mesa, the eight counties of the 1st pushed hard for a district of their own when the state was awarded two new House seats following the 2000 census. Democrats have a slight voter registration advantage in the 58,608-square-mile swath of Arizona, larger than 30 states, and nearly all locals call themselves environmentalists in a district that includes both sides of the Grand Canyon. Despite the Democrats' seeming advantage, George W. Bush captured 54 percent of the 1st's vote in 2004 while Republican Rep. Renzi was easily re-elected.

The district, which mostly follows county lines, is missing a chunk of land in its northern section to avoid placing the Hopi Nation in the same district as the Navajo Nation. The two tribes have historical land disputes. To connect the Hopi land with the western Arizona-based 2nd District, mapmakers sliced the Colorado River from the 1st where it cuts through the Grand Canyon. The district has the largest American Indian population (23 percent) in the nation.

The 1st, home to great natural beauty, tribal lands and the city of Sedona, felt its tourist economy suffer during the recession that began in the late-1990s. The 1st also faced drought and then forest fires in 2002, wounding the logging industry and straining the resources of local governments in the north.

MAJOR INDUSTRY
Tourism, copper mining, logging

CITIES
Flagstaff, 52,894; Prescott, 33,938; Casa Grande, 25,224; Prescott Valley, 23,535

NOTABLE
Arizona's most significant Civil War battle took place at Picacho Peak; Lowell Observatory, in Flagstaff, is where Clyde Tombaugh discovered Pluto in 1930; Casa Grande Ruins National Monument near Coolidge features the remains of a large prehistoric building.

Rep. Trent Franks (R)

Elected 2002; 2nd term

CAPITOL OFFICE
225-4576
www.house.gov/franks
1237 Longworth 20515-0302; fax 225-6328

COMMITTEES
Armed Services
Judiciary

HOMETOWN
Glendale

BORN
June 19, 1957, Uravan, Colo.

RELIGION
Baptist

FAMILY
Wife, Josephine Franks

EDUCATION
Ottawa U. (Ariz.), attended 1989-90

CAREER
Oil company executive; conservative think tank
president; state children's programs director

POLITICAL HIGHLIGHTS
Ariz. House, 1985-87; defeated for re-election to
Ariz. House, 1986; sought Republican nomination
for U.S. House, 1994

ELECTION RESULTS

2004 GENERAL

Trent Franks (R)	165,260	59.2%
Randy Camacho (D)	107,406	38.5%
Powell Gammill (LIBERT)	6,625	2.4%

2004 PRIMARY

Trent Franks (R)	45,261	63.6%
Rick L. Murphy (R)	25,871	36.4%

2002 GENERAL

Trent Franks (R)	100,359	59.9%
Randy Camacho (D)	61,217	36.6%
Edward R. Carlson (LIBERT)	5,919	3.5%

An opponent of abortion rights and cultural permissiveness, Franks followed the call to political activism sounded by Pat Robertson and other Christian leaders in the 1980s. He is just the kind of future officeholder they envisioned. He is not a career politician and he is devoted to a relatively narrow "values" agenda.

Before his 2002 election to Congress, Franks' only previous legislative experience was as a one-term state House representative, from 1985 to 1987. He made his living, and a lucrative one, in oil and gas exploration, which helped finance his first successful congressional race. When he did jump into local and state politics, it was to advance causes important to evangelical Christian conservatives. He headed the Arizona Family Research Institute, a group affiliated with Christian syndicated radio host James Dobson and his Focus on the Family organization, which is at the forefront of the "traditional values" movement.

In his first term in the House, Franks tried to develop a national following for an idea he successfully promoted back home: tax credits for charitable contributions to groups that provide tuition vouchers for children enrolled in private or parochial schools. Franks drafted an Arizona law in 1997 creating such scholarships, which has been challenged in federal court as an impermissible mingling of church and state. He is the sponsor of a bill in the House to create a federal tax credit for people in states that adopt a state tax credit similar to Arizona's.

Franks was a booster of the 2003 measure creating private school tuition vouchers for students in Washington, D.C.'s public schools. The single-city effort, sponsored by fellow Arizona conservative Jeff Flake, was considered an opportunity to show whether government-funded vouchers can work at a national level to raise the academic performance of low-income students.

His other signature social issue is abortion. Franks supports rolling back the landmark *Roe v. Wade* Supreme Court decision legalizing abortion and calls abortion "the greatest holocaust in the history of mankind." Back home, he was known around the statehouse for wearing a tie tack in the shape of a fetus's feet. At the outset of the 109th Congress, he was named to the Judiciary Committee, giving him an ideal forum to press his views on the issue.

Franks is among the Republicans with a skepticism of government's ability to solve thorny social problems. He opposed President Bush's 2003 expansion of the Medicare program with a new prescription drug benefit for the elderly until the very last minute, when, in a dramatic vote tally that lasted through the night, he changed his mind. Franks, along with one other Republican, C.L. "Butch" Otter of Idaho, switched his vote from no to yes, saving the bill from defeat. The turnabout came after a night of intense pressure by Bush, who lobbied Franks personally by telephone, and from Speaker J. Dennis Hastert and other GOP leaders.

Franks proved indispensible to the leadership at another moment in the 108th Congress. When associates of Majority Leader Tom DeLay were indicted in Texas in a campaign fundraising investigation, Franks helped draft a new rule allowing DeLay to keep his leadership post even if he were indicted. The rule change reversed a policy that Republicans 11 years earlier had insisted was a logical way to stem corruption in the House. At the time, they were still in the minority and clamoring for an investigation of Ways and Means Chairman Dan Rostenkowski, a Democrat from Illinois, who was ultimately indicted, convicted and sent to jail on corruption charges.

Franks acknowledged that the rule change had the appearance of reducing accountability "when really we are just ensuring justice." He said he got involved because of his great respect for DeLay but also because of the help that DeLay, one of the party's top fundraisers, had given him in the 2002 race, when Franks was able to beat out more-seasoned Republicans for the seat.

He may now be an ally of the top leadership, but he is unpopular with another powerful group within the party: the Republicans who chair the Appropriations subcommittees. He has conducted a creative if quixotic campaign to curb their authority, which he thinks leads to excessive spending. Franks has called for limiting Appropriations Committee membership to six years. Appropriators typically gain influence through seniority.

From his perch on the Budget Committee in the 108th, he became a crusader for slashing spending to reduce what he believes is a dangerously rising federal deficit. With Flake, he also has sponsored a bill to take money spent on pork barrel projects and put it into defense and homeland security budgets.

Unlike many lawmakers who decry the deficit while quietly lobbying appropriators for every federal dollar they can get, Franks focuses on just a handful of items important to his constituents. The biggest of these is Luke Air Force Base, a major hub for training fighter pilots. In 2003, he worked from his seat on the Armed Services Committee to secure $14 million for land acquisition around the base, seen locally as an important step toward keeping development from encroaching on the base and the vast airspace it uses in its training missions.

Franks lost his first attempt at a House seat to a Republican primary rival with whom he now serves in the Arizona delegation. That 1994 race for the open 4th District seat went to John Shadegg.

When Franks decided to try again in 2002, he wasn't considered a top-tier candidate in the primary, the key event in the heavily Republican district. But Franks spent $556,000, including $383,000 of his own money, and edged past Lisa Atkins, former chief of staff for retiring GOP Rep. Bob Stump, by just 797 votes in a seven-way GOP primary. He then handily defeated the Democratic candidate.

Initially in the 2004 cycle, Franks appeared the most endangered of the first-term GOP incumbents. He drew a well-financed challenger in the Republican primary, radio station owner Rick L. Murphy, who poured more than $500,000 of his own money into the contest. But Franks won by 64 percent of the vote and went on to win in November by 59 percent.

KEY VOTES

2004

No Extend federal unemployment benefits by 13 weeks
No Pass $283.2 billion, six-year federal highway and mass transit bill
Yes Approve $146 billion multi-year extension of previously enacted middle-class tax breaks
Yes Amend the Constitution to prohibit same-sex marriage
Yes Cut corporate taxes $137 billion over 10 years
Yes Reorganize U.S. intelligence agencies as proposed by Sept. 11 commission

2003

Yes Cut taxes by $330 billion through fiscal 2013
No Block Bush rule scaling back overtime pay for some white-collar federal workers
Yes Do not allow use of search warrants without first notifying subjects
Yes Allow importation of prescription drugs
Yes Create private school voucher program in Washington, D.C.
Yes Ban "partial birth" abortion except to save a woman's life
No Split $18.6 billion in Iraq aid into half-grant, half-loan
Yes Overhaul Medicare and create prescription drug benefit

CQ VOTE STUDIES

	PARTY UNITY		PRESIDENTIAL SUPPORT	
	Support	Oppose	Support	Oppose
2004	98%	2%	91%	9%
2003	97%	3%	93%	7%

INTEREST GROUPS

	AFL-CIO	ADA	CCUS	ACU
2004	0%	0%	95%	100%
2003	7%	10%	93%	88%

ARIZONA 2

Northwest and central — most of Glendale, Peoria, Lake Havasu City; Hopi reservation

Although the 2nd spans the northwestern corner of Arizona, Republicans living in the fast-growing Phoenix suburbs in the district's southeast dominate its politics. This area, which includes a small portion of the city itself, takes in suburbs such as Peoria, most of Glendale and the retirement community of Sun City. It is home to the vast majority of the 2nd's voters.

Most of the district's land is in Mohave County, where Lake Havasu City, Bullhead City and Kingman are located. Democrats maintain isolated areas of influence among American Indians in the northwest, where younger, lower-income and larger minority populations live. Overall, the district is almost 80 percent white and gave Republican George W. Bush 61 percent of the vote in the 2004 presidential election.

The 2nd also includes the Hopi reservation, an appendage separated from the surrounding Navajo reservation (located in the 1st). Historical

tensions between the tribes have led the Hopi to typically support the Republican Party, which has sided with the smaller tribe in some disputes. To reach the Hopi land in northeastern Arizona, the 2nd follows the Colorado River through the Grand Canyon, though both sides of the canyon are in the 1st.

The district's economy, once grounded in agriculture, has diversified to include manufacturing jobs in the aerospace, electronics, communications and chemical industries. Diversification helped soften the blow of the early-2000s recession.

MAJOR INDUSTRY
Retail, manufacturing, tourism

MILITARY BASES
Luke Air Force Base, 5,585 military, 2,251 civilian (2002)

CITIES
Glendale (pt.), 146,483; Peoria, 108,364; Phoenix (pt.), 47,199; Lake Havasu City, 41,938; Sun City (unincorporated), 38,309; Bullhead City, 33,769

NOTABLE
Lake Havasu City has been home to the old London Bridge since 1971; The Phoenix Coyotes hockey team moved into a new arena in Glendale in 2003.

Rep. John Shadegg (R)

Elected 1994; 6th term

CAPITOL OFFICE
225-3361
johnshadegg.house.gov
306 Cannon 20515-0303; fax 225-3462

COMMITTEES
Energy & Commerce

HOMETOWN
Phoenix

BORN
Oct. 22, 1949, Phoenix, Ariz.

RELIGION
Episcopalian

FAMILY
Wife, Shirley Shadegg; two children

EDUCATION
U. of Arizona, B.A. 1972, J.D. 1975

MILITARY SERVICE
Ariz. Air National Guard, 1969-75

CAREER
State prosecutor; lawyer

POLITICAL HIGHLIGHTS
No previous office

ELECTION RESULTS

2004 GENERAL

John Shadegg (R)	181,012	80.1%
Mark J. Yannone (LIBERT)	44,962	19.9%

2004 PRIMARY

John Shadegg (R)	unopposed

2002 GENERAL

John Shadegg (R)	104,847	67.3%
Charles Hill (D)	47,173	30.3%
Mark J. Yannone (LIBERT)	3,731	2.4%

PREVIOUS WINNING PERCENTAGES
2000 (64%); 1998 (65%); 1996 (67%); 1994 (60%)

Shadegg's rise to the fifth highest leadership post among House Republicans is a testament both to his genial manner and to the entrenched power of party conservatives.

Shadegg (SHAD-egg) arrived in Congress in 1994 as a disciple of Speaker Newt Gingrich, not only in his small-government philosophy but also in his confrontational political style. But now, the six-term congressman is both the leader of the conservative stalwarts and chairman of the Republican Policy Committee, giving him and his followers enhanced clout.

Shadegg worked behind the scenes to corral enough votes among his fellow Republicans to scare off any competition. In the end, he won the slot unanimously. As Policy Committee chair, he is in charge of research and documentation to support House GOP positions and debates on issues.

A fiscal tightwad, Shadegg is expected to bring this view to the debates over spending and social programs likely to dominate the 109th Congress. Citizens Against Government Waste, a group that seeks to hold down what it considers excessive federal spending, gave Shadegg its highest rating, a 95 percent, in 2003. Shadegg was also named a "Friend of the Taxpayer" by the National Taxpayers Union, another fiscal watchdog group.

Shadegg earned these accolades by being one of only 25 Republicans to vote against expanding the Medicare program to cover prescription drugs in 2004. He also, for fiscal reasons, opposed the $283.2 billion transportation bill and an extension of unemployment benefits for an additional 13 weeks.

Although he can be blunt, Shadegg is also energetic, amiable and well-informed on the issues. And he is extraordinarily stubborn — with one of the "strongest backbones" in the House, according to a 2002 Washingtonian magazine survey of congressional aides. Shadegg's approach — he says he would prefer to lose on principles than win on politics — led to his chairmanship from 2000 to 2002 of the caucus of about 60 Republicans who aim to reduce the role of the federal government and are not inclined toward compromise. (The group was known through the 106th Congress as the Conservative Action Team, or CATs, but then changed its name to the Republican Study Committee.)

Shadegg does not shy away from controversy. At the 2004 Republican convention in New York, he called for his state's delegates to stop buying USA Today after controversial filmmaker Michael Moore got into the proceedings with USA Today press credentials. Speaking at the delegation's breakfast, Shadegg told his state colleagues that they "ought to call and cancel your subscriptions to USA Today. Say hello! Goodbye!"

Shadegg has been useful to his party's leadership, which may have helped in his rise to a top position. In the 106th, when a band of GOP mavericks threatened to join Democrats to defeat the Republican health care agenda, Shadegg helped stave off an embarrassing defeat for the leaders by drafting a plan designed to find a middle ground on managed-care regulation. His proposal soared above two other GOP alternatives and came nearest to toppling the Democratic measure the House ultimately passed.

Speaker J. Dennis Hastert tapped Shadegg as one of his representatives to negotiate with Senate leaders on the managed-care issue. Those talks came to naught in 2000. But Shadegg secured a reputation as an eloquent spokesman for the GOP view that, with health care costs rising, any move to increase the legal rights of managed-care patients must not lead to a flood of new lawsuits, which ultimately would increase insurance prices.

Shadegg's health care proposals are market-oriented. He champions a range of initiatives aimed at employing private insurance to shrink the ranks of the uninsured. He advocates providing tax credits to help people buy insurance, allowing full tax deductibility for the self-employed, and creating medical savings accounts and new insurance risk pools for small-business workers and others.

Shadegg's Health Care Choice Act, first introduced in the 108th Congress and championed by President Bush, would allow individuals seeking to buy insurance to purchase policies that may not include mandated coverages required by their state's insurance regulators. It would also allow purchasers to shop — online, over the phone, or by mail — in other states for policies that include only those benefits that the buyers deem necessary.

A skilled lawyer who appears to relish the details of the legislative process, Shadegg has served since 1999 on the Energy and Commerce Committee. He also served on the House GOP Steering Committee, which makes committee assignments for other members. In the 108th, he was chairman of Homeland Security's Emergency Preparedness and Response Subcommittee.

Shadegg's family name is well-known in Arizona GOP circles. His late father, Stephen, was a longtime political adviser to Barry Goldwater, the five-term Arizona senator and 1964 Republican presidential nominee. The younger Shadegg developed his own political connections, working in the state attorney general's office and then serving as counsel to the House Republican Caucus in the Arizona Legislature.

The election law expertise Shadegg gained in Phoenix came in handy when he wrote a position paper for House Republican leaders on the application of law in the disputed 2000 presidential contest. He went to Florida, the locus of the dispute, and was a prominent public spokesman for George W. Bush's position.

Shadegg, who took 80 percent of the vote in the 2004 election, always has won his elections with ease. He beat his first opponent with 60 percent of the vote in 1994 in a three-way race for the House seat vacated when Republican Jon Kyl won election to the Senate. The Libertarian in that contest, Mark J. Yannone, also was Shadegg's only opponent in 2004. Yannone didn't come close either time.

KEY VOTES

2004
No   Extend federal unemployment benefits by 13 weeks
No   Pass $283.2 billion, six-year federal highway and mass transit bill
Yes   Approve $146 billion multi-year extension of previously enacted middle-class tax breaks
Yes   Amend the Constitution to prohibit same-sex marriage
Yes   Cut corporate taxes $137 billion over 10 years
Yes   Reorganize U.S. intelligence agencies as proposed by Sept. 11 commission

2003
Yes   Cut taxes by $330 billion through fiscal 2013
No   Block Bush rule scaling back overtime pay for some white-collar federal workers
No   Do not allow use of search warrants without first notifying subjects
Yes   Allow importation of prescription drugs
Yes   Create private school voucher program in Washington, D.C.
Yes   Ban "partial birth" abortion except to save a woman's life
No   Split $18.6 billion in Iraq aid into half-grant, half-loan
No   Overhaul Medicare and create prescription drug benefit

CQ VOTE STUDIES

	PARTY UNITY		PRESIDENTIAL SUPPORT	
	Support	Oppose	Support	Oppose
2004	99%	1%	97%	3%
2003	97%	3%	89%	11%
2002	98%	2%	87%	13%
2001	96%	4%	84%	16%
2000	96%	4%	22%	78%

INTEREST GROUPS

	AFL-CIO	ADA	CCUS	ACU
2004	7%	0%	95%	100%
2003	7%	20%	90%	96%
2002	11%	0%	90%	100%
2001	0%	5%	96%	96%
2000	0%	5%	80%	96%

ARIZONA 3
Northern Phoenix; Paradise Valley

Encompassing a large northern chunk of Phoenix and the hills and suburbs north of the city, the 3rd is Arizona's least minority-influenced district — 79 percent of its residents are white. Still, the district is changing with the rest of the state as the number of Hispanics increases.

Most district voters consistently support economically and socially conservative candidates at the local and federal levels. The 3rd backed George W. Bush in the previous two presidential contests, with Bush capturing 58 percent of the vote in 2004.

Democrats are concentrated in the southern part of the 3rd, where the district extends to downtown Phoenix. Seeds of liberalism also are developing in the more rural sections north of Phoenix, as young professionals move into planned communities such as New River, but they are mixed with conservative areas such as the large community of Anthem, which is more Republican.

The entire Phoenix area experienced explosive growth during the 1990s.

Divided among five congressional districts, the city itself grew by almost one-third, and even small Cave Creek north of the city grew by more than one-fourth. The area is home to many manufacturing companies, including producers of semiconductors, electronics and aerospace equipment. Aerospace manufacturer Honeywell has a division headquarters in the 3rd.

Many of the state's most affluent and politically active residents live east of Phoenix in the posh community of Paradise Valley, where the median household income is more than $150,000. The town is exclusively zoned for single-family residential use and collects no property taxes.

MAJOR INDUSTRY
Technology, manufacturing, electronics

CITIES
Phoenix (pt.), 603,604; Paradise Valley, 13,664; New River, 10,740

NOTABLE
Locally brewed Cave Creek Chili Beer has a pepper in every bottle; Carefree is home to a sundial that locals call one of the largest working sundials in the Western Hemisphere.

Rep. Ed Pastor (D)

Elected September 1991; 7th full term

CAPITOL OFFICE
225-4065
www.house.gov/pastor
2465 Rayburn 20515-0304; fax 225-1655

COMMITTEES
Appropriations

HOMETOWN
Phoenix

BORN
June 28, 1943, Claypool, Ariz.

RELIGION
Roman Catholic

FAMILY
Wife, Verma Mendez Pastor; two children

EDUCATION
Arizona State U., B.A. 1966 (chemistry), J.D. 1974

CAREER
Teacher; gubernatorial aide; public policy consultant

POLITICAL HIGHLIGHTS
Maricopa County Board of Supervisors, 1977-91

ELECTION RESULTS

2004 GENERAL

Ed Pastor (D)	77,150	70.1%
Don Karg (R)	28,238	25.7%
Gary Fallon (LIBERT)	4,639	4.2%

2004 PRIMARY

Ed Pastor (D)	unopposed

2002 GENERAL

Ed Pastor (D)	44,517	67.4%
Jonathan Barnert (R)	18,381	27.8%
Amy Gibbons (LIBERT)	3,167	4.8%

PREVIOUS WINNING PERCENTAGES
2000 (69%); 1998 (68%); 1996 (65%); 1994 (62%); 1992 (66%); 1991 Special Election (56%)

Now in his second decade in the House, Pastor is one of the highest-ranking Hispanic lawmakers in Washington, where he enjoys a prominent spot in the Democratic leadership. He has been one of his party's chief deputy whips since 1999, and he sits on the Appropriations Committee.

The party clearly recognizes his importance and prominence. Pastor (pas-TORE) was asked in the summer of 2004 by Democratic presidential nominee Sen. John Kerry to serve as a co-chairman of the Democratic National Committee along with Sen. Richard J. Durbin of Illinois and Rep. Stephanie Tubbs Jones of Ohio.

Two character traits — patience and pragmatism — have helped Pastor succeed politically. He entered the House after waiting patiently for the venerable Democrat Morris K. Udall to step down. Udall suffered from Parkinson's disease for more than a decade, but he stayed on until May 1991, when his health finally forced his resignation.

Pastor learned to be pragmatic after spending years in the minority in local government back home in Phoenix. As the first Hispanic congressman from Arizona, Pastor quickly set about becoming an insider. He was helped in this quest by the Democratic Party's desire to promote promising minority members.

Although usually mild-mannered and calm, Pastor can play the partisan ideologue when it comes to constituent issues. He criticized the Bush administration in 2004 for failing to extend unemployment compensation benefits for an additional 13 weeks. "While this will have little impact on the executives of Enron or Halliburton, there are more than 23,000 Arizonans who will be wondering how they will pay their bills," Pastor said.

Pastor received a seat on Appropriations in 1993, after election to his first full term. His seats on the Transportation-Treasury and Energy and Water Development subcommittees have enabled him to keep a steady flow of grants and federal building contracts headed toward his district.

In the 107th Congress, Pastor was able to get nearly $25 million in federal funds directed to Arizona in the energy and water spending bill. This included $17 million for Phoenix's Rio Salado project, an effort to restore natural habitat and control flooding along the Salt River bed in south Phoenix. Pastor and Arizona Republican Rep. J.D. Hayworth also secured $13 million in federal transportation dollars in 2004 to help complete Phoenix's light-rail project.

But it is the issue of immigration that commands much of Pastor's attention. In 2004, Pastor tried but failed to remove a provision in the Treasury Department spending bill that prohibited banks from allowing the use of special Mexican identity cards to establish bank accounts and gain access to other financial services. The "matricula" cards, which have been issued by the thousands by Mexican consular offices, are identification cards widely used by immigrants — including those illegally living in the United States — to set up bank accounts and obtain mortgages.

Proponents of the Treasury bill provision said the card is unreliable and allowing its use could help terrorists falsify their identities. But Pastor and other lawmakers argued that the Homeland Security Department could restrict use of the cards for immigration and other security matters but not for banking transactions.

When many lawmakers insisted that immigration and border restrictions be tightened after the Sept. 11, 2001, terrorist attacks, Pastor did not agree.

"Fear and suspicion lead to discrimination and racial profiling," he wrote in an op-ed piece in The Arizona Republic. "Attacks on freedom, in the name of terrorism or in the name of security, are attacks on our way of life." Later, Pastor introduced amnesty legislation to allow illegal immigrants who had been in the United States since before Jan. 1, 2000, to apply to be legal residents. Those who had lived in the United States for at least five years could apply for permanent residency.

Pastor was chairman of the Congressional Hispanic Caucus in 1995-96, and he has opposed occasional Republican efforts to make English the official language of the federal government. Such a law would be unconstitutional, Pastor argues, and also would not have the unifying impact that Republicans say they intend. "This legislation will further isolate non-native speakers of English and discourage them from fully integrating themselves into society," Pastor said. His wife, Verma, was the longtime director of bilingual programs for the Arizona Department of Education.

The oldest son of a copper miner, Pastor grew up in a working-class household about 85 miles east of Phoenix. He was the first member of his family to attend college. After teaching high school, he earned a law degree and ended up as an aide to Democratic Gov. Raul Castro.

Pastor was elected to the Maricopa County Board of Supervisors in 1976. During his years there — often as the only Democrat — he generally got along with the GOP majority and was able to achieve much of his legislative agenda. "I said I would never attack them personally," he told the Arizona Daily Star. "In return, I expected them to respect my positions and to listen when I made my pitch." He said his minority-party status on the board of supervisors taught him patience and sharpened his negotiating skills.

Pastor had been eyeing a run for the 2nd District ever since it was drawn in 1982 as the state's most Hispanic district. He quit his post on the board of supervisors two days after Udall's resignation to mount a full-time quest to win the subsequent special election. He was the establishment's choice, having built up a healthy war chest and high name recognition as a supervisor, and in the five-person special primary he prevailed by 5 percentage points over Tucson Mayor Tom Volgy. His 11 percentage point victory in the special election over Republican Pat Conner, a Yuma County supervisor, remains his closest House election.

Reapportionment after the 2000 census gave Arizona two additional House seats, and Pastor chose to run in the newly drawn 4th District nestled in the suburbs of Phoenix. Its population has a slightly less Hispanic makeup than his old 2nd District, but that has caused him no electoral difficulty.

KEY VOTES

2004
Yes Extend federal unemployment benefits by 13 weeks
Yes Pass $283.2 billion, six-year federal highway and mass transit bill
No   Approve $146 billion multi-year extension of previously enacted middle-class tax breaks
No   Amend the Constitution to prohibit same-sex marriage
No   Cut corporate taxes $137 billion over 10 years
Yes Reorganize U.S. intelligence agencies as proposed by Sept. 11 commission

2003
No   Cut taxes by $330 billion through fiscal 2013
Yes Block Bush rule scaling back overtime pay for some white-collar federal workers
Yes Do not allow use of search warrants without first notifying subjects
?   Allow importation of prescription drugs
No   Create private school voucher program in Washington, D.C.
No   Ban "partial birth" abortion except to save a woman's life
Yes Split $18.6 billion in Iraq aid into half-grant, half-loan
No   Overhaul Medicare and create prescription drug benefit

CQ VOTE STUDIES

	PARTY UNITY		PRESIDENTIAL SUPPORT	
	Support	Oppose	Support	Oppose
2004	93%	7%	18%	82%
2003	95%	5%	23%	77%
2002	92%	8%	28%	72%
2001	89%	11%	21%	79%
2000	90%	10%	81%	19%

INTEREST GROUPS

	AFL-CIO	ADA	CCUS	ACU
2004	100%	100%	29%	4%
2003	100%	80%	37%	25%
2002	100%	95%	40%	0%
2001	92%	100%	39%	8%
2000	100%	90%	52%	8%

ARIZONA 4
Downtown and south Phoenix; part of Glendale

Centered around Phoenix in Arizona's rapidly growing "Valley of the Sun," the Hispanic-majority 4th remains a Democratic stronghold in a generally Republican state.

The district is dominated by lower-income neighborhoods in downtown Phoenix that tend to elect Democrats. These areas have undergone a slow economic change as more white-collar workers buy up housing, but the influx has yet to shake the 4th's solidly liberal base.

The 4th's portion of the city includes the Phoenix airport (one of the nation's busiest), the state Capitol, the Heard Museum of American Indian art and culture, Mystery Castle and shopping complexes, including Arizona Center and Desert Sky Mall. Bank One Ballpark and America West Arena, home to most of the Phoenix sports teams, are here, and health care jobs also aid the economy. Area officials are working on construction of a light-rail line connecting Phoenix with

Tempe and Mesa. The initial 20-mile segment is scheduled to cost $1.3 billion and begin service by December 2008.

Glendale — shared with the 2nd District — is a conservative, prosperous community that nearly doubled its population during the 1990s. A few agricultural or undeveloped areas remain in the southwestern edge of the district, but they probably will be overtaken in the coming years as the city continues to sprawl outward.

Arizona's Hispanic voters tend to break from the Democratic Party on some social issues, opposing abortion rights and favoring some traditionally Republican "family values"-type legislation. The 4th has the state's highest percentage of Hispanic residents (58 percent) and its highest percentage of blacks (7 percent).

MAJOR INDUSTRY
Retail, government, manufacturing

CITIES
Phoenix (pt.) 558,408; Glendale (pt.), 72,329; Guadalupe, 5,228

NOTABLE
In the late 1800s, residents chose the name "Phoenix" to reflect that the town would rise from the ashes of a once-thriving Indian civilization.

Rep. J.D. Hayworth (R)

Elected 1994; 6th term

CAPITOL OFFICE
225-2190
hayworth.house.gov
2434 Rayburn 20515-0305; fax 225-3263

COMMITTEES
Resources
Ways & Means

HOMETOWN
Scottsdale

BORN
July 12, 1958, High Point, N.C.

RELIGION
Baptist

FAMILY
Wife, Mary Hayworth; three children

EDUCATION
North Carolina State U., B.A. 1980 (speech
communications & political science)

CAREER
Radio commentator; sports broadcaster; public
relations consultant; insurance agent

POLITICAL HIGHLIGHTS
No previous office

ELECTION RESULTS

2004 GENERAL

J.D. Hayworth (R)	159,455	59.5%
Elizabeth Rogers (D)	102,363	38.2%
Michael Kielsky (LIBERT)	6,189	2.3%

2004 PRIMARY

J.D. Hayworth (R)	43,166	79.3%
Roselyn O'Connell (R)	11,296	20.7%

2002 GENERAL

J.D. Hayworth (R)	103,870	61.2%
Craig Columbus (D)	61,559	36.3%
Warren Severin (LIBERT)	4,383	2.6%

PREVIOUS WINNING PERCENTAGES
2000 (61%); 1998 (53%); 1996 (48%); 1994 (55%)

Affable, boisterous and brimming with confidence, Hayworth is a loyal party advocate whose colorful, loud suits merely underscore the vehemence of his conservative views.

He is a frequent guest on radio talk shows and cable news programs such as "Crossfire," where his booming voice and take-no-prisoners debate style remind audiences of his broadcasting background. Though he underwent gastrointestinal bypass surgery in 2003 to downsize his physique, there's still nothing small about Hayworth's presence.

Hayworth, an assistant whip, has cultivated a reputation as one of the most faithful soldiers in the House GOP. He voted with his party 95 percent of the time in the 108th Congress and travels throughout the country to raise money for Republican candidates. For a man who loves partisan politics as much as Hayworth, it was only natural he would run for House Republican Conference chairman in the 108th: The job is all about selling the GOP message, a natural fit for the former sports anchor and radio commentator who thrives on deflating Democrats and scoring points in ideological debates. His lopsided loss to Deborah Pryce of Ohio was a disappointment, but even without an elected leadership position Hayworth continues to serve as a proud and enthusiastic party spokesman.

Hayworth relishes the fight with liberals. He is a devoted fan of conservative radio personality Rush Limbaugh, and one does not have to look far to find similarities in the two men's combative rhetorical styles. "While facts are stubborn things," Hayworth said during one floor speech, "we would simply point out to my friends on the left that throughout their time and the last time they were in control of this House they spent all of the Social Security surplus, they gave us the largest tax increase in American history, and they sunk us deeper into debt." In the eyes of his supporters, that fighting spirit is his greatest strength.

Hayworth has not achieved as much prominence in the legislative arena, but he is starting to make his mark. He serves on the powerful Ways and Means Committee, and used his perch there in 2002 to help push through the House a bill to encourage low- and moderate-income people to buy long-term care insurance by creating a new tax deduction for the premiums. He is a strong supporter of the GOP leadership's tax-cutting agenda.

Although Ways and Means is generally an "exclusive" committee assignment, Hayworth has a waiver that allows him also to serve on the Resources Committee, which has jurisdiction over public lands, water, Indian affairs and forests. He won enactment in 2000 of legislation authorizing the U.S. Forest Service to grant federally controlled land to local communities for construction of schools.

He chaired a bipartisan task force in 1995 that investigated the possible misuse of over $2.4 billion in Indian Trust Fund accounts. In 1997, Hayworth was one of the founders of the Congressional Native American Caucus and he continues to serve as a co-chairman.

Mostly, Hayworth favors legislation to promote conservative causes, such as a constitutional amendment he cosponsored in 2001 to permit voluntary prayer in schools. He also wants to give the legislative branch more control over the federal bureaucracy. Hayworth sponsors a bill every Congress to require both congressional and presidential approval of all future regulations issued by government agencies.

Occasionally, Hayworth has landed in hot water through a poor choice of words. During the 2002 debate on the campaign finance overhaul bill, he spoke in favor of an amendment to bar legal immigrants from contributing to political campaigns — an issue of extreme sensitivity among Hispanics, a group President Bush was trying to court. Hayworth did not help that cause with his speech, which ended: "Yes, I guess it is poisonous to disallow enemies of this state access to our political system."

Hayworth said he was not talking about legal immigrants in general, but about a notorious 1996 fundraiser at a Buddhist temple attended by Vice President Al Gore. But he was pummeled by Democrats who thought he was calling all legal residents enemies of the state.

Whatever his views of legal immigrants, Hayworth is determined to deter illegal immigration. Unlike his Arizona Republican colleagues Rep. Jeff Flake and Sen. John McCain, he opposes efforts to ease the path toward permanent residency for workers who entered the country illegally. In fact, he cosponsored a bill to authorize state and local police to round up illegal immigrants and turn them over for deportation. In 2004, he was one of just 88 House members to vote for a bill to require doctors and hospitals to report illegal aliens for deportation.

Never one to be plagued by self-doubt or second thoughts, Hayworth is more than willing to defend controversial views. He says he was prepared for people to have low expectations of him when he entered politics because of his reputation as a "somewhat irreverent, gregarious" TV personality.

After attending North Carolina State University on a football scholarship, Hayworth held sports broadcasting jobs in Cincinnati and Greenville, S.C., before landing in Phoenix in 1987. He then moved into political commentary, an outgrowth of his longstanding interest in government. A political history buff — he is an aficionado of Dwight D. Eisenhower's presidency — he can readily recount anecdotes from Arizona's colorful past.

Though Hayworth's 6th District House bid in 1994 was his first political campaign, he was already a familiar and well-liked figure to voters thanks to his seven years as a sports anchor on Phoenix's CBS affiliate and his work with area charitable events off the air. In the GOP sweep, he defeated freshman Democrat Karan English by 14 percentage points.

In a district that narrowly backed Bill Clinton in 1996, Democrats mounted aggressive challenges to Hayworth in the next three elections. Redistricting prior to the 2002 election, however, made the renumbered 5th District more reliably Republican — with more suburbs and less American Indian reservation territory. In 2004, Hayworth easily won a sixth term with 60 percent of the vote.

KEY VOTES

2004
No   Extend federal unemployment benefits by 13 weeks
Yes Pass $283.2 billion, six-year federal highway and mass transit bill
Yes Approve $146 billion multi-year extension of previously enacted middle-class tax breaks
Yes Amend the Constitution to prohibit same-sex marriage
Yes Cut corporate taxes $137 billion over 10 years
No   Reorganize U.S. intelligence agencies as proposed by Sept. 11 commission

2003
Yes Cut taxes by $330 billion through fiscal 2013
No   Block Bush rule scaling back overtime pay for some white-collar federal workers
Yes Do not allow use of search warrants without first notifying subjects
Yes Allow importation of prescription drugs
Yes Create private school voucher program in Washington, D.C.
Yes Ban "partial birth" abortion except to save a woman's life
No   Split $18.6 billion in Iraq aid into half-grant, half-loan
Yes Overhaul Medicare and create prescription drug benefit

CQ VOTE STUDIES

	PARTY UNITY		PRESIDENTIAL SUPPORT	
	Support	Oppose	Support	Oppose
2004	96%	4%	82%	18%
2003	95%	5%	94%	6%
2002	98%	2%	85%	15%
2001	98%	2%	91%	9%
2000	96%	4%	20%	80%

INTEREST GROUPS

	AFL-CIO	ADA	CCUS	ACU
2004	14%	5%	100%	96%
2003	7%	10%	97%	83%
2002	11%	0%	85%	100%
2001	8%	5%	87%	100%
2000	11%	5%	84%	100%

ARIZONA 5

Scottsdale; Tempe; part of Phoenix and Mesa

Wealth, beautiful sunsets and conservative politics abound in the 5th, which takes in a sliver of Phoenix and then spreads east to Tempe, Scottsdale and the western parts of Chandler and Mesa.

Scottsdale, known for its golf courses and tournaments, and Fountain Hills to the east draw retirees and their bank accounts — the 2000 census showed both communities had higher incomes and median ages than the state and nation.

Farther south, Tempe bucks the trend. The home of Arizona State University, its median age is under 30. Its more liberal voters slightly offset but do not heavily endanger the district's GOP bent. Overall, Republicans hold a 16-point voter registration advantage, and George W. Bush carried the district by nine points in the 2004 presidential election.

Tourism props up much of the area's economy, with resorts, parks, golf courses, rugged scenery and spring training baseball to convince travelers that the area is the right place for an upscale retreat. The district's small portion of Phoenix includes the city's zoo and the Desert Botanical Garden.

The Salt River and Fort McDowell Indian reservations are attracting guests of their own, and not just for the casinos. The Scottsdale Pavillions shopping mall, just inside the Salt River border, and the Out of Africa Wildlife Park in Fort McDowell are examples of reservations working with private businesses to develop their land.

MAJOR INDUSTRY
Tourism, education, health care

CITIES
Scottsdale, 202,705; Tempe, 158,625; Mesa (pt.), 96,622; Phoenix (pt.), 85,765; Chandler (pt.), 66,823; Fountain Hills, 20,235

NOTABLE
Fender, the guitar-maker, is based on the Salt River reservation; The fountain at Fountain Hills shoots a stream of water 560 feet into the air, which makes the Guinness World Records as "tallest fountain"; Frank Lloyd Wright's Taliesin West in Scottsdale was the architect's winter home; Taliesin Architects, based in Scottsdale, seeks to continue Wright's practices.

Rep. Jeff Flake (R)

Elected 2000; 3rd term

CAPITOL OFFICE
225-2635
jeff.flake@mail.house.gov
www.house.gov/flake
424 Cannon 20515-0306; fax 226-4386

COMMITTEES
International Relations
Judiciary
Resources

HOMETOWN
Mesa

BORN
Dec. 31, 1962, Snowflake, Ariz.

RELIGION
Mormon

FAMILY
Wife, Cheryl Flake; five children

EDUCATION
Brigham Young U., B.A. 1986 (international relations), M.A. 1987 (political science)

CAREER
Public policy institute director; African business trade representative; lobbyist

POLITICAL HIGHLIGHTS
No previous office

ELECTION RESULTS

2004 GENERAL

Jeff Flake (R)	202,822	79.4%
Craig Stritar (LIBERT)	52,695	20.6%

2004 PRIMARY

Jeff Flake (R)	33,784	59.3%
Stan Barnes (R)	23,186	40.7%

2002 GENERAL

Jeff Flake (R)	103,094	65.9%
Deborah Thomas (D)	49,355	31.6%
Andy Wagner (LIBERT)	3,888	2.5%

PREVIOUS WINNING PERCENTAGES
2000 (54%)

Flake rarely has met a federal program he wanted to vote for. In his relatively brief time on Capitol Hill, he has voted against initiatives to create a prescription drug benefit for the elderly under Medicare, to create a Department of Homeland Security in the wake of Sept. 11 and to overhaul federal education policy, a proposal of deep interest to his president.

That's his way of saying that the federal government is too big, and that it spends too much on matters better left to the states and individuals. As consistent as that seems, Flake has changed his view on one score. Having been elected in 2000 on a promise to term limit himself, a mainstay position for neoconservatives like Flake who believe that longevity breeds fealty to the status quo, he has found irresistible the prospect of a longer stay in Congress. Shortly after he was re-elected in 2004, he said that he'd made a "mistake" in limiting himself to three terms and that he would run again in 2006. "Some will say that this will be a legitimate campaign issue," Flake said. "In truth, it ought to be. But I am comfortable leaving it up to the voters."

Still, his dislike for big government spending and wasteful pork-barreling drives his decisions on the House floor. Most notably, Flake defied President Bush to vote against adding a $400 billion prescription drug benefit to the Medicare program for the elderly and disabled, in spite of heavy pressure from GOP leaders to support the presidential initiative. He argued that it would become an out-of-control entitlement, and was counter to the Republican principle of limited government. "This looks like nothing more than an extremely expensive way to buy votes," said Flake.

Before that, Flake voted against Bush's overhaul of federal education policy that for the first time tied aid to schools to performance on standardized tests. Flake says he does not see a substantial role for the federal government in education. The job of the government, he says, is to fulfill its promise to pay for the schooling of disabled students so that states can spend their money on other educational needs.

He opposed the federal bailout of the airline industry, the creation of a Homeland Security Department after the terrorist attacks, a law tightening corporate accounting standards and the omnibus spending bills in both 2003 and 2004.

He sits on the steering committee of the Republican Study Committee, a group of several dozen of the most conservative House Republicans, who share his views of limited government.

At the top of Flake's legislative agenda is reducing federal taxes. He backed an even larger tax cut than the one sought by President Bush in 2001, and he has worked to make those tax cuts, due to expire in 2011, permanent. He is no fan of the earned-income tax credit, which goes to people not earning enough to pay taxes and is often touted by Democrats. "We should stick with the principle that tax breaks go to people who owe taxes," he says.

But a close second among Flake's priorities is policy toward Cuba. He has been outspoken among Republicans in a movement to end the trade embargo with Cuba and restrictions on travel by U.S. citizens there. The issue is divisive for the party. A small group of Cuban-American lawmakers, mostly from Florida, adamantly oppose any warming trend toward Cuban leader Fidel Castro, who is a villain for people who fled the Communist regime and resettled in Florida. The embargo, Flake said, has not worked and should be replaced by a policy of robust economic engagement, which he predicts would hasten the end of 40 years of communist rule.

From his seat on the Judiciary Committee and its Subcommittee on Immigration, Border Security and Claims, Flake also is a leading voice in the Republican party's internecine immigration debate. The party is split between those who want to make it easier for illegal aliens who are working to stay and another who see illegal immigration as a national security threat and want to deport them. Flake has tried to bridge the two sides. He is a staunch supporter of President Bush's proposal to create a new guest worker visa for low-skilled foreigners, but he also favors tightening border security and forbidding illegal aliens from obtaining driver's licenses.

Although he is a hard-liner on a number of issues, Flake is easygoing and personable. He spends his free time in the House gym playing basketball and is a star of the Republicans' team in the annual congressional charity baseball game.

Flake and nine siblings grew up on the family ranch near Snowflake, about 100 miles northeast of Phoenix. Established in 1878, the town is named after its Mormon settler founders, Erastus Snow and William Flake, Flake's great-great-grandfather.

A member of the Mormon faith himself, Flake went on a two-year church mission to Zimbabwe and South Africa in 1982, an experience that he says has shaped his life. He majored in international relations at Brigham Young University. In 1989, as director of the Foundation for Democracy, Flake moved to Namibia, at the time recently separated from South Africa, to develop its constitution and help it move toward independence.

He returned to Arizona in 1992 to take the helm of the Goldwater Institute, a conservative think tank named for the late GOP Sen. Barry Goldwater, the 1964 Republican presidential nominee. The institute has worked to create charter schools and a tax credit plan that helps fund private school scholarships.

When GOP Rep. Matt Salmon adhered to his own three-term limit and retired in 2000, Flake entered the race to replace him. Salmon endorsed Flake, giving him an important boost over his four primary opponents, and Flake's 32 percent of the vote was enough to get the nomination. In the general election, buoyed by significant financial support from the Club for Growth, a fiscally conservative group advocating lower taxes, free trade and smaller government, Flake bested Democratic labor lobbyist David Mendoza.

Redistricting after the 2000 census gave the GOP a tailor-made district in the eastern Phoenix suburbs. In the 2002 election, Flake cruised past Democrat Deborah Thomas, a retired state employee, by 34 percentage points. Democrats did not field a candidate against him in 2004.

KEY VOTES

2004

No   Extend federal unemployment benefits by 13 weeks
No   Pass $283.2 billion, six-year federal highway and mass transit bill
Yes   Approve $146 billion multi-year extension of previously enacted middle-class tax breaks
Yes   Amend the Constitution to prohibit same-sex marriage
Yes   Cut corporate taxes $137 billion over 10 years
No   Reorganize U.S. intelligence agencies as proposed by Sept. 11 commission

2003

Yes   Cut taxes by $330 billion through fiscal 2013
No   Block Bush rule scaling back overtime pay for some white-collar federal workers
Yes   Do not allow use of search warrants without first notifying subjects
Yes   Allow importation of prescription drugs
Yes   Create private school voucher program in Washington, D.C.
Yes   Ban "partial birth" abortion except to save a woman's life
No   Split $18.6 billion in Iraq aid into half-grant, half-loan
No   Overhaul Medicare and create prescription drug benefit

CQ VOTE STUDIES

	PARTY UNITY		PRESIDENTIAL SUPPORT	
	Support	Oppose	Support	Oppose
2004	93%	7%	74%	26%
2003	90%	10%	70%	30%
2002	89%	11%	70%	30%
2001	90%	10%	77%	23%

INTEREST GROUPS

	AFL-CIO	ADA	CCUS	ACU
2004	13%	15%	81%	96%
2003	13%	25%	67%	92%
2002	22%	5%	65%	96%
2001	0%	5%	74%	92%

A R I Z O N A 6
Southeast Phoenix suburbs – most of Mesa and Chandler, Gilbert, Apache Junction

Rooted in the conservative leanings of an affluent, historically Mormon population, the suburban 6th favors Republican candidates. The district still has a significant population of Mormons, as well as a mix of young couples who commute to Phoenix. The area's warm sunny days have helped draw an established population of retirees from other states.

The district begins east of Phoenix, where it takes in all but the westernmost segments of Mesa and Chandler, both of which have experienced tremendous population growth over the past 20 years. Manufacturing aids the economy in Mesa, the state's third-largest city and now within the nation's top 50 in population.

Chandler, not as dependent on tourism as its neighbors, fuels its economy through retail business while attempting to attract biotechnology firms. Between the two cities is Gilbert, which has several construction-related businesses.

Redistricting following the 2000 census made the 6th — previously numbered the 1st — more conservative by slicing off the Democratic university town of Tempe and the district's portion of Phoenix. The district expanded east to take in part of largely agricultural Pinal County, including Apache Junction on the county's northern border.

Republicans now hold an almost 25-point edge in party registration, and the redrawn district gave George W. Bush 64 percent of its 2004 presidential vote — his highest percentage in the state. More than 75 percent white, the 6th has fewer minorities than the state average.

MAJOR INDUSTRY
Manufacturing, technology, retail

CITIES
Mesa (pt.), 299,753; Chandler (pt.), 109,758; Gilbert, 109,697; Apache Junction, 31,814

NOTABLE
Chandler's Ostrich Festival, held each March, features ostrich races and a parade; Mesa is the spring training home of the Chicago Cubs baseball team, which has led the Arizona Cactus League in attendance for many of the past 20 years; Mesa was founded by Mormons.

Rep. Raúl M. Grijalva (D)

Elected 2002; 2nd term

CAPITOL OFFICE
225-2435
www.house.gov/grijalva
1440 Longworth 20515-0307; fax 225-1541

COMMITTEES
Education & Workforce
Resources
Small Business

HOMETOWN
Tucson

BORN
Feb. 19, 1948, Tucson, Ariz.

RELIGION
Roman Catholic

FAMILY
Wife, Mona Grijalva; three children

EDUCATION
U. of Arizona, B.A. 1986 (sociology)

CAREER
University dean; community center director

POLITICAL HIGHLIGHTS
Tucson Unified School District Governing Board, 1974-86; Pima County Board of Supervisors, 1989-2002 (chairman, 1997, 2001-02)

ELECTION RESULTS

2004 GENERAL

Raúl M. Grijalva (D)	108,868	62.1%
Joseph "Joe" Sweeney (R)	59,066	33.7%
Dave Kaplan (LIBERT)	7,503	4.3%

2004 PRIMARY

Raúl M. Grijalva (D)	unopposed

2002 GENERAL

Raúl M. Grijalva (D)	61,256	59.0%
Ross Hieb (R)	38,474	37.1%
John L. Nemeth (LIBERT)	4,088	3.9%

Grijalva is a first generation Mexican-American whose father came to the United States with the infamous "bracero" labor program, which led to the exploitation of migrant farm workers after World War II. Grijalva (gree-HAHL-va) still lives in the working-class, heavily Latino section in south Tucson where he grew up, and he began his political career as a community organizer. At age 40, he finally got a college degree because, he says, he felt he couldn't effectively persuade at-risk teens to stay in school if he hadn't finished himself. His district staff members speak Spanish, as do half his aides in Washington.

Grijalva has a keen interest in immigration and border issues; his southwestern Arizona district shares 300 miles with Mexico and is the second-longest contiguous district after Texas' 23rd. In recent years, hundreds of people trying to evade border police have died in the vast Sonoran Desert, many of them in the brutally hot month of August. Just over the border are squalid factory towns where U.S.-owned companies have set up shop to take advantage of Mexico's cheap labor.

Grijalva has been a leading opponent of President Bush's guest worker proposal to allow illegal workers to remain in the United States for three years with no guarantee of residency or citizenship. The idea, he says, is reminiscent of the bracero program, which roughly translates to "worker" program and refers to the joint U.S.-Mexico agreement beginning in 1942 in which migrant workers flocked to low-wage farm jobs created by wartime labor shortages. Many of the workers were mistreated, housed in shacks and cheated out of wages under English-language contracts they couldn't read. The program ended under public pressure in 1964.

In the 108th Congress, Grijalva was the chief House sponsor of a Democratic alternative to Bush's plan; Sen. Edward M. Kennedy of Massachusetts sponsored its Senate counterpart. It called for amnesty plus a path to citizenship under certain conditions. Grijalva also fought against a Republican proposal allowing hospital emergency rooms to turn away undocumented immigrants in some cases, calling it "morally reprehensible." He says: "We must never forget that we are a country of immigrants."

His district is more than half Latino; it is largely poor and undereducated. When he arrived in Congress in 2002, Grijalva got a seat on the Education and Workforce Committee, where he has pushed to fully fund federal mandates to improve test scores in public schools. He opposes government vouchers for private school tuition. He also fought GOP-inspired changes to Head Start in 2003 giving states more control over the federal program for preschool-age children. He sponsored an unsuccessful amendment to increase Head Start money for children of migrant and seasonal workers, falling short in a 203-227 vote.

Among the most liberal lawmakers, Grijalva voted against Bush more than most other House members, supporting the president only 15 percent of the time in the 108th Congress. He was one of only a dozen House members in 2003 to vote against the administration's $78 billion emergency package to fund the U.S. occupation of Iraq.

As chairman of the House Democratic Environmental Task Force, he pushed the administration to crack down on mercury emissions from coal-fired plants. On health care issues, he supports efforts to expand the Clinton-era Children's Health Insurance Program to include not only poor children but their parents, a multibillion-dollar proposition that Republicans have long dismissed as unrealistic. He would also extend Medicare to people between the ages of 55 and 64, an idea popular among liberals that also hasn't gotten off the ground.

Grijalva has had more tangible success with a bill of local interest. In 2004, the House passed his bill to return to four Indian tribes 16,000 acres of land they had lost to the government in 1915 after they refused to lease the land privately for mining. The Bush administration also said it supported the legislation. There are a total of seven tribes in Grijalva's district. On his office wall, he displays a carved mask from the Yaquis.

Personally, Grijalva reflects the more casual ways of the Southwest. His friends donated neckties after he won election to the House in 2002, figuring he'd have to wear them regularly for the first time. His speech is still lightly accented by Spanish. Grijalva dislikes the nonstop fundraising of modern campaigns and has to be badgered by his staff to keep at it. Advised to hold a golf tournament to raise money, Grijalva instead threw a bowl-a-thon. Roughly a third of his campaign financing comes from labor groups.

Grijalva still lives a mile and a half from the small stucco house where he was raised. His father immigrated from Mexico as a ranch hand under the bracero program, married an American woman and settled in Tucson.

After high school, Grijalva attended the University of Arizona, but quit to get married. He and his school librarian wife, Mona, had three daughters, and Grijalva became a social worker and community activist. He was elected in 1974 to the Tucson school board, where he served 12 years, and later to the Pima County Board of Supervisors. He eventually became chairman of the county board. During his years in local government, he frequently advised young people from struggling Latino families to stay in school. To set the right example, he went back to school himself to finish nine credit hours left on his sociology degree, graduating in 1988 from the University of Arizona.

When once-a-decade redistricting created a new Hispanic-majority district in southern Arizona, Grijalva jumped into the crowded 2002 primary race. He prevailed despite stiff competition from one incumbent and two former state senators. One rival, state Sen. Elaine Richardson, raised twice as much money as he did, and another, state Sen. Jaime Gutierrez, was endorsed by the state's largest newspaper, The Arizona Republic.

In the general election, the makeup of the district ensured Grijalva's victory. It is heavily Democratic and 45 percent of eligible voters are Hispanic. He easily bested Republican Ross Hieb, a farmer and forester. In 2004, he was re-elected with 62 percent of the vote.

KEY VOTES

2004

Yes Extend federal unemployment benefits by 13 weeks

Yes Pass $283.2 billion, six-year federal highway and mass transit bill

Yes Approve $146 billion multi-year extension of previously enacted middle-class tax breaks

No Amend the Constitution to prohibit same-sex marriage

No Cut corporate taxes $137 billion over 10 years

Yes Reorganize U.S. intelligence agencies as proposed by Sept. 11 commission

2003

No Cut taxes by $330 billion through fiscal 2013

Yes Block Bush rule scaling back overtime pay for some white-collar federal workers

Yes Do not allow use of search warrants without first notifying subjects

Yes Allow importation of prescription drugs

No Create private school voucher program in Washington, D.C.

No Ban "partial birth" abortion except to save a woman's life

Yes Split $18.6 billion in Iraq aid into half-grant, half-loan

No Overhaul Medicare and create prescription drug benefit

CQ VOTE STUDIES

	PARTY UNITY		PRESIDENTIAL SUPPORT	
	Support	Oppose	Support	Oppose
2004	99%	1%	12%	88%
2003	99%	1%	16%	84%

INTEREST GROUPS

	AFL-CIO	ADA	CCUS	ACU
2004	100%	100%	10%	0%
2003	100%	100%	20%	12%

A R I Z O N A   7

Southwest — part of Tucson, Yuma, Avondale

Stretching mainly south and west from Phoenix, the Hispanic-majority 7th crosses large reservations and rural areas to take in Yuma, downtown Tucson and most of Arizona's border with Mexico. The district, most of which was in the 2nd until redistricting following the 2000 census, is a Democratic stronghold.

The 7th includes the University of Arizona in Tucson, southern Arizona's top employer, and the Mexican border town of Nogales. It also climbs up the state's border with California, taking in most of La Paz and all of Yuma counties. The economy is supported by a large population of seasonal immigrant workers, who buttress the agriculture and service industries but boost the district's poverty statistics. The 7th has more blue-collar workers and fewer college graduates than other Arizona districts.

Some conservative ranching communities exist in Yuma County and elsewhere in the district, but their political impact is largely offset by a Democratic-voting American Indian presence. The Tohono O'odham and

Gila River reservations are the 7th's largest, and American Indians make up 6 percent of the district's population, the second-highest percentage in the state. Overall, Democrats have an almost 2-to-1 advantage over Republicans in party registration, and John Kerry took 57 percent of the vote here in the 2004 presidential election.

MAJOR INDUSTRY
Agriculture, tourism, education

MILITARY BASES
Marine Corps Air Station Yuma, 5,026 military, 1,241 civilian (2003); Yuma Proving Ground (Army), 126 military, 664 civilian (2004)

CITIES
Tucson (pt.), 230,164; Yuma, 77,515; Avondale, 35,883; Phoenix (pt.), 26,069

NOTABLE
Yuma Territorial Prison — a late 19th century penitentiary — was turned into a high school, then a shelter for railroad vagrants, and now is a state historic park; The Saihati Camel Farm and Desert Animal Breeding Center in Yuma features Arabian camels; The Painted Rocks Petroglyph Site in southern Maricopa County displays rock etchings carved centuries ago.

Rep. Jim Kolbe (R)

Elected 1984; 11th term

An internationalist since his college days, Kolbe is President Bush's most important ally in the House on foreign aid issues, with the top job on the subcommittee that decides levels of U.S. aid to other countries. He is also a leader in the free-trade movement on Capitol Hill, and in the 109th Congress, he emerged as a player on one of the biggest domestic initiatives of Bush's second term — changes in the Social Security retirement system in favor of private investment accounts.

The 11-term moderate conservative from Arizona had been dabbling in Social Security long before it became Topic A. By the time Bush unveiled his plan in 2005, Kolbe (COAL-bee) had a bill ready to go that attracted a Democratic cosponsor, Allen Boyd of Florida. He was among the first Republicans to call for offsets to finance the transition to private accounts, including possible tax increases and cuts in benefits such as raising the retirement age to 67. Kolbe said, "I think it is one of the most important debates of the last 20 years."

The White House also looks to Kolbe for help on trade, including renewal of fast-track authority letting the president negotiate trade deals that cannot be amended by Congress. In 2002, Kolbe led the successful campaign to pass the fast-track bill in the House. Two years earlier, he helped round up votes when Congress granted China permanent normal trade status. In 1993, he pushed for ratification of the North American Free Trade Agreement. Kolbe was talked about in early 2005 as a possible choice for U.S. trade representative as Bush made staffing changes in his second term.

Kolbe's influence is most felt on the issue of foreign aid. He is in his third term as chairman of the Appropriations Subcommittee on Foreign Operations, which drafts the annual spending bill setting levels of direct foreign aid, contributions to international financial institutions and military sales financing. As others were jockeying for new assignments in the 109th Congress, Kolbe asked to return as chairman of the Foreign Operations Subcommittee.

In 2004, he headed off a movement led by Tom Lantos of California, the influential senior Democrat on the International Relations Committee, to slash military aid to Egypt. Lantos and other lawmakers were angry that Egypt had not assisted U.S. military operations in Iraq and Afghanistan or done enough, they insisted, to combat the spread of radical Islam. Kolbe and Secretary of State Colin L. Powell successfully pressed the argument that military aid to Egypt was a cornerstone of the 1979 Camp David peace accords and also a vital part of the effort to combat terrorism.

Kolbe is Bush's point man in the House on the Millennium Challenge Account, a new multibillion-dollar program initiated by the president to create a new category of U.S. aid for poor nations judged to be making progress in democracy, free markets and human rights.

Kolbe frequently travels overseas to hot spots affected by the decisions of his subcommittee. In 2004, he went to Sudan to investigate reports of genocide in that nation's Darfur region, and in early 2005, he visited tsunami-ravaged areas in South Asia.

His internationalist bent stretches back four decades, to a college year abroad. With a small group of students, he crisscrossed the globe, spending time in dozens of cities, living with families and attending classes. "I just look at the world, I think, differently today as a result of that experience," he said. "I've always been fascinated with world affairs and international

CAPITOL OFFICE
225-2542
www.house.gov/kolbe
237 Cannon 20515-0308; fax 225-0378

COMMITTEES
Appropriations
(Foreign Operations & Export Financing - chairman)

HOMETOWN
Tucson

BORN
June 28, 1942, Evanston, Ill.

RELIGION
Methodist

FAMILY
Divorced

EDUCATION
Northwestern U., B.A. 1965 (political science); Stanford U., M.B.A. 1967 (economics)

MILITARY SERVICE
Navy, 1965-69; Naval Reserve, 1970-77

CAREER
Land planning firm executive; gubernatorial aide

POLITICAL HIGHLIGHTS
Ariz. Senate, 1977-83; Republican nominee for U.S. House, 1982

ELECTION RESULTS

2004 GENERAL
Jim Kolbe (R)	183,363	60.4%
Eva Bacal (D)	109,963	36.2%
Robert Anderson (LIBERT)	10,443	3.4%

2004 PRIMARY
Jim Kolbe (R)	36,039	57.5%
Randy Graf (R)	26,686	42.5%

2002 GENERAL
Jim Kolbe (R)	126,930	63.3%
Mary Judge Ryan (D)	67,328	33.6%
Joe Duarte (LIBERT)	6,142	3.1%

PREVIOUS WINNING PERCENTAGES
2000 (60%); 1998 (52%); 1996 (69%); 1994 (68%); 1992 (67%); 1990 (65%); 1988 (68%); 1986 (65%); 1984 (51%)

issues, and I think that really turned me truly into an internationalist."

Kolbe breaks with the GOP on social issues, supporting abortion rights and some gun control bills. It was for this reason that he lost his bid to get into the leadership after the GOP won control of the House in 1994; he had wanted to be Republican Policy Committee chairman.

On his appropriations subcommittee, Kolbe has tried to walk a moderate line on international aid for family planning. In 2002, unable to broker a compromise with conservative Republicans who wanted to deny funds to Chinese government operatives suspected of forcing women to have abortions, Kolbe threw in the towel in frustration and handed the problem to Speaker J. Dennis Hastert to solve.

As the only openly homosexual Republican in Congress, Kolbe breaks with his party on many issues affecting gay and lesbian couples. He has pushed for legislation to punish "hate crimes" based on sexual orientation. In 2002, he won an amendment to the District of Columbia appropriations bill letting city health plans provide benefits to unmarried domestic partners. But he has supported proposed federal bans on same-sex marriage, which got him into hot water with gay rights groups. In fact, Kolbe publicly acknowledged his homosexuality in 1996 only after gay activists threatened to break the news in a magazine article. "The fact that I am this way has never, nor will it ever, change my commitment to represent all the people of Arizona's 5th District," Kolbe said. "I am the same person."

Kolbe's gay status has had a lingering, if minor, impact on his political career. He was held to 52 percent of the vote in 1998 by former Tucson Mayor Tom Volgy. At the 2000 Republican National Convention, members of the Texas delegation took off their cowboy hats and prayed during Kolbe's address on trade.

A former real estate consultant with an MBA from Stanford University, Kolbe first came to Washington as a Senate page for Arizona Republican Barry Goldwater. He later served two years as a Navy lieutenant on patrol boats in Vietnam. After six years in the state Senate, he won his first House victory in 1984, avenging a loss he had suffered two years earlier at the hands of Democrat James F. McNulty Jr. In his campaign ads, Kolbe rode a horse and reminded voters that he spent much of his youth on a cattle ranch near Sonoita, while McNulty was born and raised in Boston.

Kolbe's recent elections have been easy affairs. In 2002, he defeated his Democratic opponent by 30 percentage points in a redrawn portion of southeastern Arizona, renamed the 8th District. He won by a similar margin in 2004.

KEY VOTES

2004
No	Extend federal unemployment benefits by 13 weeks
No	Pass $283.2 billion, six-year federal highway and mass transit bill
Yes	Approve $146 billion multi-year extension of previously enacted middle-class tax breaks
No	Amend the Constitution to prohibit same-sex marriage
Yes	Cut corporate taxes $137 billion over 10 years
Yes	Reorganize U.S. intelligence agencies as proposed by Sept. 11 commission

2003
Yes	Cut taxes by $330 billion through fiscal 2013
No	Block Bush rule scaling back overtime pay for some white-collar federal workers
No	Do not allow use of search warrants without first notifying subjects
Yes	Allow importation of prescription drugs
Yes	Create private school voucher program in Washington, D.C.
No	Ban "partial birth" abortion except to save a woman's life
No	Split $18.6 billion in Iraq aid into half-grant, half-loan
Yes	Overhaul Medicare and create prescription drug benefit

CQ VOTE STUDIES

	PARTY UNITY		PRESIDENTIAL SUPPORT	
	Support	Oppose	Support	Oppose
2004	85%	15%	79%	21%
2003	90%	10%	80%	20%
2002	88%	12%	82%	18%
2001	91%	9%	84%	16%
2000	85%	15%	39%	61%

INTEREST GROUPS

	AFL-CIO	ADA	CCUS	ACU
2004	13%	20%	100%	56%
2003	7%	15%	97%	56%
2002	0%	20%	100%	80%
2001	0%	20%	96%	60%
2000	0%	20%	80%	68%

A R I Z O N A 8
Southeast – part of Tucson and northern suburbs

Located in the state's southeastern corner bordering New Mexico and Mexico, the 8th contains many swing voters and independents who often favor moderates in national elections. Most residents live in Pima County, primarily in the Tucson metropolitan area, although Cochise County makes up most of the district geographically. Both urban and rural areas grew by about 20 percent during the 1990s.

Tucson is surrounded by mountain ranges, but the majestic Santa Catalinas just north of the city are the local landmark. Population growth is heavy here as residents literally "head for the hills" and the wealthy, unincorporated areas of Casas Adobes and Catalina Foothills. These and other northern suburban communities are home to affluent, retired and military residents who moved to the area from other states in recent years and add to the district's GOP lean. Central areas of Tucson, including the University of Arizona, are in the neighboring 7th.

Democrats hold the majority in Santa Cruz and Cochise counties, which have large Hispanic populations, but Republicans lead in overall voter registration by about 5 percentage points. The 8th held the state's closest 2004 presidential contest, with George W. Bush winning 53 percent.

The various military jets that fly past Tucson on their way to or from Davis-Monthan Air Force Base reveal two of the area's economic engines: military and manufacturing. The city has a number of high-tech defense contractors and aerospace firms, including Raytheon Missile Systems, but the district is increasingly dependent on service industries, including tourism, to support its economic base. Tucson's growing suburbs have made construction an economic force as well.

MAJOR INDUSTRY
Service, manufacturing, military, aerospace, tourism, agriculture

MILITARY BASES
Davis-Monthan Air Force Base, 6,500 military, 1,970 civilian (2004); Fort Huachuca (Army), 5,484 military, 2,717 civilian (2004)

CITIES
Tucson (pt.), 256,535; Casas Adobes (unincorporated), 54,011; Catalina Foothills (unincorporated), 53,794; Sierra Vista, 37,775

NOTABLE
Tombstone, "the town too tough to die," was notorious for its boomtown lawlessness in the late 1800s.

Gov. Mike Huckabee (R)

First elected: 1998
(assumed office 1996)
Length of term: 4 years
Term expires: 1/07
Salary: $77,028
Phone: (501) 682-2345

Hometown: Little Rock
Born: Aug. 24, 1955;
Hope, Ark.
Religion: Baptist
Family: Wife, Janet Huckabee; three children
Education: Ouachita Baptist U., B.A. 1976;
Southwestern Baptist Theological Seminary,
attended 1976-77
Career: Television talk show host; television
documentary producer; pastor
Political highlights: Lieutenant governor,
1993-96

Election results:
2002 GENERAL
Mike Huckabee (R)	427,189	53.0%
Jimmie Lou Fisher (D)	378,303	46.9%

Lt. Gov. Winthrop P. Rockefeller (R)

First elected: 1996
Length of term: 4 years
Term expires: 1/07
Salary: $37,229
Phone: (501) 682-2144

STATE LEGISLATURE

General Assembly: At least 60
calendar days January-March in
odd-numbered years

House: 100 members, 2-year terms
2005 breakdown: 72D, 28R; 84 men,
16 women
Salary: $14,067
Phone: (501) 682-7771

Senate: 35 members, 4-year terms
2005 breakdown: 27D, 8R; 29 men,
6 women
Salary: $14,067
Phone: (501) 682-6107

STATE TERM LIMITS

Governor: 2 terms
House: 3 terms
Senate: 2 terms

URBAN STATISTICS

CITY	POPULATION
Little Rock	183,133
Fort Smith	80,268
North Little Rock	60,433
Fayetteville	58,047
Jonesboro	55,515

REGISTERED VOTERS

Voters do not register by party.

POPULATION

2004 population (est.)	2,752,629
2000 population	2,673,400
1990 population	2,350,725
Percent change (1990-2000)	+13.7%
Rank among states (2004)	32

Median age	36
Born in state	63.9%
Foreign born	2.8%
Violent crime rate	445/100,000
Poverty level	15.8%
Federal workers	20,543
Military	18,894

REDISTRICTING

Arkansas retained its four House
seats in reapportionment. The state
legislature drew a new map, which
the governor allowed to become law
without his signature on April 20,
2001.

MISCELLANEOUS

Web: www.arkansas.gov
Capital: Little Rock
STATE ELECTION OFFICIAL
(501) 682-5070
**DEMOCRATIC
HEADQUARTERS**
(501) 374-2361
**REPUBLICAN
HEADQUARTERS**
(501) 372-7301

District Statistics

DIST.	2004 VOTE FOR PRESIDENT BUSH	KERRY	WHITE	BLACK	ASIAN	HISP	MEDIAN INCOME	WHITE COLLAR	BLUE COLLAR	SERVICE INDUSTRY	OVER 64	UNDER 18	COLLEGE EDUCATION	RURAL	SQ. MILES
1	52%	47%	80%	17%	0%	2%	$28,940	49%	37%	14%	15%	26%	12%	56%	17,151
2	51	48	76	19	1	2	$37,221	60	26	14	12	25	23	34	5,922
3	62	36	87	2	1	6	$33,915	53	33	14	13	26	18	46	8,490
4	51	48	71	24	0	3	$29,675	48	37	15	16	25	13	55	20,505
STATE	54	45	79	16	1	3	$32,182	53	33	14	14	25	17	47	52,068
U.S.	50.7	48.3	69	12	4	13	$41,994	60	25	15	12	26	24	21	3,537,438

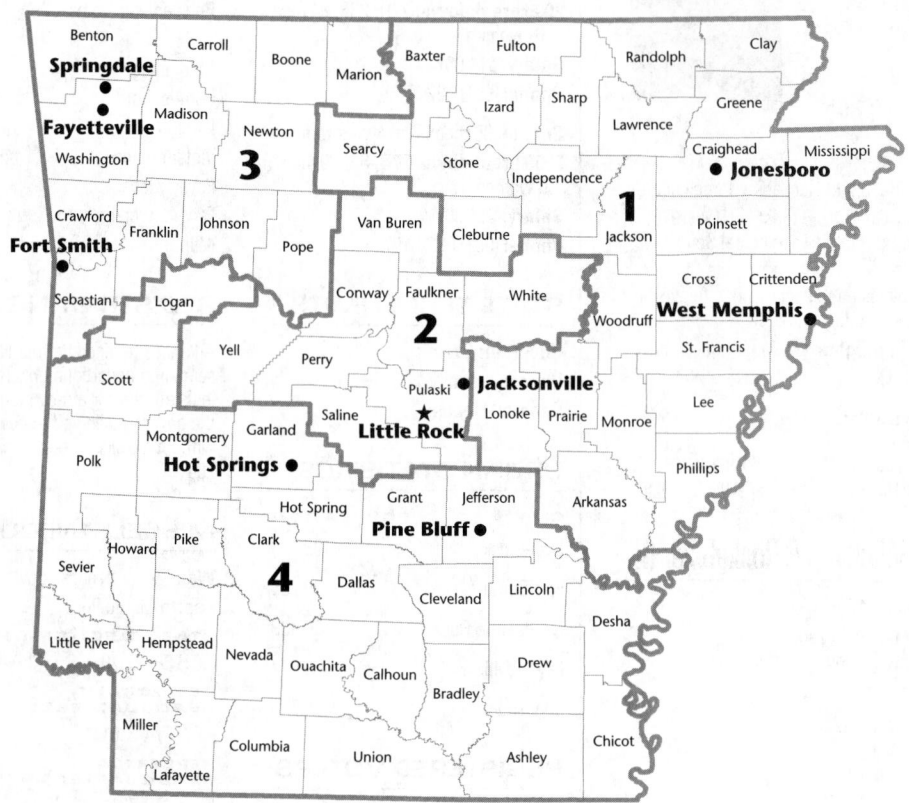

Sen. Blanche Lincoln (D)

Elected 1998; 2nd term

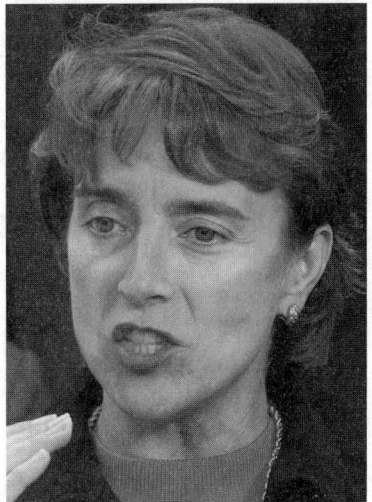

CAPITOL OFFICE
224-4843
lincoln.senate.gov
355 Dirksen 20510-0404; fax 228-1371

COMMITTEES
Agriculture, Nutrition & Forestry
Finance
Special Aging

HOMETOWN
Little Rock

BORN
Sept. 30, 1960, Helena, Ark.

RELIGION
Episcopalian

FAMILY
Husband, Steve Lincoln; two children

EDUCATION
Randolph-Macon Woman's College, B.A. 1982
(biology)

CAREER
Lobbyist; congressional aide

POLITICAL HIGHLIGHTS
U.S. House, 1993-97

ELECTION RESULTS

2004 GENERAL
Blanche Lincoln (D)	579,534	55.8%
Jim Holt (R)	458,501	44.2%

2004 PRIMARY
Blanche Lincoln (D)	231,037	83.1%
Lisa Burks (D)	47,010	16.9%

PREVIOUS WINNING PERCENTAGES
1998 (55%); 1994 House Election (53%); 1992 House
Election (70%)

Lincoln came to the Senate vowing not to let the demands of the job overwhelm her commitment to her young twin boys. Now in her second term, she has become a forceful voice on the influential Finance Committee for working families and a role model for parents trying to juggle the demands of career and family. In a city filled with workaholics, she skips an occasional business meeting to make it to a school play. "It's hard to be high and mighty when you've got peanut butter on your sleeve," she said in "Nine and Counting," a collaborative book by nine women senators.

With her boys in school and six years of experience balancing competing demands, Lincoln began the 109th Congress intent on helping farmers in the Razorback State and promoting tax incentives and health care benefits for moderate- and low-income families. She says her family still comes first, but she is now more often seen at the early morning meetings and evening events that seem to come with the job.

From her seat on the Finance panel, she has become a strong advocate for tax benefits for working families. When Republicans dropped from the 2003 tax bill $3.5 billion in refundable child tax credits, she held their feet to the fire. Conservatives said the credit amounted to welfare because families that pay no taxes qualified. Lincoln's steady attacks and eloquent defense of the benefit, which she said would help 12 million poor children, got attention. Both the House and Senate moved to restore it, although majority Republicans delayed final action until 2004. Lincoln said, "I am continually astounded that some members of Congress don't understand how challenging it is to raise a family in today's economy."

She held back her support from the 2001 tax cut until it included a provision to make a child tax credit partially refundable. And she has been involved in efforts to find compromise on proposals to permanently repeal the estate tax for family-owned businesses and farms.

Lincoln is among the Democrats advocating a greater focus on faith, family and pocketbook issues in order to appeal to rural voters in the aftermath of disappointing losses for the party in 2004. Democrats, she said, must "move beyond the 15-state strategy." She launched a legislative advocacy group, dubbed the Third Way, with Sens. Thomas R. Carper of Delaware and Evan Bayh of Indiana. Formed as a nonprofit lobbying group, its goal is to push initiatives backed by moderate Democrats.

Lincoln is a founding member of the moderate New Democrats in the Senate as well as the bipartisan Centrist Coalition. She often works closely with the state's junior senator, Democrat Mark Pryor, and other moderates. In the 2004 presidential primary season, Lincoln backed a moderate home-state ally, retired Army Gen. Wesley K. Clark, rather than her liberal colleague, Sen. John Kerry of Massachusetts.

Lincoln's outgoing personality and ability to relate to her constituents — duck hunting is among her leisure pursuits — have made her a popular politician in a state that backed President Bush in two elections. In its annual survey of staff attitudes about their bosses, Washingtonian magazine said she ranks high in the "just plain nice" category. Lincoln sided with Bush on the 2003 changes in Medicare that created a prescription drug benefit for the elderly and on the 2001 education overhaul that tied federal funds to student performance on tests. She opposed a federal constitutional amendment to ban gay marriage, but supported a state ban that Arkansas voters approved in 2004.

Raised in northeastern Arkansas, where her family has farmed for seven generations, Lincoln describes herself as a "daughter of the east Arkansas Delta" and speaks passionately about the need to improve tax breaks and services in rural areas. She looks out for the state's interests from her seat on the Agriculture Committee.

In 2002, she backed a six-year farm bill, with a $441 billion price tag, after working to raise the Senate's cap on payments to farmers. In 2001, she helped win the authorization of the eight-state Delta Regional Authority, modeled after the Appalachian Regional Commission, with initial funding of $20 million to spur economic development in the South. During a trip on Air Force One in 2001, when Bush lobbied her to support his first major tax cut, Lincoln requested disaster relief for Arkansas farmers and increased anti-poverty efforts in the Mississippi Delta region. "Agriculture is really my base, not only for my state's economy but also my heritage," she said.

In the 108th Congress, she helped cut a deal on the "Healthy Forests" law aimed at expediting forest thinning to prevent wildfires. She also pushed for a proposal to shift responsibility for migratory birds to the Agriculture Department from the U.S. Fish and Wildlife Service to help control double-crested cormorants that prey upon catfish farms, a major industry in the state.

Also in the 108th, Lincoln sat on the Ethics Committee, which led to a potentially embarrassing close call at the Democratic National Convention in 2004. She backed out of plans to host a rock concert to be paid for by lobbyists after the watchdog group Citizens for Responsibility and Ethics filed an ethics complaint alleging it would skirt a ban on "soft money" gifts.

Shortly after graduating from college, Lincoln got her start on Capitol Hill in 1982 as a receptionist for Arkansas Democratic Rep. Bill Alexander. She left after two years for a series of research jobs with lobbying firms. Then in 1991, she decided to challenge Alexander after media reports examining his ties to businessmen whose company received earmarked federal funds. Her race drew little notice until news broke that Alexander was among the top 10 abusers in the House bank overdraft scandal. She took 61 percent of the vote in the primary and coasted to victory in November. She married Steve Lincoln, an obstetrician and gynecologist, in 1993 and won re-election to the House the next year.

Seen as a rising star in Arkansas, Lincoln decided not to seek a third House term in 1996 after becoming pregnant with twins. But her career pause did not last long. When Democratic Sen. Dale Bumpers announced his retirement in 1998, Lincoln jumped at the chance to run for a Senate seat. In the general election, she benefited from a stumble by her Republican opponent, state Sen. Fay Boozman, who said that a woman was unlikely to become pregnant when she is raped because of hormonal responses in her body that he referred to as "God's little protective shield." Lincoln accused Boozman of insensitivity to rape victims, and he later apologized for the remarks. Lincoln won by 13 percentage points, becoming the youngest woman ever elected to the Senate.

She told her constituents that she planned to move to Washington with her family. "I want to watch my family grow up. I want to see their school plays. We'll be back here every holiday and every chance I get, but I'm not going to sacrifice my family for this job," she said.

In 2004, Lincoln raised $6 million for her re-election campaign. She won 56 percent of the vote to defeat Republican state Sen. Jim Holt.

Lincoln says she takes inspiration from Hattie Caraway of Arkansas, the first woman to be popularly elected to the Senate in 1932. Lincoln carried a quote from Caraway with her when she ran in 1998. It said, "If I can hold on to my sense of humor and a modicum of dignity, I shall have a wonderful time running for office whether I get there or not."

KEY VOTES

2004

Yes	Pass $318.9 billion, six-year highway and mass transit bill
Yes	Extend assault weapons ban for 10 years
Yes	Restore pay-as-you-go rules for new tax cuts and entitlement spending
No	Criminalize harm to a fetus in an attack on the mother
Yes	Increase mandatory child care funding to states by $6 billion over five years
No	Amend the Constitution to prohibit same-sex marriage
Yes	Approve $146 billion multi-year extension of previously enacted middle-class tax breaks
Yes	Reorganize U.S. intelligence agencies as proposed by Sept. 11 commission
Yes	Cut corporate taxes $137 billion over 10 years

2003

No	Delay Bush changes to Clean Air Act
No	Allow confirmation vote on Miguel A. Estrada to the U.S. Court of Appeals for the D.C. Circuit
Yes	Block a Bush proposal opening Alaska's Arctic National Wildlife Refuge to oil drilling
Yes	Limit size of Bush's proposed tax cut to $350 billion through fiscal 2013
Yes	Overhaul Medicare and create prescription drug benefit
Yes	Block Bush rule scaling back overtime pay for some white-collar federal workers
Yes	Split $20 billion in Iraq aid into half-grant, half-loan
Yes	Ban "partial birth" abortion except to save a woman's life
No	Stop proposal allowing travel to Cuba
Yes	Allow final vote on energy policy overhaul

CQ VOTE STUDIES

	PARTY UNITY		PRESIDENTIAL SUPPORT	
	Support	Oppose	Support	Oppose
2004	79%	21%	72%	28%
2003	81%	19%	61%	39%
2002	61%	39%	89%	11%
2001	79%	21%	71%	29%
2000	80%	20%	84%	16%
1999	83%	17%	80%	20%
House Service:				
1996	66%	34%	63%	37%
1995	64%	36%	63%	37%
1994	79%	21%	73%	27%
1993	87%	13%	72%	28%

INTEREST GROUPS

	AFL-CIO	ADA	CCUS	ACU
2004	100%	95%	71%	20%
2003	77%	75%	78%	20%
2002	77%	70%	75%	40%
2001	88%	85%	79%	28%
2000	50%	70%	86%	20%
1999	89%	95%	65%	12%
House Service:				
1996	57%	30%	64%	36%
1995	58%	60%	63%	20%
1994	33%	60%	83%	10%
1993	75%	65%	45%	25%

Sen. Mark Pryor (D)

Elected 2002; 1st term

CAPITOL OFFICE
224-2353
pryor.senate.gov
217 Russell 20510-0403; fax 228-0908

COMMITTEES
Commerce, Science & Transportation
Homeland Security & Governmental Affairs
Small Business & Entrepreneurship
Select Ethics

HOMETOWN
Little Rock

BORN
Jan. 10, 1963, Fayetteville, Ark.

RELIGION
Christian

FAMILY
Wife, Jill Pryor; two children

EDUCATION
U. of Arkansas, B.A. 1985 (history), J.D. 1988

CAREER
Lawyer

POLITICAL HIGHLIGHTS
Ark. House, 1991-95; sought Democratic
nomination for Ark. attorney general, 1994;
Ark. attorney general, 1999-2003

ELECTION RESULTS

2002 GENERAL

Mark Pryor (D)	433,386	53.9%
Tim Hutchinson (R)	370,735	46.1%

2002 PRIMARY

Mark Pryor (D)	unopposed

With a strong political bloodline, Pryor seems a political natural. The son of the respected, long-serving senator, David Pryor, he was elected to the Arkansas House at age 27, became state attorney general at 35 and now, in his early 40s, is among the youngest members of the Senate. Yet his influence on Capitol Hill is constrained in ways that must be frustrating for him.

A centrist, Pryor is one of only four Southern Democrats left in the Senate as the region has realigned in favor of the GOP. And, after his party lost a net of four Senate seats in the 2004 election, and the balance of power on committees shifted accordingly, Pryor had to give up his spot on the Armed Services Committee just as he was developing defense as a specialty.

As consolation, Pryor was given a seat on the Commerce, Science and Transportation Committee, an A-list assignment that gives him sway over government regulation of industry. The panel is a good perch from which to raise campaign funds from the deep-pocketed world of business. Pryor also can continue his involvement in national security issues from his seat on the Homeland Security and Governmental Affairs Committee.

He is among the moderate Democrats who believe the party will never regain its footing in the South if it doesn't do more to attract middle-class voters. Pryor is the product of the same strain of political thought that shaped the state's most successful Democrat in recent years, President Clinton, a past chairman of the Democratic Leadership Council. In late 2004, Pryor joined with a handful of other Democratic centrists to form a group called the Third Way, which distinguishes itself from the DLC and New Democrat coalitions in Congress by concentrating its efforts in the Senate. "There are a growing number of people in this country that Democrats are simply not reaching," especially in the South, Pryor said.

In the 109th Congress, Minority Leader Harry Reid gave Pryor a role in recruiting candidates in southern states and raising money for their campaigns. As part of a restructuring of the Democratic Senatorial Campaign Committee, Pryor was named regional vice chairman for the South. He is also active in a group that promotes bipartisanship and civility in the Senate, similar to an effort started in the House several years ago.

He parts with his liberal colleagues in the party on some fiscal issues and on flash point social issues such as gun control and abortion. During the campaign that saw him drive Republican incumbent Tim Hutchinson from office in 2002, Pryor declined to declare himself either "pro choice" or "pro life," as the two sides refer to themselves, because he said neither label fit. Earlier in his political career, as a candidate for attorney general, he had described himself as "pro choice."

But his record in the 108th established him as a vote for the anti-abortion movement, a disappointment to the abortion rights groups that had courted him. He supported banning a procedure its opponents call "partial birth" abortion and another measure making it a crime to injure a fetus in the course of violence against a woman. The most telling vote was on an amendment to the abortion bill. Pryor declined to affirm the principles of *Roe v. Wade*, the landmark Supreme Court case that legalized abortion. "I can't in good conscience say that *Roe v. Wade* should never be overturned," he told the Arkansas Democrat-Gazette.

Pryor calls himself a deficit hawk and says the deficit should be brought under control to keep interest rates low. When he first came to the Senate in 2003, he voted against an omnibus spending bill that contained nearly

$300 million in projects for Arkansas and for a proposal limiting a second round of tax cuts to $350 billion over 10 years. President Bush had wanted twice that much. But in 2004, Pryor voted with appropriators on most spending bills and found the siren call of tax cuts difficult to resist. He voted for a bill cutting corporate taxes $137 billion over 10 years.

Pryor in fact voted with the president 64 percent of the time. In early 2005, he was one of six Democrats who crossed party lines to support Bush's nominee for attorney general, Alberto R. Gonzales, helping end a tough, partisan confirmation battle. He is someone the White House will look to in its effort to overhaul Social Security. But Pryor says he opposes creating personal accounts in the government's retirement fund.

His record on the environment was a mixed bag in the 108th Congress. He voted against the president's proposal to open Alaska's Arctic National Wildlife Refuge to oil exploration, but he was among only five Democrats to support a Bush administration rule allowing industrial plants to upgrade without improving air pollution controls.

Pryor and his home-state partner, Democratic Sen. Blanche Lincoln, were pivotal in the administration's fight to confirm Arkansas attorney J. Leon Holmes to the federal bench. The appointment drew fire after revelations that Holmes had said in 1980 that abortion in the case of rape may not be necessary because rapes result in pregnancies "with approximately the same frequency as snowfall in Miami." Pryor and Lincoln led the battle for Holmes in spite of overwhelming Democratic opposition.

Pryor's biggest disappointment was losing the Armed Services seat. From a military-friendly state that is home to the Pine Bluff Arsenal and Little Rock Air Force Base, Pryor had immersed himself in defense issues, consistently showing up at sparsely attended committee hearings, taking briefing papers home to read, lugging around a book of Pentagon acronyms and holding face-to-face meetings with military brass on homeland security issues.

His proudest accomplishments of the 108th are the changes he was able to make to help out soldiers, including legislation that allowed them to more easily qualify for child tax credits and the Earned Income Tax Credit, paid to people whose incomes are too low to be taxed.

Pryor inherited his political gene. When his family moved to the Washington area after his father's election to the Senate in 1978, Pryor became class president at Walt Whitman High School in the affluent Maryland suburb of Bethesda. He was also a congressional page, as his father had been. Plotting a career in politics, he returned to his hometown of Fayetteville, earning undergraduate and law degrees from the University of Arkansas.

Elected to the state House two years out of law school, his budding career was set back when he lost the Democratic primary for attorney general in 1994. Shortly thereafter, he was diagnosed with sarcoma, a rare form of cancer that left him unable to walk unassisted for more than a year after surgery. But the disease went into remission, and Pryor relaunched his career. Elected attorney general in 1998, he sued tobacco companies for smoking-related health care costs and made it possible for Arkansans to block telemarketing calls.

His Senate bid turned out to be the Democrats' single recruiting success in 2002. While Pryor had strengths in his familiar name and centrist profile, Hutchinson entered as a vulnerable incumbent. In his first term, Hutchinson, a Baptist minister who had campaigned as a "traditional values" Republican, divorced his wife of 29 years and married a former Senate staff aide. In his challenge for Hutchinson's job, Pryor never spoke directly about the divorce, but frequently touted his own commitment to his religion and his family. He won with a comfortable 8 percentage point margin.

KEY VOTES

2004

Yes Pass $318.9 billion, six-year highway and mass transit bill
Yes Extend assault weapons ban for 10 years
Yes Restore pay-as-you-go rules for new tax cuts and entitlement spending
Yes Criminalize harm to a fetus in an attack on the mother
Yes Increase mandatory child care funding to states by $6 billion over five years
No Amend the Constitution to prohibit same-sex marriage
Yes Approve $146 billion multi-year extension of previously enacted middle-class tax breaks
Yes Reorganize U.S. intelligence agencies as proposed by Sept. 11 commission
Yes Cut corporate taxes $137 billion over 10 years

2003

No Delay Bush changes to Clean Air Act
No Allow confirmation vote on Miguel A. Estrada to the U.S. Court of Appeals for the D.C. Circuit
Yes Block a Bush proposal opening Alaska's Arctic National Wildlife Refuge to oil drilling
Yes Limit size of Bush's proposed tax cut to $350 billion through fiscal 2013
Yes Overhaul Medicare and create prescription drug benefit
Yes Block Bush rule scaling back overtime pay for some white-collar federal workers
Yes Split $20 billion in Iraq aid into half-grant, half-loan
Yes Ban "partial birth" abortion except to save a woman's life
No Stop proposal allowing travel to Cuba
Yes Allow final vote on energy policy overhaul

CQ VOTE STUDIES

	PARTY UNITY		PRESIDENTIAL SUPPORT	
	Support	Oppose	Support	Oppose
2004	81%	19%	68%	32%
2003	84%	16%	60%	40%

INTEREST GROUPS

	AFL-CIO	ADA	CCUS	ACU
2004	92%	85%	71%	20%
2003	85%	70%	61%	30%

Rep. Marion Berry (D)

Elected 1996; 5th term

CAPITOL OFFICE
225-4076
www.house.gov/berry
2305 Rayburn 20515-0401; fax 225-5602

COMMITTEES
Appropriations

HOMETOWN
Jonesboro

BORN
Aug. 27, 1942, Stuttgart, Ark.

RELIGION
Methodist

FAMILY
Wife, Carolyn Berry; two children

EDUCATION
U. of Arkansas, attended 1960-62 (pre-pharmacy);
U. of Arkansas, Little Rock, B.S. 1965 (pharmacy)

CAREER
Farmer; White House aide; pharmacist

POLITICAL HIGHLIGHTS
Gillett City Council, 1976-80; Ark. Soil and Water Conservation Commission, 1986-94 (chairman, 1992)

ELECTION RESULTS

2004 GENERAL

Marion Berry (D)	162,452	66.5%
Vernon Humphrey (R)	81,758	33.5%

2004 PRIMARY

Marion Berry (D)	unopposed

2002 GENERAL

Marion Berry (D)	129,701	66.8%
Tommy F. Robinson (R)	64,357	33.2%

PREVIOUS WINNING PERCENTAGES
2000 (60%); 1998 (100%); 1996 (53%)

Berry represents the poorest House district in one of the poorest states in the nation. Farming has been the focus for most of his life, starting with his childhood on a rice farm in Arkansas County, in the southeast part of his state.

With an easygoing manner and a slow, Southern drawl, Berry makes a point of playing up his rural background. He once described himself to an audience back home as nothing more than a "farmer who got more involved in politics than maybe I should have." Berry and his brothers own a soybean, rice, corn and wheat farm in Gillett, in his home county.

Berry recalls going with his father to the One Horse Store general store in Bayou Meto, where the men gathered to talk about current events and politics. Though his father and grandfather never held elective office, Berry said their involvement in civic affairs set an example for him. Later on, while he attended pharmacy school, Berry frequented a family friend's drugstore in Little Rock, where many of the state's movers and shakers often gathered to talk politics. That drugstore, Berry told the Arkansas Democrat-Gazette, "is where I cut my political teeth."

Berry worked as a pharmacist in Little Rock for two years after college. He has not practiced pharmacy since, though he has retained his license. His pharmacy background appealed to party leaders who tapped him to represent the rural and more conservative factions among House Democrats on managed-care and prescription drug issues.

When the focus in the 108th Congress shifted to the high cost of prescription drugs, Berry was sharply critical of the GOP legislation in 2003 that established a prescription drug benefit for Medicare recipients.

He was outraged when Republicans refused to let Democrats even attend meetings at which the final details of the Medicare overhaul bill were being negotiated. Berry and New York Democrat Charles B. Rangel, who were named as two of the three House Democratic conferees on the bill, dramatically barged into a room where the talks were being held. Berry said he had a brief discussion with Ways and Means Chairman Bill Thomas of California, the top House negotiator. "I did suggest I might have an idea or two worth considering, and that's when the conversation ended," Berry reported.

Berry voted against the bill, calling it "the single sorriest piece of legislation written in my lifetime." He pushed an alternate bill, which gained the support of Democratic leaders, to create a nationwide prescription drug plan to be run by Medicare. The bill also sought to force the secretary of Health and Human Services to negotiate with pharmaceutical manufacturers for lower-priced prescription drugs for seniors.

Berry also pressed in 2004 for Senate action on a House-passed bill to permit importation of cheaper drugs from Canada. Berry says that the local pharmacist is not to blame for the high cost of drugs. Drug manufacturers are the bad guys, according to Berry. "The American people pay two to three times more for medication than anywhere else in the world," he said in 2002. "We would consider other countries evil if they did that."

Even with his focus on health care, Berry continues to pay attention to agriculture issues, a necessity for his farming-dependent district. He has consistently complained about imports from Vietnam of fish that are labeled — incorrectly and unfairly, he says — as catfish. And he also criticized the Bush administration for failing to support domestic rice growers when 70,000 tons of rice destined for Iraq was purchased from Vietnam. He served for six years on the Agriculture Committee, but left it in 2003 when he won a seat on Appropriations.

Although Berry is no fan of big government and he decries the Bush administration's "mind-numbing" budget deficits, he is quick to herald federal spending that benefits his constituents. His office churns out news releases announcing federal funding for local road-building projects and the award of grants to local schools and law enforcement agencies. From his Appropriations post, Berry was able to persuade the Transportation Department in 2004 to continue federally subsidized passenger air service for Jonesboro, in the 1st District.

As an original backer of the Delta Regional Authority, established in 2000 to spur economic development in the Mississippi Delta region, Berry is disappointed in the dwindling funding the White House has sought for it.

In the 109th Congress, Berry has a seat on Appropriations' Homeland Security Subcommittee, and he has pressed the administration to be quicker in implementing national security measures that Congress has funded. He is particularly concerned about food safety and cargo screening at ports and airports.

A member of the Blue Dog Coalition, a group of conservative House Democrats, Berry takes a different tack than most in his party on certain social and budget issues. In the 108th, he voted in agreement with President Bush's position 42 percent of the time. He votes for gun owners' rights and for constitutional amendments permitting prayer in schools and requiring a two-thirds majority vote to raise taxes.

Berry began his political career in 1976, when he was elected to the Gillett City Council. In 1982, he became Bill Clinton's gubernatorial campaign coordinator in Arkansas County, a post he also held in 1986 and 1990.

As governor, Clinton in 1986 named Berry to the state Soil and Water Conservation Commission, where he served for eight years. He moved to Washington when Clinton appointed him special assistant to the president for agricultural trade and food assistance issues.

When Democrat Blanche Lincoln became pregnant with twins and decided to leave the House in 1996, Berry won a close contest to fill her seat against Republican Warren Dupwe, who had held Lincoln to 53 percent in 1994.

In a district that has not elected a Republican since Reconstruction, Berry has easily sailed through four re-election campaigns, three times winning by a better than 2-to-1 margin.

KEY VOTES

2004
Yes Extend federal unemployment benefits by 13 weeks
Yes Pass $283.2 billion, six-year federal highway and mass transit bill
No Approve $146 billion multi-year extension of previously enacted middle-class tax breaks
Yes Amend the Constitution to prohibit same-sex marriage
Yes Cut corporate taxes $137 billion over 10 years
Yes Reorganize U.S. intelligence agencies as proposed by Sept. 11 commission

2003
No Cut taxes by $330 billion through fiscal 2013
Yes Block Bush rule scaling back overtime pay for some white-collar federal workers
Yes Do not allow use of search warrants without first notifying subjects
Yes Allow importation of prescription drugs
No Create private school voucher program in Washington, D.C.
Yes Ban "partial birth" abortion except to save a woman's life
Yes Split $18.6 billion in Iraq aid into half-grant, half-loan
No Overhaul Medicare and create prescription drug benefit

CQ VOTE STUDIES

	PARTY UNITY		PRESIDENTIAL SUPPORT	
	Support	Oppose	Support	Oppose
2004	81%	19%	36%	64%
2003	79%	21%	45%	55%
2002	79%	21%	42%	58%
2001	65%	35%	40%	60%
2000	67%	33%	55%	45%

INTEREST GROUPS

	AFL-CIO	ADA	CCUS	ACU
2004	100%	60%	45%	36%
2003	93%	85%	47%	52%
2002	78%	70%	50%	32%
2001	92%	60%	43%	52%
2000	60%	35%	76%	48%

ARKANSAS 1
Northeast — Jonesboro, West Memphis

One of the nation's poorest districts, the 1st stretches across Arkansas' northeastern third, reaching from the Mississippi Delta through fertile plains and into the hilly north, where the Ozark Mountains begin.

Poverty is most notably present within the largely white, older populations in the northwest and the former sharecropping communities in the Democratic Delta. In the mid-1990s, the predominantly black Delta communities began working with Arkansas State University in Jonesboro to attract tourism and manufacturing, but have made little headway. The area receives government support in the form of the Delta Regional Authority, which seeks to increase economic development in the areas along the Mississippi River.

Some of the nation's largest rice and cotton producers farm the Delta and house their corporate headquarters in the 1st. Cattle and poultry businesses are prosperous in the north. Manufacturing is strong in several cities, including Stuttgart, Batesville and Jonesboro. One of the nation's largest steel production plants bolsters Blytheville, where the population and economy sagged after Eaker Air Force Base closed in 1992.

The 1st elects few Republicans at the state or federal level, and a Republican has not represented the district since 1875. Democratic presidential candidates carried the area in the 1990s and 2000, but despite this, George W. Bush took the 1st with 52 percent in 2004. Western Lonoke County — home to Little Rock suburbanites and some military personnel — leans Republican, as do some of the 1st's northwestern counties. The heavily Christian district is socially conservative in many areas.

MAJOR INDUSTRY
Agriculture, steel production, manufacturing

CITIES
Jonesboro, 55,515; West Memphis, 27,666; Paragould, 22,017; Blytheville, 18,272; Cabot, 15,261; Forrest City, 14,774

NOTABLE
Author John Grisham was born in Jonesboro; The world duck calling championship is held annually in Stuttgart.

Rep. Vic Snyder (D)

Elected 1996; 5th term

A family physician and a Vietnam veteran, Snyder is a thoughtful voice on both the Armed Services and Veterans' Affairs committees. But rather than introducing bills and making speeches on the House floor, Snyder is content with working behind the scenes.

As a member of the centrist New Democrat Coalition, Snyder's priorities have included balancing the budget while ensuring a strong federal role in education, health care and national defense. He pays particular attention to the well-being of his state's veterans.

In the 108th Congress, he criticized a Pentagon plan to issue a single medal for service in Afghanistan and Iraq and successfully pressed for legislation to create separate medals. "As a Vietnam veteran and former Marine, one of the first things I look for on a soldier's uniform is the campaign ribbon that notes where the soldier served," he said. "There is just a camaraderie that comes about by recognizing that campaign ribbon on a uniform." Snyder has served as the top-ranking Democrat on Armed Services' Military Personnel Subcommittee since the beginning of the 108th Congress.

In 2001, he was one of the few members of the committee to support President Bush's demand for another base-closing round, citing the repeated contentions by senior military and Pentagon civilian leaders that they were spending scarce money keeping up more bases than they needed. Yet early in his career, he and the rest of the state delegation turned back a proposal to move some of the training done at Little Rock Air Force Base to other locations — a shift that might have made the Arkansas facility more vulnerable to future rounds of base closures. The base provides more than 5,000 jobs in Snyder's district.

On the Veterans' Affairs Health Subcommittee, Snyder pressured the Defense and Veterans Affairs departments to do more to address the problems of Gulf War syndrome, a mysterious range of ailments reported by veterans of the 1991 military campaign in the Persian Gulf. He also has been persistent in his efforts to get veterans tested and treated for a serious type of hepatitis, a liver disease that affects about one-tenth of all veterans in central Arkansas, according to a Department of Veterans Affairs study.

Snyder has urged his colleagues to move cautiously on proposed changes to the Department of Veterans Affairs, under fire because of financial problems and delays in care. "It's not all doom and gloom," Snyder said of the agency in 2003, noting the VA's accomplishments in specialized fields, such as prosthetics and treating hepatitis. "There's things the VA does that are a model."

He emerged in the 108th as a leading critic of a proposed constitutional amendment to ensure congressional continuity in case of a devastating terrorist attack, possibly by giving governors the authority to fill vacant seats. "I think we need to be very cautious about amending the Constitution to take away the power of the people, even in horrendous situations, to elect the members of the people's house," he said.

With his medical background, Snyder also pays attention to Democratic efforts to broaden health care for senior citizens. He laces his remarks on prescription drug coverage for seniors or patients' problems with their health maintenance organizations with references to his personal experience.

Snyder counts as a major achievement his role in overturning a Medicare regulation that halted coverage for immunosuppressive drugs after less than four years. When some organ transplant recipients stopped taking the drugs

CAPITOL OFFICE
225-2506
www.house.gov/snyder
1330 Longworth 20515-0402; fax 225-5903

COMMITTEES
Armed Services
Veterans' Affairs

HOMETOWN
Little Rock

BORN
Sept. 27, 1947, Medford, Ore.

RELIGION
Methodist

FAMILY
Wife, Betsy Singleton

EDUCATION
Willamette U., B.A. 1975 (chemistry); U. of Oregon, M.D. 1979; U. of Arkansas, Little Rock, J.D. 1988

MILITARY SERVICE
Marine Corps, 1967-69

CAREER
Physician

POLITICAL HIGHLIGHTS
Ark. Senate, 1991-96

ELECTION RESULTS

2004 GENERAL

Vic Snyder (D)	160,834	58.2%
Marvin Parks (R)	115,655	41.8%

2004 PRIMARY

Vic Snyder (D)	unopposed

2002 GENERAL

Vic Snyder (D)	142,752	92.9%
Ed Garner ()	10,874	7.1%

PREVIOUS WINNING PERCENTAGES
2000 (58%); 1998 (58%); 1996 (52%)

because they found they could not pay for them, it sometimes led to organ rejection and the need for another costly transplant — which Medicare covered. Snyder rounded up cosponsors for a bill in the 106th Congress that changed the regulation.

Snyder also digs into foreign policy issues, partly because of his travels abroad. He supports ending the more than 40-year-old economic embargo against Cuba, a change that would likely transform the island nation into a booming market for Arkansas businesses selling poultry, rice and soybeans. Snyder contends that U.S. credibility is undermined by the glaring inconsistency of trading with communist-led China and Vietnam while trying to isolate Cuba. "All it has done is hurt the Cuban people and hurt the ability of the American people to trade with Cuba," he said of the embargo.

In 2003, Snyder underwent heart surgery for a faulty mitral valve. He recovered strongly and, in 2004, was one of just 11 House members to cast a yes or no vote on every roll call.

Born and raised in Oregon, Snyder as a young man spent much of his time in libraries — he has degrees in both medicine and law, though he has never practiced the latter discipline. After earning his medical degree at the University of Oregon, he came to Arkansas in 1979 to do his medical residency. He remained in his adoptive state, working as a family doctor.

Snyder served six years in the state Senate, where his priorities included support for small business, increased jail time for violent criminals, a crackdown on underage drinking, and a repeal of the state sales tax on food.

When Democratic incumbent Ray Thornton announced his retirement in 1996, Snyder entered the 2nd District race as an underdog, facing two tough opponents in the primary — prosecuting attorney Mark Stodola and John Edwards, a former aide to retiring U.S. Sen. David Pryor. Snyder finished second to Stodola in the primary but surged in the runoff campaign to narrowly edge out his foe.

Snyder embraced the national Democratic themes in the fall campaign, pledging to oppose GOP initiatives on Medicare, education and the environment. He took 52 percent of the vote to squeak by Republican Bud Cummins, a businessman and lawyer, while President Clinton carried the 2nd District by 18 percentage points.

In his re-election campaigns, Snyder has won by double-digit margins, and he captured 58 percent of the vote in 2004. He likes to defer fundraising until three months before the primary. He acknowledges that his approach can be risky, but he told the Arkansas Democrat-Gazette: "If it helps shorten the campaign . . . that's an improvement."

KEY VOTES

2004

Yes Extend federal unemployment benefits by 13 weeks

Yes Pass $283.2 billion, six-year federal highway and mass transit bill

Yes Approve $146 billion multi-year extension of previously enacted middle-class tax breaks

No Amend the Constitution to prohibit same-sex marriage

Yes Cut corporate taxes $137 billion over 10 years

Yes Reorganize U.S. intelligence agencies as proposed by Sept. 11 commission

2003

No Cut taxes by $330 billion through fiscal 2013

Yes Block Bush rule scaling back overtime pay for some white-collar federal workers

Yes Do not allow use of search warrants without first notifying subjects

Yes Allow importation of prescription drugs

No Create private school voucher program in Washington, D.C.

No Ban "partial birth" abortion except to save a woman's life

No Split $18.6 billion in Iraq aid into half-grant, half-loan

No Overhaul Medicare and create prescription drug benefit

CQ VOTE STUDIES

	PARTY UNITY		PRESIDENTIAL SUPPORT	
	Support	Oppose	Support	Oppose
2004	85%	15%	41%	59%
2003	84%	16%	33%	67%
2002	85%	15%	41%	59%
2001	75%	25%	33%	67%
2000	89%	11%	90%	10%

INTEREST GROUPS

	AFL-CIO	ADA	CCUS	ACU
2004	80%	95%	57%	20%
2003	79%	85%	52%	13%
2002	67%	80%	60%	12%
2001	83%	85%	38%	13%
2000	90%	70%	55%	4%

ARKANSAS 2

Central — Little Rock

Encompassing Little Rock, eight surrounding counties and part of a ninth, the 2nd is Arkansas' axis of government activity. More than half of the district's population is concentrated in the Little Rock area, where strong black, union and university populations offer support to Democrats in most elections.

The district includes the state's largest white-collar population and has the highest median income. While the district supported favored-son Bill Clinton heavily in the 1992 and 1996 presidential elections, George W. Bush carried the 2nd in 2000 with 49 percent of the vote and in 2004 with 51 percent.

Democratic support is concentrated in poor and working-class neighborhoods in east Little Rock, which is heavily black. Rural agriculture and mining communities in outlying areas also sometimes support Democrats, although social conservatism is more common.

Affluent neighborhoods in north and west Little Rock are more likely to

vote for Republicans. The GOP has gained popularity within rapidly growing suburbs in Faulkner, Saline and Pulaski counties, which are fed by affluent whites leaving Little Rock. Republicans also fare well in White County, where Church of Christ-affiliated Harding University is located.

MAJOR INDUSTRY
Government, higher education, military

MILITARY BASES
Little Rock Air Force Base, 5,600 military, 1,500 civilian (2004)

CITIES
Little Rock, 183,133; North Little Rock, 60,433; Conway, 43,167; Jacksonville, 29,916; Benton, 21,906; Sherwood, 21,511; Searcy, 18,928

NOTABLE
The Clinton Presidential Center is located along the south bank of the Arkansas River in Little Rock; Little Rock Air Force Base has the largest C-130 training and airlift facility in the world; The Arkansas state Capitol, completed in 1915, was built on the site of the state penitentiary, partly using prison labor; Gen. Douglas MacArthur was born in Little Rock; North Little Rock's "Old Mill" was seen in the opening credits of "Gone with the Wind."

Rep. John Boozman (R)

Elected 2001; 2nd full term

CAPITOL OFFICE
225-4301
www.house.gov/boozman
1519 Longworth 20515-0403; fax 225-4301

COMMITTEES
International Relations
Transportation & Infrastructure
Veterans' Affairs
  (Economic Opportunity - chairman)

HOMETOWN
Rogers

BORN
Dec. 10, 1950, Shreveport, La.

RELIGION
Baptist

FAMILY
Wife, Cathy Boozman; three children

EDUCATION
U. of Arkansas, attended 1969-72; Southern
College of Optometry, O.D. 1977

CAREER
Optometrist; cattle farm owner

POLITICAL HIGHLIGHTS
Rogers Public Schools Board of Education,
1994-2001

ELECTION RESULTS

2004 GENERAL

John Boozman (R)	160,629	59.4%
Jan Judy (D)	102,658	38.0%
Dale Morfey (I)	7,116	2.6%

2004 PRIMARY

John Boozman (R)	unopposed

2002 GENERAL

John Boozman (R)	141,478	98.9%
George N. Lyne - write-in	1,577	1.1%

PREVIOUS WINNING PERCENTAGES
2001 Special Election (56%)

Among the 18 medical professionals pursuing second careers in Congress, Boozman is the only doctor of optometry. He and his older brother founded an eye clinic in Arkansas. In fact, Fay Boozman, the more gregarious of the two and a one-time GOP nominee for the U.S. Senate, was considered more likely to get to Capitol Hill first. But that distinction went to John.

The Boozman (BOZE-man) brothers share much in common with another prominent Arkansas political family, the Hutchinsons. Boozman won the 3rd District seat after Republican Asa Hutchinson left it to head the Drug Enforcement Administration for the Bush White House. Asa's brother, Tim Hutchinson, held the seat before him, and went on to serve in the Senate. Tim Hutchinson, a minister, once led a Bible study group attended by the Boozman boys, who, like the Hutchinsons, are evangelical Christians whose faith influences their politics.

Boozman continues a long Republican tradition for the rural and small-town district covering the northwest corner of Arkansas. It's been in GOP hands for nearly 40 years; its footnote in history is its snub of Bill Clinton in 1974, when the future Democratic president was defeated in a bid for the House seat, his first loss of a political race. Arkansas has trended toward Republicans in recent decades but at a slower pace than other Southern states, due in part to Clinton's popularity there.

Nonetheless, Boozman reflects the conservative impulse of the region. On fiscal issues, he has called for abolition of the tax code and he supports President Bush's broad tax-cutting agenda. On the new array of cultural issues gaining traction in the party, he supports a constitutional amendment barring same-sex marriage and he favors allowing the display of the Ten Commandments in public places, backing an Alabama judge's refusal to remove such a monument from the state's supreme court building.

Despite his background, Boozman had little impact on health care policy in his first term. He spoke out against a bill barring optometrists from performing laser eye surgery at VA hospitals. And he sponsored a measure making non-corrective contact lenses subject to regulation as medical devices for the first time. The lenses have caused many eye injuries, especially among children.

Instead, Boozman's main focus has been on issues affecting two major 3rd District employers, Wal-Mart Stores Inc. in Bentonville and Tyson Foods Inc. in Springdale. Both companies are driving a spurt of economic growth in the area. Executives and political action committees associated with the two companies are big political contributors to Boozman.

Boozman sponsored an amendment, later withdrawn, to a mammoth six-year transportation bill in 2004 exempting short-haul truck drivers from new safety regulations that increased the number of rest hours required between shifts behind the wheel. The rules affect drivers delivering goods to Wal-Mart's many retail stores. He also joined the debate over ending the U.S. trade embargo against Cuba, a priority for the state's rice and poultry farmers, who view the country as a potentially lucrative market. Boozman says trade with Cuba will help bring internal political change there.

GOP leaders gave him a seat in his first term on the Transportation and Infrastructure Committee, from which he has been able to secure politically popular funding for the Interstate 49 project. It is a main north-south artery between Kansas City, Mo., and port cities in Louisiana, and cuts through western Arkansas. Boozman's other quest on the committee is securing federal funds for the Northwest Arkansas Regional Airport.

In his second term, Boozman was given a seat on the International Relations Committee, where in the 109th Congress he wants to focus on trade issues and ways to combat illegal drug smuggling. He has been an advocate of more federal aid to stamp out the rapid growth of methamphetamine drug labs, which have plagued rural communities.

Personally, Boozman is easygoing and unfailingly courteous. The only outward sign of his two years as an offensive tackle for the University of Arkansas' vaunted Razorbacks football team is his 6-foot, 3-inch frame. He attended the school on a football scholarship after being a standout player at Northside High School in Fort Smith, population 80,000. Even his political opponent, Democrat Jan Judy who ran unsuccessfully against him in 2004, called him "a nice guy."

Boozman was the second of three children of an Air Force master sergeant stationed at Barksdale Air Force Base in Louisiana when John was born. He was going to be a dentist until Fay, who was studying ophthalmology, convinced him to go to optometry school so they could practice together. They co-founded Boozman-Hof Regional Eye Clinic in 1977 in their hometown of Rogers.

Fay was always the more high-profile politician, serving in the state Senate and eventually being nominated to run against Democrat Blanche Lincoln in the 1998 open-seat Senate race, but losing. Meanwhile, John was elected to the Rogers school board, where he served a little more than six years. Fay characterized the brothers as "right of conservative," according to the Arkansas Democrat-Gazette.

When Asa Hutchinson was appointed by Bush to head the DEA, Fay was the obvious choice to seek the seat. But he decided to remain in Little Rock as head of the Arkansas Department of Health, so John jumped in.

He entered the four-candidate GOP field and finished first in the primary, but was forced into a runoff race by state Sen. Gunner DeLay, a distant cousin of Majority Leader Tom DeLay. Endorsed by GOP Gov. Mike Huckabee, Boozman won the runoff with 57 percent of the vote. He went on to beat the Democratic opponent in the 2001 special election with 56 percent. In 2002, Boozman's only competition was a write-in candidate.

Jan Judy, a state House member, put up a spirited challenge in 2004, but Boozman outdid her 2-to-1 in campaign fundraising and was heavily favored in the district, the most Republican of Arkansas' four congressional districts. He was re-elected with 59 percent of the vote.

KEY VOTES

2004

No Extend federal unemployment benefits by 13 weeks

Yes Pass $283.2 billion, six-year federal highway and mass transit bill

Yes Approve $146 billion multi-year extension of previously enacted middle-class tax breaks

Yes Amend the Constitution to prohibit same-sex marriage

Yes Cut corporate taxes $137 billion over 10 years

No Reorganize U.S. intelligence agencies as proposed by Sept. 11 commission

2003

Yes Cut taxes by $330 billion through fiscal 2013

No Block Bush rule scaling back overtime pay for some white-collar federal workers

Yes Do not allow use of search warrants without first notifying subjects

Yes Allow importation of prescription drugs

Yes Create private school voucher program in Washington, D.C.

Yes Ban "partial birth" abortion except to save a woman's life

No Split $18.6 billion in Iraq aid into half-grant, half-loan

Yes Overhaul Medicare and create prescription drug benefit

CQ VOTE STUDIES

	PARTY UNITY		PRESIDENTIAL SUPPORT	
	Support	Oppose	Support	Oppose
2004	96%	4%	82%	18%
2003	97%	3%	93%	7%
2002	95%	5%	85%	15%
2001	100%	0%	100%	0%

INTEREST GROUPS

	AFL-CIO	ADA	CCUS	ACU
2004	13%	10%	100%	96%
2003	7%	10%	97%	84%
2002	11%	0%	95%	96%
2001	25%	—%	100%	100%

ARKANSAS 3
Northwest – Fort Smith, Fayetteville

Arkansas' hilly northwest subscribes to a rugged conservatism unique in this Democratic state, and its Republican bent remains despite an influx of newcomers. The 3rd was the only Arkansas district to give George W. Bush more than 52 percent in the 2004 presidential election (he captured 62 percent here) and it was the state's only district to withhold hearty support from native son Bill Clinton in 1996. The 3rd has sent a Republican to Congress since the 1966 election.

Median household income, low in much of Arkansas, ranks in the bottom third of congressional districts nationwide, reflecting the 3rd's population of poor whites who live in the Ozark hills and farming communities. Residents in the Ozark mountains tend to be self-reliant and favor limited government, voting most often for Republicans.

Fayetteville, Springdale, Bentonville and Rogers in the state's northwest corner represent a wealthier part of the district, where history, religious tradition and an influx of retirees have created a solid GOP base. The 2000 census rated this corridor one of the 10 fastest-growing

metropolitan areas in the country, with 48 percent growth over the 1990s.

Though the northwest sets the political tone, the rest of the 3rd — particularly farming communities and the city of Fort Smith — is more open to electing Democrats at the state level. Fayetteville and Springdale also have some liberal-leaning areas.

Hometown giants Tyson Foods in Springdale and Wal-Mart in Bentonville sustain the 3rd's economy, as does the University of Arkansas in Fayetteville. The closure of Fort Chaffee Army Base, near Fort Smith, in the late 1990s hit the district hard, but the military is attempting to redevelop the land.

MAJOR INDUSTRY
Agriculture, livestock, retail

CITIES
Fort Smith, 80,268; Fayetteville, 58,047; Springdale, 45,798; Rogers, 38,829; Russellville, 23,682; Bentonville, 19,730

NOTABLE
Sen. J. William Fulbright, who established the Fulbright fellowships, lived in Fayetteville; The seven-story Christ of the Ozarks Statue in Eureka Springs was completed in 1966.

Rep. Mike Ross (D)

CAPITOL OFFICE
225-3772
www.house.gov/ross
314 Cannon 20515-0404; fax 225-1314

COMMITTEES
Energy & Commerce

HOMETOWN
Prescott

BORN
Aug. 2, 1961, Texarkana, Ark.

RELIGION
Methodist

FAMILY
Wife, Holly Ross; two children

EDUCATION
Texarkana Community College, attended 1979-81;
U. of Arkansas, Little Rock, B.A. 1987 (political
science)

CAREER
Pharmacy owner; wholesale drug and medical
supply company field representative; aide to
lieutenant governor

POLITICAL HIGHLIGHTS
Nevada County Quorum Court, 1983-85; Ark.
Senate, 1991-2001

ELECTION RESULTS

2004 GENERAL

Mike Ross (D)		unopposed

2004 PRIMARY

Mike Ross (D)		unopposed

2002 GENERAL

Mike Ross (D)	119,723	60.6%
Jay Dickey (R)	77,972	39.4%

PREVIOUS WINNING PERCENTAGES
2000 (51%)

Elected 2000; 3rd term

Ross spent two decades in Arkansas politics while gaining business experience as the owner of a pharmacy in the small town of Prescott. As a 21-year-old, Ross drove Bill Clinton around the state as Clinton campaigned for governor. At the same time, Ross waged his own campaign for a term on Nevada County's legislative body, the Quorum Court. Clinton and Ross both won their elections that year.

Like Clinton, Ross is a New Democrat. In the 107th Congress, he joined the New Democrat Coalition, which is made up of several dozen centrist, pro-business House Democrats.

Ross is also a member of the "Blue Dogs," an alliance of conservative House Democrats. In the 108th Congress, he agreed with President Bush's position 53 percent of the time, but he disagreed that the president should continue to cut taxes. In 2004, he told the Arkansas Democrat-Gazette: "We simply need to restore fiscal discipline to our nation's government and stop passing new tax cuts when our nation is in deficit spending and at war."

The 4th District is socially conservative, and Ross walks a path to the right when it comes to social issues. He breaks with many Democrats on abortion and gay marriage and denounces gun control legislation, although he supports laws designed to keep weapons out of schools.

Proving his allegiance to the National Rifle Association, Ross was the lead Democrat on a 2004 measure to overturn gun control laws in the District of Columbia. Ross said he was backing the bill because he wanted to restore Second Amendment rights in the nation's capital. "We're simply trying to give residents of the District of Columbia the same self-defense as residents of the 50 states," Ross told the Arkansas Democrat-Gazette. But city officials said the bill was an election-year tactic and a violation of the district's right to home rule.

In the 108th, Ross was named to the Democratic Steering Committee, which makes Democratic committee assignments, and he had a hand in the appointment of home-state colleague Marion Berry to the Appropriations Committee. In the 109th, he gained his own seat on the powerful Energy and Commerce Committee. Some Arkansas observers have described Ross as stiff and robotic in formal settings, but in a one-on-one conversation he comes across as informed and affable.

Ross says his main goal in the House is to be Arkansas' "economic ambassador." He speaks of attracting new industries to his economically lagging district, where 25 percent of the residents live below the poverty line. He also wants to add to the existing job base at the Army's Pine Bluff Arsenal, which use to make and house chemical and biological weapons.

Ross has proposed that Pine Bluff become the home of the nation's flu vaccine. He told The Atlanta Journal-Constitution that he plans to push for a government-owned, contractor-operated vaccine center in Pine Bluff, and he sent a letter to Defense Secretary Donald H. Rumsfeld asking the Pentagon to consider such a project. Contamination of flu vaccine supplies at a production plant in Britain caused a severe shortage in 2004.

The congressman is also keen to find funding for two interstate highway projects that traverse his district, improving transportation for the area's farmers and loggers. The highways — I-49, running roughly from Texarkana north to Bentonville, and I-69, arcing northeastward across the southeastern part of the district — have been authorized, but their progress depends on annual funding.

In his first two terms, Ross served on the Agriculture Committee, where he watched out for his state's peanut growers and stood up for the area's catfish farmers, who are faced with what Ross says is unfair competition from imported fish from Vietnam.

In looking out for his state's catfish farmers, Ross and members of the Arkansas and Mississippi delegations drew the ire of the National Audubon Society when they proposed a measure to allow the Agriculture Department's pest control agency the authority to kill migratory birds. The 2004 bill grew out of complaints from local catfish farmers about the double-crested cormorant, which has discovered that catfish farms are an easy place to pick up a meal. Catfish farmers are banned from shooting the birds under existing law. Ross told the Resources Committee that the Agriculture Department should have the authority to allow individuals to kill nuisance birds.

Ross has consistently refused the annual cost-of-living pay raise for lawmakers until the minimum wage is increased. He directs the pay raise to a scholarship fund for two 4th District college students.

Both of Ross' parents were schoolteachers. He went to junior college in Texarkana for a while, combining that with a job at the radio station in Hope, where he started working when he was 15.

He earned his degree in political science at 25 while working as a top aide to Arkansas' lieutenant governor, Winston Bryant. He took time off in 1988 to serve as a regional coordinator for Democrat Michael S. Dukakis' presidential campaign. After winning election to the state Senate in 1990, Ross made a living as a field representative for a wholesale drug and medical supply company. He and his wife, Holly, bought a pharmacy (Holly's Health Mart) in Prescott. His wife is the pharmacist.

In 2000, Ross entered the 4th District race, challenging four-term GOP Rep. Jay Dickey. Ross' status as the widely regarded front-runner for the Democratic nomination made him the target of attacks by his three opponents in the party's bitter primary — two of his primary foes later endorsed Dickey. He then endured a hard-fought campaign against Dickey, whose folksy manner had kept him popular despite the 4th's traditional Democratic leanings. Ross' narrow, 2 percentage point win was the Democrats' only victory over an incumbent outside California in November 2000.

In 2002, Dickey was back for a rematch, and many political observers expected the race to be close once again. But Ross eventually won handily, with 61 percent of the vote. He drew no opponent in 2004. Although there has been speculation that he would run for governor in 2006, Ross told the Arkansas Democrat-Gazette he intends to remain in Congress.

KEY VOTES

2004

Yes   Extend federal unemployment benefits by 13 weeks

Yes   Pass $283.2 billion, six-year federal highway and mass transit bill

Yes   Approve $146 billion multi-year extension of previously enacted middle-class tax breaks

Yes   Amend the Constitution to prohibit same-sex marriage

Yes   Cut corporate taxes $137 billion over 10 years

Yes   Reorganize U.S. intelligence agencies as proposed by Sept. 11 commission

2003

No   Cut taxes by $330 billion through fiscal 2013

Yes   Block Bush rule scaling back overtime pay for some white-collar federal workers

Yes   Do not allow use of search warrants without first notifying subjects

Yes   Allow importation of prescription drugs

No   Create private school voucher program in Washington, D.C.

Yes   Ban "partial birth" abortion except to save a woman's life

Yes   Split $18.6 billion in Iraq aid into half-grant, half-loan

No   Overhaul Medicare and create prescription drug benefit

CQ VOTE STUDIES

	PARTY UNITY		PRESIDENTIAL SUPPORT	
	Support	Oppose	Support	Oppose
2004	82%	18%	53%	47%
2003	81%	19%	44%	56%
2002	73%	27%	50%	50%
2001	70%	30%	37%	63%

INTEREST GROUPS

	AFL-CIO	ADA	CCUS	ACU
2004	87%	65%	62%	44%
2003	93%	80%	50%	44%
2002	78%	65%	55%	32%
2001	92%	65%	48%	36%

ARKANSAS 4
South — Pine Bluff, Hot Springs

Covering much of Arkansas' southern half, from the Mississippi River to the Texas and Oklahoma borders, the 4th is a socially conservative but Democratic district that took a Republican swing in the 1990s.

The district elected its first GOP representative of the 20th century in 1992, but overwhelmingly supported Hope-born and Hot Springs-raised Bill Clinton in both his presidential bids. The 4th narrowly supported Al Gore for president in 2000 while electing a Democrat to the House, but gave George W. Bush 51 percent of the vote in 2004. State legislators in the 4th are almost exclusively Democrats.

Rice, soybeans, cotton and rural poverty characterize the eastern edge of the 4th, where many Mississippi River communities have black-majority populations. Democrats receive their most faithful support from these areas and from blue-collar and minority populations in Little River and Lafayette counties in the west. Republicans fare better in oil- and chemical-producing southern cities such as El Dorado, as well as in military and white-collar areas near Pine Bluff and Hot Springs. The

timber industry here discourages pro-environment candidates.

The Pine Bluff Arsenal, which once produced the nation's supply of biological weapons, is home to an emergency preparedness center and a center for toxicological research. A chemical weapons disposal facility operates at the arsenal, although the base has not been successful in its attempts to be selected as the site of a vaccine production plant to guard against bioterrorism.

MAJOR INDUSTRY
Timber, agriculture, livestock

MILITARY BASES
Pine Bluff Arsenal (Army), 200 military, 1,366 civilian (2004)

CITIES
Pine Bluff, 55,085; Hot Springs, 35,750; Texarkana, 26,448; El Dorado, 21,530; Camden, 13,154

NOTABLE
Author Maya Angelou was raised in Stamps; Country singer Johnny Cash was born in Kingsland; Hot Springs, the state's premier tourist attraction, was a getaway for mobsters such as Charles "Lucky" Luciano and Al Capone in the 1930s.

CALIFORNIA

Gov. Arnold Schwarzenegger (R)

First elected: 2003
Length of term: 4 years
Term expires: 01/07
Salary: $175,000
Phone: (916) 445-2841

Hometown: Los Angeles
Born: July 30, 1947; Thal, Austria
Religion: Unspecified
Family: Wife, Maria Shriver; four children
Education: U. of Wisconsin, Superior, B.A. 1979 (business & international economics)
Career: Actor; real estate investor; bodybuilder; weight training supplies salesman
Political highlights: No previous office

Election results:
2003 SPECIAL

Arnold Schwarzenegger (R)	4,206,284	48.9%
Cruz M. Bustamante (D)	2,724,874	31.7%
Tom McClintock (R)	1,161,287	13.5%
others	263,223	3.1%
Peter Miguel Camejo (GREEN)	242,247	2.8%

Lt. Gov. Cruz M. Bustamante (D)

First elected: 1998
Length of term: 4 years
Term expires: 1/07
Salary: $131,250
Phone: (916) 445-8994

STATE LEGISLATURE

Legislature: Year-round with recess

Assembly: 80 members, 2-year terms
2005 breakdown: 48D, 32R; 55 men, 25 women
Salary: $99,000
Phone: (916) 445-3614

Senate: 40 members, 4-year terms
2005 breakdown: 25D, 15R; 28 men, 12 women
Salary: $99,000
Phone: (916) 445-4251

STATE TERM LIMITS

Governor: 2 terms
Assembly: 3 terms
Senate: 2 terms

URBAN STATISTICS

CITY	POPULATION
Los Angeles	3,694,820
San Diego	1,223,400
San Jose	894,943
San Francisco	776,733
Long Beach	461,522

REGISTERED VOTERS

Democrat	43%
Republican	34%
Unaffiliated	18%
Others	5%

POPULATION

2004 population (est.)	35,893,799
2000 population	33,871,648
1990 population	29,760,021
Percent change (1990-2000)	+13.8%
Rank among states (2004)	1

Median age	33.3
Born in state	50.2%
Foreign born	26.2%
Violent crime rate	622/100,000
Poverty level	14.2%
Federal workers	246,152
Military	228,903

REDISTRICTING

California gained one House seat in reapportionment. The state legislature drew a new 53-district map, which the governor signed on Sept. 26, 2001.

MISCELLANEOUS

Web: www.ca.gov
Capital: Sacramento
STATE ELECTION OFFICIAL
(916) 657-2166
DEMOCRATIC HEADQUARTERS
(916) 442-5707
REPUBLICAN HEADQUARTERS
(818) 841-5210

District Statistics

DIST.	2004 VOTE FOR PRESIDENT BUSH	KERRY	WHITE	BLACK	ASIAN	HISP	MEDIAN INCOME	WHITE COLLAR	BLUE COLLAR	SERVICE INDUSTRY	OVER 64	UNDER 18	COLLEGE EDUCATION	RURAL	SQ. MILES
1	38%	60%	71%	1%	4%	18%	$38,918	58%	24%	18%	13%	25%	25%	24%	11,006
2	62	37	76	1	4	14	$33,559	55	27	18	15	26	17	32	21,758
3	58	41	74	4	6	11	$51,313	68	19	13	12	26	27	14	3,374
4	61	37	84	1	2	9	$49,387	63	20	16	14	26	25	33	16,453
5	38	61	43	14	15	21	$36,719	63	20	17	11	28	21	0	147
6	28	70	76	2	4	15	$59,115	68	18	14	13	23	38	10	1,625
7	32	67	43	17	13	21	$52,778	60	23	17	10	27	22	1	349
8	14	84	43	9	29	16	$52,322	73	12	15	13	14	44	0	35
9	13	86	35	26	15	19	$44,314	69	17	14	11	23	37	0	132
10	40	58	65	6	9	15	$65,245	69	18	13	12	27	36	3	1,013
11	54	45	64	3	9	20	$61,996	68	21	11	10	29	29	10	2,277
12	27	72	48	3	29	16	$70,307	73	15	12	14	21	41	0	117
13	28	71	38	6	28	21	$62,415	67	22	11	10	25	32	1	221
14	30	68	60	3	16	18	$77,985	77	13	10	12	22	52	6	826
15	36	63	47	2	29	17	$74,947	74	17	9	10	24	42	1	286

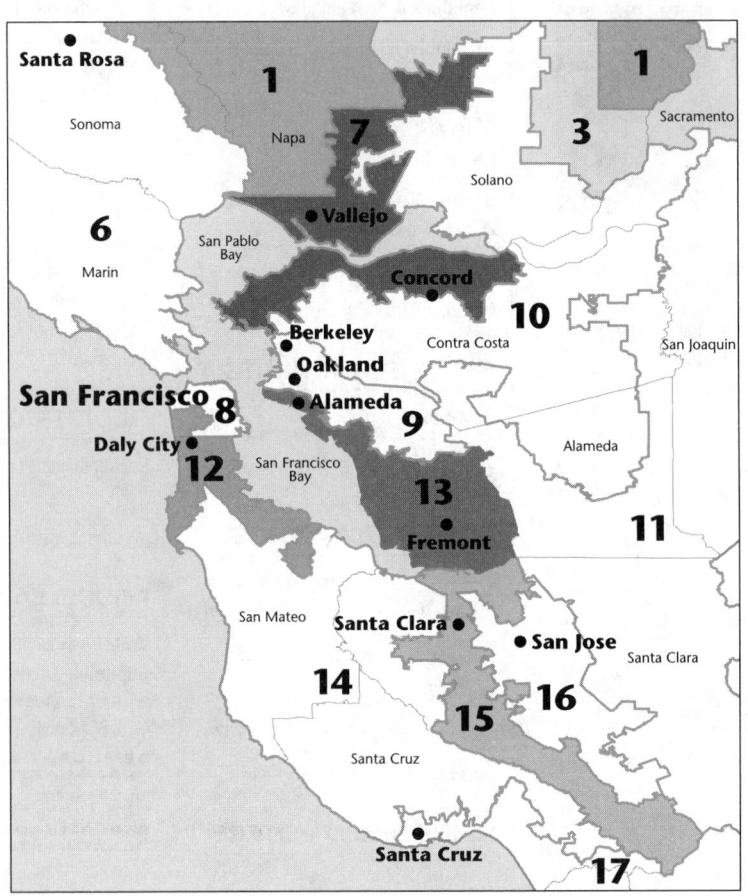

District Statistics

DIST.	2004 VOTE FOR PRESIDENT BUSH	KERRY	WHITE	BLACK	ASIAN	HISP	MEDIAN INCOME	WHITE COLLAR	BLUE COLLAR	SERVICE INDUSTRY	OVER 64	UNDER 18	COLLEGE EDUCATION	RURAL	SQ. MILES
16	36%	63%	32%	3%	23%	38%	$67,689	61%	25%	14%	8%	27%	27%	1%	230
17	33	66	46	3	5	43	$49,234	55	28	16	10	27	25	10	4,820
18	50	49	39	6	9	42	$34,211	46	37	17	10	34	10	9	3,052
19	61	38	60	3	4	28	$41,225	59	25	15	12	28	20	19	6,692
20	48	51	21	7	6	63	$26,800	38	43	19	7	35	6	9	4,982
21	65	34	46	2	5	43	$36,047	53	31	16	10	32	15	20	8,026
22	68	31	67	6	3	21	$41,801	58	25	17	11	29	18	18	10,417
23	40	58	49	2	5	42	$44,874	57	26	17	12	25	26	2	1,042
24	56	43	69	2	4	22	$61,453	68	19	14	11	28	30	6	3,883
25	59	40	57	8	4	27	$49,002	60	24	16	8	32	19	12	21,484
26	55	44	53	4	15	24	$58,968	71	17	12	11	27	32	1	752
27	39	59	45	4	11	36	$46,781	66	20	14	11	26	26	0	151
28	28	71	31	4	6	56	$40,439	58	26	16	9	29	24	0	77

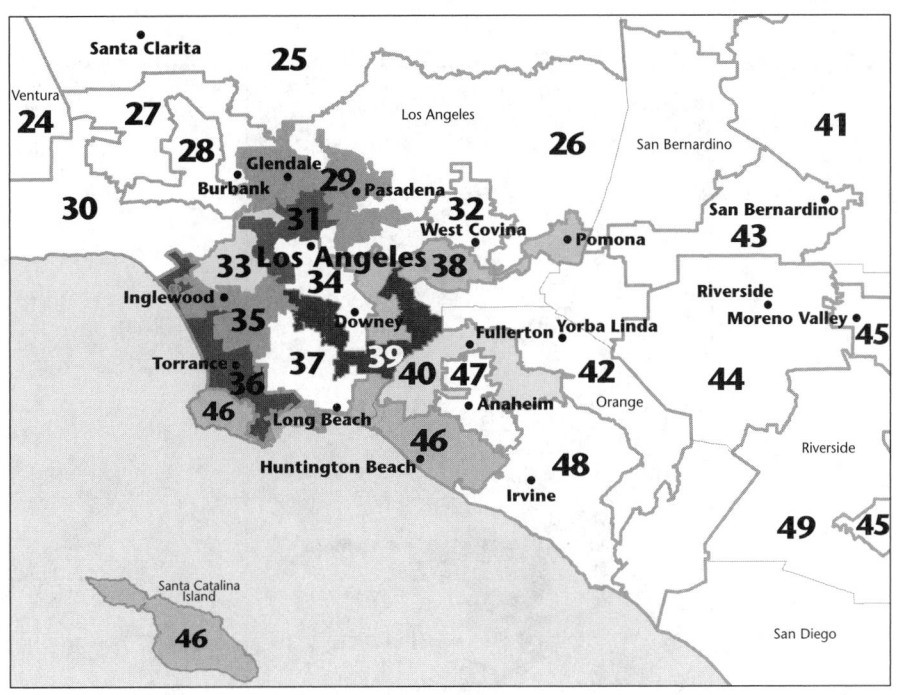

District Statistics

DIST.	2004 VOTE FOR PRESIDENT BUSH	KERRY	WHITE	BLACK	ASIAN	HISP	MEDIAN INCOME	WHITE COLLAR	BLUE COLLAR	SERVICE INDUSTRY	OVER 64	UNDER 18	COLLEGE EDUCATION	RURAL	SQ. MILES
29	37%	61%	39%	6%	24%	26%	$43,895	70%	16%	14%	13%	23%	33%	1%	101
30	33	66	76	3	9	8	$60,713	84	7	9	15	17	54	2	286
31	22	77	10	4	14	70	$26,093	44	34	22	7	30	14	0	39
32	37	62	15	3	18	62	$41,394	51	33	16	9	31	14	0	92
33	16	83	20	30	12	35	$31,655	64	18	18	10	24	27	0	48
34	30	69	11	4	5	77	$29,863	44	40	16	8	32	9	0	58
35	20	79	10	34	6	47	$32,156	53	28	19	8	33	13	0	55
36	40	59	48	4	13	30	$51,633	71	16	13	10	23	37	0	75
37	25	74	17	25	11	43	$34,006	54	29	17	8	33	15	0	75
38	34	65	14	4	10	71	$42,488	51	34	15	9	32	13	0	104
39	40	59	21	6	10	61	$45,307	55	31	14	8	33	15	0	65
40	60	39	49	2	16	30	$54,356	65	22	13	11	27	26	0	100
41	62	37	64	5	4	23	$38,721	57	25	17	14	28	18	11	13,314

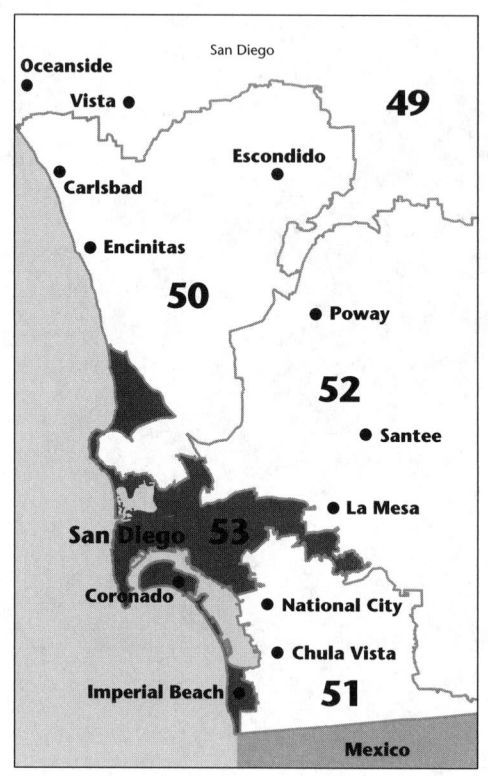

District Statistics

DIST.	2004 VOTE FOR PRESIDENT BUSH	KERRY	WHITE	BLACK	ASIAN	HISP	MEDIAN INCOME	WHITE COLLAR	BLUE COLLAR	SERVICE INDUSTRY	OVER 64	UNDER 18	COLLEGE EDUCATION	RURAL	SQ. MILES
42	62%	37%	54%	3%	16%	24%	$70,463	74%	15%	11%	8%	28%	35%	1%	314
43	41	58	23	12	3	58	$37,390	46	37	17	6	37	9	1	191
44	59	40	51	5	5	35	$51,578	59	27	14	8	31	21	2	522
45	56	43	50	6	3	38	$40,468	53	26	21	16	29	17	10	5,980
46	57	42	63	1	15	17	$61,567	73	16	12	13	22	36	0	264
47	50	49	17	1	14	65	$41,618	41	39	20	6	33	10	0	55
48	58	40	68	1	13	15	$69,663	80	10	10	12	23	47	0	212
49	62	36	58	5	3	30	$46,445	58	26	16	13	29	21	10	1,690
50	55	44	66	2	10	19	$59,813	71	16	13	12	25	40	2	300
51	46	53	21	9	12	53	$39,243	55	26	20	10	31	15	4	4,582
52	61	38	73	4	5	14	$52,940	68	18	14	11	27	29	6	2,113
53	38	61	51	7	8	29	$36,637	65	17	19	10	21	32	0	95
STATE	44	54	47	6	11	32	$47,493	63	22	15	11	27	27	6	155,959
U.S.	50.7	48.3	69	12	4	13	$41,994	60	25	15	12	26	24	21	3,537,438

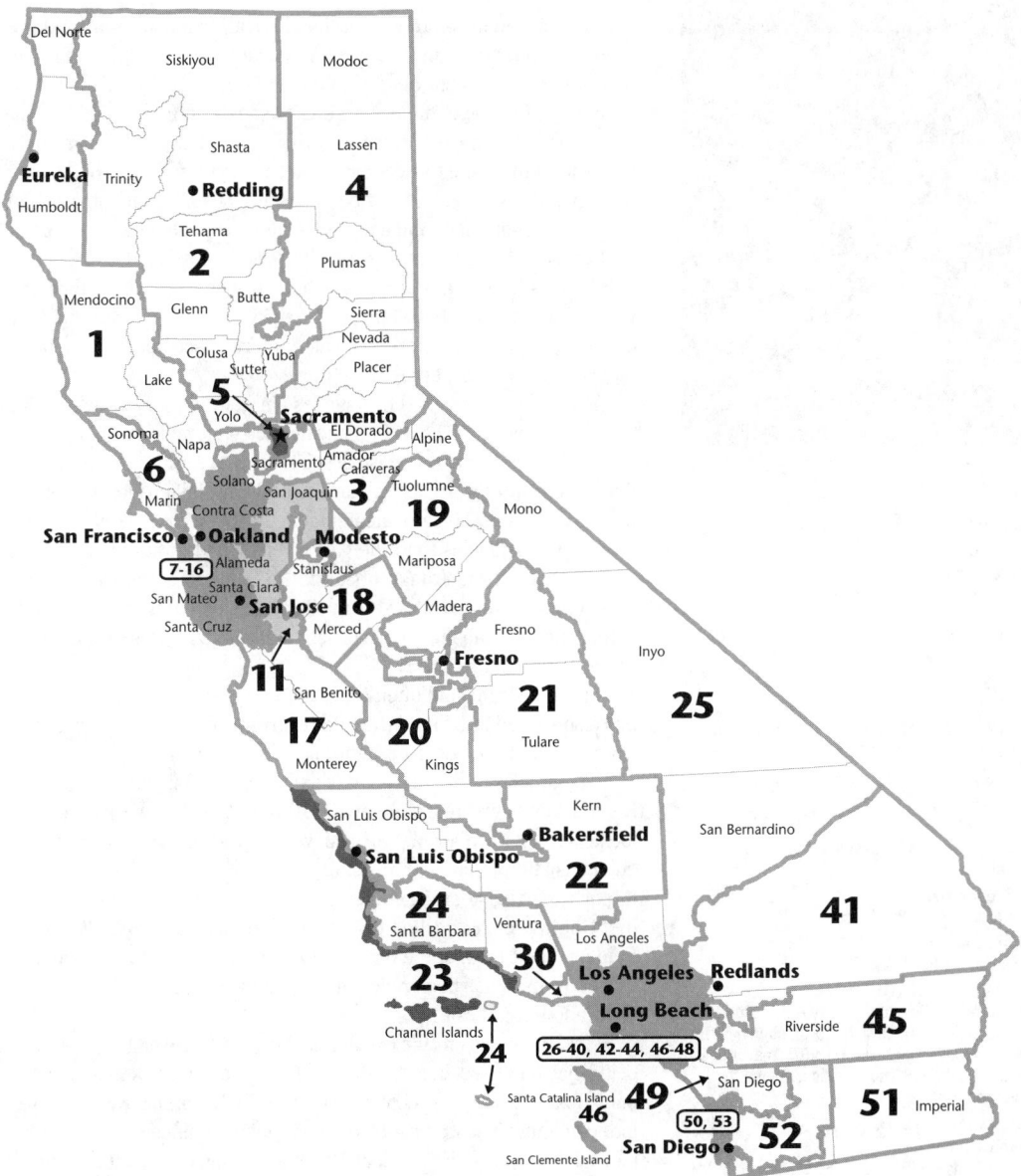

Del Norte

Siskiyou

Modoc

Shasta

Lassen

● **Eureka**

Trinity

● **Redding**

4

Humboldt

Tehama

2

Plumas

Mendocino

Glenn Butte

Sierra

1

Nevada

Colusa Yuba

Lake

Sutter Placer

5

Yolo

● **Sacramento**

Sonoma

El Dorado

Alpine

Napa

Sacramento

Amador

6

Solano

Calaveras

Marin

San Joaquin **3** Tuolumne

Contra Costa

19

Mono

San Francisco ● ● **Oakland** ● **Modesto**

7-16 Alameda

Stanislaus

Santa Clara

Mariposa

San Mateo

18

Madera

● **San Jose**

Santa Cruz

Merced

Fresno

● **Fresno**

11

San Benito

Inyo

17 **20**

21

25

Monterey Kings

Tulare

San Luis Obispo

Kern

● **Bakersfield**

San Bernardino

● **San Luis Obispo**

22

24

41

Santa Barbara

Ventura

Los Angeles

23

30

Los Angeles ● ● **Redlands**

Channel Islands

● **Long Beach**

Riverside **45**

24

26-40, 42-44, 46-48

Santa Catalina Island

49

San Diego

51 Imperial

46

50, 53

San Clemente Island

San Diego ● **52**

Sen. Dianne Feinstein (D)

Elected 1992; 2nd full term

CAPITOL OFFICE
224-3841
feinstein.senate.gov
331 Hart 20510-0504; fax 228-3954

COMMITTEES
Appropriations
Energy & Natural Resources
Judiciary
Rules & Administration
Select Intelligence

HOMETOWN
San Francisco

BORN
June 22, 1933, San Francisco, Calif.

RELIGION
Jewish

FAMILY
Husband, Richard Blum; one child, three stepchildren

EDUCATION
Stanford U., A.B. 1955 (history)

CAREER
Civic board official

POLITICAL HIGHLIGHTS
San Francisco Board of Supervisors, 1970-78 (president, 1970-71, 1974-75, 1978); candidate for mayor of San Francisco, 1971, 1975; mayor of San Francisco, 1978-89; Democratic nominee for governor, 1990

ELECTION RESULTS

2000 GENERAL

Dianne Feinstein (D)	5,932,522	55.8%
Tom Campbell (R)	3,886,853	36.6%
Medea Benjamin (GREEN)	326,828	3.1%
Gail Lightfoot (LIBERT)	187,718	1.8%
Diane Beall Templin (AMI)	134,598	1.3%

2000 PRIMARY (OPEN)

Dianne Feinstein (D)	3,759,560	51.2%
Tom Campbell (R)	1,697,208	23.1%
Ray Haynes (R)	679,034	9.2%
Bill Horn (R)	453,630	6.2%
Michael Schmier (D)	181,104	2.5%
Gail Lightfoot (LIBERT)	120,622	1.6%

PREVIOUS WINNING PERCENTAGES
1994 (47%); 1992 Special Election (54%)

Feinstein often straddles the ideological divide without making enemies, a skill that has helped her find consensus on a range of issues, but that has not catapulted her into her party's upper echelons.

Indeed, the adage that every senator sees a future president in the mirror hasn't held true for Feinstein (FINE-stine). Despite the obvious advantage she would bring to a national ticket as a representative of the country's most populous state, she has been passed over a couple of times for vice presidential nominee. And although widely respected by members of both parties, she shows no interest in a leadership position.

She sees herself a pragmatist who can move legislation through Congress. She may have been mayor of the city for over a decade, but Feinstein doesn't operate as the stereotypical "San Francisco liberal" who prizes ideological purity over getting a bill done.

That image was key to her success in getting a key provision into the 2004 overhaul of the country's spy agencies, heralded as one of the most significant bills of President Bush's first term. A senior member of the Intelligence Committee, Feinstein had introduced a bill in 2002 to create a Cabinet-level director of national intelligence with far more control over the 15 intelligence agencies than the CIA director had. It attracted a number of cosponsors but didn't take off until the Sept. 11 commission released a report in the summer of 2004 endorsing the idea. It was later folded into a comprehensive intelligence overhaul measure that passed in the final days of the 108th Congress.

Tough on crime and often sympathetic to business concerns, Feinstein has also sought and found the middle ground on issues ranging from children's safety to the environment to campaign finance.

She teamed up with her good friend Sen. Kay Bailey Hutchison, a Texas Republican, to create a nationwide "Amber Alert" network to help quickly locate abducted children. She also worked with House Republicans to rescue legislation to prevent forest fires from a partisan dispute over minority party participation in conference committees, marking a rare agreement between the parties on environmental legislation. "When Dianne Feinstein and I can agree on a bill to address the wildfire threat, it's clear that consensus has been reached," said Rep. Scott McInnis, a conservative Colorado Republican.

Feinstein was even able to walk the bipartisan line on the explosive issue of judicial nominees. In 2001, she and fellow California Democratic Sen. Barbara Boxer reached agreement with the Bush administration to create an independent, bipartisan panel to recommend nominees for California's four judicial districts. Under the deal, Boxer and Feinstein appoint half of the panelists while the other half are appointed by the White House, and no recommendation moves forward without the panel's majority support.

At the same time, she has supported, although sometimes reluctantly, her party's filibuster of 10 of the president's more conservative judicial nominees, opposing those nominees she views as out of the mainstream. On one occasion, she was the only Democratic member of the Judiciary Committee to vote for Jeff Sutton, a former Ohio solicitor general, to a seat on the 6th U.S. Circuit Court of Appeals, a move that effectively killed a likely Democratic filibuster of his nomination.

Feinstein says she developed her political mantra — "govern from the center" — while serving as San Francisco mayor and trying to work out solutions that satisfied the diverse political forces in her city. Her moderation, personal appeal and high name recognition have made her one of California's most enduring political figures. A member of the moderate Senate New Democrats and the Centrist Coalition, she is popular and respected in the Senate. She largely avoids alienating Republicans with the kind of stinging verbal assaults Boxer is known for and distances herself ideologically from another Democratic woman from the Bay area, House Minority Leader Nancy Pelosi.

A member of five committees, Feinstein has an impact on a diverse portfolio of issues, in part because California is so important electorally but also because of her ability to unemotionally conduct business in the enemy camp. In 2001, for example, when both parties were on the verge of throwing in the towel on the overhaul of campaign finance law, she teamed up with Republican Fred Thompson of Tennessee on a compromise amendment that rescued the bill.

One issue on which Feinstein takes a strong stand is gun control. "I've lived a life that has been impacted by weapons," she wrote in "Nine and Counting," a book by the nine female senators serving in 2000. "So this is not an esoteric, academic exercise for me. Nor is it a political exercise."

In November 1978, while serving on the San Francisco Board of Supervisors, Feinstein discovered the body of Mayor George Moscone after he and Harvey Milk, the city's first openly gay supervisor, were shot to death in City Hall by former Supervisor Dan White. Feinstein succeeded Moscone and won plaudits for the dignified manner in which she held the city together in the wake of the killings. Feinstein's role, recalled in the documentary "The Life and Times of Harvey Milk," has given her credibility in the gun debate. When GOP Sen. Larry E. Craig of Idaho, a National Rifle Association board member, once hinted that Feinstein did not have much weapons knowledge, she recounted how she had tried to find Milk's pulse after he was shot.

Feinstein works closely with her female colleagues. She was a prominent skeptic during the Rules Committee's investigation of a GOP challenge to Louisiana Democrat Mary L. Landrieu's narrow 1996 Senate victory. "Hell hath no fury like a man beaten by a woman," Feinstein said. "Women have to fight our way in this process all the way up. No one hands us anything."

Certainly no one handed her the Senate seat, which she first won in a special election in 1992 against Republican John Seymour, who had been appointed after Republican Sen. Pete Wilson was elected governor in 1990. Boxer was also running in 1992, and the pair, despite their differences in personality and philosophy, campaigned as "Thelma and Louise," the name of a popular female buddy movie.

Two years later, Feinstein had to defend the seat against a tough challenge from millionaire GOP Rep. Michael Huffington, who outspent her by more than 2-to-1 in what was at the time the most expensive Senate contest ever. Not until she and other Democrats turned attack ads against him — and it was revealed that Huffington had hired an illegal immigrant as a household employee — did Feinstein begin pulling ahead.

Her Republican opponent in 2000, former Rep. Tom Campbell, had trouble raising money and did little to inspire his party's conservatives, offering centrist views and even calling Feinstein an effective senator at one point in the campaign. Feinstein cruised to re-election. Also that year, Vice President Al Gore considered her for his running mate but chose Connecticut Sen. Joseph I. Lieberman to be the first Jewish vice presidential candidate from a major political party. In 1984, Democratic nominee Walter F. Mondale had given Feinstein strong consideration before selecting Rep. Geraldine Ferraro of New York to be the first female vice presidential candidate from a major party.

KEY VOTES

2004

Yes	Pass $318.9 billion, six-year highway and mass transit bill
Yes	Extend assault weapons ban for 10 years
Yes	Restore pay-as-you-go rules for new tax cuts and entitlement spending
No	Criminalize harm to a fetus in an attack on the mother
Yes	Increase mandatory child care funding to states by $6 billion over five years
No	Amend the Constitution to prohibit same-sex marriage
Yes	Approve $146 billion multi-year extension of previously enacted middle-class tax breaks
Yes	Reorganize U.S. intelligence agencies as proposed by Sept. 11 commission
No	Cut corporate taxes $137 billion over 10 years

2003

?	Delay Bush changes to Clean Air Act
No	Allow confirmation vote on Miguel A. Estrada to the U.S. Court of Appeals for the D.C. Circuit
Yes	Block a Bush proposal opening Alaska's Arctic National Wildlife Refuge to oil drilling
Yes	Limit size of Bush's proposed tax cut to $350 billion through fiscal 2013
Yes	Overhaul Medicare and create prescription drug benefit
Yes	Block Bush rule scaling back overtime pay for some white-collar federal workers
Yes	Split $20 billion in Iraq aid into half-grant, half-loan
No	Ban "partial birth" abortion except to save a woman's life
No	Stop proposal allowing travel to Cuba
No	Allow final vote on energy policy overhaul

CQ VOTE STUDIES

	PARTY UNITY		PRESIDENTIAL SUPPORT	
	Support	Oppose	Support	Oppose
2004	95%	5%	62%	38%
2003	91%	9%	49%	51%
2002	83%	17%	76%	24%
2001	85%	15%	71%	29%
2000	88%	12%	84%	16%
1999	91%	9%	87%	13%
1998	87%	13%	88%	12%
1997	86%	14%	89%	11%
1996	81%	19%	90%	10%
1995	80%	20%	84%	16%

INTEREST GROUPS

	AFL-CIO	ADA	CCUS	ACU
2004	100%	100%	65%	4%
2003	92%	90%	39%	5%
2002	92%	80%	55%	20%
2001	94%	85%	71%	12%
2000	50%	70%	54%	28%
1999	78%	100%	53%	4%
1998	88%	90%	61%	4%
1997	57%	85%	50%	4%
1996	86%	95%	38%	20%
1995	100%	95%	37%	13%

Sen. Barbara Boxer (D)

Elected 1992; 3rd term

CAPITOL OFFICE
224-3553
boxer.senate.gov
112 Hart 20510-0505; fax 228-3972

COMMITTEES
Commerce, Science & Transportation
Environment & Public Works
Foreign Relations

HOMETOWN
Millbrae

BORN
Nov. 11, 1940, Brooklyn, N.Y.

RELIGION
Jewish

FAMILY
Husband, Stewart Boxer; two children

EDUCATION
Brooklyn College, B.A. 1962 (economics)

CAREER
Congressional aide; journalist; stockbroker

POLITICAL HIGHLIGHTS
Candidate for Marin County Board of Supervisors, 1972; Marin County Board of Supervisors, 1977-83 (president, 1980); U.S. House, 1983-93

ELECTION RESULTS

2004 GENERAL

Barbara Boxer (D)	6,955,728	57.7%
Bill Jones (R)	4,555,922	37.8%
Marsha Feinland (PFP)	243,846	2.0%
James "Jim" Gray (LIBERT)	216,522	1.8%

2004 PRIMARY

Barbara Boxer (D)	unopposed

PREVIOUS WINNING PERCENTAGES
1998 (53%); 1992 (48%); 1990 House Election (68%); 1988 House Election (73%); 1986 House Election (74%); 1984 House Election (68%); 1982 House Election (52%)

In her third term in the Senate, Boxer seems in some ways to be back where she started when she first ran — a leader of protests. Her decisive re-election victory in 2004 against the tide of Republican strength in the Senate liberated the already-liberal Boxer to take even stronger feminist, environmentalist, and anti-corporate-corruption stands. Her public profile is growing, though her list of successful legislation is short and likely to remain so.

While she never abandoned her core causes, she sometimes has had to mute her tone in recent years as she ran for re-election or attempted to maneuver in the increasingly conservative Senate. No more. Once counted among the vulnerable incumbents of 2004, Boxer beat her Republican challenger by a large margin. "My political style is to be extremely candid and straight from the shoulders, and not to be mealy-mouthed or waffle," says the former 1960s-era war protester. "When I believe in something, I believe in it strongly."

On the wall of her Capitol Hill office hangs a picture of Boxer as a House member, leading six other female representatives up the steps of the Senate in 1991 to demand public hearings on law professor Anita Hill's allegations of sexual harassment against Supreme Court nominee Clarence Thomas. Looking back, she believes that that attention-grabbing stunt helped spark a voter backlash against the overwhelmingly white, male makeup of the Senate, which ultimately led to the 1992 elections being termed the "Year of the Woman." Boxer, who had represented California's 6th House District for 10 years, was elected to the Senate that year along with California's Dianne Feinstein, Patty Murray of Washington and Carol Moseley-Braun of Illinois.

In early 2005, Boxer was again protesting, this time over the usually pro forma certification of election results. During a roll call at a joint session of Congress to certify the vote count that gave President Bush his 2004 victory over Sen. John Kerry, a Massachusetts Democrat, Boxer invoked a little used prerogative to raise an objection that voters may have been denied their right to vote in Ohio, a battleground state that went for Bush. The Senate was forced to withdraw from the House chamber so the two bodies could separately debate the validity of Ohio's election results. The outcome was never in doubt— both the House and Senate ultimately voted to certify the election — but Boxer forced a debate on the issue.

For the 109th Congress, Minority Leader Harry Reid named Boxer chief deputy whip, calling her his "right hand" during tough votes on the Senate floor and helping out with some floor management responsibilities. For several years, the leadership has tried to capitalize on her nimbleness with a sound bite. She is known to raise her voice on television and in news conferences when she feels passionately about an issue, sometimes with the help of her "Boxer Box" — a portable platform that gets the 4-foot, 11-inch Boxer to microphone level.

An ardent feminist, a defender of environmental regulation and an enemy of the National Rifle Association, Boxer is often outside the majority, especially after Republicans expanded their control in 2004 from 51 to 55 seats. But she won a major environmental victory in 2003 when the Senate voted to exempt the Arctic National Wildlife Refuge from oil drilling. The issue is expected to re-emerge, setting up more battles for Boxer and environmentalists. She says, "We have to make a choice. Do we want to change the policy and go into this beautiful refuge or do we want to look at other ways to get more energy?"

Like any seasoned pol, Boxer finds time to concentrate on home-state concerns. At the end of 2004, she pushed through a tax provision sought by California's high-tech firms that grants a tax holiday on overseas earnings if the money is reinvested back home. That sort of stance gives her broad popularity in California, despite the state's more conservative leanings. Boxer gained more votes in her 2004 re-election than anyone other than the presidential candidates — 6.7 million — and won by a 20 percentage point margin over GOP challenger Bill Jones.

She has not limited her considerable passions to politics. In 2004, she was completing a novel, with author Mary-Rose Hayes, about a female politician who is elected to the Senate when her candidate-husband is killed. A blurb from the publisher, Chronicle Books, says: "On the eve of a crucial Senate vote, her personal and political worlds collide when her right-wing adversaries recruit her former lover to sabotage her credibility and career. With a fascinating, up-close view of how politics and power are shaped by personal friendships and revenge, this novel is an exciting fiction debut by an experienced senator."

In her first and most difficult re-election campaign, in 1998 against conservative GOP State Treasurer Matt Fong, The Sacramento Bee described Boxer as "a high-profile, high-energy politician with a bent for partisanship and self-promotion." Former Senate Majority Leader Bob Dole of Kansas once called her "the most partisan senator I've ever known." Her voting record puts her to the left of such well-known liberals as Edward M. Kennedy of Massachusetts and Tom Harkin of Iowa.

As a member of the Environment and Public Works Committee, she was a leader in 2001 in efforts to clean up abandoned industrial sites known as brownfields. She has pushed since the 1990s for a ban on the gasoline additive MTBE, a suspected carcinogen. And she is one of the Bush administration's harshest critics on the environment, condemning its proposed rollbacks of clean air regulations, new rules allowing more logging in national forests and its interpretation of "dolphin-safe" tuna fishing regulations.

One of 11 Jewish senators and a member of the Foreign Relations Committee, Boxer has taken on the cause of putting anti-missile technology on American commercial aircraft. In legislation and in letters, she is calling on the government to require the anti-missile devices on all new airplanes, citing attempted purchases of shoulder-fired missiles by individuals with possible links to terrorist groups.

Drawn into politics in the 1960s as a young Vietnam War protester, Boxer voted against both the 1991 Persian Gulf resolution sought by the senior George Bush and the younger Bush's 2002 use-of-force resolution against Iraq. Boxer occasionally has worked with more-moderate Republicans on lower-profile issues, such as efforts with Arlen Specter of Pennsylvania to increase health research funding.

Boxer is a stockbroker by training. But she is a child of immigrant parents and attended public schools in Brooklyn, and so sees herself as a defender of the middle class. "You can't hand anybody anything; it doesn't work that way. But you can give them a chance," Boxer says.

After six years on the Marin County Board of Supervisors, Boxer was elected to the House in 1982 as the beneficiary of one of the decade's more creative acts of redistricting. In her first Senate bid, Boxer beat out fellow House Democrat Mel Levine and Lt. Gov. Leo T. McCarthy in the primary. In November, she held off the GOP nominee, conservative TV commentator Bruce Herschensohn, by 5 percentage points.

KEY VOTES

2004

Yes — Pass $318.9 billion, six-year highway and mass transit bill

Yes — Extend assault weapons ban for 10 years

Yes — Restore pay-as-you-go rules for new tax cuts and entitlement spending

No — Criminalize harm to a fetus in an attack on the mother

Yes — Increase mandatory child care funding to states by $6 billion over five years

No — Amend the Constitution to prohibit same-sex marriage

Yes — Approve $146 billion multi-year extension of previously enacted middle-class tax breaks

Yes — Reorganize U.S. intelligence agencies as proposed by Sept. 11 commission

No — Cut corporate taxes $137 billion over 10 years

2003

Yes — Delay Bush changes to Clean Air Act

No — Allow confirmation vote on Miguel A. Estrada to the U.S. Court of Appeals for the D.C. Circuit

Yes — Block a Bush proposal opening Alaska's Arctic National Wildlife Refuge to oil drilling

Yes — Limit size of Bush's proposed tax cut to $350 billion through fiscal 2013

Yes — Overhaul Medicare and create prescription drug benefit

Yes — Block Bush rule scaling back overtime pay for some white-collar federal workers

Yes — Split $20 billion in Iraq aid into half-grant, half-loan

No — Ban "partial birth" abortion except to save a woman's life

- — Stop proposal allowing travel to Cuba

No — Allow final vote on energy policy overhaul

CQ VOTE STUDIES

	PARTY UNITY		PRESIDENTIAL SUPPORT	
	Support	Oppose	Support	Oppose
2004	96%	4%	65%	35%
2003	99%	1%	44%	56%
2002	95%	5%	65%	35%
2001	98%	2%	64%	36%
2000	100%	0%	92%	8%
1999	97%	3%	84%	16%
1998	90%	10%	90%	10%
1997	97%	3%	89%	11%
1996	94%	6%	90%	10%
1995	95%	5%	90%	10%

INTEREST GROUPS

	AFL-CIO	ADA	CCUS	ACU
2004	100%	95%	56%	4%
2003	100%	95%	22%	10%
2002	100%	90%	40%	5%
2001	100%	95%	42%	0%
2000	67%	85%	41%	4%
1999	100%	100%	47%	4%
1998	88%	95%	59%	4%
1997	86%	100%	50%	0%
1996	100%	100%	23%	5%
1995	100%	100%	26%	0%

Rep. Mike Thompson (D)

Elected 1998; 4th term

CAPITOL OFFICE
225-3311
mikethompson.house.gov
231 Cannon 20515-0501; fax 225-4335

COMMITTEES
Ways & Means

HOMETOWN
St. Helena

BORN
Jan. 24, 1951, St. Helena, Calif.

RELIGION
Roman Catholic

FAMILY
Wife, Janet Thompson; two children

EDUCATION
California State U., Chico, B.A. 1982 (political science), M.A. 1996 (public administration)

MILITARY SERVICE
Army, 1969-73

CAREER
Vintner; winery maintenance supervisor; state legislative aide; college instructor

POLITICAL HIGHLIGHTS
Calif. Senate, 1990-98

ELECTION RESULTS

2004 GENERAL

Mike Thompson (D)	189,366	66.9%
Lawrence Wiesner (R)	79,970	28.3%
Pamela Elizondo (GREEN)	13,635	4.8%

2004 PRIMARY

Mike Thompson (D)	unopposed

2002 GENERAL

Mike Thompson (D)	118,669	64.1%
Lawrence Wiesner (R)	60,013	32.4%
Kevin Bastian (LIBERT)	6,534	3.5%

PREVIOUS WINNING PERCENTAGES
2000 (65%); 1998 (62%)

Thompson, a former chairman of the California Senate Budget Committee, uses his knowledge of budget matters to challenge the Republican majority's fiscal policies. He is in an even better position to question GOP tax and trade measures with his appointment to the Ways and Means Committee in the 109th Congress.

A friend of House Democratic leader and fellow Californian Nancy Pelosi, Thompson took on a more visible role in the 108th Congress. During House debate on the budget resolution in 2004, Thompson sought approval of an amendment that would have required increased spending and new tax cuts to be offset with budget cuts. He argued that pay-as-you-go rules that did not apply to tax cuts would make no real dent in the deficit. But despite support from a number of GOP lawmakers, the Republican leadership defeated Thompson's proposal.

Thompson is a member of the conservative Blue Dog Coalition, and he is friendly toward business interests. He chairs the Democratic Congressional Campaign Committee's business council, which holds regular meetings with industry lobbyists in an effort to emphasize that Democrats understand the issues facing American businesses.

The congressman's empathy with the business community may come from his experience as a vintner in his district's thriving wine industry. He has worked to expand trade markets for California's wine and produce, and has pressed hard for federal dollars to fight insect-borne crop diseases. Thompson has even made several trips to Cuba since his election in 1998, seeking to open that nation to California's wines and rice.

The 1st District has some of northern California's most impressive scenery and most productive vineyards. Along with California Republican George P. Radanovich, Thompson is a co-founder of the Congressional Wine Caucus. The group includes lawmakers from California to New York.

Thompson has benefited from his early support of Pelosi as she sought to move into the House leadership. In 2001, he helped attract the more conservative Democrats to Pelosi's side in her successful bid for the post of Democratic whip against Steny H. Hoyer of Maryland. In 2003, he got two plum committee assignments — Budget and Transportation — as well as appointment to the Democratic Steering Committee, which makes committee assignments. He had to relinquish those seats to take the Ways and Means post in the 109th Congress.

Thompson worked closely with California Democratic Sen. Barbara Boxer in the 108th and 109th Congresses on a plan to expand federally protected wilderness along California's Northern Coast by 298,000 acres. All of the acres lie within the 1st District. The measure sought to convert 15 stretches of land owned by the U.S. Forest Service or the Bureau of Land Management into wilderness areas that would be open to most recreational activities except the use of motorized vehicles. Thompson said the wilderness designation would help boost tourism in his district, which has lost thousands of fishing and timber industry jobs.

Thompson and Boxer also teamed up in the spring of 2004 to push the Bush administration for relief from record-high gasoline prices. The two called on President Bush to divert crude oil from the nation's Strategic Petroleum Reserve into the open oil market as a way of increasing supplies and driving down gas prices at the pump. Thompson said his constituents were paying some of the highest gasoline prices in the country. "It's alarming that one community in California is paying 45 cents more per gallon than another community seven miles north in Oregon," Thompson told the San Francisco Chronicle in 2004. But the Bush administration insisted that the reserve was for emergencies, not for adjusting market prices.

On national issues, Thompson shares the same priorities as most House Democrats: education, health care and the environment. He sounds like an old-fashioned Democrat when he says, "I really believe in public service, and I really believe in government."

Thompson became interested in public service as a young man working as a maintenance supervisor at the Beringer Vineyard in Napa Valley. "I was the guy the Hispanic field laborers would come to with their problems," he says. Seeking to intervene on behalf of one Hispanic worker who had been cheated by a mechanic, Thompson recalls, "The guy in the repair shop said: 'What do you care — the guy's just a Mexican.' "

Outraged, Thompson said he realized that to be able to help people effectively, he would have to complete his education. He had dropped out of high school and joined the Army, serving as a staff sergeant and platoon leader with the 173rd Airborne Brigade in Vietnam, where he was wounded and received a Purple Heart. In his late 20s and early 30s, he got his high school diploma and earned a college degree.

A political science professor suggested that he apply for a fellowship working with the state legislature, which led to a second career as a staff member. Thompson ran for elective office himself in 1990, winning a seat in the state Senate. During his tenure in the California Senate, Thompson built coalitions across party lines on budget and other matters. In tandem with a Republican state senator, he sponsored a welfare overhaul bill that provided recipients with child care aid, job training and education to move them off the public assistance rolls.

Because of California's legislative term limits, Thompson gained increasing seniority quickly in Sacramento. But those same limits meant that he would be out of a job after the 1998 elections, so he set his sights on Congress. The prospect of facing the popular Thompson, it was widely speculated, was the reason the incumbent, Republican Rep. Frank Riggs, abandoned his seat in favor of a quixotic, late bid for the Senate. Thompson then easily defeated his underfunded Republican opponent, Napa County Supervisor Mark Luce.

Thompson has gone on to win re-election easily. Redistricting following the 2000 census made the 1st more favorable to Democrats, giving Thompson confidence that he can hold onto the seat for the foreseeable future.

KEY VOTES

2004

Yes Extend federal unemployment benefits by 13 weeks

Yes Pass $283.2 billion, six-year federal highway and mass transit bill

No Approve $146 billion multi-year extension of previously enacted middle-class tax breaks

No Amend the Constitution to prohibit same-sex marriage

Yes Cut corporate taxes $137 billion over 10 years

Yes Reorganize U.S. intelligence agencies as proposed by Sept. 11 commission

2003

No Cut taxes by $330 billion through fiscal 2013

Yes Block Bush rule scaling back overtime pay for some white-collar federal workers

Yes Do not allow use of search warrants without first notifying subjects

No Allow importation of prescription drugs

No Create private school voucher program in Washington, D.C.

No Ban "partial birth" abortion except to save a woman's life

Yes Split $18.6 billion in Iraq aid into half-grant, half-loan

No Overhaul Medicare and create prescription drug benefit

CQ VOTE STUDIES

	PARTY UNITY		PRESIDENTIAL SUPPORT	
	Support	Oppose	Support	Oppose
2004	91%	9%	24%	76%
2003	90%	10%	27%	73%
2002	93%	7%	26%	74%
2001	88%	12%	31%	69%
2000	89%	11%	81%	19%

INTEREST GROUPS

	AFL-CIO	ADA	CCUS	ACU
2004	87%	90%	48%	13%
2003	87%	90%	50%	28%
2002	100%	90%	53%	8%
2001	92%	95%	50%	8%
2000	70%	75%	66%	8%

CALIFORNIA 1
Northern Coast — Eureka; Napa, Davis

It takes about nine hours to travel the length of the 1st, a journey that starts in Yolo County, across the river from Sacramento, and ends at the Oregon border in Del Norte County, one of the district's three coastal counties. In between are wineries and majestic redwoods, for which the Northern Coast is famous.

The 1st is notable for its breadth and diversity. Even the weather patterns vary across the district, with a rainy north and arid farmland in the south. Apart from wine and timber, other dominant industries include commercial fishing in Crescent City, Eureka and Fort Bragg, and tourism. The University of California, Davis, in Yolo County is a major employer.

To the north, Mendocino, Humboldt and Del Norte counties long have been a battleground for environmentalists and the timber industry, which has suffered lately. Tensions reached a peak in 1990 with "Redwood Summer" demonstrations over the proposed logging of the Headwaters Forest, one of the last stands of virgin redwood trees. Isolated protests still occur, but have not reached the same degree of intensity.

East of Mendocino, Lake County's economy is a mix of ranching, farming and tourism, centered on Clearlake. Its relatively low cost of living, relative to Bay Area cities, makes this a retirees' haven. South of Mendocino, the 1st takes in part of wine-producing Sonoma County and all of Napa County. Half of the state's wineries are in the district.

Despite a Democratic voter registration advantage and the district's backing of the party's presidential candidates in 2000 and 2004, environmental issues, such as offshore drilling, continue to make the 1st volatile as some voters are more inclined to support alternative candidates. Green Party nominee Ralph Nader's two best counties in 2000 were in the 1st — Mendocino (15 percent) and Humboldt (13 percent). In contrast, Del Norte was the only county in the 1st to support George W. Bush in 2000, and the county repeated the feat in 2004.

MAJOR INDUSTRY
Timber, agriculture, tourism

CITIES
Napa, 72,585; Davis, 60,308; Woodland (pt.), 39,455

NOTABLE
Niebaum-Coppola is the winery owned by film director Francis Ford Coppola.

Rep. Wally Herger (R)

Elected 1986; 10th term

CAPITOL OFFICE
225-3076
www.house.gov/herger
2268 Rayburn 20515-0502; fax 225-1740

COMMITTEES
Ways & Means
(Human Resources - chairman)

HOMETOWN
Chico

BORN
May 20, 1945, Sutter County, Calif.

RELIGION
Mormon

FAMILY
Wife, Pamela Herger; nine children (one deceased)

EDUCATION
American River College, A.A. 1967; California State U., Sacramento, attended 1969

CAREER
Rancher; gas company executive

POLITICAL HIGHLIGHTS
Calif. Assembly, 1980-86

ELECTION RESULTS

2004 GENERAL

Wally Herger (R)	182,119	66.9%
Mike Johnson (D)	90,310	33.2%

2004 PRIMARY

Wally Herger (R)	unopposed

2002 GENERAL

Wally Herger (R)	117,747	65.8%
Mike Johnson (D)	52,455	29.3%
Patrice Thiessen (NL)	4,860	2.7%
Charles Martin (LIBERT)	3,923	2.2%

PREVIOUS WINNING PERCENTAGES
2000 (66%); 1998 (63%); 1996 (61%); 1994 (64%);
1992 (65%); 1990 (64%); 1988 (59%); 1986 (58%)

Herger has moved quietly and with little fanfare from the back benches of the Ways and Means Committee to become a forceful voice on welfare and family issues. Chairman of the Human Resources Subcommittee, he is the fourth-most-senior Republican on the powerful tax-writing committee. In this role, he is an important player in the debate over how much to alter the 1996 law that overhauled the nation's welfare system.

On Ways and Means, his only committee assignment, Herger has placed a high priority on building and preserving a solid family structure, which he says is a key aim of the effort to reduce the welfare rolls. Herger says the revised welfare system — which ended more than 60 years of guaranteed cash assistance and imposed a five-year time limit and new work rules on recipients — has lifted more than 2 million children out of poverty. In 2001, he was the chief sponsor of legislation, which became law, to increase funding for adoption, foster care and post-adoption services.

Herger is also the author of an alteration to the 1996 law that changed a credit which states receive for reducing their welfare caseloads, with the effect that states would have to press more public assistance recipients to find jobs and to work longer hours. Herger and other congressional Republicans insist that stricter work requirements must be part of any effort to renew the 1996 law. Democrats say only minor changes are needed. The House and the Senate tentatively agreed to continue providing $16.5 billion a year for the main welfare program, Temporary Assistance for Needy Families. But with large budget deficits looming, lawmakers may be under intense pressure to cut this amount in the coming years.

The House did pass legislation in 2003, based in part on work by Herger's Human Resources Subcommittee, calling for welfare recipients to work 40 hours a week and providing incentives to promote marriage and teenage sexual abstinence, but the measure stalled in the Senate. "What we should be doing is obvious: expecting and supporting more work instead of simply supporting more welfare checks," Herger said when the welfare law was again temporarily reauthorized in the fall of 2004.

Herger also introduced a measure in 2004 to give states more flexibility to spend federal aid on foster care and adoption services but capping future spending on such services over the next decade. Herger said the bill was a result of widespread dissatisfaction with state-operated foster care systems and several high-profile instances in which children were abused while in foster care. He hopes his proposal will expedite moving the nation's more than 500,000 foster children into safe, permanent surroundings. But his plan to cap future funding aroused concern from states and some social service organizations, which worry their finances will be stretched thin if too many children enter the system.

Although his subcommittee role has found him leading the welfare renewal effort, Herger remains visible on Western land issues. He continues to devote much of his time and effort to matters such as irrigation in the Klamath River Basin, development limitations imposed by the Endangered Species Act and timber harvesting in national forests.

Herger grew up on his family's 200-acre cattle ranch and plum farm in the Northern California town of Rio Oso. He also worked in the family's oil and gas business. Well-to-do financially, he draws heavily on his small-business and ranching background in his work on Capitol Hill.

One of Herger's main missions in Congress is to prevent environmentalists from encroaching on the rights of loggers, ranchers and private property owners in his district. His views on Western land use sit well with his Republican constituency.

The congressman chafes over what he sees as extreme environmental policies. In the 107th Congress, he directed his outrage at the "government-caused disaster" in the Klamath River basin of northern California and southern Oregon, in which water needed by farmers for irrigation was withheld to protect two species of fish. At a 2003 field hearing that the House Resources Committee held in Klamath Falls, Herger said, "This hearing has broad implications for all agriculture and rural communities in the West. Klamath farming still faces hardships resulting from the 2001 shut off."

Herger also asked the Appropriations Committee in 2003 to drop the $110,000 budgeted annually for the Klamath Fishery Management Council, an 11-member group that helps manage the annual harvest and conservation of salmon and steelhead trout in the river. He said the council had overstepped its authority by making recommendations about water management issues rather than confining itself to the fish harvest.

Herger has been happier with the decisions of the Air Force regarding its northern California bases. The Air Force in 2002 began basing the Global Hawk unmanned aerial reconnaissance plane at Beale Air Force Base in Herger's district. More than 1,600 jobs are expected to be added to Beale, which also hosts the U-2 and SR-71 spy planes, once the entire complement of planes arrives. And in the summer of 2004, the Air Force announced that a California Air National Guard intelligence unit would also move to Beale, adding about 146 jobs to the base.

Herger's voting record is solidly in the conservative camp of House Republicans, as his membership in the conservative Republican Study Committee would suggest. He sided with his party 99 percent of the time on key votes in the 108th Congress.

Herger won election to the state Assembly in 1980 and was in his third term when GOP Rep. Gene Chappie announced his retirement from the House in 1986. Linking himself to President Reagan and California's Republican governor, George Deukmejian, Herger won the general election with 58 percent of the vote. He has had little electoral difficulty since.

Redistricting in 2001 shifted Herger's district to the west — it looks much the same as it did during the 1980s — but left him with his two major population centers, Redding and Chico, and presented him with no re-election worries.

KEY VOTES

2004

No — Extend federal unemployment benefits by 13 weeks
Yes — Pass $283.2 billion, six-year federal highway and mass transit bill
Yes — Approve $146 billion multi-year extension of previously enacted middle-class tax breaks
Yes — Amend the Constitution to prohibit same-sex marriage
Yes — Cut corporate taxes $137 billion over 10 years
Yes — Reorganize U.S. intelligence agencies as proposed by Sept. 11 commission

2003

Yes — Cut taxes by $330 billion through fiscal 2013
No — Block Bush rule scaling back overtime pay for some white-collar federal workers
No — Do not allow use of search warrants without first notifying subjects
No — Allow importation of prescription drugs
Yes — Create private school voucher program in Washington, D.C.
Yes — Ban "partial birth" abortion except to save a woman's life
No — Split $18.6 billion in Iraq aid into half-grant, half-loan
Yes — Overhaul Medicare and create prescription drug benefit

CQ VOTE STUDIES

	PARTY UNITY		PRESIDENTIAL SUPPORT	
	Support	Oppose	Support	Oppose
2004	99%	1%	88%	12%
2003	98%	2%	98%	2%
2002	98%	2%	82%	18%
2001	97%	3%	90%	10%
2000	96%	4%	21%	79%

INTEREST GROUPS

	AFL-CIO	ADA	CCUS	ACU
2004	7%	5%	100%	100%
2003	0%	5%	97%	84%
2002	11%	0%	100%	100%
2001	0%	0%	96%	96%
2000	0%	0%	85%	95%

CALIFORNIA 2
North central — Redding, Chico

The mountainous 2nd forms a north-south strip down the center of the state, from the Oregon border to just north of Sacramento. It includes the Sutter-Buttes mountain range.

Agriculture dominates the 2nd, which gained five farming counties — Sutter, Colusa, Glenn, Tehama and part of Yolo — through redistricting following the 2000 census. The district is rural, with rice farms and orchards producing walnuts, olives and peaches. Much of its economic activity is centered in Shasta County, home to mining and forestry interests. Shasta Lake, the state's largest man-made reservoir, attracts tourism. Redding, the 2nd's largest city, is about 160 miles north of Sacramento in Shasta County. Both the city and county experienced strong growth through the 1980s and 1990s.

The 2nd has had to fight to save its agriculture industry from harsh weather — much of it was declared a disaster area after flooding in 1997. Wildfires account for at least one major fire every summer, especially in the northernmost counties of Shasta, Trinity and Siskiyou.

Water also is a perennial issue: Two-thirds of the state's supply comes from the upper third of the state. The timber industry has steadily declined since the 1990s, in the process diminishing some of the tension between environmental interests and the industry.

Previously abutting most of the state's border with Nevada north of Lake Tahoe, the 2nd retained its white and Republican character in redistricting, although there has been a steady influx of Sikhs in the Yuba City area, as well as an infusion of Democratic-leaning Hispanic farm workers. George W. Bush took 62 percent of the district's vote in 2004.

MAJOR INDUSTRY
Agriculture, timber, tourism, health care

MILITARY BASES
Beale Air Force Base, 3,911 military, 2,372 civilian (2004)

CITIES
Redding, 80,865; Chico, 59,954; Yuba City, 36,758

NOTABLE
The dormant Mount Shasta volcano in Siskiyou County is near the southern end of the Cascade Mountains; The Sierra Nevada Brewing Co. is in Chico; GOP presidential nominee Bob Dole fell from a stage at a rally in Chico in 1996, saying later that he had "fallen for Chico."

Rep. Dan Lungren (R)

Elected 2004; 1st term
Also served 1979-89

Lungren could hardly have imagined that he would return to the House in 2005 when he ended a decade-long tenure on Capitol Hill in 1989. Nor could he have foreseen that he would join a Republican majority entering a second decade in control of the House — or that he would do so as representative of a district based in the suburbs of Sacramento, more than 400 miles from his original constituency in Southern California.

A former state attorney general, Lungren in the 109th Congress returned to a familiar seat on the Judiciary Committee, where his previous service on the panel puts him in eighth ranking among its 23 Republicans. He also won appointments to the Budget Committee and the Homeland Security panel, where he chairs the Economic Security Subcommittee.

His signature issue when he first served in Congress was immigration: He pushed for sanctions against employers who hired illegal immigrants, but also supported limited amnesty programs for some illegal aliens. He plans to play an active role in that area again.

The son of President Nixon's personal physician, Lungren said his desire for public service was rekindled by the terrorist attacks of Sept. 11, 2001. His open-seat 2004 victory in the strongly Republican 3rd District provided both a career comeback and political vindication. He returned to politics after a six-year hiatus that followed his 20 percentage point defeat by Democrat Gray Davis in California's 1998 election for governor.

Lungren left the House, at age 42, when he was nominated by GOP Gov. George Deukmejian to be state treasurer. The Democratic-controlled state legislature rejected that nomination, but Lungren was elected as state attorney general in 1990 and was re-elected in 1994.

After his 1998 defeat, he stayed in the Sacramento area and was thus able to jump into the 2004 race after three-term Republican incumbent Doug Ose announced he would retire. Lungren mounted a late charge to claim the GOP primary against state Sen. Rico Oller and businesswoman Mary Ose, the sister of the incumbent. He won the general election with ease.

CAPITOL OFFICE
225-5716
lungren.info@mail.house.gov
www.house.gov/lungren
2448 Rayburn 20515-0503; fax 226-1298

COMMITTEES
Budget
Homeland Security
(Economic Security, Infrastructure Protection &
Cybersecurity - chairman)
Judiciary

HOMETOWN
Gold River

BORN
Sept. 22, 1946, Long Beach, Calif.

RELIGION
Roman Catholic

FAMILY
Wife, Bobbi Lungren; three children

EDUCATION
U. of Notre Dame, B.A. 1968 (English); Georgetown U., J.D. 1971

CAREER
Lawyer

POLITICAL HIGHLIGHTS
Republican nominee for U.S. House, 1976; U.S. House, 1979-89; Calif. attorney general, 1991-99; Republican nominee for governor, 1998

ELECTION RESULTS

2004 GENERAL

Dan Lungren (R)	177,738	61.9%
Gabe Castillo (D)	100,025	34.8%
Douglas Tuma (LIBERT)	9,310	3.2%

2004 PRIMARY

Dan Lungren (R)	35,595	38.9%
Rico Oller (R)	32,728	35.8%
Mary Ose (R)	21,469	23.5%
Richard Frankhuizen (R)	1,693	1.9%

1986 GENERAL

Dan Lungren (R)	140,364	72.8%
Michael P. Blackburn (D)	47,586	24.7%
Kate McClatchy (PFP)	4,761	2.5%

PREVIOUS WINNING PERCENTAGES
1984 (73%); 1982 (69%); 1980 (72%); 1978 (54%)

CALIFORNIA 3
Central — Sacramento suburbs

The 3rd stretches west from Alpine County on the Nevada border to Solano County. The district is predominately white, white-collar and Republican.

This area used to be Mother Lode country, which drew gold seekers and now attracts those seeking to leave the state's crowded cities and still work in a high-tech economy. About 85 percent of the 3rd's population comes from a chunk of Sacramento County that includes the affluent Sacramento suburbs of Citrus Heights and Rio Linda.

Wineries and agriculture dominate the 3rd's economy, especially grape, almond and prune production, except in forestry-heavy Alpine County, where mountains and skiing are prevalent. The closure of McClellan Air Force Base in 2001 dealt a blow to the area's economy, but it has been mitigated by the base's conversion into a business park (shared with the 5th), which has sought to attract high-tech activity.

Sacramento County, whose residents tend to work in state government or the technology industries that attract transplants from San Francisco, is the politically competitive heart of the district. Its surrounding areas are largely rural and Republican, and the district as a whole gave George W. Bush 58 percent of the 2004 presidential vote.

Water and flood control are important local issues, as the Sacramento and American rivers periodically flood the valley.

MAJOR INDUSTRY
Agriculture, timber, technology

CITIES
Citrus Heights, 85,071; Arden-Arcade (unincorporated) (pt.), 53,597; Folsom, 51,884; Carmichael, 49,742

NOTABLE
Angels Camp hosts the annual jumping frog contest made famous by Mark Twain.

Rep. John T. Doolittle (R)

Elected 1990; 8th term

CAPITOL OFFICE
225-2511
www.house.gov/doolittle
2410 Rayburn 20515-0504; fax 225-5444

COMMITTEES
Appropriations
House Administration
Joint Printing

HOMETOWN
Roseville

BORN
Oct. 30, 1950, Glendale, Calif.

RELIGION
Mormon

FAMILY
Wife, Julie Doolittle; two children

EDUCATION
U. of California, Santa Cruz, B.A. 1972 (history);
U. of the Pacific, J.D. 1978

CAREER
Lawyer; state legislative aide

POLITICAL HIGHLIGHTS
Calif. Senate, 1980-90

ELECTION RESULTS

2004 GENERAL

John T. Doolittle (R)	221,926	65.4%
David L. Winters (D)	117,443	34.6%

2004 PRIMARY

John T. Doolittle (R)	unopposed

2002 GENERAL

John T. Doolittle (R)	147,997	64.8%
Mark Norberg (D)	72,860	31.9%
Allen M. Roberts (LIBERT)	7,247	3.2%

PREVIOUS WINNING PERCENTAGES
2000 (63%); 1998 (63%); 1996 (60%); 1994 (61%);
1992 (50%); 1990 (51%)

As an elder statesman among House conservatives, Doolittle is in a prime position to help his constituents and advance his own causes. Now in his eighth term, he sits on the Appropriations and House Administration committees. Doolittle was elected secretary of the Republican Conference at the end of 2002 — the sixth-ranking post on the House GOP's official leadership ladder — running unopposed for the position.

Doolittle has long believed that restrictions on money in politics are a violation of the First Amendment right to free speech. Focus on disclosure, he suggests, and let the voters be the judge. He tried, unsuccessfully, to stop the overhaul of campaign finance rules in the 107th Congress. He argued that the 2002 bill banning unlimited corporate and labor donations to political parties and restricting issue advertisements was overtly unconstitutional. He also said the new restrictions were "disastrous" for the GOP's fundraising future.

He still holds this view even after the 2004 U.S. Supreme Court ruling declaring the new law constitutional. "Today's campaign finance law will continue to wreak havoc until we reinstate an open, unregulated political process," he says.

Doolittle has pushed zealously for a diminished federal role in people's lives. He decries what he sees as threats to personal freedom — sometimes even by members of his own party — in the name of a well-meaning public policy goal. Yet he is enough of an old hand to understand that things happen slowly in Washington. But that doesn't mean Doolittle likes it or is willing to adopt less-ambitious goals. He says he believes that conservatives should be aggressive in advancing their principles. In an effort to hold his party's leadership to a firm conservative line on economic and social policy issues, Doolittle in 1997 co-founded the Conservative Action Team (the CATs), now known as the Republican Study Committee.

Doolittle approaches his congressional work with the same serious-minded zeal that he evinced as a Mormon missionary in Argentina just after college. His conservative views are often on display during Appropriations panel meetings. As a member of the District of Columbia Subcommittee, he brought his social policy beliefs to bear on the city's budget, and on the Energy and Water Subcommittee, he has sought more local control over water and logging policy in the West. With the reorganization of the Appropriations Committee in the 109th Congress, Doolittle is no longer a member of the subcommittee with jurisdiction over the D.C. budget but continues to make his views known on the full committee.

During debate on the 2004 D.C. spending bill, the committee adopted Doolittle's amendment barring the city from using any money appropriated by the measure — federal subsidies or local tax dollars — to pursue a lawsuit in which the city has sought to hold gun manufacturers responsible for municipal expenses caused by gun violence. A D.C. Superior Court judge dismissed the case in 2002, but Doolittle's amendment prohibited the city from appealing.

On Energy and Water, he favors a pro-development agenda that often puts him at loggerheads with advocates of environmental protection. Doolittle has long supported completing the huge Auburn Dam in his district, which has been at the center of a bruising battle over federal water development policy. But he has slowly become enough of a Washington realist to know that most problems require some give and take. In the fall of

2003, Doolittle and California Democrat Robert T. Matsui brokered an agreement that ended the 14-year battle over Sacramento-area flood control and authorized $135 million for a number of water projects in the 4th District. Realizing that Congress was unlikely to pay for a brand-new dam, Doolittle opted for the smaller water projects to help his district.

In keeping with his open market views, Doolittle in 2004 sponsored a bill with Virginia Democrat Rick Boucher to legalize the limited, non-commercial reproduction of copyrighted material from CDs and DVDs. Under their measure, customers could legally circumvent anti-copying technologies to make a copy for their personal use. Doolittle insists that the bill doesn't weaken copyright protections. But critics of the measure say it makes it far more difficult to police illegal copying.

Raised in a conservative household in Southern California, Doolittle was 13 when he became intrigued by Barry Goldwater, the 1964 GOP presidential nominee. But his family had moved to the northern part of the state by then, and Doolittle remembers being perhaps "the only Goldwater supporter in my freshman class" at Cupertino High School.

For college, Doolittle chose the Santa Cruz campus of the University of California over Brigham Young University, where his political views would have been more in sync. But he says he is glad he went to Santa Cruz, even though, he adds, the liberal campus was in tune with the "free love, lawlessness and drugs" of the era. Doolittle was one of only 15 Young Republicans at Santa Cruz, which he says taught him to take independent stances and think for himself. "It was a fabulous experience," he says.

Goldwater had inspired in Doolittle the desire to seek office, and, after a two-year church mission to Argentina and law school, Doolittle took his résumé to Sacramento in search of a job with the state legislature.

He worked for state Sen. H.L. Richardson, who was not only an influential conservative lawmaker but also a mentor and adviser when Doolittle launched his own bid for the state Senate in 1980. Richardson persuaded Doolittle to run against an entrenched Democratic incumbent. With California favorite son Ronald Reagan heading the GOP ticket that year, Doolittle won a narrow upset. He quickly made himself known in Sacramento, particularly as a dogged proponent of expanded testing for AIDS.

In 1990, Doolittle inherited what had been a safe district from retiring Republican Rep. Norman D. Shumway, who also had positioned himself on the GOP's right flank. Doolittle narrowly beat Democrat Patricia Malberg, a former junior college teacher, that year and again in 1992. He has coasted to re-election since then in a district made more Republican by redistricting.

KEY VOTES

2004

No Extend federal unemployment benefits by 13 weeks
Yes Pass $283.2 billion, six-year federal highway and mass transit bill
Yes Approve $146 billion multi-year extension of previously enacted middle-class tax breaks
Yes Amend the Constitution to prohibit same-sex marriage
Yes Cut corporate taxes $137 billion over 10 years
Yes Reorganize U.S. intelligence agencies as proposed by Sept. 11 commission

2003

Yes Cut taxes by $330 billion through fiscal 2013
No Block Bush rule scaling back overtime pay for some white-collar federal workers
No Do not allow use of search warrants without first notifying subjects
No Allow importation of prescription drugs
Yes Create private school voucher program in Washington, D.C.
Yes Ban "partial birth" abortion except to save a woman's life
No Split $18.6 billion in Iraq aid into half-grant, half-loan
Yes Overhaul Medicare and create prescription drug benefit

CQ VOTE STUDIES

	PARTY UNITY		PRESIDENTIAL SUPPORT	
	Support	Oppose	Support	Oppose
2004	96%	4%	85%	15%
2003	98%	2%	94%	6%
2002	98%	2%	84%	16%
2001	97%	3%	91%	9%
2000	96%	4%	23%	77%

INTEREST GROUPS

	AFL-CIO	ADA	CCUS	ACU
2004	13%	0%	90%	92%
2003	7%	5%	93%	74%
2002	13%	5%	84%	91%
2001	17%	0%	91%	100%
2000	0%	5%	76%	88%

CALIFORNIA 4
Northeast — Roseville, Rocklin

Laden with rivers, lakes and the mountain ranges that give their names to Sierra and Nevada counties, the 4th moves east from the Sacramento area to Lake Tahoe and then north, along the Nevada border, up to Oregon in the state's northeast corner. The district added timber and agriculture in redistricting following the 2000 census to the old 4th's economic mainstays of mining and technology.

The mining counties of Placer and El Dorado lend the 4th its Gold Rush feel, although technology drives one of the fastest growth rates in the state. Placer, El Dorado and Nevada counties are home to facilities of big technology names like Hewlett-Packard and Oracle. These three counties, which along with a sliver of Sacramento County make up the southern part of the district, account for more than three-fourths of its population and continue to draw those who want to leave the state's crowded cities while still working in the high-tech economy.

The 4th is a popular vacation destination, with numerous ski resorts dotting the Sierra Nevada mountain range, as well as Lake Tahoe in

eastern El Dorado and Placer counties. Placer, with cheap property and abundant natural beauty, is rapidly becoming a draw for retirees. Whites make up 84 percent of the population, which gives the district the highest percentage in the state.

Redistricting following the 2000 census brought major geographic changes to the 4th. The old district occupied California's northeast-central belt, moving from Sacramento to Lake Tahoe and taking in five counties south of El Dorado. Despite the changes, the 4th remained safe Republican territory. George W. Bush took 61 percent of the vote in the 2004 presidential election, and Republicans hold a 17-point edge in party registration.

MAJOR INDUSTRY
Technology, agriculture, mining, tourism

MILITARY BASES
Sierra Army Depot, 1 military, 673 civilian (2005)

CITIES
Roseville, 79,921; Rocklin, 36,330; Orangevale (unincorporated), 26,705

NOTABLE
Squaw Valley, near Lake Tahoe, hosted the 1960 Winter Olympics.

Rep. Doris Matsui (D)

CAPITOL OFFICE
225-7163
www.house.gov/matsui
2310 Rayburn 20515-0505; fax 225-0566

COMMITTEES
Rules

HOMETOWN
Sacramento

BORN
Sept. 25, 1944, Poston, Ariz.

RELIGION
Methodist

FAMILY
Widowed; one child

EDUCATION
U. of California, Berkeley, B.A. 1966 (psychology)

CAREER
Lobbyist; White House aide; homemaker; state computer systems analyst

POLITICAL HIGHLIGHTS
No previous office

ELECTION RESULTS

2005 SPECIAL

Doris Matsui (D)	56,175	68.1%
Julie Padilla (D)	7,158	8.7%
John Thomas Flynn (R)	6,559	8.0%
Serge A. Chernay (R)	3,742	4.5%
Michael O'Brien (R)	2,591	3.1%
Shane Singh (R)	1,753	2.1%
others	1,481	1.8%
Bruce Robert Stevens (R)	1,124	1.4%
Pat Driscoll (GREEN)	976	1.2%
Leonard Padilla (I)	916	1.1%

Elected March 2005; 1st term

House Democratic leaders gave Matsui a special greeting upon her arrival in March 2005 — a seat on the Rules Committee, where she is the first freshman since 1999 to win a post on the powerful panel.

But the circumstances that brought her to Congress were not joyful: She replaced her husband, Robert T. Matsui, who died Jan. 1, 2005, just before he could be sworn in to his 14th term in the House. During the brief special-election campaign, she exhorted voters "to continue Bob's work through mine."

Matsui had never run for elected office before. Yet she has an extensive background in the policy arena. As a deputy assistant to the president and a deputy director of public liaison in the Clinton administration, she worked on an array of domestic economic policy and trade initiatives. In 1998, she became a senior adviser and director of government relations for a Washington firm whose clients included medical technology, telecommunications and financial organizations.

She can be expected to urge a stronger federal role in promoting stem cell research: Her husband died of complications of a rare stem cell disorder in which the bone marrow does not produce enough blood cells.

Matsui has signaled that, generally, she will echo the mainly liberal voting record of her husband. She backs abortion rights. And she says she would have opposed the Bush administration's 2003 tax cut law and its decision to wage war in Iraq. But, like her husband, her liberalism is tempered by her support for free-trade pacts. Still, unions will find Matsui a reliable ally on about every other issue. Her local priorities include securing funding for transportation projects and flood protection in the Sacramento area.

Matsui clinched victory early on by rallying support from leading Democratic officials and dissuading any strong candidates from entering the special-election contest. Facing 11 little-known opponents on the all-party ballot, and benefiting from the district's strong Democratic leanings, Matsui took 68 percent of the vote, well more than the majority needed to avoid a runoff.

CALIFORNIA 5
Sacramento

Two things tend to dominate the 5th — state politics and triple-digit temperatures. Located in California's hot Central Valley, the 5th is home to the state capital, Sacramento, and reaches east and south to include a few upper-middle-class suburbs such as Arden-Arcade and Elk Grove (both of which are shared with the 3rd District).

Sacramento first attracted fortune seekers as the starting point of the Gold Rush of 1849. State government now provides the lion's share of employment, although other sectors are increasing in importance.

The city's economy has improved since a statewide recession in the early 1990s, with real estate value and population numbers growing against turn-of-the-century state and national economic trends. Several big-name technology companies are major employers in the 5th.

Overall, Democrats hold a substantial edge in voter registration. Sacramento used to be a swing district, supporting Ronald Reagan and George Bush in the 1980s presidential elections and Republican Pete Wilson in the 1990 gubernatorial race. But Democrats gained strength in the last two rounds of redistricting, as some of the more affluent, GOP-leaning suburbs were stripped and parts of Rancho Cordova and North Highlands (both shared with the 3rd) were added. John Kerry captured 61 percent of the 5th's vote in the 2004 election.

Hispanics, Asians and blacks each account for at least 14 percent of the overall district's residents, although whites still form a solid plurality.

MAJOR INDUSTRY
State government, technology

CITIES
Sacramento, 407,018; Arden-Arcade (unincorporated) (pt.), 42,428; Parkway-South Sacramento (unincorporated), 36,468

NOTABLE
The California State Railroad Museum calls itself North America's most-visited railroad museum.

Rep. Lynn Woolsey (D)

Elected 1992; 7th term

CAPITOL OFFICE
225-5161
woolsey.house.gov
2263 Rayburn 20515-0506; fax 225-5163

COMMITTEES
Education & Workforce
Science

HOMETOWN
Petaluma

BORN
Nov. 3, 1937, Seattle, Wash.

RELIGION
Presbyterian

FAMILY
Divorced; four children

EDUCATION
U. of Washington, attended 1955-57 (business);
U. of San Francisco, B.S. 1980 (human resources &
organizational behavior)

CAREER
Employment placement company owner; human
resources manager

POLITICAL HIGHLIGHTS
Petaluma City Council, 1985-93

ELECTION RESULTS

2004 GENERAL

Lynn Woolsey (D)	226,423	72.7%
Paul L. Erickson (R)	85,244	27.4%

2004 PRIMARY

Lynn Woolsey (D)	99,970	84.0%
Renn Vara (D)	19,039	16.0%

2002 GENERAL

Lynn Woolsey (D)	139,750	66.7%
Paul L. Erickson (R)	62,052	29.6%
Richard Barton (LIBERT)	4,936	2.4%
Jeff Rainforth (REF)	2,825	1.4%

PREVIOUS WINNING PERCENTAGES
2000 (64%); 1998 (68%); 1996 (62%); 1994 (58%);
1992 (65%)

In a Congress where conservatives and deal-cutting pragmatists hold sway, Woolsey revels in her unambiguous liberalism. To her admirers, she represents a rare voice of conscience in Congress, speaking out against war in Iraq and in support of racial minorities, women, children, the elderly and those in need. To her detractors, she has been an ineffective backbencher, neither influential in shaping national legislation nor successful in bringing big federal money to her home in the north San Francisco Bay area.

Woolsey (WOOL-zee) will offer proposals that have no chance of adoption, to bring attention to an issue. For instance, amid President Bush's soaring wartime popularity after Sept. 11, she pressed for a vote in 2001 on a resolution condemning his nuclear arms policy. She also likes to make statements that are more spectacle than serious lawmaking. During the House debate in 2003 on Bush's bill to overhaul the Medicare program that provides federal health insurance for the elderly, Woolsey led 84 other House Democrats in a protest of AARP's support of the bill. Woolsey and the other lawmakers sent a letter to the seniors advocacy group canceling their AARP membership, or, for the younger lawmakers, promising not to join.

She excels at the witty sound bite. When the Bush administration in the fall of 2003 asked for $87 billion in supplemental spending for military and reconstruction efforts in Iraq and Afghanistan, Woolsey wanted a more detailed accounting of the spending in Iraq so lawmakers would know why the White House needed more money. "I'm not going to approve a supplemental like this," she said. "It's like marrying a guy and expecting him to change after the wedding."

Woolsey has a unique perspective on the federal safety net because she was once a single parent on welfare. At age 29, she divorced her stockbroker husband, which ended what she has described as a "Leave It To Beaver" suburban life in 1960s Marin County. To support her children — all under the age of 5 at the time — she sold her house and returned a new station wagon. To land a job as a secretary she admits she lied about her personal circumstances. Public assistance supplemented her wages until she remarried three years later. Woolsey eventually went back to college to get her degree, at age 42, and started her own human resources consulting company.

Knowing firsthand about buying groceries with food stamps and finding doctors who accepted Medi-Cal, California's Medicaid program, Woolsey arrived in Congress opposing efforts to cut people off from a system that she considers to have been her economic salvation. She was an unswerving opponent of the welfare law enacted in 1996, which set lifetime limits on benefits, and in the 107th Congress she played an active role in the debate on rewriting that statute.

Education has been her main legislative focus, and she holds seats on both the Science and Education panels. She has twice introduced her "Go Girl" legislation to encourage girls to study science and math, but the measure has gone nowhere.

Woolsey is now the top-ranking Democrat on the Education Reform Subcommittee. She has continually fought Bush administration efforts to allow faith-based groups more opportunity to receive federal block grants from anti-poverty, education and community service programs. Woolsey maintains that the language would allow religious groups to use public funds to discriminate in hiring on the basis of religion and sexual orientation. The mother of a gay man, she has also criticized what she calls a "shameful discriminatory policy toward gays in the military" promoted by Republicans in the 1990s.

She is a strident foe of what she believes are GOP efforts to favor business interests over workers' health and safety. When the Education Committee approved a measure allowing small businesses more than 15 days to contest health and safety citations after they miss the deadline to respond to the problems, Woolsey asked: "Why should workers suffer longer because of their employers' inefficiencies? It's just another way for the Bush administration to favor big business over American workers." Under existing law, employers must automatically pay a fine if they miss the deadline.

Occasionally, Woolsey will side with California Republicans on local issues, such as increasing funds for Highway 101, protecting the Golden Gate Bridge from earthquake damage, and getting federal support for California agricultural products, such as wine.

Woolsey was elected to Congress from the Petaluma City Council in 1992, the "Year of the Woman," in which a record 26 women were sent to Capitol Hill. The House seat became available when fellow Democratic liberal Barbara Boxer gave it up to run successfully for the Senate, and Woolsey's gender was an important asset as she won the nomination in an upset against eight other candidates. Woolsey was the underdog in the general election, too, until her Republican opponent, Bill Filante, known as the most liberal Republican in the state Assembly, fell ill with brain cancer and suspended his campaign a few weeks before the election.

She has since won re-election with ease. Her district, even after remapping following the 2000 census, looks much the same as in the 1990s: a progressive redoubt that takes in all of Marin and much of Sonoma counties. Many of her constituents are affluent former hippies who have retained their youthful idealism.

Yet her run for a seventh term in 2004 became complicated when news reports surfaced that she tried to persuade a Marin County judge to give a reduced sentence to an employee's son awaiting sentencing for rape. She later apologized in a letter published in the Marin Independent Journal, saying she had wanted to help a "faithful employee." But she conceded that she should not have attempted to intervene. "Given my outspoken support for both women's rights and victims' rights, my constituents and my community are right to be shocked by my action," Woolsey wrote. She won re-election with 73 percent of the vote.

KEY VOTES

2004
Yes   Extend federal unemployment benefits by 13 weeks
Yes   Pass $283.2 billion, six-year federal highway and mass transit bill
No   Approve $146 billion multi-year extension of previously enacted middle-class tax breaks
No   Amend the Constitution to prohibit same-sex marriage
No   Cut corporate taxes $137 billion over 10 years
Yes   Reorganize U.S. intelligence agencies as proposed by Sept. 11 commission

2003
No   Cut taxes by $330 billion through fiscal 2013
Yes   Block Bush rule scaling back overtime pay for some white-collar federal workers
Yes   Do not allow use of search warrants without first notifying subjects
Yes   Allow importation of prescription drugs
?   Create private school voucher program in Washington, D.C.
No   Ban "partial birth" abortion except to save a woman's life
Yes   Split $18.6 billion in Iraq aid into half-grant, half-loan
No   Overhaul Medicare and create prescription drug benefit

CQ VOTE STUDIES

	PARTY UNITY		PRESIDENTIAL SUPPORT	
	Support	Oppose	Support	Oppose
2004	98%	2%	15%	85%
2003	98%	2%	14%	86%
2002	99%	1%	25%	75%
2001	98%	2%	14%	86%
2000	98%	2%	79%	21%

INTEREST GROUPS

	AFL-CIO	ADA	CCUS	ACU
2004	93%	95%	0%	8%
2003	100%	100%	12%	13%
2002	100%	95%	35%	0%
2001	100%	100%	26%	0%
2000	100%	100%	40%	8%

CALIFORNIA 6
Northern Bay Area – Sonoma and Marin counties

Travel north across the Golden Gate Bridge and the scenery changes from the cityscape of San Francisco to the Pacific coastline and inland hills that make up the 6th. This area north of the city is home to upper-middle-class suburbanites who commute to San Francisco and the "Telecom Valley," which extends north from San Rafael to Santa Rosa.

The 6th includes all of Marin County and most of Sonoma County. The area has grown significantly since the bridge opened in 1937 and continues to prosper. In recent years, migration from the city has created a tight housing market, with median house prices in Marin and Sonoma counties at roughly half a million dollars.

Marin is home to San Quentin State Prison, San Rafael and popular getaway spots such as Point Reyes National Seashore, Sausalito and Muir Woods. To the north, Sonoma County is home to a California State University campus and Santa Rosa, the largest city in the district. Wine and dairy ranching dominate the economy here, although technology companies have made inroads. Petaluma, with Victorian architecture left untouched by the 1906 earthquake, is near the Sonoma-Marin county line.

The district's affluent residents think of themselves as progressive and tolerant of diverse views. The 6th is one of the most liberal in the Democrat-dominated Golden State. After flirting with Republicanism in the late 1970s and early 1980s, it turned solidly Democratic, giving Democrat John Kerry 70 percent of the vote in the 2004 presidential election. Democrats outnumber Republicans 2-to-1 in voter registration.

MAJOR INDUSTRY
Telecommunications, agriculture, tourism

CITIES
Santa Rosa, 147,595; San Rafael, 56,063; Petaluma, 54,548

NOTABLE
San Rafael is home to film producer and director George Lucas' companies, Industrial Light & Magic, Lucasfilm Ltd. and Skywalker Sound; Sen. Barbara Boxer, D, represented the 6th from 1983 to 1993.

Rep. George Miller (D)

Elected 1974; 16th term

CAPITOL OFFICE
225-2095
george.miller@mail.house.gov
www.house.gov/georgemiller
2205 Rayburn 20515-0507; fax 225-5609

COMMITTEES
Education & Workforce - ranking member
Resources

HOMETOWN
Martinez

BORN
May 17, 1945, Richmond, Calif.

RELIGION
Roman Catholic

FAMILY
Wife, Cynthia Miller; two children

EDUCATION
San Francisco State U., B.A. 1968; U. of California,
Davis, J.D. 1972

CAREER
Lawyer; state legislative aide

POLITICAL HIGHLIGHTS
Democratic nominee for Calif. Senate, 1969

ELECTION RESULTS

2004 GENERAL

George Miller (D)	166,831	76.1%
Charles R. Hargrave (R)	52,446	23.9%

2004 PRIMARY

George Miller (D)	unopposed

2002 GENERAL

George Miller (D)	97,849	70.7%
Charles R. Hargrave (R)	36,584	26.4%
Scott A. Wilson (LIBERT)	3,943	2.9%

PREVIOUS WINNING PERCENTAGES
2000 (76%); 1998 (77%); 1996 (72%); 1994 (70%); 1992
(70%); 1990 (61%); 1988 (68%); 1986 (67%); 1984
(66%); 1982 (67%); 1980 (63%); 1978 (63%); 1976
(75%); 1974 (56%)

A liberal firebrand shaped by the era when Democrats dominated the House, Miller is the bane of corporate interests and a strong advocate of government programs for the underprivileged. An ally of Minority Leader Nancy Pelosi — she is a fellow Californian from a district just across the San Francisco Bay — Miller is an increasingly powerful voice on education, the environment and labor issues. Pelosi made him co-chairman of the Democratic Policy Committee.

Miller, who came of political age during the Watergate scandal, often grabs attention with vitriolic floor speeches against the Republican majority. He voted with Democrats 98 percent of the time on key votes in the 108th Congress. But Miller is a founding member of the Progressive Caucus who also can be tough on his own party when, in his judgment, it drifts too far to the center. "There just can't be two Republican Parties," he says.

Miller frequently clashes with the opposing party on the labor issues close to his heart. He has railed against companies that give executives lavish retirement packages while trimming workers' pension plans. He led repeated efforts to extend unemployment benefits to laid-off workers after the economy slowed down in the early 2000s. After six months of trying, Miller in 2004 celebrated House passage of a benefits extension, saying that "this vote signals a repudiation of the president's policy of neglecting unemployed workers in America."

Miller's strategy was to introduce his jobless benefits proposal as an amendment to a community services block grant bill. He got 39 Republicans to cross the aisle to vote for it, which not only put the House on record as supporting a 26-week expansion of benefits but had the effect of splitting the usually airtight GOP caucus. Republican leaders were forced to bring up their own jobless bill, extending benefits by 13 weeks. The bill ultimately died in the Senate, where Republicans blocked it, but Miller's efforts put the spotlight on the plight of workers without jobs in an election year.

Miller is ideally situated, at least for a member of the House minority, to promote his views. He is the senior Democrat on the Education and Workforce Committee. Although he gave up his spot as top-ranking Democrat on the Resources Committee in 2001 for the top spot on the Education panel, he continues to be deeply involved in environmental issues.

He is a favorite of environmental groups. The Sierra Club once dubbed him a "green giant," and he annually wins high marks for his voting record from the League of Conservation Voters. In recent years, Miller has played a key role in opposing Republican efforts to rewrite the Endangered Species Act and to make it easier to log in national forests as a way of preventing forest fires.

Miller was an early backer of Pelosi, whom he encouraged to run first for whip, then minority leader. He didn't much care for the inclusive leadership style of her predecessor, Richard A. Gephardt of Missouri, saying it resulted in a weak party message. With Gephardt's retirement at the end of 2004, Miller is a constant pressure on the new leaders to stay true to liberal beliefs.

He has been around long enough to know that if he wants to influence policy, there are times to set aside speeches and strike deals. Miller was one of four authors of the landmark education overhaul of 2001, a bipartisan undertaking that gave President Bush many of the elements of his No Child

www.cqpress.com

Left Behind initiative. In early meetings on the legislation, Bush took to calling him "Big George" — an acknowledgement of his importance to House passage. And although willing to help pass the bill, Miller subsequently was just as quick to assail Bush for setting aside too few dollars to help public schools meet their new responsibilities.

If GOP control of the House means Miller can't write bills his way, he makes up for it with high-profile policy brawls. He was chairman of the Natural Resources Committee in 1994, when the Republicans won control of Congress, and for the subsequent six years battled the similarly blustery and sharp-elbowed GOP chairman, Don Young of Alaska, his ideological opposite. Miller not only fought Young's attempts to revise major environmental laws, he blocked some of the chairman's non-controversial proposals, just to show he was not to be easily shut out of the process. As the polarizing effects of the GOP takeover eased, Miller sometimes found it more productive to work with his nemesis.

He joined Young to push the Conservation and Reinvestment Act, which guaranteed that oil royalties would be spent for land conservation. When Young stepped down as chairman in 2000, Miller called him "a very, very caring individual" and "a real pain in the rear."

Miller's sometimes hot temper earned him a place in congressional lore in 1995 when he and Virginia Democrat James P. Moran got into a shoving match with California Republicans Robert K. Dornan and Randy "Duke" Cunningham over a bill to bar the use of funds for deploying troops in Bosnia without prior congressional approval.

He is the third George Miller in his family to earn a living in government. His grandfather, George Miller Sr., was the assistant civil engineer in Richmond. His father, George Jr., was a state senator for 20 years. Miller, whose full name is George Miller III, was a law student in 1969 when his father died. He won the Democratic nomination to succeed his father in the state Senate but lost the election.

Miller went to work as a legislative aide to state Sen. George Moscone, the Democratic floor leader and one-time mayor of San Francisco. In 1974, when Democratic Rep. Jerome Waldie decided to run for governor, Miller sought his seat in Congress.

He won a tough, three-way Democratic primary. In the general election, he exploited the Watergate scandal, which was fresh in voters' minds, disclosing his campaign finances twice a month and chiding his opponent for not doing the same. He took 56 percent of the vote and has since won re-election easily.

KEY VOTES

2004

Yes	Extend federal unemployment benefits by 13 weeks
?	Pass $283.2 billion, six-year federal highway and mass transit bill
No	Approve $146 billion multi-year extension of previously enacted middle-class tax breaks
No	Amend the Constitution to prohibit same-sex marriage
No	Cut corporate taxes $137 billion over 10 years
Yes	Reorganize U.S. intelligence agencies as proposed by Sept. 11 commission

2003

No	Cut taxes by $330 billion through fiscal 2013
Yes	Block Bush rule scaling back overtime pay for some white-collar federal workers
Yes	Do not allow use of search warrants without first notifying subjects
Yes	Allow importation of prescription drugs
No	Create private school voucher program in Washington, D.C.
No	Ban "partial birth" abortion except to save a woman's life
Yes	Split $18.6 billion in Iraq aid into half-grant, half-loan
No	Overhaul Medicare and create prescription drug benefit

CQ VOTE STUDIES

	PARTY UNITY		PRESIDENTIAL SUPPORT	
	Support	Oppose	Support	Oppose
2004	98%	2%	21%	79%
2003	99%	1%	11%	89%
2002	97%	3%	22%	78%
2001	98%	2%	23%	77%
2000	96%	4%	76%	24%

INTEREST GROUPS

	AFL-CIO	ADA	CCUS	ACU
2004	93%	100%	21%	4%
2003	100%	100%	18%	12%
2002	100%	100%	30%	4%
2001	100%	100%	27%	0%
2000	100%	95%	38%	12%

CALIFORNIA 7

Northeastern Bay Area — Vallejo, Richmond

Situated along the San Pablo Bay and home to marshes and wetlands where the Sacramento and San Joaquin deltas feed into the bay, the 7th combines industrial and suburban areas of north Contra Costa County with the western end of more rural Solano County.

In Contra Costa County, the district takes in residential Concord (shared with the 10th) and the industrial cities of Richmond and Martinez along San Pablo Bay, home to oil, steel and biotechnology. Richmond, which has a slim black plurality, was home to one of the largest World War II shipbuilding operations.

Vallejo, the largest city in the district, was the site of the Mare Island Naval Shipyard, which closed in 1996 after more than 140 years of operation. The city then converted the island into a private commercial-residential property that began accepting residents in late 2004.

Vallejo and other traditionally Democratic Solano County communities — including Green Valley and Vacaville, which were added to the northern

part of the 7th in redistricting following the 2000 census — are home to farm-support services.

Redistricting also shaved off Democratic-voting areas like Suisun City, Fairfield, Cordelia and Kensington to shore up the neighboring 10th District for Democrats, but the 7th is still a safe Democratic seat. John Kerry captured two-thirds of the 7th's 2004 presidential vote.

MAJOR INDUSTRY
Petrochemicals, steel, biotechnology, agriculture, health care

MILITARY BASES
Naval Weapons Station Seal Beach, Detachment Concord, 130 military, 470 civilian (2005)

CITIES
Vallejo, 116,760; Richmond, 99,216; Vacaville, 88,625; Pittsburg, 56,769

NOTABLE
The forerunner to the martini, the "Martinez Special," became popular in the city of Martinez during the Gold Rush; Actor Tom Hanks was born in Concord; Vallejo (twice) and Benicia both served as the state capital in the 1850s.

Rep. Nancy Pelosi (D)

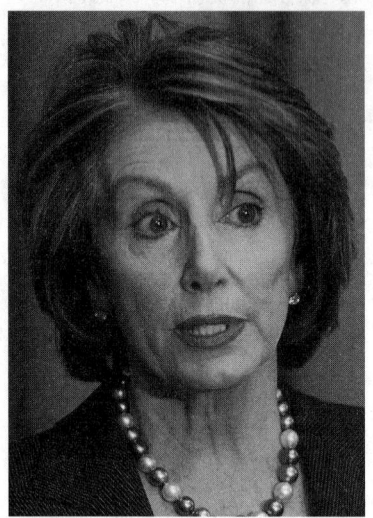

Elected June 1987; 9th full term

CAPITOL OFFICE
225-4965
sf.nancy@mail.house.gov
www.house.gov/pelosi
2371 Rayburn 20515-0508; fax 225-8259

HOMETOWN
San Francisco

BORN
March 26, 1940, Baltimore, Md.

RELIGION
Roman Catholic

FAMILY
Husband, Paul Pelosi; five children

EDUCATION
Trinity College (D.C.), A.B. 1962

CAREER
Public relations consultant; senatorial campaign committee finance chairwoman; homemaker

POLITICAL HIGHLIGHTS
Calif. Democratic Party chairwoman, 1981-83

ELECTION RESULTS

2004 GENERAL

Nancy Pelosi (D)	224,017	83.0%
Jennifer Depalma (R)	31,074	11.5%
Leilani Dowell (PF)	9,527	3.5%
Terry Baum - write-in	5,446	2.0%

2004 PRIMARY

Nancy Pelosi (D)	unopposed

2002 GENERAL

Nancy Pelosi (D)	127,684	79.6%
G. Michael German (R)	20,063	12.5%
Jay Pond (GREEN)	10,033	6.3%
Ira Spivack (LIBERT)	2,659	1.7%

PREVIOUS WINNING PERCENTAGES
2000 (84%); 1998 (86%); 1996 (84%); 1994 (82%); 1992 (82%); 1990 (77%); 1988 (76%); 1987 Special Runoff Election (63%)

Pelosi's grasp of political fundamentals and a natural dynamism have made her, over the years, an effective party activist, a master fundraiser and ultimately the first woman in history to head a major political party in Congress.

In her first term as House minority leader, Pelosi (pa-LO-see) energized and galvanized her colleagues, making them more unified than they've been in a half century. Their high-water mark was banding together to oppose President Bush's premier health initiative, a prescription drug benefit for the elderly that Pelosi said was skimpy. Without Democratic support, GOP House leaders had to very publicly twist arms on the House floor for three hours.

Still, the Republicans prevailed on the Medicare bill and also trounced Democrats in the 2004 election, resulting in a net loss of seats. Pelosi's political fate could rest on her ability to turn Democrats' solidarity on the House floor into electoral success in the 2006 midterm election.

When she was elected Democratic leader by her peers in the 108th Congress, Pelosi quickly consolidated power, showering rewards on allies and expanding her base of support by opening up new opportunities for junior members, all classic moves of a veteran power broker. She pressed several senior Democrats to part with coveted committee assignments as part of her plan to boost the representation of junior lawmakers and conservatives, and also Hispanics and blacks.

She set policy positions that could be supported by all, or nearly all Democrats, and rather than force them into line on issues that divide them, such as tax cuts, she asked for allegiance on core Democratic issues, such as education and health care. After her first two years as leader, House Democrats' party unity score on key votes was nearly 87 percent, the highest in more than 50 years.

Pelosi is an edgy partisan whose cockiness inspires friends and rankles foes. In that way, her leadership style resembles that of Majority Leader Tom DeLay probably more than either of them would care to admit. In late 2004, DeLay complained that Democrats were using an ongoing ethics case to try to destroy him and were at the same time overlooking what he called past, unspecified ethics abuses by Pelosi. She fired back that DeLay, who had been rebuked by the ethics committee, was "not only unethical but delusional."

Majority Republicans have found in her a tough opponent, in spite of her ready smile and studied graciousness. After GOP leaders wrapped up their final spending bill and left town at the close of the 108th, she had one more trick up her sleeve. When word leaked out that a provision in the bill allowed the Appropriations Committee chairmen and their staffs to see individual tax returns of everyday citizens, she refused to give the Republican leaders the authority they needed to delete it until they called lawmakers back to Washington for a special one-day session.

The low point for her came with the 2004 elections, when instead of leading House Democrats to a net gain of seats, she presided over a net loss of three. Nonetheless, she was unanimously returned as leader for the new Congress. Her fundraising zeal is one reason; she helped raise $34 million for candidates in the 2004 campaign.

Throughout her career, Pelosi has demonstrated the deft political skills learned from her father, Thomas D'Alesandro, a New Deal-era politician, former Baltimore mayor and a congressman in the 1940s. As she was growing up, copies of the daily Congressional Record were stacked underneath Pelosi's bed. Today, she speed-walks through the Capitol building as if determined to tend to every last need in a precinct paved with marble.

Pelosi took a big step toward becoming leader in 2001, when she won a pivotal race for party whip, the No. 2 Democratic leadership job, over Maryland's Steny H. Hoyer, 118-95. Her victory ended a career rivalry that began four decades earlier, when the two had worked side by side as junior aides to Sen. Daniel B. Brewster of Maryland.

When Richard A. Gephardt of Missouri stepped aside as leader after the party's losses in the 2002 election, Pelosi was a strong contender for the post. Martin Frost, a Texan with more seniority who chaired the Democratic Caucus, also wanted the job and promised leadership from the center. But Democrats seemed ready to embrace a more confrontational politics that made no apologies for liberal ideology. Just a few months earlier, Gephardt had endorsed Bush's decision to go to war with Iraq while Pelosi led opposition to the war on the floor, getting 126 Democrats to vote against a resolution giving congressional sanction to the use of force.

Ultimately, Frost bowed out of the race, concluding he could not win, and Pelosi was chosen 177-29 over Harold E. Ford Jr. of Tennessee, a late entrant who made a last-ditch appeal to conservatives. Pelosi is the first woman to be elected leader in Congress from either the Republican or Democratic Party.

She began her political career relatively late in life for one who was steeped in it as a child. After college, Pelosi changed coasts, leaving the East to move to San Francisco with investment banker Paul Pelosi. They had five children, and Pelosi stayed home for many years to be a parent, albeit a wealthy one with live-in help. She was chairwoman of the California Democratic Party in the 1980s, but she didn't run for office until she was 47 and her youngest child, now a documentary filmmaker, was in high school.

When San Francisco's principal House seat came open with the death of Democrat Sala Burton, Pelosi used her insider's contacts to capture the nomination, which was tantamount to election in one of the nation's most solidly Democratic districts. She has won re-election easily ever since.

Given the city's large Chinese-American population, Pelosi has battled in vain through three administrations to sanction China for its human rights record. She is also a strong defender of civil rights for homosexuals, another important constituency in the city. She has advocated more money to fight AIDS, welfare benefits for immigrants, debt forgiveness for poor countries and aid for international family planning groups.

KEY VOTES

2004
Yes   Extend federal unemployment benefits by 13 weeks
Yes   Pass $283.2 billion, six-year federal highway and mass transit bill
No   Approve $146 billion multi-year extension of previously enacted middle-class tax breaks
No   Amend the Constitution to prohibit same-sex marriage
No   Cut corporate taxes $137 billion over 10 years
Yes   Reorganize U.S. intelligence agencies as proposed by Sept. 11 commission

2003
No   Cut taxes by $330 billion through fiscal 2013
Yes   Block Bush rule scaling back overtime pay for some white-collar federal workers
Yes   Do not allow use of search warrants without first notifying subjects
Yes   Allow importation of prescription drugs
No   Create private school voucher program in Washington, D.C.
No   Ban "partial birth" abortion except to save a woman's life
Yes   Split $18.6 billion in Iraq aid into half-grant, half-loan
No   Overhaul Medicare and create prescription drug benefit

CQ VOTE STUDIES

	PARTY UNITY		PRESIDENTIAL SUPPORT	
	Support	Oppose	Support	Oppose
2004	97%	3%	21%	79%
2003	98%	2%	20%	80%
2002	99%	1%	23%	77%
2001	97%	3%	28%	72%
2000	96%	4%	79%	21%

INTEREST GROUPS

	AFL-CIO	ADA	CCUS	ACU
2004	93%	100%	35%	8%
2003	87%	100%	34%	12%
2002	100%	100%	37%	0%
2001	100%	100%	35%	0%
2000	100%	100%	42%	8%

CALIFORNIA 8
Most of San Francisco

Since the Gold Rush in the mid-19th century, San Francisco has attracted visitors, new residents and fortune seekers from around the globe. "The City," as it is known to natives, is famous for its landmarks, food and a diverse collection of neighborhoods, from the Italian and Hispanic centers of North Beach and the Mission District to spots such as Chinatown, hippie haven Haight-Ashbury and the gay mecca of Castro.

More than 80 percent of the city's residents live in the 8th, which forms a backward C-shape. The 12th District to the west and south takes in neighborhoods just south of Golden Gate Park and west of Twin Peaks. Whites make up 43 percent of the 8th, followed by Asians, at 29 percent.

A center for protest during the Vietnam War, the city also barred police from arresting illegal immigrants fleeing Central American bloodshed in the 1980s, in opposition to federal immigration officials. More recently, the city has helped fund the largest needle exchange program in the nation and in early 2004 allowed same-sex marriages for 29 days before a court order required the city to stop. The city also chose, however, to

cut its once-bountiful direct payments to the homeless and shift that money to create more housing and services.

The 8th is safe Democratic territory. Democrat John Kerry carried the district in 2004 with 84 percent of the presidential vote.

MAJOR INDUSTRY
Tourism, financial services, health care

CITIES
San Francisco (pt.), 639,088

NOTABLE
San Francisco was home to the nation's only declared monarch, Norton I, who named himself Emperor of the United States and Protector of Mexico in 1859; Throughout his "reign," Norton issued various proclamations, including orders to bar Congress from meeting in Washington and to construct a bridge between San Francisco and Oakland — more than 60 years before construction of the Bay Bridge; Alcatraz Island, home to the first West Coast fort and lighthouse and used as a federal maximum-security prison from 1934 to 1963, was occupied in protest by American Indians from 1969 to 1971.

Rep. Barbara Lee (D)

CAPITOL OFFICE
225-2661
barbara.lee@mail.house.gov
www.house.gov/lee
1724 Longworth 20515-0509; fax 225-9817

COMMITTEES
Financial Services
International Relations

HOMETOWN
Oakland

BORN
July 16, 1946, El Paso, Texas

RELIGION
Baptist

FAMILY
Husband, Michael Millben; two children

EDUCATION
Mills College, B.A. 1973 (psychology); U. of
California, Berkeley, M.S.W. 1975

CAREER
Congressional aide

POLITICAL HIGHLIGHTS
Calif. Assembly, 1990-96; Calif. Senate, 1996-98

ELECTION RESULTS

2004 GENERAL

Barbara Lee (D)	215,630	84.6%
Claudia Bermudez (R)	31,278	12.3%
James M. Eyer (LIBERT)	8,131	3.2%

2004 PRIMARY

Barbara Lee (D)	unopposed

2002 GENERAL

Barbara Lee (D)	135,893	81.4%
Jerald Udinsky (R)	25,333	15.2%
James M. Eyer (LIBERT)	5,685	3.4%

PREVIOUS WINNING PERCENTAGES
2000 (85%); 1998 (83%); 1998 Special Election (67%)

Elected April 1998; 4th full term

Lee's politics are shaped by her early-life recollections of discrimination. Her mother initially was refused treatment at an El Paso hospital when in labor with her. She attended a segregated school and later, she says, a riot was touched off when she was chosen the first black cheerleader at her high school in Southern California. She says many of her experiences with discrimination are similar to those of black Americans of her generation and "have fueled my disdain for injustices."

Lee represents the cities of Oakland and Berkeley, two of the most liberal communities in the state. More than one-third of Oakland's residents are black. Her voting record reflects her district, and in 2004, she voted 99 percent of the time in agreement with a majority of her party. In the 109th Congress, she is the co-chairwoman of the Progressive Caucus, the most liberal faction of House Democrats, and serves as whip for the Congressional Black Caucus.

Employing a straightforward, conversational style, she argues for the economic, health care and education needs of her constituency. Some of her constituent needs are urgent, she argues, such as recognizing the devastating impact of AIDS on the African-American community. She has been a leader in the national and global war on AIDS and drafted many of the provisions of an international AIDS measure that President Bush signed in 2003.

When the House that year passed the $15 billion international AIDS bill, it was caught up in a political fight after a GOP amendment was added to require that one-third of all AIDS prevention funding authorized by the bill be set aside for abstinence programs. Democrats accused Republicans of politicizing the fight against the disease by catering to social conservatives. Lee complained that Republicans had tinkered with a hard-fought compromise worked out in the International Relations Committee on which she sits. "Both sides made major concessions with the understanding that those dying of AIDS would trump our political differences," Lee said on the floor.

The next year, the House passed a measure drafted by Lee to create an office in the U.S. Agency for International Development to focus on the needs of AIDS orphans in the developing world. Lee called her bill "a first step to provide a more effective U.S. response to the global orphan and vulnerable children crisis."

Lee also has a seat on the Financial Services Committee, where she fought a measure, enacted in 2003, that nullified a California law protecting the privacy of personal financial information. The law bars states from regulating credit-reporting bureaus. "These groundbreaking, popular, hard-won protections which were negotiated with our financial institutions in California are threatened because of this bill," Lee said during the House debate.

Lee is a hero of the American peace movement because of her lone "no" vote in Congress on Sept. 14, 2001, against a resolution authorizing President Bush to use "all necessary and appropriate force" to retaliate against the terrorist attacks that had occurred three days earlier.

Lee said she agonized over her vote, and did not make up her mind until she attended a memorial service at the Washington National Cathedral earlier in the day. She decided on her course after hearing an invocation by the Rev. Nathan D. Baxter, the cathedral dean, who prayed that "despite our grief we may not become the evil we deplore."

Lee's vote brought in sacks of hate mail and death threats that at one point required police protection. But she has never second-guessed herself. "That was the right vote then and it's the right vote today," Lee said more than a year later. "The resolution gave the president very broad authority to use military force."

Her office was a rallying point later, in 2002, for those opposed to the war in Iraq. She said that a pre-emptive invasion to remove Saddam Hussein from power would set "a dangerous precedent." And she joined in 2003 with Dennis J. Kucinich of Ohio on a "resolution of inquiry" to require the Bush administration to turn over intelligence documents relating to any weapons of mass destruction in Iraq. The International Relations Committee had recommended the House reject the resolution. But panel Democrats continued to ask if the administration manipulated intelligence to bolster its case for war. Lee was also one of the original sponsors of a bill to establish a Cabinet-level Department of Peace.

Lee had never even registered to vote when she was faced with a course requirement at Oakland's Mills College to work for a political campaign during the presidential election year of 1972. She signed on with Democratic Rep. Shirley Chisholm of New York, the nation's first notable black candidate for president. Lee rose quickly through the ranks, eventually running Chisholm's Northern California campaign and, as she proudly recalled a quarter-century later, receiving an "A" in the course.

While earning a master's degree in social work, Lee helped start a community health center in Berkeley before going to work for Democrat Ronald V. Dellums, her predecessor in the House, in 1975. She worked for him in both California and Washington before running for the state legislature, where she served six years in the Assembly and 17 months in the Senate. When Dellums revealed his plans to resign from the House in early 1998, he endorsed Lee to succeed him and she easily won the special election.

Lee's stand against the 2001 war resolution inevitably invites comparisons to Jeanette Rankin, the Montana Republican who was the only member of Congress to vote against the U.S. entry into both world wars. But while Rankin left the House one year after each of those votes — she lost a Senate bid in 1918, and she did not run for re-election in 1942 — Lee's vote did nothing to weaken her political standing. She remains enormously popular at home, re-elected in both 2002 and 2004 with more than 80 percent of the vote.

KEY VOTES

2004

Yes   Extend federal unemployment benefits by 13 weeks

Yes   Pass $283.2 billion, six-year federal highway and mass transit bill

No   Approve $146 billion multi-year extension of previously enacted middle-class tax breaks

No   Amend the Constitution to prohibit same-sex marriage

No   Cut corporate taxes $137 billion over 10 years

Yes   Reorganize U.S. intelligence agencies as proposed by Sept. 11 commission

2003

No   Cut taxes by $330 billion through fiscal 2013

Yes   Block Bush rule scaling back overtime pay for some white-collar federal workers

Yes   Do not allow use of search warrants without first notifying subjects

Yes   Allow importation of prescription drugs

No   Create private school voucher program in Washington, D.C.

No   Ban "partial birth" abortion except to save a woman's life

Yes   Split $18.6 billion in Iraq aid into half-grant, half-loan

No   Overhaul Medicare and create prescription drug benefit

CQ VOTE STUDIES

	PARTY UNITY		PRESIDENTIAL SUPPORT	
	Support	Oppose	Support	Oppose
2004	99%	1%	15%	85%
2003	99%	1%	11%	89%
2002	99%	1%	25%	75%
2001	97%	3%	12%	88%
2000	97%	3%	82%	18%

INTEREST GROUPS

	AFL-CIO	ADA	CCUS	ACU
2004	100%	95%	5%	0%
2003	100%	100%	17%	12%
2002	100%	90%	30%	0%
2001	100%	95%	22%	0%
2000	100%	90%	33%	4%

CALIFORNIA 9
Northwest Alameda County — Oakland, Berkeley

Across the bay from San Francisco, the 9th is anchored by Oakland and Berkeley, two racially diverse and liberal communities that gained national attention for their political activism in the 1960s.

More than 60 percent of district residents live in Oakland, which is 36 percent black. The city's unemployment rate is slightly above the national average, but revitalization efforts have kept the area in good health, despite the closing of several military facilities. In the city's eastern hills, the neighborhoods tend to be wealthy and less diverse. Tension between blacks and police gave birth to the Black Panther Party in 1966.

Just north of Oakland, Berkeley is home to the flagship campus of the University of California system and looks out over the bay from the Berkeley Hills. Home to student protests in the 1960s, Berkeley still looks much the way it did then. The remainder of the district includes smaller communities such as Albany, a suburb at the north end of the district; Piedmont, a residential "suburb in the city" in Oakland's hills; and several additions from redistricting following the 2000 census: Ashland, Castro Valley, Cherryland and Fairview, which are unincorporated sections of Alameda County southeast of Oakland.

The 9th also includes the fast-growing bayside city of Emeryville, which is home to biotechnology firms, high-tech companies and the headquarters of animation studio Pixar ("Toy Story," "The Incredibles").

With a core constituency in the left-leaning cities of Oakland and Berkeley, the 9th is a Democratic stronghold. Republicans account for only 10 percent of registered voters, and John Kerry captured 86 percent of the 2004 presidential vote here — his best showing in the state.

MAJOR INDUSTRY
Biotechnology, shipping

CITIES
Oakland, 399,484; Berkeley, 102,743; Castro Valley (unincorporated) (pt.), 57,224

NOTABLE
Since 1970, Jack London Square in Oakland has featured the relocated cabin where the author, who ran for Oakland mayor twice, lived during the Yukon Gold Rush of 1897; West Oakland was a terminus for the transcontinental railroad.

Rep. Ellen O. Tauscher (D)

Elected 1996; 5th term

CAPITOL OFFICE
225-1880
www.house.gov/tauscher
1034 Longworth 20515-0510; fax 225-5914

COMMITTEES
Armed Services
Transportation & Infrastructure

HOMETOWN
Alamo

BORN
Nov. 15, 1951, Newark, N.J.

RELIGION
Roman Catholic

FAMILY
Divorced; one child

EDUCATION
Seton Hall U., B.A. 1974 (early childhood
education)

CAREER
Child care screening executive; marketing
executive; investment banker

POLITICAL HIGHLIGHTS
No previous office

ELECTION RESULTS

2004 GENERAL

Ellen O. Tauscher (D)	182,750	65.7%
Jeff Ketelson (R)	95,349	34.3%

2004 PRIMARY

Ellen O. Tauscher (D)	unopposed

2002 GENERAL

Ellen O. Tauscher (D)	126,390	75.6%
Sonia Harden (LIBERT)	40,807	24.4%

PREVIOUS WINNING PERCENTAGES
2000 (53%); 1998 (53%); 1996 (49%)

After carving out an image as a centrist, pro-business Democrat who could work with Republicans, Tauscher has been cementing another reputation, as a tough-talking critic of President Bush's national security policies.

As hostilities in Iraq persisted during 2004, Tauscher, from her seat on the House Armed Services Committee, fired barbed salvos at the administration's postwar efforts in Iraq. "This is about faulty analysis and a failed strategy," she said. "We've never had enough troops on the ground since the fall of Saddam Hussein's government to deal with the insurgency because we didn't expect one."

In particular, Tauscher (TAU — rhymes with "now" — sher) singled out the reliance on National Guard and Reserve forces as a sign that no real plan existed to stabilize the country. She introduced a bill in late 2003 to increase the size of the Army, Air Force and Marine Corps by 83,500 members over five years. It attracted 31 Democratic cosponsors, but no Republicans. In January 2005, Tauscher traveled to Iraq as part of a group to help train women running for political office.

Tauscher also led efforts to stop the Energy Department from developing a new generation of nuclear weapons, particularly when the United States is trying to persuade other nations to abandon their nuclear programs. Though she lost a close vote on an amendment to kill a controversial "bunker buster" tactical nuclear weapon sought by the White House, appropriators subsequently declined to fund the program.

She initially sought out the Armed Services assignment to watch out for the interests of the Lawrence Livermore and Sandia California National laboratories in her district, which both conduct defense-related research. But she has used the post to broaden her portfolio and develop an expertise on an issue with international heft: halting the spread of nuclear, biological and chemical weapons.

Tauscher came to the House with a wealth of experience not in government and politics but in business. In 1992, unhappy with the child care options available for her daughter, she founded a business that screens prospective child care workers. Parents, she said, needed an alternative to the kind of applicants she had encountered. "I started meeting tax fugitives and 300-pound people with no teeth," she told The Record, the newspaper that covers her childhood area home of northern New Jersey. She also published a child care guidebook.

Before that, she was a stockbroker and investment banker for 14 years. She told the San Francisco Examiner that she once confronted her boss to demand pay equal to a male colleague's and got it.

The eldest daughter in an Irish-Catholic family, Tauscher was the first person in her family to attend college, majoring in early childhood education. From Seton Hall University, she watched the World Trade Center's twin towers being built across the Hudson River. After graduating and finding it difficult to land a teaching job, she looked across the river at Wall Street and asked herself, "Why not?" By age 25, she was one of the first women to hold a seat on the New York Stock Exchange.

She says her career was good training for legislating. "I understand the art of the deal. Compromise is not a dirty word," says Tauscher, whose votes on business and labor issues frequently earn her higher rankings from the Chamber of Commerce than from the AFL-CIO.

Early in 2001, Tauscher was elected vice chairwoman of the Democratic

Leadership Council, an organization of centrist Democrats. Later that year, she was chosen as vice chairwoman of a Democratic task force on homeland security, adding to a résumé that led Washingtonian magazine to call her one of the 100 most powerful women in the capital. In the 109th, she chairs the House New Democrat Coalition of moderate, pro-business Democrats.

The San Francisco Chronicle describes her as "about the closest thing the Bay Area has to a Republican." In 2001, she was the only California Democrat to back Maryland's Steny H. Hoyer in the campaign for party whip against San Francisco's Nancy Pelosi because Hoyer, she said, more reflected her centrist views. Unfortunately for Tauscher, she picked the wrong horse. Pelosi won the whip's race and went on to become House Democratic leader; Hoyer became whip after Pelosi moved up.

In addition to her New Democrat affiliation, Tauscher belongs to the "Blue Dogs," a coalition of fiscally conservative Democrats. She favors a balanced-budget constitutional amendment and is a strong advocate of cutting taxes, particularly on capital gains and on wealth passed from one generation to the next. But on most social policy issues Tauscher is a traditional Democrat. She favors abortion rights, robust environmental protections, federal arts funding and an active federal role in improving education.

Her other committee assignment is Transportation and Infrastructure. She touts the hundreds of millions of federal dollars that have gone to the Bay Area during her tenure, and is not averse to complaining about "bureaucratic foot-dragging" by the EPA that has delayed some projects for her suburban San Francisco district.

Tauscher, the daughter of a grocery store manager, was raised in East Newark, New Jersey. She moved to Northern California in 1989 after marrying ComputerLand executive Bill Tauscher. (They have since divorced.) She got active in politics by helping Democrat Dianne Feinstein in her 1992 and 1994 Senate campaigns before launching her own quest for Congress.

In 1996, incumbent Republican Bill Baker looked vulnerable in the 10th District, having alienated some of its liberal-leaning voters with a hard line against abortion and in favor of gun owners' rights. Tauscher spent $1.7 million of her own money and outspent Baker by almost 2-to-1. She won by less than 2 percentage points.

In 1998, she easily outdistanced political novice Charles Ball, and two years later, fended off an aggressive challenge from GOP banker Claude B. Hutchison Jr. In 2002, she brushed off Libertarian challenger Sonia Harden, 3-to-1, and in 2004 defeated GOP Fairfield businessman Jeff Ketelson with a comfortable 66 percent of the vote.

KEY VOTES

2004

Yes Extend federal unemployment benefits by 13 weeks
Yes Pass $283.2 billion, six-year federal highway and mass transit bill
Yes Approve $146 billion multi-year extension of previously enacted middle-class tax breaks
No Amend the Constitution to prohibit same-sex marriage
No Cut corporate taxes $137 billion over 10 years
Yes Reorganize U.S. intelligence agencies as proposed by Sept. 11 commission

2003

No Cut taxes by $330 billion through fiscal 2013
Yes Block Bush rule scaling back overtime pay for some white-collar federal workers
Yes Do not allow use of search warrants without first notifying subjects
No Allow importation of prescription drugs
No Create private school voucher program in Washington, D.C.
No Ban "partial birth" abortion except to save a woman's life
Yes Split $18.6 billion in Iraq aid into half-grant, half-loan
No Overhaul Medicare and create prescription drug benefit

CQ VOTE STUDIES

	PARTY UNITY		PRESIDENTIAL SUPPORT	
	Support	Oppose	Support	Oppose
2004	93%	7%	35%	65%
2003	92%	8%	20%	80%
2002	86%	14%	35%	65%
2001	84%	16%	40%	60%
2000	85%	15%	78%	22%

INTEREST GROUPS

	AFL-CIO	ADA	CCUS	ACU
2004	93%	100%	48%	16%
2003	80%	90%	40%	12%
2002	78%	85%	65%	8%
2001	83%	85%	48%	4%
2000	50%	70%	71%	20%

CALIFORNIA 10

East Bay suburbs — Fairfield, Antioch, Livermore

Anyone driving through the Caldecott Tunnel across the Alameda-Contra Costa county line or on Interstate 680 during rush hour probably will be surrounded by 10th District residents on their way to and from work in San Francisco or San Jose. Separated from the rest of the Bay Area by the hills east of Oakland, the 10th's residents are mainly well-educated, well-paid professionals who work outside the district.

The 10th's residents have managed to fend off overdevelopment from their hills and hidden valleys while keeping pace with the rest of the area economically, giving the district a different feel from its more urban neighbors to the west. Almost two-thirds of residents live in the 10th's portion of Contra Costa County, including Antioch and most of Concord (shared with the 7th District).

Some of the residents here represent white flight from Oakland that is now generations old. But many newer commuters are younger and identify with San Francisco or Berkeley. The district retains a moderate political character — residents tend to be conscious of pocketbook

issues but also share their Bay Area neighbors' views on the environment and other quality-of-life issues.

The district's Solano County portion is a growing but still largely agricultural area where commuters may head south to the Bay Area or north to Sacramento. Added along with a sliver of Sacramento County during redistricting following the 2000 census, these areas made the previously competitive district more Democratic. Residents here are more working-class than their "new Democrat" suburban district-mates. Growth will soon make these areas a part of the suburbs.

MAJOR INDUSTRY
Research, health care, agriculture, service

MILITARY BASES
Travis Air Force Base, 11,328 military, 3,554 civilian (2005)

CITIES
Fairfield, 96,178; Antioch, 90,532; Livermore, 73,345; Concord (pt.), 72,540

NOTABLE
Lawrence Livermore National Laboratory is one of the country's leading centers of experimental physics research and defense analysis; Fairfield is home to the Jelly Belly jellybean factory.

Rep. Richard W. Pombo (R)

Elected 1992; 7th term

CAPITOL OFFICE
225-1947
rpombo@mail.house.gov
www.house.gov/pombo
2411 Rayburn 20515-0511; fax 226-0861

COMMITTEES
Agriculture
Resources - chairman

HOMETOWN
Tracy

BORN
Jan. 8, 1961, Tracy, Calif.

RELIGION
Roman Catholic

FAMILY
Wife, Annette Pombo; three children

EDUCATION
California State Polytechnic U., Pomona, attended
1979-81 (agriculture & business)

CAREER
Rancher

POLITICAL HIGHLIGHTS
Tracy City Council, 1990-92

ELECTION RESULTS

2004 GENERAL

Richard W. Pombo (R)	163,582	61.2%
Gerald M. McNerney (D)	103,587	38.8%

2004 PRIMARY

Richard W. Pombo (R)	unopposed

2002 GENERAL

Richard W. Pombo (R)	104,921	60.3%
Elaine Dugger Shaw (D)	69,035	39.7%

PREVIOUS WINNING PERCENTAGES
2000 (58%); 1998 (61%); 1996 (59%); 1994 (62%);
1992 (48%)

Of all the nicknames that President Bush has given people, calling Pombo "Marlboro Man" may be the most on target. Pombo is a straight-talking, conservative Western rancher, most comfortable in his cowboy boots and cowboy hat. In Congress, Pombo's agenda is just what the Marlboro Man would be pushing if he was not off rounding up strays — preserving the rights of property owners, reducing the role of the federal government, simplifying regulations and lowering taxes.

A fourth generation member of a large Central Valley family that raises dairy and beef cattle and is involved in trucking and real estate, Pombo (POM-bo) still lives on the family spread in Tracy where he grew up. He cultivates an image as a straightforward man who stakes out a position and sticks with it. Even his political foes say he is a nice guy, although they criticize his conservative views and his unwillingness to compromise.

His impact is mostly felt on environmental issues. As chairman of the Resources Committee, Pombo is an important player in the 109th Congress in President Bush's quest to open Alaska's Arctic National Wildlife Refuge to oil drilling. His pet issue on the environment is scaling back the 1973 Endangered Species Act, which Pombo says treads on the rights of private property owners. He'd like to overhaul the law, but, unable to do so in one swipe, he has been working to whittle away at it, bill by bill. One proposal Pombo supports redefines the way the government designates critical habitats for endangered plants and animals.

Pombo has also negotiated compromises to win broader support on other bills disdained by environmentalists, such as one in 2003 pushed by the White House to allow more logging on federal lands to reduce the likelihood of forest fires.

In the 108th Congress, with the strong backing of Majority Leader Tom DeLay, Pombo leapfrogged over several more-senior GOP colleagues to win election as Resources chairman. His ascension did not sit well with environmentalists, or even some of his GOP colleagues. Colorado's Joel Hefley, one of the Republicans with more seniority on the panel, quit the committee shortly thereafter.

Pombo made his feelings about the environmental movement clear when, in 1996, he co-authored "This Land Is Our Land," a book that warned of an "eco-federal coalition" of government regulators and environmental groups with an agenda that "owes more to communism than to any other philosophy." Pombo was a point man for House Republicans in their drive to rewrite the nation's environmental laws shortly after taking control of the House in 1995. Most of those efforts failed due to disagreements with fellow Republicans from the Northeast, whom he continually scuffles with. Needless to say, Pombo's ideas are getting a more friendly reception from the Bush White House than they did from the Clinton administration.

In both the 106th and 107th Congresses, Pombo opposed a plan to spend billions of dollars for land conservation programs, including purchases of private land. "I believe the federal government already owns too much land and should not come out West and buy more," he said in 2001.

To answer critics, Pombo points to some environmentally friendly positions. He asked appropriators to allocate $1 million in federal funds to save the endangered Puerto Rican parrot. He sponsored legislation that would clean up groundwater in California contaminated with traces of rocket fuel. And Pombo has long supported a ban on the MTBE additive in gasoline, which reduces harmful emissions but contaminates groundwater.

Pombo's other committee assignment is on Agriculture, a key position for his heavily agricultural Central Valley district and its dairy and wine grape industries. He has long been at the center of regional battles over dairy subsidies. In the 108th Congress, Pombo worked across the aisle with Democratic Sen. Dianne Feinstein of California to shepherd into being a long-stalled project, known as Cal-Fed, that aims to secure a steadier supply of drinking water for rapidly growing communities in Northern California.

His tenure was marred in late 2004 when The Stockton (Calif.) Record reported that Pombo spent nearly one-fourth of his campaign funds —more than $250,000 — on salaries to his wife and brother. Federal law precludes using campaign funds for personal use but does not prevent paying a family member's salary. Then, California Democrat Brad Sherman complained publicly when Pombo requested $500,000 to cover postage for national mailings for the Resource Committee's work, and Democrats objected as well that he misspent public funds by sending out 175,000 fliers that touted the Bush administration's decision to keep Yellowstone and Grand Teton National parks open to snowmobiles.

Pombo is the grandson of a Portuguese immigrant who came to the Central Valley early in the 20th century. The huge Pombo clan is well known in the area. He attended college in Southern California for a few years, while working in a slaughterhouse. Pombo did not finish at California State Polytechnic University. He instead went back to his hometown of Tracy to become partners with his father and brothers in cattle ranching. Pombo got into politics by fighting a government plan to convert an old railroad right-of-way on family land into a hiker-biker trail.

Pombo had served only two years on the Tracy City Council when he decided to run for the House in 1992 in the newly drawn 11th District. He was a clear underdog in the primary against Sacramento County Supervisor Sandra Smoley. He won by branding her a liberal. In the general election, he campaigned as a rancher out to defend his neighbors in contrast to his Democratic opponent, whom he portrayed as just another ambitious politician. Pombo prevailed by 2 percentage points and has since won re-election comfortably.

Redistricting in 2002 gave him substantial chunks of Alameda and Contra Costa counties, and Pombo's re-election hinged on his appealing to new, more liberal constituents who live closer to the San Francisco-Oakland-Berkeley urban areas. Pointing out that traffic congestion and other suburban issues affected everyone, Pombo won by more than 20 points.

KEY VOTES

2004

No	Extend federal unemployment benefits by 13 weeks
Yes	Pass $283.2 billion, six-year federal highway and mass transit bill
Yes	Approve $146 billion multi-year extension of previously enacted middle-class tax breaks
Yes	Amend the Constitution to prohibit same-sex marriage
Yes	Cut corporate taxes $137 billion over 10 years
No	Reorganize U.S. intelligence agencies as proposed by Sept. 11 commission

2003

Yes	Cut taxes by $330 billion through fiscal 2013
No	Block Bush rule scaling back overtime pay for some white-collar federal workers
Yes	Do not allow use of search warrants without first notifying subjects
No	Allow importation of prescription drugs
Yes	Create private school voucher program in Washington, D.C.
Yes	Ban "partial birth" abortion except to save a woman's life
No	Split $18.6 billion in Iraq aid into half-grant, half-loan
Yes	Overhaul Medicare and create prescription drug benefit

CQ VOTE STUDIES

	PARTY UNITY		PRESIDENTIAL SUPPORT	
	Support	Oppose	Support	Oppose
2004	96%	4%	79%	21%
2003	97%	3%	98%	2%
2002	96%	4%	84%	16%
2001	96%	4%	84%	16%
2000	95%	5%	19%	81%

INTEREST GROUPS

	AFL-CIO	ADA	CCUS	ACU
2004	27%	0%	95%	100%
2003	0%	5%	97%	92%
2002	11%	5%	85%	96%
2001	25%	10%	87%	96%
2000	10%	5%	76%	100%

CALIFORNIA 11

San Joaquin Valley; inland East Bay; part of Stockton

A mix of bedroom communities along commuter corridors east of San Francisco Bay and inland developing agricultural country, the 11th has one common thread: conservative tendencies in the voting booth. The district is wrench-shaped, with the handle running along Interstate 680 and south past San Jose, while the northern end surrounds Stockton on three sides (central Stockton is in the 18th District).

The district includes more than 40 percent of Stockton's residents and almost all of surrounding San Joaquin County, where farmland is giving way to high-end residential development. Hourlong drives to San Jose or San Francisco can more than double during rush hour. The technology boom pushed some Bay Area commuters to Stockton, and easing the gridlock remains a top concern even after boom gave way to bust. The diverse city leans Democratic, but the 11th's portion leans Republican.

Dairy products and wine grapes make up the district's biggest

agricultural exports. Woodbridge and Lodi produce 40 percent of the state's premium wine grapes — many of which are shipped to the Napa Valley for bottling. Lodi and Tracy are two main trucking centers through which the district's agricultural products travel. Interstate 205 breaks off from Interstate 5 to head west to San Francisco, making it a key transportation hub. Stockton's location as a port city on the San Joaquin River makes it a hub as well.

Residents in the rural, agricultural valley areas are sometimes at odds with their hillier suburban neighbors over water use and the smog that drifts east into the valley.

MAJOR INDUSTRY
Agriculture, technology, service

MILITARY BASES
Defense Distribution Depot San Joaquin, 6 military, 1,700 civilian (2005)

CITIES
Stockton (pt.), 104,409; Pleasanton (pt.), 58,432; Lodi, 56,999; Tracy, 56,929

NOTABLE
Stockton, named for Robert F. Stockton — who proclaimed California as U.S. territory — was the first community in California to have an American name, all others being of Spanish or Native American origin.

Rep. Tom Lantos (D)

Elected 1980; 13th term

CAPITOL OFFICE
225-3531
www.house.gov/lantos
2413 Rayburn 20515-0512; fax 225-5976

COMMITTEES
Government Reform
International Relations - ranking member

HOMETOWN
Burlingame

BORN
Feb. 1, 1928, Budapest, Hungary

RELIGION
Jewish

FAMILY
Wife, Annette Tillemann Lantos; two children

EDUCATION
U. of Washington, B.A. 1949 (economics), M.A. 1950 (economics); U. of California, Berkeley, Ph.D. 1953 (economics)

CAREER
Professor; congressional aide

POLITICAL HIGHLIGHTS
Millbrae School District Board of Trustees, 1959-66 (president, 1960-61, 1965-66)

ELECTION RESULTS

2004 GENERAL
Tom Lantos (D)	171,852	68.0%
Mike Garza (R)	52,593	20.8%
Pat Gray (GREEN)	23,038	9.1%
Harland Harrison (LIBERT)	5,116	2.0%

2004 PRIMARY
Tom Lantos (D)	63,323	73.5%
Ro Khanna (D)	17,107	19.9%
Maad Abu-Ghazalah (D)	5,678	6.6%

2002 GENERAL
Tom Lantos (D)	105,597	68.1%
Michael Moloney (R)	38,381	24.8%
Maad Abu-Ghazalah (LIBERT)	11,006	7.1%

PREVIOUS WINNING PERCENTAGES
2000 (75%); 1998 (74%); 1996 (72%); 1994 (67%); 1992 (69%); 1990 (66%); 1988 (71%); 1986 (74%); 1984 (70%); 1982 (57%); 1980 (46%)

Although he is in the minority party, Lantos is one of the House's most influential voices on foreign policy. In many areas, he is an ally of President Bush and top congressional Republicans, most notably in his support for the Iraq war. A native of Hungary, Lantos is the only Holocaust survivor in Congress and takes a hard pro-Israel line on issues involving the Middle East peace process.

His influence is also derived from his seniority on the International Relations Committee, where he is the top-ranking Democrat. Republican chairmen come and go, their power constrained by party-imposed term limits. Lantos stays. GOP Chairman Henry J. Hyde of Illinois is due to give up the gavel at the end of the 109th Congress, and although he is among the most respected lawmakers, Hyde is sometimes outflanked by Lantos.

Lantos shares with the Bush administration a muscular foreign policy that seeks to employ unquestioned military dominance and perceived moral authority to right global wrongs. The GOP-Lantos alliance has had the most impact on U.S. policy toward the Middle East. Like Republican neoconservatives, Lantos believes that a strong assertion of U.S. power can steer the region toward democracy. He backs a tougher stance against Palestinian terrorists and has criticized Saudi Arabia for financing terrorism.

When he became the senior panel Democrat in 2001, Lantos played an important behind-the-scenes role helping write the 2002 resolution authorizing war against Iraq. Then, Lantos joined with Hyde to ensure that the measure would sail through the House with Democratic support. "Had the United States and its allies confronted Hitler earlier, had we acted sooner to stymie his evil designs, the 51 million lives needlessly lost during that war could have been saved," he said.

Lantos wrote laws in the 1980s imposing sanctions on Libya, but in 2004 was the first member of Congress to call for those sanctions to be lifted after he traveled to the country for a 90-minute session with leader Muammar el-Qaddafi. Lantos was persuaded that Qaddafi's pledge to dismantle his programs to make chemical, biological and nuclear weapons was real, and the Bush administration soon went along.

The alliance with the administration is also personal. Secretary of State Condoleezza Rice befriended Lantos when she was provost at Stanford University, which lies just outside Lantos' district. Lantos himself was once a college economics professor at San Francisco State University.

However, Lantos does part company with the Republican White House. The administration rebuffed his call for cutting U.S. military aid to Egypt, saying that the financing, which started with the 1979 Camp David peace accords, was vital. Typically at the forefront of efforts to aid victims of genocide, Lantos in the 108th Congress criticized as skimpy the authorization of $300 million for humanitarian relief in Sudan. He warned that the international community may be using a double standard in Africa, citing the genocide in Rwanda in the 1990s, where most of the victims, as in Sudan, are black. Lantos was one of the first in Congress to call for a firm U.S. response to Serbia's aggression against former Yugoslavian republics during that civil war.

Hyde finds Lantos to be both a valuable and necessary ally. Shortly after he became International Relations chairman, Hyde was caught off guard when Lantos got panel Democrats and moderate Republicans to throw out some restrictions on abortion in foreign aid programs that had been championed by Hyde, an ardent anti-abortion conservative. Since then,

Hyde has rarely moved legislation without consulting Lantos.

Lantos is eloquent and intellectual — some say haughty — with the courtly air of a man bred in prewar Central Europe. He can be friendly but at times uses his bearing to his advantage when making a point. His sometimes sharp comments cause discomfort for Democratic colleagues, probably his major weakness as a leader. Lantos once described Republicans as "goose-stepping" along with whatever their leaders demanded, a reference to the gait of Nazi soldiers in Hitler's Germany.

Lantos was only 16 when the Nazis swept into Budapest, Hungary and began rounding up Jews. He was sent to a forced labor camp in Szob, a village north of the capital city, escaped, and was captured and severely beaten. He escaped a second time, this time making it back to Budapest and seeking refuge in a Wallenberg safe house, one of the apartment buildings under Swedish diplomatic protection. Because of his "Aryan" coloring — blond hair and blue eyes — Lantos was able to move around Budapest in a military cadet's uniform, acquiring food and secretly delivering it to Jews in other safe houses. Lantos recalls that he believed he was going to be killed anyway, so that he "might as well be of some use."

After house-to-house fighting for control of the city in 1945, Lantos was liberated when a Soviet soldier burst through the door of his building. He searched in vain for his mother and other members of his family, who had perished. Later he was able to locate childhood friend Annette Tillemann, a Jew who had fled to Switzerland. The two married and have been together since; Annette Lantos is a regular presence in the office as a full-time volunteer. Their experience is featured in the Steven Spielberg documentary "The Last Days."

In 1947, Lantos won a scholarship to study in the United States. He got a master's degree in economics from the University of Washington, then a doctorate at the University of California at Berkeley. The couple settled in San Francisco.

Lantos was working as a consultant to the Senate Foreign Relations Committee when Republican Bill Royer won a 1979 special House election to replace Democrat Leo J. Ryan, who was assassinated in Jonestown, Guyana by a religious cult that engineered a notorious mass suicide. Lantos left his job to begin preparing to challenge Royer for the seat.

At that time, his only elective office had been as a suburban school board president, but he took advantage of the incumbent's overconfidence and won by 3 percentage points in 1980. Lantos put down Royer's comeback attempt by 17 points in 1982 and has won with more than 65 percent of the vote since.

KEY VOTES

2004
Yes Extend federal unemployment benefits by 13 weeks
Yes Pass $283.2 billion, six-year federal highway and mass transit bill
Yes Approve $146 billion multi-year extension of previously enacted middle-class tax breaks
No   Amend the Constitution to prohibit same-sex marriage
No   Cut corporate taxes $137 billion over 10 years
Yes Reorganize U.S. intelligence agencies as proposed by Sept. 11 commission

2003
No   Cut taxes by $330 billion through fiscal 2013
Yes Block Bush rule scaling back overtime pay for some white-collar federal workers
Yes Do not allow use of search warrants without first notifying subjects
Yes Allow importation of prescription drugs
No   Create private school voucher program in Washington, D.C.
No   Ban "partial birth" abortion except to save a woman's life
Yes Split $18.6 billion in Iraq aid into half-grant, half-loan
No   Overhaul Medicare and create prescription drug benefit

CQ VOTE STUDIES

	PARTY UNITY		PRESIDENTIAL SUPPORT	
	Support	Oppose	Support	Oppose
2004	96%	4%	23%	77%
2003	96%	4%	16%	84%
2002	94%	6%	20%	80%
2001	96%	4%	26%	74%
2000	98%	2%	87%	13%

INTEREST GROUPS

	AFL-CIO	ADA	CCUS	ACU
2004	93%	95%	37%	9%
2003	100%	80%	28%	8%
2002	100%	95%	30%	4%
2001	100%	95%	30%	8%
2000	100%	85%	47%	4%

CALIFORNIA 12

Part of San Mateo County; most of western San Francisco

A mix of scenic coastal mountains and bayside commuter traffic jams, the 12th lies between its two well-known neighbors, San Francisco and the Silicon Valley.

The district includes a western section of San Francisco, but most residents live in heavily populated San Mateo County suburbs, either in Daly City or between two main commuter routes — the Junipero Serra Freeway (Interstate 280) and Bayshore Freeway (U.S. Highway 101). The 12th also covers a portion of Pacific coastline from the Great Highway in San Francisco through Pacifica to Moss Beach, and the district stretches southeast to San Carlos and part of Redwood City, about halfway to San Jose.

Despite a downturn in the 12th's high-tech economy and in Silicon Valley to the south, real estate prices have continued to rise in one of the highest-demand retail markets in the country. The district's largest

employer remains San Francisco International Airport, though a number of biotechnology firms have set up shop in the South San Francisco area, making biotechnology one of the area's leading industries. Almost 30 percent of the district's residents are Asian, with Daly City home to the district's highest concentration. The Farallon Islands, a national wildlife refuge about 30 miles west of San Francisco, also belong to the district.

Democrats hold a strong edge in the 12th's voter registration. At the southern end of the district, residents of the affluent communities of Burlingame and Hillsborough are more conservative, while voters in the San Francisco area are more Democratic. Overall, John Kerry took 72 percent of the 12th's vote in the 2004 presidential election.

MAJOR INDUSTRY
Biotechnology, airport, software

CITIES
San Francisco (pt.), 137,645; Daly City, 103,621; San Mateo, 92,482

NOTABLE
The Museum of Pez Memorabilia is in Burlingame; Daly City has the largest concentration of Filipinos outside of the Philippines; Software firm Oracle's corporate headquarters are in Redwood Shores.

Rep. Pete Stark (D)

CAPITOL OFFICE
225-5065
www.house.gov/stark
239 Cannon 20515-0513; fax 226-3805

COMMITTEES
Ways & Means
Joint Taxation

HOMETOWN
Fremont

BORN
Nov. 11, 1931, Milwaukee, Wis.

RELIGION
Unitarian

FAMILY
Wife, Deborah Roderick Stark; seven children

EDUCATION
Massachusetts Institute of Technology, B.S. 1953 (engineering); U. of California, Berkeley, M.B.A. 1960

MILITARY SERVICE
Air Force, 1955-57

CAREER
Banker

POLITICAL HIGHLIGHTS
Sought Democratic nomination for Calif. Senate, 1969

ELECTION RESULTS

2004 GENERAL

Pete Stark (D)	144,605	71.6%
George I. Bruno (R)	48,439	24.0%
Mark W. Stroberg (LIBERT)	8,877	4.4%

2004 PRIMARY

Pete Stark (D)	unopposed

2002 GENERAL

Pete Stark (D)	86,495	71.1%
Syed R. Mahmood (R)	26,852	22.1%
Mark W. Stroberg (LIBERT)	3,703	3.0%
Don Grundmann (AMI)	2,772	2.3%
John J. Bambey (REF)	1,901	1.6%

PREVIOUS WINNING PERCENTAGES
2000 (70%); 1998 (71%); 1996 (65%); 1994 (65%); 1992 (60%); 1990 (58%); 1988 (73%); 1986 (70%); 1984 (70%); 1982 (61%); 1980 (55%); 1978 (65%); 1976 (71%); 1974 (71%); 1972 (53%)

Elected 1972; 17th term

With a liberal's faith in the ability of government to improve the lot of the underprivileged, Stark for more than 30 years has been a leader of Democratic efforts to provide universal health coverage for all Americans. He is considered one of Congress' premier experts on health policy. He is the second-ranking Democrat on the powerful Ways and Means panel, and the top-ranking Democrat on its Health Subcommittee.

Stark has little patience with those who don't share his views, and his legislative efforts are sometimes undercut by an abrasive and confrontational personality. His sharp tongue makes even fellow Democrats squirm at times. When the party fared poorly in the 2002 congressional elections, Stark urged House Minority Leader Richard A. Gephardt and Senate Democratic leader Tom Daschle to resign. "Gephardt in particular has done a lousy job of running the [Democratic] caucus," he said. That same year, Stark opposed the measure allowing the use of force against Iraq and called President Bush "an inexperienced, desperate young man."

In keeping with his belief that the government should help people who can't help themselves, Stark wanted a broad overhaul of the prescription drug benefit provided under Medicare, the government-funded health care plan for seniors. Stark's vision of a Medicare drug benefit was derailed — Congress passed a more limited measure in late 2003 — and he wasted no time ripping apart the Republicans' product.

With other Democrats in tow, Stark tried to force the GOP and Bush administration officials to turn over White House estimates of how much the law would cost taxpayers, figures that were far higher than those of the Congressional Budget Office. An internal Department of Health and Human Services investigation found no wrongdoing, although it did conclude that some estimates related to the measure's cost were withheld from Congress. But, the report stated, such a practice did not violate any laws. Stark, however, was not dissuaded.

"It sounds as though the Bush administration examined itself and found it did nothing wrong," Stark said. Stark will no doubt push in the 109th Congress to repeal the Medicare drug benefit.

Stark is sometimes willing to hold his nose and work with Republicans. Since 1995, when the GOP gained the majority, he has helped win new preventative care benefits for Medicare beneficiaries and pushed Congress to reduce out-of-pocket costs for hospital outpatient services. And he won passage of a bill requiring medical facilities to use safer blood-drawing devices. But he failed to block more funding for Medicare HMOs, which he said were poorly managed. Billions of "incentive" payments to private insurers were included in the 2003 Medicare drug bill, payments that Stark has said will drive up the cost of the benefit for all Medicare beneficiaries.

Stark may be best known for two laws enacted in 1989 and 1993, known as "Stark I" and "Stark II." They strictly regulate physician referrals of Medicare patients to medical facilities in which the doctors have a financial interest, such as laboratories and physical therapy clinics.

On other key issues, Stark usually toes the Democratic line. He sided with his party 99 percent of the time in 2004. In early 2005, he came out against Bush's plan to allow workers born after 1949 to establish private accounts as part of their Social Security retirement benefit plan. Republicans say the private accounts are needed to address the retirement program's long-term funding shortfall.

Stark complained that the president in 2005 included in his budget proposal the $1.1 trillion cost of making his first-term tax cuts permanent, yet omitted any extra allowance for the Social Security plan. Addressing Treasury Secretary John W. Snow, Stark said, "Your plan is to cut benefits for Social Security and to cut taxes for the rich. That doesn't seem to be very fair."

On occasion, however, Stark's independent nature splits him from the party. In 2002, he was one of three lawmakers who declined to condemn a controversial court decision declaring the words "under God" in the Pledge of Allegiance unconstitutional.

In addition to health care, Stark is also interested in business issues, and he has served on both the Joint Economic and Joint Taxation committees. He has used those posts to criticize the Bush administration's economic policies every chance he can. In late 2004, for example, Stark released an analysis from Joint Economic Committee Democrats stating that income for the typical American household had fallen by more than $1,500 and that 2 million more people had lost their jobs due to the president's economic policies. "President Bush's hallmark accomplishment is having the worst jobs record of any president since Herbert Hoover," Stark said.

Stark grew up in Wisconsin and graduated from the Massachusetts Institute of Technology. After serving in the Air Force in the 1950s, he moved West and got a master's degree in business from the University of California at Berkeley. Though he chose a traditional line of work — at age 31 he had already founded two banks — he became a rabid opponent of the war in Vietnam. He even raised a huge neon peace symbol over one of his banks in suburban Walnut Creek.

In 1969, he made his first bid for public office, losing a primary race for a state legislative seat to George Miller, then a young law school student and now a House colleague. Three years later, Stark decided to take on another George Miller, this one an old-school conservative who had represented Oakland in Congress as a Democrat for 28 years.

Stark spent his money generously and made Miller's support of the Vietnam War a major issue on the way to a primary win. The November election was competitive, but Stark managed 53 percent of the vote.

Only once since then has Stark had a close call. Lulled by years of easy re-elections, he made only a token effort in the 1980 election. Conservative Republican William J. Kennedy, a tireless campaigner, galvanized a host of volunteers in the midst of Ronald Reagan's first presidential landslide and held Stark to 55 percent. He has won his last four elections with 70 percent of the vote or more.

KEY VOTES

2004

Yes Extend federal unemployment benefits by 13 weeks
+ Pass $283.2 billion, six-year federal highway and mass transit bill
No Approve $146 billion multi-year extension of previously enacted middle-class tax breaks
No Amend the Constitution to prohibit same-sex marriage
No Cut corporate taxes $137 billion over 10 years
Yes Reorganize U.S. intelligence agencies as proposed by Sept. 11 commission

2003

No Cut taxes by $330 billion through fiscal 2013
Yes Block Bush rule scaling back overtime pay for some white-collar federal workers
Yes Do not allow use of search warrants without first notifying subjects
Yes Allow importation of prescription drugs
No Create private school voucher program in Washington, D.C.
No Ban "partial birth" abortion except to save a woman's life
No Split $18.6 billion in Iraq aid into half-grant, half-loan
No Overhaul Medicare and create prescription drug benefit

CQ VOTE STUDIES

	PARTY UNITY		PRESIDENTIAL SUPPORT	
	Support	Oppose	Support	Oppose
2004	99%	1%	15%	85%
2003	98%	2%	11%	89%
2002	99%	1%	23%	77%
2001	97%	3%	19%	81%
2000	96%	4%	81%	19%

INTEREST GROUPS

	AFL-CIO	ADA	CCUS	ACU
2004	100%	90%	5%	0%
2003	100%	100%	17%	12%
2002	100%	100%	26%	0%
2001	100%	95%	26%	0%
2000	100%	95%	25%	4%

CALIFORNIA 13
East Bay — Fremont, Hayward, Alameda

Bordered by San Francisco Bay to the west, Silicon Valley to the south and Oakland to the north, the 13th is an industrially and culturally diverse suburban area. The district is dotted with many working-class communities and often is described as the less glamorous side of the bay, but its large Hispanic and Asian populations — including immigrants from India, China, Afghanistan and the Philippines — have flourished culturally. The area's blue-collar industry historically has given Democrats a solid base of support.

Fremont and Hayward are the two largest cities in the district. Hayward is home to a campus of the California State University system; Fremont's General Motors-Toyota joint auto plant employs almost 6,000. Both cities have become more oriented toward technology industries as Silicon Valley has extended its influence to the East Bay. The population of the Tri-City area — Newark, Fremont and Union City — has grown by more than 100,000 since 1980 and the region's technology industry has grown beside it. Computer manufacturers, including Hewlett-Packard and Sun

Microsystems, have offices there. San Leandro, just south of Oakland, is home to a Coca-Cola plant, as well as Otis Spunkmeyer's cookie empire and The North Face, which produces outdoor equipment.

Alameda's closed naval air station in the north is being converted into homes and recreational facilities. The island city features 100-year-old Victorian homes and hosts a museum aboard the *USS Hornet*, a World War II aircraft carrier. Oakland International Airport falls within the 13th's boundaries, although Oakland itself is located in the neighboring 9th.

MAJOR INDUSTRY
Electronics, industrial machinery, food product processing

CITIES
Fremont, 203,413; Hayward, 140,030; San Leandro, 79,452

NOTABLE
Ghirardelli Chocolate, the nation's longest continuously operating chocolate manufacturer, has headquarters in San Leandro; Fremont is home to Mission San Jose, which was founded by Father Fermin Lasuen in 1797.

Rep. Anna G. Eshoo (D)

Elected 1992; 7th term

CAPITOL OFFICE
225-8104
eshoo.house.gov
205 Cannon 20515-0514; fax 225-8890

COMMITTEES
Energy & Commerce
Select Intelligence

HOMETOWN
Atherton

BORN
Dec. 13, 1942, New Britain, Conn.

RELIGION
Roman Catholic

FAMILY
Divorced; two children

EDUCATION
Canada College, A.A. 1975 (English literature)

CAREER
State legislative aide

POLITICAL HIGHLIGHTS
Candidate for San Mateo County Community
College Board of Trustees, 1977; Democratic
National Committee, 1980-92; San Mateo County
Board of Supervisors, 1982-92 (president, 1986);
Democratic nominee for U.S. House, 1988

ELECTION RESULTS

2004 GENERAL

Anna G. Eshoo (D)	182,712	69.8%
John C. "Chris" Haugen (R)	69,564	26.6%
Brian Holtz (LIBERT)	9,588	3.7%

2004 PRIMARY

Anna G. Eshoo (D)	unopposed

2002 GENERAL

Anna G. Eshoo (D)	117,055	68.2%
Joseph H. Nixon (R)	48,346	28.2%
Andrew B. Carver (LIBERT)	6,277	3.7%

PREVIOUS WINNING PERCENTAGES
2000 (70%); 1998 (69%); 1996 (65%); 1994 (61%);
1992 (57%)

The daughter of immigrants who instilled in her a deep appreciation of the privileges of life in the United States, Eshoo has a talent for building relationships and bridging differences that has paid off over a House career now in its second decade.

One of her closest friends is Democratic leader Nancy Pelosi, a fellow Northern Californian whose career path in many ways resembles her own. Eshoo and Pelosi met more than 30 years ago, as homemakers and civic activists. Their shared passion for politics still spices their occasional late-night dinners together in Georgetown.

In the 108th Congress, Pelosi named Eshoo to the Intelligence Committee, and her fellow Democrats elected her as a member of the vote-getting whip team. Eshoo (EH-shoo) also holds a coveted seat on the Energy and Commerce Committee, where she works to build consensus on technology matters important to her Silicon Valley constituents. More than 80 percent of political contributions to Eshoo's war chest routinely come from business interests, according to the Center for Responsive Politics.

Eshoo's childhood prepared her for a life of public service, although she did not take that route until she was well into her 30s. Her parents were immigrants from Armenia and modern-day Iran. "In our prayers at dinner, we thanked God for the food and also thanked God for this country," says the devout Catholic. "My parents very much shaped a sense of obligation to give and to do." She passed on that sense of duty to her own two children. Her son Paul is a teacher in Laos and daughter Karen is a principal at a Catholic school. Eshoo began her work as a civic activist when her children were young, and moved into electoral politics as they grew older.

Now in her seventh term, Eshoo is a New Democrat — liberal on most issues but a firm believer in business development and risk-taking entrepreneurship. She is known for mastery of details on technology issues. She championed a law to allow the use of "electronic signatures" to seal some contracts and now touts it as a key achievement. As co-chairwoman of the House Medical Technology Caucus, Eshoo promotes biotechnology companies that are an integral part of her district's economy. She is likely to play a leading role as Congress seeks to spur a shift to electronic medical records.

Eshoo helped the high-tech industry adjust its legislative priorities after the Sept. 11, 2001, terrorist attacks to fit growing concerns about national security and privacy. She backed efforts to limit the sharing among federal agencies of information collected from borrowers, farmers and taxpayers. But she advocated looser export rules for computer hardware and encryption software, arguing that overseas buyers could get similar products from foreign manufacturers.

In the 108th Congress, Eshoo championed a bipartisan effort to block a proposed rule by the Financial Accounting Standards Board requiring employee stock options to be treated as an expense and deducted from from earnings, which would slam the bottom line of many technology companies that distribute options liberally. The bill died in the Senate, but a renewed effort loomed in the 109th.

Eshoo's pro-business stands have at times put her at odds with her party leaders. In 1995, she helped override President Clinton's veto of a measure to limit lawsuits by disgruntled investors — one of only two laws enacted over Clinton's veto. On broader legislation to limit class action lawsuits, Eshoo — after voting no in 1999 with the majority of her fellow Democrats — did not vote when the House again passed the bill in 2002, 2003 and finally, 2005.

On trade, Eshoo says that the economic downturn of 2001 influenced her decision to vote against a bill in the 107th Congress to renew the president's fast-track authority to negotiate trade agreements that Congress cannot amend. She had voted for a similar bill in 1997, for the North American Free Trade Agreement in 1993, for the creation of the World Trade Organization the next year and for permanent normal trade relations with China in 2000.

Eshoo is a reliable liberal on social issues. She favors gun control and supports abortion rights. But she and other Catholic Democrats spearheaded efforts during the 108th Congress to reach out to church leaders who fiercely oppose abortion. As some Catholic leaders declared that Democratic presidential candidate John Kerry should be denied communion because of his support for abortion rights, Eshoo and others sought to broker a truce, with partial success. In 2005, Eshoo and fellow California Democrat Ellen O. Tauscher sent a letter to the Democratic National Committee endorsing former Rep. Tim Roemer of Indiana, an abortion opponent, to be the next Democratic party chairman.

Eshoo was first drawn to Democratic politics in her native New Britain, Conn. Her father, a jeweler and watchmaker, took the family to political rallies and hung portraits of Franklin D. Roosevelt and Harry S Truman in their home. One day, as she walked home from grade school, a man in a big car drove by with a police escort, stopped and offered her a ride. Eshoo accepted the lift — from President Truman. As a high school senior, she organized more than 800 students to work for John F. Kennedy. "Back then, I really thought that I was the one who put him over the top."

The family moved to California. Eshoo married young and devoted herself to motherhood. She was active in civic groups, earned a two-year associate degree in English literature, and then, at 34, lost a bid for the local community college board of trustees.

Eshoo got an internship with Leo McCarthy, speaker of the California Assembly, and eventually became his chief of staff. Active in local party politics, she won appointment to the Democratic National Committee. In 1982, McCarthy urged her to run for the San Mateo County Board of Supervisors. That post, which she held for a decade, shaped her pragmatic philosophy.

In 1988, Eshoo ran unsuccessfully for the House against Republican Tom Campbell, taking a solid 46 percent of the vote. Four years later, in 1992, she won, boosted by Campbell's absence as he ran for the Senate and by a redrawn district map that added more Democratic voters. She has won by comfortable margins since then.

KEY VOTES

2004
Yes Extend federal unemployment benefits by 13 weeks
Yes Pass $283.2 billion, six-year federal highway and mass transit bill
Yes Approve $146 billion multi-year extension of previously enacted middle-class tax breaks
No Amend the Constitution to prohibit same-sex marriage
No Cut corporate taxes $137 billion over 10 years
Yes Reorganize U.S. intelligence agencies as proposed by Sept. 11 commission

2003
No Cut taxes by $330 billion through fiscal 2013
Yes Block Bush rule scaling back overtime pay for some white-collar federal workers
Yes Do not allow use of search warrants without first notifying subjects
No Allow importation of prescription drugs
No Create private school voucher program in Washington, D.C.
- Ban "partial birth" abortion except to save a woman's life
Yes Split $18.6 billion in Iraq aid into half-grant, half-loan
No Overhaul Medicare and create prescription drug benefit

CQ VOTE STUDIES

	PARTY UNITY		PRESIDENTIAL SUPPORT	
	Support	Oppose	Support	Oppose
2004	94%	6%	35%	65%
2003	96%	4%	20%	80%
2002	95%	5%	24%	76%
2001	90%	10%	33%	67%
2000	89%	11%	82%	18%

INTEREST GROUPS

	AFL-CIO	ADA	CCUS	ACU
2004	93%	100%	38%	12%
2003	85%	90%	24%	13%
2002	100%	100%	42%	0%
2001	100%	95%	39%	0%
2000	70%	75%	55%	8%

CALIFORNIA 14

Southern San Mateo and northwestern Santa Clara counties; most of Santa Cruz County

The 14th's economic center is Palo Alto, home to Stanford University and technology giants such as Hewlett-Packard. This Silicon Valley stronghold known for innovation has undergone tremendous economic growth since the 1980s. The orchards surrounding Stanford have given way to some of the nation's most expensive housing, even after the technology bubble burst. According to the 2000 census, the median home value in the district was $626,500 — by far the highest in the state.

The district borders the bay and the Pacific, creeping north toward the San Francisco suburbs and south into Santa Cruz County, almost to the Monterey County line. Most residents live in cities along the bay between San Francisco and San Jose, including Sunnyvale, Mountain View and Redwood City. Labor from large numbers of Asians and Hispanics aided the technology boom. Soaring housing prices, though stable in the past few years, and traffic snarls were the major results.

The 14th's innovation-minded voters are liberal on many social issues but prefer a laissez faire government that does not impede change. Environmental consciousness is high, particularly in Santa Cruz County. Conservative pockets do exist in wealthy areas such as Saratoga and Monte Sereno in Santa Clara County, but Democrats hold a 17 percentage point edge in voter registration and the district gave John Kerry 68 percent of the vote in the 2004 presidential election.

MAJOR INDUSTRY
Computers, biotechnology, defense, agriculture

MILITARY BASES
Onizuka Air Force Station, 100 military, 1,400 civilian (2004)

CITIES
Sunnyvale, 131,760; Mountain View, 70,708; Palo Alto, 58,598; Redwood City (pt.), 52,873

NOTABLE
A water tower painted as a Libby's fruit cocktail can stands where the cannery operated in Sunnyvale; Hangar One at Moffett Federal Airfield, now a NASA research station, housed a blimp for the Navy; Hewlett-Packard was founded in 1939 in a Palo Alto garage, which is now a tourist attraction; Half Moon Bay holds an annual pumpkin festival.

Rep. Michael M. Honda (D)

Elected 2000; 3rd term

CAPITOL OFFICE
225-2631
www.honda.house.gov
1713 Longworth 20515-0515; fax 225-2699

COMMITTEES
Science
Transportation & Infrastructure

HOMETOWN
San Jose

BORN
June 27, 1941, Stockton, Calif.

RELIGION
Protestant

FAMILY
Widowed; two children

EDUCATION
San Jose State U., B.S. 1969 (biological sciences),
B.A. 1970 (Spanish), M.A. 1973 (education)

CAREER
Teacher; principal; Peace Corps volunteer

POLITICAL HIGHLIGHTS
San Jose School Board, 1981-90; Santa Clara
County Board of Supervisors, 1990-96; Calif.
Assembly, 1996-2000

ELECTION RESULTS

2004 GENERAL

Michael M. Honda (D)	154,385	72.0%
Raymond L. Chukwu (R)	59,953	28.0%

2004 PRIMARY

Michael M. Honda (D)	unopposed

2002 GENERAL

Michael M. Honda (D)	87,482	65.8%
Linda Rae Hermann (R)	41,251	31.0%
Jeff Landauer (LIBERT)	4,289	3.2%

PREVIOUS WINNING PERCENTAGES
2000 (54%)

Born to Nisei farm workers in what is now called Silicon Valley, Honda was just a few months old when the Japanese launched a surprise attack on Pearl Harbor. He and his family were shipped off to an internment camp in Colorado, where they spent about two and a half years before they were able to move to Chicago when his father joined Navy intelligence.

Sixty years later, when terrorists carried out the Sept. 11, 2001, attacks against the United States, Honda was one of the most outspoken members of the House in working to ensure that other Americans were not treated like his family in 1941 only because "we looked like the enemy."

Honda wrote President Bush expressing concern about "government-sanctioned racial profiling." And he joined with fellow California Democrat Robert T. Matsui, whose family was also interned during World War II, in speaking out against reports of harassment and attacks on Arab-Americans, Muslims and members of other ethnic groups.

The age of terrorism has given new relevance to Honda's experience. He was quick to condemn remarks made in 2003 by North Carolina Republican Howard Coble, who said during a radio show that he agreed with President Roosevelt's decision to incarcerate Japanese-Americans. "We were at war. ... For many of the Japanese-Americans, it wasn't safe for them to be on the street. Some probably were intent on doing harm to us, just as some of the Arab-Americans are probably intent on doing harm to us," Coble said.

Honda said he was "outraged" that the GOP leadership made no move after Coble's remarks to persuade him to step down as chairman of the House subcommittee overseeing homeland security. "Since Sept. 11, there have been many, many civil liberties eroded away," he told the Los Angeles Times. "When you set aside the Constitution, bad things happen."

In early 2005, Honda was elected one of five vice chairmen of the Democratic National Committee. Howard Dean, the former Vermont governor and new head of the DNC, says he wants to build on the historic turnout of Asian-Americans voting for Democrats in the 2004 elections.

Representing a district with a healthy slice of California's Silicon Valley, Honda's congressional agenda is centered on the high-technology industry. He favors the repeal of export controls on high-performance computers and permanent renewal of the research and development tax credit.

In the 108th Congress, he introduced a bill calling for a beefed-up federal effort in nanotechnology research, the manipulation of matter at the level of a single atom. The measure, cosponsored with Science Committee Chairman Sherwood Boehlert of New York, passed the House in 2003. The two men say nanotechnology will spur profound technological advances over the next two decades. Honda talks of creating computers with humanlike intelligence, satellites the size of marbles, and smart medicines that hunt and destroy individual cancer cells. Honda is the top-ranking Democrat on the Science panel's Energy Subcommittee in the 109th Congress.

Although Honda is willing to work with Republicans, he took issue with Bush's economic views when the president visited the 15th District in 2003. Bush came to congratulate the employees of United Defense Inc., who designed and built the Hercules fighting vehicles being used in Iraq. The president used the opportunity to call on Congress to approve his proposed $550 billion tax cut, arguing it would stimulate the economy and help the unemployed in Silicon Valley.

Both Honda and neighboring Democrat Zoe Lofgren turned down an offer to join Bush at the defense plant. "Ever since President Bush has been in office, we have not had a balanced budget," Honda said later.

Honda also wants to find regional solutions and federal funding to deal with the downside of his district's economic boom, including traffic congestion and high housing costs. He has used his seat on the Transportation and Infrastructure Committee to press for federal funds for the mass transit system there.

Honda remembers little of his internment. He was too young, and he said his parents were reluctant to talk about it afterward. But he was a key participant in the Japanese-American community's effort that resulted in the 1988 law providing a formal apology and compensation to Japanese-Americans who were interned during World War II. That effort inspired Honda, once he reached Congress, to work for reparations for Americans who were prisoners of the Japanese during the war.

Honda said his parents were always civic-minded despite their internment experience. The family moved back to California in 1953, and his parents became strawberry sharecroppers. Honda took janitorial and delivery jobs to pay his way through San Jose State University. He was one credit shy of graduation when he joined a new overseas volunteer effort, called the Peace Corps. After a two-year stint in El Salvador, where he built schools and medical clinics, he returned to California to finish college. He took a job as a science teacher and later served as a principal.

Fluent in Spanish from his years in El Salvador, Honda developed strong ties to San Jose's Hispanic community. He went to Norman Y. Mineta, then a city councilman, to volunteer his services to the city. When Mineta was elected mayor, Honda received an appointment to the city planning commission. Mineta, who went on to serve in Congress and as a member of the Cabinet in both the Clinton and George W. Bush administrations, has remained Honda's friend and mentor.

Honda's 1971 appointment to the planning commission led to elected posts at the local school board, the county board of supervisors, and in 1996, election to the California Assembly. When moderate Republican Rep. Tom Campbell left the 15th District open in 2000 to run for the Senate, Democrats viewed it as a prime opportunity. Honda entered the race after a phone call from President Clinton convinced him that the national party would back his bid. He won the election by 12 percentage points.

Bolstered by redistricting and his ties to the Asian and Hispanic communities in a district where almost half the residents are from those constituencies, Honda has cruised to re-election since.

KEY VOTES

2004
Yes Extend federal unemployment benefits by 13 weeks
Yes Pass $283.2 billion, six-year federal highway and mass transit bill
Yes Approve $146 billion multi-year extension of previously enacted middle-class tax breaks
No Amend the Constitution to prohibit same-sex marriage
No Cut corporate taxes $137 billion over 10 years
Yes Reorganize U.S. intelligence agencies as proposed by Sept. 11 commission

2003
No Cut taxes by $330 billion through fiscal 2013
Yes Block Bush rule scaling back overtime pay for some white-collar federal workers
Yes Do not allow use of search warrants without first notifying subjects
No Allow importation of prescription drugs
No Create private school voucher program in Washington, D.C.
No Ban "partial birth" abortion except to save a woman's life
Yes Split $18.6 billion in Iraq aid into half-grant, half-loan
No Overhaul Medicare and create prescription drug benefit

CQ VOTE STUDIES

	PARTY UNITY		PRESIDENTIAL SUPPORT	
	Support	Oppose	Support	Oppose
2004	97%	3%	23%	77%
2003	97%	3%	17%	83%
2002	99%	1%	21%	79%
2001	95%	5%	24%	76%

INTEREST GROUPS

	AFL-CIO	ADA	CCUS	ACU
2004	93%	95%	39%	10%
2003	100%	95%	20%	12%
2002	100%	95%	30%	0%
2001	100%	95%	39%	0%

CALIFORNIA 15
Santa Clara County — part of San Jose

Home to one-third of San Jose's residents, the 15th touches the southern end of San Francisco Bay in the north, then descends inland through Silicon Valley to still-rural but fast-growing farm towns.

The district has a diverse population that includes the nation's second-heaviest concentration of Asian-Americans. Slightly less than 30 percent of residents are Asian, the highest percentage in any California district. Vietnamese, Chinese and Filipino Americans have flocked to the north to take white- and blue-collar jobs, while Hispanics, 17 percent of the 15th's population, make up a big part of the labor force in the south. Immigration is the top issue caseworkers face.

West of San Jose, the district includes Santa Clara, a Spanish mission in the late 1700s, and other more affluent suburbs including Campbell, Cupertino and Los Gatos. These areas house technology companies that boomed in the 1990s but have suffered higher unemployment since the tech bubble burst. Despite this, the economy remains technology-based, and Sun Microsystems is based in Santa Clara. Housing — stable but

still quite expensive — and transit troubles plague the area.

To the south, Gilroy's famous garlic farms anchor a more traditionally Democratic agricultural community. But open land is quickly being snatched up as the San Jose suburbs continue to bulge southward.

The district gave 63 percent of its vote to Democrat John Kerry in the 2004 presidential election, although if any political trend is apparent here it is an increase in independent voters who seek moderation. Generally liberal on environmental and social issues, voters also favor less government regulation of business.

MAJOR INDUSTRY
Computers, biotechnology, health care, agriculture

CITIES
San Jose (pt.), 295,018; Santa Clara, 102,361; Milpitas, 62,698

NOTABLE
Santa Clara University, founded in 1851, is California's oldest institution of higher learning; Winchester Mystery House in San Jose is a 160-room Victorian mansion famous for oddities such as staircases that lead nowhere; Apple Computer was founded in Cupertino; Gilroy is known as the "Garlic Capital of the World."

Rep. Zoe Lofgren (D)

Elected 1994; 6th term

CAPITOL OFFICE
225-3072
www.house.gov/lofgren
102 Cannon 20515-0516; fax 225-3336

COMMITTEES
Homeland Security
House Administration
Judiciary
Joint Library

HOMETOWN
San Jose

BORN
Dec. 21, 1947, San Mateo, Calif.

RELIGION
Lutheran

FAMILY
Husband, John Marshall Collins; two children

EDUCATION
Stanford U., A.B. 1970 (political science); U. of Santa Clara, J.D. 1975

CAREER
Lawyer; nonprofit housing development director; professor; congressional aide

POLITICAL HIGHLIGHTS
San Jose-Evergreen Community College District Board of Trustees, 1979-81; Santa Clara County Board of Supervisors, 1981-95

ELECTION RESULTS

2004 GENERAL

Zoe Lofgren (D)	129,222	70.9%
Douglas Adams McNea (R)	47,992	26.3%
Markus Welch (LIBERT)	5,067	2.8%

2004 PRIMARY

Zoe Lofgren (D)	unopposed

2002 GENERAL

Zoe Lofgren (D)	72,370	67.0%
Douglas Adams McNea (R)	32,182	29.8%
Dennis M. Umphress (LIBERT)	3,434	3.2%

PREVIOUS WINNING PERCENTAGES
2000 (72%); 1998 (73%); 1996 (66%); 1994 (65%)

Lofgren's legislative agenda reflects traditional Democratic social views with support for e-commerce and the business of high technology. And she is not reluctant to vote with the GOP majority on issues that help her district's technology-driven economy.

San Jose is the capital of Silicon Valley and many of Lofgren's constituents have high-tech jobs. Lofgren (first name: ZO) does not pretend to be an expert in computer technology — she was a political science major in college — but she says that representing a high-tech district requires elected officials to be knowledgeable about the industry.

On social issues, Lofgren will not shy away from a fight with Republicans. In 2004, she sought, unsuccessfully, to stop House approval of a GOP-backed measure to give distinct legal status to fetuses and embryos. The bill established a separate offense for committing a federal crime against a pregnant woman that harms the fetus she is carrying. Lofgren's proposal, offered as the Democratic alternative, would have created additional penalties for federal crimes against pregnant women without conferring a separate legal status on a fetus.

Lofgren and other opponents said the goal of the bill was to reclassify a fetus as a human, with the ultimate aim of undermining *Roe v. Wade*, the 1973 Supreme Court ruling that legalized abortion. "The real rationale behind this bill is not to protect pregnant women," said Lofgren. "It is to define a zygote . . . as a person under law."

At times, Lofgren has expressed frustration with Republican leaders, who, she says, often push bills more for show than for substance. In 2003, the Judiciary Committee, on which she has a seat, backed a measure urging the Bush administration to appeal a court ruling that held the Pledge of Allegiance unconstitutional in public schools. The move was a response to the 9th U.S. Circuit Court of Appeals ruling in 2002 that the pledge unconstitutionally endorses religion because it contains the phrase "one nation, under God." Both chambers had already voted for resolutions reaffirming their support for the Pledge of Allegiance in 2002. "Why we're spending time on this preposterous exercise is beyond me," said Lofgren, who voted present.

Immigration law was Lofgren's specialty as a lawyer early in her career, and she served on the Democrats' immigration task force in the 107th Congress. She criticized the Immigration and Naturalization Service's handling of requests for citizenship, calling it "dismal," and sought improvements in the treatment of unaccompanied children applying for asylum.

Yet her views on social issues do not prevent Lofgren from working in a more quiet way to influence the content of bills that Republicans are advancing. Lofgren has been a longtime proponent of more federal support for scientific research and development. She argues that increased funding for agencies such as the National Science Foundation is crucial in a time of growing concern over the movement of jobs overseas and the migration of U.S. students away from the fields of science and engineering. She says the nation has to invest now in basic scientific research because it takes decades for such research to mature into commercial applications.

The technology industry was particularly hard hit by big declines in stock prices in 2001. Lofgren supported House passage of a measure in 2004 to allow companies to offer stock options to employees without recording them as an expense and thus reducing reported profits for many companies.

Lofgren has a seat on the Homeland Security Committee, where she is the top-ranking Democrat on the Intelligence Subcommittee. She proposed a constitutional amendment in 2004 when the House debated the proper mechanism for ensuring the continuity of Congress after a major terrorist strike. Lofgren's proposal would have allowed for the appointment, rather than the election, of congressional replacements. But the House instead passed legislation to accelerate the existing process by setting a 45-day time limit for special elections to fill House seats whenever more than 100 seats were declared vacant by the Speaker.

Lofgren grew up in a blue-collar neighborhood in south Palo Alto. Her father was a truck driver and her mother was a secretary and later a school cafeteria cook. "I didn't meet a Republican until I went to junior high school," she says. While other mothers went door-to-door collecting money for the March of Dimes, Lofgren's mother went after "dollars for Democrats." Lofgren would spend long hours talking politics with her Swedish immigrant grandfather, and she recalls that, instead of dating or going to dances, she and her friends went to political rallies.

Lofgren went to Stanford University on a scholarship and then headed to Washington, D.C., landing an internship with Democratic Rep. Don Edwards. Convinced that she needed to go to law school when the House's legislative counsel "ripped to shreds — and for good reason" a draft of a bill she had written, she returned to California and got a law degree.

She served as the first executive director of San Jose's Community Housing Developers, a nonprofit organization involved in creating low-income housing. In 1979, a colleague urged her to run for the local community college board of trustees. She did and won. A year later, she was elected to the Santa Clara County Board of Supervisors, where she served 14 years. She was often in conflict with San Jose's Democratic mayor, Tom McEnery, who pushed downtown redevelopment. Lofgren argued that the money would have been better spent on education and human services.

When Edwards retired after 32 years, the 1994 Democratic primary saw a face-off between Lofgren and McEnery, who was no longer mayor. She benefited from an uproar that ensued when state election officials barred her from describing herself as "county supervisor/mother" on the ballot. The flap drew national attention to Lofgren's candidacy, and she went on to upset McEnery. She won handily that November and has coasted to re-election since, winning with 71 percent of the vote in 2004.

KEY VOTES

2004

Yes   Extend federal unemployment benefits by 13 weeks

Yes   Pass $283.2 billion, six-year federal highway and mass transit bill

Yes   Approve $146 billion multi-year extension of previously enacted middle-class tax breaks

No   Amend the Constitution to prohibit same-sex marriage

No   Cut corporate taxes $137 billion over 10 years

Yes   Reorganize U.S. intelligence agencies as proposed by Sept. 11 commission

2003

No   Cut taxes by $330 billion through fiscal 2013

Yes   Block Bush rule scaling back overtime pay for some white-collar federal workers

Yes   Do not allow use of search warrants without first notifying subjects

No   Allow importation of prescription drugs

?   Create private school voucher program in Washington, D.C.

No   Ban "partial birth" abortion except to save a woman's life

Yes   Split $18.6 billion in Iraq aid into half-grant, half-loan

No   Overhaul Medicare and create prescription drug benefit

CQ VOTE STUDIES

	PARTY UNITY		PRESIDENTIAL SUPPORT	
	Support	Oppose	Support	Oppose
2004	94%	6%	30%	70%
2003	96%	4%	20%	80%
2002	94%	6%	15%	85%
2001	87%	13%	30%	70%
2000	90%	10%	82%	18%

INTEREST GROUPS

	AFL-CIO	ADA	CCUS	ACU
2004	93%	95%	33%	12%
2003	87%	85%	26%	17%
2002	100%	100%	26%	0%
2001	100%	90%	35%	0%
2000	80%	85%	52%	4%

CALIFORNIA 16
Most of San Jose

The technology boom of the 1990s propelled San Jose out of San Francisco's shadow and earned it a reputation as "the capital of Silicon Valley." A metropolitan area unto itself, San Jose is home to the Bay Area's NBC affiliate and a professional hockey franchise.

San Jose is the only city in the 16th and the third-largest city in California. Two-thirds of the city falls within the 16th, and 92 percent of the district's residents live here.

Silicon Valley's tremendous growth has rubbed off on the city, creating a white-collar workforce and helping to establish it as a leading exporter of high-tech goods. An economic downturn sent unemployment soaring past 8 percent, but it was back around 5 percent by the end of 2004. Housing prices have remained high, and the county has the area's highest median income and highest rate of charitable giving.

The 16th is one of the most ethnically diverse districts in the Bay Area. Its Asian population includes the nation's second-largest Vietnamese

community, but Hispanics represent the district's largest group at 38 percent. Whites make up 32 percent of the population.

Redistricting after the 2000 census concentrated the 16th more around San Jose, removing hilly areas east of the city and southern areas including Morgan Hill (now in the 11th) and Gilroy (now in the 15th).

The 16th has been solidly Democratic for many years, and an influx of Hispanics has helped continue that trend. White-collar workers are becoming more common and could begin to shift the district's politics to the right, but John Kerry commanded 63 percent of the district's vote in the 2004 presidential election, slightly more than Al Gore in 2000.

MAJOR INDUSTRY
Technology, health care, finance

CITIES
San Jose (pt.), 590,306; Alum Rock (unincorporated), 13,479

NOTABLE
San Jose served as the state capital for a short time after California's annexation by the United States; Norman Y. Mineta San Jose International Airport is named for former Rep. and Transportation Secretary Mineta.

Rep. Sam Farr (D)

CAPITOL OFFICE
225-2861
www.farr.house.gov
1221 Longworth 20515-0517; fax 225-6791

COMMITTEES
Appropriations

HOMETOWN
Carmel

BORN
July 4, 1941, San Francisco, Calif.

RELIGION
Episcopalian

FAMILY
Wife, Shary Baldwin Farr; one child

EDUCATION
Willamette U., B.S. 1963 (biology)

CAREER
State legislative aide; Peace Corps volunteer

POLITICAL HIGHLIGHTS
Monterey County Board of Supervisors, 1975-80;
Calif. Assembly, 1980-93

ELECTION RESULTS

2004 GENERAL

Sam Farr (D)	148,958	66.7%
Mark Risley (R)	65,117	29.2%
Ray Glock-Grueneich (GREEN)	3,645	1.6%
Joe Williams (PF)	2,823	1.3%
Jim Smolen (LIBERT)	2,607	1.2%

2004 PRIMARY

Sam Farr (D)	65,809	91.1%
Art Dunn (D)	6,401	8.9%

2002 GENERAL

Sam Farr (D)	101,632	68.1%
Clint Engler (R)	40,334	27.0%
Ray Glock-Grueneich (GREEN)	4,885	3.3%
Jascha Lee (LIBERT)	2,418	1.6%

PREVIOUS WINNING PERCENTAGES
2000 (69%); 1998 (65%); 1996 (59%); 1994 (52%);
1993 Special Runoff Election (54%)

Elected June 1993; 6th full term

Farr's father was a longtime California state legislator who played a key role in Lady Bird Johnson's highway beautification effort. Now, the younger Farr is focused on efforts to save the world's oceans and protect the natural beauty of his Central Coast territory.

He has two principal passions in representing the 17th District: careful stewardship of the region's natural resources and advocacy for the military facilities in his district. While pro-military and pro-environment positions might seem a contradictory mix for a liberal Democrat, Farr does not see it that way. "The military has been very good stewards of their land out there," Farr says.

His district is not a big producer of military hardware, but rather hosts a collection of personnel-oriented facilities, allowing Farr to advocate for his military constituency while focusing on traditional Democratic issues such as education and housing. The bases found in Monterey County include the Defense Language Institute Foreign Language Center and the Naval Postgraduate School, which is a center for computer research in such areas as war games and intelligence gathering.

The 17th was dealt a blow in 1994 when Fort Ord was ordered closed. Farr has worked to ease the base's transition to civilian use, helping secure $51 million to open the Monterey Bay campus of California State University there. The base also houses a Defense Department Finance Center, a veterans' clinic and an environmental research center for the University of California at Santa Cruz.

Farr sits on the Appropriations Subcommittee on Military Quality of Life, where he works hard to direct federal funds to his district's military installations. The military construction spending bill passed by the House in 2004 included Farr's language requiring that 250 new affordable homes on Fort Ord land be sold or rented below market rate. "The housing crisis in our area is undeniable, and in order to have a strong and diverse local workforce, we need to have housing for them to live in," Farr said.

A biology major in college, Farr is eager to preserve the natural beauty of his district, which boasts rich soil, bountiful fisheries and some of the most beautiful vistas in the world. In 2002, Farr's bill to protect 55,000 acres near the Big Sur coast won approval.

As a member of the Resources Committee in the late 1990s, Farr was outspoken on ways to protect the world's oceans. He urged Congress and the Clinton administration to initiate a comprehensive review of the nation's policies on maritime and coastal matters. That wish became reality with the creation in 2000 of the U.S. Commission on Ocean Policy, a 16-member bipartisan body. The commission released its final report in September 2004 calling, among other things, for a stronger ocean agency that uses an ecosystem-based approach to better protect oceans and coasts.

A co-chairman of the Oceans Caucus, Farr has introduced a series of measures to help implement the commission's recommendations. One bill would set a clear national policy on saving the oceans and endow federal institutions with the power to implement it, focusing specifically on oceanic ecosystems.

Farr and Illinois Democratic Sen. Richard J. Durbin proposed a measure in 2004 to limit the damage done to the ocean by cruise ship pollution by creating a 12 mile-wide coastal zone in which cruise ships are prohibited from dumping. "Every week a typical 3,000 passenger cruise ship generates over a million gallons of raw sewage, gray water and oily bilge water, and at the moment it is legal for them to dump this waste almost anywhere in the ocean," Farr said when announcing the bill.

Moving inland, Farr fought in the 108th Congress to establish a new national park along California's Central Coast. Farr wanted Fort Hunter Liggett in Monterey County to qualify as a national park, but the Bush administration decided the fort and its land was still needed for Army training. The Army base — which is six times the size of the city of San Francisco — was once part of the estate of newspaper magnate William Randolph Hearst.

Across the spectrum of issues, Farr is a dependable vote for the Democratic leadership. Normally, confrontation is not a significant part of his style. He prefers to work unobtrusively, yet he can sometimes have a sharp tongue for GOP policies.

During an Appropriations Committee debate in 2003 over a supplemental spending bill for the Iraq war, some House Republicans wanted to retaliate against those countries who opposed the U.S. involvement in Iraq. Farr protested an amendment that sought to block any funds in the bill for reconstruction of postwar Iraq from going to companies located in countries that publicly opposed the United Nations Iraq resolution put forward by U.S. allies. The amendment was targeted at companies in China, Russia, Germany, France and Syria. "The way we're headed, we're not going to have any friends [in the world] tomorrow," he said.

Farr, who was born on July 4th, is proud of his work on the 1996 immigration law to encourage mass naturalization ceremonies around the country on that date. He has made a habit of participating in one of the ceremonies on his birthday each year.

After spending what he calls two "character-forming" years with the Peace Corps in Colombia following his graduation from college, Farr returned home and went to work as a staff member in the California Assembly. He later won election to the Monterey County Board of Supervisors. After five years there, he was elected to the state legislature and served the next 12 ½ years in Sacramento.

In 1993, he won a House special election to replace Democratic Rep. Leon E. Panetta, who had become President Clinton's White House budget director. Farr prevailed by 9 percentage points over Pebble Beach lawyer Republican Bill McCampbell. Farr was a strong candidate in a district already heavily Democratic. After winning a 1994 rematch by 8 percentage points, Farr has won subsequent elections by wide margins.

KEY VOTES

2004
Yes Extend federal unemployment benefits by 13 weeks
Yes Pass $283.2 billion, six-year federal highway and mass transit bill
Yes Approve $146 billion multi-year extension of previously enacted middle-class tax breaks
No Amend the Constitution to prohibit same-sex marriage
No Cut corporate taxes $137 billion over 10 years
Yes Reorganize U.S. intelligence agencies as proposed by Sept. 11 commission

2003
No Cut taxes by $330 billion through fiscal 2013
Yes Block Bush rule scaling back overtime pay for some white-collar federal workers
Yes Do not allow use of search warrants without first notifying subjects
No Allow importation of prescription drugs
No Create private school voucher program in Washington, D.C.
No Ban "partial birth" abortion except to save a woman's life
Yes Split $18.6 billion in Iraq aid into half-grant, half-loan
No Overhaul Medicare and create prescription drug benefit

CQ VOTE STUDIES

	PARTY UNITY		PRESIDENTIAL SUPPORT	
	Support	Oppose	Support	Oppose
2004	96%	4%	24%	76%
2003	98%	2%	15%	85%
2002	99%	1%	25%	75%
2001	96%	4%	24%	76%
2000	95%	5%	82%	18%

INTEREST GROUPS

	AFL-CIO	ADA	CCUS	ACU
2004	93%	100%	43%	4%
2003	100%	95%	23%	20%
2002	100%	95%	35%	0%
2001	100%	95%	43%	0%
2000	90%	95%	45%	8%

CALIFORNIA 17

Monterey, San Benito and Santa Cruz counties — Salinas, Santa Cruz

The strongly Democratic 17th includes the most populated part of upscale Santa Cruz County, with its namesake city and several sizable seaside communities. Farther south, in Monterey County, Monterey attracts tourists, and exclusive Pebble Beach is home to celebrities and Silicon Valley executives.

South of Santa Cruz County, agriculture drives the economy. Major wineries and vineyards also dot the landscape. Salinas, the seat of Monterey County and the district's largest city, is known as the nation's "salad bowl" for its fresh vegetables. The district's 43 percent Hispanic population is concentrated in the Salinas Valley, where Hispanics are beginning to win local offices. More than 60 percent of district residents live in Monterey County.

Residents in the 17th expected to suffer economically when they lost Fort Ord in 1994. But California State University Monterey Bay developed a portion of the site and continues to expand. The resulting influx of students and related jobs has helped replace the lost 17,000 military jobs. The region also has developed as a center for marine sciences, with more than a dozen major research institutions located around the Monterey Bay coastline.

Santa Cruz County is a Democratic stronghold, and the party holds a 2-to-1 voter registration edge in Monterey and San Benito counties.

MAJOR INDUSTRY
Agriculture, tourism, higher education

MILITARY BASES
Defense Language Institute Foreign Language Center/Presidio of Monterey (Army), 3,696 military, 1,634 civilian (2005); Naval Postgraduate School, 1,500 military, 1,307 civilian; Fort Hunter Liggett (Army), 1,135 military, 535 civilian (2004); Fleet Numerical Meteorology and Oceanography Center, 80 military, 135 civilian (2005)

CITIES
Salinas, 151,060; Santa Cruz, 54,593; Watsonville, 44,265; Hollister, 34,413

NOTABLE
Clint Eastwood was mayor of Carmel-by-the-Sea; The Monterey Bay National Marine Sanctuary is the nation's largest marine sanctuary.

Rep. Dennis Cardoza (D)

Elected 2002; 2nd term

CAPITOL OFFICE
225-6131
www.house.gov/cardoza
435 Cannon 20515-0518; fax 225-0819

COMMITTEES
Agriculture
International Relations
Resources

HOMETOWN
Atwater

BORN
March 31, 1959, Merced, Calif.

RELIGION
Roman Catholic

FAMILY
Wife, Kathleen McLoughlin; three children

EDUCATION
U. of Maryland, B.A. 1982 (government & politics)

CAREER
Bowling alley executive; realtor; congressional
aide; state legislative aide

POLITICAL HIGHLIGHTS
Atwater City Council, 1984-87; Merced City
Council, 1994-95; Calif. Assembly, 1996-2002

ELECTION RESULTS

2004 GENERAL

Dennis Cardoza (D)	103,732	67.5%
Charles F. Pringle Sr. (R)	49,973	32.5%

2004 PRIMARY

Dennis Cardoza (D)	unopposed

2002 GENERAL

Dennis Cardoza (D)	56,181	51.3%
Dick Monteith (R)	47,528	43.4%
Kevin H. Cripe (AMI)	3,641	3.3%
Linda M. DeGroat (LIBERT)	2,194	2.0%

Defying the stereotype of a California Democrat, Cardoza describes himself as "a raging moderate." A policy wonk, he hates campaigning but loves legislating.

For his agriculture-based, culturally conservative district in central California, he seems just the antidote to his predecessor, Democrat Gary A. Condit, a once popular incumbent who lost the seat to Cardoza in 2002 after admitting he'd had a secret affair with a young Washington intern. However, politically Cardoza is not all that different from his former friend and mentor. He is most at home with the "Blue Dogs," a coalition of House Democratic moderates founded in part by Condit, who often disagree with the party's liberal leadership in the House.

Cardoza frequently sides with Republicans on energy and environmental issues, and his votes on budget bills are driven by his distaste for federal deficits. He voted against President Bush's tax cut bill in 2003, though he does favor reductions in the inheritance tax, which disproportionately affects farmers and ranchers. Likewise on trade, he complains that American farmers are disadvantaged by free-trade pacts with countries that don't have to meet the same labor and environmental standards.

Cardoza came to the House a seasoned state legislator but finds himself in diminished circumstances. In the California Assembly, where he served for six years, he was in the majority, he led the moderate Democratic faction there and he chaired the Rules Committee. Now, as a relative newcomer in an often marginalized minority, he is unable to write legislation and get it passed the way he used to. In his first term, the only substantive bill he successfully sponsored was written by GOP Majority Whip Roy Blunt of Missouri. It forces the Agriculture Department to work more closely with local governments during crop disasters. Blunt and Cardoza's breadbasket districts had similar problems with local-federal coordination.

He should have a better chance of getting involved in major policy debates in his second term, after landing a seat on the International Relations Committee in the 109th Congress.

If working with Republicans is the only way to legislate, then Cardoza is willing to do it. He also teamed up with Rep. Adam H. Putnam, a Florida Republican, on a bill to require government school lunch programs to provide more fruit and vegetables, major crops in both of their districts.

Cardoza's best opportunities to get into the thick of things have come from his assignment on the Resources Committee. He and GOP Chairman Richard W. Pombo of California are from different parties but have much in common personally and politically. Both hail from Portuguese-American farm families in the state's Central Valley, known for its dairy, fruit and wine output, and both are ardent about protecting the interests of landowners.

Cardoza's alliance with Pombo gave him entrée into his most ambitious undertaking. He is the chief sponsor of a bill in the 109th to make it harder for the federal government to designate vast tracts of land as "critical habitats" for endangered species. It is part of a larger Republican strategy spearheaded by Pombo and the Bush administration to scale back the 31-year-old Endangered Species Act. Cardoza also sided with Pombo and other committee Republicans in 2003 in favor of Bush's proposal to open parts of the Alaskan wilderness to oil exploration.

Cardoza shares a pet concern with GOP Majority Leader Tom DeLay about the troubled foster care system in the country. Cardoza became passionate about fixing problems in foster care after he and his wife, Kathleen McLoughlin, a physician with a family practice in Merced, decided to expand their family by adoption. They already had a biological child, Brittany.

Cardoza said he was appalled that the agency the couple worked with did not take children from Los Angeles County because they were bounced among foster homes so frequently that they suffered lasting behavioral and psychological problems. Cardoza is pushing a bill that would establish a congressionally appointed commission to study foster care in the country and recommend legislative fixes. The Cardozas ultimately adopted a sibling pair, a 6-year-old boy, Joey, and a 3-year-old girl, Elaina.

Another parochial project for Cardoza is federal funding to help the new campus of the University of California system at Merced, something he worked on for years as an assemblyman. He believes that easier access to a college education could alleviate some of the district's social problems. His district includes a large immigrant population that feeds the seasonal farm labor force. It is 42 percent Hispanic, has double-digit unemployment and a big city-like drug problem.

Cardoza is the son of dairy and sweet potato farmers who later opened bowling alleys in Atwater and Merced. Interested in politics as a youth, he got a degree in government and politics from the University of Maryland, then interned for Democratic Rep. Martin Frost of Texas in 1979.

After college, he returned home to manage the family's bowling business for a time, but his real desire was to run for office. In 1984, he was elected to the Atwater City Council. He volunteered in the campaign of then-California Assemblyman Condit, who hired him on his staff in Sacramento and later in Washington, after Condit was elected to the House in 1989.

When Condit's career fell apart amid a nationally observed scandal, Cardoza decided to challenge his former boss in the Democratic primary. By that time, Condit had admitted his relationship with Chandra Levy, a young woman from Modesto who disappeared and was later found dead in a Washington park, the victim of a random assault while jogging. But Condit persisted in the primary campaign, and the relationship with Cardoza took an ugly turn.

Both of Condit's grown children circulated letters in the district labeling Cardoza a "traitor." But Cardoza had the Democratic establishment on his side. He won the primary, then prevailed over GOP state Sen. Dick Monteith by a comfortable 8 percentage points in November. In 2004, Cardoza had no primary opposition and won the general election with 68 percent of the vote.

KEY VOTES

2004
Yes	Extend federal unemployment benefits by 13 weeks
Yes	Pass $283.2 billion, six-year federal highway and mass transit bill
Yes	Approve $146 billion multi-year extension of previously enacted middle-class tax breaks
No	Amend the Constitution to prohibit same-sex marriage
No	Cut corporate taxes $137 billion over 10 years
Yes	Reorganize U.S. intelligence agencies as proposed by Sept. 11 commission

2003
No	Cut taxes by $330 billion through fiscal 2013
Yes	Block Bush rule scaling back overtime pay for some white-collar federal workers
Yes	Do not allow use of search warrants without first notifying subjects
Yes	Allow importation of prescription drugs
No	Create private school voucher program in Washington, D.C.
No	Ban "partial birth" abortion except to save a woman's life
Yes	Split $18.6 billion in Iraq aid into half-grant, half-loan
No	Overhaul Medicare and create prescription drug benefit

CQ VOTE STUDIES

	PARTY UNITY		PRESIDENTIAL SUPPORT	
	Support	Oppose	Support	Oppose
2004	81%	19%	45%	55%
2003	82%	18%	40%	60%

INTEREST GROUPS

	AFL-CIO	ADA	CCUS	ACU
2004	93%	85%	65%	25%
2003	93%	80%	50%	40%

CALIFORNIA 18

Central Valley – Merced, part of Stockton and Modesto

The politically competitive 18th takes in most of Stockton in San Joaquin County before stretching through Merced County and half of Stanislaus County, which make up the district's agricultural base, to almost reach Fresno.

Modesto, the Stanislaus County seat, has its own canning and food-processing industry, as well as the Gallo Winery, which is the second-largest winery in the United States. The city has grown substantially over the years, spurred by businesses fleeing California's congested coastal cities and by the Central Valley's successful agriculture industry.

Although still dominated by agriculture, the district now includes the central portion of the diverse and Democratic city of Stockton (shared with the 11th). The port city, on the San Joaquin River, is a transportation hub that some Bay Area commuters call home. Almost 60 percent of the city's residents — Stockton's most Democratic ground — live in the 18th.

Whites and Hispanics each make up about 40 percent of the district's overall population.

Local issues tend to revolve around water availability and the preservation of farmland. The seasonal economy has contributed to higher unemployment rates than in other parts of California.

While the location of the Central Valley-based 18th remained largely intact, redistricting after the 2000 census pushed the district's political lean to the left. Fearing that the scandal surrounding then-Rep. Gary A. Condit could move the seat into the GOP column, the Democratic-controlled state legislature redrew it from a highly competitive seat into one with a 17-point Democratic registration edge. The advantage dwindled to 10 points by 2004, and George W. Bush carried the district with 50 percent of the vote in that year's presidential election.

MAJOR INDUSTRY
Agriculture, wine, food processing

CITIES
Stockton (pt.), 139,362; Modesto (pt.), 133,975; Merced, 63,893

NOTABLE
Stockton has the largest Sikh population in the United States.

Rep. George P. Radanovich (R)

Elected 1994; 6th term

CAPITOL OFFICE
225-4540
www.house.gov/radanovich
438 Cannon 20515-0519; fax 225-3402

COMMITTEES
Energy & Commerce
Resources
(Water & Power - chairman)

HOMETOWN
Mariposa

BORN
June 20, 1955, Mariposa, Calif.

RELIGION
Roman Catholic

FAMILY
Wife, Ethie Radanovich; one child

EDUCATION
California Polytechnic State U., San Luis Obispo,
B.S. 1978 (agriculture business management)

CAREER
Vintner; bank manager; carpenter

POLITICAL HIGHLIGHTS
Mariposa County Board of Supervisors, 1989-92
(chairman, 1991); sought Republican nomination
for U.S. House, 1992

ELECTION RESULTS

2004 GENERAL

George P. Radanovich (R)	155,354	66.0%
James Lex Bufford (D)	64,047	27.2%
Larry R. Mullen (GREEN)	15,863	6.7%

2004 PRIMARY

George P. Radanovich (R)	unopposed

2002 GENERAL

George P. Radanovich (R)	106,209	67.3%
John Veen (D)	47,403	30.0%
Patrick L. McHargue (LIBERT)	4,190	2.7%

PREVIOUS WINNING PERCENTAGES
2000 (65%); 1998 (79%); 1996 (67%); 1994 (57%)

Radanovich and his rural constituents are of one mind on the limited role the government should play in their lives. His agenda is still driven by the same basic tenets that the large GOP Class of 1994 made their mantra — reduce the size and scope of government, shift authority from the federal government to state and local levels, eliminate regulations that hinder businesses and emphasize personal responsibility.

But he has backed away from one of those principles — term limits. When he was elected in 1994, Radanovich (ruh-DON-o-vitch) promised to serve just five terms. With his re-election in 2004, he's in his sixth term. He told the Fresno Bee, "There are issues that are really important to me, like water and power, and reform of the Endangered Species Act, and that hasn't happened yet," Radanovich said. "I just don't feel that my job is done yet."

Radanovich and his Western colleagues argue that Easterners (and particularly government bureaucrats) do not understand the unique issues facing the West, where the government owns huge tracts of land and where access to water is crucial. Radanovich has some say over wilderness and water policy as chairman of the Resources Committee's Water and Power Subcommittee. He told the Associated Press in 2004 that the pace of designating lands as wilderness "needs to be slowed down to keep some people from . . . abusing the intent of the law by keeping the public off public lands."

Yosemite National Park is in the 19th District, and Radanovich is wary of proposals to address park overcrowding that might hurt tourist-dependent towns and businesses near the park. He opposed portions of a National Park Service master plan to reduce crowding and restore the park after devastating floods in 1997.

Radanovich proposed his own plan for Yosemite in the 108th Congress to add 361 campsites along the Merced River and to allow for more parking. His measure also sought to remove the park's 99-year-old LeConte Memorial Lodge, a national historic landmark. The Sierra Club had opposed the addition of more campsites, and Radanovich said it was hypocritical of the conservation group to oppose his efforts to include more campsites while the club sponsored educational programs at the historic lodge. He told the Modesto Bee that the Sierra Club "needs to know how it feels" to face the possibility of losing access to a popular public space.

With his district's farmers in mind, Radanovich sponsored a measure allowing the United States to ignore an international environmental treaty calling for a ban in 2005 on methyl bromide, a popular killer of insects, weeds and diseases. Although methyl bromide is on a list of substances regulated by the treaty, Radanovich wanted Congress to exempt U.S. farmers from the ban on the pesticide until alternatives were available.

Although usually a GOP stalwart, Radanovich bucked the party in sponsoring a resolution in the 108th asking the House to recognize the killing of more than a million Armenians in Turkey from 1915 to 1923. Radanovich and California Democrat Adam B. Schiff represent districts with large populations of Armenian-Americans. The GOP leadership and the White House opposed such a vote because of Turkey's strategic importance as a Middle East ally, and the measure went nowhere.

Radanovich and fellow California lawmaker (and former vineyard owner) Mike Thompson formed the Congressional Wine Caucus to educate colleagues about wine and to join on legislative and regulatory matters pertaining to wine. Radanovich was once a vintner himself, but his family's winery closed in 2003.

News reports surfaced in the summer of 2004 suggesting that Radanovich received special treatment in a land swap with a local developer. The Fresno Bee reported on the complex financial arrangement that allowed Radanovich to reacquire a seven-acre vineyard and barn that had once belonged to his family's winery business. The newspaper said Radanovich was involved in a lucrative land swap with developer Richard Spencer, a political contributor.

Radanovich told the Associated Press that the land transfer had nothing to do with the sale of the winery. "I traded 27 acres of land with great development potential for seven land-locked acres owned by the new winery owner that were part of my family's farm where the winery was located," he said. "For the writer to conclude that somehow I got the better part of that deal defies logic."

One of eight children of a Croatian immigrant who owned and operated a clothing store in Mariposa, Radanovich spent many of his teenage years on the family's small ranch just outside town. He earned a college degree in agricultural business management, and after working a few years as a banker, a carpenter and a substitute teacher, Radanovich pursued his first love, farming.

His dream, inspired by memories of his grandfather making wine in the cellar, was to establish a winery in the Mariposa County foothills of the Sierra Nevada. He persisted, and at one time the Radanovich Winery shipped about 6,000 cases of wine annually. But facing financial losses and a large debt, the winery closed in 2003.

In building his winery, Radanovich gained firsthand familiarity with the issues of water allocation, farm labor, taxes and regulation. That led him to a seat on the Mariposa County Board of Supervisors in 1989. In 1992, he made his first bid for Congress. Mariposa is far from the district's population center in Fresno County, where he was largely unknown, but Radanovich acquitted himself well that year, losing a close race to eventual GOP nominee Tal Cloud.

Two years later, Cloud decided not to run, and Radanovich took advantage of the GOP tilt in the district caused by the post-1990 census remapping. He cruised to victory over incumbent Democratic Rep. Richard H. Lehman and has racked up formidable margins of victory since then.

In 2002, redistricting had shifted the boundaries of his district to the north, but its electorate was no less friendly, and Radanovich cruised to a 37 percentage point win. In 2004, he increased his winning margin to 39 points.

KEY VOTES

2004

No   Extend federal unemployment benefits by 13 weeks

Yes   Pass $283.2 billion, six-year federal highway and mass transit bill

Yes   Approve $146 billion multi-year extension of previously enacted middle-class tax breaks

Yes   Amend the Constitution to prohibit same-sex marriage

Yes   Cut corporate taxes $137 billion over 10 years

No   Reorganize U.S. intelligence agencies as proposed by Sept. 11 commission

2003

Yes   Cut taxes by $330 billion through fiscal 2013

No   Block Bush rule scaling back overtime pay for some white-collar federal workers

Yes   Do not allow use of search warrants without first notifying subjects

No   Allow importation of prescription drugs

Yes   Create private school voucher program in Washington, D.C.

Yes   Ban "partial birth" abortion except to save a woman's life

No   Split $18.6 billion in Iraq aid into half-grant, half-loan

Yes   Overhaul Medicare and create prescription drug benefit

CQ VOTE STUDIES

	PARTY UNITY		PRESIDENTIAL SUPPORT	
	Support	Oppose	Support	Oppose
2004	95%	5%	91%	9%
2003	97%	3%	100%	0%
2002	96%	4%	89%	11%
2001	96%	4%	93%	7%
2000	96%	4%	22%	78%

INTEREST GROUPS

	AFL-CIO	ADA	CCUS	ACU
2004	7%	0%	100%	100%
2003	0%	5%	96%	88%
2002	11%	5%	95%	88%
2001	0%	5%	95%	92%
2000	0%	5%	90%	100%

CALIFORNIA 19
Central Valley – part of Fresno and Modesto, Turlock, Madera

A fertile farm district, the 19th includes the heart of Central California's San Joaquin Valley. It takes in almost all of Madera County and part of the city of Fresno, home to large numbers of Hispanics, Hmong and Armenians. All of Mariposa and Tuolumne counties are in the district, along with about half of Stanislaus County.

The 19th is rural and Republican. The district has elected the same Republican to Congress since 1994 and has supported GOP presidential candidates since 1992. In 2004 the 19th gave George W. Bush 61 percent of the vote. Farmers and senior citizens, leery of government regulations and environmental protection laws, tend to be moderate conservatives. Farming and water issues are perpetual hot topics and are becoming more significant as population growth means less water for agricultural use.

The district's portion of Stanislaus County includes less than one-third of

Modesto's population and the growing city of Turlock. Tuolumne and Mariposa counties, which along with Madera County to the south are home to Yosemite National Park, are sparsely populated areas that account for only one-tenth of the district's population. They feature Sierra Nevada mountains, skiing and forests in the east and former Gold Rush towns such as Jamestown, Sonora and Mariposa in the west.

Tourism at Yosemite helps keep the 19th's economy afloat, though the district suffers from high unemployment because of the seasonal nature of its driving industries. The district picked up all of Yosemite, which was only partially in the old 19th, in redistricting following the 2000 census. Hispanics make up 28 percent of residents.

MAJOR INDUSTRY
Agriculture, dairy, tourism

CITIES
Fresno (pt.), 189,836; Turlock, 55,810; Modesto (pt.), 54,881; Madera, 43,207

NOTABLE
The Yosemite Valley was deeded to California in 1864 as a public trust, and Yosemite National Park was created in 1890.

Rep. Jim Costa (D)

Elected 2004; 1st term

Costa faces many of the same challenges as other freshmen, but getting to know his constituents across California's 20th District will not be among them. The state Senate district he represented for eight years completely encompasses his congressional district in the state's Central Valley.

Costa joins two other House lawmakers from the Central Valley — Republicans Richard W. Pombo and Devin Nunes — who trace their origins to Portugal's Azores islands. His appointment to the Agriculture Committee — on which his predecessor in the 20th, Democrat Cal Dooley, had also served — was wholly unsurprising: The area is one of the nation's preeminent producers of farm products. Costa's grandparents emigrated from Portugal decades ago and settled in the Central Valley as farmers, and Costa still owns a 240-acre almond orchard.

Politics, though, has been his career for practically his entire adult life. He served in the legislature for 24 years, leaving after 2002 because of a state term limit, and then came to Congress after just a two-year break.

Costa has a reputation for expertise on the concerns of local farmers, particularly water issues, though his moderate pro-business positions have not always endeared him to labor leaders and environmentalists. Costa has said he also would like to have a hand in changing the partisan tone in Washington. "I'm not pollyannaish about it, but I would like to be part of the force helping bipartisanship in Congress," he said.

Costa stayed involved in state politics after leaving the legislature by opening his own lobbying firm. Having flirted with a House run three previous times, Costa quickly declared his candidacy after Dooley announced he would not run again. He handily won the Democratic primary, but was left bruised by his opponent, former Dooley chief of staff Lisa Quigley, whose campaign raised questions about Costa's personal behavior.

Costa faced a tougher than expected challenge in November from well-funded GOP state Sen. Roy Ashburn, but he prevailed by 7 percentage points in the Democratic-leaning district.

CAPITOL OFFICE
225-3341
congressmanjimcosta@mail.house.gov
www.house.gov/costa
1004 Longworth 20515-0520; fax 225-9308

COMMITTEES
Agriculture
Resources
Science

HOMETOWN
Fresno

BORN
April 13, 1952, Fresno, Calif.

RELIGION
Roman Catholic

FAMILY
Single

EDUCATION
California State U., Fresno, B.A. 1974 (political science)

CAREER
Lobbyist; state legislative aide; congressional district aide

POLITICAL HIGHLIGHTS
Calif. Assembly, 1978-94; Democratic nominee for Calif. Senate, 1993; Calif. Senate, 1994-2002

ELECTION RESULTS

2004 GENERAL

Jim Costa (D)	61,005	53.4%
Roy Ashburn (R)	53,231	46.6%

2004 PRIMARY

Jim Costa (D)	24,338	73.2%
Lisa Quigley (D)	8,925	26.8%

CALIFORNIA 20

Central Valley — Kings County, part of Fresno and Bakersfield

The Hispanic-majority 20th reaches from Fresno to Bakersfield, through rural portions of Fresno, Kings and Kern counties. A swing district at the time of 2001 redistricting, the state legislature gave the district a distinct Democratic voter registration advantage in hopes of making it more secure. Despite this, George W. Bush came within three points of a win here in the 2004 presidential contest.

The 20th bears much of the burden of the San Joaquin Valley's urban and rural poor and is beset by unemployment and crime. It is one of California's most rural districts, and it has some of the nation's least-educated and poorest residents, many of whom are Hispanic and Hmong immigrants who work in the 20th's farming communities.

The district includes the area known as the Westlands. Here, federal water projects have spawned vast farms with battalions of workers. Motorists on Interstate 5 see nary a town while they pass fields filled with a wide variety of crops, including alfalfa, cotton, fruits, sugar beets, wheat and nuts.

Roughly 40 percent of Fresno is in the 20th, which takes in much of downtown and Hispanic areas in the southern section of the city. The downtown portion includes a multipurpose stadium — opened in 2002 and home to a minor league baseball team — which local leaders hope will give an economic boost to the city. The 20th also has attracted state and privately run prisons that assist the area's shaky economy.

MAJOR INDUSTRY
Agriculture, dairy, prisons

MILITARY BASES
Naval Air Station Lemoore, 7,062 military, 1,513 civilian (2004)

CITIES
Fresno (pt.), 154,998; Bakersfield (pt.), 43,284; Hanford, 41,686; Delano, 38,824

NOTABLE
Fresno's Mike Reynolds, whose daughter was murdered, was the catalyst behind California's "three strikes" ballot initiative.

Rep. Devin Nunes (R)

Elected 2002; 2nd term

CAPITOL OFFICE
225-2523
nunes.house.gov
1017 Longworth 20515-0521; fax 225-3404

COMMITTEES
Ways & Means

HOMETOWN
Visalia

BORN
Oct. 1, 1973, Tulare, Calif.

RELIGION
Roman Catholic

FAMILY
Wife, Elizabeth Tamariz

EDUCATION
College of the Sequoias, A.A. 1993 (agriculture);
California Polytechnic State U., San Luis Obispo,
B.S. 1995 (agricultural business), M.S. 1996
(agriculture)

CAREER
Farmer; U.S. Agriculture Department program
administrator

POLITICAL HIGHLIGHTS
College of the Sequoias Board of Trustees, 1996-
2002; sought Republican nomination for U.S.
House, 1998

ELECTION RESULTS

2004 GENERAL

Devin Nunes (R)	140,721	73.2%
Fred B. Davis (D)	51,594	26.8%

2004 PRIMARY

Devin Nunes (R)	unopposed

2002 GENERAL

Devin Nunes (R)	87,544	70.5%
David G. LaPere (D)	32,584	26.2%
Jonathan Richter (LIBERT)	4,070	3.3%

It was not ideological zeal that brought Nunes to the House before his 30th birthday, but a farmer's pragmatism. A third-generation dairyman from the unglamorous rural midsection of California, he is most concerned about building more dams for irrigation and adding more lanes to the farm-to-market roads carrying milk, fruit and wine from his prodigious agriculture-based district.

Nunes (NOO-ness) had earnestly prepared himself for a career in modern, large-scale farming. A product of the Central Valley's established Portuguese-American farm community, he got college degrees in agriculture and business with the intention of managing his family's 1,100-head dairy operation in rural Tulare County. Instead, he took a detour into politics after he won a seat on the community college board and caught the eye of local Republican Party activists.

During his fast rise in politics, Nunes made some influential friends. Ways and Means Chairman Bill Thomas, whose district abuts Nunes' 21st District, is his political mentor. In the 109th Congress, Nunes snagged a rare vacancy on the tax-writing panel despite stiff competition. Fellow Republican Pat Tiberi of Ohio had lobbied for the seat, had two years more seniority than Nunes and had the enthusiastic backing of Deborah Pryce of Ohio, the Republican Conference chairwoman.

To take the Ways and Means seat, Nunes had to give up the chairmanship of the National Parks Subcommittee of the Resources Committee. Nunes had cultivated a close relationship with GOP Chairman Richard W. Pombo, a fellow Portuguese-American from California with whom he typically sided in disputes between landowners and environmentalists.

Nunes won election to Congress in 2002 on a promise to deliver more water storage to an under-quenched slice of the state that would revert to desert if not for irrigation. His prime focus is securing federal funding to start work on a dam on the San Joaquin River, which would help chronic water shortages in Tulare County and a portion of Fresno County, two of the most agriculturally rich counties in the United States. As a freshman in 2003, he won $2 million for a feasibility study in the Interior appropriations bill. He also is intensely interested in any legislation affecting CalFed, a state-federal partnership that develops water projects. And he is an advocate for the Sequoia and Kings Canyon national parks in his district.

Nunes worked to win approval in 2004, and again in 2005, of a provision in the massive transportation bill to add work on Highway 99 from Bakersfield to Sacramento to the list of high-priority road projects, making the farm-to-market road eligible for special grants.

Nunes wants to broaden his involvement in national issues, but his focus retains a parochial flavor. For instance, he is a student of the complex workings of the European Union, particularly as they affect the ability of California's farmers to compete with their overseas counterparts who are heavily subsidized.

Nunes is frequently at odds with environmental groups who oppose commercial logging. He supports the thinning and clearing of national forests as a check on wildfires that have plagued California in recent years, including a 2002 fire that destroyed thousands of acres in Sequoia National Forest, the 1.1 million-acre park named for its giant trees.

As beautiful as parts of the district are, it suffers from high unemployment and below-average education levels, a legacy of the area's seasonal economy, its reliance on immigrants for farm work and an abundance of cheap housing for people fleeing California's high-priced coastal cities. It also has a big city-style drug problem, responsible for a large chunk of the methamphetamine supply in the United States. Nunes is pushing for more federal funds to combat increasingly organized groups producing the drugs in hidden, illegal factories.

Nunes' family hails from the Azores, the nine-island chain off the Portugal coast. His immigrant grandfather established the 640-acre family farm. His father still grows plums and oranges. Two uncles also live and work there, and Nunes and his brother, Anthony, have an alfalfa hay harvesting business. Nunes can trace his agrarian roots back several hundred years. "Everyone on the Azores had three cows, fished and made wine," he says.

The district is home to a concentration of Portuguese-Americans, many of them related by blood or marriage and most Roman Catholic. They share food traditions, festivals and other cultural elements. In 2003, Nunes married Elizabeth Tamariz, a Portuguese-American from his hometown who teaches elementary school. The two have known each other since childhood.

After graduating from California Polytechnic State University in 1996, Nunes volunteered to help a candidate for the board of the two-year College of the Sequoias, where he had attended. The candidate unexpectedly quit, and Nunes, then 22, decided to run himself and wound up ousting a seasoned incumbent. The next day Nunes, wearing work clothes and fixing his grandmother's water heater, was surprised when a local television crew drove out to interview him. He was hooked on politics.

While on the school board, he met Thomas, then the local congressman. In 1998, he agreed to an all-but-hopeless challenge to Democratic incumbent Cal Dooley in the 20th District and lost. Nunes campaigned for George W. Bush in 2000. He was rewarded for his allegiance to the party when Thomas helped him get appointed state director for the U.S. Agriculture Department's rural development program in 2001.

Reapportionment gave California an additional seat, and the 21st District was created. In 2002, Nunes beat two better-known Republicans in the primary, Fresno Mayor Jim Patterson and state Rep. Mike Briggs. His two competitors split the GOP vote in the Fresno area to Nunes' advantage. He also benefited from a Hispanic-sounding name and the solid support of Portuguese-American voters in Tulare County. He cruised to victory in the general election. Nunes drew no primary opposition in 2004 and won re-election easily.

KEY VOTES

2004

No Extend federal unemployment benefits by 13 weeks

Yes Pass $283.2 billion, six-year federal highway and mass transit bill

\+   Approve $146 billion multi-year extension of previously enacted middle-class tax breaks

Yes Amend the Constitution to prohibit same-sex marriage

Yes Cut corporate taxes $137 billion over 10 years

Yes Reorganize U.S. intelligence agencies as proposed by Sept. 11 commission

2003

Yes Cut taxes by $330 billion through fiscal 2013

No Block Bush rule scaling back overtime pay for some white-collar federal workers

No Do not allow use of search warrants without first notifying subjects

No Allow importation of prescription drugs

Yes Create private school voucher program in Washington, D.C.

Yes Ban "partial birth" abortion except to save a woman's life

No Split $18.6 billion in Iraq aid into half-grant, half-loan

Yes Overhaul Medicare and create prescription drug benefit

CQ VOTE STUDIES

	PARTY UNITY		PRESIDENTIAL SUPPORT	
	Support	Oppose	Support	Oppose
2004	95%	5%	91%	9%
2003	98%	2%	100%	0%

INTEREST GROUPS

	AFL-CIO	ADA	CCUS	ACU
2004	13%	0%	100%	96%
2003	7%	5%	100%	88%

CALIFORNIA 21
Central Valley — Tulare County, part of Fresno

The agriculture-dominated 21st is home to all of Tulare and part of Fresno counties, which vie each year for the title of top farm goods-producing county in the nation. Fresno was the winner in 2003, with more than $4 billion in agricultural commodities. In addition to about 20 percent of the city of Fresno, the district takes in some of the mountains and forests of the Sierra Nevada chain on its eastern edge.

Tulare County is the world's largest dairy-producing area, with more than $1 billion in dairy goods in 2003. But the county produces more than 250 other agricultural goods, including oranges, cattle, grapes, cotton and nuts. It is no surprise that farming and water issues are perpetual hot topics and are becoming more significant as population growth means less water for agricultural use. Unlike other areas, where supply and transportation is a concern, the big problem here is water storage. The district also faces high unemployment and below-average education rates.

The district includes the eastern, conservative portion of Fresno,

including Fresno Yosemite International Airport and the Fresno branch of California State University. It also holds the cities of Visalia and Clovis, agricultural towns that have become cities in their own right. Clovis calls itself the gateway to the Sierra Nevadas.

During redistricting following the 2000 census, state legislators created the 21st as an open seat, merging rural, conservative areas likely to elect a Republican. The district gave George W. Bush 65 percent of the vote in the 2004 presidential election, which made the 21st Bush's second-best district in the state. GOP candidates should dominate for the foreseeable future.

MAJOR INDUSTRY
Agriculture, dairy, transportation, tourism

CITIES
Visalia, 91,565; Fresno (pt.), 82,818; Clovis, 68,468; Tulare, 43,994; Porterville, 39,615

NOTABLE
Mount Whitney, at 14,494 feet, is the tallest point in the lower 48 states; Sequoia National Park was the second designated U.S. national park; The Tule River Indian Reservation east of Porterville is surrounded by the Giant Sequoia National Monument on part of three sides.

Rep. Bill Thomas (R)

Elected 1978; 14th term

CAPITOL OFFICE
225-2915
billthomas.house.gov
2208 Rayburn 20515-0522; fax 225-8798

COMMITTEES
Ways & Means - chairman
Joint Taxation - chairman

HOMETOWN
Bakersfield

BORN
Dec. 6, 1941, Wallace, Idaho

RELIGION
Baptist

FAMILY
Wife, Sharon Thomas; two children

EDUCATION
Santa Ana Community College, A.A. 1961; San
Francisco State U., B.A. 1963, M.A. 1965

CAREER
Professor

POLITICAL HIGHLIGHTS
Calif. Assembly, 1974-78

ELECTION RESULTS

2004 GENERAL

Bill Thomas (R)		unopposed

2004 PRIMARY

Bill Thomas (R)		unopposed

2002 GENERAL

Bill Thomas (R)	120,473	73.3%
Jaime A. Corvera (D)	38,988	23.7%
Frank Coates (LIBERT)	4,824	2.9%

PREVIOUS WINNING PERCENTAGES
2000 (72%); 1998 (79%); 1996 (66%); 1994 (68%);
1992 (65%); 1990 (60%); 1988 (71%); 1986 (73%);
1984 (71%); 1982 (68%); 1980 (71%); 1978 (59%)

Thomas is President Bush's MVP on Capitol Hill. Most Americans may never have heard of the chairman of the Ways and Means Committee, but he is the legislative workhorse who has drafted and helped guide to passage just about every major domestic bill of the Bush administration.

He shaped the $2 trillion in tax cuts enacted in 2001, 2002, 2003 and 2004. He did the hard work to get a prescription drug benefit added to Medicare in 2003 and to pass the trade law that gave the president fast-track power to enter trade agreements that cannot be amended by Congress. In 2004, he completed the thankless, unpopular task of putting U.S. tax laws into compliance with World Trade Organization rules by getting rid of a $50 billion tax subsidy for exporters. He got the votes for that by bargaining with individual members and special interests for goodies in a $137 billion corporate tax cut giveaway, including a buyout of big tobacco.

As Thomas completes his final term at the helm of Ways and Means in the 109th Congress, he is again at the center of the action. He has a big hand in Bush's top two domestic priorities: an overhaul of the Social Security retirement program in favor of personal investment accounts and a major tax code simplification.

Thomas is a one-man legislative shop who drafts bills single-handedly, negotiates their final versions and conducts the political arm twisting to finish the job. When signing the 2003 dividend tax cut into law, Bush said of Thomas, "He got the job done."

In his two terms as chairman, Thomas has restored the clout and prestige of the Ways and Means Committee almost to what it was a decade ago, when then-Chairman Dan Rostenkowski, an Illinois Democrat, told an audience of reporters and editors, "I am the House."

Thomas' success stems from his close coordination with the GOP whip; he keeps tabs on where members stand and whether he has the votes to pass a bill. At the same time, Thomas' peers say he is one of the most personally difficult members of Congress to deal with. He lectures, insults and cuts off colleagues. He functions on just a few hours of sleep, driving fellow lawmakers to distraction in post-midnight negotiations on legislation.

In a 2004 survey of congressional aides by Washingtonian magazine, Thomas was judged to be the most hot-tempered lawmaker in the House, but he also was voted the "Brainiest."

"He doesn't pussyfoot around," says fellow Ways and Means member Nancy L. Johnson, a Connecticut Republican. "If you've got a dumb idea, he'll tell you that you've got a dumb idea."

His legendary temper got him in trouble in 2003 when, during a testy bill-drafting session on pension legislation, Thomas called Capitol Hill Police officers to remove committee Democrats from the Ways and Means Committee library where they had gathered to protest Thomas' handling of a committee meeting. The stunt brought him and the Republicans a spate of fierce criticism for heavy-handedness. A week later, Thomas apologized on the House floor before a full chamber of his colleagues, weeping as he spoke. Thomas once said he can be overbearing because he suffers from "a very big inferiority complex."

Thomas was born on the eve of the Japanese attack on Pearl Harbor to a working-class family in the mining hills of Idaho. Soon after, his family moved to the West Coast in search of work and lived in government housing projects. Jobs were so scarce that his father, a union plumber and pipe fitter, took an 18-month contract in Saudi Arabia after World War II.

With that money, the family bought a first car and a house in Orange County, where Thomas eventually attended Santa Ana Community College. He later received bachelor's and master's degrees from San Francisco State University, becoming the first in his family to complete college. "There's no wealth in my background," said Thomas, whose only employment before his election to the state legislature in 1974 was as a community college teacher.

Thomas remains relatively less well-off than his millionaire colleagues in Congress. Other than his congressional salary of $158,100 a year, he reports no income from investments on annual disclosure reports. That helps explain why he is passionate about tax breaks that encourage savings and elimination of the estate tax, which hits family businesses being passed to the next generation especially hard.

"I understand the need and difficulty in making money," he says. "If you don't really have a starter batch, you can never really get the sourdough bread going. I'm very sensitive to enabling whatever an average person needs to accumulate their own wealth and pass it on."

After four years in the California Assembly, Thomas was elected in 1978 to a House seat that had been held since 1973 by Republican William Ketchum, who died that year following the June primary. While he had to fight to win that first nomination, he has won re-election easily since.

Thomas became Ways and Means chairman in 2001 after the retirement of Republican Bill Archer of Texas, who had the job since the first days of the GOP majority in 1995. Thomas bested Philip M. Crane of Illinois, who had 10 years more seniority but was viewed as a less energetic legislator, though not as abrasive a leader, as Thomas.

Thomas had earned a reputation for being effective as the top Republican on the Health Subcommittee. He immersed himself in health policy, rising at 4 a.m. for six months to read background material. "Basically I got a medical degree," he said.

In 1998 and 1999, Thomas served on the commission studying long-term changes to ensure Medicare's survival, but the panel could not settle on a plan that could muster the 11 votes needed to send it to Congress.

His attention to detail was useful when he was chairman of the House Administration Committee from 1995 to 2000. With Republicans in the majority, Thomas cleaned up internal practices and waste. He retooled Capitol security after two U.S. Capitol Police officers were fatally shot in 1998. He also oversaw the privatization of several House services, slashed committee staffing, and presided over the first-ever outside audit of House finances.

KEY VOTES

2004

No Extend federal unemployment benefits by 13 weeks
Yes Pass $283.2 billion, six-year federal highway and mass transit bill
Yes Approve $146 billion multi-year extension of previously enacted middle-class tax breaks
Yes Amend the Constitution to prohibit same-sex marriage
Yes Cut corporate taxes $137 billion over 10 years
Yes Reorganize U.S. intelligence agencies as proposed by Sept. 11 commission

2003

Yes Cut taxes by $330 billion through fiscal 2013
No Block Bush rule scaling back overtime pay for some white-collar federal workers
No Do not allow use of search warrants without first notifying subjects
No Allow importation of prescription drugs
Yes Create private school voucher program in Washington, D.C.
Yes Ban "partial birth" abortion except to save a woman's life
No Split $18.6 billion in Iraq aid into half-grant, half-loan
Yes Overhaul Medicare and create prescription drug benefit

CQ VOTE STUDIES

	PARTY UNITY		PRESIDENTIAL SUPPORT	
	Support	Oppose	Support	Oppose
2004	92%	8%	91%	9%
2003	96%	4%	95%	5%
2002	91%	9%	90%	10%
2001	95%	5%	90%	10%
2000	92%	8%	32%	68%

INTEREST GROUPS

	AFL-CIO	ADA	CCUS	ACU
2004	20%	5%	100%	88%
2003	7%	5%	100%	76%
2002	0%	10%	100%	80%
2001	8%	15%	100%	68%
2000	0%	10%	90%	80%

CALIFORNIA 22
Kern and San Luis Obispo counties — Bakersfield

The 22nd stretches from San Luis Obispo County near the coast inland to Ridgecrest in Kern County, dipping south into northwestern Los Angeles County. More than two-thirds of district residents live in Kern County.

Kern is known for oil production and has a strong agricultural industry. Along with the farm-oriented San Luis Obispo area (the city itself is in the coastal 23rd District), the counties produce billions of dollars each year in crops such as grapes, citrus, cotton and nuts. San Luis Obispo nurtures vineyards and cattle. Kern County also is home to a Hyundai-Kia $60 million joint "proving ground" — a facility to test vehicles — that opened in California City in 2005.

Bakersfield, some of which falls in the 20th District, is Kern County's largest city and sits in the southern end of the San Joaquin Valley. Along with Lancaster in Los Angeles County, it continues to see the most growth. Oil and agriculture also dominate the economy here, although the city is trying to diversify by promoting its growing telecommunications, financial and light manufacturing sectors.

San Luis Obispo County trends conservative, with many conservative Democrats in the northern part. Agricultural and military aviation issues remain dominant concerns for residents.

The district, previously numbered the 21st, lost its portion of Tulare County in redistricting following the 2000 census, although it remains consistently Republican. George W. Bush took 68 percent of the 22nd's 2004 presidential vote here, his highest percentage in the state.

MAJOR INDUSTRY
Agriculture, oil, military

MILITARY BASES
Edwards Air Force Base, 3,711 military, 8,559 civilian (shared with the 25th); Naval Air Warfare Center Weapons Division, China Lake, 891 military, 3,134 civilian (2004) (shared with the 25th)

CITIES
Bakersfield (pt.), 203,773; Lancaster (pt.), 65,976; Oildale, 27,885

NOTABLE
Bakersfield has been called the country music capital of the West, and Buck Owens has his Crystal Palace museum and theater there; The nation's first jet- and rocket-powered flights took off from Edwards Air Force Base; Dreyer's has a huge ice cream plant in Bakersfield.

Rep. Lois Capps (D)

Elected March 1998; 4th full term

CAPITOL OFFICE
225-3601
www.house.gov/capps
1707 Longworth 20515-0523; fax 225-5632

COMMITTEES
Budget
Energy & Commerce

HOMETOWN
Santa Barbara

BORN
Jan. 10, 1938, Ladysmith, Wis.

RELIGION
Lutheran

FAMILY
Widowed; three children (one deceased)

EDUCATION
Pacific Lutheran U., B.S. 1959 (nursing); Yale U.,
M.A. 1964 (religion); U. of California, Santa
Barbara, M.A. 1990 (education)

CAREER
Elementary school nurse; college instructor

POLITICAL HIGHLIGHTS
No previous office

ELECTION RESULTS

2004 GENERAL

Lois Capps (D)	153,980	63.0%
Donald E. Regan (R)	83,926	34.4%
Michael Favorite (LIBERT)	6,391	2.6%

2004 PRIMARY

Lois Capps (D)	unopposed

2002 GENERAL

Lois Capps (D)	95,752	59.0%
Beth Rogers (R)	62,604	38.6%
James E. Hill (LIBERT)	3,866	2.4%

PREVIOUS WINNING PERCENTAGES
2000 (53%); 1998 (55%); 1998 Special Runoff Election
(53%)

Capps has evolved from a politically inexperienced widow who claimed her late husband's seat in 1998 to a seasoned lawmaker serving her fourth term in the House. A solid Democratic vote for government spending on social programs, Capps takes the side of business more often than other liberal Democrats, in keeping with her constituency of small businesses and family farms.

A registered nurse who lost a 35-year-old daughter to lung cancer in 2000, Capps has a keen interest in health care policy. She sits on the Health Subcommittee of the Energy and Commerce Committee, where she often joins with her California colleague Democrat Henry A. Waxman to argue against GOP health initiatives.

When the Energy panel took up the GOP proposal to provide prescription drug coverage to seniors under Medicare, Capps proposed an amendment that would have required the Department of Health and Human Services to offer a nationwide prescription drug plan. Capps argued that the GOP-drafted bill provided no guarantee that seniors in rural areas would be able to obtain coverage. The bill contained only "sweeteners and enticements" to lure medical providers into rural areas, Capps said.

As the measure neared completion, Capps became more vocal in her opposition to it. In November 2003, she resigned from the senior citizens' advocacy group AARP after the organization endorsed the bill. Capps told the Ventura County Star she was "stunned and offended" by AARP's endorsement of the prescription drug plan. She characterized the legislation as a "sham," saying it would cripple the Medicare program.

Capps also questioned the value of a bill approved in 2003 by the Energy Committee, and pushed by the Bush administration, to combat bioterrorism by providing guaranteed funding for improved vaccines or drugs to fight such pathogens as smallpox, anthrax and botulinum toxin. Capps wondered whether government funding would be more appropriately directed toward public health institutions such as hospitals that would have to address a bioterror attack if one were to occur. Having treatments to fight deadly diseases "will do us no good if hospitals are closed and if doctors and nurses to administer them are not there," she said.

Despite her attacks on some GOP health policy initiatives, Capps was successful in getting the Republican-controlled House to pass her STOP Stroke bill in 2004. The measure aimed to educate the public about stroke prevention and to foster improved treatments.

The congresswoman has said her proudest moment in the 107th Congress was passage of her bill to provide federal training, grants and scholarships to address the national nursing shortage. She also has sponsored legislation to increase funding for cancer research.

Capps sometimes breaks with her party on the issue of tax cuts. During the Clinton administration, she voted to override the Democratic president's veto of Republican bills that slashed estate taxes and eliminated the marriage penalty in the tax code. In 2001, she was one of only 28 House Democrats to vote for President Bush's sweeping $1.35 trillion tax cut. Yet she voted "no" in 2003 on a GOP package of tax cuts that included a new 15 percent tax rate on dividends and capital gains.

While backing business interests, Capps' support does not extend to big oil companies that want to drill in California waters. In the 108th Congress, Capps was able to get language removed from a national energy policy bill that she said would have allowed oil and gas exploration in areas of the Outer Continental Shelf that are covered by a longstanding congressional moratorium on such exploration. She said the measure's language was "just the first step in drilling in these areas now off-limits."

Capps also proposed legislation early in the 108th to ban additional oil and gas drilling in Los Padres National Forest. She vowed to "slam the door shut" to new leases in the sprawling forest, which stretches along the Pacific Coast from Ventura County to Big Sur and is the only national forest in the state where energy development is allowed.

The daughter and granddaughter of Lutheran ministers, Capps grew up in small towns in Wisconsin and Montana. She has a master's degree in religion from Yale. She worked as a nurse for many years in Santa Barbara schools and also ran the county's teenage pregnancy counseling project.

The 22nd District had been a competitive one, split between Democrats and Republicans, when Walter Capps won election. Lois Capps helped her husband by standing in for him at campaign events in 1996 while he recovered from injuries from a car accident caused by a drunken driver. When her husband suffered a fatal heart attack less than a year into his first term, Lois Capps replaced him in a special election early in 1998.

In her election in 1998, she benefited from her late husband's political organization and from disunity among Republicans. A contest on the GOP side between conservative state Rep. Tom Bordonaro and moderate state Rep. Brooks Firestone became a bitter struggle that reflected what the party was undergoing nationally. House Speaker Newt Gingrich backed Firestone while conservative firebrands like House Whip Tom DeLay supported Bordonaro.

Capps stayed focused on local issues and stressed Democratic themes of protecting the environment and improving education and health care. She won by 9 percentage points over Bordonaro, becoming the 35th widow to win a House seat after the death of a husband.

Capps won re-election to a full term in November 1998, again besting Bordonaro, this time by 12 percentage points. In 2000, Republicans targeted her district, but she turned back Republican Mike Stoker, a former Santa Barbara County supervisor.

Her district became distinctly more Democratic after redistricting prior to the 2002 election, and Capps overwhelmingly beat Beth Rogers, a member of a wealthy fourth-generation Ventura County farming family. In 2004, Capps won easily with 63 percent of the vote.

KEY VOTES

2004

Yes Extend federal unemployment benefits by 13 weeks
Yes Pass $283.2 billion, six-year federal highway and mass transit bill
No Approve $146 billion multi-year extension of previously enacted middle-class tax breaks
No Amend the Constitution to prohibit same-sex marriage
No Cut corporate taxes $137 billion over 10 years
Yes Reorganize U.S. intelligence agencies as proposed by Sept. 11 commission

2003

No Cut taxes by $330 billion through fiscal 2013
Yes Block Bush rule scaling back overtime pay for some white-collar federal workers
Yes Do not allow use of search warrants without first notifying subjects
Yes Allow importation of prescription drugs
No Create private school voucher program in Washington, D.C.
No Ban "partial birth" abortion except to save a woman's life
Yes Split $18.6 billion in Iraq aid into half-grant, half-loan
No Overhaul Medicare and create prescription drug benefit

CQ VOTE STUDIES

	PARTY UNITY		PRESIDENTIAL SUPPORT	
	Support	Oppose	Support	Oppose
2004	98%	2%	21%	79%
2003	97%	3%	20%	80%
2002	93%	7%	32%	68%
2001	92%	8%	36%	64%
2000	89%	11%	73%	27%

INTEREST GROUPS

	AFL-CIO	ADA	CCUS	ACU
2004	100%	100%	24%	0%
2003	87%	100%	33%	16%
2002	89%	90%	45%	12%
2001	92%	85%	43%	4%
2000	70%	70%	75%	16%

CALIFORNIA 23

Central Coast – Oxnard, Santa Barbara, Santa Maria, San Luis Obispo

The 23rd is a sliver of coastline stretching from north of San Luis Obispo into Ventura County, which lies northwest of Los Angeles. Three main cities — Oxnard, Santa Barbara and San Luis Obispo — register high numbers of Democrats, especially Oxnard, which has a significant blue-collar Hispanic population. Like much of California's coast, the district is liberal on social issues.

The district's other major city, Santa Maria, is the most Republican, but wealthy members of Hollywood's elite in Santa Barbara County and students at California Polytechnic State University in San Luis Obispo and the University of California, Santa Barbara tilt the 23rd to the left.

Agriculture is a mainstay in the San Luis Obispo area, as well as in Santa Maria, which also is known for manufacturing. Oxnard is home to large biotech companies and the Port of Hueneme, the only international port on the central coast, which imports the majority of bananas and second-

most number of cars in the state. Tourism also helps this beachfront district's economy, and universities contribute to the wealth of the 23rd.

Redistricting following the 2000 census gave the district, previously numbered the 22nd, its coastal shape — at one point it narrows to the width of a strip of shoreline — and its Democratic lean. The new district gave Democrat John Kerry 58 percent of the vote in the 2004 presidential election. Hispanics make up two-fifths of the population.

MAJOR INDUSTRY
Agriculture, military, tourism

MILITARY BASES
Naval Base Ventura County, 7,646 military, 6,936 civilian (2005) (shared with the 24th); Vandenberg Air Force Base, 2,691 military, 995 civilian (2002) (shared with the 24th)

CITIES
Oxnard, 170,358; Santa Barbara, 92,325; Santa Maria, 77,423; Goleta (unincorporated), 55,204

NOTABLE
Santa Barbara was the birthplace of the Egg McMuffin; Hearst Castle, a historic house museum at San Simeon, was home to William Randolph Hearst; Channel Islands National Park.

Rep. Elton Gallegly (R)

Elected 1986; 10th term

CAPITOL OFFICE
225-5811
www.house.gov/gallegly
2427 Rayburn 20515-0524; fax 225-1100

COMMITTEES
International Relations
 (Europe & Emerging Threats - chairman)
Judiciary
Resources
Select Intelligence

HOMETOWN
Simi Valley

BORN
March 7, 1944, Huntington Park, Calif.

RELIGION
Protestant

FAMILY
Wife, Janice Gallegly; four children

EDUCATION
California State U., Los Angeles, attended 1962-63

CAREER
Real estate broker

POLITICAL HIGHLIGHTS
Simi Valley City Council, 1979-86; mayor of Simi Valley, 1980-86

ELECTION RESULTS

2004 GENERAL

Elton Gallegly (R)	178,660	62.8%
Brett Wagner (D)	96,397	33.9%
Stuart A. Bechman (GREEN)	9,321	3.3%

2004 PRIMARY

Elton Gallegly (R)	unopposed

2002 GENERAL

Elton Gallegly (R)	120,585	65.2%
Fern Rudin (D)	58,755	31.8%
Gary Harber (LIBERT)	5,666	3.1%

PREVIOUS WINNING PERCENTAGES
2000 (54%); 1998 (60%); 1996 (60%); 1994 (66%); 1992 (54%); 1990 (58%); 1988 (69%); 1986 (68%)

A traditional Western conservative who came to the House to fight federal restrictions on land use, Gallegly has had a greater impact on policy with a global reach. As a member of the International Relations Committee, his major pursuit these days is tracking emerging threats around the world, with a focus on Europe.

Gallegly (GAL-uh-glee) in the 108th Congress pushed for stricter standards for government-issued identification cards. Provisions he wrote were included in legislation to implement recommendations of the Sept. 11 Commission. But he nonetheless ended up voting against the bill because he said it did not go far enough. Conferees limited new ID restrictions to the boarding of domestic flights, which Gallegly said left the nation vulnerable to terrorists using easily forged identification documents to open bank accounts to finance their schemes, to launder money, and to enter federal buildings or nuclear sites.

"Our challenge in the 109th Congress will be to tighten our internal controls to make it more difficult for terrorists to hide among the thousands who sneak across our borders every day, then use fraudulent documents to freely move across the country," he said.

In 2005, he became chairman of International Relations' Subcommittee on Europe and Emerging Threats, with an expanded purview to monitor new terrorist threats around the world. He previously had chaired the International Terrorism Subcommittee.

Gallegly was disappointed in an earlier pursuit for a step up the ladder. The leadership passed him over for the chairmanship of the Resources Committee, which has the greatest impact on property and water rights issues important to him. He waged an aggressive campaign to become Resources chairman in the 108th when Utah's James V. Hansen retired. While careful to pay homage to the seniority of H. James Saxton of New Jersey, the highest-ranking Republican on the committee with an interest in the chairmanship, Gallegly, who ranked just below Saxton in seniority, promoted himself as a Westerner more in tune with the property rights views of Republican leaders.

But the leadership skipped over Gallegly, Saxton and three other more-senior Republicans to elevate to the chairmanship Richard W. Pombo of California, a protégé of Majority Leader Tom DeLay.

On Resources, Gallegly has looked after his state's water interests and helped landowners butting up against federal environmental laws that protect certain species of animals. Gallegly, who promotes what he calls "common sense environmentalism," says, "Endangered species and property rights are not mutually exclusive, although they would be separate bills." In the 108th Congress, Gallegly sponsored a bill to exempt military bases from some provisions of the Endangered Species Act and the Marine Mammals Protection Act, arguing that the laws impeded combat training.

Though best known for work on hot-button issues like limiting benefits to illegal immigrants and revamping environmental laws, the California Republican has an easygoing demeanor with a touch of self-deprecation. He says he tries to work with the leadership and committee chairmen and that "just throwing something up against the wall to see if it sticks is not my style."

His highest-profile initiative came out of the Judiciary Committee in 1997. Gallegly's legislation was designed to give landowners and business developers more clout in challenging local zoning laws that prevent them from building on their property. The measure, pushed by property rights advocates, drew opposition from environmentalists, historic preservationists and governors. It passed in the House but died in the Senate.

Gallegly is one of the few non-lawyers to sit on Judiciary, where he takes a hard line on illegal immigrants. He is remembered for his unsuccessful 1996 effort to allow local school districts to decide whether to provide a public school education to the children of illegal immigrants. He argued that states like California could not afford public education for those children and that the promise of free schooling was a magnet drawing illegal immigrants into the country.

While building a conservative voting record overall, Gallegly occasionally casts his lot with Democrats. As the former mayor of Simi Valley, a community close enough to Los Angeles that many of its residents are concerned about the spread of urban crime, Gallegly has voted for gun restrictions opposed by many Republicans.

He takes pride in representing the district that contains the Ronald Reagan Presidential Library. Among his prized possessions is a photo with the former president taken aboard Air Force One. The two are looking out the window at the unfinished Simi Valley site of the future library.

When he was growing up, Gallegly followed the political persuasions of his father, a lifelong Democrat. He described his father in an interview with the Los Angeles Times as "an FDR Democrat, and they're much different from the Democrats of today. He believed in government helping people who couldn't help themselves, but not those who could."

After dropping out of college, Gallegly went into the real estate business and built a successful brokerage. Frustrated in his dealings with local government, he decided to run for office himself in 1979, urged on by his business colleagues.

Gallegly won a seat on the Simi Valley City Council and served concurrently as mayor for six years before running for Congress in 1986. Touting his record of boosting Simi Valley's economic development, Gallegly defeated Tony Hope, the comedian's son, in the GOP primary and then won the general election by 40 percentage points. The area Gallegly represented in the 1990s was more competitive politically; in 2000, Al Gore carried the district and Gallegly was held to 54 percent of the vote, his lowest share ever.

Congressional district lines were redrawn for the current decade with incumbent protection in mind, and Gallegly's district, reconfigured and relabeled the 24th, is more reliably Republican. In 2004, he was re-elected with 63 percent of the vote.

KEY VOTES

2004

No   Extend federal unemployment benefits by 13 weeks

Yes   Pass $283.2 billion, six-year federal highway and mass transit bill

Yes   Approve $146 billion multi-year extension of previously enacted middle-class tax breaks

Yes   Amend the Constitution to prohibit same-sex marriage

Yes   Cut corporate taxes $137 billion over 10 years

No   Reorganize U.S. intelligence agencies as proposed by Sept. 11 commission

2003

Yes   Cut taxes by $330 billion through fiscal 2013

No   Block Bush rule scaling back overtime pay for some white-collar federal workers

No   Do not allow use of search warrants without first notifying subjects

No   Allow importation of prescription drugs

Yes   Create private school voucher program in Washington, D.C.

Yes   Ban "partial birth" abortion except to save a woman's life

No   Split $18.6 billion in Iraq aid into half-grant, half-loan

Yes   Overhaul Medicare and create prescription drug benefit

CQ VOTE STUDIES

	PARTY UNITY		PRESIDENTIAL SUPPORT	
	Support	Oppose	Support	Oppose
2004	94%	6%	82%	18%
2003	96%	4%	98%	2%
2002	94%	6%	82%	18%
2001	96%	4%	91%	9%
2000	85%	15%	35%	65%

INTEREST GROUPS

	AFL-CIO	ADA	CCUS	ACU
2004	13%	0%	100%	96%
2003	7%	5%	97%	84%
2002	11%	5%	95%	100%
2001	17%	0%	100%	88%
2000	0%	5%	85%	72%

CALIFORNIA 24

Ventura and Santa Barbara counties – Thousand Oaks, Simi Valley

Located north and west of the close-in Los Angeles suburbs, the 24th includes nearly all of Ventura County and inland Santa Barbara County.

Ventura County, where more than four-fifths of district residents live, is a mix of lower-income farming communities and more-upscale residential neighborhoods, such as Moorpark, one of district's fastest-growing cities. The county passed a slow-growth ballot initiative in 1999 in an effort to stave off urban sprawl. After absorbing some destruction from the 1994 Northridge earthquake, Ventura County now has growing electronics, finance and insurance sectors. Industries ranging from agriculture to biotechnology to construction have contributed to the county's recovery.

Because Ventura borders Los Angeles County to the south and east, it often is identified with its urban neighbor. The central and western portions of the district — mainly in Santa Barbara County — are more

agricultural, producing grapes, broccoli and strawberries, and including most of the Los Padres National Forest. Many residents are employed by hospitals and universities. San Nicolas Island and the Anacapa Islands also fall within the 24th's boundaries.

The district's reliable Republicanism comes from interior Santa Barbara — the neighboring 23rd contains the more Democratic coast. Vandenberg Air Force Base and south Ventura County cities such as Simi Valley and Thousand Oaks also contribute to the GOP base.

MAJOR INDUSTRY
Biotechnology, aerospace, service, agriculture

MILITARY BASES
Naval Base Ventura County, 7,646 military, 6,936 civilian (2005) (shared with the 23rd); Vandenberg Air Force Base, 2,691 military, 995 civilian (2002) (shared with the 23rd)

CITIES
Thousand Oaks, 117,005; Simi Valley, 111,351; Ventura (pt.), 79,416

NOTABLE
The Ronald Reagan Presidential Library is in Simi Valley; An all-white Simi Valley jury acquitted three police officers accused of beating motorist Rodney King, touching off Los Angeles riots in 1992.

Rep. Howard P. 'Buck' McKeon (R)

Elected 1992; 7th term

CAPITOL OFFICE
225-1956
mckeon.house.gov
2351 Rayburn 20515-0525; fax 226-0683

COMMITTEES
Armed Services
Education & Workforce
(21st Century Competitiveness - chairman)

HOMETOWN
Santa Clarita

BORN
Sept. 9, 1939, Los Angeles, Calif.

RELIGION
Mormon

FAMILY
Wife, Patricia McKeon; six children

EDUCATION
Brigham Young U., B.S. 1985

CAREER
Clothing store owner

POLITICAL HIGHLIGHTS
William S. Hart School Board, 1978-87; Santa
Clarita City Council, 1987-92 (mayor, 1987-88)

ELECTION RESULTS

2004 GENERAL

Howard P. "Buck" McKeon (R)	145,575	64.4%
Fred "Tim" Willoughby (D)	80,395	35.6%

2004 PRIMARY

Howard P. "Buck" McKeon (R)	unopposed

2002 GENERAL

Howard P. "Buck" McKeon (R)	80,775	65.0%
Robert "Bob" Conaway (D)	38,674	31.1%
Frank M. Consolo Jr. (LIBERT)	4,887	3.9%

PREVIOUS WINNING PERCENTAGES
2000 (62%); 1998 (75%); 1996 (62%); 1994 (65%);
1992 (52%)

McKeon's first experience in politics was serving on his local school board, and he has taken this commitment to education with him to the House. Now in his seventh term, McKeon has a great deal of influence on education issues, and also looks out for his district's defense and aerospace contractors.

While he is one of the most reliably conservative votes in the House — he voted 96 percent of the time with his party in the 108th Congress — the soft-spoken, genial McKeon operates in a non-confrontational way. He worked with Democrats on two hotly contested and partisan issues, education and job training. McKeon is the chairman of the Education and Workforce Committee's Subcommittee on 21st Century Competitiveness.

McKeon sees no gain in endless partisan squabbling on education. "We get beat up by Democrats who want 100,000 teachers, hate-crime language and gun control," he said. "And we have Republicans who want vouchers and who consider testing obtrusive."

In 2001, he was the leading sponsor of a bipartisan bill to do away with financial disincentives for workers who leave their jobs to become public school teachers. Rules governing Social Security benefits penalized workers by reducing their private sector retirement benefits. "Becoming a teacher is hard enough. I think we should do all we can to encourage teaching as a second career," McKeon said. He is also a supporter of more funding for historically black colleges.

McKeon has long been concerned with the rapidly increasing price of college tuition. He said he constantly hears complaints about college costs in his suburban Los Angeles district. "It affects every family, whether they are younger and thinking about having children or they have approached the age" when their children are going to college, McKeon said.

In the 108th Congress, when the House took up a bill to reauthorize the Higher Education Act, McKeon proposed that public colleges be put on a watch list if they increased tuition and fees by more than twice the Consumer Price Index over a three-year period. His proposal drew angry rebukes from college presidents who said they were at the mercy of the state legislatures that typically set tuition policy. McKeon then offered to remove the proposal, provided, he said, that the schools show that they would hold down tuition on their own. "I am delighted that my bill successfully sent a strong message to colleges and universities that more must be done to rein in the cost of tuition and fees," he said.

But another provision in his higher education bill raised some Democratic eyebrows. It encouraged colleges to present "dissenting sources and viewpoints" in the classroom and to "promote intellectual pluralism" in selecting outside speakers. The measure was in response to complaints by conservative college students of a liberal bias in their professors. McKeon told the Gannett News Service in August 2004 that the provision would send a message to liberal academic officials: "You're using the school in many cases to brainwash and not to educate."

Yet McKeon has also won friends in the education community. He was honored in 2002 by the National Association of Independent Colleges and Universities. "No one in Congress has done more to keep higher education accessible and affordable for millions of students of all backgrounds," the group's president said.

McKeon was also the sponsor of a measure to overhaul the nation's main worker-training program. Passed by the House in 2003, the bill, which was strongly supported by the Bush administration, consolidated programs under the Workforce Investment Act (WIA). Federal funding for job training for adults, dislocated workers and employment services was turned into a single state block grant, which concentrated control over the programs with governors.

The House measure also allowed faith-based groups to receive WIA grants even though they discriminate in hiring based on religion, which under current law makes them ineligible. Senate Democrats held up the measure because they objected to the provision, part of President Bush's faith-based initiative.

In one of his more unusual pursuits, McKeon got passed into law in the 108th Congress a bill making it illegal to buy, sell or possess dangerous large cats. McKeon said the wild and exotic animal trade had become a big underground industry in the United States

In the conservative-leaning 25th District, McKeon once observed, "Most people would just as soon the government went away." But there are some federal expenditures that the locals embrace, particularly for military projects. With many aerospace plants in his district, McKeon pushes for increased defense spending from his perch on the Armed Services Committee. The district hosts a Lockheed Martin plant and a NASA facility that refurbishes space shuttles. He champions the development of the next generation of space vehicles and fighter planes. Manufacturers in his district have thousands of jobs at stake in the projects.

Upon arriving in Washington, McKeon, a millionaire owner of a chain of Western-wear stores, organized the Congressional Boot Caucus, so that footwear aficionados from both sides of the aisle could meet, talk boots and hear presentations from manufacturers on new styles.

McKeon's initial political involvement was with his local school board. He was the first mayor of Santa Clarita after it incorporated in 1987. He says he came to Congress to get off the Santa Clarita City Council. He had been a member of the council for two terms and was only reluctantly gearing up to run for a third in 1991 when redistricting created a new House seat around his Santa Clarita base.

McKeon jumped at the chance to run and was the surprise GOP primary winner over Phillip D. Wyman, a 14-year state Assembly veteran. The victory largely determined the outcome in November. McKeon had a sizable spending edge and defeated Democratic lawyer and rancher James H. "Gil" Gilmartin by 19 percentage points. His re-elections have been easy.

KEY VOTES

2004
No Extend federal unemployment benefits by 13 weeks
Yes Pass $283.2 billion, six-year federal highway and mass transit bill
Yes Approve $146 billion multi-year extension of previously enacted middle-class tax breaks
Yes Amend the Constitution to prohibit same-sex marriage
Yes Cut corporate taxes $137 billion over 10 years
Yes Reorganize U.S. intelligence agencies as proposed by Sept. 11 commission

2003
Yes Cut taxes by $330 billion through fiscal 2013
No Block Bush rule scaling back overtime pay for some white-collar federal workers
No Do not allow use of search warrants without first notifying subjects
Yes Allow importation of prescription drugs
Yes Create private school voucher program in Washington, D.C.
Yes Ban "partial birth" abortion except to save a woman's life
?   Split $18.6 billion in Iraq aid into half-grant, half-loan
Yes Overhaul Medicare and create prescription drug benefit

CQ VOTE STUDIES

	PARTY UNITY		PRESIDENTIAL SUPPORT	
	Support	Oppose	Support	Oppose
2004	96%	4%	85%	15%
2003	95%	5%	96%	4%
2002	95%	5%	90%	10%
2001	99%	1%	98%	2%
2000	95%	5%	30%	70%

INTEREST GROUPS

	AFL-CIO	ADA	CCUS	ACU
2004	20%	0%	100%	88%
2003	7%	10%	97%	76%
2002	11%	5%	90%	88%
2001	8%	0%	100%	88%
2000	0%	5%	85%	92%

CALIFORNIA 25
Northern Los Angeles and San Bernardino counties; Inyo and Mono counties

The vast 25th stretches from east-central California on the Nevada border south along the mountains and through Death Valley before crossing the Mojave Desert and San Bernardino County into northern Los Angeles County, where it takes in the tip of the city.

Nearly three-fourths of residents live in Los Angeles County, although only 5 percent of the county's overall populace is in the district. The 25th's suburbs and desert are solidly Republican, including a mix of upper-middle-class residents and more-conservative working-class whites. Hispanics also make up more than one-fourth of the population.

Most of the land in Mono and Inyo counties, added during the last redistricting, is government-owned, and a few bedroom communities' economies rely on tourism, mining and agriculture. Santa Clarita Valley is suburban, but attracts manufacturing that cannot afford to locate in Los Angeles proper. The 25th's fastest-growing area is the Antelope Valley

desert due north of Los Angeles, home to Lancaster and Palmdale.

Economically, the 25th relies on the aerospace industry and several military bases. The district faces the challenges of managing and irrigating vast tracts of desert, much of it federally owned, and spurring its economy by attracting more industry and manufacturing jobs. Despite these obstacles, San Bernardino County saw some of the state's fastest job growth in 2004.

MAJOR INDUSTRY
Tourism, manufacturing, construction, aerospace, military

MILITARY BASES
Edwards Air Force Base, 3,711 military, 8,559 civilian (shared with the 22nd); Fort Irwin (Army), 4,960 military, 3,469 civilian; Naval Air Warfare Center Weapons Division, China Lake, 891 military, 3,134 civilian (shared with the 22nd); Marine Corps Logistics Base Barstow, 243 military, 1,492 civilian (2004)

CITIES
Santa Clarita, 151,088; Palmdale, 116,670; Victorville, 64,029; Lancaster (pt.), 52,742; Los Angeles (pt.), 22,882

NOTABLE
Badwater in Death Valley is the lowest point in the United States.

Rep. David Dreier (R)

Elected 1980; 13th term

A camera-friendly Californian plugged into the Hollywood wing of the GOP, Dreier is also a valuable asset to the House Republican leadership. Speaker J. Dennis Hastert waived a rule limiting the terms of committee chairmen to let Dreier stay on for a fourth term at the helm of the Rules Committee in the 109th Congress.

That no doubt figured in Dreier's decision to remain in the House after considering career alternatives in recent years. Dreier toyed with challenging liberal Democratic Sen. Barbara Boxer of California in 2004 but decided against the uphill campaign to unseat a popular incumbent. And he was courted as a possible replacement for the retiring Jack Valenti, the movie industry's legendary Washington lobbyist.

The House leadership arguably needed him more. He has a knack for using the rules governing debate and the amendment process to give Republicans the procedural upper hand on the House floor. Behind the scenes, he is a party loyalist who can navigate sensitive political waters. Dreier was asked to remain chairman of Rules at a time when Hastert and other top leaders were pushing for a raft of controversial changes to House rules affecting ethics complaints against members.

The changes were viewed as largely benefiting Majority Leader Tom DeLay, the House's powerful No. 2 leader, who was under political fire. He was rebuked for questionable behavior by the House ethics committee in 2004, and prosecutors in Texas were probing several political fundraising groups with ties to the Texan. Republican leaders looked to the unflappable, telegenic Dreier to help sell the proposals to skeptics in the press corps and even among some Republicans.

As Rules chairman, he is at the center of every consequential legislative battle in the House. Under pressure, he remains polite and composed. He almost always identifies colleagues on the floor not only by their home state but also by their hometown, even when he is preparing to tell them their amendment will never be discussed on the House floor.

He is at his best when playing to an audience, whether on the talk show circuit, in the well of the House, or kibitzing with the press and radio and television crews, often greeting them with a sly smile and a handshake. His impeccably pressed suits frequently land him on Washingtonian magazine's best-dressed congressmen list.

Dreier also brings an energy level noticeable even in the workaholic Capitol. His days often end long after dark, quite literally in a cigar-smoke-filled room hashing out details of a GOP-blessed script for the next day's floor proceedings.

A quarter-century after entering public life, Dreier still describes himself as a Reagan Republican who believes in the primacy of the free market and who wants government to stay out of the way of private enterprise.

He has put his legislative skills to work on some of the most important government restructurings of the post-Sept. 11 era, including the creation of the Department of Homeland Security. And as befits someone who represented Los Angeles' high-tech hub, Dreier has promoted the use of new technologies on the Hill, advocating online and interactive congressional hearings that employ e-mail, video conferencing, television and the Internet to create a virtual hearing room for witnesses across the country.

Outside the House, Dreier has had several important party roles. He was co-chairman of George W. Bush's 2000 presidential campaign in Cal-

CAPITOL OFFICE
225-2305
dreier.house.gov
233 Cannon 20515-0526; fax 225-7018

COMMITTEES
Rules - chairman

HOMETOWN
San Dimas

BORN
July 5, 1952, Kansas City, Mo.

RELIGION
Christian Scientist

FAMILY
Single

EDUCATION
Claremont Men's College, B.A. 1975 (political science); Claremont Graduate U., M.A. 1976 (American government)

CAREER
Real estate developer; university fundraiser

POLITICAL HIGHLIGHTS
Republican nominee for U.S. House, 1978

ELECTION RESULTS

2004 GENERAL
David Dreier (R)	134,596	53.6%
Cynthia M. Matthews (D)	107,522	42.8%
Randall Weissbuch (LIBERT)	9,089	3.6%

2004 PRIMARY
David Dreier (R)	53,368	83.6%
S. Sonny Sardo (R)	10,502	16.4%

2002 GENERAL
David Dreier (R)	95,360	63.8%
Marjorie Musser Mikels (D)	50,081	33.5%
Randall Weissbuch (LIBERT)	4,089	2.7%

PREVIOUS WINNING PERCENTAGES
2000 (57%); 1998 (58%); 1996 (61%); 1994 (67%); 1992 (58%); 1990 (64%); 1988 (69%); 1986 (72%); 1984 (71%); 1982 (65%); 1980 (52%)

ifornia, one of the nation's biggest electoral prizes, and he served as parliamentarian of the Republican National Convention in Philadelphia that year. Dreier's political action committee, the American Success PAC, gave more than $500,000 to candidates and colleagues in each of the last two elections.

Dreier hobnobs with a California political crowd that includes Arnold Schwarzenegger, the actor-turned-governor who relied on him for advice during his gubernatorial campaign in the state's controversial recall election in 2003. Dreier, who jogs and does 200 pushups daily, trades fitness tips with the former body-builder and does an impression of Schwarzenegger's heavy Austrian accent. He calls his involvement in the race "the most interesting 54 days of my life."

Dreier has an abiding interest in the history and the well-being of the House as an institution. He says that a relative, Richard Bland Lee of Virginia, served on the first Rules panel near the end of the 18th century.

"The difference between the House and the Senate," Dreier once said, "is that on the floor of the Senate, it's like you're in a living room. And the floor of the House of Representatives is like an arena. It's intense."

Dreier is a native of Kansas City, Mo., and remains active in his family's real estate investment firm there, which has made him one of Congress' richest members.

In his first, underfinanced campaign for the House in 1978, Dreier came within 12,000 votes of defeating Democratic incumbent James F. Lloyd. He was just 26 years old and not long out of Claremont Men's College, now Claremont McKenna, where he'd earned a graduate degree. Two years later, he swamped Lloyd in fundraising and won by 12,000 votes, aided by that year's Reagan presidential landslide.

Congressional redistricting for incumbent protection after the 2000 census made Dreier's territory more predictably Republican. But he had one of the closest elections of his career in 2004, winning with just 54 percent of the vote against a relative unknown, down from 64 percent in 2002.

The slide can probably be explained by the hot-button California issue of immigration. Local Los Angeles radio talk show hosts John Kobylt and Ken Chiampou of the "John and Ken" show held a local contest to single out lawmakers they claimed had done little to stop the flow of undocumented immigrants across the border. Dreier, who had supported Bush's proposed guest worker program to grant legal status to millions of immigrants, won, and John and Ken launched an aggressive "Fire Dreier" campaign, giving it a lot of air play.

KEY VOTES

2004

No	Extend federal unemployment benefits by 13 weeks
Yes	Pass $283.2 billion, six-year federal highway and mass transit bill
Yes	Approve $146 billion multi-year extension of previously enacted middle-class tax breaks
No	Amend the Constitution to prohibit same-sex marriage
Yes	Cut corporate taxes $137 billion over 10 years
Yes	Reorganize U.S. intelligence agencies as proposed by Sept. 11 commission

2003

Yes	Cut taxes by $330 billion through fiscal 2013
No	Block Bush rule scaling back overtime pay for some white-collar federal workers
No	Do not allow use of search warrants without first notifying subjects
No	Allow importation of prescription drugs
Yes	Create private school voucher program in Washington, D.C.
?	Ban "partial birth" abortion except to save a woman's life
No	Split $18.6 billion in Iraq aid into half-grant, half-loan
Yes	Overhaul Medicare and create prescription drug benefit

CQ VOTE STUDIES

	PARTY UNITY		PRESIDENTIAL SUPPORT	
	Support	Oppose	Support	Oppose
2004	92%	8%	94%	6%
2003	95%	5%	100%	0%
2002	93%	7%	92%	8%
2001	97%	3%	100%	0%
2000	94%	6%	30%	70%

INTEREST GROUPS

	AFL-CIO	ADA	CCUS	ACU
2004	13%	5%	100%	88%
2003	7%	5%	100%	83%
2002	11%	5%	100%	84%
2001	8%	10%	100%	84%
2000	0%	5%	90%	92%

CALIFORNIA 26
Northeastern Los Angeles suburbs

Set in the foothills of the San Gabriel Mountains, the 26th is a mix of Los Angeles bedroom communities and the mountainous Angeles National Forest, which comprises its northern half. The commuter-heavy district takes in middle- to upper-class suburbs, many of which have retained their own identities and quaint downtowns.

The district includes wealthy, Republican communities surrounding Pasadena, such as La Cañada Flintridge and San Marino, and other Los Angeles County cities such as Arcadia, Glendora, Monrovia and San Dimas. Outside La Cañada Flintridge is NASA's Jet Propulsion Laboratory, which contributes to the area's high-tech flavor along with the California Institute of Technology in Pasadena (in the 29th District) and engineering firms in Monrovia. Many of the 26th's residents commute to work in downtown Los Angeles or have technology manufacturing jobs just outside the district.

In its chunk of San Bernardino County, where orchard country has given way to rapidly developing suburbs, the district includes the Inland Valley

suburbs of Rancho Cucamonga, Upland and Montclair. Rapid development has brought young, wealthy fiscally minded Republicans to town — not unlike Orange County to the south. The valley is populated by service employers such as corporate call centers and technology groups. Most other industry is confined to small defense subcontractors and service industries, although the area has seen some growth in trade-related import and export businesses.

Like many Los Angeles suburbanites, residents here tend to be socially moderate and economically conservative. The district gave George W. Bush 55 percent of the 2004 presidential vote. While not as diverse as most of its neighbors, the district is one-fourth Hispanic.

MAJOR INDUSTRY
Service, manufacturing, health care, biotechnology

CITIES
Rancho Cucamonga, 127,743; Upland, 68,393; Arcadia, 53,054; Glendora, 49,415

NOTABLE
Santa Anita Park thoroughbred racetrack is in Arcadia; The Huntington Library, a museum and garden in San Marino, has in its collection Thomas Gainsborough's painting, The Blue Boy, and a Gutenberg Bible.

Rep. Brad Sherman (D)

Elected 1996; 5th term

In recent years, Sherman has traded on his financial background and a hawkish outlook on foreign policy to have an impact on legislation dealing with corporate scandals, the war in Iraq and the government's crackdown on terrorism. But he remains a traditional Democrat on social issues and the environment. Smart and funny, he says he has been drawn to jobs that are held in the lowest possible public esteem, which explains why he's been a certified public accountant, a lawyer and a politician.

Lately, the self-described "recovering nerd" has found that his accounting background is less a punchline than a credit line in his work in the House. Since the collapse of Enron Corp. in 2001, Sherman has found a use for his brainy form of politics in the wave of corporate accounting scandals and abuses in the mutual fund industry, and as robust budget surpluses have turned into yawning budget deficits.

The San Fernando Valley Democrat is well-positioned to make his views heard from his seat on the House Financial Services Committee. In the 108th Congress, he pushed for new federal rules forcing companies to expense stock options. And he rallied Democrats to stop an attempt in committee to tie the hands of local officials, like New York State Attorney General Eliot Spitzer, who were actively prosecuting fraud in the securities industry. Some lawmakers thought that the Securities and Exchange Commission should remain the dominant regulator. With characteristic edge, Sherman argued that while he normally agrees that a national approach is best, the SEC "has done such a phenomenally poor job," perhaps the oversight duties should go to localities and states.

A hard-liner on a balanced budget and a former member of the Budget Committee, Sherman expressed exasperation over President Bush's tax cuts at a time of deepening deficits. When Federal Reserve Chairman Alan Greenspan told Congress in 2003 that he "would prefer to find the situation in which spending was constrained, the economy was growing, and that tax cuts were capable of being initiated without creating fiscal problems," Sherman shot back: "I would prefer a world in which Julia Roberts was calling me, but that is not likely to occur."

He also takes a harder line on foreign policy than many Democrats. Sherman voted for the resolution authorizing the Iraq war and, from his seat on the International Relations Committee, called for an expanded investigative role for the CIA.

A priority of Sherman's is "to make sure bad guys don't get nuclear weapons." From his post as the senior Democrat on the International Terrorism, Nonproliferation and Human Rights Subcommittee, he has called for reinstating U.S. financing for democracy supporters in Iran, which were suspended in the 1981 accord that ended the Iranian hostage crisis. In the first meeting of the new House oversight panel in 2003, Sherman grilled State Department officials about allowing trade with Iran, when the country headed the administration's list of state sponsors of terrorism. "I'm flabbergasted that the Bush administration has continued the mistake of the Clinton administration and left the doors wide open," he said.

Sherman spearheaded a vote on the Iraq supplemental spending bill in 2003 that embarrassed the Bush administration on no-bid contracts awarded to Vice President Dick Cheney's old employer, Halliburton Co. The amendment requiring normal competitive bidding procedures for oil-related contracts in Iraq passed easily in the GOP-controlled House, surprising

CAPITOL OFFICE
225-5911
www.house.gov/sherman
1030 Longworth 20515-0527; fax 225-5879

COMMITTEES
Financial Services
International Relations
Science

HOMETOWN
Sherman Oaks

BORN
Oct. 24, 1954, Los Angeles, Calif.

RELIGION
Jewish

FAMILY
Single

EDUCATION
U. of California, Los Angeles, B.A. 1974 (political communication); Harvard U., J.D. 1979

CAREER
Accountant; lawyer

POLITICAL HIGHLIGHTS
Calif. State Board of Equalization, 1991-97 (chairman, 1991-95)

ELECTION RESULTS

2004 GENERAL
Brad Sherman (D)	125,296	62.3%
Robert M. Levy (R)	66,946	33.3%
Eric J. Carter (GREEN)	8,956	4.5%

2004 PRIMARY
Brad Sherman (D)	unopposed

2002 GENERAL
Brad Sherman (D)	79,815	62.0%
Robert M. Levy (R)	48,996	38.0%

PREVIOUS WINNING PERCENTAGES
2000 (66%); 1998 (57%); 1996 (50%)

even Sherman.

In 2004, he also took on a Republican committee chairman and fellow Californian. When House Resources Chairman Richard W. Pombo requested $500,000 for postage for national mailings touting the panel's work, Sherman noted that such spending in the previous Congress was only $3,000. He argued that unlike members of Congress, committees don't have constituents and so should not have franking privileges.

On the Science Committee, Sherman is the conservative right's worst nightmare in the emerging area of genetics policy. While describing some of his ideas as "science fiction," Sherman says he's interested in what he calls engineered intelligence and that he can imagine scenarios in which an artificially created species poses new challenges for human beings. Policy makers should be thinking about such possibilities, he says. Sherman criticized Bush's 2001 decision to back federal funding for stem cell research but only for 60 existing cell lines. "We get only as much science as the far right will allow," he griped.

Active on environmental issues, where he sticks to traditional Democratic positions, Sherman supports higher fuel efficiency requirements for cars sold in the United States and wants tax credits for people who buy hybrid cars. He says it's ironic that the federal tax code allows better tax benefits for purchases of gas-guzzling H1 Hummers and the heaviest SUVs. He has also cosponsored legislation to protect endangered species, restrict commercial logging and limit arsenic in drinking water.

One of Sherman's pet projects is altering the order of presidential succession. His legislation would ensure that the presidency remained in the hands of the same political party by allowing the president to designate either the speaker of the House or the House minority leader as second in line after the vice president, followed by either the majority or minority leader of the Senate, rather than the Senate president pro tempore.

Sherman got his start in politics as a child, stuffing envelopes for Democratic Rep. George E. Brown Jr., a longtime family friend. He was elected to the five-member California State Board of Equalization in 1990 and 1994.

When he ran for the U.S. House in 1996, Sherman had the backing of most area Democrats, including Rep. Anthony C. Beilenson, who was retiring after 10 terms. He won the nomination with 54 percent of the vote, besting six other candidates, and carried the general election by 6 percentage points. Since then, he has enjoyed wider victory margins. In 2004, he had a rematch with GOP attorney Robert M. Levy, who had taken 38 percent in 2002. Sherman prevailed decisively, by 29 points.

KEY VOTES

2004
Yes   Extend federal unemployment benefits by 13 weeks
Yes   Pass $283.2 billion, six-year federal highway and mass transit bill
Yes   Approve $146 billion multi-year extension of previously enacted middle-class tax breaks
No   Amend the Constitution to prohibit same-sex marriage
No   Cut corporate taxes $137 billion over 10 years
Yes   Reorganize U.S. intelligence agencies as proposed by Sept. 11 commission

2003
No   Cut taxes by $330 billion through fiscal 2013
Yes   Block Bush rule scaling back overtime pay for some white-collar federal workers
Yes   Do not allow use of search warrants without first notifying subjects
No   Allow importation of prescription drugs
No   Create private school voucher program in Washington, D.C.
No   Ban "partial birth" abortion except to save a woman's life
Yes   Split $18.6 billion in Iraq aid into half-grant, half-loan
No   Overhaul Medicare and create prescription drug benefit

CQ VOTE STUDIES

	PARTY UNITY		PRESIDENTIAL SUPPORT	
	Support	Oppose	Support	Oppose
2004	96%	4%	27%	73%
2003	97%	3%	16%	84%
2002	95%	5%	28%	72%
2001	92%	8%	33%	67%
2000	93%	7%	83%	17%

INTEREST GROUPS

	AFL-CIO	ADA	CCUS	ACU
2004	100%	95%	33%	4%
2003	100%	90%	30%	9%
2002	89%	100%	35%	4%
2001	92%	95%	39%	12%
2000	100%	90%	47%	20%

CALIFORNIA 27

Part of the San Fernando Valley; part of Burbank

While most of the 27th is in Los Angeles, few of the district's residents identify themselves as "Angelenos." Instead, they see themselves as part of the region's fast-growing communities: the Van Nuys, Encino and Sherman Oaks areas of Los Angeles in the San Fernando Valley north of the central city.

The Valley — primarily the 27th and 28th districts — was behind a failed ballot measure in 2002 to secede from the rest of the city amid complaints that too much of its taxes went over the mountains to city services in central Los Angeles. Though the measure was initiated by the Valley's traditional white, middle- to upper-class voters, the 27th's suburban havens have been transformed by immigrants and no longer are dominated by that group. Forty-five percent white and 36 percent Hispanic, the district also has seen a rapid increase in Asian immigrants, particularly from India and Pakistan, who have added to the district's

working-class flavor.

The flat, gridlike streets of the 27th hold the Burbank and Van Nuys airports, as well as several colleges, including California State University Northridge. Reservoirs in the northwest corner provide water to more than 10 million Los Angeles residents.

While many San Fernando Valley residents worry about traffic congestion on their commutes to downtown or west Los Angeles, quality-of-life issues including health care and air quality are major concerns as well. Immigration is one among several factors that have made the district solidly Democratic — it gave Democrat John Kerry 59 percent of the vote in the 2004 presidential election.

MAJOR INDUSTRY
Biotechnology, service

CITIES
Los Angeles (pt.), 591,573; Burbank (pt.), 45,436

NOTABLE
The San Fernando Valley is known as the pornography capital of the world.

Rep. Howard L. Berman (D)

Elected 1982; 12th term

CAPITOL OFFICE
225-4695
www.house.gov/berman
2221 Rayburn 20515-0528; fax 225-3196

COMMITTEES
International Relations
Judiciary

HOMETOWN
Valley Village

BORN
April 15, 1941, Los Angeles, Calif.

RELIGION
Jewish

FAMILY
Wife, Jan Berman; one child, one stepchild

EDUCATION
U. of California, Los Angeles, B.A. 1962
(international relations), LL.B. 1965

CAREER
Lawyer

POLITICAL HIGHLIGHTS
Calif. Assembly, 1972-82

ELECTION RESULTS

2004 GENERAL

Howard L. Berman (D)	115,303	71.0%
David R. Hernandez Jr. (R)	37,868	23.3%
Kelley L. Ross (LIBERT)	9,339	5.8%

2004 PRIMARY

Howard L. Berman (D)	33,702	81.9%
Charles R. Coleman Jr. (D)	7,448	18.1%

2002 GENERAL

Howard L. Berman (D)	73,771	71.4%
David R. Hernandez Jr. (R)	23,926	23.2%
Kelley L. Ross (LIBERT)	5,629	5.5%

PREVIOUS WINNING PERCENTAGES
2000 (84%); 1998 (82%); 1996 (66%); 1994 (63%);
1992 (61%); 1990 (61%); 1988 (70%); 1986 (65%);
1984 (63%); 1982 (60%)

A low-key liberal who assiduously guards the interests of the entertainment industry and supports the cause of Israel, Berman has built a solid reputation as an institutionalist and a serious-minded legislator who can work effectively across party lines.

The bulk of his legislative work takes place in the Judiciary and International Relations committees, where in the 109th Congress he is the second-ranking Democrat on both panels. In recent years, he has focused his efforts primarily on intellectual property rights, immigration, and U.S. relations with terrorism-sponsoring nations such as Syria and Iran. In 2002 and 2003, his concerns about the Middle East led him to support the war against Iraq and the funding to support that war, even when a majority of his fellow House Democrats voted against both.

Judiciary is seen as one of the most partisan House panels and, populated as it is by lawyers, is well known for raucous debate over social policy. But the Subcommittee on Courts, the Internet and Intellectual Property, where Berman has been the top Democrat since 1999 does not fit that mold. Disagreements are seldom overtly partisan in nature; panel members more often divide according to competing industry interests as they address problems created by rapidly developing new technologies.

Berman seems to enjoy tackling a range of complicated issues — including privacy, copyright and patent protection and business practices — that have emerged with the advent of the Internet and wireless communication.

Berman's seniority on the subcommittee is important to Southern California's many writers, composers and other content creators with a stake in guarding copyrights. He says the long-term interest of Internet, cable and satellite TV users is best served by providing incentives for people to continue to create, whether it be books, movies, music, computer software, a business method or an invention. In the 108th Congress, he introduced a bill to establish three special judgeships to determine copyright royalty rates and the distribution of royalties.

A longtime advocate for migrant farm laborers, Berman uses his Judiciary seat to champion legislation to improve the working conditions and immigrant status of farm workers and to permit the children of illegal immigrants to remain in the United States as long as they are in school. In the 108th Congress, he was a lead sponsor of a bipartisan bill to give migrant farm workers a path to permanent legal status in the United States.

After the Sept. 11, 2001, terrorist attacks, Berman pushed legislation to tighten immigration controls; improve monitoring of foreign nationals, particularly students, already in the country; and boost the use of technology to screen entrants at the border. He also favored applying asset seizure penalties that had been aimed at drug kingpins to convicted terrorists.

But Berman objected to language in the USA Patriot Act, the anti-terrorism law enacted in 2001, that permits federal authorities to detain immigrants indefinitely. This controversial practice would have been limited by a bill Berman sponsored during the 108th Congress — legislation aimed at rolling back a host of President Bush's post-Sept. 11 immigration policies that critics described as threats to civil liberties. While standing by his vote for the Patriot Act, Berman told the Los Angeles Daily News that some of Bush's anti-terror policies had become "draconian and ineffective."

On International Relations, Berman is a leader in efforts to halt the international spread of weapons of mass destruction. In 1996, he played a key role in the passage of legislation imposing sanctions on foreign companies that did business with Libya and Iran — nations closely linked with international terrorism. In the 107th, he worked to renew that sanctions law for five more years. Berman was also a strong supporter of the Syria Accountability Act, a sanctions bill passed by the 108th Congress and signed into law by Bush.

He credits his interest in public affairs to a favorite high school teacher. "My parents weren't political, so she was the person who moved me to challenge assumptions and to debate issues," he told the Daily News.

As a legislative intern while at UCLA law school, Berman worked on labor issues with Cesar Chavez's United Farm Workers. "From then on, I was hooked," he told the Daily News. He succeeded fellow Rep. Henry A. Waxman as president of the school's Federation of Young Democrats, and in 1968 he helped his friend Waxman win a seat in the California Assembly. This marked the start of the Waxman-Berman political organization, a network of like-minded politicians and activists who pooled resources to back candidates with money and organizational assistance, thereby influencing western Los Angeles County politics for years.

After graduating from college, Berman spent a year as a VISTA volunteer before practicing labor relations law in Los Angeles. In 1972, after working behind the scenes to help other Democrats win elections, it was Berman's turn to run, and he won a state Assembly seat. A consummate facilitator and tactician with a relaxed style, Berman soon rose to majority leader but lost a bid to become Speaker.

He won his seat in Congress in 1982 after state House Speaker Willie L. Brown Jr. helped draw a congressional redistricting plan that included a perfect district for Berman. Since then, he has won re-election easily.

In California redistricting for the current decade, the Golden State's House Democratic delegation hired Berman's brother, Michael, as a consultant to draft a revised map. The district lines that were eventually approved protected most incumbents, angering Southern California Hispanics who had clamored for a map that would favor election of another Hispanic. The district, which had been numbered the 26th, saw a decrease in its Hispanic population from about 65 percent to about 56 percent.

In 2002 and 2004, Berman faced the same Republican challenger, David R. Hernandez Jr. In both elections, he won with 71 percent of the vote.

KEY VOTES

2004

Yes Extend federal unemployment benefits by 13 weeks

Yes Pass $283.2 billion, six-year federal highway and mass transit bill

Yes Approve $146 billion multi-year extension of previously enacted middle-class tax breaks

No Amend the Constitution to prohibit same-sex marriage

No Cut corporate taxes $137 billion over 10 years

Yes Reorganize U.S. intelligence agencies as proposed by Sept. 11 commission

2003

No Cut taxes by $330 billion through fiscal 2013

Yes Block Bush rule scaling back overtime pay for some white-collar federal workers

Yes Do not allow use of search warrants without first notifying subjects

No Allow importation of prescription drugs

No Create private school voucher program in Washington, D.C.

No Ban "partial birth" abortion except to save a woman's life

Yes Split $18.6 billion in Iraq aid into half-grant, half-loan

No Overhaul Medicare and create prescription drug benefit

CQ VOTE STUDIES

	PARTY UNITY		PRESIDENTIAL SUPPORT	
	Support	Oppose	Support	Oppose
2004	97%	3%	31%	69%
2003	94%	6%	17%	83%
2002	96%	4%	24%	76%
2001	92%	8%	38%	62%
2000	96%	4%	94%	6%

INTEREST GROUPS

	AFL-CIO	ADA	CCUS	ACU
2004	100%	90%	29%	0%
2003	87%	5%	34%	17%
2002	100%	90%	37%	10%
2001	100%	95%	36%	4%
2000	100%	100%	50%	4%

CALIFORNIA 28
Part of the San Fernando Valley

The 28th starts in the San Fernando Valley north of Los Angeles, where it takes in the small city of San Fernando and includes the Los Angeles communities of Pacoima, Arleta, Panorama City, Van Nuys and North Hollywood. The southern border follows in part famed Mulholland Drive, taking in Encino, Sherman Oaks and Studio City in the Hollywood Hills north of Beverly Hills.

Once composed of predominately white, suburban Los Angeles communities, the area has attracted large numbers of Hispanics, who now make up 56 percent of the district's population. That majority is a major contributor to the Democratic voting tendency in the district, which gave Democrat John Kerry 71 percent of the vote in the 2004 presidential election.

The 28th's thriving commercial district, centered on financial services, is just south of Route 101, along Ventura Boulevard, where bank branch offices in office towers compete with miles of fast-food outlets, trendy restaurants and strip malls. It passes by the Sherman Oaks Galleria,

home of the "Valley girl" and recently renovated with businesses and upscale restaurants. A number of movies and TV shows have been filmed at the CBS Studio Center in Studio City, including "Hill Street Blues," "Roseanne" and "Seinfeld."

Defense industry closures and the 1994 Northridge earthquake hit the district hard. It has stayed afloat, however, fueled by the technology and entertainment industries and the growth of service industries that are increasingly driven by new immigrants. The district has some manufacturing plants, and Van Nuys, which lost a General Motors plant in 1992, got a boost from a new retail center and industrial park that opened on the old GM site in 2000.

MAJOR INDUSTRY
Service, entertainment, manufacturing, health care

CITIES
Los Angeles (pt.), 615,523; San Fernando, 23,564

NOTABLE
The Academy of Television Arts and Sciences, which presents the annual Emmy Awards, is based in North Hollywood; Actors Robert Redford and Marilyn Monroe attended Van Nuys High School; Rock & Roll Hall of Famer Ritchie Valens ("La Bamba") was a native of Pacoima.

Rep. Adam B. Schiff (D)

Elected 2000; 3rd term

CAPITOL OFFICE
225-4176
www.house.gov/schiff
326 Cannon 20515-0529; fax 225-5828

COMMITTEES
International Relations
Judiciary

HOMETOWN
Burbank

BORN
June 22, 1960, Framingham, Mass.

RELIGION
Jewish

FAMILY
Wife, Eve Schiff; two children

EDUCATION
Stanford U., A.B. 1982 (political science & pre-med); Harvard U., J.D. 1985

CAREER
Federal prosecutor; lawyer

POLITICAL HIGHLIGHTS
Assistant U.S. attorney, 1987-93; Democratic nominee for Calif. Assembly (special election), 1994; Democratic nominee for Calif. Assembly, 1994; Calif. Senate, 1996-2000

ELECTION RESULTS

2004 GENERAL

Adam B. Schiff (D)	133,670	64.6%
Harry Frank Scolinos (R)	62,871	30.4%
Philip Koebel (GREEN)	5,715	2.8%
Ted Brown (LIBERT)	4,570	2.2%

2004 PRIMARY

Adam B. Schiff (D)	unopposed

2002 GENERAL

Adam B. Schiff (D)	76,036	62.6%
Jim Scileppi (R)	40,616	33.4%
Ted Brown (LIBERT)	4,889	4.0%

PREVIOUS WINNING PERCENTAGES
2000 (53%)

Although the self-styled moderate began his career on Capitol Hill by joining the conservative Democratic Blue Dog Coalition and the centrist New Democrat group, Schiff has moved steadily toward the more liberal core of his party in the House.

In 2001, Schiff's first year in Congress, he sided with President Bush 40 percent of the time, a support score almost 10 percentage points higher than that of the average House Democrat. By the 108th Congress, however, his support for Bush had fallen to just 25 percent, slightly below that of the average House Democrat. And since 2001, Schiff's party unity scores have increased considerably as he found more in common with his fellow Democrats than with the conservative-dominated House GOP.

His votes on tax legislation typified his changing perspective. Schiff was one of 28 Democrats who voted to enact the Bush tax cuts in 2001, but he opposed the next round in 2003, saying it was "imprudent and fiscally irresponsible" to pass additional big tax cuts when the nation was at war.

One of eight former federal prosecutors in Congress, Schiff has used his positions on the Judiciary and International Relations committees to advance a range of initiatives relating to crime and national security.

In the 108th Congress, he sponsored legislation, which President Bush signed into law, to increase criminal penalties for identity theft. Schiff also introduced legislation to foster the use of DNA analysis in criminal investigations, expanding the national DNA database and boosting funding to eliminate the backlog of untested samples. Similar legislation, cosponsored by Schiff, became law late in the 108th.

In 2001, Schiff played an active role in Judiciary Committee deliberations on the counterterrorism law, known as the USA Patriot Act, that was written in the weeks following the Sept. 11, 2001, terrorist attacks. He says his experience as a prosecutor made him more comfortable than some of his colleagues with certain elements of the package; even though he backed the measure, a vital factor in his support was that some of the more controversial new law enforcement powers were to expire in 2005. Schiff said that a large part of the act should be extended, but that so far, Congress has not "stepped up its responsibility to do oversight," including a section-by-section review of the law.

In 2003, Schiff introduced legislation to authorize military tribunals for prosecuting terrorists, setting specific rules of procedure — including granting public access and providing for Supreme Court review. This, and another Schiff bill authorizing the president to detain U.S. citizens as enemy combatants, were made highly relevant by two 2004 Supreme Court rulings on emphasizing Congress' authority to set detention ground rules. "There are many unanswered questions in the court's decisions that Congress could and should answer," Schiff said.

Although his style is hardly flashy, Schiff came to Congress as something of a celebrity. His 2000 campaign in the old 27th District against two-term GOP Rep. James E. Rogan drew more attention and campaign money than many of the year's Senate races. Rogan was a prime Democratic target because of his high-profile role in the impeachment of President Clinton. Schiff, then a state senator, and Rogan raised in all more than $10 million between them — a House race record.

Given the large Armenian population in his district, Schiff immediately joined in the longstanding legislative effort to persuade the president to formally recognize as genocide the deaths of millions of Armenians that began in 1915 at the hands of the Ottoman Empire, in what is now Turkey. As a state senator, Schiff helped secure state funds for a documentary on Armenia. In the 108th, he offered an amendment to prohibit Turkey from using U.S. foreign aid dollars to lobby against a congressional resolution officially recognizing the Armenian genocide.

A central goal of Schiff's political agenda is the promotion of early childhood education, from preschool through third grade. A larger investment in helping preschool children has been proven to reduce crime, he says. In the 108th, he helped organize opposition to the Bush administration's proposed cutbacks in the Head Start program, saying the GOP-backed legislation would "close the door of the Head Start program to tens of thousands of deserving children and their families."

Schiff was born in Massachusetts. His father was a traveling salesman in the clothing business and was transferred to California when Schiff was 9. When he entered Stanford, Schiff could not decide between medicine and law, and so he majored in both pre-med and political science. He was accepted to both medical school and law school. Although his parents urged him to become a doctor, Schiff chose law school, deciding that it afforded broader opportunities for public service.

After getting his law degree at Harvard, he returned to California and clerked for a federal judge; his fascination with the cases that federal prosecutors presented, he said, led him eventually to his six years of work in the U.S. Attorney's office.

A colleague there, Tom Umberg, who was elected to the California Assembly, was the inspiration for Schiff's move into politics. "I wanted to deal with the root causes of the problems I was dealing with as a U.S. attorney," Schiff explained. He was unsuccessful at first, losing to Rogan in 1994, in both a special- and a general-election Assembly race. He rebounded in 1996, winning a state Senate district that included the old 27th Congressional District.

Schiff in 2000 again faced Rogan, who had moved up to the U.S. House in 1996. Schiff took a 9 percentage point victory in one of the year's marquee races. In 2002, running in the newly drawn 29th, which tilts even more Democratic, Schiff cruised to a 29 percentage point victory. In 2004, he bested Vietnam veteran and attorney Harry Scolinos by 34 percentage points.

Schiff's wife is named Eve, and he is amused by the attention that the "Adam and Eve" pairing gets. His wife is less amused, and they have steadfastly resisted the expected suggestions for their children's names, opting instead for Alexa and Elijah.

KEY VOTES

2004

Yes Extend federal unemployment benefits by 13 weeks

Yes Pass $283.2 billion, six-year federal highway and mass transit bill

Yes Approve $146 billion multi-year extension of previously enacted middle-class tax breaks

No Amend the Constitution to prohibit same-sex marriage

No Cut corporate taxes $137 billion over 10 years

Yes Reorganize U.S. intelligence agencies as proposed by Sept. 11 commission

2003

No Cut taxes by $330 billion through fiscal 2013

Yes Block Bush rule scaling back overtime pay for some white-collar federal workers

Yes Do not allow use of search warrants without first notifying subjects

Yes Allow importation of prescription drugs

No Create private school voucher program in Washington, D.C.

No Ban "partial birth" abortion except to save a woman's life

Yes Split $18.6 billion in Iraq aid into half-grant, half-loan

No Overhaul Medicare and create prescription drug benefit

CQ VOTE STUDIES

	PARTY UNITY		PRESIDENTIAL SUPPORT	
	Support	Oppose	Support	Oppose
2004	93%	7%	38%	62%
2003	96%	4%	16%	84%
2002	92%	8%	32%	68%
2001	83%	17%	40%	60%

INTEREST GROUPS

	AFL-CIO	ADA	CCUS	ACU
2004	93%	95%	43%	12%
2003	87%	100%	33%	16%
2002	88%	95%	45%	8%
2001	83%	85%	39%	13%

CALIFORNIA 29

Glendale; Pasadena; Alhambra; part of Burbank

Set in the foothills of the San Gabriel Mountains, the 29th includes the Los Angeles suburbs of Glendale, Pasadena, Alhambra and part of Burbank. Over the years, immigration and the growing nearby Hollywood economy have transformed once-WASPish neighborhoods, giving the district a Democratic lean.

The 29th is home to few movie stars, but many of those whose names appear farther down in movie credits live here. While a high-tech community has sprung up around the California Institute of Technology and a number of colleges, the district is primarily residential.

The area includes a wide mix of ethnicities. Monterey Park (shared with the 32nd) is upper-middle-class and known as "Little Taipei" for its Taiwanese and other Asian immigrants. Glendale is home to about 75,000 Armenians, the largest such community outside of Armenia. Alhambra is heavily Hispanic and Asian, and upscale San Gabriel has a strong Italian community. Overall, the district is about one-fourth Asian and one-fourth

Hispanic. About 60 different languages and dialects are spoken in Glendale's public schools.

Although part of the Los Angeles area, Pasadena, a lush former resort town, and Glendale have their own downtowns. Television and movie production studios drive the economy in Burbank. Landfill redevelopment is set to begin in Monterey Park, while residents of South Pasadena and Alhambra argue over whether to extend Interstate 710 through their cities.

MAJOR INDUSTRY
Entertainment, technology, engineering

CITIES
Glendale, 194,973; Pasadena, 133,936; Alhambra, 85,804; Burbank (pt.), 54,880

NOTABLE
The Rose Bowl is in Pasadena, which hosts the Tournament of Roses Parade; Burbank is home to the studios of Warner Bros., Disney and NBC; The Norton Simon Museum in Pasadena holds etchings by Rembrandt and a collection of Picasso graphics; Griffith Park is one of the nation's largest municipal parks.

Rep. Henry A. Waxman (D)

Elected 1974; 16th term

CAPITOL OFFICE
225-3976
www.house.gov/waxman
2204 Rayburn 20515-0530; fax 225-4099

COMMITTEES
Energy & Commerce
Government Reform - ranking member

HOMETOWN
Los Angeles

BORN
Sept. 12, 1939, Los Angeles, Calif.

RELIGION
Jewish

FAMILY
Wife, Janet Waxman; two children

EDUCATION
U. of California, Los Angeles, B.A. 1961 (political science), J.D. 1964

CAREER
Lawyer

POLITICAL HIGHLIGHTS
Calif. Assembly, 1968-74

ELECTION RESULTS

2004 GENERAL

Henry A. Waxman (D)	216,682	71.2%
Victor Elizalde (R)	87,465	28.8%

2004 PRIMARY

Henry A. Waxman (D)	unopposed

2002 GENERAL

Henry A. Waxman (D)	130,604	70.4%
Tony Goss (R)	54,989	29.6%

PREVIOUS WINNING PERCENTAGES
2000 (76%); 1998 (74%); 1996 (68%); 1994 (68%);
1992 (61%); 1990 (69%); 1988 (72%); 1986 (88%);
1984 (63%); 1982 (65%); 1980 (64%); 1978 (63%);
1976 (68%); 1974 (64%)

At a time when congressional oversight of the executive branch is declining due to one-party government and long-term changes in Congress, Waxman's investigative skills and partisan fervor have made him one of the few remaining lawmakers who is still devoted to that task.

He uses his role as the top-ranking Democrat on the Government Reform Committee to badger the majority Republicans to hold hearings on Bush administration policies. Waxman sometimes teams up with the committee's moderate Republican chairman, Thomas M. Davis III of Virginia, to send pointed inquiries to federal agencies on such subjects as the flu vaccine shortage. Other times, he scolds the panel over a long list of hearings he thinks it should have had, such as the failure to find weapons of mass destruction in Iraq, the abuses at the Abu Ghraib prison near Baghdad, and the awarding of lucrative contracts to Halliburton, the oil services company Dick Cheney headed before he became vice president.

And as the second-ranking Democrat on the Energy and Commerce Committee, Waxman uses techniques similar to those of John D. Dingell of Michigan, the panel's senior Democrat. Both are precise questioners during oversight hearings and force agency officials to provide extensive information. Waxman is aggressive but he employs humor and his questioning is firmly controlled, a style that can bedevil his adversaries.

Waxman is among the House's most adroit political practitioners. While he brings his extensive knowledge on a broad policy portfolio into behind-the-scenes negotiations, he can be a forceful partisan combatant in front of the television cameras. But he is patient and willing to cut deals with Republicans when necessary, as his pragmatic relationship with Davis suggests. Compromise, Waxman said, "can further your ideas and even help you improve your ideas."

Sometimes he goes beyond aggressive questioning, however. In 2004, Waxman and 18 other House members sued the Department of Health and Human Services to make public all its recent cost estimates of the options for overhauling Medicare. The lawmakers said the documents would prove the administration knew the measure it advocated in late 2003 would cost far more than the budget allowed. Democrats said the White House hid its own estimates in order to push the bill to its razor-thin enactment. The department "should have released these estimates during congressional consideration of the Medicare bill," Waxman said. "The administration's continued refusal to release this information has left us no choice."

Waxman's partisan side got the better of him in 2001, when he accused the White House of favoritism toward energy companies and suggested that the stock holdings of Karl Rove, the president's political adviser, posed potential conflicts of interest. It was this crusade that led Waxman to unwittingly place in some jeopardy the ability of Congress to oversee the workings of the executive branch.

Knowing they could not get requisite Republican backing for subpoenas, Waxman and Dingell asked the Government Accountability Office in 2001 to probe the involvement of energy companies in the formulation of administration energy policy. The GAO ended up filing an unprecedented lawsuit in 2002 seeking to compel Cheney to release records of his energy task force. In early 2003, the GAO decided not to appeal a federal judge's ruling that the congressional agency lacked the legal standing to bring such a suit — which Waxman called "a tremendous setback for open government."

Waxman's main base of operations before the Government Reform panel was the Energy and Commerce Committee, where he chaired the Health and the Environment Subcommittee for 16 years until the Republicans became the majority party in 1995. He has won many of his victories by maneuvering persistently to secure one small objective at a time, rather than making a broad frontal assault.

On occasion, Waxman has looked to cut deals with Energy and Commerce Republicans. In 2002, he supported a compromise with Chairman Billy Tauzin of Louisiana to increase funding for the Food and Drug Administration, accelerate approvals of medical devices and allow private parties to inspect factories. But Waxman opposed Tauzin on other issues in the 107th Congress, including an energy overhaul that he called a "lost opportunity" to conserve energy.

A one-time smoker, Waxman now is the leading congressional crusader against the tobacco industry. He convened the 1994 hearing during which the chief executives of the nation's seven largest tobacco companies testified under oath that they did not believe nicotine was addictive.

Waxman grew up in an apartment above the Los Angeles grocery store run by his father, who was the son of Russian immigrants and who instilled in his son an appreciation of New Deal ideals. Waxman's political career began at UCLA in the 1960s, when he and fellow student — and now House colleague — Howard L. Berman became active in California's Federation of Young Democrats. In 1968, after a term as chairman of the state federation, Waxman, with Berman's support, challenged Democratic state Assemblyman Lester McMillan in a primary. McMillan had been in office 26 years and was nearing retirement. Waxman beat him with 64 percent of the vote.

It was the beginning of the so-called Waxman-Berman machine, an informal network of like-minded politicians who pooled their resources to back candidates with money, organization and political savvy. The "machine" was functioning so smoothly in 1974 that Waxman had little trouble winning a new House seat created with him in mind. Berman waltzed into his own House seat eight years later.

Waxman's constituents in Beverly Hills and part of West Hollywood are not only politically involved, but many are also wealthy. They have been generous with their donations to Waxman's political action committee, and in turn, its contributions to other House lawmakers have broadened Waxman's influence among his colleagues. His own campaigns are formalities; he has never won re-election with less than 61 percent of the vote.

KEY VOTES

2004
Yes   Extend federal unemployment benefits by 13 weeks

?   Pass $283.2 billion, six-year federal highway and mass transit bill

No   Approve $146 billion multi-year extension of previously enacted middle-class tax breaks

No   Amend the Constitution to prohibit same-sex marriage

No   Cut corporate taxes $137 billion over 10 years

Yes   Reorganize U.S. intelligence agencies as proposed by Sept. 11 commission

2003
No   Cut taxes by $330 billion through fiscal 2013

Yes   Block Bush rule scaling back overtime pay for some white-collar federal workers

Yes   Do not allow use of search warrants without first notifying subjects

No   Allow importation of prescription drugs

?   Create private school voucher program in Washington, D.C.

No   Ban "partial birth" abortion except to save a woman's life

Yes   Split $18.6 billion in Iraq aid into half-grant, half-loan

No   Overhaul Medicare and create prescription drug benefit

CQ VOTE STUDIES

	PARTY UNITY		PRESIDENTIAL SUPPORT	
	Support	Oppose	Support	Oppose
2004	97%	3%	13%	87%
2003	97%	3%	16%	84%
2002	98%	2%	25%	75%
2001	95%	5%	32%	68%
2000	98%	2%	87%	13%

INTEREST GROUPS

	AFL-CIO	ADA	CCUS	ACU
2004	100%	100%	20%	0%
2003	85%	95%	34%	17%
2002	100%	80%	33%	5%
2001	100%	90%	36%	0%
2000	89%	90%	45%	4%

CALIFORNIA 30

West Los Angeles County – Santa Monica, West Hollywood

Boasting such glamorous locales as Beverly Hills, Malibu, Bel Air and Pacific Palisades, there are few places in the 30th that have not been immortalized by a television show or movie. The district is home to a large Jewish population, the University of California, Los Angeles, and the activist gay community of West Hollywood.

Eclectic, wealthy and Democratic describe many of the district's residents. Members of England's royal family have stayed at the Regent Beverly Wilshire hotel at the southern end of the exclusive Rodeo Drive shopping strip, and thousands annually crowd the streets of West Hollywood to witness the gay and lesbian pride parade. The district votes overwhelmingly Democratic in elections at all levels.

The district stretches north from the Santa Monica and Malibu beaches across the Santa Monica Mountains to Calabasas and Hidden Hills on the north side of the range.

The 30th is about three-fourths white and the economy is overwhelmingly white-collar. Entertainment executives lunch with financial advisers and real estate developers, and tourism brings in large amounts of money. Thousands flock annually to the legendary Grauman's Chinese Theater, where they can compare their handprints and footprints to those of the stars, or see Whoopi Goldberg's braids, preserved in cement. The area's six medical centers make health care an important economic engine.

MAJOR INDUSTRY
Entertainment, higher education, health care, tourism

CITIES
Los Angeles (pt.), 399,622; Santa Monica, 84,084; West Hollywood, 35,716

NOTABLE
Hugh Hefner's Playboy Mansion is where prominent Democrats, including presidential candidates Gary Hart, Jerry Brown and Jesse Jackson, have held fundraisers; Santa Monica Pier, an amusement park that stretches out into the ocean, was built in 1909 and features an antique carousel.

Rep. Xavier Becerra (D)

Elected 1992; 7th term

CAPITOL OFFICE
225-6235
www.house.gov/becerra
1119 Longworth 20515-0531; fax 225-2202

COMMITTEES
Ways & Means

HOMETOWN
Los Angeles

BORN
Jan. 26, 1958, Sacramento, Calif.

RELIGION
Roman Catholic

FAMILY
Wife, Carolina Reyes; three children

EDUCATION
Stanford U., A.B. 1980 (economics), J.D. 1984

CAREER
State prosecutor; state legislative aide; lawyer

POLITICAL HIGHLIGHTS
Calif. Assembly, 1990-92; candidate for mayor of Los Angeles, 2001

ELECTION RESULTS

2004 GENERAL

Xavier Becerra (D)	89,363	80.2%
Luis Vega (R)	22,048	19.8%

2004 PRIMARY

Xavier Becerra (D)	26,308	89.5%
Mervin Leon Evans (D)	3,103	10.6%

2002 GENERAL

Xavier Becerra (D)	54,569	81.2%
Luis Vega (R)	12,674	18.9%

PREVIOUS WINNING PERCENTAGES
2000 (83%); 1998 (81%); 1996 (72%); 1994 (66%); 1992 (58%)

The Stanford-educated Becerra is the first Hispanic lawmaker to sit on the Ways and Means Committee, where he focuses on trade and Social Security issues and matters of import to the movie and television business. He is also leading the drive for the Smithsonian Institution to build a National Museum of the American Latino on the Washington mall.

Becerra (full name: HAH-vee-air beh-SEH-ra) is smart, liberal and ambitious. He waged an uphill struggle in 2001 to become the first Latino mayor of Los Angeles, but wasn't able to make it past the April 10 primary in a 14-candidate field.

A member of the Progressive Caucus, the group of the most liberal Democrats in the House, Becerra voted in 2001 to enact the sweeping anti-terrorism law that most members of the caucus said went too far in restricting civil liberties. "Extraordinary times call for extraordinary measures," said Becerra. He later complained, however, about a requirement in the aviation security law enacted the same year that airport passenger and baggage screeners be U.S. citizens.

A member of Ways and Means' Social Security Subcommittee, he was quick to oppose a White House plan to revamp Social Security to allow workers to divert some of the payroll tax they now pay into the program into private investment accounts. Becerra noted in 2004 that three in four Latinos who receive Social Security benefits depend on them for half their income. "When we talk about Social Security, we need to be talking about how to protect this indispensable benefit, not about how to radically change a program that has worked and provided a guaranteed monthly check for our nation's neediest families," he told the Inland Daily Valley Bulletin.

Becerra also weighed in on a proposed free-trade agreement with five Central American nations and the Dominican Republic. The Central American Free Trade Agreement (CAFTA) would lower tariffs on U.S. farm products and consumer goods sold in the region and make it easier for those countries to export products to the U.S. market. The United States signed the agreement in 2004, but it was not ratified by Congress.

Becerra said he "believed in a CAFTA but not this CAFTA" because the legal protections for workers were not as strong as those for products and intellectual property. "I learned from NAFTA that good intentions are no substitute" for enforceable rules, Becerra told The Los Angeles Times in 2004. He supported passage of the North American Free Trade Agreement in 1994.

Representing a district in the heart of Los Angeles, Becerra looks out for the interests of the entertainment industry. He and Hollywood were disappointed in 2004 when the House passed a $137 billion corporate tax bill that provided no tax relief for the film industry. Becerra told The Daily News of Los Angeles he believed the film industry lost out because GOP leaders calculated they could get more votes by wooing Southern lawmakers and included a $10 billion tobacco buyout instead. On Ways and Means, Becerra has championed legislation to give the film industry incentives to stay in the United States to shoot their movies rather than choosing cheaper locations abroad.

On a national scale, Becerra focuses on immigration issues and promoting the creation of a National Museum of the American Latino. He says the country ought to have a museum dedicated to the nation's 38 million Hispanic Americans, and he introduced legislation in the 108th Congress to authorize $3.2 million and the creation of a bipartisan 23-member commission to plan the new museum.

Immigration issues dominated Becerra's first six years in Congress. A seat on the Judiciary Committee gave him an outlet for his views, and when he left the panel in his third term to take the seat on Ways and Means, Hispanic leaders worried they'd lost an effective advocate on the issue.

Although 70 percent Hispanic, Becerra's district also is home to a large Asian population, including much of the neighborhood known as Koreatown. Becerra can count a number of successes in behalf of his immigrant constituents. The rewrite of federal education policy enacted in 2002 included his proposal to make community libraries eligible for federal after-school funds.

His interest in immigration is personal as well as political. His father was born in the United States, his mother in Mexico, and he spent much of his early life moving back and forth across the border. Becerra says he wears his father's wedding ring to remind himself of his modest beginnings.

Becerra applied to Stanford University, he says, after coming across an application to the school in a trash can. He worked his way through college while majoring in economics, becoming the first member of his family to earn a college degree. After graduation, he took a fellowship with the California Senate. His interest in community advocacy work led him to law school, and then to a job with a legal services office in Worcester, Mass. helping mentally ill clients. Returning to California, Becerra worked briefly for a state senator and then for the state attorney general's office.

Becerra says he never envisioned a life in politics. But in 1990, urged on by friends and colleagues, he won a campaign for the California Assembly. Becerra had not yet completed his first term in Sacramento when he was recruited in 1992 for the newly drawn, overwhelmingly Hispanic 30th District seat. He outdistanced nine other candidates in the primary and easily won in November, with 58 percent of the vote, against Republican Morry Waksberg and three minor-party candidates.

In his race for Los Angeles mayor, Becerra raised and spent $1.7 million, but even that wasn't enough in the city's pricey media market. He finished fifth in the primary. Later it was discovered that his campaign was responsible for anonymous telephone calls attacking one of his main rivals, Antonio Villaraigosa. Becerra apologized, blaming his campaign staff for the transgression.

In 2002, Becerra won re-election to the House with 81 percent of the vote, and he captured 80 percent of the vote in 2004.

KEY VOTES

2004

Yes Extend federal unemployment benefits by 13 weeks

Yes Pass $283.2 billion, six-year federal highway and mass transit bill

No Approve $146 billion multi-year extension of previously enacted middle-class tax breaks

No Amend the Constitution to prohibit same-sex marriage

No Cut corporate taxes $137 billion over 10 years

Yes Reorganize U.S. intelligence agencies as proposed by Sept. 11 commission

2003

No Cut taxes by $330 billion through fiscal 2013

Yes Block Bush rule scaling back overtime pay for some white-collar federal workers

Yes Do not allow use of search warrants without first notifying subjects

Yes Allow importation of prescription drugs

No Create private school voucher program in Washington, D.C.

No Ban "partial birth" abortion except to save a woman's life

Yes Split $18.6 billion in Iraq aid into half-grant, half-loan

No Overhaul Medicare and create prescription drug benefit

CQ VOTE STUDIES

	PARTY UNITY		PRESIDENTIAL SUPPORT	
	Support	Oppose	Support	Oppose
2004	99%	1%	18%	82%
2003	98%	2%	17%	83%
2002	100%	0%	23%	77%
2001	97%	3%	27%	73%
2000	95%	5%	92%	8%

INTEREST GROUPS

	AFL-CIO	ADA	CCUS	ACU
2004	93%	95%	29%	0%
2003	87%	95%	31%	16%
2002	88%	100%	32%	0%
2001	100%	95%	40%	0%
2000	90%	90%	45%	8%

CALIFORNIA 31
Northeast and south central Los Angeles

The only district completely contained within the city of Los Angeles, the 31st is densely populated, heavily Hispanic and staunchly Democratic. It starts west of downtown Los Angeles and stretches south into south central L.A. and northeast toward Pasadena. Hispanics (70 percent) and Asians (14 percent) outnumber whites (10 percent). Voter turnout is usually low.

Rapid immigration is changing many of the district's already diverse communities. Asians, Armenians, Russians and Hispanics have been moving to the 31st, with many settling in the district's western side. This area, which includes part of East Hollywood, the mid-Wilshire area and Koreatown, was hit hard by the 1992 riots. Pico Union and Westlake are dominated by Central American immigrants. Other heavily Hispanic communities include Highland Park, Cypress Park and Glassell Park.

Directly west of Elysian Park, where Dodger Stadium is located, is the artsy and gentrifying Echo Park. A nearby area was recognized as Filipinotown in 2002. To the northeast sits Eagle Rock, a hilly, middle-class pocket of relative affluence that votes Democratic but leans more toward the political center than other parts of the 31st. The eastern side leads to Lincoln Heights and El Sereno — heavily Hispanic, blue-collar areas with a significant Mexican immigrant presence. The district also has part of south central Los Angeles east of the University of Southern California.

The 31st has the lowest median income in the state, at slightly more than $26,000. It falls mostly outside federal empowerment zone lines drawn after the riots. Entertainment studios and a slew of hospitals contribute to the economy, as do white-collar businesses along Wilshire Boulevard, a central business corridor.

MAJOR INDUSTRY
Service, entertainment, tourism, health care

CITIES
Los Angeles (pt.), 639,088

NOTABLE
Paramount Pictures is the only major motion picture studio still based in Hollywood.

Rep. Hilda L. Solis (D)

Elected 2000; 3rd term

CAPITOL OFFICE
225-5464
solis.house.gov
1725 Longworth 20515-0532; fax 225-5467

COMMITTEES
Energy & Commerce

HOMETOWN
El Monte

BORN
Oct. 20, 1957, Los Angeles, Calif.

RELIGION
Roman Catholic

FAMILY
Husband, Sam H. Sayyad

EDUCATION
California State Polytechnic U., Pomona, B.A. 1979 (political science); U. of Southern California, M.P.A. 1981

CAREER
State college preparation program director; White House aide

POLITICAL HIGHLIGHTS
Rio Hondo Community College Board of Trustees, 1985-92; Los Angeles County Insurance Commission, 1991-93; Calif. Assembly, 1992-94; Calif. Senate, 1994-2000

ELECTION RESULTS

2004 GENERAL

Hilda L. Solis (D)	119,144	85.0%
Leland Faegre (LIBERT)	21,002	15.0%

2004 PRIMARY

Hilda L. Solis (D)	unopposed

2002 GENERAL

Hilda L. Solis (D)	58,530	68.8%
Emma E. Fischbeck (R)	23,366	27.5%
Michael McGuire (LIBERT)	3,183	3.7%

PREVIOUS WINNING PERCENTAGES
2000 (79%)

Liberal, energetic and outspoken, Solis is a regular participant in Democratic presentations to the news media on topics ranging from the environment to immigration and from health insurance to domestic violence.

In the 109th Congress, she was chosen by her Democratic colleagues as a regional whip, and she was named co-chairwoman of the Congressional Women's Caucus.

Solis (soh-LEEZ) was given a coveted seat on the Energy and Commerce Committee in her second term, where in the 108th Congress she was named the top-ranking Democrat on the Environment and Hazardous Materials Subcommittee. This is a fitting post for her because she has long sought to win environmental protections for minority communities.

While in the California Legislature, she overcame strong opposition from GOP Gov. Pete Wilson and the state business community to win passage of "environmental justice" legislation, which Wilson vetoed and Democratic Gov. Gray Davis later signed. Her legislation was aimed at countering what Solis believes is a disproportionate number of waste sites and polluting factories in poor neighborhoods. Solis said she saw many examples of these dumps in her own neighborhood while growing up. In 2000, Solis won the John F. Kennedy Profile in Courage Award from the Kennedy Library for her work on environmental justice issues.

Thoughtful and workmanlike in committee, Solis has joined with Energy's senior Democrat, John D. Dingell of Michigan, in criticizing the Environmental Protection Agency for delays in cleaning up Superfund hazardous waste sites. She also looks to improve the environment in her district, and in 2003 won enactment of a bill to study recreational and environmental improvements in the San Gabriel River and San Gabriel Mountains.

The daughter of immigrants who met in a U.S. citizenship class, Solis pays particular attention to immigration issues. She was successful in the 108th in winning final approval of key portions of a bill to ease immigration and citizenship hurdles for non-citizens who serve in the U.S. military and for their relatives.

She also waged a lengthy, and ultimately successful, campaign in behalf of Maria Suarez. The woman was a victim of child sex trafficking starting when she was 16 and was imprisoned for years for her role in a murder. California Gov. Arnold Schwarzenegger eventually pardoned her, but she was due to be deported because of her conviction. Solis' fight in behalf of Suarez was in keeping with her longstanding interest in domestic violence issues. Solis also was a leader in the effort to focus attention on the slayings of hundreds of young women in the border town of Juarez, Mexico.

A member of the Progressive Caucus, the most liberal faction of House Democrats, Solis voted 99 percent of the time in agreement with her own party in the 108th Congress. In 2004, Democratic presidential nominee John Kerry picked her as a representative of the Progressive Caucus to work on the Democratic platform at the party's convention in Boston.

Solis came to the House the hard way, taking on Democratic incumbent Matthew G. Martinez in the 2000 primary. "I had butterflies," she told the Los Angeles Times of her decision to challenge Martinez, and it took several months for her to commit to the race.

One of seven children, Solis' mother is from Nicaragua and her father is from Mexico. Her father worked in blue-collar jobs and helped the Teamsters union organize at the battery recycling plant where he was employed.

Solis recalls this plant as being a polluter in her neighborhood.

The first member of her family to go to college, Solis said she was inspired by a high school counselor, who came to her home to help her fill out college and financial aid applications. She said her parents' work ethic set an example and convinced her to set her own high goals.

She worked her way through school, earning a bachelor's degree in political science and a graduate degree in public administration. Required to arrange her own internship as part of her graduate studies, Solis wrote dozens of letters and landed a dream assignment as the editor of a newsletter for the Carter administration's White House Office of Hispanic Affairs. She stayed on in Washington, working at the Office of Management and Budget's civil rights division during the early months of the Reagan administration. After returning to California, Solis took a job as director of a state program that helped disadvantaged students prepare for college.

Her first taste of elective office came in 1985, when she won election to the Rio Hondo Community College Board of Trustees. After a brief stint as an appointed member of the Los Angeles County Insurance Commission, Solis was elected to the California Assembly in 1992. She moved up to the Senate in 1994, becoming its youngest member and first Hispanic woman.

Legislative term limits would have forced Solis out of the state Senate in 2002, and so she began talking to local Democratic officials in late 1998 about taking on Martinez. He was getting criticism for being inattentive to local concerns, and his politics on issues such as abortion and gun control were considerably more conservative than Solis'. She earned the support of Sen. Barbara Boxer and former Rep. Esteban E. Torres, but only one House Democratic member — Loretta Sanchez — backed her in the primary.

Solis had high name recognition, as her 24th District Senate seat encompassed most of Martinez's congressional district. Her dynamic personality contrasted markedly with Martinez's low-key manner, and she outspent him by a considerable margin. Solis cruised to victory in the primary with 62 percent of the vote. She was the only member of the Class of 2000 who unseated a member of her own party.

The Republicans didn't field a candidate for the general election. Solis won easily in the eastern Los Angeles County Hispanic-majority district, a Democratic stronghold, capturing 79 percent of the vote against three minor-party candidates. In 2002, redistricting did not alter the Democratic and Hispanic bent of the district, now numbered the 32nd, and she won by 41 percentage points. With only a Libertarian opponent in 2004, her margin of victory was even higher.

KEY VOTES

2004

Yes Extend federal unemployment benefits by 13 weeks

Yes Pass $283.2 billion, six-year federal highway and mass transit bill

Yes Approve $146 billion multi-year extension of previously enacted middle-class tax breaks

No Amend the Constitution to prohibit same-sex marriage

No Cut corporate taxes $137 billion over 10 years

Yes Reorganize U.S. intelligence agencies as proposed by Sept. 11 commission

2003

No Cut taxes by $330 billion through fiscal 2013

Yes Block Bush rule scaling back overtime pay for some white-collar federal workers

Yes Do not allow use of search warrants without first notifying subjects

Yes Allow importation of prescription drugs

No Create private school voucher program in Washington, D.C.

No Ban "partial birth" abortion except to save a woman's life

Yes Split $18.6 billion in Iraq aid into half-grant, half-loan

No Overhaul Medicare and create prescription drug benefit

CQ VOTE STUDIES

| | PARTY UNITY | | PRESIDENTIAL SUPPORT | |
	Support	Oppose	Support	Oppose
2004	99%	1%	18%	82%
2003	99%	1%	16%	84%
2002	100%	0%	18%	82%
2001	99%	1%	17%	83%

INTEREST GROUPS

	AFL-CIO	ADA	CCUS	ACU
2004	93%	100%	25%	0%
2003	100%	100%	21%	12%
2002	100%	100%	28%	0%
2001	100%	100%	30%	0%

CALIFORNIA 32
East Los Angeles; El Monte; West Covina

The 32nd sits just east of the city of Los Angeles. It takes in the southern and central San Gabriel Valley and stretches northeast to Azusa, with several good-size cities in between. Once a largely white community, the 32nd has acquired a Hispanic majority from city residents moving to the suburbs. As a result, once-Republican enclaves have become solid Democratic domains.

The district's shrinking pockets of Republican and older white voters are in Azusa. El Monte, in the heart of the San Gabriel Valley, and Baldwin Park to the east are middle-income, blue-collar cities and the 32nd's Democratic base. El Monte also has some older white voters, mostly Democrats, and the city has a substantial new immigrant population. Monterey Park (shared with the 29th) is upper-middle class — the district's richest area — and is known as "Little Taipei" for its Taiwanese and other Asian immigrants. Another large Asian population lives in wealthy, liberal-leaning West Covina. The district has several daily Chinese-language papers.

The 32nd lacks a dominant industry, and the San Gabriel Valley has suffered from higher unemployment rates than the rest of the nation. Most residents commute outside the district to work. Once a small farming town, El Monte became home to some small aerospace factories. It is now a light manufacturing area with a huge retail auto complex. Irwindale is among the district's industrial centers.

MAJOR INDUSTRY
Service, light manufacturing

CITIES
El Monte, 115,965; West Covina, 105,080; Baldwin Park, 75,837; Rosemead, 53,505

NOTABLE
MGM's trademark roaring lion came from Gay's Lion Farm in El Monte, where animal trainer Charles Gay kept African lions until 1942; El Monte's original settlers were drawn by the California Gold Rush; The Los Angeles County Sheriff's Department is based in Monterey Park; City of Hope National Medical Center in Duarte is a research hospital specializing in cancer and other life-threatening diseases.

Rep. Diane Watson (D)

Elected June 2001; 2nd full term

CAPITOL OFFICE
225-7084
www.house.gov/watson
125 Cannon 20515-0533; fax 225-2422

COMMITTEES
Government Reform
International Relations

HOMETOWN
Los Angeles

BORN
Nov. 12, 1933, Los Angeles, Calif.

RELIGION
Roman Catholic

FAMILY
Single

EDUCATION
U. of California, Los Angeles, B.A. 1954
(education); California State U., Los Angeles, M.S.
1968 (school psychology); Harvard U., attended
1981-82; Claremont Graduate School, Ph.D. 1987
(educational administration)

CAREER
School administrator; state education department
official; teacher; school psychologist

POLITICAL HIGHLIGHTS
Los Angeles County Board of Education, 1975-78;
Calif. Senate, 1978-98; candidate for Los Angeles
County Board of Supervisors, 1992; U.S.
ambassador to the Federal States of Micronesia,
1999-2001

ELECTION RESULTS

2004 GENERAL
Diane Watson (D)	166,801	88.6%
Bob Weber (LIBERT)	21,513	11.4%

2004 PRIMARY
Diane Watson (D)	unopposed

2002 GENERAL
Diane Watson (D)	97,779	82.6%
Andrew Kim (R)	16,699	14.1%
Charles Tate (LIBERT)	3,971	3.4%

PREVIOUS WINNING PERCENTAGES
2001 Special Runoff Election (75%)

As one of the most liberal members of the minority party, Watson can be counted on to criticize sharply what she views as the misguided policies of President Bush and the GOP congressional majority. Both her voting record and her rhetoric demonstrate she does not shy from confrontation.

In her first term, while attending the United Nations World Conference Against Racism along with other members of the Congressional Black Caucus, Watson told the delegates: "America is a racist state." In the 108th Congress, Watson decried Bush's "space cowboy budget," and complained in the headline of a news release that House "Republicans Lynch Medicare in the Dead of Night."

Yet Watson is also a veteran legislator — she spent 20 years in the California Senate, most of them as a committee chairwoman — and she mixes in a dose of bipartisan pragmatism with her self-described behavior as an agitator for constituencies with no voice. Watson does not like to waste time on solely symbolic gestures. In the legislative arena, she largely shelves the rhetoric and works quietly to achieve her goals.

Watson can point to a better-than-average success rate in winning approval of her legislative offerings, largely because she concentrates her efforts on a small number of achievable legislative goals.

In the 108th, she won favorable House action on almost half of the 14 measures she authored. She won enactment of a bill to award a congressional gold medal to civil rights activist Dorothy Height and a measure to name a post office in the Koreatown section of her district after a revered Korean leader. She also obtained House approval of a resolution urging China to take meaningful steps to protect intellectual property rights and of legislation to extend the authority for the construction of a memorial to the Rev. Martin Luther King Jr. in Washington, D.C.

She also takes on more substantial legislative issues, including addressing ways to prevent certain health problems such as obesity, diabetes and HIV/AIDS. And she seeks economic development for her district by focusing on the links between youth violence, jobs, transportation and housing.

Despite her fiery rhetoric, Watson's demeanor in the International Relations and Government Reform committees has been generally low key and politic. On Government Reform, Watson continued an effort, begun while she was in the state Senate, to get rid of mercury amalgam in dental fillings, saying it causes health risks. Fighting against opponents who labeled the effort junk science, she found a powerful ally in Republican Dan Burton, who chaired Government Reform in the 107th Congress. Although the two see eye-to-eye on little else, they both agree on the dangers of mercury. In the 109th, Watson is the committee's top-ranking Democrat on the Energy and Resources Subcommittee.

The downtown Los Angeles part of her district was once the hub for the movie industry, and thousands of Watson's constituents are still involved in the entertainment industry. She was rebuffed in her bid to join the House Entertainment Industry Task Force because it was a Republican group, so she formed a bipartisan House Entertainment Caucus. She hopes the caucus will focus congressional attention on such issues as intellectual property rights and film piracy. She is also concerned about the U.S. film industry's growing practice of shooting movies at cheaper locations abroad.

In the 108th, she fought against Federal Communications Commission rules allowing for consolidation of media ownership. Watson argued that reducing the number of media outlets limited avenues of expression for creative artists.

Watson's father was a police officer and her mother was a postal worker. She says she put in time at the local post office, sorting Christmas mail for seven seasons. But Watson's career choice was education.

She earned bachelor's and master's degrees and a Ph.D. in a variety of education-related disciplines, and she was a teacher and administrator in the Los Angeles school system for more than a decade. She taught college classes while working on health issues for the state Department of Education.

She entered politics in 1975, winning election to the Los Angeles County school board — the first black woman ever elected to the post.

Three years later, she achieved another first, becoming the first black woman elected to the state Senate, where she shook up the mostly white male institution. Watson, the California Political Almanac wrote, "seemed to specialize in crashing the party and opening the windows."

Watson chaired the Senate's Health and Human Services Committee for 17 years, and she was the first non-lawyer to serve on the Judiciary Committee. She was credited with helping rebuild her community after the 1992 riots sparked by the acquittal of police officers charged with beating motorist Rodney King. She also worked to blunt the effects of the 1996 welfare overhaul law on California's poor and to help people suffering with HIV/AIDS.

After state term limits ended her Senate career in 1998, President Clinton named Watson ambassador to Micronesia, a federation of more than 600 islands in the Pacific.

When 12-term Democratic Rep. Julian C. Dixon died in December 2000, Watson says she was urged by many of Dixon's constituents to come home and run for the seat. In her special-election bid, Watson put her lifetime of political activism among Los Angeles' African-American population to good use. She took 33 percent of the vote, defeating 10 other Democrats in the April primary. The primary win virtually guaranteed victory in the overwhelmingly Democratic 32nd District. In the June general election, Watson took 75 percent of the vote, besting Republican Noel Irwin Hentschel.

Redistricting shifted the boundaries of Watson's district, renumbered the 33rd, slightly east and north, but its essential Democratic character was unchanged. She has cruised to two easy re-elections, winning with 83 percent of the vote in 2002 and 89 percent in 2004.

KEY VOTES

2004

?	Extend federal unemployment benefits by 13 weeks
Yes	Pass $283.2 billion, six-year federal highway and mass transit bill
No	Approve $146 billion multi-year extension of previously enacted middle-class tax breaks
No	Amend the Constitution to prohibit same-sex marriage
No	Cut corporate taxes $137 billion over 10 years
Yes	Reorganize U.S. intelligence agencies as proposed by Sept. 11 commission

2003

No	Cut taxes by $330 billion through fiscal 2013
Yes	Block Bush rule scaling back overtime pay for some white-collar federal workers
Yes	Do not allow use of search warrants without first notifying subjects
Yes	Allow importation of prescription drugs
No	Create private school voucher program in Washington, D.C.
No	Ban "partial birth" abortion except to save a woman's life
Yes	Split $18.6 billion in Iraq aid into half-grant, half-loan
No	Overhaul Medicare and create prescription drug benefit

CQ VOTE STUDIES

	PARTY UNITY		PRESIDENTIAL SUPPORT	
	Support	Oppose	Support	Oppose
2004	98%	2%	23%	77%
2003	98%	2%	17%	83%
2002	98%	2%	16%	84%
2001	95%	5%	17%	83%

INTEREST GROUPS

	AFL-CIO	ADA	CCUS	ACU
2004	92%	85%	16%	0%
2003	87%	100%	21%	17%
2002	100%	85%	26%	0%
2001	100%	50%	25%	0%

CALIFORNIA 33

West Los Angeles; Culver City

The 33rd is an ethnically diverse, Democratic district that begins about a mile inland from Venice Beach, runs east through Culver City and ends up in south central Los Angeles. From there it runs north through Koreatown, the "Miracle Mile" district and Hollywood.

Blacks, Hispanics and Asians account for more than three-fourths of the population, but the 33rd has no single racial majority. More than 65 percent of the district's registered voters are Democrats. Several major demographic shifts have dramatically changed the makeup. The first was in the 1960s when the district's Jewish population migrated to the area's now more upscale northwest end and the district's center became predominately black. Since the 1990s, there has been an influx of Hispanics, who now account for the largest part of the population, at almost 35 percent.

The 33rd has a solid middle class, as well as some sharply contrasting areas such as wealthy Hancock Park — where the mayor's official residence is located — and poor south central Los Angeles, which

witnessed intense racial strife during the 1992 riots.

The largest business sector is the service industry, with health care also providing employment for many. Though the 33rd is no longer the film production hub it used to be, it is home to the real Tinseltown — Hollywood — and entertainment continues to be a factor in its overall economy.

For recreation, residents and tourists flock to Exposition Park in downtown Los Angeles. In addition to the Los Angeles County Natural History Museum and the California Science Center, the park boasts the Los Angeles Memorial Coliseum, which has hosted two Olympiads.

MAJOR INDUSTRY
Service, entertainment, health care

CITIES
Los Angeles (pt.), 582,746; Culver City, 38,816; View Park-Windsor Hills (unincorporated), 10,958

NOTABLE
The University of Southern California; MGM Studios (now part of Sony Pictures Studios); The Academy Awards ceremony moved to the Kodak Theatre in 2002.

Rep. Lucille Roybal-Allard (D)

Elected 1992; 7th term

CAPITOL OFFICE
225-1766
www.house.gov/roybal-allard
2330 Rayburn 20515-0534; fax 226-0350

COMMITTEES
Appropriations
Standards of Official Conduct

HOMETOWN
East Los Angeles

BORN
June 12, 1941, Boyle Heights, Calif.

RELIGION
Roman Catholic

FAMILY
Husband, Edward T. Allard III; two children, two stepchildren

EDUCATION
California State U., Los Angeles, B.A. 1965 (speech)

CAREER
Nonprofit worker

POLITICAL HIGHLIGHTS
Calif. Assembly, 1986-92

ELECTION RESULTS

2004 GENERAL

Lucille Roybal-Allard (D)	82,282	74.5%
Wayne Miller (R)	28,175	25.5%

2004 PRIMARY

Lucille Roybal-Allard (D)	unopposed

2002 GENERAL

Lucille Roybal-Allard (D)	48,734	74.0%
Wayne Miller (R)	17,090	26.0%

PREVIOUS WINNING PERCENTAGES
2000 (85%); 1998 (87%); 1996 (82%); 1994 (81%); 1992 (63%)

Roybal-Allard is a role model for young Hispanic women. The first Mexican-American woman ever elected to Congress, she was the first woman to head the Congressional Hispanic Caucus and the first Hispanic woman appointed to the Appropriations Committee, posts she achieved in the 106th Congress. In the 109th, she will serve as whip of the Hispanic caucus.

Roybal-Allard grew up with political ambitions. Her father was Edward R. Roybal, one of only three Hispanic members of the House when he arrived in 1963. For 30 years in Congress, he fought to win greater political clout for Hispanics in his Southern California district.

Despite her political pedigree, Roybal-Allard says she grew up facing discrimination and discouragement. She recalls being punished as a child for speaking Spanish in school. She also remembers how her family would be stopped and questioned when they tried to enter hotels.

Even her own family tried to dampen her efforts to rise above her station. Her father's relatives ridiculed him for sending his daughters to college, saying all that was expected of them was marriage and children. Later, her own siblings discouraged her from entering politics, citing the difficulties their father faced.

She says the discrimination she faced as a youth has also made her particularly sensitive to the problems of immigrants to the United States. In the 108th, Roybal-Allard pressed for legislation to make it easier for children of illegal immigrants to qualify for in-state tuition rates at public universities if they met other residency criteria.

During the 107th, she fought hard but unsuccessfully to make permanent the part of the federal immigration code, known as Section 245 (i), that permits immigrants whose visas have expired to remain in the United States while their applications are processed.

On the Appropriations Committee, Roybal-Allard tends carefully to her district and the surrounding area. After joining the Homeland Security Subcommittee, she urged her colleagues to boost funding for state and local governments, including high-threat urban areas such as Los Angeles, that bear much of the cost of security measures. "Whenever an orange alert is issued, this action creates a huge hardship on localities," she said in 2003. "In Los Angeles, the last Code Orange alert [which lasted 20 days] cost $4.2 million" in additional security.

Roybal-Allard added a provision in the 2004 spending bill for Homeland Security to prevent the Homeland Security Department from privatizing immigration officers. She also inserted language to direct the Federal Aviation Administration to issue regulations for basic security training for flight attendants and to enable independent districts, such as bridge authorities, to obtain security funds.

Before entering politics, Roybal-Allard worked for the United Way and then served as an assistant director on the Alcoholism Council of East Los Angeles. In Congress, she has focused much of her legislative energy on fighting underage drinking. "While we have an extensive campaign to combat illegal drug use, the fact remains that alcohol kills more teens than all other drugs combined," she says.

She successfully won a $1 million earmark in 2001 for the Health and Human Services Department to develop new programs to curb underage drinking. In the 108th, she sponsored legislation that would create an interagency committee, chaired by the Health and Human Services secretary, to coordinate federal efforts to combat underage drinking. The proposal also aimed to increase spending on ads about the dangers of underage drinking and to fund research on the effect of underage drinking on adolescent brain development. Roybal-Allard is a member of Appropriations' Labor, Health and Human Services and Education Subcommittee.

Another of her legislative priorities has been to improve the lot of women victimized by domestic violence. Beginning in the 104th Congress, Roybal-Allard has offered legislation in every Congress to give unemployment insurance benefits to women forced to leave jobs because of domestic violence.

Roybal-Allard drew plaudits in the 105th Congress for her role in awakening the power of the California House delegation, which had been divided and ineffective. As the first elected chairman of the California Democratic delegation, she worked with her Republican counterpart, Jerry Lewis, to find issues on which the majority of the delegation could agree.

In the 108th, she agreed to take a seat on the House ethics committee at the request of her California colleague, Democratic leader Nancy Pelosi. The ethics committee is perhaps the least popular assignment in the House. Members serve for a maximum of three terms.

In her legislative work, Roybal-Allard tries to balance the related but not always overlapping needs of the two chief components of her constituency: the minority "underclass" mired in chronic poverty and a substantial Latino working class of laborers and shop owners. In recent years, Roybal-Allard and other community leaders have been working hard to encourage citizenship applications and to help speed the process.

Roybal-Allard generally has been a dependable supporter of Democratic Party positions, voting almost 99 percent of the time in agreement with a majority of her party in the 108th Congress. She often has won 100 percent favorable ratings from the AFL-CIO.

Roybal-Allard served six years in the California state Assembly before winning election to succeed her father in 1992. She jumped at the chance to run for her father's seat, drawing insubstantial opposition in the Democratic primary and winning in November by a 2-to-1 margin.

She has won with no less than 74 percent of the vote in each re-election since. During her first decade in Washington, the area of Los Angeles she represented was, at 86 percent after the 2000 census, the most populous Hispanic congressional district in the nation. Her newly redrawn district's Hispanic population is 77 percent.

KEY VOTES

2004

Yes Extend federal unemployment benefits by 13 weeks

Yes Pass $283.2 billion, six-year federal highway and mass transit bill

Yes Approve $146 billion multi-year extension of previously enacted middle-class tax breaks

No Amend the Constitution to prohibit same-sex marriage

No Cut corporate taxes $137 billion over 10 years

Yes Reorganize U.S. intelligence agencies as proposed by Sept. 11 commission

2003

No Cut taxes by $330 billion through fiscal 2013

Yes Block Bush rule scaling back overtime pay for some white-collar federal workers

Yes Do not allow use of search warrants without first notifying subjects

Yes Allow importation of prescription drugs

- Create private school voucher program in Washington, D.C.

No Ban "partial birth" abortion except to save a woman's life

Yes Split $18.6 billion in Iraq aid into half-grant, half-loan

No Overhaul Medicare and create prescription drug benefit

CQ VOTE STUDIES

	PARTY UNITY		PRESIDENTIAL SUPPORT	
	Support	Oppose	Support	Oppose
2004	98%	2%	24%	76%
2003	99%	1%	15%	85%
2002	99%	1%	22%	78%
2001	95%	5%	24%	76%
2000	98%	2%	90%	10%

INTEREST GROUPS

	AFL-CIO	ADA	CCUS	ACU
2004	100%	100%	35%	0%
2003	100%	100%	27%	12%
2002	100%	100%	35%	0%
2001	100%	100%	30%	0%
2000	100%	90%	35%	8%

CALIFORNIA 34
East central Los Angeles; Downey; Bellflower

The Democratic 34th takes in the heart and southeastern part of Los Angeles and has an overwhelming Hispanic majority. At 77 percent, the district has the largest concentration of Hispanics in California.

The local economy revolves around businesses in the revitalizing downtown area and nearby light manufacturing centers such as Vernon and Commerce. Downtown businesses include toy, jewelry and garment manufacturers and retailers. Some spaces downtown are being transformed into lofts. Many of Los Angeles' civic buildings, including city hall, courthouses and the county prison, are in the 34th.

Vernon's population, according to the 2000 census, is a mere 91 people, but during the day it jumps to more than 40,000 as workers stream into its food-processing and furniture plants. The district also is attracting new "green" industries, such as recycling companies.

One of California's poorest and least-educated districts, the 34th generally has extremely low voter turnout. John Kerry captured 69 percent of the 2004 presidential vote here — despite the district's inclusion of slightly more suburban and conservative Downey and Bellflower, located to the south where there are fewer Hispanics. Other areas include Little Tokyo and part of Pico Union and Chinatown. Despite redevelopment and many small businesses, the area has seen a rise in crime rates.

Brighter spots include the Walt Disney Concert Hall, which opened in 2003 and serves as the home of the Los Angeles Philharmonic. Transportation hub Union Station and the end of the 20-mile Alameda Corridor rail link connecting L.A. and the ports of Los Angeles and Long Beach are in the district, as is the Staples Center, home to basketball's Lakers and Clippers and hockey's Kings.

MAJOR INDUSTRY
Government, manufacturing, service, retail

CITIES
Los Angeles (pt.), 188,018; Downey, 107,323; Bellflower, 72,878

NOTABLE
The 2000 Democratic National Convention was held at the Staples Center; Downtown's El Pueblo de Los Angeles Historic Monument, including Olvera Street, is the oldest section of Los Angeles.

Rep. Maxine Waters (D)

CAPITOL OFFICE
225-2201
www.house.gov/waters
2344 Rayburn 20515-0535; fax 225-7854

COMMITTEES
Financial Services
Judiciary

HOMETOWN
Los Angeles

BORN
Aug. 15, 1938, St. Louis, Mo.

RELIGION
Christian

FAMILY
Husband, Sidney Williams; two children

EDUCATION
California State U., Los Angeles, B.A. 1970

CAREER
City council staffer; public relations firm owner;
Head Start program coordinator; telephone
service representative

POLITICAL HIGHLIGHTS
Calif. Assembly, 1976-90

ELECTION RESULTS

2004 GENERAL

Maxine Waters (D)	125,949	80.5%
Ross Moen (R)	23,591	15.1%
Gordon Michael Mego (AMI)	3,440	2.2%
Charles Tate (LIBERT)	3,427	2.2%

2004 PRIMARY

Maxine Waters (D)	unopposed

2002 GENERAL

Maxine Waters (D)	72,401	77.5%
Ross Moen (R)	18,094	19.4%
Gordon Michael Mego (AMI)	2,912	3.1%

PREVIOUS WINNING PERCENTAGES
2000 (87%); 1998 (89%); 1996 (86%); 1994 (78%);
1992 (83%); 1990 (79%)

Elected 1990; 8th term

Waters is an old-school liberal with a well-known combative streak. She is nothing short of relentless in defending the interests of her poor, minority-dominated district in South Central Los Angeles, where there are long-standing tensions between the city's police department and African-American residents.

When she is fired up about something, which is not infrequently with the Republicans running the House, Waters has been known to verbally blast her political opponents and even her allies, telling them on occasion to "shut up."

No one doubts the depth or sincerity of her commitment, but many lawmakers in both parties are put off by her temper tantrums and by the certitude with which she conveys her decidedly liberal views. Waters says that if she softens her stance and engages in the give-and-take typical of Washington politics, her constituents will feel let down.

President Bush is a favorite target. She has gone on the attack verbally for his handling of issues ranging from the war in Iraq to the economy. In 2003, Waters decried the effects of "Bush-onomics" on her district, which she said resulted in lost manufacturing jobs. "This president's arrogant catering to the needs of the wealthy is nothing more than a reverse Robin Hood philosophy of stealing from the poor to give to the rich," she said.

With Republicans in the majority, Waters seldom finds sympathy for her repeated pleas for assistance to the inner cities. Over the years, she has won a few battles to get job training and community development funding for her district and for the fight against AIDS, which she argues has become an epidemic in Los Angeles County. But she is at her rhetorical best as an insurgent, and her high-volume involvement in issues affecting the underclass at least ensures that those issues are not ignored.

She is an important player in the House Democratic leadership and an ally of Minority Leader Nancy Pelosi, also of California. She is a chief deputy whip and vice chairwoman of the leadership's Steering Committee, which makes all-important committee assignments.

Waters is also a force to be reckoned with in her 90 percent minority district. In 2004, she fought a plan by Los Angeles County to close a trauma center at King/Drew Medical Center, a public hospital established to improve local health care after riots in the Watts neighborhood in 1965. When the board of supervisors held a public hearing, she packed it with an overflow crowd that included the Rev. Jesse Jackson and Yolanda King, daughter of Martin Luther King Jr., for whom the center was named. According to the Los Angeles Times, "The supervisors appeared especially rattled by Waters, who seemed at times to have taken control of the hearing away from its chairman."

In the aftermath of the contested presidential election in 2000, Democratic leaders named Waters to head a task force on the election process. Saying that many citizens were denied their right to participate in the process, she called the election "the first major civil rights issue of the 21st century." Waters' Democrats-only panel held a series of hearings and made recommendations, and the group played an important role in keeping up pressure for eventual congressional action.

On the Judiciary Committee, Waters often jumps head first into the boisterous discussions on one of the most partisan committees on Capitol Hill. She was one of President Clinton's staunchest supporters during the panel's impeachment proceedings in 1998. And after Republican Attorney General John Ashcroft asked the panel in 2003 for even greater law enforcement powers to investigate terrorists, Waters cited a litany of complaints about the way the administration was enforcing present law, including detaining immigrants for long periods and abusing them physically. "I don't think we want to give more power to a government that seems to have abused the power it already has," she said.

The same year, Waters opposed an attempt by committee Republicans to empower a national drug "czar" to spend $1.2 billion for policing "High Intensity Trafficking Areas." Waters said drug treatment programs would be more effective and that the bill "is not worth the paper it's printed on."

Waters brings her advocacy for minorities and the poor to the Financial Services panel, where she works to stop banks from charging transaction fees to small depositors and from engaging in predatory lending practices, in which customers in low-income communities pay higher rates and fees.

Born in St. Louis as one of 13 children in a welfare family, Waters was raised in public housing projects. As a teenager, she bused tables in a segregated restaurant. Married just after high school, she moved in 1961 with her first husband and two children to Los Angeles, where she worked in a clothing factory and for the telephone company.

Waters' public career began in 1965, when she worked as a program coordinator in the new Head Start program while working her way through college. From there, she got involved in community organizing, which led her to politics. After working as a volunteer and a consultant to several candidates, she won an upset 1976 victory for a seat in the state Assembly representing many of the same neighborhoods that are now part of her congressional district.

Waters got her chance to run for Congress in 1990, when Democratic Rep. Augustus F. Hawkins retired after 14 terms. She had been preparing for the move for years. During redistricting debates in the legislature in 1982, Waters maneuvered to remove from Hawkins' district a blue-collar, mainly white suburb she saw as unfriendly territory. Her 1990 election to the House was never in doubt, and since then she has had a virtual lock on re-election every year. During Waters' first term in the House, South Central L.A. erupted in riots after white police officers were captured on videotape beating motorist Rodney King, who is black. Waters became an omnipresent figure on television, explaining to outsiders the neighborhood tensions that erupted in civil unrest. Her district was left alone in the round of redistricting that followed the 2000 census.

KEY VOTES

2004
Yes Extend federal unemployment benefits by 13 weeks
Yes Pass $283.2 billion, six-year federal highway and mass transit bill
No Approve $146 billion multi-year extension of previously enacted middle-class tax breaks
No Amend the Constitution to prohibit same-sex marriage
No Cut corporate taxes $137 billion over 10 years
Yes Reorganize U.S. intelligence agencies as proposed by Sept. 11 commission

2003
No Cut taxes by $330 billion through fiscal 2013
Yes Block Bush rule scaling back overtime pay for some white-collar federal workers
Yes Do not allow use of search warrants without first notifying subjects
Yes Allow importation of prescription drugs
No Create private school voucher program in Washington, D.C.
No Ban "partial birth" abortion except to save a woman's life
Yes Split $18.6 billion in Iraq aid into half-grant, half-loan
No Overhaul Medicare and create prescription drug benefit

CQ VOTE STUDIES

	PARTY UNITY		PRESIDENTIAL SUPPORT	
	Support	Oppose	Support	Oppose
2004	97%	3%	13%	87%
2003	98%	2%	12%	88%
2002	97%	3%	21%	79%
2001	96%	4%	12%	88%
2000	96%	4%	85%	15%

INTEREST GROUPS

	AFL-CIO	ADA	CCUS	ACU
2004	100%	95%	12%	4%
2003	100%	100%	17%	17%
2002	100%	95%	22%	0%
2001	100%	95%	23%	0%
2000	100%	85%	26%	0%

CALIFORNIA 35
South central Los Angeles; Inglewood

South central Los Angeles' 35th is one of the most secure Democratic districts in the state. Two-thirds of its voters register as Democrats, and John Kerry captured 79 percent of the vote here in the 2004 presidential election. Once predominately black, the district is seeing a huge influx of Hispanics. It still has the state's highest concentration of African-Americans at 34 percent, but Hispanics are the district's racial plurality, comprising 47 percent of the population. Gardena has a large and politically influential Japanese community.

Riots put the 35th in the headlines in 1992 in the wake of a verdict acquitting white police officers accused of beating black motorist Rodney King. Issues of poverty, joblessness and lack of basic human services remain. Police-community relations, public safety and economic development are central public policy concerns.

The district is set between downtown Los Angeles to the north, beaches to the west, Torrance to the south and the industrial Alameda Corridor to the east. Redistricting following the 2000 census added Los Angeles

International Airport, the region's largest employer. The 35th is mostly poor, but there are middle-class areas in Inglewood and the South Bay cities of Gardena and Hawthorne. Efforts to lure businesses have met with some success. In 1994, the area became part of a federal empowerment zone set up to help areas affected by the riots.

Gardena receives a strong revenue stream as one of the only cities in Los Angeles County that allows poker parlors, which account for a chunk of the city's budget. In 1999, the Los Angeles Lakers and Kings moved from the Great Western Forum in Inglewood to the new Staples Center in the nearby 34th, a disappointment for the 35th.

MAJOR INDUSTRY
Aerospace, service, manufacturing

CITIES
Los Angeles (pt.), 280,597; Inglewood, 112,580; Hawthorne, 84,112

NOTABLE
Hollywood Park racetrack is in Inglewood; Hawthorne was the birthplace of the Beach Boys and Northrop Corp., before it became aerospace giant Northrop Grumman Corp.; Central Avenue, on the district's eastern edge, was the West Coast hub of African-American entertainment during the jazz age.

Rep. Jane Harman (D)

CAPITOL OFFICE
225-8220
www.house.gov/harman
2400 Rayburn 20515-0536; fax 226-7290

COMMITTEES
Homeland Security
Select Intelligence - ranking member

HOMETOWN
Venice

BORN
June 28, 1945, Queens, N.Y.

RELIGION
Jewish

FAMILY
Husband, Sidney Harman; four children

EDUCATION
Smith College, B.A. 1966 (government); Harvard U., J.D. 1969

CAREER
Lawyer; White House aide; congressional aide

POLITICAL HIGHLIGHTS
U.S. House, 1993-99; sought Democratic nomination for governor, 1998

ELECTION RESULTS

2004 GENERAL

Jane Harman (D)	151,208	62.0%
Paul Whitehead (R)	81,666	33.5%
Alice Stek (PF)	6,105	2.5%
Mike Binkley (LIBERT)	5,065	2.1%

2004 PRIMARY

Jane Harman (D)	unopposed

2002 GENERAL

Jane Harman (D)	88,198	61.4%
Stuart Johnson (R)	50,328	35.0%
Mark McSpadden (LIBERT)	5,225	3.6%

PREVIOUS WINNING PERCENTAGES
2000 (48%); 1996 (52%); 1994 (48%); 1992 (48%)

Elected 1992; 6th term

Did not serve 1999-2001

Harman has managed within a few years to become a visible, forceful and often pithy advocate for her party in the mostly male-dominated area of national security. She is the senior Democrat on the Intelligence Committee, where she has joined in the sometimes bruising political battles over the performance of spy agencies since the Sept. 11, 2001, terrorist attacks.

After Republican committee Chairman Porter J. Goss was named CIA director in 2004, she asserted that senior agency officials resigned rather than work with Goss' "highly partisan, inexperienced" staff. "Many of us worked with that staff in the House," she said. "Frankly, on both sides of the aisle in our committee, we were happy to see them go."

Harman's signature accomplishment on Intelligence was working with Goss' successor as chairman, Michigan Republican Peter Hoekstra, to steer to enactment a law that reorganized intelligence agencies in line with recommendations of the commission that investigated the attacks. She said at the time, "Our intelligence community operates on a 1947 business model designed to defeat the Soviet Union, which was defeated in 1989. Fifteen years later, the enemy is digital, but our organizational structure remains analog."

Harman also has a seat on the Homeland Security Committee. She was an early advocate of the creation of a Homeland Security Department, months before President Bush proposed one. After the Cabinet-level department was created, she regularly took it to task for, in her view, unduly frightening the public with a color-coded threat alert system that failed to give any guidance "other than to 'remain vigilant.' "

Harman campaigned for Massachusetts Sen. John Kerry in his race against Bush in 2004, and was talked about as a possible running mate before he chose fellow Sen. John Edwards of North Carolina. Some also saw her as a candidate for Homeland Security secretary if Kerry had won.

What is surprising about Harman's ascension on homeland security issues is that during her early years in Congress, "terrorism was not on my radar," as she told an interviewer for the Harvard Law Bulletin. She served on the Intelligence and Armed Services committees, but her main interest was looking out for the large defense and aerospace companies in her district, such as Northrop Grumman.

That changed with her experience on the congressionally mandated National Commission on Terrorism. She joined the panel as one of 10 members after finding herself temporarily unemployed in 1999. She had left her House seat to run for California governor, but lost a three-way primary to Lt. Gov. Gray Davis, who went on to victory that November. Harman helped write the commission's report warning that the terrorist threat to the United States was increasing and that "today's terrorists seek to inflict mass casualties." It was released a little over a year before Sept. 11.

In 2000, Democrats pleaded with her to run for her old seat, which, during her hiatus, had been secured by a Republican, Steven T. Kuykendall. She agreed, provided she was promised she would get put back on the Intelligence panel if she won. She became the top-ranking Democrat when California's Nancy Pelosi left the panel.

Harman is among the wealthiest members of Congress; in 2004, she reported assets for herself and her second husband, electronics executive Sidney Harman, of at least $56 million. A disciplined runner and avid athlete, she can be similarly driven in her job. She has a keen memory for detail and is known for being demanding with her staff. A former aide told the Los Angeles Times that working for her is "a survival-of-the-fittest kind of game, Jane being the fittest."

Harman's approach to budget issues is similar to that of other moderate Democrats, including those in the fiscally conservative Blue Dog Coalition, of which she is a member. She also affiliates with the business-oriented New Democrat Coalition, and in 2002 she was elected president of the coalition's newly formed executive council.

Harman appeals to the swing voters in her upscale, suburban Los Angeles district with her moderate fiscal stands and liberal social views, such as support for abortion rights. At the same time, she breaks with most Democrats in voting for liberalized global trade and in strongly backing a robust defense budget. During her gubernatorial campaign, she marketed herself to Republican women who supported abortion rights as "the best Republican in the Democratic Party."

Harman's father fled Nazi Germany, then emigrated to the United States. She was born in New York City, and when she was 4, she and her family moved to Southern California, where her father, a doctor, had relocated his practice. She grew up in West Los Angeles.

She caught the politics bug in 1964 when, as a Smith College student, she did an internship in Washington. With a law degree from Harvard, she returned to Washington to work for Democratic Sen. John Tunney of California and the Senate Judiciary Committee. In 1977, she went to work in the Carter White House, then went to the Pentagon as a special counsel.

In 1991, she and her husband returned to California and settled in the 36th District, where incumbent Democrat Mel Levine was relinquishing his House seat to run for the Senate. Her move from Washington to the district was branded opportunism by the opposition, but a larger factor in the 1992 race was the anti-abortion position of Republican candidate Joan Milke Flores. Harman made the issue the centerpiece of her campaign and spent a considerable amount of her own money. She emerged with a 6 percentage point victory.

The 36th was a swing district throughout the 1990s, and her re-elections in 1994 and 1996 were hard-fought affairs. In 2000, Harman won back the seat from Kuykendall by 1.8 percentage points. Remapping before the 2002 election gave the 36th a much more Democratic tilt, ironically by removing affluent areas such as Harman's former home in Rolling Hills on the Palos Verdes Peninsula, now in the 46th District. In that election, Harman took 61 percent against attorney Stuart Johnson. In 2004, she won her most lopsided victory yet, beating teacher Paul Whitehead by more than 28 points.

KEY VOTES

2004

Yes Extend federal unemployment benefits by 13 weeks
Yes Pass $283.2 billion, six-year federal highway and mass transit bill
No Approve $146 billion multi-year extension of previously enacted middle-class tax breaks
? Amend the Constitution to prohibit same-sex marriage
No Cut corporate taxes $137 billion over 10 years
Yes Reorganize U.S. intelligence agencies as proposed by Sept. 11 commission

2003

No Cut taxes by $330 billion through fiscal 2013
? Block Bush rule scaling back overtime pay for some white-collar federal workers
No Do not allow use of search warrants without first notifying subjects
Yes Allow importation of prescription drugs
No Create private school voucher program in Washington, D.C.
No Ban "partial birth" abortion except to save a woman's life
Yes Split $18.6 billion in Iraq aid into half-grant, half-loan
No Overhaul Medicare and create prescription drug benefit

CQ VOTE STUDIES

	PARTY UNITY		PRESIDENTIAL SUPPORT	
	Support	Oppose	Support	Oppose
2004	91%	9%	34%	66%
2003	91%	9%	25%	75%
2002	83%	17%	42%	58%
2001	84%	16%	40%	60%
1998	83%	17%	78%	22%

INTEREST GROUPS

	AFL-CIO	ADA	CCUS	ACU
2004	87%	95%	55%	13%
2003	75%	85%	45%	16%
2002	50%	60%	65%	36%
2001	83%	90%	52%	20%
1998	63%	80%	83%	15%

CALIFORNIA 36

Southwest Los Angeles County — Torrance, Redondo Beach, Manhattan Beach

The 36th is home to some of Los Angeles' most famous beaches — and biggest aerospace firms. It hugs the Pacific coast south from Venice through El Segundo to Manhattan, Hermosa and Redondo beaches. Redistricting following the 2000 census removed the Republican Palos Verdes Peninsula to give the district a Democratic lean. John Kerry took 59 percent of the district's 2004 presidential vote, and Democrats hold a 12-point voter registration edge.

Venice's eclectic beaches are considered the state's most liberal havens outside of Berkeley. Manhattan Beach and Marina del Rey, with its huge private marina, are ritzier. Torrance, the district's largest whole city, is split politically. It is wealthier toward the coast, but inland sections include middle- and working-class areas that have conservative and labor-heavy pockets. New immigrants and poorer residents live just west of Interstate 110.

A number of major companies maintain headquarters in the 36th, and aerospace firms in El Segundo and Redondo Beach drive the economy. The district has some of the state's most-educated residents. Some had trouble finding work as defense and aerospace spending shrank, but many employers, such as Hughes Electronics Corp. and Northrop Grumman, have successfully converted to non-defense projects. Such efforts to diversify the economy and encourage dual-use technology resulted in an economic boost.

MAJOR INDUSTRY
Aerospace, technology, manufacturing

MILITARY BASES
Los Angeles Air Force Base, 1,300 military, 3,200 civilian (2003)

CITIES
Los Angeles (pt.), 295,808; Torrance, 137,946; Redondo Beach, 63,261; Manhattan Beach, 33,582

NOTABLE
The Hyperion sewage treatment plant in Playa del Rey, the subject of a multidecade environmental lawsuit, is now one of the cleanest plants in the Los Angeles area; Hughes and subsidiary DirecTV are based in El Segundo.

Rep. Juanita Millender-McDonald (D)

CAPITOL OFFICE
225-7924
www.house.gov/millender-mcdonald
2445 Rayburn 20515-0537; fax 225-7926

COMMITTEES
House Administration - ranking member
Small Business
Transportation & Infrastructure
Joint Library
Joint Printing - ranking member

HOMETOWN
Carson

BORN
Sept. 7, 1938, Birmingham, Ala.

RELIGION
Baptist

FAMILY
Husband, James McDonald Jr.; five children

EDUCATION
U. of Redlands, B.S. 1981 (business administration);
California State U., Los Angeles, M.A. 1988
(educational administration); U. of Southern
California, attending (public administration)

CAREER
Teacher; school program administrator

POLITICAL HIGHLIGHTS
Carson City Council, 1990-92 (mayor pro tempore,
1991-92); Calif. Assembly, 1992-96

ELECTION RESULTS

2004 GENERAL

Juanita Millender-McDonald (D)	118,823	75.1%
Vernon Van (R)	31,960	20.2%
Herb Peters (LIBERT)	7,535	4.8%

2004 PRIMARY

Juanita Millender-McDonald (D)	27,047	64.9%
Albert Robles (D)	7,800	18.7%
Peter Mathews (D)	6,802	16.3%

2002 GENERAL

Juanita Millender-McDonald (D)	63,445	72.9%
Oscar A. Velasco (R)	20,154	23.2%
Herb Peters (LIBERT)	3,413	3.9%

PREVIOUS WINNING PERCENTAGES
2000 (82%); 1998 (85%); 1996 (85%); 1996 Special
Election (27%)

Elected March 1996; 5th full term

Millender-McDonald has a compelling life story, which she uses as a basis for many of her legislative initiatives. The daughter of a minister, she married early and had five children by the time she was 26. At the age of 42, with her children older, she earned her college degree and embarked on a career as a math and English teacher, and then as an administrator, in the Los Angeles school system.

She was active in local Democratic Party politics, serving as a delegate at the 1984 and 1988 Democratic National conventions. Then, at age 51, she entered elective politics, winning a city council seat in Carson, a low-income city between Los Angeles and Long Beach.

At each step in her professional life, Millender-McDonald's forceful self-confidence has enabled her to become a powerful and noticeable presence. She has a host of ideas that she thinks would make the world a better place, and she persists, although many of them are a tough sell in a conservative-run House. Millender-McDonald is by any measure a liberal, but not an inflexible one. If cooperating with Republicans offers a chance of boosting the 37th District's struggling economy, she'll do it. Her district is one of the poorest in California.

Her interests range across the policy spectrum, from transportation projects to job training to homeland security, child care to illegal drug use, education to women's issues at home and abroad. Her rhetoric can take a hard edge when it serves her purpose, and particularly when she detects what she views as GOP indifference toward the plight of the poor.

As a member of the Transportation Committee, she joined GOP Chairman Don Young of Alaska in 2002 in challenging a proposed huge reduction in funding for highway projects, which threatened to cut California highway funds by $618 million. In the 108th Congress, she again worked across party lines to protect California funding and to steer $87.5 million for highway projects in her district. She won bipartisan backing for a $6.6 billion program in the surface transportation bill to boost projects with high national and regional significance.

Since the Sept. 11, 2001, terrorist attacks, Millender-McDonald has striven to bolster transportation security. She introduced bills to authorize increased funding for maritime security projects and to mandate the use of hardened or "blast proof" cargo containers on commercial aircraft. Her district is adjacent to two major ports, and she has repeatedly warned that growing congestion is straining them and other ports across the nation. "What I see when I go to both ports [near the district] are bumper-to-bumper trucks pretty much at a standstill," she said in 2004. "We have 35,000 to 40,000 trucks a day transporting cargo and containers, and when they come out and they get on the streets from the highway, it is literally a dead stop."

In the 107th, her transportation priorities included supporting the federal government's takeover of airport baggage and passenger screening. Having the federal government assume that responsibility, she said, would bring travelers back and ultimately protect the jobs of airport workers. She also sought to ensure that private screeners could apply for the same jobs in the newly created Transportation Security Administration.

Now in her fifth term, she has gained the seniority that puts her at the top of the Democrats serving on the House Administration Committee. The committee has authority over federal elections and the operation of the House. In the 108th, she raised concerns about the possible hacking of electronic ballot machines. "No matter how you cut this, voters are concerned about their votes being counted," she said, and she posted detailed instructions about voting on the home page of her Web site during the 2004 elections.

Millender-McDonald also sits on the Small Business Committee, where she is the senior Democrat on the panel's Tax, Finance & Exports Subcommittee. A former director of gender equity programs with the Los Angeles Unified School District, she has focused a number of her legislative efforts specifically on discrimination against women. In the 107th, she was co-chairwoman of the Congressional Caucus for Women's Issues, and in the 108th she won House support for legislation to increase Small Business Administration funding for women's business centers. She has called for specific assurances that women will receive a fair share of federal vocational education training dollars. And from her seat on Transportation's Aviation Subcommittee, she pressed for hearings on the alleged sexual harassment of female air traffic controllers.

A critic of tuition vouchers and other education ideas advanced by conservatives, Millender-McDonald has said that the GOP first should recognize the "deplorable" physical condition of many public schools and commit billions of federal dollars to repairs and renovations. Nevertheless, she voted for a Bush proposal in 2001 to require annual reading and mathematics tests as part of a reauthorization of federal education funding.

In 1999, Millender-McDonald had a post office in Compton, Calif., named for Democratic Rep. Mervyn M. Dymally, who represented much of what is now the 37th District between 1981 and 1993, and who had helped her get elected to the Carson City Council in 1990 and the state Assembly two years later. Millender-McDonald captured her House seat in a March 1996 special election after Democratic Rep. Walter R. Tucker III resigned; he had been convicted of federal extortion and tax evasion charges stemming from actions he took as mayor of Compton, before his election to Congress.

In each of her re-elections, Millender-McDonald has captured more than 70 percent of the vote. Changing demographics in the Los Angeles area threatened to jeopardize her career after the 2000 census, when the Hispanic population in her district surged to 57 percent. But the Democratic legislature drew a new district that reduced the Hispanic share of her constituency to 43 percent. The new 37th takes in much of Long Beach and other areas that in the 1990s were in the neighboring 38th District, a move that prompted its representative, moderate Republican Steve Horn, to retire in 2002.

KEY VOTES

2004

?	Extend federal unemployment benefits by 13 weeks
Yes	Pass $283.2 billion, six-year federal highway and mass transit bill
No	Approve $146 billion multi-year extension of previously enacted middle-class tax breaks
No	Amend the Constitution to prohibit same-sex marriage
?	Cut corporate taxes $137 billion over 10 years
Yes	Reorganize U.S. intelligence agencies as proposed by Sept. 11 commission

2003

No	Cut taxes by $330 billion through fiscal 2013
?	Block Bush rule scaling back overtime pay for some white-collar federal workers
Yes	Do not allow use of search warrants without first notifying subjects
No	Allow importation of prescription drugs
No	Create private school voucher program in Washington, D.C.
No	Ban "partial birth" abortion except to save a woman's life
Yes	Split $18.6 billion in Iraq aid into half-grant, half-loan
No	Overhaul Medicare and create prescription drug benefit

CQ VOTE STUDIES

	PARTY UNITY		PRESIDENTIAL SUPPORT	
	Support	Oppose	Support	Oppose
2004	95%	5%	33%	67%
2003	98%	2%	12%	88%
2002	96%	4%	27%	73%
2001	95%	5%	26%	74%
2000	98%	2%	91%	9%

INTEREST GROUPS

	AFL-CIO	ADA	CCUS	ACU
2004	92%	75%	35%	9%
2003	100%	85%	30%	14%
2002	100%	85%	44%	0%
2001	100%	90%	35%	4%
2000	100%	90%	50%	8%

CALIFORNIA 37

Southern Los Angeles County – most of Long Beach, Compton, Carson

The 37th combines some of the state's poorest and most Democratic communities with a large chunk of middle-class Long Beach. Minorities make up almost 85 percent of the population, with Hispanics as the dominant group, totalling 43 percent of residents. The district is one-fourth black and more than one-tenth Asian.

The district contains a sliver of Los Angeles itself, and then spreads to the lower- and middle-class cities of Compton and Carson south of Los Angeles. These communities boost Democratic presidential candidates to high margins of victory in the 37th. John Kerry garnered 74 percent of the vote here in the 2004 presidential election.

The district's south end contains the non-coastal portion of Long Beach (the port is in the 46th), which holds a more suburban, politically mixed community. It has a sizable Cambodian population, and more than four dozen languages are spoken in the schools.

The 37th's troubled economy suffered in the 1992 riots when fires ravaged parts of Compton. Despite redevelopment, Compton still has blocks-long stretches of abandoned buildings and vacant lots, and gang problems persist.

There are some bright spots, however. Several national retailers and fast-food chains have moved into communities once considered undevelopable, and home sales have increased. The multibillion-dollar Alameda Corridor project, which links the ports of Long Beach and Los Angeles south of the 37th to distribution areas in Los Angeles north of the district, created construction jobs for the area, and local leaders hope it will continue to provide an economic boost.

MAJOR INDUSTRY
Service, manufacturing, oil

CITIES
Long Beach (pt.), 368,591; Compton, 93,493; Carson, 89,730; Los Angeles (pt.), 33,808

NOTABLE
Toyota, which operates a manufacturing plant in Long Beach, is the title sponsor of the Grand Prix of Long Beach auto race.

Rep. Grace F. Napolitano (D)

Elected 1998; 4th term

CAPITOL OFFICE
225-5256
grace@mail.house.gov
www.napolitano.house.gov
1609 Longworth 20515-0538; fax 225-0027

COMMITTEES
International Relations
Resources

HOMETOWN
Norwalk

BORN
Dec. 4, 1936, Brownsville, Texas

RELIGION
Roman Catholic

FAMILY
Husband, Frank Napolitano; five children

EDUCATION
Brownsville H.S., graduated 1954

CAREER
Regional transportation claims agent

POLITICAL HIGHLIGHTS
Norwalk City Council, 1986-92 (mayor, 1989-90);
Calif. Assembly, 1992-98

ELECTION RESULTS

2004 GENERAL

Grace F. Napolitano (D)		unopposed

2004 PRIMARY

Grace F. Napolitano (D)	26,632	78.9%
Michael J. Manzo (D)	7,122	21.1%

2002 GENERAL

Grace F. Napolitano (D)	62,600	71.1%
Alex A. Burrola (R)	23,126	26.3%
Al Cuperus (LIBERT)	2,301	2.6%

PREVIOUS WINNING PERCENTAGES
2000 (71%); 1998 (68%)

Napolitano's grandmotherly image, enhanced by her silvery hair, can be deceptive. She can be a fierce political fighter, who is protective of the interests of her mostly Hispanic constituency.

In the 109th Congress, she will serve as chairwoman of the Congressional Hispanic Caucus. In one of her first actions on behalf of the group, she sent a letter to the Senate saying the caucus would not give its endorsement to Alberto R. Gonzales, President Bush's nominee for attorney general.

Although caucus members have always supported "the advancement of Latinos into high levels of public office," Napolitano said they could not support Gonzales because he never took the time to meet with them. Napolitano added that the Latino community continued to lack clear information on how Gonzales, as attorney general, would influence certain policies, such as the Voting Rights Act, affirmative action and due process rights of immigrants.

Napolitano sits on the Resources Committee, where she has developed a strong interest in environmental issues. In the 108th Congress, she became the senior Democrat on the Water and Power Subcommittee, helping her watch out for her district's water needs. In 2004, Congress passed a pared-back version of her bill to increase funding for cleaning up groundwater in the San Gabriel Basin, an important piece of Southern California's strategy to protect its water supply. She also weighed in on legislation to help fund the CalFed Bay-Delta Program, developed by the state of California to improve water quality and storage systems, increase its water supply and restore state fisheries.

Her biggest triumph in the 107th was persuading Bush to follow through on ensuring that the Energy Department clean up more than 10 million tons of waste left over from 30 years of uranium mining. The waste pile, near Moab, Utah, is said to be leaking thousands of gallons of radioactive uranium and other toxins daily into the Colorado River, which provides much of the West's drinking water. Bush did not include cleanup funds in his initial budget in 2001. Napolitano joined with a bipartisan coalition of lawmakers from Utah and California to successfully pressure Bush, and then Congress, to support the program.

In 2001, she joined with other Southern Californians to oppose legislation that would authorize nearly $3 billion for a program designed to restore the Sacramento-San Joaquin delta. She and other foes objected to the bill's bias in favor of farmers in California's Central Valley, which they said would come at the expense of drinking water in their area. But she showed a more pragmatic streak than some of her colleagues, winning support for an amendment to allow more than one-quarter of the money to be spent on water recycling projects in California.

Napolitano was one of 36 House Democrats who supported a 2004 resolution declaring the world safer with the removal of Saddam Hussein from power in Iraq but who voted against the 2002 law authorizing force in Iraq. She also opposed a 2003 administration request for an additional $87 billion in spending for Iraq, saying it would take away from badly needed federal funds at home.

Napolitano grew up in Brownsville, Texas, the daughter of a Mexican immigrant who raised her two children on a shoestring budget. Napolitano has cultivated a strong connection to her mother's homeland as a public official. As chairman of the state legislature's International Trade and Development Committee, she traveled to Mexico many times. In the 107th Congress, she joined the International Relations Committee.

Napolitano had been deeply immersed in the details of the 1993 North American Free Trade Agreement among the United States, Canada and Mexico, and she describes herself as a believer in the value of open commerce. Still, she must be sensitive to her constituents' unemployment concerns.

Those conflicting pressures have placed her in a difficult situation on the key trade votes during her tenure. Considered one of the last of the undecided lawmakers in 2000 — when President Clinton and big businesses pushed to grant China permanent normal trade status over the objections of labor unions and environmentalists — she eventually voted against the bill. "I know trade is good," she said afterward. "I know it's where we are going, but it's not good for the district."

Napolitano was married at age 18, and she had five children by age 23. She spent the first part of her adult life attending to their needs, while also working at the Ford Motor Co. She caught the political bug as a volunteer in Norwalk's efforts to cultivate a sister-city relationship with Hermosillo, Mexico. She first joined the group to show her children and "other youngsters on this side how lucky they were" compared to Mexican children, but became enmeshed in the project and managed the organization's budget.

In her first run for political office, Napolitano challenged the Norwalk establishment and won a seat on the city council by 28 votes. She capitalized on outrage over an expensive city council trip to Palm Springs and campaigned with $35,000 she borrowed using her home as collateral.

Napolitano served in the state legislature for six years and was mayor and councilwoman in Norwalk, her district's second-largest municipality, during the six years before that.

Nonetheless, she was overlooked when Democrat Esteban E. Torres in 1997 announced his retirement from the House. Torres threw his support to his top aide and son-in-law, James Casso. But Napolitano won by 618 votes in the primary and then took almost two-thirds of the vote to win in November. She increased her winning percentage to 71 percent in both 2000 and 2002 and was unopposed in 2004.

In Washington, she has tried to win over her political opponents in much the same way she and her husband, Frank, won customers to their Italian restaurant — through their stomachs. She prides herself on catering her own fundraisers with homemade Mexican molés, guacamole and other dishes. She says such personal involvement is the best way to express her thanks to her supporters. "I treat them like I would my family," she says.

KEY VOTES

2004

? Extend federal unemployment benefits by 13 weeks

Yes Pass $283.2 billion, six-year federal highway and mass transit bill

Yes Approve $146 billion multi-year extension of previously enacted middle-class tax breaks

No Amend the Constitution to prohibit same-sex marriage

No Cut corporate taxes $137 billion over 10 years

Yes Reorganize U.S. intelligence agencies as proposed by Sept. 11 commission

2003

No Cut taxes by $330 billion through fiscal 2013

Yes Block Bush rule scaling back overtime pay for some white-collar federal workers

Yes Do not allow use of search warrants without first notifying subjects

Yes Allow importation of prescription drugs

No Create private school voucher program in Washington, D.C.

No Ban "partial birth" abortion except to save a woman's life

Yes Split $18.6 billion in Iraq aid into half-grant, half-loan

No Overhaul Medicare and create prescription drug benefit

CQ VOTE STUDIES

	PARTY UNITY		PRESIDENTIAL SUPPORT	
	Support	Oppose	Support	Oppose
2004	98%	2%	21%	79%
2003	99%	1%	13%	87%
2002	98%	2%	21%	79%
2001	96%	4%	24%	76%
2000	95%	5%	94%	6%

INTEREST GROUPS

	AFL-CIO	ADA	CCUS	ACU
2004	100%	95%	33%	0%
2003	100%	95%	24%	12%
2002	89%	100%	40%	0%
2001	100%	90%	35%	4%
2000	100%	95%	47%	4%

CALIFORNIA 38

East Los Angeles County — Pomona, Norwalk

The Democratic 38th, once a predominately white area, has become a middle- and working-class Hispanic-majority district. A sideways "L" shape, it takes in the southeast Los Angeles County city of Norwalk, then stretches north along Interstate 5 to include nearly half of East Los Angeles. It then runs east through Montebello and Pico Rivera, goes north a bit to La Puente and then extends a thin arm parallel to the 60 Freeway into the Inland Valley to take in Pomona, the district's largest city, at the county's eastern edge.

Although mostly blue-collar, the district contains some affluent and conservative areas such as Hacienda Heights, Rowland Heights (shared with the 42nd) and a narrow sliver of Whittier.

Small businesses dominate the 38th, which contains the heart of East Los Angeles' business district. Stores generally are owned or operated by Hispanics. These near-in suburbs are in places populated by what used to be called Muppies — Mexican yuppies who have moved in and fixed up old homes.

Montebello is an upper-middle-class Hispanic area, with a lot of home-grown residents. Pico Rivera has been called a pure Middle American working community, Hispanic-style. The city received a major blow in 2000 with the closure of a Northrop Grumman B-2 plant, but part of that site was converted into a large retail development. Norwalk, the district's second-largest city, is a bedroom community. Santa Fe Springs is an industrial area with light manufacturing and oil wells.

The district's working-class residents ensure that it is reliably Democratic. John Kerry received 65 percent of the 2004 presidential vote here. California State Polytechnic University, Pomona and Cerritos College add students to the Democratic mix.

MAJOR INDUSTRY
Manufacturing, oil

CITIES
Pomona, 149,473; Norwalk, 103,298; Pico Rivera, 63,428; Montebello, 62,150

NOTABLE
The Pomona Swap Meet and Car Show is billed as the largest collection of antique cars, parts and accessories on the West Coast.

Rep. Linda T. Sánchez (D)

CAPITOL OFFICE
225-6676
www.house.gov/lindasanchez
1007 Longworth 20515-0539; fax 226-1012

COMMITTEES
Government Reform
Judiciary
Small Business

HOMETOWN
Lakewood

BORN
Jan. 28, 1969, Orange, Calif.

RELIGION
Roman Catholic

FAMILY
Divorced

EDUCATION
U. of California, Berkeley, B.A. 1991 (Spanish literature); U. of California, Los Angeles, J.D. 1995

CAREER
Union official; campaign aide; lawyer

POLITICAL HIGHLIGHTS
No previous office

ELECTION RESULTS

2004 GENERAL

Linda T. Sánchez (D)	100,132	60.7%
Tim Escobar (R)	64,832	39.3%

2004 PRIMARY

Linda T. Sánchez (D)	unopposed

2002 GENERAL

Linda T. Sánchez (D)	52,256	54.8%
Tim Escobar (R)	38,925	40.8%
Richard Newhouse (LIBERT)	4,165	4.4%

Elected 2002; 2nd term

One of the most liberal members of the House, Sánchez sees herself as a defender of working-class Americans. She is the sixth of seven children of Mexican immigrants, who, remarkably, sent two of their offspring to Congress: Linda, and her older sister, Rep. Loretta Sanchez, who represents a nearby, Anaheim-based district. The two women are the first, and so far only, sisters to serve in Congress together.

A former labor union leader, Linda Sánchez's interests in the House reflect her Hispanic-majority, blue-collar district south of Los Angeles. Instead of the standard photograph collection of grinning and famous politicians on the wall, a self-portrait of Mexican artist Frida Kahlo hangs next to Sánchez's desk.

She favors increasing the federally mandated minimum wage, and in her first term, joined in an effort by more well-known advocates like Democratic Sen. Edward M. Kennedy of Massachusetts and Rep. George Miller of California, the senior Democrat on the House Education and the Workforce Committee. Kennedy invited her to appear at a 2004 kickoff for the legislation alongside movie star Ben Affleck, who lent his famous name to the cause. The bill ultimately was blocked by GOP leaders. "No one who works full time for a living should live in poverty," said Sánchez, who grew up in working-class Anaheim wearing clothes handmade by her mother.

Another major interest is immigration policy, which led her to request a seat on the Judiciary Committee. She opposed a Bush administration initiative creating a guest worker program allowing illegal immigrants to continue working in the United States for three years. With other panel Democrats, Sánchez argued that it was a better deal for the businesses employing illegal help than for the workers, who would not have the chance to become permanent residents or citizens under the proposal and who could be deported at the end of their guest period.

On the budget, Sánchez joined other Democrats in opposing the president's planned cuts in Clinton-era social programs, including the Community-Oriented Policing Services program (COPS), which helps local governments hire more police in high-crime neighborhoods.

Some of Sánchez's House colleagues got a sense of her views on gender equality when she joined the all-male roster of players in the annual House baseball game between Democrats and Republicans. The back of her shirt bore the numerals IX, for Title IX, shorthand for the landmark 1972 law that mandated equal treatment for women in education programs, a measure that had a dramatic impact on the growth of women's sports.

Sánchez had no experience in local or state government before her election in 2002, and in her first term had yet to establish a political name for herself beyond that of "Loretta's sister." While she says she is passionate about issues affecting minorities and the poor and though Judiciary gives her a platform on relevant issues, she has not been very visible in endeavors beyond the minimum wage. Her biggest effort in her first term was a bill creating federal grants to prevent bullying in public schools, which Sánchez says is a precursor to gang violence, drug abuse and increased drop-out rates. It gained little traction, stalling in committee.

Though the sisters are from the same party, Linda, who is in her 30s, is no political clone of Loretta, in her 40s. Before coming to the House, Linda practiced civil rights and labor law; Loretta was a businesswoman with an MBA. Linda is at home with the liberal-leaning Congressional Hispanic Caucus; her sister belongs to the conservative Democrats known as the "Blue Dogs." Their personal styles are different, too. Linda, nine years younger, is a night owl; Loretta an early riser. Linda is messy, Loretta neat. They even spell their last name differently: Linda uses an accent and Loretta does not. (They pronounce it the same way: SAN-chez.)

Growing up, Linda was the more rebellious of the two. Her father, Ignacio, was a machinist and her mother, Maria Macias, a factory worker who cleaned houses for extra money. Sánchez often questioned why their traditional Latino family gave boys special status. "There was a very clear distinction between what boys could do and what girls could do," she says. "Boys were served first and girls served them. They had a lot more freedom and a lot fewer responsibilities."

Her mother told Sánchez to either accept the way things were or try to change them. She once took Sánchez to hear farm labor organizer Cesar Chavez speak. Sánchez, having worked her way through college as a nanny, security guard, bilingual teacher's aide and ESL instructor, had recently graduated with a degree in Spanish literature from the University of California at Berkeley. She was inspired by Chavez's words to go back to school for a law degree and to get involved in labor organizing. Sánchez later became executive secretary-treasurer of the AFL-CIO in Orange County, the top post in the countywide organization.

Her political activism started in high school in Anaheim. Incensed that gaffe-prone conservative Republican Robert K. Dornan represented the area in the House, Sánchez knocked on doors for Democratic challenger Dave Carter. Carter lost, but Sánchez's efforts eventually paid off. In 1996, she was the field organizer for sister Loretta's successful campaign against Dornan. "Ten years later, I was still trying to get Bob Dornan out of office," Linda Sánchez recalls with a smile.

In 2000, after the census, the California Legislature drew a new district south of downtown Los Angeles that favored a Hispanic Democratic candidate. In 2002, incumbent Republican Rep. Steve Horn declined to run for the seat, which then included only portions of his old turf. Sánchez jumped into a highly competitive Democratic primary that attracted politicians with more experience and higher profiles. She won a six-way contest with help from Loretta's fundraising network and vigorous campaigning by the Sánchez family. Her mother appealed to voters in a Spanish language television spot.

She easily won the general election. She was re-elected in 2004 with 61 percent of the vote, attracting no primary opponents and a relatively weak GOP challenger.

KEY VOTES

2004

Yes   Extend federal unemployment benefits by 13 weeks

Yes   Pass $283.2 billion, six-year federal highway and mass transit bill

Yes   Approve $146 billion multi-year extension of previously enacted middle-class tax breaks

No   Amend the Constitution to prohibit same-sex marriage

No   Cut corporate taxes $137 billion over 10 years

Yes   Reorganize U.S. intelligence agencies as proposed by Sept. 11 commission

2003

No   Cut taxes by $330 billion through fiscal 2013

Yes   Block Bush rule scaling back overtime pay for some white-collar federal workers

Yes   Do not allow use of search warrants without first notifying subjects

Yes   Allow importation of prescription drugs

No   Create private school voucher program in Washington, D.C.

No   Ban "partial birth" abortion except to save a woman's life

Yes   Split $18.6 billion in Iraq aid into half-grant, half-loan

No   Overhaul Medicare and create prescription drug benefit

CQ VOTE STUDIES

| | PARTY UNITY | | PRESIDENTIAL SUPPORT | |
	Support	Oppose	Support	Oppose
2004	99%	1%	15%	85%
2003	99%	1%	15%	85%

INTEREST GROUPS

	AFL-CIO	ADA	CCUS	ACU
2004	100%	100%	20%	0%
2003	100%	100%	24%	12%

CALIFORNIA 39

Southeast Los Angeles County — South Gate, Lakewood

The 39th is a product of the redistricting cycle following the 2000 census: State legislators carved the area out as an open seat designed to elect a Hispanic Democrat from Los Angeles County south of downtown. The district is 61 percent Hispanic and registered Democrats outnumber Republicans almost 2-to-1. Despite their external similarities, most of these communities have little interaction with one another.

The district has a strong organized-labor movement. Towns like Whittier (shared with the 42nd) and Lakewood have a number of industrial centers, and most residents work in the district or nearby rather than commuting to downtown Los Angeles, Orange County or Long Beach.

Whittier and South Whittier, on the U-shaped district's northeastern tip, are home to many second- and third-generation Latino families, and pockets of wealth exist there. La Mirada and the Asian-American-heavy Cerritos, on the eastern arm of the U, are slightly more conservative

communities that resemble cities in neighboring, richer Orange County — former farm areas now dependent on aerospace and technology jobs. Lakewood, on the southern arc of the U, is more blue-collar, while South Gate, Lynwood and Paramount, farther west, are heavily working class and include many new immigrants.

The 39th gave John Kerry 59 percent of its 2004 presidential vote, but the district is not as far left on the political spectrum as most of Los Angeles County — Kerry's victory margin here (18 points) was the smallest margin in any of the 13 districts contained entirely in the county.

MAJOR INDUSTRY
Manufacturing, aerospace

CITIES
South Gate, 96,375; Lakewood, 79,345; Lynwood, 69,845; Whittier (pt.), 56,918

NOTABLE
Whittier, where Richard M. Nixon lived and attended college, was the epicenter of L.A.'s 1987 earthquake; Paramount is home to Zamboni, maker of the ice resurfacing machines used at skating and hockey rinks; The home of the last Mexican governor of California is in Pio Pico Historical Park.

Rep. Ed Royce (R)

Elected 1992; 7th term

Royce has made his mark in Congress by championing a cause most other members have largely ignored — the promotion of robust trade with Africa. In the 108th Congress, he won a waiver from the usual Republican term limits to serve a fourth term as chairman of the International Relations Subcommittee on Africa. Royce relinquished the gavel of the Africa panel in 2005, taking the top spot on the International Terrorism and Nonproliferation Subcommittee.

As chairman of the Africa Subcommittee, Royce's successes include a 2004 law authorizing $18.6 million to help protect the African rain forest along the Congo River basin and to promote eco-tourism. In winning congressional support for the bill, Royce worked closely with Secretary of State Colin L. Powell.

In 2000, Royce helped win enactment of legislation reducing tariffs and quotas on imports from sub-Saharan Africa. That law, which also expanded the U.S. trade relationship with Caribbean nations, broke a six-year impasse on trade legislation. And in 2002, Royce won House passage of a bill that would gradually permit increased imports of African-made fabric and yarn.

Though conceived before the terrorist attacks of Sept. 11, 2001, the sub-Saharan bills grew out of Royce's view that trade is an effective way to help lift nations out of poverty and keep totalitarian regimes out of power. "For too long our African policy has been based on foreign aid," Royce said in 1998. "The United States needs to encourage African nations to move toward the free market and steer them in the direction of self-sufficiency. Markets work and subsidies don't."

Royce has laid out an ambitious agenda for the International Terrorism and Nonproliferation Subcommittee in the 109th Congress. He said the panel's focus includes the evolving threat of al-Qaeda, terrorist financing, terrorist sanctuaries and foreign forces' capacity to fight terrorism. He also plans to give attention to the proliferation threat posed by both North Korea and Iran.

Royce is not new to terrorism issues. As a member of the Financial Services Committee, he cosponsored a bill in 2004 to crack down on foreign governments whose citizens or banks finance domestic or international terrorism.

Royce travels occasionally to Africa and Asia, sometimes stirring controversy along the way. He drew criticism in early 2001, when he was part of a congressional delegation to India but left the group when it traveled to Pakistan. Critics said he bent to the will of Indian-American groups that raised funds for his election campaigns, but Royce said he did not want to legitimize President Pervez Musharraf, who had come to power in a coup. A year earlier, Royce was scolded by the government of Vietnam when he departed from his official itinerary to meet with a monk under house arrest for resisting government efforts to establish an official Communist Buddhist church.

His commitment to international cooperation and free trade reflects the conservative economic viewpoint he developed as a youth while growing up in a blue-collar, Democratic household.

In high school, he became intrigued by the free-market message in the book "Economics in One Lesson," by Henry Hazlitt. The author challenged prevailing economic thinking that gave government a central role,

CAPITOL OFFICE
225-4111
www.house.gov/royce
2202 Rayburn 20515-0540; fax 226-0335

COMMITTEES
Financial Services
International Relations
(International Terrorism & Nonproliferation - chairman)

HOMETOWN
Fullerton

BORN
Oct. 12, 1951, Los Angeles, Calif.

RELIGION
Roman Catholic

FAMILY
Wife, Marie Royce

EDUCATION
California State U., Fullerton, B.A. 1977 (accounting & finance)

CAREER
Tax manager

POLITICAL HIGHLIGHTS
Calif. Senate, 1982-92

ELECTION RESULTS

2004 GENERAL
Ed Royce (R)	147,617	67.9%
J. Tilman Williams (D)	69,684	32.1%

2004 PRIMARY
Ed Royce (R)	unopposed

2002 GENERAL
Ed Royce (R)	92,422	67.6%
Christina Avalos (D)	40,265	29.5%
Charles R. McGlawn (LIBERT)	3,955	2.9%

PREVIOUS WINNING PERCENTAGES
2000 (63%); 1998 (63%); 1996 (63%); 1994 (66%); 1992 (57%)

and that spurred Royce to read similar books on economic theory. Growing more convinced his views were on solid ground, Royce found himself defending the unorthodox viewpoints to fellow students and to teachers. He said he is glad he was drawn to unconventional economic views. "The real advantage was that people would argue with me," he said, which gave him plenty of practice articulating his positions.

In Congress, Royce has been an ardent tax-cutter, while also attacking government largesse even if it meant being at odds with his own party. His zeal has not faded, but his activism — throughout the 1990s he was the co-chairman of the Congressional Porkbusters Coalition — has subsided. With the Bush administration now producing and defending its own massive budget deficits, GOP loyalists like Royce tend to defer to White House priorities.

California lawmakers say Royce played a key role in maintaining GOP power in their state when the political map was redrawn based on the 2000 census. He joined California Republican Rep. David Dreier and House GOP campaign committee Chairman Thomas M. Davis III of Virginia to promote a plan intended to protect the 20 seats held by Republicans.

Royce spent 10 years in the California Senate, where he wrote the nation's first law making it a felony to stalk or threaten someone with injury — giving the police recourse when a stalker has not yet attacked an intended victim. He also was the guiding force behind a 1990 ballot proposition, approved by voters, setting forth rights for victims of crimes.

In Washington, Royce has continued his anti-stalking campaign, winning enactment of a measure similar to the one he sponsored in California. The federal law, signed in 1996, made it a crime to cross state lines with the intent to stalk or harass. In 1999, Royce and other lawmakers won enactment of a bill expanding the definition of stalking. In the 108th and 107th Congresses, Royce introduced a victim's rights amendment to the Constitution.

After 10 years in Sacramento, Royce jumped at the chance to run for the House in 1992 when iconoclastic Republican William E. Dannemeyer gave up his seat to run for the Senate. Royce had represented a sizable slice of the House district in the state Senate, and he drew no primary opposition. His Democratic opponent, Molly McClanahan, proved too liberal for Orange County, and Royce prevailed by almost 20 percentage points.

In redistricting before the 2002 election, the Los Angeles County portion of Royce's old 39th District was removed and the district was renumbered the 40th. Regardless of the remapping, Royce continues to win with ease, garnering 68 percent of the vote in 2004.

KEY VOTES

2004

No Extend federal unemployment benefits by 13 weeks

Yes Pass $283.2 billion, six-year federal highway and mass transit bill

Yes Approve $146 billion multi-year extension of previously enacted middle-class tax breaks

Yes Amend the Constitution to prohibit same-sex marriage

Yes Cut corporate taxes $137 billion over 10 years

No Reorganize U.S. intelligence agencies as proposed by Sept. 11 commission

2003

Yes Cut taxes by $330 billion through fiscal 2013

No Block Bush rule scaling back overtime pay for some white-collar federal workers

No Do not allow use of search warrants without first notifying subjects

Yes Allow importation of prescription drugs

Yes Create private school voucher program in Washington, D.C.

Yes Ban "partial birth" abortion except to save a woman's life

No Split $18.6 billion in Iraq aid into half-grant, half-loan

Yes Overhaul Medicare and create prescription drug benefit

CQ VOTE STUDIES

	PARTY UNITY		PRESIDENTIAL SUPPORT	
	Support	Oppose	Support	Oppose
2004	94%	6%	82%	18%
2003	95%	5%	93%	7%
2002	97%	3%	82%	18%
2001	93%	7%	84%	16%
2000	93%	7%	25%	75%

INTEREST GROUPS

	AFL-CIO	ADA	CCUS	ACU
2004	20%	15%	90%	96%
2003	7%	10%	87%	88%
2002	11%	0%	85%	100%
2001	8%	5%	74%	100%
2000	0%	0%	80%	100%

CALIFORNIA 40
North central Orange County — Orange, Fullerton

Like most of Orange County, the 40th is largely affluent and Republican, though these inland areas are less affluent than the coast. The district forms a half circle, extending north from Los Alamitos on the Los Angeles County border to take in most of Fullerton before turning southeast to reach Orange and Villa Park. It wraps around Anaheim and Garden Grove, taking in small chunks of each.

Orange, the solidly suburban district's largest city, and Fullerton are both upper middle class, while Stanton and Cypress are the district's more blue-collar communities. The median home price in the district is about $240,000, median income is high and unemployment is low. Whites make up about half of the district's population, which is seeing an influx of wealthier Hispanics. Several cities are nearly half Hispanic, while the district overall is 30 percent Hispanic and 16 percent Asian. In the 2004 presidential race, George W. Bush earned 60 percent of the 40th's vote.

Before massive growth in the 1960s and 1970s, Orange County consisted largely of orange and lemon groves, and many cities were dairy farm communities. Now the economy centers on aerospace and defense, and new technology firms have sprung up in the district.

Fullerton is home to a Raytheon facility and a Kimberly-Clark paper mill, as well as a California State University campus that is the city's major employer. Adams Rite Aerospace in Fullerton makes airplane cockpit security doors, which Congress mandated after the Sept. 11 terrorist attacks. Orange is a health care center, and the district is home to four major hospitals.

MAJOR INDUSTRY
Aerospace, defense, manufacturing, health care

CITIES
Orange, 128,821; Fullerton (pt.), 108,151; Anaheim (pt.), 87,082; Buena Park, 78,282

NOTABLE
Beach Boulevard in Buena Park features attractions such as Knott's Berry Farm — the first theme park in the United States, the Movieland Wax Museum, Ripley's Believe It or Not, Wild Bill's Wild West Dinner Extravaganza and the Medieval Times dinner and tournament.

Rep. Jerry Lewis (R)

Elected 1978; 14th term

CAPITOL OFFICE
225-5861
www.house.gov/jerrylewis
2112 Rayburn 20515-0541; fax 225-6498

COMMITTEES
Appropriations - chairman

HOMETOWN
Redlands

BORN
Oct. 21, 1934, Seattle, Wash.

RELIGION
Presbyterian

FAMILY
Wife, Arlene Lewis; four children, three stepchildren

EDUCATION
U. of California, Los Angeles, B.A. 1956
(government)

CAREER
Insurance executive

POLITICAL HIGHLIGHTS
San Bernardino School Board, 1965-68; Calif. Assembly, 1968-78; Republican nominee for Calif. Senate, 1973

ELECTION RESULTS

2004 GENERAL

Jerry Lewis (R)	181,605	83.0%
Peymon Mottahedek (LIBERT)	37,332	17.1%

2004 PRIMARY

Jerry Lewis (R)	unopposed

2002 GENERAL

Jerry Lewis (R)	91,326	67.4%
Keith A. Johnson (D)	40,155	29.6%
Kevin Craig (LIBERT)	4,052	3.0%

PREVIOUS WINNING PERCENTAGES
2000 (80%); 1998 (65%); 1996 (65%); 1994 (71%); 1992 (63%); 1990 (61%); 1988 (70%); 1986 (77%); 1984 (85%); 1982 (68%); 1980 (72%); 1978 (61%)

Lewis crowned a quarter-century of service in the House by landing his dream job. In the 109th Congress, he became chairman of the Appropriations Committee, a powerful panel that oversees about a third of the federal budget. Presiding over the annual spending bills also gives Lewis an enhanced ability to steer funding to California and to his district, which sprawls from the Los Angeles suburbs to the Nevada border.

The gavel did not come without a fight. Lewis beat out a more senior Republican lawmaker who felt he deserved the job, Ralph Regula of Ohio. House GOP leaders chose Lewis for his track record raising money for the party and for his loyalty at a time they are trying to assert more control over the appropriations process.

Lewis moved quickly to satisfy the leaders' demands for change at the uniquely bipartisan committee. He fired the longtime staff director who had worked for both Democratic and Republican chairmen. He reorganized the subcommittees in line with a plan written by Majority Leader Tom DeLay, scaling them back from 13 to 10 and reshuffling their jurisdictions. Some of Lewis' friends lost their chairmanships in the process. Senate appropriators who favored the status quo objected. But Lewis persisted, and the 109th Congress began with mismatched sets of subcommittees between the two chambers, greatly complicating the annual chore of passing the spending bills but giving DeLay and the House leadership a stronger hand.

Lewis faced another big challenge. With a growing budget deficit, the White House was seeking some of the most austere belt-tightening of domestic programs since 1996. Lewis had less room to maneuver than previous chairmen, and he was under pressure from the leaders to be less accommodating to Democrats. Within hours of learning he had been selected chairman, Lewis said he knew he would have to "reform the appropriations process and change the culture of the committee."

In addition to the regular spending bills, Lewis had to contend in 2005 with a whopping $82 billion request from the White House in supplemental funding for the war in Iraq, the fourth such request since the war began in 2003. Republicans and Democrats were growing increasingly nervous about the costs of the war.

Lewis had spent a year auditioning for the job, aggressively raising campaign contributions for fellow Republicans — more than $1.35 million in the 2004 election cycle — and promising to keep spending within GOP-written budgets, which previous chairmen had resisted. He also donated to DeLay's legal defense fund and got other members of the California delegation to do so, as DeLay was being investigated by a Texas grand jury for alleged fundraising improprieties.

Lewis vaulted over the more senior Regula and a second candidate, Kentucky Republican Harold Rogers, to succeed C.W. Bill Young, a GOP lawmaker from Florida, who relinquished the gavel under party-mandated term limits.

With a distinguishing, toothpaste-commercial smile and a buoyant personality, Lewis, a former insurance salesman, can turn on the charm. But it can disappear in an instant, as Pentagon officials learned the hard way during the six years he presided over the Defense Appropriations Subcommittee and repeatedly challenged their budgets.

He has been a force in the House in demanding that the Department of Defense modernize quicker to meet post-Cold War threats to security, even if that meant scrapping some revered projects. In 1999, he waged a losing battle to deny $1.9 billion for the Lockheed Martin F-22 jet fighter, the Air Force's premier modernization effort. It was chronically over-budget and a symbol of a whole family of programs that had been designed to fight a vanquished enemy, the Soviet Union. Ultimately, a lobbying tsunami by the Air Force and the plane's contractors persuaded Congress to approve the money. But the services got the message that Lewis was watching the way they spent their money.

Three years later, Lewis told Defense Secretary Donald H. Rumsfeld that the Bush administration's budget did not live up to Rumsfeld's call for a transformation in U.S. forces. "Hard decisions and trade-offs have not been made," he said.

In more than two decades on the Appropriations panel, Lewis generally has pushed to limit the growth of government spending. From 1995 to 1999, when he was in charge of the subcommittee that pays for housing and veterans programs, Lewis cut spending more deeply than any of the other "cardinals," as the subcommittee chairmen are known. He feels differently about defense needs, however. When he moved over to the Defense Subcommittee, Lewis doubled the amount sought by the Clinton administration in 2000 to beef up the Army's mobile fighting force.

Over the years, Lewis tried to move up the leadership ladder but was edged out by conservatives, such as Dick Armey of Texas, who were more confrontational in dealing with the Democrats. After Republicans took control of the House in 1995, Lewis strained his relations with Democratic appropriators by dutifully enforcing the new GOP leadership's cuts in domestic programs.

Lewis dates his interest in government to a trip he made to Washington in 1955. Some of his fellow UCLA students were forced to ride on a separate tourist boat on the Potomac because they were black, and Lewis decided that public service was the best way to change things. Today, he speaks of using his post to make the world safer and more peaceful for his grandchildren.

Lewis left the insurance business to enter GOP politics in the early 1960s, winning a seat on the San Bernardino School Board. After three years there, he won a state Assembly seat that he held for a decade.

Lewis' House seat is usually safe. His San Bernardino County-based district has given him at least 61 percent of the vote in 14 elections, regardless of its precise boundaries. California redistricting in 2001 to add a House seat removed some of his political territory, and his district was renumbered the 41st, but it remained essentially a GOP district.

KEY VOTES

2004
No — Extend federal unemployment benefits by 13 weeks
Yes — Pass $283.2 billion, six-year federal highway and mass transit bill
Yes — Approve $146 billion multi-year extension of previously enacted middle-class tax breaks
Yes — Amend the Constitution to prohibit same-sex marriage
Yes — Cut corporate taxes $137 billion over 10 years
Yes — Reorganize U.S. intelligence agencies as proposed by Sept. 11 commission

2003
Yes — Cut taxes by $330 billion through fiscal 2013
No — Block Bush rule scaling back overtime pay for some white-collar federal workers
No — Do not allow use of search warrants without first notifying subjects
No — Allow importation of prescription drugs
Yes — Create private school voucher program in Washington, D.C.
Yes — Ban "partial birth" abortion except to save a woman's life
No — Split $18.6 billion in Iraq aid into half-grant, half-loan
Yes — Overhaul Medicare and create prescription drug benefit

CQ VOTE STUDIES

	PARTY UNITY		PRESIDENTIAL SUPPORT	
	Support	Oppose	Support	Oppose
2004	93%	7%	91%	9%
2003	96%	4%	96%	4%
2002	92%	8%	87%	13%
2001	97%	3%	97%	3%
2000	87%	13%	36%	64%

INTEREST GROUPS

	AFL-CIO	ADA	CCUS	ACU
2004	13%	0%	100%	88%
2003	7%	5%	100%	80%
2002	11%	10%	84%	88%
2001	8%	5%	100%	80%
2000	0%	0%	80%	64%

CALIFORNIA 41
Most of San Bernardino County – Redlands

The 41st includes vast desert and mountain stretches and most of the nation's largest county, San Bernardino, but it is home to less than one-third of county residents. The district takes in some eastern Inland Valley communities and a northwestern sliver of Riverside County before crossing the San Bernardino Mountains and part of the Mojave Desert to reach the mountains along the Nevada and Arizona borders. Republicans enjoy a 16-point edge in voter registration.

Nearly everyone lives in the western quarter of the 41st, where the district's Inland Empire, Victor Valley and Riverside County areas are located. Redlands, Highland, Yucaipa and a portion of the city of San Bernardino are nestled south of the San Bernardino Mountains.

The Victor Valley high-desert cities of Hesperia and Apple Valley to the north have seen rapid growth. Affordable land and housing have made the area a magnet for Los Angeles and Orange County workers since the 1990s. The Riverside County portion of the 41st takes in the San Jacinto Valley and the areas of Banning, San Jacinto, Beaumont and Calimesa.

As the 41st heads northeast, bordered by Interstate 15 on the north and the San Bernardino-Riverside county line on the south, towns become scarce and desert, mountains and dry lakes dominate. Exits off Interstate 15 lead mostly to dirt roads. Since much of the land here is arid or mountainous, development is difficult. Local hospitals and the government remain the largest employers.

MAJOR INDUSTRY
Service, manufacturing, military

MILITARY BASES
Marine Corps Air Ground Combat Center, Twentynine Palms, 10,822 military, 1,524 civilian (2004)

CITIES
Redlands, 63,591; Hesperia, 62,582; San Bernardino (pt.), 54,789; Apple Valley, 54,239

NOTABLE
The Mojave National Preserve, designated in 1994, features the Devil's Playground dunes and the Kelso railroad depot, which was built in 1924 and closed in 1985; The depot will serve as a visitors center once renovations are complete; Roy Rogers' former ranch was in Apple Valley.

Rep. Gary G. Miller (R)

Elected 1998; 4th term

CAPITOL OFFICE
225-3201
gary.miller@mail.house.gov
www.house.gov/garymiller
1037 Longworth 20515-0542; fax 226-6962

COMMITTEES
Financial Services
Transportation & Infrastructure

HOMETOWN
Diamond Bar

BORN
Oct. 16, 1948, Huntsville, Ark.

RELIGION
Protestant

FAMILY
Wife, Cathy Miller; four children

EDUCATION
Mt. San Antonio Community College, attended 1968-70

MILITARY SERVICE
Army, 1967-68

CAREER
Real estate developer

POLITICAL HIGHLIGHTS
Diamond Bar Municipal Advisory Council, 1988-89; Diamond Bar City Council, 1989-90; sought Republican nomination for Calif. Senate, 1990; Diamond Bar City Council, 1991-95 (mayor, 1993-94); sought Republican nomination for Calif. Senate (special election), 1994; Calif. Assembly, 1995-98

ELECTION RESULTS

2004 GENERAL

Gary G. Miller (R)	167,632	68.1%
Lewis Myers (D)	78,393	31.9%

2004 PRIMARY

Gary G. Miller (R)	unopposed

2002 GENERAL

Gary G. Miller (R)	98,476	67.8%
Richard Waldron (D)	42,090	29.0%
Donald Yee (LIBERT)	4,680	3.2%

PREVIOUS WINNING PERCENTAGES
2000 (59%); 1998 (53%)

Miller's frustration with government regulations in building his housing and real estate development firm led to his involvement in public life. A self-made millionaire, Miller wants to reduce environmental and business regulations that he says hinder business. He supports government spending for infrastructure projects — highways, drinking water and wastewater treatment plants, and school construction — and backs tax cuts and worker apprenticeship programs.

A fiscal and social conservative, Miller subscribes to Republican tenets of shrinking the federal government, overhauling the tax code and advancing a "pro-family" agenda. Though ideologically he is on the far right, Miller is usually less confrontational than other lawmakers at either end of the political spectrum. Easygoing by nature, Miller has made friends and formed legislative alliances with Democrats.

During the 108th Congress, he was outspoken on an issue that particularly affects California and his district in the easterly exurbs of Los Angeles — illegal immigration. When the House in 2004 voted overwhelmingly against a measure that would have required hospital workers in emergency rooms to investigate the immigration status of their patients, Miller and seven other Republicans were the only members of the California delegation to support the legislation. The measure failed, 88-331.

Miller says that the burden of illegal immigration falls most heavily on his state. "Illegal immigration places a strain on our society and I want everyone in this body to understand, California bears the brunt of the burden of the failed immigration policies of the federal government," he said on the House floor.

From his seat on the Transportation and Infrastructure Committee, he was a staunch supporter of the committee's six-year, $283 billion transportation bill, which passed the House in 2004. Miller voted for it despite calls from other conservative Republicans to rein in spending in the face of a burgeoning federal deficit.

Under the bill, California was scheduled to receive more federal transportation dollars than any other state. Yet California Gov. Arnold Schwarzenegger, a fellow Republican and rising star in the party, complained that the state would still pay more in gasoline taxes than it got back in benefits. Miller disputed that, saying that if the dollar amounts for all the projects going to California were tallied up, the state actually got back more than it sent to the federal government.

During conference negotiations on the transportation bill, Miller added a provision to rename a stretch of the Imperial Highway in Southern California after President Nixon. Miller wanted part of the road renamed as a way to increase the visibility of the Richard M. Nixon Library, which is located in Yorba Linda in his district.

From his seat on the Financial Services Committee, Miller has also tried, on a number of fronts, to make homeownership in his district more affordable. Miller calls it the crisis of the "new homeless" — middle-class families whose incomes are below what is needed to buy a home in the district. He has a seat on the panel's Housing and Community Opportunity Subcommittee.

Miller has pushed for more federal money to treat and recycle water in California, cosponsoring a bill in 2004 authorizing the Bureau of Reclamation to fund a long-term groundwater remediation program.

Miller is generally skeptical of using government money for foreign aid. When the House in 2003 overwhelmingly approved President Bush's plan for $15 billion over five years to combat AIDS around the globe, Miller was one of 41 members, and the only lawmaker from California, to vote against it. He called the bill fiscally irresponsible and said he was "concerned that this proposal could shortchange health care needs here at home."

A Civil War history buff, Miller in 2002 won enactment of his bill to provide federal grants to states and localities to preserve battle sites.

Miller was raised by his mother and grandparents. At an early age, his family moved from Arkansas, where he was born, to Whittier, east of Los Angeles, where many other poor families from Oklahoma and Arkansas had settled. He attended community college for a while, but didn't get a degree. In the California Assembly and now in Congress, Miller has been an advocate for job training and apprenticeship programs.

After leaving school, he started a partnership with an experienced contractor, and they bid on home improvement contracts with the Department of Housing and Urban Development. He says he learned construction skills on the job, and moved on to building single-family homes and eventually to developing planned communities.

Miller began his political career on the Diamond Bar Municipal Advisory Council and then was a member of Diamond Bar's first city council after the city was incorporated in 1989. He became mayor in 1993.

Miller has made a habit of mounting electoral challenges to fellow Republicans. He lost state Senate primary bids in 1990 and 1994. Early in 1995, when voters forced a recall election of state Assemblyman Paul Horcher, who left the Republican Party and backed liberal Democrat Willie Brown for Speaker of the California Assembly, Miller ran to replace Horcher and won.

In 1998, Miller was convinced that his Diamond Bar neighbor Jay C. Kim had to be replaced in the House after his conviction on campaign finance illegalities. Miller challenged the three-term lawmaker in the GOP primary and won by almost 4,000 votes. He won the general election by 13 percentage points. Miller bankrolled his campaign with large infusions of his own money.

In 2000, his margin of victory increased to 22 percentage points. In remapping after the decennial census, the district shifted to the south and west and was renumbered the 42nd, but Miller won by 39 percentage points in 2002. He was easily re-elected in 2004.

KEY VOTES

2004

No Extend federal unemployment benefits by 13 weeks

Yes Pass $283.2 billion, six-year federal highway and mass transit bill

Yes Approve $146 billion multi-year extension of previously enacted middle-class tax breaks

Yes Amend the Constitution to prohibit same-sex marriage

Yes Cut corporate taxes $137 billion over 10 years

No Reorganize U.S. intelligence agencies as proposed by Sept. 11 commission

2003

Yes Cut taxes by $330 billion through fiscal 2013

No Block Bush rule scaling back overtime pay for some white-collar federal workers

No Do not allow use of search warrants without first notifying subjects

No Allow importation of prescription drugs

Yes Create private school voucher program in Washington, D.C.

Yes Ban "partial birth" abortion except to save a woman's life

No Split $18.6 billion in Iraq aid into half-grant, half-loan

Yes Overhaul Medicare and create prescription drug benefit

CQ VOTE STUDIES

	PARTY UNITY		PRESIDENTIAL SUPPORT	
	Support	Oppose	Support	Oppose
2004	98%	2%	85%	15%
2003	99%	1%	92%	8%
2002	99%	1%	90%	10%
2001	99%	1%	100%	0%
2000	97%	3%	25%	75%

INTEREST GROUPS

	AFL-CIO	ADA	CCUS	ACU
2004	13%	0%	100%	100%
2003	0%	5%	100%	87%
2002	0%	0%	95%	100%
2001	8%	0%	100%	100%
2000	0%	0%	95%	100%

CALIFORNIA 42

Parts of Orange, Los Angeles and San Bernardino counties — Mission Viejo, Chino

Although most of its population lives in Orange County, the Republican 42nd is centered around the area where Orange, Los Angeles and San Bernardino counties come together east of Los Angeles proper.

From there, the 42nd has a long arm that stretches southeast and then southwest farther into Orange County to Mission Viejo. Its southeasternmost city, Rancho Santa Margarita, is also its newest; its population of 47,000 incorporated in 2000. A chunk of eastern Anaheim also falls within the district's borders.

Chino and Chino Hills in San Bernardino County have an agricultural heritage, but dairy production is giving way to manufacturing and service industries. Diamond Bar, Whittier (shared with the 39th) and Rowland Heights (shared with the 38th) in Los Angeles County have large Asian populations. Hispanics and Asians also live in the northern Orange

County cities of Brea (one of the fastest-growing in the county), La Habra and Placentia (shared with the 40th), although this Orange County segment is predominately white-collar and white. Conservatism persists even among non-whites, and Republicans hold a 21 percentage point voter registration edge in the 42nd.

Overall, the district is mostly middle- and upper-class and is 24 percent Hispanic and 16 percent Asian. Unemployment is low, and housing prices, particularly in Orange County, are above average. Many district residents commute to Los Angeles or Irvine (which is located in the 48th).

MAJOR INDUSTRY
Service, manufacturing, dairy

CITIES
Mission Viejo, 93,102; Chino, 67,168; Chino Hills, 66,787; La Habra, 58,974; Yorba Linda, 58,918; Diamond Bar, 56,287; Anaheim (pt.), 55,395

NOTABLE
Yorba Linda, the birthplace and burial site of President Richard M. Nixon, is the home of the Nixon Library.

Rep. Joe Baca (D)

CAPITOL OFFICE
225-6161
www.house.gov/baca
328 Cannon 20515-0543; fax 225-8671

COMMITTEES
Agriculture
Financial Services

HOMETOWN
Rialto

BORN
Jan. 23, 1947, Belen, N.M.

RELIGION
Roman Catholic

FAMILY
Wife, Barbara Baca; four children

EDUCATION
California State U., Los Angeles, B.A. 1971
(sociology)

MILITARY SERVICE
Army, 1966-68

CAREER
Travel agency owner; corporate community
relations executive

POLITICAL HIGHLIGHTS
San Bernardino Community College District Board
of Trustees, 1979-93; sought Democratic
nomination for Calif. Assembly, 1988, 1990; Calif.
Assembly, 1992-98 (Speaker pro tempore, 1995);
Calif. Senate, 1998-99

ELECTION RESULTS

2004 GENERAL

Joe Baca (D)	86,830	66.4%
Ed Laning (R)	44,004	33.6%

2004 PRIMARY

Joe Baca (D)	unopposed

2002 GENERAL

Joe Baca (D)	45,374	66.4%
Wendy C. Neighbor (R)	20,821	30.5%
Ethel M. Mohler (LIBERT)	2,145	3.1%

PREVIOUS WINNING PERCENTAGES
2000 (60%); 1999 Special Runoff Election (51%)

Elected 1999; 3rd full term

The congressman refers to himself as "working Joe Baca," which could apply to his reputation for hard work and also to his strong support for (and from) organized labor. He has counted on the backing of unions in all of his elections, and campaign help from labor played an important role in his narrow special-election Democratic primary win in 1999. His election night victory rally was held at a local Teamsters hall.

Baca's district is close to 60 percent Hispanic and he is the first Hispanic to be elected to Congress from the part of Southern California known as the Inland Empire, a region east of Los Angeles anchored by the city of San Bernardino. In the 109th Congress, he was chosen first vice chairman of the Congressional Hispanic Caucus.

With single-minded ambition, Baca took himself from hardscrabble beginnings — he started working at age 10 as a shoeshine boy — to Congress. He would like to move up the Democratic leadership ladder. "I'm a fighter because I know what it's like to struggle," he says.

In the 108th Congress, Baca had a seat on the Democratic Steering Committee, which makes committee assignments in concert with the leadership. He was also part of the party's whip operation, helping leaders round up votes on close-call tallies. But Baca's drive can rub some of his colleagues the wrong way. He has ruffled feathers during his political ascent, and other lawmakers grumble that he hogs the credit for joint endeavors.

In 2004, Baca found himself in the unusual position of being criticized by a local union. After 12 Border Patrol agents arrested 492 illegal aliens during sweeps at shopping malls and other public places in San Bernardino and San Diego counties, Baca said the agents overstepped their authority. The sweeps caused fear and unrest in the Latino community. "I am doing everything I can to make sure that sweeps like the ones last week do not happen again," he told residents at a community meeting, according to the Los Angeles Times.

The union representing Southern California Border Patrol agents responded angrily that Baca had falsely accused the agents of racial profiling. And Baca's Republican challenger in the 2004 campaign said the incident showed the congressman supported illegal immigration, though the charge had no impact on his re-election.

Baca tends to vote with more-conservative members on some issues, including support for gun owners' rights, which was a major issue in his first race, against Marta Macias Brown, the widow of Rep. George Brown, who had been the incumbent. Baca affiliates with the "Blue Dogs," a coalition of conservative House Democrats. And he has broken with his party on environmental issues. He supports oil drilling in Alaska's Arctic National Wildlife Refuge, aligning himself with the Teamsters, who value the jobs the oil drilling would create.

At a 2004 committee hearing in his district on the protection of two local endangered species, Baca called the Endangered Species Act a "broken law," and said it was costing communities millions of dollars in lost development and new jobs.

Baca does want the federal government to help protect the water quality in his district. The House in 2004 passed his bill authorizing $50 million to help inland cities clean up perchlorate-contaminated groundwater in the Santa Ana River Watershed. Perchlorate, a chemical used in rocket fuel, had been found in at least 20 drinking-water wells.

Baca has assignments on the Financial Services and Agriculture panels. On the latter, he is the top-ranking Democrat on the Department Operations, Oversight, Nutrition, and Forestry Subcommittee. His district has a number of large citrus farms in spite of encroachment from L.A.'s exurbs and an increasing number of high-technology firms.

His wife and two of his children are teachers, and Baca has an interest in federal education policy. He supported provisions in the education overhaul of 2002 that expanded bilingual education, directed more money to migrant education and created a dropout prevention program.

Early in the 109th Congress, he pushed a resolution urging Congress or the president to declare "Native American Day" as a paid legal public holiday, and add it to the list of federal holidays.

Baca was born in tiny Belen, N.M., just south of Albuquerque. The son of a railroad laborer and the youngest of 15 children in a house where little English was spoken, Baca as a boy moved with his family to Barstow, Calif. He shined shoes starting at age 10, delivered newspapers and worked as a janitor. He was a laborer for the Santa Fe Railroad between his high school graduation and getting drafted into the Army in 1966.

When his service was done, Baca got a degree in sociology from California State University, then landed a job as a community affairs representative for a local phone company.

His political career began in 1979 with election to the San Bernardino Community College District board, where he served 14 years. After two failed attempts to oust a fellow Democrat in the state Assembly, he finally won the seat in 1992 when the incumbent retired. He was re-elected twice, and then won a state Senate seat in 1998.

By that time, he was more interested in Washington, D.C. than in Sacramento. He toyed with challenging George Brown in the Democratic primary, boasting he could beat him in every precinct.

When Brown died midway through his 18th term, Baca immediately jumped into the special-election race, though Brown's widow, Marta Macias Brown, wanted the seat. She said it was inappropriate for Baca to run just after the party had helped him win an expensive Senate contest.

He beat her in a November special-election primary in the Democratic-leaning district, then posted a 6 percentage point win over GOP businessman Elia Pirozzi. In 2000, Pirozzi was back for a rematch, but Baca crushed him by 25 points. In 2002, running in a newly drawn district more Democratic and more Hispanic than his old one, Baca took two-thirds of the vote. In 2004, he again was easily re-elected.

KEY VOTES

2004

Yes Extend federal unemployment benefits by 13 weeks

Yes Pass $283.2 billion, six-year federal highway and mass transit bill

Yes Approve $146 billion multi-year extension of previously enacted middle-class tax breaks

No Amend the Constitution to prohibit same-sex marriage

No Cut corporate taxes $137 billion over 10 years

Yes Reorganize U.S. intelligence agencies as proposed by Sept. 11 commission

2003

No Cut taxes by $330 billion through fiscal 2013

Yes Block Bush rule scaling back overtime pay for some white-collar federal workers

Yes Do not allow use of search warrants without first notifying subjects

Yes Allow importation of prescription drugs

No Create private school voucher program in Washington, D.C.

No Ban "partial birth" abortion except to save a woman's life

Yes Split $18.6 billion in Iraq aid into half-grant, half-loan

No Overhaul Medicare and create prescription drug benefit

CQ VOTE STUDIES

	PARTY UNITY		PRESIDENTIAL SUPPORT	
	Support	Oppose	Support	Oppose
2004	92%	8%	32%	68%
2003	89%	11%	30%	70%
2002	91%	9%	28%	72%
2001	89%	11%	31%	69%
2000	83%	17%	75%	25%

INTEREST GROUPS

	AFL-CIO	ADA	CCUS	ACU
2004	93%	90%	43%	12%
2003	100%	85%	40%	29%
2002	89%	95%	42%	13%
2001	100%	85%	48%	24%
2000	100%	80%	44%	16%

CALIFORNIA 43

Southwest San Bernardino County — Ontario, Fontana, most of San Bernardino

The cities of San Bernardino, Fontana and Ontario form the base of the 43rd, which is located in the heart of the Inland Valley east of Los Angeles in San Bernardino County.

The district is part of California's fastest-growing region. Some residents commute into Los Angeles along the Pomona and San Bernardino freeways. The Ontario airport, expanded in the late 1990s, is part of a growing transportation hub, and the sprawling Ontario Mills mall is here. Fontana and Rialto, farther east, also have seen explosive growth.

The 43rd is almost 60 percent Hispanic, and registered Democrats outnumber Republicans by 18 percentage points. Even as some neighboring suburbs have trended wealthier and more conservative, ethnically diverse San Bernardino and Colton (both of which are shared with the 41st) consistently vote Democratic. The district favors Democrats on all levels and gave John Kerry 58 percent of the vote in the

2004 presidential contest.

This area was a fruit-packing center in the 1930s, but today its citrus industry shares space with electronics and aerospace firms. An economic downturn fueled by a steel mill bankruptcy and then the 1994 closing of nearby Norton Air Force Base hurt, but growing technology and manufacturing industries, coupled with redevelopment of the base site, prove the economy is recovering.

Although it has prospered like its neighbors in Orange and Los Angeles counties, the district retains a diverse and working-class feel.

MAJOR INDUSTRY
Manufacturing, electronics, construction

CITIES
Ontario, 158,007; San Bernardino (pt.), 130,612; Fontana, 128,929; Rialto, 91,873; Colton (pt.), 43,349

NOTABLE
Wyatt Earp's brother, Virgil, was the first marshal of Colton; Fontana is the birthplace of the Hells Angels motorcycle club.

Rep. Ken Calvert (R)

Elected 1992; 7th term

CAPITOL OFFICE
225-1986
www.house.gov/calvert
2201 Rayburn 20515-0544; fax 225-2004

COMMITTEES
Armed Services
Resources
Science
   (Space & Aeronautics - chairman)

HOMETOWN
Corona

BORN
June 8, 1953, Corona, Calif.

RELIGION
Protestant

FAMILY
Divorced

EDUCATION
Chaffey College, A.A. 1973 (business); San Diego State U., B.A. 1975 (economics)

CAREER
Real estate executive; restaurant executive

POLITICAL HIGHLIGHTS
Sought Republican nomination for U.S. House, 1982; Riverside County Republican Party chairman, 1984-88

ELECTION RESULTS

2004 GENERAL

Ken Calvert (R)	138,768	61.6%
Louis Vandenberg (D)	78,796	35.0%
Kevin Akin (PFP)	7,559	3.4%

2004 PRIMARY

Ken Calvert (R)	49,107	85.8%
David J. Rizzo (R)	8,132	14.2%

2002 GENERAL

Ken Calvert (R)	76,686	63.7%
Louis Vandenberg (D)	38,021	31.6%
Phill Courtney (GREEN)	5,756	4.8%

PREVIOUS WINNING PERCENTAGES
2000 (74%); 1998 (56%); 1996 (55%); 1994 (55%); 1992 (47%)

Now into his second decade in Congress, Calvert has been a consistent supporter of the GOP party line and a champion of "smaller, less invasive government," with one important exception — water rights. That issue has consumed him for the past several years.

After laying the political groundwork and leveraging his position as chairman of Resources' Water and Power Subcommittee, Calvert won passage of his legislation to reauthorize and restructure the California Federal Bay-Delta Program, which aims to enhance the state's water supply, reliability and quality. The Cal-Fed legislation, passed in 2004, has been his top priority, and Calvert worked closely with a fellow Californian, Democratic Sen. Dianne Feinstein, to write a bill acceptable to both chambers. "Water is not and should not be a partisan issue," Calvert says.

The CalFed project stretches over the enormous delta that begins in the San Francisco Bay area and extends from the Sacramento Valley in the north to the San Joaquin Valley in the south, providing irrigation and drinking water for two-thirds of the state's population. Calvert has worked to rewrite the law in a way that bridges differences among farmers, homeowners and environmentalists.

Calvert represents an area with a diverse economy, where agriculture, manufacturing, the military and tourism interests can clash with environmental advocates over issues of land use and urban sprawl. From his seats on three committees — Armed Services and Science are the others — Calvert has a hand in policies that shape these conflicts. In the 109th Congress, he relinquished his chairmanship of the Water and Power Subcommittee to head Science's Space and Aeronautics Subcommittee.

Calvert is also a member of more than two dozen informal congressional organizations that reflect the varied concerns of his constituents, ranging from the Manufactured Housing Caucus (an industry leader, Fleetwood Enterprises, is headquartered in his district) to the Native American Caucus. He is one-eighth Cherokee.

A real estate agent before coming to Congress, Calvert offered legislation, which passed in 2003, to ensure that competitive adjustable-rate mortgages (ARMs) are available to first-time home buyers. "Congress has recognized the importance of more loan options to home buyers and banks," he said. In 2003, Calvert also introduced legislation, cosponsored by more than half of his House colleagues, to permanently keep banks out of the real estate business.

Calvert's conservative view of government makes him wary of tougher environmental regulations, and he says enforcement of the Endangered Species Act must be balanced with competing interests. When Democrats ran the House, he once lamented, "Rats, bugs and even weeds were more important than people. Certain bureaucrats have become so eager to list new species as endangered, they have lost sight of the intent of the Endangered Species Act and ignored human concerns."

Calvert joins other Western lawmakers who say the federal government tramples on landowners' rights in the name of environmental preservation, and he advocates legislation to protect private property rights. He is skeptical of environmentalists who warn that pollution contributes to global warming. Although he has not moderated his views, Calvert said he is trying to pick his battles more carefully.

Calvert is a native son of the area he now represents — not all that common in the rapidly growing region that is now part of the Los Angeles megalopolis. He was born in Corona, just west of Riverside. His family was in the restaurant business. Later, his father, who had changed parties to become a Republican in the mid-1960s, turned to politics, winning election to the city council and then as Corona's mayor. The younger Calvert remembers working on Richard M. Nixon's 1968 presidential campaign, and as a college student he interned in the Capitol Hill office of GOP Rep. Victor Veysey.

After college graduation, Calvert used his economics degree and interest in business to try his hand at the family business. He handled the business side of the Jolly Fox restaurant in Corona, while his brother was the chef. He expanded into other ventures — a motel, a bowling alley, other restaurants — before going into real estate.

At age 28, with "lots of time and not much money," Calvert in 1982 jumped into an open-seat race for Congress, in the old 37th District, which contained most of Riverside County. Relying on door-to-door campaigning, he did surprisingly well against a large field headed by Riverside County Supervisor Al McCandless, losing the GOP nomination by just 868 votes.

Calvert stayed active in local party affairs, significantly increasing GOP registration in Riverside County and helping run the gubernatorial campaigns of Republicans George Deukmejian and Pete Wilson. When reapportionment created a new 43rd District for the western part of Riverside County in 1992, Calvert was positioned to run again; he emerged the winner of a tough GOP primary and took a hard-fought victory in November.

Calvert's congressional tenure got off to a rough start. In his first term, a tryst with a prostitute drew widespread notice. He said his "inappropriate" behavior stemmed from depression over his recent divorce and his father's suicide.

Following the negative publicity, Calvert won the 1994 GOP primary by just 2 percentage points, but the national surge that delivered the House to the GOP carried him to victory with 55 percent of the vote. Since then, Calvert's toughest challenges have come from his own party. In 2000, he won the nomination with 58 percent. In 2002, in redistricted territory, now numbered the 44th but politically similar to his previous constituency, Calvert took 70 percent in a three-way primary and cruised to a sixth term.

When he was elected, Calvert, like other Republicans touting reform of Congress that year, pledged to limit his tenure in the House. Had he lived up to the promise, the 108th Congress would have been his last. But he changed his mind and ran again in 2004. He won with 62 percent of the vote.

KEY VOTES

2004
? Extend federal unemployment benefits by 13 weeks
Yes Pass $283.2 billion, six-year federal highway and mass transit bill
Yes Approve $146 billion multi-year extension of previously enacted middle-class tax breaks
Yes Amend the Constitution to prohibit same-sex marriage
Yes Cut corporate taxes $137 billion over 10 years
No Reorganize U.S. intelligence agencies as proposed by Sept. 11 commission

2003
Yes Cut taxes by $330 billion through fiscal 2013
No Block Bush rule scaling back overtime pay for some white-collar federal workers
Yes Do not allow use of search warrants without first notifying subjects
No Allow importation of prescription drugs
Yes Create private school voucher program in Washington, D.C.
Yes Ban "partial birth" abortion except to save a woman's life
No Split $18.6 billion in Iraq aid into half-grant, half-loan
Yes Overhaul Medicare and create prescription drug benefit

CQ VOTE STUDIES

	PARTY UNITY		PRESIDENTIAL SUPPORT	
	Support	Oppose	Support	Oppose
2004	93%	7%	82%	18%
2003	98%	2%	98%	2%
2002	96%	4%	89%	11%
2001	98%	2%	93%	7%
2000	94%	6%	31%	69%

INTEREST GROUPS

	AFL-CIO	ADA	CCUS	ACU
2004	21%	0%	100%	88%
2003	7%	5%	100%	88%
2002	11%	0%	100%	92%
2001	17%	0%	100%	91%
2000	0%	0%	80%	84%

CALIFORNIA 44

Northwestern Riverside County – Riverside, Corona

The 44th is a fast-growing residential district that lies east of Los Angeles and north of San Diego. It contains about one-third of Riverside County's residents and the southeastern portion of Orange County that borders San Diego County. Registered Republicans outnumber Democrats, and George W. Bush won the 2004 presidential vote here with 59 percent.

The district includes the city of Riverside and the rest of the burgeoning northwestern edge of Riverside County. Riverside began growing navel oranges — still one of the area's major crops — in the 19th century. While the 44th has become increasingly Republican overall, the more blue-collar Riverside communities and the areas around the University of California, Riverside lean Democratic.

The district is undergoing major growth as young, white-collar families move into its cities. The trend is especially true in Norco and Corona, where low real estate prices have produced attractive bedroom

communities for commuters into Orange and Los Angeles counties. Despite the influx, manufacturing and agriculture, including dairy, citrus, grapes, dates and avocados, contribute to the economy, although they are being driven farther east and out of the district as the Los Angeles area continues to expand. The 44th's Orange County areas include the coastal city of San Clemente, San Juan Capistrano (shared with the 48th) and Santa Ana Mountain forests.

Local officials are trying to halt illegal drug production in the Inland Empire, dubbed by some as the methamphetamine capital of the world.

MAJOR INDUSTRY
Manufacturing, agriculture, health care

MILITARY BASES
Naval Surface Warfare Center, Corona Division, 6 military, 1,349 civilian (2005)

CITIES
Riverside, 255,166; Corona, 124,966; San Clemente, 49,936

NOTABLE
Riverside's Mission Inn was where Richard and Pat Nixon were married and Ronald and Nancy Reagan stopped on their honeymoon.

Rep. Mary Bono (R)

CAPITOL OFFICE
225-5330
www.house.gov/bono
405 Cannon 20515-0545; fax 225-2961

COMMITTEES
Energy & Commerce

HOMETOWN
Palm Springs

BORN
Oct. 24, 1961, Cleveland, Ohio

RELIGION
Protestant

FAMILY
Husband, Glenn Baxley; two children

EDUCATION
U. of Southern California, B.F.A. 1984 (art history)

CAREER
Homemaker; restaurateur

POLITICAL HIGHLIGHTS
No previous office

ELECTION RESULTS

2004 GENERAL

Mary Bono (R)	153,523	66.6%
Richard J. Meyer (D)	76,967	33.4%

2004 PRIMARY

Mary Bono (R)	51,429	85.9%
John Barker (R)	8,422	14.1%

2002 GENERAL

Mary Bono (R)	87,101	65.2%
Elle K. Kurpiewski (D)	43,692	32.7%
Rod Miller-Boyer (LIBERT)	2,740	2.1%

PREVIOUS WINNING PERCENTAGES
2000 (59%); 1998 (60%); 1998 Special Election (64%)

Elected April 1998; 4th full term

Now entering her fourth term, Bono has established herself as a moderate Republican whose celebrity drawing power is matched by legislative diligence. With the memory of her first campaign — to succeed her late husband, entertainer-turned-politician Sonny Bono — receding into the past, Bono has proven to be a capable lawmaker in her own right.

Bono remains one of the most popular guests on the campaign fundraising circuit, and she makes public appearances across the country on behalf of Republican colleagues. "She has a freshness and common-sense approach that is rather unusual in people like us," Majority Leader Tom DeLay of Texas told Gannett News Service.

In recent years, Bono's activities have highlighted her expertise on issues related to technology, communications, and entertainment. An early major legislative effort was helping to pass a copyright extension bill, first championed by and eventually named after her husband. In the 108th Congress, she launched a new bipartisan Recording Arts and Sciences Caucus. "With changing technologies and emerging trends in music," she said, "there is a great need for a forum for discussion between members of Congress and artists." She had previously helped form another working group on intellectual property protection, and in 2004 authored legislation to regulate "spyware," software that monitors the behavior of computer users and collects sensitive information about them. The House passed her bill, but the Senate did not, so early in the 109th, Bono offered the bill again.

In 2003, Bono officially signed on with the Republican Main Street Partnership, a leading caucus of GOP moderates. She will stray from conservative Republican philosophy on occasion, particularly on social issues such as abortion. "I am neither pro-choice nor pro-life, and I am also both pro-choice and pro-life," she told a local paper. "I believe that's the way most Americans truly are." She also opposed the GOP's 2004 effort to amend the Constitution to ban gay marriage and expressed particular concern over a House-passed bill that sought to deny the courts authority to review the federal Defense of Marriage Act, calling it "simply not sound policy." At the 2003 California GOP convention, she offered some candid analysis of the party's appeal across the gender line. "Reaching out to women voters has got to be a constant process," she said. "I think it's something we still have to do better at. We're still failing."

In Washington, Bono has cultivated the image of a plain-speaking, unpretentious lawmaker who is ready to roll up her sleeves and get to work mastering the details of her job. She focuses on the day-to-day issues facing her Inland Empire constituents, such as high energy bills, the availability of low-income housing, access to water, and resolution of a longstanding Indian land claim. Over time, she has also proven quite successful in procuring federal dollars for a range of projects in her district.

When Bono first arrived in Congress, her goal was to continue her husband's work, notably saving the Salton Sea, a Southern California man-made lake that is threatened by increasing salinity and pollution from agricultural and industrial runoff. By the end of 1998, Congress had agreed to begin the lake's rehabilitation, and in the 108th she won House approval for $9 million for various aspects of the project, a figure later reduced by the Senate.

During the 2001 California energy crisis, Bono focused on the difficulties low-income people were having in paying their bills. She held town meetings to get out the word about federal assistance, and she has been able to win funding for the Low Income Home Energy Assistance Program, and for Housing and Urban Development-backed low-income housing.

She won passage of legislation in 2000 ratifying the settlement of an agreement to compensate the Torres Martinez Desert Cahuilla Indian tribe, which lost land when the Salton Sea was created early in the 20th century. In 2002, she secured funds for the settlement.

Bono also keeps a watchful eye on California vineyards' battle against Pierce's disease, which is spread by a small flying insect known as the glassy-winged sharpshooter, and $5.2 million was provided for the battle in 2004. Though she works to foster a positive image for herself on environmental issues — the House passed her 2003 legislation funding research on renewable energy vehicles — she voted in favor of a controversial forest fire prevention plan put forward by President Bush. Critics complained that the plan to thin out forests was designed as much to benefit the timber industry as it was to cut the risk of fire; supporters like Bono said the "Healthy Forests" initiative was just common sense. "By removing dead trees and brush from our forests, we are working responsibly to prevent future catastrophic wildfires," she said.

Bono, whose father was a surgeon and whose mother was a chemist, grew up in South Pasadena, Calif. She worked her way through college, majoring in art history, and was celebrating her graduation at Sonny Bono's restaurant when she met the owner. They hit it off and married two years later, in 1986.

At the beginning of 1998, she was a stay-at-home mom in Washington, D.C., driving her children to school and working on her martial arts skills while Sonny went off to Capitol Hill every morning. After Sonny's January 1998 death in a skiing accident, she was urged to run for her husband's seat by GOP leaders who worried that the seat might fall into Democratic hands.

Bono won a special election in April with almost two-thirds of the vote. She has not been seriously threatened in her re-election bids, and redistricting in 2001 increased the GOP tilt of the newly numbered 45th District, permitting her to post 2-to-1 re-election victories in 2002 and 2004.

California political analysts regularly mention her as a potential candidate for higher office, citing her moderate image, wide name recognition and plain-spoken manner.

Bono was linked romantically for a while with a country music drummer, providing fodder for the tabloids; but in late 2001, she married Wyoming businessman Glenn Baxley, the founder of a company that designs Western and resort clothing.

KEY VOTES

2004
No   Extend federal unemployment benefits by 13 weeks
Yes   Pass $283.2 billion, six-year federal highway and mass transit bill
Yes   Approve $146 billion multi-year extension of previously enacted middle-class tax breaks
No   Amend the Constitution to prohibit same-sex marriage
Yes   Cut corporate taxes $137 billion over 10 years
No   Reorganize U.S. intelligence agencies as proposed by Sept. 11 commission

2003
Yes   Cut taxes by $330 billion through fiscal 2013
No   Block Bush rule scaling back overtime pay for some white-collar federal workers
Yes   Do not allow use of search warrants without first notifying subjects
Yes   Allow importation of prescription drugs
Yes   Create private school voucher program in Washington, D.C.
Yes   Ban "partial birth" abortion except to save a woman's life
No   Split $18.6 billion in Iraq aid into half-grant, half-loan
Yes   Overhaul Medicare and create prescription drug benefit

CQ VOTE STUDIES

	PARTY UNITY		PRESIDENTIAL SUPPORT	
	Support	Oppose	Support	Oppose
2004	86%	14%	58%	42%
2003	91%	9%	89%	11%
2002	89%	11%	84%	16%
2001	92%	8%	84%	16%
2000	86%	14%	30%	70%

INTEREST GROUPS

	AFL-CIO	ADA	CCUS	ACU
2004	27%	35%	100%	56%
2003	7%	10%	93%	68%
2002	11%	10%	95%	71%
2001	17%	15%	100%	68%
2000	0%	5%	100%	68%

CALIFORNIA 45

Riverside County – Moreno Valley, Palm Springs

Ritzy desert resorts, a booming service industry and large, irrigated farms fuel the economy of the 45th, whose residents largely reside in one of two Riverside County areas — rapidly growing Inland Empire communities, such as Moreno Valley, Hemet and Murrieta in the west, or upscale, resort-filled Coachella Valley cities farther east.

The Palm Springs area, including Cathedral City, Indian Wells, La Quinta and Indio, attracts visitors to its numerous golf courses. Once known as playgrounds for the rich and retired, the resort cities have seen an influx of younger, middle-class families. Still, the 45th has the highest percentage of residents over age 64 (16 percent) in California.

Although the district leans Republican, pockets in Rancho Mirage and Palm Springs tend to vote Democratic. Overall, the district gave George W. Bush 56 percent of its vote in the 2004 presidential election, and Republicans hold a 10-point voter registration advantage.

The 45th has grown into a diverse community that is home to some of the richest and poorest areas in the state, with Palm Springs on one end of the economic spectrum and some of the district's American Indian reservations on the other. Many poor residents work as migrant farm laborers, or in the growing gambling industry or at tourist shops. Health care service providers and small educational institutions have begun to settle in the district, spurring an increase in professionals.

The Salton Sea — located mainly in the 51st District — attracted attention in the 1990s as one of the nation's most polluted bodies of water. Congress voted in 1998 to fund a cleanup effort in honor of the late GOP Rep. Sonny Bono, who represented the Riverside district (at the time numbered the 44th) from 1995 until his death in January 1998.

MAJOR INDUSTRY
Service, tourism, agriculture, manufacturing

CITIES
Moreno Valley, 142,381; Hemet, 58,812; Indio, 49,116; Murrieta, 44,282

NOTABLE
Gerald R. Ford retired to Rancho Mirage; Joshua Tree National Park (shared with the 41st) boasts an abundance of the namesake yuccas and other desert plants and animals; The Coachella Valley Music Festival is held annually in Indio.

Rep. Dana Rohrabacher (R)

CAPITOL OFFICE
225-2415
dana@mail.house.gov
www.house.gov/rohrabacher
2338 Rayburn 20515-0546; fax 225-0145

COMMITTEES
International Relations
  (Oversight & Investigations - chairman)
Science

HOMETOWN
Huntington Beach

BORN
June 21, 1947, Coronado, Calif.

RELIGION
Baptist

FAMILY
Wife, Rhonda Rohrabacher; three children

EDUCATION
Los Angeles Harbor College, attended 1965-67;
California State U., Long Beach, B.A. 1969 (history);
U. of Southern California, M.A. 1971 (American
studies)

CAREER
White House speechwriter; newspaper reporter

POLITICAL HIGHLIGHTS
No previous office

ELECTION RESULTS

2004 GENERAL

Dana Rohrabacher (R)	171,318	61.9%
Jim Brandt (D)	90,129	32.6%
Tom Lash (GREEN)	10,238	3.7%
Keith Gann (LIBERT)	5,005	1.8%

2004 PRIMARY

Dana Rohrabacher (R)	69,132	83.5%
Robert K. Dornan (R)	13,630	16.5%

2002 GENERAL

Dana Rohrabacher (R)	108,807	61.8%
Gerrie Schipske (D)	60,890	34.6%
Keith Gann (LIBERT)	6,488	3.7%

PREVIOUS WINNING PERCENTAGES
2000 (62%); 1998 (59%); 1996 (61%); 1994 (69%);
1992 (55%); 1990 (59%); 1988 (64%)

Elected 1988; 9th term

Rohrabacher is the colorful combination of heady dreamer, clamorous partisan and combative conservative. He brings these elements to many of his legislative goals, but particularly when he turns his eyes to the sky.

As entrepreneurs began building private aircraft capable of reaching altitudes previously seen only by government spacecraft, Rohrabacher (ROAR-ah-bah-kur) decided to help these businessmen-explorers reach space. He was driven by his own interest in space and the well-being of his district. Boeing Co.'s space division is one of the 46th's largest employers.

As chairman of the Science Committee's Space and Aeronautics Subcommittee in the 108th Congress, Rohrabacher introduced a number of measures intended to foster the development of a private space flight industry. "Before we get into anything else we need to dramatically bring down the cost of getting into space," he told the Internet news site space.com.

He introduced a measure to offer a prize of up to $100 million for the first private spacecraft to make three orbits of the Earth, but it went nowhere. But he did manage to push through Congress a law supporting the development of commercial space projects and allowing the Federal Aviation Administration to regulate private spacecraft.

President Bush signed the measure at the end of the 108th. Democratic critics said the new law offers only minimal protections for space tourists, who are expected to travel on private spacecraft in increasing numbers, even at prices that might reach $100,000 a head. But to Rohrabacher, it was more important to establish government recognition of a nascent industry critical to his district and state and, he believes, to the American dream.

His timing was excellent. Only months before President Bush signed the new law, a private aircraft known as SpaceShipOne had reached low Earth orbit, presaging a new era of space tourism.

It wasn't the first time Rohrabacher displayed uncanny timing. He was one of a few members of Congress who, after the nightmare of Sept. 11, 2001, could accurately declare "I told you so" about the dangers emanating from global terrorists. On the day of the attacks, Rohrabacher had been scheduled to meet with National Security Council officials at the White House to warn them to expect a possible terrorist attack from Osama bin Laden and the ruling Taliban regime of Afghanistan.

When Congress reconvened a few days later, he took to the House floor and described his many trips to Central Asia, including an undercover sojourn to Afghanistan just before he was sworn into Congress in 1989.

Rohrabacher has always had a particular interest in foreign affairs, and in the 109th Congress he will chair the International Relations Committee's new Oversight and Investigations Subcommittee. He will use his new position to begin a thorough investigation of the United Nations' Oil-for-Food program, he said. The U.N. program, which provided Iraq with food and medicine in exchange for the sale of its oil, is under investigation in the Senate because of questions about how the program was administered."For too long, the U.N. has been considered above reproach," Rohrabacher said. "It appears the U.N. lacks the necessary internal checks and balances for a program that oversees billions of dollars in contracts."

Rohrabacher has never been especially fond of the United Nations, once calling it "a collection of tin-pot dictatorships and corrupt regimes." On International Relations, he often promotes an "America first" brand of foreign policy, which includes arguing for stricter immigration controls.

In the 108th, he unsuccessfully sought to pass a bill that would have required hospitals to report to authorities the names of illegal aliens they treated. House leaders promised him a floor vote on the controversial measure in return for his yes vote for a 2003 measure to add a drug benefit to Medicare.

But the GOP leadership showed little enthusiasm for having hospitals turn in illegal immigrants. The party's whip organization stayed quiet, and more Republicans voted against Rohrabacher's bill than for it. Rohrabacher said he was happy just to see it given a chance on the floor. For the same reason, many immigrant advocacy groups were incensed.

Rohrabacher has been a critic of U.S. policy toward China throughout his congressional tenure, no matter whether the administration has been Republican or Democratic. He was a vigorous opponent of the law, enacted in 2000, permanently permitting Chinese goods to enter the United States under the same low tariffs afforded most countries. In 2002, he voted against a bill to give the president fast-track authority to negotiate trade agreements that Congress cannot amend, saying he did not want to diminish congressional authority.

Rohrabacher legislates with an easygoing attitude and a ready laugh. A plaque in his office reads, "Fighting for Freedom . . . and Having Fun." He represents Huntington Beach, a surfing community in coastal Southern California, and is an avid surfer. He counts writers, artists and musicians such as heavy metal vocalist Sammy Hagar, folk singer Joan Baez and rock-and-roll guitarist "Skunk" Baxter among his friends.

During his younger days, Rohrabacher was a hard-drinking, banjo-playing wanderer who worked as a house-painter. He later found steady work as a reporter and editorial writer for the conservative Orange County Register. He served as assistant press secretary for Ronald Reagan's 1976 and 1980 presidential campaigns, then became a White House speechwriter for President Reagan.

In his first bid for elective office, in 1988, Rohrabacher ran for the House seat being vacated by GOP Rep. Dan Lungren. Rohrabacher won despite primary competitors who had both name recognition and Lungren's support.

He has won every successive election with no less than 54 percent of the vote. In 2002, his newly drawn district once again included the port of Long Beach, as it did in his first two terms. But the new constituency caused him no distress at the polls and he won with 62 percent of the vote. In 2004, he beat back a primary challenge from former Rep. Robert K. Dornan and easily won the general election, again with 62 percent.

KEY VOTES

2004

No Extend federal unemployment benefits by 13 weeks

Yes Pass $283.2 billion, six-year federal highway and mass transit bill

Yes Approve $146 billion multi-year extension of previously enacted middle-class tax breaks

Yes Amend the Constitution to prohibit same-sex marriage

No Cut corporate taxes $137 billion over 10 years

No Reorganize U.S. intelligence agencies as proposed by Sept. 11 commission

2003

Yes Cut taxes by $330 billion through fiscal 2013

No Block Bush rule scaling back overtime pay for some white-collar federal workers

Yes Do not allow use of search warrants without first notifying subjects

Yes Allow importation of prescription drugs

Yes Create private school voucher program in Washington, D.C.

Yes Ban "partial birth" abortion except to save a woman's life

Yes Split $18.6 billion in Iraq aid into half-grant, half-loan

Yes Overhaul Medicare and create prescription drug benefit

CQ VOTE STUDIES

	PARTY UNITY		PRESIDENTIAL SUPPORT	
	Support	Oppose	Support	Oppose
2004	91%	9%	84%	16%
2003	92%	8%	87%	13%
2002	94%	6%	77%	23%
2001	93%	7%	86%	14%
2000	94%	6%	16%	84%

INTEREST GROUPS

	AFL-CIO	ADA	CCUS	ACU
2004	29%	15%	85%	91%
2003	13%	15%	80%	84%
2002	22%	5%	85%	96%
2001	0%	10%	78%	96%
2000	10%	10%	61%	96%

CALIFORNIA 46

Coastal Los Angeles and Orange counties — Huntington Beach, Costa Mesa

The 46th is a comfortably conservative district that runs along the coast south of Los Angeles. An eclectic mix of residents, including senior citizens, surfers and aerospace workers, live in several communities. In the northwest is an ultra-wealthy, mountainous peninsula containing Rancho Palos Verdes, Palos Verdes Estates and Rolling Hills Estates. In the center is a more blue-collar area around Long Beach Harbor. The district continues southeast into the wealthier Orange County communities of Huntington Beach and Costa Mesa.

At Seal Beach, just over the line into Orange County, two-thirds of the city's residents are 65 or older and roughly one-third live in Leisure World, a seniors community. Huntington Beach is a hub for both surfers and aerospace workers, some of whom work at a Boeing Co. plant that is a design and manufacturing facility for the space station and Delta rocket. Boeing has reduced personnel and facilities here in recent years.

Generally speaking, the coastal areas are more Republican and the inland areas slightly more Democratic. Despite its proximity to Los Angeles, the district is more than 60 percent white. The 46th's interior, which includes Costa Mesa, Fountain Valley and part of Westminster and Santa Ana, tends to be less affluent than the coastal cities. These towns are solidly middle-class residential areas. Many of the area's blue-collar workers are employed by aerospace companies within the district or in Anaheim, Torrance or Long Beach.

MAJOR INDUSTRY
Aerospace, technology, manufacturing

MILITARY BASES
Naval Weapons Station Seal Beach, 130 military, 470 civilian (2005)

CITIES
Huntington Beach, 189,594; Costa Mesa, 108,724; Long Beach (pt.), 83,666; Westminster (pt.), 60,399

NOTABLE
Huntington Beach hosts major surfing tournaments and is home to the International Surfing Museum; Catalina Island, a tourist destination, and San Clemente Island, which is owned by the Navy, are included in the 46th.

Rep. Loretta Sanchez (D)

Elected 1996; 5th term

CAPITOL OFFICE
225-2965
loretta@mail.house.gov
www.house.gov/sanchez
1230 Longworth 20515-0547; fax 225-5859

COMMITTEES
Armed Services
Homeland Security
Joint Economic

HOMETOWN
Santa Ana

BORN
Jan. 7, 1960, Lynwood, Calif.

RELIGION
Roman Catholic

FAMILY
Divorced

EDUCATION
Chapman U., B.S. 1982 (economics); American U.,
M.B.A. 1984 (finance)

CAREER
Financial adviser; strategic management
associate

POLITICAL HIGHLIGHTS
Candidate for Anaheim City Council, 1994

ELECTION RESULTS

2004 GENERAL
Loretta Sanchez (D)	65,684	60.4%
Alexandria A. Coronado (R)	43,099	39.6%

2004 PRIMARY
Loretta Sanchez (D)	unopposed

2002 GENERAL
Loretta Sanchez (D)	42,501	60.9%
Jeff Chavez (R)	24,346	34.9%
Paul Marsden (LIBERT)	2,944	4.2%

PREVIOUS WINNING PERCENTAGES
2000 (60%); 1998 (56%); 1996 (47%)

A tireless, telegenic defender of women, government social programs and organized labor, Sanchez is the senior member of the first sister duo ever to serve in Congress.

In 2002, six years after she had won her own seat in the House by upsetting conservative GOP Rep. Robert K. Dornan, Sanchez drew on her accumulated political capital to help her younger sister, Linda Sánchez, a civil rights and labor lawyer, win a seat of her own in the reconfigured 39th District in nearby Los Angeles County.

The sisters plan to publish a joint memoir recounting their experiences. They point out that they have significantly different personalities and some political differences as well.

The elder Sanchez can be aggressively partisan, and she has made headlines for stubbornly doing or saying things that go against the conventional grain. In 2000, for instance, she embarrassed fellow Democrats on the eve of their national convention in Los Angeles by refusing to cancel a fundraiser at the Playboy mansion. Though she changed the venue at the last minute, she seemed to relish the controversy. The next year, her office's pet goldfish was named "Hef" after Playboy founder Hugh Hefner. Her annual offbeat Christmas card is also a topic of conversation.

A daughter of working-class Mexican immigrants, Sanchez describes herself as growing up a "shy, quiet girl" who did not speak English. She credits government with much of her success in public life. "I am a Head Start child, a public school kid, a Pell Grant recipient," she says. She staunchly opposed the GOP's Head Start program overhaul in the 108th Congress, invoking her experience growing up poor and challenged by a speech impediment. "I know about these kids, because I am one of those kids," she said during debate on the bill. "It hurts to hear you talk about how we are not successful, or how we are losers. But we are very successful. We have had a lot of successes with Head Start," she said.

Sanchez often asserts that conservative Republicans are not committed to improving public education. When President Bush's 2003 budget proposal threatened to cut education grants, she responded, "If he can run deficits for the military, then he can run deficits to educate our children."

Thanks in part to her outspoken and spirited style, Sanchez has become a master fundraiser; in the 2004 campaign cycle, she transferred $150,000 from her own campaign funds to the House Democrats' central campaign coffers. A former Democratic National Committee co-chairwoman, Sanchez was an early ally of fellow Californian Nancy Pelosi, now the minority leader.

In the 108th, she got a seat on the newly formed Homeland Security Committee, and in both the 108th and 109th, she was the top-ranking Democrat on one of its subcommittees. She has used her seat on the Armed Services panel to focus attention on the delicate topic of sexual assault in the military and service academies — which investigations revealed was much more prevalent than previously thought. Sanchez pressed hard for a proposal requiring that the sexual assault provisions of the Uniform Code of Military Justice be revised and updated. She also sought to reverse the ban on abortions at overseas military bases and installations.

When it comes to funding programs and equipment under the Armed Services Committee's jurisdiction, Sanchez has had some reservations. But she has backed continued production of fighter planes, such as the F-22, that are important to the California economy.

The daughter of a unionized machinist father and a secretary mother who worked to organize plant workers into a union, Sanchez joined the United Food and Commercial Workers when she scooped ice cream in high school, and she had a union scholarship to college. Given such ties, she generally votes labor's way.

In 2002, she voted against reviving fast-track procedures for congressional action on trade deals. And, coming from a district with one of the largest Vietnamese communities outside Vietnam, she voted against a trade agreement with Vietnam, saying that political and human rights conditions in that country needed improvement. Her outspokenness led the Hanoi regime to refuse to allow her into the country late in 2004 when she applied for an entry visa to meet with dissidents.

Though Sanchez is allied with the Democratic left on most social issues, she follows a center-right course on fiscal policy, as a member of the Democratic "Blue Dogs." She also has sided with conservatives on such issues as amending the Constitution to outlaw flag desecration and encouraging states to prosecute violent juvenile offenders as adults.

Sanchez traces her ambitions to first-grade catechism class. A nun asked her what she wanted to be when she grew up. "I answered, 'The pope. He's the head of everyone, the one making the rules,' " Sanchez told the Orange County Register.

Sanchez's childhood shyness was so extreme that her mother took her to doctors for advice. Her father forced her to take speech and drama classes in school. Acutely aware of her parents' limited income, she worked her way through college and earned a master's degree in business administration. Feeling isolated as a Hispanic woman in the investment world, she made her first foray into politics in 1994, losing a race for an Anaheim City Council seat.

In 1996, she brazenly took on Dornan, a controversial conservative icon. After winning a four-way primary with 35 percent of the vote, she drew attention from liberal groups who played a hunch that their archenemy might not have his guard up. Thanks to the increasing number of Hispanics in the 46th District and a backlash against a ballot initiative to end most state affirmative action programs, Sanchez scored a 984-vote upset.

Dornan claimed he lost to illegal voting by non-citizens. A House task force later said it found such instances, but not enough to prove they affected the outcome. In a 1998 rematch, Sanchez defeated Dornan by 17 percentage points. Her re-elections since have been by larger margins, and redistricting in 2001 (the district is now the 47th) has not harmed her electoral prospects.

KEY VOTES

2004

Yes Extend federal unemployment benefits by 13 weeks

Yes Pass $283.2 billion, six-year federal highway and mass transit bill

Yes Approve $146 billion multi-year extension of previously enacted middle-class tax breaks

No Amend the Constitution to prohibit same-sex marriage

No Cut corporate taxes $137 billion over 10 years

Yes Reorganize U.S. intelligence agencies as proposed by Sept. 11 commission

2003

No Cut taxes by $330 billion through fiscal 2013

\+ Block Bush rule scaling back overtime pay for some white-collar federal workers

Yes Do not allow use of search warrants without first notifying subjects

No Allow importation of prescription drugs

No Create private school voucher program in Washington, D.C.

No Ban "partial birth" abortion except to save a woman's life

Yes Split $18.6 billion in Iraq aid into half-grant, half-loan

No Overhaul Medicare and create prescription drug benefit

CQ VOTE STUDIES

	PARTY UNITY		PRESIDENTIAL SUPPORT	
	Support	Oppose	Support	Oppose
2004	94%	6%	33%	67%
2003	97%	3%	22%	78%
2002	96%	4%	21%	79%
2001	88%	12%	24%	76%
2000	94%	6%	75%	25%

INTEREST GROUPS

	AFL-CIO	ADA	CCUS	ACU
2004	93%	100%	40%	12%
2003	100%	90%	34%	12%
2002	100%	100%	32%	4%
2001	92%	90%	32%	12%
2000	89%	65%	63%	17%

CALIFORNIA 47

Orange County — most of Santa Ana, Anaheim and Garden Grove

A blue-collar inland strip full of older suburban homes and younger families, the majority-Hispanic 47th is unlike its mostly affluent, Republican neighbors in Orange County. Located about 30 miles southeast of Los Angeles, it takes in part of four cities: Santa Ana, Anaheim, Garden Grove and Fullerton, where a growing number of Hispanics and other ethnic minorities are changing its demographics and creating a strong Democratic voter base.

Almost half the district's population is in Santa Ana — the Orange County seat — which has higher unemployment and more blue-collar jobs than surrounding areas. The city is one of only two in the county in which registered Democrats outnumber Republicans.

Three-fourths of Garden Grove's residents live in the 47th, which has the center (a mix of Vietnamese, Koreans and Hispanics) and east (heavily Hispanic) sections. An influx of Southeast Asian refugees has spurred a

conservative backlash from some residents who worry that increased social services will lead to higher taxes. But the Asian community, some of which is heavily Christian, also has a conservative side.

The 47th has some of Anaheim's most Democratic areas. The small part of Fullerton in the district's northern end is heavily Hispanic, although the city overall leans Republican. Al Gore won the 47th's presidential vote by 15 percentage points in 2000, but George W. Bush managed a narrow win with 50 percent of the vote in 2004.

Apart from Disneyland, no single employer drives the area's economy. Defense subcontractors and small businesses are scattered throughout the district.

MAJOR INDUSTRY
Small business, service, defense, tourism

CITIES
Santa Ana (pt.), 299,552; Anaheim (pt.), 185,537; Garden Grove (pt.), 125,336; Fullerton (pt.), 17,852

NOTABLE
The 47th's part of Anaheim is home to Disneyland, the Angels baseball team and the Mighty Ducks hockey team.

Rep. Christopher Cox (R)

CAPITOL OFFICE
225-5611
christopher.cox@mail.house.gov
cox.house.gov
2402 Rayburn 20515-0548; fax 225-9177

COMMITTEES
Homeland Security - chairman

HOMETOWN
Newport Beach

BORN
Oct. 16, 1952, St. Paul, Minn.

RELIGION
Roman Catholic

FAMILY
Wife, Rebecca Cox; three children

EDUCATION
U. of Southern California, B.A. 1973; Harvard U.,
M.B.A. 1977, J.D. 1977

CAREER
White House counsel; lawyer; professor

POLITICAL HIGHLIGHTS
No previous office

ELECTION RESULTS

2004 GENERAL

Christopher Cox (R)	189,004	65.0%
John L. Graham (D)	93,525	32.2%
Bruce Cohen (LIBERT)	8,343	2.9%

2004 PRIMARY

Christopher Cox (R)	unopposed

2002 GENERAL

Christopher Cox (R)	122,884	68.4%
John L. Graham (D)	51,058	28.4%
Joe Cobb (LIBERT)	5,607	3.1%

PREVIOUS WINNING PERCENTAGES
2000 (66%); 1998 (68%); 1996 (66%); 1994 (72%);
1992 (65%); 1990 (68%); 1988 (67%)

Elected 1988; 9th term

Cox is now the chairman of a major committee and one with a key domestic function — homeland security. The panel was given permanent status at the start of the 109th Congress, as well as greater jurisdiction over homeland security matters.

Cox has always been ambitious, yet he has struggled to convince colleagues that his wonkish, intellectual personality is suitable for jobs in the leadership. He has at times disdained the back-slapping style and overt partisan passion required to gain leadership posts, but he has shown loyalty by deferring to party leaders on key votes.

Cox's frustrating experience in the 108th Congress overseeing the fledgling Homeland Security panel made some lawmakers wonder whether he could play hardball with his Republican colleagues. His committee published numerous reports assessing the nation's security vulnerabilities, but he was consistently blocked in the 108th by more aggressive chairmen when he tried to assert his committee's jurisdiction over homeland security matters. His unwillingness to challenge other committee chairmen frustrated the panel's Democrats, and committee relations soured toward the end of the 108th.

In the 109th, Cox should have more control. His committee now has jurisdiction over the Transportation Security Administration, the largest agency under the Department of Homeland Security; border security; infrastructure protection; and some Customs functions. "This is the most extensive national security jurisdictional reorganization in Congress since 1947," Cox said. "Without question, this committee will have center stage."

Even before the 109th Congress, Cox was viewed as a national figure on homeland security policies, appearing regularly on television shows as the congressional spokesman on domestic security matters.

His priority in 2005 is to write an annual authorization bill for the Homeland Security Department, modeling the legislation after the defense authorization bill, which sets budgets, personnel and procurement policies. But many of the Homeland Security functions overlap with programs already authorized by the other House committees, and Cox will have to negotiate with his fellow chairmen to set policy and budget levels.

A technology-savvy legislator who has sponsored various Internet-related bills over the years, Cox has said cybersecurity is a major priority for his committee. But he may have to wrest oversight of the issue from both Energy and Commerce and Science, which have dealt with the issue in the past. "Ending congressional turf wars over homeland security is a pressing issue," Cox said in late 2004. "By heeding this 9/11 commission recommendation, Congress can take the next step to better secure the safety and security of the American people."

Cox had some experience with homeland security issues as he had chaired a bipartisan panel in 2002 that devised a plan to ensure the continuity of Congress after a terrorist attack. His expertise in intelligence matters made him a player on security issues after the Sept. 11, 2001, attacks. Cox was meeting with Defense Secretary Donald H. Rumsfeld when the planes hit the World Trade Center, and he had just left the Pentagon when it was struck. He was among several congressional leaders whisked away that day to an undisclosed location.

The experience reinforced his support for a missile defense system and new military strategies. The war against terrorism, he said, will not be "governed by the outdated rules of the Cold War."

Erudite and well-read, and with law and graduate business degrees from Harvard, Cox has a breadth of interests — ranging from fiscal to foreign policy — that also reflect his background as a former aide to President Reagan, a securities lawyer and a Russologist. But Cox is no mere policy wonk. His reasoned arguments have led to bipartisan triumphs, such as extending the Internet tax moratorium in the 108th Congress.

After the collapse of Enron Corp., Cox voted for the corporate accountability law of 2002, but he refused to back down from attacks on business regulation and securities lawsuits. He compared trial lawyers with rogue corporate executives "whose motive was greed." A staunch fiscal conservative and social conservative, Cox champions lower taxes, including permanent repeal of the estate tax. He once left a hospital bed after an appendectomy in 1997 so he could vote for a tax cut measure.

A longtime critic of proposals to upgrade trade relations with China, Cox joined President Clinton and GOP leaders in 2000 in supporting permanent normal trade relations with Beijing, after working for inclusion of language requiring annual reviews of China's record on human rights. On the subject of relations with China, he and Minority Leader Nancy Pelosi, a California Democrat, have worked harmoniously for years.

Cox twice considered running for Speaker when the post came up for grabs late in 1998 — after the resignations of Speaker Newt Gingrich and the man the GOP had picked to succeed him, Robert L. Livingston — but he backed away quickly when it was clear he lacked support. He chaired the Republican Policy Committee throughout the 108th Congress.

At Harvard, Cox was a law school classmate of Massachusetts Democratic Rep. Barney Frank and finished business school two years after President Bush. After graduating, Cox clerked with judges on federal appeals courts in San Francisco and Honolulu, practiced law with a Newport Beach firm, and published with his father an English version of the former official Soviet newspaper Pravda.

He became a senior associate counsel in the Reagan White House in 1986 and stayed until 1988, when Republican Robert E. Badham announced plans to retire from his Orange County House seat. In a crowded primary field, Cox separated himself by using his Washington connections. He distributed literature showing himself with Reagan and Vice President George Bush in the White House. He took 67 percent of the vote in the general election and has won with similar ease since.

KEY VOTES

2004

No Extend federal unemployment benefits by 13 weeks

Yes Pass $283.2 billion, six-year federal highway and mass transit bill

Yes Approve $146 billion multi-year extension of previously enacted middle-class tax breaks

No Amend the Constitution to prohibit same-sex marriage

Yes Cut corporate taxes $137 billion over 10 years

Yes Reorganize U.S. intelligence agencies as proposed by Sept. 11 commission

2003

Yes Cut taxes by $330 billion through fiscal 2013

No Block Bush rule scaling back overtime pay for some white-collar federal workers

No Do not allow use of search warrants without first notifying subjects

No Allow importation of prescription drugs

Yes Create private school voucher program in Washington, D.C.

Yes Ban "partial birth" abortion except to save a woman's life

No Split $18.6 billion in Iraq aid into half-grant, half-loan

Yes Overhaul Medicare and create prescription drug benefit

CQ VOTE STUDIES

	PARTY UNITY		PRESIDENTIAL SUPPORT	
	Support	Oppose	Support	Oppose
2004	97%	3%	91%	9%
2003	98%	2%	100%	0%
2002	95%	5%	86%	14%
2001	96%	4%	93%	7%
2000	95%	5%	19%	81%

INTEREST GROUPS

	AFL-CIO	ADA	CCUS	ACU
2004	7%	5%	95%	100%
2003	0%	5%	97%	88%
2002	11%	0%	89%	96%
2001	0%	5%	91%	96%
2000	0%	0%	80%	100%

CALIFORNIA 48
Southern Orange County — Irvine, Newport Beach

The 48th covers the Orange County coast from Newport Beach south through Laguna Beach to Dana Point, and it takes in a chunk of the inland county from the coast through Irvine to the foothills of the Santa Ana mountains. Registered Republicans outnumber Democrats nearly 2-to-1 here, and the district is distinguished by its large white-collar labor force and its high household income.

Newport Beach is a wealthy enclave noted for its beautiful sandy beaches, luxurious housing and solid Republicanism. Many workers commute from the north or east, where living is cheaper. Laguna Beach attracts more scuba divers than swimmers and is a more liberal enclave known as "the arts colony." Inland is Laguna Woods, home to a significant number of senior citizens, Laguna Niguel and Laguna Hills. Nearly 70 percent of district residents are white.

Smog, crime and other problems endemic to Los Angeles generally do not affect these areas, although transportation troubles are among the toughest problems, as traffic backs up and increases the risk of pollution.

Toll roads in the area have helped, but residents generally oppose a new commuter train.

While Republicans dominate the 48th, pockets of Democratic strength can be found in the district's inland sections and in the more liberal-leaning community surrounding the University of California, Irvine. The university's engineering and biomedical research programs have attracted a large number of thriving high-tech and biotechnology firms to the area, which is beginning to rival Silicon Valley.

The late-1990s closure of the El Toro and Tustin Marine Corps Air stations did not have a huge impact on the economy, but the El Toro closure did touch off a fierce battle over whether to turn it into a commercial airport. After numerous referenda, the 3,719-acre parcel is finally set to become a mix of parks and residences that includes a golf course and a museum.

MAJOR INDUSTRY
Technology, research, tourism

CITIES
Irvine, 143,072; Newport Beach, 70,032; Tustin, 67,504

NOTABLE
The television show "The O.C." depicts life in Newport Beach.

Rep. Darrell Issa (R)

CAPITOL OFFICE
225-3906
www.house.gov/issa
211 Cannon 20515-0549; fax 225-3303

COMMITTEES
Government Reform
  (Energy & Resources - chairman)
International Relations
Judiciary

HOMETOWN
Vista

BORN
Nov. 1, 1953, Cleveland, Ohio

RELIGION
Antioch Orthodox Christian Church

FAMILY
Wife, Kathy Issa; one child

EDUCATION
Kent State U., A.A. 1976 (general studies); Siena
Heights College, B.A. 1976 (business)

MILITARY SERVICE
Army, 1970-72, 1976-80; Army Reserve, 1980-88

CAREER
Car alarm company owner; electronics
manufacturing company executive

POLITICAL HIGHLIGHTS
Sought Republican nomination for U.S. Senate,
1998

ELECTION RESULTS

2004 GENERAL

Darrell Issa (R)	141,658	62.6%
Mike Byron (D)	79,057	34.9%
Lars R. Grossman (LIBERT)	5,751	2.5%

2004 PRIMARY

Darrell Issa (R)	unopposed

2002 GENERAL

Darrell Issa (R)	94,594	77.2%
Karl W. Dietrich (LIBERT)	26,891	22.0%

PREVIOUS WINNING PERCENTAGES
2000 (61%)

Elected 2000; 3rd term

Issa may not be the most prominent member of the California delegation, but he is the only one who can be called a kingmaker. It was Issa's millions that bankrolled the California recall effort in 2003, which ousted Democrat Gray Davis as governor and put Republican Arnold Schwarzenegger in his place. Although Issa wanted to replace Davis himself, he was muscled aside by Schwarzenegger, who had the greater name recognition.

A multimillionaire who made his fortune in the car alarm business, Issa (EYE-sah) spent $1.7 million on the campaign committee that forced the recall election by collecting nearly 900,000 signatures. At first, the effort divided California Republicans, some of whom thought it was counterproductive. When it became clear the recall was going to happen, several of Issa's GOP House colleagues, including David Dreier and Mary Bono, became convinced that Issa would not be a strong enough candidate to defeat Davis. They urged Schwarzenegger to run.

Issa didn't sugarcoat his opinion of that idea. He said Schwarzenegger "is too timid to engage in the brass-knuckle politics of California" and complained that "the same people who urge Arnold Schwarzenegger into the race are the same ones who didn't think there should be a recall." Eventually, though, he swallowed his pride and bowed out of the race. Schwarzenegger was handily elected when Davis lost the recall vote.

Since then, Issa has kept his name in circulation for a future run for higher office, possibly Democrat Dianne Feinstein's Senate seat if she retires in 2006. But some Republicans say the party's gratitude to Issa for forcing the recall only goes so far, and that he will have to establish a strong record of legislative achievement before mounting a successful Senate campaign.

Issa is a conservative voice on both economic and social issues, but some of his accomplishments in his first two terms were the legislative equivalent of an applause line — such as his November 2004 resolution praising the Boy Scouts. (He said it was aimed at legal challenges against group meetings on government property.) But he has also branched out into more weighty subjects such as energy policy, supporting a number of congressional initiatives aimed at increasing use of alternative fuels, including incentives for driving gasoline-electric hybrid vehicles.

In the 109th Congress, Issa continues to focus on energy policy issues as chairman of the Government Reform panel's Energy and Resources Subcommittee.

His legislation may be on the risk-averse side, but Issa is not the kind of politician who ducks controversy. Long before he engineered the recall, Issa was the frontman for business in a 1996 campaign to overturn racial and gender preferences in California state contracting and college admissions. The authors of Proposition 209, the "California Civil Rights Initiative," were having trouble finding a prominent businessman to take the lead on an issue that might get him branded a racist, but Issa took on the role and the initiative passed narrowly.

Issa also is not shy about promoting himself. In the 108th Congress, he won a seat on the Energy and Commerce Committee after campaigning for the job by distributing a computer CD touting his qualifications to members of the panel that makes assignments. He had wanted to join the panel in early 2002 when a vacancy arose, but was passed over.

Then at the start of the 109th, Issa decided to return to his former committees — Judiciary and International Relations — and to take a leave of absence from Energy and Commerce. He said he made the move so he can concentrate on intellectual property rights and immigration reform, and the U.S.-led effort to bring peace to the Middle East and democracy to Iraq.

The grandson of Lebanese immigrants, Issa has had firsthand experience with the fallout from the Sept. 11, 2001, terrorist attacks. Three weeks after the attacks, he was barred from boarding an Air France plane on an official trip to the Middle East. Issa said that while another lawmaker was permitted to board, he was stopped because "I had an Arab surname and a one-way ticket to Saudi Arabia." He started the trip the next day.

Issa was born into a working-class family in Cleveland, where his father worked as a salesman and an X-ray technician. On his 17th birthday, just two months into his senior year, Issa quit high school and joined the Army. After he had served two years, the Army paid for Issa's college education with the understanding that he would return to active duty upon graduation. He earned a degree in business and returned to the Army.

After four years, he came back to Cleveland and used his $7,000 in life savings to invest in a small car alarm business. He and his wife, Kathy, eventually took control of the business and moved it in 1985 to Vista, about 30 miles north of San Diego. He immersed himself in industry activities, and in 1999 and 2000 he was chairman of the board of the Consumer Electronics Association, an industry trade group.

In California, Issa became involved behind the scenes in local GOP politics. He briefly considered challenging 49th District Democratic Rep. Lynn Schenk in 1994, but polls showed Brian P. Bilbray would be a strong candidate and Issa remained on the sidelines. Four years later, he spent $11 million on a failed bid for the 1998 GOP nomination to challenge Democratic Sen. Barbara Boxer.

Issa was back in 2000 when Republican Ron Packard announced his retirement from the 48th District after 18 years in the House. In the reliably Republican district, which was home to President Nixon, Issa weathered a nine-candidate primary. Issa's wealth may have provided the essential edge: He sank $2 million into his primary campaign. The general election was easy, with Issa taking 61 percent of the vote to defeat Democrat Peter Kouvelis, a retired Marine officer, who spent only about $20,000.

In 2002, Democrats did not field a candidate and Issa won with 77 percent of the vote. In 2004, however, Issa faced a challenge from Democrat Mike Byron, a political science professor who campaigned against Issa's support of the Iraq war. The issue gained no traction in the conservative district, and Issa won with 63 percent of the vote.

KEY VOTES

2004

No	Extend federal unemployment benefits by 13 weeks
Yes	Pass $283.2 billion, six-year federal highway and mass transit bill
Yes	Approve $146 billion multi-year extension of previously enacted middle-class tax breaks
Yes	Amend the Constitution to prohibit same-sex marriage
Yes	Cut corporate taxes $137 billion over 10 years
No	Reorganize U.S. intelligence agencies as proposed by Sept. 11 commission

2003

Yes	Cut taxes by $330 billion through fiscal 2013
No	Block Bush rule scaling back overtime pay for some white-collar federal workers
Yes	Do not allow use of search warrants without first notifying subjects
No	Allow importation of prescription drugs
Yes	Create private school voucher program in Washington, D.C.
?	Ban "partial birth" abortion except to save a woman's life
No	Split $18.6 billion in Iraq aid into half-grant, half-loan
Yes	Overhaul Medicare and create prescription drug benefit

CQ VOTE STUDIES

	PARTY UNITY		PRESIDENTIAL SUPPORT	
	Support	Oppose	Support	Oppose
2004	95%	5%	85%	15%
2003	97%	3%	98%	2%
2002	94%	6%	85%	15%
2001	96%	4%	88%	12%

INTEREST GROUPS

	AFL-CIO	ADA	CCUS	ACU
2004	20%	0%	100%	92%
2003	7%	5%	97%	83%
2002	13%	0%	100%	96%
2001	17%	10%	100%	84%

CALIFORNIA 49
North San Diego County; West Riverside County

One of the fastest-growing areas in California, the heavily residential 49th in northwestern San Diego County and western Riverside County is home to many rapidly changing bedroom communities.

Commuters travel to jobs in San Diego (a sliver of which falls in the 49th) and, to a lesser extent, Orange County, while tourists visit the wineries in Riverside County. Almost 60 percent white and solidly conservative, the district gave George W. Bush 62 percent of the vote in the 2004 presidential election.

The 1990s saw areas like Lake Elsinore, Canyon Lake and Sun City in Riverside County turn from retirement communities into family-oriented commuter towns. Perris, which largely remains a retirement community, is the district's only city in which Democrats hold an edge.

Massive Camp Pendleton Marine Corps Base sits on the district's coast, but the local economy relies less on military contracts than its Orange County and San Diego neighbors. Sony has a plant in Rancho Bernardo

(in northeast San Diego) that makes laptop computers, among other electronics. Beach visitors to Oceanside and the Pacific Coast also boost the local economy.

Although most residents live in San Diego County, growth has been prodigious in Temecula, the heart of the district's wine industry, in Riverside County. Ballooning and skydiving are among the tourist attractions in the more rural northern parts of the district.

MAJOR INDUSTRY
Medical devices, services, manufacturing, tourism, defense

MILITARY BASES
Camp Pendleton Marine Corps Base, Air Station and Naval Hospital, 36,000 military, 24,000 civilians; Naval Weapons Station Seal Beach, Detachment Fallbrook, 130 military, 470 civilian (2005)

CITIES
Oceanside, 161,029; Vista, 89,857; Temecula, 57,716; Perris, 36,189; Fallbrook (unincorporated), 29,100; Lake Elsinore, 28,928

NOTABLE
Fallbrook is a leader in avocado production; Julian produces 10,000 apple pies a week each fall; The San Onofre nuclear power plant is on the Pacific Coast next to Camp Pendleton.

Rep. Randy 'Duke' Cunningham (R)

Elected 1990; 8th term

CAPITOL OFFICE
225-5452
www.house.gov/cunningham
2350 Rayburn 20515-0550; fax 225-2558

COMMITTEES
Appropriations
Select Intelligence
(Terrorism/Human Intelligence, Analysis & Counterintelligence - chairman)

HOMETOWN
Rancho Santa Fe

BORN
Dec. 8, 1941, Los Angeles, Calif.

RELIGION
Christian

FAMILY
Wife, Nancy Cunningham; three children

EDUCATION
U. of Missouri, B.A. 1964 (education), M.A. 1965 (education); National U., M.B.A. 1985

MILITARY SERVICE
Navy, 1966-87

CAREER
Computer software executive; Top Gun flight school instructor; teacher and coach

POLITICAL HIGHLIGHTS
No previous office

ELECTION RESULTS

2004 GENERAL

Randy "Duke" Cunningham (R)	169,025	58.4%
Francine P. Busby (D)	105,590	36.5%
Gary M. Waayers (GREEN)	6,504	2.3%
Diane Beall Templin (AMI)	4,723	1.6%
Brandon C. Osborne (LIBERT)	3,486	1.2%

2004 PRIMARY

Randy "Duke" Cunningham (R)	unopposed

2002 GENERAL

Randy "Duke" Cunningham (R)	111,095	64.3%
Del G. Stewart (D)	55,855	32.3%
Richard M. Fontanesi (LIBERT)	5,751	3.3%

PREVIOUS WINNING PERCENTAGES
2000 (64%); 1998 (61%); 1996 (65%); 1994 (67%); 1992 (56%); 1990 (46%)

A former Navy combat pilot, Cunningham's mission in the House is to protect military budgets. Gruff and straight-talking to a fault, he seems never to have really left the military. Though he appears too tough to cry, the idea of people burning the American flag moves him to tears. Like John Wayne, his nickname is "Duke."

Normally a solid conservative vote for Republican leaders, Cunningham bucks them when he feels U.S. soldiers may suffer. When the House in 2003 debated a $78 billion supplemental spending bill to pay for the Iraq war, Cunningham tried to eliminate $1 billion in economic aid to Turkey over objections from the White House. A country that refused to allow U.S. forces to attack northern Iraq from Turkish territory should get the message, he said, "that when they cost the lives of American soldiers, there's going to be a penalty." His amendment was defeated, 110-315.

Cunningham fights every year for higher defense budgets. A member of the Appropriations Defense Subcommittee, he was unhappy in 2003 with the final number of the defense spending bill though it was a record $369 billion. He and other defense hawks complained that procurement needs as well as research and development were put on hold as the amount of money for the war and reconstruction in Iraq continued to grow. "When you're running on deficits, you have to control your spending," he said. "We need some of these things, but at what price?"

Though it took him more than a decade of trying, he was more successful in the 108th Congress with a measure to give off-duty and retired police officers the right to carry concealed weapons. When President Bush signed the bill, Cunningham said, "As we have seen time and again in the law enforcement community, the oath to serve and protect our neighborhoods does not end when officers take off their uniform or retire."

When the House in 1999 debated a constitutional amendment outlawing flag desecration, Cunningham fought back tears as he implored his colleagues to vote for it. "This is not a matter of freedom of speech," he said. "There is nothing in this amendment that prevents someone from speaking or writing or doing any of the other things, but just the radical burning of the symbol that we hold dear."

Yet Cunningham more often makes news because of his choice of words or display of ill temper. During debate on a flag protection resolution he introduced in 2003, Cunningham charged that some of his fellow lawmakers routinely voted against anything related to defense, intelligence and veterans' affairs, which he called "unpatriotic."

He once intimated that opponents of the F-22 fighter jet were socialists; on another occasion, he chided the acting secretary of the Army for a "B.S." statement; and on another, he got into a shoving match with Democratic Rep. James P. Moran of Virginia.

Cunningham's other committee assignment is also related to defense and homeland security. He sits on the Intelligence Committee, which had a big role in late 2004 in revamping the intelligence services based on recommendations from the Sept. 11 commission. Cunningham raised concerns about placing the new intelligence director within the executive office of the White House, fearing the director would be micromanaged. But he ended up voting for the final bill.

After a bout with prostate cancer and surgery to treat it in 1998, Cunningham became active in efforts to boost federal funding for health research, especially prostate cancer research. In the 108th Congress, he split with many conservatives to urge Bush to allow some stem cell research, which utilizes cells from embryos and is opposed by anti-abortion forces. Cunningham signed a letter to Bush, with 205 other members, that said such research may hold the key to curing several diseases, including cancer. He told the Associated Press, "I'm pro-life . . . but this is an area where we can save lives."

A former high school teacher who is married to an education professional, Cunningham has been an advocate for giving local school boards more authority over federal education dollars. From his perch on the Appropriations Committee, Cunningham in the 108th Congress worked to increase impact aid — assistance that helps communities with substantial federal facilities such as military bases to support their schools — which is an important funding source in San Diego.

Cunningham's wife was a school administrator and former principal in the San Diego area. She moved with him to Washington when he was elected to the House and worked for the U.S. Education Department, but she returned to San Diego to take a job with the Encinitas Union school district. Cunningham moved to a houseboat on the Potomac River waterfront, where one of his nautical neighbors is New York Democratic Rep. Gary L. Ackerman.

Cunningham began his career as an Illinois high school teacher and swim coach, helping two of his athletes win Olympic medals. He joined the Navy at age 25 and during the Vietnam War became the first "ace," a combat pilot who shoots down five enemy planes. He narrowly avoided capture after his F-4 fighter was shot down over North Vietnam. Cunningham returned home with several medals for valor, including the Navy Cross. He then trained pilots at Miramar Naval Air Station north of San Diego.

After he left the military for business, his background caught the eye of another Vietnam veteran from California, GOP Rep. Duncan Hunter, who urged him to run for the House. Cunningham moved to the suburb of Chula Vista to challenge Democratic Rep. Jim Bates in 1990 in the old 44th District. Targeting evangelical Christians and conservative Democrats, he eked out a narrow victory.

After redistricting in 1992, he ran in the solidly Republican 51st and was re-elected by comfortable margins. Redistricting for 2002 did not hurt him either. His new district, numbered the 50th, still contains a healthy Republican majority, and Cunningham cruised to a 2-to-1 victory. He won by 22 percentage points in 2004.

KEY VOTES

2004
- No Extend federal unemployment benefits by 13 weeks
- Yes Pass $283.2 billion, six-year federal highway and mass transit bill
- Yes Approve $146 billion multi-year extension of previously enacted middle-class tax breaks
- Yes Amend the Constitution to prohibit same-sex marriage
- Yes Cut corporate taxes $137 billion over 10 years
- Yes Reorganize U.S. intelligence agencies as proposed by Sept. 11 commission

2003
- Yes Cut taxes by $330 billion through fiscal 2013
- No Block Bush rule scaling back overtime pay for some white-collar federal workers
- No Do not allow use of search warrants without first notifying subjects
- No Allow importation of prescription drugs
- Yes Create private school voucher program in Washington, D.C.
- Yes Ban "partial birth" abortion except to save a woman's life
- No Split $18.6 billion in Iraq aid into half-grant, half-loan
- Yes Overhaul Medicare and create prescription drug benefit

CQ VOTE STUDIES

	PARTY UNITY		PRESIDENTIAL SUPPORT	
	Support	Oppose	Support	Oppose
2004	94%	6%	85%	15%
2003	97%	3%	98%	2%
2002	97%	3%	86%	14%
2001	96%	4%	95%	5%
2000	94%	6%	26%	74%

INTEREST GROUPS

	AFL-CIO	ADA	CCUS	ACU
2004	13%	5%	100%	92%
2003	7%	5%	97%	88%
2002	11%	0%	89%	96%
2001	17%	5%	96%	96%
2000	0%	5%	95%	92%

CALIFORNIA 50
North San Diego; Escondido; Carlsbad

With its beautiful beach communities and upper-middle-class suburbs, the San Diego-area 50th is a steadily growing GOP stronghold.

The area's wealth is a testament to a booming technology industry north of San Diego that has been likened to a mini-Silicon Valley. The growth of cellular technology companies and computer firms has contributed to the area's image. Military firms and defense contractors have diversified the boom. Construction of opulent homes continues apace, and locals and tourists compete for time at a plethora of golf courses.

The 50th's conservative corridor, which runs north and south through the district along Interstate 15, includes the Marine Corps base in Miramar (shared with the 52nd), which until 1996 was home to the Navy's famed "Top Gun" fighter school. As part of downsizing, the naval air station moved to Nevada, and Marines from the closing El Toro and Tustin bases moved to Miramar.

Unlike San Diego's south side, the 50th is two-thirds white and heavily

Republican. Coastal cities such as Del Mar, Carlsbad and Encinitas, where beach replenishment and the environment are issues, add some liberals to the district, but they are outweighed by inland voters in well-off San Diego communities and Escondido, which is north of the city. Republicans have a 15 percentage point voter registration advantage in the district.

MAJOR INDUSTRY
Technology, defense, manufacturing

MILITARY BASES
Marine Corps Air Station Miramar, 9,300 military, 1,300 civilian (2004) (shared with the 52nd)

CITIES
San Diego (pt.), 262,523; Escondido, 133,559; Carlsbad, 78,247; Encinitas, 58,014; San Marcos, 54,977

NOTABLE
The Flower Fields in Carlsbad features a blooming 50-acre hillside; Carlsbad is home to several major golf equipment manufacturers, as well as the Legoland theme park; Rancho Santa Fe was the home of the Heaven's Gate cult when members committed mass suicide in 1997; The Paul Ecke Ranch produces 80 percent of the world's poinsettias.

Rep. Bob Filner (D)

CAPITOL OFFICE
225-8045
www.house.gov/filner
2428 Rayburn 20515-0551; fax 225-9073

COMMITTEES
Transportation & Infrastructure
Veterans' Affairs

HOMETOWN
Chula Vista

BORN
Sept. 4, 1942, Pittsburgh, Pa.

RELIGION
Jewish

FAMILY
Wife, Jane Merrill Filner; two children

EDUCATION
Cornell U., B.A. 1963 (chemistry); U. of Delaware,
M.A. 1969 (history); Cornell U., Ph.D. 1973 (history
of science)

CAREER
Congressional aide; college professor

POLITICAL HIGHLIGHTS
San Diego School Board, 1979-83 (president, 1982);
candidate for San Diego City Council, 1983; San
Diego City Council, 1987-92 (deputy mayor, 1991)

ELECTION RESULTS

2004 GENERAL

Bob Filner (D)	111,441	61.6%
Michael Giorgino (R)	63,526	35.1%
Michael S. Metti (LIBERT)	5,912	3.3%

2004 PRIMARY

Bob Filner (D)	33,046	76.6%
Daniel C. "Danny" Ramirez (D)	10,074	23.4%

2002 GENERAL

Bob Filner (D)	59,541	57.9%
Maria Guadalupe Garcia (R)	40,430	39.3%
Jeffrey S. Keup (LIBERT)	2,816	2.7%

PREVIOUS WINNING PERCENTAGES
2000 (68%); 1998 (99%); 1996 (62%); 1994 (57%);
1992 (57%)

Elected 1992; 7th term

A grass-roots organizer and 1960s civil rights activist, Filner is an unabashedly proud liberal. If he is at all critical of his party, it is because the Democratic leadership does not do more in the way of publicity stunts to get the party's message out to the public.

Filner wants to use political events as "organizing tools" to whip up the public's interest in policy. To that end, he and other House liberals started a small organizing group called the Moving All Democrats caucus, which goes by the moniker "MAD dogs." Lamenting the declining influence of liberals within the party, Filner said, "One day, we'll come out of the kennel."

Filner joined members of the Congressional Black Caucus in their parliamentary attempt at a January 2001 joint session to prevent Congress from certifying the Electoral College's 2000 presidential results, which formally resolved the contested election in favor of George W. Bush. Filner was so incensed by the Supreme Court ruling the previous month, which effectively decided the election, that he briefly considered introducing a resolution of impeachment in the House against some of the justices, he said.

And during California's electricity crisis at the start of the decade, which hit Filner's hometown of San Diego hard, he angrily filed court motions calling utility companies guilty of murder, extortion and grand larceny.

Despite his appetite for such political theater, Filner also has a serious side, which is most apparent in his advocacy of veterans' interests. He is second in seniority among Democrats on the Veterans' Affairs Committee.

At the start of the 109th Congress, changes at the top of the Veterans' Committee revealed fractures in Republican unity. The GOP leadership removed panel Chairman Christopher H. Smith of New Jersey, who had often complained about low funding levels for veterans' programs during his four years running the committee. Smith was replaced by Steve Buyer of Indiana, who was seen by veterans' groups as more likely to go along with the leadership's wishes.

Filner said that the GOP infighting would benefit Democrats, especially since the new chairman was opposed by many veterans' groups. "Buyer is so hostile, so virulent in his attacks on veterans that he's going to make us look great," Filner said. In 2003, Filner had strongly criticized the Bush administration's proposed spending on veterans' benefits and had called on veterans' groups to stage a march on Washington.

In the 108th, he was the top-ranking Democrat on the Health Subcommittee. Filner has worked to improve aid to homeless veterans and sponsored legislation to guarantee veterans the right to reclaim state government jobs after their military service.

Filner also made repeated bids to win benefits for Filipino veterans who served with U.S. forces in World War II. His efforts, inspired by the large Filipino community in his area, won him the gratitude of the Philippine government, especially when he was arrested with Filipino-American protesters who chained themselves to the White House fence in 1997. His efforts paid off in 2003 when his measure to improve their benefits was signed by President Bush. The legislation, which restored some benefits that had been rescinded in 1946, gave U.S.-Filipino World War II veterans full access to VA medical facilities, restored burial benefits to Philippine scouts, and boosted the compensation for Filipino veterans and their widows.

Filner also sits on the Transportation and Infrastructure Committee, where he is the top-ranking Democrat on the Coast Guard and Maritime

Transportation Subcommittee. He works with others in the state delegation to get as much money as possible for California projects in the huge surface transportation bill. In the 109th, as Congress works to reauthorize the law governing highway programs, Filner plans to push for the reopening of the San Diego-Arizona freight railway. He also wants funds for a new airport near San Diego and a high-speed rail line to go into downtown San Diego.

Of particular importance to Filner is funding for transportation projects near the Mexican border. Facilities there were strained by increased traffic under the North American Free Trade Agreement, which he opposed. The Sept. 11, 2001, terrorist attacks brought even more congestion as border security increased. Filner was pleased with the Bush administration's increase in border security staff but continued to ask for more funds and border gates south of San Diego.

Filner champions environmental protection back home. He pushed legislation to reduce the effect of sewage from Mexico on the California coast and is working to save the polluted Salton Sea, much of which is in his area.

On other issues, Filner is not afraid to buck his party when he thinks his colleagues are giving political victories to their foes. He was among the minority of Democrats who opposed the education law enacted at the end of Bush's first year in office. "Why should we give [Bush] a political victory for something that's not really going to be implemented? I don't know why the Democrats voted for it," Filner said after the president proposed less spending for education in fiscal 2003 than the law permitted.

A native Pennsylvanian, Filner's dedication to the civil rights movement led him to leave college and join the Freedom Riders in 1961. Arrested during a sit-in at a Mississippi lunch counter with John Lewis, now a House colleague from Georgia, Filner spent several months in prison. After his release, he finished college and later earned a doctorate in the history of science.

As a young academic, Filner said he had never been west of Chicago, and his colleagues thought he was "going to the frontier" when he accepted a teaching position in San Diego. "We didn't think there was civilization there," he said. He taught history at San Diego State University starting in the 1970s. After working for Hubert H. Humphrey, the former senator and vice president, and Rep. Don Fraser, both Minnesota Democrats, he spent four years on the San Diego School Board and five more on the city council.

He then ran for a newly created 50th District House seat in 1992. His single-minded devotion to fundraising and tireless campaigning helped him overcome five Democratic primary foes. The Democratic makeup of the district has allowed him a string of easy general-election victories.

KEY VOTES

2004

Yes   Extend federal unemployment benefits by 13 weeks

Yes   Pass $283.2 billion, six-year federal highway and mass transit bill

Yes   Approve $146 billion multi-year extension of previously enacted middle-class tax breaks

No   Amend the Constitution to prohibit same-sex marriage

?   Cut corporate taxes $137 billion over 10 years

Yes   Reorganize U.S. intelligence agencies as proposed by Sept. 11 commission

2003

No   Cut taxes by $330 billion through fiscal 2013

Yes   Block Bush rule scaling back overtime pay for some white-collar federal workers

Yes   Do not allow use of search warrants without first notifying subjects

Yes   Allow importation of prescription drugs

No   Create private school voucher program in Washington, D.C.

No   Ban "partial birth" abortion except to save a woman's life

Yes   Split $18.6 billion in Iraq aid into half-grant, half-loan

No   Overhaul Medicare and create prescription drug benefit

CQ VOTE STUDIES

	PARTY UNITY		PRESIDENTIAL SUPPORT	
	Support	Oppose	Support	Oppose
2004	98%	2%	23%	77%
2003	99%	1%	11%	89%
2002	99%	1%	22%	78%
2001	99%	1%	12%	88%
2000	99%	1%	88%	12%

INTEREST GROUPS

	AFL-CIO	ADA	CCUS	ACU
2004	93%	95%	22%	9%
2003	100%	100%	17%	13%
2002	89%	100%	25%	0%
2001	100%	95%	22%	0%
2000	100%	95%	27%	0%

CALIFORNIA 51

Central and southern San Diego; Imperial County

The part-urban, part-rural 51st runs the entire length of California's border with Mexico except for the western tip at the Pacific Ocean. It includes part of central San Diego and all of Imperial County, which is sometimes at odds with the city constituency. The Democratic district grew tremendously through post-census 2000 redistricting.

The district's San Diego portion, which begins south and east of downtown, is working class and heavily Hispanic, and has some of the worst of the city's problems. Much of the growth that has boosted areas north of San Diego has left the 51st behind. The Sept. 11, 2001, attacks slowed the border traffic-dependent economy — Mexican shoppers spend more than $2 billion a year at area malls — but local officials say things are returning to previous levels. In the booming residential suburb of Chula Vista, there is a sizable military and veteran population, which has produced a more even party split than in the district as a whole.

Imperial County is heavily agricultural, with an annual crop yield of about $1 billion, and about 70 percent Hispanic. Unemployment runs as high as 30 percent in some areas. Voters here are more conservative than their city cousins but still lean Democratic.

Border issues, particularly illegal immigration — which fills agricultural labor jobs — illegal drugs and wastewater treatment, are important in the Hispanic-majority 51st, which gave 53 percent to presidential nominee John Kerry in 2004. Its areas compete for water and are under pressure to reduce dependency on the Colorado River. Environmentalists object to one proposed solution — the Salton Sea (shared with the 45th) — which they say is key to the local ecosystem and to migratory birds.

MAJOR INDUSTRY
Service, manufacturing, agriculture, retail

MILITARY BASES
Naval Station San Diego (shared with the 53rd), 117,000 military, 16,000 civilian; El Centro Naval Air Facility, 300 military, 100 civilian (2005)

CITIES
San Diego (pt.), 239,457; Chula Vista, 173,556; National City, 54,260

NOTABLE
San Diego-Tijuana border crossing at San Ysidro is the world's busiest; Otay Mesa and nearby Mexican areas are called the television capital of the world for their consumer electronics manufacturing.

Rep. Duncan Hunter (R)

Elected 1980; 13th term

CAPITOL OFFICE
225-5672
www.house.gov/hunter
2265 Rayburn 20515-0552; fax 225-0235

COMMITTEES
Armed Services - chairman

HOMETOWN
El Cajon

BORN
May 31, 1948, Riverside, Calif.

RELIGION
Baptist

FAMILY
Wife, Lynne Hunter; two children

EDUCATION
U. of Montana, attended 1966-67; U. of California,
Santa Barbara, attended 1967-68; Western State
U., B.S.L. 1976, J.D. 1976

MILITARY SERVICE
Army, 1969-71

CAREER
Lawyer

POLITICAL HIGHLIGHTS
No previous office

ELECTION RESULTS

2004 GENERAL

Duncan Hunter (R)	187,799	69.2%
Brian S. Keliher (D)	74,857	27.6%
Michael Benoit (LIBERT)	8,782	3.2%

2004 PRIMARY

Duncan Hunter (R)	unopposed

2002 GENERAL

Duncan Hunter (R)	118,561	70.2%
Peter Moore-Kochlacs (D)	43,526	25.8%
Michael Benoit (LIBERT)	6,923	4.1%

PREVIOUS WINNING PERCENTAGES
2000 (65%); 1998 (76%); 1996 (65%); 1994 (64%);
1992 (53%); 1990 (73%); 1988 (74%); 1986 (77%);
1984 (75%); 1982 (69%); 1980 (53%)

Depending on one's perspective, Hunter is a one-man construction company — or wrecking crew — when it comes to national security. As the blunt, no-holds-barred chairman of the Armed Services Committee, Hunter was the prime mover in persuading the House not to cut defense funding in the 2005 budget. He also was instrumental in getting $25 billion in war spending through Congress in 2004, pushing for "Buy America" rules and against easing export controls on military technology.

But no issue elevated Hunter's public profile as much as his efforts in 2004 to block a wide-ranging intelligence overhaul bill until he was satisfied it would allow U.S. troops untrammeled access to spying data. He, along with other conservatives, regarded the creation of a new national intelligence director as a potential threat to the link between the Pentagon and intelligence provided by satellites and other means. Creation of the director's post was a key recommendation of the bipartisan panel that investigated the Sept. 11, 2001, terrorist attacks.

Despite personal lobbying by President Bush and Vice President Dick Cheney, Hunter held fast for months. He enlisted the support of the chairman of the Joint Chiefs of Staff, Gen. Richard B. Myers, who wrote a letter saying that the Pentagon preferred the House version of the bill because it gave more-limited authority to the intelligence director over budgets. Hunter also cited his interest in helping his son, Marine 1st Lt. Duncan Duane Hunter, who had fought in Iraq. During operations there, Hunter told the Los Angeles Times, his son and other troops were "pulling down lots of stuff from the intelligence platforms, the satellites that have become as important to our warfighters as reconnaissance cavalry troops were to Robert E. Lee."

Hunter is no stranger to war himself. He won a Bronze Star for participating in 25 helicopter combat assaults in Vietnam. Since entering politics, he has cemented his reputation as the embodiment of a defense hawk, with his steadfast support of President Reagan's military buildup in the 1980s and his harsh criticism of President Clinton in the 1990s for defense budgets that Hunter deemed too stingy.

He has been one of the biggest defenders of the Bush administration's efforts in Iraq, but also critical of what he calls the Pentagon's delays in requesting funds for protective equipment for the troops and in forcing contractors to increase production rates. He refused to sign off on a $2 billion Army reprogramming request until the Defense Department submitted another request to shift $161 million toward buying electronic jammers that could disable roadside bombs. Hunter also pushed the department to order ballistic glass for gun trucks from the Department of Energy's Lawrence Livermore laboratories and urged the Army to speed development of counter-mortar systems.

His self-confidence sometimes makes him an uncomfortable ally for the defense establishment. He sounds out independent experts on some issues and occasionally challenges the armed services. In the early 1990s, he battled to make the Navy explore more-novel designs and missions for nuclear-powered submarines. More recently, Hunter has pushed for a pilot program to let small companies bid to take over ongoing weapons programs, despite warnings from industry and the Pentagon that such a move would produce chaos.

A member of the defense panel since he was elected to the House at age 32, Hunter, in his mid-50s, is relatively young for one with his legislative seniority. He is the 10th-longest-serving House Republican. His sometimes boisterous informality contrasts with the courtliness of his counterpart, Senate Armed Services Chairman John W. Warner of Virginia. Still, Hunter has a solid grasp of the arguments and a forceful style of presentation.

On fiscal and social issues, Hunter casts a reliably conservative vote. A leader of the Conservative Opportunity Society, founded by former GOP Speaker Newt Gingrich in the early 1980s, Hunter began working his way up the leadership ladder, winning the chairmanship of the Republican Research Committee in 1989, the same year Gingrich became minority whip. But in 1994, he lost a bid to become chairman of the Republican Conference to Ohio's John A. Boehner, who had 10 fewer years of seniority. Since then, Hunter has focused on his Armed Services work.

On trade and border security issues, Hunter's views blend conservative populism with a concern for keeping U.S.-developed technology out of hostile hands. When the House voted in 2000 to grant China normal trade status, Hunter led a band of Republicans who warned that the vote would help Beijing rebuild its military to threaten the United States.

Hunter opposed the 1993 North American Free Trade Agreement and was against aid to Mexico after the devaluation of the peso in 1994. He has worked to upgrade fences along the Mexican border and to hire more Border Patrol agents to reduce the flow of illegal immigrants. He has introduced legislation to bar the export of natural gas to fuel pollution-causing power plants in Mexico just across the border from the 52nd District.

Those positions prompted some San Diego business executives to question whether Hunter is attuned to the needs of the area's growing economy, which has expanded beyond defense into high technology and telecommunications and is increasingly reliant on greater cooperation with Mexico. But Hunter has encountered no significant political backlash.

For three years in the late 1970s, Hunter ran a storefront legal office in San Diego's Hispanic district, often giving free legal advice to poor people. His work in the usually Democratic inner city and his tireless campaigning helped produce his 1980 upset victory over nine-term Democrat Lionel Van Deerlin. Hunter blasted Van Deerlin as "anti-defense" and promised that a pro-Pentagon stance would keep jobs in the San Diego area, which boasts the nation's largest naval base and numerous defense industries. The message helped propel Hunter to victory with 53 percent of the vote.

He secured his hold on the district in ensuing campaigns, except in 1992. Redistricting, plus Hunter's record of overdrafts at the House bank, held him to 53 percent. Since then, he has coasted to re-election.

KEY VOTES

2004
No   Extend federal unemployment benefits by 13 weeks
?   Pass $283.2 billion, six-year federal highway and mass transit bill
Yes   Approve $146 billion multi-year extension of previously enacted middle-class tax breaks
?   Amend the Constitution to prohibit same-sex marriage
Yes   Cut corporate taxes $137 billion over 10 years
Yes   Reorganize U.S. intelligence agencies as proposed by Sept. 11 commission

2003
Yes   Cut taxes by $330 billion through fiscal 2013
No   Block Bush rule scaling back overtime pay for some white-collar federal workers
No   Do not allow use of search warrants without first notifying subjects
Yes   Allow importation of prescription drugs
Yes   Create private school voucher program in Washington, D.C.
Yes   Ban "partial birth" abortion except to save a woman's life
No   Split $18.6 billion in Iraq aid into half-grant, half-loan
Yes   Overhaul Medicare and create prescription drug benefit

CQ VOTE STUDIES

	PARTY UNITY		PRESIDENTIAL SUPPORT	
	Support	Oppose	Support	Oppose
2004	95%	5%	84%	16%
2003	96%	4%	91%	9%
2002	94%	6%	78%	22%
2001	95%	5%	88%	12%
2000	94%	6%	19%	81%

INTEREST GROUPS

	AFL-CIO	ADA	CCUS	ACU
2004	7%	5%	95%	87%
2003	20%	10%	83%	83%
2002	33%	10%	75%	88%
2001	17%	5%	91%	100%
2000	10%	10%	71%	76%

CALIFORNIA 52
Eastern San Diego; inland San Diego County

The 52nd, which wraps around the east side of San Diego from Poway in the north to east of Otay Mesa in the south, is predominately made up of wealthy, conservative suburbs. It contains about 15 percent of San Diego's residents and is solidly Republican ground, complemented by growing, rich suburbs.

After years of slow economic growth, the late 1990s marked a turnaround, particularly in El Cajon, where property values and home sales rose dramatically. San Diego's large military and defense-related work force contributes to the district's conservative personality and robust economy. Although most of the area's military bases are in the 53rd, many residents commute to nearby defense and military contracting jobs. Blue- and white-collar employees alike tend to vote Republican in the almost three-fourths white district.

Poway has a more wealthy, rural feel to it than the surrounding suburban sprawl, where growth is becoming a hot issue. Just outside of Poway is an expanse of evenly developed suburbs that includes Rancho Bernardo

(shared with the 49th) and Scripps Ranch, areas within San Diego's city limits that have attracted retirees and young families alike.

The district also stretches about 100 miles east and north through mountains and protected desert parks to the San Diego County borders. Until redistricting following the 2000 census, the 52nd also had much of California's border with Mexico and all of rural Imperial County to the east. But those areas were moved into the 51st, making this district more conservative and dominated by suburban interests.

MAJOR INDUSTRY
Technology, manufacturing, defense

MILITARY BASES
Marine Corps Air Station Miramar, 9,300 military, 1,300 civilian (2004) (shared with the 50th)

CITIES
San Diego (pt.), 164,554; El Cajon, 94,869; La Mesa, 54,749; Santee, 52,975; Poway, 48,044

NOTABLE
The Unarius Academy of Science, based in El Cajon, believes UFOs will bring new technologies that will enable humanity to begin a new civilization without pollution or poverty.

Rep. Susan A. Davis (D)

Elected 2000; 3rd term

CAPITOL OFFICE
225-2040
susan.davis@mail.house.gov
www.house.gov/susandavis
1224 Longworth 20515-0553; fax 225-2948

COMMITTEES
Armed Services
Education & Workforce

HOMETOWN
San Diego

BORN
April 13, 1944, Cambridge, Mass.

RELIGION
Jewish

FAMILY
Husband, Steve Davis; two children

EDUCATION
U. of California, Berkeley, B.A. 1965 (sociology);
U. of North Carolina, M.A. 1968 (social work)

CAREER
High school leadership program director; public
television producer; social worker

POLITICAL HIGHLIGHTS
San Diego Board of Education, 1983-92 (president,
1989-92); Calif. Assembly, 1994-2000

ELECTION RESULTS

2004 GENERAL

Susan A. Davis (D)	146,449	66.1%
Darin Hunzeker (R)	63,897	28.9%
Lawrence Rockwood (GREEN)	7,523	3.4%
Adam Van Susteren (LIBERT)	3,567	1.6%

2004 PRIMARY

Susan A. Davis (D)	unopposed

2002 GENERAL

Susan A. Davis (D)	72,252	62.2%
Bill VanDeWeghe (R)	43,891	37.8%

PREVIOUS WINNING PERCENTAGES
2000 (50%)

Davis' district is home to three universities and most of San Diego's military bases. A former school board member, she says education should be the nation's first priority. But she also represents thousands of active military personnel and thousands more veterans, so Davis cannot afford to simply choose books over barracks. She wants the government to fund both.

Her committee assignments reflect the district's dichotomy as she sits on both the Armed Services and Education and Workforce committees. On Armed Services, she has been active in efforts to improve military quality of life in matters such as housing, pay and benefits. She has sponsored measures to maintain military families' eligibility for such government programs as free or reduced-cost school lunches and supplementary security income, which provides payments to the poor, elderly and disabled.

On the Education Committee, she will have a hand in the 109th Congress' reauthorization of the Higher Education Act, where she says she will address the need for adequate school loan funding. She has complained that the Bush administration's No Child Left Behind education law has been neglected financially. And she worried after hearing President Bush's 2005 State of the Union address that while he "urged the nation not to abandon the Iraqis on their road to freedom, [that] the president must be careful not to abandon the domestic needs of our nation." Davis said the future of "our economy will depend on whether our children are educated and skilled enough to compete for high-paying jobs in a highly competitive global market."

Davis had a seat in the 108th on Veterans' Affairs where she was able to see final approval of legislation that contained her provisions dealing with veterans' home loans and disability benefits. She also introduced a measure to increase protections for veterans who rely on another individual, known as a fiduciary, to manage their federal benefits. She said there has been ample evidence of fiduciaries embezzling thousands of dollars from veterans, and that her bill "will provide veterans a protective shield against the rare cases when a fiduciary does not act in good faith."

Davis affiliates with the moderate New Democrat Coalition. She supported Bush on issues such as expanded foreign trade and annual reading and math testing in elementary and middle schools. In 2004, she voted in agreement with the president's position a third of the time.

Davis took great pains to explain her vote in 2001 in favor of giving the president authority to negotiate trade agreements that would receive fast-track consideration by Congress. Several of her pro-trade New Democrat colleagues voted against the measure, arguing that the timing was wrong. Davis was among only 21 members of her party — and one of only two from California — voting yes. She said that on balance the bill would benefit her district. Still, she called it the "most agonizing vote of my first year in Washington." In 2002, she again voted yes on the bill. She also broke with her party in the 108th to back trade agreements with Chile and Singapore.

One of Davis' longstanding concerns is the regulation of diet supplements, continuing an interest that began when she was the chairwoman of a consumer protection subcommittee in the California Assembly. In the Assembly, Davis wrote bills to restrict sales of supplements containing ephedrine and to give the Food and Drug Administration more authority over supplements. An ephedrine labeling bill written by Davis passed the state legislature, only to be vetoed by Democratic Gov. Gray Davis, who said the issue was a federal matter.

Once in Congress, she took Gov. Davis' hint: She wrote bills requiring dietary supplement manufacturers to provide the FDA with a list of their products and reports of all serious adverse reactions. Late in 2003, the FDA announced it was banning the sale of ephedrine, but Davis insisted that more should be done. "It should not have taken this long," she said.

Davis was studying social work in graduate school in North Carolina when she met Steve Davis, who was studying to be a psychiatrist. After they married, they spent two years in Japan while he served in the Air Force.

When the family returned stateside and eventually settled in San Diego, Davis became active in community activities. She volunteered at her son's pre-school. She joined the League of Women Voters, serving as the president of the San Diego chapter. Davis also worked at the local public television station.

In 1983, when Bob Filner (who now represents the neighboring 51st District) left the San Diego City Board of Education to run for the city council, Davis won the election to replace him. While still on the school board, she also helped start a local fellowship program for pre-teens and teenagers to learn about how business and government work and to gain leadership skills. She did not seek re-election to the school board in 1992 and became the fellowship program's first executive director.

Two years later, she was back on the ballot, winning the first of three terms to the California Assembly. She worked on the state law that allows women to directly access an obstetrician-gynecologist, rather than first having to obtain a referral. Once in the House, she introduced similar legislation at the federal level.

A California term-limit law barred Davis from running again for the Assembly in 2000. Democrat Nancy Pelosi urged her to run for Congress instead. Pelosi invited Davis to shadow her for a day at the Capitol and provided fundraising contacts, giving Davis her own experience with mentoring.

The political vulnerability of the 49th District's GOP incumbent, Brian P. Bilbray — he had twice won with less than 50 percent of the vote — provided Davis with a window of opportunity, and she took full advantage of it in 2000, capturing a narrow, 3 percentage point victory.

Davis' vote in favor of the fast-track trade legislation cost her the support of the AFL-CIO, which had pumped almost a quarter of a million dollars into the 2000 campaign. But in 2002, even without the labor group's backing, she benefited from the newly drawn 53rd District lines that transformed her previously marginal district into a safer seat. She won with 62 percent of the vote. In 2004, again without the AFL-CIO's backing, she captured 66 percent.

KEY VOTES

2004
Yes   Extend federal unemployment benefits by 13 weeks

Yes   Pass $283.2 billion, six-year federal highway and mass transit bill

Yes   Approve $146 billion multi-year extension of previously enacted middle-class tax breaks

No   Amend the Constitution to prohibit same-sex marriage

No   Cut corporate taxes $137 billion over 10 years

Yes   Reorganize U.S. intelligence agencies as proposed by Sept. 11 commission

2003
No   Cut taxes by $330 billion through fiscal 2013

Yes   Block Bush rule scaling back overtime pay for some white-collar federal workers

Yes   Do not allow use of search warrants without first notifying subjects

Yes   Allow importation of prescription drugs

No   Create private school voucher program in Washington, D.C.

No   Ban "partial birth" abortion except to save a woman's life

Yes   Split $18.6 billion in Iraq aid into half-grant, half-loan

No   Overhaul Medicare and create prescription drug benefit

CQ VOTE STUDIES

	PARTY UNITY		PRESIDENTIAL SUPPORT	
	Support	Oppose	Support	Oppose
2004	95%	5%	33%	67%
2003	93%	7%	18%	82%
2002	92%	8%	35%	65%
2001	89%	11%	40%	60%

INTEREST GROUPS

	AFL-CIO	ADA	CCUS	ACU
2004	93%	100%	43%	4%
2003	87%	90%	33%	12%
2002	89%	90%	50%	8%
2001	83%	90%	48%	12%

CALIFORNIA 53
Downtown San Diego; Imperial Beach

The coastal 53rd is the economic engine that drives surrounding districts. It includes San Diego's downtown, large employers, coastline and most of its military bases. Redistricting following the 2000 census scooped away wealthy and Republican-leaning communities such as La Jolla and Clairemont from the north end, making the district, previously numbered the 49th, much more Democratic.

The 53rd now includes Hispanic Democratic areas east of the city such as Lemon Grove as well as a big chunk of central San Diego. It still contains some Reagan Democrats but also includes blue-collar, central city areas like North Park, City Heights, Barrio Logan and Hillcrest, one of the area's most liberal and Democratic places and the center of the city's gay community. The result is a 29 percent Hispanic district that gave John Kerry 61 percent of the vote in the 2004 presidential election.

Higher education in the district includes the University of California, San Diego on its northern tip, San Diego State University and the University of San Diego. Private companies have formed biomedical research

partnerships with the schools. The 53rd's economy has benefited from a presence of biotech and telecommunications firms, and the downtown area and military presence have kept the district diverse enough to avoid downturns.

MAJOR INDUSTRY
Telecommunications, defense, biotechnology

MILITARY BASES
Naval Station San Diego (shared with the 51st), 117,000 military, 16,000 civilian; Naval Air Station North Island/Naval Amphibious Base Coronado, 27,189 military, 7,246 civilian; Naval Base Point Loma, 5,969 military, 13,631 civilian (2005); Naval Medical Center San Diego, 3,368 military, 2,795 civilian; Marine Corps Recruit Depot San Diego, 1,500 military, 1,200 civilian (2004)

CITIES
San Diego (pt.), 542,356; Imperial Beach, 26,992; Lemon Grove, 24,918

NOTABLE
SeaWorld, the San Diego Zoo and Balboa Park, the city's cultural center, are major tourist attractions; Qualcomm Stadium, home to football's Chargers, hosted the 2003 Super Bowl; Baseball's Padres play in PETCO Park, which opened in 2004.

Gov. Bill Owens (R)

First elected: 1998
Length of term: 4 years
Term expires: 1/07
Salary: $90,000
Phone: (303) 866-2471

Hometown: Centennial
Born: Oct. 22, 1950;
Fort Worth, Texas
Religion: Roman Catholic
Family: Separated; three children
Education: Stephen F. Austin State U., B.S.
1973; U. of Texas, M.P.A. 1975
Career: Management consultant; petroleum
association director
Political highlights: Colo. House, 1983-89;
Colo. Senate, 1989-95; Colo. treasurer,
1995-99

Election results:

2002 GENERAL
Bill Owens (R)	884,583	62.6%
Rollie Heath (D)	475,372	33.6%
Ron Forthofer (GREEN)	32,099	2.3%
Ralph Shnelvar (LIBERT)	20,547	1.5%

Lt. Gov. Jane E. Norton (R)

First elected: 2002
Length of term: 4 years
Term expires: 1/07
Salary: $68,500
Phone: (303) 866-2087

STATE LEGISLATURE

General Assembly: 120 days
January-May

House: 65 members, 2-year terms
2005 breakdown: 35D, 30R; 43 men,
22 women
Salary: $30,000
Phone: (303) 866-2904

Senate: 35 members, 4-year terms
2005 breakdown: 18D, 17R; 24 men,
11 women
Salary: $30,000
Phone: (303) 866-2316

STATE TERM LIMITS

Governor: 2 terms
House: 4 consecutive terms
Senate: 2 consecutive terms

URBAN STATISTICS

CITY	POPULATION
Denver	554,636
Colorado Springs	360,890
Aurora	276,393
Lakewood	144,126
Fort Collins	118,652

REGISTERED VOTERS

Republican	37%
Unaffiliated	32%
Democrat	30%

POPULATION

2004 population (est.)	4,601,403
2000 population	4,301,261
1990 population	3,294,394
Percent change (1990-2000)	+30.6%
Rank among states (2004)	22

Median age	34.3
Born in state	41.1%
Foreign born	8.6%
Violent crime rate	334/100,000
Poverty level	9.3%
Federal workers	51,455
Military	42,802

REDISTRICTING

Colorado gained one House seat in
reapportionment. The state legislature
failed to agree on a plan and a state
district court judge adopted a new,
seven-district map on Jan. 25, 2002.

MISCELLANEOUS

Web: www.colorado.gov
Capital: Denver
STATE ELECTION OFFICIAL
(303) 894-2200
DEMOCRATIC
HEADQUARTERS
(303) 623-4762
REPUBLICAN
HEADQUARTERS
(303) 758-3333

District Statistics

DIST.	2004 VOTE FOR PRESIDENT BUSH	KERRY	WHITE	BLACK	ASIAN	HISP	MEDIAN INCOME	WHITE COLLAR	BLUE COLLAR	SERVICE INDUSTRY	OVER 64	UNDER 18	COLLEGE EDUCATION	RURAL	SQ. MILES
1	31%	68%	54%	10%	3%	30%	$39,658	64%	21%	15%	11%	22%	34%	0%	171
2	41	58	79	1	3	15	$55,204	66	21	13	7	25	39	13	5,615
3	55	44	75	1	0	21	$35,970	56	26	17	13	25	24	39	53,963
4	58	41	79	1	1	17	$43,389	60	26	14	10	26	29	25	30,898
5	66	33	77	6	2	11	$45,454	63	21	15	9	27	30	14	7,708
6	60	39	88	2	3	6	$73,393	77	13	9	7	29	47	15	4,104
7	48	51	69	6	3	20	$46,149	63	24	13	10	25	26	2	1,258
STATE	52	47	74	4	2	17	$47,203	65	22	14	10	26	33	16	103,718
U.S.	50.7	48.3	69	12	4	13	$41,994	60	25	15	12	26	24	21	3,537,438

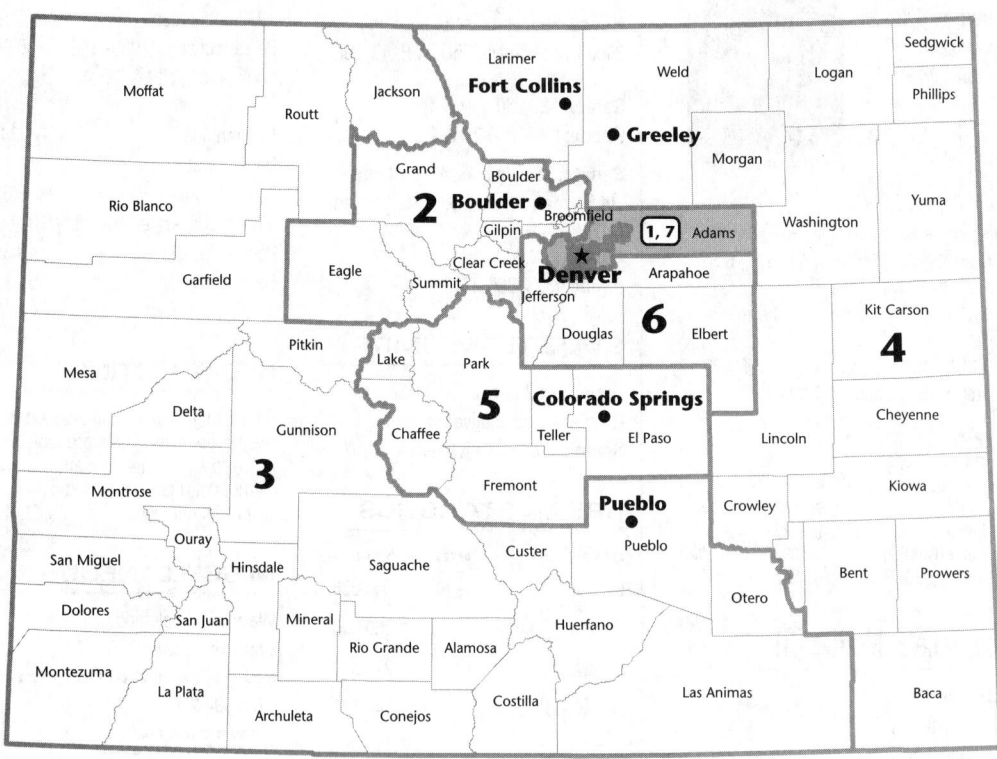

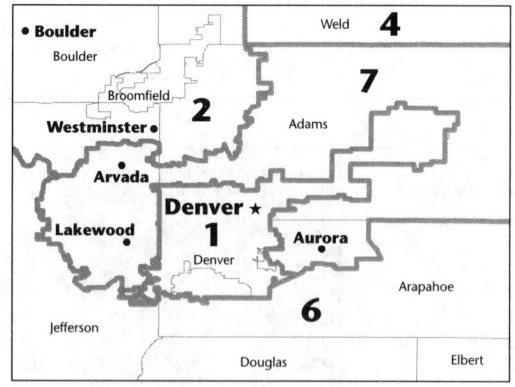

Sen. Wayne Allard (R)

Elected 1996; 2nd term

CAPITOL OFFICE
224-5941
allard.senate.gov
521 Dirksen 20510-0606; fax 224-6471

COMMITTEES
Appropriations
  (Legislative Branch - chairman)
Banking, Housing & Urban Affairs
  (Housing & Transportation - chairman)
Budget

HOMETOWN
Loveland

BORN
Dec. 2, 1943, Fort Collins, Colo.

RELIGION
Protestant

FAMILY
Wife, Joan Allard; two children

EDUCATION
Colorado State U., D.V.M. 1968

CAREER
Veterinarian

POLITICAL HIGHLIGHTS
Colo. Senate, 1983-91; U.S. House, 1991-97

ELECTION RESULTS

2002 GENERAL

Wayne Allard (R)	717,892	50.7%
Tom Strickland (D)	648,129	45.8%
Douglas Campbell (AC)	21,547	1.5%
Rick Stanley (LIBERT)	20,776	1.5%

2002 PRIMARY

Wayne Allard (R)	unopposed

PREVIOUS WINNING PERCENTAGES
1996 (51%); 1994 House Election (72%); 1992 House Election (58%); 1990 House Election (54%)

Allard's views are a good reflection of his state, which has grown increasingly conservative with the influx of high-technology entrepreneurs and suburbanites in the 1990s, but has retained a soft spot for the federal government when it comes to preserving the natural splendor of Colorado.

A product of the modern West, he is a states' rights-loving conservative with an innate skepticism of the federal government. But he sometimes is confoundingly pro-environment, to the distraction of his liberal critics who derisively describe him as "environmental lite." All in all, he appeals to the emerging class of independent-minded, conservative voter that increasingly dominates the state's politics.

A fifth-generation Coloradan raised on a ranch in one of the state's most isolated areas, Allard (AL-ard) started his career as a veterinarian. He is an amiable man with a plodding speaking style whose resolve often is underestimated by his political foes. His anti-tax and anti-regulatory positions are among the most politically conservative in the Senate. But despite the Senate's push to the right after the 2004 election, Allard was passed over for the chairmanship of the Budget Committee in favor of the more moderate Judd Gregg of New Hampshire.

Still, Allard is well-positioned to push his agenda of smaller government and strong defense. A senior member of the Budget panel, he supported President Bush's massive tax cuts in 2001 and 2003. With predictions of increasing deficits and austere budgets in the next two fiscal years, Allard is likely to be an influential figure in crafting budget resolutions.

Allard put himself on the national map in the 108th Congress by becoming the frontman in the Senate for a doomed constitutional amendment that would have defined marriage as a union of a man and a woman, effectively banning gay marriage. Allard teamed up with a fellow Colorado Republican, Rep. Marilyn Musgrave, on the amendment, which failed on a 48-50 procedural vote. He introduced the constitutional amendment again at the start of the 109th. "Activist judges and lawyers continue trying to redefine traditional marriage in literally dozens of states," he said. "The American people through their elected representatives, not unelected judges, should decide the future of marriage in our country."

While the gay marriage amendment — one of the defining issues of 2004 — raised Allard's profile in the social conservative movement, he does not want it to be his defining moment in the Senate. In fact, Allard's appointment in the 109th to the Appropriations Committee should offer him the chance to address federal spending issues. He gave up seats on Armed Services and Environment and Public Works in order to become an appropriator.

Of his service on the Environment panel, he is proudest of his legislative handiwork establishing the Great Sand Dunes National Park and converting the radioactivity-tainted Rocky Flats, a former nuclear weapons facility outside Denver, to a national wildlife refuge. At the start of the 109th Congress, he introduced a measure to establish a pristine area of land a quarter of a mile on each side of the Rio Grande River as it flows through Colorado. The bill also seeks to prevent a federal water right from being imposed on the protected area.

Yet he remains an enemy of national environmental groups, who don't like his anti-regulatory stands on clean water mandates and endangered species. The League of Conservation Voters labeled Allard one of its "dirty dozen" and supported his opponent in the 2002 election.

Allard says he tries to strike a balance between economic development and protection of the environment. "You have to be sensitive to the environment but also protect private property rights and Colorado's water rights as well," he says. "That's where I get crosswise with the environmental groups in Washington."

As the chairman of the Senate Renewable Energy and Energy Efficiency Caucus, he sponsored a bill in 2001 creating a 15 percent tax break for solar heating and electrical systems in homes. In 2000, he supported a permanent ban on commercial flights over Rocky Mountain National Park.

In the 109th, Allard remained chairman of the Banking panel's Subcommittee on Housing and Transportation. In 2000, he floated a plan to transfer most federal funds for housing and homeless programs to the states. He also noted that chairing the panel gives him the "ideal position from which to assist with Colorado's ever-increasing transportation needs" when the Senate takes up the reauthorization of highway programs in the 109th.

Allard likes to say he is party-blind when it comes to working with Colorado Democrats for the state's interests. But there is a limit to the warm feelings between him and them. When Allard ran television ads in the campaign featuring a picture of Democratic Rep. Mark Udall, who had worked with Allard on the Rocky Flats bill, Udall demanded the senator stop airing his image. Allard refused.

In his three House terms, Allard also compiled a solidly conservative record. He advocated eliminating the Education, Energy and Commerce departments and backed a constitutional amendment banning abortion.

The lawmaker subscribes to the concept of the citizen-politician. He grew up on his family's ranch, rising at dawn and working until sunset baling hay. His great-great-grandfather, a trapper and explorer, was among the first permanent settlers of northern Colorado.

Allard wanted to be a veterinarian since grade school. So after getting his degree in veterinary medicine from Colorado State University, he and his wife, Joan, a microbiologist, opened their own small-animal practice in Loveland, northwest of Denver.

Allard's first government job was as Loveland's part-time health officer. Later, he divided his time between the Colorado Senate and his veterinary practice for eight years. In 1990, Republican Hank Brown, then the 4th District representative, decided to run for the Senate, and Allard successfully sought Brown's seat.

Brown gave Allard another opening by retiring from the Senate after just one term. The 1996 GOP primary became a showdown between Allard and state Attorney General Gale A. Norton. Norton had better statewide name recognition, but Allard had better fundraising.

Both touted their conservative views. Norton hoped to attract moderates with her support for abortion rights. Allard portrayed himself as a down-to-earth, common-sense lawmaker who kept his political career in perspective, maintaining his veterinary license even though he had sold the practice in the early 1990s. Allard easily won the primary. (Norton went on to become secretary of the Interior in 2001.)

Allard created a stir in the 1996 general election when, during a televised debate with Democratic nominee Tom Strickland, he responded affirmatively to a hypothetical question about whether he would support public hanging to deter crime. Allard drew vigorous opposition from environmentalists but won strong support from conservative Christian groups, and he went on to win by 5 percentage points.

In a 2002 rematch, Strickland tried to make the environment an issue again. Allard fought back with a campaign that summed up the election as a choice between a "lawyer lobbyist or a veterinarian who loves animals."

KEY VOTES

2004
Yes   Pass $318.9 billion, six-year highway and mass transit bill
No   Extend assault weapons ban for 10 years
No   Restore pay-as-you-go rules for new tax cuts and entitlement spending
Yes   Criminalize harm to a fetus in an attack on the mother
No   Increase mandatory child care funding to states by $6 billion over five years
Yes   Amend the Constitution to prohibit same-sex marriage
Yes   Approve $146 billion multi-year extension of previously enacted middle-class tax breaks
Yes   Reorganize U.S. intelligence agencies as proposed by Sept. 11 commission
Yes   Cut corporate taxes $137 billion over 10 years

2003
No   Delay Bush changes to Clean Air Act
Yes   Allow confirmation vote on Miguel A. Estrada to the U.S. Court of Appeals for the D.C. Circuit
No   Block a Bush proposal opening Alaska's Arctic National Wildlife Refuge to oil drilling
No   Limit size of Bush's proposed tax cut to $350 billion through fiscal 2013
No   Overhaul Medicare and create prescription drug benefit
No   Block Bush rule scaling back overtime pay for some white-collar federal workers
No   Split $20 billion in Iraq aid into half-grant, half-loan
Yes   Ban "partial birth" abortion except to save a woman's life
No   Stop proposal allowing travel to Cuba
Yes   Allow final vote on energy policy overhaul

CQ VOTE STUDIES

	PARTY UNITY		PRESIDENTIAL SUPPORT	
	Support	Oppose	Support	Oppose
2004	98%	2%	98%	2%
2003	98%	2%	97%	3%
2002	91%	9%	96%	4%
2001	98%	2%	97%	3%
2000	98%	2%	35%	65%
1999	97%	3%	23%	77%
1998	97%	3%	28%	72%
1997	98%	2%	48%	52%
House Service:				
1996	94%	6%	36%	64%
1995	95%	5%	20%	80%

INTEREST GROUPS

	AFL-CIO	ADA	CCUS	ACU
2004	8%	5%	94%	96%
2003	0%	10%	100%	70%
2002	17%	5%	100%	100%
2001	6%	5%	100%	100%
2000	0%	0%	93%	100%
1999	0%	0%	100%	95%
1998	0%	5%	83%	100%
1997	0%	0%	80%	100%
House Service:				
1996	9%	10%	100%	100%
1995	0%	0%	96%	88%

Sen. Ken Salazar (D)

Elected 2004; 1st term

A centrist Democrat who strives to avoid the liberal label, Salazar won respect as an attorney and state official in Colorado. And in a state that prizes rugged individualism and homespun living, Salazar fits in perfectly, preferring a cowboy hat and bolo tie to business attire. He is a down-to-earth rancher, who is willing to work with Republicans to get things done.

Salazar made history with his 2004 victory, giving — along with Florida Republican Mel Martinez — Hispanics their first Senate presence since Democrat Joseph M. Montoya of New Mexico left in 1977. His success was important, given the weight both parties place on courting the important and fast-growing Hispanic voting bloc. But Salazar bristles at the notion that his status makes him an instant national spokesman for Hispanic issues.

"It wasn't the Hispanic community that voted me in," he told The Denver Post shortly after winning his seat. "I have to work on all the issues that affect the state of Colorado. I don't see myself working on a specific Hispanic agenda."

Still, after a White House meeting with President Bush before being sworn in, Salazar warmed to the idea of playing a prominent role on immigration and Latin American issues. Salazar's ranching background and his centrist leanings may make him a Bush ally. It's a role Salazar says he is more than willing to play.

"I told [Bush] I looked forward to working with him on a bipartisan agenda. I told him that's the way we could get things done," Salazar told the Post. "He said that the last two years it was hard to get things done since everything was so politically charged."

Salazar signaled his willingness to put partisanship aside early in the 109th Congress, when he broke with a number of Democrats to support the high-profile cabinet nominations of two of Bush's closest allies: Condoleezza Rice as secretary of State and Alberto R. Gonzales as attorney general. Even as other Democrats were lining up to condemn the nominees and tie them to what they called Bush's failures, Salazar was speaking enthusiastically in their favor. It was Salazar who introduced Gonzales at the start of his confirmation hearing before the Judiciary Committee. Salazar said he was "honored" to be presenting him and noted that "he and I come from similar backgrounds."

Salazar's early biography contributes to his image as an independent-minded politician. He was one of eight children growing up on a ranch in Colorado's mountainous San Luis Valley that his Mexican ancestors bought in 1850. Their home did not have electricity until after Salazar graduated from law school in 1981.

A Roman Catholic who favors abortion rights, Salazar nevertheless strays from his party on some issues. He supports the death penalty and has backed school voucher plans. In the debate over allowing same-sex marriage, Salazar says that marriage is between a man and a woman, but he does not support a constitutional amendment outlawing gay marriage.

Salazar sits on the Agriculture, Energy and Natural Resources and Veterans' Affairs committees. His ranching background makes him a good match for the issues addressed by the Agriculture and Energy panels. "Once you are born into a ranching and farming family, you develop a special relationship and a special sense of place through the ditches and the rivers and the trees," Salazar said during his Senate campaign.

A lifelong sportsman, Salazar believes in conservation and has been a

CAPITOL OFFICE
224-5852
www.salazar.senate.gov
702 Hart 20510-0605; fax 228-4609

COMMITTEES
Agriculture, Nutrition & Forestry
Energy & Natural Resources
Veterans' Affairs

HOMETOWN
Denver

BORN
March 2, 1955, Alamosa, Colo.

RELIGION
Roman Catholic

FAMILY
Wife, Hope Salazar; two children

EDUCATION
Colorado College, B.A. 1977 (political science);
U. of Michigan, J.D. 1981

CAREER
Lawyer; ice cream shop owner; gubernatorial aide; farmer

POLITICAL HIGHLIGHTS
Colo. Natural Resources Department executive director, 1990-94; Colo. attorney general, 1999-2005

ELECTION RESULTS

2004 GENERAL

Ken Salazar (D)	1,081,188	51.3%
Pete Coors (R)	980,668	46.5%

2004 PRIMARY

Ken Salazar (D)	173,167	73.0%
Mike Miles (D)	63,973	27.0%

strong supporter of renewable energy. He is against allowing drilling in Alaska's Arctic National Wildlife Refuge. However, he has said he supports increasing petroleum production as long as environmental concerns are adequately addressed.

On fiscal issues, Salazar is aligned with most Coloradans, who tend toward conservatism in spending decisions. He also has a unique perspective on small-business issues, derived from his experience owning a Dairy Queen in Westminster, Colo., with his wife, Hope, who runs the business. He has told interviewers it is his favorite place to eat. Salazar and his wife also have owned radio stations in Denver and Pueblo. Salazar has said he would support making some of Bush's tax cuts permanent, but only those that benefit the middle class. He supports overhauling estate tax laws, "so that family businesses can stay in the family."

On the war in Iraq, Salazar has agreed with most fellow Democrats that the war has been mishandled, but he says withdrawing troops prematurely would be devastating. Instead, he has said America must rebuild its international coalitions.

Salazar was pegged early on as a rising star by Sen. Ben Nighthorse Campbell, the Democrat-turned-Republican whose seat he ultimately won when Campbell retired. Campbell had recommended him in 1994 to head the Bureau of Land Management (BLM). That was after Salazar had distinguished himself as a successful lawyer specializing in water and resources issues, and had interrupted his quick rise at a well-heeled Denver law firm to become chief counsel for Colorado's then-Gov. Roy Romer.

Salazar got his first taste of Capitol Hill in the early 1990s as Colorado's director of natural resources, when he testified before Congress about water bills that would benefit his state. He won plaudits from both parties for crafting a program that used lottery funds for land conservation. Rather than take up Campbell's suggestion to join the federal government as the BLM chief, Salazar heeded the call of family and routine and returned to private practice. He also made time to coach his two young daughters' basketball team.

Although he is sometimes accused of grandstanding, Salazar has mostly won praise from Republicans and Democrats for being a straight shooter and sharp negotiator. He won his first elective office in 1998, as Republican Gov. Bill Owens' attorney general, and stayed on for six years. As attorney general, he led a successful effort to squelch a ballot initiative to fund $2 million in water projects that western Coloradans worried would benefit urban Denver at the expense of rural areas.

Salazar's national stature rose in 1999, when he joined Owens in a bipartisan response to the Columbine High School tragedy. The two organized a summit on youth violence and pushed through a ballot measure to limit firearms sales at gun shows. But Salazar didn't always side with state Republicans. He broke with Owens in 2003 to oppose a GOP redistricting effort, which ultimately failed.

Campbell's surprise retirement in 2004 gave Salazar an opening to run for the Senate, but he faced an uphill battle against well-financed beer magnate Pete Coors, a handsome political neophyte with unrivaled name recognition. The race was one of the closest in the country, and drew money and volunteers from far and wide. Salazar's up-from-the-bootstraps biography and independent image proved a favorable comparison to Coors' more privileged upbringing. Salazar's 5 percentage point victory was a rare bright spot for Democrats, who lost many of their most competitive 2004 contests.

Salazar has company as he settles into Washington. His older brother, John, also moved to the nation's capital to represent Colorado's 3rd District.

Rep. Diana DeGette (D)

Elected 1996; 5th term

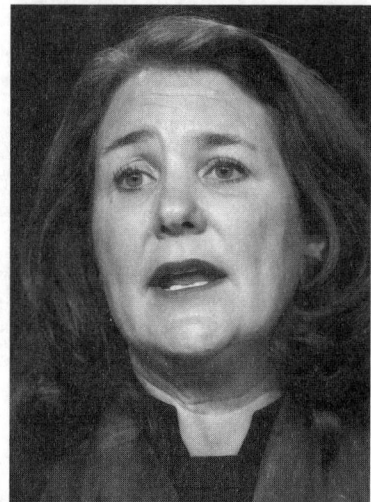

CAPITOL OFFICE
225-4431
degette@mail.house.gov
www.house.gov/degette
1527 Longworth 20515-0601; fax 225-5657

COMMITTEES
Energy & Commerce

HOMETOWN
Denver

BORN
July 29, 1957, Tachikawa, Japan

RELIGION
Presbyterian

FAMILY
Husband, Lino Lipinsky; two children

EDUCATION
Colorado College, B.A. 1979 (political science);
New York U., J.D. 1982

CAREER
Lawyer; state public defender

POLITICAL HIGHLIGHTS
Colo. House, 1993-96 (assistant minority leader,
1995-96)

ELECTION RESULTS

2004 GENERAL

Diana DeGette (D)	177,077	73.5%
Roland Chicas (R)	58,659	24.4%
George C. Lilly (AC)	5,193	2.2%

2004 PRIMARY

Diana DeGette (D)	unopposed

2002 GENERAL

Diana DeGette (D)	111,718	66.3%
Ken Chlouber (R)	49,884	29.6%
Ken Seaman (GREEN)	3,209	1.9%
Kent Leonard (LIBERT)	2,584	1.5%

PREVIOUS WINNING PERCENTAGES
2000 (69%); 1998 (67%); 1996 (57%)

Although she is now in her fifth term, DeGette has never known what it is like to be in the majority. So she tries to temper President Bush's initiatives by reaching out to moderate Republicans in an effort to find common ground. Sometimes this works and sometimes it doesn't as her own temperament can alternate between affable and fiery.

A member of the Energy and Commerce Committee, DeGette (de-GET) weighs in on issues ranging from health care to corporate scandals. In 2004, she teamed up with Delaware Republican Michael N. Castle to press for legislation allowing federally funded research on all existing stem cell lines. But in a nod to conservatives, the bill would not have permitted federally funded researchers to continue to derive new lines, which require the destruction of an embryo. "By expanding federal support for stem cell research . . . government has an opportunity to help end the suffering of millions of people with chronic or terminal diseases," she said.

DeGette also crossed the aisle to support a bill by James C. Greenwood of Pennsylvania to permit human cloning for medical research, while banning it for the purposes of starting a pregnancy.

Although neither gambit made it through the House, DeGette had more success with another medical bill in the 108th Congress. The House passed her plan to authorize $1 million to help those with juvenile diabetes by increasing patient access to islet cell transplantation, a procedure that infuses new insulin-producing cells into a patient. Her perspective is shaped by personal experience: one of her daughters has diabetes.

In the 107th, DeGette won enactment of a law to require that medical devices for children be reviewed by pediatric experts before they are put on the market. She has also pushed to give children priority on organ transplant lists.

By reaching across the aisle, DeGette has shown a deft legislative touch while at the same time proving herself a dependable liberal ally of her party's leadership. In the 109th Congress, she will serve as one of six chief deputy whips, helping Whip Steny H. Hoyer of Maryland corral House Democrats' votes while also serving on the Democratic Caucus Steering and Policy Committee and developing strategy.

DeGette made an auspicious arrival on Capitol Hill in 1997 with her appointment to Energy and Commerce; she was the only freshman Democrat named to an exclusive House panel that year. Using that assignment, DeGette soon made her presence felt on a broad array of topics: the budget, abortion rights, gun control, health care and tobacco regulation.

She was particularly fierce on corporate responsibility issues as the panel launched its investigations of business scandals, beginning with the bankruptcy of the energy behemoth Enron Corp. She also took on one of the 1st District's biggest employers, the regional telephone giant Qwest Communications International Inc. Some lawmakers would have tried to defend the hometown company; but DeGette used Qwest to demonstrate her pro-consumer views. She said Qwest's "bad business decisions have had a significant impact on our local economy, the local workforce and the community as a whole."

She is a staunch defender of legalized abortion, and she co-chairs the congressional Pro-Choice Caucus. DeGette offers an amendment annually to lift a ban on federal funding for abortions for women in federal prisons. She also has defended the controversial late-term procedure described by its critics as "partial birth" abortion. "To assume that any woman would choose this tragic procedure after carrying a healthy fetus for 8 or 9 months is offensive to the women who are facing this gruesome decision," she has said.

Her longtime support of gun control intensified after 15 people died in the 1999 rampage at Columbine High School, just outside her district. In the 107th, she fought legislation that moved through Energy and Commerce to shield gun manufacturers from lawsuits.

Although she posts a reliably liberal and partisan voting record, she is not reluctant to change her opinion when she feels it is warranted, such as on legislation to make it easier to import prescription drugs. On the House floor in 2003, she held up a plastic bag of brightly colored pills, which she said were all fakes, each with a brand name embossed on it. "I used to think I supported this legislation," she said, adding that she changed her mind after an Energy committee hearing that exposed "tons of [counterfeit] drugs coming into this country right now."

DeGette's father was serving in the Air Force and stationed in Japan when she was born, but most of her childhood was spent in the Denver area. When her parents divorced, DeGette, the eldest of five children, took some after-school jobs to help pay the bills. She recalls being profoundly affected, at age 10, by the news coverage of the assassination of the Rev. Dr. Martin Luther King Jr., which broadened her horizons and instilled in her an interest in the civil rights movement.

After earning her law degree at New York University, she was a public defender in Denver before going into private law practice, where she specialized in cases of discrimination based on disability, sex and age.

She was active in local party politics and won a seat in the Colorado House in 1992. As a freshman, DeGette won enactment of a law — upheld by the Supreme Court in 2000 — requiring protesters to stay 8 feet away from anyone within 100 feet of the entrance to a clinic where abortions are performed. She made it to the party leadership but early in 1996 resigned from the legislature to concentrate on her bid to succeed liberal Democratic Rep. Patricia Schroeder in Congress.

DeGette won a highly publicized battle with Republican nominee Joe Rogers, a lawyer and former aide to Colorado GOP Sen. Hank Brown. Rogers, who is black, got the endorsement of a group of black ministers, but DeGette was backed by Denver Mayor Wellington Webb, a black Democrat. Outspending her opponent 2-to-1, she won by 17 percentage points. Her four re-elections have been with two-thirds or more of the vote.

KEY VOTES

2004
? Extend federal unemployment benefits by 13 weeks
Yes Pass $283.2 billion, six-year federal highway and mass transit bill
No Approve $146 billion multi-year extension of previously enacted middle-class tax breaks
No Amend the Constitution to prohibit same-sex marriage
No Cut corporate taxes $137 billion over 10 years
Yes Reorganize U.S. intelligence agencies as proposed by Sept. 11 commission

2003
No Cut taxes by $330 billion through fiscal 2013
Yes Block Bush rule scaling back overtime pay for some white-collar federal workers
Yes Do not allow use of search warrants without first notifying subjects
No Allow importation of prescription drugs
? Create private school voucher program in Washington, D.C.
No Ban "partial birth" abortion except to save a woman's life
No Split $18.6 billion in Iraq aid into half-grant, half-loan
No Overhaul Medicare and create prescription drug benefit

CQ VOTE STUDIES

	PARTY UNITY		PRESIDENTIAL SUPPORT	
	Support	Oppose	Support	Oppose
2004	97%	3%	29%	71%
2003	96%	4%	30%	70%
2002	98%	2%	25%	75%
2001	96%	4%	23%	77%
2000	93%	7%	88%	12%

INTEREST GROUPS

	AFL-CIO	ADA	CCUS	ACU
2004	100%	90%	37%	0%
2003	86%	90%	31%	17%
2002	100%	95%	35%	0%
2001	100%	95%	39%	0%
2000	90%	75%	47%	8%

COLORADO 1

Denver

Mostly within the capital city of Denver, the 1st is a bastion of liberalism in a conservative-leaning state. A Republican last won Denver's House seat in 1970, and Ronald Reagan, in 1980, was the last Republican to carry Denver for president. John Kerry received 68 percent of the district's vote in the 2004 presidential election, easily his highest percentage in the state.

Denver's diversity — the fast-growing Hispanic community makes up nearly a third of the city's population while blacks make up more than a tenth — is reflected by residents' electoral decisions. Federico Peña, a Hispanic who later served in Bill Clinton's Cabinet, served eight years as mayor before Wellington Webb, an African-American, served three terms until leaving office in 2003. City officials are using the $5 billion Denver International Airport, which opened in 1995 and has become one of the nation's 10 busiest, to increase exports and lure European and Asian companies to locate or expand their business here.

Dependent on the region's oil and gas industries, Denver suffered during

the oil bust of the 1980s, but the city boomed in the 1990s. The economy became more diversified as technology and telecommunications industries revitalized downtown and surrounding areas. The former Lowry Air Force Base is now an education center; the former Fitzsimons Army Medical Center is home to the University of Colorado medical school and a bioscience research park. New baseball (1995) and football (2001) stadiums, as well as a new arena (1999), opened in Denver over the past decade.

Ninety percent of the 1st District's residents live in Denver. The rest live just south of the city, in well-off communities such as Englewood and Cherry Hills Village.

MAJOR INDUSTRY
Telecommunications, computers, health care, government

CITIES
Denver, 554,636; Englewood, 31,727

NOTABLE
The Great American Beer Festival is the nation's largest and oldest annual brewing competition; The U.S. Mint coin production facility in Denver is one of three U.S. locations that stores gold bullion and is the only one that allows visitors.

Rep. Mark Udall (D)

Elected 1998; 4th term

Udall was 10 years old when his father, the legendarily witty and energetic liberal Morris K. Udall, first won election to the House from Arizona in 1961. He shares two striking characteristics with his father: a commitment to public service and a love of the outdoors. When Udall won his House seat in 1998, he pledged to follow his father's example as a staunch environmentalist and Democratic loyalist — a vow that became more poignant when the elder Udall died a month after his son's election, following a battle with Parkinson's disease.

Now in his fourth House term, Udall is looking to expand his political horizons. He briefly entered the 2004 Colorado Senate race when Republican Sen. Ben Nighthorse Campbell retired, but backed away once state Attorney General Ken Salazar decided to run. After rejecting the idea of a run for the governorship in 2006, Udall announced in early 2005 that he would run for the Senate in 2008.

Despite, or maybe because of, his statewide aspirations, Udall seems determined to push ahead with legislation that matters both to him and to Colorado. In the 109th Congress, he gained a seat on the Armed Services Committee where he said he plans to focus on the war in Iraq, military modernization and Colorado's military installations. "As a critic of the Bush administration's policy in Iraq, I am deeply concerned about the escalating cost of our efforts there," Udall said. "If approved, the president's latest request will bring the total cost to nearly $300 billion. This amount is breathtaking, but we cannot fail to supply our troops."

Udall had voted in 2002 against authorizing President Bush to go to war against Iraq, saying he feared a large-scale conflict could result in thousands of U.S. casualties. He traveled to the region two years later and said afterward that the United States has an obligation to succeed in fostering democracy there.

Udall also sits on the Science Committee, where he is the top-ranking Democrat on the Space and Aeronautics Subcommittee. On Science, he worked with his Colorado colleagues to pass a plan to keep undeveloped a 6,000-acre zone around the contaminated and decommissioned Rocky Flats nuclear weapons plant in his district once the area is rehabilitated. Udall is also concerned about the health of the former workers at Rocky Flats, saying there "were serious administrative shortcomings in the way workers' exposure to radiation was monitored and documented." He introduced a measure early in the 109th to speed up the government's compensation and care process for Rocky Flats workers, who may have health problems as a result of their work.

Udall has also used his Science post to protect funds for Colorado's federal labs and to save the Hubble telescope. He expressed concern when the Bush administration decided not to provide funding for a Hubble repair mission when its budget was released in February 2005. He said it was "incomprehensible" that the Bush administration would provide no funding to repair the Hubble, after "all that we know about Hubble's potential to produce even more spectacular science for years to come."

Yet no issue strikes more of a chord with Udall than the environment. His father and his uncle Stewart, who was Interior secretary in the Kennedy and Johnson administrations, were instrumental in writing land preservation policy in the West. From his seat on the Resources Committee, Udall can see a portrait of his father, who chaired the panel from 1977 to 1991.

CAPITOL OFFICE
225-2161
www.house.gov/markudall
240 Cannon 20515-0602; fax 226-7840

COMMITTEES
Armed Services
Resources
Science

HOMETOWN
Eldorado Springs

BORN
July 18, 1950, Tucson, Ariz.

RELIGION
Unspecified

FAMILY
Wife, Maggie Fox; two children

EDUCATION
Williams College, B.A. 1972 (American civilization)

CAREER
Colo. Outward Bound School executive director

POLITICAL HIGHLIGHTS
Colo. House, 1997-99

ELECTION RESULTS

2004 GENERAL

Mark Udall (D)	207,900	67.2%
Stephen M. Hackman (R)	94,160	30.4%
Norm Olsen (LIBERT)	7,304	2.4%

2004 PRIMARY

Mark Udall (D)	unopposed

2002 GENERAL

Mark Udall (D)	123,504	60.1%
Sandy Hume (R)	75,564	36.8%
Norm Olsen (LIBERT)	3,579	1.7%

PREVIOUS WINNING PERCENTAGES
2000 (55%); 1998 (50%)

In the 108th Congress, Udall was co-chairman of the Renewable and Energy Efficiency Caucus. And in 2004, he cosponsored with a leading state Republican the successful movement to pass a ballot initiative to boost the amount of electricity provided by in-state utilities that is derived by renewable energy. He and his cousin, Rep. Tom Udall of New Mexico, have promoted bills to create a program to encourage volunteers to help federal agencies preserve parks, forests and other sensitive tracts.

When wildfires scorched large sections of Colorado in 2002, Udall was wary of a Bush administration plan to ease some environmental rules to allow more cutting of small trees and underbrush that can help fuel blazes. He feared such rollbacks ultimately would open the door to larger and less environmentally sensitive logging. But he later helped broker a compromise on the issue and voted for the final plan.

Udall is an accomplished mountaineer who has climbed within a few thousand feet of Mount Everest's summit. He is also the former executive director of the Colorado Outward Bound School, and he says people have to take risks and believe in causes to be true leaders.

The tall, telegenic lawmaker is popular with colleagues from both parties and regarded as thoughtful, principled and deliberative. He will work with Colorado Republicans on conservation measures, such as a 2002 law that designated more than 30,000 acres in the James Peak area as wilderness, restricting development. He also teamed with GOP Rep. Tom Tancredo to seek highway funds for improvements to the Boulder Turnpike.

In the 108th, drawing on his reputation as one of the fittest members of Congress, Udall joined with Republican colleague Zach Wamp of Tennessee to form the Congressional Fitness Caucus as a forum to encourage lawmakers to get more exercise.

On domestic policy, Udall stays close to his party, voting with fellow Democrats about 95 percent of the time.

Udall can be an aggressive campaigner. In his first House race for the seat Democrat David E. Skaggs gave up after a dozen years, Udall hammered hard when his GOP opponent, former Boulder Mayor Bob Greenlee, questioned the scientific validity of global warming. Udall also campaigned hard door-to-door to prove he was a "legitimate Coloradan" and not just trying to capitalize on a famous name. In one of the more costly House races that year, Udall prevailed by just 5,500 votes, less than 3 percent. His victory margin has steadily increased, reaching 37 percentage points in 2004.

In his House office, Udall keeps a pair of his father's size 15, white high-top sneakers, a joking reminder that he has big legislative shoes to fill.

KEY VOTES

2004
Yes	Extend federal unemployment benefits by 13 weeks
Yes	Pass $283.2 billion, six-year federal highway and mass transit bill
?	Approve $146 billion multi-year extension of previously enacted middle-class tax breaks
No	Amend the Constitution to prohibit same-sex marriage
Yes	Cut corporate taxes $137 billion over 10 years
Yes	Reorganize U.S. intelligence agencies as proposed by Sept. 11 commission

2003
No	Cut taxes by $330 billion through fiscal 2013
Yes	Block Bush rule scaling back overtime pay for some white-collar federal workers
Yes	Do not allow use of search warrants without first notifying subjects
No	Allow importation of prescription drugs
No	Create private school voucher program in Washington, D.C.
No	Ban "partial birth" abortion except to save a woman's life
Yes	Split $18.6 billion in Iraq aid into half-grant, half-loan
No	Overhaul Medicare and create prescription drug benefit

CQ VOTE STUDIES

	PARTY UNITY		PRESIDENTIAL SUPPORT	
	Support	Oppose	Support	Oppose
2004	94%	6%	32%	68%
2003	95%	5%	24%	76%
2002	93%	7%	33%	67%
2001	96%	4%	30%	70%
2000	93%	7%	77%	23%

INTEREST GROUPS

	AFL-CIO	ADA	CCUS	ACU
2004	93%	100%	53%	8%
2003	83%	80%	32%	18%
2002	89%	95%	40%	4%
2001	100%	100%	35%	0%
2000	90%	85%	47%	12%

COLORADO 2
Northwest Denver suburbs; Boulder

The liberal "granola" culture of Boulder — home to the University of Colorado and a committed corps of environmentalists — permeates much of the 2nd. But the district is mostly moderate in its political tone, exhibiting a slight but hardly overwhelming Democratic lean.

After a decade of strong growth, redistricting following the 2000 census redrew the 2nd to include more of Adams County, which is adjacent to Denver and has a blue-collar tone, and less of Boulder County, which had been entirely within the district. The 2nd also shed most of its share of fast-growing suburban Jefferson County.

Although they contain only a fraction of the 2nd's voters, Eagle, Grand and Summit counties, which were added during redistricting, form an overwhelming majority of the district's land area. Skiing is king in these mountain counties on the district's western border; the resort city of Vail is in Eagle County. The 2nd also includes some communities north of Denver in southwestern Weld County.

Environmental issues play heavily here, and because Boulder has been one of the fastest-growing cities in the state, urban sprawl has gained attention. Another concern is the Rocky Flats facility, a former nuclear plant located near the Boulder-Jefferson county line, which became a removal and cleanup site now scheduled to close by December 2006.

Education is a high priority in the 2nd, site of the state's flagship university and several federal research labs. The liberal strain in the academic community helped Green Party presidential nominee Ralph Nader garner 12 percent of the Boulder County vote in 2000, well above his statewide total of 5 percent. But newcomers — those who can overcome Boulder's slow-growth regulations and afford a home in the resulting high-priced real estate market — tend to be more fiscally conservative than voters past.

MAJOR INDUSTRY
Information technology, government laboratories, higher education

CITIES
Westminster (pt.), 100,850; Boulder, 94,673; Thornton (pt.), 82,378

NOTABLE
The atomic clock at the National Institute of Standards and Technology in Boulder is the nation's official timekeeper.

Rep. John Salazar (D)

CAPITOL OFFICE
225-4761
john.salazar@mail.house.gov
www.house.gov/salazar
1531 Longworth 20515-0603; fax 226-0622

COMMITTEES
Agriculture
Transportation & Infrastructure

HOMETOWN
Manassa

BORN
July 21, 1953, Alamosa, Colo.

RELIGION
Roman Catholic

FAMILY
Wife, Mary Lou Salazar; three children

EDUCATION
Colorado State U., attended 1971-72; Adams State College, B.S. 1981 (business)

MILITARY SERVICE
Army, 1973-76

CAREER
Farmer; rancher; seed potato business owner

POLITICAL HIGHLIGHTS
Colo. Agricultural Commission, 1999-2002; Colo. House, 2003-04

ELECTION RESULTS

2004 GENERAL

John Salazar (D)	153,500	50.6%
Greg Walcher (R)	141,376	46.6%
Jim Krug (X)	8,770	2.9%

2004 PRIMARY

John Salazar (D)	unopposed

Elected 2004; 1st term

Salazar got a bit more notice than most in the House Class of 2004, because he is half of Colorado's newly arrived lawmaking team: He won in the 3rd District on the same day that his younger brother, Democrat Ken Salazar, won election to the Senate.

The Salazars decided to share a downtown D.C. apartment, which John Salazar hinted might need housekeeping help. "I think we're both Oscars," he quipped, referring to the sloppy half of comedy's "The Odd Couple."

In succeeding retired GOP Rep. Scott McInnis in the Republican-leaning 3rd, Salazar was one of just five Democrats in 2004 to win a GOP-held seat. The Salazars' victories underscored the increasing clout of Hispanics in Colorado politics.

Salazar's top priority is ensuring that water from the snowmelt of Colorado's Western Slope is retained instead of being sent to growing populations in California and Nevada — a paramount issue for ranchers and farmers in his sprawling district, which is larger than Florida.

His committee assignments are in keeping with his interests in water and farm issues. He has seats on Agriculture and on Transportation, where he serves on the Water Resources and Environment Subcommittee.

Salazar, a fifth-generation farmer and rancher, has proposed a federally funded water easement program for Colorado's agricultural land. He is a self-styled centrist who joins most of his constituents in opposing further gun controls. As a state legislator, Salazar led efforts to allow state agencies to pool their resources to negotiate for lower prices on drug purchases.

A military veteran, Salazar has denounced cuts in veterans' health care benefits and is concerned about the demands put on families of National Guard members and reservists serving in Iraq. The latter issue is personal for Salazar: He has a son in the Colorado National Guard.

Salazar was unopposed for the Democratic nomination in 2004, while Republican Greg Walcher, a former director of the state Department of Natural Resources, survived a fractious primary. Despite a strong showing by President Bush in the district, Salazar managed a 4 percentage point win.

COLORADO 3
Western Slope; Pueblo

The expansive 3rd, which captures Colorado's entire western border and all but one county on its southern edge, displays some of the abundant variety found outside the state's urban centers: the rural poor, the resort rich, the old steel mill town and the isolated Hispanic counties.

Water and land are two of the 3rd's hottest issues. Most of the state's rivers flow down the Western Slope to Nevada and California, and farmers here would like to see more of that water stored for local use. Meanwhile, residential development has driven up property values.

A century of boom-and-bust mineral speculation — in gold, silver, uranium and shale oil — has left the Western Slope dotted with small, struggling towns. The San Luis Valley and rural areas west of Interstate 25 have been hardest hit. Profits also have shrunk in other economic mainstays, namely cattle ranching in the west and steel production in Pueblo. But with plenty of national parks and ski resorts, tourism has quickly filled the void.

Residential Colorado has spilled over the Continental Divide onto the Western Slope. Many of the newcomers came to the area to build rustic retirement homes and they tend to vote Republican. But Pueblo County, the district's most populous, is heavily unionized, more than one-third Hispanic and supports Democrats. Some other areas have a liberal strain, including San Miguel County, which includes Telluride, and Pitkin County, which takes in the Aspen ski resort. Overall, George W. Bush took 55 percent of the vote in 2004.

MAJOR INDUSTRY
Tourism, skiing, agriculture

CITIES
Pueblo, 102,121; Grand Junction, 41,986

NOTABLE
Federal Citizen Information Center in Pueblo.

Rep. Marilyn Musgrave (R)

Elected 2002; 2nd term

CAPITOL OFFICE
225-4676
rep.musgrave@mail.house.gov
www.house.gov/musgrave
1507 Longworth 20515-0604; fax 225-5870

COMMITTEES
Agriculture
Education & Workforce
Resources
Small Business
  (Workforce, Empowerment & Government
  Programs - chairwoman)

HOMETOWN
Fort Morgan

BORN
Jan. 27, 1949, Greeley, Colo.

RELIGION
Assemblies of God

FAMILY
Husband, Steve Musgrave; four children

EDUCATION
Colorado State U., B.A. 1972 (social studies)

CAREER
Homemaker; teacher

POLITICAL HIGHLIGHTS
Morgan County School Board, 1990-94; Colo.
House, 1995-99; Colo. Senate, 1999-2003

ELECTION RESULTS

2004 GENERAL

Marilyn Musgrave (R)	155,958	51.1%
Stan Matsunaka (D)	136,812	44.8%
Bob Kinsey (GREEN)	12,739	4.2%

2004 PRIMARY

Marilyn Musgrave (R)	44,649	78.1%
Bob Faust (R)	12,553	22.0%

2002 GENERAL

Marilyn Musgrave (R)	115,359	55.0%
Stan Matsunaka (D)	87,499	41.7%
John Volz (LIBERT)	7,097	3.4%

Musgrave may remind her colleagues of a doting grandmother but they don't often mistake her politics for the warm, maternal sort. She is an uncompromising social conservative from the wide open eastern third of Colorado, where people generally are skeptical of the federal government and disdainful of what they view as a too permissive society.

In her first term, Musgrave shot to prominence as the chief House sponsor of a proposed constitutional amendment banning same-sex marriage, an issue that gained unexpected momentum when President Bush endorsed it in his 2004 re-election campaign. Overnight, Musgrave was being quoted on the radio by conservative guru Rush Limbaugh and was being courted by The Wall Street Journal and other national media.

A former schoolteacher and grandmother of five who married her high school sweetheart, Musgrave is an unapologetic general in the culture wars. Her non-threatening personality serves to soften the edges of the gay marriage debate and other polarizing issues. A former colleague in the Colorado legislature recalls how once, in the heat of political battle, Musgrave produced a needle and thread and mended the unraveled hem of his suit jacket at her desk on the state Senate floor.

The liberals who hate her politics say she is always respectful and friendly, even as she refuses to budge on policy. Musgrave led the fight in her state for citizens to carry concealed weapons, and then voted against the final version of the bill because it required gun owners to pass a background check and a handgun safety course — conditions even the National Rifle Association settled for but Musgrave didn't like. As she once told the Denver Post: "If you're an elected official, if you need to be told how cute you are every week, then you're in for a very unhappy life."

She is a strong advocate of cutting taxes, limiting the Endangered Species Act in favor of private landowners and outlawing abortion except in cases of rape, incest and endangerment to the mother.

Musgrave's signature initiative would amend the Constitution to define marriage exclusively as the union of a man and a woman. She introduced the measure in May 2003, just five months into her first year in the House.

It received little attention until two crucial events occurred. The Massachusetts Supreme Judicial Court in November sanctioned gay marriage in that state. Then the following January, Bush spoke approvingly of her resolution in his State of the Union address. Musgrave told the Denver Post: "Some of the things in the culture wars are not very easily understood, but people get this one." In a 2004 House vote, her bill failed to get the two-thirds required for constitutional amendments, but it did attract 227 votes.

Bush himself got a taste of Musgrave's intransigence when he tried, without success, to get her vote on his 2003 Medicare prescription drug bill, which was a top domestic initiative of his first term. Musgrave was one of only 25 Republicans who refused to support the legislation despite an intense lobbying campaign by the White House and a rare decision by the GOP leadership to hold open the evening floor vote until nearly dawn.

The same year, she clashed publicly with Transportation and Infrastructure Chairman Don Young of Alaska, a fellow Republican, who wanted her vote for an 8-cent increase in the federal gasoline tax. Musgrave led the GOP opposition to the tax increase in the massive highway bill, then quietly requested funding for projects in her district. A furious Young told her she would get no such consideration, but Musgrave got party leaders to intervene on her behalf. Young ultimately agreed to $14 million in special projects for her district.

Musgrave's early life was a struggle against adversity in tiny rural Eaton, Colo. Her father, a laborer in a meatpacking plant, struggled with alcoholism. The family moved frequently and never seemed to have enough money. Musgrave cleaned houses and waited tables to earn a degree from Colorado State University.

She rejected the liberal campus philosophy of the 1960s, eschewed student protests and wondered at a professor who asserted that every citizen deserved a guaranteed income. She felt that people were entitled to an income but only if they worked. While still in school, she married childhood sweetheart Steve Musgrave, a Colorado Farm Bureau insurance agent; she taught school for a while but quit to raise the couple's four children.

She volunteered at a local anti-abortion center, then decided to run for the Morgan County School Board because she thought students needed more academic rigor and discipline.

She went on to serve a total of eight years in the Colorado General Assembly, first getting elected to the House in 1994 and later to the Senate. She was instrumental in passing the state's same-sex marriage law, continually reintroducing it though Democratic Gov. Roy Romer vetoed it twice. It was finally signed into law by Republican Gov. Bill Owens. She also led a push to exempt farm and ranch equipment from sales taxes, and was a steadfast defender of gun owners' rights, including the concealed weapons proposal.

When Republican Rep. Bob Schaffer announced in late 2001 that he would honor a term-limit pledge and retire, Musgrave jumped to contest for the open seat. She won the GOP nod by defeating former Weld County GOP Chairman Jeff Bedingfield, with 65 percent of the vote.

In the general campaign, Democrats put up a formidable candidate in state Senate President Stan Matsunaka of Loveland, who had blocked many of Musgrave's statehouse initiatives and who had a history of winning in Republican-leaning areas. He portrayed Musgrave as an extremist; she countered by denouncing him as the too liberal "Stan the Tax Man." Musgrave had a big fundraising advantage, with support from Gun Owners of America, the National Pro-Life Alliance and giant retailer Wal-Mart's political action committee. She won by 13 percentage points, continuing a Republican streak in the district dating to 1972.

In 2004, Matsunaka was back for a rematch. Musgrave defeated him again, winning re-election, but by a smaller, 6 percentage point margin.

KEY VOTES

2004
No Extend federal unemployment benefits by 13 weeks
Yes Pass $283.2 billion, six-year federal highway and mass transit bill
Yes Approve $146 billion multi-year extension of previously enacted middle-class tax breaks
Yes Amend the Constitution to prohibit same-sex marriage
Yes Cut corporate taxes $137 billion over 10 years
Yes Reorganize U.S. intelligence agencies as proposed by Sept. 11 commission

2003
Yes Cut taxes by $330 billion through fiscal 2013
No Block Bush rule scaling back overtime pay for some white-collar federal workers
Yes Do not allow use of search warrants without first notifying subjects
Yes Allow importation of prescription drugs
Yes Create private school voucher program in Washington, D.C.
Yes Ban "partial birth" abortion except to save a woman's life
No Split $18.6 billion in Iraq aid into half-grant, half-loan
No Overhaul Medicare and create prescription drug benefit

CQ VOTE STUDIES

	PARTY UNITY		PRESIDENTIAL SUPPORT	
	Support	Oppose	Support	Oppose
2004	98%	2%	85%	15%
2003	96%	4%	85%	15%

INTEREST GROUPS

	AFL-CIO	ADA	CCUS	ACU
2004	7%	0%	100%	100%
2003	7%	15%	93%	96%

COLORADO 4
North and east — Fort Collins, Greeley

The 4th, which covers Colorado's eastern plains and touches five other states, looks more like Kansas than Colorado. Intensive irrigation has turned these prairies where buffalo roamed into productive wheat and corn fields. Cattle production in the eastern counties ranks among the highest in the nation. But as demand for beef has fallen and wheat prices have declined, ranchers and farmers have faced hard times.

Fort Collins — the district's most populous city and home to Colorado State University — sits more than 50 miles from Boulder and Denver, but it has been able to cash in on the recent economic boom in the Front Range. Some technology industries have moved into the city, and the relatively low cost of living has attracted new residents.

The 4th has a long history of supporting GOP House members, and most of the district includes rural Republican territory. Almost every county entirely in the 4th gave George W. Bush more than two-thirds of its vote in the 2004 presidential election, with Cheyenne County awarding Bush a statewide high of 81 percent and Washington County giving him his second-highest total. Fort Collins is an exception to the district's strong GOP tilt and tends to support Democrats in local elections. Overall, Bush took 58 percent of the district's vote in 2004.

Redistricting following the 2000 census stripped the fast-growing 4th of several counties in the northwestern (Adams, Arapahoe and Elbert) and southwestern (Las Animas, most of Otero) parts of the district. The Republican-leaning northeastern portion of Boulder County, including the city of Longmont, was added.

MAJOR INDUSTRY
Agriculture, meatpacking, higher education, manufacturing

CITIES
Fort Collins, 118,652; Greeley, 76,930; Longmont, 71,093; Loveland, 50,608

NOTABLE
The Greeley Independence Stampede is a rodeo and country music festival held annually during the week of July 4th; The Kit Carson County Carousel, in Burlington, bills itself as the nation's only antique carousel that still has the original paint on the scenery and animals; The Overland Trail Museum in Sterling commemorates the route along the South Platte River that was used during 19th century western migration.

Rep. Joel Hefley (R)

Elected 1986; 10th term

CAPITOL OFFICE
225-4422
www.house.gov/hefley
2372 Rayburn 20515-0605; fax 225-1942

COMMITTEES
Armed Services
(Readiness - chairman)

HOMETOWN
Colorado Springs

BORN
April 18, 1935, Ardmore, Okla.

RELIGION
Presbyterian

FAMILY
Wife, Lynn Hefley; three children

EDUCATION
Oklahoma Baptist U., B.A. 1957; Oklahoma State U., M.S. 1962

CAREER
Community planner; management consultant

POLITICAL HIGHLIGHTS
Colo. House, 1977-79; Colo. Senate, 1979-87 (assistant majority leader, 1981-86)

ELECTION RESULTS

2004 GENERAL

Joel Hefley (R)	193,333	70.6%
Fred Hardee (D)	74,098	27.0%
Arthur "Rob" Roberts (LIBERT)	6,627	2.4%

2004 PRIMARY

Joel Hefley (R)	52,282	84.2%
Mike Payton (R)	9,785	15.8%

2002 GENERAL

Joel Hefley (R)	128,118	69.4%
Curtis Imrie (D)	45,587	24.7%
Biff Baker (LIBERT)	10,972	5.9%

PREVIOUS WINNING PERCENTAGES
2000 (83%); 1998 (73%); 1996 (72%); 1994 (100%); 1992 (71%); 1990 (66%); 1988 (75%); 1986 (70%)

After years of relative obscurity, Hefley became an unlikely irritant to House Republican leaders in the 108th Congress when, as chairman of the Committee on Standards of Official Conduct, he presided over three admonitions of Majority Leader Tom DeLay. The two men have never been friends, but the committee actions were more a reflection of an ornery independence that Hefley exhibits from time to time. Hefley said he did not want majority Republicans to rule with the same arrogance that Democrats exhibited when they were the majority party.

Republican leaders summarily ousted Hefley from his chairmanship and removed him from the committee in early 2005, saying GOP rules limited his tenure as chairman. But Hefley, who predicted his own demise, said the move smelled of political payback.

The committee's action raised doubts among Republicans that DeLay could ever ascend to the speakership when J. Dennis Hastert retires, a major setback for DeLay's career ambitions. Hefley and the committee rebuked him for appearing to link political donations to legislative favors and for directing the Federal Aviation Administration to track an aircraft used by Texas Democratic legislators to flee the state to delay a congressional redistricting plan engineered by DeLay.

Hefley said his biggest accomplishment was molding the ethics committee into a body "that goes into that room and doesn't look at any of the cases in a partisan fashion. There was a time when it was used in a partisan way." But he expressed frustration that he was not able to influence the chamber's rules. Republican leaders in 2001 rebuffed Hefley's attempts to stop or at least minimize two changes to House ethics rules. One allowed charities to give lawmakers free trips; the other permitted lobbyists to cater meals in congressional offices.

As ethics panel chairman, Hefley in 2002 also shepherded only the second expulsion of a House member since the Civil War. Democrat James A. Traficant Jr. of Ohio had been convicted of federal bribery, tax evasion and racketeering charges that year, but maintained that he was the victim of a government vendetta. He behaved with his trademark flamboyance during the ethics committee hearings, and Hefley later said that the expulsion was one of the toughest decisions he ever made because he liked the quirky Traficant.

When not passing judgment on his colleagues, Hefley tends to mostly parochial legislative matters and displays a homespun style that, along with his conservatism, has made him seemingly unbeatable back home.

Defense spending accounts for a good share of the economic activity in the 5th District, home of both the Northern Command and the North American Aerospace Defense Command (NORAD), which is charged with protecting the U.S. homeland from threats from the air. Also in his district are the Air Force Academy, Fort Carson and other installations at which more than 25,000 active-duty personnel are stationed. The district's large population of military retirees contributes to its rock-ribbed conservative personality. So Hefley's pro-Pentagon voting record, fiscal tight-fistedness, and opposition to both gay rights and abortion rights all go down well.

As chairman of the Armed Services Subcommittee on Military Installations during the Clinton administration, Hefley regularly berated the White House for proposing inadequate budgets, then won more for defense facilities and family housing than the administration requested. He also bitterly opposed Clinton's requests to close unneeded bases.

In 2001, when President Bush and Defense Secretary Donald H. Rumsfeld demanded another base-closing round, Hefley urged them to identify from the outset uniquely important bases at no risk of closure, in order to spare some communities uncertainty. His idea was not adopted.

As chairman of the Subcommittee on Readiness since 2002, Hefley has backed the Pentagon's request for limited exemptions from the Endangered Species Act and other environmental laws, which the department says interfere with realistic training.

He shares with most other Western Republicans a skepticism toward federal restrictions on land use. But his concern is practical as well as principled. From his senior seat on the Resources Committee in the 1990s, he argued that Congress has been too eager to designate new national parks while failing to maintain existing facilities. Accordingly, he secured creation of a process to review proposed additions to the parks system — a move he said would save more money for "crown jewel" parks such as Yosemite and Yellowstone. Over Hefley's vigorous objection, Speaker Hastert pushed a bill in 2001 that waived the review process in order to designate President Reagan's boyhood home in Illinois a national monument.

Hefley expressed displeasure with GOP leaders in the 108th Congress when Californian Richard W. Pombo was picked to chair the Resources panel over four more-senior members who wanted the job — Hefley among them. Hefley criticized the GOP leadership for rewarding Pombo's fundraising prowess over the seniority system, then quit the Resources panel, citing scheduling conflicts with his Armed Services subcommittee.

A former community planner and management consultant, Hefley boasts an unusual set of hobbies. The Oklahoma native acquired roping skills and participated in rodeos as a youth, and he still counts calf-roping as one of his pastimes. Hefley also is an accomplished, if decidedly partisan, political cartoonist and says that he plans to assemble a book of his favorite caricatures someday.

Hefley had served a decade in the Colorado General Assembly when Republican Ken Kramer vacated the 5th District seat to run for the Senate in 1986. Hefley and a colleague from the legislature sought to avoid a primary by flipping a coin to determine who would make the House bid. Hefley won the toss, but he drew a primary challenge anyway from millionaire Harold A. Krause, who viewed Hefley as too moderate. After surviving the primary, Hefley took 70 percent of the vote against Democratic businessman Bill Story. Since then, Hefley has won with ease.

KEY VOTES

2004

No Extend federal unemployment benefits by 13 weeks
Yes Pass $283.2 billion, six-year federal highway and mass transit bill
Yes Approve $146 billion multi-year extension of previously enacted middle-class tax breaks
Yes Amend the Constitution to prohibit same-sex marriage
Yes Cut corporate taxes $137 billion over 10 years
No Reorganize U.S. intelligence agencies as proposed by Sept. 11 commission

2003

Yes Cut taxes by $330 billion through fiscal 2013
No Block Bush rule scaling back overtime pay for some white-collar federal workers
Yes Do not allow use of search warrants without first notifying subjects
No Allow importation of prescription drugs
Yes Create private school voucher program in Washington, D.C.
Yes Ban "partial birth" abortion except to save a woman's life
No Split $18.6 billion in Iraq aid into half-grant, half-loan
Yes Overhaul Medicare and create prescription drug benefit

CQ VOTE STUDIES

	PARTY UNITY		PRESIDENTIAL SUPPORT	
	Support	Oppose	Support	Oppose
2004	91%	9%	85%	15%
2003	92%	8%	85%	15%
2002	92%	8%	85%	15%
2001	92%	8%	81%	19%
2000	93%	7%	15%	85%

INTEREST GROUPS

	AFL-CIO	ADA	CCUS	ACU
2004	33%	15%	90%	92%
2003	27%	10%	77%	80%
2002	13%	0%	78%	100%
2001	18%	5%	74%	96%
2000	10%	10%	84%	100%

COLORADO 5
South central — Colorado Springs

God and country dominate the 5th, an overwhelmingly conservative district that gave George W. Bush his highest percentage of the 2004 presidential vote (66 percent) in the state. Military installations employ tens of thousands of people in the Colorado Springs area. The popular resort town is a prime destination for retired military personnel, who come to enjoy the scenery and find like-minded neighbors. James Dobson's Focus on the Family and other evangelical organizations are based in the 5th.

Defense cutbacks threatened the district in the early 1990s when Congress tried but failed to put Fort Carson on its list of closures. Since then, the district has made itself an indispensable arm of the modern military. Colorado Springs houses the U.S. Space Command, the North American Aerospace Defense Command and a good portion of the country's satellite defense research.

The city also has broadened its economic base: Direct and indirect military expenditures account for about 40 percent of the economy,

down from 60 percent a decade ago. But much of the new industry, including superconductor and computer development, depends on the defense industry. Like much of the Front Range, the city attracts money from tourists, many of whom come to make the ascent up Pikes Peak.

More than 80 percent of district residents live in El Paso County (Colorado Springs), which has topped 535,000 residents. Redistricting following the 2000 census removed the district's portions of Douglas and Arapahoe counties near Denver and added three counties farther west.

MAJOR INDUSTRY
Military, defense, tourism, semiconductors

MILITARY BASES
Fort Carson (Army), 16,000 military, 2,700 civilian (2003); U.S. Air Force Academy, 10,104 military, 2,046 civilian (2002); Peterson Air Force Base, 5,965 military, 2,059 civilian (2003); Schriever Air Force Base, 1,400 military, 1,700 civilian; Cheyenne Mountain Air Force Station, 581 military, 251 civilian (2004)

CITIES
Colorado Springs, 360,890; Security-Widefield (unincorporated), 29,845

NOTABLE
The U.S. Olympic Headquarters is in Colorado Springs.

Rep. Tom Tancredo (R)

Elected 1998; 4th term

A stalwart champion of conservative causes, Tancredo has made his mark in Congress as its leading advocate of a tough line on U.S. immigration policy.

His campaign for tighter border controls and for steps to locate and deport illegal immigrants runs counter to the national Republican Party's efforts to woo Hispanic voters, and it angered the Bush White House. Tancredo (tan-CRAY-doe) was given a warning in 2002 by top Bush political adviser Karl Rove: "Do not darken the door of the White House."

Undeterred, Tancredo has continued to blast the administration's immigration policy. He said he did not relish the public dispute with the president, but he told the Denver Post: "If the issue didn't demand it, I wouldn't do it." He says he might enter the New Hampshire presidential primary in 2008 to highlight the issue if no one else does.

He became a familiar face on television news programs debating immigration policy, and he has posted a series of "Unbelievable but True Immigration Stories" on his official Web site. "When I got here, somebody told me, 'There's only one way to get something done — talk about it constantly.' I remember saying, 'I can do that,' " Tancredo told the Denver Post.

He could, indeed — on the House floor as well as on TV. He charged that others avoided the topic because they feared the political ramifications. "We find that this is a politically embarrassing thing. Even to bring this up on the floor of the House makes people uncomfortable," Tancredo declared in 2003. He said the Democratic Party "sees massive immigration, both illegal and legal, as a source of political support, future voters; on our side of the aisle, we see the same thing as a source of cheap labor; the administration sees the same thing as a potential source of voters for them, a wedge issue that they can use in the next campaign."

Tancredo said his interest in immigration began in the 1970s when increasing numbers of immigrants to Colorado forced the state to implement bilingual education programs. In 2004, he sharply criticized Bush's plan for creation of a new guest worker visa, calling it "dangerous and unworkable." He introduced his own alternative legislation, which would establish a moratorium on legal immigration until illegal immigrants' numbers were reduced.

The Sept. 11, 2001, terrorist attacks against the United States brought immigration and border security issues to the top of the congressional agenda. The membership of the Immigration Reform Caucus, which Tancredo chairs, has jumped from 15 to more than 75 lawmakers.

In Colorado, Tancredo proposed a state constitutional amendment that would have denied state services to illegal immigrants. The ballot initiative was withdrawn in May 2004 due to a lack of financial backing.

Tancredo's grandparents came to the United States from Italy, but he said they always regarded themselves as Americans and not as Italian-Americans.

Tancredo is conservative on other matters as well, speaking out for school vouchers, gun owners' rights and tax cuts. He wants to scrap the current income tax system and replace it with a national sales tax or a flat tax.

A former public school teacher and regional official in President Reagan's Education Department, Tancredo once advocated doing away with the Department of Education, but he now presses the federal government to make good on its promises to fund special education for disabled students.

In his first term, Tancredo signed a California group's pledge to elimi-

CAPITOL OFFICE
225-7882
www.house.gov/tancredo
1130 Longworth 20515-0606; fax 226-4623

COMMITTEES
International Relations
Resources

HOMETOWN
Littleton

BORN
Dec. 20, 1945, North Denver, Colo.

RELIGION
Presbyterian

FAMILY
Wife, Jackie Tancredo; two children

EDUCATION
U. of North Colorado, B.A. 1968

CAREER
Think tank president; teacher

POLITICAL HIGHLIGHTS
Colo. House, 1977-81; U.S. Education Department regional representative, 1981-93

ELECTION RESULTS

2004 GENERAL

Tom Tancredo (R)	212,778	59.5%
Joanna L. Conti (D)	139,870	39.1%
Jack J. Woehr (LIBERT)	3,857	1.1%

2004 PRIMARY

Tom Tancredo (R)	unopposed

2002 GENERAL

Tom Tancredo (R)	158,851	66.9%
Lance Wright (D)	71,327	30.0%
Adam D. Katz (LIBERT)	7,323	3.1%

PREVIOUS WINNING PERCENTAGES
2000 (54%); 1998 (56%)

nate all public schools, saying that "separation of school and state is essential to restore parental responsibility." He told the Denver Post that he aimed "to push the envelope of debate."

Tancredo's association with staunchly conservative causes was tested by the events of April 20, 1999, the day two students went on a shooting rampage at Columbine High School — just blocks from his suburban Denver home — killing 12 classmates and a teacher before turning their guns on themselves. In an interview with the Capitol Hill newspaper The Hill, the evangelical Presbyterian and self-proclaimed Second Amendment advocate attributed the killings to Satan. Tancredo later endorsed some gun controls, including a Colorado ballot initiative that required background checks for all firearms sales at gun shows.

The son of a truck driver and a department store clerk, Tancredo grew up in a working-class part of Denver. He became a social studies teacher, enticed by a program that paid half of his student loans if he agreed to teach for five years.

His political career began with a challenge to the junior high school class he was teaching in the 1970s: He told his 32 students that he would run for public office if each of them volunteered with a campaign. To his surprise, all of them called his bluff. The class then decided that Tancredo should run for the Colorado House.

During his four years in the state legislature, Tancredo was one of the conservatives dubbed the "House crazies" by the press and Democratic Gov. Richard Lamm for their efforts to overhaul the state's tax system.

In 1981, Tancredo began a 12-year tenure as the Education Department's regional representative. He advocated dismantling the department and downsized his own regional staff by 75 percent. He then served as president of the Libertarian Independence Institute think tank during 1993-98.

Though he had not held elective office since 1981, Tancredo edged out four other Republicans in the 1998 primary and then breezed to victory in November to succeed retiring GOP Rep. Dan Schaefer. After getting a total vote of just 54 percent in 2000, redistricting in 2002 made the 6th District more friendly to the GOP and Tancredo captured two-thirds of the vote. In 2004, against a well-funded Democratic foe, and with Tancredo's hardline immigration views a major issue, he won by 20 percentage points.

He initially pledged to serve no more than six years, which would have made the 108th Congress his last. But in early 2004, after considering a run for the Senate, he concluded "after much prayer and soul searching" that he would stand for re-election in the House.

KEY VOTES

2004
No Extend federal unemployment benefits by 13 weeks
No Pass $283.2 billion, six-year federal highway and mass transit bill
Yes Approve $146 billion multi-year extension of previously enacted middle-class tax breaks
Yes Amend the Constitution to prohibit same-sex marriage
Yes Cut corporate taxes $137 billion over 10 years
No Reorganize U.S. intelligence agencies as proposed by Sept. 11 commission

2003
Yes Cut taxes by $330 billion through fiscal 2013
No Block Bush rule scaling back overtime pay for some white-collar federal workers
Yes Do not allow use of search warrants without first notifying subjects
Yes Allow importation of prescription drugs
Yes Create private school voucher program in Washington, D.C.
Yes Ban "partial birth" abortion except to save a woman's life
No Split $18.6 billion in Iraq aid into half-grant, half-loan
No Overhaul Medicare and create prescription drug benefit

CQ VOTE STUDIES

| | PARTY UNITY | | PRESIDENTIAL SUPPORT | |
	Support	Oppose	Support	Oppose
2004	94%	6%	81%	19%
2003	90%	10%	84%	16%
2002	96%	4%	76%	24%
2001	94%	6%	77%	23%
2000	93%	7%	17%	83%

INTEREST GROUPS

	AFL-CIO	ADA	CCUS	ACU
2004	21%	10%	95%	100%
2003	20%	25%	77%	92%
2002	11%	5%	79%	100%
2001	8%	5%	70%	100%
2000	10%	5%	71%	96%

COLORADO 6
Denver suburbs – part of Aurora; Douglas County

Managing growth is a top priority for the affluent, white-collar suburbs that lie south of Denver and comprise the 6th. Highway congestion has become a serious problem as commuters living in suburban bedroom communities head into Denver every morning.

Steep housing prices on the West Coast have resulted in an influx of Californians, especially to Douglas County, which increased its population by 191 percent in the 1990s, the fastest clip in the country.

The 6th was redrawn following the 2000 census to include Douglas, which accounts for 30 percent of the district's population and solidifies it as a Republican stronghold. Douglas supported George W. Bush by a more than 2-to-1 ratio in 2004. The county is quickly filling up with young, well-educated professionals with families, and it has the state's highest median income. Technology sector growth in the suburbs has made the 6th one of the most highly educated districts.

Contrasts are evident in Arapahoe County, where a plurality of district residents reside even though the county is overwhelmingly rural. The urban, western portion of Arapahoe, which includes the county seat of Littleton just south of Denver, has many residential and retail areas. Nearly one-third of Aurora, Colorado's third most-populous city, is in the district. Columbine High School, site of a 1999 shooting that left 15 dead, is in Littleton, which makes gun control an emotional issue in the 6th.

The district's Hispanic population (slightly less than 6 percent) is the lowest percentage in the state. Minorities total 12 percent of residents, making the 6th the only district in Colorado where minorities represent less than 20 percent of the population.

MAJOR INDUSTRY
Manufacturing

CITIES
Aurora (pt.), 78,878; Highlands Ranch, 70,931; Southglenn (unincorporated), 43,520; Littleton, 40,340

NOTABLE
The "Buffalo Bill" Cody grave and museum is near Golden; The Comanche Crossing Railroad Site near Strasburg marks the place where the last spike was driven in 1870 to create the first continuous transcontinental railroad.

Rep. Bob Beauprez (R)

Elected 2002; 2nd term

CAPITOL OFFICE
225-2645
www.house.gov/beauprez
504 Cannon 20515-0607; fax 225-5278

COMMITTEES
Ways & Means

HOMETOWN
Arvada

BORN
Sept. 22, 1948, Lafayette, Colo.

RELIGION
Roman Catholic

FAMILY
Wife, Claudia Beauprez; four children

EDUCATION
U. of Colorado, B.S. 1970 (education)

CAREER
Bank owner; dairy farmer

POLITICAL HIGHLIGHTS
Colo. Republican Party chairman, 1999-2002

ELECTION RESULTS

2004 GENERAL

Bob Beauprez (R)	135,571	54.7%
Dave Thomas (D)	106,026	42.8%
Clyde J. Harkins (AC)	6,167	2.5%

2004 PRIMARY

Bob Beauprez (R)	unopposed

2002 GENERAL

Bob Beauprez (R)	81,789	47.3%
Mike Feeley (D)	81,668	47.2%
Dave Chandler (GREEN)	3,274	1.9%
Victor A. Good (REF)	3,133	1.8%
G. T. "Bud" Martin (LIBERT)	2,906	1.7%

Beauprez's biography is a classic American story. A grandson of Belgian immigrants, he worked on the family dairy farm, then sold it to start a successful community bank. As a politician — with a banker's natural conservatism — he prizes notions of self-sufficiency and a limited role for the federal government.

Beauprez (bo-PRAY) models much of his platform after the political philosophy of President Bush, who made two campaign stops for him during his hard-fought battle for election to the House in 2002. He is an avid supporter of making permanent the Bush tax cuts of 2001, and voted with the White House 95 percent of the time in the 108th Congress.

His alignment with the president makes him a perennial target of Democrats. Beauprez's district, which surrounds Denver on three sides, is one of the most competitive in the country — divided almost evenly three ways among Republicans, Democrats and independents. Even as The Denver Post endorsed him for re-election in 2004, the paper grumbled that his conservative voting record doesn't represent the range of his constituents. Beauprez said, "For the most part I've been with the administration, with our leadership. I was open about that when I was campaigning. I don't think it will change much."

Early in 2004, Beauprez toyed with the idea of running for the Senate after the unexpected retirement of Republican Sen. Ben Nighthorse Campbell. But GOP leaders, fearful of losing the seat, convinced him to stay and run for re-election. Beauprez makes no secret of wanting to make a future run for higher office. He was rewarded for his loyalty in early 2005 when the Republican leadership gave him a coveted seat on the powerful Ways and Means Committee.

Beauprez had a modest first term, not unusual for a freshman, especially one with no prior experience in local or state office. Before coming to Congress, his political background consisted of a three-year stint as chairman of Colorado's Republican Party. The House did pass his bill to allow members of the active-duty National Guard and reserves to make penalty-free early withdrawals from Individual Retirement Accounts. The measure aimed to compensate soldiers serving in Iraq at wages lower than they earned in their civilian jobs before the war and its extended tours of duty.

Because of his political vulnerability, GOP leaders appointed him to the Transportation and Infrastructure Committee as soon as he arrived in the House, where he became vice chairman of the Highways, Transit and Pipelines Subcommittee. That position allowed him to secure $45 million in transportation projects for his district, more than a third of the total awarded the entire state, though the overall transportation bill ultimately foundered in the 108th. Beauprez left the panel at the outset of the 109th in order to move to Ways and Means.

On a national scale, Beauprez's efforts in the 108th were focused on a $31 billion energy policy bill. Majority Leader Tom DeLay made him a member of the House Energy Action Team, a group for Republicans who did not sit on A-list committees with jurisdiction over the bill. Beauprez said the measure's tax breaks and incentives for oil and gas companies would create thousands of jobs in Colorado. But his efforts on the bill also had a flip side. The League of Conservation Voters, a nonpartisan environmental group, named him to its "dirty dozen" list because of his support for the bill. It also aired radio ads against him in the district during his 2004 campaign.

The Denver Post criticized him for supporting a provision in the bill to shield makers of a fuel additive called MTBE from lawsuits while taking $25,000 in campaign contributions from the manufacturers and refiners of the substance. MTBE has been found to be a carcinogen and dangerous when it gets into water supplies from leaky underground storage tanks. Beauprez defended his record on the environment, noting that he had helped secure $5 million to clean up part of the polluted Lowry bombing range.

Although he came late to politics — he was 54 when he was first elected to the House — Beauprez said it's been a passion since the early 1960s, when, as part of a junior high school class assignment, he had to make a case for John F. Kennedy becoming president. "I wasn't just fascinated by politics," Beauprez told The Denver Post. "I was drawn to it."

Beauprez's grandfather emigrated from Belgium and shoveled coal for a living before buying a small farm in Lafayette. That investment grew in the next generation into a successful dairy operation run by Beauprez's father, Joseph, who became a nationally recognized breeder of registered Hereford cattle. Beauprez himself worked on the farm after he graduated from the University of Colorado at Boulder in 1970. When the farm was sold to land developers in 1990, Beauprez used his capital to buy a failing community bank. He turned it into a thriving enterprise, called Heritage Bank, with 12 branches in suburban Denver.

Beauprez was state GOP chairman when Colorado's new 7th District was created after the 2000 census. His strong party ties enabled him to survive a tough primary contest in which Rick O'Donnell, a top aide to Republican Gov. Bill Owens, was his main competitor.

More difficult was Beauprez's general election race against Democratic former state Sen. Mike Feeley. A late surge of Republican absentee ballots propelled Beauprez to victory by a 121-vote margin — an outcome that was not officially decided until the results of a recount were announced some five weeks after the election. With the outcome in limbo, Beauprez and Feeley both attended orientation sessions in Washington, selecting seats on opposite sides of the room. The race was the second-closest in state history. Democratic incumbent Wayne Aspinall won by 29 votes over Republican Howard Schults in 1952.

The district also provided one of the few truly competitive House races in 2004. Beauprez had serious competition in Democrat Dave Thomas, the Jefferson County district attorney. Thomas ran on providing basic health care coverage for everyone and fully funding Bush's 2001 education mandate. Beauprez outspent Thomas 3-to-1 and won with 55 percent of the vote.

KEY VOTES

2004

No   Extend federal unemployment benefits by 13 weeks

Yes Pass $283.2 billion, six-year federal highway and mass transit bill

Yes Approve $146 billion multi-year extension of previously enacted middle-class tax breaks

Yes Amend the Constitution to prohibit same-sex marriage

Yes Cut corporate taxes $137 billion over 10 years

Yes Reorganize U.S. intelligence agencies as proposed by Sept. 11 commission

2003

Yes Cut taxes by $330 billion through fiscal 2013

No   Block Bush rule scaling back overtime pay for some white-collar federal workers

No   Do not allow use of search warrants without first notifying subjects

No   Allow importation of prescription drugs

Yes Create private school voucher program in Washington, D.C.

Yes Ban "partial birth" abortion except to save a woman's life

No   Split $18.6 billion in Iraq aid into half-grant, half-loan

Yes Overhaul Medicare and create prescription drug benefit

CQ VOTE STUDIES

	PARTY UNITY		PRESIDENTIAL SUPPORT	
	Support	Oppose	Support	Oppose
2004	97%	3%	91%	9%
2003	97%	3%	98%	2%

INTEREST GROUPS

	AFL-CIO	ADA	CCUS	ACU
2004	20%	5%	100%	92%
2003	0%	5%	100%	84%

COLORADO 7
Denver suburbs – Lakewood, parts of Aurora and Arvada

Awarded to fast-growing Colorado following the 2000 census, the 7th is a middle-class suburban area that surrounds Denver (and the 1st District) from the west, north and east before extending east to take in the remainder of Adams County.

The bulk of the district's population is in Jefferson County, where more than half of residents live and which forms its western edge. The 7th takes in Lakewood, a middle-class area that abuts Denver to the west, Golden, which includes the Coors Brewing Co., and nearly all of Arvada.

Minorities represent nearly a third of residents, giving the 7th the second-highest total in the state. Commerce City, a Hispanic-majority, lower-middle-class area just north of Denver, and most of the city of Aurora (shared with the 6th) in Arapahoe County are in the 7th. Aurora's black population, at 13 percent, is more than three times Colorado's percentage.

Buckley Air Force Base, a link in the Air Force Space Command satellite tracking system, has attracted aerospace firms to the area as it has expanded since 2000. The Rocky Mountain Arsenal, which once produced chemical weapons but is now a national wildlife refuge, is expected to be rid of pollutants by 2011.

The 7th is Colorado's most competitive district. John Kerry narrowly carried the area with 51 percent of the vote in the 2004 presidential election, and independents, Democrats and Republicans are nearly equal in voter registration. The slight Democratic lean of Adams and Arapahoe counties is largely offset by the GOP tilt in Jefferson.

MAJOR INDUSTRY
Telecommunications, aerospace, manufacturing

MILITARY BASES
Buckley Air Force Base, 3,626 military, 5,087 civilian (2004)

CITIES
Aurora (pt.), 197,515; Lakewood, 144,126; Arvada (pt.), 98,941; Wheat Ridge, 32,913

NOTABLE
Dinosaur Ridge near Morrison features Jurassic dinosaur bones discovered in 1877 and many Cretaceous dinosaur footprints.

CONNECTICUT

Gov. M. Jodi Rell (R)

Assumed office: 2004
Length of term: 4 years
Term expires: 1/07
Salary: $150,000
Phone: (860) 566-4840

Hometown: Brookfield
Born: June 16, 1946; Norfolk, Va.
Religion: Protestant
Family: Husband, Lou Rell; two children
Education: Old Dominion College, attended 1965-66; Western Connecticut State U., attended 1982-84
Career: Homemaker; investment firm office clerk
Political highlights: Conn. House, 1985-95 (deputy minority leader 1991-1995); lieutenant governor, 1995-2004

Recent election results:
2002 GENERAL
John G. Rowland (R)	573,958	56.1%
Bill Curry (D)	448,984	43.9%

Lt. Gov. Kevin Sullivan (D)

Assumed office: 2004
Length of term: 4 years
Term expires: 1/07
Salary: $110,000
Phone: (860) 524-7384

STATE LEGISLATURE

General Assembly: January-June in odd-numbered years; February-May in even-numbered years

House: 151 members, 2-year terms
2005 breakdown: 99D, 52R; 105 men, 46 women
Salary: $28,000
Phone: (860) 240-0400

Senate: 36 members, 2-year terms
2005 breakdown: 24D, 12R; 27 men, 9 women
Salary: $28,000
Phone: (860) 240-0500

STATE TERM LIMITS

Governor: No
House: No
Senate: No

URBAN STATISTICS

CITY	POPULATION
Bridgeport	139,529
New Haven	123,626
Hartford	121,578
Stamford	117,083

REGISTERED VOTERS

Unaffiliated	44%
Democrat	34%
Republican	22%

POPULATION

2004 population (est.)	3,503,604
2000 population	3,405,565
1990 population	3,287,116
Percent change (1990-2000)	+3.6%
Rank among states (2004)	29
Median age	37.4
Born in state	57%
Foreign born	10.9%
Violent crime rate	325/100,000
Poverty level	7.9%
Federal workers	21,296
Military	16,675

REDISTRICTING

Connecticut lost one House seat in reapportionment. The Connecticut Reapportionment Commission adopted a new, five-district map on Dec. 21, 2001.

MISCELLANEOUS

Web: www.ct.gov
Capital: Hartford
STATE ELECTION OFFICIAL
(860) 509-6100
DEMOCRATIC HEADQUARTERS
(860) 560-1775
REPUBLICAN HEADQUARTERS
(860) 547-0589

District Statistics

DIST.	2004 VOTE FOR PRESIDENT BUSH	KERRY	WHITE	BLACK	ASIAN	HISP	MEDIAN INCOME	WHITE COLLAR	BLUE COLLAR	SERVICE INDUSTRY	OVER 64	UNDER 18	COLLEGE EDUCATION	RURAL	SQ. MILES
1	39%	60%	72%	13%	2%	11%	$50,227	66%	20%	14%	15%	24%	28%	7%	653
2	44	54	89	3	2	4	$54,498	63	21	16	12	24	29	33	2,028
3	42	56	76	11	3	8	$49,752	65	21	14	15	24	28	3	459
4	46	52	71	11	3	13	$66,598	72	16	13	13	26	42	4	457
5	49.0	49.3	80	5	2	11	$53,118	63	23	14	14	25	30	14	1,248
STATE	44	54	77	9	2	9	$53,935	66	20	14	14	25	31	12	4,845
U.S.	50.7	48.3	69	12	4	13	$41,994	60	25	15	12	26	24	21	3,537,438

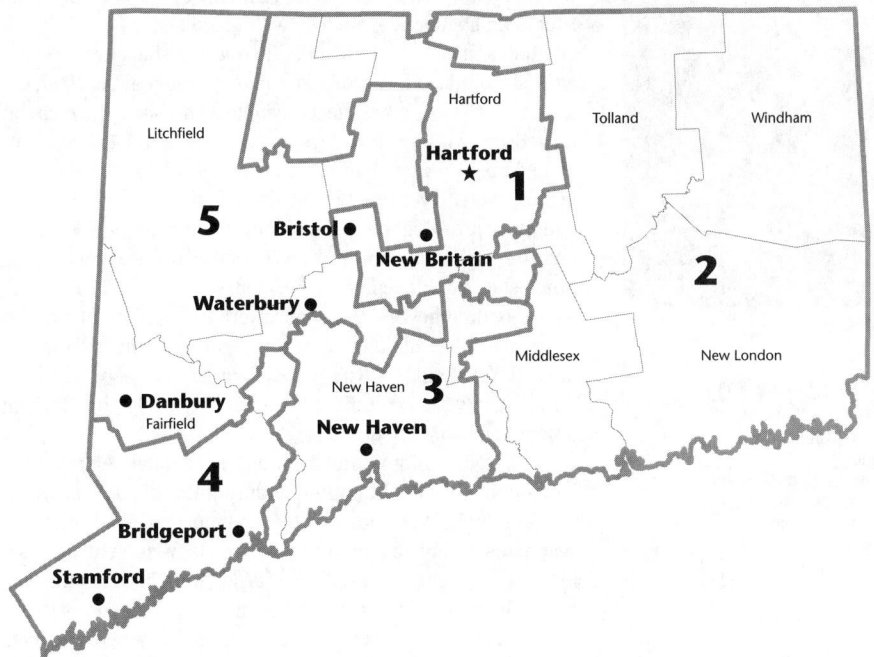

Sen. Christopher J. Dodd (D)

Elected 1980; 5th term

CAPITOL OFFICE
224-2823
dodd.senate.gov
448 Russell 20510-0702; fax 228-1683

COMMITTEES
Banking, Housing & Urban Affairs
Foreign Relations
Health, Education, Labor & Pensions
Rules & Administration - ranking member
Joint Library - ranking member

HOMETOWN
East Haddam

BORN
May 27, 1944, Willimantic, Conn.

RELIGION
Roman Catholic

FAMILY
Wife, Jackie Clegg Dodd; two children

EDUCATION
Providence College, B.A. 1966; U. of Louisville, J.D. 1972

MILITARY SERVICE
Army Reserve, 1969-75

CAREER
Lawyer; Peace Corps volunteer

POLITICAL HIGHLIGHTS
U.S. House, 1975-81

ELECTION RESULTS

2004 GENERAL

Christopher J. Dodd (D)	945,347	66.4%
Jack Orchulli (R)	457,749	32.1%

2004 PRIMARY

Christopher J. Dodd (D)	unopposed

PREVIOUS WINNING PERCENTAGES
1998 (65%); 1992 (59%); 1986 (65%); 1980 (56%); 1978
House Election (70%); 1976 House Election (65%);
1974 House Election (59%)

A veteran of a quarter-century in the Senate and the chamber's joke-loving class clown, the white-maned Dodd probably has been disappointed in his aspirations for a top leadership post or a presidential nomination. But he remains an influential liberal with an eye for a legislative deal, much like his best buddy, Sen. Edward M. Kennedy of Massachusetts, another Irish-American Democrat from a New England state.

Dodd's latest bid for a leadership role was short-lived. He explored a run against Nevada's Harry Reid for minority leader in the 109th Congress after Tom Daschle lost his re-election contest and had to give up the post. Dodd bowed out within a few days when it became clear Reid had the votes locked up. Ten years earlier, in 1994, Daschle bested Dodd for the job by just one vote. Over time, Dodd also has thought about seeking the nomination for president but his time never came. In the 2004 Democratic contest, he was overshadowed by others in the early jockeying, including home-state Sen. Joseph I. Lieberman.

"It's getting beyond the point where it's my time," he told the Hartford Courant in 2004, adding that he wasn't even sure he had the ambition to run in 2008. Yet Dodd is still a revered figure in the party. "He's got a lot of wisdom," family friend Robert F. Kennedy Jr. told the Courant. "But he's always ready for a fistfight."

His career zenith on the front line of national politics was chairing the Democratic National Committee during the Republican takeover of Congress in the 1994 elections. But he continues to be a Senate player, a liberal pragmatist willing to cross party lines on legislation he deems ideologically imperfect but close enough. After a long fight between the two parties, the Senate in early 2005 passed a bill putting new limits on class action lawsuits after Dodd and two other Democrats agreed to support it. Republicans conceded to some of their demands for changes, giving the bill a filibuster-proof 60 votes.

In the Senate corridors and off the floor, Dodd lightens the sobriety of the day's big debates with a quip or a joke, or several of them. He's often seen bantering and joshing with fellow senators or the Capitol elevator operators.

For many years, Dodd's interest in children and family issues seemed incongruous given the widespread Washington chatter about his personal life, including a period of well-publicized womanizing in the 1980s with Kennedy. (Both senators were divorced at the time.) After a decade-long courtship, Dodd married Jackie Marie Clegg, an Export-Import Bank official, in 1999, and the couple had their first child, Grace, two years later, when Dodd was 56. Their second child was born in March 2005.

Long before that, he had championed issues aimed at improving the lot of children. In 2001, he argued passionately that President Bush's education overhaul bill should include more money for schools in poor areas. He was a prime sponsor of the 1993 law requiring businesses to grant workers time off for family or medical needs, and he has been a leader in the effort to require child safety locks on handguns. In the 108th Congress, Dodd sponsored legislation to help prevent youth suicide.

Dodd has an easy, comfortable manner at work, in part derived from his background as a child of the Senate. His father, Thomas J. Dodd, was a Democratic senator from Connecticut for two terms, although his career declined after his censure in 1967 for misusing political contributions.

To this day, the senator views his father's colleagues as having treated him unfairly, and so has cast memorable votes to signal his belief that fellow senators should get the benefit of the doubt, according to the Hartford Courant. Dodd was among just eight Democrats who joined the Republican majority to confirm John Ashcroft, a former senator from Missouri, as attorney general in 2001. He also was among just three Democrats to join the minority backing confirmation of John Tower, a former GOP senator from Texas, as defense secretary in 1989.

In more recent confirmation battles not involving former colleagues, Dodd has put his party first. He voted against Bush's nominee for attorney general, Alberto R. Gonzales, who angered many Democrats by refusing to answer questions about the Bush administration's handling of detained suspected terrorists after the Sept. 11, 2001, attacks.

A member of the Foreign Relations Committee, Dodd also voted to approve Condoleezza Rice as secretary of state despite some opposition from Democrats over Bush's handling of the Iraq war. He was also one of 29 Senate Democrats who supported the resolution authorizing Bush to use military force against Iraq and later got a measure passed that required the secretary of defense to reimburse troops for protective equipment purchased with personal funds.

As the top-ranking Democrat on the Rules and Administration Committee, Dodd is a defender of Senate prerogatives. After the terrorist attacks, the House discussed how best to ensure the continuity of Congress after a catastrophe and adopted a resolution that would have established a joint House-Senate committee to review each chamber's rules. Dodd threw cold water on the plan, saying the House should have no role in Senate rules.

As chairman of Rules when Democrats controlled the Senate in 2002, Dodd worked with Republicans Mitch McConnell of Kentucky and Christopher S. Bond of Missouri to write the compromise bill to prevent a repeat of the disputed 2000 presidential contest. The measure set the first federal standards for the conduct of elections and authorized $3.9 billion over three years to help states meet the standards.

Dodd's tendency toward compromise partly reflects his need to walk the line between his ideology and the needs of industries vital to Connecticut's economy. An ardent advocate on the Banking Committee for the state's insurance industry, he helped broker a deal with the White House in 2002 on a law creating a federal program to insure commercial property and casualty firms that sell terrorism insurance.

He was less successful in 2004 in preventing the termination of the Army's $39 billion Comanche helicopter program, which relied heavily on the Sikorsky Aircraft facility in Bridgeport, Conn. for the manufacture of components. Sikorsky was dealt another blow in 2005, when the Navy awarded its contract to build Marine One helicopters to Lockheed Martin and a European consortium. Sikorsky had built the presidential helicopters since the 1950s. Dodd and Lieberman considered introducing a bill requiring that all parts of future presidential helicopters be made in the United States.

Dodd won his first House election at age 30 on a family name that still resonates with older voters in the state. He captured an open seat that had been held by a Republican in the post-Watergate election of 1974.

When Democrat Abraham Ribicoff retired six years later, Dodd became the youngest person ever elected to the Senate from Connecticut. He took 56 percent of the vote against former Sen. James L. Buckley of New York, who carried the standard of the newly resurgent conservative wing of the state GOP and whose family homestead is in Connecticut.

Dodd has since won re-elections more easily, taking almost two-thirds of the vote in his 1998 contest and again in 2004, when he defeated his GOP foe, former clothing company executive Jack Orchulli, with 66 percent.

KEY VOTES

2004
Yes Pass $318.9 billion, six-year highway and mass transit bill
Yes Extend assault weapons ban for 10 years
Yes Restore pay-as-you-go rules for new tax cuts and entitlement spending
No Criminalize harm to a fetus in an attack on the mother
Yes Increase mandatory child care funding to states by $6 billion over five years
No Amend the Constitution to prohibit same-sex marriage
Yes Approve $146 billion multi-year extension of previously enacted middle-class tax breaks
Yes Reorganize U.S. intelligence agencies as proposed by Sept. 11 commission
No Cut corporate taxes $137 billion over 10 years

2003
Yes Delay Bush changes to Clean Air Act
No Allow confirmation vote on Miguel A. Estrada to the U.S. Court of Appeals for the D.C. Circuit
Yes Block a Bush proposal opening Alaska's Arctic National Wildlife Refuge to oil drilling
Yes Limit size of Bush's proposed tax cut to $350 billion through fiscal 2013
Yes Overhaul Medicare and create prescription drug benefit
Yes Block Bush rule scaling back overtime pay for some white-collar federal workers
Yes Split $20 billion in Iraq aid into half-grant, half-loan
No Ban "partial birth" abortion except to save a woman's life
No Stop proposal allowing travel to Cuba
No Allow final vote on energy policy overhaul

CQ VOTE STUDIES

	PARTY UNITY		PRESIDENTIAL SUPPORT	
	Support	Oppose	Support	Oppose
2004	95%	5%	60%	40%
2003	95%	5%	47%	53%
2002	94%	6%	68%	32%
2001	98%	2%	66%	34%
2000	95%	5%	98%	2%
1999	90%	10%	86%	14%
1998	91%	9%	93%	7%
1997	87%	13%	94%	6%
1996	89%	11%	81%	19%
1995	87%	13%	92%	8%

INTEREST GROUPS

	AFL-CIO	ADA	CCUS	ACU
2004	100%	100%	41%	4%
2003	100%	95%	32%	15%
2002	100%	80%	40%	5%
2001	94%	95%	36%	16%
2000	75%	95%	53%	13%
1999	88%	95%	53%	0%
1998	88%	95%	61%	4%
1997	57%	90%	50%	4%
1996	100%	85%	38%	10%
1995	92%	95%	32%	4%

Sen. Joseph I. Lieberman (D)

Elected 1988; 3rd term

CAPITOL OFFICE
224-4041
lieberman.senate.gov
706 Hart 20510-0703; fax 224-9750

COMMITTEES
Armed Services
Environment & Public Works
Homeland Security & Governmental Affairs -
ranking member
Small Business & Entrepreneurship

HOMETOWN
New Haven

BORN
Feb. 24, 1942, Stamford, Conn.

RELIGION
Jewish

FAMILY
Wife, Hadassah Lieberman; four children

EDUCATION
Yale U., B.A. 1964 (politics & economics), LL.B.
1967

CAREER
Lawyer

POLITICAL HIGHLIGHTS
Conn. Senate, 1971-80 (majority leader, 1975-80);
Democratic nominee for U.S. House, 1980; Conn.
attorney general, 1983-89; Democratic nominee for
vice president, 2000; sought Democratic
nomination for president, 2004

ELECTION RESULTS

2000 GENERAL

Joseph I. Lieberman (D)	828,902	63.2%
Philip A. Giordano (R)	448,077	34.2%
William Kozak (CC)	25,509	2.0%

2000 PRIMARY

Joseph I. Lieberman (D)	unopposed

PREVIOUS WINNING PERCENTAGES
1994 (67%); 1988 (50%)

Lieberman's bid for his party's 2004 presidential nomination fell well short, but back in the Senate, he has shown he can wield influence even under a Republican majority. And he has given moderates renewed hope for a greater say in a chamber where the extremes on both sides are stronger than ever.

His role as the top-ranking Democrat on the Homeland Security and Governmental Affairs Committee affords him a powerful forum. Nine months after abandoning his presidential bid, he helped clinch the deal on one of the most significant achievements of the 108th Congress — an overhaul of the nation's intelligence agencies.

Lieberman has shed much of his persona as the engaging neophyte of the 2000 presidential campaign, when he shared the ticket with Al Gore. Lieberman charmed voters with a broad smile and gee-whiz attitude that made him appear constantly surprised and grateful to be Gore's pick. Since that campaign, the combativeness and ambition that have undergirded his political career have emerged more regularly.

During his 2004 campaign to be the Democratic presidential candidate, which he launched only after Gore said he would not run again, Lieberman argued that his centrism gave him the best chance of beating President Bush. "Democrats like me are the kinds of Democrats who can get elected," he said. "I am a center-out Democrat in the tradition of Bill Clinton."

His campaign never caught fire, and he dropped out in early February after losing in seven primary states, including Delaware, which he had targeted most heavily.

A label as centrist does not quite sum up Lieberman's politics. He takes on the character of a Southern moderate on issues such as education, health care and the economy. On other issues, including national defense and cultural mores, he resembles Bush more than any other leading Democrat. But he remains a typical Northeastern liberal when it comes to environmental protection, labor, and abortion and civil rights.

Senators of both parties describe his legislative style similarly. He is straightforward, cooperative, hard-working, well-informed, and more willing than most in Congress, they say, to reach across party lines.

In 2004, he worked closely with Republican Susan Collins of Maine, another prominent moderate and the chairwoman of the Homeland Security and Governmental Affairs Committee. Together, they pushed through the most comprehensive overhaul of the nation's intelligence community since the end of the Cold War, in spite of a conservative uprising that for months had threatened to stop it cold.

Lieberman has often used his position on the panel that was previously known as the Governmental Affairs Committee to advance his views on national security and the war on terrorism. After the Sept. 11, 2001, terrorist attacks, he was an early proponent of creating a Homeland Security Department, unveiling his proposal long before Bush embraced the idea. Lieberman also pressed the president to accept the creation of an independent commission to investigate government failures that may have opened the nation to the attacks. It was that commission's recommendation that ultimately shaped the intelligence overhaul. Lieberman also has criticized the Bush administration for what he sees as inadequate funding of the Homeland Security Department.

Changing the Social Security system, a big issue in the 109th Congress, was one area where Lieberman had found common ground with the Bush White House until he reversed course in recent years. He had spoken favorably of the idea of giving individuals the power to invest a portion of their Social Security payroll tax in the securities markets. Gore and other leading Democrats said such a plan could undermine the financial structure of the program, and after his vice presidential nomination was announced, Lieberman's office distributed a previously unpublished essay titled, "My Private Journey Away From Privatization," in which he said that "the promises and the numbers" of privatization advocates "don't add up."

Lieberman describes himself as pro-business, but on one issue in particular — the environment — he is generally on the opposite side of business groups. Most recently, he has been fighting, along with Republican John McCain of Arizona, for a measure aimed at reducing emissions of carbon dioxide and other "greenhouse" gases thought to contribute to global warming. He is an adherent of "tikkun olam," the Jewish belief that it is every person's duty to protect all of God's creations, and he cites this law when describing his advocacy of environmental stewardship.

His religious faith is a driving force for Lieberman, the first Jewish politician to be a vice presidential nominee. Most notably, he is working to write a compromise version of Bush's proposal to give faith-based organizations federal funds to provide social services.

Lieberman's centrist reputation comes in large measure from his stand on education. In 2000, he was one of nine Senate Democrats supporting a bill to create tax-deferred education savings accounts that parents could use for tutoring, supplies or private school tuition — a backdoor approach, in the view of liberal Democrats, to the GOP idea of creating vouchers that would drain money from the public schools.

The senator also sided with Republicans against trial lawyers, another Democratic constituency, in a 2005 vote on a bill putting new limits on class action lawsuits. The measure was strongly backed by insurance companies, a major industry in Connecticut.

On the Armed Services Committee, Lieberman looks out for Connecticut's defense-related industries and is more supportive of a robust military budget than many Democrats. He is among the minority of committee Democrats who support moving ahead with a national missile defense system as soon as technologically feasible.

Before the 2000 campaign, Lieberman was perhaps best known to the nation for a September 1998 speech that criticized President Clinton's behavior in the Monica Lewinsky scandal as "immoral." The senator never called for the president's resignation or advocated the lesser penalty of censure. Like all other Senate Democrats, he voted against convicting Clinton during the 1999 impeachment trial.

Lieberman always has been politically ambitious. He won a state Senate seat in 1970 — helped by 24-year-old campaign aide Clinton, who was then at Yale Law School — and soon rose to majority leader. He lost a race for the U.S. House in the Reagan landslide of 1980, but rebounded in 1982 to become Connecticut attorney general.

Six years later, Lieberman mounted a tough and sometimes negative campaign for the Senate and won a narrow upset victory over Lowell P. Weicker Jr., a three-term liberal Republican. To win, he had to rally core, liberal Democratic supporters while at the same time running to the right of Weicker on school prayer and foreign policy. In 1994, he was re-elected with 67 percent of the vote. In 2000, the Gore-Lieberman ticket carried Connecticut with 56 percent of the vote, and, although he didn't become vice president, Lieberman cruised to a third term in the Senate with 63 percent against Philip A. Giordano, the Republican mayor of Waterbury.

KEY VOTES

2004

Yes   Pass $318.9 billion, six-year highway and mass transit bill

Yes   Extend assault weapons ban for 10 years

Yes   Restore pay-as-you-go rules for new tax cuts and entitlement spending

No   Criminalize harm to a fetus in an attack on the mother

Yes   Increase mandatory child care funding to states by $6 billion over five years

No   Amend the Constitution to prohibit same-sex marriage

Yes   Approve $146 billion multi-year extension of previously enacted middle-class tax breaks

Yes   Reorganize U.S. intelligence agencies as proposed by Sept. 11 commission

Yes   Cut corporate taxes $137 billion over 10 years

2003

Yes   Delay Bush changes to Clean Air Act

No   Allow confirmation vote on Miguel A. Estrada to the U.S. Court of Appeals for the D.C. Circuit

Yes   Block a Bush proposal opening Alaska's Arctic National Wildlife Refuge to oil drilling

Yes   Limit size of Bush's proposed tax cut to $350 billion through fiscal 2013

?   Overhaul Medicare and create prescription drug benefit

Yes   Block Bush rule scaling back overtime pay for some white-collar federal workers

?   Split $20 billion in Iraq aid into half-grant, half-loan

No   Ban "partial birth" abortion except to save a woman's life

Yes   Stop proposal allowing travel to Cuba

No   Allow final vote on energy policy overhaul

CQ VOTE STUDIES

	PARTY UNITY		PRESIDENTIAL SUPPORT	
	Support	Oppose	Support	Oppose
2004	89%	11%	63%	37%
2003	95%	5%	32%	68%
2002	85%	15%	77%	23%
2001	93%	7%	69%	31%
2000	88%	12%	94%	6%
1999	87%	13%	89%	11%
1998	80%	20%	83%	17%
1997	77%	23%	93%	7%
1996	76%	24%	90%	10%
1995	72%	28%	82%	18%

INTEREST GROUPS

	AFL-CIO	ADA	CCUS	ACU
2004	83%	75%	79%	0%
2003	100%	70%	25%	0%
2002	92%	85%	60%	20%
2001	93%	95%	43%	28%
2000	80%	75%	33%	20%
1999	78%	95%	47%	0%
1998	75%	80%	56%	16%
1997	29%	75%	60%	20%
1996	86%	75%	54%	35%
1995	100%	95%	33%	10%

Rep. John B. Larson (D)

Elected 1998; 4th term

CAPITOL OFFICE
225-2265
www.house.gov/larson
1005 Longworth 20515-0701; fax 225-1031

COMMITTEES
Ways & Means

HOMETOWN
East Hartford

BORN
July 22, 1948, Hartford, Conn.

RELIGION
Roman Catholic

FAMILY
Wife, Leslie Larson; three children

EDUCATION
Central Connecticut State U., B.S. 1971 (history)

CAREER
Insurance company owner; high school teacher

POLITICAL HIGHLIGHTS
East Hartford Board of Education, 1978-79; East Hartford Town Council, 1979-83; Conn. Senate, 1983-95 (president pro tempore, 1987-95); sought Democratic nomination for governor, 1994

ELECTION RESULTS

2004 GENERAL

John B. Larson (D)	198,802	73.0%
John M. Halstead (R)	73,601	27.0%

2004 PRIMARY

John B. Larson (D)	unopposed

2002 GENERAL

John B. Larson (D)	134,698	66.8%
Phil Steele (R)	66,968	33.2%

PREVIOUS WINNING PERCENTAGES
2000 (72%); 1998 (58%)

Affable and gregarious, Larson says he was inspired to enter public service by the example of President John F. Kennedy, another Catholic from a large New England family. Yet his views reflect more of the middle of the Democratic Party than Kennedy's ever did.

Larson is a member of the New Democrat Coalition, a group of centrist Democrats. At the start of the 109th Congress, he gained a seat on the powerful Ways and Means Committee. In the 108th, Democratic leader Nancy Pelosi made Larson the top-ranking Democrat on the House Administration panel and appointed him to the Democratic Steering Committee, which makes committee assignments.

Larson has a commitment to public service and to his hometown's largest employer, Pratt & Whitney, which makes engines for military aircraft. Larson's father worked for the engine manufacturer headquartered in East Hartford, and Larson grew up with seven siblings in Hartford's Mayberry Village, a public housing project where many Pratt & Whitney employees lived. His mother, who worked at the state Capitol in Hartford and served on the East Hartford Town Council, encouraged her children to involve themselves in public life. Larson's younger brother, Timothy, is mayor of East Hartford.

In his first three terms, Larson sat on the Armed Services Committee, where he fought proposed funding cuts for the F-22 jet fighter. He also is a co-founder of the Tactical Air Caucus, which supports the funding of new jet fighters.

From his seat on the Science Committee, he championed legislation to increase funding for aerospace research and development, and for the development of fuel cell technology. In 2004, Larson and Connecticut's two Democratic senators obtained federal funding to help create a National Center for Aerospace Leadership in the 1st District. The center will conduct joint public-private research and development projects in the aerospace, aviation and defense industries.

Larson casts a dependable Democratic vote on most matters. In 2004, he voted in agreement with a majority of Democrats 95 percent of the time. He consistently votes "no" on measures to expand overseas trade that organized labor opposes. He even voted against free trade agreements with Australia and Morocco in 2004, which most Democrats favored.

Larson was successful in the 108th with his effort to have the historic Coltsville area of Hartford considered for inclusion in the national park system. Coltsville, a company town created by the gunmaker Samuel Colt, was a key site in America's industrial growth.

He had trouble pressing more partisan issues, however. The Rules Committee, for instance, refused to permit him to offer amendments to provide an alternative means of funding the war in Iraq, allow Medicare to negotiate lower prescription drug prices with drug manufacturers and increase federal funding for education programs for people with disabilities.

One of his first successes on Capitol Hill came in his first term when he sponsored legislation directing the librarian of Congress to prepare a history of the House. He headed off potential partisan bickering by signing on both Speaker J. Dennis Hastert and Minority Leader Richard A. Gephardt as cosponsors.

A former high school football coach, Larson often emphasizes the importance of teamwork, particularly in the partisan atmosphere of the House.

"There will always be rugged individualists, and we will always praise them. . . . But what gets the job done is teamwork," he once told the Southern Connecticut Business Journal.

After graduating from Central Connecticut State University, Larson taught high school history and coached for about five years. He then went into the insurance business. Stints on the local school board and town council were followed by his election in 1982 to the state Senate.

When Republicans took control of the state Senate in 1984, Larson was the only Democrat allowed to chair a committee, the Energy and Technology panel. Two years later, when the Democrats won back a majority, he was named Senate president pro tem, the state's third-highest office. He served in that post for the next eight years — making him the longest-serving president pro tem in state history.

Larson wrote Connecticut's Family and Medical Leave Act — the first such law enacted in the country. He also pushed for "family resource centers," public school buildings that are used to offer child care and family support services.

He waged an unsuccessful bid for governor in 1994, gaining the endorsements of his party leaders but losing the primary to state Comptroller Bill Curry.

Out of public office for the first time in 15 years, Larson returned to the insurance business. In 1996, he led a statewide volunteer drive, "ConneCT '96," that aimed to wire all the state's schools and libraries to the Internet. His interest in that issue continues in Congress, where he has chaired the Digital Divide Caucus, which works to make technology available to all Americans, regardless of geography or socioeconomic circumstances.

When veteran 1st District Democratic Rep. Barbara B. Kennelly announced late in 1997 that she was running for governor in 1998, Larson was the first Democrat to file for her seat. He edged past Miles S. Rapoport, the Connecticut secretary of state, in the primary and then cruised to a 17 percentage point victory in November.

In 2000, he pinned a 44 percentage point defeat on Republican Bob Backlund, a charismatic former professional wrestler with no prior political experience. He was not hurt by the fact that the 1st is so solidly liberal that it was once described by the Hartford Courant as a district in which "a Democrat could probably take a two-year nap and be re-elected."

With the 1st left largely intact by redistricting after the 2000 census, Larson has won easy re-elections in 2002 and 2004 — both times by better than a 2-to-1 ratio.

CONNECTICUT 1
Central — Hartford, Bristol

Situated midway between Boston and New York — roughly 100 miles from each — the 1st is an attractive commercial center for businesses straddling the Northeast Corridor. Insurance companies, banks and state government are the lifeblood of Hartford and its well-off suburbs.

Hartford saw a renewal in the 1990s, cleaning up its downtown and attracting several high-tech manufacturing firms. But challenges remain: While Hartford remains the most populous city in the 1st District, it experienced a 13 percent population decline in the 1990s. West Hartford, the next most populous jurisdiction, grew by 6 percent.

Hartford has an overwhelmingly minority population and is staunchly Democratic. The city gave John Kerry 80 percent of the vote in the 2004 presidential election, more than any other city or town in the state. Democrats outnumber Republicans in the 1st by more than a 2-to-1 ratio. The district gave Kerry his largest vote margin in Connecticut, and a Republican has not represented Hartford in the House since 1959.

Hispanics comprise three-fifths of Hartford residents, with most of them of Puerto Rican descent. City voters in 2001 elected Hartford's first Hispanic mayor and re-elected him in 2003.

In the 1990s, the 1st was relatively compact in shape. Connecticut lost one seat in the 2000 reapportionment, and the 1st now resembles a backward "C." The new district takes in some sparsely populated towns in northwestern Connecticut and part of Middletown, where Wesleyan University is located. The district also includes Democratic-leaning Bristol, where ESPN has its headquarters.

MAJOR INDUSTRY
Insurance, banking, defense, government

CITIES
Hartford, 121,578; West Hartford (unincorporated), 63,589; Bristol, 60,062; East Hartford (unincorporated), 49,575; Central Manchester (unincorporated), 30,595; Newington (unincorporated), 29,306

NOTABLE
The Hartford Courant, founded in 1764, is the nation's oldest newspaper in continuous circulation; Noah Webster, author of the first American dictionary, was born in West Hartford; Hartford's Wadsworth Atheneum is the nation's oldest public art museum.

KEY VOTES

2004
Yes Extend federal unemployment benefits by 13 weeks
Yes Pass $283.2 billion, six-year federal highway and mass transit bill
No Approve $146 billion multi-year extension of previously enacted middle-class tax breaks
No Amend the Constitution to prohibit same-sex marriage
No Cut corporate taxes $137 billion over 10 years
Yes Reorganize U.S. intelligence agencies as proposed by Sept. 11 commission

2003
No Cut taxes by $330 billion through fiscal 2013
Yes Block Bush rule scaling back overtime pay for some white-collar federal workers
Yes Do not allow use of search warrants without first notifying subjects
Yes Allow importation of prescription drugs
No Create private school voucher program in Washington, D.C.
No Ban "partial birth" abortion except to save a woman's life
Yes Split $18.6 billion in Iraq aid into half-grant, half-loan
No Overhaul Medicare and create prescription drug benefit

CQ VOTE STUDIES

	PARTY UNITY		PRESIDENTIAL SUPPORT	
	Support	Oppose	Support	Oppose
2004	95%	5%	24%	76%
2003	96%	4%	18%	82%
2002	95%	5%	30%	70%
2001	88%	12%	22%	78%
2000	93%	7%	85%	15%

INTEREST GROUPS

	AFL-CIO	ADA	CCUS	ACU
2004	93%	100%	38%	16%
2003	100%	100%	21%	20%
2002	100%	95%	50%	0%
2001	92%	90%	45%	8%
2000	90%	95%	57%	12%

Rep. Rob Simmons (R)

CAPITOL OFFICE
225-2076
www.house.gov/simmons
215 Cannon 20515-0702; fax 225-4977

COMMITTEES
Armed Services
Homeland Security
(Intelligence, Information Sharing & Terrorism
Risk Assessment - chairman)
Transportation & Infrastructure

HOMETOWN
Stonington

BORN
Feb. 11, 1943, Manhattan, N.Y.

RELIGION
Episcopalian

FAMILY
Wife, Heidi Simmons; two children

EDUCATION
Haverford College, B.A. 1965 (English literature);
Harvard U., M.P.A. 1979; U. of Connecticut,
attended 1988-91 (political science)

MILITARY SERVICE
Army, 1965-68; Army Reserve, 1970-2000

CAREER
Professor; congressional aide; CIA agent

POLITICAL HIGHLIGHTS
Candidate for Stonington Board of Selectmen,
1985; Stonington Republican Town Committee,
1986-92 (chairman, 1988-92); Conn. House, 1991-
2001

ELECTION RESULTS

2004 GENERAL

Rob Simmons (R)	166,412	54.2%
Jim Sullivan (D)	140,536	45.8%

2004 PRIMARY

Rob Simmons (R)	unopposed

2002 GENERAL

Rob Simmons (R)	117,434	54.1%
Joseph D. Courtney (D)	99,674	45.9%

PREVIOUS WINNING PERCENTAGES
2000 (51%)

Elected 2000; 3rd term

Simmons was an Army intelligence officer in Vietnam and a CIA spy for a decade. He has since proved he can handle another challenging task — surviving as a Republican in a Democratic-leaning district.

After toppling a Democratic incumbent in 2000 to become the first GOP lawmaker from the 2nd District since 1972, Simmons has held off two other Democratic challengers in races that have been on the national shortlist of those to watch. In both cases, his success stemmed from playing up his national security background, expressing devotion to the district's economic base and selectively bolting from his party on hot-button issues.

Simmons' experience as a CIA operations officer gave him instant credibility among his colleagues after the Sept. 11, 2001, terrorist attacks as someone who understood the nature of international terrorism. A former staff director of the Senate Intelligence Committee, he was lifted almost immediately from the relative obscurity of most House freshmen.

Fellow lawmakers sought him out during congressional inquiries into how the terrorist attacks were carried out. And when the House debated whether to authorize a military attack on Iraq, Simmons' words of caution and his support for a Democratic-drafted alternative that called for the president to work with the United Nations were surprising to some in his party.

Believing he can be more effective and outspoken if not bound by the Intelligence Committee's secrecy rules, he is not on the panel, but he works closely with its members. Simmons is a leading advocate for increasing the use of "open source" intelligence collected comprehensively from newspapers, the Internet and other public outlets. To bolster his argument, at a hearing he displayed for colleagues a set of satellite photos from a private satellite company that showed evidence of Iran's having buried portions of its Natanz nuclear facility underground. Congress, he said, has to resist the notion that, "It's not sexy because it isn't classified."

Simmons' military background — he still wears his Army dog tags — helped him land a seat on the Armed Services Committee. He has taken a special interest in submarine projects at General Dynamics' Electric Boat Corp., which is headquartered in the 2nd District. As the 109th Congress began, Simmons said one of his chief goals would be keeping the Navy submarine base in Groton open during the next round of military base closings. Another priority, he said, would be arranging for the Navy to switch sooner from buying one to two *Virginia*-class submarines each year.

During the 108th Congress, Simmons chaired the Veterans' Affairs Subcommittee on Health, and was able to win House passage of a bill that addressed a nursing shortage. The measure provided incentives for nurses to work at VA hospitals and established a program to study alternative recruitment methods. Simmons left the panel in the 109th Congress to join the Homeland Security Committee and to take over the chairmanship of the panel's Subcommittee on Intelligence, Information Sharing and Terrorism Risk Assessment.

In his first term, Simmons strayed from the party line more than any other GOP freshman. In 2004, he ranked third among House Republicans who voted most often against their party's majority. His independent ways continued during the 108th Congress, as he voted for a Democratic proposal to offer federal supplemental unemployment insurance benefits for six months to jobless workers. He also sided with organized labor groups on their push to stop passage of legislation allowing employers to grant time off, instead of extra pay, when employees work overtime.

Simmons says he was greatly influenced by his maternal grandfather, Robert Ruhl, for whom he is named. Ruhl was editor and publisher of Oregon's Medford Mail Tribune and during his tenure, the newspaper won the 1934 Pulitzer Prize for public service for its campaign against unscrupulous local politicians. Simmons worked for the paper during summer breaks and envisioned a life in public service, intending to become a journalist as well.

But the Vietnam War was under way when he graduated from college, so he enlisted rather than be drafted. He spent 19 months overseas as an Army intelligence officer, winning two Bronze Stars. He then joined the CIA, working as an operations officer for a decade, including five years on assignment in East Asia. He left the agency in 1979 after hundreds of agents were dismissed as part of a post-Vietnam downsizing.

Simmons got a master's degree in public administration from Harvard, and launched a career on Capitol Hill. He worked for two years as a legislative assistant to Rhode Island Sen. John H. Chafee, an influential Republican moderate. Two years later, in 1981, he went to work for the Senate Intelligence Committee, where he found himself facing off against top CIA officials over what became the Iran-contra scandal. He left the staff in 1985 and returned to his native Connecticut.

During five terms in the Connecticut House, he worked on transportation and education issues. But he had aspirations for Congress. When Democrat Sam Gejdenson was returned to the House for a 10th term with 61 percent of the vote — after three close elections — Simmons decided to take him on in 2000. He focused on local issues and said that the incumbent's voting record was too liberal for the district. He won one of the year's biggest upsets by 2,860 votes.

In 2002, redistricting did little to alter the 2nd District's politically competitive nature, and both national party organizations targeted the race for special attention. In the end, Simmons was held to 54 percent of the vote by the Democratic candidate, former state Rep. Joseph D. Courtney.

Democrats targeted Simmons again in 2004, with former Norwich city councilor Jim Sullivan emerging in the primary. Sullivan sought to tie Simmons to President Bush and played on the district's unhappiness with the Iraq war. Pre-election polls showed the two neck and neck. But Simmons outspent Sullivan 2-to-1 and brought luminaries such as Arizona Sen. John McCain to campaign with him. He won by an 8 percentage point margin.

KEY VOTES

2004
Yes   Extend federal unemployment benefits by 13 weeks
Yes   Pass $283.2 billion, six-year federal highway and mass transit bill
Yes   Approve $146 billion multi-year extension of previously enacted middle-class tax breaks
No   Amend the Constitution to prohibit same-sex marriage
Yes   Cut corporate taxes $137 billion over 10 years
Yes   Reorganize U.S. intelligence agencies as proposed by Sept. 11 commission

2003
Yes   Cut taxes by $330 billion through fiscal 2013
No   Block Bush rule scaling back overtime pay for some white-collar federal workers
No   Do not allow use of search warrants without first notifying subjects
No   Allow importation of prescription drugs
-   Create private school voucher program in Washington, D.C.
No   Ban "partial birth" abortion except to save a woman's life
No   Split $18.6 billion in Iraq aid into half-grant, half-loan
Yes   Overhaul Medicare and create prescription drug benefit

CQ VOTE STUDIES

	PARTY UNITY		PRESIDENTIAL SUPPORT	
	Support	Oppose	Support	Oppose
2004	73%	27%	58%	42%
2003	83%	17%	67%	33%
2002	78%	22%	78%	22%
2001	83%	17%	77%	23%

INTEREST GROUPS

	AFL-CIO	ADA	CCUS	ACU
2004	53%	55%	86%	40%
2003	27%	20%	80%	48%
2002	22%	35%	90%	68%
2001	25%	35%	91%	44%

CONNECTICUT 2
East – Norwich, New London, Storrs

The state's largest and most working-class district, the 2nd runs from the waterfront of Middlesex and New London counties north to the Massachusetts border through small towns and the main campus of the University of Connecticut in Storrs.

The defense industry continues to be a major economic force here, but it now shares some of that responsibility with the American Indian-owned Foxwoods and Mohegan Sun casinos. The economic shift started in the early 1990s, when some of the submarine contracts in New London and Groton were sent to Newport News, Va., just as Foxwoods, and later Mohegan Sun, began attracting visitors.

Defense and casino matters sit atop the district's list of political issues. The stream of gamblers and casino employees traveling through the district has strained the 2nd's highways, making transportation an election year issue. In addition, the casinos and surrounding towns have quarreled over which regulations should apply to reservation land.

Despite a series of close elections throughout the 1980s and 1990s, Democrats were able to maintain their lock on the 2nd until 2000, when Rep. Simmons became the first Republican elected since 1972. The district became slightly less Democratic in redistricting following the 2000 census, as liberal-leaning Middletown was excised from the 2nd and split up between the 1st and 3rd districts. John Kerry captured 54 percent of the 2nd's vote in the 2004 presidential election.

MAJOR INDUSTRY
Casinos, defense, health care

MILITARY BASES
New London Naval Submarine Base, 8,000 military, 2,500 civilian (2004)

CITIES
Norwich, 36,117; New London, 25,671; Willimantic (unincorporated), 15,823; Storrs (unincorporated), 10,996

NOTABLE
Foxwoods Resort and Casino, owned by the Mashantucket Pequot Tribal Nation, is the largest resort casino in the world, with annual revenue of $1 billion; New London is home to the U.S. Coast Guard Academy; The Mystic Seaport maritime museum is in Mystic.

Rep. Rosa DeLauro (D)

Elected 1990; 8th term

CAPITOL OFFICE
225-3661
www.house.gov/delauro
2262 Rayburn 20515-0703; fax 225-4890

COMMITTEES
Appropriations
Budget

HOMETOWN
New Haven

BORN
March 2, 1943, New Haven, Conn.

RELIGION
Roman Catholic

FAMILY
Husband, Stanley Greenberg; three stepchildren

EDUCATION
London School of Economics, attended 1962-63;
Marymount College (N.Y.), B.A. 1964; Columbia U.,
M.A. 1966 (international politics)

CAREER
Political activist; congressional and mayoral aide

POLITICAL HIGHLIGHTS
No previous office

ELECTION RESULTS

2004 GENERAL

Rosa DeLauro (D)	200,638	72.4%
Richter Elser (R)	69,160	25.0%
Ralph A. Ferrucci (GREEN)	7,182	2.6%

2004 PRIMARY

Rosa DeLauro (D)	unopposed

2002 GENERAL

Rosa DeLauro (D)	121,557	65.6%
Richter Elser (R)	54,757	29.5%
Charlie Pillsbury (GREEN)	9,050	4.9%

PREVIOUS WINNING PERCENTAGES
2000 (72%); 1998 (71%); 1996 (71%); 1994 (63%);
1992 (66%); 1990 (52%)

DeLauro is one of her party's fiercest liberal champions and a sharp critic of the Republican leadership in Congress. She is also a crafty politician.

As such, she was asked to chair the committee that prepared the party platform presented at the 2004 Democratic National Convention. She helped write a platform that sacrificed breadth and depth in the interest of consensus, the aim being to reflect the party's desire to foster a sense of unity. The final product clearly avoided detailed positions on issues that have long divided Democrats because as DeLauro said, "There is a uniformity around the view of the failed [George W.] Bush policies."

DeLauro (da-LAUR-o) has long been a voice for the party on national issues such as abortion rights, equal pay for women and women's health parity. She is also an outspoken ally of consumer advocates who push for food labeling and safety legislation. DeLauro knows she can speak out on national issues as long as she tends to business at home. She is hawkish on federal funding for the Black Hawk and Comanche helicopters, both products of the Stratford, Conn.-based Sikorsky Aircraft Corp.

She is easily one of the most recognizable faces in the House. Her floor speeches ooze partisanship and are often accompanied by strong podium-pounding. Her trademark clothes — bright colors, bold prints and chunky jewelry — land her on the occasional magazine worst-dressed list.

Now in her eighth term in the House, she has broken gender barriers to climb the Democratic leadership ladder. In that quest, DeLauro has had both successes and setbacks. In 107th Congress, she ran the party's communications arm as the handpicked assistant of Minority Leader Richard A. Gephardt.

As the 108th organized, she lost a race for Democratic Caucus chief to Robert Menendez of New Jersey by a lone vote, 104-103. DeLauro's appeal as a woman in leadership could not overcome Menendez's as a Hispanic. The loss marked the second time DeLauro was defeated for the position. In her first race for head of the caucus in 1998, she lost to Martin Frost of Texas. Though she is among the most influential Democrats in the House, all of her leadership roles so far have been appointed.

Providing some consolation, Minority Leader Nancy Pelosi made her the co-chairwoman of the Democratic Steering Committee, which makes committee assignments. She retains that spot for the 109th as well. DeLauro also gained a seat on the Budget Committee in addition to her slot on Appropriations.

During the 108th, DeLauro took on an even bigger opponent than the Republican leadership. A lifelong Catholic, DeLauro led her fellow Catholic representatives to speak out against church leaders who threatened to deny communion to politicians who favored abortion rights. They also urged the Catholic church to weigh in on a broader array of national issues — such as hunger, housing and wages.

DeLauro successfully championed a provision in the funding bill for the Department of Homeland Security to block the agency from giving contracts to so-called corporate expatriates that have incorporated offshore to avoid paying U.S. taxes. But she failed in her quest to expand payments to low-income parents as part of the child care tax credit.

DeLauro consistently works to ensure that her party does not take for granted the women voters who are one of its strongest constituencies. In 2000, she successfully pushed for legislation requiring insurers to pay for hospital stays after a mastectomy — ending a practice commonly known as "drive-through mastectomies." Her interest in women's health issues stems in part from her own battle with ovarian cancer several years ago. She also has advocated toughening penalties against employers who do not pay women and men equally for the same work.

All of the significant figures in DeLauro's life are passionately political. Her parents were both blue-collar activists on the New Haven City Council, and her husband is Stanley Greenberg, a prominent Democratic pollster and former adviser to President Clinton.

DeLauro developed her liberal views and political smarts growing up in Wooster Square, a tight-knit Italian neighborhood in New Haven. Her father, Ted, was an immigrant who became a New Haven alderman, and her mother, Luisa, was a factory worker who got her high school diploma studying at night. Her mother also became a city alderman.

Her parents' home was the hub of neighborhood meetings about happenings in the schools, the availability of jobs, and hassles with immigration officials. When her father decided to run for the city council, he kept a file box filled with voters' names and their concerns, then walked door-to-door to seek their votes.

As part of the first college-educated generation in her family, DeLauro graduated with honors from Marymount College in Tarrytown, N.Y., and received a master's degree in international politics from Columbia University.

In the 1960s, she became a community organizer in President Johnson's War on Poverty, then worked for the mayor of New Haven. She eventually proved her mettle running Democrat Christopher J. Dodd's first campaign for the Senate. When he won, she became his chief of staff for seven years. She expanded her political network by taking the helm of Emily's List, the powerful fundraising group promoting female candidates for higher office.

In 1990, when Democratic Rep. Bruce Morrison gave up his 3rd District seat to run for governor of Connecticut, DeLauro was ready to step out of supporting roles and become a candidate herself. Her political contacts enabled her to raise money quickly and shoo away intraparty competition.

Republicans put up state Sen. Thomas Scott, an energetic conservative opposed to gun control and abortion rights. He made some headway portraying DeLauro as a far-left radical, but her coalition of activist liberals and blue-collar voters gave her a 4 percentage point victory.

Scott came back for a rematch in 1992, but DeLauro was ready with a healthy campaign war chest. She won with 66 percent of the vote and has been re-elected easily since.

KEY VOTES

2004
Yes Extend federal unemployment benefits by 13 weeks
Yes Pass $283.2 billion, six-year federal highway and mass transit bill
No   Approve $146 billion multi-year extension of previously enacted middle-class tax breaks
No   Amend the Constitution to prohibit same-sex marriage
No   Cut corporate taxes $137 billion over 10 years
Yes Reorganize U.S. intelligence agencies as proposed by Sept. 11 commission

2003
No   Cut taxes by $330 billion through fiscal 2013
Yes Block Bush rule scaling back overtime pay for some white-collar federal workers
Yes Do not allow use of search warrants without first notifying subjects
Yes Allow importation of prescription drugs
No   Create private school voucher program in Washington, D.C.
No   Ban "partial birth" abortion except to save a woman's life
Yes Split $18.6 billion in Iraq aid into half-grant, half-loan
No   Overhaul Medicare and create prescription drug benefit

CQ VOTE STUDIES

	PARTY UNITY		PRESIDENTIAL SUPPORT	
	Support	Oppose	Support	Oppose
2004	98%	2%	21%	79%
2003	99%	1%	18%	82%
2002	96%	4%	22%	78%
2001	95%	5%	26%	74%
2000	97%	3%	87%	13%

INTEREST GROUPS

	AFL-CIO	ADA	CCUS	ACU
2004	100%	100%	29%	4%
2003	93%	100%	30%	20%
2002	100%	100%	35%	0%
2001	100%	95%	35%	0%
2000	100%	90%	42%	8%

CONNECTICUT 3
South — New Haven, Milford

Working-class, bedrock constituents of the Democratic Party mix with the liberal ivory tower elite in the 3rd. Situated on the state's southern coast, it encompasses both the working-class elements of New Haven, an active blue-collar port, and prestigious Yale University.

Although Yale is the city's largest employer, labor issues cause tension between the university and the city's blue-collar workers. All this stands in contrast to the surrounding towns where professionals, who commute throughout Connecticut and as far as New York City, reside. New Haven, like most Connecticut cities, is far poorer than its surrounding suburbs.

New Haven has a high percentage of Hispanics and blacks who traditionally support Democrats. Also, during redistricting following the 2000 census, the 3rd picked up most of the Democratic stronghold of Middletown, thereby making the district even more solidly Democratic. The outlying towns are slightly more conservative than the city, and the suburbs include many Italian-Americans.

The defense industry plays a large role in the 3rd. Sikorsky Aircraft, a helicopter manufacturer based in Stratford, depends on the military for survival, and Pratt & Whitney has a plant in North Haven. The district has had trouble attracting new industries, and was dealt a potential blow in early 2005 when the Defense Department did not award the new Marine One helicopter contract to Sikorsky. Proposed government increases in Black Hawk helicopter purchases may offset the Marine One loss.

New Haven has tried to lure tourists to its waterfront and business groups to its convention centers, with mild success. Ikea opened a giant home furnishings store in 2004 as part of the city's planned redevelopment of Long Wharf.

MAJOR INDUSTRY
Trade, manufacturing, defense

CITIES
New Haven, 123,626; West Haven, 52,360; Milford, 52,305; Stratford (unincorporated), 49,976; Middletown (pt.), 34,329; Naugatuck, 30,989

NOTABLE
Milford is home to the headquarters of the Subway sandwich shop chain; Polls conducted by Quinnipiac University in Hamden are frequently cited by national news organizations.

Rep. Christopher Shays (R)

Elected August 1987; 9th full term

CAPITOL OFFICE
225-5541
rep.shays@mail.house.gov
www.house.gov/shays
1126 Longworth 20515-0704; fax 225-9629

COMMITTEES
Financial Services
Government Reform
　(National Security, Emerging Threats &
　International Relations - chairman)
Homeland Security

HOMETOWN
Bridgeport

BORN
Oct. 18, 1945, Darien, Conn.

RELIGION
Christian Scientist

FAMILY
Wife, Betsi deRaismes Shays; one child

EDUCATION
Principia College, B.A. 1968 (American history &
political science); New York U., M.B.A. 1974
(urban affairs & economics), M.P.A. 1978

CAREER
Real estate broker; public official; Peace Corps
volunteer

POLITICAL HIGHLIGHTS
Conn. House, 1975-87; Republican candidate for
mayor of Stamford, 1983

ELECTION RESULTS

2004 GENERAL

Christopher Shays (R)	152,493	52.4%
Diane Farrell (D)	138,333	47.6%

2004 PRIMARY

Christopher Shays (R)	unopposed

2002 GENERAL

Christopher Shays (R)	113,197	64.4%
Stephanie Sanchez (D)	62,491	35.6%

PREVIOUS WINNING PERCENTAGES
2000 (58%); 1998 (69%); 1996 (60%); 1994 (74%); 1992
(67%); 1990 (77%); 1988 (72%); 1987 Special Election
(57%)

Shays stood out in his ninth term as a House member who took his oversight responsibilities seriously, even if that meant putting himself in physical danger. As chairman of the Government Reform Subcommittee on National Security, Shays visited Iraq six times in 2004 — more than any other lawmaker — to keep track of several Pentagon and State Department programs under his jurisdiction. Though many other lawmakers made the trek as well, Shays was the only Republican to criticize the tight controls that the Pentagon placed on his movements. He made defiant tours of the war zone on his own. As a result, Shays, a strong supporter of the war, knows more than anyone in the House about what U.S. troops face on the ground in Iraq.

Still, Shays' support for the war hurt him in his 2004 re-election campaign, forcing him to defend his moderate Republican candidacy much harder than usual for an incumbent. From a district that was home to many victims of the Sept. 11, 2001, terrorist attacks, he also broke from his Republican House colleagues in his outspoken support for intelligence overhaul legislation, passed in late 2004, that created a Director of National Intelligence.

But he can be a team player. In the 108th Congress, he supported the GOP tax cuts and spending reductions. During debate on the 2002 law creating the Homeland Security Department, Shays offered a key amendment on the rights of federal unionized workers, an issue that divided Republicans. His measure gave GOP moderates the chance to vote for something that seemed to favor labor, but which essentially preserved the expanded management authority the White House sought.

In 2002, Shays scored the biggest legislative coup of his career on a much different issue — enactment of new limits on the flow of money into federal campaigns, a cause he had long championed in vain. That year, influence-buying in Washington was again a hot issue as a result of the accounting scandal centered on the politically well-connected Enron Corp. Shays and Democrat Martin T. Meehan of Massachusetts capitalized on the public attention, resurrecting their legislation, and it ultimately passed the House in spite of several attempts by GOP leaders to block it.

A similar bill, sponsored by Republican John McCain of Arizona and Democrat Russell D. Feingold of Wisconsin, passed in the Senate. It became known as the McCain-Feingold law, and clamped down on "soft money" contributions, large donations from individuals and corporations that were flowing to the major parties.

Victory came with a steep price. Shays, who was next in line to replace Indiana's term-limited Dan Burton in the 108th Congress as chairman of the Government Reform Committee, was denied the gavel by the House GOP leadership, which strongly opposed his campaign finance bill. The plum instead went, pointedly, to Thomas M. Davis III of Virginia, who had endeared himself to the party by engineering the well-financed campaign organization that brought the GOP six additional House seats in 2002. Shays said, "I am a maverick. I realize that there are consequences."

As a moderate among the predominately conservative House Republicans, Shays touts a long list of issues on which he routinely goes against the grain. In the 108th Congress, he sided with the Democrats on party-line votes 25 percent of the time. And he voted against President Bush's wishes 36 percent of the time. Only one other House Republican — Jim Leach of Iowa — voted with Democrats more than Shays in the 108th, and only three Republican colleagues had lower presidential support records. His contrarian views, sometimes delivered with pained sincerity, leave colleagues grumbling that he is more interested in publicity than issues.

But many of Shays' positions flow naturally from the Rockefeller Republicanism that, while dying elsewhere in the country, still sustains dinner party conversations on the East Coast, including the tony suburbs of the 4th District. They also appeal to another of Shays' constituencies, the struggling residents of the city of Bridgeport, the state's biggest city.

Shays supports gun control and abortion rights, and he has opposed efforts to eliminate family planning funds from spending bills. He was one of only four House Republicans who opposed all of the articles of impeachment against President Clinton. He has bucked his leadership to support raising the minimum wage and banning job discrimination against gay people. After more than 60 of his constituents died in the attacks of Sept. 11, he sought, against Bush's wishes, a broad independent inquiry into government lapses in tracking terrorists.

He is particularly proud of his environmental positions, and in 2004, he was one of just 11 Republicans endorsed by the Sierra Club. "That's what really defines me as a moderate," he says. "I believe we're not going to have a world to live in if we neglect it."

Shays was a conscientious objector during the Vietnam War. After marrying right out of college, he and Betsi deRaismes Shays spent two years in the Fiji Islands as Peace Corps volunteers; she now holds a senior job at the agency.

At 29, Shays was elected to the state House in a rare Republican victory in the post-Watergate election of 1974. During his 13 years in Hartford, he developed an anti-establishment reputation. In 1985, he served several days in jail on a contempt citation after trying to make a courtroom statement accusing a judge of going easy on an attorney charged with misconduct.

The name recognition from that incident helped propel him to the House two years later, when veteran Republican Stewart B. McKinney died. With an extensive grass-roots network and tireless campaigning, Shays defeated the anointed GOP candidate in the primary and then won the special election with 57 percent of the vote.

He faced no serious election challenges until 2004, when he faced Democrat Diane Farrell, the First Selectman, or mayor, of Westport. Though redistricting in 2001 made the 4th District slightly more Republican, Farrell used Shays' support for the Iraq war against him with the 4th's many anti-war constituents. Shays won, garnering 52 percent of the vote — a relatively low showing for a longtime incumbent.

KEY VOTES

2004
Yes Extend federal unemployment benefits by 13 weeks
Yes Pass $283.2 billion, six-year federal highway and mass transit bill
Yes Approve $146 billion multi-year extension of previously enacted middle-class tax breaks
No Amend the Constitution to prohibit same-sex marriage
Yes Cut corporate taxes $137 billion over 10 years
Yes Reorganize U.S. intelligence agencies as proposed by Sept. 11 commission

2003
Yes Cut taxes by $330 billion through fiscal 2013
No Block Bush rule scaling back overtime pay for some white-collar federal workers
No Do not allow use of search warrants without first notifying subjects
Yes Allow importation of prescription drugs
Yes Create private school voucher program in Washington, D.C.
Yes Ban "partial birth" abortion except to save a woman's life
No Split $18.6 billion in Iraq aid into half-grant, half-loan
Yes Overhaul Medicare and create prescription drug benefit

CQ VOTE STUDIES

	PARTY UNITY		PRESIDENTIAL SUPPORT	
	Support	Oppose	Support	Oppose
2004	69%	31%	59%	41%
2003	78%	22%	67%	33%
2002	80%	20%	82%	18%
2001	75%	25%	65%	35%
2000	71%	29%	49%	51%

INTEREST GROUPS

	AFL-CIO	ADA	CCUS	ACU
2004	57%	70%	86%	38%
2003	27%	30%	77%	48%
2002	11%	20%	95%	76%
2001	17%	35%	83%	32%
2000	30%	40%	76%	60%

CONNECTICUT 4
Southwest — Bridgeport, Stamford

The 4th runs along Connecticut's sparkling "Gold Coast," bordering Long Island Sound, from the outskirts of New York City to Bridgeport on the district's southeast border. The contrast between working-class Bridgeport and the district's widespread wealth creates a complex world for politicians to navigate, as polo clubs rub elbows with the decayed city.

Many residents travel to jobs in New York City and Stamford, causing severe traffic problems on Interstate 95, already a congested route. Traffic issues permeate the public debate. Welfare-to-work programs also have become an issue. Having failed to place welfare recipients in good jobs in Bridgeport, the state's largest city, the local government began making moves to find employment for low-income residents in the affluent suburbs.

The 4th's political landscape is driven by the suburban elite, giving the district more registered Republicans than any other in Connecticut. Still, the 4th gave the edge to Democratic presidential candidates in 1996,

2000 and 2004. A majority of the population in the poor, urban areas votes Democratic. Darien, New Canaan and Oxford were three of the seven state jurisdictions to give George W. Bush more than 60 percent of the vote in 2004, while John Kerry's 71 percent showing in Bridgeport was his fifth-highest percentage in the state.

Republican mayors long dominated local politics. But Democrats made big inroads in 2001 when a Democrat won the race for first selectman in Greenwich and Norwalk's incumbent GOP mayor lost a re-election bid.

MAJOR INDUSTRY
Manufacturing, banking, medical

CITIES
Bridgeport, 139,529; Stamford, 117,083; Norwalk, 82,951; Trumbull (unincorporated), 34,243; Shelton (pt.), 28,192

NOTABLE
Republican Sen. Prescott Bush (1952-63), the father of the 41st president and a grandfather of the 43rd president, reared his family in Greenwich; General Electric's corporate headquarters are in Fairfield; P.T. Barnum, founder of the Ringling Bros., Barnum & Bailey Circus, made his home in Bridgeport; Bridgeport was the largest producer of ammunition for the Allied forces during both world wars.

Rep. Nancy L. Johnson (R)

Elected 1982; 12th term

CAPITOL OFFICE
225-4476
www.house.gov/nancyjohnson
2409 Rayburn 20515-0705; fax 225-4488

COMMITTEES
Ways & Means
  (Health - chairwoman)
Joint Taxation

HOMETOWN
New Britain

BORN
Jan. 5, 1935, Chicago, Ill.

RELIGION
Unitarian

FAMILY
Husband, Ted Johnson; three children

EDUCATION
Radcliffe College, B.A. 1957; U. of London, attended 1957-58

CAREER
Civic leader

POLITICAL HIGHLIGHTS
Republican candidate for New Britain Common Council, 1975; Conn. Senate, 1977-83

ELECTION RESULTS

2004 GENERAL

Nancy L. Johnson (R)	168,268	59.8%
Theresa B. Gerratana (D)	107,438	38.2%
Fernando Ramirez (WFM)	3,196	1.1%

2004 PRIMARY

Nancy L. Johnson (R)	unopposed

2002 GENERAL

Nancy L. Johnson (R)	113,626	54.3%
Jim Maloney (D)	90,616	43.3%
Joseph A. Zdonczyk (CC)	3,709	1.8%

PREVIOUS WINNING PERCENTAGES
2000 (63%); 1998 (58%); 1996 (50%); 1994 (64%); 1992 (70%); 1990 (74%); 1988 (66%); 1986 (64%); 1984 (64%); 1982 (52%)

Johnson's mix of maverick and party loyalist has added up to staying power. In 2005, she became the longest-serving House member in Connecticut's history with 12 terms.

Yet as one of the House GOP's small cadre of moderates, Johnson is invariably overruled by the more conservative Republican leadership on matters such as environmental protection, abortion rights and education funding. Still, she perseveres and is sometimes able to influence the debate.

In the 108th Congress, Johnson was the only woman in the negotiating room during the creation of the landmark Medicare law, which added a prescription drug benefit for seniors. She chairs the Ways and Means Committee's Health Subcommittee, but her role in shaping the Medicare bill was overshadowed by the powerful full committee chairman, Bill Thomas of California. Still, Johnson did have some influence. In the final version, Johnson was able to protect payments to cancer doctors, and she inserted a pilot program on disease management, which puts a coordinator in charge of patient care involving multiple specialists.

Johnson seems to enjoy a congenial relationship with the more conservative Thomas. The two often can be seen talking on the House floor. "We're both policy maniacs," she says.

Although it is not clear how much of what Johnson has to say makes its way into the chairman's draft bills, Thomas eventually bowed to her and other committee members' demands in 2003 that a corporate tax bill include a big tax cut for manufacturers, something wanted by United Technologies, which employs thousands of people in Connecticut.

And in 2002, Thomas included in two tax bills provisions sought by Johnson to crack down on companies that move their headquarters to Bermuda or other offshore tax havens. Tool and hardware maker Stanley Works, based in Johnson's district, canceled such a move in the face of a political outcry. She says Thomas "had a lot of reservations about that legislation but . . . he knew how important it was with me to address the issue."

The 108th showed Johnson's two sides: the rebellious Republican willing to challenge the party line and the cautious lawmaker careful not to isolate herself within her party. Johnson led the fight opposing the GOP leadership's effort to use the budget resolution to open the coastal plain of Alaska's Arctic National Wildlife Refuge to oil and gas exploration. As a result, the Sierra Club rewarded her with an endorsement in 2004. Johnson also earned a perfect score from NARAL Pro-Choice America, even as the GOP majority sought a ban on a procedure critics call "partial birth" abortion.

At the same time, Johnson toed the party line in supporting the exoneration of Majority Leader Tom DeLay against ethics charges in 2004. And she was so loath to criticize former Connecticut GOP Gov. John G. Rowland, who was accused in a bribery scandal, that the Hartford Courant referred to her behavior as the "the Nancy Johnson waffle."

The congresswoman is used to being squeezed from both sides. During her first three House terms, Johnson's pursuit of a prestigious committee assignment was thwarted by GOP conservatives, who took a dim view of her support for abortion rights and her calls for more diversity in the Republican Party. She landed her Ways and Means seat in 1989, but she was soundly beaten in a bid for a low-level leadership post three years later.

Johnson said she is not tempted to switch parties even as the GOP has slid to the right over the years. "The Republicans have a far greater respect for the value and importance of local power and individual responsibility to the success of our democracy than do the Democrats," Johnson says. Yet she was among the 10 Republicans who voted most often in the 108th against their party's majority, casting votes in opposition 18 percent of the time.

Johnson is careful to look after the insurance companies that are a major presence in her state — making it difficult for her to support any significant regulation of health insurers. She voted against the bipartisan managed-care overhaul bill passed by the House in 1999 and backed a more limited alternative endorsed by the GOP leadership. Johnson's Ways and Means colleague, Democrat Pete Stark of California, once called her "a whore for the insurance industry." He later apologized.

Johnson was chairwoman of the ethics committee during the 104th Congress, and events during that tenure almost ended her House career. The marquee case before the panel involved the fundraising activities of Speaker Newt Gingrich of Georgia, and her handling of the matter displeased lawmakers and constituents in both parties. Democrats accused her of dragging the case out to help the Republican Speaker; Republicans said her actions played into the Democrats' hands. She won her eighth term in 1996 by only 1,587 votes.

A Chicago native, Johnson came East to go to college. She married, raised three children and got involved in community affairs in New Britain. Her civic activism led Republicans to recruit her into politics. After losing a city council election in 1975, she won a state Senate seat the next year, waging a door-to-door campaign to defeat a Democratic incumbent by 150 votes. By 1980, her winning share was up to 62 percent of the vote.

When Democratic Rep. Toby Moffett announced he was giving up the 6th District seat to run for the Senate in 1982, Johnson moved to take his place. She captured the backing of the Republican Party establishment, and she overwhelmed a conservative opponent in the primary. In November, she defeated the badly underfunded Democrat, state Sen. Bill Curry, by 4 percentage points.

Johnson's district teeters between moderate Republican and Democratic leanings. After the close call in 1996, she pushed her percentage of the vote up to 63 in 2000. But she faced another stiff test in 2002, when Connecticut lost a House seat in reapportionment and her district was combined with that of Democratic Rep. Jim Maloney. The incumbent vs. incumbent matchup cost a fortune and drew national attention. Johnson won re-election by 11 percentage points. In a low-key 2004 race against a lesser-known competitor, Johnson sailed to victory with 60 percent of the vote.

KEY VOTES

2004
No Extend federal unemployment benefits by 13 weeks
Yes Pass $283.2 billion, six-year federal highway and mass transit bill
Yes Approve $146 billion multi-year extension of previously enacted middle-class tax breaks
No Amend the Constitution to prohibit same-sex marriage
Yes Cut corporate taxes $137 billion over 10 years
Yes Reorganize U.S. intelligence agencies as proposed by Sept. 11 commission

2003
Yes Cut taxes by $330 billion through fiscal 2013
No Block Bush rule scaling back overtime pay for some white-collar federal workers
No Do not allow use of search warrants without first notifying subjects
Yes Allow importation of prescription drugs
Yes Create private school voucher program in Washington, D.C.
No Ban "partial birth" abortion except to save a woman's life
No Split $18.6 billion in Iraq aid into half-grant, half-loan
Yes Overhaul Medicare and create prescription drug benefit

CQ VOTE STUDIES

	PARTY UNITY		PRESIDENTIAL SUPPORT	
	Support	Oppose	Support	Oppose
2004	82%	18%	65%	35%
2003	83%	17%	70%	30%
2002	75%	25%	75%	25%
2001	76%	24%	70%	30%
2000	71%	29%	51%	49%

INTEREST GROUPS

	AFL-CIO	ADA	CCUS	ACU
2004	27%	45%	100%	56%
2003	13%	35%	79%	52%
2002	11%	30%	90%	56%
2001	17%	30%	87%	32%
2000	10%	35%	90%	56%

CONNECTICUT 5
West — Danbury, New Britain, most of Waterbury

Based in the western part of the state, the 5th is a mix of bucolic farmland and mid-size industrial cities that includes nearly equal parts of the old 5th and 6th districts. The two were largely combined following the 2000 census when slow-growing Connecticut lost one House seat in reapportionment.

Waterbury is the 5th's most populous city, with about four of five city residents living in the district (the rest live in the 3rd District). The city is middle-class and racially diverse, with blacks and Hispanics together totaling 40 percent of the population. East of Waterbury, in the 5th's eastern edge, is Cheshire, an upper-income, Republican-leaning area, and Meriden, a Democratic-voting area with a large (21 percent) Hispanic population and a sizable Polish-American constituency.

North and east of Waterbury the district branches off to take in New Britain, where in 2002 directors of the toolmaking company Stanley Works voted — before reversing themselves — to reincorporate in Bermuda. New Britain, which lost population in the 1990s, has an ample Hispanic community and votes Democratic.

Danbury, located in the southwestern corner of the district, grew by 14 percent in the 1990s and has attracted immigrants from South America, the Caribbean and southeast Asia.

The 5th is a politically competitive district. John Kerry barely won the area in the 2004 presidential contest with 49 percent, his lowest percentage in the state. The GOP runs well in the medium-size and small towns in the district's center. George W. Bush carried several towns north and east of Danbury, including burgeoning New Milford and Newtown, in 2004.

MAJOR INDUSTRY
Manufacturing, health care, insurance, defense

CITIES
Waterbury (pt.), 88,624; Danbury, 74,848; New Britain, 71,538; Meriden, 58,244; Torrington (pt.), 20,202

NOTABLE
Cheshire was designated the "Bedding Plant Capital of Connecticut" by the state legislature.

DELAWARE

Gov. Ruth Ann Minner (D)

First elected: 2000
Length of term: 4 years
Term expires: 1/09
Salary: $132,500
Phone: (302) 739-4101

Hometown: Milford
Born: Jan. 17, 1935; Milford, Del.
Religion: Methodist
Family: Widowed; three children
Education: Delaware Technical and Community College, G.E.D. 1968
Career: Towing company owner; state legislative aide
Political highlights: Del. House, 1975-83; Del. Senate, 1983-93; lieutenant governor, 1993-2001

Election results:
2004 GENERAL

Ruth Ann Minner (D)	185,687	50.9%
William Swain Lee (R)	167,115	45.8%
Frank Infante (LIBERT, INDC)	12,206	3.3%

Lt. Gov. John Carney (D)

First elected: 2000
Length of term: 4 years
Term expires: 1/09
Salary: $73,000
Phone: (302) 744-4333

STATE LEGISLATURE

General Assembly: January-June

House: 41 members, two-year terms
2005 breakdown: 25R, 15D, 1I; 27 men, 14 women
Salary: $39,785
Phone: (302) 744-4087

Senate: 21 members, 4-year terms
2005 breakdown: 13D, 8R; 14 men, 7 women
Salary: $39,785
Phone: (302) 744-4087

STATE TERM LIMITS

Governor: 2 terms
House: No
Senate: No

URBAN STATISTICS

CITY	POPULATION
Wilmington	72,664
Dover	32,135
Newark	28,547
Milford	6,732
Seaford	6,699

REGISTERED VOTERS

Democrat	44%
Republican	33%
Others/unaffilated	23%

POPULATION

2004 population (est.)	830,364
2000 population	783,600
1990 population	666,168
Percent change (1990-2000)	+17.6%
Rank among states (2004)	45

Median age	36
Born in state	48.3%
Foreign born	5.7%
Violent crime rate	684/100,000
Poverty level	9.2%
Federal workers	5,438
Military	8,799

REDISTRICTING

Delaware retained its one House seat in reapportionment.

MISCELLANEOUS

Web: www.delaware.gov
Capital: Dover
STATE ELECTION OFFICIAL
(302) 739-4277
DEMOCRATIC HEADQUARTERS
(302) 328-9036
REPUBLICAN HEADQUARTERS
(302) 651-0260

District Statistics

DIST.	2004 VOTE FOR PRESIDENT BUSH	KERRY	WHITE	BLACK	ASIAN	HISP	MEDIAN INCOME	WHITE COLLAR	BLUE COLLAR	SERVICE INDUSTRY	OVER 64	UNDER 18	COLLEGE EDUCATION	RURAL	SQ. MILES
AL	46%	53%	72%	19%	2%	5%	$47,381	63%	23%	15%	13%	25%	25%	20%	1,954
STATE	46	53	72	19	2	5	$47,381	63	23	15	13	25	25	20	1,954
U.S.	50.7	48.3	69	12	4	13	$41,994	60	25	15	12	26	24	21	3,537,438

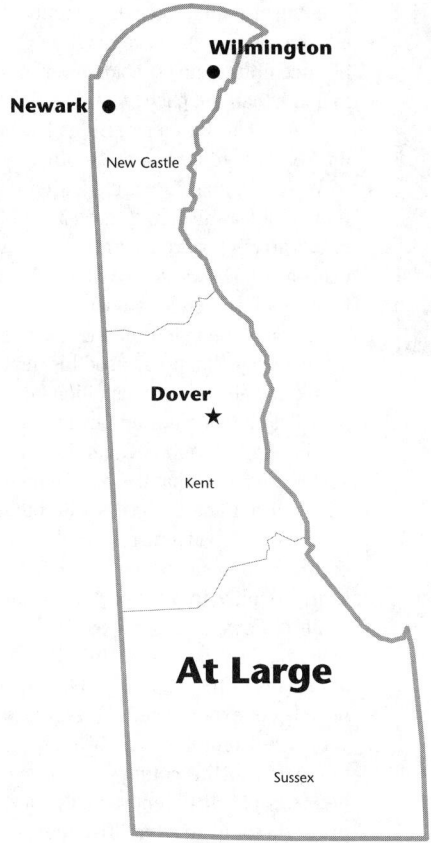

Wilmington

Newark

New Castle

Dover

Kent

At Large

Sussex

Sen. Joseph R. Biden Jr. (D)

Elected 1972; 6th term

CAPITOL OFFICE
224-5042
senator@biden.senate.gov
biden.senate.gov
201 Russell 20510-0802; fax 224-0139

COMMITTEES
Foreign Relations - ranking member
Judiciary

HOMETOWN
Wilmington

BORN
Nov. 20, 1942, Scranton, Pa.

RELIGION
Roman Catholic

FAMILY
Wife, Jill Biden; four children (one deceased)

EDUCATION
U. of Delaware, B.A. 1965 (history & political
science); Syracuse U., J.D. 1968

CAREER
Lawyer

POLITICAL HIGHLIGHTS
New Castle County Council, 1970-72

ELECTION RESULTS

2002 GENERAL

Joseph R. Biden Jr. (D)	135,253	58.2%
Raymond J. Clatworthy (R)	94,793	40.8%

2002 PRIMARY

Joseph R. Biden Jr. (D)	unopposed

PREVIOUS WINNING PERCENTAGES
1996 (60%); 1990 (63%); 1984 (60%); 1978 (58%);
1972 (50%)

For better or worse, Biden has been the Democrats' leading critic of the Bush administration's handling of the war in Iraq. He has a deeper understanding of foreign policy matters than most lawmakers, and can be eloquent in critiquing the administration while still maintaining working relationships with key officials such as Secretary of State Condoleezza Rice. But he succumbs to an occasional verbal slip that makes him seem less statesmanlike than the party would like.

Now in his sixth term, Biden has spent half his life in the Senate, a distinction earned by just three others — fellow Democrats Robert C. Byrd of West Virginia, Edward M. Kennedy of Massachusetts and Daniel K. Inouye of Hawaii. The American public, at least the portion that watches public affairs programs, knows him as a frequent guest on the Sunday television talk shows, where he can be sometimes profound and sometimes long-winded, even for a politician.

Although he voted for the 2002 resolution approving the use of force against Iraq, Biden has used his television appearances and floor speeches to castigate the administration for a lack of planning prior to the invasion, poor field intelligence and insufficient troops. As the senior Democrat on the Foreign Relations Committee and its former chairman, Biden often voices criticisms that the panel's moderate Republican chairman, Richard G. Lugar of Indiana, agrees with but is reluctant to say publicly.

Biden also has a history of deal-cutting with Republicans, on both foreign and domestic policy, which helped him during President Bush's first term to cultivate a rapport with both Rice and then-Secretary of State Colin L. Powell. He chaired the Foreign Relations panel during a transformational moment in the history of American foreign policy — the aftermath of the Sept. 11, 2001, terrorist attacks. Not only did he have decades of experience in foreign policy, but as a former chairman of the Judiciary Committee, he brought together many strands of knowledge important to the country's new war on terrorism. Indeed, on the day before Sept. 11, Biden warned in a speech that the United States faced a grave threat from a terrorist attack.

In the turbulent weeks after the attacks, Biden's Senate colleagues looked to him to help draft the resolution that gave Bush authority to wage war against al Qaeda and the Taliban regime in Afghanistan. Biden steered a course between giving Bush sufficient authority to prosecute terrorists and surrendering congressional oversight over foreign policy.

Biden had mixed results from his other high-profile endeavor, which was attempting to slow Bush's rush to war with Iraq. Biden insisted that any action required both congressional and United Nations approval, and he took credit when the president chose to at least ask Congress to sanction war. But in 2002, the president also rebuffed Biden's effort to pass legislation requiring a go-slow approach and instead bypassed his panel to cut a deal with House Democratic Leader Richard A. Gephardt of Missouri.

As chairman, Biden also pushed to enactment a law allowing the United States to forgive former Soviet debt if the funds were applied to non-proliferation programs in the former Soviet states.

Biden's tendency to say exactly what is on his mind has tripped him up on occasion. He drew barbs from Republicans in 2003 when, in making the point that Bush had to be willing to deploy ground forces in Afghanistan, he used the expression "go mano a mano" with the Afghans, a bit of commonly used slang that some of his GOP colleagues felt was flip. In 2004, Biden called the Bush administration "childish" after it failed to produce a witness for a Senate hearing on Iraq. As a critical New Republic profile put it, Biden is "legendary for speaking impulsively and leaving others to clean up the mess. . . . Not exactly the person you want out front when the country is at war."

Biden has been no less outspoken as a member of the Judiciary Committee. In 2004, he led Democrats in successfully resisting what they saw as hasty changes in criminal sentencing law during a House-Senate conference on a child crimes bill. Republicans agreed to modify the sentencing provisions so that the new restrictions on lenient sentences were limited to child and sex crimes.

Biden's stewardship at Judiciary from 1987 to 1995 will probably be best remembered for his handling of the 1991 nomination of Clarence Thomas for the Supreme Court. The nationally televised committee hearings at which professor Anita F. Hill accused Thomas of sexual harassment were an embarrassment to Biden, whose committee had not conducted more than a cursory investigation of Hill's charges until after they were leaked to the media.

But Biden also compiled a substantial legislative record wielding the Judiciary gavel, including a comprehensive anti-crime law in 1994 and an anti-terrorism law in 1996. Indeed, Biden is quick to point out that six years before the Sept. 11 attacks, he had proposed many of the provisions included in the subsequent anti-terrorism law, but that his ideas had been derailed by civil libertarians.

When Democrats regained control of the Senate in June 2001, upon the defection of Vermont's James M. Jeffords from the GOP, Biden had his pick of the Foreign Relations or Judiciary chairmanships. After a period of calculated public indecision, Biden took the Foreign Relations panel and pressed the new Judiciary chairman, Democrat Patrick J. Leahy of Vermont, to name him chairman of the Crime and Drugs Subcommittee. That allowed Biden to pursue his long-held interest in anti-narcotics efforts.

The son of a Scranton, Pa., automobile dealer, Biden overcame a childhood stutter and often speaks with charming self-deprecation. But what has made him a compelling political figure are the tragedies and dramas of his private life. He was the underdog when, as a 29-year-old county councilman, he summoned the brashness in 1972 to challenge Republican Sen. J. Caleb Boggs in a campaign run by his sister Valerie Biden Owens. Running on a dovish Vietnam platform and accusing the incumbent of being a do-nothing, he won by 3,162 votes.

Five weeks later, Biden's wife, Neilia, and their infant daughter, Amy, were killed and their two sons seriously injured in an automobile accident. Biden at first said he would not take the job he had just won. Persuaded by Democratic Leader Mike Mansfield of Montana, Biden was sworn in at the bedside of one of his sons. After 15 years building his Senate credentials and rebuilding his life, he has remarried, had another child and commutes by train from Wilmington to Washington every day.

Biden made a short presidential bid in 1988, but it resulted in his most humiliating political moment. He withdrew from the race for the Democratic nomination six months before the first primary after reports that he had plagiarized passages in speeches and in a 1965 law school paper, and had exaggerated his résumé. Later in 1988, a brain aneurysm nearly killed him.

Biden's return to good health bolstered Delaware's affections, and he won his 1990 Senate race with 63 percent of the vote. He has won with ease ever since. Biden says he is considering another presidential run in 2008.

KEY VOTES

2004

Yes Pass $318.9 billion, six-year highway and mass transit bill
Yes Extend assault weapons ban for 10 years
Yes Restore pay-as-you-go rules for new tax cuts and entitlement spending
No Criminalize harm to a fetus in an attack on the mother
Yes Increase mandatory child care funding to states by $6 billion over five years
No Amend the Constitution to prohibit same-sex marriage
Yes Approve $146 billion multi-year extension of previously enacted middle-class tax breaks
Yes Reorganize U.S. intelligence agencies as proposed by Sept. 11 commission
No Cut corporate taxes $137 billion over 10 years

2003

Yes Delay Bush changes to Clean Air Act
No Allow confirmation vote on Miguel A. Estrada to the U.S. Court of Appeals for the D.C. Circuit
Yes Block a Bush proposal opening Alaska's Arctic National Wildlife Refuge to oil drilling
Yes Limit size of Bush's proposed tax cut to $350 billion through fiscal 2013
Yes Overhaul Medicare and create prescription drug benefit
Yes Block Bush rule scaling back overtime pay for some white-collar federal workers
No Split $20 billion in Iraq aid into half-grant, half-loan
Yes Ban "partial birth" abortion except to save a woman's life
No Stop proposal allowing travel to Cuba
No Allow final vote on energy policy overhaul

CQ VOTE STUDIES

	PARTY UNITY		PRESIDENTIAL SUPPORT	
	Support	Oppose	Support	Oppose
2004	95%	5%	70%	30%
2003	90%	10%	46%	54%
2002	89%	11%	77%	23%
2001	94%	6%	65%	35%
2000	88%	12%	91%	9%
1999	93%	7%	89%	11%
1998	87%	13%	91%	9%
1997	82%	18%	84%	16%
1996	79%	21%	92%	8%
1995	87%	13%	85%	15%

INTEREST GROUPS

	AFL-CIO	ADA	CCUS	ACU
2004	100%	95%	63%	0%
2003	100%	75%	32%	26%
2002	100%	80%	50%	10%
2001	100%	100%	38%	12%
2000	63%	80%	60%	16%
1999	89%	95%	47%	4%
1998	88%	85%	56%	4%
1997	57%	70%	70%	16%
1996	86%	80%	46%	20%
1995	92%	95%	37%	17%

Sen. Thomas R. Carper (D)

Elected 2000; 1st term

CAPITOL OFFICE
224-2441
carper.senate.gov
513 Hart 20510-0803; fax 228-2190

COMMITTEES
Banking, Housing & Urban Affairs
Environment & Public Works
Homeland Security & Governmental Affairs
Special Aging

HOMETOWN
Wilmington

BORN
Jan. 23, 1947, Beckley, W.Va.

RELIGION
Presbyterian

FAMILY
Wife, Martha Carper; two children

EDUCATION
Ohio State U., B.A. 1968 (economics); U. of
Delaware, M.B.A. 1975

MILITARY SERVICE
Navy, 1968-73; Naval Reserve, 1973-92

CAREER
State economic development official

POLITICAL HIGHLIGHTS
Del. treasurer, 1977-83; U.S. House, 1983-93;
governor, 1993-2001

ELECTION RESULTS

2000 GENERAL

Thomas R. Carper (D)	181,566	55.5%
William V. Roth Jr. (R)	142,891	43.7%

2000 PRIMARY

Thomas R. Carper (D)	unopposed

PREVIOUS WINNING PERCENTAGES
1990 House Election (66%); 1988 House Election
(68%); 1986 House Election (66%); 1984 House
Election (58%); 1982 House Election (52%)

He may be a senator, but Carper thinks like a governor. He is among a handful of former state executives in the Senate who make decisions based on whether federal policy enhances government at the state level or gets in the way. His philosophy as a Democratic centrist adds to the overriding pragmatism he brings to his job in Congress.

In his career, Carper has won 11 races in a state that generally eschews ideological politics. Democratic leaders deployed him in the 109th Congress to balance liberal voices in the caucus, selecting him as one of three deputies to Whip Richard J. Durbin, a liberal from Illinois.

In 2004, Carper co-founded a centrist group called the Third Way, with the goal of giving moderates a higher profile and serving as a think tank to generate middle-of-the-road legislative proposals.

"I was a New Democrat before it was fashionable," Carper says. "I really think that we need more people in Congress who think like governors — who are results-oriented, who are not so ideologically driven, people who are impatient with gridlock, and maybe a little less partisan." In the Senate, he says, "when you're a centrist, you're in on every play."

As a young man, Carper was working for Delaware's economic development department, and had no real thoughts about a political career until one day in 1976 when he was lying on a beach, listening to the radio. A news report said Democrats could not find a candidate for state treasurer. He entered the race and at age 29, beat a strongly favored Republican. He later served two terms as governor.

Carper applies that experience every day he is in the Senate. He organizes brainstorming meetings for the eight colleagues who are also former governors. He is the chairman of the moderate Democratic Leadership Council's "best practices" committee, which scours the country for successful local programs that might work nationally. In 2004, he joined with other ex-governors in the Senate to lead a bid to sideline a four-year ban on Internet access taxation because, he argued, it would drain state treasuries of telecommunication taxes. They pushed a two-year ban instead, winning some concessions.

Carper was quick to take the lead in 2005 in opposing Bush administration attempts to trim the federal deficit with cuts to local and state governments. He is just as quick to object to bills imposing new mandates on the states without providing the federal money to pay for them.

Carper's voting record is middle-of-the-road, and he supports the Republican White House more often than most other Democrats. In the 108th Congress, he supported President Bush 57 percent of the time, making him one of the 10 Senate Democrats most apt to vote with the president.

In the 109th Congress, the White House courted him on its banner domestic initiative creating private investment accounts in the Social Security program for the first time. Carper in early 2005 was one of only two Democrats, along with Sen. Ben Nelson of Nebraska, to say he was open to considering it.

His support was crucial that year to a successful Republican bill shifting class action lawsuits from state to federal courts, which many fellow Democrats opposed because they felt the higher courts would be more hostile to plaintiffs. Carper struck a deal with Republicans to vote for it once they assured him it would not be substantially changed in the House, where Republicans want even greater restrictions on civil lawsuits. Carper also backed a bill creating a no-fault asbestos compensation trust fund. In 2004, the conservative-leaning U.S. Chamber of Commerce gave him its Legal Reform Award.

Early in his Senate career, Carper sponsored bills to increase the number of public charter schools and to encourage local school districts to offer parents a choice of which public school their children attend, ideas that eventually became part of the 2001 education overhaul.

Carper is a strong supporter of Amtrak, the federally subsidized passenger railroad. He and Democrat Joseph R. Biden Jr., the senior Delaware senator, spend nights at home in Wilmington and take an early morning Amtrak train to Washington. Carper fights an annual battle against the Bush administration's attempts to turn over unprofitable lines outside the Northeast to the states and private businesses. In 2002, he helped secure a $1.2 billion security upgrade for the railroad.

In 2004, he and the two other members of Delaware's congressional delegation successfully pressured U.S. Trade Representative Robert B. Zoellick to convince China to lift a ban on Delaware chicken following an outbreak of avian influenza.

Carper says his consensus-building skills were sharpened in his work with the National Governors Association, where he and Republican Gov. John Engler of Michigan developed a set of fundamental changes to welfare plans that formed the basis for the federal welfare overhaul of 1996.

Carper was born in West Virginia and raised in southern Virginia. When he was in high school, his family moved to Columbus, Ohio, and he went to Ohio State University on an ROTC scholarship. Years later, he told The Columbus Dispatch that until he became governor, the best job he ever had was washing dishes at an Ohio State sorority house.

In college, Carper had a political transformation. In 1964, he had campaigned for Republican presidential candidate Barry Goldwater. But by the time he was a college senior, his rightward leanings had been so eroded by his skepticism about the war in Vietnam that he was volunteering in the anti-war presidential campaign of Democratic Sen. Eugene McCarthy. Yet Carper says he wore his Navy uniform to graduation. He went on to serve in the Navy for five years, including wartime service in reconnaissance planes in Southeast Asia.

After he was discharged, Carper went to the University of Delaware in 1973 to earn a master's degree in business administration. He remained in the state to work in economic development, and not long afterward, had his fateful day at the beach that launched his political career.

In 1982, Carper jumped into a race for the House after Democrats again had trouble fielding a candidate. He made a late decision to challenge Republican Rep. Thomas B. Evans. The state's economic woes at the time and revelations that Evans was romantically involved with lobbyist Paula Parkinson boosted his campaign. His victory by 11,000 votes returned the state's House seat to Democratic control for the first time since 1966. Carper served for a decade as the small state's only House member.

He ran successfully for governor in 1993 and ultimately spent eight years in the governor's mansion. In 2000, Carper sought to return to Washington in a "battle of the titans" challenge to five-term Republican Sen. William V. Roth Jr., the Senate Finance Committee chairman who was the architect of the Roth IRA retirement plan, which created tax-free Individual Retirement Accounts.

Carper found ways to distinguish himself from Roth on health care and in other policy areas. Although he did not directly make a point of it, age was a factor. Carper was 53, Roth was 79. Voters gave Carper a surprisingly large 12 percentage point victory.

KEY VOTES

2004

Yes Pass $318.9 billion, six-year highway and mass transit bill
Yes Extend assault weapons ban for 10 years
Yes Restore pay-as-you-go rules for new tax cuts and entitlement spending
Yes Criminalize harm to a fetus in an attack on the mother
Yes Increase mandatory child care funding to states by $6 billion over five years
No   Amend the Constitution to prohibit same-sex marriage
Yes Approve $146 billion multi-year extension of previously enacted middle-class tax breaks
Yes Reorganize U.S. intelligence agencies as proposed by Sept. 11 commission
No   Cut corporate taxes $137 billion over 10 years

2003

Yes Delay Bush changes to Clean Air Act
No   Allow confirmation vote on Miguel A. Estrada to the U.S. Court of Appeals for the D.C. Circuit
Yes Block a Bush proposal opening Alaska's Arctic National Wildlife Refuge to oil drilling
Yes Limit size of Bush's proposed tax cut to $350 billion through fiscal 2013
Yes Overhaul Medicare and create prescription drug benefit
Yes Block Bush rule scaling back overtime pay for some white-collar federal workers
Yes Split $20 billion in Iraq aid into half-grant, half-loan
Yes Ban "partial birth" abortion except to save a woman's life
No   Stop proposal allowing travel to Cuba
No   Allow final vote on energy policy overhaul

CQ VOTE STUDIES

	PARTY UNITY		PRESIDENTIAL SUPPORT	
	Support	Oppose	Support	Oppose
2004	86%	14%	66%	34%
2003	81%	19%	53%	47%
2002	74%	26%	79%	21%
2001	80%	20%	72%	28%
House Service:				
1992	76%	24%	32%	68%
1991	76%	24%	37%	63%
1990	89%	11%	23%	77%
1989	85%	15%	41%	59%
1988	87%	13%	30%	70%
1987	77%	23%	32%	68%

INTEREST GROUPS

	AFL-CIO	ADA	CCUS	ACU
2004	100%	95%	71%	12%
2003	77%	75%	70%	10%
2002	85%	80%	50%	25%
2001	93%	90%	58%	24%
House Service:				
1992	67%	75%	63%	40%
1991	92%	55%	40%	20%
1990	92%	78%	21%	17%
1989	83%	80%	50%	21%
1988	77%	75%	64%	24%
1987	75%	72%	53%	9%

Rep. Michael N. Castle (R)

Elected 1992; 7th term

CAPITOL OFFICE
225-4165
www.house.gov/castle
1233 Longworth 20515-0801; fax 225-2291

COMMITTEES
Education & Workforce
(Education Reform - chairman)
Financial Services

HOMETOWN
Wilmington

BORN
July 2, 1939, Wilmington, Del.

RELIGION
Roman Catholic

FAMILY
Wife, Jane Castle

EDUCATION
Hamilton College, B.A. 1961 (economics);
Georgetown U., LL.B. 1964

CAREER
Lawyer; state prosecutor

POLITICAL HIGHLIGHTS
Del. House, 1967-69; Del. Senate, 1969-77 (minority
leader, 1976-77); lieutenant governor, 1981-85;
governor, 1985-93

ELECTION RESULTS

2004 GENERAL

Michael N. Castle (R)	245,978	69.1%
Paul Donnelly (D)	105,716	29.7%

2004 PRIMARY

Michael N. Castle (R)	unopposed

2002 GENERAL

Michael N. Castle (R)	164,605	72.1%
Micheal C. Miller Sr. (D)	61,011	26.7%
Brad C. Thomas (LIBERT)	2,789	1.2%

PREVIOUS WINNING PERCENTAGES
2000 (68%); 1998 (66%); 1996 (70%); 1994 (71%);
1992 (55%)

A leader of a dwindling band of GOP moderates in the House, Castle has found ways to make an impact by softening the edges of the ideas coming from the conservative House majority. A former governor who remains vastly popular in his home state, Castle challenges Republican leaders on issues where he feels they are too far to the right, including the size of tax cuts, education policy and federal funding for stem cell research.

Castle has found himself increasingly at odds with his party over the size of President Bush's tax cuts and the need to reduce the federal deficit. Even as he chaired the president's 2004 re-election effort in Delaware, Castle called for a re-examination of Bush's tax cuts as part of the debate in the 109th Congress about bringing the federal budget back into balance.

Castle often can be found just off the House floor, expanding on the news of the day to a clutch of reporters. He frequently is the lawmaker that journalists approach for the details when word spreads that the moderates are planning a maverick stand. In the 108th Congress, he was among the top 10 House GOP strays in bucking the president or his party leadership.

He calls himself a "pragmatist," believing that being a social moderate with fiscally conservative views is the only way to get things done in Congress. His middle-of-the-road positioning, combined with the political savvy gained from eight years in the governor's mansion, have landed Castle in the middle of some of the country's most contentious debates. On big issues, Castle often carries a substantial bloc of moderate votes with him. He is active in three centrist coalitions: the Tuesday Group of moderate Republicans, the Republican Main Street Partnership and the bipartisan House Centrist Coalition.

As chairman of the Education Reform Subcommittee, Castle is one of the architects of federal education policy. He is the chief House sponsor of legislation to allow states to take over Head Start programs, which Bush has also pushed. Though he does not adhere strictly to Republican orthodoxy on federalism, Castle says that a few programs, Head Start among them, are better operated at the local level than from Washington. Liberal critics of his plan, he grumbles, are more concerned about protecting government contracts than doing what's best for children.

As Bush and full Education and Workforce Committee Chairman John A. Boehner of Ohio embarked on a major rewrite of higher education law in the 109th Congress, Castle was someone they by necessity had to figure into their strategy. Early on, he was questioning a provision included in Boehner's proposal allowing for-profit career colleges to compete for more higher education funding. His concern is tied to scarce federal dollars flowing to for-profit companies.

Castle was a lead sponsor of the No Child Left Behind law, the 2001 legislation initiated by Bush that for the first time tied federal education aid to improvements in student test scores. Castle also shepherded through Congress a contentious bill calling for disabled students to be treated the same as non-disabled students when being punished for violations of school policy. Advocates for the disabled decried the move as a potential violation of civil rights, but Castle said it would give localities more flexibility.

One of his newest crusades is the troubling trend in childhood obesity in the United States, which Castle believes can be fought in part by providing healthier foods in schools. He sponsored a bill in the 108th Congress directing the Agriculture Department to develop nutrition guidelines for foods sold in schools and to make $30 million available for nutrition aware-ness and physical fitness programs.

Castle is deeply involved in the campaign by GOP moderates to expand embryonic stem cell research at the National Institutes of Health, which Bush and some anti-abortion rights conservatives want to strictly limit. They believe that using days-old embryos for research is tantamount to destroying a life, even if the scientific goal is to look for cures for diseases like diabetes. "Time is of the essence," Castle argues. "This is not about pre-venting a life. This is about saving a life."

After years of parting ways with conservatives on environmental issues, favoring more regulation than his GOP peers, Castle was one of just 11 House Republicans endorsed for re-election by the Sierra Club in 2004.

Amiable and relatively quiet, Castle nonetheless is forceful in his opinions and sometimes bold in confronting his leadership. In 2001, he was one of six Republicans who signed a petition to force Speaker J. Dennis Hastert to bring campaign finance legislation to the floor. Before that, in 1998, Castle was among the dozen GOP lawmakers who voted against three of the four arti-cles of impeachment against President Clinton, who was embroiled in a sex scandal involving a White House intern.

Still, Castle is an ally whom the House Speaker consults regularly. Prais-ing Hastert's consensus-building style, Castle in 1998 promoted him as a replacement for Majority Leader Dick Armey of Texas after Armey alien-ated many Republicans (Armey ultimately hung on to his job), and backed him for Speaker later that year when Hastert successfully went for the House's top job.

A fan of coin collecting, Castle has used his seat on the Financial Services Committee to promote creation of new collectible U.S. coins, including a bill that would put likenesses of the presidents on the dollar coin. Earlier, he was the principal author of the law that put commemorations of each of the 50 states on quarters.

The 6-foot, 4-inch Castle was a basketball star in high school. He caught the political bug as an adult. He got a law degree from Georgetown Uni-versity and at age 26, he became Delaware's deputy attorney general. Two years later, he began a 10-year career in the General Assembly. He even-tually became lieutenant governor and then governor for two terms.

With his stint as governor ending, Castle ran for the state's at-large con-gressional seat in 1992. He won a tough, four-way GOP primary and in November prevailed with 55 percent of the vote. With at least two-thirds of voters backing him every two years, Castle has coasted to re-election since.

KEY VOTES

2004

No Extend federal unemployment benefits by 13 weeks

No Pass $283.2 billion, six-year federal highway and mass transit bill

Yes Approve $146 billion multi-year extension of previously enacted middle-class tax breaks

No Amend the Constitution to prohibit same-sex marriage

No Cut corporate taxes $137 billion over 10 years

Yes Reorganize U.S. intelligence agencies as proposed by Sept. 11 commission

2003

Yes Cut taxes by $330 billion through fiscal 2013

No Block Bush rule scaling back overtime pay for some white-collar federal workers

Yes Do not allow use of search warrants without first notifying subjects

Yes Allow importation of prescription drugs

Yes Create private school voucher program in Washington, D.C.

Yes Ban "partial birth" abortion except to save a woman's life

No Split $18.6 billion in Iraq aid into half-grant, half-loan

Yes Overhaul Medicare and create prescription drug benefit

CQ VOTE STUDIES

	PARTY UNITY		PRESIDENTIAL SUPPORT	
	Support	Oppose	Support	Oppose
2004	79%	21%	74%	26%
2003	77%	23%	69%	31%
2002	79%	21%	78%	22%
2001	79%	21%	67%	33%
2000	74%	26%	49%	51%

INTEREST GROUPS

	AFL-CIO	ADA	CCUS	ACU
2004	35%	50%	85%	52%
2003	20%	40%	76%	40%
2002	11%	25%	95%	76%
2001	25%	30%	83%	48%
2000	20%	30%	80%	68%

DELAWARE

At large

Delaware voters supported the losing Democratic presidential nominee in each of the last two election cycles — ending the state's streak of 12-straight elections backing the winning presidential candidate — but still pursue ticket-splitting. The state is generally incumbent-friendly and has embraced Republican Rep. Castle with large majorities.

Democrats are strong in Wilmington, the state's largest city. Fifty years ago, almost half the state's population lived here, but the city's 72,664 residents now cast only about 10 percent of Delaware's vote, largely because of migration to the booming suburbs. The capital, Dover, set in the state's midsection in Kent County, also has a Democratic constituency.

The GOP's strength lies in Wilmington's suburbs and south of the Chesapeake and Delaware canal, in the poultry farms and coastal marshes of the Delmarva Peninsula. A string of beach resorts in the southeast corner draws hundreds of thousands of tourists each year. The growing number of retirees in these beach communities has made

rural Sussex County one of the state's fastest-growing areas and increased its conservative tenor.

Delaware enjoys relatively low unemployment, and its favorable tax rates attract the headquarters of many financial services companies, especially credit card firms. Thanks to liberal incorporation rules, Delaware is the on-paper home to 60 percent of the Fortune 500, which keeps the state's specialized business court busy. Wilmington is the very real home of the DuPont Company, one of Delaware's largest private employers.

MAJOR INDUSTRY
Financial services, manufacturing, tourism, chemicals

MILITARY BASES
Dover Air Force Base, 4,218 military, 1,553 civilian (2003)

CITIES
Wilmington, 72,664; Dover, 32,135; Newark, 28,547

NOTABLE
Ralph Nader's report, "The Company State" (1971), described the du Pont family's influence on Delaware — the family once owned the newspaper and held the governor's mansion; In 1787, Delaware was the first state to ratify the Constitution.

FLORIDA

Gov. Jeb Bush (R)

First elected: 1998
Length of term: 4 years
Term expires: 1/07
Salary: $124,575
Phone: (850) 488-4441

Hometown: Coral Gables
Born: Feb. 11, 1953; Midland, Texas
Religion: Roman Catholic
Family: Wife, Columba Bush; three children
Education: U. of Texas, B.A. 1973 (Latin American studies)
Career: Real estate developer; nonprofit chairman
Political highlights: Fla. secretary of commerce, 1987-89; Republican nominee for governor, 1994

Election results:
2002 GENERAL

Jeb Bush (R)	2,856,845	56.0%
Bill McBride (D)	2,201,427	43.2%

Lt. Gov. Toni Jennings (R)

Assumed office: 2003
Length of term: 4 years
Term expires: 1/07
Salary: $119,390
Phone: (850) 488-4711

STATE LEGISLATURE

Legislature: 60 days March-May; session is often extended

House: 120 members; 2-year terms
2005 breakdown: 84R, 36D; 91 men, 29 women
Salary: $29,916
Phone: (850) 488-1157

Senate: 40 members; 4-year terms
2005 breakdown: 26R, 14D; 31 men, 9 women
Salary: $29,916
Phone: (850) 487-5270

STATE TERM LIMITS

Governor: 2 terms
House: 4 consecutive terms
Senate: 2 consecutive terms

URBAN STATISTICS

CITY	POPULATION
Jacksonville	735,617
Miami	362,470
Tampa	303,447
St. Petersburg	248,232
Hialeah	226,419

REGISTERED VOTERS

Democrat	41%
Republican	38%
Unaffiliated	18%
Others	2%

POPULATION

2004 population (est.)	17,397,161
2000 population	15,982,378
1990 population	12,937,926
Percent change (1990-2000)	+23.5%
Rank among states (2004)	4

Median age	38.7
Born in state	32.7%
Foreign born	16.7%
Violent crime rate	812/100,000
Poverty level	12.5%
Federal workers	118,600
Military	106,092

REDISTRICTING

Florida gained two House seats in reapportionment. The state legislature drew a new, 25-district map, which the governor signed on March 27, 2002.

MISCELLANEOUS

Web: www.myflorida.com
Capital: Tallahassee
STATE ELECTION OFFICIAL
(850) 245-6200
DEMOCRATIC HEADQUARTERS
(850) 222-3411
REPUBLICAN HEADQUARTERS
(850) 222-7920

District Statistics

DIST.	2004 VOTE FOR PRESIDENT BUSH	KERRY	WHITE	BLACK	ASIAN	HISP	MEDIAN INCOME	WHITE COLLAR	BLUE COLLAR	SERVICE INDUSTRY	OVER 64	UNDER 18	COLLEGE EDUCATION	RURAL	SQ. MILES
1	72%	28%	78%	14%	2%	3%	$36,738	57%	25%	18%	13%	24%	20%	23%	4,642
2	54	45	72	22	1	3	$34,718	62	21	18	12	23	24	38	9,425
3	35	65	38	49	2	8	$29,785	52	27	21	11	28	13	10	1,796
4	67	32	78	14	2	4	$43,947	65	21	14	11	24	24	22	4,118
5	58	41	88	5	1	6	$34,815	55	27	17	26	20	14	36	4,044
6	61	38	79	12	2	5	$36,846	61	23	16	15	23	21	31	2,912
7	57	43	81	9	1	7	$40,525	63	21	16	18	22	25	13	1,797
8	55	44	70	7	3	18	$41,568	64	20	17	14	23	26	8	987
9	57	42	85	4	2	8	$40,742	68	18	14	20	22	25	6	634
10	51	48	88	4	2	4	$37,168	65	20	15	23	18	23	0	175
11	40	60	48	27	2	20	$33,559	61	22	17	12	25	21	0	244
12	58	42	72	13	1	12	$37,769	56	28	16	17	25	17	16	1,956
13	56	43	86	4	1	8	$40,187	59	24	18	29	18	24	11	2,599
14	61	38	84	5	1	9	$42,541	60	22	19	27	18	24	9	1,057
15	57	43	78	7	2	11	$39,397	58	22	19	20	22	22	10	2,545

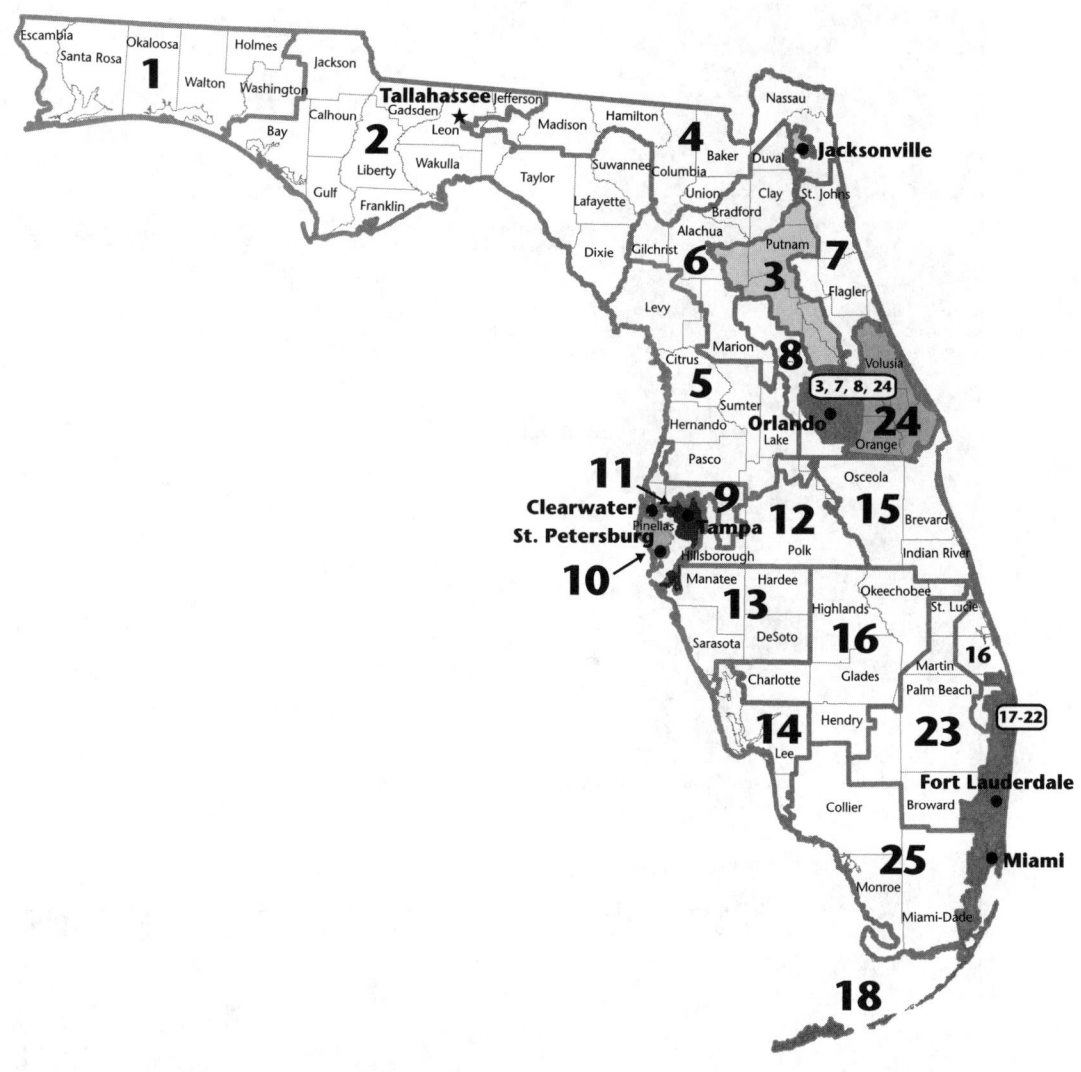

District Statistics

DIST.	2004 VOTE FOR PRESIDENT BUSH	KERRY	WHITE	BLACK	ASIAN	HISP	MEDIAN INCOME	WHITE COLLAR	BLUE COLLAR	SERVICE INDUSTRY	OVER 64	UNDER 18	COLLEGE EDUCATION	RURAL	SQ. MILES
16	55%	45%	82%	6%	1%	10%	$39,408	58%	25%	17%	25%	21%	20%	15%	4,538
17	17	83	18	55	2	21	$30,426	52	24	23	11	29	14	0	97
18	54	45	30	6	1	63	$32,298	60	21	18	18	19	26	1	355
19	33	66	77	6	2	13	$42,237	67	17	15	30	19	26	0	231
20	36	63	67	8	2	21	$44,034	69	16	14	17	21	30	0	160
21	57	43	21	7	2	70	$41,426	64	23	14	13	24	23	0	135
22	49	51	82	4	2	11	$51,200	69	16	14	21	19	34	1	268
23	21	78	29	51	1	14	$31,309	48	28	24	12	28	13	2	3,362
24	56	44	80	6	2	10	$43,954	65	20	15	15	23	26	9	1,583
25	56	44	24	10	2	62	$44,489	62	23	15	9	29	20	6	4,268
STATE	52	47	65	14	2	17	$38,819	61	22	17	18	23	22	11	53,927
U.S.	50.7	48.3	69	12	4	13	$41,994	60	25	15	12	26	24	21	3,537,438

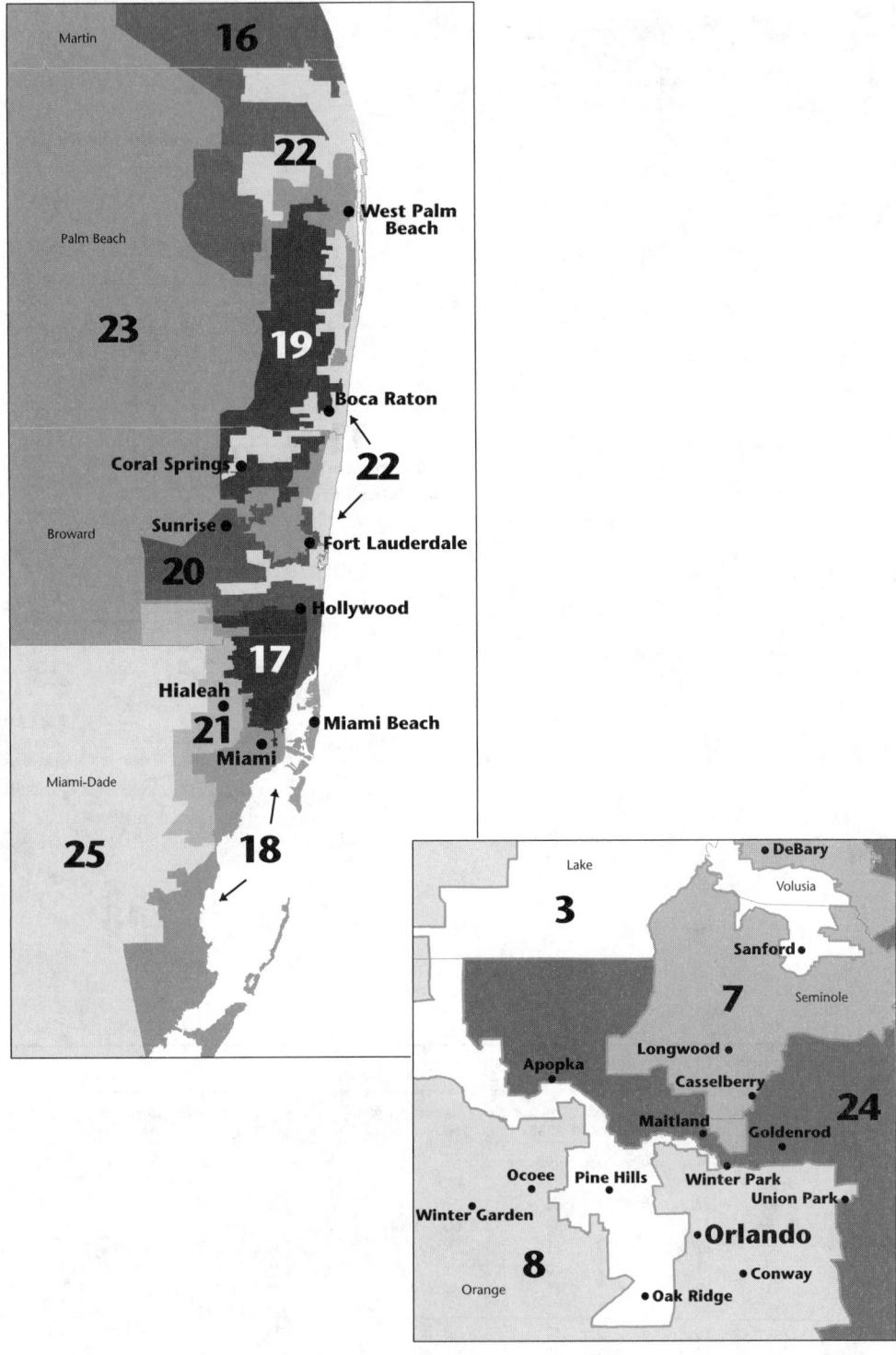

Sen. Bill Nelson (D)

Elected 2000; 1st term

As a Democratic centrist, Nelson seems tailor-made for Florida's famously divided voters, but he was often overshadowed in his first term by the state's popular senior senator, Bob Graham, also a Democrat. With Graham's retirement, Nelson has a better chance to make a name for himself as a legislator, especially as the senior Democrat on the Subcommittee on Science and Space, where his work is sure to appeal in a place that launched a man to the moon at Cape Canaveral more than three decades ago.

As a member of the centrist New Democrats, Nelson has often deviated from the more liberal party line. In the 108th Congress, he backed President Bush 58 percent of the time, more frequently than all but seven other Democrats.

Still, he is a top target of Republicans looking ahead to the 2006 election, and Nelson has much at stake in the 109th Congress. He is keeping a tight focus on Florida issues and is an outspoken advocate for the U.S. space program, an important local employer.

Nelson once flew in space himself, aboard the space shuttle *Columbia* in 1986, when he was in the House and chaired the Space Subcommittee there. Since then, he has been a vocal advocate for increases in funding for NASA and was one of the first in Congress to warn of the dangers of delaying upgrades to the shuttles, a point tragically driven home in 2003, the year the *Columbia* exploded while attempting to re-enter Earth's atmosphere during the journey home.

With Congress and Bush talking about retiring the shuttles, Nelson keeps a close eye on protecting workers on Florida's Space Coast, where NASA's Kennedy Space Center sent Neil Armstrong, Buzz Aldrin and Michael Collins on their historic trip to the moon in 1969. At the beginning of the 109th Congress, he landed the job of top-ranking Democrat on the Space Subcommittee, part of the full Commerce, Science and Transportation Committee.

In late 2004, Nelson attached an amendment to the NASA reauthorization bill requiring the agency to find workers replacement jobs within the agency. At the same time, he has pressed to accelerate the development of a space plane to ferry astronauts back and forth to the International Space Station. In 2004, when Bush proposed refocusing NASA on preparations to send humans back to the moon and on to Mars, an enthusiastic Nelson appeared with the president at the announcement at NASA headquarters. His only gripe about the Bush proposal is that it doesn't call for enough money to accomplish those goals, in his view.

Nelson also sits on Armed Services, where in 2004 he joined forces with Republican John McCain of Arizona, Democrat Hillary Rodham Clinton of New York and others to permanently add 30,000 soldiers to the Army — something Defense Secretary Donald H. Rumsfeld opposed. Nelson and others said they were dismayed by the strain on troops fighting overseas, especially in Iraq.

Closer to home, Nelson has tried to prevent the retirement of the USS *John F. Kennedy*, which is based in Florida, by introducing legislation in early 2005 that would require the Navy to maintain a fleet of at least 12 aircraft carriers.

On Foreign Relations, he has focused on Latin America, whose affairs are closely tied to Florida, a magnet for Spanish-speaking people resettling

CAPITOL OFFICE
224-5274
bill@billnelson.senate.gov
billnelson.senate.gov
716 Hart 20510-0905; fax 228-2183

COMMITTEES
Armed Services
Budget
Commerce, Science & Transportation
Foreign Relations
Special Aging

HOMETOWN
Orlando

BORN
Sept. 29, 1942, Miami, Fla.

RELIGION
Episcopalian

FAMILY
Wife, Grace H. Nelson; two children

EDUCATION
Yale U., B.A. 1965; U. of Virginia, J.D. 1968

MILITARY SERVICE
Army, 1968-70; Army Reserve, 1965-71

CAREER
Lawyer

POLITICAL HIGHLIGHTS
Fla. House, 1972-78; U.S. House, 1979-91; sought Democratic nomination for governor, 1990; Fla. treasurer and insurance commissioner, 1995-2001

ELECTION RESULTS

2000 GENERAL

Bill Nelson (D)	2,989,487	51.0%
Bill McCollum (R)	2,705,348	46.2%
Willie Logan (I)	80,830	1.4%

2000 PRIMARY

Bill Nelson (D)	692,147	77.5%
Newall J. Daughtrey (D)	105,650	11.8%
David B. Higginbottom (D)	95,492	10.7%

PREVIOUS WINNING PERCENTAGES
1988 House Election (61%); 1986 House Election (73%); 1984 House Election (61%); 1982 House Election (71%); 1980 House Election (70%); 1978 House Election (61%)

in the United States. He has promised to press for better cooperation with the region on drug interdiction, anti-terrorism efforts and trade.

On other fronts, Nelson has fought to extend a federal ban on drilling for oil or natural gas off Florida's coast, which expires in 2007. Responding to reports in several Florida newspapers, Nelson also has pressed the EPA to phase out arsenic-treated wood, which has been linked to cancer and has been used in the construction of playgrounds, waterfront decks, picnic tables and fences.

He also has pushed for a congressional investigation into how the Federal Emergency Management Agency distributes aid after hurricanes and other natural disasters, following up on reports first from Florida and then elsewhere that the agency has poured money into areas with little damage.

Appealing to Florida's large and politically powerful senior citizen population, Nelson has an interest in consumer protection and privacy issues. He has worked to prevent insurance companies, banks and other financial institutions that merge from sharing medical and financial information about customers without their explicit consent. And he sought to block pharmaceutical manufacturers from striking deals with drugstores under which they agree to persuade customers to buy alternative drugs different from those recommended by their doctors.

In the 109th Congress, he won another position for speaking to the needs of senior citizens, a seat on the Committee on Aging.

During his time in the Senate, Nelson has worked to maximize his skills as a fundraiser and has edged closer to the ranks of leadership. Leading up to the 2002 elections, he was a vice chairman of the party's Senate campaign arm, the Democratic Senatorial Campaign Committee. And he formed his own political action committee, Moving America Forward, to channel more money to Democratic candidates. At the start of the 109th Congress, Minority Leader Harry Reid named Nelson a deputy whip.

Nelson is a fifth-generation Floridian. His great-great-grandfather came to the Panhandle from Denmark in 1829. Nelson represented Brevard County in the state legislature, then ran for an open House seat in 1978 at age 36, taking conservative stands on economic issues and advocating more military spending.

In the House, he was an early member of the moderate Democratic Leadership Council, and his voting record confirmed his self-description as a New Democrat. His district included the space center, giving him an early imperative to involve himself in space issues. Yet despite the positive publicity attending his adventure as an astronaut, Nelson lost in the 1990 Democratic primary for governor, his only electoral defeat.

He was elected state insurance commissioner four years later, a high-profile position that gave him a launching pad for his Senate race. Nelson dealt with the aftermath of Hurricane Andrew, which ravaged South Florida and the state's insurance market in 1992. He also helped obtain a $206 million settlement for African-Americans who had been overcharged for life insurance and burial policies, bolstering his image as a consumer watchdog and his appeal among black voters.

From the time he announced his intention to run for the Senate, Nelson was the front-runner for the seat that Republican Connie Mack was leaving after two terms. Nelson benefited from Democratic anger at his opponent, Bill McCollum, a 10-term congressman. McCollum's conservatism on social issues and his role in President Clinton's impeachment enabled Nelson to portray him as too far to the right for Florida.

Nelson's 5 percentage point win stemmed a political tide in the state that had given the GOP control of the governorship, the legislature and most of Florida's U.S. House seats.

KEY VOTES

2004

Yes Pass $318.9 billion, six-year highway and mass transit bill
Yes Extend assault weapons ban for 10 years
Yes Restore pay-as-you-go rules for new tax cuts and entitlement spending
No   Criminalize harm to a fetus in an attack on the mother
Yes Increase mandatory child care funding to states by $6 billion over five years
No   Amend the Constitution to prohibit same-sex marriage
Yes Approve $146 billion multi-year extension of previously enacted middle-class tax breaks
Yes Reorganize U.S. intelligence agencies as proposed by Sept. 11 commission
Yes Cut corporate taxes $137 billion over 10 years

2003

Yes Delay Bush changes to Clean Air Act
Yes Allow confirmation vote on Miguel A. Estrada to the U.S. Court of Appeals for the D.C. Circuit
Yes Block a Bush proposal opening Alaska's Arctic National Wildlife Refuge to oil drilling
Yes Limit size of Bush's proposed tax cut to $350 billion through fiscal 2013
Yes Overhaul Medicare and create prescription drug benefit
Yes Block Bush rule scaling back overtime pay for some white-collar federal workers
Yes Split $20 billion in Iraq aid into half-grant, half-loan
No   Ban "partial birth" abortion except to save a woman's life
Yes Stop proposal allowing travel to Cuba
No   Allow final vote on energy policy overhaul

CQ VOTE STUDIES

	PARTY UNITY		PRESIDENTIAL SUPPORT	
	Support	Oppose	Support	Oppose
2004	92%	8%	62%	38%
2003	90%	10%	56%	44%
2002	77%	23%	78%	22%
2001	92%	8%	70%	30%
House Service:				
1990	77%	23%	40%	60%
1989	80%	20%	47%	53%
1988	72%	28%	46%	54%
1987	76%	24%	42%	58%

INTEREST GROUPS

	AFL-CIO	ADA	CCUS	ACU
2004	100%	80%	65%	4%
2003	77%	80%	48%	20%
2002	85%	70%	70%	30%
2001	100%	95%	43%	16%
House Service:				
1990	86%	50%	0%	27%
1989	91%	60%	50%	31%
1988	71%	45%	43%	56%
1987	63%	52%	53%	35%
1986	43%	15%	61%	77%
1985	47%	30%	54%	71%

Sen. Mel Martinez (R)

CAPITOL OFFICE
224-3041
www.martinez.senate.gov
317 Hart 20510-0903; fax 224-2237

COMMITTEES
Banking, Housing & Urban Affairs
Energy & Natural Resources
Foreign Relations
   (African Affairs - chairman)
Special Aging

HOMETOWN
Orlando

BORN
Oct. 23, 1946, Sagua La Grande, Cuba

RELIGION
Roman Catholic

FAMILY
Wife, Kitty Martinez; three children

EDUCATION
Orlando Junior College, A.A. 1967; Florida State U.,
B.A. 1969 (international affairs), J.D. 1973

CAREER
Lawyer

POLITICAL HIGHLIGHTS
Sought Republican nomination for lieutenant
governor, 1994; Orange County chairman, 1998-
2001; Housing and Urban Development secretary,
2001-03

ELECTION RESULTS

2004 GENERAL

Mel Martinez (R)	3,672,864	49.4%
Betty Castor (D)	3,590,201	48.3%
Dennis F. Bradley (VET)	166,642	2.2%

2004 PRIMARY

Mel Martinez (R)	522,994	44.9%
Bill McCollum (R)	360,474	30.9%
Doug Gallagher (R)	158,360	13.6%
Johnnie Byrd (R)	68,982	5.9%
Karen Saull (R)	20,365	1.8%
Sonya March (R)	17,804	1.5%
Larry Klayman (R)	13,257	1.1%

Elected 2004; 1st term

Like the life-changing 1962 airlift that carried him from Fidel Castro's Cuba to Orlando at the age of 15, Martinez's journey to the Senate has been swift and helped along by fortuitous turns. And just as Martinez arrived in the United States knowing little English and even less about his future, he comes to Congress as something of a blank slate, with no legislative record to define where he fits politically.

What is clear is that Martinez — who is the first Cuban-American to serve in the Senate and, along with his classmate Colorado Democrat Ken Salazar, the first Hispanic in more than a quarter-century — has a close relationship with President Bush. That friendship could give him a prominent seat at some of the most pressing negotiations of the 109th Congress. A week after Martinez was sworn in for his first term, he got a chance to travel around his state with Bush to showcase the president's education agenda. Martinez shares much in common with Bush and Republican congressional leaders, including his staunch social conservatism. A devout Catholic, he opposes abortion and gay marriage, and he campaigned on a pledge to help the president win confirmation of conservative federal judges.

Early in 2005, Martinez was at the forefront for Republicans in the Senate in the case of a brain-damaged Florida woman, Terri Schiavo. Martinez cosponsored a bill, quickly passed by Congress and signed into law, to give federal courts jurisdiction over her case. But the federal courts ultimately refused to order her feeding tube reinstated, as conservatives had wanted, and Schiavo died. Martinez then was embarrassed by the actions of his legal counsel, who resigned after admitting he wrote a memo citing the political advantages of the GOP weighing in on the case.

Martinez says he will support much of Bush's domestic agenda in the Senate. As a member of the Banking Committee, he is poised to pursue his goal of creating a new, more powerful regulator for the government-sponsored mortgage financiers Fannie Mae and Freddie Mac. As for the rest of his wish list, it remains a question mark. His challenge is to show he can be a policy maker of substance over style, and an independent-thinking senator rather than a yes man for the Bush administration.

Martinez's immigrant roots and up-from-the-bootstraps biography would seem to indicate a more moderate outlook. A former trial attorney who once specialized in helping poor clients and fellow immigrants win handsome settlements from companies, he made a name for himself in Orange County forging bipartisan coalitions. Now, Martinez — who spoke little about his trial lawyer past during his hard-fought campaign — says he supports limiting jury awards for "pain and suffering," although his preferred $500,000 ceiling is twice as high as the one Bush advocates. A Democrat until the Reagan administration, Martinez pushed for children's programs as a county chairman and tried to limit development to curb school crowding.

While his past may obscure some of his policy positions, Martinez's life story proved a compelling backdrop for his campaign, especially in the context of a Bush re-election bid that focused heavily on attracting Hispanic support. Martinez arrived in Florida by himself as part of "Operation Pedro Pan," a joint effort of the U.S. government and the Roman Catholic Church to spirit some 14,000 Cubans to the mainland. He hopped from one foster home to another — it was a foster mother who shortened his given name,

Melquiades, to Mel — working to save money for college and fending for himself, and later his family, with whom he was eventually reunited. Martinez later would call the program one of the first public-private "faith based" initiatives, an idea that would become dear to both him and Bush.

His journey from Cuba helped form his attitude toward international affairs. Martinez supports Bush's approach to foreign policy, from the war on terrorism to the embargo on Cuba. "My understanding of good and evil in the world was based on that experience," he said. "My understanding of America being a beacon of hope in the world, a positive force in the world, comes from that immigrant experience."

With a spot on the Foreign Relations panel, Martinez is positioned to be a valuable Bush ally on such issues as the war in Iraq. The assignment also will give Martinez a platform to trumpet his own foreign policy goals — which include efforts to rid Cuba of Castro — through funding dissident groups and outlets such as Radio Marti.

After law school, Martinez became active in the Cuban expatriate community that plays a central role in Florida's economic and political landscape. But he was a relative latecomer to politics. Martinez spent 20 years building a succession of law firms in Orlando before losing a race for the Republican lieutenant gubernatorial nomination in 1994 to Jeb Bush, who then narrowly lost to Democrat Lawton Chiles. In 1998, Martinez was elected to the office of Orange County chairman, where he won notice for the "Martinez Doctrine," his growth-management policy that tied the approval of new homes to school construction.

In 2001, Bush tapped Martinez to lead the Department of Housing and Urban Development. There, he launched a HUD Center for Faith-Based and Community Services, an office intended to help religious-oriented organizations compete for federal grants. Martinez was a forceful advocate for home ownership, one of Bush's favorite initiatives, and a highly visible administration point man on Hispanic issues.

But his effort to simplify the purchasing process for would-be homebuyers fell flat in Congress, and critics faulted him for failing to focus on issues such as increasing rental housing for poor people. Martinez also was blamed for trying to keep under wraps a study that showed evidence of mortgage discrimination during his tenure at HUD. Martinez's stay in the Cabinet was short-lived; he left at the end of 2003 to run for the Senate at Bush's urging.

Martinez is known for his charisma, approachability and talent for networking with a light and friendly touch. But he has sometimes appeared to lose his cool in fast-developing situations. In a 2000 press release, Martinez called government agents "armed thugs" for their handling of 5-year-old Elián Gonzalez, the Cuban boy who sparked an international incident when he was plucked from an inner tube in U.S. waters off of Miami. During the 2004 campaign, Martinez had to apologize to former Rep. Bill McCollum, his opponent in the Republican primary, for calling him "anti-family" and for saying in ads that McCollum sided with the "radical homosexual lobby."

In the general election, he initially refused to debate his Democratic opponent Betty Castor, the state's former education commissioner. He ran a series of blistering ads accusing Castor of being soft on terrorism because she did not suspend a professor with suspected ties to Islamic Jihad while she was president of the University of Southern Florida.

The race came down to the wire, with Martinez ultimately edging out Castor with 49 percent of the vote, capturing the support of many of Florida's conservative rural areas and weathering opposition in the state's two biggest urban areas, Tampa Bay and South Florida. The win was a coup for Bush and Republican leaders, for whom Florida was a coveted prize.

Rep. Jeff Miller (R)

CAPITOL OFFICE
225-4136
jeffmiller.house.gov
324 Cannon 20515-0901; fax 225-3414

COMMITTEES
Armed Services
Veterans' Affairs
  (Disability Assistance & Memorial Affairs -
  chairman)

HOMETOWN
Chumuckla

BORN
June 27, 1959, St. Petersburg, Fla.

RELIGION
Methodist

FAMILY
Wife, Vicki Miller; two children

EDUCATION
U. of Florida, B.A. 1984 (journalism)

CAREER
Real estate broker; state agriculture department
official; deputy county sheriff

POLITICAL HIGHLIGHTS
Fla. House, 1998-2001

ELECTION RESULTS

2004 GENERAL

Jeff Miller (R)	236,604	76.5%
Mark S. Coutu (D)	72,506	23.5%

2004 PRIMARY

Jeff Miller (R)	unopposed

2002 GENERAL

Jeff Miller (R)	152,635	74.6%
Bert Oram (D)	51,972	25.4%

PREVIOUS WINNING PERCENTAGES
2001 Special Election (66%)

Elected October 2001; 2nd full term

Miller is a low-key consensus-builder who is keen on protecting his district's numerous military installations and the veterans who live near them. More than 100,000 veterans reside in Miller's district.

A sixth-generation Floridian whose parents sold real estate and operated a cattle ranch near Clearwater, Miller instinctively understands the needs of the 1st District, which is dotted with rural farm towns, such as his hometown, Chumuckla. He appears just as comfortable in cowboy boots as a business suit.

The 1st is also home to the Pensacola Naval Air Station, the Air Force's Hurlburt Field and Eglin Air Force Base. Appropriately, Miller sits on the Armed Services Committee where in 2004 he was successful in adding an amendment to the annual defense authorization bill that eliminated the so-called widows' tax on surviving spouses of military retirees.

Under the military's Survivor Benefit Plan, enacted in the 1970s, spouses of deceased career military retirees initially receive 55 percent of the soldier's annual retirement pay, but that payment is cut to 35 percent when the spouse reaches age 62. The offset is intended to account for Social Security payments and other subsidies provided by the government. But Miller and military family advocacy groups argue that those offsets have not materialized. His measure allows military spouses over 62 to retain the full 55 percent payment. "This is restoration of fairness and equity, 32 years in the making for the surviving spouses of America's greatest generation," Miller said.

Miller also looks out for district veterans from his seat on the Veterans' Affairs Committee, where in the 109th Congress he serves as chairman of the Disability Assistance and Memorial Affairs Subcommittee, which includes jurisdiction over compensation, pensions and life insurance.

In 2003, he cosponsored a measure expanding benefits to disabled veterans by allowing military retirees to simultaneously receive both pension checks and disability benefits. This benefit — known as concurrent receipt — was ultimately rolled into that year's defense authorization bill.

Miller delivers for his district in other ways. He was able to gain federal emergency funds in the 2004 catchall appropriations bill for the replacement of the Interstate 10 bridge spanning Escambia Bay. The bridge, which was severely damaged by Hurricane Ivan in the fall of 2004, is expected to cost more than $300 million to replace.

A conservative on both social and fiscal policy, Miller is opposed to abortion and supports a constitutional amendment to ban the procedure. Reducing taxes is also a key piece of his legislative agenda, he says. He wants to make permanent the 10-year tax cut package of 2001 and enact new reductions, particularly for small companies.

As a former small-businessman, Miller is close to the business leaders in his community, many of whom rely on a robust tourism economy. Miller opposes drilling for oil and gas off the Florida coast, not only because of the potential detrimental environmental impact on beaches, but also to maintain the areas used for training exercises by pilots from Eglin Air Force Base.

In January 2003, Miller was one of just four House lawmakers to vote against an extension of unemployment benefits that had expired Dec. 28, 2002. "At what point do we quit providing a check to someone without a job?" Miller asked. "I'm afraid that extending these benefits will diminish the desire to go out and find a job," he said, according to the Associated Press.

His first legislative act in the 108th was to offer a bill to rescind the 3.1 percent cost of living pay increase that members of Congress accepted for 2003. Miller was frustrated that President Bush had allowed only a 3.1 percent pay raise for federal civilian employees, rather than the 4.1 percent increase approved for the military. "Many of our federal employees are on the front lines of the war on terrorism. The last thing we need to do is to take away the pay raise they deserve," Miller said. "Let's start with cutting the pay of members of Congress." The measure did not succeed, however.

Miller also took aim at lawmakers expelled from Congress by requiring them to forfeit the government-financed portion of their pensions. He introduced legislation in 2003 directed at Ohio Democrat James A. Traficant, who was expelled from the House in July 2002 just before he was convicted of 10 counts of bribery, racketeering and tax evasion. He is now serving eight years in prison, but he continues to receive an annual pension of more than $35,000. Miller's bill went nowhere, however.

Miller came to Congress in October 2001, after winning a special election to replace GOP Rep. Joe Scarborough who had resigned from the House to spend more time with his family. A former real estate broker and political aide, Miller arrived with an eclectic résumé. When he was in high school, he was a deejay for the local radio station. Later, he worked as a deputy sheriff and also held part-time jobs as a stock car racer and auctioneer.

Miller was bitten by the politics bug fairly early. As a journalism major at the University of Florida, he was elected president of college fraternities for Southeast Florida. This distinction came after he had become president of the university's agriculture fraternity, Alpha Gamma Rho, and then president of the school's fraternity system. He remains an enthusiastic supporter of the Florida Gators football team, a passion he shares with his two grown sons.

Fresh out of college, Miller joined the staff of Florida Agriculture Commissioner Doyle Connor. He later served as a state representative for the north Florida district that he now represents in Congress. During his stint in the Florida House, Miller chaired a committee on utilities and telecommunications.

With a district that is a Republican stronghold, Miller had no trouble winning the 2001 special election to replace Scarborough, garnering 66 percent of the vote, while Democrat Steve Briese won 28 percent. In 2002, Miller captured almost three-fourths of the ballots cast, beating Democrat Bert Oram by more than 100,000 votes. He won with similar ease in 2004.

KEY VOTES

2004

No Extend federal unemployment benefits by 13 weeks

No Pass $283.2 billion, six-year federal highway and mass transit bill

? Approve $146 billion multi-year extension of previously enacted middle-class tax breaks

Yes Amend the Constitution to prohibit same-sex marriage

Yes Cut corporate taxes $137 billion over 10 years

Yes Reorganize U.S. intelligence agencies as proposed by Sept. 11 commission

2003

Yes Cut taxes by $330 billion through fiscal 2013

No Block Bush rule scaling back overtime pay for some white-collar federal workers

Yes Do not allow use of search warrants without first notifying subjects

No Allow importation of prescription drugs

Yes Create private school voucher program in Washington, D.C.

Yes Ban "partial birth" abortion except to save a woman's life

No Split $18.6 billion in Iraq aid into half-grant, half-loan

No Overhaul Medicare and create prescription drug benefit

CQ VOTE STUDIES

	PARTY UNITY		PRESIDENTIAL SUPPORT	
	Support	Oppose	Support	Oppose
2004	99%	1%	92%	8%
2003	96%	4%	85%	15%
2002	98%	2%	85%	15%
2001	100%	0%	100%	0%

INTEREST GROUPS

	AFL-CIO	ADA	CCUS	ACU
2004	8%	5%	100%	100%
2003	7%	15%	83%	92%
2002	0%	0%	84%	100%
2001	17%	—%	78%	100%

FLORIDA 1
Panhandle — Pensacola, Fort Walton Beach

Some residents of the 1st refer to the area as "Lower Alabama," and in spirit the area is much closer to the Old South than to Florida's big cities. The district, which stretches from north of Panama City to Pensacola, has several large military bases and a mostly white population. Its Gulf Coast beaches and open spaces attract tourists and residents seeking a small-town feel. Walton and Okaloosa counties (part of which are in the 2nd) increased their populations by more than 40 percent in the 1990s.

Tourism, health care and retirement communities helped boost an economy slowed by manufacturing losses in the 1980s and early 1990s. Growth here is slower than in Florida's southern regions, but St. Joe, a paper company turned real estate giant, has started to develop largely rural northwestern Florida. Interstate 10 slips between the Blackwater River State Forest, which borders Alabama, and Eglin Air Force Base, connecting the western tip and Pensacola to the rest of the state.

The 1st is more staunchly conservative than its slight GOP registration advantage indicates. The district's Democrats are more "Dixiecrats"

than liberals, and several local and state officials from the area have switched to the GOP after decades as Democrats. The military presence also plays a significant role in politics; a large segment of the Okaloosa population is military employees. In the 2004 presidential election, George W. Bush took 78 percent in Okaloosa County — his best showing in the state. Santa Rosa County was close behind, giving Bush 77 percent of its vote. Overall, the 1st gave Bush his highest vote percentage (72 percent) of any Florida district.

MAJOR INDUSTRY
Defense, health care, tourism

MILITARY BASES
Naval Air Station Pensacola, 10,957 military, 3,547 civilian (2004); Eglin Air Force Base, 7,244 military, 3,301 civilian (2001); Hurlburt Field (Air Force), 8,000 military, 730 civilian; Naval Technical Training Center Corry Station, 2,620 military, 411 civilian; Naval Air Station Whiting Field, 1,774 military, 385 civilian (2004)

CITIES
Pensacola, 56,255; Ferry Pass, 27,176; Brent, 22,257

NOTABLE
The "Blue Angels" flight group is housed at Naval Air Station Pensacola.

Rep. Allen Boyd (D)

Elected 1996; 5th term

CAPITOL OFFICE
225-5235
www.house.gov/boyd
1227 Longworth 20515-0902; fax 225-5615

COMMITTEES
Appropriations

HOMETOWN
Monticello

BORN
June 6, 1945, Valdosta, Ga.

RELIGION
Methodist

FAMILY
Wife, Cissy Boyd; three children

EDUCATION
North Florida Junior College, A.A. 1966; Florida
State U., B.S. 1969 (accounting)

MILITARY SERVICE
Army, 1969-71

CAREER
Farmer

POLITICAL HIGHLIGHTS
Sought Democratic nomination for Jefferson
County Board of County Commissioners, 1972;
Fla. House, 1989-96

ELECTION RESULTS

2004 GENERAL

Allen Boyd (D)	201,577	61.7%
Bev Kilmer (R)	125,399	38.4%

2004 PRIMARY

Allen Boyd (D)	unopposed

2002 GENERAL

Allen Boyd (D)	152,164	66.9%
Tom McGurk (R)	75,275	33.1%

PREVIOUS WINNING PERCENTAGES
2000 (72%); 1998 (95%); 1996 (59%)

Boyd is a fifth-generation farmer in the mostly rural Florida Panhandle, and his conservatism on fiscal and social issues has enabled him to entrench himself in the 2nd District while many similar Southern districts have turned to the GOP.

He briefly joined the flock vying for retiring Democratic Sen. Bob Graham's seat. Boyd was the most conservative among the Democrats in the running. But he backed out in late 2003 after strategists said he lacked the name recognition to appeal statewide. His decision to seek re-election in the 2nd District eased Democratic fears that the Republicans could win the seat for the first time in history.

Strutting his conservative stripes at the beginning of the 109th Congress, Boyd was the first Democrat to back President Bush's plan to add personal investment accounts to Social Security, even teaming up with Republican Jim Kolbe of Arizona to draft a bill. His defection denied House Democrats a unified opposition as the issue gathered steam.

In the tax arena, however, Boyd opposes the president's agenda. He favors paying down the national debt over major tax reductions. When the nation returned to deficit spending during Bush's first term, Boyd said the $1.35 trillion, 10-year tax cut enacted in 2001 should be reconsidered. But six weeks before Election Day 2004, Boyd was in the midst of the toughest re-election fight of his congressional career, and voted for a tax cut extension package that lacked offsets in other parts of the budget.

Boyd is a member of the "Blue Dogs," the coalition of fiscally conservative House Democrats who try to exert a center-right pull on the party, especially on budget issues. Boyd founded a similar group when he was in the Florida Legislature.

His voting pattern is among the most conservative of House Democrats. In the 108th Congress, he backed President Bush's position 54 percent of the time, and he strayed from his party on almost a third of the party-line votes. He voted to give Bush the authority to wage war in Iraq and later for the $87.5 billion package to fund the effort. He supports a constitutional amendment to ban flag desecration and favors restrictions on abortions in some cases, including a ban on a procedure its critics call "partial birth" abortion. In 2000, he was one of just five Democrats who voted against legislation to increase the minimum wage, and in 1997, he was one of only six Democrats voting to eliminate the National Endowment for the Arts.

A lifelong hunter, Boyd opposes gun control legislation. He and his family have hosted annual charity fundraising dove hunts that have been criticized by animal rights protesters and some who object to the lobbyists who help pay the food and drink tab.

Although he considers himself a fiscal conservative, Boyd is not shy about pushing for government spending for his district. He increased his leverage to do so at the start of his second term in 1999, when he was awarded a coveted spot on the Appropriations Committee. He has used his assignment to the subcommittee that has jurisdiction over military construction to look out for Tyndall Air Force Base and has worked to speed runway upgrades and other improvements at Tyndall in preparation for the arrival of the Air Force's F-22 air-to-air combat planes.

Having been a junior infantry officer in Vietnam, Boyd puts a high priority on ways to retain U.S. air superiority over potential military foes. At a subcommittee hearing, he once reflected on his ground combat duty, recalling the morale boost of getting support from U.S. aircraft: "One of the greatest moments in an infantryman's life," he said, was "when he saw those fast movers coming across."

Boyd in the 109th retains a seat on the Agriculture Appropriations Subcommittee, where he has fought for farmers hurt by the citrus canker. In 2004, he cosponsored a federal grant program for six southeastern universities, including the 2nd District's Florida State University, his alma mater, to predict weather up to six months in advance, which helps farmers safeguard crops.

He also co-chairs the Rural Caucus, a bipartisan group of legislators from rural areas. In 2003, he was instrumental in killing a provision in a bill that would have forced rural communities to match funds to keep federally subsidized airlines flying to their airports.

A product of rural Jefferson County, just east of Tallahassee, Boyd was reared on a farm. He went to Florida State University just down the road, spent two years in the Army, and then returned home to help his family raise cattle, cotton, sod and peanuts. He became involved in agricultural organizations and civic groups.

A failed bid in 1972 for an open county commission seat seemed to have rid him of his inclination toward elective office, but more than a decade later, another open seat beckoned him. He won a 1989 special election to the state House and served seven years, cultivating good relations with the business community.

He first won his U.S. House seat in 1996 after the retirement of three-term Democrat Pete Peterson. Boyd demonstrated that he could hold together the 2nd's traditional Democratic coalition: Tallahassee-area voters with jobs in state and local government and higher education, African-Americans and the portion of the white electorate still clinging to an inherited aversion to the GOP, which in the region was the party of the enemy in the Civil War.

After the 2000 census, redistricting tilted the 2nd slightly toward the Republicans. Boyd won easily until 2004 when he drew a well-funded challenger in state Rep. Bev Kilmer, who tried to cast Boyd as a liberal. The national GOP sent such notables as first lady Laura Bush and Speaker J. Dennis Hastert to campaign for him. Boyd was the only incumbent Democrat in Florida with a GOP foe, and it was the state's only truly competitive congressional race. The contest got heated when Kilmer's husband sued Boyd over a campaign ad. But Boyd's popularity took him to a comfortable 62 percentage point victory in the majority Democratic district.

KEY VOTES

2004

Yes	Extend federal unemployment benefits by 13 weeks
No	Pass $283.2 billion, six-year federal highway and mass transit bill
Yes	Approve $146 billion multi-year extension of previously enacted middle-class tax breaks
Yes	Amend the Constitution to prohibit same-sex marriage
Yes	Cut corporate taxes $137 billion over 10 years
Yes	Reorganize U.S. intelligence agencies as proposed by Sept. 11 commission

2003

No	Cut taxes by $330 billion through fiscal 2013
Yes	Block Bush rule scaling back overtime pay for some white-collar federal workers
Yes	Do not allow use of search warrants without first notifying subjects
Yes	Allow importation of prescription drugs
No	Create private school voucher program in Washington, D.C.
Yes	Ban "partial birth" abortion except to save a woman's life
Yes	Split $18.6 billion in Iraq aid into half-grant, half-loan
Yes	Overhaul Medicare and create prescription drug benefit

CQ VOTE STUDIES

	PARTY UNITY		PRESIDENTIAL SUPPORT	
	Support	Oppose	Support	Oppose
2004	67%	33%	61%	39%
2003	74%	26%	50%	50%
2002	71%	29%	50%	50%
2001	70%	30%	44%	56%
2000	68%	32%	57%	43%

INTEREST GROUPS

	AFL-CIO	ADA	CCUS	ACU
2004	60%	70%	75%	46%
2003	71%	70%	71%	38%
2002	75%	70%	58%	40%
2001	82%	70%	52%	32%
2000	30%	50%	80%	40%

FLORIDA 2

Panhandle — part of Tallahassee, Panama City

The 2nd stretches around Florida's Big Bend, joining the Panhandle with the state capital of Tallahassee (a small part of which is in the 4th District) and the north-central part of the state. Taking in all or part of 16 counties, the district features tobacco and peanut farms, forests and uncongested towns. While Democratic, the 2nd is not as liberal as districts in southeast Florida.

Registered Democrats still heavily outnumber Republicans, but the GOP has made some gains, and many Democrats have conservative views on fiscal and social issues. The exception is the Tallahassee area (Leon County), home to Florida State University and Florida A&M University, where a more liberal sentiment exists. Panama City has a stronger conservative element, as do the smaller communities that ring the Gulf Coast. Black residents — the majority of whom live in the Tallahassee area or in neighboring Gadsden County — make up about one-fifth of the district's voting-age population. John Kerry took at least 60 percent of the 2004 presidential vote in Gadsden, Leon and Liberty counties, but George

W. Bush won the district with 54 percent.

The 2nd's economy is driven by its land — from the Gulf Coast beaches where oysters are harvested to farms stocked with soybeans and peanuts. Agriculture has struggled occasionally because of bad weather and low prices, but a steady base of government employees buffers any long-term economic effects. Florida's forestry industry has suffered some setbacks but maintains a strong presence. Panama City relies on tourism and the economic benefits of the military community around Tyndall Air Force Base.

MAJOR INDUSTRY
Agriculture, government, manufacturing

MILITARY BASES
Tyndall Air Force Base, 4,402 military, 637 civilian (2003)

CITIES
Tallahassee (pt.), 147,167; Panama City, 36,417; Callaway, 14,233

NOTABLE
The Suwannee River was made famous by Stephen Foster's song, "Old Folks at Home"; Liberty County has the fewest registered Republicans of any county in the state — 320 as of October 2004.

Rep. Corrine Brown (D)

Elected 1992; 7th term

CAPITOL OFFICE
225-0123
www.house.gov/corrinebrown
2444 Rayburn 20515-0903; fax 225-2256

COMMITTEES
Transportation & Infrastructure
Veterans' Affairs

HOMETOWN
Jacksonville

BORN
Nov. 11, 1946, Jacksonville, Fla.

RELIGION
Baptist

FAMILY
Divorced; one child

EDUCATION
Florida A&M U., B.S. 1969 (sociology), M.A. 1971
(education); U. of Florida, Ed.S. 1974

CAREER
College guidance counselor; travel agency owner

POLITICAL HIGHLIGHTS
Candidate for Fla. House, 1980; Fla. House, 1982-92

ELECTION RESULTS

2004 GENERAL

Corrine Brown (D)		unopposed

2004 PRIMARY

Corrine Brown (D)	46,285	81.3%
Prince Brown (D)	10,639	18.7%

2002 GENERAL

Corrine Brown (D)	88,462	59.3%
Jennifer Carroll (R)	60,747	40.7%

PREVIOUS WINNING PERCENTAGES
2000 (58%); 1998 (55%); 1996 (61%); 1994 (58%);
1992 (59%)

Known for her biting rhetoric and thoroughly liberal views, Brown is a voluble critic of Republican initiatives. But now that she has more than a dozen years in the House, she has built up sufficient seniority to do more than just speak out against proposals she dislikes.

Brown has been particularly outspoken against President Bush, saying his budget priorities have "dangerous flaws" that sacrifice a commitment to the poor and elderly in favor of defense and tax cuts. And she was an early skeptic of the president's conduct of foreign policy, in particular his focus on removing Saddam Hussein from power.

Her sharp tongue briefly cost her speaking privileges on the House floor in 2004. She accused Indiana Republican Steve Buyer and others of participating in a "coup d'état" and of stealing the contested 2000 presidential election in Florida. Unapologetic after the incident, she said, "If they're going to take my words down for telling the truth, that's OK. . . . We had a coup d'état. Straight out, they stole the election."

But Brown did apologize after another 2004 incident. During a meeting with a State Department official, she accused him and other "white men" of underfunding U.S. aid programs for Haiti. Brown said she did not mean to aim her comments at Roger F. Noriega, a Mexican-American who was assistant secretary of State for Western Hemisphere Affairs, but rather "at the policies of the Bush administration as they pertain to Haiti, which I do consider to be racist." Brown's outburst prompted Henry Bonilla of Texas, the only Mexican-American among House Republicans, to demand her resignation.

Brown may be acerbic, yet she attends to her legislative duties. In the 108th Congress, she assumed the top-ranking Democratic post on the Transportation and Infrastructure panel's Railroads Subcommittee, affording her an opportunity to weigh in on issues affecting Amtrak, the financially troubled federally subsidized passenger rail system. From her seat on Transportation, she also has been able to direct a good share of federal funding to her district and state. During the 2004 reauthorization of federal transportation programs, she served as a conferee, winning tens of millions of dollars for road and transit projects in Jacksonville and Orlando.

In the 107th, she used her position as the top-ranking Democrat on the Coast Guard and Maritime Subcommittee to press for greater security at her hometown Port of Jacksonville and other seaports around the country. She helped shape the port security law enacted in 2002.

There are several military installations near the 3rd District, including the Jacksonville Naval Air Station. Jacksonville is also home to many retired military personnel, and Brown keeps an eye on their needs as a member of the Veterans' Affairs Committee. Brown would like to see more emphasis placed on the military's human resources, such as increasing training.

She was elected first-vice chairwoman of the Congressional Black Caucus at the beginning of the 109th. She speaks out on improving access to health care for minorities and low-income people, and she has worked to make minority hiring a priority at the Transportation Security Administration since its creation in 2001.

After the 2000 election controversy in Florida — when voters, including many minorities, were turned away from some polling places and thousands of ballots were miscast or uncounted — Brown joined in the volley of criticism and began working to overhaul the election process. She backed the election standards law enacted in 2002, unlike several colleagues in the Black Caucus who felt the measure did not do enough.

Brown has a long history of fending off allegations of ethical lapses. Her 1992 primary opponent, former state Rep. Andrew E. Johnson, filed charges with the Florida Commission on Ethics claiming that Brown received illegal campaign donations and made a staff member from her state representative's office work in her travel agency.

In 1998, The St. Petersburg Times published a story saying Brown had benefited from a $10,000 check she received from the Rev. Henry J. Lyons, president of the National Baptist Convention USA Inc. Lyons had been charged in federal and state court with crimes including extortion, theft and conspiracy. Brown denied the allegation.

Also in 1998, the Committee on Standards of Official Conduct began investigating her financial dealings with a West African businessman. Just before the 2000 election, the panel ruled that Brown had "demonstrated, at the least, poor judgment." The panel decided not to take disciplinary action in large measure because key witnesses "were beyond the reach of the committee's subpoena power."

Brown was steered into politics by one of her sorority sisters at Florida A&M University, Gwendolyn Sawyer Cherry, who went on to become the first black Florida state representative. Although Brown lost her first state House race in 1980, Cherry kept after her to try again, and Brown won a seat in 1982. She served in the state House for a decade.

After a black-majority 3rd District was created by redistricting for the 1990s, Brown was one of four candidates in the district's bitter Democratic primary. She had to overcome ethics charges brought against her by one of her Democratic opponents, but survived a runoff with 64 percent of the vote. Latent acrimony helped hold her share of the vote to 59 percent in November 1992 against Republican Don Weidner.

The district has been redrawn twice since then, and for this decade African-Americans make up slightly less than half the population.

Brown has had to work for most of her general-election victories. She garnered more than three-fifths of the vote — a traditional threshold for being seen as having a safe seat — in only one of her first six races, when she got a lift from President Clinton's re-election coattails in 1996. Republicans ran a black candidate against Brown in three of her re-election campaigns, seeking to eliminate race as a factor. In 2004, Brown faced only a write-in opponent.

KEY VOTES

2004

Yes   Extend federal unemployment benefits by 13 weeks

Yes   Pass $283.2 billion, six-year federal highway and mass transit bill

No   Approve $146 billion multi-year extension of previously enacted middle-class tax breaks

?   Amend the Constitution to prohibit same-sex marriage

Yes   Cut corporate taxes $137 billion over 10 years

Yes   Reorganize U.S. intelligence agencies as proposed by Sept. 11 commission

2003

No   Cut taxes by $330 billion through fiscal 2013

Yes   Block Bush rule scaling back overtime pay for some white-collar federal workers

Yes   Do not allow use of search warrants without first notifying subjects

Yes   Allow importation of prescription drugs

No   Create private school voucher program in Washington, D.C.

No   Ban "partial birth" abortion except to save a woman's life

Yes   Split $18.6 billion in Iraq aid into half-grant, half-loan

No   Overhaul Medicare and create prescription drug benefit

CQ VOTE STUDIES

	PARTY UNITY		PRESIDENTIAL SUPPORT	
	Support	Oppose	Support	Oppose
2004	94%	6%	32%	68%
2003	95%	5%	20%	80%
2002	95%	5%	29%	71%
2001	92%	8%	24%	76%
2000	92%	8%	82%	18%

INTEREST GROUPS

	AFL-CIO	ADA	CCUS	ACU
2004	92%	90%	37%	8%
2003	100%	95%	33%	22%
2002	100%	95%	42%	0%
2001	100%	95%	43%	8%
2000	100%	80%	50%	9%

FLORIDA 3

North — parts of Jacksonville, Orlando and Gainesville

The 3rd, which bounces among three of Florida's northern cities, includes both heavily urban areas and long stretches of swamps and lakes along the St. Johns River. The racial and political demographics of the black-dominated 3rd hardly changed during redistricting following the 2000 census, although the district no longer includes the Daytona Beach area, and it now extends west from its poles of Jacksonville and Orlando to pick up voters in Gainesville, home to the University of Florida (though the university itself is in the 6th District).

Democrats dominate the 3rd — they make up more than 75 percent of registered voters. Some rural areas are home to Republicans and old-line conservative Democrats, but not enough to counter the district's strong proclivity toward Democratic candidates for federal office. John Kerry won the 2004 presidential vote here by 30 percentage points.

The 3rd includes a large portion of Putnam County. Often referred to as the Bass Fishing Capital of the World, Putnam is a blue-collar region. The 3rd does contain some tinges of conservatism, particularly in Clay County and in the Palatka area (shared with the 7th) on the St. Johns River.

Mostly blue-collar, the district relies on Naval Air Station Jacksonville (in the 4th District) and other area government facilities for jobs. CSX Corp. also is based in Jacksonville. The city's emergence as a financial center has helped the area's economic outlook, while Orlando residents work in tourism jobs at locations such as Walt Disney World (in the 8th District). Most of the areas in between have agricultural land and lack major private employers, contributing to the 3rd's poor overall economic profile.

MAJOR INDUSTRY

Defense, government, higher education, transportation

CITIES

Jacksonville (pt.), 251,892; Orlando (pt.), 61,906; Pine Hills, 41,764; Gainesville (pt.), 35,540; Oak Ridge, 22,349; Sanford (pt.), 21,786

NOTABLE

Eatonville was the hometown of Harlem Renaissance author Zora Neale Hurston; ALLTEL Stadium, home of football's Jacksonville Jaguars, hosted the Super Bowl in 2005.

Rep. Ander Crenshaw (R)

Elected 2000; 3rd term

CAPITOL OFFICE
225-2501
crenshaw.house.gov
127 Cannon 20515-0904; fax 225-2504

COMMITTEES
Appropriations
Budget

HOMETOWN
Jacksonville

BORN
Sept. 1, 1944, Jacksonville, Fla.

RELIGION
Episcopalian

FAMILY
Wife, Kitty Crenshaw; two children

EDUCATION
U. of Georgia, A.B. 1966 (political science); U. of
Florida, J.D. 1969

CAREER
Investment bank executive; lawyer

POLITICAL HIGHLIGHTS
Fla. House, 1972-78; candidate for Fla. secretary of
state, 1978; sought Republican nomination for U.S.
Senate, 1980; Fla. Senate, 1986-94 (president,
1992); sought Republican nomination for governor,
1994

ELECTION RESULTS

2004 GENERAL

Ander Crenshaw (R)		unopposed

2004 PRIMARY

Ander Crenshaw (R)	48,129	90.0%
Deborah Katz Pueschel (R)	5,368	10.0%

2002 GENERAL

Ander Crenshaw (R)		unopposed

PREVIOUS WINNING PERCENTAGES
2000 (67%)

Crenshaw is conservative across the board on fiscal and social issues, but tends to focus on finding pragmatic solutions rather than taking ideological stands. "On balance, I'd start with the proposition that government doesn't solve problems very well," he once told the Orlando Sentinel.

Easygoing and likeable, he has a knack for working with people on both sides of the aisle despite being a solid vote for the conservative Republican leadership. He voted with Republicans 97 percent of the time on votes where the parties staked out opposite positions in the 108th Congress.

With many years of seasoning in Florida's statehouse, Crenshaw caught on quickly to the steps to career advancement on Capitol Hill. In only his second term, the former college basketball player secured a seat on the powerful Appropriations Committee by doing his "pre-game homework".

He lined up support ahead of time among the Florida delegation — the fourth-largest after California, Texas and New York. And he let GOP leaders know they could count on him as a team player during tough votes, close calls and turf battles. To prove his worth, in his freshman term Crenshaw urged the Armed Services Committee to support a leadership-drafted budget that called for less spending than committee members wanted. Crenshaw generally supports larger military budgets and represents a Northeast Florida district with a large military presence.

When it comes to his district, Crenshaw has yet to see a defense spending plan that is too generous. In the 109th Congress, he joined with others in the Florida delegation in a furious attempt to keep the Navy from retiring the *USS John F. Kennedy*, an aircraft carrier docked at the Naval Station Mayport. The Pentagon proposed in early 2005 to retire one of its 12 carriers, estimating it could save over $1 billion, and it chose the *Kennedy*, the oldest and the likeliest target for retirement. Crenshaw and his home-state group introduced a bill requiring the Defense Department to maintain 12 carriers.

He was much happier in 2004 when the Navy decided to move the U.S. Naval Forces Southern Command to Mayport from a naval station in Puerto Rico. When the House voted in 2004 to delay a scheduled 2005 round of military base closings by two years, Crenshaw voted with the majority. Usually a strong supporter of the Bush administration, which wanted to honor the schedule, Crenshaw argued that the country could ill afford to close bases in the middle of the war with Iraq.

While the Navy is important to Crenshaw's district, so is the Atlantic coast as a magnet for tourists and a getaway for locals. Crenshaw worked to get federal funds for beach rehabilitation projects in the face of stiff competition from other districts in Florida that sustained heavy damage from four hurricanes in the summer of 2004. Crenshaw was able to get $15 million for erosion repair on Jacksonville's beaches.

One of Crenshaw's most enduring acts in the 108th Congress was the enactment of a law designating American Beach in Nassau County as part of the Timucuan Ecological and Historic Preserve. American Beach was a popular vacation spot for African-Americans during segregation. Originally more than 200 acres, it has shrunk to half that size because of encroaching development. "This land carries great national significance, so it is fitting we afford protections to preserve its natural character for future generations," Crenshaw said.

Crenshaw's family has been in the Jacksonville area since 1901. The son of a lawyer, he grew up comfortably middle class and was senior class president at Robert E. Lee High School. A lanky 6-foot-4, he went to the University of Georgia on a basketball scholarship, and was the third member of his family, following his father and brother, to win a letter for the Bulldogs. The first name he uses, Ander, is a shortened version of his given name Alexander; it was coined by his older brother.

Of draft age during the Vietnam War, Crenshaw served in the ROTC but avoided combat through a student deferment and then a high number in the draft lottery, according to the Sentinel.

While working on a law degree at the University of Florida, he formed a Campus Crusade for Christ chapter. He eventually found he was not interested in practicing law after all, turned to investment banking and became wealthy. He says he began thinking about running for political office after he started dating Kitty Kirk, the daughter of former Florida Gov. Claude R. Kirk Jr. The two got married.

In 1972, Crenshaw won election to the state House, where he served six years. He moved up to the state Senate in 1986. Fellow senators liked his laid-back attitude toward the job, and his nice-guy image enabled him to build trust. In 1993, Crenshaw became the first Republican to preside over the Florida Senate in 118 years, leading a chamber split evenly between the two parties. His reputation as someone who would seek consensus kept the power-sharing agreement from descending into sheer acrimony.

Despite his success in the legislature, Crenshaw lost three statewide elections — a bid for secretary of state in 1978, the Republican Senate primary in 1980 and the GOP primary for governor in 1994. In the latter race, he drew attention for condemning homosexuals, but said he would hire gay people if elected.

After leaving the state Senate in 1994, he stayed out of politics for a time until an opportunity to run for Congress came along in 2000, when GOP Rep. Tillie Fowler stuck to her term-limit pledge and retired. Crenshaw won the primary easily, which guaranteed him victory in the solidly Republican 4th District.

In once-a-decade redistricting after 2000, Crenshaw's previously compact Duval and Nassau counties district was altered. It now stretches from the Atlantic Ocean beaches of Duval and Nassau more than 150 miles west to the Leon County outskirts of Tallahassee. But the new borders did not endanger Crenshaw's electoral prospects. He easily dispatched a GOP primary foe in 2002 and had no Democratic opponent that year. He coasted to a third term in 2004.

KEY VOTES

2004

No   Extend federal unemployment benefits by 13 weeks

No   Pass $283.2 billion, six-year federal highway and mass transit bill

Yes   Approve $146 billion multi-year extension of previously enacted middle-class tax breaks

Yes   Amend the Constitution to prohibit same-sex marriage

Yes   Cut corporate taxes $137 billion over 10 years

Yes   Reorganize U.S. intelligence agencies as proposed by Sept. 11 commission

2003

Yes   Cut taxes by $330 billion through fiscal 2013

No   Block Bush rule scaling back overtime pay for some white-collar federal workers

Yes   Do not allow use of search warrants without first notifying subjects

No   Allow importation of prescription drugs

Yes   Create private school voucher program in Washington, D.C.

Yes   Ban "partial birth" abortion except to save a woman's life

No   Split $18.6 billion in Iraq aid into half-grant, half-loan

Yes   Overhaul Medicare and create prescription drug benefit

CQ VOTE STUDIES

	PARTY UNITY		PRESIDENTIAL SUPPORT	
	Support	Oppose	Support	Oppose
2004	95%	5%	88%	12%
2003	98%	2%	98%	2%
2002	98%	2%	90%	10%
2001	97%	3%	91%	9%

INTEREST GROUPS

	AFL-CIO	ADA	CCUS	ACU
2004	13%	0%	100%	92%
2003	7%	5%	97%	88%
2002	11%	0%	100%	96%
2001	17%	0%	100%	92%

FLORIDA 4
North — part of Jacksonville, sliver of Tallahassee

The solidly Republican 4th is anchored in Jacksonville and the surrounding beach communities of Duval County. It wraps around the northeast corner of the state and then runs across the northern border counties as far west as Leon County, where it narrows to a finger to take in a small eastern part of Tallahassee, the state capital.

Republicans now hold a slight but growing edge in voter registration, after decades of Democratic dominance, and many Democrats in the more rural areas of the district are old-line conservatives who now side with GOP candidates. One such example is Baker County, where Democrats hold a 3-to-1 registration advantage, but George W. Bush won 78 percent of the county's vote in the 2004 presidential election. Overall, the 4th gave Bush 67 percent of the vote.

The Jacksonville-based 4th was once a thin strip along the East Coast, but redistricting following the 2000 census gave it an east-west cast that alters the set of issues important to voters. Agriculture and inland water are now vital in a district once dominated by coastal issues. Much of the

4th shadows Interstate 10, a highway that bridges the 150 miles of rural territory between Jacksonville and Tallahassee.

Jacksonville is a major center for the financial services industry, which provides many of the jobs not associated with the Navy's strong presence in the district along the St. Johns River.

MAJOR INDUSTRY
Defense, financial services, tourism

MILITARY BASES
Naval Air Station Jacksonville, 10,000 military, 10,000 civilian; Naval Station Mayport, 13,500 military, 1,900 civilian (2004)

CITIES
Jacksonville (pt.), 396,879; Jacksonville Beach, 20,990; Atlantic Beach, 13,368; Fernandina Beach, 10,549; Lake City, 9,980

NOTABLE
Fernandina Beach is the only part of the current United States to have existed under eight flags: France, Spain (twice), England, "Patriot," "Green Cross of Florida," Mexico, Confederate and U.S.

Rep. Ginny Brown-Waite (R)

Elected 2002; 2nd term

CAPITOL OFFICE
225-1002
www.house.gov/brown-waite
414 Cannon 20515-0905; fax 226-6559

COMMITTEES
Financial Services
Government Reform
Veterans' Affairs

HOMETOWN
Crystal River

BORN
Oct. 5, 1943, Albany, N.Y.

RELIGION
Roman Catholic

FAMILY
Husband, Harvey Waite; three children

EDUCATION
State U. of New York, Albany, B.S. 1976; Russell
Sage College, M.A. 1984 (public administration)

CAREER
Health care consultant; state legislative aide

POLITICAL HIGHLIGHTS
Hernando County Board of Commissioners, 1991-
93; Fla. Senate, 1992-2002 (president pro tempore,
2001-02)

ELECTION RESULTS

2004 GENERAL

Ginny Brown-Waite (R)	240,315	65.9%
Robert G. Whittel (D)	124,140	34.1%

2004 PRIMARY

Ginny Brown-Waite (R)	unopposed

2002 GENERAL

Ginny Brown-Waite (R)	121,998	47.9%
Karen L. Thurman (D)	117,758	46.2%
Jack "Thro" Gargan (I)	8,639	3.4%
Brian Moore (I)	6,223	2.4%

A transplanted Yankee, Brown-Waite jumped into local politics in her adopted state of Florida at midlife and, in short order, rose from a seat on the county commission to a top post in the GOP-dominated statehouse.

She may appear to be a pint-size grandmother of four, but she is aggressive, driven, straight-talking, and not easily intimidated. When the Florida nursing home industry tried to slip into one of her bills a provision relaxing standards for family notification when a patient is released, Brown-Waite denounced nursing home lobbyists as "slimy bastards." At home, Brown-Waite's favorite getaway is cruising Florida's scenic coast in her red 1959 MG.

With a track record of getting bills passed in a big, populous state, she adapted quickly to legislating at the national level. She pushed through the House a bill expanding the federal guarantee for home mortgages for veterans, one of her most important constituencies. About a fifth of the population of her district is active and retired military families. Democrats complained bitterly that she stole the idea from Rep. Susan A. Davis, a California Democrat, who had been building a bipartisan coalition for a similar bill, but Brown-Waite plowed ahead.

Veterans' issues are her priority, and she has a seat on the Veterans' Affairs Committee in addition to assignments on Financial Services and Government Reform. Her signature effort her first term was a proposal to require VA hospitals to provide treatment to veterans within 30 days of their seeking care or allow them to be treated by a private medical provider.

In 2003, she received some rare criticism from veterans' groups for declining to sign a petition calling on GOP leaders to bring to the floor a bill allowing military retirees to simultaneously receive both pension checks and disability benefits. Brown-Waite declared her support for the bill but would not sign the discharge petition, which, with enough signatures, can force a bill to the floor. The procedure is frowned on by GOP leaders because it weakens their control over floor votes.

With many retirement communities in her district, the changes to Social Security proposed by President Bush are a sensitive matter for Brown-Waite. Despite loyalty to Bush and his agenda, she opposes his idea of creating a system of personal investment accounts within the program.

She also parts with the president on immigration issues, generally favoring tighter controls than the White House. Brown-Waite was among the 67 Republicans who voted in 2004 against an overhaul of intelligence-gathering agencies that Bush wanted, saying it did not go far enough in cracking down on the use of illegal identification by immigrants.

Though she calls herself a moderate, Brown-Waite often votes with conservatives on sticky social issues. She supports some restrictions on abortion and a constitutional ban on same-sex marriage. She backs gun owners' rights and carries a Colt .38-caliber handgun for self-protection.

Where she does find common ground with liberals is on issues affecting women. In the 109th Congress, she was elected co-chairwoman, along with Democrat Hilda L. Solis of California, of the Congressional Women's Caucus. Brown-Waite said she wants the caucus to focus on reauthorizing the Violence Against Women Act and to help connect women's groups and women business leaders.

A productive first term earned her favorable reviews at home except for what the Tampa Tribune dubbed an occasional "wacky streak." As congressional Republicans were fuming over France's lack of support for the

Iraq war, Brown-Waite went a step further and called for the remains of American soldiers buried overseas to be shipped back to the United States.

Brown-Waite grew up in Albany, N.Y., the daughter of a file clerk who threw her abusive husband out of the house. "I grew up poor," she told the Tampa newspaper. "I remember what it's like to be poor." She married young, divorced and later remarried her present husband, Harvey Waite, a retired state trooper. The two relocated to Florida, and Brown-Waite started her political career with election to the Hernando County Board of Commissioners.

The next stop was the Florida Legislature, where she served a decade in the Senate, rising to GOP whip and chairing major committees. She pushed bills to give patients more access to information through physician profiles and to tighten controls on health maintenance organizations. Her nursing home bill limited damages paid by the facilities as a way of curbing skyrocketing insurance rates. Her record on health care was marred, however, by a 2000 Tampa Tribune story about a too-cozy relationship with a Tampa HMO that paid her an annual salary of nearly $24,000 to "interpret" legislation that she had had a hand in passing.

She developed a pro-consumer record for fighting water and sewer rate hikes. And she backed a bill requiring mothers to wait 48 hours after giving birth before signing consent for adoption, an issue of personal interest to her. Brown-Waite adopted her daughter when the girl was 10 and living in an abusive home. The birth mother initially resisted giving her up. Her daughter is now in her mid-twenties.

When she was prevented by term limits from continuing in the state Senate, her powerful GOP allies redrew the lines of incumbent Democratic Rep. Karen L. Thurman's district to make it more favorable to a 2002 challenge by Brown-Waite. The new 5th included all of her state Senate district and excluded the liberal-leaning academic community in Alachua County, home to the University of Florida.

After an easy GOP primary win, Brown-Waite overcame a determined effort by the moderate five-term Thurman to keep her seat. She prevailed by a scant 2 percentage point margin. Two years later, Thurman declined a rematch, and Brown-Waite had only nominal Democratic opposition.

Lucky in politics, Brown-Waite has had some uncanny personal misfortunes. In 2001, she went to a Dixie Youth League baseball game to toss out the first pitch and was knocked unconscious by an errant ball thrown by a 12-year-old. In 2003, she slipped and broke her arm while leaving the Capitol, an injury that required surgery.

KEY VOTES

2004

?	Extend federal unemployment benefits by 13 weeks
No	Pass $283.2 billion, six-year federal highway and mass transit bill
Yes	Approve $146 billion multi-year extension of previously enacted middle-class tax breaks
Yes	Amend the Constitution to prohibit same-sex marriage
Yes	Cut corporate taxes $137 billion over 10 years
No	Reorganize U.S. intelligence agencies as proposed by Sept. 11 commission

2003

Yes	Cut taxes by $330 billion through fiscal 2013
No	Block Bush rule scaling back overtime pay for some white-collar federal workers
No	Do not allow use of search warrants without first notifying subjects
Yes	Allow importation of prescription drugs
Yes	Create private school voucher program in Washington, D.C.
Yes	Ban "partial birth" abortion except to save a woman's life
No	Split $18.6 billion in Iraq aid into half-grant, half-loan
Yes	Overhaul Medicare and create prescription drug benefit

CQ VOTE STUDIES

	PARTY UNITY		PRESIDENTIAL SUPPORT	
	Support	Oppose	Support	Oppose
2004	95%	5%	87%	13%
2003	95%	5%	96%	4%

INTEREST GROUPS

	AFL-CIO	ADA	CCUS	ACU
2004	14%	5%	100%	96%
2003	7%	10%	87%	83%

FLORIDA 5

Northern west coast – Pasco, Hernando counties

Located north of Tampa on Florida's west coast, the 5th includes Hernando, Citrus and part of Pasco counties and portions of five other counties. Its eastern tip, in Lake County, extends to the greater Orlando area.

During redistricting following the 2000 census, the legislature swapped Democratic strongholds for GOP bailiwicks in an effort to elect a Republican to the House. The resulting electorate has only a slight Republican tilt, with about 17 percent of voters registered as independents. Two of the most notable changes were the exclusion of Alachua County — which includes the Democratic-leaning Gainesville voters around the University of Florida — and the Pasco County coast. Mapmakers instead added more-conservative areas of Pasco. As a result of the alterations, George W. Bush beat John Kerry in the 5th District by 17 percentage points in the 2004 presidential election.

Social Security, prescription drugs and veterans' affairs are the dominant political issues in the 5th, where more than one-fourth of residents are 65 or older. Although its populace often has fought development, the district's communities have been filling up more rapidly in recent decades as additional retirees move into the area.

Tougher economic times have hit parts of the 5th, but many communities are thriving anyway. Businesses continue to buy up land in Pasco County, and industrial parks in Pasco and Hernando counties are havens for small manufacturing companies.

MAJOR INDUSTRY
Manufacturing, service, health care

CITIES
Spring Hill, 69,078; Land O' Lakes, 20,971; Homosassa Springs, 12,458

NOTABLE
Brooksville was named for Rep. Preston Brooks of South Carolina, who in 1856 bludgeoned Sen. Charles Sumner of Massachusetts with a cane after Sumner gave an anti-slavery speech in which he denounced a senator who was a relative of Brooks.

Rep. Cliff Stearns (R)

CAPITOL OFFICE
225-5744
www.house.gov/stearns
2370 Rayburn 20515-0906; fax 225-3973

COMMITTEES
Energy & Commerce
  (Commerce, Trade & Consumer Protection -
  chairman)
Veterans' Affairs

HOMETOWN
Ocala

BORN
April 16, 1941, Washington, D.C.

RELIGION
Presbyterian

FAMILY
Wife, Joan Stearns; three children

EDUCATION
George Washington U., B.S. 1963 (electrical
engineering)

MILITARY SERVICE
Air Force, 1963-67

CAREER
Hotel and restaurant executive; advertising
account executive

POLITICAL HIGHLIGHTS
No previous office

ELECTION RESULTS

2004 GENERAL

Cliff Stearns (R)	211,137	64.4%
David E. Bruderly (D)	116,680	35.6%

2004 PRIMARY

Cliff Stearns (R)	unopposed

2002 GENERAL

Cliff Stearns (R)	141,570	65.4%
David E. Bruderly (D)	75,046	34.6%

PREVIOUS WINNING PERCENTAGES
2000 (100%); 1998 (100%); 1996 (67%); 1994 (99%);
1992 (65%); 1990 (59%); 1988 (53%)

Elected 1988; 9th term

In his third term as chairman of a key subcommittee, Stearns has become a key player on such cutting-edge technology issues as "spyware" proliferation and Internet phone service as well as permitting school children with asthma to administer their own medications.

Stearns is conservative — have no doubt — but he runs the Energy and Commerce Subcommittee on Commerce, Trade and Consumer Protection in an inclusive, business-like manner. He does his homework and pragmatism is the order of the day.

That is a change from Stearns' early days on Capitol Hill. First elected in 1988, he was a forerunner of the tough-talking fiscal and social conservatives who came to Congress in droves in the 1990s. Back then, as a backbench member of the minority party, much of his effort was devoted to speaking out for conservative social causes and spearheading battles against abortion, pornography and funding for the National Endowment for the Arts.

Although his views have not changed and he still votes to narrow abortion rights and cut NEA funding, Stearns lets someone else take the lead on those issues.

Stearns is an active subcommittee chairman, however. In the 108th Congress, he convened hearings on a wide range of issues, including product safety, privacy, regulation of professional boxing, accounting standards, trade with China, highway safety, Olympic and college sports, the safety of dietary supplements, and e-commerce.

He has been in the forefront of efforts to protect the privacy of consumers who shop via the Internet and to overhaul accounting standards in the wake of a series of corporate accounting scandals. In the last three Congresses, he has drafted legislation to shield gun manufacturers and sellers from liability lawsuits for civil damages based on a gun owner's illegal use of a firearm.

In the 108th, he was a key player in the development of legislation to regulate what is commonly known as "spyware" — software that resides on many computer hard drives, unbeknownst to many users, that can divert Internet browsers, track keystrokes, monitor the Internet sites that an individual visits or bring up advertisements that can be closed only by shutting down a computer.

His conservative stripes showed through in the 108th when he championed a provision in broadcast decency legislation to make it easier for the Federal Communications Commission to fine individual performers for indecent actions. For several Congresses, he has introduced legislation to require the posting of the Ten Commandments in the House and Senate chambers.

Stearns is also fiscally conservative; on the few occasions on which he strays from the party line it is often because he objects to the price tag of some GOP proposals. In 2003, for instance, he was one of only 18 House Republicans who voted to require that half of all reconstruction aid to Iraq be in the form of loans, rather than grants.

That kind of vote has consistently earned Stearns honors from various budget watchdog groups, such as the National Taxpayers Union, the Council of Citizens Against Government Waste and Americans for Tax Reform.

The Florida Times-Union (Jacksonville), noting one of Stearns' awards, approvingly called him the "biggest tightwad" in the Florida delegation.

Stearns is also wary of moves to expand foreign trade, although he has supported trade legislation in the past if President Bush and his party need him.

Although his primary focus has been on issues before his Commerce Subcommittee, Stearns has remained a member of the Veterans' Affairs panel, where he was chairman of the Health Subcommittee from 1997-2000. In the 108th Congress, his years-long effort to get a new veterans' cemetery in the Jacksonville area was successful; his legislation to establish a new cemetery became law, as part of broader legislation that established six new veterans' cemeteries.

Stearns was born and raised in Washington, D.C., where he was a basketball and track star at Woodrow Wilson High School and his father worked as a Justice Department lawyer. During his college days at George Washington University, where he majored in electrical engineering, Stearns was part of the Air Force ROTC. He served four years in the Air Force as a specialist in aerospace engineering and satellite reconnaissance. On Capitol Hill, Stearns co-chairs the Air Force Caucus.

After his stint in the Air Force, Stearns worked in advertising before going into business for himself. He took over a dilapidated motel in Massachusetts; later, spotting what he viewed as an undervalued Howard Johnson's for sale in north central Florida, Stearns moved to the Sunshine State in the mid-1970s. He built a thriving motel and restaurant management business and involved himself in local affairs in Ocala.

He became director of the Chamber of Commerce, served on the board of a major local hospital, and joined church and civic groups. In 1988, Stearns ran for an open House seat and, through his local alliances and political savvy, was able to beat two better-connected candidates for the Republican nomination.

Although he was a heavy underdog in the general election against Democratic state House Speaker Jon Mills, Stearns' limited political background gave him a salient, populist theme: He said the time had come for "a citizen congressman." Stearns went on to out-hustle an overconfident Mills for the seat.

His last competitive race was in 1990. Democrats didn't even field a candidate against him in 1998 or 2000. Redistricting before the 2002 election did him no political harm; in his last two re-election contests, Stearns has captured almost two-thirds of the vote. His name is among a number of prominent Republicans mentioned as possible Senate candidates in 2006.

KEY VOTES

2004

No   Extend federal unemployment benefits by 13 weeks

No   Pass $283.2 billion, six-year federal highway and mass transit bill

Yes   Approve $146 billion multi-year extension of previously enacted middle-class tax breaks

Yes   Amend the Constitution to prohibit same-sex marriage

Yes   Cut corporate taxes $137 billion over 10 years

Yes   Reorganize U.S. intelligence agencies as proposed by Sept. 11 commission

2003

Yes   Cut taxes by $330 billion through fiscal 2013

No   Block Bush rule scaling back overtime pay for some white-collar federal workers

Yes   Do not allow use of search warrants without first notifying subjects

No   Allow importation of prescription drugs

Yes   Create private school voucher program in Washington, D.C.

Yes   Ban "partial birth" abortion except to save a woman's life

Yes   Split $18.6 billion in Iraq aid into half-grant, half-loan

Yes   Overhaul Medicare and create prescription drug benefit

CQ VOTE STUDIES

	PARTY UNITY		PRESIDENTIAL SUPPORT	
	Support	Oppose	Support	Oppose
2004	96%	4%	85%	15%
2003	94%	6%	91%	9%
2002	96%	4%	82%	18%
2001	93%	7%	83%	17%
2000	96%	4%	17%	83%

INTEREST GROUPS

	AFL-CIO	ADA	CCUS	ACU
2004	20%	0%	100%	96%
2003	7%	5%	90%	92%
2002	22%	5%	82%	96%
2001	18%	5%	91%	96%
2000	10%	5%	80%	100%

FLORIDA 6

North central — parts of Jacksonville, Gainesville and Ocala

The boomerang-shaped 6th takes in large swaths of rural territory, as well as western Duval County, western Gainesville and part of Ocala. The southern tip is in Leesburg, which is within Orlando's sphere in the center of the state.

The GOP has a clear edge in most federal races, but only recently did Republicans gain an advantage in voter registration. Despite this fact, voters are still willing to support conservative candidates from either major party. George W. Bush took 61 percent of the vote in the 2004 presidential election — 4 percentage points more than in 2000.

The district contains three regions with distinct interests. The northern end is centered in Jacksonville (shared with the 3rd and 4th districts), which is heavily influenced by the military. Gainesville, shared with the 3rd in the middle of the district, is home to the University of Florida and a major veterans' hospital, while the southern area is a haven for retirees.

The district includes all of two small counties — Gilchrist and Bradford — and parts of six others, including Alachua and Marion, each of which contains about one-quarter of the 6th's population. Alachua, which includes Gainesville, is the biggest Democratic outpost in the district, while Republicans have their strongest registration edge in the Clay County Jacksonville suburbs and exurbs west of the St. Johns River. George W. Bush took 76 percent of the Clay County vote in the 2004 presidential race, one of his best showings in the state.

MAJOR INDUSTRY
Higher education, health care, agriculture, forestry, defense

CITIES
Jacksonville (pt.), 86,846; Gainesville (pt.), 59,907; Lakeside, 30,927; Ocala (pt.), 29,559

NOTABLE
The Florida Museum of Natural History is located on the campus of the University of Florida in Gainesville; Camp Blanding, in Clay County, is a 73,000-acre Florida Army National Guard training center that was used for multiple purposes by the Army during World War II— including serving as a prisoner-of-war camp.

Rep. John L. Mica (R)

Elected 1992; 7th term

CAPITOL OFFICE
225-4035
www.house.gov/mica
2313 Rayburn 20515-0907; fax 226-0821

COMMITTEES
Government Reform
House Administration
Transportation & Infrastructure
(Aviation - chairman)

HOMETOWN
Winter Park

BORN
Jan. 27, 1943, Binghamton, N.Y.

RELIGION
Episcopalian

FAMILY
Wife, Pat Mica; two children

EDUCATION
Miami-Dade Community College, A.A. 1965; U. of
Florida, B.A. 1967 (political science & education)

CAREER
Cellular telephone company executive; lobbyist;
trade consultant; real estate investor;
congressional aide

POLITICAL HIGHLIGHTS
Fla. House, 1976-80; Republican nominee for Fla.
Senate, 1980

ELECTION RESULTS

2004 GENERAL

John L. Mica (R)		unopposed

2004 PRIMARY

John L. Mica (R)		unopposed

2002 GENERAL

John L. Mica (R)	142,147	59.6%
Wayne Hogan (D)	96,444	40.4%

PREVIOUS WINNING PERCENTAGES
2000 (63%); 1998 (100%); 1996 (62%); 1994 (73%);
1992 (56%)

Mica is the House leader on the aviation security issues that grew out of the Sept. 11, 2001, terrorist attacks. Since then, he has taken what had been a legislative backwater — the Aviation Subcommittee — and made it a hub of new laws and security measures that have changed the way Americans travel, from rigorous baggage screening to the arming of airline pilots. Over time, Mica has tempered his style, which he once proudly compared to that of former Speaker Newt Gingrich of Georgia, the GOP leader so brash he alienated even his political friends.

The 109th Congress may be Mica's third and final term as chairman of the subcommittee, which falls under the full Transportation and Infrastructure Committee. Republican rules mandate six-year term limits. In his time at the helm, the panel has written many of the post-Sept. 11 airline security bills. And in the 108th Congress, it contributed to a major intelligence overhaul by adding provisions speeding federal approval of devices on airplanes to foil shoulder-fired missiles and mandating a new system of identifying travelers through biometric means, such as retina scanning.

Immediately after the attacks, Mica shaped an aid and security package for the financially vulnerable airline industry. But in recent years, Mica's willingness to rescue the industry has waned. He continues to sympathize with the burdens of federally mandated security costs, but he does not want to use taxpayer money to bail out airlines that are suffering for business reasons. "The airlines now in trouble must be prepared to fend for themselves," Mica said in 2004. "Some of our airlines must either reduce their costs dramatically or they will not survive."

In earlier days, the subcommittee focused on more mundane topics such as flight delays, consumer complaints and airline mergers. Shortly after Mica took the helm in 2001, terrorism became its preoccupation. He championed the effort to arm airline pilots, and he would like to see cargo pilots armed as well. He helped write the law establishing the Transportation Security Administration under the Homeland Security Department. But as the TSA has taken shape, Mica has criticized it for being unresponsive to local concerns and for being slow to address air cargo security.

As a senior member of the full Transportation panel, Mica has been at the center of other high-profile battles, like restructuring Amtrak. He has proposed splitting off the profitable Northeast Corridor and Virginia-to-Florida Auto Train routes for management by an interstate compact of states or a private company. The other, money-losing routes across the country would continue to be subsidized by the government. On highway spending, Mica has been a strong advocate of changing the allocation of federal transportation dollars so that states like Florida — who have been paying more in gas taxes than they receive in transportation funding — get a higher percentage of federal construction grants for building roads.

In the past five Congresses, Mica has chaired three different subcommittees, covering such disparate subjects as the federal civil service and the war against drugs. As chairman of Government Reform's Civil Service Subcommittee after Republicans took control of the House in 1995, his eagerness to downsize the government and overhaul federal work rules led to a scathing denunciation by the president of a federal employees union, who called Mica "the most dangerous man in history to chair" the subcommittee. Later, Mica and the union patched things up when he supported increasing workers' health insurance.

Next he chaired Government Reform's Criminal Justice Subcommittee, where he sought bipartisan cooperation in the battle against illegal drugs. During that phase of his career, Mica coined the now well-known slogan, "Drugs Destroy Lives."

Mica has described his political style as a combination of the pushiness of Gingrich and the "political wisdom" of Robert H. Michel of Illinois, an even-tempered pragmatist who was the GOP leader from 1981 to 1995, when Republicans were still in the minority. These days, he says, the influence of Michel is more dominant. "I've tempered a bit," he says.

During one fight on the Aviation Subcommittee over whether the TSA would allow more private planes to fly into Washington's Ronald Reagan National Airport, as Mica wanted, he said: "I'm not the most powerful member of Congress. I'm not the smartest. But I am a persistent bastard."

Mica's mellowing has not altered his political views. He remains a dependable vote for the GOP leadership, with a strong pro-business rating for his votes in Congress. One area in which Mica departs from many of his Republican colleagues is his concern for environmental protection. He supports restoration of the Florida Everglades and the preservation of lands and waters in central and northern Florida.

His parochial agenda has remained constant through the years. From his seat on Transportation, he has championed commuter rail service for his district in the Orlando suburbs and pushed for a highway connecting Interstate 95 to the northern Orlando suburbs.

Mica hails from a politically active family. His younger brother, Daniel A. Mica, is a Democrat who served in the House from 1979 to 1989. But John Mica has been a Republican since high school, when he joined Youth for Nixon.

Mica served in the state legislature from 1976 to 1980. He came to Washington to be chief of staff for U.S. Sen. Paula Hawkins, a Republican who served one term. After she lost her re-election bid to Democrat Bob Graham in 1986, Mica turned to business ventures, including international trade consulting and the cellular telephone business, and became a millionaire.

Redistricting and a retirement gave him an opening to run for Congress in 1992. GOP Rep. Craig T. James decided not to seek a third House term, and the new Florida map for the 1990s gave the 7th District a clear Republican tilt. Mica won by 13 percentage points, and he has been re-elected with ease since. Though redistricting after the 2000 census shifted the boundaries, giving him some unfamiliar territory, he was able to beat his Democratic challenger by 19 points in 2002. Two years later, he was unopposed.

KEY VOTES

2004

No   Extend federal unemployment benefits by 13 weeks

Yes   Pass $283.2 billion, six-year federal highway and mass transit bill

Yes   Approve $146 billion multi-year extension of previously enacted middle-class tax breaks

Yes   Amend the Constitution to prohibit same-sex marriage

Yes   Cut corporate taxes $137 billion over 10 years

Yes   Reorganize U.S. intelligence agencies as proposed by Sept. 11 commission

2003

Yes   Cut taxes by $330 billion through fiscal 2013

No   Block Bush rule scaling back overtime pay for some white-collar federal workers

Yes   Do not allow use of search warrants without first notifying subjects

Yes   Allow importation of prescription drugs

Yes   Create private school voucher program in Washington, D.C.

Yes   Ban "partial birth" abortion except to save a woman's life

No   Split $18.6 billion in Iraq aid into half-grant, half-loan

Yes   Overhaul Medicare and create prescription drug benefit

CQ VOTE STUDIES

	PARTY UNITY		PRESIDENTIAL SUPPORT	
	Support	Oppose	Support	Oppose
2004	95%	5%	85%	15%
2003	98%	2%	98%	2%
2002	96%	4%	90%	10%
2001	98%	2%	95%	5%
2000	96%	4%	19%	81%

INTEREST GROUPS

	AFL-CIO	ADA	CCUS	ACU
2004	13%	0%	100%	84%
2003	7%	10%	97%	88%
2002	0%	0%	95%	96%
2001	17%	0%	96%	92%
2000	10%	5%	80%	88%

FLORIDA 7
East — St. John's County, Daytona Beach

The 7th follows Interstate 95 from southeast of Jacksonville to northern Daytona Beach, where it turns to follow Interstate 4 west into the Orlando area. It includes all of fast-growing Flagler and St. Johns counties, as well as most of Volusia County, parts of Putnam and Seminole counties and a tiny sliver of Orange County. Two-fifths of the district's population lives in Volusia, mostly on the strip of coast stretching from Ormond Beach to Daytona Beach.

Once a major agricultural area, Seminole County now serves as the suburban home to middle- and upper-class Orlando commuters and their families. But inland portions of the district maintain some agrarian heritage, especially in Flagler County. Daytona Beach continues to attract college students, bikers and race car fans with its beaches and sporting events, including the Daytona 500 stock car race, which is in the nearby 24th District.

The steady influx of people has meant a sustained economic boom, but also has pushed growth-management issues to the top of the local

agenda. Retirees have flocked to once-small towns closer to the ocean, drawing retail shops but not as many larger employers. The base is broadened by a growing aerospace industry near Daytona Beach, helped by Embry-Riddle Aeronautical University.

Republicans hold a slim party registration edge and have won the 7th's presidential vote since 1992. George W. Bush won the district, which was significantly altered in redistricting following the 2000 census to allow for the creation of the new 24th, with 57 percent of the vote in 2004. But some moderate Democrats also have success among the 7th's voters.

MAJOR INDUSTRY
Tourism, aerospace, service

CITIES
Daytona Beach, 53,629; Deltona, 47,033; Ormond Beach, 36,301; Palm Coast, 32,732; Wekiwa Springs, 23,169; Palm Valley, 19,860

NOTABLE
St. Augustine is the oldest continuously inhabited city in the United States; Jackie Robinson Stadium is a minor league park in Daytona Beach, where Robinson was the first black baseball player to play in a spring training game.

Rep. Ric Keller (R)

Elected 2000; 3rd term

CAPITOL OFFICE
225-2176
www.house.gov/keller
419 Cannon 20515-0908; fax 225-0999

COMMITTEES
Education & Workforce
Judiciary
Small Business

HOMETOWN
Orlando

BORN
Sept. 5, 1964, Johnson City, Tenn.

RELIGION
Methodist

FAMILY
Divorced; two children

EDUCATION
East Tennessee State U., B.S. 1986 (speech communications); Vanderbilt U., J.D. 1992

CAREER
Lawyer

POLITICAL HIGHLIGHTS
No previous office

ELECTION RESULTS

2004 GENERAL

Ric Keller (R)	172,232	60.5%
Stephen Murray (D)	112,343	39.5%

2004 PRIMARY

Ric Keller (R)	unopposed

2002 GENERAL

Ric Keller (R)	123,497	65.1%
Eddie Diaz (D)	66,099	34.9%

PREVIOUS WINNING PERCENTAGES
2000 (51%)

By most counts, Keller is a typical small-government, pro-business conservative. But he has carved a particular legislative niche as a crusader for government programs for disadvantaged children. "I have a bias in favor of poor kids," he says.

He is best known outside his Orlando district as the lawmaker behind the "cheeseburger bill," legislation in 2004 that blocked civil lawsuits against food manufacturers or venders holding them responsible for an individual's weight gain, obesity or weight-related health problem. The case that inspired the bill, a suit against McDonald's by a customer who blamed his weight gain on the company's products, was for weeks grist for talk shows and political satires. The bill passed in the House but died in the Senate.

It got him a lot of attention, but the cheeseburger bill isn't his signature issue. Keller is one of the leading champions in Congress for Pell grants, the federal grant program for college students. For the longtime Orlando resident the endeavor is personal. He was raised, along with two siblings, by a single mother on a secretary's salary, and he says Pell grants helped pay for his college education. He is so focused on the program that in 2005 he described to the Orlando Sentinel a meeting he had with President Bush in this way: "The one time I had some real one-on-one time with him, in a limo on the way to the Hard Rock (restaurant), I talked about Pell grants exclusively."

Keller introduced a bill to increase the size of Pell grants as soon as he got to the House in 2001. He then organized a Pell Grant Caucus, and as its chairman, pushed hard to raise the size of the maximum grant, succeeding in getting it moved up from $3,750 to $4,050 a year. He also fought a Department of Education proposal that he estimated would have cut grants for 84,000 students. In the 109th Congress, Keller sponsored a bill to increase the maximum grant to $6,000.

From his seat on the Education and Workforce Committee, Keller takes pride in pressing other measures he believes will enhance the dignity and well-being of disadvantaged students. One such bill requires school systems to implement a school lunch payment system that protects the privacy of students getting free or reduced-price lunches. He also worked with Nebraska GOP Rep. Tom Osborne on legislation to authorize federal grants to local mentoring programs. That legislation grew out of Keller's work before he came to Congress, when he volunteered with Orlando-area mentoring and social support organizations for troubled young people. It became law as part of the overhaul of federal aid to education in 2001.

Keller's agenda is generally conservative. Typical of the newer crop of conservatives serving in Congress, he says he believes in term limits and has pledged to serve no more than eight years in the House. He favors more tax cuts and less regulation so that businesses can create jobs. "The best way to help other poor folks is to help businesses and individuals create jobs," he told the Sentinel.

That philosophy makes him an ally in the Bush administration's fight to limit tort liability, as does his experience as a lawyer. He used his seat on the Judiciary Committee to launch his crusade in defense of fast-food restaurants sued by their overweight customers. Keller himself has struggled with weight control over the years. He went on a crash diet a few years ago after a newspaper columnist said he looked like a "ferocious cherub." He lost more than 30 pounds. Keller, who once wrote jokes for Florida Gov.

Jeb Bush, said he would resume eating desserts only when newspapers started writing nice things about him. Since his legal protection bill for the food industry passed, something else is bulging — his campaign treasury. Of the top 25 contributors to his 2004 campaign, nine were associated with the food and beverage industry.

Back home in his district, two of the largest businesses are The Walt Disney Co. and NBC Universal Inc., and Keller is strategically placed to protect their interests as a member of the Judiciary Subcommittee on Courts, the Internet and Intellectual Property. He has pressed the Justice Department to make cracking down on copyright violations a higher priority.

Previously, he successfully fought for House approval of legislation requiring attorneys for plaintiffs in class action suits to disclose their fees when cases are settled. Lawyers have walked away with millions of dollars in fees in some cases, he said, while each of the plaintiffs got a coupon for a box of cereal.

As a private lawyer in Orlando, Keller helped write two state constitutional amendments to finance the cleanup of the Florida Everglades. One, dubbed "Polluter Pays" and passed in 1996, held that sugar companies should contribute to Everglades restoration. In Congress, Keller was among the minority of Florida lawmakers who voted to reduce the sugar subsidy for the industry, a political power in the state.

Keller had just made partner at his Orlando law firm when he jumped into the 8th District House race to replace 10-term Republican Bill McCollum, who waged an unsuccessful bid for the Senate in 2000.

Though he described himself as the ideological heir to McCollum, the informal, folksy Keller is in personality the polar opposite of the serious, buttoned-down McCollum. It was Keller's first foray into politics, and he at first was not taken seriously by the political pros. He got their attention when he finished second in a three-way GOP primary, and then won an October runoff against veteran state Rep. Bill Sublette.

Democrats made a strong bid to capture the normally Republican 8th District seat by running a well-known local figure, former Orange County Commission Chairwoman Linda Chapin. But Chapin saw her once-comfortable lead in the polls shrink as Keller gathered steam with the help of conservative groups including the Club for Growth, an anti-tax organization that put over $400,000 into the campaign.

Keller won by fewer than 4,000 votes. He immediately set to work raising money to shore himself up for re-election, and his subsequent races have been much easier. In 2004, he won with nearly 61 percent of the vote.

KEY VOTES

2004

No Extend federal unemployment benefits by 13 weeks
No Pass $283.2 billion, six-year federal highway and mass transit bill
Yes Approve $146 billion multi-year extension of previously enacted middle-class tax breaks
Yes Amend the Constitution to prohibit same-sex marriage
Yes Cut corporate taxes $137 billion over 10 years
Yes Reorganize U.S. intelligence agencies as proposed by Sept. 11 commission

2003

Yes Cut taxes by $330 billion through fiscal 2013
No Block Bush rule scaling back overtime pay for some white-collar federal workers
No Do not allow use of search warrants without first notifying subjects
No Allow importation of prescription drugs
Yes Create private school voucher program in Washington, D.C.
Yes Ban "partial birth" abortion except to save a woman's life
No Split $18.6 billion in Iraq aid into half-grant, half-loan
Yes Overhaul Medicare and create prescription drug benefit

CQ VOTE STUDIES

	PARTY UNITY		PRESIDENTIAL SUPPORT	
	Support	Oppose	Support	Oppose
2004	98%	2%	91%	9%
2003	99%	1%	96%	4%
2002	99%	1%	87%	13%
2001	97%	3%	95%	5%

INTEREST GROUPS

	AFL-CIO	ADA	CCUS	ACU
2004	0%	0%	100%	100%
2003	0%	5%	96%	86%
2002	11%	0%	100%	100%
2001	9%	0%	100%	96%

FLORIDA 8
Central — most of Orlando

The 8th surrounds western Orlando and includes upscale parts of the region, a large chunk of the city, including much of the downtown area, and the Walt Disney World complex. It then pushes north to take in parts of Lake and Marion counties, giving it a rural element.

One of Florida's few landlocked districts, the 8th is thriving nonetheless, powered by the presence of Walt Disney World and the tourism industry in the Orlando area, the world's top vacation destination. Redistricting following the 2000 census removed territory in eastern Orange County and near Kissimmee.

Residents of Orlando's suburbs — from middle-class areas near the city to well-heeled Winter Park and Windermere — support conservative Republicans on social and economic issues. The population is younger, wealthier and more educated than most Florida districts. While conservative Democrats were once competitive here, Republicans now mostly prevail in Orange County elections. But the county's surging Hispanic population, which spurred its 28 percent growth in the 1990s,

has put Orange within political reach of Democratic statewide candidates. Unlike Miami-area Hispanics who are of Cuban descent and vote Republican, many Orlando-area Hispanics are of Puerto Rican stock and vote Democratic. Al Gore in 2000 was the first Democratic presidential nominee to carry Orange County since Franklin D. Roosevelt in 1944, and John Kerry captured the county in 2004.

Although tourism leads the economy, the district also relies on a growing technology sector headed by defense and aerospace contractor Lockheed Martin and Oracle Corp. Technology and research have replaced the dwindling military presence — Orlando's Naval Training Center was shut down in 1999, costing about 4,000 full-time jobs. The research park of the University of Central Florida's Institute for Simulation and Training is an economic engine.

MAJOR INDUSTRY
Tourism, technology, aerospace

CITIES
Orlando (pt.), 123,842; Ocoee (pt.), 23,591; Ocala (pt.), 16,384; Eustis, 15,106

NOTABLE
Dozens of celebrities — including golf's Tiger Woods and basketball's Shaquille O'Neal — have homes at Isleworth in Windermere.

Rep. Michael Bilirakis (R)

Elected 1982; 12th term

CAPITOL OFFICE
225-5755
www.house.gov/bilirakis
2408 Rayburn 20515-0909; fax 225-4085

COMMITTEES
Energy & Commerce
Veterans' Affairs
  (Oversight & Investigations - chairman)

HOMETOWN
Tarpon Springs

BORN
July 16, 1930, Tarpon Springs, Fla.

RELIGION
Greek Orthodox

FAMILY
Wife, Evelyn Bilirakis; two children

EDUCATION
U. of Pittsburgh, B.S. 1959 (engineering); George Washington U., attended 1959-60; U. of Florida, J.D. 1963

MILITARY SERVICE
Air Force, 1951-55

CAREER
Lawyer; county judge; restaurateur; engineer

POLITICAL HIGHLIGHTS
No previous office

ELECTION RESULTS

2004 GENERAL

Michael Bilirakis (R)		unopposed

2004 PRIMARY

Michael Bilirakis (R)	44,579	84.5%
Joseph H. Stanley (R)	8,189	15.5%

2002 GENERAL

Michael Bilirakis (R)	169,369	71.5%
Chuck Kalogianis (D)	67,623	28.5%

PREVIOUS WINNING PERCENTAGES
2000 (82%); 1998 (100%); 1996 (69%); 1994 (100%); 1992 (59%); 1990 (58%); 1988 (100%); 1986 (71%); 1984 (79%); 1982 (51%)

Bilirakis announced plans to retire at the end of the 109th Congress, wrapping up a congressional career that began more than two decades ago. He is hoping that his son, state Rep. Gus Bilirakis, will be elected to succeed him.

In his final term, Bilirakis (bil-uh-RACK-iss) will be shifting his focus somewhat from health care to veterans' affairs. He will serve as vice chairman of the Veterans' Affairs Committee and chairman of its Oversight and Investigations Subcommittee. At the same time, he has relinquished the gavel of the Energy and Commerce subcommittee with jurisdiction over health, which he held for almost half his career, despite Republican six-year term limits for chairmen. A restructuring at the beginning of the 107th Congress of what was then the Health and Environment Subcommittee removed environmental matters from the panel's jurisdiction. Billy Tauzin of Louisiana, the full committee chairman at the time, created a new Health Subcommittee for Bilirakis, resetting the term-limit clock.

The Health Subcommittee addresses Medicaid, a portion of Medicare and the regulation of health insurance, food and drugs. As a result, Bilirakis has been involved in much of the important health legislation debated on Capitol Hill over the past decade or so. However, because health care has been such a hot political topic on Capitol Hill in recent years, many decisions on legislation and strategy have been made by the party leadership. And GOP leaders have often formed separate task forces — on patients' rights and prescription drugs, for example — rather than rely on the traditional committee structure to develop legislation.

Bilirakis' work on the landmark Medicare prescription drug bill of 2003 was characteristically low-profile but loyal to the leadership's position. Some lawmakers have criticized Bilirakis for not being more aggressive, but GOP leaders seem pleased with his amenable character.

Bilirakis has found some success in shepherding through pieces of legislation that were incremental but nonetheless priorities for him. For instance, in the 107th Congress, he won approval of a bill to establish a federal scholarship program to help alleviate the national nursing shortage. And in the 108th, he won enactment of legislation authorizing grants to states and localities to help cover expenses of living organ donors.

Bilirakis did not fare as well at first on a measure that he championed in 2002 to assure doctors and hospitals that they cannot be threatened with losing federal funding if they refuse to perform abortions. The measure, which Bilirakis said merely clarified an existing "conscience clause," nevertheless sparked a partisan debate. It passed the House, but died in the Senate. But when the issue was taken up by another Florida Republican, Dave Weldon, a similar provision became law in the 2004 catchall spending bill.

A pragmatist, Bilirakis has pushed for bipartisan agreement on contentious legislation since his days as top-ranking minority member of the Health and the Environment Subcommittee. He continued that practice as subcommittee chairman, sometimes drawing criticism from more-combative Republican colleagues for being too willing to work with Democrats — particularly when GOP efforts to restrain government spending run counter to Bilirakis' sense of obligation to watch out for the interests of the many elderly residents of his district, who are wary of any tampering with their health care or retirement benefits. In the 107th, he and Democrat

Sherrod Brown of Ohio led an effort to scale back a 5.4 percent reduction in Medicare and Medicaid payments to doctors, which, Bilirakis argued, threatened senior citizens' access to medical care if doctors limited their participation in the federal programs.

Bilirakis is known for being accessible to his constituents, and he is particularly attentive to the needs of seniors, who make up almost a quarter of the 9th District's population, one of the highest percentages of any district.

On the Veterans' Affairs Committee, Bilirakis has worked to increase benefits for widows of veterans and pressed for hearings to probe allegations of sexual harassment, mismanagement and poor care at Department of Veterans Affairs medical facilities. In the 107th, he was the point man in the effort to allow veterans to receive their full retirement pay as well as disability benefits.

A champion of Greek causes, Bilirakis often delivers floor speeches commemorating special events in Greece. He never misses an opportunity to criticize the Turks, who continue to control northern Cyprus. He and his wife share the same ancestry, and her homemade Greek food is a big hit at community gatherings and at an annual party in Washington for family, friends, constituents and dignitaries, including the Greek ambassador.

The son of immigrants who moved from the Tampa Bay area to western Pennsylvania soon after he was born, Bilirakis turned down college scholarships and instead went to work in the Pittsburgh steel mills to help the family finances. He spent four years in the Air Force, and later earned an engineering degree. After working for the Federal Power Commission in Washington, he returned to Florida for law school and stayed on, working in the aerospace industry and then opening a law practice a few miles from his birthplace. He became involved in several small businesses, taught at area community colleges and served stints as an appointed local judge.

A Democrat until 1970, Bilirakis was intermittently involved in local GOP campaigns, but did not run for office himself until 1982, when he entered the race for the newly drawn 9th. Asked what had triggered his interest, Bilirakis replied, "I found myself out of challenges." In a three-way primary, the favorite, state House GOP leader Curt Kiser, made the mistake of taking his nomination for granted, while Bilirakis blanketed the district with signs saying that his was "a hard name to spell but an easy one to remember." After an upset victory, Bilirakis narrowly edged Democratic state Rep. George Sheldon by espousing conservative positions but mostly by convincing voters that he was a nice guy. He has won re-election with ease since then.

KEY VOTES

2004

No Extend federal unemployment benefits by 13 weeks

No Pass $283.2 billion, six-year federal highway and mass transit bill

Yes Approve $146 billion multi-year extension of previously enacted middle-class tax breaks

Yes Amend the Constitution to prohibit same-sex marriage

Yes Cut corporate taxes $137 billion over 10 years

Yes Reorganize U.S. intelligence agencies as proposed by Sept. 11 commission

2003

Yes Cut taxes by $330 billion through fiscal 2013

No Block Bush rule scaling back overtime pay for some white-collar federal workers

Yes Do not allow use of search warrants without first notifying subjects

No Allow importation of prescription drugs

Yes Create private school voucher program in Washington, D.C.

Yes Ban "partial birth" abortion except to save a woman's life

Yes Split $18.6 billion in Iraq aid into half-grant, half-loan

Yes Overhaul Medicare and create prescription drug benefit

CQ VOTE STUDIES

	PARTY UNITY		PRESIDENTIAL SUPPORT	
	Support	Oppose	Support	Oppose
2004	93%	7%	85%	15%
2003	96%	4%	94%	6%
2002	98%	2%	87%	13%
2001	91%	9%	86%	14%
2000	91%	9%	24%	76%

INTEREST GROUPS

	AFL-CIO	ADA	CCUS	ACU
2004	13%	5%	100%	92%
2003	0%	5%	93%	88%
2002	11%	0%	89%	100%
2001	25%	10%	91%	84%
2000	10%	5%	71%	80%

FLORIDA 9
West – suburbs north of Tampa

Suburban and rural areas north of Tampa and St. Petersburg form the bulk of the 9th, which encompasses coastal areas of Pinellas and Pasco counties as well as a large chunk of Hillsborough County.

The 9th is mostly residential, and more than one-fifth of the population is 65 or older. Clearwater, the largest city, is known as a beach resort and as the "spiritual headquarters" of the Church of Scientology, which has a large community in the city. Palm Harbor and Tarpon Springs have many Greek Orthodox residents, descendants of the area's earliest settlers.

The 9th's economy is driven by tourism, and many residents commute to Tampa and St. Petersburg. Service-oriented industries add to the mix, but the predominance of shopping centers and strip malls has created growth problems in the coastal areas. The 9th's economy has grown along with its population, although its northeast portions have lagged behind the Clearwater area. Hillsborough County is mostly suburban; Pasco County, which is bisected by Interstate 75, lacks major industry, though it has several sources of spring water.

The 9th long has been a home for mostly Republican retirees, and the GOP retains a slight edge in the district because of its dominance in Hillsborough. Many of the county's most heavily Republican precincts are in the 9th, in towns like Bloomingdale and Valrico east of I-75 and in the upscale Westchase area in western Hillsborough. The parts of Pinellas that are in the 9th also are decidedly Republican. Democrats hold their own in the 9th's share of Pasco County, where Democrats and Republicans are even in voter registration.

MAJOR INDUSTRY
Tourism, health care, technology

CITIES
Clearwater (pt.), 79,189; Palm Harbor (pt.), 30,806; East Lake, 29,394; Bayonet Point, 23,577; Plant City (pt.), 22,445; Holiday, 21,904

NOTABLE
Tarpon Springs' waters were a major source of sea sponges before they were killed off in the 1940s by toxic blooms of algae known as red tides; Jack Eckerd, founder of the Eckerd chain of drug stores that originated in Clearwater, was the Republican gubernatorial nominee in 1978, losing to Democrat Bob Graham.

Rep. C.W. Bill Young (R)

Elected 1970; 18th term

CAPITOL OFFICE
225-5961
bill.young@mail.house.gov
www.house.gov/young
2407 Rayburn 20515-0910; fax 225-9764

COMMITTEES
Appropriations
(Defense - chairman)

HOMETOWN
Indian Shores

BORN
Dec. 16, 1930, Harmarville, Pa.

RELIGION
Methodist

FAMILY
Wife, Beverly Young; three children

EDUCATION
St. Petersburg H.S., graduated 1948

MILITARY SERVICE
Fla. National Guard, 1948-57

CAREER
Insurance executive; public official

POLITICAL HIGHLIGHTS
Fla. Senate, 1960-70 (minority leader, 1966-70)

ELECTION RESULTS

2004 GENERAL

C.W. Bill Young (R)	207,175	69.3%
Robert D. "Bob" Derry (D)	91,658	30.7%

2004 PRIMARY

C.W. Bill Young (R)	unopposed

2002 GENERAL

C.W. Bill Young (R)	unopposed

PREVIOUS WINNING PERCENTAGES
2000 (76%); 1998 (100%); 1996 (67%); 1994 (100%);
1992 (57%); 1990 (100%); 1988 (73%); 1986 (100%);
1984 (80%); 1982 (100%); 1980 (100%); 1978 (79%);
1976 (65%); 1974 (76%); 1972 (76%); 1970 (67%)

Some powerful committee chairmen are reluctant to give up their gavels when GOP-imposed term limits kick in. For Young, it often seemed that the end couldn't come soon enough. At the end of his six-year term as chairman of the Appropriations Committee, Young happily returned in the 109th Congress to the job he prefers, running the subcommittee responsible for the defense budget. "I always thought that was the best job I ever had," Young said.

Young won't miss the headaches of the top spot, where he often found himself caught between his loyalties to the committee on the one hand and to the House leadership and President Bush on the other. Young is a consummate team player, however, invariably deferring to the GOP leaders and the president even as the standing of his committee eroded.

Having adapted to the reality of a tough-on-spending Republican president, Young ended 2004 in an increasingly familiar pattern, presiding over a huge and cumbersome catchall spending bill that left Democrats and some Appropriations "cardinals," as the subcommittee chairmen are called, dissatisfied with tight budget limits and leadership-mandated policy decisions.

Young pushed through more than $200 billion for the wars in Iraq and Afghanistan from 2001 to 2004. And he was able to use this clout to deliver over $13 billion in federal aid, mostly for his state, in the aftermath of a devastating quartet of hurricanes. With the presidential election approaching, Florida's electoral importance was a tactical advantage; Young persuaded the White House to add almost $2 billion to its original request, noting that delays would mean unhappy Floridians in the voting booths.

But overall, his options were more limited than in the past. He warned early in 2004 that the austere GOP budget, designed to make the party's conservatives happy, would require politically undesirable choices. However, Young and his Senate counterpart, Alaskan Republican Ted Stevens, were eager to pass the massive spending bill to avoid the experience of the two previous years, when some appropriations measures were not enacted until the next Congress convened. They bent to leaders' demands to refrain from the budgetary gimmicks often relied on by appropriators to free up extra money.

In Bush's first term, Young was a voice in the GOP ranks for additional spending at the very time that Bush was vowing to stop Congress' annual drive in that direction. Young in 2002 hoped to extract himself from a tight spending ceiling by pushing through smaller, less controversial spending bills with increases above Bush's proposed budget, while "starving" the more expensive and politically problematic bills, in the expectation that all sides would ultimately agree to add more money. But conservatives refused to go along, and Young was rebuffed when he asked Bush to support about $9 billion in additional spending.

With the GOP controlling Congress and the White House, Young could no longer count on Democratic leverage to force additional domestic discretionary spending. His non-confrontational style personifies the go-along, get-along culture of Appropriations. But it is also a product of a legislative attitude forged during 24 years in the House minority, when working with Democrats was a prerequisite for accomplishing anything. The amiable Young, the longest-serving Republican in the House, also has friendships that go way back.

In picking the first Appropriations chairman under the new GOP majority in 1995, Speaker Newt Gingrich skipped over Young and two other more senior members because he considered them too willing to increase spending. Young was denied the honor of being the first Republican chairman of House Appropriations in 40 years. Instead, he went on to chair the panel's Defense Subcommittee for four years, a choice consolation prize that gave Young great influence in his favorite policy arena, military budgets.

When Young finally took over the full committee in 1999, he allowed conservatives to dominate the early stages of appropriations negotiations until legislative reality — the need to gain President Clinton's signature — changed the playing field. Time and again, Clinton refused to sign bills he thought too stingy. As a result, Republicans had to accommodate some of the Democratic president's demands or risk a politically unacceptable government shutdown.

Closest to Young's heart is his work finding funds for bone marrow transplant research and for a federally sponsored bone marrow donor registry paid for through the defense budget. Young became interested in the issue in the 1980s after he met a 10-year-old constituent for whom bone marrow donors could not be found. After adopting the cause, Young learned in 1990 that his eldest daughter had a leukemia treatable only through such a transplant. She received bone marrow that restored her health.

On some issues, Young has a moderate streak. He has broken from the party line to support a minimum wage increase and a ban on semiautomatic assault-style weapons. And he approaches environmental issues from the perspective of a district that places a premium on protecting the coastal waters so integral to its tourism industry. He has worked to prevent offshore oil and gas drilling and has used his power to fund efforts to replenish the sand on eroding beaches.

Young was born into hardscrabble poverty in Pennsylvania's coal country during the Depression. His father, an alcoholic, abandoned his family when Young was a boy, and after his mother became ill, the family stayed with relatives in St. Petersburg, Fla. Young worked his way to success in the insurance business before going into politics in 1960, when he was elected as the sole Republican in the Florida Senate. By 1967, there were 20 others, and Young was minority leader.

In 1970, he inherited Florida's most dependable Republican House seat from William C. Cramer, who ran for the Senate. The 10th District has tilted Democratic, but more often than not, Young has been re-elected with ease. Since 1982, Democrats have fielded a candidate only in alternate elections. In 2004, Young trounced his opponent, winning 69 percent of the vote.

KEY VOTES

2004

No Extend federal unemployment benefits by 13 weeks
No Pass $283.2 billion, six-year federal highway and mass transit bill
Yes Approve $146 billion multi-year extension of previously enacted middle-class tax breaks
Yes Amend the Constitution to prohibit same-sex marriage
No Cut corporate taxes $137 billion over 10 years
Yes Reorganize U.S. intelligence agencies as proposed by Sept. 11 commission

2003

Yes Cut taxes by $330 billion through fiscal 2013
No Block Bush rule scaling back overtime pay for some white-collar federal workers
Yes Do not allow use of search warrants without first notifying subjects
Yes Allow importation of prescription drugs
Yes Create private school voucher program in Washington, D.C.
Yes Ban "partial birth" abortion except to save a woman's life
No Split $18.6 billion in Iraq aid into half-grant, half-loan
Yes Overhaul Medicare and create prescription drug benefit

CQ VOTE STUDIES

	PARTY UNITY		PRESIDENTIAL SUPPORT	
	Support	Oppose	Support	Oppose
2004	91%	9%	87%	13%
2003	95%	5%	94%	6%
2002	94%	6%	88%	12%
2001	96%	4%	91%	9%
2000	90%	10%	33%	67%

INTEREST GROUPS

	AFL-CIO	ADA	CCUS	ACU
2004	20%	10%	95%	87%
2003	7%	10%	93%	87%
2002	13%	0%	85%	96%
2001	17%	5%	91%	80%
2000	11%	5%	84%	72%

FLORIDA 10

West — most of Pinellas County, St. Petersburg

The 10th takes in about 70 percent of Pinellas County, including most of St. Petersburg and its upscale beachfront communities. From the southern portion of Pinellas, it excludes Clearwater in the central part of the county and captures Dunedin and Palm Harbor.

One of Florida's first GOP areas, the district had become increasingly Democratic over the years. During redistricting following the 2000 census, the 10th was reshaped to help Republicans stave off the trend. A significant piece of St. Petersburg, including Pinellas County's southern tip, was ceded to the neighboring, Democratic-held 11th District, and a piece north of Clearwater was added. Unlike many areas in Florida, the 10th did not see its population boom in the 1990s.

Even with the changes, Democrats and Republicans are evenly matched, although Rep. Young wins by large margins, and the 10th's loyalties regularly flip between parties in presidential elections. Al Gore would have won the new 10th by less than 5,000 votes in 2000, but George W. Bush edged out John Kerry with 51 percent in 2004.

Nearly one-fourth of the district's residents are 65 or older, and many retirees reside in Largo and the Gulf Coast towns. Younger residents tend to live in Pinellas Park and St. Petersburg to be closer to major employers and Tampa. Tourism is an economic mainstay for the district, accounting for about $2 billion per year from area hotels and attractions. The district also includes two airports — the smaller of which was kept open after voters in 2003 opted to accept federal grants and reject a development proposal for the site. Other industries, such as technology manufacturers and financial services companies, diversify the district's economy.

MAJOR INDUSTRY
Tourism, health care, retail

CITIES
St. Petersburg (pt.), 179,087; Largo, 69,371; Pinellas Park, 45,658

NOTABLE
Greyhounds have raced at St. Petersburg's Derby Lane, one of several Florida dog tracks, since the 1920s; The Salvador Dalí Museum in St. Petersburg houses a comprehensive collection of works by the Spanish surrealist painter and is raising funds to move to a new downtown facility.

Rep. Jim Davis (D)

Elected 1996; 5th term

CAPITOL OFFICE
225-3376
www.house.gov/jimdavis
409 Cannon 20515-0911; fax 225-5652

COMMITTEES
Energy & Commerce

HOMETOWN
Tampa

BORN
Oct. 11, 1957, Tampa, Fla.

RELIGION
Episcopalian

FAMILY
Wife, Peggy Bessent Davis; two children

EDUCATION
Washington and Lee U., B.A. 1979; U. of Florida, J.D. 1982

CAREER
Lawyer

POLITICAL HIGHLIGHTS
Fla. House, 1988-96 (majority leader, 1994-96)

ELECTION RESULTS

2004 GENERAL

Jim Davis (D)	191,780	85.8%
Robert E. Johnson (LIBERT)	31,579	14.1%

2004 PRIMARY

Jim Davis (D)	unopposed

2002 GENERAL

Jim Davis (D)	unopposed

PREVIOUS WINNING PERCENTAGES
2000 (85%); 1998 (65%); 1996 (58%)

Davis represents a district that is a bit of the old and the new. One of the state's most racially diverse districts, it includes both an old manufacturing base and new high-technology industries. A moderate Democrat, Davis is a good fit for the district's voters, and has not drawn a GOP opponent in the last two elections. He wants to expand his political reach to a statewide audience, and plans to run for Florida governor in 2006.

Calm and deliberative in manner, he sees himself as "a problem-solver and a peacemaker" in the legislative arena. The detail-oriented Davis uses small, colored notebooks to scribble both personal and business reminders to himself.

In the 109th Congress, Davis holds two important posts — a seat on the Energy and Commerce Committee and co-chairmanship of the New Democrat Coalition. He announced in early 2005 that he will make a bid for governor in 2006, a move he had been considering for the past year.

Davis is a fiscal conservative but hews to the Democratic view on social issues. Although he is not necessarily averse to tax cuts, Davis worries about the impact on long-term deficits. In 2003, as President Bush proposed a new round of tax cuts centered on a plan to eliminate taxes on most stock dividends to help grow the economy, Davis shunned the idea. "I will support economic stimulus, but any plan that's enacted cannot compromise our ability to fund homeland security improvements or mortgage our children's futures by driving up the deficit." He also voted in 2001 against Bush's signature $1.35 trillion, 10-year tax cut package.

He can be tough on spending measures as well, regardless of which party supports them. Davis voted against enacting the politically popular 2004 surface transportation law, which authorized significant increases in funding for highway and transit programs. When he voted against five appropriations bills at the end of 1999, he argued, "There's a lot of indefensible pork in here. It sets a bad precedent." For the same reason, he opposed a $13 billion supplemental spending bill in 2000.

In his first term, Davis said his priority was "finding a way to balance the budget while protecting our seniors" — always a concern of Florida politicians because of the state's large contingent of elderly voters. He attempted to pursue both goals in 2003 by joining other New Democrats in backing a compromise Medicare prescription drug proposal that would have helped seniors with low incomes or unusually high annual drug costs.

On Energy and Commerce, Davis helped write legislation in the 108th toughening penalties for broadcasters who violate decency standards. Provisions would allow the Federal Communications Commission to levy far greater fines on broadcasters, and also mandate a hearing on any broadcaster with three or more violations.

Although he generally takes a liberal stance on social policy issues, Davis broke with many Democrats in 2003 by voting to ban a procedure its opponents call "partial birth" abortion. Also, he backed a constitutional amendment to ban desecration of the U.S. flag. However, he joined with most of his party in 2004 in voting against a proposed constitutional amendment to ban gay marriage.

Treading where fellow Florida lawmakers are usually loath to venture, Davis went to Cuba in 2004 to assess what should be done regarding the four-decade-old economic embargo on the island nation. His visit drew criticism from some, including his Florida colleague, Republican Lincoln Diaz-Balart. But Davis won House passage in the 108th for his amendments to allow certain educational trips to Cuba and permit Americans to visit their Cuban relatives more frequently.

Davis is a strong advocate for trade liberalization. Although he is generally a supporter of organized labor, Davis broke ranks with the unions to vote for the 2002 law reviving fast-track procedures for congressional action on trade treaties and for the 2000 law permanently granting normal trade status to China — the Port of Tampa's largest trading partner. In the 108th, he was a leading voice for liberalized trade with Chile.

Education is a major concern for the congressman. In the 108th, he assailed the Florida Legislature for a plan to allow high school students to graduate early without taking certain classes. He also introduced a bill to require states to make American government and history a graduation requirement or lose federal education funds.

In the 106th, he proposed solving chronic teacher shortages by giving mid-career professionals up to $5,000 in grants to pay for teacher training. His plan won support in 2000 from the Clinton White House, which included $25 million in the budget for it. An opponent of school vouchers, Davis argues that the government instead should boost spending on charter schools. Charter schools, he says, are public schools that are open to everyone, whereas vouchers help parents send their children to private schools.

Davis was born into a Tampa family active in local politics: His father was a judge, his grandfather a mayor. Davis followed in the family tradition in 1988 when, as a lawyer and civic activist, he won the first of four terms in the state House.

When veteran Democratic Rep. Sam M. Gibbons announced plans to retire from the House in 1996, Davis was the least-known of four Democrats who campaigned to succeed him. But with his prolific fundraising, he was able to buy television advertising for the primary. He also played up his endorsements from local teacher, police and firefighter unions.

After beating former Tampa Mayor Sandy Warshaw Freedman in a runoff, Davis turned his attention to Republican Mark Sharpe, who was making his third try for the 11th District after losing to Gibbons in 1992 and 1994. Buoyed by a treasury that topped $935,000 for the entire campaign and by an easy Bill Clinton victory in the district's presidential voting, Davis won by 16 percentage points. He has continued to post comfortable victories, and in 2004 he did not face a Republican opponent.

KEY VOTES

2004

Yes	Extend federal unemployment benefits by 13 weeks
No	Pass $283.2 billion, six-year federal highway and mass transit bill
Yes	Approve $146 billion multi-year extension of previously enacted middle-class tax breaks
No	Amend the Constitution to prohibit same-sex marriage
Yes	Cut corporate taxes $137 billion over 10 years
?	Reorganize U.S. intelligence agencies as proposed by Sept. 11 commission

2003

No	Cut taxes by $330 billion through fiscal 2013
Yes	Block Bush rule scaling back overtime pay for some white-collar federal workers
Yes	Do not allow use of search warrants without first notifying subjects
No	Allow importation of prescription drugs
No	Create private school voucher program in Washington, D.C.
Yes	Ban "partial birth" abortion except to save a woman's life
No	Split $18.6 billion in Iraq aid into half-grant, half-loan
No	Overhaul Medicare and create prescription drug benefit

CQ VOTE STUDIES

	PARTY UNITY		PRESIDENTIAL SUPPORT	
	Support	Oppose	Support	Oppose
2004	89%	11%	36%	64%
2003	89%	11%	33%	67%
2002	85%	15%	48%	52%
2001	79%	21%	42%	58%
2000	85%	15%	82%	18%

INTEREST GROUPS

	AFL-CIO	ADA	CCUS	ACU
2004	87%	90%	48%	4%
2003	87%	85%	41%	25%
2002	89%	75%	65%	24%
2001	83%	80%	48%	12%
2000	70%	75%	57%	16%

FLORIDA 11
West — Tampa, south St. Petersburg

The 11th ranges from Tampa to south St. Petersburg and part of Bradenton. One of the younger and more racially diverse districts in the state, the 11th combines what is left of a traditional blue-collar manufacturing base with the newer technology and service industries that have transformed Tampa into a major Southern city. The Tampa-St. Petersburg area was a finalist to host the 2004 Republican convention, which was awarded to New York City.

The district was reconfigured in 2002 to take in some of the Democrats in the St. Petersburg area who presented a threat to the GOP's security in the neighboring Pinellas County-based 10th. Blacks and Hispanics together comprise about half of the 11th's population, with heavy concentrations of blacks in south St. Petersburg, east Tampa and parts of Bradenton, and Hispanics in west Tampa and the Egypt Lake-Leto and Town 'n' Country areas just northwest of the city. It is a heavily Democratic district that gave John Kerry 60 percent of the presidential vote in 2004.

As its economy continues to evolve, the Tampa area has attracted professional sports arenas and a steady military presence at MacDill Air Force Base. Tampa's airport and seaport make it a major shipping and transportation hub, while its traditional cigar industry is attempting a comeback from harder years. The University of South Florida, one of the state's largest schools, is on the city's northern end.

The influence of Cuban and Spanish culture is most pronounced in Ybor City, a downtown Tampa neighborhood named after the man who brought the first cigar factory to Tampa. The neighborhood's success in reinventing itself as a nighttime hot spot has given the area new life.

MAJOR INDUSTRY
Retail, health care, finance

MILITARY BASES
MacDill Air Force Base, 12,000 military, 7,000 civilian (2004)

CITIES
Tampa (pt.), 284,199; Town 'n' Country, 72,523; St. Petersburg (pt.), 69,145

NOTABLE
Native tribes named the area Tampa, which means "sticks of fire"; The U.S. Central Command and the U.S. Special Operations Command are based at MacDill Air Force Base.

Rep. Adam H. Putnam (R)

Elected 2000; 3rd term

CAPITOL OFFICE
225-1252
www.house.gov/putnam
1213 Longworth 20515-0912; fax 226-0585

COMMITTEES
Budget
Rules

HOMETOWN
Bartow

BORN
July 31, 1974, Bartow, Fla.

RELIGION
Episcopalian

FAMILY
Wife, Melissa Putnam; three children

EDUCATION
U. of Florida, B.S. 1995 (economics)

CAREER
State legislator; citrus farmer and cattle rancher

POLITICAL HIGHLIGHTS
Fla. House, 1996-2000

ELECTION RESULTS

2004 GENERAL

Adam H. Putnam (R)	179,204	64.9%
Bob Hagenmaier (D)	96,965	35.1%

2004 PRIMARY

Adam H. Putnam (R)	42,605	92.3%
Robert Wirengard (R)	3,546	7.7%

2002 GENERAL

Adam H. Putnam (R)	unopposed

PREVIOUS WINNING PERCENTAGES
2000 (57%)

In just his third term and barely into his thirties, Putnam already moves in powerful circles on Capitol Hill, having earned the confidence of Speaker J. Dennis Hastert, who, like Putnam, has usually done a good deal of thinking before he speaks.

His temperament, keen political sense, grasp of policy and loyalty to the Republican Party made him a natural choice when Hastert had to fill a vacancy on the influential Rules Committee. The timing of the appointment, near the end of the 108th Congress, gave Putnam a fast bump up in seniority on the panel — to fifth out of nine Republicans — when several senior GOP lawmakers left it at the start of the 109th Congress.

On Rules, he's had to quickly come up to speed with more-senior lawmakers in the many and layered parliamentary intricacies of managing bills on the floor. His first such assignment came in late 2004, when the leadership entrusted him to manage the rules governing debate on a high-profile measure providing money for hurricane relief in Florida.

To take the post on the leadership-run committee, Putnam had to give up assignments on Government Reform, where he was a subcommittee chairman, and on Agriculture. His departure left Florida without a Republican representative on the farm panel, which tends to be dominated by Midwesterners and their issues. But Putnam can still do the nitty-gritty work of a congressman — looking out for parochial interests. Party leaders and committee chairmen traditionally tend to the needs of Rules panelists, who give up legislative committee assignments to guard the party's priorities on the House floor.

Putnam was able to keep his seat on the Budget Committee. His Florida colleagues also elected him to represent them on the Republican Steering Committee, which makes all-important committee assignments and takes direction from the leadership.

In the 108th Congress, Putnam focused on cybersecurity as chairman of the Government Reform Subcommittee on Technology, Information Policy, Intergovernmental Relations and the Census. The government, he said, is not moving fast enough to protect the security of computer systems that manage just about every facet of life in the United States, including the economy. "Make no mistake, the threat is serious. The vulnerabilities are extensive. And the time for action is now," Putnam said at a 2004 hearing.

It's that kind of brashness mixed with steady competence that prompted one of his Republican colleagues to once describe Putnam as "26 going on 50." His bill directing federal agencies to include cybersecurity as part of their information technology planning was wrapped into a massive overhaul of the nation's intelligence community in 2004. At the height of a 2001 crisis over China's detention of a Navy plane, Putnam dispatched a letter to the Chinese ambassador sternly warning the government to return the plane and its crew, one of whom was a Putnam constituent.

Though he is normally a surefire supporter of GOP policies, Putnam has defied them when his district's interests were on the line, such as when he opposed President Bush's request for fast-track authority from Congress to sign trade deals that lawmakers could not later amend. Putnam, who hails from a prominent Central Florida citrus and cattle ranching family, opposed fast track because he felt it put the state's orange growers at risk. During one closed-door meeting with House Republicans to lobby for the legislation, Bush urged the recalcitrant in the room to reconsider. "I'm talking about you, Red," the president told the red-haired congressman.

Putnam then stared down party leaders on the floor of the House, refusing to give them his vote. Afterward, he said, "I feel like I'm going to throw up."

The next year, when House leaders revived a slightly different version of the trade bill, they negotiated with Putnam and Florida Republican Mark Foley for their support. When they didn't get it, they said they'd find the votes without their support or any input from the citrus industry.

Putnam agreed to vote for it if he could get a few tweaks to the bill that helped citrus growers. "By the time the second vote came around, I had learned there's a fine line between raising an issue and being marginalized," he said. "We came pretty close to being marginalized."

His education in the ways of Capitol Hill, where senior lawmakers like to call the shots, was tested again on the Budget Committee. When Putnam insistently pressed for a budget provision to bolster the long-term solvency of Social Security, Chairman Jim Nussle, a fellow Republican from Iowa, tartly urged Putnam to back down, saying, "I think you may want to reconsider this one, sport."

Putnam says he has loved politics all of his life. When he was 11 years old, he told his grandfather that he would run for governor some day. He was only 26 when he was elected to Congress, yet his résumé already included four years of legislative experience. Elected to the Florida Legislature in 1996, a year out of college, Putnam chaired the state House Agriculture Committee.

In 2000, Republican Rep. Charles T. Canady made way for Putnam to run for Congress when he observed a pledge to limit his service to four terms. Putnam had interned in Canady's Washington office in college.

The Democratic candidate, auto dealer Michael Stedem, tried to make Putnam's youth an issue. Putnam was careful to avoid traps that would make him seem too green for the job. He declined MTV's request to follow him on the campaign trail, saying he didn't want any "purple-hair yahoo" asking whether he wore "boxers or briefs."

Putnam won with 57 percent of the vote to Stedem's 43 percent, becoming the youngest member of Congress, a fact noted in his press releases. Four years later, he finally relinquished that distinction to North Carolina Republican Patrick McHenry, who is about 15 months younger.

Barring a statewide run, Putnam is likely to be able to hold the seat for the foreseeable future. He was unopposed for re-election in 2002 and won with 65 percent of the vote in 2004.

KEY VOTES

2004

No Extend federal unemployment benefits by 13 weeks
No Pass $283.2 billion, six-year federal highway and mass transit bill
Yes Approve $146 billion multi-year extension of previously enacted middle-class tax breaks
Yes Amend the Constitution to prohibit same-sex marriage
Yes Cut corporate taxes $137 billion over 10 years
Yes Reorganize U.S. intelligence agencies as proposed by Sept. 11 commission

2003

Yes Cut taxes by $330 billion through fiscal 2013
No Block Bush rule scaling back overtime pay for some white-collar federal workers
Yes Do not allow use of search warrants without first notifying subjects
No Allow importation of prescription drugs
Yes Create private school voucher program in Washington, D.C.
Yes Ban "partial birth" abortion except to save a woman's life
?   Split $18.6 billion in Iraq aid into half-grant, half-loan
Yes Overhaul Medicare and create prescription drug benefit

CQ VOTE STUDIES

	PARTY UNITY		PRESIDENTIAL SUPPORT	
	Support	Oppose	Support	Oppose
2004	97%	3%	91%	9%
2003	98%	2%	100%	0%
2002	98%	2%	88%	12%
2001	98%	2%	90%	10%

INTEREST GROUPS

	AFL-CIO	ADA	CCUS	ACU
2004	13%	0%	100%	100%
2003	7%	5%	97%	88%
2002	0%	0%	95%	96%
2001	18%	5%	96%	88%

FLORIDA 12
West central — Polk and Hillsborough counties

The 12th has plenty of land but much of it is covered by citrus groves and more than 500 natural lakes, as opposed to beaches and developments. Centered east of Tampa and southwest of Orlando, it includes almost all of Polk County, suburban and exurban portions of southern and eastern Hillsborough County, and a small slice of western Osceola County.

A Democratic registration advantage belies the social and economic conservatism of most residents. The GOP has the edge in the third of the district located in Hillsborough County, and the 12th has backed Republican presidential candidates since 1992. Traditional Southern Democrats probably could make state and local elections more competitive, but Republicans have had much better success recruiting top-quality candidates for important offices recently.

The 12th's economy is driven by Polk County's agricultural prowess. Polk is the state's top producer of citrus and is Florida's leader in overall farmland. Tomatoes and strawberries are cultivated in the Hillsborough

County portion of the district. Three hurricanes criss-crossed the district in 2004, but its inland location, along with massive federal aid, allowed all but the smallest farms to recover.

The 12th's economy grew steadily during the 1990s, despite some weather-related dips among citrus crops. Florida's phosphate mining industry has its home around Bartow and Mulberry, while Publix Supermarkets is headquartered in Lakeland. These industries provide consistent economic support, while citrus crops are more prone to ups and downs. Retirees are attracted to the district's significant retirement communities — including Sun City Center.

MAJOR INDUSTRY
Agriculture, mining, utilities

CITIES
Brandon (pt.), 72,878; Lakeland (pt.), 71,079; Winter Haven, 26,487

NOTABLE
Spook Hill, in Lake Wales, is a local oddity where cars parked in neutral at the base of the hill will roll up, defying gravity; Cypress Gardens Adventure Park in Winter Haven, Florida's first theme park, closed in 2003 but reopened in December 2004.

Rep. Katherine Harris (R)

Elected 2002; 2nd term

CAPITOL OFFICE
225-5015
katherine.harris@mail.house.gov
harris.house.gov
116 Cannon 20515-0913; fax 226-0828

COMMITTEES
Financial Services
Homeland Security
International Relations

HOMETOWN
Sarasota

BORN
April 5, 1957, Key West, Fla.

RELIGION
Presbyterian

FAMILY
Husband, Anders Ebbeson; one child

EDUCATION
Agnes Scott College, B.A. 1979 (history); Harvard
U., M.P.A. 1997

CAREER
Computer company marketing executive; real
estate firm executive

POLITICAL HIGHLIGHTS
Fla. Senate, 1994-98; Fla. secretary of state, 1999-
2002

ELECTION RESULTS

2004 GENERAL

Katherine Harris (R)	190,477	55.3%
Jan Schneider (D)	153,961	44.7%

2004 PRIMARY

Katherine Harris (R)	unopposed

2002 GENERAL

Katherine Harris (R)	139,048	54.8%
Jan Schneider (D)	114,739	45.2%

Harris is best known for her part in the nail-biter presidential election of 2000; as Florida's top election official, she certified George W. Bush the winner by 537 votes. The notoriety helped her land a seat in the House but hindered her recent aspirations of moving to the Senate.

Harris sat out the race for Florida's open Senate seat in 2004 after the White House privately expressed concerns that she could hurt President Bush's re-election chances by reminding voters of the bitterly polarizing campaign four years earlier. The setback for Harris is probably temporary. At the start of the 109th Congress, Harris was weighing a challenge to Democratic Sen. Bill Nelson in 2006.

Fallout from her role as Florida secretary of state in 2000 also has been personally difficult for Harris. She has been the target of death threats since she came to the House in 2002. In a frightening incident in late 2004, a 46-year-old real estate investor in Sarasota drove his Cadillac over a curb and directly at Harris as she was standing at a campaign event. The driver swerved in time to miss her and later told police he was "exercising my political expression."

Harris has had to live down the caricature of her created by Democratic enemies, the media and late-night comics. When she arrived on Capitol Hill in early 2003, she had the image of a ruthlessly partisan lightweight easily ridiculed for her snug sweaters and unsparing use of eye shadow. She was called "the Richard Nixon of Florida politics" in one unflattering newspaper feature, and Florida's best-selling pulp fiction writer Carl Hiaasen mused, "As a novelist, could I have invented Katherine Harris?"

But her House colleagues have been impressed that she is more personable than the dragon-lady image that developed after the 2000 election. A Harvard graduate with a solid résumé in state government, she has a good grasp of policy. Aggressive and energetic, Harris was described by Majority Whip Roy Blunt as "tireless on the floor" in the role of assistant in the GOP whip team.

She is a conservative and reliable vote for the man she helped make president. Harris has supported the president's tax cut proposals, government vouchers for private and parochial school tuition, and the idea of private accounts for Social Security, a priority for Bush in his second term.

Her own legislative track record is a work in progress. She managed to get one piece of legislation passed, a rarity for a junior lawmaker. She sponsored a bill that authorized $200 million over two years to help first-time homebuyers with their down payments and closing costs. The money is to be distributed to state and local governments through a program called HOME Investment Partnerships.

With a seat on the Financial Services Committee, Harris has said she wants to curb abuses in corporate boardrooms. But she is sometimes unwilling to go as far as her colleagues in giving the government more power. During consideration of a bill to give the Securities and Exchange Commission more regulatory influence, Harris objected to letting regulators seize property from the spouse of a corporate criminal. Her effort in 2004 to amend the bill in committee failed, however.

Harris paid particular attention during her inaugural term to channeling federal money back home, especially to Sarasota's lively arts community. She helped secure $1 million in 2004 appropriations to rebuild a planetarium in downtown Bradenton after it burned down.

Harris has the name recognition and devoted partisan following usually accorded to more seasoned politicians. It was not much of a stretch for her to consider running for the GOP nomination when Democratic Sen. Bob Graham left his seat open to run for president in 2004, and later retired. A St. Petersburg Times-Miami Herald poll showed her leading a field of would-be rivals. But Bush's political advisers worried that a Senate race by Harris would stir up memories of 2000 and drive avenging Democrats to the polls in a critical swing state. Bush favored former Housing Secretary Mel Martinez for the Republican nomination. Harris stayed out, and Martinez went on to win. Announcing her decision in Sarasota, Harris said: "I will be a candidate for the U.S. Senate, just not this year."

In one sense, the party brass owe it to her. She took a pass when the odds were best — an open seat — as opposed to waiting and challenging an incumbent. She said she was convinced she could have won without hurting the president. "When people look back, there are so many ways that I've been vindicated," Harris told the Miami Herald.

An heiress who is among the wealthiest House members, the Key West native is the granddaughter of Florida land tycoon Ben Hill Griffin, who amassed a fortune in citrus groves and ranching. She attended a small, private college and earned a master's degree from Harvard. As a young woman, she was interested in current events, read several newspapers a day and interned for Florida GOP Rep. Porter J. Goss, now director of the CIA.

She moved to Sarasota in the mid-1980s with her first husband, an attorney. (She is now remarried to a Swiss-born businessman and has a grown stepdaughter.) She got the notion to run for the state Senate in 1994 after being frustrated in efforts to get state help for Sarasota arts causes. While in the legislature, she sponsored a bill requiring parental consent for minors' abortions. In 1998, she won statewide office as secretary of state.

Harris was a national unknown until 2000, when she oversaw the disputed recount that gave Bush a victory in the closest race in Florida history. But she was the party's favorite to take the House seat of Republican Dan Miller, who observed his term limit pledge and retired. She raised a remarkable $3 million and campaigned with the confidence of an incumbent. She won, but with a lackluster 55 percent of the vote against the poorly financed Democrat, Jan Schneider. And she was chagrined by revelations that she'd overlooked an election law requiring her to quit her state job before qualifying to run for the House.

She has published a book revisiting the 2000 election drama, called "Center of the Storm: Practicing Principled Leadership in Times of Crisis."

KEY VOTES

2004

No Extend federal unemployment benefits by 13 weeks
No Pass $283.2 billion, six-year federal highway and mass transit bill
Yes Approve $146 billion multi-year extension of previously enacted middle-class tax breaks
Yes Amend the Constitution to prohibit same-sex marriage
Yes Cut corporate taxes $137 billion over 10 years
Yes Reorganize U.S. intelligence agencies as proposed by Sept. 11 commission

2003

Yes Cut taxes by $330 billion through fiscal 2013
No Block Bush rule scaling back overtime pay for some white-collar federal workers
Yes Do not allow use of search warrants without first notifying subjects
No Allow importation of prescription drugs
Yes Create private school voucher program in Washington, D.C.
Yes Ban "partial birth" abortion except to save a woman's life
No Split $18.6 billion in Iraq aid into half-grant, half-loan
Yes Overhaul Medicare and create prescription drug benefit

CQ VOTE STUDIES

	PARTY UNITY		PRESIDENTIAL SUPPORT	
	Support	Oppose	Support	Oppose
2004	97%	3%	94%	6%
2003	98%	2%	100%	0%

INTEREST GROUPS

	AFL-CIO	ADA	CCUS	ACU
2004	13%	0%	100%	92%
2003	7%	5%	97%	84%

FLORIDA 13
Southwest — Sarasota, most of Bradenton

Midwestern retirees flock to the Gulf Coast cities of Sarasota and Bradenton, making the 13th a reliably Republican district. Sarasota and Manatee counties have nearly 90 percent of the district's population; the more affluent tend to live near Sarasota while middle-class residents are more prevalent around Bradenton.

Most residents live near the coast, while farmland and citrus groves are inland. Sarasota County cultivates a refined image with its art museums, theater and symphony performances. It generally draws a more highly educated and wealthier class of retirees than most other west coast communities in Florida.

The 13th shares Bradenton, the county seat and retail center of Manatee County, with the 11th District. Bradenton has a more noticeable mix of incomes and ethnic groups. The 13th has the nation's highest median age, and its proportion of people 65 years and older (29 percent) makes it a popular home for older part-time residents.

The district's agricultural industry was affected by three hurricanes in 2004 that ruined the tomato and citrus crops. All four counties entirely in the 13th are among the state's top tomato producers.

Service industries, including investment companies, and trade make up much of the labor force. The district's proximity to Gulf beaches, barrier islands and a large state park makes the environment a bipartisan concern, with residents attuned to the problems of beach erosion and the effects of rapid population growth.

Republicans outnumber Democrats by nearly 40 percent in registration, and voters overwhelmingly favor GOP candidates in statewide races. Republican nominees have won the district since the 1992 presidential election.

MAJOR INDUSTRY
Health care, financial services, agriculture

CITIES
Sarasota, 52,715; Bradenton (pt.), 39,385; North Port, 22,797

NOTABLE
Former circus owner John Ringling brought his circus to the Sarasota area each winter.

Rep. Connie Mack (R)

Elected 2004; 1st term

CAPITOL OFFICE
225-2536
www.house.gov/mack
317 Cannon 20515-0914; fax 225-6820

COMMITTEES
Budget
International Relations
Transportation & Infrastructure

HOMETOWN
Fort Myers

BORN
Aug. 12, 1967, Fort Myers, Fla.

RELIGION
Roman Catholic

FAMILY
Wife, Ann Mack; two children

EDUCATION
U. of Florida, B.S. 1993 (advertising)

CAREER
Marketing consultant; health products sales representative

POLITICAL HIGHLIGHTS
Fla. House, 2000-03

ELECTION RESULTS

2004 GENERAL

Connie Mack (R)	226,662	67.6%
Robert M. Neeld (D)	108,672	32.4%

2004 PRIMARY

Connie Mack (R)	27,526	35.8%
Carole Green (R)	24,767	32.2%
Andy Coy (R)	17,089	22.2%
Frank Schwerin (R)	7,465	9.7%

Mack continues a family tradition on Capitol Hill. His current 14th District consists almost entirely of a portion of Florida's Gulf Coast that was represented from 1983 to 1989 by his father, also Connie Mack, who went on to serve in the Senate from 1989 to 2001.

He also is carrying on the tradition of going by a nickname, initiated by his great-grandfather, who was a famed baseball manager. The congressman's given name is actually Cornelius McGillicuddy IV.

Mack says he never had much interest in running for office until he started his own family. "I wanted to be where the decisions were being made so I could make sure that my children and grandchildren have opportunity," he says. During three years as a state legislator, Mack organized a group of members opposed to all measures that would have raised additional revenue, and he supports additional tax cuts in Washington.

A former health products salesman, he advocates curbing medical malpractice litigation, which he blames for rising insurance premiums and decisions by some doctors to move or curtail their practices. Yet like many Republicans in a state where health care is a dominant issue, Mack breaks with the national GOP line to support federal funding for stem cell research and permitting seniors to import prescription medications from Canada.

Two of Mack's committee assignments are Budget, where his father once served, and Transportation and Infrastructure, where he hopes to champion programs to protect the state's beaches and restore the Everglades.

When Republican Porter J. Goss decided to retire after eight terms, Mack entered the 2004 race in the overwhelmingly Republican 14th District. He eked out a primary victory in a four-way race marked by opponents' jabs that Mack, who grew up in the district but had held a state House seat in Fort Lauderdale on the other side of the state, moved back to Fort Myers only to pursue his political ambitions.

He then cruised to a lopsided general-election victory over a Democratic political unknown.

FLORIDA 14

Southwest — Cape Coral, Fort Myers, Naples

A haven for retirees and tourists, the solidly Republican 14th features Gulf Coast beaches and a rapidly expanding population centered in Lee County. It also takes in the coastal edge of Collier County and a small slice of Charlotte County. Most residents live near the coast, between the shore and Interstate 75, which runs through the entire district before turning eastward into the Everglades.

Collier County's population expanded by more than 65 percent during the 1990s, while neighboring Lee, led by Cape Coral, grew by almost a third. Originally a retirement community, Cape Coral has attracted young professionals, service industries and land developers. Wealthier retirees live around Naples, where golf courses and high-rise condominiums are plentiful and new construction helps put the area in the state's top 10 in taxable property value.

Florida Gulf Coast University, which opened in Lee County in 1997, and the nearby Everglades help promote a bustling eco-tourism industry and marine biology. The barrier islands act as a magnet for tourists — Sanibel Island is renowned for the seashells that wash up on its beaches from the Gulf of Mexico.

Small Democratic pockets exist within the district's cities, like Fort Myers and Cape Coral, but the 14th has the largest Republican registration edge in the state and regularly gives GOP candidates high vote percentages.

MAJOR INDUSTRY
Tourism, health care, agriculture

CITIES
Cape Coral, 102,286; Fort Myers, 48,208; North Fort Myers, 40,214; Lehigh Acres, 33,430; Bonita Springs, 32,797; Naples, 20,976

NOTABLE
Lee County includes the spring training homes of two major league baseball teams — the Boston Red Sox and the Minnesota Twins; The J.N. "Ding" Darling National Wildlife Refuge is on Sanibel Island.

Rep. Dave Weldon (R)

Elected 1994; 6th term

An internal medicine physician, Weldon is a strong-willed conservative who has two primary goals in Congress — advancing "family values" in public life and continuing access to outer space.

Weldon arrived in Washington as part of the revolutionary GOP Class of 1994, and he takes a back seat to no one in his defense of conservative social values. He began the 109th Congress defending a provision he had inserted in the 2004 catchall spending bill to deny federal aid to states and localities that compel health care providers, facilities or insurance companies to provide, fund or refer abortion services.

The provision significantly expanded the "conscience clause" under federal law that shields doctors and other health care providers from discrimination lawsuits when they refuse to perform abortions and cite their personal opposition to the procedure. Weldon said it would prevent situations in which cities or states deny licenses to hospitals, such as those run by the Roman Catholic Church, that refuse to perform abortions.

Two lawsuits were filed soon after the spending bill became law seeking to overturn Weldon's measure. In addition, Senate Democrats, who objected to the provision, were promised a vote in 2005 by Republican leaders on repeal legislation.

Early in 2005, Weldon was a leader in getting Congress involved in the case of a brain-damaged Florida woman, Terri Schiavo. Weldon authored bills aimed at keeping the woman, or others in similar circumstances, alive while federal courts determined the extent of her incapacitation.

Weldon also is active on the issue of human cloning. He joined with Michigan Democrat Bart Stupak in writing a bill to ban the cloning of human embryos for any purpose, including medical research. The House passed the measure in 2001 and again in 2003, but it stalled in the Senate each time. "Any attempt at human cloning, for whatever purpose, is a gross form of human experimentation that the American people oppose," Weldon said.

He is a passionate proponent of congressional efforts to ban a procedure its opponents call "partial birth" abortion, which after years of debate was outlawed in 2003. He says he became a staunch abortion foe after he and his wife, unable to have children of their own, decided to adopt.

Weldon has another legislative passion: space. Until redistricting in 2002, his "Space Coast" district included the Kennedy Space Center. However, the area economy still depends greatly on NASA and private companies attracted there by space-related work. In the 108th Congress, House GOP leaders awarded Weldon a coveted seat on the Appropriations Committee. And in the 109th, he is the vice chairman of the Science, State, Justice and Commerce Subcommittee, which has jurisdiction over NASA's budget.

NASA and its supporters were terribly shaken by the 2003 explosion of the space shuttle *Columbia*, which killed seven astronauts, and the space agency faced new questions about the practicality of the shuttle program. With a tight federal budget, the space program is always a choice target, and Weldon and other backers in Congress have battled to preserve modest increases.

Weldon likes to cite the scientific potential offered by a permanent outpost in space. It would give researchers "a fundamentally new tool to explore fields such as medicine, materials sciences, biology and astronomy," Weldon said in a letter to his House colleagues.

Weldon also looks out for the military veterans who populate his district.

CAPITOL OFFICE
225-3671
www.house.gov/weldon
2347 Rayburn 20515-0915; fax 225-3516

COMMITTEES
Appropriations

HOMETOWN
Indiatlantic

BORN
Aug. 31, 1953, Amityville, N.Y.

RELIGION
Christian

FAMILY
Wife, Nancy Weldon; two children

EDUCATION
State U. of New York, Stony Brook, B.S. 1978 (biochemistry); State U. of New York, Buffalo, M.D. 1981

MILITARY SERVICE
Army Medical Corps, 1981-87; Army Reserve, 1987-92

CAREER
Physician

POLITICAL HIGHLIGHTS
No previous office

ELECTION RESULTS

2004 GENERAL

Dave Weldon (R)	210,388	65.4%
Simon Pristoop (D)	111,538	34.7%

2004 PRIMARY

Dave Weldon (R)	unopposed

2002 GENERAL

Dave Weldon (R)	146,414	63.2%
Jim Tso (D)	85,433	36.9%

PREVIOUS WINNING PERCENTAGES
2000 (59%); 1998 (63%); 1996 (51%); 1994 (54%)

He supported building a new veterans' hospital but lowered his sights when prospects for that appeared uncertain. Instead, he won approval for a $25 million outpatient clinic and for a pilot project that permits the Department of Veterans Affairs to contract with local hospitals for inpatient care for veterans.

Weldon began his involvement in politics in the late 1980s as the co-founder of a conservative group, the Space Coast Family Forum, that endorsed candidates based on their stances on abortion, sex education and other social issues. He has continued along that path in Washington, as a member of the Values Action Team in the House, which urges GOP leaders to advance conservative, "pro-family" policies.

Religion plays an important part in Weldon's life. He says he tries to read the Bible and pray every day, and he lists among his political influences his "idol . . . Jesus Christ." Weldon's values sit well with the culturally conservative voters whose influence is growing along central Florida's East Coast.

Like many Floridians, Weldon is a transplant from the North. He grew up on Long Island, the son of a postal clerk. He worked his way through his undergraduate days as an X-ray technician, and the Army paid his way through medical school. After a stint as an Army doctor, he moved to Florida in 1987 and went into private practice.

Other than his involvement in the Space Coast Family Forum, Weldon's only taste of political life until his run for Congress came when he was president of his local homeowners association. But when two-term Democratic Rep. Jim Bacchus unexpectedly decided to retire in 1994, Weldon entered the race, overcoming criticism that he was too conservative for the district. Weldon's Family Forum ties gave him a ready-made base of support among conservatives, and he won the GOP nomination, capturing 54 percent of the vote in a runoff.

That year found the district's voters in a conservative mood, and Weldon emphasized his support for mainstream GOP fare: tax cuts, welfare reform and other aspects of the House Republicans' "Contract With America." Aided by an extensive get-out-the-vote effort conducted by groups such as the Christian Coalition, Weldon defeated Democrat Sue Munsey, a former head of the Cocoa Beach Area Chamber of Commerce, with 54 percent.

In 2000, Weldon dealt House Democratic leader Richard A. Gephardt a double defeat: Not only did he win re-election to a seat Democrats had a slim hope of grabbing; his unexpectedly large victory came over Gephardt's cousin, state Sen. Patsy Kurth. Weldon flirted with a run for the Senate in 2004 but ultimately decided against it. He then coasted to re-election.

KEY VOTES

2004

No Extend federal unemployment benefits by 13 weeks
No Pass $283.2 billion, six-year federal highway and mass transit bill
Yes Approve $146 billion multi-year extension of previously enacted middle-class tax breaks
Yes Amend the Constitution to prohibit same-sex marriage
Yes Cut corporate taxes $137 billion over 10 years
No Reorganize U.S. intelligence agencies as proposed by Sept. 11 commission

2003

Yes Cut taxes by $330 billion through fiscal 2013
No Block Bush rule scaling back overtime pay for some white-collar federal workers
Yes Do not allow use of search warrants without first notifying subjects
No Allow importation of prescription drugs
Yes Create private school voucher program in Washington, D.C.
Yes Ban "partial birth" abortion except to save a woman's life
No Split $18.6 billion in Iraq aid into half-grant, half-loan
Yes Overhaul Medicare and create prescription drug benefit

CQ VOTE STUDIES

	PARTY UNITY		PRESIDENTIAL SUPPORT	
	Support	Oppose	Support	Oppose
2004	95%	5%	88%	12%
2003	97%	3%	96%	4%
2002	98%	2%	85%	15%
2001	95%	5%	77%	23%
2000	96%	4%	19%	81%

INTEREST GROUPS

	AFL-CIO	ADA	CCUS	ACU
2004	7%	0%	100%	91%
2003	7%	5%	93%	71%
2002	11%	0%	90%	100%
2001	8%	5%	87%	92%
2000	10%	5%	76%	92%

FLORIDA 15

Central coast — Indian River County; parts of Brevard, Osceola and Polk counties

Most people in the GOP-tilting 15th live along the Atlantic Coast in Brevard and Indian River counties, primarily between the conservative strongholds of Merritt Island and Vero Beach. In addition to all of Indian River County and three-quarters of Brevard County, the 15th contains most of Osceola County and a sliver of Polk County. It is home to the Cape Canaveral Air Force Station, although redistricting following the 2000 census placed Kennedy Space Center, often associated with Cape Canaveral, in the neighboring 24th District. The Air Force Station, Patrick Air Force Base — just a few miles south — and the Kennedy Space Center are the region's economic engine, pushing a thriving technology industry and helping to insulate it from downturns.

Melbourne and Palm Bay in the northeastern portion of the district combine to form a major population center. Most cities in the 15th have seen steady growth, and a Disney complex near Vero Beach is changing the sleepy town into a high-profile resort, despite some local backlash. Voters in Indian River County passed a $50 million bond issue to preserve more land in 2004.

Fast-growing Kissimmee, a heavily Hispanic city in the district's portion of Osceola County, depends on the industry built up around Walt Disney World and other nearby tourist destinations. Democrats hold a slight registration edge in Osceola, and conservative Democrats can compete throughout the district. But the GOP holds a significant registration edge overall in the 15th, and voters have favored GOP presidential candidates since 1992. In 2004, George W. Bush captured 57 percent of the vote.

MAJOR INDUSTRY
Technology, defense, tourism

MILITARY BASES
Patrick Air Force Base, 12,000 military and civilian (2004)

CITIES
Palm Bay, 79,413; Melbourne, 71,382; Kissimmee, 47,814; Merritt Island (pt.), 27,291; Yeehaw Junction, 21,778; Vero Beach South, 20,362

NOTABLE
Kissimmee used to be known as the "cow capital of Florida"; Vero Beach is the spring training home of baseball's Los Angeles Dodgers.

Rep. Mark Foley (R)

Elected 1994; 6th term

CAPITOL OFFICE
225-5792
www.house.gov/foley
104 Cannon 20515-0916; fax 225-3132

COMMITTEES
Ways & Means

HOMETOWN
Palm Beach Gardens

BORN
Sept. 8, 1954, Newton, Mass.

RELIGION
Roman Catholic

FAMILY
Single

EDUCATION
Palm Beach Community College, attended 1973-75

CAREER
Catering company founder; real estate broker;
restaurant chain owner

POLITICAL HIGHLIGHTS
Lake Worth City Council, 1977-79; sought
Democratic nomination for Fla. House, 1980;
Lake Worth city commissioner, 1982-84; sought
Democratic nomination for Palm Beach County
Commission, 1984; Republican nominee for Fla.
House, 1986; Fla. House, 1990-92; Fla. Senate,
1992-94

ELECTION RESULTS

2004 GENERAL

Mark Foley (R)	215,563	68.0%
Jeff Fisher (D)	101,247	32.0%

2004 PRIMARY

Mark Foley (R)	unopposed

2002 GENERAL

Mark Foley (R)	176,171	78.9%
Jack McLain (CNSTP)	47,169	21.1%

PREVIOUS WINNING PERCENTAGES
2000 (60%); 1998 (100%); 1996 (64%); 1994 (58%)

Foley, who has a wealth of political experience and know-how, stands a bit apart from the ideological conservatives elected with him in the 1994 GOP sweep. He comes across as more patient and less dogmatic. He also can be more moderate on certain social issues.

Foley is one of the more visible figures in Congress, thanks to his approachable demeanor and his inclusion in Republican power circles. Whether the issue is taxes or trade, internal congressional political deals or Hollywood lobbying, Foley usually has a quotable comment. He also often knows how floor votes will fare as he is a top deputy in the Republican whip operation.

Foley has long been considered a viable statewide candidate and in 2003, he mounted a campaign for retiring Democratic Sen. Bob Graham's seat. During the campaign, however, he felt he had to address rumors about his sexuality. "I'm declaring today that I have a right to privacy, like anyone else in this country," Foley told the St. Petersburg Times in May 2003. "The fact that I'm not married has led many people to speculate, but I'm not going to be dragged into the gutter by these rumormongers." He eventually backed out of the race nearly a year before the primary, saying that his father was ill with cancer.

On some social issues, Foley strays from the majority in his party. In the 108th Congress, he voted against a leadership-backed proposed constitutional amendment banning same-sex marriage. When he is questioned about his vote, he notes that he voted for the 1996 Defense of Marriage Act, which permits states to refuse recognition of a same-sex marriage endorsed in other states.

Although he voted with his party 91 percent of the time in 2004, he gave President Bush his support only 79 percent of the time. He supports the president's plan to overhaul the Social Security system to allow individuals to set up private accounts, but he disagrees with the president over limiting federal funding of stem-cell research.

A member of the Ways and Means Committee, Foley joined the Trade Subcommittee in the 109th Congress. He is not always supportive of Bush's trade proposals. He initially opposed but later voted for reviving fast-track trade procedures, a top Bush priority that became law in 2002. Foley says he will oppose congressional approval of the Central American Free Trade Agreement, which the administration signed in 2004, if it includes sugar — a major crop in his district.

Four hurricanes ripped through Florida in the fall of 2004, and three of them blew through Foley's district. During the storms, he became a familiar face on the local television news. He worked with other members of the Florida delegation to pass a $2 billion hurricane relief bill as well as to gain an additional $11.6 billion as part of the 2004 military construction spending bill.

Walt Disney Co. and Universal Studios are powerful economic players in Florida, and Foley's work on Capitol Hill includes the chairmanship of the House Entertainment Caucus. As a leading GOP emissary to Hollywood, he has worked to build bridges between the industry and his party. In 2004, he and other movie industry supporters were only partially successful in attaining long-sought tax breaks. The corporate tax bill enacted that year allowed film studios to deduct up to $15 million in the first year of production of small and independent films, but Disney and Hollywood film companies were disappointed they did not get hundreds of millions of dollars more in tax breaks in the final legislation.

Foley's first brush with the entertainment business came in 1980 when the makers of the film "Body Heat" set up shop in Lake Worth, Fla., where he ran a restaurant called the Lettuce Patch. He got a walk-on part — most of his frames ended up on the cutting room floor, he laments — but he remembers what a boost the movie crew's business gave to the local economy. (He also snagged a bit part in a 2000 movie, "The Librarians.")

Foley, who is fiscally frugal, has played a leading role in fights to eliminate some big-ticket federal expenditures that he deemed wasteful, such as the Pentagon's B-2 bomber and a host of energy research and water projects. He criticizes deficit spending, but he has voted for Bush's tax cuts.

In the 108th, Foley was successful in attaching to the 2004 intelligence agencies overhaul law provisions to allow the Justice Department to block entry into the United States or deport from U.S. land foreign nationals who have committed acts of torture or other human rights abuses. Another of Foley's priorities is legislation to require people to give businesses 90 days' notice before suing them over noncompliance with accessibility standards in the Americans with Disabilities Act. In many cases, Foley says, businesses would comply with the law if given a chance.

Born into an Irish-Catholic family on the outskirts of Boston, Foley moved to Florida as a child and says he began his political career at age 5, distributing flyers for a local candidate. In 1975, he opened the Lettuce Patch restaurant with his mother and later became a real estate broker. He won a seat — as a Democrat — on the Lake Worth City Council two years later, at 23. After some failed bids to move up the political ladder and a President Reagan-prompted party switch to the GOP, his career began lurching forward with his election to the state House in 1990.

He moved to the state Senate two years later, where he chaired the Agriculture Committee, and just two years after that he was elected to Congress to succeed Republican Tom Lewis, who retired. Foley's image as a moderate generated some opposition from conservatives in the GOP primary, but his fundraising apparatus was impressive, and he won easily.

Foley's re-election contests have been uneventful, and the post-census redistricting improved GOP prospects in the 16th District. But Foley takes fundraising seriously. He formed a political action committee and has made substantial contributions to other GOP candidates. In 2004, he won easily with 68 percent of the vote.

KEY VOTES

2004
No   Extend federal unemployment benefits by 13 weeks
No   Pass $283.2 billion, six-year federal highway and mass transit bill
Yes   Approve $146 billion multi-year extension of previously enacted middle-class tax breaks
No   Amend the Constitution to prohibit same-sex marriage
Yes   Cut corporate taxes $137 billion over 10 years
Yes   Reorganize U.S. intelligence agencies as proposed by Sept. 11 commission

2003
Yes   Cut taxes by $330 billion through fiscal 2013
No   Block Bush rule scaling back overtime pay for some white-collar federal workers
Yes   Do not allow use of search warrants without first notifying subjects
No   Allow importation of prescription drugs
?   Create private school voucher program in Washington, D.C.
Yes   Ban "partial birth" abortion except to save a woman's life
No   Split $18.6 billion in Iraq aid into half-grant, half-loan
Yes   Overhaul Medicare and create prescription drug benefit

CQ VOTE STUDIES

	PARTY UNITY		PRESIDENTIAL SUPPORT	
	Support	Oppose	Support	Oppose
2004	91%	9%	79%	21%
2003	94%	6%	93%	7%
2002	90%	10%	90%	10%
2001	89%	11%	81%	19%
2000	81%	19%	39%	61%

INTEREST GROUPS

	AFL-CIO	ADA	CCUS	ACU
2004	13%	25%	100%	68%
2003	13%	5%	97%	76%
2002	11%	15%	95%	92%
2001	25%	30%	91%	64%
2000	0%	20%	80%	68%

FLORIDA 16

South central — Port St. Lucie, parts of Port Charlotte and Wellington

The 16th sprawls across south-central Florida, connecting wealthy east-coast communities with Charlotte Harbor on the west coast. In between, rural Floridians raise cattle and grow sugar cane, particularly around Lake Okeechobee. The district surrounds the west side of the lake and includes most of St. Lucie County's white population near the Atlantic Ocean, from southern Fort Pierce to Port St. Lucie. With the lake and beaches, environmental issues play a significant role in local politics.

The district's coast-to-coast geography was more of a curse than a blessing in 2004. Three hurricanes — Charley, Frances and Jeanne — came ashore in the 16th, causing billions of dollars in damage. Federal aid came quickly, but full recovery, particularly in the agricultural sector, may still take several years.

St. Lucie County is the most populous jurisdiction in the 16th, accounting for about one-fourth of residents. The 16th's share of St. Lucie County,

which includes all of Port St. Lucie and some of Fort Pierce and Lakewood Park, has a slight Republican lean. Martin County, which is older and even more solidly Republican, includes wealthy Jupiter Island.

Robust population growth required the 16th to shed 120,000 people in redistricting following the 2000 census. But mapmakers removed twice that much from Palm Beach County and added part of Republican-leaning Charlotte County on the state's west coast. The remaining share of Palm Beach County includes parts of Jupiter and Palm Beach Gardens, as well as most of Wellington, a growing, wealthy subdivision southwest of West Palm Beach.

The 16th had a slight Democratic tilt in the 1990s, but redistricting gave it a slight Republican edge. George W. Bush won 55 percent of the vote here in the 2004 presidential race.

MAJOR INDUSTRY
Agriculture, government, health care

CITIES
Port St. Lucie, 88,769; Port Charlotte (pt.), 39,610; Wellington (pt.), 35,797

NOTABLE
LaBelle hosts the Swamp Cabbage Festival at the end of each February.

Rep. Kendrick B. Meek (D)

Elected 2002; 2nd term

CAPITOL OFFICE
225-4506
www.house.gov/kenmeek
1039 Longworth 20515-0917; fax 226-0777

COMMITTEES
Armed Services
Homeland Security

HOMETOWN
Miami

BORN
Sept. 6, 1966, Miami, Fla.

RELIGION
Baptist

FAMILY
Wife, Leslie Dixon Meek; two children

EDUCATION
Florida A&M U., B.S. 1988 (criminal justice)

CAREER
Security firm business development aide; state trooper

POLITICAL HIGHLIGHTS
Fla. House, 1994-98; Fla. Senate, 1998-2002

ELECTION RESULTS

2004 GENERAL

Kendrick B. Meek (D)	unopposed

2004 PRIMARY

Kendrick B. Meek (D)	unopposed

2002 GENERAL

Kendrick B. Meek (D)	unopposed

A descendant of slaves, Meek represents a black-majority district in the Miami area that has been in the Meek family since its creation more than a decade ago. He is the son of Democrat Carrie P. Meek, who won the seat after the 1990 reapportionment and kept it for five terms. When she retired, Kendrick was elected without opposition in 2002 and was similarly unchallenged for re-election in 2004.

He is best known for his very public fights with Florida's governor, presidential brother Jeb Bush, over education and affirmative action during his days in the state legislature. And he's kept up his battle with the Bushes in Washington. Meek has been a vocal critic of President Bush's policies on Haitian immigrants, whom he claims are unfairly singled out for detention and deportation. Meek's district is 55 percent black and has the largest Haitian population in the United States, including residents of Miami's Little Haiti neighborhood. Many constituents have friends or relatives on the destitute island nation 600 miles off Florida's coast. Meek visits the country frequently.

When Haitian President Jean-Bertrand Aristide was toppled in a coup in 2004, Meek tried in vain to get Attorney General John Ashcroft to approve temporary protective status for people fleeing the violence. He criticized the Bush administration's policy of detaining immigrants who arrive by sea seeking asylum. Meek ultimately wants to make it easier for Haitians to emigrate but made little headway in his first term with a proposal to expand a 1998 law authored by his mother allowing Haitians who were living in the country before 1996 to receive immigration protection when applying to become permanent residents. Meek also pushed a bill giving Haitian-made apparel duty-free access to U.S. markets provided the fabric comes from countries with free-trade pacts with the United States.

Meek represents the mostly poor and working-class neighborhoods of northeast Miami-Dade and southeastern Broward counties. He is a believer in smaller class sizes in public schools as a way to stem low test scores and high drop-out rates. He introduced a bill in 2003 that continued efforts he led in Florida that resulted in a state constitutional amendment mandating class sizes from pre-school through high school. His federal legislation would give states with class-size reduction programs up to $200 million in federal matching grants to build new classrooms or to hire more teachers.

Meek was born into politics the way some children inherit the family business. His mother, the granddaughter of a slave, was the first African-American elected to Congress from Florida since Reconstruction. Kendrick remembers curling up to sleep under his mother's desk in the Florida House as she read bills late into the night. Carrie Meek, a divorced mother of three, was a strong role model, coaching young Kendrick through early learning difficulties stemming from dyslexia. When he was 12, she made him a page at the state Capitol.

Kendrick graduated from his mother's alma mater, Florida A&M University, where he studied criminal justice. He went to work as a state trooper, and with his mother's help, rose quickly to captain and got onto Democratic Lt. Gov. Buddy MacKay's security detail.

After just five years on the force, in 1994, he decided to challenge a veteran state Democratic House member who was a leader on women's issues. Rep. Elaine Gordon retired, avoiding a primary battle, and Meek was elected. In 1998, Meek, at age 32, elbowed out another Democratic incumbent to capture his mother's old state Senate seat.

Though he got there on Carrie Meek's coattails, Kendrick skillfully made his own reputation in state government. When Gov. Bush refused to meet with him to discuss a proposal to eliminate minority preferences in state contracts and university admissions, Meek staged a well-publicized, overnight "sit in" at Bush's office. The move galvanized opponents, leading to the state's largest ever protest march on the Capitol.

Capitalizing on the momentum, Meek traveled the state promoting an "Arrive with Five" campaign urging women and minorities to register to vote in 2000 and to bring five new voters with them. It helped turn out the largest number of black voters in state history, according to the Orlando Sentinel, in an election that became famous for the recount that made George Bush president.

Meek then reconstituted his forces into the successful campaign to amend the state constitution in 2002 to make smaller classes mandatory, overcoming fierce opposition from Gov. Bush.

In 2002, Carrie Meek announced her retirement less than two weeks before the candidate filing deadline, giving a jump start to her son. Would-be challengers stayed away, and Meek was easily elected.

Hoping to take advantage of Meek's abundant political skills, Democratic House leaders made him a co-vice chairman of the Democratic Congressional Campaign Committee, which raises money for House candidates. And they gave him a spot on the newly created Homeland Security Committee, giving him a say in the post-Sept. 11 revamping of the Immigration and Naturalization Service, the U.S. Customs Service and the Coast Guard.

The port of Miami, where nearly four million people a year pass through on cruises, is just outside his district and is a major employer there, as is Miami International Airport. Nationally, Meek wants to replace the nation's emergency notification system, which relies heavily on radio and television broadcasts, with one that would alert people by telephone, including cell phones. It has the advantage, he says, of reaching more Americans, especially during power outages, and letting the government zero in on threats to specific cities, counties or states.

Meek's other committee assignment is Armed Services, which oversees Florida's many military installations.

U.S.-Cuba relations also figure in Meek's portfolio, though the Cuban-American population in his district is not as dominant as it is in other South Florida districts. He is a staunch foe of Cuba's Fidel Castro, making him a sometimes ally of Cuban-American Republicans from the region.

KEY VOTES

2004

Yes Extend federal unemployment benefits by 13 weeks

Yes Pass $283.2 billion, six-year federal highway and mass transit bill

Yes Approve $146 billion multi-year extension of previously enacted middle-class tax breaks

? Amend the Constitution to prohibit same-sex marriage

No Cut corporate taxes $137 billion over 10 years

Yes Reorganize U.S. intelligence agencies as proposed by Sept. 11 commission

2003

No Cut taxes by $330 billion through fiscal 2013

Yes Block Bush rule scaling back overtime pay for some white-collar federal workers

? Do not allow use of search warrants without first notifying subjects

No Allow importation of prescription drugs

No Create private school voucher program in Washington, D.C.

No Ban "partial birth" abortion except to save a woman's life

Yes Split $18.6 billion in Iraq aid into half-grant, half-loan

No Overhaul Medicare and create prescription drug benefit

CQ VOTE STUDIES

	PARTY UNITY		PRESIDENTIAL SUPPORT	
	Support	Oppose	Support	Oppose
2004	94%	6%	39%	61%
2003	93%	7%	26%	74%

INTEREST GROUPS

	AFL-CIO	ADA	CCUS	ACU
2004	93%	85%	45%	9%
2003	87%	85%	47%	23%

FLORIDA 17
Southeast — parts of Miami and Hollywood

The black-majority 17th, once a long strip running from the Broward County border through Miami to points south, became more compact during redistricting following the 2000 census. The district now encompasses an array of neighborhoods, including some well-to-do areas and some of the region's most destitute, but is confined to northeast Miami-Dade County and southeast Broward County.

The district has the state's highest percentage of black residents (55 percent), including many originally from the West Indies. Whites and Hispanics each make up about one-fifth of the residents.

Overtown, once the hub of African-American wealth in the region, spent decades in decline. But that area, along with others in the district, is part of Miami-Dade's federal empowerment zone, and revitalization efforts are ongoing. Officials are encouraging public-private partnerships as a means to rebuild communities.

Infrastructure is a big part of the picture in the 17th: Miami International Airport is located just outside the district, and another airport in Opa-Locka serves as a base for civilian pilots. Interstate 95 and Route 1 wind through the district. Health concerns are a major topic for residents, many of whom are uninsured. In addition, the HIV/AIDS epidemic has hit the 17th hard, particularly in the black community.

Democrats are a lock at all levels in the 17th, where Republican candidates in statewide races often get less than 25 percent of the vote. John Kerry won 83 percent here in the 2004 presidential race — his best showing in the state.

MAJOR INDUSTRY
Transportation, service, entertainment

CITIES
Miami (pt.), 81,688; Hollywood (pt.), 57,267; North Miami (pt.), 50,514; Miramar (pt.), 41,272; Carol City (pt.), 35,858

NOTABLE
Overtown's Lyric Theater, which for decades hosted eminent black entertainers, closed for construction in 2003 and is expected to re-open in 2006; Opa-Locka's architecture is based on an Arabian theme.

Rep. Ileana Ros-Lehtinen (R)

Elected August 1989; 8th full term

CAPITOL OFFICE
225-3931
www.house.gov/ros-lehtinen
2160 Rayburn 20515-0918; fax 225-5620

COMMITTEES
Budget
Government Reform
International Relations
(Middle East & Central Asia - chairwoman)

HOMETOWN
Miami

BORN
July 15, 1952, Havana, Cuba

RELIGION
Roman Catholic

FAMILY
Husband, Dexter Lehtinen; two children, two
stepchildren

EDUCATION
Miami-Dade Community College, A.A. 1972
(English); Florida International U., B.A. 1975
(English & education), M.S. 1976-86 (education);
U. of Miami, Ph.D. 2004 (education)

CAREER
Teacher; private school administrator

POLITICAL HIGHLIGHTS
Fla. House, 1982-86; Fla. Senate, 1986-89

ELECTION RESULTS

2004 GENERAL

Ileana Ros-Lehtinen (R)	143,647	64.7%
Sam Sheldon (D)	78,281	35.3%

2004 PRIMARY

Ileana Ros-Lehtinen (R)	unopposed

2002 GENERAL

Ileana Ros-Lehtinen (R)	103,512	69.1%
Ray Chote (D)	42,852	28.6%
Orin Opperman (I)	3,423	2.3%

PREVIOUS WINNING PERCENTAGES
2000 (100%); 1998 (100%); 1996 (100%); 1994 (100%);
1992 (67%); 1990 (60%); 1989 Special Election (53%)

As the first Cuban-American and the first Hispanic woman elected to Congress, Ros-Lehtinen spent her early years in the House focused on U.S. policy toward Cuba and on immigration but has increasingly expanded her portfolio to other international arenas as well. She would like to take over as chairwoman of the International Relations Committee when Republican Henry J. Hyde of Illinois steps down.

She is a growing favorite of the American pro-Israel lobby and is often mentioned as a leading candidate to replace Hyde, who in 2007 hits the six-year term limit on chairmanships imposed under GOP rules. As chairwoman of the Subcommittee on the Middle East and Central Asia, Ros-Lehtinen (full name: il-ee-AH-na ross-LAY-tin-nen) has targeted countries suspected of supporting terrorists. She advocates a harder line in pursuing Iran over the issue of weapons of mass destruction and Saudi Arabia over lingering concerns about whether it is financing terrorist groups. She also backs legislation aimed at aiding victims of Palestinian terrorism.

Despite her departure from conservative orthodoxy on some issues, Ros-Lehtinen has cultivated strong relationships with party leaders, including Majority Leader Tom DeLay, with whom she shares strong support of Israel. Such bonds could bolster her campaign for chairwoman. She also established in 2004 a political action committee, IRL-PAC, to build goodwill with colleagues with donations to their campaigns.

While terrorism and Israel have been her focus in recent years, Ros-Lehtinen has long preached the wisdom of keeping Cuba and President Fidel Castro isolated. Divisions within the Republican Party on the issue have forced a change in her arguments, if not her position, in recent years.

After a broad majority of the House voted in 2002 to lift the 42-year-old ban on travel by U.S. citizens to Cuba, Ros-Lehtinen and her allies declared that they had "lost the moral high ground" in their campaign to continue the economic embargo against the island nation. So they modified their arguments and began to talk less about Castro's communism and more about how doing business with his country would be bad for the U.S. businesses because they would have few legal protections.

Grain and fruit producers are among the most eager to sell their products to Cuba, and they have clout with lawmakers. Still, the Bush White House and congressional GOP leaders have helped to keep the embargo in place by preventing amendments to end it from being added to appropriations bills for several years. The president and his brother, Florida's Republican Gov. Jeb Bush, have been eager to maintain good relations with the state's large, GOP-leaning Cuban community that is mostly anti-Castro in sentiment.

Ros-Lehtinen's expanding list of interests grew out of her work on the Cuba issue, which motivated her to come to Congress over 15 years ago. While she pressed Cuba on its treatment of political dissidents from her perch as chairwoman of the International Relations panel's Human Rights Subcommittee in the early 2000s, she also highlighted the plight of dissidents in countries like Pakistan, Northern Ireland and the Congo. Her efforts drew praise from human rights groups.

Her prominent role in the Elián González episode in 1999 and 2000 caused some consternation in her party. Social conservatives wanted the 5-year-old boy to be returned to his father in Cuba after he was fished out of the sea by rescuers helping a disabled boat full of refugees. Elián's mother drowned in the tragedy. Ros-Lehtinen and other Florida politicians made the case a cause célèbre, insisting the boy be allowed to stay with his U.S. relatives.

Ros-Lehtinen visited Elián several times, even attending his birthday party, and her efforts received the ultimate accolade for a Cuban-American legislator — a direct personal attack from Cuba's state-run newspaper, Granma, which called her a "ferocious wolf disguised as a woman." She had "loba feroz" (shortened to "loba frz") stamped on a vanity license plate.

Ros-Lehtinen also has clashed with some in her party who have tried to push restrictive immigration policies. She opposed measures to overhaul the welfare system, curb illegal immigration and designate English as the official U.S. language. Ros-Lehtinen and fellow Floridian Lincoln Diaz-Balart, also a Cuban-American, were the only Republicans to vote against the final version of a welfare overhaul bill in 1996, warning of an "anti-immigrant sentiment."

Ros-Lehtinen often has been cold to lowering trade barriers, voting in 1995 against granting President Clinton the power to negotiate expedited trade agreements and in 2000 against permanently granting China normal trade status. She later reversed course, supporting fast-track trade negotiating authority for President Bush.

An educator by trade, Ros-Lehtinen fulfilled a 14-year dream by completing a doctorate in education in 2004. The topic of her dissertation — the perspectives of members of the House of Representatives on educational testing.

After growing up in Miami, Ros-Lehtinen became a teacher and ran a bilingual private school in South Florida. In 1982, at age 30, she was the first Hispanic elected to the state legislature.

In a 1989 special election to replace the late Democratic Rep. Claude Pepper, Ros-Lehtinen easily defeated three other candidates for the Republican nomination. With generous support from the national party, she went on to beat Democrat Gerald Richman, a Jewish Miami Beach lawyer with limited political experience. Stressing her support for Israel, she traveled there during the campaign. But her victory, with 53 percent of the vote, was narrower than expected.

She prepared well for her re-election a year later, and several formidable Democrats declined to challenge her. She won with 60 percent that year. Reapportionment in 2002 gave her a more demographically diverse district that includes the Florida Keys, a prime tourist attraction. Ros-Lehtinen wanted the territory included because it is also a common destination for Cuban refugees seeking asylum in the United States.

KEY VOTES

2004
No Extend federal unemployment benefits by 13 weeks
No Pass $283.2 billion, six-year federal highway and mass transit bill
Yes Approve $146 billion multi-year extension of previously enacted middle-class tax breaks
? Amend the Constitution to prohibit same-sex marriage
No Cut corporate taxes $137 billion over 10 years
Yes Reorganize U.S. intelligence agencies as proposed by Sept. 11 commission

2003
Yes Cut taxes by $330 billion through fiscal 2013
No Block Bush rule scaling back overtime pay for some white-collar federal workers
Yes Do not allow use of search warrants without first notifying subjects
No Allow importation of prescription drugs
Yes Create private school voucher program in Washington, D.C.
Yes Ban "partial birth" abortion except to save a woman's life
No Split $18.6 billion in Iraq aid into half-grant, half-loan
Yes Overhaul Medicare and create prescription drug benefit

CQ VOTE STUDIES

	PARTY UNITY		PRESIDENTIAL SUPPORT	
	Support	Oppose	Support	Oppose
2004	89%	11%	84%	16%
2003	93%	7%	96%	4%
2002	93%	7%	85%	15%
2001	94%	6%	87%	13%
2000	86%	14%	30%	70%

INTEREST GROUPS

	AFL-CIO	ADA	CCUS	ACU
2004	14%	15%	95%	80%
2003	13%	5%	90%	78%
2002	11%	10%	75%	88%
2001	17%	10%	86%	71%
2000	30%	15%	71%	64%

FLORIDA 18
Southeast — most of Miami; Florida Keys

The 18th features the glitz of downtown Miami and the southern part of Miami Beach, but its political base comes from the Latin-dominated areas west of downtown — although it gave up some Hispanic suburbs when a third GOP-leaning, Hispanic-majority South Florida district was drawn during redistricting following the 2000 census. From Miami, the 18th winds its way south along the coast and then follows U.S. 1 through the Florida Keys. More than three-fifths of the district's residents are Hispanic and many are stridently anti-Castro.

The district has a wide mix of areas, from the downtrodden sections of Little Havana to wealthy Coral Gables (home to the University of Miami), Key Biscayne and Fisher Island. Residents tend to be conservative on foreign policy issues but more in line with Democrats on welfare and other social issues. A strong economy that does not rely solely on tourism has translated into little opposition for incumbents, including Rep. Ros-Lehtinen, who has won easily here for more than a decade.

The Keys, particularly Key West, have a significant gay and lesbian population in addition to older natives who adhere to the independence and environmentalism of the "Conch Republic."

The Port of Miami and Miami International Airport, which is in the 21st District, are major transportation centers that feed thriving trade and tourism industries. Concerns about port security have mounted since Sept. 11, as has the Port of Miami's traffic, particularly with the Far East. The port's trade with China drastically increased from 2001 through 2004, and increases are expected to continue. Local officials are concerned the federal government will not provide enough funds to step up security to meet the needs of the port.

MAJOR INDUSTRY
Trade, transportation, tourism

CITIES
Miami (pt.), 270,214; Miami Beach (pt.), 75,172; Coral Gables, 42,249; Westchester, 30,271; Key West, 25,478; Coral Terrace, 24,380

NOTABLE
Little Havana dominoes players gather at "Domino Park" — actually named Maximo Gomez Park; A giant sculpted hand stretches out toward the sky at the Holocaust Memorial in Miami Beach.

Rep. Robert Wexler (D)

Elected 1996; 5th term

CAPITOL OFFICE
225-3001
www.house.gov/wexler
213 Cannon 20515-0919; fax 225-5974

COMMITTEES
International Relations
Judiciary

HOMETOWN
Boca Raton

BORN
Jan. 2, 1961, Queens, N.Y.

RELIGION
Jewish

FAMILY
Wife, Laurie Wexler; three children

EDUCATION
Emory U., attended 1978-79; U. of Florida, B.A. 1982
(political science); George Washington U., J.D.
1985

CAREER
Lawyer

POLITICAL HIGHLIGHTS
Fla. Senate, 1990-96

ELECTION RESULTS

2004 GENERAL

Robert Wexler (D)		unopposed

2004 PRIMARY

Robert Wexler (D)		unopposed

2002 GENERAL

Robert Wexler (D)	156,747	72.2%
Jack Merkl (R)	60,477	27.8%

PREVIOUS WINNING PERCENTAGES
2000 (72%); 1998 (100%); 1996 (66%)

Wexler has seldom seen a subject that doesn't merit a sound bite. Ever since he arrived on Capitol Hill, he has been a regular in front of the television cameras, advancing his views on subjects ranging from prescription drug prices to U.S. policy on Iraq to Palm Beach County's difficulties in administering elections in 2000 and 2002.

But it is on the subject of the Middle East that Wexler, who sits on the International Relations Committee, has been most vocal. A staunch defender of Israel, he applauded the Bush administration's insistence that the Palestinians oust Yasser Arafat and renounce terrorism. He also urges the administration to take tough actions against nations in the Middle East and South Asia — even erstwhile U.S. allies — when it is in the interest of the United States.

In the 108th Congress, he cosponsored the "Saudi Arabia Accountability Act," aimed at correcting what Wexler sees as the kingdom's non-cooperation in the war on terror. "There are substantial elements of the royal family that do not view the United States as an ally against terrorism," Wexler told the Miami Herald following a visit to the kingdom in 2003. "Saudi Arabia is a far greater threat to Americans than Iraq ever was."

For the Florida Democrat, whose district includes the heavily Jewish communities of Boca Raton and Palm Beach, Middle East policy is virtually local politics. "That is the stuff I love talking about," Wexler says.

Although he voted in October 2002 to authorize the use of military force against Iraq, Wexler has lambasted the Bush administration's handling of pre-war intelligence and its rationale for the conflict. "Iraq was not an imminent threat to America," he said. "There were no chemical, biological or nuclear weapons. . . . The only mushroom cloud resulting from the war in Iraq is that represented by the Bush administration's barrage of deception and lies."

Florida's voting problems in 2000 and 2002 infuriated Wexler. He filed lawsuits challenging the reliability of new touchscreen voting machines in the state and introduced legislation in Congress requiring all computerized voting machines to print paper receipts. Calling for an investigation into "glitches" in Florida's post-2000 system, Wexler told the Florida Attorney General that there is a "cloud of suspicion hanging over Tallahassee." After the 2004 election, Wexler asked Congress' Government Accountability Office to investigate voting irregularities.

Wexler has consistently fought against the Republican tax cuts. In 2003, he introduced a bill linking $87 billion in emergency military funding for Iraq "directly to a reduction in tax cuts that have already been passed." A year earlier, and again in the 108th, he proposed rescinding part of the $1.3 billion tax cut passed by Congress to pay for a $300 billion to $350 billion prescription drug program. The Democratic Party, Wexler said, "abdicates its responsibility when we criticize [President] Bush's tax cuts without having the courage to repeal it."

Wexler fought Bush's Medicare prescription drug plan with all his rhetorical might, and when the AARP, the nation's largest seniors group, decided to back the Bush initiative, Wexler introduced legislation lambasting the organization for "abandoning seniors by supporting the Republican Medicare prescription drug bill."

A member of the Judiciary Committee, Wexler first made a media splash during the Clinton impeachment. His staff estimates that he was interviewed on television about 100 times during the six months the impeachment wars raged in Congress. "I got to do in one term what it might have taken 10 terms to do," said Wexler, who rated it an almost entirely positive experience. Not everyone was a fan, however: Political writer Ronald Brownstein of the Los Angeles Times once labeled Wexler "the human advertisement for the mute button."

Wexler takes criticism in stride, even treating it at times as a badge of honor. He proudly noted that the National Rifle Association targeted him in the 2002 election campaign as one of the "F troop" of lawmakers whose voting records were given failing grades by the gun group. "If the NRA is afraid of me, then I must be doing a good job working to make America's streets safer," he said. In 2003, he introduced legislation making it illegal to sell an individual customer more than one firearm in a 30-day period.

Wexler is a frequent traveler. He serves as the top-ranking Democrat on the International Relations panel's Europe Subcommittee and has traveled to the continent to meet with NATO officials. He has visited India, Turkey and Taiwan and is the co-founder and co-chairman of the Taiwan and Turkey caucuses. Wexler also often flies back and forth between Saudi Arabia and Israel to engage in unofficial shuttle diplomacy.

Born in Queens, Wexler was 10 when his family moved to South Florida. After earning his law degree at George Washington University, he returned to Florida and practiced law in Boca Raton.

In 1990, he unseated a 16-year veteran of the state Senate. During the ensuing six years, Wexler won generally favorable reviews, but he also attracted criticism for some controversial proposals.

As chairman of the state Senate's Criminal Justice Committee, Wexler proposed castration (via a chemical process, not surgery) for two-time rapists and electrocution for a third rape conviction. He also proposed that women who gave birth to so-called cocaine babies be prevented from having more children. His castration-of-rapists bill was vehemently criticized. The head of the Florida chapter of the American Civil Liberties Union said, "He wants to adopt Islamic-style justice." But Wexler told the Orlando Sentinel, "What I'm proposing is just common sense."

When four-term Democratic Rep. Harry A. Johnston announced he would not seek re-election to his 19th District seat in 1996, Wexler leaped at the opening. In the ensuing four-way primary, he won a plurality of the vote, then handily defeated state Senate Majority Leader Peter Weinstein in the runoff. He rolled up two-thirds of the general-election vote against Republican Beverly Kennedy, a Pompano Beach financial consultant, and has won re-election easily since. In 2004, no Republican filed against him.

KEY VOTES

2004

Yes Extend federal unemployment benefits by 13 weeks

No Pass $283.2 billion, six-year federal highway and mass transit bill

Yes Approve $146 billion multi-year extension of previously enacted middle-class tax breaks

No Amend the Constitution to prohibit same-sex marriage

No Cut corporate taxes $137 billion over 10 years

Yes Reorganize U.S. intelligence agencies as proposed by Sept. 11 commission

2003

No Cut taxes by $330 billion through fiscal 2013

Yes Block Bush rule scaling back overtime pay for some white-collar federal workers

Yes Do not allow use of search warrants without first notifying subjects

Yes Allow importation of prescription drugs

No Create private school voucher program in Washington, D.C.

No Ban "partial birth" abortion except to save a woman's life

Yes Split $18.6 billion in Iraq aid into half-grant, half-loan

No Overhaul Medicare and create prescription drug benefit

CQ VOTE STUDIES

	PARTY UNITY		PRESIDENTIAL SUPPORT	
	Support	Oppose	Support	Oppose
2004	97%	3%	32%	68%
2003	97%	3%	22%	78%
2002	89%	11%	29%	71%
2001	94%	6%	27%	73%
2000	91%	9%	79%	21%

INTEREST GROUPS

	AFL-CIO	ADA	CCUS	ACU
2004	85%	95%	37%	0%
2003	100%	95%	27%	16%
2002	100%	100%	32%	9%
2001	100%	100%	30%	4%
2000	100%	85%	52%	17%

FLORIDA 19

Southeast – parts of Coral Springs, Margate and Boca Raton

Two-thirds of the heavily Democratic 19th's residents live in Palm Beach County and one-third live in Broward County, mostly west of Interstate 95, where subdivisions dot the landscape. The 19th stretches from West Palm Beach as far south as Margate and includes parts of Boca Raton and Deerfield Beach. Older, upper-middle-class residents make it one of the most educated and white-collar districts in the state.

More than three-fourths white, the 19th supports Democrats by overwhelming margins at the state and national levels. John Kerry won the district with 66 percent of the vote in the 2004 presidential election. Retirees, including many Jewish condominium residents, provide a consistent base of support throughout much of the district — his third-best showing in the state.

The 19th has the highest percentage of residents age 65 or older (30 percent) of any district in the nation, and elderly voters comprise more

than 80 percent of the electorate in the 19th's portion of Palm Beach County. Accordingly, the "condo commandos" who run condominium associations serve as local power brokers. Redistricting following the 2000 census removed some wealthy residents of gated communities in Boca Raton, adding to the 19th's Democratic tilt.

The portion of Boca Raton included in the 19th long has been home to corporate headquarters. Sensormatic Electronics Corp. (acquired by Tyco International in 2001) and Rexall Sundown, a vitamin producer, have major facilities there.

MAJOR INDUSTRY
Health care, electronics, financial services

CITIES
Coral Springs (pt.), 74,195; Margate (pt.), 42,284; Greenacres, 27,569; Tamarac (pt.), 25,756; Coconut Creek (pt.), 24,901

NOTABLE
A photo editor for The Sun, a supermarket tabloid, contracted the first fatal case of anthrax in 2001 while working at the newspaper's Boca Raton office; Boca Raton, known for its pink municipal buildings and the Spanish revival architecture of Addison Mizner, has started to paint its buildings a neutral color.

Rep. Debbie Wasserman-Schultz (D)

Elected 2004; 1st term

CAPITOL OFFICE
225-7931
www.house.gov/schultz

118 Cannon 20515-0920; fax 225-8456

COMMITTEES
Financial Services

HOMETOWN
Weston

BORN
Sept. 27, 1966, Queens, N.Y.

RELIGION
Jewish

FAMILY
Husband, Steve Schultz; three children

EDUCATION
U. of Florida, B.A. 1988 (political science), M.A. 1990 (political science)

CAREER
University program administrator; college instructor; state legislative aide

POLITICAL HIGHLIGHTS
Fla. House, 1992-2000 (Democratic leader pro tempore, 2000); Fla. Senate, 2000-04

ELECTION RESULTS

2004 GENERAL

Debbie Wasserman-Schultz (D)	191,195	70.2%
Margaret Hostetter (R)	81,213	29.8%

2004 PRIMARY

Debbie Wasserman-Schultz (D)	unopposed

A state legislator for a dozen years, Wasserman-Schultz made a name for herself as an outspoken liberal activist. Among the bills she sponsored was one to require dry cleaners to charge women the same prices as men.

Yet in terms of style, she promises a softer approach than that of her predecessor, Democrat Peter Deutsch, who left the seat open in 2004 to make a bid for the Senate. While Deutsch was known as a hard-driving partisan, Schultz tries to build relationships across party lines.

"Although I am liberal philosophically, I think you don't always have to wear that on your sleeve. There is a lot to be said in terms of being nice," says Wasserman-Schultz, who was Deutsch's chief of staff when he served in the state House. She says she "never really wanted to do anything other than be a member of a legislative body."

She intends to push for increased funding for a variety of health care and economic assistance measures. Homeland security also ranks as a top priority, as Florida is home to several of the nation's busiest seaports and is a major entry point for overseas visitors.

Early in 2005, she was a visible Democratic spokeswoman — both on the House floor and on television — in the debate over how to handle the case of a brain-damaged Florida woman, Terri Schiavo. Wasserman-Schultz argued that Congress should stay out of the family tragedy.

Even before she took office, Wasserman-Schultz was a team player: Unopposed in her primary and a shoo-in to hold the overwhelmingly Democratic 20th District, she donated $100,000 from her campaign treasury to help other House candidates during the 2004 cycle — exceeding amounts given even by many senior House Democrats. Once in office, she was named the freshman representative to the Democratic Steering Committee, which makes committee assignments.

Name recognition and an early fundraising push deterred any potential Democratic primary foes and her general-election win over Republican Margaret Hostetter, a social conservative activist, was never in doubt.

FLORIDA 20

Southeast – parts of Hollywood, Sunrise and Davie

Middle-class suburbs mix with beach communities as the 20th snakes through heavily Democratic territory in Broward and Miami-Dade counties from as far north as Village Park to as far south as Miami Beach. The district takes in a slice of Fort Lauderdale and accounts for about one-third of Broward's population, much of it in suburbs such as Sunrise, Plantation and Davie. Western Broward teems with shopping centers and development as many former Miami residents have moved north in search of suburban life.

Although it takes in those western Broward suburbs, the 20th wraps around the eastern side of the Miami area. It twists through portions of Hollywood and Hallandale and moves south into Aventura, with its growing community of young professionals, and North Miami before jumping the Intracoastal

Waterway to take in Bal Harbor and a chunk of Miami Beach.

Two-thirds of residents are white and about one-fifth are Hispanic. Some liberal-leaning areas, such as most of Wilton Manors, were added in redistricting following the 2000 census. Wilton Manors has a significant gay and lesbian community, and Dania Beach is becoming a more prominent gay resort area. Jewish retirees also contribute to the district's overall Democratic bent.

Davie, with its cattle ranches, has retained some of its rural feel. Plantation has more expensive homes and light industry. Democrats tend to win elections in Broward, where they rack up especially large margins in the 20th's parts of Sunrise and Lauderhill.

MAJOR INDUSTRY
Tourism, business services, retail

CITIES
Hollywood (pt.), 81,921; Sunrise (pt.), 71,670; Davie (pt.), 70,142; Plantation (pt.), 66,264

NOTABLE
Wilton Manors has a gay-majority city council.

Rep. Lincoln Diaz-Balart (R)

CAPITOL OFFICE
225-4211
www.house.gov/diaz-balart
2244 Rayburn 20515-0921; fax 225-8576

COMMITTEES
Rules

HOMETOWN
Miami

BORN
Aug. 13, 1954, Havana, Cuba

RELIGION
Roman Catholic

FAMILY
Wife, Cristina Diaz-Balart; two children

EDUCATION
U. of South Florida, B.A. 1976 (international relations); Case Western Reserve U., J.D. 1979

CAREER
Lawyer; state prosecutor

POLITICAL HIGHLIGHTS
Democratic nominee for Fla. House, 1982; Fla. House, 1986-89; Fla. Senate, 1989-92

ELECTION RESULTS

2004 GENERAL

Lincoln Diaz-Balart (R)	146,507	72.8%
Frank J. Gonzalez (LIBERT)	54,736	27.2%

2004 PRIMARY

Lincoln Diaz-Balart (R)	unopposed

2002 GENERAL

Lincoln Diaz-Balart (R)	unopposed

PREVIOUS WINNING PERCENTAGES
2000 (100%); 1998 (75%); 1996 (100%); 1994 (100%); 1992 (100%)

Elected 1992; 7th term

Diaz-Balart's politics are defined by his personal roots and his political base. He hails from a family of pre-revolution politicians in Cuba, and he represents an anti-Castro, Cuban-American community in south Florida. Fidel Castro has even sent spies to penetrate his district offices.

It is not only Castro whom Diaz-Balart (DEE-az ba-LART) and the three other Cuban-American members of the House — his congressman brother, Mario, their Republican colleague from Miami, Ileana Ros-Lehtinen, and Democrat Robert Menendez of New Jersey — are fighting. They also face growing pressures from farm-state lawmakers and others to lift the four-decade-old U.S. embargo on trade with Cuba.

"Those of us who want to keep the embargo as leverage to force a democratic transition are in a race against time," Diaz-Balart said in 2002.

So far, he has been able to count on steady support from the White House to withstand the assault. President Bush's political aides credited Diaz-Balart's Cuban-American constituents for putting Bush over the top in Florida in the 2000 presidential election. And they came through again for Bush in 2004, as Bush came through for them.

Bush's staunch anti-Castro stand has given Diaz-Balart and his compatriots the upper hand in the ongoing congressional battle over the embargo. In 2003, the White House threatened to veto the year-end catchall spending bill if a provision easing travel to Cuba, opposed by Diaz-Balart and his anti-Castro camp, was not deleted. The tactic worked; the provision was removed. A year later, during the height of the presidential campaign, GOP Rep. Jeff Flake of Arizona, leader of the drive to lift the travel ban, didn't even bother offering his proposal on the House floor. "We have been fighting Mr. Flake for years now," Diaz-Balart said. "He knows he doesn't have the votes this year. This is a great victory."

The victory held throughout 2004. All attempts to ease the trade embargo were blocked by White House veto threats.

Diaz-Balart's successes reached beyond the halls of Congress. In 2001, Attorney General John Ashcroft yielded to pleas from him and Ros-Lehtinen to try to strip Eriberto Mederos, a Cuban-American in Miami, of his U.S. citizenship for allegedly torturing political prisoners at a psychiatric hospital in Havana in the 1970s. It was the first such case in more than two decades.

Diaz-Balart is a skillful inside player; drawing on his background as a prosecutor, he can be persuasive in face-to-face meetings. He is a key operator in the arcane world of House rules and congressional organization. He is the second-ranking Republican on the Rules Committee, where he has a say in setting the ground rules for debate on the House floor. He may well be in line to chair the panel in the 110th Congress.

Because of his Rules Committee assignment, Diaz-Balart frequently leads House floor debates, a plus for Republicans eager to showcase one of only four Hispanic members of their party in the House in the 109th Congress.

Like all Rules members, Diaz-Balart is a dependable party loyalist on most issues. He also is an effective fundraiser for the GOP; in 2004, he ponied up $200,000 for the House Republicans' major campaign fundraising effort.

Diaz-Balart has used his influence as a GOP insider — and the competition between the parties to woo Hispanic voters — to push for liberalized immigration policies that he says are the "great unifier" among all Latinos, not just Cuban-Americans. This is a plus in a district that includes a substantial number of other Latinos.

He played a key role during the 107th Congress in persuading House GOP leaders to drop efforts to make it more difficult for legal immigrants to obtain food stamps. He also has sought to forestall U.S. deportation of thousands of refugees from Central and South America.

But in the 108th and early in the 109th, Diaz-Balart was in the distinct minority of House Republicans who opposed homeland security-related legislation to crack down on illegal immigrants and tighten restrictions on asylum. He was one of eight House Republicans who voted against a 2004 bill that contained the immigration language Diaz-Balart opposed. That language was later dropped, but resurfaced in a measure passed by the House in early 2005, with Diaz-Balart again voting with the minority in opposition.

Florida's Cuban-American community is heavily Republican, but the working-class nature of his constituency can lead Diaz-Balart to stray from the GOP line on occasion. He was one of the few GOP House candidates in 1994 who declined to sign the "Contract With America" campaign platform, and he has bucked his party on a number of social programs, including the 1996 welfare overhaul, which imposed new restrictions on benefits to legal as well as illegal immigrants.

Diaz-Balart's grandfather, father and uncle served in Cuba's House before the family fled to the United States in 1959, the year of the revolution, when the future congressman was 5 years old. His father's sister was married to Castro in the late 1940s and early 1950s, but they divorced and there was a political falling-out between the families long before Castro took control.

After law school, Diaz-Balart worked for a Miami legal services organization that provided free legal help for the poor. He served as a Dade County prosecutor in the early 1980s under Janet Reno, whom he frequently criticized during her time as attorney general under President Clinton.

A Democrat when he first ran, unsuccessfully, in 1982 for the Florida Legislature, Diaz-Balart was a co-chairman of the Democrats for Reagan campaign in Florida in 1984 and switched to the GOP in 1985, easily winning a state House seat in 1986. He served three years in the House and three in the state Senate.

When the courts redrew Florida's congressional maps after the 1990 census, a second Hispanic-majority district was created. Diaz-Balart easily bested a fellow Cuban-American state senator in a two-way Republican primary. He drew no Democratic foe that November, and since then has been re-elected with little or no competition.

KEY VOTES

2004

No	Extend federal unemployment benefits by 13 weeks
No	Pass $283.2 billion, six-year federal highway and mass transit bill
Yes	Approve $146 billion multi-year extension of previously enacted middle-class tax breaks
?	Amend the Constitution to prohibit same-sex marriage
No	Cut corporate taxes $137 billion over 10 years
Yes	Reorganize U.S. intelligence agencies as proposed by Sept. 11 commission

2003

Yes	Cut taxes by $330 billion through fiscal 2013
No	Block Bush rule scaling back overtime pay for some white-collar federal workers
No	Do not allow use of search warrants without first notifying subjects
No	Allow importation of prescription drugs
Yes	Create private school voucher program in Washington, D.C.
Yes	Ban "partial birth" abortion except to save a woman's life
No	Split $18.6 billion in Iraq aid into half-grant, half-loan
Yes	Overhaul Medicare and create prescription drug benefit

CQ VOTE STUDIES

	PARTY UNITY		PRESIDENTIAL SUPPORT	
	Support	Oppose	Support	Oppose
2004	90%	10%	91%	9%
2003	95%	5%	94%	6%
2002	94%	6%	87%	13%
2001	94%	6%	88%	12%
2000	84%	16%	35%	65%

INTEREST GROUPS

	AFL-CIO	ADA	CCUS	ACU
2004	7%	10%	84%	83%
2003	13%	5%	90%	71%
2002	14%	15%	83%	88%
2001	8%	5%	86%	84%
2000	40%	20%	65%	56%

FLORIDA 21
Southeast — most of Hialeah and Kendall

The Hispanic-dominated 21st is a dependable Republican district that includes middle-class suburbs in central-west Miami-Dade County, from part of Miami Lakes in the north through most of Hialeah in its center and much of Kendall to the south. It includes one-fourth of Miami-Dade's population and a slice of southwestern Broward County. Traditionally, the district's politics center around opposition to Fidel Castro. But economic and foreign policy conservatism are balanced somewhat by residents' more moderate views on labor and social policy matters.

Many residents commute from Hialeah, a vibrant, blue-collar residential area filled with Cuban-Americans, to other parts of the 21st. Transportation-related businesses, including Carnival Cruise Lines, have set up facilities close to Miami International Airport, which was moved into the 21st during redistricting following the 2000 census. Officials say the area is well-positioned to capitalize on trade pacts with Latin American countries.

The 21st also picks up parts of Miramar and Pembroke Pines, which boast many young professionals from Latin America. South Florida's healthy economic scene during the 1990s meant more jobs and homes for the 21st and neighboring districts.

The district's large, suburban Cuban-American community accounts for its Republican bent in statewide and federal elections. Few areas in Florida are as heavily Republican as Hialeah, which has a large contingent of elderly Cuban-American voters and which gave Republican Gov. Jeb Bush more than 80 percent of the vote in the 2002 election. Bob Dole only narrowly won the district in 1996, but George W. Bush carried the 21st by 16 percentage points in 2000 and by 14 points in 2004.

MAJOR INDUSTRY
Trade, technology, small business

CITIES
Hialeah (pt.), 208,552; Kendall (pt.), 59,676; Pembroke Pines (pt.), 54,426; Fountainbleau (pt.), 52,244; Country Club, 36,310; University Park, 26,538

NOTABLE
Hialeah boasts 15,000 multilingual businesses; Amelia Earhart's final flight began in 1937 in Hialeah.

Rep. E. Clay Shaw Jr. (R)

Elected 1980; 13th term

CAPITOL OFFICE
225-3026
shaw.house.gov
1236 Longworth 20515-0922; fax 225-8398

COMMITTEES
Ways & Means
(Trade - chairman)
Joint Taxation

HOMETOWN
Fort Lauderdale

BORN
April 19, 1939, Miami, Fla.

RELIGION
Roman Catholic

FAMILY
Wife, Emilie Shaw; four children

EDUCATION
Stetson U., B.S. 1961 (business); U. of Alabama,
M.B.A. 1963 (accounting); Stetson U., J.D. 1966

CAREER
Nurseryman; lawyer; city prosecutor

POLITICAL HIGHLIGHTS
Fort Lauderdale associate municipal judge, 1969-
71; Fort Lauderdale City Commission, 1971-73; vice
mayor of Fort Lauderdale, 1973-75; mayor of Fort
Lauderdale, 1975-81

ELECTION RESULTS

2004 GENERAL

E. Clay Shaw Jr. (R)	192,581	62.8%
Robin Rorapaugh (D)	108,258	35.3%
Jack McLain (CNSTP)	5,260	1.7%

2004 PRIMARY

E. Clay Shaw Jr. (R)	unopposed

2002 GENERAL

E. Clay Shaw Jr. (R)	131,930	60.8%
Carol Roberts (D)	83,265	38.4%

PREVIOUS WINNING PERCENTAGES
2000 (50%); 1998 (100%); 1996 (62%); 1994 (63%);
1992 (52%); 1990 (98%); 1988 (66%); 1986 (100%);
1984 (66%); 1982 (57%); 1980 (55%)

With President Bush's desire for a revamping of the Social Security system in his second term, Shaw may find himself in great demand. He represents one of the largest percentages of elderly constituents of any congressman and has long been a weather vane on the issue of overhauling Social Security. Although he clung to his seat in 2000 by only 599 votes, Shaw continued the politically charged debate about Social Security's future and won re-election handily in 2004.

Shaw has been a central figure in the debate for years, particularly as chairman of the Ways and Means Subcommittee on Social Security from 1999-2005. The 108th Congress was his last holding that gavel, but he remains a member of the subcommittee and does not plan to step back from the debate. "I probably know more about Social Security than just anyone else in Congress. I'm not going to let all of that go to waste," he said.

He now takes the helm at the Trade Subcommittee and is among the four Republicans most often mentioned as candidates to succeed Chairman Bill Thomas of California, who would be required by GOP term limits to yield the Ways and Means gavel in 2007. "I can work with people, put people together and get deals done," Shaw says when asked about the characteristics that would make him a good chairman.

A lawyer as well as an accountant, Shaw has earned a reputation in the House for mastering complex topics involving taxation and pensions, and he has made a concerted effort to explain his proposals to the seniors in his district, where one in five residents is 65 or older. "It's not something I can run from, as many members do," he said.

His 63 percent landslide in 2004 was eased by redistricting, but Shaw's continued success in the district has chipped away at the idea that touting an overhaul for Social Security, the federal retirement income benefit, constitutes a third rail of politics. He acknowledges that an overhaul is "not going to be a slam dunk" but expresses hope that his constituents are beginning to warm to it once they understand the reasons for a change.

Nevertheless, Republican proposals to allow workers to invest some of their payroll taxes in individual investment accounts went nowhere in the 108th as a tough election season was ramping up. The president's re-election, however, cleared away some of the political concerns about tackling an overhaul of the entitlement program.

If Bush does endorse Shaw's proposal — to move Social Security into a system of private accounts while still paying current benefits — as part of his "ownership society" platform, members of his party may still be reluctant to take on the $1 trillion, 10-year estimated cost of the plan at a time of record deficits.

In the 108th, Shaw also sought to reduce fraud in the Social Security system with a bill that would protect Social Security beneficiaries from abuses by "representative payees" — surrogates appointed by the Social Security Administration who manage the financial affairs of almost 7 million recipients of the benefits. The legislation, which also bars benefit payments to illegal immigrants and felons, was signed into law early in 2004. Despite broad agreement on the bill, Shaw drew the ire of Texas Democrats who opposed a provision closing a loophole that had allowed state government workers — many of whom do not pay into the Social Security system — to qualify for larger Social Security survivor benefits when a spouse dies.

Shaw, who began receiving his own Social Security benefits when he turned 65 in 2004, holds much of the GOP's institutional memory on another major social policy change: the 1996 rewrite of the welfare system. As chairman of the Ways and Means Human Resources Subcommittee in the 104th Congress, he was one of the lawmakers who molded President Clinton's promise to "end welfare as we know it" into the 1996 law that almost all Republicans and many Democrats supported. Although he no longer chairs the panel that oversees welfare, Shaw was an important behind-the-scenes force in urging Congress to preserve most of those changes as it worked to update the law in 2003.

He endorsed Bush's proposal to impose a longer, 40-hour workweek requirement to qualify for welfare benefits, without counting vocational training, and shepherded that bill through the House. The bill hit snags in the Senate and the reauthorization will have to be considered again in the 109th Congress.

His work on welfare was in keeping with Shaw's reputation for trying to craft legislation that will attract bipartisan backing. During the lengthy and often contentious welfare debate of the 104th Congress, Shaw made sure Democrats' viewpoints got a fair hearing. But he also helped advance the GOP position that localities and states should have more authority over welfare policy, a view anchored in his 12 years' experience in municipal government, including six years as the mayor of Fort Lauderdale.

Shaw was operated on for lung cancer in January 2003, but the procedure did not slow him down much: He spent his recovery time lobbying colleagues for a provision in the 2002 wrap-up spending law to have the government assume the estimated $20 million cost of cleaning up anthrax contamination at a tabloid newspaper company in Boca Raton that was the target of mail sabotage in 2001. Also close to home, Shaw helped secure more than $10 billion in disaster relief funding for recovery efforts from four hurricanes in 2004 that devastated wide swaths of the state.

After stints as a municipal judge, city commissioner, vice mayor and mayor of Fort Lauderdale, Shaw was unopposed for the GOP nomination when he first ran for the House in 1980. He capitalized on Democratic squabbling to secure what was then the 12th District. Democratic primary voters dumped 70-year-old Rep. Edward J. Stack for a younger candidate, former state Rep. Alan Becker. Bragging that during his tenure as mayor he had cut spending, broadened the economic base and helped give Fort Lauderdale a more cosmopolitan image, Shaw won with 55 percent of the vote.

He was re-elected relatively easily until 2000, when Democratic state Rep. Elaine Bloom pounced on his plan for revising Social Security.

KEY VOTES

2004
No   Extend federal unemployment benefits by 13 weeks

No   Pass $283.2 billion, six-year federal highway and mass transit bill

Yes   Approve $146 billion multi-year extension of previously enacted middle-class tax breaks

Yes   Amend the Constitution to prohibit same-sex marriage

Yes   Cut corporate taxes $137 billion over 10 years

Yes   Reorganize U.S. intelligence agencies as proposed by Sept. 11 commission

2003
Yes   Cut taxes by $330 billion through fiscal 2013

No   Block Bush rule scaling back overtime pay for some white-collar federal workers

Yes   Do not allow use of search warrants without first notifying subjects

Yes   Allow importation of prescription drugs

Yes   Create private school voucher program in Washington, D.C.

Yes   Ban "partial birth" abortion except to save a woman's life

No   Split $18.6 billion in Iraq aid into half-grant, half-loan

Yes   Overhaul Medicare and create prescription drug benefit

CQ VOTE STUDIES

	PARTY UNITY		PRESIDENTIAL SUPPORT	
	Support	Oppose	Support	Oppose
2004	93%	7%	82%	18%
2003	94%	6%	93%	7%
2002	93%	7%	92%	8%
2001	92%	8%	95%	5%
2000	87%	13%	31%	69%

INTEREST GROUPS

	AFL-CIO	ADA	CCUS	ACU
2004	13%	10%	100%	80%
2003	13%	10%	90%	76%
2002	11%	10%	95%	88%
2001	8%	10%	100%	76%
2000	0%	10%	80%	68%

FLORIDA 22
Southeast – coastal Broward and Palm Beach counties, parts of Fort Lauderdale and Boca Raton

The 22nd follows picturesque Route A1A down the Southeast coast from northern Palm Beach County to Fort Lauderdale in Broward County. Although its projections reach inland in places to pick up middle-class suburbs and gated communities, the district is mostly identifiable by its upscale beachfront cities and towns, including parts of Boca Raton. The 22nd no longer has the highest percentage of elderly residents in the state after redistricting following the 2000 census, but one-fifth of its population is 65 or older.

The district's residents are mostly well-off and overwhelmingly white. Republicans count Palm Beach, Pompano Beach and Fort Lauderdale as their base. Many of the old 22nd's Democratic strongholds — including all of the district's territory in Miami-Dade County — were excised during redistricting to help bolster GOP candidates here.

Both Palm Beach, where a majority of residents live, and Broward

counties lean Democratic, but redistricting lassoed in enough Republican precincts to transform the 22nd from a Democratic-leaning district that favored Al Gore by 21 percentage points in the 2000 presidential election into a politically competitive battleground that would have backed Gore by just 5 points. In 2004, John Kerry won the 22nd by only 2 percentage points. Rep. Shaw, who won by fewer than 600 votes under the old lines in 2000, captured more than 60 percent of the vote in the new district in 2002 and 2004.

Exclusive hotels and shopping centers lie within the district, while the ports of Palm Beach and Fort Lauderdale attract shipping and cruise line business. The area's elderly population supports several large hospitals. The wealth of many district residents helps insulate them from economic pressures, but the area depends heavily on tourism.

MAJOR INDUSTRY
Health care, tourism, shipping

CITIES
Fort Lauderdale (pt.), 61,509; Boca Raton (pt.), 55,946; Coral Springs (pt.), 43,354; Pompano Beach (pt.), 34,925; Palm Beach Gardens (pt.), 30,649

NOTABLE
The International Swimming Hall of Fame Museum is in Fort Lauderdale.

Rep. Alcee L. Hastings (D)

Elected 1992; 7th term

CAPITOL OFFICE
225-1313
alceehastings.house.gov
2353 Rayburn 20515-0923; fax 225-1171

COMMITTEES
Rules
Select Intelligence

HOMETOWN
Miramar

BORN
Sept. 5, 1936, Altamonte Springs, Fla.

RELIGION
African Methodist Episcopal

FAMILY
Divorced; three children

EDUCATION
Fisk U., B.S. 1958 (zoology & botany); Howard U., attended 1958-60 (law); Florida A&M U., J.D. 1963

CAREER
Judge; lawyer

POLITICAL HIGHLIGHTS
Sought Democratic nomination for U.S. Senate, 1970; U.S. District Court judge, 1979-89; Democratic nominee for Fla. secretary of state, 1990

ELECTION RESULTS

2004 GENERAL

Alcee L. Hastings (D)		unopposed

2004 PRIMARY

Alcee L. Hastings (D)	49,284	74.2%
Keith A. Clayborne (D)	17,106	25.8%

2002 GENERAL

Alcee L. Hastings (D)	96,347	77.5%
Charles Laurie (R)	27,986	22.5%

PREVIOUS WINNING PERCENTAGES
2000 (76%); 1998 (100%); 1996 (73%); 1994 (100%); 1992 (59%)

A charismatic charmer and vocal partisan, Hastings has had more than his share of political lives. He is well known as a champion of liberal causes, an inside player in the House and an expert on overseas elections. But any biography of Hastings will also include his House impeachment in 1988 and his removal from office as a federal trial court judge for allegedly extorting a bribe.

Hastings' partisan penchants are visible in almost all of his statements in the House. When the GOP leadership at the end of the 108th Congress brought to the floor a catchall spending bill that wrapped together nine appropriations bills, Democrats complained they were forced to vote quickly without being able to read the massive bill's entire text. "This process smells," Hastings said. "And the odor wafts from sea to shining sea."

Two hours before President Bush gave his 2005 State of the Union address, Hastings released a statement challenging the president "to focus on helping those most in need." He said the president "should inform the wealthy that they're going to have to make do with what they've got for a while." And then, Hastings added, the president should "tell the corporations and executives who bankrolled his re-election campaign and record-breaking $40 million inauguration spectacle that America's no longer for sale."

Hastings is one of four Democrats on the powerful Rules Committee. He uses the seat on Rules to unleash his fiery oratorical style to protest the substance of Republican legislation as well as the floor procedures pushed by the GOP leadership. When his committee protests are in vain, as they often are, Hastings takes his anger out to the House floor and often sets the rhetorical tone for the Democratic side of the debate.

Hastings is the second-ranking Democrat on the Intelligence Committee. On Intelligence, his questions were among the most pointed in the House about the veracity of the Bush administration's intelligence assessments of Iraq's possession of weapons of mass destruction. Hastings has also pushed for more cultural and ethnic diversity in recruiting new spies. The House version of the 2004 intelligence authorization bill included a Hastings amendment to create a pilot project to improve recruitment of minorities and women to intelligence agencies.

Hastings is interested in overseas cooperation and justice. He led a bipartisan coalition of 27 House members in calling on the Justice Department to settle the "Hungarian Gold Train" case in which Holocaust survivors held claims on assets taken from them by the Nazis. The case was settled in 2004, to Hastings' satisfaction. He said the settlement provided an opportunity for the United States "to once again confirm its leadership in ensuring that Holocaust survivors receive proper restitution for their losses."

In the summer of 2004, Hastings was appointed president of the Organization for Security and Cooperation in Europe, a 55-nation organization of mostly European nations that focuses on security issues, ranging from arms control and diplomacy to human rights and election monitoring.

As a liberal Democrat from Florida, Hastings was none too happy with the results of the past two presidential elections. In the 107th Congress, he led a walkout by members of the Congressional Black Caucus to protest President George W. Bush's victory over Al Gore, who, as vice president, presided over the House's formal election session. "We did all we could,"

Hastings called out to Gore. "The chair thanks the gentleman from Flori-da," the vice president replied with a smile. Hastings was also among the 31 House members to vote to challenge the results of Ohio's 2004 presi-dential vote, and thus the presidential election, when the electoral votes were counted in Congress.

Hastings arrived in the House in 1993 determined to impress the law-makers who had impeached him five years before as courteous, respect-ful and hard-working. "Succeeding is the best revenge," he once said. "My goal was to get beyond people viewing me as an impeached judge."

To that end, he concentrated on issues of particular concern to his con-stituents — funding for Medicare, job training, Head Start and sugar sub-sidies — and on developing an expertise in foreign affairs. The congress-man's local activism includes resisting what he sees as efforts by some white Florida Democrats to shift the state party to a right-of-center stance, diminishing the influence of black voters. He has several times urged blacks to consider voting for Republicans as a means of sending the party a signal that it should not take black support for granted.

The only child of under-educated parents who mostly toiled as domes-tic workers, Hastings earned a degree in zoology and botany at Fisk Uni-versity and was accepted to medical school, but he chose to pursue a law career instead.

In 1979, President Carter nominated him to fill a U.S. District Court seat in Miami and he became the first black federal judge in Florida. In 1983, a jury acquitted Hastings of charges that he solicited a $150,000 bribe in exchange for granting a lenient sentence, but a federal judicial panel later concluded he had lied and made up evidence to secure that verdict. The vote was 413-3 in the House to impeach him and 69-26 in the Senate to remove him from office. In 1997, by which time Hastings was in his third term in the House, there were reports that the FBI had misled Congress and the courts on forensic tests used as evidence in the case and that an agent had falsely testified against Hastings.

Though he lost a bid for Florida secretary of state in 1990, two years later Hastings won a majority in the precincts of the new 23rd District, drawn for the 1990s with a slight black majority. State Rep. Lois Frankel, a liberal white Democrat, took 35 percent of the vote to his 28 percent in the primary, but Hastings won the nomination in a runoff with 58 percent. He prevailed in November with 59 percent against GOP real estate developer Ed Fielding, and in his six subsequent re-elections he has never polled below 73 percent. He was unopposed in the 2004 general election.

KEY VOTES

2004
Yes   Extend federal unemployment benefits by 13 weeks
No   Pass $283.2 billion, six-year federal highway and mass transit bill
No   Approve $146 billion multi-year extension of previously enacted middle-class tax breaks
?   Amend the Constitution to prohibit same-sex marriage
Yes   Cut corporate taxes $137 billion over 10 years
?   Reorganize U.S. intelligence agencies as proposed by Sept. 11 commission

2003
No   Cut taxes by $330 billion through fiscal 2013
Yes   Block Bush rule scaling back overtime pay for some white-collar federal workers
Yes   Do not allow use of search warrants without first notifying subjects
Yes   Allow importation of prescription drugs
No   Create private school voucher program in Washington, D.C.
No   Ban "partial birth" abortion except to save a woman's life
Yes   Split $18.6 billion in Iraq aid into half-grant, half-loan
No   Overhaul Medicare and create prescription drug benefit

CQ VOTE STUDIES

	PARTY UNITY		PRESIDENTIAL SUPPORT	
	Support	Oppose	Support	Oppose
2004	97%	3%	23%	77%
2003	96%	4%	23%	77%
2002	93%	7%	27%	73%
2001	91%	9%	18%	82%
2000	95%	5%	82%	18%

INTEREST GROUPS

	AFL-CIO	ADA	CCUS	ACU
2004	92%	55%	21%	0%
2003	100%	100%	19%	17%
2002	100%	95%	42%	0%
2001	100%	100%	29%	8%
2000	100%	80%	55%	4%

FLORIDA 23
Southeast — parts of Fort Lauderdale, West Palm Beach and Lauderhill

One of two black-majority districts in the state, the heavily Democratic 23rd stretches westward from working-class Fort Pierce to the eastern shores of Lake Okeechobee and back east toward some of the coastal hubs, such as West Palm Beach and Fort Lauderdale. Most residents live in Broward County, and much of the area west of Interstate 95 is rural and unpopulated. A significant portion of the Everglades was added to the 23rd in redistricting following the 2000 census. The eastern borders of the 23rd tend to be several blocks off the coast, with the neighboring 22nd taking in much of the prime beachfront property.

Most urban areas in the 23rd — such as Lauderhill, Lauderdale Lakes, Riviera Beach and portions of West Palm Beach — contain largely black neighborhoods and attract local government employees, educators and other middle-class professionals. The 23rd is growing more diverse, drawing in people from around the world. Hispanics make up 14 percent of the population. Citrus, sugar cane and rice growers work the large but sparsely populated rural portions of the district. The 23rd lacks a major employment sector, and the vulnerability of citrus crops to bad weather contributes to making it one of the poorest districts in the state. Luckily the area was spared the worst of the 2004 hurricanes.

Democrats outnumber Republicans by a ratio of nearly 4-to-1, and voters routinely give Democratic candidates more than 75 percent of the vote in competitive statewide elections. Indeed, many heavily black precincts — including some in western Fort Lauderdale and Lauderdale Lakes — give Democratic candidates more than 90 percent of the vote. Overall, the district gave John Kerry 78 percent of the presidential vote in 2004.

MAJOR INDUSTRY
Agriculture, local government, small business

CITIES
Fort Lauderdale (pt.), 57,387; West Palm Beach (pt.), 52,330; Lauderhill (pt.), 47,371; North Lauderdale, 32,264; Lauderdale Lakes (pt.), 30,895

NOTABLE
Lake Okeechobee, part of which is in the 23rd, is the second-largest freshwater lake contained wholly within the United States; Lauderdale Lakes has more than 20 churches within its four square miles.

Rep. Tom Feeney (R)

Elected 2002; 2nd term

CAPITOL OFFICE
225-2706
www.house.gov/feeney
323 Cannon 20515-0924; fax 226-6299

COMMITTEES
Financial Services
Judiciary
Science

HOMETOWN
Oviedo

BORN
May 21, 1958, Abington, Pa.

RELIGION
Presbyterian

FAMILY
Wife, Ellen Stewart Feeney; two children

EDUCATION
Pennsylvania State U., B.A. 1980 (political science); U. of Pittsburgh, J.D. 1983

CAREER
Lawyer

POLITICAL HIGHLIGHTS
Fla. House, 1990-94; Republican nominee for lieutenant governor, 1994; Fla. House, 1996-2002 (Speaker, 2000-02)

ELECTION RESULTS

2004 GENERAL
Tom Feeney (R)		unopposed

2004 PRIMARY
Tom Feeney (R)		unopposed

2002 GENERAL
Tom Feeney (R)	135,576	61.8%
Harry Jacobs (D)	83,667	38.2%

Brash and ambitious, Feeney is a new star in the House Republican Party. He is sometimes compared to Tom DeLay, the hardball-playing majority leader, and he has his eye on bigger prizes in Washington, perhaps a spot in the leadership or a Senate seat. Infatuated with politics since grade school, when Richard Nixon was his hero, Feeney rose to power at a precocious pace in the Florida Legislature, ultimately becoming House Speaker and a pal of Republican Gov. Jeb Bush, the president's brother.

Feeney's talent for a pithy quote gets him more than the usual share of national media exposure for one new to Capitol Hill. He also has the attention of senior GOP leaders. A prolific fundraiser, Feeney in his first term was named to the executive committee of the National Republican Congressional Committee, which helps elect fellow Republicans.

A self-described "Reagan Republican," Feeney is conservative on social issues; he favors prayer in the schools and opposes abortion even in cases of rape. But he says he has a libertarian streak on economic and regulatory policy. He is a favorite of both the Christian Coalition and the Club for Growth, an influential conservative group advocating lower taxes and smaller government. In his office, Feeney keeps an early edition of economist Adam Smith's seminal 1776 book "Wealth of Nations."

His belief in a limited role for government led to his joining only 24 other House Republicans in voting against President Bush's top domestic priority in 2003, an expansion of Medicare that added a prescription drug benefit to the government's health care program for the elderly and the disabled. The political pressure was immense. Feeney turned down a personal entreaty from Bush over the phone as the president hastened home from a foreign trip to salvage his bill during a squeaker, predawn vote.

Feeney's revolt was lauded by leading conservatives outside of Congress, but he sacrificed his Eagle Scout image with the leadership. He also bucked his party for reasons of fiscal restraint during the 2003 debate on funding for the stabilization of Iraq. Though he ultimately voted for Bush's aid package, he called for making part of it a loan that would have to be repaid with proceeds from Iraq's oil reserves. In early 2005, he helped lead opposition to the size of another of a series of special spending bills for Iraq.

A sharp legislative tactician thanks to his years in the statehouse, Feeney is unfazed by the nitty-gritty of legislating. In 2003, he shepherded to completion a bill favored by Judiciary Chairman F. James Sensenbrenner Jr. of Wisconsin that curbed judicial discretion in sentencing. Dubbed the Feeney Amendment, it was staunchly opposed by the American Bar Association and the American Civil Liberties Union and was even criticized by Supreme Court Chief Justice William H. Rehnquist. Getting it signed into law was an accomplishment for a freshman. In the 109th Congress, the matter is once again on Feeney's radar screen after an early 2005 Supreme Court ruling rendered federal sentencing guidelines optional for judges. Feeney called the court's decision "egregious."

Feeney also was picked by Attorney General John Ashcroft to sponsor a bill giving federal investigators power to obtain the records of terrorism suspects without search warrants. The bill was loudly booed by civil libertarians, including some in the Republican Party.

With the proposed retirement of the space shuttle beginning in 2010, Feeney's district, which is home to the Kennedy Space Center, stands to lose thousands of jobs. Despite his advocacy of a lean federal budget, he is a big booster of Bush's call for manned missions to the moon and to Mars, which potentially could replace lost jobs on the Space Coast.

Feeney grew up in Glenside, a suburb of Philadelphia, the son of a community college dean and elementary school teacher. He played ice hockey and got hooked on politics at age 10, after portraying Nixon in a mock school election in 1968.

Liberalism may have been the fashionable campus philosophy during Feeney's undergraduate years at Penn State, but he was enamored of a California Republican named Ronald Reagan. After graduation, he chose a law school — the University of Pittsburgh — for its reputation for turning out prominent Pennsylvania politicians. But with only middling grades in law school, Feeney abandoned his political plans and moved to Florida, where the economy was booming. He became a real estate lawyer, and his wife, Ellen, his law school sweetheart, became an engineer with a space contractor. The couple had two children.

Politics was still a fascination, however. "I was unsure whether a transplanted Yankee could make it in the Deep South," Feeney recalls. "Then I get to Orlando and find out everybody's a transplanted Yankee." At age 32, he won his first election, to the Florida House in 1990.

Feeney's political career took off after he caught the eye of Jeb Bush, who was being talked about as a future governor and was leading an effort to establish government vouchers for education in Florida, which happened to be Feeney's top issue.

In 1994, Bush picked Feeney to join him on the ticket as his lieutenant governor, though Feeney's legislative experience stretched a mere four years. Bush lost that time, but he and Feeney forged a strong political bond. Bush eventually became governor, and in 2000 Feeney rose to Florida House Speaker. He cemented his friend-of-the-Bushes status in the famously contested 2000 presidential election. After the state Supreme Court ruled against Bush, Feeney asserted that the House had the power to appoint presidential electors for Bush. The U.S. Supreme Court later gave Bush the victory, rendering Feeney's move unnecessary.

When Florida got two new congressional seats as a result of reapportionment in 2000, Feeney used his power as House Speaker to make sure one of the new districts was tailor-made for him. Despite a ferocious contest with Democrat Harry Jacobs, a personal-injury lawyer, Feeney won with a comfortable 62 percent of the vote. The campaign was highly negative, with Feeney calling Jacobs an ambulance-chaser and Jacobs questioning Feeney's ethics. He was unopposed in the 2004 election.

KEY VOTES

2004
No	Extend federal unemployment benefits by 13 weeks
No	Pass $283.2 billion, six-year federal highway and mass transit bill
Yes	Approve $146 billion multi-year extension of previously enacted middle-class tax breaks
Yes	Amend the Constitution to prohibit same-sex marriage
Yes	Cut corporate taxes $137 billion over 10 years
No	Reorganize U.S. intelligence agencies as proposed by Sept. 11 commission

2003
Yes	Cut taxes by $330 billion through fiscal 2013
No	Block Bush rule scaling back overtime pay for some white-collar federal workers
No	Do not allow use of search warrants without first notifying subjects
No	Allow importation of prescription drugs
Yes	Create private school voucher program in Washington, D.C.
Yes	Ban "partial birth" abortion except to save a woman's life
Yes	Split $18.6 billion in Iraq aid into half-grant, half-loan
No	Overhaul Medicare and create prescription drug benefit

CQ VOTE STUDIES

	PARTY UNITY		PRESIDENTIAL SUPPORT	
	Support	Oppose	Support	Oppose
2004	99%	1%	88%	12%
2003	98%	2%	91%	9%

INTEREST GROUPS

	AFL-CIO	ADA	CCUS	ACU
2004	7%	0%	100%	100%
2003	8%	10%	93%	96%

FLORIDA 24

East central — Orlando suburbs, part of Space Coast

Created following the 2000 census, the 24th takes in much of the area between the Republican-leaning Orlando suburbs and the so-called Space Coast, drawing nearly equally from Orange, Seminole and Volusia counties, with just a bit less than one-fifth of its population coming from its portion of Brevard County.

Fashioned out of slices of the old Republican-held 7th, 8th and 15th districts, the 24th is a potentially competitive district with a small but distinct Republican lean. The GOP nominee has won each of the last four presidential contests here. George W. Bush captured 52 percent of the vote in 2000 and then increased his percentage by 4 points in 2004.

The Space Coast, home of the Kennedy Space Center, is an economic driver in the region, providing a tourist attraction and a base for technology companies. Space shuttle flights were scheduled to resume in 2005, more than two years after the *Columbia* shuttle disaster.

North of the Space Coast are popular beach communities and the city of Daytona Beach, most of which is in the neighboring 7th District. College students and bikers flock to Daytona's famous coastline during spring and summer.

The 24th takes in one of Daytona Beach's jewels — Daytona International Speedway, which is home to NASCAR's Daytona 500 stock car race.

The district, which has a relatively young population for Florida, sweeps west to pick up suburban communities outside Orlando, including most of Altamonte Springs and all of Oviedo.

MAJOR INDUSTRY
Aerospace, technology, tourism

CITIES
Port Orange, 45,823; Titusville, 40,670; Altamonte Springs (pt.), 30,130; Oviedo, 26,316; Deltona (pt.), 22,510

NOTABLE
Star Systems, an electronic payments network utilizing ATMs and retailers, is based in Maitland (shared with the 7th).

Rep. Mario Diaz-Balart (R)

Elected 2002; 2nd term

CAPITOL OFFICE
225-2778
www.house.gov/mariodiaz-balart
313 Cannon 20515-0925; fax 226-0346

COMMITTEES
Budget
Transportation & Infrastructure

HOMETOWN
Miami

BORN
Sept. 25, 1961, Fort Lauderdale, Fla.

RELIGION
Roman Catholic

FAMILY
Wife, Tia Diaz-Balart

EDUCATION
U. of South Florida, attended 1979-82

CAREER
Marketing firm executive; mayoral aide

POLITICAL HIGHLIGHTS
Fla. House, 1988-92; Fla. Senate, 1992-2000;
Fla. House, 2000-02

ELECTION RESULTS

2004 GENERAL

Mario Diaz-Balart (R)		unopposed

2004 PRIMARY

Mario Diaz-Balart (R)		unopposed

2002 GENERAL

Mario Diaz-Balart (R)	81,845	64.7%
Annie Betancourt (D)	44,757	35.4%

Not yet 45, Diaz-Balart describes anything positive as "awesome" or "cool." He is the next generation Cuban-American lawmaker, and though his views on Cuba are as passionately anti-Castro as those of his older and better-known brother, House Republican Lincoln Diaz-Balart of Florida, his focus is elsewhere. He is more interested in issues such as expanding the availability of health insurance and reining in government spending.

Although his brother was born in Cuba and lived there until the Diaz-Balart (DEE-az ba-LART) family was forced into exile by Fidel Castro, Mario was born in Fort Lauderdale. His district is heavily Cuban, but less so than the two other Hispanic-majority districts in South Florida, represented by Lincoln and fellow Republican Ileana Ros-Lehtinen. Mario Diaz-Balart's constituents are roughly half Cuban-American and are a mix of city dwellers, suburbanites, farmers and Latino immigrant families.

As a Florida House member heading the legislature's post-census reapportionment in 2000, Diaz-Balart drew the district himself, carving out a Republican slice of Miami-Dade County and rural areas to the west. Non-Cubans in gated communities miles from Miami's borders initially objected to being included, so Diaz-Balart has had to win over constituents who care more about their tax brackets than Castro.

Diaz-Balart wants to promote a conservative Hispanic voice in the House on immigration and other issues. In his first term, he started the Congressional Hispanic Conference, intended to be a counterweight to the liberal-dominated Congressional Hispanic Caucus, which has about 20 members. The new group has just seven, and about half are Portuguese-American lawmakers the Census Bureau does not consider to be Hispanic.

During the 2003 battle over President Bush's nomination of Miguel Estrada to a federal judgeship, Diaz-Balart led efforts to build support for the Honduran-born nominee in the House. "Left-wing Democrats are trying to define what it means to be Hispanic," he said. Estrada dropped his bid after a filibuster by Senate Democrats. But the happy result for Diaz-Balart was a burst of national television exposure and the chance to impress GOP leaders.

In 2005, Diaz-Balart joined other Cuban-American lawmakers in breaking ranks with the leadership and voting with Democrats against a bill that tightened rules for immigrants trying to obtain asylum.

Diaz-Balart is typical of the energetic, idealistic newcomers ready to take on entrenched political interests dependent on federal spending. He says cutting waste and fraud in government spending is a priority, along with increased access to health insurance. He advocates establishing a $3,000 tax credit for people who buy their own policies.

An important parochial topic is the $7.8 billion Everglades restoration project. Within his district are vast tracts of Florida swamp, including Everglades National Park. The U.S. Army Corps of Engineers project seeks to restore an ecosystem that little by little has been destroyed by development.

Diaz-Balart faced his first tough test as a junior House member in 2003 when senior Republicans on the Appropriations Committee restricted release of Everglades money — and he was unaware of the threat until the bill was less than 24 hours from a scheduled floor vote. His brother, who is close to House GOP leaders and sits on the Rules Committee, held up the bill while Mario scurried to assuage concerns about the mammoth project. He was able to reopen the funding spigot — a close call that gave him a victory to tout back home.

He is quick-talking and gregarious in contrast to the more reserved Lincoln. The two are among four sibling pairs in Congress; the others are House Democrats Linda T. and Loretta Sanchez of California, Colorado Democrats Sen. Ken Salazar and Rep. John Salazar and Sen. Carl Levin and Rep. Sander M. Levin, both Michigan Democrats.

To some degree, Diaz-Balart will always be influenced by the politics of his family, sometimes called the Cuban Kennedys. His father, Rafael Diaz-Balart, was once majority leader of the Cuban House, and his aunt was Castro's first wife and mother of his son. The Diaz-Balarts were a wealthy and politically prominent family under Cuban leader Fulgencio Batista, before Castro toppled Batista's government in 1959. Their home was looted and burned as the family vacationed in Paris.

Author Ann Louise Bardach described the Diaz-Balarts' relationship with Castro this way: "The principal players are all related. You have this 45-year political conundrum, plus a family blood feud on top of it." Mario Diaz-Balart once told The Miami Herald: "We didn't go to sporting events. We talked politics. We'd have lunches or dinners at people's homes and talk about history. That's how we grew up. That's how we are."

The youngest of four brothers, Diaz-Balart entered the family industry early. He dropped out of the University of South Florida to work for the campaign of Miami Mayor Xavier Suarez. In 1988, he was elected to the Florida House, and four years later, to the state Senate. As the Senate's chief budget writer, he advocated deep cuts in spending.

Forced out of the Senate by term limits in 2000, he ran successfully to return to the state House, which was not the step back it appeared to be. Florida got two new seats in Congress as a result of the once-a-decade census. Diaz-Balart was appointed by Florida House Speaker Tom Feeney to head the panel drawing a new congressional map. In some old-fashioned logrolling, Diaz-Balart drew a Hispanic-majority district for himself and another GOP-leaning district in central Florida that Feeney ultimately won.

Still, Diaz-Balart drew a serious challenger in his first House race. Annie Betancourt, a Democratic state representative and also a Cuban-American, challenged him in a contest that became a referendum on Cuba policy. Diaz-Balart supported the status quo of sanctions while Betancourt, although equally anti-Castro, called for loosening economic and travel restrictions.

Diaz-Balart outspent Betancourt 6-to-1, and his tough talk on Castro appealed to Cuban-American voters. He won with 65 percent of the vote. In the 2004 election two years later, he was unopposed.

KEY VOTES

2004

No   Extend federal unemployment benefits by 13 weeks

No   Pass $283.2 billion, six-year federal highway and mass transit bill

Yes   Approve $146 billion multi-year extension of previously enacted middle-class tax breaks

?   Amend the Constitution to prohibit same-sex marriage

No   Cut corporate taxes $137 billion over 10 years

Yes   Reorganize U.S. intelligence agencies as proposed by Sept. 11 commission

2003

Yes   Cut taxes by $330 billion through fiscal 2013

No   Block Bush rule scaling back overtime pay for some white-collar federal workers

No   Do not allow use of search warrants without first notifying subjects

No   Allow importation of prescription drugs

Yes   Create private school voucher program in Washington, D.C.

Yes   Ban "partial birth" abortion except to save a woman's life

No   Split $18.6 billion in Iraq aid into half-grant, half-loan

Yes   Overhaul Medicare and create prescription drug benefit

CQ VOTE STUDIES

	PARTY UNITY		PRESIDENTIAL SUPPORT	
	Support	Oppose	Support	Oppose
2004	94%	6%	94%	6%
2003	97%	3%	98%	2%

INTEREST GROUPS

	AFL-CIO	ADA	CCUS	ACU
2004	7%	5%	95%	96%
2003	7%	10%	93%	88%

FLORIDA 25
South – western Miami-Dade County, the Everglades

The 25th takes in a broad swath of land covering the western portion of Miami-Dade County, most of Collier County and almost all of Monroe County. One of two seats Florida gained following the 2000 census, it is geographically centered in Everglades National Park and Big Cypress National Preserve.

The district was constructed to elect a Republican of Cuban descent. A majority of residents are Hispanic — many of them Cuban-American — and Republicans have a 41 percent to 34 percent registration edge over Democrats. Although Bill Clinton won the district's area with a plurality in his 1996 re-election bid, Republicans have won the area in most statewide elections, especially those involving members of the Bush family. The 2004 presidential election was no different, as George W. Bush won the district with 56 percent of the vote.

Nearly 90 percent of the district's population lives in Miami-Dade County,

much of it on the western edge of the Miami region and in communities south of the city.

National parks give the 25th an ecosystem and an array of wildlife — everything from manatees to panthers — not commonly found in North America. Restoration of the Everglades, oil drilling and the pace of development promise to remain contentious issues here for some time.

Republican support for a hard line against Fidel Castro-led Cuba has helped the GOP forge a longstanding alliance with South Florida's large Cuban-American community.

MAJOR INDUSTRY
Tourism

CITIES
Kendale Lakes, 56,901; Tamiami, 54,788; The Hammocks, 47,379; Kendall West, 38,034; South Miami Heights, 33,522; Homestead, 31,909

NOTABLE
Everglades National Park covers 1.5 million acres — which is just a small portion of the Everglades; The Coral Castle, located in Homestead, is a castle made from 1,100-tons of coral.

GEORGIA

Gov. Sonny Perdue (R)

First elected: 2002
Length of term: 4 years
Term expires: 1/07
Salary: $128,903
Phone: (404) 656-1776

Hometown: Bonaire
Born: Dec. 20, 1946; Perry, Ga.
Religion: Baptist
Family: Wife, Mary Perdue; four children
Education: U. of Georgia, D.V.M. 1971
Military Service: Air Force, 1971-74
Career: Fertilizer and grain business owner; veterinarian
Political highlights: Houston County Planning and Zoning Board, 1978-90; Ga. Senate, 1991-2001 (president pro tempore, 1997-99)

Election results:
2002 GENERAL
Sonny Perdue (R)	1,042,221	51.4%
Roy Barnes (D)	937,335	46.2%
Garrett Hayes (LIBERT)	47,968	2.4%

Lt. Gov. Mark Taylor (D)

First elected: 1998
Length of term: 4 years
Term expires: 1/07
Salary: $84,748
Phone: (404) 656-5030

STATE LEGISLATURE

General Assembly: January-March, limit of 40 days

House: 180 members, 2-year terms
2005 breakdown: 99R, 80D, 1I; 143 men, 37 women
Salary: $16,524
Phone: (404) 656-0305

Senate: 56 members, 2-year terms
2005 breakdown: 34R, 22D; 49 men, 7 women
Salary: $16,524
Phone: (404) 656-0028

STATE TERM LIMITS

Governor: 2 terms
House: No
Senate: No

URBAN STATISTICS

CITY	POPULATION
Atlanta	416,474
Augusta-Richmond County	199,775
Columbus	186,291
Savannah	131,510
Athens-Clarke County	101,489

REGISTERED VOTERS

Voters do not register by party.

POPULATION

2004 population (est.)	8,829,383
2000 population	8,186,453
1990 population	6,478,216
Percent change (1990-2000)	+26.4%
Rank among states (2004)	9

Median age	33.4
Born in state	57.8%
Foreign born	7.1%
Violent crime rate	505/100,000
Poverty level	13%
Federal workers	93,207
Military	96,952

REDISTRICTING

Georgia gained two House seats in reapportionment. The legislature drew a new, 13-district map, which the governor signed on Oct. 1, 2001.

MISCELLANEOUS

Web: www.georgia.gov
Capital: Atlanta
STATE ELECTION OFFICIAL
(404) 656-2871
DEMOCRATIC HEADQUARTERS
(404) 870-8201
REPUBLICAN HEADQUARTERS
(404) 257-5559

District Statistics

DIST.	2004 VOTE FOR PRESIDENT BUSH	KERRY	WHITE	BLACK	ASIAN	HISP	MEDIAN INCOME	WHITE COLLAR	BLUE COLLAR	SERVICE INDUSTRY	OVER 64	UNDER 18	COLLEGE EDUCATION	RURAL	SQ. MILES
1	68%	31%	71%	23%	1%	4%	$36,158	53%	32%	15%	11%	28%	18%	42%	11,232
2	53	46	50	44	1	3	$29,354	50	33	17	12	28	14	41	9,724
3	56	44	56	40	1	3	$31,433	49	34	17	12	26	13	51	10,915
4	28	71	32	53	4	9	$49,307	67	20	13	8	25	36	0	251
5	27	72	34	56	2	6	$39,725	68	17	15	9	22	37	0	252
6	70	29	83	7	4	5	$75,611	80	11	9	7	28	51	2	435
7	73	26	82	7	4	5	$63,455	69	21	10	6	29	32	14	1,195
8	73	27	83	13	1	2	$52,406	61	28	12	9	27	23	42	3,512
9	72	27	81	14	1	3	$39,987	53	34	13	12	26	19	66	6,947
10	76	23	85	3	1	9	$42,031	51	38	11	10	26	16	48	3,741
11	55	44	62	28	1	7	$37,582	52	34	14	11	26	17	28	3,701
12	46	53	52	42	1	3	$31,108	54	29	18	11	25	19	26	5,224
13	37	62	42	41	5	10	$43,429	56	30	14	7	28	19	8	777
STATE	58	41	63	28	2	5	$42,433	59	27	13	10	27	24	28	57,906
U.S.	50.7	48.3	69	12	4	13	$41,994	60	25	15	12	26	24	21	3,537,438

www.cq.com

275

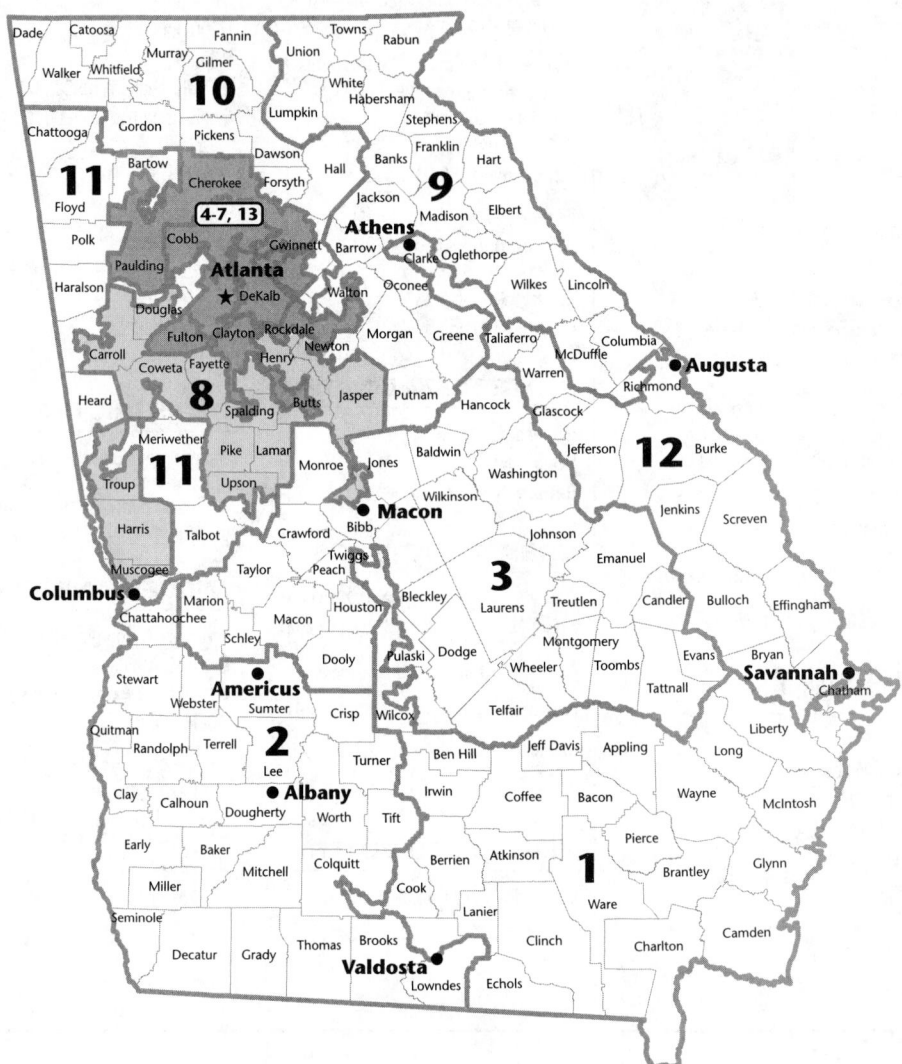

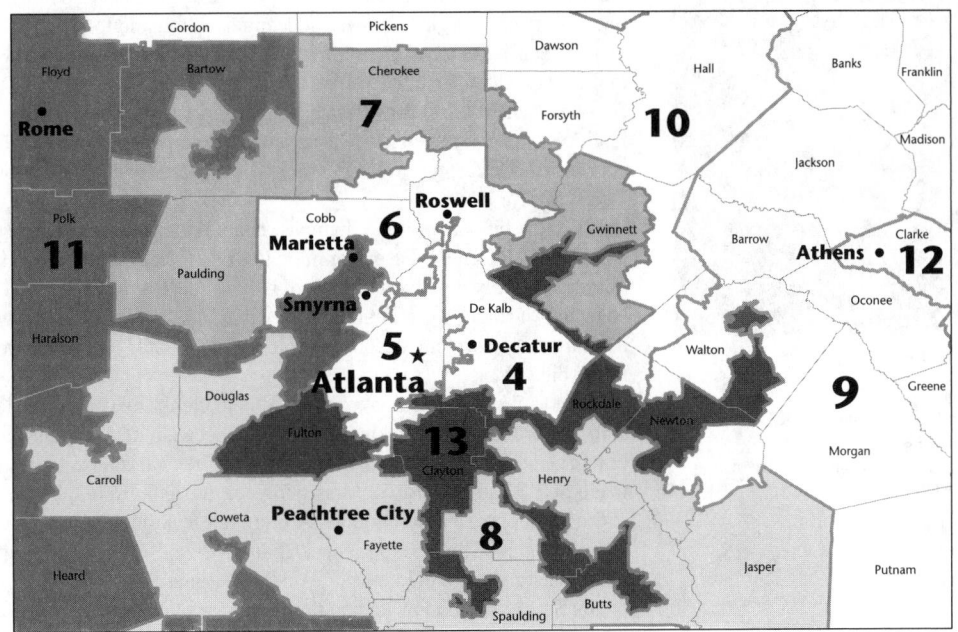

Sen. Saxby Chambliss (R)

Elected 2002; 1st term

CAPITOL OFFICE
224-3521
chambliss.senate.gov
416 Russell 20510-1005; fax 224-0103

COMMITTEES
Agriculture, Nutrition & Forestry - chairman
Armed Services
Rules & Administration
Select Intelligence
Joint Printing

HOMETOWN
Moultrie

BORN
Nov. 10, 1943, Warrenton, N.C.

RELIGION
Episcopalian

FAMILY
Wife, Julianne Chambliss; two children

EDUCATION
Louisiana Tech U., attended 1961-62; U. of
Georgia, B.B.A. 1966 (business administration);
U. of Tennessee, J.D. 1968

CAREER
Lawyer; hotel owner; firefighter; construction
worker

POLITICAL HIGHLIGHTS
Sought Republican nomination for U.S. House,
1992; U.S. House, 1995-2003

ELECTION RESULTS

2002 GENERAL

Saxby Chambliss (R)	1,071,352	52.7%
Max Cleland (D)	932,422	45.9%
Claude Thomas (LIBERT)	27,830	1.4%

2002 PRIMARY

Saxby Chambliss (R)	300,371	61.1%
Bob Irvin (R)	132,132	26.9%
Robert "Bob" Brown (R)	59,109	12.0%

PREVIOUS WINNING PERCENTAGES
2000 House Election (59%); 1998 House Election
(62%); 1996 House Election (53%); 1994 House
Election (63%)

After just two years in the Senate, Chambliss ascended to the helm of the Agriculture Committee in the 109th Congress, helped by the retirement of another senator and by his eight years of seniority in the House. He is in a better spot than ever to steer federal resources to his agriculture-heavy home state of Georgia, a grower of peanuts, cotton and tobacco.

The chairman's gavel gives him a key role in negotiations over revisions to the $249 billion farm bill that was passed in 2002. Chambliss (full name: SAX-bee CHAM-bliss) is especially concerned about peanut farmers, who he thinks were wronged in the farm law. The old peanut subsidy program was ended and farmers were guaranteed no more than coverage of their losses for five years.

When the bill was written, Chambliss chaired the House Agriculture Sub-committee on General Farm Commodities and Risk Management. He was not afraid to mix it up with leaders of his own party when the interests of Georgia's farmers were at stake. But Chambliss was unable to save the peanut subsidy system, despite his role as a negotiator on the final version of the bill.

The former small-town lawyer was able to climb the committee leadership ladder relatively quickly in the Senate because Republicans ahead of him in seniority held other leadership posts. The chairmanship came open when Sen. Thad Cochran of Mississippi left Agriculture to take the gavel of the higher-profile Appropriations Committee, clearing the way for Chambliss. Given his House experience, Chambliss said, "I feel very confident of my background and knowledge on these issues."

His Senate promotion was no doubt helped by the fact that in 2002 he secured one of the most important Republican victories by defeating incumbent Democrat Max Cleland. He quickly positioned himself in the Senate as a loyal GOP foot soldier, eager to help advance President Bush's legislative agenda. He supported the president and his party 98 percent of the time on pivotal votes in the 108th Congress.

And he picked up where he left off in the House — advocating generous spending on the military, prodding the government's spy agencies and defending federal help for Southern farmers.

Chambliss took assignments to three committees, Armed Services, Intelligence and Agriculture, directly paralleling those he had in the House. He also was named to the Rules and Administration Committee, which tends to the Senate's logistical needs. For a time, he was on the Judiciary Committee and immersed himself in advancing Bush's nominees for the federal judiciary, one of the most polarizing items on the closely divided Senate's agenda in the run-up to the 2004 election. He left that committee at the outset of the 109th Congress.

On Armed Services, Chambliss looks out for the needs of the state's 13 military installations, which have blossomed since World War II, thanks in part to a nearly continuous presence of a Georgian on the committee. Cleland spent his one term on the panel — and was insufficiently attentive to Georgia's needs, in the view of candidate Chambliss. Cleland succeeded Sam Nunn, who chaired the panel for eight years ending in 1994; before him, Richard B. Russell was the chairman at the height of the Cold War in the 1950s and 1960s.

Chambliss wants to protect Georgia facilities from future rounds of base closings. As a civic activist before coming to Congress, he helped keep

www.cqpress.com

Robins Air Force Base open during an earlier, 1993 round. And as a House member, he tussled with GOP leaders and President Clinton over a proposal to keep Texas and California maintenance bases functioning rather than closing them and moving the work to Georgia, which was planned as part of the 1995 round.

When Chambliss headed the Judiciary Subcommittee on Immigration, Border Security and Citizenship in the 108th Congress, he quietly worked to help businesses by making it easier for foreigners with high-technology backgrounds to get visas.

He added to the fiscal 2005 catchall spending bill a provision that allowed more foreign graduate students at American universities to work in the United States. Another provision aimed to stop abuses by employers finding novel ways of getting around limits on the number of foreign workers they can bring into the country.

An avid quail, duck and dove hunter, Chambliss is a member of the Congressional Sportsmen's Caucus and sponsored legislation to establish a federal policy to promote hunting. In the year after college, Chambliss worked as a firefighter and as a construction worker to pay for law school. Other items on his civic résumé include coaching YMCA basketball and Little League baseball. He was a second-baseman on the University of Georgia baseball team.

The son of an Episcopal priest, Chambliss says his family's frequent moves when he was a boy helped him learn to make friends quickly, an asset in his political career. Chambliss spent more than two decades in business and with civic groups in southern Georgia, where he was an attorney specializing in agriculture law, a motel owner in Moultrie and an activist in local economic development efforts.

Chambliss lost his first bid for public office, when in 1992 he sought the Republican nomination to challenge Democratic Rep. J. Roy Rowland. But when Rowland retired in 1994, Chambliss captured an easy pickup for the GOP in that landslide year by defeating Democrat Craig Mathis, a lawyer and the son of former Rep. Dawson Mathis. He was the first Republican to represent the rural middle Georgia district since Reconstruction.

Having passed on entreaties that he run for the Senate against Democrat Zell Miller in 2000, he lost a four-way race that fall to become House Budget Committee chairman, setting the stage for him to challenge Cleland. Three days after the Sept. 11, 2001, terrorist attacks, Chambliss' nascent Senate campaign got an important boost when he was picked by Speaker J. Dennis Hastert to chair a new Intelligence Subcommittee on Terrorism and Homeland Security. The panel was assigned one of the hottest topics on the national agenda — recommending ways the CIA, FBI and National Security Agency could prevent future attacks.

However, Chambliss had one slip that could have cost him dearly in the election had he not turned things around. In an offhand remark viewed as insensitive, he quipped that one route to security would be for local sheriffs to "arrest every Muslim that comes across the state line."

Nevertheless, Chambliss went on the attack against Cleland on the terrorism issue, alleging that the incumbent had gone soft on defense by opposing portions of Bush's plans for a Department of Homeland Security. Chambliss was criticized by Democrats who said he unfairly impugned Cleland as unpatriotic. Although Chambliss had been recruited by the White House, many doubted that he could defeat Cleland, a moderate and one of the most prominent disabled veterans of the Vietnam War. Chambliss' focused campaign, combined with a massive Republican voter turnout effort, propelled him to victory by an unexpectedly wide 7 percentage point margin.

KEY VOTES

2004

No	Pass $318.9 billion, six-year highway and mass transit bill
No	Extend assault weapons ban for 10 years
No	Restore pay-as-you-go rules for new tax cuts and entitlement spending
Yes	Criminalize harm to a fetus in an attack on the mother
No	Increase mandatory child care funding to states by $6 billion over five years
Yes	Amend the Constitution to prohibit same-sex marriage
Yes	Approve $146 billion multi-year extension of previously enacted middle-class tax breaks
Yes	Reorganize U.S. intelligence agencies as proposed by Sept. 11 commission
?	Cut corporate taxes $137 billion over 10 years

2003

No	Delay Bush changes to Clean Air Act
Yes	Allow confirmation vote on Miguel A. Estrada to the U.S. Court of Appeals for the D.C. Circuit
No	Block a Bush proposal opening Alaska's Arctic National Wildlife Refuge to oil drilling
No	Limit size of Bush's proposed tax cut to $350 billion through fiscal 2013
Yes	Overhaul Medicare and create prescription drug benefit
No	Block Bush rule scaling back overtime pay for some white-collar federal workers
Yes	Split $20 billion in Iraq aid into half-grant, half-loan
Yes	Ban "partial birth" abortion except to save a woman's life
Yes	Stop proposal allowing travel to Cuba
Yes	Allow final vote on energy policy overhaul

CQ VOTE STUDIES

	PARTY UNITY		PRESIDENTIAL SUPPORT	
	Support	Oppose	Support	Oppose
2004	99%	1%	100%	0%
2003	97%	3%	97%	3%
House Service:				
2002	98%	2%	90%	10%
2001	98%	2%	93%	7%
2000	95%	5%	24%	76%
1999	94%	6%	26%	74%
1998	95%	5%	22%	78%
1997	96%	4%	26%	74%
1996	96%	4%	35%	65%
1995	98%	2%	17%	83%

INTEREST GROUPS

	AFL-CIO	ADA	CCUS	ACU
2004	0%	5%	93%	96%
2003	15%	5%	91%	90%
House Service:				
2002	0%	0%	90%	100%
2001	17%	0%	95%	100%
2000	0%	0%	90%	91%
1999	33%	10%	80%	80%
1998	0%	0%	94%	96%
1997	0%	5%	88%	88%
1996	0%	0%	100%	100%
1995	0%	0%	100%	96%

Sen. Johnny Isakson (R)

Elected 2004; 1st term

CAPITOL OFFICE
224-3643
www.isakson.senate.gov
120 Russell 20510-1006; fax 228-2090

COMMITTEES
Environment & Public Works
Health, Education, Labor & Pensions
   (Employment & Workplace Safety - chairman)
Small Business & Entrepreneurship
Veterans' Affairs

HOMETOWN
Marietta

BORN
Dec. 28, 1944, Atlanta, Ga.

RELIGION
Methodist

FAMILY
Wife, Dianne Isakson; three children

EDUCATION
U. of Georgia, B.B.A. 1966

MILITARY SERVICE
Ga. Air National Guard, 1966-72

CAREER
Real estate company president

POLITICAL HIGHLIGHTS
Candidate for Cobb County Commission, 1974;
Ga. House, 1977-90 (Republican leader, 1983-90);
Republican nominee for governor, 1990; Ga.
Senate, 1993-96; sought Republican nomination
for U.S. Senate, 1996; Ga. Board of Education
chairman, 1996-99; U.S. House, 1999-2005

ELECTION RESULTS

2004 GENERAL

Johnny Isakson (R)	1,864,202	57.9%
Denise L. Majette (D)	1,287,690	40.0%
Allen Buckley (LIBERT)	69,051	2.1%

2004 PRIMARY

Johnny Isakson (R)	346,670	53.3%
Herman Cain (R)	170,370	26.2%
Mac Collins (R)	133,952	20.6%

PREVIOUS WINNING PERCENTAGES
2002 House Election (80%); 2000 House Election
(75%); 1999 Special House Election (65%)

A pragmatic consensus-builder who has demonstrated a taste for bipartisan dealmaking, Johnny Isakson combines a staunchly conservative outlook with a quiet, even-tempered style. His years as a leader in Georgia politics and then in the House were characterized by a passion for education reform, which has made him a leading driver in Congress for President Bush's education policy.

Elected to the Senate in 2004, he was one of the Republican Party's heroes who expanded their majority to a comfortable 55 seats. Isakson came with experience on Capitol Hill. He was the House member who succeeded GOP firebrand Newt Gingrich when the Speaker was forced out of power by his own party.

The Atlanta-bred Isakson resolutely resists political labels, and his record and background make him difficult to pigeonhole. He considers himself a "compassionate conservative" and says that Republicans have no monopoly on good ideas. He is regarded as a loyal GOP vote, but has broken with his party on some bedrock issues. For instance, he has voted for the abortion rights position in some cases, opposing a constitutional amendment to ban abortion and voting to permit abortions in U.S. military facilities overseas provided the patient pays for the procedure.

Isakson affiliates with the Republican Main Street Partnership, a group of moderate GOP lawmakers who say they favor a pragmatic center within the Republican Party. "Johnny is not an extremist. Johnny is a moderate," former Georgia Gov. Roy Barnes, a Democrat, told The Atlanta Journal-Constitution.

Isakson is a multimillionaire real estate agency executive who is generally pro-business, but he says that corporate America deserved what it got with the added regulation of the Sarbanes-Oxley accounting overhaul. "Labels become clothes, and the next thing, it's your wardrobe, and the next thing, you're voting to fulfill your wardrobe rather than what your heart and your head tells you," Isakson says. "I like to think through every issue. And I'm not going to be like a lemming marching over the cliff to fulfill a generic description."

Isakson proved his consensus-building mettle in the House, where he helped push for compromise in the contentious debate over Bush's No Child Left Behind initiative. The legislation tied federal aid to schools to improvements in student performance on annual standardized tests. As a member of a House-Senate committee that negotiated the final version of the bill, Isakson persuaded colleagues to give schools more flexibility in using federal money and to allow them to transfer money among a variety of programs.

Chairman of the Georgia Board of Education from 1996 to 1999, Isakson got his preferred assignment on the Senate's Health, Education, Labor and Pensions Committee, where he chairs the Employment and Workplace Safety Subcommittee. In the 109th Congress, he was also appointed to the Environment and Public Works Committee, the Veterans' Affairs panel and the Small Business and Entrepreneurship Committee.

His passion for schools comes from a childhood steeped in deep respect for education, instilled by a parent who never completed his own schooling. Isakson's father, Edwin Andrew Isakson, who dropped out of high school, often told his son he was destined to be the first Isakson ever to attend college. As the two would walk from one end of the Georgia Tech campus to the other to attend football games, Isakson's father would point to the buildings and say, "One day, you're going to go to a school like this."

Though he is a conservative, Isakson says he is not a slave to ideology. He sides faithfully with GOP leaders on tax-cutting bills, and his background as a wealthy executive puts him on the side of business in most cases. At other times, he is more fiscally conservative than his Republican leaders. Isakson rails at every opportunity against the widely accepted practice of larding spending measures with last-minute earmarks — often called "pork" — to smooth enactment of the annual appropriations bills. He registered his opposition in the House by voting against catchall spending measures, which he argued made it easier to stuff pet projects into the federal budget. He introduced a bill mandating that negotiators submit a list 24 hours before floor action of all 11th-hour items added to spending bills.

Isakson opposes gun control, and on national security issues, is a strong Bush defender. As the House debated in 2002 whether to authorize the administration to use force against Iraq, Isakson called Bush's approach a "doctrine of liberation."

Isakson began his focus on education early in his House career. Though he was the lowest-ranking Republican on the Education and the Workforce Committee in the 106th Congress, he was the driving force behind a party proposal to help states pay for federally mandated school modernization costs like asbestos removal and outfitting buildings for disabled students. Committee Republicans were resisting Democratic proposals for the federal government to shoulder the cost of school repairs, but recognizing the potential political impact of the school construction issue, Isakson persuaded Republican leaders they would lose the debate without their own proposal.

Meanwhile, he kept an eye on district concerns as most House members must. Isakson promoted federal grants for programs like one in Dalton, Ga., in which Mexican teachers are hired to teach immigrant students who cannot speak English. And he used his other committee assignment, on the Transportation and Infrastructure panel, to get more money for traffic-clogged Atlanta. He also badgered Georgia officials to bring Atlanta into compliance with the Clean Air Act, a requirement for restoring the highway funds.

Isakson has cut a national profile only recently, but he has long been a fixture in Georgia politics. He was in the Georgia General Assembly for 17 years, and in 1990, was the GOP candidate for governor. He was defeated by the incumbent, Zell Miller, the Democrat whom he replaced in the Senate.

When Gingrich resigned under fire from his Republican colleagues after the party's loss of seats in the 1998 midterm elections, Isakson was the state schools chairman and the immediate front-runner to succeed Gingrich. With huge advantages in name identification and campaign funds, Isakson took 65 percent of the vote against five opponents in the special election in 1999. He cruised to easy re-election wins in 2000 and 2002.

In 2004, Isakson was forced again to battle the "liberal" label, beating back primary challenges from two more-conservative Republicans — businessman Herman Cain and 8th District Rep. Mac Collins. Isakson took 53 percent of the vote, enough to avoid a run-off. He handily beat his Democratic opposition, former Rep. Denise L. Majette, with 58 percent of the vote.

Isakson and Saxby Chambliss, the state's senior senator, share a friendship that dates back to their days as students at the University of Georgia in 1962. "We know a lot on each other we can never tell," Isakson says with a smile, noting that their sorority-sister wives also have been fast friends since 1963. Chambliss helped in Isakson's unsuccessful campaign for governor against Miller.

KEY VOTES

House Service:
2004

No   Extend federal unemployment benefits by 13 weeks

No   Pass $283.2 billion, six-year federal highway and mass transit bill

Yes   Approve $146 billion multi-year extension of previously enacted middle-class tax breaks

Yes   Amend the Constitution to prohibit same-sex marriage

Yes   Cut corporate taxes $137 billion over 10 years

Yes   Reorganize U.S. intelligence agencies as proposed by Sept. 11 commission

2003

Yes   Cut taxes by $330 billion through fiscal 2013

No   Block Bush rule scaling back overtime pay for some white-collar federal workers

No   Do not allow use of search warrants without first notifying subjects

No   Allow importation of prescription drugs

Yes   Create private school voucher program in Washington, D.C.

Yes   Ban "partial birth" abortion except to save a woman's life

No   Split $18.6 billion in Iraq aid into half-grant, half-loan

Yes   Overhaul Medicare and create prescription drug benefit

CQ VOTE STUDIES

House Service:

	PARTY UNITY		PRESIDENTIAL SUPPORT	
	Support	Oppose	Support	Oppose
2004	99%	1%	89%	11%
2003	99%	1%	96%	4%
2002	94%	6%	85%	15%
2001	97%	3%	90%	10%
2000	91%	9%	30%	70%
1999	87%	13%	29%	71%

INTEREST GROUPS

House Service:

	AFL-CIO	ADA	CCUS	ACU
2004	8%	5%	100%	95%
2003	0%	5%	100%	84%
2002	0%	5%	100%	96%
2001	9%	5%	100%	88%
2000	0%	5%	85%	72%
1999	13%	10%	91%	66%

Rep. Jack Kingston (R)

Elected 1992; 7th term

CAPITOL OFFICE
225-5831
jack.kingston@mail.house.gov
www.house.gov/kingston
2242 Rayburn 20515-1001; fax 226-2269

COMMITTEES
Appropriations

HOMETOWN
Savannah

BORN
April 24, 1955, Bryan, Texas

RELIGION
Episcopalian

FAMILY
Wife, Libby Kingston; four children

EDUCATION
U. of Georgia, B.A. 1978 (economics)

CAREER
Insurance broker

POLITICAL HIGHLIGHTS
Ga. House, 1984-92

ELECTION RESULTS

2004 GENERAL

Jack Kingston (R)		unopposed

2004 PRIMARY

Jack Kingston (R)		unopposed

2002 GENERAL

Jack Kingston (R)	103,661	72.1%
Don Smart (D)	40,026	27.9%

PREVIOUS WINNING PERCENTAGES
2000 (69%); 1998 (100%); 1996 (68%); 1994 (77%);
1992 (58%)

A zealous but affable partisan, Kingston uses his dual roles as party messenger and Appropriations Committee member to talk-the-talk and walk-the-walk of fiscal conservatism. While he is a devoted member of the House leadership team, he doesn't shy away from taking on those that outrank him.

Kingston won an easy bid after the November 2004 elections to continue as vice chairman of the Republican Conference, a party organization that among other things seeks to enhance the GOP's public image. The job was a logical step from his previous post as chairman of the House GOP's "Theme Team," a group of lawmakers responsible for spreading the party's message, mostly in speeches on the floor before and after the day's legislative business. He had been the group's chairman since 1997.

Kingston has won kudos for his quick wit, which he frequently uses to zing liberal Democratic proposals. He was a guest several times, for instance, on "Politically Incorrect," a late-night talk show that aired on ABC. The show's liberal host, Bill Maher, said he appreciated Kingston's ability to express his conservative views as well as his one-liners.

Colleagues also praise him for his creative approach to communications and an innate ability to relate to everyday people. Kingston, one GOP aide said, knows how to connect with "Joe Six-pack."

As head of the Theme Team, he told his colleagues to keep their message short and simple. "It's not lofty or esoteric, it's understandable," he said of their rhetorical goal. He was also the impetus behind the Teddy Roosevelt award, a new award to recognize members who conduct town hall meetings, pen opinion editorials and give floor speeches.

A challenge, he said, is to overcome the notion that the GOP does not understand or care about the impact of its policies on those with modest or small incomes.

The informal and easygoing Republican takes a harder line on the Appropriations Committee, where in the 108th Congress he chaired the subcommittee in charge of funding for Congress and its affiliated agencies. He used the bill, which pays for lawmakers' own operations, to set an example of restraint in the hope that other chairmen would follow. His fiscal 2005 measure, in fact, was one of the few spending bills that came close to honoring President Bush's request for increases of less than 1 percent in non-defense, non-homeland security discretionary spending — a point of pride for Kingston. "We held the line," he said at the time. "I think Congress has to lead the way." Cutting spending, he added, "makes it easier for us to fight the fight."

In the 109th, a reshuffling of the Appropriations panel's structure did away with the Legislative Branch Subcommittee, depriving Kingston of a gavel. But he got a nice consolation price: a seat on the Defense Subcommittee.

Kingston is seen frequently on the floor attacking Democratic stands and seldom strays from his party's position. In the 108th Congress, for example, he backed the president 93 percent of the time and sided with the GOP on 97 percent of the votes that pitted one party against the other.

Still, Kingston does not shy away from a good fight against his leaders. His 2004 quest for legislation to let farmers cash out of the federal tobacco quota system put him at odds with fellow members of the Republican leadership. He joined forces with a bipartisan team of tobacco-state lawmakers to persuade Majority Leader Tom DeLay and other leaders to back the $10 billion buyout. They were reluctant, but ultimately relented and incorporated the buyout in the corporate tax overhaul measure that was enacted in 2004.

Kingston is not reluctant to acknowledge that the war in Iraq could drag down elements of the Bush agenda in the 109th Congress. "A popular president is going to get more of his legislation done than an unpopular president," said Kingston. "We need to kind of get to the point where people can see the light at the end of the tunnel in Iraq. And that is going to be a ball and chain around his legislative foot." In 2003, Kingston bucked both the White House and DeLay to vote for legislation that would make it easier to import prescription drugs.

On the Agriculture Appropriations Subcommittee, Kingston has been especially protective of the state's peanut and cotton farmers. This position has sometimes put him at odds with those Republicans who view federal crop subsidy programs as antithetical to free enterprise.

Kingston also caters to his district by seeking funding for government programs that support the south Georgia economy. He has sought federal assistance to deepen the harbors at Savannah and Brunswick and money for a visitors center and repair work on structures on Cumberland Island, site of a historic slave settlement.

Kingston cuts his own personal cost of living by using his Capitol Hill office as a bedroom when he is in Washington. He enjoys a good laugh and his office has the feel of a teenage boy's bedroom — with sports paraphernalia decorating virtually every wall.

Born in Texas, where his father was an art professor, Kingston and his family spent a few months in Ethiopia before they settled in Georgia while he was still in diapers. Kingston claims Georgia as his home state, telling a reporter once, "If you're potty-trained in a state, I think that gives you native status."

After earning an undergraduate degree in economics, Kingston moved to Savannah to sell insurance. He won his first election in 1984 to the state House, where he served eight years. When Democrat Lindsay Thomas retired in 1992, Kingston was well-positioned to woo voters into the Republican column in a House race; many of them already had been voting Republican for president. Kingston drew minor primary opposition, then dispatched Democrat Barbara Christmas, a school principal. His 58 percent share of the vote that year remains his lowest election percentage.

Redistricting after the 2000 census put both Kingston and his 8th District GOP colleague Saxby Chambliss in the 1st District, but Chambliss decided to run for the Senate. The new map gave the 1st an even more Republican flavor; Kingston won by 44 percentage points in 2002 and was unopposed in 2004.

KEY VOTES

2004

No Extend federal unemployment benefits by 13 weeks

No Pass $283.2 billion, six-year federal highway and mass transit bill

Yes Approve $146 billion multi-year extension of previously enacted middle-class tax breaks

Yes Amend the Constitution to prohibit same-sex marriage

Yes Cut corporate taxes $137 billion over 10 years

No Reorganize U.S. intelligence agencies as proposed by Sept. 11 commission

2003

Yes Cut taxes by $330 billion through fiscal 2013

No Block Bush rule scaling back overtime pay for some white-collar federal workers

Yes Do not allow use of search warrants without first notifying subjects

Yes Allow importation of prescription drugs

Yes Create private school voucher program in Washington, D.C.

Yes Ban "partial birth" abortion except to save a woman's life

No Split $18.6 billion in Iraq aid into half-grant, half-loan

Yes Overhaul Medicare and create prescription drug benefit

CQ VOTE STUDIES

	PARTY UNITY		PRESIDENTIAL SUPPORT	
	Support	Oppose	Support	Oppose
2004	97%	3%	91%	9%
2003	98%	2%	94%	6%
2002	98%	2%	85%	15%
2001	98%	2%	93%	7%
2000	95%	5%	17%	83%

INTEREST GROUPS

	AFL-CIO	ADA	CCUS	ACU
2004	0%	0%	100%	96%
2003	0%	10%	97%	88%
2002	0%	0%	85%	96%
2001	8%	5%	95%	100%
2000	10%	5%	80%	100%

GEORGIA 1

Southeast – Savannah suburbs, part of Valdosta

The 1st takes in a swath of southeast Georgia and its entire coastline, stretching from South Carolina to Florida. In redistricting following the 2000 census, the 1st became a Republican-leaning district with a substantial military population. Like much of the rest of Georgia, the district is ancestrally Democratic but trends Republican in federal races. George W. Bush received 68 percent of the vote here in 2004.

The 1st has no population center; redistricting removed the urban, Democratic areas of Savannah that were the nucleus of the old 1st. The district now has large, mostly rural chunks, reaching into the Republican suburbs of Savannah and parts of Valdosta. It also travels north just east of Interstate 75, taking in parts of Warner Robins, the Republican areas outside of Macon and Robins Air Force Base. The district includes five of the state's 12 major military bases, and 23 percent of residents are black.

Despite the hardships caused area farmers by several years of drought and then large amounts of rain from 2004 hurricanes, peanuts, onions, cotton, tobacco and other crops help sustain the economy, as do timber,

defense, shrimping and tourism. The district's ports and coastline make trade and coastal conservation dominant issues.

Georgia's coast is becoming a popular destination for retirees and is seeing an influx of new residents settling between Hilton Head, S.C., and Florida. This growing part of the population adds to the Republican lean of the district, outnumbering older, agricultural Democrats.

MAJOR INDUSTRY
Agriculture, military, manufacturing

MILITARY BASES
Fort Stewart (Army), 17,517 military, 2,908 civilian (shared with the 3rd and the 12th); Robins Air Force Base, 6,452 military, 13,247 civilian (2003); Kings Bay Naval Submarine Base, 4,426 military, 3,645 civilian (2004); Hunter Army Airfield, 4,905 military, 577 civilian (2003); Moody Air Force Base, 3,715 military, 339 civilian (2004)

CITIES
Hinesville, 30,392; Brunswick, 15,600; Valdosta (pt.), 15,442

NOTABLE
The Okefenokee Swamp, which covers 436,000 acres, is home to an estimated 35,000 alligators and 234 species of birds.

Rep. Sanford D. Bishop Jr. (D)

Elected 1992; 7th term

CAPITOL OFFICE
225-3631
bishop.email@mail.house.gov
www.house.gov/bishop
2429 Rayburn 20515-1002; fax 225-2203

COMMITTEES
Appropriations

HOMETOWN
Columbus

BORN
Feb. 4, 1947, Mobile, Ala.

RELIGION
Baptist

FAMILY
Wife, Vivian Creighton Bishop; one stepchild

EDUCATION
Morehouse College, B.A. 1968 (political science);
Emory U., J.D. 1971

MILITARY SERVICE
Army, 1971

CAREER
Lawyer

POLITICAL HIGHLIGHTS
Ga. House, 1977-91; Ga. Senate, 1991-93

ELECTION RESULTS

2004 GENERAL

Sanford D. Bishop Jr. (D)	129,984	66.8%
Dave Eversman (R)	64,645	33.2%

2004 PRIMARY

Sanford D. Bishop Jr. (D)	unopposed

2002 GENERAL

Sanford D. Bishop Jr. (D)	unopposed

PREVIOUS WINNING PERCENTAGES
2000 (53%); 1998 (57%); 1996 (54%); 1994 (66%);
1992 (64%)

Bishop consistently casts votes that show him to be the most conservative black member of Congress, displaying a middle-of-the-road political philosophy that cuts across a variety of economic and social issues. He breaks ranks with his fellow Democrats more often than any other member of the Congressional Black Caucus, and he is by far the caucus member who casts the most votes in support of President Bush.

He fits in comfortably with the Blue Dog Coalition of conservative House Democrats, where he, Harold E. Ford Jr. of Tennessee and David Scott, also of Georgia, are the only black members. He has won commendations from the National Federation of Independent Business and the American Legion for his legislative stands.

In the 108th Congress, Bishop was one of the first Democrats to indicate he would vote for Bush's corporate tax overhaul bill and one of just 34 Democrats who voted to permit oil drilling in the Arctic National Wildlife Refuge. He was one of just 36 from his party who voted for a proposed constitutional amendment to ban same-sex marriage.

With his independent voting record, Bishop has resisted racial pigeonholing throughout his congressional career. Attention to his constituents' agriculture and military interests has enabled him to build a base of support beyond the black community. And on certain core Democratic issues, Bishop votes with his party. He supports abortion rights and has taken labor's side in disputes with the business-oriented Republican majority.

Bishop and another Blue Dog, Marion Berry of Arkansas, were named to the Appropriations Committee in 2003 as part of an effort by Minority Leader Nancy Pelosi to award choice committee assignments to all factions of the party. To take the seat, Bishop had to leave the Agriculture and Intelligence panels. He had served on Intelligence since 1997 and had been in line to be top-ranking Democrat in the 108th Congress.

He might have had the top spot on the Intelligence dais in the 107th, but he ranked just below Pelosi on the committee, and she declined to step down when she became party whip in 2001. Still, Bishop voted for Pelosi for Speaker at the start of the 108th, despite his unhappiness over Intelligence and the pressure he and several other Blue Dogs got from some conservative groups to withhold support from her.

In 2004, Bishop used his post on Appropriations to help restore money for dredging the Apalachicola-Chattahoochee-Flint river basin on the Georgia-Alabama border to preserve the route for barge traffic and to enhance recreational use. The Bush administration had proposed practically zeroing out the project as wasteful. Some Florida legislators opposed the project on environmental grounds.

Building on his work on the Intelligence panel, Bishop was named in late 2001 to the House Democrats' Homeland Security Task Force. He chaired a subcommittee that developed recommendations for protecting the country's infrastructure — including refineries, power plants, government buildings and computer networks — from terrorist attacks.

Bishop has always supported a healthy defense budget and looked out for the interests of the 2nd District's Fort Benning, the Army's huge infantry training base, as well as Moody Air Force Base, which was in the 2nd before redistricting put it just across the 1st District line in 2001.

On Agriculture, Bishop played a crucial role in protecting peanut farmers when their subsidy program was overhauled during debate on the

2002 farm bill. More peanuts are grown in the 2nd District than in any other congressional district — considerably more than a quarter of the nation's output. The farm bill did away with the peanut quota, which was becoming less valuable in the face of imports from Mexico under the North American Free Trade Agreement. In addition to a cash payment as a buy-out of the peanut quota, Bishop was able to include a new market support program and requirements that foreign peanuts be labeled. He also supported more funding to help small and disadvantaged farmers.

Bishop grew up in Mobile, Ala., where his parents were both educators. His father was the president of a community college that is now named for him — Bishop State Community College — and his mother was the college librarian. The younger Bishop made a name for himself as a civil rights lawyer in Columbus, Ga., before winning election to the state legislature in 1976, where he served for 16 years.

Bishop was on the Reapportionment Committee that, with stern urgings from the Justice Department, in 1992 drew new congressional district maps that made the 2nd District the third black-majority district in the state. Columbus business leaders persuaded Bishop to seek the new seat and helped finance his challenge to white Democratic Rep. Charles Hatcher, who had been identified as one of the chief abusers of the House's private bank, with 819 overdrafts. In a primary runoff against Hatcher, Bishop won the nomination with 53 percent of the vote; in November, he coasted past Republican physician Jim Dudley.

In 1995, a federal court ruled the boundaries of the 2nd to be an unconstitutional "racial gerrymander" and handed down a new map, altering the racial composition of his constituency and putting Columbus in the 3rd District. The black share of the population in the redrawn 2nd dropped from 51 percent to 39 percent. Bishop moved about 90 miles southeast to Albany, in the center of the 2nd.

He weathered some tough re-election fights in 1996, 1998 and 2000. In his closest battle, in 2000, Bishop narrowly defeated former Senate aide Dylan Glenn, who is also black.

But redistricting following the 2000 census was good to Bishop, putting part of Muscogee County, his longtime home, back in the 2nd District and increasing the black share of the population to 44 percent. The resulting Democratic district scared off potential challengers for a time, and Bishop was unopposed in both the 2002 primary and general election. He was again unopposed in the 2004 primary and easily held on to the seat in the general election against former broadcaster and businessman Dave Eversman.

KEY VOTES

2004
Yes Extend federal unemployment benefits by 13 weeks
Yes Pass $283.2 billion, six-year federal highway and mass transit bill
\+ Approve $146 billion multi-year extension of previously enacted middle-class tax breaks
Yes Amend the Constitution to prohibit same-sex marriage
Yes Cut corporate taxes $137 billion over 10 years
Yes Reorganize U.S. intelligence agencies as proposed by Sept. 11 commission

2003
No Cut taxes by $330 billion through fiscal 2013
Yes Block Bush rule scaling back overtime pay for some white-collar federal workers
Yes Do not allow use of search warrants without first notifying subjects
Yes Allow importation of prescription drugs
No Create private school voucher program in Washington, D.C.
Yes Ban "partial birth" abortion except to save a woman's life
Yes Split $18.6 billion in Iraq aid into half-grant, half-loan
No Overhaul Medicare and create prescription drug benefit

CQ VOTE STUDIES

	PARTY UNITY		PRESIDENTIAL SUPPORT	
	Support	Oppose	Support	Oppose
2004	78%	22%	57%	43%
2003	80%	20%	44%	56%
2002	80%	20%	52%	48%
2001	71%	29%	50%	50%
2000	65%	35%	55%	45%

INTEREST GROUPS

	AFL-CIO	ADA	CCUS	ACU
2004	69%	55%	79%	35%
2003	100%	75%	57%	44%
2002	78%	75%	55%	40%
2001	100%	70%	65%	39%
2000	60%	50%	78%	43%

GEORGIA 2

Southwest – Albany, part of Columbus and Valdosta

Georgia's 2nd takes in the state's entire southwest corner and extends south from Columbus to the Florida border. It contains parts of Columbus and Valdosta and all of Albany, Bainbridge and Thomasville.

Although it was once a black-majority district, redistricting in 1995 reduced its black population, changing it from a strongly Democratic area to one in which Republicans were competitive. Redistricting following the 2000 census made the 2nd significantly more Democratic again, adding predominately black areas of Columbus to the district. Forty-four percent of the voting age population is black.

Democrats hold most local offices and are strong in the northwestern counties that have higher black populations. Pockets of GOP strength exist in Lee County, in the central part of the 2nd, as well as in Thomasville and other southern parts of the district. Dougherty County, with Albany as the county seat, is the district's most populous and is reliably Democratic. Nonetheless, George W. Bush carried the 2nd with 53 percent of the district's presidential vote in 2004, increasing his winning percentage by 3 percentage points from the 2000 presidential election.

The 2nd's largely rural and heavily agricultural regions have struggled economically for decades and are heavily dependent on farm loan assistance. Farming and livestock are key to the economy, and the district grows more peanuts than any other place in the United States.

MAJOR INDUSTRY
Agriculture, military, manufacturing, health care

MILITARY BASES
Fort Benning (Army), 49,149 military, 7,140 civilian (shared with the 11th); Marine Corps Logistics Base, 516 military, 1,854 civilian (2004)

CITIES
Columbus (pt.), 83,973; Albany, 76,939; Valdosta (pt.), 28,282

NOTABLE
Jackie Robinson, who broke baseball's color barrier in 1947, was born in Cairo; Plains is the hometown of former President Jimmy Carter.

Rep. Jim Marshall (D)

Elected 2002; 2nd term

A war hero who dropped out of Princeton to fight in Vietnam, Marshall is a gung-ho supporter of the military, a defender of the flag, an avid hunter and a conservative Democrat. He may not be as visible as former Georgia Sen. Zell Miller for defying party orthodoxy, but he is equally rebellious. Their similarities invite speculation that Marshall may have a Senate race in his future.

The son and grandson of Army generals, Marshall has been one of President Bush's most reliable Democratic boosters of the war in Iraq. He has attacked critics of the war, including the media, for being indirectly responsible for the deaths of American soldiers. Negativity about the U.S. role, he says, weakens Iraqi resolve for self-governance and emboldens insurgents. In 2003, he infuriated fellow Democrats who opposed the war by crashing their press conference to say it was wrong to hold lengthy discussions during the U.S. military strike on Iraq. Rep. John Lewis, dean of the Georgia delegation, called the breech of protocol "unthinkable."

In his first term, Marshall pushed hard for a proposal to allow veterans to receive both disability pay and retirement pay. At the time, military retirees' pension benefits were reduced, dollar for dollar, by the amount of disability income they receive. Marshall circulated a petition demanding that his concurrent benefits bill be brought to a vote. Although he didn't get the required 218 signatures, he did put pressure on Republican leaders, who ultimately included a concurrent benefits provision in a 2004 defense spending bill.

The military drives the economy in Marshall's middle Georgia district, home to Fort Stewart where the 3rd Infantry Division is based. Just over the district line is Fort Benning, where the famed Army Infantry school is located, and Robins Air Force Base is next door in the 1st District. Much of the rest of the 3rd is agricultural, producing peaches, cotton, pecans, tobacco and the sweet Vidalia onion. It is anchored by Macon, population 97,000, where Marshall was once mayor. His two committees reflect those demographics — Armed Services and Agriculture.

Like Miller was, Marshall is sometimes a more reliable vote for the Republican president than for his own party. He was among the dozen House Democrats most apt to vote against their party in 2004, voting nearly 30 percent of the time against Democratic wishes on key votes and 53 percent of the time in agreement with the president.

The most significant example came on a bill creating a prescription drug benefit under Medicare. Democrats widely opposed the 2003 Bush initiative because they said it fell short of providing senior citizens with a meaningful benefit. House GOP leaders kept the vote open all night when it looked like the bill would fail. It passed only after Marshall and five other lawmakers switched their votes from no to yes.

A military brat, Marshall was born in Ithaca, N.Y. but grew up on Army bases around the world. His family moved 22 times. He was a national merit scholar in high school in Mobile, Ala. and was admitted to Princeton University. In 1968, he left school to become an Army ranger. Marshall said that in light of his upbringing, he felt it was wrong for him to sit out the war on an academic deferment. He was wounded twice in combat and earned a Purple Heart.

When his service ended in 1970, Marshall finished his degree in politics at Princeton and then worked a series jobs, including as a wilderness

CAPITOL OFFICE
225-6531
jim.marshall@mail.house.gov
www.house.gov/marshall
515 Cannon 20515-1003; fax 225-3013

COMMITTEES
Agriculture
Armed Services

HOMETOWN
Macon

BORN
March 31, 1948, Ithaca, N.Y.

RELIGION
Roman Catholic

FAMILY
Wife, Camille Marshall; two children

EDUCATION
Princeton U., A.B. 1972 (politics); Boston U., J.D. 1977

MILITARY SERVICE
Army, 1968-70

CAREER
Lawyer; law professor; logging business owner

POLITICAL HIGHLIGHTS
Mayor of Macon, 1995-99; Democratic nominee for U.S. House, 2000

ELECTION RESULTS

2004 GENERAL

Jim Marshall (D)	136,273	62.9%
Calder Clay (R)	80,435	37.1%

2004 PRIMARY

Jim Marshall (D)	unopposed

2002 GENERAL

Jim Marshall (D)	75,394	50.5%
Calder Clay (R)	73,866	49.5%

instructor, a short-order cook, a welder and a high school economics teacher. He also owned and operated a small logging business in Idaho. In that job, his leg was badly injured by a falling tree. While recovering, Marshall earned a law degree from Boston University, where he met his wife, Camille, also a law student. (Her father, John Hope, a Weather Channel meteorologist, named Hurricane Camille for her.)

The two moved South, where her family roots were, and Marshall joined the faculty of Mercer University's law school in Macon. In 1995, at age 47, he ran for office for the first time, becoming mayor of Macon. In that role, he was credited with shoring up the city financially. A fitness buff and jogger, he earned local public affection in 1997 by chasing down a man who had broken into the women's locker room at his health club. Apparently in superior shape, Marshall overtook the suspect, who was later arrested.

Marshall first ran for the House in 2000, challenging GOP Rep. Saxby Chambliss. He lost by 18 percentage points, despite a colorful campaign stunt. When Senate Majority Leader Trent Lott of Mississippi threatened to move military contracts out of Georgia if Republicans lost the Senate race that year, Marshall called a press conference and brought a live donkey. "I just want to invite Sen. Lott to kiss my donkey," he said.

In 2002, Marshall was back, running in a redrawn district that includes Macon and has a slight Democratic edge. With Chambliss running for the Senate, Marshall's Republican opponent was Calder Clay, a Macon city councilman. Marshall edged out Clay by only 1,528 votes, in the third-closest House race that year.

Marshall looked vulnerable in 2004. Polls showed him in a dead heat in a rematch with Clay. The Republican was well-financed, and Vice President Dick Cheney put in an appearance for him. But Clay failed to make a compelling case for ousting Marshall. For instance, Clay criticized the incumbent's record on veterans' concerns, an issue on which Marshall occupied safe ground after his efforts on military retiree benefits. Marshall surprised even himself when he won with 63 percent of the vote, a margin of almost 56,000 votes.

But Republicans have gained control of the statehouse and are plotting their revenge in 2005, drawing up a new map that changes the district boundaries to make it more GOP-friendly. Democrats are threatening to contest the map in federal court.

Marshall has survived several bouts of skin cancer, a condition he attributes to his exposure to the herbicide Agent Orange in Vietnam. In 2003, he had successful surgery to treat prostate cancer.

KEY VOTES

2004

Yes Extend federal unemployment benefits by 13 weeks
Yes Pass $283.2 billion, six-year federal highway and mass transit bill
Yes Approve $146 billion multi-year extension of previously enacted middle-class tax breaks
Yes Amend the Constitution to prohibit same-sex marriage
Yes Cut corporate taxes $137 billion over 10 years
Yes Reorganize U.S. intelligence agencies as proposed by Sept. 11 commission

2003

Yes Cut taxes by $330 billion through fiscal 2013
Yes Block Bush rule scaling back overtime pay for some white-collar federal workers
Yes Do not allow use of search warrants without first notifying subjects
Yes Allow importation of prescription drugs
No Create private school voucher program in Washington, D.C.
Yes Ban "partial birth" abortion except to save a woman's life
? Split $18.6 billion in Iraq aid into half-grant, half-loan
Yes Overhaul Medicare and create prescription drug benefit

CQ VOTE STUDIES

	PARTY UNITY		PRESIDENTIAL SUPPORT	
	Support	Oppose	Support	Oppose
2004	69%	31%	53%	47%
2003	73%	27%	53%	47%

INTEREST GROUPS

	AFL-CIO	ADA	CCUS	ACU
2004	80%	55%	55%	48%
2003	87%	70%	48%	24%

GEORGIA 3
Middle Georgia – Macon

Created to encompass the rural heart of Georgia, the 3rd takes in mostly agricultural counties in the center of the state. Farm issues are paramount here, increasingly so after drought gripped the area from the late 1990s into 2002, putting the area's economy in peril. But rain from 2004 hurricanes appears to have ended the drought fears at least temporarily.

The district stretches from Marion County in the west to Hancock County in the north, while Telfair and Tattnall counties flank its southern border. Peaches, pecans and cotton are primary crops in the center of the district. Peanuts dominate the southern area, and onions and tobacco are prevalent in the southeast. Forestry also is a major industry. Aerospace jobs and textile manufacturing have helped sustain the economy, though some textile plants have closed in recent years.

The 3rd was drawn in redistricting after the 2000 census to elect a Democrat. But like much of the South, voters will support Republicans, and the 3rd can be politically competitive — George W. Bush received

56 percent of the vote here in the 2004 presidential election. Blacks make up 40 percent of the district's population.

The 3rd is almost split in two by a gash up its center, in which the 1st District takes in Warner Robins Air Force Base and Republican suburbs south of Macon. The 8th also descends into the area, taking in Republican suburbs north of Macon. The 3rd incorporates the rest of Macon, including the heavily Democratic city center.

MAJOR INDUSTRY
Agriculture, distribution, aerospace, timber

MILITARY BASES
Fort Stewart (Army), 17,517 military, 2,908 civilian (2003) (shared with the 1st and 12th)

CITIES
Macon (pt.), 89,507; Warner Robins (pt.), 38,969; Milledgeville, 18,757

NOTABLE
Milledgeville served as the state capital from 1803 until 1868, when the capital was moved to Atlanta during Reconstruction; Vidalia is known for its sweet onions; Claxton proudly calls itself the Fruitcake Capital of the World.

Rep. Cynthia A. McKinney (D)

Elected 1992; 6th term
Did not serve 2003-05

During her first tenure in Congress, from 1993 to 2003, McKinney was a confrontational advocate for liberal causes. She gained a following on the left by criticizing policies she saw as hurting minorities, union members and the poor. And she reserved a special passion for international human rights, occasionally striking alliances with Republicans to limit U.S. arms sales to authoritarian regimes and to push for Third World debt forgiveness.

But McKinney had to make a comeback in 2004 after a two-year hiatus that can be attributed, in part, to another aspect of her persona: a tendency to make remarks that alienated many of her constituents. Her implication on a talk radio program that the Bush administration may have had advance knowledge of the Sept. 11, 2001, terrorist attacks raised an uproar, which contributed to her defeat in the 2002 Democratic primary by Denise L. Majette.

Ironically, it was Majette who set the stage for McKinney's unexpectedly quick return to Washington. After a little more than a year in Congress, Majette made a surprise decision to run for the Senate — a long-shot bid that would result in her loss to Republican Johnny Isakson. McKinney wasted no time joining the House race in the suburban Atlanta 4th. Despite doubts raised by her 2002 stumble, her well-known name and strong support base among the district's black majority enabled her to win the primary over five opponents with 51 percent of the vote. She then carried the Democratic stronghold with 64 percent against Republican Catherine Davis.

McKinney's positions have changed little during her time out of office. Regaining a seat she had formerly held on the Armed Services panel and taking a new seat on Budget, she advocates an immediate withdrawal of American troops from Iraq, expanded protection for the disadvantaged and increased funding for a host of health, education and veterans' programs.

She had an unusual start in politics. Her father, a veteran civil rights leader and Georgia legislator, decided to get back at a political rival by putting her name on the ballot against him — without her knowledge. She lost soundly, but her interest was piqued and she won a state House seat two years later.

CAPITOL OFFICE
225-1605
www.house.gov/mckinney
320 Cannon 20515-1004; fax 226-0691

COMMITTEES
Armed Services
Budget

HOMETOWN
Decatur

BORN
March 17, 1955, Atlanta, Ga.

RELIGION
Roman Catholic

FAMILY
Divorced; one child

EDUCATION
U. of Southern California, B.A. 1978 (international relations); Tufts U., M.A. 1994 (law & diplomacy); U. of California, Berkeley, attending

CAREER
Professor

POLITICAL HIGHLIGHTS
Democratic nominee for Ga. House, 1986; Ga. House, 1989-93; U.S. House, 1993-2003; defeated in primary for re-election to U.S. House, 2002

ELECTION RESULTS

2004 GENERAL

Cynthia A. McKinney (D)	157,461	63.8%
Catherine Davis (R)	89,509	36.2%

2004 PRIMARY

Cynthia A. McKinney (D)	48,512	50.8%
Liane Levetan (D)	19,723	20.6%
Cathy Woolard (D)	18,164	19.0%
Connie Stokes (D)	4,972	5.2%
Nadine Thomas (D)	2,938	3.1%
Chris Vaughn (D)	1,280	1.3%

PREVIOUS WINNING PERCENTAGES
2000 (61%); 1998 (61%); 1996 (58%); 1994 (66%); 1992 (73%)

GEORGIA 4
Atlanta suburbs — DeKalb County

The DeKalb County-based 4th is decidedly Democratic. One of Georgia's two black-majority districts, African-Americans make up 53 percent of residents.

DeKalb County, which sits just east of Atlanta, accounts for almost 97 percent of the district's population and is the most Democratic county in the state. Democratic candidates find success in the county's racially diverse central and western portions, while Republicans run well in northern DeKalb's more white, affluent areas. Overall, John Kerry captured 71 percent of the 4th's 2004 presidential vote — his second-best showing in the state.

Like the rest of the Atlanta area, south DeKalb — which has one of the nation's most affluent concentrations of blacks — is seeing rapid growth. This growth has changed the tenor of the 4th, bringing more moderate, business-oriented African-Americans into the district and lessening the influence of more-liberal voices.

Jobs in the 4th center around health care and higher education. Emory University, home to a university hospital, is a major employer. The Centers for Disease Control and Prevention also employs a sizable number of the area's health care workers. Decatur was a 19th century commercial hub until it lost out as a railroad center to Atlanta, but it still has many government-related jobs.

MAJOR INDUSTRY
Retail, health care, government

CITIES
North Atlanta, 38,579; Redan, 33,841; Dunwoody, 32,808; Candler-McAfee, 28,294

NOTABLE
Stone Mountain Park features a huge granite outcropping into which a sculpture of Robert E. Lee and other Confederate heroes is carved.

Rep. John Lewis (D)

CAPITOL OFFICE
225-3801
www.house.gov/johnlewis
343 Cannon 20515-1005; fax 225-0351

COMMITTEES
Ways & Means

HOMETOWN
Atlanta

BORN
Feb. 21, 1940, Troy, Ala.

RELIGION
Baptist

FAMILY
Wife, Lillian Lewis; one child

EDUCATION
American Baptist Theological Seminary, B.A. 1961
(theology); Fisk U., B.A. 1963 (religion &
philosophy)

CAREER
Civil rights activist

POLITICAL HIGHLIGHTS
Sought Democratic nomination for U.S. House
(special election), 1977; Atlanta City Council,
1982-86

ELECTION RESULTS

2004 GENERAL

John Lewis (D)	unopposed

2004 PRIMARY

John Lewis (D)	unopposed

2002 GENERAL

John Lewis (D)	unopposed

PREVIOUS WINNING PERCENTAGES
2000 (77%); 1998 (79%); 1996 (100%); 1994 (69%);
1992 (72%); 1990 (76%); 1988 (78%); 1986 (75%)

Elected 1986; 10th term

In Congress, Lewis is seen as the keeper of the flame of the civil rights movement. He became famous as one of the leaders of the 1965 "Bloody Sunday" protest in Selma, Ala., an event that helped propel passage of the landmark Voting Rights Act. Now he leads members of Congress each year on a tour of civil rights sites in the South. Senate Majority Leader Bill Frist made the pilgrimage in 2004.

By the usual measure, Lewis is not a productive lawmaker. He doesn't introduce many bills or push for amendments to other people's legislation. But he is the conscience of House liberal Democrats and his colleagues seek him out to speak at their hometown events. And the bills he does advance are in keeping with his civil rights background.

His legislation creating the National Museum of African American History and Culture was signed into law by President Bush in 2003 after years of effort. "In 1963, I was on the outside looking in. I couldn't even vote," Lewis said in a July 2003 speech commemorating the 40th anniversary of the March on Washington, where he was one of the speakers. Now, he said, "I'm on the inside making laws."

Lewis is also in the House Democratic leadership, serving as the senior chief deputy whip, and a member of the Ways and Means Committee. He has sponsored legislation to reduce racial disparities in health care, and he often speaks with emotion about the need for better medical services for the poor and the uninsured. He finds much to dislike in Republican tax policy and argues that liberalized trade undermines labor rights in the Third World. As Congress approved sweeping new powers for law enforcement in the aftermath of the Sept. 11, 2001, terrorist attacks, Lewis voted no, worrying that the new domestic surveillance powers could mark a return to the days when the government spied on him and other civil rights leaders.

His preacher's voice, with its thundering timbre and a cadence that sounds eerily like the Rev. Martin Luther King Jr.'s, is one of the House's most familiar. Lewis is one of the few in the chamber with a past worthy of a book. His autobiography, "Walking in the Wind," recounts the day in March 1965 when he stood at the front of hundreds of marchers on the Edmund Pettus Bridge in Selma and faced down state troopers without moving a muscle. The police attacked the peaceful crowd, and images from the "Bloody Sunday" march helped jolt Congress into giving minorities full voting rights by passing the Voting Rights Act. Lewis himself suffered a severe concussion from the crack of a trooper's billy club that day.

Earnest and serious, Lewis writes in his book: "I've never been the kind of person who naturally attracts the limelight. I'm not a handsome guy. I'm not flamboyant. I'm not what you would call elegant. . . . I simply have never been the kind of guy who draws attention."

But activist groups and Democratic Party leaders call on him for everything from ribbon-cutting ceremonies at housing projects to high stakes fundraising dinners. Mississippi lawmaker Trent Lott, trying to salvage his job as Senate Republican leader, sought forgiveness from Lewis in late 2002 after his off-the-cuff remarks praising Sen. Strom Thurmond's 1948 pro-segregation presidential campaign ignited a firestorm. Lewis indicated he might be willing to give Lott a second chance, but the uproar was so great Lott had to step down.

Since 1997, Lewis has been one of the leaders of the Faith and Politics

Institute, an interfaith, nonpartisan organization that sponsors forums on racial issues. For many years, he co-chaired the institute with Republican Rep. Amo Houghton, who retired in 2004. Their audiences have heard from such speakers as Secretary of State Colin L. Powell and civil rights leader Jim Lawson, Lewis' mentor in the nonviolent protest tactics that drove the movement. The institute also sponsors the annual civil rights pilgrimage to Selma, where Lewis recreates his famous walk across the bridge.

One of 10 children of sharecroppers, Lewis recalls that he was shy as a boy attending segregated schools in rural Alabama. He was inspired by hearing King's sermons on the radio and developed a sense of outrage at racial incidents, such as the brutal lynching of 15-year-old Emmett Till in Mississippi in 1955. Lewis was the same age as Till at the time.

Later, as a student at the American Baptist Theological Seminary in Nashville, he began attending Lawson's workshops on nonviolent resistance against segregation, driven in part by the knowledge that African-American high school students were challenging the system in Little Rock, Ark. Lewis said he developed a sense of mission during that time and a belief that if others were putting themselves on the line for the cause, then so should he.

He put his inhibitions aside and joined the emerging civil rights movement. He says he was "forced to grow up" as he and others took responsibility for the groups of people who sat in at lunch counters. As a Freedom Rider, Lewis was one of the protesters who took dangerous, integrated bus rides through the Deep South in 1961. He became chairman of the Student Nonviolent Coordinating Committee in 1963. "I think the movement liberated me," Lewis says. "And I think being in Congress liberated me more."

He first ran for Congress in 1977, for the seat Andrew Young left to become U.N. ambassador. He lost to Wyche Fowler, who went on to serve 10 years in the House and six in the Senate. Lewis went to Washington to head the federal volunteer agency ACTION. Returning to Atlanta, he won a seat on the city council in 1981. He made his next bid for the House in 1986, when Fowler ran for the Senate. After winning a tough battle against state Sen. Julian Bond for the Democratic nomination, Lewis breezed to a 3-to-1 victory in November. He has won re-election with ease. In 2002 and 2004, the GOP did not bother to field a candidate.

Though he still is a shy man, Lewis says, the act of campaigning in Atlanta draws him out, and the battles in Congress embolden him by spurring him to "get in the way" — a civil rights expression for physically placing oneself in the way of injustice and forcing change.

KEY VOTES

2004

Yes   Extend federal unemployment benefits by 13 weeks
Yes   Pass $283.2 billion, six-year federal highway and mass transit bill
No   Approve $146 billion multi-year extension of previously enacted middle-class tax breaks
No   Amend the Constitution to prohibit same-sex marriage
No   Cut corporate taxes $137 billion over 10 years
Yes   Reorganize U.S. intelligence agencies as proposed by Sept. 11 commission

2003

No   Cut taxes by $330 billion through fiscal 2013
Yes   Block Bush rule scaling back overtime pay for some white-collar federal workers
Yes   Do not allow use of search warrants without first notifying subjects
Yes   Allow importation of prescription drugs
No   Create private school voucher program in Washington, D.C.
No   Ban "partial birth" abortion except to save a woman's life
Yes   Split $18.6 billion in Iraq aid into half-grant, half-loan
No   Overhaul Medicare and create prescription drug benefit

CQ VOTE STUDIES

	PARTY UNITY		PRESIDENTIAL SUPPORT	
	Support	Oppose	Support	Oppose
2004	98%	2%	18%	82%
2003	99%	1%	13%	87%
2002	96%	4%	21%	79%
2001	97%	3%	15%	85%
2000	96%	4%	80%	20%

INTEREST GROUPS

	AFL-CIO	ADA	CCUS	ACU
2004	100%	100%	10%	4%
2003	100%	90%	17%	13%
2002	100%	80%	31%	0%
2001	100%	100%	26%	0%
2000	100%	95%	42%	4%

GEORGIA 5

Atlanta

The heart of the 5th lies in downtown Atlanta, the symbolic capital of the New South and the commercial center of the Southeast. The district takes in almost all of the city of Atlanta and much of surrounding Fulton County. The most populous county in Georgia, Fulton is reliably Democratic. A few pockets of GOP strength exist in the district's wealthier northern suburbs, such as Buckhead.

The 5th is one of two black-majority districts in the state. Its 56 percent black population — concentrated mostly in the southern part of the district — keeps it a Democratic bastion, though whites have flooded into the recently revitalized Midtown area. A large gay population in Midtown also influences local politics. John Kerry received 72 percent of the 5th's 2004 presidential vote, his highest percentage in Georgia.

During the 1990s, Atlanta saw a 13 percent increase in white residents, while the black population declined by 3 percent. Overall, the city's population grew by about 6 percent. New apartment buildings and condominiums are going up almost daily as the city attempts to keep up with the increase.

Along with Atlanta's downtown business district, Hartsfield-Jackson Atlanta International Airport in Clayton County is the 5th's major economic generator. The airport, a small part of which is located in the 13th District, is one of the nation's busiest and employs more than 55,000 people. The 5th's strategic location also has made it the headquarters for transportation-related industries, distribution companies and other major firms. At the same time, air pollution, gridlock and urban sprawl from the expanding economy are a concern.

MAJOR INDUSTRY
Transportation, distribution

MILITARY BASES
Fort McPherson (Army), 1,329 military, 2,064 civilian (2004)

CITIES
Atlanta (pt.), 403,925; Sandy Springs (pt.), 44,738; East Point, 39,595; Smyrna (pt.), 26,781; College Park (pt.), 18,348; North Druid Hills, 16,132

NOTABLE
Martin Luther King Jr. was born in Atlanta and served as a pastor of Ebenezer Baptist Church; Atlanta hosted the 1996 Summer Olympics; Coca-Cola and CNN headquarters are in Atlanta.

Rep. Tom Price (R)

Elected 2004; 1st term

Price represents a generation of Republicans who spearheaded the party's drive to take power in conservative-leaning but traditionally Democratic Georgia. He served as Georgia's first-ever Republican state Senate majority leader after the GOP won control of the chamber in 2002.

The effectiveness of the efforts waged by Price and his peers were apparent during the 2004 open-seat House race in the 6th District. Price had to outduel serious competition for the Republican nomination to succeed Republican incumbent Johnny Isakson, who was staging a successful bid for the Senate. But Price's primary runoff win guaranteed a trip to Washington: The 6th, in north suburban Atlanta, has become such a Republican stronghold that the Democrats did not even field a candidate for the race.

Price's conservatism on most social and fiscal issues will fit comfortably into the Republican majority on Capitol Hill.

An orthopedic surgeon, Price joins many physician-politicians in his desire to limit doctors' exposure to malpractice lawsuits. But Price calls himself an advocate of "big idea" conservatism, and says he would prefer that efforts to limit doctors' liability become part of a more sweeping package to reduce health care costs. In his view, individuals should be allowed to buy medical insurance in the free market, with employers and the government continuing to subsidize whatever plan an individual chooses.

He advocates an equally sweeping tax code overhaul. He has expressed support for a proposal to replace virtually all taxes — including income, corporate, dividend and capital gains — with a 23 percent national sales tax.

But like predecessor Isakson, Price comes off more as an affable "country club" Republican than a conservative firebrand. That is a good fit for his district, one of the nation's wealthiest enclaves.

Price spent years as a behind-the-scenes GOP organizer and fundraiser, then became a candidate himself in 1996 at the behest of a retiring state senator who urged him to run for her seat.

CAPITOL OFFICE
225-4501
www.house.gov/tomprice
506 Cannon 20515-1006; fax 225-4656

COMMITTEES
Education & Workforce
Financial Services

HOMETOWN
Roswell

BORN
Oct. 8, 1954, Lansing, Mich.

RELIGION
Presbyterian

FAMILY
Wife, Elizabeth Clark Price; one child

EDUCATION
U. of Michigan, B.A. 1976 (general studies), M.D. 1979

CAREER
Surgeon

POLITICAL HIGHLIGHTS
Ga. Senate, 1997-2005 (minority whip, 1999-2002; majority leader, 2003)

ELECTION RESULTS

2004 GENERAL

Tom Price (R)		unopposed

2004 PRIMARY RUNOFF

Tom Price (R)	28,180	54.1%
Robert B. Lamutt (R)	23,959	46.0%

2004 PRIMARY

Tom Price (R)	29,144	35.2%
Robert B. Lamutt (R)	23,176	28.0%
Chuck Clay (R)	17,705	21.4%
Roger Hines (R)	7,645	9.2%
Al Beverly (R)	3,187	3.9%
Chris Chatwood (R)	991	1.2%
Kevin Johns (R)	974	1.2%

GEORGIA 6

Atlanta suburbs — Roswell, part of Marietta

Anchored in Atlanta's burgeoning northern suburbs, the 6th covers parts of three counties that are home to Republican voters who largely work in technology and other white-collar occupations.

The mostly white 6th is one of Georgia's most affluent, educated and Republican districts. Office parks, malls and housing subdivisions dominate the landscape. This area, referred to as the Golden Crescent, is sandwiched between three major highways — Interstate 75, Interstate 85 and the Interstate 285 perimeter highway. Cobb County, northwest of Atlanta, accounts for more than half of the district's vote, and many of its residents work at Lockheed Martin in the nearby 11th.

Along with its defense industry, Marietta (shared with the 11th) provides Cobb County

with its own thriving commercial center. Numerous corporations have office space in the "Platinum Triangle," shared with the 5th, a huge employment center. But the growth and prospering economy also have brought gridlock and air pollution, causing some businesses to reconsider locating here.

In the central part of the 6th are solidly GOP suburbs in northern Fulton County. Alpharetta was once home to large farms that since have been converted into suburban developments. Roswell, formerly a cotton-milling center, is now a booming bedroom community in Fulton County.

MAJOR INDUSTRY
Defense, finance, technology

CITIES
Roswell (pt.), 71,848; Sandy Springs (pt.), 41,043; Alpharetta, 34,854; Kennesaw, 21,675; Marietta (pt.), 18,614; Acworth, 13,422

NOTABLE
Former Republican Rep. Newt Gingrich represented the 6th from 1979-99 and served as House Speaker from 1995-99.

Rep. John Linder (R)

Elected 1992; 7th term

For the soft-spoken Linder, the brass ring continues to hang just beyond his grasp. He was in line to chair the Rules Committee in the 109th Congress, until Speaker J. Dennis Hastert granted a term limit waiver to Chairman David Dreier and allowed him a fourth two-year stint with the gavel. So Linder relinquished his Rules post to take a seat on the Ways and Means Committee.

It was not a bad consolation prize. On Ways and Means, he is on the front line of one of the biggest issues of the Congress, the debate over fundamental changes in Social Security to introduce private market forces. And he can press his case for replacing the income tax with a national sales tax, his signature issue.

Linder's proposal to institute a 23 percent national sales tax as a replacement for all federal income, estate and payroll taxes won him an ally in Majority Leader Tom DeLay, who flirted briefly with the idea of putting the measure to a vote on the House floor in 2004. The bill would almost certainly have failed, but the idea was to call attention to the issue and to try to build support for overhauling the tax code in the 109th Congress.

If Linder manages to find the spotlight in the tax debate, it will mark his return to prominence after a stumble from the top GOP ranks in the late 1990s. His fortunes declined when his closest political ally, House Speaker Newt Gingrich, was forced to resign in 1998; Linder lost the chairmanship of the National Republican Congressional Committee (NRCC), the organization that helps recruit and fund GOP candidates for the House.

He spent a good deal of time in the 107th Congress fighting to keep his seat. Redistricting threw him into a redrawn district and a primary contest in 2002 against Rep. Bob Barr, a fellow conservative with a higher national profile. Campaigning hard on his plan to eliminate the Internal Revenue Service, Linder prevailed by an unexpectedly large margin.

Linder is as conservative a Republican as they come. He regularly scores perfect, 100 percent ratings from the U.S. Chamber of Commerce and zeros from the AFL-CIO. His tax plan, first introduced in 1999, calls for abolition of the Internal Revenue Service; his proposed national sales tax would be administered primarily by the states. But he has been an ardent supporter of President Bush's tax proposals as well, including the $137 billion corporate tax cut in 2004 and the $1.35 trillion tax cut in 2001.

Linder is equally conservative on social issues. He opposes abortion and cosponsored legislation that became law in 2003 banning a procedure that opponents call "partial birth" abortion. He is against most new gun control proposals and in 2002 voted in favor of arming commercial pilots with handguns to discourage terrorists.

In his previous post as the No. 3 Republican on Rules, Linder typically supported the leadership, but was outspoken at times on the need to cut deals with Democrats to avert floor fights. Through his quiet backing of GOP leaders, and his thoughtful work on issues such as the sales tax, Linder won respect as a team player. In 2003, he left his own birthday dinner to return to the House to provide the tie-breaking vote to adopt an amendment to the District of Columbia spending bill creating a program of private school vouchers.

The political alliance between Linder and Gingrich dated to the mid-1970s, when the two worked to rebuild the Georgia Republican Party. After Gingrich led Republicans to their historic takeover of Congress in 1995, the

CAPITOL OFFICE
225-4272
linder.house.gov
1026 Longworth 20515-1007; fax 225-4696

COMMITTEES
Homeland Security
(Prevention of Nuclear & Biological Attack - chairman)
Ways & Means

HOMETOWN
Duluth

BORN
Sept. 9, 1942, Deer River, Minn.

RELIGION
Presbyterian

FAMILY
Wife, Lynne Linder; two children

EDUCATION
U. of Minnesota, Duluth, B.S. 1963; U. of Minnesota, D.D.S. 1967

MILITARY SERVICE
Air Force, 1967-69

CAREER
Financial executive; dentist

POLITICAL HIGHLIGHTS
Ga. House, 1975-81; Republican nominee for Ga. Senate, 1980; Ga. House, 1983-91; Republican nominee for U.S. House, 1990

ELECTION RESULTS

2004 GENERAL
John Linder (R)		unopposed

2004 PRIMARY
John Linder (R)		unopposed

2002 GENERAL
John Linder (R)	138,997	78.9%
Michael R. Berlon (D)	37,124	21.1%

PREVIOUS WINNING PERCENTAGES
2000 (100%); 1998 (69%); 1996 (64%); 1994 (58%); 1992 (51%)

new Speaker rewarded Linder by putting him in charge of the leaders' primary campaign committee. When the GOP instead lost five seats in 1998, the rank and file's long-simmering dissatisfaction with Gingrich's leadership, his controversial public comments and his ethics problems peaked. Without a strong base among House Republicans to call his own, Linder was swept out of the leadership, losing a bid to remain in the NRCC top post to Virginia's Thomas M. Davis III.

Linder grew up in a small Minnesota town, the son of a car salesman. He worked his way through college at the University of Minnesota in Duluth, starting in pre-med but switching to dentistry after being inspired by observing dentists at a speech clinic working with children with cleft palates.

After graduating from dental school, Linder joined the Air Force, where he practiced dentistry in San Antonio. Linder and his wife then moved to suburban Atlanta. He set up a dentistry practice, but was increasingly interested in politics. He subscribed to the Congressional Record, a daily digest of activities on the House and Senate floors, and was fascinated, he says, by the good ideas he found in the Extension of Remarks section, where lawmakers expound on issues of the day.

Linder ran successfully for a seat in the Georgia House in 1974 and wound up serving a total of 14 years in the state legislature. In 1977, he founded a lending institution that specialized in providing financial assistance to small businesses, and eventually he left dentistry. While in the state House, he earned a reputation for battling the Democratic leadership.

Linder first ran for Congress in 1990, losing a tight battle with Democratic Rep. Ben Jones in the 4th District. Two years later, redistricting gave the district a more Republican tilt, and Linder tried again. He narrowly edged out state Sen. Cathey Steinberg, with 51 percent of the vote, while Jones sought re-election in the 10th District.

After a Supreme Court decision invalidated Georgia's congressional map as racial gerrymandering, Linder in 1995 wound up representing a redrawn 11th District. It included some of the Atlanta suburbs and rural areas.

He enjoyed easy re-elections until forced to face off against Barr in the 2002 primary in the newly drawn 7th District. Barr was known for his role as a leader in the House GOP effort to impeach President Clinton and as an outspoken critic of the president on television talk shows. But Republican voters ultimately rejected Barr's acerbic style and polarizing politics in favor of the buttoned-down Linder, who prevailed by 29 percentage points. Linder went on to win in November with 79 percent of the vote. He was unopposed in the 2004 primary and general elections.

KEY VOTES

2004
?	Extend federal unemployment benefits by 13 weeks
No	Pass $283.2 billion, six-year federal highway and mass transit bill
Yes	Approve $146 billion multi-year extension of previously enacted middle-class tax breaks
Yes	Amend the Constitution to prohibit same-sex marriage
Yes	Cut corporate taxes $137 billion over 10 years
Yes	Reorganize U.S. intelligence agencies as proposed by Sept. 11 commission

2003
Yes	Cut taxes by $330 billion through fiscal 2013
No	Block Bush rule scaling back overtime pay for some white-collar federal workers
Yes	Do not allow use of search warrants without first notifying subjects
No	Allow importation of prescription drugs
Yes	Create private school voucher program in Washington, D.C.
Yes	Ban "partial birth" abortion except to save a woman's life
No	Split $18.6 billion in Iraq aid into half-grant, half-loan
Yes	Overhaul Medicare and create prescription drug benefit

CQ VOTE STUDIES

	PARTY UNITY		PRESIDENTIAL SUPPORT	
	Support	Oppose	Support	Oppose
2004	98%	2%	94%	6%
2003	98%	2%	100%	0%
2002	98%	2%	90%	10%
2001	99%	1%	98%	2%
2000	96%	4%	22%	78%

INTEREST GROUPS

	AFL-CIO	ADA	CCUS	ACU
2004	7%	0%	100%	100%
2003	0%	5%	100%	88%
2002	11%	0%	100%	100%
2001	8%	0%	100%	96%
2000	0%	0%	90%	87%

GEORGIA 7
North of Atlanta — outer Atlanta suburbs

The 7th takes in overflow from many of the Atlanta suburbs contained in the 6th District. Forming a horseshoe shape around the top of Atlanta, the district is characterized by rapid suburban growth, including many newcomers to the state. As the suburbs close to the city become increasingly populated, the areas represented by the 7th are becoming outer suburbs. Many of the towns are transforming from rural to suburban.

In addition to those who commute to Atlanta, many who live in the district work at Lockheed Martin in the nearby 11th or at one of a host of technology companies in Norcross. The homebuilding industry is burgeoning as the explosion of housing developments and wealthy subdivisions extends farther north from the city.

Voters in the 7th range from social conservatives living in rural areas to fiscal conservatives living in suburban areas. Redistricting following the 2000 census shifted the district's politics further right, as many Democratic and swing voters were removed, leaving a solid GOP base.

In 2004, George W. Bush received 73 percent of the presidential vote in the 7th, his second-highest percentage in the state. The bulk of voters live in Gwinnett County, considered the most-moderate and fastest-growing county in the district, although Bush received almost twice as many Gwinnett County votes as Democratic nominee John Kerry in 2004.

Water use is a major issue in the area. Rain from the 2004 hurricanes appears to have at least temporarily ended Georgia's recent battles with drought, but the expanding population here is depleting the water supply. Lake Lanier (shared with the 10th) and Allatoona Lake are major bodies of water in the district.

MAJOR INDUSTRY
Technology, retail, homebuilding, manufacturing

CITIES
Duluth, 22,122; Lawrenceville (pt.), 18,269; Snellville (pt.), 15,346

NOTABLE
Mall of Georgia, in Buford, covers 2 million square feet and features themed courtyards that represent areas of the state; Duluth elected Georgia's first woman mayor, Alice H. Strickland, in 1921; She promised to "clean up Duluth and rid it of demon rum."

Rep. Lynn Westmoreland (R)

Elected 2004; 1st term

Westmoreland passed up a chance to become the first Republican Speaker in the Georgia House to run for Congress. The chamber's minority leader when he decided to run for the open 8th District seat, Westmoreland left just as his party surged into the majority. But the same powerful GOP trend allowed Westmoreland to cruise to an easy general-election victory in his race to succeed Republican Mac Collins, who left the House seat for a Senate bid that failed.

A homebuilder, Westmoreland will fit neatly into the dominant conservative wing of the congressional Republican Party. He opposes abortion, advocates gun owners' rights and strongly supports the GOP agenda of reducing taxes and federal regulation of private enterprise. Soon after his arrival, he led a push to get Georgia to redraw its congressional district lines.

If he sticks to his sharp opposition to what he sees as runaway federal spending, Westmoreland may find himself tangling with his party's leadership over earmarks that lawmakers put into spending bills to support projects in their district. He said that he probably would have opposed the 2003 Medicare prescription drug law as being too costly.

Nonetheless, Westmoreland will pursue several parochial matters during his first term. He got his preferred assignment, to the Transportation and Infrastructure panel, a post he hopes to use to work to relieve congestion on roads in the fast-growing parts of his district just south of Atlanta. On the Aviation Subcommittee, he can look out for the interests of thousands of constituents employed by the city's airport and Atlanta-based Delta Airlines.

Like many Southern Republicans, Westmoreland grew up in a family of conservative Democrats. He says he committed to the GOP only after he decided to pursue a state Senate seat. He failed in the 1988 primary and 1990 general election, but won his state House seat in 1992.

In 2004, Westmoreland won a GOP runoff over Dylan Glenn, a former White House and gubernatorial aide who was bidding to become the House's only black Republican.

CAPITOL OFFICE
225-5901
www.house.gov/westmoreland
1118 Longworth 20515-1008; fax 225-2515

COMMITTEES
Government Reform
Small Business
Transportation & Infrastructure

HOMETOWN
Grantville

BORN
April 2, 1950, Atlanta, Ga.

RELIGION
Baptist

FAMILY
Wife, Joan Westmoreland; three children

EDUCATION
Georgia State U., attended 1969-71

CAREER
Construction company owner; real estate developer

POLITICAL HIGHLIGHTS
Sought Republican nomination for Ga. Senate, 1988; Republican nominee for Ga. Senate, 1990; Ga. House, 1993-2005 (minority leader, 2001-03)

ELECTION RESULTS

2004 GENERAL

Lynn Westmoreland (R)	227,524	75.6%
Silvia Delamar (D)	73,632	24.5%

2004 PRIMARY RUNOFF

Lynn Westmoreland (R)	34,250	55.5%
Dylan Glenn (R)	27,485	44.5%

2004 PRIMARY

Lynn Westmoreland (R)	43,005	45.9%
Dylan Glenn (R)	35,276	37.6%
Mike D. Crotts (R)	10,596	11.3%
Tom Mills (R)	4,926	5.3%

GEORGIA 8

West – suburbs of Atlanta, Columbus and Macon

Created in redistricting following the 2000 census, the 8th was drawn to elect a Republican. Mostly within the rough triangle of Macon, Columbus and the south-central suburbs of Atlanta, the 8th jumps all around western Georgia, taking in Republican suburbs of those cities. The 11th and 13th districts wind in and around the 8th, encompassing Democratic areas.

Much of the 8th used to be agricultural but is now suburban, although many rural areas remain. Textile and poultry processing plants dot the landscape, and the timber industry flourishes here. The home building industry also is becoming a larger force in the suburbs, as additional housing developments and malls are constructed.

South of Atlanta, the district includes suburbs that were cut out of the heavily Democratic 13th. Peachtree City, in Fayette

County, is a planned community 15 miles south of Atlanta that attracts commuters and homebuilders. Fayette County is home to many workers at nearby Hartsfield-Jackson Atlanta International Airport. Henry County, east of Fayette, is the second-fastest-growing county in the state.

Farther east, the district encompasses all of rural Jasper County and snakes into Bibb County, covering the Republican suburbs north of Macon. Some workers from Robins Air Force Base, in the 1st District, live in the 8th, along with commuters to Macon.

The district's western edge includes rural Carroll and Coweta counties and extends south into northern Muscogee County and its immediate suburbs of Columbus.

MAJOR INDUSTRY
Textiles, agriculture, timber, poultry processing, home building

CITIES
Columbus (pt.), 53,778; Peachtree City, 31,580; Douglasville (pt.), 13,553; Fayetteville, 11,148

NOTABLE
Callaway Gardens holds the Sky High Hot Air Balloon Festival every Labor Day.

Rep. Charlie Norwood (R)

Elected 1994; 6th term

CAPITOL OFFICE
225-4101
www.house.gov/norwood
2452 Rayburn 20515-1009; fax 226-0776

COMMITTEES
Education & Workforce
  (Workforce Protections - chairman)
Energy & Commerce

HOMETOWN
Augusta

BORN
July 27, 1941, Valdosta, Ga.

RELIGION
Methodist

FAMILY
Wife, Gloria Norwood; two children

EDUCATION
Georgia Southern U., B.S. 1964 (biology);
Georgetown U., D.D.S. 1967

MILITARY SERVICE
Army, 1967-69

CAREER
Dentist

POLITICAL HIGHLIGHTS
No previous office

ELECTION RESULTS

2004 GENERAL

Charlie Norwood (R)	197,869	74.3%
Bob Ellis (D)	68,462	25.7%

2004 PRIMARY

Charlie Norwood (R)	unopposed

2002 GENERAL

Charlie Norwood (R)	123,313	72.8%
Barry Gordon Irwin (D)	45,974	27.2%

PREVIOUS WINNING PERCENTAGES
2000 (63%); 1998 (60%); 1996 (52%); 1994 (65%)

For much of his congressional career, Norwood was known mainly as the leading House Republican advocate of a "patients' bill of rights." He received enormous attention for his maneuvering on legislation to give people more leverage over their medical insurance plans — first working with Democrats and against the House Republican leadership for two years, then reversing field and cutting a deal in secret with President Bush in 2001.

In doing so, however, Norwood alienated key players on both sides. The issue eventually faded anyway, as health insurance companies backed off on many of the harshest practices that built resentment against managed care in the 1990s. When the Supreme Court invalidated 10 state patients' rights laws in June 2004, Norwood said the ruling would "reinvigorate our efforts to press on in the battle to deliver patients' rights once and for all." He is unlikely, however, to regain the spotlight he once had, as the political urgency has lessened and his allies in Congress no longer trust him enough to work with him.

Instead, Norwood, an earnest and plain-spoken Georgian who was a dentist before he came to Congress in the GOP Class of 1994, probably will stick with more traditional Republican issues through the rest of his congressional career. In the 108th Congress, for example, he briefly regained the spotlight on a new issue: reining in the Occupational Safety and Health Administration, which many conservatives say is an overly bureaucratic agency that imposes unreasonable rules on businesses.

In 2004, the House passed four overhaul bills written by Norwood, in his role as chairman of the Education and the Workforce Subcommittee on Workforce Protections. Among other things, the bills waived deadlines for businesses to respond to citations and required OSHA to pay the legal fees of small businesses that successfully defended themselves against an agency citation. The Senate never acted on the measures, though, and they died at the end of the year.

A tobacco chewer with a love of fishing and duck hunting, Norwood's broad interests in Congress may spring from the fact that his political experience came late in life. He had never held public office before his election in 1994 at age 53. He ran on the platform that local and state governments are generally better problem solvers than federal bureaucrats. As a dentist, he said, he knew plenty about unnecessary and onerous federal regulation.

From his seat on the Energy and Commerce panel's Health Subcommittee, Norwood continues to be active in health care debates affecting Medicare and Medicaid. Indeed, one of his Medicare proposals in 2003, months before the Medicare prescription drug bill passed Congress, went far beyond the ideas even the most market-oriented Republicans were willing to consider. In a paper to his fellow Republicans on the subcommittee, Norwood suggested his party phase out the current Medicare fee-for-service program. Seniors born before a certain date would have been allowed to have fee-for-service as an option, but those born after that date would not. "We're going to have to do [Medicare] differently or we're going to have to break the bank," Norwood said at the time.

Norwood initially became influential on the managed care issue by working with the leadership, helping to write a GOP package that the House passed in 1998. But when the legislation died in the Senate, he resolved to take a more aggressive stance in the following Congress.

He at first tried to work within the system but concluded that top Republicans were inhospitable to compromise. With the Commerce Committee's top-ranking Democrat, John D. Dingell of Michigan, as his partner, Norwood promoted a bill under which patients could have sued their health plans over coverage decisions — an idea anathema to loyal GOP business and insurance interests. When the House passed the plan with 275 votes, a furious Speaker J. Dennis Hastert refused to appoint Norwood as one of the negotiators with the Senate, and the legislation died again at the end of 2000.

In 2001, Norwood strayed on the issue anew, this time abandoning the Dingell fold. Torn between his Democratic allies on the issue and Bush, whom he considered a friend, Norwood gambled that picking the president would boost momentum for his cause. Their surprise accord allowed a bill with a GOP stamp to pass the House, but the measure died once more when priorities shifted after the Sept. 11, 2001, terrorist attacks.

Norwood has dealt with health care issues on a personal level as well. He had a single-lung transplant operation in 2004. Four years earlier, he was in a car accident that shattered several ribs and bones in his hands.

Norwood's rebellious streak extends to other issues, particularly trade. He opposed Bush's campaign in 2002 for the power to negotiate trade deals on a fast track. And he worked actively against the GOP leadership and President Clinton in 2000 to oppose enactment of the law permanently granting China normal trade status.

But despite his high-profile defections, Norwood is generally a loyal party foot soldier. In each of his first four terms, he stood with Republicans on party-line votes at least 95 percent of the time. And he voted with his party 98 percent of the time in the 108th Congress.

He opposes abortion, supports school vouchers and school prayer, and is a staunch advocate for the rights of gun owners — a position that he says was cemented by an incident when he was 16 years old. He and a high school friend were playing with a .22-caliber pistol when it discharged while in Norwood's hands, killing the other boy. Norwood said the experience convinced him that no amount of gun control could have prevented such an accident.

After serving as a combat medic in Vietnam, Norwood opened his dental practice. His election two decades later — he trounced one-term incumbent Democrat Don Johnson by a 2-to-1 margin in the 1994 GOP landslide — made him the first Republican to represent the Augusta area in the House since Reconstruction. With the exception of 1996, he has retained his seat by generally comfortable margins.

KEY VOTES

2004

No	Extend federal unemployment benefits by 13 weeks
No	Pass $283.2 billion, six-year federal highway and mass transit bill
Yes	Approve $146 billion multi-year extension of previously enacted middle-class tax breaks
Yes	Amend the Constitution to prohibit same-sex marriage
?	Cut corporate taxes $137 billion over 10 years
?	Reorganize U.S. intelligence agencies as proposed by Sept. 11 commission

2003

Yes	Cut taxes by $330 billion through fiscal 2013
No	Block Bush rule scaling back overtime pay for some white-collar federal workers
No	Do not allow use of search warrants without first notifying subjects
No	Allow importation of prescription drugs
Yes	Create private school voucher program in Washington, D.C.
Yes	Ban "partial birth" abortion except to save a woman's life
No	Split $18.6 billion in Iraq aid into half-grant, half-loan
No	Overhaul Medicare and create prescription drug benefit

CQ VOTE STUDIES

	PARTY UNITY		PRESIDENTIAL SUPPORT	
	Support	Oppose	Support	Oppose
2004	99%	1%	87%	13%
2003	97%	3%	85%	15%
2002	96%	4%	82%	18%
2001	96%	4%	88%	12%
2000	97%	3%	17%	83%

INTEREST GROUPS

	AFL-CIO	ADA	CCUS	ACU
2004	7%	0%	100%	100%
2003	27%	10%	87%	92%
2002	22%	5%	68%	96%
2001	25%	10%	81%	96%
2000	10%	5%	71%	100%

GEORGIA 9
Northeast — part of Augusta

The 9th starts in northeastern Georgia, encompassing agricultural and mountain areas, and travels down the South Carolina border to take in parts of Augusta. It also extends west to take in some suburbs east of Atlanta.

Created following the 2000 census, the 9th is solidly Republican at the federal level. An arm from the neighboring 12th cuts north into the center of the district to strip out liberal Athens and the University of Georgia. A growing suburban population contributes to the GOP bent, and as a result George W. Bush received 72 percent of the district's vote in the 2004 presidential election — a 4 percent increase from his percentage in 2000.

Suburban areas around Augusta and Athens are less developed than those bordering Atlanta. The district takes in part of the city of Augusta as well, including much of the Augusta National Golf Club (shared with the 12th). Many of the 9th's suburbs are rural in character, dotted with dairy farms and ranches. The mountainous northern region is the most

rural, with dairy, timber and mining industries sustaining the economy. The area also depends on tourism dollars from visitors to a chain of lakes on the South Carolina border: Lake Russell, Lake Thurmond and Lake Hartwell.

The Savannah River valley makes water a major issue. Legislators representing this part of the state often have fought against exporting water to Atlanta, hoping to keep the resources on their own turf.

MAJOR INDUSTRY
Agriculture, tourism, retail

MILITARY BASES
Fort Gordon (Army), 12,003 military, 6,511 civilian (2004) (shared with the 12th)

CITIES
Augusta-Richmond (pt.), 36,679; Martinez, 27,749; Evans, 17,727

NOTABLE
Augusta National Golf Club (shared with the 12th) hosts the annual Masters golf tournament; The movies "Deliverance" and "Smokey and the Bandit" were set in Rabun County; Helen, a hamlet in White County, is a replica of a Bavarian village; Elberton is known as the granite capital of the world.

Rep. Nathan Deal (R)

Elected 1992; 7th term

CAPITOL OFFICE
225-5211
congressmandeal@mail.house.gov
www.house.gov/deal
2133 Rayburn 20515-1010; fax 225-8272

COMMITTEES
Energy & Commerce
  (Health - chairman)

HOMETOWN
Gainesville

BORN
Aug. 25, 1942, Millen, Ga.

RELIGION
Baptist

FAMILY
Wife, Sandra Dunagan Deal; four children

EDUCATION
Mercer U., B.A. 1964, J.D. 1966

MILITARY SERVICE
Army, 1966-68

CAREER
Lawyer; state prosecutor

POLITICAL HIGHLIGHTS
Hall County Juvenile Court judge, 1971-72; Hall
County attorney, 1977-79; Ga. Senate, 1981-93
(served as a Democrat; president pro tempore,
1991-93)

ELECTION RESULTS

2004 GENERAL
Nathan Deal (R)   unopposed
2004 PRIMARY
Nathan Deal (R)   unopposed
2002 GENERAL
Nathan Deal (R)   unopposed

PREVIOUS WINNING PERCENTAGES *
2000 (75%); 1998 (100%); 1996 (66%); 1994 (58%);
1992 (59%)
*Elected as a Democrat 1992-1994

Deal has now served as a Republican more than five times as long as he sat in the House as a Democrat. His conservative views have barely shifted along the way, suggesting that his party switch was more about marketing himself to his rural North Georgia constituents than about signaling an altered ideology.

Deal changed sides near the beginning of his second term in 1995, three months after the House came under GOP control for the first time in 40 years. Deal declared at the time that "the Democratic Party's attitude wasn't in tune with me or my constituents' beliefs."

The switch only enhanced Deal's political security at home. He won both his elections to the House as a Democrat with less than 60 percent of the vote, a threshold often used in assessing whether a lawmaker can be considered safe in his next re-election bid. His share of the vote has never dipped below about two-thirds in the five elections since, and Deal was unopposed in both his 2002 and 2004 elections. They took place in a redrawn and renumbered district — it was the 9th in the 1990s — that ambles southward toward Atlanta but has retained its overwhelmingly conservative, and national Republican, loyalties. Demonstrating this loyalty, Deal in 2004 voted in agreement with a majority of his party 100 percent of the time.

Deal's legislative efforts have mostly been behind the scenes on the Energy and Commerce Committee, the panel to which he was assigned by the Republicans as a reward for his new allegiance. Deal is seldom seen on the House floor except for votes, and many of the appearances he does make are as the presiding officer.

But he is certain to be more visible in the 109th as the new chairman of the panel's Health Subcommittee. The GOP leadership will want to push a diverse health care agenda highlighted by medical malpractice legislation, proposed revisions of the Medicaid program and new market-based incentives to help the uninsured. The first steps of many of these measures will be taken in Deal's subcommittee.

Deal will also have to contend with California Democrat Henry A. Waxman, who chaired the Health and the Environment Subcommittee for 16 years before the GOP took over in 1995, and the subcommittee's top-ranking Democrat, Sherrod Brown of Ohio. Both Democrats have a strong command of health care issues and will promote their party line by advocating step-by-step expansions of health care coverage while needling the Republicans over issues such as the prescription drug benefit for seniors. Deal's demeanor is low-key and approachable, however, and his regular-guy persona may fend off any severe partisan bickering.

Deal briefly found himself in the national spotlight in 2003 when Speaker J. Dennis Hastert slipped a provision for him into that year's catchall spending package to allow beef and poultry producers to give their animals non-organic feed and still label the meat as organic. Deal, who had been pushing for the organic chicken feed exemption on behalf of Baldwin-based Fieldale Farms in his district, said the provision was an effort to ease the standards for organic producers, which he said were too strict. "They are penalizing people who are already in the business and want to stay in the business," he said. Amid an outcry from organic food producers, lawmakers subsequently repealed Deal's provision.

Deal looks out for the 10th District's businesses in other ways. In 2003, he added a provision to the House-passed energy bill to authorize a one-time grant to study the burning of used carpet as a fuel to make Portland cement, the key ingredient in concrete. The idea was important to Dalton, home to three of the world's largest carpet companies.

At first glance, Deal's landlocked and mostly rural district might seem an unlikely hot spot for concern about immigration. But the poultry and carpet businesses rely on foreign workers — illegal and legal — and Deal has long served on a GOP immigration task force. His particular interest lies in beefing up enforcement against illegal immigrants, including those who enter the United States legally but stay longer than permitted. After the Sept. 11, 2001, terrorist attacks, he was even more adamant that the Immigration and Naturalization Service improve its processes for approving visas, not just to weed out potential terrorists but also to make sure immigrants are legally entitled to be in the United States. His position on illegal immigration has put him at odds with the Bush administration, which has pressed to ease some immigration laws.

While the 10th District includes part of the rapidly growing Atlanta metropolitan area, its heart remains rural, so issues such as logging and satellite television access are important. In the 106th Congress, Deal was a leader on legislation to help local counties whose revenues from timber harvesting on federal lands have dwindled. In the 108th, he floated a plan to encourage cable and satellite companies to offer a la carte programming, allowing subscribers to choose and pay for individual channels instead of packages.

Deal is the only child of two public school teachers (his wife is a teacher as well), and although his parents were not active in politics, they impressed on him the importance of being active in public life. "After all, teaching is a type of public service," he says.

He was a successful high school and college debater, and he went on to law school. Fulfilling a commitment he made as a four-year member of the ROTC during college, he joined the Army and served two years in the Judge Advocate General corps before opening his law practice back in Gainesville. He served as a prosecutor and a juvenile court judge and then, at the urging of friends, ran successfully for an open state Senate seat in 1980.

Deal had had a string of effortless re-elections there by the time Ed Jenkins, a fellow conservative Democrat, announced in 1992 that he was retiring from the House. Deal's GOP opponent that year was Daniel Becker, who made abortion the focus of a "morality in government" campaign. Becker's appeal proved to be limited and he managed only 41 percent of the vote.

KEY VOTES

2004

No   Extend federal unemployment benefits by 13 weeks

No   Pass $283.2 billion, six-year federal highway and mass transit bill

?   Approve $146 billion multi-year extension of previously enacted middle-class tax breaks

Yes   Amend the Constitution to prohibit same-sex marriage

Yes   Cut corporate taxes $137 billion over 10 years

No   Reorganize U.S. intelligence agencies as proposed by Sept. 11 commission

2003

Yes   Cut taxes by $330 billion through fiscal 2013

No   Block Bush rule scaling back overtime pay for some white-collar federal workers

No   Do not allow use of search warrants without first notifying subjects

No   Allow importation of prescription drugs

Yes   Create private school voucher program in Washington, D.C.

Yes   Ban "partial birth" abortion except to save a woman's life

No   Split $18.6 billion in Iraq aid into half-grant, half-loan

Yes   Overhaul Medicare and create prescription drug benefit

CQ VOTE STUDIES

	PARTY UNITY		PRESIDENTIAL SUPPORT	
	Support	Oppose	Support	Oppose
2004	100%	0%	87%	13%
2003	99%	1%	93%	7%
2002	96%	4%	82%	18%
2001	98%	2%	93%	7%
2000	95%	5%	15%	85%

INTEREST GROUPS

	AFL-CIO	ADA	CCUS	ACU
2004	7%	0%	94%	100%
2003	20%	5%	93%	84%
2002	11%	0%	90%	100%
2001	9%	5%	90%	100%
2000	10%	5%	71%	96%

GEORGIA 10
North — Dalton, Gainesville

Anchored by North Georgia's mountains, the 10th runs across the western half of the state's northern border. It includes the Cloudland Canyon, the man-made Lake Lanier and several growing Atlanta suburbs, as well as bedroom communities outside of Chattanooga, Tenn.

Residents are overwhelmingly white and strongly Republican; only 3 percent of the district's population is black. While Democrats have long dominated local politics, the GOP allegiance in some north-central counties is unwavering and dates to the Civil War. George W. Bush received 76 percent of the district's vote in the 2004 presidential election — his highest percentage in the state and a 5 percent increase from his 2000 share of the vote.

Economically, the 10th has benefited from a population boom. A surge of new residents in the south has brought white-collar and service-sector jobs to the district but is straining local water resources. Many of the new residents are Hispanic immigrants who work in the district's poultry processing and carpet-making industries in Hall and Whitfield counties.

Tourist dollars also play a role in the economy, as visitors flock to Lake Sidney Lanier (shared with the 7th) on the 10th's eastern edge. Roughly 8 million people annually visit the lake, which was constructed in the 1950s by the U.S. Army Corps of Engineers.

The district also dips down into the Atlanta area, where it takes in Republican suburbs north and east of the city, most of them dominated by housing subdivisions and shopping malls.

MAJOR INDUSTRY
Poultry processing, carpet manufacturing, textiles

CITIES
Dalton, 27,912; Gainesville, 25,578; Calhoun, 10,667; Fort Oglethorpe, 6,940

NOTABLE
Dalton is known as the carpet capital of the world; Gainesville, dubbed the poultry capital of the world, displays the Georgia Poultry Federation's monument to the industry in the center of town: an obelisk with a chicken statue on top; Springer Mountain is the southern terminus of the Appalachian National Scenic Trail, which is 2,174 miles long and extends to Maine.

Rep. Phil Gingrey (R)

Elected 2002; 2nd term

An obstetrician who boasts of delivering 5,200 babies before he came to Congress, Gingrey is a strict anti-abortion rights Republican. The issue is at the top of the portfolio of family issues that interest him. He also focuses on federal education policy and — not surprisingly given his earlier career — wants to limit medical malpractice lawsuits.

Gingrey also gained the notice of GOP leaders who were happy with his 2002 win in a district drawn for a Democrat. Speaker J. Dennis Hastert put him on the Rules Committee at the start of the 109th Congress, and he was also asked to join the Republican Policy Committee.

Gingrey, who ran for the House on the slogan "He Delivers," had a relatively productive first term, getting two minor bills through the House. Most junior lawmakers struggle just to get a word in edgewise at committee hearings. But someone who counts babies as a career statistic can be said to be goal-oriented, and Gingrey isn't happy unless he's crossing items off his to-do list. "As a physician, I've got the personality where I like to do something and move on to the next case. You don't like to have people slow you down," he once told Family Practice News.

His most far-reaching effort was a bill setting stricter standards for reporting and measuring the effectiveness of teacher training programs at the college level. Gingrey's bill builds on President Bush's 2001 overhaul of public education, the No Child Left Behind Act, by making federal grants to colleges and universities contingent on producing teachers who are highly qualified in their core subjects.

Gingrey, a former Marietta school board chairman, was less enthusiastic about the government dabbling in school cafeterias. During a 2004 debate in the Education and Workforce Committee on changes to the school lunch program to help curb childhood obesity, Gingrey said that a Democratic attempt to restrict sales of sweet and fatty foods in public schools was government intrusion. Control over what children eat should be left to parents, he said.

He also sponsored a measure, which passed the House, to create within the EPA a research and development program for "green" chemistry, an emerging field of making products that generate the least amount of hazardous waste.

Gingrey says one of his main reasons for seeking a seat in the House is his desire to curb medical malpractice lawsuits, which result in doctors paying higher insurance premiums and force some to abandon their practices. He has faced some medical concerns of his own. In December 2002, Gingrey had double coronary bypass surgery. Once his health rebounded, he resumed a rigorous exercise schedule; he is up at 5 a.m. to be at the House gym when it opens at 5:30.

Gingrey is one of the House's staunchest opponents of abortion, even in cases of rape or incest. He also quickly joined Bush in calling for a constitutional ban on same-sex marriage, an issue the president used to rally social conservatives in his 2004 re-election campaign. Local Democrats grumbled that Gingrey had become a "rubber stamp and yes man" for Bush, the Atlanta Journal-Constitution reported. Gingrey, who voted in agreement with Bush 85 percent of the time in 2004, shot back: "If the president continues to stand for traditional values we all treasure in Georgia, then I'll rubber stamp him until the ink runs dry."

On fiscal issues, he supports abolishing the Internal Revenue Service

CAPITOL OFFICE
225-2931
gingrey.ga@mail.house.gov
www.house.gov/gingrey
119 Cannon 20515-1011; fax 225-2944

COMMITTEES
Rules

HOMETOWN
Marietta

BORN
July 10, 1942, Augusta, Ga.

RELIGION
Roman Catholic

FAMILY
Wife, Billie Gingrey; four children

EDUCATION
Georgia Institute of Technology, B.S. 1965 (chemistry); Medical College of Georgia, M.D. 1969

CAREER
Physician

POLITICAL HIGHLIGHTS
Marietta Board of Education, 1993-97 (chairman, 1994-97); Ga. Senate, 1999-2003

ELECTION RESULTS

2004 GENERAL

Phil Gingrey (R)	120,696	57.4%
Rick Crawford (D)	89,591	42.6%

2004 PRIMARY

Phil Gingrey (R)	unopposed

2002 GENERAL

Phil Gingrey (R)	69,427	51.6%
Roger Kahn (D)	65,007	48.4%

and wants a national retail sales tax enacted to replace the federal income tax. One of his parochial priorities is continued funding of the F-22 fighter plane. He also lobbies for full production of the 300 planes ordered from Lockheed Martin's Marietta plant, one of his district's largest employers.

He is truly a local boy. Gingrey worked his way through undergraduate studies at the Georgia Institute of Technology with a factory job. He intended to become an engineer but after visiting an operating room with a family friend who was a neurosurgeon, he switched gears and pursued medicine at the Medical College of Georgia. He went into obstetrics because "I like the upbeat-ness of delivering babies and having that situation almost always a happy one," he once told the Journal-Constitution.

After serving on the school board when his children were in school (the four Gingrey children are now grown), he went on to two terms in the Georgia Senate while continuing with his medical practice. In the legislature, he became well-known for advocating the tightening of teen driving laws, including a 10 p.m. curfew on teen drivers. Gingrey said he was motivated by reading the obituaries of teenagers he had helped deliver as babies.

In 2001, he toyed with running against Democratic incumbent Sen. Max Cleland. After redistricting gave Georgia two new seats in the House as a result of population growth, he decided instead to run for the House.

The Democratic legislature had designed the 11th District to favor one of their own, so much so that Republican Rep. Bob Barr, who then represented a portion of it, decided to take his chances on running in the GOP primary against another incumbent Republican, John Linder.

With Barr out of the way, Gingrey jumped in and won a primary contest for the new district, which covers an area of exurbs and small towns southwest of Atlanta. He had a hard fight in the general election against Roger Kahn, a wealthy wholesale liquor distributor, who lent his own campaign $2.5 million. The Journal-Constitution called the race "expensive and dirty." Gingrey got help from the American Medical Association, which paid for polling and radio ads.

Gingrey won with 52 percent of the vote, mainly by appealing to right-leaning and religious conservatives from rural areas. But the Georgia Ethics Commission found him guilty of violating state ethics codes for funneling money from his state campaign committee to his congressional race. He paid a $250 fine and returned $3,500 in contributions.

By the time of his 2004 race, Gingrey had caught on to fundraising. He amassed $1.5 million in 2003, and won easily over Rick Crawford with over 57 percent of the vote.

KEY VOTES

2004

No   Extend federal unemployment benefits by 13 weeks

No   Pass $283.2 billion, six-year federal highway and mass transit bill

Yes   Approve $146 billion multi-year extension of previously enacted middle-class tax breaks

Yes   Amend the Constitution to prohibit same-sex marriage

Yes   Cut corporate taxes $137 billion over 10 years

No   Reorganize U.S. intelligence agencies as proposed by Sept. 11 commission

2003

Yes   Cut taxes by $330 billion through fiscal 2013

No   Block Bush rule scaling back overtime pay for some white-collar federal workers

No   Do not allow use of search warrants without first notifying subjects

No   Allow importation of prescription drugs

Yes   Create private school voucher program in Washington, D.C.

Yes   Ban "partial birth" abortion except to save a woman's life

No   Split $18.6 billion in Iraq aid into half-grant, half-loan

Yes   Overhaul Medicare and create prescription drug benefit

CQ VOTE STUDIES

	PARTY UNITY		PRESIDENTIAL SUPPORT	
	Support	Oppose	Support	Oppose
2004	98%	2%	85%	15%
2003	99%	1%	95%	5%

INTEREST GROUPS

	AFL-CIO	ADA	CCUS	ACU
2004	7%	5%	100%	96%
2003	0%	5%	100%	84%

GEORGIA 11

Northwest — Rome, parts of Columbus and Marietta

Running south along the Alabama border from northwest Georgia to Columbus, the oddly shaped 11th stretches east to take in Atlanta's northwestern suburbs and to connect several Democratic areas. While the district includes all or part of 17 counties, the majority of its voters live in three counties — Cobb (suburbs of Atlanta and part of Marietta), Floyd (Rome) and Muscogee (Columbus).

The 11th was drawn following the 2000 census to lean Democratic. Although 28 percent of the district's residents are black and generally support Democrats, the white population tends to be socially conservative and supportive of GOP candidates. George W. Bush captured 55 percent of the vote here in the 2004 presidential election.

Cobb County is a collection of largely white-collar, middle-income suburbs with a rapidly growing minority population. The 11th takes in southern parts of the county and much of Marietta (shared with the 6th).

Small businesses and corporate headquarters, as well as military- and aerospace-related jobs in Marietta, spark the economy. Lockheed Martin is one of the top employers. Other major industries include electrical wire in Carroll County and carpet manufacturing in the north.

Areas outside the district's three cities are largely agricultural, and some small towns are reliant on textile trades. The beef and timber industries and a few manufacturers provide jobs for workers along the border.

MAJOR INDUSTRY
Defense, carpet manufacturing, electronics

MILITARY BASES
Fort Benning (Army), 49,149 military, 7,140 civilian (shared with the 2nd) (2004); Naval Air Station Atlanta, 1,233 military, 139 civilian (2005)

CITIES
Columbus (pt.), 48,030; Marietta (pt.), 40,133; Rome, 34,980; Mableton (pt.), 28,140

NOTABLE
Like its Italian namesake, Rome is built on seven hills.

Rep. John Barrow (D)

CAPITOL OFFICE
225-2823
www.house.gov/barrow
226 Cannon 20515-1012; fax 225-3377

COMMITTEES
Agriculture
Education & Workforce
Small Business

HOMETOWN
Athens

BORN
Oct. 31, 1955, Athens, Ga.

RELIGION
Baptist

FAMILY
Wife, Victoria Pentlarge; two children

EDUCATION
U. of Georgia, B.A. 1976 (history & political science); Harvard U., J.D. 1979

CAREER
Lawyer

POLITICAL HIGHLIGHTS
Sought Democratic nomination for Ga. House, 1986; Athens-Clarke County Commission, 1991-2005

ELECTION RESULTS

2004 GENERAL

John Barrow (D)	113,036	51.8%
Max Burns (R)	105,132	48.2%

2004 PRIMARY

John Barrow (D)	28,110	51.5%
Doug Haines (D)	15,808	28.9%
Tony Center (D)	8,122	14.9%
Caine Cortellino (D)	2,585	4.7%

Elected 2004; 1st term

In ousting one-term Rep. Max Burns, Barrow was one of only two Democrats who managed to unseat a GOP incumbent in 2004.

Barrow (BEAR-oh), who refers to himself as a "flaming moderate," affiliates with the "Blue Dogs," a group of fiscally conservative Democrats. His campaign focused on health care issues and he says his top congressional priority is to alter the 2003 Medicare prescription drug bill to ensure that oncologists receive adequate compensation for treating cancer patients.

Barrow also says that consumers should be permitted to reimport prescription drugs from Canada, and that the government should be able to negotiate bulk purchase prices from pharmaceutical firms.

Barrow won an assignment to the Education and Workforce Committee, a good fit for his district, as it is home to the University of Georgia, the Medical College of Georgia and other schools. He says Congress should work on improving existing education programs and increasing federal school funding instead of drafting major new legislation.

An assignment to the Agriculture Committee could help Barrow build job security in the wide-ranging 12th District. While the Democratic base — including most of the district's sizable black population — is in the cities of Athens, Augusta and Savannah, the conservative bent of voters in more-rural areas presents a challenge to Democratic candidates.

Barrow worked as a trial lawyer in Athens and spent 14 years as a Clarke County commissioner.

In 2004, Barrow ran in a district that was supposed to elect a Democrat; it had been drawn before the 2002 election by the Democrats who then controlled the state legislature. And although the conservative Burns pulled off a surprise victory in 2002, Democratic strategists argued that his win over an ethically flawed Democratic nominee was a fluke.

Barrow took 51 percent of the vote in the four-way 2004 Democratic primary, and with strong backing from national Democratic officials, he staved off the well-financed and aggressive Burns by just 4 percentage points.

GEORGIA 12

East – Athens, most of Augusta and Savannah

The 12th resembles the Statue of Liberty, with Athens at the torch, Augusta at the head, and Savannah at the feet. It covers the southern half of Georgia's border with South Carolina, extending down from Augusta into Chatham County to cover most of the city of Savannah. The district's arm travels through agricultural communities to take in Athens and the University of Georgia's main campus.

Drawn during redistricting following the 2000 census to elect a Democrat, the 12th encompasses Savannah's city center, including the inner city and historic areas. While all of Savannah was included in the old 1st District, the new map split the city to separate predominantly Democratic and Republican areas. Forty-two percent of the 12th's population is black.

Effingham, a rapidly growing Savannah suburb, is the most Republican part of the

district. Farther north, the 12th takes in the urban areas of Augusta. Most of Augusta National Golf Club is in the 9th, but the 13th hole, part of "Amen Corner," is in the 12th.

The agricultural areas south of Athens are heavily African-American, specializing in row farming and timber production. Textile factories had a presence here, but many have shut down in recent years. The Medical College of Georgia is in the district.

MAJOR INDUSTRY
Agriculture, manufacturing, timber

MILITARY BASES
Fort Stewart (Army), 17,517 military, 2,908 civilian (2003) (shared with the 1st and 3rd); Fort Gordon (Army), 12,003 military, 6,511 civilian (shared with the 9th); Navy Supply Corps School, 115 military, 188 civilian (2004)

CITIES
Augusta-Richmond (pt.), 158,503; Savannah (pt.), 126,598; Athens-Clarke, 101,489

NOTABLE
Both R.E.M. and the B-52's had their first public performances in Athens in the 1980s and both bands have supported the city.

Rep. David Scott (D)

Elected 2002; 2nd term

Scott defies standard political assumptions. A centrist Democrat, he is neither consistently liberal nor always loyal to the party that dominates among African-American voters. Scott voted for President Bush's tax cuts as well as the GOP's Medicare prescription drug plan, facing down Democratic leaders who opposed the bills. "He who controls the center controls the political debate," Scott says. "You can't lead from the left, you can't lead from the right."

Scott got to Congress in spite of his party, not because of it. Establishment Democrats in this suburban Atlanta district backed a rival in the 2002 primary when Scott, after years of dues-paying including more than 25 years in the Georgia General Assembly, decided to run for the new 13th District seat. Scott won the nomination with strong support from affluent suburbanites, business leaders, doctors and big health care companies.

Over the years, Scott was closely associated with Atlanta's black and liberal leaders — former Mayors Andrew Young and Maynard Jackson and Jimmy Carter, the governor who became president — but he calculated correctly that only a centrist could win the district. The new 13th is a mix of urban and rural areas and nearly even numbers of black and white voters.

When he arrived in Washington, Scott joined the group of conservative Democrats called the Blue Dog Coalition. He earned the disapproval of his party leadership by changing his no vote to yes on the 2003 Medicare bill, helping Bush eke out a slender victory. Though fellow Democrats called the bill a sham that failed to do much to help seniors, Scott joined just five other lawmakers in flipping their votes during a tight and protracted vote that GOP leaders gaveled to a close just before dawn.

Scott was also one of only seven Democrats to vote for Bush's $350 billion, 10-year tax bill in 2003. He also favors a flat tax, an idea typically pushed by conservatives that would replace the present graduated income tax with a single rate for everyone. The tax is regressive but Scott argues it would greatly simplify the labyrinthine tax code. "The tax cut was not just for white folks paying taxes," Scott says. "I have a district where a lot of African-Americans with money are paying taxes. It pains me greatly to vote against my party, but I have to dance with those that brought me."

On the Financial Services Committee, Scott is equally independent. He protested proposed Republican cuts in housing programs for the poor, but he sided with Republicans on a bill favoring brokerage firms and investment banks when states seek to punish them for corporate fraud.

Scott's background is a lesson in adaptation. Born in Aynor, S.C., an impoverished country town, he attended elementary school in Pennsylvania and moved with his parents in the sixth grade to Scarsdale, N.Y., where his father and mother went to work for a wealthy family as a chauffeur and maid. An only child, he was also the only black child in his school. His classmates had money; he lived in an apartment over the garage on the estate owned by his parents' employer.

Civil rights protests raged across the country, and although Scott says he encountered surprisingly little overt bigotry among Scarsdale's upper crust, his racial isolation was stressful. "I am who I am today because of that experience," he said. "I learned at a very young age how to have confidence in myself and how to get along with people who don't look like me."

Scott finished high school in Daytona Beach, Florida and went on to

CAPITOL OFFICE
225-2939
david.scott@mail.house.gov
www.house.gov/davidscott
417 Cannon 20515-1013; fax 225-4628

COMMITTEES
Agriculture
Financial Services

HOMETOWN
Atlanta

BORN
June 27, 1946, Aynor, S.C.

RELIGION
Baptist

FAMILY
Wife, Alfredia Scott; two children

EDUCATION
Florida A&M U., B.A. 1967 (English & speech);
U. of Pennsylvania, M.B.A. 1969

CAREER
Advertising agency owner; recruiting firm executive; defense contracting company manager

POLITICAL HIGHLIGHTS
Ga. House, 1975-83; Ga. Senate, 1983-2003

ELECTION RESULTS

2004 GENERAL

David Scott (D)		unopposed

2004 PRIMARY

David Scott (D)	42,498	83.6%
William Ogletree (D)	8,340	16.4%

2002 GENERAL

David Scott (D)	70,011	59.6%
Clay Cox (R)	47,405	40.4%

Florida A&M University. During an internship in Washington with the U.S. Labor Department, Scott by chance met George W. Taylor, the noted labor-management expert. Impressed by the young man, Taylor suggested he apply to the University of Pennsylvania's Wharton School of Finance, where Taylor was on the faculty. "Well maybe I will," Scott recalls telling Taylor. "What's the Wharton school?"

With a Wharton MBA in hand, Scott in the early 1970s was attracted to Atlanta and its emerging group of black leaders. He was a volunteer with Young's campaign for the House in 1972. In 1979, on a whim, Scott produced a tribute to black poet Langston Hughes, voicing the narrative himself and setting a dozen of Hughes' works to dance, music and dramatic interpretation. Georgia public television aired the program.

Scott won his first election to the Georgia House in 1974 and stayed in the legislature for 28 years, 20 of those in the Senate. He chaired the Senate Rules Committee, leading the Atlanta Journal-Constitution in 1993 to describe him as "the second most powerful black politician in the state, behind only the mayor of Atlanta." The mayor then was Maynard Jackson.

A religious man who sometimes sees the hand of divine intervention in his legislative successes, Scott is best remembered for authoring the Georgia law requiring a moment of silence at the beginning of the public school day. He has sponsored a national version of the bill in the House. He says the moment of silence has the effect of calming children and giving them "inner strength." Scott quotes liberally from both the Bible and Shakespeare.

Scott was a prime force behind several major bills in the state legislature. He clashed frequently with the National Rifle Association, pushing to passage a law requiring background checks for handgun purchases. Scott wrote the state's sex-education law and fended off conservatives who tried to restrict the curricula to sixth grade and beyond. He once stopped Waste Management Inc., the garbage-hauling giant, from expanding a landfill in a poor black neighborhood that already had several dumps.

In 2002, Scott won a decisive primary victory for the new 13th District, avoiding a September runoff, in spite of the party's decision to put its influence and resources behind state Sen. Greg Hecht. He also outpolled David Worley, former state Democratic party chairman, who had twice run against former GOP House Speaker Newt Gingrich.

Scott easily defeated businessman Clay Cox in the general election. His campaign featured ads by his wife's brother, baseball great Hank Aaron, holder of the record for career home runs. Scott was unopposed in 2004.

KEY VOTES

2004

Yes Extend federal unemployment benefits by 13 weeks

Yes Pass $283.2 billion, six-year federal highway and mass transit bill

Yes Approve $146 billion multi-year extension of previously enacted middle-class tax breaks

Yes Amend the Constitution to prohibit same-sex marriage

Yes Cut corporate taxes $137 billion over 10 years

Yes Reorganize U.S. intelligence agencies as proposed by Sept. 11 commission

2003

Yes Cut taxes by $330 billion through fiscal 2013

Yes Block Bush rule scaling back overtime pay for some white-collar federal workers

Yes Do not allow use of search warrants without first notifying subjects

No Allow importation of prescription drugs

No Create private school voucher program in Washington, D.C.

No Ban "partial birth" abortion except to save a woman's life

Yes Split $18.6 billion in Iraq aid into half-grant, half-loan

Yes Overhaul Medicare and create prescription drug benefit

CQ VOTE STUDIES

	PARTY UNITY		PRESIDENTIAL SUPPORT	
	Support	Oppose	Support	Oppose
2004	79%	21%	47%	53%
2003	76%	24%	38%	62%

INTEREST GROUPS

	AFL-CIO	ADA	CCUS	ACU
2004	86%	75%	78%	30%
2003	87%	75%	60%	32%

GEORGIA 13

Southern Atlanta suburbs – parts of Clayton, Gwinnett and Fulton counties

One of two new districts created in Georgia following the 2000 census, the 13th covers a spidery area south of Atlanta with tentacles extending outward from the city. The district was created by Democratic state legislators to represent the growing black population on the outskirts of Atlanta.

The district has a slim white plurality: 42 percent of the 13th's population is white, while 41 percent is African-American. Roughly 10 percent of residents are Hispanic, though voter turnout is much lower among that population. Solidly Democratic, 62 percent of residents voted for John Kerry in the 2004 presidential election.

The 13th takes in an array of middle-income urban, suburban and rural areas. Many residents in the urban areas — the two fingers that run along Interstate 85, north of Atlanta in Gwinnett County and south of the city in Fulton County — live in apartment communities and commute to

Atlanta. The heart of the district is suburban Clayton County, which formerly was populated by blue-collar white residents and is now a haven for African-American families moving south from Atlanta. The 13th's fingers run through some Republican areas to reach rural, Democratic-leaning towns at the district's fingertips.

The 13th includes a small section of Atlanta and a small part of Hartsfield-Jackson Atlanta International Airport. The airport, one of the nation's busiest, helps bolster the economy.

MAJOR INDUSTRY
Agriculture, distribution, aerospace

MILITARY BASES
Fort Gillem (Army), 398 military, 1,796 civilian (2004)

CITIES
Forest Park, 21,447; Griffin (pt.), 17,783; Atlanta (pt.), 12,515; Riverdale, 12,478

NOTABLE
Jonesboro was the setting for Tara, the plantation in Margaret Mitchell's novel "Gone With the Wind"; The TV show "Dukes of Hazzard" was filmed in Covington.

HAWAII

Gov. Linda Lingle (R)

First elected: 2002
Length of term: 4 years
Term expires: 12/06
Salary: $94,780
Phone: (808) 586-0034

Hometown: Honolulu
Born: June 4, 1953;
St. Louis, Mo.
Religion: Jewish
Family: Divorced
Education: California State U., Northridge,
B.A. 1975 (journalism)
Career: Newspaper owner; journalist
Political highlights: Maui County Council,
1981-91; mayor of Maui, 1991-98; Republican
nominee for governor, 1998; Hawaii
Republican Party chairwoman, 1999-2002

Election results:

2002 GENERAL
Linda Lingle (R)	197,009	51.6%
Mazie Hirono (D)	179,647	47.0%

Lt. Gov. James 'Duke' Aiona (R)

First elected: 2002
Length of term: 4 years
Term expires: 12/06
Salary: $90,041
Phone: (808) 586-0255

STATE LEGISLATURE

Legislature: 60 days January-April

House: 51 members, 2-year terms
2005 breakdown: 41D, 10R; 35 men,
16 women
Salary: $34,200
Phone: (808) 586-6400

Senate: 25 members, 4-year terms
2005 breakdown: 20D, 5R; 19 men,
6 women
Salary: $34,200
Phone: (808) 586-6720

STATE TERM LIMITS

Governor: 2 consecutive terms
House: No
Senate: No

URBAN STATISTICS

CITY	POPULATION
Honolulu	371,657
Hilo	40,759
Kailua	36,513
Kaneohe	34,970
Waipahu	33,108

REGISTERED VOTERS

Voters do not register by party.

POPULATION

2004 population (est.)	1,262,840
2000 population	1,211,537
1990 population	1,108,229
Percent change (1990-2000)	+9.3%
Rank among states (2004)	42

Median age	36.2
Born in state	56.9%
Foreign born	17.5%
Violent crime rate	244/100,000
Poverty level	10.7%
Federal workers	29,276
Military	53,632

REDISTRICTING

Hawaii retained its two House seats
in reapportionment. The Hawaii
Reapportionment Commission
adopted a new map on Nov. 30, 2001.

MISCELLANEOUS

Web: www.hawaii.gov
Capital: Honolulu
STATE ELECTION OFFICIAL
(808) 453-8683
**DEMOCRATIC
HEADQUARTERS**
(808) 596-2980
**REPUBLICAN
HEADQUARTERS**
(808) 593-8180

District Statistics

DIST.	2004 VOTE FOR PRESIDENT BUSH	KERRY	WHITE	BLACK	ASIAN	HISP	MEDIAN INCOME	WHITE COLLAR	BLUE COLLAR	SERVICE INDUSTRY	OVER 64	UNDER 18	COLLEGE EDUCATION	RURAL	SQ. MILES
1	47%	52%	18%	2%	54%	5%	$50,798	64%	16%	20%	15%	22%	29%	1%	191
2	44	56	28	2	28	9	$48,686	57	21	22	11	27	23	16	6,232
STATE	45	54	23	2	41	7	$49,820	60	19	21	13	24	26	9	6,423
U.S.	50.7	48.3	69	12	4	13	$41,994	60	25	15	12	26	24	21	3,537,438

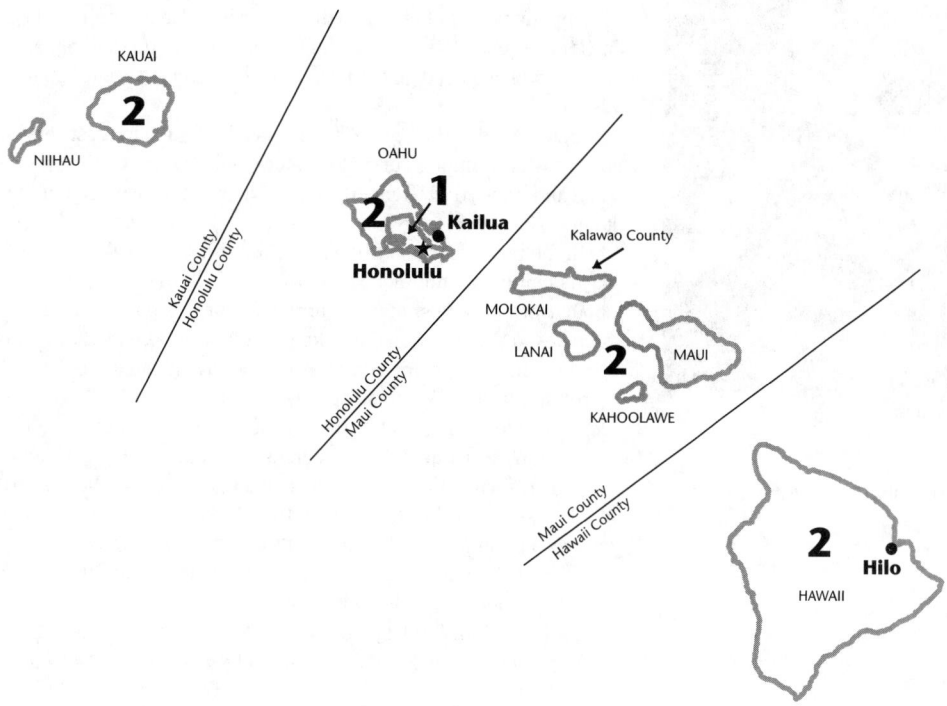

Sen. Daniel K. Inouye (D)

Elected 1962; 8th term

CAPITOL OFFICE
224-3934
senator@inouye.senate.gov
inouye.senate.gov
722 Hart 20510-1102; fax 224-6747

COMMITTEES
Appropriations
Commerce, Science & Transportation - ranking member
Indian Affairs
Rules & Administration
Joint Printing

HOMETOWN
Honolulu

BORN
Sept. 7, 1924, Honolulu, Hawaii

RELIGION
Methodist

FAMILY
Wife, Margaret Shinobu Inouye; one child

EDUCATION
U. of Hawaii, A.B. 1950 (government & economics);
George Washington U., J.D. 1952

MILITARY SERVICE
Army, 1943-47

CAREER
Lawyer; city prosecutor

POLITICAL HIGHLIGHTS
Hawaii Territorial House, 1954-58 (majority leader);
Hawaii Territorial Senate, 1958-59; U.S. House,
1959-63

ELECTION RESULTS

2004 GENERAL

Daniel K. Inouye (D)	313,629	75.5%
Cam Cavasso (R)	87,172	21.0%
Jim Brewer (NON)	9,269	2.2%
Jeff Mallan (LIBERT)	5,277	1.3%

2004 PRIMARY

Daniel K. Inouye (D)	157,367	93.8%
Brian Evans (D)	8,051	4.8%
Eddie Yoon (D)	2,437	1.5%

PREVIOUS WINNING PERCENTAGES
1998 (79%); 1992 (57%); 1986 (74%); 1980 (78%); 1974
(83%); 1968 (83%); 1962 (69%); 1960 House Election
(74%); 1959 Special House Election (68%)

A deeply private man in a highly public job, Inouye is a living link between Hawaii's past as a U.S. territory and its future as the nation's vibrant, multicultural bridge to the Pacific Rim. He has represented Hawaii in Congress since the archipelago joined the union in 1959, and he has done so with a quiet dignity that belies his behind-the-scenes influence with his colleagues.

First elected in 1962, by 2005 he was the fourth-longest-serving senator in history. Among current senators, only Robert C. Byrd of West Virginia and Edward M. Kennedy of Massachusetts have been in the Senate longer.

On the rare occasions when Inouye (ih-NO-ay) speaks out publicly, his words command attention. In 2004, he led the resistance to a politically popular proposal to shift some of the Pentagon's power over intelligence agencies to a new national intelligence director. The idea was among the recommendations of the commission that investigated the Sept. 11, 2001, terrorist attacks. "We must be careful not to sever the link between the Defense Department and its intelligence agencies," Inouye said in a floor speech. "We must not take the defense secretary out of the loop."

Similarly, when the Senate was debating in 2002 whether to grant President Bush the authority to attack Iraq, Inouye made headlines when he took exception to a Bush comment that Democrats were not sufficiently concerned about national security. Inouye, who lost an arm while fighting Nazi Germany in World War II and won the Congressional Medal of Honor in 2000 for bravery, rose on the Senate floor to protest.

"It grieves me when my president makes statements that would divide this nation," he said. "This is not a time for Democrats and Republicans to say we got more medals than you, we've lost more limbs than you, we've shed more blood than you."

The first Japanese-American elected to Congress, Inouye believes strongly in the notion of honor — one of the attributes that identify him as the product of an earlier political era, when collegiality was valued over partisan combativeness and reverence for the Senate as an institution was the norm. He declined to cast a tie-breaking vote in favor of a Democratic amendment to the 2001 Bush tax bill in order to keep his promise to "pair" his votes that day with his friend Ted Stevens, a Republican who would have voted the other way but was home in Alaska speaking at a granddaughter's high school graduation ceremony.

Inouye and Stevens have developed exceptionally close ties as senators from the most recently admitted states and as longstanding senior members of the Appropriations Committee. In the 109th Congress, Stevens became chairman and Inouye the senior Democrat of the Commerce, Science and Transportation Committee, which changed the panel's dynamic. Whereas committee meetings under former chairman John McCain of Arizona were freewheeling events, with deals hashed out through last-minute amendments, Stevens and Inouye like to move significant legislation after differences of opinion have been dealt with behind the scenes.

Inouye shares with Stevens an interest in shifting military priorities away from a longstanding concentration on Europe and toward the Pacific. The two also see eye to eye on issues affecting indigenous populations. The prospect that native Alaskans might benefit from oil exploration in the Arctic National Wildlife Refuge caused Inouye to support Stevens' unsuccessful efforts in 2003 to open the refuge to oil drilling. Most Democrats opposed the controversial Bush administration proposal, saying it could damage Alaska's fragile wildlife and environment.

With his ascension on Commerce, Inouye stepped aside in the 109th Congress as top-ranking Democrat on the Indian Affairs panel. But he was expected to continue to advance legislation important to American Indians and native Hawaiians.

Though Inouye typically votes the Democratic party line, his colleagues have come to rely on him to handle delicate tasks that require the appearance of impartiality and unquestioned probity. He was at the center of two congressional investigations of executive branch misdeeds. His 1987 appointment to chair the Senate committee investigating the Iran-contra affair stemmed not only from his evenhanded manner but also from the esteem accorded him during the 1973 Watergate hearings, which led to the resignation of President Nixon. Inouye earned a reputation as a tough but judicious interrogator of Nixon's aides and associates. When Chairman Harry Reid of Nevada recused himself in 2002, Inouye stepped in to head the Ethics Committee's investigation of fellow Democrat Robert G. Torricelli of New Jersey.

On Appropriations, Inouye has secured billions of dollars in federal spending for his state, including $497 million in defense funds in 2005. His efforts have made him a prime target of the nonprofit watchdog group Citizens Against Government Waste, which has attacked him for annually adding funding for Hawaii not sought by the White House. Inouye is unapologetic about helping to boost the economy back home. "The criticism is to me an indication that I am doing the job I was elected to do," he says.

Despite his popularity and longevity, Inouye has had trouble ascending the Senate leadership ladder. His 1989 bid for majority leader attracted only 14 of the 55 Democratic votes. Inouye never really expanded his base of support beyond old hands and colleagues on the Appropriations Committee.

Inouye is revered by Hawaii's large Japanese-American community. In 1943, as an 18-year-old pre-med student at the University of Hawaii, he enlisted in the famed "Go for Broke" all-nisei 442nd Regimental Combat Team and fought across Italy and France. When he advanced alone to take out a machine gun that had pinned down his men, he lost his right arm and spent 20 months in military hospitals. At the Percy Jones Hospital in Michigan, he met another recuperating soldier with an arm injury — Bob Dole of Kansas, who later became Senate majority leader. Dole told Inouye he planned to be in Congress someday.

Prevented by his injury from becoming a surgeon, Inouye decided he too would try politics. He won his first election in 1954, to Hawaii's territorial House. Inouye helped guide Hawaii to statehood in 1959, and was elected that year as the state's first U.S. House member. In 1962, Inouye won election to the Senate, with 69 percent of the vote.

His next four wins were landslides over modest GOP opposition. But in 1992, Inouye's pedestal was shaken by state Sen. Rick Reed, his Republican opponent. Reed ran a radio ad featuring claims by Inouye's barber that Inouye had made unwanted sexual advances. Inouye called the accusation "unmitigated lies," and the Ethics Committee dropped a review of the charges. But the bad press likely contributed to his lowest winning percentage ever in a congressional race, 57 percent.

Inouye's political decline proved short-lived, however. His re-election numbers returned to form in 1998, when he drew 79 percent. He was re-elected with an overwhelming 76 percent in the 2004 election.

KEY VOTES

2004

Yes Pass $318.9 billion, six-year highway and mass transit bill
Yes Extend assault weapons ban for 10 years
Yes Restore pay-as-you-go rules for new tax cuts and entitlement spending
No Criminalize harm to a fetus in an attack on the mother
Yes Increase mandatory child care funding to states by $6 billion over five years
No Amend the Constitution to prohibit same-sex marriage
? Approve $146 billion multi-year extension of previously enacted middle-class tax breaks
Yes Reorganize U.S. intelligence agencies as proposed by Sept. 11 commission
Yes Cut corporate taxes $137 billion over 10 years

2003

? Delay Bush changes to Clean Air Act
No Allow confirmation vote on Miguel A. Estrada to the U.S. Court of Appeals for the D.C. Circuit
No Block a Bush proposal opening Alaska's Arctic National Wildlife Refuge to oil drilling
Yes Limit size of Bush's proposed tax cut to $350 billion through fiscal 2013
Yes Overhaul Medicare and create prescription drug benefit
Yes Block Bush rule scaling back overtime pay for some white-collar federal workers
No Split $20 billion in Iraq aid into half-grant, half-loan
No Ban "partial birth" abortion except to save a woman's life
No Stop proposal allowing travel to Cuba
No Allow final vote on energy policy overhaul

CQ VOTE STUDIES

	PARTY UNITY		PRESIDENTIAL SUPPORT	
	Support	Oppose	Support	Oppose
2004	95%	5%	59%	41%
2003	93%	7%	48%	52%
2002	90%	10%	76%	24%
2001	98%	2%	66%	34%
2000	91%	9%	94%	6%
1999	91%	9%	86%	14%
1998	93%	7%	87%	13%
1997	91%	9%	87%	13%
1996	87%	13%	86%	14%
1995	84%	16%	85%	15%

INTEREST GROUPS

	AFL-CIO	ADA	CCUS	ACU
2004	100%	100%	50%	8%
2003	100%	85%	40%	15%
2002	92%	80%	41%	0%
2001	100%	90%	43%	9%
2000	60%	60%	69%	23%
1999	88%	95%	50%	0%
1998	88%	80%	44%	9%
1997	83%	75%	50%	4%
1996	86%	85%	33%	11%
1995	100%	95%	41%	0%

Sen. Daniel K. Akaka (D)

Elected 1990; 2nd full term
Appointed April 1990

CAPITOL OFFICE
224-6361
senator@akaka.senate.gov
akaka.senate.gov
141 Hart 20510-1103; fax 224-2126

COMMITTEES
Armed Services
Energy & Natural Resources
Homeland Security & Governmental Affairs
Indian Affairs
Veterans' Affairs - ranking member
Select Ethics

HOMETOWN
Honolulu

BORN
Sept. 11, 1924, Honolulu, Hawaii

RELIGION
Congregationalist

FAMILY
Wife, Millie Akaka; five children

EDUCATION
U. of Hawaii, B.Ed. 1952, M.Ed. 1966

MILITARY SERVICE
Army Corps of Engineers, 1945-47

CAREER
Gubernatorial aide; state economic grants official;
elementary school principal and teacher

POLITICAL HIGHLIGHTS
Sought Democratic nomination for lieutenant
governor, 1974; U.S. House, 1977-90

ELECTION RESULTS

2000 GENERAL

Daniel K. Akaka (D)	251,215	72.7%
John S. Carroll (R)	84,701	24.5%
Lauri A. Clegg (NL)	4,220	1.2%

2000 PRIMARY

Daniel K. Akaka (D)	150,507	90.2%
Arturo P. Reyes (D)	16,312	9.8%

PREVIOUS WINNING PERCENTAGES
1994 (72%); 1990 Special Election (54%); 1988
House Election (89%); 1986 House Election (76%);
1984 House Election (82%); 1982 House Election
(89%); 1980 House Election (90%); 1978 House
Election (86%); 1976 House Election (80%)

He keeps one of the lowest profiles of anyone in the Senate. His name, Akaka, comes first on every roll call vote, but that is pretty much the extent of his fame on Capitol Hill. At home, however, the senator is seen as an active member of a cohesive state delegation that protects Hawaii's interests.

The only native Hawaiian ever to serve in Congress (his mother is Hawaiian and his father is of Chinese and Hawaiian ancestry), Akaka (uh-KAH-kuh) gets involved in the nitty-gritty of the issues important to his state — some as serious as preserving the islands' role in national security, and others less weighty, such as creating a postage stamp with the likeness of surfing and swimming legend Duke Kahanamoku.

He has been a champion of the rights of native Hawaiians. For years, Akaka has tried to pass legislation that would recognize natives as a distinct indigenous group with federally guaranteed rights, achieving self-determination and self-governance similar to what is now enjoyed by American Indians and native Alaskans. He drafted the measure in 2000 and introduced a similar bill in 2001, only to find it blocked by conservative Republicans on the Senate floor.

In the 108th Congress, the bill won approval in the Indian Affairs Committee, only to be blocked by Majority Leader Bill Frist when Akaka tried to add it as an amendment to a measure limiting class action lawsuits. "For five years we have worked to enact this bill which has effectively been blocked from Senate consideration by a handful of senators who refuse to acknowledge native Hawaiians as indigenous peoples," a frustrated Akaka said in a Senate floor speech. He offered the bill again in the 109th.

As a member of the Armed Services Committee, Akaka took part in one of the most closely watched events of the 108th Congress: the May 2004 hearing in which Defense Secretary Donald H. Rumsfeld and other top officials were grilled over the abuse of Iraqi prisoners. Akaka proved himself capable of needling the military chiefs with blunt questions. "How is it that an entire brigade could be deployed to Iraq and not trained for their mission?" he asked Gen. Richard B. Myers, the chairman of the Joint Chiefs of Staff.

In 2004, Akaka cosponsored a bill by two other members of the Armed Services panel, Rhode Island Democrat Jack Reed and Nebraska Republican Chuck Hagel, to permanently add 30,000 soldiers to the Army. But the measure languished in the Senate.

Akaka has tackled other national issues as well. Outraged by a series of trading abuses in the mutual fund industry, in November 2003 he became the first senator to introduce legislation to curtail conflicts of interest on mutual fund boards. The Senate took no action on the bill.

After the nation was briefly rattled by an appearance of "mad cow" disease in the United States, Akaka added an amendment to the 2004 agricultural spending bill to bar funding of the inspection process that approves the meat of downed animals for human consumption. But the House defeated a similar amendment, and the provision was dropped in conference.

Akaka often builds legislation from the ground up, meeting with scientists and local officials to gather information, then building support on the federal level. He has a quiet, deliberative working method — described by one Pacific islander official as "island-style" — more in tune with traditional Hawaiian ways than with the modern media operations run by many in the Senate.

The 12-hour plane rides from Washington to Honolulu make it difficult for Akaka to return home, but he is never far from his roots. Every morning, he meets with visiting constituents over coffee and pastries.

The senator has long promoted the rights of indigenous peoples, especially native Hawaiians. An Akaka law enacted in the 104th Congress compensates native Hawaiians by transferring federal land to a trust in return for lands seized by the United States during the state's territorial period. The law builds on a measure that Akaka helped steer through the Senate in 1992: an apology to Hawaiians for the 1893 U.S. overthrow of the native government. But when that apology helped fuel an independence movement in Hawaii, Akaka the conciliator was quick to clarify that his intention was quite the opposite. "I look at the apology resolution as the first step toward healing, not creating new barriers," he said in 1998.

Akaka is a loyal Democrat, but his commitment to native peoples can supersede his party ties. In 2002, he cited the Inupiat Eskimos' desire for economic development as his main reason for eschewing the concerns of environmentalists and supporting President Bush's proposal to allow oil drilling in Alaska's Arctic National Wildlife Refuge. When Akaka voted to permit drilling, Senate Democratic Leader Tom Daschle went through convoluted maneuvers to ensure that Akaka, the second-most-senior Democrat on the Energy Committee, was not on the conference committee named to write a compromise House-Senate energy bill.

A protector of Hawaii's sugar industry, Akaka has successfully fought recurrent efforts to do away with federal sugar subsidy programs. In 1996 and again in 2001, he opposed efforts by New Hampshire Republican Judd Gregg to lessen the government's support of sugar producers. In 1990, Akaka won a larger victory for sugar subsidies against Democrat Bill Bradley of New Jersey, a lanky former basketball star. Of that fight, Akaka told a newspaper, "I'm only 5-feet-7, but I slam-dunked him."

He has not always been so steadfast. In 1984, the House Democratic leadership was one vote short when it sought to block President Reagan's request for production of the MX missile. With time running out, Illinois Democrat Marty Russo located Akaka, who had been recorded as a pro-MX vote, lifted him out of a phone booth and escorted — some witnesses said carried — him into the chamber. Akaka then changed his vote, giving the anti-MX forces a key victory.

Akaka's career is a study in the quiet but steady perseverance of a quintessential team player. He rose through the Honolulu education bureaucracy before entering politics in 1971 as the appointed head of the state Office of Economic Opportunity. In 1976, he captured the 2nd District seat after a difficult primary contest. He climbed to the middle tier of seniority on the House Appropriations Committee, where he concentrated almost entirely on fulfilling parochial needs.

When Democrat Spark M. Matsunaga died in April 1990, Akaka was a logical choice to fill the Senate vacancy. Not only was he on good terms with Democratic Gov. John Waihee III, who made the appointment, he was also close to the state Democratic Party leadership and had received support throughout his career from Japanese-Americans, a crucial voting bloc.

However, with Akaka facing a special election in November 1990 to fill the remaining four years of Matsunaga's term, there was a degree of trepidation about his ability to hold the seat in the face of a challenge by Republican Rep. Patricia F. Saiki. Akaka had been a rather sedate figure during his House career and was not readily identifiable to many Hawaiians. But by playing to his strengths — his low-key personality and his ability to deliver federal largess to Hawaii — he prevailed with a surprisingly solid 54 percent of the vote. He won his next two Senate elections far more easily.

KEY VOTES

2004

Yes	Pass $318.9 billion, six-year highway and mass transit bill
Yes	Extend assault weapons ban for 10 years
Yes	Restore pay-as-you-go rules for new tax cuts and entitlement spending
No	Criminalize harm to a fetus in an attack on the mother
Yes	Increase mandatory child care funding to states by $6 billion over five years
No	Amend the Constitution to prohibit same-sex marriage
?	Approve $146 billion multi-year extension of previously enacted middle-class tax breaks
Yes	Reorganize U.S. intelligence agencies as proposed by Sept. 11 commission
No	Cut corporate taxes $137 billion over 10 years

2003

Yes	Delay Bush changes to Clean Air Act
No	Allow confirmation vote on Miguel A. Estrada to the U.S. Court of Appeals for the D.C. Circuit
No	Block a Bush proposal opening Alaska's Arctic National Wildlife Refuge to oil drilling
Yes	Limit size of Bush's proposed tax cut to $350 billion through fiscal 2013
Yes	Overhaul Medicare and create prescription drug benefit
Yes	Block Bush rule scaling back overtime pay for some white-collar federal workers
Yes	Split $20 billion in Iraq aid into half-grant, half-loan
No	Ban "partial birth" abortion except to save a woman's life
No	Stop proposal allowing travel to Cuba
No	Allow final vote on energy policy overhaul

CQ VOTE STUDIES

	PARTY UNITY		PRESIDENTIAL SUPPORT	
	Support	Oppose	Support	Oppose
2004	97%	3%	56%	44%
2003	97%	3%	51%	49%
2002	91%	9%	63%	37%
2001	98%	2%	70%	30%
2000	98%	2%	97%	3%
1999	96%	4%	89%	11%
1998	96%	4%	91%	9%
1997	97%	3%	90%	10%
1996	95%	5%	88%	12%
1995	95%	5%	89%	11%

INTEREST GROUPS

	AFL-CIO	ADA	CCUS	ACU
2004	100%	95%	29%	5%
2003	100%	90%	30%	11%
2002	100%	80%	53%	0%
2001	100%	95%	50%	13%
2000	86%	85%	46%	12%
1999	89%	100%	41%	4%
1998	100%	85%	41%	10%
1997	71%	95%	60%	4%
1996	100%	95%	31%	5%
1995	100%	95%	24%	0%

Rep. Neil Abercrombie (D)

Elected 1990; 8th full term
Also served Sept. 1986-Jan. 1987

CAPITOL OFFICE
225-2726
neil.abercrombie@mail.house.gov
www.house.gov/abercrombie
1502 Longworth 20515-1101; fax 225-4580

COMMITTEES
Armed Services
Resources

HOMETOWN
Honolulu

BORN
June 26, 1938, Buffalo, N.Y.

RELIGION
Unspecified

FAMILY
Wife, Nancie Caraway

EDUCATION
Union College, B.A. 1959; U. of Hawaii, M.A. 1964,
Ph.D. 1974 (American studies)

CAREER
Educator

POLITICAL HIGHLIGHTS
Sought Democratic nomination for U.S. Senate,
1970; Hawaii House, 1974-78; Hawaii Senate, 1978-
86; U.S. House, 1986-87; defeated in primary for
re-election to U.S. House, 1986; Honolulu City
Council, 1988-90

ELECTION RESULTS

2004 GENERAL

Neil Abercrombie (D)	128,567	63.0%
Dalton Tanonaka (R)	69,371	34.0%
Elyssa Young (LIBERT)	6,243	3.1%

2004 PRIMARY

Neil Abercrombie (D)	unopposed

2002 GENERAL

Neil Abercrombie (D)	131,673	72.9%
Mark Terry (R)	45,032	24.9%
James H. Bracken (LIBERT)	4,028	2.2%

PREVIOUS WINNING PERCENTAGES
2000 (69%); 1998 (62%); 1996 (50%); 1994 (54%);
1992 (73%); 1990 (61%); 1986 Special Election (30%)

When Abercrombie made his congressional debut years ago, he seemed to have stepped out of a 1960s anti-Vietnam War time capsule. In the marbled decorum of the Capitol, his outspoken demeanor — and his long hair — were visual and verbal cues of a lawmaker pushing the leftward edge of the ideological envelope at every turn.

Minus the ponytail (it was shorn in 1997), Abercrombie retains much of his early intensity. And he has a new war to oppose — the one in Iraq. But his opposition to that conflict has not kept him from looking out for Hawaii's interests in a robust Pentagon budget, and as a senior member of the Armed Services Committee, he is in a position to deliver.

In the 108th Congress, he continued procuring hundreds of millions of dollars in funding for military research and construction in his district's numerous bases and installations, which include Pearl Harbor. "There are always fierce battles over the money," he told the Honolulu Advertiser, "and I'll be fighting hard to protect every penny for Hawaii." Abercrombie's advocacy has not gone unnoticed: In 2002, a new tugboat that services Navy vessels at Pearl Harbor was named after him.

Despite his strong support for military spending, the burly Hawaii lawmaker has little use for much of the Bush administration's defense policy. He was a persistent critic of the administration's handling of postwar Iraq, and in 2003 voted against emergency supplemental funding for operations there and in Afghanistan. Abercrombie repeatedly expressed frustration with the GOP's tactic of framing Iraq-related legislation in terms of support for U.S. troops. Employing Vietnam-era vocabulary, he declared, "Supporting our troops does not mean sticking them in a no-exit quagmire, which is exactly what the Bush policy does." In 2004, he complained that Republicans were using support-the-troops resolutions "as blackmail, like they're holding the troops hostage."

Abercrombie also criticized the Pentagon's reliance on National Guard and Reserve soldiers in prosecuting the war. "The draft has returned to this country, except it's by default," he told CNN in 2003. "We're drafting by default through the Guard and Reserve."

Though his days as a Vietnam anti-war protester are behind him, Abercrombie still voices skepticism on the overall wisdom of using military force when other options are available. He backed the military operations in Afghanistan after the Sept. 11, 2001, terrorist attacks, but he warned against getting U.S. troops involved in counterinsurgency operations in the Philippines. And in 2002, he voted against authorizing President Bush to go to war against Iraq.

Abercrombie's liberal leanings show through in the details of military regulation as well as these broader questions of foreign policy. In 2003, he pushed — unsuccessfully — to strengthen endangered species protection on lands owned by the military.

Abercrombie sometimes talks like the professor he once was: When a federal appeals court ruled that schoolchildren could not be required to recite the Pledge of Allegiance because it contains the phrase "under God," Abercrombie joined all but three House members in voting to condemn the decision. But Abercrombie explained his vote in terms of the sociological importance of rituals such as the pledge in promoting values such as freedom and patriotism.

Some of his most striking deviations from the liberal line are on tax policies important to the travel and tourism industries that account for a large share of his state's employment. Abercrombie has pushed hard for legislation allowing a tax deduction for the full cost of business meals and entertainment as well as for travel costs of an accompanying spouse on a business trip. He also backed the long GOP-led campaign to repeal the estate tax, which he said is harmful to Hawaii's many family-owned businesses.

The 2001 tax cut law included an Abercrombie-sponsored provision allowing shareholders in the Campbell Estate — Hawaii's seventh-largest private landowner — up to 14 years to pay the taxes they will owe when the trust is dissolved in 2007.

Still, on most issues, Abercrombie is a pro-labor Democrat. In the 108th, he opposed a Labor Department rewrite of rules governing overtime pay, accusing the administration of "siding with the big-money interests that put them in power," and arguing that the change would have a major negative impact on the incomes of military families. He was no less caustic in blasting the Republican Medicare prescription drug plan, calling it "a betrayal of senior citizens." And in 2002, he voted against the House version of a bill to establish the Department of Homeland Security, objecting to provisions waiving certain Civil Service protections for employees of the new department.

Another priority for Abercrombie has been protecting civilian federal employees against what he sees as a "pro-privatization" bias in the Bush administration's process for deciding whether to outsource work.

He has also pushed legislation that would recognize native Hawaiians as a distinct indigenous group with the right to self-determination.

The man who now represents Waikiki got his start in Buffalo, N.Y. After college, he taught school for a time before moving to Hawaii for graduate school. He became a practitioner of protest politics, taking 13 percent of the 1970 Democratic Senate primary vote as an anti-Vietnam War candidate. Four years later, he won election to the state House.

After 11-plus years in the legislature, Abercrombie briefly served in the House when he won a special election in 1986 to fill a vacancy. But he narrowly lost the primary election for a full term, which was held the same day. He got a second chance when the seat opened up in 1990, winning the Democratic primary with 46 percent of the vote and cruising to an easy victory in November.

He faced difficult re-election battles in 1994 and 1996 and struggled to fend off charges that he was an extreme liberal. Since then, however, he has won by comfortable margins.

KEY VOTES

2004
Yes Extend federal unemployment benefits by 13 weeks
Yes Pass $283.2 billion, six-year federal highway and mass transit bill
Yes Approve $146 billion multi-year extension of previously enacted middle-class tax breaks
No Amend the Constitution to prohibit same-sex marriage
No Cut corporate taxes $137 billion over 10 years
? Reorganize U.S. intelligence agencies as proposed by Sept. 11 commission

2003
No Cut taxes by $330 billion through fiscal 2013
Yes Block Bush rule scaling back overtime pay for some white-collar federal workers
No Do not allow use of search warrants without first notifying subjects
Yes Allow importation of prescription drugs
No Create private school voucher program in Washington, D.C.
No Ban "partial birth" abortion except to save a woman's life
Yes Split $18.6 billion in Iraq aid into half-grant, half-loan
No Overhaul Medicare and create prescription drug benefit

CQ VOTE STUDIES

	PARTY UNITY		PRESIDENTIAL SUPPORT	
	Support	Oppose	Support	Oppose
2004	94%	6%	15%	85%
2003	94%	6%	16%	84%
2002	89%	11%	32%	68%
2001	79%	21%	35%	65%
2000	86%	14%	72%	28%

INTEREST GROUPS

	AFL-CIO	ADA	CCUS	ACU
2004	93%	85%	32%	0%
2003	100%	95%	30%	16%
2002	100%	85%	45%	12%
2001	92%	90%	39%	8%
2000	90%	80%	42%	12%

HAWAII 1
Oahu — Honolulu, Waipahu, Pearl City

Located on the southern coast of Oahu Island, the compact 1st takes in the narrow plain south of the Koolau mountain range, encompassing the city of Honolulu — the engine that drives all of Hawaii. Redistricting following the 2000 census added only one town, Waipahu, which lies west of Honolulu. Pearl Harbor is the district's unforgettable landmark.

Honolulu is Hawaii's capital, home to most of its business and about one-third of its people. To the east lies Waikiki and the heart of Hawaii's leading industry: tourism. The state experienced a downturn in the mid-1990s as Asia's economic problems meant fewer Japanese visitors and less investment in the state. The Sept. 11 attacks also hurt tourism, but it has largely rebounded. The district's other major economic plank — the military — managed to escape major cuts and is holding steady.

The 1st is a Democratic stronghold that has elected only one Republican to Congress in its history. But George W. Bush held John Kerry to 52 percent here in the 2004 presidential election, showing that a Republican can make the vote close.

Japanese-Americans — particularly of the older generation — dominate the Democratic Party and are joined by many other non-white constituents to form the majority of the 1st's residents. Locally, Democrats also do very well, although some moderate Republican enclaves exist in the suburbs of East Honolulu and Waikiki. But even in traditionally GOP areas, Democratic Rep. Abercrombie garners support.

MAJOR INDUSTRY
Tourism, military, construction

MILITARY BASES
Hickam Air Force Base, 5,205 military, 1,945 civilian (2004); Fort Shafter, 3,000 military, 1,950 civilian (2005); Pearl Harbor Naval Shipyard and IMF, 525 military, 3,757 civilian (2003); Tripler Army Medical Center, 1,500 military, 1,500 civilian; Pearl Harbor Naval Submarine Base, 2,500 military, 175 civilian; Pearl Harbor Naval Station, 675 military, 543 civilian; Camp H.M. Smith, 730 military, 160 civilian (2004)

CITIES
Honolulu, 371,657; Waipahu, 33,108; Pearl City, 30,976; Waimalu, 29,371

NOTABLE
Iolani Palace in Honolulu calls itself the only royal palace in the United States.

Rep. Ed Case (D)

CAPITOL OFFICE
225-4906
ed.case@mail.house.gov
www.house.gov/case
115 Cannon 20515-1102; fax 225-4987

COMMITTEES
Agriculture
Budget
Small Business

HOMETOWN
Kaneohe

BORN
Sept. 27, 1952, Hilo, Hawaii

RELIGION
Protestant

FAMILY
Wife, Audrey Case; four children

EDUCATION
Williams College, B.A. 1975 (psychology); U. of California, Hastings College of the Law, J.D. 1981

CAREER
Lawyer; congressional aide

POLITICAL HIGHLIGHTS
Manoa Neighborhood Board, 1985-89; Democratic nominee for Hawaii House, 1986, 1988; Hawaii House, 1995-2002 (majority leader, 1999-2001); sought Democratic nomination for governor, 2002

ELECTION RESULTS

2004 GENERAL

Ed Case (D)	133,317	62.8%
Mike Gabbard (R)	79,072	37.2%

2004 PRIMARY

Ed Case (D)	73,705	94.7%
John Gentile (D)	4,121	5.3%

2003 SPECIAL

Ed Case (D)	33,002	43.7%
Matt Matsunaga (D)	23,050	30.5%
Colleen Hanabusa (D)	6,046	8.0%
others	4,681	6.2%
Barbara Marumoto (R)	4,497	6.0%
Bob McDermott (R)	4,298	5.7%

PREVIOUS WINNING PERCENTAGES
2002 Special Election (51%)

Elected 2002; 2nd full term

Case is the youngest member of the state's four-person delegation by 14 years. He is also the first newcomer to the delegation in more than a decade. He ran on a pledge to shake up the state's long-dominant Democratic establishment.

Case says his views — liberal on social issues, centrist on economic ones — are most closely aligned with the New Democrats, a group of political moderates. He is also a member of the "Blue Dogs," with whom he shares the ideal of ending deficit spending and keeping the federal budget in balance even if it means forgoing tax cuts and spending increases. He opposes President Bush's tax policies, saying, "The president's message is that we can have our cake and eat it too. We can have both deep across-the-board reductions in personal, business, estate and other taxes, and we can also dramatically boost federal spending. . . . It doesn't work that way."

Case is one of only two House members from Hawaii and represents most of the land area in the island chain, including most of Oahu outside Honolulu and all of the other Hawaiian islands. (The 1st District is concentrated in Honolulu, the state's largest city.) As a consequence, Case has strong views on environmental protection. Isolated geographically 2,500 miles from California's coast, Hawaii has more endangered species per square mile than any location on earth.

Case says one of his main goals is to preserve the islands' coastal areas, which aside from their natural beauty, are important to the state's tourism industry, the mainstay of its economy. He sponsored a bill in his first term to add sections of Maui's north shore to the National Park Service. Case also wants to prohibit the export of threatened coral reef species and to impose national standards for wastewater discharges from cruise ships.

He was among the Democrats who strongly opposed the GOP's energy policy legislation. He called the Republican-written bill in 2003 "a disgrace," which was geared toward "rewarding special friends and powerful insider interests with a truly disgusting array of tax breaks and subsidies, immunities from liability and exemptions from troublesome environmental protections and protections from competition."

His seat on the Agriculture Committee helps him look out for another major economic force in Hawaii, agriculture, particularly the cattle ranches, coffee farms and sugar and pineapple plantations of the 2nd District.

A highly contentious issue for the island state is the Jones Act, a little-known section of the Merchant Marine Act of 1920 that requires that all cargo moved between two U.S. seaports be shipped by a U.S.-flagged ship built in a U.S. shipyard. The law was enacted to preserve a strong national merchant marine, but Case says it's an anachronism and should be repealed. It has produced a monopoly on shipping to and from the islands, where 90 percent of life's necessities arrive by boat. A handful of shipping companies overcharge farmers and ranchers, making them uncompetitive with those on the mainland, Case says. The state's cattle industry is dying, he says, because it can't get products to market fast enough at a reasonable price.

Other leading politicians in Hawaii want to maintain the law, and they are backed by two companies that dominate the local shipping market, Matson Navigation and CSX Lines.

In his first term, Case sat on the Education and Workforce Committee, where he expressed interest in federal education policy and refinements to the Bush administration's 2001 No Child Left Behind Act. Standardized tests show Hawaii's public school system to be one of the worst performers in the nation, and the schools are greatly affected by the law, which is targeted at forcing schools to raise test scores. Case left the Education Committee in the 109th Congress for a seat on the Budget panel.

He has also taken up another longstanding issue for Hawaiians: the proposal to grant federal recognition of native Hawaiians as an indigenous people. They make up 12 percent of a population of 1.2 million.

Case says he was interested in politics as a boy growing up in Hilo, Hawaii's second-largest city and the largest urban area on the island of Hawaii. He was educated on the mainland, earning a degree in psychology from Williams College in Massachusetts and a law degree from the University of California's Hastings College of Law in San Francisco. He became a partner in Hawaii's largest law firm, Carlsmith Ball, and says his life apart from politics has made him a better legislator. Case, whose cousin is Steve Case, founder of AOL, says he moves "easily between the world of business and the world of government."

In between college and law school, Case worked for three years on the staff of the late Sen. Spark M. Matsunaga, a Hawaii Democrat, and says Matsunaga was a mentor. When he returned home to Hawaii, Case ran successfully for the state House, served seven years and eventually became majority leader. While in the legislature, he fought the state's powerful employees' union for increased efficiency and reductions in the soaring costs of its health care fund.

In 2002, Case narrowly lost a long-shot bid for the Democratic gubernatorial nomination. But he leveraged that effort to become the front-runner to succeed Patsy T. Mink, the first non-white woman elected to Congress. Mink died unexpectedly in September 2002 of viral pneumonia brought on by chickenpox.

In a special election to fill out the final weeks of Mink's 12th term, Case gained an outright majority of 51 percent of the vote, despite a field of some three dozen candidates that included Mink's husband, John, the sentimental favorite who campaigned on a promise to keep her office staff intact. Case served only briefly, but his victory allowed him to run as the incumbent in the January 2003 special election to fill Mink's seat in the 108th Congress. (She had won re-election posthumously in November.) In a field of 44 candidates, he bested runner-up Matt Matsunaga, a former state senator and Spark Matsunaga's son, by 13 percentage points.

Case won re-election easily with 63 percent of the vote in 2004 and says he would like to run for the Senate someday.

KEY VOTES

2004
Yes Extend federal unemployment benefits by 13 weeks
Yes Pass $283.2 billion, six-year federal highway and mass transit bill
Yes Approve $146 billion multi-year extension of previously enacted middle-class tax breaks
No Amend the Constitution to prohibit same-sex marriage
No Cut corporate taxes $137 billion over 10 years
? Reorganize U.S. intelligence agencies as proposed by Sept. 11 commission

2003
No Cut taxes by $330 billion through fiscal 2013
Yes Block Bush rule scaling back overtime pay for some white-collar federal workers
Yes Do not allow use of search warrants without first notifying subjects
Yes Allow importation of prescription drugs
No Create private school voucher program in Washington, D.C.
No Ban "partial birth" abortion except to save a woman's life
No Split $18.6 billion in Iraq aid into half-grant, half-loan
No Overhaul Medicare and create prescription drug benefit

CQ VOTE STUDIES

	PARTY UNITY		PRESIDENTIAL SUPPORT	
	Support	Oppose	Support	Oppose
2004	81%	19%	30%	70%
2003	86%	14%	35%	65%

INTEREST GROUPS

	AFL-CIO	ADA	CCUS	ACU
2004	80%	90%	50%	20%
2003	86%	95%	48%	28%

HAWAII 2
Suburban and Outer Oahu; 'Neighbor Islands'

Some visitors call these Pacific islands paradise. With sandy beaches, volcanoes, tropical rain forests and deserts, the 2nd is amazing in its geographic diversity. The district includes part of Oahu and all of the other seven major islands that make up the state.

The 2nd's economy struggled through rough times in the 1990s with both of its major industries, tourism and agriculture, in crisis. The more luxury-oriented tourism offered in the 2nd was not as hard-hit as Honolulu. But the Japanese yen's depreciation and Asia's economic woes resulted in Asian visitors spending less in the latter part of the decade — a worrisome development in a state that welcomes more than one-fourth of its tourists from Japan. A wave of sugar plantation closures also shook the economy, but growers are diversifying by adding more coffee, macadamia nuts and bananas. Tax incentives have helped attract biotechnology and information technology companies.

The 2nd has large Asian sections and is heavily Democratic. While there are some predominantly white, conservative-leaning communities on

Oahu and Maui, these areas usually are not strong enough to push Republicans to victory in federal races. Economic problems can give the GOP grounds to make inroads at the local level, but the 2nd has kept Democrats in office, and John Kerry captured 56 percent of the district's 2004 presidential vote. Republican Gov. Linda Lingle did well in Hawaii and Honolulu counties and poorly in Kauai County in her 2002 victory.

MAJOR INDUSTRY
Tourism, agriculture, military

MILITARY BASES
Schofield Barracks (Army), 16,500 military, 3,950 civilian (2005); Marine Corps Base Hawaii, 7,014 military, 1,905 civilian (2004); Naval Computer and Telecommunications Area Master Station Pacific, 769 military, 257 civilian; Lualualei Naval Magazine, 200 military, 435 civilian (2003)

CITIES
Hilo, 40,759; Kailua (unincorporated), 36,513; Kaneohe, 34,970; Kahului, 20,146

NOTABLE
Kauai's Mt. Waialeale, the wettest spot in the United States, averages 460 inches of rain annually; The world's largest active volcano, Mauna Loa, is located on the island Hawaii.

IDAHO

Gov. Dirk Kempthorne (R)

First elected: 1998
Length of term: 4 years
Term expires: 1/07
Salary: $98,700
Phone: (208) 334-2100

Hometown: Boise
Born: Oct. 29, 1951;
San Diego, Calif.
Religion: Methodist
Family: Wife, Patricia Kempthorne; two children
Education: U. of Idaho, B.A. 1975 (political science)
Career: Public affairs manager; securities representative; political consultant; building association executive
Political highlights: Mayor of Boise, 1986-92; U.S. Senate, 1993-99

Election results:
2002 GENERAL

Dirk Kempthorne (R)	231,566	56.3%
Jerry M. Brady (D)	171,711	41.7%
Daniel L.J. Adams (LIBERT)	8,187	2.0%

Lt. Gov. Jim Risch (R)

First elected: 2002
Length of term: 4 years
Term expires: 1/07
Salary: $26,750
Phone: (208) 334-2200

STATE LEGISLATURE

Legislature: January-March

House: 70 members, 2-year terms
2005 breakdown: 57R, 13D; 47 men, 23 women
Salary: $15,646; $99/day in session
Phone: (208) 332-1140

Senate: 35 members, 2-year terms
2005 breakdown: 28R, 7D; 31 men, 4 women
Salary: $15,646; $99/day in session
Phone: (208) 332-1309

STATE TERM LIMITS

Governor: No
House: No
Senate: No

URBAN STATISTICS

CITY	POPULATION
Boise	185,787
Nampa	51,867
Pocatello	51,466
Idaho Falls	50,730
Meridian	34,919

REGISTERED VOTERS

Voters do not register by party.

POPULATION

2004 population (est.)	1,393,262
2000 population	1,293,953
1990 population	1,006,749
Percent change (1990-2000)	+28.5%
Rank among states (2004)	39

Median age	33.2
Born in state	47.2%
Foreign born	5%
Violent crime rate	253/100,000
Poverty level	11.8%
Federal workers	12,939
Military	9,730

REDISTRICTING

Idaho retained its two House seats in reapportionment. The Idaho Commission on Redistricting adopted a new map on Aug. 22, 2001.

MISCELLANEOUS

Web: www.idaho.gov
Capital: Boise
STATE ELECTION OFFICIAL
(208) 334-2852
DEMOCRATIC HEADQUARTERS
(208) 336-1815
REPUBLICAN HEADQUARTERS
(208) 343-6405

District Statistics

DIST.	2004 VOTE FOR PRESIDENT BUSH	KERRY	WHITE	BLACK	ASIAN	HISP	MEDIAN INCOME	WHITE COLLAR	BLUE COLLAR	SERVICE INDUSTRY	OVER 64	UNDER 18	COLLEGE EDUCATION	RURAL	SQ. MILES
1	68%	30%	89%	0%	1%	7%	$38,364	56%	28%	15%	12%	28%	20%	34%	39,525
2	68	30	87	0	1	9	$36,934	57	27	16	11	29	23	33	43,222
STATE	68	30	88	0	1	8	$37,572	57	28	16	11	29	22	34	82,747
U.S.	50.7	48.3	69	12	4	13	$41,994	60	25	15	12	26	24	21	3,537,438

Sen. Larry E. Craig (R)

Elected 1990; 3rd term

CAPITOL OFFICE
224-2752
craig.senate.gov
520 Hart 20510-1203; fax 228-1067

COMMITTEES
Appropriations
Energy & Natural Resources
    (Public Lands & Forests - chairman)
Veterans' Affairs - chairman
Special Aging

HOMETOWN
Eagle

BORN
July 20, 1945, Council, Idaho

RELIGION
Methodist

FAMILY
Wife, Suzanne Craig; three children

EDUCATION
U. of Idaho, B.A. 1969 (political science); George
Washington U., attended 1969-70 (U.S. foreign
policy)

MILITARY SERVICE
Idaho National Guard, 1970-72

CAREER
Farmer; rancher

POLITICAL HIGHLIGHTS
Idaho Senate, 1975-81; U.S. House, 1981-91

ELECTION RESULTS

2002 GENERAL

Larry E. Craig (R)	266,215	65.2%
Alan Blinken (D)	132,975	32.6%
Donovan Bramwell (LIBERT)	9,354	2.3%

2002 PRIMARY

Larry E. Craig (R)	unopposed

PREVIOUS WINNING PERCENTAGES
1996 (57%); 1990 (61%); 1988 House Election (66%);
1986 House Election (65%); 1984 House Election
(69%); 1982 House Election (54%); 1980 House
Election (54%)

The Republican Party is of two minds on immigration policy, and Larry E. Craig has become a Senate leader for the more liberal position, in contrast to his strictly conservative leanings on most other issues.

Craig has single-mindedly taken up the plight of thousands of illegal immigrant farm workers and the farms that rely on their labor, and pushed the Bush White House to make a bill he has sponsored the lead immigration legislation of the 109th Congress. The measure gives legal status to farmworkers currently working off the books and, as President Bush has proposed, creates a new guest worker program for illegal aliens. "It is one of my top priorities in the new Congress," Craig says.

Craig represents a viewpoint on illegal immigration that he believes is gaining strength in the Republican Party. With more than 9 million illegal foreigners estimated to be living and working in the country, the idea of deporting them all is seen by these Republicans, and nearly all Democrats, as impractical and potentially devastating to the economy.

These lawmakers say that while border security should be strengthened, the nation should also make it easier for foreigners to enter and stay in the country when they seek to fill jobs Americans don't want. Further, they consider America to be facing a humanitarian crisis on its southwestern border, where hundreds of immigrants are believed to die each year trying to sneak into the country through the desert.

But liberalized immigration policy is still a hard sell among many Republicans, particularly House GOP leaders, who see it as offering "amnesty" to people who have broken the law to enter the country. Craig's push on immigration has also brought him into conflict with the White House. In July 2004, he tried to attach the measure to a class action reform bill. But the administration, uneasy taking up the issue in an election year, pressed Majority Leader Bill Frist to pull the underlying bill from the floor rather than allow votes on several controversial amendments, including Craig's proposal.

His unwavering conservatism, combined with flawless diction and masterful debating skills, lifted Craig to the chairmanship of the Republican Policy Committee, the fourth-ranking GOP leadership position, at the start of his second term in 1997. He had to give up the post in the 108th Congress because of party-imposed leadership term limits.

In the 109th Congress, he took the gavel of the Veterans' Affairs Committee, which oversees the second-largest department in the government. He said he wants to serve a new generation of veterans from the Iraq and Afghanistan wars, particularly disabled ones. To take that job, he stepped down as chairman of the Aging Committee, a special committee that does not write legislation.

Land-use issues have long been Craig's calling card. As a member of the Energy and Natural Resources Committee and chairman of the panel's Public Lands and Forests Subcommittee, he has fought efforts by Democrats and some moderate Republicans to limit or ban grazing, mining, drilling and road-building on the millions of acres owned by the U.S. government. But where pioneers like his ancestors tamed the West for gold, timber and other resources, Craig sees a new wave of "amenity migrants" arriving in search of an outdoor lifestyle.

Throughout his congressional career, Craig has taken aim at environmental laws — most notably the Endangered Species Act — that he says trample on private property rights and inhibit job growth. Craig advocates a Bush administration proposal called Healthy Forests designed to make it easier to thin underbrush, small trees and some commercially valuable old-growth trees in national forests. But after a career built by aggressively pursuing those issues, Craig finds himself working with a Republican president who largely shares his views on the matter. Environmental issues, as a result, have receded from the top of his agenda. "We've made a lot of progress in bringing balance and common sense to land management," he said.

Craig joined the Appropriations Committee in 1997, a seat he still holds. He used that influential post, with limited success, to fight the Clinton administration's penchant to regulate public lands. In the 108th, he was one of a bipartisan coalition of Western senators who successfully fought an effort by their Eastern peers to insert an extension of an expiring milk subsidy into a catchall spending bill passed in the final days of the 2004 legislative session. Craig and his allies said the subsidy favored small dairy farms in the East over the larger operations that dominate in the West.

Craig has championed other bipartisan efforts — at times in opposition to his party. He made a public break with the president in 2002, when the Senate debated Bush's legislation giving the president fast-track authority to negotiate trade agreements that Congress must approve or reject without amendment. Craig teamed with Minnesota Democrat Mark Dayton to win adoption of a provision giving the Senate power to vote separately on parts of trade pacts that weaken U.S. anti-dumping laws. Bush threatened to veto the bill unless the provision was removed, and in the end, Craig settled for a requirement that trade negotiators keep anti-dumping laws intact if possible.

Craig is on the board of the National Rifle Association and in the Senate he zealously guards the rights of gun owners. After a student massacre at Colorado's Columbine High School in 1999, he led the campaign against proposals to require background checks at gun shows. In 2002, Craig teamed with fellow Republican John McCain of Arizona and two Democrats, Charles E. Schumer of New York and Edward M. Kennedy of Massachusetts, to push legislation strengthening instant background checks. (They called themselves the "Odd Quad.")

Craig showed an early inclination toward politics. Born on his family's ranch, which was homesteaded in 1899 by his grandfather, he headed the Idaho Young Republicans and was national vice president of the Future Farmers of America. In 1974, he won election to the state Senate, and has never lost an election since.

In 1980, when conservative Steve Symms vacated his U.S. House seat to run for the Senate, Craig prevailed in a tough primary and was a solid favorite going into the general election. But Democratic rival Glenn W. Nichols drew attention by walking the length of the district, from Canada to Nevada, and held Craig to 54 percent of the vote.

The retirement of Republican James A. McClure after three terms in 1990 gave Craig his opportunity to advance to the Senate. He easily bested state Attorney General Jim Jones in the GOP primary, winning 59 percent of the vote. In the general election, Craig beat Democrat Ron Twilegar, a former state legislator and Boise City Council member, with 61 percent.

In 1996, Craig's Democratic opponent was Walt Minnick, a former executive at a Boise lumber company and a one-time aide in the Nixon White House. Craig campaigned vigorously and captured 57 percent. He had even less trouble winning a third term in 2002, collecting 65 percent of the vote against Democrat Alan Blinken, who had been President Clinton's ambassador to Belgium, and Libertarian Donovan Bramwell.

KEY VOTES

2004

No	Pass $318.9 billion, six-year highway and mass transit bill
No	Extend assault weapons ban for 10 years
No	Restore pay-as-you-go rules for new tax cuts and entitlement spending
Yes	Criminalize harm to a fetus in an attack on the mother
No	Increase mandatory child care funding to states by $6 billion over five years
Yes	Amend the Constitution to prohibit same-sex marriage
Yes	Approve $146 billion multi-year extension of previously enacted middle-class tax breaks
Yes	Reorganize U.S. intelligence agencies as proposed by Sept. 11 commission
Yes	Cut corporate taxes $137 billion over 10 years

2003

No	Delay Bush changes to Clean Air Act
Yes	Allow confirmation vote on Miguel A. Estrada to the U.S. Court of Appeals for the D.C. Circuit
No	Block a Bush proposal opening Alaska's Arctic National Wildlife Refuge to oil drilling
No	Limit size of Bush's proposed tax cut to $350 billion through fiscal 2013
Yes	Overhaul Medicare and create prescription drug benefit
No	Block Bush rule scaling back overtime pay for some white-collar federal workers
No	Split $20 billion in Iraq aid into half-grant, half-loan
Yes	Ban "partial birth" abortion except to save a woman's life
No	Stop proposal allowing travel to Cuba
Yes	Allow final vote on energy policy overhaul

CQ VOTE STUDIES

	PARTY UNITY		PRESIDENTIAL SUPPORT	
	Support	Oppose	Support	Oppose
2004	98%	2%	96%	4%
2003	98%	2%	97%	3%
2002	93%	7%	95%	5%
2001	96%	4%	97%	3%
2000	100%	0%	40%	60%
1999	97%	3%	29%	71%
1998	99%	1%	29%	71%
1997	97%	3%	54%	46%
1996	98%	2%	32%	68%
1995	98%	2%	20%	80%

INTEREST GROUPS

	AFL-CIO	ADA	CCUS	ACU
2004	8%	5%	88%	96%
2003	15%	5%	91%	90%
2002	8%	5%	90%	100%
2001	13%	0%	100%	96%
2000	0%	0%	93%	100%
1999	0%	0%	88%	96%
1998	0%	5%	100%	84%
1997	0%	5%	100%	84%
1996	0%	0%	100%	95%
1995	0%	0%	100%	96%

Sen. Michael D. Crapo (R)

Elected 1998; 2nd term

CAPITOL OFFICE
224-6142
crapo.senate.gov
239 Dirksen 20510-1205; fax 228-1375

COMMITTEES
Agriculture, Nutrition & Forestry
  (Forestry, Conservation & Rural Revitalization -
  chairman)
Banking, Housing & Urban Affairs
  (International Trade & Finance - chairman)
Budget
Finance
Indian Affairs

HOMETOWN
Idaho Falls

BORN
May 20, 1951, Idaho Falls, Idaho

RELIGION
Mormon

FAMILY
Wife, Susan Crapo; five children

EDUCATION
Brigham Young U., B.A. 1973 (political science);
Harvard U., J.D. 1977

CAREER
Lawyer

POLITICAL HIGHLIGHTS
Idaho Senate, 1985-93 (president pro tempore,
1989-93); U.S. House, 1993-99

ELECTION RESULTS

2004 GENERAL
Michael D. Crapo (R)   499,796   99.2%
Scott F. McClure (D) - write-in   4,136   0.8%

2004 PRIMARY
Michael D. Crapo (R)   unopposed

PREVIOUS WINNING PERCENTAGES
1998 (70%); 1996 House Election (69%); 1994 House
Election (75%); 1992 House Election (61%)

Low-key and well-liked on Capitol Hill, Crapo is continuing his career ascent, winning a seat in the 109th Congress on the Finance Committee, while at the same time planning to play a central role in Western land and resources issues, even after relinquishing a key subcommittee chairmanship.

Crapo (CRAY-poe) was also given a small post in the 109th near the bottom of the Senate GOP leadership ladder — the chairmanship of the Committee on Committees, which makes some of the decisions, subject to leadership and party approval, on committee assignments for fellow Republicans.

Conservative in his political philosophy and moderate in his demeanor, Crapo was aptly described in 2003 by former Idaho GOP Sen. James A. McClure in the Idaho Statesman newspaper. "He's not flamboyant, he's not seeking headlines, he is thoughtful, and he works," McClure said. "That's a good combination. You're not threatening anybody, you're not pushing anybody, you're not embarrassing anybody. They can count on you to listen and give a thoughtful response. Those things are appreciated by other senators."

And Boise State University political scientist Jim Weatherby notes that Crapo's "voting record is probably as conservative as other members of the [Idaho] delegation, but he certainly is not seen as an ideologue." Crapo is viewed as "more of a problem solver," Weatherby told the Spokane (Wash.) Spokesman Review.

Crapo appears reluctant to personalize political disagreements, and he usually can count on a receptive audience when he seeks to cross party lines to gain a compromise or cosponsors. He is described by many of his colleagues as "a nice guy."

His mild manner belies an ambition, fueled in part by his dedication to a deceased older brother, that is reflected in the climb that Crapo has made up the political ladder. A cum laude graduate of Harvard Law School, he was elected to the state Senate at age 33 and chosen its president pro tempore just four years later. He won the 2nd District seat in 1992 and was then tapped to be the freshman class representative to the GOP leadership. He was given a much sought-after seat on the House Energy and Commerce Committee in his first term.

As he began his public life, Crapo was guided by his desire to fulfill dreams his oldest brother, Terry, could not. An Idaho state legislator and wunderkind who was also his mentor and law partner, Terry Crapo died just two weeks after he was diagnosed with leukemia in 1982. In a written response to an Idaho newspaper's question in 1996 about the motivations of political candidates, Crapo said, "I began to reflect on how Terry might face this battle if the roles were reversed. I knew without a doubt that he would be in there fighting until the very last moment."

Crapo faced his own trial with cancer in 2000, when doctors diagnosed prostate cancer and operated. Since then, he has sponsored health screening booths at fairs across the state. Early in 2005, the cancer returned, and Crapo began radiation treatments.

When he was given the Finance Committee assignment, Crapo had to relinquish his seat on Environment and Public Works, where in the 108th he had chaired the Fisheries, Wildlife and Water Subcommittee. He did not make the decision lightly because an overhaul of the Endangered Species Act has been a priority of his for years. Crapo sought out the new Environment Committee leaders and received assurances that his participation on the issue would be welcome.

Crapo has always taken an interest in water issues, ranging from pollution from agricultural runoff to helping small communities afford improvements to their water systems to providing water rights for farmers.

On the Agriculture Committee in the 108th, he took the lead role in legislation, which became law, that authorized the thinning of 20 million acres of national forests and restricted challenges to thinning projects. The measure was aimed at preventing wildfires.

As Congress in 2004 prepared to consider a trade agreement between the United States and Australia, Crapo joined other Idaho lawmakers in writing a letter to President Bush warning of the pact's potential for dire consequences for the dairy industry, although he eventually voted for the agreement. Like many Western legislators, Crapo is wary of Canadian policies toward timber and agricultural trade with the United States. He bucked the majority of his party and opposed legislation to implement both the 1993 North American Free Trade Agreement and the 1994 General Agreement on Tariffs and Trade. Since then, he has voted to enact the 2000 law making permanent the normalized U.S.-China trade relationship and the 2002 law giving the president fast-track authority to negotiate trade deals.

Crapo is generally supportive of party positions and of the president, voting for both well more than 90 percent of the time.

There were a few occasions in the 108th when he strayed, however. He voted against measures to limit medical malpractice awards (it would have pre-empted an Idaho law) and to provide tax incentives for charitable donations. He also was in the GOP minority on lifting the ban on travel to Cuba.

The youngest of six children of an Idaho Falls postmaster and his homemaker wife, Crapo graduated from Brigham Young University with a degree in political science. He was an intern with GOP Rep. Orval Hansen of Idaho during the summer that the Watergate scandal began and later watched the televised hearings with great interest. "It bothered me to see that happening . . . but I was also fascinated with the political process and the fact that our system had a mechanism" to deal with the crisis, he later told the Spokesman Review.

Crapo thought about becoming a doctor and after graduating from college spent a year in a pre-med program. But he changed his mind after gaining admission to Harvard Law School. After graduating and working as a law clerk, Crapo returned to his hometown to practice law.

A devout Mormon, Crapo says his experiences with the church, which gives its lay leaders considerable responsibilities in dealing with personal and community issues, helped prepare him for public office. Friendly and casual, he is more at ease wearing boots, jeans and a plaid shirt. He says he is sorry that his days of riding dirt bikes, a favorite pastime in college, are now behind him.

In 1992, he ran for the House seat being vacated by Democrat Richard Stallings, who ran unsuccessfully for the Senate. In the GOP-leaning 2nd, Crapo was aided by George Bush's presence as the GOP presidential candidate, and he defeated Democrat J.D. Williams by 26 percentage points.

Crapo never has had a difficult time winning re-election. When Republican Sen. Dirk Kempthorne decided to run for governor in 1998, Crapo quickly became the ordained front-runner as his successor. Crapo's general popularity and a strong Republican tide enabled him to crush Bill Mauk, a former Democratic state chairman, by more than 40 points.

In 2004, for the first time in the state's history, the Democratic Party declined to even field a Senate candidate. An opponent — Jerome businessman Scott F. McClure — did surface late in the campaign. McClure, saying that democracy was not well-served if voters had no choice at all, ran as a write-in candidate. Crapo captured 99 percent of the vote.

KEY VOTES

2004

Yes Pass $318.9 billion, six-year highway and mass transit bill
No   Extend assault weapons ban for 10 years
No   Restore pay-as-you-go rules for new tax cuts and entitlement spending
Yes Criminalize harm to a fetus in an attack on the mother
No   Increase mandatory child care funding to states by $6 billion over five years
Yes Amend the Constitution to prohibit same-sex marriage
Yes Approve $146 billion multi-year extension of previously enacted middle-class tax breaks
Yes Reorganize U.S. intelligence agencies as proposed by Sept. 11 commission
Yes Cut corporate taxes $137 billion over 10 years

2003

No   Delay Bush changes to Clean Air Act
Yes Allow confirmation vote on Miguel A. Estrada to the U.S. Court of Appeals for the D.C. Circuit
No   Block a Bush proposal opening Alaska's Arctic National Wildlife Refuge to oil drilling
No   Limit size of Bush's proposed tax cut to $350 billion through fiscal 2013
Yes Overhaul Medicare and create prescription drug benefit
No   Block Bush rule scaling back overtime pay for some white-collar federal workers
No   Split $20 billion in Iraq aid into half-grant, half-loan
Yes Ban "partial birth" abortion except to save a woman's life
No   Stop proposal allowing travel to Cuba
Yes Allow final vote on energy policy overhaul

CQ VOTE STUDIES

	PARTY UNITY		PRESIDENTIAL SUPPORT	
	Support	Oppose	Support	Oppose
2004	96%	4%	90%	10%
2003	98%	2%	97%	3%
2002	92%	8%	96%	4%
2001	94%	6%	96%	4%
2000	100%	0%	41%	59%
1999	97%	3%	30%	70%
House Service:				
1998	89%	11%	30%	70%
1997	94%	6%	20%	80%
1996	95%	5%	30%	70%
1995	97%	3%	21%	79%

INTEREST GROUPS

	AFL-CIO	ADA	CCUS	ACU
2004	8%	10%	94%	92%
2003	15%	5%	91%	89%
2002	9%	10%	94%	94%
2001	19%	10%	100%	92%
2000	0%	0%	93%	100%
1999	0%	0%	88%	100%
House Service:				
1998	22%	10%	94%	83%
1997	13%	0%	70%	92%
1996	0%	0%	100%	95%
1995	0%	5%	100%	92%

Rep. C. L. 'Butch' Otter (R)

Elected 2000; 3rd term

CAPITOL OFFICE
225-6611
www.house.gov/otter
1711 Longworth 20515-1201; fax 225-3029

COMMITTEES
Energy & Commerce

HOMETOWN
Star

BORN
May 3, 1942, Caldwell, Idaho

RELIGION
Roman Catholic

FAMILY
Divorced; four children

EDUCATION
College of Idaho, B.A. 1967 (political science)

MILITARY SERVICE
Idaho National Guard, 1967-73

CAREER
Agribusiness company executive; oil company partner

POLITICAL HIGHLIGHTS
Idaho House, 1973-77; sought Republican nomination for governor, 1978; lieutenant governor, 1987-2001

ELECTION RESULTS

2004 GENERAL

C. L. "Butch" Otter (R)	207,662	69.6%
Naomi Preston (D)	90,927	30.5%

2004 PRIMARY

C. L. "Butch" Otter (R)	48,986	78.5%
Jim A. "Big Jim" Pratt (R)	13,433	21.5%

2002 GENERAL

C. L. "Butch" Otter (R)	120,743	58.6%
Betty Richardson (D)	80,269	38.9%
Steve Gothard (LIBERT)	5,129	2.5%

PREVIOUS WINNING PERCENTAGES
2000 (65%)

The 109th Congress is likely be Otter's last. He was laying plans to run for Idaho governor in early 2005, raising money and forming a campaign committee for a race to succeed Republican Gov. Dirk Kempthorne.

Otter staged a close but unsuccessful bid for the GOP gubernatorial nomination in 1978, when he was 36 years old, and later was Idaho's lieutenant governor for 14 years. He was expected to face Lt. Gov. Jim Risch, a savvy grass-roots campaigner and strong fundraiser.

Otter's libertarian beliefs seem to go over well with Idaho voters, who elected him to state offices several times before sending him to Washington in 2000. He advocates a limited role for the federal government, and tries to keep Washington from restricting private property rights, infringing on civil liberties in the name of investigating terrorists and forcing states to raise the legal drinking age.

A back-slapping, guitar-strumming cowboy at heart, Otter's personal appeal explains how he has been able to sustain Idahoans' support despite a drunken driving conviction and a divorce from his wife of 30 years.

Ironically, Otter's time in the House will likely be best remembered for the decisive vote he cast in favor of a major expansion of the Medicare entitlement program to include a prescription drug benefit for the elderly. Otter opposed the bill as too costly and an unwarranted expansion of the government's role in health care, and he at first voted against it. Then, President Bush and top GOP leaders launched an all-out pressure campaign to win over Republicans whose support they needed to pass the bill, one of the president's top legislative priorities of the 108th Congress.

Bush phoned Otter and a handful of other GOP members while Speaker J. Dennis Hastert held the vote open for nearly three hours, into the night and early hours of the morning. "He asked me what my problem was," Otter recalled. "My problem was we didn't pay for it."

Ultimately, Otter agreed to switch his vote to yes, one of a handful of votes that gave Bush a narrow victory. Later, Otter said it was not the president's appeal to him that prompted him to switch but rather the fear that Democrats would prevail with an even more expensive bill. He said he was won over by the argument that if the House rejected the conference agreement, the chamber's Democrats would likely be able to gather enough signatures on a discharge petition to force a vote on a more generous Senate bill. "I've seen those discharge petitions move pretty rapidly when they see that deals are being cut," Otter said after the vote. "If we lost [the Republican] bill, we weren't going to like what we'd end up with."

Otter was one of just three Republicans who voted in 2001 against legislation that gave law enforcement agencies new tools to investigate terrorists, which he said gave the government more power "than our Founding Fathers could ever have dreamt." In 2003, he failed in his attempt to scale back a provision of the Patriot Act giving federal agents new powers to conduct searches without notifying the targets in advance.

Much of Idaho's land is under federal control, and like many Western lawmakers, Otter is an ardent advocate of state management of federal lands. A millionaire businessman and rancher, Otter has had his own run-ins with the federal government. He was fined $50,000 by the Environmental Protection Agency in 2001 for filling in wetlands on his ranch along the Boise River. It was his third EPA citation. "I think the EPA is way out of control," he told the Spokane Spokesman-Review, adding that he does not believe he has done anything wrong.

One of his priorities in Congress is to require the federal government to complete studies of potential wilderness areas within 10 years. He contends that some wilderness studies drag on and meanwhile the land is effectively off-limits for many uses.

Sixth in a family of nine children, Otter grew up in Caldwell, just west of Boise. He dropped out of high school to help his mother run the family farm when his father and brother were injured. Mounting medical bills forced the Otters to sell the farm, and he went back to school, studying at a Catholic monastery for two years before giving up the idea of entering the priesthood. He continued his studies at the College of Idaho, becoming the first member of his family to complete college.

While there, he met Gay Simplot. They married and Otter went to work for her father at the Boise-based J.R. Simplot agribusiness company.

Otter's father was a union electrician, and his family members were Democrats. But he remembers comparing Democratic and Republican campaign literature as he prepared to vote for the first time in 1964. He told the Spokesman-Review that he recalls thinking, "Boy, my dad's not going to like this very well, but I don't think I'm a Democrat. I feel more like a Barry Goldwater Republican."

In 1972, at the urging of both his father-in-law and a well-known libertarian, Ralph Smeed, Otter ran for the state House on a platform of reducing the size of government. He served two terms, and in 1986, ran for the first of his four terms as the state's lieutenant governor. In office less than two months, Otter took the chance to demonstrate his libertarian approach as acting governor while his boss, Democratic Gov. Cecil D. Andrus, was briefly out of the state. He vetoed a bill passed to raise the state's legal drinking age from 19 to 21. At the time, Idaho was under pressure from the federal government to raise the drinking age or lose millions of dollars in highway money. The legislature passed the bill again, and Andrus signed it.

Otter's divorce from Simplot and a drunken driving conviction put an end to his thoughts of running for governor in 1994. He decided to run again for lieutenant governor and was re-elected two more times.

In 2000, when outspoken conservative Rep. Helen Chenoweth-Hage fulfilled her pledge to limit her House service to three terms, Otter entered the race to succeed her and overcame seven GOP opponents in the primary. He then breezed to an easy general-election victory by a ratio of more than 2-to-1. In 2002, he beat former U.S. Attorney Betty Richardson by 20 percentage points. He improved that margin to 39 percentage points in 2004.

KEY VOTES

2004

No Extend federal unemployment benefits by 13 weeks

No Pass $283.2 billion, six-year federal highway and mass transit bill

Yes Approve $146 billion multi-year extension of previously enacted middle-class tax breaks

Yes Amend the Constitution to prohibit same-sex marriage

Yes Cut corporate taxes $137 billion over 10 years

No Reorganize U.S. intelligence agencies as proposed by Sept. 11 commission

2003

Yes Cut taxes by $330 billion through fiscal 2013

No Block Bush rule scaling back overtime pay for some white-collar federal workers

Yes Do not allow use of search warrants without first notifying subjects

Yes Allow importation of prescription drugs

Yes Create private school voucher program in Washington, D.C.

Yes Ban "partial birth" abortion except to save a woman's life

No Split $18.6 billion in Iraq aid into half-grant, half-loan

Yes Overhaul Medicare and create prescription drug benefit

CQ VOTE STUDIES

	PARTY UNITY		PRESIDENTIAL SUPPORT	
	Support	Oppose	Support	Oppose
2004	94%	6%	74%	26%
2003	92%	8%	87%	13%
2002	94%	6%	87%	13%
2001	96%	4%	81%	19%

INTEREST GROUPS

	AFL-CIO	ADA	CCUS	ACU
2004	0%	5%	95%	100%
2003	0%	20%	97%	88%
2002	0%	0%	90%	96%
2001	8%	0%	87%	96%

IDAHO 1
West — Nampa, Panhandle, part of Boise

Stretching the 500-mile height of western Idaho, from British Columbia in the north to Nevada in the south, the 1st is mostly rural, punctuated by urban pockets. White-collar workers in Idaho's capital, Boise (shared with the 2nd), combine with agricultural voters to give it a GOP base. Redistricting after the 2000 census had little effect on the district, with the 1st losing a small part of Boise.

Boise and its surroundings contain about one-fourth of the district's population and house the headquarters of many lumber, paper, food processing, electronics and construction companies. The strongest Democratic voting bloc is found among the timber and metal miners in the panhandle and around Coeur d'Alene, but Democrats are outnumbered in nearly every other part of the district.

The 1st's midsize cities have attracted new technology businesses, such as Hewlett-Packard in Boise, and created new white-collar jobs. Some technology companies also reside along the Interstate 90 corridor in the northern part of the district. Nampa, west of Boise, has experienced high growth due to cheaper housing and a solid job market, and officials hope a proposed expansion of Interstate 84 will decrease congestion. Some small towns have not fared as well, as the 1st has become increasingly urbanized. Small timber mills have suffered, although the mining industry has seen price increases. Many rural communities are attempting to attract tourists to the state's forests, lakes and mountains.

Republicans dominate the district. Since 1967, Democrats have held the congressional seat for only four years (1991-95). In both the 2000 and 2004 presidential elections, George W. Bush swept every county in the 1st.

MAJOR INDUSTRY
Manufacturing, agriculture, timber

CITIES
Boise City (pt.), 59,680; Nampa, 51,867; Meridian, 34,919; Coeur d'Alene, 34,514; Lewiston, 30,904; Caldwell, 25,967; Moscow, 21,291

NOTABLE
The Sunshine Mine Memorial near Kellogg in Shoshone County memorializes the 1972 Sunshine Mine fire, which killed 91 miners; At nearly 20 carats, one of the largest diamonds found in the United States was discovered near McCall.

Rep. Mike Simpson (R)

Elected 1998; 4th term

CAPITOL OFFICE
225-5531
www.house.gov/simpson
1339 Longworth 20515-1202; fax 225-8216

COMMITTEES
Appropriations
Budget

HOMETOWN
Blackfoot

BORN
Sept. 8, 1950, Burley, Idaho

RELIGION
Mormon

FAMILY
Wife, Kathy Simpson

EDUCATION
Utah State U., attended 1968-72 (pre-dentistry);
Washington U. (Mo.), D.D.S. 1977; Utah State U.,
B.S. 2002 (pre-dentistry)

CAREER
Dentist

POLITICAL HIGHLIGHTS
Blackfoot City Council, 1980-84; Idaho House,
1985-99 (Speaker, 1993-99)

ELECTION RESULTS

2004 GENERAL

Mike Simpson (R)	193,704	70.7%
Lin Whitworth (D)	80,133	29.3%

2004 PRIMARY

Mike Simpson (R)	unopposed

2002 GENERAL

Mike Simpson (R)	135,605	68.2%
Edward W. Kinghorn (D)	57,769	29.1%
John H. Lewis (LIBERT)	5,508	2.8%

PREVIOUS WINNING PERCENTAGES
2000 (71%); 1998 (53%)

A conservative small-town dentist, Simpson says he abides by a 12-point set of "Simpson's Rules," which include "hear both sides before judging" and "never, never make an enemy needlessly." He has looked to understand other viewpoints by briefly joining the American Civil Liberties Union and the Idaho Conservation League, and he regularly attends meetings with environmental groups with whom he often disagrees.

In the 108th Congress, Simpson won appointment to the Appropriations Committee, a panel where bipartisan relationships are important, as they can provide votes for spending on hometown projects. In the 109th, he is vice chairman of the Interior, Environment and Related Agencies Subcommittee, and he also sits on the panel that funds energy and water development programs. From these posts, he is able to look out for local priorities, including the Idaho National Engineering and Environmental Laboratory.

Simpson in the 109th will need his skills at consensus-building to move legislation important to him: overhauling how public lands in central Idaho can be used. He weighed in on this idea at the end of 2004 with a bill to create three new wilderness areas. Although environmentalists applauded this aspect of the measure, they raised concerns about provisions to give away some federal land for development and allow off-road uses on other federal land. Simpson said he is trying to promote development, assist ranchers and protect wilderness, and his efforts won an initial round of generally respectable reviews from often opposing Idaho interests.

Simpson says he represents the views of rural Western lawmakers, whose perspectives on water and land-use issues are often misunderstood by Easterners. He says Westerners "must resist the temptation to turn local decision-making power over to the federal government in return for assistance in funding."

To take the Appropriations post in 2003, he had to relinquish his other assignments, including the Veterans' Affairs Committee. Yet he continued to concern himself with veterans' issues, and in the 108th Congress won passage of a bill to mandate that the Department of Labor place staff in overseas veterans' assistance offices. He now serves on the Appropriations subcommittee with jurisdiction over military quality of life and veterans' affairs.

On another issue of importance to him, Simpson tried in the 108th to split the U.S. Court of Appeals for the 9th Circuit into three separate circuits. He won House passage of an amendment in 2004 that would have placed a number of Western states, including Idaho, into one of two newly created circuits. The San Francisco-based 9th Circuit has long drawn the ire of conservatives who view it as the most liberal appellate court in the country. Simpson insisted that he wanted to break up the 9th Circuit not because of its decisions, but because its sheer size makes it too unwieldy to be efficient. "It is inevitable, inevitable, that the 9th Circuit will be split," Simpson said.

Simpson casts a conservative vote on most social and economic issues. But in the 108th, he was one of only 18 Republicans to vote for an amendment by Vermont independent Bernard Sanders that would have prevented the Justice Department from obtaining library and bookseller records as part of an investigation of suspected terrorists. The amendment, which failed on a tie vote, proved that some Republicans, like Simpson, are uneasy about the curbs on civil liberties under the post-Sept. 11, 2001, Patriot Act.

During his first term, Simpson set an ambitious goal of meeting every one of his 434 House peers. He actually met with about 350 lawmakers, a feat that underscored his commitment to working equally with ideological soul mates and partisan opposites. "A legislative body functions on relationships. You may have the best idea in the world, but if you can't convince 218 people to agree with you, you're out of luck," he told the Idaho Statesman soon after arriving in Congress.

Simpson had intended to work for free in Washington, D.C. dental clinics, but he found that licensing requirements made that too complicated. He also discovered that he did not have time to see patients during his visits back home, so he reluctantly sold his share of a dental practice.

Simpson grew up in the eastern Idaho town of Blackfoot, where his father and uncle had a dental practice. He met his wife in high school, and they both attended Utah State University. (Simpson did not earn his degree until 2002, however, when he arranged to have some credits from dental school at Washington University in St. Louis transferred to Utah State.)

Returning to Blackfoot to join the family dental business, Simpson decided to run for a city council seat, a nonpartisan job, only after he noticed no one else was. He says that his interest in politics was first sparked by a high school teacher who was a staunch Democrat, but when he decided to run for the state legislature four years later, Simpson had to choose a party affiliation and concluded he was more comfortable with the GOP.

Simpson started out with a reputation as an occasionally angry maverick, but he mellowed and made a name for himself in Boise, rising through the ranks in the state House and serving as Speaker during his last six years there. He gave some thought to seeking the governorship in 1998 but decided against it when Republican Sen. Dirk Kempthorne chose to run. Republican Rep. Michael D. Crapo made a bid for Kempthorne's Senate seat, which created an opening for Simpson in the 2nd District. He won a four-way GOP primary despite criticism from social conservatives that he was insufficiently ardent on their issues.

During the campaign, Simpson was more worried about voters learning of his memberships in the ACLU and the Idaho Conservation League than of his use of marijuana in college 30 years earlier. He made no effort to hide the fact that he is a lapsed Mormon who once smoked and still drinks occasionally. But these revelations seemed to have little effect on the heavily Mormon, but also Republican, electorate. He went on to defeat conservative Democrat Richard Stallings, who had held the seat from 1985 to 1993, by 8 percentage points. He has easily won re-election since. He has not ruled out a future run for governor.

KEY VOTES

2004
No Extend federal unemployment benefits by 13 weeks
No Pass $283.2 billion, six-year federal highway and mass transit bill
Yes Approve $146 billion multi-year extension of previously enacted middle-class tax breaks
Yes Amend the Constitution to prohibit same-sex marriage
Yes Cut corporate taxes $137 billion over 10 years
No Reorganize U.S. intelligence agencies as proposed by Sept. 11 commission

2003
Yes Cut taxes by $330 billion through fiscal 2013
No Block Bush rule scaling back overtime pay for some white-collar federal workers
Yes Do not allow use of search warrants without first notifying subjects
Yes Allow importation of prescription drugs
No Create private school voucher program in Washington, D.C.
Yes Ban "partial birth" abortion except to save a woman's life
No Split $18.6 billion in Iraq aid into half-grant, half-loan
Yes Overhaul Medicare and create prescription drug benefit

CQ VOTE STUDIES

	PARTY UNITY		PRESIDENTIAL SUPPORT	
	Support	Oppose	Support	Oppose
2004	94%	6%	79%	21%
2003	94%	6%	95%	5%
2002	95%	5%	92%	8%
2001	98%	2%	88%	12%
2000	94%	6%	29%	71%

INTEREST GROUPS

	AFL-CIO	ADA	CCUS	ACU
2004	7%	0%	95%	92%
2003	7%	10%	97%	92%
2002	11%	0%	100%	92%
2001	17%	5%	100%	84%
2000	0%	0%	90%	88%

IDAHO 2
East – Pocatello, Idaho Falls, part of Boise

Covering eastern and central Idaho, the 2nd includes part of Boise, a few midsize towns and a vast swath of agricultural land irrigated by the Snake River. To the west, in Elmore County, is Mountain Home Air Force Base, but most of the district subsists on agriculture, primarily potatoes, sugar beets and grain. Blackfoot, in Bingham County, is known as the potato-producing capital of the world.

The 2nd's fortunes have risen and fallen with its agriculture. Some farms have benefited from the 2002 farm law that reinstated federal subsidies for staple crops, and farmers have expanded into dairy, beef and cheese processing, especially in Twin Falls and Jerome counties. The 2nd's manufacturing economy revolves around food processing, including Ore-Ida's frozen french fries. The district also is home to technology firms, including Micron, which provide thousands of jobs.

Tourism is the district's third-leading industry. With natural wonders such as Shoshone Falls, and ski resorts such as Sun Valley, the 2nd attracts a steady stream of vacationers.

The district consistently votes Republican at the state and national level. Members of The Church of Jesus Christ of Latter-day Saints make up the largest religious group, and like most Mormon areas, the district is strongly conservative. Since 1992, only Blaine County, with its resorts, has voted Democratic in presidential elections; this was not unexpected in 2004, since John Kerry and his wife own a vacation home in Sun Valley. Kerry increased the Democratic percentage of the presidential vote in Blaine County by 12 points in 2004.

MAJOR INDUSTRY
Agriculture, food processing, tourism

MILITARY BASES
Mountain Home Air Force Base, 4,400 military, 820 civilian (2004)

CITIES
Boise City (pt.), 126,107; Pocatello, 51,466; Idaho Falls, 50,730; Twin Falls, 34,469; Rexburg, 17,257

NOTABLE
The vast majority of all commercial trout sold in the United States is produced in the Hagerman Valley near Twin Falls; Sun Valley was America's first ski resort; In 1955, Arco became the first town powered solely by atomic energy — for one hour.

Gov. Rod R. Blagojevich (D)

First elected: 2002
Length of term: 4 years
Term expires: 1/07
Salary: $150,691
Phone: (217) 782-0244

Hometown: Chicago
Born: Dec. 10, 1956; Chicago, Ill.
Religion: Eastern Orthodox
Family: Wife, Patricia Blagojevich; two children
Education: Northwestern U., B.A. 1979 (history); Pepperdine U., J.D. 1983
Career: Lawyer
Political highlights: Assistant Cook County state's attorney, 1986-88; Ill. House, 1993-97; U.S. House, 1997-2003

Election results:
2002 GENERAL

Rod R. Blagojevich (D)	1,847,040	52.2%
Jim Ryan (R)	1,594,960	45.1%
Cal Skinner (LIBERT)	73,794	2.1%

Lt. Gov. Pat Quinn (D)

First elected: 2002
Length of term: 4 years
Term expires: 1/07
Salary: $115,235
Phone: (217) 782-7884

STATE LEGISLATURE

General Assembly: January-May
House: 118 members, 2-year terms
2005 breakdown: 65D, 53R; 82 men, 36 women
Salary: $57,619
Phone: (217) 782-8223

Senate: 59 members, rotates between 2 and 4-year terms
2005 breakdown: 34D, 27R, 1I; 45 men, 14 women
Salary: $57,619
Phone: (217) 782-5715

STATE TERM LIMITS

Governor: No
House: No
Senate: No

URBAN STATISTICS

CITY	POPULATION
Chicago	2,896,016
Rockford	150,115
Aurora	142,990
Naperville	128,358
Peoria	112,936

REGISTERED VOTERS

Voters do not register by party.

POPULATION

2004 population (est.)	12,713,634
2000 population	12,419,293
1990 population	11,430,602
Percent change (1990-2000)	+8.6%
Rank among states (2004)	5

Median age	34.7
Born in state	67.1%
Foreign born	12.3%
Violent crime rate	657/100,000
Poverty level	10.7%
Federal workers	91,284
Military	57,753

REDISTRICTING

Illinois lost one House seat in reapportionment. The state legislature drew a new, 19-district map, which the governor signed on May 31, 2001.

MISCELLANEOUS

Web: www.illinois.gov
Capital: Springfield
STATE ELECTION OFFICIAL
(217) 782-4141
DEMOCRATIC HEADQUARTERS
(217) 546-7404
REPUBLICAN HEADQUARTERS
(217) 525-0011

District Statistics

DIST.	2004 VOTE FOR PRESIDENT BUSH	KERRY	WHITE	BLACK	ASIAN	HISP	MEDIAN INCOME	WHITE COLLAR	BLUE COLLAR	SERVICE INDUSTRY	OVER 64	UNDER 18	COLLEGE EDUCATION	RURAL	SQ. MILES
1	17%	83%	27%	65%	1%	5%	$37,222	61%	22%	17%	13%	28%	19%	0%	98
2	16	84	26	62	1	10	$41,330	60	24	16	12	29	18	0	185
3	41	59	68	6	3	21	$48,048	58	28	14	14	26	21	0	124
4	21	79	18	4	2	74	$35,935	43	39	17	6	32	14	0	39
5	33	67	66	2	6	23	$48,531	65	22	14	12	20	34	0	57
6	53	46	75	3	8	12	$62,640	70	20	10	10	26	35	0	213
7	16	83	27	62	4	6	$40,361	71	16	14	10	27	32	0	56
8	55	44	79	3	6	11	$62,762	67	22	11	8	28	32	4	618
9	31	68	62	11	12	12	$46,531	70	16	14	16	21	40	0	75
10	47	52	75	5	6	12	$71,663	76	15	10	12	27	48	0	250
11	53	46	84	8	1	7	$47,800	55	30	15	12	27	19	22	4,241
12	48	52	80	16	1	2	$35,198	55	27	18	14	25	17	23	4,425
13	55	45	82	5	7	5	$71,686	75	16	9	9	28	42	1	355
14	55	44	74	5	2	18	$56,314	60	27	13	9	29	26	14	2,852
15	58	41	88	6	2	2	$38,583	58	27	15	14	23	23	36	10,072

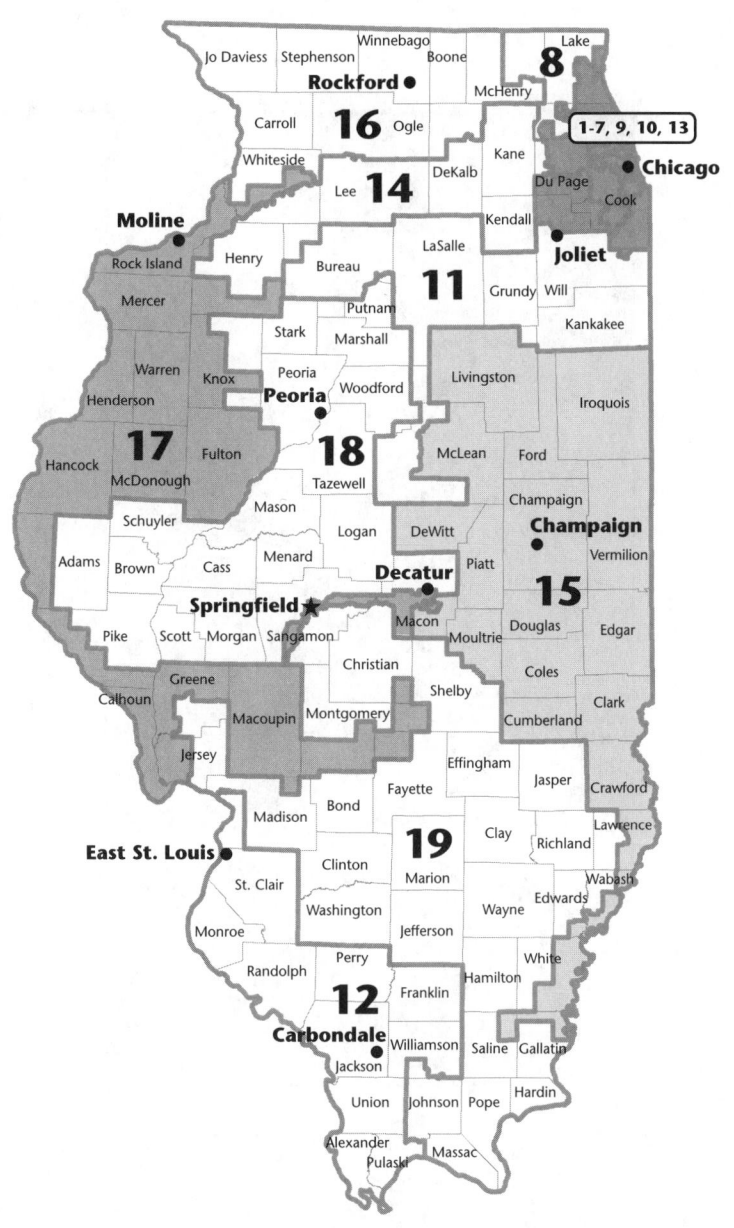

District Statistics

DIST.	2004 VOTE FOR PRESIDENT BUSH	KERRY	WHITE	BLACK	ASIAN	HISP	MEDIAN INCOME	WHITE COLLAR	BLUE COLLAR	SERVICE INDUSTRY	OVER 64	UNDER 18	COLLEGE EDUCATION	RURAL	SQ. MILES
16	55%	44%	86%	5%	1%	6%	$48,960	57%	30%	13%	12%	28%	21%	22%	4,098
17	48	51	87	7	1	4	$35,066	52	31	18	16	24	15	29	8,120
18	58	42	90	6	1	2	$41,934	59	25	15	15	24	21	32	8,186
19	61	39	94	3	0	1	$38,955	55	29	16	15	24	17	48	11,519
STATE	44	55	68	15	3	12	$46,590	62	24	14	12	26	26	12	55,584
U.S.	50.7	48.3	69	12	4	13	$41,994	60	25	15	12	26	24	21	3,537,438

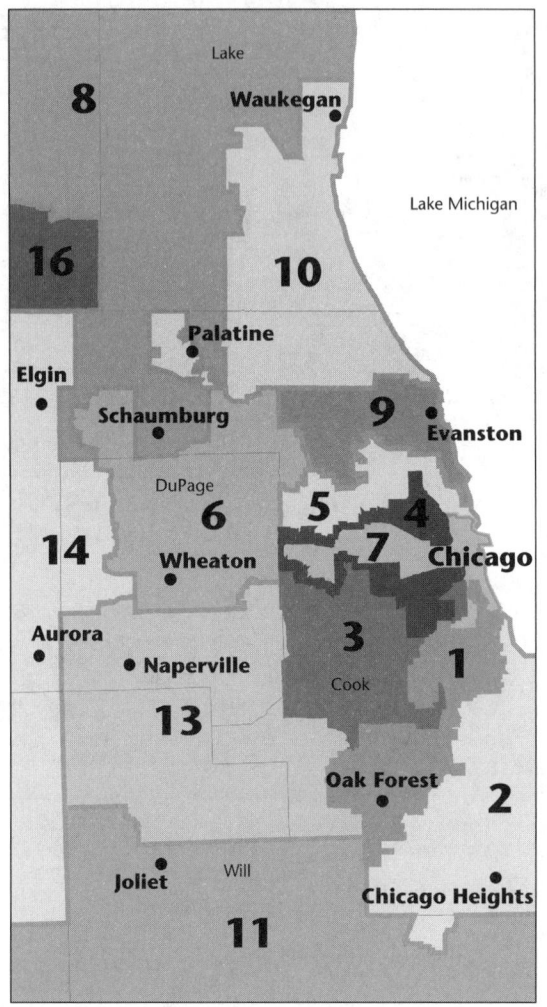

Sen. Richard J. Durbin (D)

Elected 1996; 2nd term

CAPITOL OFFICE
224-2152
dick@durbin.senate.gov
durbin.senate.gov
332 Dirksen 20510-1304; fax 228-0400

COMMITTEES
Appropriations
Judiciary
Rules & Administration

HOMETOWN
Springfield

BORN
Nov. 21, 1944, East St. Louis, Ill.

RELIGION
Roman Catholic

FAMILY
Wife, Loretta Schaefer Durbin; three children

EDUCATION
Georgetown U., B.S.F.S. 1966 (international affairs
& economics), J.D. 1969

CAREER
Gubernatorial and state legislative aide; lawyer

POLITICAL HIGHLIGHTS
Democratic nominee for Ill. Senate, 1976;
Democratic nominee for lieutenant governor, 1978;
U.S. House, 1983-97

ELECTION RESULTS

2002 GENERAL

Richard J. Durbin (D)	2,103,766	60.3%
Jim Durkin (R)	1,325,703	38.0%
Steven Burgauer (LIBERT)	57,382	1.7%

2002 PRIMARY

Richard J. Durbin (D)	unopposed

PREVIOUS WINNING PERCENTAGES
1996 (56%); 1994 House Election (55%); 1992 House
Election (57%); 1990 House Election (66%); 1988
House Election (69%); 1986 House Election (68%);
1984 House Election (61%); 1982 House Election
(50%)

As minority whip, the telegenic Durbin is the Democrats' main messenger in the Senate. He has a knack for matching his rhetoric to the occasion — catchy when the subject is broad political themes, detailed when the subject is the nuts and bolts of legislation. He can shift gears between details and the big picture in a way few members of Congress can.

It is a point of pride in his home state that Durbin in 2005 became the first senator from Illinois to make it to the top ranks of leadership since Republican Everett McKinley Dirksen was the minority leader from 1959 until 1969. Nevertheless, Durbin was overshadowed at the outset of the 109th Congress by the political phenomenon of Barack Obama, the state's new junior senator and star of the 2004 election who delivered a knockout speech at the Democratic convention. It was Obama, not Durbin, who suddenly was on everyone's watch list for a future presidential race.

On Capitol Hill on any given day, however, Durbin is the more visible of the two Illinois senators. He is either on or near the floor just about every moment the Senate is in session, managing floor operations for Minority Leader Harry Reid. He is the No. 2 leader for the Democrats, having beaten out their caucus' Policy Committee chairman, Byron L. Dorgan of North Dakota. Dorgan was better known for his mastery of policy, but after their dismal showing at the polls in 2004, Democrats were looking for someone with Durbin's communication skills.

He is one of the Senate's best debaters and is frequently sought out by television talk show schedulers. Noting the absence of bipartisan items on the Republican agenda for the 109th Congress, Durbin quipped that the GOP motto is: "Remember: We are all in this alone."

Democratic nominee John Kerry tapped Durbin to coordinate the party's message between his campaign and Congress in the run-up to the election. In the Senate, Durbin runs a weekly "Speaker's Group" to set the issues the party will talk about publicly that week. As a representative of an urban constituency, Durbin also provides regional balance to Reid, who is from Nevada and is new to the minority leader's job.

The 13 years Durbin spent as parliamentarian of the Illinois Senate helped him to master the rules and practices of the U.S. Senate, making him a natural to lead Democratic opposition to several of President Bush's judicial nominees. When Republicans accused Democrats of blocking one of Bush's picks in 2004 because he was a Catholic, Durbin, also a Catholic, angrily insisted there were no such motives at work. "Whether you are Jewish, Catholic, Protestant or Muslim, it is appropriate to ask any nominee for a judicial position: 'Where do you stand on the death penalty?' That is a political issue. It is a social issue. And yes, it is also a religious issue," he said.

Durbin was one of the main targets of two Senate Republican aides who purloined thousands of Judiciary Committee computer files on judicial nominees between 2001 and 2003. He got the Senate sergeant-at-arms to investigate, and those findings were referred for federal prosecution.

His elevation to whip signaled that Democrats were ready to do battle in the 109th Congress with the conservative Republicans who control the Senate. When Bush unveiled in 2005 plans for an overhaul of Social Security that would include private savings accounts, Durbin in a Senate floor speech declared it a "non-starter," making the battle lines clear.

Since 1997, Durbin has never failed to back his party at least 95 percent of the time that the two parties have been in opposition, and he typically is a reliable liberal vote. In the past several years, he has championed, among other issues, restoring Food Stamps to legal immigrants, making them eligible for a public benefit they had lost with the 1996 welfare overhaul, and providing unemployment compensation to part-time workers who normally do not qualify.

Strongly pro-union, Durbin sometimes strays from labor on trade. He took heat from unions in 1993 for supporting the North American Free Trade Agreement, and again in 2000 for backing the Clinton administration on granting China permanent normal trade status. But beginning in 2002, he was back with the unions, opposing reviving fast-track procedures for congressional consideration of trade deals and cosponsoring a measure to impose a high tariff on imported Chinese goods unless China adopted a market-based exchange rate.

When the issues facing Congress radically changed with the Sept. 11, 2001, terrorist attacks, Durbin brought himself up to speed quickly. Already an advocate for stricter food safety regulations, he began to focus on thwarting bioterrorism after mysterious anthrax-laden envelopes started to turn up in the U.S. mail system. After security guards at Chicago's O'Hare International Airport nearly let a passenger board a flight with knives and a stun gun, Durbin got a law through requiring more extensive background checks of airport workers and the use of new technology to detect explosives.

By the time he came to the Senate in 1997, Durbin had seven House terms under his belt. His precocious grasp of procedure and rules persuaded leaders to let him preside over contentious House debates in his first term, rare in its day for a freshman. He developed alliances with two other up-and-coming Democrats, Richard A. Gephardt of Missouri, who eventually became Democratic leader, and Tony Coelho of California, who became party whip in the House.

Durbin led the successful House effort in the late 1980s to ban smoking on most domestic airline flights. Later, as chairman and then top-ranking Democrat on the House Agriculture Appropriations Subcommittee, he tried unsuccessfully to scale back government support for tobacco farmers and to exempt tobacco-related cases from new rules making it harder to bring class action lawsuits. Durbin was just 14 years old when his chain-smoking father died of lung cancer, and he has dedicated much of his congressional career to crusading against tobacco use. "I am not unique," he says. "I know it's a big issue to millions of Americans and their families who have lost loved ones to tobacco."

Durbin jumped into politics as soon as he left college with undergraduate and law degrees from Georgetown University. He went back home and had a number of jobs in politics, including state Senate parliamentarian and aide to Lt. Gov. Paul Simon, who went on to serve 22 year in Congress.

In 1982, Durbin unseated 11-term GOP Rep. Paul N. Findley by 1,410 votes in a Springfield-based House district. He won re-election six times by comfortable, if not overwhelming, margins.

When his old mentor, Simon, announced he would not seek re-election to the Senate in 1996, Durbin got into the race. With endorsements from Simon and top Illinois Democrats, Durbin had little trouble winning the primary. In the general election, he faced off against state Rep. Al Salvi, a little-known conservative who campaigned as a staunch foe of abortion rights and defender of gun ownership. Durbin won the election by 15 percentage points.

By 2002, Durbin's seat was safe enough that he coasted to a second term. No top-tier Republican considered the race seriously and he ended up defeating GOP state Rep. Jim Durkin by 22 points.

KEY VOTES

2004

Yes Pass $318.9 billion, six-year highway and mass transit bill

Yes Extend assault weapons ban for 10 years

Yes Restore pay-as-you-go rules for new tax cuts and entitlement spending

No Criminalize harm to a fetus in an attack on the mother

Yes Increase mandatory child care funding to states by $6 billion over five years

No Amend the Constitution to prohibit same-sex marriage

Yes Approve $146 billion multi-year extension of previously enacted middle-class tax breaks

Yes Reorganize U.S. intelligence agencies as proposed by Sept. 11 commission

No Cut corporate taxes $137 billion over 10 years

2003

Yes Delay Bush changes to Clean Air Act

No Allow confirmation vote on Miguel A. Estrada to the U.S. Court of Appeals for the D.C. Circuit

Yes Block a Bush proposal opening Alaska's Arctic National Wildlife Refuge to oil drilling

Yes Limit size of Bush's proposed tax cut to $350 billion through fiscal 2013

Yes Overhaul Medicare and create prescription drug benefit

Yes Block Bush rule scaling back overtime pay for some white-collar federal workers

Yes Split $20 billion in Iraq aid into half-grant, half-loan

No Ban "partial birth" abortion except to save a woman's life

No Stop proposal allowing travel to Cuba

No Allow final vote on energy policy overhaul

CQ VOTE STUDIES

	PARTY UNITY		PRESIDENTIAL SUPPORT	
	Support	Oppose	Support	Oppose
2004	96%	4%	54%	46%
2003	97%	3%	46%	54%
2002	97%	3%	67%	33%
2001	95%	5%	62%	38%
2000	99%	1%	97%	3%
1999	95%	5%	87%	13%
1998	95%	5%	90%	10%
1997	97%	3%	92%	8%
House Service:				
1996	91%	9%	82%	18%
1995	93%	7%	83%	17%

INTEREST GROUPS

	AFL-CIO	ADA	CCUS	ACU
2004	92%	95%	47%	4%
2003	85%	95%	35%	10%
2002	100%	95%	50%	0%
2001	94%	95%	31%	0%
2000	75%	95%	50%	4%
1999	89%	100%	35%	4%
1998	100%	95%	50%	8%
1997	100%	100%	40%	4%
House Service:				
1996	91%	80%	27%	0%
1995	100%	85%	25%	8%

Sen. Barack Obama (D)

Elected 2004; 1st term

CAPITOL OFFICE
224-2854
obama.senate.gov
713 Hart 20510-1305; fax 228-1372

COMMITTEES
Environment & Public Works
Foreign Relations
Veterans' Affairs

HOMETOWN
Chicago

BORN
Aug. 4, 1961, Honolulu, Hawaii

RELIGION
United Church of Christ

FAMILY
Wife, Michelle Obama; two children

EDUCATION
Occidental College, attended 1979-81; Columbia U.,
B.A. 1983 (political science); Harvard U., J.D. 1991

CAREER
Lawyer; voter registration and education project
director; community outreach organizer; business
reporter

POLITICAL HIGHLIGHTS
Ill. Senate, 1997-2004; sought Democratic
nomination for U.S. House, 2000

ELECTION RESULTS

2004 GENERAL

Barack Obama (D)	3,597,456	70.0%
Alan L. Keyes (R)	1,390,690	27.1%
Albert J. Franzen (I)	81,164	1.6%
Jerry Kohn (LIBERT)	69,253	1.4%

2004 PRIMARY

Barack Obama (D)	655,923	52.8%
Daniel Hynes (D)	294,717	23.7%
Blair Hull (D)	134,453	10.8%
Maria Pappas (D)	74,987	6.0%
Gery Chico (D)	53,433	4.3%
Nancy Skinner (D)	16,098	1.3%
Joyce Washington (D)	13,375	1.1%

Obama arrived on Capitol Hill with the kind of star wattage other politicians dream of. The story of his election to the Senate in 2004 stands out even in a place where overachievers are a dime a dozen and a former first lady keeps office hours. Obama is a rare combination of intelligence, political skill, good looks and charisma. When he shot to national prominence with a knock-out keynote speech at the party's convention, the only surprise was that the 42-year-old career politician had not been noticed sooner.

Named for his native African father, Obama (full name: buh-ROCK o-BAH-mah) started the year as a state official relatively unknown outside of Illinois. Handed a bit of luck by Republicans, who bungled their recruiting and failed to put up a strong candidate against him, Obama made maximum use of his considerable natural assets, developed a strong state following and then introduced himself to a national audience with a skillfully delivered speech at the Democratic National Convention in Boston, challenging Americans to have "the audacity of hope."

Democrats who have hungered for a winner since Bill Clinton left office seized on the Obama drama. Before he cast a single vote as a U.S. senator in 2005, he was being mobbed at Washington restaurants and hounded for public appearances and press interviews. "Obama '08" bumper stickers cropped up around the country.

That much attention for a newcomer can be threatening to the egos of other senators, and Obama quickly adopted the model used with great effect by Democratic Sen. Hillary Rodham Clinton of New York when she came to the Senate in 2001 as a former first lady. He lowered his profile as much as he could by declining television interviews. He accepted a cramped, windowless office without complaint and burrowed in to learn the chamber's arcane rules.

Behind the scenes, he focused on raising money, always a good way to make friends in Congress. Pouncing on his potential as a fundraiser, Minority Leader Harry Reid named him at the start of the 109th Congress as a vice chairman of the Democratic Senatorial Campaign Committee.

Obama is a liberal, but not one on the furthest end of party ideology. He supports abortion rights and expanded health care for the poor and opposes President Bush's tax cuts and the war in Iraq. In early 2005, he voted with liberal Democrats to oppose oil drilling in the Alaskan wilderness.

But he is against same-sex marriage and favors work requirements and time limits for welfare recipients. One of his first votes, in early 2005, was in favor of a Republican bill that discourages some class action lawsuits and limits attorneys' fees in such lawsuits.

"I am rooted in the African-American community, but I am not limited to it," Obama likes to say.

As he did in his campaign, Obama is trying in his first term to cultivate a common-man image. He describes helping his wife, Michelle, with the laundry and using her as a check against letting fame go to his head. "As my wife reminds me, I better not screw up," he says.

Yet it is also true that Obama is a supremely confident man aware of his potential in the Democratic Party. The Chicago Sun-Times took him to task during the campaign for a "passion for secrecy" because he refused to disclose his travel outside of Illinois. He raised a quarter of his $14 million war chest outside of his home state, including a fundraiser on Martha's Vineyard, the tony resort island off Cape Cod. He also took a chartered flight to Omaha, Neb., to have lunch with billionaire businessman Warren Buffett and Buffett's daughter, the newspaper said.

The Senate's only African-American member and only the third black senator since Reconstruction, Obama is aware enough of his own marketability to have reissued in 2004 an almost forgotten memoir he wrote nearly a decade ago, titled "Dreams from My Father: A Story of Race and Inheritance." It shot to the top of The New York Times bestseller list and stayed there for several months. He signed a contract to write another book, drawing an advance of $1.9 million.

The son of a white mother from Kansas and a black Kenyan father, Obama, whose first name in Swahili means "blessed by God," was raised in Hawaii by his mother and maternal grandparents. His father left the family to attend Harvard when Obama was 2, and the couple divorced. Determined that her son advance in life, Obama's mother, Ann Dunham, sent him to Punahou Academy, an elite private school in Honolulu. He went on to earn degrees from Columbia University and Harvard Law School, where he became the first African-American president of the Harvard Law Review.

His early adulthood was marked by confusion about his place in African-American society and a period of using drugs and alcohol. Obama went to work on Wall Street for a time, and when that did not suit him, he applied for community organizer jobs around the country and landed one in the hard-pressed black neighborhoods on Chicago's South Side.

There, he went from activist to politician, running for state representative and spending about eight years in the Illinois General Assembly. Obama is credited with bills that created a state income tax credit for the working poor and required police agencies to videotape interrogations and confessions in all murder cases.

In 2000, Obama made his first run at a seat in Congress, challenging Democratic Rep. Bobby Rush. He was trounced by the popular incumbent and former civil rights leader. A few years later, he was not on anyone's radar screen to run for the Senate seat vacated by retiring GOP Sen. Peter G. Fitzgerald. The Democratic primary attracted six other candidates. Out of nowhere, Obama dominated the contest with 53 percent of the vote.

In the fall campaign, he had a tough opponent in multimillionaire Jack Ryan. Then, a series of setbacks for the GOP turned fortune Obama's way. Ryan dropped out amid allegations he had pressured his wife to go to sex clubs. Desperate for a quick replacement, Republicans settled on Alan L. Keyes, a bombastic social conservative who moved from Maryland to Illinois to run.

Suddenly, Obama was favored to capture the seat. Presidential nominee John Kerry of Massachusetts asked him to give the keynote speech on the second night of the party's convention. Obama called on Americans to put aside ideological and cultural differences. And he took the requisite partisan shot at Bush, saying the country must "never ever go to war without enough troops to win the war." The address kicked off what one GOP operative later bemoaned as the "Obamapalooza."

With his exotic good looks and ability to connect with a crowd, Obama inspired comparisons to President Kennedy. He snagged an appearance on the Late Show with David Letterman and was profiled by The New Yorker. In endorsing him, the Chicago Tribune said that when he gets up to speak "opponents know they are about to hear the best argument the other side has to offer."

Obama won with 70 percent of the vote. His heroes, he says, are Gandhi, Martin Luther King Jr., Picasso and jazz musician John Coltrane. "I'm enamored with people who change the framework, who don't take something as a given, but scramble it," Obama says.

Rep. Bobby L. Rush (D)

Elected 1992; 7th term

CAPITOL OFFICE
225-4372
www.house.gov/rush
2416 Rayburn 20515-1301; fax 226-0333

COMMITTEES
Energy & Commerce

HOMETOWN
Chicago

BORN
Nov. 23, 1946, Albany, Ga.

RELIGION
Protestant

FAMILY
Wife, Carolyn Rush; five children (one deceased)

EDUCATION
Roosevelt U., B.A. 1973 (political science); U. of
Illinois, Chicago, attended 1975-77 (political
science), M.A. 1994 (political science); McCormick
Seminary, M.A. 1998 (theological studies)

MILITARY SERVICE
Army, 1963-68

CAREER
Insurance broker; political aide

POLITICAL HIGHLIGHTS
Candidate for Chicago City Council, 1975; sought
Democratic nomination for Ill. House, 1978;
Chicago City Council, 1983-93; candidate for mayor
of Chicago, 1999

ELECTION RESULTS

2004 GENERAL

Bobby L. Rush (D)	212,109	84.9%
Raymond G. Wardingley (R)	37,840	15.1%

2004 PRIMARY

Bobby L. Rush (D)	unopposed

2002 GENERAL

Bobby L. Rush (D)	149,068	81.2%
Raymond G. Wardingley (R)	29,776	16.2%
Dorothy G. Tsatsos (LIBERT)	4,812	2.6%

PREVIOUS WINNING PERCENTAGES
2000 (88%); 1998 (87%); 1996 (86%); 1994 (76%);
1992 (83%)

Rush is among the most liberal members of the House, active in both the Progressive Caucus and the Congressional Black Caucus. But his ability to make alliances with lawmakers who stand nowhere near him on the ideological spectrum is a hallmark of his approach to politics and marks an evolution from his early days as a member of the radical Black Panthers.

In addressing the shortage of health care workers in urban hospitals, for example, Rush allied himself with a prominent conservative, Republican home-state colleague Henry J. Hyde, on a bill to establish a special visa classification for foreign nurses. During the summer of 2001, Rush teamed with Republican Roy Blunt of Missouri to introduce a bill aimed at stabilizing gasoline prices.

Rush focuses on his South Side Chicago constituents, among the city's poorest residents, but is also trying to expand his issues portfolio. In 2004, he was arrested outside the Sudanese Embassy in Washington during a protest in which he accused that country's government of practicing genocide. Also in 2004, he aggressively pursued the half-century-old unpunished murder in Mississippi of a Chicago-born 14-year-old, Emmett Till, whose death helped spark the civil rights movement.

He introduced a resolution calling for a renewed investigation, then praised the Justice Department when it reopened the case. Rush escalated his call for action in November 2004 with a new resolution cosponsored by New York Democrat Charles B. Rangel. In the Senate, Rush's resolution drew bipartisan sponsors: New York Democrat Charles E. Schumer and Missouri Republican Jim Talent.

Rush's life took numerous twists and turns before landing him in Congress. Born in southern Georgia, he grew up in Chicago, where his mother moved when he was 7 after her marriage broke up. She worked as a Republican activist because whites dominated the city's Democratic machine. Rush volunteered for the Army, but when he became disillusioned by a commanding officer whom he viewed as racist, he joined the Student Non-Violent Coordinating Committee.

He soon founded the Illinois chapter of the militant Black Panthers organization. Rush coordinated a Panthers-run program that provided free breakfasts for children and a medical clinic that developed a mass screening effort for sickle cell anemia. When he was in his 20s, Rush was imprisoned for six months for illegal possession of weapons.

In Congress, however, he has been an advocate of strict restrictions on firearms. His commitment to tighter gun restrictions has been strengthened by personal experience. In 1999, his son Huey (named after Black Panther leader Huey Newton) was shot and killed in a Chicago sidewalk robbery. The assailants were identified, arrested and convicted in 2002. But more hardship struck the Rush family that year. Rush's nephew was charged with murder in what police said was a drug deal gone bad. "These kinds of stories have no winners, only losers, and occur far too often in our communities," Rush said.

Rush has spoken out against the death penalty, particularly in Illinois, where several people on death row subsequently were proven innocent. But in 2003, his amendment to the annual Justice Department spending bill, which would have barred the federal government from seeking the death penalty, failed on an 85-339 vote.

After graduating from college, Rush quit the Panthers, sold insurance and entered local politics, challenging the party machinery and losing races for the Chicago City Council and the state House. In 1983, however, he was elected to the council on the coattails of 1st District Democratic Rep. Harold Washington, elected in an upset as Chicago's first black mayor.

Rush was elected to Congress in 1992, ousting Democrat Charles A. Hayes, who had replaced Washington in the House but who was susceptible to Rush's charge that he had not provided sufficient leadership in Congress. A gifted political organizer, Rush quickly impressed his party leaders and by his second term had a seat on the coveted Commerce Committee, now called the Energy and Commerce Committee, which writes energy policy and oversees regulation of business and industry.

In the 107th Congress, he was the driving force behind a provision in the broadband deregulation bill to require the regional Bell companies to offer high-speed Internet service to low-income areas. The House passed a bill in 2002 that included the proposal, but the legislation died in the Senate.

Rush is active in the Congressional Black Caucus; he was its secretary and lost to Maryland Democrat Elijah E. Cummings for the chairmanship in the 108th Congress. Melvin Watt of North Carolina took over in the 109th Congress. Rush was one of two House members to endorse former Illinois Sen. Carol Moseley-Braun for president in 2003.

Because of his past association with the Black Panthers, the media instantly focused on Rush after the 1992 election, making him a TV celebrity before his term even began. But Rush seldom mentions that part of his past, except on issues concerning increased police powers. He was a vocal opponent of legislation swept to enactment soon after the Sept. 11, 2001, terrorist attacks that increased law enforcement's ability to investigate and prosecute suspected terrorists. "I feel like I'm in a time warp," Rush told the Chicago Tribune. "So much of what Bush and [Attorney General John] Ashcroft are saying sounds identical to the language the FBI used 32 years ago" to investigate the Black Panthers and other groups.

Rush has won every general election with ease. However, he had a poor showing in his 1999 challenge to the re-election of Democrat Richard M. Daley as mayor, receiving just 28 percent in the primary. In the race, Rush accused Daley of neglecting the city's poorer neighborhoods. Following that defeat, Rush had to face an emboldened field of challengers in 2000 but was renominated with 61 percent of the vote. In that campaign, he defeated Barack Obama, the future senator who joined Rush in the Illinois delegation of the 109th Congress. In both 2002 and 2004, Rush ran uncontested in the party primary and easily won the general election.

KEY VOTES

2004

Yes	Extend federal unemployment benefits by 13 weeks
Yes	Pass $283.2 billion, six-year federal highway and mass transit bill
No	Approve $146 billion multi-year extension of previously enacted middle-class tax breaks
No	Amend the Constitution to prohibit same-sex marriage
No	Cut corporate taxes $137 billion over 10 years
Yes	Reorganize U.S. intelligence agencies as proposed by Sept. 11 commission

2003

No	Cut taxes by $330 billion through fiscal 2013
Yes	Block Bush rule scaling back overtime pay for some white-collar federal workers
Yes	Do not allow use of search warrants without first notifying subjects
No	Allow importation of prescription drugs
No	Create private school voucher program in Washington, D.C.
No	Ban "partial birth" abortion except to save a woman's life
Yes	Split $18.6 billion in Iraq aid into half-grant, half-loan
No	Overhaul Medicare and create prescription drug benefit

CQ VOTE STUDIES

	PARTY UNITY		PRESIDENTIAL SUPPORT	
	Support	Oppose	Support	Oppose
2004	97%	3%	21%	79%
2003	96%	4%	15%	85%
2002	95%	5%	28%	72%
2001	91%	9%	26%	74%
2000	98%	2%	91%	9%

INTEREST GROUPS

	AFL-CIO	ADA	CCUS	ACU
2004	100%	100%	24%	0%
2003	100%	95%	29%	12%
2002	100%	85%	50%	0%
2001	100%	75%	35%	10%
2000	100%	90%	36%	0%

ILLINOIS 1
Chicago — South Side and southwest

The nation's first black-majority district, the 1st covers much of Chicago's South Side. It begins at 26th Street in the historic black hub and spreads out to the south and west through mainly residential areas. The district narrows through the southwestern neighborhoods of Washington Heights, Beverly and Morgan Park, then expands outside the city to scoop up close-in suburbs. About 70 percent of the 1st's residents live in Chicago (down from 90 percent under the district's 1990s configuration).

Long a relatively compact district, the 1st's boundaries have expanded gradually in the past few decades to adjust for declining populations in some of the area's most economically distressed neighborhoods. Redistricting following the 2000 census stretched the 1st as far south as Cook County's border with Will County.

When the steel industry left the South Side in the 1970s, it decimated the district's middle class and many black-owned businesses. Now the 1st is home to some of the city's largest subsidized housing projects, and about 20 percent of the population lives in poverty. The district still has several solidly middle-class black neighborhoods, including Chatham and Avalon Park. The north end takes in part of Bronzeville, which has attracted many black-owned businesses and young black professionals who move in and rehabilitate old houses instead of leaving the city. Blue Island, a southwest suburb, is 38 percent Hispanic and 24 percent black.

The 1st, represented by black congressmen since 1929, has the nation's largest percentage of African-Americans (65 percent). White voters are concentrated outside the city or in some southwestern neighborhoods. The 1st is one of the state's most Democratic districts, and it gave 2004 presidential nominee John Kerry his third-best showing in Illinois with 83 percent.

MAJOR INDUSTRY
Hospitals, higher education, manufacturing

CITIES
Chicago (pt.), 451,488; Oak Forest (pt.), 28,041; Orland Park (pt.), 27,342; Tinley Park (pt.), 23,863; Blue Island (pt.), 23,436; Evergreen Park, 20,821

NOTABLE
The 1st is home to the national headquarters of Jesse Jackson's Rainbow/PUSH Coalition; The University of Chicago is in the Hyde Park neighborhood.

Rep. Jesse L. Jackson Jr. (D)

Elected December 1995; 5th full term

CAPITOL OFFICE
225-0773
www.house.gov/jackson
2419 Rayburn 20515-1302; fax 225-0899

COMMITTEES
Appropriations

HOMETOWN
Chicago

BORN
March 11, 1965, Greenville, S.C.

RELIGION
Baptist

FAMILY
Wife, Sandi Jackson; two children

EDUCATION
North Carolina A&T U., B.S. 1987 (business management); Chicago Theological Seminary, M.A. 1990 (theology); U. of Illinois, J.D. 1993

CAREER
Lawyer

POLITICAL HIGHLIGHTS
No previous office

ELECTION RESULTS

2004 GENERAL

Jesse L. Jackson Jr. (D)	207,535	88.5%
Stephanie Sailor (LIBERT)	26,990	11.5%

2004 PRIMARY

Jesse L. Jackson Jr. (D)	106,506	88.6%
Mel Reynolds (D)	7,103	5.9%
Anthony W. Williams (D)	5,159	4.3%
Everette Drayden Shumpert (D)	1,516	1.3%

2002 GENERAL

Jesse L. Jackson Jr. (D)	151,443	82.3%
Doug Nelson (R)	32,567	17.7%

PREVIOUS WINNING PERCENTAGES
2000 (90%); 1998 (89%); 1996 (94%); 1995 Special Election (76%)

After nine years in the House, Jackson now appears more willing to step forward as an advocate and spokesman for the liberal values of his party. Jackson has neither his famous father's looming physical presence nor the cadences of the civil rights leader's oratory, but he is full of energy and shares a passion for bringing economic parity to his South Side and suburban Chicago constituents.

Early in 2005, Jackson stepped out front on the question of voting irregularities in the 2004 presidential election. When Congress met in a joint session to count the electoral votes, he joined with two other African-American House Democrats — John Conyers Jr. of Michigan and Stephanie Tubbs Jones of Ohio — to protest what they considered serious and widespread voting irregularities in Ohio. After California Democratic Sen. Barbara Boxer joined them in the challenge, both chambers were then required to hold a two-hour debate on the balloting. Jackson said the debate was an opportunity to "highlight the problems in Ohio — which are very prevalent virtually everywhere else in the country as well — that disenfranchised innumerable Ohio voters."

Jackson was also a strong voice during the 108th Congress in criticizing the Bush administration. When Deputy Secretary of Defense Paul Wolfowitz appeared before the Foreign Operations Appropriations Subcommittee in the spring of 2004, he understated the number of U.S. soldiers who had died in Iraq. Jackson told Newsday that Wolfowitz's gaffe showed an "almost wanton disregard for human life in the field." Jackson had voted against the resolution authorizing the president to go to war in Iraq.

In his second term, Jackson won a seat on the Appropriations Committee. He has learned to take a less partisan approach on the panel that doles out federal funds, saying, "We need some guarantees that whatever dialogue we're in with the Republicans does not result in our not being able to deliver for our people."

Jackson also has taken a greater interest in legislation outside appropriators' purview. When the House in 2004 passed a measure to extend through September 2015 a trade law permitting duty-free treatment of African imports, Jackson objected that the bill extended what he called "outrageous conditionalities" that African countries had to meet to be eligible for trade benefits. He argued it was discriminatory to require African countries to certify that their internal policies do not run counter to U.S. foreign policy objectives, while other trade bills did not impose such requirements.

Jackson takes voting seriously: He has missed just one roll call vote in his House career. He says he was talking to a reporter in the Rayburn Building and did not hear the bells signifying a vote on March 1, 2001. He rushed to the floor, but was too late. Upset about the missed vote, Jackson vowed not to miss any more.

As the son of one of the nation's most prominent civil rights leaders, Jackson says he sees America "through the eyes of race," but he adds, "I believe that Americans hear all political dialogue through the hearing aid of the economy."

To that end, Jackson, along with staff member Frank Watkins, wrote a book, "A More Perfect Union: Advancing New American Rights," in which they advanced the theory that the regional differences between the North and the South have played a key role in shaping the kind of country the United States is now — politically, economically and socially. The divide between

North and South still shapes the views of many lawmakers on whether states' rights should take precedence over federal authority, Jackson contends. He writes that this regional split is far more relevant to the future of the country than the differing ideologies of the political parties, the role of labor unions or the women's movement, or the impact of immigration.

Jackson has acknowledged that he is both blessed and cursed with the expectations that come with being the son of the Rev. Jesse L. Jackson. Many people have expected him to travel the country, speaking, marching and trying to build his own national reputation. "They thought I'd be a young man in a hurry. . . . But I'm not in a hurry, except to fix some things in my district." He proudly points to funds he has obtained for local projects, such as safe drinking water and an $8 million flood control project in Ford Heights.

Jackson also has been the leading advocate for the construction of a third airport in the Chicago area, which he says will provide economic expansion for his district. He has proposed that the airport be built on rural land outside of Peotone, just south of Jackson's district, and that it aim to attract discount carriers. His plan has run into opposition from Chicago Democratic Mayor Richard M. Daley, however, who favors an expansion of Chicago's O'Hare Airport. The debate over whether to build a third regional airport was revived in 2004 after delays at O'Hare reached an all-time high. Jackson said he had lined up an estimated $200 million from private investors, which would cover the cost of the terminal, runway and a parking lot.

CBS News once filmed Jackson vacuuming the carpet in his Capitol Hill office, and Jackson confessed he does it all the time. "It's relaxing for me. It's a way for me to think and reflect," he said. Jackson has earned a black belt in tae kwon do.

A lawyer who graduated from Washington, D.C.'s elite St. Alban's School, Jackson presents himself as a vibrant member of a new generation of black leadership. He followed in his father's footsteps, serving as vice president at-large of Operation PUSH (People United to Serve Humanity) and as national field director for the Rainbow Coalition.

Jackson came to Congress in a 1995 special election to replace Democrat Mel Reynolds, who resigned after being convicted of sexual misconduct. Jackson countered criticism that he was too young for the job by arguing that being the son of Jesse Jackson amounted to a lifetime of political experience. After winning a hard-fought primary against state Sen. Emil Jones Jr., Jackson had no difficulty in the general election, and his subsequent re-elections have been a breeze.

KEY VOTES

2004

Yes Extend federal unemployment benefits by 13 weeks

Yes Pass $283.2 billion, six-year federal highway and mass transit bill

No Approve $146 billion multi-year extension of previously enacted middle-class tax breaks

No Amend the Constitution to prohibit same-sex marriage

No Cut corporate taxes $137 billion over 10 years

Yes Reorganize U.S. intelligence agencies as proposed by Sept. 11 commission

2003

No Cut taxes by $330 billion through fiscal 2013

Yes Block Bush rule scaling back overtime pay for some white-collar federal workers

Yes Do not allow use of search warrants without first notifying subjects

Yes Allow importation of prescription drugs

No Create private school voucher program in Washington, D.C.

No Ban "partial birth" abortion except to save a woman's life

Yes Split $18.6 billion in Iraq aid into half-grant, half-loan

No Overhaul Medicare and create prescription drug benefit

CQ VOTE STUDIES

	PARTY UNITY		PRESIDENTIAL SUPPORT	
	Support	Oppose	Support	Oppose
2004	98%	2%	15%	85%
2003	98%	2%	9%	91%
2002	96%	4%	25%	75%
2001	95%	5%	16%	84%
2000	96%	4%	83%	17%

INTEREST GROUPS

	AFL-CIO	ADA	CCUS	ACU
2004	100%	100%	14%	0%
2003	100%	100%	17%	12%
2002	100%	90%	25%	0%
2001	100%	95%	23%	0%
2000	100%	100%	23%	4%

ILLINOIS 2
Chicago — far South Side; Chicago Heights

The 2nd begins in Chicago's South Side along Lake Michigan and extends south along the Indiana border and southwest to take in Chicago Heights and Cook County suburbs. Redistricting following the 2000 census extended the southern border into University Park in Will County.

About 40 percent of district residents live in Chicago. The 2nd runs from the Hyde Park area near the University of Chicago south through such neighborhoods as South Shore, South Chicago, East Side, Roseland and Pullman. East Side is heavily Hispanic.

U.S. Steel was once a dominant employer in the 2nd. When the steel industry collapsed in the late 1970s, it devastated the district's industrial-based economy. Ford Motor Co. is one of the few large manufacturing businesses remaining in the district. A proposed new airport in nearby Peotone (in the 11th District) could rejuvenate the 2nd's economy, although a final plan and federal approval have yet to materialize. Advocates hope the airport would attract corporate headquarters,

hotels, distributors and other new businesses. Unemployment remains high in the district, and many residents have fled the South Side to find jobs. Before redistricting, the 2nd had the smallest population of any Illinois district.

In Chicago's south suburbs it is not unusual to find heavily black areas like Harvey, Dolton and Ford Heights, or largely white areas like Homewood, Flossmoor and Thornton. Other areas are more racially mixed — in Chicago Heights, whites and blacks are about equal in population, and one-fourth of residents are Hispanic.

Overall, the 2nd's 62 percent black population and working-class base shape a staunchly Democratic district that gave John Kerry his highest Illinois vote percentage (84 percent) in the 2004 presidential race.

MAJOR INDUSTRY
Automotive and wire manufacturing, health care

CITIES
Chicago (pt.), 265,814; Calumet City, 39,071; Chicago Heights, 32,776

NOTABLE
Pullman, now part of Chicago near Lake Calumet, originally was a factory town built by the Pullman Palace Car Co., maker of railroad cars.

Rep. Daniel Lipinski (D)

Elected 2004; 1st term

CAPITOL OFFICE
225-5701
www.house.gov/lipinski
1217 Longworth 20515-1303; fax 225-1012

COMMITTEES
Science
Small Business

HOMETOWN
Western Springs

BORN
July 15, 1966, Chicago, Ill.

RELIGION
Roman Catholic

FAMILY
Wife, Judy Lipinski

EDUCATION
Northwestern U., B.S. 1988 (mechanical engineering); Stanford U., M.S. 1989 (engineering-economic systems); Duke U., Ph.D. 1998 (political science)

CAREER
Professor; congressional aide; campaign aide

POLITICAL HIGHLIGHTS
No previous office

ELECTION RESULTS

2004 GENERAL

Daniel Lipinski (D)	167,034	72.6%
Ryan Chlada (R)	57,845	25.2%
Krista Grimm - write-in	5,077	2.2%

Lipinski easily strolled into Congress in the 2004 election, benefiting from a familiar name and the strong Democratic leanings of Illinois' 3rd District. He succeeded his father, William O. Lipinski, who retired after 22 years and ensured that his son would be the Democratic nominee to succeed him.

Like his father, Lipinski is an economic populist, a conservative on some social issues, an admirer of Republican legend Ronald Reagan and devoted to the transportation issues important to Chicago and its inner suburbs. "My positions on issues are very similar to my father's positions, and I don't feel like I need to make any apologies for that," Lipinski said.

There are generational differences, though. The elder Lipinski attended college for two years and trained for Congress as a city councilman and ward boss. The newcomer holds a master's degree in economic engineering and a doctorate in political science — but never before ran for office.

Lipinski worked on numerous Illinois campaigns, though, and served as a congressional aide to both Rod R. Blagojevich, now the governor, and former House Minority Leader Richard A. Gephardt of Missouri.

Lipinski did not get a hoped-for freshman assignment to the Transportation Committee, on which his father served during his entire tenure in the House. He was put on the Science Committee and on the Small Business Committee, where he was made top-ranking Democrat on that panel's Workforce, Empowerment and Government Programs Subcommittee.

Lipinski said he also wants to focus on health care, particularly on making prescription drugs more affordable.

Lipinski probably had the easiest path to Congress of any candidate for an open House seat in 2004. His father had filed to run for re-election and was unopposed in the March Democratic primary. But he announced his retirement during the August congressional recess. As permitted by state law, a committee of 3rd District Democrats, which included Rep. Lipinski and several of his allies, met and unanimously selected Daniel Lipinski to fill the vacated slot. In November, Lipinski defeated Republican political unknown Ryan Chlada with 73 percent of the vote.

ILLINOIS 3

Chicago — southwest side; south and west suburbs

The 3rd covers the southwest corner of Chicago and adjacent suburbs, part of a working-class region known as the Bungalow Belt that is stocked with voters of Eastern European, Italian and Irish descent.

Redistricting following the 2000 census added more of Chicago; city residents comprise about 40 percent of the district population. The 3rd includes the historically Irish neighborhood of Bridgeport, which is the political base of the powerful Daley family, and southwest Chicago neighborhoods such as Beverly, West Lawn, Clearing and Garfield Ridge (where Midway Airport is located). The West Lawn and West Eldson neighborhoods have experienced rapid Hispanic growth. The 3rd has more Hispanics than all but two districts in Illinois.

Crisscrossed by highways, railroads and the Chicago Sanitary and Ship Canal, the 3rd is a center of manufacturing and distribution. Expansion at Midway has broadened the district's retail and service base and created new jobs for district residents.

In national elections, the 3rd typically votes Democratic, but not by the same wide margins as other Chicago-based districts. Many working- and middle-class voters lean to the right on social issues, and there is an ample GOP vote in the district's more affluent western Cook County suburbs.

MAJOR INDUSTRY
Metals and other heavy manufacturing, trucking, warehouses

CITIES
Chicago (pt.), 266,264; Oak Lawn, 55,245; Berwyn (pt.), 51,179; Burbank, 27,902; Brookfield (pt.), 18,980; Palos Hills, 17,665

NOTABLE
The Berwyn Houby Festival, celebrating Czech heritage, is named after the Czech word for mushroom.

Rep. Luis V. Gutierrez (D)

Elected 1992; 7th term

CAPITOL OFFICE
225-8203
luisgutierrez.house.gov
2367 Rayburn 20515-1304; fax 225-7810

COMMITTEES
Financial Services
Veterans' Affairs

HOMETOWN
Chicago

BORN
Dec. 10, 1953, Chicago, Ill.

RELIGION
Roman Catholic

FAMILY
Wife, Soraida Arocho Gutierrez; two children

EDUCATION
Northeastern Illinois U., B.A. 1975 (liberal arts)

CAREER
Teacher; social worker

POLITICAL HIGHLIGHTS
Chicago City Council, 1986-93

ELECTION RESULTS

2004 GENERAL

Luis V. Gutierrez (D)	104,761	83.7%
Tony Cisneros (R)	15,536	12.4%
Jake Whitmer (LIBERT)	4,845	3.9%

2004 PRIMARY

Luis V. Gutierrez (D)	unopposed

2002 GENERAL

Luis V. Gutierrez (D)	67,339	79.7%
Anthony J. Lopez-Cisneros (R)	12,778	15.1%
Marjorie Kohls (LIBERT)	4,396	5.2%

PREVIOUS WINNING PERCENTAGES
2000 (89%); 1998 (82%); 1996 (94%); 1994 (75%); 1992 (78%)

Gutierrez spent his early years in Congress as the liberal outsider who railed at the GOP majority, his own leadership and even the institution. Now in his seventh term, he has mellowed. He has learned the art of legislating, while working hard to provide opportunities for the people of his Hispanic-majority district.

This doesn't mean he has gone quietly into the night. He still argues that GOP proposals on the environment, education, labor-management relations and immigration policy are a threat to his constituents, but he is now more likely to counter with a legislative plan than with a few choice words.

The first Hispanic member of Congress from Illinois, Gutierrez (full name: loo-EES goo-tee-AIR-ez) represents one of the poorest, least-educated districts in the nation. A 2002 Chicago Sun-Times editorial called Gutierrez "arguably . . . the most influential Latino political leader in Chicago history." He can be passionate in his defense of society's underdogs, and his central issue in Congress is easing immigration limits.

Gutierrez is the chairman of the Congressional Hispanic Caucus' Task Force on Immigration and Citizenship. In 2004, he introduced immigration reform legislation, along with New Jersey Democratic Rep. Robert D. Menendez and Massachusetts Democratic Sen. Edward M. Kennedy, to offer undocumented immigrant workers and their families a path to permanent resident status and, later, citizenship. The bill aimed to make it easier for spouses and children of legal immigrants to enter the country, reducing a years-long backlog of such requests.

The measure was a Democratic alternative to a proposal by President Bush to offer undocumented immigrants a temporary "guest worker" visa, with no guarantee of a green card. "Unlike the president's plan that says come, work and adios, our legislation respects workers," Gutierrez said. But he added that he was willing to work with Bush to craft a reform plan. "The president of the United States has made an offer," Gutierrez said. "We're responding. Let's engage in some constructive dialogue." Neither measure moved in the 108th Congress, however.

Gutierrez criticized the Bush administration when oversight of immigration benefits was moved to the Department of Homeland Security, which he said is slow in processing immigrants' citizenship and benefits applications. The department also proposed raising application fees, but Gutierrez said the department needs a systemic overhaul before asking immigrants to pay more. "It's like someone selling a defective car that is being recalled and then increasing the price," Gutierrez told the Chicago Tribune.

Gutierrez also takes a hands-on approach in helping thousands of immigrants become citizens. A decade ago, he became the first congressman allowed to complete immigration applications, reports the Tribune. Shortly after his election to Congress in 1992, when hundreds of thousands of legal residents became eligible for citizenship under the 1986 Immigration Reform and Control Act, Gutierrez held a number of workshops for constituents explaining how to complete the necessary paperwork. Since launching the workshops, which he has taken to other cities, his office has helped more than 30,000 people, he said.

"They pay property taxes. They pay federal income taxes," Gutierrez told the Tribune. "They should be able to vote and decide who represents them."

Gutierrez is on the same two committees he has sat on since coming to Congress in 1993: Financial Services and Veterans' Affairs. He is the top-ranking Democrat on Financial Services' Oversight and Investigations Subcommittee. In the 108th, he won approval of a measure to commission a study analyzing the current credit scoring system by businesses. The study, to be conducted by the Federal Trade Commission and the Federal Reserve, is designed to examine whether the use of credit scores and credit-based insurance scores could result in discrimination based on geography, income, ethnicity, religion, age, sex or marital status.

The son of Puerto Rican immigrants, Gutierrez likes to remind lawmakers of the difficulties faced by non-white Americans. He often cites something that happened to him at the Capitol in 1996. Returning to his office from a reception with his daughter and niece, Gutierrez was confronted by a security officer who questioned whether he indeed was a member of Congress. The officer made matters worse by being rude and insulting, Gutierrez says.

Gutierrez's first year in the House was marked by his nationally televised criticism of Congress, which drew angry responses even from Democratic colleagues. Gutierrez denounced Congress' shortcomings in an appearance on the CBS program "60 Minutes." He drew raves from congressional critics, and his office logged more than 500 phone calls and faxes praising his integrity and candor. But his House colleagues judged his performance to be self-serving, especially for someone who came up through the rough-and-tumble of Chicago city politics.

Born in Chicago, Gutierrez returned there after high school in Puerto Rico to attend college. He worked for more than a decade as a teacher, social worker and community activist. In 1983, he backed the insurgent mayoral bid of Democrat Harold Washington, who defeated incumbent Mayor Jane Byrne and Illinois States Attorney Richard M. Daley, son of the longtime mayor, in the Democratic primary. Washington became Chicago's first African-American mayor. In 1986, Gutierrez was elected to the City Council, where he was nicknamed "El Gallito," Spanish for "the little fighting rooster," for his tenacity.

After Washington died and Daley became mayor, he and Gutierrez reconciled. When the oddly shaped Hispanic-majority 4th District was created for the 1992 election, Daley backed Gutierrez for the seat. Daley's support practically guaranteed Gutierrez the non-Hispanic white vote, and he won easily in the heavily Democratic district. Since then, he generally has faced a primary challenge but has breezed to re-election in the fall.

KEY VOTES

2004
? Extend federal unemployment benefits by 13 weeks
Yes Pass $283.2 billion, six-year federal highway and mass transit bill
No Approve $146 billion multi-year extension of previously enacted middle-class tax breaks
No Amend the Constitution to prohibit same-sex marriage
No Cut corporate taxes $137 billion over 10 years
Yes Reorganize U.S. intelligence agencies as proposed by Sept. 11 commission

2003
No Cut taxes by $330 billion through fiscal 2013
Yes Block Bush rule scaling back overtime pay for some white-collar federal workers
Yes Do not allow use of search warrants without first notifying subjects
? Allow importation of prescription drugs
No Create private school voucher program in Washington, D.C.
No Ban "partial birth" abortion except to save a woman's life
Yes Split $18.6 billion in Iraq aid into half-grant, half-loan
No Overhaul Medicare and create prescription drug benefit

CQ VOTE STUDIES

	PARTY UNITY		PRESIDENTIAL SUPPORT	
	Support	Oppose	Support	Oppose
2004	99%	1%	24%	76%
2003	97%	3%	14%	86%
2002	95%	5%	31%	69%
2001	95%	5%	28%	72%
2000	96%	4%	84%	16%

INTEREST GROUPS

	AFL-CIO	ADA	CCUS	ACU
2004	100%	90%	22%	0%
2003	100%	90%	31%	12%
2002	100%	95%	42%	0%
2001	100%	95%	35%	16%
2000	100%	90%	38%	9%

ILLINOIS 4

Chicago — parts of North Side, southwest side

Surrounding the black-majority 7th District in the center of Chicago, the horseshoe-shaped 4th was drawn to unite the city's Hispanic neighborhoods into one voting bloc. Slightly less than 90 percent of district residents live in Chicago.

The district, created after the 1990 census revealed that the city's Hispanic population had passed 500,000, is three-fourths Hispanic, and after slight boundary revisions following the 2000 census includes 45 percent of Cook County's 1.1 million Hispanics. Solidly Democratic, the 4th is plagued by low voter turnout.

A narrow strip of land — about 10 miles in length and running along railroad tracks, highways and cemeteries — attaches the Puerto Rican neighborhood of Logan Square in the northern part of the 4th to Mexican-American communities in Little Village and Pilsen in the southern part. In 1998, the Supreme Court declined to hear a suit alleging that the district had been unconstitutionally drawn with race as the major factor.

More than 90 percent of residents are Hispanic in parts of the Lower West Side and South Lawndale neighborhoods around Cermak Road. Hispanic growth also has been impressive in some close-in suburbs: Cicero, a once heavily Slavic town infamous for being the center of operations for Al Capone's mob and the site of a 1966 race riot, is now more than three-fourths Hispanic. Stone Park, located in the district's northwestern corner (near the DuPage County line), was once largely Italian but is now four-fifths Hispanic.

The 4th has the state's largest percentage of blue-collar workers, and includes significant immigrant populations in both its Hispanic communities and adjacent Ukrainian and Polish neighborhoods. It also takes in part of Back of the Yards, an area in Chicago that declined when the city's famed stockyards closed in the early 1970s.

MAJOR INDUSTRY
Light manufacturing, county administration, electronics

CITIES
Chicago (pt.), 560,373; Cicero (pt.), 73,209; Melrose Park (pt.), 5,756

NOTABLE
The Mexican Fine Arts Center Museum is located in the Lower West Side neighborhood.

Rep. Rahm Emanuel (D)

Elected 2002; 2nd term

CAPITOL OFFICE
225-4061
rahm.emanuel@mail.house.gov
www.house.gov/emanuel
1319 Longworth 20515-1305; fax 225-5603

COMMITTEES
Ways & Means

HOMETOWN
Chicago

BORN
Nov. 29, 1959, Chicago, Ill.

RELIGION
Jewish

FAMILY
Wife, Amy Rule; three children

EDUCATION
Sarah Lawrence College, B.A. 1981 (liberal arts);
Northwestern U., M.A. 1985 (speech &
communication)

CAREER
Investment bank executive; senior White House
official; campaign aide and finance director

POLITICAL HIGHLIGHTS
No previous office

ELECTION RESULTS

2004 GENERAL

Rahm Emanuel (D)	158,400	76.2%
Bruce Best (R)	49,530	23.8%

2004 PRIMARY

Rahm Emanuel (D)	60,821	83.2%
Mark A. Fredrickson (D)	12,255	16.8%

2002 GENERAL

Rahm Emanuel (D)	106,514	66.8%
Mark A. Augusti (R)	46,008	28.9%
Frank Gonzalez (LIBERT)	6,913	4.3%

As junior House members go, Emanuel is in a league of his own. A former top official in the Clinton administration, he knows policy, understands how to use the media, excels at fundraising and ranks among the party's smartest strategists. The former president describes him as a breath of fresh air "blowing at gale force speed."

Against a backdrop of competing big egos, Emanuel's celebrity, combined with his personal aggressiveness, can be offputting to some colleagues. But those qualities have also made him unusually effective for a newcomer without benefit of seniority or a committee chairmanship. He was rewarded by Minority Leader Nancy Pelosi with two plums at the outset of the 109th Congress — a seat on the Ways and Means Committee and the chairmanship of the Democratic Congressional Campaign Committee (DCCC), the party organization that works to elect Democrats to the House and an important first rung on the leadership ladder.

"I'm not a patient person. I've never disguised that," Emanuel says. "Nobody on the Northwest side of Chicago elected me because they thought I was a patient guy."

Emanuel represents a district that takes in the trendy, rowhouse neighborhoods along Chicago's lakefront but is dominated by the sprawling working-class sections to the northwest of downtown, where Polish, and increasingly Spanish, is a first language for many residents. Having grown up in a well-heeled suburb, Emanuel had to fend off suggestions in his first campaign in 2002 that he had moved to the district out of political opportunism. Since being in office, he has balanced his interest in national policy with an energetic list of initiatives aimed at the people back home. They include support for a move to give historic designation to the bungalow, the spare, peaked roof dwellings built by European immigrants that dominate the city's housing. And he has a staff member in his district office translate press releases into Polish.

Emanuel's biggest achievement in his first term was on the issue of drug reimportation, a controversial bill allowing purchases of U.S. drugs from foreign countries, where they are often cheaper because of government price controls. The bill hadn't drawn a Democratic cosponsor until Emanuel jumped on it. He enlivened the debate with a frontal media strategy. When the pharmaceutical industry aired radio ads decrying alleged safety hazards of reimportation, Emanuel countered by purchasing ads rebutting the industry. When the House passed the bill in 2003, it was a triumph for its longtime GOP sponsors but also for its new Democratic cosponsor.

Emanuel's famous name makes the rare political blunder stand out. In February 2004, he was quoted in a New York Times story saying his party likely would not win majority control of the House — a prediction that angered party leaders trying to raise money for fall campaigns. That it came from President Clinton's former finance director made things worse. "I said it, and I eat it," Emanuel said later.

He is one of four children of a Chicago pediatrician. His father, Benjamin, is a native of what is now Israel and fought in the Zionist movement in the 1940s; he emigrated to the United States in 1959 after marrying Emanuel's mother, Marsha, an American Jew and civil rights activist whom he had met during his medical training. Emanuel's family experience inspires a passionate interest in Middle East policy.

At New Trier High School, Emanuel was small for a boy — he's still just

5 feet 8 inches tall and 150 pounds — and drawn to soccer. He took a ballet class to improve his agility and liked it so much that he continued to study dance while getting a liberal arts degree at Sarah Lawrence College in New York.

Emanuel discovered politics by accident. During a semester off, he worked on the campaign staff of a Democratic House candidate in a district near Springfield, Ill. and befriended David Wilhelm, another young, idealistic campaign worker. Emanuel returned to Chicago to get a master's degree in speech and communication and to pursue a political career.

He worked on the 1984 Senate campaign of Illinois Democrat Paul Simon, then as national campaign director for the DCCC and later as a fundraiser in the first campaign of Chicago Mayor Richard M. Daley, Jr. By 1991, Wilhelm had become campaign manager for the fledgling presidential campaign of Arkansas Gov. Bill Clinton, then struggling to raise money. Wilhelm recruited Emanuel to head fundraising, and his old friend turned the under-performing operation into the vaunted Clinton money machine.

Clinton took Emanuel with him to the White House as political director. Emanuel was only 33 and a star, but smart as he was, he was blunt to a fault and lacked people skills. When he alienated other senior aides, he was demoted to manager of special legislative efforts. Emanuel worked hard to rehabilitate himself. He successfully spearheaded Clinton's efforts to pass the North American Free Trade Agreement, an overhaul of the welfare system and a ban on assault-style weapons. When senior adviser George Stephanopoulos left in 1996, Emanuel was given the job along with an office just steps from the Oval Office. In Clinton's second term, he helped defend the president during the Monica Lewinsky scandal.

Emanuel left Washington in 1999 and became an investment banker, though he had no training in that field. Drawing on his government connections, he built a stable of clients who had been major donors to Democratic campaigns, raking in $16 million in under three years, the Chicago Tribune reported. Having made his fortune, he jumped into the 2002 contest for the seat being vacated by three-term Democratic Rep. Rod R. Blagojevich, who ran, successfully, for governor.

Emanuel's biggest obstacle was primary opponent Nancy Kaszak, a former state representative with a Polish surname who depicted him as a carpetbagger. But Emanuel had the backing of Daley, the city's popular mayor, and of the labor unions. He also got walking-around help from a police sergeant uncle in a district where many police officers and firefighters live. He won easily and in 2004, facing only token opposition, cruised to re-election.

KEY VOTES

2004

Yes Extend federal unemployment benefits by 13 weeks

Yes Pass $283.2 billion, six-year federal highway and mass transit bill

No Approve $146 billion multi-year extension of previously enacted middle-class tax breaks

No Amend the Constitution to prohibit same-sex marriage

No Cut corporate taxes $137 billion over 10 years

Yes Reorganize U.S. intelligence agencies as proposed by Sept. 11 commission

2003

No Cut taxes by $330 billion through fiscal 2013

Yes Block Bush rule scaling back overtime pay for some white-collar federal workers

Yes Do not allow use of search warrants without first notifying subjects

Yes Allow importation of prescription drugs

No Create private school voucher program in Washington, D.C.

No Ban "partial birth" abortion except to save a woman's life

Yes Split $18.6 billion in Iraq aid into half-grant, half-loan

No Overhaul Medicare and create prescription drug benefit

CQ VOTE STUDIES

	PARTY UNITY		PRESIDENTIAL SUPPORT	
	Support	Oppose	Support	Oppose
2004	97%	3%	18%	82%
2003	95%	5%	26%	74%

INTEREST GROUPS

	AFL-CIO	ADA	CCUS	ACU
2004	100%	100%	29%	0%
2003	87%	95%	39%	24%

ILLINOIS 5
Chicago — North Side

The 5th spans the North Side of Chicago, from Lake Michigan to near O'Hare International Airport (located in the 6th District). One of the city's few remaining active industrial sectors runs through the middle of the district, along the north branch of the Chicago River. The district's 2 percent black population is the lowest in the state.

On the east side, the 5th includes most of Lincoln Park, a wealthy community of "lakefront liberals" known for their expensive homes and opposition to Democratic machine politics. Voters here rarely support establishment candidates in the primary but then vote Democratic in general elections.

The west side of the district covers part of the "Bungalow Belt," a strip of 1930s brick homes built by Central and Eastern European families. This section of town is still dominated by middle- and working-class German and Polish neighborhoods, but has seen an increasing number of Hispanic newcomers. Voters here also lean Democratic, generally supporting the organization's primary candidates, but sometimes vote for

Republicans in the general election.

The combination of these voting habits makes for a constituency that leans Democratic. The west's working-class base routinely supports candidates trumpeting populist-style economic causes. But far-west side neighborhoods also have been known to elect a few Republicans to local offices. On the federal level, the 5th has supported Democratic presidential candidates since 1992. John Kerry garnered 67 percent of the district's vote in 2004.

MAJOR INDUSTRY
Warehousing and storage, electronics, manufacturing, health care

CITIES
Chicago (pt.), 549,762; Elmwood Park (pt.), 23,741; Franklin Park, 19,434

NOTABLE
Wrigley Field is home to baseball's Chicago Cubs; Famous gangster death sites: the S.M.C. Cartage Co. garage, where Al Capone ordered rival "Bugs" Moran's gangsters shot in the 1929 St. Valentine's Day Massacre, and the Biograph Theatre, where federal agents gunned down outlaw John Dillinger in 1934.

Rep. Henry J. Hyde (R)

Elected 1974; 16th term

CAPITOL OFFICE
225-4561
www.house.gov/hyde
2110 Rayburn 20515-1306; fax 225-1166

COMMITTEES
International Relations - chairman
Judiciary

HOMETOWN
Wood Dale

BORN
April 18, 1924, Chicago, Ill.

RELIGION
Roman Catholic

FAMILY
Widowed; four children

EDUCATION
Duke U., attended 1943-44; Georgetown U., B.S. 1947 (history); Loyola U., J.D. 1949

MILITARY SERVICE
Navy, 1944-46; Naval Reserve, 1946-68

CAREER
Lawyer

POLITICAL HIGHLIGHTS
Republican nominee for U.S. House, 1962;
Ill. House, 1967-75 (majority leader, 1971-73)

ELECTION RESULTS

2004 GENERAL

Henry J. Hyde (R)	139,627	55.8%
Christine Cegelis (D)	110,470	44.2%

2004 PRIMARY

Henry J. Hyde (R)	unopposed

2002 GENERAL

Henry J. Hyde (R)	113,174	65.1%
Tom Berry (D)	60,698	34.9%

PREVIOUS WINNING PERCENTAGES
2000 (59%); 1998 (67%); 1996 (64%); 1994 (73%);
1992 (66%); 1990 (67%); 1988 (74%); 1986 (75%);
1984 (75%); 1982 (68%); 1980 (67%); 1978 (66%);
1976 (61%); 1974 (53%)

In his final term in the House, Hyde is among the most revered members of Congress. Although he has been slowed by age and arthritis, few can match him in the sheer power of his oratory or the agility of his intellect. Best known for his command of legal issues and his opposition to abortion, Hyde in recent years has been a player in major foreign policy fights as chairman of the International Relations Committee.

Now in his 80s, Hyde announced in 2005 that he will retire at the end of the 109th Congress in 2006. With that, the House will lose one of its most eloquent voices, and the foreign relations panel will get a new chairman from among a field of senior Republicans.

In his fourth decade in Congress, Hyde is still capable of inflicting moments of great rhetorical pain on members of the minority party who take issue with his loyally Republican and mostly conservative views. He was the author of the meticulously worded resolution in 2004 declaring the world safer since the removal of Saddam Hussein from power. The resolution had no real effect, but was a neat trap for Democrats, who were becoming increasingly critical of President Bush's handling of the war in Iraq. A majority of them supported Hyde's resolution, calculating that it was safer politically to vote for it than against it.

When one Democrat tried to turn the floor debate to shortages of body armor for the U.S. troops in Iraq, Hyde noted that the lawmaker had voted against a special spending bill for the war. "To talk out of one side of your mouth for a vigorous military and that it should be supplied, and then to deny them the wherewithal to do it seems to me standing on two stools," Hyde said. "It's a way to get a political hernia."

Among his colleagues, Hyde is respected as one of the sharpest legal minds on Capitol Hill, a genuinely nice man and a defender of the institution. In legislative battles, he pounces on flaws in foes' arguments with all the repartee and sarcasm he once used as a Chicago trial lawyer.

Hyde is also appreciated for an old-fashioned charm. On the Judiciary Committee, he proposed in 2004 to do away with a technical law that prevents commercial establishments with satellite TV from showing the superstation WGN. All sports taverns, Hyde insisted, should be able to broadcast Cubs baseball games, be they served by cable or satellite. "Watching day baseball from beautiful Wrigley Field is one of life's simple and enduring pleasures," he said.

Judiciary is where Hyde probably spent the best days of his career, arguing constitutional points and writing abortion policy. As its chairman, Hyde in 1998 led the historic impeachment of President Clinton on charges related to his affair with a White House intern; Hyde later served as lead prosecutor in the Senate trial.

When GOP colleagues counseled against zealous pursuit of the popular president, Hyde insisted that the nation's chief law enforcement officer should be removed from office for undermining "the rule of law." Hyde became a favorite target of Democratic partisans, who revealed that he had carried on a long affair with a married woman when he was in his 40s. He dismissed the chapter in his life as "youthful indiscretion."

On the legislative front, he is best known for the "Hyde amendment," the law that bars federal funding for abortions. It has since been altered to create exceptions for cases involving incest or rape or endangerment to the woman, but has otherwise withstood assaults from abortion rights forces over the years. Hyde also champions legislation to further restrict abortion, including making it a crime to take a minor across state lines for an abortion without notifying her parents, and requiring doctors to tell women seeking abortions after 20 weeks about the capacity of the fetus to feel pain. He supported the Family and Medical Leave Act because he saw it as helpful to people choosing to have children.

GOP term limits compelled Hyde in 2001 to give up the Judiciary gavel for the helm of International Relations. Republican members there tend to be more centrist than in the House as a whole, and they joined with Democrats to hand Hyde an early defeat by voting to overturn some anti-abortion restrictions on foreign aid. Subsequently, he made sure he had the support of the long-serving senior Democrat on the panel, Tom Lantos of California, before moving legislation.

Hyde and Lantos agree on many issues, including the war in Iraq, strong support for Israel and economic aid to Afghanistan. With Lantos, he pushed through a bill to repay U.S. debt to the United Nations. And the two launched the drive to boost funding to combat AIDS overseas, which resulted in Bush signing in 2003 a $15 billion aid package. However, Hyde had to give up his provision that none of the money go to groups that discuss abortion options with patients. On other issues, he is also sometimes sidelined by a president who seems to prefer to tackle the most significant foreign policy issues directly with the House Republican leaders.

While Hyde has not had to worry much about parochial concerns, he places much importance on the proposed construction of a third airport to serve the Chicago area. He opposed the 2000 federal aviation law because it allowed more flights at O'Hare Airport, which is in his suburban district.

Hyde grew up in Chicago as an Irish Catholic Democrat. As a young man in 1952, he cast off the political label he was born with to become a Republican. Elected to the state House in 1966, he eventually rose to majority leader but lost a bid for Speaker.

In 1974, longtime GOP Rep. Harold Collier retired from his suburban Chicago House seat. Capitalizing on his fundraising prowess and his army of precinct workers, Hyde bucked the post-Watergate tide and won with 53 percent of the vote. He has been invincible ever since.

Courtly, with a distinguishing full head of white hair, he has suffered arthritis and back problems in recent years, and now sometimes uses a wheelchair to get around. "Maybe I lost a step or two," Hyde told the Chicago Tribune while campaigning for re-election in 2004. But, he added, "I don't think God is through with me yet."

KEY VOTES

2004
No Extend federal unemployment benefits by 13 weeks
Yes Pass $283.2 billion, six-year federal highway and mass transit bill
Yes Approve $146 billion multi-year extension of previously enacted middle-class tax breaks
Yes Amend the Constitution to prohibit same-sex marriage
Yes Cut corporate taxes $137 billion over 10 years
Yes Reorganize U.S. intelligence agencies as proposed by Sept. 11 commission

2003
Yes Cut taxes by $330 billion through fiscal 2013
No Block Bush rule scaling back overtime pay for some white-collar federal workers
No Do not allow use of search warrants without first notifying subjects
Yes Allow importation of prescription drugs
Yes Create private school voucher program in Washington, D.C.
?   Ban "partial birth" abortion except to save a woman's life
No Split $18.6 billion in Iraq aid into half-grant, half-loan
Yes Overhaul Medicare and create prescription drug benefit

CQ VOTE STUDIES

	PARTY UNITY		PRESIDENTIAL SUPPORT	
	Support	Oppose	Support	Oppose
2004	90%	10%	79%	21%
2003	97%	3%	96%	4%
2002	97%	3%	92%	8%
2001	95%	5%	88%	12%
2000	89%	11%	35%	65%

INTEREST GROUPS

	AFL-CIO	ADA	CCUS	ACU
2004	27%	15%	95%	75%
2003	8%	10%	93%	83%
2002	13%	0%	100%	88%
2001	17%	5%	96%	92%
2000	20%	10%	71%	76%

ILLINOIS 6
Northwest and west Chicago suburbs

Just west of Chicago, the 6th includes northern DuPage County and part of northwest Cook County. It is full of older, mostly built-out bedroom communities along commuter rail lines running into the city. Many of these suburbs have been revitalizing their downtown districts.

Most residents of the 6th traditionally have commuted to Chicago, but some now travel to booming northwest satellite cities. The district's eastern boundary is O'Hare International Airport (an extension of the city of Chicago), which is one of the nation's busiest airports and the focus of the 6th's commercial district. Hotels and other travel-related businesses, and companies seeking close airport access, are located in the area.

The district has a reputation as a Republican bastion, historically working in opposition to Chicago's Democrats. It includes slightly more than half of DuPage County, which accounts for three-fourths of the population. DuPage is decidedly Republican, but has become more competitive — George W. Bush carried the county by 13 percentage points in 2000, but won by only 10 points in 2004. Overall, Bush won the 6th with 53 percent

of the vote in 2004.

The 6th is one-eighth Hispanic, and DuPage is becoming more racially diverse. Addison and Bensenville have many Hispanic residents, and Asians and Hispanics each tally 20 percent in Glendale Heights. Many Hispanics came to the district when agriculture was a dominant industry and then stayed as Chicago's suburbs crept westward, taking over farmland, in the 1970s and 1980s.

The Cook County portions of the district also have a conservative lean. Under redistricting following the 2000 census, the 6th ceded nearly all of Maine township (Des Plaines, Park Ridge) to the 9th District and gained most of Hanover township (the westernmost township in Cook) from the 8th District.

MAJOR INDUSTRY
Airport, light manufacturing, health care

CITIES
Wheaton, 55,416; Elmhurst, 42,762; Lombard, 42,322; Carol Stream, 40,438

NOTABLE
United Airlines headquarters is in Elk Grove Village.

Rep. Danny K. Davis (D)

Elected 1996; 5th term

CAPITOL OFFICE
225-5006
www.house.gov/davis
1526 Longworth 20515-1307; fax 225-5641

COMMITTEES
Education & Workforce
Government Reform
Small Business

HOMETOWN
Chicago

BORN
Sept. 6, 1941, Parkdale, Ark.

RELIGION
Baptist

FAMILY
Wife, Vera Davis; two children

EDUCATION
Arkansas AM&N College, B.A. 1961 (history & education); Chicago State U., M.A. 1968 (guidance); Union Institute, Ph.D. 1977 (public administration)

CAREER
Health care association executive; teacher; postal clerk

POLITICAL HIGHLIGHTS
Chicago City Council, 1979-90; sought Democratic nomination for U.S. House, 1984, 1986; Cook County Commission, 1990-97; sought Democratic nominiation for mayor of Chicago, 1991

ELECTION RESULTS

2004 GENERAL

Danny K. Davis (D)	221,133	86.1%
Antonio Davis-Fairman (R)	35,603	13.9%

2004 PRIMARY

Danny K. Davis (D)	84,950	82.2%
Anita Rivkin-Carothers (D)	15,190	14.7%
Robert Dallas (D)	3,191	3.1%

2002 GENERAL

Danny K. Davis (D)	137,933	83.2%
Mark Tunney (R)	25,280	15.3%
Martin Pankau (LIBERT)	2,543	1.5%

PREVIOUS WINNING PERCENTAGES
2000 (86%); 1998 (93%); 1996 (82%)

A gregarious, enthusiastic man with a deep, melodious voice, Davis laces his talk with tidbits of personal philosophy, drawing heavily on his childhood as one of 11 children born to sharecroppers who picked cotton in southeastern Arkansas, one of the poorest regions of the country. He says he and his brothers and sisters went to a segregated school only four or five months of the year, spending the rest of the time in the fields.

Sometimes stubborn when pressing his priorities, Davis says he learned perseverance from his father and empathy from his mother. "They instilled whatever drive and desire I may have had," he notes.

His liberal views allow him to work comfortably in the Congressional Progressive Caucus, and he votes a consistently liberal line on most social policy issues. But Davis also draws on his church-going upbringing to examine policy questions. He backs the principle, if not the specifics, of President Bush's faith-based initiative to provide new tax breaks for charitable giving and to permit federal funding of religious groups that provide social services. Many social advances for blacks — since and including the abolition of slavery — have their origins in the church, he says.

At other times, he flays conservatives with sharp rhetoric. Of a GOP amendment in 2003 that would have placed restrictions on the use of federal funding to distribute condoms, Davis said, "By denying young people contraceptives we are writing death sentences for thousands of kids."

Davis is willing to take on legislative issues that other members might find pedestrian. A good example is his work in the 108th Congress to change the name of the General Accounting Office to the Government Accountability Office and to give it more flexibility to deal with its workers. "GAO has been determined to be one of the best places to work in the federal government," Davis said. "There are many agencies that could model themselves after GAO." But he expressed some concerns about the trend of giving departments more leeway over their workers, and he won support for an amendment requiring the GAO to submit reports on how it uses its new flexibility. Davis is the senior Democrat on the Government Reform panel's Federal Workforce and Agency Organization Subcommittee.

Davis also used his seat on Government Reform to work to increase participation in the 2000 census, particularly in low-income areas. He pressed the U.S. Postal Service (where he once worked as a clerk) to move more ethnic minorities into management jobs. In 2001, he was among the first who called on Congress to honor postal workers who died after handling anthrax-tainted mail, and he said the incident should spur Congress to look at improving the postal service in general.

He now has a seat on the committee's Criminal Justice, Drug Policy and Human Resources Subcommittee, where he is likely to pursue an issue he knows will require a long battle: the effort to integrate ex-convicts into their communities with jobs, housing and voting rights. "All of the issues associated with poverty are pronounced in my district," Davis says. "Rather than run from it, or hope someone else is going to do it, we took a vote that the ex-offender issue is going to be the top issue."

After winning a seat on the Education and the Workforce Committee in the 108th, Davis floated a plan to give stipends to Head Start teachers. He also has a seat on the Small Business Committee.

His district in the heart of Chicago is different in some obvious ways from his rural roots, but Davis says he sees many of the same problems in both

www.cqpress.com

places. He pleads for "economic policies that will also create jobs for which people can actually work and earn a decent wage, a livable wage." He has pushed legislation to improve transportation, housing, health care and education for his heterogeneous district, which includes not only huge public housing projects but also some well-to-do suburbs, luxury high rises and the downtown Chicago business center.

Davis joined in a bill to require local and state governments to reduce taxes and regulatory requirements on companies operating in designated urban and rural renewal areas. In the Congressional Black Caucus, where he is the secretary in the 109th, Davis has pushed for a serious look at police brutality and racial profiling, seeking "equal application of the law" — which he sees as a major focus in the future of the ongoing civil rights struggle.

Davis says he went off to college in Arkansas with the idea of becoming a teacher. After graduation, with $50 given to him by his father, Davis set off for California where a job awaited. But his money ran out, and he got no farther than Chicago. He stayed with an older sister for a time, working in the post office and at other jobs before landing a teaching job. Davis soon realized he wanted to be more involved in the community, and his activism eventually led him to become president of the National Association of Community Health Centers. In 1979, Davis headed a committee of neighborhood leaders looking for a candidate to challenge the Democratic political machine in a city council race, but he failed to turn up anyone. "So I said, 'what the hell,' and decided to run myself," he said.

Davis won — the first black alderman who was not part of the regular party machinery — and served until 1990, when he became a Cook County commissioner. On the city council in the early 1980s, Davis was a close associate of Harold Washington, a former House member and the city's first black mayor, who also had challenged the Democratic machine.

In 1984, Davis opposed 7th District Rep. Cardiss Collins in the Democratic primary; he lost by 10 percentage points but held her to less than a majority. Davis opposed Collins again in 1986 but lost decisively. And in 1991, Davis was the decided underdog in a Democratic primary campaign for mayor against the incumbent, Richard M. Daley.

Davis never gave up. When Collins announced plans to retire in 1996, Davis jumped into the race. He faced a crowded primary field and opposition from some elements of the party machine, but he cleared those hurdles and won with ease that November. He has since enjoyed large winning margins.

KEY VOTES

2004

Yes Extend federal unemployment benefits by 13 weeks

Yes Pass $283.2 billion, six-year federal highway and mass transit bill

No Approve $146 billion multi-year extension of previously enacted middle-class tax breaks

? Amend the Constitution to prohibit same-sex marriage

Yes Cut corporate taxes $137 billion over 10 years

Yes Reorganize U.S. intelligence agencies as proposed by Sept. 11 commission

2003

No Cut taxes by $330 billion through fiscal 2013

Yes Block Bush rule scaling back overtime pay for some white-collar federal workers

Yes Do not allow use of search warrants without first notifying subjects

Yes Allow importation of prescription drugs

No Create private school voucher program in Washington, D.C.

No Ban "partial birth" abortion except to save a woman's life

Yes Split $18.6 billion in Iraq aid into half-grant, half-loan

No Overhaul Medicare and create prescription drug benefit

CQ VOTE STUDIES

	PARTY UNITY		PRESIDENTIAL SUPPORT	
	Support	Oppose	Support	Oppose
2004	98%	2%	16%	84%
2003	99%	1%	13%	87%
2002	96%	4%	24%	76%
2001	97%	3%	17%	83%
2000	97%	3%	88%	12%

INTEREST GROUPS

	AFL-CIO	ADA	CCUS	ACU
2004	87%	90%	30%	0%
2003	100%	100%	19%	12%
2002	100%	90%	42%	0%
2001	100%	100%	35%	4%
2000	100%	100%	33%	4%

ILLINOIS 7

Chicago – downtown, West Side; west suburbs

East to west, the 7th stretches from the Loop, Chicago's downtown business district, almost to the DuPage County line, taking in the well-to-do western suburbs of Oak Park and River Forest. North to south, the district runs from the upscale Lincoln Park neighborhood to 57th Street on the South Side.

The eastern end of the 7th houses some of Chicago's gems, including the Sears Tower, the plush high-rises of River North, several museums and about a dozen colleges and universities. Chicago's "Magnificent Mile" on Michigan Avenue includes some prestigious shops and first-rate hotels and museums. Business giants such as Boeing, Sara Lee and Quaker Foods and Beverages have their corporate headquarters in the 7th.

But most of the district lives in the poverty-stricken neighborhoods that stretch from the western Loop to the edge of the county. Except for a few communities of middle-class blacks, the West Side has had problems with gang violence, unemployment and crumbling infrastructure. The

situation has changed in the West Loop, once dominated by the Cabrini-Green housing project, where once-dilapidated buildings now house lofts, galleries and a vibrant night life. A large park also is planned for the area.

The district fills with white commuters during the day, but more than 60 percent of the district's residents are black. A reliably Democratic district across the ballot, the only genuine political contests in the 7th are the Democratic primaries. John Kerry won 83 percent of the 2004 presidential vote here — his second-highest percentage in the state.

MAJOR INDUSTRY
Insurance, banking, accounting

CITIES
Chicago (pt.), 502,445; Oak Park, 52,524; Maywood (pt.), 24,895

NOTABLE
The United Center, arena for the Chicago Bulls and Blackhawks, Soldier Field, home to the Chicago Bears and Fire, and U.S. Cellular Field (formerly known as Comiskey Park), stadium of the Chicago White Sox, are in the district; The Ernest Hemingway birthplace and museum are in Oak Park; Oprah Winfrey's Harpo Productions is in Chicago; Architect Frank Lloyd Wright's home and studio are in Oak Park.

Rep. Melissa Bean (D)

Elected 2004; 1st term

One usually must look in the Republican cloakroom to find a lawmaker who says she is influenced by the thinking of economists Adam Smith of long-ago Scotland and conservative Milton Friedman of the modern-day University of Chicago. But Democrat Bean, a self-described "fiscal conservative," is an exception.

A suburban businesswoman for 20 years, Bean could not have won her House seat in 2004 had she not proven herself sufficiently centrist to the Republican-leaning constituency north and west of Chicago. Those voters delivered Bean perhaps the biggest House upset of 2004, a 3 percentage point victory over veteran Republican incumbent Philip M. Crane.

Bean now faces a significant challenge: proving that her victory, in a rematch of her 2002 political debut, was more about her qualities than just voter weariness with Crane, who had represented the region since 1969.

She believes that her committee assignments, Financial Services and Small Business, will provide a solid platform for her. "I've always said I'd like to be a voice for the small- and medium-size business community," Bean said. She says the 2003 tax cuts included too little relief for small businesses.

Bean says she will advocate a tighter rein on spending than most of her Democratic colleagues: She opposed both the GOP-drafted 2003 Medicare prescription drug law and an alternative Democratic plan as too expensive. Budgetary concerns also underpin Bean's opposition to a system of private accounts under Social Security, which she said is "not even remotely fiscally responsible."

Some of Bean's more localized interests include environmental protections for the Great Lakes and transportation initiatives for the 8th District, which is burdened by commuter traffic problems.

After collecting just 43 percent in her long-shot bid against Crane in 2002, Bean came into 2004 armed with a far larger campaign treasury and stronger national party support. She convinced many voters that Crane was more interested in foreign travel than the concerns of his constituents.

CAPITOL OFFICE
225-3711
www.house.gov/bean
512 Cannon 20515-1308; fax 225-7830

COMMITTEES
Financial Services
Small Business

HOMETOWN
Barrington

BORN
Jan. 22, 1962, Chicago, Ill.

RELIGION
Serbian Orthodox

FAMILY
Husband, Alan Bean; two children

EDUCATION
Oakton Community College, A.A. 1982 (business);
Roosevelt U., B.A. 2002 (political science)

CAREER
Technology consulting firm president;
telecommunications sales manager

POLITICAL HIGHLIGHTS
Democratic nominee for U.S. House, 2002

ELECTION RESULTS

2004 GENERAL

Melissa Bean (D)	139,792	51.7%
Philip M. Crane (R)	130,601	48.3%

2004 PRIMARY

Melissa Bean (D)	26,740	78.1%
William C. Scheurer (D)	7,518	21.9%

ILLINOIS 8

Northwest Cook County; parts of Lake and McHenry counties

Most of the 8th's population lies in the affluent, well-established suburbs northwest of Chicago, although population growth has spurred new developments farther north through western Lake County and into the Chain-O-Lakes vacation communities near the Wisconsin border.

The district became a huge employment center in the late 1980s, drawing commuters away from Chicago. The 8th is still struggling with the traffic problems that come with rapid development and suburban sprawl.

As in other northwestern Chicago suburban districts, some of the 8th's cities, such as Palatine (which is shared with the 10th) and Schaumburg, have lured corporate headquarters. Motorola is based in Schaumburg. The biggest development boom in Cook County has been abetted by access to interstates and proximity to O'Hare International Airport (in the 6th District).

Redistricting following the 2000 census gave the 8th more of Lake County, where a slight majority of district residents now live. This area is mostly upscale and well-educated; in the southwest Lake townships of Cuba and Ela, the median family income is more than $100,000. Redistricting also added the northeastern part of fast-growing McHenry County, located west of Lake.

Despite Rep. Bean's 2004 victory, the 8th still has a strong Republican tradition — it gave George W. Bush 55 percent of the vote in 2004 — that has been moderated only slightly by newcomers and a small but growing minority population. Hispanics make up one-tenth of district residents.

MAJOR INDUSTRY
Health care, insurance, retail

CITIES
Schaumburg (pt.), 71,577; Palatine (pt.), 47,077; Hoffman Estates (pt.), 39,568

NOTABLE
The Volo Illinois Auto Museum features classic and celebrity cars.

Rep. Jan Schakowsky (D)

Elected 1998; 4th term

CAPITOL OFFICE
225-2111
jan.schakowsky@mail.house.gov
www.house.gov/schakowsky
1027 Longworth 20515-1309; fax 226-6890

COMMITTEES
Energy & Commerce

HOMETOWN
Evanston

BORN
May 26, 1944, Chicago, Ill.

RELIGION
Jewish

FAMILY
Husband, Robert Creamer; three children

EDUCATION
U. of Illinois, B.S. 1965 (elementary education)

CAREER
Senior citizens group director; consumer advocate; teacher

POLITICAL HIGHLIGHTS
Candidate for Cook County Commission, 1986;
Ill. House, 1991-99 (floor leader, 1994-99)

ELECTION RESULTS

2004 GENERAL

Jan Schakowsky (D)	175,282	75.7%
Kurt J. Eckhardt (R)	56,135	24.3%

2004 PRIMARY

Jan Schakowsky (D)	unopposed

2002 GENERAL

Jan Schakowsky (D)	118,642	70.3%
Nicholas M. Duric (R)	45,307	26.8%
Stephanie Sailor (LIBERT)	4,887	2.9%

PREVIOUS WINNING PERCENTAGES
2000 (76%); 1998 (75%)

Schakowsky is a firm believer in using the power of government to improve citizens' lives. She describes Medicare as a spectacular success and wants to expand it to pay the medical bills of all Americans. As befits a former elementary school teacher, she clamors for a stronger federal investment in public education.

A member of the Congressional Progressive Caucus, a group of the most liberal House Democrats, Schakowsky supports gun control and abortion rights. And she remains an outspoken advocate of pushing the agenda to the left. "It's more important than ever for there to be a very clear, unapologetic progressive voice," she has said.

Schakowsky (shuh-KOW-ski) is one of the most loyal House Democrats. Since 2001, she has backed her party 99 percent of the time on votes that pitted the two parties against each other. She was an early supporter of Nancy Pelosi of California, who was elected Democratic whip in 2002 and then moved up to minority leader in the 108th Congress.

Schakowsky gained a coveted assignment to the Energy and Commerce Committee in the 108th. She is now the top-ranking Democrat on the Commerce, Trade and Consumer Protection Subcommittee. She also is one of seven chief deputy whips. The subcommittee post enables her to continue the work she began three decades ago on behalf of consumers. She has introduced legislation to end automatic-teller surcharges and excessive bank fees as well as a measure to crack down on lenders who prey on the poor and elderly by charging high rates and fees for mortgage loans.

She is also wary of handing over too much authority to the government. In early 2005, when GOP leaders revived legislation from the 108th to give federal regulators more authority to punish broadcasters and performers for sexually explicit or vulgar programming, Schakowsky said the measure would give the government too much power. "We are heading down a slippery slope when Big Brother decides what constitutes free speech and artistic expression," said Schakowsky, who was one of two Democrats on Energy and Commerce voting against the bill.

Schakowsky does not mince words in her criticism of the House Republican leadership. In the 108th when the chamber voted on legislation that would have required hospitals to collect data to determine whether a patient was an illegal immigrant, Schakowsky said Republicans had reached an all-time low. "We've been asked to vote on a lot of really bad ideas presented by the majority, but this is clearly one of the worst," she said.

Schakowsky has been a persistent critic of American intervention in Iraq, voting against the resolution authorizing the war there. She is particularly worried about the increased reliance by the Pentagon on the use of civilian contractors in Iraq.

Schakowsky has been a longtime critic of the often-obscure process by which private companies receive government contracts, and she worries about the secrecy that surrounds Defense Department contracting. She has introduced legislation to expand congressional oversight and access to major contracts signed with private firms. "I'm sure many important functions are done by these private contractors," she says. "But at the same time, the process masks just what the U.S. commitment is in places like Iraq and allows many of these activities to literally fly under the radar of the Congress and the consciousness of the American people."

Although she has supported the Bush administration's fight against terrorism in Afghanistan, she said it must be coupled with increased foreign aid to economically distressed nations. "That has to be included in the calculation of the war on terrorism," she said. "There is no security in the world without economic justice."

Schakowsky does not just espouse progressive causes. A veteran activist of more than 25 years, she seeks to teach organizing skills to others. With her husband, Robert Creamer, a longtime Chicago political organizer, she set up a training program for political advocates that has been replicated nationwide. The program brought volunteers to Chicago to a "campaign school," where they were given instruction and political tools and then put to work on several House races.

Schakowsky also helped organize in 1989 the famous town hall meeting protest that featured seniors booing Ways and Means Committee Chairman Dan Rostenkowski, also an Illinois Democrat, because he had supported the 1988 law that provided benefits for drugs and catastrophic illnesses but required seniors to help shoulder the costs. In the face of protests, Congress overturned that law in 1989. As the House in 2003 neared passage of a Medicare prescription drug bill, Schakowsky, who was advising liberal activists planning protests because they thought the drug benefit was not generous enough, quipped, "As Yogi Berra said, it's déjà vu all over again."

Schakowsky's activist approach began as a stay-at-home mother in the early 1970s, when she helped launch a successful nationwide campaign to require freshness dates on food products. She was elected to the Illinois House in 1990, where she fought for labor unions, family leave benefits and changes in medical insurance law sought by consumer groups. She worked on toughening Illinois' hate crimes law and guaranteeing homeless people the right to vote. She became chairwoman of the state House Labor and Commerce Committee and Democratic floor leader.

In seeking to replace Sidney R. Yates, a liberal Democrat who held the 9th District seat for 48 years before retiring, Schakowsky easily won the Democratic district in 1998 after besting state Sen. Howard W. Carroll and Hyatt hotel heir Jay "J.B." Pritzker, both centrist Democrats, in the primary. She has won each of her general elections with over 70 percent of the vote.

She has drawn attention within Democratic circles for her fundraising prowess. Without any serious challengers in her own elections, Schakowsky has been able to devote substantial effort to her party's attempt to regain the House. She was by far the biggest party fundraiser among first-term House members in 2000 and one of the biggest among all Democrats.

KEY VOTES

2004

Yes	Extend federal unemployment benefits by 13 weeks
Yes	Pass $283.2 billion, six-year federal highway and mass transit bill
No	Approve $146 billion multi-year extension of previously enacted middle-class tax breaks
No	Amend the Constitution to prohibit same-sex marriage
No	Cut corporate taxes $137 billion over 10 years
Yes	Reorganize U.S. intelligence agencies as proposed by Sept. 11 commission

2003

No	Cut taxes by $330 billion through fiscal 2013
Yes	Block Bush rule scaling back overtime pay for some white-collar federal workers
Yes	Do not allow use of search warrants without first notifying subjects
Yes	Allow importation of prescription drugs
No	Create private school voucher program in Washington, D.C.
No	Ban "partial birth" abortion except to save a woman's life
Yes	Split $18.6 billion in Iraq aid into half-grant, half-loan
No	Overhaul Medicare and create prescription drug benefit

CQ VOTE STUDIES

	PARTY UNITY		PRESIDENTIAL SUPPORT	
	Support	Oppose	Support	Oppose
2004	99%	1%	12%	88%
2003	99%	1%	15%	85%
2002	99%	1%	25%	75%
2001	99%	1%	17%	83%
2000	97%	3%	85%	15%

INTEREST GROUPS

	AFL-CIO	ADA	CCUS	ACU
2004	100%	100%	5%	0%
2003	100%	100%	20%	12%
2002	100%	100%	30%	0%
2001	100%	100%	27%	0%
2000	100%	85%	40%	4%

ILLINOIS 9

Chicago – North Side lakefront; Evanston

The 9th starts in upscale Wilmette (shared with the 10th), runs south through the liberal suburbs of Evanston and Skokie and Chicago's multi-ethnic North Side, and then drops into one of the city's most prosperous lakefront neighborhoods. It also extends west to industrial and blue-collar Des Plaines and Rosemont (both shared with the 6th).

Roughly two-thirds of the district's population is white, with the remainder almost evenly divided among Asians, blacks and Hispanics. More than one in five who live in Skokie, Morton Grove and Lincolnwood are Asian.

Slightly less than half of the district's population lives in Chicago. The neighborhoods of Rogers Park, Edgewater and Uptown once housed Eastern European and Irish immigrants; they are now an eclectic mix of Asian, European and African immigrants. Rogers Park, tucked in the city's northeast corner, takes in the campus of Loyola University. Uptown has undergone rapid gentrification and residents are at odds over the future of what was a working-class enclave. Southeast Asians have

opened shops and restaurants, revitalizing the area's economy.

Lakeview, the district's southernmost point, includes a large gay population. The area near Wrigley Field (which lies in the adjacent 5th District) is a mecca for affluent young professionals and is home to a hot real estate market.

Most of the other Chicagoans in the 9th live in the far northwestern part of the city, near O'Hare International Airport (which is located in the neighboring 6th).

The mix of immigrants, affluent urbanites and Northwestern University students makes the 9th solidly Democratic. Although the "lakefront liberals" tend not to vote for machine candidates, they reliably support Democrats. The district's suburbs contain a sizable Jewish population.

MAJOR INDUSTRY
Health care, insurance, light manufacturing

CITIES
Chicago (pt.), 299,868; Evanston, 74,239; Skokie, 63,348; Des Plaines (pt.), 39,632; Park Ridge, 37,775; Niles, 30,068; Morton Grove, 22,451

NOTABLE
The North Shore Center for the Performing Arts is in Skokie.

Rep. Mark Steven Kirk (R)

Elected 2000; 3rd term

Kirk hails from a part of suburban Chicago that is as conservative on pocketbook issues as well-to-do suburbs anywhere, but that can't quite throw off the Democratic impulses of the city that spawned them. Kirk is the co-chairman of the Tuesday Group of moderate Republicans, and says his goal is to keep the party from moving too far to the right and to get it back to its "Teddy Roosevelt" environmental roots.

Representing close-in communities populated by the grown-up children and grandchildren of the heavily Democratic city, Kirk parts with Republican doctrine on a number of big social issues. He supports stem cell research, opposes a constitutional amendment to ban same-sex marriage and voted against tax breaks for corporations in 2004.

He also has been an obstacle for the Republican leadership and its attempts to quietly tinker with the House's ethics standards. When leaders tried at the outset of the 109th Congress to change the ethics rules to protect Majority Leader Tom DeLay, who was under investigation in a political fundraising probe in Texas, Kirk threatened to vote against it and to try to take others with him. The leadership backed down when the brewing revolt by Kirk and several other Republicans threatened to become a publicity fiasco.

Kirk is a relative newcomer who commands respect. He is well-educated and polished. Whip Roy Blunt made Kirk one of his deputies, to help the leadership round up votes on hotly contested bills. He also got a seat on the Appropriations Committee in early 2003 after only one term in the House, something that lawmakers typically wait years to get.

Now in his third term, Kirk is versed in international issues, having been an intelligence officer in the Naval Reserve for more than a dozen years. That gives him cachet on a priority issue — fighting terrorism and protecting the homeland. With the Navy, Kirk did seven tours of duty in hot spots around the world, including Panama, Haiti, Bosnia and Iraq. He's got a degree from the London School of Economics, he once worked for a member of Parliament, and he has traveled in more than 40 countries.

Kirk previously was legislative counsel for the House International Relations Committee and worked at the World Bank. His boss on International Relations, former New York Republican Rep. Benjamin A. Gilman, says that Kirk "has a great leadership potential. Give him as many responsibilities as possible."

Kirk's idea of attacking a heroin problem in the Chicago suburbs was to travel to Afghanistan in 2005 to bolster President Hamid Karzai's promise to stem the country's large output of heroin, an effort that has a $700 million commitment in aid from the United States. Kirk considers such root treatment of the problem key to stopping not only addiction but the giant profits from the heroin trade suspected to be going to fugitive Osama bin Laden, mastermind of the Sept. 11, 2001, terrorist attacks.

In 2002, Kirk was one of nine House members chosen by President Bush to work on the resolution authorizing the use of force against Iraq. On an aviation security bill enacted after the attacks, Kirk contributed provisions requiring airport baggage screeners to be U.S. citizens and a system for trained personnel to handle emergency calls from airplanes.

Kirk is politically moderate across a wide range of domestic issues, and breaks with the leadership on some high-profile issues. In the 108th Congress, he voted against cutting corporate taxes for an array of special inter-

CAPITOL OFFICE
225-4835
www.house.gov/kirk
1717 Longworth 20515-1310; fax 225-0837

COMMITTEES
Appropriations

HOMETOWN
Highland Park

BORN
Sept. 15, 1959, Champaign, Ill.

RELIGION
Congregationalist

FAMILY
Wife, Kimberly Vertolli-Kirk

EDUCATION
Cornell U., B.A. 1981 (history); London School of Economics, M.S. 1982; Georgetown U., J.D. 1992

MILITARY SERVICE
Naval Reserve, 1989-present

CAREER
Congressional committee counsel; congressional aide; lawyer; U.S. State Department aide; World Bank officer

POLITICAL HIGHLIGHTS
No previous office

ELECTION RESULTS

2004 GENERAL

Mark Steven Kirk (R)	177,493	64.1%
Lee Goodman (D)	99,218	35.9%

2004 PRIMARY

Mark Steven Kirk (R)	unopposed

2002 GENERAL

Mark Steven Kirk (R)	128,611	68.8%
Henry H. "Hank" Perritt Jr. (D)	58,300	31.2%

PREVIOUS WINNING PERCENTAGES
2000 (51%)

ests and amending the Constitution to prohibit same-sex marriage. In the previous Congress, he was one of only nine Republicans who voted against a bill to outlaw a procedure that opponents call "partial birth" abortion. He also strongly backs the use of stem cells in medical research. He voted to maintain the prohibition on drilling for oil in Alaska's Arctic National Wildlife Refuge, and he supported campaign finance overhaul legislation.

Among the key parochial issues for him are securing appropriations for an expansion of the Metra commuter rail system, which connects the suburbs in his district to the Loop. He also has teamed with Democrat Rahm Emanuel, the former Clinton White House aide from a Chicago-based district, to push for pollution cleanup of the Great Lakes. Anything affecting the Great Lakes Naval Station gets Kirk's attention, too. Though much of the district is middle class, it has pockets of blue-collar workers and low-income minorities. Kirk convinced the owner of the Chicago Bulls to build a community basketball facility in North Chicago, an economically struggling city in his district, to give young people an after-school activity.

The son of a telephone company executive, Kirk grew up in Kenilworth, a wealthy suburb on Chicago's North Shore along Lake Michigan. A brush with death at age 16 — he nearly drowned in the lake during a boating accident — shaped his future. "To be given a second chance means it has to mean something," he told the Chicago Tribune. "For me, that means making a difference through public service."

After graduating from New Trier High School, Kirk built an impressive résumé, going on to Cornell University, a stint in Mexico learning to speak fluent Spanish, combat service in Kosovo and a career in military intelligence. He then spent several years on the staff of Rep. John Edward Porter, the Republican he succeeded in the House in 2000.

When Porter retired, Kirk jumped into a primary contest with 10 other Republicans. Though not the front-runner, Kirk impressed voters with his grasp of policy, and was helped by Porter's endorsement. He beat his closest competitor, printing company heiress Shawn Margaret Donnelley, by 16 percentage points. In the general election, he faced a formidable opponent in state Rep. Lauren Beth Gash, but prevailed by 2 percentage points.

To buttress his chances for re-election in 2002, Kirk undertook an aggressive fundraising effort in his first term. The new district mapped out by the state legislature following the 2000 census gave him a slightly more Republican constituency. Buoyed by endorsements from the Sierra Club, Planned Parenthood and the Illinois Education Association, Kirk won handily with 69 percent of the vote. In the 2004 election, he easily won again.

KEY VOTES

2004

No   Extend federal unemployment benefits by 13 weeks

Yes   Pass $283.2 billion, six-year federal highway and mass transit bill

Yes   Approve $146 billion multi-year extension of previously enacted middle-class tax breaks

No   Amend the Constitution to prohibit same-sex marriage

No   Cut corporate taxes $137 billion over 10 years

Yes   Reorganize U.S. intelligence agencies as proposed by Sept. 11 commission

2003

Yes   Cut taxes by $330 billion through fiscal 2013

No   Block Bush rule scaling back overtime pay for some white-collar federal workers

Yes   Do not allow use of search warrants without first notifying subjects

No   Allow importation of prescription drugs

Yes   Create private school voucher program in Washington, D.C.

?   Ban "partial birth" abortion except to save a woman's life

No   Split $18.6 billion in Iraq aid into half-grant, half-loan

Yes   Overhaul Medicare and create prescription drug benefit

CQ VOTE STUDIES

	PARTY UNITY		PRESIDENTIAL SUPPORT	
	Support	Oppose	Support	Oppose
2004	84%	16%	63%	37%
2003	87%	13%	81%	19%
2002	85%	15%	85%	15%
2001	85%	15%	74%	26%

INTEREST GROUPS

	AFL-CIO	ADA	CCUS	ACU
2004	29%	45%	90%	63%
2003	7%	10%	89%	58%
2002	11%	20%	95%	76%
2001	25%	25%	83%	48%

ILLINOIS 10

North and northwest Chicago suburbs — Waukegan

The mostly upscale 10th hugs Lake Michigan, taking in southeast Lake County and northeast Cook County. Along the lakefront, Chicagoland's old-money elite live in exclusive towns like Wilmette (shared with the 9th), Kenilworth and Winnetka.

In the northern part of the district, the industrial sector, in Waukegan and North Chicago, found new life in 1994 when nearby Great Lakes Naval Training Center became the nation's only naval recruit training facility. Most of the district's minorities live in Waukegan, which is about 45 percent Hispanic and 20 percent black. Minorities also make up a majority in North Chicago, located just south of Waukegan. The 10th also has a large Jewish constituency.

Suburban and working-class residents combine to make the 10th a moderate "swing" district — fiscally conservative but socially liberal, especially on abortion rights and gun control. With its proximity to Lake

Michigan, environmental protection is a major issue.

The 10th's portion of Cook County is slightly more populous than its portion of Lake County. In redistricting following the 2000 census, the 10th shed part of Wilmette to the south and some communities on the Wisconsin border, which had been the district's northern boundary. The western border was extended to pick up part of Palatine and Inverness. The revised 10th is slightly more Republican than its 1990s configuration, although residents within the new lines would have narrowly backed Bill Clinton in 1996 and Al Gore in 2000, and did back John Kerry in 2004.

MAJOR INDUSTRY
Pharmaceutical research, insurance, military

MILITARY BASES
Naval Training Center Great Lakes, 4,050 military, 2,452 civilian (2004)

CITIES
Waukegan (pt.), 79,726; Arlington Heights (pt.), 69,414; Buffalo Grove, 42,909; North Chicago, 35,918; Wheeling, 34,496; Northbrook, 33,435

NOTABLE
Berto Center, the Chicago Bulls basketball training facility, is in Deerfield; The Chicago Botanic Garden is in Glencoe.

Rep. Jerry Weller (R)

Elected 1994; 6th term

A member of the agitating class of Republicans that won the majority for their party in the House over a decade ago, Weller has been persistent in promoting tax breaks for businesses and married couples.

He is an expert on Latin American issues. In 2004, Weller made headlines with his marriage to Guatemalan legislator Zury Rios Sosa, daughter of the former Guatemalan dictator, Efrain Rios Montt. A Democratic rival and the Chicago Sun-Times urged him to resign his seat on the International Relations Committee, arguing that his marriage would present a conflict of interest on issues affecting U.S. policy in Latin America. Weller insisted there was no conflict and refused to leave the panel. He said he would not vote on bills related to Guatemala. The Federal Election Commission issued a ruling the same year to allow Weller's wife, a foreign national, to be an unpaid campaign adviser for him.

Close to Speaker J. Dennis Hastert, who is from a neighboring district, Weller has made himself useful in the leadership's party-building efforts. He raises money for Republican incumbents and candidates and is active in the GOP campaign to increase its support among Hispanic Americans. As finance chairman of the National Republican Congressional Committee, Weller helped the party raise a record $163 million for 2002 campaigns, but was thwarted in his quest to move up. He would have liked to take charge of the NRCC, which is a leadership role, but House Republicans instead gave the job to New York's Thomas M. Reynolds for the 2004 elections.

As consolation, the leadership gave Weller a seat on International Relations in addition to one on the Ways and Means Committee, a post that normally precludes a member from holding other committee assignments. Weller also was named a deputy whip and retained his seat on the Republican Policy Committee.

In the 109th Congress, Weller continues to push for faster write-offs for business investment. He won a provision to cut excise taxes for a manufacturer of fishing tackle boxes in his district as part of a GOP corporate tax bill in 2004, which was filled with tax goodies for special interests.

Weller does not like to waver once he has staked out a position, and his penchant for repetition sometimes tries the patience of even his allies.

When in 2001 he presented to House tax writers a plan to prevent a two-earner married couple from owing more taxes than they would have as two singles, Weller had his usual props — poster-size photos of a young couple from Joliet, Ill., Shad and Michelle Hallihan, who had to pay what was referred to as a marriage tax penalty. But before Weller could give a well-rehearsed speech about their plight, Republican Ways and Means Chairman Bill Thomas of California jokingly declared that Weller's time had expired, adding, "I believe I know them."

In 2004, he pushed successfully for House passage of a permanent extension of tax breaks for married couples. The proposal stalled in the Senate, but Congress later passed a short-term version as part of a larger package of tax breaks for families. Because the Bush tax cuts of 2001 are set to expire after 2010, Weller's crusade is not over; he is pushing legislation in the 109th Congress to extend the provisions indefinitely.

Weller came to Congress as part of the Republican takeover Class of 1994 and soon won some plum assignments. With Hastert's backing, in his freshman term he served on the Steering Committee, which makes GOP

CAPITOL OFFICE
225-3635
www.house.gov/weller
108 Cannon 20515-1311; fax 225-3521

COMMITTEES
International Relations
Ways & Means

HOMETOWN
Morris

BORN
July 7, 1957, Streator, Ill.

RELIGION
Christian

FAMILY
Wife, Zury Rios Sosa

EDUCATION
Joliet Junior College, attended 1977; U. of Illinois, B.S. 1979 (agriculture)

CAREER
Hog farmer; U.S. Agriculture Department aide; congressional aide; health and beauty products salesman

POLITICAL HIGHLIGHTS
Republican nominee for Ill. House, 1986; Ill. House, 1989-95

ELECTION RESULTS

2004 GENERAL

Jerry Weller (R)	173,057	58.7%
Tari Renner (D)	121,903	41.3%

2004 PRIMARY

Jerry Weller (R)	unopposed

2002 GENERAL

Jerry Weller (R)	124,192	64.3%
Keith S. Van Duyne (D)	68,893	35.7%

PREVIOUS WINNING PERCENTAGES
2000 (56%); 1998 (59%); 1996 (52%); 1994 (61%)

committee assignments. Two years later, Weller won his coveted Ways and Means seat and was elected president of his sophomore class. But a bid to climb the leadership ranks failed when he finished last in a four-way race for Republican Conference secretary.

Weller turned his energies to his main policy goal, minimizing the marriage penalty. His proposal became a mainstay of GOP tax bills in the late 1990s that were blocked by President Clinton. Once President Bush took office, the measure became part of Bush's $1.35 trillion tax cut package of 2001.

Trade is the one rare policy area where Weller bucks his party. In 1998, he was one of only two Ways and Means Republicans who opposed giving Clinton fast-track authority to negotiate trade agreements that cannot be amended by Congress, but he voted in 2002 to give Bush such authority.

Even though redistricting after the 2000 census gave the 11th District many more Republicans, Weller still represents many blue-collar workers. As a result, he tends to be sympathetic to issues important to organized labor. He has voted to increase the minimum wage and has backed efforts to extend unemployment benefits.

One of his key district issues is the establishment of a third Chicago-area airport in Peotone. It's a rare point of disagreement with Hastert, who wants to enlarge Chicago's O'Hare Airport instead. Weller had more success persuading the Army to turn over the Joliet Arsenal for local use as a prairie preserve and veterans' cemetery. Another of his interests is legalized gambling. Weller chaired the Gaming Caucus in the 108th Congress and has been an advocate for the riverboat casinos in his district.

Raised on a hog farm, Weller worked as a congressional aide and an Agriculture Department staff member before running for the Illinois House in 1986. Declared the winner by four votes, he took office in January. But when a recount showed Weller losing by four votes, the young legislator was sent home. He won the seat two years later, however, and he stayed there until his election to the House in 1994.

When Democrat George E. Sangmeister retired after four terms, Weller picked up the seat for the GOP with a surprisingly easy 3-to-2 victory over Democratic state Rep. Frank Giglio.

He held off his stiffest Democratic challenge two years later, from former state Rep. Clem Balanoff, winning by less than 4 percentage points. But in 2002, with his district redrawn, Weller won his biggest majority ever. And in 2004, Weller took 59 percent of the vote to defeat Democrat Tari Renner, a political science professor at Illinois Wesleyan University.

KEY VOTES

2004

No Extend federal unemployment benefits by 13 weeks

Yes Pass $283.2 billion, six-year federal highway and mass transit bill

Yes Approve $146 billion multi-year extension of previously enacted middle-class tax breaks

Yes Amend the Constitution to prohibit same-sex marriage

Yes Cut corporate taxes $137 billion over 10 years

Yes Reorganize U.S. intelligence agencies as proposed by Sept. 11 commission

2003

Yes Cut taxes by $330 billion through fiscal 2013

No Block Bush rule scaling back overtime pay for some white-collar federal workers

No Do not allow use of search warrants without first notifying subjects

No Allow importation of prescription drugs

Yes Create private school voucher program in Washington, D.C.

Yes Ban "partial birth" abortion except to save a woman's life

No Split $18.6 billion in Iraq aid into half-grant, half-loan

Yes Overhaul Medicare and create prescription drug benefit

CQ VOTE STUDIES

	PARTY UNITY		PRESIDENTIAL SUPPORT	
	Support	Oppose	Support	Oppose
2004	92%	8%	88%	12%
2003	95%	5%	100%	0%
2002	96%	4%	88%	12%
2001	96%	4%	93%	7%
2000	86%	14%	41%	59%

INTEREST GROUPS

	AFL-CIO	ADA	CCUS	ACU
2004	20%	15%	100%	84%
2003	7%	5%	97%	84%
2002	11%	5%	95%	92%
2001	17%	0%	100%	92%
2000	22%	15%	68%	66%

ILLINOIS 11

South Chicago exurbs – Joliet; part of Bloomington-Normal

Beginning south of Chicago in suburban Will County, the 11th heads west through the old industrial city of Joliet and into farming country, with a sliver making a southward turn in LaSalle County to run parallel to Interstate 39 as it heads to Bloomington-Normal.

Will County (shared mostly with the 13th District) is the district's most populous jurisdiction and has seen an influx of young suburban families. The county had a 41 percent growth rate in the 1990s and gave George W. Bush 52 percent of its presidential vote in 2004 after narrowly backing Bush in 2000. The county is at the nexus of a debated plan to build a third Chicago metro-area airport in Peotone. Residents in the 11th's northern reaches say a new airport would boost the suburbs, although rural residents worry it may disrupt their way of life.

South of Will, the 11th includes Kankakee County before assuming a more rural posture west of those two counties as it takes in a small

portion of Livingston County, all of Grundy and LaSalle counties and most of Bureau County before its jaunt south to Bloomington.

Redistricting following the 2000 census made the district less urban and suburban by moving the old 11th's racially diverse Cook County portions into the 2nd District and by adding the southern leg to McLean County's Bloomington-Normal region, which is home to Illinois State University and is shared with the 15th District.

The 11th remains politically competitive on the numbers, but the removal of Democratic-leaning southern Cook County lessened the district's Democratic influence. While the old 11th voted for Al Gore in the 2000 presidential election by 8 percentage points, the new district backed Bush in 2004 by 7 points.

MAJOR INDUSTRY
Farm equipment manufacturing, agriculture

CITIES
Joliet (pt.), 105,052; Normal (pt.), 30,662; Bloomington (pt.), 30,298; Kankakee, 27,491; Ottawa, 18,307

NOTABLE
The Midewin National Tallgrass Prairie is in Will County.

Rep. Jerry F. Costello (D)

Elected August 1988; 9th full term

CAPITOL OFFICE
225-5661
www.house.gov/costello
2269 Rayburn 20515-1312; fax 225-0285

COMMITTEES
Science
Transportation & Infrastructure

HOMETOWN
Belleville

BORN
Sept. 25, 1949, East St. Louis, Ill.

RELIGION
Roman Catholic

FAMILY
Wife, Georgia Cockrum Costello; three children

EDUCATION
Belleville Area College, A.A. 1971; Maryville
College of the Sacred Heart, B.A. 1973

CAREER
Law enforcement official

POLITICAL HIGHLIGHTS
St. Clair County Board chairman, 1980-88

ELECTION RESULTS

2004 GENERAL

Jerry F. Costello (D)	198,962	69.5%
Erin R. Zweigart (R)	82,677	28.9%
Walter B. Steel (LIBERT)	4,794	1.7%

2004 PRIMARY

Jerry F. Costello (D)	56,397	90.0%
Kenneth Charles Weizer (D)	6,265	10.0%

2002 GENERAL

Jerry F. Costello (D)	131,580	69.3%
David Sadler (R)	58,440	30.8%

PREVIOUS WINNING PERCENTAGES
2000 (100%); 1998 (60%); 1996 (72%); 1994 (66%);
1992 (71%); 1990 (66%); 1988 (53%); 1988 Special
Election (51%)

Costello is the man to go to on all matters of air, rail and road for the Illinois delegation. As the top-ranking Democrat on the Transportation Committee's Aviation Subcommittee, he will have to watch out for transportation needs not only in southern Illinois but also the entire state and Chicago, including the proposed expansion of O'Hare International Airport.

An elected official who has long represented the struggling industrial towns of southwest Illinois, Costello realized long ago that the dwindling steel mill, stockyard and coal mining jobs that were the traditional backbone of the district's economy were not likely to return. He believes that improving the region's transportation infrastructure will retain and attract new jobs. And he has set about doing just that, with some success.

He has brought millions of federal dollars to his district and the region for industrial parks, visitors centers and transportation projects. He helped steer nearly $600 million in federal funding for the MetroLink light rail, which connects the "Metro East" area of Illinois with St. Louis. He also is trying to develop MidAmerica St. Louis Airport just north of Scott Air Force Base as a "feeder" destination for Lambert-St. Louis International Airport, despite difficulties attracting regularly scheduled commercial passenger service. Costello hopes linking MidAmerica with Lambert via the light rail system will make the smaller airfield more viable.

He and Illinois Republican John Shimkus are also leading efforts, backed by Speaker J. Dennis Hastert, to place a clean-coal research facility in southern Illinois, as a boon to downstate's ailing coal industry.

Costello seeks to direct as much of the federal pie to the 12th District as he can. In addition to his work on infrastructure needs, he won approval of legislation to set aside federal land for a visitors center devoted to the journey of explorers Meriwether Lewis and William Clark, near the site where the expedition departed on its westward journey in 1804. The center opened in 2002.

He continues to look out for the interests of Scott Air Force Base, a candidate in past rounds of military base closings and a vulnerable target in the round of selections to begin during the 109th Congress. In the aftermath of the Sept. 11, 2001, terrorist attacks, Costello argued that keeping Air Force assets deployed across centrally located installations such as Scott is preferable to concentrating them in fewer locations.

Costello, who rarely speaks on the House floor, is not a completely dependable vote for party leaders. He has supported the party line about 80 percent of the time in recent years, and in the 108th Congress backed President Bush's position 41 percent of the time. He is a staunch labor ally, opposing overseas trade agreements that he says will cost U.S. jobs.

On social policy issues, Costello reflects his constituency's cultural conservatism. He opposes abortion and supports gun owners' rights. In the 108th, he bucked most of his party by supporting a ban on a procedure opponents call "partial birth" abortion, which became law, and a proposed constitutional amendment to ban same-sex marriage, which failed.

He also has received his share of unfavorable publicity. Media reports in 2002 revealed that Illinois Secretary of State Jesse White hired Costello's 26-year-old son for a $50,000-a-year job over a more experienced candidate after Costello had called on behalf of his son. Costello described the incident as a routine job reference call, adding that he had not directly spoken to White about his son's candidacy. He attributed the flap, in part, to a long-running feud with his hometown newspaper, the Belleville News-Democrat, which obtained state documents on the hiring.

In 1997, he was named an "unindicted co-conspirator" in the trial of his childhood friend and former business partner Amiel Cueto, who was convicted of trying to block the federal investigation of a convicted racketeer. Costello denied wrongdoing in the Cueto matter.

At the trial, government witnesses testified that Costello was a silent partner in two casino deals and that he helped pass a bill in Congress to aid an Indian tribe that owned the land where one of the casinos was to be built. Costello was not implicated in any crime and said that being named an unindicted co-conspirator was merely a prosecutorial tool to ensure that certain testimony was admissible.

Republicans have never tired of reminding voters of the connection, but to no avail. The GOP did not even field a candidate against him in 2000; in 2004, he bested nominal opposition by some 40 percentage points.

Costello grew up in East St. Louis in a politically active family. In 1960, when he was 11, the young Irish Catholic Costello was intrigued by the campaign appearance in his hometown of another Irish Catholic — John F. Kennedy, who was running for president.

While attending a local community college, Costello began a career in law enforcement during which he rose from court bailiff to become administrator of the region's court system. In 1980, he was elected chairman of the St. Clair County Board. He became well-known in his heavily Democratic region, serving at one point as chairman of the metropolitan St. Louis Council of Governments.

His high profile made him heir apparent to the elderly Democratic House veteran Melvin Price, who did not seek re-election in 1988. But in the primary, Madison County Auditor Pete Fields portrayed Costello as an old-style, hardball "boss" in the county Democratic machine. Costello survived because of a huge financial advantage but with only a 46 percent plurality.

When Price died in April, Costello squared off against Republican college official Robert H. Gaffner in a special election. Gaffner suggested voters call Costello and quiz him about his ethics. Costello barely won the special election, then went on to win in November with 53 percent of the vote.

He was not seriously challenged again until 1998, when Republican Bill Price, an orthopedic surgeon and the son of Melvin Price, announced his candidacy. Costello overcame the questions about his connections with Cueto and charged that Price represented a threat to Social Security and Medicare. Costello took 60 percent of the vote.

KEY VOTES

2004
Yes Extend federal unemployment benefits by 13 weeks
Yes Pass $283.2 billion, six-year federal highway and mass transit bill
Yes Approve $146 billion multi-year extension of previously enacted middle-class tax breaks
Yes Amend the Constitution to prohibit same-sex marriage
No Cut corporate taxes $137 billion over 10 years
Yes Reorganize U.S. intelligence agencies as proposed by Sept. 11 commission

2003
No Cut taxes by $330 billion through fiscal 2013
Yes Block Bush rule scaling back overtime pay for some white-collar federal workers
Yes Do not allow use of search warrants without first notifying subjects
Yes Allow importation of prescription drugs
No Create private school voucher program in Washington, D.C.
Yes Ban "partial birth" abortion except to save a woman's life
Yes Split $18.6 billion in Iraq aid into half-grant, half-loan
No Overhaul Medicare and create prescription drug benefit

CQ VOTE STUDIES

	PARTY UNITY		PRESIDENTIAL SUPPORT	
	Support	Oppose	Support	Oppose
2004	82%	18%	41%	59%
2003	84%	16%	41%	59%
2002	80%	20%	40%	60%
2001	72%	28%	37%	63%
2000	76%	24%	52%	48%

INTEREST GROUPS

	AFL-CIO	ADA	CCUS	ACU
2004	93%	70%	38%	36%
2003	93%	80%	38%	48%
2002	100%	70%	50%	36%
2001	100%	80%	48%	44%
2000	90%	55%	47%	33%

ILLINOIS 12
Southwest – Belleville, East St. Louis, Carbondale

The 12th begins in the St. Louis suburbs along the Mississippi River and extends south along the river to the end of the state, where the Mississippi and Ohio rivers converge near Cairo.

Illinois' worst urban blight isn't in Chicago — it is 300 miles southwest in East St. Louis, where severe white flight and industrial decay nearly bankrupted the city. In the late 1980s, the city cut off most municipal services, including trash collection. Federal and state intervention, coupled with new revenue from casino gambling, restored most city services by the mid-1990s, but residents still face high unemployment and poverty.

Other cities in the 12th also stand on precarious ground. Alton had to bolster its industrial base with riverboat gambling. Residents of Belleville, where nearby Scott Air Force Base is the largest employer, worry about defense cutbacks. Coal mining has almost disappeared from the hilly, southern end of the district with the mechanization of the industry and enactment of the 1990 Clean Air Act. Higher education remains one of

the few steadfast employers: Jackson County's economy is bolstered by Southern Illinois University in Carbondale, which has 21,000 students.

The district's economic anxiety and relatively large minority population (blacks make up 16 percent) make it solid Democratic turf. Rod R. Blagojevich carried nine of the 11 counties wholly or partly in the 12th in his 2002 race for governor, although in 2004 John Kerry carried only four counties. St. Clair County, which includes East St. Louis, is the only Illinois county other than Chicago-based Cook to vote Democratic in the past seven presidential elections. Some corn and hog farmers in western counties lean Republican, but they are too few to sway the district.

MAJOR INDUSTRY
Manufacturing, higher education, gambling, agriculture

MILITARY BASES
Scott Air Force Base, 5,753 military, 5,431 civilian (2004)

CITIES
Belleville, 41,410; East St. Louis, 31,542; Granite City, 31,301; Alton, 30,496; O'Fallon, 21,910; Carbondale, 20,681

NOTABLE
Cahokia Mounds, a prehistoric civilization, was designated by the United Nations as a World Heritage Site in 1982.

Rep. Judy Biggert (R)

Elected 1998; 4th term

CAPITOL OFFICE
225-3515
www.house.gov/biggert
1317 Longworth 20515-1313; fax 225-9420

COMMITTEES
Education & Workforce
Financial Services
Science
  (Energy - chairwoman)
Standards of Official Conduct

HOMETOWN
Hinsdale

BORN
Aug. 15, 1937, Chicago, Ill.

RELIGION
Episcopalian

FAMILY
Husband, Rody Biggert; four children

EDUCATION
Stanford U., A.B. 1959 (international relations);
Northwestern U., J.D. 1963

CAREER
Lawyer

POLITICAL HIGHLIGHTS
Hinsdale Board of Education, 1982-85 (president,
1983-85); Village of Hinsdale Plan Commission,
1989-93; Ill. House, 1993-99

ELECTION RESULTS

2004 GENERAL

Judy Biggert (R)	200,472	65.0%
Gloria Schor Andersen (D)	107,836	35.0%

2004 PRIMARY

Judy Biggert (R)	unopposed

2002 GENERAL

Judy Biggert (R)	139,546	70.3%
Thomas Mason (D)	59,069	29.7%

PREVIOUS WINNING PERCENTAGES
2000 (66%); 1998 (61%)

Now in her fourth term, Biggert has emerged as a major foe of the nation's labor unions, which successfully faced her down in the 108th Congress over her controversial effort to rewrite overtime rules.

Biggert's "flextime" legislation would have allowed employers to give workers compensatory time off instead of premium overtime pay. She argued that this would be especially valuable for women juggling the competing demands of work and family who wanted to be able to spend more time with their children.

But women's groups and unions opposed the bill, saying it could spell the end of the 40-hour workweek, allowing employers to effectively coerce employees to work overtime without additional pay and without the ability to schedule the time off when they wanted it. So many moderate Republicans threatened to join Democrats in voting against the measure that House GOP leaders pulled it off the floor schedule in 2003.

Though she affiliates with GOP moderates in the Tuesday Group and the Republican Main Street Partnership, Biggert has taken a conservative line on many issues. She did not support the 2002 campaign finance law, voted against creation of the independent Sept. 11 commission and supported opening Alaska's Arctic National Wildlife Refuge to oil drilling. She does, however, back efforts to broaden educational opportunities and to protect many abortion rights — though in 2003 she voted in favor of banning a procedure opponents call "partial birth" abortion.

Biggert has been dogged in her work on a number of child-related issues, including schooling for homeless children, helping children who have eating disorders and financing school construction.

She was able to get her measure providing schooling for homeless children included in the education law enacted in 2002. Her portion of the statute authorized $70 million to help ensure that homeless children can be schooled — either in the closest facility or by staying in the school they attended before becoming homeless — without facing delays and red tape in winning admission. Biggert also wrote a second provision, providing more money for training teachers of math and science.

In the 107th Congress, Biggert co-chaired the Congressional Caucus on Women's Issues. When the plight of women and children in Afghanistan received widespread notice, the caucus made them its top priority. Biggert helped to win U.S. education and health care aid to help Afghan women and children cope with the woeful conditions in their war-torn country.

In 1999, Fortune magazine identified Biggert as one of the congressional newcomers most likely to become a star. But she has been unsuccessful trying to prove the prophecy. She first ran for Republican Conference secretary in 2001, reminding her colleagues that she had advanced to the leadership of the Illinois House in just her second term there and that she had been a prolific fundraiser for the National Republican Congressional Committee in 2000. She lost to Barbara Cubin of Wyoming, 123-76.

At the start of the 108th Congress, Biggert made a second and short-lived bid for the secretary's job, dropping out when she concluded Californian John T. Doolittle had the election wrapped up.

Biggert presents herself as a team player. In the 107th, Speaker J. Dennis Hastert asked her to serve on the ethics committee in addition to her three other committees — Financial Services, Education and the Workforce, and Science. It is an unpopular assignment, but Biggert took it on, and in the 109th Congress remained on the panel even as it underwent a significant GOP membership shakeup.

On the Science panel, she chairs the Energy Subcommittee, whose jurisdiction includes the Argonne and Fermi national laboratories. Argonne plays a key role in fuel cell research, and Biggert has sought to ensure this research continues despite President Bush's high-profile support of hydrogen-fueled car engines. In the 108th, she won enactment of legislation to require the Energy Department to build high-end computer labs for academic and government researchers and promote a long-range plan for providing high-performance computers to the broad research community.

Biggert is from a generation when the career choices pursued by women were limited. She recalls that her sister originally said she wanted to be a nurse and considered medical school only when their father, a business executive, told her that girls could be doctors too. Biggert said when she applied to a master's in business degree program, she received a letter from the school informing her that women were not accepted, but that she was welcome to take a few night classes.

She enrolled in law school instead. After clerking for a federal judge, Biggert ran her own home-based law practice — specializing in real estate and estate planning — for 20 years, while raising four children.

She also involved herself in countless community organizations and boards, dealing with such concerns as education, health care and crime.

Her community activities eventually led her to serve on the Hinsdale planning commission and the board of education, including a stint as president of the latter group from 1983 to 1985. Elected to the Illinois House in 1992, she focused on women's and children's issues and was elected assistant Republican leader after just one term in Springfield.

Biggert was the handpicked successor of Republican Harris W. Fawell, who retired in 1998. She defeated five men vying for the GOP nomination and went on to win the seat with 61 percent of the vote.

Biggert pledged to observe a six-year term limit when she first ran for Congress. But soon after arriving in Washington, she retracted the pledge, saying she had not been aware of the powerful seniority system in Congress. In 2004, she passed up entreaties to run for the Senate, even after party leaders were desperate to replace a GOP primary winner who suddenly withdrew. Biggert's solidly Republican 13th District — its tilt was maintained by redistricting — gave her 70 percent of the vote in 2002 and 65 percent in 2004.

KEY VOTES

2004

No   Extend federal unemployment benefits by 13 weeks

Yes   Pass $283.2 billion, six-year federal highway and mass transit bill

Yes   Approve $146 billion multi-year extension of previously enacted middle-class tax breaks

No   Amend the Constitution to prohibit same-sex marriage

Yes   Cut corporate taxes $137 billion over 10 years

Yes   Reorganize U.S. intelligence agencies as proposed by Sept. 11 commission

2003

Yes   Cut taxes by $330 billion through fiscal 2013

No   Block Bush rule scaling back overtime pay for some white-collar federal workers

Yes   Do not allow use of search warrants without first notifying subjects

No   Allow importation of prescription drugs

No   Create private school voucher program in Washington, D.C.

Yes   Ban "partial birth" abortion except to save a woman's life

No   Split $18.6 billion in Iraq aid into half-grant, half-loan

Yes   Overhaul Medicare and create prescription drug benefit

CQ VOTE STUDIES

	PARTY UNITY		PRESIDENTIAL SUPPORT	
	Support	Oppose	Support	Oppose
2004	88%	12%	74%	26%
2003	90%	10%	85%	15%
2002	89%	11%	82%	18%
2001	90%	10%	84%	16%
2000	82%	18%	43%	57%

INTEREST GROUPS

	AFL-CIO	ADA	CCUS	ACU
2004	13%	35%	100%	64%
2003	13%	10%	100%	60%
2002	11%	15%	100%	84%
2001	17%	20%	100%	56%
2000	0%	20%	100%	68%

ILLINOIS 13
Southwest Chicago suburbs – Naperville

More than half of the suburban Chicago-based 13th's population lives in the southern part of booming DuPage County. The district's most populous city is Naperville, which has tripled its population since 1980. Sprawling subdivisions and a newly refurbished downtown characterize this fairly young suburb.

Argonne National Laboratory, in southeast DuPage, and Fermi National Accelerator Laboratory, just over the border in the 14th District, have made the area a scientific research hub and provide a prime source of jobs for district residents.

Naperville and Oak Brook have become leading business centers outside Chicago and are home to a growing number of corporate headquarters. Oak Brook, home to headquarters for McDonald's, is about 10 miles south of O'Hare International Airport and sits near the nexus of Interstates 88, 294 and 290, which has abetted its development. These cities increasingly draw in commuters, creating serious traffic problems in suburban communities.

Nearly one-third of the population lives in northern Will County communities such as Bolingbrook and Romeoville. The rest live in the southwestern corner of Cook. Redistricting following the 2000 census required the 13th, Illinois' fastest-growing district in the 1990s, to shed more than 100,000 people (mostly to the 1st and 11th districts).

Voters in the 13th tend to be white-collar executive types, loyal to free enterprise. It is a reliably Republican district that backed George W. Bush with 55 percent of the vote in both the 2000 and 2004 presidential elections. Many residents, however, hold moderate views on family and women's issues (such as equal pay and child care) and environmental protection.

MAJOR INDUSTRY
Scientific research, health care, insurance

CITIES
Naperville, 128,358; Bolingbrook, 56,321; Downers Grove (pt.), 45,139; Aurora (pt.), 40,846; Woodridge, 30,934; Orland Park (pt.), 23,729

NOTABLE
Hamburger University, McDonald's management training center, is located in Oak Brook.

Rep. J. Dennis Hastert (R)

Elected 1986; 10th term

CAPITOL OFFICE
225-2976
www.house.gov/hastert
235 Cannon 20515-1314; fax 225-0697

COMMITTEES
Speaker of the House — no committee
assignments

HOMETOWN
Plano

BORN
Jan. 2, 1942, Aurora, Ill.

RELIGION
Methodist

FAMILY
Wife, Jean Hastert; two children

EDUCATION
Wheaton College (Ill.), A.B. 1964 (economics);
Northern Illinois U., M.A. 1967 (education)

CAREER
Teacher; restaurateur

POLITICAL HIGHLIGHTS
Ill. House, 1981-86

ELECTION RESULTS

2004 GENERAL

J. Dennis Hastert (R)	191,618	68.6%
Ruben K. Zamora (D)	87,590	31.4%

2004 PRIMARY

J. Dennis Hastert (R)	unopposed

2002 GENERAL

J. Dennis Hastert (R)	135,198	74.1%
Laurence J. Quick (D)	47,165	25.9%

PREVIOUS WINNING PERCENTAGES
2000 (74%); 1998 (70%); 1996 (64%); 1994 (76%);
1992 (67%); 1990 (67%); 1988 (74%); 1986 (52%)

In six years as Speaker of the House, Hastert has transformed himself from the affable "Denny," the popular and low-key former high school wrestling coach, into an increasingly hard-edged partisan who goes to extraordinary lengths to prevail on votes. His style suits the Bush administration, which relies on Hastert to push its conservative legislation in the House to balance the compromises it has to make in the Senate.

After the 2004 election, Republicans had their biggest majority in the House since 1995, the Senate had a larger and more conservative GOP majority, and President Bush had just been elected to a second term. The combination gave Hastert more breathing room than he has had since he became Speaker in 1999. And it looked as though he was going to need every inch.

The president was counting on him to shepherd through the House a major restructuring of Social Security that was a hard sell with the public. Even some Republicans balked at Bush's idea of introducing private savings accounts into the government-run retirement program.

At the same time, Hastert was trying, without much early success, to keep his troops focused on legislation amid an unseemly debate on the ethical behavior of his No. 2 man in the leadership, Majority Leader Tom DeLay. Hastert himself fueled the controversy when he stepped in and summarily ejected three Republican members of the House ethics committee, a shake-up widely viewed as punishment for their votes to publicly admonish DeLay in 2004 for, among other infractions, trying to bargain for a Republican congressman's vote for a Medicare prescription drug benefit. The legislation was a top priority for both the president and Hastert.

Hastert appointed loyalists to the panel, installed one of his allies as chairman, and persuaded Republicans to approve new ethics rules helpful to DeLay. Democrats on the usually bipartisan committee boycotted, and the panel came to a standstill until Republicans agreed to restore the old rules. It was not Hastert's finest hour. At private meetings, GOP lawmakers complained that constituents took a dim view of the ethics imbroglio.

Two of Hastert's actions on legislation stand out above others in recent years. During an extraordinary all-night session of the House in 2003, he held open the roll call vote on the prescription drug bill until he had the votes to pass it. The next year, he delayed a vote on an overhaul of the intelligence community until he could get a majority of Republicans to back it, even though the bill could have passed with the help of Democratic votes.

In the first instance, Hastert held open the vote for three hours while he cajoled, lobbied and pleaded with conservative Republicans who opposed the bill because it was a major expansion of a government program. Just before dawn, he got the final votes he needed and the bill passed.

Democrats accused him of cheating, but Hastert insisted the normal 15-minute span for a vote was a minimum under House rules, not a maximum. His interest in the Medicare bill ran deep — Hastert had made health care a signature issue from his first days in the House. He said that he'd worked so many years on overhauling Medicare that "I don't think that waiting an additional three hours to get it done is too much."

With the intelligence bill, Hastert declined to schedule a House vote on the final version in November 2004 after two committee chairmen refused to support the proposed compromise. The bill would have passed with Democratic votes, but Hastert refused to force Republicans to vote on a measure that the majority of them did not endorse. Behind the scenes, however, he and chief of staff Scott Palmer worked hard to move the negotiations along, helping to sell compromises to wary House members. Later, Congress approved the legislation overwhelmingly.

A former coach and high school civics teacher, Hastert has a regular-guy manner that puts the troops at ease. His 2004 autobiography is full of awestruck references to his rise to the job third in line to the presidency. In a 2003 speech, Hastert listed the principles that guide his decisions. He said he tries to be a good listener, to keep his word, to let committees write their own legislation, and to rule fairly — but not against the will of the majority. His motto is: "Please the majority of the majority." He said he puts all of his energy into running the House.

Hastert's close working relationship with DeLay dates to 1995, when Republicans became the majority party in the House. Newt Gingrich of Georgia became Speaker and DeLay was elected whip, though Gingrich didn't particularly care for DeLay and wanted one of his allies for the job. Hastert ran DeLay's successful upset campaign for whip, and DeLay in turn made Hastert his chief deputy, an appointed post.

In 1998, Gingrich resigned the speakership after he lost the confidence of most House Republicans. Although the party had many promising young leaders, there was no ready replacement. Robert L. Livingston, the influential Appropriations Committee chairman, withdrew after admitting to an extramarital affair. Other potential candidates, notably DeLay and Majority Leader Dick Armey of Texas, were more seasoned than Hastert, but their standing among Republicans was diminished by an earlier, secret attempt to oust Gingrich and grab power for themselves. Hastert emerged as the consensus choice — and DeLay helped him round up the votes to win.

Hastert was elected to the post after just a dozen years in the House, the fastest rise for a Speaker since 1891, when Charles Crisp of Georgia got the job after eight years in Congress. In December 2000, his staff quietly prepared him to step in as acting president if the electoral standoff between George W. Bush and Al Gore was not resolved by inauguration day.

Hastert was a high school social studies teacher and wrestling coach for 16 years before being appointed in 1981 to the state legislature to fill a vacancy. He served in the Illinois General Assembly for six years. When GOP Rep. John E. Grotberg retired from the U.S. House because of illness in 1986, Hastert was elected to succeed him with 52 percent of the vote. He has drawn at least two-thirds of the vote in all but one election since.

KEY VOTES

2004

No   Extend federal unemployment benefits by 13 weeks

S   Pass $283.2 billion, six-year federal highway and mass transit bill

Yes   Approve $146 billion multi-year extension of previously enacted middle-class tax breaks

Yes   Amend the Constitution to prohibit same-sex marriage

Yes   Cut corporate taxes $137 billion over 10 years

Yes   Reorganize U.S. intelligence agencies as proposed by Sept. 11 commission

2003

Yes   Cut taxes by $330 billion through fiscal 2013

No   Block Bush rule scaling back overtime pay for some white-collar federal workers

S   Do not allow use of search warrants without first notifying subjects

No   Allow importation of prescription drugs

S   Create private school voucher program in Washington, D.C.

Yes   Ban "partial birth" abortion except to save a woman's life

No   Split $18.6 billion in Iraq aid into half-grant, half-loan

Yes   Overhaul Medicare and create prescription drug benefit

CQ VOTE STUDIES

	PARTY UNITY		PRESIDENTIAL SUPPORT	
	Support	Oppose	Support	Oppose
2004	100%	0%	100%	0%
2003	100%	0%	100%	0%
2002	100%	0%	100%	0%
2001	100%	0%	100%	0%
2000	100%	0%	28%	72%

INTEREST GROUPS

	AFL-CIO	ADA	CCUS	ACU
2004	0%	0%	100%	100%
2003	0%	0%	100%	75%
2002	0%	—	100%	8%
2001	0%	0%	100%	100%
2000	0%	0%	81%	100%

I L L I N O I S   1 4
North Central — Aurora, Elgin, DeKalb

Most people in the 14th live on the district's eastern side, in established towns along the Fox River valley. West of the river, prairies and farms stretch to the district's end in Henry County, nearly to the Mississippi River. Rich in hay, soybeans and corn, the flat landscape is interrupted only by Northern Illinois University in DeKalb.

The district's population center is Kane County, a fast-growing area on the outskirts of metropolitan Chicago. The district's largest cities, Aurora and Elgin, suffered a period of heavy manufacturing decline in the 1980s but have recovered by promoting industrial parks and opening riverboat casinos. One of Aurora's major employers is the heavy-equipment manufacturer Caterpillar. The cities also have benefited from job growth in nearby Naperville and Schaumburg, suburban cities that have emerged as business centers outside Chicago.

Both Elgin and Aurora are about one-third Hispanic, a vestige of the days when DuPage County farms were cultivated by migrant labor. Those farms have now been paved over and built upon, but many of the migrant

workers remained in the area. Only three other Illinois districts — the Chicago-area 3rd, 4th and 5th — have a greater Hispanic population than the 14th, which is almost one-fifth Hispanic.

While the minority influence tends to help Democrats, the 14th overall has a strong Republican tilt, due mostly to the GOP leanings of Kane County, Kendall County (which includes Speaker Hastert's hometown area of Plano and Yorkville), and northwestern DuPage County. GOP-friendly suburban and rural voters far outnumber the cities' blue-collar and minority Democrats. As a result, George W. Bush carried the district by 12 percentage points in the 2000 presidential election and by 11 points in 2004.

MAJOR INDUSTRY

Farm machinery and other manufacturing, riverboat gambling, agriculture

CITIES

Aurora (pt.), 102,144; Elgin (pt.), 74,013; DeKalb, 39,018; Carpentersville, 30,586; St. Charles, 27,896; Batavia, 23,866

NOTABLE

Former President Ronald Reagan's birthplace in Tampico and boyhood home in Dixon are operated as local museums.

Rep. Timothy V. Johnson (R)

Elected 2000; 3rd term

CAPITOL OFFICE
225-2371
www.house.gov/timjohnson
1229 Longworth 20515-1315; fax 226-0791

COMMITTEES
Agriculture
Science
Transportation & Infrastructure

HOMETOWN
Urbana

BORN
July 23, 1946, Champaign, Ill.

RELIGION
Assemblies of God

FAMILY
Divorced; nine children

EDUCATION
U.S. Military Academy, attended 1964; U. of Illinois, B.A. 1969, J.D. 1972

CAREER
Lawyer; realtor

POLITICAL HIGHLIGHTS
Urbana City Council, 1971-75; Ill. House, 1977-2000

ELECTION RESULTS

2004 GENERAL

Timothy V. Johnson (R)	178,114	61.1%
David Gill (D)	113,625	39.0%

2004 PRIMARY

Timothy V. Johnson (R)	unopposed

2002 GENERAL

Timothy V. Johnson (R)	134,650	65.2%
Joshua T. Hartke (D)	64,131	31.0%
Carl Estabrook (GREEN)	7,836	3.8%

PREVIOUS WINNING PERCENTAGES
2000 (53%)

Johnson is frequently out of step with the conservatives that dominate his party. In the 108th Congress, he was the sixth-least-loyal Republican when it came to votes on issues that divided the two parties. And he opposed President Bush more often than all but six of his GOP colleagues, voting in agreement with the president only 62 percent of the time in 2004. He is a member of the Main Street Partnership, a group of moderate and pro-business Republicans.

Many of his oppositional positions are on environmental matters. Johnson is a leader in the effort to ban MTBE, a gasoline additive blamed for polluting groundwater. He has voted against drilling for oil in Alaska's Arctic National Wildlife Refuge and for the protection of national park and offshore areas from drilling. He was one of only 11 Republicans to win an endorsement from the Sierra Club in 2004.

Johnson wants more use of two MTBE rivals: ethanol, which is made from corn, and biodiesel, which is derived from soybeans. Both plants are grown in abundance in the 15th District. Johnson also works to increase funding for Agriculture Department export promotion activities; nearly half of the corn, soybeans and other grains grown in Illinois are exported.

Johnson in the 108th Congress also split from most in his party on votes to restructure the Head Start program, permit the Labor Department to modify overtime pay rules, authorize additional unemployment benefits, and prevent library and bookseller records of suspected terrorists from being turned over to the Justice Department.

But Johnson agrees with the majority of Republicans on social issues. He is opposed to abortion and gun control. He does, however, support stem cell research in certain circumstances. Johnson's father had diabetes, and his grandfather suffered from Parkinson's disease. He voted in 2004 for a constitutional amendment to ban same-sex marriage.

His willingness to join with Democrats on certain votes demonstrates his interest in building comity between the parties. He bemoans the rancorous atmosphere in the House, telling the Bloomington Pantagraph in late 2004 that the lack of civility is "offensive to me." He said: "Both sides are guilty. I'd like to see more pressure from the press and the public to stop it."

At the beginning of the 109th, Johnson and New York Democrat Steve Israel announced they were forming a "Center Aisle Caucus," which would encourage members to respect other points of view and rebuke lawmakers who take an uncivil tone.

Agriculture policy is Johnson's leading interest, since crops and food processing are the economic lifeblood for thousands of his constituents. He landed a seat on the Agriculture Committee in his first term. He also sits on the Science and Transportation committees.

Johnson spends a good part of his day in the House gym, swimming laps or pounding out the miles on a treadmill or stationary bike while catching up on his reading or making some of the dozens of phone calls he makes to constituents every day.

He says he hopes his self-discipline in taking care of his body can serve as an example for others in an era when Americans' lifestyles are often blamed for illness, premature death and diminished productivity. Johnson's multitasking while on the treadmill is a perfect illustration of his organized daily routine as well as his self-described compulsion to make phone calls, sometimes several hundred a day.

Johnson also has what he admits are "very, very eccentric eating habits." He skips breakfast and lunch and survives on a diet of fruit, rice cakes, granola, vitamin supplements, fresh squeezed juice and a kind of farmer's cheese. "I eat the same thing every single meal of my life," he told Illinois Magazine. His thin physique evokes an occasional observation that he resembles another central Illinois politician — Abraham Lincoln. The resemblance was perhaps more striking when Johnson had a beard. He shaved it off in late 2001.

Johnson grew up in a political family. His mother and her parents were active in McLean County GOP politics. His father, though originally a Democrat, switched parties and served on the Urbana City Council. Johnson says he began passing out campaign literature when he was 3 or 4 years old.

He became a GOP precinct committeeman at age 21, while he was still in college. By 24, he was on the Urbana City Council, and at 30, he was elected to the Illinois House, where he stayed for 24 years. Outside the legislature, Johnson worked in real estate and founded a law practice.

During his long tenure in Springfield, Johnson worked to toughen penalties for drunken driving and sex offenses. He briefly considered running for Congress in 1992 against Republican Thomas W. Ewing, then just a freshman. By 2000, Johnson was looking for something new, and he leapt into the 15th District race when Ewing announced his retirement.

Known as an indefatigable campaigner who is now undefeated in 16 general elections, Johnson was the first candidate to jump into the race. But the GOP primary field grew to four, and three of the most influential Illinois Republicans backed different candidates. Gov. George Ryan endorsed Johnson, Speaker J. Dennis Hastert backed state Rep. Bill Brady, and incumbent Ewing supported his son, Sam. Running on high name recognition and ample personal funds, Johnson won the contest with 44 percent of the vote.

The 15th leans Republican and Johnson entered the fall race as a strong favorite. But he faced a tougher-than-expected battle with his Democratic foe, university instructor Mike Kelleher, a first-time candidate and former Capitol Hill aide. Johnson prevailed, though with a modest 53 percent.

Redistricting before the 2002 election put Democratic Rep. David Phelps' home in the 15th District, but Phelps elected to run against Republican John Shimkus in the 19th instead. When Kelleher declined to run again, Johnson cruised to a 2-to-1 victory over political novice Joshua T. Hartke. In 2004, Johnson enjoyed a 22 percentage point victory.

He had promised to limit himself to three terms, but right before the 2002 election he revoked that pledge.

KEY VOTES

2004

Yes Extend federal unemployment benefits by 13 weeks

Yes Pass $283.2 billion, six-year federal highway and mass transit bill

Yes Approve $146 billion multi-year extension of previously enacted middle-class tax breaks

Yes Amend the Constitution to prohibit same-sex marriage

Yes Cut corporate taxes $137 billion over 10 years

Yes Reorganize U.S. intelligence agencies as proposed by Sept. 11 commission

2003

Yes Cut taxes by $330 billion through fiscal 2013

Yes Block Bush rule scaling back overtime pay for some white-collar federal workers

Yes Do not allow use of search warrants without first notifying subjects

No Allow importation of prescription drugs

No Create private school voucher program in Washington, D.C.

Yes Ban "partial birth" abortion except to save a woman's life

No Split $18.6 billion in Iraq aid into half-grant, half-loan

Yes Overhaul Medicare and create prescription drug benefit

CQ VOTE STUDIES

	PARTY UNITY		PRESIDENTIAL SUPPORT	
	Support	Oppose	Support	Oppose
2004	77%	23%	62%	38%
2003	82%	18%	74%	26%
2002	85%	15%	80%	20%
2001	85%	15%	74%	26%

INTEREST GROUPS

	AFL-CIO	ADA	CCUS	ACU
2004	60%	40%	86%	64%
2003	47%	30%	79%	60%
2002	11%	15%	85%	76%
2001	33%	15%	74%	68%

ILLINOIS 15
East central — Champaign, Bloomington, Danville

Agriculture is the dominant industry in the 15th, which takes in all or part of 22 counties. Corn and soybean fields cover much of this area, and the crop yields are the state's highest in the counties south of Champaign, the district's main population center. Farmers produce feed and raw material for food products manufactured just over the border at Decatur-based Archer Daniels Midland Co. in the 17th District.

Scattered amid the farms are several midsize towns, including Danville, that are centered around agribusiness and manufacturing. Higher education is big business in this district, with 39,000 students at the University of Illinois flagship campus in Urbana-Champaign. Bloomington-Normal has Illinois State and Illinois Wesleyan universities, which are just outside the district in the 11th. Bloomington, home to State Farm Insurance, leads downstate Illinois in insurance and finance.

Redistricting following the 2000 census altered the 15th's boundaries after slow growth in downstate Illinois cost the state one seat in reapportionment. Mapmakers dismantled the southeastern 19th District,

and the remnants that were attached to the 15th form a long, narrow appendage that hugs the Indiana border. North to south, the 15th runs for more than 250 miles.

The district has a solid GOP lean, and Republicans typically run strongest in counties north of Champaign, including Iroquois and Ford. Both counties gave George W. Bush in his two presidential runs, as well as 2002 gubernatorial nominee Jim Ryan, at least 60 percent of the vote, although both men lost the state each time. Champaign County's academic community helps keep Democrats competitive, and Champaign was the only county east of Decatur and south of Chicago that Bush lost in Illinois in 2004, although by a slim margin. As a result, Bush won the 15th with 58 percent of the vote in 2004.

MAJOR INDUSTRY
Agriculture, higher education, food processing

CITIES
Champaign, 67,518; Urbana, 36,395; Bloomington (pt.), 34,510; Danville, 33,904; Charleston, 21,039; Mattoon, 18,291

NOTABLE
The Lincoln Log Cabin State Historic Site in Coles County preserves the last home of Abraham Lincoln's father and stepmother.

Rep. Donald Manzullo (R)

Elected 1992; 7th term

CAPITOL OFFICE
225-5676
www.house.gov/manzullo
2228 Rayburn 20515-1316; fax 225-5284

COMMITTEES
Financial Services
Small Business - chairman

HOMETOWN
Egan

BORN
March 24, 1944, Rockford, Ill.

RELIGION
Baptist

FAMILY
Wife, Freda Manzullo; three children

EDUCATION
American U., B.A. 1967 (political science);
Marquette U., J.D. 1970

CAREER
Lawyer

POLITICAL HIGHLIGHTS
Sought Republican nomination for U.S. House,
1990

ELECTION RESULTS

2004 GENERAL

Donald Manzullo (R)	204,350	69.1%
John Kutsch (D)	91,452	30.9%

2004 PRIMARY

Donald Manzullo (R)	unopposed

2002 GENERAL

Donald Manzullo (R)	133,339	70.6%
John Kutsch (D)	55,488	29.4%

PREVIOUS WINNING PERCENTAGES
2000 (67%); 1998 (100%); 1996 (60%); 1994 (71%);
1992 (56%)

After more than a decade in the House, Manzullo seems ready to toss off backbencher status. A champion of small businesses and manufacturers, he has made a series of brazen moves that changed the course of legislative affairs. Manzullo is sometimes dismissed as a loose canon, and the committee he chairs — Small Business — is often overlooked. But from that perch, Manzullo has managed to make a lot of noise lately.

In 2003 and 2004, Manzullo helped lead a rare GOP rebellion against Republican Ways and Means Chairman Bill Thomas of California, forcing the powerful chairman to rewrite his corporate tax bill to include a generous tax break for manufacturers and small businesses that Manzullo wanted. In 2002, Manzullo subpoenaed the head of the Centers for Medicare and Medicaid, Thomas A. Scully, when he refused to testify before his panel. The two fights solidified Manzullo's reputation as a maverick willing to buck his party and the president on initiatives he regards as threats to small business.

His deeply felt views on protecting entrepreneurs date to his boyhood, when his family lived in a one-room apartment above their struggling grocery store in Rockford. Manzullo's father extended store credit to new arrivals from displaced persons camps in Europe, Manzullo recalls, and was a "one-man social services agency," who helped families insulate their homes with cardboard and organized community boxing tournaments.

Over the years, he watched the once vibrant city of the industrial heartland disintegrate as machine tool, automobile parts and tire plants closed their doors. Manufacturing job losses have pushed the unemployment rate to 11 percent, one of the highest in the nation. Manzullo feels that his job is to try to reverse that tide.

In the corporate tax fight of the 108th Congress, Manzullo succeeded by hiring an savvy tax aide, Jim Clark, who had worked under Thomas and served as GOP tax counsel on the Ways and Means Committee for years. With the blessing of Speaker J. Dennis Hastert, who also wanted to protect manufacturing interests in the state, Manzullo forged an alliance with Democrats and rounded up GOP lawmakers to deny Thomas a majority.

At one point, Thomas had made enough compromises to satisfy Hastert, but not Manzullo, and Thomas reluctantly dispatched an emissary to placate him. In the end, the bill included $77 billion in tax breaks for manufacturers and a package of tax breaks for small businesses, both of which Manzullo had wanted, and a scaled-back version of the tax breaks for multinationals that Thomas favored.

As Small Business chairman, Manzullo made a splash by confronting Scully, the medicare and medicaid chief, in a rare public standoff between a House Republican and the Bush administration. When Scully refused to testify in 2002 on the same panel with medical industry witnesses who'd been critical of his agency, Manzullo subpoenaed him. When Scully then defied the subpoena, the chairman threatened a contempt of Congress citation. Scully relented and apologized to the committee.

In 2005, Manzullo objected to IBM's proposed sale of its personal computing subsidiary to a Chinese company. The same year, he canceled a Small Business Committee meeting rather than let Democrats get the upper hand and force Republicans to take difficult votes.

Trade is another issue Manzullo jumps into with zeal. He believes that the way to help small firms survive competition against big companies and foreign rivals is to give them access to government contracts and foreign markets, while reducing regulation.

Manzullo is a strong backer of the Export-Import Bank and the Overseas Private Investment Corporation, two government agencies that assist businesses in expanding exports and are sometimes criticized as "corporate welfare." Manzullo argues that they are an essential counterbalance to foreign governments that invest much more heavily than the United States in helping their businesses increase exports.

He has championed a bill he calls "America's Jobs First," which encourages procurement officers and purchasing agents to buy supplies from American companies. And Manzullo was a sharp critic of Bush's 2002 steel tariffs, which raised costs for users of steel in his district. He lobbied the administration to pressure China to end the low fixed exchange rate for its currency, the yuan, which makes Chinese goods less expensive in the United States and U.S. goods more expensive in China.

Manzullo supports his party over 90 percent of the time on major votes in the House. But he has defied GOP leaders on a few notable occasions, including casting a no vote in 2002 on an early version of a Medicare prescription drug benefit. He said it would hurt independent pharmacists.

A member of the Republican Study Committee, a conservative group that boasts 100 members, Manzullo is among the House's most conservative members, particularly on social issues.

Early in his career, he helped start crisis pregnancy centers in Rockford and picketed clinics that performed abortions. His wife, Freda Manzullo, a microbiologist, taught the couple's three children at home until the eighth grade, when they went to a small Christian high school in suburban Virginia. Manzullo says that it was the best way to keep everyone together given his hectic work schedule. When Congress is in recess, the family heads for their small beef cattle farm in Illinois.

Manzullo recalls deciding, at age 4, that he wanted to be a lawyer. At age 10, he decided he wanted to be in Congress. He spent 20 years as a small-town lawyer handling family cases. When Republican Rep. Lynn Martin decided to try for the Senate in 1990, Manzullo ran for her seat, campaigned door-to-door, and got a respectable 46 percent of the vote in the GOP primary. Democrat John W. Cox, Jr. won that fall in the general election.

In 1992, Manzullo tried again, winning the GOP primary with 56 percent of the vote. In November, the district reverted to its traditional GOP form; Manzullo ejected Cox by 12 percentage points. He has not been seriously challenged since.

KEY VOTES

2004

No Extend federal unemployment benefits by 13 weeks
Yes Pass $283.2 billion, six-year federal highway and mass transit bill
Yes Approve $146 billion multi-year extension of previously enacted middle-class tax breaks
Yes Amend the Constitution to prohibit same-sex marriage
Yes Cut corporate taxes $137 billion over 10 years
No Reorganize U.S. intelligence agencies as proposed by Sept. 11 commission

2003

Yes Cut taxes by $330 billion through fiscal 2013
No Block Bush rule scaling back overtime pay for some white-collar federal workers
Yes Do not allow use of search warrants without first notifying subjects
Yes Allow importation of prescription drugs
Yes Create private school voucher program in Washington, D.C.
Yes Ban "partial birth" abortion except to save a woman's life
No Split $18.6 billion in Iraq aid into half-grant, half-loan
Yes Overhaul Medicare and create prescription drug benefit

CQ VOTE STUDIES

	PARTY UNITY		PRESIDENTIAL SUPPORT	
	Support	Oppose	Support	Oppose
2004	93%	7%	84%	16%
2003	95%	5%	95%	5%
2002	95%	5%	82%	18%
2001	94%	6%	77%	23%
2000	95%	5%	22%	78%

INTEREST GROUPS

	AFL-CIO	ADA	CCUS	ACU
2004	14%	5%	100%	100%
2003	13%	10%	97%	88%
2002	13%	5%	95%	100%
2001	17%	0%	96%	92%
2000	0%	5%	90%	95%

ILLINOIS 16
North — Rockford, part of McHenry County

The 16th spans most of the Illinois-Wisconsin border, taking in Rockford and covering the rolling northern prairie where family farmers grow corn and raise dairy cows.

At its eastern end, the district includes most of McHenry County, the fastest-growing county in Illinois during the 1990s at 42 percent. Located at the edge of Chicago's flourishing northwest counties, McHenry is quickly filling up with new suburban bedroom communities. Solidly GOP, the county voted for George W. Bush by 20 percentage points in the 2004 presidential election. To the west is Boone County, which also is fast-growing and Republican-leaning.

About one-fourth of the district's voters live in Rockford (Winnebago County), an industrial hub and the state's second-largest city. Once the self-styled tool and die capital of the world, in the 1980s it became a poster child of Rust Belt decline, with unemployment often exceeding 20 percent. The city recovered by upgrading to technology manufacturing and expanding its exports to China, Mexico and Canada.

Other counties in the 16th are among Illinois' leading dairy producers. Jo Daviess County, in the northwest corner, is a state leader in raising beef cattle and producing hay. Galena, in rolling hills near the Mississippi River, has a tourist-based economy.

Redistricting following the 2000 census made the 16th somewhat more rural by shedding part of McHenry to the 8th District and adding parts of the counties to the southwest.

More than 90 percent of the district's black residents live in Rockford, giving the city a base of loyal Democrats. But the 16th covers mostly conservative, Republican territory. Only once in the 20th century did district voters elect a Democrat to the House.

MAJOR INDUSTRY
Manufacturing, aircraft and machine parts, agriculture, trade

CITIES
Rockford,150,115; Crystal Lake (pt.), 37,740; Freeport, 26,443; Lake in the Hills, 23,152; Belvidere, 20,820; Machesney Park, 20,759

NOTABLE
The Ulysses S. Grant Home is in Galena; Rockford is known as the world's largest producer of fasteners.

Rep. Lane Evans (D)

CAPITOL OFFICE
225-5905
lane.evans@mail.house.gov
www.house.gov/evans
2211 Rayburn 20515-1317; fax 225-5396

COMMITTEES
Armed Services
Veterans' Affairs - ranking member

HOMETOWN
Rock Island

BORN
Aug. 4, 1951, Rock Island, Ill.

RELIGION
Roman Catholic

FAMILY
Single

EDUCATION
Augustana College (Ill.), B.A. 1974 (political science); Georgetown U., J.D. 1978

MILITARY SERVICE
Marine Corps, 1969-71

CAREER
Lawyer

POLITICAL HIGHLIGHTS
No previous office

ELECTION RESULTS

2004 GENERAL

Lane Evans (D)	172,320	60.7%
Andrea Lane Zinga (R)	111,680	39.3%

2004 PRIMARY

Lane Evans (D)	unopposed

2002 GENERAL

Lane Evans (D)	127,093	62.4%
Peter Calderone (R)	76,519	37.6%

PREVIOUS WINNING PERCENTAGES
2000 (55%); 1998 (52%); 1996 (52%); 1994 (55%); 1992 (60%); 1990 (67%); 1988 (65%); 1986 (56%); 1984 (57%); 1982 (53%)

Elected 1982; 12th term

Almost a quarter-century ago, when "Reaganomics" was a dirty word and the 1982 recession had many Republican candidates on the run, a feisty young Evans urged the 17th District's struggling farmers and factory workers to "send Reagan a message," and that they did, switching the district from Republican to Democratic hands.

Evans has kept it there all these years, weathering some tough re-election battles in the 1990s, campaigns made even more challenging by the Parkinson's disease he has grappled with since 1995. But Evans has fought through the adversity, and got a big break in the last round of redistricting, which pushed the 17th more solidly into the Democratic column.

Evans points to his parents — his father was a firefighter, his mother a nurse — as the inspiration for his political views, saying, "They saved people's lives. I fight for ordinary people and I identify with ordinary people." Before coming to Congress, he was a legal services lawyer and a counsel for the NAACP and ACLU; he supported Edward M. Kennedy's primary challenge against President Carter for the 1980 presidential nomination. Evans has been an outspoken economic populist in Congress, reliably earning 100 percent ratings from the AFL-CIO.

In 1998, Evans revealed that he had been suffering from Parkinson's disease for three years, prompting questions about his ability to keep up with the rigorous House schedule. But Evans says his condition has stabilized enough to allow him to continue his work. In fact, the regular jogger argues that his illness "has made me an even better congressman. I understand the difficulties people face every day."

The centerpiece of Evans' legislative career has been his work on veterans' programs. As the top-ranking Democrat on the Veterans' Affairs Committee since 1997, Evans has worked tirelessly to beef up benefits for others who have served in uniform. Veterans' matters traditionally have been less partisan than other issues in Congress, and Evans has generally worked well with panel Republicans, including Christopher H. Smith of New Jersey, who chaired the committee in the 107th and 108th Congresses.

When the House passed legislation in November 2004 expanding a range of veterans' benefits, Evans praised Smith, saying, "Every time we try to do something good, his name is always in the forefront of the action." Unfortunately for Smith, he was not so warmly regarded by his own party's leaders, who came to see him as more attuned to his veterans' constituency than to the struggle to rein in the deficit. They ousted Smith from the chair for the 109th, giving the gavel to Steve Buyer of Indiana.

Even during Smith's tenure leading the committee, Evans did not hesitate to criticize Republicans when he believed they were holding back on benefits needed by veterans. He fumed in late 2004 when legislation funding veterans' programs was stalled and GOP talk of the need for belt-tightening was in the air. Though the veterans' legislation later passed, he still had no kind words for the White House. "It is unfortunate that these critical measures were held up for so long," said Evans, "especially when we have service members coming home from Iraq and Afghanistan in need of health care and transition benefits. It's another example of how this administration simply does not understand that the costs of war include the continued care of our veterans and military families."

Evans was a Marine from 1969 to 1971, although he was not assigned to Vietnam. Early in his House career, he emerged as a leading proponent of federal programs benefiting Vietnam veterans, at a time when the older leaders of Veterans' Affairs were still focused mostly on the concerns of those who fought in World War II and Korea. Evans was a crusader for veterans suffering from diseases linked to Agent Orange, a defoliant used during the Vietnam War. His four-year effort to gain medical compensation for these veterans paid off when his bill was enacted in the 102nd Congress.

In 1992, Evans sought to buck the seniority system and take the gavel of the Veterans' panel, after years of locking horns with Chairman G.V. "Sonny" Montgomery of Mississippi. Younger veterans perceived Montgomery as dragging his feet on compensation for Agent Orange-related diseases. In a secret ballot of House Democrats, Evans fell four votes short in his bid to oust Montgomery, who had held the gavel for a dozen years.

Evans also serves on the Armed Services Committee, and he has joined with Vermont's Democratic Sen. Patrick J. Leahy to mobilize U.S. government support for an international agreement to ban the use of land mines.

The impact of Evans' struggle with Parkinson's is evident in his stand on controversial social issues, such as President Bush's decision in 2001 to fund research only on stem cells already extracted from human embryos — an endorsement of limited research that pleased neither the scientific community nor abortion foes. While opponents of legal abortion wanted an outright ban on such research, Evans said it held out hope for curing his and other crippling conditions. "I know many people feel strongly about the right to life. But for me, there's also a right to live," he said.

In 1982, Evans emerged from his community legal clinic in Rock Island to make his first run for public office. It was an effort that seemed futile until the March Republican primary, when former state Sen. Kenneth G. McMillan, a New Right stalwart, defeated moderate eight-term Rep. Tom Railsback. That set up a clear ideological choice in November, one that benefited Evans in the recession year. With his "send Reagan a message" theme, Evans won with 53 percent of the vote.

From 1994 to 2000, Evans was one of the more endangered House incumbents. A combination of hard work, an engaging manner, prodigious fundraising, and an active constituent service effort enabled him to hold onto the seat. After the 2000 census, the Illinois General Assembly — required to wipe away one House seat because of reapportionment — remade the district, moving out many of the rural areas and small towns where Evans had struggled and replacing them with Democratic-leaning urban neighborhoods.

In his last two re-election contests, Evans has topped 60 percent.

KEY VOTES

2004
Yes Extend federal unemployment benefits by 13 weeks
Yes Pass $283.2 billion, six-year federal highway and mass transit bill
Yes Approve $146 billion multi-year extension of previously enacted middle-class tax breaks
No   Amend the Constitution to prohibit same-sex marriage
No   Cut corporate taxes $137 billion over 10 years
Yes Reorganize U.S. intelligence agencies as proposed by Sept. 11 commission

2003
No   Cut taxes by $330 billion through fiscal 2013
Yes Block Bush rule scaling back overtime pay for some white-collar federal workers
Yes Do not allow use of search warrants without first notifying subjects
Yes Allow importation of prescription drugs
No   Create private school voucher program in Washington, D.C.
?   Ban "partial birth" abortion except to save a woman's life
Yes Split $18.6 billion in Iraq aid into half-grant, half-loan
No   Overhaul Medicare and create prescription drug benefit

CQ VOTE STUDIES

	PARTY UNITY		PRESIDENTIAL SUPPORT	
	Support	Oppose	Support	Oppose
2004	97%	3%	21%	79%
2003	96%	4%	15%	85%
2002	97%	3%	24%	76%
2001	93%	7%	26%	74%
2000	94%	6%	76%	24%

INTEREST GROUPS

	AFL-CIO	ADA	CCUS	ACU
2004	100%	95%	38%	4%
2003	100%	95%	30%	8%
2002	100%	100%	40%	0%
2001	100%	100%	27%	0%
2000	100%	95%	38%	8%

ILLINOIS 17

West — Moline, Rock Island; parts of Decatur and Springfield

The 17th is a vivid demonstration of the extremes Illinois mapmakers went to following the 2000 census to draw safe districts for incumbent House members. In the 1990s, the 17th was a relatively compact district that split just two counties. The redrawn 17th is a geographic monstrosity, taking in nine full counties and parts of 14 others, hugging much of Illinois' border with the Mississippi River but reaching with tentacle-like appendages as far inland as Springfield and Decatur.

In 1837, John Deere developed the first self-cleaning steel plow in the present-day 17th, which includes rich farmland along the Mississippi and the cities of Rock Island and Moline, two of the four industrial Quad Cities that straddle the river into Iowa. Defense cutbacks drained jobs from one of the 17th's industrial mainstays, the Rock Island Arsenal, but military operations in Iraq have required additional hires for two years in a row.

Corn, soybeans and hogs fuel most of the rest of the district's economy.

Even the industrial sector depends on agriculture. It is dominated by the nation's two largest farm equipment manufacturers, and Archer Daniels Midland Co. is based in the 17th's portion of Decatur. Sliding farm profits have forced the Quad Cities to recruit new types of manufacturing.

Redistricting gave the 17th, a politically competitive district in the 1990s, a Democratic tilt. John Kerry captured 51 percent of the vote here in the 2004 presidential election. The Democratic vote in Rock Island, coupled with the Democratic lean of the parts of Springfield and Decatur that were drawn into the district, are enough to overcome the Republican tendencies of some rural areas.

MAJOR INDUSTRY
Farm equipment manufacturing, agriculture, defense

MILITARY BASES
Rock Island Arsenal (Army), 135 military, 6,012 civilian (2004)

CITIES
Decatur (pt.), 58,701; Moline, 43,768; Quincy, 40,366; Rock Island, 39,684; Galesburg, 33,706; Springfield (pt.), 28,952; East Moline, 20,333

NOTABLE
Bishop Hill, a village in Henry County, was established in 1846 by Swedish religious dissidents searching for a "utopia on the prairie."

Rep. Ray LaHood (R)

CAPITOL OFFICE
225-6201
www.house.gov/lahood
1424 Longworth 20515-1318; fax 225-9249

COMMITTEES
Appropriations
Select Intelligence

HOMETOWN
Peoria

BORN
Dec. 6, 1945, Peoria, Ill.

RELIGION
Roman Catholic

FAMILY
Wife, Kathy LaHood; four children

EDUCATION
Spoon River Community College, attended 1963-65;
Bradley U., B.S. 1971 (education)

CAREER
Congressional aide; youth bureau director; urban
planning commission director; teacher

POLITICAL HIGHLIGHTS
Ill. House, 1982-83; defeated for election to Ill.
House, 1982

ELECTION RESULTS

2004 GENERAL

Ray LaHood (R)	216,047	70.2%
Steve Waterworth (D)	91,548	29.8%

2004 PRIMARY

Ray LaHood (R)	unopposed

2002 GENERAL

Ray LaHood (R)	unopposed

PREVIOUS WINNING PERCENTAGES
2000 (67%); 1998 (100%); 1996 (59%); 1994 (60%)

Elected 1994; 6th term

LaHood is the resident master of parliamentary procedure. He presides over the House in a manner both forceful and evenhanded and is often tapped by Speaker J. Dennis Hastert to take the chair during contentious floor proceedings. The GOP leadership is confident that LaHood's quick and confident rulings help maintain order during emotionally charged debates. He was the one called on to wield the gavel in 1998 as the House debated the impeachment of President Clinton.

His prowess in managing floor debate has not translated to increased power within the GOP leadership, however. LaHood is now in his second decade as a member of the House, and he spent another decade before his 1994 election as the chief of staff to Republican Leader Robert H. Michel. Like his former boss, LaHood comes from the moderate side of the Republican Party. He occasionally seems out of step with the hard-charging conservatives who sit in more of the seats on the House floor these days. While many of his colleagues in the Class of 1994 still revel in their outsider backgrounds, LaHood has never shied from his role as an insider.

LaHood was passed over as chairman of the Intelligence Committee in 2004 even though he had more seniority on the panel than Peter Hoekstra of Michigan, who was tapped by Hastert for the post. Hoekstra, however, outranks LaHood in overall House seniority, having been elected two years before him. LaHood will remain on both the Appropriations Committee and Intelligence, where he chaired two subcommittees in the 108th — Intelligence Policy and National Security and Terrorism and Homeland Security.

LaHood also failed in the 108th to move up the party ranks when it was clear that Tom DeLay would move from party whip to majority leader. LaHood launched a campaign for whip but when his bid failed to gain traction after three months, he gave up and endorsed DeLay's anointed successor, Roy Blunt of Missouri.

Despite his failure to gain a committee or party leadership position, LaHood remains part of a small, informal group of Republican advisers to Hastert. The two are close friends, having served in the state legislature together. LaHood usually is a reliable vote for the party on core issues. Yet at times, he splits from the GOP leadership.

When the House and Senate Intelligence panels joined forces in 2002 to investigate intelligence-related failures before the Sept. 11, 2001, terrorist attacks, LaHood criticized the White House for refusing to declassify records that, in his view, would have revealed how much the White House knew prior to the attacks. At the same time, LaHood unsuccessfully fought creation of the independent commission to investigate government lapses before the attacks, terming it "a set-up deal to blame the president."

LaHood subsequently voted no in 2004 on a measure reorganizing the nation's 15 intelligence agencies and creating a new position of national intelligence director. He was one of 67 Republicans to vote against the bill, and one of only three members of the Illinois delegation to vote no. LaHood said the reorganization measure would add a new and unneeded layer of bureaucracy to the federal government. "I think we've secured America pretty well," LaHood told The Bloomington Pantagraph. "I just think we're going to hold out hope to people that this is going to solve the problems."

Although LaHood may not always vote the way the GOP leadership wants, he occasionally will be the frontman for certain party needs. LaHood tried to find a legislative way in 2004 to shelve an ethics complaint filed against DeLay. He offered an amendment, which failed in committee, to that year's legislative branch spending bill to prohibit lame-duck lawmakers from filing complaints with the House ethics committee.

The move came one day after freshman Democrat Chris Bell of Texas filed a complaint accusing DeLay of improper and illegal behavior. Bell lost his bid for a second House term in a March Democratic primary forced by the off-year congressional redistricting engineered largely by DeLay. LaHood's proposed rules change would have applied to Bell and blocked his complaint. Allowing a departing member of Congress to file an ethics complaint is a form of "political gotcha" that "sets a very bad precedent," LaHood said.

In the late 1990s, LaHood sponsored legislation to abolish the Electoral College and allow the president to be chosen by the popular vote. "The existence of the College needs to be addressed before we are embroiled in a crisis in which a president is elected without winning the popular vote," he said in 1997, three years before Al Gore won the popular vote but George W. Bush was elected by virtue of his narrow Electoral College majority.

LaHood sits on Appropriations' Agriculture Subcommittee, which is important to his district's farmers who grow or sell corn and soybeans. Among other things, he has pressed for broader use of ethanol, the corn-based fuel additive. LaHood complained in 2004 that the Senate was holding up an energy policy bill, which included House-passed provisions emphasizing the use of ethanol and biodiesel, two products important to the Illinois economy. "We have waited for a decade for a comprehensive energy policy in this country, and people are paying the price at the pump for not having that policy enacted," LaHood said.

The grandson of an immigrant from Lebanon and a one-time junior high school teacher, LaHood watches out for minority rights. He has worried about the level of sophistication among his colleagues in their knowledge of the Middle East. "There is a pretty fair understanding about Israel and the Palestinians," he says, "but there is only a sketchy understanding of other countries in the region, including Syria, Egypt and Lebanon."

Echoing the move by outgoing Republican Gov. George Ryan to commute all death sentences in Illinois in 2003, LaHood has pushed legislation to improve death row prisoners' access to DNA testing that might prove their innocence. There is speculation that LaHood will one day make a move to gain the governor's mansion in Springfield.

LaHood first declared his candidacy for Congress in 1993, one day after Michel announced his retirement after 30 years in the House. He won with 60 percent of the vote and has never faced a serious challenge since.

KEY VOTES

2004

No Extend federal unemployment benefits by 13 weeks
Yes Pass $283.2 billion, six-year federal highway and mass transit bill
Yes Approve $146 billion multi-year extension of previously enacted middle-class tax breaks
Yes Amend the Constitution to prohibit same-sex marriage
No Cut corporate taxes $137 billion over 10 years
No Reorganize U.S. intelligence agencies as proposed by Sept. 11 commission

2003

Yes Cut taxes by $330 billion through fiscal 2013
No Block Bush rule scaling back overtime pay for some white-collar federal workers
Yes Do not allow use of search warrants without first notifying subjects
Yes Allow importation of prescription drugs
?   Create private school voucher program in Washington, D.C.
Yes Ban "partial birth" abortion except to save a woman's life
No Split $18.6 billion in Iraq aid into half-grant, half-loan
Yes Overhaul Medicare and create prescription drug benefit

CQ VOTE STUDIES

	PARTY UNITY		PRESIDENTIAL SUPPORT	
	Support	Oppose	Support	Oppose
2004	86%	14%	75%	25%
2003	90%	10%	89%	11%
2002	92%	8%	82%	18%
2001	90%	10%	74%	26%
2000	87%	13%	32%	68%

INTEREST GROUPS

	AFL-CIO	ADA	CCUS	ACU
2004	40%	20%	85%	71%
2003	29%	15%	89%	72%
2002	11%	0%	89%	92%
2001	33%	15%	86%	72%
2000	10%	15%	95%	72%

ILLINOIS 18

Central – Peoria, part of Springfield and Decatur

When Richard M. Nixon spoke to the silent majority, his message hit home in Peoria, an American Everytown filled with hard-working, conservative, middle-class folks.

More than thirty years later, Peoria is a politically competitive region in a sea of mostly rural Republicanism. A large black population on the south side and a substantial union constituency allow Democratic candidates to prevail in Peoria, as John Kerry did in the city and its namesake county in the 2004 presidential election, although his countywide margin of victory was less than 100 votes. Republicans run stronger on the north side, and 2002 GOP gubernatorial nominee Jim Ryan's strong showing there helped him carry the city and county.

The 18th takes in all or part of 20 counties in central and western Illinois, with Peoria County accounting for nearly 30 percent of the population. In the south, the 18th takes in the northern part of Springfield, the state capital, some Republican-leaning suburbs north and west of the city, and rural turf that stretches west of the capital almost to the Mississippi

River. In its southeastern reaches, the 18th runs to north Decatur.

In much of this predominately agricultural district, voters worry about crop prices, ethanol, free trade and estate taxes. But the district's economic health still depends largely on Peoria-based Caterpillar Inc., which manufactures earth-moving equipment and other heavy machinery.

The Republican lean of the rural areas, primarily those north and east of Peoria and north of Springfield, tips the 18th to the GOP. Woodford County, which abuts Peoria to the east, gave George W. Bush 68 percent of its vote in the 2004 presidential election, as did Logan County.

MAJOR INDUSTRY

Construction machinery, ethanol and grain products, agriculture

CITIES

Peoria, 112,936; Springfield (pt.), 57,209; Pekin, 33,857; East Peoria, 22,638; Jacksonville, 18,940; Decatur (pt.), 15,571

NOTABLE

Pekin (Tazewell County) was the hometown of former Senate Minority Leader Everett McKinley Dirksen; Abraham Lincoln's tomb in Springfield is a state historic site.

Rep. John Shimkus (R)

Elected 1996; 5th term

CAPITOL OFFICE
225-5271
www.house.gov/shimkus
513 Cannon 20515-1319; fax 225-5880

COMMITTEES
Energy & Commerce

HOMETOWN
Collinsville

BORN
Feb. 21, 1958, Collinsville, Ill.

RELIGION
Lutheran

FAMILY
Wife, Karen Shimkus; three children

EDUCATION
U.S. Military Academy, B.S. 1980; Southern Illinois
U., M.B.A. 1997

MILITARY SERVICE
Army, 1980-86; Army Reserve, 1986-present

CAREER
Teacher

POLITICAL HIGHLIGHTS
Candidate for Madison County Board, 1988;
Collinsville Township Board of Trustees, 1989-93;
Madison County treasurer, 1990-97; Republican
nominee for U.S. House, 1992

ELECTION RESULTS

2004 GENERAL

John Shimkus (R)	213,451	69.4%
Tim Bagwell (D)	94,303	30.6%

2004 PRIMARY

John Shimkus (R)	unopposed

2002 GENERAL

John Shimkus (R)	133,956	54.8%
David Phelps (D)	110,517	45.2%

PREVIOUS WINNING PERCENTAGES
2000 (63%); 1998 (61%); 1996 (50%)

A graduate of West Point, Shimkus is a lieutenant colonel in the U.S. Army Reserves. He admits to carrying a generous load of guilt about not fighting in the war in Iraq, which he voted to authorize in 2002.

But he has also come to terms with his strengths and at the moment, he says, his strengths do not include the military skills he would need to be a useful participant in the war. He says he has not trained regularly or rigorously enough since joining Congress to be as sharp as is needed in Iraq.

"I just personally had to struggle with it because I'm an infantry man, and I went to military school — West Point — where you are trained to lead," he said in 2003. "When you lead, you have to lead by example. When you are about to send troops into war, there's a lot of guilt on my part about not shucking the civilian clothes and putting on a military uniform."

Instead, he has strongly supported the war as a lawmaker and by visiting Iraq and meeting with the troops.

Burly and athletic, Shimkus is a combination of serious competitor and affable colleague, whether on the field or on the House floor. A baseball catcher in his junior varsity days at West Point, he is the star GOP pitcher in the annual congressional baseball game. In 2004, he won for the third year in a row, and in two of those games, he was named the Most Valuable Player.

A deeply committed social conservative, he is often out front on politically charged issues. He is among the most outspoken House opponents of a procedure referred to by its critics as "partial birth" abortion. "As a pro-life Christian, I find partial-birth abortion a most cruel and gruesome act against another living human being," Shimkus has said.

Yet he is also interested in working in a bipartisan fashion on less controversial issues. In the 108th Congress, he teamed up with California Democrat Anna G. Eshoo to encourage states to upgrade 911 services for mobile phones, enabling emergency operators to pinpoint the location of a cell phone caller. He also won support from both parties for legislation to promote the placement of automatic external defibrillators in schools.

Shimkus is a pragmatic conservative in the same mold as another Illinois Republican, Speaker J. Dennis Hastert. In 2000, he played a central role in efforts to craft a bipartisan package that would have paired a Democratic-backed minimum wage hike with Republican-backed tax cuts. In 2001, he listed an increase in the minimum wage as one of his top legislative priorities, although no increase was passed. In 2004, he was one of 39 Republicans who supported a Democratic amendment to extend unemployment insurance benefits for jobless workers.

GOP leaders had Shimkus' narrow 1996 victory in mind when they awarded him a choice seat in the 105th Congress on the Energy and Commerce Committee. The panel's broad jurisdiction gives its members contacts with lobbying interests eager to contribute to incumbents' re-election campaigns. Shimkus landed the prize with help from Hastert, who used his status as a senior member of the committee to champion Shimkus' cause.

When the 109th Congress takes up comprehensive energy legislation, Shimkus likely will use his committee position to be a voice for ethanol, a gasoline additive made from corn that is used to reduce emissions. He also supports legislation to promote an alternative fuel called biodiesel, which is refined from soybeans, a crop grown in his district. "Biodiesel is good for the environment, good for family farmers and good for the economy," he says. "Meanwhile, soybean farmers are given a new market in which to sell their product."

Shimkus repays his leadership's kind treatment by voting a reliably Republican line even on trade, a tough issue in southern Illinois. The district has a large population of factory workers wary of foreign competition. But Shimkus also wants to promote agricultural exports from his district and state. Illinois ranks among the top 10 states in agricultural exports.

Shimkus backed the White House in 2001 on a bill to give the president fast-track trade negotiating authority. Under fast-track, trade agreements are sent to Congress for an up-or-down vote and cannot be amended. The measure was favored by agriculture interests. Shimkus also backed stiff tariffs on imported steel, sought by domestic steel producers.

A fourth-generation Lithuanian, Shimkus is co-chairman of the House Baltic Caucus. A U.S. delegate to the NATO Parliamentary Assembly, he was active in the 107th in supporting NATO expansion to include the Baltic states of Lithuania, Latvia and Estonia.

Shimkus graduated from West Point, served in the Army from 1980 to 1986, and then returned to his Illinois hometown of Collinsville. After teaching high school history and government, he entered local politics, winning election in 1989 to the Collinsville Township Board of Trustees.

The next year, he won the post of Madison County treasurer, and he was easily re-elected in 1994. In 1992, he challenged Democratic Rep. Richard J. Durbin, who had represented the 20th for the previous 10 years. Shimkus took 44 percent of the vote in a losing effort. When Durbin made a move for the Senate in 1996, Shimkus again mounted a House campaign.

In the general election, he faced state Rep. Jay C. Hoffman, who emphasized his work on anti-crime legislation in the state legislature. Shimkus portrayed Hoffman as an opponent of tax relief and billed himself as a pro-business voice who would roll back taxes and government regulations. Although President Clinton carried the district by 7 percentage points, Shimkus managed to win narrowly by 1,238 votes.

In 2002, when reapportionment cost Illinois one of its House seats, the new congressional map threw Shimkus and Democrat David Phelps together in the new 19th District. The district's demographics favored Shimkus, and he won the incumbent vs. incumbent matchup by almost 10 percentage points. He won with more than two-thirds of the vote in 2004 against businessman and teacher Tim Bagwell. In early 2005, he announced he would abide by his term limits pledge and serve only 12 years in the House. The 2006 election will be his last.

KEY VOTES

2004
Yes   Extend federal unemployment benefits by 13 weeks

Yes   Pass $283.2 billion, six-year federal highway and mass transit bill

Yes   Approve $146 billion multi-year extension of previously enacted middle-class tax breaks

Yes   Amend the Constitution to prohibit same-sex marriage

Yes   Cut corporate taxes $137 billion over 10 years

Yes   Reorganize U.S. intelligence agencies as proposed by Sept. 11 commission

2003
Yes   Cut taxes by $330 billion through fiscal 2013

No   Block Bush rule scaling back overtime pay for some white-collar federal workers

Yes   Do not allow use of search warrants without first notifying subjects

No   Allow importation of prescription drugs

Yes   Create private school voucher program in Washington, D.C.

Yes   Ban "partial birth" abortion except to save a woman's life

No   Split $18.6 billion in Iraq aid into half-grant, half-loan

Yes   Overhaul Medicare and create prescription drug benefit

CQ VOTE STUDIES

	PARTY UNITY		PRESIDENTIAL SUPPORT	
	Support	Oppose	Support	Oppose
2004	91%	9%	76%	24%
2003	95%	5%	89%	11%
2002	94%	6%	80%	20%
2001	95%	5%	86%	14%
2000	93%	7%	29%	71%

INTEREST GROUPS

	AFL-CIO	ADA	CCUS	ACU
2004	43%	20%	95%	88%
2003	27%	10%	90%	80%
2002	11%	0%	90%	100%
2001	25%	5%	100%	92%
2000	20%	10%	80%	80%

ILLINOIS 19

South – southern rural counties; part of Springfield

Following a decade of slow population growth, Illinois lost one of its 20 House districts in reapportionment following the 2000 census. In general, the new map merged the 19th and 20th districts, creating a sprawling district in southern Illinois that meanders across the state and takes in all or part of 30 counties.

The northern counties cover typical Midwestern country — acres of corn and soybean fields dotted by small towns. This area leans Republican, as do more-populous areas such as the 19th's share of Madison County and the Sangamon County suburbs of Springfield, the state capital.

The southern half looks more like Appalachia than Midwestern prairie. Its hilly, forested counties depend on timber and coal mining. Unemployment is an endemic problem in much of the region. Mechanization of mining has caused job losses and reduced demand for

the region's high-sulfur coal. Pope County, the state's least populous, is almost entirely within the Shawnee National Forest.

The district has an ancestrally conservative Democratic tradition, but went Republican in the last two presidential elections. It backed George W. Bush with 61 percent of the vote in 2004, which made the district Bush's best in the state. While the economic populism of the region can help conservative Democrats win, voters will cast a GOP ballot when they perceive Democrats as too liberal on cultural issues. Wayne County (74 percent) and Effingham County (72 percent) were Bush's two best Illinois counties. Edwards County, which is shared with the 15th District, gave Bush 72 percent of its vote as well.

MAJOR INDUSTRY
Agriculture, coal mining, manufacturing, food products

CITIES
Springfield (pt.), 25,293; Collinsville (pt.), 21,803; Edwardsville (pt.), 21,478

NOTABLE
Metropolis (Massac County) was declared the official hometown of Superman by the Illinois House in 1972 — the town is closer to Birmingham, Ala., than to Chicago.

INDIANA

Gov. Mitch Daniels (R)

First elected: 2004
Length of term: 4 years
Term expires: 1/09
Salary: $95,000
Phone: (317) 232-4567

Hometown: Indianapolis
Born: April 7, 1949; Monongahela, Pa.
Religion: Presbyterian
Family: Wife, Cheri Daniels; four children
Education: Princeton U., A.B. 1971 (urban studies); Indiana U., attended 1975-76 (law); Georgetown U., J.D. 1979
Career: Pharmaceutical company executive; public policy institute executive; lawyer; White House aide; congressional and campaign aide; mayoral aide
Political highlights: U.S. Office of Management and Budget director, 2001-03

Election results:

2004 GENERAL
Mitch Daniels (R)	1,302,912	53.2%
Joseph E. Kernan (D)	1,113,900	45.5%
Ken Gividen (LIBERT)	31,664	1.3%

Lt. Gov. Rebecca Skillman (R)

First elected: 2004
Length of term: 4 years
Term expires: 1/09
Salary: $76,000
Phone: (317) 232-4545

STATE LEGISLATURE

General Assembly: January-April in odd-numbered years; January-March in even-numbered years

House: 100 members, 2-year terms
2005 breakdown: 52R, 48D; 86 men, 14 women
Salary: $11,600
Phone: (317) 232-9600

Senate: 50 members, 4-year terms
2005 breakdown: 33R, 17D; 39 men, 11 women
Salary: $11,600
Phone: (317) 232-9400

STATE TERM LIMITS

Governor: 2 terms
House: No
Senate: No

URBAN STATISTICS

CITY	POPULATION
Indianapolis	791,926
Fort Wayne	205,727
Evansville	121,582
South Bend	107,789
Gary	102,746

REGISTERED VOTERS

Voters do not register by party.

POPULATION

2004 population (est.)	6,237,569
2000 population	6,080,485
1990 population	5,544,159
Percent change (1990-2000)	+9.7%
Rank among states (2004)	14

Median age	35.2
Born in state	69.3%
Foreign born	3.1%
Violent crime rate	349/100,000
Poverty level	9.5%
Federal workers	37,567
Military	22,639

REDISTRICTING

Indiana lost one House seat in reapportionment. The state legislature failed to agree on a plan and so the governor signed an executive order adopting the new, nine-district map on May 16, 2001.

MISCELLANEOUS

Web: www.in.gov
Capital: Indianapolis
STATE ELECTION OFFICIAL
(317) 232-3939
DEMOCRATIC HEADQUARTERS
(317) 231-7100
REPUBLICAN HEADQUARTERS
(317) 635-7561

District Statistics

DIST.	2004 VOTE FOR PRESIDENT BUSH	KERRY	WHITE	BLACK	ASIAN	HISP	MEDIAN INCOME	WHITE COLLAR	BLUE COLLAR	SERVICE INDUSTRY	OVER 64	UNDER 18	COLLEGE EDUCATION	RURAL	SQ. MILES
1	44%	55%	70%	18%	1%	10%	$44,087	53%	31%	15%	13%	27%	17%	13%	2,209
2	56	43	84	8	1	5	$40,381	51	35	14	13	26	17	27	3,679
3	68	31	88	6	1	4	$44,013	52	36	12	11	28	18	35	3,240
4	69	30	94	1	1	3	$45,947	57	30	13	11	26	22	32	4,016
5	71	28	93	3	1	2	$52,800	63	25	12	11	27	31	26	3,266
6	64	35	93	4	0	1	$39,002	50	35	15	14	25	15	41	5,550
7	41	58	63	29	1	4	$36,522	58	26	16	11	26	21	0	262
8	62	38	94	4	1	1	$36,732	52	32	16	14	24	16	42	7,042
9	59	40	94	2	1	2	$39,011	51	35	14	12	24	17	48	6,603
STATE	60	39	86	8	1	4	$41,567	54	32	14	12	26	19	29	35,867
U.S.	50.7	48.3	69	12	4	13	$41,994	60	25	15	12	26	24	21	3,537,438

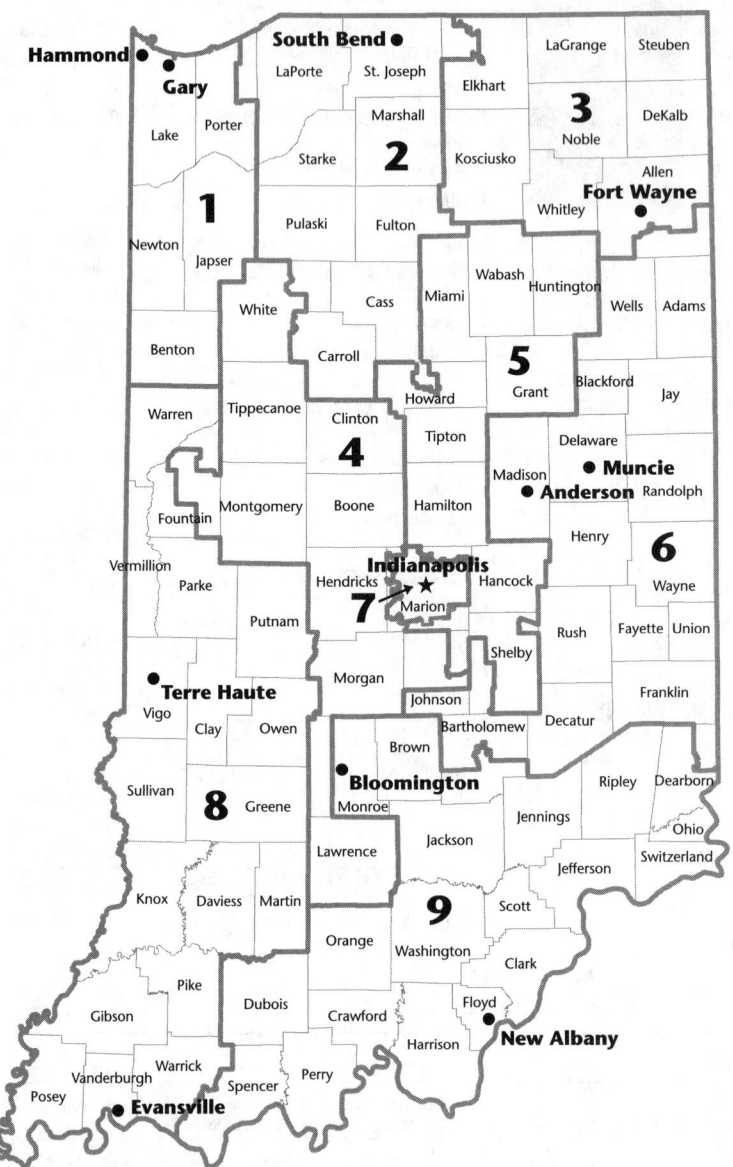

Sen. Richard G. Lugar (R)

Elected 1976; 5th term

CAPITOL OFFICE
224-4814
senator_lugar@lugar.senate.gov
lugar.senate.gov
306 Hart 20510-1401; fax 228-0360

COMMITTEES
Agriculture, Nutrition & Forestry
Foreign Relations - chairman

HOMETOWN
Indianapolis

BORN
April 4, 1932, Indianapolis, Ind.

RELIGION
Methodist

FAMILY
Wife, Charlene Lugar; four children

EDUCATION
Denison U., B.A. 1954; Oxford U., M.A. 1956
(Rhodes scholar)

MILITARY SERVICE
Navy, 1957-60

CAREER
Farm manager; manufacturing executive

POLITICAL HIGHLIGHTS
Indianapolis School Board, 1964-67; mayor of
Indianapolis, 1968-75; Republican nominee for
U.S. Senate, 1974; sought Republican nomination
for president, 1996

ELECTION RESULTS

2000 GENERAL

Richard G. Lugar (R)	1,427,944	66.6%
David L. Johnson (D)	683,273	31.9%
Paul Hager (LIBERT)	33,992	1.6%

2000 PRIMARY

Richard G. Lugar (R)	unopposed

PREVIOUS WINNING PERCENTAGES
1994 (67%); 1988 (68%); 1982 (54%); 1976 (59%)

For a man who's been thought of as too nice to get ahead in politics and too cerebral to hold people's attention for very long, Lugar has command-ed a good deal of attention as a pointed questioner of President Bush's for-eign policy decisions. With a constant smile and an avuncular voice he rarely raises, he might seem to be the last senator to cause problems for the White House. But with his knowledge of foreign policy and his prag-matic streak, the chairman of the Foreign Relations Committee is a barom-eter of Bush's Iraq policy, serving as an early warning when the president is about to encounter misgivings from members of both parties.

That was the case in 2003, when, as the U.S. mission in Iraq seemed to be foundering, Lugar declared that it was time for the administration and Congress to "level" with the American people about what it would take to stabilize Iraq. Lugar announced he would hold hearings on the adminis-tration's plans for postwar Iraq, and bluntly dismissed the message Bush and senior officials had been delivering that the military operation would be over quickly and cleanly.

"This idea that we will be in just as long as we need to and not a day more, we've got to get over that rhetoric. It is rubbish!" Lugar said. "We're going to be there a long time." The following week, Bush publicly acknowledged that the United States was engaged in a "massive and long-term under-taking" in Iraq.

In 2003, Lugar got a chance to disprove the old cliché that there are no second acts in American politics. He had waited for 16 years to return as chairman of the Foreign Relations panel, a post he held in 1985 and 1986, while Republicans briefly were in the majority. He was finally able to reclaim the job he loves after the 2002 election, with the retirement of Jesse Helms of North Carolina.

Lugar made clear his priority was to restore the prestige of a committee whose luster had faded since the end of the Cold War. But his efforts to get a foreign assistance authorization bill through Congress for the first time since his previous chairmanship were unsuccessful in the 108th Congress. And the White House sometimes stonewalls his demands for information about planning and cost estimates for the war.

His signature issue is nuclear arms nonproliferation. He has worked to strengthen the Nunn-Lugar cooperative threat reduction program, crafted in 1991 by him and Sen. Sam Nunn, a Georgia Democrat, to help the coun-tries of the former Soviet Union secure and dispose of weapons of mass destruction. During its first 10 years in effect, the Nunn-Lugar policy elim-inated more than 5,000 Soviet nuclear warheads and earned the two sena-tors a Nobel Peace Prize nomination.

In the 108th Congress, Lugar called for an enhanced role for the State Department and USAID in rebuilding Iraq, Afghanistan and other war-torn nations such as Sudan. He has proposed giving the State Department more control over reconstruction efforts and creating a $100 million emer-gency fund for nation-building programs.

Politics is an intellectual calling for Lugar, who cites his access to intel-ligence briefings and classified foreign policy documents as a favorite aspect of being a senator. With all the energy and self-discipline of a long-distance runner — in his early 70s, he still runs 12 to 15 miles a week — he has racked up an impressive list of accomplishments: Phi Beta Kappa at Denison University, where he was co-president of the student body with his wife-to-be, Charlene Smeltzer; Rhodes Scholar at Oxford; naval intelligence officer; mayor of Indianapolis; longest-serving senator in Indiana history; and architect of an overhaul in federal agriculture policy.

Regarded as a virtual icon back home, Lugar manages to blend his Capitol Hill image as an elder statesman with a reputation for close attention to state issues. Although he admits that the intricacies of foreign policy do not capture the imagination of Indiana voters, his meticulous work attending to constituent service gives him license to steer his own course in Washington.

That latitude has allowed Lugar to participate in some of the dramatic foreign policy events of the past three decades. In 1986, he headed a U.S. delegation monitoring the Philippine contest between President Ferdinand E. Marcos and challenger Corazon C. Aquino. Lugar helped persuade President Reagan that Marcos had stolen the election and should step down. The same year, Lugar dealt Reagan one of his worst foreign policy defeats when he joined with Democrats in voting for sanctions against South Africa. When Reagan vetoed the measure, Lugar led the successful effort to override his veto.

An unabashed proponent of a strong U.S. global presence, Lugar has advocated bold actions aimed at stabilizing volatile regions. During the Persian Gulf conflict of 1990 and 1991, he gained national attention for suggesting that Iraqi leader Saddam Hussein "must either leave or be removed." Ten years later, Lugar supported Bush's efforts to force a confrontation with Saddam, but argued publicly and privately that the confrontation should occur through the United Nations.

On the domestic front, Lugar, as chairman of the Agriculture Committee from 1995 to 2001, employed his own experience as a farmer to shape agriculture policy. For 46 years, he has run a 604-acre corn, soybean and walnut farm that belonged to his father. He pushed for Senate passage in 1996 of a sweeping Republican farm bill replacing New Deal-era crop subsidies with a seven-year schedule of fixed payments, moving farmers toward a free-market system. But pressure from farmers prompted Congress in 2002 to undo most of the changes.

He is a solid conservative on most issues, favoring tax cuts and military spending and opposing abortion in most cases. In the 108th Congress, he voted with the president on key votes 97 percent of the time, a reflection of his belief in a strong presidency. Lugar breaks with his party on gun-related issues; he was one of only 10 Republicans in 2004 voting to extend the federal assault-weapons ban.

Lugar has suffered his share of political setbacks. When the GOP lost control of the Senate in the 1986 election, Helms asserted his seniority to take the top Republican spot on Foreign Relations, and Lugar lost a fight challenging the seniority system. Later, when Republicans regained the majority in the 1994 election, Helms became chairman.

Briefly considered as a vice presidential prospect in 1980, Lugar was stung eight years later when the No. 2 spot on the GOP ticket went to the junior senator from Indiana, Dan Quayle. Lugar also ran an abbreviated presidential campaign in 1996 but was doomed by his complex policy speeches on international affairs and by his modest gifts as a campaigner. He meets crowds rather stiffly, and his style borders on lecturing.

He has always impressed Indiana voters as a man of substance, though. Even in 1974, running for the Senate in a Watergate-dominated year with a reputation as "Richard Nixon's favorite mayor," Lugar came within a respectable 75,000 votes of Democratic incumbent Birch Bayh (whose son, Evan, is now Indiana's junior senator). In 1976, against a much weaker Democratic incumbent, Vance Hartke, Lugar won handily, and he has been re-elected four times.

KEY VOTES

2004

Yes Pass $318.9 billion, six-year highway and mass transit bill

Yes Extend assault weapons ban for 10 years

No Restore pay-as-you-go rules for new tax cuts and entitlement spending

Yes Criminalize harm to a fetus in an attack on the mother

Yes Increase mandatory child care funding to states by $6 billion over five years

Yes Amend the Constitution to prohibit same-sex marriage

Yes Approve $146 billion multi-year extension of previously enacted middle-class tax breaks

Yes Reorganize U.S. intelligence agencies as proposed by Sept. 11 commission

Yes Cut corporate taxes $137 billion over 10 years

2003

No Delay Bush changes to Clean Air Act

Yes Allow confirmation vote on Miguel A. Estrada to the U.S. Court of Appeals for the D.C. Circuit

No Block a Bush proposal opening Alaska's Arctic National Wildlife Refuge to oil drilling

No Limit size of Bush's proposed tax cut to $350 billion through fiscal 2013

Yes Overhaul Medicare and create prescription drug benefit

No Block Bush rule scaling back overtime pay for some white-collar federal workers

No Split $20 billion in Iraq aid into half-grant, half-loan

Yes Ban "partial birth" abortion except to save a woman's life

Yes Stop proposal allowing travel to Cuba

Yes Allow final vote on energy policy overhaul

CQ VOTE STUDIES

	PARTY UNITY		PRESIDENTIAL SUPPORT	
	Support	Oppose	Support	Oppose
2004	94%	6%	93%	7%
2003	97%	3%	98%	2%
2002	91%	9%	100%	0%
2001	92%	8%	100%	0%
2000	86%	14%	65%	35%
1999	88%	12%	40%	60%
1998	84%	16%	54%	46%
1997	83%	17%	62%	38%
1996	90%	10%	31%	69%
1995	92%	8%	28%	72%

INTEREST GROUPS

	AFL-CIO	ADA	CCUS	ACU
2004	8%	20%	100%	84%
2003	0%	10%	96%	80%
2002	31%	5%	95%	90%
2001	13%	15%	100%	92%
2000	0%	10%	100%	84%
1999	0%	5%	100%	88%
1998	0%	0%	94%	68%
1997	0%	30%	90%	64%
1996	0%	5%	85%	95%
1995	0%	5%	100%	77%

Sen. Evan Bayh (D)

CAPITOL OFFICE
224-5623
bayh.senate.gov
463 Russell 20510-1404; fax 228-1377

COMMITTEES
Armed Services
Banking, Housing & Urban Affairs
Small Business & Entrepreneurship
Select Intelligence
Special Aging

HOMETOWN
Indianapolis

BORN
Dec. 26, 1955, Shirkieville, Ind.

RELIGION
Episcopalian

FAMILY
Wife, Susan Bayh; two children

EDUCATION
Indiana U., B.S. 1978 (business economics);
U. of Virginia, J.D. 1981

CAREER
Lawyer

POLITICAL HIGHLIGHTS
Ind. secretary of state, 1986-89; governor, 1989-97

ELECTION RESULTS

2004 GENERAL

Evan Bayh (D)	1,496,976	61.7%
Marvin B. Scott (R)	903,913	37.2%
Albert Barger (LIBERT)	27,344	1.1%

2004 PRIMARY

Evan Bayh (D)	unopposed

PREVIOUS WINNING PERCENTAGES
1998 (64%)

Elected 1998; 2nd term

Bayh is cut from the mold of the centrists who rose to prominence in Democratic politics in the 1990s. As the chairman of the Democratic Leadership Council, the leading organization of party moderates, he is in a good position to shape policies edging the party away from its traditional liberalism.

His high-profile role at the leadership council, which once introduced a Southern state governor named Bill Clinton to a national audience, positions Bayh (BY) as a politically moderate candidate for the Democratic presidential nomination in 2008, and he has not ruled out a bid. If the intense scrutiny following his early 2005 vote against Secretary of State Condoleezza Rice is an indicator — some saw it as a play to the liberal base of his party — the political motive behind his votes in the 109th Congress will be the topic of much speculation.

During his first Senate term, Bayh made a point of seeking compromises that blur party lines and partisan credit. Though his father, Birch Bayh, was one of the Senate's leading liberal Democratic voices during an 18-year career, the younger Bayh is much more in tune with the Hoosier State's conservative bent. He says he always looks for the center, because that is where deals are made. Back home, he is sometimes referred to as the "Republicrat." In 2004, he co-founded a group called the Third Way with the goal of giving moderates a greater role and serving as a think tank to generate middle-of-the-road legislative proposals.

If his opposition to Rice startled some in Washington who viewed him as a Democrat in name only, Bayh's record of siding with the party mainstream has precedent. He was one of the first to oppose President Bush's choice of John Ashcroft to be attorney general, saying his views were strident, and he was an early critic of the president's tax cut in 2001, voting against the $1.35 trillion, 10-year bill.

On one important issue that could affect presidential politics in 2008 — the war in Iraq — Bayh seems to be having second thoughts about his early, enthusiastic backing of the Bush administration.

Bayh was among the first Democrats to call for pre-emptive action against Iraq to prevent Saddam Hussein from developing weapons of mass destruction. "They're waiting for a threat to materialize," he said of those who urged caution. "I'm not sure we'll find a smoking gun here, but if we wait until it's cocked and loaded, it's probably too late." Bayh also backed a resolution that recommended but did not require that Bush consult with the world community before taking action.

As the war dragged on, and Baghdad took longer than expected to transition to a new government, Bayh's support for the war softened. In 2003, he offered an amendment to an Iraq aid package to make half of it a loan that would have to be repaid, a move Bush adamantly opposed. By late 2004, Bayh said he was convinced the administration had mishandled the war. He called for the resignation of Defense Secretary Donald H. Rumsfeld, and when Rice's nomination came up for a vote on the Senate floor, he joined 12 mostly liberal Democrats in voting against her. Bayh explained that the vote against Rice was a vote for accountability, and about "principle, not politics."

Bayh generally takes a cautious approach to politics. He tends to inch ahead rather than rush forward, preferring to examine all sides of an issue before taking a stand. His floor speeches are rare and prosaic events, filled with calls for compromise and a reliance on "Hoosier values." While many fellow senators gave impassioned speeches before voting on President Clinton's fate in the 1999 impeachment trial, Bayh, who voted to acquit, delivered remarks that sounded like a legal brief.

Critics say that his caution comes from his attempts to accumulate political capital rather than risk his neck on bold initiatives. "I'll never have the political capital or popularity of Evan Bayh," Indiana state Rep. Mark Kruzan, a Democrat, told The Indianapolis Star in 1996, as Bayh was ending his two terms as governor. "But I've often sensed that polling information and pressure from advisers was helping to steer the ship."

In the 108th Congress, Bayh pushed legislation designed to promote responsible fatherhood, an objective no one was likely to quibble with. He and conservative GOP Sen. Rick Santorum of Pennsylvania tried but failed to attach to a welfare bill $100 million to educate men about taking care of their children and $200 million to promote marriage through education and counseling programs for low-income couples. Children without meaningful relationships with their fathers are more susceptible to dropping out of school or committing suicide, contends Bayh, and preventing that is the next logical step in welfare policy.

Bayh has also been a main Democratic backer of Bush's faith-based initiatives, and a forceful advocate of boosting federal spending to education but tying the aid to performance. He championed legislation, which was enacted into law, aimed at protecting senior citizens from fraud, including deceptive sweepstakes offers, investment schemes and telemarketing come-ons.

Bayh's movie-star good looks and cross-party appeal keep his favorability ratings high back home in Indiana. And it drives speculation that he has his sights set on the White House. He briefly considered a 2004 campaign but concluded his children were too young for him to be an absent father for the better part of two years. Bayh is the father of school-age twins, Beau (Birch Evans IV) and Nicholas.

Opposition from abortion rights groups who questioned his suitability for a vice presidential slot in 2000 had weakened by 2004, when the groups were desperate to oust Bush. Bayh also published the requisite pre-campaign memoir; in it, he recalls his childhood as the namesake son of a senator and his journey from popular two-term governor to senator. For 2008, he says he has "not ruled anything in or out."

Born in the small town of Shirkieville, Ind., Bayh moved to Washington at age 7, when his father was elected to the Senate. While attending the elite St. Albans School, among his babysitters was Lynda Bird Johnson, the president's older daughter. Bayh met his wife, Susan, while she was a summer intern for the House Ways and Means Committee. While in law school, he managed his father's losing campaign for a fourth term in 1980, when Birch Bayh was swept out in the Reagan landslide.

After clerking for a federal judge and practicing law, at age 30 Bayh was elected Indiana secretary of state. Two years later, in 1988, he became the youngest governor in the nation and stayed popular for eight years, in part by riding the crest of a robust economy.

He delivered the keynote address at the 1996 Democratic convention. Term limits barred him from running for governor again, so Bayh began preparing to challenge GOP incumbent Sen. Daniel R. Coats, who decided to retire in 1998 rather than face Bayh. In November, Bayh trounced Mayor Paul Helmke of Fort Wayne by a nearly 2-to-1 margin.

He briefly considered mounting a bid to return to the governor's mansion in 2004 but then decided to stay in Washington. He won re-election that year with 62 percent of the vote.

KEY VOTES

2004

Yes Pass $318.9 billion, six-year highway and mass transit bill
Yes Extend assault weapons ban for 10 years
Yes Restore pay-as-you-go rules for new tax cuts and entitlement spending
No   Criminalize harm to a fetus in an attack on the mother
Yes Increase mandatory child care funding to states by $6 billion over five years
No   Amend the Constitution to prohibit same-sex marriage
Yes Approve $146 billion multi-year extension of previously enacted middle-class tax breaks
Yes Reorganize U.S. intelligence agencies as proposed by Sept. 11 commission
Yes Cut corporate taxes $137 billion over 10 years

2003

Yes Delay Bush changes to Clean Air Act
No   Allow confirmation vote on Miguel A. Estrada to the U.S. Court of Appeals for the D.C. Circuit
Yes Block a Bush proposal opening Alaska's Arctic National Wildlife Refuge to oil drilling
Yes Limit size of Bush's proposed tax cut to $350 billion through fiscal 2013
Yes Overhaul Medicare and create prescription drug benefit
Yes Block Bush rule scaling back overtime pay for some white-collar federal workers
Yes Split $20 billion in Iraq aid into half-grant, half-loan
Yes Ban "partial birth" abortion except to save a woman's life
No   Stop proposal allowing travel to Cuba
No   Allow final vote on energy policy overhaul

CQ VOTE STUDIES

	PARTY UNITY		PRESIDENTIAL SUPPORT	
	Support	Oppose	Support	Oppose
2004	78%	22%	64%	36%
2003	82%	18%	55%	45%
2002	70%	30%	79%	21%
2001	82%	18%	69%	31%
2000	92%	8%	98%	2%
1999	88%	12%	89%	11%

INTEREST GROUPS

	AFL-CIO	ADA	CCUS	ACU
2004	100%	90%	65%	20%
2003	85%	75%	43%	30%
2002	85%	70%	65%	30%
2001	100%	100%	50%	32%
2000	75%	80%	60%	16%
1999	89%	90%	59%	12%

Rep. Peter J. Visclosky (D)

Elected 1984; 11th term

CAPITOL OFFICE
225-2461
www.house.gov/visclosky
2256 Rayburn 20515-1401; fax 225-2493

COMMITTEES
Appropriations

HOMETOWN
Merrillville

BORN
Aug. 13, 1949, Gary, Ind.

RELIGION
Roman Catholic

FAMILY
Divorced; two children

EDUCATION
Indiana U. Northwest, B.S. 1970 (accounting); U. of
Notre Dame, J.D. 1973; Georgetown U., LL.M. 1982

CAREER
Lawyer; congressional aide

POLITICAL HIGHLIGHTS
No previous office

ELECTION RESULTS

2004 GENERAL

Peter J. Visclosky (D)	178,406	68.3%
Mark J. Leyva (R)	82,858	31.7%

2004 PRIMARY

Peter J. Visclosky (D)	unopposed

2002 GENERAL

Peter J. Visclosky (D)	90,443	66.9%
Mark J. Leyva (R)	41,909	31.0%
Timothy P. Brennan (LIBERT)	2,759	2.0%

PREVIOUS WINNING PERCENTAGES
2000 (72%); 1998 (73%); 1996 (69%); 1994 (56%);
1992 (69%); 1990 (66%); 1988 (77%); 1986 (73%);
1984 (71%)

Visclosky flies below the radar on most issues in the House and that is probably the way he likes it. His seat on the Appropriations Committee satisfies his first ambition as a lawmaker and he works continually to achieve his second — reviving the nation's ailing steel industry.

Visclosky (vis-KLOSS-key) waited patiently for a slot on Appropriations and finally made it onto the panel in October 1991 — six years, nine months and nine days after he made his first bid for such an appointment, Visclosky later recalled, revealing just how focused he was on the goal.

The second matter — championing the steel industry — Visclosky approaches with energy and zeal in the hope he can slow or even reverse the continued decline of steel, which was the main industry of his northwestern district. Though steelmaking jobs in northwestern Indiana have plummeted from about 70,000 two decades ago to fewer than half as many now, Visclosky's blue-collar district produces more steel than any other area in the country— more than 12 percent of the nation's total output. His father was an ironworker.

Visclosky's low-key approach and sharp focus on a short list of issues keeps him out of the spotlight. A detail-minded legislator, he is devoted to the idea that politics is about resolving disputes through discussion and compromise. And he is an unassuming man whose infrequent floor speeches are likely to be tributes to people back home or to a civic organization.

But he is willing to fight over steel tariffs. Visclosky has battled with presidents — both Democratic and Republican — who he believes have not done nearly enough to protect the domestic steel industry from unfair foreign competition.

In 2002, he urged President Bush to place tariffs of 40 percent on foreign steel imports, saying anything less would be "meaningless and unacceptable." Bush imposed lesser tariffs and then, just 21 months later, revoked them. Realizing what was coming, Visclosky had urged Bush to retain the tariffs, arguing that the president "must decide whether he is with America's workers, or against them." Visclosky and his allies in the Congressional Steel Caucus introduced legislation to reinstate the tariffs, but to no avail.

As the vice chairman of the Steel Caucus since 2000, Visclosky has pushed legislation under which the government would help pay the health and pension costs of steel company retirees.

Visclosky has generally opposed trade liberalization. He voted in 1993 against the North American Free Trade Agreement, in 2000 against making China a permanent normal U.S. trade partner, and in 2001 against reviving fast-track procedures for congressional action on trade deals.

Not surprisingly, organized labor looks favorably on him: Since 1998, he has received a 100 percent score in the AFL-CIO's annual report card on congressional voting behavior.

Visclosky's other abiding interest in Congress is leveraging his seniority on the Appropriations Committee to deliver money for Indiana transportation and infrastructure projects and to diversify the economy of his district. He is the only Hoosier on the Appropriations panel, and he must watch out for his colleagues as well as seek funding for his own district's needs. In the 109th Congress, he is the top-ranking Democrat on the Energy and Water Development Subcommittee.

In the last two Congresses, he has sought millions of dollars for improvements to the Gary/Chicago Airport to help make it a more viable alternative to crowded O'Hare and Midway airports in Chicago. He also backs the extension of commuter rail lines from Chicago, redevelopment efforts along the Lake Michigan shore and a technology "incubator" center affiliated with Purdue University.

His secondary legislative initiatives have included local crime-fighting efforts and steps to permit floating casinos in Gary, his district's population center, in the hope of spurring more lakeshore development.

Visclosky secured funds in 1996 to provide 600 bulletproof vests to northwest Indiana law enforcement officers. Then, learning the problem was a national one — an estimated 25 percent of U.S. police officers do not have access to the vests — Visclosky in 1998 joined with New Jersey Republican Frank A. LoBiondo to authorize a new Justice Department grant program. He worked to reauthorize the program in 2004 and to keep the funding in place.

In representing his reliably Democratic district, Visclosky generally votes the party line. But he is a fiscal conservative who will break with his leadership on some budgetary matters. Visclosky declares that the government has "a moral responsibility" to balance the budget.

He also has shown a conservative bent on some social issues, such as his support of a ban on a procedure that opponents call "partial birth" abortion.

Visclosky is a Catholic seminary dropout who later went on to complete two degrees at Catholic institutions, Notre Dame and Georgetown. He has spent most of his adult life in politics. After finishing law school in 1973 at Notre Dame, he linked his fortunes to Adam Benjamin Jr., then a state senator and rising political star in Indiana. Visclosky coordinated Benjamin's successful campaign for Congress in 1976 and served as one of his top aides in Washington for the next six years.

When Benjamin died in September 1982, Democrats were without a candidate for the November election. As the 1st District Democratic chairman, Richard G. Hatcher — Gary's longtime mayor — was in a position to choose the Democratic nominee, and he picked Katie Hall, a state senator and loyal ally. She won easily, but when she sought renomination in 1984, Visclosky and another candidate challenged her.

Visclosky put on dozens of $2 "dog and bean" dinners to attract the young, the elderly and the unemployed. His "Slovak kid" background helped, as did the memory that older voters had of the candidate's father, John, Gary's mayor in 1962 and 1963. Visclosky bested Hall in the primary by 2 percentage points, then swamped the Republican in November. He has had little trouble winning his subsequent 10 re-elections.

KEY VOTES

2004

Yes Extend federal unemployment benefits by 13 weeks

Yes Pass $283.2 billion, six-year federal highway and mass transit bill

No Approve $146 billion multi-year extension of previously enacted middle-class tax breaks

No Amend the Constitution to prohibit same-sex marriage

No Cut corporate taxes $137 billion over 10 years

Yes Reorganize U.S. intelligence agencies as proposed by Sept. 11 commission

2003

No Cut taxes by $330 billion through fiscal 2013

Yes Block Bush rule scaling back overtime pay for some white-collar federal workers

Yes Do not allow use of search warrants without first notifying subjects

No Allow importation of prescription drugs

No Create private school voucher program in Washington, D.C.

Yes Ban "partial birth" abortion except to save a woman's life

Yes Split $18.6 billion in Iraq aid into half-grant, half-loan

No Overhaul Medicare and create prescription drug benefit

CQ VOTE STUDIES

	PARTY UNITY		PRESIDENTIAL SUPPORT	
	Support	Oppose	Support	Oppose
2004	90%	10%	19%	81%
2003	91%	9%	25%	75%
2002	92%	8%	22%	78%
2001	86%	14%	33%	67%
2000	92%	8%	75%	25%

INTEREST GROUPS

	AFL-CIO	ADA	CCUS	ACU
2004	100%	95%	35%	4%
2003	100%	85%	37%	24%
2002	100%	90%	35%	12%
2001	100%	85%	39%	17%
2000	100%	75%	33%	12%

INDIANA 1
Northwest – Gary, Hammond

Bordered to the north by Lake Michigan and to the west by Illinois, the 1st is home to steelworkers, a large union presence and some minority populations that offer Democrats solid support. More steel is produced here than in any other district in the nation — more than 30,000 steelworkers reside in Gary, Hammond and East Chicago. Most of the 1st's population lives in the far northwest corner, where more than 80 percent of Gary residents are black and more than half of East Chicago residents are Hispanic. The 1st also is home to many Eastern European ethnic neighborhoods.

Residents around Gary still struggle with the effects of unemployment, suburban flight and urban decay that began when the steel industry took a dive in the early 1980s. As recently as 1970, Gary and Fort Wayne (located in the 3rd) were equal in population. Thirty years later, Gary had only half the population of Fort Wayne.

Another crisis hit in 1998 when cheap, imported steel flooded the U.S. market in record amounts. At least one steel company went out of business and there were thousands of layoffs. The district has attracted some lake boat gambling, but so far it is not a replacement for steel's place in the economy.

Democrats carry congressional and presidential elections by strong margins. Republicans have a meager base in growing Porter County and in Lake County suburbs such as Crown Point and Merrillville, where an influx of white Chicago commuters has raised incomes.

Redistricting following the 2000 census added southern Lake County and three rural counties, and altered the district's portion of Porter County. Lake, which gave John Kerry 61 percent of its 2004 presidential vote, was the state's only county to give Kerry more than 58 percent of the vote.

MAJOR INDUSTRY
Steel, manufacturing, gambling

CITIES
Gary, 102,746; Hammond, 83,048; Portage, 33,496; East Chicago, 32,414; Merrillville, 30,560; Valparaiso (pt.), 27,362; Hobart, 25,363

NOTABLE
Indiana Dunes National Lakeshore; Singer Michael Jackson was raised in Gary; John Dillinger's infamous jailbreak occurred in Crown Point.

Rep. Chris Chocola (R)

Elected 2002; 2nd term

CAPITOL OFFICE
225-3915
www.house.gov/chocola
510 Cannon 20515-1402; fax 225-6798

COMMITTEES
Ways & Means

HOMETOWN
Bristol

BORN
Feb. 24, 1962, Jackson, Mich.

RELIGION
Presbyterian

FAMILY
Wife, Sarah Chocola; two children

EDUCATION
Hillsdale College, B.A. 1984 (business administration & political economy); Thomas M. Cooley Law School, J.D. 1988

CAREER
Agricultural manufacturing company executive; lawyer; cleaning materials company credit manager; foreign exchange trader

POLITICAL HIGHLIGHTS
Republican nominee for U.S. House, 2000

ELECTION RESULTS

2004 GENERAL

Chris Chocola (R)	140,496	54.2%
Joe Donnelly (D)	115,513	44.5%
Douglas Barnes (LIBERT)	3,346	1.3%

2004 PRIMARY

Chris Chocola (R)	36,847	84.0%
Tony Zirkle (R)	7,043	16.1%

2002 GENERAL

Chris Chocola (R)	95,081	50.5%
Jill Long Thompson (D)	86,253	45.8%
Sharon Metheny (LIBERT)	7,112	3.8%

Chocola is a wealthy businessman from the heartland who made his fortune producing feeders for chickens and pigs before coming to the House as a "citizen legislator." Typical of the crop of anti-Washington lawmakers who arrived in the last decade, he has pledged to limit himself to no more than five terms, or 10 years.

His political independence as a self-described outsider is restricted in one sense. He owes a debt of gratitude to President Bush, who went out of his way to help elect Chocola (cha-KO-luh) in the swing district along Indiana's northern border. Political moderates had dominated the region until the conservative Chocola came along in 2002.

In his first term, he became one of the most pro-Bush members of the House, supporting the president 100 percent of the time in pivotal votes in 2003 and over 90 percent of the time in 2004. He was an early and avid booster of overhauling Social Security by allowing beneficiaries to invest a portion of the money themselves, a priority issue for the president in his second term. During Chocola's first race for the House in 2000, he was quoted by the Elkhart Truth newspaper, saying, "Bush's plan of individual investment of 2 percent of the money is a start. Eventually, I'd like to see the entire system privatized."

Tax policy, especially as it affects business growth, is Chocola's main interest. He got a coveted seat on the Ways and Means Committee in the 109th Congress. He supports making permanent the sweeping tax cuts of 2001. And he has sponsored a bill giving small employers up to $100,000 in tax credits for creating new jobs. He also favors expanding tax breaks on savings for college expenses.

In his first term, Chocola jumped into the debate over extreme protest measures adopted by some groups advocating for environmental protection. He introduced a bill making it a federal crime to damage property in order to influence public opinion on environmental issues.

Chocola was unable to get any of his bills passed, which is not atypical for a freshman. The Indianapolis Star, the state's largest newspaper, gave him a lukewarm appraisal when it endorsed him for re-election in 2004. Chocola, the paper said, "has recorded a solid although unremarkable first term."

He has tended to focus on parochial needs, as many freshmen do. Before leaving to take the Ways and Means spot, he was on the Transportation panel, where he worked to get a $1 million upgrade for the Hoosier Heartland Highway, an important farm-to-market road in Indiana, and to secure federal funds for the rebuilding of U.S. 31 between South Bend and Indianapolis, a project that is expected to cost $1 billion and take at least 10 years.

On Transportation's Aviation Subcommittee, he successfully added a provision to the reauthorization bill for the Federal Aviation Administration to crack down on government credit card abuse by FAA employees, which Chocola said had cost more than $5 million. The measure directs the FAA to adopt General Accountability Office recommendations to increase the employees' accountability.

A native Midwesterner, Chocola grew up in Michigan and excelled in school. He was in the top 10 of his senior class in high school, then went on to graduate summa cum laude from Hillsdale College, a small, private school in Michigan that emphasizes "moral values" and maintains the online archive of writings by William F. Buckley, one of the nation's leading conservative thinkers.

Chocola got a law degree from Thomas M. Cooley Law School in 1988 but spent most of his career in business. He joined a company founded by his grandfather, Howard S. Brembeck, that makes feeders for poultry and swine producers. Rising through a series of managerial positions, he became chief executive officer of CTB International Corp. in 1994. He helped the firm double in size to annual revenues of over $250 million, extend its customer base into 100 countries and go from a family-owned business to a publicly held company traded on the NASDAQ. Chocola, who left the company when he came to the House, is one of that chamber's wealthiest members, listing assets of over $15 million on annual disclosure forms.

He first ran for the House in 2000, challenging Rep. Tim Roemer, a moderate five-term Democrat. Chocola, then 38 years old, did amazingly well for an upstart. He raised $1.1 million, including over $500,000 of his own money. He portrayed Roemer as a career politician and himself as a citizen legislator willing to take a term limit pledge. Chocola even came up with a catchy campaign slogan, handing out bottles of a chocolate drink called "Chocola" at his events. He came within 4 percentage points of beating Roemer.

Two years later, with the results of the once-a-decade census, Democrats in control of remapping drew a district evenly split between the two parties and receptive to a moderate like Roemer. But Roemer by then had decided to retire. So Chocola jumped at the chance to run for the open seat in the newly drawn 2nd District.

Democrats were able to attract a seasoned competitor in Jill Long Thompson, who had served three terms in Indiana's old 4th District, which covered some of the same ground as the new 2nd. That set up one of the most competitive races of 2002, with the national parties stepping into the duel. Bush dropped in for a fundraiser, as did Vice President Dick Cheney and Speaker J. Dennis Hastert. Thompson tried to make an issue of Chocola living just outside the district boundaries, turning the tables on Chocola's attacks on Roemer in 2000 for his decision to move his family to Washington. Chocola prevailed, with 51 percent of the vote.

In 2004, his Democratic opponent was lawyer Joe Donnelly. The challenger was unable to compete with Chocola in the fundraising race, and Chocola won with a convincing 54 percent.

Chocola's bad luck in drawing for office space as a freshman gave him a cramped, inconvenient office suite on the fifth floor of the Cannon House Office Building. But he discovered that the office once belonged to Richard M. Nixon, a House member from 1947 to 1950 and, although he could have sought a better office in the 109th, Chocola decided to stay put.

KEY VOTES

2004

No   Extend federal unemployment benefits by 13 weeks

Yes   Pass $283.2 billion, six-year federal highway and mass transit bill

Yes   Approve $146 billion multi-year extension of previously enacted middle-class tax breaks

Yes   Amend the Constitution to prohibit same-sex marriage

Yes   Cut corporate taxes $137 billion over 10 years

Yes   Reorganize U.S. intelligence agencies as proposed by Sept. 11 commission

2003

Yes   Cut taxes by $330 billion through fiscal 2013

No   Block Bush rule scaling back overtime pay for some white-collar federal workers

No   Do not allow use of search warrants without first notifying subjects

No   Allow importation of prescription drugs

Yes   Create private school voucher program in Washington, D.C.

Yes   Ban "partial birth" abortion except to save a woman's life

No   Split $18.6 billion in Iraq aid into half-grant, half-loan

Yes   Overhaul Medicare and create prescription drug benefit

CQ VOTE STUDIES

	PARTY UNITY		PRESIDENTIAL SUPPORT	
	Support	Oppose	Support	Oppose
2004	99%	1%	91%	9%
2003	98%	2%	100%	0%

INTEREST GROUPS

	AFL-CIO	ADA	CCUS	ACU
2004	13%	5%	100%	96%
2003	0%	5%	100%	88%

INDIANA 2
North central — South Bend, parts of Elkhart and Kokomo

The 2nd touches a southeastern corner of Lake Michigan and stretches across Indiana's northern border, but also drops south to Kokomo. Traditionally a politically competitive area, it has been considered a barometer of national political trends.

The district takes in St. Joseph County (South Bend), which is home to an ideologically diverse and economically disparate population. Here, the wealthy, Catholic Notre Dame community is joined by low-income, minority populations downtown, as well as blue-collar communities east of the city. Farther west, Michigan City's steel-producing areas and blue-collar La Porte provide solid Democratic support.

Farming and business in Elkhart County (shared with the 3rd) — a national center for the manufactured housing industry — create a faithful conservative constituency. Elkhart's large Amish population helps make it the state's leading milk producer.

The 2nd takes in some rural, Republican-leaning counties in north-central Indiana. Redistricting following the 2000 census extended the district (numbered the 3rd in the 1990s) south to Kokomo in Howard County. Kokomo (shared with the 5th) is dependent on the automobile industry, with Delphi and Daimler Chrysler as the area's dominant employers, and has a working-class, Democratic orientation.

These changes made the 2nd less Republican-leaning than the old 3rd, but George W. Bush still managed to win 11 of the 12 counties at least partially in the 2nd in the 2004 presidential election — his best was Fulton County with 69 percent. LaPorte was one of only four Indiana counties won by John Kerry in 2004, and overall Bush won the 2nd District with 56 percent of the vote.

MAJOR INDUSTRY
Manufacturing, higher education, agriculture

CITIES
South Bend, 107,789; Elkhart (pt.), 48,783; Mishawaka, 46,557; Michigan City, 32,900

NOTABLE
The College Football Hall of Fame and Studebaker National Museum are located in South Bend.

Rep. Mark Souder (R)

CAPITOL OFFICE
225-4436
souder@mail.house.gov
www.house.gov/souder
2231 Rayburn 20515-1403; fax 225-3479

COMMITTEES
Education & Workforce
Government Reform
  (Criminal Justice, Drug Policy & Human
  Resources - chairman)
Homeland Security

HOMETOWN
Fort Wayne

BORN
July 18, 1950, Fort Wayne, Ind.

RELIGION
Evangelical

FAMILY
Wife, Diane Souder; three children

EDUCATION
Indiana U., B.S. 1972 (business administration);
U. of Notre Dame, M.B.A. 1974

CAREER
Congressional aide; furniture company executive;
general store owner

POLITICAL HIGHLIGHTS
No previous office

ELECTION RESULTS

2004 GENERAL

Mark Souder (R)	171,389	69.2%
Maria M. Parra (D)	76,232	30.8%

2004 PRIMARY

Mark Souder (R)	46,583	79.2%
William R. Larsen (R)	12,210	20.8%

2002 GENERAL

Mark Souder (R)	92,566	63.1%
Jay Rigdon (D)	50,509	34.5%
Michael Donlan (LIBERT)	3,531	2.4%

PREVIOUS WINNING PERCENTAGES
2000 (62%); 1998 (63%); 1996 (58%); 1994 (55%)

Elected 1994; 6th term

Souder says that religious faith guides his politics. And while he typically votes a conservative line, he sometimes feels compelled by his beliefs to side with liberals on issues such as environmental protection and government support for drug treatment.

"If you scratch behind any of my positions, you find my religious beliefs," Souder (SOW — rhymes with "now" — dur) says. If he votes with Democrats for tougher environmental regulation, for instance, it is because "as a Christian, part of what you do is be a steward of all creation," he says.

His most high-profile issue in the 108th Congress was a bill to replace the image of Franklin Roosevelt on the dime with President Reagan's, an initiative that got a lot of attention after Reagan died in 2004. Democrats objected, as did Reagan's widow, Nancy Reagan, who said her husband would have wanted FDR to stay on the 10-cent piece. Souder deferred to her wishes.

Another of his ideas that year was hotly debated. Souder led a push in the House to overturn strict gun control laws in Washington, D.C., prompting the district's delegate in Congress, Eleanor Holmes Norton, to call him an "incorrigible extremist." The bill lifted the city's ban on private ownership of handguns and ammunition. The measure passed the House but got nowhere in the Senate. Souder defended the bill on the grounds that the ban encroached on the constitutional right to bear arms and that it failed to stem violence while leaving victims of crime defenseless.

A former congressional aide, Souder often works behind the scenes. Amiable and wonkish, he immerses himself in the details of his issues and is rarely caught flat-footed on the facts. His passion for policy, however, has not translated into leadership roles. He has no appetite for the year-round fundraising demanded of leaders. "I don't like to raise money, and I never will," Souder says. "I'd much rather read a book, read a bill or sit through a three-hour hearing."

Long active in anti-drug efforts, Souder chairs the Government Reform Subcommittee on Criminal Justice, Drug Policy and Human Resources. He supports interdiction to stop drug smuggling — he has taken several trips to Colombia to study the problem — but believes the federal government should also fund prevention programs.

He sponsored a bill in the 108th Congress to ease limits on the number of drug-addicted patients that physician groups can treat with medications designed to counter addiction. The measure was aimed at increasing the use of Buprenorphine, which has proven successful in treating heroin addicts. In the 109th Congress, Souder focused on the growing methamphetamine trade, which has become a problem in Indiana and several other states. He also was looking into the heroin trade out of Afghanistan, which is believed to be helping finance the terrorist activities of Osama bin Laden and his followers.

Souder, who came to the House with the radicalized Class of 1994, notes that in spite of frequent setbacks, conservatives scored significant victories in recent years in changing the welfare system and slashing federal income taxes. "If you're expecting in government dramatic changes constantly, you'll be frustrated," he says. "If you capitalize on key moments of transition in politics, you'll move government."

Souder's work on a faith-based charities initiative in President Bush's first term produced incremental results for the religious right. The bill was intended to remove barriers preventing religiously influenced groups from getting federal money for their programs helping the disadvantaged and the poor. Souder, in private communication with the White House, had argued that the original proposal was too ambitious and had urged early compromise with liberal Democrats and civil rights groups. When Bush decided to press ahead, Souder fought for the president's plan, which stalled in Congress.

The Souders were among the earliest settlers of Allen County, Ind., in the 1840s. The family's original harness shop grew into a series of family businesses in Grabill that made the Souder name well-known. The modern-day Souders, mostly religious conservatives, generally were not inclined to step into the temporal realm of politics. That changed the day then-Rep. Daniel R. Coats, another Indiana conservative Republican and later a member of the Senate, dropped by the family store to buy some furniture and met Mark Souder.

Coats believed in ideas that appealed to Souder, such as using the tax code to further conservative causes. In 1985, Souder became Coats' staff director on the Select Committee on Children, Youth and Families. Souder later was deputy chief of staff in Coats' Senate office.

In 1994, Souder decided to run for Coats' former House seat. He faced a tough, six-candidate primary. All the major contenders in the GOP field that year were staunchly conservative, and Souder's low-key demeanor made him appear less hard-line.

After winning the primary, Souder went on the attack early, starting with summer radio ads that portrayed the incumbent, Democratic Rep. Jill L. Long, as a Washington insider beholden to special interests and a loyalist for the Clinton administration. The strategy paid off — and Souder beat Long by 11 percentage points.

In 1998, Souder declared his opposition to impeaching President Clinton, saying he should be prosecuted as a private citizen. The stance earned him a serious primary opponent in 2000, but Souder eventually bested Allen County chief deputy prosecutor Michael Loomis. He attracted serious primary competition again in 2002, this time as a result of redistricting, but Souder handily defeated former Fort Wayne Mayor Paul Helmke.

In 2004, Souder drew only a token primary challenge and he dispatched engineer William R. Larsen handily. His general election was noteworthy for producing one of the stranger events of the campaign season. His Democratic challenger, insurance agent Maria M. Parra, fled a late-October debate after stage fright set in when, she said, she was "overwhelmed" by the presence of television cameras. She had little chance of winning anyway, and Souder took 69 percent of the vote.

KEY VOTES

2004
No   Extend federal unemployment benefits by 13 weeks
No   Pass $283.2 billion, six-year federal highway and mass transit bill
Yes   Approve $146 billion multi-year extension of previously enacted middle-class tax breaks
Yes   Amend the Constitution to prohibit same-sex marriage
Yes   Cut corporate taxes $137 billion over 10 years
Yes   Reorganize U.S. intelligence agencies as proposed by Sept. 11 commission

2003
Yes   Cut taxes by $330 billion through fiscal 2013
No   Block Bush rule scaling back overtime pay for some white-collar federal workers
No   Do not allow use of search warrants without first notifying subjects
No   Allow importation of prescription drugs
Yes   Create private school voucher program in Washington, D.C.
Yes   Ban "partial birth" abortion except to save a woman's life
?   Split $18.6 billion in Iraq aid into half-grant, half-loan
Yes   Overhaul Medicare and create prescription drug benefit

CQ VOTE STUDIES

	PARTY UNITY		PRESIDENTIAL SUPPORT	
	Support	Oppose	Support	Oppose
2004	94%	6%	79%	21%
2003	97%	3%	98%	2%
2002	94%	6%	89%	11%
2001	96%	4%	86%	14%
2000	91%	9%	19%	81%

INTEREST GROUPS

	AFL-CIO	ADA	CCUS	ACU
2004	13%	5%	100%	88%
2003	7%	5%	100%	88%
2002	11%	10%	85%	88%
2001	9%	10%	91%	96%
2000	10%	10%	71%	88%

INDIANA 3
Northeast – Fort Wayne

Agricultural communities with deep-rooted religious beliefs shape the character of the 3rd, a solidly Republican district in Indiana's northeast corner. The district's long tradition of social conservatism begins in the large Amish communities to the northwest, which are not overtly politically active but form and reflect the area's traditional values. Rural voters bolster the state's Republican leanings.

The 3rd's population center is Allen County, which includes Fort Wayne and accounts for nearly half of the district population. Fort Wayne, the state's most populous city after Indianapolis, has white-collar suburban neighborhoods and German-Americans that cement the 3rd's conservative loyalties. Like many midsize Midwestern cities, Fort Wayne has a substantial manufacturing sector. While the surrounding area has lost thousands of manufacturing jobs since the late 1990s, the region has been cushioned somewhat by a strong white-collar service sector. Technology and financial-service jobs have attracted professionals into Allen County, which had a slightly higher growth rate in the 1990s than

Indiana at large. Noble County, northwest of Allen, grew by 22 percent in the 1990s.

After Allen, the district's next most-populous counties are Elkhart (shared with the 2nd) and Kosciusko, which were added to the 3rd in redistricting following the 2000 census. Both counties are solidly conservative: Kosciusko gave George W. Bush a statewide high of 78 percent of the vote in the 2004 presidential election. East of Elkhart is LaGrange County, where nearly one-third of residents speak a language at home other than English; the county's Amish population speaks a German dialect.

Democrats find support in minority and blue-collar neighborhoods in Fort Wayne, but little backing elsewhere. In 2004, George W. Bush won every county in the 3rd with at least 63 percent of the vote.

MAJOR INDUSTRY
Manufacturing, agriculture, health care

CITIES
Fort Wayne (pt.), 202,769; Goshen, 26,611

NOTABLE
Author and naturalist Gene Stratton-Porter's former home is a state historical site on Sylvan Lake in Noble County.

Rep. Steve **Buyer** (R)

CAPITOL OFFICE
225-5037
www.house.gov/buyer
2230 Rayburn 20515-1404; fax 225-2267

COMMITTEES
Energy & Commerce
Veterans' Affairs - chairman

HOMETOWN
Monticello

BORN
Nov. 26, 1958, Rensselaer, Ind.

RELIGION
Methodist

FAMILY
Wife, Joni Buyer; two children

EDUCATION
The Citadel, B.S. 1980 (business administration);
Valparaiso U., J.D. 1984

MILITARY SERVICE
Army Reserve, 1980-84; Army, 1984-87; Army
Reserve, 1987-present

CAREER
Lawyer; Army prosecutor

POLITICAL HIGHLIGHTS
No previous office

ELECTION RESULTS

2004 GENERAL

Steve Buyer (R)	190,445	69.5%
David Sanders (D)	77,574	28.3%
Kevin R. Fleming (LIBERT)	6,117	2.2%

2004 PRIMARY

Steve Buyer (R)	52,921	65.8%
Dennis Hardy (R)	10,862	13.5%
Mike Campbell (R)	8,403	10.4%
Brian D. Paasch (R)	8,305	10.3%

2002 GENERAL

Steve Buyer (R)	112,760	71.4%
Bill Abbott (D)	41,314	26.2%
Jerry L. Susong (LIBERT)	3,934	2.5%

PREVIOUS WINNING PERCENTAGES
2000 (61%); 1998 (63%); 1996 (65%); 1994 (70%);
1992 (51%)

Elected 1992; 7th term

Intense and loyal to his party, Buyer was named chairman of the Veterans' Affairs Committee in the 109th Congress, a plum awarded in part because the Republican leadership likes him and in part because the former occupant fell out of favor. House leaders ousted Christopher H. Smith of New Jersey from the chairmanship after he fought them to increase spending for veterans' programs. Buyer took his place.

Yet the choice of Buyer (BOO-yer), a Persian Gulf War veteran and a colonel in the Army Reserve, worried some of the veterans' groups that had grown to appreciate Smith's devotion to more spending. Buyer in the past has criticized veterans' groups for politicizing issues and "measuring compassion by the dollar."

Veterans' organizations oppose any step back from the 1996 expansion of eligibility for outpatient care to all veterans, not just those with severe, service-connected disabilities. Buyer has said he plans to focus on the "core constituency . . . to ensure that VA benefits and health care are sustainable in the future." He defines core constituency as the disabled and indigent, and told the Indianapolis Star in 2005, "That's who comes first."

During hearings in the 108th Congress, Buyer was more sympathetic to the views of the Bush administration and the House leadership than Smith. When Veterans Affairs Secretary Anthony J. Principi told lawmakers early in 2004 that the VA received $1.2 billion less than it requested from the White House, Smith vowed to put the money back into the agency's budget. Buyer, on the other hand, reminded legislators that Congress had enacted laws over two decades that changed the VA from a specialized health care service to an outpatient network for all veterans, regardless of how they were injured. The changes, he said, have left many veterans using VA facilities for all or most of their health care needs, which has become costly for the government.

Now in his seventh term, Buyer is a tough-talking conservative who enjoys sparring with liberals on abortion, gun control and other polarizing issues. His high-volume partisanship has been off-putting to some.

Late in 2000, with the outcome of the presidential race hanging in the balance, Buyer spent nine days in Florida pressing local officials to count military ballots mailed from overseas, most of which were presumed to be for President Bush and many of which had been ruled invalid on technical grounds. Florida Democratic Rep. Peter Deutsch filed a complaint with the House ethics committee, alleging that Buyer, who was chairman of the Armed Services Subcommittee on Military Personnel at the time, had used his contacts with the Pentagon to obtain information on military absentee voters and passed it on to Republican party officials in Florida. The complaint against Buyer was dismissed, but the panel concluded that one of his subcommittee aides had improperly passed along government information for political purposes.

In 2001, Buyer took the unusual step of giving up his seniority on the Armed Services Committee and starting over at the bottom of the ladder on the Energy and Commerce Committee. He said he wanted to switch committees because he had accomplished his goals on Armed Services — altering the military's retirement system, changing its pay tables and creating the Tricare for Life medical and prescription drug benefit.

Buyer came to Congress fresh from duty with the Army Reserve in the Persian Gulf War, where he was a lawyer specializing in the treatment of prisoners, detained civilians and refugees. He was still in the reserves when the United States went to war with Iraq in 2003, and was notified that he would be called for active duty. But the Pentagon decided that the presence of a congressman in the region would cause security problems and his activation was canceled.

During his tour of duty in the first Iraq war in 1991, Buyer was near an enemy munitions depot when it was destroyed by U.S. forces. He suffered a series of mysterious illnesses for years afterward. He said at a congressional hearing in 1993 that a month after he returned home from the Gulf, he noticed he became exhausted jogging even short distances. He also suffered kidney problems, two bouts of pneumonia and spent much of the last month of his 1992 campaign in bed. In 2000, Buyer was notified by the Defense Department that he likely had been exposed to chemical agents that drifted in the smoke cloud from the depot.

Buyer's father, brother and sister are dentists, but he majored in business administration at The Citadel, the military college of South Carolina. Buyer's active duty was deferred while he attended law school in Indiana. He became an Army lawyer, first on active duty and then as a reservist.

When he returned from the war, Buyer ran for Congress against three-term Democrat Jim Jontz. Buyer criticized Jontz's vote in 1991 against giving President George Bush authority to commit troops to the Gulf. He also drew attention to Jontz's four overdrafts at the private bank for House members. The scandal hurt the careers of many lawmakers who overdrew their accounts. Buyer's 4,500-vote win was among the biggest House race upsets of 1992. He easily won his next four re-election bids.

Then, reapportionment after the 2000 census took one House seat away from Indiana, forcing a substantial redrawing of the political lines to account for the reduction to nine districts. Buyer's 5th District was parceled out among six districts. Only 3 percent of his former constituents were put in the 4th, but his hometown was there, so Buyer decided to run for re-election there in 2002. To introduce himself to his new constituents, he staged a 260-mile run across the new district. He declared the journey a success, reporting that he went through two pairs of shoes and encountered one angry pit bull and 51 dead opossums.

Buyer's energetic approach to the campaign was a contrast to his chief GOP opponent, first-term Rep. Brian Kerns, who put up a lackluster fight. Buyer won the primary by 25 percentage points. He cruised to a 45 percentage point win in November. In 2004, he crushed Democrat David Sanders, a Purdue University biology professor, by 41 percentage points.

KEY VOTES

2004
No   Extend federal unemployment benefits by 13 weeks
Yes   Pass $283.2 billion, six-year federal highway and mass transit bill
Yes   Approve $146 billion multi-year extension of previously enacted middle-class tax breaks
Yes   Amend the Constitution to prohibit same-sex marriage
Yes   Cut corporate taxes $137 billion over 10 years
Yes   Reorganize U.S. intelligence agencies as proposed by Sept. 11 commission

2003
Yes   Cut taxes by $330 billion through fiscal 2013
No   Block Bush rule scaling back overtime pay for some white-collar federal workers
No   Do not allow use of search warrants without first notifying subjects
No   Allow importation of prescription drugs
Yes   Create private school voucher program in Washington, D.C.
Yes   Ban "partial birth" abortion except to save a woman's life
No   Split $18.6 billion in Iraq aid into half-grant, half-loan
Yes   Overhaul Medicare and create prescription drug benefit

CQ VOTE STUDIES

	PARTY UNITY		PRESIDENTIAL SUPPORT	
	Support	Oppose	Support	Oppose
2004	96%	4%	87%	13%
2003	97%	3%	96%	4%
2002	97%	3%	83%	17%
2001	97%	3%	93%	7%
2000	94%	6%	22%	78%

INTEREST GROUPS

	AFL-CIO	ADA	CCUS	ACU
2004	13%	5%	100%	96%
2003	7%	10%	97%	92%
2002	13%	0%	94%	91%
2001	18%	0%	96%	96%
2000	10%	5%	85%	84%

I N D I A N A 4

West central — Indianapolis suburbs, Lafayette

Traversing the 4th by car requires a 175-mile trip through a slender district that takes in a mixture of farmland, small towns and suburbs. It spans from White County, which is roughly halfway between Chicago and Indianapolis, south to Lawrence County, which is about halfway between Indianapolis and Louisville.

Montgomery, White (shared with the 2nd District) and Boone counties are the top three Indiana counties in terms of soybean production. All three also rank among the state's top seven counties in corn production. Tippecanoe County, located between White and Montgomery, takes in Lafayette and West Lafayette. The latter is home to the main campus of Purdue University, which has an enrollment of more than 38,000. The school's engineering bent helps give Tippecanoe, the district's most populous county, a conservative hue.

South and east of fast-growing, GOP-friendly Boone and Hendricks counties, the 4th takes in a western sliver of Marion County (Indianapolis) and curves south of Indianapolis to take in most of

Johnson County, which is filling up with young, well-educated families.

Moving west and south, the district encompasses all of mostly rural Morgan County before narrowing considerably to take in western Monroe County (but not Bloomington, which is in the 9th District). South of Monroe is Lawrence County.

The 4th includes some of the most overwhelmingly Republican territory in Indiana. In the 2004 election, Montgomery and Boone gave George W. Bush 75 percent of the vote. Bush did not lose a single county entirely in the 4th in 2000 or 2004.

MAJOR INDUSTRY
Higher education, agriculture, manufacturing

CITIES
Lafayette, 56,397; Indianapolis (pt.), 39,244; Greenwood, 36,037

NOTABLE
The General Lew Wallace Study and Museum, which honors the Ben-Hur author, is in Crawfordsville; Tippecanoe Battlefield was where troops led by then-governor, and later president, William Henry Harrison fought off an American Indian attack in 1811.

www.cqpress.com

Rep. Dan Burton (R)

Elected 1982; 12th term

One of the House's most ferocious partisans during the Clinton years, Burton has become marginalized by party leaders. Left to himself, the man who once described himself as the "pit bull" of the House Republicans has not hesitated to occasionally wander down his own maverick path.

Burton still avidly pursues his party's domestic priorities, such as Social Security privatization and revamping the tax code. But in recent years, he has chased foreign policy aims that put him at odds with fellow Republicans, such as taking up Pakistan's cause in its dispute with India over Kashmir. He also called attention to alleged kidnappings of Americans in Saudi Arabia when the Bush White House was taking a softer line on the country, and he has championed Taiwan over China, a point of division in the GOP.

Early in the 108th Congress, party leaders blocked him from assuming the chairmanship of the International Relations South Asia Subcommittee, though his seniority in the House put him in line to take it, because he was thought to be too pro-Pakistan. At the start of the 109th, he finally got a subcommittee chairmanship on the panel, but with jurisdiction over the Western Hemisphere, the half of the globe where his agenda will be least distressing to his colleagues.

Burton in the 108th Congress was forced by GOP term limit rules to give up the gavel of the full Government Reform Committee, which he had used as an investigative cudgel on the Clinton White House. So he stepped out of the spotlight. But he did have a role in one of the big health issues of the Congress, a drug reimportation bill allowing U.S. citizens to buy American-made drugs from other countries, where price controls make them cheaper. Burton later helped lead the floor debate with the bill's chief sponsor, Minnesota Republican Gil Gutknecht.

The legislation passed the House in 2003 but stalled in the Senate. During a hearing on the issue, Burton bashed the Federal Drug Administration for raising safety questions about the practice among senior citizens. "You scare the hell out of them," he scolded.

Some of Burton's diminished stature can be traced to his revelation in 1998 that he fathered a son out of wedlock in the early 1980s. At the time of his disclosure, he was chairman of Government Reform and leading the House investigation of President Clinton's attempts to cover up a sexual relationship with a young White House intern.

He used his chairmanship to pummel the Clinton White House with subpoenas and investigations into campaign fundraising and other areas. Most famously, he suggested that presidential counsel Vincent W. Foster Jr.'s suicide in 1994 was a murder. He conducted his own investigation in his backyard with the help of a homicide detective, firing a gun into what he would describe only as "a head-like object" — reportedly a pumpkin or a watermelon — to see if the sound could be heard at a distance. Burton once called Clinton a "scumbag" and his Democratic critics "squealing pigs."

Burton's zealous partisanship was viewed as a liability. House GOP leaders quickly moved in 2002 to take the job of writing the authorizing legislation to create a Department of Homeland Security away from the Government Reform Committee. But in a sign of how distant those days are now, one of Burton's chief allies on the drug reimportation bill was former Clinton top adviser Rahm Emanuel, now a Democratic House member from Illinois. "It's great to work with you without my lawyer present," Emanuel quipped to Burton.

CAPITOL OFFICE
225-2276
www.house.gov/burton
2185 Rayburn 20515-1405; fax 225-0016

COMMITTEES
Government Reform
International Relations
 (Western Hemisphere - chairman)
Veterans' Affairs

HOMETOWN
Indianapolis

BORN
June 21, 1938, Indianapolis, Ind.

RELIGION
Christian

FAMILY
Widowed; four children

EDUCATION
Indiana U., attended 1958-59; Cincinnati Bible College, attended 1959-60

MILITARY SERVICE
Army, 1956-57; Army Reserve, 1957-62

CAREER
Real estate and insurance agent

POLITICAL HIGHLIGHTS
Ind. House, 1967-69; Ind. Senate, 1969-71; Republican nominee for U.S. House, 1970; sought Republican nomination for U.S. House, 1972; Ind. House, 1977-81; Ind. Senate, 1981-83

ELECTION RESULTS

2004 GENERAL

Dan Burton (R)	228,718	71.8%
Katherine Fox Carr (D)	82,637	26.0%
Rick Hodkin (LIBERT)	7,008	2.2%

2004 PRIMARY

Dan Burton (R)	83,136	86.4%
George Thomas Holland (R)	8,825	9.2%
Victor Dean Wakley (R)	4,287	4.5%

2002 GENERAL

Dan Burton (R)	129,442	72.0%
Katherine Fox Carr (D)	45,283	25.2%

PREVIOUS WINNING PERCENTAGES
2000 (70%); 1998 (72%); 1996 (75%); 1994 (77%); 1992 (72%); 1990 (63%); 1988 (73%); 1986 (68%); 1984 (73%); 1982 (65%)

Although the White House is in GOP hands, Burton still tends to challenge the executive branch. In the 108th Congress, he often voted against the president's positions on key issues; among Indiana's six GOP House members, only John Hostettler voted with President Bush less frequently. On one issue though, the war in Iraq, he is strongly with the president; on the talk show circuit he has defended Bush's decision to forcibly remove Saddam Hussein from power. He remains one of the House's most conservative members, a past co-founder of the Conservative Action Team, or CATs as they called themselves. The group today is known as the Republican Study Committee.

Burton's tenacity and combativeness developed from a difficult early life. His 6-foot, 8-inch tall father regularly beat him and his mother and was eventually jailed for abuse. His family lived in hotels and trailer parks, and by the time he was 12, Burton had lived in 38 states, Mexico and Canada. "I never stopped worrying that Dad would come back after he got out of jail," he told People magazine in 1994. "One day, when I was 13, he did. I was baby-sitting my younger brother and sister when I saw him come up the front walk. I was petrified and yelled, 'Don't come up here.' . . . I grabbed a shotgun we kept beside the front door. When he saw the gun, he turned around. I'm glad he did because I might have shot him."

After a stint in the Army and later attending Cincinnati Bible College, Burton worked as an insurance agent. At that time, he considered himself an independent but often voted Democratic. Then in 1964 he read an interview with Norman Thomas, a socialist presidential candidate who espoused the idea that the socialist philosophy was infiltrating American politics through the Democratic Party. Burton went to the local library and, reading the Congressional Record, studied the legislation Democrats supported. Concluding that Thomas was right, Burton called the local GOP and joined. Two years later, at age 28, he won a seat in the state legislature as a Republican.

Burton first made national headlines in 1987 when he proposed mandatory blood tests for everyone in the United States to track the AIDS virus. One former House Democrat told reporters that Burton refuses to eat soup in restaurants for fear of being infected with the disease.

His flamboyant conservatism remains a good fit for his wealthy suburban district. He has won his past seven re-elections with more than 70 percent of the vote, even though Indiana's congressional map for this decade made his constituency slightly less Republican. He briefly flirted with a run for governor in 2003 before supporting the eventual winner, Mitch Daniels.

KEY VOTES

2004

No Extend federal unemployment benefits by 13 weeks

Yes Pass $283.2 billion, six-year federal highway and mass transit bill

Yes Approve $146 billion multi-year extension of previously enacted middle-class tax breaks

Yes Amend the Constitution to prohibit same-sex marriage

Yes Cut corporate taxes $137 billion over 10 years

Yes Reorganize U.S. intelligence agencies as proposed by Sept. 11 commission

2003

Yes Cut taxes by $330 billion through fiscal 2013

No Block Bush rule scaling back overtime pay for some white-collar federal workers

No Do not allow use of search warrants without first notifying subjects

Yes Allow importation of prescription drugs

Yes Create private school voucher program in Washington, D.C.

Yes Ban "partial birth" abortion except to save a woman's life

Yes Split $18.6 billion in Iraq aid into half-grant, half-loan

No Overhaul Medicare and create prescription drug benefit

CQ VOTE STUDIES

	PARTY UNITY		PRESIDENTIAL SUPPORT	
	Support	Oppose	Support	Oppose
2004	96%	4%	76%	24%
2003	94%	6%	86%	14%
2002	97%	3%	84%	16%
2001	97%	3%	87%	13%
2000	98%	2%	17%	83%

INTEREST GROUPS

	AFL-CIO	ADA	CCUS	ACU
2004	21%	0%	95%	100%
2003	13%	20%	93%	92%
2002	13%	0%	80%	100%
2001	9%	5%	87%	100%
2000	13%	5%	89%	91%

INDIANA 5

East central — part of Indianapolis and suburbs

Dominated by Indianapolis suburbanites and rural farmers, the 5th is Indiana's wealthiest district and is staunchly Republican turf. The trend might well continue; the suburbanites, who are rapidly taking the region's countryside, have been a largely GOP constituency.

The district's most affluent residents and its few minorities live in northern Indianapolis (Marion County) and in the Hamilton County suburbs of Carmel, Fishers and Noblesville. Here, growing populations of white-collar workers in electronics and financial services bring median incomes well above state and national averages. Hamilton's median family income, $80,000 in 1999, was the state's highest and was nearly $20,000 above the next-highest county, Hancock (which is east of Indianapolis and also in the 5th District).

Hamilton, Marion and Hancock counties make up more than half of the 5th's population. Southeast of Indianapolis, the district also takes in most of Shelby County and northeastern Johnson County.

The suburban affluence does not extend to the northern part of the district, which is more middle-class. Miami County lost population in the 1990s, in part because of the 1994 realignment of what is now Grissom Air Reserve Base. Wabash and Grant, adjacent to Miami, also lost population in the 1990s. The district also takes in most of Howard County, including parts of working-class Kokomo (shared with the 2nd).

While the rural communities are not as affluent as their suburban counterparts, they too are solidly Republican. In the 2004 presidential election, George W. Bush won every county at least partly within the 5th, and his overall 71 percent made the 5th his best district in the state.

MAJOR INDUSTRY
Financial services, electronics, agriculture

CITIES
Indianapolis (pt.), 130,195; Fishers, 37,835; Carmel, 37,733; Marion, 31,320

NOTABLE
The Dan Quayle Center and U.S. Vice Presidential Museum is in Quayle's hometown of Huntington; Peru is the birthplace of Cole Porter and the site of the International Circus Hall of Fame; The Elwood Haynes Museum, in Kokomo, honors the inventor who was among the first to build a gasoline-powered automobile.

Rep. Mike Pence (R)

Elected 2000; 3rd term

There is nothing middle-of-the-road about Pence, who is one of the most conservative members of Congress. As a former talk radio host who says Rush Limbaugh was the inspiration for his radio career, Pence is among the most articulate communicators of the conservative message, both on talk radio shows in his district and on cable news channels nationwide.

Pence can usually be relied on to support the GOP leadership and President Bush, except when he stakes out positions to the right of them, such as when he led the charge in 2003 against a $400 billion-plus measure to provide a prescription drug benefit under Medicare. He said the costly drug benefit should have been accompanied by broader Medicare overhaul and should have focused on the poor instead of all seniors. A conservative revolt almost scuttled the bill.

His conservative colleagues rewarded him in 2004 with the chairmanship of the Republican Study Committee, a group of almost 100 lawmakers that represents a powerful bloc when it chooses to assert itself.

Conservatives sometimes bit their tongues in the 108th Congress — especially as the deficit spiraled upward — so as not to damage Bush's re-election bid. Now that Election Day has passed, a buoyant Pence is poised to lead a more organized and assertive conservative caucus. "House conservatives believe it's time to put our fiscal house in order," Pence says.

To that end, Pence opposed the 2004 highway bill as too profligate. While he and fellow conservatives were forced later that year to vote to increase the debt limit, they did so only after insisting that House GOP leaders hold to appropriations "caps" during end-of-session negotiations over a catchall spending bill. Pence was also among the dozen fiscal conservatives who insisted, throughout the 107th, on holding Republican leaders responsible for keeping government spending down. In 2001, Pence voted against a large education bill because, he said, it called for a 22 percent increase in federal spending. In 2002, Pence and his allies forced the leadership to adjust its timetable for considering annual spending bills, a move many of his GOP colleagues criticized.

A social conservative as well, Pence is staunchly anti-abortion and he opposes embryonic stem cell research. He was active in the debate on a constitutional amendment to ban same-sex marriage. Despite his zeal in promoting his views, he has a soft-spoken, placid manner. He remains in good graces with his party's leaders despite his periodic opposition to their policies.

When he arrived in the House in 2001, Pence was named to the GOP whip team. In the 108th Congress, he was promoted to deputy whip and was given a seat on the Republican Policy Committee.

The 6th District has a large rural constituency, and Pence tends to the interests of the farming community from his seat on the Agriculture Committee. He also sits on Judiciary, and supported committee Chairman F. James Sensenbrenner Jr. in a bid to attach language to a major bill overhauling U.S. intelligence programs to prohibit states from issuing driver's licenses to illegal aliens.

Although Arizona Republican Sen. John McCain campaigned for Pence in 2000, the two had a falling-out over McCain's push for campaign finance legislation. Pence eventually accused McCain of working too closely with the Democrats. The Indianapolis Star reported that Pence

CAPITOL OFFICE
225-3021
mikepence.house.gov
426 Cannon 20515-1406; fax 225-3382

COMMITTEES
Agriculture
International Relations
Judiciary

HOMETOWN
Columbus

BORN
June 7, 1959, Columbus, Ind.

RELIGION
Christian

FAMILY
Wife, Karen Pence; three children

EDUCATION
Hanover College, B.A. 1981 (history); Indiana U., J.D. 1986

CAREER
Radio and television broadcaster; think tank president; lawyer

POLITICAL HIGHLIGHTS
Republican nominee for U.S. House, 1988, 1990

ELECTION RESULTS

2004 GENERAL

Mike Pence (R)	182,529	67.1%
Melina Ann "Mel" Fox (D)	85,123	31.3%
Chad "Wick" Roots (LIBERT)	4,397	1.6%

2004 PRIMARY

Mike Pence (R)	unopposed

2002 GENERAL

Mike Pence (R)	118,436	63.8%
Melina Ann "Mel" Fox (D)	63,871	34.4%
Doris Robertson (LIBERT)	3,346	1.8%

PREVIOUS WINNING PERCENTAGES
2000 (51%)

told his GOP colleagues, "McCain is so deep in bed with the Democrats that his feet are coming out of the bottom of the sheets." Pence joined as a plaintiff in a lawsuit challenging the constitutionality of the campaign finance law enacted in 2002.

Drawing on his radio experience, Pence has set up a small radio studio in his House office where he records commentaries that are available on his Web site. He devotes several hours most weeks to appearing on local talk radio programs, and he encourages his colleagues to follow suit. "You've got to be willing to go in there and turn your face like flint to the wind," Pence says. "And I think too few of my colleagues in the conservative caucus are willing to do that."

A Democrat in his younger days, Pence made a run for the House in 1988 at age 29 with a challenge to veteran Democratic Rep. Philip R. Sharp. He lost by 6 percentage points. Two years later, he tried again, this time losing by almost 19 points. In the latter race, Pence ran a harshly negative campaign against Sharp. Pence later wrote an article, "Confessions of a Negative Campaigner," in which he said, "Negative campaigning, I now know, is wrong." He added, "It is wrong, quite simply, to squander a candidate's priceless moment in history . . . on partisan bickering."

It was during that period that Limbaugh captured Pence's imagination. "I was inspired by those dulcet tones to seek a career in radio and television," he recalls. Pence's first radio show aired in 1989 in Rushville, Ind. He eventually built up a syndicated talk show that was heard on 18 stations across the state. On many of those stations, he said, he was Limbaugh's "warm-up act."

Pence's years as a radio broadcaster and as host of a public affairs television show in Indianapolis kept his name before the public. When he decided in 2000 to run for the seat of GOP Rep. David M. McIntosh, who ran unsuccessfully for governor, Pence easily beat state Rep. Jeff Linder and four other opponents in the GOP primary. He then topped Democratic lawyer Bob Rock by 12 percentage points in November.

Redistricting after the 2000 census helped Pence. State Democrats who controlled the remapping process sought to bolster vulnerable Democratic Rep. Baron P. Hill in the neighboring 9th District. In shaping the new 6th District, the Democrats gave Pence some of Hill's Republican-leaning rural territory in southeastern Indiana. They put forth an active challenger in Melina Ann "Mel" Fox, a farmer and party activist running for office for the first time, but Pence took a 29 percentage point victory in a race that was noted for its civility. In a 2004 rematch, Pence upped his margin to 36 points.

KEY VOTES

2004

No	Extend federal unemployment benefits by 13 weeks
No	Pass $283.2 billion, six-year federal highway and mass transit bill
Yes	Approve $146 billion multi-year extension of previously enacted middle-class tax breaks
Yes	Amend the Constitution to prohibit same-sex marriage
Yes	Cut corporate taxes $137 billion over 10 years
Yes	Reorganize U.S. intelligence agencies as proposed by Sept. 11 commission

2003

Yes	Cut taxes by $330 billion through fiscal 2013
No	Block Bush rule scaling back overtime pay for some white-collar federal workers
No	Do not allow use of search warrants without first notifying subjects
No	Allow importation of prescription drugs
Yes	Create private school voucher program in Washington, D.C.
Yes	Ban "partial birth" abortion except to save a woman's life
No	Split $18.6 billion in Iraq aid into half-grant, half-loan
No	Overhaul Medicare and create prescription drug benefit

CQ VOTE STUDIES

	PARTY UNITY		PRESIDENTIAL SUPPORT	
	Support	Oppose	Support	Oppose
2004	99%	1%	94%	6%
2003	98%	2%	94%	6%
2002	99%	1%	84%	16%
2001	97%	3%	91%	9%

INTEREST GROUPS

	AFL-CIO	ADA	CCUS	ACU
2004	0%	0%	100%	100%
2003	7%	10%	96%	100%
2002	11%	5%	84%	100%
2001	0%	0%	96%	100%

INDIANA 6
East – Muncie, Anderson, Richmond

Covering most of Indiana's eastern border with Ohio, the 6th is a mix of farm, midsize city and suburban populations. The district's major population centers are Muncie and Anderson, in the center of the district.

In the 1920s, Muncie was the model for "Middletown," a study of small-town American life. Today, it is home to Ball State University, as well as automotive plants. MAGNA Drivetrain announced in 2004 that it plans to build parts for General Motors vehicles at a plant in Muncie that is expected to bring 420 new jobs to the area. The city's economy can be unsteady, as it was for much of the 1990s, with unemployment rates well above the state average. Delaware and adjacent Blackford were among the 11 Indiana counties that lost population in the 1990s. Anderson, another former auto manufacturing hub, also has seen industrial decline.

South and east of Muncie and Anderson, the 6th takes in Wayne and Henry counties, where the percentage of residents over age 65 is among the highest in Indiana. Richmond, in Wayne County, is the main city on

the 6th's eastern edge. Rush County is a top state producer of corn and soybeans.

Redistricting following the 2000 census elongated the district. The new 6th extends as far south as Dearborn County, just a few miles from the Ohio River, and stretches as far north as Allen County, just south of Fort Wayne.

The 6th has a Democratic past but now leans conservative, in part because the decline of manufacturing weakened the district's Democratic labor base. Bill Clinton carried Delaware and Madison counties, where Muncie and Anderson are located respectively, in the 1996 presidential election, but George W. Bush carried all 19 counties that lie wholly or partly in the 6th in both 2000 and 2004.

MAJOR INDUSTRY
Auto manufacturing, agriculture, light industry

CITIES
Muncie, 67,430; Anderson, 59,734; Richmond, 39,124

NOTABLE
The Indiana Basketball Hall of Fame is in New Castle; David Letterman is an alumnus of Ball State University.

Rep. Julia Carson (D)

CAPITOL OFFICE
225-4011
rep.carson@mail.house.gov
www.house.gov/carson
1535 Longworth 20515-1407; fax 225-5633

COMMITTEES
Financial Services
Transportation & Infrastructure

HOMETOWN
Indianapolis

BORN
July 8, 1938, Louisville, Ky.

RELIGION
Baptist

FAMILY
Divorced; two children

EDUCATION
Martin U., attended 1994-95 (political science)

CAREER
Clothing store owner; human resources manager; congressional district aide

POLITICAL HIGHLIGHTS
Ind. House, 1973-77; Ind. Senate, 1977-91; Center Township trustee, 1991-97

ELECTION RESULTS

2004 GENERAL

Julia Carson (D)	121,303	54.4%
Andrew Horning (R)	97,491	43.7%
Barry Campbell (LIBERT)	4,381	2.0%

2004 PRIMARY

Julia Carson (D)	30,915	89.4%
Bobby Hidalgo (D)	3,652	10.6%

2002 GENERAL

Julia Carson (D)	77,478	53.1%
Brose McVey (R)	64,379	44.1%
Andrew Horning (LIBERT)	3,919	2.7%

PREVIOUS WINNING PERCENTAGES
2000 (59%); 1998 (58%); 1996 (53%)

Elected 1996; 5th term

A loyal Democrat who has worked to help low-income people emerge from poverty, Carson generally aligns with fellow members of the Progressive Caucus, the most liberal faction of the House Democrats. Although she fought her own way to success, she believes government social programs can and should provide a helping hand to those in need.

Carson has been a fairly reliable supporter of organized labor, environmental protections, abortion rights, gun control and health care programs. From her seat on the Financial Services Committee, she has resisted such GOP initiatives as an overhaul of the federal public housing program, which included a requirement that unemployed tenants perform eight hours of community service per month.

Carson's personal background has informed her policy views. Born to a teenage single mother, she waited tables, delivered newspapers and did farm labor to earn money as a youth. Later, as a divorced young mother of two, she pinched every penny. While Carson's self-reliance might seem to fit right in with the philosophy of the typical Republican, her experiences have led her to very different conclusions about how to help the poor.

Right before her election to Congress, she held the job of Center Township trustee, administering municipal social services to low-income people in downtown Indianapolis. "We got people off of welfare and put them into jobs and into training and into educational experiences," Carson recalled. "We did not do that by being cruel." She uses adjectives like "cruel" and "regressive" to describe many GOP proposals.

But there are exceptions to Carson's partisanship. In the 108th Congress, she crossed party lines to work with her fellow Hoosier, GOP Sen. Richard G. Lugar, in authoring legislation that would streamline the Medicaid process for low-income children. She has worked with Lugar in the past on the issue.

At the start of the 108th, Carson traded the seat she had held on the Veterans' Affairs panel since her freshman year for assignment to the Transportation and Infrastructure Committee, which crafted a multibillion-dollar surface transportation authorization bill. She used her seat to secure funding for the Indianapolis bus system and highway network, as well as community cleanup and redevelopment projects for her urban district. The measure died in the 108th, but has been reintroduced in early 2005.

In 2002, Carson opposed President Bush's request for broad authority to wage war against Iraq. She has continued to attack Bush's policies — both foreign and domestic — and early in 2005 joined 30 other House Democrats in voting not to certify the presidential election vote tally in Ohio.

Her record on trade liberalization has been mixed. She joined most Democrats in 2002 against Bush's successful bid to revive fast-track procedures for congressional action on trade agreements, and opposed free-trade treaties like those passed in 2003 with Singapore and Chile. But in 2000, she bowed to intense lobbying by the Clinton White House, put aside her concerns about human rights violations and voted to make permanent the normal trade relations between the United States and China.

She argued that Bush had "perpetrated a fraud upon the people" by maintaining that the budget could accommodate not only his tax cuts but also adequate social spending and a reduction of the national debt. She opposed making the Bush tax cuts permanent, noting that Vice President Dick Cheney received $31,000 in tax deductions. "I just think we need to find something that's more fair and equitable," she told the Indianapolis Star.

Carson characterized it as "incomprehensible" when Republicans sought to close the Legal Services Corporation in the 1990s and leave legal representation for the indigent in the hands of private attorneys. She has said that providing government vouchers that parents can use to pay tuition at private or religious schools is a "cruel hoax" on the public school system. Like all but four of her fellow Democrats, she voted no when Congress created such a voucher program in 2003 in the District of Columbia.

In 1999, Carson won enactment of a measure awarding the Congressional Gold Medal to civil rights figure Rosa Parks. The bill initially won little support beyond members of the Congressional Black Caucus, but Carson stirred up media coverage and eventually enlisted more than 300 cosponsors in her successful campaign for the measure.

In both 2002 and 2003, she introduced, but failed to win enactment of, legislation to make all of her state, rather than just haphazard portions of it, subject to daylight-saving time. She argued that the measure was needed to improve energy efficiency and reduce pollution.

Carson began her congressional career as a secretary, and then a district aide, for Democratic Rep. Andrew Jacobs Jr. of Indianapolis. In 1972, she won the first of two state House terms, and in 1976 she moved up to the state Senate, where she served until 1991. During her years in the General Assembly, she worked as human resources director at Cummins Engine and later opened a dress shop that failed and left her saddled with debt. (She had her state Senate wages garnished to partially pay off the debts.)

While she was Center Township trustee, the office's overhead went up. But she improved the agency's financial standing overall, while reducing taxes and halving the roster of people receiving financial assistance.

When Jacobs retired in 1996 after 15 terms, he endorsed Carson to succeed him, helping her win a difficult nomination battle and hold off a vigorous Republican attempt to capture the 10th District. She won her next two re-election contests by comfortable margins. Redistricting for this decade made her district — which had been labeled the 10th — somewhat less Democratic. Her 9 percentage point victory in 2002 was her closest since her initial win in 1996.

Carson has battled a number of ailments through the years, including heart disease (she had bypass surgery in 1997), high blood pressure, asthma and diabetes. She missed almost a third of the House roll call votes in 2004 and had to answer tough campaign questions about her health. Nevertheless, her 2004 re-election was by 11 percentage points.

KEY VOTES

2004

Yes Extend federal unemployment benefits by 13 weeks

Yes Pass $283.2 billion, six-year federal highway and mass transit bill

Yes Approve $146 billion multi-year extension of previously enacted middle-class tax breaks

No Amend the Constitution to prohibit same-sex marriage

No Cut corporate taxes $137 billion over 10 years

Yes Reorganize U.S. intelligence agencies as proposed by Sept. 11 commission

2003

No Cut taxes by $330 billion through fiscal 2013

Yes Block Bush rule scaling back overtime pay for some white-collar federal workers

Yes Do not allow use of search warrants without first notifying subjects

Yes Allow importation of prescription drugs

No Create private school voucher program in Washington, D.C.

No Ban "partial birth" abortion except to save a woman's life

Yes Split $18.6 billion in Iraq aid into half-grant, half-loan

No Overhaul Medicare and create prescription drug benefit

CQ VOTE STUDIES

	PARTY UNITY		PRESIDENTIAL SUPPORT	
	Support	Oppose	Support	Oppose
2004	97%	3%	17%	83%
2003	97%	3%	20%	80%
2002	96%	4%	19%	81%
2001	95%	5%	26%	74%
2000	96%	4%	84%	16%

INTEREST GROUPS

	AFL-CIO	ADA	CCUS	ACU
2004	100%	75%	29%	0%
2003	93%	95%	33%	38%
2002	100%	100%	37%	0%
2001	100%	100%	35%	4%
2000	90%	90%	40%	4%

INDIANA 7
Most of Indianapolis

Indiana's largest concentration of minorities lives in the urban 7th, which has the state's lowest median income but also is home to a large white-collar workforce. Almost four times bigger than Fort Wayne, the state's next most-populous city, Indianapolis is the state's capital as well as its banking and commercial center. Heavy industry also plays a role in the city's economy, with a few automotive plants hanging on despite industry downturns.

Redistricting following the 2000 census changed the district's number (from 10 to 7) and slightly reduced the district's black population and Democratic lean. But even with those changes, the 7th gave John Kerry 58 percent of the vote in the 2004 presidential election — his highest percentage in the state — and the district's substantial minority influence makes it hard for a Republican to win.

Large minority populations, particularly blacks, in central Indianapolis form the 7th's core. The joint Indiana University-Purdue University campus is here, and some neighborhoods are up to 65 percent black. In the city's northern tier, white-collar residents are some of the wealthiest in the state and are more receptive to Republican candidates. In the southern part of the district, blue-collar, mostly white populations built around the city's manufacturing industry are more socially conservative and generally supported Republicans on the local level in the 1990s.

Indianapolis has a reputation for being one of the nation's more conservative metropolitan areas. Sen. Richard G. Lugar, William Hudnut and Stephen Goldsmith kept the mayor's office in GOP hands for 32 years, until Democrat Bart Peterson took office in 2000. City voters re-elected Peterson in 2003.

MAJOR INDUSTRY
Manufacturing, health care, higher education

CITIES
Indianapolis (pt.), 612,431; Lawrence (pt.), 27,868

NOTABLE
Indianapolis Motor Speedway; President Benjamin Harrison, John Dillinger, poet James Whitcomb Riley, three vice presidents and 10 Indiana governors are buried in the Crown Hill Cemetery.

Rep. John Hostettler (R)

Elected 1994; 6th term

CAPITOL OFFICE
225-4636
john.hostettler@mail.house.gov
www.house.gov/hostettler
1214 Longworth 20515-1408; fax 225-3284

COMMITTEES
Armed Services
Judiciary
  (Immigration, Border Security & Claims -
  chairman)

HOMETOWN
Blairsville

BORN
July 19, 1961, Evansville, Ind.

RELIGION
General Baptist

FAMILY
Wife, Elizabeth Ann Hostettler; four children

EDUCATION
Rose-Hulman Institute of Technology, B.S. 1983
(mechanical engineering)

CAREER
Mechanical engineer

POLITICAL HIGHLIGHTS
No previous office

ELECTION RESULTS

2004 GENERAL

John Hostettler (R)	145,576	53.4%
Jon P. Jennings (D)	121,522	44.6%
Mark Garvin (LIBERT)	5,680	2.1%

2004 PRIMARY

John Hostettler (R)	unopposed

2002 GENERAL

John Hostettler (R)	98,952	51.3%
Bryan L. Hartke (D)	88,763	46.0%
Pam Williams (LIBERT)	5,150	2.7%

PREVIOUS WINNING PERCENTAGES
2000 (53%); 1998 (52%); 1996 (50%); 1994 (52%)

A decade after he swept into Washington with the revolutionary 1994 class of GOP freshmen, Hostettler remains a true believer in the group's core conservative principles — smaller government, strict adherence to the letter of the Constitution, gun owners' rights and opposition to abortion.

His conservatism often trumps his loyalty to President Bush or the Republican leadership. In the 108th Congress, Hostettler (HO-stet-lur) opposed Bush more often than all but eight other House Republicans. He was one of only six House Republicans to vote against authorizing the president to wage war against Iraq in 2002.

Hostettler goes his own way on budget issues in particular. He voted against a number of spending bills in 2003 and 2004 because he said they were too big. He also voted against the leadership-backed budget resolutions in those years, and opposed Bush's 2003 Medicare prescription drug bill as too costly.

From the moment he arrived, he made it clear that he would not be a loyalist at any cost. During his first term, Hostettler split openly with Speaker Newt Gingrich, contending early that Gingrich's ethics woes and general unpopularity made him a hindrance to the GOP message. Hostettler joined a small band of rebels who tried to force Gingrich from the speakership in 1997, several months before Gingrich acknowledged his depleted support among Republicans by stepping down voluntarily.

From his seat on the Judiciary Committee, Hostettler is consistent in his belief that the Constitution should not be amended with every new current in politics. That results in an occasional alliance with Democrats. In 2004, he was one of 27 House Republicans who opposed a proposed constitutional amendment to ban gay marriage, even though he believes in the underlying notion of banning such unions. Previously, he voted with Democratic lawmakers against constitutional amendments requiring a balanced budget and imposing term limits on service in the House.

In 2004, he sponsored legislation that prevented federal courts, including the Supreme Court, from having jurisdiction over the legislative branch's "Defense of Marriage Act," a 1996 law that gave states the option of not recognizing same-sex marriages performed in other states. His bill passed the House, but was not taken up by the Senate.

Since 2003, Hostettler has chaired Judiciary's Immigration Subcommittee. With full committee Chairman F. James Sensenbrenner Jr. of Wisconsin, he fought for tougher border security and immigration laws to address terrorism threats during 2004 debate of a comprehensive overhaul of intelligence agencies. Some of the provisions were adopted by the House, but later removed from the final version of the bill. In response, Hostettler joined a minority of House Republicans voting against it.

Hostettler is an avid defender of gun owners' rights, but was embarrassed in 2004 when he was caught carrying a loaded handgun in an airport. Two years prior to the incident, he had introduced legislation to provide for state-to-state reciprocity in permitting people to carry concealed weapons.

In April 2004, Hostettler was detained at the Louisville airport when a loaded handgun was found in his carry-on bag. He called the incident a "stupid mistake," explaining that he had carried the gun while traveling through his district during a congressional recess and forgot that it was in his bag. Hostettler pleaded guilty to carrying a concealed deadly weapon and got a 60-day suspended sentence.

From his seat on the Armed Services Committee, Hostettler supports Republican efforts to boost Pentagon spending and also watches out for the Crane Naval Surface Warfare Center in his district. He was among the lawmakers who unsuccessfully tried in the 108th Congress to delay the 2005 round of military base closings.

Although he opposes spending for many domestic programs, he does lobby for spending for Indiana. Hostettler has worked with a group of lawmakers pressing for completion of Interstate 69, the highway that stretches from the Canadian border in Michigan to the Mexican border. When completed, the highway will run through his district.

Before coming to Congress, Hostettler was a mechanical engineer by trade and active in his church, serving on the board of deacons of the Twelfth Avenue General Baptist Church in Evansville and teaching Bible classes there.

Hostettler grew up with nine siblings in a house with one bathroom in the southern Indiana county where he now lives. "I'm the eighth of 10 children," he told the newspaper Newsday. "In a family that size, you had to fight to get anything you got. Struggle is not new to me."

After getting an engineering degree from the Rose-Hulman Institute of Technology in Terre Haute, he married his high school sweetheart and went to work for Southern Indiana Gas & Electric Co.

The election of Bill Clinton in 1992 got him interested in politics — and not because he was a fan of the new president. Two years later, Hostettler decided to challenge six-term Democratic Rep. Frank McCloskey. He had little money, but relying on a grass-roots organization drawn primarily from evangelical churches, won the GOP primary. He went on to defeat McCloskey by almost 5 percentage points in the watershed election for Republicans. His victory celebration cake read, "To God Give the Glory."

Hostettler has struggled in each of his re-election races, never capturing more than the 53 percent he got in 2004. Close races in the 8th District predate Hostettler, and it's been known locally as the "Bloody 8th" for its perennially close calls. But Hostettler has managed to hold onto the seat, although Democrats continue to target him.

Redistricting for the 2002 election changed the district's geography — adding Terre Haute and dropping Bloomington — but did little to alter the 8th's competitiveness. In 2004, Hostettler faced Jon P. Jennings, a senior official in the Clinton administration's Justice Department and a scout for the NBA's Boston Celtics. He won by 9 percentage points — his highest margin yet.

KEY VOTES

2004

No Extend federal unemployment benefits by 13 weeks

Yes Pass $283.2 billion, six-year federal highway and mass transit bill

Yes Approve $146 billion multi-year extension of previously enacted middle-class tax breaks

No Amend the Constitution to prohibit same-sex marriage

Yes Cut corporate taxes $137 billion over 10 years

No Reorganize U.S. intelligence agencies as proposed by Sept. 11 commission

2003

Yes Cut taxes by $330 billion through fiscal 2013

No Block Bush rule scaling back overtime pay for some white-collar federal workers

No Do not allow use of search warrants without first notifying subjects

No Allow importation of prescription drugs

Yes Create private school voucher program in Washington, D.C.

Yes Ban "partial birth" abortion except to save a woman's life

No Split $18.6 billion in Iraq aid into half-grant, half-loan

No Overhaul Medicare and create prescription drug benefit

CQ VOTE STUDIES

	PARTY UNITY		PRESIDENTIAL SUPPORT	
	Support	Oppose	Support	Oppose
2004	93%	7%	62%	38%
2003	92%	8%	76%	24%
2002	88%	12%	72%	28%
2001	94%	6%	85%	15%
2000	92%	8%	17%	83%

INTEREST GROUPS

	AFL-CIO	ADA	CCUS	ACU
2004	33%	20%	81%	88%
2003	40%	35%	87%	84%
2002	22%	15%	80%	84%
2001	11%	15%	85%	92%
2000	30%	15%	76%	88%

INDIANA 8
West — Evansville, Terre Haute

Indiana's southwest corner, formed by the converging Wabash and Ohio rivers, houses the 8th, a district characterized by laborers and social conservatives. Evansville, an Ohio River port and the state's third-largest city, is southern Indiana's industrial center. It is located in Vanderburgh County, the district's most populous, and is home to the 8th's only substantial minority and liberal populations.

North of Evansville the district takes on a more rural and culturally conservative flavor. Gibson and Knox counties are among Indiana's top corn producing areas. Nearly one in six people in Daviess County, east of Knox, speak a language other than English at home. The county also has a large Amish population. Martin County, east of Daviess, includes the Naval Surface Warfare Center in Crane.

Owen County, northwest of Bloomington and about 50 miles southwest of Indianapolis, has just 22,000 residents but had a higher population growth rate in the 1990s than all but three other Indiana counties. West of Owen is Vigo County, the district's other major population center and

home of Indiana State University in Terre Haute. Redistricting following the 2000 census extended the district's northern boundary to Warren County, which is closer to Chicago than to Evansville.

Known in political circles as the "Bloody Eighth" for its aggressive and close elections, including a 1984 barnburner in which four votes separated the candidates, the 8th's manufacturing base and history as a mining center long gave Democrats an edge. But cultural issues, including gun control, moved the district to the right, and George W. Bush carried every county here en route to winning the district with 62 percent of the 2004 presidential vote.

MAJOR INDUSTRY
Manufacturing, agriculture, higher education

MILITARY BASES
Naval Surface Warfare Center, Crane Division, 61 military, 3,955 civilian (2003)

CITIES
Evansville, 121,582; Terre Haute, 59,614; Vincennes, 18,701

NOTABLE
Labor leader Jimmy Hoffa was born in Brazil.

Rep. Mike Sodrel (R)

CAPITOL OFFICE
225-5315
www.house.gov/sodrel
1508 Longworth 20515-1409; fax 226-6866

COMMITTEES
Science
Small Business
Transportation & Infrastructure

HOMETOWN
New Albany

BORN
Dec. 17, 1945, Louisville, Ky.

RELIGION
Christian

FAMILY
Wife, Keta Sodrel; two children

EDUCATION
New Albany High School, graduated 1963

MILITARY SERVICE
Ind. National Guard, 1966-73

CAREER
Trucking, shipping and motor coach company owner

POLITICAL HIGHLIGHTS
Republican nominee for U.S. House, 2002

ELECTION RESULTS

2004 GENERAL
Mike Sodrel (R)	142,197	49.5%
Baron P. Hill (D)	140,772	49.0%
Al Cox (LIBERT)	4,541	1.6%

2004 PRIMARY
Mike Sodrel (R)	unopposed

Elected 2004; 1st term

"Jobs, taxes and values" was something of a campaign-trail mantra for trucking company owner Sodrel as he cruised southeastern Indiana, driving his own 18-wheeler on a 2004 tour that allowed him to win a rematch with Democratic Rep. Baron P. Hill in the second-closest House contest of 2004.

Sodrel (SOD-drell) also made use of more-traditional methods of communicating when he was given podium time at the 2004 Republican National Convention in New York. "I know America's stronger when we create family-supporting jobs here in America. I know America's stronger when government takes less money from our nation's families. And I know America's stronger when we defend traditional moral values," he said.

A consummate Republican Party man whose fundraisers featured Vice President Dick Cheney and Speaker J. Dennis Hastert, Sodrel said he looks forward to working with the leadership to permanently repeal the inheritance tax and the so-called marriage penalty.

Sodrel's social conservatism is manifest in his opposition to abortion and gun control measures and support for constitutional amendments to ban same-sex marriage and desecration of the American flag.

As the owner of three trucking and bus companies, Sodrel was an easy choice for the Transportation and Infrastructure Committee. He represents a district that should benefit from a $1.9 billion project to link southeastern Indiana and Louisville, Ky., with two new bridges over the Ohio River.

Sodrel geared up for a rematch with Hill soon after losing by 5 percentage points in his 2002 political debut. And he benefited from a more vigorous campaign organization than in his first race, as well as ample financial aid from the national Republicans and a top-of-the-ticket boost from President Bush, who did well in the conservative-leaning 9th District.

Still, Hill's deep local roots and reputation as a centrist Democrat made the outcome a cliffhanger. Sodrel won by 1,425 votes. His victory marked the first GOP triumph in the 9th in four decades; it also was the only 2004 general-election defeat of a Democratic House member outside of Texas.

INDIANA 9
Southeast – Bloomington, New Albany

Bordering the Ohio River to the south, the 9th shares socially conservative roots and, more recently, competitive politics with other river valley districts. Manufacturing forms the economic foundation, although agriculture and retail trade also are prevalent in Indiana's southeastern quadrant.

The 9th's northeastern counties are seeing an influx of Cincinnati migrants, who have started to change the district from rural to slightly suburban. To the south, Clark and Floyd counties are adding residents due to Louisville metropolitan area growth. Clark is the 9th's most populous county.

Much of Monroe, the next most-populous county, was drawn into the 9th following the 2000 census, including Bloomington. Indiana University's presence gives the city a Democratic lean. The 9th's part of Monroe gave John Kerry his second-best showing in the state in the 2004 presidential race.

While the university makes Monroe one of Indiana's best-educated counties, the 9th as a whole is blue-collar with a low percentage of college graduates. Unemployment in some counties, including Orange and Crawford, can run substantially above the state's otherwise low average, and areas of rural poverty exist in the district. Crawford has the state's second-highest poverty rate and the longest commute time: many residents work due east in Louisville.

While the 9th has a Democratic heritage, the area's deep conservatism on cultural issues propelled Bush to double-digit victories in 2000 and 2004.

MAJOR INDUSTRY
Manufacturing, agriculture, retail

CITIES
Bloomington (pt.), 66,459; New Albany, 37,603; Jeffersonville, 27,362

NOTABLE
Larry Bird is from French Lick; Corydon was Indiana's first state capital (1816-25).

IOWA

Gov. Tom Vilsack (D)

First elected: 1998
Length of term: 4 years
Term expires: 1/07
Salary: $107,482
Phone: (515) 281-5211

Hometown: Mt. Pleasant
Born: Dec. 13, 1950; Pittsburgh, Pa.
Religion: Roman Catholic
Family: Wife, Christie Vilsack; two children
Education: Hamilton College (N.Y.), A.B. 1972; Albany Law School, J.D. 1975
Career: Lawyer
Political highlights: Mayor of Mt. Pleasant, 1987-92; Iowa Senate, 1993-99

Election results:
2002 GENERAL

Tom Vilsack (D)	540,449	52.7%
Doug Gross (R)	456,612	44.5%
Jay Robinson (GREEN)	14,628	1.4%
Clyde Cleveland (LIBERT)	13,098	1.3%

Lt. Gov. Sally Pederson (D)

First elected: 1998
Length of term: 4 years
Term expires: 1/07
Salary: $76,698
Phone: (515) 281-0225

STATE LEGISLATURE

General Assembly: January-May

House: 100 members, 2-year terms
2005 breakdown: 51R, 49D; 76 men, 24 women
Salary: $21,381
Phone: (515) 281-3221

Senate: 50 members, 4-year terms
2005 breakdown: 25D, 25R; 45 men, 5 women
Salary: $21,381
Phone: (515) 281-3371

STATE TERM LIMITS

Governor: No
House: No
Senate: No

URBAN STATISTICS

CITY	POPULATION
Des Moines	198,682
Cedar Rapids	120,758
Davenport	98,359
Sioux City	85,013
Waterloo	68,747

REGISTERED VOTERS

Unaffiliated	39%
Republican	31%
Democrat	30%

POPULATION

2004 population (est.)	2,954,451
2000 population	2,926,324
1990 population	2,776,755
Percent change (1990-2000)	+5.4%
Rank among states (2004)	30

Median age	36.6
Born in state	74.8%
Foreign born	3.1%
Violent crime rate	266/100,000
Poverty level	9.1%
Federal workers	18,928
Military	14,329

REDISTRICTING

Iowa retained its five seats in reapportionment. The Legislative Service Bureau drew a new map, which the state legislature approved and the governor signed on June 22, 2001.

MISCELLANEOUS

Web: www.iowa.gov
Capital: Des Moines
STATE ELECTION OFFICIAL
(515) 281-5865
DEMOCRATIC HEADQUARTERS
(515) 244-7292
REPUBLICAN HEADQUARTERS
(515) 282-8105

District Statistics

DIST.	2004 VOTE FOR PRESIDENT BUSH	KERRY	WHITE	BLACK	ASIAN	HISP	MEDIAN INCOME	WHITE COLLAR	BLUE COLLAR	SERVICE INDUSTRY	OVER 64	UNDER 18	COLLEGE EDUCATION	RURAL	SQ. MILES
1	46%	53%	92%	4%	1%	2%	$38,727	56%	29%	15%	14%	25%	20%	34%	7,217
2	44	55	92	2	2	3	$40,121	59	27	14	13	24	25	34	7,566
3	49.7	49.6	90	3	2	3	$43,176	62	24	14	13	26	25	27	6,979
4	51	48	95	1	1	3	$38,242	56	29	15	16	24	20	49	15,760
5	60	39	94	1	1	4	$36,773	53	31	16	17	26	16	51	18,348
STATE	50	49	93	2	1	3	$39,469	57	28	15	15	25	21	39	55,869
U.S.	50.7	48.3	69	12	4	13	$41,994	60	25	15	12	26	24	21	3,537,438

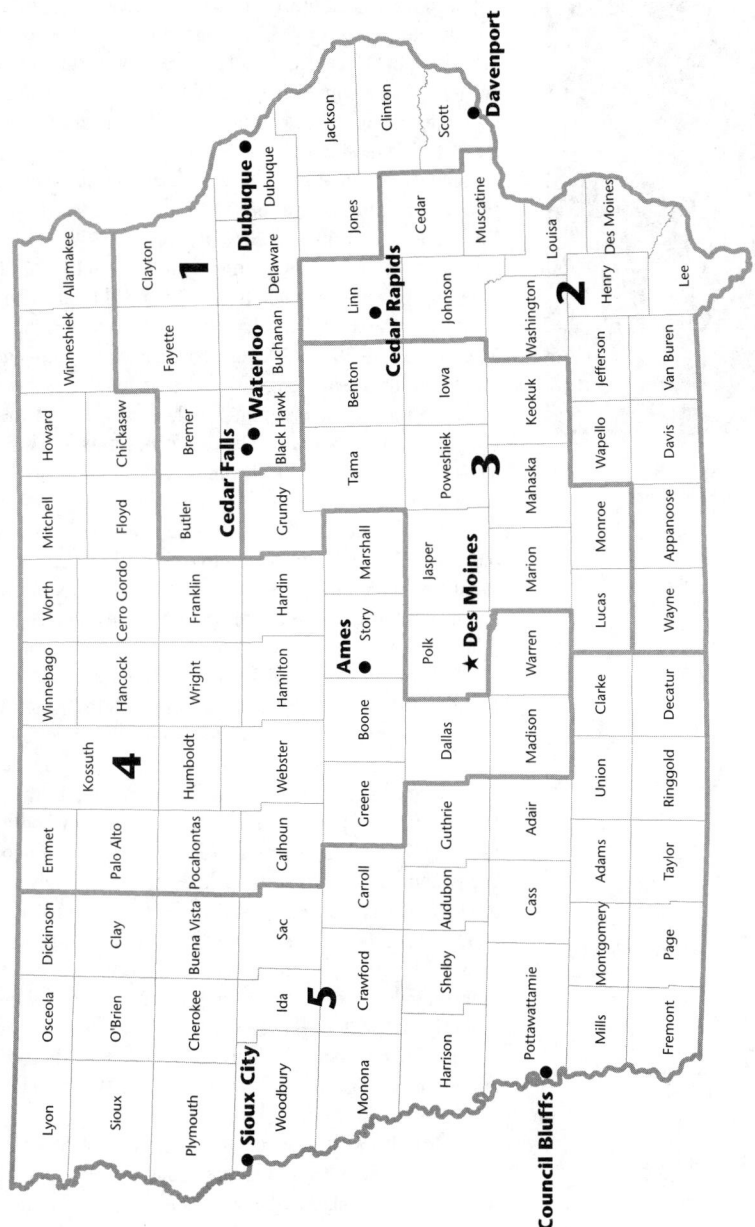

Sen. Charles E. Grassley (R)

Elected 1980; 5th term

CAPITOL OFFICE
224-3744
chuck_grassley@grassley.senate.gov
grassley.senate.gov
135 Hart 20510-1501; fax 224-6020

COMMITTEES
Agriculture, Nutrition & Forestry
Budget
Finance - chairman
Judiciary
  (Immigration, Border Security & Citizenship)
Joint Taxation

HOMETOWN
New Hartford

BORN
Sept. 17, 1933, New Hartford, Iowa

RELIGION
Baptist

FAMILY
Wife, Barbara Grassley; five children

EDUCATION
U. of Northern Iowa, B.A. 1955, M.A. 1956 (political science); U. of Iowa, attended 1957-58 (graduate studies)

CAREER
Farmer

POLITICAL HIGHLIGHTS
Republican nominee for Iowa House, 1956; Iowa House, 1959-75; U.S. House, 1975-81

ELECTION RESULTS

2004 GENERAL

Charles E. Grassley (R)	1,038,175	70.2%
Arthur Small (D)	412,365	27.9%
Christy Welty (LIBERT)	15,218	1.0%

2004 PRIMARY

Charles E. Grassley (R)	unopposed

PREVIOUS WINNING PERCENTAGES
1998 (68%); 1992 (70%); 1986 (66%); 1980 (54%);
1978 House Election (75%); 1976 House Election
(57%); 1974 House Election (51%)

One of two farmers in the U.S. Senate, Grassley has an independent streak that drives the White House to distraction. His fiscal conservatism demands that future tax cuts be offset with compensating revenue increases. The prairie populist in him lashes out at the Food and Drug Administration for being too soft on big pharmaceutical companies. He is the champion of FBI whistle-blowers.

Because as Finance chairman Grassley happens to head up the most powerful Senate committee, which oversees taxes, Medicare, Social Security, trade and welfare policy, he often feels the heat from Pennsylvania Avenue as well as from his more ideological colleagues, who accuse him of being the chief obstacle to the Bush economic agenda.

At the same time, Grassley's insistence on working with Democrats and forging policies through consensus translates into legislative accomplishments. In the 109th Congress, Grassley played a pivotal role in brokering a compromise to enact limits on class action suits and advanced an overhaul of bankruptcy laws. "The difference between being an ideologue and a realistic conservative is, I want to get things done. In order to get things done, you can't be a consistent ideologue," Grassley says.

At the outset of the 109th, Grassley told the Bush administration that he didn't agree with its approach to overhauling the Social Security program to introduce private investment. Rather, he said, he wanted a bill to boost tax breaks for retirement savings and make changes to private pension systems. The White House was not pleased, especially after Grassley returned to Washington from a visit to Iowa in early 2005 and said publicly that President Bush's plan was not selling with the American public.

On the Finance panel, Grassley has been able to draw support for tax measures from moderates in both parties, especially those from rural states. Max Baucus of Montana, the panel's top-ranking Democrat, is a constant ally. In a sea of bitter partisanship in the Senate, they operate the committee as a nonpartisan island, sharing office staff and issuing joint statements.

Agreements between the pair helped clear the way for some of Bush's top legislative achievements: the 10-year, $1.35 trillion tax cut of 2001, the 2002 law renewing the president's fast-track authority to negotiate trade deals that cannot be amended by Congress, the 2003 tax cut of $330 billion that reduced dividend and capital gains rates, and the 2003 law that added prescription drug coverage to Medicare.

Back in 2003, Grassley initially questioned whether Bush's proposal to eliminate taxation of corporate dividends was politically viable but later reversed course. "I think I should have kept my mouth shut back in January," Grassley said after meeting with the president.

Later, in 2004, Grassley successfully helped assemble a $137 billion corporate tax cut bill. Treasury Secretary John W. Snow condemned it for being packed with special interest provisions and for containing tax policies that the administration did not support, such as a $77 billion tax break for manufacturers. Nonetheless, Grassley's tax legislation, which happened to include a few targeted tax breaks for Iowa constituencies, became law.

But overall, Grassley backed the president on Senate floor votes 98 percent of the time during the 108th Congress. He is a social conservative who opposes abortion and gun control. When it comes to approving conservative judges, for example, Grassley votes the straight party line.

Grassley is not a lawyer — "I'm just a farmer from Butler County," he likes

www.cqpress.com

to say — but on the Judiciary Committee he holds his own by mastering legislative details and building coalitions on his priorities. Since 1997, these have included a campaign to rewrite bankruptcy law, primarily to make it harder for people to wipe away their debts in bankruptcy court.

Although no one at the Capitol views him as a riveting speechmaker, he is considered among the most persistent of senators. Through much of his congressional career, Grassley has led high-profile investigations of government waste and misconduct. "Frankly, it takes too much time to pass legislation on some issues," he says. "With oversight, it's direct and immediate, and you see results much more quickly."

Working with Judiciary Chairman Patrick J. Leahy, a Vermont Democrat, in 2001 and 2002 he probed allegations that rank-and-file FBI employees were being held to tougher standards of conduct than bureau managers. Grassley also pushed successfully in 2002 to extend whistle-blower protection requirements to the new Department of Homeland Security.

He is most proud of his role as government watchdog. During the 1980s, he publicized some extraordinary Pentagon expenditures, including $7,600 for a coffeemaker and $700 for a toilet seat. In the 108th Congress, he staged dramatic hearings where anonymous witnesses sitting behind screens recounted complex schemes by U.S. corporations to shelter billions of dollars from taxation. Cracking down on tax abuse became Grassley's crusade. In the 109th Congress, he turned his attention to the FDA and whether the agency is approving unsafe drugs.

He has also worked on overhauling the IRS and trimming the number of federal judgeships. He has made working conditions on Capitol Hill itself a priority, pushing the 1995 law making Congress abide by the labor and safety rules it imposes on businesses. He has tried to require public disclosure of "holds" placed on legislation by individual senators, which halt action on a bill. And following the 2001 anthrax attack, in which individual lawmakers were mailed anonymous letters tainted with the toxin, Grassley investigated the health effects of the chemicals used in the cleanup itself.

Grassley backs aggressive enforcement of antitrust laws. He has expressed alarm at the rate of mergers in the meat processing industry and has pushed the Agriculture Department to take a tougher stand against anti-competitive practices. With Iowa's other senator, Democrat Tom Harkin, he has moved to spur more airline competition, in part by writing into a 2000 law the guarantee of two slots at Washington's crowded Reagan National Airport for a carrier offering nonstop service to Des Moines.

The son of Waterloo-area farmers, Grassley is proud of his deep rural roots. He still returns to work the family corn and soybean fields on weekends in the spring and fall, and has been known to haul grain with a cell phone tucked inside his cap so he can feel the vibrations of an incoming call. He views himself as one of the few farmer-statesmen left in a country founded by them and is not one to put on airs or attempt to spin.

He began predicting a career in politics for himself while he was in high school, although he initially dreamed only of a seat in the Iowa House. After graduating from the University of Northern Iowa, he did graduate work at two Iowa universities and paid the bills by working in a factory, where he was a Machinists union member. A few years later, he and his wife, Barbara, took over his family's grain and livestock operation. (Indiana Sen. Richard Lugar is the Senate's other farmer.)

At the age of 25, he began a 16-year stint in the Iowa House, where he rose to become chairman of the Appropriations Committee. He moved to Congress as the successor of H.R. Gross, a revered Republican figure in the state who retired in 1974. Six years later, he moved to the Senate, unseating liberal Democrat John C. Culver. He has won with ease ever since.

KEY VOTES

2004

Yes Pass $318.9 billion, six-year highway and mass transit bill
No Extend assault weapons ban for 10 years
No Restore pay-as-you-go rules for new tax cuts and entitlement spending
Yes Criminalize harm to a fetus in an attack on the mother
Yes Increase mandatory child care funding to states by $6 billion over five years
Yes Amend the Constitution to prohibit same-sex marriage
Yes Approve $146 billion multi-year extension of previously enacted middle-class tax breaks
Yes Reorganize U.S. intelligence agencies as proposed by Sept. 11 commission
Yes Cut corporate taxes $137 billion over 10 years

2003

No Delay Bush changes to Clean Air Act
Yes Allow confirmation vote on Miguel A. Estrada to the U.S. Court of Appeals for the D.C. Circuit
No Block a Bush proposal opening Alaska's Arctic National Wildlife Refuge to oil drilling
No Limit size of Bush's proposed tax cut to $350 billion through fiscal 2013
Yes Overhaul Medicare and create prescription drug benefit
No Block Bush rule scaling back overtime pay for some white-collar federal workers
No Split $20 billion in Iraq aid into half-grant, half-loan
Yes Ban "partial birth" abortion except to save a woman's life
Yes Stop proposal allowing travel to Cuba
Yes Allow final vote on energy policy overhaul

CQ VOTE STUDIES

	PARTY UNITY		PRESIDENTIAL SUPPORT	
	Support	Oppose	Support	Oppose
2004	97%	3%	94%	6%
2003	96%	4%	99%	1%
2002	88%	12%	95%	5%
2001	93%	7%	99%	1%
2000	94%	6%	42%	58%
1999	90%	10%	33%	67%
1998	86%	14%	39%	61%
1997	91%	9%	60%	40%
1996	92%	8%	32%	68%
1995	92%	8%	26%	74%

INTEREST GROUPS

	AFL-CIO	ADA	CCUS	ACU
2004	17%	20%	100%	96%
2003	0%	5%	100%	80%
2002	15%	10%	95%	95%
2001	13%	5%	100%	92%
2000	0%	0%	100%	96%
1999	0%	0%	94%	92%
1998	0%	5%	83%	80%
1997	0%	5%	100%	80%
1996	0%	15%	92%	90%
1995	0%	5%	100%	91%

Sen. Tom Harkin (D)

Elected 1984; 4th term

CAPITOL OFFICE
224-3254
harkin.senate.gov
731 Hart 20510-1502; fax 224-9369

COMMITTEES
Agriculture, Nutrition & Forestry - ranking member
Appropriations
Health, Education, Labor & Pensions
Small Business & Entrepreneurship

HOMETOWN
Cumming

BORN
Nov. 19, 1939, Cumming, Iowa

RELIGION
Roman Catholic

FAMILY
Wife, Ruth Harkin; two children

EDUCATION
Iowa State U., B.S. 1962 (government &
economics); Catholic U. of America, J.D. 1972

MILITARY SERVICE
Navy, 1962-67; Naval Reserve, 1968-74

CAREER
Lawyer; congressional aide

POLITICAL HIGHLIGHTS
Democratic nominee for U.S. House, 1972; U.S.
House, 1975-85; sought Democratic nomination
for president, 1992

ELECTION RESULTS

2002 GENERAL

Tom Harkin (D)	554,278	54.2%
Greg Ganske (R)	447,892	43.8%
Timothy A. Harthan (GREEN)	11,340	1.1%

2002 PRIMARY

Tom Harkin (D)	unopposed

PREVIOUS WINNING PERCENTAGES
1996 (52%); 1990 (54%); 1984 (56%); 1982 House
Election (59%); 1980 House Election (60%); 1978
House Election (59%); 1976 House Election (65%);
1974 House Election (51%)

After more than two decades in the Senate, Harkin still lives his convictions as one of a dwindling number of influential liberals in Congress. As his party has increasingly moderated its policies to try to appeal to independent voters, Harkin has remained unbowed.

"What used to be known as the center has moved to the right, and I think that's unhealthy for the country," Harkin says. "The so-called conservative tax and social policies of the right really make us a more divided society. They put more and more emphasis on those few who have a lot."

Though old-school liberals are often sidelined these days, Harkin's influence is felt on a wide range of issues, from changes in Social Security to farm subsidies. He frequently joins with moderates to strike deals, the result often being more left-leaning legislation.

Early in the 109th Congress, Harkin took up the fight against President Bush's proposed overhaul of the Social Security program, warning that children, surviving spouses and the disabled would see their benefits shrink under the president's plan to allow workers to divert some of their payroll taxes into personal investment accounts.

He compared Bush's proposal unfavorably with his own landmark legislation in 1990, the Americans With Disabilities Act. "We said, 'Look, people with disabilities aren't going to be shunted aside. When we talk about public policy, and changes to public policy, they're not going to be an afterthought.' And they're an afterthought right now," Harkin said.

Late in the 108th Congress, Harkin helped stall action on a corporate tax bill. He was upset that a majority of senators had reneged on a deal to give the Food and Drug Administration authority to regulate tobacco products as a condition for a $10 billion buyout for tobacco farmers, which was tacked on to the tax bill. The tax bill and buyout ultimately became law.

With active support from the AFL-CIO labor union, Harkin tried unsuccessfully in both 2003 and 2004 to thwart new Labor Department rules that would take away overtime pay for some federal workers. As the senior Democrat on the Appropriations subcommittee that funds the Labor Department and other government offices, he was able to block the rules from going forward in the Senate version of each spending bill. But in both years, Harkin's ban was later removed at the White House's request during year-end negotiations over the catchall spending bill.

Harkin was a vocal foe of the president's $1.35 trillion tax cut in 2001, which he said unduly favored the wealthy over the middle and lower classes. A small group of Senate Democrats voted for the tax cut, but Harkin remained steadfast.

A rare spot of political ambiguity for him is trade. A strong friend of labor, he nonetheless finds himself voting for free-trade agreements in deference to Iowa farmers and their demands for favorable export rules.

With Nebraska Republican Chuck Hagel, Harkin is a leader in the fight for full funding for special-education programs, which the federal government mandates but pays for only in part. He also frequently teams with his friend, Republican Arlen Specter of Pennsylvania, who shares his intense interest in health care policy. Working together in recent years, they doubled funding for medical research at the National Institutes of Health, and cosponsored a bill to allow human embryos to be used in stem cell research aimed at curing diseases but not at cloning humans.

Harkin's signal achievement was the Americans With Disabilities Act, which extended broad civil rights protections to an estimated 54 million Americans with mental and physical disabilities. Harkin says he was inspired by his deaf brother, Frank, and he gave part of his floor speech in sign language in Frank's honor.

Given Iowa's importance in the Farm Belt, agriculture is another of Harkin's interests. And his leadership in this area helped him fend off a serious Republican challenge to his seat. Harkin was facing a tough contest in 2002 against GOP Rep. Greg Ganske. Then, Harkin got the chairmanship of the Agriculture Committee in 2001, when the Democrats briefly held the majority. He was a major force behind a six-year farm bill that restored some certainty for farmers by ensuring continued government subsidies.

Enactment of the bill just before the election helped. Considered one of the most vulnerable incumbents because of Iowa's swing politics, Harkin defeated Ganske by 10 percentage points despite a last-minute appeal to voters by Bush. With the win, he became the longest-serving Democratic senator in Iowa history.

The son of a coal miner, Harkin grew up in a small, crowded house in the town of Cumming. His mother, a Slovenian immigrant, died when he was 10. He worked his way through college and law school, and spent five years in Vietnam as a Navy pilot.

In 1969, he was hired by Iowa Democratic Rep. Neal Smith as an aide on the House select committee investigating the U.S. military's progress in Vietnam. He made a name for himself with his discovery of South Vietnam's "tiger cages." By outwitting a South Vietnamese official on a guided tour of a prison camp, Harkin found, behind a hidden door, hundreds of men, women and children crammed into underground cells. The cells had open grates on top through which guards poured skin-searing doses of lime. Harkin photographed the political prisoners and tape-recorded their stories.

Skittish members of the committee sought to suppress his documentation of abuses by America's ally. But Harkin insisted on going public, and his photographs and story in Life magazine energized the anti-war movement in this country and forced South Vietnam to shutter the tiger cages. The move cost the 30-year-old Harkin his job, but a few years later he found his way back to Capitol Hill.

Harkin first ran for Congress in 1972, against entrenched GOP incumbent William Scherle. He attracted publicity with his gimmick of "work days," toiling alongside farmers, teachers and welfare caseworkers — a technique still used in campaigns today. He lost narrowly but tried again and toppled Scherle by a slim margin in 1974, this time building a stronger organization and raising more money. In four House re-elections, he captured about 60 percent of the vote.

His Senate campaigns have been tougher. He won his seat in 1984 by ousting GOP Sen. Roger W. Jepsen with 56 percent of the vote. In 1990, GOP challenger Rep. Tom Tauke threatened Harkin by accusing him of abusing congressional mailing privileges and voting for excessive spending. Harkin eventually won by 9 percentage points. In 1996, he won a third term by defeating GOP Rep. Jim Ross Lightfoot by 5 percentage points.

Harkin ran briefly for the Democratic nomination for president in 1992, winning the Iowa caucuses handily but staggering in subsequent primaries. In 2000, Democratic presidential nominee Al Gore considered making Harkin his running mate but settled on Democratic Sen. Joseph I. Lieberman of Connecticut.

Harkin says he no longer wants to run for president. But he wants to continue to influence the Democratic Party, and perhaps move it back to the left.

KEY VOTES

2004

Yes	Pass $318.9 billion, six-year highway and mass transit bill
Yes	Extend assault weapons ban for 10 years
Yes	Restore pay-as-you-go rules for new tax cuts and entitlement spending
No	Criminalize harm to a fetus in an attack on the mother
Yes	Increase mandatory child care funding to states by $6 billion over five years
No	Amend the Constitution to prohibit same-sex marriage
Yes	Approve $146 billion multi-year extension of previously enacted middle-class tax breaks
Yes	Reorganize U.S. intelligence agencies as proposed by Sept. 11 commission
Yes	Cut corporate taxes $137 billion over 10 years

2003

?	Delay Bush changes to Clean Air Act
No	Allow confirmation vote on Miguel A. Estrada to the U.S. Court of Appeals for the D.C. Circuit
Yes	Block a Bush proposal opening Alaska's Arctic National Wildlife Refuge to oil drilling
Yes	Limit size of Bush's proposed tax cut to $350 billion through fiscal 2013
No	Overhaul Medicare and create prescription drug benefit
Yes	Block Bush rule scaling back overtime pay for some white-collar federal workers
Yes	Split $20 billion in Iraq aid into half-grant, half-loan
No	Ban "partial birth" abortion except to save a woman's life
No	Stop proposal allowing travel to Cuba
Yes	Allow final vote on energy policy overhaul

CQ VOTE STUDIES

	PARTY UNITY		PRESIDENTIAL SUPPORT	
	Support	Oppose	Support	Oppose
2004	94%	6%	52%	48%
2003	98%	2%	46%	54%
2002	92%	8%	69%	31%
2001	97%	3%	63%	37%
2000	97%	3%	92%	8%
1999	97%	3%	91%	9%
1998	98%	2%	88%	12%
1997	92%	8%	87%	13%
1996	91%	9%	85%	15%
1995	91%	9%	90%	10%

INTEREST GROUPS

	AFL-CIO	ADA	CCUS	ACU
2004	100%	100%	59%	8%
2003	100%	95%	32%	15%
2002	100%	80%	45%	15%
2001	100%	100%	38%	8%
2000	75%	95%	57%	4%
1999	89%	100%	47%	4%
1998	100%	95%	50%	5%
1997	71%	85%	70%	12%
1996	86%	80%	38%	10%
1995	92%	95%	44%	9%

Rep. Jim Nussle (R)

Elected 1990; 8th term

Nussle has matured and mellowed since coming to the House as part of the firebrand Class of 1990. Now, as he enters his eighth term in the House, and his third and last as chairman of the Budget Committee, Nussle is positioning himself for bigger things: a run for Iowa's Terrace Hill governor's mansion.

He has some advantages as a proven and articulate candidate with a record of performing well in Democratic areas.

But the Budget chairmanship does not provide the greatest platform from which to seek state office, especially in Nussle's case. The deficit has ballooned under his watch as a recession, tax cuts and heavy spending on defense, the Iraq war, and homeland security have combined to turn record surpluses into record deficits.

The 109th Congress could prove to be the most challenging yet of Nussle's tenure, as President Bush and fiscal conservatives in the House promise to try to attack the deficit. Given the makeup of the federal budget, that could mean taking a hard look at expensive but politically sensitive entitlement programs such as Medicare and Medicaid. Any attempts to cut such spending would originate in the Budget panel, and the effort might not sit well with Hawkeye State voters.

Nussle has settled in as a reliable GOP leadership ally on fiscal policy. Since becoming Budget chairman in 2001, he has smoothed some of the rough edges of his demeanor and legislative style that, earlier in his career, drew the ire not just of Democrats but also of House Republican leaders.

Nussle bested three other contenders to take the Budget gavel, including two who had more seniority on the panel. He promptly returned the favor to Republican leaders early in 2001 by writing a budget resolution much to their liking, closely following Bush's initial budget proposal and setting the stage for the $1.35 trillion tax cut enacted that spring.

In his second term as chairman, Nussle continued to write House budgets faithful to Bush blueprints, but the GOP's narrow control of the Senate meant that in 2003 moderate Senate Republicans had pivotal influence — at the expense of House conservatives such as Nussle — in drafting the budget resolution. In 2004, an impasse between Senate moderates and the House scotched the budget process altogether.

With the Budget panel simply a rubber stamp for Bush, Nussle has struggled to find ways to make an imprint. In 2003, he launched a bid to identify "waste, fraud and abuse" in the federal budget and an initiative to cut 1 percent from mandatory programs. The former failed to produce significant savings while the mandatory cuts flopped badly and were dropped. He later observed that many of his GOP colleagues said they wanted to cut the deficit but could not stomach the steps needed to do so.

In 2004, panel conservatives restive over the budget deficit prevailed upon GOP leaders to schedule a debate on legislation to impose new appropriations "caps" and other budget process "reform" proposals. Nussle was unenthusiastic about the measure's prospects, and his warnings proved prophetic as the powerful Appropriations Committee rallied against the effort, killing it decisively.

Nussle is seen by many colleagues as less divisive than his predecessor, John R. Kasich of Ohio, who offered the minority party little substantive input on the budgets written during his six-year tenure. Democrats acknowledge that Nussle is running a more open shop than did Kasich,

CAPITOL OFFICE
225-2911
nussleia@mail.house.gov
www.house.gov/nussle
303 Cannon 20515-1501; fax 225-9129

COMMITTEES
Budget - chairman
Ways & Means

HOMETOWN
Manchester

BORN
June 27, 1960, Des Moines, Iowa

RELIGION
Lutheran

FAMILY
Wife, Karen Nussle; two children

EDUCATION
Luther College, B.A. 1983 (political science);
Drake U., J.D. 1985

CAREER
Lawyer

POLITICAL HIGHLIGHTS
Delaware County attorney, 1986-90

ELECTION RESULTS

2004 GENERAL

Jim Nussle (R)	159,993	55.2%
Bill Gluba (D)	125,490	43.3%

2004 PRIMARY

Jim Nussle (R)	unopposed

2002 GENERAL

Jim Nussle (R)	112,280	57.2%
Ann Hutchinson (D)	83,779	42.7%

PREVIOUS WINNING PERCENTAGES
2000 (55%); 1998 (55%); 1996 (53%); 1994 (56%);
1992 (50%); 1990 (50%)

allowing them more influence and more resources. And he has improved his relationship with the news media.

Nussle also sits on the influential Ways and Means Committee, where he is poised to be a player on efforts in the 109th to overhaul Social Security and the tax code, which he says is needlessly complex. Nussle, whose eldest child has Down syndrome, is also a strong supporter of federal special education programs and the Special Olympics.

Like many of his colleagues, Nussle has learned to fight for items of clear interest back home, and he earns praise for his constituent service. As a representative of farm country, he favors increasing agricultural exports — he is a solid vote for trade liberalization — and has worked to expand domestic markets for ethanol, a fuel additive made from corn.

In the past, Nussle has had a more rocky relationship with members of both parties. He still is remembered for the time in 1991 when, during a floor speech, he placed a brown paper bag over his head to decry the Democratic leadership's decision not to make public the roster of lawmakers who had overdrawn their accounts at the private bank for House members. The moment — telecast by C-SPAN and extensively covered by the national media — came to symbolize the image problem Congress then faced. It also was viewed, in both cloakrooms, as demeaning grandstanding particularly inappropriate from a colleague.

Nussle was then one of the "Gang of Seven," a group of Republican freshmen in the 102nd Congress who agitated for changes in the way the Democratic-run House operated.

Nussle was interested in government and politics from an early age; he was a 30-year-old lawyer with just one term as a county attorney under his belt when he ran in 1990 for the House seat that Republican Tom Tauke (for whom Nussle once interned) gave up to run for the Senate. Nussle eked out a 1,642-vote victory. Two years later, he had to run against another incumbent, Democrat Dave Nagle, when reapportionment cost Iowa a House seat. Nussle again squeaked by.

Although he seemed to be one of the more vulnerable GOP incumbents in 2002, Nussle ended up scoring a decisive victory over Democrat Ann Hutchinson, the mayor of Bettendorf, who sought to make the race a referendum on the struggling economy. His 57 percent share of the vote in 2002 was a career high.

In 2004, his race failed to hit the radar screen of most politics watchers and he won comfortably with 55 percent, leaving roughly $300,000 in campaign funds for a likely gubernatorial run.

KEY VOTES

2004

No Extend federal unemployment benefits by 13 weeks

Yes Pass $283.2 billion, six-year federal highway and mass transit bill

Yes Approve $146 billion multi-year extension of previously enacted middle-class tax breaks

Yes Amend the Constitution to prohibit same-sex marriage

Yes Cut corporate taxes $137 billion over 10 years

Yes Reorganize U.S. intelligence agencies as proposed by Sept. 11 commission

2003

Yes Cut taxes by $330 billion through fiscal 2013

Yes Block Bush rule scaling back overtime pay for some white-collar federal workers

Yes Do not allow use of search warrants without first notifying subjects

No Allow importation of prescription drugs

Yes Create private school voucher program in Washington, D.C.

Yes Ban "partial birth" abortion except to save a woman's life

No Split $18.6 billion in Iraq aid into half-grant, half-loan

Yes Overhaul Medicare and create prescription drug benefit

CQ VOTE STUDIES

	PARTY UNITY		PRESIDENTIAL SUPPORT	
	Support	Oppose	Support	Oppose
2004	93%	7%	88%	12%
2003	95%	5%	91%	9%
2002	93%	7%	88%	12%
2001	95%	5%	88%	12%
2000	93%	7%	25%	75%

INTEREST GROUPS

	AFL-CIO	ADA	CCUS	ACU
2004	27%	15%	95%	80%
2003	20%	15%	90%	84%
2002	11%	0%	100%	92%
2001	17%	0%	100%	88%
2000	10%	15%	95%	84%

IOWA 1

East – Davenport, Waterloo, Dubuque

The 1st takes in half of Iowa's Mississippi River counties and is dominated by three midsize industrial cities: Davenport, Waterloo and Dubuque.

Davenport and Bettendorf in Scott County — Iowa's half of the Quad Cities that straddle the river into Illinois — are old, industrial river cities whose economies suffered badly during the 1980s but are recovering by capitalizing on tourists drawn to riverboat gambling. Waterloo, slightly more than 100 miles northwest of Davenport, grew up around the farm-implement and meatpacking industries. While hogs still are slaughtered here, the economy diversified in the 1990s to include finance and insurance. Neighboring Cedar Falls relies on the influence of the University of Northern Iowa.

Dubuque, built against the bluffs facing the Mississippi River, is Iowa's oldest city. Its economic base shifted in the 1990s from manufacturing and meatpacking to service, including insurance, finance and telecommunications.

Democrats slightly outnumber Republicans in the 1st, but voters have tended to demonstrate their independence at the polls in recent years. Black Hawk County, with Cedar Falls and Waterloo, has a strong Democratic base from its labor and academic communities. Scott County narrowly voted for John Kerry in the 2004 presidential election but has a centrist Republican tradition. Democrats have the advantage in Clinton County, located north of Scott. Overall, Kerry carried the district with 53 percent of the vote.

Dubuque County, which is heavily Catholic, and Jackson County just to the south were Kerry's best counties in the 1st. Dubuque has a culturally conservative lean, though, and Rep. Nussle has consistently outperformed Republican presidential candidates there. Many of the rest of the 1st's residents live in rural areas that by and large are Republican-leaning but politically competitive.

MAJOR INDUSTRY
Farm machinery, meatpacking, health care, agriculture

CITIES
Davenport, 98,359; Waterloo, 68,747; Dubuque, 57,686; Cedar Falls, 36,145

NOTABLE
Dyersville is home to the baseball field in the movie "Field of Dreams."

Rep. Jim Leach (R)

Elected 1976; 15th term

Leach looks like a rumpled college professor and speaks in an erudite manner. His knowledge of economic theory was developed at Princeton, Johns Hopkins and the London School of Economics. Yet Leach is one of the Capitol's gentler souls; he treats friend and foe in the same measured, polite way and approaches issues with more than the usual introspection.

He is also a man who goes his own way. In the 108th Congress, he strayed from his party and voted with the Democrats 35 percent of the time — more often than any other Republican. And he supported President Bush's position just 53 percent of the time, a lower score than all but one other House Republican, Ron Paul of Texas. He was one of 11 Republicans endorsed by the Sierra Club in 2004.

Leach was chairman of the Banking Committee for six years, but was forced to give up the gavel in 2001 because of GOP term limits. At the time, he was No. 2 in GOP seniority on International Relations and had hoped to take the helm, but the position went instead to Henry J. Hyde of Illinois, who was No. 3 in seniority and had served six years as Judiciary chairman. Leach was given the chairmanship of International Relations' Asia and the Pacific Subcommittee. The snub is emblematic of Leach's situation after more than a quarter-century in the House. He has rarely shied away from disagreeing with his party, and his search for bipartisanship has at times come at the expense of the GOP agenda.

Not surprisingly, Leach is also something of a maverick on matters of foreign policy. In 2002, he was one of only six House Republicans to vote against the resolution authorizing Bush to launch a military campaign against Iraq. Unlike other Republicans, he did not see America's first pre-emptive war as a paradigm for future conflict. And in 2003, he became the first Republican to call for a withdrawal of U.S. forces from Iraq.

By turning his focus to foreign affairs, Leach in some ways has returned to his roots. He was a Foreign Service officer in 1971 and 1972 and played a high-level role in negotiating a number of international treaties — including the Biological and Toxic Weapons Convention of 1972 — while working for the Arms Control and Disarmament Agency.

Over the years, Leach has held leadership posts on a number of significant international panels, including Parliamentarians for Global Action, an international nonprofit organization of elected leaders from more than 100 nations, and the U.S. Commission on Improving the Effectiveness of the United Nations.

As chairman of the subcommittee dealing most closely with Asia, he has focused on North Korea's nuclear presence. In the 108th Congress, Leach sponsored a measure to authorize $96 million over four years for programs to promote human rights and democracy in North Korea, protect its refugees and provide aid to North Koreans both inside and outside that country's borders. The measure became law in October 2004.

Leach also led a bipartisan congressional group to the tsunami-ravaged areas of Thailand, Indonesia and Sri Lanka early in 2005.

International concerns were less of a priority for Leach during his time chairing the Banking Committee. He was a principal architect of the landmark law enacted in the 106th Congress that lowered the regulatory barriers that had separated banks, brokerages and insurers since the Depression. The path to a deal on the bill was notoriously complicated until the end — the affected industries squabbled as they vied for competitive advantage,

CAPITOL OFFICE
225-6576
www.house.gov/leach
2186 Rayburn 20515-1502; fax 226-1278

COMMITTEES
Financial Services
International Relations
  (Asia & the Pacific - chairman)

HOMETOWN
Iowa City

BORN
Oct. 15, 1942, Davenport, Iowa

RELIGION
Episcopalian

FAMILY
Wife, Elisabeth Ann "Deba" Leach; two children

EDUCATION
Princeton U., A.B. 1964 (political science); Johns Hopkins U., M.A. 1966 (Soviet politics); London School of Economics, attended 1966-68 (economics & Soviet politics)

CAREER
Propane gas company executive; Foreign Service officer; congressional aide

POLITICAL HIGHLIGHTS
Republican nominee for U.S. House, 1974

ELECTION RESULTS

2004 GENERAL

Jim Leach (R)	176,684	58.9%
Dave Franker (D)	117,405	39.2%
Kevin Litten (LIBERT)	5,586	1.9%

2004 PRIMARY

Jim Leach (R)	unopposed

2002 GENERAL

Jim Leach (R)	108,130	52.2%
Julie Thomas (D)	94,767	45.7%
Kevin Litten (LIBERT)	4,178	2.0%

PREVIOUS WINNING PERCENTAGES
2000 (62%); 1998 (57%); 1996 (53%); 1994 (60%); 1992 (68%); 1990 (100%); 1988 (61%); 1986 (66%); 1984 (67%); 1982 (59%); 1980 (64%); 1978 (64%); 1976 (52%)

and the Federal Reserve and the Treasury fought over regulatory power — yet Leach succeeded where many others had failed in decades of previous attempts.

Leach's independent streak was evident early on. Although his job in the Foreign Service had nothing to do with Watergate, when he was 31 he resigned in protest over President Nixon's "Saturday night massacre" firing of Archibald Cox, the special prosecutor.

In the House, Leach joined nine other Republicans at the start of the 105th Congress in casting their votes for Speaker for people other than Newt Gingrich, the GOP incumbent whose conduct was then the subject of a House ethics committee investigation. Leach voted for retired House Minority Leader Robert H. Michel of Illinois. (Two of the other dissidents voted for Leach.)

Leach's career started in 1965 as an aide to Republican Rep. Donald H. Rumsfeld of Illinois. (The pair became close enough that Rumsfeld's daughter once stayed with the Leach family for a year.) Four decades on, Leach says that he respects tremendously Rumsfeld's work as secretary of defense, although they often disagree on foreign affairs.

Leach lost his first bid for the House, in 1974, against Democratic incumbent Edward Mezvinsky. But he won their 1976 rematch and was easily re-elected until 1996, when he was held to 53 percent of the vote by Democrats portraying him as having lost his moderation in the GOP "revolution."

Leach was touted for a top State Department or Treasury post in the Bush administration, but his chances were hurt by the Democratic nature of eastern Iowa. Al Gore carried the 1st District, which Leach was representing at the time, by 10 percentage points in 2000.

Redistricting for this decade — which was handled by a nonpartisan state legislative agency — then put Leach and his Republican colleague Jim Nussle in a newly configured 1st.

The district would have favored Nussle in the 2002 GOP primary, so Leach moved from Davenport to Iowa City, a Democratic stronghold dominated by the University of Iowa. One-third of voters in the 2nd District were new to him — and he kept to his practice of refusing contributions from political action committees or people outside Iowa — but Leach squeezed past family physician Julie Thomas, touted by Democrats for her health care expertise and endearing image.

Leach handily won his 2004 re-election by 20 percentage points. When he does retire, though, Leach does not plan to stay in Washington. "I can spell Nirvana for you," he says. "IOWA CITY."

KEY VOTES

2004
Yes   Extend federal unemployment benefits by 13 weeks
Yes   Pass $283.2 billion, six-year federal highway and mass transit bill
Yes   Approve $146 billion multi-year extension of previously enacted middle-class tax breaks
No   Amend the Constitution to prohibit same-sex marriage
Yes   Cut corporate taxes $137 billion over 10 years
Yes   Reorganize U.S. intelligence agencies as proposed by Sept. 11 commission

2003
No   Cut taxes by $330 billion through fiscal 2013
Yes   Block Bush rule scaling back overtime pay for some white-collar federal workers
Yes   Do not allow use of search warrants without first notifying subjects
Yes   Allow importation of prescription drugs
?   Create private school voucher program in Washington, D.C.
Yes   Ban "partial birth" abortion except to save a woman's life
No   Split $18.6 billion in Iraq aid into half-grant, half-loan
Yes   Overhaul Medicare and create prescription drug benefit

CQ VOTE STUDIES

	PARTY UNITY		PRESIDENTIAL SUPPORT	
	Support	Oppose	Support	Oppose
2004	66%	34%	47%	53%
2003	65%	35%	57%	43%
2002	71%	29%	70%	30%
2001	73%	27%	60%	40%
2000	73%	27%	45%	55%

INTEREST GROUPS

	AFL-CIO	ADA	CCUS	ACU
2004	42%	55%	94%	43%
2003	53%	50%	70%	44%
2002	11%	30%	85%	56%
2001	42%	45%	78%	25%
2000	20%	30%	80%	58%

IOWA 2
Southeast — Cedar Rapids, Iowa City

The 2nd, a Democratic-leaning region of 15 southeastern Iowa counties, takes in part of the state's eastern border with the Mississippi River and about half of the state's southern border with Missouri.

In the district's north is Cedar Rapids (Linn County), the most populous city in the state after the capital of Des Moines. Long a center for grain processing, Cedar Rapids has weathered hard economic times recently with help from telecommunication equipment firms, which are still recovering from the end of the late 1990s technology boom.

Iowa City (Johnson County), located south of Cedar Rapids, is home to the University of Iowa and a growing number of high-tech companies. The academic community gives Iowa City a strong liberal tilt, and Johnson was John Kerry's best county in 2004, as he won 64 percent of the presidential vote there. Johnson has not backed a Republican presidential nominee since Richard M. Nixon in 1960.

The 2nd's other population center runs along the Mississippi River in the district's southeast, in Des Moines and Lee counties. Unions retain some influence in the area, but an economy once centered on manufacturing is headed toward tourism and riverboat gambling.

The counties that form the district's southwestern arm are predominately rural; the economy here relies on exporting agricultural products, including corn, tomatoes, soybeans and pork. With the exception of Wapello County (Ottumwa), this area leans Republican.

Linn, Johnson and the river counties together give the 2nd a decidedly Democratic tilt, and the district gave Kerry his best showing in the state (55 percent) in 2004. But Republican Rep. Leach has held onto the district by mixing fiscal conservatism with moderate-to-liberal social views.

MAJOR INDUSTRY
Technology, telecommunications, health care, grain processing

CITIES
Cedar Rapids, 120,758; Iowa City, 62,220; Burlington, 26,839; Marion, 26,294; Ottumwa, 24,998; Muscatine, 22,697

NOTABLE
Cedar Rapids' government buildings are located on an island in the center of the city.

Rep. Leonard L. Boswell (D)

Elected 1996; 5th term

CAPITOL OFFICE
225-3806
rep.boswell.ia03@mail.house.gov
www.house.gov/boswell
1427 Longworth 20515-1503; fax 225-5608

COMMITTEES
Agriculture
Transportation & Infrastructure
Select Intelligence

HOMETOWN
Des Moines

BORN
Jan. 10, 1934, Harrison County, Mo.

RELIGION
Community of Christ

FAMILY
Wife, Dody Boswell; three children

EDUCATION
Graceland College, B.A. 1969 (business
administration)

MILITARY SERVICE
Army, 1956-76

CAREER
Farmer

POLITICAL HIGHLIGHTS
Iowa Senate, 1985-97 (president, 1992-97); sought
Democratic nomination for U.S. House, 1986;
Iowa Democratic Central Committee, 1992-96;
Democratic nominee for lieutenant governor, 1994

ELECTION RESULTS

2004 GENERAL

Leonard L. Boswell (D)	168,007	55.2%
Stan Thompson (R)	136,099	44.7%

2004 PRIMARY

Leonard L. Boswell (D)	unopposed

2002 GENERAL

Leonard L. Boswell (D)	115,367	53.4%
Stan Thompson (R)	97,285	45.0%
Jeffrey J. Smith (LIBERT)	2,689	1.3%

PREVIOUS WINNING PERCENTAGES
2000 (63%); 1998 (57%); 1996 (49%)

The only Democrat in Iowa's House delegation, Boswell is an easygoing politician with a knack for representing constituents from both ends of the party spectrum. He started his House career as a rural conservative from southern Iowa, but redistricting in 2002 compelled him to move to Des Moines. Once there, he was able to show the state's most liberal Democrats that he could protect their interests as well.

Boswell's voting record shows him to be a moderate-to-conservative Democrat. In 2004, he sided with his party on crucial votes 83 percent of the time, and he supported President Bush 39 percent of the time. He tends to be socially conservative, voting in his first four years against some gun control measures and in favor of a ban on a procedure its opponents call "partial birth" abortion.

In the 107th Congress, Boswell rebuffed overtures from the GOP to switch parties, and from then on his votes took on a more Democratic cast. He and Sen. Tom Harkin, the other Democrat in the state delegation, were the only Iowans to oppose the $1.35 trillion tax cut of 2001 and the 2002 law granting the president fast-track trade negotiating power.

Boswell's varied background enables him to offer expertise in a number of fields, particularly military affairs, agriculture and the appropriations process. His legislative career began in 1985 in the state Senate, where he chaired the Appropriations Committee and eventually became president.

Drafted in 1956, when he was 22, Boswell became a helicopter pilot and did two tours in Vietnam, earning a pair of Distinguished Flying Crosses and a pair of Bronze Stars. Upon his retirement as a lieutenant colonel, Boswell returned home to farm cattle on 475 acres in his native Decatur County. His involvement in community affairs spurred his neighbors to urge him to enter politics, first as a member of the local farmers' co-op and grain elevator board and then in the General Assembly.

That breadth and depth of experience set him apart from his classmates when he arrived in Washington in 1997, at 63 the oldest House freshman in the 105th Congress. Boswell's age, calm demeanor and career credentials brought him early respect from Democratic leaders, who put him on the party panel that makes committee assignments.

With his military experience, Boswell was also given a seat on the Intelligence Committee. He is the top-ranking Democrat on the panel's Terrorism/Human Intelligence, Analysis and Counterintelligence Subcommittee, where he has been particularly critical of the Bush administration's financing of its counterterrorism programs. Boswell doesn't like the idea of making a down payment on counterterrorism funding and then asking for the rest of the money later in the year, a plan the White House proposed in 2004. Boswell wrote an amendment to that year's intelligence bill that would have significantly increased the authorization for counterterrorism spending. Democrats said the amount in the GOP-written bill, which was classified, was less than one-third of what was needed.

"Full funding for the war on terrorism should not have been decided on a partisan vote," said Boswell. And he criticized the administration's practice of funding intelligence agencies piecemeal. "Agency leaders have told us this practice disrupts their ability to plan operations," Boswell added.

Together with Republican Tom Osborne of Nebraska, Boswell has sought to alter the Medicare system for reimbursing health care providers. The pair want to ensure that no state gets payments more than 5 percent above or below the national average. Boswell voted in 2003 against the GOP Medicare overhaul bill, which provided a prescription drug benefit for seniors. In a December 2003 letter to the editor of the Des Moines Register, Boswell said, "Iowans have long suffered due to our state's status as last in the nation in Medicare payments. I am deeply troubled by the negligible impact the recently passed prescription drug bill will have on that ranking," he said. "Estimates show it will not mean a thing."

On the Transportation Committee, Boswell works to improve commercial airline service to Des Moines, which like many medium-size cities must deal with limited options and high fares. He was a negotiator in 2000 on an aviation law that authorized funds for airport construction and designated money for more than a dozen airports in the 3rd District.

Boswell also serves on the Agriculture Committee. He was the only Iowan to vote against the original six-year farm bill rewrite passed by the House in 2001. He said it did not provide enough for small family farms and it did not take steps to minimize livestock ownership by meatpackers in order to improve market access for smaller operators. But when the final bill was written without ameliorating some of his concerns, he declared it the "best deal" possible for Iowa farmers and voted for its enactment in 2002.

In 1996, Boswell gave in to the coaxing of supporters and entered the race for the 3rd District seat just two days before the filing deadline. The Republican incumbent, Jim Ross Lightfoot, was giving up the seat after a dozen years to run against Harkin for the Senate.

Boswell won the primary easily, capitalizing on his name recognition from years in the state legislature and campaigns for lieutenant governor in 1994 and for Congress in 1986 — when he lost the Democratic nomination for the right to oppose Lightfoot. Against Mike Mahaffey, a county prosecutor and former state GOP chairman, Boswell eked out a November win with the endorsement of the Iowa Farm Bureau, unusual for a Democrat.

In the 2002 race against Republican lawyer Stan Thompson, who co-chaired George W. Bush's Iowa campaign in 2000, Boswell was attacked as a liberal who opposed school prayer. Boswell countered that he was for voluntary school prayer. He used his hefty campaign war chest to counter campaign appearances by Bush administration heavyweights in behalf of Thompson and won with 53 percent of the vote.

In 2004, he faced a rematch with Thompson but won again easily with over 55 percent. Boswell initially said he would serve only four terms; but he rethought that pledge.

KEY VOTES

2004
Yes   Extend federal unemployment benefits by 13 weeks
Yes   Pass $283.2 billion, six-year federal highway and mass transit bill
Yes   Approve $146 billion multi-year extension of previously enacted middle-class tax breaks
No   Amend the Constitution to prohibit same-sex marriage
Yes   Cut corporate taxes $137 billion over 10 years
?   Reorganize U.S. intelligence agencies as proposed by Sept. 11 commission

2003
No   Cut taxes by $330 billion through fiscal 2013
Yes   Block Bush rule scaling back overtime pay for some white-collar federal workers
Yes   Do not allow use of search warrants without first notifying subjects
Yes   Allow importation of prescription drugs
No   Create private school voucher program in Washington, D.C.
?   Ban "partial birth" abortion except to save a woman's life
Yes   Split $18.6 billion in Iraq aid into half-grant, half-loan
No   Overhaul Medicare and create prescription drug benefit

CQ VOTE STUDIES

	PARTY UNITY		PRESIDENTIAL SUPPORT	
	Support	Oppose	Support	Oppose
2004	83%	17%	39%	61%
2003	85%	15%	42%	58%
2002	81%	19%	40%	60%
2001	78%	22%	37%	63%
2000	69%	31%	60%	40%

INTEREST GROUPS

	AFL-CIO	ADA	CCUS	ACU
2004	87%	80%	55%	20%
2003	80%	80%	45%	23%
2002	78%	80%	55%	32%
2001	92%	85%	48%	24%
2000	70%	55%	65%	41%

IOWA 3
Central and east central — Des Moines

The 12-county 3rd is somewhat microcosmic of the Hawkeye state. It includes relatively well-off urban and suburban areas, as well as rural counties, industrial cities and scattered towns with hopes for economic development. It is roughly one-third urban, suburban and rural.

The district is anchored in Des Moines, the state's largest city and the region's commercial, financial and governmental center. Almost two-thirds of the district's residents live in Des Moines and the surrounding towns in Polk County. The capital has flourished since the 1980s, partly because of its diverse, white-collar employment base and its partial independence from agriculture. There is a sizable African-American and Hispanic population north of downtown, between Interstate 235 and Drake University.

Outside of Polk the 3rd takes on a more rural and conservative flavor. No other county has more than 40,000 residents, and George W. Bush won seven of the district's 11 other counties in the 2004 presidential election. Mahaska and Grundy counties are among the most heavily Republican

territories in Iowa.

But the 3rd is competitive in its voting — it gave Bush a slightly less than 50 percent plurality in 2004. Poweshiek, Tama and Benton counties also were all but tied in the 2004 race — each siding with John Kerry by less than 100 votes. The influence of Des Moines and surrounding Polk County gives the 3rd its slight Democratic lean. Polk has been more reliably Democratic than many parts of the nation, even supporting Democratic presidential nominees in the GOP presidential landslides of 1984 and 1988. Polk has not given a Republican presidential candidate a majority of its votes since Richard M. Nixon in 1972.

MAJOR INDUSTRY
Insurance, health care, manufacturing

CITIES
Des Moines, 198,682; West Des Moines (pt.), 42,525; Urbandale (pt.), 28,745; Ankeny, 27,117; Newton, 15,579

NOTABLE
F.L. Maytag built the first mechanized washer in Newton; Legendary Western lawman and gunfighter Wyatt Earp grew up in Pella; Pella is home to window and door manufacturer Pella Corp.

Rep. Tom Latham (R)

CAPITOL OFFICE
225-5476
tom.latham@mail.house.gov
www.house.gov/latham
2447 Rayburn 20515-1504; fax 225-3301

COMMITTEES
Appropriations

HOMETOWN
Alexander

BORN
July 14, 1948, Hampton, Iowa

RELIGION
Lutheran

FAMILY
Wife, Kathy Latham; three children

EDUCATION
Wartburg College, attended 1967; Iowa State U.,
attended 1967-70 (agriculture & business)

CAREER
Seed company executive; insurance agency
marketing representative; insurance agent;
bank teller

POLITICAL HIGHLIGHTS
Franklin County Republican Party chairman,
1984-91

ELECTION RESULTS

2004 GENERAL

Tom Latham (R)	181,294	60.9%
Paul W. Johnson (D)	116,121	39.0%

2004 PRIMARY

Tom Latham (R)		unopposed

2002 GENERAL

Tom Latham (R)	115,430	54.8%
John Norris (D)	90,784	43.1%
Terry L. Wilson (LIBERT)	2,952	1.4%

PREVIOUS WINNING PERCENTAGES
2000 (69%); 1998 (99%); 1996 (65%); 1994 (61%)

Elected 1994; 6th term

Latham has worked in Congress for the past 10 years with his eyes firmly fixed on his constituents in the small towns and farms of north central Iowa, home to some of the nation's most productive farmland. Latham and his brothers own three farms and a family seed company.

But Latham also has another important role. As the only Iowan on the Appropriations Committee, he must look out for the entire state delegation in getting money sent home. He sits on the spending panel's Agriculture Subcommittee.

From there he has been able to direct millions of dollars to the National Animal Disease Center, a livestock health research facility in Ames, which Latham says is "a huge thing for the state of Iowa." The facility, which Latham says is "like the CDC [Centers for Disease Control] only for livestock," tests for such newsworthy diseases as mad cow and anthrax.

In the 108th Congress, he was able to include in the House-passed version of the agriculture spending bill $178 million toward a total project cost of $406 million for a major upgrade of the facility. Final funding was trimmed to $122 million. Obtaining funding to complete the upgrade will continue to be a priority of his in the 109th.

Ames is home to several other federally funded agriculture research facilities as well, and Latham has been able to direct funds their way, including to a lab that researches the use of corn and soybeans for pharmaceuticals.

Latham also wants to lift U.S. embargoes on the export of food and medicine to countries, such as Cuba, that are under U.S. economic sanctions. "Embargoes have always destroyed the farmers and never really punished the people they were aimed at," he argues.

Latham says he is a fiscal conservative, although he has received lukewarm ratings from such watchdog organizations as the Concord Coalition, Citizens Against Government Waste and the National Taxpayers Union. In 2004, he complained about the year-end omnibus spending bill, characterizing it as "one of the most horrific monsters that should terrify any American with a belief in fiscal common sense" and noting that "where there is an omnibus, there is usually 'pork barrel' spending."

Yet he said that the bill included many important provisions for Iowa — "vital funds that support agriculture, education, transportation, health care, conservation, and homeland security functions throughout the state of Iowa."

One of Latham's priorities in Congress is to roll back federal regulations and taxes, to create "a smaller and smarter federal government," according to his official biography. To that end, he has worked to permanently repeal the estate tax. He says that large estate tax bills have forced some heirs to sell the family farm. He voted in 2004 for all of President Bush's tax cut proposals.

Latham is usually loyal to the House GOP leadership. He supports the party line almost 95 percent of the time when the two parties are pitted against each other. In the 109th Congress, as he has been since the 105th, Latham is on the Republican Steering Committee, which makes committee assignments, and the Republican Policy Committee.

But he did stray from the fold late in 2004 when House Republicans met to propose rules for the 109th. Latham was in the minority of his colleagues who opposed a rules change that would have permitted party leaders to keep their post even if they were indicted.

The change, aimed at keeping Majority Leader Tom DeLay in that job in the event that a Texas grand jury indicted him in connection with a campaign finance probe, was initially approved by the GOP caucus, before leaders later determined it was not good for the party's image. Latham later explained his vote opposing the rule change: "As elected leaders . . . we need to ensure that our work is done with the utmost confidence of the American people."

Latham grew up on a farm doing the usual chores and helping in the family seed business. He stayed close to home in his first 20 years — attending Wartburg College about 50 miles east of his hometown of Alexander and then going to Iowa State University, about 60 miles south in Ames. Today, he jokes that he lives in the suburbs — his home is a mile from downtown Alexander, population in 2000: 165.

His interest in politics was sparked by a trip he took in 1990, as a member of a farm delegation that visited Russia and Poland. Latham says he was appalled at the primitive agricultural methods and machinery, and he blames much of that on the totalitarian governments that he says not only mismanaged the economy but "destroyed individual freedom and dignity." He remembers one Polish farmer who tearfully told him that farmers hadn't owned their land since the Nazis seized it in World War II.

Latham decided that a government that so profoundly intruded in individuals' lives and controlled what they did with their land was something to be feared and resisted. He can date his resolve to run for public office to that realization.

Back in Iowa, he chaired the Franklin County Republican Party for seven years but rebuffed entreaties to run for the legislature: The seasonal nature of his seed business conflicted with state legislative sessions. In 1994, however, when GOP Rep. Fred Grandy gave up the 5th District seat to seek the governorship, Latham decided to run. He was a good fit for the district in a strong GOP year, and he breezed to election.

Latham won re-election easily in 1996, 1998 and 2000, but in 2002 new district lines drafted by a nonpartisan state agency made the district more competitive. The new map put Latham's home in the 4th District; but more than half of his constituents were in the 5th, and it was viewed as more favorable to a Republican than the 4th.

Nonetheless, Latham elected to run in the 4th. He was well-known to many of the new constituents, dating back to his days as a traveling salesman for the family seed business. He wound up winning by almost 12 percentage points against Democrat John Norris, a former state party chairman, in a race that attracted considerable national attention. In 2004, he cruised to a 22 percentage point victory.

KEY VOTES

2004

No Extend federal unemployment benefits by 13 weeks
Yes Pass $283.2 billion, six-year federal highway and mass transit bill
Yes Approve $146 billion multi-year extension of previously enacted middle-class tax breaks
Yes Amend the Constitution to prohibit same-sex marriage
Yes Cut corporate taxes $137 billion over 10 years
Yes Reorganize U.S. intelligence agencies as proposed by Sept. 11 commission

2003

Yes Cut taxes by $330 billion through fiscal 2013
No Block Bush rule scaling back overtime pay for some white-collar federal workers
Yes Do not allow use of search warrants without first notifying subjects
No Allow importation of prescription drugs
Yes Create private school voucher program in Washington, D.C.
Yes Ban "partial birth" abortion except to save a woman's life
No Split $18.6 billion in Iraq aid into half-grant, half-loan
Yes Overhaul Medicare and create prescription drug benefit

CQ VOTE STUDIES

	PARTY UNITY		PRESIDENTIAL SUPPORT	
	Support	Oppose	Support	Oppose
2004	92%	8%	88%	12%
2003	95%	5%	93%	7%
2002	92%	8%	85%	15%
2001	97%	3%	90%	10%
2000	94%	6%	26%	74%

INTEREST GROUPS

	AFL-CIO	ADA	CCUS	ACU
2004	20%	10%	100%	72%
2003	13%	5%	97%	84%
2002	11%	5%	100%	88%
2001	8%	0%	100%	91%
2000	10%	5%	95%	88%

IOWA 4

North and central — Ames, Mason City

The vast 4th takes up most of the state's northern border and dips deeply south, past the state capital of Des Moines (in the 3rd District), dividing Republican-leaning western Iowa and Democratic-leaning eastern Iowa.

Ames is the district's most populous city and is home to Iowa State University, about 30 miles north of Des Moines. Ames leans Democratic, but does not have a strong liberal strain. The city, which accounts for almost two-thirds of Story County residents, backed John Kerry by just 4 percentage points in the 2004 presidential election.

Democrats fare well in Cerro Gordo County, which includes Mason City, the 4th's next most-populous city. Two-thirds of Mason City's employers are involved in manufacturing. Another urban center is Fort Dodge in Webster County, where there are many Irish Catholic Democrats. The city, an industrial center that has relied on gypsum factories to support the area's economy, also emerged as a leader in veterinary pharmaceuticals.

But overall, the 4th has a slight GOP lean. George W. Bush won the district with 51 percent in 2004, capturing 15 of the 20 counties that have fewer than 20,000 residents.

The southern reaches of the district buttonhook counterclockwise around Des Moines to take in the Republican-leaning counties of Dallas, Madison and Warren. Dallas is a big exception to Iowa's sluggish population growth; suburban growth west of Des Moines fueled Dallas' 37 percent growth rate in the 1990s, by far the fastest clip in the state. Warren (13 percent) and Madison (12 percent) also registered impressive growth.

MAJOR INDUSTRY
Meatpacking, health care, veterinary pharmaceuticals, agriculture

CITIES
Ames, 50,731; Mason City, 29,172; Marshalltown, 26,009; Fort Dodge, 25,136; Indianola, 12,998; Boone, 12,803

NOTABLE
Film star John Wayne was born in Winterset; Madison County's covered bridges were popularized in Robert James Waller's book; Mason City inspired native son Meredith Willson to compose the musical "The Music Man."

Rep. Steve King (R)

Elected 2002; 2nd term

CAPITOL OFFICE
225-4426
steve.king@mail.house.gov
www.house.gov/steveking
1432 Longworth 20515-1505; fax 225-3193

COMMITTEES
Agriculture
Judiciary
Small Business

HOMETOWN
Kiron

BORN
May 28, 1949, Storm Lake, Iowa

RELIGION
Roman Catholic

FAMILY
Wife, Marilyn King; three children

EDUCATION
Northwest Missouri State U., attended 1967-70

CAREER
Construction company owner

POLITICAL HIGHLIGHTS
Iowa Senate, 1997-2002

ELECTION RESULTS

2004 GENERAL

Steve King (R)	168,583	63.3%
E. Joyce Schulte (D)	97,597	36.6%

2004 PRIMARY

Steve King (R)	unopposed

2002 GENERAL

Steve King (R)	113,257	62.2%
Paul Shomshor (D)	68,853	37.8%

A former small-business owner, whose construction firm did earth excavating, King says he was driven into politics out of frustration with federal regulations imposed on his mom-and-pop operation. King calls himself a "family values" Republican, and he is prone to sharp appraisals of liberal views in the culture wars. When a state judge in Sioux City granted a homosexual couple a divorce in 2003, King fumed: "Unicorns, leprechauns, gay marriages in Iowa — these are all things you will never find because they just don't exist." Longtime Des Moines Register political columnist David Yepsen dubbed King "the Pat Buchanan of Iowa."

Born in tiny Storm Lake, King has deep roots in the district, which covers the predominately rural western third of Iowa. King's maternal great-grandparents were among the original homesteaders in the region after the Civil War. The two largest cities are Sioux City and Council Bluffs, both to the far west on the border with Nebraska.

King was 47 before he campaigned for office the first time. He spent most of his career developing King Construction Company, an earth-moving firm he founded in 1975 that specializes in soil erosion solutions for farmers. He employed usually no more than five people and his annual sales were about $700,000. (He has since sold the business to his son.) He became angry at ever-increasing federal taxes, government regulations and IRS audits of his business. "After they picked my pocket, I went to work and sat there every day, thinking about how to get rid of them," he says.

In 1996, he won a seat in the Iowa Senate, where he became known for a culturally conservative agenda. His "God and Country" law requires Iowa public schools to teach that the United States has "derived its strength from Biblical values." He sponsored a bill, which was signed into law, making English the state's official language. In 2000, he fought an executive order by Democratic Gov. Tom Vilsack banning discrimination against homosexuals in state jobs, which he took to the Iowa Supreme Court and won. Vilsack's order was overturned, ending one of King's frequent clashes with the governor.

After his election to the House in 2002, King continued to be an agitator for conservative causes. His rhetorical sharpness belies his "kindly uncle" manner. King is meticulously polite and self-deprecating, but he would have been at home with the grenade-throwing tactics of the Newt Gingrich era in the latter half of the 1990s. He continues to advocate for an end to the Internal Revenue Service, which he would replace with a national sales tax. King says he also wants to get rid of the Civil Rights Commission because the bias complaints it typically handles belong in the courts.

King generally dislikes federal entitlement programs and initially resisted supporting President Bush's 2003 health initiative — expansion of the Medicare program to create a prescription drug benefit for the elderly. He agreed to vote for the bill under heavy pressure from GOP leaders, who needed every last vote. He finally agreed to vote yes after getting a phone call from Vice President Dick Cheney. King received a small concession from Republican leaders in return: Medicare reimbursements to Iowa hospitals would be increased under certain conditions.

A supporter of a national right-to-work law limiting union activity, King also wants to repeal the 1931 Davis-Bacon Act, a Depression-era law that requires federal contractors to pay "local prevailing wages."

King also favors cracking down on illegal immigration though Iowa has one of the nation's smallest minority populations. He says he opposes amnesty for illegal workers in the United States because it encourages more people to try to enter the country to get in line for the next round of amnesty. In the 109th Congress, he has a seat on the Judiciary Committee's Immigration Subcommittee. On foreign policy, he follows other conservatives in harboring a deep suspicion of the United Nations, which he calls a "third world class envy society." He wants to reduce dramatically the share of its budget provided by the United States, currently about 22 percent.

King has been a staunch supporter of the Bush administration's policy in Iraq, with sometimes colorful word choices. After revelations that U.S. military guards at the Abu Ghraib prison in Iraq had abused prisoners with physical torture and forced sexual acts, King lashed out at the critics, likening the incidents to college hazing. The Des Moines Register, the most influential newspaper in the state, said his remarks were "an embarrassment" to Iowa. King once waded into a young crowd protesting the Iraq war in Washington because, he said, he was curious about them. "The vast majority of them were communists, socialists and radicals," he told a local reporter.

King has yet to get a major bill passed, although he has had some luck with district-focused legislation. With a seat on the Agriculture Committee, he was able in 2003 to get a provision included in an energy policy bill providing a tax credit for small ethanol producers. His language was geared toward making the half-dozen small producers in his district more competitive with ethanol giants Archer Daniels Midland and Cargill.

A new state district map drafted by a nonpartisan state agency in 2002 put 5th District Rep. Tom Latham's home in the 4th District; but more than half of his constituents remained in the 5th. Latham elected to run in the 4th, leaving the 5th seat open.

As the most Republican district in the state, the real contest was the primary. Then a state senator, King had to overcome formidable competition from Republican House Speaker Brent Siegrist of Council Bluffs and fellow GOP state Sen. John Redwine, a doctor who was as adamantly opposed to abortion as King. Also in the primary was car wash owner Jeff Ballenger, who spent $400,000 of his own money.

No candidate received the required 35 percent of the vote to prevail, although King led the field with 30 percent. The outcome was decided by a nominating convention. King led on each of three ballots, finally beating Siegrist, 272-253. From there, King easily defeated Democrat Paul Shomshor, who tried to depict him as too conservative for the district. King won with 62 percent of the vote and was re-elected in 2004 with 63 percent.

KEY VOTES

2004
- No Extend federal unemployment benefits by 13 weeks
- Yes Pass $283.2 billion, six-year federal highway and mass transit bill
- Yes Approve $146 billion multi-year extension of previously enacted middle-class tax breaks
- Yes Amend the Constitution to prohibit same-sex marriage
- Yes Cut corporate taxes $137 billion over 10 years
- No Reorganize U.S. intelligence agencies as proposed by Sept. 11 commission

2003
- Yes Cut taxes by $330 billion through fiscal 2013
- No Block Bush rule scaling back overtime pay for some white-collar federal workers
- Yes Do not allow use of search warrants without first notifying subjects
- Yes Allow importation of prescription drugs
- Yes Create private school voucher program in Washington, D.C.
- Yes Ban "partial birth" abortion except to save a woman's life
- No Split $18.6 billion in Iraq aid into half-grant, half-loan
- Yes Overhaul Medicare and create prescription drug benefit

CQ VOTE STUDIES

	PARTY UNITY		PRESIDENTIAL SUPPORT	
	Support	Oppose	Support	Oppose
2004	99%	1%	85%	15%
2003	98%	2%	91%	9%

INTEREST GROUPS

	AFL-CIO	ADA	CCUS	ACU
2004	13%	5%	100%	96%
2003	0%	10%	96%	88%

IOWA 5
West — Sioux City, Council Bluffs

The 32-county 5th takes in miles of fertile soil and gently undulating hills in the western part of the state. The bountiful land has allowed the region to remain more like the Iowa of old than any other part of the state.

Sioux City, the district's largest metropolitan center, has developed into a service center for a region that includes part of Nebraska and South Dakota. Some Sioux City businesses have moved across the river to take advantage of more-favorable tax laws in other states, but Woodbury County has sprouted numerous bedroom communities where many workers live. Sioux City long has leaned Republican, and surrounding rural towns are home to many independent farmers who tend to vote Republican.

The district's second-largest city, Council Bluffs, also is located on the state's western border, though farther south. Built against bluffs, the city was a bustling crossroads for three westward trails in the early 1800s, and five railroads later met there. Today, many workers cross the Missouri River to work for Omaha businesses that have been lured to

Nebraska by lower tax rates.

Southwest Iowa is less wedded to social conservatism than the northwest region and is more likely to back GOP-establishment candidates. This area gave big percentages to George W. Bush in the 2000 caucuses, and it backed state House Speaker Brent Siegrist in the 2002 5th District primary over more-conservative challengers.

Overall, the solidly Republican district gave Bush 60 percent of the vote in the 2004 presidential election, making it his best district in the state by a wide margin. Bush's seven best counties were in the 5th, and the district includes every county in which Bush exceeded 65 percent of the vote, led by Sioux County with 86 percent.

MAJOR INDUSTRY
Meatpacking, agriculture

CITIES
Sioux City, 85,013; Council Bluffs, 58,268; Spencer, 11,317

NOTABLE
The annual Donna Reed Festival is held in the actress' hometown of Denison; The largest rural Danish settlement in the United States is in the area around Elk Horn and Kimballton.

Gov. Kathleen Sebelius (D)

First elected: 2002
Length of term: 4 years
Term expires: 1/07
Salary: $101,280
Phone: (785) 296-3232

Hometown: Topeka
Born: May 15, 1948; Cincinnati, Ohio
Religion: Roman Catholic
Family: Husband, Gary Sebelius; two children
Education: Trinity College (D.C.), B.A. 1970 (political science); U. of Kansas, M.P.A. 1977
Career: Law association director; state corrections department official
Political highlights: Kansas Governmental Ethics Commission, 1975-77; Kan. House, 1987-95; Kan. insurance commissioner, 1995-2003

Election results:
2002 GENERAL

Kathleen Sebelius (D)	441,858	52.9%
Tim Shallenburger (R)	376,830	45.1%
Ted Pettibone (REF)	8,907	1.1%
Ira Dennis Hawver (LIBERT)	8,097	1.0%

Lt. Gov. John E. Moore (D)

First elected: 2002
Length of term: 4 years
Term expires: 1/07
Salary: $98,000
Phone: (785) 296-2213

STATE LEGISLATURE

Legislature: January to spring, limit of 90 days in even-numbered years

House: 125 members, 2-year terms
2005 breakdown: 83R, 42D; 85 men, 40 women
Salary: $81/day in session; $91/day expenses; $6,480/year allowance
Phone: (785) 296-7633

Senate: 40 members, 4-year terms
2005 breakdown: 30R, 10D; 27 men, 13 women
Salary: $81/day in session; $91/day expenses; $6,480/year allowance
Phone: (785) 296-7344

STATE TERM LIMITS

Governor: 2 terms
House: No
Senate: No

URBAN STATISTICS

CITY	POPULATION
Wichita	344,284
Overland Park	149,080
Kansas City	146,866
Topeka	122,377

REGISTERED VOTERS

Republican	46%
Democrat	27%
Unaffiliated/others	27%

POPULATION

2004 population (est.)	2,735,502
2000 population	2,688,418
1990 population	2,477,574
Percent change (1990-2000)	+8.5%
Rank among states (2004)	33
Median age	35.2
Born in state	59.5%
Foreign born	5%
Violent crime rate	389/100,000
Poverty level	9.9%
Federal workers	25,639
Military	29,103

REDISTRICTING

Kansas retained its four House seats in reapportionment. The state legislature drew a new map, which the governor signed on May 31, 2002.

MISCELLANEOUS

Web: www.accesskansas.org
Capital: Topeka
STATE ELECTION OFFICIAL
(785) 296-4561
DEMOCRATIC HEADQUARTERS
(785) 234-0425
REPUBLICAN HEADQUARTERS
(785) 234-3456

District Statistics

DIST.	2004 VOTE FOR PRESIDENT BUSH	KERRY	WHITE	BLACK	ASIAN	HISP	MEDIAN INCOME	WHITE COLLAR	BLUE COLLAR	SERVICE INDUSTRY	OVER 64	UNDER 18	COLLEGE EDUCATION	RURAL	SQ. MILES
1	72%	26%	85%	2%	1%	11%	$34,869	53%	31%	16%	16%	26%	18%	48%	57,373
2	59	39	87	5	1	4	$37,855	58	27	16	14	25	23	40	14,134
3	55	44	80	9	3	7	$51,118	70	17	12	10	27	39	5	778
4	64	34	81	7	2	7	$40,917	57	29	14	13	28	23	21	9,531
STATE	62	37	83	6	2	7	$40,624	60	26	14	13	27	26	29	81,815
U.S.	50.7	48.3	69	12	4	13	$41,994	60	25	15	12	26	24	21	3,537,438

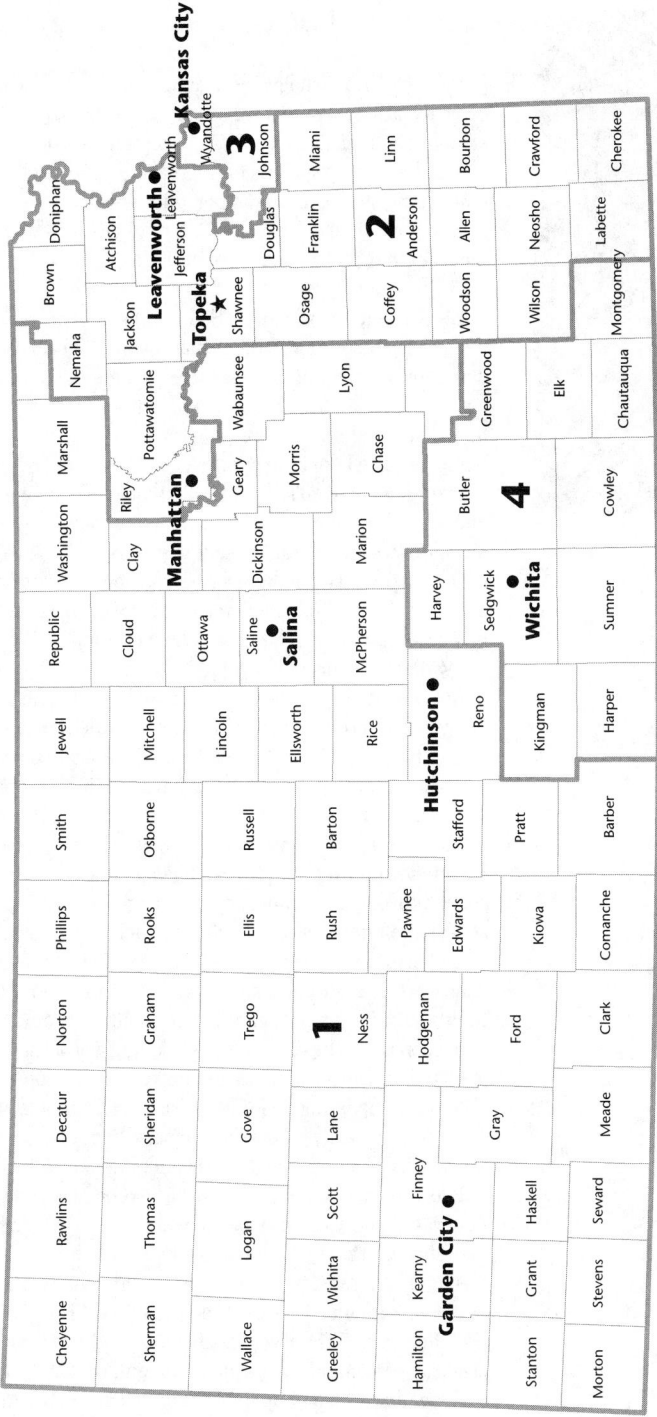

Sen. Sam Brownback (R)

Elected 1996; 2nd full term

CAPITOL OFFICE
224-6521
sam_brownback@brownback.senate.gov
brownback.senate.gov
303 Hart 20510-1604; fax 228-1265

COMMITTEES
Appropriations
(District of Columbia - chairman)
Judiciary
(Constitution, Civil Rights & Property Rights -
chairman)
Joint Economic

HOMETOWN
Topeka

BORN
Sept. 12, 1956, Garnett, Kan.

RELIGION
Roman Catholic

FAMILY
Wife, Mary Brownback; five children

EDUCATION
Kansas State U., B.S. 1979 (agricultural
economics); U. of Kansas, J.D. 1982

CAREER
Lawyer; professor; White House fellow;
broadcaster

POLITICAL HIGHLIGHTS
Kan. secretary of Agriculture, 1986-93; U.S. House,
1995-96

ELECTION RESULTS

2004 GENERAL

Sam Brownback (R)	780,863	69.2%
Lee Jones (D)	310,337	27.5%
Steven A. Rosile (LIBERT)	21,842	1.9%
George Cook (REF)	15,980	1.4%

2004 PRIMARY

Sam Brownback (R)	286,839	87.0%
Arch Naramore (R)	42,880	13.0%

PREVIOUS WINNING PERCENTAGES
1998 (65%); 1996 Special Election (54%); 1994 House
Election (66%)

Brownback is usually found at the center of the action on issues of interest to social conservatives. His time in the Senate has been marked by passionate denunciations of what he views as the decay of American culture, and he has led campaigns for media indecency laws and against the use of embryonic stem cells and cloning for research.

His quest to align policy with his religious views is evident in his work on everything from putting restrictions on abortion to intervening in the crisis in Sudan.

Brownback is a prominent Senate opponent of research using embryonic stem cells, the primordial cells that scientists believe may eventually unlock cures for a variety of diseases. He equates the use of stem cells with taking a human life because they are extracted from days-old embryos, and he has likened the research to slavery, saying it uses one class of human beings for the benefit of another.

President Reagan's death in 2004 from Alzheimer's disease rekindled interest in boosting federal support for stem cell research, particularly after his widow, Nancy Reagan, said she favored it. But Brownback remained steadfast, promising to fight any expansion of the policy President Bush put in place in 2001 allowing federal funding of stem cell research using embryos that have already been destroyed, but not to finance future harvesting of cells. Brownback has also pressed for a ban on all forms of human cloning.

In the 108th Congress, and again in the 109th, he introduced bills requiring women who seek an abortion after 20 weeks of pregnancy to sign a form saying they have been "fully informed" that a fetus can feel pain.

As head of the GOP Values Action Team in the Senate, Brownback regularly meets with the Family Research Council and the conservative Catholic group American Society for the Defense of Tradition, Family and Property. He attends midweek Bible readings and prayer sessions and has close personal and political connections to religious conservative activists. In July 2002, he left the Methodist church to become a Roman Catholic.

In the 109th Congress, Brownback returned to the Judiciary Committee, after a two-year absence, and got the chairmanship of the Constitution, Civil Rights and Property Rights Subcommittee. From there, he can have an impact on issues he cares about, including a proposed constitutional amendment to ban same-sex marriage. Brownback also took the helm of the Appropriations Subcommittee for the District of Columbia, which gives him a say in the many social policies that conservatives in Congress like to impose on the district as a first step toward taking them nationwide.

Brownback blames Hollywood for some of society's ills. He prompted a Federal Trade Commission investigation of whether the entertainment industry markets violent and sexually explicit movies and songs to teenagers. "There are more social workers than serial murderers in America. There are more pastors than prostitutes. But you'd never know it from TV," he says. "When we watch more and more violence, profanity and sleaze, we eventually grow more violent, profane and coarse."

Brownback turned up the heat on television broadcasters after the infamous Super Bowl halftime show in 2004 in which pop singer Janet Jackson bared a breast. His bill increasing indecency fines for broadcasters tenfold to $275,000 per incident stalled in the Senate after it was paired with a controversial proposal related to media ownership rules. Brownback continued to push his bill in the 109th Congress.

On foreign policy issues, Brownback traveled to Sudan in 2004 and came back convinced that ethnic cleansing was taking place. He authored a resolution describing the situation in Darfur as "genocide" and called on other nations to join the United States in taking action. But he qualified the proposal, saying that limited U.S. military involvement should be part of a broader force under U.N. or NATO auspices.

Despite complaints about China's human rights record, he voted for the 2000 law granting that nation permanent normal trade status. The prospects of more grain exports are eagerly embraced by his state's corn and wheat farmers.

At the time of the Sept. 11, 2001, terrorist attacks, Brownback was the top-ranking Republican on the Foreign Relations Committee's Near Eastern and South Asian Affairs Subcommittee. He developed an expertise on Afghanistan and the Muslim world, and helped push to enactment that year a law waiving for two years sanctions on Pakistan, a key Bush administration ally in its war on terrorism. And long before Bush focused on Saddam Hussein, Brownback was pressing for a tougher policy against the Iraqi leader. "I don't want to see Saddam outlast another U.S. president," he said in 1999.

The senator has adopted children from China and Guatemala. Ironically, he came under criticism from some adoption advocates for opposing Senate ratification of the Hague Convention on Intercountry Adoption, a treaty designed to impose standards on the often chaotic international adoption process. The treaty, Brownback contended, would create an unwieldy and costly adoption bureaucracy.

The low point of Brownback's congressional career was in 1996, when his own campaign fundraising came under scrutiny during congressional inquiries into improprieties by the Democratic National Committee. Brownback's in-laws had funneled money to his campaign in excess of legal limits by using third-party groups and were later fined by the Federal Election Commission. Then, he angered Asian-American groups by affecting accented English — supposedly of someone who is Chinese-American — at a Senate hearing. While questioning the DNC finance director about the alleged promise of a bonus to fundraiser John Huang for good work, Brownback said, "So, no raise money, no get bonus." Brownback quickly apologized, but he was upbraided by the groups and by leading Democrats for "racial stereotyping."

Brownback has been inclined toward politics since he was president of his eighth-grade class. He was student body president at Kansas State University, a national officer of the Future Farmers of America, a White House fellow in the U.S. Trade Representative's office in the administration of the first President Bush, and Kansas secretary of agriculture for six years. Brownback planned a bid for governor in 1994 but decided on a House race instead when Democratic incumbent Jim Slattery gave up his 2nd District seat to run for the governorship. In that year's GOP tidal wave, Brownback easily defeated the state's two-term Democratic governor, John Carlin.

When Bob Dole became the GOP's nominee for president and resigned from the Senate in 1996, Brownback announced he would seek the seat. But Gov. Bill Graves appointed GOP Lt. Gov. Sheila Frahm to the post until a special election could be held. Brownback beat the more moderate Frahm by 13 percentage points in a primary by appealing to business groups and social conservatives. In November, he narrowly defeated stockbroker Jill Docking, a member of a well-known Kansas political family, with 54 percent of the vote.

Kansas Republicans urged Brownback to run for governor in 2002, but he decided to stay in the Senate. In 2004, he was re-elected easily with 69 percent.

KEY VOTES

2004

No Pass $318.9 billion, six-year highway and mass transit bill
No Extend assault weapons ban for 10 years
No Restore pay-as-you-go rules for new tax cuts and entitlement spending
Yes Criminalize harm to a fetus in an attack on the mother
Yes Increase mandatory child care funding to states by $6 billion over five years
Yes Amend the Constitution to prohibit same-sex marriage
Yes Approve $146 billion multi-year extension of previously enacted middle-class tax breaks
Yes Reorganize U.S. intelligence agencies as proposed by Sept. 11 commission
Yes Cut corporate taxes $137 billion over 10 years

2003

No Delay Bush changes to Clean Air Act
Yes Allow confirmation vote on Miguel A. Estrada to the U.S. Court of Appeals for the D.C. Circuit
No Block a Bush proposal opening Alaska's Arctic National Wildlife Refuge to oil drilling
No Limit size of Bush's proposed tax cut to $350 billion through fiscal 2013
Yes Overhaul Medicare and create prescription drug benefit
No Block Bush rule scaling back overtime pay for some white-collar federal workers
Yes Split $20 billion in Iraq aid into half-grant, half-loan
Yes Ban "partial birth" abortion except to save a woman's life
No Stop proposal allowing travel to Cuba
Yes Allow final vote on energy policy overhaul

CQ VOTE STUDIES

	PARTY UNITY		PRESIDENTIAL SUPPORT	
	Support	Oppose	Support	Oppose
2004	98%	2%	98%	2%
2003	96%	4%	97%	3%
2002	94%	6%	98%	2%
2001	94%	6%	99%	1%
2000	98%	2%	40%	60%
1999	95%	5%	31%	69%
1998	96%	4%	37%	63%
1997	96%	4%	56%	44%
House Service:				
1996	92%	8%	32%	68%
1995	96%	4%	22%	78%

INTEREST GROUPS

	AFL-CIO	ADA	CCUS	ACU
2004	0%	15%	94%	96%
2003	0%	5%	100%	80%
2002	15%	5%	100%	100%
2001	19%	0%	93%	96%
2000	0%	0%	100%	100%
1999	0%	5%	94%	95%
1998	0%	0%	94%	92%
1997	0%	0%	100%	100%
House Service:				
1996	0%	5%	93%	100%
1995	8%	0%	100%	92%

Sen. Pat Roberts (R)

Elected 1996; 2nd term

Among the most quotable of senators, Roberts is known for his pithy and sometimes sarcastic tongue. In overseeing the new power structure in the intelligence community, Roberts has a more diplomatic role to play in soothing tensions between the CIA and its military intelligence counterparts, which do not always get along.

Roberts was largely sidelined during the biggest restructuring of the nation's intelligence community in 60 years, which was enacted by Congress at the close of the 108th Congress. His committee was bypassed in favor of the Governmental Affairs Committee, which wrote the legislation. Roberts supported a more radical dismantling of the intelligence agencies, but his ideas did not prevail. Majority Leader Bill Frist decided to keep governmental restructuring in the hands of moderate Republican Susan Collins of Maine, who chairs Governmental Affairs.

But Roberts now has some new tools to try to enhance the Intelligence Committee's authority. As the Senate reorganized for the 109th Congress, Intelligence was upgraded to an "A" committee, making it a top-tier panel with more say in originating bills and overseeing the changes brought about by the 2004 legislation. At the same time, the Senate did away with term limits for the Intelligence chairman, which enhanced Roberts' power. Anyone who thinks to cross him has to consider that he could be in the driver's seat for a long time.

Roberts has had a sometimes rocky relationship with the committee's top-ranking Democrat, Vice Chairman John D. Rockefeller IV of West Virginia. They fought over the nomination of Porter J. Goss, a former House member from Florida and former chairman of the House Intelligence panel, to be director of the CIA. Rockefeller judged Goss to be too political for the job, but Roberts led Goss supporters in pushing his nomination through the Senate.

Roberts is known for unleashing verbal zingers on the floor and off, often voted "Funniest Senator" in Washingtonian magazine's annual survey of congressional staff. Lamenting his lack of input into the intelligence overhaul during Senate debate, Robert said, "I'm like a one-legged chicken." In 2000, he labeled anti-trade organizations as "the representatives of Ralph Nader, Ross Perot, Pat Buchanan and other various wackos." The next year, he said asking the federal agency that administers Medicare and Medicaid for help would be akin to "asking the Boston Strangler for a necklace."

Roberts sometimes challenges the party line on national security issues. He guided a committee inquiry into Iraq-related intelligence that concluded the CIA relied on flawed and outdated intelligence regarding Saddam Hussein's weapons of mass destruction.

Though he does not tout the fact, few members have as good a claim as Roberts to foreseeing the threat of a terrorist attack before Sept. 11, 2001. As the first chairman of the Armed Services Subcommittee on Emerging Threats and Capabilities, which focuses on the terrorism threat, Roberts in 1999 started pressing the Pentagon and Congress to get beyond a Cold War mentality and to prepare for military attacks that would use novel weapons. He urged preparedness for a gamut of possible terrorist assaults — attacks on civilian populations with nuclear, chemical or biological weapons and cyberattacks on critical computer networks.

While he is a reliable GOP vote on such issues as abortion rights and cutting taxes, he is less confrontational than some younger Republicans. Rob-

CAPITOL OFFICE
224-4774
roberts.senate.gov
109 Hart 20510-1605; fax 224-3514

COMMITTEES
Agriculture, Nutrition & Forestry
Armed Services
Health, Education, Labor & Pensions
Select Ethics
Select Intelligence - chairman

HOMETOWN
Dodge City

BORN
April 20, 1936, Topeka, Kan.

RELIGION
Methodist

FAMILY
Wife, Franki Roberts; three children

EDUCATION
Kansas State U., B.A. 1958 (journalism)

MILITARY SERVICE
Marine Corps, 1958-62

CAREER
Congressional aide; newspaper owner; reporter

POLITICAL HIGHLIGHTS
U.S. House, 1981-97

ELECTION RESULTS

2002 GENERAL

Pat Roberts (R)	641,075	82.5%
Steven A. Rosile (LIBERT)	70,725	9.1%
George Cook (REF)	65,050	8.4%

2002 PRIMARY

Pat Roberts (R)	233,642	83.7%
Thomas L. "Tom" Oyler (R)	45,491	16.3%

PREVIOUS WINNING PERCENTAGES
1996 (62%); 1994 House Election (77%); 1992 House Election (68%); 1990 House Election (63%); 1988 House Election (100%); 1986 House Election (77%); 1984 House Election (76%); 1982 House Election (68%); 1980 House Election (62%)

erts often tries to build alliances with Democrats on the security issues that interest him. Rep. Barney Frank of Massachusetts, a liberal Democrat with no fondness for Republicans, once told the Kansas City Star, "He's not one of the impossible ideologues."

To stay close to the corn and wheat farmers and cattle ranchers of his state, Roberts sits on the Agriculture Committee. Like many farm-state Republicans, he has an internationalist view on trade that emphasizes exports. He worries that U.S. economic sanctions against other countries are hurting the farm economy. Roberts was an ardent proponent of the 2002 law giving President Bush authority to negotiate new trade agreements that cannot be amended by Congress.

Roberts is an old hand at the legislative power game, and despite his current high profile on national security, he has a long record on issues dear to Kansans. He served eight terms in the House, where he was known as "The Aggie" for his pivotal role in the farm policy debate that resulted in the 1996 Freedom to Farm law. It was a major legislative achievement for him though much of it subsequently was undone by Congress. The legislation replaced traditional farm subsidies with a system of declining payments to farmers, under the assumption that strong overseas markets for commodities would offset smaller government payments. But prices slumped worldwide, and Congress wound up bailing out farmers year after year.

Since 1999, Roberts has been on the Ethics Committee, where he was the chairman from late 1999 to mid-2001. In 2002, he helped mete out the harshest punishment of a senator in years when Democrat Robert G. Torricelli was severely admonished for accepting gifts from a campaign donor.

Roberts has deep ties to the military and continues to be loyal to the Marines, often beginning speeches by calling himself "this ex-Marine." His father was a Marine, and an uncle was a military attaché to the U.S. embassy in China who survived the 1937 sinking by Japanese planes of the U.S. gunboat *Panay*. Roberts' office is decorated with Marine regalia though it's been over 40 years since his service.

Roberts earned a journalism degree from Kansas State University, intending to follow a family tradition in the news business. His great-grandfather, Wesley Roberts, had moved to the Kansas Territory from Ohio with "a Bible, a six-shooter and printing press in tow," according to a 1996 profile of Roberts in the Star.

After graduation, Roberts was drafted, so he joined the Marines. Returning home in 1962, he worked as a reporter and then co-owned a weekly newspaper in the Phoenix suburbs. He learned about zoning boards, city councils, boards of education, and developed, as he told the Star later, "a healthy respect and a degree of cynicism in a lot of federal programs."

He first came to Washington to work as a Senate aide and later ran the office of Republican Rep. Keith G. Sebelius of Kansas. When Sebelius announced his retirement in 1980, Roberts was ready. He cruised to victory in the general election, capitalizing on Sebelius' popularity and referring to "our record" so frequently he sounded like an incumbent.

As he became one of the most popular politicians in Kansas, Roberts was often likened to Majority Leader Bob Dole, another Kansan known for a caustic tone and conservative outlook.

Roberts initially balked at making a Senate bid in 1996 when Republican Nancy Landon Kassebaum retired, saying he wanted to focus on shepherding the farm bill into law. But he eventually entered the race and handily won the GOP nod. Facing Democratic state Treasurer Sally Thompson in the fall, he won with 62 percent of the vote. In 2002, Democrats didn't field a candidate.

KEY VOTES

2004

Yes   Pass $318.9 billion, six-year highway and mass transit bill

No   Extend assault weapons ban for 10 years

No   Restore pay-as-you-go rules for new tax cuts and entitlement spending

Yes   Criminalize harm to a fetus in an attack on the mother

Yes   Increase mandatory child care funding to states by $6 billion over five years

Yes   Amend the Constitution to prohibit same-sex marriage

Yes   Approve $146 billion multi-year extension of previously enacted middle-class tax breaks

Yes   Reorganize U.S. intelligence agencies as proposed by Sept. 11 commission

Yes   Cut corporate taxes $137 billion over 10 years

2003

No   Delay Bush changes to Clean Air Act

Yes   Allow confirmation vote on Miguel A. Estrada to the U.S. Court of Appeals for the D.C. Circuit

No   Block a Bush proposal opening Alaska's Arctic National Wildlife Refuge to oil drilling

No   Limit size of Bush's proposed tax cut to $350 billion through fiscal 2013

Yes   Overhaul Medicare and create prescription drug benefit

No   Block Bush rule scaling back overtime pay for some white-collar federal workers

No   Split $20 billion in Iraq aid into half-grant, half-loan

Yes   Ban "partial birth" abortion except to save a woman's life

No   Stop proposal allowing travel to Cuba

Yes   Allow final vote on energy policy overhaul

CQ VOTE STUDIES

	PARTY UNITY		PRESIDENTIAL SUPPORT	
	Support	Oppose	Support	Oppose
2004	99%	1%	92%	8%
2003	96%	4%	97%	3%
2002	96%	4%	96%	4%
2001	95%	5%	99%	1%
2000	97%	3%	38%	62%
1999	94%	6%	29%	71%
1998	95%	5%	35%	65%
1997	90%	10%	59%	41%
House Service:				
1996	92%	8%	37%	63%
1995	96%	4%	19%	81%

INTEREST GROUPS

	AFL-CIO	ADA	CCUS	ACU
2004	17%	15%	100%	92%
2003	0%	15%	100%	90%
2002	15%	0%	100%	100%
2001	13%	0%	93%	100%
2000	0%	0%	100%	92%
1999	0%	0%	94%	88%
1998	0%	0%	100%	84%
1997	0%	15%	90%	68%
House Service:				
1996	0%	5%	94%	95%
1995	0%	0%	96%	80%

Rep. Jerry Moran (R)

Elected 1996; 5th term

CAPITOL OFFICE
225-2715
www.house.gov/moranks01
2443 Rayburn 20515-1601; fax 225-5124

COMMITTEES
Agriculture
  (General Farm Commodities & Risk
  Management - chairman)
Transportation & Infrastructure
Veterans' Affairs

HOMETOWN
Hays

BORN
May 29, 1954, Great Bend, Kan.

RELIGION
Protestant

FAMILY
Wife, Robba Moran; two children

EDUCATION
Fort Hays State U., attended 1972-73; U. of Kansas,
B.S. 1976 (economics), J.D. 1981

CAREER
Lawyer; banker

POLITICAL HIGHLIGHTS
Kan. Senate, 1989-97 (vice president, 1993-95;
majority leader, 1995-97)

ELECTION RESULTS

2004 GENERAL

Jerry Moran (R)	239,776	90.7%
Jack W. Warner (LIBERT)	24,517	9.3%

2004 PRIMARY

Jerry Moran (R)	unopposed

2002 GENERAL

Jerry Moran (R)	189,976	91.1%
Jack W. Warner (LIBERT)	18,585	8.9%

PREVIOUS WINNING PERCENTAGES
2000 (89%); 1998 (81%); 1996 (73%)

Every year, Moran drives a rental car through the 69 flat Kansas counties that make up the sprawling 1st District, known locally as the Big First. His far-flung "listening tour" is a custom begun three decades ago by one of his predecessors, and it leads him to such places as the Kansas Barbed Wire Museum in La Crosse and Our Daily Bread Bake Shoppe and Bistro in Barnes. Most often, Moran hears complaints about low crop prices, which explains why his focus in Washington is trying to pry open foreign markets for U.S. commodities.

From his seat on the Agriculture Committee, Moran also tries to help corn and wheat farmers in western Kansas by pushing to boost subsidies to shelter farmers from the effects of drought or plummeting wheat prices. "Ninety-eight percent of the mouths to feed are outside the United States, and many of them are hungry," Moran told the Topeka Capital-Journal newspaper. "So if there is going to be profitability on the farm, in large part it's going to come about as the result of the United States getting aggressive about exports."

Early in the 109th Congress, Moran introduced legislation to ease restrictions on trade with Cuba, a priority for many GOP farm advocates despite opposition from President Bush. He chairs a key subcommittee on Agriculture — the General Farm Commodities and Risk Management Subcommittee.

During the last major revision of the farm law, in 2002, Moran worked on the addition of provisions to increase production of ethanol, a fuel additive made from corn, and to speed the installation of broadband cable across rural America, which many see as essential to small-town economic survival.

Moran has worked behind the scenes within the Republican Conference, the group of all House Republicans, to gain influence in the years since he was first elected in 1996. He served for a time on the Republican Steering Committee, which decides the party's committee assignments. Moran is a senior member of the House Veterans' Affairs Committee's Health Subcommittee and also has served as a co-chairman of the 181-lawmaker Rural Health Care Coalition.

Moran stuck with party leaders 92 percent of the time on major votes in the 108th Congress, but he strayed on one issue important to Bush and Speaker J. Dennis Hastert. In 2003, he opposed the president's Medicare prescription drug bill as too costly and not good for his rural constituents. Though not naming Moran, Hastert complained in a 2004 autobiography about a fourth-term "prairie state" member who "voted no, then ran and hid." Moran, who won plaudits from conservative and libertarian groups for his vote, told the Associated Press he didn't think Hastert was talking about him even though others read it that way.

By and large, Moran's big issues tend to be parochial. When the Bush administration, in response to the terrorism threat, stopped a program that gave visas to foreign doctors who promised to work in rural outposts, Moran rallied opposition among rural lawmakers.The administration ultimately agreed to resume processing applications, including from doctors destined for Kansas, and in 2004 Moran won a two-year extension of the program, keeping it going through 2006.

He also sought in 2003 to advance legislation re-opening Ronald Reagan Washington National Airport to private planes. Kansas is home to the Cessna Aircraft Co., a division of Textron Inc., and also to Raytheon Aircraft. As a member of the Transportation and Infrastructure Committee in the 109th Congress, Moran is pushing for more rural roadbuilding. In 2000, he backed a measure to promote the use of communications technology to improve rural medicine by allowing Medicare reimbursement for care and consultation performed via interactive television hookups.

At 53,275 square miles, Moran's is among the nation's largest congressional districts. In the redistricting following the 2000 census, the Republican legislature redrew the boundaries in an attempt to weaken the Kansas delegation's lone Democrat, Dennis Moore in the 3rd District, and so added a little more territory to Moran's district. But he has had no trouble getting re-elected. Moran in fact has not had a Democratic opponent since 1998.

Moran is a native of the district, where his father labored in the oil fields and his mother worked as a secretary at an electric utility. As a high school student body officer, Moran was in charge of inviting the local congressman, Republican Keith G. Sebelius, to speak at a fundraising dinner. They kept in touch, and several years later Moran went off to Washington as an intern for Sebelius, originator of the "listening tour" tradition in the 1st District. It was the summer of 1974, the height of the Watergate scandal, and Moran remembers feeling like an eyewitness to history as the House Judiciary Committee held hearings to consider the impeachment of President Nixon.

In 1976, Moran graduated from the University of Kansas with a degree in economics and took a job as a banker. He earned his law degree five years later and opened his own practice in Hays. In 1988, he made a longshot race for the state Senate against an 18-year incumbent and won by just a few hundred votes. He was unopposed for a second term in 1992.

Moran went on to become chairman of the state Senate Judiciary Committee and then ascended to majority leader in 1995, thanks to his ability to appeal to both the conservative and moderate wings of the Kansas GOP.

He ran for Congress in 1996 when Republican Pat Roberts left the House seat to succeed Nancy Landon Kassebaum in the Senate. Moran quickly became the front-runner, portraying himself as a pragmatic conservative. In a district with a long Republican tradition, and with Kansas Republican Bob Dole topping the GOP ticket as its presidential nominee, Moran rolled to an easy victory with 73 percent of the vote against John Divine, the former mayor of Salina.

Against Libertarian Jack W. Warner, Moran won re-election resoundingly in 2004. He is often mentioned as a potential candidate for governor in 2006.

KEY VOTES

2004

No Extend federal unemployment benefits by 13 weeks
Yes Pass $283.2 billion, six-year federal highway and mass transit bill
Yes Approve $146 billion multi-year extension of previously enacted middle-class tax breaks
Yes Amend the Constitution to prohibit same-sex marriage
Yes Cut corporate taxes $137 billion over 10 years
Yes Reorganize U.S. intelligence agencies as proposed by Sept. 11 commission

2003

Yes Cut taxes by $330 billion through fiscal 2013
No Block Bush rule scaling back overtime pay for some white-collar federal workers
Yes Do not allow use of search warrants without first notifying subjects
Yes Allow importation of prescription drugs
Yes Create private school voucher program in Washington, D.C.
Yes Ban "partial birth" abortion except to save a woman's life
No Split $18.6 billion in Iraq aid into half-grant, half-loan
No Overhaul Medicare and create prescription drug benefit

CQ VOTE STUDIES

	PARTY UNITY		PRESIDENTIAL SUPPORT	
	Support	Oppose	Support	Oppose
2004	92%	8%	68%	32%
2003	92%	8%	82%	18%
2002	89%	11%	72%	28%
2001	90%	10%	77%	23%
2000	93%	7%	25%	75%

INTEREST GROUPS

	AFL-CIO	ADA	CCUS	ACU
2004	21%	10%	95%	92%
2003	27%	25%	90%	92%
2002	0%	5%	90%	96%
2001	25%	5%	96%	88%
2000	0%	0%	90%	92%

KANSAS 1

West and central — Salina, Hutchinson, Garden City, Emporia

The fiscally conservative 1st takes in all of western Kansas and stretches east across farmland to reach Nemaha County in the north and Emporia in the center, covering most of rural Kansas in the process. The district covers 70 percent of the state and in land area is bigger than most U.S. states (including 25 of the 26 states east of the Mississippi River).

The 1st's economy is wedded to agriculture, an industry that suffered from weather disasters in the 1980s and falling commodity prices in the 1990s. More and more rural residents have packed their bags for the city to escape the tough farming life.

The largest population center is in the district's eastern portion. Salina (Saline County) is a traditional farm-market town, but has an industrial element — Raytheon has a factory here. Hutchinson, site of the Kansas State Fair, is dominated by farm- and food-related businesses. Junction City is home to many civilian workers who commute to Fort Riley in the

2nd District. In the west, towns such as Garden City and Dodge City rely on meatpacking and tourism. Thriving beef processing plants continue to draw Mexican and Asian immigrants.

The 1st is comfortably Republican, although it did exhibit an independent streak in the 1992 presidential election, giving Ross Perot 29 percent of the vote. The district overwhelmingly voted for George W. Bush in the 2004 presidential contest, giving him his highest percentage in the state (72 percent). The GOP also dominates local offices, except in Hays, where Fort Hays State University is located, and in Hutchinson.

MAJOR INDUSTRY
Agriculture, manufacturing, oil and gas

CITIES
Salina, 45,679; Hutchinson, 40,787; Garden City, 28,451; Emporia, 26,760; Dodge City, 25,176; Hays, 20,013; Liberal, 19,666; Junction City, 18,886

NOTABLE
Dwight D. Eisenhower's burial place and presidential library are in Abilene; Former Senate Majority Leader and 1996 Republican presidential nominee Bob Dole was born and raised in Russell.

Rep. Jim Ryun (R)

Elected 1996; 5th term

CAPITOL OFFICE
225-6601
ryun.house.gov
1110 Longworth 20515-1602; fax 225-7986

COMMITTEES
Armed Services
Budget
Financial Services

HOMETOWN
Jefferson County

BORN
April 29, 1947, Wichita, Kan.

RELIGION
Presbyterian

FAMILY
Wife, Anne Ryun; four children

EDUCATION
U. of Kansas, B.A. 1970 (photojournalism)

CAREER
Motivational speaker; author; product consultant;
Olympic athlete

POLITICAL HIGHLIGHTS
No previous office

ELECTION RESULTS

2004 GENERAL

Jim Ryun (R)	165,325	56.2%
Nancy Boyda (D)	121,532	41.3%
Ira Dennis Hawver (LIBERT)	7,579	2.6%

2004 PRIMARY

Jim Ryun (R)	unopposed

2002 GENERAL

Jim Ryun (R)	127,477	60.4%
Dan Lykins (D)	79,160	37.5%
Arthur L. Clack (LIBERT)	4,340	2.1%

PREVIOUS WINNING PERCENTAGES
2000 (67%); 1998 (61%); 1996 (52%)

It's been a long time since Ryun has clocked under 4 minutes for a mile. The former teenage running phenomenon today is a conservative GOP loyalist serving his fifth term in the House. Popular among Kansas conservatives, who are waging an ongoing battle with the moderate wing of the party, he is a champion of causes ranging from property rights to services for the hearing impaired.

Before he arrived in the House in 1997, people in eastern Kansas knew his name as well as any state officeholder's. Ryun was the first high school miler to break the 4-minute barrier. He was on the cover of Sports Illustrated as its Sportsman of the Year in 1966, won the Sullivan Award as the nation's top amateur athlete in 1967, held the world record for the mile (3:51:1) for seven years, and was on three U.S. Olympic teams — all by the age of 25.

In the quarter-century after his competitive athletics career ended, Ryun worked with sports camps, gave motivational speeches drawing on athletics and religion, and worked with a hearing aid manufacturer to help hearing-impaired children. (He has a hearing impairment himself.) Ryun dabbled in politics, mostly working in behalf of other candidates who shared his conservative views.

He won his House seat when Majority Leader Bob Dole resigned from the Senate to run for president in 1996 and the 2nd District's incumbent, Republican Sam Brownback, left to run successfully for Dole's seat.

On national issues, Ryun's priorities and philosophy generally mirror those of the GOP leadership — lower taxes, restraints on domestic spending, more robust defense spending and fewer federal regulations. He has a near-perfect record of supporting his party. His annual rating for voting with GOP leaders on key votes usually does not dip below 98 percent. On the rare occasions he has been at odds with the GOP mainstream, Ryun has almost always been on its right. He was one of 25 Republicans to oppose the Medicare prescription drug bill in 2003 because it was too expensive and did not do enough to restrain future costs.

Loyalty was not enough to move him into the ranks of leadership. In the 108th Congress, Ryun lost his bid to become chairman of the House Republican Conference, finishing a poor third behind Deborah Pryce of Ohio and J.D. Hayworth of Arizona.

He is carving out a niche with causes that get scant attention. Ryun has prevented the Bureau of Citizenship and Immigration from administering a rewritten oath that, starting in 2003, was to be taken by naturalized citizens. The bureau said the 50-plus-year-old oath needed to be updated with clear and modern language, but Ryun said the new words transformed "an absolute commitment . . . into a conditional statement and thereby weaken our citizenship." Ryun won a temporary delay in implementing the new oath and favors permanent legislation to require more resolute language.

Ryun also would like to trim the sails of the Supreme Court. In a move with support only in the most conservative of quarters, he is pushing a nonbinding resolution asking the Supreme Court to stop taking international laws or laws from other countries into account when it interprets the Constitution. He points to several death penalty and gay rights cases, in which justices said they were influenced by legal practices elsewhere. "The American people have had no opportunity to vote on any of these laws, and, in fact, many international laws are often developed by United Nations bureaucrats, without any democratic input," Ryun says.

An ardent foe of abortion rights, Ryun opposes federal funding for embryonic stem cell research, noting in a 2001 floor speech that he would prefer instead for embryos created in fertility clinics to be allowed to grow into babies, who could then be adopted. Ryun often refers to the importance of his Christian faith, and in 2002 he and his two sons collaborated on a book, "Heroes Among Us," which was featured in Christian bookstores.

From his seat in the middle tier of GOP seats on the Armed Services Committee, Ryun's principal focus is looking out for the troops at Fort Riley and Fort Leavenworth and for local defense contractors.

Another parochial pursuit is seeking to amend the "rails-to-trails" act to give the former owners of land under abandoned railroad tracks a chance to get the land back or be paid for it. Currently, many unused railbeds are converted to recreational trails, and while Ryun says he has made use of such trails as a runner, he argues that the original landowners deserve help against the "Goliath that's denying them all their rights."

In 2001, Ryun saw enactment of his legislation creating a commission to commemorate the 50th anniversary of the most important Supreme Court decision arising from Kansas, the *Brown v. Board of Education* school desegregation decision. He joined President Bush on stage at a ceremony in Topeka on the actual anniversary, May 17, 2004.

Ryun launched his career with the backing of conservatives in Kansas' divided GOP, prevailing easily in 1996 in a three-way primary against two more-moderate candidates. In the fall, he won by 7 percentage points over Democratic lawyer John Frieden. Three subsequent races were far easier.

But in 2004, Nancy Boyda, a pharmaceutical company executive who had the year before become a Democrat because she felt the GOP had grown too extreme, threw a scare into Ryun with a well-financed challenge. Ryun fought back, winning some national notice when he aired an attack ad featuring Osama bin Laden and complaining about Boyda's anti-war activities. She did better than any of Ryun's opponents since his maiden race, but Ryun beat her handily, by 15 points.

In May 2001, a Reston, Va., prep runner shattered Ryun's high school mile record of 36 years. Ryun says he never regarded himself as a phenomenon. He had failed to make the basketball and baseball teams, and once described himself as "a nerd" who began running as a teenager to find acceptance. Ryun continues to run recreationally, but still faster than most. In an annual Washington fundraising race that attracts many lawmakers, he covers the three-mile course in about 20 minutes.

KEY VOTES

2004

No	Extend federal unemployment benefits by 13 weeks
Yes	Pass $283.2 billion, six-year federal highway and mass transit bill
Yes	Approve $146 billion multi-year extension of previously enacted middle-class tax breaks
Yes	Amend the Constitution to prohibit same-sex marriage
Yes	Cut corporate taxes $137 billion over 10 years
Yes	Reorganize U.S. intelligence agencies as proposed by Sept. 11 commission

2003

Yes	Cut taxes by $330 billion through fiscal 2013
No	Block Bush rule scaling back overtime pay for some white-collar federal workers
No	Do not allow use of search warrants without first notifying subjects
No	Allow importation of prescription drugs
Yes	Create private school voucher program in Washington, D.C.
Yes	Ban "partial birth" abortion except to save a woman's life
No	Split $18.6 billion in Iraq aid into half-grant, half-loan
No	Overhaul Medicare and create prescription drug benefit

CQ VOTE STUDIES

	PARTY UNITY		PRESIDENTIAL SUPPORT	
	Support	Oppose	Support	Oppose
2004	98%	2%	88%	12%
2003	98%	2%	91%	9%
2002	98%	2%	88%	12%
2001	99%	1%	91%	9%
2000	98%	2%	25%	75%

INTEREST GROUPS

	AFL-CIO	ADA	CCUS	ACU
2004	20%	5%	100%	96%
2003	7%	15%	97%	96%
2002	11%	0%	95%	100%
2001	8%	0%	96%	100%
2000	0%	0%	90%	100%

KANSAS 2

East – Topeka, Manhattan, Leavenworth

The 2nd runs the length of the state in east Kansas from Nebraska to Oklahoma, passing west of the Kansas City area. This moderately conservative district is a combination of rural farm communities and urbanized areas, including the state capital of Topeka. One-fourth of district residents live in Topeka or surrounding Shawnee County.

Republicans do well in the district's rural regions, while Democrats are more successful in Topeka and the state's blue-collar southeast corner. Although the 2nd is conservative, it is not overwhelmingly Republican. The district favored Democrat Kathleen Sebelius in the 2002 governor's election, but George W. Bush won the district with 59 percent of the vote in the 2004 presidential election.

The 2nd's economy has experienced slow but steady growth, and unemployment is low. Most of the jobs revolve around agriculture, particularly wheat. State government is Topeka's largest employer. Fort Riley and Fort Leavenworth also aid the 2nd's economy, though Fort Riley suffered a round of cutbacks in the mid-1990s.

Redistricting following the 2000 census added part of Lawrence — the Democratic-leaning home of the University of Kansas (the university itself is in the 3rd District) — but the political impact was offset by the 2nd's acquisition of conservative Miami County. The district also includes Manhattan, home to Kansas State University.

MAJOR INDUSTRY
Agriculture, defense, higher education, government

MILITARY BASES
Fort Riley (Army), 10,300 military, 4,800 civilian; Fort Leavenworth (Army), 2,884 military, 2,346 civilian (2004)

CITIES
Topeka, 122,377; Manhattan, 44,831; Leavenworth, 35,420; Lawrence (pt.), 25,768; Pittsburg, 19,243

NOTABLE
Robert Stroud, the "Birdman of Alcatraz," served 30 years in the federal penitentiary in Leavenworth before being transferred to Alcatraz; The Kansas Museum of History is in Topeka; Mine Creek Battlefield in Pleasanton was the site of Kansas' only major Civil War battle.

Rep. Dennis Moore (D)

Elected 1998; 4th term

CAPITOL OFFICE
225-2865
www.house.gov/moore
1727 Longworth 20515-1603; fax 225-2807

COMMITTEES
Budget
Financial Services

HOMETOWN
Lenexa

BORN
Nov. 8, 1945, Anthony, Kan.

RELIGION
Protestant

FAMILY
Wife, Stephene Moore; seven children

EDUCATION
Southern Methodist U., attended 1965; U. of
Kansas, B.A. 1967; Washburn U., J.D. 1970

MILITARY SERVICE
Army, 1970; Army Reserve, 1970-73

CAREER
Lawyer

POLITICAL HIGHLIGHTS
Johnson County district attorney, 1977-89;
Democratic nominee for Kan. attorney general,
1986

ELECTION RESULTS

2004 GENERAL

Dennis Moore (D)	184,050	54.8%
Kris Kobach (R)	145,542	43.4%

2004 PRIMARY

Dennis Moore (D)	unopposed

2002 GENERAL

Dennis Moore (D)	110,095	50.2%
Adam Taff (R)	102,882	46.9%
Dawn Bly (REF)	5,046	2.3%

PREVIOUS WINNING PERCENTAGES
2000 (50%); 1998 (52%)

The lone Democrat in the House from Kansas, Moore has to fight harder than most to hang onto his seat in the Republican-friendly suburbs of Kansas City. Moore has survived politically largely because of his willingness to go along with the Republicans — and President Bush, who twice carried Moore's district — on issues like tax cuts and the war in Iraq.

In 2004, he finally managed to garner nearly 55 percent of the vote — affording him a career-high winning margin of 11 percentage points. A former county prosecutor, he fended off a staunchly conservative law professor who served on the staff of former Attorney General John Ashcroft. But Republicans are unlikely to take their sights off this competitive congressional district. Before the last election, Moore had three close re-election victories; he defies local historical trends by being the first Democrat to survive re-election in nearly seven decades.

Despite the conservative lean of his constituents, Moore is a reliable vote for Democratic Party leaders on a handful of core issues, including gun control measures. Married to a nurse, he also generally supports them on health care initiatives.

In the 108th Congress, Moore voted against Bush's legislation to create a prescription drug benefit for Medicare recipients. Calling the bill "flawed" for putting "profits of special interests ahead of a real benefit for seniors," Moore objected in particular to a provision barring the federal government from negotiating with drug companies for lower prices. Moore favors giving the secretary of Health and Human Services negotiating authority.

Moore belongs to both the centrist New Democrat Coalition and the "Blue Dogs," a coalition of the most conservative House Democrats. He has focused on health and education issues for the latter group, and he supported his Blue Dog colleague, Harold E. Ford Jr. of Tennessee, in his unsuccessful race against Nancy Pelosi of California to become Democratic leader at the outset of the 108th Congress.

From his seat on the Budget Committee, Moore initially supported the president's aggressive tax cut agenda but backed off after the government started running large deficits. He voted for Bush's 2001 plan to cut taxes by $1.35 trillion through 2010, noting that it included several individual tax breaks he favored and arguing that tax cuts were appropriate at a time of government surpluses. But when the government slipped into yearly deficits, Moore voted against making the tax cuts permanent.

In 2003, he opposed Bush's second major tax cut, which provided $350 billion in tax breaks over 11 years. Just before the 2004 elections, however, he backed a package that would extend some of the cuts already enacted, albeit with serious reservations about its cost.

Moore stood with the president on one important issue, the war in Iraq. He voted for the 2002 resolution giving congressional authorization for the use of force to topple Iraqi President Saddam Hussein from power. In general, Moore voted with the Republican president about a third of the time on key votes in the 108th Congress.

Like many of his generation, Moore was drawn to politics by the civil rights movement and the war in Vietnam. In 1965, he was inspired by Sen. J. William Fulbright's convocation speech about the war at his college, Southern Methodist University. The same year, friends visiting his dorm encouraged him to join them on their drive to Selma, Ala., to take part in a civil rights march. To his chagrin, Moore took his father's advice and skipped the trip. He says he is glad that later, as a congressman, he was able to return to the scene of the historic march with former civil rights leader John Lewis, a Democratic House colleague from Georgia, to participate in a re-enactment.

Moore compares his political career with that of his father, a three-term county prosecutor who ran unsuccessfully for Congress in 1958 and 1960. A framed "Walter Moore for Congress" poster hangs in his Capitol Hill office. But campaigning for dad "did not give me the bug," he recalls. "In fact, if anything, going door-to-door handing out cards for my dad was not something I enjoyed that much." But he adds, "If you're going to be successful in politics, gradually you have to overcome that."

For a dozen years, Moore was the Johnson County district attorney, and he was known for his personal touch. Barbara Daniels, the mother of a teenager murdered by three men, asked Moore to testify whenever one of the killers came up for parole. "If I call, he answers," Daniels told The Kansas City Star. "He's really been a good friend." Moore also took the lead in creating a county victims assistance program.

Moore has played guitar since high school, favoring country rock, the blues and classical music, and he once shared the stage at a Farm Aid concert with Willie Nelson and David Crosby. He made a memorable campaign commercial during his 1998 race in which he humorously interspersed his positions on issues with guitar licks.

The 3rd District had long been represented by GOP moderates, but in 1998 Moore was able to unseat the conservative Republican Vince Snowbarger after one term. Moore entered the race when he saw that Snowbarger had not raised much money in his first year in office, a mistake Moore was careful not to make. He raised more than $1.5 million for his 2000 race against state Rep. Phill Kline, another conservative.

In 2002, all of the odds seemed to be against Moore. Not only had his district been redrawn to be slightly more Republican, but GOP nominee Adam Taff was also more of a moderate than past challengers. Moore organized a major get-out-the-vote drive in friendly Democratic areas, and he may have benefited from the National Republican Congressional Committee's decision not to pump money into Taff's race until late in the campaign.

Early in 2003, Moore said that he had "looked hard" at a possible race, but had decided not to challenge GOP Sen. Sam Brownback in 2004. He opted instead to seek re-election to a fourth term.

KEY VOTES

2004

Yes Extend federal unemployment benefits by 13 weeks

Yes Pass $283.2 billion, six-year federal highway and mass transit bill

Yes Approve $146 billion multi-year extension of previously enacted middle-class tax breaks

No Amend the Constitution to prohibit same-sex marriage

Yes Cut corporate taxes $137 billion over 10 years

Yes Reorganize U.S. intelligence agencies as proposed by Sept. 11 commission

2003

No Cut taxes by $330 billion through fiscal 2013

Yes Block Bush rule scaling back overtime pay for some white-collar federal workers

Yes Do not allow use of search warrants without first notifying subjects

Yes Allow importation of prescription drugs

No Create private school voucher program in Washington, D.C.

No Ban "partial birth" abortion except to save a woman's life

Yes Split $18.6 billion in Iraq aid into half-grant, half-loan

No Overhaul Medicare and create prescription drug benefit

CQ VOTE STUDIES

	PARTY UNITY		PRESIDENTIAL SUPPORT	
	Support	Oppose	Support	Oppose
2004	83%	17%	38%	62%
2003	87%	13%	29%	71%
2002	82%	18%	40%	60%
2001	77%	23%	40%	60%
2000	76%	24%	68%	32%

INTEREST GROUPS

	AFL-CIO	ADA	CCUS	ACU
2004	87%	90%	62%	20%
2003	80%	90%	52%	28%
2002	78%	85%	60%	20%
2001	75%	85%	57%	20%
2000	50%	65%	66%	24%

KANSAS 3

Kansas City region – Overland Park, eastern Lawrence

Eastern Kansas' 3rd differs markedly from the state's other districts. Compact, it is almost entirely within the sphere of Kansas City, Mo., and most residents live either in Kansas City, Kan., or in Johnson County suburbs. It boasts three of the state's five most-populous cities.

The district is hardly uniform in its economic character. Poverty and unemployment are prevalent in Wyandotte County and Kansas City itself. Overshadowed by its namesake across the Missouri River, Kansas City, Kan., is an industrial town that has had its share of Rust Belt blues because of factory closures and the long-term decline of urban stockyards. But Kansas City maintains a large industrial base and has attracted some growth in its biotechnology sector.

Johnson County is one of the state's richest, with company headquarters, suburban developments and a strong service sector. While Kansas City lost population in the 1990s, many Johnson County areas are booming. Overland Park grew by one-third, passing Topeka and Kansas City to become the state's second-largest city, and Olathe grew by nearly 50 percent during the decade.

Heading west, the 3rd takes in the eastern part of Douglas County and two-thirds of Lawrence (shared with the 2nd). Lawrence is home to the University of Kansas, which falls within the 3rd's boundaries, and is considered the most liberal area in the state.

Large, wealthy Johnson County is a Republican stronghold, and it gives the 3rd a GOP-lean. But Democratic strength in Wyandotte and parts of Douglas keep the district competitive. The counties were the only two in Kansas won by John Kerry in the 2004 presidential election.

MAJOR INDUSTRY

Long-distance phone service, auto manufacturing, service

CITIES

Overland Park, 149,080; Kansas City, 146,866; Olathe, 92,962; Lawrence (pt.), 54,330; Shawnee, 47,996; Lenexa, 40,238; Leawood, 27,656

NOTABLE

James Naismith, inventor of basketball, was the University of Kansas' first coach and the only one with a losing record.

Rep. Todd Tiahrt (R)

Elected 1994; 6th term

CAPITOL OFFICE
225-6216
www.house.gov/tiahrt
2441 Rayburn 20515-1604; fax 225-3489

COMMITTEES
Appropriations
Select Intelligence

HOMETOWN
Goddard

BORN
June 15, 1951, Vermillion, S.D.

RELIGION
Assemblies of God

FAMILY
Wife, Vicki Tiahrt; three children (one deceased)

EDUCATION
South Dakota School of Mines and Technology,
attended 1969-71; Evangel College, B.A. 1975
(management); Southwest Missouri State U.,
M.B.A. 1989 (marketing)

CAREER
College instructor; airline company project
manager

POLITICAL HIGHLIGHTS
Republican nominee for Kan. House, 1990; Kan.
Senate, 1993-95

ELECTION RESULTS

2004 GENERAL

Todd Tiahrt (R)	173,151	66.1%
Michael R. Kinard (D)	81,388	31.1%
David Loomis (LIBERT)	7,376	2.8%

2004 PRIMARY

Todd Tiahrt (R)	unopposed

2002 GENERAL

Todd Tiahrt (R)	115,691	60.6%
Carlos Nolla (D)	70,656	37.0%
Maike Warren (LIBERT)	4,616	2.4%

PREVIOUS WINNING PERCENTAGES
2000 (54%); 1998 (58%); 1996 (50%); 1994 (53%)

Tiahrt worked as a contract manager with Boeing Co. before coming to Congress, and he has spent much of his time in the House making sure the aircraft giant continues to receive Defense Department funds. He serves on the Appropriations Committee, and although he sometimes argues for spending restraint, he has used his seat to win an array of federal contracts and grants for his district, particularly for defense, transportation and water development projects, and disaster relief for farmers.

Early in 2005, Boeing announced it was selling its commercial operations in Wichita to Canadian conglomerate Onex Corp., causing some anxiety but also optimism, as Onex said it intended to invest more than $1 billion in the facility and to seek to increase its production. That sale did not affect Boeing's military production operations in Wichita, a source of employment for about 3,500 workers.

On the Defense Appropriations Subcommittee, which he joined in the 107th Congress, Tiahrt (TEE-hart) has teamed with Washington Democrat Norm Dicks to win approval of a plan allowing the Air Force to lease 100 Boeing 767 aircraft for use as aerial refueling tankers. The modifications on the planes were to be done at Boeing's Wichita facility. But the Pentagon announced in 2004 that it was putting the tanker deal on hold until it completed more studies on the need for the planes and possible alternatives. Tiahrt warned that the tanker contract could go to Boeing's main rival, the European Aeronautic Defence and Space Co., which had expressed interest in the contract.

Tiahrt and Dicks managed to add provisions to the House version of the 2004 defense authorization bill ordering the Pentagon to sign a contract for the planes by March 2005, but their additions were removed during final House-Senate negotiations. In the 109th, Tiahrt can be expected to fight any move by the Pentagon to award the contract to a foreign company.

Tiahrt touted that he was able to direct $68 million in federal funds for defense projects in south-central Kansas when the House passed the final version of the 2004 defense spending bill. "These 'earmarks' were not originally in the president's budget and were added" through my efforts, he said in a statement. "These projects not only are critical to our national security, they employ Kansans and help strengthen our local economy."

Tiahrt clearly believes government funds should be invested in military matters, particularly in Kansas, but he is less convinced there is a need for government involvement in other areas. As his hometown newspaper, the Wichita Eagle, once observed, Tiahrt "has turned out to be just as advertised. A fiscal conservative, a social conservative, a religious conservative." Yet on occasion, Tiahrt's insistence on pursuing his conservative agenda has given his own leadership heartburn.

He has sought to advance conservative principles by adding social policy proposals to the annual appropriations bills. In 2004, he inserted provisions in one bill to limit the disclosure of federally stored information about firearms that are used in crimes. Tiahrt's appropriations amendments also have targeted U.S. funding for foreign family planning organizations, needle-exchange programs for drug abusers, and adoptions by gay couples.

The GOP leadership has responded to Tiahrt's insistent style by making him one of them. In the 107th Congress, he was appointed one of 18 deputy whips, requiring him to persuade other lawmakers to back the party's agenda and giving him less time to engage in floor fights on conservative social policy amendments.

Tiahrt faced a difficult return to the House after the 2004 August recess, as his 16-year-old son, Luke, had committed suicide in July. The day after Tiahrt returned, Congress passed a measure to authorize more money for suicide prevention programs. The bill was named after Garrett Lee Smith, Oregon GOP Sen. Gordon H. Smith's son, who took his own life in 2003.

Born in South Dakota, Tiahrt grew up on a family farm in the southeast part of the state. His father served on the local school board. Tiahrt played football in college and is one of the stars of the annual congressional charity baseball and basketball games. He enrolled at the South Dakota School of Mines and Technology but transferred to Evangel College in Springfield, Mo., which describes itself as a Christian liberal arts university. It is run by the Assemblies of God church, of which Tiahrt is a member.

After college, Tiahrt embarked on a career in the aerospace industry with Boeing. As a contract manager, he was involved in talks between Boeing and the federal government on a number of projects, including NASA's space station, Air Force One and many military aircraft.

Tiahrt originally registered as a Democrat. His grandfather had impressed him with the story of how the federal government had helped with the purchase of the family farm during the Depression. Tiahrt says he did not give his party affiliation much thought until he set out to run for the Kansas House in 1990. He decided then that the Republican Party was a closer match for his strong religious views and switched parties.

Tiahrt lost that race for the state House, succumbing in a recount after initial tallies had shown him with a 24-vote lead. He remained active in local politics, and two years later he was elected to the state Senate, where he was best-known for pushing legislation allowing people to carry concealed weapons.

In 1994, Tiahrt decided to wage a long-shot challenge to popular nine-term Democratic Rep. Dan Glickman. Glickman's polls throughout the summer showed him with a lead in the 30 percentage point range; but Tiahrt mobilized a grass-roots network that drew heavily from the ranks of the anti-abortion movement, in which his wife was active, and which had engaged in protests in Wichita. Tiahrt chipped away at Glickman, linking him to the unpopular Clinton administration. He ended up winning by 6 points.

He had a serious re-election battle in 1996, eventually defeating moderate Democrat Randy Rathbun, former U.S. attorney, by just 3 points. Democrats harbor some hope of capturing the district again, but Tiahrt has won his subsequent re-elections by comfortable margins.

KEY VOTES

2004

No	Extend federal unemployment benefits by 13 weeks
Yes	Pass $283.2 billion, six-year federal highway and mass transit bill
Yes	Approve $146 billion multi-year extension of previously enacted middle-class tax breaks
Yes	Amend the Constitution to prohibit same-sex marriage
Yes	Cut corporate taxes $137 billion over 10 years
Yes	Reorganize U.S. intelligence agencies as proposed by Sept. 11 commission

2003

Yes	Cut taxes by $330 billion through fiscal 2013
No	Block Bush rule scaling back overtime pay for some white-collar federal workers
No	Do not allow use of search warrants without first notifying subjects
No	Allow importation of prescription drugs
Yes	Create private school voucher program in Washington, D.C.
Yes	Ban "partial birth" abortion except to save a woman's life
No	Split $18.6 billion in Iraq aid into half-grant, half-loan
Yes	Overhaul Medicare and create prescription drug benefit

CQ VOTE STUDIES

	PARTY UNITY		PRESIDENTIAL SUPPORT	
	Support	Oppose	Support	Oppose
2004	96%	4%	85%	15%
2003	99%	1%	98%	2%
2002	96%	4%	88%	12%
2001	97%	3%	88%	12%
2000	94%	6%	24%	76%

INTEREST GROUPS

	AFL-CIO	ADA	CCUS	ACU
2004	13%	5%	100%	92%
2003	14%	5%	100%	88%
2002	11%	5%	95%	96%
2001	0%	0%	96%	96%
2000	0%	0%	95%	91%

KANSAS 4
South central — Wichita

Seeing an airplane is about as commonplace as seeing a bird to residents of the 4th. The moderately conservative district is centered on the state's largest city, Wichita, with its large aviation industry. Much of the rest of the 4th is farmland.

Residents hope the aviation industry that Wichita and the district depend on will recover from the economic decline intensified by the Sept. 11, 2001, terrorist attacks. In addition, Boeing, one of the state's largest employers, is selling its Wichita commercial aviation plant to Onex Corp., a Canadian investment firm. Onex announced in early 2005 that it hopes to boost production at the Wichita plant, perhaps reversing recent job losses and turning the Boeing sale into a positive for the area's economy.

Boeing is keeping its Wichita defense aviation business, and Cessna, Raytheon Aircraft and Bombardier Aerospace are among the other airplane manufacturers that have operations in the area. Although the industry has helped keep the economy healthy, aviation business downturns have led the city to look for ways to diversify. Wichita also

benefits from a regional medical center and universities.

Sumner County, on the Oklahoma border, is one of Kansas' leading wheat-growing counties. Wheat also is important in Harper and Kingman counties to the west. Cattle graze in sparsely populated Greenwood, Elk and Chautauqua counties to the east.

Changes to the district during 1990s redistricting opened the door for Republicans to win the 4th in 1994 and keep it since then. Map changes following the 2000 census did not alter the 4th's political outlook. Locally, Republicans usually win here, but Democrats capture some offices. Cowley County, in the south-central part of the district, tilts more Democratic. George W. Bush took 64 percent of the 4th's vote in 2004.

MAJOR INDUSTRY
Aviation, defense, agriculture

MILITARY BASES
McConnell Air Force Base, 2,781 military, 914 civilian (2004)

CITIES
Wichita, 344,284; Derby, 17,807; Newton, 17,190

NOTABLE
Old Cowtown Museum recreates Sedgwick County life, circa 1865-1880.

KENTUCKY

Gov. Ernie Fletcher (R)

First elected: 2003
Length of term: 4 years
Term expires: 01/08
Salary: $109,146
Phone: (502) 564-2611

Hometown: Lexington
Born: Nov. 12, 1952;
Mount Sterling, Ky.
Religion: Baptist
Family: Wife, Glenna Fletcher; two children
Education: U. of Kentucky, B.S 1974
(mechanical engineering), M.D. 1984
Military Service: Air Force, 1974-80
Career: Physician
Political highlights: Ky. House, 1995-96;
Republican nominee for U.S. House, 1996;
U.S. House, 1999-2003

Election results:

2003 GENERAL

Ernie Fletcher (R)	596,284	55.0%
Ben Chandler (D)	487,159	45.0%

Lt. Gov. Stephen Pence (R)

First elected: 2003
Length of term: 4 years
Term expires: 01/08
Salary: $92,790
Phone: (502) 564-2611

STATE LEGISLATURE

General Assembly: January-April in
even-numbered years, limit of 60 days;
January-March in odd-numbered
years, limit of 30 days

House: 100 members, 2-year terms
2005 breakdown: 57R, 43D; 89 men,
11 women
Salary: $170/day in session;
$1,617/month out of session
Phone: (502) 564-8100

Senate: 38 members, 4-year terms
2005 breakdown: 22R, 15D, 1I; 32
men, 6 women
Salary: $170/day in session;
$1,617/month out of session
Phone: (502) 564-8100

STATE TERM LIMITS

Governor: 2 terms
House: No
Senate: No

URBAN STATISTICS

CITY	POPULATION
Lexington-Fayette	260,512
Louisville Metro	674,032
Owensboro	54,067

REGISTERED VOTERS

Democrat	57%
Republican	36%
Unaffiliated/others	6%

POPULATION

2004 population (est.)	4,145,922
2000 population	4,041,769
1990 population	3,685,296
Percent change (1990-2000)	+9.7%
Rank among states (2004)	26

Median age	35.9
Born in state	73.7%
Foreign born	2%
Violent crime rate	295/100,000
Poverty level	15.8%
Federal workers	36,234
Military	50,134

REDISTRICTING

Kentucky retained its six House seats
in reapportionment. The state
legislature drew a new map, which
the governor signed on Jan. 31, 2002.

MISCELLANEOUS

Web: www.kentucky.gov
Capital: Frankfort
STATE ELECTION OFFICIAL
(502) 573-7100
**DEMOCRATIC
HEADQUARTERS**
(502) 695-4828
**REPUBLICAN
HEADQUARTERS**
(502) 875-5130

District Statistics

DIST.	2004 VOTE FOR PRESIDENT BUSH	KERRY	WHITE	BLACK	ASIAN	HISP	MEDIAN INCOME	WHITE COLLAR	BLUE COLLAR	SERVICE INDUSTRY	OVER 64	UNDER 18	COLLEGE EDUCATION	RURAL	SQ. MILES
1	63%	36%	90%	7%	0%	1%	$30,360	47%	39%	15%	15%	24%	12%	63	11,683
2	65	34	91	6	1	2	$35,724	50	36	14	12	26	14	53	7,567
3	49	51	76	19	1	2	$39,468	62	24	14	14	24	25	2	367
4	63	36	95	2	0	1	$40,150	56	30	14	12	26	18	40	5,679
5	61	39	97	1	0	1	$21,915	48	36	15	12	25	10	79	10,676
6	58	41	87	8	1	2	$37,544	59	27	14	11	23	25	29	3,757
STATE	60	40	89	7	1	1	$33,672	54	32	14	13	25	17	44	39,728
U.S.	50.7	48.3	69	12	4	13	$41,994	60	25	15	12	26	24	21	3,537,438

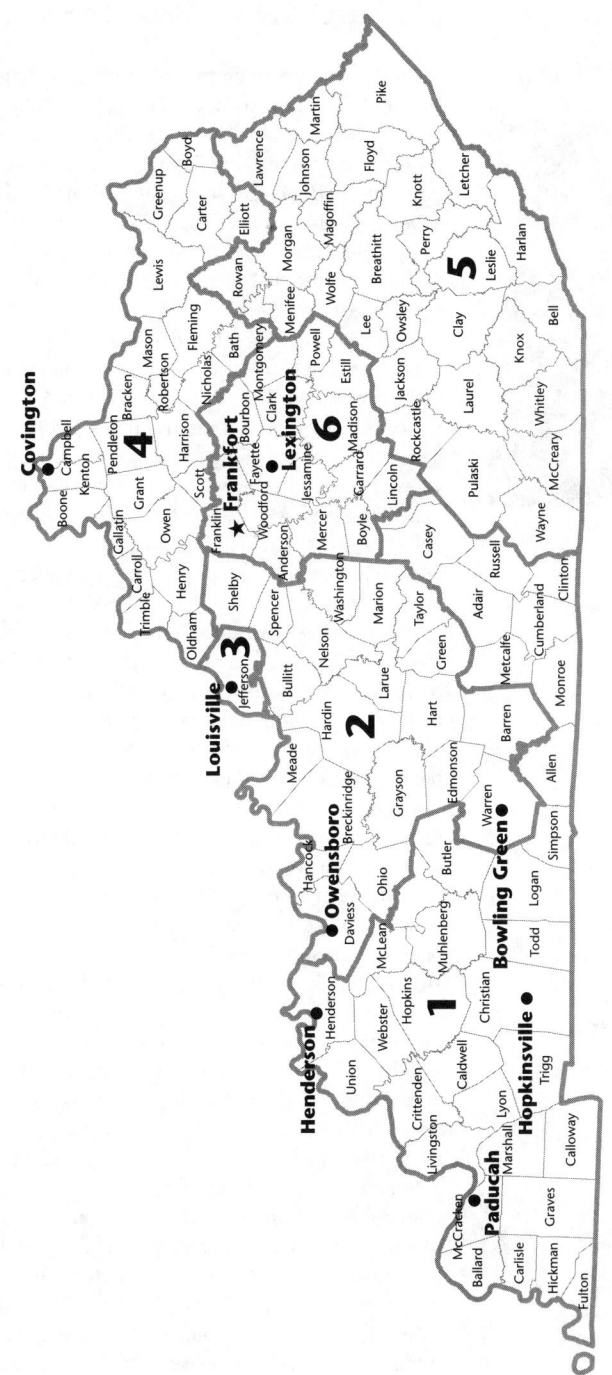

Sen. Mitch McConnell (R)

Elected 1984; 4th term

McConnell can be aggressive and unyielding in his conservatism, and at times he has been a divisive figure, frequently opting to stand by his principles rather than take the more politically prudent position. He showed that most strongly in his long fight against overhauling the nation's campaign finance laws. But he is also a realist and an effective backstage operator with a well-regulated ego, willing to bargain when necessary to advance his party's goals. As GOP whip — the Senate's No. 2 Republican — he is the leading candidate to become leader in 2007, when Majority Leader Bill Frist plans to leave the Senate.

In the independent-minded and closely divided Senate, the whip's job is to be the tough cop when it comes to rounding up votes while also tending to the care and feeding of his colleagues' preferences in policy and logistics. It means being highly partisan at times, fighting to keep his colleagues unified, while also serving as a bridge builder, reaching for the Democratic votes the GOP often needs to form majorities for President Bush's agenda.

Senate Republican leaders have "almost all carrot, and no stick," McConnell says, so he and Frist "spend a lot of time pleading and cajoling, bringing about the maximum degree of cooperation, knowing that there's not a great deal of punishment that can be doled out."

McConnell was elevated to the leadership in the 108th Congress even though, during his four years as chairman of the Senate Republican campaign organization, the roster of GOP senators declined from 55 to 50. After outflanking a pair of rivals behind the scenes, he was unopposed for election as whip. He succeeded Oklahoma's Don Nickles, who had to step down because of GOP-mandated term limits. Since then, McConnell has been a staunch ally to Frist, a heart surgeon who helped ensure that he would continue to have the Kentuckian by his side by persuading him in 2003 to undergo heart bypass surgery.

From 1999 through 2002, McConnell chaired the Rules Committee, which handles internal Senate housekeeping matters as well as campaign finance and election legislation. And since 1993, he has had a strong hand in determining levels of U.S. foreign aid from his perch as chairman of the Appropriations Subcommittee on Foreign Operations. In the 107th, McConnell also took a forceful role in guiding Middle East policy. As one of Israel's strongest supporters, he introduced legislation with California Democrat Dianne Feinstein to sever ties with the Palestinian Authority. He also has been a leading advocate for increased U.S. aid to Ukraine, Georgia and Armenia, seeing them as bulwarks against a potentially resurgent Russia.

In the 108th Congress, McConnell pushed successfully to extend trade sanctions against Myanmar to protest the brutally anti-democratic regime that runs the country. The effort pitted him against business allies who oppose unilateral trade sanctions. He said he was inspired to take on the fight a decade ago by the story of the country's leading democratic activist, Aung San Suu Kyi, whose peaceful protests against her country's repressive regime won her the Nobel Peace Prize in 1991.

He also helped cut a bipartisan deal to allow the Food and Drug Administration to regulate tobacco products in exchange for a federal buyout to free tobacco farmers in his state and elsewhere from a half-century of price supports and strict growing allotments. McConnell, however, was no fan of FDA regulation; he saw it as the only way to get the buyout through

CAPITOL OFFICE
224-2541
senator@mcconnell.senate.gov
mcconnell.senate.gov
361A Russell 20510-1702; fax 224-2499

COMMITTEES
Agriculture, Nutrition & Forestry
(Production & Price Competitiveness - chairman)
Appropriations
(State, Foreign Operations & Related Programs - chairman)
Rules & Administration

HOMETOWN
Louisville

BORN
Feb. 20, 1942, Sheffield, Ala.

RELIGION
Baptist

FAMILY
Wife, Elaine L. Chao; three children

EDUCATION
U. of Louisville, B.A. 1964; U. of Kentucky, J.D. 1967

CAREER
Lawyer, U.S. Justice Department official; congressional aide

POLITICAL HIGHLIGHTS
Jefferson County judge-executive, 1978-85

ELECTION RESULTS

2002 GENERAL

Mitch McConnell (R)	731,679	64.7%
Lois Combs Weinberg (D)	399,634	35.3%

2002 PRIMARY

Mitch McConnell (R)	unopposed

PREVIOUS WINNING PERCENTAGES
1996 (55%); 1990 (52%); 1984 (50%)

the Senate. And he did not protest when the buyout went through without the regulation, at the insistence of the House, in late 2004.

But McConnell is best known for his fight against new restrictions on campaign fundraising and advertising, which he says trample on the constitutional right of groups and individuals to speak out freely and participate in the political process. He blocked a rewrite of campaign finance rules for 15 years, mounting more than 20 filibusters against various iterations of the legislation. When he finally lost in Congress in 2002, he assembled some of the nation's best legal minds and took the battle to the Supreme Court, which narrowly upheld the measure in late 2003.

He was vilified by government watchdog groups and others as the chief defender of a corrupt status quo. At times, he seemed to relish that notoriety, even though it may be a negative in a future majority leader.

But even those who have fought him on campaign finance describe him as approachable and willing to reach out to senators with divergent philosophies. Most notably, he brokered a major bipartisan compromise in 2002 on legislation to overhaul the nation's election system. His deal — between Democrats who wanted to make it easier to vote and Republicans who wanted to make it harder to cheat — led to the nation's first federal standards for the conduct of elections. In the 109th, McConnell is again focusing on election reform, introducing a bill to combat voter fraud.

Although it is less well-known than his campaign finance fight, McConnell has made a forceful stand against what he views as money-hungry trial lawyers. He was among those who won new restrictions on civil lawsuits in the 2002 law creating a federal terrorism insurance program. He has fought to limit malpractice lawsuit damages and lawyers' fees and to restrict unsolicited contact by personal injury lawyers with victims or their families. Such initiatives, which defenders call "tort reform," are also high on Bush's agenda.

Having overcome polio as a child, McConnell doesn't lack for toughness or tenacity. His rise is due at least in part to his taking on unpopular jobs. In 1995, he chaired the Ethics Committee when it voted to expel Republican Bob Packwood of Oregon over charges of sexual misconduct. Packwood subsequently resigned.

McConnell was student body president in high school and college and president of his law school class. After earning his law degree in 1967, he worked for Republican Sen. Marlow W. Cook of Kentucky and then served as a deputy assistant attorney general in the Ford administration. He served two terms as the chief executive of Jefferson County, now called Louisville Metro, before waging his winning 1984 Senate race.

His campaign against two-term Democratic incumbent Walter D. Huddleston struggled until McConnell hit upon a clever, homey gimmick to get across the idea that the incumbent had limited influence and was often absent from committee meetings. McConnell aired television advertising showing bloodhounds sniffing around Washington in search of the incumbent. Aided by President Reagan's long re-election coattails, McConnell won by four-tenths of a percentage point.

In 1990, McConnell was tabbed as one of the most vulnerable Republicans up for re-election. He brought back the TV bloodhounds, this time to bark up the fact that he had made 99 percent of the votes cast during his first term. He won with 52 percent of the vote. McConnell's margin of victory has grown in each of his subsequent races. He took 55 percent in 1996 against former Lt. Gov. Steven L. Beshear, and 65 percent in 2002 against Lois Combs Weinberg, an education activist. Midway through his second term, he married Elaine L. Chao, who became part of Bush's Cabinet when she was sworn in as secretary of labor in 2001.

KEY VOTES

2004

No   Pass $318.9 billion, six-year highway and mass transit bill

No   Extend assault weapons ban for 10 years

No   Restore pay-as-you-go rules for new tax cuts and entitlement spending

Yes Criminalize harm to a fetus in an attack on the mother

No   Increase mandatory child care funding to states by $6 billion over five years

Yes Amend the Constitution to prohibit same-sex marriage

Yes Approve $146 billion multi-year extension of previously enacted middle-class tax breaks

Yes Reorganize U.S. intelligence agencies as proposed by Sept. 11 commission

Yes Cut corporate taxes $137 billion over 10 years

2003

No   Delay Bush changes to Clean Air Act

Yes Allow confirmation vote on Miguel A. Estrada to the U.S. Court of Appeals for the D.C. Circuit

No   Block a Bush proposal opening Alaska's Arctic National Wildlife Refuge to oil drilling

No   Limit size of Bush's proposed tax cut to $350 billion through fiscal 2013

Yes Overhaul Medicare and create prescription drug benefit

No   Block Bush rule scaling back overtime pay for some white-collar federal workers

No   Split $20 billion in Iraq aid into half-grant, half-loan

Yes Ban "partial birth" abortion except to save a woman's life

Yes Stop proposal allowing travel to Cuba

Yes Allow final vote on energy policy overhaul

CQ VOTE STUDIES

	PARTY UNITY		PRESIDENTIAL SUPPORT	
	Support	Oppose	Support	Oppose
2004	99%	1%	98%	2%
2003	99%	1%	100%	0%
2002	97%	3%	96%	4%
2001	98%	2%	97%	3%
2000	99%	1%	42%	58%
1999	95%	5%	33%	67%
1998	95%	5%	39%	61%
1997	97%	3%	59%	41%
1996	95%	5%	39%	61%
1995	95%	5%	24%	76%

INTEREST GROUPS

	AFL-CIO	ADA	CCUS	ACU
2004	8%	15%	94%	96%
2003	0%	10%	100%	84%
2002	23%	0%	95%	100%
2001	6%	5%	93%	96%
2000	0%	5%	92%	100%
1999	0%	0%	88%	84%
1998	0%	0%	94%	92%
1997	0%	5%	100%	88%
1996	14%	10%	85%	95%
1995	0%	0%	100%	91%

Sen. Jim Bunning (R)

Elected 1998; 2nd term

As an eight-time All-Star pitcher, Jim Bunning has had his share of wins in front of cheering fans, but his election victories have been more like one-run nail-biters at the bottom of the ninth inning.

He secured his Senate seat in 1998 by fewer than 7,000 votes, and was re-elected in 2004 with a bit wider margin — 22,652 votes out of more than 1.7 million ballots cast — but against a relatively unknown state senator who should have been an easy mark for Bunning.

The squeakers are a testament to the strong feelings evoked by Bunning's stubborn and competitive political style — the same style that left batters swinging ineffectually during his baseball heyday. Those who support him laud his diligence and conservative convictions. His detractors see him as needlessly abrasive and prone to the kind of impolitic comments that contributed to his weak showing in the last election. During remarks to a Republican audience, Bunning told a joke in which he commented that his opponent, Daniel Mongiardo, an Italian-American state senator, resembled one of Saddam Hussein's sons. The widely circulated comment was an embarrassment for Bunning.

Yet even his critics acknowledge that Bunning can't be written off as a mere jock thriving in Congress on his sports-world celebrity. With a degree in economics from Xavier University, he seems as much at ease tangling with Federal Reserve Chairman Alan Greenspan over monetary policy as he does reminiscing about his halcyon days with the Philadelphia Phillies.

Bunning is a booster of President Bush's agenda, especially on energy and tax policy and on changes to the Social Security retirement program. He is positioned to have a hand in nearly all of those hot-button domestic issues from his seats on the Finance Committee, the Energy and Natural Resources Committee and the Budget Committee. He also chairs Banking, Housing and Urban Affairs' Subcommittee on Economic Policy.

A former House member, Bunning was chairman of the Ways and Means Social Security Subcommittee from 1995 to 1998 and favored using the budget surplus to shore up the Social Security trust fund. With the surplus gone, Bunning has backed Bush's proposal to allow younger workers to privately invest a portion of what they pay into the program.

He is a fierce defender of the Bush economic policies that critics say are responsible for mounting deficits. He defended the president in 2004 when Greenspan suggested that Bush's tax cuts had a role in deficit spending. The Fed chief, he said, was offering views on "many things outside the Fed's charter" and was too quick to support interest rate increases. "There is a good chance that I will be the only member of the U.S. Senate not to support your renomination," he told Greenspan.

In 2004, he upbraided the Energy Department for what he considered an abysmal performance helping former atomic weapons workers win medical compensation. The department has received $95 million for the program but has paid only four of 24,000 claims, he said. He sponsored an amendment to the defense authorization bill that would transfer the program to the Labor Department.

When it comes to advocacy on behalf of Kentucky's economic interests, Bunning has yet to match the reputation of his Senate colleague, Mitch McConnell, who has a 14-year head start on Bunning and a seat on the Appropriations Committee. But he has been effective defending home-

CAPITOL OFFICE
224-4343
bunning.senate.gov
316 Hart 20510-1703; fax 228-1373

COMMITTEES
Banking, Housing & Urban Affairs
 (Economic Policy - chairman)
Budget
Energy & Natural Resources
Finance

HOMETOWN
Southgate

BORN
Oct. 23, 1931, Southgate, Ky.

RELIGION
Roman Catholic

FAMILY
Wife, Mary Bunning; nine children

EDUCATION
Xavier U., B.S. 1953 (economics)

CAREER
Investment broker; sports agent; professional baseball player

POLITICAL HIGHLIGHTS
Fort Thomas City Council, 1977-79; Ky. Senate, 1979-83; Republican nominee for governor, 1983; U.S. House, 1987-99

ELECTION RESULTS

2004 GENERAL

Jim Bunning (R)	873,507	50.7%
Daniel Mongiardo (D)	850,855	49.3%

2004 PRIMARY

Jim Bunning (R)	96,545	84.0%
Barry Metcalf (R)	18,395	16.0%

PREVIOUS WINNING PERCENTAGES
1998 (50%); 1996 House Election (68%); 1994 House Election (74%); 1992 House Election (62%); 1990 House Election (69%); 1988 House Election (74%); 1986 House Election (55%)

state interests in other ways. Bunning was a leading supporter in the 108th Congress of a 10-year, $10 billion buyout for tobacco farmers included in the corporate tax overhaul. And Bunning wants to help revive Kentucky's coal industry by fighting for clean coal incentives in any energy bill that might come before the 109th Congress.

Though he gave up his seat on the Armed Services Committee at the start of the 108th for other assignments, Bunning actively fights for funds for Fort Campbell, Fort Knox and the Blue Grass Army Depot. He opposed the round of military base closures set for 2005, saying the Pentagon has failed to prove that earlier rounds saved the government much money.

A strong opponent of abortion and gun control, Bunning fits in comfortably with the Senate's ideological conservatives. His voting record typically rates 90 percent-plus scores from the American Conservative Union. But he occasionally displays a populist streak on trade. Although in 2002 he voted to give Bush fast-track trade negotiating authority, in 2000 he objected to permanently granting China normal trade status and in 1993 he opposed the North American Free Trade Agreement.

The father of nine children, Bunning has a personal interest in foster care and adoption issues. Two of his daughters have adopted children. In 2002, Bunning's son David, who had been a federal prosecutor, won confirmation at age 35 as a U.S. District Court judge in Covington.

Bunning was born and reared in the Kentucky suburbs of Cincinnati. His major league career spanned 17 years, primarily with the Phillies and the Detroit Tigers. He played in both the American and National leagues and was the first pitcher to record 100 wins and 1,000 strikeouts in each league. He had 224 career wins and pitched two no-hitters. Bunning was inducted into the Hall of Fame in 1996, and the Phillies retired his No. 14 uniform five years later. He managed minor league teams for several seasons, then returned to Kentucky to work as an agent to professional athletes.

Reflecting on his sports career years later, when the Senate was split between the two parties in 2001, Bunning said, "I'm in the Hall of Fame. My number is retired. The next thing to do is die. We'll hold off on that for a while, especially since there is a tie in the Senate."

He won a seat on the Fort Thomas City Council in 1977, and two years later, unseated a longtime Democratic state senator. Bunning eventually rose to Republican floor leader. He ran for governor in 1983, losing to Democratic Lt. Gov. Martha Layne Collins while garnering a respectable 44 percent of the vote in a state that usually elects Democratic governors.

In 1986, GOP officials enlisted Bunning to run for the seat of retiring Republican Rep. Gene Snyder in the 4th District, an area connecting the Louisville and Cincinnati suburbs. Bunning won with 55 percent, and then was re-elected five times.

The 1998 Senate election to succeed retiring Democrat Wendell H. Ford pitted Bunning against Democrat Scotty Baesler, a three-term House member from the adjacent 6th District. Outside groups including the Christian Coalition intervened to attack Baesler's support of abortion rights. Bunning ultimately won the general election by 6,766 votes out of more than 1.1 million cast. It was the second-smallest victory margin in the 1998 Senate races.

In 2004, he faced Mongiardo, a physician and state senator who started out far behind Bunning in both name recognition and cash. In a campaign that was highly negative on both sides, Mongiardo managed to narrow the gap as some of Bunning's actions raised eyebrows.

Bunning was trounced in the major urban centers of Louisville and Lexington, but he reaped votes from rural conservatives who came out to vote in favor of a state constitutional amendment banning gay marriage, which Bunning made a signature issue.

KEY VOTES

2004

Yes Pass $318.9 billion, six-year highway and mass transit bill
No Extend assault weapons ban for 10 years
No Restore pay-as-you-go rules for new tax cuts and entitlement spending
Yes Criminalize harm to a fetus in an attack on the mother
Yes Increase mandatory child care funding to states by $6 billion over five years
Yes Amend the Constitution to prohibit same-sex marriage
Yes Approve $146 billion multi-year extension of previously enacted middle-class tax breaks
Yes Reorganize U.S. intelligence agencies as proposed by Sept. 11 commission
Yes Cut corporate taxes $137 billion over 10 years

2003

No Delay Bush changes to Clean Air Act
Yes Allow confirmation vote on Miguel A. Estrada to the U.S. Court of Appeals for the D.C. Circuit
No Block a Bush proposal opening Alaska's Arctic National Wildlife Refuge to oil drilling
No Limit size of Bush's proposed tax cut to $350 billion through fiscal 2013
Yes Overhaul Medicare and create prescription drug benefit
No Block Bush rule scaling back overtime pay for some white-collar federal workers
No Split $20 billion in Iraq aid into half-grant, half-loan
Yes Ban "partial birth" abortion except to save a woman's life
Yes Stop proposal allowing travel to Cuba
Yes Allow final vote on energy policy overhaul

CQ VOTE STUDIES

	PARTY UNITY		PRESIDENTIAL SUPPORT	
	Support	Oppose	Support	Oppose
2004	98%	2%	94%	6%
2003	99%	1%	100%	0%
2002	97%	3%	96%	4%
2001	97%	3%	96%	4%
2000	98%	2%	33%	67%
1999	95%	5%	24%	76%
House Service:				
1998	92%	8%	20%	80%
1997	95%	5%	27%	73%
1996	96%	4%	33%	67%
1995	98%	2%	19%	81%

INTEREST GROUPS

	AFL-CIO	ADA	CCUS	ACU
2004	17%	15%	100%	100%
2003	0%	10%	100%	85%
2002	31%	0%	95%	100%
2001	13%	0%	93%	100%
2000	13%	5%	78%	100%
1999	11%	0%	82%	100%
House Service:				
1998	0%	0%	94%	92%
1997	0%	0%	90%	92%
1996	9%	5%	81%	100%
1995	0%	0%	96%	92%

Rep. Edward Whitfield (R)

Elected 1994; 6th term

CAPITOL OFFICE
225-3115
www.house.gov/whitfield
301 Cannon 20515-1701; fax 225-3547

COMMITTEES
Energy & Commerce
(Oversight & Investigations - chairman)

HOMETOWN
Hopkinsville

BORN
May 25, 1943, Hopkinsville, Ky.

RELIGION
Methodist

FAMILY
Wife, Constance Whitfield; one child

EDUCATION
U. of Kentucky, B.S. 1965 (business); Wesley
Theological Seminary, attended 1966; U. of
Kentucky, J.D. 1969

MILITARY SERVICE
Army Reserve, 1967-73

CAREER
Lawyer; oil distributor; railroad executive

POLITICAL HIGHLIGHTS
Ky. House, 1974-75 (served as a Democrat)

ELECTION RESULTS

2004 GENERAL

Edward Whitfield (R)	175,972	67.4%
Billy R. Cartwright (D)	85,229	32.6%

2004 PRIMARY

Edward Whitfield (R)	unopposed

2002 GENERAL

Edward Whitfield (R)	117,600	65.3%
Klint Alexander (D)	62,617	34.8%

PREVIOUS WINNING PERCENTAGES
2000 (58%); 1998 (55%); 1996 (54%); 1994 (51%)

Tobacco may be on the endangered industry list, but it will always have a fierce defender as long as Whitfield is in Congress. From a western Kentucky district that has been economically dependent on tobacco since the days of slavery, he uses his accruing influence on the Energy and Commerce Committee to push for federal help for tobacco and to keep the Food and Drug Administration from regulating the impact of its products on American health.

Whitfield began his second decade in the House in the 109th Congress, giving him enough seniority to be in charge of an important subcommittee, the Energy and Commerce Subcommittee on Oversight and Investigations. In the past, the panel has examined high-profile issues such as the collapse and financial misdeeds of energy giant Enron Corp. and the insider trading scandal involving domestic arts maven Martha Stewart and ImClone Systems Inc. The panel also has oversight of the FDA, which has tried over the years to restrict tobacco products because of their adverse effects on health.

Whitfield won a slot on Energy and Commerce in his first term, in 1995, when the GOP took over the majority in the House and an influential Republican colleague from another tobacco state, Thomas J. Bliley Jr. of Virginia, was looking to bring friends of the industry onto the committee, which he chaired. When the Clinton administration in the latter half of the 1990s sued tobacco companies for selling hazardous products, Whitfield called it a "punitive and vindictive pursuit of a legal business and farmers who grow a legal crop."

In 2004, Whitfield pushed for provisions in a comprehensive corporate tax bill giving tobacco farmers a 10-year, $10 billion buyout. Congress passed the bill and President Bush signed it. The 70-year-old tobacco program previously imposed acreage allotments and marketing quotas designed to keep supplies in line with demand at market prices. But farmers in recent years had complained that the quotas made it too hard to compete with foreign tobacco farmers.

The Senate had originally wanted to tie the tobacco buyout with a move to allow the FDA to regulate tobacco. Whitfield, with other House members from tobacco states, objected, and the condition was dropped from the bill. Whitfield praised the buyout plan, saying the money would allow farmers to repay loans, buy equipment or diversify their farming operations.

During his years on Energy and Commerce, Whitfield has been a consistent supporter of another industry important to his district, coal-powered electricity. In 2003, he helped shape the House-passed version of the energy bill, which included provisions from bills he had sponsored giving federal money and tax credits to encourage research, development and investment in "clean coal" technology aimed at making coal burn with fewer harmful emissions.

Whitfield also has been active in shaping health care legislation, advocating free-market solutions during debates on patients' rights and creation of a Medicare drug benefit. He and California Democrat Lois Capps led the effort in the House for one of the few significant health bills passed in the 107th Congress, the Nurse Reinvestment Act, designed to increase the nation's capacity to train nurses and to encourage practicing nurses to remain in the profession.

Whitfield's bill to allow electronic monitoring of prescription drugs passed the House in 2004. He said the bill aimed to discourage the over-prescribing of medicines and "doctor shopping" by drug addicts. The measure would authorize funds for states to create databases of prescriptions for controlled substances, which would be accessible by doctors and pharmacies.

Whitfield usually votes with the GOP majority but has deviated on occasion, such as when he opposed a Republican plan to provide government vouchers for private and parochial school tuition.

He supported legislation compensating nuclear plant workers for past exposure to radiation, which helped employees at the uranium enrichment plant at Paducah, in the 1st District. Although GOP leaders were initially reluctant to act because of the compensation bill's price tag, Whitfield and his allies eventually were able to win a $150,000 lump-sum payment and lifetime medical benefits for ailing workers, with the government forced to bear the burden of proof to show that workers were not eligible. The package also included $78 million for cleanup at the Paducah facility.

Among Whitfield's local legislative endeavors was money for a new lock at the Kentucky Dam to accommodate barge traffic and funds for the U.S. Forest Service to oversee the popular Land Between the Lakes recreation area. Land Between the Lakes had been managed by the Tennessee Valley Authority, but Whitfield and other area lawmakers were able to ease the transition to Forest Service management. He also secured funds in the 2004 catchall appropriations bill to help local law enforcement agencies target and dismantle methamphetamine drug labs in Kentucky.

Whitfield is the first Republican to represent the 1st District, and in each election, he has added to his margin of victory and tightened his hold on a seat in historically Democratic territory.

Born in Hopkinsville, near the Tennessee border, Whitfield practiced law and ran an oil distribution company in western Kentucky. He found an early political mentor in Democrat Edward Breathitt, a longtime family friend who was Kentucky's governor in the 1960s. With Breathitt's encouragement, Whitfield won a state House seat, but then left the state to move east. In Washington, D.C., he was a top railroad executive, a job he landed with some help from Breathitt. In the early 1990s, he was a lawyer for the Interstate Commerce Commission.

After being out of elective office for almost 20 years, Whitfield was convinced to run in 1994, this time as a Republican, by Kentucky GOP Sen. Mitch McConnell. Whitfield's challenge to one-term Democratic Rep. Tom Barlow looked like an uphill battle, even to McConnell, given the district's deep Democratic roots. But Whitfield won that race with 51 percent of the vote and has not faced a serious challenge since.

KEY VOTES

2004

No Extend federal unemployment benefits by 13 weeks

Yes Pass $283.2 billion, six-year federal highway and mass transit bill

Yes Approve $146 billion multi-year extension of previously enacted middle-class tax breaks

Yes Amend the Constitution to prohibit same-sex marriage

Yes Cut corporate taxes $137 billion over 10 years

Yes Reorganize U.S. intelligence agencies as proposed by Sept. 11 commission

2003

Yes Cut taxes by $330 billion through fiscal 2013

No Block Bush rule scaling back overtime pay for some white-collar federal workers

Yes Do not allow use of search warrants without first notifying subjects

No Allow importation of prescription drugs

? Create private school voucher program in Washington, D.C.

Yes Ban "partial birth" abortion except to save a woman's life

No Split $18.6 billion in Iraq aid into half-grant, half-loan

Yes Overhaul Medicare and create prescription drug benefit

CQ VOTE STUDIES

	PARTY UNITY		PRESIDENTIAL SUPPORT	
	Support	Oppose	Support	Oppose
2004	91%	9%	85%	15%
2003	94%	6%	94%	6%
2002	94%	6%	87%	13%
2001	96%	4%	93%	7%
2000	90%	10%	29%	71%

INTEREST GROUPS

	AFL-CIO	ADA	CCUS	ACU
2004	14%	5%	100%	88%
2003	21%	10%	100%	84%
2002	0%	0%	94%	100%
2001	8%	0%	100%	96%
2000	0%	0%	90%	87%

KENTUCKY 1
West — Hopkinsville, Henderson, Paducah

Located in the western part of the Bluegrass state, Kentucky's rural 1st is a hub of agricultural activity. Here, slaves once helped cultivate cotton and tobacco crops, and tobacco still dominates the economy, particularly in the counties south of the Ohio River city of Henderson, although its future is uncertain. The 1st also has seen a steady decline in its coal industry to the north, but a new ethanol plant in Hopkinsville may be a boost to the economy — especially for corn growers.

The Ohio River port of Paducah (McCracken County) traditionally has been the political and population center of western Kentucky, but its population has been surpassed by Hopkinsville (Christian County), an agricultural market center dependent on nearby Fort Campbell, and by Henderson.

While the 1st has seen its coal and mining industries fade precipitously, Hopkins County has weathered the loss by evolving into a regional industrial and medical center. Tourism and recreation also play a role in the economy, especially near the Land Between the Lakes recreation

area, where management functions in 1999 were transferred from the Tennessee Valley Authority to the Forest Service.

The 1st's Confederate legacy traditionally translated into Democratic votes, but the 1994 GOP wave sent the district's first Republican to Congress. While conservative Democrats continue to dominate local offices in western Kentucky, the region votes for Republican presidential candidates. George W. Bush carried all of the district's 34 counties in the 2004 election, including Ballard and Muhlenberg counties, which last voted for a GOP presidential candidate in 1972.

MAJOR INDUSTRY
Tobacco, agriculture, manufacturing

MILITARY BASES
Fort Campbell, 26,046 military, 4,111 civilian (2004) (shared with Tennessee's 7th District)

CITIES
Hopkinsville, 30,089; Henderson, 27,373; Paducah, 26,307

NOTABLE
The Jefferson Davis Monument, located at his birthplace in Fairview, is a 351-foot obelisk; The nation's only plant that turns uranium into nuclear fuel is operated by USEC Inc. in Paducah.

Rep. Ron Lewis (R)

CAPITOL OFFICE
225-3501
www.house.gov/ronlewis
2418 Rayburn 20515-1702; fax 226-2019

COMMITTEES
Ways & Means

HOMETOWN
Cecilia

BORN
Sept. 14, 1946, Greenup County, Ky.

RELIGION
Baptist

FAMILY
Wife, Kayi Lewis; two children

EDUCATION
Morehead State U., attended 1964-67; U. of
Kentucky, B.A. 1969 (political science & history);
Southern Baptist Theological Seminary, attended
1980 (divinity); Morehead State U., M.A. 1981
(higher education)

MILITARY SERVICE
Navy, 1972

CAREER
Christian bookstore owner; minister; college
instructor; oil company sales representative

POLITICAL HIGHLIGHTS
Sought Republican nomination for Ky. House, 1971

ELECTION RESULTS

2004 GENERAL

Ron Lewis (R)	185,394	67.9%
Adam Smith (D)	87,585	32.1%

2004 PRIMARY

Ron Lewis (R)	unopposed

2002 GENERAL

Ron Lewis (R)	122,773	69.6%
David L. Williams (D)	51,431	29.2%
Robert Guy Dyer (LIBERT)	2,084	1.2%

PREVIOUS WINNING PERCENTAGES
2000 (68%); 1998 (64%); 1996 (58%); 1994 (60%);
1994 Special Election (55%)

Elected May 1994; 6th full term

With a decade of legislating under his belt, Lewis achieved a notably higher profile during the 108th Congress. His forays into the politically sensitive areas of economic policy and constitutional law carried him beyond the relatively limited focus on parochial interests and conservative social policies that marked his first few years on Capitol Hill.

In his initial years in the House, Lewis, a former minister and owner of a Christian bookstore, often used the pulpit of the House floor to sermonize about the decline of moral values in contemporary America. While he still feels strongly about family values, his focus of late has been on the difficult economic situation faced by many of his constituents. He has used his seat on the Ways and Means Committee to address those concerns.

In 2004, Lewis, the son of a tobacco farmer, helped win passage of a $10 billion buyout of tobacco farmers to encourage crop diversification. The bill "delivers long-awaited relief to hard-hit farmers in Kentucky and across the nation," Lewis said. He defended the buyout from critics who called it a boon for large growers, saying it would help the 8,000 tobacco growers in his district. "Recipient payments are a simple case of economics: Those who have invested more also have had more to lose; those less, less," Lewis said.

A free-trade advocate, Lewis worked to persuade colleagues that communities can surmount its adverse effects. He traveled to a town in his central Kentucky district with two prominent Republican colleagues on the House Ways and Means Committee, seeking to illustrate for them how a once-industrialized community can figure out how to survive in an age of globalization.

In Campbellsville, a Fruit of the Loom plant shut down in 1997 and the manufacturing was moved to plants in Latin America and the Caribbean, causing hundreds of Lewis' constituents to lose their jobs. But now, Lewis says, Campbellsville is a hub of job creation, with 13 recently arrived companies that collectively employ 3,700 — including manufacturers, distributors such as Amazon.com, and international companies such as Murakami, an auto parts producer.

Lewis held up Campbellsville as "a warning to any community" not to "put all your eggs in one basket, and diversify your economy." Ultimately, he said, liberalized trade can free up communities that have come to rely on a single major employer, and protectionist trade policies in the long run can harm those whom they were intended to assist.

Lewis, who has a perfect career score from the Christian Coalition, has served in leadership posts in such conservative groups as the Conservative Opportunity Society, the House Family Caucus and the House Pro-Life Caucus. Lewis lays a large share of the blame for what he believes is a decline in moral values on the Democratic Party, but he also casts aspersions on the judgments of the courts. In 2004, with a national debate raging over the propriety of state court decisions allowing gay marriage, Lewis introduced controversial legislation to allow a two-thirds majority in Congress to overrule the Supreme Court in any case in which the high court declared an act of Congress unconstitutional. "America's judicial branch has become increasingly overreaching and disconnected from the values of everyday Americans," he said. "Congress, as the people's branch of representative government, should take steps to equally affirm our authority to interpret constitutional issues."

Although he is a fiscal conservative on most issues, Lewis is a defender of the Appalachian Regional Commission (ARC), a Great Society program to build roads and spur economic development in 13 Appalachian states. Lewis grew up in Appalachia. "I remember the little one-lane roads, the dusty dirt roads, the lack of utilities, the small one-room schools," he told his House colleagues. The ARC, he said, had brought "tremendous improvement" to Eastern Kentucky and "now there are nice highways, nice schools, utilities reaching into the homes, paved highways." In 2002, Lewis wrote legislation to add three Kentucky counties to those eligible for assistance from the ARC.

Lewis also champions the development of alternative fuels that make use of crops grown in his district. Backed by Kentucky farm organizations, he has introduced legislation to promote increased use of ethanol and biodiesel, made from corn and soybeans.

Lewis says that he is "one politician who can truly claim he was born in a log cabin." He worked his way through college, which included doing stints at a steel company, a hospital and the highway department.

After graduation, Lewis was a salesman before beginning a five-year teaching job at a small Louisville business college. He later attended a seminary and became an ordained Baptist minister. He also operated a Christian bookstore. He had never before held office when he sought the 1994 GOP nomination for a race against Democratic Rep. William H. Natcher. When Natcher died that March, in his 41st year in the House, party officials chose Lewis to run in the resulting special election.

Although the tobacco country of western central Kentucky had been represented by Democrats for more than a century, Democratic voters did not have to make a big ideological leap to support Lewis, because the culturally conservative views he holds long have been the local norm. The unassuming Lewis made a favorable impression on many skeptical Democratic voters, who had expected him to be more doctrinaire. He tied his Democratic opponent, former state Sen. Joseph Prather, to the unpopular Clinton White House. With about $200,000 from the national GOP, Lewis won with 55 percent of the vote, an outcome that gave a hint of the Republican electoral tide that would sweep the GOP into control of the House that fall.

In the fall general-election contest, Lewis was the winner with 60 percent and he has won re-election easily since.

Lewis had pledged to serve no more than four terms, but in 1998 he said the promise had been a mistake. "It's not fair for people to invest six or eight years in a representative who would be a lame duck his last two years and could not be as effective as he should be or could be," he said.

KEY VOTES

2004
No Extend federal unemployment benefits by 13 weeks
Yes Pass $283.2 billion, six-year federal highway and mass transit bill
Yes Approve $146 billion multi-year extension of previously enacted middle-class tax breaks
Yes Amend the Constitution to prohibit same-sex marriage
Yes Cut corporate taxes $137 billion over 10 years
No Reorganize U.S. intelligence agencies as proposed by Sept. 11 commission

2003
Yes Cut taxes by $330 billion through fiscal 2013
No Block Bush rule scaling back overtime pay for some white-collar federal workers
Yes Do not allow use of search warrants without first notifying subjects
No Allow importation of prescription drugs
Yes Create private school voucher program in Washington, D.C.
Yes Ban "partial birth" abortion except to save a woman's life
No Split $18.6 billion in Iraq aid into half-grant, half-loan
Yes Overhaul Medicare and create prescription drug benefit

CQ VOTE STUDIES

	PARTY UNITY		PRESIDENTIAL SUPPORT	
	Support	Oppose	Support	Oppose
2004	96%	4%	82%	18%
2003	96%	4%	90%	10%
2002	98%	2%	85%	15%
2001	98%	2%	93%	7%
2000	94%	6%	25%	75%

INTEREST GROUPS

	AFL-CIO	ADA	CCUS	ACU
2004	27%	5%	95%	84%
2003	13%	15%	97%	84%
2002	11%	0%	90%	96%
2001	8%	0%	96%	100%
2000	0%	0%	90%	96%

KENTUCKY 2
West central — Owensboro, Bowling Green

The mostly rural 2nd, anchored in Kentucky's west-central heartland, takes in some suburban areas near Louisville and runs through rolling tobacco country, ending in the river country to the west.

While tobacco remains the district's dominant crop, the 2nd's economy relies on more than agriculture. Oil and coal help make Owensboro western Kentucky's leading trade center, while the General Motors Corvette plant in Bowling Green also provides jobs. Although substantially smaller than either Louisville Metro or Lexington-Fayette, the two cities are the state's third and fourth most populous. Away from the main population areas, the economic picture has been somewhat grim. In Taylor County, the closing of a textile plant in the late 1990s helped ratchet its unemployment rate above 20 percent at one point. An Amazon.com facility has helped steady the area.

The eastern portion of the district includes several of the distilleries that comprise Kentucky's "Bourbon Trail." Bardstown, in Nelson County, bills itself as the bourbon capital of the world, and there even is a whiskey

museum in the city. Redistricting following the 2000 census brought the 2nd's northern boundary to Shelby County, which is sandwiched between Louisville and the state capital of Frankfort.

The 2nd includes the birthplace of Abraham Lincoln (in Larue County), the first Republican president, and district voters now side with the GOP in federal elections after a long period of Democratic dominance. In the 2004 presidential election, George W. Bush won all 19 counties that lie wholly within the 2nd, and just two gave him less than 60 percent of the vote. The 2nd was Bush's best district (65 percent) in Kentucky in 2004.

MAJOR INDUSTRY
Tobacco, tourism, manufacturing

MILITARY BASES
Fort Knox, 5,761 military, 2,626 civilian (2004)

CITIES
Owensboro, 54,067; Bowling Green, 49,296; Elizabethtown, 22,542

NOTABLE
The U.S. Bullion Depository, or "Gold Vault," at Fort Knox houses the largest portion of the U.S. gold reserve; Bardstown includes Federal Hill Mansion, which inspired Stephen Foster to compose the ballad "My Old Kentucky Home" and is on the state's commemorative quarter.

Rep. Anne M. Northup (R)

Elected 1996; 5th term

CAPITOL OFFICE
225-5401
northup.house.gov
2459 Rayburn 20515-1703; fax 225-5776

COMMITTEES
Appropriations

HOMETOWN
Louisville Metro

BORN
Jan. 22, 1948, Louisville, Ky.

RELIGION
Roman Catholic

FAMILY
Husband, Robert Wood Northup; six children

EDUCATION
Saint Mary's College (Ind.), B.A. 1970 (economics & business)

CAREER
Teacher

POLITICAL HIGHLIGHTS
Ky. House, 1987-96

ELECTION RESULTS

2004 GENERAL

Anne M. Northup (R)	197,736	60.3%
Tony Miller (D)	124,040	37.8%
George C. Dick (LIBERT)	6,363	1.9%

2004 PRIMARY

Anne M. Northup (R)	unopposed

2002 GENERAL

Anne M. Northup (R)	118,228	51.6%
Jack Conway (D)	110,846	48.4%

PREVIOUS WINNING PERCENTAGES
2000 (53%); 1998 (52%); 1996 (50%)

Northup represents one of the most heavily Democratic House districts held by a Republican. Yet her conservative voting record and embrace of President Bush's agenda have not stopped her from defeating some of the best candidates state Democrats can put in her path.

In fact, in 2004 she won re-election by over 22 percentage points against Tony Miller, the Jefferson County Circuit Court clerk. That gave her a more secure hold on a district where registered Democrats outnumber Republicans by a ratio of about 2-to-1 and where she'd never before won re-election with more than 53 percent of the vote.

Northup came to Congress with a background that makes her a Republican campaign strategist's dream. She is a telegenic mother of six, a seasoned legislator and an articulate proponent of pragmatic politics — in other words, a made-to-order candidate for a party that often has image problems with women voters. She was identified early as a potential GOP star, was given a prized seat on the Appropriations Committee as a freshman and is frequently tapped to give the "working mother" perspective. At the 2004 Republican convention, she introduced and appeared in a video touting the Bush administration's aid for families that adopt. Two of Northup's children are adopted; one is African-American, the other is of mixed race.

"All soccer moms don't think alike," Northup told The Christian Science Monitor. "I do not believe the Republican philosophy and perspective is in general anti-minority, anti-women . . . but it is certainly portrayed that way."

Having survived four close re-election contests, she puts a lower priority on her aspirations for moving up in the Republican leadership ranks than on tending to her district. In 2004, Northup secured $96.3 million for 77 Louisville Metro projects in the fiscal 2005 catchall appropriations bill. The projects included more than $4 million for Louisville waterfront development, $3.2 million for education, job training and social service projects and $2 million for Ohio River bridges. She has received local raves for her work on keeping money flowing to the two bridge projects, which are to ease traffic congestion in the area. Northup also arranged for expedited environmental review so the work could begin without the typical bureaucratic delays.

In the process, she has won some support from Democrats, including former state Attorney General Chris Gorman, who ran against Northup in 1998, and Louisville Councilwoman Denise Brantley, whose district is 62 percent African-American.

To bring what she calls a family ethic to policy debates, Northup often prefaces her remarks with, "As a mother of six children." When adding her support to the GOP education overhaul bill in 2002, she said that she sold quilts to pay for tutoring for several of her children who had learning disabilities. She ascribes her willingness to compromise to growing up in a large family. Northup traveled to China in 2002 to help persuade the government to lift its cap on the number of Chinese children foreigners can adopt.

Northup, a former teacher, wrote legislation creating the National Reading Panel, which was charged with determining which federally funded reading programs were most effective. The findings were incorporated into the education revamp, and Bush praised her efforts.

Northup is pro-business, and her voting record has grown increasingly conservative over the years. She played a lead role in the 2000 battle over the Occupational Safety and Health Administration's rule requiring businesses to set up programs to prevent repetitive motion injuries. She argued that the rule would be too expensive for most businesses and "simply isn't feasible." The regulation was of particular interest to United Parcel Service, which has a large distribution hub in Louisville and many workers who perform repetitive tasks.

In 1998, Northup ran for vice chairman of the House Republican caucus, finishing second in a field of four to Tillie Fowler of Florida. She did win appointment, however, as one of six vice chairmen of the National Republican Congressional Committee, the organization that seeks to elect Republicans to the House. When Fowler announced her retirement, Northup planned to run for vice chairman again in 2000. But when Deborah Pryce of Ohio entered the race, Northup switched and campaigned for secretary of the Republican Conference. One day before the balloting she dropped out of the leadership sweepstakes altogether, saying she needed to focus on holding her House seat.

Northup has one brother and nine sisters, including Olympic champion swimmer Mary T. Meagher. Her father was involved in local Republican politics. When her youngest child started school, Northup rekindled her own interest in politics — she had been active in student government in high school and college — by taking a part-time job in the state legislature. She was elected to the state House in 1987. Her record there was conservative but with an independent streak. For example, even though tobacco is essential to Kentucky's economy, Northup led an effort to impose stricter laws against tobacco sales to children. In 2004, she voted for a corporate tax bill containing a $10 billion tobacco buyout.

With the help of religious conservatives, Northup, who opposes abortion rights and same-sex marriage, won her House seat by 1,299 votes in 1996. She defeated freshman Democrat Mike Ward, making her the only GOP challenger to oust a Democrat in a district President Clinton carried that year. Democrats have put up top-tier candidates against her ever since: Gorman in 1998; state Rep. Eleanor Jordan, the only black woman in the state legislature, in 2000; and telegenic, well-funded lawyer Jack Conway in 2002.

In 2004, when Northup faced Miller, the Democratic county clerk, his main theme was that Northup's social conservatism and support for the war in Iraq were out of step with voters. But in three debates, Northup hammered away at Miller's command of national issues and reminded voters of the money she brought into the district.

KEY VOTES

2004

No Extend federal unemployment benefits by 13 weeks
Yes Pass $283.2 billion, six-year federal highway and mass transit bill
Yes Approve $146 billion multi-year extension of previously enacted middle-class tax breaks
Yes Amend the Constitution to prohibit same-sex marriage
Yes Cut corporate taxes $137 billion over 10 years
Yes Reorganize U.S. intelligence agencies as proposed by Sept. 11 commission

2003

Yes Cut taxes by $330 billion through fiscal 2013
No Block Bush rule scaling back overtime pay for some white-collar federal workers
No Do not allow use of search warrants without first notifying subjects
Yes Allow importation of prescription drugs
Yes Create private school voucher program in Washington, D.C.
Yes Ban "partial birth" abortion except to save a woman's life
No Split $18.6 billion in Iraq aid into half-grant, half-loan
Yes Overhaul Medicare and create prescription drug benefit

CQ VOTE STUDIES

	PARTY UNITY		PRESIDENTIAL SUPPORT	
	Support	Oppose	Support	Oppose
2004	92%	8%	85%	15%
2003	96%	4%	94%	6%
2002	95%	5%	90%	10%
2001	99%	1%	98%	2%
2000	89%	11%	32%	68%

INTEREST GROUPS

	AFL-CIO	ADA	CCUS	ACU
2004	27%	5%	100%	83%
2003	0%	10%	97%	84%
2002	11%	0%	100%	88%
2001	8%	0%	100%	96%
2000	0%	0%	95%	72%

KENTUCKY 3
Louisville Metro

With the Ohio River forming its western border, the 3rd sprawls across ethnically and economically diverse neighborhoods in the newly formed jurisdiction of Louisville Metro — the result of a 2003 merger between Jefferson County and its largest city, Louisville.

Compared with the rest of the state, Louisville Metro has a sizable black population (one-third of the state's blacks live here), as well as a large Catholic community, a legacy of a massive German immigration in the mid-19th century.

Despite some job losses from industrial decline, labor strength runs deep among the blue-collar, white residents of Louisville's South End. Blacks, who live near downtown in the West End, also make up a strong Democratic voting bloc. Republicans live in the affluent East End by the Ohio River. The bulk of the 3rd's recent population growth came in the northeastern and southeastern areas.

Although tobacco is a part of the 3rd's hearty economy, other sectors, such as the service industry, have rivaled it. Louisville claims a booming health care industry. United Parcel Service, which operates an air-freight hub out of Louisville International Airport, announced plans in early 2005 to hire 300 new pilots. Two Ford assembly plants provide thousands of jobs. Tourism, which was already big, was boosted by the 1998 opening of a massive floating casino on the Indiana bank of the Ohio River.

The 3rd is Kentucky's most Democratic district, but nonetheless is politically competitive. Democrats run well at the local level, especially in downtown Louisville. But more-upscale areas favor Republicans, and the increasing muscle of white-collar suburbanites appears to be swinging the 3rd closer to the GOP. John Kerry won the 3rd with 51 percent of the presidential vote in 2004.

MAJOR INDUSTRY
Service, manufacturing, trade, tobacco

CITIES
Louisville Metro, 674,032

NOTABLE
The Kentucky Derby, called "the greatest two minutes in sports," is held at Churchill Downs in south Louisville; Louisville is the birthplace of the cheeseburger (1934) and is home to the Louisville Slugger Museum.

Rep. Geoff Davis (R)

CAPITOL OFFICE
225-3465
www.house.gov/geoffdavis
1541 Longworth 20515-1704; fax 225-0003

COMMITTEES
Armed Services
Financial Services

HOMETOWN
Hebron

BORN
Oct. 26, 1958, Montreal, Canada

RELIGION
Baptist

FAMILY
Wife, Pat Davis; six children

EDUCATION
U.S. Military Academy, B.S. 1981

MILITARY SERVICE
Army, 1976-87

CAREER
Manufacturing productivity consulting firm owner;
aerospace technology consultant

POLITICAL HIGHLIGHTS
Republican nominee for U.S. House, 2002

ELECTION RESULTS

2004 GENERAL

Geoff Davis (R)	160,982	54.4%
Nick Clooney (D)	129,876	43.9%
Michael E. Slider (I)	5,069	1.7%

2004 PRIMARY

Geoff Davis (R)	13,957	58.0%
Kevin L. Murphy (R)	7,672	31.9%
John Kelly King (R)	2,434	10.1%

Elected 2004; 1st term

In an era when the ranks of military veterans in Congress are dwindling, Davis can bring long Army service to bear in discussions and policy making about the military. His background made him a lock for the Armed Services Committee, on which he is one of five Republican freshmen.

Davis graduated from West Point, where he studied Arabic and the cultures of Southwest Asia and Eastern Europe. Later in his decade-plus Army career, he was a flight commander with the 82nd Airborne.

Davis' post-military career as a business consultant also makes him a good fit for the Financial Services Committee, where he works on issues ranging from insurance to financial market regulation.

Davis uses the words "conservative" and "populist" to characterize his views on the role of government. Limited government is desirable, he says. But personal experiences have sensitized him to the help government can provide: Social Security survivor benefits enabled his family to make ends meet after his stepfather died, and a government-subsidized loan made it possible for his mother to buy a house.

Davis is strongly opposed to abortion and to efforts to restrict gun ownership. He supports extending tax cuts and proposes to reduce health care costs by curbing lawsuits and offering tax credits that would help individuals purchase insurance.

Davis made his political debut in 2002 by nearly defeating Democratic Rep. Ken Lucas, whose conservative views had enabled him to prevail in Kentucky's strongly Republican 4th District. After the 4 percentage point defeat, Davis immediately began preparing for a second campaign. In late 2003, Lucas announced that he would not seek re-election.

Davis comfortably won the Republican primary and squared off against Democratic nominee Nick Clooney — the father of actor George Clooney — who was almost universally known as a longtime local newscaster and columnist. A close race was forecast, but the strong Republican underpinnings of the district helped Davis post a solid 10 percentage point victory.

KENTUCKY 4
North — Covington, Florence, Ashland

The 4th travels across northern Kentucky, from the industrial city of Ashland along the Ohio River, past tobacco farms and small towns, through the Ohio commuters' region before reaching the suburbs northeast of Louisville. Roughly half of the residents live in Cincinnati's suburbs, which helps explain the district's dual economic personality and its consistently conservative politics.

Covington and the northern part of the 4th have enjoyed steady economic growth, partly because of Cincinnati-Northern Kentucky International Airport, which is located in Boone County. Covington also serves as a regional processing center for the IRS. Boone increased its population by about 50 percent in the 1990s, and Boone, Campbell and Kenton counties account for just less than half of the 4th's population.

At the district's western end is Oldham

County, which abuts Louisville Metro and has the highest median income in the state. Oldham joins the Cincinnati-area counties in voting reliably Republican.

The economic picture is gloomier in the eastern counties. Ashland struggled to cope with businesses relocating and downsizing, and the city has become a declining industrial hub. Boyd County, which includes Ashland, was the only county in the 4th to lose population in the 1990s.

The district steadfastly backs Republican presidential candidates. George W. Bush took 63 percent of the vote in the 4th, and John Kerry carried just three counties — Elliott, which has voted Democratic for president since before 1920, Bath and Carter, which Bush narrowly lost.

MAJOR INDUSTRY
Service, manufacturing, health care

CITIES
Covington, 43,370; Florence, 23,551; Ashland, 21,981; Newport, 17,048; Erlanger, 16,676

NOTABLE
Kentucky Speedway racetrack near Sparta.

Rep. Harold **Rogers** (R)

Elected 1980; 13th term

CAPITOL OFFICE
225-4601
talk2hal@mail.house.gov
www.house.gov/rogers
2406 Rayburn 20515-1705; fax 225-0940

COMMITTEES
Appropriations
    (Homeland Security - chairman)

HOMETOWN
Somerset

BORN
Dec. 31, 1937, Barrier, Ky.

RELIGION
Baptist

FAMILY
Wife, Cynthia Doyle Rogers; three children

EDUCATION
Western Kentucky U., attended 1956-57; U. of
Kentucky, B.A. 1962, LL.B. 1964

MILITARY SERVICE
Ky. National Guard, 1956-57; N.C. National Guard,
1957-58; Ky. National Guard, 1958-63

CAREER
Lawyer

POLITICAL HIGHLIGHTS
Pulaski and Rockcastle counties commonwealth
attorney, 1969-80; Republican nominee for
lieutenant governor, 1979

ELECTION RESULTS

2004 GENERAL

Harold Rogers (R)		unopposed

2004 PRIMARY

Harold Rogers (R)	26,909	91.3%
Billy Ray Wilson (R)	2,566	8.7%

2002 GENERAL

Harold Rogers (R)	137,986	78.3%
Sidney "Jane" Bailey-Bamer (D)	38,254	21.7%

PREVIOUS WINNING PERCENTAGES
2000 (74%); 1998 (78%); 1996 (100%); 1994 (79%);
1992 (55%); 1990 (100%); 1988 (100%); 1986 (100%);
1984 (76%); 1982 (65%); 1980 (68%)

Rogers' iron fist in warding off members' specific requests in the appropriations process was not enough to help him ascend to the chairmanship of the full Appropriations Committee at the start of the 109th Congress. That slot went to Jerry Lewis of California, and Rogers will once again steward spending for the still-evolving Department of Homeland Security.

Rogers tends toward a pragmatic conservatism. He is an easygoing, old-style Republican pol who understands the art of cutting a legislative deal. He has been the chairman of three different Appropriations subcommittees since joining the panel in his second term in 1983.

As chairman of the new Homeland Security Subcommittee in the 108th, Rogers regularly disappointed his colleagues by refusing to slip specific funding requests — despite receiving hundreds of them — into the bills. The panel was created to provide funding for the Department of Homeland Security, which is made up of pieces of 22 other agencies and has about 180,000 employees.

Despite holding the line on other earmarks, Rogers has not completely turned a blind eye to his own district. In each of the past two Homeland Security spending bills, Rogers has slipped in language that calls for DHS to use a specific optical laser technology for new immigrant identification cards. The language does not mention any specific company, but the firm that uses this technology and makes these cards, SEI Technology Inc., has a manufacturing facility in Rogers' eastern Kentucky district.

And Rogers in 2004 announced the creation of the National Institute for Hometown Security, a nonprofit research and development organization to be housed in Rogers' hometown of Somerset, which will focus on developing security solutions for smaller cities and rural areas. Rogers said the institute will not only help fight terrorism but also bring new jobs and economic development to southern and eastern Kentucky.

Rogers has sometimes shown a penchant for aggressive oversight, especially with government agencies he believes are too inefficient or bureaucratic. In the past four years, the Transportation Security Administration was the focus of his ire. Rogers has consistently charged that the TSA does a poor job and wants too many screeners.

He was chairman of Appropriations' Transportation Subcommittee in the 107th Congress, when the TSA was created after the Sept. 11, 2001, terrorist attacks. During floor debate on legislation to create the new agency, Rogers supported calls to place passenger and baggage screening under the federal government, but he opposed hiring new federal workers to handle those tasks. Republicans lost that battle, and Rogers ended up supporting the final version of the bill, which allowed the new agency to hire and manage the baggage screeners.

He then took aim at the new agency, which was originally part of the Transportation Department, for paying law enforcement officers too much and submitting budget requests that appeared dubious — including a request for 3,400 employees to handle passenger clothing when it was removed for screening and 1,400 workers to tell passengers to remove cellular devices when they pass through the metal detectors. "We will not give them money to hire a standing army of almost 70,000 people to take off your shoes, check your briefcase three times, and perform intensive checks of white-haired grandmothers in wheelchairs," Rogers said.

The 2002 law creating the Department of Homeland Security settled a longstanding debate, in which Rogers played a leading role, over how to improve the performance of the Immigration and Naturalization Service. The agency was split in half, with one bureau to guard the nation's borders and another to process immigration paperwork. Both bureaus were placed in the new security agency. Rogers had promoted such a plan, with little success, during the six years he was chairman of Appropriations' Commerce, Justice and State Subcommittee, which provided funding for the INS.

Rogers has been enough of a watchdog against bureaucratic waste that he was safe at the start of the 108th, when the more fiscally conservative GOP leadership won the power to decide who would remain Appropriations subcommittee chairmen, known as "cardinals."

Off the committee, Rogers has not been afraid to go against the partisan grain when parochial concerns have conflicted with the leadership's wishes. This has proved especially true on trade. Southeastern Kentucky's declining coal and tobacco industries have made the 5th the poorest district in the state, and the poorest in the country represented by a Republican. As a consequence, Rogers has voted against three of the four marquee trade liberalization laws of the past decade.

Rogers was pleased with a $10 billion buyout of tobacco farmers included in a 2004 measure overhauling corporate taxes. The buyout abolished the federal quota system and reimbursed farmers for their losses. Tobacco farmers had disliked the quotas, saying they made it harder to compete with foreign tobacco growers. The buyout "frees farmers from the archaic tobacco system and allows them to choose whether or not to continue growing or to look into other commodities," Rogers said.

After earning undergraduate and law degrees at the University of Kentucky, Rogers made a name for himself in the southeastern part of the state as a civic activist, promoting industrial development. In 1969, he took over as the commonwealth's attorney in that part of the state and continued to play a conspicuous role in politics as prosecutor for Pulaski and Rockcastle counties. Although he lost a 1979 campaign for lieutenant governor, the name recognition he earned paid off when he ran for the House in 1980 to succeed retiring Republican Tim Lee Carter. Rogers won a 10-person GOP primary and then waltzed to victory in November with 68 percent of the vote.

He has posted a lower vote percentage only twice, most notably in 1992 when, running in a district that was made more Democratic by redistricting after the 1990 census, he was held to 55 percent. Redistricting for this decade should keep the seat safely in Rogers' hands. Democrats did not even field a candidate in 2004.

KEY VOTES

2004

No Extend federal unemployment benefits by 13 weeks

Yes Pass $283.2 billion, six-year federal highway and mass transit bill

Yes Approve $146 billion multi-year extension of previously enacted middle-class tax breaks

Yes Amend the Constitution to prohibit same-sex marriage

Yes Cut corporate taxes $137 billion over 10 years

Yes Reorganize U.S. intelligence agencies as proposed by Sept. 11 commission

2003

Yes Cut taxes by $330 billion through fiscal 2013

No Block Bush rule scaling back overtime pay for some white-collar federal workers

No Do not allow use of search warrants without first notifying subjects

No Allow importation of prescription drugs

Yes Create private school voucher program in Washington, D.C.

Yes Ban "partial birth" abortion except to save a woman's life

No Split $18.6 billion in Iraq aid into half-grant, half-loan

Yes Overhaul Medicare and create prescription drug benefit

CQ VOTE STUDIES

	PARTY UNITY		PRESIDENTIAL SUPPORT	
	Support	Oppose	Support	Oppose
2004	95%	5%	88%	12%
2003	98%	2%	95%	5%
2002	95%	5%	87%	13%
2001	96%	4%	93%	7%
2000	91%	9%	23%	77%

INTEREST GROUPS

	AFL-CIO	ADA	CCUS	ACU
2004	20%	0%	100%	88%
2003	7%	5%	97%	84%
2002	13%	0%	100%	88%
2001	17%	10%	91%	88%
2000	10%	5%	76%	80%

KENTUCKY 5
East and southeast – Somerset, Middlesboro

No area of Kentucky has lower levels of income and education than the rural 5th, which takes in eastern Kentucky's hardscrabble coal country and whose largest city, Somerset, has a population of 11,000.

Coal mining once was a thriving industry in this sparsely populated, Appalachian region, but its decline has brought even harder times to the region's mountain people. Mining still provides thousands of jobs in the area — particularly in high-producing coal areas such as Pike, Perry, Harlan and Knott counties — but the eastern counties are trying to diversify their economies. Some community leaders are trying to attract tourists by highlighting the area's country music heritage, building new arts centers and showcasing the area's coal history.

Population in the western section is concentrated in Pulaski and Laurel counties. Like the rest of the west, Somerset relies heavily on tourism and recreation. Lake Cumberland is nearby, as is the Big South Fork National River and Recreation Area. The Daniel Boone National Forest extends from Rowan County in the north to the Tennessee border.

The 5th is secure GOP territory — Democrats have not represented the southeast Kentucky district since 1889. Republicans run particularly well in the more populous central and western areas. In 2004, Jackson County gave George W. Bush 84 percent of its vote, and most of the other counties in the district's western region gave Bush vote shares in the mid-70 percent range. Overall, Bush carried the district with 61 percent of the vote.

Democrats maintain a strong presence in the far eastern coal counties, where the United Mine Workers of America union is strong. Nine of the 12 Kentucky counties John Kerry won in 2004 are in the 5th, and Democratic voter registration tops 90 percent in some of the counties. Despite the disadvantage, Bush won Morgan County in 2000 and 2004.

MAJOR INDUSTRY
Health care, service, tourism, coal

CITIES
Somerset, 11,352; Middlesboro, 10,384; Corbin, 7,742; Pikeville, 6,295

NOTABLE
The 5th has the nation's highest percentage of white residents (97 percent); Colonel Harland Sanders began making what would later be known as Kentucky Fried Chicken at his service station in Corbin.

Rep. Ben Chandler (D)

Elected February 2004; 1st full term

CAPITOL OFFICE
225-4706
chandler.house.gov
1504 Longworth 20515-1706; fax 225-2122

COMMITTEES
Agriculture
International Relations
Transportation & Infrastructure

HOMETOWN
Versailles

BORN
Sept. 12, 1959, Lexington, Ky.

RELIGION
Presbyterian

FAMILY
Wife, Jennifer Chandler; three children

EDUCATION
U. of Kentucky, B.A. 1983 (history), J.D. 1986

CAREER
Lawyer

POLITICAL HIGHLIGHTS
Ky. auditor, 1992-96; Ky. attorney general, 1996-2004; Democratic nominee for governor, 2003

ELECTION RESULTS

2004 GENERAL

Ben Chandler (D)	175,355	58.6%
Tom Buford (R)	119,716	40.0%

2004 PRIMARY

Ben Chandler (D)	unopposed

2004 SPECIAL

Ben Chandler (D)	84,168	55.2%
Alice Forgy Kerr (R)	65,474	42.9%
Mark Gailey (LIBERT)	2,952	1.9%

Chandler's presence in the House must be reassuring to fellow Democrats. When he wrested the seat from Republican hands in a 2004 special election, his victory represented a sweet, rare Democratic takeback of a district in the South after a string of disappointing congressional elections that held Democrats to minority status in the House.

The 6th district, which includes Frankfort and Lexington and much of the state's horse-breeding country, went for George W. Bush in the last two presidential elections. Chandler has deep roots in the GOP-friendly state and is a proven vote-getter statewide, having won two terms as attorney general and one as state auditor. His grandfather and namesake, A.B. "Happy" Chandler, was a two-time governor and a U.S. senator and may be best remembered for his five-year stint as commissioner of Major League Baseball.

When he arrived in the 108th Congress, Democratic leaders showered Chandler with what few plums they had to bestow, giving him his pick of available committee seats. Then in the 109th, they gave him a seat on the Transportation and Infrastructure Committee, which controls the flow of highway and bridge money to the folks back home. Chandler also is on the Agriculture Committee.

Those assignments put him in the middle of battles over two big reauthorization bills that leaders slated for the 109th Congress — a new farm bill and a huge transportation and mass transit bill that stalled in the last Congress. Chandler's office boasts that he is the only member from the state's House delegation on the Agriculture panel.

Chandler is more independent than liberal Democratic leaders would like, however. He voted with his party on major votes just 79 percent of the time in the 108th Congress, compared with scores in the mid- or high-90s for most rank-and-file members. In 2004, only 21 Democrats broke with their party more often. "I disagree with a lot of things that the national Democrats do. I disagree with plenty of things that the Republicans do," he says. "The point is, on an issue, I'm going to be my own man."

A member of the Blue Dog Coalition of moderate to conservative Democrats, Chandler departs from most House Democrats in his opposition to gun control and his support for the war in Iraq, though he has grown increasingly critical of President Bush's conduct of the war.

He voted in favor of a proposed constitutional amendment to ban same-sex marriage, the most emotionally charged issue of his brief tenure in the 108th. Chandler characterizes his position on abortion rights as the "right-hand end of pro-choice," supporting a ban on the procedure critics call "partial birth" abortion, but opposing an outright ban on abortion. He favors less restrictive rules for stem cell research, which uses cells from days-old human embryos, generally left over from in-vitro fertilization, that otherwise would be destroyed.

Chandler is more closely aligned with Democratic leaders in his views on economic policy. He opposes the tax cuts for higher-income individuals that were enacted in 2001 and 2003, arguing that tax relief should be skewed toward middle- and lower-income taxpayers because "those are the very people who would have plugged it right back into the economy."

On trade, Chandler said trade agreements have to be more closely analyzed by Congress to ensure they do not erode U.S. manufacturing jobs. He has cosponsored legislation aimed at slowing the number of U.S. jobs going overseas, teaming with one of the most left-leaning members of

Congress, independent Bernie Sanders of Vermont.

He is a leading voice on the potentially costly issue of whether states should be allowed to use tax breaks as a lure for business. The Cincinnati-based 6th U.S. Circuit Court of Appeals struck down an Ohio law in late 2004 that helped bring a DaimlerChrysler plant to Toledo. GOP Sen. George V. Voinovich of Ohio and Chandler introduced legislation to ensure such incentives continue.

Like many in his party, Chandler has backed the positions of labor unions and environmental groups, which has earned him endorsements from the League of Conservation Voters and the Sierra Club. He also would have opposed Bush's Medicare prescription drug bill that Congress dealt with just before his arrival.

On a parochial issue, Chandler found himself at the center of a heated budget dispute with the Bush administration. Bush's fiscal 2006 budget proposed reducing funds for destroying chemical weapons stockpiles at the Blue Grass Army Depot just southeast of Richmond. The weapons have long been a concern to the surrounding communities in Chandler's district.

Chandler was elected auditor in 1991 and won elections for attorney general in 1995 and 1999. As the state's top law enforcement officer, he oversaw the establishment of the state's "do not call" telemarketing list.

He made a play for governor in 2003, but was defeated by Republican Rep. Ernie Fletcher. So Chandler turned around and ran in the special-election contest for the House seat vacated by Fletcher.

Chandler's race against GOP state Sen. Alice Forgy Kerr drew widespread attention. The candidates were financially competitive. Both national parties as well as advocacy groups, recognizing that the contest would be perceived as a bellwether, spent heavily to promote them. The nine-week campaign cost more than $4 million. Chandler won by 12 percentage points. A little more than eight months later, he handily won election to a full term.

Fletcher went on to have a tough first term as governor. His budget and tax reform plans were rejected by the legislature, and state employees protested his changes in their health benefits. Chandler meanwhile was being celebrated as a party hero for capturing Fletcher's old seat.

Chandler says he thinks he got the better deal. "I love this job. I wouldn't trade," he told the Lexington Herald-Leader in 2004. "Ernie might want to, but I don't think I'd let him."

Chandler lives in Woodford County — which boasts some of the finest thoroughbred horse farms in the world — on land that has been in the family nearly as long as Kentucky has been a state.

KEY VOTES

2004

Yes Pass $283.2 billion, six-year federal highway and mass transit bill

Yes Approve $146 billion multi-year extension of previously enacted middle-class tax breaks

Yes Amend the Constitution to prohibit same-sex marriage

Yes Cut corporate taxes $137 billion over 10 years

Yes Reorganize U.S. intelligence agencies as proposed by Sept. 11 commission

CQ VOTE STUDIES

	PARTY UNITY		PRESIDENTIAL SUPPORT	
	Support	Oppose	Support	Oppose
2004	79%	21%	45%	55%

INTEREST GROUPS

	AFL-CIO	ADA	CCUS	ACU
2004	86%	70%	55%	32%

KENTUCKY 6
East central — Lexington, Frankfort

The 6th embodies the culture and economic pursuits that most outsiders associate with the state of Kentucky. This is the heart of the Bluegrass region, which spawns Kentucky Derby champions and is host to considerable tobacco and liquor interests.

A patchwork of urban, suburban and rural areas, the 6th experienced steady economic growth in the 1990s. Lexington, the district's largest city, continues to have a strong equine industry and is known as the thoroughbred capital of the world. The city is home to the University of Kentucky, where the basketball team plays at Rupp Arena. A Toyota manufacturing facility in Georgetown, just north of Lexington, is one of the largest employers in the state.

Tobacco, always a highly charged subject in this region, held strong in the 1990s despite mounting concerns about its future. Kentucky's top two producers of burley tobacco in 2004 — Bourbon and Fayette counties — are in the 6th District.

The 6th swung sharply to George W. Bush in the 2000 presidential election, after narrowly backing Bill Clinton in 1996, and stayed with Bush in 2004. District voters tend to be socially conservative, especially on gun control and gay marriage, but will support candidates from either major party. Control over the House seat has changed three times since 1990.

Government workers in Frankfort contribute to Franklin County's Democratic lean, although the county voted for Bush in 2004 after being the only county in the 6th to back Al Gore in 2000. Democratic support dips in Woodford and Scott counties, which border Franklin and have some of the highest incomes in Kentucky. The GOP runs up big margins in the farmland south of Lexington — Bush took districtwide highs of 72 percent in Garrard County and 70 percent in Jessamine County in 2004.

MAJOR INDUSTRY
Manufacturing, service, tobacco, retail

MILITARY BASES
Blue Grass Army Depot, 9 military, 936 civilian (2005)

CITIES
Lexington-Fayette, 260,512; Frankfort, 27,741; Richmond, 27,152

NOTABLE
The whiskey bourbon was named after Bourbon County.

LOUISIANA

Gov. Kathleen Babineaux Blanco (D)

First elected: 2003
Length of term: 4 years
Term expires: 1/08
Salary: $95,000
Phone: (225) 342-7015

Hometown: Lafayette
Born: Dec. 15, 1942;
Coteau, La.
Religion: Roman Catholic
Family: Husband, Raymond Blanco; six
children (one deceased)
Education: U. of Southwestern Louisiana,
B.S. 1964 (business education)
Career: Political marketing firm partner; U.S.
Census Bureau district manager; homemaker;
teacher
Political highlights: La. House, 1984-89;
La. Public Service Commission, 1989-95
(chairwoman, 1993-94); lieutenant governor,
1996-2004

Election results:
2003 GENERAL RUNOFF
Kathleen Babineaux Blanco (D) 731,358 52.0%
Bobby Jindal (R) 676,484 48.1%

Lt. Gov. Mitch Landrieu (D)

First elected: 2003
Length of term: 4 years
Term expires: 1/08
Salary: $85,000
Phone: (225) 342-7009

STATE LEGISLATURE

Legislature: March-June in odd-
numbered years; April-June in even-
numbered years

House: 105 members, 4-year terms
2005 breakdown: 67D, 37R, 1I; 87
men, 18 women
Salary: $16,800
Phone: (225) 342-6945

Senate: 39 members, 4-year terms
2005 breakdown: 24D, 15R; 33 men,
6 women
Salary: $16,800
Phone: (225) 342-2040

STATE TERM LIMITS

Governor: 2 terms
House: 3 consecutive terms
Senate: 3 consecutive terms

URBAN STATISTICS

CITY	POPULATION
New Orleans	484,674
Baton Rouge	227,818
Shreveport	200,145
Lafayette	110,257
Lake Charles	71,757

REGISTERED VOTERS

Democrat	55%
Republican	24%
Unaffiliated/others	20%

POPULATION

2004 population (est.)	4,515,770
2000 population	4,468,976
1990 population	4,219,973
Percent change (1990-2000)	+5.9%
Rank among states (2004)	24
Median age	34
Born in state	79.4%
Foreign born	2.6%
Violent crime rate	681/100,000
Poverty level	19.6%
Federal workers	34,590
Military	41,392

REDISTRICTING

Louisiana retained its seven House
seats in reapportionment. The state
legislature drew a new map, which
the governor signed on Oct. 19, 2001.

MISCELLANEOUS

Web: www.louisiana.gov
Capital: Baton Rouge
STATE ELECTION OFFICIAL
(225) 922-0900
**DEMOCRATIC
HEADQUARTERS**
(225) 336-4155
**REPUBLICAN
HEADQUARTERS**
(225) 928-2998

District Statistics

DIST.	2004 VOTE FOR PRESIDENT BUSH	KERRY	WHITE	BLACK	ASIAN	HISP	MEDIAN INCOME	WHITE COLLAR	BLUE COLLAR	SERVICE INDUSTRY	OVER 64	UNDER 18	COLLEGE EDUCATION	RURAL	SQ. MILES
1	70%	29%	80%	13%	2%	5%	$40,948	65%	21%	14%	13%	25%	27%	20%	2,402
2	24	75	28	64	3	4	$27,514	56	22	22	10	28	19	1	266
3	58	41	70	25	1	2	$34,463	50	35	15	11	29	11	27	7,010
4	59	40	62	33	1	2	$31,085	53	29	18	13	27	17	41	10,765
5	62	37	63	34	1	1	$27,453	54	29	18	13	27	16	47	13,775
6	59	40	63	33	1	2	$37,931	61	24	15	10	27	24	24	3,076
7	60	39	72	25	1	1	$31,453	55	29	17	12	28	17	31	6,268
STATE	57	42	63	32	1	2	$32,566	57	27	17	12	27	19	27	43,562
U.S.	50.7	48.3	69	12	4	13	$41,994	60	25	15	12	26	24	21	3,537,438

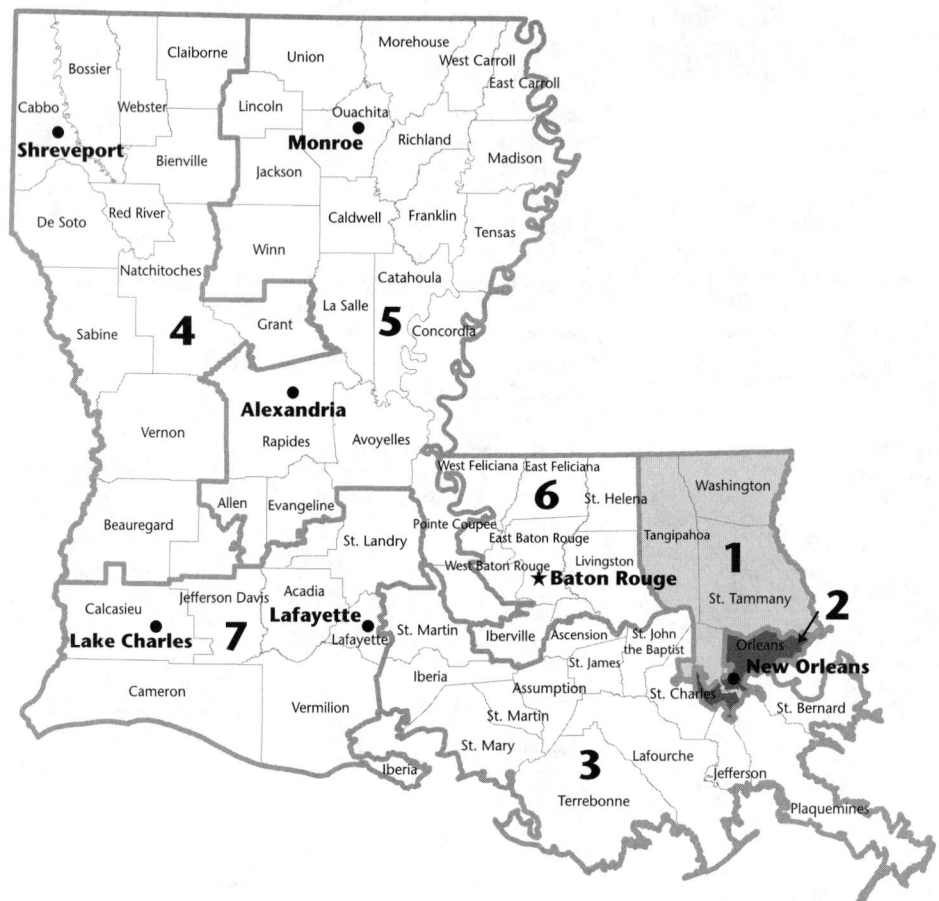

Sen. Mary L. Landrieu (D)

Elected 1996; 2nd term

CAPITOL OFFICE
224-5824
senator@landrieu.senate.gov
landrieu.senate.gov
724 Hart 20510-1804; fax 224-9735

COMMITTEES
Appropriations
Energy & Natural Resources
Small Business & Entrepreneurship

HOMETOWN
New Orleans

BORN
Nov. 23, 1955, Arlington, Va.

RELIGION
Roman Catholic

FAMILY
Husband, Frank Snellings; two children

EDUCATION
Louisiana State U., B.A. 1977 (sociology)

CAREER
Realtor

POLITICAL HIGHLIGHTS
La. House, 1980-88; La. treasurer, 1988-96;
candidate for governor, 1995

ELECTION RESULTS

2002 GENERAL RUNOFF

Mary L. Landrieu (D)	638,654	51.7%
Suzanne Haik Terrell (R)	596,642	48.3%

2002 GENERAL

Mary L. Landrieu (D)	573,347	46.0%
Suzanne Haik Terrell (R)	339,506	27.2%
John Cooksey (R)	171,752	13.8%
Tony Perkins (R)	119,776	9.6%
Raymond Brown (D)	23,553	1.9%
others	18,399	1.4%

PREVIOUS WINNING PERCENTAGES
1996 (50%)

With the retirement of John B. Breaux, Landrieu has become her state's senior senator. Like Breaux, she is a moderate Democrat who departs from her party on many crucial votes — a practice that helps get her elected in a conservative Southern state, but often makes the liberals who dominate the party wary of her next move. Landrieu says she considers herself part of the Senate's "sensible center."

Late in the 108th Congress, Landrieu (LAN-drew) forced lawmakers to stay in town through the Columbus Day weekend as she vowed to use every procedural tactic she knew to protest the removal of one of her provisions from corporate tax legislation. Calling it a case of "Mary against Goliath," Landrieu delayed the final vote on the measure until GOP leaders reinstated her proposal to give companies a $2 billion tax credit for keeping National Guard members and military reservists on payrolls while they fight in Iraq and Afghanistan. At the time, Louisiana had the 11th largest number of National Guard reservists on active duty.

Landrieu used similar tactics in the 2003 Senate debate over legislation to make it easier to remove class action lawsuits from state courts and send them to federal courts, where the rules are generally not as friendly to plaintiffs. When Majority Leader Bill Frist refused to include a list of changes that Landrieu wanted, she voted against shutting off floor debate, although supporters of the measure had long counted Landrieu as one of their allies. Frist later struck a deal with Landrieu and two other Democrats in return for their support.

Landrieu affiliates with both the Senate New Democrats and the bipartisan Centrist Coalition. "Too often here in Washington, the loudest voices are the ones on the far left and far right," she said in 2000 as the New Democrats organized. "That is why this group was formed, to give voice to those in the sensible center."

She has little patience for some of the social issues that preoccupy conservatives and on which there seems no identifiable middle ground. When the Senate considered a proposal to amend the Constitution to ban same-sex marriage, Landrieu was one of 50 senators voting against moving the issue forward. Her office was bombarded with calls, mostly from angry supporters. Although her home state has banned same-sex marriage, Landrieu said amending the Constitution would violate the document's underlying principle of limiting the role of government in people's lives. "More than anything else, this debate over the Federal Marriage Amendment has been a divisive, politically motivated distraction from other critical issues," Landrieu said.

That position, along with her opposition to federal vouchers for private school tuition for low-income families, may cost Landrieu some support in her heavily Roman Catholic state. The church hierarchy favored the idea, and a pro-voucher group ran advertisements in the New Orleans Times-Picayune criticizing Landrieu by publicizing the fact that Landrieu's two children attend a private school in Washington, D.C. Landrieu argued that private schools that accepted the vouchers should have to meet the same academic standards set for public schools by the Bush administration's No Child Left Behind policy, which imposed tough new testing requirements on schools. Though she lost that fight, she helped include a condition that the new federal funds target school districts with the highest concentrations of poor children.

Landrieu's politics often confound the efforts of her party to weaken President Bush and the Republicans who control Congress. In 2002, she voted for the $1.35 trillion Bush tax cut and sided with Republicans in a vote to permanently repeal the estate tax, muddying the Democratic message that the tax cut favored the wealthy, was fundamentally unfair and would balloon the federal deficit. Landrieu also sided with Republicans on opening Alaska's Arctic National Wildlife Refuge to oil and gas exploration. And she cosponsored a measure with Republican Sam Brownback of Kansas that would have banned all human cloning, opposing Democrats and some Republicans who wanted to allow the practice for biomedical research.

But Landrieu's support for Republican initiatives, especially those from the White House, may be a thing of the past. The president worked hard to defeat her when she sought re-election in 2002, and Landrieu still resents the intrusion into her race. "I'm not saying that I'm not going to work on issues of concern to my state, but if this president is re-elected, it will take a lot more than words to get me to team up with him again," Landrieu said just before Bush won a second term in November 2004.

A daughter of colorful New Orleans, where her father was once mayor, Landrieu combines politics and social charm in the best tradition of Breaux and other Cajun state politicians. When Energy and Natural Resources Committee Chairman Frank H. Murkowski wouldn't budge in opposing her idea of earmarking offshore drilling revenue for conservation programs, Landrieu took the notoriously dour Republican to dinner at Commander's Palace, one of the city's oldest and best loved restaurants in the French Quarter. Landrieu and other supporters had to settle for a more modest approach subject to annual appropriations, but even that partial victory was unexpected.

Despite party differences, Landrieu shares a strong bond with her female colleagues in the Senate. In 2000, she collaborated on a book, "Nine and Counting," with her eight female Senate colleagues in the 106th Congress. After that, she announced that she would not campaign against any of those women — Democrat or Republican.

Landrieu's political grit comes naturally. She hails from a noted Louisiana political family; she is the oldest of nine children of Moon Landrieu, who was New Orleans mayor for eight years and secretary of the Department of Housing and Urban Development in the Carter administration. She has also survived the state's not so genteel politics.

After serving in the state legislature and as Louisiana treasurer, Landrieu made an unsuccessful run for governor in 1995. A year later, when she sought to fill the seat of retiring Democratic Sen. J. Bennett Johnston, she won by the slimmest margin ever in a Louisiana Senate race — just 5,788 votes out of 1.7 million cast. The outcome was challenged by the loser, conservative Louis "Woody" Jenkins, who alleged voter fraud. Republicans on the Senate Rules Committee voted for a broad investigation, and a bitter and divisive probe dragged on until the panel voted to end it almost a year after the election.

When she sought re-election in 2002, Landrieu was forced into a runoff because she fell short of the 50 percent needed under state law to claim victory in Louisiana's unique nonpartisan primary. She had finished first, with 46 percent, in the nine-candidate field, which included three well-known Republicans: Suzanne Haik Terrell, the state elections commissioner; Rep. John Cooksey; and state Rep. Tony Perkins. In the runoff, she increased the size of her 1996 victory seven-fold, to 42,012 votes. Bush campaigned for Terrell, but some analysts said that his efforts looked like overkill and actually may have helped her.

KEY VOTES

2004

Yes Pass $318.9 billion, six-year highway and mass transit bill
No Extend assault weapons ban for 10 years
Yes Restore pay-as-you-go rules for new tax cuts and entitlement spending
Yes Criminalize harm to a fetus in an attack on the mother
Yes Increase mandatory child care funding to states by $6 billion over five years
No Amend the Constitution to prohibit same-sex marriage
Yes Approve $146 billion multi-year extension of previously enacted middle-class tax breaks
Yes Reorganize U.S. intelligence agencies as proposed by Sept. 11 commission
Yes Cut corporate taxes $137 billion over 10 years

2003

No Delay Bush changes to Clean Air Act
No Allow confirmation vote on Miguel A. Estrada to the U.S. Court of Appeals for the D.C. Circuit
No Block a Bush proposal opening Alaska's Arctic National Wildlife Refuge to oil drilling
Yes Limit size of Bush's proposed tax cut to $350 billion through fiscal 2013
Yes Overhaul Medicare and create prescription drug benefit
Yes Block Bush rule scaling back overtime pay for some white-collar federal workers
Yes Split $20 billion in Iraq aid into half-grant, half-loan
Yes Ban "partial birth" abortion except to save a woman's life
No Stop proposal allowing travel to Cuba
Yes Allow final vote on energy policy overhaul

CQ VOTE STUDIES

	PARTY UNITY		PRESIDENTIAL SUPPORT	
	Support	Oppose	Support	Oppose
2004	81%	19%	68%	32%
2003	78%	22%	58%	42%
2002	65%	35%	84%	16%
2001	81%	19%	74%	26%
2000	88%	12%	85%	15%
1999	81%	19%	86%	14%
1998	89%	11%	86%	14%
1997	77%	23%	87%	13%

INTEREST GROUPS

	AFL-CIO	ADA	CCUS	ACU
2004	100%	85%	71%	32%
2003	77%	60%	78%	20%
2002	83%	70%	84%	35%
2001	88%	85%	69%	28%
2000	63%	80%	73%	16%
1999	67%	95%	59%	4%
1998	88%	90%	67%	8%
1997	29%	70%	70%	16%

Sen. David Vitter (R)

Elected 2004; 1st term

Vitter is the first popularly elected Republican senator in Louisiana history, and his style contrasts sharply with that of his Democratic predecessor, John B. Breaux. Where Breaux thrived politically through dealmaking and compromise, Vitter has a track record of solid loyalty to President Bush and Republican leaders.

Yet it may be risky to assume that Vitter will maintain the style he developed in more than five years in the House. In just his first few months in the Senate, he showed signs of becoming a more independent voice.

In early 2005, Vitter fulfilled a campaign promise by introducing a bill to allow for the purchase of American-made prescription drugs imported from overseas, where they can be purchased more cheaply than in the United States. Senate GOP leaders and the White House oppose the measure, but it has drawn wide, bipartisan support. Vitter also has pledged to oppose a guest worker program backed by the Bush administration that would allow some undocumented workers to remain in the United States legally. And like some other Republicans, he has openly criticized Secretary of Defense Donald H. Rumsfeld's handling of the war in Iraq.

When he was a member of the House, Vitter was apt to buck his party when Louisiana's interests were at risk. He broke with Bush by opposing the Central American Free Trade Agreement on grounds it would hurt the state's sugar farmers. He also joined other Louisiana lawmakers taking a position against steel tariffs imposed in 2002 by the Bush administration because of the potential fallout for the Port of New Orleans, which derives 40 percent of its revenue from steel shipments. The tariffs were rescinded in 2003 after the World Trade Organization declared them illegal and threatened to impose duties on some U.S. exports.

Vitter is also a strong defender of Louisiana's farming and energy interests and of what he calls "Louisiana values," namely conservative stands on social issues, such as opposition to abortion rights and same-sex marriage. Vitter also has railed against political corruption, which he says has tarnished Louisiana's image.

Vitter has expressed interest in getting on the Senate Appropriations Committee, where he could continue to push for spending on a $14 billion Louisiana coastline restoration project that he advocated as a member of the House Appropriations panel.

In the 109th Congress, Vitter drew some plum committee assignments for a freshman senator. He got seats on the Commerce, Science and Transportation Committee, the Environment and Public Works Committee and the Small Business and Entrepreneurship panel. That leaves him well-positioned to push proposals for Louisiana, one of the country's poorest states.

On issues not affecting Louisiana, Vitter has been generally loyal to the White House and his party. He votes with his party on key votes most of the time, and in 2004, he supported Bush 94 percent of the time on issues where the president took a position. Among the administration priorities he supports are legislation to make tax cuts permanent and to place strict limits on lawsuits and jury awards. He has said he will likely support all of the president's judicial nominations.

Vitter is seen as smart but brash, and his rejection of go-along-to-get-along politics has turned off some potential allies in his party. Republican state House Speaker Pro Tempore C.E. "Peppi" Bruneau Jr. once said Vit-

CAPITOL OFFICE
224-4623
vitter.senate.gov
516 Hart 20510-1803; fax 228-2577

COMMITTEES
Commerce, Science & Transportation
 (Global Climate Change & Impacts - chairman)
Environment & Public Works
Small Business & Entrepreneurship

HOMETOWN
Metairie

BORN
May 3, 1961, New Orleans, La.

RELIGION
Roman Catholic

FAMILY
Wife, Wendy Baldwin Vitter; four children

EDUCATION
Harvard U., A.B. 1983; Oxford U., B.A. 1985 (Rhodes scholar); Tulane U., J.D. 1988

CAREER
Lawyer; professor

POLITICAL HIGHLIGHTS
La. House, 1992-99; U.S. House, 1999-2005

ELECTION RESULTS

2004 GENERAL

David Vitter (R)	943,014	51.0%
Chris John (D)	542,150	29.3%
John Kennedy (D)	275,821	14.9%
Arthur A. Morrell (D)	47,222	2.6%
others	39,849	2.2%

2002 GENERAL HOUSE

David Vitter (R)	147,117	81.5%
Monica L. Monica (R)	20,268	11.2%
Robert "Bob" Namer (R)	7,229	4.0%
Ian P. Hawkhurst (I)	5,956	3.3%

PREVIOUS WINNING PERCENTAGES
2000 House Election (80%); 1999 Special House Runoff Election (51%)

ter was "incapable of working with anybody." Vitter says he is criticized because he challenges the status quo. "I've rocked the boat and that's caused some resentment," he says. "But that's only in the political establishment."

When he was in the state legislature, Vitter filed an ethics complaint against a close friend of former Louisiana Gov. Edwin Edwards, and then spearheaded a recall petition effort against Edwards. He won passage of a measure limiting the terms of state lawmakers, while also opposing a pay raise for them. And he led a successful fight to end a scholarship program at Tulane University that allowed state legislators to choose recipients, denouncing the program as an abuse of power.

Vitter carried on a longstanding feud with former Republican Gov. Mike Foster over legalized gambling, which Vitter opposed. Former Rep. Billy Tauzin, an influential state Republican, counseled Vitter about the need for better personal relationships when he was elected to the House in 1999, and Vitter seemed to heed the advice. When he took office, he told The New Orleans Times Picayune that if people "are expecting some grand confrontational style, they will be sorely disappointed."

Vitter worked to mend fences with Foster, who ultimately endorsed him in his Senate race. His relationship with the state's senior senator, Democrat Mary L. Landrieu, grew bitter during the campaign but Vitter wasn't entirely to blame. Landrieu was outspoken in opposing him and promoting his Democratic opponent. After the 2004 election, Breaux hosted a peacemaking breakfast attended by both Vitter and Landrieu.

Vitter's first experience with congressional politics was as an intern for the late Joe Moakley, a liberal Massachusetts House member, while in college. Vitter graduated magna cum laude from Harvard University, and later got a law degree from Tulane University. He is also a Rhodes Scholar, one of four in the Senate. Early in his career, Vitter practiced law and also taught at both Tulane and Loyola universities.

In 1991, he ran for state office, saying he wanted to do something about the low reputation of Louisiana politics. He won the state House seat vacated by former Ku Klux Klan leader David Duke, who ran unsuccessfully for governor. Vitter was in the legislature for a little more than seven years.

His predecessor in Congress was Robert L. Livingston, who was chairman of the Appropriations Committee for four years and was picked by his GOP colleagues at the end of 1998 to replace Newt Gingrich as Speaker in the next Congress. But the next month Livingston decided to resign from the House after admitting to extramarital affairs, and Vitter narrowly won a special election in 1999 to succeed him.

In 2004, Vitter ran for the Senate seat left open by Breaux's retirement. He had a tough fight against Breaux's protégé, House Democrat Chris John. In Louisiana, all candidates, regardless of party, are on the same ballot for the primary, which coincides with Election Day. Vitter faced two independents and four Democrats, including John.

He was favored going in, but the question was whether his competitors would hold him to less than 50 percent of the vote and force a Dec. 4 runoff between the two top vote-getters. Vitter had won the state GOP's backing of his candidacy and no other Republicans entered the race. Meanwhile, John had to compete against other strong Democrats. Vitter got a rare, outright victory by winning a majority of the votes and capturing the seat without a runoff.

Louisiana has not had a Republican senator since William Pitt Kellogg, who began service in 1868 but was elected to the job by the state legislature, not directly by voters. The 17th Amendment, ratified in 1913, calls for direct election of senators.

KEY VOTES

House Service:
2004

No	Extend federal unemployment benefits by 13 weeks
Yes	Pass $283.2 billion, six-year federal highway and mass transit bill
?	Approve $146 billion multi-year extension of previously enacted middle-class tax breaks
Yes	Amend the Constitution to prohibit same-sex marriage
Yes	Cut corporate taxes $137 billion over 10 years
Yes	Reorganize U.S. intelligence agencies as proposed by Sept. 11 commission

2003

Yes	Cut taxes by $330 billion through fiscal 2013
No	Block Bush rule scaling back overtime pay for some white-collar federal workers
No	Do not allow use of search warrants without first notifying subjects
Yes	Allow importation of prescription drugs
Yes	Create private school voucher program in Washington, D.C.
Yes	Ban "partial birth" abortion except to save a woman's life
No	Split $18.6 billion in Iraq aid into half-grant, half-loan
Yes	Overhaul Medicare and create prescription drug benefit

CQ VOTE STUDIES

House Service:

	PARTY UNITY		PRESIDENTIAL SUPPORT	
	Support	Oppose	Support	Oppose
2004	98%	2%	94%	6%
2003	99%	1%	96%	4%
2002	99%	1%	85%	15%
2001	98%	2%	93%	7%
2000	92%	8%	25%	75%
1999	92%	8%	20%	80%

INTEREST GROUPS

House Service:

	AFL-CIO	ADA	CCUS	ACU
2004	7%	5%	100%	96%
2003	0%	10%	97%	88%
2002	11%	0%	95%	100%
2001	8%	0%	100%	100%
2000	0%	0%	85%	88%
1999	14%	5%	88%	83%

Rep. Bobby Jindal (R)

CAPITOL OFFICE
225-3015
www.house.gov/jindal
1205 Longworth 20515-1801; fax 225-0739

COMMITTEES
Education & Workforce
Homeland Security
Resources

HOMETOWN
Kenner

BORN
June 10, 1971, Baton Rouge, La.

RELIGION
Roman Catholic

FAMILY
Wife, Supriya Jindal; two children

EDUCATION
Brown U., Sc.B. 1991 (biology & public policy);
Oxford U., M.Litt. 1994 (Rhodes scholar)

CAREER
State university system president; management
consultant

POLITICAL HIGHLIGHTS
La. Health and Hospitals Department secretary,
1996-98; U.S. Health and Human Services
assistant secretary for planning and evaluation,
2001-03; candidate for governor, 2003

ELECTION RESULTS

2004 GENERAL

Bobby Jindal (R)	225,708	78.4%
Roy Armstrong (D)	19,266	6.7%
M.V. "Vinny" Mendoza (D)	12,779	4.4%
Daniel Zimmerman (D)	12,135	4.2%
Jerry Watts (D)	10,034	3.5%
Mike Rogers (R)	7,975	2.8%

Elected 2004; 1st term

Arriving on Capitol Hill in 2005 at just 33 years of age, Jindal had already compiled an impressive résumé in policy and politics.

In 1996, when he was just 25, the former Rhodes Scholar was named secretary of the Health and Hospital Department in his home state of Louisiana. He first came to Washington in 2001 to serve as an assistant secretary in the Health and Human Services Department in the Bush administration.

Jindal (JIN-dle) went back home to enter politics at an unusually high level, making a strong bid for governor of Louisiana in 2003. Though he fell short — losing the runoff to Democrat Kathleen Babineaux Blanco by 52 percent to 48 percent — the contest left him in a strong position for a future race.

The opportunity was not long in coming: In 2004, Republican Rep. David Vitter left the 1st District seat open for what would be a successful bid for the Senate. Though Jindal had to move to suburban New Orleans from Baton Rouge to run in the 1st, the foundation he had laid the year before immediately established him as the overwhelming favorite in the Republican stronghold district. He went on to win with 78 percent of the vote.

His win was a breakthrough in the 1st, which has a staunchly conservative constituency and few minorities. Jindal, whose parents emigrated from India, is the only lawmaker of that background in the 109th Congress, and only the second ever: Dalip Singh Saund, a California Democrat born in India in 1899, served in the House from 1957 to 1963.

Jindal's rise continued even before he was sworn in, with his election as president of the House Republican Class of 2004: Jindal, benefiting from little competition in his race and more money than he needed, had contributed to the campaign treasuries of many of his fellow GOP newcomers.

The freshman lawmaker did not get everything he hoped for. His wish list included a seat on either the Energy and Commerce or the Ways and Means panel. Instead, he was given assignments to the Education and Workforce, Homeland Security, and Resources committees.

LOUISIANA 1
East — Metairie, part of Florida Parishes

A short distance from festive downtown New Orleans, the conservative 1st skims the edges of the city and reaches north across Lake Pontchartrain to the Mississippi border. The mostly white-collar population is the wealthiest and most educated in the state. Blacks make up 13 percent of the 1st's population — making it the only district in the state with less than 24 percent.

The 1st's population center is on the south side of the lake and includes the upscale Metairie suburbs. The area is packed with white-collar conservatives.

North of the lake, the 1st includes three of the "Florida Parishes," so named because they were part of Spanish Florida until 1810. Once a community of seasonal homes for residents escaping New Orleans, the north shore is now booming, full of suburbanites who commute across Lake Pontchartrain

Causeway to New Orleans. St. Tammany Parish was the fastest-growing area in the 1st during the 1990s. Local developments include petrochemical and oil industries, and leaders hope to attract technology firms related to the expansion of the Avondale Shipyard in the 2nd. The northern parishes are still heavily agricultural, producing mainly cotton, corn and soybeans.

Democrats held the 1st for more than a century before Republicans took over in 1977. Now, residents warmly welcome the GOP on all levels. George W. Bush took 70 percent of the district's 2004 presidential vote, making the 1st the only Louisiana district to give him more than 62 percent. But Democrats do win a few local offices in rural Washington and Tangipahoa parishes.

MAJOR INDUSTRY
Petrochemicals, oil, agriculture, tourism

CITIES
Metairie (pt.), 140,916; Kenner (pt.), 46,007; New Orleans (pt.), 37,451; Slidell, 25,695

NOTABLE
Lake Pontchartrain Causeway is the world's longest highway bridge over water.

Rep. William J. Jefferson (D)

Elected 1990; 8th term

CAPITOL OFFICE
225-6636
jeffersonmc@mail.house.gov
www.house.gov/jefferson
2113 Rayburn 20515-1802; fax 225-1988

COMMITTEES
Budget
Ways & Means

HOMETOWN
New Orleans

BORN
March 14, 1947, Lake Providence, La.

RELIGION
Baptist

FAMILY
Wife, Andrea Green Jefferson; five children

EDUCATION
Southern U. and A&M College, B.A. 1969 (English & political science); Harvard U., J.D. 1972; Georgetown U., LL.M. 1996 (taxation)

MILITARY SERVICE
Army, 1969-75

CAREER
Lawyer; congressional aide

POLITICAL HIGHLIGHTS
La. Senate, 1980-91; candidate for mayor of New Orleans, 1982, 1986; candidate for governor, 1999

ELECTION RESULTS

2004 GENERAL

William J. Jefferson (D)	173,510	79.0%
Arthur L. "Art" Schwertz (R)	46,097	21.0%

2002 GENERAL

William J. Jefferson (D)	90,310	63.5%
Irma Muse Dixon (D)	28,480	20.0%
Silky Sullivan (R)	15,440	10.9%
Clarence "Buddy" Hunt (D)	4,137	2.9%
Wayne E. Clement (I)	3,789	2.7%

PREVIOUS WINNING PERCENTAGES
2000 (100%); 1998 (86%); 1996 (100%); 1994 (100%); 1992 (100%); 1990 (53%)

A tax attorney educated at Harvard and Georgetown, Jefferson is one of the more conservative members of the generally liberal Congressional Black Caucus. His frequent support for business interests sets him apart from most of that group. Raised in rural northeast Louisiana in a family of 10 children, he has gained impressive insider's credentials over the years, including spots on the Ways and Means and Budget Committees.

With his relatively moderate politics and a strong record as a free trader, Jefferson is a likely target in the 109th Congress if President Bush follows through on his re-election vow to reach out to Democrats and members of the black caucus. In the 108th Congress, Jefferson backed Bush in one out of three key votes; only three other black caucus members voted with Bush more often.

The top-ranking Democrat on Ways and Means, Charles B. Rangel of New York, described Jefferson for the New Orleans Times-Picayune as "no nonsense . . . a very serious legislator." Notably industrious, Jefferson went to night school for three years after being elected to Congress. He graduated from Georgetown with a master's of law in taxation. Rangel often refers to Jefferson as "my tax counsel."

His biggest career disappointment in recent years was not being chosen for a leadership role. In 2003, new House Democratic leader Nancy Pelosi picked fellow Californian Robert T. Matsui over Jefferson to head the party's House re-election organization, the Democratic Congressional Campaign Committee. Jefferson had worked to show his mettle with energetic fundraising for the party in the run-up to the 2002 election, and he had the backing of many members of the Congressional Black Caucus.

The most loyal proponent of trade liberalization among black lawmakers, Jefferson and Harold E. Ford Jr. of Tennessee were the only African-Americans among the 25 House Democrats who voted to enact the 2002 law giving the president authority to negotiate trade deals that Congress may not amend. He also voted in 2000 to make permanent the normal U.S.-China trade relationship, and in 1994 to create the World Trade Organization; in 1993, he embraced the North American Free Trade Agreement.

However, he is not enthusiastic about Bush's top trade priority in the 109th Congress, the Central America Free Trade Agreement. Most members of the Louisiana delegation object to the pact because it would loosen import quotas for sugar, jeopardizing a mainstay of the state's economy.

Oil and gas interests are big business in Louisiana; Jefferson is a firm supporter of the energy industry and voted to allow oil drilling in Alaska's Arctic National Wildlife Refuge. He also criticized Bush's decision in 2001 to impose tariffs on steel imports at the behest of domestic steelmakers. He said the tariffs threatened the maritime and port industries, particularly in New Orleans where steel shipments are the port's leading revenue source. But only 18 Democrats and 12 Republicans voted for his resolution to overturn Bush's tariff policy.

Jefferson supported a $137 billion corporate tax cut bill in 2004 that most Democrats opposed, largely because it included his provision to reduce taxes paid by U.S.-flagged vessels. The change imposes a "tonnage tax" on ships instead of a tax on the income they generate, translating into huge savings for New Orleans shippers.

His alliances with the Republicans are not limited to business issues. In recent years, Jefferson has backed constitutional amendments to ban flag burning and same-sex marriage, voted to ban a procedure its opponents call "partial birth" abortion and supported a GOP plan to repeal estate taxes.

As chairman of the Congressional Black Caucus Foundation, Jefferson led a foundation initiative aimed at increasing homeownership by minorities. The program also helped would-be homeowners navigate the process of finding an affordable mortgage.

Jefferson was born and brought up in poverty in far northeast Louisiana, where he earned money by chopping cotton. His mother was adamant about the need for education, and Jefferson proved to be a high achiever. He was class president in high school and student body president at Southern University in Baton Rouge. He won a scholarship to Harvard Law School. He went on to clerk for a federal judge in Louisiana and then worked as an aide to Democratic Sen. J. Bennett Johnston Jr. of Louisiana. He moved to New Orleans in 1976 to practice law.

Elected to the state Senate in 1979, Jefferson represented a racially mixed New Orleans district that included much of the affluent Uptown area. He developed a reputation as a nuts-and-bolts expert on fiscal matters and a promoter of economic development. He waged unsuccessful campaigns to become mayor of New Orleans in 1982 and 1986, but because of the timing of the elections he did not have to give up his Senate seat.

When Democratic Rep. Lindy Boggs retired in 1990 after 18 years, Jefferson finished first in the crowded primary and in the runoff narrowly defeated lawyer Marc Morial, the son of New Orleans' first black mayor, Ernest N. "Dutch" Morial. Jefferson has since won re-election handily.

Some other political ventures have not panned out as well. In 1999, he ran for governor against GOP incumbent Mike Foster, only to lose by more than 30 percentage points. In 2002, he played a high-profile, hands-on role in the unsuccessful mayoral campaign of Richard Pennington.

In 2004, the news was bad for Louisiana Democrats in general. Jefferson split with retiring Sen. John B. Breaux and Sen. Mary L. Landrieu over who had the best shot at keeping Breaux's seat Democratic. Breaux and Landrieu backed Rep. Chris John, but Jefferson supported state Treasurer John Kennedy. The divided allegiances helped make David Vitter the first GOP senator from Louisiana since Reconstruction.

Shortly before the election, Democratic Rep. Rodney Alexander, who won his 5th District seat with Jefferson's help in rallying blacks behind him, switched to the GOP. The losses mean that Louisiana's delegation of House and Senate members went from five Democrats and four Republicans at the start of the 108th Congress, to six Republicans and three Democrats.

KEY VOTES

2004

Yes Extend federal unemployment benefits by 13 weeks
Yes Pass $283.2 billion, six-year federal highway and mass transit bill
Yes Approve $146 billion multi-year extension of previously enacted middle-class tax breaks
Yes Amend the Constitution to prohibit same-sex marriage
Yes Cut corporate taxes $137 billion over 10 years
Yes Reorganize U.S. intelligence agencies as proposed by Sept. 11 commission

2003

No Cut taxes by $330 billion through fiscal 2013
Yes Block Bush rule scaling back overtime pay for some white-collar federal workers
Yes Do not allow use of search warrants without first notifying subjects
— Allow importation of prescription drugs
No Create private school voucher program in Washington, D.C.
Yes Ban "partial birth" abortion except to save a woman's life
Yes Split $18.6 billion in Iraq aid into half-grant, half-loan
No Overhaul Medicare and create prescription drug benefit

CQ VOTE STUDIES

	PARTY UNITY		PRESIDENTIAL SUPPORT	
	Support	Oppose	Support	Oppose
2004	94%	6%	32%	68%
2003	91%	9%	33%	67%
2002	92%	8%	40%	60%
2001	87%	13%	44%	56%
2000	90%	10%	80%	20%

INTEREST GROUPS

	AFL-CIO	ADA	CCUS	ACU
2004	80%	80%	57%	17%
2003	87%	90%	46%	32%
2002	86%	75%	58%	20%
2001	91%	80%	70%	21%
2000	89%	70%	66%	13%

LOUISIANA 2

New Orleans

French street names, strands of Spanish moss and snake-bearing, fortune-telling voodoo queens add to New Orleans' unique cultural mix. But beyond its reputation as the "Big Easy," the comfortably Democratic 2nd, which takes in much of the city and some middle-class suburbs, has dealt with serious issues. While the crime rate has fallen, widespread poverty continues to cause some flight from the city. Since its peak in 1960, New Orleans' population has declined by almost one-fourth.

Famed for its food and jazz traditions, New Orleans is one of the most popular tourist destinations in the country. Mardi Gras and the annual Jazz & Heritage Festival alone attract millions of visitors and billions of dollars each year.

Other staples of the 2nd's economic diet — the New Orleans port, shipbuilding and petroleum industries — have held strong in recent years. The Avondale shipyard, recently purchased by defense contractor Northrop Grumman, built a new technology center that has created jobs and drawn businesses to the area. Meanwhile, after a decade of

decline, the oil and gas industry experienced a resurgence in the 1990s that has leveled off in recent years.

Three rounds of redistricting in the 1990s left the 2nd as Louisiana's only black-majority district. Changes following the 2000 census did not alter that status, and the district is currently 64 percent black. Democratic presidential candidates do exceptionally well here — Al Gore received 76 percent of the vote in 2000 and John Kerry captured 75 percent in 2004, making the 2nd the only Louisiana district either man won.

MAJOR INDUSTRY
Tourism, shipbuilding, oil and gas

MILITARY BASES
Naval Support Activity New Orleans, 2,986 military, 1,313 civilian (2004)

CITIES
New Orleans (pt.), 447,223; Marrero (pt.), 35,796; Kenner (pt.), 24,510

NOTABLE
The St. Charles Streetcar Line, created in 1835, is the oldest continuously operating line in the world; Lindy Boggs, mother of newscaster Cokie Roberts and widow of Rep. Hale Boggs, was elected to the U.S. House in 1973 and held the 2nd until Rep. Jefferson was elected in 1990.

Rep. Charlie Melancon (D)

Elected 2004; 1st term

CAPITOL OFFICE
225-4031
www.house.gov/melancon
404 Cannon 20515-1803; fax 225-0563

COMMITTEES
Agriculture
Resources
Science

HOMETOWN
Napoleonville

BORN
Oct. 3, 1947, Napoleonville, La.

RELIGION
Roman Catholic

FAMILY
Wife, Peachy Melancon; two children

EDUCATION
U. of Southwestern Louisiana, B.S. 1971
(agribusiness)

CAREER
Sugar cane trade group president; insurance
company owner; storage and housing rental
company owner; ice cream shop owner; multi-
county planning and development director

POLITICAL HIGHLIGHTS
Candidate for La. House, 1975; La. House, 1987-93

Melancon pulled off a rare feat — a Democratic takeback of a Southern district that had gone Republican — by edging Republican lobbyist Billy Tauzin III by 569 votes in the closest congressional election of 2004.

A former state lawmaker, Melancon (meh-LAW-sawn) has ambitions for his House career. He hopes for a future assignment to the exclusive Energy and Commerce Committee, once chaired by his predecessor in southeastern Louisiana's 3rd District, retired Republican Billy Tauzin, the father of the man Melancon defeated.

For now, though, Melancon has assignments — on the Agriculture and Resources committees — that should be relevant to his home base. Agriculture makes up a big part of the economy in the 3rd, and Melancon is a former president of the American Sugar Cane League. The Resources Committee oversees issues that affect the oil and gas industries, also Louisiana mainstays. He has a third assignment, to the Science panel.

Melancon will have to maintain a local focus if he is to last long enough to rise through the congressional ranks. Most of his district's voters are conservatives who often favor Republican candidates.

Melancon says one of his top priorities is creating and protecting jobs in southern Louisiana, in part by strengthening its education system. He vowed to try to block passage of the Central American Free Trade Agreement, which he said could lead to decreased sugar prices and job losses.

He wants to look out for the state's tourism industry. As a state representative, Melancon was the driving force behind the Louisiana Tourism Taxing District, which dedicated a portion of state sales tax to tourism promotion.

Melancon won by promising to maintain a rightward agenda. He emphasizes his conservative views on social issues, saying he opposes abortion, supports gun owners' rights and wants to maintain the definition of marriage as being only between a man and a woman. Melancon garnered only 24 percent of the first-round vote in November, but that was enough for second place and a spot in the Dec. 4 runoff against Tauzin.

ELECTION RESULTS

2004 GENERAL RUNOFF

Charlie Melancon (D)	57,611	50.2%
Billy Tauzin III (R)	57,042	49.8%

2004 GENERAL

Billy Tauzin III (R)	84,680	32.0%
Charlie Melancon (D)	63,328	23.9%
Craig Romero (R)	61,132	23.1%
Damon J. Baldone (D)	25,783	9.7%
C. Degruise Caccioppi (D)	19,347	7.3%
Kevin D. Chiasson (R)	10,350	3.9%

LOUISIANA 3

South central — New Iberia, Houma, Chalmette

A maze of interconnected bayous, swamps and marshes, the southern 3rd District runs along the coast of the Gulf of Mexico and takes in the Mississippi River delta and the eastern half of Cajun country. Folks here know the intricate details of catching and cleaning fish, a major industry in the 3rd, and are adept at stockpiling canned goods and plywood during hurricane season. River Road, a highway running the length of the Mississippi River, originates in the 3rd and is lined by symbols of the Old South — antebellum sugar plantations.

After a decade of decline, the 3rd rebounded somewhat in the 1990s, due in large part to the oil and gas industry, which is especially big in parishes along the Gulf. The district helps the state lead the nation in crawfish, catfish, blue crab and shrimp production. Farther inland, petrochemical plants along the Mississippi struggle with declining overseas demand. Sugar cane, which dominated the regional economy into the 20th century, continues to be profitable. Employment remains seasonal, and the unemployment rate soars in the off-season.

Democrats dominated the region for most of a century, but the Catholic 3rd now favors Republicans. The historical tendency of the district, however, remains: Conservative Democrats fare well in local elections.

MAJOR INDUSTRY
Oil and gas, petrochemicals, fishing, shipbuilding, sugar cane

MILITARY BASES
Naval Air Station Joint Reserve Base New Orleans, 1,200 military, 1,100 civilian (2004)

CITIES
New Iberia, 32,623; Houma, 32,393; Chalmette, 32,069; Laplace, 27,684

NOTABLE
Morgan City hosts the Louisiana Shrimp & Petroleum Festival each Labor Day; New Iberia is home to the Conrad Rice Mill, the oldest working rice mill in the United States.

Rep. Jim McCrery (R)

Elected April 1988; 9th full term

CAPITOL OFFICE
225-2777
jim.mccrery@mail.house.gov
www.house.gov/mccrery
2104 Rayburn 20515-1804; fax 225-8039

COMMITTEES
Ways & Means
(Social Security - chairman)

HOMETOWN
Shreveport

BORN
Sept. 18, 1949, Shreveport, La.

RELIGION
Methodist

FAMILY
Wife, Johnette McCrery; two children

EDUCATION
Louisiana Tech U., B.A. 1971 (English & history);
Louisiana State U., J.D. 1975

CAREER
Lobbyist; lawyer; congressional aide

POLITICAL HIGHLIGHTS
Candidate for Leesville City Council, 1978

ELECTION RESULTS

2004 GENERAL

Jim McCrery (R)		unopposed

2002 GENERAL

Jim McCrery (R)	114,649	71.6%
John Milkovich (D)	42,340	26.5%
Bill Jacobs (I)	3,104	1.9%

PREVIOUS WINNING PERCENTAGES
2000 (71%); 1998 (100%); 1996 (100%); 1994 (100%);
1992 (63%); 1990 (100%); 1988 (100%); 1988 Special
Runoff Election (51%)

McCrery is not one for impassioned speeches on the House floor or for political theatrics. But while his style is to be more accountant than showman, McCrery's behind-the-scenes expertise has made him a player on an impressive list of legislative issues.

As chairman of the Ways and Means Subcommittee on Social Security, McCrery handles one of the most politically sensitive aspects of President Bush's second-term agenda — a plan to introduce market forces into the program by allowing younger workers to put some of their Social Security payroll taxes into personal investment accounts. Previously, McCrery was chairman of the Select Revenue Measures Subcommittee, a role in which he shepherded through the president's tax cuts in 2001, the economic stimulus package that followed the Sept. 11, 2001, terrorist attacks, and the 2004 corporate tax law.

McCrery's name often is mentioned when talk turns to who will chair the Ways and Means Committee starting in 2007, when his close ally, Chairman Bill Thomas of California, will be compelled by GOP term limits to yield the gavel. For more than a decade, McCrery has worked closely with Thomas, who hand-picked him for the Select Revenue Subcommittee chairmanship at the start of the 107th Congress in 2001.

McCrery has cemented his political standing among Republicans by doling out campaign funds. During the 2004 campaign, his political action committee raised almost $1.3 million; he gave more than a half million dollars to colleagues, who are likely to remember his generosity when he eventually seeks the Ways and Means chairmanship.

Preventing insolvency of the Social Security, Medicare and Medicaid programs is McCrery's top interest. He is a key supporter of Bush's plan to revamp Social Security in the 109th Congress. The president wants to let younger workers divert 4 percent of their wages into personal investment accounts; benefits would be cut by an unspecified amount in return.

A member of the Ways and Means Health Subcommittee, McCrery has similar ideas about placing parts of Medicare in the private sector. He would like to transform the giant government health care program into a system of subsidized private health insurance plans that senior citizens could choose among in much the same way workers choose among plans offered by employers. His solution to Congress' long-elusive goal of providing health coverage to all Americans would be to require everyone to purchase insurance and to equalize the size of premiums, regardless of a person's age, sex or medical history, to spread the risks broadly.

Like Thomas, McCrery immerses himself in the details of issues. He sometimes displays the zeal of a convert (he began his political career as a Democrat), and at other times he is as pragmatic as a chief operating officer. While he can be a fiercely loyal partisan, his even-tempered nature allows him to work with Democrats more frequently than the more combative Thomas. "It's not a good-cop, bad-cop routine," McCrery says. "But each of us is aware that the other has strengths and weaknesses, and we do try to complement those as best we can."

McCrery says significant compromises are needed on issues such as Social Security and Medicare. "If we want to save the private health care system, Republicans are going to have to accept some things that normally would be contrary to our basic philosophy," he told the Atlantic Monthly magazine.

While he has a large role in national issues, McCrery must also look out for the interests of Fort Polk and Barksdale Air Force Base in his district. And, during the rewrite of the highway law in the 109th Congress, he is working to accelerate spending on Interstate 49, which is being expanded, and on Interstate 69, a newly designated Michigan-to-Mexico highway that cuts across the 4th District.

McCrery's fascination with politics began at a young age. At 11, he displayed a homemade "Nixon for president" sign in his front yard during the 1960 campaign. As a slight, fair-haired young man, McCrery won election as high school student body president by defeating a popular quarterback. He set up his first telephone bank and talked to 800 other students.

After graduating from law school, McCrery joined a firm in Leesville, where he grew up, then put in two years as an assistant city attorney in Shreveport, where he was born. As a Democrat, in 1981, he signed on with Louisiana Democratic Rep. Buddy Roemer, working first in his district office in Shreveport and then as Roemer's legislative director in Washington. McCrery returned to Louisiana in 1984 to lobby for Georgia-Pacific Corp. in the state capital.

In 1987, he joined the list of Southern conservative Democrats switching to the GOP. After Roemer became governor, McCrery jumped into the 1988 special election to succeed him. Although initially the least-known candidate, he stood out as the only Republican and impressed voters with his knowledge of issues. He finished first in the primary and took 51 percent of the vote to defeat Democratic state Sen. Foster L. Campbell Jr. in the general-election runoff.

His most significant re-election challenge came in 1992, when redistricting matched him against fellow incumbent Jerry Huckaby, an eight-term Democrat. Huckaby chaired the Agriculture Subcommittee on Cotton, Rice and Sugar — commodities of great importance to Louisiana — but he was put at a disadvantage by the demographics of the new district and also had 88 overdrafts at the private bank for House members. McCrery won with 63 percent and has not been as seriously challenged since.

With his own re-election prospects assured, McCrery has focused on helping fellow Republicans win their races. In addition to contributing hefty sums from his political action committee in recent years, he served as the incumbent retention director of the National Republican Congressional Committee from 1997 to 2002. In 2005, he serves on the executive committee of the organization, the main fundraising arm of the House GOP.

KEY VOTES

2004
- ? Extend federal unemployment benefits by 13 weeks
- Yes Pass $283.2 billion, six-year federal highway and mass transit bill
- Yes Approve $146 billion multi-year extension of previously enacted middle-class tax breaks
- Yes Amend the Constitution to prohibit same-sex marriage
- Yes Cut corporate taxes $137 billion over 10 years
- Yes Reorganize U.S. intelligence agencies as proposed by Sept. 11 commission

2003
- Yes Cut taxes by $330 billion through fiscal 2013
- No Block Bush rule scaling back overtime pay for some white-collar federal workers
- Yes Do not allow use of search warrants without first notifying subjects
- No Allow importation of prescription drugs
- Yes Create private school voucher program in Washington, D.C.
- Yes Ban "partial birth" abortion except to save a woman's life
- No Split $18.6 billion in Iraq aid into half-grant, half-loan
- Yes Overhaul Medicare and create prescription drug benefit

CQ VOTE STUDIES

	PARTY UNITY		PRESIDENTIAL SUPPORT	
	Support	Oppose	Support	Oppose
2004	98%	2%	97%	3%
2003	97%	3%	100%	0%
2002	97%	3%	87%	13%
2001	98%	2%	98%	2%
2000	90%	10%	27%	73%

INTEREST GROUPS

	AFL-CIO	ADA	CCUS	ACU
2004	8%	5%	100%	96%
2003	0%	5%	97%	88%
2002	13%	0%	100%	92%
2001	8%	5%	100%	92%
2000	0%	5%	95%	83%

LOUISIANA 4
Northwest and west — Shreveport, Bossier City

Removed from the Cajun influence that much of Louisiana is known for, the mostly white-collar 4th identifies more with Dallas than New Orleans. Covering most of western Louisiana, the conservative district takes in Shreveport at its north end and wanders into timber country in Beauregard and Allen parishes in the south.

The oil industry that fueled the economy in the 4th fizzled in the 1980s. But Shreveport and Bossier City responded to a 1995 gambling proposal that allowed for 15 casinos in the state; five riverboat casinos now are docked on the Red River, which separates the two cities. A wave of riverfront renewal, accompanied by a large influx of retail and service industries, has helped drive the economy in recent years.

Other industries remain intact: General Motors has invested millions in a new Shreveport facility, and the city has remained a health care hub for northern Louisiana as well as for eastern Texas and southern Arkansas. Barksdale Air Force Base near Bossier City also is a major employer for both cities. Forestry and poultry production scattered throughout the 4th

add to the economy.

Redistricted three times in the 1990s, the old 4th briefly had a black majority, but African-Americans now make up a third of the population. The area sent conservative Democrats to Congress from 1874 until a 1988 special election. The GOP incumbent has won comfortably since (briefly in the old 5th), even though registered Democrats outnumber Republicans. Locally, the 4th still favors Democrats, although the suburbs around Shreveport and Bossier City have elected some Republicans in recent elections.

MAJOR INDUSTRY
Military, riverboat gambling, health care, timber

MILITARY BASES
Fort Polk (Army), 10,668 military, 7,276 civilian; Barksdale Air Force Base, 7,878 military, 1,153 civilian (2004)

CITIES
Shreveport, 200,145; Bossier City, 56,461; Natchitoches, 17,865

NOTABLE
Bank robbers Bonnie and Clyde were gunned down south of Gibsland in 1934 — the town re-enacts the shooting every year.

Rep. Rodney Alexander (R)

Elected 2002; 2nd term

CAPITOL OFFICE
225-8490
rodney.alexander@mail.house.gov
www.house.gov/alexander
316 Cannon 20515-1805; fax 225-5639

COMMITTEES
Appropriations

HOMETOWN
Quitman

BORN
Dec. 5, 1946, Quitman, La.

RELIGION
Baptist

FAMILY
Wife, Nancy Alexander; three children

EDUCATION
Louisiana Tech U., attended 1965

MILITARY SERVICE
Air Force Reserve, 1965-71

CAREER
Insurance agent; road construction contractor

POLITICAL HIGHLIGHTS
Jackson Parish Police Jury, 1972-87 (president, 1980-87); La. House, 1988-2002 (served as a Democrat)

ELECTION RESULTS *

2004 GENERAL

Rodney Alexander (R)	141,495	59.4%
Zelma "Tisa" Blakes (D)	58,591	24.6%
John W. "Jock" Scott (R)	37,971	16.0%

2002 GENERAL RUNOFF

Rodney Alexander (D)	86,718	50.3%
Lee Fletcher (R)	85,744	49.7%

2002 GENERAL

Rodney Alexander (D)	52,952	28.7%
Lee Fletcher (R)	45,278	24.5%
Clyde C. Holloway (R)	42,573	23.1%
Robert J. Barham (R)	34,533	18.7%
Sam Houston Melton Jr. (D)	4,595	2.5%
Jack Wright (R)	3,581	1.9%

*Elected as a Democrat 2002

Alexander's claim to fame is his last-minute party switch from Democrat to Republican in 2004. The maneuver effectively left him with no real competition in the election that fall and earned him the lasting enmity of former friends in the Democratic Party. But it ensured him great popularity with GOP leaders who hand out committee assignments and other plums. In the 109th Congress, he was given a rare open seat on the Appropriations Committee, which will no doubt help him send federal dollars back to his impoverished district in northeast Louisiana.

He is culturally conservative and so fits right in with his new Republican colleagues on issues such as abortion rights and same-sex marriage, both of which he opposes. He is also a supporter of gun owners' rights. But Alexander is a populist from a state that practically invented the breed, and he often votes like the Democrat he once was. He harps on the need for government to do better at providing health care and a good public education to the disadvantaged. "If a mother can't buy medicine for a crying child, she doesn't care how many warheads Saddam Hussein has," he told The Monroe (La.) News-Star. "I care about people who can't pay to see a doctor and overworked teachers in country schools where the roof leaks."

He is best known for a bold strategy just as he was beginning his first re-election campaign in 2004. On Aug. 4, he filed as a Democrat — he had been elected two years earlier as a Democrat — but two days later refiled as a Republican, just minutes before the filing deadline. That prevented Democrats from countering with a strong challenger. Alexander pretty much had the campaign to himself.

Senior Louisiana Democrats howled. Sen. Mary Landrieu, who had campaigned for Alexander in his first race, called him a "coward." William J. Jefferson, the only black member from Louisiana, stopped him off the House floor to complain that he had betrayed the African-American voters who make up a third of the district. Threatened by Minority Whip Steny H. Hoyer of Maryland with a lawsuit, Alexander began returning campaign donations he had gotten from Democrats.

Amid the tempest, Alexander kept his head down and just endured. He offered some tepid explanations about never quite fitting in with the Democrats, though he had been one all of his political life, including his 14 years in the Louisiana statehouse. "We never argued about Democrats versus Republicans in Baton Rouge. But on the national level, that's the way it is," he told the Monroe paper in 2003. "I want to represent everybody — Republicans, Democrats, Independents. I am not a die-hard party man. I just happened to be registered as a Democrat."

His temporary discomfort was grandly rewarded by his new party. Speaker J. Dennis Hastert named him to the Transportation Committee in September 2004 just after his party switch. (He relinquished that seat in the 109th when he got on Appropriations.) Two weeks before the election, Hastert promised Alexander $10 million in federal funds for a new terminal building for the Monroe Regional Airport. Such sums got attention in the economically struggling district, which makes up about a third of Louisiana's land area but has some of its poorest rural parishes in the state. "We've never seen the inside of the pork barrel, much less hopped a ride on a gravy train," The Monroe News-Star said.

The hoopla was unusual for Alexander, whose personal style is low-key. He is quiet and soft-spoken and his intelligence and grasp of issues is often underestimated, said longtime Monroe, La. newspaper political writer John Hill, adding that he "could get along with a cougar."

In his first term, when he was still a Democrat, Alexander supported some of President Bush's major initiatives, including the creation of a prescription drug benefit in the federal Medicare program. On many issues, Alexander stayed true to Democratic principles. He voted with labor on key votes, opposing Bush administration proposals to privatize a portion of the federal workforce and to impose limits on overtime rules. A protectionist when it comes to sugar, he opposes free trade agreements that interfere with Louisiana's dominance as the nation's third-leading producer of sugar.

Alexander is especially eager to see the government expand its role in health care and education. In Louisiana, he chaired the House Committee on Health and Welfare and cosponsored a bill creating a health insurance program for poor children. From his seat on Appropriations, he is well-positioned to keep a campaign pledge to fund health care improvements. He opposes government vouchers for private school tuition, saying he prefers to bolster the quality of foundering public schools in his district. Of his constituents, Alexander told The Monroe News-Star, "They're good people who will succeed with a chance. I want to help them get that chance."

Alexander, a former construction contractor who dropped out of Louisiana Technical University, decided to run for the House after GOP incumbent John Cooksey announced he was leaving to run for the Senate, a race he ultimately lost. At age 56, Alexander had spent much of his adult life in politics, first as a member of the Jackson Parish Police Jury, the Louisiana equivalent of a county board of supervisors, and later in the state House.

He led a field of seven candidates in the state's open primary, in which members of both major parties can run. But he didn't get the majority needed under state law to avoid a runoff. He was considered the underdog in the weeks leading to the runoff, behind Republican Lee Fletcher, a former top aide to Cooksey and no Washington rookie. Fletcher was showered with attention from national Republicans, and he outspent Alexander 2-to-1. Helped by a surge in Democratic voting in Landrieu's Senate race that year, Alexander beat Fletcher by a mere 974 votes.

His close call may have inspired his party switch two years later. Having set up ideal political conditions, he defeated Democrat Zelma "Tisa" Blakes, a stay-at-home mother who had never run for office before, with 59 percent of the vote. Gordon Harvey, political historian at the University of Louisiana at Monroe, told The Monroe News-Star: "Barring some unforeseen event, this is his seat for a long time. This is a conservative district."

KEY VOTES

2004

Yes Extend federal unemployment benefits by 13 weeks

Yes Pass $283.2 billion, six-year federal highway and mass transit bill

Yes Approve $146 billion multi-year extension of previously enacted middle-class tax breaks

Yes Amend the Constitution to prohibit same-sex marriage

Yes Cut corporate taxes $137 billion over 10 years

Yes Reorganize U.S. intelligence agencies as proposed by Sept. 11 commission

2003

Yes Cut taxes by $330 billion through fiscal 2013

Yes Block Bush rule scaling back overtime pay for some white-collar federal workers

Yes Do not allow use of search warrants without first notifying subjects

No Allow importation of prescription drugs

No Create private school voucher program in Washington, D.C.

Yes Ban "partial birth" abortion except to save a woman's life

Yes Split $18.6 billion in Iraq aid into half-grant, half-loan

Yes Overhaul Medicare and create prescription drug benefit

CQ VOTE STUDIES

	PARTY UNITY		PRESIDENTIAL SUPPORT	
	Support	Oppose	Support	Oppose
2004	97%	3%	67%	33%
2003	69%	31%	56%	44%

INTEREST GROUPS

	AFL-CIO	ADA	CCUS	ACU
2004	80%	40%	70%	48%
2003	87%	60%	67%	48%

LOUISIANA 5
Northeast and central — Monroe, Alexandria

Taking in most of northeastern and central Louisiana, the 5th stretches from the delta parishes along the Mississippi River to central Louisiana — a region known as the Crossroads for its mix of American Indians, Cajuns and European settlers. While conservative throughout, the 5th is plagued by pockets of poverty and unemployment despite numerous efforts to bring more economic opportunities to the district.

Although the rich, black soil along the Mississippi River produces much of the state's cotton and soybeans, poor education and transportation systems slow economic growth — poverty and unemployment in the delta parishes can affect as many as one-fourth of the residents. A move toward larger farms has altered the economy of Monroe, the 5th's largest city. Located between the delta farms in the east and the small lumber and paper mills that dot the western parishes, Monroe now depends increasingly on health care, service and retail industries.

The central part of the state is focused around Alexandria in Rapides Parish. Although military base closings in the 1990s hurt the regional economy, the 1992 conversion of England Air Force Base into an industrial park has helped the area.

This historically Democratic district leans Republican, but voters will still support conservatives of either party. About one-third of the district's residents are African-American, and Democrats hold many local offices. Most residents classify themselves as conservative Democrats, but the Baptists and Pentecostals in the north are more likely to vote for Republicans than the Catholics are in the south. George W. Bush took 57 percent of the 5th's vote in the 2000 presidential election and improved his winning percentage by 5 points in 2004.

MAJOR INDUSTRY
Agriculture, health care

CITIES
Monroe, 53,107; Alexandria, 46,342; Ruston, 20,546

NOTABLE
Former Gov. and Sen. Huey Long was born in Winn Parish in 1893; Delta Air Lines started in Monroe and was based there until moving to Atlanta in 1941; Winn Parish was the only parish not to secede during the Civil War.

Rep. Richard H. Baker (R)

Elected 1986; 10th term

CAPITOL OFFICE
225-3901
www.house.gov/baker
341 Cannon 20515-1806; fax 225-7313

COMMITTEES
Financial Services
(Capital Markets, Insurance & GSEs - chairman)
Transportation & Infrastructure
Veterans' Affairs

HOMETOWN
Baton Rouge

BORN
May 22, 1948, New Orleans, La.

RELIGION
Methodist

FAMILY
Wife, Kay Baker; two children

EDUCATION
Louisiana State U., B.A. 1971 (political science)

CAREER
Real estate broker

POLITICAL HIGHLIGHTS
La. House, 1972-86 (served as a Democrat,
1972-85)

ELECTION RESULTS

2004 GENERAL

Richard H. Baker (R)	189,106	72.2%
Rufus Holt Craig Jr. (D)	50,732	19.4%
Edward Anthony Galmon (D)	22,031	8.4%

2002 GENERAL

Richard H. Baker (R)	146,932	84.0%
Rick Moscatello (I)	27,898	16.0%

PREVIOUS WINNING PERCENTAGES
2000 (68%); 1998 (51%); 1996 (100%); 1994 (100%);
1992 (51%); 1990 (100%); 1988 (100%); 1986 (100%)

Unlike the uniquely flamboyant politicians Louisiana is known for, Baker is not a natural glad-hander. His passion is the dry banking and finance issues that fall to the Financial Services Committee; he chairs a subcommittee that sounds like a graduate course in economics: capital markets, insurance and government-sponsored enterprises. As Baker acknowledges, "99.9 percent of what I do is of no interest to the people in my district."

But anyone who has ever shopped for a home mortgage has felt Baker's unseen power as the House point man on oversight of mortgage super siblings Fannie Mae and Freddie Mac, the financiers of nearly half of the nation's home loans. In the 109th Congress, he is at the forefront of efforts to more closely regulate the two government-sponsored enterprises, which are chartered by Congress.

Baker's appearance is staid and his manner exudes decorum, a reflection of his upbringing as a minister's son. But he is known to be a tough interviewer of witnesses called before the committee. He was the most vociferous critic of Fannie and Freddie even before the scandals involving alleged accounting improprieties in the 108th Congress brought other lawmakers into his corner. Investors view the duo as having the implicit backing of the U.S. Treasury, and if they were to lapse, Baker warns, taxpayers would have to bail them out.

With a wide portfolio covering the securities and insurance industries, capital markets, and the secondary mortgage market, Baker's performance as subcommittee chairman is a tryout for taking the helm of the full committee; Michael G. Oxley of Ohio will step down at the end of the 109th Congress as a result of GOP-imposed term limits. In 2000, Baker had angled for the chairmanship of the House Banking Committee, but when the panel's jurisdiction was expanded and renamed Financial Services, Oxley was named chairman and Baker had to settle for continuing as a subcommittee chairman.

Baker has cultivated a close working relationship with Oxley, which could make for an easy transition on the panel and be a plus for Baker when the Republican leadership names a new chairman. He has teamed up with Oxley on major legislation to bolster corporate accountability and to create a government safety net for the insurance industry as it writes terrorism policies. In the 109th Congress, Baker and Oxley want to overhaul insurance regulation by streamlining state government bureaucracy. Baker sponsored several of the committee's high-profile bills in the 108th Congress, such as a measure aimed at blocking the Financial Accounting Standards Board from forcing companies to treat stock options as an expense.

Baker's serious style puts him at odds with the popular perception of the backslapping Louisiana politician. He is not a regular at Louisiana State University football games or other venues for political hobnobbing. He prefers to spend his off hours at home with his family. Most lawmakers love television cameras, but Baker didn't even bother to hire a press secretary until a 1998 re-election scare prompted him to toot his own horn more often.

Baker's solemnity is matched by his conservatism. The liberal Americans for Democratic Action gave Baker a 5 percent score in 2003 after 12 consecutive years of 0 percent, while the Chamber of Commerce gives him a career grade of 95 percent. Baker's philosophy of business regulation is "to make sure whatever A can do to B under the rules, B can do to A," and he says his main goal is to prevent another bailout of an economic sector akin to the savings and loan debacle of the late 1980s and early 1990s.

Baker is a staunch believer that the federal government, and not the states, should regulate the securities industry. In his view, New York state Attorney General Eliot Spitzer overreached when he investigated the alleged conflict-of-interest culture among analysts at Wall Street banks, which ultimately led to a $1.4 billion settlement from 10 banks and to changes in national securities rules. Baker wrote to the attorneys general of the other 49 states urging them not to follow Spitzer's example.

He introduced a bill in 2003 giving the Securities and Exchange Commission new powers to crack down on corporate fraud. One provision limiting the scope of state enforcement actions, the "anti-Spitzer" clause, caused Democrats and state attorneys general to balk. The bill languished in the 108th Congress, but the regulation battle continued.

Back home, Baker was the driving force behind the creation of a training camp for at-risk youngsters and a health facility for veterans on the grounds of an old federal leprosy hospital that he had transferred to state control. And for years he worked to secure federal funding for a $163 million flood diversion canal north of Baton Rouge.

By the age of 23, Baker had graduated from LSU and started his own real estate business. He credits his father, a Methodist minister and World War II pilot, for guiding him philosophically and his mother-in-law for getting him into politics. Baker at first considered following in his father's footsteps, but he concluded that pastoral life required a more patient man. He was encouraged by his mother-in-law, who worked in local campaigns and organized political fundraisers over sandwiches and fruit punch at parlor parties.

He won election to the Louisiana state House when he was just 23, and made a name for himself by writing a law creating objective criteria for allocating state highway funds, an activity that had been based on political favoritism. In 1985, Baker, then a Democrat, switched to the GOP, a practical move that instantly made him the favorite to capture the House seat being vacated by Republican W. Henson Moore, who was running for the Senate.

In 1992, reapportionment cost Louisiana a House seat, and Baker was re-elected by only 2,700 votes after he was forced to run in the same district as GOP Rep. Clyde C. Holloway. Baker's only other close call was in 1998, when he prevailed by 2,800 votes in a race against Democrat Marjorie McKeithen, the daughter and granddaughter of big players in Louisiana politics. In 2002, Baker was the beneficiary of redistricting, and his turf became more securely Republican. He was re-elected easily in 2002 and 2004.

KEY VOTES

2004
No	Extend federal unemployment benefits by 13 weeks
Yes	Pass $283.2 billion, six-year federal highway and mass transit bill
Yes	Approve $146 billion multi-year extension of previously enacted middle-class tax breaks
Yes	Amend the Constitution to prohibit same-sex marriage
Yes	Cut corporate taxes $137 billion over 10 years
Yes	Reorganize U.S. intelligence agencies as proposed by Sept. 11 commission

2003
Yes	Cut taxes by $330 billion through fiscal 2013
No	Block Bush rule scaling back overtime pay for some white-collar federal workers
Yes	Do not allow use of search warrants without first notifying subjects
No	Allow importation of prescription drugs
Yes	Create private school voucher program in Washington, D.C.
Yes	Ban "partial birth" abortion except to save a woman's life
No	Split $18.6 billion in Iraq aid into half-grant, half-loan
Yes	Overhaul Medicare and create prescription drug benefit

CQ VOTE STUDIES

	PARTY UNITY		PRESIDENTIAL SUPPORT	
	Support	Oppose	Support	Oppose
2004	95%	5%	94%	6%
2003	98%	2%	98%	2%
2002	96%	4%	82%	18%
2001	99%	1%	100%	0%
2000	90%	10%	26%	74%

INTEREST GROUPS

	AFL-CIO	ADA	CCUS	ACU
2004	13%	5%	100%	88%
2003	0%	5%	100%	88%
2002	11%	0%	95%	100%
2001	9%	0%	100%	96%
2000	0%	0%	85%	75%

LOUISIANA 6

East central — Baton Rouge

Centered around the state capital of Baton Rouge, the socially conservative 6th takes in a slew of petrochemical plants along the Mississippi River as well as rural parishes along the Mississippi border. Baton Rouge's economic and population growth has spilled over into neighboring parishes, which attract commuters with superior schools and lower crime rates.

The decline of the domestic oil industry in the 1980s made Baton Rouge's government and university employees even more vital to the district's economy — Southern and Louisiana State universities are both located in the city. While oil and petrochemicals rebounded in the 1990s, local officials were concerned with the exodus of white-collar workers. A 1996 "Plan Baton Rouge" to redevelop downtown brought more tourism to the area — aided by the addition of two docked riverboat casinos. Although the port is no longer the centerpiece of the 6th's economy, it remains important.

Agriculture fuels the rural parishes on the outskirts of the district —

sugar cane is produced in the west, while the northeastern part is lined with paper mills and potato farms.

As in most of the South, socially conservative suburban and rural voters have shifted toward the GOP. But the minority and blue-collar residents of Baton Rouge still vote Democratic. Rounds of redistricting in the 1990s gave the 6th more and more of Baton Rouge, transforming it into a politically competitive district. Democrats fare well locally in the northern and western parts of the 6th, while East Baton Rouge, Livingston and Ascension parishes consistently vote Republican. George W. Bush received 59 percent of the district's vote in 2004.

MAJOR INDUSTRY
Government, higher education, petrochemicals

CITIES
Baton Rouge, 227,818; Shenandoah, 17,070; Baker, 13,793

NOTABLE
The state capitol, completed in 1932, is the tallest in the United States; Gov. Huey Long, who led the fight for the new capitol, was assassinated there in 1935 and is buried on the capitol grounds; The five-campus Southern University System is the only historically black university system in the country.

Rep. Charles Boustany Jr. (R)

Elected 2004; 1st term

Boustany, a surgeon, made a mid-life entry into politics at a high level, as his 2004 bid for the open 7th District House seat was his first run for public office.

Boustany (boo-STAN-knee) emphasizes his strongly conservative positions. His views on abortion place him to the right even within the conservative ranks of House Republicans: He says he is "100 percent pro-life" without exception.

He favors President Bush's pro-business agenda, including making permanent tax cuts for individuals and businesses that Bush signed into law during his first term. But he has criticized the Republican-controlled Congress for its deficit spending and said fiscal responsibility will be one of his key themes as a House member.

Boustany says he will work to make health care more accessible in one of the nation's poorest states. He advocates tax breaks to help people buy health care insurance and favors expanding the number of federally qualified clinics in rural Louisiana.

Boustany did not receive committee seats directly relevant to his background in health care, but he did get a couple of posts that apply to concerns back home. Representing a district that borders the Gulf of Mexico and faces coastal erosion problems, Boustany was named vice chairman of the Transportation and Infrastructure Subcommittee on Water Resources and Environment. His Agriculture Committee seat may play well with the farm constituency inland. He also serves on the Education and Workforce panel.

Boustany's win, in a region that had elected only Democrats to the House since 1884, was aided by a rift in Democratic ranks that arose in the primary. Boustany finished first in a five-way all-candidate primary and then beat conservative Democratic state Sen. Willie Landry Mount, by a 10 percentage point margin, in the Dec. 4 runoff to succeed Chris John, who left the House seat open to wage an unsuccessful bid for the Senate.

CAPITOL OFFICE
225-2031
www.house.gov/boustany
1117 Longworth 20515-1807; fax 225-5724

COMMITTEES
Agriculture
Education & Workforce
Transportation & Infrastructure

HOMETOWN
Lafayette

BORN
Feb. 21, 1956, Lafayette, La.

RELIGION
Episcopalian

FAMILY
Wife, Bridget Boustany; two children

EDUCATION
U. of Southwestern Louisiana, B.S. 1978 (biology); Louisiana State U., M.D. 1982

CAREER
Surgeon

POLITICAL HIGHLIGHTS
No previous office

ELECTION RESULTS

2004 GENERAL RUNOFF

Charles Boustany Jr. (R)	75,039	55.0%
Willie Landry Mount (D)	61,493	45.0%

2004 GENERAL

Charles Boustany Jr. (R)	105,761	38.6%
Willie Landry Mount (D)	69,079	25.2%
Don Cravins (D)	67,389	24.6%
David Thibodaux (R)	26,526	9.7%
Malcolm R. Carriere (D)	5,177	1.9%

LOUISIANA 7

Southwest — Lafayette, Lake Charles

Anchored by blue-collar Lake Charles in the west, white-collar Lafayette in the east and the Gulf of Mexico in the south, the 7th takes in both coastal and city life. A sizable Catholic citizenry bolsters the district's socially conservative leanings, and blacks make up one-fourth of the population.

The 7th's economy is firmly centered around agriculture and oil and gas production. After the statewide petroleum depression in the 1980s, local officials worked to diversify the economy. But with recovery in the 1990s, attention has refocused on the offshore and inland oil wells. The rural parishes between Lafayette and Lake Charles produce rice and soybeans. Rice farmers also have had success raising crawfish in fallow rice fields.

Dotted with waterfowl and wildlife refuges, the 7th's Gulf edge serves commercial and sports fishermen. Lake Charles, a refining and chemical-producing hub in Calcasieu Parish, offers a sharp industrial contrast to the district's coastal and rural areas.

Despite the 7th's conservative tenor, the area tended to vote for moderate Democrats, and, until 2004, had sent a Democrat to Congress in every election since 1884. Lafayette Parish, in the eastern part of the district, is the most Republican-leaning area.

Three stabs at redistricting in the 1990s did little to change the 7th, and changes following the 2000 census also left the district largely intact. George W. Bush captured 60 percent of the 7th's presidential vote in 2004.

MAJOR INDUSTRY
Agriculture, oil and gas, petrochemicals, fishing

CITIES
Lafayette, 110,257; Lake Charles, 71,757

NOTABLE
Former Gov. Edwin W. Edwards, who is Rep. Boustany's wife's uncle, represented the 7th; Rayne, the self-proclaimed frog capital of the world, hosts an annual frog festival.

Gov. John Baldacci (D)

First elected: 2002
Length of term: 4 years
Term expires: 1/07
Salary: $70,000
Phone: (207) 287-3531

Hometown: Bangor
Born: Jan. 30, 1955; Bangor, Maine
Religion: Roman Catholic
Family: Wife, Karen Baldacci; one child
Education: U. of Maine, B.A. 1986 (history)
Career: Restaurant operator
Political Highlights: Bangor City Council, 1978-81; Maine Senate, 1982-94; U.S. House, 1995-2003

Election Results:

2002 GENERAL

John Baldacci (D)	238,179	47.1%
Peter E. Cianchette (R)	209,496	41.5%
Jonathan K. Carter (GI)	46,903	9.3%
John M. Michael (I)	10,612	2.1%

Senate President Beth Edmonds (D)

(no lieutenant governor)
Phone: (207) 287-1500

STATE LEGISLATURE

Legislature: January-June in odd-numbered years; January-April in even-numbered years

House: 151 members, 2-year terms
2005 breakdown: 76D, 73R, 1I, 1 Green; 118 men, 33 women
Salary: $19,686/2-year term
Phone: (207) 287-1400

Senate: 35 members, 2-year terms
2005 breakdown: 19D, 16R; 24 men, 11 women
Salary: $19,686/2-year term
Phone: (207) 287-1540

STATE TERM LIMITS

Governor: 2 consecutive terms
House: 4 consecutive terms
Senate: 4 consecutive terms

URBAN STATISTICS

CITY	POPULATION
Portland	64,249
Lewiston	35,690
Bangor	31,473
South Portland	23,325
Auburn	23,203

REGISTERED VOTERS

Unaffiliated/others	40%
Democrat	31%
Republican	29%

POPULATION

2004 population (est.)	1,317,253
2000 population	1,274,923
1990 population	1,227,928
Percent change (1990-2000)	+3.8%
Rank among states (2004)	40
Median age	38.6
Born in state	67.3%
Foreign born	2.9%
Violent crime rate	110/100,000
Poverty level	10.9%
Federal workers	13,542
Military	10,200

REDISTRICTING

Maine retained its two House seats in reapportionment. Maine's constitution calls for redistricting in the third year of each decade and the state Supreme Judicial Court implemented a map on July 2, 2003.

MISCELLANEOUS

Web: www.maine.gov
Capital: Augusta
STATE ELECTION OFFICIAL
(207) 624-7650
DEMOCRATIC HEADQUARTERS
(207) 622-6233
REPUBLICAN HEADQUARTERS
(207) 622-6247

District Statistics

DIST.	2004 VOTE FOR PRESIDENT BUSH	KERRY	WHITE	BLACK	ASIAN	HISP	MEDIAN INCOME	WHITE COLLAR	BLUE COLLAR	SERVICE INDUSTRY	OVER 64	UNDER 18	COLLEGE EDUCATION	RURAL	SQ. MILES
1	43%	55%	96%	1%	1%	1%	$42,044	61%	24%	14%	14%	24%	28%	51%	3,535
2	46	52	97	0	0	1	$32,678	53	31	16	15	23	18	71	27,244
STATE	45	54	96	1	1	1	$37,240	57	27	15	14	24	23	60	30,862
U.S.	50.7	48.3	69	12	4	13	$41,994	60	25	15	12	26	24	21	3,537,438

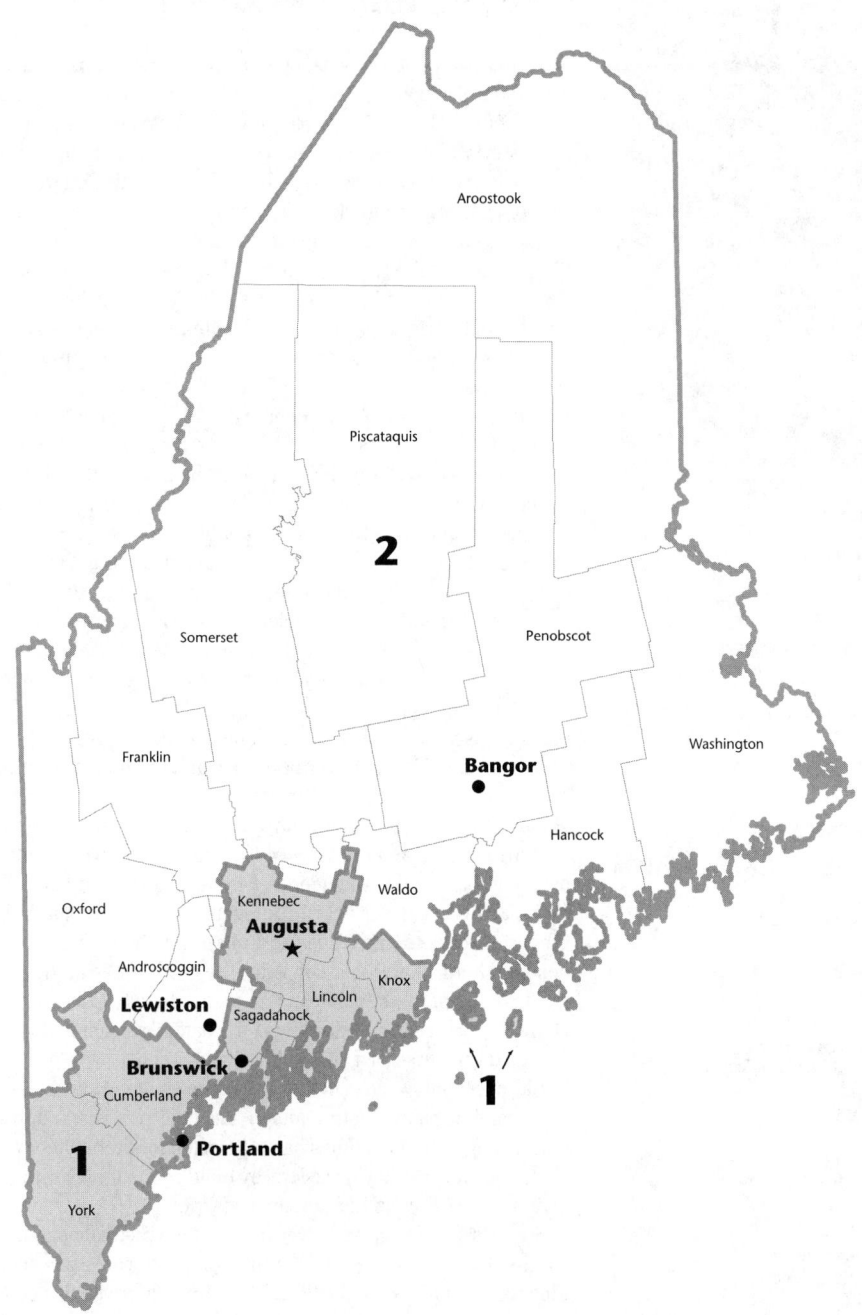

Sen. Olympia J. Snowe (R)

Elected 1994; 2nd term

CAPITOL OFFICE
224-5344
olympia@snowe.senate.gov
snowe.senate.gov
154 Russell 20510-1903; fax 224-1946

COMMITTEES
Commerce, Science & Transportation
  (Fisheries & the Coast Guard - chairwoman)
Finance
Small Business & Entrepreneurship - chairwoman
Select Intelligence

HOMETOWN
Falmouth

BORN
Feb. 21, 1947, Augusta, Maine

RELIGION
Greek Orthodox

FAMILY
Husband, John R. McKernan Jr.

EDUCATION
U. of Maine, B.A. 1969 (political science)

CAREER
Congressional district aide; city employee

POLITICAL HIGHLIGHTS
Maine House, 1973-77; Maine Senate, 1977-79;
U.S. House, 1979-95

ELECTION RESULTS

2000 GENERAL

Olympia J. Snowe (R)	437,689	68.9%
Mark Lawrence (D)	197,183	31.1%

2000 PRIMARY

Olympia J. Snowe (R)	unopposed

PREVIOUS WINNING PERCENTAGES
1994 (60%); 1992 House Election (49%); 1990 House
Election (51%); 1988 House Election (66%); 1986
House Election (77%); 1984 House Election (76%);
1982 House Election (67%); 1980 House Election
(79%); 1978 House Election (51%)

Snowe is one of the Senate's most powerful and influential centrists, a role she relishes and plays wisely. She has been a force on nearly every piece of major legislation in recent years, from tax cuts to homeland security. Her fiscally conservative and socially moderate priorities help determine whether Republicans are unified in the 109th Congress, with its infusion of conservative freshmen.

Snowe has served in Congress for more than a quarter of a century, winning election to the House in 1978 and then joining the Senate in 1995 after the GOP takeover. In that time, she says, she has watched her party drift steadily to the right, paying too little attention to deficits and too much to divisive social issues such as abortion. "To be a dominant Republican majority, we've got to have a mix of philosophies under the Republican majority," she said in 2004. "People don't live by ideology alone. They live by solutions. We've got to be relevant to the average American."

The rapidly escalating federal deficit has changed Snowe's thinking on tax cuts. When President Reagan slashed taxes in 1981, she says, the timing was right because the American public really was overtaxed. And when President Bush pushed his sweeping tax cut plan in 2001, Snowe played along, persuading her colleagues to broaden a provision on child tax credits. But by 2003, with deficit projections soaring, Snowe was one of the centrists who forced Congress to hold Bush's next tax cut to $350 billion.

And by the next year, she and other Senate Republican moderates were so insistent on applying pay-as-you-go rules to tax cuts — not just spending increases, as GOP leaders wanted — that Congress was unable to adopt its annual budget. "Cutting taxes and fighting for a balanced budget are now mutually exclusive," Snowe said. "That's what's changed. We've just shifted to the mantra of tax cuts at the expense of fiscal responsibility."

With a casual, approachable style, Snowe is known as a modest senator in a chamber filled with big egos. She is popular with her colleagues, and both parties court her heavily, knowing she is well-regarded. She enjoys preparing for committee hearings, often spending hours at the task. Aides describe her as tough but fair. After the GOP sweep in the 2004 elections, she was one of the Republicans most insistent that the party reach out to Democrats and compromise to get the nation's business done. "To do less, we run a great risk of a political backlash," she said.

Although Snowe does not always get everything she wants, she is often successful at slipping strategically targeted provisions into final legislation. Though she sometimes has to threaten to withhold her vote to prevail, she succeeds on many occasions by building coalitions with centrist Democrats and relying on her personal charm.

Snowe's knowledge and savvy have brought her national stature. She was the first Republican woman ever to sit on the Senate's powerful tax-writing Finance Committee. In the 2002 Miss America pageant, a contestant cited Snowe as a role model, along with Bush administration national security adviser Condoleezza Rice. Washingtonian Magazine in 2001 named her one of the city's 100 most powerful women.

As chairwoman of the Small Business Committee, Snowe wants to use her post to encourage female entrepreneurs and to pursue a wide-ranging legislative agenda. Over 90 percent of Maine's 37,000 employers are businesses with fewer than 20 employees. Snowe also chairs the Commerce Committee's panel on Fisheries and the Coast Guard, where a top priority of hers is the reauthorization of the Magnuson-Stevens fisheries conservation law. The law is important to Maine, with its 3,500 miles of coastline, and the state's fishing industry. Snowe also continues to look out for the interests of Bath Iron Works, the giant builder of Navy ships that is the state's largest employer.

Along with Democrat Joseph I. Lieberman of Connecticut, Snowe co-chairs the Centrist Coalition, a bipartisan group of senators who look for common ground on issues such as tax policy and campaign finance reform. She has pushed Republican leaders to focus more on the party's moderates, and has made clear to them that she thinks they could do a better job of reaching across the aisle.

She demonstrated her independence during tense negotiations on legislation to create a homeland security department. Snowe, fellow Maine Republican Susan Collins and Republican Lincoln Chafee of Rhode Island took issue with special-interest provisions in the bill to help shield vaccine manufacturers from lawsuits. The three withheld their votes for the bill until they won assurances from House and Senate GOP leaders that the provisions would be stripped from the law early in the 108th Congress, which they were.

Though she strongly supports abortion rights, Snowe tries to broker compromises with conservatives, joining with Democrats in seeking an alternative to the GOP's desired ban on a procedure opponents call "partial birth" abortion. She was unsuccessful and voted against the bill that Bush signed into law in 2003. She also has joined with Democrats on a proposal requiring federal workers' health insurance plans to pay for contraceptives. On environmental matters, she opposes drilling in Alaska's Arctic National Wildlife Refuge, like most Democrats, and wants to require that sport utility vehicles get better gas mileage.

Snowe arrived in the Senate in the election that gave control of both chambers of Congress to the GOP, and she was notable as the only newly elected Senate Republican moderate. But she also stood out for having a personal story as compelling as many of the military heroes she joined there.

The daughter of first- and second-generation Greek immigrants, Snowe was orphaned at age 9 and raised by an aunt and uncle in the small town of Auburn, Maine. She put herself on a political track early on, first as a campaign worker for Sen. Margaret Chase Smith in 1972 and for William S. Cohen's first campaign for the U.S. House the same year. She was married to state Rep. Peter Snowe and running Cohen's district office in Lewiston in 1973 when Peter was killed in an automobile accident. A month later, she was elected to succeed him in the state House. She won election to the Maine Senate in 1976, and two years later, won a close race to succeed Cohen in the U.S. House when Cohen moved on to the Senate.

While Snowe was representing the 2nd District, another personable moderate Republican, John R. McKernan Jr., won the 1st District seat in 1982. Four years later, he was elected to the first of two terms as governor. He won Snowe's heart along the way, and the two were married in 1989.

After winning election to the House, Snowe enjoyed a series of easy victories until 1990, when a deepening recession led to voter restlessness. She eventually defeated Democratic state Rep. Patrick K. McGowan, 51 percent to 49 percent. A 1992 rematch was even closer; she won with a 49 percent plurality.

Despite the close outcomes, Snowe was the presumed GOP nominee when Senate Majority Leader George J. Mitchell, a Democrat, announced his surprise retirement early in 1994. She prevailed with 60 percent of the vote. In 2000, she overwhelmed state Senate President Mark Lawrence with nearly 69 percent.

KEY VOTES

2004

Yes	Pass $318.9 billion, six-year highway and mass transit bill
Yes	Extend assault weapons ban for 10 years
Yes	Restore pay-as-you-go rules for new tax cuts and entitlement spending
No	Criminalize harm to a fetus in an attack on the mother
Yes	Increase mandatory child care funding to states by $6 billion over five years
No	Amend the Constitution to prohibit same-sex marriage
No	Approve $146 billion multi-year extension of previously enacted middle-class tax breaks
Yes	Reorganize U.S. intelligence agencies as proposed by Sept. 11 commission
Yes	Cut corporate taxes $137 billion over 10 years

2003

Yes	Delay Bush changes to Clean Air Act
Yes	Allow confirmation vote on Miguel A. Estrada to the U.S. Court of Appeals for the D.C. Circuit
Yes	Block a Bush proposal opening Alaska's Arctic National Wildlife Refuge to oil drilling
Yes	Limit size of Bush's proposed tax cut to $350 billion through fiscal 2013
Yes	Overhaul Medicare and create prescription drug benefit
Yes	Block Bush rule scaling back overtime pay for some white-collar federal workers
Yes	Split $20 billion in Iraq aid into half-grant, half-loan
No	Ban "partial birth" abortion except to save a woman's life
Yes	Stop proposal allowing travel to Cuba
No	Allow final vote on energy policy overhaul

CQ VOTE STUDIES

	PARTY UNITY		PRESIDENTIAL SUPPORT	
	Support	Oppose	Support	Oppose
2004	71%	29%	74%	26%
2003	75%	25%	82%	18%
2002	57%	43%	90%	10%
2001	64%	36%	84%	16%
2000	71%	29%	62%	38%
1999	69%	31%	49%	51%
1998	65%	35%	55%	45%
1997	59%	41%	78%	22%
1996	72%	28%	53%	47%
1995	70%	30%	42%	58%

INTEREST GROUPS

	AFL-CIO	ADA	CCUS	ACU
2004	67%	65%	71%	60%
2003	0%	55%	65%	45%
2002	31%	30%	85%	65%
2001	50%	40%	79%	60%
2000	0%	30%	73%	80%
1999	33%	45%	59%	60%
1998	38%	35%	78%	40%
1997	43%	55%	70%	44%
1996	29%	35%	77%	70%
1995	25%	40%	84%	39%

Sen. Susan Collins (R)

Elected 1996; 2nd term

Collins has managed to maintain her independent ways while never raising serious questions about her party loyalty. And in a Senate fraught with partisan tensions, she usually avoids the fray. Her well-earned reputation as a Republican centrist has brought her security at home in Maine, where political moderation is cherished and where Democrats are highly competitive.

In the 108th Congress, Majority Leader Bill Frist asked Collins to draft legislation in response to the Sept. 11 commission recommendation that the government overhaul its intelligence agencies. Democrats did not object, and Collins, who chairs the Homeland Security and Governmental Affairs Committee, joined forces with the panel's top-ranking Democrat, Joseph I. Lieberman of Connecticut, to develop legislation and shepherd it through Congress.

The two crafted a measure that included the new position of director of national intelligence to oversee the country's 15 spy agencies and compel them to share their intelligence about threats to national security. The bill passed the Senate 96-2 but clashed with a far different House version that proposed more-limited powers for the intelligence director. Collins assessed the split as nothing more than a turf battle, as House GOP conservatives loyal to the Pentagon sought to stop the measure. "The forces of the status quo are preventing change," Collins said as the bill lingered in legislative limbo. In the end, President Bush and top administration aides pushed Congress to act, and the measure passed in the final days of the 2004 session.

Collins was able to navigate skillfully the treacherous turf battles while moving the intelligence overhaul bill, but in 2005 she will face new skirmishes over the jurisdictional issues plaguing homeland security oversight. Her committee has been given some Department of Homeland Security responsibilities, but transportation security, the largest area, was assigned to the Commerce Committee.

As one of a handful of top Republican woman lawmakers, Collins increasingly finds herself showcased by her party's national leaders as they try to expand the appeal of the party to moderate and swing voters. Collins' growing stature was symbolized by her rise to the helm of Governmental Affairs in the 108th Congress. At the time, she was only the third woman in history to chair a permanent Senate committee.

Collins is not afraid to use her stature to question those in power. She has been critical of Defense Secretary Donald H. Rumsfeld's management of the war in Iraq. A member of the Armed Services Committee, Collins sent a toughly worded letter to Rumsfeld in late 2004, accusing the Pentagon of falling short in its efforts to build or refit armored vehicles. Noting that field commanders had received 5,910 of the 8,105 factory-armored Humvees they said they needed, Collins wrote: "The Department of Defense still has been unable to ensure that our troops have the equipment they need to perform their mission as safely as possible."

In her role as chairwoman of the Homeland Security panel, Collins will continue her focus on issues affecting government workers. She has championed legislation to improve protections for federal employees who expose fraud, waste and wrongdoing from inside the government. In the 108th, Collins moved two measures to benefit federal workers through Congress and onto Bush's desk. One bill, cosponsored with Democrat Daniel K. Akaka of Hawaii, gives federal employees broader access to dental and vision insur-

CAPITOL OFFICE
224-2523
collins.senate.gov
461 Dirksen 20510-1904; fax 224-2693

COMMITTEES
Armed Services
Homeland Security & Governmental Affairs - chairwoman
Special Aging

HOMETOWN
Bangor

BORN
Dec. 7, 1952, Caribou, Maine

RELIGION
Roman Catholic

FAMILY
Single

EDUCATION
St. Lawrence U., B.A. 1975 (government)

CAREER
Business center director; congressional aide

POLITICAL HIGHLIGHTS
Maine commissioner of financial regulation, 1987-91; Small Business Administration official, 1992-93; Maine deputy treasurer, 1993; Republican nominee for governor, 1994

ELECTION RESULTS

2002 GENERAL

Susan Collins (R)	295,041	58.4%
Chellie Pingree (D)	209,858	41.6%

2002 PRIMARY

Susan Collins (R)	unopposed

PREVIOUS WINNING PERCENTAGES
1996 (49%)

ance. The second gives federal workers more flexibility in using the federal retirement savings program. Early in 2005, Collins said she would prefer to see how new personnel systems at the departments of Defense and Homeland Security work before making changes at all federal agencies — as the Bush administration has said it would like to do.

Collins' strict attention to the nuts and bolts of governing is in keeping with her background as a former congressional aide and state regulator. She also has displayed shrewd political skills, winning concessions from conservatives when her support was critical to move a bill through the narrowly divided Congress.

Her approach served her well in the 107th Congress when the Democrats who then controlled the Senate were fighting the Bush administration over its proposal to create a Homeland Security Department with rules to limit civil service protections. Collins kept her vote closely guarded until she gained concessions from the White House on two major issues: labor rights and coastal resources.

She got a promise from the administration to set up a grievance process for workers denied union protections on national security grounds. She also won assurances that the Coast Guard's responsibilities for preventing terrorism would not diminish resources for fisheries oversight, boating safety and other functions vital to her coastal state. By conducting her negotiations discreetly and not publicly confronting the administration, she never raised doubts about her party loyalty.

On fiscal policy, Collins generally sides with the political right, in support of a balanced-budget constitutional amendment and a requirement that any increase in taxes be approved by a two-thirds majority vote of Congress. She has been skeptical of tax cut plans that threaten to impose long-range budget deficit pressures.

But on some social policies, Collins is likely to join fellow Maine Republican Sen. Olympia J. Snowe and other centrists who urge a go-slow approach. That resonates in a state where independents are the biggest voting bloc, and where Democratic registrants outnumber Republicans.

Politics is in Collins' blood: Both her parents served terms as mayor of the small northern Maine town of Caribou. Her father, grandfather, great-grandfather and great-great-grandfather served as Maine legislators. Collins visited the U.S. Capitol as a high school senior and spent two hours talking with a Republican woman trailblazer, Maine Sen. Margaret Chase Smith. "I remember leaving her office and thinking that if she can be in the Senate, women can do anything. It really was in some ways a transformational experience," Collins has said.

After college, Collins returned to Washington in the mid-1970s and worked for a dozen years as an adviser on business issues to Maine Republican Sen. William S. Cohen. She then served as commissioner of Maine's Department of Professional and Financial Regulation.

Collins' first venture as a political candidate was disappointing. She won the 1994 Republican nomination for governor but ran far behind victorious independent Angus King and Democratic nominee Joseph E. Brennan, a former governor and House member.

After Cohen announced that he would retire in 1996, Collins climbed back in the ring. A clearly improved campaigner, she won the GOP primary handily. In the general election, she faced Brennan. Collins defeated Brennan by 5 percentage points in a year in which Democrats won both of Maine's House districts and the presidential contest. In 2002, Collins focused on issues, such as health care, education and consumer protection, that have traditionally benefited Democrats, and easily beat challenger Chellie Pingree, a former state senator, by 17 points.

KEY VOTES

2004
Yes Pass $318.9 billion, six-year highway and mass transit bill
Yes Extend assault weapons ban for 10 years
Yes Restore pay-as-you-go rules for new tax cuts and entitlement spending
Yes Criminalize harm to a fetus in an attack on the mother
Yes Increase mandatory child care funding to states by $6 billion over five years
No   Amend the Constitution to prohibit same-sex marriage
Yes Approve $146 billion multi-year extension of previously enacted middle-class tax breaks
Yes Reorganize U.S. intelligence agencies as proposed by Sept. 11 commission
No   Cut corporate taxes $137 billion over 10 years

2003
Yes Delay Bush changes to Clean Air Act
Yes Allow confirmation vote on Miguel A. Estrada to the U.S. Court of Appeals for the D.C. Circuit
Yes Block a Bush proposal opening Alaska's Arctic National Wildlife Refuge to oil drilling
No   Limit size of Bush's proposed tax cut to $350 billion through fiscal 2013
Yes Overhaul Medicare and create prescription drug benefit
No   Block Bush rule scaling back overtime pay for some white-collar federal workers
Yes Split $20 billion in Iraq aid into half-grant, half-loan
No   Ban "partial birth" abortion except to save a woman's life
No   Stop proposal allowing travel to Cuba
No   Allow final vote on energy policy overhaul

CQ VOTE STUDIES

	PARTY UNITY		PRESIDENTIAL SUPPORT	
	Support	Oppose	Support	Oppose
2004	78%	22%	82%	18%
2003	78%	22%	87%	13%
2002	57%	43%	88%	12%
2001	67%	33%	88%	12%
2000	74%	26%	57%	42%
1999	74%	26%	49%	51%
1998	67%	33%	63%	37%
1997	61%	39%	76%	24%

INTEREST GROUPS

	AFL-CIO	ADA	CCUS	ACU
2004	50%	45%	94%	68%
2003	31%	45%	78%	35%
2002	31%	35%	85%	55%
2001	50%	35%	79%	64%
2000	0%	25%	80%	76%
1999	11%	25%	76%	64%
1998	38%	35%	78%	36%
1997	14%	50%	80%	48%

Rep. Tom Allen (D)

Elected 1996; 5th term

An articulate and attractive spokesman for liberal Democrats, Allen has a knack for being at the center of particularly contentious debates. His new spot on the Budget Committee in the 109th Congress lets him add tax and spending issues to a list that already includes health care, education and clean air policy.

Allen joined the committee just as the White House and Congress began grappling with the consequences of $400 billion-plus annual budget deficits blamed on tax cuts, an economic downturn, the war in Iraq and post-Sept. 11 homeland security spending. The squeeze is certain to mean yearlong battles over spending priorities, with the first round each year being fought in the Budget panel.

Maine is a poor state with an older population, so, with the other three members of the state's small delegation, Allen fights fiercely to preserve federal programs that provide assistance and jobs. Two of the most important are the Medicaid program and shipbuilding contracts for Bath Iron Works and the Portsmouth Naval Shipyard in nearby New Hampshire.

As a member of the Energy and Commerce Committee, which has jurisdiction over both Medicaid and Medicare, Allen is frequently at the fore of health care policy fights. He regards the high cost of prescription drugs as his signature issue and is involved in a bipartisan effort to allow imports of U.S.-made prescription drugs from foreign countries, where they are often cheaper because of government price controls. Allen also opposed President Bush's Medicare prescription drug measure in 2003, arguing that the plan should have allowed the government to use its leverage as a large purchaser of drugs to bargain with pharmaceutical companies for lower prices.

Allen says the importance of the drug-cost issue became clear to him at a town meeting in 1997, during his first term. After a retired firefighter spoke about his $300 monthly bill for prescription drugs, Allen enlisted the Democratic staff of the Government Reform Committee, where he served, to investigate. The panel's subsequent reports were among the earliest to show that senior citizens without prescription plans often spent a large portion of their income on medicines.

In 2003, Allen joined the fight over education spending with an amendment that suspended the president's No Child Left Behind policy until the law was fully funded. Allen's proposal was defeated during debate on a schools spending bill. But it served to highlight Democrats' claims that without enough money to help troubled schools, the new testing requirements aimed at helping low-income children catch up with their more affluent peers would be meaningless.

As a member of the Energy Committee's Energy and Air Quality Subcommittee, Allen is positioned to tackle another of Maine's chief concerns, air pollution. Prevailing winds blow much of the air pollution produced in the Midwest to New England, especially to Maine, and lawmakers of both parties tend to be surprisingly united in demanding tough regulations. Allen wants Congress to defeat Bush's "Clear Skies" initiative, which he says is weaker than current law. Allen is also a leader in efforts to overturn EPA rules, issued in 2005, regulating mercury emissions from power plants. He argues that the crackdown on mercury must be far tougher because of the health risks it poses to children and women of child-bearing age.

His liberalism did not prevent Allen from embracing more-hawkish posi-

CAPITOL OFFICE
225-6116
rep.tomallen@mail.house.gov
www.house.gov/allen
1127 Longworth 20515-1901; fax 225-5590

COMMITTEES
Budget
Energy & Commerce

HOMETOWN
Portland

BORN
April 16, 1945, Portland, Maine

RELIGION
Protestant

FAMILY
Wife, Diana Allen; two children

EDUCATION
Bowdoin College, B.A. 1967 (English); Oxford U., B.Phil. 1970 (Rhodes scholar); Harvard U., J.D. 1974

CAREER
Policy consultant; lawyer; congressional aide

POLITICAL HIGHLIGHTS
Portland City Council, 1989-95 (mayor, 1991-92); sought Democratic nomination for governor, 1994

ELECTION RESULTS

2004 GENERAL
Tom Allen (D)	219,077	59.7%
Charles E. Summers Jr. (R)	147,663	40.3%

2004 PRIMARY
Tom Allen (D)	unopposed

2002 GENERAL
Tom Allen (D)	172,646	63.8%
Steven Joyce (R)	97,931	36.2%

PREVIOUS WINNING PERCENTAGES
2000 (60%); 1998 (60%); 1996 (55%)

tions on the Armed Services Committee, where he spent his first three terms. His district includes the Bath Iron Works, Maine's largest private employer and one of the six commercial shipyards in the nation building vessels for the Navy. Like more-conservative members from other ship-building districts, Allen says the Bush administration is buying too few ships to meet the goal of keeping a fleet of more than 300 vessels.

Allen also is fighting to stave off potential closures of two locally important facilities, a Navy air base in Brunswick and the Portsmouth Naval Shipyard in Kittery.

On the biggest defense issue of the day, Allen sides with other Democrats in opposing the war in Iraq, which he calls "a major miscalculation" by the Bush administration. He also opposes Bush's push to deploy a nationwide anti-missile defense system.

Allen cut his teeth on one of the hottest issues before Congress in the past decade — campaign finance. As co-chairman of the freshman task force on the issue in the 105th Congress (1997-1998), Allen pushed to ban "soft money," the unlimited contributions that were becoming a dominant force in federal elections. Allen stayed active in the cause, generally behind the scenes, until changes to campaign finance law were enacted in 2002, with a ban on soft money at the core.

Allen comes from a political family. His father and grandfather were both on the Portland City Council, and his mother was active in politics as well. He was an exceptional student, a Rhodes scholar who went on to get a law degree from Harvard. During his college years, Allen worked in 1970 for Democratic Sen. Edmund S. Muskie, both on a campaign in Maine and on Muskie's Senate staff.

After practicing law for almost 20 years in Portland, Allen's first elective office was as a member of the Portland City Council, where he served for six years, including one year as the council-elected mayor. Allen chaired Bill Clinton's presidential campaign in Maine in 1992 and was an adviser on agriculture issues during Clinton's transition.

After an unsuccessful 1994 bid for the Democratic gubernatorial nomination, Allen in 1996 challenged freshman GOP Rep. James B. Longley Jr. With a million-dollar assist from the AFL-CIO, the Sierra Club and other groups that ran campaign ads in his behalf, Allen mobilized core Democratic supporters while successfully tying Longley to the "extreme" Republican "Contract With America" agenda. He won by 11 percentage points. He has won by at least 20 points three times since, and barely missed that mark in the 2004 race.

KEY VOTES

2004

Yes Extend federal unemployment benefits by 13 weeks

Yes Pass $283.2 billion, six-year federal highway and mass transit bill

Yes Approve $146 billion multi-year extension of previously enacted middle-class tax breaks

No Amend the Constitution to prohibit same-sex marriage

No Cut corporate taxes $137 billion over 10 years

Yes Reorganize U.S. intelligence agencies as proposed by Sept. 11 commission

2003

No Cut taxes by $330 billion through fiscal 2013

Yes Block Bush rule scaling back overtime pay for some white-collar federal workers

Yes Do not allow use of search warrants without first notifying subjects

Yes Allow importation of prescription drugs

No Create private school voucher program in Washington, D.C.

No Ban "partial birth" abortion except to save a woman's life

No Split $18.6 billion in Iraq aid into half-grant, half-loan

No Overhaul Medicare and create prescription drug benefit

CQ VOTE STUDIES

	PARTY UNITY		PRESIDENTIAL SUPPORT	
	Support	Oppose	Support	Oppose
2004	95%	5%	41%	59%
2003	95%	5%	20%	80%
2002	95%	5%	36%	64%
2001	96%	4%	28%	72%
2000	94%	6%	84%	16%

INTEREST GROUPS

	AFL-CIO	ADA	CCUS	ACU
2004	93%	100%	38%	8%
2003	100%	95%	30%	12%
2002	100%	95%	53%	0%
2001	100%	95%	30%	0%
2000	90%	85%	52%	4%

MAINE 1
South — Portland, Augusta

Rural oceanfront property draws residents to the 1st, a district incorporating the southern reaches of Maine that are also bustling with new technology jobs. Residents of Maine's largest city, Portland, are moving into outlying areas, replacing farmland and uninterrupted forests with single-family homes.

Although textile- and shoe-manufacturing plants have been downsized or closed, a high-tech boom has kept unemployment low. Companies seeking a strong infrastructure and a high quality of life have moved to southern Maine, where Interstate 95 offers a straight shot to Boston. Well-to-do and largely seasonal residents live on the coast, where former President George Bush travels for retreats at his Kennebunkport estate.

Tourism is important in the lower part of the state, as residents from across New England and Canada head to popular beaches and shopping areas along the York County coast. The military's influence also is strong in the 1st.

The district's traditional Yankee Republican tendencies have given way over the years to a more solidly Democratic voting preference in presidential elections. In 2004, voters in the 1st favored John Kerry by 12 percentage points. On the local level, divisions between Democrats and Republicans are few. But the lack of party strength has not translated into lower rates of political participation. Two-thirds of the state's voting age population turned out in the last presidential election, one of the highest rates in the nation.

MAJOR INDUSTRY
Military shipbuilding, fishing, technology, tourism

MILITARY BASES
Portsmouth Naval Shipyard, 115 military, 5,008 civilian; Brunswick Naval Air Station, 4,008 military, 702 civilian (2004)

CITIES
Portland, 64,249; South Portland, 23,324; Biddeford, 20,942; Augusta, 18,560; Saco, 16,822; Westbrook, 16,142

NOTABLE
Portland businessman Neal Dow, the "father of prohibition," helped push through the 1851 "Maine Law," which banned the sale of liquor in Maine; Dow was the Prohibition Party's presidential candidate in 1880.

Rep. Michael H. Michaud (D)

Elected 2002; 2nd term

CAPITOL OFFICE
225-6306
www.house.gov/michaud
437 Cannon 20515-1902; fax 225-2943

COMMITTEES
Small Business
Transportation & Infrastructure
Veterans' Affairs

HOMETOWN
East Millinocket

BORN
Jan. 18, 1955, Millinocket, Maine

RELIGION
Roman Catholic

FAMILY
Single

EDUCATION
Schenck H.S., graduated 1973

CAREER
Paper mill worker

POLITICAL HIGHLIGHTS
Maine House, 1981-94; Maine Senate, 1995-2002
(president, 2001)

ELECTION RESULTS

2004 GENERAL

Michael H. Michaud (D)	199,303	58.0%
Brian N. Hamel (R)	135,547	39.5%
Carl Cooley (SE)	8,586	2.5%

2004 PRIMARY

Michael H. Michaud (D)	unopposed

2002 GENERAL

Michael H. Michaud (D)	116,868	52.0%
Kevin L. Raye (R)	107,849	48.0%

Most members of Congress claim to be on the side of the working man in America, but Michaud is one of the few who can say he's actually been one. He was a union card-carrying paper mill worker for three decades before being elected to the House in 2002.

While many of his House colleagues were pursuing their college degrees, Michaud (ME-shoo) was punching a clock at the Great Northern Paper Co. in Millinocket, Maine. From that experience comes a political orientation strongly in favor of worker protections and greater government involvement in paying for health care as well as a deep skepticism of globalized trade, which he blames for the loss of thousands of good-paying jobs in his home state.

The importance of those issues to his district was evident in Michaud's first term. Three days after he was sworn in, the Great Northern company filed for bankruptcy protection and shuttered its two paper mills, including the one in East Millinocket, where Michaud and three generations of Michauds had worked. His first weeks as a congressman were consumed by the fallout from the surge in unemployment in the district. He cosponsored a bill to extend the length of federal unemployment assistance and to boost the tax deductibility of health care costs. Michaud also helped get $900,000 for the Millinocket Regional Hospital to treat uninsured workers.

His background makes him an important symbol for House Democrats on labor issues. In 2004, party leaders chose him to lead opposition on the floor to a Bush administration initiative limiting some workers' eligibility for overtime pay. The same year, Michaud introduced a bill to improve benefits provided in the Trade Adjustment Assistance program by allowing workers to be reimbursed with a refundable tax credit for 100 percent of their health care costs rather than 65 percent.

With other Democrats, he opposes the proliferation of free trade deals and blames the 1993 North American Free Trade Agreement, which liberalized trade with Mexico, for a steep decline in Maine's manufacturing base and unemployment rates of 30 percent in some parts of the state. "If there is one thing America cannot afford to keep getting wrong, it is trade," Michaud says. He has introduced a bill to repeal fast-track authority, which allows the president to enter into trade deals that Congress must approve or reject but may not amend.

Though he votes with Democrats most of the time, Michaud departs on abortion rights. He opposes abortion except to save the life of the woman. He is one of the few Democrats from the North to affiliate with the "Blue Dogs," a coalition of conservative Democrats.

His major area of interest is health care, especially spiraling drug prices. In the 108th Congress, Michaud introduced a bill to nationalize a policy he helped create in Maine while he was in the state legislature. Known as America Rx, it calls for the federal government to negotiate lower prices for prescription drugs. Congress soundly rejected similar ideas in 2003 when it passed President Bush's prescription drug plan for seniors enrolled in Medicare, after a lengthy debate about whether the government should use its buying power to secure lower prices from drug companies. Michaud was among the members of Congress who protested high prices by crossing into Canada from his border state with seniors taking advantage of the lower prices in that country.

Important local issues for Michaud include the environment and border security. He fought to stop proposed cuts in funding for the Forest Legacy program, which helps states protect forest areas from development. From his seat on the Transportation and Infrastructure Committee, he has worked to get more funding for border security, a big state concern. He helped secure money to build Border Patrol stations in Calais and Madawaska, which is expected to alleviate traffic congestion and improve security.

Michaud grew up in the small rural town of Medway, close to the mill. After graduating from high school in 1973, he considered college to study criminal justice, thinking he'd become a state trooper. But Great Northern beckoned with good wages and health benefits, and Michaud followed in the steps of his father, who had worked at the mill for over 40 years, and his grandfather, who had worked there most of his life. Michaud's five siblings had also pulled shifts at the company at different times in their lives. Michaud became a paper finisher, working on the final stages of papermaking at the mill. He remains a member of PACE Local #1-0037.

Michaud decided to run for the state legislature because of his concern for the polluting of the Penobscot River — which his employer contributed to. In 1980, he ran successfully for a seat in the Maine House, taking advantage of a clause in his union contract that allowed workers to keep their jobs while serving in the legislature. He worked at the mill when the legislature was not in session, and when it was, he chaired the Environment Committee and wrote bills to clean up the river.

His political career prospered. Michaud served seven terms in the House, then ran for the Maine Senate in 1994. He eventually moved up to chair the budget-writing committee, giving him a hand in drafting two state budgets that cut taxes while also mandating a big boost in education spending, including money for what is now called the Michael H. Michaud Technology Center at the University of Maine. When he became Senate president, he took a leave of absence from the mill.

In 2002, Democratic Rep. John Baldacci ran successfully for governor, leaving open the 2nd District seat. Michaud's support from organized labor helped him eke out a narrow victory over Republican Kevin L. Raye, former chief of staff for Olympia J. Snowe, who represented the district from 1979 to 1995 and is now Maine's senior senator.

In 2004, Michaud won re-election by a wide margin against Brian N. Hamel, director of a group redeveloping the defunct Loring Air Force Base. Michaud's job was made easier after state courts sanctioned a redistricting plan that left the district lines largely intact. A competing Republican plan would have made it more difficult for Michaud to defend his seat.

KEY VOTES

2004

Yes Extend federal unemployment benefits by 13 weeks
Yes Pass $283.2 billion, six-year federal highway and mass transit bill
Yes Approve $146 billion multi-year extension of previously enacted middle-class tax breaks
No Amend the Constitution to prohibit same-sex marriage
No Cut corporate taxes $137 billion over 10 years
Yes Reorganize U.S. intelligence agencies as proposed by Sept. 11 commission

2003

No Cut taxes by $330 billion through fiscal 2013
Yes Block Bush rule scaling back overtime pay for some white-collar federal workers
Yes Do not allow use of search warrants without first notifying subjects
Yes Allow importation of prescription drugs
No Create private school voucher program in Washington, D.C.
Yes Ban "partial birth" abortion except to save a woman's life
Yes Split $18.6 billion in Iraq aid into half-grant, half-loan
No Overhaul Medicare and create prescription drug benefit

CQ VOTE STUDIES

	PARTY UNITY		PRESIDENTIAL SUPPORT	
	Support	Oppose	Support	Oppose
2004	88%	12%	38%	62%
2003	90%	10%	31%	69%

INTEREST GROUPS

	AFL-CIO	ADA	CCUS	ACU
2004	93%	90%	48%	20%
2003	100%	95%	40%	40%

MAINE 2
North – Lewiston, Bangor, Presque Isle

Millions of acres of trees surround the small towns of northern Maine's 2nd, one of the most politically independent districts in the nation. The largest district in a state east of the Mississippi, the 2nd attracts millions of visitors to Acadia National Park, Baxter State Park and Maine's many lakes and ski resorts.

A billion-dollar lobster industry dominates the east coast, and the timber industry reigns in the rest of the 2nd. Sparsely populated in parts, the region is less wealthy than the 1st, which has benefited from technology jobs. Aroostook County, on the Canadian border, lost more than 10,000 people after Loring Air Force Base closed in the 1990s, although revitalization efforts have brought 1,000 new jobs to the 8,700-acre base.

As the national economy has become more service-based, the 2nd has felt the pinch. Manufacturing jobs, especially in shoes and textiles, have gone overseas, and residents are heading south for jobs. Farming is in decline as well, though the district remains one of the largest producers of potatoes and blueberries in the country.

Redistricting prior to the 2004 election made the 2nd slightly more Democratic by adding part of Kennebec County, including Waterville, an aging manufacturing town that is now shifting to a service-based economy.

A weak party system throughout the state and a higher proportion of rural voters have helped make the 2nd the more competitive of Maine's two congressional districts. Voters here gave a 6 percentage point edge to John Kerry in the 2004 presidential election — one-half of the advantage he enjoyed in the 1st District. Crossing party lines is common, and in 1992, the 2nd gave Ross Perot more votes than George Bush in the presidential election.

MAJOR INDUSTRY
Logging, fishing, textiles, tourism, agriculture, higher education

CITIES
Lewiston, 35,690; Bangor, 31,473; Auburn, 23,203; Waterville, 15,605; Presque Isle, 9,511

NOTABLE
Author Stephen King lives in Bangor; Abraham Lincoln's first vice president, Hannibal Hamlin, was born in Paris Hill; E.B. White, author of "Charlotte's Web" and "Stuart Little," lived on a farm in North Brooklin.

MARYLAND

Gov. Robert L. Ehrlich Jr. (R)

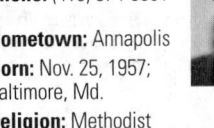

First elected: 2002
Length of term: 4 years
Term expires: 1/07
Salary: $145,000
Phone: (410) 974-3901

Hometown: Annapolis
Born: Nov. 25, 1957;
Baltimore, Md.
Religion: Methodist
Family: Wife, Kendel Sibiski Ehrlich;
two children
Education: Princeton U., A.B. 1979; Wake
Forest U., J.D. 1982
Career: Lawyer
Political highlights: Md. House, 1987-95;
U.S. House, 1995-2003

Election results:
2002 GENERAL
Robert L. Ehrlich Jr. (R) 879,592 51.6%
Kathleen Kennedy Townsend (D) 813,422 47.7%

Lt. Gov. Michael S. Steele (R)

First elected: 2002
Length of term: 4 years
Term expires: 1/07
Salary: $116,667
Phone: (410) 974-3901

STATE LEGISLATURE

General Assembly: 90 days
January-April

House: 141 members, 4-year terms
2005 breakdown: 98D, 43R; 92 men,
49 women
Salary: $40,500
Phone: (410) 841-3800

Senate: 47 members, 4-year terms
2005 breakdown: 33D, 14R; 32 men,
15 women
Salary: $40,500
Phone: (410) 841-3700

STATE TERM LIMITS

Governor: 2 terms
House: No
Senate: No

URBAN STATISTICS

CITY	POPULATION
Baltimore	651,154
Frederick	52,767
Gaithersburg	52,613
Bowie	50,269
Rockville	47,388

REGISTERED VOTERS

Democrat	55%
Republican	29%
Unaffiliated/others	15%

POPULATION

2004 population (est.)	5,558,058
2000 population	5,296,486
1990 population	4,781,468
Percent change (1990-2000)	+10.8%
Rank among states (2004)	19

Median age	36
Born in state	49.3%
Foreign born	9.8%
Violent crime rate	787/100,000
Poverty level	8.5%
Federal workers	151,044
Military	50,137

REDISTRICTING

Maryland retained its eight House
seats in reapportionment. The state
legislature drew a new map, which
the governor signed on May 6, 2002.

MISCELLANEOUS

Web: www.maryland.gov
Capital: Annapolis
STATE ELECTION OFFICIAL
(410) 269-2840
DEMOCRATIC
HEADQUARTERS
(410) 269-8818
REPUBLICAN
HEADQUARTERS
(410) 269-0113

District Statistics

DIST.	2004 VOTE FOR PRESIDENT BUSH	KERRY	WHITE	BLACK	ASIAN	HISP	MEDIAN INCOME	WHITE COLLAR	BLUE COLLAR	SERVICE INDUSTRY	OVER 64	UNDER 18	COLLEGE EDUCATION	RURAL	SQ. MILES
1	62%	36%	85%	11%	1%	2%	$51,918	63%	23%	14%	13%	25%	27%	36%	3,653
2	45	54	66	27	2	2	$44,309	61	23	15	12	26	20	2	355
3	45	54	76	16	3	3	$52,906	72	16	12	13	23	37	1	293
4	21	78	28	57	6	8	$57,727	71	15	14	7	28	33	2	315
5	42	57	60	30	4	3	$62,661	68	19	13	9	26	29	25	1,504
6	65	34	92	5	1	1	$50,957	61	24	14	12	26	24	39	3,062
7	26	73	34	59	4	2	$38,885	67	16	17	12	26	28	5	294
8	30	69	56	16	11	14	$68,306	77	11	12	12	24	54	1	297
STATE	43	56	62	28	4	4	$52,868	68	18	14	11	26	31	14	9,774
U.S.	50.7	48.3	69	12	4	13	$41,994	60	25	15	12	26	24	21	3,537,438

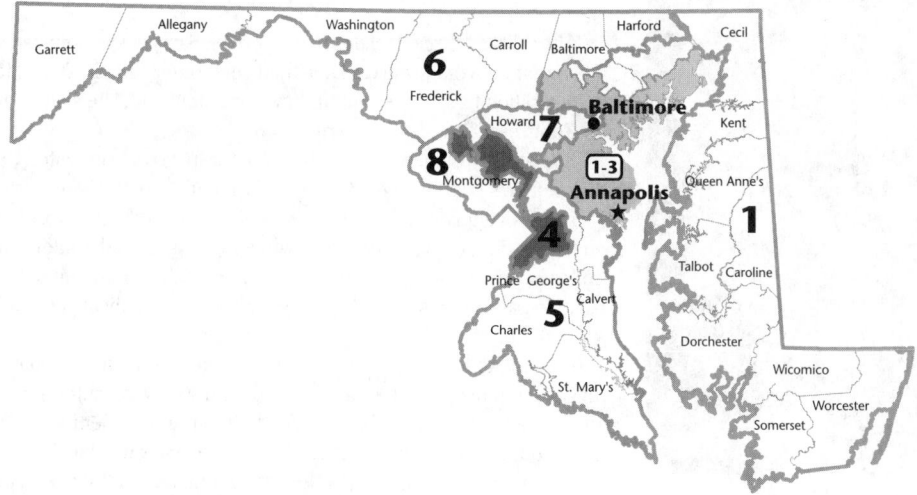

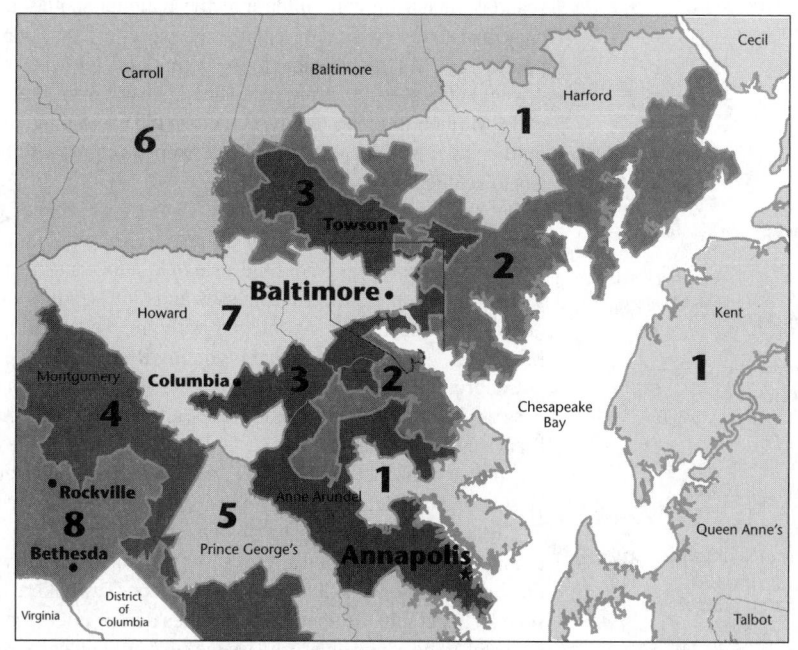

Sen. Paul S. Sarbanes (D)

Elected 1976; 5th term

CAPITOL OFFICE
224-4524
sarbanes.senate.gov
309 Hart 20510-2002; fax 224-1651

COMMITTEES
Banking, Housing & Urban Affairs - ranking
  member
Budget
Foreign Relations
Joint Economic

HOMETOWN
Baltimore

BORN
Feb. 3, 1933, Salisbury, Md.

RELIGION
Greek Orthodox

FAMILY
Wife, Christine Sarbanes; three children

EDUCATION
Princeton U., A.B. 1954 (public & international
affairs); Oxford U., B.A. 1957 (Rhodes scholar);
Harvard U., LL.B. 1960

CAREER
Lawyer; White House aide

POLITICAL HIGHLIGHTS
Md. House, 1967-71; U.S. House, 1971-77

ELECTION RESULTS

2000 GENERAL

Paul S. Sarbanes (D)	1,230,013	63.2%
Paul Rappaport (R)	715,178	36.7%

2000 PRIMARY

Paul S. Sarbanes (D)	384,748	83.2%
George English (D)	45,984	10.0%
Sidney Altman (D)	31,502	6.8%

PREVIOUS WINNING PERCENTAGES
1994 (59%); 1988 (62%); 1982 (64%); 1976 (57%);
1974 House Election (84%); 1972 House Election
(70%); 1970 House Election (70%)

After almost three decades in the Senate, Sarbanes announced in March 2005 that he would retire rather than seek re-election in 2006. "It was not my ambition to stay there until they carried me out," he said of his tenure in Congress. "It was just the right time."

Sarbanes is the longest-serving senator in Maryland history, and he is the Senate's sixth-most-senior Democrat in the 109th Congress.

In his five terms, Sarbanes has lived comfortably in a world of precise details and quiet insistence. And while he possesses the intellectual skills to leave opponents sputtering, he generally shows little appetite for legislative gamesmanship, relying instead on a methodical approach to policy making.

A liberal to his core, Sarbanes was the only Democratic senator in 2004 to side with his party 100 percent of the time on votes pitting most Democrats against most Republicans. As the top-ranking member of the Banking, Housing and Urban Affairs Committee, Sarbanes has been a no-frills legislator and an authority on the arcane nuances of finance. A noted academic with degrees from Princeton, Oxford and Harvard, Sarbanes is more at home in the substance of an issue than with the political and publicity-seeking displays of some of his better-known colleagues.

His workhorse style suits the Banking panel, where incremental steps are the norm. It can yield results, too. In 2002, the Enron Corp. accounting scandal thrust the committee into the national spotlight. Sarbanes was chairman at the time and the sponsor of sweeping legislation to combat corporate fraud. As the bill came to the committee, lobbyists were convinced it would at best win narrow, party-line approval from the majority Democrats. Momentum for a tough regulatory bill was fading, and Republicans on the panel had delayed the bill and were working with business lobbyists to scuttle it altogether.

But the legislation was approved, 17-4, after Sarbanes did something increasingly rare in the modern Congress. Not only did he strike a late-night deal by reaching across the aisle to Republicans, he did so with such stealth that both K Street businesses and GOP leaders were caught off-guard. He also quietly negotiated with the Senate's only accountant, Michael B. Enzi, a conservative Wyoming Republican.

Congress ultimately passed the bill that has come to be known in the business world as the Sarbanes-Oxley rules, after its Senate sponsor and Republican House sponsor Michael G. Oxley of Ohio. It imposed new rules on accounting firms that audit publicly traded companies and mandated new disclosure and conflict-of-interest reporting requirements for companies.

The strategy in that legislative battle epitomized Sarbanes, whom the Baltimore Sun once described as the "silver fox" and someone who works "quietly but with shrewd skillfulness." While other lawmakers used the Enron scandal to get into the spotlight, Sarbanes quietly undertook a painstaking series of 10 hearings on arcane issues surrounding corporate governance and accounting.

In 2004, Sarbanes resisted a GOP House effort to prevent new controls on stock options from taking effect. The House measure would have blocked a Financial Accounting Standards Board rule to require companies to account for stock options as an expense, which could lead some firms to report losses instead of gains on their income statements. Technology companies, which often compensate workers with stock options, wanted the bill. But Sarbanes said the independence of the accounting standards board was vital to ensuring the integrity of corporate financial reports.

When he announced his intention to retire in 2006, Sarbanes said he first intended to wrap up some unfinished business. He said he would work over the remaining 22 months of his Senate career "to oppose the tragic and misguided policies of this administration, especially the current radical attempt to undermine the Social Security system."

And, as a senior member of the Foreign Relations Committee, Sarbanes in 2005 said he had "serious reservations" about the nomination of John R. Bolton to be the U.S. ambassador to the United Nations. Sarbanes and other Democrats said Bolton's nomination broadcasts the wrong message to other countries about the White House's willingness to practice multilateralism. Bolton has been an outspoken critic of the United Nations.

For someone with a long career in politics, Sarbanes has often appeared uninterested in campaigning. He can come off as diffident in dealing with his colleagues and prickly in his relations with advocacy groups. He usually has little use for media attention. But he is a straightforward Democratic vote, a signature advantage in a state with nearly twice as many Democrats as Republicans.

Nor did Sarbanes' detached manner hurt him at the voting booth as he worked throughout his tenure to keep federal jobs in the state, improve public housing programs and ensure the privacy of personal financial information — all issues important to his constituents. Sarbanes earns high marks for his attention to local issues, too, such as protection of the Chesapeake Bay. In 2004, Sarbanes and Republican Rep. Wayne T. Gilchrest took on GOP Gov. Robert L. Ehrlich Jr., questioning Ehrlich's plan to introduce Asian oysters into the bay to replace native oysters.

Democratic leaders have acknowledged that Sarbanes' low-octane reputation can come in handy on partisan issues. In 1987, he was selected for the panel investigating the Iran-contra arms-for-hostages scandal. In 1995, he was the top Democrat on the Senate Whitewater Committee, where he challenged Republican Alfonse M. D'Amato of New York at every opportunity.

Minority Leader Harry Reid in the 109th Congress detailed Sarbanes to a new job in the leadership. He serves as chairman of a "ranking member outreach" team, designed to speak on behalf of the party's senior members on the Senate committees.

The son of Greek immigrant parents, Sarbanes grew up on Maryland's Eastern Shore, went to Princeton and won a Rhodes scholarship to Oxford. After graduating from Harvard Law School in 1960 — where he befriended Michael S. Dukakis, the 1988 Democratic presidential nominee — Sarbanes practiced law briefly before jumping into public life as an administrative assistant in President Kennedy's Council of Economic Advisers. He practiced law again and won a state House seat in 1966.

Running as an anti-war, anti-machine insurgent, Sarbanes headed for Congress in 1970 by winning a primary challenge to Democratic Rep. George H. Fallon, the aging chairman of the Public Works Committee, who had represented Baltimore in the House for 13 terms. With Democrats enjoying a nearly 4-to-1 registration advantage in the multiethnic 4th District, Sarbanes won the seat with ease in the fall.

He moved to the Senate by unseating one-term Republican J. Glenn Beall Jr. in 1976. Republicans put Sarbanes on their 1982 target list, but he raised money aggressively and state GOP leaders failed to enlist a big-name challenger. In 1988, he trounced Alan L. Keyes, a former State Department official and more recently a presidential candidate. In 1994, Sarbanes defeated national GOP Chairman Bill Brock. And in 2000, he triumphed easily over Republican attorney Paul Rappaport.

KEY VOTES

2004

Yes Pass $318.9 billion, six-year highway and mass transit bill
Yes Extend assault weapons ban for 10 years
Yes Restore pay-as-you-go rules for new tax cuts and entitlement spending
No Criminalize harm to a fetus in an attack on the mother
Yes Increase mandatory child care funding to states by $6 billion over five years
No Amend the Constitution to prohibit same-sex marriage
Yes Approve $146 billion multi-year extension of previously enacted middle-class tax breaks
Yes Reorganize U.S. intelligence agencies as proposed by Sept. 11 commission
No Cut corporate taxes $137 billion over 10 years

2003

Yes Delay Bush changes to Clean Air Act
No Allow confirmation vote on Miguel A. Estrada to the U.S. Court of Appeals for the D.C. Circuit
Yes Block a Bush proposal opening Alaska's Arctic National Wildlife Refuge to oil drilling
Yes Limit size of Bush's proposed tax cut to $350 billion through fiscal 2013
No Overhaul Medicare and create prescription drug benefit
Yes Block Bush rule scaling back overtime pay for some white-collar federal workers
Yes Split $20 billion in Iraq aid into half-grant, half-loan
No Ban "partial birth" abortion except to save a woman's life
No Stop proposal allowing travel to Cuba
No Allow final vote on energy policy overhaul

CQ VOTE STUDIES

	PARTY UNITY		PRESIDENTIAL SUPPORT	
	Support	Oppose	Support	Oppose
2004	100%	0%	59%	41%
2003	99%	1%	46%	54%
2002	98%	2%	65%	35%
2001	99%	1%	63%	37%
2000	99%	1%	95%	5%
1999	97%	3%	86%	14%
1998	99%	1%	92%	8%
1997	98%	2%	87%	13%
1996	94%	6%	90%	10%
1995	96%	4%	90%	10%

INTEREST GROUPS

	AFL-CIO	ADA	CCUS	ACU
2004	100%	100%	35%	0%
2003	100%	100%	27%	10%
2002	100%	100%	40%	0%
2001	100%	95%	36%	8%
2000	88%	95%	40%	12%
1999	100%	100%	35%	4%
1998	100%	95%	44%	4%
1997	100%	100%	30%	0%
1996	100%	95%	23%	0%
1995	100%	100%	21%	0%

Sen. Barbara A. Mikulski (D)

Elected 1986; 4th term

CAPITOL OFFICE
224-4654
mikulski.senate.gov
503 Hart 20510-2003; fax 224-8858

COMMITTEES
Appropriations
Health, Education, Labor & Pensions
Select Intelligence

HOMETOWN
Baltimore

BORN
July 20, 1936, Baltimore, Md.

RELIGION
Roman Catholic

FAMILY
Single

EDUCATION
Mount Saint Agnes College, B.A. 1958 (sociology);
U. of Maryland, M.S.W. 1965

CAREER
Social worker

POLITICAL HIGHLIGHTS
Baltimore City Council, 1971-77; Democratic
nominee for U.S. Senate, 1974; U.S. House, 1977-87

ELECTION RESULTS

2004 GENERAL

Barbara A. Mikulski (D)	1,504,691	64.8%
E.J. Pipkin (R)	783,055	33.7%
Maria Allwine (GREEN)	24,816	1.1%

2004 PRIMARY

Barbara A. Mikulski (D)	408,848	89.9%
A. Robert Kaufman (D)	32,127	7.1%
Sidney Altman (D)	13,901	3.1%

PREVIOUS WINNING PERCENTAGES
1998 (71%); 1992 (71%); 1986 (61%); 1984 House
Election (68%); 1982 House Election (74%); 1980
House Election (76%); 1978 House Election (100%);
1976 House Election (75%)

Mikulski provides the human face for qualities often associated with minority party lawmakers. She's tough and persistent, aggressive and nononsense, much like the east Baltimore neighborhood where she was raised. But Mikulski also knows how to compromise to achieve goals, even if they turn out to be not exactly what she wanted. Those qualities may be useful to the junior senator from Maryland in the 109th Congress, where Democrats are at their worst numeric disadvantage in 40 years.

While other Democrats struggled or lost in the 2004 election, Mikulski sailed easily to a fourth term, winning by an almost 2-to-1 margin. Part of her appeal can be traced to her seniority. She is the longest-serving woman in the Senate and a senior member of the Appropriations Committee.

Mikulski also has seats on the Health, Education, Labor and Pensions Committee and the Intelligence panel. She had more time for committee work after deciding in late 2004 to step down as caucus secretary, the No. 3 Democratic leadership post that she held for a decade.

As the Senate's senior woman, Mikulski takes seriously her self-assigned job mentoring the women who have come after her. In that role, she reveals a side of her personality that seems a closer match to her early days as a social worker in Baltimore than her dominant image as a feisty, blue-collar, partisan, liberal lawmaker. But there is a hard-edged purpose to the women's bonding: to get beyond the good intentions that spurred them to public life and develop strategies to get things done.

That's the way Mikulski shaped her own career. She first got involved in politics in a neighborhood battle to stop a highway project. At one point, she recalls, she jumped on a table and gave a fiery speech and everyone in the room cheered. But, she says, she has learned that there also has to be a plan, to "operationalize good intentions."

"If you only talk and don't produce . . . you contribute to the cynicism," she wrote in "Nine and Counting," a collaborative book written by the nine women serving in the Senate in 2000. "When I was a social worker, I wanted to help people, but it was difficult to do because I didn't have all of the resources I wanted. Now I am a social worker with power."

From the time she arrived in 1987 until 1992, Mikulski and Republican Nancy Landon Kassebaum of Kansas were the only two women in the Senate. As the ranks jumped to five in 1993, to nine in 1999 and to 14 in 2003, Mikulski offered the incoming women her own introductory seminars and dispensed advice on everything from organizing their offices to setting long-range goals. In the book, Mikulski recalls, "I didn't come to politics by the traditional male route, being in a nice law firm or belonging to the right clubs. Like most of the women I've known in politics, I got involved because I saw a community need."

The senator's record has rarely disappointed feminist groups. She is a strong supporter of abortion rights and has tried to ensure that federal health care plans provide abortion coverage. She helped push to enactment the 1990 law that created the women's health research office at the National Institutes of Health. And in 1995, she was the first member of the Ethics Committee to call for public hearings on sexual harassment allegations against Republican Bob Packwood of Oregon, a turning point in a three-year case that ultimately led to Packwood's resignation from the Senate.

She still fights hard for local interests, including finding money to relieve the state's congested roads, leading efforts to clean up the Chesapeake Bay and finding ways to protect the state's economy. When a General Motors plant closed in November 2004 in Baltimore, Mikulski promised to help laid-off workers find new jobs and recruit a new business to the old plant. She has been a longtime supporter of NASA, which maintains a major presence in her state at the Goddard Space Flight Center, a space research facility that employs nearly 9,000 people.

From her spot on the Appropriations panel, Mikulski secured $3.5 million in 2004 to upgrade a popular route to Maryland's beaches, which attract vacationers from Baltimore, Philadelphia and Washington, D.C. In all, $18 million has been earmarked for the project, but she has had to work each year to have more of the money released. So the road is getting fixed section by section. If voters missed the point, Mikulski reinforced it during her campaign. She ended her TV ads with the tag line, "100 percent Maryland."

As the top-ranking Democrat for many years on the Appropriations subcommittee that drafts the annual spending bill for housing, veterans, space, environment and science programs, Mikulski was not shy about sprinkling money for Maryland throughout the bill. That panel was disbanded in the 109th in a reshuffling and she took the top Democratic post on the panel that drafts the spending bill for science programs (including NASA) as well as the departments of Commerce and Justice.

Mikulski grew up in the working-class Baltimore neighborhood of Highlandtown. Her parents ran a grocery store called Willy's Market across the street from their row house. Nearby, her Polish immigrant grandmother operated a bakery legendary for its jelly doughnuts and raisin bread.

Inspired by a movie about Marie Curie, Mikulski decided to become a chemist. But reality set in when she got to college. "I got a C in chemistry and an A in social sciences. I decided that I would go with my strengths," she says. She got a master's degree in social work in 1965. When parts of her neighborhood were torched in anger after the 1968 assassination of the Rev. Martin Luther King Jr., social worker Mikulski delivered food to the needy during the riots, sometimes by riding atop a tank.

She jumped into a multiethnic, multiracial fight against a freeway that would have leveled several city neighborhoods. Building on the successful battle against the highway, Mikulski won a city council seat in 1971 and became prominent in the feminist movement.

In the post-Watergate election of 1974, she took advantage of the public backlash against Republicans by challenging incumbent Sen. Charles McC. Mathias Jr. She lost, but got a respectable 43 percent of the vote. That positioned her for 1976, when Democrat Paul S. Sarbanes gave up his seat as Baltimore's congressman to run for the Senate. Mikulski won and went on to serve five terms in the House. There, from her seat on the Energy and Commerce Committee, she was known as a champion of consumer causes. She also attracted notice on the national scene, including some support for her selection as Walter F. Mondale's running mate in 1984; the nod went to another congresswoman, New York's Geraldine Ferraro.

Mikulski won her Senate seat in 1986, when Mathias retired. She easily defeated Rep. Michael D. Barnes and outgoing Gov. Harry R. Hughes in the primary. Republicans nominated conservative Linda Chavez, a staff director of the U.S. Commission on Civil Rights under President Reagan. Mikulski won by 22 percentage points. She has racked up 40-plus point victories since, over black conservative activist Alan L. Keyes in 1992 and again in 1998.

Mikulski has teamed with writer Marylouise Oates to pen two mystery novels, both featuring Eleanor Gorzack, a Pennsylvania senator. When Gorzack is appointed to the Senate after her husband's death, she seeks the counsel of Hilda Mendelssohn, a more senior Senate colleague. The advice she receives sounds like an introductory seminar offered by Mikulski.

KEY VOTES

2004

Yes Pass $318.9 billion, six-year highway and mass transit bill

Yes Extend assault weapons ban for 10 years

Yes Restore pay-as-you-go rules for new tax cuts and entitlement spending

No Criminalize harm to a fetus in an attack on the mother

Yes Increase mandatory child care funding to states by $6 billion over five years

No Amend the Constitution to prohibit same-sex marriage

Yes Approve $146 billion multi-year extension of previously enacted middle-class tax breaks

Yes Reorganize U.S. intelligence agencies as proposed by Sept. 11 commission

Yes Cut corporate taxes $137 billion over 10 years

2003

Yes Delay Bush changes to Clean Air Act

No Allow confirmation vote on Miguel A. Estrada to the U.S. Court of Appeals for the D.C. Circuit

Yes Block a Bush proposal opening Alaska's Arctic National Wildlife Refuge to oil drilling

Yes Limit size of Bush's proposed tax cut to $350 billion through fiscal 2013

Yes Overhaul Medicare and create prescription drug benefit

Yes Block Bush rule scaling back overtime pay for some white-collar federal workers

Yes Split $20 billion in Iraq aid into half-grant, half-loan

No Ban "partial birth" abortion except to save a woman's life

No Stop proposal allowing travel to Cuba

No Allow final vote on energy policy overhaul

CQ VOTE STUDIES

	PARTY UNITY		PRESIDENTIAL SUPPORT	
	Support	Oppose	Support	Oppose
2004	96%	4%	61%	39%
2003	97%	3%	44%	56%
2002	96%	4%	68%	32%
2001	98%	2%	66%	34%
2000	97%	3%	92%	8%
1999	96%	4%	86%	14%
1998	97%	3%	91%	9%
1997	92%	8%	91%	9%
1996	92%	8%	90%	10%
1995	87%	13%	89%	11%

INTEREST GROUPS

	AFL-CIO	ADA	CCUS	ACU
2004	100%	100%	56%	8%
2003	100%	90%	39%	15%
2002	100%	100%	47%	0%
2001	100%	95%	43%	12%
2000	88%	95%	46%	8%
1999	89%	100%	59%	4%
1998	100%	90%	53%	4%
1997	86%	95%	44%	4%
1996	86%	95%	23%	0%
1995	100%	90%	39%	4%

Rep. Wayne T. Gilchrest (R)

Elected 1990; 8th term

CAPITOL OFFICE
225-5311
www.house.gov/gilchrest
2245 Rayburn 20515-2001; fax 225-0254

COMMITTEES
Resources
  (Fisheries & Oceans - chairman)
Science
Transportation & Infrastructure

HOMETOWN
Kennedyville

BORN
April 15, 1946, Rahway, N.J.

RELIGION
Methodist

FAMILY
Wife, Barbara Gilchrest; three children

EDUCATION
Wesley College, A.A. 1971; Delaware State U., B.A.
1973 (history); Loyola College (Md.), attended 1990

MILITARY SERVICE
Marine Corps, 1964-68

CAREER
Teacher

POLITICAL HIGHLIGHTS
Republican nominee for U.S. House, 1988

ELECTION RESULTS

2004 GENERAL

Wayne T. Gilchrest (R)	245,149	75.8%
Kostas Alexakis (D)	77,872	24.1%

2004 PRIMARY

Wayne T. Gilchrest (R)	23,590	61.9%
Richard F. Colburn (R)	14,508	38.1%

2002 GENERAL

Wayne T. Gilchrest (R)	192,004	76.7%
Ann D. Tamlyn (D)	57,986	23.2%

PREVIOUS WINNING PERCENTAGES
2000 (64%); 1998 (69%); 1996 (62%); 1994 (68%);
1992 (51%); 1990 (57%)

An avid outdoorsman who makes no secret of the fact that he prefers wandering the wilderness to strolling the halls of the Capitol, Gilchrest seems almost entirely without affectation. A quiet and quirky Republican from Maryland's Eastern Shore, he has a reputation as one of his party's leading environmentalists in Congress.

The former public school teacher and house painter has demonstrated his willingness to defy his party on some issues — he has favored gun control and abortion rights, and champions environmental regulation so much that he was endorsed by the Sierra Club in 2004 — while hewing to conservative principles on fiscal policy and education.

His wide-eyed demeanor, wrinkled shirts and sometimes bent or broken eyeglasses all convey the image of a man who stumbled into public life and is a little bewildered to find that he is still there. He still occasionally refers to himself as an "accidental" congressman.

Gilchrest is not afraid to challenge the White House or GOP leaders. In the 107th Congress, Gilchrest voted against President Bush 27 percent of the time, more often than all but eight other House Republicans. In the 108th, he was more loyal to the president, but still voted against Bush's position 23 percent of the time.

Although he supported the invasion of Iraq, Gilchrest was one of the first Republicans to speak out against the U.S. military's abuse of detainees evidenced in photographs from the Abu Ghraib prison. He summed up his emotions forcefully for the Associated Press: "Disgust, anger, rage, sadness."

Gilchrest votes with the GOP majority on labor issues, and despite his background as a public school teacher he supports conservatives' push to give parents taxpayer-financed vouchers to pay for private school education. He says competition will force public schools to improve.

GOP leaders, eager to keep party moderates in the fold, made Gilchrest vice chairman of the Republican Policy Committee at the start of the 109th Congress. It is not the policy position he might have wanted, but it was the one he was granted. Gilchrest was sufficiently aware of the dynamics within his own caucus that he did not enter the race to chair the Resources Committee in the 108th Congress; his environmental views and moderate stands on other issues left him no prospect of winning. Instead, he retained the chairmanship of the Fisheries and Oceans Subcommittee — a forum for addressing his top priority, the preservation of the Chesapeake Bay. He is in his final two years at that post.

Undeterred by conservative House GOP leaders, Gilchrest continues to push for stronger environmental regulations. He has fought attempts by fellow Republicans to scale back substantially the 1973 Endangered Species Act, once telling the Baltimore Sun, "Somebody has to stand up for the critters."

He is the co-chairman, with Massachusetts Democrat Rep. John W. Olver, of the House caucus on global climate change. He has introduced legislation to limit emissions of greenhouse gases, including carbon dioxide, which the White House does not support. He regularly holds forums in his district on global warming — for instance, co-hosting with the Chesapeake Climate Action Network a screening in 2004 of a movie that projected how climate change could affect the eastern United States.

Gilchrest is no ivory-tower analyst. After a deadly tsunami devastated South Asia in late 2004, he quickly scheduled a tour of the region. Upon his return, he used his position on the Science Committee to call for expansion of the U.S. Tsunami Warning System, which is supposed to warn Americans if a similar wave threatened the United States.

When Congress debated the farm bill in 2002, Gilchrest banded with environmentalists to try to divert billions of dollars from commodity subsidy payments into conservation programs, such as those that pay farmers to idle environmentally sensitive land and to protect wildlife and wetlands. The effort was unsuccessful, but it marked the first time in years that suburban and Northeastern lawmakers had worked so actively and come so close to shaping agriculture policy against the wishes of Farm Belt lawmakers. Gilchrest did come away from the 2002 farm bill with a federal pilot program to send agricultural conservation funds to the most environmentally sensitive land on the Chesapeake's eastern Delmarva Peninsula.

Born in New Jersey, Gilchrest joined the Marine Corps right out of high school. He plays down the 1967 battle that won him the Bronze Star and the chest and shoulder wound that earned him a Purple Heart, portraying his conduct as more foolhardy than brave. He attended several colleges, mixing in a job as a chicken plucker in Maine and studying rural poverty in Kentucky. After graduating from Delaware State University, he held a series of teaching jobs, ending up on Maryland's Eastern Shore in 1979.

Gilchrest did two stints with the Forest Service in Idaho and supplemented his teacher's income by moonlighting as a house painter. When he first ran for the House in 1988, he rushed to Annapolis in paint-covered clothes to file for election after he read in a newspaper that the GOP was having trouble finding a candidate. He lost that first bid against Rep. Roy Dyson, a conservative Democrat. But he won their 1990 rematch. Dyson had been weakened by reports of ties to a Pentagon procurement scandal and revelations that, despite his hawkish stance on military matters, he had been a conscientious objector during the Vietnam War.

Gilchrest's only general-election scare was two years later, when redistricting pitted him against three-term Democratic Rep. Tom McMillen, a basketball star with the University of Maryland, the U.S. Olympic team and the Washington Bullets. Portraying McMillen as a rich Washington insider and himself as an average guy, Gilchrest won with 51 percent of the vote.

In 2002, the conservative Club for Growth made one of its first efforts to unseat a moderate incumbent Republican by backing attorney Dave Fischer, who captured 36 percent of the GOP primary vote against Gilchrest. Another conservative, state Sen. Richard F. Colburn, whom Gilchrest had defeated in the 1990 primary, tried again in the 2004, scoring 38 percent. Both years, Gilchrest swept the general election with three-quarters of the vote.

KEY VOTES

2004

No Extend federal unemployment benefits by 13 weeks
Yes Pass $283.2 billion, six-year federal highway and mass transit bill
Yes Approve $146 billion multi-year extension of previously enacted middle-class tax breaks
No Amend the Constitution to prohibit same-sex marriage
Yes Cut corporate taxes $137 billion over 10 years
Yes Reorganize U.S. intelligence agencies as proposed by Sept. 11 commission

2003

Yes Cut taxes by $330 billion through fiscal 2013
No Block Bush rule scaling back overtime pay for some white-collar federal workers
No Do not allow use of search warrants without first notifying subjects
Yes Allow importation of prescription drugs
Yes Create private school voucher program in Washington, D.C.
Yes Ban "partial birth" abortion except to save a woman's life
No Split $18.6 billion in Iraq aid into half-grant, half-loan
Yes Overhaul Medicare and create prescription drug benefit

CQ VOTE STUDIES

| | PARTY UNITY | | PRESIDENTIAL SUPPORT | |
	Support	Oppose	Support	Oppose
2004	85%	15%	74%	26%
2003	88%	12%	80%	20%
2002	86%	14%	80%	20%
2001	86%	14%	67%	33%
2000	79%	21%	50%	50%

INTEREST GROUPS

	AFL-CIO	ADA	CCUS	ACU
2004	27%	35%	95%	56%
2003	7%	25%	82%	63%
2002	13%	10%	94%	78%
2001	17%	25%	87%	48%
2000	20%	15%	80%	58%

MARYLAND 1
East – Eastern Shore, part of Anne Arundel County

The 1st includes the rural counties of the Eastern Shore and, across the Chesapeake Bay, some of the fast-growing suburbs of Anne Arundel County. It also moves across the Susquehanna River in the northeastern part of the state and claims large chunks of Harford County, including Bel Air, and Baltimore County.

Although the district's regions are different in many ways, they share a conservative lean that benefits Republicans. The 1st supported the Republican candidate in the last four presidential elections. During redistricting following the 2000 census, some GOP-leaning voters were pushed into the 1st from the 2nd and 3rd districts.

The Eastern Shore, which holds about three-fifths of the district's population, has a steady economic grounding in agriculture. The central, more rural, part of the Eastern Shore is GOP heartland. The northern counties, closer to Baltimore and Philadelphia, and southern counties, with larger black and working-class populations, are more Democratic. Ocean City is a popular beach town that swells with visitors during the summer months.

Across the bay, some conservative parts of Anne Arundel County remain in the district. Annapolis, the Democratic-leaning state capital, was removed during redistricting. Part of Baltimore's fast-growing, GOP-leaning northern suburbs also are included in the 1st.

MAJOR INDUSTRY
Agriculture, manufacturing, tourism

MILITARY BASES
U.S. Naval Academy/Annapolis Naval Station, 1,063 military, 1,709 civilian (2005) (shared with 3rd District)

CITIES
Bel Air South (unincorporated) (pt.), 35,353; Severna Park (unincorporated) (pt.), 26,646; Bel Air North (unincorporated) (pt.), 25,372; Salisbury, 23,743; Arnold (unincorporated), 23,422

NOTABLE
Wild ponies can be seen roaming Assateague Island, a barrier island on the Atlantic Ocean; Residents of Smith Island, which calls itself Maryland's only inhabited offshore island in the Chesapeake Bay, speak an Elizabethan English-based dialect.

Rep. C.A. Dutch Ruppersberger (D)

Elected 2002; 2nd term

CAPITOL OFFICE
225-3061
dutch.house.gov
1630 Longworth 20515-2002; fax 225-3094

COMMITTEES
Government Reform
Select Intelligence

HOMETOWN
Cockeysville

BORN
Jan. 31, 1946, Baltimore, Md.

RELIGION
Methodist

FAMILY
Wife, Kay Ruppersberger; two children

EDUCATION
U. of Maryland, attended 1963-67; U. of Baltimore, J.D. 1970

CAREER
Collection agency owner; lawyer; county prosecutor

POLITICAL HIGHLIGHTS
Democratic nominee for Md. Senate, 1978; Baltimore County Council, 1985-94; Baltimore County executive, 1994-2002

ELECTION RESULTS

2004 GENERAL

C.A. Dutch Ruppersberger (D)	164,751	66.6%
Jane Brooks (R)	75,812	30.7%
Keith Salkowski (GREEN)	6,508	2.6%

2004 PRIMARY

C.A. Dutch Ruppersberger (D)	unopposed

2002 GENERAL

C.A. Dutch Ruppersberger (D)	105,718	54.2%
Helen Delich Bentley (R)	88,954	45.6%

He was born Charles Albert Ruppersberger III, but goes by the nickname "Dutch." Unlike recent waves of younger, more-wonkish lawmakers, he is an affable former county prosecutor who is at ease with the back-slapping nature of the business. "I love campaigns. I love getting out with the people," Ruppersberger says. "I love town hall meetings."

He had wanted to become the governor of Maryland, which was to be his political reward for two successful terms as Baltimore County executive, the county's top job. But he was edged out in 2002 by Kathleen Kennedy Townsend, the lieutenant governor with the politically golden middle name. Ruppersberger seemed to have no way to move up until fellow Democrats, who controlled the state legislature, came to his rescue with a remapped 2nd District, which included heavily Democratic parts of Baltimore and its suburbs. He beat a well-liked Republican to win the seat.

Ruppersberger arrived in the House in 2003 with some powerful friends. Minority Leader Nancy Pelosi, whose father was once the mayor of Baltimore, gave him a plum seat on the Intelligence Committee, making him the second-ever freshman on the panel. Pelosi also chose him to second her nomination for leader. Democratic Whip Steny H. Hoyer is a home-state ally who encouraged him to run for the House. He also sits on the Democratic Steering Committee, which makes committee assignments.

In his first term, Ruppersberger has cultivated homeland security issues as a niche. His district is less than an hour's drive from Washington, D.C. and is home to the Baltimore-Washington International Airport, the Port of Baltimore and the National Security Agency, the code-breaking arm of the country's spy network. He has championed more spending for first-responders — the local, county and state personnel such as police and rescue squads that would be first at the scene of a terrorist attack.

Ruppersberger said he knows from experience that local governments are strained each time the federal government posts a heightened terrorism alert. "Every time the code went up we had to double our resources," he said.

After hearing complaints from U.S. troops arriving at BWI that they had to pay for connecting flights home out of their own pockets, Ruppersberger called attention to the problem with an offbeat program that allowed civilians to donate their frequent flier miles to soldiers via a Web site. Major airlines cooperated, and Ruppersberger's "Operation Hero Miles," which was run by an aide out of his office, received a spate of favorable stories in the press. At his instigation, Congress added a provision to a 2004 supplemental spending bill directing the Pentagon to pay the whole airfare bill for troops returning from Afghanistan and Iraq for rest and recuperation.

In an important parochial battle, Ruppersberger fought successfully to stop plans for a 1,750-bed federal prison in the town of Dundalk, a largely Democratic blue-collar suburb in his district.

On national issues, he mostly votes with his party, agreeing in 2004 with a majority of his party 88 percent of the time. Though he supports abortion rights in most instances, he voted in 2003 for a ban on a procedure its critics call "partial birth" abortion. He was among only 62 Democrats to do so.

The son of a Baltimore manufacturing salesman and a school teacher, Ruppersberger has been called "Dutch" since birth, when the doctor who delivered him described him as a "big, blonde Dutchman." (His hair has since changed to black.) As practical a politician as they come, he later adopted the nickname legally when he realized "Ruppersberger" was too long to be readily seen on a bumper sticker.

A strong athlete as a youth, he played lacrosse at the University of Maryland and made the U.S. team in 1967. During college summers, he was a lifeguard in Ocean City, and then worked his way through night school at the University of Baltimore Law School as an insurance claims adjuster.

Ruppersberger began his career as a Baltimore County assistant state's attorney but made a life change after a near-fatal car accident in 1975. He says that the doctor who patched him up urged him to go into public service. Ruppersberger first tried and failed to get the party's nomination for a Maryland Senate seat. He then set his sights on a role in local government, and he was elected in 1985 to the Baltimore County Council. In 1994, he won the top job as Baltimore County executive.

He was an adept manager, steering the county to triple-A bond ratings while also building new schools, adding parks and building new roads. Under his stewardship, Governing Magazine called Baltimore one of the nation's four best-managed counties in 2001.

The next year Ruppersberger planned to run for governor, but he was haunted by events that took place two years earlier. In 2000, he had aggressively pushed a state bill that would have allowed the county to condemn private property for urban revitalization. People in the affected areas fought back with a referendum that passed by a margin of 2-to-1, an embarrassing renunciation for the county executive. Then in November 2000, the Baltimore Sun reported an alleged sweetheart deal in which Ruppersberger steered tax-exempt bonds and government grants to an apartment rental firm with which he had personal business dealings. The firm was the major client of a private collection agency owned by Ruppersberger.

Ruppersberger called the report flawed and said he had broken no laws. But he was weakened as the governor's race geared up. And he faced a potentially brutal primary fight with a well-financed Townsend, daughter of the late Sen. Robert F. Kennedy. Hoyer and other party elders urged him to run instead for the newly redrawn House district, where Democratic strength had gone from 53 percent to 64 percent and where incumbent Republican Robert L. Ehrlich Jr. was stepping down to run for governor.

Republicans countered by putting up popular former Rep. Helen Delich Bentley, who had represented the 2nd from 1985 to 1995. Voters' familiarity with Ruppersberger helped him prevail by almost 9 percentage points.

KEY VOTES

2004

?	Extend federal unemployment benefits by 13 weeks
Yes	Pass $283.2 billion, six-year federal highway and mass transit bill
Yes	Approve $146 billion multi-year extension of previously enacted middle-class tax breaks
No	Amend the Constitution to prohibit same-sex marriage
Yes	Cut corporate taxes $137 billion over 10 years
Yes	Reorganize U.S. intelligence agencies as proposed by Sept. 11 commission

2003

No	Cut taxes by $330 billion through fiscal 2013
Yes	Block Bush rule scaling back overtime pay for some white-collar federal workers
Yes	Do not allow use of search warrants without first notifying subjects
Yes	Allow importation of prescription drugs
No	Create private school voucher program in Washington, D.C.
Yes	Ban "partial birth" abortion except to save a woman's life
Yes	Split $18.6 billion in Iraq aid into half-grant, half-loan
No	Overhaul Medicare and create prescription drug benefit

CQ VOTE STUDIES

	PARTY UNITY		PRESIDENTIAL SUPPORT	
	Support	Oppose	Support	Oppose
2004	88%	12%	44%	56%
2003	89%	11%	23%	77%

INTEREST GROUPS

	AFL-CIO	ADA	CCUS	ACU
2004	86%	90%	55%	12%
2003	93%	90%	33%	24%

MARYLAND 2
Part of Baltimore and suburbs — Dundalk, Essex

The 2nd includes northern and eastern parts of Baltimore, suburbs in most directions around the city and most of the territory east of Interstate 95 between Baltimore and the Susquehanna River.

Redrawn during redistricting following the 2000 census to increase Democratic strength, the 2nd ranges northeast from Baltimore along the Chesapeake Bay coastline of Baltimore and Harford counties and south into Anne Arundel County, where it picks up Baltimore-Washington International Airport and Fort George G. Meade (including the National Security Agency). The district's northwest branch moves through the GOP-heavy northern suburbs and then hooks into largely African-American suburbs west of Baltimore, such as Randallstown. Blacks make up 27 percent of the 2nd's population.

In eastern Baltimore County, the blue-collar industrial sector — including Dundalk — has struggled with unemployment. But Bethlehem Steel, one of the county's major employers, opened a new mill in 2000 at its Sparrows Point complex, which is seen as a valuable asset for the area's economy. A General Motors plant in White Marsh expanded in 2000 and currently employs several hundred people.

The 2nd generally supports Democrats. District residents gave John Kerry 54 percent of the vote in the 2004 presidential election — 3 percentage points less than Al Gore received here in 2000. But many Democrats in the Baltimore suburbs have favored GOP candidates in House races.

MAJOR INDUSTRY
Manufacturing, defense, product distribution

MILITARY BASES
Fort George G. Meade (Army), 12,961 military, 25,891 civilian (2005); Aberdeen Proving Ground (Army), 5,000 military, 7,500 civilian (2004)

CITIES
Baltimore (pt.), 111,715; Dundalk (unincorporated), 62,306; Essex (unincorporated), 39,078; Randallstown (unincorporated) (pt.), 29,097

NOTABLE
The stadium complex in Aberdeen is home to Cal Ripken Baseball, a youth division of the amateur Babe Ruth League, and minor league baseball's Aberdeen IronBirds, a team owned by Ripken.

Rep. Benjamin L. Cardin (D)

Elected 1986; 10th term

CAPITOL OFFICE
225-4016
rep.cardin@mail.house.gov
www.house.gov/cardin
2207 Rayburn 20515-2003; fax 225-9219

COMMITTEES
Ways & Means

HOMETOWN
Baltimore

BORN
Oct. 5, 1943, Baltimore, Md.

RELIGION
Jewish

FAMILY
Wife, Myrna Edelman Cardin; two children (one deceased)

EDUCATION
U. of Pittsburgh, B.A. 1964 (economics); U. of Maryland, LL.B. 1967

CAREER
Lawyer

POLITICAL HIGHLIGHTS
Md. House, 1967-87 (Speaker, 1979-87)

ELECTION RESULTS

2004 GENERAL

Benjamin L. Cardin (D)	182,066	63.4%
Robert P. Duckworth (R)	97,008	33.8%
Patsy Allen (GREEN)	7,895	2.8%

2004 PRIMARY

Benjamin L. Cardin (D)	52,398	89.5%
John Rea (D)	6,163	10.5%

2002 GENERAL

Benjamin L. Cardin (D)	145,589	65.7%
Scott Alan Conwell (R)	75,721	34.2%

PREVIOUS WINNING PERCENTAGES
2000 (76%); 1998 (78%); 1996 (67%); 1994 (71%); 1992 (74%); 1990 (70%); 1988 (73%); 1986 (79%)

Cardin's political philosophy is difficult to pigeonhole; he characterizes himself as a fiscally conservative progressive. But it seems to work for Maryland's liberal-leaning voters. Cardin said in early 2005 that he would run for the seat of retiring Democratic Sen. Paul S. Sarbanes in 2006.

His signature issue over the last few years has been increasing workers' retirement savings and income, and he advocates balancing the federal budget. He is a staunch defender of the current income tax system. On social issues he votes a liberal line, opposing a proposed constitutional amendment banning same-sex marriage and supporting abortion rights and a ban on searches of library and bookseller records in terrorism investigations.

With a degree in economics, he takes a straightforward, non-ideological approach to the nation's problems. An acknowledged expert on such complicated issues as pension regulation and Social Security, Cardin is proud to wear the label "policy wonk." He likes the details of legislating.

Cardin is the senior Democrat on the Ways and Means Subcommittee on Trade. He and Chairman E. Clay Shaw Jr., a Florida Republican, have both supported free-trade legislation in the past, though Cardin opposed a 2002 bill giving the president greater power to negotiate trade agreements.

The two will play central roles in the debate over congressional approval of the Central American Free Trade Agreement. In 2005, Cardin already signaled a concern many Democrats have about CAFTA's potential impact on labor conditions, saying, "It is critical that the United States take a leadership role internationally in advancing environmental and labor standards in its trade negotiations."

Cardin walks a careful line on trade issues. Organized labor is a force in Baltimore, but international commerce also plays a key role in the port city. He wants to promote trade while guarding against the shift of U.S. jobs overseas. He voted to put the North American Free Trade Agreement in place in 1993 and to create the World Trade Organization in 1994. He agreed to grant China normal trade status in 2000 after initially opposing the measure on human rights grounds. But two years later, he voted against granting President Bush special authority to negotiate trade deals that Congress can approve or reject but not amend.

Cardin has on occasion drawn fire from some Democrats for his collaboration with Republicans, especially for his work with Ohio Republican Rob Portman, the main conduit between the Bush White House and House GOP leaders during Bush's first term. In the 108th Congress, the two lawmakers developed an alternative to Bush's ambitious plan to restructure Social Security and allow younger workers to divert a share of their payroll tax payments into personal retirement accounts.

Cardin first worked with Portman in 1993 on minor changes in hospice regulation. Later, they teamed up to draft language that formed the basis of a 1998 law overhauling the IRS.

But he does not always agree with the Republicans. On Ways and Means, he has argued against GOP efforts to replace the income tax with a consumption tax or other alternative and against tax-sheltered education savings accounts that parents could use for private school expenses. He also has been a regular critic of the bulk of Bush's tax proposals.

Democratic leaders need not worry about Cardin's loyalty. In 2004, he voted in agreement with his party 94 percent of the time, his highest party unity score since 1994.

He also sided with most Democrats in late 2003 against the law expanding Medicare to include prescription drug coverage. Cardin has worked steadily since the measure's passage to emphasize what he sees as its weaknesses, including a reliance on private insurance to provide coverage and possible threats to drug coverage that retirees have from former employers. "I predict that a growing number of retired Americans are going to find their health benefits in serious jeopardy," Cardin has said. "I also predict that because the new Medicare law relies solely on private insurers and does not offer a defined benefit within Medicare, that continuity of coverage is not guaranteed for any senior." He introduced legislation to alter the bill in the 108th Congress, but in the Republican-controlled House, the measure had little hope of survival.

On home-state issues, Cardin has had a hand in preserving the Coast Guard base at Curtis Bay and restoring Fort McHenry in Baltimore. He helped secure funding for Amtrak and development assistance for a light rail system in Baltimore.

Cardin's father and uncle held office in Maryland in the 1950s, and on the strength of his family name Cardin began his uninterrupted string of election victories one month after turning 23. Cardin says that he has "worked hard to warrant his seat ever since," and in Annapolis as well as Washington he has participated in some of the most complex questions of the day.

Cardin arrived in Annapolis in 1967, several months before graduating first in his class at the University of Maryland Law School. While representing the white-collar, heavily Jewish precincts of northwest Baltimore, he earned a reputation as a master conciliator and a budgetary expert. By age 32, he was chairman of the state House Ways and Means Committee, and four years later he became the youngest Speaker in the history of the House of Delegates. During his eight years in that job, he promoted extra spending on education, mass transit and bipartisan compromise on banking regulations and pension law.

Cardin hoped to run for governor in 1986, but when Baltimore Mayor William Donald Schaefer decided to seek the job (he won and served eight years), Cardin shifted his sights to the House seat that Barbara A. Mikulski was vacating to run for Senate. He won in a rout, has done so ever since and remains a potent figure on the Maryland political stage.

His flirtation with a 1998 gubernatorial candidacy had the incumbent Democrat and his leading GOP challenger on edge.

KEY VOTES

2004

Yes Extend federal unemployment benefits by 13 weeks

Yes Pass $283.2 billion, six-year federal highway and mass transit bill

Yes Approve $146 billion multi-year extension of previously enacted middle-class tax breaks

No Amend the Constitution to prohibit same-sex marriage

No Cut corporate taxes $137 billion over 10 years

Yes Reorganize U.S. intelligence agencies as proposed by Sept. 11 commission

2003

No Cut taxes by $330 billion through fiscal 2013

Yes Block Bush rule scaling back overtime pay for some white-collar federal workers

Yes Do not allow use of search warrants without first notifying subjects

No Allow importation of prescription drugs

No Create private school voucher program in Washington, D.C.

No Ban "partial birth" abortion except to save a woman's life

Yes Split $18.6 billion in Iraq aid into half-grant, half-loan

No Overhaul Medicare and create prescription drug benefit

CQ VOTE STUDIES

	PARTY UNITY		PRESIDENTIAL SUPPORT	
	Support	Oppose	Support	Oppose
2004	94%	6%	35%	65%
2003	93%	7%	24%	76%
2002	90%	10%	35%	65%
2001	89%	11%	35%	65%
2000	92%	8%	94%	6%

INTEREST GROUPS

	AFL-CIO	ADA	CCUS	ACU
2004	100%	95%	43%	0%
2003	87%	90%	37%	20%
2002	100%	95%	55%	0%
2001	100%	100%	35%	4%
2000	90%	90%	42%	8%

MARYLAND 3
Part of Baltimore; eastern Columbia; Annapolis

Like a Z-shaped lightning bolt, the 3rd District flashes through three of Maryland's largest urban centers — Baltimore, Columbia and Annapolis.

Starting in the traditionally Jewish suburbs northwest of Baltimore, the district snakes east, then south, to pick up parts of northeastern Baltimore's suburbs and parts of downtown Baltimore, including Fells Point and the stadiums that house Baltimore's major-league sports teams: baseball's Orioles and football's Ravens. Many of eastern Baltimore's ethnic neighborhoods are included in the district, but it lost much of downtown to the neighboring 7th in redistricting following the 2000 census. The 3rd then twists south and west through suburban Arbutus and Elkridge on its way to the eastern part of Columbia. Finally, the district moves southeast to Annapolis.

State and local governments provide employment in Annapolis, which is both the state capital and the Anne Arundel County seat, while technology, financial services and health care businesses push the economy of the Columbia area. Fort George G. Meade — including the

National Security Agency — and Baltimore-Washington International Airport, which are both located in the neighboring 2nd District, attract defense-related companies to the region.

The district includes some GOP-leaning areas in Anne Arundel and Baltimore counties, such as Towson, but was designed to favor Democratic candidates for federal office. John Kerry won 54 percent of the 3rd's 2004 presidential vote.

MAJOR INDUSTRY
Government, technology, defense-related business

MILITARY BASES
U.S. Naval Academy/Annapolis Naval Station, 1,063 military, 1,709 civilian (2005) (shared with 1st District)

CITIES
Baltimore (pt.), 168,687; Columbia (unincorporated) (pt.), 40,311; Annapolis, 35,838; Pikesville (unincorporated), 29,123

NOTABLE
The Preakness Stakes, the second event in horse racing's Triple Crown, is held at Pimlico in northwestern Baltimore; Both of Maryland's senators, Democrats Paul S. Sarbanes and Barbara A. Mikulski, represented the 3rd before their election to the Senate.

Rep. Albert R. Wynn (D)

Elected 1992; 7th term

CAPITOL OFFICE
225-8699
www.house.gov/wynn
434 Cannon 20515-2004; fax 225-8714

COMMITTEES
Energy & Commerce

HOMETOWN
Mitchellville

BORN
Sept. 10, 1951, Philadelphia, Pa.

RELIGION
Baptist

FAMILY
Wife, Gaines Clore Wynn; one child, one stepchild

EDUCATION
U. of Pittsburgh, B.S. 1973 (political science);
Howard U., attended 1973-74 (public
administration); Georgetown U., J.D. 1977

CAREER
Lawyer

POLITICAL HIGHLIGHTS
Md. House, 1983-87; Md. Senate, 1987-93

ELECTION RESULTS

2004 GENERAL

Albert R. Wynn (D)	196,809	75.2%
John McKinnis (R)	52,907	20.2%
Theresa M. Dudley (GREEN)	11,885	4.5%

2004 PRIMARY

Albert R. Wynn (D)	48,643	84.0%
George E. McDermott (D)	9,268	16.0%

2002 GENERAL

Albert R. Wynn (D)	131,644	78.6%
John B. Kimble (R)	34,890	20.8%

PREVIOUS WINNING PERCENTAGES
2000 (87%); 1998 (86%); 1996 (85%); 1994 (75%);
1992 (75%)

An intense, high-energy politician, Wynn does not immerse himself in the details of legislating. His skills lie in the broader art of politics.

Although he has a seat on the powerful Energy and Commerce Committee, his legislative efforts focus more on what he can do for Maryland in general and the 4th District in particular. His office touts the $208 million in federal funding included in the 2004 catchall spending bill for projects in and around the 4th District, including $800,000 for the Intercounty Connector, a new highway to connect the I-270 corridor in Montgomery County with the I-95/U.S. 1 corridor in Prince George's County; $1 million to reduce pollution in the Anacostia River; and $200,000 for a study of the Potomac River.

When Wynn first came to Congress more than a decade ago, he represented a district drawn by state General Assembly Democrats to maximize the clout of minority voters. But the same redistricting process that propelled a record number of African-Americans into office nationwide in 1992 also helped Republicans win control of the House in the next election.

When district lines were redrawn for this decade, Wynn put his party loyalty ahead of his personal political security. He encouraged mapmakers to take some suburban Democrats from his 4th District and include them in the 8th District, which helped force neighboring Republican Constance A. Morella from office in 2002. Democrats still suffered a net loss of House seats that year.

If Wynn is discouraged by the national political trend, he is encouraged by the local political scene. He earned a reputation as a kingmaker in 1998, when he used his voter mobilization skills to help Democrat Parris N. Glendening win re-election as governor by a healthy margin. In 2002, Wynn played a dominant role in Prince George's County politics, offering key endorsements of the new county executive, Jack Johnson, and most of the new county council members.

Wynn has looked out for his district on one of the most divisive issues in Maryland politics — whether to legalize gambling. GOP Maryland Gov. Robert L. Ehrlich Jr. came into office promoting the use of slot machines as a way to cure the state's budget ills. Ehrlich ruled out the construction of casinos in the state, however.

But Wynn says he would rather have a casino attached to a four-star hotel in Prince George's County than slot machines. A casino would provide an economic incentive for the region and create thousands of jobs with union wages and lucrative construction contracts, Wynn says. He told The Washington Post in 2004 that a top-quality casino would bring in big spenders from across the country, and their gambling losses would generate hundreds of millions of dollars a year for county schools and other civic needs. "If the state is going to force gaming on us, then we need to insist that it be high-end gaming, creating an economic engine," he told the newspaper. Simply legalizing slot machines at racetracks would be unacceptable, he said.

Bordering the nation's capital on the north, east and south, the 4th was the nation's first black-majority district dominated by middle-class suburbanites. As a result, its residents' priorities differ from those of many other districts where most people are African-American. Many of Wynn's constituents are small-business owners who contract with the federal government, and he tends to be more pro-business than many of his colleagues in the Congressional Black Caucus.

Wynn was one of only four Black Caucus members to vote for the 2002 resolution authorizing President Bush to launch a military campaign against Iraq. Wynn said he was concerned about the safety of more than 70,000 federal workers who are his constituents and could become terrorist targets at their workplaces.

But in 2004 he told a Muslim group that his vote was a mistake. Wynn said the war resolution was based on intelligence about Iraq's purported weapons of mass destruction that turned out to be wrong. Wynn said he believed that the removal of Saddam Hussein had improved some aspects of life in Iraq. But the information given to Congress to support the war was "inaccurate" and "overstated," he said. "I regret that vote based on what I know now," he told The Washington Post.

Wynn's strong political base has helped him move up in the ranks of the Black Caucus; he ran its political action committee for both the 2002 and 2004 campaigns. He has also served as a Democratic regional whip.

Wynn is not one to curb his tongue when it comes to the GOP or the Bush administration. During the 2004 Democratic Convention, Wynn said that while Democrats would challenge Bush on several fronts, including the war in Iraq, education, the deficit and jobs, it really just comes down to one issue. "This guy is incompetent," Wynn told U.S. News and World Report. "Nothing good has happened on his watch."

Born in Philadelphia, Wynn spent his early years in North Carolina, where his father farmed and his mother taught school. When he was 7, his father was hired by the Department of Agriculture and the family moved back north, first to Washington, D.C. and later to the Maryland suburbs. Wynn attended segregated schools until he was in the ninth grade. He was elected president of his high school senior class. "I have always been pretty good at mobilizing," Wynn recalls.

Wynn excelled at the trombone and was a debater at the University of Pittsburgh. After earning a law degree from Georgetown University in 1977, Wynn ran the Prince George's County Consumer Protection Commission. He became involved in local politics, working on other candidates' campaigns. In 1982, his door-to-door campaigning skills and party contacts helped him unseat an incumbent state representative.

After 10 years in Annapolis, Wynn was one of 13 Democrats who lined up for the newly drawn 4th District. He won the primary, which was tantamount to election, with 1,300 more votes than Alexander Williams Jr., the Prince George's County prosecutor. That remains his only tough race.

KEY VOTES

2004
Yes Extend federal unemployment benefits by 13 weeks
Yes Pass $283.2 billion, six-year federal highway and mass transit bill
Yes Approve $146 billion multi-year extension of previously enacted middle-class tax breaks
No   Amend the Constitution to prohibit same-sex marriage
Yes Cut corporate taxes $137 billion over 10 years
Yes Reorganize U.S. intelligence agencies as proposed by Sept. 11 commission

2003
No   Cut taxes by $330 billion through fiscal 2013
Yes Block Bush rule scaling back overtime pay for some white-collar federal workers
Yes Do not allow use of search warrants without first notifying subjects
Yes Allow importation of prescription drugs
No   Create private school voucher program in Washington, D.C.
No   Ban "partial birth" abortion except to save a woman's life
Yes Split $18.6 billion in Iraq aid into half-grant, half-loan
No   Overhaul Medicare and create prescription drug benefit

CQ VOTE STUDIES

| | PARTY UNITY | | PRESIDENTIAL SUPPORT | |
	Support	Oppose	Support	Oppose
2004	88%	12%	38%	62%
2003	91%	9%	20%	80%
2002	87%	13%	32%	68%
2001	88%	12%	31%	69%
2000	95%	5%	84%	16%

INTEREST GROUPS

	AFL-CIO	ADA	CCUS	ACU
2004	80%	95%	71%	20%
2003	100%	90%	43%	20%
2002	100%	85%	50%	8%
2001	100%	90%	35%	4%
2000	100%	85%	57%	12%

MARYLAND 4
Inner Prince George's County; part of Montgomery County

The first suburban district in the nation with a black majority, the 4th includes Washington, D.C.'s eastern suburbs in Prince George's County and a sizable swath of northern Montgomery County. Democrats have a strong hold on the district's largely middle-class, black population.

The 4th's thriving economy is built on small business and the spillover of technology firms from Montgomery County and Northern Virginia. The district has major parts of the Prince George's County High Technology Triangle, which is home to companies such as Raytheon and is anchored by the University of Maryland and NASA (both nearby in the 5th). Prince George's County is a national leader in black business formation, home ownership and education. Many of its residents are federal employees who have moved out of Washington, and the 4th has the nation's highest percentage of government employees (29 percent).

But some of Prince George's County's low-income areas inside the

Capital Beltway, which surrounds Washington, share the capital's problems of drug trafficking and violent crime.

Mapmakers altered the 4th in redistricting following the 2000 census in order to make the neighboring 8th District more Democratic. They exchanged some of the 4th's heavily minority neighborhoods in western Prince George's County and eastern Montgomery County for farther-out Montgomery County suburbs and exurbs, like Burtonsville, Olney and Sandy Spring. Nearly 40 percent of the new 4th's population resides in Montgomery County, and 57 percent of residents are black.

MAJOR INDUSTRY
Retail grocery, computers, recreation, technology

MILITARY BASES
Andrews Air Force Base, 6,096 military, 1,900 civilian (2005); Adelphi Army Research Laboratory, 58 military, 2,024 civilian (2004)

CITIES
Silver Spring (unincorporated) (pt.), 46,910; Oxon Hill-Glassmanor (unincorporated), 35,355; Suitland-Silver Hill (unincorporated), 33,515

NOTABLE
Air Force One is kept at Andrews Air Force Base; FedEx Field is the home of the NFL's Washington Redskins.

Rep. Steny H. Hoyer (D)

Elected May 1981; 12th full term

CAPITOL OFFICE
225-4131
www.house.gov/hoyer
1705 Longworth 20515-2005; fax 225-4300

COMMITTEES
Appropriations

HOMETOWN
Mechanicsville

BORN
June 14, 1939, Manhattan, N.Y.

RELIGION
Baptist

FAMILY
Widowed; three children

EDUCATION
U. of Maryland, B.S. 1963 (political science);
Georgetown U., J.D. 1966

CAREER
Lawyer

POLITICAL HIGHLIGHTS
Md. Senate, 1967-79 (president, 1975-79); sought
Democratic nomination for lieutenant governor,
1978; Md. Board of Higher Education, 1978-81

ELECTION RESULTS

2004 GENERAL

Steny H. Hoyer (D)	204,867	68.7%
Brad Jewitt (R)	87,189	29.2%
Bob S. Auerbach (GREEN)	4,224	1.4%

2004 PRIMARY

Steny H. Hoyer (D)	unopposed

2002 GENERAL

Steny H. Hoyer (D)	137,903	69.3%
Joseph T. Crawford (R)	60,758	30.5%

PREVIOUS WINNING PERCENTAGES
2000 (65%); 1998 (65%); 1996 (57%); 1994 (59%);
1992 (53%); 1990 (81%); 1988 (79%); 1986 (82%);
1984 (72%); 1982 (80%); 1981 Special Election (55%)

A smart, seasoned and savvy lawmaker, Hoyer is needed by his Democratic colleagues more than ever. After three consecutive dispiriting elections and a decade in the minority, House Democrats are struggling to find success both at the ballot box and in thwarting the GOP agenda.

Hoyer is now the No. 2 Democrat in the House leadership. And he has learned to make the best of an unusual situation — being deputy to the very rival who defeated him in an earlier race for the post.

Hoyer lost a hard-fought race for the minority whip position in the fall of 2001 to Californian Nancy Pelosi. Ordinarily, that might have spelled the end of his leadership aspirations, but Hoyer was soon presented with an opportunity to take the job after Pelosi moved up to be minority leader at the beginning of the 108th Congress.

Despite a sometimes uncomfortable transition, Hoyer has settled nicely into the job. As whip, Hoyer serves as the top vote counter for his party, but perhaps as important, he is a liaison to lawmakers who have their doubts about having a liberal San Franciscan as the public face of the party, especially more-moderate members who were his core supporters in the race against Pelosi.

Charming and impeccably dressed, Hoyer has well-honed skills as an inside operator and a smoothness in front of the cameras that makes him a favorite party spokesman. Known for his diligence, Hoyer is willing to reach out to new members and veteran lawmakers alike. And he is a prodigious fundraiser and party builder — he often calls winning Democratic candidates on primary night. His political action committee, AmeriPAC, is one of the most active leadership PACs among House Democrats.

Hoyer has worked to expand the whip's role beyond the customary duties of vote-counting and persuasion. He sees his job as cultivating support for the party's positions earlier in the process, long before legislation hits the floor. "Steny has created a higher level of strategic thinking maybe than we've seen in recent years on the other side," Hoyer's GOP counterpart, Roy Blunt of Missouri, told the Washington Post. Hoyer is respected by Republicans and, given the poisonous relationship between GOP leaders and Pelosi, is sometimes a conduit between the warring camps.

But he can also have sharp words for the majority party. When the House in 2004 passed a GOP measure providing a host of new tax breaks for corporations, Hoyer fumed, "I've served 23 years, and this is the worst tax bill I've seen on the floor of the House. This bill is an appalling orgy in self-indulgence, a legislative abomination and a national embarrassment."

Hoyer was once the top-ranking Democrat on the House Administration Committee, which handles internal housekeeping and Capitol security issues. His service on that panel led to Hoyer's greatest legislative achievement: enactment of a law that set the first national standards for the conduct of elections. Hoyer and Chairman Bob Ney, an Ohio Republican, negotiated tirelessly with Senate leaders in both parties to overcome partisan suspicions and strike a deal in 2002.

With a seat on the Appropriations Committee, Hoyer fights relentlessly for the federal workers who make up a large voting bloc in his district. He regularly combines with Washington-area Republicans to award them pay raises beyond those proposed by President Bush. He rebuffed entreaties to give up the committee when he became whip because of the value of the post to his constituents. "I have a primary responsibility: to work for the people who hired me," Hoyer said. "And where I serve them is on the committee."

He has fought efforts by the Bush administration to allow private contractors to take over part of the work of the federal government. He proposed language in 2004 during subcommittee consideration of a spending bill for the Transportation and Treasury departments to bar the privatization of some federal jobs unless a contractor could show a savings of 10 percent or $10 million, whichever was less. His language did not make it into the final bill, however.

Hoyer's rise to the whip position was a welcome reversal of fortune after a series of unsuccessful attempts to move up the ladder. Pelosi had soundly defeated him, 118-95, in the 2001 race for the whip position. And that was Hoyer's second failed bid for the job. He had lost to David E. Bonior of Michigan 10 years earlier, 160-109.

A third opportunity for him to run for whip arose in late 2002 when Pelosi became the favorite to step up to minority leader, succeeding Richard A. Gephardt, who was leaving the post to run for president. Hoyer had anticipated such a scenario; he had never truly stopped campaigning for the job. By the time the party election rolled around, he had the votes lined up. This time, Hoyer had no opposition.

Hoyer generally votes a pro-labor, pro-environment line, and is a strong proponent of abortion rights. He is more routinely pro-defense than most House Democrats. He split with the majority of his peers in 2002 to vote to authorize the use of military force against Iraq.

Hoyer showed leadership potential long before his service in Congress. He was president of the Maryland Young Democrats, and in 1963, was named the University of Maryland's "Outstanding Male Graduate." Three years later, he graduated from Georgetown Law School and immediately won election, at age 27, to the Maryland Senate. A few years later, when he turned 35, he became that body's youngest president ever.

He was 41 when he won his House seat in a special election to replace Democrat Gladys Noon Spellman, who was in an irreversible coma.

A self-described "John Kennedy Democrat," Hoyer throughout the 1980s had no trouble holding his seat in the mostly liberal, heavily Democratic district in suburban Prince George's County outside of Washington, D.C. Hoyer began moderating his views after redistricting in the 1990s added a conservative swath of southern Maryland to his district.

Held to 53 percent of the vote in 1992, he has since gained higher victory margins. To do so, he shifted his ideology toward the center on some issues. By his 2002 and 2004 elections, he was once again topping 65 percent.

KEY VOTES

2004

Yes   Extend federal unemployment benefits by 13 weeks

Yes   Pass $283.2 billion, six-year federal highway and mass transit bill

No   Approve $146 billion multi-year extension of previously enacted middle-class tax breaks

No   Amend the Constitution to prohibit same-sex marriage

No   Cut corporate taxes $137 billion over 10 years

Yes   Reorganize U.S. intelligence agencies as proposed by Sept. 11 commission

2003

No   Cut taxes by $330 billion through fiscal 2013

Yes   Block Bush rule scaling back overtime pay for some white-collar federal workers

Yes   Do not allow use of search warrants without first notifying subjects

Yes   Allow importation of prescription drugs

No   Create private school voucher program in Washington, D.C.

No   Ban "partial birth" abortion except to save a woman's life

No   Split $18.6 billion in Iraq aid into half-grant, half-loan

No   Overhaul Medicare and create prescription drug benefit

CQ VOTE STUDIES

	PARTY UNITY		PRESIDENTIAL SUPPORT	
	Support	Oppose	Support	Oppose
2004	95%	5%	24%	76%
2003	92%	8%	24%	76%
2002	89%	11%	32%	68%
2001	91%	9%	30%	70%
2000	93%	7%	90%	10%

INTEREST GROUPS

	AFL-CIO	ADA	CCUS	ACU
2004	100%	100%	38%	0%
2003	87%	90%	40%	20%
2002	100%	95%	42%	4%
2001	100%	95%	43%	9%
2000	90%	80%	47%	12%

MARYLAND 5
Outer Prince George's County; southern Maryland

The 5th includes part of Prince George's County, southern Anne Arundel County and all of the three rapidly growing southern counties of Charles, Calvert and St. Mary's. The mix of liberals in Prince George's County and conservative Democrats and Republicans throughout much of the rest of the district gives the 5th a broad array of political interests.

Prince George's County, which accounts for half the district's population — and nearly 60 percent of its registered Democrats — includes many liberal black communities and College Park, home of the University of Maryland's main campus. "P.G." County, as locals call it, was the only county in the 5th to back Bill Clinton in 1996, allowing Democrats to carry the district. In 2004, a growing black population helped John Kerry take largely exurban Charles County while winning the 5th handily. The GOP holds a slight registration edge among the 5th's Calvert and Anne Arundel residents, but Democrats have the advantage in other counties.

The district is enjoying a moderate amount of economic success due to a technology boom, both in Prince George's County and in Southern

Maryland. Many residents and companies have left the Washington, D.C., metropolitan area for the southern counties, attracted by the abundance of land and the military presence. Its proximity to Washington gives the 5th the nation's second-highest percentage of government workers (28.8 percent), behind the neighboring 4th District. The Tri-County area retains its Southern rural character, however, with tobacco as its major crop and a conservative, but strongly Democratic, tradition.

MAJOR INDUSTRY
Defense, agriculture, technology

MILITARY BASES
Naval Air Station Patuxent River, 3,000 military, 7,000 civilian (2005); Naval Surface Warfare Center, Indian Head Division, 2 military, 1,488 civilian (2004)

CITIES
Bowie (pt.), 47,714; St. Charles (unincorporated), 33,379; Clinton (unincorporated), 26,064; College Park, 24,657

NOTABLE
NASA Goddard Space Flight Center; Cliffs along the Chesapeake Bay in Calvert County contain more than 600 species of fossils; St. Mary's was the first capital of Maryland.

Rep. Roscoe G. Bartlett (R)

Elected 1992; 7th term

CAPITOL OFFICE
225-2721
bartlett.house.gov
2412 Rayburn 20515-2006; fax 225-2193

COMMITTEES
Armed Services
  (Projection Forces - chairman)
Science
Small Business

HOMETOWN
Frederick

BORN
June 3, 1926, Moreland, Ky.

RELIGION
Seventh-day Adventist

FAMILY
Wife, Ellen Bartlett; 10 children

EDUCATION
Columbia Union College, B.S. 1947 (theology &
biology); U. of Maryland, M.S. 1948 (physiology),
Ph.D. 1952 (physiology)

CAREER
Real estate developer; scientific research
company owner; farmer; biomedical engineer;
professor

POLITICAL HIGHLIGHTS
Sought Republican nomination for U.S. Senate,
1980; Republican nominee for U.S. House, 1982

ELECTION RESULTS

2004 GENERAL

Roscoe G. Bartlett (R)	206,076	67.4%
Kenneth T. Bosley (D)	90,108	29.5%
Gregory Hemingway (GREEN)	9,324	3.1%

2004 PRIMARY

Roscoe G. Bartlett (R)	31,867	70.3%
Scott L. Rolle (R)	13,481	29.7%

2002 GENERAL

Roscoe G. Bartlett (R)	147,825	66.1%
Donald M. DeArmon (D)	75,575	33.8%

PREVIOUS WINNING PERCENTAGES
2000 (61%); 1998 (63%); 1996 (57%); 1994 (66%);
1992 (54%)

Bartlett's outlook on life was shaped by his father, a tenant farmer who refused any assistance from the government as he raised his children during the Great Depression. Since then, Bartlett has maintained a conservative political philosophy based on self-reliance and a strict constructionist reading of the Constitution.

The self-styled citizen-legislator, who commutes about 50 miles every day to Capitol Hill from his farm near Frederick, Md., was considerably older than many of the conservative young Republican firebrands who joined the House in the 1990s. But he is every bit their equal in ideological fervor.

During the past 12 years, Bartlett has been a reliable proponent of the House Republican agenda, voting to scale back government and reduce taxes. His Main Street conservatism, rooted in his hardscrabble childhood, strongly held religious beliefs and his experience as a small-businessman, has made him a standout in an increasingly Democratic state. A Washington Post magazine profile in October 2004 described his answer to constituents who ask what he would do about the deficit. "Stop spending money for things that are unconstitutional," he says, including education, philanthropy, and non-military health care. "If you can't find it in Article 1, you can't do it."

That same strict view of the Constitution occasionally leads Bartlett to part ways with his Republican colleagues. In 2002, he was one of 27 House Republicans who voted, unsuccessfully, against giving the president fast-track authority to negotiate trade agreements that Congress can accept or reject but not amend. "I don't think you can give to the president power [to regulate foreign trade] constitutionally given to Congress," he told a reporter, pulling a copy of the Constitution out of his coat pocket.

A member of the Armed Services Committee, Bartlett became a key player on military policy in 2003 when he was named chairman of the new Projection Forces Subcommittee, which handles aircraft construction and shipbuilding issues. As chairman, Bartlett has spoken out about his own concerns but ultimately has fallen in line. In 2004, for example, when the Air Force requested a new generation of refueling tankers from the Boeing Co., Bartlett resisted at first. He said the Air Force itself acknowledged the current tankers could last for decades, but he eventually included $95 million for the tankers at the instruction of Armed Services Chairman Duncan Hunter of California. (The final bill included the money but did not allow any planes to be leased.)

The abuse of Iraqi prisoners at the Abu Ghraib prison near Baghdad put an uncomfortable spotlight on Bartlett's district, which includes Cresaptown, Md., the headquarters of the Army's 372nd Military Police Company, home to several of the reservists implicated in the scandal. Bartlett, who believed high-ranking officials ordered the abuse, was careful not to come down too hard on the reservists. "America's Constitution guarantees American citizens the presumption of innocence until proven guilty in a court of law," he said when the abuse was revealed in May 2004. More investigation was needed, he said, to determine who was responsible for "systemic failures in management and leadership that created the environment in which heinous abuses occurred."

Usually a stalwart defense hawk, Bartlett is an equally staunch libertarian who regretted his 2001 vote for the so-called USA-PATRIOT Act, enacted after the Sept. 11 terrorist attacks to give the government sweeping new powers to track, arrest and prosecute suspected terrorists. "Probably the least patriotic thing I've done since I got here," he lamented in an interview several months later. "If the price of catching another terrorist or two is an erosion of our civil liberties, they will have won."

In 2003, Bartlett tried to make amends by voting to block a provision of the law that lets the government execute search warrants without notifying the subjects first. He also voted against the 2004 overhaul of the intelligence community, saying it "did not go nearly far enough" to protect civil liberties or strengthen the enforcement of U.S. immigration laws. His support for gun owners' rights leads him to introduce a measure every Congress stipulating that Americans have the right to use firearms to defend their families and homes.

Bartlett's independence is particularly striking on technical issues that engage his flair for science. On the Science Committee, he is well-versed in the subject of global energy resources. Unlike most in his party, he opposes drilling for oil in Alaska's Arctic National Wildlife Refuge, saying there is not enough oil there to help end the nation's dependence on foreign oil.

Born on his grandfather's farm in Kentucky, Bartlett saw his father work as a tenant farmer in western Pennsylvania during the Depression. He originally intended to become a minister but instead pursued graduate education in physiology at the University of Maryland, earning a master's degree and a doctorate in physiology.

He taught in California and Washington, D.C., and did research for the National Institutes of Health and the Navy's School of Aviation Medicine, where his mechanical skill led him into engineering. He holds 20 patents for his invention of respiratory support and safety devices used by pilots, astronauts and rescue workers. Bartlett was honored in 1999 for his lifetime service by the American Institute of Aeronautics and Astronautics.

In 1961, Bartlett moved to a dairy farm in Frederick County and continued to work at the Johns Hopkins Applied Physics Laboratory. He later entered the home building business.

He made an unsuccessful House bid in 1982 but returned a decade later, after closing his home building firm and leaving his teaching career. He narrowly won a three-way GOP primary in 1992 and expected a tough general-election battle against conservative Democrat Beverly B. Byron, a seven-term incumbent, who had held Bartlett to just 26 percent of the vote in 1982. But Byron was upset in the primary by challenger Thomas H. Hattery; in November, Bartlett capitalized on confusion in the Democratic ranks to beat Hattery by 8 percentage points. His re-elections have been easy.

KEY VOTES

2004
- No Extend federal unemployment benefits by 13 weeks
- Yes Pass $283.2 billion, six-year federal highway and mass transit bill
- Yes Approve $146 billion multi-year extension of previously enacted middle-class tax breaks
- Yes Amend the Constitution to prohibit same-sex marriage
- Yes Cut corporate taxes $137 billion over 10 years
- No Reorganize U.S. intelligence agencies as proposed by Sept. 11 commission

2003
- Yes Cut taxes by $330 billion through fiscal 2013
- No Block Bush rule scaling back overtime pay for some white-collar federal workers
- Yes Do not allow use of search warrants without first notifying subjects
- Yes Allow importation of prescription drugs
- Yes Create private school voucher program in Washington, D.C.
- Yes Ban "partial birth" abortion except to save a woman's life
- No Split $18.6 billion in Iraq aid into half-grant, half-loan
- Yes Overhaul Medicare and create prescription drug benefit

CQ VOTE STUDIES

	PARTY UNITY		PRESIDENTIAL SUPPORT	
	Support	Oppose	Support	Oppose
2004	93%	7%	76%	24%
2003	92%	8%	89%	11%
2002	94%	6%	79%	21%
2001	91%	9%	74%	26%
2000	97%	3%	17%	83%

INTEREST GROUPS

	AFL-CIO	ADA	CCUS	ACU
2004	20%	10%	90%	92%
2003	20%	20%	90%	88%
2002	22%	10%	80%	96%
2001	17%	15%	78%	88%
2000	10%	5%	71%	100%

MARYLAND 6
North and west — Frederick, Hagerstown

The 6th reaches across the northern tier of the state from Western Maryland to the Susquehanna River. It takes in all of Garrett, Allegany, Washington, Frederick and Carroll counties, as well as significant portions of Baltimore and Harford counties and a small, exurban slice of Montgomery County. The 6th has a rural tradition and a conservative bent that benefits the GOP. Though Frederick and Carroll counties are thriving economically, the demise of old-line industry has left the Appalachian Mountain area struggling. Some local leaders have tried to promote the region as a destination for vacationers.

Frederick and Carroll are experiencing rapid growth from new residents escaping the city and inner suburbs and commuting to Baltimore and Washington, D.C. Carroll County, however, still has an agricultural economy and remains a Republican stronghold.

During redistricting following the 2000 census, northern portions of Baltimore and Harford counties, where Republicans and old-line conservative Democrats reign, were taken out of the 2nd and folded into

the 6th, bolstering the GOP's hold here. The new 6th gave George W. Bush his highest vote percentage in any Maryland district in both the 2000 (61 percent) and 2004 (65 percent) presidential elections.

The three western counties are less populous and remain solidly conservative. Washington County, with its strong manufacturing base, is the only one experiencing economic prosperity. With companies such as Kelly-Springfield closing their operations, Allegany and Garrett counties both are struggling and have become dependent on tourism.

MAJOR INDUSTRY
Manufacturing, technology, agriculture, tourism

MILITARY BASES
Fort Detrick (Army), 1,500 military, 2,700 civilian (2004)

CITIES
Frederick, 52,767; Hagerstown, 36,687; Eldersburg (unincorporated), 27,741; Cumberland, 21,518; Westminster, 16,731

NOTABLE
Camp David, the president's retreat; Whittaker Chambers' pumpkin patch in Westminster produced evidence for Richard M. Nixon during the Alger Hiss trial; Fort Detrick specializes in biomedical research and development.

Rep. Elijah E. Cummings (D)

Elected April 1996; 5th full term

CAPITOL OFFICE
225-4741
www.house.gov/cummings
2235 Rayburn 20515-2007; fax 225-3178

COMMITTEES
Government Reform
Transportation & Infrastructure
Joint Economic

HOMETOWN
Baltimore

BORN
Jan. 18, 1951, Baltimore, Md.

RELIGION
Baptist

FAMILY
Divorced; three children

EDUCATION
Howard U., B.A. 1973 (political science); U. of
Maryland, J.D. 1976

CAREER
Lawyer

POLITICAL HIGHLIGHTS
Md. House, 1983-96 (Speaker pro tempore, 1995)

ELECTION RESULTS

2004 GENERAL

Elijah E. Cummings (D)	179,189	73.4%
Tony Salazar (R)	60,102	24.6%
Virginia T. Rodino (GREEN)	4,727	1.9%

2004 PRIMARY

Elijah E. Cummings (D)	53,015	91.4%
Charles C. McPeek (D)	4,972	8.6%

2002 GENERAL

Elijah E. Cummings (D)	137,047	73.5%
Joseph E. Ward (R)	49,172	26.4%

PREVIOUS WINNING PERCENTAGES
2000 (87%); 1998 (86%); 1996 (83%); 1996 Special
Election (81%)

After keeping a relatively low profile during his first three terms in the House, Cummings in the 108th Congress served a two-year term as chairman of the Congressional Black Caucus. He soon became one of President Bush's most scathing and frequently quoted critics.

"Americans of good conscience cannot overlook the sharp contrast between the president's words and his deeds," Cummings said in 2004. "The critical question is this: Can America trust this president?"

In assailing Bush, Cummings left no policy area unmentioned — from health care and taxes to foreign policy and the war in Iraq. Addressing Bush's education plan, passed with bipartisan support in 2001 but never fully funded, Cummings accused Bush of empty rhetoric: "Pious declarations about 'leaving no child behind' . . . do not educate one American."

Speaking on behalf of the Black Caucus, Cummings in 2004 called for the resignation of Defense Secretary Donald H. Rumsfeld after disclosures that U.S. military police and military intelligence personnel had abused Iraqi detainees at the Abu Ghraib prison. He also complained about the administration's refusal to get deeply involved in the chaotic situation in Haiti.

Elected caucus chairman in December 2002, Cummings was thrust immediately into the national spotlight. Just a week before, Republican Sen. Trent Lott of Mississippi, who was about to assume the majority leader's post, had suggested that the country would have been better off had Strom Thurmond been elected president in 1948, when he ran on a segregationist platform. The furor ultimately cost Lott his leadership post.

Cummings then led the Black Caucus in protesting Bush's decision to renominate Lott's personal friend, federal District Judge Charles W. Pickering Sr., for the 5th Circuit Court of Appeals. The Democratic-controlled Senate Judiciary Committee had rejected Pickering's nomination in March 2002, criticizing his civil rights record. Caucus members said Bush's decision to renominate Pickering in 2003 "fails to live up to" the spirit of Bush's condemnation of Lott's remarks about Thurmond.

Cummings complained sharply in 2003 that Bush was shutting off dialogue with the all-Democratic Black Caucus. On the same day that Bush was meeting with a group of African-American clergy to boost his faith-based community initiatives, Cummings announced, "The CBC has requested a meeting with the president for over two and a half years and, unfortunately, each time he has refused."

When Bush met with the Black Caucus early in 2005 — after Cummings' chairmanship had ended — he was not sanguine about the outcome: "I don't think anything changed other than we had a very cordial meeting."

Although the Black Caucus is dominated by liberals, its members do not march in lockstep. For example, even though Cummings and most of his colleagues vehemently opposed the war in Iraq, four caucus members voted for it. "This is the first time in our history when we've had such opposing opinions," Cummings told the Baltimore Sun in 2004, "but it reflects black Americans in general. We don't all think the same thing all the time."

His colleagues also credit Cummings for concentrating as chairman on issues that unite them.

A public official for two decades, Cummings has seen his political successes marred by personal financial problems. Owing thousands of dollars in back taxes and other debts when he arrived at the Capitol, he warded off foreclosure proceedings on his house and spent two winters without heat because he could not afford to fix his furnace.

He blamed his shaky finances on conditions that dated back many years — starting his own law firm, trying to support three children, lacking car insurance when he got into an accident — but he told The Baltimore Sun in 1999 that he had finally paid off most of his debts. "I have a moral conscience that is real central," he told the Sun. "I didn't ask the federal government or anyone else to do me any favors."

Cummings, whose mostly urban district has a black majority, says the communities he represents need ample federal assistance to combat illegal drugs and violent crime, improve education and health care, and stimulate economic development. In 2002, Cummings won expanded federal support for a nursing program at Coppin State College in Baltimore. He also has won federal grants for Morgan State University and money to rehabilitate several Baltimore-area school playgrounds.

A member of the Congressional Steel Caucus, Cummings introduced legislation in 2002 to provide health insurance aid for retired steel workers. About 13,000 Bethlehem Steel Corp. retirees live in Baltimore. Cummings also looks for other ways to help his constituents. He holds job fairs and seminars to help them learn about college aid programs.

A Baltimore native, Cummings was one of seven children in a working-class family. His parents had migrated from South Carolina, where they were sharecroppers. "As a young boy in south Baltimore . . . we did not have many opportunities," he recalls. "We did not play on grass. We played on asphalt." But he says he was set on a productive course by "two very strong parents," who scrimped and saved to buy their own home in a city neighborhood that was integrating.

He graduated Phi Beta Kappa from Howard University and earned a law degree from the University of Maryland in 1976. Six years later, he was elected to the state House. During 13 years there, he rose to the chamber's second-ranking position, at the time the highest Maryland office ever held by an African-American. In 1996, he outpaced 26 other Democrats and five Republicans to replace Democrat Kweisi Mfume, who resigned from the House to become president of the NAACP. Since then, Cummings' November election tally has never dropped below 70 percent — a consistency of support that has led to his name being mentioned continually as a possible candidate for mayor of Baltimore. And, after Mfume stepped down at the NAACP at the end of 2004, Cummings was mentioned as a possible successor. Both Mfume and Cummings may opt to run in 2006 for the open Senate seat created by Democratic Sen. Paul S. Sarbanes' retirement.

KEY VOTES

2004
Yes Extend federal unemployment benefits by 13 weeks
Yes Pass $283.2 billion, six-year federal highway and mass transit bill
Yes Approve $146 billion multi-year extension of previously enacted middle-class tax breaks
No Amend the Constitution to prohibit same-sex marriage
No Cut corporate taxes $137 billion over 10 years
Yes Reorganize U.S. intelligence agencies as proposed by Sept. 11 commission

2003
No Cut taxes by $330 billion through fiscal 2013
Yes Block Bush rule scaling back overtime pay for some white-collar federal workers
Yes Do not allow use of search warrants without first notifying subjects
Yes Allow importation of prescription drugs
No Create private school voucher program in Washington, D.C.
No Ban "partial birth" abortion except to save a woman's life
Yes Split $18.6 billion in Iraq aid into half-grant, half-loan
No Overhaul Medicare and create prescription drug benefit

CQ VOTE STUDIES

| | PARTY UNITY | | PRESIDENTIAL SUPPORT | |
	Support	Oppose	Support	Oppose
2004	98%	2%	21%	79%
2003	97%	3%	14%	86%
2002	95%	5%	25%	75%
2001	95%	5%	19%	81%
2000	97%	3%	88%	12%

INTEREST GROUPS

	AFL-CIO	ADA	CCUS	ACU
2004	100%	100%	30%	0%
2003	100%	90%	25%	18%
2002	100%	95%	45%	0%
2001	100%	95%	27%	4%
2000	100%	85%	47%	4%

MARYLAND 7
Downtown Baltimore; part of Columbia

The 7th takes in both the low-income neighborhoods of West Baltimore and much of downtown, including the bustling retail center of the Inner Harbor. The 7th follows the black migration west to include Baltimore County's middle-class southwestern suburbs, and it also includes the bulk of Howard County, including the western portion of Columbia, a liberal-leaning planned community between Baltimore and Washington.

The 7th's black majority, the most in the state at 59 percent, gives Democrats a distinct advantage in national and local contests through much of the district. But Republicans regularly win on the local level in the more rural parts of Howard County.

Efforts to improve Baltimore's poor neighborhoods have been slow, and urban problems, such as crime, drug abuse, teen pregnancy and unemployment, have prompted many of the city's middle-class residents to head to the suburbs.

But the picture within the city is not all bleak. Many of Baltimore's most

identifiable landmarks and businesses are in the 7th. The gentrified Mount Vernon area, home of the Walters Art Museum and the Peabody Institute, are within its boundaries. Farther north are Johns Hopkins University and the Baltimore Museum of Art.

In addition to the revitalized Inner Harbor waterfront, the old retail section west of the downtown hub still survives; Lexington Market and the Baltimore Arena are here. There are middle-class black communities along Liberty Heights Road in West Baltimore.

Just southwest of the city, the University of Maryland, Baltimore County and its adjacent research area are attracting technology firms.

MAJOR INDUSTRY
Health care, manufacturing, technology

CITIES
Baltimore (pt.), 370,752; Ellicott City (unincorporated) (pt.), 56,231; Columbia (unincorporated) (pt.), 47,943; Catonsville (unincorporated), 39,820; Woodlawn (unincorporated), 36,079

NOTABLE
The 7th's portion of Baltimore is home to NAACP national headquarters, author Edgar Allan Poe's gravesite and the National Aquarium.

Rep. Chris Van Hollen (D)

Elected 2002; 2nd term

CAPITOL OFFICE
225-5341
chris.vanhollen@mail.house.gov
www.house.gov/vanhollen
1419 Longworth 20515-2008; fax 225-0375

COMMITTEES
Education & Workforce
Government Reform
Judiciary

HOMETOWN
Kensington

BORN
Jan. 10, 1959, Karachi, Pakistan

RELIGION
Episcopalian

FAMILY
Wife, Katherine Wilkens Van Hollen; three children

EDUCATION
Swarthmore College, B.A. 1983 (philosophy);
Harvard U., M.P.P. 1985; Georgetown U., J.D. 1990

CAREER
Lawyer; gubernatorial aide; congressional aide

POLITICAL HIGHLIGHTS
Md. House, 1991-95; Md. Senate, 1995-2003

ELECTION RESULTS

2004 GENERAL

Chris Van Hollen (D)	215,129	74.8%
Chuck Floyd (R)	71,989	25.0%

2004 PRIMARY

Chris Van Hollen (D)	67,805	91.1%
Deborah A. Vollmer (D)	4,847	6.5%
Lih Y. Young (D)	1,784	2.4%

2002 GENERAL

Chris Van Hollen (D)	112,788	51.7%
Constance A. Morella (R)	103,587	47.5%

Well-educated and well-traveled, Van Hollen's résumé is a good match for his district, a swath of demographically elite suburbs just outside Washington, D.C. In his short time in the House, he has cultivated an interest in education and foreign policy. Van Hollen is capable of searing analysis in the latter arena; his critique in 2003 of the Bush administration's handling of the war in Iraq received national attention.

In the 109th Congress, the Georgetown University-educated lawyer got a seat on the Judiciary Committee from Minority Leader Nancy Pelosi, who waived a two-panel limit set by the party to let him take a third assignment. He also was named to head a 10-member group on the Democratic Congressional Campaign Committee that meets weekly to plot candidate recruitment for the 2006 election.

Van Hollen's top domestic issue is improving public schools, which has appeal in the generally affluent, white-collar area he represents. Many constituents work in the capital city's main industry — politics and government — and still others in science, technology and the emerging biotech field.

In his first term, Van Hollen used his seat on the Education Committee to press the Bush administration to boost education funding, including for President Bush's own signature No Child Left Behind Act, which set tough new testing standards for public schools. He was also a leading proponent of making aid for special-needs students mandatory, which would up the federal contribution from 18 percent to 40 percent for programs under the Individuals with Disabilities Education Act. Though doomed in the Republican-controlled House, his efforts helped highlight what he said was the GOP's unwillingness to pay for promised improvements in schools.

Van Hollen also sits on the Government Reform Committee, where he had more tangible success with another issue of vital interest to his district: a Bush proposal to give some federal jobs to private contractors. Taking Republican leaders by surprise, Van Hollen pushed through the House an amendment to the 2004 Transportation-Treasury spending bill that blocked funding for the so-called outsourcing initiative. His proposal gained 26 GOP votes, prevailing 220-198. An identical Senate measure failed to pass by one vote, and Van Hollen's amendment was weakened in the final bill.

He was perhaps a bigger thorn for Bush on Iraq policy. The views of most freshman House members don't usually figure prominently in matters of war and peace, but Van Hollen's carried weight. In the late 1980s, when he was a young aide to the Senate Foreign Relations Committee, he traveled to the Iraq-Turkish border to interview rebel ethnic Kurds about Saddam Hussein's use of chemical weapons against them. His and colleague Peter Galbraith's report resulted in an ultimately unsuccessful attempt in Congress to impose economic sanctions against Iraq. (Galbraith went on to broker peace agreements in Bosnia and Croatia.)

In speeches on the House floor and at the University of Maryland, Van Hollen said the unilateral invasion of Iraq had squandered international sympathy for the United States after the Sept. 11, 2001, terrorist attacks, and that the Iraq war would not result in more democracy in the Middle East. "It is just as easy to imagine a scenario where difficulties in Iraq fuel resentment of occupying American troops and inflame the region against us," he said in widely quoted remarks.

Van Hollen takes a liberal tack on social issues, favoring abortion rights and restrictions on the availability of guns. He fought without result in 2003 to stop a bill shielding gun dealers and manufacturers from lawsuits by gun-crime victims and another measure exempting gun sale statistics from public disclosure under the Freedom of Information Act. Six of the 10 people killed by snipers in random attacks in the Washington area in October 2002 lived in his district.

Van Hollen is also in step with liberals on tax policy. The GOP's attempt to further cut taxes in 2003 while boosting spending on Iraq was "reckless," he said.

The son of a Foreign Service officer, Van Hollen was born in Pakistan and lived in Turkey and Sri Lanka, where his father was ambassador. His mother is an expert on Russia. When he reached his teens, he went back to the states to Middlesex boarding school in Concord, Mass. From there, Van Hollen landed at Swarthmore College and then at Harvard's prestigious Kennedy School of Government, where he earned a master's degree in public policy and national security studies.

Doors on Capitol Hill quickly opened for him, and Van Hollen was hired on the staff of Maryland Sen. Charles McC. Mathias Jr. When Mathias retired in 1986, Van Hollen moved to a job on the Foreign Relations Committee as an arms control and NATO specialist.

He then launched his own political career by winning a Maryland House seat in 1990, and spent a total of 12 years in the Maryland House and Senate. He distinguished himself by successfully pushing for a state law mandating trigger locks on guns, two cigarette tax increases opposed by the tobacco lobby and a big boost in funding for Montgomery County schools. He also led a drive to block drilling for gas in the Chesapeake Bay.

A promotion to Congress seemed out of reach, however, as Republican Constance A. Morella proved in every election that she could overcome the Democratic impulses of Van Hollen's home turf with political moderation. She was one of the most liberal House Republicans. But redistricting changed things in 2000. Minority neighborhoods in Prince George's County, which abuts Montgomery, were added to bolster Democratic registration, and suddenly the district looked better for Van Hollen.

First, he had to take on fellow Democrats in a four-way primary, defeating by a breath his most serious rival, Maryland state Rep. Mark K. Shriver, a nephew of President Kennedy. He and Morella then waged one of the most expensive and closely watched contests of the 2000 election. Each spent about $3 million. Van Hollen eked out a 4 percentage point win. In 2004, he won handily with 75 percent of the vote. He may run for the seat of retiring Democratic Sen. Paul S. Sarbanes in 2006.

KEY VOTES

2004
Yes Extend federal unemployment benefits by 13 weeks
Yes Pass $283.2 billion, six-year federal highway and mass transit bill
Yes Approve $146 billion multi-year extension of previously enacted middle-class tax breaks
No   Amend the Constitution to prohibit same-sex marriage
No   Cut corporate taxes $137 billion over 10 years
Yes Reorganize U.S. intelligence agencies as proposed by Sept. 11 commission

2003
No   Cut taxes by $330 billion through fiscal 2013
Yes Block Bush rule scaling back overtime pay for some white-collar federal workers
Yes Do not allow use of search warrants without first notifying subjects
Yes Allow importation of prescription drugs
No   Create private school voucher program in Washington, D.C.
No   Ban "partial birth" abortion except to save a woman's life
No   Split $18.6 billion in Iraq aid into half-grant, half-loan
No   Overhaul Medicare and create prescription drug benefit

CQ VOTE STUDIES

	PARTY UNITY		PRESIDENTIAL SUPPORT	
	Support	Oppose	Support	Oppose
2004	96%	4%	35%	65%
2003	97%	3%	22%	78%

INTEREST GROUPS

	AFL-CIO	ADA	CCUS	ACU
2004	100%	100%	38%	4%
2003	87%	95%	33%	16%

MARYLAND 8

Part of Montgomery County — Bethesda, Gaithersburg, Rockville

The 8th contains wealthy Montgomery County suburbs northwest of Washington, D.C., such as Bethesda, Chevy Chase and Potomac, as well as less-affluent suburbs in eastern Montgomery and western Prince George's County. It also includes rural areas northwest of Potomac and the Interstate 270 technology corridor, a hotbed for high-tech and biotechnology companies that runs through Rockville and Gaithersburg.

The district was redrawn to elect a Democrat following the 2000 census. Mapmakers removed some GOP-leaning areas in northern Montgomery County and added liberal Takoma Park, as well as heavily black and Hispanic neighborhoods in western Prince George's County. The 8th has the highest percentage of Asians (11 percent) and Hispanics (14 percent) of any Maryland district, and its support for John Kerry in the 2004 presidential election — 69 percent of the vote — was beaten in Maryland only by the state's two black-majority districts.

Government is the dominant employer in the 8th, where federal agencies abound and Rockville is the Montgomery County seat. The large contingent of educated professionals supports a thriving economy that is bolstered by a wide array of big-name business interests, including Lockheed Martin, Marriott and IBM.

Potomac, in the western part of the district, is known for its horse farms and expensive estates. In the far west, officials struggle to preserve an agricultural heritage.

MAJOR INDUSTRY
Government, technology, service, retail

MILITARY BASES
National Geospatial-Intelligence Agency, 6,500 civilian (2004); National Naval Medical Center, 2,307 military, 1,329 civilian (2003); Naval Surface Warfare Center, Carderock Division, 6 military, 1,500 civilian (2004)

CITIES
Wheaton-Glenmont (unincorporated), 57,694; Bethesda (unincorporated), 55,277; Gaithersburg, 52,613; Rockville, 47,388

NOTABLE
Author F. Scott Fitzgerald is buried in Rockville.

MASSACHUSETTS

Gov. Mitt Romney (R)

First elected: 2002
Length of term: 4 years
Term expires: 1/07
Salary: $135,000
Phone: (617) 725-4005

Hometown: Belmont
Born: March 12, 1947;
Detroit, Mich.
Religion: Mormon
Family: Wife, Ann Davies; five children
Education: Stanford U., attended 1965-66;
Brigham Young U., B.A. 1971 (English);
Harvard U., M.B.A. 1975, J.D. 1975
Career: Salt Lake City Olympic organizing
committee president; venture capitalist
Political highlights: Republican nominee
for U.S. Senate, 1994

Election results:
2002 GENERAL

Mitt Romney (R)	1,091,988	49.8%
Shannon P. O'Brien (D)	985,981	44.9%
Jill Stein (GREEN)	76,530	3.5%
Carla Howell (LIBERT)	23,044	1.1%

Lt. Gov. Kerry Healey (R)

First elected: 2002
Length of term: 4 years
Term expires: 1/07
Salary: $120,000
Phone: (617) 725-4005

STATE LEGISLATURE

General Court: Usually year-round,
but meeting time varies

House: 160 members, 2-year terms
2005 breakdown: 136D, 21R,
3 vacancies; 117 men, 40 women
Salary: $55,000
Phone: (617) 722-2356

Senate: 40 members, 2-year terms
2005 breakdown: 34D, 6R; 30 male,
10 female
Salary: $63,070
Phone: (617) 722-1276

STATE TERM LIMITS

Governor: 2 terms
House: No
Senate: No

URBAN STATISTICS

CITY	POPULATION
Boston	589,141
Worcester	172,648
Springfield	152,082
Lowell	105,167
Cambridge	101,355

REGISTERED VOTERS

Unenrolled	49%
Democrat	37%
Republican	13%
Others	1%

POPULATION

2004 population (est.)	6,416,505
2000 population	6,349,097
1990 population	6,016,425
Percent change (1990-2000)	+5.5%
Rank among states (2004)	13

Median age	36.5
Born in state	66.1%
Foreign born	12.2%
Violent crime rate	476/100,000
Poverty level	9.3%
Federal workers	53,161
Military	23,516

REDISTRICTING

Massachusetts retained its 10 House
seats in reapportionment. The state
legislature drew a new map, which
the governor allowed to become law
without her signature on Feb. 11,
2002.

MISCELLANEOUS

Web: www.mass.gov
Capital: Boston
STATE ELECTION OFFICIAL
(617) 727-2828
**DEMOCRATIC
HEADQUARTERS**
(617) 472-0637
**REPUBLICAN
HEADQUARTERS**
(617) 523-5005

District Statistics

DIST.	2004 VOTE FOR PRESIDENT BUSH	KERRY	WHITE	BLACK	ASIAN	HISP	MEDIAN INCOME	WHITE COLLAR	BLUE COLLAR	SERVICE INDUSTRY	OVER 64	UNDER 18	COLLEGE EDUCATION	RURAL	SQ. MILES
1	35%	63%	89%	2%	2%	6%	$42,570	60%	24%	16%	14%	24%	25%	31%	3,101
2	40	59	82	5	1	9	$44,386	61	24	15	14	26	23	15	922
3	40	59	86	3	3	6	$50,223	66	21	14	13	25	31	7	581
4	34	65	88	2	3	3	$53,169	68	20	13	14	24	37	12	732
5	41	57	80	2	5	12	$56,217	67	21	12	11	27	34	7	566
6	41	58	90	2	2	4	$57,826	70	18	13	14	24	35	5	480
7	33	66	84	3	6	5	$56,110	73	14	13	16	21	40	0	170
8	16	82	49	22	8	16	$39,300	71	13	17	9	18	40	0	41
9	38	61	79	8	4	5	$55,407	69	17	14	14	24	34	2	313
10	43	56	92	2	3	1	$51,928	67	18	15	17	23	34	8	934
STATE	37	62	82	5	4	7	$50,502	67	19	14	14	24	33	9	7,840
U.S.	50.7	48.3	69	12	4	13	$41,994	60	25	15	12	26	24	21	3,537,438

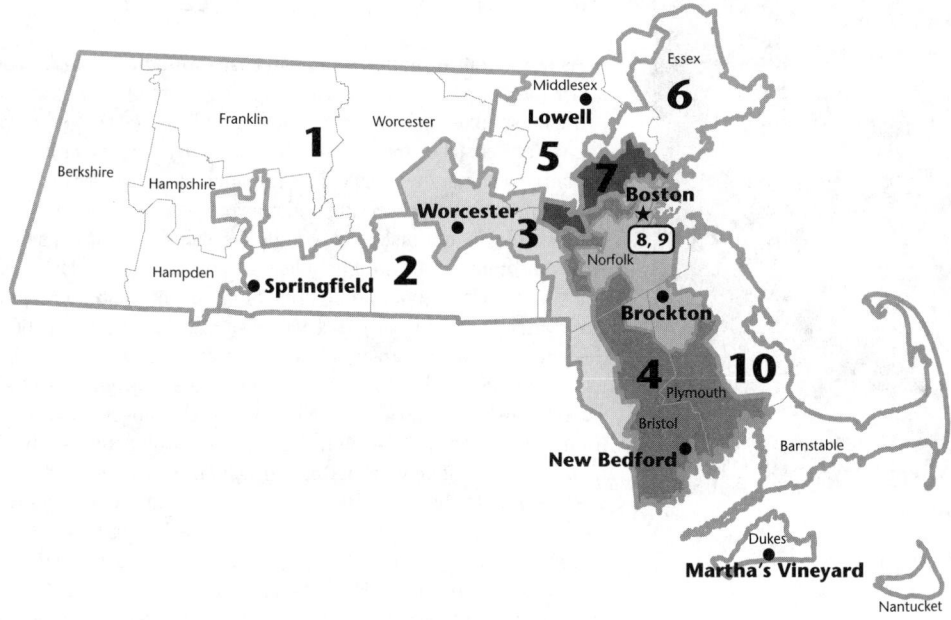

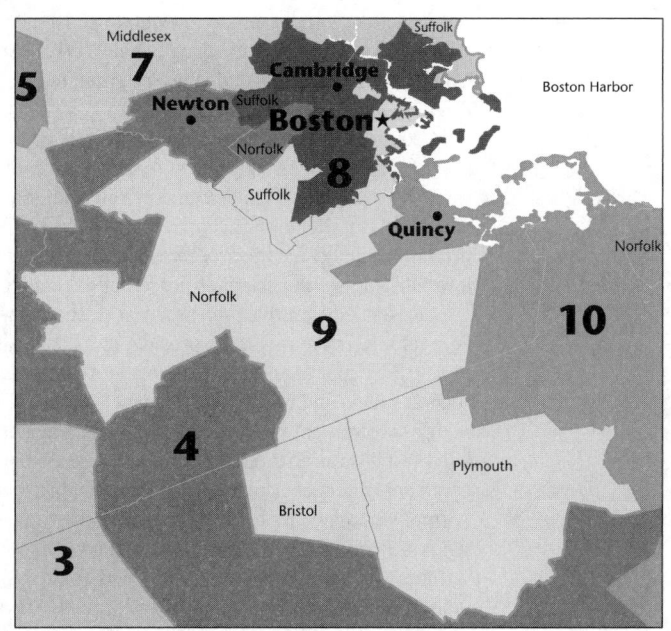

Sen. Edward M. Kennedy (D)

Elected 1962; 7th full term

CAPITOL OFFICE
224-4543
senator@kennedy.senate.gov
kennedy.senate.gov
317 Russell 20510-2101; fax 224-2417

COMMITTEES
Armed Services
Health, Education, Labor & Pensions - ranking
  member
Judiciary
Joint Economic

HOMETOWN
Hyannis Port

BORN
Feb. 22, 1932, Boston, Mass.

RELIGION
Roman Catholic

FAMILY
Wife, Victoria Reggie Kennedy; three children, two
stepchildren

EDUCATION
Harvard U., A.B. 1956 (government); International
Law School, The Hague (The Netherlands),
attended 1958; U. of Virginia, LL.B. 1959

MILITARY SERVICE
Army, 1951-53

CAREER
Lawyer

POLITICAL HIGHLIGHTS
Suffolk County assistant district attorney, 1961-62;
sought Democratic nomination for president, 1980

ELECTION RESULTS

2000 GENERAL

Edward M. Kennedy (D)	1,889,494	72.7%
Jack E. Robinson III (R)	334,341	12.9%
Carla Howell (LIBERT)	308,860	11.9%
Philip Lawler (CNSTP)	42,113	1.6%

2000 PRIMARY

Edward M. Kennedy (D)	236,883	99.0%
write-ins	2,467	1.0%

PREVIOUS WINNING PERCENTAGES
1994 (58%); 1988 (65%); 1982 (61%); 1976 (69%);
1970 (62%); 1964 (74%); 1962 Special Election (55%)

As Democrats struggle to come to terms with their status as a minority party, Kennedy towers as one of their most forceful spokesmen, and one of the most influential legislators on Capitol Hill. He is the embodiment of Democrats' nostalgia for his family's political dynasty, and as he settles into his fifth decade in the Senate, he is an anchor for his party's liberal base. But his passion for preserving and improving social programs should not be mistaken for intransigence. Kennedy retains a keen sense of how and when to compromise with Republicans to transform bills into laws.

Kennedy has been a leading critic of President Bush's foreign policies, a role he capped off in early 2005 with a vote against the nomination of Condoleezza Rice to be secretary of state. He called Rice the "principal architect of our failed policy" in Iraq. As some Democrats tempered their opposition to Bush's Iraq policy — wary of being tagged by Republicans as unpatriotic — Kennedy intensified his criticism. He called the war "Bush's Vietnam." In a 2004 floor speech, Kennedy said the president had misled Congress before the invasion. "Before the war, week after week after week after week, we were told lie after lie after lie after lie," he said.

For all of his passionate rhetoric, Kennedy has demonstrated a flare for pragmatic deal-making on issues that he cares about. During the 108th Congress, he played a pivotal role in negotiations on Bush's Medicare overhaul. A longtime proponent of adding prescription drugs to the federal health program for senior citizens and the disabled, Kennedy's support for the bill brought along other Democrats who opposed allowing private insurance companies to administer the drug benefit. "With a Republican president and Congress, this is the best deal we're going to get," Kennedy told the Los Angeles Times in November 2003.

In 2001, he teamed up with Bush to win enactment of a law tying federal school aid more directly to test results. "I've come to admire him," Bush said. "He's a smart, capable senator. You want him on your side, I can tell you that." But the following year, when Bush and Republicans backed off promises to fully fund the programs, Kennedy called the education law "hollow talk" and set the stage for fierce budget battles over the program.

Still, Kennedy is as partisan as any at election time. He threw himself into Sen. John Kerry's run for the presidency in 2004, dispatching former aides to help the junior Massachusetts senator's campaign and joining him on the road at rallies and fundraising events. Some strategists fretted that Kennedy's involvement would turn swing voters against Kerry. Others speculated that it was a chance to avenge his own crushing loss in the 1980 Democratic presidential primaries. But Kennedy brushed off such theories and seemed energized by his leading role in the campaign, even shedding 40 pounds as he stumped around the country.

After the painful defeat of Kerry and congressional Democrats at the polls, Kennedy called on his party colleagues to revamp the way they articulated their ideals and goals, in an effort to deprive Republicans of the politically potent monopoly they seemed to have claimed on moral values.

Kennedy's public image has long been defined by family triumph, tragedy and scandal. But he has built a very different reputation at the Capitol, where he is now the third-longest-serving senator. The power of his rhetoric in favor of organized labor, health care for all and environmental protection wins grudging admiration even from opponents. Republicans still favor him as their metaphor for the wrong approach to federal governance

— the "Ted Kennedy liberal" label remains the most cutting epithet they can sling — but they have found him to be a Democrat with whom they can deal. Despite their philosophical differences, one of Kennedy's most productive and friendly alliances has been with conservative Utah Republican Orrin G. Hatch, the chairman of the Judiciary Committee.

Kennedy long ago understood the iron law of the Senate: Little can be accomplished without the 60 votes needed to overcome filibusters, the endless speeches aimed at delaying and ultimately killing a bill. And that requires compromises that cross party lines. Former New York Times reporter Adam Clymer wrote in a 1999 biography, "Kennedy has built a career on that understanding, winning victories over three decades on civil rights, election law, health care, crime and other subjects, in a series of alliances with key Republicans from Howard Baker . . . to Strom Thurmond."

For all his willingness to cut a deal when half a loaf appears within his grasp, Kennedy still fights losing battles with zeal, seeking patients' rights protections, minimum wage increases, a ban on employment discrimination against gays and more. From his desk at the rear of the Senate, he can raise the somnolent with his thunderous roar, his face reddening and his voice needing no electronic amplification.

Kennedy is also known for a penchant for reckless behavior, although, now in his early 70s, he seems to have mellowed. There was the 1969 auto accident at Chappaquiddick in which the passenger in his car, Mary Jo Kopechne, drowned; the long period of pub-crawling in the 1980s; the 1991 revelry with his son Patrick and nephew William Kennedy Smith at a Florida nightclub, where Smith met a woman who subsequently accused him of rape. (Smith was acquitted after a highly publicized trial.) But Kennedy's personal life stabilized after 1992, when he was married for the second time, to Washington attorney Victoria Reggie.

Doubts about Kennedy's judgment fueled Republican hopes of defeating him in 1994, when Republican venture capitalist Mitt Romney (now a Massachusetts governor harboring presidential ambitions) tapped his personal fortune to mount a campaign tagging the senator as tired and haggard. Kennedy fought back, touring the state delivering federal checks and painting Romney as unprepared for Congress. Bucking the year's GOP tide, Kennedy won with 58 percent of the vote. In 2000, he won his seventh full term with 73 percent against another wealthy businessman, Jack E. Robinson III. He has not announced his plans for the future, but many analysts believe Kennedy will seek re-election for the last time in 2006.

The youngest of nine children of Rose Fitzgerald, a congressman's daughter, and Joseph P. Kennedy, an ambassador to Britain and the first chairman of the Securities and Exchange Commission, Kennedy was first elected in 1962, at age 30, to fill the remaining two years of President John F. Kennedy's Senate term. The president had arranged for family friend Benjamin A. Smith to be appointed until his youngest brother was old enough under the Constitution to serve.

After John Kennedy was assassinated in 1963 and Sen. Robert F. Kennedy of New York was assassinated while seeking the Democratic presidential nomination in 1968, Kennedy felt intense pressure to take up his brothers' fallen banner. But when he challenged President Carter in 1980, memories of Chappaquiddick were still too fresh, and the candidate failed to articulate a clear idea of why he wanted to be president.

For many, the most memorable moment of Kennedy's campaign came at its finale, in his concession speech at the Democratic National Convention. "For all those whose cares have been our concern," Kennedy intoned, "the work goes on, the cause endures, the hope still lives, and the dream shall never die."

KEY VOTES

2004

Yes   Pass $318.9 billion, six-year highway and mass transit bill

Yes   Extend assault weapons ban for 10 years

Yes   Restore pay-as-you-go rules for new tax cuts and entitlement spending

No   Criminalize harm to a fetus in an attack on the mother

Yes   Increase mandatory child care funding to states by $6 billion over five years

No   Amend the Constitution to prohibit same-sex marriage

?   Approve $146 billion multi-year extension of previously enacted middle-class tax breaks

Yes   Reorganize U.S. intelligence agencies as proposed by Sept. 11 commission

No   Cut corporate taxes $137 billion over 10 years

2003

Yes   Delay Bush changes to Clean Air Act

No   Allow confirmation vote on Miguel A. Estrada to the U.S. Court of Appeals for the D.C. Circuit

Yes   Block a Bush proposal opening Alaska's Arctic National Wildlife Refuge to oil drilling

Yes   Limit size of Bush's proposed tax cut to $350 billion through fiscal 2013

Yes   Overhaul Medicare and create prescription drug benefit

Yes   Block Bush rule scaling back overtime pay for some white-collar federal workers

Yes   Split $20 billion in Iraq aid into half-grant, half-loan

No   Ban "partial birth" abortion except to save a woman's life

No   Stop proposal allowing travel to Cuba

No   Allow final vote on energy policy overhaul

CQ VOTE STUDIES

	PARTY UNITY		PRESIDENTIAL SUPPORT	
	Support	Oppose	Support	Oppose
2004	98%	2%	59%	41%
2003	97%	3%	47%	53%
2002	97%	3%	64%	36%
2001	97%	3%	66%	34%
2000	98%	2%	94%	6%
1999	97%	3%	93%	7%
1998	100%	0%	96%	4%
1997	97%	3%	88%	12%
1996	94%	6%	88%	12%
1995	96%	4%	92%	8%

INTEREST GROUPS

	AFL-CIO	ADA	CCUS	ACU
2004	100%	100%	31%	0%
2003	100%	95%	26%	10%
2002	100%	100%	29%	0%
2001	100%	100%	38%	4%
2000	86%	90%	40%	12%
1999	88%	95%	47%	4%
1998	100%	95%	47%	0%
1997	100%	100%	40%	4%
1996	100%	90%	38%	0%
1995	100%	100%	33%	4%

Sen. John Kerry (D)

Elected 1984; 4th term

Before he launched his campaign for the presidency, Kerry was known as a thoughtful senator with valuable foreign policy knowledge and investigative skills, but one without a lot of legislative accomplishments to his name. But he returned to the Senate with a wealth of policy proposals developed for his campaign on a full range of national issues. Even as Senate Democrats' reduced number gives them little power to enact an agenda of their own, Kerry's presidential run offers him an opportunity to become a better and more aggressive legislator than he was before.

Rather than simply returning to the position of top-ranking Democrat on the Small Business Committee, Kerry has turned his Senate office into a kind of permanent campaign against President Bush, against his Republican colleagues, and for another possible White House bid in 2008 — a scenario he has done nothing to discourage. He has kept his old campaign Web site running as an online organizing tool and created a political action committee called Keeping America's Promise, which allows him to raise money for other candidates and keep his own profile high at the same time.

He has also turned his campaign platform into a legislative agenda. Barely two weeks after the election, Kerry announced that his first bill in the 109th Congress would be a measure to provide health insurance to all children, based on part of his campaign health care plan. Before his presidential run, Kerry had largely deferred to the senior senator from Massachusetts, Democrat Edward M. Kennedy, on health care issues. Kerry now puts more energy into the effort, at least on the surface. He rounded up signatures for an online petition supporting the bill and threatened to campaign in 2006 against any senator who opposed it.

Kerry wants the public to see him as a changed man, more of a populist than he was before he hit the campaign trail. He says he engineered 35,000 phone calls to Senate Majority Leader Bill Frist and House Speaker J. Dennis Hastert demanding support for a new effort to set federal standards for elections — a response to the lingering distrust among many Democrats of the voting machines and processes that were used in 2004. He also introduced a measure, based on another campaign proposal, to overhaul the military by adding 40,000 troops and to help military families by giving a tax credit to small businesses that make up the wages reservists lose when they go on active duty.

Kerry's return to the Senate, where he has already spent 20 years of his political life, has been awkward on some levels. He is pushing against a larger Republican majority, full of senators who issued blistering attacks against him as surrogates for the Bush campaign. His initial efforts were seen in some circles as competition with the new Democratic leadership, particularly Minority Leader Harry Reid, who does not have the television presence or the national fame Kerry gained from the campaign. And many of the post-election commentaries were brutal to Kerry, calling him an overly cautious campaigner and an unlikeable candidate.

But most Senate Democrats were more charitable to their colleague. They say they respect the fact that he won 59 million votes, more than any previous Democratic presidential nominee. And Kerry's star power is likely to make him a popular frontman for bills important to the party. Still, Democrats say Kerry will have to put more focus into his Senate work than he has in the past — and they note pointedly that he will still be seen as one of 100 senators, not the party's leader.

CAPITOL OFFICE
224-2742
kerry.senate.gov
304 Russell 20510-2102; fax 224-8525

COMMITTEES
Commerce, Science & Transportation
Finance
Foreign Relations
Small Business & Entrepreneurship -ranking member

HOMETOWN
Boston

BORN
Dec. 11, 1943, Denver, Colo.

RELIGION
Roman Catholic

FAMILY
Wife, Teresa Heinz; two children, three stepchildren

EDUCATION
Yale U., B.A. 1966 (political science); Boston College, J.D. 1976

MILITARY SERVICE
Navy, 1966-70

CAREER
Lawyer; county prosecutor

POLITICAL HIGHLIGHTS
Democratic nominee for U.S. House, 1972; lieutenant governor, 1983-85; Democratic nominee for president, 2004

ELECTION RESULTS

2002 GENERAL

John Kerry (D)	1,605,976	80.0%
Michael E. Cloud (LIBERT)	369,807	18.4%
Randall Forsberg - write-in	24,898	1.2%

2002 PRIMARY

John Kerry (D)	unopposed

PREVIOUS WINNING PERCENTAGES
1996 (52%); 1990 (57%); 1984 (55%)

Kerry has always struggled with an aloof, blue-blood image, which was not helped by a widely broadcast videotape of him windsurfing during a break from the presidential campaign. Largely because of the inherited wealth of his wife, Teresa Heinz, he is one of the 50 richest members of Congress, with a net worth estimated by the Los Angeles Times to be somewhere between $900 million and $3.2 billion.

In addition to his position as the No. 1 Democrat on Small Business, Kerry holds seats on other committees that could provide him a platform for his expertise. He sits on the Foreign Relations Committee, where he enjoys good relations with the senior Democrat, Joseph R. Biden Jr. of Delaware, and Republican Chuck Hagel of Nebraska, both of whom have echoed Kerry's calls for the Bush administration to improve the United States' relations with the international community. He also is a member of the Finance Committee — the staging ground for debates on Social Security, health care and tax policy — and the Commerce Committee.

Kerry's foreign policy background is important to a Democratic Party that is trying to gain more credibility on the subject, as is his background as a veteran of the Vietnam War. Although Kerry's war record was not as helpful to the presidential campaign as he had hoped, it led to one of his most notable achievements in the Senate.

As chairman of the Senate Select Committee on POW/MIA Affairs in the 102nd Congress, Kerry joined forces with Republican John McCain of Arizona — a fellow Vietnam veteran whom Kerry sounded out as a potential running mate in 2004 — on a report that found no evidence that any missing soldiers were still alive in Vietnam. The report paved the way for President Clinton to normalize diplomatic relations with the country in 1995.

Kerry, a former prosecutor, is also known for his oversight investigations, notably his inquiry into the Bank of Credit and Commerce International scandal in the late 1980s and early 1990s. The probe did not unearth the most damning information about the bank, but Kerry was widely credited for being first on the scene and paving the way for other investigations. His loyalists say it also put his compassionate side on display. His staff urged him to be tougher on Democratic power broker Clark Clifford, who was caught up in the scandal and was unable to recall specific names and dates in his 1991 testimony. "He couldn't remember," Kerry responded. "I'm not going to humiliate an old man."

After rising to the rank of lieutenant in the Navy, Kerry became one of the nation's most prominent demonstrators against the Vietnam War when he returned to the United States. He got front-page coverage in April 1971 when he asked the Senate Foreign Relations Committee, "How do you ask a man to be the last man to die for a mistake?" He tried to exploit the publicity by moving to Lowell and running for an open House seat in 1972. He won the primary, but lost in the fall to Republican Paul Cronin.

After his defeat, he went to law school and then worked as an assistant district attorney in Middlesex County. In 1982, he was elected lieutenant governor in a challenge to the Democratic establishment. Two years later, he beat Democratic Rep. James M. Shannon for the nomination to replace retiring Sen. Paul E. Tsongas. He won the general election over conservative businessman Raymond Shamie with 55 percent of the vote.

In 1996, he faced his toughest challenge yet from William F. Weld, then the state's popular GOP governor. On the campaign trail, Weld's affable, down-to-earth style contrasted well with Kerry's stiff persona. But Kerry's late spending and solid performance in a series of debates carried him to victory by 7 percentage points. In 2002, Republicans did not even bother to run a candidate against him.

KEY VOTES

2004

+	Pass $318.9 billion, six-year highway and mass transit bill
Yes	Extend assault weapons ban for 10 years
Yes	Restore pay-as-you-go rules for new tax cuts and entitlement spending
No	Criminalize harm to a fetus in an attack on the mother
+	Increase mandatory child care funding to states by $6 billion over five years
?	Amend the Constitution to prohibit same-sex marriage
?	Approve $146 billion multi-year extension of previously enacted middle-class tax breaks
?	Reorganize U.S. intelligence agencies as proposed by Sept. 11 commission
?	Cut corporate taxes $137 billion over 10 years

2003

Yes	Delay Bush changes to Clean Air Act
No	Allow confirmation vote on Miguel A. Estrada to the U.S. Court of Appeals for the D.C. Circuit
Yes	Block a Bush proposal opening Alaska's Arctic National Wildlife Refuge to oil drilling
Yes	Limit size of Bush's proposed tax cut to $350 billion through fiscal 2013
?	Overhaul Medicare and create prescription drug benefit
Yes	Block Bush rule scaling back overtime pay for some white-collar federal workers
Yes	Split $20 billion in Iraq aid into half-grant, half-loan
No	Ban "partial birth" abortion except to save a woman's life
—	Stop proposal allowing travel to Cuba
—	Allow final vote on energy policy overhaul

CQ VOTE STUDIES

	PARTY UNITY		PRESIDENTIAL SUPPORT	
	Support	Oppose	Support	Oppose
2004	100%	0%	50%	50%
2003	100%	0%	30%	70%
2002	92%	8%	72%	28%
2001	98%	2%	65%	35%
2000	96%	4%	97%	3%
1999	95%	5%	93%	7%
1998	95%	5%	94%	6%
1997	97%	3%	87%	13%
1996	92%	8%	92%	8%
1995	92%	8%	87%	13%

INTEREST GROUPS

	AFL-CIO	ADA	CCUS	ACU
2004	100%	25%	—	0%
2003	100%	85%	0%	13%
2002	92%	85%	55%	20%
2001	100%	95%	38%	4%
2000	75%	90%	53%	12%
1999	78%	95%	53%	0%
1998	100%	95%	50%	4%
1997	71%	95%	50%	0%
1996	86%	95%	31%	5%
1995	100%	95%	32%	4%

Rep. John W. Olver (D)

CAPITOL OFFICE
225-5335
www.house.gov/olver
1111 Longworth 20515-2101; fax 226-1224

COMMITTEES
Appropriations

HOMETOWN
Amherst

BORN
Sept. 3, 1936, Honesdale, Pa.

RELIGION
Unspecified

FAMILY
Wife, Rose Olver; one child

EDUCATION
Rensselaer Polytechnic Institute, B.S. 1955 (chemistry); Tufts U., M.S. 1956 (chemistry); Massachusetts Institute of Technology, Ph.D. 1961 (chemistry)

CAREER
Professor

POLITICAL HIGHLIGHTS
Mass. House, 1969-73; Mass. Senate, 1973-91

ELECTION RESULTS

2004 GENERAL

John W. Olver (D)		unopposed

2004 PRIMARY

John W. Olver (D)		unopposed

2002 GENERAL

John W. Olver (D)	137,841	67.6%
Matthew W. Kinnaman (R)	66,061	32.4%

PREVIOUS WINNING PERCENTAGES
2000 (68%); 1998 (72%); 1996 (53%); 1994 (99%); 1992 (52%); 1991 Special Election (50%)

Elected June 1991; 7th full term

Olver is a solitary, nose-to-the-task legislator who is rarely out front on legislation. In his 14 years in Congress, he has introduced 29 bills. Only two have become law.

Yet Olver is the only member of the Massachusetts House delegation on the Appropriations Committee, where he is the top-ranking Democrat on the Treasury, Transportation, HUD, the Judiciary and the District of Columbia Subcommittee, and he knows how to get money sent home.

He says using his Appropriations seat to help his district and state is more important than introducing bills. "I co-sign numbers of bills, but as an appropriator, my legislative product is mostly in what I can do for my district or help to do for Massachusetts — how I'm able to help other people in my delegation to get things they would like," he told The Berkshire Eagle in early 2005. In 2004, for example, he secured $2.4 million in the huge end-of-the-year catchall spending bill for several research projects at the University of Massachusetts at Amherst, located in the 1st District.

Olver has long been a protector of Amtrak, the national passenger rail system, and he wants to increase the railroad's annual operating subsidy. He has consistently opposed the Bush administration's plan to end subsidies to Amtrak absent congressional passage of a restructuring plan. "Amtrak is held to an unfair standard that no other rail system in the world is held to," Olver said in 2004. "No large private or public intercity passenger rail system in the world has been profitable or been able to survive without public subsidies."

He succeeded in amending the 2004 Transportation spending bill to eliminate a 24-month phase-in of safety compliance requirements for trucks entering the United States from Mexico and Canada. He argued that shippers from those countries already had had plenty of time to bring their vehicles up to U.S. safety standards.

A former chemistry professor, Olver is a staunch supporter of environmental causes. He continually presses the Bush administration to do more to reduce greenhouse gas emissions and to increase automobile fuel economy. Olver and Maryland Republican Wayne T. Gilchrest formed and co-chair the House's Climate Change Caucus, in which members work to develop bipartisan agreements on climate issues.

Olver, Gilchrest and other caucus members introduced a bill in early 2005 to set caps on the amount of carbon dioxide emitted from the burning of fossil fuels, believed to be one of the main sources of global warming. The carbon dioxide emissions cause a heat-trapping blanket to form in the atmosphere, raising temperatures, Olver said. The measure also creates a market-based system encouraging profitable opportunities for companies to cut emissions.

Olver has a quiet and low-key personality, but he enjoys a challenge. He is an avid outdoorsman who still spends much of his free time hiking, rock climbing, wind surfing or cross-country skiing. He has worked for continued funding of the Silvio O. Conte National Wildlife Refuge along the Connecticut River, named after his predecessor in the House. Olver in 2002 won enactment of legislation requiring a study to determine whether a number of hiking trails in Connecticut and Massachusetts should be added to the National Trails System. During a hearing on the bill, Olver showed up with his own enlarged photos of scenic spots along the trails and gave a mini-seminar on the geologic and botanic highlights of the area.

Olver says it is the government's responsibility to solve society's problems and to play a part in economic development. He has called on the Bush administration to release all the funds under the Low Income Home Energy Assistance Program, a federal initiative that helps low-income families pay their energy bills. The program received $300 million in the 2004 catchall appropriations bill, Olver said, and while the president released $100 million of the funds in December, the remainder of the money is still being held. "LIHEAP helps lower-income families pay their energy bills, a service that is particularly valuable given the rise in heating costs this winter," Olver said. "Families shouldn't have to choose between heating their home and buying food."

Olver is a member of the Progressive Caucus, a group of the most liberal House Democrats. When the House voted to reject a challenge to Ohio's electoral votes, thus upholding the 2004 re-election of President Bush, Olver was one of 31 Democrats, and one of only two in his delegation, to vote to sustain the challenge. In the 108th Congress, he voted in agreement with his party 98 percent of the time.

Olver has pushed for funding to build and run a number of community health centers. As a member of the Rural Health Care Coalition, he has sought Medicare funds for hospitals and medical providers.

Born on a farm in Pennsylvania, Olver headed north for graduate school, earning a doctorate from the Massachusetts Institute of Technology at age 24. He taught chemistry at the University of Massachusetts' Amherst campus for eight years before making his first foray into elective politics by winning a state House race in 1968.

Four years later, he bucked the national GOP trend, unseating an incumbent Republican state senator. He stayed in the state Senate until 1991 when Conte, a liberal Republican, died in the middle of his 17th term.

Olver won a 10-way Democratic primary with surprising ease, then he collected endorsements from his defeated rivals as well as from union members, teachers, environmentalists, women's groups and abortion rights supporters. He won the special election by fewer than 2,000 votes, marking the first time since 1892 that the area had sent a Democrat to the House. After that, he alternated close races in 1992 and 1996 (when he defeated Jane Swift, who would later serve as governor) with re-election romps in 1994 and 1998.

The 2000 election broke that pattern, when Olver won by 39 percentage points. His territory left largely intact by redistricting, he won by 35 points in 2002 and was unopposed in 2004.

KEY VOTES

2004

Yes Extend federal unemployment benefits by 13 weeks

Yes Pass $283.2 billion, six-year federal highway and mass transit bill

No Approve $146 billion multi-year extension of previously enacted middle-class tax breaks

No Amend the Constitution to prohibit same-sex marriage

No Cut corporate taxes $137 billion over 10 years

Yes Reorganize U.S. intelligence agencies as proposed by Sept. 11 commission

2003

No Cut taxes by $330 billion through fiscal 2013

Yes Block Bush rule scaling back overtime pay for some white-collar federal workers

Yes Do not allow use of search warrants without first notifying subjects

Yes Allow importation of prescription drugs

No Create private school voucher program in Washington, D.C.

No Ban "partial birth" abortion except to save a woman's life

Yes Split $18.6 billion in Iraq aid into half-grant, half-loan

No Overhaul Medicare and create prescription drug benefit

CQ VOTE STUDIES

	PARTY UNITY		PRESIDENTIAL SUPPORT	
	Support	Oppose	Support	Oppose
2004	98%	2%	21%	79%
2003	99%	1%	15%	85%
2002	99%	1%	27%	73%
2001	98%	2%	12%	88%
2000	97%	3%	83%	17%

INTEREST GROUPS

	AFL-CIO	ADA	CCUS	ACU
2004	100%	100%	19%	0%
2003	100%	100%	23%	16%
2002	100%	95%	37%	0%
2001	100%	100%	23%	0%
2000	100%	90%	38%	4%

MASSACHUSETTS 1
West – Pittsfield, Leominster, Westfield, Amherst

The oranges of autumn, the whites of winter and the greens of spring and summer attract vacationers to the 1st. The Berkshire Mountains of western Massachusetts once protected American Indians from encroaching whites. But three hundred years later, the area serves as home to a shrinking blue-collar, but stable, rural population.

Tourist areas include the kind of serene New England towns depicted in films, books and Norman Rockwell paintings. Tanglewood, the summer home of the Boston Symphony Orchestra, also attracts music fans to its outdoor theater in Lenox. The Yankee Candle Company, one of the largest manufacturers of scented candles, is based in South Deerfield.

After decades as a dominant textile mill area and the world's top plastics producer, factory closures and downsizing decimated the region during the recession of the late 1980s and early 1990s. Pittsfield and Fitchburg suffered the most. While the economy of Pittsfield is diversifying, General Electric reduced its defense-related workforce there from 11,000 in the 1980s to 2,000 a decade later. A strong retail and plastics industry has

spurred growth in Leominster, a western outgrowth of the Boston suburbs that sits on the crossing of two major highways at the eastern edge of the district.

Once a Republican stronghold, the 1st was held by liberal GOP Rep. Silvio O. Conte for more than three decades until his death in 1991. Some rural areas east of Interstate 91 support Republicans, but the sparse population is overwhelmed by Democratic union voters in the northeast and university liberals around Amherst, where the state's flagship university is located. Seven of the 13 cities and towns in which 2002 Democratic gubernatorial nominee Shannon O'Brien received at least two-thirds of the vote are in the 1st. John Kerry took 63 percent of the 2004 presidential vote here, and five of Kerry's top ten cities or towns are in the district.

MAJOR INDUSTRY
Plastics, paper, tourism, higher education

CITIES
Pittsfield, 45,793; Leominster, 41,303; Westfield, 40,072; Holyoke, 39,838; Fitchburg, 39,102; Amherst (unincorporated), 34,874

NOTABLE
John Chapman, known as Johnny Appleseed, was born in Leominster.

Rep. Richard E. Neal (D)

Elected 1988; 9th term

CAPITOL OFFICE
225-5601
www.house.gov/neal
2266 Rayburn 20515-2102; fax 225-8112

COMMITTEES
Budget
Ways & Means

HOMETOWN
Springfield

BORN
Feb. 14, 1949, Worcester, Mass.

RELIGION
Roman Catholic

FAMILY
Wife, Maureen Neal; four children

EDUCATION
American International College, B.A. 1972 (political science); U. of Hartford, M.P.A. 1976

CAREER
College lecturer; teacher; mayoral aide

POLITICAL HIGHLIGHTS
Springfield City Council, 1978-84 (president, 1979); mayor of Springfield, 1984-89

ELECTION RESULTS

2004 GENERAL

Richard E. Neal (D)	217,682	98.7%
write-ins	2,802	1.3%

2004 PRIMARY

Richard E. Neal (D)	unopposed

2002 GENERAL

Richard E. Neal (D)	unopposed

PREVIOUS WINNING PERCENTAGES
2000 (99%); 1998 (98%); 1996 (72%); 1994 (59%); 1992 (53%); 1990 (100%); 1988 (80%)

As a key player on tax and Social Security issues, Neal is likely to be busy in the 109th Congress. A member of both the Budget and Ways and Means committees, his legislative priorities in recent years have been to reform the alternative minimum tax and prevent or punish businesses who escape U.S. taxes by moving their headquarters out of the country.

In opposing President Bush's tax cuts of 2001 and 2003, Neal repeatedly argued — presciently as it turns out — that the new, lower tax rates would force millions more people to pay the alternative minimum tax. The AMT was originally designed to ensure that the very richest people would have to pay some tax despite all the credits and deductions they might claim. Instead of catching only the wealthiest Americans, more and more middle-class taxpayers are now being snared by the AMT because the income levels that trigger it have not been revised to reflect inflation.

Some key Republicans now see the need to address the AMT issue as an opportunity to press for broader tax reform, a priority for Bush in his second term, and Neal is likely to be involved in those deliberations.

He has tried different tactics to deal with companies that set up offices outside of the country, sometimes by just renting a mailbox, to avoid U.S. taxes. The most recent was his measure to bar such companies from bidding for lucrative homeland security contracts. The bill passed the House in the 108th but failed in the Senate.

Neal also is likely to be a key player in Bush's other domestic priority: creating private accounts within Social Security. He told the Boston Herald that Democrats, who almost uniformly view personal accounts as a threat to Social Security, asked him to switch from Ways and Means' Trade Subcommittee to the Social Security panel for the 109th because of his personal experience. Neal and his two younger sisters received Social Security survivor benefits after the death of their parents. He compares the benefits to jumping on a trampoline: "You hit it and you bounce back up."

When he served on the Trade Subcommittee, Neal was a swing vote. Siding with labor and environmental groups, he opposed the 2002 fast-track law giving the president authority to negotiate trade agreements that Congress can approve or reject but not amend. He also voted against the 1993 North American Free Trade Agreement. But in 2000, he voted to grant China permanent normal trade status, one of only two in the Massachusetts House delegation to do so. He could be a crucial vote for trade agreements in the 109th, especially one with Central America.

Neal is a reflection of 2nd District social values and he votes a more conservative line on certain social policy issues. Residents of Springfield tend to be blue-collar and Irish Catholic and are not as liberal as other voters in the state. Neal opposes federal funding of abortions and voted in favor of the 2003 ban on what opponents call "partial birth" abortion. He also supports a constitutional amendment allowing Congress to outlaw desecration of the U.S. flag. Yet in 2004, he voted against amending the Constitution to prohibit same-sex marriage.

Neal has been a leader of congressional efforts to keep the United States involved in the search for peace in Northern Ireland. His paternal grandparents are from Ireland, while his maternal grandparents are from Northern Ireland, and Neal is co-chairman of the Ad Hoc Congressional Committee on Irish Affairs.

Neal is known for being particularly respectful of the House, its traditions and procedures. He drew some attention in 2001 when he appeared to be thwarting the effort of his Massachusetts colleague and Washington roommate, Martin T. Meehan, to bring campaign finance legislation to the floor. When GOP leaders refused to bring up the bill, Meehan and his Republican cosponsor, Christopher Shays of Connecticut, sought to force the bill to a vote by getting a majority of members to sign a discharge petition. Though he supported the measure, Neal initially declined to sign, arguing that legislative chaos would result if such grass-roots campaigns were to succeed on a regular basis. Still, he promised Meehan that if he gained 217 signatures, he would provide the pivotal 218th — which is what happened in early 2002.

What the golf course is for many businessmen and civic leaders, the basketball court is for Neal — a place to develop personal relationships that go beyond political interests and to cut a deal now and then while working up a healthy sweat. Neal spends plenty of time in the members-only House gymnasium and at the Springfield YMCA competing in what his staff describes as "spirited" full court games. As a former high school player and the father of two sons good enough to play at the college level, Neal's passion for the game goes well beyond any sense of obligation he may feel as the representative of the city where basketball was invented.

Neal also has an affection for baseball. He is a member of the Minor League Baseball Caucus and sponsored legislation in 2004 to posthumously present Jackie Robinson, who broke the color barrier in the major leagues, a Congressional Gold Medal.

Neal says he has always been fascinated by politics. He majored in political science in college, and later he was the co-chairman of George McGovern's 1972 presidential campaign in western Massachusetts. After serving as an aide to Springfield Mayor William C. Sullivan, he won three elections to the city council. He also taught history and government at a high school and at area colleges. In 1983, he won the first of three elections as Springfield mayor, drawing favorable notices for stimulating downtown rehabilitation and neighborhood revitalization.

In 1988, when Democrat Edward P. Boland announced his retirement after 36 years in the House, Neal was quick off the mark. He won the nomination unopposed and crushed a weak GOP foe. He faced a couple of stiff challenges in the early 1990s — especially in 1994 when anti-incumbent fever was running high and Neal was being chastised for 87 overdrafts at the now-defunct private bank for House members. But Republicans have not fielded a challenger since 1996.

KEY VOTES

2004

Yes Extend federal unemployment benefits by 13 weeks

Yes Pass $283.2 billion, six-year federal highway and mass transit bill

No Approve $146 billion multi-year extension of previously enacted middle-class tax breaks

No Amend the Constitution to prohibit same-sex marriage

No Cut corporate taxes $137 billion over 10 years

Yes Reorganize U.S. intelligence agencies as proposed by Sept. 11 commission

2003

No Cut taxes by $330 billion through fiscal 2013

Yes Block Bush rule scaling back overtime pay for some white-collar federal workers

Yes Do not allow use of search warrants without first notifying subjects

Yes Allow importation of prescription drugs

No Create private school voucher program in Washington, D.C.

Yes Ban "partial birth" abortion except to save a woman's life

Yes Split $18.6 billion in Iraq aid into half-grant, half-loan

No Overhaul Medicare and create prescription drug benefit

CQ VOTE STUDIES

	PARTY UNITY		PRESIDENTIAL SUPPORT	
	Support	Oppose	Support	Oppose
2004	98%	2%	24%	76%
2003	95%	5%	30%	70%
2002	96%	4%	28%	72%
2001	92%	8%	26%	74%
2000	92%	8%	83%	17%

INTEREST GROUPS

	AFL-CIO	ADA	CCUS	ACU
2004	100%	95%	33%	4%
2003	80%	95%	33%	24%
2002	88%	90%	37%	4%
2001	92%	85%	27%	13%
2000	90%	80%	38%	8%

MASSACHUSETTS 2
South central — Springfield, Chicopee, Northampton

The rolling hills and thick forests of the 2nd extend along the state's southern border from Springfield and Northampton in the west to Bellingham in the east. Springfield dwarfs all other communities in the 2nd; small, rural towns and intermittent farms fill out the rest of south-central Massachusetts.

Much of Springfield's economic success in the 1990s was tied to its history as a hub for inventions, although the region's future rests with the insurance and health care industries — most notably Mass Mutual and Baystate Health System — which have replaced some of the city's shrinking manufacturing base. Service and government jobs, some of which are generated by Chicopee's Westover Air Reserve Base, are important to the region's economy. The expansion of the Basketball Hall of Fame in 2002 and restoration of the civic center should bring more visitors to Springfield.

Hispanics — many of whom moved to the 2nd in the 1950s to work in the tobacco fields — once gravitated to Springfield's North End but are now more dispersed through the city. Most African-Americans live near the city's center.

Residents in and around Springfield, many of whom are blue collar and Irish Catholic, vote Democratic and dominate the district's elections. Smith College produces a strongly liberal vote in Northampton, and as a result the area gave Green Party presidential nominee Ralph Nader more votes than George W. Bush in 2000, and gave John Kerry his highest percentage in the district in 2004. Despite this strong Democratic lean, some Republicans can be competitive, particularly among small-town and rural voters. Mitt Romney, the 2002 GOP gubernatorial nominee, narrowly won the 2nd, and in 2004 East Brookfield was Bush's best city or town in Massachusetts — Bush took 57 percent of the vote there.

MAJOR INDUSTRY
Insurance, health care, higher education, tourism

CITIES
Springfield, 152,082; Chicopee, 54,653; Northampton, 28,978

NOTABLE
Important local inventions include the gasoline-powered car (1893).

Rep. Jim McGovern (D)

CAPITOL OFFICE
225-6101
www.house.gov/mcgovern
430 Cannon 20515-2103; fax 225-5759

COMMITTEES
Rules

HOMETOWN
Worcester

BORN
Nov. 20, 1959, Worcester, Mass.

RELIGION
Roman Catholic

FAMILY
Wife, Lisa McGovern; two children

EDUCATION
American U., B.A. 1981 (history), M.P.A. 1984

CAREER
Congressional aide; campaign aide

POLITICAL HIGHLIGHTS
Sought Democratic nomination for U.S. House, 1994

ELECTION RESULTS

2004 GENERAL

Jim McGovern (D)	192,036	70.5%
Ronald A. Crews (R)	80,197	29.4%

2004 PRIMARY

Jim McGovern (D)	unopposed

2002 GENERAL

Jim McGovern (D)	155,697	98.8%
write-ins	1,848	1.2%

PREVIOUS WINNING PERCENTAGES
2000 (99%); 1998 (57%); 1996 (53%)

Elected 1996; 5th term

McGovern entered Congress in 1997 far ahead of the curve, with an extensive knowledge of many of the arcane and important House rules for turning good intentions into law.

The reason: He spent nearly two decades behind the scenes on Capitol Hill, first as a college-age aide to South Dakota senator and presidential candidate George McGovern (no relation), and later to Joe Moakley, who chaired the Rules Committee for five and a half years and was dean of the Massachusetts House delegation at his death in 2001.

McGovern, who is known as a legislative tactician, developed an appreciation for the importance of both grand vision and pragmatism in politics. "McGovern taught me it was OK to be an idealist," he told the Boston Globe. "Moakley taught me how to get things done."

When Moakley died, McGovern moved quickly to gain his mentor's seat on the Rules Committee, a powerful arm of the leadership because of its power to set the parameters for floor debate. He was granted his request, but was asked to leave in mid-2001 to allow Democrat Alcee L. Hastings of Florida to take the seat. He returned a year later. In the 109th Congress, he is the top-ranking Democrat on the Rules and Organization of the House Subcommittee.

He's proved to be an able bare-knuckles battler in the often tartly partisan debates of the committee. Yet sometimes his passions have neared the edge of propriety. Early in the 109th, when the House passed a measure making it difficult for illegal immigrants to use driver's licenses as identification, McGovern called some backers of the bill "immigrant haters."

And he had sharp words for the Republican leadership when it tried to enact a series of rule changes at the start of the 109th. One of the proposed changes said that if an ethics complaint was not acted upon within 45 days it would no longer be considered. McGovern said that under these rules, the ethics panel chairman could ultimately kill any ethics complaint simply by stonewalling until the 45 days are up. "This should be a place where honesty and integrity are the standard, not a place where the rules are changed merely to protect a powerful few from their own ethical shortcomings," McGovern said. The GOP leadership ultimately killed the rules package.

McGovern proudly embraces multiple humanitarian causes. He's a co-sponsor of the Torture Outsourcing Prevention Act, which would prohibit the United States from turning immigrants over to other countries where they likely will be tortured. He is a critic of the administration's softened stance on American use of land mines. He joined with North Carolina Republican Sen. Elizabeth Dole to promote an international school lunch program — a particularly apt pairing since the program's biggest boosters are George McGovern, a longtime ambassador to the World Food Program, and Dole's husband, former Senate Majority Leader Robert Dole.

McGovern also takes a keen interest in foreign affairs, particularly in Latin America. He has traveled to Cuba twice; in 2002, he was among the 17 Democrats and 17 Republicans to form the Cuba Working Group, which pressed for elimination of the ban on travel to Cuba and removal of financing restrictions on food sales to the island.

While he was a top aide to Moakley, McGovern was a key staff member on a 1990 House task force that looked into the murders the year before of six Jesuit priests and two women in El Salvador. Several of the Salvadoran military officers who were implicated in the case had graduated from the U.S. Army School of the Americas at Fort Benning, which trains Latin American military officers. Since then, McGovern has persistently tried to eliminate funding for the school, which he says "continues to train military officers who harm and kill the innocent people of Latin America." The school was reorganized and renamed the Western Hemispheric Institute for Security Cooperation in 2000 but remains in business.

McGovern belongs to the Progressive Caucus, the most left-leaning faction of House Democrats. But he works with lawmakers in both parties on nuts-and-bolts issues of economic development, education and health care. He has fought to improve Medicare payments for home health care and increase Pell Grants for college students.

During his childhood in Worcester — his father ran a liquor store and his mother was a dance teacher — the McGoverns followed politics closely, especially where the Kennedys were involved. When Sen. Robert F. Kennedy was assassinated in 1968, he recalls, "My father gathered us around the kitchen table and we wrote sympathy cards to Ethel."

McGovern had his first brush with politics in junior high school in 1972, when he found himself defending presidential candidate George McGovern because they shared the same last name. He then became involved in the campaign. Later, as an American University student, he worked in McGovern's Senate office. In 1984, when the South Dakotan launched another presidential bid, Jim McGovern was his campaign manager in Massachusetts and made the nominating speech at the Democratic National Convention in San Francisco. The elder McGovern returned the favor in 1996 and campaigned for Jim McGovern in Massachusetts.

McGovern went to work for Moakley in 1981 and served on his personal staff and in the Rules Committee office until 1996.

He unsuccessfully sought the Democratic nod for the 3rd District seat in 1994. In 1996, in something of an upset, he defeated two-term Republican Peter I. Blute by 8 percentage points. In 1998, Republicans viewed McGovern as vulnerable, but he beat moderate state Sen. Matthew J. Amorello by 15 points. The incumbent faced no GOP opposition in his next two re-elections and trounced a nominal Republican candidate in 2004.

McGovern may be making a tradition out of staff members becoming lawmakers. Ed Augustus, who was McGovern's chief of staff for six years, was elected state senator in Massachusetts the same day McGovern was elected to a fifth term in 2004. In a peculiar twist, the GOP candidate Augustus defeated was Robi Blute, the wife of the incumbent McGovern ousted to win the seat eight years earlier.

KEY VOTES

2004

Yes Extend federal unemployment benefits by 13 weeks

Yes Pass $283.2 billion, six-year federal highway and mass transit bill

Yes Approve $146 billion multi-year extension of previously enacted middle-class tax breaks

No Amend the Constitution to prohibit same-sex marriage

No Cut corporate taxes $137 billion over 10 years

Yes Reorganize U.S. intelligence agencies as proposed by Sept. 11 commission

2003

No Cut taxes by $330 billion through fiscal 2013

Yes Block Bush rule scaling back overtime pay for some white-collar federal workers

Yes Do not allow use of search warrants without first notifying subjects

Yes Allow importation of prescription drugs

No Create private school voucher program in Washington, D.C.

No Ban "partial birth" abortion except to save a woman's life

Yes Split $18.6 billion in Iraq aid into half-grant, half-loan

No Overhaul Medicare and create prescription drug benefit

CQ VOTE STUDIES

	PARTY UNITY		PRESIDENTIAL SUPPORT	
	Support	Oppose	Support	Oppose
2004	98%	2%	21%	79%
2003	99%	1%	16%	84%
2002	99%	1%	22%	78%
2001	97%	3%	16%	84%
2000	98%	2%	86%	14%

INTEREST GROUPS

	AFL-CIO	ADA	CCUS	ACU
2004	93%	100%	38%	4%
2003	100%	100%	23%	12%
2002	100%	100%	30%	0%
2001	100%	90%	35%	4%
2000	100%	100%	33%	0%

MASSACHUSETTS 3
Central and south — Worcester, Attleboro, part of Fall River

The 3rd District cuts a diagonal sliver from the mountains of Princeton to the fishing community of Fall River, winding its way from areas north and west of Boston almost to the Atlantic Ocean south of the city.

Worcester, a working-class city with a strong biotechnology presence, is the 3rd's population hub and has been revitalizing its downtown. A late-1990s project centralizing its respected hospitals, research institutes and some drug manufacturing plants into a medical center has sparked economic development. Still, Worcester registered slow population growth in the 1990s. Hispanics and blacks are displacing whites. Communities to the north and south are filling up with suburbanites who commute to jobs in Boston or Providence, R.I.

At the district's southern end, Fall River (shared with the 4th District) has long been a bastion of blue-collar white ethnic Democrats. The city has long had one of the highest unemployment rates in the state.

The Democratic dominance in Worcester and Fall River allows Democrats to overcome the ring of Republican support that binds the towns surrounding Worcester, including Paxton, Holden, the Boylstons and Shrewsbury. George W. Bush failed to carry a single city or town in the 3rd in the 2000 presidential election, but managed to squeak out wins in Rutland and Wrentham with 50 percent of the vote in 2004.

Despite the dominance of Democratic presidential candidates, the 3rd can support moderate-to-liberal Republicans, as shown by its backing of Mitt Romney in the 2002 gubernatorial election. Romney won every city and town in the 3rd except Fall River, Worcester and two others.

MAJOR INDUSTRY
Biotechnology, health care, heavy manufacturing, retail

CITIES
Worcester, 172,648; Fall River (pt.), 53,704; Attleboro, 42,068

NOTABLE
Worcester boasts two important "firsts," more than two centuries apart: the publication of the first American novel, William Hill Brown's "The Power of Sympathy," in 1789, and the successful cloning of human embryos by a Worcester-based biotech company in 2001.

Rep. Barney Frank (D)

Elected 1980; 13th term

CAPITOL OFFICE
225-5931
www.house.gov/frank
2252 Rayburn 20515-2104; fax 225-0182

COMMITTEES
Financial Services - ranking member

HOMETOWN
Newton

BORN
March 31, 1940, Bayonne, N.J.

RELIGION
Jewish

FAMILY
Partner, Sergio Pombo

EDUCATION
Harvard U., A.B. 1962 (government), J.D. 1977

CAREER
Lawyer; mayoral and congressional aide

POLITICAL HIGHLIGHTS
Mass. House, 1973-81

ELECTION RESULTS

2004 GENERAL

Barney Frank (D)	219,260	77.7%
Charles A. Morse (I)	62,293	22.1%

2004 PRIMARY

Barney Frank (D)	unopposed

2002 GENERAL

Barney Frank (D)	166,125	99.0%
write-ins	1,691	1.0%

PREVIOUS WINNING PERCENTAGES
2000 (75%); 1998 (98%); 1996 (72%); 1994 (100%);
1992 (68%); 1990 (66%); 1988 (70%); 1986 (89%);
1984 (74%); 1982 (60%); 1980 (52%)

In an era when floor "debate" is often just a recitation of boilerplate rhetoric, Frank is spontaneous combustion, passionately making his liberal case with off-the-cuff, rapid-fire — and tightly reasoned — arguments. He is easily the most entertaining speaker in the House.

But Frank is not just the resident wit; after 24 years in the House, he has amassed an encyclopedic knowledge of public policy and parliamentary rules, which he employs with precision in his battles. Frank is considered by many congressional staff members to be the funniest and smartest member of Congress.

He is also the top-ranking Democrat on the Financial Services Committee. In the 108th Congress, at the request of Minority Leader Nancy Pelosi, he left the No. 2 Democratic slot on the Judiciary Committee, where he had long served as one of the most effective and thoughtful committee members. On Financial Services, Frank has sought to steer the panel's attention to housing issues such as President Bush's attempts to curtail spending on rent assistance for low-income families. He also became a defender of the giant government-backed mortgage financiers Fannie Mae and Freddie Mac, which help keep money for mortgages cheap and plentiful but have been assailed by critics for accounting troubles.

When Frank learned that the Department of Housing and Urban Development was to receive one of the biggest cuts in Bush's 2006 budget, much of it because of a plan to shift the Community Development Block Grant program from HUD to the Commerce Department, he said the administration's proposal would neglect the poor. "It's clearly the first step toward getting the federal government out of all these programs," he said. The community development grants provide money for affordable housing, public improvements in poor communities and homeless shelters.

And when the spending bill for the departments of Veterans Affairs and Housing and Urban Development cleared the Senate as part of the catchall spending bill for 2005, Frank also complained that the Republicans had cut housing programs to pay for other domestic needs, such as increases in NASA's budget. Democrats charged that low-income and affordable housing programs are under attack from Republicans and are being tapped to pay for Bush's moon and Mars missions. "It's bad," Frank said. "It's not the disaster that the administration wanted, but it's part of a slow and steady decline in affordable housing." For the administration, Frank said, "HUD is a piggy bank to fund other priorities."

Frank has never allowed his committee assignments — or lack thereof — to circumscribe his intellectual engagement or his activism. And he will often catch members, particularly Republican members, off-guard with his razor-sharp sarcasm. He will chide the GOP majority for dictating policy to the states even as they claim the mantle of states' rights champions. He savors opportunities to make fun of rifts in the Republican party, once observing: "The right hand doesn't know what the far right hand is doing."

Frank, who was the first member of Congress ever to announce his homosexuality, pushed for a censure of President Clinton rather than impeachment as Congress in 1998 debated how to address his affair with a White House intern. Frank spoke from experience: The House reprimanded him in 1990 after revelations that a male prostitute Frank had hired as a household employee was running a prostitution business from Frank's apartment.

His willingness to use himself as an example illustrates the matter-of-fact way Frank has handled controversy about his personal life. "I answer every other question I'm asked," he said in disclosing his sexual orientation in 1987. And he does not shy away from alluding to his personal life during floor debates.

As the House in 2004 debated a proposed constitutional amendment to ban same-sex marriage, Texas Republican John Carter, a former judge, argued for the amendment by noting that he had presided over the dissolution of 20,000 marriages in his former career. "It is a shame that we have to go through this attack on marriage, but to add a further attack on marriage by redefining the definition of marriage would be an abomination to our children," Carter said.

Frank quickly rose to challenge Carter. "I just wonder, in how many of those [cases] was the cause of the dissolution some gay relationship?" he asked. "Am I responsible, as a gay man, for any of those 20,000 dissolutions? Would he tell us in how many of those 20,000 dissolutions was the existence of a gay marriage or gay civil union the cause?" About a half-dozen, Carter admitted. The amendment failed, despite the GOP leadership's support, when 27 Republicans voted against it.

But for all the attention he attracts by provoking the GOP, Frank also is willing to work with Republicans to reach compromise. "If you're not able to work closely with people you despise, you can't really work here," he told The Boston Globe, as he worked with conservatives in a bid to prevent enactment of the 2000 law normalizing the U.S.-China trade relationship.

He has also fostered a collegial relationship with Financial Services Chairman Michael G. Oxley, an Ohio Republican; the two sponsored a bill together to renew a lapsed federal flood insurance program.

After growing up in Bayonne, N.J., Frank went to Harvard and stuck around to teach government and do graduate work. Between 1968 and 1971, he worked for Boston Mayor Kevin White and was administrative assistant to Democratic Rep. Michael Harrington of Massachusetts, gaining contacts that helped him win a seat in the state House. He had been there eight years when Democratic Rep. Robert F. Drinan, a liberal Catholic priest, bowed to a papal prohibition on clergymen holding public office. Frank won the seat with 52 percent of the vote against a Republican who portrayed him as too liberal.

His hardest re-election battle was his first, when Frank in 1982 ran against GOP Rep. Margaret M. Heckler. He won with 60 percent. His closest contest since was after the 1990 prostitution scandal, when he won with 66 percent. In 2004, facing an independent challenger, he took 78 percent.

KEY VOTES

2004

Yes Extend federal unemployment benefits by 13 weeks

Yes Pass $283.2 billion, six-year federal highway and mass transit bill

No Approve $146 billion multi-year extension of previously enacted middle-class tax breaks

No Amend the Constitution to prohibit same-sex marriage

No Cut corporate taxes $137 billion over 10 years

Yes Reorganize U.S. intelligence agencies as proposed by Sept. 11 commission

2003

No Cut taxes by $330 billion through fiscal 2013

Yes Block Bush rule scaling back overtime pay for some white-collar federal workers

Yes Do not allow use of search warrants without first notifying subjects

Yes Allow importation of prescription drugs

? Create private school voucher program in Washington, D.C.

No Ban "partial birth" abortion except to save a woman's life

Yes Split $18.6 billion in Iraq aid into half-grant, half-loan

No Overhaul Medicare and create prescription drug benefit

CQ VOTE STUDIES

	PARTY UNITY		PRESIDENTIAL SUPPORT	
	Support	Oppose	Support	Oppose
2004	98%	2%	16%	84%
2003	98%	2%	16%	84%
2002	97%	3%	14%	86%
2001	97%	3%	9%	91%
2000	94%	6%	84%	16%

INTEREST GROUPS

	AFL-CIO	ADA	CCUS	ACU
2004	100%	100%	20%	4%
2003	100%	100%	23%	16%
2002	100%	100%	26%	8%
2001	100%	100%	22%	0%
2000	100%	95%	33%	12%

MASSACHUSETTS 4

New Bedford; Boston suburbs – Newton; Taunton; part of Fall River

Downtowns replete with 18th- and 19th-century town hall buildings dot the Yankee communities in the 4th, several of which have celebrated their 300th or 350th anniversaries. The district encompasses thickly settled Boston suburbs, rural cranberry bogs and urban New Bedford and Fall River (shared with the 3rd District).

The economic health of the 4th reflects a split between the northern and southern tiers of the district. The northern well-to-do towns and Boston suburbs benefited from a strong economy in the 1990s, due in large part to the Route 128 technology corridor, although moderate unemployment started to affect the area at the end of the 1990s. The southern fishing and former textile mill communities, including Fall River and New Bedford, struggled to stave off double-digit unemployment as the textile industry declined to almost nothing and commercial fishermen faced sparse catches. In the 4th's center, the cranberry bogs in Middleboro

and biotechnology firms farther north provide a strong economic base.

The blue-collar, immigrant-laden southern section of the district gives the 4th a strong Democratic lean. New Bedford, which has the lowest median household income in the state, and Fall River are heavily Portuguese and vote solidly Democratic. So does the district's wealthiest community, Westport, located south of Fall River and west of New Bedford. The wealthy northwestern towns of Wellesley, Dover and Sherborn are more likely to support Republicans, but the well-to-do and densely populated Newton and Brookline opt for liberal Democrats.

MAJOR INDUSTRY

Fishing, cranberries, health care, textile manufacturing

CITIES

New Bedford, 93,768; Newton, 83,829; Brookline (unincorporated), 57,107; Taunton, 55,976; Fall River (pt.), 38,234; Dartmouth (unincorporated), 30,666; Wellesley (unincorporated), 26,613

NOTABLE

Fig Newtons originated in Newton; Former Gov. Michael S. Dukakis commuted downtown by trolley from his home in Brookline; Ocean Spray is headquartered in Lakeville-Middleboro.

Rep. Martin T. Meehan (D)

Elected 1992; 7th term

CAPITOL OFFICE
225-3411
martin.meehan@mail.house.gov
www.house.gov/meehan
2229 Rayburn 20515-2105; fax 226-0771

COMMITTEES
Armed Services
Judiciary

HOMETOWN
Lowell

BORN
Dec. 30, 1956, Lowell, Mass.

RELIGION
Roman Catholic

FAMILY
Wife, Ellen Murphy; two children

EDUCATION
U. of Massachusetts, Lowell, B.S. 1978 (political science & education); Suffolk U., M.P.A. 1981, J.D. 1986

CAREER
County prosecutor; state securities investigator; state legislative aide; congressional aide

POLITICAL HIGHLIGHTS
No previous office

ELECTION RESULTS

2004 GENERAL

Martin T. Meehan (D)	179,652	67.0%
Thomas P. Tierney (R)	88,232	32.9%

2004 PRIMARY

Martin T. Meehan (D)	unopposed

2002 GENERAL

Martin T. Meehan (D)	122,562	60.2%
Charles McCarthy (R)	69,337	34.0%
Ilana Freedman (LIBERT)	11,729	5.8%

PREVIOUS WINNING PERCENTAGES
2000 (98%); 1998 (71%); 1996 (99%); 1994 (70%); 1992 (52%)

Meehan has repeatedly taken on the moneyed interests in politics, and in recent years, with the aid of several key allies, he has scored a few wins.

At the beginning of the 109th Congress, the self-described "street kid from Lowell" was back on the case. Joined by Connecticut Republican Christopher Shays, Meehan sued the Federal Election Commission for the way it was enforcing the 2002 campaign finance law that banned unlimited corporate and labor donations to political parties and restricted issue advertisements. After a seven-year crusade, the two had helped push the law to enactment, along with Arizona Republican John McCain and Wisconsin Democrat Russell D. Feingold in the Senate.

Meehan and his allies in 2005 also sponsored legislation to close a loophole left in the 2002 law that allowed so-called 527 organizations (named after an applicable section of the tax code) to collect vast sums in unregulated money and spend it on political advertising. Speaker J. Dennis Hastert, who proclaimed that the 2002 bill would "end democracy as we know it," endorsed the effort to rein in unaffiliated 527 groups.

Proof that Meehan can be a scrappy fighter came at a Brookings Institution forum in January 2005, when he challenged the White House and stepped out ahead of the position held by most other Democrats by calling for an "exit strategy" for Iraq and a cut in the number of U.S. troops there to 30,000 by early 2006. Senior Massachusetts Sen. Edward M. Kennedy later joined the call for troop withdrawals.

From his seat on Armed Services, Meehan weighs in on controversial military issues. He and fellow Democrat Ellen O. Tauscher of California tried unsuccessfully in 2004 to cut spending on nuclear weapons programs. The following month, during floor debate on the energy-water appropriations bill, Meehan and Democrat Adam B. Schiff of California offered a proposal to increase funding for a program that cleans up highly enriched uranium at reactor sites in Russia and elsewhere, but it was rejected.

Meehan often finds himself vying for attention in a state where even the No. 2 senator is so well-known that he can be the Democratic nominee for president. With the possibility that John Kerry would vacate his seat and move to Pennsylvania Avenue, Meehan raised more than $4 million in the 2004 election cycle and sat on most of it for a possible Senate campaign that never materialized. He would likely have contended against House Democratic colleagues Barney Frank and Edward J. Markey.

A Senate run would have tested his support just a few years after Meehan had to lobby his state's legislature to save his House district. In 2002, Meehan successfully persuaded the Massachusetts House to reject the efforts of Speaker Tom Finneran to make Meehan and fellow Democratic Rep. John Tierney face off over the same House seat as part of redistricting. Meehan had irked Finneran by supporting a Massachusetts initiative giving public funds to candidates for statewide office if they agreed to limit their spending and did not accept contributions above $100. Meehan, who sold his car and mortgaged his house to finance his first race for Congress, supports government-financed campaigns.

Although the map eventually was shaped so that Meehan and Tierney could run in separate districts, Meehan's efforts cost him a chance to be governor in 2002. Finneran had said he wanted to change the boundaries because Meehan, ahead in gubernatorial polls, was unlikely to seek re-election. When his congressional district was challenged, Meehan pledged to forgo the statewide race and run again for Congress.

The fast-talking Meehan is the son of working-class Irish Americans. When President Kennedy came on television in the 1960s, he recalls, the Meehan household fell silent. Meehan named his first son Robert Francis after the president's younger brother who was attorney general.

Meehan is candid about how personal experience influences his legislative priorities. When he is not winning money for Lowell and Lawrence, old textile towns attempting to switch to high-tech enterprises, Meehan focuses on an issue close to his heart: discouraging tobacco use. He describes how his father, a typesetter at the Lowell newspaper, was so addicted that he "smoked a cigarette on the way home from being told he was going to die if he didn't stop."

The elder Meehan eventually quit, but his son has spent much of his congressional career attempting to expose the motives of tobacco companies and finding ways to keep teenagers away from cigarettes. In 1994, after tobacco executives testified that nicotine was not addictive, Meehan drafted a 111-page memo asking Attorney General Janet Reno to convene a grand jury to consider perjury and fraud charges. Later, he and Utah Republican James V. Hansen introduced several anti-smoking bills, including one to remove nicotine gradually from all tobacco products sold in the United States and another to ban sales of tobacco over the Internet.

Although Meehan is within the mainstream of his party, his voting record defies easy labeling. Like an earlier 5th District congressman, Democrat Paul E. Tsongas, Meehan is a social policy liberal and a budget cutter. He often rates among the most fiscally responsible members of Congress in the Concord Coalition's annual survey of votes. Concord, site of the famous early Revolutionary War battle, is in the 5th District and where Tsongas and New Hampshire Republican Sen. Warren B. Rudman in 1992 launched the coalition to press for a balanced federal budget.

In Meehan's first election to the House in 1992, he ousted four-term incumbent Chester G. Atkins in the Democratic primary by branding him an unsavory political insider. Meehan struck a chord with voters when he assailed Atkins for supporting a House pay raise and for having 127 House bank overdrafts. In November, Meehan took 52 percent of the vote over former GOP Rep. Paul W. Cronin, at a time when the seat had a slight Republican edge.

On his way to winning his House seat, Meehan pledged to serve only four terms in Congress. He reneged on the pledge in 2000 but easily won re-election. In 2004, he won with 67 percent.

KEY VOTES

2004

Yes	Extend federal unemployment benefits by 13 weeks
Yes	Pass $283.2 billion, six-year federal highway and mass transit bill
No	Approve $146 billion multi-year extension of previously enacted middle-class tax breaks
No	Amend the Constitution to prohibit same-sex marriage
No	Cut corporate taxes $137 billion over 10 years
Yes	Reorganize U.S. intelligence agencies as proposed by Sept. 11 commission

2003

No	Cut taxes by $330 billion through fiscal 2013
Yes	Block Bush rule scaling back overtime pay for some white-collar federal workers
Yes	Do not allow use of search warrants without first notifying subjects
Yes	Allow importation of prescription drugs
No	Create private school voucher program in Washington, D.C.
No	Ban "partial birth" abortion except to save a woman's life
Yes	Split $18.6 billion in Iraq aid into half-grant, half-loan
No	Overhaul Medicare and create prescription drug benefit

CQ VOTE STUDIES

	PARTY UNITY		PRESIDENTIAL SUPPORT	
	Support	Oppose	Support	Oppose
2004	98%	2%	22%	78%
2003	96%	4%	20%	80%
2002	98%	2%	26%	74%
2001	97%	3%	29%	71%
2000	92%	8%	81%	19%

INTEREST GROUPS

	AFL-CIO	ADA	CCUS	ACU
2004	93%	100%	22%	4%
2003	87%	100%	31%	20%
2002	100%	75%	44%	9%
2001	100%	90%	29%	0%
2000	90%	90%	45%	12%

MASSACHUSETTS 5
North central — Lowell, Lawrence, Haverhill

More than a generation ago, billowing smokestacks put Lawrence and Lowell among the nation's leading industrial centers. Today, the cities remain population hubs for the 5th, but the wealthy suburbs and rural communities — home to technology workers and some of the nation's most prestigious prep schools — give the district a more upscale flavor.

Textiles are still vital to struggling Lawrence, where immigration has put its sizable Hispanic population — comprised mostly of Dominicans and Puerto Ricans — in the majority.

Lowell and surrounding suburbs, meanwhile, continue to reinvent themselves as they rebound from declines in textiles and 1990s job losses at Digital Equipment Corporation, which later merged with Compaq, and Wang Laboratories, which were major area employers. The subsequent Internet boom attracted software firms and other technology companies, and the upswing spurred growth in small towns, as aging buildings that once housed textile mills, and then defense contractors, became home to start-ups and financial services firms.

While political rivalries between European immigrants are giving way to contests featuring Puerto Ricans, Dominicans and Cambodians, the blue-collar and low-income minority residents of Lowell and Lawrence vote strongly Democratic, as do many well-educated suburban liberals.

The southern part of the 5th is generally wealthy, with Carlisle, Sudbury, Harvard and Bolton all registering six-figure median household incomes. These areas demonstrated their political independence by backing Democrat Al Gore in the 2000 presidential election, Republican Mitt Romney in the 2002 gubernatorial election and Democrat John Kerry in the 2004 presidential election.

MAJOR INDUSTRY
Computer software, defense, textiles

CITIES
Lowell, 105,167; Lawrence, 72,043; Haverhill, 58,969; Methuen, 43,789; Billerica (unincorporated), 38,981; Chelmsford (unincorporated), 33,858

NOTABLE
Concord was the site of the first day of fighting in the Revolutionary War on April 19, 1775 (now celebrated each year as Patriots Day); Paul Revere's ride and the first Revolutionary battles in towns in the 5th and 7th districts are re-enacted every year.

Rep. John F. Tierney (D)

Elected 1996; 5th term

CAPITOL OFFICE
225-8020
www.house.gov/tierney
120 Cannon 20515-2106; fax 225-5915

COMMITTEES
Education & Workforce
Select Intelligence

HOMETOWN
Salem

BORN
Sept. 18, 1951, Salem, Mass.

RELIGION
Unspecified

FAMILY
Wife, Patrice Tierney

EDUCATION
Salem State College, B.A. 1973 (political science);
Suffolk U., J.D. 1976

CAREER
Lawyer; chamber of commerce official

POLITICAL HIGHLIGHTS
Democratic nominee for U.S. House, 1994

ELECTION RESULTS

2004 GENERAL

John F. Tierney (D)	213,458	69.9%
Steven P. O'Malley Jr. (R)	91,597	30.0%

2004 PRIMARY

John F. Tierney (D)	unopposed

2002 GENERAL

John F. Tierney (D)	162,900	68.3%
Mark C. Smith (R)	75,462	31.6%

PREVIOUS WINNING PERCENTAGES
2000 (71%); 1998 (55%); 1996 (48%)

Tierney is vocal about the need to improve access to health care, protect retirees' benefits, encourage conservation and strengthen public schools. Each Congress, he presses some of the same proposals to achieve those goals — with pretty much the same frustrating results.

Unfortunately for Tierney, he has spent his entire House career as a liberal Democrat in a chamber run by conservative Republicans. That leaves him frequently tilting at windmills, legislatively speaking.

The rhetoric he aims at the GOP probably doesn't help. In comments in 2004 about the new Medicare prescription drug law, Tierney said that "Republicans have consistently misrepresented the facts" and put "corporate interests over the needs of America's seniors." During a 2002 House debate on a spending package for military and homeland security programs, Tierney castigated GOP leaders for insinuating that Democrats who opposed portions of the bill were not patriotic. "That was disgraceful, even for a majority that has made the disparagement of the democratic process an art form," Tierney said.

Tierney's liberal initiatives and rhetorical jibes were once seen as bold moves for a man whose first election victory came by a slim 371 votes against a Republican incumbent. But in his fifth term, he now enjoys the comforts of incumbency and widespread support in his district.

Tierney has introduced a "Clean Money, Clean Elections" bill each Congress since he arrived in 1997. The bill provides for public financing and free broadcast time for candidates who agree not to use personal funds or accept contributions, and it limits expenditures by political parties. Some of the bill's provisions were included in the Shays-Meehan elections legislation that passed in 2002. Tierney is now pushing for enactment of the remaining provisions, but with little hope of success anytime soon.

The same holds true for his bills to prevent companies from canceling or reducing their retirees' health benefits and to provide incentives to states to develop universal health care programs: No Republican support, no committee consideration.

But there are exceptions. On national security and criminal justice issues, for instance, he sometimes attracts interest from the other side of the aisle. And some of his education initiatives, such as proposals to offer incentives to encourage top college graduates to enter teaching, have advanced as part of broader legislation.

Tierney is increasingly interested in national security issues. At the start of the 109th Congress, he won a seat on the Intelligence Committee, taking a leave of absence from the Government Reform panel on which he had served eight years. In his previous assignment, he was a member of Government Reform's National Security Subcommittee and participated in the legislative creation of the Department of Homeland Security and the Sept. 11 commission.

Tierney has worked to boost funding for first-responder communications training and equipment. In 2002, he cosponsored a bipartisan bill that required the intelligence community to share homeland security information with local officials and directed the president to set up procedures for declassifying that type of information so that state officials can remain informed about threats. In the 109th, he is expected to continue to promote funding for first-responders and military personnel.

Tierney is the only New Englander on the Education and Workforce

Committee, where he champions measures to make college more affordable by increasing federal funding for Pell grants, maintaining low-interest student loans, and adding incentives to encourage middle-class students to attend college. He also wants to use federal money to help local school districts hire more teachers so that class sizes in elementary and secondary schools can be reduced.

In 2002, he used his seat on the Education and Workforce panel to obtain a $3 million grant for job training and placement for about 800 workers who lost jobs at a closed Lucent Technologies plant in his district.

Although Tierney served a year as president of the Salem Chamber of Commerce, he does not usually see eye to eye with the U.S. Chamber of Commerce, backing the business group's position less than a quarter of the time. The National Federation of Independent Business says it approves of fewer than 10 percent of Tierney's votes.

Tierney first became interested in politics as a boy growing up in Salem. His uncle served as a ward councilor in Peabody, and Tierney used to campaign with him door-to-door in the community. He worked to put himself through college, where he majored in political science. After law school, he worked for a private law practice and became active in Salem civic affairs.

Although the 6th District contains much of the territory of the oddly shaped district that spawned the term "gerrymander" two centuries ago, it is now one of the most regularly shaped and compact of the state's 10 House districts. In redistricting after the 2000 census, state House Speaker Thomas Finneran, who was feuding with Democratic Rep. Martin T. Meehan, initially proposed a plan that would have thrown Tierney and Meehan together in a substantially redrawn 6th. That plan did not fly, however, and the district's new boundaries are little different from what they have been since the early 1990s.

After pondering an electoral bid for years, Tierney launched his first campaign in 1994 and came within 4 percentage points of defeating freshman GOP Rep. Peter G. Torkildsen, whose ability to keep the seat was aided by that year's Republican tide.

Tierney tried again in 1996, and with President Clinton sweeping up a 28 percentage point win in the district, he eked out a 371-vote win. Torkildsen was back for a rematch in 1998, stressing his moderate stands on such issues as abortion and gay rights. GOP party strategists targeted the race as a priority, but Tierney won by 12 points. He has breezed to lopsided re-election wins since then.

KEY VOTES

2004
Yes Extend federal unemployment benefits by 13 weeks
Yes Pass $283.2 billion, six-year federal highway and mass transit bill
No Approve $146 billion multi-year extension of previously enacted middle-class tax breaks
No Amend the Constitution to prohibit same-sex marriage
No Cut corporate taxes $137 billion over 10 years
Yes Reorganize U.S. intelligence agencies as proposed by Sept. 11 commission

2003
No Cut taxes by $330 billion through fiscal 2013
Yes Block Bush rule scaling back overtime pay for some white-collar federal workers
Yes Do not allow use of search warrants without first notifying subjects
Yes Allow importation of prescription drugs
No Create private school voucher program in Washington, D.C.
No Ban "partial birth" abortion except to save a woman's life
Yes Split $18.6 billion in Iraq aid into half-grant, half-loan
No Overhaul Medicare and create prescription drug benefit

CQ VOTE STUDIES

	PARTY UNITY		PRESIDENTIAL SUPPORT	
	Support	Oppose	Support	Oppose
2004	99%	1%	12%	88%
2003	99%	1%	15%	85%
2002	99%	1%	23%	77%
2001	98%	2%	19%	81%
2000	97%	3%	81%	19%

INTEREST GROUPS

	AFL-CIO	ADA	CCUS	ACU
2004	100%	100%	19%	0%
2003	100%	100%	23%	12%
2002	100%	100%	32%	0%
2001	100%	100%	26%	0%
2000	100%	95%	28%	4%

MASSACHUSETTS 6
North Shore – Lynn, Peabody

Pristine beaches line the cool ocean of Boston's North Shore, home to some of the state's largest homes. Country clubs, fox hunting and polo matches are popular diversions for residents of the northern inland, where the population is sparse but wealthy.

The population is denser along the Route 128 technology corridor, which cuts through the southern part of the district. Like much of Massachusetts in the 1990s, communities along Route 128 turned from manufacturing to an information-based economy. Fueled in part by Boston's universities, technology firms have flourished from Burlington (where Sun Microsystems has offices) to Gloucester, which also supports a major fishing industry. Burlington has a major new industrial park, reflecting the continued growth of the district's economy.

Lynn, the 6th's largest community, is home to aerospace and defense contractors and includes a General Electric jet engine plant. Urban dwellers are concentrated mostly in Lynn and Peabody and provide blue-collar and minority votes for Democrats. Other population centers in

the district include the adjacent coastal cities of Beverly, which residents describe as the birthplace of the Navy because its first commissioned ship sailed from the city's harbor, and Salem, which has a rich history as the locale of the 1692 witch trials. Salem is middle-class and has a Democratic slant, while Beverly is more politically independent.

Republicans can do well in upscale towns such as Boxford, Lynnfield, Topsfield and Wenham, which gave 2002 GOP gubernatorial nominee Mitt Romney more than two-thirds of the vote and narrowly backed George W. Bush in the 2004 presidential election. While the district has a Democratic tilt, it is not overwhelming, and the GOP can win by attracting independent-minded "unenrolled" voters.

MAJOR INDUSTRY
Computer software, defense, fishing

MILITARY BASES
Hanscom Air Force Base, 1,554 military, 1,532 civilian (2003)

CITIES
Lynn, 89,050; Peabody, 48,129; Salem, 40,407; Beverly, 39,862

NOTABLE
The 6th includes territory that spawned the original "gerrymander," a state legislative district named for Gov. Elbridge Gerry in 1812.

Rep. Edward J. Markey (D)

Elected 1976; 15th full term

CAPITOL OFFICE
225-2836
www.house.gov/markey
2108 Rayburn 20515-2107; fax 226-0092

COMMITTEES
Energy & Commerce
Homeland Security
Resources

HOMETOWN
Malden

BORN
July 11, 1946, Malden, Mass.

RELIGION
Roman Catholic

FAMILY
Wife, Susan Blumenthal

EDUCATION
Boston College, B.A. 1968, J.D. 1972

MILITARY SERVICE
Army Reserve, 1968-73

CAREER
Lawyer

POLITICAL HIGHLIGHTS
Mass. House, 1973-77

ELECTION RESULTS

2004 GENERAL

Edward J. Markey (D)	202,399	73.6%
Kenneth G. Chase (R)	60,334	21.9%
James O. Hall (I)	12,139	4.4%

2004 PRIMARY

Edward J. Markey (D)	unopposed

2002 GENERAL

Edward J. Markey (D)	170,968	98.2%
write-ins	2,206	1.3%

PREVIOUS WINNING PERCENTAGES
2000 (99%); 1998 (71%); 1996 (70%); 1994 (64%); 1992
(62%); 1990 (100%); 1988 (100%); 1986 (100%); 1984
(71%); 1982 (78%); 1980 (100%); 1978 (85%); 1976
Combined General and Special Election (77%)

Perhaps no other Democrat on Capitol Hill was as dismayed as Markey by John Kerry's failure in 2004 to unseat President Bush. Markey headed up Kerry's whip team in Congress, winning colleagues' endorsements even as the Massachusetts senator trailed in early primary polls. And Markey had been regarded as a leading candidate for Kerry's Senate seat if he moved to the White House.

Markey is now one of the most influential Democrats in Congress. During the 108th Congress, he broadened his legislative portfolio as an expert on technology issues and an advocate for consumer protection to become one of Bush's most barbed critics on responding to domestic terrorism.

A milk truck driver's son who has been a member of Congress since he was 30, Markey is the dean of the Massachusetts House delegation and is tenth overall in Democratic seniority in the chamber. His seniority has afforded him influence on a pair of committees that between them touch almost every aspect of domestic policy. He is the No. 3 Democrat on Energy and Commerce, and he has served more time on the Resources Committee than anyone else in the 109th Congress.

Markey also landed a prized spot in the 108th Congress on the new Homeland Security Committee. He wasted little time in prodding the White House to move more aggressively against terrorism, particularly on requiring physical screening of all cargo on passenger planes. He accused the administration, airlines, cargo carriers and airport vendors of being unwilling to spend the money to do so even though it would make flying safer. His air cargo amendment on the 2003 Homeland Security appropriations bill won overwhelming support in the House but was later removed in conference.

Markey also pressed the administration to make good on its commitment to distribute potassium iodide as an anti-radiation drug in the event of an attack on a nuclear power plant. And he argued for safety improvements at liquefied natural gas (LNG) terminals, saying they represent another prime terrorist target. Homeland Security and Coast Guard officials initially said that the polystyrene foam in LNG tankers was not flammable, but later admitted they were mistaken. "The fact that [they] could be so completely wrong about the fact that LNG carrier vessels use a highly flammable foam insulation shows how much we need to do to ensure federal regulators are more knowledgeable about potential hazards associated with LNG," he said.

Since 1987, Markey has been the top-ranking Democrat on the Energy and Commerce subcommittee that deals with telecommunications issues. On the panel, he indulges his longstanding fascination with electronic gizmos and communications devices; promotes the interests of companies and workers in the high-tech Route 128 corridor in his district; and champions the personal privacy concerns of the information age.

Markey has gained some of his most noted victories and learned new coalition-building skills since the Republican takeover took away most of his legislative clout. With Dan Burton, a conservative Indiana Republican, he pushed the requirement for "v-chip" circuitry in new televisions to allow parents to block violent or sexually explicit programs. In the 108th, he worked with Pennsylvania Republican Joe Pitts on a bill to protect consumers from having their mobile phone numbers listed in a national wireless number directory without their permission. He also has championed a requirement that online businesses obtain consent before sharing customers' personal information with others.

Because of their broad legislative portfolio, members of Energy and Commerce are magnets for campaign dollars, and Markey is no exception. What was unusual about him is that for years he took money only from individuals, not political action committees.

Markey's proven ability to raise cash prompted Minority Leader Nancy Pelosi to offer Markey the chairmanship of the House Democratic campaign organization in the run-up to the 2004 election. After word of the offer was leaked to The Boston Globe, to Pelosi's annoyance, Markey turned her down. He also began accepting PAC money in his 2004 re-election campaign, at one point collecting more money from telecommunications and high-tech companies than Michigan Republican Fred Upton, chairman of the telecommunications panel.

Markey deploys a wry wit and well-honed sarcasm to skewer opponents and to make his points. Addressing Federal Communications Commission Chairman Michael K. Powell, the son of Secretary of State Colin L. Powell, Markey said in 2001, "People are always asking me to compare you to your father. What I always tell them is you're just as smart as your father, but you have a lot more power to affect the world." A longtime crusader against domestic uses of nuclear energy, he once scoffed at proponents of building new reactors by invoking a line from an old "Saturday Night Live" skit: "Nuclear power is like General Francisco Franco: It's still dead."

But his humor sometimes serves a purely personal purpose. When his beloved Boston Red Sox won the 2004 World Series after 86 years of futility, ending what had become known as "the Curse," Markey proudly took to the House floor to recite a poem of his own modeled after the classic last stanza in "Casey at the Bat." Its ending: "And Red Sox Nation smiles and laughs, and little children shout/And there is pure joy in Beantown — the Curse has struck out."

Elected to the state House at 26, he served two terms, battling his party's leadership on occasion. Once, they retaliated by kicking him off the Judiciary Committee, and one opponent went so far as to throw the furniture from Markey's office into the hallway.

Markey came to Congress in 1976 by winning a special election to succeed Democrat Torbert H. Macdonald, who died. Markey's only tough campaign since then was in 1984, when his opponent questioned his commitment to the job after Markey briefly ran for the Senate seat opened by the retirement of Democrat Paul E. Tsongas.

KEY VOTES

2004
Yes   Extend federal unemployment benefits by 13 weeks
Yes   Pass $283.2 billion, six-year federal highway and mass transit bill
No   Approve $146 billion multi-year extension of previously enacted middle-class tax breaks
No   Amend the Constitution to prohibit same-sex marriage
No   Cut corporate taxes $137 billion over 10 years
Yes   Reorganize U.S. intelligence agencies as proposed by Sept. 11 commission

2003
No   Cut taxes by $330 billion through fiscal 2013
Yes   Block Bush rule scaling back overtime pay for some white-collar federal workers
Yes   Do not allow use of search warrants without first notifying subjects
Yes   Allow importation of prescription drugs
No   Create private school voucher program in Washington, D.C.
No   Ban "partial birth" abortion except to save a woman's life
Yes   Split $18.6 billion in Iraq aid into half-grant, half-loan
No   Overhaul Medicare and create prescription drug benefit

CQ VOTE STUDIES

	PARTY UNITY		PRESIDENTIAL SUPPORT	
	Support	Oppose	Support	Oppose
2004	98%	2%	15%	85%
2003	99%	1%	13%	87%
2002	99%	1%	25%	75%
2001	96%	4%	26%	74%
2000	98%	2%	88%	12%

INTEREST GROUPS

	AFL-CIO	ADA	CCUS	ACU
2004	100%	100%	10%	0%
2003	100%	100%	20%	12%
2002	100%	100%	30%	4%
2001	100%	100%	36%	4%
2000	100%	85%	29%	4%

MASSACHUSETTS 7
Northwest Boston suburbs — Framingham

The affluent strip along Route 128-Interstate 95, a Silicon Valley of the East, shapes the 7th's character. The district, which includes some of the state's most well-to-do communities, stretches east from an urban retail center on Route 9 in Framingham to Route 128 as it rings Boston, then moves east through Medford and Malden to reach the middle-class coastal town of Revere.

For decades, Revere has attracted vacationers to its beaches, but overall, the 7th's economy is driven by a strong software and Internet industry. Many Medford and Malden residents commute to blue-collar jobs in Boston, and Malden has a rapidly growing Asian community.

The area takes pride in its history; each year, Lexington re-enacts Paul Revere's ride and the first Revolutionary War battles (which took place in towns in the 7th and 5th districts) on Patriots Day.

The 7th's political roots are a mix of Protestant Yankee Republicans and Irish Democrats. But like all Massachusetts districts, the 7th votes

Democratic in federal races. Redistricting following the 2000 census only increased the 7th's already strong Democratic lean. Al Gore won the 2000 presidential vote here, as did John Kerry in 2004 with 66 percent of the vote. George W. Bush's best showing in the district in 2004 was in Woburn, where he received only 43 percent of the vote.

The wealthy sections of the 7th vary from the more conservative Weston to the liberal Lincoln. Democrats also draw votes from a blue-collar, middle-class base in Framingham and in the eastern part of the district, including Revere, Everett and Malden.

MAJOR INDUSTRY
Computer software, telecommunications, defense

MILITARY BASES
Army Soldier Systems Center (Natick), 99 military, 1,126 civilian (2005)

CITIES
Framingham (unincorporated), 66,910; Waltham, 59,226; Malden, 56,340; Medford, 55,765; Revere, 47,283; Arlington (unincorporated), 42,389

NOTABLE
James Pierpont is said to have written "Jingle Bells" in 1850 while visiting Medford Square; The only known American father and son to die in the Vietnam War were from Stoneham.

Rep. Michael E. Capuano (D)

Elected 1998; 4th term

CAPITOL OFFICE
225-5111
www.house.gov/capuano
1530 Longworth 20515-2108; fax 225-9322

COMMITTEES
Financial Services
Transportation & Infrastructure

HOMETOWN
Somerville

BORN
Jan. 9, 1952, Somerville, Mass.

RELIGION
Roman Catholic

FAMILY
Wife, Barbara Teebagy Capuano; two children

EDUCATION
Dartmouth College, B.A. 1973 (psychology);
Boston College, J.D. 1977

CAREER
Lawyer; state legislative aide

POLITICAL HIGHLIGHTS
Somerville Board of Aldermen, 1977-79; candidate
for mayor of Somerville, 1979, 1981; Somerville
Board of Aldermen, 1985-89; mayor of Somerville,
1990-99; sought Democratic nomination for Mass.
secretary of state, 1994

ELECTION RESULTS

2004 GENERAL

Michael E. Capuano (D)	165,852	98.7%
write-ins	2,229	1.3%

2004 PRIMARY

Michael E. Capuano (D)	unopposed

2002 GENERAL

Michael E. Capuano (D)	unopposed

PREVIOUS WINNING PERCENTAGES
2000 (99%); 1998 (82%)

Capuano is a sharp-tongued partisan who often shows little patience for the priorities of his Republican colleagues who run the House. A former Massachusetts alderman and a suburban mayor, Capuano has street smarts that belie his Ivy League education, and on occasion he uses rough language that accentuates his brash personality.

He is a member of the Democratic leadership team as a regional whip and sits on the Democratic Steering Committee, which makes committee assignments.

Trained as a tax attorney, he willingly dives into the minutiae of budget and tax issues. Capuano (KAP-you-AH-no) sits on the Financial Services Committee, where he has been particularly critical of President Bush's 2005 budget for housing programs. He said that Bush's budget would dismantle the Community Development Block Grant (CDBG) program, which in 2004 brought more than $120 million in economic development funding to Massachusetts cities and towns.

Capuano said Bush has proposed eliminating the CDBG program and replacing it with a similar program run by the Department of Commerce while cutting its funding by at least 35 percent. He said Bush's budget would also change the way the money is distributed so that it can no longer be used for affordable housing initiatives. "Our cities and towns are already struggling under the weight of reduced state aid," he said. "Cutting the CDBG program will force communities to make very difficult funding choices, and many valuable initiatives may not survive."

Capuano is clearly interested in helping his constituents afford a home. A bill passed by the House during his first term included his provision to allow teachers and uniformed municipal workers to buy homes through subsidized housing programs — even if their incomes were above the poverty level.

He also wants to help people cope in the new age of terrorism. He added an amendment when Financial Services sought to extend terrorism insurance coverage for another two years. The Terrorism Risk Insurance Act was passed in 2002 to help stabilize the commercial property and casualty insurance markets after the Sept. 11, 2001, terrorist attacks. The program requires the government to cover 90 percent of terrorism-related losses once insured losses reach trigger levels. Capuano's amendment extended this coverage to group life insurance policies. "As Congress works to extend this critical legislation, it is important that we not only protect bricks and mortar, but the men and women working in those buildings," he said. In 2001, he pushed to include the families of the victims of the anthrax attacks among those compensated after the Sept. 11 attacks.

Capuano forged a national profile with his comments on the accounting scandals that helped to shape the 2001 legislative agenda. When officials of Global Crossing Ltd., a bankrupt communications company, appeared before Financial Services, newspapers across the country reported Capuano's unambiguous indictment. "The whole thing you're talking about is nothing more than a much more fancy and larger Ponzi scheme," he said. In 2004, his concerns about the financial services industry were closer to home as he pressed Bank of America to live up to its assurances about maintaining jobs in the Boston region after swallowing up Fleet Bank.

Capuano also sits on the Transportation and Infrastructure Committee, where he can help direct federal funds to Boston's Big Dig construction project, which is placing Boston's central highway system underground.

Capuano now seems to have settled into his role as a legislator, opting out in early 2005 in a bid for governor against GOP incumbent Mitt Romney. Capuano said he was not prepared to sacrifice his personal and professional life to mount a campaign for governor. "It takes up your entire life for two years," Capuano told the Boston Globe. He said he would focus his energy in Washington on fighting GOP efforts to overhaul Social Security and on winning transportation funding for the state.

A member of the Congressional Progressive Caucus, a group of the most left-leaning House Democrats, Capuano opposed a constitutional amendment banning same-sex marriage. He voted against authorizing Bush to wage war in Iraq and opposed the Patriot Act, saying it was a threat to civil liberties.

Capuano won the 8th District seat after Joseph P. Kennedy II, the son of Robert F. Kennedy and nephew of John F. Kennedy, gave it up after six terms. The House seat was the first political post President Kennedy ever won. Further back, the Kennedy brothers' grandfather, John F. Fitzgerald, represented the district at the turn of the century.

Capuano is the product of a more modest political dynasty: His father was the first Italian-American elected to local office in the city of Somerville. While Capuano is half-Irish, his Italian-American surname is a change from the Irish identification of the Kennedys and others who have held the seat since World War II: James Michael Curley and former Speaker Thomas P. "Tip" O'Neill Jr. Capuano inherited O'Neill's mammoth desk when another Boston Democrat, Rep. Joe Moakley, died in 2001.

Capuano must navigate in a district where political tensions continually work their way to the surface. As mayor of Somerville, he drew criticism from detractors who described his style as "tyrannical" and said he managed the city like a ward boss, hiring friends and relatives and running enemies out of public agencies. Capuano called the attacks on his leadership style "a sign of a good executive."

Capuano triumphed in a 10-person Democratic donnybrook created by Kennedy's unexpected 1998 retirement in the solidly Democratic district. The presumed front-runner was Raymond L. Flynn, a former Boston mayor and ambassador to the Vatican who had abandoned a flagging run for governor. But Capuano needled Flynn on his education and housing policies as mayor; others attacked Flynn's anti-abortion position. Although greatly outspent by two other candidates, Capuano was lifted to victory by a strong turnout in Somerville. He breezed by a Republican opponent that November, and the GOP has not fielded a candidate since.

KEY VOTES

2004

Yes Extend federal unemployment benefits by 13 weeks
Yes Pass $283.2 billion, six-year federal highway and mass transit bill
No Approve $146 billion multi-year extension of previously enacted middle-class tax breaks
No Amend the Constitution to prohibit same-sex marriage
No Cut corporate taxes $137 billion over 10 years
Yes Reorganize U.S. intelligence agencies as proposed by Sept. 11 commission

2003

No Cut taxes by $330 billion through fiscal 2013
Yes Block Bush rule scaling back overtime pay for some white-collar federal workers
Yes Do not allow use of search warrants without first notifying subjects
Yes Allow importation of prescription drugs
No Create private school voucher program in Washington, D.C.
No Ban "partial birth" abortion except to save a woman's life
Yes Split $18.6 billion in Iraq aid into half-grant, half-loan
No Overhaul Medicare and create prescription drug benefit

CQ VOTE STUDIES

	PARTY UNITY		PRESIDENTIAL SUPPORT	
	Support	Oppose	Support	Oppose
2004	96%	4%	24%	76%
2003	97%	3%	19%	81%
2002	98%	2%	21%	79%
2001	96%	4%	17%	83%
2000	98%	2%	87%	13%

INTEREST GROUPS

	AFL-CIO	ADA	CCUS	ACU
2004	93%	90%	19%	4%
2003	100%	100%	20%	16%
2002	89%	95%	28%	4%
2001	100%	95%	32%	4%
2000	100%	100%	33%	0%

MASSACHUSETTS 8

Part of Boston and suburbs — Cambridge, Somerville

The 8th combines Boston's historic Revolutionary War sites with neighborhoods that reflect its evolving future. From the North End and South End — the neighboring 9th takes in places in between like Beacon Hill and the financial district — the 8th grabs much of the city west of Interstate 93. In doing so, it picks up the Back Bay area, Chinatown and many largely black and Hispanic neighborhoods in areas like Roxbury, Dorchester and Jamaica Plain, making it the state's only district where a majority of residents are minorities.

Among the many Beantown sights found in the 8th are the Old North Church, Bunker Hill, the U.S.S. Constitution and Logan International Airport (shared with the 7th). Most of the land involved in the "Big Dig," a long-running transportation project, is in the 8th.

Two of the world's most respected universities — Harvard and the Massachusetts Institute of Technology — lie across the Charles River in Cambridge. Typifying the district's monolithically liberal politics, Cambridge gave George W. Bush just 13 percent of the vote in the 2000 presidential election — a showing topped by Green Party nominee Ralph Nader. Bush received just 13 percent again in 2004. Unsurprisingly, John Kerry received 82 percent of the district's vote in 2004, a state high.

The district also takes in dozens of other colleges, which drive much of the economy, whether through blue-collar service employees who work at the schools and teaching hospitals or through biotechnology software firms that employ local talent. Somerville, just north of Cambridge, has a thriving arts community, while Chelsea, with more-affordable housing and blue-collar jobs, has seen its Hispanic population expand to comprise one-half of the city's residents.

MAJOR INDUSTRY
Biotechnology, higher education, health care, tourism

CITIES
Boston (pt.), 420,922; Cambridge, 101,355; Somerville, 77,478

NOTABLE
The 8th is the descendant of the district once represented by John F. Kennedy (1947-53) and Thomas P. "Tip" O'Neill Jr. (1953-87); Fenway Park is home to baseball's Boston Red Sox, who won the 2004 World Series.

Rep. Stephen F. Lynch (D)

Elected October 2001; 2nd full term

CAPITOL OFFICE
225-8273
stephen.lynch@mail.house.gov
www.house.gov/lynch
319 Cannon 20515-2109; fax 225-3984

COMMITTEES
Financial Services
Government Reform

HOMETOWN
Boston

BORN
March 31, 1955, Boston, Mass.

RELIGION
Roman Catholic

FAMILY
Wife, Margaret Lynch; one child

EDUCATION
Wentworth Institute of Technology, B.S. 1988
(construction management); Boston College, J.D.
1991; Harvard U., M.A. 1998 (public administration)

CAREER
Lawyer; ironworker

POLITICAL HIGHLIGHTS
Mass. House, 1995-96; Mass. Senate, 1996-2001

ELECTION RESULTS

2004 GENERAL
Stephen F. Lynch (D)   unopposed
2004 PRIMARY
Stephen F. Lynch (D)   unopposed
2002 GENERAL
Stephen F. Lynch (D)   unopposed

PREVIOUS WINNING PERCENTAGES
2001 Special Election (65%)

Lynch has an uncommon life story. He grew up in one of South Boston's poorest housing projects, and he labored as an ironworker for 18 years while putting himself through school, including earning a law degree from Boston College and a master's degree from Harvard University. During his time as an ironworker, he served as president of his local union.

His background also separates him from the stereotype of the typical northeast liberal. A Roman Catholic, Lynch opposes abortion and voted for the legislation banning the procedure opponents call "partial birth" abortion. Yet he voted against a constitutional amendment to prohibit same-sex marriage and has expressed support for an extension of medical benefits to domestic partners. Lynch describes himself as a moderate. In the 108th Congress, he voted with a majority of his party 91 percent of the time and in agreement with President Bush's position 33 percent of the time.

Lynch also voted in 2002 to authorize war against Iraq. Lynch said he was not impressed by the diplomatic skills of the Bush administration, but was nevertheless convinced Saddam Hussein should not be allowed to build weapons of mass destruction.

For him, the decisive moment came when he and other wavering Democrats were briefed by David Kay, the U.N. weapons inspector under President Clinton. Kay's view at the time, according to Lynch, was that even though the Iraqis "had destroyed what they had built at that time, they had not destroyed their ability to just build it all back up again."

After the war started, it was Kay, as Bush's chief weapons inspector, who declared that "we were almost all wrong" about the threat Iraq's weapons posed. Lynch does not quite say he would have voted against the war resolution had he known the truth about the weapons. But he is angry about the fact that none were found. He says Congress "was misled, either intentionally or unintentionally" into thinking Saddam posed an immediate threat and there was no more time for diplomacy. "We committed our troops prematurely," he said. "It is almost a commandment in this country that we do not put our sons and daughters in harm's way unless it is absolutely necessary, unless we have exhausted all other options. That did not happen here."

On most fiscal votes, Lynch fits comfortably in the party mainstream. In 2003, he voted with virtually all House Democrats against Bush's $350 billion tax cut and against the Republican Medicare measure providing prescription drug benefits for seniors. He has traveled to Cuba and is a strong advocate of lifting the economic sanctions against that country.

As a former labor leader, Lynch voted in 2003 to block Bush's plans to limit eligibility for overtime pay. He also opposed the law enacted in 2002 granting the president fast-track authority to negotiate trade deals Congress must approve or reject but may not amend. He consistently earns high ratings from the AFL-CIO for his labor votes.

Lynch served on the Veterans' Affairs Committee until the end of the 107th Congress, where he looked after the interests of the three VA medical facilities in his district and its shelter for homeless veterans. He retained his focus on veterans' issues in the 108th, after trading his Veterans' Affairs seat for a spot on Financial Services. Along with Jack Quinn, a moderate Republican from New York, he introduced legislation to improve staffing levels at VA hospitals, which he said were so chronically inadequate that the lack of staff was endangering veterans' lives.

Early in 2005, Lynch blasted Bush's budget proposal, saying it included cuts in funding for veterans' health care. Lynch said the administration's budget would double the co-payments for prescriptions from $7 to $15 for a 30-day supply and require veterans to pay a new $250 fee to access the VA medical system. Lynch said: "I can't understand how the president can continue to advocate tax cuts for the rich and yet he will not stand with veterans who have made enormous sacrifices for this country."

Lynch sits on the Government Reform panel, where in the 109th he became the top-ranking Democrat on the Regulatory Affairs Subcommittee.

Lynch came to the House after winning a special election in the fall of 2001 to replace an especially beloved congressman: Joe Moakley, a Democrat who held the seat from 1973 until his death from leukemia. Lynch won the Democratic nomination for the 9th District seat on Sept. 11, 2001. The events of that day have left their mark on him. He was already campaigning as a Democrat with an independent streak, but after the terrorist attacks, he became more willing than most in his caucus to err on the side of using force to head off terrorist threats.

Lynch's father was an ironworker for 40 years. At age 30, Lynch was elected as the youngest president ever of the Ironworkers Local 7. At the same time, he attended law school, which was his ticket out of the unstable and often dangerous work of his trade. He joined a law firm, continuing a practice he had begun in law school of representing housing project residents for free. His pro bono interests eventually prompted friends to encourage him to run for the Massachusetts Legislature.

Lynch unseated incumbent state Rep. Paul Gannon in 1994, and in April 1996 he won a special election to fill the state Senate seat of Senate President William M. Bulger, who became president of the University of Massachusetts system. That position gave Lynch a solid launching pad to run for Congress when Moakley died soon after his 15th term began.

It was not a clear shot, however. He was up against six Democratic opponents, several of whom criticized him for his opposition to abortion. And two of his opponents raised questions about an incident from Lynch's days as an attorney, when he defended 14 white teenagers accused of physically and verbally abusing a white girl and her Hispanic boyfriend. But Lynch benefited from his personal story of working his way out of poverty, as well as the publicity from an act of generosity: He donated 60 percent of his liver to his brother-in-law, who had liver cancer.

Lynch won the primary with 39 percent of the vote and then went on to defeat Republican state Sen. Jo Ann Sprague with 65 percent. In 2002 and 2004, no Republican challenged him for re-election.

KEY VOTES

2004

Yes Extend federal unemployment benefits by 13 weeks

Yes Pass $283.2 billion, six-year federal highway and mass transit bill

Yes Approve $146 billion multi-year extension of previously enacted middle-class tax breaks

No   Amend the Constitution to prohibit same-sex marriage

No   Cut corporate taxes $137 billion over 10 years

Yes Reorganize U.S. intelligence agencies as proposed by Sept. 11 commission

2003

No   Cut taxes by $330 billion through fiscal 2013

Yes Block Bush rule scaling back overtime pay for some white-collar federal workers

Yes Do not allow use of search warrants without first notifying subjects

Yes Allow importation of prescription drugs

No   Create private school voucher program in Washington, D.C.

Yes Ban "partial birth" abortion except to save a woman's life

Yes Split $18.6 billion in Iraq aid into half-grant, half-loan

No   Overhaul Medicare and create prescription drug benefit

CQ VOTE STUDIES

	PARTY UNITY		PRESIDENTIAL SUPPORT	
	Support	Oppose	Support	Oppose
2004	91%	9%	42%	58%
2003	91%	9%	27%	73%
2002	94%	6%	33%	67%
2001	97%	3%	37%	63%

INTEREST GROUPS

	AFL-CIO	ADA	CCUS	ACU
2004	93%	85%	43%	28%
2003	100%	85%	27%	33%
2002	100%	90%	40%	13%
2001	100%	—	44%	0%

MASSACHUSETTS 9
Part of Boston; southern suburbs — Brockton, Braintree

The 9th begins with a central swath of downtown Boston, covering Beacon Hill, the West End and the financial district. The statehouse and brokerage houses — the 9th is home to one of the world's largest centers for mutual fund investing — are dominant in this part of Boston. They share the area with sprawling Boston Common park and several of New England's major tourist attractions. Faneuil Hall Marketplace anchors the retail industry. Some of the wealthiest neighborhoods in the state are along the Charles River.

From central Boston the district hops the Fort Point Channel into South Boston — long referred to as "Southie" — and closely hugs Interstate 93 on its way into Milton. It connects through Dedham to West Roxbury, a mostly white suburban enclave in the southwestern part of Boston.

The "Brahmin" homes of Beacon Hill are counterbalanced by the poor and working-class neighborhoods of traditionally Irish Southie and

middle-class suburban communities south and west of the city. Though solidly Democratic, Southie's political tradition is one of supporting pro-labor Democrats who are more conservative on social issues.

The 9th's areas outside of Boston are relatively conservative for Massachusetts. While the district's suburbs have helped elect Republicans to the governor's mansion in recent years, the district's mostly blue-collar base in Boston and Brockton keeps it solidly Democratic in federal elections.

MAJOR INDUSTRY
Financial services, government, tourism

CITIES
Boston (pt.), 168,219; Brockton, 94,304; Braintree (unincorporated), 33,698; Randolph (unincorporated), 30,963; Norwood (unincorporated), 28,587

NOTABLE
Patriots tossed boxes of tea into Boston Harbor during the Boston Tea Party in 1773, a catalyst for the Revolutionary War; The John F. Kennedy Library and Museum is in Boston; A new federal courthouse in South Boston was named for the late Rep. Joe Moakley, who represented the district from 1973 until his death in 2001.

Rep. Bill Delahunt (D)

CAPITOL OFFICE
225-3111
william.delahunt@mail.house.gov
www.house.gov/delahunt
2454 Rayburn 20515-2110; fax 225-5658

COMMITTEES
International Relations
Judiciary

HOMETOWN
Quincy

BORN
July 18, 1941, Quincy, Mass.

RELIGION
Roman Catholic

FAMILY
Divorced; two children

EDUCATION
Middlebury College, B.A. 1963; Boston College, J.D. 1967

MILITARY SERVICE
Coast Guard, 1963; Coast Guard Reserve, 1963-71

CAREER
Lawyer

POLITICAL HIGHLIGHTS
Quincy City Council, 1971-73; Mass. House, 1973-75; Norfolk County district attorney, 1975-97

ELECTION RESULTS

2004 GENERAL

Bill Delahunt (D)	222,013	65.9%
Michael J. Jones (R)	114,879	34.1%

2004 PRIMARY

Bill Delahunt (D)	unopposed

2002 GENERAL

Bill Delahunt (D)	179,238	69.2%
Luiz Gonzaga (R)	79,624	30.7%

PREVIOUS WINNING PERCENTAGES
2000 (74%); 1998 (70%); 1996 (54%)

Elected 1996; 5th term

A reliable liberal vote and an important Democratic voice on the International Relations and Judiciary committees, Delahunt is an affable Yankee pol in an age dominated by a more caustic partisanship. Although unafraid to level sharp criticisms when he feels it is warranted, Delahunt (DELL-a-hunt) has a knack for cultivating relationships with colleagues who have far different ideological outlooks. International Relations Committee Chairman Henry J. Hyde of Illinois says Delahunt brings with him "a maturity, leavened with a good sense of humor."

In the 108th Congress, he joined with Republican Ray LaHood of Illinois to win bipartisan House passage of legislation that sought to expand and improve forensic laboratories, clear a backlog of untested biological evidence in criminal cases and give death row inmates access to post-conviction DNA testing. Delahunt and LaHood built support slowly, working to overcome skittishness on both the left and the right. Their efforts were bolstered by a nationwide wave of criticism of the death penalty and two Supreme Court rulings in June 2002 that restricted the use of the death penalty, reversing a trend of the court. The legislation became law as part of a broader measure at the end of the 108th.

In another bipartisan initiative during the 108th, Delahunt and conservative Oklahoma Republican Ernest Istook introduced legislation to lift the moratorium on Internet taxes. "States that are confronting their worst fiscal crisis since the great Depression cannot continue to forgo billions in sales-tax revenues," he said.

Delahunt was tapped in 2004 for one bipartisan chore that no member relishes: a prominent role in a House ethics investigation of whether GOP leaders improperly pressured Republican Nick Smith to vote for the GOP Medicare prescription drug plan. The panel admonished Majority Leader Tom DeLay.

Delahunt was inspired to enter politics by John F. Kennedy. While a student at Middlebury College, he was co-chairman of a Vermont college students-for-Kennedy group. The other chairman (and a fraternity brother of Delahunt's) was the late Ronald H. Brown, secretary of Commerce under President Clinton.

Delahunt spent more than 20 years as a district attorney just south of Boston, and his experience as a prosecutor has made him an influential voice for his party on Judiciary. "Billy has locked up more people than everyone else on the committee put together," Barney Frank of Massachusetts, for years the panel's No. 2 Democrat, told The Boston Globe. "He is a liberal with his head on his shoulders."

Delahunt has worked to toughen the Clean Air Act and continue enforcement of environmental standards at military facilities, and in 2003, he secured $2 million in grants for environmental protection on Cape Cod. He also led an effort to block electricity-generating windmills in Nantucket Sound, supporting local residents who objected to the project and warned that it would put endangered birds at risk.

On International Relations, Delahunt helped organize a bipartisan 52-member Cuba Working Group to press for an end to the four-decade trade embargo against the island nation. In 2003, Delahunt joined Republican Jeff Flake of Arizona and others in a successful effort to add to a spending bill a provision ending the Cuba travel ban — only to have the proposal dropped in conference in the face of a veto threat inspired by pressure from the powerful anti-Castro Florida delegation.

Delahunt is also an active member of the "Boston Group," an interparliamentary exchange between Congress and members of the Venezuelan National Assembly.

Delahunt, who adopted an abandoned Vietnamese baby girl in 1975, has been a force behind legislation to ease overseas adoptions. In 2000, he won a major victory with passage of his bill to grant automatic citizenship to children adopted from abroad, as well as to foreign-born children of U.S. parents.

Although "politics may make odd bedfellows," Delahunt's bedfellows are reliable liberals, too — as was made clear by "The Little House on the Hill," a short-lived television show put together by comedian Al Franken in 2002. It portrayed the domestic hijinks of Delahunt and his three Democratic housemates, Sens. Charles E. Schumer of New York and Richard J. Durbin of Illinois and Rep. George Miller of California.

Delahunt's fondness for baseball, particularly the Boston Red Sox, has crept into his political work. At a 1999 reception for Venezuelan President Hugo Chávez, Delahunt sought to court the controversial leftist with an unusual gift: a framed baseball card of Luis Aparicio, a Venezuelan and Hall of Fame shortstop who played for the Red Sox. And in 2003, International Relations Chairman Hyde broke into Delahunt's aggressive questioning of a Defense Department official by saying, "I think a more relevant question is how long do we have to wait for the Red Sox to win the pennant." "Only the gods know that," Delahunt said, as laughter enveloped the room.

A Quincy native, Delahunt became a city councilman at age 30. Elected to the state House in 1972, he shared an office with a couple of other Beacon Hill rookies, Edward J. Markey and Frank, now senior members of the state's congressional delegation. Two years later, however, Gov. Michael S. Dukakis named him the district attorney for suburban Norfolk County, of which Quincy is the major municipality.

In 1996, when Democrat Gerry E. Studds announced his retirement from the House after a dozen terms, Delahunt was regarded as the Democratic front-runner from the start. But in a hard-fought September primary, he trailed state Rep. Phil Johnston by about 300 votes. Delahunt went to court, charging that ballots that should have been counted for him were mistakenly counted as blank. A state judge concurred, and Delahunt was certified the primary winner just 28 days before Election Day. He went on to win the general election by 13 percentage points and has had no trouble retaining his seat since. Redistricting following the 2000 census preserved his core constituencies, and in 2002 and 2004 he was re-elected by wide margins.

KEY VOTES

2004

Yes Extend federal unemployment benefits by 13 weeks

Yes Pass $283.2 billion, six-year federal highway and mass transit bill

? Approve $146 billion multi-year extension of previously enacted middle-class tax breaks

No Amend the Constitution to prohibit same-sex marriage

No Cut corporate taxes $137 billion over 10 years

Yes Reorganize U.S. intelligence agencies as proposed by Sept. 11 commission

2003

No Cut taxes by $330 billion through fiscal 2013

Yes Block Bush rule scaling back overtime pay for some white-collar federal workers

Yes Do not allow use of search warrants without first notifying subjects

Yes Allow importation of prescription drugs

No Create private school voucher program in Washington, D.C.

No Ban "partial birth" abortion except to save a woman's life

Yes Split $18.6 billion in Iraq aid into half-grant, half-loan

No Overhaul Medicare and create prescription drug benefit

CQ VOTE STUDIES

	PARTY UNITY		PRESIDENTIAL SUPPORT	
	Support	Oppose	Support	Oppose
2004	98%	2%	19%	81%
2003	98%	2%	10%	90%
2002	97%	3%	24%	76%
2001	94%	6%	21%	79%
2000	95%	5%	80%	20%

INTEREST GROUPS

	AFL-CIO	ADA	CCUS	ACU
2004	93%	95%	33%	0%
2003	100%	95%	14%	13%
2002	100%	90%	39%	0%
2001	100%	95%	26%	4%
2000	89%	85%	47%	8%

MASSACHUSETTS 10
South Shore — Quincy, Cape Cod, islands

Cool coastal breezes in the summer and warm ocean air in the winter attract retirees and tourists to the 10th, where most towns border the ocean. The area that spawned the nation's puritanical streak and the Thanksgiving holiday still retains a Yankee flavor, but the northern part of the 10th has attracted residents from Boston's ethnic neighborhoods. A rail line from Boston to several South Shore communities is contributing to the area's population boom. The old 10th was the fastest-growing Massachusetts district in the 1990s.

Other than tourism, maritime technology and research are burgeoning industries along the Cape, especially in Woods Hole. To the north, a booming software industry helped the area recover from a recession in the early 1990s.

The mainland coastal towns of the 10th are commonly referred to as the South Shore. With the exception of a handful of thriving cranberry bogs, most of the South Shore towns consist of bedroom developments for Boston's professionals or Quincy's blue-collar workers. The state's most

liberal population lives on the far end of Cape Cod, where Provincetown, a predominately gay artists' colony, thrives. Provincetown gave 75 percent of the vote to Democrat Shannon O'Brien in the 2002 gubernatorial race, her statewide high, and 87 percent to John Kerry in 2004, his second-highest state total.

But those totals belie the 10th's overall political character, which is more politically independent than Democratic. The state's least heavily Democratic district in both the 2000 and 2004 presidential races, the 10th opted for Republican Mitt Romney by 17 points in the 2002 gubernatorial race, thanks to GOP strength in communities southeast of Quincy and northwest of Plymouth.

MAJOR INDUSTRY
Marine technology, biotechnology, health care, tourism

CITIES
Quincy, 88,025; Weymouth, 53,988; Plymouth (unincorporated), 51,701; Barnstable, 47,821; Falmouth (unincorporated), 32,660

NOTABLE
Presidents John Adams (1797-1801) and John Quincy Adams (1825-1829) were from Quincy; Plymouth Rock; The John Alden House in Duxbury is named for the Pilgrim who sailed on the Mayflower.

Gov. Jennifer M. Granholm (D)

First elected: 2002
Length of term: 4 years
Term expires: 1/07
Salary: $177,000
Phone: (517) 373-3400

Hometown: Lansing
Born: Feb. 5, 1959; Richmond, Canada
Religion: Roman Catholic
Family: Husband, Daniel G. Mulhern; three children
Education: U. of California, Berkeley, B.A. 1984 (political science & French); Harvard U., J.D. 1987
Career: Federal prosecutor; campaign aide; lawyer
Political highlights: Wayne County Corporation Counsel, 1994-98; Mich. attorney general, 1999-2003

Election results:
2002 GENERAL
Jennifer M. Granholm (D)	1,633,796	51.4%
Dick Posthumus (R)	1,506,104	47.4%

Lt. Gov. John Cherry (D)

First elected: 2002
Length of term: 4 years
Term expires: 1/07
Salary: $123,900
Phone: (517) 373-3400

STATE LEGISLATURE

Legislature: Year-round with recess

House: 110 members, 2-year terms
2005 breakdown: 58R, 52D; 91 men, 19 women
Salary: $79,650; $12,000/year expenses
Phone: (517) 373-0135

Senate: 38 members, 4-year terms
2005 breakdown: 22R, 16D; 27 men, 11 women
Salary: $79,650; $12,000/year expenses
Phone: (517) 373-2400

STATE TERM LIMITS

Governor: 2 terms
House: 3 terms
Senate: 2 terms

URBAN STATISTICS

CITY	POPULATION
Detroit	951,270
Grand Rapids	197,800
Warren	138,247
Flint	124,943
Sterling Heights	124,471

REGISTERED VOTERS

Voters do not register by party.

POPULATION

2004 population (est.)	10,112,620
2000 population	9,938,444
1990 population	9,295,297
Percent change (1990-2000)	+6.9%
Rank among states (2004)	8

Median age	35.5
Born in state	75.4%
Foreign born	5.3%
Violent crime rate	555/100,000
Poverty level	10.5%
Federal workers	54,604
Military	21,833

REDISTRICTING

Michigan lost one House seat in reapportionment. The state legislature drew a new, 15-district map, which the governor signed on Sept. 11, 2001.

MISCELLANEOUS

Web: www.michigan.gov
Capital: Lansing
STATE ELECTION OFFICIAL
(517) 373-2540
DEMOCRATIC HEADQUARTERS
(517) 371-5410
REPUBLICAN HEADQUARTERS
(517) 487-5413

District Statistics

DIST.	2004 VOTE FOR PRESIDENT BUSH	2004 VOTE FOR PRESIDENT KERRY	WHITE	BLACK	ASIAN	HISP	MEDIAN INCOME	WHITE COLLAR	BLUE COLLAR	SERVICE INDUSTRY	OVER 64	UNDER 18	COLLEGE EDUCATION	RURAL	SQ. MILES
1	53%	46%	94%	1%	0%	1%	$34,076	51%	30%	19%	17%	23%	16%	67%	24,887
2	60	39	87	4	1	5	$42,589	51	34	15	12	28	18	44	5,365
3	59	40	82	8	2	6	$45,936	57	30	13	11	28	24	23	1,854
4	55	44	93	2	1	2	$39,020	54	29	17	14	25	19	59	7,451
5	41	59	75	18	1	4	$39,675	51	32	17	12	27	15	21	1,754
6	53	46	84	9	1	4	$40,943	53	32	15	12	26	21	42	3,331
7	54	45	88	6	1	3	$45,181	54	32	15	12	26	19	46	4,295
8	54	45	88	5	2	3	$52,510	63	23	14	9	26	29	30	2,254
9	50	49	81	8	6	3	$65,358	75	15	10	12	24	44	1	311
10	56	43	94	1	1	2	$52,690	55	32	13	11	27	17	34	3,549
11	52	47	90	4	3	2	$59,177	65	24	12	12	25	29	3	399
12	39	60	82	12	2	1	$46,784	60	27	14	16	23	20	0	160

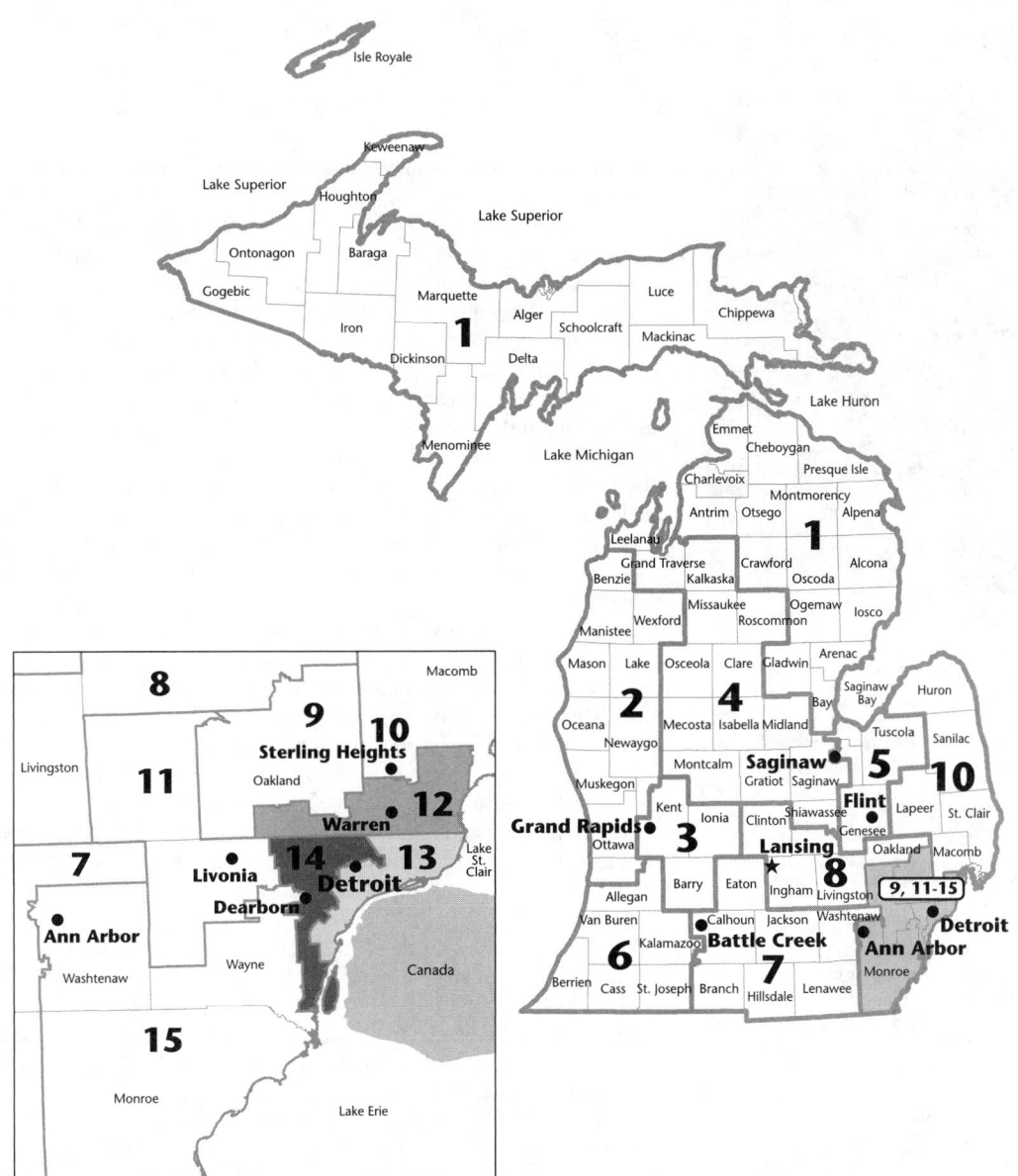

District Statistics

DIST.	2004 VOTE FOR PRESIDENT BUSH	KERRY	WHITE	BLACK	ASIAN	HISP	MEDIAN INCOME	WHITE COLLAR	BLUE COLLAR	SERVICE INDUSTRY	OVER 64	UNDER 18	COLLEGE EDUCATION	RURAL	SQ. MILES
13	19%	80%	29%	60%	1%	7%	$31,165	51%	29%	20%	11%	30%	14%	0%	108
14	18	82	32	61	1	2	$36,099	53	29	18	12	29	14	0	123
15	38	61	79	12	4	3	$48,963	59	26	14	10	25	28	12	961
STATE	48	51	79	14	2	3	$44,667	57	28	15	12	26	22	25	56,804
U.S.	50.7	48.3	69	12	4	13	$41,994	60	25	15	12	26	24	21	3,537,438

Sen. Carl Levin (D)

Elected 1978; 5th term

Levin's trademarks — the reading glasses on the tip of his nose, the famously rumpled style, the genial way he has of compelling truth from balky congressional witnesses — are as familiar at the Armed Services Committee as a general's stars. He is one of the Democrats' leading critics of the war in Iraq, and no friend of Bush administration foreign policy.

As the senior Democrat on the panel, Levin highlighted the administration's failure to account for Iraq's alleged weapons of mass destruction, which President Bush cited as a reason for the war. Levin particularly singled out former CIA Director George J. Tenet for not being assertive enough before the war in stopping senior administration officials from making dire statements about Iraq, especially about its alleged ties to al Qaeda and attempts to reconstitute its nuclear program — claims that U.S. intelligence had not substantiated. More accountability, Levin said, "might have undermined the false sense of urgency for proceeding to war and could have contributed to delay, neither of which fit the administration's policy goals."

Levin also used his post to try to block administration plans for deploying a national missile shield, saying the effort violates laws governing weapons development. He unsuccessfully tried to use the 2005 defense authorization bill to shift $515.5 million from the program to other priorities, such as efforts to keep nuclear materials out of the hands of terrorists.

Though he may not have as much influence as he did when Democrats controlled the Senate in 2001 and 2002, Levin is not averse to using the filibuster to wage an aggressive defense for the Democrats. "We can stop, we can prevent, we can clarify issues," he told the Detroit Free Press. "The Senate is an unusual place because 41 senators can at least stop bad stuff from happening."

Levin made good on the threat in 2004 by teaming with fellow Michigan Democratic Sen. Debbie Stabenow to block the nominations of three of Bush's selections for the 6th U.S. Circuit Court of Appeals, all of whom were from Michigan. Levin said the White House did not adequately consult them beforehand. He and Stabenow also argued that the Republican-controlled Senate unfairly bottled up two of President Clinton's 6th Circuit nominees, Helene N. White and Kathleen McCree Lewis.

Levin's comprehension of the complicated issues he deals with is the foundation of his clout. He leverages that expertise by taking his opponents' arguments seriously and digging methodically for inconsistencies. And he does it with amiable tenacity. He is a dogged but genial interrogator in committee hearings and negotiator in legislative drafting sessions.

On international affairs, his bedrock premise is that collaboration with allies is essential — not for idealistic reasons but because of hard-nosed, pragmatic calculations. For instance, even after Bush yielded to Democrats' demands and sought congressional backing for war against Iraq in 2002, Levin opposed the legislation, calling it a "blank check" for Bush to act unilaterally in the absence of an imminent threat to the United States. If Bush attacked without specific U.N. authorization, Levin warned, other countries might refuse the use of essential bases and airspace. Moreover, he said, potential allies might be less willing to help shoulder the burden of reconstructing Iraq after the war.

By similar reasoning, Levin was skeptical of the missile system's technical feasibility. And he warned — long before Sept. 11, 2001 — that a

CAPITOL OFFICE
224-6221
levin.senate.gov
269 Russell 20510-2202; fax 224-1388

COMMITTEES
Armed Services - ranking member
Homeland Security & Governmental Affairs
Small Business & Entrepreneurship
Select Intelligence

HOMETOWN
Detroit

BORN
June 28, 1934, Detroit, Mich.

RELIGION
Jewish

FAMILY
Wife, Barbara Levin; three children

EDUCATION
Swarthmore College, B.A. 1956 (political science);
Harvard U., LL.B. 1959

CAREER
Lawyer

POLITICAL HIGHLIGHTS
Michigan Civil Rights Commission general counsel, 1964-67; Detroit chief appellate defender, 1968-69; Detroit City Council, 1970-77 (president, 1974-77)

ELECTION RESULTS

2002 GENERAL

Carl Levin (D)	1,896,614	60.6%
Andrew Raczkowski (R)	1,185,545	37.9%

2002 PRIMARY

Carl Levin (D)	unopposed

PREVIOUS WINNING PERCENTAGES
1996 (58%); 1990 (57%); 1984 (52%); 1978 (52%)

defense against a rogue state's ballistic missiles would be useless against far more likely terrorist attacks. But his fundamental argument was that if the United States deployed a missile defense without regard to the views of other countries, they might respond with new weapons of their own, paradoxically making the United States less secure with a missile defense than without one.

On another major issue, Levin was of the same mind as the president. Bush demanded that Congress authorize another round of military base closings, which Levin had long supported. Clinton had undercut his own chances of winning additional closures by maneuvering in 1995, before his re-election campaign, to save jobs at bases to be closed in Texas and California. Enraged Republicans vowed never to let the president preside over base closures. Levin and Republican John McCain of Arizona pushed to resume base closures after Clinton left office, but they were unsuccessful. Backed by Defense Secretary Donald H. Rumsfeld, in 2001 Levin secured another round of base closings, although it took a Bush veto threat to overcome GOP opposition in the House.

On social issues, Levin stands left of center. He voted against banning a procedure its opponents call "partial birth" abortion, and he opposes the ban on abortions at overseas military hospitals. While he supported barring job discrimination on the basis of sexual orientation, he did vote to prohibit federal recognition of same-sex marriage. He was among the most ardent advocates of the gun control package Congress considered after the 1999 teenage shooting spree at Columbine High School in Colorado, but the plan ultimately was scuttled by disagreement.

In 2002, Levin's most conspicuous departure from liberal orthodoxy came when he joined the successful opposition, along with 18 other Democrats, to a Senate proposal to increase significantly the average automobile mileage that U.S. auto manufacturers would be required to achieve. The measure would have disrupted Detroit's marketing of the current generation of minivans and SUVs, and was vehemently opposed by the industry, which remains the economic anchor of Levin's home state.

In the 1960s, Levin was general counsel to the Michigan Civil Rights Commission. He started his career in elective office in the 1970s with a seat on the Detroit City Council, where he teamed with Mayor Coleman A. Young to demolish thousands of abandoned buildings.

In 1978, Levin won his Senate seat, defeating Republican incumbent Robert P. Griffin, who had initially planned to retire after losing a bid to become party leader the previous year. By the time he reversed course and decided to run, Griffin had missed one-third of the Senate votes over an entire year. Levin said Griffin was obviously tired of the job, and the voters agreed that Griffin deserved a rest. Levin won by 4 percentage points.

Levin, whose older brother Sander represents Michigan in the House, has an avuncular manner, but he can play political hardball. In 1984, he aired an ad showing his GOP opponent, former astronaut Jack Lousma, warming up a Japanese audience a year earlier by telling them about the Toyota he owned — an obvious faux pas in a state where the phrase "Japanese car" translates as joblessness. President Reagan carried Michigan with 59 percent of the vote, but Levin held on to win with 52 percent.

In his three succeeding re-election efforts, Levin's margin of victory has steadily improved. By 2002, he was well enough entrenched that several GOP heavyweights declined to make what they assumed to be a futile run. At one point, Republicans considered nominating a one-time contestant in the TV reality game show "Survivor." Ultimately, state Rep. Andrew Raczkowski took up the GOP banner, but he garnered just 38 percent of the vote.

KEY VOTES

2004

Yes Pass $318.9 billion, six-year highway and mass transit bill

Yes Extend assault weapons ban for 10 years

Yes Restore pay-as-you-go rules for new tax cuts and entitlement spending

No Criminalize harm to a fetus in an attack on the mother

Yes Increase mandatory child care funding to states by $6 billion over five years

No Amend the Constitution to prohibit same-sex marriage

Yes Approve $146 billion multi-year extension of previously enacted middle-class tax breaks

Yes Reorganize U.S. intelligence agencies as proposed by Sept. 11 commission

No Cut corporate taxes $137 billion over 10 years

2003

Yes Delay Bush changes to Clean Air Act

No Allow confirmation vote on Miguel A. Estrada to the U.S. Court of Appeals for the D.C. Circuit

Yes Block a Bush proposal opening Alaska's Arctic National Wildlife Refuge to oil drilling

Yes Limit size of Bush's proposed tax cut to $350 billion through fiscal 2013

No Overhaul Medicare and create prescription drug benefit

Yes Block Bush rule scaling back overtime pay for some white-collar federal workers

Yes Split $20 billion in Iraq aid into half-grant, half-loan

No Ban "partial birth" abortion except to save a woman's life

No Stop proposal allowing travel to Cuba

No Allow final vote on energy policy overhaul

CQ VOTE STUDIES

	PARTY UNITY		PRESIDENTIAL SUPPORT	
	Support	Oppose	Support	Oppose
2004	96%	4%	60%	40%
2003	98%	2%	50%	50%
2002	95%	5%	66%	34%
2001	98%	2%	65%	35%
2000	97%	3%	92%	8%
1999	97%	3%	89%	11%
1998	98%	2%	93%	7%
1997	95%	5%	90%	10%
1996	94%	6%	86%	14%
1995	97%	3%	89%	11%

INTEREST GROUPS

	AFL-CIO	ADA	CCUS	ACU
2004	100%	100%	41%	0%
2003	85%	100%	39%	25%
2002	100%	95%	40%	0%
2001	100%	100%	36%	8%
2000	75%	90%	66%	12%
1999	89%	95%	53%	4%
1998	100%	90%	44%	0%
1997	86%	95%	50%	0%
1996	86%	85%	23%	5%
1995	100%	100%	26%	0%

Sen. Debbie Stabenow (D)

Elected 2000; 1st term

CAPITOL OFFICE
224-4822
senator@stabenow.senate.gov
stabenow.senate.gov
133 Hart 20510-2204; fax 228-0325

COMMITTEES
Agriculture, Nutrition & Forestry
Banking, Housing & Urban Affairs
Budget

HOMETOWN
Lansing

BORN
April 29, 1950, Clare, Mich.

RELIGION
United Methodist

FAMILY
Husband, Tom Athans; two children

EDUCATION
Michigan State U., B.A. 1972, M.S.W. 1975

CAREER
Leadership training consultant

POLITICAL HIGHLIGHTS
Ingham County Commission, 1975-78 (chairwoman,
1977-1978); Mich. House, 1979-91; Mich. Senate,
1991-94; sought Democratic nomination for
governor, 1994; Democratic nominee for lieutenant
governor, 1994; U.S. House, 1997-2001

ELECTION RESULTS

2000 GENERAL

Debbie Stabenow (D)	2,061,952	49.5%
Spencer Abraham (R)	1,994,693	47.9%

2000 PRIMARY

Debbie Stabenow (D)	unopposed

PREVIOUS WINNING PERCENTAGES
1998 House Election (57%); 1996 House Election
(54%)

Stabenow is a liberal and a feminist but without the edginess of a Barbara Boxer, the brash California Democrat. She is a polished pol who's been at the game most of her life. She picks issues that resonate with Democratic voters and frequently gains the tactical advantage over the opposition, like the time she road a bus across the Canadian border to illustrate the plight of elderly constituents taking desperate measures to find medicines they could afford. When the fight is over, Stabenow often will turn a political enemy into a political friend.

As the 109th Congress began, Stabenow (STAB-uh-now) was chosen by her peers to serve as Senate Democratic Conference secretary, the third-highest leadership position for the minority party in the Senate. In the 108th, she was vice chairwoman of the Democratic Senatorial Campaign Committee, the party's main fundraising arm for Senate candidates, and she chaired the Women's Senate Network, which provides money for women running for the Senate. She is a member of the centrist New Democrats.

Stabenow led Senate Democrats in one of the most hard-fought political debates in recent years, the creation of a prescription drug benefit as part of the Medicare program for the elderly. While the battle did not go her way, and President Bush and the Republicans were able to pass their version of a drug bill in 2003, the debate served to highlight her political smarts as Stabenow geared up for a 2006 re-election bid.

After two terms in the House, Stabenow narrowly unseated Republican incumbent Sen. Spencer Abraham in 2000, becoming the first woman senator elected from Michigan. Health care issues were the primary focus of her campaign, with Stabenow ushering busloads of Michigan seniors to Canada where they could buy their medication for far less than in the United States. Since her election, Stabenow has consistently challenged prescription drugmakers, a powerful industry that heavily supports Republicans.

Stabenow is also out front in the bipartisan drive to allow consumers to import U.S.-made drugs from Canada and to make it easier for generic drugs, which usually sell for less than their brand-name counterparts, to get to the marketplace. In 2002, Stabenow helped pass a bill to allow such imports but it carried a condition that the secretary of health and human services certify the drugs as safe, which is unlikely.

In 2003, the Senate repealed provisions in the law creating the Homeland Security Department to help shield vaccine makers from lawsuits. Stabenow had aggressively opposed those provisions and their removal was a "great victory" over special interests, she said.

Another concern for Stabenow is foreign steel imports. Thousands of her constituents work in the steel industry in Michigan's Upper Peninsula, and to protect those jobs, Stabenow pushed Bush in 2002 to slap a four-year, 50 percent tariff on imported steel. She praised Bush's decision to levy a 30 percent tariff, but was disappointed it was not higher. Anything less than 40 percent, she said, is like "splitting the baby, which is not good enough."

Stabenow has shown a willingness to join with Republicans on a number of issues. In the Senate, she partnered with Republican Olympia J. Snowe of Maine in a failed attempt to pass legislation that would have delayed future tax cuts if expected budget surpluses did not materialize. Stabenow also was one of three Budget Committee Democrats to support an effort by Republican Pete V. Domenici of New Mexico to extend existing budget caps for another year.

In the House, Stabenow voted for GOP-sponsored measures to restructure the nation's public housing system and to encourage states to prosecute violent juvenile offenders as adults. She also supported a GOP-backed constitutional amendment to outlaw desecration of the U.S. flag.

Yet Stabenow has been true to traditional Democratic positions on such matters as abortion rights, education, gun control and public funding for the arts. She has shown strong support for labor, a key Democratic constituency. In 2003, she fought to delay, for one year, the allotment of $5 billion of the $20 billion sought by the Bush administration for rebuilding in Iraq, insisting the money should be spent instead on U.S. school construction, veterans' health care, community health clinics and transportation projects. In 2002, she voted against giving Bush fast-track authority to negotiate trade agreements that Congress cannot amend, which labor strongly opposed.

Stabenow, along with home-state Democratic colleague Carl Levin, also clashed with Bush over the president's judicial nominees. She and Levin have prevented most of Bush's nominees for the 6th U.S. Circuit Court of Appeals, which includes Michigan, from getting a hearing in the Judiciary Committee. Their goal was to stonewall the Bush nominees until President Clinton's picks for the court, blocked by Republicans during Clinton's two terms, received hearings.

Stabenow in 2002 opposed a Bush administration plan to permanently store nuclear waste at a national repository at Yucca Mountain in Nevada, arguing that the material would still have to be kept in "cooling pools" in the Great Lakes region for at least five years. She said the administration's proposal for transporting the waste was unclear and could pose security risks in the states the waste would pass through, including Michigan.

One of Stabenow's first actions as a freshman senator was to help the man she had defeated, Abraham, win Senate confirmation as Bush's secretary of energy. She introduced Abraham to the Senate Energy Committee, which votes on the appointment.

Stabenow's political career has spanned more than half her life. She established herself as a mover in Michigan politics by winning a seat on the Ingham County Commission in 1975 at age 25. She went on to serve 12 years in the Michigan House and a term in the state Senate.

She had one unhappy year in politics. In 1994, she lost the Democratic gubernatorial primary to veteran Democratic Rep. Howard Wolpe. She then accepted Wolpe's invitation to join his ticket as a candidate for lieutenant governor. But incumbent GOP Gov. John Engler swept to re-election in what turned out to be a good year for Republicans.

Stabenow made a comeback in 1996, ending Republican Rep. Dick Chrysler's one-term tenure in the politically competitive 8th District. She was easily re-elected to the seat in 1998.

That win set up Stabenow's Senate challenge to Abraham. Neither candidate had primary opposition. Stabenow was a vice chairwoman of the Democratic presidential convention in Los Angeles — an indication of the importance that her party placed on her takeover bid. Abraham launched a summertime campaign blitz that gave him a big lead in polls, and some Democratic strategists fretted that they might have to write off the race. But Stabenow and allied groups staged a late counteroffensive that enabled her campaign to peak at the right time.

Stabenow had a campaign chest of $8 million. She was the top recipient of money from EMILY's list, a political action committee that supports Democratic women candidates. And she benefited from a strong turnout by blacks and union members. Still, Stabenow just hung on, winning by less than 2 percentage points.

KEY VOTES

2004

Yes Pass $318.9 billion, six-year highway and mass transit bill

Yes Extend assault weapons ban for 10 years

Yes Restore pay-as-you-go rules for new tax cuts and entitlement spending

No Criminalize harm to a fetus in an attack on the mother

Yes Increase mandatory child care funding to states by $6 billion over five years

No Amend the Constitution to prohibit same-sex marriage

Yes Approve $146 billion multi-year extension of previously enacted middle-class tax breaks

Yes Reorganize U.S. intelligence agencies as proposed by Sept. 11 commission

Yes Cut corporate taxes $137 billion over 10 years

2003

Yes Delay Bush changes to Clean Air Act

No Allow confirmation vote on Miguel A. Estrada to the U.S. Court of Appeals for the D.C. Circuit

Yes Block a Bush proposal opening Alaska's Arctic National Wildlife Refuge to oil drilling

Yes Limit size of Bush's proposed tax cut to $350 billion through fiscal 2013

Yes Overhaul Medicare and create prescription drug benefit

Yes Block Bush rule scaling back overtime pay for some white-collar federal workers

Yes Split $20 billion in Iraq aid into half-grant, half-loan

No Ban "partial birth" abortion except to save a woman's life

No Stop proposal allowing travel to Cuba

No Allow final vote on energy policy overhaul

CQ VOTE STUDIES

	PARTY UNITY		PRESIDENTIAL SUPPORT	
	Support	Oppose	Support	Oppose
2004	96%	4%	58%	42%
2003	97%	3%	49%	51%
2002	95%	5%	66%	34%
2001	96%	4%	64%	36%
House Service:				
2000	82%	18%	74%	26%
1999	87%	13%	78%	22%
1998	87%	13%	78%	22%
1997	88%	12%	81%	19%

INTEREST GROUPS

	AFL-CIO	ADA	CCUS	ACU
2004	100%	100%	65%	8%
2003	85%	95%	39%	20%
2002	100%	95%	45%	0%
2001	100%	100%	43%	8%
House Service:				
2000	90%	90%	47%	16%
1999	78%	95%	44%	4%
1998	90%	100%	61%	9%
1997	100%	95%	50%	12%

Rep. Bart Stupak (D)

Elected 1992; 7th term

CAPITOL OFFICE
225-4735
www.house.gov/stupak
2352 Rayburn 20515-2201; fax 225-4744

COMMITTEES
Energy & Commerce

HOMETOWN
Menominee

BORN
Feb. 29, 1952, Milwaukee, Wis.

RELIGION
Roman Catholic

FAMILY
Wife, Laurie Stupak; two children (one deceased)

EDUCATION
Northwestern Michigan Community College, A.A. 1972; Saginaw Valley State College, B.S. 1977 (criminal justice); Thomas M. Cooley Law School, J.D. 1981

CAREER
Lawyer; state trooper; patrolman

POLITICAL HIGHLIGHTS
Mich. House, 1989-91; sought Democratic nomination for Mich. Senate, 1990

ELECTION RESULTS

2004 GENERAL

Bart Stupak (D)	211,571	65.6%
Don Hooper (R)	105,706	32.8%

2004 PRIMARY

Bart Stupak (D)	unopposed

2002 GENERAL

Bart Stupak (D)	150,701	67.7%
Don Hooper (R)	69,254	31.1%
John W. Loosemore (LIBERT)	2,732	1.2%

PREVIOUS WINNING PERCENTAGES
2000 (58%); 1998 (59%); 1996 (71%); 1994 (57%); 1992 (54%)

With the House an increasingly polarized institution, Stupak has become a more reliable vote for the Democratic leadership, supporting his party 91 percent of the time on key votes in 2004. But, befitting someone from Michigan's frigid and self-reliant Upper Peninsula, he has a tendency to go his own way often enough to preserve his standing as a centrist back home in the rural reaches of the 1st District.

A former police officer and state trooper, a supporter of gun owners, an opponent of abortion rights and a steadfast ally of organized labor, Stupak (STU-pack) appeals to many social conservatives while pleasing union-label Democrats with his populist views on trade and economic policy.

His social conservatism was on display in the 108th Congress when the House passed legislation Stupak wrote with Dave Weldon, a Florida Republican, to make it illegal to clone a human embryo or to import cloned embryos or any product derived from them. The House passed a similar bill by Stupak and Weldon in 2001, but the Senate never debated either measure.

Stupak has bolstered his political standing back home with his work on the Energy and Commerce Committee, where he opposed lifting rules on media ownership, which he fears will limit options for his far-flung constituents. From his seat on the Health Subcommittee, Stupak pressed for the Food and Drug Administration to impose tighter regulation of the acne medication Accutane. He believes Accutane was the reason his son B.J. — a popular high school athlete and student leader who aspired to replace his father in the House — committed suicide at age 17 in 2000.

Stupak was able to get a two-year committee investigation about the drug's effects that lent credence to his belief. And while his bill to restrict the drug and support additional tests on its link to suicide and depression went nowhere in the 108th Congress, the FDA in November 2004 ordered doctors and pharmacies to inform patients about the drug's risks and get their informed consent before dispensing it.

Stupak, who was a law enforcement officer for 12 years, is the founder of the Congressional Law Enforcement Caucus. He often focuses on neighborhood crime prevention, including community and school policing. In the 107th Congress, he won enactment of his legislation to limit public access to body armor, which emboldens some criminals to engage in shootouts with police.

In the wake of the Sept. 11 commission's finding that local law enforcement and emergency response services often cannot communicate effectively, Stupak has been a leading advocate of federal aid to improve first-responder communications systems. The intelligence overhaul law enacted in 2004 called on Congress to pass legislation setting aside certain broadcast frequencies for emergency services, required the Department of Homeland Security to work to enhance communications, and authorized $118 million over five years for the program. Early in the 109th, Stupak offered legislation to establish a permanent grant program to help improve emergency communications among first responders.

Though Stupak has been a member of the National Rifle Association, in the wake of the shootings at Colorado's Columbine High School in 1999 he voted for the strictest of several proposals to require background checks at gun shows. The move drew opposition from many in northern Michigan, where gun ownership is common and hunting is a popular pastime. The NRA, which had endorsed Stupak in the past, backed his Republican challenger in 2000 and has not endorsed a candidate for the 1st District seat since then. In 2004, Stupak voted for a bill to repeal a ban on gun ownership in the District of Columbia.

As redrawn and enlarged after the 2000 census, the 1st District is 24,887 square miles — almost 45 percent of the state's land area and the third-largest district east of the Mississippi River. Touching three of the Great Lakes, the district has 1,556 miles of freshwater shoreline — more than any other district in the continental United States. And Stupak walks a fine line on environmental issues. Economically struggling communities in the district would like to attract more industry, but encouraging development threatens the natural environment, which attracts much-needed tourist dollars.

In the late 1990s, Stupak voted with Republicans to continue road building subsidies for the logging industry. In 2002, he opposed efforts to ban road building in one-third of U.S. national forests. And he criticized the National Park Service for proposing a ban on snowmobiles in its parks — environmentalists fault the recreational vehicles for the noise and pollution they create. He argued that each park should set its own policy.

But Stupak sided with environmentalists in the 107th when he won enactment of a federal ban on oil drilling beneath the Great Lakes, matched soon after with a ban enacted by the Michigan Legislature. More recently, he has worked to protect water quality in the lakes.

As a lifelong resident of the Upper Peninsula (known by locals as the U.P.), Stupak prides himself on his "Yooper" background. While serving as an Escanaba police officer, he earned an undergraduate degree in criminal justice. Still a trooper, he got a law degree, which served him well after his forced retirement from the state police in 1984, due to an injury sustained in the line of duty. He entered private law practice and got involved in local civic and political affairs. He won a state House seat in 1988 but gave it up after two years for a state Senate bid, in which he narrowly lost the Democratic primary.

Stupak's opportunity to try for Congress came in 1992, when Republican Rep. Robert W. Davis retired after seven terms. Davis' departure was hastened when the House ethics committee labeled him one of 22 abusers of the private bank then maintained for House members. Stupak defeated former Republican Rep. Philip E. Ruppe with 54 percent of the vote. In subsequent elections in the 1990s, he managed only once to poll more than 60 percent.

But decennial redistricting for this decade created a slightly more Democratic 1st District and Stupak's road to re-election has become easier. He won with 68 percent in 2002 and 66 percent in 2004.

KEY VOTES

2004
Yes Extend federal unemployment benefits by 13 weeks
Yes Pass $283.2 billion, six-year federal highway and mass transit bill
Yes Approve $146 billion multi-year extension of previously enacted middle-class tax breaks
No   Amend the Constitution to prohibit same-sex marriage
No   Cut corporate taxes $137 billion over 10 years
Yes Reorganize U.S. intelligence agencies as proposed by Sept. 11 commission

2003
No   Cut taxes by $330 billion through fiscal 2013
Yes Block Bush rule scaling back overtime pay for some white-collar federal workers
Yes Do not allow use of search warrants without first notifying subjects
Yes Allow importation of prescription drugs
No   Create private school voucher program in Washington, D.C.
Yes Ban "partial birth" abortion except to save a woman's life
Yes Split $18.6 billion in Iraq aid into half-grant, half-loan
No   Overhaul Medicare and create prescription drug benefit

CQ VOTE STUDIES

	PARTY UNITY		PRESIDENTIAL SUPPORT	
	Support	Oppose	Support	Oppose
2004	91%	9%	41%	59%
2003	86%	14%	38%	62%
2002	89%	11%	33%	67%
2001	81%	19%	31%	69%
2000	83%	17%	67%	33%

INTEREST GROUPS

	AFL-CIO	ADA	CCUS	ACU
2004	93%	80%	38%	16%
2003	100%	85%	29%	42%
2002	100%	80%	45%	16%
2001	100%	75%	38%	38%
2000	100%	65%	30%	22%

MICHIGAN 1
Upper Peninsula; northern Lower Michigan

Rolling, forested hills and some Upper Peninsula (U.P.) mountains that get hundreds of inches of snow make the 1st one of the few places suited to skiing in the Midwest. Beaches and resorts around Petoskey also lure vacationers from Detroit, Chicago and Cleveland, feeding the area's tourist industry. The district's economy relies on these ample natural resources, especially since its traditional economic foundations eroded in the 1990s.

The U.P., surrounded by three of the Great Lakes and connected to the rest of the state by the Mackinac Bridge, is still recovering from the closure of K. I. Sawyer Air Force Base in the 1990s. Mining, which once drew immigrants to remote parts of the state, has not been a growth industry since the early 20th century. NAFTA has effectively killed most remaining copper, paper and iron production.

Tourism and timber products are the only growth industries. Snowmobiling makes up at least 40 percent of winter revenues for restaurants and hotels. Slow population growth in northern Michigan

and the U.P. gradually has led to the expansion of the district's territory so that now it encompasses more than 40 percent of the state's land mass. After the 2000 census, the 1st lost some northwestern counties, including Grand Traverse, but gained northeastern counties along the Saginaw Bay. The 1st reaches nearly as far south as Bay City, which is in the 5th.

There is a strong current of social conservatism in the 1st, particularly with regard to gun rights, that contributes to the Republican shift in recent years, although Democrats still dominate local politics. George W. Bush made major inroads in the area in the 2000 presidential election, and in 2004, the 1st was the only Michigan district to back a presidential candidate, Bush, and a House candidate, Rep. Stupak, from different political parties. The northern counties at the top of the "mitten" tend to support Republicans, although blue-collar Arenac and Saginaw counties at the southern end of the district balance the political landscape.

MAJOR INDUSTRY
Logging, tourism, mining, auto parts

CITIES
Marquette, 19,661; Sault Ste. Marie, 16,542; Escanaba, 13,140

NOTABLE
Isle Royale National Park; The National Ski Hall of Fame is in Ishpeming.

Rep. Peter Hoekstra (R)

Elected 1992; 7th term

CAPITOL OFFICE
225-4401
hoekstra.house.gov
2234 Rayburn 20515-2202; fax 226-0779

COMMITTEES
Transportation & Infrastructure
Select Intelligence - chairman

HOMETOWN
Holland

BORN
Oct. 30, 1953, Groningen, Netherlands

RELIGION
Christian Reformed Church

FAMILY
Wife, Diane Hoekstra; three children

EDUCATION
Hope College, B.A. 1975 (political science); U. of
Michigan, M.B.A. 1977

CAREER
Furniture company executive

POLITICAL HIGHLIGHTS
No previous office

ELECTION RESULTS

2004 GENERAL

Peter Hoekstra (R)	225,343	69.3%
Kimon Kotos (D)	94,040	28.9%

2004 PRIMARY

Peter Hoekstra (R)	unopposed

2002 GENERAL

Peter Hoekstra (R)	156,937	70.4%
Jeffrey A. Wrisley (D)	61,749	27.7%
Laurie L. Aleck (LIBERT)	2,680	1.2%

PREVIOUS WINNING PERCENTAGES
2000 (64%); 1998 (69%); 1996 (65%); 1994 (75%);
1992 (63%)

Hoekstra has undergone something of a transformation after more than a decade in Washington. Once a business executive who disdained government's regulatory ways and who pledged to serve no more than six terms, he now chairs a high-profile committee and is keeping his political future open.

After Intelligence Committee Chairman Porter J. Goss became CIA director in 2004, Speaker J. Dennis Hastert chose Hoekstra (HOOK-struh) to replace Goss as head of the panel. Hastert was impressed not only by Hoekstra's work as chairman of Intelligence's Technical and Tactical Subcommittee and repeated trips to Iraq, but also by his political generosity toward GOP colleagues. Although he once refused to accept money from political action committees, Hoekstra donated $106,000 to Republican candidates with funds from his own PAC, the Milead Fund, in the last two election cycles and thousands more from his individual campaign account.

Hoekstra took over the committee as lawmakers were struggling to enact a massive intelligence overhaul bill in response to the recommendations of the commission that investigated the Sept. 11, 2001, terrorist attacks. He formed an alliance with Intelligence's top-ranking Democrat, Jane Harman of California, along with Senate Governmental Affairs Chairwoman Susan Collins of Maine and that panel's top-ranking Democrat, Joseph I. Lieberman of Connecticut. By working "60 and 70 hours a week," in Hoekstra's estimate, the four were able to satisfy key conservatives and successfully steer the legislation to President Bush's desk.

Hoekstra's challenge now is to ensure that the Bush administration adheres to the law. As the 109th Congress began, he said he would form an Intelligence subcommittee to monitor its implementation. He also vowed to require the CIA and other agencies to develop strategic long-range future plans. In doing so, he said he would try not to overreact to the day's headlines. "On the stuff you do here, you've got to be very even-keeled," he said. "You can't react too emotionally to the things you're dealing with."

Beyond his service on the Intelligence Committee, Hoekstra's background on national security issues remains thin in contrast to others who have held the panel's top job. But he does have solid experience as an executive branch watchdog. As chairman of the Education and Workforce panel's Oversight Subcommittee for six years, he examined the books of the Labor and Education departments and of President Clinton's AmeriCorps community service program. He also headed a probe of election corruption within the Teamsters union for which he was criticized by members of both parties — Democrats argued he was seeking partisan advantage while Republicans complained he wasn't being political enough.

In investigating the Labor and Education departments, Hoekstra came up with what he believed were damning tales of federal agencies unable to document how they were spending taxpayer money. He hoped that public outrage would bolster his efforts to reform government spending practices. But with dozens of congressional investigations vying for public notice — many of them much sexier than his businesslike probes — Hoekstra found that his work was largely overlooked.

In 2000, the Michigan Teamsters endorsed Hoekstra and he helped nurture a political relationship between the union and the White House. That led to the union's backing of Bush's proposal to drill for oil in Alaska's Arctic National Wildlife Refuge, which the union said would create jobs. In 2002 and 2004, the Teamsters again backed Hoekstra.

Hoekstra's voting record is solidly conservative. In the 108th, he backed the Republican position on 96 percent of his votes and voted in support of Bush's positions 91 percent of the time. He received a "True Blue" award in 2004 from the Family Research Council for his 100 percent voting record on issues of importance to the group.

While he believes in his party's core conservative message, Hoekstra has gone his own way on some high-profile issues. He voted against Bush's request in 2002 for fast-track trade negotiating authority, worried that new trade deals could disadvantage western Michigan's fruit and vegetable farmers. Most publicly, in 2001 he unsuccessfully fought to kill a central tenet of Bush's education overhaul proposal: mandatory annual testing in reading and math in grades 3 through 8. Hoekstra viewed the testing as an inappropriate federal mandate.

When news about illegal and unethical corporate conduct hit Capitol Hill with full force during the 107th Congress, Hoekstra, a former furniture company executive, was angry. He sent leading business executives around the country a draft of his proposed "Shareholders' Bill of Rights," an ethics and accountability code to be practiced by corporate chiefs. To his chagrin, some executives demurred.

Hoekstra was born in the Netherlands and immigrated to the United States with his family when he was 3, settling in the town of Holland in a heavily Dutch part of Michigan. After receiving an MBA from the University of Michigan, Hoekstra embarked on an executive career.

In 1992, Hoekstra decided he could do a better job than 13-term Republican Rep. Guy Vander Jagt — for whom Hoekstra once interned. Hoekstra accused Vander Jagt of neglecting his constituents' needs in favor of enjoying the Washington high life and raising money for the National Republican Congressional Committee, which he chaired. Hoekstra ousted Vander Jagt in the GOP primary by 6 percentage points. In November, he won the seat handily and has not been challenged seriously since.

Hoekstra had said he would serve no more than six terms, but in December 2002 he announced he would run for re-election in 2004. He said his term limit pledge had been a mistake, but denied becoming a captive of Capitol Hill. He pointed out that he does not own or rent property in Washington, D.C., but instead sleeps in his office while the House is in session. He spends the remainder of his time in Michigan. "People say, 'He may have served 12 years, but he's still the same Pete we sent to Washington,' " he said. "People in general are becoming disillusioned with term limits."

KEY VOTES

2004

No	Extend federal unemployment benefits by 13 weeks
Yes	Pass $283.2 billion, six-year federal highway and mass transit bill
Yes	Approve $146 billion multi-year extension of previously enacted middle-class tax breaks
Yes	Amend the Constitution to prohibit same-sex marriage
Yes	Cut corporate taxes $137 billion over 10 years
Yes	Reorganize U.S. intelligence agencies as proposed by Sept. 11 commission

2003

Yes	Cut taxes by $330 billion through fiscal 2013
No	Block Bush rule scaling back overtime pay for some white-collar federal workers
No	Do not allow use of search warrants without first notifying subjects
Yes	Allow importation of prescription drugs
Yes	Create private school voucher program in Washington, D.C.
Yes	Ban "partial birth" abortion except to save a woman's life
No	Split $18.6 billion in Iraq aid into half-grant, half-loan
Yes	Overhaul Medicare and create prescription drug benefit

CQ VOTE STUDIES

	PARTY UNITY		PRESIDENTIAL SUPPORT	
	Support	Oppose	Support	Oppose
2004	98%	2%	90%	10%
2003	95%	5%	92%	8%
2002	91%	9%	88%	12%
2001	91%	9%	74%	26%
2000	93%	7%	23%	77%

INTEREST GROUPS

	AFL-CIO	ADA	CCUS	ACU
2004	15%	5%	95%	96%
2003	23%	10%	88%	77%
2002	11%	5%	85%	92%
2001	17%	10%	91%	88%
2000	10%	10%	90%	88%

MICHIGAN 2
West — Muskegon, Holland

The 2nd stretches 140 miles along Lake Michigan, covering counties full of cherry trees and asparagus farms. Pioneers, most of them Dutch, were drawn to the region by rich logging opportunities. Like other parts of Michigan, the manufacturing economy has declined but still dominates the most populated counties, including Ottawa, Muskegon and Allegan. Dutch independence has made the 2nd one of the most staunchly Republican districts in Michigan, and the district gave George W. Bush his highest 2004 vote percentage (60 percent) in the state.

This Republicanism is led by Ottawa County, which gave Bush a statewide high of 72 percent of the vote in the 2004 presidential election. Ottawa added more than 50,000 residents in the 1990s, more than all but three other Michigan counties, and grew by 27 percent. More than 35 percent of district residents live in Ottawa County.

Support for Democratic candidates can be found among minority voters in the district's largest city, Muskegon, which has struggled to keep manufacturing jobs. But local tax incentives have drawn in new

automotive parts suppliers, helping the economy rebound. Western Michigan also hosts several of the nation's top office furniture makers, including Herman Miller in Zeeland and Haworth in Holland.

Holland, south of Muskegon, is a conservative, Dutch-settled port town that draws tourists from all over the Midwest. It is the westernmost point of the "Dutch Triangle," formed by Holland, Grand Rapids and Kalamazoo. The early 20th century lifestyle is recreated in Dutch Village theme park, featuring wooden shoes and klompen dancers. Holland's annual tulip festival draws hundreds of thousands of visitors every May.

Redistricting following the 2000 census did not significantly alter the 2nd's borders. The new map added Benzie County, a fast-growing area in northwest Michigan, and reconfigured the boundaries in the south.

MAJOR INDUSTRY
Metal, furniture, tourism, agriculture

CITIES
Muskegon, 40,105; Holland, 35,048; Norton Shores, 22,527

NOTABLE
The world's largest weather vane is in Montague; Oceana County hosts the National Asparagus Festival.

Rep. Vernon J. Ehlers (R)

Elected December 1993; 6th full term

After Republicans captured control of the House in the 1994 elections, Speaker-to-be Newt Gingrich of Georgia announced on national television that a little-known freshman from Grand Rapids, Mich., would direct an effort to bring the House into the Internet age.

Ehlers (AY-lurz) was certainly qualified for the job — overqualified, in fact. The first research physicist elected to Congress, he had been using computers since 1957, when he was pursuing his Ph.D. specializing in the structure of the atomic nucleus.

He quickly discovered that the House was not on the cutting edge of technology. "When I got here," Ehlers recalled, "it was easier to send an e-mail to Moscow than to send it 20 feet down the hall to a colleague." The project, which eventually consumed more than 700 hours of Ehlers' time, helped establish him as the go-to guy on science and technology issues.

"He has added influence because he is a scientist," Science Committee Chairman Sherwood Boehlert, a New York Republican, says of Ehlers, who sits on the panel. "With Vern, usually it's me asking a question and then listening."

As Ehlers has learned, credibility helps — but it is not always enough to win the day. When asked, in an interview published by the American Physical Association, what he would like people to know about him, Ehlers answered, "Well, I'm a nice guy." He added, "So sometimes I feel like a misfit in Congress. There are other nice people there, don't misunderstand me, but it's a pretty tough place. It's a little hard for someone from the world of physics to get used to."

Ehlers, who in 1998 headed a review of national science policy, frets that the United States is not devoting enough resources to basic science — or to science education. "If kids in school now want a good job in the future, they had better know the basics of science, mathematics and engineering," Ehlers says. "Most of them are not learning that in elementary and secondary schools right now."

Schooled at home until college because of a severe asthma condition, Ehlers travels extensively to schools and universities to promote science education. "I often tell high school kids, 'Don't laugh at the nerds. If you're not a nerd, you're likely to be working for one in the future,' " he quips. Ehlers was able to add a provision to President Bush's 2001 education bill that ensures students are tested on science as well as reading and math, and in 2003 he successfully offered a measure to expand the National Science Foundation's K-12 education programs.

In the 108th Congress, Ehlers and fellow physicist-legislator Rush D. Holt, a New Jersey Democrat, led a group of 155 lawmakers urging House appropriators to follow through with a plan to double the National Science Foundation's budget by 2007. The group contends that foundation-supported research has led to more than 100 Nobel Prizes and spawned innovations such as Internet browsers, lasers, wireless phones and global positioning technology. In 2003, Ehlers and Holt were also successful in boosting funding for a national training program for math and science teachers to $101 million, an eight-fold increase from the year before.

Ehlers is a scientist, but he is also the son of a minister and a devout Christian himself. The Basic Dictionary of Science and the Holy Bible sit side by side on his office shelf.

Ehlers' work as an environmental activist helped launch his political career

CAPITOL OFFICE
225-3831
www.house.gov/ehlers
1714 Longworth 20515-2203; fax 225-5144

COMMITTEES
Education & Workforce
House Administration
Science
  (Environment, Technology & Standards - chairman)
Transportation & Infrastructure
Joint Library

HOMETOWN
Grand Rapids

BORN
Feb. 6, 1934, Pipestone, Minn.

RELIGION
Christian Reformed Church

FAMILY
Wife, Jo Ehlers; four children

EDUCATION
Calvin College, attended 1952-55 (physics); U. of California, Berkeley, A.B. 1956 (physics), Ph.D. 1960 (physics)

CAREER
Professor; physicist

POLITICAL HIGHLIGHTS
Kent County Commission, 1975-83 (chairman, 1979-82); Mich. House, 1983-85; Mich. Senate, 1985-93 (president pro tempore, 1990-93)

ELECTION RESULTS

2004 GENERAL
Vernon J. Ehlers (R)	214,465	66.6%
Peter H. Hickey (D)	101,395	31.5%
Warren Adams (LIBERT)	3,695	1.2%

2004 PRIMARY
Vernon J. Ehlers (R)	unopposed

2002 GENERAL
Vernon J. Ehlers (R)	153,131	70.0%
Kathryn D. Lynnes (D)	61,987	28.3%
Tom Quinn (LIBERT)	2,613	1.2%

PREVIOUS WINNING PERCENTAGES
2000 (65%); 1998 (73%); 1996 (69%); 1994 (74%); 1993 Special Election (67%)

as a county commissioner in Michigan in the mid-1970s. In 2001, he voted against Bush's plan to drill for oil in Alaska's Arctic National Wildlife Refuge. That stand, and his support for increasing fuel efficiency standards for sport utility vehicles — an unpopular position in auto-centric Michigan — won him the Sierra Club's endorsement in the 2002 election. But he voted for the final energy bill that included the Arctic refuge drilling, and he backed Bush's controversial decision not to sign the Kyoto Protocol to limit industrial emissions, arguing that the treaty unfairly exempted China and other developing nations. In 2004, the Sierra Club did not repeat its endorsement.

Ehlers is a strong opponent of cloning, and he avoided taking a stand when Bush decided in 2001 to allow federal funding for stem cell research under limited circumstances.

He also appears uncomfortable when asked whether his votes for Bush's tax cuts conflicted with his desire to win more congressional funding for science. "This is basically a grand experiment to see if we can get ourselves out of a recession," Ehlers said. "You can increase federal tax revenue more by improving the economy than by raising taxes. The question is, can we increase revenues even more by lowering taxes?"

In the 108th, Ehlers used his seat on the Transportation and Infrastructure Committee to urge greater funding for transportation-related research. He said the results would pay off in a variety of areas, from identifying the best surface for a roadway to developing creative uses of technology to minimize congestion. With budget constraints looming large, Ehlers argued, "If the research is good, it's going to save a lot of money."

After receiving his doctorate in physics from Berkeley at 26, Ehlers stayed as a lecturer and research physicist for six years. In 1966, he traded that liberal atmosphere for conservative, religious-oriented Calvin College in Grand Rapids, where he had studied as an undergraduate.

In 1982, Ehlers won election to the state House, succeeding Republican Paul B. Henry, a former colleague at Calvin, who had moved to the state Senate. Over the next dozen years, Ehlers followed Henry up the political ladder, succeeding him in the state Senate and finally in Congress.

In 1993, Ehlers was president pro tempore of the Michigan Senate. Nearly 60 years old, he was looking for new challenges and weighing a 1994 campaign for the Senate seat then held by Democrat Donald W. Riegle Jr. But when Henry died of brain cancer that July, Ehlers launched a House bid and quickly moved to the front of an eight-person Republican pack. He won with 67 percent of the vote in the special election and has never faced a significant challenge to his re-election.

KEY VOTES

2004
No Extend federal unemployment benefits by 13 weeks
Yes Pass $283.2 billion, six-year federal highway and mass transit bill
Yes Approve $146 billion multi-year extension of previously enacted middle-class tax breaks
Yes Amend the Constitution to prohibit same-sex marriage
Yes Cut corporate taxes $137 billion over 10 years
Yes Reorganize U.S. intelligence agencies as proposed by Sept. 11 commission

2003
Yes Cut taxes by $330 billion through fiscal 2013
No Block Bush rule scaling back overtime pay for some white-collar federal workers
Yes Do not allow use of search warrants without first notifying subjects
Yes Allow importation of prescription drugs
Yes Create private school voucher program in Washington, D.C.
Yes Ban "partial birth" abortion except to save a woman's life
No Split $18.6 billion in Iraq aid into half-grant, half-loan
Yes Overhaul Medicare and create prescription drug benefit

CQ VOTE STUDIES

	PARTY UNITY		PRESIDENTIAL SUPPORT	
	Support	Oppose	Support	Oppose
2004	86%	14%	79%	21%
2003	84%	16%	85%	15%
2002	85%	15%	87%	13%
2001	88%	12%	81%	19%
2000	78%	22%	38%	62%

INTEREST GROUPS

	AFL-CIO	ADA	CCUS	ACU
2004	27%	20%	100%	67%
2003	7%	15%	87%	68%
2002	11%	15%	95%	80%
2001	8%	10%	91%	68%
2000	20%	20%	80%	64%

MICHIGAN 3
West central — Grand Rapids

Grand Rapids, Michigan's second-most-populous city, teems with auto plants and metals manufacturing, but it's a world away from Detroit. Conservative Dutch Republicans — not auto union Democrats — control the district, making the 3rd one of Michigan's heaviest GOP regions. Its staunch conservatism is rivaled only by the neighboring 2nd, and in the 2004 presidential election, the 3rd gave George W. Bush his second-highest vote percentage in the state (59 percent).

Also unlike Detroit, Grand Rapids has escaped complete dependence on the auto industry. The city is a leading producer of metal office furniture, in addition to making avionics systems, tools and home appliances. The city's economy prospered in the 1970s when modular furniture became popular, but it suffered in the early 1990s when companies began to downsize their managerial staffs and cut back on office space. In a major effort to revitalize downtown Grand Rapids, the city built a new arena and recruited three minor league sports teams. It also is slated to be the new location for Michigan State University's medical school.

Gerald R. Ford made his way to the House and then the presidency from Grand Rapids (the area airport is named for the 38th president), and his brand of small-government Republicanism and fiscal restraint still holds sway in the 3rd. One of the district's largest employers, Amway, based in Ada, consistently contributes to Republicans around the nation. This direct sales company, which markets personal- and home-care products, promotes its philosophy of private philanthropy by donating generously to area universities, hospitals and churches.

More than 80 percent of residents live in Kent County, which grew by 15 percent in the 1990s largely because of rapid growth outside of Grand Rapids, which grew by just 5 percent. The rest live in Ionia and Barry counties, located east and southeast of Kent, respectively.

MAJOR INDUSTRY
Office furniture, auto parts, metals manufacturing

CITIES
Grand Rapids, 197,800; Wyoming, 69,368; Kentwood, 45,255; Walker, 21,842; Forest Hills (unincorporated), 20,942

NOTABLE
The Norton Mound Group, one of the best-preserved burial centers of the Hopewell culture, is in Grand Rapids.

Rep. Dave Camp (R)

Elected 1990; 8th term

CAPITOL OFFICE
225-3561
www.house.gov/camp
137 Cannon 20515-2204; fax 225-9679

COMMITTEES
Ways & Means
(Select Revenue Measures - chairman)

HOMETOWN
Midland

BORN
July 9, 1953, Midland, Mich.

RELIGION
Roman Catholic

FAMILY
Wife, Nancy Camp; three children

EDUCATION
Albion College, B.A. 1975 (economics); U. of San Diego, J.D. 1978

CAREER
Lawyer; congressional aide

POLITICAL HIGHLIGHTS
Mich. House, 1989-91

ELECTION RESULTS

2004 GENERAL

Dave Camp (R)	205,274	64.4%
Mike Huckleberry (D)	110,885	34.8%

2004 PRIMARY

Dave Camp (R)	unopposed

2002 GENERAL

Dave Camp (R)	149,090	68.2%
Lawrence D. Hollenbeck (D)	65,950	30.2%
Sterling Johnson (GREEN)	2,261	1.0%

PREVIOUS WINNING PERCENTAGES
2000 (68%); 1998 (91%); 1996 (65%); 1994 (73%); 1992 (63%); 1990 (65%)

While not as vocal as some in his party, Camp maintains a firmly conservative point of departure on most issues. With an understated political style and a steadfast loyalty to his party leadership, Camp has steadily moved up the ranks in the House. He has worked his way onto the top row of the Ways and Means Committee dais, where in the 109th Congress he serves as the chairman of the Select Revenue Measures Subcommittee.

When he arrived in the House in 1991, Camp was on the leading edge of the wave of youthful Republican conservatives who since have flooded the chamber. But while many of those lawmakers have continued to cultivate their images as political outsiders, Camp has made his mark in Congress a more old-fashioned way — landing a choice committee assignment, digging into complex legislative issues and taking on a variety of chores for party elders.

Camp ran J. Dennis Hastert's whirlwind campaign to become Speaker at the end of 1998 and remains a part of the Speaker's inner circle. He also holds several other, more formal leadership posts. He is a deputy majority whip and serves on the GOP Steering Committee, which makes committee assignments for the party.

But it is on Ways and Means, where Camp has served since his second term, that he has been most influential. He had a key role in the enactment of the 1996 law overhauling the welfare system; he had a hand in writing laws to expand adoptions; and he has been a leader in the GOP's quest to make permanent the package of tax cuts enacted in 2001.

In the 109th, the committee will consider President Bush's proposal to set up private accounts as part of Social Security. Camp says he favors the president's plan to give workers the option of seeking a greater overall return in the future through the combination of private investment accounts and a lower guaranteed benefit. "Once we begin to give individuals more control over their retirement, we will take a giant step toward protecting the long-term security of Social Security," Camp told the Gannett News Service in early 2004.

Ways and Means members are also trying to figure out how to staunch corporate pension plan insolvencies that are placing a severe financial strain on the federal agency that insures private pensions. Camp supported the 2004 law allowing employers to reduce their pension contributions by more than $80 billion during 2004-2005. The bill was designed to give struggling companies temporary relief while Congress works on a long-term solution. "This legislation makes important common sense changes to help keep workers' pensions intact and companies in business," said Camp.

Although Camp usually votes a fairly straight party line, in early 2004 he was one of 39 Republicans to vote for a Democratic amendment extending for six months a federal program offering 13 weeks of supplemental unemployment benefits to jobless workers who have exhausted their state benefits.

And when it came time to vote on the final version of the intelligence agencies overhaul bill, Camp was one of 67 Republicans to vote no. The measure, based on recommendations from the Sept. 11 commission, reorganized the 15 U.S. intelligence agencies under a new director of national intelligence. A member of the Homeland Security Committee in the 108th, Camp said he objected to the omission from the final bill of certain provisions regarding detention of terrorists and illegal aliens thought to be a security risk and the failure to grant border patrol agents greater authority to deport dangerous illegal aliens.

Camp has relied on his experience as a domestic law attorney in Michigan to play a leading role in writing laws to promote the adoption of children in foster care. In 2003, his measure to give states financial incentives to increase the number of adoptions each year, particularly of older children and those with special needs, was signed into law. Camp's bill offered states $4,000 extra for each child adopted beyond the previous year's level.

As a measure of his frugal way with federal monies, Camp has long promoted legislation to apply any lawmaker's unused office and staff funds to paying down the deficit or the national debt, and during his tenure he has returned to the Treasury more than $1 million in unused office account money, though lawmakers are not required to do so. He also donates his congressional cost-of-living pay increases to scholarships for college students every other year.

Camp's office in Washington features a rack of several dozen men's neckties — a curiosity for visiting constituents, who paw through the collection looking for a tie that represents a favorite school or organization. He began building the collection when The Detroit News reported that Camp had arrived in Congress with just three ties and invited readers to supplement the congressman's collection.

Camp's interest in politics began at an early age, and he got his initial hands-on experience volunteering on the local judicial campaign of a lawyer for whom he was interning.

After practicing law for five years, Camp became chief of staff for Republican Bill Schuette, a childhood friend, during Schuette's first term in the House. Camp returned to Michigan in 1986 to manage Schuette's re-election campaign and resume his law career. But in 1988, Camp ran for and won an open state House seat based in Midland, his hometown. He had barely found his chair in the legislature when GOP strategists persuaded Schuette to run for the Senate against Democrat Carl Levin in 1990 and suggested that Camp would make a fine successor to Schuette in the House.

Aided by Schuette's endorsement, Camp eked out a close primary victory against four opponents. The Democrats nominated Joan L. Dennison, who espoused support for some of the ideas of political extremist Lyndon H. LaRouche Jr. Camp coasted to victory with 65 percent of the vote. He has won re-election easily since, rolling up a 30 percentage point margin in 2004 over Democrat Mike Huckleberry, a small-business owner.

KEY VOTES

2004

Yes Extend federal unemployment benefits by 13 weeks
Yes Pass $283.2 billion, six-year federal highway and mass transit bill
Yes Approve $146 billion multi-year extension of previously enacted middle-class tax breaks
Yes Amend the Constitution to prohibit same-sex marriage
Yes Cut corporate taxes $137 billion over 10 years
No Reorganize U.S. intelligence agencies as proposed by Sept. 11 commission

2003

Yes Cut taxes by $330 billion through fiscal 2013
No Block Bush rule scaling back overtime pay for some white-collar federal workers
No Do not allow use of search warrants without first notifying subjects
No Allow importation of prescription drugs
Yes Create private school voucher program in Washington, D.C.
Yes Ban "partial birth" abortion except to save a woman's life
No Split $18.6 billion in Iraq aid into half-grant, half-loan
Yes Overhaul Medicare and create prescription drug benefit

CQ VOTE STUDIES

	PARTY UNITY		PRESIDENTIAL SUPPORT	
	Support	Oppose	Support	Oppose
2004	94%	6%	82%	18%
2003	97%	3%	94%	6%
2002	95%	5%	85%	15%
2001	96%	4%	91%	9%
2000	91%	9%	24%	76%

INTEREST GROUPS

	AFL-CIO	ADA	CCUS	ACU
2004	27%	10%	100%	88%
2003	7%	5%	100%	84%
2002	11%	0%	100%	96%
2001	17%	0%	100%	96%
2000	0%	5%	90%	84%

MICHIGAN 4
North central — Midland, Traverse City

Forests and farms cover much of the 14 central Michigan counties that lie wholly or partly in the 4th, which is the state's second-largest district in land area. The white pine forests north of Midland, the district's largest city, were once some of the most bountiful logging lands in the state. Now, retirees and vacationers build second homes in the sparsely populated woods, and tourists come to ski, camp and hunt in these remote areas.

Midland, on the district's eastern border, is home to Dow Chemical and Dow Corning, makers of chemicals, plastics and silicone products. Dow Chemical headquarters sits on a 2,150-acre campus in Midland, giving the city more engineers, chemists and metallurgists per capita than any other city in the nation. The area escaped the brunt of Dow's corporate restructuring, and continues to benefit from the company's philanthropy, with churches, schools and libraries built by the Dow fortune.

West and south of Midland, the district turns agricultural. Farmers — who till fields of sugar beets, dry beans, corn, wheat and oats — worry about free trade, price supports and crop insurance. The number of farms and small towns throughout the 4th gives it a Republican lean.

Redistricting following the 2000 census gave the 4th some solidly Republican, sparsely populated but fast-growing counties in northwest Michigan. The proximity to Lake Michigan and distance from noisy population centers makes the area especially attractive to retirees. Leelanau County, in the northwestern corner, grew by 28 percent in the 1990s, and Grand Traverse County (Traverse City), grew by 21 percent. Almost every county in the 4th that is west and north of Midland saw its population grow by at least 15 percent.

MAJOR INDUSTRY
Agriculture, chemical and plastics manufacturing, tourism

CITIES
Midland (pt.), 41,463; Mount Pleasant, 25,946; Owosso, 15,713; Traverse City, 14,532

NOTABLE
Interlochen Center for the Arts, south of Traverse City, includes a camp and an academy for students of the arts; Prominent Interlochen alumni include CBS News correspondent Mike Wallace, actors Tom Hulce and Linda Hunt, and soprano Jessye Norman.

Rep. Dale E. Kildee (D)

CAPITOL OFFICE
225-3611
www.house.gov/kildee
2107 Rayburn 20515-2205; fax 225-6393

COMMITTEES
Education & Workforce
Resources

HOMETOWN
Flint

BORN
Sept. 16, 1929, Flint, Mich.

RELIGION
Roman Catholic

FAMILY
Wife, Gayle Kildee; three children

EDUCATION
Sacred Heart Seminary, B.A. 1952; U. of Detroit,
attended 1954 (teaching certificate); U. of
Peshawar (Pakistan), attended 1958-59 (Rotary
fellowship); U. of Michigan, M.A. 1961 (history)

CAREER
Teacher

POLITICAL HIGHLIGHTS
Mich. House, 1965-75; Mich. Senate, 1975-77

ELECTION RESULTS

2004 GENERAL

Dale E. Kildee (D)	208,163	67.2%
Myrah Kirkwood (R)	96,934	31.3%

2004 PRIMARY

Dale E. Kildee (D)	unopposed

2002 GENERAL

Dale E. Kildee (D)	158,709	91.6%
Clint Foster (LIBERT)	9,344	5.4%
Harley Mikkelson (GREEN)	5,188	3.0%

PREVIOUS WINNING PERCENTAGES
2000 (61%); 1998 (56%); 1996 (59%); 1994 (51%);
1992 (54%); 1990 (68%); 1988 (76%); 1986 (80%);
1984 (93%); 1982 (75%); 1980 (93%); 1978 (77%);
1976 (70%)

Elected 1976; 15th term

Kildee's political views are an organic outgrowth of his roots. The son of an autoworker who hails from the home of General Motors Corp., he is a fierce protector of the auto industry and labor unions. He is a seminary graduate who taught Latin after abandoning plans to become a Roman Catholic priest, the foundation for his strong opposition to abortion and staunch support for education. He is committed to using government as a force to help the downtrodden, after being raised with a profound concern for the condition of American Indians.

As the No. 2 Democrat on both the Education and Workforce and Resources committees, Kildee is well-placed to press all of his causes.

Kildee entered politics in 1964 when he won election to the state House. It was the era of the civil rights movement and President Johnson's Great Society war on poverty, and Kildee remains a staunch liberal on most issues unrelated to abortion. He voted against the 2003 Medicare overhaul and opposes President Bush's proposal to allow younger workers to divert part of their Social Security payroll taxes into private investment accounts.

Convinced that trade agreements of the past decade or so have contributed to job losses at home and failed to improve labor standards abroad, Kildee in the 108th Congress voted against pacts with Chile, Singapore and Australia. He also opposed the 2002 revival of fast-track trade negotiating authority.

Like fellow Michigan Democrat John D. Dingell, Kildee requires his congressional employees who drive to work to do so in a car manufactured by members of the United Auto Workers. "If I walked into an office of a member from Florida, I would not expect to see oranges from Brazil in a big bowl there," Kildee once said on Fox News. "We tend to be sensitive to the needs of our people in our districts."

Kildee has championed many women's issues and in 2002 even sought to join the all-female Congressional Caucus for Women's Issues. He was gently rebuffed. "Mr. Kildee had expressed an interest early on," said an aide to California Democrat Juanita Millender-McDonald, then the caucus co-chairwoman. "But regrettably, he's of the wrong gender."

Kildee splits with most Democrats on an issue vital to women — abortion. In the 108th, he supported legislation outlawing a procedure critics call "partial birth" abortion and another bill making it a crime to injure or kill a fetus during a violent offense — laws that most of his Democratic colleagues said would undermine the Supreme Court's 1973 *Roe v. Wade* decision.

He voted for the 1996 law that imposed the first-ever work requirements on welfare recipients — anathema to most liberals. In 2001, Kildee was a negotiator on the final terms of Bush's No Child Left Behind education overhaul, helping to block an effort to combine drug-abuse prevention and after-school programs into one block grant to states.

Like a majority of House Democrats, Kildee voted in 2002 against the use of military force in Iraq. But in March 2004, one year after the U.S.-led invasion, he voted for a resolution declaring that the nation and the world "have been made safer with the removal of Saddam Hussein and his regime from power in Iraq." He was one of about three dozen Democrats to support the resolution after voting 17 months earlier against the war.

The hometown of Kildee's father is near the Grand Traverse Indian reservation, and as a child, Kildee was impressed with his father's concern for the well-being of its residents. A previous generation of Kildees had traded with Indians. As a state legislator, Kildee wrote a law allowing Michigan's American Indians to attend its state colleges for free. In his suit pocket are copies not only of the Constitution but also of the landmark 1832 Supreme Court decision that gave the federal government exclusive jurisdiction over Indian affairs, and thus responsibility for Indians' welfare.

In the House, that jurisdiction is generally exercised by the Resources Committee. When lawmakers in 1997 started talking about taxing Indian-run gambling operations, Kildee founded the Native American Caucus. In honor of all his efforts, the Grand Traverse Band of Ottawa and Chippewa Indians in 1998 named April 15 "Dale Kildee Day."

Kildee can champion individuals as well as groups. He worked for five years to secure a presidential pardon — granted on President Clinton's final day in office — for one of his former ninth-grade civics students, a local businessman convicted of international money laundering in 1981. The case captured Kildee's interest after the federal judge who sentenced the businessman petitioned the Justice Department for the pardon.

Starting in late 1985, Kildee voted yes or no on more than 6,000 consecutive roll call votes on the House floor, the longest streak of any active member. By Congressional Quarterly's strict accounting, the streak ended in June 1998, when he joined more than 60 lawmakers in voting "present" on a campaign finance proposal. The Detroit News contends the streak did not end until October 2000, at 8,141, when Kildee was in an Education Committee meeting and missed a routine vote to approve the congressional journal. Kildee did not miss a single roll call in the 107th or 108th Congress.

After a decade in the state House, Kildee won a state Senate seat in 1974. He was elected to Congress with 70 percent of the vote two years later to succeed Democrat Donald W. Riegle Jr., who left the House for a successful bid for the Senate. He coasted through subsequent contests until 1992 and 1994, when Republican Megan O'Neill, who had worked in the White House under President George Bush, ran strong campaigns. In the 1992 race, Kildee had to answer for 100 overdrafts at the private bank for House members; more generally, redistricting for the 1990s had left him a redrawn 9th District in which almost half the people were new to him.

Redistricting for this decade again made Kildee potentially vulnerable. The GOP-controlled legislature drew a map that pitted Kildee against five-term incumbent Democrat James A. Barcia in a redrawn 5th District. But Barcia ran for the state Senate rather than take on his more senior colleague in a 2002 primary. Kildee put a convincing lock on the seat in the general election and won easily again in 2004.

KEY VOTES

2004

Yes Extend federal unemployment benefits by 13 weeks
Yes Pass $283.2 billion, six-year federal highway and mass transit bill
Yes Approve $146 billion multi-year extension of previously enacted middle-class tax breaks
No   Amend the Constitution to prohibit same-sex marriage
No   Cut corporate taxes $137 billion over 10 years
Yes Reorganize U.S. intelligence agencies as proposed by Sept. 11 commission

2003

No   Cut taxes by $330 billion through fiscal 2013
Yes Block Bush rule scaling back overtime pay for some white-collar federal workers
Yes Do not allow use of search warrants without first notifying subjects
Yes Allow importation of prescription drugs
No   Create private school voucher program in Washington, D.C.
Yes Ban "partial birth" abortion except to save a woman's life
Yes Split $18.6 billion in Iraq aid into half-grant, half-loan
No   Overhaul Medicare and create prescription drug benefit

CQ VOTE STUDIES

	PARTY UNITY		PRESIDENTIAL SUPPORT	
	Support	Oppose	Support	Oppose
2004	93%	7%	35%	65%
2003	92%	8%	29%	71%
2002	89%	11%	38%	62%
2001	88%	12%	37%	63%
2000	87%	13%	72%	28%

INTEREST GROUPS

	AFL-CIO	ADA	CCUS	ACU
2004	100%	90%	38%	16%
2003	100%	90%	27%	32%
2002	100%	80%	40%	8%
2001	100%	85%	35%	32%
2000	100%	75%	42%	20%

MICHIGAN 5
East – Flint, Saginaw, Bay City

Flint, the birthplace of General Motors in 1908, gave rise to the modern labor movement 30 years later when sit-down strikes at two Flint plants forced the auto giant to recognize the power of the United Auto Workers (UAW) union. North of Flint and surrounding Genesee County, the 5th takes in Saginaw and Bay City and includes Tuscola County — part of Michigan's "Thumb."

From the turn of the century until the late 1960s, Flint, the largest city in the 5th, grew alongside the U.S. auto industry. Then the 1970s oil shock and an increase in inexpensive imports undercut demand for GM cars and drove the economy into a downward spiral. The industry recovered from the slump, but Flint has not. The city has continually struggled and lost population. In 2002, the city's finances were in such disrepair that the state took Flint into receivership. The city regained control in 2004, and some small auto-related companies have supplemented GM jobs that have left the city.

The district's blue-collar voters are populist on economics and more conservative on cultural issues, but they identify strongly with the Democratic Party. Genesee County, which accounts for two-thirds of the district's population, is strongly influenced by the UAW and gave 60 percent of its vote to John Kerry in the 2004 presidential election, his third-best showing in Michigan. Kerry received 83 percent in Flint, which is predominantly black. Auto workers and Democratic voters also are plentiful in Saginaw, which gave Kerry almost three-fourths of the vote.

Redistricting following the 2000 census cut counties from the old 5th's north and east. Mapmakers expanded the district's southern border to include the remainder of Genesee County, including Flint. The county had been split between the 5th, 8th and 9th districts in the 1990s.

MAJOR INDUSTRY
Auto parts manufacturing, agriculture, sugar processing

CITIES
Flint, 124,943; Saginaw, 61,799; Bay City, 36,817; Burton, 30,308

NOTABLE
Famous natives include Stevie Wonder (Saginaw) and Madonna (Bay City); Bay City was once known as the "Lumber Capital of the World"; Flint native Michael Moore's documentary film, "Roger & Me," chronicled the effect of GM's layoffs in the 1980s.

Rep. Fred Upton (R)

Elected 1986; 10th term

Upton is a genial pragmatist who takes his time making decisions and views himself as a natural-born compromiser who can work with Democrats. As the chairman of an influential subcommittee, he has to stay in the good graces of the GOP leadership. But he nonetheless often aligns himself with the House's dwindling band of moderate Republicans.

With some fairly conspicuous departures from the party line in the 108th Congress, Upton wound up in the bottom fifth of Republicans in his allegiance to the party on votes that pitted a majority of Republicans against a majority of Democrats.

In his 50s, Upton is showing a few wrinkles but still looks too boyish to be in his 10th term. By telling everyone he meets to "just call me Fred," he perpetuates that image. President Bush first dubbed him "Freddy Boy" and later shortened the nickname to "Freddy."

In 2003, Upton ended a streak of 3,587 consecutive votes cast (dating back to mid-1997). At the time, he was the leader among those with unbroken voting participation records. Upton missed eight recorded votes while in Iraq as part of a congressional delegation.

Upton is in his third and final two-year term as chairman of the Energy panel's Subcommittee on Telecommunications and the Internet, a post that has given him an influential voice on communications issues. As the 109th Congress prepared to tackle a rewrite of the 1996 Telecommunications Act, Upton said his focus would be "deregulatory parity" for all elements of the industry. "Why stymie one method when another provider is not held to the same standards in terms of regulation?" Upton asked in earlier discussions on the matter.

In the 108th Congress and again early in the 109th, Upton steered legislation through the House to stiffen fines that the Federal Communications Commission could impose for broadcast indecency. "Using the public airwaves comes with the responsibility to follow the FCC decency standards," he said. He also has pushed to restrict junk e-mail and to auction off some government-owned spectrum so telecom firms could use it. In 2002, he shepherded to enactment a law creating a ".kids" domain on the Internet that would be free of pornography and other potentially harmful materials. And he renewed his call to recording industry executives to improve the labeling of violent or sexually explicit material.

While he usually sides with Bush and the GOP leadership, Upton is not afraid to go his own way. In 2004, he was one of just 12 House Republicans supporting a budget amendment by conservative "Blue Dog" Democrats to require offsets for new tax cuts as well as new entitlement spending. He was one of 16 Republicans voting against a package of corporate tax cuts later in the year. And he was one of 22 GOP members who voted to overturn Bush administration overtime rules that critics said could cost millions of workers their eligibility for premium pay.

In 2002, Upton was among 20 Republican moderates who protested to Speaker J. Dennis Hastert when, at the insistence of conservatives, Hastert halted action on the year's biggest domestic spending bill until its price tag was reduced to an amount acceptable to Bush. In the end, some domestic programs — especially for education — were increased.

Upton also bucked party leaders to vote for the campaign finance overhaul of 2002. And he has sided with a minority of Republicans in voting for tighter curbs on firearms purchases at gun shows.

CAPITOL OFFICE
225-3761
tellupton@mail.house.gov
www.house.gov/upton
2183 Rayburn 20515-2206; fax 225-4986

COMMITTEES
Energy & Commerce
(Telecommunications and the Internet - chairman)

HOMETOWN
St. Joseph

BORN
April 23, 1953, St. Joseph, Mich.

RELIGION
Protestant

FAMILY
Wife, Amey Upton; two children

EDUCATION
U. of Michigan, B.A. 1975 (journalism)

CAREER
Congressional aide; White House budget analyst

POLITICAL HIGHLIGHTS
No previous office

ELECTION RESULTS

2004 GENERAL

Fred Upton (R)	197,425	65.3%
Scott Elliot (D)	97,978	32.4%

2004 PRIMARY

Fred Upton (R)	unopposed

2002 GENERAL

Fred Upton (R)	126,936	69.2%
Gary C. Giguere Jr. (D)	53,793	29.3%
Richard M. Overton (REF)	2,788	1.5%

PREVIOUS WINNING PERCENTAGES
2000 (68%); 1998 (70%); 1996 (68%); 1994 (73%);
1992 (62%); 1990 (58%); 1988 (71%); 1986 (62%)

In 2001, when the administration's energy plan left open the possibility of drilling for oil and gas in the Great Lakes, Upton helped pass a ban on such exploration. He told the White House from the House floor, "Gentlemen, you should look elsewhere."

When public outrage swelled in 2000 over the deaths of more than 100 people using vehicles equipped with Firestone tires, Upton, a member of the Energy and Commerce Committee since his third term, won passage of a bill to impose prison terms on auto industry officials if they withhold information about defects.

Though he watches federal spending, Upton once blocked the Coast Guard's plans to save money by dismantling the Great Lakes foghorn network. He said he owed the horns a debt of gratitude: Once, out sailing with friends when a fog rolled in, Upton and his shipmates were led home by the foghorns' blasts.

Upton comes from one of Michigan's wealthier Republican families; his grandfather helped found Whirlpool Corp., which is based in Upton's district. A sense of social responsibility was instilled in the young Upton early on. His parents took care of as many as two dozen foster children at various times, and one of Upton's first jobs was in a day care center.

He was first elected to Congress in 1986 after ousting incumbent Mark D. Siljander, a Christian conservative activist, in a Republican primary. But Upton's credentials as a fiscal conservative were solid: He had spent nearly a decade working for David A. Stockman, first on Stockman's 1976 campaign, then in Washington on his congressional staff and finally at the Office of Management and Budget, where Stockman was President Reagan's budget director and Upton was the budget office's liaison to Capitol Hill.

In Congress, Upton became a deputy to Newt Gingrich when Gingrich was elected GOP whip in 1989, and the next year joined Gingrich in castigating President George Bush for agreeing to raise taxes as part of a deal to reduce the deficit. Upton resigned as a deputy whip in 1993 because he disliked Gingrich's confrontational style.

Upton's political positioning has helped give him a virtual lock on his House seat; he has won his past six November elections with better than 65 percent of the vote. But in 2002, he drew a primary challenge from state Sen. Dale L. Shugars, who charged that Upton was not conservative enough, especially on some abortion-related issues. Upton criticized Shugars for waging a negative campaign, and he urged voters to reject such tactics. They did, renominating Upton with 66 percent of the vote. In 2004, he was unchallenged in the GOP primary.

KEY VOTES

2004

Yes Extend federal unemployment benefits by 13 weeks

Yes Pass $283.2 billion, six-year federal highway and mass transit bill

Yes Approve $146 billion multi-year extension of previously enacted middle-class tax breaks

Yes Amend the Constitution to prohibit same-sex marriage

No Cut corporate taxes $137 billion over 10 years

Yes Reorganize U.S. intelligence agencies as proposed by Sept. 11 commission

2003

Yes Cut taxes by $330 billion through fiscal 2013

Yes Block Bush rule scaling back overtime pay for some white-collar federal workers

No Do not allow use of search warrants without first notifying subjects

No Allow importation of prescription drugs

Yes Create private school voucher program in Washington, D.C.

Yes Ban "partial birth" abortion except to save a woman's life

No Split $18.6 billion in Iraq aid into half-grant, half-loan

Yes Overhaul Medicare and create prescription drug benefit

CQ VOTE STUDIES

	PARTY UNITY		PRESIDENTIAL SUPPORT	
	Support	Oppose	Support	Oppose
2004	88%	12%	82%	18%
2003	86%	14%	91%	9%
2002	92%	8%	82%	18%
2001	88%	12%	77%	23%
2000	79%	21%	39%	61%

INTEREST GROUPS

	AFL-CIO	ADA	CCUS	ACU
2004	47%	35%	90%	76%
2003	27%	10%	93%	76%
2002	11%	5%	95%	92%
2001	25%	10%	100%	76%
2000	10%	25%	85%	60%

MICHIGAN 6
Southwest – Kalamazoo, Portage, Benton Harbor

Lush forests in Michigan's southwest corner make the 6th a prime spot for tourists and orchards. Cherries and peaches grow in the fruit belt that extends north from St. Joseph and Benton Harbor — once a stop on the Underground Railroad — through Van Buren County. Many affluent Chicagoans keep second homes in the wooded area along the Lake Michigan shoreline, which has become known as "Harbor County."

Kalamazoo, the 6th's most-populous city, has a strong and diverse manufacturing economy. Cities throughout the district have escaped dependence on Detroit's automaker economy.

Home appliance manufacturer Whirlpool is based in Benton Harbor, and pharmaceutical maker Pfizer is in Kalamazoo and has the largest of its 78 plants worldwide in Portage. Education is another economic pillar, led by Western Michigan University's 27,000 students.

Kalamazoo's blue-collar workforce makes it one of the few Democratic parts of the 6th; John Kerry carried the city by a 34 percentage point margin in the 2004 presidential election, helping him narrowly win Kalamazoo County.

But the city's voters are no match for the Republican influences in the district — namely, its conservative Dutch heritage, white-collar corporate managers and rural conservatives. Berrien County, the district's second-most-populous county, gave George W. Bush 55 percent of the vote, although heavily black Benton Harbor went for Kerry by a better than 6-to-1 margin.

The 6th also includes all of Republican-leaning Van Buren, St. Joseph and Cass counties — the latter abuts the Indiana state line near South Bend and Elkhart. Redistricting gave the district more of Allegan County, a solidly Republican lake county between Kalamazoo and Grand Rapids.

MAJOR INDUSTRY
Manufacturing, higher education, agriculture, tourism

CITIES
Kalamazoo, 77,145; Portage, 44,897; Niles, 12,204; Sturgis, 11,285

NOTABLE
The first outdoor pedestrian shopping mall in the United States was built in Kalamazoo in 1959.

Rep. Joe Schwarz (R)

Elected 2004; 1st term

Schwarz was 67 years old when he was sworn in, making him the oldest member of the House Class of 2004. He also was among the most experienced, with 16 years as an influential state senator.

Yet he understands that he is on Congress' bottom rung: "I understand the system is built on seniority and I'll take what committee assignments I get and do the best I can," he said.

He did fairly well on that front. Agriculture and food processing are major industries in the 7th District, and Schwarz (pronounced SCHWARTZ) was given a seat on the Agriculture Committee. A CIA attaché before switching to a career in medicine, Schwarz also was placed on Armed Services.

Schwarz may need to establish himself quickly if he is to forestall electoral problems back home in 2006 — from within his own party. As a moderate Republican, he is more likely in his GOP-leaning district to face a challenge from the right in a Republican primary than from a Democrat.

Schwarz supports abortion rights, is willing to consider tax increases and strongly advocates increased federal presence in several areas, particularly higher education and transportation. An ear, nose and throat doctor for 30 years, he holds centrist views on health care accessibility and embryonic stem cell research — an area in which he says the United States risks falling behind the rest of the world unless federal spending is increased.

But he takes a position much more in line with Republican leaders on revising the nation's medical malpractice laws, which he says lead to frivolous lawsuits and force doctors to demur from treating patients.

In 2000, Schwarz ran Arizona GOP Sen. John McCain's presidential primary campaign in Michigan. Two years later, he sought the Republican nomination for governor but lost to a conservative candidate.

In 2004, he finished first in a six-way GOP primary against five more-conservative candidates, including Brad Smith, the son of the retiring six-term incumbent, Nick Smith. Schwarz then coasted to victory in November over little-known Democrat Sharon Renier.

CAPITOL OFFICE
225-6276
www.house.gov/schwarz
128 Cannon 20515-2207; fax 225-6281

COMMITTEES
Agriculture
Armed Services
Science

HOMETOWN
Battle Creek

BORN
Nov. 15, 1937, Chicago, Ill.

RELIGION
Roman Catholic

FAMILY
Divorced; one child

EDUCATION
U. of Michigan, B.A. 1959 (history); Wayne State U., M.D. 1964

MILITARY SERVICE
Navy, 1965-67

CAREER
Physician; Southeast Asia CIA attaché

POLITICAL HIGHLIGHTS
Battle Creek City Commission, 1979-87 (mayor, 1985-87); Mich. Senate, 1987-2003 (president pro tempore, 1993-2003); sought Republican nomination for U.S. House, 1992; sought Republican nomination for governor, 2002

ELECTION RESULTS

2004 GENERAL

Joe Schwarz (R)	176,053	58.4%
Sharon Renier (D)	109,527	36.3%
Dave Horn (USTAX)	9,032	3.0%
Jason Seagraves (GREEN)	3,996	1.3%
Kenneth L. Proctor (LIBERT)	3,034	1.0%

2004 PRIMARY

Joe Schwarz (R)	20,440	27.8%
Brad Smith (R)	16,488	22.4%
Tim Walberg (R)	12,973	17.7%
Clark Bisbee (R)	10,301	14.0%
Gene DeRossett (R)	8,379	11.4%
Paul DeWeese (R)	4,886	6.7%

MICHIGAN 7

South central — Battle Creek, Jackson

The southern Michigan counties that make up the 7th take in small towns, farming communities and a few mid-size cities. Kellogg's Tony the Tiger makes his home in Battle Creek, the district's largest city. The cereal giant is not only one of the city's largest employers, but it also maintains one of the nation's top philanthropic organizations, donating some gifts to the Battle Creek area.

Outside Battle Creek, auto parts manufacturing drives small-town economies, especially in Jackson. Agriculture dominates most of the rest of the 7th, with soybeans and corn as the staple crops. The farming counties of Branch, Eaton, Hillsdale, Jackson and Lenawee have been fertile ground for the GOP, and George W. Bush carried all five in the 2000 and 2004 presidential elections, even though he lost the state both times.

Rural and small-town voters tend to overwhelm the influence of the cities' blue-collar population, but even Democrats tend to be socially conservative. Unlike Detroit's auto workers, many of those living here have roots in the surrounding GOP countryside. Hillsdale County is home to Hillsdale College, which does not accept federal funding and has a free-market orientation.

The district's political and social culture has been shaped by Quaker settlements that made the area a station on the Underground Railroad and left many residents sensitive to issues such as racial segregation and the Vietnam War.

MAJOR INDUSTRY
Agriculture, food processing, auto parts manufacturing, health care

CITIES
Battle Creek, 53,364; Jackson, 36,316

NOTABLE
Sojourner Truth lived in Battle Creek; Battle Creek's annual Cereal Festival culminates in the world's longest breakfast table.

Rep. Mike Rogers (R)

Elected 2000; 3rd term

In two terms, Rogers has transformed himself from vulnerable new-comer to leadership-track rising star. After winning his seat by a heart-stopping 111 votes, the affable, high-energy former FBI agent threw himself into the gritty business of raising political contributions, not only to help secure his own seat but to help other endangered House Republicans. These days, he's winning elections with 60 percent of the vote or more and is on track to take over the party's major fundraising arm in the House, the National Republican Congressional Committee.

In the 2004 election cycle, he was finance chairman of the organization, and co-chaired the NRCC's "Battleground" effort, which banked $16 million for colleagues in tough races. That achievement makes him a top candidate to take over for NRCC Chairman Thomas M. Reynolds of New York, who is heading the group for the run-up to the 2006 mid-term election. The NRCC chairman is a member of the GOP leadership.

House Majority Whip Roy Blunt of Missouri, who once led the Battleground effort himself, had considered Rogers for the job as his chief deputy in 2002 but instead chose Eric Cantor of Virginia.

Rogers' prize was appointment by the leadership to the Energy and Commerce Committee, one of the most active and important panels. He was also named one of 18 deputy majority whips.

An Army veteran and a member of the Intelligence Committee, Rogers initially urged a go-slow approach when President Bush sought congressional authorization for the war in Iraq. Once he felt his concerns were satisfied, Rogers voted for the 2002 war resolution. His own military service, and the fact that one of his brothers is a colonel with the 101st Airborne, gave him extra credibility on the issue.

At Speaker J. Dennis Hastert's request, Rogers has traveled extensively to the Middle East and conflict areas such as Afghanistan and Iraq. He was a member of the first official congressional delegation to Iraq following the invasion and has returned to the country three times.

To take his Energy and Commerce seat in early 2003 — where his priorities include regulating garbage shipments from Canada — Rogers had to relinquish his spots on the Transportation and Financial Services panels.

The Sept. 11, 2001, terrorist attacks took place in Rogers' first year in the House and put a premium on his background as a former FBI special agent. He has showcased his knowledge about intelligence gathering and counterterrorism as a member of the Intelligence panel.

Because he has firsthand experience in wiretapping, Rogers was asked for his input as the Justice Department developed its anti-terrorism package, including proposals to broaden wiretap authority. As the plan moved toward enactment, his colleagues also sought out Rogers for guidance.

He also called for police, firefighters and medical technicians to be given vaccinations against anthrax attacks by terrorists. Rogers had a parochial interest in the proposal as well — BioPort Corp., located in the 8th District, was embroiled in a lengthy dispute with the Food and Drug Administration as it sought approval to make an anthrax vaccine.

On Financial Services, he and Chairman Michael G. Oxley of Ohio, a fellow FBI veteran, developed a bill to permit more than 250 federal, state and private regulatory organizations to coordinate their databases, including the FBI's fingerprint files, to combat fraud. Of particular interest was the collection of data on money laundering, which has been linked to illegal drug

CAPITOL OFFICE
225-4872
www.mikerogers.house.gov
133 Cannon 20515-2208; fax 225-5820

COMMITTEES
Energy & Commerce
Select Intelligence

HOMETOWN
Brighton

BORN
June 2, 1963, Livonia, Mich.

RELIGION
Methodist

FAMILY
Wife, Diane Rogers; two children

EDUCATION
Adrian College, B.A. 1985 (sociology & criminal justice)

MILITARY SERVICE
Army, 1985-88

CAREER
Home construction company owner; FBI agent

POLITICAL HIGHLIGHTS
Mich. Senate, 1995-2001 (majority floor leader, 1999-2001)

ELECTION RESULTS

2004 GENERAL

Mike Rogers (R)	207,925	61.1%
Robert Alexander (D)	125,619	36.9%
Will Tyler White (LIBERT)	3,591	1.1%

2004 PRIMARY

Mike Rogers (R)	unopposed

2002 GENERAL

Mike Rogers (R)	156,525	67.9%
Frank McAlpine (D)	70,920	30.8%
Thomas Yeutter (LIBERT)	3,152	1.4%

PREVIOUS WINNING PERCENTAGES
2000 (49%)

operations and terrorism.

Although usually a team player, Rogers opposed Ways and Means Chairman Bill Thomas of California when he tried to add a provision to a 2004 corporate tax bill that would have allowed the Internal Revenue Service to hire private debt collectors.

Rogers also drafted legislation to offer grants to help first-time homebuyers come up with down payments. His efforts to make housing more affordable have roots in his family's business. He, his father and his brothers own a company that assembles modular homes, and he lives in one of the company's dwellings.

Rogers grew up in Livingston County, just west of Detroit. His father was a high school vice principal and football coach, and a town supervisor. His mother ran a local chamber of commerce and served on the county commission. The youngest of five boys, Rogers says he wanted to be an FBI agent from the time he was in his teens.

He majored in sociology and criminal justice at Adrian College. At the same time, he enrolled in Army ROTC at the University of Michigan. After graduation, he spent three years in the Army and then entered the FBI Academy. He finished at the top of his class, earning a coveted assignment to the field office in Chicago, where he was responsible for unraveling a complex case involving public officials in the Chicago suburb of Cicero.

In 1994, after moving back to Michigan to raise his family, Rogers jumped into a race for the state Senate. A longtime GOP incumbent had decided to retire, and in the strongly Republican district, Rogers cruised to victory. He was re-elected in 1998 and served as majority floor leader in 1999 and 2000.

When Democrat Debbie Stabenow decided to give up the 8th District seat to run for the Senate in 2000, Rogers made a bid and faced state Senate colleague, Democrat Dianne Byrum, in the general election. Their expensive but civil campaign in the swing district went down to the wire and beyond — Rogers' victory was not official until December, when Byrum conceded after a partial recount failed to erase her opponent's slim lead. It was the closest House election that year.

Rogers immediately set out to solidify his hold on the district. He raised nearly $750,000 in his first six months in office. Additionally, the redrawing of Michigan's congressional map added thousands of GOP voters to the 8th District. Byrum declined to run again, and Rogers had an almost free ride against Democratic attorney Frank McAlpine, who entered the race on the last possible day and raised little money. Rogers won a second term with 68 percent of the vote and his third term in 2004 with 61 percent.

KEY VOTES

2004

Yes Extend federal unemployment benefits by 13 weeks

No Pass $283.2 billion, six-year federal highway and mass transit bill

Yes Approve $146 billion multi-year extension of previously enacted middle-class tax breaks

Yes Amend the Constitution to prohibit same-sex marriage

Yes Cut corporate taxes $137 billion over 10 years

Yes Reorganize U.S. intelligence agencies as proposed by Sept. 11 commission

2003

Yes Cut taxes by $330 billion through fiscal 2013

No Block Bush rule scaling back overtime pay for some white-collar federal workers

No Do not allow use of search warrants without first notifying subjects

No Allow importation of prescription drugs

Yes Create private school voucher program in Washington, D.C.

Yes Ban "partial birth" abortion except to save a woman's life

No Split $18.6 billion in Iraq aid into half-grant, half-loan

Yes Overhaul Medicare and create prescription drug benefit

CQ VOTE STUDIES

	PARTY UNITY		PRESIDENTIAL SUPPORT	
	Support	Oppose	Support	Oppose
2004	95%	5%	97%	3%
2003	98%	2%	96%	4%
2002	96%	4%	85%	15%
2001	95%	5%	88%	12%

INTEREST GROUPS

	AFL-CIO	ADA	CCUS	ACU
2004	20%	10%	100%	92%
2003	7%	5%	100%	84%
2002	0%	0%	90%	92%
2001	17%	5%	96%	84%

MICHIGAN 8

Central – Lansing

Michigan's capital district, where Ransom Eli Olds founded Olds Motor Vehicle Co. in 1897, covers Lansing, East Lansing and some agricultural communities to the east. The local dominance of General Motors, which makes Chevrolets, Cadillacs, Pontiacs and other brands, is matched only by state government. Together, they employ thousands of people in the 8th.

Michigan State, the nation's first land-grant university, gave birth to the district's second-largest city, East Lansing. State government workers, university students, faculty and autoworkers make Ingham County strongly Democratic. In the 2004 presidential election, John Kerry took 58 percent in Ingham, his fourth-best county showing in Michigan.

Ingham's liberal leanings are counterbalanced by the strong GOP tendencies of Livingston County, a fast-growing area just to the east. Livingston increased its population by 36 percent in the 1990s and has been absorbing whites leaving Detroit, Flint, Lansing and Pontiac. In contrast to Livingston, Ingham lost population in the 1990s. Combined, the

two counties account for two-thirds of residents in the 8th District.

Most of the rest of the 8th's voters live in northern Oakland County, an upscale region that is closer to Flint and Detroit than to Lansing. The 8th also includes Clinton County, just north of Lansing, and parts of Shiawassee County, located between Lansing and Flint.

In redistricting following the 2000 census, Republican mapmakers drew more of Oakland into the 8th to give a GOP lean to a district that was highly competitive in the 1990s. The old 8th's share of Genesee County, including many Democratic voters, was shifted to the 5th District.

MAJOR INDUSTRY
State government, auto manufacturing, higher education

CITIES
Lansing (pt.), 114,321; East Lansing, 46,525; Okemos (unincorporated), 22,805

NOTABLE
Basketball star Earvin "Magic" Johnson hails from Lansing and played college ball at Michigan State University; Howell celebrates the honeydew harvest with its annual Melon Festival.

Rep. Joe Knollenberg (R)

CAPITOL OFFICE
225-5802
www.house.gov/knollenberg
2349 Rayburn 20515-2209; fax 226-2356

COMMITTEES
Appropriations
    (Transportation, Treasury, HUD, the Judiciary &
    District of Columbia - chairman)

HOMETOWN
Bloomfield Township

BORN
Nov. 28, 1933, Mattoon, Ill.

RELIGION
Roman Catholic

FAMILY
Wife, Sandie Knollenberg; two children

EDUCATION
Eastern Illinois U., B.S. 1955 (social science)

MILITARY SERVICE
Army, 1955-57

CAREER
Insurance broker

POLITICAL HIGHLIGHTS
Oakland County Republican Party chairman,
1978-86

ELECTION RESULTS

2004 GENERAL

Joe Knollenberg (R)	199,210	58.5%
Steven Reifman (D)	134,764	39.5%
Robert Schubring (LIBERT)	6,825	2.0%

2004 PRIMARY

Joe Knollenberg (R)	unopposed

2002 GENERAL

Joe Knollenberg (R)	141,102	58.1%
David Fink (D)	96,856	39.9%
Robert Schubring (LIBERT)	4,922	2.0%

PREVIOUS WINNING PERCENTAGES
2000 (56%); 1998 (64%); 1996 (61%); 1994 (68%);
1992 (58%)

Elected 1992; 7th term

Knollenberg is from the old school of GOP politics, with conservative political views that are rooted in the long business career he had before coming to Washington. He is also one of the influential "cardinals," as the subcommittee chairmen on Appropriations are known, and so is well-positioned to deliver federal funds to his suburban Detroit district.

The seven-term congressman's easygoing style is suited to the bipartisan deal-making that characterizes the Appropriations Committee. His support for the traditions of the panel, however, was sure to be tested in the 109th Congress by GOP leaders trying to assert more control over federal spending. In 2005, he became chairman of the panel that funds the departments of Transportation, Treasury and Housing as well as the federal judiciary and District of Columbia budgets.

In the 108th Congress, Knollenberg served as chairman of the Military Construction Subcommittee, responsible for what is traditionally one of the most popular and easy-to-pass spending bills due to its rich array of grants for lawmakers' home districts. But throughout 2003, Knollenberg struggled to write a bill with nearly $1.3 billion less to work with than in 2002. The result was a 15-week impasse for the conference committee, as lawmakers toiled over painful cuts and the possibility that their actions would make life harder for troops overseas. Knollenberg eventually fashioned a compromise that trimmed several programs and leveraged government funds to finance privately built military housing.

Earlier, in his single term as chairman of the District of Columbia Appropriations Subcommittee, Knollenberg won kudos for his efforts to produce annual spending bills. The bill funding the capital city's budget has often been the focus of partisan battles over proposed conservative mandates on the liberal District government, such as the perennial fight over publicly funded vouchers for private school tuition. Knollenberg reduced the number of such policy initiatives from 67 in 2000 to 34 in 2001. Rep. Eleanor Holmes Norton, the city's Democratic delegate, called the subcommittee's work "the smoothest in my 12 years in Congress." (In the 109th, the Appropriations subcommittees were reorganized and the District's funding is no longer appropriated in a separate bill in the House.)

Knollenberg is best known for his crusade against what he regards as frivolous over-regulation by the government. He once pushed to do away with federal standards that have limited post-1992 toilets to 1.6 gallons per flush, less than half the volume of the previous standard, and others that restricted the output of new showerheads. In 2000, Knollenberg was able to get a House subcommittee vote on his bill. He lost, 12-13, but said he remained committed to the fight.

In 2005, Knollenberg sponsored legislation to crack down on foreign firms that make counterfeit manufactured goods such as car parts. His bill seeks not only to prosecute counterfeiters but also to destroy their equipment to prevent further crimes. The auto companies have complained that counterfeiting in countries, such as China, has grown into a $200 billion annual drain on their bottom line and presents a danger to consumers. "When you talk about a brake pad that is not the real McCoy, it may last only 10 percent of its supposed lifetime, which could create catastrophic problems," Knollenberg told the Washington Automotive Press Association.

Knollenberg took a leading role in opposing the steel tariffs imposed in 2002 by President Bush. Knollenberg's district contains one of the country's highest concentrations of auto-parts manufacturers, which were affected by steep increases in steel prices. Like most Michigan lawmakers, Knollenberg strongly opposes raising automotive fuel economy standards. He has used his Appropriations seat to provide research grants for fuel-efficient technologies, but he contends that the government should not mandate new technologies until they are ready for commercial use.

While he rails against wasteful spending, Knollenberg has sought federal funds for pet projects such as artificial kidney research at the University of Michigan and the cleanup of the Rouge River. And he annually seeks to secure funding for local roads projects.

His Military Construction chairmanship paid off for facilities in Michigan. He secured $27.6 million for the Army National Guard Aviation Support Facility in Grand Ledge in 2004, and $9.7 million for the Selfridge Air National Guard base that year.

Knollenberg's opposition to abortion and his backing of other conservative social initiatives earn him high ratings from groups such as the Christian Coalition and the American Conservative Union. Knollenberg, whose son Steve is gay, earns low marks for his voting record from the Human Rights Campaign, an issue advocacy group for homosexuals. Knollenberg says that his son's "sexual orientation is a personal matter" and that he "unequivocally" supports him "with all the love and respect that a family possibly can."

The fifth of 13 children reared on a farm in central Illinois, Knollenberg graduated from Eastern Illinois University. After two years in the Army, he moved to the Detroit area in 1959 to work as an Allstate Insurance agent, eventually opening his own branch office. His community activities in the north Detroit suburbs included chairing a local PTA, chairing the Oakland County GOP organization and heading the campaign of Republican Rep. William S. Broomfield.

When Broomfield retired in 1992 after 18 terms, Knollenberg won the GOP nomination in a three-way race. He then defeated Democrat Walter O. Briggs IV, nephew of former Democratic Sen. Philip A. Hart, by 18 percentage points in the upscale Republican 11th District. His next four re-election wins came easily; his smallest victory margin was 15 points in 2000.

After redistricting for this decade, Knollenberg sought re-election in the 9th District, with a constituency that was 60 percent new. In 2002, he was matched dollar for dollar by wealthy Democratic lawyer David Fink in one of the most expensive House races in Michigan history, but he won by 18 points. In 2004, he upped his winning margin to 19 points.

KEY VOTES

2004

No   Extend federal unemployment benefits by 13 weeks

Yes   Pass $283.2 billion, six-year federal highway and mass transit bill

Yes   Approve $146 billion multi-year extension of previously enacted middle-class tax breaks

No   Amend the Constitution to prohibit same-sex marriage

Yes   Cut corporate taxes $137 billion over 10 years

Yes   Reorganize U.S. intelligence agencies as proposed by Sept. 11 commission

2003

Yes   Cut taxes by $330 billion through fiscal 2013

No   Block Bush rule scaling back overtime pay for some white-collar federal workers

No   Do not allow use of search warrants without first notifying subjects

No   Allow importation of prescription drugs

Yes   Create private school voucher program in Washington, D.C.

Yes   Ban "partial birth" abortion except to save a woman's life

No   Split $18.6 billion in Iraq aid into half-grant, half-loan

Yes   Overhaul Medicare and create prescription drug benefit

CQ VOTE STUDIES

	PARTY UNITY		PRESIDENTIAL SUPPORT	
	Support	Oppose	Support	Oppose
2004	94%	6%	88%	12%
2003	97%	3%	100%	0%
2002	96%	4%	92%	8%
2001	99%	1%	98%	2%
2000	92%	8%	32%	68%

INTEREST GROUPS

	AFL-CIO	ADA	CCUS	ACU
2004	13%	5%	100%	84%
2003	7%	5%	100%	84%
2002	0%	0%	100%	88%
2001	8%	0%	100%	92%
2000	0%	0%	90%	80%

MICHIGAN 9

Suburban Detroit – eastern Oakland County

Michigan's 9th — the wealthiest and most-educated district in the state — is wholly contained within Oakland County, one of the most affluent counties in the nation and home to the American headquarters for DaimlerChrysler in Auburn Hills and Kmart in Troy. The district includes more than half of Oakland County residents.

Communities such as Farmington Hills, north of the northern Detroit boundary cut by 8 Mile Road, form a corridor between Grand River Avenue and the Northwestern Highway that has served as one of the major routes for white exodus from Detroit. Troy, in the southeast corner of the district, has benefited from growth in high-tech automotive research and design, and is also a major office center. The area has a large Asian population.

Troy, Bloomfield and Rochester Hills give the district its Republican lean, but Democrats fare well in Pontiac, where blacks are a plurality and where John Kerry won 79 percent of the 2004 presidential vote. He also won Farmington Hills, the most-populous city in the district, and West

Bloomfield by comfortable margins.

Republican candidates have slipped somewhat in Oakland County. In the 1980s, Ronald Reagan and George Bush ran 6 to 8 percentage points ahead of their statewide vote share. In 2004, George W. Bush received 49 percent in losing the Oakland County vote, which was barely higher than his 48 percent showing statewide, but he did win the 9th with 50 percent of the vote. The district, as redrawn following the 2000 census, contains part of the old 9th, 11th and 12th districts.

MAJOR INDUSTRY

Auto manufacturing, engineering, health care, insurance

CITIES

Farmington Hills, 82,111; Troy, 80,959; Rochester Hills, 68,825; Pontiac, 66,337; Waterford (pt.) (unincorporated), 66,316; West Bloomfield (unincorporated), 64,862; Royal Oak (pt.), 54,536

NOTABLE

The first Holocaust museum built in the United States is in West Bloomfield; The Rev. Charles Coughlin broadcast his controversial weekly radio programs from the Shrine of the Little Flower church in Royal Oak in the 1930s.

Rep. Candice S. Miller (R)

Elected 2002; 2nd term

Miller prefers Hush Puppies to Manolos and is perhaps the only member of the House who doesn't mind being called an "Old Goat," a title she earned from fellow Michigan watermen for sailing a choppy course across Lake Huron a benchmark 25 times. An assertive party loyalist with a salty tongue, she was admonished in her first term by the ethics committee for threatening political retaliation against a fellow Republican who refused to support a major GOP-backed health care bill.

Miller had a relatively high profile in 2004 as President Bush's campaign chairman in Michigan, an important swing state courted heavily by both presidential candidates. She had arrived in the House two years earlier already a well-established statewide political player, having served two terms as secretary of state. After being passed over by her party for the nomination for governor, she was accommodated in 2002 with a newly redrawn congressional district that included her political base in the state's "Thumb" region northeast of Detroit.

Miller immediately landed on Washington's rising star watch list, but the 2004 rebuke from the Committee on Standards of Official Conduct was a setback. The ethics panel said Miller went too far when, during the pitched battle over Bush's Medicare prescription drug plan, she cornered fellow Republican Nick Smith, also from Michigan, on the floor and threatened to use her influence in his son's congressional campaign unless Smith supported the legislation. At the time, Brad Smith was seeking to take his retiring father's place, a race he ultimately lost.

The elder Smith complained to the ethics panel of pressure from Miller and Republican leaders. Miller did not dispute the findings, but told the Detroit Free Press, in a reference to Smith's martial arts training: "If a black belt can be intimidated by an overweight, middle-age woman, that's too bad."

The congresswoman says she's a social and fiscal conservative. But hailing as she does from the nation's automobile-making hub, she sometimes sides with big labor. Her grown daughter is a Ford assembly worker who belongs to the United Auto Workers. Miller joined 38 other Republicans in voting for a Democratic proposal in 2004 to extend federal unemployment benefits for 13 weeks. She is a vocal opponent of raising fuel efficiency standards for cars and SUVs.

In most instances, Miller can be counted on as a GOP team player. She has adamantly supported making the president's tax cuts permanent. She is an energetic fundraiser and was chosen by the leadership for its "message action" team, which is responsible for instant responses to assertions by Democrats. In the 109th Congress, she has a seat on the House Administration Committee, a panel where party loyalty is generally a prerequisite.

Miller's major committee assignment is Armed Services, where she fiercely protects the interests of Selfridge Air National Guard Base in her district. Her husband, Donald Miller, a circuit judge, is a former commander of the base. She wants to have Selfridge become the Midwest hub of the Department of Homeland Security.

Another parochial concern is the Great Lakes. Miller is in the middle of any fight over water rights, as landlocked states to the west eye the lakes as a potential solution to water shortages.

In Michigan, Miller is a perhaps improbable icon of feminist ideals, shattering as she has a number of gender barriers in politics and in one

CAPITOL OFFICE
225-2106
candicemiller.house.gov
228 Cannon 20515-2210; fax 226-1169

COMMITTEES
Armed Services
Government Reform
  (Regulatory Affairs - chairwoman)
House Administration
Joint Library

HOMETOWN
Harrison Township

BORN
May 7, 1954, Detroit, Mich.

RELIGION
Presbyterian

FAMILY
Husband, Donald Miller; one child

EDUCATION
Macomb Community College, attended 1973-74;
Northwood Institute, attended 1974

CAREER
Boat saleswoman

POLITICAL HIGHLIGHTS
Harrison Township Board of Trustees, 1979-80;
Harrison Township supervisor, 1980-92;
Republican nominee for U.S. House, 1986;
Macomb County treasurer, 1993-95; Mich.
secretary of state, 1995-2002

ELECTION RESULTS

2004 GENERAL

Candice S. Miller (R)	227,720	68.6%
Rob Casey (D)	98,029	29.5%
Phoebe A. Basso (LIBERT)	3,966	1.2%

2004 PRIMARY

Candice S. Miller (R)	unopposed

2002 GENERAL

Candice S. Miller (R)	137,339	63.3%
Carl J. Marlinga (D)	77,053	35.5%
Renae Coon (LIBERT)	2,536	1.2%

of the state's most popular sports. For, when Miller was growing up in 1960s suburban Detroit, her father, who owned a marina, discouraged his daughter's growing interest in sailboat racing because he deemed it a better sport for boys, particularly her older brother, Gary. "In my family, women's liberation was not discussed," she once told a newspaper profiler. "You were supposed to get married and do your thing."

She joined a high school boating crew anyway. When the local yacht club barred her and other women from the annual Port Huron-to-Mackinac Island regatta, they raised Cain until they were allowed in, becoming the first all-female crew to compete in the prestigious 300-mile race. They called their boat the Sayonara. Years later, fellow race veterans admitted her to their Old Goat Society, when she completed her 25th race.

Miller attended a community college but dropped out to sell boats for the family business. By 25, she was a divorced single mother with a toddler. (She later remarried.) When the local township board proposed a tax increase on marinas, she became a "noisy activist" and surprised herself by finding "that whole experience very stimulating."

Miller was elected to the township board and just a year later unseated the incumbent Harrison Township supervisor, becoming the first woman to hold the job. In 1994, she was elected Michigan's first female secretary of state, and in two terms was recognized for making the technologically backward office more efficient and for instituting fraud-proof driver's licenses.

Miller had long eyed a seat in Congress but was blocked by the popularity of Democratic Rep. David E. Bonior, whom she had lost to in 1986 when she was relatively green. Though Miller was the favorite to take on Bonior again in 2000, she was more interested in preparing a run for governor. When Republican Gov. and party powerhouse John Engler backed Lt. Gov. Dick Posthumus for governor instead, Miller stayed out of both contests. (Posthumus eventually lost to the Democratic candidate, state Attorney General Jennifer Granholm.)

The Republican-controlled legislature made it up to her in 2002 with a redrawn congressional district that included several GOP-leaning counties and Miller's base in Macomb County, the symbolic home of the Reagan Democrats of the 1980s and increasingly friendly turf for Republicans today.

Her Democratic opponent was popular Macomb County Prosecuting Attorney Carl J. Marlinga. The race was supposed to be tight, but Miller, who enjoyed solid statewide name recognition and greatly outpaced Marlinga in fundraising, won with 63 percent of the vote. She drew only marginal competition from Democrats in 2004.

KEY VOTES

2004
Yes Extend federal unemployment benefits by 13 weeks
Yes Pass $283.2 billion, six-year federal highway and mass transit bill
Yes Approve $146 billion multi-year extension of previously enacted middle-class tax breaks
Yes Amend the Constitution to prohibit same-sex marriage
Yes Cut corporate taxes $137 billion over 10 years
Yes Reorganize U.S. intelligence agencies as proposed by Sept. 11 commission

2003
Yes Cut taxes by $330 billion through fiscal 2013
No   Block Bush rule scaling back overtime pay for some white-collar federal workers
No   Do not allow use of search warrants without first notifying subjects
Yes Allow importation of prescription drugs
Yes Create private school voucher program in Washington, D.C.
Yes Ban "partial birth" abortion except to save a woman's life
No   Split $18.6 billion in Iraq aid into half-grant, half-loan
Yes Overhaul Medicare and create prescription drug benefit

CQ VOTE STUDIES

	PARTY UNITY		PRESIDENTIAL SUPPORT	
	Support	Oppose	Support	Oppose
2004	93%	7%	85%	15%
2003	96%	4%	95%	5%

INTEREST GROUPS

	AFL-CIO	ADA	CCUS	ACU
2004	27%	10%	100%	84%
2003	13%	10%	97%	83%

MICHIGAN 10
Southeast — northern Macomb County, Port Huron, most of Michigan 'Thumb'

Stretching from Sterling Heights in the Macomb County suburbs north of Detroit to the Michigan "Thumb," the 10th combines suburban, lakefront and rural communities. Although statewide candidates who carry Macomb, an electoral bellwether where half of the 10th's residents live, usually win the state, that did not hold true in 2004, as George W. Bush won the county, but lost Michigan.

Macomb, while still home to some auto plants, largely has shed its blue-collar past and "Reagan Democrat" reputation and is becoming more white-collar and upscale. Democrats have made major inroads in northern-state suburban counties such as Macomb. But Republican lawmakers who controlled Michigan's redistricting process following the 2000 census were careful to draw Macomb's most solidly Republican territories, including Shelby, Macomb and Washington townships, into the 10th. They put Democratic-leaning southern Macomb into the 12th.

North of Macomb is St. Clair County, a politically competitive region where one-fourth of district residents live. Port Huron, a source of blue-collar Democratic votes, has grown with the expansion of Detroit's metropolitan area. Water quality issues are important to residents along Lake Huron and Lake St. Clair. The 10th also has thriving small businesses based on the boating industry.

The rest of the district has a rural feel, with communities that are dependent on fruit, soybeans, corn and dairy products. The 10th has some of the most productive navy bean and sugar beet fields in the state. Sanilac County leads Michigan in dairy production.

MAJOR INDUSTRY
Auto manufacturing, agriculture, recreation

CITIES
Sterling Heights (pt.), 86,536; Shelby (unincorporated), 65,159; Port Huron, 32,338

NOTABLE
The U.S. Senate's famous navy bean soup uses Michigan navy beans exclusively; The annual Bacardi Bayview Mackinac Race, a freshwater sailing race on Lake Huron, begins in Port Huron.

Rep. Thaddeus McCotter (R)

Elected 2002; 2nd term

CAPITOL OFFICE
225-8171
thaddeus.mccotter@mail.house.gov
mccotter.house.gov
1632 Longworth 20515-2211; fax 225-2667

COMMITTEES
Budget
International Relations
Small Business
Joint Economic

HOMETOWN
Livonia

BORN
Aug. 22, 1965, Detroit, Mich.

RELIGION
Roman Catholic

FAMILY
Wife, Rita McCotter; three children

EDUCATION
U. of Detroit, B.A. 1987 (political science), J.D. 1990

CAREER
Lawyer

POLITICAL HIGHLIGHTS
Schoolcraft College Board of Trustees, 1989-92;
Wayne County Commission, 1993-98; Mich.
Senate, 1999-2002

ELECTION RESULTS

2004 GENERAL

Thaddeus McCotter (R)	186,431	57.0%
Phillip Truran (D)	134,301	41.0%
Charles I. Basso (LIBERT)	6,484	2.0%

2004 PRIMARY

Thaddeus McCotter (R)	unopposed

2002 GENERAL

Thaddeus McCotter (R)	126,050	57.2%
Kevin Kelley (D)	87,402	39.7%
William Boyd (GREEN)	4,243	1.9%
Daniel E. Malone (USTAX)	2,710	1.2%

Since his days in state and local government, McCotter has followed a fiscally conservative path, favoring lower taxes and smaller government. In this way, he is like many of his fellow Republicans who say they want to get the government out of people's pocketbooks. McCotter favors making permanent the tax cuts President Bush pushed to enactment in 2001. "In our community, we do not want to pay more taxes to the federal government," he says.

But he differs from many of his GOP colleagues in that he also wants to give workers certain labor protections. He was among the small minority of Republicans to break ranks and support measures in both 2003 and 2004 to extend unemployment benefits an additional 13 weeks. He said workers in his district need the benefits to weather the ups and downs of economic cycles. "We have a lot of people who want to work very badly and they can't, through no fault of their own. My constituents don't enjoy taking unemployment compensation. It's a necessity," he said.

During his second term, McCotter is likely to stay focused on home-state issues. He is worried about Michigan's struggling economy with its dependence on manufacturing. He says Michigan needs to continue to diversify its economy and forestall a "brain drain" of college graduates leaving the state in search of employment.

As might be expected of a lawmaker whose district is near Detroit, McCotter champions the auto industry above other business interests when they are in conflict. To that end, he joined other Republican members of the Michigan delegation to urge Bush to drop foreign tariffs that protect steel foundries in Pennsylvania and other states but raise prices for Detroit car manufacturers that purchase large quantities of steel from abroad. He also argues against tougher fuel economy standards for vehicles, saying they are "unfunded mandates" that would set off a round of layoffs and lead to the day when "my district's economic vitality will become ancient history."

As a freshman, McCotter was appointed to seats on the Budget and International Relations committees. He says he is interested in how American foreign policy affects the U.S. economy. Later in the 108th Congress, he also gained a seat on the Small Business Committee. Small businesses spawned by the automotive industry are "critical," he says, to the economy of the 11th District.

McCotter wants to require that more of the content in military weapons be produced in the United States. "We need to manufacture our own weaponry and not outsource it to other parts of the world," he told the Detroit News.

A self-described conservationist, McCotter cosponsored a Great Lakes protection bill when he was in the state legislature, and he has brought that interest to Washington. He is a cosponsor of a bipartisan measure to clean up the five Midwestern lakes that serve the region as supplier of drinking water, recreational activities and cargo shipping corridors. The sponsors seek financing to restore polluted waters and reduce the frequency of beach closings and fish contamination alerts.

A lifelong resident of the 11th District, located north and west of Detroit, McCotter spent many years as a semi-professional musician playing guitar in several bands, including one called Sir Funk-a-Lot and the Knights of the Terrestrial Jam.

His parents were both special education teachers in the Detroit public schools. His mother, Joan, was elected to the Livonia City Council in 1985 — a campaign he helped manage. She later became the city clerk. McCotter still lives in Livonia with his wife, who is a registered nurse, and their three children.

Persuaded by a friend to get involved in the 1988 presidential campaign, McCotter went to the Republican National Convention as a delegate pledged to the senior George Bush. After graduating from law school, he worked as a solo practitioner, then made a successful bid for a seat on the Wayne County Commission in 1992. He was elected to the state Senate in 1998.

While on the county commission, he was the driving force behind a measure still in effect that requires 60 percent voter approval for any tax increase. He also worked to repeal more than 50 arcane state laws, including one that required city and township clerks to pay the bearer of a dead rat the price of one dime per head.

When he ran for the House in 2002, McCotter was the beneficiary of a Republican-controlled redistricting process. Then a state senator, he was vice chairman of the Senate Reapportionment Committee, which oversaw the remapping. The 11th District was created to promote McCotter's candidacy, as it includes his entire state Senate district. The 11th could be more politically competitive because of the presence of a fair number of Democrats in the Wayne County portion, but the party has failed to recruit top-notch Democratic candidates.

In the 2002 primary, McCotter handily beat businessman David C. Hagerty. McCotter's kickoff event drew national attention, with then-House Majority Leader Dick Armey of Texas making an appearance. The two had met while working on a 1994 congressional campaign in Michigan. "You step back and say, 'Wow, he's here for me,'" said McCotter. "I thought that was pretty awe-inspiring."

In the general election, he easily fended off Democratic nominee Kevin Kelley, a township supervisor who had a long political résumé but was a late entry to the race. The McCotter campaign gained a significant infusion of cash in October, when Bush headlined a fundraising dinner that netted $500,000. On the other hand, the Kelley campaign was not able to buy television ads until late in the race and had to rely on direct mail to reach voters. In the end, McCotter had $1.2 million to spend, almost twice as much as Kelley.

In 2004, McCotter easily defeated the Democratic nominee, local union president Phillip Truran, by 16 percentage points.

KEY VOTES

2004

Yes Extend federal unemployment benefits by 13 weeks

Yes Pass $283.2 billion, six-year federal highway and mass transit bill

Yes Approve $146 billion multi-year extension of previously enacted middle-class tax breaks

Yes Amend the Constitution to prohibit same-sex marriage

Yes Cut corporate taxes $137 billion over 10 years

Yes Reorganize U.S. intelligence agencies as proposed by Sept. 11 commission

2003

Yes Cut taxes by $330 billion through fiscal 2013

No Block Bush rule scaling back overtime pay for some white-collar federal workers

Yes Do not allow use of search warrants without first notifying subjects

No Allow importation of prescription drugs

Yes Create private school voucher program in Washington, D.C.

Yes Ban "partial birth" abortion except to save a woman's life

No Split $18.6 billion in Iraq aid into half-grant, half-loan

Yes Overhaul Medicare and create prescription drug benefit

CQ VOTE STUDIES

	PARTY UNITY		PRESIDENTIAL SUPPORT	
	Support	Oppose	Support	Oppose
2004	91%	9%	82%	18%
2003	96%	4%	96%	4%

INTEREST GROUPS

	AFL-CIO	ADA	CCUS	ACU
2004	27%	15%	95%	88%
2003	7%	50%	100%	88%

MICHIGAN 11
Southeast — Livonia, Westland, Novi

The 11th, which takes in suburbs west and north of Detroit, stands out as a Republican-leaning area in a region renowned for its support of pro-labor Democrats. Auto manufacturing is important here, with several Ford facilities among the area plants.

Although Detroit's presence makes Wayne County, where 70 percent of the district's residents live, a Democratic stronghold, the 11th's portion of Wayne is politically competitive. Residents here split their presidential votes almost evenly in 2004 between George W. Bush and John Kerry.

Communities in the district have been trying to shed their image as decentralized suburbs. Plymouth has seen a revitalization of its downtown with the addition of mixed-use buildings containing lofts and retail outlets. In Canton Township, a $360 million housing development is aimed at breaking the mold of the traditional subdivision.

Republicans run well in upper-middle-class communities such as Livonia, the most populous city in the district, and Canton, a rapidly

developing residential area in western Wayne County, east of Ann Arbor (located in the 15th). While Wayne County overall lost population in the 1990s, Canton boomed, increasing its population by more than one-third. Northville and Plymouth townships, upscale areas just west of Livonia, also are growing rapidly. Bush took 58 percent of the 2004 vote in Plymouth and 61 percent of the vote in Northville.

Democrats run better in more middle-class areas such as Redford Township, just west of Detroit, and Westland, an area south of Livonia that gave 58 percent to Kerry in 2004.

The 11th also covers southwestern Oakland County, which is more Republican-leaning. Novi, the most populous Oakland County jurisdiction in the 11th, grew by 47 percent in the 1990s.

MAJOR INDUSTRY
Auto manufacturing, engineering, health care, insurance

CITIES
Livonia, 100,545; Westland, 86,602; Canton (unincorporated), 76,366

NOTABLE
Novi, first settled around 1825, is said to have been named for being the sixth stop — VI in Roman numerals — on a stagecoach route.

Rep. Sander M. Levin (D)

Elected 1982; 12th term

CAPITOL OFFICE
225-4961
www.house.gov/levin
2300 Rayburn 20515-2212; fax 226-1033

COMMITTEES
Ways & Means

HOMETOWN
Royal Oak

BORN
Sept. 6, 1931, Detroit, Mich.

RELIGION
Jewish

FAMILY
Wife, Victoria Levin; four children

EDUCATION
U. of Chicago, B.A. 1952; Columbia U., M.A. 1954
(international relations); Harvard U., LL.B. 1957

CAREER
Lawyer; U.S. Agency for International
Development official

POLITICAL HIGHLIGHTS
Oakland Board of Supervisors, 1961-64; Mich.
Senate, 1965-71 (minority leader, 1969-70);
Michigan Democratic Party chairman, 1968-69;
Democratic nominee for governor, 1970, 1974

ELECTION RESULTS

2004 GENERAL

Sander M. Levin (D)	210,827	69.3%
Randell J. Shafer (R)	88,256	29.0%
Dick Gach (LIBERT)	5,051	1.7%

2004 PRIMARY

Sander M. Levin (D)	unopposed

2002 GENERAL

Sander M. Levin (D)	140,970	68.3%
Harvey R. Dean (R)	61,502	29.8%
Dick Gach (LIBERT)	2,694	1.3%

PREVIOUS WINNING PERCENTAGES
2000 (64%); 1998 (56%); 1996 (57%); 1994 (52%);
1992 (53%); 1990 (70%); 1988 (70%); 1986 (76%);
1984 (100%); 1982 (67%)

As the Democratic point man on fending off GOP changes to the Social Security system, Levin has taken on a high-profile role in the 109th Congress. As the top-ranking Democrat on Ways and Means' Social Security Subcommittee, Levin has made it clear he intends to challenge President Bush's assumptions on how to shore up Social Security.

Bush has proposed allowing younger workers to open private accounts in which to invest part of their Social Security payroll tax, but Levin says Bush's broader intent is to tear down existing New Deal programs. "They want to dismantle Social Security and replace it with private accounts, even if there is no assurance that anybody would be better off and even if many would be worse off," he told the Los Angeles Times in early 2005. "It's a Darwinian, survival-of-the-fittest, everybody-on-their-own philosophy."

Mild-mannered yet tenacious, Levin has the look and the speaking style of a distracted college professor. He is known for throwing his intellectual might into understanding the details of legislation — and their practical implication. Before moving to the Social Security panel, Levin was the top-ranking Democrat on the Trade Subcommittee, where he established himself as the wise man on the complex topic of international trade agreements. Often by the end of lengthy hearings, Levin looks so rumpled, with his white hair strewn about wildly, that he appears to be physically wrestling with the answers to his complex questions.

Throughout the 108th Congress, Levin hammered home the importance of paying more attention to the impact trade agreements were having on U.S. workers. Michigan has felt an acute upsurge in the loss of well-paying manufacturing jobs, many in Levin's own district.

Even with his attention directed toward Social Security issues, Levin is expected to play a leading role in the 109th as lawmakers debate a free trade agreement with Central America. In the 108th, even as he voted to support liberalized trade with Chile and Singapore, Levin warned that the Central American agreement was entirely different because of poor labor laws in most Latin American countries.

Levin also took a hard line on steel imports, praising Bush's decision to impose tariffs in March 2002. Levin lobbied to keep the duties in place in late 2003, even though many suburban Detroit auto parts suppliers claimed they were hurt because of rising steel prices. To Levin, the issue was about fair trade, about preserving the right to retaliate against countries who were "dumping" subsidized steel into the United States.

Levin has also become a strong critic of the way U.S. trade with China has evolved, saying the Bush administration has not taken notice as the Asian giant has moved aggressively into high technology here while keeping U.S. imports at a minimum. "As the trade deficit soars, alarms are sounding for U.S. workers and businesses, yet the Bush administration continues to hit 'snooze,' " Levin said.

Levin was a central player in securing enactment of the 2000 law making China a permanent normal U.S. trading partner. Passage by the House was deeply in doubt until Levin and Nebraska Republican Doug Bereuter struck a deal to include language establishing a congressional-executive branch commission to monitor China's behavior on human rights and compliance with trade rules. Levin later was appointed to the commission he helped to create, and his work with the group has formed the basis for much of his later criticism.

In 2001, Levin came out against one of the Bush administration's first-term priorities: reviving procedures that compel Congress to approve or reject, without amendment, the trade deals struck by the president. Levin wanted the legislation to guarantee that enforceable labor rights and environmental quality standards would be required of each nation participating in any trade deal moved along such a fast track. When he did not like the finished product, he voted against it and took many Democrats with him.

Levin split his vote on the two big trade laws enacted in the 1990s. He opposed the 1993 measure implementing the North American Free Trade Agreement, saying the new benefits to Mexico would "tilt the playing field against American workers." But he voted the next year for the law endorsing a global trade agreement and creating the World Trade Organization, saying it would be a net benefit to the domestic economy.

Levin, who has won considerable respect as a judicious legislator, looks for common ground with conservatives. For example, Levin joined with Ohio Republican Rob Portman in legislation to combat illegal drugs, including a bipartisan matching grant initiative, the Drug-Free Communities Act. By 2004, the program supported the operations of 713 community anti-drug coalitions throughout the country.

Levin represents one of the most renowned political proving grounds in the nation: Macomb County outside Detroit, where the term "Reagan Democrat" was coined. After four years as an appointed supervisor in Oakland County, Levin in 1964 won his first elective office, a suburban Detroit state Senate seat. He was minority leader in Lansing, served as state Democratic Party chairman in the late 1960s and was viewed as a rising star when he was the party's gubernatorial nominee in 1970 and 1974. But his low-key manner did not shine in the statewide races, and he lost both.

After a stint as assistant administrator in the U.S. Agency for International Development, Levin ran for the House seat of retiring Democratic Rep. William M. Brodhead in 1982. With his well-known surname — his younger brother, Carl, had been in the Senate almost four years by then — and support from the party establishment, Levin overcame five primary opponents and then won the general election with two-thirds of the vote.

Levin has survived challenges at the polls because he is a prolific fundraiser and stays involved in 12th District community affairs. The Republican-led state legislature redrew Levin's district for this decade to make it more Democratic, and in 2002 Levin easily prevailed with 68 percent of the vote. He increased his share of the vote to 69 percent in 2004, his best showing since 1990.

KEY VOTES

2004

Yes   Extend federal unemployment benefits by 13 weeks

Yes   Pass $283.2 billion, six-year federal highway and mass transit bill

Yes   Approve $146 billion multi-year extension of previously enacted middle-class tax breaks

No   Amend the Constitution to prohibit same-sex marriage

No   Cut corporate taxes $137 billion over 10 years

Yes   Reorganize U.S. intelligence agencies as proposed by Sept. 11 commission

2003

No   Cut taxes by $330 billion through fiscal 2013

Yes   Block Bush rule scaling back overtime pay for some white-collar federal workers

Yes   Do not allow use of search warrants without first notifying subjects

Yes   Allow importation of prescription drugs

No   Create private school voucher program in Washington, D.C.

No   Ban "partial birth" abortion except to save a woman's life

Yes   Split $18.6 billion in Iraq aid into half-grant, half-loan

No   Overhaul Medicare and create prescription drug benefit

CQ VOTE STUDIES

	PARTY UNITY		PRESIDENTIAL SUPPORT	
	Support	Oppose	Support	Oppose
2004	95%	5%	26%	74%
2003	93%	7%	22%	78%
2002	95%	5%	28%	72%
2001	93%	7%	30%	70%
2000	93%	7%	90%	10%

INTEREST GROUPS

	AFL-CIO	ADA	CCUS	ACU
2004	100%	100%	38%	0%
2003	87%	90%	37%	20%
2002	100%	95%	40%	0%
2001	100%	95%	43%	4%
2000	90%	90%	52%	8%

MICHIGAN 12
Suburban Detroit — Warren, Clinton, Southfield

Well-settled suburbs north of 8 Mile Road, Detroit's northern boundary, form Michigan's 12th. The district is fertile ground for Democratic candidates and depends heavily on automobile manufacturing, making the United Auto Workers union a potent political force.

Roughly 70 percent of district residents live in Macomb County, once a largely blue-collar area that typified the "Reagan Democrats," those socially conservative, ancestrally Democratic blue-collar voters who had strong union loyalties but overwhelmingly backed Republican presidential candidates in the 1980s. Macomb has since become more white-collar, and although the county overall narrowly supported George W. Bush in the 2004 presidential election, the 12th's portion of the county gave John Kerry 54 percent of the vote.

The district is lined with auto manufacturing facilities. Warren, the district's most populous city and a traditional Democratic stronghold, is home to the General Motors Technical Center, a 330-acre design and engineering campus. The Army's Tank-automotive and Armaments

Command also is based in Warren. The city gave John Kerry 56 percent of the vote in 2004.

The western part of the district takes in several areas in southern Oakland County, near the Detroit boundary, that are heavily Democratic and African-American: Southfield, which has become a haven for black urban professionals escaping Detroit's crime, Lathrup Village, Oak Park and Royal Oak. Other Oakland County communities in the 12th include Ferndale, Hazel Park and Madison Heights, which also are solidly Democratic but mostly white.

Redistricting following the 2000 census pushed the Democratic district further into the Democrats' column. Republican mapmakers removed some GOP-leaning areas to improve their chances in adjacent districts.

MAJOR INDUSTRY
Auto manufacturing, auto and tank research and design

CITIES
Warren, 138,247; Clinton (unincorporated), 95,648; Southfield, 78,296; St. Clair Shores, 63,096; Roseville, 48,129; Sterling Heights (pt.), 37,935

NOTABLE
The Detroit Zoo is in Royal Oak.

Rep. Carolyn Cheeks Kilpatrick (D)

Elected 1996; 5th term

CAPITOL OFFICE
225-2261
www.house.gov/kilpatrick
1610 Longworth 20515-2213; fax 225-5730

COMMITTEES
Appropriations

HOMETOWN
Detroit

BORN
June 25, 1945, Detroit, Mich.

RELIGION
African Methodist Episcopal

FAMILY
Divorced; two children

EDUCATION
Ferris State U., A.A. 1965; Western Michigan U.,
B.S. 1968 (education); U. of Michigan, M.A. 1972
(education)

CAREER
Teacher

POLITICAL HIGHLIGHTS
Mich. House, 1979-97; candidate for Detroit City
Council, 1991; sought Democratic nomination for
Mich. Senate, 1994

ELECTION RESULTS

2004 GENERAL

Carolyn Cheeks Kilpatrick (D)	173,246	78.2%
Cynthia Cassell (R)	40,935	18.5%
Thomas Lavigne (GREEN)	4,261	1.9%
Eric B. Gordon (LIBERT)	3,211	1.5%

2004 PRIMARY

Carolyn Cheeks Kilpatrick (D)	unopposed

2002 GENERAL

Carolyn Cheeks Kilpatrick (D)	120,869	91.6%
Raymond H. Warner (LIBERT)	11,072	8.4%

PREVIOUS WINNING PERCENTAGES
2000 (89%); 1998 (87%); 1996 (88%)

Kilpatrick once said her district "has the best and worst of America in it." She is blunt about the challenges facing the center-city Detroit neighborhoods that she represents — and about her view that the federal government should play a key role in addressing those problems. She is now in her fourth term on the Appropriations Committee, where she has a seat on the Transportation Subcommittee, and she has focused a great deal on steering federal dollars to her district.

Transportation is at the top of Kilpatrick's long list of needs that call out for government attention in her district, by far the poorest in the state. She has helped in the development of a coordinated Detroit-area transportation strategy that includes a sizable commitment to mass transit, something that has been sorely lacking in the "Motor City." In the 108th Congress, she helped secure more than $7 million toward a new downtown bus station.

Since the Sept. 11, 2001, terrorist attacks, she also has worked to get federal aid for border security and customs operations, including money for equipment to scan trucks for contraband as they cross into the United States on Ambassador Bridge, which spans the Detroit River and connects Detroit with Windsor, Ontario.

Kilpatrick's district includes wide swaths of impoverished center-city neighborhoods and is overwhelmingly Democratic. Unlike many lawmakers, who seek to portray their constituency only in positive terms, Kilpatrick is frank about the problems facing her district, including high infant mortality, high unemployment, significant school drop-out rates, blighted neighborhoods and substandard housing.

Mindful of her constituents' needs and their dependence on federal programs, Kilpatrick is one of Congress' more steadfast liberal voices, though slightly less so than her Democratic colleague from Detroit, John Conyers Jr. In 2001, she cast one of the 66 votes in the House against the final version of the anti-terrorism package written in response to the terrorist attacks, arguing that its enactment severely curtailed civil liberties. She also voted against the package of aid to the airline industry, which was crippled after the attacks, because, she said, "It contains nothing for 100,000 employees who were laid off."

She does break from the liberal ranks when it comes to automobile fuel economy standards, which are anathema to the Detroit-area automobile industry.

Kilpatrick has undertaken a crusade to get corporate America and the federal government to spend more of their advertising dollars with women- and minority-owned media outlets and advertising agencies. In 2000, using a General Accounting Office study as ammunition, she and New Jersey Democrat Robert Menendez helped persuade President Clinton to sign an executive order aimed at giving minority firms a bigger piece of the federal ad budget. Kilpatrick has been working since to codify the Clinton order.

The congresswoman has taken a lead role in the Congressional Black Caucus. She was chosen as a vice chairwoman of the group at the start of the 109th Congress, and during the 2004 elections, she helped organize debates sponsored by the caucus for the Democratic presidential candidates.

Kilpatrick is responsible for a family political legacy. Her son, Kwame, who was her campaign manager at an early age, succeeded her in the state House when she came to Congress and then, in 2001, was elected mayor of Detroit at the age of 31. The new mayor credited his mother and father (a leading Wayne County government official) for instilling in him the obligations of public service.

Mother and son faced some recent criticism, too: At the end of 2004, the Detroit Free Press reported that proponents of a new tunnel under the Detroit River had accused Kilpatrick and her son of blocking the project to protect Ambassador Bridge owner and political supporter, Manuel "Matty" Maroun, who now has a monopoly on cross-border truck traffic. The newspaper also reported that a political action committee the congresswoman had formed — and which was partly funded by Maroun — had funneled more money to the congresswoman's family and friends than to candidates.

Kilpatrick says she favors a second crossing but has questions about the tunnel plans, including the effects on Detroit neighborhoods that would be disrupted by the project and the resulting traffic. As for her PAC's expenditures, her office says all were legitimate political expenses.

A Detroit native, Kilpatrick holds a master's degree in education. She taught business and vocational classes in the Detroit public schools for eight years. Often, in floor debate, she makes her points by discussing the needs of children. She won the first of nine terms in the state House, a full-time job, in 1978. In Lansing, she was the first black woman to serve on the Appropriations Committee, and she once led a coalition of Democratic and Republican lawmakers seeking to block a proposal by popular Republican Gov. John Engler to halt state funding for local transportation programs. But she generally was not regarded as a key player on most issues.

She has hit a few bumps in her political career: She lost a 1991 bid for the Detroit City Council when questions arose about whether she was sufficiently independent from Mayor Coleman Young; and she failed, after changing her mind several times, to win a spot on the 1994 state Senate ballot.

In 1996, when Democratic Rep. Barbara-Rose Collins became the subject of separate investigations by the House ethics committee and the Justice Department into allegations of ethical and financial misconduct, Kilpatrick stepped forward to challenge her one-time political ally. She won a majority of the primary vote and beat Collins by 20 percentage points. The November outcome was a foregone conclusion in the heavily Democratic district. Kilpatrick has since won re-election with ease.

KEY VOTES

2004

Yes	Extend federal unemployment benefits by 13 weeks
Yes	Pass $283.2 billion, six-year federal highway and mass transit bill
No	Approve $146 billion multi-year extension of previously enacted middle-class tax breaks
No	Amend the Constitution to prohibit same-sex marriage
No	Cut corporate taxes $137 billion over 10 years
Yes	Reorganize U.S. intelligence agencies as proposed by Sept. 11 commission

2003

No	Cut taxes by $330 billion through fiscal 2013
Yes	Block Bush rule scaling back overtime pay for some white-collar federal workers
Yes	Do not allow use of search warrants without first notifying subjects
Yes	Allow importation of prescription drugs
No	Create private school voucher program in Washington, D.C.
No	Ban "partial birth" abortion except to save a woman's life
Yes	Split $18.6 billion in Iraq aid into half-grant, half-loan
No	Overhaul Medicare and create prescription drug benefit

CQ VOTE STUDIES

	PARTY UNITY		PRESIDENTIAL SUPPORT	
	Support	Oppose	Support	Oppose
2004	96%	4%	28%	72%
2003	97%	3%	17%	83%
2002	98%	2%	27%	73%
2001	93%	7%	15%	85%
2000	96%	4%	83%	17%

INTEREST GROUPS

	AFL-CIO	ADA	CCUS	ACU
2004	100%	95%	29%	4%
2003	100%	100%	24%	16%
2002	100%	95%	42%	0%
2001	100%	100%	39%	4%
2000	100%	85%	42%	8%

MICHIGAN 13

Part of Detroit; Lincoln Park; Wyandotte

General Motors helped build Detroit through a thriving U.S. auto industry over the first half of the 20th century. The 1967 riots and the 1970s oil crisis decimated the city's economy and turned Detroit into a virtual war zone. The 13th suffered the worst of the riots in terms of property damage and deaths, and for a time, Detroit was known as the "Beirut of America." The city still has a tough reputation and relatively high taxes, and many of the affluent suburbs that surround Detroit have become regional office centers that have lured companies away from the city.

Detroit is divided between the 13th and 14th districts, with a slightly larger share of the city's population living in the 13th. The 13th is a black-majority district, and about three-fourths of its residents live in Detroit. The city steadily declined in population in the 1990s, and fell below 1 million in the 2000 census.

Detroit remains overwhelmingly Democratic, and John Kerry won the 13th's portion of the city with 93 percent of the vote in the 2004 election. Pockets of poverty exist, and the 13th has the state's highest percentage

of households with incomes under $10,000. Wealthy communities to the northeast, such as Grosse Pointe, also are losing population.

Downtown Detroit and the waterfront, covered by the 13th, have been a target for intensive redevelopment. There are two new sporting venues downtown that are part of a massive entertainment complex — Comerica Park opened in 2000 for baseball's Detroit Tigers, and Ford Field opened in 2002 for the National Football League's Detroit Lions. There also are several new casinos and GM and Compuware have relocated their respective headquarters downtown.

Redistricting following the 2000 census renumbered the district from the 15th to the 13th and added the cities of Wyandotte and Lincoln Park, but the changes did not shift the district's overwhelmingly Democratic tilt.

MAJOR INDUSTRY
Auto and auto parts manufacturing, government

CITIES
Detroit (pt.), 511,449; Lincoln Park, 40,008; Wyandotte, 28,006

NOTABLE
The Charles H. Wright Museum of African-American History is in the 13th; Detroit's Ford Field will host the 2006 Super Bowl.

Rep. John Conyers Jr. (D)

CAPITOL OFFICE
225-5126
www.house.gov/conyers
2426 Rayburn 20515-2214; fax 225-0072

COMMITTEES
Judiciary - ranking member

HOMETOWN
Detroit

BORN
May 16, 1929, Detroit, Mich.

RELIGION
Baptist

FAMILY
Wife, Monica Conyers; two children

EDUCATION
Wayne State U., B.A. 1957, LL.B. 1958

MILITARY SERVICE
Mich. National Guard, 1948-50; Army, 1950-54; Army Reserve, 1954-57

CAREER
Lawyer; congressional aide

POLITICAL HIGHLIGHTS
Candidate for mayor of Detroit, 1989, 1993

ELECTION RESULTS

2004 GENERAL

John Conyers Jr. (D)	213,681	83.9%
Veronica Pedraza (R)	35,089	13.8%

2004 PRIMARY

John Conyers Jr. (D)	unopposed

2002 GENERAL

John Conyers Jr. (D)	145,285	83.2%
Dave Stone (R)	26,544	15.2%

PREVIOUS WINNING PERCENTAGES
2000 (89%); 1998 (87%); 1996 (86%); 1994 (81%); 1992 (82%); 1990 (89%); 1988 (91%); 1986 (89%); 1984 (89%); 1982 (97%); 1980 (95%); 1978 (93%); 1976 (92%); 1974 (91%); 1972 (88%); 1970 (88%); 1968 (100%); 1966 (84%); 1964 (84%)

Elected 1964; 21st term

After four decades in Congress, Conyers still positions himself as a champion of the downtrodden, just as he did when he was swept into office alongside Lyndon B. Johnson in 1964. He spends much of his time trying to thwart what he views as GOP efforts to weaken individual rights at the behest of business or law enforcement.

Conyers has served longer than any other House member except John D. Dingell, his fellow Detroit-area Democrat. And like Dingell, he has frequently found it difficult to adapt to life under Republican control.

But since 2001, he has at least found it more pleasant to operate as the top-ranking Democrat on the Judiciary Committee. Conyers has worked closely behind the scenes with Republican Chairman F. James Sensenbrenner Jr. of Wisconsin, despite their frequent public disagreements over policy. That is in contrast to the much stormier six-year relationship that Conyers had with the previous Republican chairman, Henry J. Hyde of Illinois.

Conyers worked with Sensenbrenner in 2001 on a plan to give law enforcement greater legal leeway to fight terrorism in the aftermath of the attacks of Sept. 11. But the House Republican leadership abruptly scrapped the bipartisan bill in favor of its own version, which was quickly rammed through the House. Conyers opposed both that version and the subsequent compromise with the Senate that became law.

The next year, Conyers also opposed the legislation establishing the Department of Homeland Security, saying that it did too little to maintain civil service and union protections for federal workers.

In 2004, Conyers repeatedly pressed the Bush administration to turn over memos and other documents outlining its deliberations over the treatment of detained terrorism suspects. He criticized GOP efforts to limit judges' discretion. And he spoke out strongly against legislation Republicans rushed through Congress in early 2005 seeking to reverse a decision by Florida courts to allow removal of a feeding tube that was keeping a brain-damaged Florida woman named Terri Schiavo alive. "We are no longer a nation of laws but have been reduced to a nation of men," Conyers said.

For all their political differences, Conyers and Sensenbrenner agree that Congress has a constitutional responsibility to serve as a check on the executive branch and that the Judiciary panel must exercise its oversight responsibilities to prevent congressional appropriators from making all the important decisions about how the Justice Department spends its money. With limited success, the two have pressed the Justice Department to account for how it is using powers under the 2001 anti-terrorism law known as the USA Patriot Act.

Having fought almost every social policy battle at least once before, Conyers has become less fiery in his delivery of late but his voice remains strongly partisan. So does his voting record. In 2004, he opposed President Bush 93 percent of the time. And he sided with fellow Democrats 98 percent of the time on votes in which the two parties were in opposition.

A co-founder of the Congressional Black Caucus, Conyers has consistently championed the causes of civil rights, minorities and the poor. He introduced legislation to make the birthday of the Rev. Dr. Martin Luther King Jr. a national holiday four days after the civil rights leader's assassination in 1968, and he pushed the bill until it was enacted in 1983. In 2001, he introduced a bill to ban racial profiling by law enforcement.

In each Congress for more than a decade, Conyers has introduced legislation to set up a commission to study whether the federal government owes reparations to African-American descendants of slaves. His bill has yet to receive a hearing.

Conyers won the gratitude of other Democrats for his vociferous defense of President Clinton during the 1998 impeachment proceedings. He accused Republicans of a politically inspired attempt to remove a twice-elected president on trivial grounds related to his affair with a White House intern. By that time, Conyers was the only remaining Judiciary Committee member from 1974, when the panel had voted to impeach President Nixon for obstruction of justice and abuse of his official powers. Conyers had been on the Nixon administration's infamous "enemies list."

Conyers voted against the 2002 resolution authorizing the use of military force against Iraq, arguing that "we should avoid the horrors of war unless war is really necessary." He has joined with New York Democrat Charles B. Rangel in suggesting that the military draft should be revived, which he said might appropriately dampen enthusiasm for war.

After serving with the Army in Korea, Conyers went home to Detroit and became involved in politics while in law school there. The creation in 1964 of a second black-majority congressional district in the city provided an opening for Conyers, who won a primary race against accountant Richard H. Austin by 108 votes. He won the Democratic district in a rout that November and has won his 20 subsequent terms the same way.

In the House, Conyers has often seemed less interested in legislative brokerage than in being a liberal voice of protest. Twice in the early 1970s, he waged symbolic campaigns for Speaker against Carl Albert of Oklahoma, whom he accused of "stagnation and reaction." And his two quixotic bids to become mayor of Detroit did not enhance his reputation. In 1989, he challenged Mayor Coleman A. Young and finished third in a primary. A 1993 run also failed.

As the 108th Congress ended, the House ethics committee was considering a complaint that Conyers had used his Detroit district office to conduct campaign activity. The panel was expected to rule on the allegation, which Conyers denied, in the 109th Congress.

Conyers has a strong interest in jazz and frequently takes time out to listen to music in his office, where posters of jazz artists are displayed. In 1987, he successfully sponsored a House resolution declaring jazz a "rare and valuable national American treasure." A Washington, D.C., jazz club, HR-57, was named for the resolution.

KEY VOTES

2004
?	Extend federal unemployment benefits by 13 weeks
Yes	Pass $283.2 billion, six-year federal highway and mass transit bill
No	Approve $146 billion multi-year extension of previously enacted middle-class tax breaks
No	Amend the Constitution to prohibit same-sex marriage
No	Cut corporate taxes $137 billion over 10 years
Yes	Reorganize U.S. intelligence agencies as proposed by Sept. 11 commission

2003
No	Cut taxes by $330 billion through fiscal 2013
Yes	Block Bush rule scaling back overtime pay for some white-collar federal workers
?	Do not allow use of search warrants without first notifying subjects
Yes	Allow importation of prescription drugs
No	Create private school voucher program in Washington, D.C.
No	Ban "partial birth" abortion except to save a woman's life
Yes	Split $18.6 billion in Iraq aid into half-grant, half-loan
No	Overhaul Medicare and create prescription drug benefit

CQ VOTE STUDIES

	PARTY UNITY		PRESIDENTIAL SUPPORT	
	Support	Oppose	Support	Oppose
2004	98%	2%	7%	93%
2003	98%	2%	10%	90%
2002	99%	1%	21%	79%
2001	96%	4%	7%	93%
2000	98%	2%	85%	15%

INTEREST GROUPS

	AFL-CIO	ADA	CCUS	ACU
2004	100%	90%	11%	0%
2003	100%	90%	19%	15%
2002	100%	100%	21%	0%
2001	100%	90%	23%	4%
2000	100%	95%	30%	0%

MICHIGAN 14
Parts of Detroit and Dearborn

The auto industry kept Detroit humming for most of this century. The early factories drew people from rural Michigan, Appalachia, the South and Eastern Europe. Then race riots during the summer of 1967 and the oil crisis of the early 1970s sparked an evacuation of the Motor City. Many residents fled to the suburbs, and automakers moved to Mexico and non-union U.S. towns, leaving Detroit with some of the poorest and most crime-ridden neighborhoods in the nation. In 1960, 1.7 million people lived in Detroit; in 2000, its population was 951,000, and more recent census estimates put the population at less than 900,000.

The 14th covers the residential neighborhoods that sprang up north of Detroit's auto plants. It includes slightly less than half of Detroit, which accounts for two-thirds of the district's total population. Although the city's property levels have risen in some areas, demolition of blighted areas has slowed and the murder rate has spiked. The city's finances also are in disarray — a potential problem in an area with a large public sector workforce.

As redrawn following the 2000 census, the 14th includes two-thirds of Dearborn, which is home to Ford Motor Co. and its River Rouge factory — once the largest in the world. Dearborn has a large Arab-American population, with 30 percent of city residents claiming Arab ancestry. The district also includes two cities enveloped by Detroit: Hamtramck, an ethnically diverse enclave, and Highland Park, an overwhelmingly black area that in 2000 had the highest poverty rate (38 percent) in metropolitan Detroit.

The 14th has one of the nation's highest percentages of black residents (61 percent), and is safely Democratic. Detroit's unyielding Democratic bent keeps Republicans from carrying the seat or Wayne County, and John Kerry took 82 percent of the 14th's presidential vote in 2004.

MAJOR INDUSTRY
Auto and auto parts manufacturing, health care

CITIES
Detroit (pt.), 439,821; Dearborn (pt), 64,759; Southgate, 30,136; Allen Park, 29,376; Hamtramck, 22,976

NOTABLE
Woodward Avenue, between 6 Mile and 7 Mile roads, was the nation's first paved road (1909).

Rep. John D. Dingell (D)

Elected December 1955; 25th full term

CAPITOL OFFICE
225-4071
www.house.gov/dingell
2328 Rayburn 20515-2215; fax 226-0371

COMMITTEES
Energy & Commerce - ranking member

HOMETOWN
Dearborn

BORN
July 8, 1926, Colorado Springs, Colo.

RELIGION
Roman Catholic

FAMILY
Wife, Debbie Dingell; four children

EDUCATION
Georgetown U., B.S. 1949 (chemistry), J.D. 1952

MILITARY SERVICE
Army, 1944-46

CAREER
County prosecutor

POLITICAL HIGHLIGHTS
No previous office

ELECTION RESULTS

2004 GENERAL

John D. Dingell (D)	218,409	70.9%
Dawn Anne Reamer (R)	81,828	26.6%
Gregory Stempfle (LIBERT)	3,400	1.1%

2004 PRIMARY

John D. Dingell (D)	unopposed

2002 GENERAL

John D. Dingell (D)	136,518	72.2%
Martin Kaltenbach (R)	48,626	25.7%
Gregory Stempfle (LIBERT)	3,919	2.1%

PREVIOUS WINNING PERCENTAGES
2000 (71%); 1998 (67%); 1996 (62%); 1994 (59%);
1992 (65%); 1990 (67%); 1988 (97%); 1986 (78%);
1984 (64%); 1982 (74%); 1980 (70%); 1978 (77%);
1976 (76%); 1974 (78%); 1972 (68%); 1970 (79%);
1968 (74%); 1966 (63%); 1964 (73%); 1962 (83%);
1960 (79%); 1958 (79%); 1956 (74%); 1955 Special
Election (76%)

Dingell has become known for many things, but two stand out. One is his longevity. The other is his reputation for aggressive oversight. First elected in 1955, Dingell entered his 50th year in Congress at the start of the 109th Congress. He is the longest currently serving member of the House.

Dingell keeps tabs on the executive branch — whether in GOP or Democratic hands — through a constant stream of letters known as "Dingell-grams," detailed and time-consuming document requests he presents to federal agencies. Those were especially potent weapons during his long reign as chairman of the powerful Energy and Commerce Committee, from 1981 through 1994, which ended when Republicans gained the majority. At the time, Dingell also chaired the panel's Subcommittee on Oversight and Investigations, a position he used to instill fear in bureaucrats and, his critics said, ruin reputations unfairly.

Republicans give him grudging respect for mastering the techniques needed to make Congress an effective watchdog. Even as a member of the minority party, Dingell has been able to embarrass the Bush administration into responding to his requests, rather than dismissing them with form letters, as it initially tried to do. President Bush told Dingell he was the "biggest pain in the ass" on Capitol Hill, according to a 2002 story in the Detroit Free Press.

Dingell says the Republican majority has a few things to learn about oversight and believes they have pulled their punches to avoid embarrassing Bush. "We always sent the staff out and said, 'You find the facts, and we'll figure out what the politics are,' " Dingell said in May 2004. "This crowd sends the staff out and says, 'Find the politics, and we'll cook the facts to fit the politics.' That's not a very good way to do oversight."

In one glaring instance, his oversight crusade backfired. With Democrat Henry A. Waxman of California, his colleague on Energy and Commerce, Dingell asked the General Accounting Office in 2001 to probe the involvement of energy companies in the formulation of the Bush administration's energy policy. The GAO ended up filing an unprecedented lawsuit to compel Vice President Dick Cheney to release records. But the quest ended in 2003, when the GAO (now named the Government Accountability Office) declined to appeal a federal judge's ruling that the agency lacked the legal standing to bring such a suit — a possible setback for Congress' investigatory reach.

As he approached 80 years old, Dingell's complex personality and keen political sense still inspired fear. If his imposing frame is not enough to intimidate guileless visitors or political foes who visit his office, a stuffed menagerie of animals that once crossed Dingell's path might do the trick. Although the avid hunter resigned from the National Rifle Association board in 1994 during debate on a crime bill, his aggressive and successful pursuit of big game is key to understanding his cunning, occasional mercilessness and his reputation for ruthless accretion of power. He says he has adopted as his own the aphorism the Corleone family made famous in "The Godfather, Part II": "Keep your friends close, but your enemies closer."

It is a style he learned from his father, John D. Dingell Sr., a New Deal champion of national health insurance who was a Detroit congressman for 22 years until his death in 1955, when the son took over. Dingell picked up the cause of health care. He introduces a national health insurance bill at the start of every Congress, and worked with Republican Charlie Norwood of Georgia in the late-1990s to pass a patients' bill of rights, an effort that lost steam in 2001 after Norwood abandoned Dingell to cut a deal with Bush. Dingell was in the House in 1965 when Congress launched the Medicare health care program for the elderly and disabled.

As Energy and Commerce chairman, Dingell built a fiefdom, running the committee with an iron fist and becoming a potent symbol of the Old Bull Democratic chairmen who made life miserable for the minority. He amassed the broadest committee jurisdiction of any chairman in the post-war era, covering energy, health, communications and several regulatory agencies. Republicans hated his imperious style, but they saw him as a leadership model to emulate when they took control in 1995.

Although in the minority since then, Dingell has frequently outwitted, outmaneuvered and outlasted Republicans on major issues. Against his fervent opposition, he watched Republicans tear down the Depression-era regulatory barriers that had separated banks, brokerages and insurance companies. But he proved to GOP leaders he would not be ignored, blocking ideas he opposed, such as electric utility deregulation, and writing legislation on issues ranging from telecommunications to drinking water quality.

Aside from his views on abortion rights and gun control, both of which he opposes, Dingell on most issues stands with liberal Democrats, supporting civil rights, Great Society programs and expansion of the federal government's role. Even on health care, though, he has been known to part ways with his Democratic colleagues, as he did in 2003 on a bill to allow cheaper prescription drugs to be imported from other countries. "It will allow this country to be flooded with unsafe, counterfeit drugs, drugs that will not do what they should, drugs that are unsafe; drugs that will kill the American people," he said during floor debate.

In 25 general elections, he has slipped to less than 60 percent of the vote only once, when the GOP won control of Congress in 1994. But in his 2002 primary race, he had a close call that almost ended his nearly half-century of service. When post-census reapportionment took a House seat away from Michigan and the Republican-controlled state legislature redrew the congressional map for this decade, Dingell was forced to run against another incumbent House Democrat, eight-year veteran Lynn Rivers. Feminists, environmentalists and gun control advocates teamed up with Rivers and gave Dingell the fight of his political life. But he fought back — and won the primary with 59 percent — with a hefty campaign war chest and a muscular coalition of National Rifle Association members, the auto industry and its union members, business lobbyists and longtime grass-roots activists.

KEY VOTES

2004

Yes Extend federal unemployment benefits by 13 weeks

Yes Pass $283.2 billion, six-year federal highway and mass transit bill

Yes Approve $146 billion multi-year extension of previously enacted middle-class tax breaks

No Amend the Constitution to prohibit same-sex marriage

No Cut corporate taxes $137 billion over 10 years

Yes Reorganize U.S. intelligence agencies as proposed by Sept. 11 commission

2003

No Cut taxes by $330 billion through fiscal 2013

Yes Block Bush rule scaling back overtime pay for some white-collar federal workers

Yes Do not allow use of search warrants without first notifying subjects

No Allow importation of prescription drugs

No Create private school voucher program in Washington, D.C.

Yes Ban "partial birth" abortion except to save a woman's life

Yes Split $18.6 billion in Iraq aid into half-grant, half-loan

No Overhaul Medicare and create prescription drug benefit

CQ VOTE STUDIES

	PARTY UNITY		PRESIDENTIAL SUPPORT	
	Support	Oppose	Support	Oppose
2004	94%	6%	27%	73%
2003	91%	9%	28%	72%
2002	96%	4%	26%	74%
2001	88%	12%	29%	71%
2000	89%	11%	81%	19%

INTEREST GROUPS

	AFL-CIO	ADA	CCUS	ACU
2004	100%	95%	33%	4%
2003	100%	85%	31%	28%
2002	100%	90%	42%	4%
2001	100%	95%	41%	24%
2000	100%	80%	33%	16%

MICHIGAN 15

Southeast – Ann Arbor, Taylor, parts of Dearborn and Dearborn Heights

Situated on the flat land west and south of Detroit, the 15th contains a mix of auto workers, engineers and academics. As redrawn following the 2000 census, the 15th is a Democratic bastion that takes in parts of the old 13th, based in Ann Arbor, and the old 16th, based in Wayne County outside Detroit.

Interstate 94, which joins the eastern and western ends of the 15th in the north, has emerged as an engineering and research corridor where robotics companies who are developing ways to automate auto manufacturing have helped turn Detroit assembly line jobs into highly skilled, computerized work.

At the district's northwestern corner is Ann Arbor, the district's most populous city and home to the University of Michigan's academic community. Ann Arbor votes reliably Democratic, and John Kerry took 76 percent of the vote here in the 2004 presidential election. Ypsilanti, a

working-class town southeast of Ann Arbor, is home to Eastern Michigan University and also reliably backs Democratic candidates.

A little more than 40 percent of the district's residents live in the blue-collar, reliably Democratic suburbs of Wayne County. The 15th's most populous city here is Taylor, which is just east of Detroit Metropolitan Wayne County Airport in Romulus. Dearborn, the western third of which is in the 15th, Dearborn Heights (shared with the 11th) and Inkster form the district's northeast corner.

Monroe County, south of Wayne and Washtenaw counties, borders Lake Erie to the east and the Toledo, Ohio, area to the south. George W. Bush narrowly carried the county in the 2004 presidential election.

MAJOR INDUSTRY
Auto and parts manufacturing, higher education, medical research, steel

CITIES
Ann Arbor, 114,024; Taylor, 65,868; Dearborn Heights (pt.), 44,694; Dearborn (pt.), 33,016; Inkster, 30,115; Romulus, 22,979; Ypsilanti, 22,362

NOTABLE
The National Oceanic and Atmospheric Administration's Great Lakes Environmental Research Laboratory is in Ann Arbor.

Gov. Tim Pawlenty (R)

First elected: 2002
Length of term: 4 years
Term expires: 1/07
Salary: $120,311
Phone: (651) 296-3391

Hometown: Eagan
Born: Nov. 27, 1960;
South St. Paul, Minn.
Religion: Protestant
Family: Wife, Mary Pawlenty; two children
Education: U. of Minnesota, B.A. 1983
(political science), J.D. 1986
Career: Internet consulting firm executive;
lawyer
Political Highlights: Eagan Planning
Commission, 1988-89; Eagan City Council,
1990-92; Minn. House, 1993-2003

Election results:
2002 GENERAL

Tim Pawlenty (R)	999,473	44.4%
Roger Moe (D)	821,268	36.5%
Timothy J. Penny (INDC)	364,534	16.2%
Ken Pentel (GREEN)	50,589	2.3%

Lt. Gov. Carol Molnau (R)

First elected: 2002
Length of term: 4 years
Term expires: 1/07
Salary: $78,197
Phone: (651) 296-3391

STATE LEGISLATURE

Legislature: January-May in odd-
numbered years; February-May in
even-numbered years

House: 134 members, 2-year terms
2005 breakdown: 68R, 66D;
97 men, 37 women
Salary: $31,140; $66/day in session
Phone: (651) 296-2146

Senate: 67 members, 4-year terms
2005 breakdown: 35D, 31R, 1I;
44 men, 23 women
Salary: $31,140; $66/day in session
Phone: (651) 296-0504

STATE TERM LIMITS

Governor: No
House: No
Senate: No

URBAN STATISTICS

CITY	POPULATION
Minneapolis	382,618
St. Paul	287,151
Duluth	86,918
Rochester	85,806
Bloomington	85,172

REGISTERED VOTERS

Voters do not register by party.

POPULATION

2004 population (est.)	5,100,958
2000 population	4,919,479
1990 population	4,375,099
Percent change (1990-2000)	+12.4%
Rank among states (2004)	21

Median age	35.4
Born in state	70.2%
Foreign born	5.3%
Violent crime rate	281/100,000
Poverty level	7.9%
Federal workers	32,833
Military	19,625

REDISTRICTING

Minnesota retained its eight House
seats in reapportionment. The state
legislature failed to agree on a plan
and a state Supreme Court special
redistricting panel adopted a new map
on March 19, 2002.

MISCELLANEOUS

Web: www.state.mn.us
Capital: St. Paul
STATE ELECTION OFFICIAL
(651) 215-1440
**DEMOCRATIC
HEADQUARTERS**
(651) 293-1200
**REPUBLICAN
HEADQUARTERS**
(651) 222-0022

District Statistics

DIST.	2004 VOTE FOR PRESIDENT BUSH	KERRY	WHITE	BLACK	ASIAN	HISP	MEDIAN INCOME	WHITE COLLAR	BLUE COLLAR	SERVICE INDUSTRY	OVER 64	UNDER 18	COLLEGE EDUCATION	RURAL	SQ. MILES
1	51%	47%	93%	1%	2%	3%	$40,941	57%	28%	15%	15%	25%	22%	44%	13,322
2	54	45	92	2	2	3	$61,344	65	23	12	8	30	31	20	3,035
3	51	48	89	4	4	2	$63,816	73	17	10	10	27	40	4	468
4	37	62	78	6	8	5	$46,811	67	19	14	12	26	33	0	202
5	28	71	71	13	5	6	$41,569	67	18	15	12	22	35	0	124
6	57	42	95	1	1	1	$56,862	60	27	12	8	29	25	36	3,081
7	55	43	93	0	1	3	$36,453	53	31	16	17	26	16	66	31,796
8	46	53	95	1	0	1	$37,911	53	30	17	16	25	18	63	27,583
STATE	48	51	88	3	3	3	$47,111	62	24	14	12	26	27	29	79,610
U.S.	50.7	48.3	69	12	4	13	$41,994	60	25	15	12	26	24	21	3,537,438

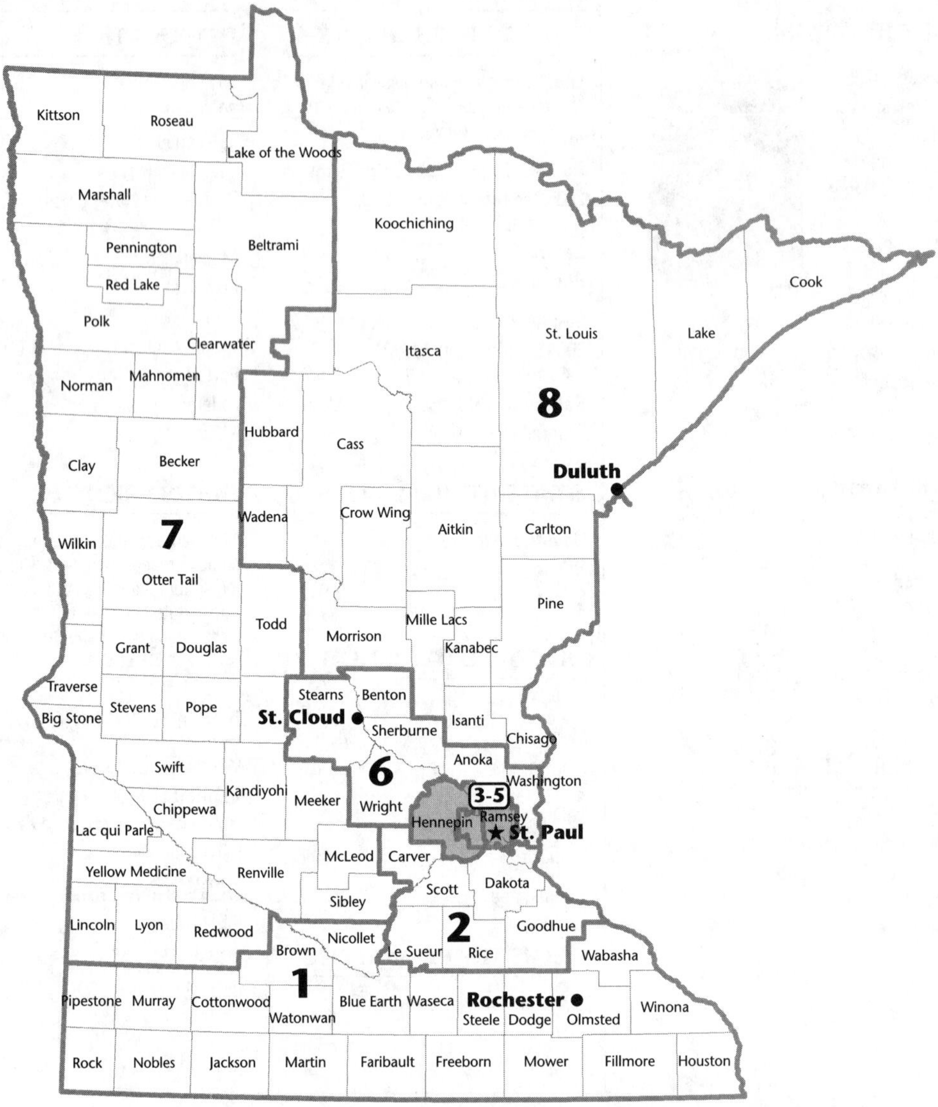

Kittson
Roseau
Lake of the Woods
Marshall
Pennington
Beltrami
Koochiching
Red Lake
Polk
Clearwater
Cook
Norman
Mahnomen
Itasca
St. Louis
Lake
Clay
Becker
Hubbard
Cass
8
Wilkin
Wadena
Crow Wing
Aitkin
Carlton
Duluth ●
7
Otter Tail
Pine
Grant
Douglas
Todd
Morrison
Mille Lacs
Kanabec
Traverse
Stevens
Pope
Stearns
Benton
St. Cloud ●
Sherburne
Isanti
Chisago
Big Stone
Swift
Anoka
Washington
Chippewa
Kandiyohi
Meeker
Wright
6
3-5
Lac qui Parle
Hennepin
Ramsey **★ St. Paul**
Yellow Medicine
Renville
McLeod
Carver
Lincoln
Lyon
Redwood
Sibley
Scott
Dakota
Nicollet
2
Goodhue
Brown
Le Sueur
Rice
Wabasha
Pipestone
Murray
Cottonwood
1
Blue Earth
Waseca
Rochester ●
Winona
Watonwan
Steele
Dodge
Olmsted
Rock
Nobles
Jackson
Martin
Faribault
Freeborn
Mower
Fillmore
Houston

Wright
6
Anoka
Washington
Hennepin
● **Coon Rapids**
Brooklyn Park
Ramsey
3
4
Plymouth
Minneapolis
★ St. Paul
5
Minnetonka
Eden Prairie
Bloomington
● **Eagan**
Carver
2
Scott
Dakota

Sen. Mark Dayton (D)

CAPITOL OFFICE
224-3244
dayton.senate.gov
123 Russell 20510-2305; fax 228-2186

COMMITTEES
Agriculture, Nutrition & Forestry
Armed Services
Homeland Security & Governmental Affairs
Rules & Administration
Joint Printing

HOMETOWN
Minneapolis

BORN
Jan. 26, 1947, Minneapolis, Minn.

RELIGION
Presbyterian

FAMILY
Divorced; two children

EDUCATION
Yale U., B.A. 1969 (psychology)

CAREER
Investment company president; runaway youth
home director; congressional and gubernatorial
aide; social worker; teacher

POLITICAL HIGHLIGHTS
Minn. commissioner of economic development,
1978; Democratic nominee for U.S. Senate, 1982;
Minn. commissioner of energy and economic
development, 1983-86; Minn. auditor, 1991-95;
sought Democratic nomination for governor, 1998

ELECTION RESULTS

2000 GENERAL

Mark Dayton (D)	1,181,553	48.8%
Rod Grams (R)	1,047,474	43.3%
James Gibson (INDC)	140,583	5.8%
others	49,910	2.1%

2000 PRIMARY

Mark Dayton (D)	178,972	41.3%
Michael Ciresi (D)	96,874	22.4%
Jerry R. Janezich (D)	90,074	20.8%
Rebecca Yanisch (D)	63,289	14.6%
others	4,190	1.0%

Elected 2000; 1st term

At the beginning of his fifth year in the Senate, Dayton announced that he would not seek re-election to a second term in 2006. "I do not believe that I am the best candidate to lead the party to victory next year," Dayton said. "I cannot stand to do the constant fundraising necessary to wage a successful campaign, and I cannot be an effective senator while also being a nearly full-time candidate."

His announcement was not a surprise as Republicans had already targeted him as a vulnerable incumbent. A Minneapolis Star Tribune poll in early 2005 showed his favorable rating among Minnesotans had slipped 15 percentage points to 43 percent during 2004. Dayton told the Associated Press he wanted to avoid a re-election process in which "the Republican strategy is to destroy you personally in order to defeat you politically."

Dayton at times seems ill-suited to the profession of U.S. senator. Awkward and stiff in crowds, he displays little affinity for the back-slapping camaraderie of the Capitol corridors. Born into privilege and heir to the Target Corp. retailing fortune, Dayton has devoted his life to public service and liberal causes in the tradition of Minnesota's Democratic icons Hubert H. Humphrey and Walter F. Mondale.

Dayton's ideology and voting record are reminiscent of Paul Wellstone, one of the most liberal members of the Senate until his death in October 2002. Dayton, however, has not sought the spotlight that Wellstone often attracted. He espouses universal health care, opposes tax cuts and has used his own Senate salary to pay for seniors to travel to Canada to purchase cheaper prescription drugs.

True to his liberal beliefs, Dayton has been a constant critic of the Bush administration's handling of the war in Iraq. He voted against the resolution authorizing the war, and he has used his seat on the Armed Services Committee to criticize the administration's conflicting reports on Iraq. At a committee hearing in early 2005, he was visibly upset over the Pentagon's inconsistent estimates of the number of Iraqi security forces that had been trained. After 15 months of training, the Iraqi army is at 9,500, he said, "and many of them are non-functional." He added, "This is an indefensibly poor outcome for all this money and all this effort. We ought to know at this point when we're able to get out."

He was also one of 13 senators to vote against the confirmation of Condoleezza Rice to be secretary of State. During her confirmation hearing, Dayton accused Rice of "hiding the truth" about "matters of life and death, war and peace." He said she and other administration officials had "lied repeatedly, blatantly, intentionally" about prewar intelligence, treatment of detainees, and other issues. "My vote [against Rice] is my statement that this administration lying must stop now," he declared.

Dayton became the object of some ridicule when he closed his Capitol Hill office and moved his staff because of security concerns for three weeks leading up to the 2004 elections. He said the move was in response to a classified security briefing he received as a lawmaker, but no other senator followed his lead and many members took him to task for alarming the public. Dayton defended his decision, saying, "I cannot leave Washington for the relative safety of Minnesota and leave the people I employ exposed to risks of which I have been made aware."

One of Dayton's signature issues in the 108th Congress was pressing to allow seniors to purchase prescription drugs from Canada, where they are usually cheaper. Dayton donated his Senate salary to a Minnesota seniors' group so it could provide free travel on the "Rx Express" for seniors to travel north to buy drugs. When that bus was stopped at the border in October 2003 and inspected by Food and Drug Administration officials, Dayton demanded assurances that border agents were not implementing a "new practice of harassment and intimidation."

Dayton was unhappy with the 2004 spending bill for labor, health and human services and education because poor children in Minnesota stood to receive less money under the measure. Under a new Education Department policy for distribution of Title I funds, which go to low-income schools, 10 states, including Minnesota, stood to lose as much as 10 percent of their usual funding. Dayton noted that his state received $12.3 million less in Title I funding for fiscal 2004 than the previous year, even though the number of low-income students in his state increased by more than 3,600.

"Once again, this legislative process has impoverished the truly needy while it enriches the truly greedy," Dayton said. "Poor schoolchildren don't have full-time lobbyists to prowl the halls of Congress and serve their interests."

Dayton has been an eager pupil of West Virginia's senior senator, Democrat Robert C. Byrd, in learning the Senate's rules and customs. When Democrats were in the majority, Dayton was one of the chamber's most attentive and diligent presiding officers — a job generally seen as a thankless task.

Dayton has not been shy about following Byrd's lead and using a single senator's power to delay floor action on some of Bush's nominations, either to express his opposition to the confirmation or to obtain other concessions. In the spring of 2002, for example, he lifted his objections to the confirmation of a new head of the Air National Guard only after the organization agreed to give the 148th Fighter Wing in Duluth newer F-16C fighter jets to replace its aging fleet.

Dayton's liberal leanings go back to his college days at Yale. While his parents supported Republican Richard M. Nixon for president in 1960 and 1968, Dayton's political hero was Robert F. Kennedy. He protested the Vietnam War and applied the family fortune to left-wing causes. His rebelliousness led the young Dayton to be investigated by the FBI, targeted by the IRS and named to Nixon's enemies list.

His great-grandfather George Dayton started a dry goods store in Minneapolis in 1902 that grew into the nation's fifth-largest retailer, encompassing the Marshall Field's, Mervyn's and Target chains. Dayton Hudson Corp. became Target in 2000.

Dayton briefly dabbled in the family business, but he quickly gravitated to public service, working as a science teacher in New York City's Lower East Side and as a counselor of runaway children in Boston. He served as an aide to Mondale and did a stint as state economic development commissioner. He was the state auditor for four years.

Dayton first ran for the Senate in 1982, spending $7 million and garnering 47 percent of the vote against GOP incumbent David Durenberger. Frugal Minnesotans derided him as a rich boy who tried to buy a Senate seat. Dayton also failed in a 1998 bid to win the Democratic gubernatorial nomination.

In 2000, Dayton spent $12 million from his own accounts to win election to the Senate by 6 percentage points against one-term conservative Republican Rod Grams. Once again criticized for his heavy campaign spending, Dayton countered that because he had plenty of his own money, he would not be beholden to special interest groups. "Persistence pays," he says. "I think eventually people saw that I've been committed to public service."

KEY VOTES

2004
Yes   Pass $318.9 billion, six-year highway and mass transit bill
Yes   Extend assault weapons ban for 10 years
Yes   Restore pay-as-you-go rules for new tax cuts and entitlement spending
Yes   Criminalize harm to a fetus in an attack on the mother
Yes   Increase mandatory child care funding to states by $6 billion over five years
No   Amend the Constitution to prohibit same-sex marriage
Yes   Approve $146 billion multi-year extension of previously enacted middle-class tax breaks
Yes   Reorganize U.S. intelligence agencies as proposed by Sept. 11 commission
Yes   Cut corporate taxes $137 billion over 10 years

2003
Yes   Delay Bush changes to Clean Air Act
No   Allow confirmation vote on Miguel A. Estrada to the U.S. Court of Appeals for the D.C. Circuit
Yes   Block a Bush proposal opening Alaska's Arctic National Wildlife Refuge to oil drilling
Yes   Limit size of Bush's proposed tax cut to $350 billion through fiscal 2013
Yes   Overhaul Medicare and create prescription drug benefit
Yes   Block Bush rule scaling back overtime pay for some white-collar federal workers
Yes   Split $20 billion in Iraq aid into half-grant, half-loan
No   Ban "partial birth" abortion except to save a woman's life
No   Stop proposal allowing travel to Cuba
Yes   Allow final vote on energy policy overhaul

CQ VOTE STUDIES

	PARTY UNITY		PRESIDENTIAL SUPPORT	
	Support	Oppose	Support	Oppose
2004	91%	9%	60%	40%
2003	94%	6%	49%	51%
2002	95%	5%	68%	32%
2001	99%	1%	60%	40%

INTEREST GROUPS

	AFL-CIO	ADA	CCUS	ACU
2004	100%	95%	53%	12%
2003	100%	75%	35%	20%
2002	100%	95%	45%	11%
2001	100%	100%	36%	4%

Sen. Norm Coleman (R)

Elected 2002; 1st term

He was at Woodstock, he was a rock band roadie, and he organized a student strike after the 1970 shootings at Kent State. Not a typical résumé for a Republican, but for Coleman, politics has been an evolution. His defining trait in Congress is his pragmatism. Neither party can predict how he will vote.

A prime example is his position on the controversial issue of opening Alaska's Arctic National Wildlife Refuge to oil drilling. Democrats who wanted his support for a ban on drilling as well as Republicans who favored opening the land up for energy exploration could not be sure where Coleman would stand in his early months in the Senate. That is because Coleman let it be known that a drilling bill that also contained assistance for Minnesota's energy interests could influence his position. "If I have a chance to deliver for my constituents, I will do that," he told the Minneapolis Star Tribune. "For some, ANWR's a religion. It's not for me. . . . I want to be measured by what I deliver. I really do. That's who I am."

In the end, he voted twice to ban drilling, once in 2003 and again in 2005.

Coleman tries to position himself as a moderate voice within the Republican Party, which is something he may have to achieve to obtain electoral security in politically competitive Minnesota.

In 2002, President Bush hand-picked Coleman to challenge liberal Sen. Paul Wellstone, with whom Coleman once was allied. Less than two weeks before the election, Wellstone was killed in an airplane crash. After the tragedy, the conventional wisdom was that the seat would stay Democratic, considering the outpouring of public sympathy for the loss of Wellstone and the fame of the replacement Democrat in the race, Walter F. Mondale, the former vice president. But Coleman eked out a win by just 2 percentage points and helped the GOP clinch control of the Senate for the 108th Congress.

Coleman lines up with Bush on most defense, trade and tax issues, including support for reduced regulation of business and for fast-track authority that allows the president to negotiate trade pacts that may not be amended by Congress. Coleman supported White House proposals for creating a federal prescription drug benefit through the Medicare program, establishing the Homeland Security Department, waging war against Iraq and permitting workers to privately invest some of their Social Security payroll taxes. He supports making permanent the 2001 Bush tax cut. Yet Coleman said the second wave of tax cuts the president proposed in 2003 were too costly and would not stimulate the economy quickly enough. He joined 10 moderate senators to draft an alternative plan.

Coleman scored an early coup as a freshman when he was named chairman of the Governmental Affairs panel's Permanent Subcommittee on Investigations, one of the more powerful forums in Congress for inquiries into government, business and political malfeasance. Coleman in 2004 and 2005 guided a subcommittee investigation that dug up evidence that Saddam Hussein skimmed billions of dollars from a United Nations program that permitted Iraqi oil sales only to pay for food, medicine and other essentials. He called for the resignation of U.N. Secretary General Kofi Annan, saying he should be held accountable for failing to stop corruption in the program.

As a freshman senator, Coleman also competed for a career-enhancing leadership role. He ran for chairman of the party's fundraising arm in the Senate, the National Republican Senatorial Committee. He lost by one vote, to Elizabeth Dole of North Carolina.

With his New York accent, styled hair and glinting smile, Coleman

CAPITOL OFFICE
224-5641
coleman.senate.gov
320 Hart 20510-2303; fax 224-1152

COMMITTEES
Agriculture, Nutrition & Forestry
Foreign Relations
(Western Hemisphere, Peace Corps & Narcotics Affairs - chairman)
Homeland Security & Governmental Affairs
(Permanent Investigations - chairman)
Small Business & Entrepreneurship

HOMETOWN
St. Paul

BORN
Aug. 17, 1949, Brooklyn, N.Y.

RELIGION
Jewish

FAMILY
Wife, Laurie Coleman; four children (two deceased)

EDUCATION
Hofstra U., B.A. 1971 (political science); Brooklyn Law School, attended 1972-74; U. of Iowa, J.D. 1976

CAREER
Lawyer; state prosecutor and solicitor general; city welfare aide

POLITICAL HIGHLIGHTS
Sought Democratic nomination for mayor of St. Paul, 1989; mayor of St. Paul, 1994-2002 (served as a Democrat 1994-96); Republican nominee for governor, 1998

ELECTION RESULTS

2002 GENERAL

Norm Coleman (R)	1,116,697	49.5%
Walter F. Mondale (D)	1,067,246	47.3%
Jim Moore (INDC)	45,139	2.0%

2002 PRIMARY

Norm Coleman (R)	195,630	94.4%
Jack Shepard (R)	11,678	5.6%

might seem an unlikely breadbasket politician but he sits on the Agriculture Committee and has a large portfolio of farm issues. Coleman wants to expand farm loans and create a grant program for rural small businesses. He has spoken in support of alternative energy sources, particularly ethanol and biodiesel made from Minnesota corn and soybeans. He backed energy legislation during the 108th Congress that had the potential to double ethanol production over 10 years.

Coleman, a Brooklyn native, grew up part of a large, extended family. His high school classmate was New York Democratic Sen. Charles E. Schumer. In the 1960s, Coleman was a liberal, attended the famed hippie music festival known as Woodstock, and traveled with the band Ten Years After.

While student body president at Hofstra University in Hempstead, N.Y., on Long Island, he led anti-war protests and organized a student strike in 1970 after protesters at Kent State University were shot by members of the Ohio National Guard. He brokered a compromise with the administration that averted the complete shutdown of the school. After graduation, a mentor who had become a vice president at the University of Iowa's law school offered Coleman the chance to attend tuition-free by working as a graduate assistant. He earned his law degree and was recruited by the Minnesota attorney general, where he became a prosecutor.

From the beginning of his political career in 1989, he did not fit comfortably with Democratic Party leaders, and he failed to get the party's endorsement to run for mayor of St. Paul that year. Four years later, he ran against the party's endorsed candidate and won. Coleman has always been more conservative than Minnesota's Democratic-Farmer-Labor Party on fiscal and social issues. He opposes abortion and supports "pro-family" issues, a result he says of losing two of his four children in infancy to the incurable genetic disorder known as Zellweger syndrome. The deaths, he has said, gave him resolve to value every life.

As mayor of St. Paul during the economic boom of the 1990s, Coleman developed increasingly pro-business sentiments while working to revitalize the city. Democrats, he said, defended the "status quo" favoring labor, while he tried to keep a lid on wages and benefits.

In December 1996, Coleman switched parties, officially became a Republican, and was re-elected the following year. Democrats accused him of political opportunism, as it was widely anticipated he was preparing to run for governor in 1998. As expected, he entered the governor's race as the GOP nominee, only to be defeated by Reform Party candidate Jesse Ventura. Yet the statewide name recognition Coleman developed in that race — and his potential to cut into the Democratic vote in St. Paul and other cities — convinced GOP strategists that he was their pick to take on Wellstone in 2002.

Coleman ran on his eight years as mayor, during which the city enjoyed job growth, downtown revitalization, and the return of major league hockey to Minnesota for the first time since the North Stars left for Dallas in 1993 — all accomplished without a raise in property taxes. Coleman said his bipartisan approach would make him more effective than Wellstone, who was known more for standing by his principles than for getting bills passed.

The contest seemed deadlocked when Wellstone, his wife, daughter, three aides and two pilots died in the crash of their campaign plane in northern Minnesota. Democrats replaced Wellstone on the ballot with Mondale, a Minnesota political icon who was vice president under President Carter and the 1984 Democratic presidential nominee.

Many Democrats expected a replay of Missouri's Senate race in 2000, when Democrat Mel Carnahan died in a campaign plane crash and was elected posthumously. But the tide turned when a televised memorial for Wellstone turned overtly partisan and triggered a backlash against Mondale.

KEY VOTES

2004

Yes	Pass $318.9 billion, six-year highway and mass transit bill
No	Extend assault weapons ban for 10 years
No	Restore pay-as-you-go rules for new tax cuts and entitlement spending
Yes	Criminalize harm to a fetus in an attack on the mother
Yes	Increase mandatory child care funding to states by $6 billion over five years
Yes	Amend the Constitution to prohibit same-sex marriage
Yes	Approve $146 billion multi-year extension of previously enacted middle-class tax breaks
Yes	Reorganize U.S. intelligence agencies as proposed by Sept. 11 commission
Yes	Cut corporate taxes $137 billion over 10 years

2003

No	Delay Bush changes to Clean Air Act
Yes	Allow confirmation vote on Miguel A. Estrada to the U.S. Court of Appeals for the D.C. Circuit
Yes	Block a Bush proposal opening Alaska's Arctic National Wildlife Refuge to oil drilling
No	Limit size of Bush's proposed tax cut to $350 billion through fiscal 2013
Yes	Overhaul Medicare and create prescription drug benefit
No	Block Bush rule scaling back overtime pay for some white-collar federal workers
No	Split $20 billion in Iraq aid into half-grant, half-loan
Yes	Ban "partial birth" abortion except to save a woman's life
Yes	Stop proposal allowing travel to Cuba
Yes	Allow final vote on energy policy overhaul

CQ VOTE STUDIES

	PARTY UNITY		PRESIDENTIAL SUPPORT	
	Support	Oppose	Support	Oppose
2004	91%	9%	92%	8%
2003	92%	8%	98%	2%

INTEREST GROUPS

	AFL-CIO	ADA	CCUS	ACU
2004	25%	30%	100%	84%
2003	0%	15%	91%	85%

Rep. Gil Gutknecht (R)

Elected 1994; 6th term

Usually easygoing and good-natured, Gutknecht is irritated that prescription drugs manufactured in the United States often are sold at much lower prices in other countries than here at home. He resisted pressure from his party leadership and introduced a measure in the 108th Congress to lower prescription drug costs by allowing the importation of cheaper drugs from abroad.

Gutknecht (GOOT-neck) has charts and studies ever-ready to pull out to demonstrate to other members, the public and the press how much more Americans pay for their drugs than the rest of the world. He also has studied up on anti-counterfeit technologies to ward off opponents who say importing drugs is unsafe.

Gutknecht won a victory in 2003 when the House passed, 243-186, his bill to allow the importation of drugs from 25 industrialized nations. That vote came after Missouri Republican Jo Ann Emerson was persuaded to switch her vote from no to yes on the GOP Medicare bill providing prescription drug coverage for seniors after the leadership promised her a floor vote on the drug importation bill.

The victory, however, was short-lived. The drug importation language was dropped in final congressional negotiations after pressure from the White House. Gutknecht and Emerson voted no on the final version of the bill, and then left the floor quickly to avoid a repeat of the arm-twisting.

Gutknecht sits on the Agriculture Committee, where in the 109th he is the chairman of the Department Operations, Oversight, Nutrition and Forestry Subcommittee. This is a good slot for him as the 1st District is a largely rural area where corn, soybeans and sugar beets are grown and dairy cattle and hogs are raised. Gutknecht is known to have a weakness for Spam, the oft-derided processed meat loaf produced by Hormel Foods Corp. located in his district. He passes out tins to his colleagues and in 2000 persuaded the Library of Congress to hold an exhibit on the product's place in American life.

Gutknecht, who likes to remind his constituents that his name means "good hired hand" in German, goes to great lengths to lobby for the agricultural interests in his district, which is also home to the Jolly Green Giant of processed-vegetable fame. Gutknecht and other Midwestern lawmakers scored a victory in the 2002 farm law, which included a three-and-a-half year, $1.3 billion dairy price support program. He defends genetically modified food products that have come under fire from some environmental groups.

Gutknecht is a common-sense fellow who doesn't put on airs. In his down-to-earth way, he believes that careful control of government spending will be the key to eventually bringing about the return of surpluses. "The demand for spending is enormous," he said. "Those of us who believe we have to continue to apply fiscal discipline are many times outnumbered."

That belief resulted in a rare breach in the united front of GOP House members when Gutknecht raised concerns over President Bush's $2.2 trillion 2004 budget proposal that included a $1.49 trillion tax package. Gutknecht supports tax cuts, but had reservations when it was being done against a backdrop of rising deficits. "It's going to be very difficult for me, at least, to justify to my constituents that we need additional tax relief at a time we're trying to fight a war, we're trying to provide prescription drugs, we're trying to improve domestic security," he said.

A deficit hawk who sat on the Budget Committee for four terms before departing at the start of the 109th because of term limits, Gutknecht threat-

CAPITOL OFFICE
225-2472
gil@mail.house.gov
www.gil.house.gov
425 Cannon 20515-2301; fax 225-3246

COMMITTEES
Agriculture
(Department Operations, Oversight, Nutrition & Forestry - chairman)
Government Reform
Science

HOMETOWN
Rochester

BORN
March 20, 1951, Cedar Falls, Iowa

RELIGION
Roman Catholic

FAMILY
Wife, Mary Gutknecht; three children

EDUCATION
U. of Northern Iowa, B.A. 1973 (business)

CAREER
Real estate broker; school supplies salesman; auctioneer; computer software salesman

POLITICAL HIGHLIGHTS
Minn. House, 1983-95

ELECTION RESULTS

2004 GENERAL

Gil Gutknecht (R)	193,132	59.6%
Leigh Pomeroy (D)	115,088	35.5%
Greg Mikkelson (INDC)	15,569	4.8%

2004 PRIMARY

Gil Gutknecht (R)	unopposed

2002 GENERAL

Gil Gutknecht (R)	163,570	61.5%
Steve Andreasen (D)	92,165	34.7%
Greg Mikkelson (GREEN)	9,964	3.8%

PREVIOUS WINNING PERCENTAGES
2000 (56%); 1998 (55%); 1996 (53%); 1994 (55%)

ened to oppose the 2004 congressional budget resolution because it did not control spending as much as he would have liked. The leadership won his support only after agreeing to hold a floor vote on legislation to require Congress to stick to its budget or risk across-the-board spending cuts. After a marathon debate, that legislation was defeated, 146-268.

Early in 2005, Gutknecht was one of 12 House Republicans to vote no on the GOP-drafted budget resolution, saying that GOP leaders and the Bush administration were "in denial," in refusing to acknowledge the costs of the new Medicare prescription drug benefit.

Gutknecht, who likes to read military histories and can cite details from biographies of Abraham Lincoln and Winston Churchill, is more skeptical than many in his party about large increases in military spending. He says he believes in a strong defense, but "just look at the Defense Department and the amount of waste and duplication and mismanagement that we see."

Gutknecht has invested much energy in an effort that is politically appealing, though it bothers some of his colleagues: cutting back on House members' pensions. He wants to bar members from accruing additional pension benefits after they have served six terms, which would be an incentive for members to leave after a dozen years in office.

A native of Cedar Falls, Iowa, and a graduate of the University of Northern Iowa there, Gutknecht was active in Republican campaigns from an early age. He is a skilled pitchman — for years, he sold school supplies, and then worked as an auctioneer. After college, a sales job took him to southeastern Minnesota. He won a seat in the Minnesota House at 31 and spent a dozen years there as a loyal team player in the Independent-Republican caucus, attracting attention for his considerable oratorical ability and rising to the post of minority whip.

After exploring a bid for an open Senate seat in 1994, he shifted his focus to winning a House seat when Democrat Timothy J. Penny decided to leave Congress after six terms. With his base in the district's leading population center, Rochester, and his ties to the GOP hierarchy, Gutknecht easily got the party's nod and overwhelmed former Republican Rep. Arlen I. Erdahl's comeback bid in the primary. In the general election, Gutknecht won with 55 percent of the vote against state Sen. John C. Hottinger.

As the 1st District was configured in the 1990s, it was a classic swing district, and Gutknecht never captured more than 56 percent in his first four elections. The map drawn following the 2000 census gave the 1st a slightly greater GOP lean, but it is still a competitive district. Gutknecht took 60 percent against Democrat Leigh Pomeroy in 2004.

KEY VOTES

2004

No Extend federal unemployment benefits by 13 weeks

No Pass $283.2 billion, six-year federal highway and mass transit bill

Yes Approve $146 billion multi-year extension of previously enacted middle-class tax breaks

Yes Amend the Constitution to prohibit same-sex marriage

Yes Cut corporate taxes $137 billion over 10 years

No Reorganize U.S. intelligence agencies as proposed by Sept. 11 commission

2003

Yes Cut taxes by $330 billion through fiscal 2013

No Block Bush rule scaling back overtime pay for some white-collar federal workers

Yes Do not allow use of search warrants without first notifying subjects

Yes Allow importation of prescription drugs

Yes Create private school voucher program in Washington, D.C.

Yes Ban "partial birth" abortion except to save a woman's life

No Split $18.6 billion in Iraq aid into half-grant, half-loan

No Overhaul Medicare and create prescription drug benefit

CQ VOTE STUDIES

	PARTY UNITY		PRESIDENTIAL SUPPORT	
	Support	Oppose	Support	Oppose
2004	97%	3%	82%	18%
2003	93%	7%	87%	13%
2002	94%	6%	78%	22%
2001	94%	6%	84%	16%
2000	92%	8%	24%	76%

INTEREST GROUPS

	AFL-CIO	ADA	CCUS	ACU
2004	13%	5%	90%	92%
2003	21%	15%	89%	84%
2002	22%	0%	85%	100%
2001	17%	0%	83%	96%
2000	0%	5%	80%	92%

MINNESOTA 1
South — Rochester, Mankato

One of Minnesota's three rural districts, the 1st runs across the state's entire southern border from South Dakota to the Mississippi River, cut horizontally by Interstate 90 and vertically by Interstate 35. While the rural areas continue to lose population, cities such as Rochester, home to the Mayo Clinic and an IBM facility, and Mankato thrive. But the district's economy is dominated by agriculture and food processing, and a push is under way to establish a university in Rochester.

Corn, soybeans, sugar beets, hogs and dairy are staples of the agricultural economy. Food processing — from fresh turkey to canned soups — is more prevalent in the western half of the district, where there is no town with more than 20,000 people. Although still more than 90 percent white, Spanish, Hmong, Lao and Somali immigrants have come to take agricultural jobs in towns such as Worthington, which has the state's second-highest enrollment of non-English speakers in its schools, following St. Paul.

While many towns and small farmers support the Democratic-Farmer-

Labor Party, Republicans have made gains by preaching fiscal conservatism and stressing rural and farm issues. George W. Bush took 51 percent of the district's vote in the 2004 presidential election.

Larger farms — particularly dairy — in the east support Republicans. Redistricting following the 2000 census added western farmlands but maintained the district's competitive composition and slight Republican lean. Rochester, once solidly Republican, has begun to support some Democrats. Blue-collar workers from the Austin-based Hormel meat-packing company, as well as the city of Albert Lea, form a Democratic stronghold. College communities in Mankato (Minnesota State University) and Winona (Winona State University) also support Democrats.

MAJOR INDUSTRY
Agriculture, food processing, health care

CITIES
Rochester, 85,806; Mankato, 32,427; Winona, 27,069; Austin, 23,314; Owatonna, 22,434

NOTABLE
Austin, the birthplace of Spam, is home to the Spam Museum.

Rep. John Kline (R)

CAPITOL OFFICE
225-2271
www.house.gov/kline
1429 Longworth 20515-2302; fax 225-2595

COMMITTEES
Armed Services
Education & Workforce

HOMETOWN
Lakeville

BORN
Sept. 6, 1947, Allentown, Pa.

RELIGION
Methodist

FAMILY
Wife, Vicky Kline; two children

EDUCATION
Rice U., B.A. 1969 (biology); Shippensburg U., M.S. 1988 (public administration)

MILITARY SERVICE
Marine Corps, 1969-94

CAREER
Think tank executive; farmer; management consultant; Marine officer

POLITICAL HIGHLIGHTS
Republican nominee for U.S. House, 1998, 2000

ELECTION RESULTS

2004 GENERAL

John Kline (R)	206,313	56.4%
Teresa Daly (D)	147,527	40.3%
Doug Williams (INDC)	11,822	3.2%

2004 PRIMARY

John Kline (R)	unopposed

2002 GENERAL

John Kline (R)	152,970	53.3%
Bill Luther (D)	121,121	42.2%
Samuel D. Garst (NNT)	12,430	4.3%

Elected 2002; 2nd term

With the nation at war, military issues are the focus for Kline, a retired Marine who carried the "football" — a briefcase containing the codes that would be used to launch a nuclear attack — for Presidents Carter and Reagan. He is one of the Bush administration's staunchest defenders of the war in Iraq. When critics compare it unfavorably to the U.S. experience in Vietnam, Kline says the history lesson should be about withdrawing troops before the war is won. A similar pull-out from Iraq would be a "horrible breach of faith," the Vietnam veteran says. "I'm not going to let that happen."

As a member of the Armed Services Committee, Kline has surveyed conditions and visited troops in Afghanistan and Iraq and returned encouraged by progress made and with renewed resolve to maintain the American military presence there as long as needed. He is one of the few members of Congress with a child scheduled for deployment. His son is an Army helicopter pilot. "I'm worried about him," he says. "But I'm worried about them all."

Kline cuts an impressive figure. He has a straight-arrow military bearing befitting his 25 years in the service along with an easygoing charm that serves him well in the political arena. The military probably contributed to Kline's salient political trait — persistence. He lost two bids for the House to the same Democrat before finally winning a seat in 2002 in a newly drawn, GOP-leaning district concentrated in the Twin Cities suburbs.

Kline's concerns about reductions in personnel and spending for the armed forces inspired his interest in political office. His service was important job-training experience. "My opinion is solicited and I'm brought into conversations earlier than if I didn't have that experience," he says.

Kline was one of the conservative Republicans who joined Armed Services Committee Chairman Duncan Hunter of California in digging in their heels and refusing to approve the Sept. 11 Commission's recommended restructuring of intelligence agencies until they were confident that Defense Department battlefield needs would not be jeopardized. He is adamant about the need to increase troop strength and joined committee Democrats to block a proposal by Defense Secretary Donald Rumsfeld seeking more leeway to force the retirement of senior officers.

In 2005, Kline led the debate on the House floor on a resolution urging the administration to challenge a court ruling that could stop military recruiters from visiting university campuses. And, just a few months into office, he ushered through legislation extending a law excusing active duty personnel from making payments on college loans.

Kline is a strong fiscal and social conservative. He wants to see the 2001 tax cuts made permanent and believes that the Social Security system should be overhauled to allow workers to invest some of their payroll contributions as they choose. Klein opposes abortion except in cases of rape or incest. His record earned him a "True Blue Award" from The Family Research Council, which favors traditional marriage and anti-abortion positions.

A tragic loss suffered by a family in his district moved him to press for tougher regulations over the rapidly developing human tissue industry. The 23-year-old son of a Minnesota couple had died following what should have been routine knee surgery for an arthritic condition because tissue used in the surgery was not properly refrigerated.

Kline grew up in Texas, where his father owned a small-town newspaper. His mother managed the Corpus Christi Symphony Orchestra for 40 years.

He joined the ROTC at Rice University in Houston while earning a biology degree and later received a master's in public administration from Shippensburg University in Pennsylvania.

During his career with the Marines, in addition to carrying the "football," Kline was a helicopter pilot in Vietnam, commanded aviation forces in Somalia, and flew the presidential helicopter Marine One. He also worked at Marine headquarters as a program development officer, responsible for developing a long-range spending plan. In 1994, he retired with the rank of colonel, settled in Lakeville, Minn. with his wife, and helped his father-in-law manage the family farm in Houston County, at the southeastern tip of the state.

In 1998, he contemplated running for Congress, and sought the counsel of friend James Baker, Reagan's former chief of staff whom he met during his tour of duty at the White House. Baker administered a "dose of reality," telling Kline, "Well, you don't have your party's nomination, you are running against an incumbent, and you don't have any money. Other than that, you're in good shape."

Kline spent months making visits to delegates whose support he would need at the nominating convention. "I would walk up and ring their doorbells," he says. "Sometimes I would be invited in. Sometimes we'd be standing in the doorway talking. Sometimes I'd leave them a note."

Kline got the GOP nomination in 1998 at an old-fashioned, Minnesota-style convention held in a local junior high school. Abortion politics played a role. Both Kline and his opponent, state senator Linda Runbeck, opposed abortion rights, but state anti-abortion activists were riled that Runbeck had failed to back one of their positions four years earlier, so they lobbied for Kline. He lost in the general election to Democratic incumbent Rep. Bill Luther. In 2000, he challenged Luther again, this time getting help from national Republican committees. He lost again, but only by 5,000 votes.

After the census that year, redistricting paired Luther with GOP Rep. Mark Kennedy in the new 6th District. Luther moved his residence to the redrawn 2nd District, which held only about 39 percent of his former constituency and was far more Republican than before. Kline challenged him again. Luther tried to portray Kline as an "extremist," and the state Democratic Party ran a radio ad claiming he would "end Social Security as we know it." But Kline's message of lower taxes, smaller government and a strong military resonated with voters of the 2nd District.

In 2004, Kline easily won re-election against Democrat Teresa Daly, a city council member from Burnsville.

KEY VOTES

2004

No Extend federal unemployment benefits by 13 weeks

No Pass $283.2 billion, six-year federal highway and mass transit bill

Yes Approve $146 billion multi-year extension of previously enacted middle-class tax breaks

Yes Amend the Constitution to prohibit same-sex marriage

Yes Cut corporate taxes $137 billion over 10 years

Yes Reorganize U.S. intelligence agencies as proposed by Sept. 11 commission

2003

Yes Cut taxes by $330 billion through fiscal 2013

No Block Bush rule scaling back overtime pay for some white-collar federal workers

No Do not allow use of search warrants without first notifying subjects

No Allow importation of prescription drugs

Yes Create private school voucher program in Washington, D.C.

Yes Ban "partial birth" abortion except to save a woman's life

No Split $18.6 billion in Iraq aid into half-grant, half-loan

Yes Overhaul Medicare and create prescription drug benefit

CQ VOTE STUDIES

	PARTY UNITY		PRESIDENTIAL SUPPORT	
	Support	Oppose	Support	Oppose
2004	99%	1%	94%	6%
2003	98%	2%	98%	2%

INTEREST GROUPS

	AFL-CIO	ADA	CCUS	ACU
2004	7%	5%	100%	96%
2003	0%	5%	100%	84%

MINNESOTA 2
Southern Twin Cities suburbs

Located south of the Twin Cities, the 2nd includes all or part of seven rapidly growing counties. Transformed from largely rural to suburb-dominated during redistricting following the 2000 census, the district now reflects the 1990s population influx to the Minneapolis-St. Paul area.

Residents can hop on Interstate 35 and shoot into the Twin Cities from Scott, the fastest-growing county in the state, or Dakota county. New, expensive housing developments underscore the area's higher incomes, and population increases in Carver, Scott and particularly Dakota (shared with the 4th District) have made these counties younger and wealthier.

Goodhue, Le Sueur and Rice counties retain an agricultural feel, although people are beginning to move here as well. The cost of living has not yet skyrocketed in these rural areas, however.

Scott and Carver counties propel conservative Republicans to office, while Dakota County has some working-class areas that are faithful Democratic-Farmer-Labor Party supporters. But their political voice is competing with growing numbers of young families, who tend to vote socially progressive but fiscally conservative.

The Rice County towns of Northfield — home to St. Olaf and Carleton colleges — and Faribault also provide Democratic votes, while Goodhue County remains a conservative farming area.

Despite a downturn in the airline industry, Northwest Airlines, which makes its headquarters in Eagan, remains an economic linchpin for the region, and the company is promoting an $860 million airport expansion plan at the nearby Minneapolis airport (located in the 5th). Casinos are big business for the Shakopee Mdewakanton Sioux tribe in Prior Lake.

MAJOR INDUSTRY
Manufacturing, casinos, aviation

CITIES
Eagan, 63,557; Burnsville, 60,220; Apple Valley, 45,527; Lakeville, 43,128

NOTABLE
The late Sen. Paul Wellstone was a political science professor at Carleton College before beginning his political career; Green Giant food manufacturer was founded in Le Sueur.

Rep. Jim Ramstad (R)

Elected 1990; 8th term

CAPITOL OFFICE
225-2871
mn03@mail.house.gov
www.house.gov/ramstad
103 Cannon 20515-2303; fax 225-6351

COMMITTEES
Ways & Means
    (Oversight - chairman)

HOMETOWN
Minnetonka

BORN
May 6, 1946, Jamestown, N.D.

RELIGION
Protestant

FAMILY
Single

EDUCATION
U. of Minnesota, B.A. 1968; George Washington U., J.D. 1973

MILITARY SERVICE
Army Reserve, 1968-74

CAREER
Lawyer; professor; congressional and state legislative aide

POLITICAL HIGHLIGHTS
Minn. Senate, 1981-91

ELECTION RESULTS

2004 GENERAL

Jim Ramstad (R)	231,871	64.6%
Deborah Watts (D)	126,665	35.3%

2004 PRIMARY

Jim Ramstad (R)	19,232	89.9%
Burton Hanson (R)	2,159	10.1%

2002 GENERAL

Jim Ramstad (R)	213,334	72.0%
Darryl Tyree Stanton (D)	82,575	27.9%

PREVIOUS WINNING PERCENTAGES
2000 (68%); 1998 (72%); 1996 (70%); 1994 (73%); 1992 (64%); 1990 (67%)

Ramstad represents Minnesota's most affluent district. The 3rd is upscale, suburban and leans Republican, and district voters tend to be more moderate on social issues. They show a strong desire for environmental protections and are more inclined to back abortion rights. Ramstad does his best to reflect their interests.

He has worked with a group of other moderates to produce a compromise rewrite of the Endangered Species Act, and he has battled proposals to allow increased motorboat traffic through northern Minnesota's Boundary Waters wilderness area. He was one of only 11 Republican congressional candidates endorsed by the Sierra Club in 2004.

He also steers a more moderate course than many of his Republican colleagues on abortion, backing legalized abortion but also supporting "reasonable limits" on access to the procedure. He voted to ban a procedure opponents call "partial birth" abortion, labeling it "repulsive and extreme." He supports federal funding for embryonic stem cell research, he says, in part to prevent the private sector from deciding the related legal and moral issues.

In the 108th Congress, Ramstad voted against President Bush's position 25 percent of the time, making him one of the 20 least loyal House Republicans. He has acknowledged that it isn't always easy being a centrist in the often ideologically polarized House. But with a genial personality and a non-confrontational approach, Ramstad is easily accepted by the more hard-line members in his party.

It is on the Ways and Means Committee that Ramstad is likely to have the most influence in the 109th, as he has assumed the chairmanship of its Oversight Subcommittee. While he has loyally supported Bush's tax cuts and GOP budget resolutions, he was less pleased with Bush's 2005 budget proposal because of its failure to address the problem of the alternative minimum tax. Originally enacted in 1969 to make sure the super-rich did not take too many deductions and pay too little tax, the AMT was never properly adjusted for inflation, and therefore, many middle-class taxpayers now have to pay it every year.

Ramstad in 2005 said he was "disappointed" the White House essentially kicked the AMT issue down Pennsylvania Avenue to the Capitol, instead of fixing it in the president's budget. He noted that many constituents in his home state are feeling the AMT bite. "Congress needs to address it," Ramstad said, adding that he wished the president had included at least a one-year adjustment of the AMT to hold the number of filers affected at less than 4 million. Ramstad was concerned about other aspects of Bush's budget. He told the Minneapolis Star Tribune in 2005, "While I agree with the budget priorities of homeland security and economic growth, I must say I am concerned about the deep cuts to education and law enforcement."

Ramstad has been quieter about the president's proposal to allow private accounts as part of Social Security. "It's kind of a game of chicken right now, who goes first. We believe the president needs to offer a specific plan," Ramstad told the Star Tribune early in 2005. "He's obviously reticent to do that and wants Congress to go first. But it seems to me he has the bully pulpit and he's in a better position to educate the general public."

Ramstad is also interested in trade issues, and early in the 109th, he introduced a bill to repeal the so-called Byrd amendment, which distributes duties collected in cases involving unfair trade practices directly to the aggrieved companies. Ramstad said such an arrangement provides incentives for companies to seek anti-dumping and countervailing duty rewards rather than searching for new markets for their products. The World Trade Organization has threatened sanctions if the measure is not repealed. "The Byrd amendment is bad trade policy and bad fiscal policy and ought to be scrapped," Ramstad said.

Ramstad, whose district is home to several medical companies, uses his Ways and Means seat to pursue his interest in health issues. Concerned that Medicare, the federal medical insurance program for the elderly and disabled, sometimes takes years to approve reimbursement for new medical devices, he has introduced legislation to speed up the process. He voted for the GOP's 2003 Medicare bill to provide prescription drug coverage for seniors. But that same year, he also went against GOP leaders and voted in favor of a measure to allow the importation of cheaper drugs.

Ramstad takes his voting seriously and was one of only 11 House members who voted yes or no on every roll call vote held in 2004.

A recovering alcoholic, Ramstad is keenly interested in boosting treatment for drug and alcohol addicts, and has repeatedly pressed bipartisan legislation that would require insurance companies to cover the costs of such care.

Ramstad speaks freely about his struggles with addiction. He says he started drinking as a college senior, and that he recognized he needed to do something about his addiction in 1981 when he woke up in jail in Sioux Falls, S.D., after a night of drinking, fighting and a blackout. "Every day, I have to recover," he has said. "Every day I do healthy, positive things so I won't take another drink."

Government has been an interest of Ramstad's since boyhood. For years, his Web page carried the famous photo of a young Bill Clinton shaking hands with President Kennedy at the White House in 1963. Also in that photo is Ramstad, who was with Clinton in the American Legion Boys Nation contingent that day.

Ramstad came to Washington to study law at George Washington University and work as an aide to GOP Rep. Tom Kleppe of North Dakota. In 1980, he won a seat in the Minnesota Senate, serving there until he ran for the 3rd District seat vacated in 1990 by veteran Republican Bill Frenzel.

His abortion rights stance put him at odds with many at the party convention, but he defeated four candidates after seven ballots. Ramstad won in November with 67 percent of the vote against Democratic investment executive Lewis DeMars and has won easily since. In 2004, he won with 65 percent, but it was his lowest vote share since his first re-election in 1992.

KEY VOTES

2004

No Extend federal unemployment benefits by 13 weeks
Yes Pass $283.2 billion, six-year federal highway and mass transit bill
Yes Approve $146 billion multi-year extension of previously enacted middle-class tax breaks
Yes Amend the Constitution to prohibit same-sex marriage
Yes Cut corporate taxes $137 billion over 10 years
Yes Reorganize U.S. intelligence agencies as proposed by Sept. 11 commission

2003

Yes Cut taxes by $330 billion through fiscal 2013
No Block Bush rule scaling back overtime pay for some white-collar federal workers
No Do not allow use of search warrants without first notifying subjects
Yes Allow importation of prescription drugs
No Create private school voucher program in Washington, D.C.
Yes Ban "partial birth" abortion except to save a woman's life
Yes Split $18.6 billion in Iraq aid into half-grant, half-loan
Yes Overhaul Medicare and create prescription drug benefit

CQ VOTE STUDIES

	PARTY UNITY		PRESIDENTIAL SUPPORT	
	Support	Oppose	Support	Oppose
2004	91%	9%	74%	26%
2003	80%	20%	76%	24%
2002	84%	16%	82%	18%
2001	77%	23%	65%	35%
2000	78%	22%	41%	59%

INTEREST GROUPS

	AFL-CIO	ADA	CCUS	ACU
2004	7%	25%	100%	76%
2003	20%	25%	90%	56%
2002	11%	15%	95%	92%
2001	17%	20%	87%	52%
2000	10%	30%	90%	68%

MINNESOTA 3

Hennepin County suburbs — Bloomington, Brooklyn Park, Plymouth

Minnesota's most affluent district, the 3rd encompasses Minneapolis' western suburbs, where large white-collar populations are grounded in fiscal conservatism but adhere to moderate views on social issues, particularly abortion.

With an abundant technology industry, white-collar workers, golf courses and middle-class homes, the 3rd is a classic picture of suburban living. Several Fortune 500 corporations, such as State Farm Insurance, have their headquarters in the district, and many residents commute to large companies just outside the 3rd, such as Northwest Airlines and General Mills. Traffic snarls for commuters driving east from the Lake Minnetonka area have worsened considerably because of sustained regional growth.

Brooklyn Park was governed in the early 1990s by Mayor Jesse Ventura, who later became governor with the 3rd's electoral blessing, although

the white-collar areas did not favor him. Unlike the faster-growing, more conservative outlying suburbs in the 2nd and 6th districts, the 3rd has sent moderate Republicans to the U.S. House since 1970. The district also elects Republicans to the state legislature, but supported Bill Clinton for president in 1992 and 1996. George W. Bush defeated John Kerry 51 percent to 48 percent here in the 2004 presidential election.

Brooklyn Park, Coon Rapids (shared with the 6th) and Brooklyn Center's blue-collar residents are older, conservative Democratic-Farmer-Labor Party voters, but the affluent, Republican south and west portions of the 3rd cast most of the votes, giving the district a tilt to the right.

MAJOR INDUSTRY
Electronics, manufacturing, food processing

CITIES
Bloomington, 85,172; Brooklyn Park, 67,388; Plymouth, 65,894; Coon Rapids (pt.), 58,396; Eden Prairie, 54,901; Minnetonka, 51,301

NOTABLE
Southdale, in Edina, was the nation's first fully enclosed shopping mall (1956); The Mall of America in Bloomington, the nation's largest shopping mall at 4.2 million square feet, attracts up to 40 million visitors a year and employs nearly 12,000.

Rep. Betty McCollum (D)

Elected 2000; 3rd term

CAPITOL OFFICE
225-6631
www.mccollum.house.gov
1029 Longworth 20515-2304; fax 225-1968

COMMITTEES
Education & Workforce
International Relations

HOMETOWN
St. Paul

BORN
July 12, 1954, Minneapolis, Minn.

RELIGION
Roman Catholic

FAMILY
Divorced; two children

EDUCATION
Inver Hills Community College, A.A. 1980; College of St. Catherine, B.A. 1987 (education)

CAREER
Teacher; retail saleswoman

POLITICAL HIGHLIGHTS
Candidate for North St. Paul City Council, 1984; North St. Paul City Council, 1987-92; Minn. House, 1993-2001

ELECTION RESULTS

2004 GENERAL

Betty McCollum (D)	182,387	57.5%
Patrice Bataglia (R)	105,467	33.2%
Peter F. Vento (INDC)	29,099	9.2%

2004 PRIMARY

Betty McCollum (D)	unopposed

2002 GENERAL

Betty McCollum (D)	164,597	62.2%
Clyde Billington (R)	89,705	33.9%
Scott J. Raskiewicz (GREEN)	9,919	3.8%

PREVIOUS WINNING PERCENTAGES
2000 (48%)

The first woman to represent Minnesota in the House in more than 40 years, McCollum's liberal views seem to sit well with the mostly liberal residents of St. Paul. In her first two terms, McCollum mainly sought to continue the work of her predecessor, environmentalist Bruce F. Vento. She asked for and gained a seat on the Resources Committee.

Now in her third term, McCollum has broadened her focus by becoming a quiet, but serious player on a number of international issues. In 2003, she left Resources for the International Relations Committee.

McCollum has closely associated herself with another woman in the House — Minority Leader Nancy Pelosi. When Pelosi ran for party whip in 2001, she asked McCollum to give the nominating speech. When Pelosi ascended to Democratic leader in the 108th Congress, she named McCollum to the Steering Committee, which makes committee assignments. McCollum's upper Midwest colleagues also selected her to be their regional whip.

On International Relations, McCollum is a vocal opponent of the war in Iraq. She was one of 126 Democrats to vote against the 2002 war resolution. She told the Minneapolis Star Tribune that what she heard in classified briefings in 2002 led her to believe there was no need to rush to war. She said she was then "stunned" to hear Condoleezza Rice, President Bush's national security adviser at the time, talk of ties between Saddam Hussein and the al Qaeda terrorist network and of disarming Iraq before it attacked the United States. She told the newspaper she suspected the administration was "starting to mislead and manipulate the American public."

McCollum has twice been to Baghdad to assess the war firsthand. On her last trip in August 2004, she told the Saint Paul Pioneer Press that Iraq continues to battle a growing insurgency, general lawlessness, widespread unemployment and a distrustful citizenry — all of which are overwhelming any more-hopeful signs. "We have to be straight with the American people about what's going on there, the amount of American lives being lost, the amount of taxpayer dollars being spent," McCollum said.

She has also traveled twice to Africa to work on the global AIDS crisis. McCollum told the Associated Press that the fight to combat the spread of AIDS is "a wonderful opportunity for the United States to be seen as a nation that nurtures people." McCollum won passage in 2003 of an amendment to require that at least 10 percent of U.S. funding to fight AIDS internationally be spent on orphans and vulnerable children.

McCollum has also been at the forefront of gaining federal money to help in the resettlement of Hmong refugees from Laos in Minnesota. She secured $19 million in the 2004 catchall spending bill for the Hmong refugees. St. Paul is home to one of the highest concentrations of the Hmong people of any U.S. city.

McCollum was also the lead sponsor of a bill passed by both chambers in 2004 to normalize trade relations with Laos. The measure bitterly divided the Hmong community. Opponents said the current regime in Laos is persecuting the Hmong people there and should not be rewarded with a trade agreement. But McCollum said by ending the isolation of Laos the United States would have more influence over the country's government.

A former substitute teacher, McCollum has a seat on the Education and Workforce Committee. She has complained that the Bush administration has grossly underfunded its No Child Left Behind initiative, a major rewrite of education policy that for the first time tied federal aid to performance on student achievement tests. McCollum was one of only six House Democrats in 2001 to vote against the final bill.

McCollum has a solid Democratic voting record, backing her party on 97 percent of the votes on which the two parties were opposed in the 108th Congress. She has a career rating of 100 percent from the liberal Americans for Democratic Action. "I don't see anything wrong with saying I'm a liberal," McCollum told the Saint Paul Pioneer Press in 2004.

McCollum says her public policy views were shaped by her upbringing in a penny-pinching middle-class household, and by her background as a teacher and sales clerk. She says her retail background — she worked at such stores as J.C. Penney, Sears and Dayton's — taught her a lesson that has proven equally valuable in politics. "Retail teaches you to listen to people. It's not about what I want to give you. It's about what you need to make your life better," she told the Star Tribune.

McCollum was born and raised in the Twin Cities area. She studied at a community college and received her bachelor's degree when she was 32, at about the time she was venturing into politics. She says she decided to become politically active when, as the mother of young children, she approached the city manager of North St. Paul to demand repairs to playground equipment. She ran for city council, lost that first bid, but won in a second attempt. She moved to the legislature six years later, beating two incumbents thrown into the same district by decennial redistricting.

Despite her nearly 14 years in elective office, McCollum says she had not thought of running for Congress until Vento announced in 2000 that he would not run for a 13th term and revealed that he had a rare form of lung cancer. Although six other Democrats were vying for the seat, McCollum gained an essential edge in the September primary when she won the state Democratic Party's endorsement at its convention in June.

McCollum drew a seasoned Republican foe in state Sen. Linda Runbeck, but her biggest worry seemed to be the possible siphoning of Democratic votes by independent candidate Tom Foley, a former Democrat and longtime Ramsey County attorney. But Foley, who ran as a fiscal conservative, appeared to draw votes from both candidates. Though McCollum missed a majority with 48 percent of the vote, she easily outran Runbeck, who took 31 percent. Foley finished with 21 percent.

In 2002, McCollum was re-elected with 62 percent of the vote. And in 2004, she took 58 percent against her Republican challenger, Patrice Bataglia, a Dakota County commissioner.

KEY VOTES

2004

Yes	Extend federal unemployment benefits by 13 weeks
Yes	Pass $283.2 billion, six-year federal highway and mass transit bill
No	Approve $146 billion multi-year extension of previously enacted middle-class tax breaks
No	Amend the Constitution to prohibit same-sex marriage
No	Cut corporate taxes $137 billion over 10 years
Yes	Reorganize U.S. intelligence agencies as proposed by Sept. 11 commission

2003

No	Cut taxes by $330 billion through fiscal 2013
Yes	Block Bush rule scaling back overtime pay for some white-collar federal workers
Yes	Do not allow use of search warrants without first notifying subjects
Yes	Allow importation of prescription drugs
No	Create private school voucher program in Washington, D.C.
No	Ban "partial birth" abortion except to save a woman's life
Yes	Split $18.6 billion in Iraq aid into half-grant, half-loan
No	Overhaul Medicare and create prescription drug benefit

CQ VOTE STUDIES

	PARTY UNITY		PRESIDENTIAL SUPPORT	
	Support	Oppose	Support	Oppose
2004	97%	3%	21%	79%
2003	97%	3%	18%	82%
2002	98%	2%	25%	75%
2001	96%	4%	28%	72%

INTEREST GROUPS

	AFL-CIO	ADA	CCUS	ACU
2004	93%	100%	24%	0%
2003	100%	100%	24%	12%
2002	89%	100%	40%	4%
2001	100%	100%	39%	4%

MINNESOTA 4
Ramsey County — St. Paul and suburbs

St. Paul's liberal university communities, bedroom neighborhoods, state government and labor populations provide a consistent stronghold for the Democratic-Farmer-Labor Party. Represented in Congress by a Democrat since 1949, voters in the 4th — slightly less than half of whom live in St. Paul — have elected DFL candidates at all levels of government. But as with much of central Minnesota, the district has an independent streak, as demonstrated by support for Ross Perot in the 1992 presidential election and Jesse Ventura in the 1998 gubernatorial race.

St. Paul gained population in the 1990s, although it grew much slower than surrounding areas. The district includes independent and moderate voters in parts of fast-growing Washington County and affluent northern suburbs such as North Oaks and White Bear Lake.

St. Paul is a traditionally Democratic city with a large German and Irish-Catholic population. The city developed as a major port and railroading center and still has a strong labor tradition. Today, blue-collar, black and Hispanic communities contribute to the city's Democratic flavor. It also is a center of Hmong culture in the United States. Forty-one percent of students in St. Paul's schools speak a first language other than English.

Home to the state capital and the headquarters of 3M, the 4th has a large percentage of white-collar workers who live in middle- and high-income neighborhoods. Several colleges, including the University of Minnesota's agriculture school, are located in affluent communities around St. Paul. The limited Republican base is in the growing suburbs to the north of the city that have drawn city residents and newcomers.

MAJOR INDUSTRY
State government, higher education, manufacturing

CITIES
St. Paul, 287,151; Maplewood, 34,947; Roseville, 33,690; Oakdale, 26,653; Shoreview, 25,924; White Bear Lake, 24,325; New Brighton, 22,206

NOTABLE
Supreme Court Justices Warren E. Burger and Harry A. Blackmun grew up in St. Paul; St. Paul was originally called Pig's Eye Landing, after bootlegger Pierre "Pig's Eye" Parrant; In 2002, the area elected Mee Moua to the state Senate, making her the first Hmong state legislator in the United States.

Rep. Martin Olav Sabo (D)

Elected 1978; 14th term

CAPITOL OFFICE
225-4755
sabo.house.gov
2336 Rayburn 20515-2305; fax 225-4886

COMMITTEES
Appropriations

HOMETOWN
Minneapolis

BORN
Feb. 28, 1938, Crosby, N.D.

RELIGION
Lutheran

FAMILY
Wife, Sylvia Lee Sabo; two children

EDUCATION
Augsburg College, B.A. 1959 (history); U. of
Minnesota, attended 1960

CAREER
Public official

POLITICAL HIGHLIGHTS
Minn. House, 1961-79 (minority leader, 1969-73;
Speaker, 1973-79)

ELECTION RESULTS

2004 GENERAL

Martin Olav Sabo (D)	218,434	69.7%
Daniel Nielsen Mathias (R)	76,600	24.4%
Jay Pond (GREEN)	17,984	5.7%

2004 PRIMARY

Martin Olav Sabo (D)	23,047	91.1%
Dick Franson (D)	2,264	8.9%

2002 GENERAL

Martin Olav Sabo (D)	171,572	67.0%
Daniel Nielsen Mathias (R)	66,271	25.9%
Tim Davis (GR)	17,825	7.0%

PREVIOUS WINNING PERCENTAGES
2000 (69%); 1998 (67%); 1996 (64%); 1994 (62%);
1992 (63%); 1990 (73%); 1988 (72%); 1986 (73%);
1984 (70%); 1982 (66%); 1980 (70%); 1978 (62%)

No one would ever describe this stoic son of Norwegian Lutheran immigrants as "fiery," but in his politics, Sabo is as liberal as they come. He has been moved in recent years to deliver some pretty stern critiques of the policies of the Republican White House.

"Crass self-interest and a lack of leadership are producing massive debt for future generations so that we can give lavish tax giveaways to the most wealthy," Sabo wrote in the Minneapolis Star Tribune after the 2004 election. "The president contends we can fight wars and give tax cuts to millionaires and big business without endangering our long-term prosperity, Social Security and Medicare benefits. Republican rhetoric does not match reality."

He also challenged the president early in the 109th Congress by introducing his own plan for overhauling Social Security. President Bush has made changing the current Social Security system to allow younger workers to create private accounts a centerpiece of his second term. Sabo's legislation takes a different tack. He wants the federal government to pay Social Security's trust funds enough interest to keep them from being exhausted until 2080, which would ensure the government paid the full benefits promised to retirees under current law until at least that date.

"When I first started in politics, the words 'elderly' and 'poor' were virtually synonymous," Sabo said. "Social Security has changed that, and has become the base foundation for retirement planning for most Americans. To take and begin a systematic destruction of that plan based on conservative long-term economic estimates is just simply wrong."

At the start of the 108th, the new Democratic leadership under Nancy Pelosi rewarded Sabo with the job of top-ranking Democrat on the Appropriations Committee's new Homeland Security Subcommittee. In that role, he has also criticized the Bush administration's efforts to keep the nation safe.

Sabo is especially worried that not enough resources are going to "first responders" — local police, fire and emergency workers who are likely to be first on the scene if there is any future terrorist attack. When Bush released his budget plan in February 2005, he asked Congress to slash the first-responder grants to state and local agencies as a way of keeping the budget numbers down. But lawmakers usually protect grant programs that bring money home to their states. "The cuts to first-responders are totally inappropriate," said Sabo. "I suspect that'll have trouble getting the votes." Port security and safeguarding the transportation of hazardous materials are other Sabo concerns.

Before moving to the Homeland Security Subcommittee, Sabo was the top-ranking Democrat on the Appropriations subcommittee overseeing transportation. During his long tenure in the House — he now ranks 15th in seniority among the chamber's 200-plus Democrats — he has brought to Minnesota millions of dollars for transit and environmental projects.

Few can work a spending bill as well as Sabo; his low-key manner, persistence and deep knowledge of the federal budget help him succeed even as a member of the House minority. Thanks to his quiet lobbying, the massive catchall spending bill passed at the end of the 108th included millions for Minnesota projects, including $1 million to help the Norwegian American Foundation promote the centennial celebration of Norway's peaceful 1905 independence from Sweden.

Sabo is a believer in government's ability to improve the lot of working Americans. But it is hard to imagine that some of his proposals will become law. He would change the tax laws to discourage "excessive executive pay." He wants to limit the tax deductibility of an executive's pay to 25 times the amount paid a company's lowest-paid worker, which he says would send the message "that those who work on the factory floor are as important to a company's success as those who work in the executive suite."

Sabo also would guarantee health insurance to all Americans through a single-payer, tax-financed system. He likes to quote former Minnesota Republican Gov. Elmer L. Andersen, who said, "Taxes are the way people join hands to get good things done. That's the tradition in Minnesota."

Sabo was an important contributor to the elimination of the budget deficit in the late 1990s. As chairman of the Budget Committee in the 103rd Congress, he helped build the case for President Clinton's tax-raising, deficit-cutting budget plan. Its passage in 1993, without a single Republican vote, was a factor in spurring economic growth and bringing the budget into surplus by the time Clinton left office. "Unfortunately," Sabo said later, "the Bush White House squandered the $5.6 trillion surplus it inherited from President Bill Clinton and has racked up record annual deficits."

Sabo has a legendary quickness with numbers. He left Budget Committee aides gaping once when he was handed a long table of numbers. He glanced down the columns, handed it back and said, "It doesn't add up."

His favorite numbers are baseball statistics. A huge Minnesota Twins fan, he listens to broadcasts of games over the Internet on his office computer. He also coaches the Democrats' team in the annual congressional baseball game.

Sabo's political values are rooted in his upbringing. He was born of Norwegian immigrant parents on a North Dakota farm. (His last name means "farm by the sea.") His family donated land for the community's school, where his mother volunteered as a cook; Sabo was valedictorian of a graduating class of three. He recalls how grateful his family was to finally get electricity from the Roosevelt-era Rural Electrification Administration.

Sabo was first elected to the state House at age 22, serving for 18 years, including six as Speaker. When Democrat Donald Fraser left the U.S. House for an unsuccessful Senate bid in 1978, Sabo easily won his party's nomination and was elected comfortably in the dependably Democratic 5th District. His re-election races have been routine, except for an intraparty challenge in 1992 when a faction of liberals complained that Sabo had opposed across-the-board defense cuts. But Sabo won the primary with ease.

KEY VOTES

2004

Yes Extend federal unemployment benefits by 13 weeks

Yes Pass $283.2 billion, six-year federal highway and mass transit bill

No Approve $146 billion multi-year extension of previously enacted middle-class tax breaks

No Amend the Constitution to prohibit same-sex marriage

No Cut corporate taxes $137 billion over 10 years

No Reorganize U.S. intelligence agencies as proposed by Sept. 11 commission

2003

No Cut taxes by $330 billion through fiscal 2013

Yes Block Bush rule scaling back overtime pay for some white-collar federal workers

Yes Do not allow use of search warrants without first notifying subjects

Yes Allow importation of prescription drugs

No Create private school voucher program in Washington, D.C.

? Ban "partial birth" abortion except to save a woman's life

Yes Split $18.6 billion in Iraq aid into half-grant, half-loan

No Overhaul Medicare and create prescription drug benefit

CQ VOTE STUDIES

	PARTY UNITY		PRESIDENTIAL SUPPORT	
	Support	Oppose	Support	Oppose
2004	94%	6%	18%	82%
2003	92%	8%	17%	83%
2002	96%	4%	25%	75%
2001	91%	9%	14%	86%
2000	96%	4%	90%	10%

INTEREST GROUPS

	AFL-CIO	ADA	CCUS	ACU
2004	100%	100%	24%	0%
2003	93%	95%	23%	17%
2002	89%	100%	35%	0%
2001	92%	100%	26%	0%
2000	90%	100%	38%	0%

MINNESOTA 5
Minneapolis and suburbs

Established at the northernmost navigable point on the Mississippi River, Minneapolis accounts for most of the 5th's vote and has supported liberal Rep. Sabo since 1978. Redistricting following the 2000 census may have made the district even more Democratic, moving the affluent suburb of Edina into the 3rd and adding first-ring northern suburbs. For the first time in a half-century, Minneapolis gained population in the 1990s, although it grew much slower than surrounding areas.

Minneapolis is home to many large corporations, such as General Mills, Target Corp. and U.S. Bancorp. The 5th attracted well-educated white-collar workers in the economic boom of the 1990s, but the shift has not changed the area's liberal-mindedness. Minneapolis has the highest number of theater seats per capita in the United States outside of New York City. This strong arts community's liberal lean is bolstered by the University of Minnesota in eastern Minneapolis. Residents who flock to the area's many lakes also support environmental protections. John Kerry received 71 percent of the 5th's vote in the 2004 presidential

election — his best showing in the state.

Traffic and the lack of affordable housing have become large problems here. Though Minneapolis was dubbed "murderapolis" by the New York Times in 1996, the city has managed to cut crime and redevelop downtown riverfront areas.

Although Minneapolis is known for its Scandinavian heritage, the 5th is the state's most racially diverse district. Asian and black communities — including a sizable Somali population — contribute to the district's Democratic-Farmer-Labor voter rolls. The district's poorer communities lie north of downtown.

MAJOR INDUSTRY
Corporate administration, banking, higher education

CITIES
Minneapolis, 382,618; St. Louis Park, 44,126; Richfield, 34,439

NOTABLE
The Minneapolis Sculpture Garden at Walker Art Center features an enormous metal spoon holding a cherry; Democrat Hubert H. Humphrey was elected mayor of Minneapolis in 1945; Minneapolis was the locale of the "Mary Tyler Moore Show."

Rep. Mark Kennedy (R)

CAPITOL OFFICE
225-2331
mark.kennedy@mail.house.gov
markkennedy.house.gov
1415 Longworth 20515-2306; fax 225-6475

COMMITTEES
Financial Services
Transportation & Infrastructure

HOMETOWN
Watertown

BORN
April 11, 1957, Benson, Minn.

RELIGION
Roman Catholic

FAMILY
Wife, Debbie Kennedy; four children

EDUCATION
Saint John's U. (Minn.), B.A. 1978 (accounting);
U. of Michigan, M.B.A. 1983

CAREER
Giftware company financial executive; food
company financial director; accountant

POLITICAL HIGHLIGHTS
No previous office

ELECTION RESULTS

2004 GENERAL

Mark Kennedy (R)	203,669	54.0%
Patty Wetterling (D)	173,309	45.9%

2004 PRIMARY

Mark Kennedy (R)	unopposed

2002 GENERAL

Mark Kennedy (R)	164,747	57.3%
Janet Robert (D)	100,738	35.1%
Dan Becker (INDC)	21,484	7.5%

PREVIOUS WINNING PERCENTAGES
2000 (48%)

Elected 2000; 3rd term

Kennedy, a dedicated conservative and loyal Bush supporter with a folksy, down-to-earth personality, in February 2005 announced he was running for the Senate in 2006, a pronouncement that came as no surprise to those who had been keeping an eye on him.

His entry into the race came just after Democrat Mark Dayton announced he would not seek re-election, but it is likely Kennedy would have run regardless of Dayton's decision.

During the 108th Congress, Kennedy was often seen at Minnesota events far from his suburban Twin Cities district. He began speaking out on a range of issues beyond the confines of his committee assignments, and even traveled to Iraq in 2003 for a firsthand look at the conflict there.

In 2004, Kennedy emerged as a champion of the planned 2005 round of military base closings, taking on the Armed Services Committee in the process. Although he has no particular military expertise, Kennedy vigorously defended the Bush administration's proposed closings, arguing that they are necessary now more than ever to ensure efficiency in the nation's use of its military resources. "The critical nature of our war on terrorism and our military actions in Iraq and Afghanistan demand we go forward," he told his colleagues. Although he lost a floor fight on the issue, Kennedy ultimately prevailed when President Bush and the Senate insisted that the House drop its attempt to delay the 2005 round.

Kennedy could afford to champion the closings: There are no military facilities in the 6th District, and relatively few anywhere in Minnesota.

Kennedy made a splash of a different kind earlier in the 108th, when he won adoption of an amendment to the fiscal 2003 Iraq war supplemental spending bill that barred French, German, Russian and Syrian companies from getting U.S. funding for the postwar reconstruction of Iraq. At the time, public resentment was running high against countries that criticized Bush's decision to go to war.

Kennedy has been able to look out for the interests of his district and the state from his seat on the Transportation and Infrastructure Committee, which drafted a six-year surface transportation bill during the 108th Congress. In his first term, he hosted both Republican Tom Petri of Wisconsin, the chairman of the Highway Subcommittee, and Transportation Secretary Norman Y. Mineta, showing them his district's transportation needs; Mineta was so taken with the freshman lawmaker's pitch that he gave him the nickname "Roads" Kennedy.

In the 108th, Kennedy emerged as a champion of toll roads as a solution to the nation's chronically underfunded highway system, introducing legislation to end the prohibition on tolls on interstate highways that were not originally toll roads. "This is the only viable source of funding that has the broad base of support," Kennedy said.

While almost always a dependable vote for his party and Bush, Kennedy in 2001 voted against allowing drilling in Alaska's Arctic National Wildlife Refuge and against the president's No Child Left Behind education bill. Most members of the Minnesota delegation opposed the education measure, objecting to its intrusion on local controls.

Kennedy was named to the Financial Services Committee in the 108th Congress, a good fit with his background as an accountant and corporate financial officer. He has been a consistent advocate of the Bush tax-cutting agenda and of laissez-faire economics, in general. In 2003, he introduced a resolution proposing a "Free Enterprise Education Week" in public schools.

In his initial campaign, Kennedy jokingly urged voters to send him to Congress to prove there are Kennedys who are Republicans. He had a grandmother named Rose, and he comes from a large Roman Catholic family with plenty of involvement in politics: His grandfather was mayor of Murdoch, in rural Swift county, and his father was on the county school board. But that is where any similarity with the Massachusetts family ends. All of Mark Kennedy's relatives in public life have been Republicans.

Kennedy has three brothers and three sisters, and he spent much of his childhood in Pequot Lakes, a small town in the north-central part of the state where his father was the local banker and sat on the school board for 27 years.

Kennedy was a sports star in high school and active in the 4-H Club. In college, he worked on Republican Rudy Boschwitz's successful 1978 Senate campaign, and he says he always knew that one day he would run for office because of his family's history of involvement in politics.

That day came in 2000. Kennedy decided to make his electoral debut in a race for the House against four-term Democratic incumbent David Minge. Minge's incumbency almost rescued him, but the election night tally showed Kennedy the winner by 155 votes. Minge asked for a recount, but withdrew the request more than a month later when it became clear he would not reverse the outcome. The race was the second-closest House race of 2000.

That made Kennedy one of two Republicans to unseat a House Democratic incumbent in 2000. He moved aggressively to supplement his campaign war chest as soon as he took office.

In 2002, a new congressional map drawn by a state court dramatically relocated the 2nd District, which Kennedy then represented, and put his house just across the border in the newly configured 6th District. Kennedy told the St. Paul Pioneer Press that a group of friends had offered to "hoist up my home and drag it" the necessary half-mile, but he decided instead to run in the 6th. His house is on 60 acres of land in Watertown, about 40 miles west of Minneapolis. He rents some of the land out for farming and rhapsodizes about the wildlife that wanders through his property.

In 2002, Kennedy faced well-funded Democrat Janet Robert, an attorney who was spending mainly her own money. The campaign was bruising, but Kennedy cruised to a 22 percentage point victory. In 2004, he bested child safety advocate Patty Wetterling by a margin of 8 points.

KEY VOTES

2004

No   Extend federal unemployment benefits by 13 weeks

Yes   Pass $283.2 billion, six-year federal highway and mass transit bill

Yes   Approve $146 billion multi-year extension of previously enacted middle-class tax breaks

Yes   Amend the Constitution to prohibit same-sex marriage

Yes   Cut corporate taxes $137 billion over 10 years

Yes   Reorganize U.S. intelligence agencies as proposed by Sept. 11 commission

2003

Yes   Cut taxes by $330 billion through fiscal 2013

No   Block Bush rule scaling back overtime pay for some white-collar federal workers

No   Do not allow use of search warrants without first notifying subjects

No   Allow importation of prescription drugs

Yes   Create private school voucher program in Washington, D.C.

Yes   Ban "partial birth" abortion except to save a woman's life

No   Split $18.6 billion in Iraq aid into half-grant, half-loan

Yes   Overhaul Medicare and create prescription drug benefit

CQ VOTE STUDIES

	PARTY UNITY		PRESIDENTIAL SUPPORT	
	Support	Oppose	Support	Oppose
2004	97%	3%	97%	3%
2003	97%	3%	98%	2%
2002	97%	3%	90%	10%
2001	93%	7%	86%	14%

INTEREST GROUPS

	AFL-CIO	ADA	CCUS	ACU
2004	13%	5%	100%	92%
2003	0%	5%	93%	80%
2002	11%	0%	95%	96%
2001	17%	10%	91%	88%

MINNESOTA 6
North and east Twin Cities suburbs; St. Cloud

One of Minnesota's three suburban-oriented districts, the 6th stretches from east and north of the Twin Cities through conservative, developing areas northwest to St. Cloud. The district is tied together by Interstate 94, which runs from St. Cloud through the Twin Cities to Wisconsin, and the burgeoning Northstar Corridor that runs along the Mississippi River. Officials hope a planned 40-mile commuter train line to link Big Lake in Sherburne County with the Twin Cities will help alleviate traffic congestion along the corridor and create jobs.

Development has not yet made St. Cloud a Twin Cities suburb, although the former granite quarrying city is one of the fastest-growing in the state. Home to a mix of blue-collar Democrats and white-collar Republicans, it lies within heavily Catholic Stearns County.

Anoka and Wright counties, to the north and west of Minneapolis and its first-ring suburbs, include new, wealthy suburban developments and also exurban hobby farms. Washington County, to the east and north of St. Paul, includes Woodbury (a small part of which is in the 2nd), which

doubled in population in the 1990s, and the cosmopolitan small town of Stillwater on the St. Croix River, which marks the Wisconsin border. Sherburne County grew by more than 50 percent in the 1990s.

The 6th is a competitive district with a slight GOP lean, but surprisingly it provided George W. Bush with his best showing in the state in the 2004 presidential election. Young, high-income families that fuel the region's growth tend to favor fiscal conservatism, except on social issues such as public safety and education. Transplants from the north are more liberal on spending but are often socially conservative. Blue-collar communities in the suburbs of Anoka and Washington counties are faithful Democratic-Farmer-Labor Party supporters, although as a whole, both counties narrowly sided with Bush in 2004. Independent Jesse Ventura won every county in the 6th during his 1998 gubernatorial bid.

MAJOR INDUSTRY
Corporate administration, manufacturing

CITIES
St. Cloud, 59,107; Blaine, 44,942; Woodbury (pt.), 44,767; Andover, 26,588; Ramsey, 18,510

NOTABLE
Writer and radio show host Garrison Keillor was born in Anoka.

Rep. Collin C. Peterson (D)

Elected 1990; 8th term

CAPITOL OFFICE
225-2165
collinpeterson.house.gov
2159 Rayburn 20515-2307; fax 225-1593

COMMITTEES
Agriculture - ranking member

HOMETOWN
Detroit Lakes

BORN
June 29, 1944, Fargo, N.D.

RELIGION
Lutheran

FAMILY
Divorced; three children

EDUCATION
Moorhead State U., B.A. 1966 (accounting)

MILITARY SERVICE
Minn. National Guard, 1963-69

CAREER
Accountant

POLITICAL HIGHLIGHTS
Minn. Senate, 1977-87; sought Democratic
nomination for U.S. House, 1982; Democratic
nominee for U.S. House, 1984, 1986; sought
Democratic nomination for U.S. House, 1988

ELECTION RESULTS

2004 GENERAL

Collin C. Peterson (D)	207,628	66.1%
David E. Sturrock (R)	106,349	33.8%

2004 PRIMARY

Collin C. Peterson (D)	unopposed

2002 GENERAL

Collin C. Peterson (D)	170,234	65.3%
Dan Stevens (R)	90,342	34.6%

PREVIOUS WINNING PERCENTAGES
2000 (69%); 1998 (72%); 1996 (68%); 1994 (51%);
1992 (50%); 1990 (54%)

Peterson overcame questions about his devotion to his party and gained the top Democratic spot on the Agriculture Committee in the 109th Congress. "It turned out to be not that big of a deal," Peterson said. "Only three or four [Democrats] voted against me on the Steering Committee. . . . I'm looking forward to getting to work."

His colleagues' concerns were not unfounded as Peterson consistently votes in opposition to many of his party's positions. In 2004, he opposed the position of a majority of Democrats 37 percent of the time, ranking him among the top five Democrats who voted most often against their party. That same year, he voted in agreement with President Bush 50 percent of the time.

But this is not to say that Peterson is always happy with the president. When Bush released his budget proposal in early 2005, Peterson was angry about cuts to farm programs. He said it doesn't make sense for Bush to target farm spending for cuts because the Bush administration had agreed to stick with the payments included in the last farm bill until 2007, so any changes would be breaking a promise.

"I don't think the farm bill should be monkeyed with," Peterson told the Associated Press, adding that the farm bill programs have cost $15 billion less than was originally estimated, a big savings for the government. "We weren't part of the problem, so why should we be part of the solution?" he said. When Peterson gained the top minority slot on the committee, he promised to fight for rural America, which he said is "often forgotten by the federal government."

Peterson was part of the House-Senate conference committee that wrote the final 2002 farm bill boosting spending by $73.5 billion over 10 years. The measure reversed a 1996 law designed to wean farmers from federal price supports, a longtime goal of fiscal conservatives. Peterson declared the bill a triumph, even as the federal budget slipped back into deficit.

Although he dislikes most federal spending, he defends government support for farm subsidies that are important in agriculture-dependent regions. He likes to share in the credit for defeating the perennial amendment to the annual agriculture appropriations bill to kill the sugar price-support program. Sugar beets are a major crop in the western part of the 7th District. He has already come out in opposition to the Bush administration's 2004 plan for a trade agreement with Central America, which Peterson worries will increase sugar imports and undercut the price of domestic sugar.

Peterson tends to follow big labor's preferences on international trade, voting in 2002 against granting the president fast-track authority to negotiate trade agreements that Congress cannot amend. And in 2000, he opposed granting China permanent normal trade status.

On other farm matters, he has been less successful and was not able to protect upper Midwestern dairy farmers from national pricing structures that favor producers in other regions. He introduced bills in 2004 and 2005 to establish a national beef identification system to help track and quarantine livestock with highly contagious infectious diseases.

A founding member of the Blue Dog Coalition, a group of fiscally conservative Democrats, Peterson says what the Blue Dogs want is a balanced federal budget, and they will chide Bush about his tax cuts if they lead to a higher deficit. He was one of just 10 Democrats who voted in 2001 for a $958 billion package of tax cuts proposed by Bush. But he declined to go along with a larger proposal calling for $1.6 trillion in tax cuts over 10 years. Peterson also backed an unsuccessful amendment that would have delayed or canceled parts of the tax cuts if Congress failed to pass spending cuts to keep the budget in balance.

When Republicans came back in 2002 with proposals to make the tax cuts permanent, Peterson voted no. And as the budget deficit ballooned, Peterson in 2004 voiced regrets for backing the initial round of tax cuts.

Peterson also will vote with Republicans on health care issues. He was one of just eight Democrats in 2002 who voted for a GOP bill creating a drug benefit for Medicare beneficiaries by relying on private insurers, and one of only nine who voted in favor of the 2003 Republican Medicare bill providing prescription drug coverage for seniors.

But Peterson probably confounds his fellow Democrats the most by his stands on social issues. He opposes abortion and gun control, and he likes the idea of a constitutional amendment on school prayer.

Peterson draws high marks from the National Rifle Association. An avid sportsman, he is the co-chairman of the Congressional Sportsmen's Caucus and once boasted he has "more dead animals on my wall than anybody in this Congress, except for [Alaska Republican] Don Young."

In 2003, he opposed a measure to curb the use of "bear baiting," where hunters use human food to bring bears in range and then shoot them. Peterson argued that bear baiting was a way to keep the bear population down. "We have three times as many bears now as we did back when they were not protected," he said. "In Minnesota, last year, we shot 2,915 bears; 2,900 were shot over bait."

A pilot and a musician, Peterson was a trombonist in the Army National Guard band for six years. He enjoys performing as a country-rock guitarist and singer at small venues, such as fundraisers for House Democrats. He once appeared with country singer Willie Nelson at a Farm Aid concert.

Before his election to the House, Peterson served for 10 years in the Minnesota Senate. In the 1980s, he made four unsuccessful bids for a House seat; in two of those attempts, he failed to get even the Democratic nomination.

Peterson decided to run again in 1990 when Republican Rep. Arlan Stangeland faced criticism over using his House credit card to charge several calls to or from the phone of a female Virginia lobbyist. Peterson was careful to present himself as a "new Collin Peterson," and he took 54 percent of the vote. After scratching out close re-election victories in 1992 and 1994, Peterson has since won with better than 65 percent of the vote.

KEY VOTES

2004
Yes Extend federal unemployment benefits by 13 weeks
Yes Pass $283.2 billion, six-year federal highway and mass transit bill
Yes Approve $146 billion multi-year extension of previously enacted middle-class tax breaks
Yes Amend the Constitution to prohibit same-sex marriage
Yes Cut corporate taxes $137 billion over 10 years
Yes Reorganize U.S. intelligence agencies as proposed by Sept. 11 commission

2003
No Cut taxes by $330 billion through fiscal 2013
Yes Block Bush rule scaling back overtime pay for some white-collar federal workers
Yes Do not allow use of search warrants without first notifying subjects
Yes Allow importation of prescription drugs
No Create private school voucher program in Washington, D.C.
Yes Ban "partial birth" abortion except to save a woman's life
Yes Split $18.6 billion in Iraq aid into half-grant, half-loan
Yes Overhaul Medicare and create prescription drug benefit

CQ VOTE STUDIES

	PARTY UNITY		PRESIDENTIAL SUPPORT	
	Support	Oppose	Support	Oppose
2004	63%	37%	50%	50%
2003	65%	35%	58%	42%
2002	64%	36%	54%	46%
2001	63%	37%	42%	58%
2000	60%	40%	49%	51%

INTEREST GROUPS

	AFL-CIO	ADA	CCUS	ACU
2004	80%	55%	76%	52%
2003	87%	70%	70%	50%
2002	56%	45%	70%	48%
2001	75%	50%	55%	43%
2000	60%	60%	52%	32%

MINNESOTA 7
West – Moorhead, Willmar

Stretching 330 miles from north to south, the vast 7th spans almost all of the state's western third. It shifts from flat prairie in the west to hills, lakes and heavy forests in the middle of the state. Besides Willmar in the southern part of the district, the 7th's main population centers, Moorhead and East Grand Forks, are on the Red River, which forms the border between Minnesota and North Dakota, and have much larger companion cities across the border.

While the river irrigates some of the nation's blackest soil, floods in 1997 and 2001 capped a decade of agricultural struggle in the area. Although it lost some population, East Grand Forks largely has been rebuilt since 1997. Sugar beets and sunflowers are the dominant crops in the fertile west, while soybeans, wheat, corn and other staples are more prevalent in the east and south. The district also is a top producer of turkeys. Concern over the sugar market, the floods, drought and crop disease has left farmers looking to diversify and has sent younger residents fleeing. The Prairie Correctional Facility, a private prison taking inmates from

across the country, is located in Appleton.

The district's manufacturing firms lend some stability to the area. The 7th produces hockey sticks, windows, skis and snowmobiles. Lakes in the north and east drive many resorts catering to retirees.

The district gave George W. Bush 55 percent of the vote in each of his presidential elections, making the 7th Bush's strongest Minnesota district in 2000 and his second-best district in the state in 2004. But residents will support candidates from either party, and the 7th is often the state's most competitive district in statewide races. Traditional small-farm and labor support for Democrats still exists, but these voters tend to oppose gun control and abortion.

MAJOR INDUSTRY
Agriculture, light manufacturing, recreation

CITIES
Moorhead, 32,177; Willmar, 18,351; Fergus Falls, 13,471

NOTABLE
Writer Sinclair Lewis, the first American to win the Nobel Prize in Literature, grew up in Sauk Center; Walnut Grove was the childhood home of "Little House on the Prairie" author Laura Ingalls Wilder.

Rep. James L. Oberstar (D)

Elected 1974; 16th term

CAPITOL OFFICE
225-6211
www.house.gov/oberstar
2365 Rayburn 20515-2308; fax 225-0699

COMMITTEES
Transportation & Infrastructure - ranking member

HOMETOWN
Chisholm

BORN
Sept. 10, 1934, Chisholm, Minn.

RELIGION
Roman Catholic

FAMILY
Wife, Jean Oberstar; six children

EDUCATION
College of St. Thomas, B.A. 1956 (French &
political science); College of Europe (Belgium),
M.A. 1957 (comparative government)

CAREER
Language teacher; congressional aide

POLITICAL HIGHLIGHTS
Sought Democratic nomination for U.S. Senate,
1984

ELECTION RESULTS

2004 GENERAL

James L. Oberstar (D)	228,586	65.2%
Mark Groettum (R)	112,693	32.2%
Van Presley (GREEN)	8,933	2.6%

2004 PRIMARY

James L. Oberstar (D)	37,353	85.5%
Michael H. Johnson (D)	6,314	14.5%

2002 GENERAL

James L. Oberstar (D)	194,909	68.7%
Robert Lemen (R)	88,673	31.2%

PREVIOUS WINNING PERCENTAGES
2000 (68%); 1998 (66%); 1996 (67%); 1994 (66%);
1992 (59%); 1990 (73%); 1988 (75%); 1986 (73%);
1984 (67%); 1982 (77%); 1980 (70%); 1978 (87%);
1976 (100%); 1974 (62%)

Oberstar is a policy wonk and world traveler, who can converse in six different languages. He began to work in the House before some members of the 109th Congress were even born, having spent 11 years as a top congressional aide before he was elected in his own right in 1974.

Oberstar now ranks seventh among House Democrats in seniority and is one of only three Democratic "Watergate babies" remaining in the House. He remains a New Deal liberal, but he parts ways with many of his Democratic colleagues on certain social issues.

His background, interests and legislative experience are well-suited to the Transportation and Infrastructure Committee, where he has been the top-ranking Democrat since 1995. That role will keep him busy in the 109th, when the committee once again tries to reauthorize a 1998 surface transportation law that stalled during the 108th.

Oberstar believes that generous federal spending on the nation's transportation and infrastructure needs is key to maintaining America's global competitiveness. At a 2005 committee meeting on the highway bill, Oberstar commented on the extensive government spending on highways and rail networks he saw during a 2004 trip to China. "China is investing $150 billion to build the equivalent of our interstate highway system in the next 15 years," he said, warning that as a result, Chinese goods "are going to be less expensive when they come to our shores" because they will move more quickly through their own country.

Oberstar and the chairman of the Transportation Committee, Republican Don Young of Alaska, usually work in concert to help members gain federal funding for their districts' transportation and infrastructure needs. When the highway bill was considered in the 108th, Young was compelled by his own party to trim back his original plan of paying for the bill's projects with a gasoline tax increase. Oberstar was as unhappy with the bill's reduced price tag as Young. He voted for Young's watered-down bills only after lobbing sharp barbs at the Bush administration, who he said goaded House Republicans into embracing a compromise he called a "tragedy" and "a shame."

Oberstar also joined forces with Young to defend the committee against efforts to shrink its jurisdiction. They argued together that their panel should not be whittled away by President Bush's plan to consolidate 22 agencies into the new Department of Homeland Security. Transportation Committee members voted against efforts to move the Federal Emergency Management Agency and the Coast Guard into the new department, but they lost that battle. They fought against jurisdictional incursions by the new Homeland Security Committee with more success. The Transportation panel maintained oversight of the Coast Guard, the Federal Emergency Management Agency, and aviation policy relating to safety and regulation.

The son of a blue-collar mining family whose father was a union official, Oberstar is a fierce ally of unions. He repeatedly sought ways to help airline workers laid off in the aftermath of the Sept. 11, 2001, terrorist attacks. He also pushed to strengthen aviation security and bail out the ailing airline industry.

A dedicated bicyclist who enjoys hobnobbing with bicycle advocacy groups in his home state, Oberstar included in the 1998 transportation law numerous provisions to encourage biking and enhance bicycle safety and education and protected their inclusion in the law's reauthorization.

Oberstar strays from the liberal wing of the Democrats on abortion and gun owners' rights. In 2004, he was one of 52 Democrats who voted in favor of striking down the District of Columbia's gun control law. A devout Roman Catholic, he has proposed a constitutional amendment to ban abortion except in cases where the woman's life is in danger. But during Massachusetts Sen. John Kerry's presidential campaign, Oberstar co-signed a letter to the Catholic Archbishop of Washington, Theodore McCarrick, protesting bishops who said they would deny communion to politicians who supported abortion rights.

Oberstar is an advocate of adoption and co-chairs the Congressional Coalition on Adoption; his oldest child was adopted. He wants more federal funding for breast cancer research. His first wife died in 1991 after an eight-year battle with the disease, and he has since married a woman who lost her first husband to cancer. He has pushed for legislation to provide financial relief, including a tax credit, to caregivers of sick family members.

He generally sides with Democrats in fighting Republican efforts to scale back environmental protections. In 2002, he introduced legislation aimed at overturning a Supreme Court decision that in his view had diminished the protection of wetlands. He said the decision went against nearly 30 years of interpretation and opened "an opportunity for waters across the nation to be destroyed and degraded."

Oberstar takes delight in demonstrating his facility with foreign languages, including French and Creole, which he taught to U.S. Navy personnel in Haiti in the early 1960s before coming to Washington. When the French Ambassador Jean-David Levitte hosted a reception in 2005 for the Congressional French Caucus, which Oberstar co-chairs, Oberstar delivered a speech in both English and French. The congressman, who has a graduate degree from the College of Europe in Brussels, also speaks some Spanish, Italian, Slovenian and Serbo-Croatian.

Oberstar's father was an iron ore miner and union official who worked in both underground mine shafts and open pits, where Oberstar also labored as a teenager. His mother worked in a shirt factory.

Oberstar's mentor and predecessor in the House was Democrat John A. Blatnik, who rose to the chairmanship of what was then called the Public Works and Transportation Committee. As Blatnik's chief aide, Oberstar learned how to bring federal largess back home. And Blatnik was never shy about earmarking funds to benefit his colleagues' districts.

When Blatnik retired and sought to anoint Oberstar as his successor in 1974, a rival Democratic faction led by Minnesota's Perpich political dynasty sought to derail the plan. But Oberstar won the primary and has been elected with at least 59 percent of the vote ever since.

KEY VOTES

2004

Yes	Extend federal unemployment benefits by 13 weeks
Yes	Pass $283.2 billion, six-year federal highway and mass transit bill
No	Approve $146 billion multi-year extension of previously enacted middle-class tax breaks
?	Amend the Constitution to prohibit same-sex marriage
No	Cut corporate taxes $137 billion over 10 years
No	Reorganize U.S. intelligence agencies as proposed by Sept. 11 commission

2003

No	Cut taxes by $330 billion through fiscal 2013
Yes	Block Bush rule scaling back overtime pay for some white-collar federal workers
Yes	Do not allow use of search warrants without first notifying subjects
Yes	Allow importation of prescription drugs
No	Create private school voucher program in Washington, D.C.
Yes	Ban "partial birth" abortion except to save a woman's life
?	Split $18.6 billion in Iraq aid into half-grant, half-loan
No	Overhaul Medicare and create prescription drug benefit

CQ VOTE STUDIES

	PARTY UNITY		PRESIDENTIAL SUPPORT	
	Support	Oppose	Support	Oppose
2004	91%	9%	27%	73%
2003	91%	9%	33%	67%
2002	94%	6%	28%	72%
2001	87%	13%	34%	66%
2000	92%	8%	80%	20%

INTEREST GROUPS

	AFL-CIO	ADA	CCUS	ACU
2004	93%	75%	14%	12%
2003	100%	85%	24%	44%
2002	100%	80%	26%	4%
2001	100%	75%	35%	24%
2000	100%	75%	25%	8%

MINNESOTA 8
Northeast – Duluth, Iron Range

The expansive 8th covers Minnesota's northeast quadrant, including Duluth and the Iron Range — taconite mining communities that stretch across the middle of the state through Cass, Crow Wing and St. Louis counties. It is the only one of Minnesota's three rural districts to include any of the Minneapolis-St. Paul metro area, although that area makes up only 12 percent of its population.

Logging and mining still provide a solid base for the region, but the workforce is less than half of what it was in the 1980s. After a poor 2003, however, demand for taconite and limestone skyrocketed in 2004 — a boom that is expected to last several years. These blue-collar workers with strong ties to labor cement the 8th's long affiliation with the Democratic-Farmer-Labor Party. The 8th has not sent a Republican to Congress since the 1944 election.

Duluth is the shipping point for much of the grain from the Plains states, and is the westernmost deep sea port to the Atlantic. Both the city and rural areas are Democratic, but voters favor a hands-off approach to

federal land management and tend to oppose gun control and abortion.

The southern end of the district grew in the 1990s by attracting Twin Cities commuters. The GOP is making inroads in this rapidly expanding area, where voters will stray from the 8th's solid Democratic stance.

The district has the most varied terrain in the state, from farms in the south and west through the Iron Range and a watery northern border to rugged terrain in the northeastern arrowhead region. Huge tracts of land are designated as state and national forests, and the Boundary Waters Canoe Area Wilderness along the Canadian border is noted for its motor-free beauty.

MAJOR INDUSTRY
Mining, timber, recreation

CITIES
Duluth, 86,918; Hibbing, 17,071; Brainerd, 13,178

NOTABLE
The gas station designed by Frank Lloyd Wright is in Cloquet; The U.S. Hockey Hall of Fame is in Eveleth; Little Falls was the boyhood home of aviator Charles Lindbergh; International Falls calls itself "the icebox of the nation" and claims to be the coldest spot in the lower 48 states.

MISSISSIPPI

Gov. Haley Barbour (R)

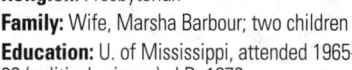

First elected: 2003
Length of term: 4 years
Term expires: 1/08
Salary: $122,000
Phone: (601) 359-3150

Hometown: Yazoo City
Born: Oct. 21, 1947;
Yazoo City, Miss.
Religion: Presbyterian
Family: Wife, Marsha Barbour; two children
Education: U. of Mississippi, attended 1965-69 (political science), J.D. 1973
Career: Lobbyist; lawyer; White House aide; party official
Political highlights: Republican nominee for U.S. Senate, 1982; Republican National Committee chairman, 1993-97

Election results:
2003 GENERAL
Haley Barbour (R)	470,404	52.6%
Ronnie Musgrove (D)	409,787	45.8%
others	14,296	1.6%

Lt. Gov. Amy Tuck (R)

First elected: 1999*
Length of term: 4 years
Term expires: 1/08
Salary: $60,000
Phone: (601) 359-3200
*Elected as a Democrat

STATE LEGISLATURE

Legislature: 90 days January-April

House: 122 members, 4-year terms
2005 breakdown: 75D, 47R; 104 men, 18 women
Salary: $10,000; $1,500/month out of session; $91/day in session
Phone: (601) 359-3360

Senate: 52 members, 4-year terms
2005 breakdown: 28D, 24R; 48 men, 4 women
Salary: $10,000; $1,500/month out of session; $91/day in session
Phone: (601) 359-3202

STATE TERM LIMITS

Governor: 2 terms
House: No
Senate: No

URBAN STATISTICS

CITY	POPULATION
Jackson	184,256
Gulfport	71,127
Biloxi	50,644
Hattiesburg	44,779
Greenville	41,633

REGISTERED VOTERS

Voters do not register by party.

POPULATION

2004 population (est.)	2,902,966
2000 population	2,844,658
1990 population	2,573,216
Percent change (1990-2000)	+10.5%
Rank among states (2004)	31

Median age	33.8
Born in state	74.3%
Foreign born	1.4%
Violent crime rate	361/100,000
Poverty level	19.9%
Federal workers	25,318
Military	35,850

REDISTRICTING

Mississippi lost one House seat in reapportionment. The state legislature failed to agree on a plan and a three-judge federal panel implemented a new, four-district map on Feb. 4, 2002.

MISCELLANEOUS

Web: www.state.ms.us
Capital: Jackson
STATE ELECTION OFFICIAL
(601) 359-6357
DEMOCRATIC HEADQUARTERS
(601) 969-2913
REPUBLICAN HEADQUARTERS
(601) 948-5191

District Statistics

DIST.	2004 VOTE FOR PRESIDENT BUSH	KERRY	WHITE	BLACK	ASIAN	HISP	MEDIAN INCOME	WHITE COLLAR	BLUE COLLAR	SERVICE INDUSTRY	OVER 64	UNDER 18	COLLEGE EDUCATION	RURAL	SQ. MILES
1	62%	37%	71%	26%	0%	1%	$32,535	49%	39%	12%	12%	27%	14%	62%	11,413
2	40	58	35	63	0	1	$26,894	52	31	17	11	29	17	37	13,625
3	65	34	64	33	1	1	$31,907	57	30	13	13	26	20	60	13,168
4	68	31	73	22	1	2	$33,023	52	31	17	12	27	17	46	8,701
STATE	59	39	61	36	1	1	$31,330	52	33	15	12	27	17	51	46,907
U.S.	50.7	48.3	69	12	4	13	$41,994	60	25	15	12	26	24	21	3,537,438

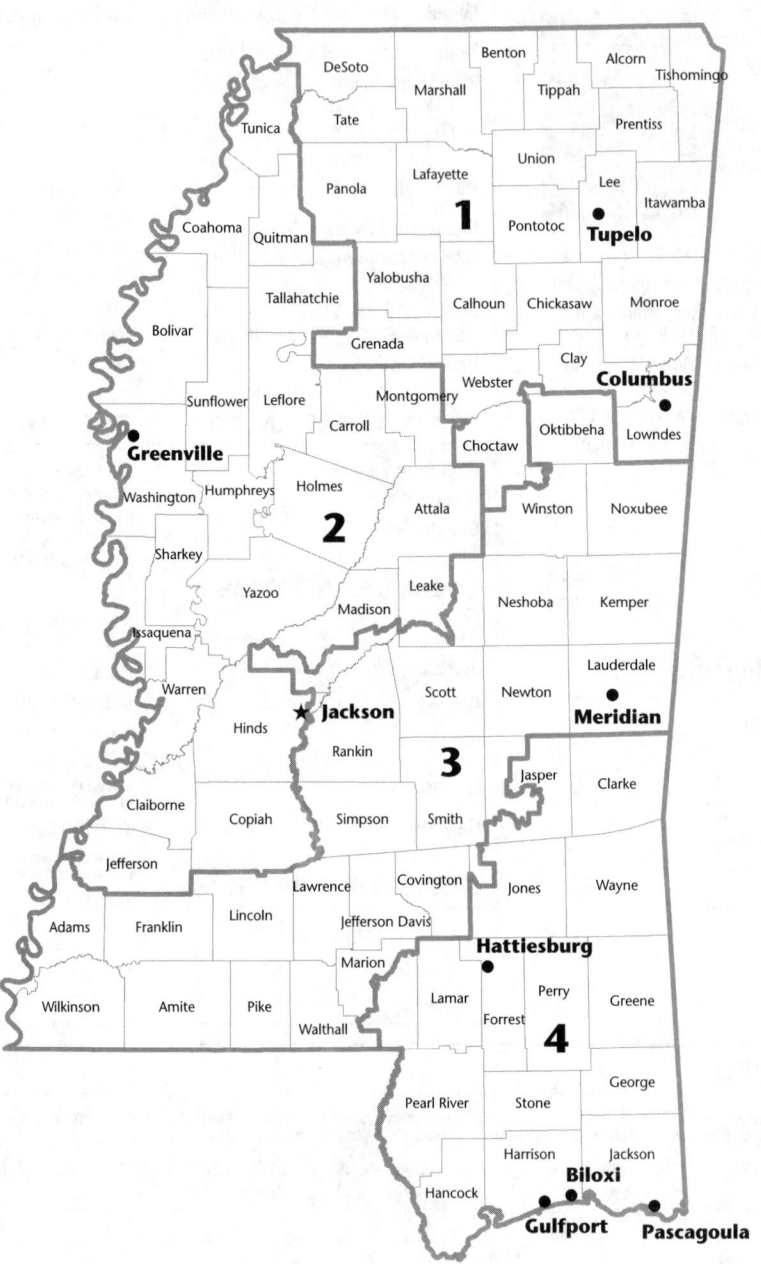

Sen. Thad Cochran (R)

CAPITOL OFFICE
224-5054
cochran.senate.gov
113 Dirksen 20510-2402; fax 224-9450

COMMITTEES
Agriculture, Nutrition & Forestry
Appropriations - chairman
Rules & Administration
Joint Library
Joint Printing

HOMETOWN
Jackson

BORN
Dec. 7, 1937, Pontotoc, Miss.

RELIGION
Baptist

FAMILY
Wife, Rose Cochran; two children

EDUCATION
U. of Mississippi, B.A. 1959 (psychology); Trinity
College (U. of Dublin, Ireland), attended 1963-64
(international law); U. of Mississippi, J.D. 1965

MILITARY SERVICE
Navy, 1959-61

CAREER
Lawyer

POLITICAL HIGHLIGHTS
U.S. House, 1973-78

ELECTION RESULTS

2002 GENERAL

Thad Cochran (R)	533,269	84.6%
Shawn O'Hara (REF)	97,226	15.4%

2002 PRIMARY

Thad Cochran (R)	unopposed

PREVIOUS WINNING PERCENTAGES
1996 (71%); 1990 (100%); 1984 (61%); 1978 (45%);
1976 House Election (76%); 1974 House Election
(70%); 1972 House Election (48%)

Elected 1978; 5th term

The genteel and inscrutable Cochran ascended to the chairmanship of the Appropriations Committee at the outset of the 109th Congress, the pinnacle of his slow, steady rise through the GOP ranks.

Cochran's challenge is to get bills to the floor in an orderly fashion amid tighter than ever budget constraints — a task his predecessor, Republican Ted Stevens of Alaska, had difficulty doing in the 108th Congress. The quiet Mississippian brings a low-key and predictable style to the committee, a stark contrast to his brusque predecessor.

After taking the gavel, Cochran was immediately confronted with a tough test of his leadership abilities. At the direction of House Majority Leader Tom DeLay, the House undertook a major restructuring of its appropriations subcommittees, paring the number from 13 to 10 and shuffling jurisdictions. That put pressure on Cochran to follow suit, or risk longer delays and added difficulties in moving bills. The House and Senate panels traditionally have operated as pairs with almost identical subcommittee jurisdictions, a design that eases negotiations between the chambers as they attempt to reconcile their differences on the spending bills.

Cochran's turf-conscious fellow "cardinals," as the Appropriations subcommittee chairmen are known, resisted following the House's lead. Cochran quietly brokered a compromise. The Senate met the House halfway by giving up one subcommittee and making some jurisdictional changes; Cochran gave up his Homeland Security Subcommittee gavel to accommodate another senator, which eased the pain for several colleagues, who would still get powerful subcommittee slots. The dispute ended, and he was able to avoid what might have been a nasty family feud.

Urbane and thoughtful, Cochran's Southern manner stands out in the modern Senate, where sharp, partisan rhetoric more often holds sway. That in part is why he remained in the background in years past while Mississippi's junior senator, Trent Lott, and other younger Republican conservatives brought their more confrontational style to the chamber.

He and Lott are longtime rivals, dating back to their college days at the University of Mississippi. As Lott moved quickly up the Senate leadership in the late 1990s, Cochran's influence as a facilitator within the GOP was often underestimated. Lott was forced out as Republican leader in 2002 after a furor over a racially divisive remark.

Cochran ran the Agriculture Committee in 2003 and 2004. He also chaired Appropriations' new Homeland Security Subcommittee, steering through a closely divided Senate the department's first two budgets. When Stevens gave up the gavel of the full Appropriations Committee under GOP-imposed term limits in 2005, it was finally Cochran's turn.

For 22 years, he was either the chairman or the top-ranking Republican on the Agriculture Appropriations Subcommittee. In 2002, he was at the center of the rewrite of the law that authorizes federal agriculture subsidies and conservation and nutrition programs.

Otherwise, his stint as Agriculture chairman was uneventful. He held few markups, in part because Charles E. Grassley, an Iowa Republican, threatened to amend any bill coming out of the panel with a provision to lower the maximum a farmer could receive in federal subsidies. Grassley wanted to free up money for other farm programs. Cochran opposed such limits. Mississippi's cotton and rice crops are more expensive to grow than some Midwestern crops and thus receive higher subsidies.

It was Cochran's change of heart that proved a turning point in the long drive to alter campaign finance law. His announcement in January 2001 that he had switched sides and would support the bill that GOP leaders opposed began a steady erosion of Republican opposition; the law was enacted 14 months later. "It became obvious to me that the influence of soft money and independent groups was overwhelming the efforts of candidates," Cochran said.

Elected to the House in President Nixon's re-election landslide of 1972, Cochran established himself as one of the bright lights among the new breed of GOP conservatives who were dissolving the Democrats' "Solid South." But while Nixon's vaunted "Southern Strategy" included a none-too-subtle pitch to whites unhappy about the empowerment of blacks, Cochran avoided alienating black constituents. Though his electoral base was the Jackson area's younger, upwardly mobile white population, he made an effort to maintain contact with the black communities that made up almost half of his constituency.

Yet Cochran is no liberal. In 1990, he was able to oust moderate John H. Chafee of Rhode Island as secretary of the Republican Conference — the third-ranking slot in the Senate GOP hierarchy — because the group's increasingly numerous conservatives were unhappy with Chafee's defection on a range of lightning rod issues for the party.

Still, his approach has been largely conciliatory as he focuses on the pragmatic aspects of legislating. He has plied his skills in the parceling out of federal money to his state, particularly for agriculture programs. In a 2004 package of emergency funding for hurricane and drought victims, Cochran made sure there was $9 million for the "reseeding, rehabilitation and restoration of oyster reefs," which are cultivated in Mississippi. Moreover, he makes sure that his cotton, peanut, rice and sugar farmers get emergency federal relief when they ask for it.

A rivalry between Cochran and Lott probably was inevitable, given that both are smart, attractive politicians in the same party in a relatively small state and that they are nearly contemporaries. Cochran was four years ahead of Lott at Ole Miss, where both were presidents of fraternities as well as cheerleaders — an elected position that was the starting point in many a Mississippi political career.

The son of two educators, Cochran was known even in college as diplomatic and quiet. He was an honor student who later made partner in his Jackson law firm when he was less than three years out of school.

Cochran had been active in local party politics during his law career and was a key state figure in Nixon's 1968 campaign. In 1972, when Democratic Rep. Charles R. Griffin retired, Cochran narrowly won the open seat. Lott was elected to the House the same year, and the two young congressmen soon became the leaders of warring factions within the state party. The pragmatists, led by Cochran, and the ideologues, led by Lott, feuded with increasing intensity for the better part of two decades.

Although Lott wanted to run in 1978, when long-serving Democrat James O. Eastland retired, Cochran muscled him out of the way and became Mississippi's first GOP senator in a century. He won with 45 percent of the vote, as an independent black candidate drew much of the black vote away from Democrat Maurice Dantin, a former Columbia mayor.

All of Cochran's Senate re-elections have been cakewalks. Democrats did not even field a challenger in 1990 or 2002. The only election he has lost along the way was in 1996: When Bob Dole left the Senate to concentrate on his presidential campaign, the two candidates for majority leader were Mississippi's senators. Lott, then the GOP whip, was first out of the gate in rounding up support and won, 44-8.

KEY VOTES

2004
Yes	Pass $318.9 billion, six-year highway and mass transit bill
No	Extend assault weapons ban for 10 years
No	Restore pay-as-you-go rules for new tax cuts and entitlement spending
Yes	Criminalize harm to a fetus in an attack on the mother
Yes	Increase mandatory child care funding to states by $6 billion over five years
Yes	Amend the Constitution to prohibit same-sex marriage
Yes	Approve $146 billion multi-year extension of previously enacted middle-class tax breaks
Yes	Reorganize U.S. intelligence agencies as proposed by Sept. 11 commission
Yes	Cut corporate taxes $137 billion over 10 years

2003
No	Delay Bush changes to Clean Air Act
Yes	Allow confirmation vote on Miguel A. Estrada to the U.S. Court of Appeals for the D.C. Circuit
No	Block a Bush proposal opening Alaska's Arctic National Wildlife Refuge to oil drilling
No	Limit size of Bush's proposed tax cut to $350 billion through fiscal 2013
Yes	Overhaul Medicare and create prescription drug benefit
No	Block Bush rule scaling back overtime pay for some white-collar federal workers
No	Split $20 billion in Iraq aid into half-grant, half-loan
Yes	Ban "partial birth" abortion except to save a woman's life
Yes	Stop proposal allowing travel to Cuba
Yes	Allow final vote on energy policy overhaul

CQ VOTE STUDIES

	PARTY UNITY		PRESIDENTIAL SUPPORT	
	Support	Oppose	Support	Oppose
2004	98%	2%	92%	8%
2003	98%	2%	98%	2%
2002	86%	14%	96%	4%
2001	84%	16%	96%	4%
2000	98%	2%	45%	55%
1999	94%	6%	38%	62%
1998	86%	14%	53%	47%
1997	82%	18%	68%	32%
1996	93%	7%	40%	60%
1995	93%	7%	34%	66%

INTEREST GROUPS

	AFL-CIO	ADA	CCUS	ACU
2004	8%	15%	100%	92%
2003	0%	5%	100%	85%
2002	23%	25%	100%	90%
2001	25%	15%	86%	88%
2000	0%	0%	100%	92%
1999	0%	0%	88%	84%
1998	0%	0%	100%	76%
1997	0%	15%	90%	56%
1996	0%	5%	91%	94%
1995	8%	0%	95%	83%

Sen. Trent Lott (R)

CAPITOL OFFICE
224-6253
senatorlott@lott.senate.gov
lott.senate.gov
487 Russell 20510-2403; fax 224-2262

COMMITTEES
Commerce, Science & Transportation
   (Surface Transportation & Merchant Marine -
   chairman)
Finance
Rules & Administration - chairman
Select Intelligence
Joint Library - chairman
Joint Printing
Joint Taxation

HOMETOWN
Pascagoula

BORN
Oct. 9, 1941, Grenada County, Miss.

RELIGION
Baptist

FAMILY
Wife, Patricia Elizabeth Lott; two children

EDUCATION
U. of Mississippi, B.P.A. 1963 (public
administration), J.D. 1967

CAREER
Lawyer; congressional aide

POLITICAL HIGHLIGHTS
U.S. House, 1973-89

ELECTION RESULTS

2000 GENERAL

Trent Lott (R)	654,941	65.9%
Troy Brown (D)	314,090	31.6%

2000 PRIMARY

Trent Lott (R)	unopposed

PREVIOUS WINNING PERCENTAGES
1994 (69%); 1988 (54%); 1986 House Election (82%);
1984 House Election (85%); 1982 House Election
(79%); 1980 House Election (74%); 1978 House
Election (100%); 1976 House Election (68%); 1974
House Election (73%); 1972 House Election (55%)

Elected 1988; 3rd term

After getting booted from the Senate leadership, Lott has pulled off one of the more unlikely resurrections in the modern Congress. He has remade himself into a maverick, a favorite of reporters who chase him down the Senate corridors for his candid views on issues and internal Senate Republican politics. They know what his nervous colleagues also know: You never can tell what Lott will say next.

That, of course, is the characteristic that led to Lott's fall from grace. In six and a half years as Senate Republican leader, including about five years as majority leader from 1996 through 2001, Lott was faithful to the party line but also had a habit of speaking off-the-cuff. Usually, this did little damage, but in December 2002, the impact was devastating. In a birthday speech for retiring GOP Sen. Strom Thurmond of South Carolina, Lott made a remark that seemed to praise Thurmond's segregationist campaign for president in 1948. Embarrassed Republicans moved against him, and Lott was forced out of the leadership.

Now, Lott has settled into a more low-key Senate career. He chairs the Rules and Administration Committee, a post he was given by the new leadership to cushion his fall. He also heads the Commerce Committee's Subcommittee on Surface Transportation and Merchant Marine, providing him the opportunity to have an impact on the huge surface transportation bill to be reauthorized in the 109th Congress. He has used his influence to serve the more traditional role of steering federal funds to his state, winning aid for Mississippi's shipbuilding industry and funds for an economic development center at the University of Southern Mississippi.

Lott has the cheerful, carefree air of a politician who has already lost everything that he can lose and has still survived. "I'm a free agent these days," Lott said in 2004. "I can be anywhere I want." He plans to run for re-election in 2006, a move that would have been unthinkable at the height of the controversy over his Thurmond speech, when it was not clear he would serve out the rest of his term.

In his new role, Lott has worked with Democrats, teaming up with Byron L. Dorgan of North Dakota on a resolution opposing the Bush administration's rule allowing greater consolidation of media ownership. He backed moderate Arlen Specter of Pennsylvania to head the Judiciary Committee in the 109th, defending him against social conservatives who thought he was not committed to putting anti-abortion judges on the federal bench. And Lott worked with other moderates on the 2004 overhaul of the intelligence agencies, whipping votes and helping to settle disputes.

There is little doubt that Lott is still a committed conservative. He favors the "nuclear option" on judges, the Republican effort to change the chamber's rules in order to end Democrats' ability to filibuster conservative nominees. He opposed the 2003 Medicare prescription drug bill as too expensive, only reluctantly casting the deciding vote against a Democratic attempt to kill the bill.

But Lott is no longer a reliable party-line voter. In the 108th Congress, his record was about in the middle of the Senate Republican rankings for votes that pitted a majority of Republicans against a majority of Democrats — a notable change from his leadership days, when he usually ranked near the top.

Lott effectively ended his leadership career on Dec. 5, 2002, when he gave an impromptu speech at a party celebrating Thurmond's 100th birthday. "I want to say this about my state: When Strom Thurmond ran for president, we voted for him. We're proud of it," Lott said. "And if the rest of the country had followed our lead, we wouldn't have had all these problems over all these years, either."

His remarks ignited a political firestorm. He issued several public apologies and even appeared on Black Entertainment Television to declare his support for affirmative action policies. But Republicans, angry at seeing the party cast as insensitive to minorities, distanced themselves, and President Bush called his remarks "offensive." Behind the scenes, the White House maneuvered to replace him with Bill Frist of Tennessee, a Bush ally and a polished politician who better symbolized the New South, especially for younger Republicans. After Frist announced he would challenge Lott at a special GOP caucus to reconsider the party's leadership, Lott, his political options exhausted, stepped down.

Since then, Lott has tried to avoid second-guessing Frist's decisions, though occasionally he will. In 2004, as the Senate attempted to broaden the jurisdiction of the Governmental Affairs Committee to include homeland security, Lott wondered why Frist let so many panel chairmen protect their turf. "I'm trying to be as nice as I can," Lott said, "but I don't think the leadership can basically say 'I'm agnostic and, you know, I can go either way.' You have to lead." Still, Lott sponsored a change in GOP conference rules that gave Frist more power in the 109th by letting him fill half of all vacancies on the most prestigious committees.

Lott remains a study in contrasts. The son of a shipyard worker, he favors pinstriped suits and tightly knotted silk ties. A courtly Southerner, he talks faster than many of his Northern colleagues. A committed conservative, he often tried as majority leader to cut deals with former Democratic Leader Tom Daschle to keep the Senate moving.

A single-minded focus on forcing bills to passage, and a sometimes dictatorial approach, created internal strife within his party. It was Lott's threat of retribution against those who strayed on Bush's first tax cut proposal that backfired badly for the Republicans. Moderate James M. Jeffords of Vermont quit the GOP in a huff, became an independent and sided with the Democrats, handing that party control of the Senate in June 2001.

When Lott arrived on the Capitol's north side in 1989, he was part of a wave of aggressive conservatives moving over from the House eager to push a more overtly conservative agenda in the clubby Senate. Lott won election as Republican Conference secretary in 1993, and two years later he ousted the more moderate Alan K. Simpson of Wyoming to become whip. Eighteen months after that, when Majority Leader Bob Dole resigned to focus on his 1996 presidential campaign, Lott sought the top job, vowing more-aggressive leadership. His opponent was longtime political rival Thad Cochran, the senior senator from Mississippi. The mild-tempered Cochran offered the GOP a chance to vote against the changes in political style. The party voted for change and for Lott, 44-8.

Lott has been a political animal at least since his days at the University of Mississippi, where he was a cheerleader and president of the Interfraternity Council. He came to Washington in 1968 as the top aide to House Rules Committee Chairman William M. Colmer, a Mississippi Democrat. When Colmer retired in 1972, Lott switched parties and ran as a Republican to succeed him. He won with 55 percent of the vote against Democratic state Sen. Ben Stone and was easily re-elected seven times. In 1981, he became the first House Republican whip from the Deep South.

When Democrat John C. Stennis retired in 1988 after 41 years in the Senate, Lott was elected with 54 percent over Democratic Rep. Wayne Dowdy. Democrats have put up a minimal fight in Lott's two subsequent contests.

KEY VOTES

2004
Yes Pass $318.9 billion, six-year highway and mass transit bill
No   Extend assault weapons ban for 10 years
No   Restore pay-as-you-go rules for new tax cuts and entitlement spending
Yes Criminalize harm to a fetus in an attack on the mother
No   Increase mandatory child care funding to states by $6 billion over five years
Yes Amend the Constitution to prohibit same-sex marriage
Yes Approve $146 billion multi-year extension of previously enacted middle-class tax breaks
Yes Reorganize U.S. intelligence agencies as proposed by Sept. 11 commission
Yes Cut corporate taxes $137 billion over 10 years

2003
No   Delay Bush changes to Clean Air Act
Yes Allow confirmation vote on Miguel A. Estrada to the U.S. Court of Appeals for the D.C. Circuit
No   Block a Bush proposal opening Alaska's Arctic National Wildlife Refuge to oil drilling
No   Limit size of Bush's proposed tax cut to $350 billion through fiscal 2013
No   Overhaul Medicare and create prescription drug benefit
No   Block Bush rule scaling back overtime pay for some white-collar federal workers
No   Split $20 billion in Iraq aid into half-grant, half-loan
Yes Ban "partial birth" abortion except to save a woman's life
Yes Stop proposal allowing travel to Cuba
Yes Allow final vote on energy policy overhaul

CQ VOTE STUDIES

	PARTY UNITY		PRESIDENTIAL SUPPORT	
	Support	Oppose	Support	Oppose
2004	94%	6%	94%	6%
2003	98%	2%	97%	3%
2002	98%	2%	100%	0%
2001	98%	2%	96%	4%
2000	98%	2%	45%	55%
1999	97%	3%	32%	68%
1998	96%	4%	39%	61%
1997	94%	6%	56%	44%
1996	97%	3%	34%	66%
1995	98%	2%	23%	77%

INTEREST GROUPS

	AFL-CIO	ADA	CCUS	ACU
2004	17%	5%	100%	96%
2003	0%	10%	96%	89%
2002	15%	0%	100%	100%
2001	0%	0%	85%	96%
2000	0%	5%	93%	100%
1999	0%	0%	82%	96%
1998	0%	0%	94%	92%
1997	0%	5%	90%	72%
1996	0%	5%	85%	100%
1995	0%	0%	100%	96%

Rep. Roger Wicker (R)

CAPITOL OFFICE
225-4306
roger.wicker@mail.house.gov
www.house.gov/wicker
2455 Rayburn 20515-2401; fax 225-3549

COMMITTEES
Appropriations
Budget

HOMETOWN
Tupelo

BORN
July 5, 1951, Pontotoc, Miss.

RELIGION
Southern Baptist

FAMILY
Wife, Gayle Wicker; three children

EDUCATION
U. of Mississippi, B.A. 1973 (political science & journalism), J.D. 1975

MILITARY SERVICE
Air Force, 1976-80; Air Force Reserve, 1980-2004

CAREER
County public defender; lawyer; congressional aide

POLITICAL HIGHLIGHTS
Miss. Senate, 1988-94

ELECTION RESULTS

2004 GENERAL

Roger Wicker (R)	219,328	78.9%
Barbara Dale Washer (REF)	58,256	21.1%

2004 PRIMARY

Roger Wicker (R)	unopposed

2002 GENERAL

Roger Wicker (R)	95,404	71.4%
Rex N. Weathers (D)	32,318	24.2%
Brenda Blackburn (REF)	3,477	2.6%
Harold M. Taylor (LIBERT)	2,368	1.8%

PREVIOUS WINNING PERCENTAGES
2000 (70%); 1998 (67%); 1996 (68%); 1994 (63%)

Elected 1994; 6th term

Wicker was president of the historic "Republican revolution" class of 1994, but he is far from a firebrand. He prefers the quiet work in the trenches of the Appropriations Committee where he can provide for his district — something he has done quite effectively during the past decade.

With the help of fellow Mississippi Republican and former boss Sen. Trent Lott, Wicker is trying to turn his impoverished state into a magnet for high-tech defense jobs by sending millions of dollars into his district to encourage research, provide tax breaks and build infrastructure. His seat on Appropriations' Defense Subcommittee helps him with this goal.

"Twenty years ago, who would have dreamed that aircraft plants would spring out of the forests and soybean fields of Mississippi. . . . We are well positioned in the Congress and through the resources in this region to continue developing this enormous potential," Wicker said in 2004.

While such successes have led to Mississippi consistently landing on the list of "12 Porkiest States" put out by Citizens Against Government Waste, Wicker regards himself as a fiscal conservative willing to rein in federal spending. In 1999, he backed a proposal to impose an across-the-board spending cut, declaring, "There are no winners and losers, and I don't know of any accounts that couldn't take a small hit."

Wicker is proud to have been a leader of the Class of '94 and attended a 10th anniversary reunion intended to rekindle some of the intellectual fires of a decade ago, but he never viewed taking control of the House for the first time in 40 years as a revolution. "I didn't come to Washington to burn all the buildings down. We were all unfairly painted with the same brush," he said in 1998. "Most of us in our own ways are much more pragmatic and results-oriented."

Yet he also remains a loyal and conservative Republican. Wicker rarely breaks with party leaders on votes and is consistently given high scores by the American Conservative Union — not to mention a lifetime rating of 1 from the liberal Americans for Democratic Action.

Wicker scored one of his major legislative victories in the 108th Congress. Appalled by the poor understanding most high school students have of American history, Wicker joined with Republican Lamar Alexander of Tennessee in a two-year effort to create special academies that would teach history to both high school students and teachers. "If we expect future generations to appreciate what it means to be an American, we must teach them," he told The Clarion-Ledger of Jackson, Miss.

The bill passed and was signed by President Bush in 2004. The victory was not unalloyed, however — $25 million intended to fund the academies was stripped out after conservative groups objected to the measure because they feared the curricula would have a liberal bias. Grants for the academies must now come out of scarce general education funds.

Wicker is also mastering the use of the appropriations process to further non-fiscal goals. He wrote language setting National Institutes of Health guidelines to block federal funding of embryonic stem cell research until Bush announced a new policy in 2001 that allowed studies using only a limited number of embryos that already had been harvested.

As a member of the subcommittee that funds the Health and Human Services, Education and Labor departments, Wicker takes a special interest in beefing up funding for disease research. He helped lead efforts to double the NIH budget over five years and has championed spending more to fight polio, provide for Muscular Dystrophy research and help improve the lives of cancer survivors.

Wicker also makes certain that his constituents know about every district road improvement he has helped win money for and every contract he has helped steer to his alma mater, the University of Mississippi. In 2000, Wicker, Lott and Republican Sen. Thad Cochran of Mississippi persuaded a reluctant NIH to create a new National Institute of Biomedical Imaging and Bioengineering with an initial appropriation of $112 million and with the ultimate goal of landing an institute campus at Ole Miss.

Wicker's seniority on Appropriations should have put him next in line to join the "college of cardinals," the subcommittee chairmen who develop the drafts of the annual spending bills, but new committee Chairman Jerry Lewis and Majority Leader Tom DeLay succeeded in reducing the number of cardinals from 13 to 10. That pushed Wicker further back in line.

Wicker is an easygoing, approachable man who sings in his church choir, acts in community theater groups and once chaired the Mississippi Senate's Public Health and Welfare Committee even though the Democrats controlled the chamber.

Raised in a political family — his father was a county attorney, a state senator and then a circuit judge for 20 years — Wicker organized the local Teenage Republican club in high school. Although his father was a Democrat, as was virtually every office-holder in the South in those days, Wicker says, "There's not a dime's worth of difference in his philosophy of government and mine."

He was the first Republican ever to be elected student body president at Ole Miss. While still in college, he was a delegate to the 1972 Republican National Convention and came to know a young Trent Lott as the latter was making his first run for Congress. Wicker was in the Air Force ROTC and after law school served four years on active duty as a prosecutor before going to work for Lott in Washington in 1980. He came home to practice law and, in 1987, won his own state Senate seat. In Jackson, he helped write Mississippi's strict abortion law and push through an education overhaul that included a controversial school-choice provision.

When Democrat Jamie L. Whitten retired in 1994 after 53 years in the House — the longest service in the chamber's history — the conservative-minded 1st District was ripe for GOP picking. Wicker emphasized his legislative experience and edged out Grant Fox, a former Cochran aide, for the Republican nomination. In November, he won with 63 percent of the vote, and he has not been seriously challenged since.

KEY VOTES

2004

No Extend federal unemployment benefits by 13 weeks
Yes Pass $283.2 billion, six-year federal highway and mass transit bill
Yes Approve $146 billion multi-year extension of previously enacted middle-class tax breaks
Yes Amend the Constitution to prohibit same-sex marriage
Yes Cut corporate taxes $137 billion over 10 years
Yes Reorganize U.S. intelligence agencies as proposed by Sept. 11 commission

2003

Yes Cut taxes by $330 billion through fiscal 2013
No Block Bush rule scaling back overtime pay for some white-collar federal workers
Yes Do not allow use of search warrants without first notifying subjects
Yes Allow importation of prescription drugs
Yes Create private school voucher program in Washington, D.C.
Yes Ban "partial birth" abortion except to save a woman's life
No Split $18.6 billion in Iraq aid into half-grant, half-loan
Yes Overhaul Medicare and create prescription drug benefit

CQ VOTE STUDIES

	PARTY UNITY		PRESIDENTIAL SUPPORT	
	Support	Oppose	Support	Oppose
2004	95%	5%	86%	14%
2003	97%	3%	96%	4%
2002	99%	1%	85%	15%
2001	99%	1%	95%	5%
2000	93%	7%	22%	78%

INTEREST GROUPS

	AFL-CIO	ADA	CCUS	ACU
2004	8%	0%	100%	87%
2003	0%	10%	97%	88%
2002	11%	0%	90%	100%
2001	8%	0%	96%	96%
2000	0%	0%	85%	84%

MISSISSIPPI 1
North — Tupelo, Southaven, Columbus

The northeastern Hill Country and rich farmland on the edge of the Delta region in northwestern Mississippi support an agricultural economy in the 1st, while manufacturing dominates in Lee County (Tupelo) and surrounding areas.

The region has made several efforts in recent years to bolster manufacturing, including securing federal funds for a center to help develop locally owned businesses that is scheduled to open in 2006. A 2004 law to designate U.S. 78 as Interstate 22 as soon as the road reaches Interstate standards is expected to draw manufacturing jobs, and officials are hopeful Toyota will expand into the district this decade. Tupelo, the 1st's largest city, is a major producer of upholstered furniture, and the University of Mississippi is located in Oxford.

In the district's northwestern corner, De Soto County is becoming a haven for residents who commute to Memphis over the Tennessee border. De Soto is the district's most populous county and its fastest growing — its population expanded by nearly 50 percent in the 1990s.

Just to the east, Marshall and Benton counties are home to many of the district's African-Americans, a group that makes up more than one-fourth of the district's population. Redistricting following the 2000 census attached Lowndes County, which includes Columbus and Columbus Air Force Base, to the district's extreme southeast corner.

Democrats — including Jamie L. Whitten, the longest-serving House member — held the congressional seat for more than a century until Republicans captured it in 1994. Voters here have gradually turned away from Democrats in federal elections, favoring GOP presidential candidates. Democrats still dominate state and local elections, stemming from the party's provincial political monopoly since Reconstruction.

MAJOR INDUSTRY
Furniture, agriculture, manufacturing

MILITARY BASES
Columbus Air Force Base, 1,492 military, 1,319 civilian (2003)

CITIES
Tupelo, 34,211; Southaven, 28,977; Columbus, 25,944; Olive Branch, 21,054

NOTABLE
Tupelo hosts a biannual national furniture market that draws enough visitors to temporarily double the local population.

Rep. Bennie Thompson (D)

Elected April 1993; 6th full term

CAPITOL OFFICE
225-5876
benniethompson.house.gov
2432 Rayburn 20515-2402; fax 225-5898

COMMITTEES
Homeland Security - ranking member

HOMETOWN
Bolton

BORN
Jan. 28, 1948, Bolton, Miss.

RELIGION
Methodist

FAMILY
Wife, London Thompson; one child

EDUCATION
Tougaloo College, B.A. 1968 (political science);
Jackson State College, M.S. 1972 (educational
administration)

CAREER
Teacher

POLITICAL HIGHLIGHTS
Bolton Board of Aldermen, 1969-73; mayor of
Bolton, 1973-79; Hinds County Board of
Supervisors, 1980-93

ELECTION RESULTS

2004 GENERAL

Bennie Thompson (D)	154,526	58.4%
Clinton B. LeSueur (R)	107,647	40.7%

2004 PRIMARY

Bennie Thompson (D)	unopposed

2002 GENERAL

Bennie Thompson (D)	89,913	55.1%
Clinton B. LeSueur (R)	69,711	42.8%
Lee F. Dilworth (REF)	3,426	2.1%

PREVIOUS WINNING PERCENTAGES
2000 (65%); 1998 (71%); 1996 (60%); 1994 (54%);
1993 Special Runoff Election (55%)

Thompson has spent more than half his life in public service. In 1968, at age 20, he ran successfully for alderman in his native Bolton, Miss., but white officials prevented him from taking the seat until a court order forced the town to relent. His early experience as a black politician in Mississippi and the makeup of his constituency — largely black, rural and poor — have made him a champion of civil rights issues in Congress.

But as the 109th Congress got under way, Thompson found himself in a new role. He is now the top-ranking Democrat on the Homeland Security Committee, which became a permanent committee in early 2005. He and California Republican Christopher Cox, the committee's chairman, will run a high-profile committee with jurisdiction over the Transportation Security Administration, border security, infrastructure protection, and some Customs functions. "This committee has a solemn responsibility to conduct meaningful oversight of the Department of Homeland Security and take whatever steps necessary to ensure terrorism never occurs on our soil again," Thompson told the Federal Times.

Yet Thompson's ascension on the committee does little to help his district. In fact, as a result he was forced to leave the Agriculture Committee, where he was also near the top in seniority. The Agriculture panel is a better match for his district, which faces few terrorist risks but depends heavily on farming. On Homeland Security, he will look out for the interests of rural districts, such as his own, as the panel considers changes to the formula for allocating homeland security grants, to give greater weight to the risks of terrorism. That may put him at odds with Cox and big-city Democrats, however.

He started his tenure at the committee by cleaning house, letting go the minority staff director, general counsel and communications director with little notice. He said he was undertaking a "total evaluation" of the committee staff, and was looking for the "best and brightest folk" to work for him. But Thompson, who replaced Texas Democrat Jim Turner as the top-ranking Democrat after Turner retired, also had publicly complained in 2003 about Turner's decision not to hire more minorities for top staff positions.

Thompson's rural, black-majority 2nd District is one of the poorest in the nation. He has been able to secure some federal funding to improve the region's infrastructure, rural housing and health care. When the Congressional Black Caucus met with President Bush early in 2005, Thompson complained that rural access to health care is dwindling in his state. "The insurance companies do not want to insure doctors in medically underserved areas, and that is a major issue for rural America," Thompson told The Washington Times. "And when you tie in blacks in [rural] areas, the disparities go off the charts."

He has joined other Black Caucus members from largely rural districts in protesting that the Agriculture Department has long been guilty of discriminating against blacks in the administration of federal farm and loan programs. In 2001, he introduced legislation to compensate black farmers for such discrimination.

Although his state's political landscape has changed since Thompson's first election, as many blacks now hold office, in Thompson's view too much has stayed the same. He still feels that minorities wage an uphill battle against the wealthy and the powerful, and he has called for aggressive federal action to combat discrimination. Even his own party does not escape criticism; he says African-Americans "have been taken for granted."

But he saves most of his barbs for Republicans. When home-state senator Trent Lott lauded Strom Thurmond's segregationist 1948 presidential campaign, Thompson, the state's only black congressman, condemned the remarks, and noted that Lott had never sought him out in the decade they had both served in Congress. When Thompson hears the conservative House GOP majority malign affirmative action, he bristles. He once told his colleagues, "For most of us who are over 45, we never had new textbooks in our community, we never had the opportunity to play in a public playground or swim in a public swimming pool, and so some of us take very seriously the notion of affirmative action because this was the only opportunity that many of us ever received."

Thompson spends much of his time in Washington trying to get federal funds sent home to the 2nd District. Even with a Republican House majority and president, Thompson has continued to lobby for federal money. In 2002, $6.2 million in federal grants was awarded to Central Mississippi Inc., which runs a Head Start program in Winona.

Born in 1948, Thompson was educated in segregated elementary and secondary schools in Mississippi. At Tougaloo College, he met civil rights activist Fannie Lou Hamer, who inspired him to pursue a political career. Thompson graduated from Tougaloo in 1968 and that same year won a seat on the Bolton Board of Aldermen. Four years later, he was elected mayor of Bolton. At 32, he took a seat on the board of supervisors for Hinds County, which includes the state capital, Jackson. His pioneering record led President Clinton to name Thompson as one of 100 "unsung African-Americans" honored at the 2004 opening of his presidential library.

The House seat Thompson won in a 1993 special election had been held since 1987 by Mike Espy, Mississippi's first African-American in Congress since Reconstruction. Espy resigned in January 1993 to become Clinton's secretary of Agriculture. In the special election, the first-place finisher in the initial balloting was Republican Hayes Dent, an adviser to GOP Gov. Kirk Fordice. Dent took 34 percent of the vote; Thompson ran second with 28 percent. Thompson prevailed in the runoff with 55 percent.

In his 1994 bid for a full term, Thompson faced Bill Jordan, a black attorney and ordained minister. Thompson outspent Jordan and won by 15 percentage points. His next three re-elections were by comfortable margins. In 2002, he defeated Clinton B. LeSueur, an underfunded and little-known candidate, with 55 percent. And in 2004, he bested LeSueur in a rematch, collecting 58 percent.

KEY VOTES

2004
Yes Extend federal unemployment benefits by 13 weeks
Yes Pass $283.2 billion, six-year federal highway and mass transit bill
?   Approve $146 billion multi-year extension of previously enacted middle-class tax breaks
Yes Amend the Constitution to prohibit same-sex marriage
Yes Cut corporate taxes $137 billion over 10 years
Yes Reorganize U.S. intelligence agencies as proposed by Sept. 11 commission

2003
No   Cut taxes by $330 billion through fiscal 2013
Yes Block Bush rule scaling back overtime pay for some white-collar federal workers
Yes Do not allow use of search warrants without first notifying subjects
No   Allow importation of prescription drugs
No   Create private school voucher program in Washington, D.C.
No   Ban "partial birth" abortion except to save a woman's life
Yes Split $18.6 billion in Iraq aid into half-grant, half-loan
No   Overhaul Medicare and create prescription drug benefit

CQ VOTE STUDIES

	PARTY UNITY		PRESIDENTIAL SUPPORT	
	Support	Oppose	Support	Oppose
2004	92%	8%	33%	67%
2003	94%	6%	25%	75%
2002	94%	6%	22%	78%
2001	87%	13%	29%	71%
2000	92%	8%	77%	23%

INTEREST GROUPS

	AFL-CIO	ADA	CCUS	ACU
2004	87%	85%	45%	8%
2003	100%	90%	43%	20%
2002	100%	90%	55%	8%
2001	100%	85%	48%	12%
2000	100%	90%	50%	8%

MISSISSIPPI 2
West central — Jackson, Mississippi Delta

The 2nd combines most of Jackson, the state's capital and largest city, with the nutrient-rich flatlands of the Mississippi Delta. The agricultural economy stemming from the Delta has promoted landowner/tenant relationships that have made the 2nd one of the poorest districts in the nation. Parts of the Delta still lack centralized running water.

Most of the district lies west of Interstate 55 and north of Interstate 20. Traveling west from Jackson, it moves into Vicksburg on the Louisiana border. Just north of the city, the road drops 15 feet in Issaquena County, marking the beginning of the flat Delta, where some of the nation's most fertile soil supports cotton and soybeans. Although some low-income white residents call the 2nd home, it is the only black-majority district in a state with the highest percentage of black residents in the nation.

The 2nd's economic underpinnings come from a variety of sources. Some successes include Vicksburg, where a mixture of tourism, casinos and a Mississippi River port have fostered local prosperity, and a Nissan assembly plant outside Canton, just north of Jackson. Progress like this,

however, is not universal. Popular casinos in Tunica County have helped erase its standing as the nation's poorest county, but many workers commute from outside the district. Manufacturing jobs have been lost to Mexico over the past decade, but government, service and small-scale manufacturing jobs have kept unemployment in check in Jackson. The collapse of WorldCom (now MCI) hit the district hard — after the financial scandal erupted in 2002, the company moved its headquarters to Virginia and eliminated more than 2,000 jobs. The fate of the remaining employees is unclear in the wake of Verizon's 2005 deal to acquire MCI.

Democratic since 1987, the 2nd's politics are dominated by the African-American vote, although Republicans hold small areas around Jackson and the district's northeast.

MAJOR INDUSTRY
Agriculture, government, casinos

CITIES
Jackson (pt.), 152,424; Greenville, 41,633; Vicksburg, 26,407; Clinton, 23,347; Clarksdale, 20,645; Greenwood, 18,425

NOTABLE
Blues music was born in the Delta: Pioneer Muddy Waters was born in Rolling Fork in 1915, and legend B.B. King was born in Indianola in 1925.

Rep. Charles W. 'Chip' Pickering Jr. (R)

Elected 1996; 5th term

CAPITOL OFFICE
225-5031
www.house.gov/pickering
229 Cannon 20515-2403; fax 225-5797

COMMITTEES
Energy & Commerce

HOMETOWN
Laurel

BORN
Aug. 10, 1963, Laurel, Miss.

RELIGION
Baptist

FAMILY
Wife, Leisha Jane Pickering; five children

EDUCATION
Mississippi College, attended 1981-82; U. of Mississippi, B.A. 1986 (business administration); Baylor U., M.B.A. 1989

CAREER
Congressional aide; U.S. Agriculture Department official

POLITICAL HIGHLIGHTS
No previous office

ELECTION RESULTS

2004 GENERAL

Charles W. Pickering Jr. (R)	234,874	80.1%
Jim Giles (I)	40,426	13.8%
Lamonica L. Magee (REF)	18,068	6.2%

2004 PRIMARY

Charles W. Pickering Jr. (R)	unopposed

2002 GENERAL

Charles W. Pickering Jr. (R)	139,329	63.6%
Ronnie Shows (D)	76,184	34.8%

PREVIOUS WINNING PERCENTAGES
2000 (73%); 1998 (85%); 1996 (61%)

A fresh-faced conservative from a prominent Mississippi Republican family, Pickering is a man on the rise. After five terms in the House, he has established a reputation as an effective legislator and a reliable party operative. But he may not be applying his skills to the House much longer.

Pickering is widely viewed as a likely successor to his mentor and long-time family friend, Trent Lott, if the former GOP Senate leader decides to retire after the 109th Congress.

During the 108th, Pickering served as assistant House majority whip and played a key role in helping the party leadership convince wayward Republicans to support President Bush's Medicare prescription drug plan.

He also spent a good deal of time lobbying senators in behalf of his father, Charles W. Pickering Sr., one of Bush's most controversial judicial nominees. The elder Pickering's record on civil rights helped sink his nomination to the 5th Circuit Court of Appeals in both 2002 and 2003, leading Bush to give him a temporary recess appointment while Congress was on break in early 2004.

The junior Pickering's previous jobs — two years as an Agriculture Department political appointee followed by four years as a legislative aide to Lott — helped him master the legislative process quickly and choose issues on which to make his name. So, too, did his political support from the rest of the "Mississippi mafia" of Thad Cochran, the state's senior senator, and Gov. Haley Barbour, a former Republican National Committee chairman.

Serving as Mississippi co-chairman of Bush's campaigns in both 2000 and 2004, Pickering has been a strong supporter of the president. He vigorously promoted the Bush tax cuts and embraced the president's call for a constitutional amendment defining marriage as the union of a man and a woman. In 2004, he cosponsored the House version of the amendment. "Protecting the institution of marriage guards the very social fabric of our country," he said. "The encouragement of marriage will be fruitless if the very foundation of marriage is destroyed." In 2002, when a federal court ruled that it was unconstitutional to require schoolchildren to recite the Pledge of Allegiance because of its phrase "under God," Pickering introduced a constitutional amendment to explicitly allow the pledge to be recited anywhere, including in schools.

From his seat on the Energy and Commerce Committee, where he holds the honorary title of vice chairman, Pickering has been able to use the expertise he developed as the telecommunications aide for Lott. He was one of Lott's pivotal staff players during the debate over the 1996 overhaul of telecommunications law. In the 108th, Pickering and GOP Senator John E. Sununu of New Hampshire introduced legislation that would assert federal jurisdiction over the growing Internet phone industry, barring states from taxing and regulating it. "We're pre-empting any type of regulatory intrusion" by states, Pickering said. That is one of many issues to be addressed during a rewrite of the telecommunications law in the 109th.

In 2002, the big telecommunications fight was over whether to allow the four regional Bell companies to offer broadband Internet services over telephone lines without first opening their local markets to competitors, an important requirement of 1996 law. MCI WorldCom, then a long-distance company headquartered near Pickering's district just outside of Jackson, opposed the bill, and Pickering sided with them. He argued that it would kill competition in the telecommunications market, a position at odds with

Republican Billy Tauzin of Louisiana, a main sponsor of the bill and the Energy and Commerce chairman at the time. Though the House easily passed a bill, the Senate did not act.

Pickering's technical expertise and political savvy caught the attention of business leaders who testified before him in congressional hearings. In July 2003, Pickering announced he was turning down an offer to lobby for the Cellular Telecommunications and Internet Association at a million-dollar-plus salary. "I feel a calling to public service," he said. The White House reportedly encouraged him to remain in Congress, suggesting he had a bright future.

Pickering, who says he is a seventh-generation Mississippian, comes from a prominent Jones County family, of which his father remains the patriarch. But he says he "kind of rebelled against" politics as a youth. He went to small, Baptist-run Mississippi College for three semesters, then worked for a year on the family dairy and catfish farm before heading to the University of Mississippi to study business. After college, Pickering was a trailblazer in establishing a Baptist missionary presence beyond the Iron Curtain, in Hungary. He then returned to another Baptist institution, Baylor University, for a master's degree with an emphasis on international business.

In the Agriculture Department under President George Bush, he specialized in export promotion. Pickering started a family — his five sons are prominently featured in his campaigns and he tells constituents that if they can't give him their vote, they should at least offer their sympathy — and Lott offered him a staff job.

There is a tradition in Mississippi of congressional aides moving into elective office; Lott did so, as did 1st District Republican Rep. Roger Wicker. So when Democrat G.V. "Sonny" Montgomery retired, Pickering jumped at the chance to join that group. His political contacts and well-known name propelled him to first place in the nine-candidate 1996 GOP primary, and he won the runoff against former state Rep. Bill Crawford. In November, Pickering took 61 percent of the vote against Democrat John Arthur Eaves Jr., a lawyer who also grew up in a political family.

Because Mississippi lost a seat in post-2000 census reapportionment, a federal court redistricting plan forced Pickering into a race against Democrat Ronnie Shows, a four-year House veteran. The district lines favored the GOP and Pickering won by 29 percentage points — the most lopsided of the four general-election matchups between incumbents in 2002. After a legal challenge to the redistricting plan that went all the way to the Supreme Court, the 3rd retains its GOP tilt, and Pickering won easily in 2004.

KEY VOTES

2004
No   Extend federal unemployment benefits by 13 weeks
Yes   Pass $283.2 billion, six-year federal highway and mass transit bill
Yes   Approve $146 billion multi-year extension of previously enacted middle-class tax breaks
Yes   Amend the Constitution to prohibit same-sex marriage
Yes   Cut corporate taxes $137 billion over 10 years
Yes   Reorganize U.S. intelligence agencies as proposed by Sept. 11 commission

2003
Yes   Cut taxes by $330 billion through fiscal 2013
No   Block Bush rule scaling back overtime pay for some white-collar federal workers
Yes   Do not allow use of search warrants without first notifying subjects
No   Allow importation of prescription drugs
?   Create private school voucher program in Washington, D.C.
+   Ban "partial birth" abortion except to save a woman's life
No   Split $18.6 billion in Iraq aid into half-grant, half-loan
Yes   Overhaul Medicare and create prescription drug benefit

CQ VOTE STUDIES

	PARTY UNITY		PRESIDENTIAL SUPPORT	
	Support	Oppose	Support	Oppose
2004	94%	6%	85%	15%
2003	95%	5%	96%	4%
2002	97%	3%	85%	15%
2001	95%	5%	84%	16%
2000	97%	3%	25%	75%

INTEREST GROUPS

	AFL-CIO	ADA	CCUS	ACU
2004	20%	5%	100%	92%
2003	0%	5%	97%	83%
2002	11%	0%	90%	100%
2001	17%	5%	91%	96%
2000	0%	0%	90%	100%

MISSISSIPPI 3

East central to southwest — Jackson suburbs

The 3rd sprawls across 28 counties, moving from Oktibbeha and Noxubee counties in the east central part of the state to the Mississippi River in the southwest corner. The GOP stronghold picks up Jackson's northeast corner and some of its mostly white northern and eastern suburbs.

Timber is dominant in the 3rd, but health care and defense also are important industries, especially in Meridian. A new Nissan plant — just outside the district in the neighboring 2nd — is expected to boost the Jackson-area economy. Small rural communities, filled with poultry and dairy farms, are prevalent. Rankin County is one of the fastest-growing regions of the state, spurred by nearby Jackson residents moving to the suburbs. Kemper and Noxubee counties on the eastern border include areas as poor as the Delta.

The recession of the late 1980s and early 1990s decimated Natchez's oil and gas industry, but tourism helped the southwestern outpost's economy stay afloat; the small river city, with its antebellum homes and dockside casinos, attracts nearly 150,000 visitors per year.

Republicans now dominate the federal politics of the 3rd, as Democrats did for most of the 20th century. George W. Bush took 65 percent of the vote in 2004. The new 3rd, created in redistricting following the 2000 census, combines the old 3rd and 4th districts to create a GOP district.

MAJOR INDUSTRY
Timber, poultry, agriculture, defense

MILITARY BASES
Naval Air Station Meridian, 5,222 military, 759 civilian (2004)

CITIES
Meridian, 39,968; Jackson (pt.), 31,832; Pearl, 21,961; Starkville, 21,869

NOTABLE
Some call Natchez, the oldest settled city on the Mississippi River (1716), the "City of Five Flags" — it has been controlled by the French, British, Spanish, the Confederacy and the United States; Neshoba County is known as the site of an annual fair in Philadelphia, and as the place where three civil rights workers were murdered by members of the Ku Klux Klan in 1964, an event partly fictionalized for the movie "Mississippi Burning."

Rep. Gene Taylor (D)

Elected October 1989; 8th full term

One of the most conservative Democrats in the House, Taylor is a staunch defender of the military who fights year in and year out against base closings and program cutbacks.

A decade ago, Taylor helped pull together a coalition of other conservative House Democrats, known as the "Blue Dogs." In the 108th Congress, Taylor broke party ranks and sided with the GOP on nearly a third of all floor votes that pitted most Democrats against most Republicans — and he backed President Bush's position half of the time. Instead of voting for the Democratic nominee for Speaker in the last three Congresses, Taylor has cast a protest vote for his Pennsylvania Democratic colleague, John P. Murtha.

But ever since Bush and Defense Secretary Donald H. Rumsfeld began to push in 2001 for more military base closures, Taylor has been one of their most voluble opponents. It is a fight that is likely to consume him during the first part of the 109th Congress, when a new round of closures is expected. A senior member of the Armed Services Committee, Taylor argues it is wrong to close bases during a war on terrorism. He has tried everything from outraged floor speeches to a parliamentary guerrilla war during debate on the 2002 defense authorization bill to a last-gasp effort in 2004 on that same measure, all to no avail. His proposals to cancel the new round of base closings drew veto threats, spelling defeat once again.

Taylor's Mississippi Gulf Coast district is heavily dependent on federal defense spending. It is home to Keesler Air Force Base, the naval station in Pascagoula, the naval construction center in Gulfport and Ingalls Shipbuilding, the state's largest private employer. (In 2002, he played a key role in a Biloxi City Council decision to reject a proposed high-rise condominium near the flight path of Keesler, which could have increased the base's vulnerability to closure.)

Taylor is an energetic champion not only of his district's military interests, but also its blue-collar factory workers and socially conservative values. He is in step with the GOP majority on many issues — banning flag desecration, cutting off federal arts subsidies, protecting gun owners' rights and curbing environmental regulation.

But like many Democrats, Taylor pursues a protectionist course on trade, arguing that working people are hurt by trade liberalization while the monied establishment benefits. He has been critical of the Bush administration, as well as his free-trader colleagues. "The ones I'm really mad at," Taylor said in 2003, were those who "looked out for the big multinational corporations at the expense of average Mississippians and average citizens." Taylor has opposed every significant trade law enacted while he has been in Congress, including the 1993 North American Free Trade Agreement and the 2002 legislation restoring the president's fast-track trade negotiating authority.

In 1998, Taylor was the only Democrat who voted in favor of all articles of impeachment the House brought against President Clinton. He has waged campaigns, annoying to members on both sides of the aisle, to limit the amount of speechmaking on the House floor and the range of perks for congressional leaders. Although he is now over 50, Taylor still looks like an angry young man, and he is rarely more angry than when he decries federal deficits, which he abhors.

Taylor strongly opposed the 10-year, $1.35 trillion Bush tax cut of 2001.

CAPITOL OFFICE
225-5772
www.house.gov/genetaylor
2311 Rayburn 20515-2404; fax 225-7074

COMMITTEES
Armed Services
Transportation & Infrastructure

HOMETOWN
Bay St. Louis

BORN
Sept. 17, 1953, New Orleans, La.

RELIGION
Roman Catholic

FAMILY
Wife, Margaret Taylor; three children

EDUCATION
Tulane U., B.A. 1976 (history & political science); U. of Southern Mississippi, Gulf Park, attended 1978-80 (business & economics)

MILITARY SERVICE
Coast Guard Reserve, 1971-84

CAREER
Box company sales representative

POLITICAL HIGHLIGHTS
Bay St. Louis City Council, 1981-83; Miss. Senate, 1983-89; Democratic nominee for U.S. House, 1988

ELECTION RESULTS

2004 GENERAL

Gene Taylor (D)	179,979	64.2%
Michael Lott (R)	96,740	34.5%
Tracy Lou O'Hara Hill (REF)	3,663	1.3%

2004 PRIMARY

Gene Taylor (D)	unopposed

2002 GENERAL

Gene Taylor (D)	121,742	75.2%
Karl Mertz (R)	34,373	21.2%
Wayne Parker (LIBERT)	3,311	2.1%
Thomas R. Huffmaster (REF)	2,442	1.5%

PREVIOUS WINNING PERCENTAGES
2000 (79%); 1998 (78%); 1996 (58%); 1994 (60%); 1992 (63%); 1990 (81%); 1989 Special Runoff Election (65%)

"Quit sticking my kids with your bills," Taylor said a year later, when deficits were back and congressional Republicans were pushing to make the 2001 cuts permanent. "I liked you guys so much better when you were for a balanced budget." In 2003, he voted against the second round of Bush tax cuts as well. At one point that year, Taylor enlisted 16 young pages on the House floor to hold large cards that spelled out the amount that had been added to the debt since Bush took office — $914,878,724,867, at that time. When Republicans objected, he repeated the display with fellow lawmakers as his assistants.

At times, Taylor has been caustic on the campaign trail. In 2002, he suggested that his GOP opponent, Karl Mertz, belonged in a mental hospital.

Observing him only in public, one could assume that Taylor is a humorless man. "If he was like he appears on TV, none of us would work for the S.O.B.," an aide once said. But in private, Taylor is an easygoing, fun-loving guy, according to those who know him, particularly those who have attended his annual Mardi Gras party on Capitol Hill, complete with miniature floats, outlandish costumes, liquid refreshment and his homemade jambalaya.

During 13 years in the Coast Guard Reserves, Taylor twice won commendations for his work skippering a 41-foot patrol boat on the Mississippi River, and he continues to have an interest in things nautical. Earlier in his congressional career he lived on a boat while in Washington. Taylor protects the interests of his district's shrimpers and fishermen, urges increased Coast Guard funding, and promotes measures to help the U.S. shipbuilding and cruise ship industries compete against foreign companies.

Taylor went to Catholic schools, and he recalls the nuns wheeling in a television set so the students could watch the inauguration of the first Catholic president, John F. Kennedy. Taylor was only 7 years old, but he recalls that moment as the beginning of his interest in politics.

He majored in political science and history at Tulane and then was a salesman for a box company. In 1981, he won a seat on the Bay St. Louis City Council, and two years later he started a six-year turn in the state Senate.

The Democratic Party had little interest in Taylor's first campaign for Congress, for the seat Republican Trent Lott left open in 1988 to run for the Senate. But he surprised them with a strong, 45 percent showing against Republican Larkin Smith. Less than a year later, Smith died in a plane crash. In the special-election campaign, national Democratic support was again slim, but Taylor prevailed over Lott's longtime aide Tom Anderson Jr. and Democratic Attorney General Mike Moore. He has won with ease since.

KEY VOTES

2004

Yes Extend federal unemployment benefits by 13 weeks

Yes Pass $283.2 billion, six-year federal highway and mass transit bill

No Approve $146 billion multi-year extension of previously enacted middle-class tax breaks

Yes Amend the Constitution to prohibit same-sex marriage

Yes Cut corporate taxes $137 billion over 10 years

Yes Reorganize U.S. intelligence agencies as proposed by Sept. 11 commission

2003

No Cut taxes by $330 billion through fiscal 2013

Yes Block Bush rule scaling back overtime pay for some white-collar federal workers

Yes Do not allow use of search warrants without first notifying subjects

Yes Allow importation of prescription drugs

Yes Create private school voucher program in Washington, D.C.

Yes Ban "partial birth" abortion except to save a woman's life

Yes Split $18.6 billion in Iraq aid into half-grant, half-loan

No Overhaul Medicare and create prescription drug benefit

CQ VOTE STUDIES

	PARTY UNITY		PRESIDENTIAL SUPPORT	
	Support	Oppose	Support	Oppose
2004	67%	33%	45%	55%
2003	71%	29%	53%	47%
2002	63%	37%	45%	55%
2001	56%	44%	45%	55%
2000	57%	43%	40%	60%

INTEREST GROUPS

	AFL-CIO	ADA	CCUS	ACU
2004	67%	60%	52%	54%
2003	87%	65%	47%	68%
2002	67%	50%	45%	48%
2001	64%	55%	39%	64%
2000	60%	45%	38%	56%

MISSISSIPPI 4
Southeast — Gulf Coast, Hattiesburg

The pristine white Gulf Coast beaches of the 4th are surrounded by casino resorts that have popped up since Hancock and Harrison counties changed their gaming laws in 1992. Despite slow statewide population growth during the 1990s, many parts of the 4th, including Hancock, experienced population booms. Small forested rural communities dominate where strip malls and suburban sprawl do not. The district's healthy economy and general lack of poverty differentiate it from the rest of the state.

The military, defense-related businesses — most notably Northrop Grumman's Ingalls shipbuilding yard in Pascagoula — and casinos are the dominant industries. Large medical facilities at Keesler Air Force Base and the University of Southern Mississippi, as well as new golf courses, have attracted retirees to the region.

A conservative Democrat holds the 4th's congressional seat, but the district tends to swing between the parties locally. GOP presidential candidates have won the district in each election since 1992, and George

W. Bush earned his highest 2004 vote percentage (68 percent) in the state here.

The 4th, which includes the core of the old 5th District, picked up Clarke County, the rest of Wayne County and parts of Marion, Jones and Jasper counties in redistricting following the 2000 census, but the additions are unlikely to change the political outlook of the district.

MAJOR INDUSTRY
Military, shipbuilding, casinos

MILITARY BASES
Keesler Air Force Base, 13,295 military, 3,620 civilian (2003); Naval Construction Training Center Gulfport, 3,664 military, 827 civilian (2004); Naval Oceanographic Office, 42 military, 1,117 civilian; Naval Station Pascagoula, 398 military, 185 civilian (2005)

CITIES
Gulfport, 71,127; Biloxi, 50,644; Hattiesburg, 44,779; Pascagoula, 26,200

NOTABLE
Sen. Trent Lott was the only Republican since 1877 to hold the area's congressional seat for more than one year — he held it from 1973 until 1989; Harrison County claims to have the largest manmade beach in the nation at 26 miles.

MISSOURI

Gov. Matt Blunt (R)

First elected: 2004
Length of term: 4 years
Term expires: 1/09
Salary: $120,087
Phone: (573) 751-3222

Hometown: Springfield
Born: Nov. 20, 1970; Strafford, Mo.
Religion: Baptist
Family: Wife, Melanie Blunt; one child
Education: U.S. Naval Academy, B.S. 1993 (history)
Military Service: Navy, 1993-98; Naval Reserve, 1998-present
Career: Coffee company market researcher
Political highlights: Mo. House, 1999-2001; Mo. secretary of state, 2001-05

Election results:

2004 GENERAL
Matt Blunt (R)	1,382,419	50.8%
Claire McCaskill (D)	1,301,442	47.9%
others	35,738	1.3%

Lt. Gov. Peter Kinder (R)

First elected: 2004
Length of term: 4 years
Term expires: 1/09
Salary: $77,184
Phone: (573) 751-4727

STATE LEGISLATURE

General Assembly: January-May

House: 163 members, 2-year terms
2005 breakdown: 98R, 64D, 1 vacancy; 126 men, 36 women
Salary: $31,351
Phone: (573) 751-3659

Senate: 34 members, 4-year terms
2005 breakdown: 23R, 11D; 28 men, 6 women
Salary: $31,351
Phone: (573) 751-3766

STATE TERM LIMITS

Governor: 2 terms
House: 4 terms
Senate: 2 terms

URBAN STATISTICS

CITY	POPULATION
Kansas City	441,545
St. Louis	348,189
Springfield	151,580
Independence	113,288
Columbia	84,531

REGISTERED VOTERS

Voters do not register by party.

POPULATION

2004 population (est.)	5,754,618
2000 population	5,595,211
1990 population	5,117,073
Percent change (1990-2000)	+9.3%
Rank among states (2004)	17

Median age	36.1
Born in state	67.8%
Foreign born	2.7%
Violent crime rate	490/100,000
Poverty level	11.7%
Federal workers	57,783
Military	38,091

REDISTRICTING

Missouri retained its nine House seats in reapportionment. The state legislature drew a new map, which the governor signed on June 1, 2001.

MISCELLANEOUS

Web: www.state.mo.us
Capital: Jefferson City
STATE ELECTION OFFICIAL
(573) 751-2301
DEMOCRATIC HEADQUARTERS
(573) 636-5241
REPUBLICAN HEADQUARTERS
(573) 636-3146

District Statistics

DIST.	2004 VOTE FOR PRESIDENT BUSH	KERRY	WHITE	BLACK	ASIAN	HISP	MEDIAN INCOME	WHITE COLLAR	BLUE COLLAR	SERVICE INDUSTRY	OVER 64	UNDER 18	COLLEGE EDUCATION	RURAL	SQ. MILES
1	25%	75%	46%	50%	2%	1%	$36,314	62%	21%	17%	14%	26%	22%	1%	217
2	60	40	93	2	2	1	$61,416	71	18	11	11	27	38	8	1,248
3	43	57	86	9	2	2	$41,091	60	24	15	13	25	23	13	1,247
4	64	35	92	3	1	2	$34,541	51	33	16	14	25	16	60	14,544
5	40	59	66	24	1	6	$38,311	62	23	15	13	26	23	4	512
6	57	42	92	3	1	2	$41,225	59	27	15	13	25	21	34	13,032
7	67	32	93	1	1	3	$32,929	55	29	16	14	24	19	41	5,480
8	63	36	92	4	0	1	$27,865	48	36	16	16	25	12	60	18,681
9	59	41	93	4	1	1	$36,693	54	31	15	13	25	20	54	13,925
STATE	53	46	84	11	1	2	$37,934	58	27	15	14	26	22	31	68,886
U.S.	50.7	48.3	69	12	4	13	$41,994	60	25	15	12	26	24	21	3,537,438

Sen. Christopher S. Bond (R)

Elected 1986; 4th term

CAPITOL OFFICE
224-5721
bond.senate.gov
274 Russell 20510-2503; fax 224-8149

COMMITTEES
Appropriations
  (Transportation, Treasury, the Judiciary & HUD -
  chairman)
Environment & Public Works
  (Transportation & Infrastructure - chairman)
Small Business & Entrepreneurship
Select Intelligence

HOMETOWN
Mexico

BORN
March 6, 1939, St. Louis, Mo.

RELIGION
Presbyterian

FAMILY
Wife, Linda Bond; one child

EDUCATION
Princeton U., A.B. 1960; U. of Virginia, LL.B. 1963

CAREER
Lawyer

POLITICAL HIGHLIGHTS
Republican nominee for U.S. House, 1968; Mo.
auditor, 1971-73; governor, 1973-77; defeated for
re-election as governor, 1976; governor, 1981-85

ELECTION RESULTS

2004 GENERAL

Christopher S. Bond (R)	1,518,089	56.1%
Nancy Farmer (D)	1,158,261	42.8%

2004 PRIMARY

Christopher S. Bond (R)	541,998	88.1%
Mike Steger (R)	73,354	11.9%

PREVIOUS WINNING PERCENTAGES
1998 (53%); 1992 (52%); 1986 (53%)

After 18 years in the Senate, Bond has carved out a comfortable niche. He has abandoned any leadership aspirations and has instead cemented his reputation as a pragmatic "Old Bull" who views legislation as a malleable product to be shaped according to the practical and political necessities of the moment rather than a work cast in a rigid ideological mold.

Bond votes a loyal leadership line but lacks the harder edge of more-junior Republicans, many of whom graduated from the House. His legislative efforts — on the Appropriations and Environment and Public Works committees — are focused almost entirely on Missouri. Bond's singleness of purpose was illustrated in 2003 when he declined the chairmanship of the Small Business Committee to take over the gavel of the Transportation and Infrastructure Subcommittee of Environment and Public Works. That move positioned Bond to claim a central role in crafting a major surface transportation bill to deliver vast amounts of federal dollars to Missouri at the very time he sought a fourth term.

But the post proved frustrating as a clash occurred between generous lawmakers and a more parsimonious President Bush over the level of highway funding. The measure stalled in the 108th Congress. Bond was a leader of a large pack of Senate Republicans who locked horns with the White House over the measure. He helped craft a $319 billion Senate bill that was considerably more expensive than the White House said it could accept. Bush's re-election win and fresh deficit concerns only added to the White House's leverage as negotiations resumed in the 109th.

Bond won a fourth term at 65, staying on at an age when some lawmakers choose to leave the Senate to earn money while still relatively young. He has seen significant changes in his personal life, however: In 2002, Bond married his second wife, Linda Pell, a GOP political consultant about 20 years his junior. After safely winning re-election, he and his wife purchased a $1.6 million home in Washington's exclusive Spring Valley neighborhood. Bond also lost considerable weight on a low-carb diet.

Still known by his childhood nickname, "Kit," Bond is known for his love of cigars and for the Senate gym; he has been known to arrive at the Senate in sweaty athletic garb when votes interrupt his workouts.

Behind his sometimes gruff exterior, Bond is a soft-edged conservative, happy to spend money on government programs that benefit his state and willing to cooperate with Democrats if necessary to do so. He has a reputation as a low-key workhorse, yet his fellow Republicans have been reluctant to elect him to a leadership post; he has lost three attempts to become chairman of the Senate Republican caucus.

Bond appears to delight in the work of the Appropriations Committee. Beginning in 1997, he was the top-ranking Republican on the subcommittee that writes the second-largest of the annual domestic spending bills — covering veterans', housing, space, environmental and science programs. As chairman, he forged a fast and friendly relationship with the panel's top-ranking Democrat, Barbara A. Mikulski of Maryland.

But he will take on new appropriations territory in the 109th. When the jurisdictions of the subcommittees were shuffled, Bond moved to become chairman of the Transportation, Treasury, the Judiciary and Housing and Urban Development Subcommittee, where he will work with Washington Democrat Patty Murray.

As a senior appropriator, Bond annually delivers a raft of federal projects to Missouri. And he is not shy about using policy add-ons to appropriations legislation to block others who take steps that could harm Missouri's interests. In 2004, he successfully defended new Missouri River regulations from upriver rivals seeking to restrict river flows, capping a longstanding effort in which he turned defeat into victory. In 2003, he used a spending bill to try to defend Briggs & Stratton Corp., which employs 6,000 Missourians making small gasoline engines, from California air pollution rules.

Bond is unashamed about bringing home the bacon. When the watchdog group Citizens Against Government Waste gave him a "License to Pork" in 1999 for having brought home more than $50 million in federal dollars the year before, Bond was more proud than offended. "If they think it's pork, it's an awfully healthy diet for the people of Missouri, and I'm proud to participate in it," Bond told the Associated Press. "Just tell 'em, 'In the next batch, I'll bring along my own barbecue sauce.'"

In standing up for Missouri, Bond has sometimes found himself in the midst of major controversy. While much of the nation was focused on the Florida ballot snafus that threw the 2000 presidential election into disarray, St. Louis was reeling from findings that thousands of its voters were registered in more than one place. Missouri Republicans were convinced that fraud had cost them a Senate seat and the governor's mansion.

When the 107th Congress produced an election law overhaul in 2002, it contained a Bond provision requiring voters to show proof of residence either when they register or when they vote. Although he publicly fumed at several points along the way, Bond negotiated with the Democrats for six months on language each side could live with.

Despite his occasional forays into bipartisanship, Bond votes a conservative line. He receives low marks from labor and high ones from the Chamber of Commerce. He generally supports Bush — the highway bill notwithstanding — on roll call votes. But he also crossed the White House in 2004 by producing a VA-HUD spending bill that contained $2 billion in budget-busting "emergency" spending for veterans and NASA. That generated a Bush veto threat, and when Bond's handiwork was rolled into the catchall spending bill, the extra money was gone.

Bond has never won an overwhelming election victory in Missouri, but his 2004 re-election performance was his best yet. Democrats touted Missouri state Treasurer Nancy Farmer, but Bond put her away by 13 percentage points. That was only the second time he had won an election by more than 10 points; his first victory in 1970 was the only prior occasion.

Bond broke into politics in 1968, unsuccessfully seeking a seat in the House from northeastern Missouri. But two years later, he won the office of state auditor. In 1972, he was elected the state's first GOP governor since World War II — and, at 33, he was immediately labeled a rising Republican star. In 1976, he lost a re-election bid to Democrat Joseph P. Teasdale, but he avenged that loss in 1980.

In 1986, Bond battled Democratic Lt. Gov. Harriett Woods in a bitter contest for the Senate seat being vacated after three terms by Democrat Thomas F. Eagleton. Bond ran as a budget-conscious conservative and painted Woods as a liberal with values out of sync with most Missourians. She called Bond a passive governor, an aloof aristocrat and a likely rubber stamp for President Reagan. Bond won with 53 percent of the vote.

In 1992, Bond's opponent, St. Louis County Council member Geri Rothman-Serot, sought to capitalize on the "Year of the Woman" tide. But Bond's campaign treasury was four times larger than Rothman-Serot's, and he prevailed with 52 percent — Missouri's only victorious statewide GOP candidate that year. Six years later, the Democrats touted Missouri Attorney General Jay Nixon, but Bond won with 53 percent.

KEY VOTES

2004

Yes Pass $318.9 billion, six-year highway and mass transit bill

No Extend assault weapons ban for 10 years

No Restore pay-as-you-go rules for new tax cuts and entitlement spending

Yes Criminalize harm to a fetus in an attack on the mother

Yes Increase mandatory child care funding to states by $6 billion over five years

Yes Amend the Constitution to prohibit same-sex marriage

Yes Approve $146 billion multi-year extension of previously enacted middle-class tax breaks

Yes Reorganize U.S. intelligence agencies as proposed by Sept. 11 commission

Yes Cut corporate taxes $137 billion over 10 years

2003

No Delay Bush changes to Clean Air Act

Yes Allow confirmation vote on Miguel A. Estrada to the U.S. Court of Appeals for the D.C. Circuit

No Block a Bush proposal opening Alaska's Arctic National Wildlife Refuge to oil drilling

No Limit size of Bush's proposed tax cut to $350 billion through fiscal 2013

Yes Overhaul Medicare and create prescription drug benefit

No Block Bush rule scaling back overtime pay for some white-collar federal workers

No Split $20 billion in Iraq aid into half-grant, half-loan

Yes Ban "partial birth" abortion except to save a woman's life

? Stop proposal allowing travel to Cuba

Yes Allow final vote on energy policy overhaul

CQ VOTE STUDIES

	PARTY UNITY		PRESIDENTIAL SUPPORT	
	Support	Oppose	Support	Oppose
2004	94%	6%	92%	8%
2003	97%	3%	97%	3%
2002	89%	11%	98%	2%
2001	94%	6%	99%	1%
2000	96%	4%	46%	54%
1999	93%	7%	34%	66%
1998	88%	12%	38%	62%
1997	89%	11%	62%	38%
1996	95%	5%	37%	63%
1995	93%	7%	36%	64%

INTEREST GROUPS

	AFL-CIO	ADA	CCUS	ACU
2004	42%	20%	100%	96%
2003	8%	5%	100%	80%
2002	15%	10%	100%	84%
2001	19%	10%	93%	88%
2000	0%	0%	100%	92%
1999	0%	0%	94%	84%
1998	13%	15%	89%	72%
1997	0%	15%	100%	76%
1996	29%	10%	100%	90%
1995	8%	5%	100%	70%

Sen. Jim Talent (R)

CAPITOL OFFICE
224-6154
talent.senate.gov
493 Russell 20510-2505; fax 228-1518

COMMITTEES
Agriculture, Nutrition & Forestry
(Marketing, Inspection & Product Promotion -
chairman)
Armed Services
(Seapower - chairman)
Energy & Natural Resources
Special Aging

HOMETOWN
Chesterfield

BORN
Oct. 18, 1956, Des Peres, Mo.

RELIGION
Presbyterian

FAMILY
Wife, Brenda Lyons Talent; three children

EDUCATION
Washington U., B.A. 1978 (political science); U. of
Chicago, J.D. 1981

CAREER
Lobbyist; lawyer

POLITICAL HIGHLIGHTS
Mo. House, 1985-93 (minority leader, 1989-93); U.S.
House, 1993-2001; Republican nominee for
governor, 2000

ELECTION RESULTS

2002 SPECIAL

Jim Talent (R)	935,032	49.8%
Jean Carnahan (D)	913,778	48.7%

2002 PRIMARY SPECIAL

Jim Talent (R)	395,994	89.6%
Joseph A. May (R)	18,525	4.2%
Doris Bass Landfather (R)	14,074	3.2%
Scott Craig Babbitt (R)	7,705	1.7%
Martin Lindstedt (R)	5,773	1.3%

PREVIOUS WINNING PERCENTAGES
1998 House Election (70%); 1996 House Election
(61%); 1994 House Election (67%); 1992 House
Election (50%)

Elected 2002; 1st term

Talent belongs to the crop of conservatives who got their start in the House in the early and mid-1990s and constantly seethed over the way the more methodical Senate slowed down or scaled back their proposals for redefining the role of the federal government. But as they say, if you can't beat 'em, join 'em. Talent was elected to the Senate in 2002.

He brings to his work in Congress his core philosophy of transferring authority over domestic programs to the states, a view shared by the Bush administration. As one of the originators of the welfare overhaul in 1996 while in the House, Talent used that experience as a basis to call for further devolution from the federal to state levels. He is an avid supporter of White House proposals to hand over to the states the administration of programs such as Head Start, the early education program for poor children. "I like the idea of getting control over the provision of services as close as we can to the people who are receiving the services," Talent says.

Though generally wary of federal spending, he has backed the administration's escalating requests to fund the war in Iraq. Concerns over the burgeoning deficit are secondary, he says. "Well, yes, the deficit is a problem," he says. "We are in a war. Members who do not believe that should read about it. It is in the papers every day."

He also carves out a big exception for federal spending on highways and mass transit projects that are generally popular with voters. When a six-year transportation bill stalled in Congress in 2004 because President Bush said it cost too much, Talent advocated a proposal to have the government use its bonding authority to borrow the money. Along with Ron Wyden, an Oregon Democrat, he pushed for a bill allowing the use of construction bonds for transportation projects.

The Talent-Wyden plan, dubbed by its originators "Build America Bonds," called for a federally chartered nonprofit corporation authorized to issue $50 billion in tax credit bonds for transit, rail, seaport, airport and waterway projects. States were to provide a 20 percent match. Investors in the bonds would receive federal tax credits instead of cash interest payments. The White House did not buy the idea, however, and threatened a veto.

Talent also teamed up with a more liberal colleague on another big issue — health care for the uninsured. In 2004, he and moderate GOP Sen. Olympia J. Snowe of Maine cosponsored a bill to allow small businesses to pool their money to buy health insurance through groups called association health plans. The idea is one of several floated in Congress as a way to solve the problem of the large segment of uninsured Americans. It is a solution, he says, that "doesn't cost the taxpayer a dime."

Talent narrowly prevailed in one of the bellwether Senate races of 2002 by hewing to the same conservative stands on taxes, regulation, defense and social policy that defined his eight years in the House, and his close but unsuccessful 2000 campaign to be governor of Missouri.

His election to the Senate was one of the notable political comebacks of recent years. He defeated incumbent Democrat Jean Carnahan in a special election. Carnahan had been appointed to the seat in place of her husband, Gov. Mel Carnahan, who died in a plane crash three weeks before his posthumous election to the Senate in 2000. Carnahan's appointment as senator lasted until the next general election.

Missouri is one of the nation's principal swing states, and as a candidate,

Talent promised to seek bipartisan compromises. Yet, he has long associated mainly with the conservative activist wing of the Republican Party and was a close adviser to the GOP leadership in the House.

In the Senate, Talent gained the gavel of two subcommittees. On Agriculture, he chairs the Marketing panel, an obvious fit for a senator whose constituents live in the buckle of the farm belt. On Armed Services, he chairs the Seapower panel, with little apparent parochial benefit to a landlocked state.

Talent favors more tax cuts, including making permanent many of the tax measures enacted in Bush's 2001 tax bill. He is an enemy of workplace ergonomics rules and other regulations that he believes are onerous and costly for small businesses. In the House, he opposed the 1993 law guaranteeing job security for workers who take time off for family or medical reasons.

Talent was among the early advocates of the welfare overhaul that Republicans worked out with President Clinton in 1996. While in the House, Talent also sponsored legislation to cut off federal assistance for unmarried mothers younger than 21 and eventually for those under 25 — a plan even more stringent than that proposed in the "Contract With America," the conservative agenda adopted by House GOP candidates in their triumphant 1994 campaign.

Talent is particularly conservative on social issues. He has opposed a law that makes it a federal offense to use force or threats to prevent women from entering abortion clinics, and he opposes additional gun control.

From his seat on the Energy and Natural Resources Committee, Talent has promised to support construction of a national nuclear waste repository at Yucca Mountain in Nevada. He voted in early 2005 in favor of oil exploration in Alaska's Arctic National Wildlife Refuge, a Bush proposal that environmentalists vehemently oppose.

Talent was born just outside St. Louis and went to college in the city. He earned a law degree at the University of Chicago and clerked for Judge Richard A. Posner, a prominent conservative on the 7th Circuit Court of Appeals. He was 28 when he won a state House seat. He spent eight years in the legislature, four of them as minority leader, at one point bucking Republican Gov. John Ashcroft's proposal for a tax increase to support education programs.

After winning a Republican primary against George Herbert Walker III, a cousin of President George H.W. Bush, Talent was elected to the House in 1992. He defeated one-term Democrat Joan Kelly Horn in the 2nd District, covering the mostly affluent St. Louis suburbs. He gave up his House seat in 2000 to run for governor, but lost by 21,445 votes to the Democratic state treasurer, Bob Holden.

Soon afterward, Talent went to work for Arent Fox, a Washington law and lobbying firm, a job Democrats said amounted to an improper subsidy for his Senate campaign. Talent represented small businesses and grain processors, among other clients, but he said he complied with a one-year prohibition on former members directly lobbying Congress. He also said he had not decided to run for the Senate when he took the job.

But Republicans were already looking to Talent as their best candidate against Jean Carnahan. Well-known as an adviser to her husband throughout his career, she was sustained by his lingering popularity and sympathy over her personal loss.

But she had only two years to establish her own legislative and policy record, and often found herself caught between the push of the Senate Democratic leadership and the pull of the centrist political impulses of her state. This time Talent won — and by almost the same margin that he had lost by two years before: 21,254 votes.

KEY VOTES

2004

Yes Pass $318.9 billion, six-year highway and mass transit bill
No Extend assault weapons ban for 10 years
No Restore pay-as-you-go rules for new tax cuts and entitlement spending
Yes Criminalize harm to a fetus in an attack on the mother
Yes Increase mandatory child care funding to states by $6 billion over five years
Yes Amend the Constitution to prohibit same-sex marriage
Yes Approve $146 billion multi-year extension of previously enacted middle-class tax breaks
Yes Reorganize U.S. intelligence agencies as proposed by Sept. 11 commission
Yes Cut corporate taxes $137 billion over 10 years

2003

No Delay Bush changes to Clean Air Act
Yes Allow confirmation vote on Miguel A. Estrada to the U.S. Court of Appeals for the D.C. Circuit
No Block a Bush proposal opening Alaska's Arctic National Wildlife Refuge to oil drilling
No Limit size of Bush's proposed tax cut to $350 billion through fiscal 2013
Yes Overhaul Medicare and create prescription drug benefit
No Block Bush rule scaling back overtime pay for some white-collar federal workers
No Split $20 billion in Iraq aid into half-grant, half-loan
Yes Ban "partial birth" abortion except to save a woman's life
No Stop proposal allowing travel to Cuba
Yes Allow final vote on energy policy overhaul

CQ VOTE STUDIES

	PARTY UNITY		PRESIDENTIAL SUPPORT	
	Support	Oppose	Support	Oppose
2004	96%	4%	94%	6%
2003	96%	4%	98%	2%
House Service:				
2000	94%	6%	23%	77%
1999	91%	9%	22%	78%
1998	93%	7%	20%	80%
1997	95%	5%	27%	73%
1996	93%	7%	32%	68%
1995	98%	2%	15%	85%
1994	95%	5%	51%	49%
1993	93%	7%	34%	66%

INTEREST GROUPS

	AFL-CIO	ADA	CCUS	ACU
2004	33%	20%	100%	96%
2003	0%	5%	100%	85%
House Service:				
2000	0%	10%	78%	91%
1999	11%	15%	92%	84%
1998	0%	5%	100%	96%
1997	0%	5%	80%	100%
1996	9%	10%	100%	100%
1995	0%	0%	100%	96%
1994	0%	5%	100%	95%
1993	8%	10%	82%	96%

Rep. William Lacy Clay (D)

Elected 2000; 3rd term

CAPITOL OFFICE
225-2406
www.house.gov/clay
131 Cannon 20515-2501; fax 225-1725

COMMITTEES
Financial Services
Government Reform

HOMETOWN
St. Louis

BORN
July 27, 1956, St. Louis, Mo.

RELIGION
Roman Catholic

FAMILY
Wife, Ivie Lewellen Clay; two children

EDUCATION
U. of Maryland, B.S. 1983 (government & politics)

CAREER
Real estate agent; paralegal; congressional aide

POLITICAL HIGHLIGHTS
Mo. House, 1983-91; Mo. Senate, 1991-2000

ELECTION RESULTS

2004 GENERAL

William Lacy Clay (D)	213,658	75.3%
Leslie L. Farr II (R)	64,791	22.8%
Terry Chadwick (LIBERT)	3,937	1.4%

2004 PRIMARY

William Lacy Clay (D)	unopposed

2002 GENERAL

William Lacy Clay (D)	133,946	70.1%
Richard Schwadron (R)	51,755	27.1%
James "Jim" Higgins (LIBERT)	5,354	2.8%

PREVIOUS WINNING PERCENTAGES
2000 (75%)

Although his own elections have been relatively effortless — he has never failed to win at least 70 percent of the vote in his three House races — Clay nevertheless has been deeply involved in issues surrounding the conduct of campaigns and elections during his congressional career.

Clay succeeded his namesake father, William L. Clay, who stepped down in 2000 after 32 years in the House. The younger Clay, who is known by his middle name, shares his father's liberal agenda. He is a member of the Congressional Progressive Caucus, a group of about five dozen of the most liberal House lawmakers.

Although Clay is an avid cook and a golf fanatic, his mother told a local newspaper that politics "has been his life. That's the only thing he knows."

He serves on the Financial Services Committee, where he works to make housing more affordable and to crack down on what he views as unfair lending practices in low-income communities. He has introduced legislation in both the 108th and 109th Congresses to provide tax breaks for homeowners who remove lead-based paint hazards.

But Clay has spent much of his time monitoring the nation's electoral process, which he believes is not always implemented fairly, particularly in poor and predominately Democratic neighborhoods. He complained about the long lines and voting irregularities in Ohio in 2004, and he joined in a lawsuit that kept polls open extra hours in St. Louis in 2000 to permit voters caught in long lines to cast ballots. In the early 2000s, he also served on a Congressional Black Caucus working group on voting rights and the electoral process.

He has had scathing words about the way campaigns and elections are conducted, and he has applied his scorn to Democrats as well as Republicans. He complained in a 2005 St. Louis Post-Dispatch interview about the "extortion" tactics of Democratic leaders, who he said pressured him to raise campaign funds on behalf of the Democratic Congressional Campaign Committee — the campaign arm of House Democrats. Clay said that choice committee assignments are linked to how well lawmakers pony up their "dues." He also said he didn't think the DCCC's performance in recent elections showed the group deserved the money.

But Clay also believes there has been progress: After the 2004 election, he said St. Louis had improved its own voting performance 100 percent.

Another of Clay's priorities is to spur economic development in urban St. Louis County — where crime and a troubled public school system have contributed to a steady decline in population. In 2001, Clay was able to earmark $5 million in the defense spending bill for cleanup work at the abandoned St. Louis Army Ammunition Plant. The 21-acre site is in a prime location for commercial development and will be a valuable piece of real estate once the toxic wastes have been removed. He and other area lawmakers are also keeping tabs on the Ford Motor Co. Hazelwood plant in the district, where 900 workers were laid off in 2005. Ford has said it plans eventually to close it.

Economic development is a family effort. Clay's wife, Ivie, works for the St. Louis Development Corp., the city's economic development agency.

Clay serves on the Government Reform Committee, where in the 109th he is the top-ranking Democrat on the Federalism and the Census Subcommittee. In his first term, he sought a congressional probe of nursing home conditions in his district after four people died of heat stress in 2001. The inquiry, by the committee's Democratic staff, found that all 30 of the homes that care for Medicaid or Medicare recipients had violated federal safety and health standards, and that half of them had serious violations.

Clay was 12 when his father was elected to Congress, and he spent his teenage years in suburban Maryland, attending high school in Silver Spring and college at the University of Maryland in College Park. To pay for his college education, Clay was a House of Representatives doorman for six years. The hours he spent watching the action from the cloakrooms and the Speaker's lobby gave him ample insight into the ways of Congress. Clay's experience so impressed his colleagues in the Democratic Class of 2000 that they elected him class president for the 107th Congress.

A government and politics major, Clay also earned a paralegal certificate. He was just starting law school at Howard University when an opening in the Missouri House drew him back to St. Louis to run in a special election.

He spent the next 17 years in the General Assembly, serving eight years in the state House before winning a 1991 special election for a state Senate vacancy. He supplemented his part-time legislator's salary by working in real estate and as a paralegal.

In Jefferson City, Clay helped push through measures benefiting welfare recipients, imposing new penalties for hate crimes and creating tax breaks for those saving for education and home ownership. When the Ku Klux Klan announced that its members would "adopt" a stretch of Interstate 55 to keep it clean, Clay orchestrated legislative action to name that segment of the road after civil rights icon Rosa Parks.

Clay was the presumed heir to the 1st District seat from the moment his father announced his retirement. The younger Clay both embraced his father and declared his independence when he entered the race to succeed him. "Although I am not my father, I am my father's son, in that we share the same values . . . and commitment to principles, such as fairness and justice," said Clay. He won easily, with 75 percent of the vote.

In 2001, as the state legislature tackled the decennial chore of drawing new congressional district boundaries, Clay declared himself ashamed of the way the Democratic Party was "leading the charge to dilute minority strength." At the core of that allegation was a dispute over how to draw the boundaries between the constituents of Clay and Democratic Leader Richard A. Gephardt. The two ultimately reached an agreement under which the black population of the 1st District was reduced to half the district total, down from the three-fifths it had reached by the late 1990s.

That caused Clay no electoral distress: He garnered 70 percent of the vote in 2002 and 75 percent in 2004.

KEY VOTES

2004

Yes	Extend federal unemployment benefits by 13 weeks
Yes	Pass $283.2 billion, six-year federal highway and mass transit bill
No	Approve $146 billion multi-year extension of previously enacted middle-class tax breaks
No	Amend the Constitution to prohibit same-sex marriage
No	Cut corporate taxes $137 billion over 10 years
Yes	Reorganize U.S. intelligence agencies as proposed by Sept. 11 commission

2003

No	Cut taxes by $330 billion through fiscal 2013
Yes	Block Bush rule scaling back overtime pay for some white-collar federal workers
Yes	Do not allow use of search warrants without first notifying subjects
Yes	Allow importation of prescription drugs
No	Create private school voucher program in Washington, D.C.
No	Ban "partial birth" abortion except to save a woman's life
?	Split $18.6 billion in Iraq aid into half-grant, half-loan
No	Overhaul Medicare and create prescription drug benefit

CQ VOTE STUDIES

	PARTY UNITY		PRESIDENTIAL SUPPORT	
	Support	Oppose	Support	Oppose
2004	97%	3%	24%	76%
2003	98%	2%	16%	84%
2002	94%	6%	32%	68%
2001	95%	5%	21%	79%

INTEREST GROUPS

	AFL-CIO	ADA	CCUS	ACU
2004	87%	100%	35%	8%
2003	100%	95%	32%	13%
2002	100%	80%	44%	4%
2001	100%	100%	35%	8%

MISSOURI 1
North St. Louis; northeast St. Louis County

Flanked by the Mississippi and Missouri rivers, the St. Louis-based 1st is a mixture of poor center-city communities and middle-class suburbs. Redistricting following the 2000 census extended the district farther west in St. Louis County to offset a population decline fueled by crime and deteriorating housing conditions.

The 1st takes in the northern half of St. Louis, including most of the city's popular attractions, such as the Gateway Arch and Forest Park, which attracts more than 12 million visitors a year. Many of the area's largest employers are scattered throughout the 1st, including BJC HealthCare, one of the largest nonprofit health care organizations in the United States.

Suburbs in St. Louis County include the region's main airport, one of the nation's 10 busiest, and a Boeing Co. jet plant added in redistricting. Residents are concerned by Ford Motor Co.'s plan to close its Hazelwood assembly plant — an agreement in 2003 that temporarily halted the closure is set to expire in 2007.

By far the state's most heavily Democratic district, the 1st gave John Kerry 75 percent of its vote in the 2004 presidential election. Local and state contests almost always favor Democrats. The black population, which stood at just under 60 percent after the 1990 census, has decreased considerably, although African-Americans still make up almost 50 percent of district voters.

Deep state budget cuts have led to cutbacks in city spending, making education, health care and housing key issues for voters at the polls. Allegations of voting fraud in the 2000 Senate and gubernatorial elections thrust St. Louis into the national debate over an election standards bill, and made officials eager to replace the district's aging voting equipment.

MAJOR INDUSTRY
Manufacturing, aircraft, higher education

CITIES
St. Louis (pt.), 163,020; Florissant, 50,497; Hazelwood, 26,206; University City (pt.), 24,075; Ferguson, 22,406

NOTABLE
The Missouri History Museum, St. Louis Art Museum, St. Louis Zoo and St. Louis Science Center are located in 1400-acre Forest Park, which calls itself the nation's seventh-largest urban park.

Rep. Todd Akin (R)

Elected 2000; 3rd term

Akin could be the poster child for the American Conservative Union. The bills he cosponsored early in the 109th Congress are a veritable wish list of the Republican right — placing restrictions on abortion, toughening enforcement of obscenity laws, limiting regulations on small businesses, making the elimination of the federal inheritance tax permanent, and putting former President Ronald Reagan on the $50 bill.

Akin also has led the effort to ensure the courts can never strike the words "under God" from the Pledge of Allegiance.

Akin is steadfastly opposed to same-sex marriage and gun control. He served on the board of Missouri Right to Life. His six children have been educated at home, and he wants to give parents more choice over the schools their children attend. He also advocates local control over school testing.

Not surprisingly, he has earned scores of 100 percent from the American Conservative Union for three of the four years he has served in Congress. The liberal interest group, Americans for Democratic Action, has twice given Akin a rating of 0 percent.

The role of government, Akin says, is to make distinctions between good and bad ideas and to be the servant of the people. He wants to curb the size and scope of the federal government by seeking a constitutional amendment to restrict the growth of revenue flowing to the Treasury. Akin is suspicious of much of federal spending, with the exception of money for the military.

Akin, like many other lawmakers, was outraged when the 9th U.S. Circuit Court ruled in 2002 that it was unconstitutional to have the Pledge of Allegiance recited in public schools because of the words "under God." But while the issue died out for many when the Supreme Court struck down the decision, Akin feared the ruling — which was not on the overall constitutional question — meant the pledge continues "to be jeopardized by fringe groups and an activist judiciary."

He authored the "Pledge Protection Act" — which the House passed in late 2004 but the Senate never took up — to take the pledge out of the courts' legal reach. Akin is pushing the measure again in the 109th. Conservatives such as Akin view the 9th Circuit's decision as emblematic of what is wrong with the courts: too activist and too eager to impose culturally liberal values on the rest of the nation.

A former Army lieutenant, Akin sits on the Armed Services Committee. From that perch, he has assiduously worked to look out for the interests of Boeing Co., which has large plants in St. Charles County, in the 2nd District, as well as in St. Louis, in the 1st.

In 2004, he helped ensure the defense authorization bill included $357 million in funding for research on Boeing's new electronic attack aircraft, intended to update jamming and electronic attack capabilities. In 2001, as the Pentagon weighed bids from Boeing and Lockheed Martin Corp. for a contract to build the Joint Strike Fighter, Akin and Missouri Republican Sen. Christopher S. Bond called for both companies to share the work. Akin argued that the loser might drop out of the jet fighter business, hurting national security in the long run. Lockheed won the contract, but firms in the St. Louis area wound up getting some peripheral work from the job. Boeing also won a contract with South Korea for another jet fighter.

Akin was one of the few House members — Republican or Democrat — to side with President Bush in 2004 on the need to keep spending down in

CAPITOL OFFICE
225-2561
rep.akin@mail.house.gov
www.house.gov/akin
117 Cannon 20515-2502; fax 225-2563

COMMITTEES
Armed Services
Science
Small Business
(Regulatory Reform & Oversight - chairman)

HOMETOWN
Town & Country

BORN
July 5, 1947, Manhattan, N.Y.

RELIGION
Christian

FAMILY
Wife, Lulli Akin; six children

EDUCATION
Worcester Polytechnic Institute, B.S. 1971
(engineering); Covenant Theological Seminary,
M.Div. 1985

MILITARY SERVICE
Army, 1972; Army Reserve, 1972-80

CAREER
University lecturer; steel company manager;
computer company marketing executive

POLITICAL HIGHLIGHTS
Mo. House, 1989-2000

ELECTION RESULTS

2004 GENERAL

Todd Akin (R)	228,725	65.4%
George D. "Boots" Weber (D)	115,366	33.0%
Darla R. Maloney (LIBERT)	4,822	1.4%

2004 PRIMARY

Todd Akin (R)	unopposed

2002 GENERAL

Todd Akin (R)	167,057	67.1%
John Hogan (D)	77,223	31.0%
Darla R. Maloney (LIBERT)	4,548	1.8%

PREVIOUS WINNING PERCENTAGES
2000 (55%)

a massive surface transportation bill. Akin said he opposed the measure, which Bush threatened to veto, even though it contained projects he sought for his district, "because of basic flaws in the legislation which are fiscally irresponsible and a poor use of taxpayers' money." The measure died in the 108th, but it was revived early in the 109th.

Akin also sits on the Small Business Committee, and became chairman of the Regulatory Reform and Oversight Subcommittee in the 109th. As chairman, he is likely to try to reduce federal regulation of small businesses.

Akin's great-grandfather founded the Laclede Steel Co. of St. Louis, and his father worked there as well. Akin grew up in the St. Louis area but went to college in Massachusetts, where he studied engineering and joined the Army ROTC. After serving as an Army combat engineer, Akin sold large computers for IBM in Massachusetts, where he met his wife, Lulli. After four years, Akin returned to Missouri. He worked for a while at Laclede Steel and then decided to enter divinity school.

Akin says the blend of his engineering and seminary training gives him the scientific problem-solving skills and the theological reference points to help him study the "mechanics of how our system was put together."

As a member of the Missouri House for about 12 years, he unsuccessfully sued the state after the legislature approved a schools bill that included $310 million in tax increases. Later, wary of the social impact of expanded gambling, he brought suit against the state's approval of "riverboat" casino licenses for several vessels permanently anchored in manmade ponds near the Missouri River. The court battle eventually led to a referendum on the issue that, while permitting such arrangements, served to tighten state regulation of the industry.

Akin's reputation as a doctrinaire state legislator spurred opponents to label him as ideologically isolated when he launched his campaign for the House seat being vacated by Republican Jim Talent, who left Congress in 2000 to run for governor. But ardent grassroots support enabled Akin to narrowly prevail in a five-way primary, defeating former St. Louis County Executive Gene McNary by 56 votes. Many observers credited Akin's victory to bad weather on Election Day that hurt turnout for McNary. Akin told the St. Louis Post-Dispatch, "My base will show up in earthquakes."

The Democratic nominee, state Sen. Ted House, who holds conservative views on social issues such as abortion, characterized Akin's views on health care and education as "far extreme," but an energetic campaign style and the district's GOP leanings carried Akin to a 13 percentage point victory. He has won with over 65 percent of the vote in his past two elections.

KEY VOTES

2004

No Extend federal unemployment benefits by 13 weeks

No Pass $283.2 billion, six-year federal highway and mass transit bill

Yes Approve $146 billion multi-year extension of previously enacted middle-class tax breaks

Yes Amend the Constitution to prohibit same-sex marriage

Yes Cut corporate taxes $137 billion over 10 years

Yes Reorganize U.S. intelligence agencies as proposed by Sept. 11 commission

2003

Yes Cut taxes by $330 billion through fiscal 2013

No Block Bush rule scaling back overtime pay for some white-collar federal workers

Yes Do not allow use of search warrants without first notifying subjects

No Allow importation of prescription drugs

Yes Create private school voucher program in Washington, D.C.

Yes Ban "partial birth" abortion except to save a woman's life

No Split $18.6 billion in Iraq aid into half-grant, half-loan

No Overhaul Medicare and create prescription drug benefit

CQ VOTE STUDIES

	PARTY UNITY		PRESIDENTIAL SUPPORT	
	Support	Oppose	Support	Oppose
2004	99%	1%	94%	6%
2003	97%	3%	89%	11%
2002	98%	2%	90%	10%
2001	97%	3%	86%	14%

INTEREST GROUPS

	AFL-CIO	ADA	CCUS	ACU
2004	7%	0%	95%	100%
2003	29%	5%	90%	88%
2002	11%	0%	85%	100%
2001	0%	5%	91%	100%

MISSOURI 2

West St. Louis County; north and east St. Charles County — St. Charles

Composed mostly of upper-middle-class white suburbanites, the 2nd is one of the state's richest and fastest-growing districts. Western St. Louis and St. Charles counties continue to prosper from a westward migration started by mass population departures from St. Louis in the 1980s.

Commuter traffic into the St. Louis business district remains heavy, but local residents are increasingly finding lucrative jobs away from the city. Boeing Co. employs many 2nd District residents, although redistricting following the 2000 census moved the company's main manufacturing facility into the neighboring 1st District. DaimlerChrysler and a General Motors plant in Wentzville are major employers, along with biotechnology and financial services companies. A dwindling but diverse agriculture industry supports the northern fringes around the Mississippi-Missouri river junction.

Although Democrats held the 2nd during most of the latter part of the

20th century, Republicans have dominated in recent years. GOP presidential candidates have won the district in each election since 1992, and Republicans have an edge in state and local races.

Wealthy communities such as Ladue and Frontenac are unshakably Republican, and the removal of union-laden Florissant, St. Ann and Bridgeton during redistricting moved the district further into the GOP column. Lincoln County, added in redistricting, threw a Democratic-leaning constituency into the mix, but the 2nd gave George W. Bush 60 percent of its vote in the 2004 presidential race, after awarding Bush 58 percent in 2000.

MAJOR INDUSTRY
Auto manufacturing, biotechnology, agriculture

CITIES
St. Charles, 60,321; St. Peters (pt.), 50,001; Chesterfield, 46,802; O'Fallon (pt.), 44,949; Wildwood, 32,884; Ballwin, 31,283

NOTABLE
Route 66 State Park near Eureka is located on what was Times Beach, the site of an environmental disaster where soil became tainted with dioxin.

Rep. Russ Carnahan (D)

Elected 2004; 1st term

CAPITOL OFFICE
225-2671
www.house.gov/carnahan
1232 Longworth 20515-2503; fax 225-7452

COMMITTEES
Science
Transportation & Infrastructure

HOMETOWN
St. Louis

BORN
July 10, 1958, Columbia, Mo.

RELIGION
Methodist

FAMILY
Wife, Debra Carnahan; two children

EDUCATION
U. of Missouri, B.S. 1979 (public administration),
J.D. 1983

CAREER
Lawyer; campaign aide; state legislative aide

POLITICAL HIGHLIGHTS
Democratic nominee for U.S. House, 1990;
Mo. House, 2001-05

ELECTION RESULTS

2004 GENERAL

Russ Carnahan (D)	146,894	52.9%
Bill Federer (R)	125,422	45.1%
Kevin C. Babcock (LIBERT)	4,367	1.6%

2004 PRIMARY

Russ Carnahan (D)	24,507	22.9%
Jeff Smith (D)	22,783	21.3%
Steve Stoll (D)	19,372	18.1%
Joan Barry (D)	18,922	17.7%
Mariano V. Favazza (D)	9,647	9.0%
Mark Smith (D)	7,400	6.9%
Jo Ann Karll (D)	2,667	2.5%
others	1,703	1.6%

Carnahan has an impressive pedigree. He is the third generation of his family to serve in Congress, beginning with his grandfather, A.S.J. Carnahan, who served in the House from 1945 to 1947 and from 1949 to 1961.

And his mother, Jean, served in the Senate from 2001 to 2002, filling in for her late husband, Mel, the popular governor of Missouri, who was elected posthumously in 2000, just weeks after he died in an airplane crash while campaigning for the Senate. Jean was appointed to replace him.

"My last name has always been and always will be a two-edged sword, but the positives outweigh the negatives," said Russ Carnahan, who lost a long-shot 1990 House challenge to veteran Republican Bill Emerson in a conservative southeastern Missouri district, but bounced back in 2004 — after four years in the state House — to win the St. Louis-area seat left open by Democrat Richard A. Gephardt, the former House minority leader.

Health care is an abiding concern for Carnahan. When his wife had complications during her second pregnancy, the bills started adding up. "It's one thing to talk about health care in abstract terms," said Carnahan, who later spent nine years as an attorney at BJC HealthCare in St. Louis. "Certainly, my personal experience has shaped me."

Carnahan will be a reliable vote for the Democratic leadership on most issues. He supports stem cell research, expanding medical services to the uninsured, allowing the importation of prescription drugs from Canada and increasing the minimum wage. His seat on the Transportation and Infrastructure Committee is a good fit for Carnahan, an avid traveler and a fan of antique cars and motorcycles. He also is on the Science Committee.

In 2004, Carnahan's name recognition helped him edge college instructor Jeff Smith in the 10-candidate Democratic scramble to succeed Gephardt. In the general election, Carnahan faced Republican Bill Federer, an author who had twice run unsuccessfully against Gephardt. Carnahan took 53 percent of the vote and won by 8 percentage points on the same day that his sister Robin was elected Missouri secretary of state.

MISSOURI 3

South St. Louis; southeast St. Louis County; Jefferson and Ste. Genevieve counties

Bordered on the east by the Mississippi River, the 3rd includes the southern half of St. Louis, as well as older, established suburbs and newer, sprawling ones. Most of the suburban middle-class residents commute to St. Louis County's business district, although there are traces of small-scale farming, manufacturing and river trading.

Whereas St. Louis as a whole (shared with the 1st District) has declined in population, south St. Louis' residential areas, including large Italian and German neighborhoods, have remained stable. To the south, Jefferson County has been one of the state's fastest-growing areas since 1980. Bedroom communities such as Arnold and Imperial continue to prosper.

Many suburban residents work outside the district, but Anheuser-Busch, headquartered in the 3rd's portion of St. Louis, is a major provider of jobs to the region, and the National Geospatial-Intelligence Agency has facilities in the district. Farther south, on the fringes of Ste. Genevieve County, small farming complements a sizable trading industry along the Mississippi River, where chemical facilities also are located.

The district's blue-collar base favors Democrats, although the GOP finds significant support in middle-class communities such as Arnold, and a large Catholic contingent gives the district an anti-abortion tilt. Redistricting following the 2000 census removed some traditionally conservative areas, such as Sunset Hills. The 3rd gave John Kerry 57 percent of the vote in the 2004 presidential election.

MAJOR INDUSTRY
Beer manufacturing, defense, health care

CITIES
St. Louis (pt.), 185,169; Oakville (unincorporated), 35,309

NOTABLE
St. Louis' Missouri Botanical Garden.

Rep. Ike Skelton (D)

Elected 1976; 15th term

CAPITOL OFFICE
225-2876
www.house.gov/skelton
2206 Rayburn 20515-2504; fax 225-2695

COMMITTEES
Armed Services - ranking member

HOMETOWN
Lexington

BORN
Dec. 20, 1931, Lexington, Mo.

RELIGION
Christian Church

FAMILY
Wife, Susan Skelton; three children

EDUCATION
Wentworth Military Academy, A.A. 1951; U. of Edinburgh (United Kingdom), attended 1953; U. of Missouri, A.B. 1953 (history), LL.B. 1956

CAREER
Lawyer; state prosecutor

POLITICAL HIGHLIGHTS
Lafayette County prosecuting attorney, 1957-60; Mo. Senate, 1971-77

ELECTION RESULTS

2004 GENERAL

Ike Skelton (D)	190,800	66.2%
James A. Noland Jr. (R)	93,334	32.4%

2004 PRIMARY

Ike Skelton (D)	unopposed

2002 GENERAL

Ike Skelton (D)	142,204	67.6%
James A. Noland Jr. (R)	64,451	30.7%
Daniel Roy Nelson (LIBERT)	3,583	1.7%

PREVIOUS WINNING PERCENTAGES
2000 (67%); 1998 (71%); 1996 (64%); 1994 (68%); 1992 (70%); 1990 (62%); 1988 (72%); 1986 (100%); 1984 (67%); 1982 (55%); 1980 (68%); 1978 (73%); 1976 (56%)

Skelton is the leading Democratic voice on defense. As the top-ranking Democrat on the Armed Services Committee since 1998, Skelton's hawkish views have given Democrats some political cover against their party's post-Vietnam reputation for being soft on defense.

A reliable supporter of high defense budgets with a particular concern for the welfare of the troops and their combat-readiness, Skelton backed President Bush's 2002 request for authority to go to war with Iraq. But as the war continued to drag on and turned into a grinding battle against an increasingly deadly insurgency, Skelton became concerned that the Pentagon was spreading U.S. troops too thin.

With panel Chairman Duncan Hunter of California, Skelton pushed for more troops, arguing that burnout rates among active duty personnel threatened to reduce troop strength to dangerously low levels. "You can only deploy them so often," Skelton said before passage of the 2004 defense authorization bill that added 39,000 soldiers and Marines to the armed forces. Skelton and Hunter also teamed up on a bill that expedited the acquisition of armor to protect soldiers and vehicles in Iraq and Afghanistan.

Skelton also struggles with the desire of the Defense Department to increase its troop strength in Iraq by extending the tour of duty for the soldiers who are already there. Defense Secretary Donald H. Rumsfeld approved a request in late 2004 to boost the number of U.S. troops in Iraq from about 138,000 to 150,000 by extending the tour of two Army brigades and a Marine unit. "The decision to extend these units beyond their standard one-year deployment and to bring in additional troops is necessary to establish a stable security environment in Iraq if upcoming elections are to be held on schedule," Skelton said in December 2004. "However, these measures — particularly the deployment of two battalions from the 82nd Airborne normally held as a strategic reserve — make clear that we are stretching our forces close to the breaking point."

Skelton has helped shape hard-nosed, practical critiques of Bush's defense proposals behind which Democrats of widely varying ideological stripes could rally. Weeks before the House voted to authorize the war with Iraq, Skelton was badgering Bush to lay out a strategy for encouraging the emergence of a politically stable post-war regime in Iraq. "I have no doubt that our military would decisively defeat Iraq's forces and remove Saddam," he wrote the president, "but like the proverbial dog chasing the car, we must consider what we would do after we caught it."

Ultimately, nearly two-thirds of House Democrats voted against the Iraq resolution. But unlike Bush's initial proposal, Skelton contended, the resolution that was adopted reflected the Democrats' preference for acting multilaterally, if possible, and for staying the course after a military victory to rebuild a peaceable Iraq.

Skelton has also supported Bush's decision to deploy a nationwide anti-missile defense system. Skelton and other Democratic centrists backed the eventual deployment of a system that could fend off small numbers of missiles launched by North Korea or other rogue states. But they insisted the system undergo adequate testing before deployment and that it not be funded at the expense of more-pressing defense requirements, particularly pay and other factors bearing on the troops' quality of life.

"I see the need to increase budgets for re-enlistment bonuses, special pays, recruiting and family housing," Skelton said, commenting on Bush's decision to deploy the first phase of a missile defense by 2004. This call for "increased funding to deploy an untested missile defense system gives me concern about their priorities," he said.

Although a childhood bout with polio kept Skelton from military service, he has had a lifelong interest in military history. And much of his desire to maintain military readiness stems from his study of the years between the World Wars — years that saw the allies disarm too much too soon. In the 1980s, Skelton was convinced the military was not producing the kind of strategic thinkers who won World War II, and helped push through legislation that changed the emphasis in war colleges from management skills to strategic thinking.

Skelton often viewed President Clinton's defense budgets as anemic and goaded the administration to request more money and more troops. But he also parried some GOP attacks on Clinton. In common with many Republicans, Skelton warned that Clinton was wearing out U.S. forces by frequently sending them overseas while cutting manpower. But he opposed congressional efforts to force a pullout once troops were in the field.

On most social issues, Skelton is in tune with his constituents and at odds with his more liberal Democratic colleagues. He has opposed abortion in most cases, voted to repeal the ban on certain semiautomatic assault-style weapons and supported amending the Constitution to prohibit same-sex marriage. On votes pitting most Democrats against most Republicans, he stuck with his party only 77 percent of the time in the 108th Congress, while voting in agreement with Bush 64 percent of the time.

Skelton's father, a friend of Harry S Truman's, brought his son to Washington for the 1949 inauguration. Truman has continued to occupy a central role in Skelton's political life: He was endorsed by Truman's widow, chaired a joint session of Congress on the day it observed Truman's 100th birthday, and fought a Smithsonian exhibit on the dropping of the first atomic bomb because he viewed it as unfairly questioning Truman's motives toward the Japanese. Truman's birthplace is located in the 4th District.

After six years in the state Senate, Skelton ran for the House in 1976, seeking to succeed retiring Democrat William Randall. As a rural state legislator with a narrow political base, Skelton did not look particularly well-positioned when the campaign began, but he won with 56 percent of the vote. That was his closest race, except for a 1982 post-redistricting contest when he was forced to run against GOP freshman Rep. Wendell Bailey. Skelton benefited from greater familiarity with the new district's voters, and he won with 55 percent. He has won with more than 60 percent ever since.

KEY VOTES

2004

Yes Extend federal unemployment benefits by 13 weeks
Yes Pass $283.2 billion, six-year federal highway and mass transit bill
Yes Approve $146 billion multi-year extension of previously enacted middle-class tax breaks
Yes Amend the Constitution to prohibit same-sex marriage
Yes Cut corporate taxes $137 billion over 10 years
Yes Reorganize U.S. intelligence agencies as proposed by Sept. 11 commission

2003

No Cut taxes by $330 billion through fiscal 2013
Yes Block Bush rule scaling back overtime pay for some white-collar federal workers
Yes Do not allow use of search warrants without first notifying subjects
Yes Allow importation of prescription drugs
No Create private school voucher program in Washington, D.C.
Yes Ban "partial birth" abortion except to save a woman's life
No Split $18.6 billion in Iraq aid into half-grant, half-loan
No Overhaul Medicare and create prescription drug benefit

CQ VOTE STUDIES

	PARTY UNITY		PRESIDENTIAL SUPPORT	
	Support	Oppose	Support	Oppose
2004	80%	20%	68%	32%
2003	75%	25%	62%	38%
2002	73%	27%	58%	42%
2001	61%	39%	56%	44%
2000	70%	30%	61%	39%

INTEREST GROUPS

	AFL-CIO	ADA	CCUS	ACU
2004	93%	65%	60%	48%
2003	80%	80%	60%	64%
2002	67%	60%	70%	32%
2001	67%	50%	64%	64%
2000	80%	40%	66%	40%

MISSOURI 4
West central — Kansas City suburbs, Jefferson City

Laden with lakes, rivers and farmland, the 4th follows the Missouri River on much of its northern border. Besides portions of southeast Kansas City suburbs, state capital Jefferson City and medium-size Sedalia, the district typifies rural and small-town Missouri.

Most residents work at small-scale farming — row crops, soybeans and livestock — or moderate-size manufacturing of household goods. The farming communities generally have recovered from "hundred-year" Missouri River floods in 1993 and 1995. Tourism helps the rural areas. In Camden County, the Lake of the Ozarks region (shared with the 9th), with modern hotels and retail outlets, attracts 300,000 boaters a weekend during peak times. The lake areas also draw many retirees.

The 4th's piece of the Kansas City suburbs has not grown as fast as the area north of the city (in the 6th), and the suburbs are not as affluent, but they provide some blue-collar manufacturing jobs. Across the district, in Jefferson City, state government employs more than 15,000 people.

Congressional elections favor Democrats in the western counties while Republican votes can be tilled in the east, especially in Webster and Camden counties, and in counties in the southwest, such as Cedar and Barton, which were added from the old 7th during redistricting following the 2000 census. The district may be trending Republican — GOP state legislators heavily outnumber their Democratic counterparts in the state districts covering the 4th, and George W. Bush took 64 percent of the 4th's vote in the 2004 presidential election, winning all 25 counties either wholly or partially in the district.

MAJOR INDUSTRY
Government, defense, agriculture, manufacturing

MILITARY BASES
Fort Leonard Wood, 4,544 military, 2,527 civilian (2004); Whiteman Air Force Base, 4,948 military, 2,059 civilian (2003)

CITIES
Jefferson City (pt.), 39,611; Sedalia, 20,339; Warrensburg, 16,340

NOTABLE
President Harry S Truman was born in Lamar; Sedalia hosts the Scott Joplin Ragtime Festival each June; The restored home of George Caleb Bingham in Arrow Rock honors the late American artist.

Rep. Emanuel Cleaver II (D)

Elected 2004; 1st term

With a background that includes work as a pastor, civil rights leader, talk-show host and former mayor, Cleaver is familiar to voters in the Kansas City-based 5th District. Elected at 60, with two decades of local government service under his belt, Cleaver also is one of the most seasoned newcomers.

But even this practiced politician was overwhelmed on his first day in the House. "It was a frighteningly beautiful moment," Cleaver said of his swearing-in, according to the Kansas City Star. "Frightening because of the awesome responsibility. I was standing there thinking, 'This is scary.' At same time, I was saying, 'I'm happy to be here.' "

Cleaver, who got a seat on the Financial Services Committee, has an agenda that includes higher taxes for high-income taxpayers, health care coverage for average citizens that matches the benefits members of Congress receive, and increased funding for education. His wife until early 2005 was the chief administrative officer for the Kansas City School District.

Cleaver opposes continued American troop presence in Iraq. "There is no question that the people in northwest Missouri are no longer just opposed to the war, they are now against its continuation," he said during the campaign.

Seeking to succeed retired five-term Democratic Rep. Karen McCarthy in a district that favors Democrats, Cleaver faced Republican businesswoman Jeanne Patterson, who spent more than $2.8 million from her own wealth — much of it on ads that raised questions about Cleaver's professional and personal ethics. Cleaver denied Patterson's charges and accused her of trying to buy the seat. He emphasized his record as mayor from 1991 to 1999, when he helped bring firms such as Citicorp and Harley Davidson to the region, and won by a comfortable 13 percentage point margin.

Following in the footsteps of black Democrat Alan Wheat, who held the seat from 1983 to 1995, Cleaver represents a district with the smallest black population of any district represented by an African-American (24 percent of the total population).

CAPITOL OFFICE
225-4535
www.house.gov/cleaver
1641 Longworth 20515-2505; fax 225-4403

COMMITTEES
Financial Services

HOMETOWN
Kansas City

BORN
Oct. 26, 1944, Waxahachie, Texas

RELIGION
Methodist

FAMILY
Wife, Dianne Cleaver; four children

EDUCATION
Murray State College (Okla.), attended 1963-64;
Prairie View A&M College, B.S. 1972 (sociology);
Saint Paul School of Theology, M.Div. 1974

CAREER
Pastor; radio talk show host; civil rights group chapter founder; charitable group manager

POLITICAL HIGHLIGHTS
Sought Democratic nomination for Mo. House, 1970; sought Democratic nomination for Kansas City Council, 1975; Kansas City Council, 1979-91; mayor of Kansas City, 1991-99

ELECTION RESULTS

2004 GENERAL

Emanuel Cleaver II (D)	161,727	55.2%
Jeanne Patterson (R)	123,431	42.1%
Rick Bailie (LIBERT)	5,827	2.0%

2004 PRIMARY

Emanuel Cleaver II (D)	72,810	60.0%
Jamie Metzl (D)	48,607	40.0%

MISSOURI 5

Kansas City and suburbs

Mostly middle-class Democratic residents live in Kansas City and the Jackson and Cass County suburbs that make up the 5th. Although the city's suburban growth is greatest in its Kansas portion, Missouri communities have prospered as well.

A diverse economic base has helped Kansas City grow from a cow town into a transportation and telecommunications hub. Steel and automobile facilities highlight a solid industrial base. Many residents travel out of the district to work at companies such as Sprint Communications and General Motors. The federal government also is a large employer, as is Hallmark Cards. The city remains a viable market for feeder cattle and winter wheat, although less so than in years past.

Resurgence in high-end loft communities has lured younger, well-to-do residents to the city. Still, the contrasting neighborhoods on opposite sides of Troost Avenue display the city's economic disparity, which largely runs along racial lines. Taking in nearly all of the city's black neighborhoods, the 5th has a 24 percent black population. About half its voters are in Kansas City, half in the suburbs. Offshoot cities such as Lee's Summit and the 5th's portion of Cass County experienced rapid growth during the first half of the 1990s. The city of Independence (a small part of which is in the 6th) still accounts for about one-fifth of the district's vote.

The 5th is reliably Democratic and socially moderate. Democrats have held the Kansas City seat since 1931, and John Kerry captured 59 percent of the district's vote in the 2004 presidential election.

MAJOR INDUSTRY
Auto manufacturing, agriculture

MILITARY BASES
Marine Corps Support Activity, 190 military, 140 civilian (2004)

CITIES
Kansas City (pt.), 322,910; Independence (pt.), 110,822; Lee's Summit (pt.), 65,498

NOTABLE
Harry S Truman hailed from Independence.

Rep. Sam Graves (R)

Elected 2000; 3rd term

CAPITOL OFFICE
225-7041
sam.graves@mail.house.gov
www.house.gov/graves
1513 Longworth 20515-2506; fax 225-8221

COMMITTEES
Agriculture
Small Business
 (Rural Enterprises, Agriculture & Technology -
  chairman)
Transportation & Infrastructure

HOMETOWN
Tarkio

BORN
Nov. 7, 1963, Fairfax, Mo.

RELIGION
Baptist

FAMILY
Wife, Lesley Graves; three children

EDUCATION
U. of Missouri, B.S. 1986 (agronomy)

CAREER
Farmer

POLITICAL HIGHLIGHTS
Mo. House, 1993-95; Mo. Senate, 1995-2000

ELECTION RESULTS

2004 GENERAL

Sam Graves (R)	196,516	63.8%
Charles S. Broomfield (D)	106,987	34.8%
Erik Buck (LIBERT)	4,352	1.4%

2004 PRIMARY

Sam Graves (R)	unopposed

2002 GENERAL

Sam Graves (R)	131,151	63.0%
Cathy Rinehart (D)	73,202	35.2%
Erik Buck (LIBERT)	3,735	1.8%

PREVIOUS WINNING PERCENTAGES
2000 (51%)

Graves is not a man of half measures. He has called for a halt in all immigration until the nation can account for foreigners already here. He has sponsored a bill to terminate the federal income tax code at the end of 2007. And he has demanded that the United States government stop acquiring land for national parks and forests.

As a member of the Small Business Committee, he has proposed the first major exemptions to the 1965 Highway Beautification Act because he fears small businesses are being hurt by its billboard ban. "The Highway Beautification Act is an ugly obstacle for small businesses," Graves said in 2003. "If we continue to take away billboards because someone in Washington decides what is pretty to look at, small businesses will continue to suffer."

Graves chairs the Small Business panel's Subcommittee on Rural Enterprises, Agriculture and Technology.

A fiscal conservative, Graves raised eyebrows by obtaining a $273,000 grant in 2002 to help the Kansas City suburb of Blue Springs combat Goth culture among local teens. The town gave half of the money back in 2004 because it could not find enough of a problem to combat.

During his two years in the Missouri House and six in the state Senate, Graves also made headlines occasionally — staging a filibuster that threatened a school desegregation bill that he thought did not contain enough for rural districts, successfully easing state automobile inspection requirements and proposing that prisoners be required to work on chain gangs.

Graves is best known, however, for his commitment to farming. A lifelong resident of tiny Tarkio, in the northwest corner of the state, he returned to the family farm there after he graduated with a degree in agronomy from the University of Missouri in 1986. He is part of the sixth generation of Graveses to till the soil there.

His dedication to farming despite the continuing exodus of farmers from the land was noteworthy enough that NBC's "Today" show featured him in 1987 to tell viewers why he had chosen a career in farming. He said he wanted to continue his family's heritage, and he intended to make money from farming. With Graves now in Congress, his younger brother, Danny, and his father, Sam Sr., are in charge of the farm's day-to-day operations, raising corn, soybeans and cattle.

Although he now spends most of his days in the marble halls of Congress, Graves is still a farmer at heart — he can wax rhapsodic about the many uses of baling wire and about climbing up on the old 1968 John Deere 4020 tractor that his grandfather had bought new.

Graves became involved in politics through the Missouri Farm Bureau. In his hometown of Tarkio, he was active in the bureau — winning recognition as the organization's national outstanding young farmer — and in the Atchison County young farmer and rancher committee.

Graves argues that farmers are at the mercy of many factors beyond their control — including the national policy of providing low-cost food to consumers — so federal government involvement is essential. Graves sits on the Agriculture Committee, and when the panel considered a major overhaul of farm programs in 2002, he won inclusion of a provision to boost farmers' earnings by easing their entry into other stages of food production, such as food processing and the transportation of crops.

Graves was a leader in the fight to block the Corps of Engineers from changing its management of the Missouri River to create a "spring rise" that mimics the natural flow of the river. Critics of the proposal say it poses threats to agriculture and river barge traffic.

Although agricultural issues top Graves' agenda, he proudly points to two of his proposals that were included in the large education bill that became law in 2002. One was a requirement that 95 percent of federal education dollars be spent in the classroom and the other provided protection for teachers from frivolous lawsuits arising from disciplining students. The 95 percent requirement was one of Graves' campaign pledges. His wife, Lesley, is a kindergarten teacher.

Graves has vowed to make immigration a top issue in the 109th Congress. Rather than allowing more immigrants to work here legally, as President Bush has proposed, Graves would halt immigration entirely until the government can better control its borders and track immigrants already in the country. "No one ever fixes a leaky faucet while the water is running," Graves said when he made the proposal in 2003.

The Graves family has been active in northwest Missouri public affairs for many years. Graves' great-grandfather (also named Sam) was a stalwart Democrat and served on the county commission. Most family members were Democrats (conservative Democrats, Graves hastens to point out) until they, like many other area residents, gravitated to the GOP.

Graves' younger brother, Todd, was appointed by Bush to be the U.S. attorney for western Missouri, shortly after Sam Graves entered the House. Todd Graves had worked for a Republican attorney general, managed a statewide GOP campaign for attorney general, won election as Platte County prosecutor, and was the 2000 GOP nominee for state treasurer.

Just six months before the 2000 election, Sam Graves appeared to be headed again to the state Senate in Jefferson City. He had no intention of running for Congress, because Pat Danner — a popular conservative Democrat who had held the 6th District seat for four terms — had filed for re-election.

But Danner unexpectedly announced in May that she would retire. The filing period for candidates for the seat was reopened, and GOP officials coaxed eight-year state legislator Graves into entering the race. He quickly overshadowed several lesser-known Republican hopefuls.

The Democrats nominated the congresswoman's son, Steve Danner. But Graves' assertive campaign and conservative politics gave him momentum in a district that, outside of its portion of Kansas City, consists mainly of small towns and farms. Although historically Democratic, the district had been competitive, but is now considered to be strongly Republican. Graves won easily in 2002 and 2004.

KEY VOTES

2004

No   Extend federal unemployment benefits by 13 weeks

Yes   Pass $283.2 billion, six-year federal highway and mass transit bill

+   Approve $146 billion multi-year extension of previously enacted middle-class tax breaks

Yes   Amend the Constitution to prohibit same-sex marriage

Yes   Cut corporate taxes $137 billion over 10 years

Yes   Reorganize U.S. intelligence agencies as proposed by Sept. 11 commission

2003

Yes   Cut taxes by $330 billion through fiscal 2013

No   Block Bush rule scaling back overtime pay for some white-collar federal workers

No   Do not allow use of search warrants without first notifying subjects

No   Allow importation of prescription drugs

No   Create private school voucher program in Washington, D.C.

Yes   Ban "partial birth" abortion except to save a woman's life

No   Split $18.6 billion in Iraq aid into half-grant, half-loan

Yes   Overhaul Medicare and create prescription drug benefit

CQ VOTE STUDIES

	PARTY UNITY		PRESIDENTIAL SUPPORT	
	Support	Oppose	Support	Oppose
2004	93%	7%	79%	21%
2003	96%	4%	92%	8%
2002	95%	5%	79%	21%
2001	96%	4%	90%	10%

INTEREST GROUPS

	AFL-CIO	ADA	CCUS	ACU
2004	20%	10%	100%	92%
2003	0%	5%	100%	83%
2002	11%	0%	95%	100%
2001	17%	5%	100%	88%

MISSOURI 6
Northwest — St. Joseph, part of Kansas City

A mixture of suburbanites and farmers, the 6th is bordered by Iowa to the north, Nebraska and Kansas to the west, and the Missouri River to the west and most of the south.

Kansas City's suburban boom in the 1980s provided steady growth for the middle-class residents of Platte, Clay and eastern Jackson counties, who work mainly for the city's steel, transportation and communications companies. Kansas City International Airport in Platte County and American Airlines also are large employers, and the Kansas City area is home to Farmland, a large farm cooperative, and the Dairy Farmers of America, a large cooperative milk supplier. The suburbs have attracted some insurance, financial services and agribusiness companies.

Outside of the metropolitan area, the river town of St. Joseph serves as the economic hub. In the 1990s, the economy began to speed up, but agrarian life still prevails in most of the district's counties, where corn and livestock are pervasive. New processing plants have created a growing market for soybeans as well.

Although historically Democratic, the district was competitive during the last quarter of the 20th century, and now seems strongly in GOP hands. Democrat Bill Clinton won the 1992 and 1996 presidential elections here, but GOP Senate candidates did well during the same period, and George W. Bush carried the district with 52 percent of the presidential vote in 2000. Bush won all 26 of the district's counties in 2004, earning 57 percent of the overall vote in the process. Republicans seeking state office also have fared better recently, especially in the northern, rural areas.

MAJOR INDUSTRY
Agriculture, international shipping, manufacturing

CITIES
Kansas City (pt.), 118,635; St. Joseph, 73,990; Blue Springs (pt.), 39,698; Gladstone, 26,365; Liberty, 26,232

NOTABLE
Jesse James was raised near Kearney and is buried there; The Jesse James Home in St. Joseph was where the outlaw was shot and killed in 1882; The Pony Express carried mail between St. Joseph and California from April 1860 through October 1861.

Rep. Roy Blunt (R)

CAPITOL OFFICE
225-6536
blunt.house.gov
217 Cannon 20515-2507; fax 225-5604

COMMITTEES
Energy & Commerce

HOMETOWN
Strafford

BORN
Jan. 10, 1950, Niangua, Mo.

RELIGION
Baptist

FAMILY
Wife, Abigail Blunt; three children

EDUCATION
Southwest Baptist U., B.A. 1970 (history);
Southwest Missouri State U., M.A. 1972 (history &
government)

CAREER
University president; teacher

POLITICAL HIGHLIGHTS
Greene County clerk, 1973-84; Republican nominee
for lieutenant governor, 1980; Mo. secretary of
state, 1985-93; sought Republican nomination for
governor, 1992

ELECTION RESULTS

2004 GENERAL

Roy Blunt (R)	210,080	70.5%
Jim Newberry (D)	84,356	28.3%

2004 PRIMARY

Roy Blunt (R)	unopposed

2002 GENERAL

Roy Blunt (R)	149,519	74.8%
Ron Lapham (D)	45,964	23.0%
Doug Burlison (LIBERT)	4,378	2.2%

PREVIOUS WINNING PERCENTAGES
2000 (74%); 1998 (73%); 1996 (65%)

Elected 1996; 5th term

Blunt's first term as the House Republican whip was not always a smooth ride. He was blamed for an embarrassing failure on a GOP legislative priority and by media reports that he had quietly tried to help a tobacco company with a provision in a bill. His formerly critical role as the leadership's liaison to the Bush administration diminished as other Republicans developed their own relationships with the White House.

Still, he remained popular enough with the rank-and-file to be re-elected to the third-ranking leadership post in the 109th Congress. It says something about his low-key style that Blunt, the man officially responsible for rounding up votes for bills, has not been perceived as a strong-arm whip at a time the GOP leadership goes to great lengths to win votes. Those tactics are more often associated with Majority Leader Tom DeLay. Blunt has carved out a role as the leader who listens to House members' concerns and then tries to figure out what the leadership can do to win their votes.

His style is markedly different from that of DeLay, Blunt's former mentor and a former whip. Blunt's colleagues say his approach is to win votes from Republican holdouts by agreeing to do favors for them on other bills, not by threatening them. "What the whip needs to understand is what members want to accomplish while they're here, what things about their district define the way they do their job here, what things about their philosophy define the way they do their job here," he said in 2003. "Often, you [are] able to say, 'I've been to your district, and this is not a vote that's a problem for you in your district.'"

That approach has won the gratitude of rank-and-file Republicans, but it has not always endeared him to other GOP leaders. In 2003, the House leadership had to pull from the floor a bill that would have allowed businesses to offer workers compensatory time instead of overtime pay. Speaker J. Dennis Hastert and DeLay felt that Blunt had not worked hard enough to round up the votes to pass it.

Blunt was also the subject of a Washington Post story reporting that he tried to slip a measure benefiting Philip Morris USA into the 2002 legislation creating the Department of Homeland Security. Hastert's chief of staff stripped out the provision, which would have made it more difficult to sell tobacco products over the Internet, a practice that cut into Philip Morris' profits. Blunt's attempt was considered especially ill-advised because he was in a romantic relationship at the time with Philip Morris lobbyist Abigail Perlman, whom he later married in October 2003.

In his early days as whip, Blunt served as an important link between House Republicans and President Bush, a role that dated to 2000, when he was the House GOP liaison to Bush's first campaign for president. By the end of 2004, however, Hastert and other Republican leaders had developed their own close ties to Bush, so Blunt spent more of his time dealing with House members. "There's something to be said for not being the conduit," he said.

The key to keeping Republicans united is what Blunt calls "listening sessions." He brings in a dozen lawmakers representing opposing sides of an issue and creates in his office a microcosm of the discordant GOP. He believes that the experience helps moderates and conservatives appreciate how difficult the road to reconciliation can be.

Blunt himself is a committed conservative; he typically gets approval ratings in the 90s from the American Conservative Union.

Blunt rose fast through the ranks by allying himself with DeLay. He was

DeLay's appointive chief deputy whip from 1999 until 2003, a role that helped him move up to the elective post of whip at the start of the 108th Congress. Blunt also has a seat on the influential Republican Steering Committee, where he helps dole out choice committee assignments.

He set about building his own loyalty base by allocating campaign funds to vulnerable lawmakers — a strategy used with great success by DeLay in his own rise to power. Blunt's political action committee, Rely on Your Beliefs (RoyB for short), delivered $700,000 to GOP candidates and groups in the 2004 election cycle.

Though DeLay helped Blunt's career along considerably by making Blunt his chief deputy, there is friction between the two now. They are competing unofficially to be chosen by Republicans as Speaker when Hastert retires. Blunt is viewed as a possible alternative to DeLay, whose considerable power was diminished early in the 109th Congress by an investigation of his fundraising by Texas officials and by media reports of his close ties to a lobbyist.

The Blunt name is well-known in Missouri. In 2004, his son, Matt Blunt, was elected governor, a job his father had sought unsuccessfully 12 years earlier. In 1992, the elder Blunt was defeated for the GOP gubernatorial nomination after serving as Missouri's secretary of state.

The son of a dairy farmer and a state legislator, Blunt was raised on a farm near Springfield. He still lives on a farm near there, and each summer conducts an agricultural tour of the district, visiting farms and ranches and bringing in foreign trade representatives from Asia.

Blunt's first job after college was as a high school government and history teacher. He was active in politics at an early age, working in 1972 on an unsuccessful congressional bid by conservative Republican John Ashcroft, who went on to become governor, senator and then U.S. attorney general. A year later, Blunt was appointed Greene County clerk by GOP Gov. Christopher S. Bond, now a senator. Blunt was re-elected to that post twice.

He won the first of two terms as secretary of state in 1984. That set the stage for his campaign for governor in 1992. After losing the GOP primary, Blunt accepted the presidency of his alma mater, Southwest Baptist University. But he jumped back into politics when GOP Rep. Mel Hancock announced his retirement in 1996. Blunt won a narrow primary victory over Gary Nodler, a former congressional aide. In the general election, Blunt cruised to victory with 65 percent of the vote in the reliably Republican district. He has been easily re-elected since.

KEY VOTES

2004

No Extend federal unemployment benefits by 13 weeks

No Pass $283.2 billion, six-year federal highway and mass transit bill

Yes Approve $146 billion multi-year extension of previously enacted middle-class tax breaks

Yes Amend the Constitution to prohibit same-sex marriage

Yes Cut corporate taxes $137 billion over 10 years

Yes Reorganize U.S. intelligence agencies as proposed by Sept. 11 commission

2003

Yes Cut taxes by $330 billion through fiscal 2013

No Block Bush rule scaling back overtime pay for some white-collar federal workers

Yes Do not allow use of search warrants without first notifying subjects

No Allow importation of prescription drugs

Yes Create private school voucher program in Washington, D.C.

Yes Ban "partial birth" abortion except to save a woman's life

No Split $18.6 billion in Iraq aid into half-grant, half-loan

Yes Overhaul Medicare and create prescription drug benefit

CQ VOTE STUDIES

	PARTY UNITY		PRESIDENTIAL SUPPORT	
	Support	Oppose	Support	Oppose
2004	97%	3%	100%	0%
2003	98%	2%	100%	0%
2002	98%	2%	91%	9%
2001	98%	2%	95%	5%
2000	98%	2%	25%	75%

INTEREST GROUPS

	AFL-CIO	ADA	CCUS	ACU
2004	7%	0%	100%	96%
2003	0%	5%	97%	88%
2002	14%	0%	100%	100%
2001	17%	5%	95%	96%
2000	0%	0%	90%	96%

MISSOURI 7
Southwest — Springfield, Joplin

Two decades of rapid growth helped lift southwestern Missouri from a rural hideaway to a burgeoning resort and industrial region. Since the 1970s, this part of Missouri has outpaced the rest of the state in population growth, increasing its numbers by 24 percent in the 1990s.

Springfield, in Greene County, is the 7th's industrial and commercial center and has become a manufacturing hub. More than 40 percent of district residents live in Greene or neighboring Christian County on the 7th's eastern edge. Large hospital facilities in Springfield draw patients from as far as Arkansas. The district's other population center, Joplin, is across the district in Jasper County. Once a lead and zinc mining town, it is now a manufacturing and trucking center.

Branson, in the southeast corner, leads the 7th's thriving tourism industry as a magnet for country music fans. A town of 6,000, it draws more than six million visitors a year and boasts more than 40 theaters, including the Andy Williams and Mel Tillis theaters. The area also relies on the resort industry surrounding Table Rock and Taneycomo lakes.

The southwest corner of the district supports beef and dairy cattle, along with poultry. Many of the small, rural communities in the Ozarks have not quite yielded to development. Expansion along U.S. Highway 71, which runs from Kansas City into Arkansas, is expected to improve the area's accessibility and economic prospects.

The 7th long has been a GOP bastion. The Assemblies of God, based in Springfield, is among the active religious groups that reflect the area's devout, conservative population. Springfield has become slightly more Democratic since the 1980s, partly because of an influx of new residents, but the city still leans Republican. The 7th gave George W. Bush 67 percent of the vote in the 2004 election — his best showing in the state.

MAJOR INDUSTRY
Manufacturing, agriculture, tourism

CITIES
Springfield, 151,580; Joplin, 45,504; Carthage, 12,668; Nixa, 12,124

NOTABLE
Springfield is home to Fantastic Caverns, which calls itself the nation's only ride-through cave; George Washington Carver's boyhood home is now a national monument in Diamond; Precious Moments Inspiration Park, devoted to the inspirational figurines, is in Carthage.

Rep. Jo Ann Emerson (R)

Elected 1996; 5th full term

CAPITOL OFFICE
225-4404
www.house.gov/emerson
2440 Rayburn 20515-2508; fax 226-0326

COMMITTEES
Appropriations

HOMETOWN
Cape Girardeau

BORN
Sept. 16, 1950, Washington, D.C.

RELIGION
Presbyterian

FAMILY
Husband, Ron Gladney; two children, six stepchildren

EDUCATION
Ohio Wesleyan U., B.A. 1972 (political science)

CAREER
Public affairs executive; lobbyist

POLITICAL HIGHLIGHTS
No previous office

ELECTION RESULTS

2004 GENERAL

Jo Ann Emerson (R)	194,039	72.2%
Dean Henderson (D)	71,543	26.6%

2004 PRIMARY

Jo Ann Emerson (R)	65,052	88.6%
Richard Allen Kline (R)	8,401	11.4%

2002 GENERAL

Jo Ann Emerson (R)	135,144	71.8%
Gene Curtis (D)	50,686	26.9%
Eric Van Oostrom (LIBERT)	2,491	1.3%

PREVIOUS WINNING PERCENTAGES *
2000 (69%); 1998 (63%); 1996 (50%); 1996 Special Election (63%)
* Elected as an independent 1996

Raised in the suburbs of Washington, D.C., Emerson was a city girl who worked as a lobbyist on Capitol Hill after college. Twenty-five years later, she is still working in the Capitol but now as a representative of a southeastern Missouri congressional district with some of the nation's most abundant farmland. Emerson has become a self-taught expert on agriculture policy since she succeeded her husband, Bill Emerson, in the 8th District after he died of lung cancer in 1996.

She took on both the Clinton and Bush administrations in pushing to open up the Cuban market to help farmers. "When my farmers say that Congress and the administration have made it impossible to sell rice to Cuba, I'm going to learn all I can about that and try to fix it."

She also joined with North Carolina Democrat Eva Clayton in 2000 to revive the disbanded Congressional Rural Caucus to ensure that rural areas are considered in federal policy decisions and spending bills. Emerson sits on the Appropriations Committee and on its Agriculture Subcommittee. She learned from her husband the importance of delivering federal dollars to her district, as symbolized by his legacy project, a new $100 million Mississippi River bridge linking Missouri and Illinois that was named for him.

Emerson can be blunt, and she makes no apologies for reaching across party lines to solve problems important to her constituents. Her centerpiece issue is the high cost of prescription drugs. She and Minnesota Republican Gil Gutknecht led the effort in 2003 to allow the importation of prescription drugs approved by U.S. regulators that are sold more cheaply abroad. With prescription drug costs soaring, Emerson said lawmakers needed to "stop listening to the scare tactics of drug companies" and pay more attention to the needs of average citizens.

In 2003, Emerson withheld her support of a Medicare bill providing prescription drug coverage for senior citizens until GOP leaders agreed to permit a floor vote on a measure allowing drug imports from 25 industrialized countries. Her changed vote allowed the Medicare bill to pass.

A month later, the House passed the drug importation bill with a higher number of GOP votes than expected. Eighty-seven Republicans defied the leadership to vote for the bill. "I will not stand by while senior citizens take a back seat to the drug industry," Emerson said. "Our credibility is on the line tonight." Yet when the Medicare bill went to conference, the drug importation provisions were dropped. The bill eventually died.

Later, in the fall, she defied President Bush on one of the biggest votes of 2003, again on a Medicare prescription drug bill that failed to include her drug imports provision. During a dramatic, night-long vote, Emerson voted no and then hid behind a banister on the Democratic side of the chamber while Republican Whip Roy Blunt, on an arm-twisting mission, searched for her in vain. "At that point, it was high drama. I didn't want to miss anything," Emerson said later. "They didn't talk to me because they didn't find me."

Emerson ducks her party and the president on other issues. In 2004, she supported Bush's position just 61 percent of the time, compared with scores in the 90s for the most loyal members.

She was among 39 House Republicans who voted for a Democratic amendment to offer federal supplemental unemployment benefits for six months to jobless workers. The move reversed a decision by Republican leaders to allow a supplemental insurance program to expire. Emerson and 10 other Republicans crossed party lines later in 2004 to support a non-binding Democratic motion intended to put the House in favor of making both tax cuts and spending subject to pay-as-you-go rules. Republican leaders eventually secured a 209-209 tie on the motion, enough to kill it.

Early in 2005, she was one of 12 House Republicans who voted against the GOP-drafted budget resolution, after leading the opposition to the plan's proposed cuts in farm programs.

Although she voted for the 2002 resolution authorizing the war in Iraq, Emerson said in 2004 she fears for the soldiers from her district as well as for her stepdaughter Jessica, an Army captain who was recently reassigned to Iraq despite having been scheduled to return home from a tour of duty in Europe. "When you send people [into] battle, you know you're going to lose some of them. All you have to do is put the face of your own child on the face of the soldiers," Emerson said. "I'm very proud of my stepdaughter, but it's heart-wrenching to send her off."

Despite Emerson's willingness on occasion to challenge her party's positions, she continues to have good relations with her GOP colleagues. She stumped with former Missouri GOP Rep. Jim Talent during his successful 2002 Senate campaign against incumbent Democrat Jean Carnahan. And Blunt, of the neighboring 7th District, introduced her to constituents he had lost to Emerson through redistricting.

Emerson grew up in Bethesda, Md., where she learned Republican principles from her father, Ab Hermann, who was for many years the executive director of the Republican National Committee. Emerson says her father also taught her how to get along with Democrats, including family friend Hale Boggs, the powerful Louisiana representative who rose to majority leader before he disappeared on a plane flight in Alaska in 1972. Emerson remained friends with Boggs' widow, Lindy, and drew inspiration from her successful race to succeed her husband after his death.

After graduating from Ohio Wesleyan, Emerson returned to the Washington area, where she worked for the National Republican Congressional Committee and then began a career as a lobbyist. In Washington, she met Bill Emerson, a former congressional staffer who also was a lobbyist.

Bill Emerson, first elected in 1980, was a candidate for a ninth House term when he died. In the race to succeed him, Jo Ann Emerson ran as an independent because the filing deadline for the primary had closed. She won with 50 percent of the vote, finishing 13 percentage points ahead of Democrat Emily Firebaugh and 39 points ahead of the official GOP candidate, Richard A. Kline. Emerson's re-elections have been by strong margins. In 2000, she married St. Louis Democratic labor lawyer Ron Gladney.

KEY VOTES

2004

Yes   Extend federal unemployment benefits by 13 weeks

Yes   Pass $283.2 billion, six-year federal highway and mass transit bill

Yes   Approve $146 billion multi-year extension of previously enacted middle-class tax breaks

Yes   Amend the Constitution to prohibit same-sex marriage

Yes   Cut corporate taxes $137 billion over 10 years

Yes   Reorganize U.S. intelligence agencies as proposed by Sept. 11 commission

2003

?   Cut taxes by $330 billion through fiscal 2013

No   Block Bush rule scaling back overtime pay for some white-collar federal workers

Yes   Do not allow use of search warrants without first notifying subjects

Yes   Allow importation of prescription drugs

Yes   Create private school voucher program in Washington, D.C.

Yes   Ban "partial birth" abortion except to save a woman's life

No   Split $18.6 billion in Iraq aid into half-grant, half-loan

No   Overhaul Medicare and create prescription drug benefit

CQ VOTE STUDIES

	PARTY UNITY		PRESIDENTIAL SUPPORT	
	Support	Oppose	Support	Oppose
2004	89%	11%	61%	39%
2003	91%	9%	93%	7%
2002	93%	7%	81%	19%
2001	91%	9%	83%	17%
2000	91%	9%	24%	76%

INTEREST GROUPS

	AFL-CIO	ADA	CCUS	ACU
2004	50%	20%	86%	76%
2003	31%	10%	92%	95%
2002	22%	0%	95%	96%
2001	17%	5%	91%	83%
2000	10%	0%	80%	80%

MISSOURI 8

Southeast — Cape Girardeau, Ozark Plateau

Some of the state's most bountiful farmland can be found in the 8th, which takes in the mountains, forests and Mississippi Valley towns of Missouri's southeastern corner.

The district spans the political spectrum from solidly Republican counties in the west and northeast along the Mississippi River to "Yellow Dog" Democratic territory in the southeast area, dubbed the boot heel because of its shape. Voters tend to be socially conservative on issues such as abortion and gun control and leery of environmental regulations, and the GOP has made inroads in the boot heel in elections for offices higher than the county level.

The 8th is slowly recovering from a decline in the textile industry since the 1980s. Agriculture and lead mining fuel the central counties, while the boot heel is a former wheat-growing region that now produces soybean, corn, cotton and rice.

Major growth centers in the district include the northern counties of

Phelps and St. Francois, which have been boosted by light manufacturing and defense subcontracts. Lumber also features heavily in the 8th's industry, and four-fifths of Mark Twain National Forest's 1.5 million acres lies in the 8th.

Frequent flooding and earthquakes from the New Madrid fault line that runs through southeastern Missouri make the 8th a disaster-prone region, although reinforced levees and highways have reduced the risk. The last major flooding from the Mississippi River was in 2002 and 1995, but preparation for smaller floods is still an annual spring ritual in the border towns.

MAJOR INDUSTRY
Agriculture, lead mining, lumber

CITIES
Cape Girardeau, 35,349; Sikeston, 16,992; Poplar Bluff, 16,651; Rolla, 16,367

NOTABLE
The Census Bureau estimates that the population center of the United States is near Edgar Springs; Laura Ingalls Wilder wrote her "Little House" series of books in Mansfield; The New Madrid region has more earthquakes than any other part of the United States east of the Rocky Mountains.

Rep. Kenny Hulshof (R)

Elected 1996; 5th term

CAPITOL OFFICE
225-2956
hulshof.house.gov
412 Cannon 20515-2509; fax 225-5712

COMMITTEES
Budget
Ways & Means

HOMETOWN
Columbia

BORN
May 22, 1958, Sikeston, Mo.

RELIGION
Roman Catholic

FAMILY
Wife, Renee Hulshof; two children

EDUCATION
U. of Missouri, B.S. 1980 (agriculture economics);
U. of Mississippi, J.D. 1983

CAREER
State and city prosecutor; public defender

POLITICAL HIGHLIGHTS
Sought Republican nomination for Boone County
prosecutor, 1992; Republican nominee for U.S.
House, 1994

ELECTION RESULTS

2004 GENERAL

Kenny Hulshof (R)	193,429	64.6%
Linda Jacobsen (D)	101,343	33.8%
Tamara A. Millay (LIBERT)	3,228	1.1%

2004 PRIMARY

Kenny Hulshof (R)	unopposed

2002 GENERAL

Kenny Hulshof (R)	146,032	68.2%
Donald M. Deichman (D)	61,126	28.6%
Keith Brekhus (GREEN)	4,262	2.0%
John Mruzik (LIBERT)	2,705	1.3%

PREVIOUS WINNING PERCENTAGES
2000 (59%); 1998 (62%); 1996 (49%)

Hulshof was a state prosecutor before he entered politics, and his willingness to apply his investigative skills to the ethics complaints against Majority Leader Tom DeLay in the 108th Congress put him at odds with the House leadership and helped get him unceremoniously dumped from the ethics committee at the start of the 109th.

But Hulshof (HULLZ-hoff) is still a rising star with statewide ambitions in Missouri, and the dust-up is likely to enhance his reputation as a straight-shooter willing to put principle above partisanship. What's more, as a member of the high-profile Ways and Means Committee, Hulshof will be instrumental in efforts to shape and deliver two of President Bush's top priorities: carving out private accounts in Social Security and tax reform.

Hulshof headed the ethics subcommittee that investigated DeLay's role in trying to switch the vote of Michigan Republican Nick Smith during a three-hour vote on the final Medicare prescription drug bill in 2003. The Committee on Standards of Official Conduct formally reprimanded DeLay in October 2004 for offering to endorse Smith's son, who was running for his father's seat, if the retiring Smith voted yes. That was one of three reprimands the panel gave DeLay in a matter of months. When word spread that Speaker J. Dennis Hastert was thinking of removing committee Chairman Joel Hefley of Colorado, Hulshof said Hefley should be allowed to stay. Those moves cost him his seat.

"I strongly believe that my actions . . . were in keeping with the best traditions of the U.S. House of Representatives. I wholeheartedly stand behind my subcommittee's findings and do not apologize for my actions," he said in a statement issued after the committee shakeup.

Hulshof generally hews to conservative principles. From his perch on Ways and Means, he has been a leading proponent of making Bush's tax cuts permanent and of creating tax-advantaged savings accounts for education and for farmers. He introduced Bush's limited proposal for altering campaign finance law and was tapped in 2001 to head the Republican Policy Committee's panel on retirement security capital markets and tax policy.

Hulshof articulated party policy so eloquently that he was picked to be the Bush campaign's formal spokesman in Missouri in 2004 and went to Boston to be the GOP killjoy during the Democratic convention.

He has been a major player in farm states' campaign to use tax credits to create markets for renewable fuels, such as ethanol and biodiesel, both of which are derived from agricultural products. He finally succeeded in winning the tax credit for biodiesel — largely made from soybeans, a leading Missouri crop — as part of a corporate tax bill in 2004.

As a freshman, Hulshof even took on the powerful chairman of his committee at the time, Republican Bill Archer of Texas, when Archer tried to phase out the ethanol tax break. When Archer abandoned the plan the next year, Hulshof — as a negotiator on that year's big rewrite of highway and mass transit law — and other farm-state lawmakers were able to win a seven-year extension of the ethanol credit. He prevailed again in the 2004 corporate tax bill, when the ethanol break was improved and extended to 2010.

Hulshof grew up on a farm near the boot heel of southeastern Missouri and still recalls getting an uncomfortably personal lesson in how politics influences agriculture when his parents almost lost their farm in the early 1980s because of the U.S. embargo on grain sales to the Soviet Union.

Hulshof has been gaining influence steadily in Washington since the day he defeated Democrat Harold L. Volkmer, a two-decade veteran in a district that had last sent a Republican to Washington in 1920. Not only did he receive an immediate appointment to Ways and Means, a rare plum for a freshman, but his first-term GOP colleagues elected him class president. Hulshof made a concerted effort in that role to define himself and his peers as not only conservative but also pragmatic and cooperative — and not given to the kind of ideological brinkmanship that characterized the class first elected in 1994, when the GOP won control of Congress.

Soon after the 105th Congress convened, Hulshof was a leading force behind the first in a series of biannual and bipartisan "civility" retreats, where the objective is for Republicans and Democrats to get acquainted with each other in a non-confrontational setting. In the same vein, Hulshof's wife, Renee, formed a support group with the wife of a state Democratic figure for spouses of servicemen, including her brother, deployed to the Middle East for the Iraq war.

Hulshof has flirted with seeking higher office. The state's senior GOP officeholder, Sen. Christopher S. Bond, and other prominent Republicans tried in 2001 to persuade Hulshof to challenge Democrat Jean Carnahan's bid for a full term in the Senate. He demurred, citing family reasons. After his easy win in 2002, Hulshof briefly considered a run for governor in 2004. But the birth of a daughter, the death of his father, and his mother's desire to keep the family farm operating convinced Hulshof, an only child, to focus on personal matters for now.

A former high school athlete, Hulshof stars as first baseman for the Republicans in the annual charity baseball game against the Democrats, and as a guard and a forward on the congressional basketball team that plays a team of lobbyists for charity. He also sings and plays the drums in his church choir.

An agricultural economics graduate of the University of Missouri, Hulshof went on to the University of Mississippi for law school. Upon graduation, he worked as a public defender and then as a prosecutor in Cape Girardeau County before moving to Columbia to work for the state attorney general.

Hulshof was a fill-in candidate in 1994 against Volkmer, tapped by party leaders when the GOP front-runner bowed out after the filing deadline. Despite being a political neophyte with no name recognition, Hulshof lost by just 5 percentage points. When he tried again in 1996, he first overcame a stiff primary challenge from wealthy ophthalmologist Harry Eggleston, then edged Volkmer by slightly less than 6,000 votes in November.

KEY VOTES

2004

No Extend federal unemployment benefits by 13 weeks

? Pass $283.2 billion, six-year federal highway and mass transit bill

Yes Approve $146 billion multi-year extension of previously enacted middle-class tax breaks

Yes Amend the Constitution to prohibit same-sex marriage

Yes Cut corporate taxes $137 billion over 10 years

Yes Reorganize U.S. intelligence agencies as proposed by Sept. 11 commission

2003

Yes Cut taxes by $330 billion through fiscal 2013

No Block Bush rule scaling back overtime pay for some white-collar federal workers

No Do not allow use of search warrants without first notifying subjects

No Allow importation of prescription drugs

Yes Create private school voucher program in Washington, D.C.

Yes Ban "partial birth" abortion except to save a woman's life

Yes Split $18.6 billion in Iraq aid into half-grant, half-loan

Yes Overhaul Medicare and create prescription drug benefit

CQ VOTE STUDIES

	PARTY UNITY		PRESIDENTIAL SUPPORT	
	Support	Oppose	Support	Oppose
2004	96%	4%	94%	6%
2003	96%	4%	98%	2%
2002	95%	5%	88%	12%
2001	94%	6%	95%	5%
2000	96%	4%	19%	81%

INTEREST GROUPS

	AFL-CIO	ADA	CCUS	ACU
2004	8%	5%	100%	91%
2003	7%	5%	100%	88%
2002	11%	10%	100%	96%
2001	17%	5%	100%	92%
2000	0%	5%	85%	96%

MISSOURI 9
Northeast — Columbia, St. Louis exurbs

Besides Columbia and some western St. Louis suburbs, the 9th consists of small towns spread among farmlands. Residents include many middle-class, socially conservative Democrats, but the arrival of new wealth has led to rapid suburban growth and a rise in Republican-leaning areas.

The 9th splits St. Charles County with the neighboring 2nd District and encompasses all of nearby Warren and Franklin counties. A General Motors plant and a Boeing Co. hub in nearby districts provide jobs, but much of the area's growth has come from small businesses. A wine industry that dates back to the 19th century provides income for Gasconade and surrounding counties.

Columbia, a steadily growing and mostly middle-class city across the district from St. Charles County, is home to the University of Missouri's flagship campus and a handful of medical facilities, including the Harry S Truman Memorial Veterans Hospital. Despite a significant exodus of young people from farming families, the district's economy still thrives on

cattle, soybean, corn and winter wheat.

Traditionally Democratic, the 9th is becoming increasingly Republican with the growth of suburban St. Louis and the decline of "Yellow Dog" Democrats in rural communities. Before 1996, voters elected a Republican member of Congress only once in the 20th century, in 1920. Still mostly Democratic at the local level, the district expanded southwest in redistricting following the 2000 census to gain new counties that have contributed to a GOP base for state offices. George W. Bush carried the district with 59 percent of the vote in the 2004 presidential election.

MAJOR INDUSTRY
Higher education, electronics, agriculture

CITIES
Columbia, 84,531; Hannibal, 17,757; Kirksville, 16,988; Washington, 13,243

NOTABLE
Samuel Clemens (Mark Twain) was born in the town of Florida in Monroe County and grew up in Hannibal, which attracts visitors to Twain's boyhood home; Westminster College in Fulton was the site of Winston Churchill's "Iron Curtain" speech after World War II; The August A. Busch wildlife area in St. Charles County was purchased by the state in 1947 after Busch's widow made a donation toward the purchase.

Gov. Brian Schweitzer (D)

First elected: 2004
Length of term: 4 years
Term expires: 1/09
Salary: $96,462
Phone: (406) 444-3111

Hometown: Whitefish
Born: Sept. 4, 1955; Havre, Mont.
Religion: Roman Catholic
Family: Wife, Nancy Schweitzer; three children
Education: Colorado State U., B.S. 1978 (international agronomy); Montana State U., Bozeman, M.S. 1980 (soil science)
Career: Farmer; rancher; agronomist
Political highlights: Democratic nominee for U.S. Senate, 2000

Election results:
2004 GENERAL

Brian Schweitzer (D)	225,016	50.4%
Bob Brown (R)	205,313	46.0%
Bob Kelleher (GREEN)	8,393	1.9%
Stanley R. Jones (LIBERT)	7,424	1.7%

Lt. Gov. John Bohlinger (R)

First elected: 2004
Length of term: 4 years
Term expires: 1/09
Salary: $66,724
Phone: (406) 444-3111

STATE LEGISLATURE

Legislature: January-April in odd-numbered years, limit of 90 days

House: 100 members, 2-year terms
2005 breakdown: 50D, 50R; 69 men, 31 women
Salary: $77/ day in session; $94/day in session allowance
Phone: (406) 444-4819

Senate: 50 members, 4-year terms
2005 breakdown: 27D, 23R; 43 men, 7 women
Salary: $77/day in session; $94/day in session allowance
Phone: (406) 444-4880

STATE TERM LIMITS

Governor: 2 terms in a 16-year period
House: 4 terms in a 16-year period
Senate: 2 terms in a 16-year period

URBAN STATISTICS

CITY	POPULATION
Billings	89,847
Missoula	57,053
Great Falls	56,690
Butte-Silver Bow	34,606
Bozeman	27,509

REGISTERED VOTERS

Voters do not register by party.

POPULATION

2004 population (est.)	926,865
2000 population	902,195
1990 population	799,065
Percent change (1990-2000)	+12.9%
Rank among states (2004)	44

Median age	37.5
Born in state	56.1%
Foreign born	1.8%
Violent crime rate	241/100,000
Poverty level	14.6%
Federal workers	13,044
Military	8,349

REDISTRICTING

Montana retained its one House seat in reapportionment.

MISCELLANEOUS

Web: www.state.mt.us
Capital: Helena
STATE ELECTION OFFICIAL
(406) 444-4732
DEMOCRATIC HEADQUARTERS
(406) 442-9520
REPUBLICAN HEADQUARTERS
(406) 442-6469

District Statistics

DIST.	2004 VOTE FOR PRESIDENT BUSH	KERRY	WHITE	BLACK	ASIAN	HISP	MEDIAN INCOME	WHITE COLLAR	BLUE COLLAR	SERVICE INDUSTRY	OVER 64	UNDER 18	COLLEGE EDUCATION	RURAL	SQ. MILES
AL	59%	39%	90%	0%	1%	2%	$33,024	59%	24%	17%	13%	26%	24%	46%	145,552
STATE	59	39	90	0	1	2	$33,024	59	24	17	13	26	24	46	145,552
U.S.	50.7	48.3	69	12	4	13	$41,994	60	25	15	12	26	24	21	3,537,438

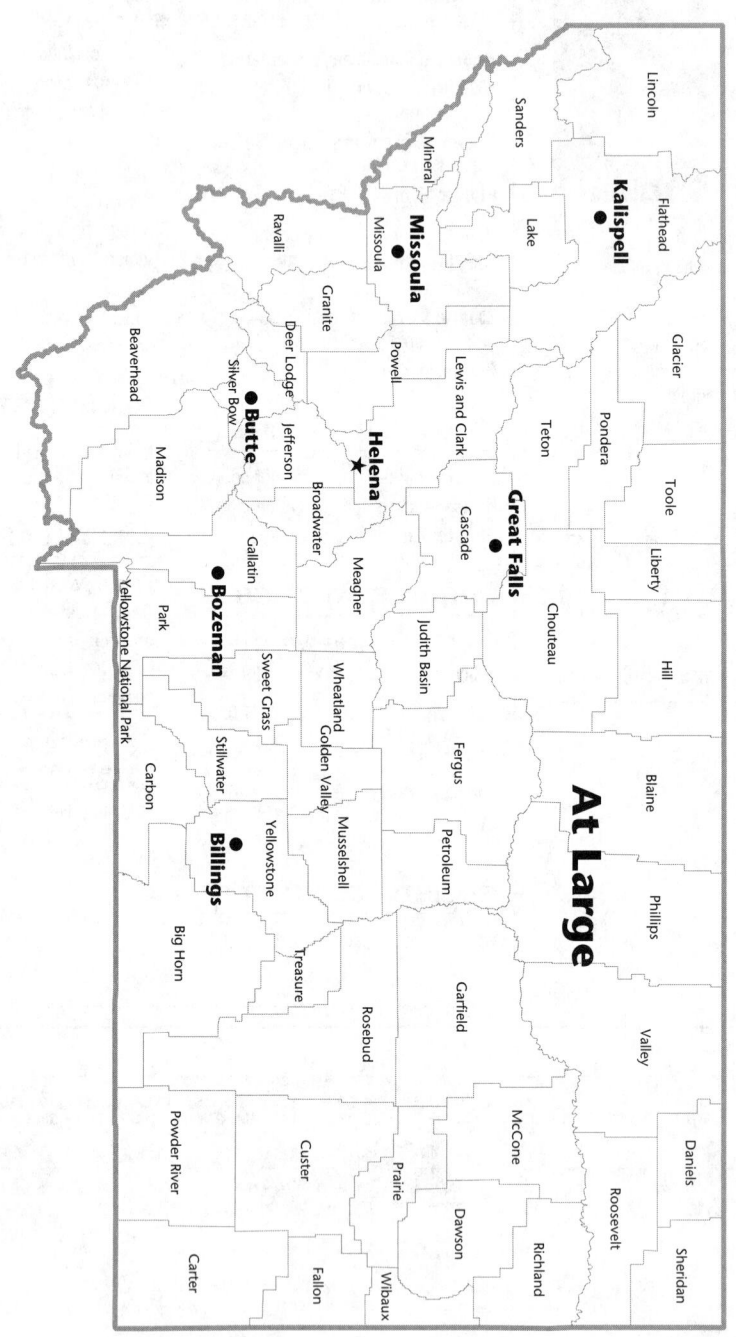

Sen. Max Baucus (D)

CAPITOL OFFICE
224-2651
max@baucus.senate.gov
baucus.senate.gov
511 Hart 20510-2602; fax 228-3790

COMMITTEES
Agriculture, Nutrition & Forestry
Environment & Public Works
Finance - ranking member
Joint Taxation

HOMETOWN
Helena

BORN
Dec. 11, 1941, Helena, Mont.

RELIGION
United Church of Christ

FAMILY
Wife, Wanda Baucus; one child

EDUCATION
Stanford U., A.B. 1964 (economics), LL.B. 1967

CAREER
Lawyer

POLITICAL HIGHLIGHTS
Mont. House, 1973-75; U.S. House, 1975-78

ELECTION RESULTS

2002 GENERAL

Max Baucus (D)	204,853	62.7%
Mike Taylor (R)	103,611	31.7%
Stanley R. Jones (LIBERT)	10,420	3.2%
Bob Kelleher (GR)	7,653	2.3%

2002 PRIMARY

Max Baucus (D)	unopposed

PREVIOUS WINNING PERCENTAGES
1996 (50%); 1990 (68%); 1984 (57%); 1978 (56%); 1976
House Election (66%); 1974 House Election (55%)

Elected 1978; 5th term

The cold shoulder that Baucus sometimes received from his fellow Democrats for siding with Republicans on economic and health care policy was nothing compared to everything else he endured in the 108th Congress — a motorcycle accident, heart surgery to implant a pacemaker, and a major injury to his head when he fell during a 50-mile ultramarathon (the latter required an operation in which two small holes were drilled into his skull).

Baucus is clearly a survivor. And none of these out-of-the-ordinary episodes seems to have distracted him from his energetic legislative work as one of the most senior tax writers in the Senate. Not only does Baucus attempt physical feats that men half his age would never contemplate, as a Democrat he walks an extraordinarily fine line to keep winning elections as Montana trends increasingly Republican and conservative.

Many in his party remain skeptical of Baucus' loyalty since he collaborated with the Bush administration and congressional Republicans on the 2003 Medicare overhaul and the 2001 tax cut. Baucus was one of only two Democrats in the final negotiations. His participation was also critical in passing the $350 billion tax cut of 2003 and the $146 billion tax cut of 2004, both of which were GOP priorities.

At the same time, his conservative legislative record gave Baucus a landslide election to a fifth term in 2002, an astonishing achievement for a Democrat in today's Rocky Mountain West. And Baucus looks to be front and center on a number of important issues in the 109th Congress.

Despite his party's wariness, Democratic Leader Harry Reid tapped Baucus to be the lead Democratic Senate negotiator on any changes to the Social Security system. The move demonstrated Reid's respect for the committee system; Baucus is the most senior Democratic member of the Finance Committee, which has jurisdiction over the Social Security program. In exchange, Baucus vowed not to endorse President Bush's plan to divert Social Security payroll taxes into private investment accounts.

In fact, at a Finance Committee hearing in early 2005, Baucus singled out for criticism the personal accounts plan proposed by Bush. "The kind of plan the president seems to be suggesting would mean deep benefit cuts for retirees," Baucus said. "And it would also mean massive increases in debt for the federal government."

Baucus is also a senior member of the Environment and Public Works Committee, where he is the top-ranking Democrat on the Transportation and Infrastructure Subcommittee. That panel is often the starting point for the reauthorization of highway and mass transit funds, and so Baucus is in a prime position to steer highway dollars to Montana during the rewrite of the surface transportation law scheduled for the 109th.

Baucus works well with Finance Chairman Charles E. Grassley of Iowa, and the two share a desire to protect the interests of rural communities. Baucus was not happy with the cuts to agriculture spending proposed in the Senate's 2005 budget resolution, and he tried to remove them when the Senate voted on the budget plan early in the 109th. Baucus said the cuts were not proportionate to agriculture's share of the budget and would reduce the baseline for the next farm law, due in 2007. "Agriculture is a small portion of the federal budget, and it is expected to shoulder huge cuts," Baucus said. His amendment failed, however.

Nothing better illustrates Baucus' willingness to work with the other party than his co-writing of the $1.35 trillion tax cut enacted in the spring of 2001, Bush's biggest domestic policy victory during his first year in office. As the top-ranking Democrat on Finance at the time, Baucus worked closely with Grassley and the White House to move the bill seamlessly through a Senate split 50-50 between Republicans and Democrats. Montana voters embraced the tax relief. But their senator's collaboration irked Democrats nationwide, because the party's ability to criticize Bush's tax cut in the 2002 campaign was hobbled by the fact that Baucus' deal had won the votes of 12 Democratic senators.

Baucus' ideological inconsistencies reflect the historic political divide in his sparsely populated state. Democrats traditionally have dominated in the stunningly picturesque mountainous western half, while Republicans rule in the open ranchland of the eastern half. Baucus also must juggle the interests of the conservative ranching and business communities with those of the unionized miners and educators who make up his base. In 2001, he was one of six Democrats to vote for a measure overturning Clinton administration ergonomics regulations — rules promoted by organized labor but opposed by business. That same year, however, he voted with the rest of his party to approve patients' bill of rights legislation that business and insurance groups fought.

Like many Western lawmakers, Baucus wants to protect the rights of gun owners, and he angered many constituents when he voted in 1993 for the Brady law, which mandated a waiting period and a background check before the purchase of a handgun. But in 1999, Baucus was the only Senate Democrat who voted no on the key amendment to that year's gun control bill that would have required background checks for firearms purchases at gun shows. And Baucus joined forces in 2005 with GOP Sen. Larry Craig of Idaho to introduce legislation that would protect firearms manufacturers from lawsuits.

Because of the conservative nature of his state, Baucus tends to hew closer to the liberal side of his party between elections. In the 108th Congress, he voted with his party 73 percent of the time on votes that pitted majorities of the two parties against each other, up 6 percentage points from his score in the 107th, when he was running for re-election.

Baucus' brother and sister-in-law now run the sprawling family ranch north of Helena. Even though the Sieben Ranch Co. bears the senator's middle name, it was clear early on that Baucus was going to take a different career path. He entered public life after finishing Stanford Law School in 1967, serving as an attorney for the Securities and Exchange Commission in Washington for three years. He returned home to Montana in 1971 to coordinate the state's constitutional convention, and the next year he won a seat in the state legislature.

Two years later, he dislodged a two-term Republican incumbent to win a House seat in the post-Watergate election of 1974. He arrived in the Senate at the end of 1978, four days after his 37th birthday, after winning a primary against Paul Hatfield, a Democrat who had been appointed to the seat.

Holding his seat in the Senate has not always been easy, and in 1996 Baucus won by fewer than 20,000 votes over Republican Denny Rehberg, then the lieutenant governor and now Montana's sole House member.

Bush carried Montana by 25 percentage points in 2000, and Republicans tried hard to recruit popular former Gov. Marc Racicot to run against Baucus in 2002. Racicot demurred — he was later named Republican National Committee chairman — and Baucus cruised to victory with 63 percent of the vote against GOP state Sen. Mike Taylor. He was confident enough of victory that he was spotted jogging along the Potomac River on some weekend afternoons close to the election.

KEY VOTES

2004

Yes Pass $318.9 billion, six-year highway and mass transit bill
No   Extend assault weapons ban for 10 years
Yes Restore pay-as-you-go rules for new tax cuts and entitlement spending
No   Criminalize harm to a fetus in an attack on the mother
Yes Increase mandatory child care funding to states by $6 billion over five years
No   Amend the Constitution to prohibit same-sex marriage
Yes Approve $146 billion multi-year extension of previously enacted middle-class tax breaks
Yes Reorganize U.S. intelligence agencies as proposed by Sept. 11 commission
Yes Cut corporate taxes $137 billion over 10 years

2003

Yes Delay Bush changes to Clean Air Act
No   Allow confirmation vote on Miguel A. Estrada to the U.S. Court of Appeals for the D.C. Circuit
Yes Block a Bush proposal opening Alaska's Arctic National Wildlife Refuge to oil drilling
Yes Limit size of Bush's proposed tax cut to $350 billion through fiscal 2013
Yes Overhaul Medicare and create prescription drug benefit
Yes Block Bush rule scaling back overtime pay for some white-collar federal workers
Yes Split $20 billion in Iraq aid into half-grant, half-loan
No   Ban "partial birth" abortion except to save a woman's life
No   Stop proposal allowing travel to Cuba
Yes Allow final vote on energy policy overhaul

CQ VOTE STUDIES

	PARTY UNITY		PRESIDENTIAL SUPPORT	
	Support	Oppose	Support	Oppose
2004	72%	28%	57%	43%
2003	74%	26%	54%	46%
2002	67%	33%	88%	12%
2001	67%	33%	71%	29%
2000	88%	12%	97%	3%
1999	87%	13%	81%	19%
1998	84%	16%	81%	19%
1997	73%	27%	87%	13%
1996	73%	27%	90%	10%
1995	68%	32%	79%	21%

INTEREST GROUPS

	AFL-CIO	ADA	CCUS	ACU
2004	92%	85%	71%	29%
2003	62%	85%	74%	15%
2002	69%	75%	70%	37%
2001	81%	80%	71%	28%
2000	75%	85%	46%	16%
1999	78%	95%	59%	4%
1998	75%	80%	56%	5%
1997	29%	65%	70%	4%
1996	71%	85%	46%	20%
1995	83%	75%	47%	13%

Sen. Conrad Burns (R)

Elected 1988; 3rd term

CAPITOL OFFICE
224-2644
burns.senate.gov
187 Dirksen 20510-2603; fax 224-8594

COMMITTEES
Appropriations
 (Interior - chairman)
Commerce, Science & Transportation
 (Aviation - chairman)
Energy & Natural Resources
Small Business & Entrepreneurship
Special Aging

HOMETOWN
Billings

BORN
Jan. 25, 1935, Gallatin, Mo.

RELIGION
Lutheran

FAMILY
Wife, Phyllis Burns; two children

EDUCATION
U. of Missouri, attended 1952-54 (agriculture)

MILITARY SERVICE
Marine Corps, 1955-57

CAREER
Radio owner and broadcaster; auctioneer; agricultural magazine sales representative; airline ground operations employee

POLITICAL HIGHLIGHTS
Yellowstone County Commission, 1987-89

ELECTION RESULTS

2000 GENERAL

Conrad Burns (R)	208,082	50.6%
Brian Schweitzer (D)	194,430	47.2%
Gary Lee (REF)	9,089	2.2%

2000 PRIMARY

Conrad Burns (R)	unopposed

PREVIOUS WINNING PERCENTAGES
1994 (62%); 1988 (52%)

Burns is a man of contrasts. A prototypical Montana cowboy with his boots, big belt buckles, folksy speaking style and scenes of cattle drives hanging on his office walls, he also is the Senate standard-bearer for bringing the nation's communications laws into the digital age. As Congress continues to grapple with the effects of rapid change in the telecommunications, entertainment and computer industries, Burns has often placed himself at the center of the debates.

Early in the 109th Congress, Burns unveiled a technology agenda that includes reviving a failed attempt from the 108th to ban unsolicited spyware from computers, making enhanced 911 services available to people using the Internet to place phone calls, fighting identity theft, and ensuring rural access to high-speed Internet and other advanced communications services. "It is no longer a world where we can distinguish between voice, video and data," Burns said when introducing his legislative agenda. "Everything now is in the indistinguishable form of ones and zeroes. This will pose new challenges as we continue forward with reform legislation."

Burns' background as a radio broadcaster helped him see, long before many of his colleagues, the importance of embracing and fostering new communications technologies. In 1996, Burns chaired the first interactive hearing on Capitol Hill and several times he has been cited as one of the Senate's most Net-friendly members. He founded the Congressional Internet Caucus that same year with Vermont Democrat Patrick J. Leahy. Burns has been its co-chairman ever since. For seven years, Burns was either the chairman or top-ranking minority member of the Commerce Committee's Communications Subcommittee.

In the 109th, he takes on a new challenge as he moves over to chair Commerce's Aviation Subcommittee. Burns has always paid particular attention to rural issues, and as chairman he is likely to push for more federal assistance for small rural airports.

He has been able specifically to address his rural constituents' needs from his seat on the Appropriations Committee, where he is chairman of the Interior Subcommittee. Burns announced in late 2004 that he had succeeded in securing $194 million for Montana in that year's huge catchall spending bill. Burns sides with the farmers and cattlemen of his state, who complain that large meatpackers do not offer them fair prices, and that railroads hold them captive to high shipping rates. In 2001, he pushed for generous emergency drought aid in the face of budget constraints, saying, "I am unable to overlook an industry that is as important to America as the military."

Modern communication is of particular importance in sparsely populated states such as Montana. In fact, many of the most technology-savvy senators — including Burns and Leahy, and Republicans Michael B. Enzi of Wyoming and Ted Stevens of Alaska — represent mostly rural states located far from the nation's traditional communications and technology centers. Burns argues that such technology is vital to the economic well-being of Montana, by providing its residents the same access to information and electronic commerce opportunities as residents of more-populous states. Long-distance learning and telemedicine are also important in rural areas, where professors and doctors are especially scarce.

Burns has sided firmly with broadcasters in their fight to slow down the speed at which they have to surrender the analog spectrum they now use in exchange for access to a higher-frequency digital spectrum. Burns' position angered fellow Republican John McCain of Arizona in 2004 when McCain tried to push through the Senate a provision that would free up the analog spectrum sooner so the government could auction it off to cellular providers. He also tangled with mass-marketers in 2003 in helping to secure enactment of anti-spam legislation, which allows recipients of unwanted e-mail solicitations to take their name off mailing lists and penalizes e-mail marketers that do not comply. The measure was criticized by privacy advocates who said the law was not tough enough.

Burns' effort to increase Internet access, including wireless broadband, even involved the 2002 rewrite of the farm bill. Burns was a leader in the effort to include funds in the measure for grants or loans from the Department of Agriculture's Rural Utilities Service to spur deployment of broadband service in rural areas.

In 2005, Burns joined the Special Committee on Aging, where he joined the debate on the future of Social Security. Burns was among those congressional Republicans who did not immediately side with President Bush, but he did not join the president's critics, either. "President Bush's plan may not be exactly the right way to go about it, but perhaps there are parts that will be beneficial, and we can implement them along with suggestions from Montanans," he told the Helena Independent Record. "To simply stick your fingers in your ears and say, 'No way, I'm not listening,' is to do a disservice to the generations to follow."

After the terrorist attacks of Sept. 11, 2001, Burns' military background — he served three years in the Marine Corps — helped shape his view that airline pilots should be given weapons to defend the cockpit from would-be hijackers. He played a leading role in the law enacted in 2002 to that end. He also argued that the United States should stop importing "rogue oil" from Middle East nations that use the revenue to support terrorists. And he convinced the Treasury Department to issue "Patriot Bonds" to help fund the war on terrorism and rebuild New York City and the Pentagon.

Burns grew up on a small Missouri farm, where his mother was a Democratic Party worker. He first went to Montana as a teenager for a summer job as a firefighter. He studied agriculture at the University of Missouri for two years and then enlisted in the Marines. In 1962, he got a job with an agricultural magazine and moved to Billings. He later worked for the Billings Livestock Commission and did radio and television farm and ranch reports before co-founding the Northern Agricultural Network, which began with four radio stations.

After winning election as a Yellowstone County Commissioner in 1986, he sold his interest in the network, which by then had grown to more than three dozen radio and television stations in Montana and Wyoming.

Soon, Burns' name was mentioned as a potential challenger in 1988 to two-term Democratic Sen. John Melcher. Despite being tagged as an underdog with no expertise on national or international issues, his broadcasting life gave him wide name recognition. With strong backing from the Senate GOP campaign organization and President Reagan's timely veto of a wilderness bill Melcher wrote — giving credence to Burns' view that the incumbent lacked clout in Washington — Burns won with 52 percent of the vote. It was the biggest Senate upset of the year.

He breezed to a second term in 1994 with 62 percent against Jack Mudd, a former University of Montana law school dean. But in 2000, he won by only 3 percentage points against farmer Brian Schweitzer, a political neophyte who focused his campaign on the high cost of prescription drugs. Not long after he celebrated his 70th birthday, Burns announced that he would run for re-election in 2006.

KEY VOTES

2004

Yes   Pass $318.9 billion, six-year highway and mass transit bill

No   Extend assault weapons ban for 10 years

No   Restore pay-as-you-go rules for new tax cuts and entitlement spending

Yes   Criminalize harm to a fetus in an attack on the mother

No   Increase mandatory child care funding to states by $6 billion over five years

Yes   Amend the Constitution to prohibit same-sex marriage

Yes   Approve $146 billion multi-year extension of previously enacted middle-class tax breaks

Yes   Reorganize U.S. intelligence agencies as proposed by Sept. 11 commission

Yes   Cut corporate taxes $137 billion over 10 years

2003

No   Delay Bush changes to Clean Air Act

Yes   Allow confirmation vote on Miguel A. Estrada to the U.S. Court of Appeals for the D.C. Circuit

No   Block a Bush proposal opening Alaska's Arctic National Wildlife Refuge to oil drilling

No   Limit size of Bush's proposed tax cut to $350 billion through fiscal 2013

Yes   Overhaul Medicare and create prescription drug benefit

No   Block Bush rule scaling back overtime pay for some white-collar federal workers

No   Split $20 billion in Iraq aid into half-grant, half-loan

Yes   Ban "partial birth" abortion except to save a woman's life

?   Stop proposal allowing travel to Cuba

Yes   Allow final vote on energy policy overhaul

CQ VOTE STUDIES

	PARTY UNITY		PRESIDENTIAL SUPPORT	
	Support	Oppose	Support	Oppose
2004	97%	3%	94%	6%
2003	98%	2%	99%	1%
2002	88%	12%	93%	7%
2001	96%	4%	97%	3%
2000	90%	10%	51%	49%
1999	94%	6%	24%	76%
1998	94%	6%	38%	62%
1997	94%	6%	57%	43%
1996	97%	3%	29%	71%
1995	95%	5%	26%	74%

INTEREST GROUPS

	AFL-CIO	ADA	CCUS	ACU
2004	8%	5%	100%	100%
2003	0%	10%	100%	80%
2002	31%	10%	90%	100%
2001	19%	10%	100%	96%
2000	0%	5%	93%	87%
1999	11%	0%	88%	96%
1998	0%	0%	100%	84%
1997	14%	15%	78%	88%
1996	0%	5%	85%	100%
1995	0%	0%	100%	83%

Rep. Denny Rehberg (R)

Elected 2000; 3rd term

CAPITOL OFFICE
225-3211
denny.rehberg@mail.house.gov
www.house.gov/rehberg
516 Cannon 20515-2601; fax 225-5687

COMMITTEES
Appropriations

HOMETOWN
Billings

BORN
Oct. 5, 1955, Billings, Mont.

RELIGION
Episcopalian

FAMILY
Wife, Janice Lenhardt Rehberg; three children

EDUCATION
Montana State U., attended 1973-74; Washington State U., B.A. 1977 (political science)

CAREER
Rancher; congressional aide; realtor

POLITICAL HIGHLIGHTS
Mont. House, 1985-91; lieutenant governor, 1991-97; Republican nominee for U.S. Senate, 1996

ELECTION RESULTS

2004 GENERAL

Denny Rehberg (R)	286,076	64.4%
Tracy Velazquez (D)	145,606	32.8%
Mike Fellows (LIBERT)	12,548	2.8%

2004 PRIMARY

Denny Rehberg (R)	unopposed

2002 GENERAL

Denny Rehberg (R)	214,100	64.6%
Steve Kelly (D)	108,233	32.7%
Mike Fellows (LIBERT)	8,988	2.7%

PREVIOUS WINNING PERCENTAGES
2000 (52%)

A loyal soldier for the Republican leadership on most issues, Rehberg reaped his reward at the start of the 109th Congress when he won a coveted seat on the Appropriations Committee. As he has done since he first arrived on Capitol Hill, he plans to use his position to address the concerns of his vast, largely rural state.

"This is obviously good for Montana," Rehberg (REE-berg) said at the time of his appointment, noting that the position will enable him to "take care of important Montana priorities" even as he tries to "help bring some added fiscal discipline" to the federal budget. Rehberg had to give up his posts on the Agriculture, Transportation and Infrastructure, and Resources committees to take the seat on Appropriations.

Montana stretches more than 500 miles east to west and 250 miles north to south, a vast expanse with many small, widely scattered population centers. As the state's lone congressman, Rehberg drives thousands of miles each year and represents more constituents than any of his colleagues in the House: an estimated 927,000 in mid-2004. Even though Montana's population grew by 13 percent in the 1990s, it did not grow enough to win back the House seat it lost in the 1990 reapportionment.

To respond to the needs of so many people — the typical member represents about two-thirds as many — Rehberg has kept a broad base of knowledge, a skill he says he learned during his six years as Montana's lieutenant governor in the 1990s.

Pro-business, pro-development and socially conservative, Rehberg typically backs Republican leaders and the White House. But he will cross party lines if he sees a threat to his state's parochial interests. He opposed Australia trade legislation in the 108th because he feared more beef imports would threaten the livelihood of Montana ranchers. He voted to delay the scheduled 2005 round of military base closures out of concern for Malmstrom Air Force Base. And he supported legislation to allow the importation of cheaper prescription drugs from Canada; Montanans often cross the border to find affordable medicines. "I have to vote my state," he says.

A fifth-generation rancher, Rehberg earlier used his seat on the Agriculture Committee to fight for implementation of a country-of-origin labeling law that would distinguish U.S.-produced beef from imports. He also opposed a ban on the sale and slaughter of so-called downer cattle, calling it an overreaction to the threat of mad cow disease.

In the 107th Congress, he set out to help farmers and ranchers cope with the West's devastating drought and to open agricultural markets to foreign trade. During committee debate on the rewrite of the farm bill, Rehberg won inclusion of a plan aimed at helping farmers participate in business ventures beyond producing raw commodities. He also pushed for more funding in a 2001 agriculture assistance bill than President Bush wanted, saying, "I fear that many producers in my state may not make it to the next farm bill."

As a member of the Resources Committee, Rehberg protested a Clinton administration ban on snowmobile access to Yellowstone National Park and its neighbor, Grand Teton. The Bush administration eased the rules before the ban took effect, permitting continued snowmobiling in the national parks.

Rural states such as Montana face unique challenges in providing economic development, education and health care opportunities. As lieutenant governor, Rehberg chaired the state's Rural Development Council. In Congress, he has lobbied to strengthen the public school system, calling on the federal government to pay its agreed-upon share for special education for disabled students. He also wants to provide rural areas with modern health care that is convenient and affordable and to address the nationwide problem of the uninsured.

Rehberg says he has a keen personal interest in seeing Congress enact a permanent repeal of the estate tax because his family had to sell part of its ranch holdings to pay taxes due after his great-grandmother died in 1976.

Rehberg grew up on his family's beef cattle and cashmere goat ranch, competing in gymnastics and playing the drums. He was among the lawmakers in the "Congressional All-Stars" band that played a benefit concert to raise money for relief efforts after the Sept. 11, 2001, terrorist attacks.

His mother taught elementary school, and his father ran the ranch and worked a number of other jobs to help support the family. Rehberg's father, Jack, was the GOP nominee for a House seat in 1970, but took just 36 percent of the vote against Democrat John Melcher.

After earning a degree in political science, Rehberg worked as an intern in the Montana Senate, sold real estate for two years, and then moved to Washington in 1979 to join the staff of GOP Rep. Ron Marlenee of Montana. He returned to the family ranch three years later and ended up serving six years in the state House. He managed political campaigns for Marlenee in 1986 and Republican Conrad Burns in his successful Senate bid in 1988.

Rehberg was appointed lieutenant governor in 1991 when Lt. Gov. Allen Kolstad quit to join the administration of President George Bush. Rehberg was elected to a four-year term in 1992. In 1996, he came within 5 percentage points of defeating Democratic Sen. Max Baucus, who outspent him by almost 3-to-1.

In 2000, he was unopposed for the House nomination when Republican Rep. Rick Hill retired after two House terms, citing poor health. Rehberg looked to be the underdog against Democratic state school superintendent Nancy Keenan, but after a somewhat vitriolic campaign, he won by 5 points.

During that race, Rehberg removed himself from the management of the family ranch by arranging to move its 600 goats to the Baucus family ranch. The two families now share the profits from the operation.

National GOP strategists sounded out Rehberg about another race against Baucus in 2002, but he nixed that idea and was essentially given a pass by the Democrats for election to his second and third House terms.

In 2002 and 2004, befitting his largest-in-the-House constituency, Rehberg received the most votes of any House candidate.

KEY VOTES

2004

No Extend federal unemployment benefits by 13 weeks
Yes Pass $283.2 billion, six-year federal highway and mass transit bill
Yes Approve $146 billion multi-year extension of previously enacted middle-class tax breaks
Yes Amend the Constitution to prohibit same-sex marriage
Yes Cut corporate taxes $137 billion over 10 years
No Reorganize U.S. intelligence agencies as proposed by Sept. 11 commission

2003

Yes Cut taxes by $330 billion through fiscal 2013
No Block Bush rule scaling back overtime pay for some white-collar federal workers
Yes Do not allow use of search warrants without first notifying subjects
Yes Allow importation of prescription drugs
Yes Create private school voucher program in Washington, D.C.
Yes Ban "partial birth" abortion except to save a woman's life
No Split $18.6 billion in Iraq aid into half-grant, half-loan
Yes Overhaul Medicare and create prescription drug benefit

CQ VOTE STUDIES

	PARTY UNITY		PRESIDENTIAL SUPPORT	
	Support	Oppose	Support	Oppose
2004	96%	4%	76%	24%
2003	95%	5%	93%	7%
2002	95%	5%	85%	15%
2001	96%	4%	88%	12%

INTEREST GROUPS

	AFL-CIO	ADA	CCUS	ACU
2004	13%	5%	95%	96%
2003	7%	10%	93%	84%
2002	11%	0%	95%	100%
2001	17%	5%	100%	84%

MONTANA
At large

Montana's Big Sky country has long been a place where pioneers traveled to strike it rich. Once explored by Lewis and Clark and later by fur trappers and gold seekers, Montana is now a prime destination for celebrities and telecommuters who want to buy their own small piece of the frontier.

After the 1990 census, Montana lost one of its two U.S. House seats. The resulting statewide district combines the state's politically independent halves into one unpredictable voting bloc. The western, mountainous half of the state leans Democratic, with an environmental base and a union tradition in mining and lumber mills. It also is home to the state's university community in Missoula. The area has been shifting to support more natural resources-based development in recent years. The eastern half, a flat plain where wheat and cattle are raised, follows a tradition of rural Republicanism.

Despite these differences, both halves can be conservative and independent. The state elected Jeannette Rankin, the first woman in

Congress, in 1916. While only six of the state's 56 counties sided with John Kerry in the 2004 presidential election, many voters split their tickets, and the result was a Democratic governor and full Democratic control of the state legislature. Overall, George W. Bush captured 59 percent of the state's presidential vote in 2004.

With an economy based on natural resources, Montana finds itself exploiting its terrain while also striving to protect it. In ballot initiatives, voters have rejected some environmental regulations. Yet Butte, the site of years of mining, is the center of a massive superfund clean-up effort.

MAJOR INDUSTRY
Agriculture, tourism, forestry

MILITARY BASES
Malmstrom Air Force Base, 3,699 military, 1,987 civilian (2005)

CITIES
Billings, 89,847; Missoula, 57,053; Great Falls, 56,690; Butte-Silver Bow, 34,606; Bozeman, 27,509; Helena, 25,780

NOTABLE
Glacier National Park is located in the northwestern part of the state; Jordan was the site of a 1996 standoff between federal authorities and an anti-tax group called The Freemen.

NEBRASKA

Gov. Dave Heineman (R)

Assumed office: 2005
Length of term: 4 years
Term expires: 1/07
Salary: $85,000
Phone: (402) 471-2244

Hometown: Fremont
Born: May 12, 1945;
Falls City, Neb.
Religion: Eastern Orthodox
Family: Wife, Sally Ganem; one child
Education: U.S. Military Academy, B.S. 1970
(economics)
Military Service: Army, 1970-75
Career: Congressional aide; health and
beauty products company salesman
Political highlights: Neb. Republican Party
executive director, 1979-81; Fremont City
Council, 1990-94; Neb. treasurer, 1995-2001;
lieutenant governor, 2001-05

Recent election results:
2002 GENERAL

Mike Johanns (R)	330,349	68.7%
Stormy Dean (D)	132,348	27.5%
Paul A. Rosberg (NEB)	18,294	3.8%

Lt. Gov. Rick Sheehy (R)

Assumed office: 2005
Length of term: 4 years
Term expires: 1/07
Salary: $60,000
Phone: (402) 471-2256

STATE LEGISLATURE

Unicameral Legislature: 90 days in
odd-numbered years; 60 days in
even-numbered years

Legislature: 49 nonpartisan
members, 4-year terms
2005 breakdown: 37 men,
12 women
Salary: $12,000
Phone: (402) 471-2271

STATE TERM LIMITS

Governor: 2 consecutive terms
Legislature: 2 consecutive terms

URBAN STATISTICS

CITY	POPULATION
Omaha	390,007
Lincoln	225,581
Bellevue	44,382
Grand Island	42,940
Kearney	27,431

REGISTERED VOTERS

Republican	50%
Democrat	34%
Nonpartisan	15%

POPULATION

2004 population (est.)	1,747,214
2000 population	1,711,263
1990 population	1,578,385
Percent change (1990-2000)	+8.4%
Rank among states (2004)	38

Median age	35.3
Born in state	67.1%
Foreign born	4.4%
Violent crime rate	328/100,000
Poverty level	9.7%
Federal workers	15,620
Military	15,040

REDISTRICTING

Nebraska retained its three House
seats in reapportionment. The state
legislature drew a new map, which
the governor signed on May 30, 2001.

MISCELLANEOUS

Web: www.nebraska.gov
Capital: Lincoln
STATE ELECTION OFFICIAL
(402) 471-2555
**DEMOCRATIC
HEADQUARTERS**
(402) 434-2180
**REPUBLICAN
HEADQUARTERS**
(402) 475-2122

District Statistics

DIST.	2004 VOTE FOR PRESIDENT BUSH	KERRY	WHITE	BLACK	ASIAN	HISP	MEDIAN INCOME	WHITE COLLAR	BLUE COLLAR	SERVICE INDUSTRY	OVER 64	UNDER 18	COLLEGE EDUCATION	RURAL	SQ. MILES
1	63%	36%	91%	1%	2%	4%	$40,021	58%	27%	15%	13%	25%	24%	35%	11,951
2	61	38	80	10	2	6	$45,235	67	20	13	10	27	31	2	411
3	75	24	92	0	0	6	$33,866	54	31	15	17	26	17	54	64,511
STATE	66	33	87	4	1	6	$39,250	59	26	15	14	26	24	30	76,872
U.S.	50.7	48.3	69	12	4	13	$41,994	60	25	15	12	26	24	21	3,537,438

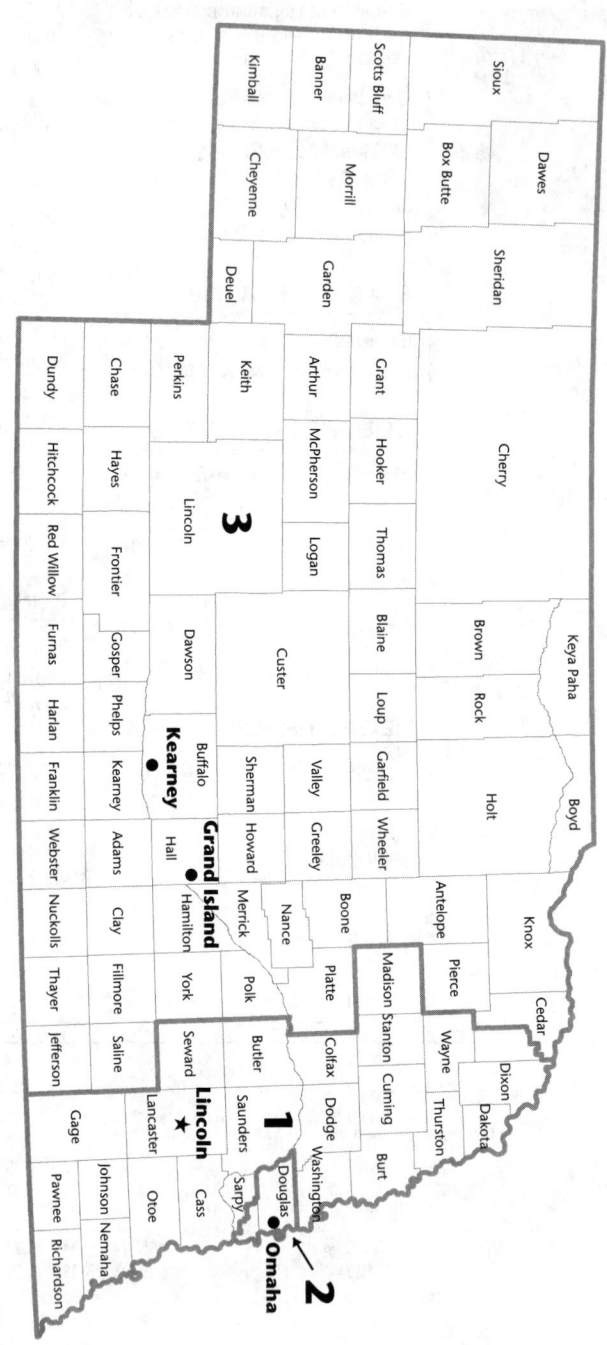

Sen. Chuck Hagel (R)

Elected 1996; 2nd term

Hagel has made little secret of his interest in running for president in 2008. A fiercely independent Republican who regularly makes the rounds of the Sunday talk shows, the second-term senator has carved out a national profile as a supporter of the Iraq war but a thoughtful critic of the way the Bush administration has handled it.

A major point of disagreement between the two leaders is reinstatement of the draft. President Bush spent a good deal of his 2004 re-election campaign denying Democratic charges that he plans to bring back the draft. Hagel actually proposed it as a senior member of the Foreign Relations Committee. He believes that U.S. troops are spread too thin among U.S. engagements in Iraq, Afghanistan and the Balkans. "There is not an American — unless you've been asleep for the last few years — who isn't aware of what we are engaged in today," he said in 2004. "If that's the case, why shouldn't we ask all of our citizens to bear some responsibility, to pay some price?"

That's the kind of bluntness and disregard for political consequences that could make Hagel a tough sell in a national campaign. Then again, the same qualities made a popular celebrity out of John McCain of Arizona, another maverick Republican and former presidential candidate to whom Hagel is often compared. The two senators have much in common: heroic service in Vietnam, plain-spoken candor and impatience with the status quo. Hagel has been called "McCain without the attitude."

The two differ in another significant way. Hagel supports a business-oriented conservatism, sometimes at odds with McCain's populist impulses. Hagel embraces the longstanding Republican tenets of tax cuts and reductions in federal government spending. With a perspective rooted in business, he stresses the importance of internationalism, and of "dynamic, global, interconnected" markets. Hagel has little patience for the foreign policy views of some on the GOP right who support economic sanctions on foreign nations guilty of human rights abuses. He has encouraged Bush to build more alliances with foreign governments in the Iraq occupation.

Hagel has the ability to work across party lines. To address the problem of overstretched armed forces, he cosponsored legislation in 2004 with Democrat Jack Reed of Rhode Island to expand the Army permanently by adding 30,000 active-duty soldiers.

Hagel and McCain broke ranks with the Republican Party to support an independent investigation of why the intelligence before the Iraq war turned out to be so wrong. Their defections put pressure on Bush to drop his opposition to the probe. Hagel hasn't backed away from his support of the war, but he was also one of the few Republicans, before it began, to warn of the importance of planning for the aftermath.

An affable and articulate self-made millionaire and decorated Vietnam veteran, Hagel had never held elective office before his long-shot 1996 victory in a Senate race over popular Democratic Gov. Ben Nelson. (Nelson won the state's other Senate seat when it came open in 2000.) Hagel got off to a fast start in Washington. He made a fortuitous early decision to accept a request from Indiana Republican Richard G. Lugar, a senior member of the Foreign Relations Committee, to join the panel at a time few lawmakers were interested in foreign affairs. A series of retirements and election losses allowed Hagel to rise quickly to the top of the committee hierarchy, putting him in an influential position to affect policy after the Sept. 11,

CAPITOL OFFICE
224-4224
chuck_hagel@hagel.senate.gov
hagel.senate.gov
248 Russell 20510-2705; fax 224-5213

COMMITTEES
Banking, Housing & Urban Affairs
   (Securities & Investment - chairman)
Foreign Relations
   (International Economic Policy, Export & Trade
   Promotion - chairman)
Rules & Administration
Select Intelligence

HOMETOWN
Omaha

BORN
Oct. 4, 1946, North Platte, Neb.

RELIGION
Episcopalian

FAMILY
Wife, Lilibet Hagel; two children

EDUCATION
U. of Nebraska, Omaha, B.A. 1971 (history)

MILITARY SERVICE
Army, 1967-68

CAREER
Investment bank executive; cellular telephone company founder; lobbyist; congressional aide; radio talk show host

POLITICAL HIGHLIGHTS
Veterans Administration deputy administrator, 1981-82

ELECTION RESULTS

2002 GENERAL

Chuck Hagel (R)	397,438	82.8%
Charlie A. Matulka (D)	70,290	14.6%
John J. Graziano (LIBERT)	7,423	1.6%
Phil Chase (I)	5,066	1.1%

2002 PRIMARY

Chuck Hagel (R)	unopposed

PREVIOUS WINNING PERCENTAGES
1996 (56%)

2001, terrorist attacks placed a premium on foreign policy expertise.

Hagel expanded his knowledge by traveling extensively overseas, meeting with top foreign leaders and slogging through tedious hours of committee hearings. That commitment, and his close ideological affinity with Lugar's "realist" brand of foreign policy, helped the panel's two senior Republicans forge a close working relationship. He also can usually find common ground with the panel's top-ranking Democrat, Joseph R. Biden Jr. of Delaware.

In the 108th Congress, Hagel, once considered by Bush as a potential running mate, was more likely to square off against the president than the Democrats. Their differences did not always involve foreign policy. Hagel is a fiscal conservative and was one of nine Senate Republicans who voted in 2003 against the final version of the Medicare prescription drug bill, one of Bush's top domestic priorities. Although he voted for an earlier version, Hagel said the final plan was too expensive and insisted the true costs would soar beyond estimates.

During the 2004 Republican convention, where Bush was nominated for a second term, Hagel made the rounds of the Iowa and New Hampshire delegations, one of the gathering signs that he is considering running when Bush steps down. He told the Omaha World-Herald that although his focus is the Senate, he will "along the way and on parallel tracks" assess his viability as a candidate for president in 2008.

Hagel's compelling personal story contributed to his rapid political rise. He grew up in a small town in Nebraska, where he started working as a carhop at a drive-in restaurant when he was 9 years old. After his father died when he was 16, Hagel, as the oldest child, helped supervise his younger siblings. In high school, he successfully ran for student council president, attracting attention by tying a live chicken to the hood of his car and driving around blaring out his positions.

Later, Hagel enlisted in the Army and spent a year as an infantryman in Vietnam, serving side by side with his brother, Tom. Hagel was seriously wounded twice and received two Purple Hearts. He suffered burns, which required a decade to heal completely, when an enemy mine exploded underneath his armored personnel carrier. His brother was in the same carrier and knocked unconscious. Hagel pulled him to safety.

After graduating from college in 1971, he landed a job with Republican Rep. John Y. McCollister of Nebraska and rose to become his top aide. Hagel then became a lobbyist for the Firestone Tire & Rubber Company and campaigned heavily in 1980 for Ronald Reagan, who rewarded him with a top job at the Veterans Administration. He left government in 1982 to start a business on a financial shoestring, selling his seven-year-old Buick and two insurance bonds and investing his net worth of $5,000 in a cellular phone company that he began with two partners. That company, Vanguard Cellular Systems Inc., became the country's second-largest independent cell phone company and made Hagel a multimillionaire. Hagel received the 2001 Horatio Alger Award, which recognizes self-made business leaders who have overcome adversity.

He entered the 1996 Senate primary as the underdog against state Attorney General Don Stenberg but spent lavishly from his personal funds and won the nomination with more than 60 percent of the vote. In the fall, Hagel made his centerpiece issue tax cuts as a stimulant of economic growth, something he contended would do more to address problems in society than any government program. Helped by GOP criticism that Nelson was breaking an earlier pledge to serve out his term as governor, Hagel won by 14 percentage points. In 2002, Hagel's victory margin of 68 points over Democrat Charlie A. Matulka was the largest in Nebraska Senate election history.

KEY VOTES

2004
No Pass $318.9 billion, six-year highway and mass transit bill
No Extend assault weapons ban for 10 years
No Restore pay-as-you-go rules for new tax cuts and entitlement spending
Yes Criminalize harm to a fetus in an attack on the mother
Yes Increase mandatory child care funding to states by $6 billion over five years
Yes Amend the Constitution to prohibit same-sex marriage
Yes Approve $146 billion multi-year extension of previously enacted middle-class tax breaks
Yes Reorganize U.S. intelligence agencies as proposed by Sept. 11 commission
Yes Cut corporate taxes $137 billion over 10 years

2003
No Delay Bush changes to Clean Air Act
Yes Allow confirmation vote on Miguel A. Estrada to the U.S. Court of Appeals for the D.C. Circuit
No Block a Bush proposal opening Alaska's Arctic National Wildlife Refuge to oil drilling
No Limit size of Bush's proposed tax cut to $350 billion through fiscal 2013
Yes Overhaul Medicare and create prescription drug benefit
No Block Bush rule scaling back overtime pay for some white-collar federal workers
No Split $20 billion in Iraq aid into half-grant, half-loan
Yes Ban "partial birth" abortion except to save a woman's life
No Stop proposal allowing travel to Cuba
Yes Allow final vote on energy policy overhaul

CQ VOTE STUDIES

	PARTY UNITY		PRESIDENTIAL SUPPORT	
	Support	Oppose	Support	Oppose
2004	93%	7%	94%	6%
2003	96%	4%	98%	2%
2002	94%	6%	98%	2%
2001	92%	8%	96%	4%
2000	94%	6%	49%	51%
1999	92%	8%	36%	64%
1998	89%	11%	42%	58%
1997	92%	8%	59%	41%

INTEREST GROUPS

	AFL-CIO	ADA	CCUS	ACU
2004	9%	20%	93%	87%
2003	8%	15%	87%	100%
2002	23%	10%	95%	95%
2001	25%	25%	100%	84%
2000	0%	0%	100%	88%
1999	0%	5%	100%	88%
1998	0%	0%	94%	72%
1997	0%	5%	100%	80%

Sen. Ben Nelson (D)

Elected 2000; 1st term

Four years into his first term, the affable and independent Nelson has positioned himself as a key player on issues ranging from tax cuts to energy policy, and he seeks to leverage his much sought-after vote into victories for his home state.

In a Senate so closely divided, Nelson's willingness to cross party lines has given him an unusual amount of power for a freshman. He estimates that he has met with President Bush at least a half-dozen times, including flying with him twice on Air Force One. The retirement of Louisiana Democratic dealmaker John B. Breaux may increase Nelson's influence as Bush pushes an ambitious second-term agenda and looks for Democrats willing to listen. Bush, who is known for bestowing nicknames, first called Nelson "Nelly" and then "Benny," but the senator, saying he preferred a more "macho" moniker, convinced the president to call him "Benator."

While Nelson sometimes complains of being worked over by the president or party leaders, he generally plays down the role such lobbying has in his decisions. He invoked his standard line — "The only pressure I feel is internal pressure to do what's right" — when deciding whether to support a ban on "soft money" campaign contributions to political parties. He eventually sided with Republicans on that issue, one of only two Senate Democrats to vote against the law enacted in 2002.

Following the 2004 election, Nelson was named vice chairman of the Senate Centrist Coalition, a bipartisan group of moderates. Nelson has warned his Democratic colleagues about the potential political perils of blocking certain GOP measures, such as the energy bill that stalled in the 108th Congress. Indeed, Nelson bucks the party line regularly. In 2004, he voted only 52 percent of the time with a majority of Democrats on votes opposed by a majority of Republicans, and he sided with Bush 82 percent of the time — more than any other Democrat besides Georgia conservative Zell Miller, who retired at the end of the 108th Congress.

Nelson has not burned his bridges with Democratic leaders, however; they named him to the Commerce, Science and Transportation and Rules committees at the start of the 109th. Nelson hopes to use the Commerce post to advocate for rural transportation and health care issues. He also has seats on the Agriculture and Armed Services panels, and he is the top-ranking Democrat on Armed Services' Personnel Subcommittee. On Agriculture, Nelson wants to focus congressional attention on the drought that has plagued Nebraska farmers.

Nelson's willingness to cross the aisle is indicative of the majority of Nebraskans, who tend to have a strong conservative and independent streak. His understanding of the state's political dynamic is constantly on display. In 2003, Nelson joined 10 other Democrats in voting for the GOP Medicare prescription drug benefit bill. He was one of only three Democrats to vote to allow the Senate to take up a constitutional amendment banning same-sex marriage. Nelson also worked to break the logjam on the GOP energy bill, which included one of his priorities: subsidies for renewable energy sources such as ethanol, and solar and wind power.

Republican leaders routinely sound out Nelson when they need an extra vote for tax cut legislation — and he is often ready to deal. Before agreeing to support a $330 billion package of tax cuts in 2003, he helped engineer enactment of a $20 billion package of aid to states that included funding for Medicaid coverage for low-income families.

CAPITOL OFFICE
224-6551
senator@bennelson.senate.gov
bennelson.senate.gov
720 Hart 20510-2706; fax 228-0012

COMMITTEES
Agriculture, Nutrition & Forestry
Armed Services
Commerce, Science & Transportation
Rules & Administration

HOMETOWN
Omaha

BORN
May 17, 1941, McCook, Neb.

RELIGION
Methodist

FAMILY
Wife, Diane Nelson; four children

EDUCATION
U. of Nebraska, B.A. 1963 (philosophy), M.A. 1965 (philosophy), J.D. 1970

CAREER
Lawyer; insurance company executive

POLITICAL HIGHLIGHTS
Neb. director of insurance, 1975-76; governor, 1991-99; Democratic nominee for U.S. Senate, 1996

ELECTION RESULTS

2000 GENERAL
Ben Nelson (D)	353,093	51.0%
Don Stenberg (R)	337,977	48.8%

2000 PRIMARY
Ben Nelson (D)	105,661	92.1%
Al Hamburg (D)	8,482	7.4%

Nelson's Democratic stripes show clearly when the Senate considers changes to Social Security, Medicare or farm programs. He has said he is a strong supporter of federal entitlement programs for the elderly. And he was an avid proponent of the Democrats' $410 billion plan to boost farm incomes, though he lamented that too many wealthy farmers would benefit from its payments.

Nelson's support for many conservative proposals has led some in the Republican Party to view him as a possible convert. Efforts to persuade Nelson to switch became more frequent after Vermont's James M. Jeffords left the GOP in 2001 to become an independent. Nelson has given no sign that he is any more interested in changing parties than he was when approached by the Nebraska GOP. "I've had people talking to me about that for a decade or more," he says matter-of-factly.

Nelson prides himself on being a practical joker. As governor, he participated in a segment of the TV show "Candid Camera" in which he told visitors to his office that he was planning to change the state's name to "something much more modern . . . something like Zenmar or Quentron." He also held a party for others named Ben Nelson. Twelve from Nebraska, 10 from other states and one dog attended. The senator goes by his middle name — his first name is Earl — but he still gets phone calls for other Ben Nelsons.

He returns to Nebraska often but was forced to make some unwanted trips in 2002 to testify on the state's behalf in a lawsuit filed by a company denied a license for a low-level radioactive waste facility. The company alleged that Nelson improperly used his political power to ensure the license would not be granted. Nebraska has agreed to pay $141 million to settle the issue, but Nelson still defends state regulators' decision to deny the license.

Unlike some politicians whose glad-handing style propels them into public office, Nelson's rise to the Senate is mostly the product of perseverance. Since age 17, when he was elected governor of a model Nebraska high school legislature, Nelson has yearned for statewide office. The election of his high school superintendent and debate coach, Ralph Brooks, to be Nebraska's governor persuaded Nelson that "you didn't have to be from a big city to have an opportunity in politics."

Nelson was reared in McCook, a remote small town where his mother, Birdella, started a local taxpayers' watchdog group. Her attention to how tax revenue was spent was not lost on her son. "Watching the purse strings is the most important basic thing you can do in government," he says.

Although Nelson has held politics in high esteem since an early age, he considered joining the ministry while at the University of Nebraska. He opted instead for law school and, upon graduation, began a long career in insurance law. He ran an insurance company, headed a national association of insurance regulators and directed his state's insurance department. In 1990, he launched his first statewide bid for office, surviving the Democratic primary for governor by just 42 votes. He went on to defeat the incumbent, Republican Kay Orr, by 4,000 votes.

After eight years as governor, he returned in 1999 to his law firm, Kaufman-Nelson-Pattee, where he helped states develop Washington lobbying strategies. But when Democratic Sen. Bob Kerrey announced he would retire the next year, Nelson was a shoo-in for the Democratic nomination to be his successor. He then defeated the Republican candidate, Attorney General Don Stenberg, by 2 percentage points — the closest Senate election in Nebraska history. Nelson's Senate record will be scrutinized in 2006 by Nebraska voters — who overwhelmingly backed Bush in the 2004 election.

KEY VOTES

2004
+ Pass $318.9 billion, six-year highway and mass transit bill
No Extend assault weapons ban for 10 years
Yes Restore pay-as-you-go rules for new tax cuts and entitlement spending
Yes Criminalize harm to a fetus in an attack on the mother
Yes Increase mandatory child care funding to states by $6 billion over five years
Yes Amend the Constitution to prohibit same-sex marriage
Yes Approve $146 billion multi-year extension of previously enacted middle-class tax breaks
Yes Reorganize U.S. intelligence agencies as proposed by Sept. 11 commission
Yes Cut corporate taxes $137 billion over 10 years

2003
Yes Delay Bush changes to Clean Air Act
Yes Allow confirmation vote on Miguel A. Estrada to the U.S. Court of Appeals for the D.C. Circuit
Yes Block a Bush proposal opening Alaska's Arctic National Wildlife Refuge to oil drilling
Yes Limit size of Bush's proposed tax cut to $350 billion through fiscal 2013
Yes Overhaul Medicare and create prescription drug benefit
Yes Block Bush rule scaling back overtime pay for some white-collar federal workers
Yes Split $20 billion in Iraq aid into half-grant, half-loan
Yes Ban "partial birth" abortion except to save a woman's life
No Stop proposal allowing travel to Cuba
Yes Allow final vote on energy policy overhaul

CQ VOTE STUDIES

	PARTY UNITY		PRESIDENTIAL SUPPORT	
	Support	Oppose	Support	Oppose
2004	52%	48%	82%	18%
2003	57%	43%	80%	20%
2002	51%	49%	91%	9%
2001	58%	42%	74%	26%

INTEREST GROUPS

	AFL-CIO	ADA	CCUS	ACU
2004	82%	65%	81%	52%
2003	62%	45%	86%	42%
2002	62%	50%	63%	55%
2001	81%	70%	71%	56%

Rep. Jeff Fortenberry (R)

Elected 2004; 1st term

CAPITOL OFFICE
225-4806
www.house.gov/fortenberry
1517 Longworth 20515-2701; fax 225-5686

COMMITTEES
Agriculture
International Relations
Small Business

HOMETOWN
Lincoln

BORN
Dec. 27, 1960, Baton Rouge, La.

RELIGION
Roman Catholic

FAMILY
Wife, Celeste Gregory; four children

EDUCATION
Louisiana State U., B.A. 1982 (economics);
Georgetown U., M.P.P. 1986; Franciscan U. of
Steubenville, M.Div. 1996 (theology)

CAREER
Publishing firm public relations manager and sales
representative; economist; congressional aide

POLITICAL HIGHLIGHTS
Lincoln City Council, 1997-2001

ELECTION RESULTS

2004 GENERAL

Jeff Fortenberry (R)	143,756	54.2%
Matt Connealy (D)	113,971	43.0%
Steven R. Larrick (GREEN)	7,345	2.8%

2004 PRIMARY

Jeff Fortenberry (R)	18,735	39.2%
Curt Bromm (R)	15,708	32.9%
Greg Ruehle (R)	10,077	21.1%
Bob Van Valkenburg (R)	1,044	2.2%
Daniel Manning (R)	1,027	2.2%
Greg Walburn (R)	696	1.5%

Fortenberry shares an unexpected interest with his predecessor, Doug Bereuter: a passion for foreign policy that earned him a seat on the International Relations Committee, on which Bereuter had been a senior member. Fortenberry says that when he was in the fifth grade, he wrote to Richard Nixon about the president's trip to China.

But the mild-mannered Fortenberry follows a more tenaciously conservative line than Bereuter, a prominent Republican moderate and leading voice in international affairs who stepped down in 2004 after nearly 26 years in the House.

Fortenberry has a particular interest in the transformations of Iraq and Afghanistan. He said the United States underestimated the difficulty for these nations to transform into a Western-style democracy. "We may have been naive because they have different economic and societal values and levels of resources than us, and it may take some time," he said.

Fortenberry has a more conventional — for a Nebraska lawmaker — assignment on the Agriculture panel, where he plans to promote agriculture-based energy production and trade policies that benefit farm producers.

And with a seat on Small Business, Fortenberry says he wants to help small businesses by creating a "business investment account," which would provide tax breaks to help people start or expand a business.

Bereuter's decision to retire — he actually resigned his seat early, in late August 2004 — created a free-for-all in the Republican primary, the first such competitive intraparty contest in more than a quarter-century. Fortenberry peaked late in the campaign and surged past Curt Bromm, the Speaker of Nebraska's unicameral legislature and Bereuter's choice as successor. Bromm's voting record was hammered by the Club for Growth, a conservative anti-tax organization.

In the solidly GOP 1st District, Fortenberry won by 11 percentage points in November against Democratic state Sen. Matt Connealy, who played down his party affiliation and touted his background as a farmer.

NEBRASKA 1

East — Lincoln, Fremont

The 1st takes in eastern Nebraska, excluding Omaha and its suburbs. The region includes the state's capital, Lincoln, and the University of Nebraska's Memorial Stadium, which could qualify as the state's third-largest city when filled to its 74,000-seat capacity. Despite the area's small-town reputation, growing industry in Lincoln, Norfolk and South Sioux City is helping to make the eastern portion of the state more urban.

Lincoln, in particular, is thriving and has seen major growth led by the expanding state and city governments and the university. Hospitals and a banking and insurance industry also help sustain the city's economy.

The region depends on agriculture, but with a modern twist. Traditional crop and hog farming is supplemented by other agribusiness, such as meat processing, food packaging and fertilizer production. Polling and telemarketing companies in the area add to the white-collar job opportunities.

Flood control also is a problem here.

Although the district was home to populist William Jennings Bryan and many of his supporters at the turn of the 20th century, the 1st now votes consistently Republican at all levels. The University of Nebraska's main campus in Lincoln makes the city more liberal, but voter registration favors the GOP in both the city and surrounding Lancaster County. The strongest Democratic areas are in the northeast, in Dakota County, with a sizable blue-collar contingent, and in Thurston County, made up of the Winnebago and Omaha Indian reservations. Democratic-leaning Saline County was moved from the 1st District to the western 3rd in redistricting following the 2000 census.

MAJOR INDUSTRY
Agriculture, meat processing, health care, government, higher education

CITIES
Lincoln, 225,581; Fremont, 25,174; Norfolk, 23,516; Beatrice, 12,496

NOTABLE
The late Johnny Carson, former host of "The Tonight Show," grew up in Norfolk.

Rep. Lee Terry (R)

Elected 1998; 4th term

Fresh-faced and cheery, Terry is a solid conservative who knows how to keep his Omaha constituents happy. He has been re-elected three times by impressive margins of at least 25 percentage points.

He seems less well known within his own party, however. Vice President Dick Cheney twice referred to him as "Terry Lee" at a July 2003 fundraiser in Terry's district. But Terry is a loyal partisan who votes consistently with the House GOP leadership, earning a 95 percent party unity score in the 108th Congress. In recognition of his loyalty, GOP leaders gave Terry a bottom-rung post on the leadership ladder, an assignment as one of several dozen assistant whips.

Unlike the more combative conservatives who came to the House earlier in the 1990s, Terry has positioned himself as a pragmatist. "I want to fight the good fight on abortion, but that doesn't mean I drag down an appropriations bill," he told The Omaha World-Herald after his election.

Yet Terry casts a conservative vote on most social issues. He has denounced a procedure opponents call "partial birth" abortion, and he voted in 2004 in favor of a constitutional amendment to ban same-sex marriage. But he struggles with the question of gun owners' rights. Although he voted in 1999 against mandatory trigger locks, he said early in 2000 he could support such a step, as well as waiting periods for purchases at gun shows, because he was dismayed by the nation's repeated school shootings. And as a former trial lawyer, Terry does not always vote with his party in favor of changing tort laws.

Terry was given a seat in the 107th on the Energy and Commerce Committee, which has jurisdiction over a broad swath of the American economy, from the railroads to the Internet. He has used his assignment to push initiatives aimed at helping Nebraskans, such as legislation to create a rural affairs advisory board at the Federal Communications Commission.

In 2003, Terry was one of just eight lawmakers to vote against legislation allowing creation of a federal "do not call" list for telemarketers. His vote prompted calls from angry constituents, and he appeared in numerous national media outlets to explain his vote. "It's about jobs, jobs, jobs, jobs," Terry told National Public Radio. He said 39,000 people in his Omaha district are employed, directly or indirectly, by telemarketers. "That do not call list is taking bread off of somebody's table," he added.

In the 108th, Terry sponsored a bill to broaden the number of rural states that would receive federal subsidies for telecommunications services to include Nebraska.

No 2nd District representative can ignore Offutt Air Force Base, located just south of Omaha. Employing more than 10,000 military and civilian personnel, it is as much a part of the community as Creighton University or the Mutual of Omaha insurance company. Offutt is the home of the U.S. Strategic Command, where any nuclear war would be planned, and President Bush went there for part of the day following the Sept. 11, 2001, terrorist attacks. Terry has looked out for the base's interests, including helping to secure $11 million in 2002 for a new fire and crash rescue station.

In the 108th Congress, he was one of only 24 House Republicans with military bases in their districts to vote for maintaining the current schedule of base closures slated to begin in 2005 rather than postponing the closures for two years. Offutt is not considered a likely candidate for closure.

CAPITOL OFFICE
225-4155
leeterry.house.gov
1524 Longworth 20515-2702; fax 226-5452

COMMITTEES
Energy & Commerce

HOMETOWN
Valley

BORN
Jan. 29, 1962, Omaha, Neb.

RELIGION
Methodist

FAMILY
Wife, Robyn Terry; three children

EDUCATION
U. of Nebraska, B.S. 1984 (political science);
Creighton U., J.D. 1987

CAREER
Lawyer

POLITICAL HIGHLIGHTS
Omaha City Council, 1991-99 (president, 1994-95)

ELECTION RESULTS

2004 GENERAL

Lee Terry (R)	152,608	61.1%
Nancy Thompson (D)	90,292	36.2%
John J. Graziano (LIBERT)	4,656	1.9%

2004 PRIMARY

Lee Terry (R)	unopposed

2002 GENERAL

Lee Terry (R)	89,917	63.3%
Jim Simon (D)	46,843	33.0%
Doug Paterson (GREEN)	3,236	2.3%
Dave Stock (LIBERT)	2,018	1.4%

PREVIOUS WINNING PERCENTAGES
2000 (66%); 1998 (66%)

Omaha is home to the headquarters of Union Pacific Railroad, making rail issues a concern of Terry's. He was a sponsor of the law enacted in 2001, at the behest of both labor and management, to restructure the federal railroad pension system to allow some of the funds to be invested in stocks and bonds.

Though the 2nd District is the state's most urban and suburban, Terry keeps an eye on agricultural issues. When the 107th took up a rewrite of farm law, he expressed an interest in maintaining the free-market philosophy of the statute enacted in 1996. But in the end, he voted to enact a replacement in 2002 that reverted to providing substantial farm subsidies. And he has sponsored a measure to provide federal subsidies to companies and groups that use hydrogen fuel cells to power their facilities.

Terry is a hometown boy who learned politics from his parents. At age 10, he analyzed President Nixon's landslide victory for his folks on election night 1972. His father was a famous local news anchor and elections commissioner of Douglas County, which surrounds Omaha, who was also the 1976 Republican nominee for the House seat that his son now holds. Terry's mother ran unsuccessfully for the county board six years later.

By that time, Terry was at the state university in Lincoln, having mapped a life plan for himself centered on a career in politics. Unlike so many Nebraskans, who devote their suppertime discussions to the joys and sorrows of Husker football, talk around the Terry table was often about the wayward ways of a liberal Congress. Four years after earning his law degree at Omaha's Creighton University, Terry was on the city council, and during eight years there he rose to be the group's president and played a role in lowering property taxes.

In 1998, Terry's position on the Omaha City Council made him the clear front-runner for the House seat that Republican Jon Christensen was vacating after two terms to wage an ultimately unsuccessful run for governor. Terry won the four-way primary by 10 percentage points and then triumphed by 31 points in November over underfunded Democrat Mike Scott, a newscaster.

Democrats in 2002 held out some hope for victory in Jim Simon, a wealthy former AOL executive. But Terry won with 63 percent of the vote and almost matched that in 2004, earning 61 percent to defeat Democrat Nancy Thompson.

When he first ran for office, Terry pledged to serve no more than three terms, but he backed away from that promise soon after arriving in Washington. He said he quickly realized the benefits that come with seniority.

KEY VOTES

2004

No Extend federal unemployment benefits by 13 weeks
Yes Pass $283.2 billion, six-year federal highway and mass transit bill
Yes Approve $146 billion multi-year extension of previously enacted middle-class tax breaks
Yes Amend the Constitution to prohibit same-sex marriage
Yes Cut corporate taxes $137 billion over 10 years
Yes Reorganize U.S. intelligence agencies as proposed by Sept. 11 commission

2003

Yes Cut taxes by $330 billion through fiscal 2013
No Block Bush rule scaling back overtime pay for some white-collar federal workers
Yes Do not allow use of search warrants without first notifying subjects
No Allow importation of prescription drugs
Yes Create private school voucher program in Washington, D.C.
Yes Ban "partial birth" abortion except to save a woman's life
No Split $18.6 billion in Iraq aid into half-grant, half-loan
Yes Overhaul Medicare and create prescription drug benefit

CQ VOTE STUDIES

	PARTY UNITY		PRESIDENTIAL SUPPORT	
	Support	Oppose	Support	Oppose
2004	93%	7%	88%	12%
2003	96%	4%	89%	11%
2002	92%	8%	84%	16%
2001	95%	5%	91%	9%
2000	96%	4%	25%	75%

INTEREST GROUPS

	AFL-CIO	ADA	CCUS	ACU
2004	29%	0%	90%	92%
2003	0%	5%	97%	76%
2002	11%	5%	85%	88%
2001	8%	0%	91%	96%
2000	0%	5%	95%	96%

NEBRASKA 2
East – Omaha and suburbs

Formerly the eastern terminus of the Union Pacific Railroad, Omaha is the heart of the 2nd. Omaha grew up as a blue-collar city: a railroad center, a Missouri River port and a place where cattle became steaks. To outsiders, this broad-shouldered, gritty image remains. But the city has become mainly a place of downtown office buildings and white-collar jobs in agriculture and insurance businesses. It also is known as the nation's 1-800 capital, thanks to a glut of telecommunications and credit processing companies.

As its core has filled with people through the years, the 2nd has become more compact. The district lost its slice of Cass County and much of Sarpy County in redistricting following the 2000 census, and now contains just Douglas County and eastern Sarpy County.

Although the district votes consistently Republican, Omaha's dwindling blue-collar base still supports some Democrats, and victory in the city's south side is essential for Democrats to win statewide. The 2nd has always been anti-abortion, but social conservatives are gaining ground

once held by more-moderate European immigrants.

Douglas County is reliably Republican, having voted for the GOP presidential candidate every time but once since Harry S Truman. Omaha is home to three-fourths of Nebraska's growing black population, but the state's first black candidate for Congress lost the district by more than 30 percentage points in 1998. George W. Bush took 61 percent of the 2nd's vote in the 2004 presidential election, his lowest tally in the state.

MAJOR INDUSTRY
Toll-free phone service centers, food processing

MILITARY BASES
Offutt Air Force Base, 8,359 military, 2,134 civilian (2004)

CITIES
Omaha, 390,007; Bellevue, 44,382; Papillion, 16,363

NOTABLE
Gerald R. Ford and political activist Malcolm X were born in Omaha; Father Flanagan's Boys Town, incorporated in 1936, was the only village in the nation run by children; Billionaire investor Warren Buffett lives in Omaha — his father, Republican Howard Buffett, represented Omaha in the House from 1943 to 1949 and 1951 to 1953.

Rep. Tom Osborne (R)

Elected 2000; 3rd term

Now in his third term, Osborne is still better known as the legendary football coach of the Nebraska Cornhuskers than as a House member — cheerfully so. "You don't need to do that," the Omaha World-Herald quoted Osborne as telling a wildly cheering crowd in 2004. "I'm not the football coach anymore. I'm just a politician."

Osborne planned to try to leverage his popularity at home in a bid for Nebraska governor in 2006. He said in early 2005 that he would make the race, after first ruling out a challenge to Democratic Sen. Ben Nelson.

His legislative interests are just about what you would expect from a respected college coach from a farm state: an overpowering concern for protecting and promoting the interests of both young people and the rural way of life.

Osborne has had considerable success on the first front, leading the effort to pass measures banning anabolic steroids and punishing overeager sports agents. Some of his priorities in the 109th Congress include coordinating the numerous federal youth programs, promoting mentoring of young people, banning legalized gambling on college sporting events, and pushing the NCAA to forbid beer advertising during college games.

The results of his fight for farmers and others in the largely rural 3rd District, which includes some of the country's poorest counties, are more mixed. While farm-state lawmakers have boosted rural health programs and won drought relief for the long-parched Midwest, the persistent federal budget deficits have made rural programs the target of steep cuts.

"Federal programs pertaining to agriculture, vocational education, community service block grants, air service and veterans are all very important to the livelihood of Nebraskans in my congressional district and throughout rural America," Osborne said after President Bush proposed a budget in early 2005 that would reduce or eliminate many programs in those areas.

Osborne's committee assignments reflect the interests of a community that relies heavily on farm, highway, education and job training programs. He is on the Agriculture and the Education and Workforce committees and added Transportation and Infrastructure in the 109th, when Congress will consider a long-delayed six-year highway and mass transit bill.

Osborne says he applies many of his coaching techniques to his new life on Capitol Hill. He believes that communicating ideas, formulating a plan and fostering teamwork toward a common goal are applicable in coaching and in Congress. Although both endeavors are highly competitive, he says, coaching offered more immediate feedback. "As a coach, you call a play and it's done in five seconds," he told USA Today. In the House, however, "you have to be much more patient."

Also, in football the location of the goal line is beyond dispute, he says, while in legislating that line keeps moving. For instance, Osborne thought one of his top agenda items — the Mentoring for Success program — was included in the federal education policy overhaul enacted at the end of his first year in office. The program was allocated $17.5 million for its first year, and Osborne saw its future as secure. But a few months later, Bush's budget made no mention of the mentoring program. He persevered, however, and Bush highlighted the program in his 2003 State of the Union address and asked for $450 million over three years.

Osborne is a firm believer in the benefits of national service and is a lead-

CAPITOL OFFICE
225-6435
www.house.gov/osborne
507 Cannon 20515-2703; fax 226-1385

COMMITTEES
Agriculture
Education & Workforce
Transportation & Infrastructure

HOMETOWN
Lemoyne

BORN
Feb. 23, 1937, Hastings, Neb.

RELIGION
Methodist

FAMILY
Wife, Nancy Osborne; three children

EDUCATION
Hastings College, B.A. 1959 (history); U. of Nebraska, M.A. 1963 (educational psychology), Ph.D. 1965 (educational psychology)

MILITARY SERVICE
Neb. National Guard, 1960-66

CAREER
College football coach; professional football player

POLITICAL HIGHLIGHTS
No previous office

ELECTION RESULTS

2004 GENERAL

Tom Osborne (R)	218,751	87.5%
Donna J. Anderson (D)	26,434	10.6%
Robert A. Rosberg (NEB)	3,396	1.4%

2004 PRIMARY

Tom Osborne (R)	unopposed

2002 GENERAL

Tom Osborne (R)	163,939	93.2%
Jerry Hickman (LIBERT)	12,017	6.8%

PREVIOUS WINNING PERCENTAGES
2000 (82%)

ing opponent of efforts by the Bush administration and GOP leadership to cut or eliminate the Clinton-era AmeriCorps volunteer program.

He is also an unabashed critic of the coarseness of popular culture and, as co-chairman of the Sex and Violence in the Media Caucus, is a leading advocate for toughening broadcast indecency laws and cracking down on violence on television.

Osborne's agenda on the Agriculture Committee includes efforts to bolster the farm economy and bring new businesses to rural areas. He says that electronic commerce could thrive in rural locations if computer broadband access were improved, and he preaches the virtues of "niche farming," such as goats for the growing immigrant population or organic beef. Like many rural legislators, he also votes for liberalized trade to expand crop exports. But he opposed a trade pact with Australia in 2004, largely because he thinks the U.S. market could be threatened by cheap Australian beef.

Osborne casts a generally conservative vote and seldom strays from the positions taken by the GOP leadership and Bush. But when it came to overhauling the campaign finance system, he was one of nine GOP freshmen — and 41 House Republicans altogether — to vote for the measure enacted in 2002 over strenuous leadership objections.

A high school sports star in Hastings, Neb., Osborne played football for Hastings College and then played three seasons with the Washington Redskins and San Francisco 49ers. He returned to the University of Nebraska as a graduate assistant football coach while pursuing a master's degree in educational psychology. He stayed at the Lincoln campus, working his way through the assistant coaching ranks while earning a doctorate in educational psychology.

He became head coach in 1973, and over the next 25 seasons he led the Cornhuskers to three national crowns and 13 conference championships. Osborne retired from coaching after the 1997 season and was inducted into the College Football Hall of Fame in 1998. He soon realized that fishing and other retirement activities were not enough for him. Two years later, when Republican Bill Barrett called it quits after five House terms, Osborne decided to run, because he "still has some energy left."

His Democratic foe, real estate agent Rollie Reynolds, acknowledged he had little chance for victory in heavily Republican western Nebraska, especially against "a worldwide hero" whose "face recognition is about like Muhammad Ali." Osborne won with 82 percent of the vote. He had little or no opposition in his subsequent elections.

KEY VOTES

2004

No	Extend federal unemployment benefits by 13 weeks
Yes	Pass $283.2 billion, six-year federal highway and mass transit bill
?	Approve $146 billion multi-year extension of previously enacted middle-class tax breaks
Yes	Amend the Constitution to prohibit same-sex marriage
Yes	Cut corporate taxes $137 billion over 10 years
Yes	Reorganize U.S. intelligence agencies as proposed by Sept. 11 commission

2003

Yes	Cut taxes by $330 billion through fiscal 2013
No	Block Bush rule scaling back overtime pay for some white-collar federal workers
Yes	Do not allow use of search warrants without first notifying subjects
Yes	Allow importation of prescription drugs
Yes	Create private school voucher program in Washington, D.C.
Yes	Ban "partial birth" abortion except to save a woman's life
No	Split $18.6 billion in Iraq aid into half-grant, half-loan
Yes	Overhaul Medicare and create prescription drug benefit

CQ VOTE STUDIES

	PARTY UNITY		PRESIDENTIAL SUPPORT	
	Support	Oppose	Support	Oppose
2004	91%	9%	79%	21%
2003	94%	6%	95%	5%
2002	89%	11%	88%	12%
2001	94%	6%	88%	12%

INTEREST GROUPS

	AFL-CIO	ADA	CCUS	ACU
2004	20%	10%	95%	84%
2003	13%	15%	93%	76%
2002	11%	10%	90%	80%
2001	17%	5%	100%	84%

NEBRASKA 3
West — Grand Island, North Platte, Scottsbluff

Scouting what would later become the Oregon Trail, early 19th century explorers described this section of the country as the "Great American Desert." Most of the 3rd's land is arid, and most of the district's population lives along the meager Platte River.

Grand Island, North Platte and Scottsbluff each serve as regional centers, providing for the retail and health care needs of the surrounding counties. Industry and manufacturing also locate around these areas, as well as in Columbus, Hastings and Kearney. The rest of the land in the district's 69 counties is left to cattle ranchers and sugar beet and wheat farmers. The economy is susceptible to changes in the region's climate. Droughts in the early part of the 1990s battered western Nebraska. The district has a number of the nation's poorest counties.

The 3rd is fiercely independent politically — it gave more votes to Ross Perot than Bill Clinton in 1992 — but the majority is conservative and strongly Republican. George W. Bush carried the district in 2004 with 75 percent of the vote — his highest showing in the state. Reflecting the

area's isolation, most voters are against government intervention. The 1st and 2nd districts dominate state politics, leaving the 3rd resentful that despite its massive land area, its interests, such as farm subsidies and property taxes, are not top priorities.

Saline County, a Democratic-leaning pocket, was added to the 3rd in redistricting following the 2000 census, but the change should not alter the district's outlook.

MAJOR INDUSTRY
Agriculture, food processing, tourism

CITIES
Grand Island, 42,940; Kearney, 27,431; Hastings, 24,064; North Platte, 23,878; Columbus, 20,971; Scottsbluff, 14,732

NOTABLE
Pulitzer Prize-winning author Willa Cather grew up in Red Cloud and based several of her novels in the central-southern region of the state; Carhenge, a full-size replica of Britain's Stonehenge made of cars, stands in Alliance; Fort Robinson near Crawford, now a state park, served as a German prisoner-of-war camp during World War II; The Great Platte River Road Archway Monument, across Interstate 80 near Kearney, was built to memorialize westward expansion.

Gov. Kenny Guinn (R)

First elected: 1998
Length of term: 4 years
Term expires: 1/07
Salary: $117,000
Phone: (775) 684-5670

Hometown: Las Vegas
Born: Aug. 24, 1936; Garland, Ark.
Religion: Protestant
Family: Wife, Dema Guinn; two children
Education: California State U., Fresno, B.A. 1957, M.A. 1958 (physical education); Utah State U., Ph.D. 1970 (education)
Career: Bank chairman; interim university president; utility company chairman; school superintendent
Political highlights: No previous office
Election results:

2002 GENERAL
Kenny Guinn (R)	344,001	68.2%
Joe Neal (D)	110,935	22.0%
"None of these candidates"	23,674	4.7%
Dick Geyer (LIBERT)	8,104	1.6%
David G. Holmgren (IA)	7,047	1.4%
Jerry L. Norton (I)	5,543	1.1%
A. Charles Laws (GREEN)	4,775	1.0%

Lt. Gov. Lorraine Hunt (R)

First elected: 1998
Length of term: 4 years
Term expires: 1/07
Salary: $50,000
Phone: (775) 684-5637

STATE LEGISLATURE

Legislature: February-June in odd-numbered years, limit of 120 days

Assembly: 42 members, 2-year terms
2005 breakdown: 26D, 16R; 27 men, 15 women
Salary: $130/day in session; $91/day allowance
Phone: (775) 684-8555

Senate: 21 members, 4-year terms
2005 breakdown: 12R, 9D; 15 men, 6 women
Salary: $130/day in session; $91/day allowance
Phone: (775) 684-1437

STATE TERM LIMITS

Governor: 2 terms
Assembly: 6 terms
Senate: 3 terms

URBAN STATISTICS

CITY	POPULATION
Las Vegas	478,434
Reno	180,480
Henderson	175,381
North Las Vegas	115,488

REGISTERED VOTERS

Republican	40%
Democrat	40%
Nonpartisan/others	19%

POPULATION

2004 population (est.)	2,334,771
2000 population	1,998,257
1990 population	1,201,833
Percent change (1990-2000)	+66.3%
Rank among states (2004)	35

Median age	35
Born in state	21.3%
Foreign born	15.8%
Violent crime rate	524/100,000
Poverty level	10.5%
Federal workers	14,701
Military	11,932

REDISTRICTING

Nevada gained one House seat in reapportionment. The state legislature drew a new, three-district map, which the governor signed on June 15, 2001.

MISCELLANEOUS

Web: www.nv.gov
Capital: Carson City
STATE ELECTION OFFICIAL
(775) 684-5705
DEMOCRATIC HEADQUARTERS
(702) 737-8683
REPUBLICAN HEADQUARTERS
(702) 258-9182

District Statistics

DIST.	2004 VOTE FOR PRESIDENT BUSH	KERRY	WHITE	BLACK	ASIAN	HISP	MEDIAN INCOME	WHITE COLLAR	BLUE COLLAR	SERVICE INDUSTRY	OVER 64	UNDER 18	COLLEGE EDUCATION	RURAL	SQ. MILES
1	42%	57%	52%	12%	5%	28%	$39,480	48%	23%	29%	10%	27%	15%	0%	177
2	57	41	75	2	3	15	$43,879	55	25	20	11	26	19	21	105,079
3	50	49	69	5	6	16	$50,749	57	18	25	12	24	20	4	4,570
STATE	50	48	65	7	4	20	$44,581	53	22	25	11	26	18	8	109,826
U.S.	50.7	48.3	69	12	4	13	$41,994	60	25	15	12	26	24	21	3,537,438

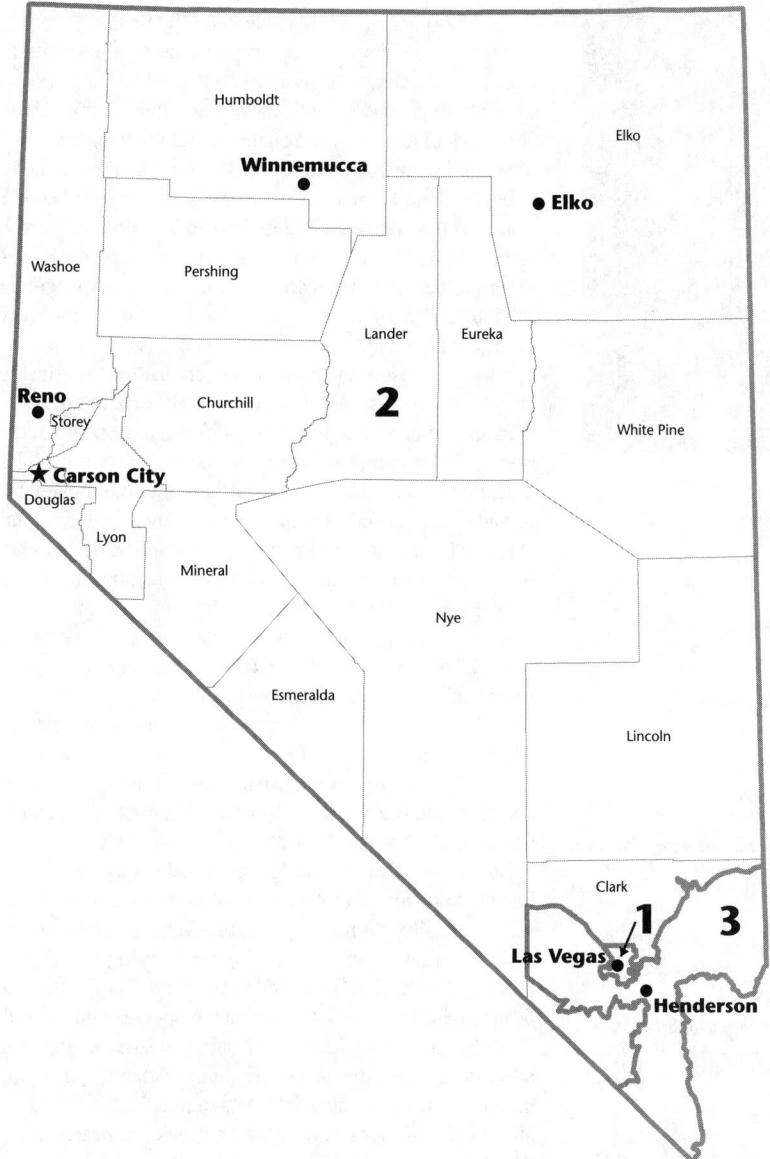

Humboldt

Elko

Winnemucca
●

● **Elko**

Washoe

Pershing

Lander   Eureka

Reno
●
Storey

Churchill

2

White Pine

★ **Carson City**

Douglas

Lyon

Mineral

Nye

Esmeralda

Lincoln

Clark

1   **3**

Las Vegas
●

● **Henderson**

Sen. Harry Reid (D)

Elected 1986; 4th term

CAPITOL OFFICE
224-3542
senator_reid@reid.senate.gov
reid.senate.gov
528 Hart 20510-2803; fax 224-7327

COMMITTEES
Appropriations

HOMETOWN
Searchlight

BORN
Dec. 2, 1939, Searchlight, Nev.

RELIGION
Mormon

FAMILY
Wife, Landra Reid; five children

EDUCATION
Southern Utah State College, A.S. 1959; Utah State
U., B.A. 1961 (history & political science); George
Washington U., J.D. 1964; U. of Nevada, Las Vegas,
attended 1969-70

CAREER
Lawyer

POLITICAL HIGHLIGHTS
Nev. Assembly, 1969-71; lieutenant governor,
1971-75; Democratic nominee for U.S. Senate,
1974; candidate for mayor of Las Vegas, 1975;
Nevada Gaming Commission chairman, 1977-81;
U.S. House, 1983-87

ELECTION RESULTS

2004 GENERAL

Harry Reid (D)	494,805	61.1%
Richard Ziser (R)	284,640	35.1%
None of these candidates	12,968	1.6%
Thomas L. Hurst (LIBERT)	9,559	1.2%

2004 PRIMARY

Harry Reid (D)	unopposed

PREVIOUS WINNING PERCENTAGES
1998 (48%); 1992 (51%); 1986 (50%); 1984 House
Election (56%); 1982 House Election (58%)

Reid has earned his shot at leading the Senate Democrats. As the Democratic whip for six years, he was the trusted top lieutenant of the previous leader, South Dakota's Tom Daschle. Reid worked yeoman's hours monitoring floor activity, counting votes and handling much of the prosaic but vital work of keeping the Senate running day to day.

When Daschle lost his bid in 2004 for a fourth Senate term, Reid quickly became the Democrats' consensus choice to succeed him as minority leader. But while no one questions Reid's skill and savvy at the Senate's inside game, Democrats, as the party out of power, are also now looking to him to be a national leader, to frame the party's agenda effectively and sell it to the American public. In that role, the taciturn, even shy Nevadan is largely untested.

For that reason, the Democrats' choice for their new whip, Richard J. Durbin of Illinois, seemed particularly propitious. Durbin is a skilled debater and has considerable experience as a spokesman for his party. He is expected to complement the new leader. For his part, Reid can be tough in the face of a challenge — he is a onetime amateur boxer who, as a Nevada state official early in his career, investigated organized crime. Reid also has the security of knowing that he has at last cemented his political position back home. After several close elections in his Republican-leaning state, he won a fourth term in 2004 with a solid majority.

Reid hails from a conservative state, and although he rarely bucks his party, he does go his own way on a couple of issues. A practicing Mormon, he typically votes with Republicans in favor of restrictions on abortion. In 1999, he was one of two Democrats to oppose an amendment expressing support for the Supreme Court's 1973 *Roe v. Wade* decision legalizing abortion. In 2003, he voted for a ban on a procedure opponents call "partial birth" abortion, and in 2004, he supported a bill making it a federal crime to harm a fetus in the course of an attack on the mother.

Reid has cultivated working relationships with Republicans, which have been helpful during the Senate's frequent partisan meltdowns. As whip, he was responsible for helping pressure Democrats to resist offering politically charged amendments or employing delaying tactics. When he became minority leader, GOP Whip Mitch McConnell of Kentucky and other Republicans praised him as someone they respected and trusted.

At the same time, McConnell said that in no way does he consider Reid a "patsy." Indeed, the Nevadan is not reluctant to play hardball when party imperatives or his state's interests demand it. In 2003, he held up the Senate's business, alone and without a break, for nearly nine hours to protest what he said was the GOP majority's disrespect for the rights of the minority party. He held forth on everything from the economy and judicial nominees to the history of his hometown, Searchlight, Nev., reading passages from a book he wrote about the town.

In 2005, Reid fought back when Majority Leader Bill Frist and Republicans threatened to change the rules to prevent similar filibusters of President Bush's conservative judicial nominees. "If the rules are changed so that the Senate becomes another House of Representatives, I don't think you're going to see a lot of things happen around here," Reid warned.

He is not the ideal politician. Reid is an average debater. He prefers reading books to attending fundraising dinners. He often avoids reporters, and he shuns the nonstop self-promotion that consumes many lawmakers. "I don't like parades. I don't like banquets. I don't like public gatherings," says Reid, who spends his free time with his wife, five children and grandchildren.

Environmentalists generally like Reid, and several national groups have helped him in his races back home. In 2001, he cosponsored the successful "brownfields" bill boosting the federal commitment to cleaning up contaminated industrial sites. But ranchers and miners hold sway in Nevada, and Reid often defends their interests on land-use issues.

By far, his biggest effort in behalf of his constituents is trying to stop the opening of a national nuclear waste repository at Yucca Mountain, 100 miles northwest of Las Vegas. Reid suffered a serious defeat in 2002 when Congress endorsed Bush's decision to store 77,000 tons of spent reactor fuel under the mountain's volcanic rock. Reid lobbied fellow senators hard, telling them their votes mattered to him personally. But the key Senate vote was a filibuster-proof 60-39. In 2003, he was able to cut the funding for the program from nearly $600 million to $460 million.

Organized labor is also an important constituency in Nevada, and Reid has sided with the unions on big trade votes in recent years. In 2000, he opposed permanently granting China normal trade status.

Reid grew up in a cabin without indoor plumbing in Searchlight, a tiny mining town. His mother was a high school dropout. His father was a hard-drinking miner who later killed himself. Searchlight did not have a high school, so Reid boarded with other families in Henderson, about 40 miles north, to attend school there. He worked his way through college, moonlighting as a Capitol police officer while attending law school at George Washington University in Washington, D.C. He took up boxing and became an amateur middleweight who sometimes sparred with the pros in exhibition fights.

With his law degree in hand, Reid returned to Henderson to be city attorney. At age 28, he won election to the Nevada state Assembly. His political mentor was Democrat Mike O'Callaghan, who had met Reid when he was a civics teacher at Reid's high school and later his boxing coach. When O'Callaghan became governor in 1970, Reid was elected his lieutenant governor, the youngest in state history. In 1974, Reid lost a close race for the U.S. Senate to Republican Paul Laxalt.

O'Callaghan named him chairman of the Nevada Gaming Commission to oversee the state's top industry at a time when it was heavily influenced by organized crime. Reid later told the Las Vegas Review-Journal, "They put bombs on my car, there were threatening phone calls at night, people tried to bribe me and went to jail."

In 1982, Reid ran successfully for the first of two terms in the U.S. House. He still had his heart set on the Senate, however, and in 1986, he tried again. He carried only two of the state's 16 counties against Rep. Jim Santini, a Democrat turned Republican. But one of those was Clark County, Reid's political base and home to the majority of Nevada voters in or near Las Vegas. Reid won with 50 percent of the vote.

In 1992, Democrat Charles Woods, a wealthy broadcast executive, held Reid to 53 percent in the primary. In the general election, Reid outspent GOP rancher Demar Dahl 5-to-1 and pulled off the win with 51 percent.

In his 1998 campaign, Reid won by only 428 votes over Republican John Ensign, a House member from Las Vegas. Their contest was bitter. Reid called Ensign "an embarrassment to the state," and Ensign's advertising described Reid as an "old card shark." After Ensign was elected in 2000 to the state's other Senate seat, the two reconciled and these days frequently cosponsor legislation in the state's interest.

In 2004, Reid easily defeated Republican Richard Ziser, an anti-gay marriage activist, for a fourth term.

KEY VOTES

2004
Yes Pass $318.9 billion, six-year highway and mass transit bill
No Extend assault weapons ban for 10 years
Yes Restore pay-as-you-go rules for new tax cuts and entitlement spending
Yes Criminalize harm to a fetus in an attack on the mother
Yes Increase mandatory child care funding to states by $6 billion over five years
No Amend the Constitution to prohibit same-sex marriage
Yes Approve $146 billion multi-year extension of previously enacted middle-class tax breaks
Yes Reorganize U.S. intelligence agencies as proposed by Sept. 11 commission
Yes Cut corporate taxes $137 billion over 10 years

2003
Yes Delay Bush changes to Clean Air Act
No Allow confirmation vote on Miguel A. Estrada to the U.S. Court of Appeals for the D.C. Circuit
Yes Block a Bush proposal opening Alaska's Arctic National Wildlife Refuge to oil drilling
Yes Limit size of Bush's proposed tax cut to $350 billion through fiscal 2013
Yes Overhaul Medicare and create prescription drug benefit
Yes Block Bush rule scaling back overtime pay for some white-collar federal workers
Yes Split $20 billion in Iraq aid into half-grant, half-loan
Yes Ban "partial birth" abortion except to save a woman's life
Yes Stop proposal allowing travel to Cuba
No Allow final vote on energy policy overhaul

CQ VOTE STUDIES

	PARTY UNITY		PRESIDENTIAL SUPPORT	
	Support	Oppose	Support	Oppose
2004	83%	17%	61%	39%
2003	95%	5%	53%	47%
2002	94%	6%	71%	29%
2001	96%	4%	65%	35%
2000	94%	6%	92%	8%
1999	92%	8%	82%	18%
1998	81%	19%	79%	21%
1997	83%	17%	84%	16%
1996	79%	21%	78%	22%
1995	74%	26%	75%	25%

INTEREST GROUPS

	AFL-CIO	ADA	CCUS	ACU
2004	100%	90%	53%	21%
2003	100%	70%	35%	21%
2002	100%	85%	45%	10%
2001	100%	100%	43%	20%
2000	88%	90%	40%	12%
1999	100%	90%	35%	12%
1998	75%	90%	56%	20%
1997	86%	85%	50%	8%
1996	71%	85%	31%	15%
1995	100%	80%	37%	9%

Sen. John Ensign (R)

Elected 2000; 1st term

Ensign came to Congress as part of the Republican takeover in 1995, and he adheres to the strain of fiscal conservatism that distinguished many of the newcomers in that watershed political year. He disdains big government spending and is not afraid to vote against it. On money issues, he is more likely to cast his lot with maverick Republican Sen. John McCain and his campaign against wasteful spending than he is with GOP Senate leader Bill Frist and party-backed bills laden with home-state projects.

In 2004, Ensign was one of only four Republicans who voted against passing an $820 billion catchall spending bill written mainly by GOP leaders and the White House that would have brought a bitterly fought budget debate to an end. Before that, he voted with most Democrats and against almost all Republicans to keep alive a filibuster of the bill. "Now is a time to curtail runaway government spending," Ensign said.

Ensign also dealt a blow to Frist's efforts to revive a stalled energy bill in the 108th Congress by declaring he would join six other wayward Republicans in filibustering it, calling its subsidies for ethanol and nuclear power too costly. And in November 2003, Ensign was one of only nine Senate Republicans to oppose President Bush's landmark Medicare prescription drug plan, saying that over 10 years it would far exceed the $400 billion price tag cited by its authors.

"The decisions we make today about how the government spends money have serious ramifications for future generations, and we must always be mindful of that," Ensign said in 2005. The National Taxpayers Union gave him its highest score among senators for fiscal restraint in 2004, the second straight year he was so recognized.

Ensign has forged an unusually close relationship with the state's senior senator, Harry Reid — considering that Reid is not just a Democrat, but the leader of the Democrats in the Senate. The two work together on Nevada-specific legislation, so closely that Nevada political commentator Jon Ralston refers to the pair as "Harry Ensign." Their easygoing relationship is remarkable given Reid's razor-thin victory over Ensign in an acrimonious 1998 race. "We crack up all the time," Ensign told U.S. News & World Report in 2004.

Ensign suggested to Bush in 2003 that Reid's son, Leif, be among the candidates considered for a federal judgeship, but withdrew the name after other Republicans balked.

Ensign and Reid share a conviction about stopping the administration from establishing a nuclear waste storage facility at Yucca Mountain, 90 miles northwest of Las Vegas. Opposition to the repository has long been a unifying force for Nevada lawmakers.

Ensign found himself in the crosshairs of the standoff in 2002, after the House overwhelmingly ratified an Energy Department recommendation that waste from 38 states be shipped to the site. In the months leading up to the Senate vote, Ensign worked the Capitol like a lobbyist, toting an inch-thick briefing book of news articles and documents about the storage project and delivering an aggressive one-on-one pitch tailored to each of his Republican colleagues' regions and interests. He was unable to stop senators from endorsing the plan, but continues to use his position on the Budget Committee to try to limit funding for the Yucca Mountain project.

Ensign has so far fared better in his efforts to protect the state's gaming industry, an economic mainstay. From his seat on the Commerce, Science

CAPITOL OFFICE
224-6244
ensign.senate.gov
364 Russell 20510-2805; fax 228-2193

COMMITTEES
Armed Services
  (Readiness & Management Support - chairman)
Budget
Commerce, Science & Transportation
  (Technology, Innovation & Competitiveness - chairman)
Health, Education, Labor & Pensions
Veterans' Affairs

HOMETOWN
Las Vegas

BORN
March 25, 1958, Roseville, Calif.

RELIGION
Christian

FAMILY
Wife, Darlene Ensign; three children

EDUCATION
U. of Nevada, Las Vegas, attended 1976-79;
Oregon State U., B.S. 1981; Colorado State U.,
D.V.M. 1985

CAREER
Veterinarian; casino manager

POLITICAL HIGHLIGHTS
U.S. House, 1995-99; sought Republican
nomination for U.S. Senate, 1998

ELECTION RESULTS

2000 GENERAL
John Ensign (R)	330,687	55.1%
Ed Bernstein (D)	238,260	39.7%
write-ins	11,503	1.9%
Kathryn Rusco (GREEN)	10,286	1.7%

2000 PRIMARY
John Ensign (R)	95,904	88.0%
Richard Hamzik (R)	6,202	5.7%
write-ins	5,290	4.9%
Fernando Platin (R)	1,543	1.4%

PREVIOUS WINNING PERCENTAGES
1996 House Election (50%); 1994 House Election
(48%)

and Transportation Committee, he has been able to fight a rearguard action against legislation outlawing gambling on college sports, which is legal in Nevada. And Ensign has made it a top priority to limit the growth of Internet gambling, a practice that has cut into casinos' revenues.

Ensign's links to the influential Nevada industry go beyond political necessity. He is a former casino manager and his stepfather had been chairman and CEO of Mandalay Resort Group until it completed a $7.9 billion merger with casino giant MGM Mirage in spring 2005.

In the 108th Congress, Ensign worked on a number of other issues before the Commerce panel, including legislation to curb indecent broadcasting that would toughen fines for violations by companies and performers. He also was a main supporter of the bill creating a national "do not call registry" protecting consumers from unwanted telephone solicitations.

Ensign has emerged as a leader on technology issues. In early 2005, incoming Commerce Chairman Ted Stevens of Alaska named him chairman of the panel's newly created Technology, Innovation and Competitiveness Subcommittee. He has received generous political contributions from high-tech companies.

Outside of his fights on home-state matters, Ensign has sought to increase his influence on a broader set of issues. In April 2003, he sought to capitalize on Republican anger at Germany and France for their refusal to join the Iraq war coalition by pushing an amendment that would have prevented companies in those two nations from helping to rebuild Iraq. He described the countries' actions as "despicable," but withdrew the proposal at the urging of the White House.

With Republican Judd Gregg of New Hampshire, Ensign wants to impose a $250,000 cap on "pain and suffering" awards in medical malpractice lawsuits, an idea Bush has supported but many lawmakers oppose. Ensign says the legislation would reduce frivolous suits and lower the costs of malpractice insurance that doctors say are driving them out of their practices.

Ensign, whose mane of thick silver hair looks like a senatorial coif from central casting, is one of the Senate's better athletes. He has been named most valuable player in several congressional charity baseball and basketball games, and in 2004 posted the fifth-fastest time of congressional entrants in an annual 3-mile charity running race, with a time of 20:41.

After getting a degree in veterinary medicine, Ensign opened the first 24-hour animal hospital in Las Vegas and was the general manager at two Las Vegas casinos. GOP leaders urged him to run for the House in 1994 and, although he was a political novice, he assembled an impressive organization of volunteers and embarked on an energetic precinct-walking effort. In the Republicans' sweep that year, he overcame a large Democratic registration advantage to squeeze past four-term Democrat James Bilbray in the Las Vegas-based 1st District by just 1,436 votes.

As a freshman, he landed a spot on the Ways and Means Committee, where he took an active part in the overhaul of the nation's welfare system that was one of the major achievements of the Republicans' first years in the majority. To bolster his argument for the law, he cited his own autobiography: When he was a preschooler, his biological father abandoned his family. Although she qualified for public assistance, his mother took a $12-a-day job making change in a Reno casino.

Ensign left the House to challenge Reid in 1998, losing by just 428 votes. Then, in early 1999, Democrat Richard H. Bryan announced he wouldn't seek a third Senate term. Though Democrat Ed Bernstein, an attorney, was an aggressive foe, Ensign was able to spend twice as much money. He won with 55 percent of the vote in 2000. He is heavily favored for re-election in 2006 and would like to have a role in the GOP leadership.

KEY VOTES

2004

No   Pass $318.9 billion, six-year highway and mass transit bill
No   Extend assault weapons ban for 10 years
No   Restore pay-as-you-go rules for new tax cuts and entitlement spending
Yes Criminalize harm to a fetus in an attack on the mother
No   Increase mandatory child care funding to states by $6 billion over five years
Yes Amend the Constitution to prohibit same-sex marriage
Yes Approve $146 billion multi-year extension of previously enacted middle-class tax breaks
Yes Reorganize U.S. intelligence agencies as proposed by Sept. 11 commission
Yes Cut corporate taxes $137 billion over 10 years

2003

No   Delay Bush changes to Clean Air Act
Yes Allow confirmation vote on Miguel A. Estrada to the U.S. Court of Appeals for the D.C. Circuit
No   Block a Bush proposal opening Alaska's Arctic National Wildlife Refuge to oil drilling
No   Limit size of Bush's proposed tax cut to $350 billion through fiscal 2013
No   Overhaul Medicare and create prescription drug benefit
No   Block Bush rule scaling back overtime pay for some white-collar federal workers
Yes Split $20 billion in Iraq aid into half-grant, half-loan
Yes Ban "partial birth" abortion except to save a woman's life
Yes Stop proposal allowing travel to Cuba
Yes Allow final vote on energy policy overhaul

CQ VOTE STUDIES

	PARTY UNITY		PRESIDENTIAL SUPPORT	
	Support	Oppose	Support	Oppose
2004	90%	10%	100%	0%
2003	95%	5%	98%	2%
2002	90%	10%	96%	4%
2001	88%	12%	97%	3%
House Service:				
1998	82%	18%	27%	73%
1997	87%	13%	30%	70%
1996	80%	20%	40%	60%
1995	89%	11%	18%	82%

INTEREST GROUPS

	AFL-CIO	ADA	CCUS	ACU
2004	9%	15%	75%	92%
2003	0%	10%	91%	100%
2002	15%	15%	95%	85%
2001	19%	20%	93%	84%
House Service:				
1998	20%	25%	83%	88%
1997	0%	5%	80%	100%
1996	18%	5%	88%	85%
1995	0%	0%	100%	96%

Rep. Shelley Berkley (D)

Elected 1998; 4th term

CAPITOL OFFICE
225-5965
www.house.gov/berkley
439 Cannon 20515-2801; fax 225-3119

COMMITTEES
International Relations
Transportation & Infrastructure
Veterans' Affairs

HOMETOWN
Las Vegas

BORN
Jan. 20, 1951, Manhattan, N.Y.

RELIGION
Jewish

FAMILY
Husband, Larry Lehrner; two children, two stepchildren

EDUCATION
U. of Nevada, Las Vegas, B.A. 1972 (political science); U. of San Diego, J.D. 1976

CAREER
Lawyer

POLITICAL HIGHLIGHTS
Nev. Assembly, 1983-85; University and Community College System of Nevada Board of Regents, 1990-98

ELECTION RESULTS

2004 GENERAL

Shelley Berkley (D)	133,569	66.0%
Russ Mickelson (R)	63,005	31.1%
Jim Duensing (LIBERT)	5,862	2.9%

2004 PRIMARY

Shelley Berkley (D)	27,765	83.2%
Ann Reynolds (D)	3,208	9.6%
Brian Kral (D)	2,412	7.2%

2002 GENERAL

Shelley Berkley (D)	64,312	53.7%
Lynette Boggs-McDonald (R)	51,148	42.7%
Steven Dempsey (I)	2,861	2.4%
W. Lane Startin (GR)	1,393	1.2%

PREVIOUS WINNING PERCENTAGES
2000 (52%); 1998 (49%)

Now in her fourth term in the House, Berkley is beginning to shed some of the flamboyant image she brought with her from the neon world of Las Vegas. "I tend to have a very effusive personality," she said soon after her election in 1998, when Nevada's governor predicted that everyone on Capitol Hill would know about Berkley within a month of her arrival.

Indeed, she quickly made headlines, showing up at a news conference wearing high-heeled tennis shoes, for example, and holding her 1999 wedding at Bally's casino — attended by no fewer than 19 bridesmaids.

But Berkley has worked hard to prove she is a serious legislator. She doggedly tends to parochial concerns, joining others in her congressional delegation in their longstanding fight to keep nuclear waste out of a proposed site at Yucca Mountain, about 90 miles northwest of Las Vegas.

Nevadans suffered a major setback on the issue in 2002, when a bill was enacted allowing nuclear waste storage at Yucca Mountain. But the battle has continued in the courts. Berkley and other Nevadans got a major break in 2004, when judges ruled that the plan to build the waste dump was built on shaky science. Berkley and her colleagues are now trying to block any legislation that would sidestep the federal appeals court decision. "I will line up in front of the railroad ties to keep nuclear waste from going to Yucca Mountain," she has said.

Berkley had hoped by now to have a seat on the Ways and Means Committee. When he was minority leader, Richard A. Gephardt signaled his interest in giving her the plum assignment. But when Gephardt stepped aside after the party's 2002 election losses and Nancy Pelosi became party leader, she picked two other Democrats. Berkley was passed over again in 2004, leaving her on the Veterans' Affairs, International Relations and Transportation and Infrastructure panels.

That is not to say Berkley is on the outs with party leaders. Pelosi has helped steer millions of dollars in appropriations to projects in southern Nevada. And, when she was still Democratic whip, Pelosi made Berkley one of her 24 regional assistants. Berkley was promoted to senior regional whip in the 109th Congress. In addition, she was asked to help draft the party platform in advance of the Democratic National Convention in 2004, a role she used to add language declaring Yucca Mountain an unsafe repository for nuclear waste.

In the 109th, Berkley became the top-ranking Democrat on Veterans' Affairs' new Disability Assistance and Memorial Affairs Subcommittee, with jurisdiction ranging from compensation paid to veterans to burial benefits, life insurance, VA claims and veterans' cemeteries. "I am working to build bipartisan support for increasing VA burial benefits so that families who have just lost a loved one are not also facing thousands of dollars in out-of-pocket funeral expenses," she said. She has also pressed aggressively for increases in veterans' health benefits and to allow veterans "concurrent receipt" of both full retirement pay and full disability benefits.

On International Relations, Berkley serves on the Middle East and Central Asia Subcommittee, allowing her to pursue her interest in Israel.

Berkley's longstanding interest in politics is fueled, she says, by her desire to give something back after her parents emigrated to the United States from Eastern Europe. She moved to Las Vegas at age 6, later attending the University of Nevada at Las Vegas, where she served as student body president before graduating with a political science degree.

After earning a law degree in San Diego, Berkley returned to Las Vegas to start a career. She spent two years in the state Assembly, but became better known as a state university regent, a position that helped her become familiar with education issues. A former vice president of government and legal affairs for the Sands Hotel, she is also a former board chairwoman of the Nevada Hotel and Motel Association.

Although Berkley was known as a Democratic Party activist in her home state, she bills herself as a moderate who can work with Republicans, as well. She is a member of the centrist New Democrat Coalition.

In 2002, she backed the resolution that authorized President Bush to invade Iraq and later supported an $87 million supplemental bill to fund the war, although she told her local paper that she resents the administration for what she characterized as lies about Iraq's weapons of mass destruction. She later called for the ouster of Defense Secretary Donald H. Rumsfeld because of the Abu Ghraib prison abuse scandal and for his seemingly flippant comments to frontline soldiers who asked about the lack of armored vehicles and other needed equipment in Iraq.

Berkley describes herself as an opponent of gun control, a position echoed by many Western politicians. But she voted against a House bill in 2004 that would have lifted a ban on the private possession of hand guns in the District of Columbia and another in 2003 that would have nullified lawsuits by dozens of cities against gun manufacturers for crimes related to firearms. She has said in the past that votes in favor of gun safety do not conflict with her belief that the federal government must not prevent citizens from owning guns.

Diagnosed with an advanced case of osteoporosis at about the time she was first elected to the House, Berkley has championed legislation to require insurance coverage for bone mass measurements.

Berkley first won election to the House in 1998 when Republican John Ensign gave up his 1st District seat to run for the Senate — unsuccessfully, that year. (Ensign later won election to the Senate, in 2000.) She squeaked by Republican Don Chairez, a former county judge, by just 3 percentage points after battling ethics questions involving memos she had written several years before advising a legal client to make campaign contributions to judges as a way to curry favor.

In 2000, fending off the same ethics questions, Berkley defeated GOP state Sen. Jon Porter (now her 3rd District colleague) by 8 points. Redistricting following the 2000 census left her with a more urban, Democratic constituency and she won in 2002 and 2004 by ever wider margins.

KEY VOTES

2004

Yes Extend federal unemployment benefits by 13 weeks

Yes Pass $283.2 billion, six-year federal highway and mass transit bill

Yes Approve $146 billion multi-year extension of previously enacted middle-class tax breaks

No Amend the Constitution to prohibit same-sex marriage

Yes Cut corporate taxes $137 billion over 10 years

Yes Reorganize U.S. intelligence agencies as proposed by Sept. 11 commission

2003

No Cut taxes by $330 billion through fiscal 2013

Yes Block Bush rule scaling back overtime pay for some white-collar federal workers

? Do not allow use of search warrants without first notifying subjects

Yes Allow importation of prescription drugs

No Create private school voucher program in Washington, D.C.

No Ban "partial birth" abortion except to save a woman's life

Yes Split $18.6 billion in Iraq aid into half-grant, half-loan

No Overhaul Medicare and create prescription drug benefit

CQ VOTE STUDIES

	PARTY UNITY		PRESIDENTIAL SUPPORT	
	Support	Oppose	Support	Oppose
2004	93%	7%	41%	59%
2003	93%	7%	27%	73%
2002	87%	13%	42%	58%
2001	88%	12%	37%	63%
2000	81%	19%	63%	37%

INTEREST GROUPS

	AFL-CIO	ADA	CCUS	ACU
2004	93%	95%	60%	8%
2003	100%	85%	36%	27%
2002	89%	85%	50%	16%
2001	92%	90%	43%	12%
2000	80%	65%	57%	28%

NEVADA 1

Las Vegas

Neon lights and the chance of easy money continue to reel pleasure seekers into the 1st, which includes Las Vegas and its immediate areas. The city, the state's largest, experienced phenomenal growth in the 1990s; the metropolitan area has been the fastest growing in the nation. One of the downsides is that traffic congestion is now a major concern.

Gambling and tourism drive the 1st's economy. With a healthy economy in the late 1990s, large and small gaming companies continued to thrive. Several new luxury resorts were built on Las Vegas Boulevard, the newest part of the famed "Strip."

The Sept. 11, 2001, terrorist attacks sharply hurt tourism, forcing many workers out of jobs as visitors stayed away. It took years for the number of visitors to match 2000 levels, but in 2004 more than 37 million people visited Las Vegas, with an economic impact of $33.7 billion. Discussion in California about opening more casinos has worried the industry here, but local leaders are excited over the Las Vegas Monorail, a four-mile line opened in 2004 that runs along the east side of the Strip.

Besides the gambling industry, the 1st also attracts tourists to its surrounding national parks and desert topography. The area's record growth has made home building an important industry as well, and the city relies on distribution and trade because of its central Western location.

The 1st used to be a competitive swing district that attracted quite a bit of national attention and money, but it became significantly more Democratic in redistricting after the 2000 census when many of the rapidly growing suburbs of the city were placed in the new 3rd District. Although some pockets of Republicans live in the district, the 1st has a strong Democratic base in unionized service workers. The 1st was the only district 2004 presidential nominee John Kerry won in the state.

MAJOR INDUSTRY
Tourism, casinos, conventions

CITIES
Las Vegas (pt.), 362,908; North Las Vegas, 115,488; Paradise (unincorporated) (pt.), 77,893

NOTABLE
The Little White Wedding Chapel on Las Vegas Boulevard has a drive-through window for weddings.

Rep. Jim Gibbons (R)

Elected 1996; 5th term

A decorated fighter pilot and staunch conservative, Gibbons occasionally riles House GOP leaders but remains a popular figure back home. His views reflect the people of rural Nevada and a district that includes desert and just about everything in the state outside of Las Vegas and its suburbs. He adheres to the Western philosophy that government should interfere in citizens' lives as little as possible.

Gibbons lobbies in support of the mining industry from his seat on the Resources Committee. Almost 90 percent of the land in his district is owned by the government, and federal water, grazing and mining policies play a large role in the economic life of the state. Gibbons holds bachelor's and master's degrees in geology and mining, in addition to a law degree.

At the start of the 109th Congress, he was given the helm of the panel's Energy and Mineral Resources Subcommittee. He is also co-chairman of the Congressional Mining Caucus. Gibbons aims to get Congress to act on an overhaul of mining laws that would benefit mining companies. Any revision, he said, should include changes to allow mines to leave behind such infrastructure as power lines and water lines that communities could use to attract other types of industry to develop there in the future. Current law requires the companies to clear and restore the land.

Gibbons takes a strong interest in education. In 2004, he teamed with his wife Dawn Gibbons, a member of the state assembly, to put before state voters a successful ballot measure called "Education First." It requires lawmakers to analyze and approve education spending before the rest of the state budget. This was a response to lawmakers delaying the schools budget in 2003 because of a deadlock over taxes.

Gibbons has not always endeared himself to Republicans in Washington. He clashes with his GOP colleagues on the marquee issue in Nevada politics — the push to establish a national, high-level radioactive waste site at Yucca Mountain, 90 miles northwest of Las Vegas. In 2002, when the House voted in favor of President Bush's decision to put the waste dump at Yucca, Gibbons labored mightily to convince lawmakers the project was unsafe. He also argued that Nevadans should not be forced to accept waste they did not generate and do not want. After the vote, he vowed to work with the rest of the state delegation to block further progress in court. He has also tried to chip away at the project's funding.

Gibbons also has been pitted against fellow Republicans in his avid defense of Nevada's gambling industry. He has fought proposals to outlaw gambling on college sports, to ban automated teller machines from casinos, to withhold a portion of bingo and keno winnings for federal income taxes and to tax casino workers for the value of employer-provided meals. In 2004, Nevada political commentator Jon Ralston said that some in the "GOP elite" regard him as "a mercurial maverick at best and a loose cannon at worst."

Gibbons' party leaders bypassed him at a key moment in his House career. In 2004, he was a senior member of the Intelligence Committee and had hopes of being given the gavel after GOP Chairman Porter J. Goss was appointed as CIA director. But Speaker J. Dennis Hastert tapped Peter Hoekstra of Michigan, an aggressive fundraiser for the party. At the start of the 109th, Gibbons was required to leave the Intelligence Committee because of GOP term limits.

He still sits on the Homeland Security Committee, but had to give up his gavel on the panel on intelligence and counterterrorism. He was among the

CAPITOL OFFICE
225-6155
www.house.gov/gibbons
100 Cannon 20515-2802; fax 225-5679

COMMITTEES
Armed Services
Homeland Security
Resources
(Energy & Mineral Resources - chairman)

HOMETOWN
Reno

BORN
Dec. 16, 1944, Sparks, Nev.

RELIGION
Mormon

FAMILY
Wife, Dawn Gibbons; three children

EDUCATION
U. of Nevada, Reno, B.S. 1967 (geology), M.S. 1973 (mining geology); Southwestern U., J.D. 1979

MILITARY SERVICE
Air Force, 1967-71; Nev. Air National Guard, 1975-95

CAREER
Airline pilot; lawyer; geologist

POLITICAL HIGHLIGHTS
Nev. Assembly, 1989-94 (minority whip, 1993); Republican nominee for governor, 1994

ELECTION RESULTS

2004 GENERAL

Jim Gibbons (R)	195,466	67.2%
Angie G. Cochran (D)	79,978	27.5%
Janine Hansen (IA)	10,638	3.7%
Brendan Trainor (LIBERT)	4,997	1.7%

2004 PRIMARY

Jim Gibbons (R)	unopposed

2002 GENERAL

Jim Gibbons (R)	149,574	74.3%
Travis O. Souza (D)	40,189	20.0%
Janine Hansen (IA)	7,240	3.6%
Brendan Trainor (LIBERT)	3,413	1.7%

PREVIOUS WINNING PERCENTAGES
2000 (65%); 1998 (81%); 1996 (59%)

first to support the creation of the Homeland Security Department after the Sept. 11, 2001, terrorist attacks. He also deals with terrorism issues as a member of the Armed Services Committee.

National Republicans have recognized Gibbons' political appeal even if they don't always like his positions. In 2003, White House political adviser Karl Rove tried to persuade him to run against Democratic Sen. Harry Reid, who had a history of razor-thin re-election margins. Gibbons was seen as the premium GOP prospect. He had won easily in all four of his House races, and was well-known in both of the state's major media markets, Las Vegas and Reno. Gibbons declined that race, in part due to his fundraising disadvantage at the time — he had just more than $500,000 on hand compared with Reid's $3.1 million. (Reid became Senate minority leader in the 109th Congress.)

In early 2005, Gibbons was mulling a bid for governor in 2006, while his wife said she wanted to succeed her husband in the House. While contemplating his political future, Gibbons faced some embarrassing national publicity. In March 2005, he delivered a speech inveighing against "liberal, tree-hugging, Birkenstock-wearing, hippie, tie-dyed liberals" who support abortion rights and oppose the war in Iraq. A local newspaper, the Elko Daily Press, reported that the speech was lifted from a copyrighted address by Alabama State Auditor Beth Chapman a year earlier. Gibbons apologized for what he termed the inadvertent recycling of Chapman's words.

Gibbons was born in Sparks, just outside of Reno. His father was a laborer for the Southern Pacific Railroad, and the family had little money. Their house was located along the flight path of the local airport, and Gibbons dreamed of being a pilot. Faced with a draft notice after college graduation, Gibbons joined the Air Force. A combat pilot, he flew A-37 close-air support planes during a tour in Vietnam.

After his service, Gibbons wanted to become a commercial pilot, but the airlines weren't hiring. So he pursued a master's degree in mining geology before deciding that he "didn't want to be packing rocks up a hill like my dad did." He earned a law degree and then got an offer to be a pilot; he flew for Western Airlines and Delta Airlines the better part of two decades. In the last four Congresses, he has offered legislation to raise the mandatory retirement age for commercial pilots from 60 to 65. Recalled to active duty during the Gulf War, Gibbons won a Distinguished Flying Cross.

In 1988, Gibbons won the first of three elections to the Nevada state Assembly. After losing a 1994 race for governor to incumbent Democrat Bob Miller, Gibbons ran successfully for the 2nd District in 1996. He has won with at least 65 percent of the vote ever since.

KEY VOTES

2004

No Extend federal unemployment benefits by 13 weeks

Yes Pass $283.2 billion, six-year federal highway and mass transit bill

Yes Approve $146 billion multi-year extension of previously enacted middle-class tax breaks

No Amend the Constitution to prohibit same-sex marriage

Yes Cut corporate taxes $137 billion over 10 years

Yes Reorganize U.S. intelligence agencies as proposed by Sept. 11 commission

2003

Yes Cut taxes by $330 billion through fiscal 2013

— Block Bush rule scaling back overtime pay for some white-collar federal workers

No Do not allow use of search warrants without first notifying subjects

No Allow importation of prescription drugs

Yes Create private school voucher program in Washington, D.C.

Yes Ban "partial birth" abortion except to save a woman's life

No Split $18.6 billion in Iraq aid into half-grant, half-loan

Yes Overhaul Medicare and create prescription drug benefit

CQ VOTE STUDIES

	PARTY UNITY		PRESIDENTIAL SUPPORT	
	Support	Oppose	Support	Oppose
2004	95%	5%	84%	16%
2003	96%	4%	94%	6%
2002	96%	4%	88%	12%
2001	97%	3%	93%	7%
2000	92%	8%	29%	71%

INTEREST GROUPS

	AFL-CIO	ADA	CCUS	ACU
2004	20%	10%	95%	96%
2003	8%	5%	97%	80%
2002	11%	5%	90%	92%
2001	17%	5%	96%	96%
2000	20%	30%	61%	88%

NEVADA 2
Reno, Carson City and the 'Cow Counties'

The conservative-leaning 2nd takes in everything outside of Las Vegas and its suburbs — almost all of the state's vast rural areas. Reno and the capital, Carson City, anchor the 2nd in the west, and in the district's "Cow Counties," agriculture, mining and ranching dominate. Nearly 90 percent of the district's land is federally owned.

In the 1800s, the gold rush attracted fortune seekers to Reno. Fortune seekers now are more inclined to try their luck in the city's casinos or head to Lake Tahoe. Gambling has not fared as well in Reno in recent years, and the industry is concerned that customers will flock to new Indian reservation casinos in California. Yucca Mountain, the proposed national nuclear waste storage site located northwest of Las Vegas in Nye County, also has been a contentious issue in the 2nd.

The 2nd has sent Republicans to Congress since its creation in 1982. It votes mostly Republican in local elections and is becoming increasingly conservative. Redistricting following the 2000 census further increased the district's Republican voting base by removing some urban territory in Clark County to create the new 3rd District. In 2004, George W. Bush garnered 57 percent of the presidential vote in the 2nd District, which was his highest total in the state.

Although the 3rd was drawn to take in most of the Las Vegas suburbs, the 2nd dips into two areas of Clark County in the southern part of the state. It takes in Nellis Air Force Base and much of the northern part of Clark, as well as a few suburban communities in the southwestern area of the county.

MAJOR INDUSTRY
Gambling, mining, manufacturing, warehousing

MILITARY BASES
Nellis Air Force Base, 8,251 military, 288 civilian; Naval Air Station Fallon, 1,100 military, 1,800 civilian (2004)

CITIES
Reno, 180,480; Sparks, 66,346; Carson City, 52,457; Pahrump (unincorporated), 24,631

NOTABLE
White King, a 10-foot, 4-inch tall polar bear on display in Elko that died in 1957, is said to be the world's largest polar bear; The Washington Post Magazine named Battle Mountain "the armpit of America" in 2001.

Rep. Jon Porter (R)

CAPITOL OFFICE
225-3252
www.house.gov/porter
218 Cannon 20515-2803; fax 225-2185

COMMITTEES
Education & Workforce
Government Reform
  (Federal Workforce & Agency Organization -
  chairman)
Transportation & Infrastructure

HOMETOWN
Henderson

BORN
May 16, 1955, Fort Dodge, Iowa

RELIGION
Roman Catholic

FAMILY
Wife, Laurie Porter; two children

EDUCATION
Briar Cliff College, attended 1973-77 (theology)

CAREER
Farm insurance company branch manager and
agent; electronics repairman and distributor

POLITICAL HIGHLIGHTS
City Council of Boulder City, 1983-93 (mayor, 1987-
1991); Nev. Senate, 1995-2002; Republican nominee
for U.S. House, 2000

ELECTION RESULTS

2004 GENERAL

Jon Porter (R)	162,240	54.5%
Tom Gallagher (D)	120,365	40.4%
Joseph P. Silvestre (LIBERT)	9,260	3.1%
Richard O'Dell (X)	6,053	2.0%

2004 PRIMARY

Jon Porter (R)	unopposed

2002 GENERAL

Jon Porter (R)	100,378	56.1%
Dario Herrera (D)	66,659	37.2%
Pete O'Neil (I)	6,842	3.8%
Neil Scott (LIBERT)	3,421	1.9%

Elected 2002; 2nd term

Porter must be one of the GOP's proudest achievements of the last two elections. He won in a brand-new district added after Nevada's growth spurt in the 1990s. He not only gave his party a toe in the door on valuable new political turf in the West, he overcame a strong Democratic challenge in 2004, putting down what was probably the opposition's best chance of snatching away the swing district. The 3rd is evenly divided between the two parties and based in the Las Vegas suburbs.

For all of this, the one-time farm insurance salesman who never finished college has been, and likely will continue to be, handsomely rewarded by GOP leaders. They chose him to sponsor two important bills in the 108th Congress, one a White House initiative to revamp job training programs and another a measure to extend a popular tax credit for parents.

Porter's one disappointment was failing to secure the seat he wanted on the Ways and Means Committee at the start of the 109th. Nevada's politically powerful gaming industry lobbied hard in his behalf, hoping to get an advocate on the panel sympathetic to tax breaks for organized gambling. He is a strong contender for any future openings on the committee.

Porter may have been disappointed in not getting a seat on the powerful tax and trade panel, but he was clearly happy to be out front on some high-profile GOP legislation. He sits on the Education and Workforce Committee, where he was the chief sponsor of a bill in 2005 creating stipends of up to $3,000 to help jobless workers pay for education, transportation and child care as part of their job search, giving them discretion in how to use the money and allowing them to keep the unused balance once they found jobs.

Democrats assailed the bill as a first step toward dismantling traditional, government-run job retraining programs. Nevertheless, Porter's bill passed the House. In 2004, he sponsored another GOP bill making permanent a tax credit of $1,000 per child. That bill also passed the House, but stalled in the Senate.

Porter also made headway on a matter of intense interest back home. The House passed a bill that included his provision directing the Pentagon to investigate the potential health threat of a toxin called perchlorate that leaked from a defense factory and contaminated drinking water supplies in Nevada.

For his part, Porter returned the favor by helping the party on pivotal votes, and by being reliable in a pinch. He voted for a bill to give soldiers in Iraq and Afghanistan a salary bonus, but switched his vote to no after GOP leaders, who were strongly opposed to the measure, told him they suspected the Democrats were using it to convince the public that the war in Iraq was underfunded. When Porter and another Republican switched, the bill died on a tie vote.

The 800-pound gorilla in the room for any lawmaker from Nevada, Republican or Democrat, is the massive Yucca Mountain nuclear waste storage project, and Porter has devoted a lot of attention to it. Harry Reid, elevated to Senate Democratic leader for the 109th Congress, is the undisputed leader of Nevada's opposition to the project, but upon his arrival in Washington Porter jumped into the fray. He fought proposals to fund the repository, a favorite stalling tactic of Nevada politicians and environmentalists.

In testimony before the Energy and Commerce Committee in 2004, Porter called the project a "fiasco." He said, "Instead of admitting their mistakes, successive administrations, Republican and Democrat, decided to continue dumping billions of dollars into studies to turn a molehill into a mountain recipient of nuclear waste."

Porter teamed with Democrat Mark Udall of Colorado on an amendment to redirect money from the Yucca project to renewable energy programs, which are as popular in Nevada as the waste dump is unpopular. With 300 days a year of sunshine, the state stands to benefit from breakthroughs in solar energy as well as geothermal and wind energy studies.

Though he once challenged her for her House seat and lost, Porter also found ways to work closely with Democrat Shelley Berkley, whose Las Vegas-based district abuts his. He and Berkley team up on issues related to drunken driving. Porter's daughter Nicole, now 24, was seriously injured in a crash with a drunken driver when she was a teenager.

In part, Porter is bipartisan because he is so darned nice. A political columnist for the Las Vegas Review-Journal wrote in 2004 that he is "the man everybody wants at the backyard barbecue."

But that doesn't mean he can't run a tough campaign. National Democrats targeted him for defeat in 2004 when he faced his first re-election test. His opponent, Democrat Tom Gallagher, was a Harvard Law graduate and former top executive with Hilton Hotels who sank $700,000 of his own money into the race. Gallagher accused Porter of not working hard enough to stop the Yucca Mountain project in Congress. Porter fought back, and won with a surprisingly comfortable 55 percent of the vote.

Porter was born in Iowa and attended Briar Cliff College in Sioux City but didn't finish a degree. He married an elementary school teacher and settled in Henderson, Nev., where he worked as a farm insurance agent, eventually managing 40 agents. He first held elective office as a Boulder City councilman in 1983. He served on the council for a decade, and was mayor for about four years, before moving to the state Senate in 1995.

His first race for the House ended unhappily for him in 2000, when he took on Berkley in the 1st District and lost. But he got a respectable 44 percent share of the vote, making him attractive as a candidate in 2002, after the once-a-decade reapportionment gave Nevada a third House seat. The district was drawn to be evenly divided between Republicans and Democrats.

Democrats hoped the low-key Porter would be eclipsed by their energetic candidate, Clark County Commissioner Dario Herrera. But Herrera was politically damaged by ethics questions, and Porter won by 19 percentage points. Future challengers might bear in mind that Porter is literally a long-distance runner. After taking up the sport a few years ago, Porter in 2003 completed the 26-mile Marine Corps Marathon in 5 hours and 40 minutes.

KEY VOTES

2004

No	Extend federal unemployment benefits by 13 weeks
Yes	Pass $283.2 billion, six-year federal highway and mass transit bill
Yes	Approve $146 billion multi-year extension of previously enacted middle-class tax breaks
Yes	Amend the Constitution to prohibit same-sex marriage
Yes	Cut corporate taxes $137 billion over 10 years
Yes	Reorganize U.S. intelligence agencies as proposed by Sept. 11 commission

2003

Yes	Cut taxes by $330 billion through fiscal 2013
No	Block Bush rule scaling back overtime pay for some white-collar federal workers
Yes	Do not allow use of search warrants without first notifying subjects
No	Allow importation of prescription drugs
Yes	Create private school voucher program in Washington, D.C.
Yes	Ban "partial birth" abortion except to save a woman's life
No	Split $18.6 billion in Iraq aid into half-grant, half-loan
Yes	Overhaul Medicare and create prescription drug benefit

CQ VOTE STUDIES

	PARTY UNITY		PRESIDENTIAL SUPPORT	
	Support	Oppose	Support	Oppose
2004	83%	17%	82%	18%
2003	94%	6%	98%	2%

INTEREST GROUPS

	AFL-CIO	ADA	CCUS	ACU
2004	27%	15%	100%	76%
2003	13%	5%	100%	88%

NEVADA 3
Las Vegas suburbs

Roughly pinwheel-shaped, the 3rd District is located in Clark County, which has absorbed much of the 66 percent population gain that made Nevada the nation's fastest-growing state in the 1990s. The district includes a chunk of Las Vegas, but it is mainly composed of suburbs such as Henderson and Boulder City.

Although most of the city's casinos are located in the urban 1st District, the 3rd is home to many who work in the gambling industry and are part of the area's strong union structure. The district has a 16 percent Hispanic population. It also contains McCarran International Airport, one of the 10 busiest in the country.

The 3rd was drawn to be a partisan swing district. When it was created in redistricting following the 2000 census, its party registration was 42 percent Democratic and 42 percent Republican, with the rest of the voters unaffiliated. Al Gore narrowly beat George W. Bush in the 2000 presidential election here by 48.4 percent to 47.8 percent, but Bush edged John Kerry in 2004 by 49.9 percent to 48.6 percent.

Republicans may have an advantage in the future, as the GOP suburban areas are expanding rapidly. The district takes in most of the suburbs, including Summerlin to the west, a massive planned community along the western rim of Las Vegas Valley. These areas are populated with many white-collar new arrivals to the state, as well as one of the fastest-growing elderly populations in the country.

To the east, along the Arizona border near Utah, the population is largely Mormon — an influence that has spread into suburbs such as Henderson. In the south, the district contains lightly populated mining communities around Laughlin on the Arizona border.

CITIES
Henderson, 175,381; Spring Valley (unincorporated), 117,390; Las Vegas (pt.), 115,526; Paradise (unincorporated) (pt.), 108,177

MAJOR INDUSTRY
Mining, gambling, ranching

NOTABLE
Hoover Dam, about 30 miles southeast of Las Vegas, often is called one of the greatest engineering works in history.

Gov. John Lynch (D)

First elected: 2004
Length of term: 2 years
Term expires: 1/07
Salary: $103,000
Phone: (603) 271-2121

Hometown: Hopkinton
Born: Nov. 25, 1952; Waltham, Mass.
Religion: Roman Catholic
Family: Wife, Susan Lynch; three children
Education: U. of New Hampshire, B.A. 1974 (English); Harvard U., M.B.A. 1979; Georgetown U., J.D. 1984
Career: Business consulting firm owner; furniture manufacturing company president; college admissions director; state party executive director
Political highlights: No previous office

Election results:

2004 GENERAL
John Lynch (D)	339,927	51.0%
Craig Benson (R)	325,514	48.9%

Senate President Thomas Eaton (R)

(no lieutenant governor)
Phone: (603) 271-2111

STATE LEGISLATURE

General Court: January-June

House: 400 members, 2-year terms
2005 breakdown: 251R, 147D, 2 vacancies; 273 men, 125 women
Salary: $200/2-year term
Phone: (603) 271-3661

Senate: 24 members, 2-year terms
2005 breakdown: 16R, 8D; 19 men, 5 women
Salary: $200/2-year term
Phone: (603) 271-2111

STATE TERM LIMITS

Governor: No
House: No
Senate: No

URBAN STATISTICS

CITY	POPULATION
Manchester	107,006
Nashua	86,605
Concord	40,687
Derry	34,021
Rochester	28,461

REGISTERED VOTERS

Unaffiliated	42%
Republican	31%
Democrat	27%

POPULATION

2004 population (est.)	1,299,500
2000 population	1,235,786
1990 population	1,109,252
Percent change (1990-2000)	+11.4%
Rank among states (2004)	41

Median age	37.1
Born in state	43.3%
Foreign born	4.4%
Violent crime rate	175/100,000
Poverty level	6.5%
Federal workers	7,933
Military	4,435

REDISTRICTING

New Hampshire retained its two House seats in reapportionment. The state legislature drew a new map, which the governor signed on April 8, 2002.

MISCELLANEOUS

Web: www.nh.gov
Capital: Concord
STATE ELECTION OFFICIAL
(603) 271-3242
DEMOCRATIC HEADQUARTERS
(603) 225-6899
REPUBLICAN HEADQUARTERS
(603) 225-9341

District Statistics

DIST.	2004 VOTE FOR PRESIDENT BUSH	KERRY	WHITE	BLACK	ASIAN	HISP	MEDIAN INCOME	WHITE COLLAR	BLUE COLLAR	SERVICE INDUSTRY	OVER 64	UNDER 18	COLLEGE EDUCATION	RURAL	SQ. MILES
1	51%	48%	95%	1%	1%	2%	$50,135	63%	24%	13%	12%	25%	29%	33%	2,449
2	47	52	95	1	1	2	$48,762	62	25	13	12	25	29	48	6,519
STATE	49	50	95	1	1	2	$49,467	62	25	13	12	25	29	41	8,968
U.S.	50.7	48.3	69	12	4	13	$41,994	60	25	15	12	26	24	21	3,537,438

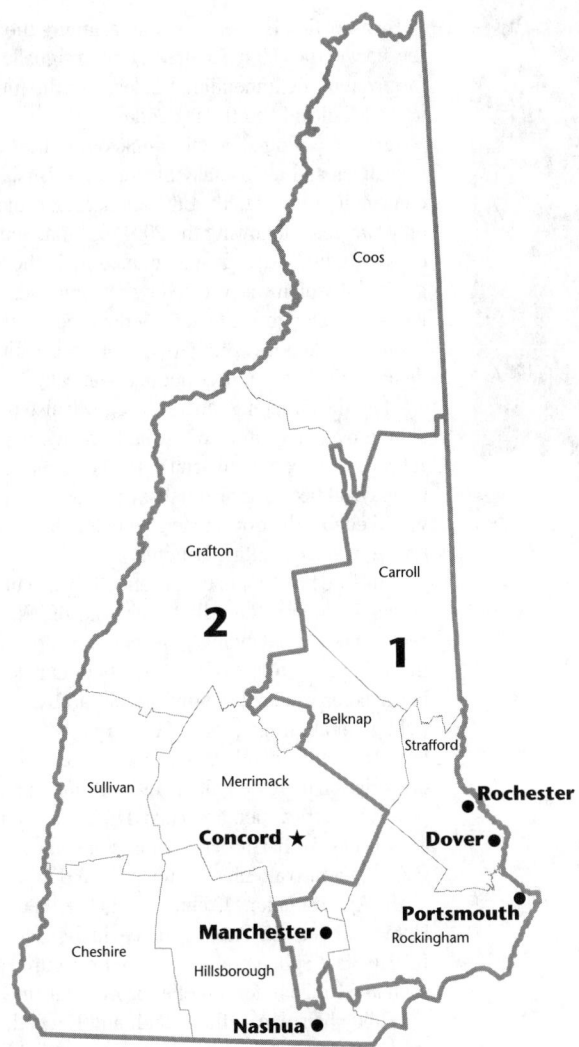

Sen. Judd Gregg (R)

Elected 1992; 3rd term

CAPITOL OFFICE
224-3324
gregg.senate.gov
393 Russell 20510-2904; fax 224-4952

COMMITTEES
Appropriations
  (Homeland Security - chairman)
Budget - chairman
Health, Education, Labor & Pensions

HOMETOWN
Rye

BORN
Feb. 14, 1947, Nashua, N.H.

RELIGION
Congregationalist

FAMILY
Wife, Kathleen Gregg; three children

EDUCATION
Columbia U., A.B. 1969; Boston U., J.D. 1972, LL.M. 1975

CAREER
Lawyer

POLITICAL HIGHLIGHTS
N.H. Governor's Executive Council, 1979-81; U.S. House, 1981-89; governor, 1989-93

ELECTION RESULTS

2004 GENERAL
Judd Gregg (R)	434,847	66.2%
Doris "Granny D" Haddock (D)	221,549	33.7%

2004 PRIMARY
Judd Gregg (R)	60,597	91.6%
Tom Alciere (R)	2,682	4.1%
Michael Tipa (R)	2,563	3.9%

PREVIOUS WINNING PERCENTAGES
1998 (68%); 1992 (48%); 1986 House Election (74%); 1984 House Election (76%); 1982 House Election (71%); 1980 House Election (64%)

By asserting his seniority and claiming the Budget Committee gavel at the start of the 109th Congress, Gregg signalled that he intends to be at the forefront of the impending battles over the future of Social Security, Medicare, Medicaid and the tax code.

An acknowledged budget wonk, one of the Senate's staunchest fiscal conservatives and a close ally of President Bush, Gregg gave up his post as chairman of the Health, Education, Labor and Pensions Committee after only two years following the 2004 election. Sensing an opportunity for success with the GOP's expanded majority in the Senate, Gregg took the Budget job — which was vacated by retiring Oklahoma Republican Don Nickles — and pledged to tackle a federal deficit that he says is far too high.

Gregg takes the Budget post at a difficult juncture. He believes that deficit reduction requires putting politically sacrosanct programs like Medicaid on the chopping block. Gregg will also be a lead player in the volatile debate over the future of Social Security, having teamed with Democrat John B. Breaux of Louisiana in the late 1990s to propose using a portion of the payroll tax for individual savings accounts. Such a step, the pair said, would enable the government to maintain the program's solvency without raising taxes or cutting benefits.

While he has supported recent GOP tax cuts, Gregg worked with Democrats, including Russell D. Feingold of Wisconsin, during the 107th to renew budget-balancing enforcement mechanisms that would, in part, make it harder to cut taxes. Such budget rules are currently out of vogue in the congressional Republican hierarchy.

In general, Gregg is one of Congress' few consistent spending hawks. He joined a handful of other fiscal conservatives in voting against the Medicare prescription drug benefit bill in 2003, and has bucked some in the GOP by proposing strict spending caps. He has tried, unsuccessfully, to eliminate a tax break for hard-rock mining companies.

Gregg is also a senior member of the Budget Committee's traditional rival — the Appropriations Committee. In the 109th, he assumed the chair of the Homeland Security Subcommittee. In the 108th, he chaired the Commerce-Justice-State Subcommittee, where he secured special projects for his state, such as $1 million for street improvements in North Conway in 2004.

While chairman of the Health and Education Committee, his top-ranking Democratic member was Massachusetts' Edward M. Kennedy — a fellow New Englander with diametrically opposite views on most of the major social policy issues of the day and a far different temperament. But Kennedy and Gregg managed to forge a solid working relationship. During the 108th, the two men worked together to enact legislation of mutual concern — a rewrite of the law governing special education for the nation's 6.7 million disabled students.

In 2001, Gregg and Kennedy, working with their counterparts from the House Education and Workforce Committee, overcame partisan differences to write the final version of Bush's education overhaul initiative. Subsequently, Gregg was instrumental in obtaining $2 billion more than Bush had initially sought for education programs.

Still, only nine GOP senators voted in agreement with Bush more often than Gregg in 2004; he did so 98 percent of the time.

Gregg is also conservative on social issues, where he has battled legislation designed to ban job discrimination against homosexuals, arguing that a federal law should not overturn state rulings on the matter. He has also been a longtime ally of anti-abortion forces. As governor from 1989 to 1993, he vetoed bills that would have bolstered abortion rights provisions in New Hampshire law. In the Senate, he has voted to ban a procedure opponents call "partial birth" abortion.

Gregg will occasionally stray from the party line on regional matters, particularly on environmental protection. In late 2003, Gregg and four other Northeastern Republicans joined Democrats to block the White House-backed energy bill over a provision that would waive liability for producers of methyl tertiary butyl ether (MTBE), a fuel additive that has been found to contaminate groundwater in New Hampshire. That and other provisions made the bill "a clear, gratuitous attack on New England," Gregg said. Earlier that year, Gregg joined Democrats in an unsuccessful effort to delay new administration rules weakening air pollution requirements.

In 2004, despite White House opposition, Gregg introduced legislation to allow consumers to import cheaper drugs from some developed countries. But he was cagey on the issue; his bill did not go as far as Democrats would like and Gregg did not press for action on the bill.

Gregg is a man of some reserve, not often given to backroom bonhomie. When presidential candidate George W. Bush picked Gregg to play the part of his opponent, Al Gore, for debating practice in the fall of 2000, campaign aides told The Washington Post that Gregg was the right person for the job because he was smart, stiff and dour — the very characteristics that GOP operatives delighted in ascribing to Gore. In 2004, Gregg once again played the part of the Democratic nominee, this time John Kerry.

The son of a former GOP governor of New Hampshire — Hugh Gregg, who served from 1953 to 1955 — Gregg has spent most of his life in public service. He practiced law only a short time before launching his political career in 1978, when he unseated a Republican incumbent to join the five-member state executive council. Two years later, he won the House seat of retiring Republican James C. Cleveland. His training as a tax attorney helped win him a seat on the Ways and Means Committee, but he manifested a straight-laced Yankee distaste for deal-cutting and had little role in the tax code overhaul of 1986.

Two years later, he left Congress for the first of a pair of two-year terms as governor. In each race, he took at least 60 percent of the vote.

When Gregg sought to return to Washington in 1992, he ran into stiff opposition. New Hampshire's economic woes fired up an angry electorate, helping Bill Clinton carry the state for president and putting pro-business Democrat John Rauh in a position to give Gregg his toughest electoral fight as they vied to succeed Republican Sen. Warren B. Rudman, who was stepping down after two terms.

Gregg acknowledged the state's economic hardships while noting that he had kept a tight lid on spending and remained staunchly opposed to state income and sales taxes. He lost most of the counties in his old congressional district on the rural western side of New Hampshire, but he carried the populous southeast corner and the GOP "North Country" and prevailed by 3 percentage points.

Gregg won an easy re-election in 1998, even after his opponent, George Condodemetraky, accused him of draft-dodging. Gregg vehemently denied the accusations — he received a valid medical deferment, he said — and refused to debate his opponent on television. Gregg walked away with 68 percent of the vote. In 2004, Gregg defeated Doris "Granny D" Haddock with 66 percent. Haddock had gained attention in 1999 by walking 3,200 miles across the country to highlight the need to reform campaign financing practices. She was 89 years old at the time.

KEY VOTES

2004

No   Pass $318.9 billion, six-year highway and mass transit bill
Yes Extend assault weapons ban for 10 years
No   Restore pay-as-you-go rules for new tax cuts and entitlement spending
?   Criminalize harm to a fetus in an attack on the mother
No   Increase mandatory child care funding to states by $6 billion over five years
Yes Amend the Constitution to prohibit same-sex marriage
Yes Approve $146 billion multi-year extension of previously enacted middle-class tax breaks
Yes Reorganize U.S. intelligence agencies as proposed by Sept. 11 commission
No   Cut corporate taxes $137 billion over 10 years

2003

Yes Delay Bush changes to Clean Air Act
Yes Allow confirmation vote on Miguel A. Estrada to the U.S. Court of Appeals for the D.C. Circuit
No   Block a Bush proposal opening Alaska's Arctic National Wildlife Refuge to oil drilling
No   Limit size of Bush's proposed tax cut to $350 billion through fiscal 2013
No   Overhaul Medicare and create prescription drug benefit
No   Block Bush rule scaling back overtime pay for some white-collar federal workers
No   Split $20 billion in Iraq aid into half-grant, half-loan
Yes Ban "partial birth" abortion except to save a woman's life
Yes Stop proposal allowing travel to Cuba
No   Allow final vote on energy policy overhaul

CQ VOTE STUDIES

	PARTY UNITY		PRESIDENTIAL SUPPORT	
	Support	Oppose	Support	Oppose
2004	94%	6%	98%	2%
2003	92%	8%	93%	7%
2002	81%	19%	96%	4%
2001	96%	4%	100%	0%
2000	98%	2%	38%	62%
1999	94%	6%	33%	67%
1998	91%	9%	43%	57%
1997	87%	13%	63%	37%
1996	91%	9%	34%	66%
1995	94%	6%	22%	78%

INTEREST GROUPS

	AFL-CIO	ADA	CCUS	ACU
2004	0%	15%	88%	88%
2003	0%	15%	78%	85%
2002	15%	10%	100%	85%
2001	13%	0%	100%	88%
2000	0%	0%	86%	100%
1999	0%	0%	76%	91%
1998	0%	5%	89%	76%
1997	0%	10%	100%	76%
1996	0%	5%	92%	75%
1995	0%	0%	95%	87%

Sen. John E. Sununu (R)

Elected 2002; 1st term

CAPITOL OFFICE
224-2841
sununu.senate.gov
111 Russell 20510-2903; fax 228-4131

COMMITTEES
Banking, Housing & Urban Affairs
Commerce, Science & Transportation
(Ocean Policy Study - chairman)
Foreign Relations
(International Operations & Terrorism -
chairman)
Joint Economic

HOMETOWN
Waterville Valley

BORN
Sept. 10, 1964, Boston, Mass.

RELIGION
Roman Catholic

FAMILY
Wife, Kitty Sununu; three children

EDUCATION
Massachusetts Institute of Technology, B.S. 1987
(mechanical engineering), M.S. 1987 (mechanical
engineering); Harvard U., M.B.A. 1991

CAREER
Corporate financial officer; management
consultant; mechanical engineer

POLITICAL HIGHLIGHTS
U.S. House, 1997-2003

ELECTION RESULTS

2002 GENERAL

John E. Sununu (R)	227,229	50.8%
Jeanne Shaheen (D)	207,478	46.4%
Clarence G. Blevens (LIBERT)	9,835	2.2%

2002 PRIMARY

John E. Sununu (R)	81,920	53.5%
Robert C. Smith (R)	68,608	44.8%
Kenneth Scot Stremsky (R)	2,694	1.8%

PREVIOUS WINNING PERCENTAGES
2000 House Election (52%); 1998 House Election
(67%); 1996 House Election (50%)

The name Sununu is to New Hampshire what Bush is to Texas. The Senate's youngest member, Sununu is the son of a famous political father, John H. Sununu, the state's governor from 1983 to 1989 and then chief of staff to the first President Bush for three years.

Like the Bushes, the Sununus are conservative-leaning Republicans. In the Senate, Sununu (suh-NU-nu) votes mostly along party lines, but can veer off course on fiscal matters. He was among a small group of conservative Republicans who voted against the administration's Medicare prescription drug plan in 2003, fearing its costs would escalate beyond already hefty projections over time. "There aren't many cost containment measures in this legislation that would ensure long-term solvency," he said. "We shouldn't be bankrupting future generations of retirees."

In the 109th Congress, Sununu is on board with President Bush's centerpiece domestic issue: revamping the Social Security program to allow people to put some of their tax dollars into private accounts. He also joins the president in favoring less taxation and government spending, a bedrock belief of New Hampshire Republicans. Sununu favors a flat tax, arguing that the federal government uses the current tax code to "engineer the way we live."

Sununu says he does not seek legislative advice from his father, and that he speaks to him "no more or no less than anyone else who has a good relationship with their father." But he is not shy about stating that he has personal ties to the upper echelons of the current administration, including Bush himself. He says he has "a great personal relationship" with White House Chief of Staff Andrew H. Card Jr.

As a member of the Sununu clan, he may come to politics naturally, but he is not a natural politician. Sununu credits his background in mechanical engineering with giving him an analytical approach to problem-solving that separates him from career politicians in Washington. And, unlike some of his harder-line conservative colleagues, Sununu does not regard compromise as capitulation. "There's nothing contradictory about being fiscally conservative and pragmatic," he said.

Soft-spoken and reserved in public settings, Sununu nonchalantly strolled the halls of the House during his six years there, usually with his hands in his pockets. He did not make incendiary floor speeches and he rarely attended news conferences. Passersby took him for a 30-something congressional aide. But his measured approach made him a bridge-builder between the conflicting worlds of his two committees: Budget, where Republicans try to hold down spending, and Appropriations, where members of both parties like to spend on projects for the folks back home. Sununu says he likes the greater freedom he has in the Senate to shape policy. "In the Senate, given the openness of the rules, it's easier for an individual to shape legislation that doesn't necessarily move through committee," he says.

Though low in seniority on the Commerce, Science, and Transportation Committee, Sununu has drawn on his engineering and business background to carve out a specialty in telecommunications. The latest version of the law governing the rapidly changing industry was written in 1996 and is ripe for revision. The issue has given Sununu's career traction with his elders, as he demonstrates an ability to keep up with new technologies and the corresponding need to alter regulatory schemes. He has focused on such issues as computer-based telephone services, the potential for law enforcement agencies to wiretap computer lines, and telecommunications service to rural areas.

With a seat on the Foreign Relations Committee, Sununu along with Vermont Democratic Sen. Patrick J. Leahy are the congressional members of the United States delegation to the United Nations. The subcommittee he chairs, the International Operations and Terrorism panel, has oversight of U.N. programs.

Sununu has been out front on an environmental issue that is particularly sensitive in New Hampshire — anger that Northeastern states have become the "tailpipe of America," with some of the worst air pollution in the country, caused by air currents that carry emissions from Midwestern power plants and cause acid rain to fall farther east. He worked against the White House by joining other Northeastern Republicans and most Democrats early in 2003 in an unsuccessful bid to delay a Bush administration rule that weakens air pollution regulations.

On other key environmental issues without a specific impact on New England, such as oil drilling in Alaska or global warming, Republican leaders have been able to count on Sununu's support of the GOP line.

Sununu was elected to the Senate at age 38, defeating incumbent Republican Sen. Robert C. Smith in the primary and incumbent Democratic Gov. Jeanne Shaheen in the general election.

While in junior high school, Sununu observed firsthand his mother's work as a school board member; her experiences in that capacity taught him the importance and difficulties of public service. As a youth, he had an aptitude for science and math, which he turned into engineering degrees at the Massachusetts Institute of Technology (MIT) and a business degree at Harvard. He landed a job as chief financial officer for Teletrol Systems Inc., an innovative heating and cooling equipment maker in New Hampshire owned by Dean Kamen, inventor of the Segway Human Transporter, a motorized two-wheel scooter.

Sununu's opportunity to enter the family business came in 1996, when after three terms Republican Bill Zeliff gave up the 1st District House seat to run unsuccessfully for the GOP gubernatorial nomination. Sununu benefited from his name and won a seven-person GOP primary by 476 votes. In the general election, Sununu edged Joseph F. Keefe, the state Democratic chairman, by 3 percentage points.

Sununu cruised to a second term in 1998 with 67 percent. But in 2000, he did not campaign aggressively and won by only 8 points against Democratic state Rep. Martha Fuller Clark.

Although his modest victory in that race raised some eyebrows, GOP operatives turned to Sununu soon afterward, when they sensed incumbent Smith's vulnerability could hamper the party's ability to win back control of the Senate in 2002. Smith, an aggressive and unpredictable conservative, had flummoxed party strategists by embarking in 1999 on a quixotic presidential bid, which he began as a Republican and ended as an independent.

Sununu jumped into the Senate race in the fall of 2001. Smith attacked him for waging a battle that would leave Republicans divided after the primary. Sununu countered that Republicans needed to put forward their strongest candidate to take on Shaheen, who had been a popular governor, and touted endorsements he had received from some of Smith's Republican colleagues in the Senate.

Sununu won the GOP nomination in September by 9 points — the first person to unseat an elected senator in a primary since 1992. His high-profile victory eight weeks before the general election gave him a bounce in public opinion polls. Shaheen closed the gap in October, but a strong turnout of Republican voters helped propel Sununu to a 4-point victory.

KEY VOTES

2004

No Pass $318.9 billion, six-year highway and mass transit bill
No Extend assault weapons ban for 10 years
No Restore pay-as-you-go rules for new tax cuts and entitlement spending
Yes Criminalize harm to a fetus in an attack on the mother
No Increase mandatory child care funding to states by $6 billion over five years
No Amend the Constitution to prohibit same-sex marriage
Yes Approve $146 billion multi-year extension of previously enacted middle-class tax breaks
Yes Reorganize U.S. intelligence agencies as proposed by Sept. 11 commission
?   Cut corporate taxes $137 billion over 10 years

2003

Yes Delay Bush changes to Clean Air Act
Yes Allow confirmation vote on Miguel A. Estrada to the U.S. Court of Appeals for the D.C. Circuit
No Block a Bush proposal opening Alaska's Arctic National Wildlife Refuge to oil drilling
No Limit size of Bush's proposed tax cut to $350 billion through fiscal 2013
No Overhaul Medicare and create prescription drug benefit
No Block Bush rule scaling back overtime pay for some white-collar federal workers
No Split $20 billion in Iraq aid into half-grant, half-loan
Yes Ban "partial birth" abortion except to save a woman's life
No Stop proposal allowing travel to Cuba
No Allow final vote on energy policy overhaul

CQ VOTE STUDIES

	PARTY UNITY		PRESIDENTIAL SUPPORT	
	Support	Oppose	Support	Oppose
2004	94%	6%	96%	4%
2003	96%	4%	95%	5%
House Service:				
2002	93%	7%	92%	8%
2001	93%	7%	95%	5%
2000	95%	5%	28%	72%
1999	95%	5%	18%	82%
1998	91%	9%	25%	75%
1997	95%	5%	29%	71%

INTEREST GROUPS

	AFL-CIO	ADA	CCUS	ACU
2004	0%	10%	93%	100%
2003	0%	15%	83%	95%
House Service:				
2002	13%	0%	90%	92%
2001	0%	0%	100%	92%
2000	10%	10%	85%	96%
1999	0%	0%	88%	100%
1998	0%	0%	94%	92%
1997	0%	5%	100%	92%

Rep. Jeb Bradley (R)

CAPITOL OFFICE
225-5456
www.house.gov/bradley
1218 Longworth 20515-2901; fax 225-5822

COMMITTEES
Armed Services
Budget
Small Business
(Tax, Finance & Exports - chairman)
Veterans' Affairs

HOMETOWN
Wolfeboro

BORN
Oct. 20, 1952, Rumford, Maine

RELIGION
Episcopalian

FAMILY
Wife, Barbara Bradley; four children

EDUCATION
Tufts U., B.A. 1974 (sociology)

CAREER
Real estate developer; natural food store owner;
magician; painting company owner

POLITICAL HIGHLIGHTS
Wolfeboro Planning Board, 1986-90; Wolfeboro
Budget Committee, 1990-93; N.H. House, 1990-2002

ELECTION RESULTS

2004 GENERAL

Jeb Bradley (R)	204,836	63.3%
Justin Nadeau (D)	118,226	36.6%

2004 PRIMARY

Jeb Bradley (R)	27,285	89.5%
R. "Bob" Tillman Bevill (R)	3,076	10.1%

2002 GENERAL

Jeb Bradley (R)	128,993	58.1%
Martha Fuller Clark (D)	85,426	38.5%
Dan Belforti (LIBERT)	7,387	3.3%

Elected 2002; 2nd term

Bradley arrived in the House in 2003 with a reputation as one of the more moderate GOP freshmen. His blend of fiscal conservatism and moderate social views is dwindling nationwide, but it remains a viable strain in the Northeast. He says that a fiscal philosophy of "lower taxes and lower spending wherever possible" can help spur the nation's economic growth.

Bradley underscored his moderate views by joining the centrist Republican Main Street Partnership group.

With a seat on the Armed Services Committee, he will fight for the future of the Portsmouth Naval Shipyard, which employs about 1,600 people in his district. The shipyard could be vulnerable in the next round of base closures. "Keeping the shipyard fully operational is vitally important to our national security and New Hampshire's economy," Bradley said.

Bradley also sits on the Veterans' Affairs Committee, where he has worked to expand veterans' benefits, pushing for improved pensions and successfully extending education benefits for survivors and dependents of National Guard members called for active duty.

Bradley has honored the New England tradition of town hall meetings by hosting 70 such forums during his first term. At these small town gatherings, he has explained his view supporting American intervention in Iraq and listened to voters' worries about education, veterans' benefits and, especially, the troops in Iraq.

"It's gut-wrenching when our men and women are getting killed over there, and certainly that's very emotional and people are concerned," he said. "I can't minimize that, but at the same time most people I'm talking to feel that we have to finish the mission."

Bradley was named chairman of the Small Business Subcommittee on Tax, Finance and Exports. He intends to use his post to work to keep a lid on taxes and litigation claims against small businesses. He also wants to promote trade with other nations. "Small businesses are the backbone of New Hampshire's economy, producing the majority of new jobs in the state," he said. For the 109th Congress, Bradley has added the Budget Committee to his list of committee assignments.

Bradley tends to take a more moderate stance than many in his party on social and environmental issues. He says he supports abortion rights but voted yes on a measure to ban a procedure critics call "partial birth" abortion. Bradley says he believes the ban on the procedure will not threaten existing abortion rights. On the issue of using stem cells for medical research, Bradley supports making stem cells available as long as the embryonic specimens are created in fertility clinics and would otherwise be discarded.

He opposes school vouchers, unless, as he told the Manchester Union Leader, the school district is "clearly failing"; yet, in 2003 he voted to authorize a private school voucher program in Washington, D.C. Bradley is also against opening Alaska's Arctic National Wildlife Refuge to oil exploration.

A priority for Bradley upon his arrival in Washington was to push for a federal commitment to fund 40 percent of the cost of mandated special education programs — as promised to local school districts almost 30 years ago. That has proved difficult to accomplish, but he was successful with a measure to help smaller states cover the administrative cost of complying with special education requirements.

During his first term in office, Bradley sided with a majority of Republicans against a majority of Democrats 91 percent of the time. He support-ed President Bush's position 85 percent of the time.

An avid outdoorsman with a tough constitution, Bradley has climbed all of New Hampshire's tallest peaks, accomplishing a lifelong goal. Shortly after his first re-election in 2004, he hiked to the summit of Cannon Moun-tain, the 48th and final White Mountain peak reaching 4,000 feet or more that he had set out to climb.

A daily dip in the family lake is also integral to his fitness regimen — whenever possible. "When the water is below 40 degrees, it feels like your skin is burning. If you focus on that mentally, you feel warm," Bradley said. "I've been doing it for years. If you can do that, you can do anything."

Bradley grew up in Wolfeboro, where he worked in his parents' hard-ware store. A graduate of Tufts University, he has worked as a magician, developed real estate, and was the owner of a painting business and a nat-ural food store.

He worked his way up in politics, doing a stint on the city planning board in a town of 5,000 beside Lake Winnipesaukee, and serving a dozen years in the state House. While in the state legislature, he played a key role in ushering in the deregulation of electricity in New Hampshire, as chair-man of the state House Committee on Science, Technology and Energy.

He says his greatest surprise in making the transition from state to fed-eral lawmaker is the pace at which things happen in Washington, D.C. "It is relentless in a way I was not experienced with," he told a local Rotary Club in an appearance covered by The Laconia Citizen.

Bradley captured the 1st District seat by breaking open what had appeared to be a close race, trouncing Democratic state Rep. Martha Fuller Clark by almost 20 percentage points.

His easy win belied the nervousness some Republicans felt about hold-ing the seat that Republican John E. Sununu gave up to pursue a Senate race. Clark was well-funded and had come within 8 points of Sununu in 2000. But Bradley's state legislative record helped propel him to victory in an eight-candidate primary, and in the fall his Republican Party backers effectively portrayed Clark as too liberal for the district.

In the 2004 primary, Bradley shrugged off a challenge from businessman R. "Bob" Tillman Bevill, winning 90 percent of the vote. Bevill ran to the right of Bradley, especially on social issues. But his argument that the incumbent was not conservative enough drew little support. In November, Bradley beat his Democratic challenger, lawyer Justin Nadeau, with 63 per-cent of the vote.

KEY VOTES

2004

No Extend federal unemployment benefits by 13 weeks
Yes Pass $283.2 billion, six-year federal highway and mass transit bill
Yes Approve $146 billion multi-year extension of previously enacted middle-class tax breaks
Yes Amend the Constitution to prohibit same-sex marriage
No Cut corporate taxes $137 billion over 10 years
Yes Reorganize U.S. intelligence agencies as proposed by Sept. 11 commission

2003

Yes Cut taxes by $330 billion through fiscal 2013
No Block Bush rule scaling back overtime pay for some white-collar federal workers
No Do not allow use of search warrants without first notifying subjects
No Allow importation of prescription drugs
Yes Create private school voucher program in Washington, D.C.
Yes Ban "partial birth" abortion except to save a woman's life
No Split $18.6 billion in Iraq aid into half-grant, half-loan
Yes Overhaul Medicare and create prescription drug benefit

CQ VOTE STUDIES

	PARTY UNITY		PRESIDENTIAL SUPPORT	
	Support	Oppose	Support	Oppose
2004	87%	13%	85%	15%
2003	93%	7%	85%	15%

INTEREST GROUPS

	AFL-CIO	ADA	CCUS	ACU
2004	20%	30%	90%	76%
2003	7%	10%	90%	72%

NEW HAMPSHIRE 1
East — Manchester, Rochester, Dover

Nestled in the southeast corner of the state, the 1st covers about one-fourth of New Hampshire's land yet contains 12 of the 17 most populous communities, including the largest, Manchester.

Most people live in and around Manchester or in Rockingham County along the coast. Some residents of southeastern towns, such as Dover, Portsmouth, Hampton and Exeter, commute to Boston.

Manchester, which boasts many technology and manufacturing companies, grew slowly in the 1990s. But the city is surrounded by rapidly growing areas such as upper-income Bedford to the southwest and Hooksett to the north.

In the eastern part of the district, the Portsmouth Naval Shipyard, across the state line in Kittery, Maine, employs many district residents and has served as an economic anchor. Portsmouth experienced a big population drop in the 1990s, in part due to the closing of Pease Air Force Base.

Democratic-leaning Strafford County, where Durham (home to the University of New Hampshire) and Dover are located, gives Democrats healthy margins at the polls. Carroll County, in the northern end of the district, is a rural, GOP-friendly area that thrives primarily on tourism and farming.

The 1st exhibits a Republican lean, albeit a small one. Republicans do well in medium- and smaller-size towns, but the GOP no longer rolls up big margins in population centers such as Manchester, where city voters re-elected their Democratic mayor in 2003. Despite this, George W. Bush managed to narrowly win the district overall with 51 percent of the 2004 presidential vote.

MAJOR INDUSTRY
Health care, insurance, computer manufacturing

CITIES
Manchester, 107,006; Rochester, 28,461; Dover, 26,884; Derry, 22,661; Portsmouth, 20,784

NOTABLE
Franklin Pierce, the 14th president, was born in Hillsborough; Robert Frost operated a farm in Derry that is now a state historic site.

Rep. Charles Bass (R)

Elected 1994; 6th term

Bass is a near perfect reflection of the independent and libertarian brand of conservatism that makes New Hampshire so politically distinctive and unpredictable.

As befitting a lawmaker from the only state in the nation without a sales or income tax, Bass is an anti-tax conservative who has generally supported President Bush and party leaders on tax cuts and other fiscal issues. But he tends to be more moderate on certain social and environmental issues.

Bass is not opposed to tax cuts but he wants them offset by other cuts in spending. He opposed a 2004 corporate tax bill because, among other perceived flaws, it was bloated by inclusion of a $10 billion buyout of tobacco farmers, which he called "an outrageous use of taxpayer money."

Bass was one of 11 Republicans in 2004 to cross the leadership and support a non-binding Democratic motion intended to put the House on record in favor of making both tax cuts and mandatory spending subject to pay-as-you-go rules. Bass had earlier angered his leadership by becoming one of the decisive final four lawmakers who forced a vote on the 2002 campaign finance overhaul bill opposed by most Republicans.

A former member of the Budget Committee, Bass has backed a two-year budget cycle, in which money would be appropriated only in alternate years. He also urged Bush to veto the 2002 farm bill on grounds that it was too expensive and would help big corporate farms and "drive family farmers out." Bass owns a farm in New Hampshire.

But he fiercely defends some vulnerable spending programs, especially the Low Income Heating and Energy Assistance Program for the poor. The program is particularly important to poor families in the Northeast where long, cold winters can make heating bills run high. He has also argued that the federal government should pay its promised 40 percent share of special education funding in public schools.

Bass sits on the Energy and Commerce Committee, where he tends to the diverse needs of his district's consumers and business interests, which include defense, electronics, computer and health care companies. On the Telecommunications and the Internet Subcommittee, he supports the effort to permit the regional Bell Telephone companies to transmit high-speed Internet traffic over telephone lines outside their service regions without first having to open their local phone systems to competition. He pushed this idea in the 108th Congress, but was convinced by committee leaders to hold off and offer it again in the 109th.

Bass and Illinois Republican Mark Steven Kirk are co-chairmen of the moderate Republican Main Street Partnership for the 109th. They could find themselves on a collision course with the GOP leadership on a variety of issues, including budget reforms, stem cell research and drilling in Alaska's Arctic National Wildlife Refuge. Bass also opposed the GOP effort in 2004 to amend the Constitution to prohibit same-sex marriage.

Bass voted in agreement with Bush's position just 74 percent of the time in the 108th, differing with the president enough that only 15 Republicans strayed more often than he did.

But he agrees with most Republicans that the government often discourages economic development by saddling business with too many regulations. Harboring a fascination with gadgets that dates to his childhood, he is a champion of one of his state's most prominent businessmen, inventor Dean Kamen, who has dubbed Bass the "gearhead congressman."

CAPITOL OFFICE
225-5206
cbass@mail.house.gov
www.house.gov/bass
2421 Rayburn 20515-2902; fax 225-2946

COMMITTEES
Energy & Commerce

HOMETOWN
Peterborough

BORN
Jan. 8, 1952, Boston, Mass.

RELIGION
Episcopalian

FAMILY
Wife, Lisa L. Bass; two children

EDUCATION
Dartmouth College, A.B. 1974

CAREER
Congressional aide; architectural products executive

POLITICAL HIGHLIGHTS
Sought Republican nomination for U.S. House, 1980; N.H. House, 1982-88; N.H. Senate, 1988-92; defeated in primary for re-election to N.H. Senate, 1992

ELECTION RESULTS

2004 GENERAL

Charles Bass (R)	191,188	58.3%
Paul Hodes (D)	125,280	38.2%
Richard B. Kahn (LIBERT)	11,311	3.5%

2004 PRIMARY

Charles Bass (R)	25,414	71.2%
Mark Brady (R)	10,167	28.5%

2002 GENERAL

Charles Bass (R)	125,804	56.8%
Katrina Swett (D)	90,479	40.9%
John Babiarz (LIBERT)	5,051	2.3%

PREVIOUS WINNING PERCENTAGES
2000 (56%); 1998 (53%); 1996 (50%); 1994 (51%)

Bass backs legislation to allow Kamen's motorized two-wheel scooter, the Segway Human Transporter, to roll on federally funded paths and sidewalks in states that have approved its use. He also hopes to clear any regulatory hurdles for another Kamen invention: a powerful electric generator for homes and businesses that could provide a cheap alternative source of electricity. "We don't want technology to be blocked by the stroke of a bureaucrat's pen," Bass said.

Bass keeps chickens and a collection of antique cars, including his prize Ford Model A, on his family farm. His chickens can regularly be heard in the background when he is doing radio interviews from his home.

He was born into a political family. From 1955 to 1963 his father, Perkins Bass, held the congressional seat he now occupies. His grandfather, Robert P. Bass, was the state's governor from 1911 to 1913. Bass still keeps a banner that he says inspired him to run for the House in 1994. Made by his two children, it bears their handprints and a slogan: "The future of the world is in hands so small."

After graduating from Dartmouth, Bass served first as a field worker for Republican Rep. William S. Cohen of Maine and then was chief of staff for GOP Rep. David F. Emery of Maine. His first attempt to win a seat in Congress was in 1980, when Republican Rep. James C. Cleveland retired. But Bass was outmaneuvered by another of the state's political "blue bloods," Judd Gregg, whose father had been governor in the 1950s.

Two years later, while chairman of a company that fabricates decorative facades for buildings, Bass won election to the state House, where he served six years. In 1988, he won a seat in the state Senate, where he wrote the New Hampshire law on voluntary campaign spending limits.

In 1992, Bass lost his state Senate seat when a conservative beat him in the GOP primary. He tried for Congress again two years later, winning his party's nomination with just 29 percent of the vote; two conservatives divided nearly half of the total. In November, the Republican takeover tide helped Bass oust Democratic Rep. Dick Swett by 5 percentage points.

In both 1996 and 1998, Bass drew primary challenges from conservatives and went on to post narrow victories in the fall. In 2000, he avoided a primary challenge and took 56 percent against a well-funded Democratic newcomer, Barney Brannen.

In 2002, Bass was outspent by his opponent, Democrat Katrina Swett, the wife of the man he unseated in 1994 and a daughter of Rep. Tom Lantos of California, but he won with 57 percent. In 2004, he beat Paul Hodes, a former state assistant attorney general, by 20 points.

KEY VOTES

2004

No Extend federal unemployment benefits by 13 weeks

Yes Pass $283.2 billion, six-year federal highway and mass transit bill

Yes Approve $146 billion multi-year extension of previously enacted middle-class tax breaks

No Amend the Constitution to prohibit same-sex marriage

No Cut corporate taxes $137 billion over 10 years

Yes Reorganize U.S. intelligence agencies as proposed by Sept. 11 commission

2003

Yes Cut taxes by $330 billion through fiscal 2013

No Block Bush rule scaling back overtime pay for some white-collar federal workers

No Do not allow use of search warrants without first notifying subjects

Yes Allow importation of prescription drugs

Yes Create private school voucher program in Washington, D.C.

Yes Ban "partial birth" abortion except to save a woman's life

No Split $18.6 billion in Iraq aid into half-grant, half-loan

Yes Overhaul Medicare and create prescription drug benefit

CQ VOTE STUDIES

| | PARTY UNITY | | PRESIDENTIAL SUPPORT | |
	Support	Oppose	Support	Oppose
2004	85%	15%	68%	32%
2003	91%	9%	78%	22%
2002	85%	15%	82%	18%
2001	85%	15%	79%	21%
2000	85%	15%	34%	66%

INTEREST GROUPS

	AFL-CIO	ADA	CCUS	ACU
2004	27%	45%	86%	56%
2003	7%	20%	87%	64%
2002	0%	15%	90%	80%
2001	17%	25%	91%	60%
2000	0%	20%	90%	75%

NEW HAMPSHIRE 2
West — Nashua, Concord

The 2nd encompasses the entire western half of New Hampshire and most of the state's southern border with Massachusetts, extending from white-collar territory in the southern tier to the mountains and forests of the sparsely populated "North Country."

The district has an economy as varied as its population. Many of the upwardly mobile refugees who fled Massachusetts' higher tax rates reside along the populous southern tier of the district in towns such as Salem, Windham and Atkinson, but still work across the state line. Nashua, the 2nd's most populous city, has experienced ups and downs with industries deeply involved in computers and electronics.

The economy of the heavily forested North Country is closely tied to paper manufacturing and wood products. In the far northern reaches of the state, about 20 miles from the border with Quebec, is tiny Dixville Notch, where residents cast the nation's first votes at the stroke of midnight Election Day. In between lie smaller blue-collar towns, many of which depend on tourist dollars from lake visitors and skiers.

Once rock-ribbed Republican, the 2nd has become more competitive in recent years. John Kerry won the district's presidential vote in 2004, as did Al Gore in 2000, thanks to the Democratic lean of Nashua and the liberalism of Concord, the state capital, and the college towns of Hanover and Keene. Other population centers are politically competitive, and the northern counties tend to lean Republican.

Redistricting following the 2000 census made minimal changes to the 2nd, which retained all of its territory from the 1990s map but added the Merrimack County towns of Epsom and Pittsfield, just east of Concord.

MAJOR INDUSTRY
Electronics, computer technology, health care

CITIES
Nashua, 86,605; Concord, 40,687; Keene, 22,563; Claremont, 13,151

NOTABLE
The "Old Man of the Mountain" stone profile — the source for the state emblem — was in Franconia Notch State Park in the White Mountains until its collapse on May 3, 2003; The State House in Concord is the oldest U.S. legislative building in which both houses continue to sit in their original chambers; The Daniel Webster Birthplace is in Franklin.

Acting Gov. Richard J. Codey (D) *

Assumed office: 2004
Length of term: 4 years
Term expires: 1/06
Salary: $175,000
Phone: (609) 777-2500

Hometown: West Orange
Born: Nov. 27, 1946; Orange, N.J.
Religion: Roman Catholic
Family: Wife, Mary Jo Codey; two children
Education: Fairleigh Dickinson U., B.A. 1981 (education)
Career: Insurance company owner; teacher; funeral director
Political highlights: N.J. Assembly, 1974-82; N.J. Senate, 1982-present (minority leader, 1998-2002; co-president, 2002-04; president, 2004-present)

Recent election results:

2001 GENERAL

James E. McGreevey (D)	1,256,853	56.4%
Bret Schundler (R)	928,174	41.7%
Bill Schluter (I)	24,084	1.1%

Senate President
Richard J. Codey (D) *

(no lieutenant governor)
Phone: (609) 292-5213

* Codey assumed office Nov. 16, 2004, following the resignation of James E. McGreevey, D, and, according to the New Jersey Constitution, serves as acting governor while remaining Senate president.

STATE LEGISLATURE

Legislature: Year-round with recess

Assembly: 80 members, 2-year terms
2005 breakdown: 47D, 33R; 67 men, 13 women
Salary: $49,000
Phone: (609) 292-4840

Senate: 40 members, 4-year terms
2005 breakdown: 22D, 18R; 35 men, 5 women
Salary: $49,000
Phone: (609) 292-4840

STATE TERM LIMITS

Governor: 2 consecutive terms
Assembly: No
Senate: No

URBAN STATISTICS

CITY	POPULATION
Newark	273,546
Jersey City	240,055
Paterson	149,222
Elizabeth	120,568
Edison	97,687

REGISTERED VOTERS

Unaffiliated	59%
Democrat	23%
Republican	18%

POPULATION

2004 population (est.)	8,698,879
2000 population	8,414,350
1990 population	7,730,188
Percent change (1990-2000)	+8.9%
Rank among states (2004)	10

Median age	36.7
Born in state	53.4%
Foreign born	17.5%
Violent crime rate	384/100,000
Poverty level	8.5%
Federal workers	64,174
Military	27,982

REDISTRICTING

New Jersey retained its 13 House seats in reapportionment. The New Jersey Redistricting Commission adopted a new map on Oct. 26, 2001

MISCELLANEOUS

Web: www.state.nj.us
Capital: Trenton
STATE ELECTION OFFICIAL
(609) 292-3760
DEMOCRATIC HEADQUARTERS
(609) 392-3367
REPUBLICAN HEADQUARTERS
(609) 989-7300

District Statistics

DIST.	2004 VOTE FOR PRESIDENT BUSH	KERRY	WHITE	BLACK	ASIAN	HISP	MEDIAN INCOME	WHITE COLLAR	BLUE COLLAR	SERVICE INDUSTRY	OVER 64	UNDER 18	COLLEGE EDUCATION	RURAL	SQ. MILES
1	39%	60%	71%	16%	3%	8%	$47,473	62%	23%	15%	12%	27%	21%	1%	335
2	50	49	72	14	2	10	$44,173	54	24	23	14	25	18	21	1,982
3	51	48	83	9	3	4	$55,282	68	19	14	17	24	27	4	926
4	56	43	81	8	2	8	$54,073	65	20	14	16	25	25	7	719
5	57	42	86	1	7	4	$72,781	73	16	11	13	26	39	17	1,099
6	43	56	62	16	8	12	$55,681	66	20	14	12	24	30	0	196
7	53	46	79	4	8	7	$74,823	74	16	10	13	25	42	10	595
8	41	58	54	13	5	26	$51,954	64	23	13	13	25	28	0	107
9	41	58	61	7	11	19	$52,437	67	20	13	15	21	30	0	93
10	18	81	21	57	4	15	$38,177	58	24	18	11	27	18	0	66
11	57	42	83	3	6	7	$79,009	76	14	10	12	25	45	7	610
12	45	54	72	11	9	5	$69,668	76	14	10	13	25	42	7	633
13	31	68	32	11	6	48	$37,129	56	28	16	11	23	21	0	57
STATE	46	53	66	13	6	13	$55,146	66	20	14	13	25	30	6	7,417
U.S.	50.7	48.3	69	12	4	13	$41,994	60	25	15	12	26	24	21	3,537,438

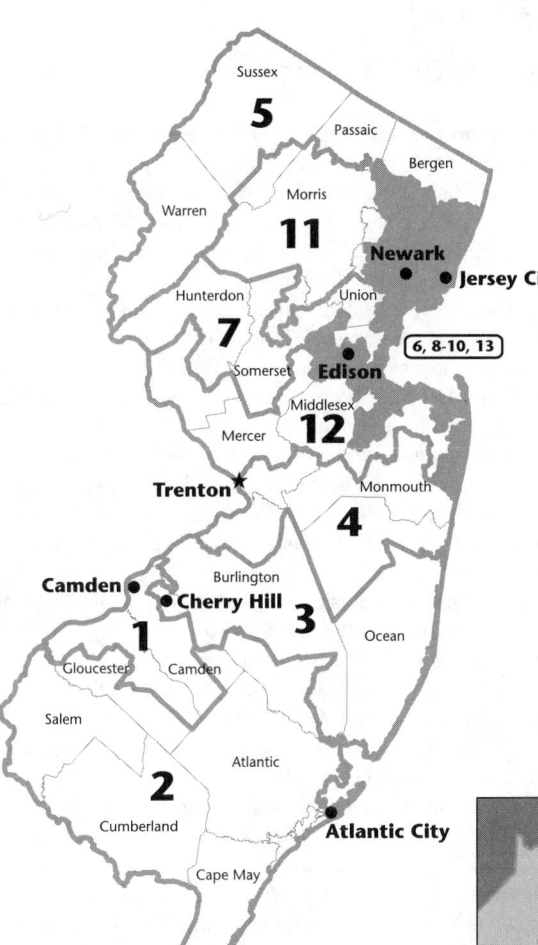

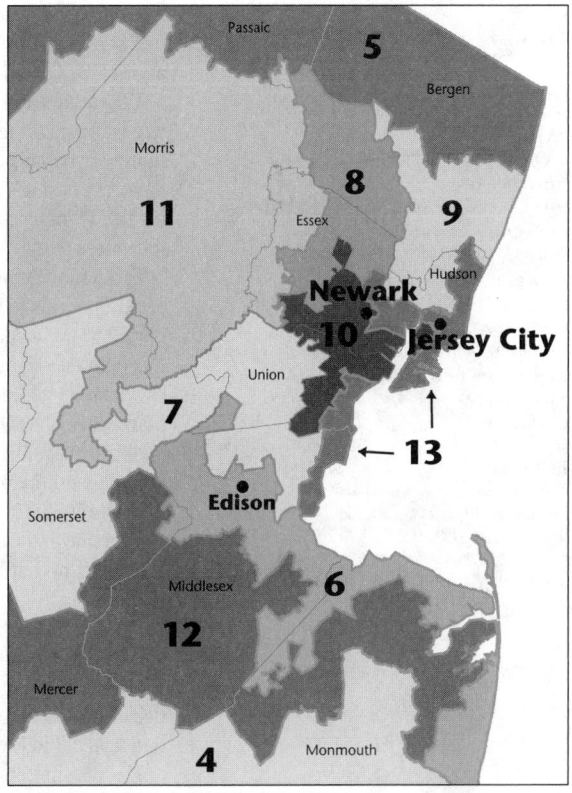

Sen. Jon Corzine (D)

CAPITOL OFFICE
224-4744
corzine.senate.gov
502 Hart 20510-3004; fax 228-2197

COMMITTEES
Banking, Housing & Urban Affairs
Budget
Energy & Natural Resources
Select Intelligence

HOMETOWN
Hoboken

BORN
Jan. 1, 1947, Taylorville, Ill.

RELIGION
Christian non-denominational

FAMILY
Divorced; three children

EDUCATION
U. of Illinois, B.A. 1969; U. of Chicago, M.B.A. 1973

MILITARY SERVICE
Marine Corps Reserve, 1969-75

CAREER
Investment bank CEO, manager; bond trader

POLITICAL HIGHLIGHTS
No previous office

ELECTION RESULTS

2000 GENERAL

Jon Corzine (D)	1,511,237	50.1%
Bob Franks (R)	1,420,267	47.1%
Bruce Afran (I)	32,841	1.1%

2000 PRIMARY

Jon Corzine (D)	251,216	58.0%
James J. Florio (D)	182,212	42.0%

Elected 2000; 1st term

Corzine holds not only an enormous Wall Street fortune but also unwaveringly progressive political views. Like the Roosevelts, Kennedys and his Senate colleague Frank R. Lautenberg, he has convinced the party faithful that, despite his wealth, he has the interests of the working class at heart. He has taken on virtually all the issues important to the business community — and taken the opposite side.

The 109th Congress marked the final leg of Corzine's first term, and he was looking to his next career move. He launched a bid for New Jersey governor in 2005 after the job came open unexpectedly. The incumbent, Democratic Gov. James E. McGreevey, gave up the office after admitting to a homosexual extramarital affair. Corzine's interest in serving as governor was well-known in state political circles, and he became the instant front-runner on the Democratic side. After Corzine (COR-zyne) announced his bid, the acting governor, Richard J. Codey, soon announced he would not seek election to the job. But Republicans, emboldened by McGreevey's downfall, were expected to put up a fight for the seat.

There was speculation in Washington and in New Jersey that Corzine was looking to go back home after Senate Democrats' disappointing showing at the polls in 2004. They lost a net of four seats under his watch as chairman of the Democratic Senatorial Campaign Committee, though he raised $83 million to help Democratic Senate candidates. Also, his party had faced long odds from the start. Democrats were defending 19 seats, including five in the Republican-leaning South, to the GOP's 15 in a year when an incumbent Republican president was up for re-election. "There was a perfect storm against him," Charles E. Schumer of New York, his successor at the DSCC, told The New York Times.

When he arrived at the Capitol, the former investment banking executive was known primarily for spending more than $60 million of his own money to win his Senate seat, a self-financing record. From his start in the Senate, Corzine's business credentials made him a natural top spokesman for the Democratic leadership on a panoply of economic and regulatory measures. He quickly established himself as an economic populist.

From his seat on the Banking Committee, Corzine joined with other Senate Democrats to introduce an early version of a bill to crack down on corporate fraud in 2002, well before the telecommunications giant WorldCom Inc. conceded it had improperly accounted for billions of dollars in expenses. Corzine was tapped by then-Majority Leader Tom Daschle as a spokesman for Senate Democrats in promoting the toughest measure that was politically possible, and he played a major hand in shaping the bill that finally landed on the president's desk.

In the 108th Congress, responding to a wave of mutual fund trading abuses, Corzine and Connecticut Democrat Christopher J. Dodd introduced legislation aimed at improving regulation and oversight of the mutual fund industry.

Corzine has staunchly opposed President Bush's proposal to divert some Social Security payroll taxes to set up individual investment accounts. In 2001, he opposed Bush's proposals for the deepest tax cuts in two decades. And he has led the opposition to measures to reduce or eliminate financial aid to low-income college students.

He has spoken out increasingly on a range of other issues. Corzine has fought to force the chemical industry to upgrade security at its plants and submit its plans to federal agencies for oversight. He has accused the Bush administration and GOP leaders in Congress of caving in to pressure from the chemical industry to avoid tougher regulation. Corzine's stance is rooted in his concern for New Jersey, home to many large chemical plants. In 2005, after a number of trains carrying hazardous chemicals derailed, he said he favored legislation to tighten standards and oversight for freight trains carrying hazardous materials.

With the 109th Congress, Corzine took a spot on the Intelligence Committee, which he hoped would help him in his quest to strengthen security at chemical and nuclear plants. He also got a seat on the Energy and Natural Resources Committee.

Although he left the Foreign Relations Committee in the 109th to take the other committee assignments, Corzine continued his involvement in the situation in Sudan, offering legislation to impose sanctions against that government for the genocide in the western region of Darfur, where Arab Muslim militias, backed by the Sudanese government, are terrorizing the black African Muslim population.

Like Lautenberg — who held that Senate seat before him, and who returned to sit beside him in the 108th Congress — Corzine is a staunch supporter of gun control. He backs proposals to license and register all firearms, ban sales of firearms at gun shows, impose safety standards on gun manufacturers, and limit individuals' handgun purchases to one each month.

Corzine is not the product of inherited wealth. He grew up on a small farm in the central Illinois community of Willey's Station. His father farmed and sold insurance; his mother was a teacher. Corzine says he took his first job at age 13 to help the family make ends meet.

After graduating Phi Beta Kappa from the University of Illinois, Corzine enlisted in the Marine Corps Reserve, where he rose to the rank of sergeant. After his active duty, he began working as a portfolio analyst at the Continental Illinois National Bank in Chicago. He earned a graduate business degree from the University of Chicago and went to work at Bank Ohio, a regional bank in Columbus.

In 1975, Corzine moved to New Jersey after he was hired as a bond trader at Goldman Sachs. He became a partner in 1980 and was chosen chairman and chief executive officer in 1994, when Goldman Sachs was one of the world's most competitive and profitable investment banks. He left in 1999 after converting the firm from a private partnership to a public company. Corzine continues to serve as a trustee of an array of arts and educational institutions.

When Lautenberg announced that he was retiring after three terms in 2000, Corzine's willingness to spend freely from his personal fortune was the principal reason he was able to win his first campaign for public office.

Corzine was not known to New Jersey voters when he entered the race, and he did not make an easy transition from business to politics. He came across as both plain-spoken and ill at ease. Yet his appeal as a fresh face — along with his big spending — enabled him to trounce his Democratic primary opponent, James J. Florio, by 16 percentage points. After 15 years in the House, Florio had been defeated after one term as governor because of an unpopular tax increase, and he wasn't able to resurrect his image.

The Republican nominee was Rep. Bob Franks. He trailed badly in polls throughout much of the race, but was able to make it a close contest with a drumbeat of themes: that Corzine was trying to "buy" a Senate seat, that he was reluctant to release his tax returns, and that he lacked experience in public life. But Corzine used his outsize campaign treasury to dominate the television airwaves, and he prevailed by 3 percentage points.

KEY VOTES

2004
- Yes Pass $318.9 billion, six-year highway and mass transit bill
- Yes Extend assault weapons ban for 10 years
- Yes Restore pay-as-you-go rules for new tax cuts and entitlement spending
- No Criminalize harm to a fetus in an attack on the mother
- Yes Increase mandatory child care funding to states by $6 billion over five years
- No Amend the Constitution to prohibit same-sex marriage
- Yes Approve $146 billion multi-year extension of previously enacted middle-class tax breaks
- Yes Reorganize U.S. intelligence agencies as proposed by Sept. 11 commission
- No Cut corporate taxes $137 billion over 10 years

2003
- Yes Delay Bush changes to Clean Air Act
- No Allow confirmation vote on Miguel A. Estrada to the U.S. Court of Appeals for the D.C. Circuit
- Yes Block a Bush proposal opening Alaska's Arctic National Wildlife Refuge to oil drilling
- Yes Limit size of Bush's proposed tax cut to $350 billion through fiscal 2013
- Yes Overhaul Medicare and create prescription drug benefit
- Yes Block Bush rule scaling back overtime pay for some white-collar federal workers
- Yes Split $20 billion in Iraq aid into half-grant, half-loan
- No Ban "partial birth" abortion except to save a woman's life
- Yes Stop proposal allowing travel to Cuba
- No Allow final vote on energy policy overhaul

CQ VOTE STUDIES

	PARTY UNITY		PRESIDENTIAL SUPPORT	
	Support	Oppose	Support	Oppose
2004	96%	4%	57%	43%
2003	96%	4%	43%	57%
2002	96%	4%	64%	36%
2001	96%	4%	63%	37%

INTEREST GROUPS

	AFL-CIO	ADA	CCUS	ACU
2004	100%	100%	47%	4%
2003	100%	90%	27%	15%
2002	100%	100%	50%	5%
2001	100%	100%	36%	0%

Sen. Frank R. Lautenberg (D)

Elected 1982; 4th term
Did not serve 2001-2003

The second time around is the charm for Lautenberg, the man Democrats called back from retirement when they were in danger of losing the seat to the Republicans in 2002. Lautenberg has the unique combination of many years of experience, few political concerns, and few prospects for leadership on a major committee. So he feels free to speak his mind and is making his mark as one of the fiercest critics of the Bush administration.

"He did not come back to be a shrinking violet," says Tim Yehl, Lautenberg's chief of staff.

When Republicans in 2004 questioned the defense record of Democratic presidential candidate John Kerry, a Massachusetts senator and Vietnam veteran, Lautenberg stunned some colleagues by dragging a giant cartoon of a chicken hawk to the Senate floor and mocking Vice President Dick Cheney, who did not serve in the Vietnam War. "We know who the chicken hawks are," bellowed Lautenberg from the well. "They talk tough on national defense and military issues and cast aspersions on others. When it was their turn to serve, where were they? AWOL, that's where they were."

Later in the 108th Congress, he demanded that Attorney General John Ashcroft appoint a special counsel to investigate no-bid contracts the government made with Halliburton Co. — formerly headed by Cheney — for Iraq reconstruction. The rejuvenated party warrior also called for investigations of alleged misuse of office and taxpayer dollars to promote the White House agenda on Social Security, prescription drugs, and the president's signature education program, No Child Left Behind.

Lautenberg is enjoying himself so much, he says he wants to stick around. He plans to run again in 2008, when he will be 84.

Lautenberg retired from public life in 2000, bringing down the curtain on an 18-year Senate career. He was summoned back when New Jersey Democratic Sen. Robert G. Torricelli was forced to abandon his bid for re-election amid revelations of improper dealings with a campaign donor. It was just five weeks before the election. The party furiously courted replacement candidates, including New Jersey Rep. Robert Menendez, a rising star in the House. But they all declined the race, and Democrats feared losing the seat to wealthy Republican businessman Doug Forrester.

Age 78 at the time, Lautenberg was perhaps an older candidate than party leaders would have preferred, but he was well-known and still popular in New Jersey. He agreed to take on Forrester. With a month to go before the election, Lautenberg was essentially excused from fundraising obligations, the aspect of congressional life most distasteful to him. The race ended in a rout, with Lautenberg winning by 10 percentage points.

Democrats were grateful, but not so much that they restored the seniority he had accrued during his first stint in the Senate. Lautenberg lost the perquisites and greater authority over policy decisions afforded more-senior members and was as low in rank on his committees as any other freshman, though he did land a seat on the powerful Commerce, Science and Transportation Committee. Had he run for and won a fourth consecutive term in 2000, he would have been the top-ranking Democrat on either the Budget Committee or the Environment and Public Works Committee. He rejoined the Environment panel in the 109th Congress, but with a ranking near the bottom. He also would have been fifth in Democratic seniority on the Appropriations Committee, where he was the top-ranking Dem-

CAPITOL OFFICE
224-3224
lautenberg.senate.gov
324 Hart 20510-3003; fax 228-4054

COMMITTEES
Commerce, Science & Transportation
Environment & Public Works
Homeland Security & Governmental Affairs

HOMETOWN
Cliffside Park

BORN
Jan. 23, 1924, Paterson, N.J.

RELIGION
Jewish

FAMILY
Wife, Bonnie Englebardt; four children

EDUCATION
Columbia U., B.S. 1949 (economics)

MILITARY SERVICE
Army, 1942-46

CAREER
Paycheck processing firm founder

POLITICAL HIGHLIGHTS
No previous office

ELECTION RESULTS

2002 GENERAL
Frank R. Lautenberg (D)	1,138,193	53.9%
Doug Forrester (R)	928,439	44.0%
Ted Glick (GREEN)	24,308	1.2%

1994 GENERAL
Frank R. Lautenberg (D)	1,033,487	50.3%
Garabed "Chuck" Haytaian (R)	966,244	47.0%

PREVIOUS WINNING PERCENTAGES
1988 (54%); 1982 (51%)

ocrat on the Transportation Subcommittee for 14 years.

The rapport between senators serving New Jersey has dramatically improved with the departure of Torricelli, no ally of Lautenberg's. In the late 1990s, when Lautenberg and Torricelli were their state's senators, they barely spoke, in large part because Lautenberg viewed his first-term colleague as insufficiently deferential and overly brash. Lobbyists complained that straightforward parochial issues were going unacknowledged because the two would not sign off on them together.

Lautenberg has more in common with fellow Democrat Jon Corzine, the state's senior senator. Both are self-made millionaires and have reliably liberal voting records. Corzine asked Lautenberg to chair his 2005 campaign for governor of New Jersey.

During his first Senate tenure, Lautenberg was known for taking on two of Washington's most influential forces — the tobacco and gun lobbies. A former two-pack-a-day smoker, he was the driving force in the Senate behind the 1989 law that banned smoking on domestic airline flights. And he subsequently led the crusade to restrict smoking in most federal buildings. In 1997, he pushed through language barring anyone convicted of domestic violence, including spousal or child abuse, from possessing a firearm. And he won a Senate vote in 1999 to require background checks on all people who buy firearms at gun shows.

He takes more-conservative stands on fiscal matters. From his senior seat on the Budget Committee, Lautenberg gave crucial Democratic congressional backing to the 1997 budget-balancing deal that had been struck mainly between President Clinton and the GOP.

Lautenberg's popularity at home grew as he proved a tenacious advocate of home-state interests as well, leading the charge to protect subsidies for Amtrak, whose major Northeast route goes through his state. In 1998, he pressed the Clinton administration to back away from plans to lower the passenger railroad's government support.

Born in Paterson, Lautenberg is the son of Polish and Russian immigrants. His parents moved their family a dozen times in their constant search for work. His father, Sam, worked in the silk mills, sold coal and once ran a tavern. When his father died of cancer, Lautenberg, then a teenager, worked nights and weekends to help the family stay afloat.

After high school, Lautenberg enlisted and served in the Army Signal Corps in Europe during World War II. When he returned, he enrolled in Columbia University on the GI Bill, graduating with an economics degree in 1949. With two boyhood friends from his old neighborhood, he started a payroll services company, Automatic Data Processing, and turned it into one of the world's largest computing services companies.

While the business grew, Lautenberg dabbled in politics as a Democratic activist and fundraiser. His $90,000 contribution to George McGovern's 1972 campaign earned him a place on President Nixon's enemies list.

In 1982, he decided to run for the open New Jersey Senate seat after veteran Democratic incumbent Harrison A. Williams Jr. was convicted in the Abscam corruption probe. Spending $4 million of his own money, an unusually large sum in that era, Lautenberg took 51 percent of the vote to defeat Republican Rep. Millicent Fenwick.

In 1988, he won with 54 percent against an aggressive challenge from Republican Pete Dawkins, once the Army's youngest brigadier general. Lautenberg survived the 1994 GOP tide with a 3 percentage point victory over conservative state Assembly Speaker Garabed "Chuck" Haytaian.

He declined to seek re-election in 2000, saying he was retiring from politics for good. To mark his service in Congress, a New Jersey Transit commuter rail station was named in his honor.

KEY VOTES

2004
Yes Pass $318.9 billion, six-year highway and mass transit bill
Yes Extend assault weapons ban for 10 years
Yes Restore pay-as-you-go rules for new tax cuts and entitlement spending
No Criminalize harm to a fetus in an attack on the mother
Yes Increase mandatory child care funding to states by $6 billion over five years
No Amend the Constitution to prohibit same-sex marriage
Yes Approve $146 billion multi-year extension of previously enacted middle-class tax breaks
Yes Reorganize U.S. intelligence agencies as proposed by Sept. 11 commission
? Cut corporate taxes $137 billion over 10 years

2003
Yes Delay Bush changes to Clean Air Act
No Allow confirmation vote on Miguel A. Estrada to the U.S. Court of Appeals for the D.C. Circuit
Yes Block a Bush proposal opening Alaska's Arctic National Wildlife Refuge to oil drilling
Yes Limit size of Bush's proposed tax cut to $350 billion through fiscal 2013
Yes Overhaul Medicare and create prescription drug benefit
Yes Block Bush rule scaling back overtime pay for some white-collar federal workers
Yes Split $20 billion in Iraq aid into half-grant, half-loan
No Ban "partial birth" abortion except to save a woman's life
Yes Stop proposal allowing travel to Cuba
No Allow final vote on energy policy overhaul

CQ VOTE STUDIES

	PARTY UNITY		PRESIDENTIAL SUPPORT	
	Support	Oppose	Support	Oppose
2004	96%	4%	57%	43%
2003	97%	3%	44%	56%
2000	98%	2%	98%	2%
1999	96%	4%	93%	7%
1998	97%	3%	90%	10%
1997	94%	6%	87%	13%
1996	93%	7%	90%	10%
1995	94%	6%	87%	13%
1994	84%	16%	82%	18%
1993	86%	14%	85%	15%

INTEREST GROUPS

	AFL-CIO	ADA	CCUS	ACU
2004	100%	100%	38%	0%
2003	100%	95%	26%	15%
2000	75%	90%	46%	4%
1999	78%	100%	44%	0%
1998	88%	95%	50%	4%
1997	71%	95%	60%	0%
1996	100%	95%	15%	0%
1995	100%	100%	16%	0%
1994	88%	95%	30%	4%
1993	82%	95%	45%	24%

Rep. Robert E. Andrews (D)

Elected 1990; 8th full term

CAPITOL OFFICE
225-6501
www.house.gov/andrews
2439 Rayburn 20515-3001; fax 225-6583

COMMITTEES
Armed Services
Education & Workforce

HOMETOWN
Haddon Heights

BORN
Aug. 4, 1957, Camden, N.J.

RELIGION
Episcopalian

FAMILY
Wife, Camille Spinello Andrews; two children

EDUCATION
Bucknell U., B.A. 1979 (political science); Cornell U., J.D. 1982

CAREER
Lawyer; professor

POLITICAL HIGHLIGHTS
Camden County Board of Freeholders, 1987-90 (director, 1988-90); sought Democratic nomination for governor, 1997

ELECTION RESULTS

2004 GENERAL

Robert E. Andrews (D)	201,163	75.0%
S. Daniel Hutchison (R)	66,109	24.7%

2004 PRIMARY

Robert E. Andrews (D)	unopposed

2002 GENERAL

Robert E. Andrews (D)	121,846	92.7%
Timothy Haas (LIBERT)	9,543	7.3%

PREVIOUS WINNING PERCENTAGES
2000 (76%); 1998 (73%); 1996 (76%); 1994 (72%); 1992 (67%); 1990 (54%); 1990 Special Election (55%)

Andrews, who has earned a reputation as a smart, fresh-thinking lawmaker who can frame classic Democratic arguments in new ways, keeps looking for ways to move up in New Jersey politics. He could be trying again soon — this time for the Senate. Or perhaps not; the choice is not entirely his to make.

Andrews in early 2005 bypassed a second chance to run for New Jersey's Democratic gubernatorial nomination, instead endorsing Democratic Sen. Jon Corzine, who would, if elected, appoint his own successor. His move helped convince acting Gov. Richard J. Codey to abandon any thought of a primary contest against Corzine. Codey had become governor after Democrat James E. McGreevey was forced to resign following a personal scandal that emerged in 2004.

Andrews and McGreevey had been rivals for years; the congressman was bitterly disappointed when he narrowly lost the gubernatorial nomination to McGreevey in 1997. By helping Corzine, Andrews may have opened a path to the Senate instead. But others in the New Jersey delegation covet the seat, too, including Frank Pallone Jr., who endorsed Corzine before Andrews did.

Andrews' willingness to defer to Corzine, and his rising standing in the party on Capitol Hill, contrast with an early reputation he built as a talented but power-hungry lone wolf with his own agenda. After his 1997 loss to McGreevey, he withdrew for a time from party politics and had harsh words not only for some party leaders but for the political system, saying that "people who control vast sums of money have undue leverage." But since then, he has worked more actively with others on core issues and become more vocal in Democratic Caucus meetings, where he is credited with insightful arguments that have helped fine-tune party positions.

As Congress takes on the hot-button issue of Social Security, Andrews is determined to play a strong role in the debate. He will also have a chance to influence an anticipated overhaul of the private pension system from his seat on the Education and Workforce Committee. He is the top-ranking Democrat on the panel's Subcommittee on Employer-Employee Relations.

In the summer of 2004, Andrews showed an interest in trying to bridge the partisan divide on some pension issues. At a hearing, he said most lawmakers agree that workers should have a choice of staying with a traditional defined pension plan or switching to a "cash-balance" plan, but said steps needed to be taken to avoid hurting older workers. He maintained that converting standard pensions to cash-balance plans required caution because "it's the only kind of pension change I can think of where the employee might wind up poorer than he might otherwise be."

Andrews took the lead on another important issue, opposing a Republican bill to allow businesses to offer their workers access to professional investment advice for their retirement savings. He sponsored an alternative that would have required firms with a conflict of interest to refer workers to another firm for advice. His plan was defeated, and the Republican bill passed, but the Senate never acted.

Andrews also was a member of the conference committee that wrote the final version of the sweeping education overhaul bill in 2001.

Andrews was an early advocate of the creation of a House committee to oversee the Department of Homeland Security, and in the 108th Congress, when such a panel was formed, Andrews took a leave of absence from the

Armed Services Committee to serve on it. He gave up the seat in the 109th, returning to Armed Services. He is somewhat hawkish on foreign policy, and supported the U.S. invasion of Iraq.

Andrews does not schmooze with his colleagues very much, but he is pleasant and approachable and displays a dry sense of humor. "I guess they want to build a mud castle," he once said of a Delaware River dredging project that would have deposited most of the sludge in his district. At night, he usually takes the train home to Haddon Heights to be with his wife and two young daughters; he says they have been instrumental in making him less of a workaholic.

The son of a former shipyard worker, Andrews generally takes the side of organized labor, opposing free-trade agreements he says could cost U.S. workers their jobs. He is a fairly conventional Northeastern Democrat, supporting environmental protection, abortion rights and gun control.

When Andrews was a 14-year-old in the Jersey suburbs of Philadelphia, his father lost his shipyard job. His mother went to work as a secretary, and his father eventually got a janitor's job. In an interview with Gannett News Service, Andrews recalled telling his newly unemployed father: "Maybe there's someone in the government who could help you." When his father dismissed the suggestion as unlikely, Andrews remembers thinking: "What were they doing, if not helping people like him?"

The first in his family to go to college, Andrews was a teaching assistant in his senior year at Bucknell and wrote this question as the entire final exam for an introductory political science class: "Politics is everything. Explain."

After a half-dozen years practicing law, Andrews at age 29 won a seat on the Camden County governing board. He became known as a young reformer and two years later was chosen to head the board.

He was a protégé of liberal Democratic Rep. James J. Florio. After Florio was elected governor in 1989, Andrews took his place in the House, winning a 1990 special election (and a full term the same day) despite voter anger at Florio over a big state tax increase that year. Andrews refrained from directly repudiating the governor but took a "no new taxes" pledge for his first term.

Andrews easily won three re-elections, making him the initial favorite in the 1997 gubernatorial race. His narrow loss has had no carry-over effect in his subsequent House bids, but the ill will between Andrews and McGreevey lingered. When Sen. Robert G. Torricelli dropped his 2002 re-election bid five weeks before Election Day, the governor vetoed the idea of making Andrews the replacement Democratic nominee.

KEY VOTES

2004

Yes Extend federal unemployment benefits by 13 weeks

Yes Pass $283.2 billion, six-year federal highway and mass transit bill

No Approve $146 billion multi-year extension of previously enacted middle-class tax breaks

No Amend the Constitution to prohibit same-sex marriage

No Cut corporate taxes $137 billion over 10 years

Yes Reorganize U.S. intelligence agencies as proposed by Sept. 11 commission

2003

No Cut taxes by $330 billion through fiscal 2013

Yes Block Bush rule scaling back overtime pay for some white-collar federal workers

Yes Do not allow use of search warrants without first notifying subjects

No Allow importation of prescription drugs

No Create private school voucher program in Washington, D.C.

No Ban "partial birth" abortion except to save a woman's life

Yes Split $18.6 billion in Iraq aid into half-grant, half-loan

No Overhaul Medicare and create prescription drug benefit

CQ VOTE STUDIES

	PARTY UNITY		PRESIDENTIAL SUPPORT	
	Support	Oppose	Support	Oppose
2004	94%	6%	26%	74%
2003	93%	7%	26%	74%
2002	88%	12%	41%	59%
2001	88%	12%	35%	65%
2000	88%	12%	75%	25%

INTEREST GROUPS

	AFL-CIO	ADA	CCUS	ACU
2004	93%	95%	24%	0%
2003	100%	75%	38%	16%
2002	89%	90%	32%	8%
2001	100%	90%	41%	20%
2000	90%	75%	38%	20%

NEW JERSEY 1
Southwest – Camden, Pennsauken

Across the Delaware River from Philadelphia, in southwestern New Jersey, the 1st is a Democratic stronghold. The largest concentration of its population lives in the troubled city of Camden, one of the poorest in the nation. Almost two-thirds of the district's residents live in Camden County, with most of the rest in Gloucester County and a handful in the southwestern edge of Burlington County.

For decades, Camden has been plagued by the departure of residents and businesses, a shrinking tax base, surging unemployment and crime, particularly drug trafficking. A research firm named Camden the most dangerous city in the United States in 2005. The state government assumed control of the city's finances and in 2002 approved a $175 million plan to redevelop and revitalize the area.

There are some good signs for the city. A 25,000-seat outdoor amphitheater and an aquarium, which is expanding, have attracted more tourists to Camden's waterfront, which is starting to generate interest from corporations, thanks in part to tax incentives set up by the state.

The city also joined its port facilities with Philadelphia's to create one of the largest on the Eastern Seaboard, and the EPA launched a redevelopment initiative to clean up industrial waste. Camden also is home to the Campbell Soup Company.

As distressed as the city is, the southern suburbs that fill out the 1st — like Gloucester and Collingswood — are developing. Voorhees Township also grew at a steady clip in the 1990s.

Blacks and Hispanics form a majority of the population in Camden, while many whites live in the surrounding suburbs. Overall, blacks make up 16 percent of district residents and Hispanics total 8 percent. The 1st has a large working-class contingent, and John Kerry took 60 percent of the vote here in the 2004 presidential election.

MAJOR INDUSTRY
Shipping, manufacturing, education, health care

CITIES
Camden, 79,904; Pennsauken (unincorporated), 35,737; Glassboro, 19,068; Lindenwold, 17,414

NOTABLE
Poet Walt Whitman lived in Camden at the time of his death.

Rep. Frank A. LoBiondo (R)

Elected 1994; 6th term

CAPITOL OFFICE
225-6572
www.house.gov/lobiondo
225 Cannon 20515-3002; fax 225-3318

COMMITTEES
Armed Services
Transportation & Infrastructure
  (Coast Guard & Maritime Transportation -
  chairman)

HOMETOWN
Ventnor

BORN
May 12, 1946, Bridgeton, N.J.

RELIGION
Roman Catholic

FAMILY
Wife, Tina Ercole; two children

EDUCATION
Saint Joseph's U., B.S. 1968 (business administration)

CAREER
Trucking company operations manager

POLITICAL HIGHLIGHTS
Cumberland County Board of Freeholders, 1985-87;
N.J. Assembly, 1988-94; Republican nominee for
U.S. House, 1992

ELECTION RESULTS

2004 GENERAL

Frank A. LoBiondo (R)	172,779	65.1%
Timothy J. Robb (D)	86,792	32.7%

2004 PRIMARY

Frank A. LoBiondo (R)	unopposed

2002 GENERAL

Frank A. LoBiondo (R)	116,834	69.2%
Steven A. Farkas (D)	47,735	28.3%
Roger Merle (LIBERT)	1,739	1.0%
Michael J. Matthews (GREEN)	1,720	1.0%

PREVIOUS WINNING PERCENTAGES
2000 (66%); 1998 (66%); 1996 (60%); 1994 (65%)

Like a lot of other Republicans who made term limit pledges when they first ran for Congress, LoBiondo has changed his mind about an initial vow to serve no more than 12 years in the House. But he made sure he told constituents of that change of heart well in advance of his original departure date at the end of the 109th Congress.

"I didn't fully understand what personal relationships and seniority could mean to the district," he told The Associated Press in 2003, when he said he no longer planned to observe his self-imposed term limit. New Jersey Democrats criticized his decision, predictably, but voters showed no discernible concern about it, re-electing him in 2004 by a wide margin.

In 2001, LoBiondo (lo-bee-ON-dough) began to capitalize on the seniority he was accumulating, taking the gavel of the Transportation Committee's Coast Guard and Maritime Transportation Subcommittee. That position gives him oversight of the Coast Guard's base at Cape May.

And as chairman, he has been unabashed in pushing for more money for the service, including its long-term funding plan, known as Deepwater. Throughout the 108th Congress, LoBiondo was a driving force behind reauthorization of the Coast Guard. The legislation stalled in 2003 over a House provision that would have required the Coast Guard to approve security plans for foreign vessels entering U.S. ports. The Senate version did not have the item, though LoBiondo supported it, and once the conferees removed it, the bill moved quickly and was signed in 2004 by President Bush.

The chairmanship also gave LoBiondo a chance to get involved in the homeland security debate after the Sept. 11, 2001, terrorist attacks. He cosponsored a port security bill requiring the Coast Guard to conduct vulnerability assessments of U.S. ports while evaluating the effectiveness of security at some foreign ones.

He won a seat on the Armed Services Committee in the 108th Congress — a reward from GOP leaders who were pleased with his 2001 decision to forgo challenging Democratic Sen. Robert G. Torricelli — a move that would have left his 2nd District seat vulnerable to a Democratic takeover.

In some respects, LoBiondo fits in well with his conservative colleagues in the GOP Class of 1994. On fiscal policy, abortion and gun control, he hews to the right. The National Rifle Association has been a key backer of all of his House races. But he is more moderate than the majority of his party, and he has bucked the leadership on several major votes. He supported the 2002 campaign finance overhaul law even though House GOP leaders strongly opposed it. And he sided with Democrats in a losing effort to block a Labor Department regulation altering eligibility for overtime pay.

In return, LoBiondo has received substantial support from labor unions, who like his record on increasing the minimum wage, opposing foreign trade agreements, and backing the Davis-Bacon wage law, which requires federal construction contractors to pay workers the prevailing local wage.

Even though he ranked in the bottom 10 in party loyalty on votes in the 108th Congress, LoBiondo says he does not seek to be a maverick. Rather, his departures from the party line are simply a response to district interests. An economically diverse area, the 2nd District includes small farms and the beach communities of Cape May and Atlantic City, with its large hotels and casinos and its crime-ridden poorer sections. LoBiondo's legislative efforts include coastal protection, tourism, gambling and agriculture. In 2004, he was one of only 11 Republicans to win endorsement from the Sierra Club.

As a co-founder of the Congressional Gaming Caucus, LoBiondo watches out for the interests of Atlantic City's gambling establishments in the face of increasing competition from the Internet.

LoBiondo is a strong advocate of spending restraint and has voted against a number of programs that many Republicans support, including NASA's International Space Station. He opposes price supports for peanuts, sugar and tobacco; he also has criticized as "corporate welfare" the Market Promotion Program, which provides subsidies to companies to advertise their products overseas.

But whether he is voting against programs treasured by many of his colleagues or in favor of labor-friendly legislation opposed by most Republicans, LoBiondo remains low-key and prefers to work quietly behind the scenes. Reporters who cover him regularly say he can come across as aloof.

LoBiondo's grandfather and father, both immigrants, established a trucking company in South Jersey to transport farm produce to market, and today LoBiondo represents the district that accounts for more than 40 percent of the Garden State's agricultural production.

LoBiondo grew up in the small South Jersey town of Rosenhayn in what would be a dream environment for many young boys — working around the trucks at LoBiondo Brothers Motor Express Inc., while spending time on local farms owned by other members of his extended family. His father was involved in local politics and served as mayor of Deerfield Township. He instilled in his son the idea that public involvement, in civic organizations as well as in politics, is an important aspect of life. But the LoBiondo children also were expected to join the family business, and for 26 years after college, LoBiondo worked in the family's trucking company.

In the early 1980s, LoBiondo ran for the Cumberland County Board of Freeholders. He served one term and was ready to run for another when party leaders convinced him to run instead for an unexpected open seat in the General Assembly. He served in the statehouse for almost seven years.

Then, in 1992, he challenged longtime Democratic Rep. William J. Hughes, whose moderate image and personal popularity offset the GOP's advantage in voter registration. LoBiondo lost, capturing just 41 percent of the vote. Two years later, Hughes retired and LoBiondo tried again. He easily overcame the better-funded William L. Gormley, longtime Atlantic County GOP boss and a member of the state Senate, by tagging him as a "closet Democrat." He went on to defeat a little-known Democrat, Louis N. Magazzu, in the general election. LoBiondo has won re-election with ease since then.

KEY VOTES

2004
Yes Extend federal unemployment benefits by 13 weeks

Yes Pass $283.2 billion, six-year federal highway and mass transit bill

Yes Approve $146 billion multi-year extension of previously enacted middle-class tax breaks

Yes Amend the Constitution to prohibit same-sex marriage

Yes Cut corporate taxes $137 billion over 10 years

Yes Reorganize U.S. intelligence agencies as proposed by Sept. 11 commission

2003
Yes Cut taxes by $330 billion through fiscal 2013

Yes Block Bush rule scaling back overtime pay for some white-collar federal workers

No Do not allow use of search warrants without first notifying subjects

No Allow importation of prescription drugs

No Create private school voucher program in Washington, D.C.

Yes Ban "partial birth" abortion except to save a woman's life

No Split $18.6 billion in Iraq aid into half-grant, half-loan

Yes Overhaul Medicare and create prescription drug benefit

CQ VOTE STUDIES

	PARTY UNITY		PRESIDENTIAL SUPPORT	
	Support	Oppose	Support	Oppose
2004	82%	18%	68%	32%
2003	84%	16%	76%	24%
2002	84%	16%	80%	20%
2001	82%	18%	79%	21%
2000	77%	23%	35%	65%

INTEREST GROUPS

	AFL-CIO	ADA	CCUS	ACU
2004	60%	30%	76%	60%
2003	53%	25%	70%	64%
2002	22%	15%	75%	80%
2001	42%	30%	70%	60%
2000	30%	20%	57%	64%

NEW JERSEY 2
South — Atlantic City, Vineland

One of the state's most politically and economically diverse districts, the 2nd stretches from the Philadelphia suburbs in Gloucester County to the beach communities of Ocean City and Cape May, taking in much of the southern tier of the state. This is a Republican-leaning district, and locals generally support smaller government and oppose gun control. However, Democrats fare well in statewide elections and have a stronghold in south Cumberland County and in some of the district's more industrial towns. The 2nd was the closest of New Jersey's congressional districts in the 2004 presidential election, handing George W. Bush a 1 percent victory.

The western corner of the 2nd is largely rural Salem County, home to a nuclear energy plant run by PSEG. The district's center includes Cumberland and Atlantic counties, where farmers' markets and small agrarian communities grow peaches, blueberries, cranberries, tomatoes and soybeans. South Cumberland County is the 2nd's most industrial area, although the economy is shifting from glass and plastics

manufacturing to service. Cumberland and Cape May counties have been plagued with an unemployment rate higher than the state average.

The 2nd includes one of the nation's most well-known gambling resort destinations, Atlantic City, where hotels and casinos create huge numbers of jobs, but where the poorer parts of the city are ravaged by crime and urban blight. Tourism is the cash crop in shore communities, where environmental and economic issues are one and the same.

The Delaware River's busy port and one of the nation's largest petroleum centers also contribute to the economy.

MAJOR INDUSTRY
Gambling, tourism, agriculture, petroleum, manufacturing

CITIES
Vineland, 56,271; Atlantic City, 40,517; Millville, 26,847; Bridgeton, 22,771

NOTABLE
The main federal air marshal training facility is in Pomona at Atlantic City International Airport; Delaware Memorial Bridge, the world's longest twin suspension bridge, crosses the Delaware River from Salem County; Cape May Lighthouse, at the southern tip of New Jersey, was built in 1859 and is still in operation.

Rep. H. James Saxton (R)

Elected 1984; 11th full term

Saxton, now beginning his third decade in the House, is directing his energies to economics, homeland security and defense policy, issues that dovetail nicely with the concerns of his district. But that focus is more by default than design.

The New Jersey lawmaker is the most senior Republican on the Resources Committee without another full legislative committee chairmanship. But when the Resources gavel came up for grabs at the start of the 108th Congress, Saxton did not even try to claim it. He knew he had two strikes against him that all but guaranteed he would lose: He is an Easterner on a committee long led by Westerners, and he is a pro-environment moderate in a party of conservative property rights advocates. In fact, Saxton is one of just 11 Republicans endorsed by the Sierra Club in 2004.

As a consolation prize, Saxton chairs the Joint Economic Committee in the 109th and also wields the gavel of the Armed Services Subcommittee on Terrorism, Unconventional Threats and Capabilities. The panel oversees the U.S. Special Operations Command, including Navy Seals, Army Rangers, Green Berets and other elite forces.

Saxton frequently grills the Pentagon's decision-makers about their strategic choices and prods the military brass to provide better equipment to U.S. forces in Iraq and elsewhere. In the 108th, he sharply questioned the value of the Stryker combat vehicle in Iraq, saying it offered inadequate protection to the troops because it is vulnerable to rocket-propelled grenades, a weapon of choice for the insurgents. And he pressed for speedier acquisition of items like body armor. "Lives can be at stake," he said. "We need to move to a faster acquisition process during wartime. The peacetime process simply takes too long."

Saxton has long been interested in the role of the military in homeland security. He served in the 107th as chairman of a special oversight panel on terrorism and has become an influential voice on homeland defense.

As chairman of Armed Services' Military Installations Subcommittee in the 107th, Saxton championed more defense spending and advocated expanded roles for the 3rd District's Fort Dix and McGuire Air Force Base to strengthen homeland security. He joined fellow committee members in a vain effort to stave off the 2005 round of base closures, arguing that domestic bases should be retained as assets to fight terrorism. He was bracing for battle to protect New Jersey bases, arguing that the reservists being deployed to Iraq and Afghanistan needed them for training. He held news conferences, issued press releases and rallied community leaders — all before the list of proposed closures came out.

On the economic front, Saxton is a critic of the International Monetary Fund, objecting to the size of the U.S. contribution to the fund. He is known for tough questions about how that money is spent.

He is a fiscal conservative who advocates for increased tax incentives for savings. He sponsored a bill in the 107th to exclude from an individual's taxable income up to $3,000 in mutual fund capital gains distributions, and pushed for elimination of a requirement that retirees begin withdrawing funds from tax-deferred individual retirement accounts at age 70 1/2. He also promotes the use of inflation targets by the Federal Reserve when it sets monetary rules, arguing that explicit price stability goals will make it easier for the central bank to duplicate the successes of Federal Reserve Chairman Alan Greenspan after he retires. But Greenspan has opposed setting such targets.

CAPITOL OFFICE
225-4765
www.house.gov/saxton
2217 Rayburn 20515-3003; fax 225-0778

COMMITTEES
Armed Services
(Terrorism, Unconventional Threats & Capabilities - chairman)
Resources
Joint Economic - chairman

HOMETOWN
Mount Holly

BORN
Jan. 22, 1943, Nicholson, Pa.

RELIGION
Methodist

FAMILY
Divorced; two children

EDUCATION
East Stroudsburg State College, B.A. 1965 (education); Temple U., attended 1967-68 (education)

CAREER
Real estate broker; teacher

POLITICAL HIGHLIGHTS
N.J. Assembly, 1976-82; N.J. Senate, 1982-84

ELECTION RESULTS

2004 GENERAL

H. James Saxton (R)	195,938	63.4%
Herb Conaway (D)	107,034	34.7%
Edward "Rob" Forchion (LMP)	4,914	1.6%

2004 PRIMARY

H. James Saxton (R)	unopposed

2002 GENERAL

H. James Saxton (R)	123,375	65.0%
Richard Strada (D)	64,364	33.9%

PREVIOUS WINNING PERCENTAGES
2000 (57%); 1998 (62%); 1996 (64%); 1994 (66%); 1992 (59%); 1990 (58%); 1988 (69%); 1986 (65%); 1984 (61%); 1984 Special Election (62%)

Saxton is the No. 3 Republican on the Resources panel and one of the GOP's most prominent "greens." He has fought the Western Republicans who favor mining, logging, oil and gas drilling, and grazing on public lands over environmental protection. He criticizes the Bush administration's pollution policies. And the Sierra Club calls him "a steadfast leader" for his defense of wilderness areas, including Alaska's Arctic National Wildlife Refuge.

On the committee, Saxton watches for coastal interests important to a constituency that stretches from the Philadelphia suburbs across Barnegat Bay to the Jersey Shore. In the 107th, he pushed for new time and area restrictions on commercial long-line fishermen to protect migratory white marlin. He won passage of legislation in 2000 of a law directing the EPA to develop new standards for pollutants in coastal waters. And he has been a leading advocate for imposing tighter regulations on the noise and water pollution generated by personal watercraft.

On social issues, Saxton generally opposes abortion, but he has backed some gun control measures, including a ban on certain types of assault-style weapons. In the 108th, Saxton was one of only 22 Republicans voting against legislation that sought to repeal the municipal gun control laws of Washington, D.C. He opposed creation of a private school voucher program for the District, and he sided with Democrats in voting to block new overtime pay rules that critics said could cost millions of workers their eligibility for premium pay.

A former real estate broker and elementary school teacher, Saxton served in the state legislature for eight years before making a bid for the House. He struggled to win the nomination for the seat left open in 1984 with the death of another environmentally friendly Republican in the House, Edwin B. Forsythe. Saxton had support from the strong GOP organization in Burlington County, but he faced two rivals from Ocean and Camden counties. Saxton ran ads on Philadelphia TV stations to attract voters in Camden County and drew support from his large state Senate constituency. After surviving the primary, he had little trouble winning the special election to complete Forsythe's term and the general election on the same day.

Saxton had tough re-election races in 1990, when he took 58 percent of the vote against former Cherry Hill City Council member John H. Adler, and in 2000, when longtime Cherry Hill Mayor Susan Bass Levin held him to 57 percent. He won his 11th full term by nearly 30 percentage points in 2004 in a district slightly reconfigured in 2001 but drawn with incumbent protection in mind.

KEY VOTES

2004

Yes	Extend federal unemployment benefits by 13 weeks
?	Pass $283.2 billion, six-year federal highway and mass transit bill
Yes	Approve $146 billion multi-year extension of previously enacted middle-class tax breaks
Yes	Amend the Constitution to prohibit same-sex marriage
Yes	Cut corporate taxes $137 billion over 10 years
Yes	Reorganize U.S. intelligence agencies as proposed by Sept. 11 commission

2003

Yes	Cut taxes by $330 billion through fiscal 2013
Yes	Block Bush rule scaling back overtime pay for some white-collar federal workers
No	Do not allow use of search warrants without first notifying subjects
No	Allow importation of prescription drugs
No	Create private school voucher program in Washington, D.C.
Yes	Ban "partial birth" abortion except to save a woman's life
No	Split $18.6 billion in Iraq aid into half-grant, half-loan
Yes	Overhaul Medicare and create prescription drug benefit

CQ VOTE STUDIES

	PARTY UNITY		PRESIDENTIAL SUPPORT	
	Support	Oppose	Support	Oppose
2004	84%	16%	76%	24%
2003	88%	12%	84%	16%
2002	91%	9%	87%	13%
2001	89%	11%	82%	18%
2000	78%	22%	40%	60%

INTEREST GROUPS

	AFL-CIO	ADA	CCUS	ACU
2004	50%	35%	81%	64%
2003	38%	20%	79%	72%
2002	13%	0%	90%	92%
2001	33%	15%	82%	64%
2000	30%	20%	61%	56%

NEW JERSEY 3
South central — Cherry Hill, Toms River

Covering one of New Jersey's oldest and wealthiest areas, the 3rd crosses the south-central section of the state, while also taking in the entire political spectrum, from the solidly Republican southern shores of Ocean County to the staunchly Democratic Cherry Hill area in Camden County.

Industrial growth dominates the short strip of land in Burlington County that abuts the Delaware River and encompasses the affluent, Republican-leaning suburbs of Cinnaminson, Delran and Moorestown. Other parts of Burlington County are Democratic and, combined with the district's small share of Camden County, can make elections competitive. However, heavily Republican Ocean County gives the district a slight GOP lean. George W. Bush won the district by less than 3 percentage points in the 2004 presidential election.

McGuire Air Force Base and Fort Dix (shared with the 4th District) make defense a salient issue in the 3rd. Communities around Toms River are concerned that offshore waste disposal and other environmental issues may affect their beach tourist industry. Local officials, most of whom are Republicans, emphasize their "green" credentials.

The district has lots of wealthy elderly voters, many of whom live in retirement communities along Route 70, and has the lowest percentage of Hispanic residents of any district in the state. Municipal and school budgets, as well as tax rates, are among the lowest in the state — due in part to the high turnout by elderly voters.

MAJOR INDUSTRY
Retail sales, health care, agriculture

MILITARY BASES
Fort Dix (Army), 10,668 military, 1,955 civilian (2004) (shared with the 4th); McGuire Air Force Base, 5,944 military, 1,689 civilian (2005)

CITIES
Toms River (unincorporated), 86,327; Springdale (unincorporated), 14,409; Holiday City-Berkeley (unincorporated), 13,884

NOTABLE
Burlington County, three-fourths of which is in the 3rd District, is the second-largest cranberry-producing county in the nation; Toms River was one of two American teams to win the Little League World Series in the 1990s.

Rep. Christopher H. Smith (R)

Elected 1980; 13th term

CAPITOL OFFICE
225-3765
www.house.gov/chrissmith
2373 Rayburn 20515-3004; fax 225-7768

COMMITTEES
International Relations
  (Africa, Global Human Rights & International
  Operations - chairman)

HOMETOWN
Hamilton

BORN
March 4, 1953, Rahway, N.J.

RELIGION
Roman Catholic

FAMILY
Wife, Marie Smith; four children

EDUCATION
Trenton State College, B.A. 1975 (business)

CAREER
Sporting goods executive; state anti-abortion
group director

POLITICAL HIGHLIGHTS
Republican nominee for U.S. House, 1978

ELECTION RESULTS

2004 GENERAL

Christopher H. Smith (R)	192,671	67.0%
Amy Vasquez (D)	92,826	32.3%

2004 PRIMARY

Christopher H. Smith (R)	unopposed

2002 GENERAL

Christopher H. Smith (R)	115,293	66.2%
Mary Brennan (D)	55,967	32.1%

PREVIOUS WINNING PERCENTAGES
2000 (63%); 1998 (62%); 1996 (64%); 1994 (68%);
1992 (62%); 1990 (63%); 1988 (66%); 1986 (61%);
1984 (61%); 1982 (53%); 1980 (57%)

Despite losing his committee chairmanship and much of his clout in the 109th Congress, Smith remains a national leader in the anti-abortion movement. Abortion recurs as an issue every Congress, and every time, Smith can be found manning the barricades, whether trying to prevent federal funds from paying for the abortions of poor women, or to stop foreign aid to agencies that counsel women about abortion, or to protect the legal rights of abortion protesters.

Smith spearheaded a major victory for anti-abortion groups in the 108th Congress with the passage of the ban on a procedure that doctors call "dilation and extraction," but that Smith and his allies described as "partial birth" abortion. And while that issue is still facing court tests, it was a big win for Smith and his allies in Congress after years of trying unsuccessfully to outlaw the procedure.

Smith's latest crusade is The Unborn Child Pain Awareness Act, which requires that women seeking abortions be told that a fetus feels pain. Smith does not shy away from hyperbole in his speeches on the subject, asserting that a fetus feels "excruciating pain, two to four times more pain than you or I would feel from the same type of assault." Doctors disagree on whether that is true.

But Smith's unceremonious removal as chairman of the Veterans' Affairs Committee at the start of the 109th Congress stood as a stark reminder that even a stalwart on a core Republican issue can get slapped down if he affronts the GOP leadership too often. In Smith's case, his energetic and steadfast opposition to abortion was not enough to protect him. Speaker J. Dennis Hastert took Smith's gavel away after he fought hard to increase veterans' benefits when leaders were urging tighter budgets. He defied the leadership on other occasions, once refusing to support them in a vote on a measure setting out ground rules for debate on the House floor. Rank-and-file members are expected to vote for the rules of debate as dictated by Hastert and the leadership-controlled Rules Committee.

Smith was replaced as chairman by the more fiscally conservative Steve Buyer of Indiana. But Henry J. Hyde of Illinois, a popular Republican and a fellow anti-abortion crusader, softened Smith's fall by giving him a key subcommittee chairmanship on the International Relations Committee, which Hyde chairs. Smith now heads the Africa, Global Human Rights and International Operations Subcommittee — a panel Hyde created in the 109th Congress with Smith's interests in mind. Smith has long been active in human rights issues and also has pushed for establishment of a federal program to help victims of torture around the world.

Announcing the reorganization, Hyde said in a statement, "Under Chris Smith's leadership, the former Human Rights and International Operations Subcommittee was a powerhouse subcommittee producing major legislative initiatives including the first ever anti-trafficking legislation, embassy security upgrades and critical reforms to the State Department. Joining these comprehensive jurisdictions with authority for the important continent of Africa gives this subcommittee significant latitude to chart, reform and reshape foreign policy initiatives."

Still, veterans' groups were dismayed at losing Smith as their champion, and while Smith sought to put the best face on his position, he suffered a blow to his prestige and power.

Smith's stances — hard-line on abortion and support for veterans, labor and human rights — fit his New Jersey district's political realities and his deeply held Roman Catholic beliefs.

In 1998, he won enactment of a law establishing a federal program to help victims of torture both in the United States and abroad. Smith has continued his human rights work as co-chairman of the Congressional Commission on Security and Cooperation in Europe, an organization set up to monitor the progress of human rights in Europe after the signing of the 1975 Helsinki Final Act between the United States and the Soviet Union.

Smith has a special interest in the rights of children and has sponsored legislation to monitor child labor conditions abroad and crack down on abuses. He often refers in conversation to his own four children, whose photographs are prominently displayed in his congressional office. In 2000, he won enactment of a law to combat trafficking in women and children, who are often forced into prostitution. The statute also doubled the authorized funding for the Violence Against Women Act.

Shaken by the Sept. 11, 2001, terrorist attacks and by anthrax-laced letters to Congress believed to have originated in Trenton, in his district, Smith sponsored and worked hard to pass legislation giving the Department of Veterans Affairs a role in the war on terrorism. The measure established four centers at veterans' hospitals to research and develop responses to biological, chemical or radiological attacks.

Veterans' support has always been an ingredient in a potent political mix that has allowed Smith to win election to the House more than a dozen times, despite repeated attempts by his political opponents to paint him as obsessed with abortion to the exclusion of other societal issues. Under Smith, the Veterans' Affairs Committee grew from a legislative backwater to a prolific producer of bills to boost spending for veterans' programs, offer more job training for homeless vets and provide the largest-ever increase for educational funding under the GI bill.

Smith has secured his position with diligent constituent work. He is known to run one of the most effective constituent service operations in the House. And he pays attention to the needs of blue-collar workers and their unions. On labor matters, the environment and gun control, Smith often breaks from his party. He voted in the 108th, for example, to extend unemployment benefits an extra 13 weeks, a pro-labor position.

Smith was executive director of the New Jersey Right to Life Committee before coming to Congress, at age 27, after beating 13-term Democrat Frank Thompson Jr. Thompson had been tainted by the Abscam bribery scandal. Smith has faced only token opposition at the polls in recent years.

KEY VOTES

2004
Yes Extend federal unemployment benefits by 13 weeks
Yes Pass $283.2 billion, six-year federal highway and mass transit bill
Yes Approve $146 billion multi-year extension of previously enacted middle-class tax breaks
Yes Amend the Constitution to prohibit same-sex marriage
Yes Cut corporate taxes $137 billion over 10 years
Yes Reorganize U.S. intelligence agencies as proposed by Sept. 11 commission

2003
Yes Cut taxes by $330 billion through fiscal 2013
Yes Block Bush rule scaling back overtime pay for some white-collar federal workers
Yes Do not allow use of search warrants without first notifying subjects
Yes Allow importation of prescription drugs
Yes Create private school voucher program in Washington, D.C.
Yes Ban "partial birth" abortion except to save a woman's life
No   Split $18.6 billion in Iraq aid into half-grant, half-loan
Yes Overhaul Medicare and create prescription drug benefit

CQ VOTE STUDIES

	PARTY UNITY		PRESIDENTIAL SUPPORT	
	Support	Oppose	Support	Oppose
2004	77%	23%	67%	33%
2003	85%	15%	78%	22%
2002	89%	11%	80%	20%
2001	84%	16%	70%	30%
2000	73%	27%	42%	58%

INTEREST GROUPS

	AFL-CIO	ADA	CCUS	ACU
2004	67%	40%	76%	54%
2003	33%	30%	69%	71%
2002	22%	10%	80%	80%
2001	50%	30%	61%	56%
2000	50%	30%	47%	64%

NEW JERSEY 4
Central — part of Trenton, Lakewood

The 4th spreads across the center of the state, where the Garden State begins its transition from South to North Jersey, extending from Trenton and the Delaware River to the Jersey Shore and coastal communities such as Point Pleasant and Spring Lake.

The district includes much of the southern and eastern portions of Trenton, the state capital. While those areas vote Democratic, they do not lean quite as strongly as other parts of the city, which are shared with the 12th District to the north.

Most of Trenton's white residents live in the 4th, which includes the historically Italian neighborhood of Chambersburg. But the area is not without diversity — more than 25 percent of the 4th's Trenton population is black and 30 percent is Hispanic.

Military bases are important to the economy, but the district does not rely solely on defense. Trenton and its suburbs have a diverse range of businesses, and the towns along the Jersey Shore in Ocean and

Monmouth counties depend heavily on tourism.

Ocean and Monmouth counties in the district's eastern half dominate the geography of the 4th and shape its politics. George W. Bush beat John Kerry by a 12 percentage point margin in the 4th, and he topped 60 percent in the portions of both counties included in the district. Some municipalities in Monmouth gave Bush more than 70 percent of the vote. Redistricting following the 2000 census made the district far more favorable to Republicans with the removal of half of Trenton, although voters can still exhibit an independent streak in local elections.

MAJOR INDUSTRY
State government, tourism, manufacturing

MILITARY BASES
Fort Dix (Army), 10,668 military, 1,995 civilian (shared with the 3rd); Naval Air Systems Command Lakehurst, 523 military, 1,907 civilian (2004)

CITIES
Trenton (pt.), 37,745; Lakewood (unincorporated), 36,065; Mercerville-Hamilton Square (unincorporated), 26,419; Point Pleasant, 19,306

NOTABLE
Trenton, a Revolutionary War battleground, was temporarily the U.S. capital; Bruce Springsteen hails from Freehold.

Rep. Scott Garrett (R)

Elected 2002; 2nd term

CAPITOL OFFICE
225-4465
www.house.gov/garrett
1318 Longworth 20515-3005; fax 225-9048

COMMITTEES
Budget
Financial Services

HOMETOWN
Wantage

BORN
July 9, 1959, Englewood, N.J.

RELIGION
Protestant

FAMILY
Wife, Mary Ellen Garrett; two children

EDUCATION
Montclair State College, B.A. 1981 (political science); Rutgers U., J.D. 1984

CAREER
Lawyer

POLITICAL HIGHLIGHTS
N.J. Assembly, 1990-2003; sought Republican nomination for U.S. House, 1998, 2000

ELECTION RESULTS

2004 GENERAL

Scott Garrett (R)	171,220	57.6%
Anne Wolfe (D)	122,259	41.1%

2004 PRIMARY

Scott Garrett (R)	unopposed

2002 GENERAL

Scott Garrett (R)	118,881	59.5%
Anne Sumers (D)	76,504	38.3%
Michael J. Cino (LTI)	4,466	2.2%

Garrett's adherence to conservative ideals can make even like-minded GOP leaders nostalgic for the time the suburban New Jersey district sent moderate Republican Marge Roukema back to them every two years. Appeals for party loyalty at critical times are often wasted on Garrett. He opposed the GOP's Medicare prescription drug bill, though it was one of the biggest domestic initiatives of President Bush's first term. And he votes against budget legislation he finds onerous, though it leaves the majority party looking as though it's struggling with the basic task of financing the government.

With equally strong views on social issues, Garrett is at home in the "traditional values" coalition responsible for turning an otherwise closely divided electorate in Bush's favor in 2004. He is in a good position to press for action on the issues that engage him, such as prohibitions on same-sex marriage, stem cell research and abortion.

But unlike many of his fellow House conservatives, Garrett cannot afford to dismiss the party's centrists out of hand. His North Jersey district is in the heart of the urban Northeast. Conservative voters in farming villages and new exurban developments in the western portion of the district, where Garrett has his political base, are offset by socially moderate suburbanites of Bergen County who commute to jobs in New York City.

Though he can't often bring himself to vote with moderates, he has inched away from some of the positions he held in challenging Roukema for the seat. He once advocated government-paid tuition vouchers for private school students but now says a tax credit for private school tuition would suffice. He has retreated from his call to abolish the Department of Education and the Internal Revenue Service, staples of the anti-establishment Republican politics of the mid-1990s. Garrett sometimes stops by meetings of House Republican moderates who call themselves the Tuesday Group. "I think I'm sort of in the middle," he told the Bergen Record in 2002 after years of portraying Roukema as too liberal for the district.

On most issues, however, he votes with the most conservative House members. He is a tax-cutting diehard who believes higher taxes pose a bigger threat to the economy than deficit spending. He says the government's red ink can be wiped out by controlling the spending side of the ledger. A a member of the Budget Committee, he opposed the GOP-backed budget in 2004, saying, "We have a spending problem in Washington, not a tax problem."

A devout evangelical Christian, Garrett opposes abortion even in cases of rape and incest. He favors an exception for the life of the woman. Garrett and his wife, Mary Ellen, have two teenage daughters. He is outspoken in the campaign to amend the Constitution to ban same-sex marriage. "Our kids need strong families, and strong families work best when kids have a mom and a dad at home, engaged in their lives," he says.

Garrett avoids overindulging in pet spending programs, focusing instead on selected projects that are more appropriately areas of interest for the federal government. He helped target $50 million in homeland security spending for New Jersey, which, with its proximity to Manhattan, is especially sensitive to the terrorism threat. And he cosponsored with GOP Rep. Rodney Frelinghuysen of New Jersey a $25 million bill to preserve open space in the Highlands, a region of hills and mountains through northern New Jersey that is an important source of drinking water but also a target for builders pushing the bounds of exurbia. He otherwise gets low scores from environmental groups who don't like his support for oil and gas drilling in Alaska's Arctic National Wildlife Refuge and for maintaining present fuel economy standards for SUVs, which the groups want to raise.

State Democrats initially mocked Garrett for fealty to the Bush White House, but his vote against the president's Medicare prescription drug bill in 2003 quieted those critics. Speaker J. Dennis Hastert exerted tremendous pressure on junior lawmakers to support the initiative and Bush himself phoned Garrett to plead for his vote, but he refused.

He is the youngest of four children of an executive salesman for Uniroyal and a stay-at-home mom who, in search of a more bucolic life, moved from the rapidly building suburbs in Bergen County to a 100-acre farm in Wantage. The land today is still in family hands; Garrett's older brother raises Christmas trees. He took an early interest in civics, publishing an alternative high school newspaper that raised questions about how the school administration was spending its money. After getting his law degree, Garrett worked for midsize firms specializing in insurance, then jumped into politics at the state level. He spent a bit more than a dozen years in the New Jersey legislature, where he sponsored a widely debated bill promoting the right to carry a concealed weapon.

In 1998, he took on Roukema, a pro-abortion rights moderate with 22 years in the House. He lost the primary but got the attention of national conservative groups, including the Club for Growth, an influential anti-tax group that spent over $250,000 in his behalf two years later. Again, he lost, but by only 2,000 votes. By 2002, the pressure from the right and battles with the conservative House leadership had taken their toll on Roukema, and she declined to run for re-election, paving the way for Garrett.

Luckily for him, two Republican moderates — state Assemblyman David C. Russo and state Sen. Gerald Cardinale — wanted the seat as well and they split the moderate vote in Bergen County, which accounts for half the district's votes. Garrett swept two more-rural, conservative counties and prevailed. He had a tough general-election opponent in ophthalmologist Anne Sumers. But GOP leaders came to his aid, with the National Republican Congressional Committee spending heavily on issue ads attacking Sumers. Garrett won with 60 percent of the vote.

Bitterness between moderate and conservative factions lingered after the election, and in early 2004, Russo considered running again. But he opted out, and Garrett prevailed over Democrat Anne Wolfe, a Bergen County Improvement Authority commissioner, winning 58 percent of the vote.

KEY VOTES

2004

No Extend federal unemployment benefits by 13 weeks

Yes Pass $283.2 billion, six-year federal highway and mass transit bill

? Approve $146 billion multi-year extension of previously enacted middle-class tax breaks

Yes Amend the Constitution to prohibit same-sex marriage

Yes Cut corporate taxes $137 billion over 10 years

Yes Reorganize U.S. intelligence agencies as proposed by Sept. 11 commission

2003

Yes Cut taxes by $330 billion through fiscal 2013

No Block Bush rule scaling back overtime pay for some white-collar federal workers

No Do not allow use of search warrants without first notifying subjects

Yes Allow importation of prescription drugs

Yes Create private school voucher program in Washington, D.C.

Yes Ban "partial birth" abortion except to save a woman's life

No Split $18.6 billion in Iraq aid into half-grant, half-loan

No Overhaul Medicare and create prescription drug benefit

CQ VOTE STUDIES

	PARTY UNITY		PRESIDENTIAL SUPPORT	
	Support	Oppose	Support	Oppose
2004	98%	2%	88%	12%
2003	97%	3%	89%	11%

INTEREST GROUPS

	AFL-CIO	ADA	CCUS	ACU
2004	7%	5%	95%	100%
2003	13%	12%	93%	96%

NEW JERSEY 5
North and west — Bergenfield, Paramus

Although the 5th stretches across northern New Jersey, three-fifths of its population is packed into northern Bergen County, which is home to affluent, Republican-leaning voters, many of whom commute into New York City. The rest of the district is scenic and hilly, and includes the state's small portion of the Appalachian Trail.

The 5th's property values and income levels are among the highest in the state, and no municipality here has more than 30,000 residents. The 5th also has the smallest minority population of New Jersey's 13 districts.

Saddle River, in wealthy Bergen County, is home to multimillion-dollar homes. But Bergen County's tony suburbs contrast with a more rural, small-town feel in neighboring Passaic County, which includes Great Falls State Park and attractions dating back to the colonial era. The scenic back country of Sussex and Warren counties traditionally has been rural but grew by about 10 percent in the 1990s as young professionals from New York City moved to the area. Warren County continues to experience significant housing development.

The 5th tends to vote Republican, but Democrats are successful in some pockets, including Phillipsburg in south Warren County, the only county to lie entirely within the district's boundaries. George W. Bush did very well in the 5th in 2004 — perhaps as a result of many residents being directly affected by the Sept. 11, 2001, terrorist attacks. The Bergen County portion of the district favored Bush by 8 percentage points, and his margin was even more lopsided in the 5th's part of the three outlying counties. Overall, Bush captured 57 percent of the district's 2004 vote, his second-best showing in the state. Despite the GOP strength, most voters continue to register as independents.

MAJOR INDUSTRY
Pharmaceuticals, electronics, shipping

CITIES
West Milford (unincorporated), 26,410; Bergenfield, 26,247; Paramus, 25,737; Ridgewood, 24,936

NOTABLE
Richard M. Nixon retired to Park Ridge; The Hertz rental car company is based in Park Ridge; M&M/Mars is based in Hackettstown; Skylands Park in Augusta is home to baseball's New Jersey Cardinals, a minor league affiliate of the St. Louis Cardinals.

Rep. Frank Pallone Jr. (D)

Elected 1988; 9th full term

CAPITOL OFFICE
225-4671
www.house.gov/pallone
420 Cannon 20515-3006; fax 225-9665

COMMITTEES
Energy & Commerce
Resources

HOMETOWN
Long Branch

BORN
Oct. 30, 1951, Long Branch, N.J.

RELIGION
Roman Catholic

FAMILY
Wife, Sarah Pallone; three children

EDUCATION
Middlebury College, B.A. 1973 (history & French);
Tufts U., M.A. 1974 (international relations);
Rutgers U., J.D. 1978

CAREER
Lawyer

POLITICAL HIGHLIGHTS
Long Branch City Council, 1982-88; N.J. Senate,
1984-88

ELECTION RESULTS

2004 GENERAL

Frank Pallone Jr. (D)	153,981	66.9%
Sylvester Fernandez (R)	70,942	30.8%
Virginia A. Flynn (LIBERT)	2,829	1.2%
Mac Dara Francis X. Lyden (X)	2,399	1.0%

2004 PRIMARY

Frank Pallone Jr. (D)	unopposed

2002 GENERAL

Frank Pallone Jr. (D)	91,379	66.5%
Ric Medrow (R)	42,479	30.9%
Richard D. Strong (GREEN)	1,819	1.3%

PREVIOUS WINNING PERCENTAGES
2000 (68%); 1998 (57%); 1996 (61%); 1994 (60%);
1992 (52%); 1990 (49%); 1988 (52%); 1988 Special
Election (52%)

Pallone entered the 109th Congress hoping to switch chambers before the two-year session comes to an end. After New Jersey Democratic Sen. Jon Corzine announced he was running for governor in the 2005 election, Pallone promptly endorsed him and said he hoped Corzine would name him to the Senate vacancy if he won election as governor. "I'm campaigning to be appointed, so to speak," Pallone said at a news conference.

He's not the only one. Fellow New Jersey Democratic Reps. Robert E. Andrews, Robert Menendez and Steven R. Rothman also were displaying interest in Corzine's seat. Pallone and Menendez both weighed Senate bids in late 2002, when Sen. Robert G. Torricelli dropped his re-election bid that summer after he was rebuked by his colleagues for ethical lapses. But they demurred, and party leaders instead lured Senate veteran Frank R. Lautenberg out of retirement for a new term. Pallone also considered a Senate bid in 2000 but backed off as party leaders urged him to seek re-election as part of their push to regain control of the House.

Pallone (puh-LOAN) serves on several party leadership committees, including the Democratic Policy Committee, where he is communications chairman, coordinating the party's message on the floor. He is frequently on the floor at the end of the day, speaking out on a wide range of topics after almost all other lawmakers have left the chamber. Since 1995, he also has been a co-chairman of both the Democratic Task Force on Health Care Reform and the House Democratic Environmental Task Force.

Pallone vigorously promotes Democratic views on health care and environmental issues, addressing both topics from his seats on the Energy and Commerce and Resources committees. At the start of the 108th Congress, he gave up the top-ranking Democratic slot on Energy and Commerce's Subcommittee on the Environment and Hazardous Materials to claim a seat on its Health Subcommittee. He is now the top-ranking Democrat on the Resources panel's Fisheries and Oceans Subcommittee.

Pallone fought hard against the Republican Medicare overhaul of 2003, denouncing its prescription drug benefit as inadequate and assailing other provisions as little more than a handout to private health plans. During committee consideration of the bill, he held up a large cardboard doughnut to illustrate the Democrats' protests against a gap in coverage that will leave seniors with above-average drug costs paying thousands of dollars in out-of-pocket expenses. He also took issue with subsidies provided to private health insurers to encourage them to offer coverage to seniors, saying the GOP plan "bribes HMOs with billions of dollars in the hopes they'll provide seniors assistance, allows pharmaceutical companies to continue to charge high prices and privatizes Medicare down the line.... I refuse to force seniors to swallow this poison pill."

Pallone often portrays Republicans as determined, in his view, "to gut environmental laws" such as the clean water act, the Clean Air Act, the superfund hazardous waste law and the Safe Drinking Water Act. A native of the Jersey Shore town of Long Branch, he represents a significant swath of the coastline. His top legislative priorities usually include coastal environmental issues, a cause he brought with him to Washington from his days as a member of the state Senate, where he sponsored bills to limit ocean dumping of garbage and sewage sludge. In the 108th Congress, Pallone introduced legislation to reinstate a tax that would ensure polluters rather than taxpayers pay for superfund cleanups. And he has fought President

www.cqpress.com

Bush's attempts to scale back the number of superfund sites in New Jersey.

He has promoted continuation of the federal program to bulk up ocean beaches with additional sand. But he has opposed plans to mine sand and gravel in the Atlantic — he argued that would hurt marine life — and he and others in the New Jersey delegation have opposed a Bush administration proposal to study the economic and environmental impact of allowing oil drilling off the Jersey coast. Pallone has called for an end to the use of the gasoline additive MTBE, which has contaminated drinking water supplies. In part because of his concerns about the potential environmental damage from expanded global trade, he has opposed all major trade liberalization laws enacted since his arrival. That included separate trade pacts in the 108th Congress with Singapore, Chile and Australia.

Pallone tends to the interests of the sizable Indian-American community in the 6th District. He is one of the founders of the House India Caucus, along with several other New Jersey lawmakers. In 2003, Pallone joined eight of his colleagues in filing an amicus brief on behalf of the more than 20,000 victims of the 1984 Union Carbide chemical disaster in Bhopal, India, after a U.S. district judge in New York dismissed claims against Dow Chemical, parent company of Union Carbide.

Pallone has also taken a special interest in Armenian issues because of a large district presence and a longstanding curiosity about the area. In 2004, he and Michigan Republican Joe Knollenberg, as co-chairmen of the Congressional Caucus on Armenian Issues, wrote to Bush urging that he call on Turkey to lift its blockade against Armenia, in effect since 1994.

Pallone inherited his interest in politics from his father, who was a police officer in Long Branch and a longtime activist in local Democratic politics, including the campaigns of Democratic Rep. James J. Howard. Howard urged the younger Pallone, a maritime lawyer, to run for the Long Branch City Council in 1982. One year later, Pallone won a state Senate seat.

In March 1988, Howard died of a heart attack. Many Democratic insiders, including Howard's widow, lined up behind Pallone. In November, he won two elections on the same day — a special election to fill the vacancy and a full term in his own right — each by only 5 percentage points. He has faced several other electoral challenges since then, the closest of which came in 1990 when he squeaked by with a margin of just 4,258 votes.

New Jersey lost a House seat in reapportionment for the 1990s, and Pallone had to scramble again to hold his redrawn district. But redistricting after the 2000 census protected all the state's incumbents, and he coasted in 2002 and 2004.

KEY VOTES

2004

Yes Extend federal unemployment benefits by 13 weeks
Yes Pass $283.2 billion, six-year federal highway and mass transit bill
No Approve $146 billion multi-year extension of previously enacted middle-class tax breaks
No Amend the Constitution to prohibit same-sex marriage
No Cut corporate taxes $137 billion over 10 years
Yes Reorganize U.S. intelligence agencies as proposed by Sept. 11 commission

2003

No Cut taxes by $330 billion through fiscal 2013
Yes Block Bush rule scaling back overtime pay for some white-collar federal workers
Yes Do not allow use of search warrants without first notifying subjects
Yes Allow importation of prescription drugs
No Create private school voucher program in Washington, D.C.
No Ban "partial birth" abortion except to save a woman's life
Yes Split $18.6 billion in Iraq aid into half-grant, half-loan
No Overhaul Medicare and create prescription drug benefit

CQ VOTE STUDIES

	PARTY UNITY		PRESIDENTIAL SUPPORT	
	Support	Oppose	Support	Oppose
2004	96%	4%	18%	82%
2003	97%	3%	22%	78%
2002	95%	5%	30%	70%
2001	93%	7%	28%	72%
2000	91%	9%	77%	23%

INTEREST GROUPS

	AFL-CIO	ADA	CCUS	ACU
2004	93%	95%	24%	4%
2003	100%	95%	30%	20%
2002	89%	100%	35%	4%
2001	100%	95%	30%	16%
2000	100%	85%	30%	12%

NEW JERSEY 6

East central — New Brunswick, Plainfield, part of Edison

Wedged in the heart of the suburbs south of New York and Newark, the 6th combines industrial communities in Middlesex County with a long, thin stretch that incorporates beach towns in Monmouth County.

Like much of the state, the district was previously politically competitive but has leaned toward Democrats in recent years. A carefully constructed remap following the 2000 census added one municipality from Union County — solidly Democratic Plainfield — and most of Somerset in Somerset County in an attempt to pull the 6th further to the left. John Kerry took 56 percent of the district's presidential vote in 2004.

In the southwestern corner, New Brunswick consolidates two Democratic voting blocs — students from Rutgers University and African-Americans. Nearby Piscataway and the wealthier suburb of Highland Park also favor Democrats.

Middle-class and independent-voting residents cluster around Edison (shared with the 7th), which is home to various corporate offices and some manufacturing. Two-thirds of Edison's population lives in the 6th. Exceptionally fast growth in this area after World War II established Middlesex County as the state's leader in industrial growth.

In Monmouth County, the problems of Asbury Park, a vacation site made famous by rocker Bruce Springsteen, are an exception to the area's generally sunny outlook. Yet hope exists even here, thanks to a 10-year, $1.25 billion waterfront redevelopment plan that broke ground in 2004, and some success in reducing the city's infamous narcotics trade. Kerry won 82 percent of the vote in Asbury Park in 2004, but overall he captured only 50 percent of the vote in the 6th's portion of Monmouth.

MAJOR INDUSTRY
Higher education, technology, pharmaceuticals, manufacturing

CITIES
Edison (unincorporated) (pt.), 65,782; New Brunswick, 48,573; Plainfield, 47,829; Sayreville, 40,377; Long Branch, 31,340

NOTABLE
Edison was named after inventor Thomas Edison; The Sandy Hook Light, opened in 1764, is the nation's oldest standing lighthouse.

Rep. Mike Ferguson (R)

Elected 2000; 3rd term

CAPITOL OFFICE
225-5361
www.house.gov/ferguson
214 Cannon 20515-3007; fax 225-9460

COMMITTEES
Energy & Commerce

HOMETOWN
Warren

BORN
July 22, 1970, Ridgewood, N.J.

RELIGION
Roman Catholic

FAMILY
Wife, Maureen Ferguson; four children

EDUCATION
U. of Notre Dame, B.A. 1992 (government);
Georgetown U., M.P.P. 1995 (education policy)

CAREER
College instructor; education consulting firm owner

POLITICAL HIGHLIGHTS
Republican nominee for U.S. House, 1998

ELECTION RESULTS

2004 GENERAL

Mike Ferguson (R)	162,597	56.9%
Steve Brozak (D)	119,081	41.7%

2004 PRIMARY

Mike Ferguson (R)	unopposed

2002 GENERAL

Mike Ferguson (R)	106,055	58.0%
Tim Carden (D)	74,879	40.9%
Darren Young (LIBERT)	2,068	1.1%

PREVIOUS WINNING PERCENTAGES
2000 (52%)

Now beginning his third term, Ferguson represents a district in central New Jersey where the electorate is split almost down the middle. He carefully steers a legislative course reflecting that political reality. He staked out a position as a GOP moderate in his first term and joined the Main Street Partnership, a group of about 50 Republican House members and a dozen GOP senators whose goal is "to serve as a voice for centrist Republicans."

Over his first two terms, Ferguson voted with a majority of his party against a majority of Democrats about 88 percent of the time, in the bottom quarter of all of his chamber's Republicans. Although his support for President Bush placed him in the middle ranks of House Republicans in his first term, he parted ways with the White House more often in the 108th Congress, particularly in 2004, when he ranked in the bottom 20 of House Republicans in backing the president.

Still, House GOP leaders and the White House allow Ferguson plenty of leeway in the interest of keeping his seat in Republican control. To bolster his standing back home, the leadership gave him a seat on the powerful Energy and Commerce Committee in the 108th Congress.

Ferguson is often pigeonholed as a conservative because of his strong opposition to abortion, even in the case of rape or incest. He shrugs off such stereotyping, suggesting his critics look again. "I don't fit into an ideological box. I am a practical person. I use my life experiences to form opinions on issues," he said. For example, in January 2005, he traveled to Southeast Asia to examine devastation from a Dec. 26, 2004, tsunami and suggested that to help Sri Lanka, one of the hardest hit nations, the United States should adjust trade rules with that nation on such things as textiles.

Ferguson favors more federal aid for education and tougher federal protection of the environment, stands more often associated with Democrats. The first piece of legislation he introduced called for increased federal funding of the Individuals with Disabilities Education Act, a proposal he pushed again in the 108th. He also has urged increased funding for Pell Grants for college students and for teacher training and reading programs.

He has voted to continue a prohibition on drilling in the Arctic National Wildlife Refuge and the Great Lakes, delay drilling in the Gulf of Mexico, bar new energy leases within national monuments, prohibit the Interior Department from changing regulations on hard-rock mining and increase funding for alternative energy programs.

On labor issues, Ferguson was one of 13 House Republicans who voted against the repeal in 2001 of workplace ergonomics standards issued at the end of the Clinton administration. He supports an increase in the minimum wage and approves of the Davis-Bacon prevailing wage standards that apply to workers on federally funded construction projects.

Eighty-one people from the 7th District died in the Sept. 11, 2001, terrorist attacks, and Ferguson and his wife visited all of their families. Ferguson said he told the families he would do everything he could to make sure something like Sept. 11 never happened again. In both the 108th and 109th Congresses, he cosponsored legislation to direct more homeland security funding to areas facing the highest risks.

Ferguson has succeeded in getting federal funds for local transportation projects. In 2004, he worked to secure $3 million for improvements to Route 22, an important highway in his district. He was one of 21 Republicans to ask for increased funding for Amtrak, a very popular service in the Northeast.

With major drug companies such as Pfizer, Inc. and Bristol-Myers Squibb Co. maintaining facilities in the 7th District, Ferguson has been careful not to upset them. In 2003, he voted against legislation allowing importation of prescription drugs from 25 industrial countries. Pharmaceutical companies said those products might not be safe.

In early 2003, at a time when doctors were engaged in a work slowdown to protest rising malpractice insurance premiums, Ferguson signed on as a cosponsor of legislation offered by Pennsylvania Republican James C. Greenwood to cap malpractice awards.

Ferguson's first exposure to life in the nation's capital came as a high school senior, in the Washington Workshops seminar program. That led him to major in government at Notre Dame, where he lost a race for student body president. As a senior, he became a mentor to a 2nd grade child of poor Polish immigrants; his experience guided him toward public service.

After getting his master's degree in public policy, specializing in education policy, he eventually decided he was "more interested in making policy than analyzing it." He first ran for the House in 1998, in the neighboring 6th District, where he was helped by the fundraising prowess of his father, politically well-connected public relations executive Thomas Ferguson. Although he spent more than $1 million, he lost to incumbent Democrat Frank Pallone Jr. by almost 17 percentage points.

Undeterred, Ferguson moved to the 7th District, where Republican Bob Franks was abandoning the seat to run for the Senate in 2000. Ferguson confronted the carpetbagger label directly. "It's because I want to go to Congress, because I want to serve," he said when asked why he moved. "It's not fun to pack up your family over Christmas and move them in a haphazard way. That's not something anyone would do for fun."

He beat out three rivals — including Tom Kean Jr., son of the former New Jersey governor — for the GOP nomination. In November, he defeated the former mayor of Fanwood, Maryanne S. Connelly. Ferguson's argument that his views were mainstream helped him to a 6 percentage point win.

Redistricting after the 2000 census helped all of New Jersey's House incumbents, but Ferguson may have benefited the most. In his last two campaigns, he won by 17 and 15 points, respectively.

Ferguson got into some campaign finance difficulties when in 2003, he was fined $210,000 for improperly funneling more than a half-million dollars from his parents to his campaign in 2000. He told the Gannett News Service that he was "dumbfounded" by the fine and could have won a court appeal, but he accepted the decision to avoid further distraction and legal fees.

KEY VOTES

2004

No	Extend federal unemployment benefits by 13 weeks
Yes	Pass $283.2 billion, six-year federal highway and mass transit bill
Yes	Approve $146 billion multi-year extension of previously enacted middle-class tax breaks
Yes	Amend the Constitution to prohibit same-sex marriage
Yes	Cut corporate taxes $137 billion over 10 years
Yes	Reorganize U.S. intelligence agencies as proposed by Sept. 11 commission

2003

Yes	Cut taxes by $330 billion through fiscal 2013
No	Block Bush rule scaling back overtime pay for some white-collar federal workers
?	Do not allow use of search warrants without first notifying subjects
No	Allow importation of prescription drugs
Yes	Create private school voucher program in Washington, D.C.
Yes	Ban "partial birth" abortion except to save a woman's life
No	Split $18.6 billion in Iraq aid into half-grant, half-loan
Yes	Overhaul Medicare and create prescription drug benefit

CQ VOTE STUDIES

	PARTY UNITY		PRESIDENTIAL SUPPORT	
	Support	Oppose	Support	Oppose
2004	85%	15%	71%	29%
2003	93%	7%	90%	10%
2002	87%	13%	88%	12%
2001	87%	13%	88%	12%

INTEREST GROUPS

	AFL-CIO	ADA	CCUS	ACU
2004	36%	30%	95%	67%
2003	20%	0%	90%	75%
2002	11%	5%	85%	84%
2001	33%	20%	87%	58%

NEW JERSEY 7
North central — Woodbridge Township

All four of the 7th's counties boast long histories, with charters dating back centuries. During the Revolutionary War, New Providence residents dumped the town's supply of salt into a brook to prevent the British from taking it.

Today, the district is composed of bedroom communities that serve as a starting point for those commuting to Newark and New York City. It crosses north-central New Jersey while taking in parts of four counties, resulting in a competitive district where moderate Republicanism holds sway.

Although the western areas of the district are less densely populated, the entire 7th has experienced some corporate and industrial growth. Parts of Somerset and Hunterdon counties, once dotted by horse farms, have been developed into office parks and shopping malls. Both counties, particularly Hunterdon, have remained safely Republican.

Drug manufacturers fuel the economy, led by Merck & Co. in Whitehouse Station. Telecommunications giant Lucent Technologies is based in Murray Hill (Union County).

The district has several of New Jersey's superfund toxic waste sites, and residents tend to be environmentally conscious. Other important local issues include aircraft noise from nearby Newark Liberty International Airport (in the 10th and 13th districts) and money for infrastructure.

Redistricting following the 2000 census removed Democratic areas such as Plainfield and added wealthy, heavily Republican areas in Somerset and Hunterdon counties. The new district's lean toward the GOP was evident in the 2004 presidential election, when George W. Bush captured 53 percent of the vote. The 7th contains most of Democratic Union County, although the district's portion is highly competitive.

MAJOR INDUSTRY
Pharmaceuticals, manufacturing, telecommunications

CITIES
Edison (unincorporated) (pt.), 31,905; Westfield, 29,644; Union (unincorporated) (pt.), 27,066; Scotch Plains (unincorporated), 22,732

NOTABLE
The U.S. equestrian team's headquarters is in Gladstone.

Rep. Bill Pascrell Jr. (D)

Elected 1996; 5th term

CAPITOL OFFICE
225-5751
bill.pascrell@mail.house.gov
pascrell.house.gov
2464 Rayburn 20515-3008; fax 225-5782

COMMITTEES
Homeland Security
Transportation & Infrastructure

HOMETOWN
Paterson

BORN
Jan. 25, 1937, Paterson, N.J.

RELIGION
Roman Catholic

FAMILY
Wife, Elsie Marie Pascrell; three children

EDUCATION
Fordham U., B.A. 1959 (journalism), M.A. 1961
(philosophy)

MILITARY SERVICE
Army, 1961; Army Reserve, 1962-67

CAREER
City official; teacher

POLITICAL HIGHLIGHTS
Paterson Board of Education, 1977-81 (president, 1981); N.J. Assembly, 1988-97; mayor of Paterson, 1990-97

ELECTION RESULTS

2004 GENERAL

Bill Pascrell Jr. (D)	152,001	69.5%
George Ajjan (R)	62,747	28.7%
Joseph A. Fortunato (GREEN)	4,072	1.9%

2004 PRIMARY

Bill Pascrell Jr. (D)	unopposed

2002 GENERAL

Bill Pascrell Jr. (D)	88,101	66.8%
Jared Silverman (R)	40,318	30.6%
Joseph A. Fortunato (GREEN)	3,400	2.6%

PREVIOUS WINNING PERCENTAGES
2000 (67%); 1998 (62%); 1996 (51%)

Pascrell's focus in Congress remains right where it has been from the day he arrived: on his district. The working-class town of Paterson, the heart of the territory he represents, is where his Italian immigrant grandparents settled. It is where he served as head of the school board, mayor and a state legislator. And it is where he still has his home, a modest house in a middle-class neighborhood. So his claim to being close to the constituency he represents is difficult to refute.

As mayor and in the General Assembly, Pascrell (pass-KRELL) devoted his attention to jobs, public safety and education. In Congress, his legislative priorities include highways and other transportation projects, assistance for firefighters, prescription drug coverage for the elderly, and shoring up Social Security and Medicare. He generally backs Democratic Party positions on matters such as gun control and education funding. But he has voted for tougher penalties for juvenile offenders, a Republican-written overhaul of the nation's public housing system and a ban on the medical procedure described by its opponents as "partial birth" abortion.

Perhaps his proudest legislative accomplishment is a 2000 law he shepherded through Congress creating a new federal program to direct hundreds of millions of dollars to hire, train and equip local firefighters. He won reauthorization of the program in 2004. He also sponsored a measure in 2001 to provide federal mortgage assistance to volunteer firefighters and introduced a bill to require colleges receiving federal funds to publish fire safety reports.

After the Sept. 11, 2001, terrorist attacks on the World Trade Center and the Pentagon, Pascrell proposed a bill to allow taxpayers to designate $3 of their federal tax payment to fund homeland security efforts. He chaired a House Democratic bioterrorism task force established after the attacks. Appointed to the Homeland Security Committee in the 108th Congress, he became top-ranking Democrat in the 109th of the panel's Emergency Preparedness, Science, and Technology Subcommittee, where he champions more funding for firefighters and other first-responders.

Also a member of the Transportation and Infrastructure Committee, Pascrell made sure the six-year surface transportation bill passed by the House in the 109th Congress contained funding for road and bridge projects in the 8th District. And he won adoption of a House floor amendment allowing New Jersey and other states to ban companies that have donated to political candidates or parties from participating in federal highway contracts. New Jersey, fighting corruption allegations, had enacted legislation barring award of state contracts worth more than $17,500 to those who had donated to state or county political parties in the previous 18 months.

An Army veteran, Pascrell sponsored legislation to require the Veterans Affairs Department to more fully inform veterans of available federal benefits, and a bill to exempt small businesses owned by recently discharged veterans from paying certain loan fees. He leaped to the defense of New Jersey Republican Christopher H. Smith, an ardent advocate of increased funding for veterans' programs, when House GOP leaders stripped Smith of the Veterans' Affairs Committee chairmanship at the start of the 109th Congress. "At a time of war, firing the chief advocate for veterans is the wrong signal to send to our fighting men and women," Pascrell said. "For the Republican leadership in the House of the people to arbitrarily remove Congressman Smith as chairman is an outright abomination. Because

www.cqpress.com

Chris is his own person and speaks out on issues, he should be commended."

Inspired by the plight of a constituent, Pascrell was a co-founder in 2001 of the Congressional Brain Injury Task Force, a bipartisan effort to steer federal funding to brain injury research and heighten awareness of the more than 1 million traumatic brain injuries that occur in the United States every year. As co-chairmen of the group, he and Republican Todd R. Platts of Pennsylvania introduced a resolution in 2005 to designate a National Brain Injury Awareness Month.

Pascrell, whose father worked for the railroad, was the first member of his family to go to high school, and his neighborhood pals razzed him when he went off to college. He worked his way through Fordham University, earning a bachelor's degree in journalism and a master's in philosophy. Pascrell then embarked on a 12-year career as a high school teacher in neighboring Paramus, and along the way did a stint in the Army. In 1974, he began working for the city of Paterson, first as director of the public works department and then heading up the planning and development office. At the same time, he got involved in local politics, as a campaign volunteer for Democratic Rep. Robert A. Roe and others. He was appointed to the Paterson Board of Education and was eventually elected its president.

He won a seat in the state General Assembly in 1987 and simultaneously served as mayor of Paterson beginning in 1990. As mayor, Pascrell promoted tough law enforcement measures, particularly in drug trafficking. To make it more difficult for dealers to communicate with their customers, he personally ripped out the lines and receivers of pay telephones that had not been issued a city permit. In 1996, his New Jersey mayoral colleagues of both parties elected him "mayor of the year."

Pascrell was his party's choice to take on Rep. Bill Martini in 1996, two years after the freshman Republican's narrow victory had ended 34 years of Democratic hegemony in the 8th District. The national party gave Pascrell a boost, inviting him to speak at the 1996 Democratic National Convention. The AFL-CIO targeted the race as a key labor battlefield. Pascrell needed every bit of help he could get: He toppled Martini by just 6,200 votes. In acknowledgment of his tenuous hold on the seat, Pascrell immediately began amassing a war chest for 1998, which dissuaded Martini from running. Since then, Pascrell's re-election contests have been routine.

He may pursue a different challenge soon. He is one of several House Democrats weighing a run for Democratic Sen. Jon Corzine's seat in 2006 if Corzine succeeds in capturing the governor's mansion in 2005.

KEY VOTES

2004

+	Extend federal unemployment benefits by 13 weeks
Yes	Pass $283.2 billion, six-year federal highway and mass transit bill
Yes	Approve $146 billion multi-year extension of previously enacted middle-class tax breaks
No	Amend the Constitution to prohibit same-sex marriage
No	Cut corporate taxes $137 billion over 10 years
Yes	Reorganize U.S. intelligence agencies as proposed by Sept. 11 commission

2003

No	Cut taxes by $330 billion through fiscal 2013
Yes	Block Bush rule scaling back overtime pay for some white-collar federal workers
Yes	Do not allow use of search warrants without first notifying subjects
No	Allow importation of prescription drugs
No	Create private school voucher program in Washington, D.C.
Yes	Ban "partial birth" abortion except to save a woman's life
Yes	Split $18.6 billion in Iraq aid into half-grant, half-loan
No	Overhaul Medicare and create prescription drug benefit

CQ VOTE STUDIES

	PARTY UNITY		PRESIDENTIAL SUPPORT	
	Support	Oppose	Support	Oppose
2004	94%	6%	31%	69%
2003	92%	8%	30%	70%
2002	89%	11%	48%	52%
2001	87%	13%	37%	63%
2000	84%	16%	66%	34%

INTEREST GROUPS

	AFL-CIO	ADA	CCUS	ACU
2004	100%	90%	40%	4%
2003	100%	80%	33%	24%
2002	100%	90%	50%	12%
2001	100%	95%	39%	20%
2000	100%	75%	35%	20%

NEW JERSEY 8
Northeast — Paterson, Clifton, Passaic

The 8th is a diverse combination of urban centers and suburban towns that begins in Pompton Lakes and moves south through the southern portion of Passaic County into northern Essex County, extending into parts of Livingston, West Orange and South Orange, just to the west of Newark. It includes Paterson, the state's third-largest city, as well as Clifton and Passaic.

Paterson was once known for silk mills that made it a leading textile producer in the late 19th century. But after labor strife and the introduction of rayon and other materials, the city experienced a serious economic downturn from which it never fully recovered. Redevelopment projects that have lifted the prospects of Trenton and Newark have eluded Paterson, and its socioeconomic problems remain chronic. Clifton, Paterson and Passaic all have been plagued by child poverty, and Passaic's child poverty rate increased 50 percent in the 1990s.

These struggling communities have provided Democrats with a solid base in recent years — particularly Paterson, which has a deep-seated labor tradition. Overall, the district is more than one-fourth Hispanic and 13 percent black, but Paterson, home to dozens of ethnic groups, is half Hispanic and nearly one-third black.

Republicans fare better in the district's Essex County portion, which is mostly suburban and includes wealthy Montclair (shared with the 10th) and the blue-collar and middle-class towns of Nutley and Belleville. Italian Catholics make up a large segment of this area, and there also are pockets of Jewish voters in the district. Many residents commute into Newark or New York.

MAJOR INDUSTRY
Pharmaceuticals, manufacturing, communications

CITIES
Paterson, 149,222; Clifton, 78,672; Passaic, 67,861; Wayne (unincorporated), 54,069; Bloomfield (unincorporated), 47,683; West Orange (unincorporated) (pt.), 43,835; Belleville (unincorporated), 35,928

NOTABLE
Samuel Colt patented his first Colt revolver in Paterson and opened his first factory there in 1836; Toys "R" Us is headquartered in Wayne; The tough methods principal Joe Clark employed at Paterson's Eastside High School were portrayed by Morgan Freeman in the movie "Lean on Me."

Rep. Steven R. Rothman (D)

Elected 1996; 5th term

Improving the quality of life in a congested, noisy and polluted suburb of New York that also happens to have its own airport is no easy task. But that's what Rothman is seeking to do for his northern New Jersey district from his seat on the Appropriations Committee.

Rothman is a member of the Transportation Subcommittee, which not only helps him land millions of dollars for highway and mass transit projects for the densely populated district, but to rein in activity at the bustling Teterboro Airport. Because it is so convenient to Manhattan, there are repeated efforts to increase traffic there from corporate and small chartered jets. In 2003, Rothman won a ban on scheduled charter flights, which amounted to regular air service minus many of the usual safety and security regulations, and a limit on the size of aircraft to no more than 100,000 pounds. He had won earlier restrictions on noise and evening flights.

But in early 2005, a corporate jet with eight passengers and three crew skidded off the runway onto Route 46 at rush hour, injuring 20 people. Rothman vowed further crackdowns. "The FAA, who now have total control over the number of flights and the time of day aircraft can come into and out of Teterboro must understand that a new, better balance must be struck," he said the day of the February accident. "In the name of our people's safety and quality of life, aircraft at Teterboro must be reduced."

In the years after the Sept. 11, 2001, terrorist attacks, which crippled the tangled web of mass transit systems that had converged around the World Trade Center, Rothman worked to obtain hundreds of millions of dollars for the New York-New Jersey area to restore and expand commuter rail and ferry service. He also helped obtain money for light rail projects in Bergen County, particularly the Hudson-Bergen mass transit project, and for a variety of highway improvements.

He has weighed in against train noise, offering a bill every year since 1999 to give local authorities more power to regulate trains passing through their jurisdictions. While the measure has not succeeded, he did win $300,000 in 2004 for a Rutgers University noise study in Teaneck. That's the first step toward tougher federal regulations on noise.

Another of Rothman's goals is the preservation of the remaining 8,400 acres of undeveloped land in the Meadowlands, by the stadium where the Giants and Jets play their National Football League home games. He would like to see the land become a park, with bird-watching platforms and nature trails throughout the wetlands. He obtained some federal money to begin buying the land, and he also has arranged for several federal agencies to study the feasibility of protecting the rest, which otherwise would be a prime target for development.

In addition to the Transportation panel, Rothman serves on the Foreign Operations and Export Financing Subcommittee of House Appropriations. He is a strong supporter of Israel, and voted in 2002 to authorize the war against Iraq. But 15 months later, he voted against a resolution declaring that the world had been made safer by the removal of Saddam Hussein. He was one of nine Democrats making such a switch.

While praising the goals of President Bush's global AIDS initiative, Rothman questions its heavy emphasis on abstinence and marital fidelity over condom use in AIDS prevention. "Why wouldn't it be productive to know which one [method] is most effective?" he asked the program coordinator in 2005. "I find it startling you don't know which one is most effective."

CAPITOL OFFICE
225-5061
www.house.gov/rothman
2303 Rayburn 20515-3009; fax 225-5851

COMMITTEES
Appropriations

HOMETOWN
Fair Lawn

BORN
Oct. 14, 1952, Englewood, N.J.

RELIGION
Jewish

FAMILY
Divorced; two children

EDUCATION
Syracuse U., B.A. 1974 (political philosophy);
Washington U., J.D. 1977

CAREER
Lawyer

POLITICAL HIGHLIGHTS
Mayor of Englewood, 1983-89; Democratic nominee for Bergen County Board of Freeholders, 1989; Bergen County Surrogate Court judge, 1993-96

ELECTION RESULTS

2004 GENERAL

Steven R. Rothman (D)	146,038	67.5%
Edward Trawinski (R)	68,564	31.7%

2004 PRIMARY

Steven R. Rothman (D)	unopposed

2002 GENERAL

Steven R. Rothman (D)	97,108	69.8%
Joseph Glass (R)	42,088	30.2%

PREVIOUS WINNING PERCENTAGES
2000 (68%); 1998 (65%); 1996 (56%)

Rothman votes with the majority of his party on issues such as abortion rights, environmental protection, gun control and health care. He has, however, made an occasional foray into Republican territory. He was in the minority of Democrats who voted in favor of a proposed constitutional amendment to ban desecration of the U.S. flag. "People can find plenty of ways to denigrate this country and still maintain their freedom of speech, but they can do it without desecrating the flag," Rothman told a veterans' gathering.

Colleagues describe Rothman as soft-spoken and thoughtful. An assessment offered midway through his first term by now-retired California Democratic Rep. Cal Dooley still applies. Dooley told The Bergen Record that Rothman is the type of lawmaker who will "get underneath the hood and get their hands dirty and really get things done."

Rothman served for three years as a Bergen County Surrogate Court judge and has voted with the GOP on occasion to require tougher treatment in the courts of violent juvenile offenders. He supports the death penalty.

He was a member of the Judiciary Committee during his first two terms and won recognition during the panel's impeachment proceedings against President Clinton in 1998 as a voice of calm and reason. He did not excuse Clinton's behavior in the sex scandal that led to his impeachment, but he was critical of the extensive investigation of the president by special counsel Kenneth W. Starr.

A divorced father of two, Rothman is not secretive about wanting to marry again. In 2004, he took out a personal ad with an online Jewish dating service. The ad identified him only as Steve3366 and a Libra, but under profession he wrote: "U.S. Congress."

Rothman was born in Englewood. After leaving New Jersey for college and law school, he returned in 1978 to practice law. He immediately got involved in local Democratic Party politics. In 1983, he won the Englewood mayoralty and served in that post, working to balance the city's budget and reduce crime. He gave up the job in 1989 for an unsuccessful bid for Bergen County freeholder, or councilman. He won his next campaign, for the Surrogate Court judgeship, in 1993.

He decided to run for Congress in 1996, when Robert G. Torricelli gave up his House seat that year to run for the Senate seat of retiring Democrat Bill Bradley. Rothman took 80 percent of the primary vote and 56 percent in the general election. He has won re-election easily ever since, and was one of several New Jersey Democrats eyeing a 2006 Senate bid if Sen. Jon Corzine wins his 2005 gubernatorial race.

KEY VOTES

2004

Yes Extend federal unemployment benefits by 13 weeks

Yes Pass $283.2 billion, six-year federal highway and mass transit bill

Yes Approve $146 billion multi-year extension of previously enacted middle-class tax breaks

No Amend the Constitution to prohibit same-sex marriage

No Cut corporate taxes $137 billion over 10 years

Yes Reorganize U.S. intelligence agencies as proposed by Sept. 11 commission

2003

No Cut taxes by $330 billion through fiscal 2013

Yes Block Bush rule scaling back overtime pay for some white-collar federal workers

Yes Do not allow use of search warrants without first notifying subjects

No Allow importation of prescription drugs

No Create private school voucher program in Washington, D.C.

No Ban "partial birth" abortion except to save a woman's life

Yes Split $18.6 billion in Iraq aid into half-grant, half-loan

No Overhaul Medicare and create prescription drug benefit

CQ VOTE STUDIES

	PARTY UNITY		PRESIDENTIAL SUPPORT	
	Support	Oppose	Support	Oppose
2004	94%	6%	31%	69%
2003	90%	10%	25%	75%
2002	87%	13%	32%	68%
2001	91%	9%	27%	73%
2000	89%	11%	80%	20%

INTEREST GROUPS

	AFL-CIO	ADA	CCUS	ACU
2004	93%	95%	30%	5%
2003	100%	80%	38%	20%
2002	89%	95%	42%	12%
2001	100%	85%	26%	13%
2000	100%	90%	38%	12%

NEW JERSEY 9
Northeast — Hackensack, part of Jersey City

Across the Hudson from northern Manhattan, the 9th is a predominately wealthy but overwhelmingly Democratic district that takes in southeastern Bergen County before dipping into parts of Hudson County and the suburbs adjacent to Newark. The most prestigious neighborhoods to live in lie in the north, including Englewood and Fort Lee; the district becomes more blue-collar and middle-class as it runs south into Lyndhurst and Jersey City.

Redevelopment has strengthened the district's already solid economy. Anchored by the Meadowlands Sports Complex in East Rutherford, the southern part of the district has seen increased commercial and residential development. But the future of the Meadowlands, which includes Continental Airlines Arena, Giants Stadium and Meadowlands Racetrack, may be in doubt. Football's Jets hope to move to a new stadium in Manhattan, basketball's Nets are planning a move to Brooklyn and hockey's Devils and soccer's MetroStars may head south to Newark and Harrison.

The most divisive issue facing the Meadowlands is tied to the persistent concern among residents about wetlands space that, so far, has kept growth in check. A $1.3 billion office, retail and entertainment complex called Xanadu has been approved by local government officials, but faces legal roadblocks from environmental groups.

The 9th's part of Bergen is Democratic, as the county's Republican areas are in the 5th District. Englewood and Hackensack both gave John Kerry more than 70 percent of the 2004 presidential vote, with Teaneck close behind. The strong Hispanic population around Jersey City (shared with the 10th and 13th) and sizable proportions of black, Jewish and Asian voters also contribute to the Democrats' strength here. Kerry took 58 percent of the 9th's vote in 2004 after Al Gore took 65 percent in 2000.

MAJOR INDUSTRY
Manufacturing, health care, shipping, stadium events

CITIES
Jersey City (pt.), 58,129; Hackensack, 42,677; Teaneck (unincorporated), 39,260; Kearny (pt.), 38,250; Fort Lee, 35,461; Fair Lawn, 31,637

NOTABLE
Teterboro Airport is home to the Aviation Hall of Fame and Museum of New Jersey; Lipton is based in Englewood Cliffs.

Rep. Donald M. Payne (D)

Elected 1988; 9th term

CAPITOL OFFICE
225-3436
donald.payne@mail.house.gov
www.house.gov/payne
2209 Rayburn 20515-3010; fax 225-4160

COMMITTEES
Education & Workforce
International Relations

HOMETOWN
Newark

BORN
July 16, 1934, Newark, N.J.

RELIGION
Baptist

FAMILY
Widowed; three children

EDUCATION
Seton Hall U., B.A. 1957 (social studies)

CAREER
Computer forms company executive; company community affairs director; teacher

POLITICAL HIGHLIGHTS
Essex County Board of Freeholders, 1972-78; sought Democratic nomination for Essex County executive, 1978; sought Democratic nomination for U.S. House, 1980; Newark Municipal Council, 1982-88; sought Democratic nomination for U.S. House, 1986

ELECTION RESULTS

2004 GENERAL

Donald M. Payne (D)	155,697	96.9%
Toy-Ling Washington (GREEN)	2,927	1.8%
Sara J. Lobman (S)	2,089	1.3%

2004 PRIMARY

Donald M. Payne (D)	unopposed

2002 GENERAL

Donald M. Payne (D)	86,433	84.5%
Andrew Wirtz (R)	15,913	15.6%

PREVIOUS WINNING PERCENTAGES
2000 (88%); 1998 (84%); 1996 (84%); 1994 (76%); 1992 (78%); 1990 (81%); 1988 (77%)

Payne's career has been marked by an unwavering commitment to addressing the problems of Africa. While other lawmakers pursue more popular causes, he continues to fight for heightened U.S. attention and aid to the world's poorest continent.

In recent years, he has made a special effort to win new sanctions against the government of Sudan. In 2001, Payne chained himself to the gates of the Sudanese embassy to protest that country's brutal civil war. In 2004, he won House adoption of a resolution declaring the ethnic cleansing under way in the western Sudan region of Darfur a genocide and calling on the world to join the United States in taking steps to stop it. As supporters of the resolution cited the world's failure to respond to the Holocaust during World War II and to slaughters in Cambodia and Rwanda, Payne declared, "We're not going to look the other way in 2004."

Payne serves as the top-ranking Democrat on International Relations' Africa Subcommittee, travels regularly to the continent and has pushed administration after administration to pay more attention to relations with the continent and to provide more aid to the region. With his seniority, he could have chaired a subcommittee on the Education and Workforce Committee, where he ranks fourth among Democratic members. He has chosen to stick with the Africa Subcommittee.

During the committee downsizing begun by the Democrats in the 103rd Congress and continued by the Republicans in the 104th, Payne was a key figure in the successful effort to maintain the Africa Subcommittee as a distinct entity. During the 107th, he objected when Republicans chose to have Egypt — the largest recipient of aid on the continent — fall under the jurisdiction of the Middle East and South Asia Subcommittee instead of his panel.

Payne's behind-the-scenes influence reached a high point during the Clinton administration. He persuaded President Clinton to travel to Africa and accompanied him on a 1998 visit to the continent. In 2000, he helped in the negotiations that led to enactment of a law expanding trade with the nations of sub-Saharan Africa.

Under President Bush, Payne's access to the White House has been largely symbolic. He attended a state dinner in honor of Kenya's president and was the only Congressional Black Caucus member to attend a briefing by Bush after his 2003 visit to Africa; several other Black Caucus members declined. Bush also appointed Payne as a congressional delegate to the United Nations in 2003.

One of the most liberal members of the House, Payne in 2004 opposed Bush 91 percent of the time, second-most-often of any House Democrat. He works to defend traditional Democratic domestic priorities and has applied his concern for human rights abroad to problems closer to home, deploring police brutality, racial profiling and the burning of black churches.

From his seat on the Education and Workforce panel, Payne has fought to continue targeting federal funds to low-income districts, in the face of Republican plans to give states more flexibility. He argues that the nation's economic prosperity "has not spread to our inner cities," and that the government should not be abandoning its responsibility to help all of its citizens in the rush to balance the budget.

Payne is generally a low-key operator. "I would not call myself electrifying," he said more than a decade ago. "But I think there is a lot of dignity in being able to achieve things without having to create rapture."

Payne's strategy of quiet persuasiveness faced one its biggest tests in 1995, when he became chairman of the Congressional Black Caucus just as the newly in-control GOP cut off congressional funding for such groups. Payne helped raise money privately to maintain caucus operations. In 2003, and again in 2005, Democratic leader Nancy Pelosi appointed Payne to the Steering Committee, which determines Democratic committee assignments.

Payne credits much of his own success in life to an organization known as The Leaguers, and to its founders, Reynold and Mary Burch, both leading members of the Newark black community. Burch used her contacts with Seton Hall University to help Payne win a four-year scholarship to the school. Payne was the first president of The Leaguers, which celebrated its 50th anniversary in 1999. The group's goals are to provide Newark inner-city teenagers with encouragement, education and work opportunities, and social outlets.

A high school history teacher and football coach after college, Payne moved into business in 1963 as community affairs director for the Newark-based Prudential Insurance Co. Later, he was vice president of a computer forms company founded by his brother.

The head of a "storefront YMCA" in Newark in the late 1950s, Payne became the first black president of the National Council of YMCAs in 1970 and later served two four-year terms as chairman of the YMCA's International Committee on Refugees. While participating in these activities, the widowed Payne was raising his three children and building his political career. He served six years as an Essex County freeholder, essentially a county councilman, and another six on the Newark Municipal Council.

Perseverance enabled Payne to pull himself up from poverty, and it also took perseverance — and three campaigns — to win election in the black-majority 10th District. His path was blocked by legendary Democrat Peter W. Rodino Jr., who had held the seat since 1949. As chairman of the Judiciary Committee, Rodino achieved fame during the 1974 impeachment proceedings against President Nixon, but it was Rodino's steadfast advocacy of civil rights legislation that earned him the votes of the district's blacks.

Nevertheless, Payne tried in 1980 and 1986 to unseat Rodino, arguing that a black person could better represent the district. Rodino prevailed both times. When Rodino decided to retire in 1988, party officials got behind Payne. He easily defeated city council colleague Ralph T. Grant Jr. in the primary, and his November victory was a formality in this over-whelmingly Democratic district. He became the first black representative from New Jersey and has won easily ever since.

KEY VOTES

2004
Yes Extend federal unemployment benefits by 13 weeks

Yes Pass $283.2 billion, six-year federal highway and mass transit bill

No   Approve $146 billion multi-year extension of previously enacted middle-class tax breaks

No   Amend the Constitution to prohibit same-sex marriage

No   Cut corporate taxes $137 billion over 10 years

\+   Reorganize U.S. intelligence agencies as proposed by Sept. 11 commission

2003
No   Cut taxes by $330 billion through fiscal 2013

?   Block Bush rule scaling back overtime pay for some white-collar federal workers

Yes Do not allow use of search warrants without first notifying subjects

No   Allow importation of prescription drugs

No   Create private school voucher program in Washington, D.C.

No   Ban "partial birth" abortion except to save a woman's life

Yes Split $18.6 billion in Iraq aid into half-grant, half-loan

No   Overhaul Medicare and create prescription drug benefit

CQ VOTE STUDIES

	PARTY UNITY		PRESIDENTIAL SUPPORT	
	Support	Oppose	Support	Oppose
2004	99%	1%	9%	91%
2003	98%	2%	20%	80%
2002	98%	2%	16%	84%
2001	98%	2%	12%	88%
2000	97%	3%	86%	14%

INTEREST GROUPS

	AFL-CIO	ADA	CCUS	ACU
2004	100%	95%	5%	0%
2003	100%	80%	25%	17%
2002	100%	90%	30%	0%
2001	100%	100%	22%	0%
2000	100%	95%	33%	0%

NEW JERSEY 10
Northeast — parts of Newark and Jersey City

Covering a multiracial, urban region centered in Newark, the black-majority 10th provides a solid base for Democrats. Outside Newark (which is shared with the 13th), the district extends into Essex County's working-class suburbs of Irvington, East Orange and Orange. It also takes in portions of Jersey City (shared with the 9th and 13th districts) and Elizabeth (shared with the 13th).

The 10th's portion of Newark is made up of the largely black central, south and west wards of the city. The central ward was decimated in the 1967 riots and has been slow to recover. Although deep poverty continues to be a problem in some spots, efforts to revitalize the area have had some success. The area is now home to University Heights Science Park, a collaboration between three universities and start-up technology companies. Rutgers University and the New Jersey Institute of Technology have embarked on an $84 million plan to construct dormitories at their Newark branches in an effort to convince students to live on what have been regarded as commuter campuses.

A performing arts center that opened in 1997 is helping, as are new retail outlets in Essex County. Newark Liberty International Airport (a small part of which is in the 13th) is a transportation hub for travelers to New York City. Port Newark-Elizabeth (in the 13th) also provides jobs for the region.

Large area employer Continental Airlines has suffered since the Sept. 11, 2001, terrorist attacks, but has avoided bankruptcy, unlike some of its competitors. Another large employer, Prudential Financial, saw its headquarters named as one of the few targets in a 2004 terrorism alert.

The district votes consistently Democratic at all levels, though Rahway includes some Republicans. John Kerry posted his highest percentage in the state here in the 2004 presidential election, winning 81 percent of the district's vote.

MAJOR INDUSTRY
Aviation, shipping, insurance, higher education, pharmaceuticals

CITIES
Newark (pt.), 155,413; Elizabeth (pt.), 74,984; East Orange, 69,824; Jersey City (pt.), 63,725; Irvington (unincorporated), 60,695

NOTABLE
Thomas Edison's first shop opened in Newark in 1871.

Rep. Rodney Frelinghuysen (R)

Elected 1994; 6th term

CAPITOL OFFICE
225-5034
rodney.frelinghuysen@mail.house.gov
frelinghuysen.house.gov
2442 Rayburn 20515-3011; fax 225-3186

COMMITTEES
Appropriations

HOMETOWN
Harding

BORN
April 29, 1946, Manhattan, N.Y.

RELIGION
Episcopalian

FAMILY
Wife, Virginia T. Frelinghuysen; two children

EDUCATION
Hobart College, B.A. 1969; Trinity College (Conn.),
attended 1971 (American history)

MILITARY SERVICE
Army, 1969-71

CAREER
County board aide

POLITICAL HIGHLIGHTS
Morris County Board of Freeholders, 1974-83
(director, 1980); sought Republican nomination for
U.S. House, 1982; N.J. Assembly, 1983-94; sought
Republican nomination for U.S. House, 1990

ELECTION RESULTS

2004 GENERAL

Rodney Frelinghuysen (R)	200,915	67.9%
James W. Buell (D)	91,811	31.0%

2004 PRIMARY

Rodney Frelinghuysen (R)	unopposed

2002 GENERAL

Rodney Frelinghuysen (R)	132,938	72.4%
Vij Pawar (D)	48,477	26.4%
Richard S. Roth (LIBERT)	2,263	1.2%

PREVIOUS WINNING PERCENTAGES
2000 (68%); 1998 (68%); 1996 (66%); 1994 (71%)

After inching patiently up the seniority ladder on the Appropriations Committee, Frelinghuysen finally laid claim to a subcommittee gavel at the start of the 108th Congress. At the start of the 109th, he saw it taken away.

There was nothing personal about the grab-back. Frelinghuysen (FREE-ling-high-zen) just suffered collateral damage from Majority Leader Tom DeLay insisting that the Appropriations Committee be restructured and its subcommittees reduced from 13 to 10. As the most junior of the subcommittee chairmen, Frelinghuysen was a loser in the musical chairs game, along with two other "cardinals," as the panel leaders are called.

The New Jersey blueblood, one of the wealthiest members of Congress, comes from a long line of public servants dating to the Revolutionary War; he is the sixth member of his family to serve in Congress.

In the 108th Congress, he voted with the conservative majority of his party almost 90 percent of the time on votes pitting the two parties against each other. That was a notable change from some of his earlier years in Congress, when his party support was in the mid-70 percent range. Frelinghuysen sides with moderates on selected environmental, gun control and abortion-related issues, but even there he can be inconsistent. In his first term, he opposed legislation to outlaw a procedure opponents call "partial birth" abortion. In his second term and thereafter, he supported it. In 1997, he voted against use of federal funds for private school vouchers. In 2003, he voted to create a voucher program — the first ever to receive federal funding — in the District of Columbia.

Frelinghuysen is a more consistent moderate on environmental issues, backing conservation efforts and anti-pollution regulations, stands that sit well with his upscale, suburban constituents. He has worked hard to preserve the Highlands, areas of mountainous and scenic watershed lands in northern New Jersey, New York, Pennsylvania and Connecticut. The federal purchase of lands in the Sterling Forest in 1996 was due to his efforts, and in the 107th, Frelinghuysen won additional funds to set aside more of the Highlands. In 2004, he won enactment of the Highlands Conservation Act authorizing federal funds for land conservation partnerships in the four-state region. Frelinghuysen also continues to secure millions in federal funds for the expansion of the Morristown National Historical Park and the Great Swamp Wildlife Refuge, cleanups of toxic waste at superfund sites, flood protection, wetlands purchases, and the preservation of the state's 127 miles of shoreline.

Frelinghuysen has made consumer privacy one of his top issues, whether it is protecting personal information that consumers provide in Internet transactions or requiring cell phone users' consent for the location of their calls to be tracked. The first five bills he introduced in the 109th Congress all dealt with privacy protection.

Despite the loss of his chairmanship of the now-defunct District of Columbia Subcommittee, Frelinghuysen remains on the Appropriations Committee. As the only Republican member from New Jersey (there is also one Democrat), he is most responsible for securing funds for Garden State priorities. He has pursued federal dollars for local mass transit projects, New York Harbor dredging and changes in Veterans Affairs Department funding formulas to direct more health care spending to New Jersey. Since the terrorist attacks of Sept. 11, 2001, he has been in the forefront of directing federal money to New York and New Jersey, areas he argues have been proven to be at highest risk of attack.

He sits on the panel's Defense Subcommittee, where he keeps a watchful eye on the Army's Picatinny Arsenal in the 11th District. He also serves on the Energy and Water Development panel. Even before the Sept. 11 attacks and the spread of anthrax through the mail, Frelinghuysen emphasized the possible threat of terrorism as the impetus for more spending at New Jersey's military establishments, including "smart" weapons research at the Picatinny Arsenal and communications research at Fort Monmouth.

In 2002, Frelinghuysen led the fight to preserve one of the oldest trees on the Capitol grounds, an English elm that was endangered by work on a new visitors center. Some of his ancestors may well have enjoyed the shade of that ancient English elm: The first Frelinghuysen served in the Continental Congress; another was a senator and also secretary of state; one ran for vice president on a ticket with Henry Clay; and Frelinghuysen's father, Peter H. Frelinghuysen, served in the House for 22 years, until 1975.

Noting that he was 6 years old when his father first ran for Congress, Frelinghuysen observed in a newspaper interview, "A lot of what you do in life is the direct result of those who bring you up. It either drives you toward this life or drives you away."

Frelinghuysen began his political career after college and an Army stint in Vietnam, going to work for Dean Gallo, then a Morris County freeholder and later a member of the House. Frelinghuysen became a freeholder himself in 1974. In 1982, he lost a GOP primary for the 12th District seat, but in 1983, he won a state Assembly seat. In 1990, he failed again in a contest for the 12th District, running third in the Republican primary won by Dick Zimmer, who went on to serve three terms in the House.

When Frelinghuysen finally won election to the House in 1994, the victory was bittersweet, because it followed the death of his friend and mentor Gallo. Ill health had forced Gallo in August 1994 to abandon his campaign for a sixth term. Gallo anointed Frelinghuysen, who had been managing the re-election bid, as his successor.

After New Jersey GOP insiders overwhelmingly ratified Gallo's choice at a special nominating convention, Frelinghuysen sailed to victory in the Republican-dominated 11th. Gallo died two days before the November election, which Frelinghuysen won with 71 percent of the vote over Democrat Frank Herbert, a former state senator. He has easily won re-election since then, although there has been some talk of a challenge from the conservative wing of the GOP.

KEY VOTES

2004

No Extend federal unemployment benefits by 13 weeks

Yes Pass $283.2 billion, six-year federal highway and mass transit bill

Yes Approve $146 billion multi-year extension of previously enacted middle-class tax breaks

No Amend the Constitution to prohibit same-sex marriage

Yes Cut corporate taxes $137 billion over 10 years

Yes Reorganize U.S. intelligence agencies as proposed by Sept. 11 commission

2003

Yes Cut taxes by $330 billion through fiscal 2013

No Block Bush rule scaling back overtime pay for some white-collar federal workers

No Do not allow use of search warrants without first notifying subjects

No Allow importation of prescription drugs

Yes Create private school voucher program in Washington, D.C.

Yes Ban "partial birth" abortion except to save a woman's life

No Split $18.6 billion in Iraq aid into half-grant, half-loan

Yes Overhaul Medicare and create prescription drug benefit

CQ VOTE STUDIES

	PARTY UNITY		PRESIDENTIAL SUPPORT	
	Support	Oppose	Support	Oppose
2004	88%	12%	79%	21%
2003	91%	9%	85%	15%
2002	84%	16%	85%	15%
2001	89%	11%	88%	12%
2000	73%	27%	48%	52%

INTEREST GROUPS

	AFL-CIO	ADA	CCUS	ACU
2004	20%	25%	100%	67%
2003	13%	10%	93%	64%
2002	11%	15%	95%	80%
2001	0%	20%	91%	60%
2000	10%	25%	71%	56%

NEW JERSEY 11

North central — Morris County

Exclusive, pastoral estates and Fortune 500 firms make the 11th one of the most privileged districts in the nation. Located in northern New Jersey and centered in Morris County, the district has the nation's second-highest median income.

The area's voters have been economically conservative for some time, but the district now appears to be shifting to the right on social issues as well. The 11th is one of the most solidly Republican districts in the northeast, and George W. Bush captured 57 percent of the vote here in the 2004 presidential election, his highest total in the state.

After some downsizing in the telecommunications industry, office space in the 11th is beginning to fill up again. Citigroup moved hundreds of jobs to Morris County from Manhattan in 2004, joining an already strong corporate presence in the district that includes giants like Nabisco in East Hanover and AT&T. Pharmaceutical companies have found the area attractive, with Pfizer (Morris Plains) and Novartis (East Hanover) basing major operations in the district and Wyeth headquartered in Madison.

Still, attempts are underway to diversify the area's economy, which was set back by corporate layoffs. Morris County officials hope to draw tourists to historic parks, dwellings and other sites. The change comes as job growth in the area has tapered to 15 percent over the past decade after running at 122 percent over the previous 30 years, and as suburban growth has given way to faster expansion in New York City and other urban areas.

In addition to all of Morris County, the district takes in chunks of Essex County in the east, Somerset County in the south, Sussex County in the northwest and a sliver of Passaic County in the northeast.

MAJOR INDUSTRY
Pharmaceuticals, finance, telecommunications, manufacturing

MILITARY BASES
Picatinny Arsenal (Army), 41 military, 2,945 civilian (2004)

CITIES
Morristown, 18,544; Dover, 18,188; Madison, 16,530; Livingston (unincorporated), 16,224

NOTABLE
Bertrand Island Amusement Park on Lake Hopatcong was a major tourist destination in the 1920s and into the 1950s — it closed in 1983.

Rep. Rush D. Holt (D)

Elected 1998; 4th term

CAPITOL OFFICE
225-5801
holt.house.gov
1019 Longworth 20515-3012; fax 225-6025

COMMITTEES
Education & Workforce
Select Intelligence

HOMETOWN
Hopewell

BORN
Oct. 15, 1948, Weston, W.Va.

RELIGION
Quaker

FAMILY
Wife, Margaret Lancefield; three children

EDUCATION
Carleton College, B.A. 1970 (physics); New York U.,
M.S. 1980 (physics), Ph.D. 1981 (physics)

CAREER
University research assistant director; physics
professor

POLITICAL HIGHLIGHTS
Sought Democratic nomination for U.S. House,
1996

ELECTION RESULTS

2004 GENERAL

Rush D. Holt (D)	171,691	59.3%
Bill Spadea (R)	115,014	39.7%

2004 PRIMARY

Rush D. Holt (D)	unopposed

2002 GENERAL

Rush D. Holt (D)	104,806	61.0%
DeForest "Buster" Soaries (R)	62,938	36.7%
Carl J. Mayer (GREEN)	1,871	1.1%

PREVIOUS WINNING PERCENTAGES
2000 (49%); 1998 (50%)

A research physicist by training, Holt is not averse to venturing into some of the most explosive areas of politics. From intelligence oversight to election reform, he has prodded his colleagues in Congress to take a more active role in ensuring that individual rights are protected and American values are upheld.

He has forcefully questioned the Bush administration's credibility on intelligence matters, and he championed an upgrade of new electronic voting machines introduced in many states as a result of an election reform law prompted by the 2000 Florida recount imbroglio.

Named to the Intelligence Committee in the 108th Congress, Holt in 2004 demanded that the White House give Congress the results of a Justice Department investigation into leaks made to columnist Robert Novak of the identity of covert CIA operative Valerie Plame. Plame, whose cover was blown in 2003, is the wife of former Ambassador Joseph C. Wilson IV, who accused the White House of overstating intelligence findings on Iraq's nuclear programs before the war. Democrats describe the leak of Plame's identity as an effort to punish Wilson for his views.

Holt's resolution of inquiry to compel the Bush administration to turn over all relevant records about the disclosure was squashed by all four GOP-led committees with jurisdiction in the matter. Holt never expected otherwise but said, "I am disappointed by the absence of public outrage."

Holt has raised broader concerns about the Bush administration's secrecy and use of intelligence. Urging stronger congressional oversight, he warned of the increased risk of a fiasco such as the 1961 Bay of Pigs invasion, in which the CIA unsuccessfully tried to land a counter-revolutionary force in Cuba. "With these operations, it's hard to know where the checks and balances are," Holt said. "Rogue operations could become the order of the day if Congress is not more vigilant." He was one of just two Intelligence Committee members to vote against the intelligence section of the overhaul bill that was introduced after the Sept. 11 commission's report.

On his other big issue of the 108th, Holt urged Congress to revisit the 2002 election reform law to require all voting machines to produce paper records that could be used to verify votes. "These new machines are vulnerable to massive fraud," he wrote in a Washington Post op-ed. The legislation did not advance, but the issue remained a hot one through the 2004 elections. Afterward, Holt joined other lawmakers in demanding a Government Accountability Office investigation of complaints from voters about malfunctioning electronic voting machines, failures to count absentee ballots, and other reported voting problems. In the 109th Congress, he has again offered his paper-trail legislation.

Not surprisingly, given his background, Holt has used his seat on the Education and Workforce Committee to encourage support for research and development, and to promote math and science education. In the 108th, he sought increased federal job-training grants in high-tech manufacturing. He also proposed a measure to help teachers gain "real world" experience in math and science research centers and businesses that they could then bring back to the classroom.

Another of his priorities has been to reinstate the Office of Technology Assessment, which advised Congress on scientific and technology issues for a quarter-century before the GOP-run Congress closed it in 1995. For this effort, Holt was named by Scientific American magazine in 2002 as one of its 50 "visionaries from the worlds of research, industry and politics whose accomplishments point toward a brighter technological future."

Holt's doctoral dissertation was on the outer layer of the sun, and he holds a patent for improving the efficiency of solar ponds, a source of thermal energy. As a former assistant director of the Princeton Plasma Physics Laboratory, he likes to hand out bumper stickers proclaiming, "My congressman *is* a rocket scientist."

Holt says he picked up his interest in science at an early age from his mother, who earned a master's degree in zoology and taught science at a junior college. He also learned politics at home. His mother was a West Virginia state legislator and secretary of state; his father, Rush Dew Holt, served 13 years as a state legislator and was elected to the U.S. Senate at age 29. He had to wait six months to take office, because under the Constitution, senators must be at least 30 years old.

The younger Holt was a Congressional Science Fellow in the office of Pennsylvania Democratic Rep. Bob Edgar in the early 1980s and consulted with the State Department on arms control, space activities and international science. He told the Newark Star-Ledger that his impetus for running for office was a distaste for the "shortsightedness and mean-spiritedness of the Gingrich Congress."

Holt is a five-time champion of the TV quiz show "Jeopardy" and is bemused by the attention that brings. After his 1998 election, he told the Charleston, W.Va., Daily Mail that he didn't think his game show success was particularly relevant to the campaign but from the interest it received from journalists, "it must be the most significant thing I've done."

Holt first ran for the House in 1996, losing in the Democratic primary to David N. Del Vecchio, who in turn lost a close race to Republican Michael Pappas. Two years later, Holt portrayed socially conservative Pappas as too far to the right for the district. His 5,000-vote victory made Holt one of the GOP's most-targeted incumbents in 2000. His campaign against moderate Republican Dick Zimmer, who had held the House seat for three terms ending in 1996, was bitter, and the outcome was in doubt for three weeks after Election Day. Holt was eventually declared the victor by 651 votes.

The GOP kept the 12th District on its target list for 2002 and offered up an attractive candidate, DeForest "Buster" Soaries, an African-American Baptist minister who had served as New Jersey's secretary of state. Benefiting slightly from redistricting, Holt won with 61 percent of the vote. In 2004, he defeated Bill Spadea, a former Marine and national chairman of the College Republicans, with 59 percent.

KEY VOTES

2004
Yes Extend federal unemployment benefits by 13 weeks
Yes Pass $283.2 billion, six-year federal highway and mass transit bill
No Approve $146 billion multi-year extension of previously enacted middle-class tax breaks
No Amend the Constitution to prohibit same-sex marriage
No Cut corporate taxes $137 billion over 10 years
Yes Reorganize U.S. intelligence agencies as proposed by Sept. 11 commission

2003
No Cut taxes by $330 billion through fiscal 2013
Yes Block Bush rule scaling back overtime pay for some white-collar federal workers
Yes Do not allow use of search warrants without first notifying subjects
No Allow importation of prescription drugs
No Create private school voucher program in Washington, D.C.
No Ban "partial birth" abortion except to save a woman's life
Yes Split $18.6 billion in Iraq aid into half-grant, half-loan
No Overhaul Medicare and create prescription drug benefit

CQ VOTE STUDIES

	PARTY UNITY		PRESIDENTIAL SUPPORT	
	Support	Oppose	Support	Oppose
2004	98%	2%	26%	74%
2003	97%	3%	22%	78%
2002	94%	6%	30%	70%
2001	92%	8%	35%	65%
2000	88%	12%	67%	33%

INTEREST GROUPS

	AFL-CIO	ADA	CCUS	ACU
2004	93%	95%	19%	4%
2003	93%	95%	23%	8%
2002	100%	90%	40%	8%
2001	92%	90%	43%	0%
2000	80%	80%	47%	16%

N E W   J E R S E Y   1 2

Central — part of Trenton, East Brunswick, Princeton

Set in the middle of the state, the 12th begins in Hunterdon County, hitting ethnically diverse Trenton (shared with the 4th) and East Brunswick as it winds east to Monmouth County. It ends in shore communities such as Rumson just short of the Atlantic Ocean.

Despite its jagged shape, many of the district's towns are similar. Office parks dominate the landscape in these affluent and white communities. But there are pockets of blue-collar diversity. Redistricting following the 2000 census made the 12th more Democratic by exchanging part of predominantly white Hunterdon County for a sizable portion of the state capital, Trenton, where more than 70 percent of the residents are black. Plainsboro in Middlesex County has a large Asian population.

The 12th has benefited from economic growth, although midsize towns such as Ewing must contend with the side effects of suburban sprawl. In addition to the Capitol, the district also boasts the governor's official residence, the stately and imposing Drumthwacket in Princeton. Delaware River towns, such as Frenchtown and Lambertville, offer quaint antique shops and bed and breakfasts.

Old money and suburban affluence made the area historically Republican, except for a small Democratic constituency anchored by Princeton's academic community. An influx of independents has made the district competitive despite the state's Democratic tide and the advantage the party gained in redistricting. John Kerry took 54 percent of the 12th's vote in the 2004 presidential election, although George W. Bush did carry the district's portions of Hunterdon and Monmouth counties.

MAJOR INDUSTRY
Higher education, military, pharmaceuticals

MILITARY BASES
Fort Monmouth (Army), 467 military, 4,574 civilian (2004)

CITIES
Trenton (pt.), 47,658; East Brunswick (unincorporated), 46,756; North Brunswick (unincorporated), 36,287; Ewing (unincorporated), 35,707

NOTABLE
The Lenox Inc. china company, founded in Trenton, is based in Lawrenceville.

Rep. Robert Menendez (D)

Elected 1992; 7th term

CAPITOL OFFICE
225-7919
menendez.house.gov
2238 Rayburn 20515-3013; fax 226-0792

COMMITTEES
International Relations
Transportation & Infrastructure

HOMETOWN
Hoboken

BORN
Jan. 1, 1954, Manhattan, N.Y.

RELIGION
Roman Catholic

FAMILY
Separated; two children

EDUCATION
St. Peter's College, B.A. 1976 (political science & urban studies); Rutgers U., J.D. 1979

CAREER
Lawyer

POLITICAL HIGHLIGHTS
Union City Board of Education, 1974-82; mayor of Union City, 1986-92; N.J. Assembly, 1987-91; N.J. Senate, 1991-93

ELECTION RESULTS

2004 GENERAL
Robert Menendez (D)	121,018	75.9%
Richard W. Piatkowski (R)	35,288	22.1%

2004 PRIMARY
Robert Menendez (D)	34,807	87.2%
Steven Fulop (D)	5,099	12.8%

2002 GENERAL
Robert Menendez (D)	72,605	78.3%
James Geron (R)	16,852	18.2%
Pat Henry Faulkner (GREEN)	1,195	1.3%

PREVIOUS WINNING PERCENTAGES
2000 (79%); 1998 (80%); 1996 (79%); 1994 (71%); 1992 (64%)

As chairman of the House Democratic Caucus, Menendez is the highest-ranking Hispanic in the history of Congress, occupying the No. 3 spot in the minority leadership. He is a powerful voice on the gamut of Latino issues, yet does not want to be thought of exclusively as a Hispanic leader. Rather, Menendez cultivates a larger role for himself as a Democratic statesman. He once warned a New Jersey public television station that he would refuse interview requests if they continued to question him only on ethnic issues such as immigration.

His ambitions are for higher office. He's dreamed of the Senate, and he was well-positioned to get there if Sen. Jon Corzine of New Jersey wins his bid for governor in the fall of 2005. Menendez was among the leading candidates to be appointed to Corzine's job if the seat opened up.

But even without the Senate, Menendez has made his mark in Congress. He is the first Hispanic elected to Congress from New Jersey, the only Cuban-American Democrat in Congress and one of the party's best spokesmen. As the battle for the loyalty of Hispanic voters rages between Republicans and Democrats, Menendez is among the Democrats' most powerful weapons.

His political standing at home is strong, too, save for some negative fallout from his decision to get involved in the morass of Democratic Gov. James E. McGreevey's resignation, following revelations in August 2004 of a homosexual extramarital affair. Menendez quietly urged McGreevey to resign immediately, before his self-imposed deadline of Nov. 15, 2004. Then, a local television station reported that Menendez himself had had an extramarital affair, with a woman. Party leaders urged Menendez to back off, and he wrote a letter supporting McGreevey's decision to delay his resignation, while never acknowledging the reports.

Getting the chairmanship of the Democratic Caucus was no easy trick as the House Democrats organized for the 108th Congress. Menendez beat veteran Rosa DeLauro of Connecticut by a single vote. In besting DeLauro, a favorite of those who wanted more gender diversity in the leadership, Menendez argued that Democrats needed to have a Hispanic in the top echelon if they were going to effectively court the fastest-growing ethnic voting bloc. Several Hispanic groups outside Congress promoted Menendez's candidacy, warning that his defeat would send the wrong message to Hispanic voters. Also, Menendez's leadership political action committee donated $689,000 to Democratic candidates for Congress in 2002, three times as much as DeLauro's PAC.

A confluence of two odd circumstances helped him in the final stretch. Menendez and DeLauro agreed to permit Colorado Democrat Mike Feeley to vote, though his standing as a House member was shaky because the election results were in doubt. (After a lengthy recount, he lost to Republican Bob Beauprez.) Feeley backed Menendez, while one of DeLauro's supporters, Darlene Hooley of Oregon, missed the vote because of knee surgery.

As the top Democrat on the International Relations Western Hemisphere Subcommittee, Menendez is an important voice in shaping Latin American policy. He often joins with the House's three other Cuban-Americans, all Republicans, in criticizing the Castro regime. He was a valued adviser to President Clinton on the politics of the Cuban-American community. And he criticized President Bush for what he called pandering to Cuban-exile voters in Florida when the president announced a plan in mid-2004 to use military aircraft to reduce Cuban jamming of American broadcasts to the island nation.

Menendez is a liberal and a believer in activist government. He sides with organized labor, backs abortion rights, supports gun control and faults Republicans as proponents of tax breaks for the wealthy. Menendez blasted Bush's 2001 tax cut proposal for ignoring "families who depend on a paycheck, not an inheritance."

Menendez often speaks for the party on immigration issues. In the 108th Congress, he helped lead a successful drive against a bill to force hospitals to report to the government data about their immigrant patients, including their names, employers, immigration status and biometric identifiers such as fingerprints and photos.

With a seat on the Transportation Committee, Menendez's major parochial issue is security. Many who escaped the terrorist attacks on the World Trade Center in New York City on Sept. 11, 2001, were ferried across the Hudson River for medical treatment in Menendez's district. Two hundred of his constituents were killed. His district also includes part of Newark Liberty International Airport, the origin of United Airlines Flight 93, which was hijacked by the terrorists and then retaken by rebel passengers before crashing in rural Pennsylvania, killing all aboard.

A native New Yorker and the son of Cuban immigrants, Menendez won election to the Union City school board in 1974 while still in college. He was elected mayor of Union City in 1986 and to the state legislature in 1987, serving in both offices simultaneously. He was named to fill a state Senate vacancy in early 1991 and that November won the seat.

Redistricting for the 1990s nearly doubled the Hispanic population in the 13th District. In 1992, when Democratic Rep. Frank J. Guarini decided to retire after 14 years, Menendez emerged as the front-runner for the seat. He won the primary with 68 percent of the vote and the general election with 64 percent. He has done very well in subsequent re-elections, with vote shares approaching 80 percent. Redistricting after the 2000 census kept the 13th almost half Hispanic and overwhelmingly Democratic.

While making his mark in the House, Menendez had kept an eye on his childhood dream of serving in the Senate, raising millions of dollars for a future campaign. He planned to run for an open seat in 2000, but dropped out when Democratic Sen. Robert G. Torricelli instead backed Corzine, who went on to win. After Torricelli was rebuked by the Senate Ethics Committee and dropped his bid for a second term in September 2002, state party leaders approached Menendez about becoming the replacement nominee, but he turned them down.

KEY VOTES

2004

Yes	Extend federal unemployment benefits by 13 weeks
Yes	Pass $283.2 billion, six-year federal highway and mass transit bill
No	Approve $146 billion multi-year extension of previously enacted middle-class tax breaks
?	Amend the Constitution to prohibit same-sex marriage
No	Cut corporate taxes $137 billion over 10 years
Yes	Reorganize U.S. intelligence agencies as proposed by Sept. 11 commission

2003

No	Cut taxes by $330 billion through fiscal 2013
Yes	Block Bush rule scaling back overtime pay for some white-collar federal workers
Yes	Do not allow use of search warrants without first notifying subjects
No	Allow importation of prescription drugs
No	Create private school voucher program in Washington, D.C.
No	Ban "partial birth" abortion except to save a woman's life
Yes	Split $18.6 billion in Iraq aid into half-grant, half-loan
No	Overhaul Medicare and create prescription drug benefit

CQ VOTE STUDIES

	PARTY UNITY		PRESIDENTIAL SUPPORT	
	Support	Oppose	Support	Oppose
2004	93%	8%	34%	66%
2003	93%	7%	24%	76%
2002	87%	13%	28%	72%
2001	89%	11%	30%	70%
2000	91%	9%	78%	22%

INTEREST GROUPS

	AFL-CIO	ADA	CCUS	ACU
2004	93%	85%	35%	8%
2003	93%	0%	37%	20%
2002	89%	95%	42%	8%
2001	100%	95%	35%	16%
2000	100%	95%	38%	8%

NEW JERSEY 13

Northeast – parts of Jersey City and Newark

Within sight of some of the nation's best-known landmarks, including the Statue of Liberty and Manhattan's skyscrapers, the 13th covers a long, thin swath from North Bergen to Perth Amboy along the Hudson River, Newark Bay and Arthur Kill. The district takes in parts of Jersey City and Newark, linking together Hispanic neighborhoods to create a Hispanic plurality (48 percent).

Russian, Indian, Korean and Filipino communities add to the district's diversity and its overwhelming Democratic vote. A Middle Eastern community is beginning to form, while much of the Cuban population is moving north to Bergen County. John Kerry won 68 percent of the 13th's vote in the 2004 presidential election.

The large Hispanic population is a key factor in plans by the region's Major League Soccer team, the MetroStars, to construct a 25,000-seat stadium in Harrison. The stadium deal, which has not been finalized, is part of a $160 million redevelopment plan that includes cafes, bars, apartments, lofts and a parking deck for the many commuters who hop on trains into Manhattan.

The district, a transportation hub, includes Port Newark-Elizabeth and a small part of Newark Liberty International Airport, most of which is in the 10th. Several lines, including Hudson-Bergen Light Rail, carry commuters across the district, and PATH trains, ferries and tunnels bring passengers to and from New York.

Hoboken has seen gentrification, as young professionals and financial services companies have moved across the river from Manhattan. Officials are hoping to turn long-suffering Jersey City, which is shared with the 9th and 10th districts, into "Wall Street West."

MAJOR INDUSTRY
Transportation, health care, retail, financial securities

CITIES
Jersey City (pt.), 118,201; Newark (pt.), 118,133; Union City, 67,088; Bayonne (pt.), 56,465; Perth Amboy, 47,303; West New York, 45,768

NOTABLE
Ellis Island; Bayonne Bridge, the world's longest steel arch bridge from 1931 until 1977, connects Bayonne and Staten Island over the Kill Van Kull; Frank Sinatra was born and raised in Hoboken.

NEW MEXICO

Gov. Bill Richardson (D)

First elected: 2002
Length of term: 4 years
Term expires: 1/07
Salary: $110,000
Phone: (505) 476-2200

Hometown: Santa Fe
Born: Nov. 15, 1947;
Pasadena, Calif.
Religion: Roman Catholic
Family: Wife, Barbara Richardson
Education: Tufts U., B.A. 1970 (political science & French), M.A. 1971 (international relations)
Career: International trade consultant; state party official; congressional aide
Political highlights: Democratic nominee for U.S. House, 1980; U.S. House, 1983-97; United Nations ambassador, 1997-98; Energy secretary, 1998-2001

Election results:
2002 GENERAL

Bill Richardson (D)	268,674	55.5%
John A. Sanchez (R)	189,090	39.1%
David E. Bacon (GREEN)	26,465	5.5%

Lt. Gov. Diane Denish (D)

First elected: 2002
Length of term: 4 years
Term expires: 1/07
Salary: $85,000
Phone: (800) 432-4406

STATE LEGISLATURE

Legislature: 60 days January-March in odd-numbered years; 30 days January-February in even-numbered years

House: 70 members, 2-year terms
2005 breakdown: 42D, 28R; 47 men, 23 women
Salary: $141/day
Phone: (505) 986-4751

Senate: 42 members, 4-year terms
2005 breakdown: 24D, 18R; 31 men, 11 women
Salary: $141/day
Phone: (505) 986-4714

STATE TERM LIMITS

Governor: 2 consecutive terms
House: No
Senate: No

URBAN STATISTICS

CITY	POPULATION
Albuquerque	448,607
Las Cruces	74,267
Santa Fe	62,203
Rio Rancho	51,765
Roswell	45,293

REGISTERED VOTERS

Democrat	50%
Republican	32%
Unaffiliated	15%

POPULATION

2004 population (est.)	1,903,289
2000 population	1,819,046
1990 population	1,515,069
Percent change (1990-2000)	+20.1%
Rank among states (2004)	36
Median age	34.6
Born in state	51.5%
Foreign born	8.2%
Violent crime rate	758/100,000
Poverty level	18.4%
Federal workers	28,772
Military	17,163

REDISTRICTING

New Mexico retained its three House seats in reapportionment. GOP Gov. Gary E. Johnson vetoed the state legislature's plan and a state judge adopted a new map on Jan. 2, 2002.

MISCELLANEOUS

Web: www.state.nm.us
Capital: Santa Fe
STATE ELECTION OFFICIAL
(505) 827-3621
DEMOCRATIC HEADQUARTERS
(505) 830-3650
REPUBLICAN HEADQUARTERS
(505) 298-3662

District Statistics

DIST.	2004 VOTE FOR PRESIDENT BUSH	KERRY	WHITE	BLACK	ASIAN	HISP	MEDIAN INCOME	WHITE COLLAR	BLUE COLLAR	SERVICE INDUSTRY	OVER 64	UNDER 18	COLLEGE EDUCATION	RURAL	SQ. MILES
1	48%	51%	49%	2%	2%	43%	$38,413	65%	19%	16%	11%	26%	30%	9%	4,717
2	58	41	44	2	1	47	$29,269	53	29	18	13	29	17	29	69,493
3	45	54	41	1	1	36	$35,058	60	23	17	11	29	24	37	47,146
STATE	50	49	45	2	1	42	$34,133	60	23	17	12	28	24	25	121,356
U.S.	50.7	48.3	69	12	4	13	$41,994	60	25	15	12	26	24	21	3,537,438

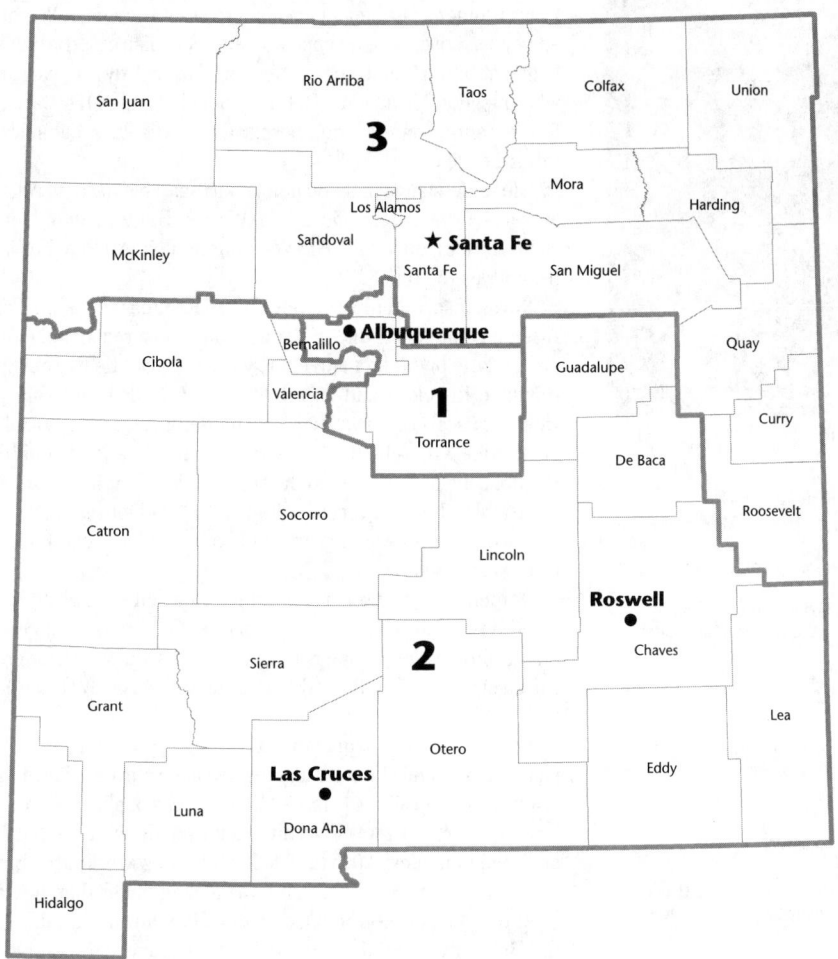

Sen. Pete V. Domenici (R)

Elected 1972; 6th term

CAPITOL OFFICE
224-6621
domenici.senate.gov
328 Hart 20510-3101; fax 228-0900

COMMITTEES
Appropriations
  (Energy & Water - chairman)
Budget
Energy & Natural Resources - chairman
Homeland Security & Governmental Affairs
Indian Affairs

HOMETOWN
Albuquerque

BORN
May 7, 1932, Albuquerque, N.M.

RELIGION
Roman Catholic

FAMILY
Wife, Nancy Domenici; eight children

EDUCATION
U. of Albuquerque, attended 1950-52; U. of New
Mexico, B.S. 1954 (education); U. of Denver, LL.B.
1958

CAREER
Lawyer

POLITICAL HIGHLIGHTS
Albuquerque City Commission, 1966-70 (chairman
and ex-officio mayor, 1967-70); Republican
nominee for governor, 1970

ELECTION RESULTS

2002 GENERAL

Pete V. Domenici (R)	314,193	65.0%
Gloria Tristani (D)	168,863	35.0%

2002 PRIMARY

Pete V. Domenici (R)	unopposed

PREVIOUS WINNING PERCENTAGES
1996 (65%); 1990 (73%); 1984 (72%); 1978 (53%);
1972 (54%)

Even as he has accumulated power in a Senate career of more than 30 years, Domenici has maintained a regular-guy image in Washington. A driven yet sensitive man, he appears genuinely distressed when a colleague is angry at him. He does not suffer criticism lightly and can bristle at those who question his actions. But he is deeply loyal to his staff, treating them like extended family members, and he displays considerable respect toward colleagues.

"He understands that you don't do irreparable harm to relationships with anyone," former Republican Sen. Warren B. Rudman of New Hampshire, a close friend, once told The Washington Post. "If Pete has a fault, it's that he worries too much."

Now the second-most-senior Senate Republican, behind Ted Stevens of Alaska, Domenici is one of Capitol Hill's most respected elder statesmen, particularly on budget and energy matters. But he has never been able to translate his clout and credibility into a GOP leadership post. A hardworking fiscal conservative with a moderate streak on social issues, Domenici (doe-MEN-ih-chee) has continually been left behind as Senate Republicans have moved to the right to pick their leaders. He watched his close ally Bob Dole overtake him in a 1990 bid for majority leader and later lost two races for the chairmanship of the Republican Policy Committee, in 1990 and 2000.

Domenici nevertheless is highly regarded enough to have been considered twice for vice president. In 1988, George Bush included Domenici on his shortlist of prospects; 12 years later, Majority Leader Trent Lott of Mississippi publicly floated his name to George W. Bush for consideration as his running mate.

The years have begun to catch up with Domenici. He suffers from painful elbow and shoulder injuries and from chronic arthritis in his hip and lower back. The ailments forced him to occasionally ride around in a motorized scooter and to awkwardly shake hands with his left hand. But he declared in January 2005 that, following a new workout regimen and treatment by arthritis specialists, he was feeling better than he had in years.

At the start of the 108th Congress, Domenici relinquished the gavel of the Budget Committee. He had been the panel's top-ranking Republican for 22 years, making a name for himself with his dedication to fiscal discipline and balanced budgets. But GOP term limits would have forced him to step down in the 109th, so Domenici opted not to wait, instead claiming the open chairmanship of the Energy and Natural Resources Committee. Within three months, he pushed through a comprehensive energy bill, the first to clear the panel in 11 years. But he was unable to get a final version through the full Senate, even after drafting a new measure that dropped several contentious provisions. Democrats were incensed that they were kept out of negotiations on crafting the new version, and it never overcame a threatened filibuster.

Domenici was expected to try again in the 109th, and also to continue his longtime efforts as Congress' chief apostle for nuclear power, an energy source he says has been unjustly maligned. "Nuclear power is safe, if not safer than some of the other energy sources, and it is environmentally sound," he said in 2001. He published a book on the subject in 2004.

He also promotes his energy agenda as chairman of the Energy and Water Appropriations Subcommittee. Two of the Energy Department's nuclear weapons laboratories, Sandia and Los Alamos, are in his state, and he has been such an ardent protector of their funding that some employees refer to him as "St. Pete."

He also has been a leading supporter of the Bush administration's plans to modernize the nation's nuclear weapons arsenal, fighting off efforts by critics in the 108th Congress to delete Energy Department funding for research on new nuclear weapons, including a "bunker buster" intended to take out underground facilities. He was bracing to fight that battle all over again in the 109th — and to take on House appropriators who have sought to cut money for his beloved weapons labs.

Domenici can work with a broad spectrum of lawmakers. In years past, he teamed with conservative Phil Gramm, a Texas Republican, on Social Security legislation and worked with liberal Paul Wellstone, a Minnesota Democrat, on mental health issues. Domenici has a daughter who suffers from schizophrenia, and her struggles caused him to lead a push to make health insurers treat mental illness like any other ailment.

While he has voted with the majority of his party more often in recent years than he did during some earlier periods, Domenici doesn't shy away from tangling with some of his more conservative colleagues. He opposed their push for "dynamic scoring" of tax cuts, which assumes that cuts will produce so much economic growth that revenue losses to the Treasury will be mitigated. And as an appropriator, he has been less willing than many of his colleagues to make deep cuts in domestic programs.

He learned fiscal restraint from his father, an Italian immigrant grocer. When Domenici was accepted into law school, his father agreed to finance his education but demanded to be repaid if his son brought home an "F."

Domenici first was thrust into the limelight on budget issues in the 1980s, when the GOP controlled the Senate and he served his first stint as Budget Committee chairman, leading the panel in its three-way battles with the Reagan administration and the Democratic-controlled House. He was more interested in balancing the budget than in providing the fiscal stimulus sought by "supply side" conservatives. Indeed, President Reagan's budget director David A. Stockman called him a "Hooverite."

During the Clinton administration, Domenici helped produce a 1997 deal to balance the budget by fiscal 2002. The sprawling pact offered tax cuts that had long been sought by Republicans plus limited new money for selected Democratic priorities such as health care for children.

Enduringly popular with voters across the spectrum of his state's diverse population, he has not faced an even remotely difficult re-election race in more than 20 years. He goes to great lengths not to be perceived as an out-of-touch Beltway insider, a label that a number of opponents have tried unsuccessfully to pin on him.

One of five children, Domenici worked in his father's wholesale grocery business as a youth. He was a good enough pitcher in college to receive a contract from a Brooklyn Dodgers farm team in 1954. But he gave up baseball after a season, taught math for a year and then went to law school.

As an Albuquerque city official in the late 1960s, he prided himself on holding neighborhood meetings to hear residents' complaints. After four years in city government, he ran for governor in 1970, losing to Democrat Bruce King by 5 percentage points.

Undeterred, Domenici came back in 1972, this time running for the Senate seat being vacated by Democrat Clinton P. Anderson. He linked his Democratic foe, banker and former state Rep. Jack Daniels, to the unpopular presidential candidacy of George McGovern and won, with 54 percent of the vote. He struggled to win re-election in 1978, but since then, he has had little trouble holding his seat. He took 65 percent in 2002.

KEY VOTES

2004

Yes	Pass $318.9 billion, six-year highway and mass transit bill
No	Extend assault weapons ban for 10 years
No	Restore pay-as-you-go rules for new tax cuts and entitlement spending
Yes	Criminalize harm to a fetus in an attack on the mother
?	Increase mandatory child care funding to states by $6 billion over five years
Yes	Amend the Constitution to prohibit same-sex marriage
Yes	Approve $146 billion multi-year extension of previously enacted middle-class tax breaks
Yes	Reorganize U.S. intelligence agencies as proposed by Sept. 11 commission
Yes	Cut corporate taxes $137 billion over 10 years

2003

No	Delay Bush changes to Clean Air Act
Yes	Allow confirmation vote on Miguel A. Estrada to the U.S. Court of Appeals for the D.C. Circuit
No	Block a Bush proposal opening Alaska's Arctic National Wildlife Refuge to oil drilling
No	Limit size of Bush's proposed tax cut to $350 billion through fiscal 2013
Yes	Overhaul Medicare and create prescription drug benefit
No	Block Bush rule scaling back overtime pay for some white-collar federal workers
No	Split $20 billion in Iraq aid into half-grant, half-loan
Yes	Ban "partial birth" abortion except to save a woman's life
Yes	Stop proposal allowing travel to Cuba
Yes	Allow final vote on energy policy overhaul

CQ VOTE STUDIES

	PARTY UNITY		PRESIDENTIAL SUPPORT	
	Support	Oppose	Support	Oppose
2004	97%	3%	94%	6%
2003	96%	4%	97%	3%
2002	89%	11%	96%	4%
2001	89%	11%	96%	4%
2000	94%	6%	51%	49%
1999	93%	7%	33%	67%
1998	83%	17%	57%	43%
1997	85%	15%	67%	33%
1996	90%	10%	42%	58%
1995	93%	7%	26%	74%

INTEREST GROUPS

	AFL-CIO	ADA	CCUS	ACU
2004	17%	15%	100%	95%
2003	0%	5%	100%	85%
2002	25%	15%	100%	88%
2001	21%	10%	100%	90%
2000	0%	0%	100%	95%
1999	11%	5%	94%	88%
1998	13%	5%	100%	70%
1997	0%	25%	100%	60%
1996	14%	20%	83%	85%
1995	8%	5%	100%	78%

Sen. Jeff Bingaman (D)

Elected 1982; 4th term

CAPITOL OFFICE
224-5521
senator_bingaman@bingaman.senate.gov
bingaman.senate.gov
703 Hart 20510-3102; fax 224-2852

COMMITTEES
Energy & Natural Resources - ranking member
Finance
Health, Education, Labor & Pensions
Joint Economic

HOMETOWN
Sante Fe

BORN
Oct. 3, 1943, El Paso, Texas

RELIGION
Methodist

FAMILY
Wife, Anne Kovacovich Bingaman; one child

EDUCATION
Harvard U., A.B. 1965 (government); Stanford U.,
J.D. 1968

MILITARY SERVICE
Army Reserve, 1968-74

CAREER
Lawyer

POLITICAL HIGHLIGHTS
N.M. attorney general, 1979-83

ELECTION RESULTS

2000 GENERAL

Jeff Bingaman (D)	363,744	61.7%
Bill Redmond (R)	225,517	38.3%

2000 PRIMARY

Jeff Bingaman (D)	unopposed

PREVIOUS WINNING PERCENTAGES
1994 (54%); 1988 (63%); 1982 (54%)

In a Senate whose members often resemble the hard-charging Captain Kirk of television's "Star Trek," Bingaman seems more like the show's Mr. Spock: cerebral, logical and seemingly without ego in his willingness to let others take credit for legislative accomplishments.

Bingaman is among those Democrats more at ease with the intricacies of policy than the glamour of politics. He avoids the television talk-show circuit, rarely takes part in news conferences and often lets other New Mexico lawmakers put out press releases on statewide matters.

As the top-ranking Democrat on the Energy and Natural Resources Committee, Bingaman has avoided the spotlight even in the debate over a high-profile national energy policy. He allowed Democratic colleagues with presidential ambitions such as Massachusetts' John Kerry and Connecticut's Joseph I. Lieberman to grab the headlines on such issues as drilling for oil in Alaska's Arctic National Wildlife Refuge and raising automobile fuel efficiency standards.

National energy policy legislation remains important to him, and in the 108th Congress, Bingaman forged ahead on an energy bill in his low-key fashion, eventually helping to get a series of energy tax-related provisions broken out of the bill and passed into law. The tax breaks were a 10-year, $13 billion package aimed at bolstering energy production and providing tax credits for renewable energy technologies. The tax provisions became part of a measure to alter the corporate tax code.

As work on the energy bill progressed, Bingaman uncharacteristically rebuked his home-state Republican colleague Pete V. Domenici, who is the committee's chairman. Bingaman accused Domenici of shutting him and other Democrats out of negotiations on the final version of the bill. Bingaman wanted popular components of the package — such as changes to the nation's electricity grid — to be handled separately from controversial ones, such as liability protection for some fuel producers. Domenici wanted to pass the bill as a whole. Even so, the two men continued their respectful relationship in other areas, such as furthering energy research, and they were able to get panel approval of numerous public lands bills.

As the 109th began, Bingaman said he would focus on re-emphasizing America's commitment to training students to work in technology-related fields. "I'm going to try to get on the national agenda the issue of how to maintain U.S. leadership in science and technology," he told the Albuquerque Journal.

In addition to mastering such complex topics as technology and nuclear weapons, Bingaman has delved into issues at the core of Democratic concerns, including education and pensions. He was able to include several education provisions in the huge catchall spending measure passed at the end of the 108th, including funds for dropout prevention, Advanced Placement classes and a program that gives grants to large high schools that want to create "smaller learning communities" on their campuses. "I'm working to give schools the funding they need to be aggressive about identifying students at risk of dropping out and working to keep them in the classroom," Bingaman told the Journal in 2004.

From his seat on the Health, Education, Labor and Pensions Committee, Bingaman was able to incorporate several provisions into the 2003 Medicare prescription drug benefit law, including one that offered higher payments to hospitals that treat uninsured patients and another that improves

Medicare reimbursement rates for doctors serving in rural states.

Bingaman also has been active on nutrition issues. He has teamed with Majority Leader Bill Frist to introduce legislation aimed at reducing obesity among children and adolescents. He added a provision to the 2004 child nutrition law that tripled funding for a program to promote healthful eating and physical activity in public schools.

With Democrats forced to reduce their membership on committees in the 108th after Republicans gained the majority, Bingaman had to relinquish his seat on the Armed Services Committee. His workmanlike devotion to detail on the committee earned him comparisons to the panel's venerated retired chairman, Democrat Sam Nunn of Georgia. Bingaman kept a watchful eye on New Mexico's military bases and was a strong proponent of putting defense technologies to use in the private sector. That position is popular in New Mexico — home to two of the Energy Department's national laboratories, Sandia and Los Alamos, which have sought new missions with the end of the Cold War.

A member of the powerful Finance Committee, Bingaman is the top-ranking Democrat on the International Trade Subcommittee.

He has taken on a variety of unglamorous but important assignments in the Senate. Bingaman served on task forces studying high-wage job creation, Social Security, and the settlement between tobacco companies and the states. He was tapped by Minority Leader Harry Reid to be vice chairman of an effort to ensure that ranking committee members work together smoothly. He also serves on the Democratic Steering and Coordination Committee, which helps make committee assignments.

Almost without exception, though, Bingaman has let other lawmakers grab the spotlight on issues. "He never seeks to advance himself; he never says, 'Look at me,' " said North Dakota Democrat Kent Conrad, citing Bingaman as among those he turns to for advice on difficult issues. "I find him to be one of the colleagues I respect the most."

A pragmatic, results-oriented lawmaker, Bingaman has compiled a moderate-to-liberal voting record as a senator. He supported President Bush's position 54 percent of the time in the 108th Congress and voted with a majority of Democrats against a majority of Republicans 91 percent of the time. Like many of his colleagues, he has lamented the growing partisanship in the Senate.

Bingaman's family helped point him toward a political career. He grew up in the New Mexico mining town of Silver City, the son of a professor and the nephew of John Bingaman, a confidant of the state's 24-year Democratic senator, Clinton Anderson. While at Stanford University Law School, Bingaman worked for Democratic Sen. Robert F. Kennedy's 1968 presidential campaign. Returning to New Mexico, he served as counsel to the 1969 state constitutional convention, joined a politically connected law firm and ran successfully for attorney general in 1978.

When he launched his 1982 Senate campaign, he was little-known outside the political and legal communities but politically unscarred. He won 54 percent of the vote to topple incumbent GOP Sen. Harrison H. Schmitt, a former Apollo astronaut, who appeared more interested in pet subjects such as 21st century technology than in the state's struggling economy.

Only one re-election race since has featured a serious challenger — Colin McMillan, a former Pentagon official, who used much of his own money in 1994 to aggressively criticize Bingaman for his stance on fees for grazing on public lands and his support for President Clinton's budget policy. But McMillan could not make sufficient inroads in Democratic counties, and Bingaman won with 54 percent. He won easily in 2000 with 62 percent and has said he will run again in 2006.

KEY VOTES

2004
Yes Pass $318.9 billion, six-year highway and mass transit bill
Yes Extend assault weapons ban for 10 years
Yes Restore pay-as-you-go rules for new tax cuts and entitlement spending
Yes Criminalize harm to a fetus in an attack on the mother
Yes Increase mandatory child care funding to states by $6 billion over five years
No   Amend the Constitution to prohibit same-sex marriage
Yes Approve $146 billion multi-year extension of previously enacted middle-class tax breaks
Yes Reorganize U.S. intelligence agencies as proposed by Sept. 11 commission
Yes Cut corporate taxes $137 billion over 10 years

2003
Yes Delay Bush changes to Clean Air Act
No   Allow confirmation vote on Miguel A. Estrada to the U.S. Court of Appeals for the D.C. Circuit
Yes Block a Bush proposal opening Alaska's Arctic National Wildlife Refuge to oil drilling
Yes Limit size of Bush's proposed tax cut to $350 billion through fiscal 2013
Yes Overhaul Medicare and create prescription drug benefit
Yes Block Bush rule scaling back overtime pay for some white-collar federal workers
Yes Split $20 billion in Iraq aid into half-grant, half-loan
No   Ban "partial birth" abortion except to save a woman's life
No   Stop proposal allowing travel to Cuba
No   Allow final vote on energy policy overhaul

CQ VOTE STUDIES

	PARTY UNITY		PRESIDENTIAL SUPPORT	
	Support	Oppose	Support	Oppose
2004	90%	10%	64%	36%
2003	91%	9%	50%	50%
2002	78%	22%	79%	21%
2001	91%	9%	68%	32%
2000	87%	13%	95%	5%
1999	88%	12%	84%	16%
1998	87%	13%	87%	13%
1997	88%	12%	92%	8%
1996	88%	12%	84%	16%
1995	84%	16%	91%	9%

INTEREST GROUPS

	AFL-CIO	ADA	CCUS	ACU
2004	92%	90%	71%	12%
2003	85%	95%	48%	10%
2002	92%	90%	60%	17%
2001	100%	90%	50%	29%
2000	75%	85%	64%	16%
1999	78%	100%	59%	4%
1998	75%	85%	56%	0%
1997	57%	90%	60%	0%
1996	100%	95%	15%	0%
1995	100%	90%	42%	0%

Rep. Heather A. Wilson (R)

Elected June 1998; 4th full term

CAPITOL OFFICE
225-6316
ask.heather@mail.house.gov
wilson.house.gov
318 Cannon 20515-3101; fax 225-4975

COMMITTEES
Energy & Commerce
Select Intelligence
  (Technical & Tactical Intelligence - chairwoman)

HOMETOWN
Albuquerque

BORN
Dec. 30, 1960, Keene, N.H.

RELIGION
Methodist

FAMILY
Husband, Jay Hone; three children

EDUCATION
U.S. Air Force Academy, B.S. 1982 (international politics); Oxford U., M.Phil. 1984 (Rhodes scholar), D.Phil. 1985 (international relations)

MILITARY SERVICE
Air Force, 1978-89

CAREER
Management consultant; National Security Council staff member

POLITICAL HIGHLIGHTS
N.M. Children, Youth and Families secretary, 1995-98

ELECTION RESULTS

2004 GENERAL

Heather A. Wilson (R)	147,372	54.4%
Richard Romero (D)	123,339	45.5%

2004 PRIMARY

Heather A. Wilson (R)	unopposed

2002 GENERAL

Heather A. Wilson (R)	95,711	55.3%
Richard Romero (D)	77,234	44.7%

PREVIOUS WINNING PERCENTAGES
2000 (50%); 1998 (48%); 1998 Special Election (45%)

Wilson has solidified her political standing at home and her influence within the House. A former Air Force officer who is the first woman military veteran to serve in Congress, she is ordinarily a reliable ally of the White House and the GOP leadership. But in her own quiet way, she has demonstrated that she will buck them both when her own convictions or the interests of her district conflict with the party line.

In a Republican Conference that marches largely in lockstep, she voted against her fellow partisans 21 percent of the time in 2004 on votes that pitted Republicans against Democrats. That was enough to put her in seventh place on the top 10 list of GOP dissidents. She has had run-ins with Energy and Commerce panel Chairman Joe L. Barton, a Texas Republican, who she says told her she was "too independent." For the past two Congresses, Wilson served on both the Energy and Armed Services committees. She says Barton would not let her serve on both panels in the 109th, prompting her to drop Armed Services and return to the Intelligence Committee, which she last served on in 2000.

Wilson is steeped in the military issues that most concern her defense-dominated district. Her hometown paper once described her as someone who "with short-cropped hair and her back ramrod straight . . . looks like she still would be at home in the Air Force blues she wore until 1989."

A number of her dissents have come on defense issues. In 2003, Wilson co-authored a letter with Democrat Jim Cooper of Tennessee urging President Bush to "significantly increase" the size of the active-duty military, saying the armed forces were overextended in Iraq and Afghanistan. More than 100 members signed the letter, including Armed Services Committee Chairman Duncan Hunter of California. A year later, Wilson broke ranks with her fellow Republicans on the panel, voting for a Democratic proposal to force the Defense Department to turn over all available material on the investigation of alleged prison abuses in Iraq.

Also in 2004, Wilson voted against the House version of the big intelligence overhaul bill, criticizing some provisions as an intrusion on civil liberties. But she voted for the final measure after Bush and GOP leaders made a last-minute push for the legislation.

Wilson, who delivers serious speeches in her signature low, even tone, also has taken on the Bush administration to protect and promote the energy industry, an all-important force in her state. Her mentor is Republican Pete V. Domenici, New Mexico's senior senator, who chairs the Energy and Natural Resources Committee. Domenici played a strong role in plucking Wilson from her spot as secretary of New Mexico's Children, Youth and Families Department and propelling her toward Congress in 1998, calling her "the most brilliantly qualified candidate" then running for the House.

In the 107th and 108th Congresses, she chaired the Republican Policy Committee's National Security and Foreign Affairs panel, where she helped hone the party's message on defense issues after the terrorist attacks of Sept. 11, 2001, and in the preparation for an invasion of Iraq. Her panel spent nearly a year on a report that challenged the government to do a better job of sustaining its nuclear weapons complex, investing more in research and development, and refining anti-proliferation programs.

On the Energy and Commerce panel, she can fight for the interests of Sandia National Laboratories, a Department of Energy research facility whose focus is national security. Sandia is a major employer in her district.

In 2001, Wilson voted against the annual defense authorization measure because it established a timetable for a new round of military base closures culminating in 2005. In 2004, she joined other Armed Services members in a futile attempt to stave off the 2005 closures. Kirtland Air Force Base, in Albuquerque, is another big district employer.

Nuclear power is big business in New Mexico and, in concert with Domenici, Wilson has worked to boost nuclear's role in U.S. energy policy. In the 107th, she won House passage of a provision, crucial to the industry's survival, to extend the federal nuclear liability system that provides compensation in the event of a nuclear accident, and to cap the industry's payments.

On Energy and Commerce, Wilson has spearheaded congressional efforts to regulate junk e-mail, or spam. Leading a coalition of lawmakers who favored strict regulation, she helped strengthen the provisions of an "anti-spam" law enacted in 2003.

She sought to bolster resources for education, joining a bipartisan group in the 107th that called for increasing Head Start spending by more than $330 million and advocating a tax credit for teachers in low-income areas. As the debate on rewriting welfare law started in 2002, Wilson and other GOP women pressed for a $2 billion increase in child care block grants.

Wilson was a high school junior in New Hampshire when the Air Force Academy opened its doors to women, and she decided she wanted to be a pilot, like her father and grandfather. She graduated from the academy in 1982, the third class that included women. She never got a pilot's license, however, as she went to Oxford as a Rhodes scholar. There, she earned master's and doctoral degrees in international relations.

After serving in the Air Force in Europe, Wilson took a job in 1989 with the National Security Council under President George Bush. In 1991, she married and moved to New Mexico. She started a consulting firm and joined GOP Gov. Gary E. Johnson's Cabinet in 1995.

She resigned that post early in 1998 to run for the House when Republican Steven H. Schiff, who was battling skin cancer, said he would retire. She entered the race with the endorsements of Schiff and Domenici. When Schiff died in March, Wilson became the GOP nominee for the special election to finish his term. She prevailed by 5 percentage points against multimillionaire businessman and Democratic state Sen. Phillip J. Maloof. She won election to a full term by 7 points.

In 2002, in territory that retained its Democratic lean after redistricting, Wilson won by 11 points over state Sen. Richard Romero. She bested him again in their 2004 rematch, this time by 9 points.

KEY VOTES

2004
Yes Extend federal unemployment benefits by 13 weeks
Yes Pass $283.2 billion, six-year federal highway and mass transit bill
Yes Approve $146 billion multi-year extension of previously enacted middle-class tax breaks
Yes Amend the Constitution to prohibit same-sex marriage
No Cut corporate taxes $137 billion over 10 years
Yes Reorganize U.S. intelligence agencies as proposed by Sept. 11 commission

2003
Yes Cut taxes by $330 billion through fiscal 2013
No Block Bush rule scaling back overtime pay for some white-collar federal workers
No Do not allow use of search warrants without first notifying subjects
Yes Allow importation of prescription drugs
Yes Create private school voucher program in Washington, D.C.
Yes Ban "partial birth" abortion except to save a woman's life
No Split $18.6 billion in Iraq aid into half-grant, half-loan
Yes Overhaul Medicare and create prescription drug benefit

CQ VOTE STUDIES

	PARTY UNITY		PRESIDENTIAL SUPPORT	
	Support	Oppose	Support	Oppose
2004	79%	21%	88%	12%
2003	91%	9%	89%	11%
2002	90%	10%	90%	10%
2001	94%	6%	88%	12%
2000	87%	13%	33%	67%

INTEREST GROUPS

	AFL-CIO	ADA	CCUS	ACU
2004	33%	25%	95%	84%
2003	13%	20%	93%	72%
2002	11%	5%	100%	84%
2001	17%	5%	91%	84%
2000	10%	10%	80%	80%

NEW MEXICO 1
Central – Albuquerque

Built around Albuquerque, New Mexico's largest city, the 1st is the only urban district in a sparsely populated, desert state. Since the Manhattan Project set the region on a technology-driven course in the 1940s, Albuquerque has grown from 35,000 people before WWII to more than 440,000 in 2000.

Sandia National Laboratories — born out of the Manhattan Project — is the basis for a steady defense industry. Sandia, which employs more than 8,000 people, coordinates with the two other major employers in the district, the University of New Mexico and Kirtland Air Force Base, to conduct nuclear and national security research. Sandia's success has contributed to a surge in computer, laser and other technology firms in the area, including Muse Technologies, Emcore, Phillips Laboratory at Kirtland and nearby Intel (located in the 3rd). The city's concentration of technology companies draws a disproportionate number of PhDs.

Although the 1st became slightly more conservative as a result of redistricting following the 2000 census, the large government workforce and predominately Hispanic South Valley provide registered Democrats with an edge. Democrats hold most local offices and Hispanics, who make up 43 percent of the 1st's population, overwhelmingly favor Democrats. The Green Party also makes a strong showing, reaching double-digit percentages in some congressional races. But the GOP has held the congressional seat since its creation in 1968, with the area traditionally sending fiscally conservative, defense-oriented moderate Republicans to Congress. Much of the GOP vote comes from the mainly white, upper-middle-class Northeast Heights section of Albuquerque.

MAJOR INDUSTRY
Higher education, scientific research, government, defense

MILITARY BASES
Kirtland Air Force Base, 5,240 military, 17,125 civilian (2003)

CITIES
Albuquerque (pt.), 442,365; South Valley (unincorporated) (pt.), 39,060; North Valley (unincorporated), 11,923

NOTABLE
Albuquerque's annual International Balloon Fiesta is the world's largest hot air balloon event; The National Atomic Museum in Albuquerque is owned by the Department of Energy and operated by Sandia Labs.

Rep. Steve Pearce (R)

CAPITOL OFFICE
225-2365
pearce.house.gov
1607 Longworth 20515-3102; fax 225-9559

COMMITTEES
Financial Services
Homeland Security
Resources

HOMETOWN
Hobbs

BORN
Aug. 24, 1947, Lamesa, Texas

RELIGION
Baptist

FAMILY
Wife, Cynthia Pearce; one child

EDUCATION
New Mexico State U., B.B.A. 1970 (economics);
Eastern New Mexico U., M.B.A. 1991

MILITARY SERVICE
Air Force, 1971-76

CAREER
Oil well services company owner; corporate pilot

POLITICAL HIGHLIGHTS
N.M. House, 1997-2001; sought Republican
nomination for U.S. Senate, 2000

ELECTION RESULTS

2004 GENERAL

Steve Pearce (R)	130,498	60.2%
Gary King (D)	86,292	39.8%

2004 PRIMARY

Steve Pearce (R)	unopposed

2002 GENERAL

Steve Pearce (R)	79,631	56.2%
John Arthur Smith (D)	61,916	43.7%

Elected 2002; 2nd term

People in the rural West often look out for their neighbors, and it is Pearce's good fortune that his rural district abuts the West Texas oil-patch area where President Bush got his political start. Pearce's loyalty to Bush and his agenda helped him win his seat in 2002 and keep it two years later, despite his district's Democratic edge.

A self-described "very conservative" politician, Pearce is a strong supporter of Bush's economic program and his pre-emptive action against Iraq. A former owner of an oil well parts business, Pearce believes public lands should be open to greater oil and gas exploration along with other commercial uses.

But as a border-state congressman, Pearce disagrees with some in his party who want to sharply cut the flow of immigrants from Mexico and other countries. "I've got good conservative friends of mine who say we should lock the borders down and that we should stop all immigration," he said in early 2005. "My response to them is, 'You don't understand that we don't have enough workers.'"

From his seat on the Resources Committee, Pearce concerns himself with water policy, an important Western issue. Among his priorities is to seek funding for a program at the New Mexico Institute of Mining and Technology for an advanced water purification and filtration system that he hopes could remove salt from water in much greater quantities than currently possible.

Pearce has made no secret of his desire to eventually serve on the Appropriations Committee, where his like-minded predecessor, Republican Joe Skeen, was able to steer millions of federal dollars for farming, ranching and energy projects to the district each year. But in the 109th Congress, he was forced to settle for new posts to two other committees — Homeland Security and Financial Services. In the 108th, Republican leaders named him an assistant whip and tapped him for duty on task forces studying prescription drugs, natural gas and other energy issues.

Like most freshmen, Pearce was preoccupied in his first term with helping people from his district navigate the federal bureaucracy. "We've really paid attention to our constituents, and that's the thing I think I'm proudest of," Pearce said in late 2004.

Legislatively, he also kept his focus on local issues. He added language to a bill the House passed calling for a reduction in the royalties that potash companies pay the federal government, seeking to help local companies that mine the fertilizer chemical. He also added funds to the 2004 surface transportation bill for the four-lane widening of U.S. Highway 62-180 from Carlsbad to the Texas state line.

Pearce joined with others in the New Mexico delegation in fighting the Air Force's plans to retire F-117 Stealth fighters stationed at Holloman Air Force Base. To protect Holloman and other New Mexico bases, he introduced a bill in April 2004 to force the Bureau of Land Management to turn over to the Pentagon millions of acres of land it owns on military bases. He said the bureau's ownership on military installations "puts us at a distinct disadvantage" when the Pentagon looks to close bases.

Pearce is no stranger to the Air Force. He is a veteran of the service and served in Vietnam. He owns a Mooney airplane that he flies for fun these days, although he also has been a corporate pilot.

Pearce shares with many in his party his conservative views on social issues. He opposes more gun control and expanded abortion rights, and he wants to amend the Constitution to prohibit same-sex marriage. He says he rises at 4:30 a.m. daily to read the Bible.

Pearce jumped into the 2nd District race after Skeen's failing health led to his retirement in 2002. Although conservative-leaning, the 2nd has a large Hispanic population that helps yield a Democratic voter registration edge. And the socially conservative views of the Democratic nominee, state Sen. John Arthur Smith, gave the party hope that he might have crossover appeal. But Pearce — a two-term state House member — had a money advantage and help from the Bush administration, and he won by 12 percentage points.

In 2004, Pearce squared off against an even better-known Democrat — Gary King, a businessman, lawyer and state legislator for 12 years with deep New Mexico political roots. His father, Bruce King, was the longest-serving governor in state history, with three separate four-year terms as governor in the 1970s, 1980s and 1990s.

The year before the election, King moved into a rented house in Carlsbad, in the district's southeast corner, and began putting what he said was more than 100,000 miles on his car traveling around the vast 69,000-square-mile district, which includes part of 18 New Mexico counties. He campaigned on improving health care and the economy and on fixing Bush's No Child Left Behind education law, which he said amounted to an unfunded mandate.

King also went on the offensive against Pearce, criticizing the incumbent for voting against a $1,500 bonus for active military serving in Iraq and Afghanistan, and for voting against Democratic initiatives to expand health care for reservists.

But Pearce struck back hard, running a campaign ad that called the attacks misleading. His spokesman noted that though Pearce voted against the Democrat-led $1,500 bonus for troops, he later voted for a defense appropriations bill that included an annual $2,700 salary increase for all troops.

Pearce sought to portray King as a carpetbagger and — taking a well-worn page from the GOP campaign playbook — a tax-and-spend liberal. He ran an ad that said King "just moved here to run for Congress," and that accused King of voting for higher taxes and fees "time and time again."

King was unable to gain much traction in a swing state that the Bush campaign desperately sought to add to the presidential victory column after barely losing it in 2000. With Bush and Vice President Dick Cheney making numerous campaign stops in New Mexico, Pearce won with 60 percent.

KEY VOTES

2004

No Extend federal unemployment benefits by 13 weeks

Yes Pass $283.2 billion, six-year federal highway and mass transit bill

Yes Approve $146 billion multi-year extension of previously enacted middle-class tax breaks

Yes Amend the Constitution to prohibit same-sex marriage

Yes Cut corporate taxes $137 billion over 10 years

Yes Reorganize U.S. intelligence agencies as proposed by Sept. 11 commission

2003

Yes Cut taxes by $330 billion through fiscal 2013

No Block Bush rule scaling back overtime pay for some white-collar federal workers

No Do not allow use of search warrants without first notifying subjects

No Allow importation of prescription drugs

Yes Create private school voucher program in Washington, D.C.

Yes Ban "partial birth" abortion except to save a woman's life

No Split $18.6 billion in Iraq aid into half-grant, half-loan

Yes Overhaul Medicare and create prescription drug benefit

CQ VOTE STUDIES

	PARTY UNITY		PRESIDENTIAL SUPPORT	
	Support	Oppose	Support	Oppose
2004	94%	6%	91%	9%
2003	98%	2%	98%	2%

INTEREST GROUPS

	AFL-CIO	ADA	CCUS	ACU
2004	13%	0%	95%	96%
2003	0%	5%	97%	88%

NEW MEXICO 2
South — Las Cruces, Roswell, Little Texas

Before hosting the first atomic bomb explosion in 1945, the mostly rural 2nd, covering the southern half of the state, looked like the old American West. Since then, the area has attracted nuclear research and waste facilities to the Chihuahua Desert's deep salt beds and remote location. The first permanent underground low-level nuclear waste repository opened in abandoned salt mines near Carlsbad in 1999.

Towns in the 2nd have built a stable economy on traditional Western industries: copper and lead mining in the Mexican Highlands along the Arizona border, and oil and gas, as well as cattle and sheep ranching, in the southeastern corner of the state, dubbed Little Texas after the Texans who settled the region in the early 20th century. The northern New Mexico technology industry has spilled over into the 2nd, supported by New Mexico State and other universities. Severe water shortages have prevented large-scale industrial development and larger corporate farming, although the northern part of the district is a major producer of pistachios.

Beginning in the 1970s, ranchers and conservative Democrats steered away from a long liberal tradition. Democrats hold the vast majority of local offices, but the district is competitive at the national level. In the 2004 presidential election, the 2nd was New Mexico's only congressional district won by George W. Bush, who captured 58 percent here.

MAJOR INDUSTRY
Agriculture, mining, oil and gas production

MILITARY BASES
Holloman Air Force Base, 4,608 military, 2,160 civilian (2003); White Sands Missile Range, 490 military, 6,100 civilian (2004)

CITIES
Las Cruces, 74,267; Roswell, 45,293; Alamogordo, 35,582; Hobbs, 28,657; Carlsbad, 25,625

NOTABLE
White Sands National Monument is the world's largest gypsum dune field; Roswell hosts an annual UFO festival near the site where a UFO allegedly crashed in 1947; Ted Turner, one of the nation's largest private landowners, owns more than 1.1 million acres in New Mexico, much of it in the 2nd; Hatch calls itself the "Chile Capital of the World" and holds an annual chile festival.

Rep. Tom Udall (D)

CAPITOL OFFICE
225-6190
tom.udall@mail.house.gov
www.house.gov/tomudall
1414 Longworth 20515-3103; fax 226-1331

COMMITTEES
Resources
Small Business
Veterans' Affairs

HOMETOWN
Santa Fe

BORN
May 18, 1948, Tuscon, Ariz.

RELIGION
Mormon

FAMILY
Wife, Jill Z. Cooper; one stepchild

EDUCATION
Prescott College, B.A. 1970 (government & political science); Cambridge U., B.L.L. 1975; U. of New Mexico, J.D. 1977

CAREER
Lawyer

POLITICAL HIGHLIGHTS
Assistant U.S. attorney, 1978-81; sought Democratic nomination for U.S. House, 1982; Democratic nominee for U.S. House, 1988; N.M. attorney general, 1991-99

ELECTION RESULTS

2004 GENERAL

Tom Udall (D)	175,269	68.7%
Gregory M. Tucker (R)	79,935	31.3%

2004 PRIMARY

Tom Udall (D)	unopposed

2002 GENERAL

Tom Udall (D)	unopposed

PREVIOUS WINNING PERCENTAGES
2000 (67%); 1998 (53%)

Elected 1998; 4th term

Public service is a family business for the Udalls, and the New Mexico congressman has carried on the tradition. As the first cousin of a current congressman, the nephew of a former congressman, and the son of a former congressman and Interior secretary, Udall can claim a political legacy beyond almost any Democrat whose last name is not Kennedy. And like the rest of his clan, he can also claim the mantle of an environmentalist.

Udall and his Colorado cousin, Democrat Mark Udall, were elected to the House on the same day in 1998, bringing to Congress a second generation of their family. Tom's father, Stewart, represented Arizona in the House in the late 1950s before serving as secretary of Interior under presidents Kennedy and Johnson. Morris K. Udall, Tom's uncle and Mark's father, succeeded his brother, Stewart, in the House in 1961 and was a prominent force there for the next 30 years, gaining particular attention as an advocate for environmental protection. "From the time I was six, I heard my father and uncle talk about public service," Tom recalls.

There's another Udall cousin in the current Congress as well — a second cousin — but the name and party identification are different: Republican Sen. Gordon H. Smith of Oregon. His mother and the Udall brothers' fathers were first cousins.

Tom and Mark Udall are avid mountaineers. Both sit on the Resources Committee, and they have paired up on legislation affecting environmental issues, usually finding themselves on the losing side. In the 108th Congress, the Udalls introduced a bill to revamp and streamline fire-prevention management on federal land. They also joined forces against President Bush's "Healthy Forests" legislation in 2003, but to no avail.

In 2003, the New Mexico Udall also proposed legislation seeking to stop the administration's plans to loosen requirements for the Forest Service to seek public input and conduct environmental and scientific reviews in writing forest management plans. "They have swept the scientists out of the system," he said. Despite his efforts, the forest plan was adopted in 2004.

Although Udall maintains a near-perfect voting participation record, he finds time to host many town meetings with his constituents. In a series of gatherings during the 108th, Udall spoke out against the USA Patriot Act, the anti-terror law pushed through Congress by the administration in the wake of the Sept. 11, 2001, terrorist attacks. Bush "preyed on a vulnerable and fearful country," Udall said, commending a New Mexico county for passing a local ordinance defying the act, which critics say infringes on civil liberties. Udall was one of just 66 House members who voted against the measure in 2001.

Joining with Independent Bernard Sanders of Vermont, Udall cosponsored legislation in the 108th to counteract provisions of the Patriot Act affecting access to library and bookstore patrons' records. "The threat of terrorism should not be used as an excuse for 'Big Brother' to tread on our most cherished constitutionally guaranteed civil liberties," he said. But the proposal, offered as an amendment to a spending bill, was narrowly defeated on the House floor.

He has worked on other priorities as well, including health care, releasing a study showing discrepancies in prescription drug prices in his district. He also joined with California's George Miller, the Education Committee's top-ranking Democrat, on the No Child Left Behind education law passed by Congress in 2001. Udall considers Miller, a liberal firebrand who nonetheless is skilled in the art of dealmaking, one of the colleagues he most admires.

Udall takes pains to stay in touch with his constituents, who range from nuclear scientists at Los Alamos National Laboratory to wealthy liberals in Santa Fe to rural Hispanics and Indians living in areas where unemployment remains fixed above 40 percent. He maintains six offices across his sprawling district, which encompasses northern New Mexico and is roughly the size of Pennsylvania. "I believe very much in access," he says. "The main thing for me is striving to reach new people and get new ideas."

He also carefully tends to issues of local interest, working with others in the state's delegation in 2000, for instance, to get the federal government to purchase the picturesque 95,000-acre Baca Ranch in his district. Udall, who speaks Spanish, also reintroduced a measure his predecessor, Republican Bill Redmond, had sponsored creating a commission to review the claims of heirs to Hispanic land grants. In 2004, Udall received the Government Accountability Office's first-ever comprehensive study of all land grant claims in New Mexico — requested four years earlier by Udall and New Mexico's senators, Democrat Jeff Bingaman and Republican Pete V. Domenici.

At the start of the 108th Congress, Udall was elected by regional colleagues to the Steering and Policy Committee, which makes Democratic committee assignments.

Continuing a practice he started as attorney general, the New Mexican has relied on his wife, Jill Z. Cooper, also an attorney, as a political confidante. The couple's daughter, Amanda Cooper, also seems to have the family's political genes: In 2003, she signed on as a district political director for New Mexico Democratic Gov. Bill Richardson.

Udall has carved out a safe niche for himself in the 3rd District, which is easily New Mexico's most liberal. His 1998 House campaign was his third try: He lost a 1982 Democratic primary for the seat to Richardson, who went on to win and serve for more than 14 years. In 1988, Udall was the Democratic nominee in the adjacent 1st District but lost to Republican Steven H. Schiff. In 1998, Udall returned to the 3rd, as local Democrats were eager to oust Redmond, a conservative Republican minister who had won a three-way special election in May 1997 to replace Richardson when he left to become President Clinton's U.N. ambassador.

Udall won an eight-candidate Democratic primary. In the general election, he attacked Redmond as being too conservative and won by a comfortable, 10 percentage point margin. He cruised to victory in 2000, and his district lines were altered only slightly by redistricting following the 2000 census. Udall was unopposed in 2002, and won re-election in 2004 with more than two-thirds of the vote.

KEY VOTES

2004

Yes   Extend federal unemployment benefits by 13 weeks

Yes   Pass $283.2 billion, six-year federal highway and mass transit bill

Yes   Approve $146 billion multi-year extension of previously enacted middle-class tax breaks

No   Amend the Constitution to prohibit same-sex marriage

No   Cut corporate taxes $137 billion over 10 years

Yes   Reorganize U.S. intelligence agencies as proposed by Sept. 11 commission

2003

No   Cut taxes by $330 billion through fiscal 2013

Yes   Block Bush rule scaling back overtime pay for some white-collar federal workers

Yes   Do not allow use of search warrants without first notifying subjects

Yes   Allow importation of prescription drugs

No   Create private school voucher program in Washington, D.C.

No   Ban "partial birth" abortion except to save a woman's life

Yes   Split $18.6 billion in Iraq aid into half-grant, half-loan

No   Overhaul Medicare and create prescription drug benefit

CQ VOTE STUDIES

	PARTY UNITY		PRESIDENTIAL SUPPORT	
	Support	Oppose	Support	Oppose
2004	95%	5%	21%	79%
2003	97%	3%	18%	82%
2002	98%	2%	20%	80%
2001	96%	4%	23%	77%
2000	91%	9%	77%	23%

INTEREST GROUPS

	AFL-CIO	ADA	CCUS	ACU
2004	93%	100%	29%	8%
2003	100%	100%	23%	12%
2002	89%	100%	35%	0%
2001	100%	100%	30%	4%
2000	90%	80%	35%	9%

NEW MEXICO 3
North — Santa Fe, Rio Rancho, Farmington

Since artist Georgia O'Keeffe began painting northern New Mexico in 1929, the 3rd District's breathtaking scenery and unique Spanish and American Indian heritage have attracted thousands of artists and beauty seekers. Today, galleries and ski resorts still attract tourists, while an influx of retirees made the district the most rapidly growing part of the state in the 1990s.

But the 3rd is a district of extremes. Alongside the bountiful art trade is extraordinary poverty. Gallup, in McKinley County, boasts many millionaires, while the county itself remains one of the poorest in the nation. Large American Indian populations in the northwest struggle with modest farming and ranching ventures, while the same area provides lofty incomes for oil and gas producers. Many western reservations are plagued with alcoholism, and Rio Arriba County in the north has one of the highest drug mortality rates in the nation.

Hispanics and American Indians — alongside a wealthy, liberal base in the state capital of Santa Fe — give Democrats a 2-to-1 edge in voter

registration. Conservative pockets exist in areas such as Rio Rancho, where Intel employs more than 5,500 workers; Los Alamos National Laboratory, where the A-bomb was developed during WWII; and among energy producers in San Juan County in the district's northwest.

MAJOR INDUSTRY
State government, ranching, farming, tourism

MILITARY BASES
Cannon Air Force Base, 3,400 military, 597 civilian (2005)

CITIES
Santa Fe, 62,203; Rio Rancho (pt.), 46,701; Farmington, 37,844; Clovis, 32,667; Gallup, 20,209

NOTABLE
Santa Fe, the nation's second-oldest city, was founded in 1607; Roughly 100 tribes show their work at the Santa Fe Indian Market each August; The Aztec Ruins National Monument in Aztec features structures and artifacts from the 1100s and 1200s; Camel Rock, near Tesuque, is a natural sandstone formation that the elements have eroded into the shape of camel; U.S. Route 666, which ran north from Gallup into Colorado and Utah, was known as the "devil's highway" before it was renumbered as U.S. Route 491 in 2005.

NEW YORK

Gov. George E. Pataki (R)

First elected: 1994
Length of term: 4 years
Term expires: 1/07
Salary: $179,000
Phone: (518) 474-8390

Hometown: Garrison
Born: June 24, 1945; Peekskill, N.Y.
Religion: Roman Catholic
Family: Wife, Elizabeth "Libby" Pataki; four children
Education: Yale U., B.A. 1967; Columbia U., J.D. 1970
Career: Lawyer; farm owner
Political highlights: Mayor of Peekskill, 1982-84; N.Y. Assembly, 1985-92; N.Y. Senate, 1993-95

Election results:

2002 GENERAL

George E. Pataki (R, C)	2,262,255	49.4%
H. Carl McCall (D, WFM)	1,534,064	33.5%
Tom Golisano (INDC)	654,016	14.3%
Gerard J. Cronin (RTL)	44,195	1.0%

Lt. Gov. Mary Donohue (R)

First elected: 1998
Length of term: 4 years
Term expires: 1/07
Salary: $151,500
Phone: (518) 474-4623

STATE LEGISLATURE

Legislature: Officially year-round; main session January-June

Assembly: 150 members, 2-year terms

2005 breakdown: 104D, 46R; 110 men, 40 women

Salary: $79,500
Phone: (518) 455-4218

Senate: 62 members, 2-year terms

2005 breakdown: 35R, 27D; 52 men, 10 women

Salary: $79,500
Phone: (518) 455-3216

STATE TERM LIMITS

Governor: No
Assembly: No
Senate: No

URBAN STATISTICS

CITY	POPULATION
New York City	8,008,278
Buffalo	292,648
Rochester	219,773
Yonkers	196,086
Syracuse	147,306

REGISTERED VOTERS

Democrat	47%
Republican	27%
Unaffiliated/others	26%

POPULATION

2004 population (est.)	19,227,088
2000 population	18,976,457
1990 population	17,990,455
Percent change (1990-2000)	+5.5%
Rank among states (2004)	3

Median age	35.9
Born in state	65.3%
Foreign born	20.4%
Violent crime rate	554/100,000
Poverty level	14.6%
Federal workers	133,980
Military	57,987

REDISTRICTING

New York lost two House seats in reapportionment. The state legislature drew a new, 29-district map, which the governor signed on June 5, 2002.

MISCELLANEOUS

Web: www.state.ny.us
Capital: Albany
STATE ELECTION OFFICIAL
(518) 474-6220
DEMOCRATIC HEADQUARTERS
(212) 725-8825
REPUBLICAN HEADQUARTERS
(518) 462-2601

District Statistics

DIST.	2004 VOTE FOR PRESIDENT BUSH	KERRY	WHITE	BLACK	ASIAN	HISP	MEDIAN INCOME	WHITE COLLAR	BLUE COLLAR	SERVICE INDUSTRY	OVER 64	UNDER 18	COLLEGE EDUCATION	RURAL	SQ. MILES
1	49%	49%	84%	4%	2%	8%	$61,884	64%	21%	15%	12%	26%	27%	6%	646
2	45	53	72	10	3	14	$71,147	66	20	14	12	27	31	0	239
3	52	47	87	2	3	7	$70,561	69	17	14	15	24	31	0	183
4	44	55	62	18	4	14	$66,799	68	17	15	14	25	31	0	90
5	36	63	44	5	24	23	$51,156	65	18	17	15	22	34	0	66
6	15	84	13	52	9	17	$43,546	57	21	22	11	27	18	0	40
7	25	74	28	17	13	40	$36,990	57	21	22	13	24	20	0	26
8	27	72	69	5	11	12	$47,061	79	10	11	14	18	48	0	15
9	44	56	64	4	15	14	$45,426	68	18	14	17	21	31	0	37
10	13	86	16	60	3	17	$30,212	60	18	22	10	30	18	0	18
11	13	86	21	59	4	12	$34,082	61	16	23	9	27	25	0	12
12	19	80	23	9	16	49	$29,195	51	22	21	9	26	17	0	19
13	55	45	71	6	9	11	$50,092	65	18	17	13	24	24	0	65
14	24	74	66	5	11	14	$57,152	82	8	10	13	13	57	0	13
15	9	90	16	31	3	48	$27,934	64	15	21	11	24	25	0	10

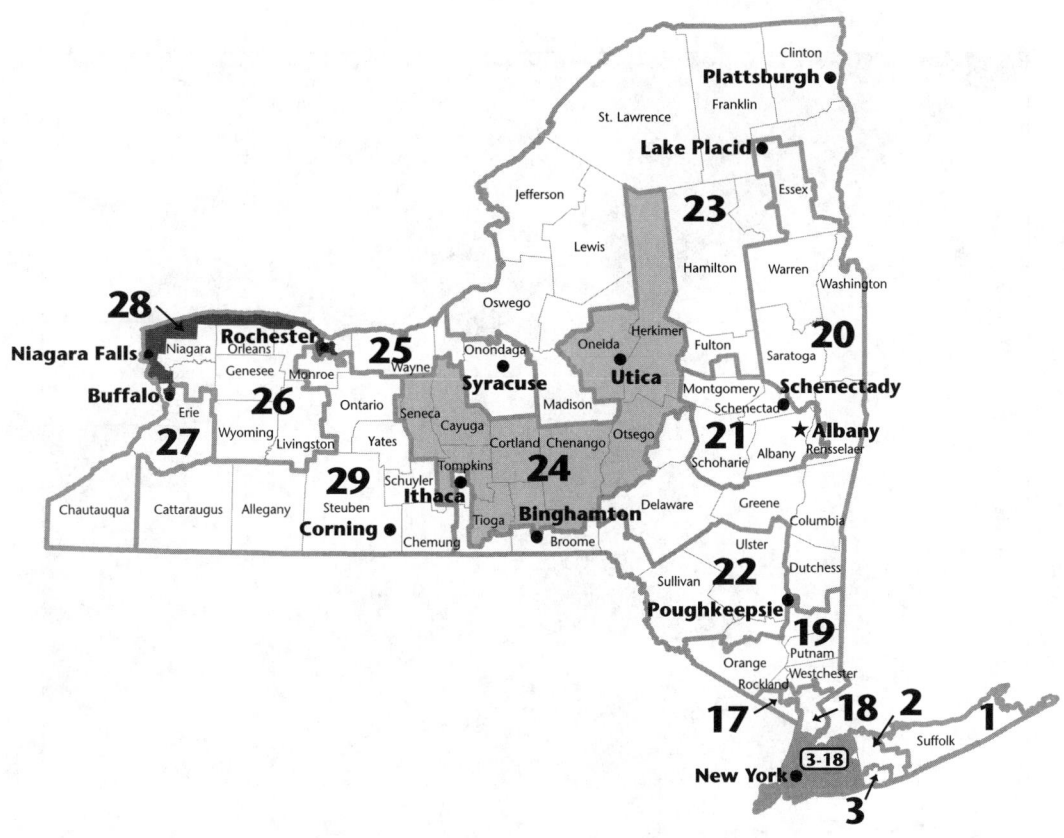

District Statistics

DIST.	2004 VOTE FOR PRESIDENT BUSH	KERRY	WHITE	BLACK	ASIAN	HISP	MEDIAN INCOME	WHITE COLLAR	BLUE COLLAR	SERVICE INDUSTRY	OVER 64	UNDER 18	COLLEGE EDUCATION	RURAL	SQ. MILES
16	10%	89%	3%	30%	2%	63%	$19,311	46%	24%	30%	7%	35%	8%	0%	12
17	33	66	41	30	5	20	$44,868	65	16	19	13	27	29	0	127
18	42	57	67	9	5	16	$68,887	73	13	14	14	25	44	1	222
19	53	45	84	5	2	8	$64,337	67	19	14	11	27	32	21	1,401
20	53	45	93	2	1	2	$44,239	61	24	15	14	24	25	55	7,018
21	43	55	85	7	2	2	$40,254	66	19	15	15	23	27	16	1,935
22	45	53	80	8	3	8	$38,586	61	22	17	14	24	24	32	3,246
23	51	47	93	3	1	2	$35,434	52	29	19	12	25	16	65	13,235
24	52	46	92	3	1	2	$36,082	57	25	17	15	24	19	49	6,164
25	48	50	87	7	2	2	$43,188	65	21	14	14	26	28	21	1,620
26	55	43	92	3	2	2	$46,653	62	24	14	14	25	26	29	2,731
27	44	53	89	4	1	5	$36,884	58	26	16	16	24	20	18	1,830
28	36	62	62	29	1	6	$31,751	58	23	18	14	26	21	7	534
29	56	42	93	3	2	1	$41,875	61	24	15	14	25	26	42	5,660
STATE	40	58	62	15	5	15	$43,393	64	20	17	13	25	27	13	47,214
U.S.	50.7	48.3	69	12	4	13	$41,994	60	25	15	12	26	24	21	3,537,438

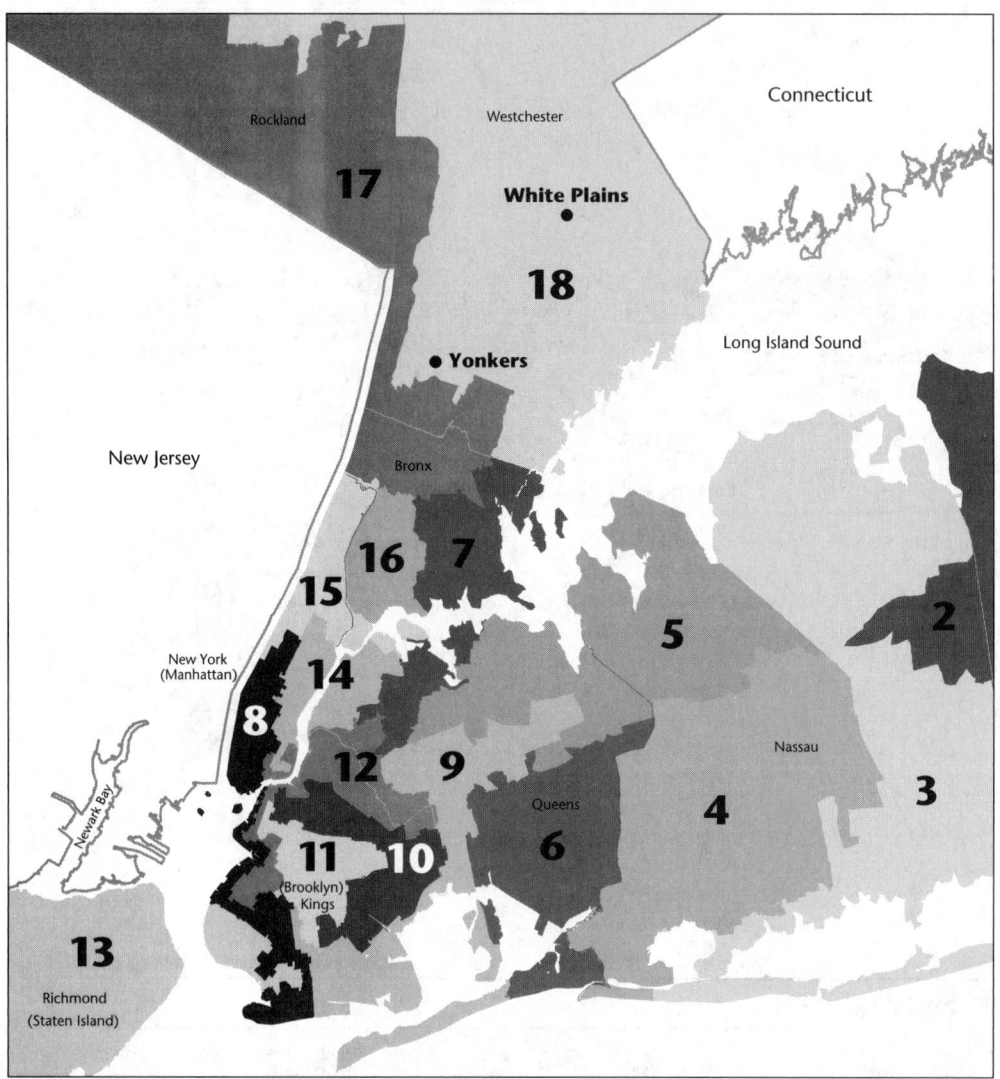

Sen. Charles E. Schumer (D)

Elected 1998; 2nd term

A prolific fundraiser, sharp-tongued communicator and skilled legislator, Schumer is testing his skills in what promises to be the most difficult challenge of his career — guiding Democrats in their quest to win the six seats they need to take majority control in 2006. The role seems tailor-made for Schumer, an articulate ambassador for his party who speaks with authority on a wide range of issues via frequent television appearances, reliably clever quotes and his office's incessant stream of news releases.

Schumer is also uniquely situated as a representative of the country's financial hub and has shown he is capable of raising the huge sums common in modern Senate campaigns. In the 2004 election cycle, he accrued more than $27 million for his own shoo-in bid for re-election, more than any other Senate candidate. He earned goodwill from colleagues by pouring about $2.5 million into state and national party committees.

Despite his qualifications, Schumer did not exactly jump at the chance to take the helm of the Democratic Senatorial Campaign Committee, a job that typically earns the occupant high praise if the party wins and an inordinate amount of blame when it loses. He had been mulling whether to run in the 2006 contest for New York governor when incoming Senate Minority Leader Harry Reid called to offer him the leadership position.

Reid sweetened the deal by offering to give Schumer control over the party message as the communications point person as well as the opportunity to trade his seat on the Energy and Natural Resources Committee for a more coveted spot on the Finance panel. Schumer accepted, and avoided what could have been a bruising primary against state Attorney General Eliot Spitzer.

Schumer has his work ahead of him. In 2006, the Democrats have more seats to defend than the Republicans. But they have history on their side, as the president's party tends to suffer most in the sixth year of an administration's tenure, a phenomenon known as the six-year itch.

Outside the political arena, Schumer weighs in on high-profile issues such as the future of Social Security and the president's judicial appointments, though he is sometimes overshadowed by home-state colleague and former first lady Hillary Rodham Clinton.

As a new member of the Finance Committee, Schumer brings a liberal tilt to the debate over introducing private savings accounts into the Social Security program, and he serves as a counterweight to the panel's more moderate senior Democrat, Max Baucus of Montana. His appointment came as relief to Wall Street lobbyists, who felt their interests were underrepresented in the 108th Congress, when the panel lacked its customary senator from New York or New Jersey.

A veteran member of the Judiciary Committee, as he was during his 18-year House career, Schumer has led his party's opposition to President Bush's judicial nominees. He believes that senators should take into consideration a potential federal judge's ideology, a view contrary to the traditional notion that presidents should get wide latitude to shape the federal courts. Schumer staked out his role in the confirmation wars from the opening days of the Bush administration, when he battled the nomination of John Ashcroft, a former colleague on Judiciary, to be attorney general. He declared that the fight against Ashcroft was "a shot across the bow" aimed at discouraging the president from making similarly divisive judicial nominations in the future.

CAPITOL OFFICE
224-6542
schumer.senate.gov
313 Hart 20510-3203; fax 228-1218

COMMITTEES
Banking, Housing & Urban Affairs
Finance
Judiciary
Rules & Administration
Joint Library

HOMETOWN
Brooklyn

BORN
Nov. 23, 1950, Brooklyn, N.Y.

RELIGION
Jewish

FAMILY
Wife, Iris Weinshall; two children

EDUCATION
Harvard U., A.B. 1971, J.D. 1974

CAREER
Lawyer

POLITICAL HIGHLIGHTS
N.Y. Assembly, 1975-81; U.S. House, 1981-99

ELECTION RESULTS

2004 GENERAL

C. Schumer (D, INDC, WFM)	4,769,824	71.2%
Howard Mills (R)	1,625,069	24.2%
Marilyn F. O'Grady (C)	220,960	3.3%

2004 PRIMARY

C. Schumer (D)	unopposed

PREVIOUS WINNING PERCENTAGES
1998 (55%); 1996 House Election (75%); 1994 House Election (73%); 1992 House Election (89%); 1990 House Election (80%); 1988 House Election (78%); 1986 House Election (93%); 1984 House Election (72%); 1982 House Election (79%); 1980 House Election (77%)

Bush was undeterred. In the 108th Congress, he appointed numerous conservatives to the bench, prompting Schumer and his colleagues to filibuster 10 they considered "out of the mainstream." Outraged Republicans decried what they viewed as a partisan move to deny senators their constitutional right to give advice and consent — via an up-or-down floor vote — on the president's nominees.

In the 107th Congress, Schumer partnered with Arizona Republican Jon Kyl on a bill to ease the authorization for warrants under the Foreign Intelligence Surveillance Act. The effort was typical of Schumer's longstanding support for giving law enforcement more power to pursue criminals. In the House, where he chaired the Judiciary Crime Subcommittee for four years, he was a main sponsor of the 1994 anti-crime law that put 100,000 new police officers on the beat, banned 19 assault weapons and created a "three strikes" mandatory life sentence for repeat violent offenders.

An ardent gun control advocate, Schumer was the chief sponsor of the 1993 Brady law requiring a background check for the purchase of any handgun. When the National Rifle Association once called him "the criminal's best friend," Schumer shot back: "I wear this like a badge of honor."

He is a crusader for crime victims. In 2002, Schumer lambasted the Justice Department for requiring rape victims to help pay for the collection of forensic evidence against their attackers, which he likened to "asking the family of a homicide victim to pay for the autopsy."

Schumer's reach on issues is broad. In 2003, he pushed hard to add to the economic stimulus package a $40 billion boost in direct aid to state and local governments. He also proposed a $10 billion plan to outfit all commercial airliners with anti-missile equipment. And he resurrected a bill with Republican John McCain of Arizona to speed generic drugs to market by making it more difficult for brand-name drugmakers to extend their patents.

On the Banking Committee, Schumer tries to serve both business interests and average New Yorkers. He worked to reverse a federal plan that would have required investment banks to set up alternate headquarters outside New York as a contingency in case of another terrorist attack. He has pressed to reduce transaction fees paid by the securities industry while also working for more protection for consumers with bad credit, prompting the American Banker newsletter to describe Schumer as "one of the few members of the often-polarized Senate Banking and Judiciary committees that can make both industry and community groups happy."

Brooklyn-born and bred, Schumer was elected to represent the borough in the state Assembly just before he turned 24, the fall after his graduation from Harvard Law School. Six years later, he was easily elected to Congress with the endorsement of Elizabeth Holtzman, who gave up her Brooklyn House seat to be the 1980 Democratic nominee for the Senate.

She lost that year to Republican Alfonse M. D'Amato. In 1998, after 18 years in the House, Schumer took on D'Amato, winning the Democratic nomination with 51 percent of the vote against former Rep. Geraldine A. Ferraro, the 1984 vice presidential nominee, and New York City Public Advocate Mark Green.

In the fall, D'Amato branded Schumer as too liberal and attacked him for missing more than 100 floor votes while campaigning. Schumer deflected D'Amato's charges, pointing to his anti-crime and gun control efforts. He also recounted D'Amato's history of ethics problems. Though D'Amato spent more than $24 million, Schumer was competitive, spending almost $17 million. He won by almost 500,000 votes.

He easily topped that in 2004, winning with 71 percent against an underfunded opponent, Republican assemblyman Howard Mills.

KEY VOTES

2004

Yes Pass $318.9 billion, six-year highway and mass transit bill

Yes Extend assault weapons ban for 10 years

Yes Restore pay-as-you-go rules for new tax cuts and entitlement spending

No Criminalize harm to a fetus in an attack on the mother

Yes Increase mandatory child care funding to states by $6 billion over five years

No Amend the Constitution to prohibit same-sex marriage

Yes Approve $146 billion multi-year extension of previously enacted middle-class tax breaks

Yes Reorganize U.S. intelligence agencies as proposed by Sept. 11 commission

Yes Cut corporate taxes $137 billion over 10 years

2003

Yes Delay Bush changes to Clean Air Act

No Allow confirmation vote on Miguel A. Estrada to the U.S. Court of Appeals for the D.C. Circuit

Yes Block a Bush proposal opening Alaska's Arctic National Wildlife Refuge to oil drilling

Yes Limit size of Bush's proposed tax cut to $350 billion through fiscal 2013

Yes Overhaul Medicare and create prescription drug benefit

Yes Block Bush rule scaling back overtime pay for some white-collar federal workers

Yes Split $20 billion in Iraq aid into half-grant, half-loan

No Ban "partial birth" abortion except to save a woman's life

No Stop proposal allowing travel to Cuba

No Allow final vote on energy policy overhaul

CQ VOTE STUDIES

	PARTY UNITY		PRESIDENTIAL SUPPORT	
	Support	Oppose	Support	Oppose
2004	91%	9%	62%	38%
2003	96%	4%	47%	53%
2002	95%	5%	68%	32%
2001	92%	8%	65%	35%
2000	97%	3%	98%	2%
1999	94%	6%	91%	9%
House Service:				
1998	94%	6%	85%	15%
1997	90%	10%	83%	17%
1996	91%	9%	83%	17%
1995	89%	11%	87%	13%

INTEREST GROUPS

	AFL-CIO	ADA	CCUS	ACU
2004	100%	100%	65%	12%
2003	85%	95%	39%	10%
2002	92%	85%	50%	10%
2001	100%	95%	43%	16%
2000	75%	95%	53%	12%
1999	89%	100%	53%	4%
House Service:				
1998	100%	100%	36%	9%
1997	100%	85%	40%	19%
1996	90%	90%	31%	5%
1995	100%	80%	32%	4%

Sen. Hillary Rodham Clinton (D)

Elected 2000; 1st term

CAPITOL OFFICE
224-4451
clinton.senate.gov
476 Russell 20510-3204; fax 228-0282

COMMITTEES
Armed Services
Environment & Public Works
Health, Education, Labor & Pensions
Special Aging

HOMETOWN
Chappaqua

BORN
Oct. 26, 1947, Chicago, Ill.

RELIGION
Methodist

FAMILY
Husband, Bill Clinton; one child

EDUCATION
Wellesley College, B.A. 1969; Yale U., J.D. 1973

CAREER
First lady; lawyer; law school professor;
congressional aide

POLITICAL HIGHLIGHTS
No previous office

ELECTION RESULTS

2000 GENERAL

Hillary R. Clinton (D, L, WFM)	3,747,310	55.3%
Rick A. Lazio (R, C)	2,915,730	43.0%

2000 PRIMARY

Hillary R. Clinton (D)	565,353	82.0%
Mark McMahon (D)	124,315	18.0%

To the surprise of her critics and many Republicans, Clinton has used her first term in the Senate to transform herself into a more broadly appealing national figure, and with the passage of time, has shed some of the baggage from her past as the love-her-or-hate-her former first lady.

Her political evolution was evident in 2005, as she began talking more about faith and prayer, and counseling tolerance of those opposed to abortion and gay marriage on moral grounds. She says she is committed to running for re-election in New York when her first term is up in 2006, but she nonetheless is positioned to be a serious contender on the national stage. Clinton is among the handful of Democrats with the stature to compete for the nomination for president in 2008.

Clinton and those close to her deny that she has changed; like her husband, they say, she has always been a centrist "New Democrat," who draws convictions and inspiration from her religious beliefs. But there can be little doubt that Clinton's transformation from scandal-prone lightning rod to well-respected legislator and party powerbroker is well underway.

Public polls after the 2004 elections showed that the proportion of New Yorkers with a negative view of Clinton had dropped substantially. The number of state Republicans saying they approve of her performance has risen sharply to just under 50 percent, according to a February 2005 New York Times poll.

Those gains may be the result of Clinton's determination to balance her celebrity among Democrats — which she has exploited to raise money and trumpet the party message — with her role as a first-term New York senator facing parochial challenges.

In early 2005, Clinton joined several more-senior Democrats, including Minority Leader Harry Reid, on a Social Security "road show" designed to rival President Bush's cross-country push to win enactment of his plan to add personal retirement accounts to the program. A few weeks earlier, after some closely watched pondering, Clinton supported Bush's nomination of Michael Chertoff to be secretary of homeland security, putting aside her old grudge against a man who once led the Whitewater investigation into the Clintons' real estate dealings. Chertoff's "repeated expressions of support for policies that are essential to the security of New Yorkers are decisive factors" in the decision, she said.

Clinton also confounded expectations that she would hog the spotlight in the 2004 presidential race in order to smooth her own White House path. Instead, she was a loyal soldier working in behalf of Sen. John Kerry's unsuccessful bid, using both her celebrity to raise money for Kerry and her considerable skills as a political strategist to help guide the party.

Indeed, Clinton has won admiration from colleagues in both parties for her fierce defense of New York's interests. After the terrorist attacks of Sept. 11, 2001, she lobbied persistently, if unsuccessfully, to steer more homeland security funds to big cities facing more-serious risks. She has crusaded in behalf of Fort Drum, near the northern tip of New York, fighting to keep the base from being closed. Such work has won her accolades from Empire State Republicans including Rep. John M. McHugh, who represents the base, Rep. Thomas M. Reynolds and Rep. Peter T. King, all of whom have praised Clinton's work in behalf of her adopted state.

Clinton also has reached out to some Republicans who were arch-enemies of her husband's administration. She joined House Majority Leader Tom

DeLay, a zealous proponent of impeaching President Clinton, on legislation to revamp the foster care system. In 2003, she teamed with GOP Sen. Lindsey Graham of South Carolina — one of the House managers who presented the impeachment case against her husband — to add a provision to the defense authorization bill creating health insurance subsidies for the families of National Guard and Reserve members on active duty.

Clinton has made the most of her seat on the Armed Services Committee, a plum she secured in the 108th Congress. The post allowed her to fill in what had been a gaping hole in her portfolio — military and foreign affairs — and get involved in the most pressing issue of the day: the war in Iraq. Clinton joined many of her Democratic colleagues in 2002 to support the resolution allowing Bush to invade Iraq, but she has been a vocal critic of the president's handling of the conflict.

On the Health, Education, Labor and Pensions Committee, Clinton has focused on improving teacher training and easing nursing shortages. But one of her biggest setbacks has come on a health care bill. Her initiative in the 107th Congress to require drugmakers to conduct pediatric safety tests when their products are prescribed for children stalled in committee. It is no secret that Clinton is eyeing an assignment to one of the more coveted committees — either Finance or Appropriations.

Despite her efforts to be a model freshman senator, she has never strayed far from the limelight. She was one of six Democrats, for example, who won the "golden gavel" in 2002 for having presided over the Senate for 100 hours. Her memoir, "Living History," for which she received a reported advance of $8 million, became the fastest-selling non-fiction book ever. And Democratic officials got a blunt reminder that Clinton was not just another senator when they passed her over for a speaking role at the 2004 party convention in Boston. Women Democrats and New York officials objected loudly, and Clinton was given a prime time role introducing her husband on the first night.

Clinton's biography is one of the most familiar in current American politics. Raised in the well-heeled Chicago suburb of Park Ridge, Hillary Rodham was ambitious, with the smarts to back it up. She got into Yale University, a fateful event that resulted in her meeting, and falling in love with, fellow student Bill Clinton, her equal in intelligence and ambition. The two married and returned to his native Arkansas to launch his political career.

Their first attempt to get Bill Clinton elected failed, when he lost a 1974 House race. But as a political unit, they were a disciplined and savvy team, even though as a couple they famously fought and Clinton's career was shadowed by chronic rumors of dalliances with other women.

He went on to become Arkansas governor and a leader of the centrist movement in the Democratic Party; she was his top adviser and activist first lady. They brought that operating mode to Washington in 1992. Hillary Clinton had an enormous impact on Oval Office decisions in President Clinton's two terms, including an ill-fated attempt in 1993 to revamp the health care system. She stood by him publicly in his darkest hour, impeachment proceedings in 1998 stemming from his attempt to cover up an affair with a White House intern.

Once her husband finished his second term, Clinton was free to pursue a political career of her own. Though she'd never lived in New York, she announced she would move there and run for the Senate. She had tremendous advantages as a former first lady in the Democratic-leaning state, but Republicans pounced on the fact that she had never lived there and accused her of sheer political ambition. They had a strong and seasoned candidate in Rep. Rick Lazio, but Clinton won handily by 12 percentage points. She is the first former first lady to serve in Congress.

KEY VOTES

2004

Yes Pass $318.9 billion, six-year highway and mass transit bill

Yes Extend assault weapons ban for 10 years

Yes Restore pay-as-you-go rules for new tax cuts and entitlement spending

No Criminalize harm to a fetus in an attack on the mother

Yes Increase mandatory child care funding to states by $6 billion over five years

No Amend the Constitution to prohibit same-sex marriage

Yes Approve $146 billion multi-year extension of previously enacted middle-class tax breaks

Yes Reorganize U.S. intelligence agencies as proposed by Sept. 11 commission

Yes Cut corporate taxes $137 billion over 10 years

2003

Yes Delay Bush changes to Clean Air Act

No Allow confirmation vote on Miguel A. Estrada to the U.S. Court of Appeals for the D.C. Circuit

Yes Block a Bush proposal opening Alaska's Arctic National Wildlife Refuge to oil drilling

Yes Limit size of Bush's proposed tax cut to $350 billion through fiscal 2013

No Overhaul Medicare and create prescription drug benefit

Yes Block Bush rule scaling back overtime pay for some white-collar federal workers

Yes Split $20 billion in Iraq aid into half-grant, half-loan

No Ban "partial birth" abortion except to save a woman's life

No Stop proposal allowing travel to Cuba

No Allow final vote on energy policy overhaul

CQ VOTE STUDIES

	PARTY UNITY		PRESIDENTIAL SUPPORT	
	Support	Oppose	Support	Oppose
2004	96%	4%	61%	39%
2003	98%	2%	47%	53%
2002	93%	7%	67%	33%
2001	97%	3%	61%	39%

INTEREST GROUPS

	AFL-CIO	ADA	CCUS	ACU
2004	100%	95%	50%	0%
2003	85%	95%	35%	10%
2002	92%	95%	45%	10%
2001	100%	95%	43%	12%

Rep. Timothy H. Bishop (D)

Elected 2002; 2nd term

CAPITOL OFFICE
225-3826
tim.bishop@mail.house.gov
www.house.gov/timbishop
1133 Longworth 20515-3201; fax 225-3143

COMMITTEES
Education & Workforce
Transportation & Infrastructure

HOMETOWN
Southampton

BORN
June 1, 1950, Southampton, N.Y.

RELIGION
Roman Catholic

FAMILY
Wife, Kathryn Bishop; two children

EDUCATION
College of the Holy Cross, B.A. 1972; Long Island
U., M.P.A. 1981

CAREER
College provost and administrator

POLITICAL HIGHLIGHTS
No previous office

ELECTION RESULTS

2004 GENERAL

Timothy H. Bishop (D, INDC, WFM)	156,354	56.2%
Bill Manger (R, C)	121,855	43.8%

2004 PRIMARY

Timothy H. Bishop (D)	unopposed

2002 GENERAL

Timothy H. Bishop (D, WFM)	84,276	50.2%
Felix J. Grucci Jr. (R, C, INDC, RTL)	81,524	48.6%
Lorna Salzman (GREEN)	1,991	1.2%

Bishop is the accidental congressman. A political neophyte when he was elected in 2002, he got his seat largely because a formerly safe incumbent bungled his own campaign. But Bishop is catching up with the seasoned pros in a hurry.

As a liberal from a Republican-leaning district on Long Island, he has subordinated some of his views to appeal to middle-of-the-road voters and has put elbow grease into constituent service. And he has shown he can raise money like a political veteran, the kind that scares away the hard competition. Republicans ceded what was perhaps their best chance at recovering the seat in 2004, when Bishop was re-elected convincingly.

Bishop's passion is education. He spent nearly 30 years as an administrator at a small college on Long Island, half of those as provost. He jumped into politics relatively late in life and without much of a political résumé. He was 52 when he challenged incumbent Republican Felix J. Grucci Jr. and won.

He is able to pursue his legislative priorities from his seat on the Education and Workforce Committee, a second-choice assignment for some but not for a lawmaker with a strong interest in both subjects. He is a crusader for more federal funds to help schools adapt to the No Child Left Behind law, the Bush administration initiative imposing new testing requirements and sink-or-swim standards on public schools. He also wants the government to pay its promised 40 percent share of the tab for programs for disabled students under the Individuals with Disabilities Education Act.

Bishop gathered signatures in his first term on a petition to try to force the Republican leadership to bring an education funding bill to the floor. But it was largely a symbolic move aimed at highlighting the issue. Such petitions by the minority party are rarely successful since they require a majority of the House — 218 members — to sign. Bishop also introduced a bill to institute nationally a program he began as a college provost. It matches students to jobs where they can learn professional skills or start careers, with private companies paying the salaries.

The son of a telephone lineman, Bishop is also a friend of organized labor. In the 108th Congress, he pushed a proposal in the Education Committee to increase the minimum wage from $5.15 to $7 an hour and another to require company pension boards to have employee representation. He actively opposed the Bush administration's plan to scale back worker protections for overtime pay. During debate, Bishop described how his father worked over 80 hours a week, depending on overtime wages to put five children through college.

His pet fiscal issue is repeal of the alternative minimum tax, which was designed to ensure that wealthy taxpayers pay at least some taxes but in effect has forced many middle-class taxpayers to pay more. His constituents are disproportionately affected, mainly because the law does not allow deductions for property taxes, which are sky high in the New York City area.

The 1st District covers the eastern half of Long Island's "fishtail," a place of economic extremes that has working-class suburbs like Smithtown but also the tony Hamptons, where the city's business elite summer. The area also includes coastal villages where fishing is still a mainstay and concentrations of artists attracted by the light and cliffs overlooking the sea.

Bishop has deep roots in the district. His father's family came to Southampton from Southampton, England, in 1643, and his great-great-grandfather was mayor of the town. He still lives a block from the house where he grew up. His mother's family were potato farmers, and Bishop has warm memories of weekends helping out during harvest time.

After getting a master's degree in public administration, Bishop in 1973 took a job as an admissions counselor at Southampton College, and worked his way up with jobs as dean of enrollment and director of financial aid. He eventually became provost of the school, where half the students are, like Bishop, the first in their families to get college degrees.

When he decided to take on Grucci in 2002, Bishop's only political experience was a stint as chairman of the Southampton Town Board of Ethics. It seemed a quixotic campaign against an incumbent who had all the advantages. Grucci, former president of Fireworks by Grucci, was well-known, well-financed and a Republican in a district where the GOP enjoyed a 3-to-2 edge over Democrats. But Bishop had some things going for him, especially a 30-year friendship with entertainment mogul Robert F.X. Sillerman, who had a home in the Hamptons. Sillerman,who became chancellor at Southampton College in 1993, was Bishop's campaign chairman and tapped Hollywood and Hamptons money circles to help him.

Then Grucci made a serious misstep. He ran an ad wrongly accusing Bishop of covering up a student rape while he was provost, a charge based on an old, discredited article in a student newspaper. Bishop won public sympathy as a result. He also was able to hurt Grucci on an important local issue, environmental protection, by publicizing a county health department report identifying the Grucci fireworks factory in Yaphank as a likely source of pollution in local drinking water wells.

Once in office, Bishop worked smartly to make himself less dispensable to voters, who have a history of trading in congressmen like cars. Since 1999, the seat has changed hands three times. Bishop doubled the aides doing constituent service, and won from Democratic leaders a coveted seat on the Transportation and Infrastructure Committee, where he has been able to lobby for grants for his district. He was also able to secure $240 million for Brookhaven National Laboratory, a major physics research facility in the 1st. And he raised an impressive $2 million in campaign funds.

The one blemish on his first term was a media revelation that he accepted from Sillerman a gift of $21,000 for college costs for his daughter, Meghan. Bishop said his friend has never asked for a legislative favor.

His re-election was secured when the Republicans' best candidate, John Jay LaVelle, supervisor of Brookhaven, stayed out of the race for personal reasons. Bishop was able to easily defeat William Manger, a former federal transportation official who was a Southampton village trustee.

KEY VOTES

2004
Yes Extend federal unemployment benefits by 13 weeks

Yes Pass $283.2 billion, six-year federal highway and mass transit bill

Yes Approve $146 billion multi-year extension of previously enacted middle-class tax breaks

No Amend the Constitution to prohibit same-sex marriage

No Cut corporate taxes $137 billion over 10 years

Yes Reorganize U.S. intelligence agencies as proposed by Sept. 11 commission

2003
No Cut taxes by $330 billion through fiscal 2013

Yes Block Bush rule scaling back overtime pay for some white-collar federal workers

Yes Do not allow use of search warrants without first notifying subjects

Yes Allow importation of prescription drugs

No Create private school voucher program in Washington, D.C.

No Ban "partial birth" abortion except to save a woman's life

Yes Split $18.6 billion in Iraq aid into half-grant, half-loan

No Overhaul Medicare and create prescription drug benefit

CQ VOTE STUDIES

	PARTY UNITY		PRESIDENTIAL SUPPORT	
	Support	Oppose	Support	Oppose
2004	95%	5%	32%	68%
2003	96%	4%	18%	82%

INTEREST GROUPS

	AFL-CIO	ADA	CCUS	ACU
2004	100%	100%	48%	4%
2003	100%	90%	30%	16%

NEW YORK 1

Eastern Suffolk County — Hamptons, Smithtown, Brookhaven

Covering the eastern two-thirds of Long Island's Suffolk County, the 1st reaches out into the Atlantic Ocean. At its far eastern end, the district takes in the elite estates of some of New York's wealthiest in the Hamptons and Shelter Island. The rural end of the island has retained its pastoral character, with fishing villages, farms and wineries scattered throughout. Many duck farms have disappeared, but Long Island's wine industry has expanded rapidly, growing from one winery in the mid-1970s to more than two dozen producing about 500,000 cases a year.

Moving west, the 1st takes in some blue-collar towns, populated by conservative Irish-Catholics and Italian-Americans. Farther west, Smithtown and Brookhaven have boomed with suburban growth. Defense once dominated the economy, but many of those jobs have been replaced by scientific research, attracted by the State University of New York at Stony Brook and Brookhaven National Laboratory.

The 1st's lingering rural temperament and small-town feel make it more likely to lean to the right than many other districts near New York City. Registration favors Republicans, but the district's brand of conservatism remains moderate, with many residents supporting more-liberal views on abortion and gun control. Environmental issues rank high, as many towns depend on the ocean for fish and tourism.

Republicans dominate at the local level, but Democrats make the 1st competitive in federal elections. Voters have sent a Democrat to the House in six of the previous 10 elections. George W. Bush and John Kerry each took 49 percent of the 1st's 2004 presidential vote, with Bush winning narrowly.

MAJOR INDUSTRY
Higher education, medicine, research

CITIES
Coram (unincorporated), 34,923; Centereach (unincorporated), 27,285; Shirley (unincorporated), 25,395; Medford (unincorporated), 21,985

NOTABLE
The Montauk Point Lighthouse, built in 1796, was the first lighthouse in New York State; The Big Duck, a duck-shaped structure and shop built in 1931 that stands 20 feet tall, graces Route 24 in Flanders.

Rep. Steve Israel (D)

Elected 2000; 3rd term

Israel was only nine months into his career in Congress on Sept. 11, 2001, when 112 of his constituents died in the terrorist attack on the World Trade Center. Fifteen months after that, he was named to the Armed Services Committee; as the only New York Democrat on the panel, he has staked out a decidedly hawkish position. He argues that from a political perspective, it makes sense for his party to advocate an aggressive foreign policy and a strong military.

"If we don't make them feel safe 35 miles from Ground Zero, they're not going to pay as much attention to us on those other issues," Israel said of the electorate in 2003 when he endorsed former NATO Commander Wesley K. Clark for president. In the 109th Congress, he chairs the House Democrats' Task Force on Defense and Military.

In the 108th Congress, Israel's most visible legislative crusade to that end was his bill to require airlines to equip their planes with anti-missile technology. The flight paths of John F. Kennedy International Airport are above his Long Island district, and Israel became concerned about the proliferation of shoulder-fired missiles after one was launched at an Israeli airplane as it took off from a Kenyan airport in 2002.

The missile did not hit the aircraft, but the issue has been a topic of discussion in Congress ever since. Israel's measure stalled as lawmakers began to ponder the cost to the airline industry — $10 billion, by Israel's estimate. So Israel began work with Republican John L. Mica, chairman of Transportation's Aviation Subcommittee, on a scaled-down version that would not mandate any immediate action by airlines. As part of an overhaul of the nation's intelligence apparatus, lawmakers included provisions directing the Federal Aviation Administration to develop anti-missile technologies and urging the president to pursue non-proliferation of shoulder-fired missiles.

When he first arrived in the House, Israel set out to work across party lines. He often teamed up with his Long Island neighbor, Republican Felix Grucci Jr., on issues of local concern. And in his first year, he backed President Bush almost half the time on roll call votes where the president had staked out a position. But in the 108th Congress, Israel's support for the president dwindled; he backed Bush just 31 percent of the time — a score not much higher than the 28 percent average for House Democrats.

Nevertheless, he remains interested in cooperation across party lines. At the beginning of the 109th, he joined with Republican Timothy V. Johnson of Illinois to form a "Center Aisle Caucus." Israel is also a member of the centrist New Democrat Coalition and the more conservative Blue Dog Coalition. He is the only New Yorker and one of only three Northeastern lawmakers in the Blue Dogs.

Though he is active on international security issues, Israel has said that health care is one of his top legislative concerns. He co-chairs the House Cancer Caucus, and has supported medical research projects at local facilities. In the 108th, he introduced legislation to strengthen the power of the Food and Drug Administration to crack down on counterfeit drugs. Assertive and energetic, Israel buttonholed Bush late in 2001 about the Medicare prescription drug issue when the president visited Capitol Hill to pass along Christmas wishes. "I just planted myself at the exit of the room. He was going to have to knock me down to get past," Israel later boasted to The New York Times.

CAPITOL OFFICE
225-3335
www.house.gov/israel
432 Cannon 20515-3202; fax 225-4669

COMMITTEES
Armed Services
Financial Services

HOMETOWN
Huntington

BORN
May 30, 1958, Brooklyn, N.Y.

RELIGION
Jewish

FAMILY
Wife, Marlene Budd; two children

EDUCATION
Nassau Community College, A.A. 1978 (liberal arts); Syracuse U., attended 1978-79; George Washington U., B.A. 1982 (political science)

CAREER
Public relations and marketing firm manager; assistant county executive; university fundraising director; Jewish advocacy group county director; congressional aide

POLITICAL HIGHLIGHTS
Democratic nominee for Suffolk County Legislature, 1987; Huntington Town Board, 1993-2001 (majority leader, 1997-2001)

ELECTION RESULTS

2004 GENERAL

Steve Israel (D, INDC, WFM)	161,593	66.6%
Richard Hoffmann (R, C)	80,950	33.4%

2004 PRIMARY

Steve Israel (D)	unopposed

2002 GENERAL

Steve Israel (D, INDC, WFM)	85,451	58.5%
Joseph P. Finley (R, C, RTL)	59,117	40.5%
John Keenan (GREEN)	1,558	1.1%

PREVIOUS WINNING PERCENTAGES
2000 (48%)

Israel's path to Congress opened up when New York Mayor Rudolph W. Giuliani announced that he had prostate cancer and was giving up his bid for the Senate in 2000. The 2nd District's four-term congressman, Rick A. Lazio, stepped in to take the GOP Senate nomination and Israel — a prominent municipal official on Long Island — immediately launched a campaign for the open seat. He won then and in 2002 with relative ease.

As a freshman congressman, he was the only one appointed to the Democratic Steering Committee, which doles out committee assignments. Later, just after the terrorist attacks, party leaders also put him on their Homeland Security Task Force. On the Financial Services panel, Israel has worked to ensure the availability of affordable housing, a longtime interest and an issue of concern to suburban Long Islanders.

Israel became involved in politics in high school, riding his bicycle after school to the campaign headquarters of Democrat Franklin Ornstein, who in 1974 waged an unsuccessful challenge to GOP Rep. Norman F. Lent. As a political science student at George Washington University, Israel worked part time for California Democratic Rep. Robert T. Matsui and then spent three years with Rep. Richard L. Ottinger, a New York Democrat.

Israel returned to Long Island in 1983, where he worked as a fundraiser for Touro College, a Jewish-sponsored institution. In 1987, he lost a bid for the Suffolk County legislature. He later formed his own fundraising and public relations firm, and was also the director of the Institute on the Holocaust and the Law, which is affiliated with Touro and the American Jewish Congress. He stayed active in local politics, winning a seat on the Huntington Town Board in a 1993 special election. During his seven years on the town board, Israel worked with Republicans to put the town on a sound financial footing. He was the first local official to offer information about his activities on the Internet, establishing his own Web page.

During his years in Long Island politics, Israel said, he always had in mind a return to Washington. "I learned as a congressional aide how effective you can be, and I always hoped to have the opportunity," he told Newsday.

His chance came in 2000 when Lazio entered the Senate race to challenge Democrat Hillary Rodham Clinton. Israel narrowly beat out Suffolk County legislator David Bishop for the Democratic nod. Israel's hold on the seat seemed tenuous in 2002. There was talk that redistricting might put him and Grucci in the same district. There was also the specter of a challenge from the popular Lazio, whom GOP strategists were urging to make a comeback. Neither event came to pass and Israel won re-election comfortably with just over 58 percent of the vote. He won with nearly 67 percent in 2004.

KEY VOTES

2004

Yes Extend federal unemployment benefits by 13 weeks

Yes Pass $283.2 billion, six-year federal highway and mass transit bill

Yes Approve $146 billion multi-year extension of previously enacted middle-class tax breaks

No Amend the Constitution to prohibit same-sex marriage

No Cut corporate taxes $137 billion over 10 years

Yes Reorganize U.S. intelligence agencies as proposed by Sept. 11 commission

2003

No Cut taxes by $330 billion through fiscal 2013

Yes Block Bush rule scaling back overtime pay for some white-collar federal workers

Yes Do not allow use of search warrants without first notifying subjects

Yes Allow importation of prescription drugs

No Create private school voucher program in Washington, D.C.

No Ban "partial birth" abortion except to save a woman's life

Yes Split $18.6 billion in Iraq aid into half-grant, half-loan

No Overhaul Medicare and create prescription drug benefit

CQ VOTE STUDIES

	PARTY UNITY		PRESIDENTIAL SUPPORT	
	Support	Oppose	Support	Oppose
2004	92%	8%	30%	70%
2003	90%	10%	31%	69%
2002	83%	17%	41%	59%
2001	82%	18%	48%	52%

INTEREST GROUPS

	AFL-CIO	ADA	CCUS	ACU
2004	93%	100%	47%	13%
2003	80%	90%	47%	20%
2002	67%	75%	58%	32%
2001	75%	90%	43%	8%

NEW YORK 2
Long Island — Brentwood, Commack

Taking in the central part of Long Island and covering almost all of western Suffolk County, the 2nd is full of suburban communities that popped up all over the county's potato fields during the post-World War II suburban boom. Now the 2nd, which also takes in a small piece of east-central Nassau County, has a burgeoning computer sector and the state's highest median income.

Much of the district's white-collar workforce commutes to New York City, and the indigenous industry has long been blue-collar. Defense plants hummed during the height of the Cold War, but cutbacks brought job losses. Computer and electronics firms have helped fill the void. The 2nd houses a relatively diverse population, mixing well-to-do communities like Dix Hills with solidly middle- and working-class neighborhoods. During the summer, many New Yorkers flock to Fire Island, a beach community that lies partly in the 2nd.

Redistricting following the 2000 census gave the 2nd all of Huntington — which it previously shared with the 5th — and stripped it of more-

conservative coastal communities in Islip and Babylon to the south. The 2nd also acquired most of Plainview and part of Jericho in Nassau County, both of which have large Jewish populations.

With a nearly 30 percent minority population, a significant Jewish community and a blue-collar base, the 2nd has a substantial, but not overwhelming, Democratic vote. A Republican held the seat for most of the 1990s before it reverted to Democratic control in 2000. The district remains competitive, but redistricting did push it leftward. John Kerry captured 53 percent of the vote here in the 2004 presidential election.

MAJOR INDUSTRY
Computers, electronics, service

CITIES
Brentwood (unincorporated), 53,917; Commack (unincorporated), 36,363; Central Islip (unincorporated), 31,950; Huntington Station (unincorporated), 29,910

NOTABLE
Fire Island National Seashore separates the Atlantic Ocean from the Great South Bay; Islip Long Island MacArthur Airport is near Ronkonkoma; The Walt Whitman Birthplace State Historic Site and Interpretive Center is in West Hills (South Huntington).

Rep. Peter T. King (R)

CAPITOL OFFICE
225-7896
pete.king@mail.house.gov
www.house.gov/king
436 Cannon 20515-3203; fax 226-2279

COMMITTEES
Financial Services
Homeland Security
   (Emergency Preparedness, Science &
   Technology - chairman)
International Relations

HOMETOWN
Seaford

BORN
April 5, 1944, Manhattan, N.Y.

RELIGION
Roman Catholic

FAMILY
Wife, Rosemary King; two children

EDUCATION
St. Francis College, B.A. 1965 (history); U. of Notre
Dame, J.D. 1968

MILITARY SERVICE
N.Y. National Guard, 1968-73

CAREER
Lawyer

POLITICAL HIGHLIGHTS
Hempstead Town Council, 1978-81; Nassau County
comptroller, 1981-93; Republican nominee for N.Y.
attorney general, 1986

ELECTION RESULTS

2004 GENERAL

Peter T. King (R, INDC, C)	171,259	63.0%
Blair H. Mathies Jr. (D)	100,737	37.0%

2004 PRIMARY

Peter T. King (R)	8,110	83.6%
Robert Previdi (R)	1,564	16.1%

2002 GENERAL

Peter T. King (R, C, INDC, RTL)	121,537	71.9%
Stuart L. Finz (D)	46,022	27.2%

PREVIOUS WINNING PERCENTAGES
2000 (60%); 1998 (64%); 1996 (55%); 1994 (59%);
1992 (50%)

Elected 1992; 7th term

King is just enough of a GOP maverick to get his name into the newspapers and on the air frequently, and just enough of a conservative to keep himself in the good graces of the Republican establishment. He's one of the few members of Congress to have pictures of himself with both Bill Clinton and George W. Bush on his wall. He backed John McCain in the 2000 primaries, but gets along well enough with President Bush, who gave him a nickname — "Pedro" — as he sometimes does for people he likes.

King seems to enjoy being a bit unpredictable, though his voting record is more conservative than his outspokenness would indicate. He enjoys stirring up controversy. He stepped into the middle of the U.S.-Europe feud by labeling France a "third-rate country," and suggesting in 2003 that French leaders go to Baghdad "to instruct the Iraqis in how to surrender." He angered Muslims, including many in his district, by suggesting in a radio interview that most were "loyal Americans," but their mosques were run by extremists. Muslim leaders charged that he made the comment to sell books, a reference to King's sideline as a novel writer. His latest book deals with radical Muslims.

In the 109th Congress, King gave up his chairmanship of a Financial Services subcommittee to become chairman of the Homeland Security Emergency Preparedness, Science and Technology Subcommittee, a panel more tailored to his interests. The son of a New York City police officer, King staunchly supports law enforcement. He lost several friends from his Long Island district in the Sept. 11, 2001, terrorist attacks, and has an avid interest in coordination between the federal government and local police and firefighters in combating terrorism.

In the international arena, King has played a significant role in the effort to bring peace to Northern Ireland, an experience he draws on in his fiction writing. Over the years, he has made several trips to Northern Ireland to protest British policies and to press for an end to British rule. He developed a close relationship with Gerry Adams, the leader of Sinn Fein, the political wing of the Irish Republican Army. That friendship led to his serving as an intermediary between Adams and British Prime Minister Tony Blair and later being credited with helping bring about the 1998 Good Friday peace accord.

His interest in Irish affairs — his parents are from Ireland — also brought him close to President Clinton and Sen. Hillary Rodham Clinton, the former first lady. King worked closely with the Clinton White House on the issue. He and members of his family later flew with Clinton on Air Force One to Ireland for festivities celebrating the accord.

King argued strenuously in 1998 against Clinton's impeachment by the House, and was one of only four Republicans who voted against all four articles of impeachment. He and the Clintons continue to have a warm relationship, which would seem to discount any future attempt by King to unseat the incumbent New York senator. But his name often surfaces in connection with higher office.

King can be exceedingly loyal. He backed former New York City Police Commissioner Bernard Kerik's nomination for Homeland Security secretary even as Kerik came under fire from critics and ultimately dropped out.

Despite his occasional conflicts with the House Republican leadership, King votes with his party on most fiscal and social issues, supporting expanded trade opportunities and school vouchers, while opposing abortion. In the 108th Congress, he sided with his party 89 percent of the time.

On other issues, King is difficult to predict. He supports drilling in Alaska's Arctic National Wildlife Refuge, saying, "You can't always cave in to the environmental wackos." But he joins with Democrats to back increased automotive fuel economy standards, and he favors some gun control measures. He also supported labor unions' efforts to raise the minimum wage, to require employers to meet ergonomic standards for their workers and to impose steel import quotas.

King bemoans the declining ranks of Northeast Republicans in the House, saying he believes that "to be a real national party, you can't isolate yourself from any region." In the last decade or so, he says, the GOP has had "a voice and face that scared off many [voters] in the Northeast. There was a judgmental tone, a harshness."

A veteran of the rough-and-tumble politics of Nassau County, King says confrontation and partisanship are natural elements of legislating. And to stay in practice, he recently took up boxing for recreation, shedding 30 pounds in a year. "This is the one sport where you are out there on your own. There is nowhere to run; nowhere to hide. I think it takes extraordinary courage," King told Newsday. "There are other individual sports like tennis, but if you lose in boxing you get your head split open, you lose your teeth and the whole world sees." He has teamed up with McCain to sponsor legislation to establish national guidelines regulating the boxing industry.

King grew up in a blue-collar Queens neighborhood. He borrowed money to attend Notre Dame's law school. Afterward, he interned (along with Rudolph Giuliani) at Richard Nixon's New York law firm. He entered public life in 1972 as a deputy Nassau County attorney and eventually became the county comptroller, serving three terms. During his tenure, King lost a 1986 run for New York attorney general.

When veteran GOP Rep. Norman F. Lent announced in 1992 that he would not seek re-election, King moved with characteristic dispatch to establish himself as Lent's successor, contending that his government experience would help him get things done in Washington.

After coasting through the primary, King narrowly survived a contest against the better-funded Democrat, Steve A. Orlins. In the GOP-leaning district, King's long history of involvement in local civic and political affairs helped him win by 3 percentage points. He routinely wins re-election with margins exceeding 20 percentage points. After winning in 2002 by 45 points, he seriously considered running in 2004 against Democratic Sen. Charles E. Schumer, but bowed out in the face of Schumer's large war chest.

KEY VOTES

2004
Yes Extend federal unemployment benefits by 13 weeks
Yes Pass $283.2 billion, six-year federal highway and mass transit bill
Yes Approve $146 billion multi-year extension of previously enacted middle-class tax breaks
Yes Amend the Constitution to prohibit same-sex marriage
Yes Cut corporate taxes $137 billion over 10 years
Yes Reorganize U.S. intelligence agencies as proposed by Sept. 11 commission

2003
Yes Cut taxes by $330 billion through fiscal 2013
Yes Block Bush rule scaling back overtime pay for some white-collar federal workers
No Do not allow use of search warrants without first notifying subjects
No Allow importation of prescription drugs
Yes Create private school voucher program in Washington, D.C.
Yes Ban "partial birth" abortion except to save a woman's life
No Split $18.6 billion in Iraq aid into half-grant, half-loan
Yes Overhaul Medicare and create prescription drug benefit

CQ VOTE STUDIES

	PARTY UNITY		PRESIDENTIAL SUPPORT	
	Support	Oppose	Support	Oppose
2004	83%	17%	77%	23%
2003	93%	7%	89%	11%
2002	92%	8%	84%	16%
2001	92%	8%	93%	7%
2000	77%	23%	45%	55%

INTEREST GROUPS

	AFL-CIO	ADA	CCUS	ACU
2004	50%	25%	80%	71%
2003	27%	15%	83%	72%
2002	0%	10%	85%	83%
2001	27%	10%	83%	84%
2000	40%	15%	55%	64%

NEW YORK 3

Long Island — Levittown, Hicksville, Long Beach

Most of Long Island's eastern Nassau County and the south shore of western Suffolk County make up the 3rd, where extravagant estates mingle with some of the nation's oldest middle-class suburbs. The district boasts New York State's second-highest median income.

The Republican Party has long been a potent force in the 3rd, and redistricting following the 2000 census strengthened the party's hand even further by adding southwestern Suffolk. The addition was headlined by the acquisition of coastal portions of Islip and Babylon. Even with the district's significant labor presence from construction and professional unions, most of the 3rd's elected officials are Republicans, although Democrats have made some gains in Nassau County overall. Pockets of Democratic support in Plainview and Jericho, where many of the residents are Jewish, were moved into the neighboring 2nd District in redistricting.

Democratic presidential candidates usually carry the district's territory, but George W. Bush won the 3rd in 2004 with 52 percent of the vote after losing here in 2000. The district easily favors Republicans in state and congressional races.

The economy faltered in the 1980s when aircraft and electronics manufacturing giant Northrup Grumman downsized following post-Cold War defense cutbacks. But the 3rd has rebounded, expanding its information technology base and enjoying a low unemployment rate.

The district is overwhelmingly white, with the lowest percentage of black residents (2 percent) in the state and the lowest percentage of Hispanics (7 percent) in the New York City area.

MAJOR INDUSTRY
Information technology, higher education

CITIES
Levittown (unincorporated), 53,067; Hicksville (unincorporated) (pt.), 39,670; Long Beach, 35,462; West Islip (unincorporated) (pt.), 27,171; Lindenhurst (pt.), 27,162; Glen Cove, 26,622

NOTABLE
Bethpage State Park hosted the 2002 U.S. Open golf tournament; President Theodore Roosevelt's Sagamore Hill estate is in Oyster Bay; Roosevelt's grave is at nearby Youngs Memorial Cemetery.

Rep. Carolyn McCarthy (D)

Elected 1996; 5th term

Although her partisan roots are shallow — she did not officially register to vote as a Democrat until April 2003, six years into her tenure in Congress — McCarthy appears to fit comfortably in the mainstream of her party. Now in her fifth term, she has branched out beyond her signature issue, gun control, and is moving up within the Democratic Caucus. She is an assistant whip and serves on the Steering Committee, the leadership-dominated panel that makes committee assignments for the House Democrats.

McCarthy once joked to Newsday that being an assistant whip is somewhat similar to being a nurse, which was her career for more than 30 years before she entered politics. "We're just sent out to take the temperature of our fellow Democrats, and report back to the 'doctor,' " she said.

Her background as a nurse — and her own experience with tragedy — helped her provide grief counseling to the many families in her district who lost loved ones in the Sept. 11, 2001, terrorist attacks. "I know what these victims are going through. . . . They're not going to find closure," she said two years after the attacks. "You don't know how it's going to hit you on any given day. I prepare the victims for that."

In December 1993, a deranged gunman opened fire on a Long Island Rail Road commuter train. Among the victims were McCarthy's husband, Dennis, who was killed, and her adult son, Kevin, who was seriously wounded.

In the 108th Congress, McCarthy gave up a seat on the Budget Committee after one term to take a place on the Financial Services Committee, a panel with jurisdiction over many of the businesses that employ her commuter constituency. She also serves on the Education and Workforce Committee, where she played an active role in the 107th as the panel drafted President Bush's No Child Left Behind overhaul of federal elementary and secondary education programs. McCarthy joined forces with Dale Kildee, a Michigan Democrat, and Mark Souder, an Indiana Republican, to defeat an attempt to consolidate drug-abuse prevention and after-school programs into a single block grant.

Having struggled with dyslexia as a child, McCarthy has pressed for more federal aid to school districts to help cope with the costs of educating learning-disabled children. She has backed multibillion-dollar Democratic plans to pay for new teachers and renovate aging schools, while opposing GOP proposals for school vouchers.

She has begun to take a greater interest in international affairs, traveling to Iraq in October 2003 with a group of seven other congresswomen to see how the war was affecting Iraqi women and children. She has also spoken out against the international trafficking of women.

She backed abortion rights and environmental protections, and is a steady friend of labor. But she sometimes tilts toward conservatism: She supports constitutional amendments to ban desecration of the U.S. flag and require a two-thirds congressional majority to raise federal taxes. She also has voted to repeal the estate tax, although she opposed Bush's 2003 tax cuts and the 2003 Medicare bill.

McCarthy likely always will be first and foremost identified with the tragedy that propelled her into public life and inspired her continuing crusade for tougher gun controls. "I've come to peace with the fact that that will be in my obituary," she told The Associated Press.

When her congressman, freshman Republican Daniel Frisa, voted in 1996 to eliminate a 1994 ban on semiautomatic weapons, McCarthy was

CAPITOL OFFICE
225-5516
www.house.gov/carolynmccarthy
106 Cannon 20515-3204; fax 225-5758

COMMITTEES
Education & Workforce
Financial Services

HOMETOWN
Mineola

BORN
Jan. 5, 1944, Brooklyn, N.Y.

RELIGION
Roman Catholic

FAMILY
Widowed; one child

EDUCATION
Glen Cove Nursing School, L.P.N. 1964

CAREER
Nurse

POLITICAL HIGHLIGHTS
No previous office

ELECTION RESULTS

2004 GENERAL

Carolyn McCarthy (D, INDC, WFM)	159,969	63.0%
James A. Garner (R, C)	94,141	37.1%

2004 PRIMARY

Carolyn McCarthy (D)	unopposed

2002 GENERAL

Carolyn McCarthy (D, INDC, WFM)	94,806	56.3%
Marilyn F. O'Grady (R, C, RTL)	72,882	43.2%

PREVIOUS WINNING PERCENTAGES
2000 (61%); 1998 (53%); 1996 (57%)

incensed. Local GOP officials squelched her inquiries about mounting a primary challenge to Frisa, so she quit the Republican Party and launched a Democratic campaign to unseat him.

She raised more than $1 million and outspent Frisa, whom she described as out of the mainstream and in the mold of Speaker Newt Gingrich. She campaigned on gun control and health policy, and Frisa seemed at a loss for an effective response. McCarthy won by 17 percentage points. In 2000, she bumped her margin to 22 points. Facing a tougher challenge in 2002, she still won by 13 points over GOP ophthalmologist Marilyn F. O'Grady. She trounced African-American Republican mayor James A. Garner in 2004.

McCarthy's personal tragedy gives her speeches on gun control unusual emotional force. When she rose to speak on the House floor at 1 a.m. June 18, 1999, a hush fell over the chamber. With tears flowing down her cheeks, McCarthy implored her colleagues to support her amendment to toughen background check requirements for would-be purchasers at gun shows. "I am Irish and I am not supposed to cry in front of anyone. But I made a promise a long time ago" to her late husband and her son, she said. "If there was anything that I could do to prevent one family from going through what I have gone through, then I have done my job."

McCarthy thought she had connected with her colleagues, particularly in the aftermath of the mass shooting at Columbine High School in Colorado. But her amendment lost, as have nearly all of her gun control efforts since then. She suffered another significant setback in the 108th Congress when House Republicans blocked an extension of an assault weapons ban that had been in place for 10 years. "I know I get very emotional about it," she said as the ban neared an end. "The problem is I know the effect it's going to have in this country as it comes down the road. I know there are going to be a lot more families, they're going to be, unfortunately, in the same position that I was in. And we're going to see a lot more of our police officers, unfortunately, gunned down."

Despite all the frustrations, she is determined to keep trying, especially after the birth of her first grandson, named for her slain husband. True to form, she introduced a bill early in the 109th Congress to reinstate the assault weapons ban. She also introduced measures to ban gun purchases by anyone on the government's "do not fly" list and to provide grants to states to upgrade and automate their criminal records to permit instant background checks on more gun buyers.

"I've come to the realization this is going to take a while," she told Newsday in 2000.

KEY VOTES

2004

Yes Extend federal unemployment benefits by 13 weeks

Yes Pass $283.2 billion, six-year federal highway and mass transit bill

Yes Approve $146 billion multi-year extension of previously enacted middle-class tax breaks

No Amend the Constitution to prohibit same-sex marriage

No Cut corporate taxes $137 billion over 10 years

Yes Reorganize U.S. intelligence agencies as proposed by Sept. 11 commission

2003

No Cut taxes by $330 billion through fiscal 2013

Yes Block Bush rule scaling back overtime pay for some white-collar federal workers

Yes Do not allow use of search warrants without first notifying subjects

Yes Allow importation of prescription drugs

No Create private school voucher program in Washington, D.C.

No Ban "partial birth" abortion except to save a woman's life

Yes Split $18.6 billion in Iraq aid into half-grant, half-loan

No Overhaul Medicare and create prescription drug benefit

CQ VOTE STUDIES

	PARTY UNITY		PRESIDENTIAL SUPPORT	
	Support	Oppose	Support	Oppose
2004	94%	6%	32%	68%
2003	91%	9%	28%	72%
2002	84%	16%	45%	55%
2001	83%	17%	44%	56%
2000	84%	16%	68%	32%

INTEREST GROUPS

	AFL-CIO	ADA	CCUS	ACU
2004	93%	100%	45%	12%
2003	93%	85%	40%	24%
2002	67%	80%	60%	32%
2001	83%	85%	48%	17%
2000	70%	65%	65%	24%

NEW YORK 4
Southwest Nassau County — Hempstead

The 4th's diverse array of residents includes wealthy New York City suburbanites and Wall Street commuters, as well as low- and middle-income residents. The district consumes the southwest corner of Long Island's Nassau County and borders eastern Queens.

With the largest minority population of Long Island's four congressional districts, the 4th has a Democratic base, particularly in Hempstead and Uniondale, which include large black and Hispanic communities. The affluent and largely Jewish "Five Towns" (Inwood, Lawrence, Cedarhurst, Woodmere and Hewlett), in the 4th's southwestern corner, also lean Democratic. But overall voter registration slightly favors Republicans.

District politics were competitive in the 1990s, with independent and socially moderate voters electing four different representatives during the decade. The 4th elected Republicans until 1996, when voters chose pro-gun control Democratic Rep. McCarthy; they have re-elected her to four more terms. The district has supported Democratic presidential

nominees since 1992, with John Kerry taking 55 percent of the 4th's vote in 2004.

Economic turmoil here began in the 1980s with the decline of the defense industry, on which Long Island was heavily dependent. The 4th continues to rebuild and diversify, focusing on technology and small businesses. A number of working-class residents are employed by John F. Kennedy International Airport (across the district line in Queens' 6th District), Belmont Park race track, and large shopping centers such as Roosevelt Field Mall in Garden City.

Pocketbook issues and unique regional concerns — such as airplane noise — dominate political discussion in the 4th and help keep it competitive on the local level.

MAJOR INDUSTRY
Health care, technology, higher education

CITIES
Hempstead, 56,554; East Meadow (unincorporated), 37,461; Valley Stream, 36,368; Freeport (pt.), 34,958; Elmont (unincorporated), 32,657

NOTABLE
Nassau Coliseum is home to the New York Islanders hockey team.

Rep. Gary L. Ackerman (D)

Elected March 1983; 11th full term

CAPITOL OFFICE
225-2601
gary_ackerman@mail.house.gov
www.house.gov/ackerman
2243 Rayburn 20515-3205; fax 225-1589

COMMITTEES
Financial Services
International Relations

HOMETOWN
Queens

BORN
Nov. 19, 1942, Brooklyn, N.Y.

RELIGION
Jewish

FAMILY
Wife, Rita Ackerman; three children

EDUCATION
Queens College, B.A. 1965

CAREER
Teacher; newspaper publisher and editor;
advertising executive

POLITICAL HIGHLIGHTS
Sought Democratic nomination for New York City
Council at large, 1977; N.Y. Senate, 1979-83

ELECTION RESULTS

2004 GENERAL

Gary Ackerman (D, INDC, WFM)	119,726	71.3%
Stephen Graves (R, C)	46,867	27.9%

2004 PRIMARY

Gary Ackerman (D)	unopposed

2002 GENERAL

Gary Ackerman (D, INDC, L, WFM)	68,773	92.3%
Perry S. Reich (C)	5,718	7.7%

PREVIOUS WINNING PERCENTAGES
2000 (68%); 1998 (65%); 1996 (64%); 1994 (55%);
1992 (52%); 1990 (100%); 1988 (100%); 1986 (77%);
1984 (69%); 1983 Special Election (50%)

Known for his acid wit and agility with parliamentary procedures, Ackerman has a proven ability to promote his liberal views, funnel federal dollars to his Long Island district, and generally get the goat of the Republican majority.

His staunchly liberal views on education, health care and the environment seldom prevail, but his humor helps him be heard above the fray. During the tense moments before lawmakers voted in 1998 on whether to launch an impeachment inquiry against President Clinton, Ackerman said, "I move that when the House adjourn, we do so to Salem, a quaint village in the Commonwealth of Massachusetts, whose history beckons us thence." His reference to the site of the infamous 17th century witch trials drew hisses from Republicans but elicited a wry smile from GOP Speaker Newt Gingrich.

Ackerman's caustic broadsides are sometimes aimed at corporate chieftains and others he suspects of abuses of power. Typical was his rebuke of Bernard J. Ebbers, former chief executive officer of WorldCom Inc., during a 2002 hearing on alleged accounting manipulation by the telecommunications giant. "Do you sleep well at night?" Ackerman demanded as Ebbers sat tight-lipped at the witness table.

When the House took up a constitutional amendment in 1999 to ban desecration of the U.S. flag, Ackerman came to the floor wearing a tie depicting the flag and said his neckwear would be banned under the amendment. In an interview on the Howard Stern radio show, he described himself as "naked and draped in the flag." The real threat, he said, was not the occasional burning of a flag, "but the permanent banning of the burners."

Ackerman, who sports a white carnation boutonniere, scoffs at pretension and convention. His residence in Washington is a houseboat on the Potomac called the Unsinkable II. He says the original Unsinkable wasn't.

The top Democrat on the International Relations Middle East Subcommittee, Ackerman is a respected voice on foreign policy. He often travels overseas and cites his firsthand experiences when urging policy change.

Since the terrorist attacks of Sept. 11, 2001, Ackerman has forged an unlikely alliance with conservative Republicans to build support for Israel's hard-line policies toward the Palestinians. In 2004, Ackerman cosponsored a bipartisan resolution supporting Israel's controversial construction of a "security fence" along the border of Palestinian-controlled areas. In 2002, he joined with Republicans Tom DeLay of Texas and Roy Blunt of Missouri, both Christian conservatives, on a bill that would have severed ties between the United States and Yasser Arafat's Palestinian Authority. Ackerman also co-sponsored a resolution expressing solidarity with Israel.

Ackerman also has pushed President Bush to take a harder line with terror-supporting states such as Syria, backing a sanctions bill in the 108th and accusing the administration of "empty threats and business as usual." He has been no less critical of U.S.-Pakistani relations, despite that country's cooperation in the war on terrorism. "In Pakistan," Ackerman said in 2004, "we are hitching our wagon to a very questionable horse."

Ackerman contends that to promote global security, the United States must remain actively engaged in dialogue even with nations such as China and North Korea that are allegedly involved in weapons proliferation. Breaking with his allies in labor, he voted in 2000 to grant China permanent normal trade status. Similarly, he voted against a 1998 proposal to ban the export of U.S. satellites to China. He has also successfully battled efforts by conservatives to cut aid to India.

Even as he pursues his foreign policy interests, Ackerman tends to the parochial concerns of his sprawling, diverse 5th District. He saved the U.S. Coast Guard station at Eatons Neck from threatened closure; he pushed for resolution of the 1994 Long Island Rail Road strike; and he lobbies relentlessly for funds to clean up Long Island Sound. His Internet Web site still proudly proclaims that in 2002 the 5th was No. 1 in New York state in the amount of federal spending — $9.5 billion. When Newsday rated 10 Long Island and Queens members of Congress in 2004, Ackerman drew the top score.

Despite his liberalism, Ackerman can work with ideological opposites, as he showed in 1996 when he joined GOP conservative Tom Coburn of Oklahoma in passing a measure to provide mandatory AIDS testing of newborns. "You have to be willing to compromise," Ackerman told Newsday in 1998. "Part of the problem is there is a group of Republicans down here who believe they are locked in a battle, not between good and bad, but between good and evil. Those who believe that way, they can't compromise with evil."

Ackerman, a former social studies teacher, first ventured into public policy in 1969, when, as a new father, he successfully sued the New York City Board of Education for the right of a father to receive unpaid leave. At the time, time off to care for newborns was offered only to women. He subsequently had run-ins with the Queens Democratic machine as a publisher of a weekly newspaper (of which he now owns a share). He challenged a city council incumbent in 1977 and lost.

But the next year, he captured a state Senate seat. After Democratic Rep. Benjamin S. Rosenthal died in 1983, Ackerman convinced Democratic leaders to support him in the special-election race against a wealthy independent, pollster Douglas Schoen, and a less competitive GOP candidate. Ackerman won with 50 percent of the vote and cruised through four re-elections in the then-7th District, a mainly urban constituency that included many loyally Democratic Jewish and Hispanic voters.

In redistricting for the 1992 election, some of Ackerman's Queens base was replaced with conservative, suburban areas in Nassau and Suffolk counties, throwing him into Long Island's 5th District. Ackerman was also hurt by revelations that he had 111 overdrafts at the House Bank, during the scandal over special checking privileges for lawmakers. But he prevailed by 7 percentage points over GOP Suffolk County Legislator Allan E. Binder by rolling up a big margin in what remained of his Queens district. Changes before the 2002 election made the 5th more Democratic, and he has coasted to re-election since then.

KEY VOTES

2004

Yes   Extend federal unemployment benefits by 13 weeks

Yes   Pass $283.2 billion, six-year federal highway and mass transit bill

Yes   Approve $146 billion multi-year extension of previously enacted middle-class tax breaks

No   Amend the Constitution to prohibit same-sex marriage

No   Cut corporate taxes $137 billion over 10 years

Yes   Reorganize U.S. intelligence agencies as proposed by Sept. 11 commission

2003

No   Cut taxes by $330 billion through fiscal 2013

Yes   Block Bush rule scaling back overtime pay for some white-collar federal workers

Yes   Do not allow use of search warrants without first notifying subjects

Yes   Allow importation of prescription drugs

?   Create private school voucher program in Washington, D.C.

No   Ban "partial birth" abortion except to save a woman's life

Yes   Split $18.6 billion in Iraq aid into half-grant, half-loan

No   Overhaul Medicare and create prescription drug benefit

CQ VOTE STUDIES

	PARTY UNITY		PRESIDENTIAL SUPPORT	
	Support	Oppose	Support	Oppose
2004	99%	1%	30%	70%
2003	95%	5%	23%	77%
2002	93%	7%	32%	68%
2001	94%	6%	29%	71%
2000	96%	4%	94%	6%

INTEREST GROUPS

	AFL-CIO	ADA	CCUS	ACU
2004	93%	95%	41%	4%
2003	100%	95%	26%	17%
2002	100%	95%	37%	4%
2001	100%	80%	35%	4%
2000	90%	80%	41%	13%

NEW YORK 5

Northeast Queens; northwest Nassau County

The 5th stretches east from south of LaGuardia Airport in Queens into northwestern Nassau County, reaching Roslyn and East Hills. Redistricting following the 2000 census made significant changes to the district, which previously had skirted Long Island Sound's North Shore into Suffolk County to take in part of Huntington. By removing Suffolk and adding more of Queens, the new district is more Democratic. Almost 80 percent of the 5th's residents live in Queens, with 20 percent in Nassau.

The minority population grew substantially with redistricting, particularly in Hispanic and Asian communities. Half of New York City's Asians live in Queens, and Elmhurst, downtown Flushing, Murray Hill and Queensboro Hill have a heavy Asian presence. The neighborhoods of North Corona and South Corona have a strong Hispanic influence.

Although pockets of low-income neighborhoods exist in the 5th, northeastern Queens has affluent areas such as the Douglaston and Little Neck neighborhoods near the Nassau County line. Before fanning eastward into Nassau, the district buttonhooks to the south and west along the Grand Central Parkway to take in some communities around St. John's University (which itself is in the 6th District).

Many of the district's residents commute to white-collar jobs outside the 5th, but the local economy is boosted by the U.S. Merchant Marine Academy at Kings Point, Shea Stadium (home to the Mets baseball team) and the USTA National Tennis Center in Flushing Meadows-Corona Park, where the U.S. Open tennis tournament is held each year.

Nassau tends to be politically competitive, but the strong Democratic tilt of Queens contributes to the district's more than 2-to-1 Democratic registration advantage.

MAJOR INDUSTRY
Higher education, health care, small business

CITIES
New York (pt.), 517,889; Port Washington (unincorporated), 15,215; Great Neck, 9,538

NOTABLE
In 1662, religious freedom advocate John Bowne was arrested for allowing Quakers to worship in his Flushing home, which is now one of the oldest remaining structures in New York State.

Rep. Gregory W. Meeks (D)

Elected February 1998; 4th full term

CAPITOL OFFICE
225-3461
congmeeks@mail.house.gov
www.house.gov/meeks
1710 Longworth 20515-3206; fax 226-4169

COMMITTEES
Financial Services
International Relations

HOMETOWN
Queens

BORN
Sept. 25, 1953, Harlem, N.Y.

RELIGION
Baptist

FAMILY
Wife, Simone-Marie Meeks; three children

EDUCATION
Adelphi U., B.A. 1975; Howard U., J.D. 1978

CAREER
Workers' compensation board judge; lawyer;
city prosecutor

POLITICAL HIGHLIGHTS
N.Y. Assembly, 1993-98

ELECTION RESULTS

2004 GENERAL
Gregory W. Meeks (D, WFM)		unopposed

2004 PRIMARY
Gregory W. Meeks (D)		unopposed

2002 GENERAL
Gregory W. Meeks (D, L, WFM)	72,799	96.5%
Rey Clarke (INDC)	2,632	3.5%

PREVIOUS WINNING PERCENTAGES
2000 (100%); 1998 (100%); 1998 Special Election
(56%)

A vocal liberal partisan, Meeks is a man on the move, both on Capitol Hill and beyond. He was one of the first members of Congress to endorse John Kerry, and he served as national co-chairman of the Kerry-Edwards campaign. He was part of a 20-person Democratic "truth squad" that criss-crossed the battleground states in 2004 to denounce President Bush's "misleadership" and defend the Democratic ticket.

Just weeks after the election, Meeks was named to the New York State Democratic Steering Committee. "He is bright, articulate and one of the present and future leaders in New York City and Washington," state party chairman Herman "Denny" Farrell told Newsday. In December 2004, Meeks announced he was running for vice chairman of the Democratic National Committee, telling the New York Sun he wanted the party leadership to focus more intensely on state and local rebuilding efforts, including in Republican-dominated areas. "The DNC cannot be an organization that works just every four years to nominate a candidate for president," Meeks told the Sun. "We can't allow so many states to go uncontested." But Meeks abandoned his long-shot bid before the vote.

At the start of the 108th Congress, Meeks sought the vice chairmanship of the House Democratic Caucus. But on the day of the balloting, he and another candidate, Zoe Lofgren of California, conceded defeat to James E. Clyburn of South Carolina before the votes were tabulated.

Meeks is deeply involved with his party's black activist constituency. He has been arrested for protesting the under-representation of minority law clerks at the Supreme Court, and after four New York City police officers shot and killed a Guinean immigrant in 1999, he joined other black leaders in protesting police violence against minorities.

Reared in the public housing of East Harlem, Meeks says affordable child care, economic development, and education are essential ingredients for helping his constituents improve their lot. His district, which includes John F. Kennedy International Airport, was hit hard by the economic after-shocks of the Sept. 11, 2001, terrorist attacks. Though Democrats were unable to obtain aid for the thousands of airline workers who faced layoffs after the attacks, Meeks backed the law providing up to $15 billion in aid for the airlines. He and other New York lawmakers also championed US Airways' successful effort to obtain a $900 million federal loan guarantee under the law. In the 108th, he secured $22 million to help soundproof schools in the Queens neighborhoods surrounding Kennedy Airport.

His seat on the Financial Services Committee is Meeks' main forum for promoting affordable housing. He has consistently opposed proposals to tighten regulation of Fannie Mae and Freddie Mac, the government-chartered mortgage giants, and introduced legislation in 2004 to repeal a controversial community service requirement for public housing residents.

A member of the International Relations Committee, Meeks has blasted Bush's Iraq policy as strategically misguided and financially disastrous. "America cannot afford the price tag that the president has put on this Iraqi misadventure," he said in 2003. "The money that we will be spending will be money that we will be taking from the middle-class and working-class people of this great nation, and the poor who are already paying for this war, especially with their sons and daughters." Returning from an official visit to Iraq in 2003, Meeks accused the Bush administration of hiding the truth. "They have a dog and pony show going on," he told Newsday, "so they wanted to make sure we only saw good things there."

Meeks has been a swing vote on trade. During the 2000 debate on whether to make permanent the normal U.S.-China trade relationship, he took a trip arranged by the Clinton administration to observe the Chinese economy. He returned and agreed to vote yes, partly because he concluded the society was not as oppressive as he had believed — and partly because of the prospect of increased trade going through JFK. He opposed the 2002 law expanding the administration's trade negotiating authority, but in 2004 voted in favor of stand-alone free-trade agreements with Chile and Singapore.

Meeks says he owes his interest in public affairs to his mother, who resumed her education when her four children were in their teens and inspired him to become involved alongside her in community improvement projects. His idol was legendary civil rights attorney and Supreme Court Justice Thurgood Marshall. "From the time that I could remember, I wanted to be a lawyer," Meeks told Newsday. "I always admired Thurgood Marshall and I learned from my parents what he was doing to make life better for people of color."

After graduating from Howard University Law School, Meeks began his career as a Queens County assistant district attorney and narcotics crime prosecutor. After a brief stint on the state Commission of Investigation, which probes wrongdoing by state officials and organized crime figures, Meeks was appointed as a state workers' compensation judge and later moved up to the position of supervising law judge. During those years, Meeks became involved in a variety of community matters — neighborhood cleanups, street repairs, traffic problems, and street safety — in the working-class neighborhood of Far Rockaway, where his parents were eventually able to move.

Meeks says he always thought his involvement in politics would be behind the scenes, but community activist colleagues persuaded him to run for office. In 1992, he won the first of three terms to the state Assembly, where he held seats on a range of committees that oversaw state codes, the judiciary, insurance, small business and government operations.

When Democrat Floyd H. Flake resigned his 6th District seat late in 1997 to lead an influential African Methodist Episcopal church in Jamaica, Queens, he endorsed Meeks to be his successor. Propelled by additional key endorsements, Meeks got Democratic leaders' backing in the February 1998 special election. He captured 56 percent of the vote in that five-way contest. He was unopposed in the election for a full term in November and has not drawn Republican opposition in any of his subsequent elections.

KEY VOTES

2004

Yes Extend federal unemployment benefits by 13 weeks

Yes Pass $283.2 billion, six-year federal highway and mass transit bill

Yes Approve $146 billion multi-year extension of previously enacted middle-class tax breaks

? Amend the Constitution to prohibit same-sex marriage

Yes Cut corporate taxes $137 billion over 10 years

Yes Reorganize U.S. intelligence agencies as proposed by Sept. 11 commission

2003

No Cut taxes by $330 billion through fiscal 2013

Yes Block Bush rule scaling back overtime pay for some white-collar federal workers

Yes Do not allow use of search warrants without first notifying subjects

No Allow importation of prescription drugs

No Create private school voucher program in Washington, D.C.

No Ban "partial birth" abortion except to save a woman's life

Yes Split $18.6 billion in Iraq aid into half-grant, half-loan

No Overhaul Medicare and create prescription drug benefit

CQ VOTE STUDIES

| | PARTY UNITY | | PRESIDENTIAL SUPPORT | |
	Support	Oppose	Support	Oppose
2004	94%	6%	37%	63%
2003	93%	7%	25%	75%
2002	94%	6%	26%	74%
2001	94%	6%	20%	80%
2000	95%	5%	92%	8%

INTEREST GROUPS

	AFL-CIO	ADA	CCUS	ACU
2004	93%	75%	55%	9%
2003	87%	95%	45%	16%
2002	89%	85%	45%	4%
2001	100%	85%	36%	5%
2000	90%	95%	50%	8%

NEW YORK 6

Southeast Queens – Jamaica, St. Albans

A black-majority, mostly middle-class area, the 6th is economically focused around John F. Kennedy International Airport on Jamaica Bay in southeastern Queens. It is the only district wholly within the 2.2 million-resident borough of Queens.

Redistricting following the 2000 census only marginally changed the lines of the 6th, which is bound roughly by Cross Bay Boulevard to the west, Grand Central Parkway to the north and the Nassau County line to the east. South of the airport, across Jamaica Bay, the 6th takes in part of Rockaway, including Edgemere and Far Rockaway. Included in the 6th's boundaries are St. John's University, located in the far north, and Aqueduct Racetrack, in the far west.

More than a generation ago, communities such as Springfield Gardens and St. Albans were settled by a burgeoning Irish and Italian Roman Catholic middle class. Today, while the economic profile of these areas is not much different, the demographics are completely changed — most of the residents are black.

The 6th is one of the nation's most economically sound black-majority districts, although some areas, such as South Jamaica, have been troubled by unemployment and other urban ills. JFK Airport, the 6th's largest employer, provides a steady job base and, combined with health care, municipal government and construction jobs, helps create a strong union constituency.

With a sizable Hispanic constituency to go along with its black majority, the district is overwhelmingly Democratic. John Kerry won 84 percent of the vote here in the 2004 presidential election, and Democrats outnumber Republicans 8-to-1 in voter registration.

MAJOR INDUSTRY
Airport, health care, education

CITIES
New York (pt.), 654,361

NOTABLE
Roy Wilkins Park in Jamaica is named for the civil rights leader; Residents of the 6th have the nation's longest average travel time to work — more than 47 minutes, according to the 2000 census; King Park in Jamaica was the farm of Rufus King, a delegate to the Constitutional Convention in Philadelphia and later a Federalist senator from New York.

Rep. Joseph Crowley (D)

Elected 1998; 4th term

CAPITOL OFFICE
225-3965
write2joecrowley@mail.house.gov
crowley.house.gov
312 Cannon 20515-3207; fax 225-1909

COMMITTEES
Financial Services
International Relations

HOMETOWN
Queens

BORN
March 16, 1962, Queens, N.Y.

RELIGION
Roman Catholic

FAMILY
Wife, Kasey Crowley; two children

EDUCATION
Queens College, B.A. 1985 (communications & political science)

CAREER
State legislator

POLITICAL HIGHLIGHTS
N.Y. Assembly, 1987-99

ELECTION RESULTS

2004 GENERAL

Joseph Crowley (D, WFM)	104,275	80.9%
Joseph Cinquemain (R, C)	24,548	19.1%

2004 PRIMARY

Joseph Crowley (D)	15,738	63.4%
Dennis Coleman (D)	4,716	19.0%
Aniello V. Grimaldi (D)	2,280	9.2%
Curtis Brooks (D)	2,102	8.5%

2002 GENERAL

Joseph Crowley (D, WFM)	50,967	73.3%
Kevin Brawley (R, C)	18,572	26.7%

PREVIOUS WINNING PERCENTAGES
2000 (72%); 1998 (69%)

Now in his fourth term, the gregarious Crowley has emerged as an easygoing but vigorous defender of the Democratic Party line, someone to be reckoned with inside the minority party.

Upon his arrival on Capitol Hill in 1999, Crowley (KRAU-lee) lobbied his peers to win election to one of four six-month terms as president of the Democratic freshman class, a leadership role that gave him access to top party officials. He credits such political networking as a factor in his selection for a seat on the Financial Services panel in the 107th Congress, a post he sought avidly.

At the start of the 108th, he became one of seven chief deputy whips, helping to round up votes and enforce party discipline. He also was named to the party's Steering Committee, which makes Democratic committee assignments. "Joe influences people not with his formidable size [he's a burly 6-feet, 4-inches], but with his personality and sense of humor," New York colleague Anthony Weiner told Newsday.

As the 109th Congress organized, Crowley made the shortlist to head the Democratic Congressional Campaign Committee, the party organization that works to elect Democrats to the House and an important first rung on the leadership ladder. (The DCCC chairmanship ultimately went to Rahm Emanuel of Illinois.) And he was an early candidate for vice chairman of the Democratic Caucus in the 110th Congress.

Crowley occasionally strays from his fellow House Democrats on trade and foreign policy issues. Although he voted against presidential fast-track trade negotiating authority in 2002, he backed free-trade pacts with Chile and Singapore in the 108th Congress, putting him at odds with his party. And in 2002, he voted to authorize President Bush to use force against Iraq.

A member of the International Relations Committee, Crowley is a staunch defender of Israel. He argued in 2003 against conditioning aid to the Jewish state on its approach to the Palestinian peace process. "The United States must not stand in the way of Israel protecting its citizens from terrorists who threaten them," he said. "Israel did not ask us to restrain ourselves when we acted against the terrorists responsible for the 9/11 attacks, and we should not ask that from them." In 2004, Crowley joined other New York lawmakers to offer an amendment prohibiting aid to Saudi Arabia, calling that nation "soft on Al Qaeda," the terrorist network.

Like other New Yorkers, Crowley has spent substantial time on issues stemming from the Sept. 11, 2001, terrorist attacks — ranging from foreign aid policy and intelligence to homeland security. Based on congressional field hearings, town hall meetings and information from local officials, he wrote a 100-page blueprint on New York City's security needs to guard against future attacks. In 2004, he introduced legislation to boost support for the city's first-responders, which he says continue to be massively underfunded.

Crowley estimates that 105 families in his district, including his own, lost a family member in the collapse of the World Trade Center towers: His cousin, firefighter John Moran, died in the attacks. Crowley, whose district includes Queens and part of the Bronx, worked to ensure compensation for victims' families, health care monitoring of those exposed to toxic dust, and recognition for the efforts of rescue workers.

On a more mundane level, he has tried to help his constituents battle incessant traffic congestion, noise and air pollution. In the 108th, Crowley secured millions for local transportation improvements. In 2000, he won money for security improvements and approval of a study of noise and air pollution in the vicinity of La Guardia airport, as well as $40 million to help soundproof local schools.

Crowley, whose mother is from Northern Ireland, has worked vigorously to boost the peace process in Northern Ireland. In the 108th, he helped secure $18.5 million for community and political development efforts aimed at bridging the divide between long-feuding Protestants and Catholics. He is also co-chairman of the India Caucus; his district has a large South Asian population, and his travels have included visits to India and Bangladesh.

Though personally opposed to abortion, he has faced off with the Republican majority over legislative language conditioning foreign aid on the receiving nation's abortion policies.

A guitar player, Crowley once belonged to a band called "The Budget Blues" with three friends from his days in the New York Assembly. He has been known to perform a perfect imitation of Van Morrison singing "Wild Nights." He occasionally sings in public, including the national anthem once before a New York Knicks basketball game.

Reared in a political family, Crowley says that one of his earliest memories is handing out pamphlets with his family for Democrat Mario M. Cuomo after church. His uncle, Walter Crowley, was a well-known Queens politician who served on the New York City Council. First elected to the state Assembly just a year after his graduation from college, Crowley spent 12 years in Albany. He made news in 1996 when he offered legislation to require New York schools to teach about starvation in Ireland during the 1840s potato famine.

His predecessor in the 7th District, Democrat Thomas J. Manton, was a longtime friend of Crowley's father and uncle. Manton surprised his fellow Democrats in 1998 when he announced his retirement several days after the election filing deadline. That allowed party officials, including Manton, the Queens Democratic chairman, to handpick Crowley as the nominee. Crowley then swamped the Republican candidate, corporate security manager James J. Dillon, in the general election.

But Manton's tactics angered other Democrats who had wanted a shot at the seat. Several vowed to unseat Crowley in the 2000 Democratic primary, and, after months of wrangling, they united behind Queens Councilman Walter McCaffrey. Crowley, however, used his incumbency to cement his hold on the seat. He was so effective that McCaffrey pulled out of the race right before the September primary, citing campaign funding difficulties. Crowley coasted to victory in the general election, winning more than 70 percent of the vote. He has won his last two elections with ease.

KEY VOTES

2004

Yes Extend federal unemployment benefits by 13 weeks

Yes Pass $283.2 billion, six-year federal highway and mass transit bill

Yes Approve $146 billion multi-year extension of previously enacted middle-class tax breaks

No Amend the Constitution to prohibit same-sex marriage

Yes Cut corporate taxes $137 billion over 10 years

Yes Reorganize U.S. intelligence agencies as proposed by Sept. 11 commission

2003

No Cut taxes by $330 billion through fiscal 2013

Yes Block Bush rule scaling back overtime pay for some white-collar federal workers

Yes Do not allow use of search warrants without first notifying subjects

Yes Allow importation of prescription drugs

No Create private school voucher program in Washington, D.C.

Yes Ban "partial birth" abortion except to save a woman's life

Yes Split $18.6 billion in Iraq aid into half-grant, half-loan

No Overhaul Medicare and create prescription drug benefit

CQ VOTE STUDIES

	PARTY UNITY		PRESIDENTIAL SUPPORT	
	Support	Oppose	Support	Oppose
2004	93%	7%	30%	70%
2003	92%	8%	27%	73%
2002	93%	7%	39%	61%
2001	89%	11%	30%	70%
2000	91%	9%	82%	18%

INTEREST GROUPS

	AFL-CIO	ADA	CCUS	ACU
2004	93%	90%	55%	9%
2003	80%	95%	37%	20%
2002	78%	95%	50%	8%
2001	91%	80%	43%	20%
2000	100%	85%	38%	20%

NEW YORK 7
Part of Queens and the Bronx

Few districts in the nation are as ethnically and racially diverse as the 7th, which takes in part of northern Queens and the eastern part of the Bronx. Blacks, Hispanics and Asians each compose more than 10 percent of the population, with Hispanics a clear plurality of residents at 40 percent.

The rapid-growth 7th was one of the few New York districts to see substantial change in redistricting following the 2000 census. Under the district's 1990s configuration, nearly three-fourths of the registered votes came out of Queens. Now, two-thirds of registered voters come from the Bronx.

The district climbs north from near the intersection of the Brooklyn-Queens and Long Island expressways (in the neighboring 12th) to take in Woodside, Jackson Heights, East Elmhurst and LaGuardia Airport. This fast-growing area is heavily Hispanic and spurred much of Queens' 14 percent population growth rate in the 1990s.

The district continues northeast to the College Point neighborhood, then jumps across the Whitestone Bridge to envelop parts of the Bronx, reaching as far west as the Bronx Zoo and the New York Botanical Garden and as far north as Co-op City and the Westchester County line. The Bronx portion of the district includes Morris Park and Pelham Bay, which have an Italian influence. While the Bronx overall has economic struggles, the areas around Eastchester Bay have some of the borough's highest incomes.

Like most New York City districts, the 7th strongly supports Democrats, although a bit less monolithically. It is mostly middle class and residential, but steady growth tied to the city has spurred new businesses. LaGuardia makes the Queens area a transportation hub, and the health care industry is a major employer in the Bronx.

MAJOR INDUSTRY
Airport, health care, service

CITIES
New York (pt.), 654,360

NOTABLE
The Maritime Industry Museum and SUNY Maritime College are at Fort Schuyler in Throgs Neck, where the East River meets Long Island Sound.

Rep. Jerrold Nadler (D)

Elected 1992; 7th full term

CAPITOL OFFICE
225-5635
www.house.gov/nadler
2334 Rayburn 20515-3208; fax 225-6923

COMMITTEES
Judiciary
Transportation & Infrastructure

HOMETOWN
Manhattan

BORN
June 13, 1947, Brooklyn, N.Y.

RELIGION
Jewish

FAMILY
Wife, Joyce L. Miller; one child

EDUCATION
Columbia U., A.B. 1969 (government); Fordham U., J.D. 1978

CAREER
Lawyer; state legislative aide

POLITICAL HIGHLIGHTS
N.Y. Assembly, 1976-92; candidate for Manhattan borough president, 1985; candidate for New York City comptroller, 1989

ELECTION RESULTS

2004 GENERAL

Jerrold Nadler (D, WFM)	162,082	80.5%
Peter Hort (R,C,INDC)	39,240	19.5%

2004 PRIMARY

Jerrold Nadler (D)	unopposed

2002 GENERAL

Jerrold Nadler (D, L, WFM)	81,002	76.1%
Jim Farrin (R, INDC)	19,674	18.5%
Alan Jay Gerber (C)	3,361	3.2%
Dan Wentzel (GREEN)	1,918	1.8%

PREVIOUS WINNING PERCENTAGES
2000 (81%); 1998 (86%); 1996 (82%); 1994 (82%); 1992 (81%); 1992 Special Election (100%)

The World Trade Center's twin towers were a landmark of the 8th District. Their destruction on Sept. 11, 2001, changed forever the district's landscape and constituents. As their representative, Nadler has spent the last four years working to rebuild the area and help the victims.

He is persistently annoyed by what he calls "malfeasance" by the EPA in responding to concerns about air contaminants and other environmental degradation that resulted from the collapse of the skyscrapers. "EPA continues to ignore the health and safety needs of people living near Ground Zero, despite its legal obligation to act," Nadler said in early 2005. "More than three years have passed since 9/11, but the environmental issues at Ground Zero are far from resolved."

After the terrorist attacks, Nadler (NAD-ler) and conservative Republican Donald Manzullo of Illinois led a successful effort to change federal law to allow benefits paid out for firefighters, police and chaplains to be directed to whoever is listed on a victim's life insurance policy, thus allowing gay partners to collect on the policies.

Nadler is an unapologetic liberal in one of the nation's most liberal districts. The 8th stretches from Manhattan's Upper West Side through Greenwich Village and into Brooklyn, and it is home to one of the largest concentrations of liberal Jewish voters and gay and lesbian political activists in America. Whether the argument is against legislation to restrict abortion services, prohibit same-sex marriage or ban flag burning, Nadler is a leader among Democrats fighting for civil liberties and individual rights.

He is often the foremost Democratic spokesman in Judiciary Committee meetings, always at the ready with an amendment or an argument, or both, as the panel considers Republican proposals to alter social policy, the Constitution, the criminal justice system, consumer regulations or civil rights.

The top-ranking Democrat on Judiciary's Constitution Subcommittee, Nadler has long been a passionate foe of a proposed constitutional amendment to outlaw desecration of the U. S. flag. "The crass political use of the flag to question the patriotism of those who value our fundamental freedoms is a greater insult to those who died in the service of our nation than even the burning of the flag," he said. He is also an advocate for gay rights. When the House in 2004 considered a constitutional amendment to ban same-sex marriage, Nadler said the House was "playing politics with bigotry."

A member of the Progressive Caucus, the most liberal faction of House Democrats, Nadler is quick to join in partisan debate. Just weeks after the Sept. 11 attacks, he was one of just 66 House members to oppose a sweeping 2001 anti-terrorism bill, which gave the government enhanced authority to spy on suspected terrorists.

And when the House in early 2005 passed a measure to tighten some restrictions on asylum for immigrants, Nadler tried to strip out the provisions. Under the legislation, applicants for asylum would be required to prove that a "central reason" for their persecution was race, religion, nationality, membership in a particular social group, or political opinion. The bill also gave immigration judges broader authority to weigh the credibility of people seeking asylum in the United States. Supporters of the bill said it was designed to keep terrorists from exploiting the nation's asylum laws.

But Nadler said the language would impose an unfair, high barrier for refugees seeking asylum, who might be forced to seek corroborating evidence from their persecutors. Nadler called the asylum provisions "reckless, paranoid, and overly stringent." His amendment was defeated, however.

Nadler was also upset with what he called "voting irregularities" in Ohio during the 2004 presidential election. "The right to vote has been stolen from qualified voters — stolen through corruption, through political cynicism, through incompetence and through technical malfunction," he said.

From his seat on the Transportation and Infrastructure Committee, Nadler's long-range goal is to increase freight rail service to New York City by building a new tunnel under New York Harbor to connect Brooklyn with Bayonne, N.J. He says the tunnel would foster economic development, reduce air pollution and lower consumer costs in the city.

Nadler made an immediate impression when he arrived in the House in 1993. He persuaded his Democratic colleagues to approve an organizational overhaul that spreads out party power. The "Nadler rule" prohibits the top-ranking Democrat on a full committee from also holding the party's No. 1 seat on a subcommittee.

Born in Brooklyn, Nadler spent his early years on a New Jersey poultry farm. His family moved back to New York City after the farm failed. He earned a degree in government from Columbia and a law degree from Fordham, which he attended at night while working at an off-track betting office during the day.

Politics has been a lifelong passion for Nadler. In high school, he became friends with Dick Morris — who was later to gain fame and then notoriety as a political consultant to President Clinton — and roomed with Morris at Columbia. Nadler organized students against the Vietnam War to campaign for Eugene McCarthy in the 1968 New Hampshire Democratic presidential primary. He was an aide to a New York state senator and he campaigned for liberal Democrat Ted Weiss' election to Congress. In 1976, Nadler won a seat in the state Assembly. He served there for 16 years.

When Weiss died on the eve of the 1992 Democratic primary, voters renominated him nonetheless, giving party officials the right to pick a successor. That set off a scramble among the ample cadre of Democratic activists, with six candidates jumping into the frenetic nine-day race for the nomination. While others, such as former Rep. Bella S. Abzug, were better known to the public, Nadler had longstanding ties to the insiders who would cast the votes. He got the nomination and went on to win the special election and the general election for a full term on the same day.

In the overwhelmingly Democratic district, the nature of which was not altered by post-2000 census redistricting, Nadler's lowest re-election score was in 2002, when he earned 76 percent of the vote.

KEY VOTES

2004

Yes Extend federal unemployment benefits by 13 weeks

Yes Pass $283.2 billion, six-year federal highway and mass transit bill

Yes Approve $146 billion multi-year extension of previously enacted middle-class tax breaks

No Amend the Constitution to prohibit same-sex marriage

No Cut corporate taxes $137 billion over 10 years

Yes Reorganize U.S. intelligence agencies as proposed by Sept. 11 commission

2003

No Cut taxes by $330 billion through fiscal 2013

Yes Block Bush rule scaling back overtime pay for some white-collar federal workers

Yes Do not allow use of search warrants without first notifying subjects

Yes Allow importation of prescription drugs

No Create private school voucher program in Washington, D.C.

No Ban "partial birth" abortion except to save a woman's life

Yes Split $18.6 billion in Iraq aid into half-grant, half-loan

No Overhaul Medicare and create prescription drug benefit

CQ VOTE STUDIES

	PARTY UNITY		PRESIDENTIAL SUPPORT	
	Support	Oppose	Support	Oppose
2004	99%	1%	18%	82%
2003	99%	1%	13%	87%
2002	97%	3%	18%	82%
2001	98%	2%	21%	79%
2000	95%	5%	84%	16%

INTEREST GROUPS

	AFL-CIO	ADA	CCUS	ACU
2004	100%	100%	29%	0%
2003	100%	100%	21%	12%
2002	100%	95%	26%	0%
2001	100%	95%	26%	0%
2000	100%	95%	28%	4%

NEW YORK 8
West Side Manhattan; Borough Park; Coney Island

Starting just west of Central Park, the 8th moves south through Manhattan's West Side, taking in part of the Theater District and Times Square, then Chelsea, Greenwich Village, SoHo and Wall Street. It continues across the East River to skim Brooklyn's western waterfront, followed by some working-class areas, much of Brighton Beach and some of Brooklyn's south coastline in Coney Island.

It was in the 8th that terrorists crashed commercial airliners into the twin towers of the World Trade Center on Sept. 11, 2001, killing thousands of people and leveling the buildings. Despite the generally varied interests of the winding district, the logistics of rebuilding Lower Manhattan will dominate political and economic discussion here for some time to come.

Manhattan's heavily Democratic West Side has sent liberal representatives to Congress for decades. The Brooklyn portion, added in 1992 redistricting, increased the district's diversity.

The manufacturing industry that once sustained Brooklyn has been

neglected in a surge of white-collar financial growth, although most of Brooklyn's well-to-do neighborhoods are in other districts.

The 8th's politically active communities — gay, Jewish, minority, artistic and student — have supported Democratic presidential candidates overwhelmingly in recent years. Some GOP voters live in Brooklyn's middle-class neighborhoods, like Borough Park and Bensonhurst, and back candidates with more-conservative views. George W. Bush actually won the district's Brooklyn portion with 53 percent of the 2004 presidential vote, but overall John Kerry took 72 percent of the 8th's vote. Bush did not carry a single precinct in the 8th's part of Manhattan.

MAJOR INDUSTRY
Finance, tourism, manufacturing, small business

CITIES
New York (pt.), 654,360

NOTABLE
The Statue of Liberty, Empire State Building, Governors Island, South Street Seaport, American Museum of Natural History, Lincoln Center, Penn Station, Madison Square Garden, City Hall, New York University and Coney Island's KeySpan Park, home to minor-league baseball's Brooklyn Cyclones, are in the 8th.

Rep. Anthony Weiner (D)

Elected 1998; 4th term

CAPITOL OFFICE
225-6616
weiner@mail.house.gov
www.house.gov/weiner
1122 Longworth 20515-3209; fax 226-7253

COMMITTEES
Judiciary
Transportation & Infrastructure

HOMETOWN
Queens

BORN
Sept. 4, 1964, Brooklyn, N.Y.

RELIGION
Jewish

FAMILY
Single

EDUCATION
State U. of New York, Plattsburgh, B.A. 1985

CAREER
Congressional aide

POLITICAL HIGHLIGHTS
New York City Council, 1992-99

ELECTION RESULTS

2004 GENERAL

Anthony Weiner (D, WFM)	113,025	71.3%
Gerard J. Cronin (R, C, INDC)	45,451	28.7%

2004 PRIMARY

Anthony Weiner (D)	unopposed

2002 GENERAL

Anthony Weiner (D, L, WFM)	60,737	65.7%
Alfred F. Donohue (R, C)	31,698	34.3%

PREVIOUS WINNING PERCENTAGES
2000 (68%); 1998 (66%)

Weiner fits the stereotype of the New York City politician perfectly: He's brash, loud, a close-in brawler, and a master of the city's intensely local and personal style of politics.

A candidate for New York City mayor in 2005, Weiner (WEE-ner) happily positions himself at the center of local disputes. That can mean battling a new stadium site one day, objecting to the closing of the gym at his old high school on another and trying on a third to resolve a fight over whether a local restaurant should be forced to remove flower-filled planters. (Weiner put out a press release taking the side of the flowers.)

The New York City media, predictably, delight in being able to describe Weiner as a "political hot dog" and to exclaim "Weiner on a roll!"

Weiner has an upfront style that he is not shy about using with his own constituents. He favors a new stadium to help attract the Olympics in 2012, but wants it built in Queens, while Mayor Michael Bloomberg is pushing for the West Side of Manhattan. In 2005, Weiner encountered a group of iron-workers who sided with Bloomberg and heckled Weiner. "What are you, a bunch of rich Upper East Siders?" asked Weiner, according to Newsday. He went and spoke with the protesters, who surrounded him and began chanting "Stadium!" Weiner punctuated each chant with: "In Queens!"

Like many New York City-area lawmakers, much of Weiner's work in the House has been in response to the Sept. 11, 2001, terrorist attacks. A member of the Judiciary Committee, he added language to the 2002 law creating the Department of Homeland Security to permit federal authorities to share security intelligence with local law enforcement. He is also a strident advocate of funneling anti-terrorism and security funds to New York and other cities considered likely targets of attacks instead of spreading money around to a list of cities that has grown from seven to 50.

"If we are at the point where the terrorists are targeting the Charlotte [North Carolina] Raptor Museum, or whatever it is they have down there, then we are in big trouble," Weiner told The New York Times, objecting to proposals in President Bush's 2004 budget. "That was not what this program was intended for."

Weiner also cosponsored a House bill by fellow New Yorker, Republican Sherwood Boehlert, to create special teams within the National Institute of Standards and Technology to investigate building failures and protect potentially valuable evidence. Weiner argued that bureaucratic infighting and mishandled evidence had impeded the probe into why the World Trade Center's twin towers collapsed so readily.

Always ready to take on Bush's policies, Weiner is a favorite of the cable news shows. As some Democrats shied away from challenging Bush on national security in 2002, Weiner in a Fox News interview questioned the success of the war on terrorism: "Show me a victory," he declared.

The Sept. 11 terrorist attacks also deepened Weiner's activism on issues relating to the Middle East. His district is heavily Jewish and Weiner is a persistent advocate of Israel and relentless foe of its perceived enemies. The 2002 State Department authorization law included a Weiner provision requiring department recognition of Jerusalem as the capital of Israel. Palestinian leader Yasser Arafat denounced the provision, and Bush has declined to enforce it.

When Arafat was reported to be near death in 2004, Weiner issued a statement that said, "The world is better off without him. The loss of Arafat is a gain for peace." Arguing that Saudi Arabia has provided better than half of the funding for the anti-Israel terrorist group Hamas, Weiner is pushing legislation to ax all U.S. aid to the Saudis.

Young, energetic and ambitious, Weiner found his footing quickly in the House. And although he is a solid Democratic liberal, Weiner has on occasion worked with Judiciary Republicans. He helped write a deal with Republicans in 2000 on a law making it more difficult for the government to seize private property from suspected criminals.

Weiner is a champion of consumer interests — parochial and national. As a representative for a substantial elderly population, he has proposed a bill to give bigger annual cost-of-living increases for Social Security beneficiaries in the most expensive cities. Since Sept. 11, he has pushed a bill requiring the New York City subway system to be equipped so cell phone users could make a 911 call in any of its underground stations.

Weiner also sits on the Transportation and Infrastructure Committee and its Aviation Subcommittee. As a 34-year-old freshman, he won approval in 1999 of $30 million over three years to encourage aircraft builders to design quieter engines — a key concern for his constituents who live beneath the takeoff and final approach paths of both LaGuardia and Kennedy airports. Weiner also joined with other New York-area lawmakers to prevent more takeoffs and landings at those airports; their success locked in the existing numbers until 2007.

Weiner came to politics with a run for student government at the State University of New York at Plattsburgh. His first campaign gave him a chance to hone his self-deprecating sense of humor. Among his slogans was "Vote for Weiner. He'll be frank."

After college, he served for six years as a congressional aide in New York Democratic Sen. Charles E. Schumer's Brooklyn and Washington offices when Schumer was in the U.S. House. Then in 1991, at age 27, he became the youngest person at the time ever elected to the New York City Council. He worked with at-risk teenagers to create an anti-graffiti cleanup group known as "Weiner's Cleaners." Seven years later, he was among the youngest members of the 106th Congress and was elected by his freshman class to the Democratic whip organization.

Though he was seen as Schumer's protégé, Weiner did not have an easy path to his party's nomination when the incumbent made his 1998 Senate run. Weiner won the Democratic nomination in a tight four-way primary by 489 votes. But he coasted in the strongly Democratic district in November and has taken more than 65 percent of the vote since then.

KEY VOTES

2004

Yes	Extend federal unemployment benefits by 13 weeks
Yes	Pass $283.2 billion, six-year federal highway and mass transit bill
Yes	Approve $146 billion multi-year extension of previously enacted middle-class tax breaks
No	Amend the Constitution to prohibit same-sex marriage
No	Cut corporate taxes $137 billion over 10 years
Yes	Reorganize U.S. intelligence agencies as proposed by Sept. 11 commission

2003

No	Cut taxes by $330 billion through fiscal 2013
Yes	Block Bush rule scaling back overtime pay for some white-collar federal workers
Yes	Do not allow use of search warrants without first notifying subjects
Yes	Allow importation of prescription drugs
No	Create private school voucher program in Washington, D.C.
No	Ban "partial birth" abortion except to save a woman's life
Yes	Split $18.6 billion in Iraq aid into half-grant, half-loan
No	Overhaul Medicare and create prescription drug benefit

CQ VOTE STUDIES

	PARTY UNITY		PRESIDENTIAL SUPPORT	
	Support	Oppose	Support	Oppose
2004	99%	1%	30%	70%
2003	97%	3%	22%	78%
2002	95%	5%	24%	76%
2001	95%	5%	26%	74%
2000	94%	6%	90%	10%

INTEREST GROUPS

	AFL-CIO	ADA	CCUS	ACU
2004	100%	100%	38%	4%
2003	87%	100%	30%	17%
2002	100%	100%	32%	8%
2001	100%	95%	35%	0%
2000	90%	85%	40%	8%

NEW YORK 9
Parts of Brooklyn and Queens — Forest Hills, Rockaway, Sheepshead Bay

The Democratic-leaning 9th takes in north-central and western Queens and segues into southeastern Brooklyn. The district was divided almost equally between Brooklyn and Queens in the late 1990s, but redistricting following the 2000 census left the 9th with 70 percent of its registered voters living in Queens.

The new map extended the 9th farther east in Queens, past the Grand Central Parkway and through the Hillcrest and Fresh Meadows neighborhoods to the edge of Oakland Gardens, which is only a few exits from Nassau County on the Long Island Expressway. Many of Queens' wealthiest communities are in the northern part of the 9th. Median household incomes in this area top $100,000.

The 9th narrows and runs south from Forest Park, taking in part of the Woodhaven, Ozone Park and Lindenwood neighborhoods. A decade ago, these areas were mostly white. Hispanics now outnumber whites,

and the Asian population is rapidly expanding.

The 9th also takes in much of the Rockaway area in far southwestern Queens along the Atlantic Ocean. In Brooklyn, the district includes Floyd Bennett Field and most of Gateway National Recreation Area on Jamaica Bay. Farther west, the Sheepshead Bay area has seen an influx of Russian immigrants.

Although Al Gore topped two-thirds of the presidential vote here in 2000, the aftermath of the Sept. 11, 2001, terrorist attacks moved the Brooklyn portion to the right. George W. Bush carried the Brooklyn part with 53 percent of the vote in 2004, and overall John Kerry was held to his second-lowest percentage (56 percent) of any district entirely in the city.

MAJOR INDUSTRY
Service, finance, insurance, manufacturing

CITIES
New York (pt.), 654,360

NOTABLE
Kings Plaza Shopping Center, billed as the first indoor mall in New York City, opened in 1970 near Mill Basin; American Airlines Flight 587, bound for the Dominican Republic, crashed into Belle Harbor on Nov. 12, 2001.

Rep. Edolphus Towns (D)

Elected 1982; 12th term

CAPITOL OFFICE
225-5936
www.house.gov/towns
2232 Rayburn 20515-3210; fax 225-1018

COMMITTEES
Energy & Commerce
Government Reform

HOMETOWN
Brooklyn

BORN
July 21, 1934, Chadbourn, N.C.

RELIGION
Baptist

FAMILY
Wife, Gwendolyn Towns; two children

EDUCATION
North Carolina A&T State U., B.S. 1956; Adelphi U., M.S.W. 1973

MILITARY SERVICE
Army, 1956-58

CAREER
Professor; hospital administrator

POLITICAL HIGHLIGHTS
Brooklyn borough deputy president, 1976-82

ELECTION RESULTS

2004 GENERAL

Edolphus Towns (D, WFM)	136,113	91.5%
Harvey R. Clarke (R)	11,099	7.5%
Mariana Blume (C)	1,554	1.1%

2004 PRIMARY

Edolphus Towns (D)	unopposed

2002 GENERAL

Edolphus Towns (D, L)	73,859	97.8%
Herbert F. Ryan (C)	1,639	2.2%

PREVIOUS WINNING PERCENTAGES
2000 (90%); 1998 (92%); 1996 (91%); 1994 (89%); 1992 (96%); 1990 (93%); 1988 (89%); 1986 (89%); 1984 (85%); 1982 (84%)

On the Democratic side of the dais of the prestigious Energy and Commerce Committee sit some of the House's most prominent and active legislators — John D. Dingell of Michigan, Henry A. Waxman of California and Edward J. Markey of Massachusetts. Sitting alongside them is the considerably less well-known Towns, the committee's No. 5 Democrat.

The spotlight rarely shines on Towns, who in 2004 turned 70 and won his 12th House term. Yet he can look back on a career in which he has scored some notable legislative successes, helped bring considerable largess to his Brooklyn district, and built a strong enough local political base to fuel speculation that when he retires, he will be able to engineer the succession to Congress of his son, New York Assemblyman Darryl Towns.

Towns' most prominent legislative accomplishment came when the 101st Congress passed the Student Right to Know Act, requiring colleges to report the graduation rates of their scholarship athletes. Media had begun to focus attention on college sports programs that seemed more concerned about drawing paying customers to games than about ensuring their athletes met graduation requirements. "If we can have reporting as to the on-time arrivals of airlines," Towns said, "surely we can let student-athletes know whether they are likely to receive a useful college degree if they sign a letter of intent at "X" University." The bill became law in 1990.

Keeping up his interest in student athletes, Towns in the 107th cosponsored legislation to bring sports agents under the auspices of the Federal Trade Commission, allowing unscrupulous agents to be sued in state courts for misleading student athletes or offering them bribes or gifts.

Towns' district is home to many low-income and working-class people who are trying to grab or hold onto the ladder of economic success. Towns wants the federal government to increase educational opportunities, improve health services and accelerate economic development.

From his seat on Energy and Commerce's Subcommittee on Telecommunications and the Internet, Towns has tried to bridge the "digital divide," supporting a measure in the 108th to foster the use of technology at "minority-serving institutions" — colleges and universities that historically and predominately have served black, Hispanic, and other minority groups. He cosponsored the same bill in the 109th.

Over the years, he has helped secure federal funding for numerous projects in Brooklyn. In the 107th, for example, he procured $153 million for a federal courthouse and acquired a $150 million reconstruction bond for the borough's Interfaith Hospital. In the 2004 catchall spending bill, Brooklyn received money for the Kings County Hospital Center to develop and operate a resource center for diabetes and cardiovascular disease, which are especially prevalent among blacks and Latinos.

Although Towns gained some notice — and peeved some Democrats — when he endorsed Republican Rudolph Giuliani for re-election as mayor of New York City in 1997, he votes a liberal, pro-labor line in the House. When the Census Bureau in September 2004 released data showing an increase in the number of Americans living in poverty and uninsured, Towns lamented, "It is just another sad sign that the current economic policies of this administration are not working."

Towns' first choice for president in 2004 was the Rev. Al Sharpton, because he "is telling it like it is," Towns said. He agreed with Sharpton's view that the Bush administration should have spent the Iraq war money on improving education and health care at home.

From his seat on the Government Reform Committee, Towns keeps a watchful eye on the new Department of Homeland Security. "We must make every effort to ensure the department is run effectively and efficiently," he said. In the 109th, he became the top-ranking Democrat on the Government Management, Finance and Accountability Subcommittee.

Towns has heard criticism that he has not achieved as much on Capitol Hill as might be expected from a lawmaker with his longevity. In 2000, The New York Times endorsed his challenger in the Democratic primary, commenting that "after 18 years, [Towns'] record in Congress has been minimal and his support for tobacco and other special interests is troubling."

The son of a sharecropper in North Carolina, where tobacco is a major crop, Towns argues that anti-tobacco legislation affects small farmers and the large manufacturers. He only stopped taking campaign donations from the tobacco industry in 2000 after considerable pressure.

In an overwhelmingly Democratic district such as the 10th, the Democratic primary is the real election. The 2000 primary, in which Towns beat Harvard-trained lawyer Barry Ford by 14 percentage points, was fought amid grumblings that Towns was going too far in trying to position his son, Darryl, as heir to the district seat.

Towns was born in southeastern North Carolina and graduated from historically black North Carolina A & T in Greensboro. After a two-year stint in the Army, he worked as a teacher and hospital administrator and earned a master's degree in social work from Adelphi University, in Long Island, N.Y. In 1976, he was appointed Brooklyn Borough deputy president.

His chance to run for the House came in 1982 after redistricting gave the 11th District an almost even split of blacks and Hispanics. The new district included some Brooklyn territory that had been represented by white Democratic Rep. Frederick W. Richmond, but an indictment on charges of income tax evasion and possession of marijuana led him to resign.

In the turbulent world of Brooklyn politics, Towns benefited from a lack of enemies. He drew support from party regulars and from a rival faction calling for a change. Towns fended off two Hispanic primary contenders to win nomination with 50 percent of the vote, then won easily in November. Redistricting in 1992 put him in a newly drawn but just as Democratic 10th District, where he faced tough primary battles three times, including in 2000. The latest round of redistricting did him no harm, and he ran unopposed in the Democratic primaries of 2002 and 2004.

KEY VOTES

2004
Yes   Extend federal unemployment benefits by 13 weeks

Yes   Pass $283.2 billion, six-year federal highway and mass transit bill

No   Approve $146 billion multi-year extension of previously enacted middle-class tax breaks

No   Amend the Constitution to prohibit same-sex marriage

?   Cut corporate taxes $137 billion over 10 years

Yes   Reorganize U.S. intelligence agencies as proposed by Sept. 11 commission

2003
No   Cut taxes by $330 billion through fiscal 2013

Yes   Block Bush rule scaling back overtime pay for some white-collar federal workers

Yes   Do not allow use of search warrants without first notifying subjects

No   Allow importation of prescription drugs

No   Create private school voucher program in Washington, D.C.

No   Ban "partial birth" abortion except to save a woman's life

Yes   Split $18.6 billion in Iraq aid into half-grant, half-loan

No   Overhaul Medicare and create prescription drug benefit

CQ VOTE STUDIES

	PARTY UNITY		PRESIDENTIAL SUPPORT	
	Support	Oppose	Support	Oppose
2004	96%	4%	15%	85%
2003	96%	4%	20%	80%
2002	94%	6%	32%	68%
2001	91%	9%	34%	66%
2000	97%	3%	89%	11%

INTEREST GROUPS

	AFL-CIO	ADA	CCUS	ACU
2004	100%	90%	33%	0%
2003	100%	80%	33%	18%
2002	100%	80%	40%	4%
2001	100%	65%	50%	14%
2000	100%	95%	50%	4%

NEW YORK 10

Part of Brooklyn — Bedford-Stuyvesant, Canarsie, Downtown Brooklyn, East New York

The 10th begins just inland of Brooklyn's industrial waterfront and heads east before bounding back southwest after reaching the Queens border. The district encompasses one of New York's most economically and ethnically diverse constituencies, but is homogeneously Democratic, with a 13-to-1 Democratic registration advantage. John Kerry took 86 percent of the area's vote in the 2004 presidential contest.

Redistricting following the 2000 census brought the black-majority 10th west of Flatbush Avenue to include part of Midwood in south-central Brooklyn. East of this area, the district takes in growing Georgetown and Canarsie. Canarsie's racial composition has changed dramatically, as many blacks of Caribbean descent are moving to an area that was once predominately white. Many of these families have solid middle-class incomes, which is the exception rather than the rule for most of the district. At its northwestern corner, the 10th cups the Brooklyn Navy Yard (located in the 12th) to take in Fort Greene and part of Williamsburg — diverse areas with large black and Hispanic populations.

Joblessness has aggravated poverty, violent crime and racial tensions in some working-class and low-income communities like East New York and Bedford-Stuyvesant. Erosion in the 10th's manufacturing base has caused unemployment, although government jobs in Downtown Brooklyn, which includes Borough Hall and several court facilities, and education jobs at the district's colleges, which include Brooklyn College and Long Island University-Brooklyn, aid the economy.

George W. Bush found some small pockets of support in the 10th in 2004 among Jewish voters in Williamsburg and Midwood, but these areas pale in comparison to the overwhelmingly Democratic voting patterns of the rest of the district.

MAJOR INDUSTRY
Government, higher education, small business, pharmaceuticals

CITIES
New York (pt.), 654,361

NOTABLE
Spike Lee's film, "Do The Right Thing," is set in Bedford-Stuyvesant.

Rep. Major R. Owens (D)

Elected 1982; 12th term

This is the 12th and final House term for Owens, a passionate liberal who has made a unique contribution to congressional discourse as the "Rappin' Rep," penning rap lyrics to assail the conservative initiatives of the Republican majority and to mock those whom he sees as enemies of the working class. "I am one of those who is not ashamed to be called a liberal," Owens says. "In fact, I am proud of it. I am a liberal, I am progressive, all of those kinds of things that people seem to shrink away from. Our group has not disappeared."

Owens says he brings the rhythm of the streets to the Capitol with his rap poems, which are printed in the Congressional Record and on his congressional Web site; he calls them "an outlet for political frustrations." Among his offerings in the 108th Congress was "Stop the War," a scathing denunciation of the war in Iraq. An excerpt: "Stop the War / We need the cash! /...Give Medicaid families /All of Rumsfeld's stash...Welfare mothers rush to cry / Soldiers from the ranks of the poor will be the first to die."

Owens announced in 2003 that he would seek re-election just once more, but two Democrats with designs on the 11th District seat did not wait until 2006 to run. They challenged Owens in the 2004 primary and together split more than 50 percent of the vote. But Owens was renominated with 45 percent, and soon after his November re-election (a given in the overwhelmingly Democratic district), Owens' son Chris, a former local school board member, said he would run in 2006 to succeed his father.

Owens spent the first half of his House career in the majority, rising to become chairman of the Education and Labor panel's Subcommittee on Select Education and Civil Rights. In the 102nd Congress (1991-1992), he pushed through legislation reauthorizing grants for states to maximize job opportunities for the disabled by funding independent living centers, rehabilitative training centers and other programs. Another successful Owens initiative reauthorized funding for education for the deaf.

When Republicans took control of the House in 1995, they abolished Owens' panel as part of a broad reorganization of House committees. Owens shifted to become the top-ranking Democrat on the Education and Workforce panel's Workforce Protections Subcommittee, where he has fought what he sees as GOP attacks on organized labor and efforts to relax health and safety regulations on business. He has supported minimum wage increases, blocked attempts to eliminate cash payments for overtime and protested the effort to dismantle the Occupational Safety and Health Administration. A former librarian, he has fought for more library funding in education bills.

The past decade has been a tough time for Owens and those in Congress who share his liberal ideals and objectives. He fumed in 2004 at Republicans' refusal to increase the minimum wage to $7, saying that rate would "lift seven million working families and children out of poverty." Pounding on one of his favorite targets, Owens said, "Corporate CEO's have given themselves whopping, six- and seven-digit pay raises as workers paid entry-level wages continue to struggle. It is both unconscionable and un-American to have such a huge gap between the wages of hard-working men and women and their corporate bosses."

Owens is a member of the Progressive Caucus, the most liberal faction of House Democrats. A staunch proponent of gun control, he has proposed rewriting or even repealing the Second Amendment, which guar-

CAPITOL OFFICE
225-6231
major.owens@mail.house.gov
www.house.gov/owens
2309 Rayburn 20515-3211; fax 226-0112

COMMITTEES
Education & Workforce
Government Reform

HOMETOWN
Brooklyn

BORN
June 28, 1936, Memphis, Tenn.

RELIGION
Baptist

FAMILY
Wife, Maria Cuprill-Owens; five children

EDUCATION
Morehouse College, B.A. 1956 (math); Atlanta U., M.L.S. 1957

CAREER
City community development commissioner; librarian

POLITICAL HIGHLIGHTS
N.Y. Senate, 1975-83

ELECTION RESULTS

2004 GENERAL

Major R. Owens (D, WFM)	144,999	94.0%
Lorraine Stevens (INDC)	4,721	3.1%
Sol Lieberman (C)	4,478	2.9%

2004 PRIMARY

Major R. Owens (D)	14,715	45.4%
Yvette D. Clarke (D)	9,370	28.9%
Tracy L. Boyland (D)	7,121	22.0%
Gabriel A. Pearse (D)	1,179	3.6%

2002 GENERAL

Major R. Owens (D, WFM)	76,917	86.6%
Susan Cleary (R, INDC)	11,149	12.6%

PREVIOUS WINNING PERCENTAGES
2000 (87%); 1998 (90%); 1996 (92%); 1994 (89%); 1992 (94%); 1990 (95%); 1988 (93%); 1986 (91%); 1984 (91%); 1982 (91%)

antees the right of Americans to bear arms. In 2003, he became the first member of the Congressional Black Caucus to endorse the presidential candidacy of Democratic Vermont Gov. Howard Dean.

After Democrats lost the 2004 presidential election — a race in which some black voters defected to President Bush because they shared his opposition to same-sex marriage — Owens expressed alarm. "I am frightened by what is happening," he told The Los Angeles Times. "Our party is in grave danger. This Republican movement is going to expand exponentially unless we do something."

The 11th District is home to a large Caribbean immigrant population, and Owens advocates policies to aid immigrating Haitians. He has sponsored legislation to prevent the Immigration and Naturalization Service from deporting people with American-born children under 18 and to allow children under 12 without parents to become U.S. citizens.

Born in Memphis and educated in the South, Owens was a community organizer in Brooklyn's economically depressed Brownsville section in the 1960s. There he was tapped by Mayor John V. Lindsay to head New York City's anti-poverty program. He made his first bid for elected office in 1974, winning a state Senate seat that he held for eight years.

When Owens set his sights on the House in 1982 — on the retirement of Democrat Shirley Chisholm after seven terms — he faced a tough opponent in Vander Beatty, who as deputy Democratic leader in the state Senate had built a patronage empire in the Brooklyn black community. But Owens capitalized on Beatty's unsavory connections and his own reputation for honesty. He eked out a narrow primary win, and in November won the seat with ease.

His re-elections were routine until 2000, when, with his district tilting increasingly toward West Indian immigrants, he had a tough primary against city council member Una Clarke, who was born in Jamaica. Clarke contended that Owens had failed to win a federal empowerment zone for the district and did not respond to constituents who needed help with immigration procedures or other matters. Owens enlisted help from prominent Democrats, including first lady and New York Senate candidate Hillary Rodham Clinton, and won the primary by almost 9 percentage points.

The 2002 election was uneventful for Owens, but when he said in 2003 that he would leave Congress after the 2006 election, two young city council members, Yvette D. Clarke and Tracy L. Boyland, tried to usher him from office sooner. Clarke, the daughter of Owens' 2000 primary challenger, won 29 percent, and Boyland took 22 percent. Owens limped to renomination with a plurality of the vote.

KEY VOTES

2004

Yes Extend federal unemployment benefits by 13 weeks

Yes Pass $283.2 billion, six-year federal highway and mass transit bill

No Approve $146 billion multi-year extension of previously enacted middle-class tax breaks

No Amend the Constitution to prohibit same-sex marriage

No Cut corporate taxes $137 billion over 10 years

Yes Reorganize U.S. intelligence agencies as proposed by Sept. 11 commission

2003

No Cut taxes by $330 billion through fiscal 2013

+ Block Bush rule scaling back overtime pay for some white-collar federal workers

Yes Do not allow use of search warrants without first notifying subjects

Yes Allow importation of prescription drugs

No Create private school voucher program in Washington, D.C.

No Ban "partial birth" abortion except to save a woman's life

Yes Split $18.6 billion in Iraq aid into half-grant, half-loan

No Overhaul Medicare and create prescription drug benefit

CQ VOTE STUDIES

	PARTY UNITY		PRESIDENTIAL SUPPORT	
	Support	Oppose	Support	Oppose
2004	99%	1%	18%	82%
2003	98%	2%	12%	88%
2002	98%	2%	21%	79%
2001	98%	2%	17%	83%
2000	98%	2%	88%	12%

INTEREST GROUPS

	AFL-CIO	ADA	CCUS	ACU
2004	93%	100%	15%	0%
2003	100%	100%	21%	12%
2002	100%	90%	25%	4%
2001	100%	95%	19%	4%
2000	100%	90%	42%	0%

NEW YORK 11

Part of Brooklyn — Flatbush, Crown Heights, Brownsville, Park Slope

A black-majority residential district in central Brooklyn, the 11th is predominately working-class but also contains some of the borough's wealthiest neighborhoods.

Redistricting following the 2000 census did not significantly alter the district's boundaries, other than to extend it westward through Carroll Gardens into parts of Cobble Hill and Brooklyn Heights to compensate for slow population growth in the 1990s. The changes did not affect the district's reliably Democratic vote — Democrats outnumber Republicans by a 12-to-1 ratio. George W. Bush finished with only 13 percent of the vote here in the 2004 presidential election.

At the heart of the district is Flatbush, a working-class black and Hispanic neighborhood that has become home to numerous Caribbean immigrants from Jamaica, Haiti, the Dominican Republic and Trinidad and Tobago. The 11th's West Indian Carnival Parade attracts hundreds of

thousands of visitors each year, a feature that economic development officials hope to exploit to draw tourists into Brooklyn.

In the district's north is Crown Heights, made infamous in 1991 when a car driven by an orthodox rabbi's assistant struck and killed a black child, setting off four days of riots between African-Americans and Hasidic Jews.

While New York City gained population in the 1990s, the Crown Heights region lost population during that period. Brownsville, east of Crown Heights, also is heavily black. Pockets of affluence in the 11th include Park Slope, just northwest of Prospect Park, and part of Brooklyn Heights near the Brooklyn Bridge.

MAJOR INDUSTRY
Health care, retail

CITIES
New York (pt.), 654,361

NOTABLE
Ebbets Field, where the Brooklyn Dodgers played from 1913 to 1957, was demolished in 1960 and is now a housing complex; The Brooklyn Museum of Art and Brooklyn Botanic Garden are in the 11th.

Rep. Nydia M. Velázquez (D)

CAPITOL OFFICE
225-2361
www.house.gov/velazquez
2241 Rayburn 20515-3212; fax 226-0327

COMMITTEES
Financial Services
Small Business - ranking member

HOMETOWN
Brooklyn

BORN
March 28, 1953, Yabucoa, P.R.

RELIGION
Roman Catholic

FAMILY
Husband, Paul Bader

EDUCATION
U. of Puerto Rico, B.A. 1974 (political science);
New York U., M.A. 1976 (political science)

CAREER
Puerto Rican Community Affairs Department
director; professor; congressional aide

POLITICAL HIGHLIGHTS
New York City Council, 1984-85; defeated for
re-election to New York City Council, 1984

ELECTION RESULTS

2004 GENERAL

Nydia M. Velázquez (D, WFM)	107,796	86.3%
Paul A. Rodriguez (R, C)	17,166	13.7%

2004 PRIMARY

Nydia M. Velázquez (D)	unopposed

2002 GENERAL

Nydia M. Velázquez (D, WFM)	48,408	95.8%
Cesar Estevez (C)	2,119	4.2%

PREVIOUS WINNING PERCENTAGES
2000 (86%); 1998 (84%); 1996 (85%); 1994 (92%);
1992 (77%)

Elected 1992; 7th term

Velázquez was raised in the sugar cane region in southeastern Puerto Rico with her twin sister and seven other siblings. Her father cut cane and her mother helped the family make ends meet by selling food to other cane workers. Her father also ran a small business that made cinder blocks, and he had to deal with the regulations, labor standards and taxes faced by all small businesses.

His daughter is now the top-ranking Democrat on the Small Business Committee, and the first Hispanic woman to be the ranking member of a House committee. From her top slot, Velázquez (full name: NID-ee–uh veh-LASS-kez) is determined to do more for small businesses, especially those owned by minorities and women. She has pushed to increase the share of government business that goes to small firms, to help small-business owners provide health insurance and pensions for their employees, and to direct them to loans and other sources of capital.

Although Velázquez is a solid Democratic vote, she broke with her party leadership in 2003 on a bill to streamline regulations for small businesses that pool their money to buy health insurance through groups called association health plans. By pooling together, small businesses can increase their purchasing power with insurance companies. The legislation, which passed the House 262-162, was opposed by Democratic leaders because it allowed the groups to sidestep state mandates requiring insurance companies to cover certain diseases and screenings.

Velázquez endorsed the Bush administration's association health plan proposal, but she also maintained that the president's push for a series of tax cuts as his main effort to spur economic vitality has done little to help small firms. She said health care and energy costs are making it difficult for small businesses to survive. "Once again, for all of the rhetoric, the promises aren't being kept," she said.

She was instrumental in helping the committee gain an elusive Small Business Administration reauthorization bill, which was included in the catchall spending bill passed at the end of the 108th Congress.

Velázquez works well with committee Chairman Donald Manzullo of Illinois. They both believe the federal government should provide more contracts for small businesses. "For many small businesses, an iron curtain hangs around federal procurement offices that reads: 'Small businesses need not apply,' " she laments.

In 2004, she released the fifth annual report compiled by the Small Business Democratic members rating the performance of 22 federal agencies in ensuring that smaller firms receive their share of government contracts. Despite a larger pie for these agencies, and in spite of Bush administration efforts to boost federal contracting with small businesses, the Democrats gave a grade of "D" to the government's use of small businesses.

Taken together, the portions of the three boroughs that make up Velázquez's district are home to the second-highest percentage of blue-collar workers of any congressional district in New York, so she pays particular attention to government and private programs aimed at helping people improve their lives through better access to education, health care, housing and jobs.

Velázquez also sits on the Financial Services Committee, where she is the only New York City Democrat on its Housing and Community Opportunity Subcommittee. She won the panel's endorsement to require a plan for counseling families who receive housing assistance on how to avoid fore-closures — many of which are a result of unscrupulous lenders charging high interest rates, she said.

The first woman of Puerto Rican descent to be elected to Congress, Velázquez represents more than 100,000 Puerto Rican constituents and so she also focuses on matters affecting the island commonwealth. She joined other Puerto Rican lawmakers in demanding that the Navy stop using the island of Vieques, just off Puerto Rico, for bombing practice and was once arrested during a protest of the shelling.

She also has a keen interest in immigration issues. From 1986 until her election to the House, she worked as a liaison between the Puerto Rican government and Latino communities in the United States. Most of the casework in her district office relates to immigration matters, she says.

Although her father had only a third-grade education, Velázquez says he sparked her interest in politics. She told The New York Times that he delivered passionate speeches from the back of a flatbed truck and found-ed a political party in their hometown of Yabucoa. "I always wanted to be like my father," she told The Times.

After graduating from the University of Puerto Rico with a degree in polit-ical science — the first in her family to receive a college diploma — Velázquez came to New York City for graduate school. She then taught Puerto Rican studies at Hunter College, worked as a special assistant to Democratic Rep. Edolphus Towns and served briefly on the New York City Council before becoming liaison between the Puerto Rican government and Latino communities in the United States in 1986.

Her local name recognition increased significantly before her 1992 House race, when she ran a Hispanic voter registration effort financed by the Puerto Rican government. Critics said she targeted the Brooklyn sec-tions that later became part of a redrawn, Hispanic-majority district.

Her biggest obstacle in the Democratic primary was nine-term incum-bent Stephen J. Solarz, whose district had been dismantled in the redis-tricting. Solarz hired Hispanic advisers and learned a few Spanish phras-es, but he was an unknown to many in the new district and branded a wealthy carpetbagger. Velázquez defeated him by 5 percentage points in the primary, then captured 77 percent of the vote in November.

Velázquez has won six more times with at least 84 percent of the vote, even though the Hispanic population in the 12th District was cut from a majority to a strong plurality during 1997 court-ordered redistricting. In 2004, she again won easily, collecting 86 percent.

KEY VOTES

2004
Yes   Extend federal unemployment benefits by 13 weeks
Yes   Pass $283.2 billion, six-year federal highway and mass transit bill
Yes   Approve $146 billion multi-year extension of previously enacted middle-class tax breaks
No   Amend the Constitution to prohibit same-sex marriage
No   Cut corporate taxes $137 billion over 10 years
Yes   Reorganize U.S. intelligence agencies as proposed by Sept. 11 commission

2003
No   Cut taxes by $330 billion through fiscal 2013
Yes   Block Bush rule scaling back overtime pay for some white-collar federal workers
Yes   Do not allow use of search warrants without first notifying subjects
Yes   Allow importation of prescription drugs
No   Create private school voucher program in Washington, D.C.
No   Ban "partial birth" abortion except to save a woman's life
Yes   Split $18.6 billion in Iraq aid into half-grant, half-loan
No   Overhaul Medicare and create prescription drug benefit

CQ VOTE STUDIES

	PARTY UNITY		PRESIDENTIAL SUPPORT	
	Support	Oppose	Support	Oppose
2004	96%	4%	15%	85%
2003	97%	3%	22%	78%
2002	99%	1%	24%	76%
2001	96%	4%	26%	74%
2000	97%	3%	85%	15%

INTEREST GROUPS

	AFL-CIO	ADA	CCUS	ACU
2004	87%	100%	32%	8%
2003	100%	90%	25%	14%
2002	89%	95%	35%	0%
2001	92%	90%	35%	0%
2000	100%	90%	40%	4%

NEW YORK 12

Lower East Side of Manhattan; parts of Brooklyn and Queens

The 12th, which takes in parts of Manhattan, Brooklyn and Queens, was created in 1992 to form a Hispanic-majority district under the Voting Rights Act. Once known as the Bullwinkle District because of its resemblance to the cartoon moose, a court-ordered redistricting in 1997 resulted in a more compact shape and a decreased Hispanic population. Marginal changes following the 2000 census retained its basic contours and pegged its Hispanic population at 49 percent.

Even with a significant immigrant population that is not eligible to vote and low turnout among Hispanic voters, the 12th elected and continues to send a Puerto Rican representative to Congress. The district's numerous working-class and minority residents make it a Democratic bastion.

Two-thirds of the 12th's registered voters live in Brooklyn. In its southwestern corner, the district begins in Sunset Park, which has a large Hispanic population, then segues north along the East River and jumps across the Brooklyn and Manhattan bridges into Manhattan to take in Chinatown, part of Little Italy and the Lower East Side. Nearly one in five registered voters lives in Manhattan.

Back in northern Brooklyn (the 12th also includes the Williamsburg Bridge), it takes in Greenpoint, which has a large Polish population, and moves east along the Brooklyn-Queens border to the heavily Hispanic neighborhoods of East Williamsburg, Bushwick and Cypress Hills. In Queens, the 12th takes in parts of the Sunnyside and Woodside neighborhoods, which are experiencing rapid Hispanic growth.

MAJOR INDUSTRY
Health care, manufacturing, service

CITIES
New York (pt.), 654,360

NOTABLE
Brooklyn's Green-Wood Cemetery, where the more than 560,000 interred include Leonard Bernstein, Horace Greeley and notorious 19th century New York politician William M. "Boss" Tweed; Brooklyn Navy Yard; The Brooklyn Heights Promenade, built over the Brooklyn-Queens Expressway, looks out at the lower Manhattan skyline.

Rep. Vito J. Fossella (R)

Elected 1997; 4th full term

CAPITOL OFFICE
225-3371
vito.fossella@mail.house.gov
www.house.gov/fossella
1239 Longworth 20515-3213; fax 226-1272

COMMITTEES
Energy & Commerce
Financial Services

HOMETOWN
Staten Island

BORN
March 9, 1965, South Beach, N.Y.

RELIGION
Roman Catholic

FAMILY
Wife, Mary Pat Fossella; three children

EDUCATION
U. of Pennsylvania, B.S. 1987; Fordham U.,
J.D. 1993

CAREER
Management consultant; lawyer

POLITICAL HIGHLIGHTS
New York City Council, 1994-97

ELECTION RESULTS

2004 GENERAL

Vito J. Fossella (R, C)	112,934	59.0%
Frank J. Barbaro (D, INDC, WFM)	78,500	41.0%

2004 PRIMARY

Vito J. Fossella (R)	unopposed

2002 GENERAL

Vito J. Fossella (R, C, RTL)	72,204	69.6%
Arne M. Mattsson (D, L, WFM)	29,366	28.3%
Anita Lerman (INDC)	1,427	1.4%

PREVIOUS WINNING PERCENTAGES
2000 (65%); 1998 (65%); 1997 Special Election (61%)

As the only Republican in Congress representing a borough of New York City, Fossella walks a fine line. More pragmatic than many of his conservative Republican colleagues, he remains firmly fixed on helping his Staten Island constituents. The 13th District, which also takes in part of Brooklyn, has the largest percentage of non-Hispanic white residents of any of the New York City-area districts.

Yet Fossella (full name: VEE-toe Fuh-SELL-ah) is more conservative than other Northeastern Republicans, who tend to be labor-friendly, pro-abortion rights moderates. In the 108th Congress, he voted with his party 92 percent of the time, backing all of President Bush's tax cuts and a GOP effort to amend the Constitution to ban same-sex marriage. He opposes abortion rights and supports oil drilling in Alaska's Arctic National Wildlife Refuge.

He did break with his party in 2004 on a vote to extend unemployment benefits for an additional 13 weeks as one of only 39 Republicans to vote for the extension. But the leadership can count on Fossella to back them up when needed. Fossella was one of 10 vote switchers who killed an amendment to the 2004 overhaul of the nation's intelligence agencies that would have broadened the category of illegal immigrants to be deported immediately and without review.

He has seats on two major committees, Financial Services and Energy and Commerce. He received special permission from Speaker J. Dennis Hastert to get the two posts since Energy and Commerce is normally an "exclusive" committee.

Fossella seems to be a quintessential New Yorker — glib, telegenic and brash. He was prominently featured at the 2004 Republican convention in New York. And he was public in urging Colin Powell, a New York City native and Bush's secretary of state during his first term, to run for the Senate against Democrat Hillary Rodham Clinton, only days after Powell left his post. "I am a simple guy," says Fossella, whom the New York Daily News has described as having a "self-deprecating, smart-aleck" style. "My job every day is defined by how I can best serve the people of Brooklyn and Staten Island."

One of Fossella's priorities since the Sept. 11, 2001, terrorist attacks has been to establish a national memorial at the Fresh Kills landfill on Staten Island, a closed facility that was temporarily reopened as the place for sorting debris from the World Trade Center, including the incinerated remains of victims. Those remains are to be interred at the Trade Center memorial, but Fossella still is convinced that the Fresh Kills site should be recognized.

Fossella lost several friends and high school classmates on Sept. 11, as well as 30 fellow parishioners from St. Clare's Roman Catholic Church on Staten Island. It would be hard to find a family in Fossella's district that was not personally touched by the attacks.

From his seat on Financial Services, Fossella is building a portfolio on issues that have an impact on Wall Street, where many of his constituents work. And on matters affecting the financial center, he is willing to defy his party leadership. For example, he was one of six Republicans on Financial Services who voted against legislation — which passed the House with a majority of GOP votes — to stop an effort to require companies to account for stock options as an expense. He said he believes that expensing options is the right thing to do, philosophically, for the financial markets.

In 2001, Fossella enjoyed a first taste of success in helping Wall Street when the House passed his bill slashing federal fees on stock trades, a move he said would help spur market activity. The bill also increased salaries for employees of the Securities and Exchange Commission, when the agency was in the middle of a political storm over corporate ethics.

Fossella also has taken a particular interest in some of the policies of the United Nations. He sponsored a bill in 2003 to trim United States funding for the U.N. if a country listed by the State Department as a sponsor of state terrorism wins leadership of a U.N. body. He introduced the measure as a way to protest the rotation of Iraq into the leadership of the U.N.'s Conference on Disarmament and Libya's move to head the Human Rights Commission. "We have to send a signal to the U.N. that there has to be accountability," Fossella said. "You have to ask whether they are in Manhattan or on Mars."

When he arrived on Capitol Hill in late 1997 after a special-election victory, Fossella won assignment to the Transportation and Infrastructure Committee. He secured $32 million for new ferries between Staten Island and Manhattan, the first new vessels in many years.

Fossella hails from a well-known Italian-American political family on Staten Island, and he is close to another one, the Molinaris. Fossella's father, Vito Sr., served in Mayor Ed Koch's administration; an uncle, Frank Fossella, was a New York City Council member. From 1935 until his death in 1944, Fossella's great-grandfather James O'Leary was a Democratic House member from New York. Though he comes from a long line of Democrats, Fossella's conservatism prompted him to switch parties in 1990.

When Susan Molinari announced in 1997 that she was resigning from the House for a career in television, her father, Guy, a former House member himself and the Staten Island GOP borough president, immediately tapped Fossella as the heir apparent, referring to him as "my son."

Fossella already had a respectable political résumé. A Fordham University-trained lawyer and graduate of the University of Pennsylvania, he was on the city council — in the same seat once held by his uncle. As part of an overmatched GOP minority, Fossella had won notice in the conservative and insular borough of Staten Island by securing the island's first new public schools.

During the 1997 special-election campaign for the House seat, which coincided with the New York mayoral race, Fossella marched alongside GOP Mayor Rudolph W. Giuliani's re-election bandwagon. Giuliani's landslide margins within the district helped propel Fossella to an easy victory. He won his next three elections with over 60 percent of the vote. In 2004, he faced a lively contest with New York Democratic assemblyman Frank J. Barbaro as an opponent. Fossella won by 18 percentage points.

KEY VOTES

2004
Yes Extend federal unemployment benefits by 13 weeks
Yes Pass $283.2 billion, six-year federal highway and mass transit bill
Yes Approve $146 billion multi-year extension of previously enacted middle-class tax breaks
Yes Amend the Constitution to prohibit same-sex marriage
Yes Cut corporate taxes $137 billion over 10 years
Yes Reorganize U.S. intelligence agencies as proposed by Sept. 11 commission

2003
Yes Cut taxes by $330 billion through fiscal 2013
? Block Bush rule scaling back overtime pay for some white-collar federal workers
No Do not allow use of search warrants without first notifying subjects
No Allow importation of prescription drugs
Yes Create private school voucher program in Washington, D.C.
Yes Ban "partial birth" abortion except to save a woman's life
No Split $18.6 billion in Iraq aid into half-grant, half-loan
Yes Overhaul Medicare and create prescription drug benefit

CQ VOTE STUDIES

	PARTY UNITY		PRESIDENTIAL SUPPORT	
	Support	Oppose	Support	Oppose
2004	88%	12%	84%	16%
2003	95%	5%	98%	2%
2002	94%	6%	87%	13%
2001	92%	8%	93%	7%
2000	91%	9%	26%	74%

INTEREST GROUPS

	AFL-CIO	ADA	CCUS	ACU
2004	43%	20%	90%	78%
2003	20%	15%	96%	82%
2002	11%	0%	95%	92%
2001	9%	0%	100%	88%
2000	0%	0%	80%	80%

NEW YORK 13
Staten Island; part of southwest Brooklyn

Staten Island's large retired population and white, upper-middle-class suburban residents make the 13th more amenable to Republicans than any other New York City district. The 13th's predominately Catholic and Italian-American conservatives that live on both sides of the Verrazano Narrows Bridge, which connects Staten Island and Brooklyn, have sent Republicans to the House since 1982. Al Gore carried Staten Island in the 2000 presidential election, but Republican Michael R. Bloomberg took 77 percent in his 2001 mayoral victory, and George W. Bush took 56 percent of the borough's vote in 2004. Overall, the 13th gave Bush 55 percent of the vote, making it the only New York City district the president carried.

Staten Island was so disenchanted with New York City's Democratic leadership that in 1993 residents overwhelmingly approved a referendum to secede from the city, though the state legislature blocked its enactment. Chief among Staten Island's complaints had been the presence of the Fresh Kills landfill, which the city sanitation department closed in March 2001 but was temporarily reopened following the Sept.

11, 2001, terrorist attacks to receive and process most of the debris.

The least diverse of the five boroughs, Staten Island is the only one in which whites make up a majority of the residents (71 percent). The Hispanic and black populations are concentrated mostly in the borough's northeastern neighborhoods. There is an Asian presence in some of the borough's north-central neighborhoods.

Almost three-fourths of residents live in Staten Island. The Brooklyn portion extends from the Verrazano into Bay Ridge, Dyker Heights and part of Bensonhurst, before buttonhooking south of Cropsey Avenue and moving east to Ocean Parkway, taking in the Gravesend neighborhood.

MAJOR INDUSTRY
Health care, retail, communications

MILITARY BASES
Fort Hamilton (Army), 561 military, 351 civilian (2004)

CITIES
New York (pt.), 654,631

NOTABLE
Bay Ridge was the setting for the 1977 disco movie "Saturday Night Fever."

Rep. Carolyn B. Maloney (D)

Elected 1992; 7th term

CAPITOL OFFICE
225-7944
rep.carolyn.maloney@mail.house.gov
www.house.gov/maloney
2331 Rayburn 20515-3214; fax 225-4709

COMMITTEES
Financial Services
Government Reform
Joint Economic

HOMETOWN
Manhattan

BORN
Feb. 19, 1948, Greensboro, N.C.

RELIGION
Presbyterian

FAMILY
Husband, Clifton H.W. Maloney; two children

EDUCATION
Greensboro College, A.B. 1968

CAREER
State legislative aide; teacher

POLITICAL HIGHLIGHTS
New York City Council, 1982-93

ELECTION RESULTS

2004 GENERAL

Carolyn Maloney (D, INDC, WFM)	186,688	81.1%
Anton Srdanovic (R, C)	43,623	18.9%

2004 PRIMARY

Carolyn Maloney (D)	unopposed

2002 GENERAL

Carolyn Maloney (D, INDC, L, WFM)	95,931	75.3%
Anton Srdanovic (R, C)	31,548	24.8%

PREVIOUS WINNING PERCENTAGES
2000 (74%); 1998 (77%); 1996 (72%); 1994 (64%);
1992 (50%)

In the 108th Congress, Maloney reached beyond her usual roles as liberal gadfly and persistent Bush administration critic, helping win enactment of a sweeping bill to reorganize U.S. intelligence operations. The measure followed many of the recommendations of the independent commission that reviewed intelligence failures surrounding the Sept. 11, 2001, terrorist attacks, and included creation of a strong national intelligence director with authority over the budgets of all U.S. spy agencies.

Maloney joined Connecticut Republican Christopher Shays, her colleague on the Government Reform Committee, to sponsor a bipartisan intelligence overhaul bill that mirrored Senate-passed legislation and drew vigorous opposition from House GOP leaders. Their bill went nowhere at first in the House, and the Rules Committee blocked them from offering it on the floor as an amendment. But the support that Maloney and Shays helped develop gave impetus to House-Senate conferees, whose final bill resembled the approach taken by the Senate and the Shays-Maloney bill.

She is tireless in her efforts in behalf of her New York City constituents and was particularly critical of the Bush administration after the Sept. 11 attacks on the World Trade Center. Maloney, who represents Queens and a good portion of the east side of Manhattan, was the first to accuse President Bush of reneging on his promise of $20 billion in federal funds to help rebuild New York City. She also teamed up with New York Democratic Sen. Hillary Rodham Clinton to complain about the Federal Emergency Management Agency's poor response to victims of the attacks.

She relishes taking on White House officials in behalf of Democratic Party principles. In early 2004, she chided the president's chief economist, N. Gregory Mankiw, for the economy's weak job growth figures, which at the time fell far short of the administration's forecast. And she rebuked Mankiw for saying that the shifting of U.S. jobs overseas, while painful in the short term, ultimately will help the economy.

Maloney has long been an advocate for abortion rights and is devoted to the causes of women worldwide. She demonstrated the plight of Afghan women under the Taliban by coming to the House floor in a head-to-toe blue burqa. Her point partly backfired when Islamic groups condemned her for being insensitive to the women who voluntarily wear those garments for religious reasons.

She condemned Bush over his decision to cut U.S. contributions to the U.N. Population Fund, which helps to deliver birth control information and services to women in Third World nations, saying that the funding cut "sends a message that when push comes to shove, the administration's right-wing base comes first."

Maloney introduces scores of bills, many representing priorities for the Caucus for Women's Issues, which she used to co-chair. In each of the past five Congresses, Maloney introduced an equal rights constitutional amendment, though without much success. Her high mark for cosponsors was 211 in the 107th Congress, well short of the two-thirds needed.

Her legislation to permit breast-feeding on federal property, which she introduced after some nursing women were asked to leave the Capitol, federal museums and parks, was signed into law in 1999. A few other bills sponsored by Maloney have become law, including one to reduce fees charged by the Securities and Exchange Commission. Others passed the House, such as one to allow wiretaps to combat child pornography and sexual exploitation. In the 108th Congress, Maloney's resolution honoring former President Clinton on his birthday was adopted by the House.

On the Government Reform Committee, she puts her New York City Council expertise on procurement and government contracting policies to use. She was the city government's top watchdog against government waste, chairing the Committee on Contracts.

In the 105th Congress (1997-1998), Democratic leaders gave Maloney responsibility for making the case that the GOP was playing politics with the 2000 census. As the top-ranking Democrat on the Census Subcommittee, she waged battle with Republicans on whether the Census Bureau should be permitted to use statistical sampling to augment the traditional head count. Sampling is a scientific estimate of population in areas where counting methods do not yield a complete tally.

Calling it "the civil rights issue of the 1990s," Maloney accused the GOP of blocking sampling because it might boost the count of minorities and give Democrats an edge in redistricting. She lost her battle on sampling in court and in Congress, but won money for extra census takers to go door-to-door to make the head count as complete as possible.

Maloney also has a seat on the Financial Services Committee, where she focuses on holding down credit card interest rates, protecting the elderly from financial fraud and giving senior citizens in public housing the right to own household pets. In the 109th, she is the top-ranking Democrat on the Domestic and International Monetary Policy, Trade and Technology Subcommittee.

Maloney hails from Greensboro, N.C. She came to New York City for a visit in her early 20s and stayed, eventually teaching adult education in East Harlem and joining the city's vast educational bureaucracy. Maloney says she realized that government had a larger impact than any teacher on the education of the city's youth, and she moved to Albany to work for the state legislature. Five years later, she was elected to the New York City Council, where she served about 10 years.

When Maloney ran against seven-term GOP Rep. Bill Green in 1992, media hype about the "Year of the Woman" lent momentum to her underdog challenge. She also benefited from redistricting, which forced Green to campaign on some unfamiliar turf. She beat him narrowly, 50 percent to 48 percent.

Maloney has not had a primary opponent since 1994, and her general-election victories since 1992 have been runaways. In 2004, she won with 81 percent of the vote.

KEY VOTES

2004

Yes	Extend federal unemployment benefits by 13 weeks
Yes	Pass $283.2 billion, six-year federal highway and mass transit bill
+	Approve $146 billion multi-year extension of previously enacted middle-class tax breaks
No	Amend the Constitution to prohibit same-sex marriage
No	Cut corporate taxes $137 billion over 10 years
Yes	Reorganize U.S. intelligence agencies as proposed by Sept. 11 commission

2003

No	Cut taxes by $330 billion through fiscal 2013
Yes	Block Bush rule scaling back overtime pay for some white-collar federal workers
Yes	Do not allow use of search warrants without first notifying subjects
Yes	Allow importation of prescription drugs
No	Create private school voucher program in Washington, D.C.
No	Ban "partial birth" abortion except to save a woman's life
Yes	Split $18.6 billion in Iraq aid into half-grant, half-loan
No	Overhaul Medicare and create prescription drug benefit

CQ VOTE STUDIES

	PARTY UNITY		PRESIDENTIAL SUPPORT	
	Support	Oppose	Support	Oppose
2004	97%	3%	28%	72%
2003	96%	4%	25%	75%
2002	93%	7%	34%	66%
2001	90%	10%	33%	67%
2000	92%	8%	82%	18%

INTEREST GROUPS

	AFL-CIO	ADA	CCUS	ACU
2004	100%	100%	45%	4%
2003	80%	95%	33%	16%
2002	89%	100%	53%	4%
2001	92%	95%	35%	0%
2000	90%	90%	45%	12%

NEW YORK 14
East Side of Manhattan; western Queens

Wealthy Republicans engineered politics on Manhattan's East Side when this "Silk Stocking District" was created. But starting in the 1960s, the old-money elite was gradually supplanted by "limousine liberals," highly educated young professionals devoted to the arts. The 14th has the nation's highest percentage of residents with at least a bachelor's degree (57 percent) and the highest percentage who walk to work.

Republicans can still compete locally, and the 14th supported GOP Mayor Rudolph Giuliani in 1997. But the district sent a Democrat to Congress in 1992, and its residents have given overwhelming support to Democratic presidential candidates in recent years.

Taking in all of Central Park in the district's northwest corner, the 14th's western edge then roughly follows Broadway south toward Union Square before narrowing to reach the Lower East Side. Landmarks include Carnegie Hall, Rockefeller Center, Grand Central Terminal, the United Nations, the Chrysler Building, Trump Tower and Fifth Avenue's Museum Mile, which includes the Metropolitan Museum of Art.

But the tony neighborhoods of Manhattan's East Side do not tell the whole story of a district that crosses Roosevelt Island to pick up ethnic working-class sections of Queens, such as Astoria, and some poorer sections. Long Island City, once an industrial powerhouse, experienced decline but is seeing some resurgence as a haven for artists. It is also home to Queens West — a massive new commercial and residential development along the riverfront.

Although revised in redistricting following the 2000 census, the Queens portion of the 14th still includes most of the borough's northwestern edge. In the 1980s and 1990s, the region attracted immigrants from abroad, particularly Greeks, Asians and Hispanics. Now it draws Manhattanites in search of more-affordable housing.

MAJOR INDUSTRY
Finance, publishing, communications, advertising, health care, tourism

CITIES
New York (pt.), 654,361

NOTABLE
The American Museum of the Moving Image is in Astoria; Republican John V. Lindsay and Democrat Edward I. Koch held the East Side congressional seat at the time each was elected mayor of New York.

Rep. Charles B. Rangel (D)

Elected 1970; 18th term

CAPITOL OFFICE
225-4365
www.house.gov/rangel
2354 Rayburn 20515-3215; fax 225-0816

COMMITTEES
Ways & Means - ranking member
Joint Taxation - ranking member

HOMETOWN
Manhattan

BORN
June 11, 1930, Manhattan, N.Y.

RELIGION
Roman Catholic

FAMILY
Wife, Alma Rangel; two children

EDUCATION
New York U., B.S. 1957; St. John's U., LL.B. 1960

MILITARY SERVICE
Army, 1948-52

CAREER
Lawyer

POLITICAL HIGHLIGHTS
Assistant U.S. attorney, 1961-62; N.Y. Assembly, 1967-71; sought Democratic nomination for N.Y. City Council president, 1969

ELECTION RESULTS

2004 GENERAL

Charles B. Rangel (D, WFM)	161,351	91.1%
Kenneth P. Jefferson Jr. (R)	12,355	7.0%
Jessie Fields (INDC)	3,345	1.9%

2004 PRIMARY

Charles B. Rangel (D)	19,087	76.0%
Ruben Dario Vargas (D)	3,254	13.0%
Geoffrey G. Johnson (D)	2,778	11.1%

2002 GENERAL

Charles B. Rangel (D, WFM)	84,367	88.5%
Jessie Fields (R, INDC)	11,008	11.5%

PREVIOUS WINNING PERCENTAGES
2000 (92%); 1998 (93%); 1996 (91%); 1994 (97%); 1992 (95%); 1990 (97%); 1988 (97%); 1986 (96%); 1984 (97%); 1982 (97%); 1980 (96%); 1978 (96%); 1976 (97%); 1974 (97%); 1972 (96%); 1970 (87%)

With Republicans secure in their majority, Rangel has had to set aside his dream of becoming chairman of the House Ways and Means Committee anytime soon. The clever, quip-loving dean of the powerful New York delegation has adjusted by making the opposition's life as miserable as he can from his perch as the senior Democrat on the panel.

He is an unapologetic liberal who takes up the cause of people he says are left behind by Republican policies. Representing a poor district in Harlem, he weighs in with gusto on everything from the distribution of tax cut benefits to the president's plan to introduce private accounts into Social Security.

First elected in 1970, he is tied with C.W. "Bill" Young of Florida for fourth-longest-serving member of the House, and his seniority inspires a certain fearlessness. He relishes publicly embarrassing Republicans, and takes glee in torpedoing their bills behind the scenes when he is able to. A natural wit, quick with a rejoinder or a pun, the raspy-voiced Rangel is one of a handful of lawmakers who could survive question time in the British House of Commons. His sly delivery and bombastic punch lines once inspired an aide to describe him as "a black Jackie Gleason."

He regularly appears on the conservative Fox television news network, where he serves as the voice of opposition.

After the U.S. invasion of Iraq in 2003, Rangel spoke out against it. A Korean War veteran, he proposed legislation to reinstate the military draft, arguing that a disproportionate number of enlisted soldiers are poor or minorities "while the most privileged Americans are underrepresented or absent." Just before the 2004 elections, GOP leaders called his bluff by bringing the politically unpopular bill to the floor. Rangel voted against it. He organized an Internet petition to impeach Defense Secretary Donald H. Rumsfeld.

His relationship with his main nemesis among Republicans, Ways and Means Chairman Bill Thomas of California, is rocky, with each accusing the other of intransigence. In 2003, it was Rangel who came up with the idea of gathering committee Democrats in the library of the Ways and Means hearing room to protest being given little time to read a complicated bill drafted by Republicans. Thomas took the heavy-handed step of calling in the Capitol Police to evict Rangel and his group, and the tactic was widely condemned as over the top. Thomas had to apologize to the Democrats, breaking into tears as he did so, in a speech on the House floor.

Later that year, Rangel joined forces with Republican Philip M. Crane of Illinois to undermine Thomas' bill to cut taxes for multinational corporations. Crane, who was passed over by GOP leaders for the Ways and Means chairmanship in favor of Thomas in 2001, agreed to co-write with Rangel a rival bill that would give domestic manufacturers a break instead. In the end, Thomas was forced to swallow Rangel's bill.

Ways and Means is a powerful committee in charge of tax writing, trade, Medicare, Social Security and welfare policy. Like Democrats who served on the committee before him, Rangel is pro-business and quick to support many targeted tax cuts. He has long tried to convince the GOP majority that federal tax-exempt bonds for school construction, a potential boon for Wall Street, are a good idea. Corporate lobbyists have come to know Rangel more frequently as a deal-cutting pragmatist, with lawyerly powers of persuasion, than as a liberal ideologue.

Rangel helped engineer the 2002 economic stimulus bill, which paired narrow GOP tax breaks for business with a Democratic proposal extending unemployment benefits for laid-off workers. And he bucked labor unions to endorse permanent normalized trade relations with China, giving the business lobby one of its top priorities in 2000. Rangel also has a longstanding friendly relationship with Republican Charles E. Grassley of Iowa, the Senate Finance Committee chairman.

He's had the most success legislatively with efforts to spur economic development in downtrodden neighborhoods. Rangel was a principal author of the 1993 "empowerment zones" law providing tax credits to businesses that move into blighted areas and of the 1986 tax credit for developers who build low-income housing.

Rangel had worked doggedly since 1995 in Democratic efforts to win back the majority, going on the road to help raise money and organize get-out-the-vote campaigns. But he has lost some of his enthusiasm as the GOP has become entrenched over the past decade. His fundraising slowed to about $2 million in 2004 — a good sum but just a fraction of what he collected for the 2000 campaign.

A founder of the Congressional Black Caucus, Rangel has a reliably liberal record on social policy. He champions gun control, affirmative action and abortion rights, and he was a passionate critic of the 1996 law ending welfare's status as an entitlement. He has backed a commission to promote reparations for descendants of former slaves.

Raised by his seamstress mother and her family in Harlem, Rangel dropped out of high school at 16, later joined the Army and won a Purple Heart and Bronze Star in the Korean War after surviving firefights that claimed much of his unit. Once back home, he finished high school and went to college and law school on the G.I. Bill. He says he was inspired to get into politics after he successfully appealed to Tammany Hall bosses to allow his grandfather to keep his job operating elevators at city hall.

Rangel served four years in the state Assembly, then ran for the U.S. House in 1970. He ousted Rep. Adam Clayton Powell Jr. in the Democratic primary, ending one of the most flamboyant congressional careers of modern times. Rangel has had only one significant challenger since; Powell's son and namesake opposed him in the 1994 primary. By 2004, Rangel was being re-elected with over 90 percent of the vote.

Rangel's time in Congress has not been without setbacks. He was among the last members cleared of wrongdoing in the House bank scandal in the early 1990s, and in 1999 he was entangled in a financial scandal at Harlem's historic Apollo Theater. The state of New York dropped a lawsuit against Rangel and others on the theater board, saying they acted in good faith.

KEY VOTES

2004
Yes Extend federal unemployment benefits by 13 weeks
Yes Pass $283.2 billion, six-year federal highway and mass transit bill
Yes Approve $146 billion multi-year extension of previously enacted middle-class tax breaks
? Amend the Constitution to prohibit same-sex marriage
No Cut corporate taxes $137 billion over 10 years
Yes Reorganize U.S. intelligence agencies as proposed by Sept. 11 commission

2003
No Cut taxes by $330 billion through fiscal 2013
Yes Block Bush rule scaling back overtime pay for some white-collar federal workers
Yes Do not allow use of search warrants without first notifying subjects
Yes Allow importation of prescription drugs
? Create private school voucher program in Washington, D.C.
No Ban "partial birth" abortion except to save a woman's life
Yes Split $18.6 billion in Iraq aid into half-grant, half-loan
No Overhaul Medicare and create prescription drug benefit

CQ VOTE STUDIES

	PARTY UNITY		PRESIDENTIAL SUPPORT	
	Support	Oppose	Support	Oppose
2004	98%	2%	19%	81%
2003	96%	4%	21%	79%
2002	98%	2%	24%	76%
2001	91%	9%	23%	77%
2000	93%	7%	97%	3%

INTEREST GROUPS

	AFL-CIO	ADA	CCUS	ACU
2004	93%	95%	30%	0%
2003	83%	85%	25%	19%
2002	100%	95%	32%	0%
2001	100%	90%	25%	4%
2000	90%	90%	41%	4%

NEW YORK 15

Northern Manhattan — Harlem, Washington Heights

Harlem was a nexus of black political and cultural power during its heyday in the 1920s and 1930s. But by the time the district was created in 1944, the Great Depression, an influx of poor migrants and race riots had contributed to severe decline. Two highly popular black Democrats — Adam Clayton Powell Jr. and Rep. Rangel — have controlled the 15th since its creation; Powell served 12 terms and part of a 13th; Rangel has been elected 18 times. A solidly Democratic district, John Kerry received 89.7 percent of the vote here in the 2004 presidential election, making the 15th his best district in the country.

The past 20 years have brought substantial change to the 15th, with Puerto Rican and Dominican immigration supplanting the district's African-American majority. Hispanics now far outnumber non-Hispanic blacks, but low voter participation among Hispanics means the smaller black population (31 percent of residents) continues to dominate the district's politics.

Harlem's 1996 designation as a federal empowerment zone has brought the beginning of an economic resurgence. Refurbished brownstones, new restaurants, national retail chains and prominent corporations are moving into the area. In early 2001, Harlem also received a public relations boon when Bill Clinton decided to lease office space in a building on 125th Street, the area's main thoroughfare.

The district's hospitals and colleges, along with many small businesses, provide much of the employment. But for less-educated residents, many of the jobs are out of reach. The district's doctors, lawyers and other professionals reside in Harlem's affluent black neighborhoods like Strivers Row, the white, affluent Upper West Side or around Columbia University in Morningside Heights.

MAJOR INDUSTRY
Health care, higher education, retail

CITIES
New York (pt.), 654,361

NOTABLE
Legendary venues such as the Cotton Club and the Apollo Theater drew jazz greats and comedians; The district includes Randalls, Wards and Rikers islands.

Rep. José E. Serrano (D)

Elected March 1990; 8th full term

CAPITOL OFFICE
225-4361
jserrano@mail.house.gov
www.house.gov/serrano
2227 Rayburn 20515-3216; fax 225-6001

COMMITTEES
Appropriations

HOMETOWN
Bronx

BORN
Oct. 24, 1943, Mayaguez, P.R.

RELIGION
Roman Catholic

FAMILY
Wife, Mary Staucet; five children

EDUCATION
Dodge Vocational H.S., graduated 1961; Lehman College, attended 1979-80

MILITARY SERVICE
Army Medical Corps, 1964-66

CAREER
School district administrator; banker

POLITICAL HIGHLIGHTS
N.Y. Assembly, 1975-90; sought Democratic nomination for Bronx borough president, 1985

ELECTION RESULTS

2004 GENERAL

José E. Serrano (D, WFM)	111,638	95.2%
Ali Mohamed (R, C)	5,610	4.8%

2004 PRIMARY

José E. Serrano (D)	unopposed

2002 GENERAL

José E. Serrano (D, WFM)	50,716	92.1%
Frank Dellavalle (R, C)	4,366	7.9%

PREVIOUS WINNING PERCENTAGES
2000 (96%); 1998 (95%); 1996 (96%); 1994 (96%); 1992 (91%); 1990 (93%); 1990 Special Election (92%)

An eight-term House member, Serrano is a consummate Democratic Party insider and unabashed liberal who makes no bones about the direction he would choose if he ran the show.

"Being low-carb Republicans isn't going to win us elections," Serrano told The New York Sun after the 2004 election left the GOP in control of both the White House and Congress. "We need to do what we do best — be real Democrats . . . the party of FDR and the New Deal, the Great Society, Social Security and environmental protection."

Serrano works to influence his party, care for his Bronx district and advance the cause of Hispanic-Americans from his post on the Appropriations Committee and as a vice chairman of the Democratic Steering and Policy Committee, which makes committee assignments and advises the leadership on policy matters.

Serrano (full name: ho-ZAY sa-RAH-no, with a rolled 'R') grew up in the Millbrook Houses, a public housing project in the Bronx. As the representative of one of the poorest and most Democratic districts in the nation, Serrano says his principal legislative priority "is ensuring that the South Bronx gets its fair share for education, jobs, housing and economic development."

He had long been the top-ranking Democrat on the subcommittee that directs spending for the Commerce, Justice and State departments and several federal agencies. But in the 109th Congress, he was bumped as the senior Democrat when GOP leaders reduced the number of subcommittees from 13 to 10. He also is a member of the Homeland Security Subcommittee, of particular concern to terrorism-conscious New York City.

Serrano's voting record is solidly Democratic. In the 108th Congress, he had a party unity score of 97 percent. He wins high marks from the liberal Americans for Democratic Action while often receiving perfect 0s from the American Conservative Union.

The Puerto Rican-born Serrano weighs in on issues of importance to the island commonwealth, whose delegate to Congress has no vote on the House floor. Close to 200,000 of Serrano's 16th District constituents are of Puerto Rican descent. Many support his high-profile battle to ease the Cuban trade embargo and travel restrictions. He believes citizens of the island should be allowed to decide whether Puerto Rico should be granted statehood or independence.

On Appropriations, Serrano was able to obtain funding for a scholarship program aimed at training students in the Bronx for careers in foreign affairs. He has also obtained federal money to clean up the Bronx River, plant trees in the borough and reduce air pollution from trucks, believed to be a contributing factor in the high incidence of asthma among his constituents. Serrano has helped San Juan win federal funds for its light-rail system, while failing to get funds for New York City for its long-dormant Second Avenue subway route. Newsday quoted a lawmaker complaining, "Is he the congressman for the Bronx or for Puerto Rico?"

Serrano's passion for Puerto Rico caused him embarrassment in 2004. He had arranged a $1.7 million appropriation to establish an institute — called House of Artful Expression — to document the contributions of New Yorkers of Puerto Rican descent, and he had hand-picked the director and other officers. But the New York Daily News reported in August that more than $1 million had been spent with little accomplished. Serrano blocked further appropriations and said he regretted helping the organization.

In 2002, when the House voted on a feel-good resolution marking the 50th anniversary of the constitution of the Puerto Rican commonwealth, Serrano demurred. While the relationship between Puerto Rico and the United States "has had some wonderful moments, it has never stopped, in my opinion, being a colonial relationship," he said. Serrano was pleased when 31 of his colleagues also voted against the measure, as he thought he would cast the lone dissenting vote.

In 2000, Serrano was arrested outside the White House for protesting the Navy's continued use of the island of Vieques, off the coast of Puerto Rico, for training exercises using live bombs. On the Vieques issue and some others, Serrano has aligned himself with black activist Al Sharpton, and he endorsed Sharpton's 2004 presidential bid in the Democratic primaries.

Serrano also is a strong advocate of liberalized immigration laws, backing extension of a program that allows some immigrants to apply for residency even if they are in the country illegally. In 2001, he won approval of a measure granting posthumous citizenship to victims of the Sept. 11, 2001, terrorist attacks who had been in the process of becoming citizens.

Since the mid-1990s, Serrano has offered "English-plus" legislation, which encourages all residents of the United States not only to become proficient in English but also to preserve or gain skills in other languages as well. The measure began as a response to proposals to make English the official language, reflecting what Serrano views as an English-only attitude. "Multilingualism is an asset, not a liability," he says.

His parents emigrated from Puerto Rico when he was 7, and Serrano says he learned English by listening to Frank Sinatra records that his father brought back from the Army. Serrano became a big fan, amassing a large collection of Sinatra records and sponsoring the 1997 measure that awarded Sinatra a congressional gold medal.

Serrano graduated from a vocational high school, served in the Army, and then took a job in a New York City bank and began making political contacts, which helped him win a state Assembly seat in 1974. His tenure in Albany, including service as chairman of the Assembly Education Committee, made him a fixture in New York Hispanic politics. His son, José Marco Serrano, was elected to the New York City Council in 2001 and the state Senate in 2004.

When Democratic Rep. Robert Garcia resigned his seat in 1990 after he was convicted of defense contract extortion, Serrano moved quickly to stake his claim. He breezed to victory with 92 percent of the vote in the special election and won a full term with 93 percent that November. He has won all his subsequent re-elections with at least 91 percent.

KEY VOTES

2004

Yes Extend federal unemployment benefits by 13 weeks

Yes Pass $283.2 billion, six-year federal highway and mass transit bill

Yes Approve $146 billion multi-year extension of previously enacted middle-class tax breaks

No Amend the Constitution to prohibit same-sex marriage

No Cut corporate taxes $137 billion over 10 years

Yes Reorganize U.S. intelligence agencies as proposed by Sept. 11 commission

2003

No Cut taxes by $330 billion through fiscal 2013

Yes Block Bush rule scaling back overtime pay for some white-collar federal workers

Yes Do not allow use of search warrants without first notifying subjects

Yes Allow importation of prescription drugs

No Create private school voucher program in Washington, D.C.

No Ban "partial birth" abortion except to save a woman's life

Yes Split $18.6 billion in Iraq aid into half-grant, half-loan

No Overhaul Medicare and create prescription drug benefit

CQ VOTE STUDIES

	PARTY UNITY		PRESIDENTIAL SUPPORT	
	Support	Oppose	Support	Oppose
2004	98%	2%	12%	88%
2003	96%	4%	22%	78%
2002	96%	4%	26%	74%
2001	92%	8%	29%	71%
2000	93%	7%	90%	10%

INTEREST GROUPS

	AFL-CIO	ADA	CCUS	ACU
2004	100%	100%	30%	0%
2003	100%	90%	21%	23%
2002	100%	90%	37%	0%
2001	92%	85%	35%	0%
2000	90%	90%	42%	0%

NEW YORK 16
South Bronx

The 16th, which covers the distressed neighborhoods of the South Bronx, is the nation's poorest district in terms of median income. One-third of families live on a household income of less than $10,000, and the area is plagued by urban ills and low rates of home ownership. But some South Bronx neighborhoods have started to turn around, thanks to grass-roots community work and federal empowerment zone money.

The South Bronx, overtaken by a post-World War II influx of Hispanics to New York City, has since 1970 elected men of Puerto Rican origin to the House. The Puerto Rican influence has long been strong in the 16th, although the district also is home to many African and South and Central American immigrants. The district's 3 percent non-Hispanic white population is the lowest in the nation.

The 16th is one of the most strongly Democratic districts in the nation — it was John Kerry's second-best district in the 2004 presidential election, behind only the neighboring 15th — but like many districts with large minority and immigrant populations, voter turnout is low. Redistricting

following the 2000 census made the 16th a bit longer and narrower in shape, and the district now reaches almost as far north as the convergence of the Harlem and Hudson rivers.

Like frontier settlements, several downtown developments of single-family homes and low-rise housing have been built on vacated lots by subsidized economic development organizations, and they are occupied by people who grew up in the district, worked their way out and are now returning to help rebuild the neighborhoods.

Light-manufacturing firms also have set up shop, replacing some of the heavy industry that moved out decades ago. Local baseball fans and businesses hope the New York Yankees do not make good on threats to move the team from the Bronx. Fordham University is in the 16th as well.

MAJOR INDUSTRY
Health care, light manufacturing

CITIES
New York (pt.), 654,360

NOTABLE
The Edgar Allan Poe Cottage in the Bronx (the writer's last home) is owned by New York City.

Rep. Eliot L. Engel (D)

Elected 1988; 9th term

CAPITOL OFFICE
225-2464
www.house.gov/engel
2161 Rayburn 20515-3217; fax 225-5513

COMMITTEES
Energy & Commerce
International Relations

HOMETOWN
Bronx

BORN
Feb. 18, 1947, Bronx, N.Y.

RELIGION
Jewish

FAMILY
Wife, Patricia Ennis Engel; three children

EDUCATION
Hunter-Lehman College, B.A. 1969 (history); City U.
of New York, Lehman College, M.A. 1973 (guidance
& counseling); New York Law School, J.D. 1987

CAREER
Teacher; guidance counselor

POLITICAL HIGHLIGHTS
Bronx Democratic district leader, 1974-77; N.Y.
Assembly, 1977-88

ELECTION RESULTS

2004 GENERAL

Eliot L. Engel (D, WFM)	140,530	76.2%
Matthew I. Brennan (R)	40,524	22.0%
Kevin Brawley (C)	3,482	1.9%

2004 PRIMARY

Eliot L. Engel (D)	18,854	58.9%
Kevin M. McAdams (D)	6,416	20.0%
write-ins	3,543	11.1%
Jessica Flagg (D)	3,225	10.1%

2002 GENERAL

Eliot L. Engel (D, L, WFM)	77,535	62.6%
C. Scott Vanderhoef (R, C, INDC)	42,634	34.4%
Arthur L. Gallagher (RTL)	1,931	1.6%
Elizabeth Shanklin (GREEN)	1,743	1.4%

PREVIOUS WINNING PERCENTAGES
2000 (90%); 1998 (88%); 1996 (85%); 1994 (78%);
1992 (80%); 1990 (61%); 1988 (56%)

A lifelong resident of the Bronx who embodies the fierce parochial pride of a New Yorker born and bred, Engel mixes unflagging attention to constituent concerns with a sweeping global perspective. One minute he is railing against fare increases by the Metropolitan Transit Authority or increases in local cable rates. The next he is championing most-favored-nation trade status for Albania or accusing the Saudi government of aiding terrorist attacks against Americans.

Foreign affairs has long been one of Engel's principal interests. A vocal member of the International Relations Committee, Engel takes the position of a liberal interventionist. He argues that the United States should seek to stop humanitarian tragedies, and he supported President Bush's decision to go to war against Saddam Hussein. Engel has advocated continued U.S. sanctions against Iran, and he was an early proponent of U.S. intervention in the civil war in Yugoslavia. In 1993, he joined a bipartisan group of lawmakers who urged the Clinton administration to take sides in Bosnia against the Serbs, who were being accused of "ethnic cleansing," the forced removal of Muslims.

In 2000, he opposed granting China normal trade status because of the country's human rights abuses. "Are we only for the almighty dollar or are we for morality and doing what's right?" he asked.

During the 108th Congress, Engel teamed up with Republican Ileana Ros-Lehtinen of Florida to shepherd through Congress a sanctions bill targeting Syria, battling the persistent misgivings of the State Department. He calls the measure "one of my greatest legislative victories."

Five months after signing the bill into law, Bush used it to impose tough sanctions on Syria. His executive order banned all exports to Syria, with the exception of food and medicine. Bush labeled Syrian government activities "an extraordinary threat to the national security of the United States."

Engel, like many of his constituents, is Jewish, and he is a strong supporter of Israel. He was the prime sponsor of a congressional resolution recognizing Jerusalem as the "undivided capital of Israel" — a controversial stand given that city's religious significance to the Palestinian minority.

In keeping with his district's leanings, Engel follows a traditionally Democratic course. He sides with labor unions, fights for civil rights and defends the United Nations, the Corporation for Public Broadcasting and the National Endowment for the Humanities against GOP attacks. In his career, he has supported the Democratic Party position more than 90 percent of the time.

Engel sits on the Energy and Commerce Committee, where he is active on legislation related to health care, illegal drugs, housing, and the availability and price of energy. He sometimes quotes his mother, who he says is "my best adviser in terms of health care, particularly the importance of prescription drug coverage and Medicare."

For much of his tenure in Washington, Engel has been content to stand in the background and attend to constituent service and the nuts-and-bolts of legislation. But on one day every year, he has a brief moment on the national stage: He arrives early in the House chamber for the annual State of the Union address to be sure to grab an aisle seat so he can greet the president and renew acquaintances with a number of ambassadors. He began the practice as a freshman when he greeted President George Bush and continued with it when George W. Bush gained the White House.

After he greeted Bush in 2003, he said, "The constituents love it. And as long as they love it, I love it."

Constituent service is second nature to Engel, who grew up in the Bronx and earned his political spurs in local Democratic clubs. An Engel aide proudly points to a 1996 Wall Street Journal profile where the writer noted that Engel is known in his working-class district as "The Mayor," a tribute to his attention to voters' everyday concerns, such as overcrowded subways or broken traffic lights.

Engel's father was a welder, but father and son were both interested in politics and world affairs, and they walked picket lines together. He says he has always been a political junkie and adds that as a boy he memorized the names of all 100 senators then serving. Engel attended New York City public schools, where he later worked as a teacher and guidance counselor. He was elected to the state Assembly in 1977, when he defeated the candidate endorsed by the Democratic Party.

In the Assembly, he worked on housing and substance abuse issues and established his credentials in the "reform" wing of the Bronx Democratic organization. Thus, it was not completely unexpected when he announced in 1988 that he was giving up his Assembly seat to challenge Democratic Rep. Mario Biaggi, who was then on trial for bribery, conspiracy and extortion. In August, Biaggi was convicted and resigned his seat. His name remained on the ballot, however, for both the primary and the general election (the latter because he regularly received the endorsement of district Republicans). Engel won both contests, taking 56 percent of the vote in the general election to Biaggi's 27 percent.

He easily rebuffed a Biaggi comeback attempt in 1992, but as minorities have made up a rising proportion of his district's population, he has felt growing pressure from Hispanic and black challengers. Engel is one of the few non-minority lawmakers who represents a district in which a majority of the populace belongs to a racial or ethnic minority. In 2000, Engel survived a nasty and racially tinged primary challenge from state Sen. Larry Seabrook, who is black and who received backing from Bronx Democratic Party leader Roberto Ramirez. Engel managed to win with 50 percent.

His district was remapped in 2002 to include parts of Rockland and Westchester counties, but parts of the Bronx were removed. Engel had no primary opposition that year, but in 2004 he confronted two primary challengers plus write-in candidates, prevailing with 59 percent of the vote and coasting to a general-election win with 76 percent.

KEY VOTES

2004

Yes Extend federal unemployment benefits by 13 weeks

Yes Pass $283.2 billion, six-year federal highway and mass transit bill

Yes Approve $146 billion multi-year extension of previously enacted middle-class tax breaks

No Amend the Constitution to prohibit same-sex marriage

No Cut corporate taxes $137 billion over 10 years

Yes Reorganize U.S. intelligence agencies as proposed by Sept. 11 commission

2003

No Cut taxes by $330 billion through fiscal 2013

Yes Block Bush rule scaling back overtime pay for some white-collar federal workers

Yes Do not allow use of search warrants without first notifying subjects

Yes Allow importation of prescription drugs

No Create private school voucher program in Washington, D.C.

No Ban "partial birth" abortion except to save a woman's life

Yes Split $18.6 billion in Iraq aid into half-grant, half-loan

No Overhaul Medicare and create prescription drug benefit

CQ VOTE STUDIES

	PARTY UNITY		PRESIDENTIAL SUPPORT	
	Support	Oppose	Support	Oppose
2004	96%	4%	36%	64%
2003	94%	6%	24%	76%
2002	89%	11%	44%	56%
2001	94%	6%	35%	65%
2000	94%	6%	87%	13%

INTEREST GROUPS

	AFL-CIO	ADA	CCUS	ACU
2004	93%	90%	35%	4%
2003	100%	95%	30%	20%
2002	100%	90%	50%	12%
2001	100%	85%	32%	4%
2000	100%	85%	38%	22%

NEW YORK 17

North Bronx; part of Westchester and Rockland counties — Mount Vernon, part of Yonkers

The 17th is an economically, racially and ethnically diverse territory that takes in the northwestern part of the Bronx and parts of Westchester and Rockland counties northwest of New York City. Blacks and Hispanics together constitute a majority of residents in the district.

Riverdale, a heavily Jewish neighborhood, sits at the western edge of the Bronx and is one of New York's most affluent areas. East of Riverdale, on the other side of Van Cortlandt Park and Woodlawn Cemetery, there is a large black population. The 17th reaches almost as far east as the mammoth Co-op City apartment complex (in the 7th District). About 45 percent of district residents live in the Bronx.

In Westchester County, home to one-fourth of the 17th's residents, the district takes in all of Mount Vernon, which is heavily black, some black and Hispanic communities in western Yonkers, and predominately white

communities, many of Italian and Irish descent, in southeastern Yonkers.

The 17th narrows significantly in northern Yonkers, meandering north along Route 9 and the Hudson River to cross the Tappan Zee Bridge into Rockland County, parts of which were appended to the 17th in redistricting following the 2000 census. Rockland leans Democratic, but not overwhelmingly so.

The new district lines excised some of the Bronx's Democratic faithful, but John Kerry nonetheless took 66 percent of the 17th's vote in the 2004 presidential election — tallying 81 percent of the vote in the district's portion of the Bronx — and Democrats hold a substantial registration edge over the GOP.

MAJOR INDUSTRY
Health care, higher education, city government

CITIES
New York (pt.), 292,423; Yonkers (pt.), 87,617; Mount Vernon, 68,381; Spring Valley, 25,464

NOTABLE
Duke Ellington, Elizabeth Cady Stanton, F.W. Woolworth, Nellie Bly and "Bat" Masterson are among those buried in Woodlawn Cemetery.

Rep. Nita M. Lowey (D)

Elected 1988; 9th term

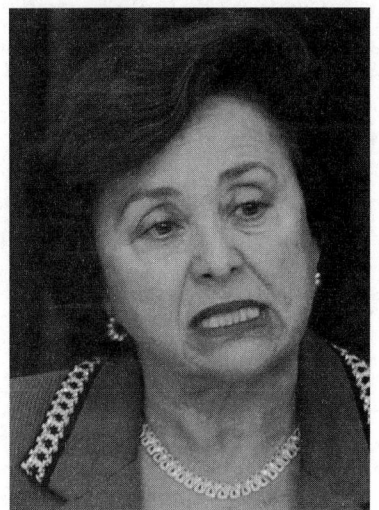

CAPITOL OFFICE
225-6506
www.house.gov/lowey
2329 Rayburn 20515-3218; fax 225-0546

COMMITTEES
Appropriations
Homeland Security

HOMETOWN
Harrison

BORN
July 5, 1937, Bronx, N.Y.

RELIGION
Jewish

FAMILY
Husband, Stephen Lowey; three children

EDUCATION
Mount Holyoke College, B.A. 1959 (marketing)

CAREER
State government aide; homemaker

POLITICAL HIGHLIGHTS
N.Y. assistant secretary of state, 1985-87

ELECTION RESULTS

2004 GENERAL

Nita M. Lowey (D, INDC, WFM)	170,715	69.8%
Richard A. Hoffman (R)	73,975	30.2%

2004 PRIMARY

Nita M. Lowey (D)	unopposed

2002 GENERAL

Nita M. Lowey (D, WFM)	98,957	92.0%
Michael J. Reynolds (RTL)	8,558	8.0%

PREVIOUS WINNING PERCENTAGES
2000 (67%); 1998 (83%); 1996 (64%); 1994 (57%); 1992 (56%); 1990 (63%); 1988 (50%)

Lowey's outward appearance as a doting grandmother belies her inner steel and political savvy. From her senior position on the Appropriations Committee, she doles out federal money with toughness and political finesse. At election time, she is one of her party's most prolific fundraisers.

Two of her constituents are more well-known than she is — Bill and Hillary Rodham Clinton, who now live in Chappaqua, N.Y. Overshadowed by the two politically, Lowey (LOW-ee) has handled the situation with grace, say fellow Democrats and even a few Republicans.

Lowey's hopes of advancing to the Senate in 2000 were dashed when Hillary Rodham Clinton moved to New York and entered the race to replace retiring Democratic Sen. Daniel Patrick Moynihan. Loyal Lowey stepped aside and has since developed strong ties with the Clintons. In 2004, the congresswoman and the senator teamed up to introduce a bill to make basic education for children worldwide a major goal of U.S. foreign policy.

During her 16 years in the House, the high-energy Lowey has been a leading advocate for women's rights and liberal causes. As the top-ranking Democrat on Appropriations' Foreign Operations Subcommittee, she has pushed for U.S. support for international family planning programs.

In the 108th Congress, Lowey teamed with Republican Mark Steven Kirk of Illinois to offer an amendment to the foreign aid bill restoring funding to the U.N. Population Fund and rescinding the so-called Mexico City policy, a Reagan administration-era rule revived by President Bush that bans U.S. aid to overseas organizations that perform or promote abortions. The Bush administration said some of the organizations were helping China enforce its one-child-per-family policy by indirectly funding coerced abortions. Lowey's measure failed, as it had in previous years.

Lowey says that anti-abortion forces are chipping away bit by bit at the basic right to an abortion. She tried without success in the 108th Congress to stop a bill giving a fetus legal rights in federal cases. The legislation, she said, "is not about shielding pregnant women. It is and always has been about undermining freedom of choice."

Lowey did succeed in adding money to world AIDS funding, when House Republicans followed Bush's call for more U.S. aid to combat the disease globally. And in 1998, she enjoyed an unexpected triumph by winning coverage for contraception for federal workers whose insurance plans cover pharmaceuticals.

In one of her more unusual legislative alliances, Lowey joined conservative Republicans in 2005 in an effort to cut back on Bush's request for more money to fight the war in Iraq. But she had no praise for her temporary allies. "Let's face it, Republicans are trying to create an illusion that they have fiscal discipline," Lowey said. "But they're only shaving the budget in increments."

While Lowey proudly wears her liberal credentials, she also is an inside player who maneuvers skillfully through the appropriations process. She knows how to deal, whether the issue is aid to Israel or money for projects in New York. She won the coveted seat on the Appropriations panel in 1993 by aggressively lobbying the Democratic leadership.

She got a seat on the Homeland Security Committee in the 108th Congress, giving her a post to secure funds to protect a state particularly sensitive to security issues.

In 2004, Lowey and two of her Republican colleagues from New York,

John Sweeney and Sue Kelly, founded the Hudson River Congressional Caucus with eight other lawmakers. Later that year, Lowey secured $500,000 for the Hudson River National Heritage Area.

One of her major achievements of the 108th was to see a law enacted that requires the food industry to more clearly label products that contain the eight most common allergens: milk, eggs, fish, shellfish, tree nuts, peanuts, wheat and soybeans. Lowey has been pushing for such labeling since 2000.

A dutiful fundraiser, Lowey in 2000 helped raise $6 million for the House Democrats' effort to recruit and elect women candidates and also gave more than $160,000 from her own campaign treasury to other Democrats. Two years later, she was picked by leaders to head the Democratic Congressional Campaign Committee, which raises money and recruits candidates for House races. She set fundraising records that year.

Lowey got her start in politics more than 30 years ago. She was a homemaker in Queens when she volunteered in a neighbor's 1974 campaign for lieutenant governor. The neighbor was Mario M. Cuomo. Though Cuomo lost that primary race, new Democratic Gov. Hugh L. Carey appointed him secretary of state, and he in turn hired Lowey to work in his department's anti-poverty division.

By the mid-1980s, Cuomo was governor and Lowey was the top aide to new Secretary of State Gail Shaffer. Lowey made an impressive debut in electoral politics in 1988 when she unseated two-term GOP Rep. Joseph J. DioGuardi in the then-20th District. Lowey survived a primary against Hamilton Fish III, publisher of The Nation magazine and son of a GOP House member, and against businessman Dennis Mehiel. She raised $1.3 million, a huge sum for a challenger.

In the general election, DioGuardi outspent her. But his campaign was damaged by a newspaper account of a pass-through scheme involving a New Rochelle auto dealer funneling $57,000 in corporate contributions to DioGuardi's campaign through his employees. Lowey won narrowly.

DioGuardi returned for a rematch in 1990, but by then Lowey's legislative work, constituent service and fundraising skills made her the front-runner, and she won decisively. Since then, she has outdistanced all competition. Lowey's campaigns have benefited from her personal wealth, largely derived from her husband's law firm of Lowey Dannenberg Bemporad & Selinger.

As a result of reapportionment after the 2000 census, New York lost two districts. The new map drawn by the state legislature gave Lowey a larger share of New York City's northern suburbs. The GOP declined to field a candidate in 2002, and she won handily again in 2004.

KEY VOTES

2004

Yes Extend federal unemployment benefits by 13 weeks

Yes Pass $283.2 billion, six-year federal highway and mass transit bill

Yes Approve $146 billion multi-year extension of previously enacted middle-class tax breaks

No Amend the Constitution to prohibit same-sex marriage

No Cut corporate taxes $137 billion over 10 years

Yes Reorganize U.S. intelligence agencies as proposed by Sept. 11 commission

2003

No Cut taxes by $330 billion through fiscal 2013

Yes Block Bush rule scaling back overtime pay for some white-collar federal workers

Yes Do not allow use of search warrants without first notifying subjects

Yes Allow importation of prescription drugs

No Create private school voucher program in Washington, D.C.

No Ban "partial birth" abortion except to save a woman's life

Yes Split $18.6 billion in Iraq aid into half-grant, half-loan

No Overhaul Medicare and create prescription drug benefit

CQ VOTE STUDIES

	PARTY UNITY		PRESIDENTIAL SUPPORT	
	Support	Oppose	Support	Oppose
2004	95%	5%	35%	65%
2003	94%	6%	24%	76%
2002	94%	6%	26%	74%
2001	96%	4%	28%	72%
2000	94%	6%	91%	9%

INTEREST GROUPS

	AFL-CIO	ADA	CCUS	ACU
2004	100%	100%	47%	4%
2003	87%	95%	33%	16%
2002	100%	90%	40%	4%
2001	100%	95%	38%	0%
2000	90%	75%	52%	9%

NEW YORK 18

Most of Westchester County — New Rochelle, most of Yonkers

The 18th encompasses most of southern and central Westchester County, excluding parts of Yonkers bordering the Hudson River and the Bronx, and all of Mount Vernon. The district hops the Hudson to pick up most of New City and Congers and all of Haverstraw in Rockland County. Redistricting following the 2000 census pushed the district out of New York City, where it had taken in a swath of the Bronx and Queens.

The 18th is a well-to-do residential district that leans Democratic, but not overwhelmingly. Westchester County has a Republican base, and wealthy New York suburbs such as Scarsdale and Mamaroneck are the district's hallmark. Many of the district's residents enjoy an easy commute to white-collar jobs in Manhattan.

But the district also takes in working-class communities, including Port Chester and urban sections of White Plains and New Rochelle. These areas, coupled with some affluent Democratic areas, are more than

enough to offset the GOP base. John Kerry carried the district with 57 percent of the vote in the 2004 presidential election. The 18th has more than half of the residents of Yonkers, Westchester's most-populous city. It also includes Ossining, site of Sing Sing prison — its location north of the city on the Hudson River led New Yorkers to refer to prison-bound criminals being "sent up the river."

Hospitals and colleges provide employment opportunities in the district, and officials are trying to attract more technology firms to the region, particularly around Yonkers. Purchase is home to PepsiCo., IBM's corporate headquarters are in Armonk and Reader's Digest is based in Pleasantville.

MAJOR INDUSTRY
Health care, higher education

CITIES
Yonkers (pt.), 108,469; New Rochelle, 72,182; White Plains, 53,077

NOTABLE
North Tarrytown was renamed Sleepy Hollow in honor of the Washington Irving story set there; Thomas Paine Cottage and Museum is in New Rochelle; Former President Bill Clinton and Sen. Hillary Rodham Clinton have a home in Chappaqua.

Rep. Sue W. Kelly (R)

Elected 1994; 6th term

With political views shaped by a wide array of real-world experience before she entered politics, it is not surprising that Kelly practices a pragmatic brand of politics, one in which her voting record offers most interest groups something to praise and something to criticize.

"I've been called a liberal, a strong centrist and a member of the vast right-wing conspiracy," she once told Gannett News Service. Sometimes, groups on the same side of the ideological divide have very different views of Kelly's performance. In 2002 and 2004, for example, Kelly was endorsed by the League of Conservation Voters but not by the Sierra Club. In 2002, she was endorsed by the Republican Pro-Choice Coalition, even as the Westchester Coalition for Legal Abortion lamented that Kelly "has joined the anti-choice majority . . . and in so doing both baffled and alienated the pro-choice women who elected her."

Her voting pattern does reflect a slight shift to the right since she first came to Congress. In both the 107th Congress and the 108th, she sided with the conservative majority of her fellow Republicans on 85 percent of votes that pitted the two parties against each other. That put her among the bottom 20 House Republicans for party unity scores, but it was still a higher score than she recorded in some of her early years in the House.

Indeed, she has moved into the Republican mainstream on several bellwether votes in recent years. In her first term, for example, she voted against banning a procedure opponents call "partial birth" abortion, but since then she has voted for such legislation. In 1998 and 1999, she voted in favor of campaign finance overhaul legislation offered by Republican Christopher Shays of Connecticut and Democrat Martin T. Meehan of Massachusetts. In 2002, she stood with the GOP leadership and voted against the Shays-Meehan measure that became law.

She took the side of labor unions and backed an increase in the minimum wage in 1996, but voted against a similar plan in 2000. Similarly, she sided with unions, environmentalists and a majority of Democrats in 1998 by voting against reviving fast-track presidential trade negotiating authority. When President Bush pushed a similar proposal in 2002, she voted yes.

The gay rights group Human Rights Campaign gave Kelly an 83 in the 107th Congress, but her score plunged to 33 in the 108th. On one of the most important gay rights votes in years, Kelly voted for a constitutional amendment to ban gay marriage.

Like many New York and New Jersey lawmakers Kelly developed an intense interest and expertise in terrorism after the Sept. 11, 2001, attacks. She chairs the Oversight and Investigations Subcommittee of the Financial Services Committee and is using the panel to try to shore up laws aimed at choking off financial lifelines of terrorist groups. In July 2004, she formed a bipartisan Congressional Anti-terrorist Financing Task Force. At the start of the 109th Congress, Kelly accused Saudi Arabia of moving too slowly to crack down on financing operations and made clear she would keep track of administration efforts to pressure the Saudi government.

The daughter of a doctor, Kelly studied botany and bacteriology in college and then worked as a medical researcher. She married and raised four children. She co-founded a local chapter of the League of Women Voters, served as a PTA president, and volunteered as a rape crisis counselor and patients' advocate at a New York City hospital. She taught junior high school science and math, had a florist shop and ran a business that reha-

CAPITOL OFFICE
225-5441
suekelly.house.gov
2182 Rayburn 20515-3219; fax 225-3289

COMMITTEES
Financial Services
  (Oversight & Investigations - chairwoman)
Small Business
Transportation & Infrastructure

HOMETOWN
Katonah

BORN
Sept. 26, 1936, Lima, Ohio

RELIGION
Presbyterian

FAMILY
Husband, Edward W. Kelly; four children

EDUCATION
Denison U., B.A. 1958 (science); Pace Law School, attended 1976-77; Sarah Lawrence College, M.A. 1985 (health advocacy)

CAREER
Professor; teacher; hospital administrative aide; medical researcher; retailer

POLITICAL HIGHLIGHTS
No previous office

ELECTION RESULTS

2004 GENERAL

Sue W. Kelly (R, INDC, C)	175,401	66.7%
Michael Jaliman (D)	87,429	33.3%

2004 PRIMARY

Sue W. Kelly (R)	unopposed

2002 GENERAL

Sue W. Kelly (R, C, INDC)	121,129	70.0%
Janine M.H. Selendy (D)	44,967	26.0%
Christine M. Tighe (RTL)	4,374	2.5%
Jonathan M. Wright (GREEN)	2,642	1.5%

PREVIOUS WINNING PERCENTAGES
2000 (61%); 1998 (62%); 1996 (46%); 1994 (52%)

bilitated real estate. She took two years of law school classes, earned a master's degree in health advocacy and was a part-time professor at Sarah Lawrence College.

Her legislative agenda reflects her eclectic background. She is pushing to create a national registry of people convicted of child abuse and neglect to try to ensure children are not placed with abusers who have moved to a different state. In the 107th, she worked to increase Medicare payments to hospitals in the 19th District, and she joined with Democratic Sen. Hillary Rodham Clinton on legislation to rectify a national nursing shortage. Kelly sponsored legislation to broaden insurance coverage of breast cancer treatments, including reconstructive breast surgery. Her bill to renew the special breast cancer stamp — which costs more than a regular first-class stamp, with the extra money going to breast cancer research — became law in 2001 as part of a larger measure.

Kelly works hard at trying to protect the remaining open spaces in her Hudson River Valley district. In 2004, she and New Jersey Republican Rodney Frelinghuysen succeeded in passing legislation to conserve land and water resources in the Northeast Highlands region in New York, New Jersey, Pennsylvania and Connecticut. The Highlands region supplies and protects drinking water for more than 15 million residents from New York to Philadelphia.

Although Kelly had worked in the campaigns of Republicans at the local, state and national level, she did not run for office until 1994, when moderate Republican Hamilton Fish retired after 26 years in the House. Positioning herself as the moderate in the race, she won the seven-person GOP primary with 23 percent of the vote. Two more-conservative candidates trailed narrowly. In the fall, her Democratic opponent was Hamilton Fish Jr., son of the GOP incumbent, who was seeking to perpetuate a line of Hamilton Fishes in Congress dating to 1843. The Conservative and Right to Life parties' nominee was Joseph J. DioGuardi, one of the losers of the GOP primary, who had represented a nearby House district from 1985 to 1989. Kelly won with 52 percent of the vote.

DioGuardi ran again in 1996 and helped hold Kelly to a 46 percent plurality win. But starting in 1998, she has been unopposed in the primary and has won with comfortable margins in each general election. She did so even after post-census reapportionment cost New York two House seats, and the state legislature placed Kelly and 30-year Republican Rep. Benjamin A. Gilman in the same district. Gilman briefly weighed a party switch to run against Kelly but decided instead to retire.

KEY VOTES

2004

Yes Extend federal unemployment benefits by 13 weeks

Yes Pass $283.2 billion, six-year federal highway and mass transit bill

Yes Approve $146 billion multi-year extension of previously enacted middle-class tax breaks

Yes Amend the Constitution to prohibit same-sex marriage

Yes Cut corporate taxes $137 billion over 10 years

Yes Reorganize U.S. intelligence agencies as proposed by Sept. 11 commission

2003

Yes Cut taxes by $330 billion through fiscal 2013

Yes Block Bush rule scaling back overtime pay for some white-collar federal workers

No Do not allow use of search warrants without first notifying subjects

No Allow importation of prescription drugs

Yes Create private school voucher program in Washington, D.C.

Yes Ban "partial birth" abortion except to save a woman's life

No Split $18.6 billion in Iraq aid into half-grant, half-loan

Yes Overhaul Medicare and create prescription drug benefit

CQ VOTE STUDIES

	PARTY UNITY		PRESIDENTIAL SUPPORT	
	Support	Oppose	Support	Oppose
2004	84%	16%	71%	29%
2003	86%	14%	76%	24%
2002	90%	10%	80%	20%
2001	80%	20%	77%	23%
2000	75%	25%	46%	54%

INTEREST GROUPS

	AFL-CIO	ADA	CCUS	ACU
2004	33%	40%	86%	56%
2003	33%	15%	77%	60%
2002	11%	20%	85%	88%
2001	25%	25%	91%	40%
2000	20%	35%	76%	56%

NEW YORK 19
Hudson Valley — Peekskill, West Point

Wedged between Connecticut and New Jersey, the 19th follows a sizable portion of the Hudson River. On the east side of the river, the 19th spans the southern tier of Dutchess County, all of Putnam County and the northern section of Westchester County. It also takes in some land west of the Hudson in Orange County and the northern edge of Rockland County.

The southeastern, Westchester County, portion of the district is known for its elegant exurban homes and horse country that attract wealthy professionals and celebrities from Manhattan, where some residents work. The median family income approaches $200,000 in some places. Nearly 85 percent of the district's residents are white. Racially, ethnically and economically diverse Peekskill, with a working- and middle-class base, sits on the eastern shore of the Hudson River in northwestern Westchester.

The wealth in the southern part of the district and the rural character of its northern and western reaches — which extend to the foothills of the

Catskill Mountains — help give the 19th a solidly Republican tilt. George W. Bush did not capture a majority of the district's presidential vote in 2000, but still won the 19th with 49 percent of the vote. In 2004, he took 53 percent of the district's presidential vote.

Drawn by the groundwork built by IBM — a longtime presence in Yorktown — technical and research firms have moved into the lower Hudson Valley. Dutchess County, Putnam County and Orange County, where farmers grow onions, lettuce and celery, are more rural. The U.S. Military Academy at West Point, which celebrated its bicentennial in 2002, also aids the district's economy.

MAJOR INDUSTRY
Computers, telecommunications, agriculture

MILITARY BASES
U.S. Military Academy, 885 military, 3,163 civilian (2004)

CITIES
Peekskill, 22,441; Jefferson Valley-Yorktown, 14,891; Beacon, 13,808

NOTABLE
The home and farm of John Jay, Continental Congress president and first chief justice of the United States, is in Katonah.

Rep. John E. Sweeney (R)

Elected 1998; 4th term

Sweeney is a rising star in the House despite a mild independent streak that he loves to tout to voters back home. Like many Northeastern Republicans, he sometimes splits with President Bush and the GOP leadership on specific issues. "I don't go to the floor and vote for things just because it's good for my team," he told the Albany Times-Union editorial board in October 2004.

Gregarious and approachable, Sweeney makes a point of cultivating good relationships with fellow lawmakers. He often joins forces with New York Republican Thomas M. Reynolds, whom he has known for years. And he has made friends across the aisle, earning praise from New York Democrat José E. Serrano, an Appropriations Committee colleague.

Sweeney has built bipartisan support for a range of objectives, including four that promise to occupy much of his time in the 109th Congress: a ban on slaughtering horses for food; cracking down on the use of steroids and similar drugs; targeting homeland security funds to likely targets, such as New York City, instead of nationwide; and finding ways to encourage more students to pursue math and science in college and graduate school.

He is pressing GOP leaders to show more independence from the White House. "Quite candidly, we've ceded some of our agenda to the White House in the last few years," he said after the 2004 elections. "In '06, the midterm elections with a lame-duck presidency, we need to make a compelling case to the American people that we deserve to be re-elected."

Sweeney is the subject of recurring speculation about his political ambitions, and he does not discourage suggestions that he might be interested in higher office. While there were some noises about a possible challenge to popular Democratic Sen. Charles E. Schumer in 2004, it never materialized.

It seems you can't be a politician in New York without being involved in at least a minor controversy or two, and Sweeney is no exception.

The Times-Union discovered in early 2004 that a former state trooper who once owned some strip clubs, including a nude juice bar in Albany, was drawing paychecks from both Sweeney's campaign and his congressional payroll to provide security and be his driver. Harwood McCart was Sweeney's largest single campaign expense in 2001 and 2002, when he was paid $50,400 in wages and reimbursed $33,800 for various expenses. The newspaper said McCart earned $34,100 as a staff assistant on Sweeney's federal payroll during the same period. While eyebrows were raised, the issue disappeared when McCart resigned.

Sweeney has had his ups and downs with "green" groups. While he opposes drilling for oil in an Alaska wildlife refuge and has criticized Bush's air pollution policies, he often opposes other items on the environmentalists' agenda. When the League of Conservation Voters gave him a 15 percent score in 2003 and 18 percent in 2004, Sweeney accused the group of favoring Democrats — even though it had endorsed two of his New York GOP colleagues with far higher scores, Sherwood Boehlert and Sue W. Kelly.

"I view myself as a moderate Republican on environmental issues," Sweeney told the Times-Union. "I am certainly not a pave-the-world-over Republican and I'm not knee-jerk pro-industry."

Although he was raised in a union household and served for two years as the New York state labor commissioner, he generally — but not always — holds pro-business views. In the 108th, Sweeney bucked Bush and most

CAPITOL OFFICE
225-5614
john.sweeney@mail.house.gov
www.house.gov/sweeney
416 Cannon 20515-3220; fax 225-6234

COMMITTEES
Appropriations

HOMETOWN
Clifton Park

BORN
Aug. 9, 1955, Troy, N.Y.

RELIGION
Roman Catholic

FAMILY
Wife, Gayle Ford; three children

EDUCATION
Hudson Valley Community College, A.A. 1978 (liberal arts); Russell Sage College, B.A. 1981 (political science & criminal justice); Western New England College, J.D. 1990

CAREER
Gubernatorial and county government aide; lawyer; county public safety program director

POLITICAL HIGHLIGHTS
N.Y. Republican Party executive director, 1992-95; N.Y. labor commissioner, 1995-97

ELECTION RESULTS

2004 GENERAL

John E. Sweeney (R, INDC, C)	188,753	65.8%
Doris F. Kelly (D)	96,630	33.7%

2004 PRIMARY

John E. Sweeney (R)	unopposed

2002 GENERAL

John E. Sweeney (R, C)	140,238	73.3%
Frank Stoppenbach (D)	45,878	24.0%
Margaret Lewis (GREEN)	5,162	2.7%

PREVIOUS WINNING PERCENTAGES
2000 (68%); 1998 (55%)

Republicans by supporting an extension of unemployment benefits and trying to kill new overtime regulations. But in 2000, he opposed an increase in the minimum wage. His voting scores from the AFL-CIO can swing wildly, from 56 in 1999, to 11 in 2002, to 53 in 2004.

One of Sweeney's major accomplishments in the 108th was pushing through a ban on performance-enhancing drugs for athletes, as well as the sale of the dietary supplement ephedra. He pursued the steroid issue again in the 109th, demanding that Major League Baseball crack down harder on steroid use by players.

In his first term, Sweeney served on the Transportation and Infrastructure Committee, which helped him deliver much-needed funding for Albany's airport, a main link to the rest of the world for many of his constituents. He has continued to promote his district's transportation interests since winning a seat in 2001 on the Appropriations Committee, where he serves on the Transportation Subcommittee. He is using that post to battle Bush's efforts to slash funding for Amtrak.

Sweeney's early years were spent in a public housing project in Troy. His father worked in a shirt factory and was a local union official, and his mother worked at a hospital. He says both gave him a strong work ethic and the notion that children should strive to do better than their parents.

He attended the local community college off and on, getting his two-year degree at the age of 22 and then earning a bachelor's degree through night classes at Russell Sage College. Sweeney's first job out of college was as head of a local drunken-driving prevention program. He later was an aide to the Rensselaer County executive. Deciding to become a lawyer, he commuted several hours a day to law school in Springfield, Mass., about 85 miles each way, and earned his law degree in 1990. He was 34.

He had become friends with William Powers, a local GOP official, who Sweeney says was his political mentor. Powers became state party chairman, and Sweeney became the party's lawyer and then its executive director. When Republican George E. Pataki became governor in 1995, he named Sweeney to head the state's labor department. Sweeney quickly cleaned house, aiming to show that the department should not be viewed as pro-labor and anti-business. Later, he became one of Pataki's personal aides.

When 10-term GOP Rep. Gerald B.H. Solomon announced his retirement from the 22nd District in 1998, he handpicked Sweeney as his successor. Sweeney sailed through the four-candidate GOP primary and won comfortably over Democratic publisher and Red Hook Councilwoman Jean Parvin Bordewich. He has breezed to re-election ever since.

KEY VOTES

2004

Yes Extend federal unemployment benefits by 13 weeks

Yes Pass $283.2 billion, six-year federal highway and mass transit bill

Yes Approve $146 billion multi-year extension of previously enacted middle-class tax breaks

No Amend the Constitution to prohibit same-sex marriage

Yes Cut corporate taxes $137 billion over 10 years

No Reorganize U.S. intelligence agencies as proposed by Sept. 11 commission

2003

Yes Cut taxes by $330 billion through fiscal 2013

Yes Block Bush rule scaling back overtime pay for some white-collar federal workers

No Do not allow use of search warrants without first notifying subjects

No Allow importation of prescription drugs

Yes Create private school voucher program in Washington, D.C.

Yes Ban "partial birth" abortion except to save a woman's life

No Split $18.6 billion in Iraq aid into half-grant, half-loan

Yes Overhaul Medicare and create prescription drug benefit

CQ VOTE STUDIES

	PARTY UNITY		PRESIDENTIAL SUPPORT	
	Support	Oppose	Support	Oppose
2004	88%	12%	71%	29%
2003	91%	9%	81%	19%
2002	91%	9%	85%	15%
2001	92%	8%	83%	17%
2000	89%	11%	32%	68%

INTEREST GROUPS

	AFL-CIO	ADA	CCUS	ACU
2004	53%	25%	81%	72%
2003	47%	20%	79%	72%
2002	11%	5%	95%	88%
2001	18%	15%	96%	68%
2000	20%	10%	76%	72%

NEW YORK 20
North Hudson Valley – Saratoga Springs, Glens Falls

The 20th runs along the state's eastern border, starting just outside Poughkeepsie and stretching into the Adirondack Mountains. It covers much of the primarily residential Hudson River Valley, including the site of the Battle of Saratoga, America's first significant victory against the British in the Revolutionary War. A western branch of the 20th picks up rural territory as far west as Delaware and Otsego counties.

The district's population hub is in its center, in the Albany-Schenectady-Troy metropolitan area. The district includes none of those cities (they are all in the 21st), but does claim much of their GOP suburbia. The three cities helped fuel a suburban boom in southern Saratoga County in the 1980s. Saratoga Springs, synonymous with world-class horse racing, attracts tourists during the summer months.

The district follows Interstate 87 north into mountainous, scenic Adirondack Park and the resort areas of Lake George and Essex County.

Lake Placid, site of the 1932 and 1980 Winter Olympics, is in Essex County at the northern tip of the district.

The southern end is made up of mainly rural and mountainous territory in Otsego, Delaware, Greene, Columbia and northern Dutchess counties. It includes mansions built along the Hudson River by the nation's elite, including the Vanderbilts, Martin Van Buren and Franklin Delano Roosevelt.

A heavy presence of unionized state workers outside Albany makes labor an important constituency, but dairy farmers and small-town voters give the GOP a solid edge. The 20th (previously the 22nd) has the lowest minority percentage in the state, and gave George W. Bush 53 percent of the vote in the 2004 presidential election.

MAJOR INDUSTRY
Agriculture, tourism, paper manufacturing

CITIES
Saratoga Springs, 26,186; Glens Falls, 14,354

NOTABLE
Franklin Roosevelt lost Dutchess County, site of his Hyde Park home, in seven of nine general elections in which he competed.

www.cqpress.com

Rep. Michael R. McNulty (D)

Elected 1988; 9th term

CAPITOL OFFICE
225-5076
mike.mcnulty@mail.house.gov
www.house.gov/mcnulty
2210 Rayburn 20515-3221; fax 225-5077

COMMITTEES
Ways & Means

HOMETOWN
Green Island

BORN
Sept. 16, 1947, Troy, N.Y.

RELIGION
Roman Catholic

FAMILY
Wife, Nancy Ann McNulty; four children

EDUCATION
College of the Holy Cross, B.A. 1969 (political science)

CAREER
Public official

POLITICAL HIGHLIGHTS
Green Island supervisor, 1970-77; Democratic nominee for N.Y. Assembly, 1976; mayor of Green Island, 1977-83; N.Y. Assembly, 1983-89

ELECTION RESULTS

2004 GENERAL

M. McNulty (D, C, INDC, WFM)	194,033	70.8%
Warren Redlich (R)	80,121	29.2%

2004 PRIMARY

M. McNulty (D)	unopposed

2002 GENERAL

M. McNulty (D, C, INDC, WFM)	161,329	75.1%
Charles B. Rosenstein (R)	53,525	24.9%

PREVIOUS WINNING PERCENTAGES
2000 (74%); 1998 (74%); 1996 (66%); 1994 (67%); 1992 (63%); 1990 (64%); 1988 (62%)

McNulty flies so far under the radar on Capitol Hill that he is all but undetectable. He sits on the powerful Ways and Means Committee, but he rarely opens his mouth during its deliberations. He goes to the House floor faithfully to vote but seldom speaks. And when he does, it is usually to lead the daily Pledge of Allegiance.

In that rarest of congressional attitudes, McNulty even told the Albany Times-Union that he has "no aspirations to a higher office." He prefers to tend to business in the Capitol's backrooms and to focus on constituent service.

A typical piece of legislation for McNulty was a resolution he sponsored early in the 109th Congress that would recognize Dr. Richard Shuckburgh, a British Army surgeon, as the primary author of the lyrics to "Yankee Doodle." Why? Shuckburgh is said to have written the ditty during the 1750s after viewing provincial forces near Fort Crailo, located in the city of Rensselaer, N.Y., which just happens to be in his district. He also has sponsored legislation to allow tandem trailers to use Interstate 787 between the New York State Thruway and Church Street in Albany.

McNulty dipped a toe into national issues in the 108th Congress by introducing a bill to authorize first-responder money to go directly to cities rather than statehouses. But his idea was rejected in the final bill. More typical of his efforts — and more successful — was a bill authorizing the establishment in his district of the Kate Mullany National Historic Site in Troy, N.Y., in honor of the woman who organized and led the first all-female labor union at the nation's first commercial laundry. Three of McNulty's constituents had pushed for the designation — and he duly praised them, by name, as the bill neared enactment.

McNulty won his seat on Ways and Means after his first two terms in the House, during which he served as a vote-counter in the Democratic whip organization. The committee is home to numerous outsize egos on both sides of the aisle — with the exception of McNulty, who is the top-ranking Democrat on the Select Revenue Measures Subcommittee.

McNulty always has been an organization man. He is the scion of a Democratic dynasty in the gritty blue-collar town of Green Island. At 22, he was elected town supervisor, a post his grandfather and father had held. After six years as mayor and six more in the state Assembly, he was hand-picked by the Albany area's Democratic bosses in 1988 to take the state capital's seat in Congress. He has never been seriously challenged for the seat and virtually never has been opposed in a primary.

In his last election, the only ripple of controversy stemmed from a family matter. His opponent questioned McNulty's decision to pay his brother close to $35,000 over two years to serve as his campaign treasurer. That amount was McNulty's second-largest campaign expense, after a $50,000 contribution to the Democratic Congressional Campaign Committee. McNulty acknowledged that paying the campaign treasurer was somewhat unusual, but not illegal.

McNulty is a reliable Democratic vote on most issues and rock-solid in his backing of organized labor's causes. In keeping with that loyalty, he voted against three of the principal trade liberalization laws of the past decade-plus: the 1993 codification of the North American Free Trade Agreement, the 2000 statute permanently granting China normal trade status, and the 2002 fast-track measure giving the president authority to negotiate trade agreements that Congress can approve or reject but cannot amend. Maintaining his pattern, he opposed the three bilateral trade deals of the 108th Congress — with Australia, Singapore and Chile.

McNulty also was a vocal opponent of the 2001 law allowing the president to extend normal trade relations status to Vietnam. McNulty, whose brother Bill was killed in the Vietnam War, argued that the country should not be rewarded with that economic benefit because it had insufficiently accounted for U.S. military personnel still missing since the conflict.

He sometimes differs with his party on social issues, especially those involving abortion. He voted to outlaw a procedure described as "partial birth" abortion by its opponents. He would prohibit federal workers' health plans from paying for abortions, and would prevent public funding of the procedure except in cases of rape, incest or danger to the life of the woman. He voted for the 1996 law barring federal recognition of same-sex marriages, but against a constitutional amendment in the 108th Congress to ban gay unions.

The McNulty name has been a force in local upstate New York politics since 1914, when the congressman's grandfather, John J. McNulty, was elected Green Island tax collector. He went on to serve as town supervisor, county board chairman and county sheriff. The congressman's father, Jack McNulty Jr., served as town supervisor starting in 1949 and was mayor until the end of 2002. He was succeeded as mayor of Green Island by his daughter, the congressman's sister, Ellen McNulty-Ryan.

In his long political career, McNulty has waged only one unsuccessful campaign, a 1976 challenge to a GOP assemblyman. But he bounced back to win the first of his three terms in the legislature in 1982. While an assemblyman, McNulty once introduced legislation to make Uncle Sam the official state patriot. The icon is believed to have been modeled after Sam Wilson, a meatpacker from Troy, which is in McNulty's district.

McNulty's opening to move to Washington came with the sudden retirement in 1988 of 30-year Democratic incumbent Samuel S. Stratton, whose health was failing. Within hours of the announcement, the district's Democratic leaders met and chose McNulty to replace him on the ballot. McNulty defeated local Republican official Peter Bakal with 62 percent of the vote — his lowest share ever in a congressional general election.

Following the 2000 census, the 21st District was enlarged slightly because of reapportionment, in which New York gave up two House seats. But its solid Democratic cast was not altered. In 2004, McNulty won a ninth term, defeating his underfunded opponent, Republican Warren Redlich, by a whopping 42 percentage points.

KEY VOTES

2004

Yes Extend federal unemployment benefits by 13 weeks

Yes Pass $283.2 billion, six-year federal highway and mass transit bill

Yes Approve $146 billion multi-year extension of previously enacted middle-class tax breaks

No Amend the Constitution to prohibit same-sex marriage

No Cut corporate taxes $137 billion over 10 years

Yes Reorganize U.S. intelligence agencies as proposed by Sept. 11 commission

2003

No Cut taxes by $330 billion through fiscal 2013

Yes Block Bush rule scaling back overtime pay for some white-collar federal workers

Yes Do not allow use of search warrants without first notifying subjects

Yes Allow importation of prescription drugs

No Create private school voucher program in Washington, D.C.

Yes Ban "partial birth" abortion except to save a woman's life

Yes Split $18.6 billion in Iraq aid into half-grant, half-loan

No Overhaul Medicare and create prescription drug benefit

CQ VOTE STUDIES

	PARTY UNITY		PRESIDENTIAL SUPPORT	
	Support	Oppose	Support	Oppose
2004	91%	9%	29%	71%
2003	92%	8%	30%	70%
2002	90%	10%	28%	72%
2001	87%	13%	36%	64%
2000	88%	12%	75%	25%

INTEREST GROUPS

	AFL-CIO	ADA	CCUS	ACU
2004	100%	90%	33%	16%
2003	100%	90%	24%	28%
2002	100%	85%	30%	12%
2001	100%	80%	32%	24%
2000	100%	55%	57%	17%

NEW YORK 21

Capital District — Albany, Schenectady, Troy

As the terminus of the Erie Canal, which connects the Great Lakes to the Hudson River, New York's Capital District was one of the state's earliest industrial centers. Blue-collar workers and state employees give the Albany-Schenectady-Troy area a substantial union population and a solidly Democratic vote — unusual for an upstate district.

Albany is home to one of the nation's last big-city political machines, formed in 1921. During the heyday of Daniel O'Connell and Mayor Erastus Corning II, the Albany machine used to ensure Democratic victories throughout the area, but it now holds less sway over the area's ever-expanding suburbs. Few of the district's Democrats can be described as liberal. Most are quite conservative when it comes to social issues. Indeed, Rep. McNulty runs on the Conservative and Independence party lines, in addition to the Democratic Party line.

The 21st was expanded during redistricting following the 2000 census and now includes all of Albany, Schenectady, Schoharie and Montgomery counties, as well as parts of Fulton, Saratoga and

Rensselaer counties.

Despite large-scale industrial losses in the 1980s and 1990s, manufacturing remains a force. Job losses have been mitigated by an intensive effort to recruit small manufacturing and technology firms. Retail and wholesale jobs saw a real boom during the 1990s, and service jobs now account for about one-third of non-farm employment.

MAJOR INDUSTRY
State government, service, manufacturing, retail

MILITARY BASES
Watervliet Arsenal (Army), 1 military, 609 civilian (2005)

CITIES
Albany, 95,658; Schenectady, 61,821; Troy, 49,170; Rotterdam, 20,536

NOTABLE
The Mohawk and Hudson Rail Road, chartered in 1826 and opened in 1831, ran between Albany and Schenectady and was the state's first railroad; Samuel Wilson, a meatpacker who provided the Army with much of its rations during the War of 1812, is believed to be the inspiration for "Uncle Sam" and is buried in Troy; The original Shaker settlement was established in Watervliet in 1776.

Rep. Maurice D. Hinchey (D)

Elected 1992; 7th term

CAPITOL OFFICE
225-6335
www.house.gov/hinchey
2431 Rayburn 20515-3222; fax 226-0774

COMMITTEES
Appropriations
Joint Economic

HOMETOWN
Hurley

BORN
Oct. 27, 1938, Manhattan, N.Y.

RELIGION
Roman Catholic

FAMILY
Separated; three children

EDUCATION
State U. of New York, New Paltz, B.S. 1968
(political science & English), M.A. 1970 (English)

MILITARY SERVICE
Navy, 1956-59

CAREER
State education department employee; state
highway toll collector; cement and paper mill
equipment operator

POLITICAL HIGHLIGHTS
Democratic nominee for N.Y. Assembly, 1972;
N.Y. Assembly, 1975-93

ELECTION RESULTS

2004 GENERAL

M. Hinchey (D, C, INDC, WFM)	167,489	67.2%
William A. Brenner (R)	81,881	32.8%

2004 PRIMARY

M. Hinchey (D)	unopposed

2002 GENERAL

M. Hinchey (D, INDC, L, WFM)	113,280	64.2%
Eric Hall (R, C)	58,008	32.9%
Steven Greenfield (GREEN)	2,723	1.5%
Paul J. Laux (RTL)	2,473	1.4%

PREVIOUS WINNING PERCENTAGES
2000 (62%); 1998 (62%); 1996 (55%); 1994 (49%);
1992 (50%)

Notably tart-tongued, even for a New York politician, Hinchey is one of the Bush administration's harshest critics — especially when it comes to what he regards as excessive kowtowing to business interests.

As a member of the Appropriations Subcommittee on Agriculture, Rural Development, FDA and Related Agencies, Hinchey in the 108th Congress was among those leading attacks on the Food and Drug Administration for its handling of prescription drugs, including the painkiller Vioxx, which was removed from the market because of potentially lethal side effects. He also blamed the flu vaccine shortage of 2004-05 on FDA missteps.

When the agency tried to stem criticism by creating a new drug safety review board in February 2005, Hinchey angrily dismissed it as "a farce." "The real problem with the FDA is that it remains far too closely tied to the pharmaceutical industry," he said. "The entire culture at the FDA needs to change and that is not something a fake 'independent' panel can fix."

Hinchey was at the forefront of efforts in the 108th Congress to overturn a Federal Communications Commission rule loosening ownership restrictions and allowing greater concentration of media holdings by large corporations. He said the FCC was producing "a new censorship in America" that meant "a select few will determine what information and entertainment the public will have access to. This decision flies in the face of democracy and is clearly not in the best interest of the American people."

He was one of just 16 House members (15 of them Democrats) to vote against a 2004 resolution marking the third anniversary of the Sept. 11, 2001, terrorist attacks, objecting to language that he saw as an attempt to link the war in Iraq to the fight against terrorism. That link, he said, is "blatantly false."

Hinchey's bare-knuckle style has made him a target of the right. He infuriated conservatives in early 2005 when he suggested — without evidence — that presidential adviser Karl Rove had a role in misleading CBS News when it used apparently forged documents in a story about George W. Bush's National Guard service during the Vietnam War. A conservative syndicated columnist referred to Hinchey as "the unhinged tin-foil hat wearer who continues to assert that White House adviser Karl Rove planted the bogus National Guard memos that Dan Rather wrapped himself in at CBS News."

Hinchey's politics reflect his working-class roots. He has a 99 percent career rating from the AFL-CIO, and he has never received less than a 95 percent rating from the liberal Americans for Democratic Action. He has a 95 percent lifetime rating from the League of Conservation Voters. He is also a member of the Progressive Caucus, the most liberal of the policy groups in the House. He is generally a dependable vote for Democratic Party positions, and in the 108th Congress, he was elected one of 12 regional whips.

Hinchey can deviate from the majority of his party on gun issues. In 1996, he was the only New York Democrat to vote to repeal a ban on certain semiautomatic assault-style weapons. Yet he supported the 1993 Brady bill, which calls for a five-day waiting period for handgun purchases; and in 2004, he voted against repealing the District of Columbia's gun control law. Hinchey drew unwelcome attention during his first House term when he was charged with carrying a loaded handgun in his baggage at Ronald Reagan Washington National Airport. He eventually pleaded no contest and was given a suspended sentence.

An Appropriations member since 1999, Hinchey works there with members of both parties to advance his region's interests. After the Sept. 11, 2001, terrorist attacks, Hinchey and New York Republican John E. Sweeney, who is also on Appropriations, led an effort to secure more aid for New York City in the fiscal 2002 defense spending bill than the Bush administration and GOP leaders wanted to provide. Their efforts eventually failed.

On the Agriculture Appropriations panel, Hinchey works to open Cuba to agricultural exports from the United States, a move that also has support of many farm-state Republicans and would provide an important new market for farmers in his own district. He also serves on the Interior Appropriations Subcommittee, where he pursues his environmental interests.

Environmental policies remain Hinchey's passion. An environmental fight in the 1970s over the development of a huge power plant on the Hudson River was the primary reason for his entry into electoral politics. In the state Assembly, Hinchey chaired the Environmental Conservation Committee investigating the "Love Canal" contamination scandal and drafting bills to combat acid rain and to create the Hudson River Valley Greenway. Once in Congress, Hinchey won passage of a bill to designate much of the Greenway region as a National Heritage Area. He also has been involved in a long-running effort to require General Electric to clean up toxic polychlorinated biphenyls, or PCBs, discharged into the Hudson River from its plant north of Albany.

Hinchey grew up in a working-class home, joined the Navy out of high school, worked in a local cement plant for five years and then paid his way through college by working nights collecting tolls on the New York State Thruway. In the House, he is noticed for his silver hair, pin-striped suits and elegant silk ties.

Hinchey's parents had been active in local party politics, and after his graduation from college, he was encouraged to get involved in behind-the-scenes political activities while starting a career in education. He lost his first bid for the state Assembly, in 1972, but came back two years later to begin an 18-year tenure in Albany.

In 1992, when nine-term Democratic Rep. Matthew F. McHugh retired, Hinchey went after the seat. He started as the Democratic primary underdog, facing Binghamton Mayor Juanita M. Crabb. He prevailed by pushing a plan to revitalize the economy of the recession-hit region. In November, he edged Republican Bob Moppert, a six-year county legislator, by 8,819 votes. He survived a 1994 rematch by an even closer margin of slightly more than 1,200 votes. Since then, however, he has rolled up more comfortable margins.

KEY VOTES

2004
Yes Extend federal unemployment benefits by 13 weeks
Yes Pass $283.2 billion, six-year federal highway and mass transit bill
Yes Approve $146 billion multi-year extension of previously enacted middle-class tax breaks
No   Amend the Constitution to prohibit same-sex marriage
No   Cut corporate taxes $137 billion over 10 years
Yes Reorganize U.S. intelligence agencies as proposed by Sept. 11 commission

2003
No   Cut taxes by $330 billion through fiscal 2013
Yes Block Bush rule scaling back overtime pay for some white-collar federal workers
Yes Do not allow use of search warrants without first notifying subjects
Yes Allow importation of prescription drugs
No   Create private school voucher program in Washington, D.C.
No   Ban "partial birth" abortion except to save a woman's life
Yes Split $18.6 billion in Iraq aid into half-grant, half-loan
No   Overhaul Medicare and create prescription drug benefit

CQ VOTE STUDIES

	PARTY UNITY		PRESIDENTIAL SUPPORT	
	Support	Oppose	Support	Oppose
2004	99%	1%	20%	80%
2003	98%	2%	16%	84%
2002	99%	1%	20%	80%
2001	96%	4%	21%	79%
2000	98%	2%	94%	6%

INTEREST GROUPS

	AFL-CIO	ADA	CCUS	ACU
2004	100%	95%	25%	0%
2003	100%	95%	28%	12%
2002	100%	100%	30%	4%
2001	100%	100%	26%	0%
2000	100%	95%	23%	0%

NEW YORK 22

South central — Binghamton, Poughkeepsie, Ithaca

The elongated 22nd reaches from the hills above Cayuga Lake to the east bank of the Hudson River. Most residents are found at those extremes: the Ithaca and Binghamton areas in the west and the Hudson Valley region, including Poughkeepsie, Newburgh and Kingston, on the eastern edge.

In general, the district is rural, with a large portion of the Catskill Mountains in the center and apple and dairy farms throughout. Taking in all of Sullivan and Ulster counties and parts of six others, the mixture of cities and farmland creates a politically competitive environment, although Democrats enjoy a slight advantage.

Ithaca, in the 22nd's far northwest, is home to Cornell University, Ithaca College and a corps of liberal activists. Residents elected a socialist mayor three times in the 1990s. Overall, John Kerry took 53 percent of the district's 2004 presidential vote.

The district extends along the Pennsylvania border from Tioga County to

Sullivan County, taking in Broome County's Triple Cities — Binghamton, Johnson City and Endicott. Once an industrial hub, Binghamton saw a decline in manufacturing jobs during the 1980s and 1990s, and the economy has been hit hard by recessions. Defense companies are still a major force, although IBM, which at one time was headquartered in Endicott, has significantly reduced operations in the area. Officials now hope to use the state university in Binghamton as an anchor for economic development.

The Catskills' Borscht Belt, a prominent Jewish resort area, declined as tourists began vacationing in more exotic locales. Officials hope to lure tourists back with casinos that have been approved by the state.

MAJOR INDUSTRY
Higher education, agriculture, electronics

CITIES
Binghamton, 47,380; Poughkeepsie, 29,871; Ithaca, 29,287

NOTABLE
Gen. George Washington had his headquarters and residence in Newburgh from 1782 to 1783; Bethel was the site of the marathon Woodstock rock concert in 1969; Mohonk Mountain House, near New Paltz, has hosted four presidents since its opening in 1869.

Rep. John M. McHugh (R)

Elected 1992; 7th term

CAPITOL OFFICE
225-4611
www.house.gov/mchugh
2333 Rayburn 20515-3223; fax 226-0621

COMMITTEES
Armed Services
(Military Personnel - chairman)
Government Reform
Select Intelligence

HOMETOWN
Pierrepont Manor

BORN
Sept. 29, 1948, Watertown, N.Y.

RELIGION
Roman Catholic

FAMILY
Divorced

EDUCATION
Utica College of Syracuse U., B.A. 1970 (political science); State U. of New York, Albany, M.P.A. 1977

CAREER
State legislative aide; city official; insurance broker

POLITICAL HIGHLIGHTS
N.Y. Senate, 1985-93

ELECTION RESULTS

2004 GENERAL

John McHugh (R, C, INDC, WFM)	160,079	70.7%
Robert J. Johnson (D)	66,448	29.3%

2004 PRIMARY

John McHugh (R)	unopposed

2002 GENERAL

John McHugh (R, C)	unopposed

PREVIOUS WINNING PERCENTAGES
2000 (74%); 1998 (79%); 1996 (71%); 1994 (79%); 1992 (61%)

As chairman of the Armed Services panel's personnel subcommittee for a third straight Congress, McHugh is on the front lines in the debate over the number of troops the Army needs to maintain a sufficient force in Iraq and Afghanistan. In 2004, he helped secure a permanent increase of 20,000 in active duty Army troops and said he would seek to add 10,000 more in 2005.

McHugh is at home with the nuts-and-bolts work of governing and writing legislation, but he prefers to stay behind the scenes and has little need for television face time. His colleagues describe him as a "worker bee," and he is often spotted sitting just off the House floor, puffing on a cigar and doing his legislative homework.

McHugh did find himself in the spotlight in the 108th Congress, when some Democrats raised the possibility that the Bush administration might want to reinstate the military draft, which had been scuttled at the end of the Vietnam War. To quash the rumors, House GOP leaders forced a floor vote on a bill sponsored by Democrat Charles B. Rangel of New York that called for a renewed draft. McHugh led the Republican side of the debate, emphasizing that the White House had no intention of abandoning the all-volunteer force, and the bill was overwhelmingly defeated.

A career politician, McHugh began working in government soon after graduating from college with a degree in political science. As might be expected from someone who has made public service his career, McHugh seeks not to dismantle or shrink the federal government but to make it work better. His effort to reorganize the U.S. Postal Service is a good example. As chairman of Government Reform's Postal Service Subcommittee from 1995 to 2001, McHugh labored in vain to advance legislation to help the Postal Service remain competitive in an era when technology has transformed the way people communicate. The committee defeated the legislation in 2002 after heavy lobbying against the bill by the United Parcel Service.

He continues to pursue the issue. McHugh says that new technologies, including e-mail, faxing and the Internet, have supplanted the Postal Service in transmitting documents that were once the mainstay of the mail business, while electronic billing and private mail and package delivery companies threaten the future of the Postal Service unless it can adapt.

In the 108th Congress, he headed a special Government Reform Committee panel on the Postal Service and was sponsor of yet another overhaul bill that won bipartisan support in two House committees. But White House opposition kept the legislation off the floor. The chief obstacle was a provision intended to help the Postal Service's finances by transferring to the Treasury responsibility for about $27 billion in benefits paid military retirees who had become postal workers. Once again in the 109th, he offered overhaul legislation, which won committee approval early in 2005.

McHugh still seeks cooperation with Democrats and does not have a notably ideological voting record. He supports labor on a number of issues and has won AFL-CIO endorsement several times. But on fiscal policy and most social issues, he casts a dependably Republican vote.

McHugh's vast upstate district is one of New York's poorest. It is heavily dependent on defense spending at Fort Drum and on agriculture, particularly dairy farming and apple growing, all areas in which the federal government plays a key role. In the 107th, McHugh offered a package of economic development bills dealing with agriculture, tourism and technology, such as increasing rural access to the Internet.

The 10th Mountain Division, based at Fort Drum, was one of the first Army units deployed in Afghanistan in 2001 to help topple the Taliban and search for al Qaeda terrorists. McHugh has been able to direct funding to maintain Fort Drum's standing as one of the Army's most modern bases. He argues that the 1995 military base closures were not always based on sound criteria, and he pushed hard to prevent another round. Having failed in that quest, in the 107th he played an influential role on Armed Services in developing more-specific guidelines for the base-closing commission to follow before proposing that installations be shut in 2005.

McHugh and his New York GOP colleagues John E. Sweeney and Sherwood Boehlert are concerned about the effect of acid rain on the Adirondack region, joining forces each Congress to offer legislation aimed at reducing emissions from power plants.

Throughout his House career, McHugh has voted against giving the president fast-track trade negotiating authority, saying he does not think the dairy industry would be adequately protected in the resulting trade liberalization agreements. He and his dairy industry allies were satisfied with the farm bill written in the 107th. While it did not include an interstate compact for Northeast dairy farmers to help them compete with Midwest milk producers, it did add a national income support program for dairy farmers.

McHugh grew up in a middle-class family in Watertown, and after college and a brief stint as an insurance broker, he got a job as an assistant to the city manager in Watertown. He moved to the staff of state Sen. H. Douglas Barclay, where his duties included serving as a liaison to local governments in the district — a job that helped McHugh prepare for a successful run for the state Senate when Barclay retired in 1984.

When Republican Rep. David O'B. Martin decided to retire in 1992 after a dozen years in the House, McHugh jumped into the race. He won the primary over a more conservative opponent, Morrison J. Hosley Jr., a local business owner and Hamilton town supervisor. That was tantamount to winning election in the historically Republican North Country; he won his first term with 61 percent of the vote and has done better than that ever since.

Redistricting for this decade was surprisingly favorable to McHugh. New York lost two seats in reapportionment, and several plans for a revised map would have put McHugh in the same district with other incumbents or drastically altered his constituency. But in the end, the state legislature gave McHugh everything he wanted. No one ran against him in 2002, and he won in 2004 with almost 71 percent.

KEY VOTES

2004

+	Extend federal unemployment benefits by 13 weeks
Yes	Pass $283.2 billion, six-year federal highway and mass transit bill
Yes	Approve $146 billion multi-year extension of previously enacted middle-class tax breaks
Yes	Amend the Constitution to prohibit same-sex marriage
Yes	Cut corporate taxes $137 billion over 10 years
Yes	Reorganize U.S. intelligence agencies as proposed by Sept. 11 commission

2003

Yes	Cut taxes by $330 billion through fiscal 2013
Yes	Block Bush rule scaling back overtime pay for some white-collar federal workers
Yes	Do not allow use of search warrants without first notifying subjects
Yes	Allow importation of prescription drugs
No	Create private school voucher program in Washington, D.C.
Yes	Ban "partial birth" abortion except to save a woman's life
No	Split $18.6 billion in Iraq aid into half-grant, half-loan
Yes	Overhaul Medicare and create prescription drug benefit

CQ VOTE STUDIES

	PARTY UNITY		PRESIDENTIAL SUPPORT	
	Support	Oppose	Support	Oppose
2004	87%	13%	76%	24%
2003	88%	12%	83%	17%
2002	90%	10%	85%	15%
2001	89%	11%	88%	12%
2000	87%	13%	34%	66%

INTEREST GROUPS

	AFL-CIO	ADA	CCUS	ACU
2004	50%	20%	90%	64%
2003	67%	35%	68%	67%
2002	22%	15%	85%	79%
2001	42%	15%	91%	68%
2000	20%	5%	80%	73%

NEW YORK 23
North — Watertown, Plattsburgh, Oswego

The vast 23rd covers more than one-fourth of the state, bordering Lake Champlain, the St. Lawrence Seaway and Lake Ontario. The waterways provide an inexpensive source of electricity, which has lured some heavy industry to the district and given it a number of blue-collar voters. But most of the district is rural, full of small towns, dairy farms, maple syrup producers and colleges. It reaches south to Oneida Lake and Madison County.

Fort Drum (near Watertown, the district's largest city) is one of the largest and most modern Army facilities on the East Coast. It thus far has been safe from post-Cold War base closures, but district residents did experience some economic hardship when Plattsburgh Air Force Base shut down in 1995. A business park has sprung from its ashes, attracting roughly 60 tenants.

Still, unemployment remains a problem throughout the district, as harsh winters and high transportation costs make attracting jobs difficult. Bright spots include seasonal tourism — the 23rd covers much of the

Adirondack Mountains. The proximity to waterways and forests made paper production a major industry for a long while, but many mills have been forced to close their doors, although Georgia Pacific retains its presence in Plattsburgh. Officials see the expansion of broadband Internet access as a means of stoking economic development.

The northeastern corner of the state has sent Republicans to the House since the 1872 election. Republicans hold a registration edge and George W. Bush took 51 percent of the vote here in the 2004 presidential election, but Democrats have had increasing success at the local level in recent years.

MAJOR INDUSTRY
Agriculture, manufacturing, tourism, defense

MILITARY BASES
Fort Drum, 12,117 military, 2,548 civilian (2003)

CITIES
Watertown, 26,705; Plattsburgh, 18,816; Oswego, 17,954

NOTABLE
In 1775, Ethan Allen led the Green Mountain Boys — and Benedict Arnold — in seizing Fort Ticonderoga from the British; Whiteface Mountain is a top East Coast skiing destination.

Rep. Sherwood Boehlert (R)

Elected 1982; 12th term

CAPITOL OFFICE
225-3665
www.house.gov/boehlert
2246 Rayburn 20515-3224; fax 225-1891

COMMITTEES
Science - chairman
Transportation & Infrastructure

HOMETOWN
New Hartford

BORN
Sept. 28, 1936, Utica, N.Y.

RELIGION
Roman Catholic

FAMILY
Wife, Marianne Willey Boehlert; four children

EDUCATION
Utica College, A.B. 1961 (public relations)

MILITARY SERVICE
Army, 1956-58

CAREER
Congressional aide; public relations executive

POLITICAL HIGHLIGHTS
Sought Republican nomination for U.S. House,
1972; Oneida County executive, 1979-82

ELECTION RESULTS

2004 GENERAL

Sherwood Boehlert (R, INDC)	143,000	56.9%
Jeffrey A. Miller (D)	85,140	33.9%
David L. Walrath (C)	23,228	9.2%

2004 PRIMARY

Sherwood Boehlert (R)	22,908	58.9%
David L. Walrath (R)	15,394	39.6%
write-in (R)	588	1.5%

2002 GENERAL

Sherwood Boehlert (R)	108,017	70.7%
David L. Walrath (C)	32,991	21.6%
Mark Dunau (GREEN)	6,660	4.4%
Kathleen M. Peters (RTL)	5,109	3.3%

PREVIOUS WINNING PERCENTAGES
2000 (61%); 1998 (81%); 1996 (64%); 1994 (71%);
1992 (64%); 1990 (84%); 1988 (100%); 1986 (69%);
1984 (73%); 1982 (56%)

Boehlert — "Sherry" to virtually everyone — has managed not only to survive but also to thrive as an unvarnished moderate in an increasingly conservative House. Known best for his strong pro-environment positions, he is someone the Bush White House has to keep a sharp eye on. Respected among his peers, Boehlert has the ability to influence the votes of about 30 GOP moderates on "green" issues.

Approachable and low-key, Boehlert (BO-lert) is a former congressional staffer and a forceful debater with a ready command of the facts. Though often at war with the conservative-dominated GOP leadership, he knows when to strike a deal and so is never at risk of being considered irrelevant. He tells district audiences good-naturedly: "When I vote against the Republican leadership, you can assume they're wrong."

Boehlert dismisses occasional criticisms from political opponents that he is too liberal to be a Republican in the current Congress or that he is to the left of most of his constituents. He told the Syracuse Post-Standard that his effectiveness has nothing to do with being liberal, moderate or conservative. "It's my ability to bring people together in a common cause," he said.

He obviously loves his role as chairman of the Science Committee, a position he assumed at the outset of the 107th Congress. He has steered the second-tier committee into new territory, such as anti-terrorism and cyberspace policy. He boosted the professionalism of the staff by hiring scientists for key subcommittees and has tried to ensure that the panel's recommendations are based on science, not ideology. Boehlert envisions extending the panel's mission to efforts to upgrade science, math and technology education.

As the 109th Congress began, Boehlert concentrated on determining the future of the Hubble space telescope in light of a National Research Council report saying a space shuttle mission should be launched to service the Hubble, which is at risk of going dark as early as 2007.

When his seniority gave him a shot at chairing the Intelligence Committee in 2004, after Republican Porter J. Goss of Florida was chosen as the new chief of the CIA, Boehlert said he had no interest in the job and wanted to stay at Science. He left Intelligence at the end of the 108th.

Under House rules, Boehlert will be required to give up the Science panel gavel at the end of the 109th. In the 110th, he could assume leadership of the more powerful Transportation and Infrastructure Committee, whose chairman, Don Young of Alaska, is also term-limited. As a senior member of Transportation, Boehlert has been a leader of the FAIR Coalition, which seeks to protect the distribution formula for federal highway aid against efforts to adjust it, changes that could cost New York hundreds of millions of dollars.

Boehlert is mostly at odds with President Bush and the GOP on environmental issues. In direct conflict with Bush, Boehlert supports restrictions on carbon dioxide emissions, opposes drilling for oil in Alaska's Arctic National Wildlife Refuge and has pushed for tougher fuel emissions standards for sport utility vehicles. He has tried without success to ensure more money for the cleanup of the nation's worst toxic waste sites.

He honed his role as protector of the environment during the heyday of Republican anti-regulatory fervor under Speaker Newt Gingrich. In 1995, Boehlert rallied a coalition of Democrats and GOP moderates against efforts to scale back clean air and clean water laws. He helped kill 17 controversial provisions that made funding for EPA programs contingent on new curbs on the agency's regulatory powers. The episode angered GOP Westerners, who see him as insensitive to the economic realities of their region.

The issue has a parochial side for Boehlert. Upstate New York voters in his district favor more stringent controls on emissions that originate at power plants in the Midwest but cause acid rain, smog and haze in the Northeast. "If I weren't an environmentalist, my constituents would find someone else to represent them," Boehlert told The Washington Post.

On fiscal policy, Boehlert generally concurs with his party's conservative majority. But in other areas, he often votes with Democrats. He has supported increasing the minimum wage and sided with unions on labor matters. He also favors some new controls on guns and voted against easing restrictions on the purchase of weapons at gun shows.

Boehlert was a Capitol Hill aide for 15 years. His own political ambitions were deferred for a decade after an initial defeat in 1972. That year, he had hoped to succeed his boss, retiring GOP Rep. Alexander Pirnie, but he lost to Donald J. Mitchell, an assemblyman, in a Republican primary. Boehlert swallowed his disappointment and went to work for Mitchell. In 1979, he ran for Oneida County executive and won.

By 1982, Mitchell was ready to retire. Boehlert was driving along a highway in Oneida County when he heard the news. He pulled into a rest stop, called a radio station and announced his candidacy. He came out of the chute with support from labor unions, who liked his positions as county executive. After winning the Republican primary comfortably, Boehlert capitalized on a huge organizational and financial advantage to defeat Democrat Anita Maxwell with 56 percent of the vote.

But Boehlert's left-of-center Republican philosophy leaves him vulnerable to a conservative primary challenge. In 2002, he survived a surprising close call at the hands of David L. Walrath, a Cayuga County legislator. Boehlert hung on to win, with 53 percent. Shortly after undergoing triple-bypass surgery in 2004, he increased his vote total in a primary rematch with Walrath, to 59 percent, and then collected 57 percent in the general election to defeat Democratic college professor Jeffrey A. Miller and Walrath, who ran as a Conservative.

A rabid baseball fan, Boehlert aptly represents a district that houses the Baseball Hall of Fame in Cooperstown. At one time, he owned a small share of the minor league Utica Blue Sox, and the walls of his office are lined with baseball memorabilia. That passion has helped cement his friendship with Bush, who formerly owned a piece of the Texas Rangers. Boehlert gave the president his first tour of the Hall of Fame.

KEY VOTES

2004
Yes Extend federal unemployment benefits by 13 weeks
Yes Pass $283.2 billion, six-year federal highway and mass transit bill
Yes Approve $146 billion multi-year extension of previously enacted middle-class tax breaks
? Amend the Constitution to prohibit same-sex marriage
? Cut corporate taxes $137 billion over 10 years
? Reorganize U.S. intelligence agencies as proposed by Sept. 11 commission

2003
Yes Cut taxes by $330 billion through fiscal 2013
Yes Block Bush rule scaling back overtime pay for some white-collar federal workers
No Do not allow use of search warrants without first notifying subjects
No Allow importation of prescription drugs
No Create private school voucher program in Washington, D.C.
Yes Ban "partial birth" abortion except to save a woman's life
No Split $18.6 billion in Iraq aid into half-grant, half-loan
Yes Overhaul Medicare and create prescription drug benefit

CQ VOTE STUDIES

	PARTY UNITY		PRESIDENTIAL SUPPORT	
	Support	Oppose	Support	Oppose
2004	81%	19%	68%	32%
2003	81%	19%	70%	30%
2002	79%	21%	78%	22%
2001	79%	21%	74%	26%
2000	68%	32%	61%	39%

INTEREST GROUPS

	AFL-CIO	ADA	CCUS	ACU
2004	53%	40%	84%	50%
2003	47%	25%	80%	48%
2002	11%	25%	90%	64%
2001	33%	35%	83%	32%
2000	30%	40%	80%	40%

NEW YORK 24
Central — Utica, Rome, Auburn

The J-shaped 24th starts at the western edge of the Adirondack Mountains, sweeps through the central part of the state — south of Syracuse and north of Binghamton — and extends into the Finger Lakes region. Pristine countryside is dotted by the small towns and rural hamlets of central New York. James Fenimore Cooper's tales of the frontier days gave central New York its nickname, the "Leatherstocking Region." Along with dairy farms, the 24th contains halls of fame and other historical gems, including the Women's Rights Convention and the National Women's Hall of Fame in Seneca Falls and the National Baseball Hall of Fame in Cooperstown.

Utica and Rome, aging industrial cities on the Mohawk River, suffered as manufacturing jobs left the state, but blue-collar jobs remain critical to these cities and give the 24th many of its Democratic voters.

The region took a major hit when Griffiss Air Force Base closed in 1995. An effort to turn the Mohawk River Valley into a technology information center — aided by the Air Force's Rome research laboratory, which works with many of the state's universities — has replaced some of those jobs.

The 24th also is home to the Oneida Indian Nation, which runs a profitable casino in Verona and has a long-running lawsuit against the state to reclaim its native lands. Oneida officials are worried about state proposals to allow out-of-state tribes to open casinos in New York, particularly in the Catskills.

The district's natural beauty gives voters a proclivity for earth-friendly policies, but they are traditional Yankee Republicans. The 24th gives solid support to Republican congressional candidates, and voters awarded 52 percent of the vote to George W. Bush in the 2004 presidential election.

MAJOR INDUSTRY
Higher education, agriculture, tourism, manufacturing

CITIES
Utica, 60,651; Rome, 34,950; Auburn, 28,574; Cortland, 18,740

NOTABLE
The National Soccer Hall of Fame is in Oneonta, and the National Distance Running Hall of Fame is in Utica.

Rep. James T. Walsh (R)

Elected 1988; 9th term

CAPITOL OFFICE
225-3701
rep.james.walsh@mail.house.gov
www.house.gov/walsh
2369 Rayburn 20515-3225; fax 225-4042

COMMITTEES
Appropriations
   (Military Quality of Life & Veterans Affairs -
   chairman)

HOMETOWN
Syracuse

BORN
June 19, 1947, Syracuse, N.Y.

RELIGION
Roman Catholic

FAMILY
Wife, DeDe Ryan Walsh; three children

EDUCATION
St. Bonaventure U., B.A. 1970 (history)

CAREER
Marketing executive; social worker; Peace Corps
volunteer

POLITICAL HIGHLIGHTS
Syracuse Common Council, 1978-88 (president,
1986-88); sought nomination for Onondaga County
executive, 1987

ELECTION RESULTS

2004 GENERAL

James T. Walsh (R, INDC, C)	189,063	90.4%
Howie Hawkins (GREEN)	20,106	9.6%

2004 PRIMARY

James T. Walsh (R)	unopposed

2002 GENERAL

James T. Walsh (R, C, INDC)	144,610	72.3%
Stephanie Aldersley (D)	53,290	26.6%
Francis J. Gavin (WFM)	2,131	1.1%

PREVIOUS WINNING PERCENTAGES
2000 (69%); 1998 (69%); 1996 (55%); 1994 (58%);
1992 (56%); 1990 (63%); 1988 (57%)

By bucking his party's leaders in the 108th Congress, ignoring their spending priorities and packing the appropriations bill he oversaw with more than 1,300 earmarks, Walsh helped spark a determination by House GOP leaders to force a reorganization of the Appropriations Committee in the 109th Congress. Not surprisingly, he came out a loser in the shuffle.

The Appropriations subcommittee Walsh chaired for six years — which funded veterans' affairs, housing and urban development programs, NASA and the EPA — was dismantled. He wound up with the gavel at a reconstituted military construction panel, where he served as the No. 2 Republican in the 108th Congress. The panel now has jurisdiction over veterans' affairs and military health care as well as the more traditional military housing and base facilities. Its new title: Military Quality of Life and Veterans Affairs.

Whatever the name, Walsh's new power base is much narrower than his old one. As chairman of the VA-HUD panel, he was able to steer generous funding to veterans', housing and environmental programs in his district and New York, making him one of the most influential members of the Empire State's delegation. As a member of the Agriculture Appropriations Subcommittee as well, he was able to look out for upstate dairy farmers and other agricultural producers.

But in the 108th Congress, Walsh's panel was nothing but trouble to House leaders. Constrained by a budget cap he felt was unfair, Walsh wrote a bill that increased spending for veterans' programs, but cut NASA spending by $1 billion to stay under his panel's overall limit. That did not sit well with Majority Leader Tom DeLay, who represents many employees of the Johnson Space Center in his Houston area district. Walsh's bill would never get a floor vote, DeLay declared. It never did.

Instead, the VA-HUD bill and eight others were rolled into a massive catchall spending package that was quickly written and passed in the waning hours of the 108th Congress. Hanky-panky ensued; top appropriators quietly slipped controversial measures into the package, including one provision that would have allowed the Appropriations chairmen and their staffs access to individual tax returns. An uproar forced removal of the offending provision.

In organizing for the 109th Congress, House GOP leaders saw to it that three of the 13 Appropriations subcommittees, including VA-HUD, were eliminated and their turf redistributed in ways they said were more logical.

In addition to chairing the new military life and veterans' affairs panel in the 109th, Walsh will serve for the first time on the Labor, Health and Human Services, and Education Subcommittee, which handles the second-largest spending bill after defense. He gave up his Agriculture panel seat.

Walsh used his old subcommittee chairmanship to help Syracuse and other parts of central New York suffering economic decline, and he most assuredly will continue that practice from his new vantage point. He notes that the practice of earmarking funds for local needs has a long congressional tradition. "Does it have warts? Yes. Are there abuses? Yes, there are," he told the Syracuse Herald American. "But it's as good a process as you can find because it gives members an opportunity to directly impact on problems and concerns they have in their districts."

Walsh assumed a high profile defending New York's interests after the the Sept. 11, 2001, terrorist attacks. Over White House objections, he and others in the delegation led a campaign for $9.7 billion in emergency spending, as part of Congress' pledge to provide $20 billion for recovery and rebuilding efforts. After being rebuffed in the Appropriations Committee, the New Yorkers threatened to stall the defense appropriations bill unless they received a House vote on their proposal. That brought the White House to the negotiating table, and the two sides eventually came to an agreement on aid for New York.

Walsh has endorsed funding increases for the Peace Corps, where he spent two years teaching rice-growing techniques in Nepal. He also quietly opposed GOP efforts to eliminate AmeriCorps, the national service program modeled in some ways after the Peace Corps. The program's funding was covered by the VA-HUD bill, and whenever the House has voted to cut it, Walsh has worked behind the scenes to restore it. In the 109th, even though he no longer had direct charge of the program, he was girding for battle to save community development block grants, which President Bush proposed cutting deeply. "I adamantly oppose weakening the CDBG program," Walsh said early in 2005.

His colleagues on Appropriations view Walsh as a fair and effective legislator open to bipartisan cooperation. He enjoyed a particularly close working relationship with the former top-ranking Democrat on VA-HUD, Alan M. Mollohan of West Virginia. And David R. Obey of Wisconsin, the irascible No. 1 Democrat on the full committee, has called Walsh "a first-class legislator."

Walsh ranks in the middle of the GOP pack in his support for Bush, but he is more moderate than a majority of his GOP colleagues. In the 108th Congress, his party unity score put him in the bottom third of House Republicans on votes pitting the two parties against each other.

In 2002, Walsh broke with his party to vote for an overhaul of campaign finance laws. He also voted against the revival of fast-track authority that allows the president to negotiate trade deals that Congress can accept or reject, but not amend. But in the following two years, Walsh voted in favor of bilateral trade pacts with Australia, Singapore and Chile.

In 2005, he was reappointed chairman of the congressional Friends of Ireland, a post he has held since 1995. He has often traveled to Ireland on peace efforts.

Walsh got a close view of politics at an early age: His father was mayor of Syracuse and served in the House. The younger Walsh served more than a decade on the Syracuse City Council, including some three years as council president. He entered Congress on his first try in 1988, when four-term GOP incumbent George C. Wortley was nudged into retirement by local party leaders. He has since won re-election handily, rolling up 90 percent of the vote over his 2004 challenger, Green Party candidate Howie Hawkins.

KEY VOTES

2004
Yes Extend federal unemployment benefits by 13 weeks
Yes Pass $283.2 billion, six-year federal highway and mass transit bill
Yes Approve $146 billion multi-year extension of previously enacted middle-class tax breaks
Yes Amend the Constitution to prohibit same-sex marriage
Yes Cut corporate taxes $137 billion over 10 years
Yes Reorganize U.S. intelligence agencies as proposed by Sept. 11 commission

2003
Yes Cut taxes by $330 billion through fiscal 2013
No   Block Bush rule scaling back overtime pay for some white-collar federal workers
No   Do not allow use of search warrants without first notifying subjects
No   Allow importation of prescription drugs
Yes Create private school voucher program in Washington, D.C.
?   Ban "partial birth" abortion except to save a woman's life
No   Split $18.6 billion in Iraq aid into half-grant, half-loan
Yes Overhaul Medicare and create prescription drug benefit

CQ VOTE STUDIES

	PARTY UNITY		PRESIDENTIAL SUPPORT	
	Support	Oppose	Support	Oppose
2004	87%	13%	85%	15%
2003	94%	6%	93%	7%
2002	88%	12%	87%	13%
2001	92%	8%	88%	12%
2000	79%	21%	43%	57%

INTEREST GROUPS

	AFL-CIO	ADA	CCUS	ACU
2004	40%	20%	90%	67%
2003	14%	5%	93%	75%
2002	22%	15%	84%	75%
2001	10%	10%	91%	76%
2000	10%	20%	85%	56%

NEW YORK 25
North central — Syracuse, most of Irondequoit

Located in the center of the state, Syracuse is the only major city and economic hub of the 25th, which stretches from Onondaga County west along Lake Ontario to Irondequoit, a suburb of Rochester. Small towns and farms fill the rest of the area in this politically diverse district.

Throughout the 1980s and 1990s, the region suffered a steep decline in manufacturing jobs, although employment in higher education and service professions, particularly health care, has helped mitigate that erosion. State officials are working to turn upstate New York cities into university-based technology centers, and they hope Syracuse (home to Syracuse University) will become a hub for environmental systems. Outside Syracuse, small towns rely on dairy farming.

In this previously strong Republican territory, the area's GOP organization once held the loyalties of Irish, Italian, Polish and Jewish constituencies in and around Syracuse. The electorate's Republican leanings were reinforced by the typical upstate antipathy toward Democratic New York City. Yet economic stagnation in the 1990s and the decline of the city's

industrial sector have helped the Democratic Party gain ground. Minorities and blue-collar workers contribute to the Democratic vote in Syracuse, as does an upscale Jewish population in DeWitt.

Redistricting following the 2000 census added parts of Monroe County and all of Wayne County, padding the sizable GOP base. The revised 25th gave a slight majority to John Kerry in the 2004 presidential election, but by a smaller margin than under the old lines.

MAJOR INDUSTRY
Agriculture, service, manufacturing, higher education

CITIES
Syracuse, 147,306; Irondequoit (pt.), 32,661; Fairmount, 10,795

NOTABLE
The name Syracuse was proposed by village postmaster John Wilkinson because of the similarities between the area and a description of ancient Siracusa in Sicily — both had salt-water springs and a town to the north called Salina; Syracuse is called the "Salt City"; The Brannock Device, used to measure feet for shoe size, was invented by Syracuse native Charles F. Brannock, and the company is based in Liverpool, a Syracuse suburb; Joseph Smith, founder of the Mormon Church, grew up and had his first visions in Palmyra.

Rep. Thomas M. Reynolds (R)

Elected 1998; 4th term

CAPITOL OFFICE
225-5265
www.house.gov/reynolds
332 Cannon 20515-3226; fax 225-5910

COMMITTEES
House Administration
Ways & Means
Joint Printing

HOMETOWN
Springville

BORN
Sept. 3, 1950, Belfonte, Pa.

RELIGION
Presbyterian

FAMILY
Wife, Donna Reynolds; four children

EDUCATION
Griffith Institute H.S., graduated 1968; Kent State
U., attended 1968-69 (business)

MILITARY SERVICE
N.Y. Air National Guard, 1970-76

CAREER
Real estate and insurance broker; state legislative
aide

POLITICAL HIGHLIGHTS
Concord Town Council, 1974-82; Erie County
Legislature, 1982-88 (Republican leader, 1987-88);
N.Y. Assembly, 1989-99 (minority leader, 1995-98)

ELECTION RESULTS

2004 GENERAL

Thomas M. Reynolds (R, INDC, C)	157,466	55.6%
Jack Davis (D, WFM)	125,613	44.4%

2004 PRIMARY

Thomas M. Reynolds (R)	unopposed

2002 GENERAL

Thomas M. Reynolds (R, C, INDC)	135,089	73.6%
Ayesha F. Nariman (D)	41,140	22.4%
Shawn Harris (RTL)	4,084	2.2%
Paul E. Fallon (GREEN)	3,146	1.7%

PREVIOUS WINNING PERCENTAGES
2000 (69%); 1998 (57%)

Reynolds is a trusted and influential member of the House Republican leadership, with the portfolio to match. He's chairman of the National Republican Congressional Committee, a deputy majority whip and a member of the powerful Ways and Means Committee. His success as NRCC chairman — he helped his party widen its majority in the House in the 2004 elections — also has earned him the deep gratitude of his colleagues. He is often mentioned as a possible future Speaker.

"He's taught me more about real politics than almost anyone," Speaker J. Dennis Hastert told the Buffalo News. "That's because he came up the New York way. I depend on him a lot."

Reynolds, who was elected by acclamation at the start of the 109th Congress to a second two-year stint as NRCC chairman, is as partisan as they come. Unlike many lawmakers who say they are not politicians, Reynolds embraces the role, once calling politics and government his "vocation, avocation and hobby." After the 2004 elections, he gloated over the Republican victories, saying they were "personally damaging" to House Democratic leader Nancy Pelosi, and claimed a mandate for Republicans to move ahead full tilt with their agenda.

But he also has shown he is willing to work across party lines, particularly within his own state delegation. He told The New York Times that he considers Sen. Hillary Rodham Clinton, his state's junior senator, to be a valuable ally in his efforts to steer federal aid to western New York.

Reynolds says the needs of his upstate constituents are his priority, and he is intent on helping apple growers and dairy farmers, both important to his district. In the 109th, for example, he is leading the fight to protect and expand a federal subsidy for milk producers. He has spoken out against European Union trade rules that he says would hurt apple growers. With Democrat Rahm Emanuel of Illinois, who is now his counterpart at the Democratic Congressional Campaign Committee, he has cosponsored legislation to fund a five-year $4 billion effort to clean up the Great Lakes and combat invasive animal species, such as the big-head carp.

And he has focused on the health care needs of veterans. One of the first bills he introduced in the 109th was aimed at ensuring blind veterans can collect state aid while still receiving their full Social Security benefits.

Reynolds has been on the rise in the House leadership nearly from the moment he arrived in Washington in 1999. In his first term, he became the second Republican freshman appointed to the Rules Committee in 75 years. He also was the only freshman named as one of 18 GOP deputy whips. Reynolds said his work in Tom DeLay's whip organization helped him understand the behind-the-scenes intricacies of legislating.

He gave up his seat on Rules in the 109th, however, to take a seat on Ways and Means. He said he wanted to be sure New York had someone in the majority on that panel, which handles some of the highest-profile issues in the Congress, such as Social Security and tax legislation.

Reynolds angered many back home when he opted to stand with his party leadership in 2001 and help the GOP pass an anti-terrorism supplemental spending bill that contained less money than New Yorkers said they had been promised for terrorism recovery aid. But his loyalty earned him credit with the GOP leadership and the White House. And Reynolds pressed for help for New York in other ways, including supporting a package of tax breaks to encourage redevelopment in lower Manhattan.

Reynolds had shown fundraising and organizational acumen as a party leader in western New York and in the state Assembly. It was no surprise, therefore, when Hastert chose Reynolds as co-chairman for Battleground 2000, an unprecedented effort by the NRCC to raise money to help embattled incumbents, challengers and open-seat candidates. Reynolds pressed lawmakers who had large cash reserves and safe seats to write checks; he talked others into conducting special fundraisers.

He kept up the pressure as NRCC chairman: On his watch, the party committee raised $185 million during the 2004 campaign season, despite a new ban on unregulated "soft money" contributions. At the start of the 109th, he helped leaders lean on Republicans who had not anted up their assigned quotas to the party committee during the elections.

Reynolds grew up in southern Erie County. He entered Kent State University as a business major, but left when his mother became ill. He returned home to help his traveling salesman father raise his younger siblings. He never went back to college. He worked in the real estate and insurance businesses before becoming an aide to a state assemblyman at the age of 22. A year later, he was elected to the Concord Town Council, in southern Erie County.

After eight years, he moved up to the Erie County Legislature, following the elective path of GOP Rep. Bill Paxon, whom he had met through their service in the Young Republicans, and who had just won election to the state Assembly. In 1988, when Paxon ran for Congress, Reynolds won election to fill Paxon's seat in the state Assembly. During his decade in Albany, Reynolds earned a reputation as a hard-working conservative.

In 1994, as the Republican Party leader in Erie County, long a Democratic stronghold, Reynolds was instrumental in moving the county to the GOP column as George E. Pataki was elected governor. He was on Pataki's transition team. In 1995, Reynolds was chosen leader of the Assembly's GOP minority, a position he held until he ran for Congress in 1998 when Paxon retired.

Throughout Paxon's House career, Reynolds had served as his campaign manager, and Paxon returned the favor by managing Reynolds' House campaign. Reynolds easily won a 15 percentage point victory over history professor Bill Cook, even though he didn't live in the district.

Despite significant redistricting due to the loss of two House seats after the 2000 census, Reynolds found himself in a solidly, albeit renumbered, GOP district. In 2002, he won re-election by better than 3-to-1. In 2004, he faced a tougher fight from a wealthy Republican-turned-Democrat named Jack Davis, but in the end, Reynolds won with 56 percent of the vote.

KEY VOTES

2004

No   Extend federal unemployment benefits by 13 weeks

Yes   Pass $283.2 billion, six-year federal highway and mass transit bill

Yes   Approve $146 billion multi-year extension of previously enacted middle-class tax breaks

Yes   Amend the Constitution to prohibit same-sex marriage

Yes   Cut corporate taxes $137 billion over 10 years

Yes   Reorganize U.S. intelligence agencies as proposed by Sept. 11 commission

2003

Yes   Cut taxes by $330 billion through fiscal 2013

No   Block Bush rule scaling back overtime pay for some white-collar federal workers

No   Do not allow use of search warrants without first notifying subjects

No   Allow importation of prescription drugs

Yes   Create private school voucher program in Washington, D.C.

Yes   Ban "partial birth" abortion except to save a woman's life

No   Split $18.6 billion in Iraq aid into half-grant, half-loan

Yes   Overhaul Medicare and create prescription drug benefit

CQ VOTE STUDIES

	PARTY UNITY		PRESIDENTIAL SUPPORT	
	Support	Oppose	Support	Oppose
2004	96%	4%	88%	12%
2003	97%	3%	100%	0%
2002	96%	4%	92%	8%
2001	94%	6%	93%	7%
2000	93%	7%	25%	75%

INTEREST GROUPS

	AFL-CIO	ADA	CCUS	ACU
2004	20%	5%	100%	92%
2003	7%	5%	100%	80%
2002	11%	0%	100%	92%
2001	17%	5%	96%	88%
2000	0%	0%	85%	84%

NEW YORK 26
Suburban Buffalo and Rochester, rural west

The Republican-leaning 26th spreads from the Buffalo to the Rochester suburbs, scooping up mainly rural areas in between and to the south. It takes in all or part of seven counties, but slightly less than half of the residents live in Niagara and Erie counties in the district's western part.

The population is anchored in Amherst, a white-collar suburb northeast of Buffalo. The State University of New York at Buffalo and corporate office parks are mainstays. Amherst voted for John Kerry in the 2004 presidential election, but Lancaster, a town to the southeast, voted narrowly for George W. Bush. Less-populous areas in northeastern Erie, including Clarence and Newstead, lean Republican and backed Bush by wider margins.

The 26th's share of Niagara County, including Lockport and North Tonawanda, was added during redistricting following the 2000 census, which renumbered the district from the 27th. As in Erie, the Niagara portion is politically competitive, with registered Republicans only slightly outnumbering Democrats.

The New York State Thruway links Erie County to the Rochester suburbs of western Monroe County, which include Greece and have a Republican lean.

Between Buffalo and Rochester are the dairy, vegetable and grain farms of rural western New York. Wyoming County is solidly Republican and heavily agricultural, with an abundance of dairy farms. Wyoming also has a facility that is not so bucolic: the state penitentiary at Attica, which in 1971 had one of the worst prison riots in U.S. history. Livingston County, east of Wyoming, includes Conesus Lake, which is at the western edge of New York's Finger Lakes region, and part of the Genesee River, which flows north into Rochester. Overall, the 26th gave Bush 55 percent of its 2004 presidential vote.

MAJOR INDUSTRY
Manufacturing, agriculture, service

CITIES
North Tonawanda, 33,262; Lockport, 22,279; Batavia, 16,256

NOTABLE
The Herschell Carrousel Factory Museum in North Tonawanda hosts about 20,000 visitors a year; The Jell-O museum in LeRoy celebrates the beginnings of the famous gelatin dessert.

Rep. Brian Higgins (D)

Elected 2004; 1st term

CAPITOL OFFICE
225-3306
www.house.gov/higgins
431 Cannon 20515-3227; fax 226-0347

COMMITTEES
Government Reform
Transportation & Infrastructure

HOMETOWN
Buffalo

BORN
Oct. 6, 1959, Buffalo, N.Y.

RELIGION
Roman Catholic

FAMILY
Wife, Mary Jane Hannon; two children

EDUCATION
State U. of New York, Buffalo, B.A. 1984 (political science), M.A. 1985 (history); Harvard U., M.P.A. 1996 (public policy & administration)

CAREER
County council chief of staff; state legislative aide

POLITICAL HIGHLIGHTS
Buffalo Common Council, 1988-94; Democratic nominee for Erie County comptroller, 1993; N.Y. Assembly, 1999-2004

ELECTION RESULTS

2004 GENERAL

Brian Higgins (D, INDC, WFM)	143,332	50.7%
Nancy Naples (R, C)	139,558	49.3%

2004 PRIMARY

Brian Higgins (D)	18,790	44.4%
Paul T. Clark (D)	11,150	26.4%
Michael J. Collesano (D)	5,042	11.9%
Mark W. Thomas (D)	3,961	9.4%
write-in	1,962	4.6%
Peter Crotty (D)	1,401	3.3%

Higgins' blue-collar heritage — his father and uncles were bricklayers and active in local unions — and his own background as an experienced local and state legislator (and before that as a legislative aide) shape his views and his priorities on Capitol Hill.

Higgins, who describes himself as a moderate, spent more than a decade in elective office as a Buffalo council member and state legislator. He plans to continue his efforts to spur economic growth and restore and develop the Buffalo waterfront.

He sought and received an appointment to the Transportation and Infrastructure Committee, an important panel for a region that lies at the juncture of major highways and Great Lakes waterways and which is a major portal for trade with Canada. Higgins also got a seat on Government Reform.

His district's proximity to Canada contributes to Higgins' advocacy of allowing seniors to import prescription drugs from across the border. "Ten miles from where I am standing right now, drugs are $60 to $70 cheaper than they are here in the United States," he said during the campaign. He said one of his priorities would be to push for a "real" prescription drug benefit that allows the government to negotiate volume discounts to bring down costs. He also said he wants Congress to repeal President Bush's tax cuts for the nation's wealthiest individuals.

His narrow (less than 4,000 votes) victory in 2004 ended a dozen years of frustration for his fellow Democrats in his Buffalo-based district — a period that coincided with the congressional tenure of Jack Quinn, a Republican moderate who had dominated the Democratic-leaning constituency with a voting record that earned him solid support from organized labor.

Quinn's decision to retire from the House provided the opening for Higgins, who had a strong pro-labor record in the state Assembly during his three terms. The decision by most unions to back him over his Republican rival, Erie County Comptroller Nancy Naples, was a key factor in the outcome of the race.

NEW YORK 27

West — most of Buffalo, south and east suburbs

Tucked along the shores of Lake Erie in western New York, the 27th contains all of Erie County south of Buffalo and all but the northeastern portion of the city itself. Most of Buffalo's minority residents are in the 28th.

The region has battled to shed its high unemployment rate and Rust Belt image. Auto manufacturing remains important in the area, and the city has a large concentration of blue-collar workers. Buffalo has seen an increase in finance, insurance and real estate industry jobs — driven mostly by two thriving banks, HSBC and M&T. As part of a larger plan to help the beleaguered economy of upstate New York, officials hope university-based research will turn the Buffalo region into a bioinformatics center, promoting the use of computer technology to study genomes, proteins and biomolecules.

Local leaders see the waterfront as the locus for Buffalo's renaissance. Sports teams, particularly football's Buffalo Bills, who play in Orchard Park, are the pride of the city. The rest of Erie County and Chautauqua County, a grape-growing region, are mostly rural.

The 27th was made slightly less Democratic in redistricting following the 2000 census. An incumbent-protection plan added the GOP stronghold of Chautauqua County to the old 30th, which was renumbered the 27th. Residents have shown a willingness to select moderate Republicans with union sympathies, but in 2004 they elected a Democrat to the House for the first time since 1990 and gave John Kerry 53 percent of the presidential vote.

MAJOR INDUSTRY
Auto manufacturing, government, agriculture, tourism

CITIES
Buffalo (pt.), 163,179; Cheektowaga, 79,988; West Seneca, 45,943; Jamestown, 31,730

NOTABLE
Westfield, home to a Welch's plant, calls itself the "Grape Juice Capital of the World."

Rep. Louise M. Slaughter (D)

Elected 1986; 10th term

CAPITOL OFFICE
225-3615
www.slaughter.house.gov
2469 Rayburn 20515-3228; fax 225-7822

COMMITTEES
Rules - ranking member

HOMETOWN
Fairport

BORN
Aug. 14, 1929, Harlan County, Ky.

RELIGION
Episcopalian

FAMILY
Husband, Robert Slaughter; three children

EDUCATION
U. of Kentucky, B.S. 1951 (microbiology),
M.P.H. 1953

CAREER
State government aide; market researcher;
microbiologist

POLITICAL HIGHLIGHTS
Monroe County Legislature, 1975-79; N.Y.
Assembly, 1983-87

ELECTION RESULTS

2004 GENERAL

Louise M. Slaughter (D, WFM)	159,655	72.6%
Michael D. Laba (R, C)	54,543	24.8%
Francina J. Cartonia (INDC)	5,678	2.6%

2004 PRIMARY

Louise M. Slaughter (D)	19,966	78.9%
Francina J. Cartonia (D)	3,202	12.7%
write-ins	2,149	8.5%

2002 GENERAL

Louise M. Slaughter (D, WFM)	99,057	62.5%
Henry F. Wojtaszek (R, C, INDC)	59,547	37.5%

PREVIOUS WINNING PERCENTAGES
2000 (66%); 1998 (65%); 1996 (57%); 1994 (57%);
1992 (55%); 1990 (59%); 1988 (57%); 1986 (51%)

The phrase "Steel Magnolia" could have been invented for Slaughter. When she opens her mouth, she drips the Southern-accented charm of her old Kentucky home. But when she's on a legislative campaign — especially about Medicare, genetic discrimination or other health issues — she reflects the steel of her Rust Belt district in upstate New York.

Slaughter is an influential voice within her party. She has served in the House longer than any other Democratic woman except Marcy Kaptur of Ohio, elected four years before her. As chairwoman of the Democratic Congressional Women's Caucus, she addressed the Democratic National Convention in Boston in 2004. She is the top-ranking Democrat on the Rules Committee and a member of the Democratic Steering Committee, which effectively determines committee assignments. But she suffered one setback in the 109th Congress, when House Republican leaders downsized the Homeland Security Committee and she lost her seat on that panel.

Slaughter is an expert on many medical issues, reflecting her background as a bacteriologist with a master's degree in public health. And she doesn't mince words when she thinks complex issues are being given short shrift. During consideration of the Medicare prescription drug bill in the 108th Congress, Slaughter sarcastically noted that the House was to debate the issue for only three hours — compared with two weeks of Senate discussion. "We are not naming a post office here. We are considering . . . the most important change to Medicare since its creation," she said.

Slaughter has fought a long battle against genetic discrimination. Early in the 109th Congress, she was gearing up to do so again, after the Senate unanimously passed its version of a bill barring employers and insurers from discriminating against people based on their genetic profile. Opposition in the House, stemming from business lobbying and committee jurisdictional conflicts, had stalled the measure repeatedly in that chamber.

"For nearly a decade, I have championed this legislation because the American people have a right to expect that when they make the decision to undergo genetic testing, their private genetic information will be protected from abuse," Slaughter said. "Two presidents, two Senates, and legions of Americans have endorsed this bill. It's time for the House to act."

In addition to her interest in health care, Slaughter is a strong advocate of the arts and co-chairs the Congressional Arts Caucus. In 2004, she won adoption of a House floor amendment boosting funds for the National Endowment for the Arts by $10 million and for the National Endowment for the Humanities by $3.5 million.

Slaughter lives in a suburb of Rochester where she has spent most of her adult life, but she was brought up in the mountains of Kentucky's Harlan County, a genuine coal miner's daughter. When she came to Congress in 1987, House Democratic leaders quickly took a liking to her warmth, grit and liberal views. They gave her a seat on the Rules Committee in 1989 and on the Budget Committee in 1991. But her rise through the party then slowed. She lost a bid for vice chairman of the Democratic Caucus in the 104th. And she was edged out in the 105th for the top-ranking Democratic slot on the Budget Committee. She left the panel after that defeat as her term expired.

In 2002, while Nancy Pelosi of California (now House minority leader) was still Democratic whip, she named Slaughter as her point person on "issues that concern women," from abortion rights to health care and education; in the 108th, she was the Democratic co-chairwoman of the Congressional Caucus for Women's Issues. Slaughter is front and center in a fight against GOP efforts to restrict abortion and family planning funds. She once called a Republican plan to curtail family planning aid to developing countries "inhumane," and she attacked as "shameful" the majority party's successful effort to ban a procedure opponents call "partial birth" abortion.

Her legislative successes include the establishment of a national task force to ensure that children get proper care in the event of a terrorist attack, and a bill to increase education about the health risks of the anti-miscarriage drug DES, which has caused cancer and abnormalities in the children of some women who took the drug.

While working on national issues, Slaughter also carefully tends to the interests of major employers in her district, including Eastman Kodak and Xerox. Slaughter also remains involved in the district's fight to win more frequent and less expensive airline service. She helped lure low-cost carrier JetBlue to Rochester in 2000 and AirTran Airways in 2002. In 2005, she was gearing up to fight a proposal to eliminate airport tower service between midnight and 5 a.m. at Greater Rochester International Airport.

Slaughter moved to New York in the 1950s, when her husband went to work as an executive with a local corporation. Her first brush with public policy came in 1971 when she joined with some neighbors to try to save a stand of trees from development. "I thought in my best Kentucky fashion that if I would put on my best dress and go and be very nice and polite and ask them to save this forest that they would say, 'Well, why not?'" she later told the Associated Press. "And they just handed me my hat."

The episode sparked an interest in politics. She served as a Monroe County legislator and as an assistant to Mario Cuomo, then New York's secretary of state. In 1982, she ousted a Republican incumbent to move to the state Assembly, where she served four years before winning her seat in the House with 51 percent of the vote against conservative first-term Republican Fred J. Eckert. Actor Richard Gere, with whom she shared an interest in Central American issues, campaigned door-to-door with her. (They are friends still; he headlined a 2002 fundraiser for her.)

Not until 1998, in her seventh House election, did Slaughter begin to draw better than 60 percent. Reapportionment after the 2000 census cost New York two House seats, and the state legislature placed Slaughter in the same district as 14-term Democrat John J. LaFalce. When efforts to alter the remap failed, LaFalce retired rather than face Slaughter in a primary. She won by 25 percentage points in November and quickly began cultivating new parts of her district in Buffalo and in Niagara Falls. She won by 48 points in 2004.

KEY VOTES

2004

Yes Extend federal unemployment benefits by 13 weeks

Yes Pass $283.2 billion, six-year federal highway and mass transit bill

Yes Approve $146 billion multi-year extension of previously enacted middle-class tax breaks

No Amend the Constitution to prohibit same-sex marriage

? Cut corporate taxes $137 billion over 10 years

Yes Reorganize U.S. intelligence agencies as proposed by Sept. 11 commission

2003

No Cut taxes by $330 billion through fiscal 2013

Yes Block Bush rule scaling back overtime pay for some white-collar federal workers

Yes Do not allow use of search warrants without first notifying subjects

Yes Allow importation of prescription drugs

No Create private school voucher program in Washington, D.C.

No Ban "partial birth" abortion except to save a woman's life

Yes Split $18.6 billion in Iraq aid into half-grant, half-loan

No Overhaul Medicare and create prescription drug benefit

CQ VOTE STUDIES

	PARTY UNITY		PRESIDENTIAL SUPPORT	
	Support	Oppose	Support	Oppose
2004	98%	2%	24%	76%
2003	98%	2%	11%	89%
2002	98%	2%	16%	84%
2001	96%	4%	29%	71%
2000	96%	4%	87%	13%

INTEREST GROUPS

	AFL-CIO	ADA	CCUS	ACU
2004	100%	95%	44%	0%
2003	100%	100%	27%	12%
2002	100%	100%	22%	0%
2001	100%	95%	35%	0%
2000	100%	90%	38%	4%

NEW YORK 28

Northwest — Rochester, part of Buffalo

A small strip of land along the shore of Lake Ontario serves as a connector for the ends — Buffalo and Rochester — of the telephone receiver-shaped 28th. The old Rochester-based 28th and Buffalo-based 29th were merged during redistricting following the 2000 census to create one district that encompasses the northeastern portion of Buffalo, all of Niagara Falls and almost all of Rochester, giving the new 28th most of the Democratic-rich voting areas in western New York.

Blacks make up 29 percent of the population, and minorities combined total 38 percent, giving the 28th a far higher proportion of minority residents than any other New York district north of Westchester County.

While manufacturing powered by the Niagara River long has been the base of Buffalo's economy, Rochester has been a technology center. Both cities are trying to recover from economic decline in the 1990s.

Optic and imaging manufacturing firms drive Rochester's economy, joined by technology start-up companies that benefit from proximity to the area's major corporations, Eastman Kodak and Xerox Corp., and academic institutions.

Rochester suffered from high unemployment during the 1990s, but the situation has improved. While much of the slack in the manufacturing sector has been picked up by the service industries, the lower salaries have exacerbated the problems of Rochester's low-income residents.

Unlike many northeastern cities with blue-collar bases, the Rochester area long held to a moderate Republican tradition typical of upstate New York. But it has begun to lean the other way. Both the old 28th and old 29th supported Democratic presidential candidates in 1992, 1996 and 2000. Al Gore won the new district by 30 percentage points in 2000, and John Kerry took 62 percent of the vote in the 2004 presidential election.

MAJOR INDUSTRY
Service, manufacturing, tourism

CITIES
Rochester (pt.), 219,729; Buffalo (pt.), 129,469; Niagara Falls, 55,593

NOTABLE
About 50,000 honeymooners visit Niagara Falls each year; The Rochester home of women's rights activist Susan B. Anthony is now a museum.

Rep. John R. 'Randy' Kuhl Jr. (R)

Elected 2004; 1st term

CAPITOL OFFICE
225-3161
www.house.gov/kuhl
1505 Longworth 20515-3229; fax 225-5574

COMMITTEES
Agriculture
Education & Workforce
Transportation & Infrastructure

HOMETOWN
Hammondsport

BORN
April 19, 1943, Bath, N.Y.

RELIGION
Episcopalian

FAMILY
Divorced; three children

EDUCATION
Union College, B.S. 1966 (civil engineering);
Syracuse U., J.D. 1969

CAREER
Lawyer

POLITICAL HIGHLIGHTS
N.Y. Assembly, 1981-87; N.Y. Senate, 1987-2004

ELECTION RESULTS

2004 GENERAL

John R. "Randy" Kuhl Jr. (R)	136,883	50.7%
Samara Barend (D, WFM)	110,241	40.8%
Mark W. Assini (C)	17,272	6.4%
John Ciampoli (INDC)	5,819	2.2%

2004 PRIMARY

John R. "Randy" Kuhl Jr. (R)	25,552	64.0%
Mark W. Assini (R)	13,303	33.3%
write-ins	1,074	2.7%

Sworn into Congress as a 61-year-old freshman, Kuhl is one of the oldest and most legislatively experienced members of the Class of 2004, with 24 years in the state legislature, including 18 in the state Senate, on his résumé.

Kuhl's freshman-term committee assignments — Transportation and Infrastructure, Education and Workforce, and Agriculture — replicate his state-level experience to a remarkable degree. He chaired analogous committees at different points of his state legislative career.

Kuhl (KOOL) says his top priority on Capitol Hill is local job creation in a district where employment options have narrowed recently: The region's two largest employers, Corning Inc. and Eastman Kodak Co., have reduced payrolls.

He also hopes to cement his reputation for constituent service, and perhaps make his political future more secure, by holding a town hall meeting each year in each of the 143 towns that dot the 5,600 square miles he represents.

Kuhl is more conservative than his predecessor, Amo Houghton, a prominent moderate who co-founded the Republican Main Street Partnership. Kuhl voted against abortion rights, gun control and tax increases as a state lawmaker.

Nevertheless, Houghton, who retired after nine terms, strongly endorsed Kuhl, giving him a centrist image. And, with support from organized labor — which viewed him as one of the friendlier Republicans in the state Senate and saw chances for a Democratic victory in the GOP-tilting 29th District as highly unlikely — Kuhl established himself early on as the front-runner in the 2004 race.

He fended off a challenge from the right in the GOP primary and was never seriously threatened in the general election. But the outcome was closer than expected: He defeated Samara Barend, a Democratic first-time candidate, by just 10 percentage points, largely because he was bruised by the release of information from his previously sealed divorce documents.

NEW YORK 29
Southern Tier – Elmira, Corning; Rochester suburbs

The 29th blankets much of the southwestern portion of New York known as the Southern Tier, encompassing a mix of forests, lakes, farms and small towns. It also reaches north to take in Rochester suburbs.

The district has a large presence of blue-collar workers and is home to diverse manufacturing interests including glassware, furniture and diesel engines. Agriculture also helps drive the economy, mostly through dairy farms and wineries. The Finger Lakes and surrounding parks draw thousands of visitors annually. Like much of the upstate region, the district's population was stagnant in the 1990s, with four counties losing population and the other four registering single-digit growth.

The 29th curls north and west to take in southern parts of Monroe County outside Rochester, where a plurality of the district's residents live. It wraps around the west, south and east sides of the city, taking in mostly GOP-leaning towns such as Chili, Pittsford and Perinton.

The 29th's westernmost point is Cattaraugus County, a rural area that includes Allegany State Park and St. Bonaventure University. To the east, the GOP holds a better than 2-to-1 registration advantage over Democrats in Allegany, Steuben and Yates counties. Steuben County contains Corning, one of the better-known U.S. company towns due to its glass products and costly crystal pieces.

Republicans hold an edge over Democrats in voter registration, and George W. Bush had his best showing in the state here in both the 2000 and 2004 presidential elections. The 29th also has the lowest percentage of Hispanic residents in any New York district.

MAJOR INDUSTRY
Agriculture, manufacturing, tourism

CITIES
Elmira, 30,940; Brighton (pt.), 25,869

NOTABLE
The Corning Museum of Glass is a major tourist attraction.

NORTH CAROLINA

Gov. Michael F. Easley (D)

First elected: 2000
Length of term: 4 years
Term expires: 1/09
Salary: $121,391
Phone: (919) 733-4240

Hometown: Rocky Mount
Born: March 23, 1950; Nash County, N.C.
Religion: Roman Catholic
Family: Wife, Mary Easley; one child
Education: U. of North Carolina, B.A. 1972 (political science); North Carolina Central U., J.D. 1976
Career: Lawyer
Political highlights: Brunswick, Bladen and Columbus County district attorney, 1982-92; sought Democratic nomination for U.S. Senate, 1990; N.C. attorney general, 1993-2001

Election results:
2004 GENERAL

Michael F. Easley (D)	1,939,154	55.6%
Patrick J. Ballantine (R)	1,495,021	42.9%
Barbara J. Howe (LIBERT)	52,513	1.5%

Lt. Gov. Beverly Perdue (D)

First elected: 2000
Length of term: 4 years
Term expires: 1/09
Salary: $107,000
Phone: (919) 733-7350

STATE LEGISLATURE

General Assembly: January-June

House: 120 members, 2-year terms
2005 breakdown: 63D, 57R; 88 men, 32 women
Salary: $13,951; $104/day in session
Phone: (919) 733-4111

Senate: 50 members, 2-year terms
2005 breakdown: 29D, 21R; 42 men, 8 women
Salary: $13,951; $104/day in session
Phone: (919) 733-4111

STATE TERM LIMITS

Governor: 2 consecutive terms
House: No
Senate: No

URBAN STATISTICS

CITY	POPULATION
Charlotte	540,828
Raleigh	276,093
Greensboro	223,891
Durham	187,035
Winston-Salem	185,776

REGISTERED VOTERS

Democrat	47%
Republican	34%
Unaffiliated	19%

POPULATION

2004 population (est.)	8,541,221
2000 population	8,049,313
1990 population	6,628,637
Percent change (1990-2000)	+21.4%
Rank among states (2004)	11

Median age	35.3
Born in state	63%
Foreign born	5.3%
Violent crime rate	498/100,000
Poverty level	12.3%
Federal workers	60,331
Military	118,281

REDISTRICTING

North Carolina gained one House seat in reapportionment. The state legislature drew a new 13-district map. The governor had no role in the process and the map was enacted on Dec. 5, 2001.

MISCELLANEOUS

Web: www.ncgov.com
Capital: Raleigh
STATE ELECTION OFFICIAL
(919) 733-7173
DEMOCRATIC HEADQUARTERS
(919) 821-2777
REPUBLICAN HEADQUARTERS
(919) 828-6423

District Statistics

DIST.	2004 VOTE FOR PRESIDENT BUSH	KERRY	WHITE	BLACK	ASIAN	HISP	MEDIAN INCOME	WHITE COLLAR	BLUE COLLAR	SERVICE INDUSTRY	OVER 64	UNDER 18	COLLEGE EDUCATION	RURAL	SQ. MILES
1	43%	57%	44%	50%	0%	3%	$28,410	46%	37%	18%	14%	26%	12%	52%	7,199
2	55	45	59	30	1	8	$36,510	52	34	14	10	26	16	50	3,956
3	68	32	76	17	1	4	$37,510	56	29	15	12	24	20	47	6,192
4	44	55	69	21	4	5	$53,847	75	14	11	8	25	48	17	1,253
5	67	33	88	7	1	4	$39,710	54	34	12	13	23	20	57	4,402
6	69	30	85	9	1	4	$43,503	56	33	11	14	24	23	48	2,944
7	56	44	63	23	0	4	$33,998	50	34	16	13	25	18	55	6,087
8	54	45	62	27	2	7	$38,390	53	33	14	11	26	18	31	3,283
9	63	36	83	10	2	4	$55,059	69	20	10	10	25	36	16	991
10	67	33	85	9	1	3	$37,649	45	42	12	13	24	14	50	3,302
11	57	43	90	5	0	3	$34,720	52	32	16	18	21	21	56	6,025
12	37	63	45	45	2	7	$35,775	52	32	16	11	26	19	11	821
13	47	53	63	27	2	6	$41,060	60	26	13	11	23	27	26	2,256
STATE	56	44	70	21	1	5	$39,184	56	31	14	12	24	23	40	48,711
U.S.	50.7	48.3	69	12	4	13	$41,994	60	25	15	12	26	24	21	3,537,438

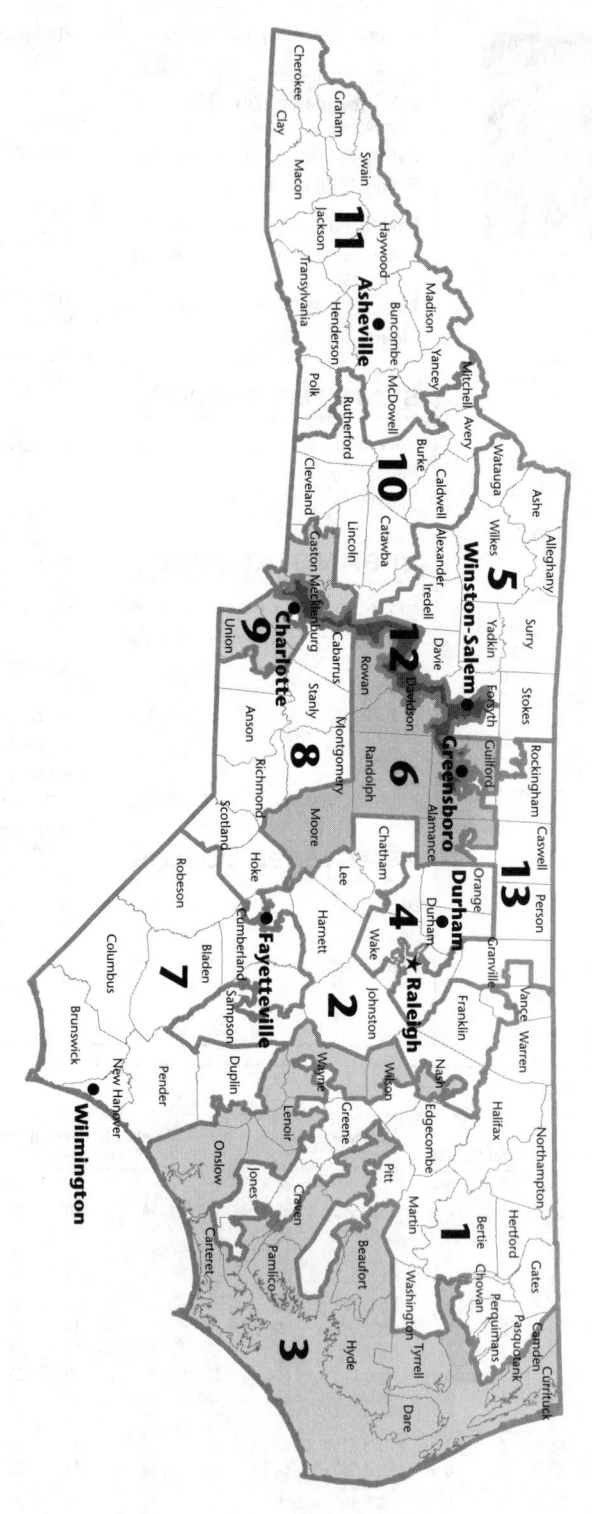

Sen. Elizabeth Dole (R)

Elected 2002; 1st term

CAPITOL OFFICE
224-6342
dole.senate.gov
555 Dirksen 20510-3301; fax 224-1100

COMMITTEES
Armed Services
Banking, Housing & Urban Affairs
Special Aging

HOMETOWN
Salisbury

BORN
July 29, 1936, Salisbury, N.C.

RELIGION
Presbyterian

FAMILY
Husband, Bob Dole

EDUCATION
Duke U., B.A. 1958 (political science); Harvard U., M.A. 1960 (education & government), J.D. 1965

CAREER
American Red Cross president; lawyer; White House aide

POLITICAL HIGHLIGHTS
Federal Trade Commission, 1973-79; Transportation secretary, 1983-87; Labor secretary, 1989-90; sought Republican nomination for president, 2000

ELECTION RESULTS

2002 GENERAL

Elizabeth Dole (R)	1,248,664	53.6%
Erskine Bowles (D)	1,047,983	45.0%
Sean Haugh (LIBERT)	33,807	1.5%

2002 PRIMARY

Elizabeth Dole (R)	342,631	80.4%
Jim Snyder (R)	60,477	14.2%
Jim Parker (R)	8,752	2.1%
Ada M. Fisher (R)	6,045	1.4%

Although she does not promote herself as a feminist, Dole is a pioneer among women and boasts one of the strongest résumés in politics. She worked in the administrations of six presidents and is talked about as a potential Republican nominee for president in the future. Dole beat a strong Democratic opponent to win her Senate seat in 2002.

Engaging and oozing Southern charm, she brings a more politically temperate tone to the Senate than did her five-term predecessor, conservative Republican firebrand Jesse Helms. And she has settled smoothly into a place she already knew well as the wife of Majority Leader Bob Dole of Kansas, the 1996 Republican nominee for president.

Senate GOP leaders in 2005 named her chairwoman of the National Republican Senatorial Committee, the party's main fundraising arm in the Senate and a first step on the leadership ladder. With her skill at raising money, her ability to attract female candidates, and her appeal as a headliner, she defeated Norm Coleman of Minnesota by one vote, 28-27.

President Bush is also aware of her ability to attract attention. He took Dole on his initial tours around the country to rally support for his proposed overhaul of Social Security. Dole was among the earliest high-profile figures in the party to embrace private Social Security accounts, standing by it even when she came under fire in her tough 2002 Senate campaign against Democrat Erskine Bowles, once an adviser to President Clinton. Dole famously replied to attacks from Bowles by holding up a blank piece of paper, saying Bowles had no plan.

Dole was featured at the 2004 Republican convention, and had spoken at previous conventions in 1984, 1996 and 2000. In 1996, she introduced her husband, when he was running for president against Clinton.

Even an underarm deodorant company has tried to capitalize on Dole's appeal. The Women's Museum of Dallas in 2004 joined with the maker of Arrid Total deodorant to honor Dole and four other women in an event that they called "Arrid Total Women of Today."

She has been married to Bob Dole since 1975, and lived most of the intervening years in the nation's capital. She twice headed a Cabinet agency, was president of the American Red Cross for eight years, and was a potential presidential candidate in 2000.

If she has a political flaw, it is that she sometimes comes across in a crowd as a creature of Washington, with a certain stiffness and formality perhaps appropriate for a Georgetown dinner, but less of a selling point at a North Carolina community barbecue. Her fans say she is polished, but others in the party complain that as a messenger for Republican policy proposals, she is too scripted.

On the Senate floor, Dole is often methodical and chooses her words carefully, but seems to have relaxed enough to stray occasionally from prepared remarks. On her visits to the state, she has adopted a folksy tone that has helped working-class voters warm to her. She holds constituent events and makes a point of traveling to each of the state's 100 counties.

She has done her duty as a freshman to familiarize herself with parochial issues, and to defend her state's interests when necessary. As soon as she got to Congress, Dole secured a seat on the Armed Services Committee, a pivotal position for a state with several military bases. And she's on the Banking Committee as well, which is a good match with Charlotte's interests as a regional financial center.

Though she has backed the Bush administration's pro-trade agenda, including giving him expanded powers to negotiate trade deals, she had bashed China for denying North Carolina workers a "level playing field" in international trade. "Many of North Carolina's economic woes related to manufacturing can be summed up in one word," Dole says in her speeches back home. "One word. And I know you know what it is: China."

She favors making the president's tax cuts permanent, saying that cutting taxes and reducing regulation on business will help lower the state's higher-than-average unemployment and the decline of the once-thriving textile industry. On most issues, Dole toes the Republican line. She supported her party 96 percent of the time on major issues in the 108th Congress. She also supported the military intervention in Iraq.

After graduating from Harvard Law School, Dole began her Washington career as a consumer affairs aide to President Johnson and then to President Nixon. She then served as a member of the Federal Trade Commission under Presidents Ford and Carter and as assistant for public liaison in the Reagan administration. Originally a Democrat, she switched her party affiliation when she married Dole.

In February 1983, she became the first woman to serve as secretary of the Transportation Department. In January 1989, she was sworn in as secretary of the Labor Department under the first President Bush. She did not enter the private sector until 1991, when she became president of the American Red Cross.

Though she was regarded in the run-up to 2000 as the first woman to make a serious bid for the presidency, critics derided her campaign appearances as overly controlled and said she was unable to connect well with voters. She abandoned her campaign in October 1999, before a single primary or caucus was held, citing the overwhelming fundraising advantage that party front-runner George W. Bush had established. But her name crops up on most lists of potential candidates for the Republican nomination in 2008, when Bush leaves office.

Dole had not lived in North Carolina since she graduated from Duke University in 1958, and in the 2002 Senate campaign some opponents tried to portray her as a Washington insider and a carpetbagger. But this criticism was blunted by the fact that Democratic nominee Bowles' main political credential also meant that he had spent his recent years elsewhere, as chief of staff to Clinton.

Despite her reliably Republican rhetoric, Dole often had to walk a fine line between emphasizing her GOP credentials and trying not to alienate middle-of-the-road voters and conservative Democrats.

One case in point was her position on the Family and Medical Leave Act, which guarantees workers time off to attend to major personal matters. Though she opposed the measure when Clinton signed it into law in 1993 and when she ran for president in 1999, she said in 2002 that it had proven itself over 10 years and that she would like to see it expanded.

Dole benefited from having only minor opposition in the September 2002 Republican primary, while Bowles had serious opposition for the Democratic nomination. That allowed Dole to spend the summer touring the state and accruing almost universally positive publicity, especially from many small newspapers that published adoring accounts of her visits to their towns.

Rural voters had much to do with her impressive 9 percentage point win over Bowles, as did the strong early endorsement she received from former political rival Bush. Her 53.6 percent vote tally was the highest percentage any North Carolina Senate candidate had received since 1978.

KEY VOTES

2004
Yes Pass $318.9 billion, six-year highway and mass transit bill
No Extend assault weapons ban for 10 years
No Restore pay-as-you-go rules for new tax cuts and entitlement spending
Yes Criminalize harm to a fetus in an attack on the mother
Yes Increase mandatory child care funding to states by $6 billion over five years
Yes Amend the Constitution to prohibit same-sex marriage
Yes Approve $146 billion multi-year extension of previously enacted middle-class tax breaks
Yes Reorganize U.S. intelligence agencies as proposed by Sept. 11 commission
Yes Cut corporate taxes $137 billion over 10 years

2003
No Delay Bush changes to Clean Air Act
Yes Allow confirmation vote on Miguel A. Estrada to the U.S. Court of Appeals for the D.C. Circuit
No Block a Bush proposal opening Alaska's Arctic National Wildlife Refuge to oil drilling
No Limit size of Bush's proposed tax cut to $350 billion through fiscal 2013
Yes Overhaul Medicare and create prescription drug benefit
No Block Bush rule scaling back overtime pay for some white-collar federal workers
No Split $20 billion in Iraq aid into half-grant, half-loan
Yes Ban "partial birth" abortion except to save a woman's life
Yes Stop proposal allowing travel to Cuba
Yes Allow final vote on energy policy overhaul

CQ VOTE STUDIES

	PARTY UNITY		PRESIDENTIAL SUPPORT	
	Support	Oppose	Support	Oppose
2004	94%	6%	92%	8%
2003	96%	4%	98%	2%

INTEREST GROUPS

	AFL-CIO	ADA	CCUS	ACU
2004	33%	25%	100%	92%
2003	8%	15%	91%	80%

Sen. Richard M. Burr (R)

Elected 2004; 1st term

CAPITOL OFFICE
224-3154
burr.senate.gov
217 Russell 20510-3306; fax 228-1374

COMMITTEES
Energy & Natural Resources
Health, Education, Labor & Pensions
(Bioterrorism & Public Health Preparedness -
chairman)
Indian Affairs
Veterans' Affairs

HOMETOWN
Winston-Salem

BORN
Nov. 30, 1955, Charlottesville, Va.

RELIGION
Methodist

FAMILY
Wife, Brooke Burr; two children

EDUCATION
Wake Forest U., B.A. 1978 (communications)

CAREER
Marketing manager; kitchen appliance salesman

POLITICAL HIGHLIGHTS
Republican nominee for U.S. House, 1992; U.S.
House, 1995-2005

ELECTION RESULTS

2004 GENERAL

Richard M. Burr (R)	1,791,450	51.6%
Erskine Bowles (D)	1,632,527	47.0%
Tom Bailey (LIBERT)	47,743	1.4%

2004 PRIMARY

Richard M. Burr (R)	302,319	87.9%
John Ross Hendrix (R)	25,971	7.6%
Albert Lee Wiley Jr. (R)	15,585	4.5%

PREVIOUS WINNING PERCENTAGES
2002 House Election (70%); 2000 House Election
(93%); 1998 House Election (68%); 1996 House Election (62%); 1994 House Election (57%)

After a decade in the House, Burr brings a record on energy, health care and telecommunications to the Senate, but it's his easygoing style that has made him a trusted Bush administration ally and a go-to player for Republican leaders. The college football-playing son of a Presbyterian minister likes to chauffeur himself and roll up his sleeves for jobs such as scooping ice cream on the campaign trail. He rarely misses a chance to squeeze in a golf game between committee meetings.

Far from being a legislative lightweight, he has seats on the powerful Energy and Natural Resources and Health, Education, Labor and Pensions committees. On the latter panel, he is the chairman of the Bioterrorism and Public Health Preparedness Subcommittee.

The former appliance salesman has a flair for translating complex policy issues into easy-to-understand terms. He played a prominent role in winning passage in 1997 of legislation to speed Food and Drug Administration approval of new drugs and medical devices, such as pacemakers. During his three-year push to pass the bill, Burr kept in his back pocket a Sensor Pad, a lubricated polyurethane pad designed to help women with breast self-exams that took 12 years to win FDA approval. "It probably displayed more than anything else I could find the lack of common sense in the federal government," Burr told the Winston-Salem Journal.

Although Burr is every bit as conservative as others in the GOP Class of 1994, his patience and pragmatism in molding the FDA bill to facilitate congressional and presidential backing showed that he was more interested in legislating than some of his classmates, who styled themselves "revolutionaries" and insisted on adhering to their core conservative principles rather than compromising.

Burr came to Congress promising to balance the federal budget at a time of large annual deficits in the mid-1990s. But in 1997, when he got the chance to vote on a major budget bill that balanced the budget in part with steep spending cuts, Burr was among the small group of Republicans who voted against the legislation. He said he worried that the bill cut too much from government health care programs.

Burr concentrated his efforts in the House on holding down the growth of prescription drug prices, improving rural health care, and enhancing food safety warnings and biomedical research, as well as on trying to stem the defection of teachers and nurses from their professions into higher-paying high-tech jobs. In the House, he worked on those issues on the Energy and Commerce Committee as the hand-picked jack-of-all-trades lieutenant of Chairman Billy Tauzin, a powerful Louisiana Republican.

He worked with other Republicans to develop a proposal to curb the high cost of prescription drugs for Medicare beneficiaries, declaring that younger generations had an obligation to help seniors finance their medical needs.

After the Sept. 11, 2001, terrorist attacks, Burr, as the chairman of an Intelligence subcommittee on bioterrorism, was a chief negotiator on legislation enacted in 2002 to strengthen the nation's defenses against a biological or chemical attack.

His deep involvement in health care issues is driven in part by a desire to watch out for his state's medical technology, medical education and pharmaceutical industries. North Carolina has been trying for more than a decade to convert its economic base from the old mainstays of tobacco, textiles and furniture to the high-tech and financial industries now clustered around the state's two metropolises, Raleigh and Charlotte. Burr faces a challenge in helping to nurture the new economy while struggling to ensure that U.S. trade policies protect the old.

His hometown is Winston-Salem, home to the R.J. Reynolds Tobacco Co. Burr defends the interests not only of cigarette manufacturers but of the state's farmers who depend on tobacco for their livelihood. During his Senate campaign, Burr touted his role in winning passage of a tobacco buy-out measure in 2004 that steered $3.8 billion to state tobacco farmers, while fighting off FDA regulation opposed by the industry.

Burr says the right approach to tobacco's financial woes is to increase government assistance for tobacco exports and to help tobacco farmers transition out of the business. Burr quit smoking cigarettes in 1998 after making a televised vow to do so.

He also watches out for the textile industry, a vital part of his state's economy. However, Burr did support legislation in 2002 to give the president fast-track authority to negotiate trade agreements that Congress may not amend. But he has consistently opposed expanding trade with China. And while he said at the time of its approval that he supported the North American Free Trade Agreement — which passed before he came to Congress — Burr reversed his stance the day he filed to run for the open 2004 Senate seat, saying the trade pact had been a mistake. Then he attacked his Democratic opponent, Erskine Bowles, once a chief of staff to President Clinton, for his role in pushing the trade pact.

Encouraged by a number of Republicans back home to run for governor in 2000, Burr took a pass. The governor's job was too administrative, he said, for someone who still gets goose bumps when he sees the illuminated Capitol dome as he flies into Washington at night. He considered a Senate run in 2002, but deferred to Elizabeth Dole, the former Cabinet secretary and wife of 1996 GOP presidential contender Bob Dole. Elizabeth Dole went on to win the seat and is now the state's senior senator.

Burr began preparing to run for Democrat John Edwards' Senate seat more than a year in advance of the 2004 election, a rarity for the spontaneity-loving Burr. In the past, his career had been driven by spur-of-the-moment decisions. In 1991, Burr surprised his wife by coming home one day from his job as a kitchen appliance salesman and announcing he wanted to run for Congress. Burr recalls, "I'd never been active politically, and I certainly didn't even know how much a congressman made."

He lost that race against Democrat Stephen L. Neal in 1992, but garnered 46 percent of the vote. After a stint as co-chairman of North Carolina Taxpayers United, and angered by the 1993 congressional vote to raise taxes, he was back in 1994. Neal decided to retire, and Burr won with 57 percent against state Sen. A.P. "Sandy" Sands, Burr's closest House election.

Burr weathered criticism for an initially lackluster Senate campaign in 2004, believing, with trademark self-assuredness, that his legislative record would earn him a following. Campaign visits from President Bush, whose coattails were particularly long in North Carolina, did not hurt. Burr won with 52 percent of the vote to Bowles' 47 percent.

Born in Virginia, Burr moved to Winston-Salem when he was 6. His father was a Presbyterian minister. He played football at Wake Forest University and then went into sales, pushing Amana by day and teaching housewives how to cook with their newfangled microwave ovens at night.

Burr says he loves to campaign for re-election. One technique he favors is a periodic "take this job and try it" program, in which he asks constituents to invite him to work alongside them in their jobs. He's flipped hamburgers, delivered parcels and observed open-heart surgery.

KEY VOTES

House Service:
2004
Yes Extend federal unemployment benefits by 13 weeks

Yes Pass $283.2 billion, six-year federal highway and mass transit bill

Yes Approve $146 billion multi-year extension of previously enacted middle-class tax breaks

Yes Amend the Constitution to prohibit same-sex marriage

Yes Cut corporate taxes $137 billion over 10 years

? Reorganize U.S. intelligence agencies as proposed by Sept. 11 commission

2003
Yes Cut taxes by $330 billion through fiscal 2013

No Block Bush rule scaling back overtime pay for some white-collar federal workers

Yes Do not allow use of search warrants without first notifying subjects

No Allow importation of prescription drugs

? Create private school voucher program in Washington, D.C.

Yes Ban "partial birth" abortion except to save a woman's life

No Split $18.6 billion in Iraq aid into half-grant, half-loan

Yes Overhaul Medicare and create prescription drug benefit

CQ VOTE STUDIES

House Service:

	PARTY UNITY		PRESIDENTIAL SUPPORT	
	Support	Oppose	Support	Oppose
2004	92%	8%	79%	21%
2003	94%	6%	96%	4%
2002	95%	5%	92%	8%
2001	95%	5%	93%	7%
2000	92%	8%	22%	78%
1999	93%	7%	17%	83%
1998	92%	8%	24%	76%
1997	94%	6%	28%	72%
1996	96%	4%	32%	68%
1995	96%	4%	21%	79%

INTEREST GROUPS

House Service:

	AFL-CIO	ADA	CCUS	ACU
2004	33%	10%	94%	87%
2003	27%	15%	93%	84%
2002	11%	0%	100%	96%
2001	17%	10%	96%	88%
2000	10%	5%	80%	88%
1999	33%	5%	84%	87%
1998	10%	5%	82%	92%
1997	13%	10%	90%	92%
1996	9%	5%	88%	100%
1995	8%	0%	96%	88%

Rep. G.K. Butterfield (D)

CAPITOL OFFICE
225-3101
www.house.gov/butterfield
413 Cannon 20515-3301; fax 225-3354

COMMITTEES
Agriculture
Armed Services

HOMETOWN
Wilson

BORN
April 27, 1947, Wilson, N.C.

RELIGION
Baptist

FAMILY
Divorced; two children

EDUCATION
North Carolina Central U., B.A. 1971 (political science & sociology), J.D. 1974

MILITARY SERVICE
Army, 1968-70

CAREER
Lawyer; child care center owner

POLITICAL HIGHLIGHTS
Candidate for Wilson City Council, 1976; N.C. Superior Court judge, 1989-2001; N.C. Supreme Court, 2001-02; defeated for election to N.C. Supreme Court, 2002; N.C. Superior Court judge, 2003-04

ELECTION RESULTS

2004 GENERAL

G.K. Butterfield (D)	137,667	64.0%
Greg Dority (R)	77,508	36.0%

2004 SPECIAL

G.K. Butterfield (D)	48,567	71.1%
Greg Dority (R)	18,491	27.1%
Tom Eisenmenger (LIBERT)	1,201	1.8%

2004 PRIMARY

G.K. Butterfield (D)	43,257	71.5%
Samuel S. "Sam" Davis III (D)	7,577	12.5%
Christine L. Fitch (D)	4,301	7.1%
Donald "Don" Davis (D)	3,296	5.4%
Darryl Smith (D)	2,111	3.5%

Elected July 2004; 1st full term

Butterfield had been sworn in for less than a month when he found himself going toe to toe with one of the most powerful and unyielding institutions in the country, the Pentagon. The Navy chose a swath of land in his district to build an airstrip, where it planned to conduct 32,000 practice flights a year for pilots of F/A-18 Super Hornet jets.

No way, said Butterfield, who succeeded in zeroing out money for the airstrip in the House version of the defense authorization bill. He also called for an investigation into whether the Navy followed its own rules in selecting the site. His response made it clear that he will be a fierce advocate for the poorest and most heavily black district in North Carolina.

Butterfield is now in a better position to take up the cause: He was appointed in the 109th Congress to a seat on the Armed Services Committee.

The former state judge was also leading in 2005 an effort to push the Federal Communications Commission and the Bush administration to move more slowly toward an all-digital cable television system. Although a huge step technologically, such a system requires a change in cable equipment that could cost customers $250 each. "Unfortunately, in poor rural places like eastern North Carolina, this could leave a lot of people in the dark when it comes to watching television," said Butterfield, who won a special election in July 2004 to fill the seat of Democratic Rep. Frank W. Ballance Jr., who retired because of illness.

The district claims more tobacco farmers than any other in the country, and Butterfield was given a seat on the Agriculture Committee upon his arrival in Congress. He was an advocate of the buyout program for tobacco farmers that passed in late 2004. His office immediately got busy helping constituents figure out how to apply for the aid. His Web site routinely posted updates about a court battle affecting the amount farmers ultimately receive.

Butterfield also jumped into an important local issue after more than 300 retirees in his district lost their savings to a Rocky Mount businessman, whose license to sell securities had expired three years earlier. Butterfield asked the FBI to take on the case.

In his district's fight with the Pentagon, residents and environmentalists have had some successes in challenging the project in federal court — the proposed site is near a wildlife refuge that is the winter home to tens of thousands of migratory birds. Several small towns also are nearby. Opponents charged in court that Navy officials pushed for the site despite internal concerns over its environmental impact.

After Butterfield succeeded in getting the proposal, called the "Outlying Landing Field," dropped from the House defense bill, he had to settle for a compromise. The final version of the 2005 bill, agreed to by the House and Senate, set aside $30 million, a third of what the Pentagon sought and what the Senate had approved in its version of the bill.

Butterfield's political education began in the 1950s. His namesake father, George Kenneth Butterfield, won a city council seat in their small hometown of Wilson. His father was just the fourth African-American to hold political office in the state since Reconstruction. But in 1957, when his family was vacationing in New York, town officials replaced ward-by-ward elections — which had allowed the elder Butterfield to win among a black-majority constituency — with at-large elections. That eliminated chances for Butterfield's father or any other black candidate to succeed.

"I saw how the political system was manipulated to obtain an unfair result," he said. "Having seen that injustice has made me want to be involved politically."

His path to the House was smoothed by connections he started making more than three decades ago, when he served as a foot soldier for blacks seeking political equality in North Carolina. In college, he volunteered to manage a voter registration drive for the 1968 congressional bid of Eva Clayton, a well-known community activist. She lost the Democratic nomination, but a quarter-century later she became one of the first African-Americans elected to Congress from the state since Reconstruction.

Butterfield failed in his own city council bid in 1976. But he won election as a Superior Court judge in 1988 and held that job until Democratic Gov. Michael F. Easley elevated him to the state Supreme Court in 2001. After Butterfield lost a bid in 2002 for election to that seat in his own right, Easley reinstated him on the lower court.

Butterfield was a good friend of another young, ambitious eastern North Carolina black politician, Ballance, who gave Butterfield his first job after law school, in a firm he ran with Clayton's husband. Ballance succeeded Clayton when she retired from the House in 2002.

Party officials easily tapped Butterfield as the successor when Ballance announced he would retire in 2004 because of declining health. Butterfield defeated Republican Greg Dority in the July 20 special election by 44 percentage points in the decidedly Democratic district. His margin fell to 28 points in a repeat match-up for a full term in November, when more than three times as many people voted because of the presidential race.

Within months of arriving in Congress, Butterfield found himself involved in one of the biggest parochial battles, not at home, but in the nation's capital — what to name the new major league team that brought baseball back to Washington in 2005 after an absence of 35 years.

Traditionalists favored the old name, the Senators. But that was nixed by city officials, who wanted nothing to do with the name because the city has no voting representative in Congress, a sore spot with city residents and leaders. Democratic Mayor Anthony A. Williams suggested the Washington Grays, after the Homestead Grays, a Negro League team that played in Washington during the 1940s.

Butterfield liked the idea, and circulated a letter to fellow House members and to baseball and team officials urging them to adopt the name. The Grays' star slugger and first baseman, Buck Leonard, grew up in his district, in Rocky Mount. The team ended up being called the Nationals.

KEY VOTES

2004

Yes Approve $146 billion multi-year extension of previously enacted middle-class tax breaks

No Amend the Constitution to prohibit same-sex marriage

Yes Cut corporate taxes $137 billion over 10 years

Yes Reorganize U.S. intelligence agencies as proposed by Sept. 11 commission

CQ VOTE STUDIES

	PARTY UNITY		PRESIDENTIAL SUPPORT	
	Support	Oppose	Support	Oppose
2004	87%	13%	27%	73%

INTEREST GROUPS

	AFL-CIO	ADA	CCUS	ACU
2004	—	35%	57%	0%

NORTH CAROLINA 1

Northeast – parts of Goldsboro, Rocky Mount and Greenville

Situated among the tobacco fields and Baptist churches of eastern North Carolina, the 1st is a poor, rural Democratic stronghold. It has the lowest education and income levels of any North Carolina congressional district.

The 1st, which takes in all of 13 counties and parts of 10 others, is the only black-majority district in the state — 50 percent of residents are black. The main body of the district rests along the Virginia border, with appendages winding south to take in parts of several of the region's commercial centers — Goldsboro, Greenville and Kinston. Redistricting following the 2000 census kept the 1st's basic shape intact.

The area's economy is based overwhelmingly on manufacturing and agriculture. Cotton and peanut fields prevail in the northern counties, while tobacco, hogs and poultry dominate farther south. Manufacturing, primarily of textiles and lumber products, is scattered throughout.

Registered Democrats outnumber Republicans by more than 4-to-1 in the 1st. Many white voters claim the Democratic roots of their forefathers, but often support GOP candidates at the state and national level. Republicans also find support in coastal areas such as Perquimans and Chowan counties.

But Democrats dominate overall. In the 2004 gubernatorial race, Edgecombe County was Democratic Gov. Michael F. Easley's best county, and the other four counties in Easley's top five also are in the 1st, north of Edgecombe. The district supported John Kerry by a 14 percentage point margin in the 2004 presidential election.

MAJOR INDUSTRY
Agriculture, manufacturing, health care

MILITARY BASES
Seymour Johnson Air Force Base, 6,409 military, 1,091 civilian (2003)

CITIES
Goldsboro (pt.), 36,187; Rocky Mount (pt.), 32,062; Wilson (pt.), 25,068; Greenville (pt.), 22,028

NOTABLE
Caleb Bradham started selling "Brad's Drink" in 1898 at his New Bern drug store — the beverage is now known as Pepsi Cola.

Rep. Bob Etheridge (D)

Elected 1996; 5th term

CAPITOL OFFICE
225-4531
www.house.gov/etheridge
1533 Longworth 20515-3302; fax 225-5662

COMMITTEES
Agriculture
Homeland Security

HOMETOWN
Lillington

BORN
Aug. 7, 1941, Sampson County, N.C.

RELIGION
Presbyterian

FAMILY
Wife, Faye Cameron Etheridge; three children

EDUCATION
Campbell U., B.S. 1965 (business administration)

MILITARY SERVICE
Army, 1965-67

CAREER
Hardware store owner; tobacco farmer

POLITICAL HIGHLIGHTS
Harnett County Commission, 1973-77 (chairman, 1975-77); N.C. House, 1979-87; N.C. superintendent of Public Instruction, 1989-96

ELECTION RESULTS

2004 GENERAL

Bob Etheridge (D)	145,079	62.3%
Billy J. Creech (R)	87,811	37.7%

2004 PRIMARY

Bob Etheridge (D)	unopposed

2002 GENERAL

Bob Etheridge (D)	100,121	65.4%
Joseph L. Ellen (R)	50,965	33.3%
Gary Minter (LIBERT)	2,098	1.4%

PREVIOUS WINNING PERCENTAGES
2000 (58%); 1998 (57%); 1996 (53%)

In an era of easy mobility, when many in Congress represent states or House districts far from their childhood homes, Etheridge is a proud exception. He is a native of the 2nd District, and except for a two-year stint in the military, he has lived there virtually his entire life.

His district is a dichotomy: It is home to the state capital of Raleigh and its high-tech Research Triangle Park as well as more-rural counties where family tobacco and hog farms dot the landscape. Etheridge comes from the latter part of the district. He has been a hardware store owner, a part-time tobacco farmer, a Sunday school teacher and a Boy Scout leader. And for the past three decades, he has been a politician, too — holding local, state and national office.

Etheridge is a centrist Southern Democrat who votes with the majority of his party on most issues but is a conservative on many social issues and a strong supporter of free trade. A member of the moderate, pro-business New Democrat Coalition, he supported President Bush's position 47 percent of the time in the 107th Congress and 38 percent in the 108th. It is never far from his mind that the 2nd District has voted for Republican presidential candidates in each of the last three elections. When he attacks Republicans, it is generally over issues that resonate in his district, such as GOP attempts to restrict spending for disaster relief or education.

Etheridge was the only Democrat in the North Carolina delegation voting in 2002 to give Bush fast-track trade negotiating authority, which limits Congress' role in trade agreements. North Carolina's powerful textile lobby, which fears job losses from free-trade pacts, vowed retribution at the voting booth. But the 2nd District is not so concerned with textiles. Etheridge has a strong base among tobacco farmers and other farm interests, and the Raleigh area is focused on attracting new technology firms. Etheridge has voted accordingly, and in the 108th he continued his support for free-trade agreements, backing pacts with Chile, Singapore and Australia.

He watches out for farmers from his perch on the Agriculture Committee, and was pleased when Congress in 2004 enacted a buyout for tobacco farmers as part of a corporate tax cut bill. The measure will bring $3.9 billion to farmers in North Carolina. Etheridge, a part-time tobacco farmer himself, is one of eight members of Congress who will benefit from the deal. The Environmental Working group estimated Etheridge will receive $31,000 under the plan.

Etheridge has also pressed for a trade agreement to allow tobacco farmers to export their product to China. In 2000, he voted for legislation permanently granting China normal trade relations with the United States. "Gaining access to China, the largest market in the world, will only help our state and our nation expand our economic leadership and extend our ideals of liberty, democracy and freedom to those who have been shut off from such basic rights and values for far too long," he said.

Etheridge has fought the perennial effort in the House to curtail spending on the federal price-support program for peanuts, another key crop in North Carolina. Critics of the federal peanut program say it inflates the price of peanuts at the expense of consumers. Etheridge played a key role in the 2002 farm bill overhaul of the peanut program, which replaced quotas with marketing loans, direct payments and counter-cyclical payments to provide funds when market prices fall.

Before coming to Congress, Etheridge was the top official in North

Carolina's public school system for almost eight years. He has spoken frequently and at length on the House floor of his desire to "build on what is working well in our public schools, rather than scapegoating public school principals, teachers, parents and children."

He supported Bush's No Child Left Behind Act in 2001, but filed a bill in the 108th Congress to prohibit enforcement of the mandatory testing and standards law until it was fully funded. He opposes private school tuition voucher plans that "will only divert attention away from improving public schools." He believes the federal government should devote more dollars to the repair and construction of schools. "I have seen multimillion-dollar prisons next door to crummy, crumbling, decaying public schools," Etheridge once said, "and then we have the gall to tell our children that education is important. They can see the difference in where we put our money." In the 108th and 109th Congresses, he pushed legislation to provide a $2,000 annual tax credit to teachers, principals and other staff who work in schools with high proportions of low-income pupils.

On the Science Committee in the 107th, Etheridge won approval of his bill to improve hurricane forecasting, especially for inland areas where flooding can be a serious problem. He took a leave from the Science panel in the 108th Congress when he was appointed to the Homeland Security Committee, where he continues to serve.

Born, raised and educated in east-central North Carolina, Etheridge first entered politics in 1972. He won election to the Harnett County Commission, serving for four years, the last two as chairman. In 1978, he won the first of four terms in the state House, where he rose to chair the Appropriations Committee. Then he moved to statewide office, holding the school superintendency for about eight years.

That background made Etheridge the choice of 2nd District Democrats in 1996 to take on freshman Republican David Funderburk, who had been a zealous supporter of the House GOP's conservative agenda in the 104th Congress. Following the national Democratic script, Etheridge called Funderburk a threat to entitlement programs such as Social Security, Medicare and Medicaid. Etheridge's deep local roots helped him win with 53 percent of the vote.

In 1998, conservative state Sen. Dan Page and the national GOP went after Etheridge aggressively, seeking to tie him to President Clinton and his White House sex scandal. But Etheridge had given Republicans little opportunity to tag him as a liberal, and he won by 16 percentage points. He has coasted ever since.

KEY VOTES

2004

Yes Extend federal unemployment benefits by 13 weeks

Yes Pass $283.2 billion, six-year federal highway and mass transit bill

Yes Approve $146 billion multi-year extension of previously enacted middle-class tax breaks

Yes Amend the Constitution to prohibit same-sex marriage

Yes Cut corporate taxes $137 billion over 10 years

Yes Reorganize U.S. intelligence agencies as proposed by Sept. 11 commission

2003

No Cut taxes by $330 billion through fiscal 2013

Yes Block Bush rule scaling back overtime pay for some white-collar federal workers

Yes Do not allow use of search warrants without first notifying subjects

No Allow importation of prescription drugs

No Create private school voucher program in Washington, D.C.

Yes Ban "partial birth" abortion except to save a woman's life

Yes Split $18.6 billion in Iraq aid into half-grant, half-loan

No Overhaul Medicare and create prescription drug benefit

CQ VOTE STUDIES

	PARTY UNITY		PRESIDENTIAL SUPPORT	
	Support	Oppose	Support	Oppose
2004	85%	15%	47%	53%
2003	90%	10%	33%	67%
2002	87%	13%	50%	50%
2001	83%	17%	44%	56%
2000	84%	16%	65%	35%

INTEREST GROUPS

	AFL-CIO	ADA	CCUS	ACU
2004	87%	85%	52%	20%
2003	87%	90%	47%	32%
2002	78%	80%	60%	24%
2001	92%	85%	57%	36%
2000	70%	60%	66%	28%

NORTH CAROLINA 2

Central – parts of Raleigh and Fayetteville

From the thriving state capital of Raleigh, the 2nd pinwheels east, north and south to take in several surrounding rural counties and part of Fayetteville. While the high-tech Research Triangle Park, the area's economic hub, lies in the neighboring 4th, its influence radiates through the low hills of this eastern Piedmont district.

Research Triangle techies, university academics and government employees live in Raleigh (shared with the 4th and 13th districts) and form the basis of the district's Democratic tilt. Much of the region consists of booming and increasingly urban bedroom communities such as Garner. Sprawl has begun to infiltrate surrounding counties as well, but they still rely primarily on tobacco farming (especially in Johnston and Harnett counties) and blue-collar manufacturing jobs. Redistricting after the 2000 census added a strong military presence, as the 2nd now contains Pope Air Force Base and part of Fort Bragg, located at the southwestern edge of the district.

Redistricting also lessened the 2nd's conservative lean by excising parts

of Wake and Nash counties and adding a black-majority section of Fayetteville. The 2nd contains the mostly black and strongly Democratic southeastern part of Raleigh, and has a higher percentage of Hispanic residents (8 percent) than any other district in the state. While the Democrats' 24-point district registration advantage exaggerates the party's strength — Republicans run well in areas such as Johnston County despite the Democratic edge — the GOP has a tough time here.

MAJOR INDUSTRY
State government, higher education, agriculture, manufacturing

MILITARY BASES
Fort Bragg (Army), 41,458 military, 4,431 civilian (shared with the 8th District); Pope Air Force Base, 6,381 military, 774 civilian (2004)

CITIES
Fayetteville (pt.), 49,899; Raleigh (pt.), 45,368; Fort Bragg (unincorporated), 29,183; Sanford, 23,220

NOTABLE
A highway sign outside Sanford claims that it is the brick capital of the United States; The Harnett County town of Erwin grew up around a denim plant, formerly called itself the "denim capital of the world," and still holds a fall festival called "Denim Days."

Rep. Walter B. Jones (R)

Elected 1994; 6th term

Nothing he has done during more than a decade in Congress has come close to garnering the kind of worldwide media attention Jones received for a suggestion he made in March 2003 that was promptly adopted by the House cafeteria: the renaming of french fries as "freedom fries" to protest France's refusal to support the U.S. decision to invade Iraq.

Jones doesn't usually seek or receive nearly so much publicity. He serves on three committees, but in his sixth term still holds no subcommittee gavel. He champions the interests of his eastern North Carolina district, including the protection of its popular Outer Banks beaches and its inland farms. He looks out for its military bases, including Camp Lejeune, from his post on the Armed Services Committee. And he hews to a hard conservative line on almost everything that doesn't directly benefit his district. Only a dozen Republicans bucked the president more often in the 108th Congress, and only 18 voted more often against a majority of their GOP colleagues on votes pitting the two parties against each other.

Jones spent his early adulthood following in his father's footsteps, first into the family business and then into politics. But he has charted his own course in the House, one far to the right of his father, Walter B. Jones Sr., a Democrat who died in 1992 as he was preparing to retire after 26 years in Congress. The younger Jones ran for his father's 1st District seat that year as a Democrat but lost a primary runoff to Eva Clayton. He switched parties the next year and won the neighboring 3rd District seat in 1994.

Unlike his father, a committee chairman accustomed to pragmatic, result-oriented dealings, the younger Jones is one of the few unreconstructed "true believers" of the GOP takeover Class of 1994. He still sees little virtue in compromise. In 2004, he urged fellow fiscal conservatives to form a "suicide squad" that would not vote in favor of spending increases under any circumstances, an example he had set a year earlier when he refused to vote for the GOP's Medicare prescription drug bill despite hours of leadership arm-twisting.

A member of the Republican Study Committee, the House GOP's most conservative members, Jones usually garners ratings of 95 percent or more from the American Conservative Union. (His father's annual scores were closer to 20 percent at the end of his career.)

Jones has backed measures to make English the nation's official language, to allow prayer in public schools, to provide vouchers to help parents pay for private school tuition, and to outlaw same-sex marriage. He frequently takes to the House floor to demand tax cuts and advocates a phaseout of the tax code.

He has tried since the 107th Congress to ensure that religious leaders can preach or speak from the pulpit about political candidates or topics. Jones says a little-known 1954 law means that religious leaders risk losing their tax-exempt status if they campaign for specific candidates. He wants to repeal that provision. His bill was defeated in the House in 2002, but Jones introduced it again in the 108th and 109th Congresses.

On the Armed Services Committee, Jones looks out for the military installations of the 3rd District and has written a number of bills aimed at improving pay, benefits and housing for military personnel and veterans, including one in the 106th Congress to give a $500 tax credit to military families who are eligible for food stamps. He undertook a crusade in the 106th to block a Pentagon requirement that armed forces personnel be given an

CAPITOL OFFICE
225-3415
congjones@mail.house.gov
www.house.gov/jones
422 Cannon 20515-3303; fax 225-3286

COMMITTEES
Armed Services
Financial Services
Resources

HOMETOWN
Farmville

BORN
Feb. 10, 1943, Farmville, N.C.

RELIGION
Roman Catholic

FAMILY
Wife, Joe Anne Jones; one child

EDUCATION
North Carolina State U., attended 1962-65 (history); Atlantic Christian College, B.A. 1967 (history)

MILITARY SERVICE
N.C. National Guard, 1967-71

CAREER
Lighting company executive; insurance benefits company executive; office supply company executive

POLITICAL HIGHLIGHTS
N.C. House, 1983-93 (served as a Democrat); sought Democratic nomination for U.S. House, 1992

ELECTION RESULTS

2004 GENERAL

Walter B. Jones (R)	171,863	70.7%
Roger A. Eaton (D)	71,227	29.3%

2004 PRIMARY

Walter B. Jones (R)	unopposed

2002 GENERAL

Walter B. Jones (R)	131,448	90.7%
Gary Goodson (LIBERT)	13,486	9.3%

PREVIOUS WINNING PERCENTAGES
2000 (61%); 1998 (62%); 1996 (63%); 1994 (53%)

anthrax vaccination. Citing reports casting doubt on the safety of the vaccine, Jones proposed legislation to make the vaccination voluntary.

In the 108th Congress, he sided with Democrats in urging an investigation of overcharges by Halliburton, Vice President Cheney's old company, for work performed in Iraq. "It's our responsibility to show the taxpayers whether this was an innocent mistake or contrived," he said.

Jones is a member of the Resources Committee and has joined Democrats who represent coastal districts in fighting to retain a ban on offshore oil and gas drilling. He also was involved in the decade-long battle to preserve the 1870 lighthouse at Cape Hatteras. He pushed to build a stronger seawall to protect the landmark against beach erosion, but it was eventually decided that the lighthouse should be moved.

Jones proudly cites his success in winning enactment of a 1998 law designed to preserve the wild horses of Shackleford Banks, a part of the Cape Lookout National Seashore. His measure required the National Park Service to work with a local foundation to ensure that the equine population stays above 100. In the 108th Congress and again in the 109th, he pushed a revision through the House setting a new minimum of 110 and a target population of 120 to 130 horses, saying scientific studies had shown that population range to be the optimal size to maintain the herd's long-term viability.

On most issues, Jones is a staunch fiscal conservative, often more so than his party's leaders. He voted against the popular six-year transportation authorization bill in 1998 and its successor in 2004. He also opposed the massive end-of-year catchall spending bill in 1998, criticized by conservatives for breaking spending caps agreed to in 1997.

Despite such tight-fistedness, Jones backs federal programs that are important to his district, such as the price-support program for peanut growers. He also has been vocal in protecting another important crop in his district — tobacco. During the Clinton administration, he said the Food and Drug Administration was conducting a "witch hunt" against tobacco farmers. But he was satisfied with a bailout for tobacco farmers included in the 2004 corporate tax bill that would pour billions of dollars into North Carolina without subjecting tobacco to FDA regulation.

After graduating from college in 1967, Jones became an executive with the family's office supply company, later moving on to other business ventures. It was not until he was almost 40 that he sought elective office. He started out small, winning a seat in the state House, where he served for a decade. He won his 1994 race for the House with 53 percent of the vote and has been re-elected easily ever since.

KEY VOTES

2004

Yes Extend federal unemployment benefits by 13 weeks
No   Pass $283.2 billion, six-year federal highway and mass transit bill
Yes Approve $146 billion multi-year extension of previously enacted middle-class tax breaks
Yes Amend the Constitution to prohibit same-sex marriage
Yes Cut corporate taxes $137 billion over 10 years
No   Reorganize U.S. intelligence agencies as proposed by Sept. 11 commission

2003

Yes Cut taxes by $330 billion through fiscal 2013
No   Block Bush rule scaling back overtime pay for some white-collar federal workers
Yes Do not allow use of search warrants without first notifying subjects
Yes Allow importation of prescription drugs
Yes Create private school voucher program in Washington, D.C.
Yes Ban "partial birth" abortion except to save a woman's life
Yes Split $18.6 billion in Iraq aid into half-grant, half-loan
No   Overhaul Medicare and create prescription drug benefit

CQ VOTE STUDIES

	PARTY UNITY		PRESIDENTIAL SUPPORT	
	Support	Oppose	Support	Oppose
2004	86%	14%	75%	25%
2003	86%	14%	73%	27%
2002	89%	11%	72%	28%
2001	88%	12%	78%	22%
2000	92%	8%	19%	81%

INTEREST GROUPS

	AFL-CIO	ADA	CCUS	ACU
2004	36%	30%	70%	79%
2003	33%	25%	70%	92%
2002	22%	10%	63%	96%
2001	18%	10%	80%	92%
2000	10%	5%	61%	96%

NORTH CAROLINA 3

East — Jacksonville, part of Greenville, Outer Banks

The 3rd runs along the eastern shore from the Virginia border to north of Wilmington, sweeping from the fragile barrier islands of the Outer Banks to the tobacco and peanut fields of the coastal plain. It is a large swath of rural land inlaid with waterways, affluent vacation towns and military facilities; the closest thing to skyscrapers here are historic lighthouses that dot the shoreline.

Many residents earn their living through fishing, farming and tourism. The district's military bases have a large impact on the economy, notably Camp Lejeune, which deployed a high percentage of its Marines abroad following the Sept. 11, 2001, terrorist attacks. At the southern end, two fingers of land stretch northwest, taking in turkey, hog and wheat farms.

Redistricting following the 2000 census did not significantly overhaul the district's jagged shape. One leg of the 3rd stretches from Onslow County in the south, where Jacksonville and Camp Lejeune are located, all the

way north to Nash County, including part of Rocky Mount.

The remap enhanced the 3rd's conservative bent by ceding to the 1st some northeastern counties with large black populations, even though registered Democrats still barely outnumber registered Republicans. The 3rd supports GOP candidates on the federal level, and George W. Bush took 68 percent of the vote here. The district's portions of Lenoir and Jones counties were Bush's second- and third-best counties in the state.

MAJOR INDUSTRY
Military, agriculture, tourism

MILITARY BASES
Camp Lejeune Marine Corps Base, 41,500 military, 4,861 civilian (2000); Cherry Point Marine Corps Air Station and Naval Air Depot, 8,987 military, 5,771 civilian; New River Marine Corps Air Station, 5,510 military, 376 civilian (2004)

CITIES
Jacksonville, 66,715; Greenville (pt.), 38,448; Wilson (pt.), 19,337

NOTABLE
Kitty Hawk is where Wilbur and Orville Wright made their first flight; Dare County is named for Virginia Dare, the first child born of English parents in America (1587).

Rep. David E. Price (D)

Elected 1986; 9th term
Did not serve 1995-97

A former political science professor, Price is a perfect fit for a district that is home to 11 colleges and universities, including Duke, where he once taught. The son of a high school principal father and an English teacher mother, he is a lifelong educator who has used his years in Congress to promote learning at every level.

The 4th District is home to the Raleigh-Durham-Chapel Hill Research Triangle Park, where many academics and Northern transplants have come to work. With its highly educated constituency, it is one of the South's more politically progressive districts, and on a wide range of issues Price has compiled a more liberal voting record than the typical Southern Democrat. But he carefully tempers his liberalism with the occasional vote in support of tobacco growers and other local interests. In 2004, for example, he was among the minority of Democrats who voted for a corporate tax bill that carried a $10 billion buyout for tobacco farmers.

Not surprisingly, given his personal background and district makeup, Price cites education as a top priority. "We need 2.3 million teachers in the next 10 years in this country, and I don't think we have any idea where they're coming from," Price said. In 2004, the House passed a bill containing much of his Teaching Fellows Act, legislation to provide college scholarships to students who agree to become public school teachers. In 2002, he sought to improve technical education and training programs at community colleges in a reauthorization of the Advanced Technology Education program at the National Science Foundation, which a Price-authored bill established in 1993. Earlier in his career, in 1997, Price scored a major victory when Congress passed legislation he had been advocating for several years that made interest on student loans tax deductible and permitted penalty-free withdrawals from IRAs for education expenses.

Price has used his seat on the Appropriations Committee to tend to his district's needs, securing millions of dollars of grants and support for the 4th's many research facilities, both private and public, and for more-mundane needs such as refurbishing Chapel Hill's buses and helping build a new wastewater treatment facility in Efland. As the Bush administration has sought to restrain the growth of many domestic research enterprises and shift additional funds toward defense, Price has fought to maintain research funding for non-defense purposes.

In the 108th Congress, for example, he secured more than $1.5 million for biochemical research and nursing school programs at North Carolina Central University. In 2001, he earmarked funds for a new $500,000 magnetic resonance imaging facility at Durham County Regional Hospital, $250,000 to enhance technology at rural and low-income North Carolina schools, and another $250,000 for technology grants to the North Carolina Community College System. And in 1999, he landed $49 million for an Environmental Protection Agency facility in the Research Triangle.

Price serves on the Homeland Security Appropriations Subcommittee, created in the 108th Congress. He has used that position to good effect, snagging nearly $500,000 in federal grants to help law enforcement departments in his district update their technology.

Price is more inclined than most House Democrats to support free-trade agreements. He voted for legislation in 2000 granting China permanent normal trade status, contending the measure would bolster U.S. jobs through increased exports. "Our markets are already largely open, so all the opening

CAPITOL OFFICE
225-1784
price.house.gov
2162 Rayburn 20515-3304; fax 225-2014

COMMITTEES
Appropriations

HOMETOWN
Chapel Hill

BORN
Aug. 17, 1940, Erwin, Tenn.

RELIGION
Baptist

FAMILY
Wife, Lisa Price; two children

EDUCATION
Mars Hill College, attended 1957-59; U. of North Carolina, B.A. 1961 (American history & math); Yale U., B.D. 1964 (theology), Ph.D. 1969 (political science)

CAREER
Professor

POLITICAL HIGHLIGHTS
N.C. Democratic Party chairman, 1983-84; U.S. House, 1987-95; defeated for re-election to U.S. House, 1994

ELECTION RESULTS

2004 GENERAL

David E. Price (D)	217,441	64.1%
Todd A. Batchelor (R)	121,717	35.9%

2004 PRIMARY

David E. Price (D)	unopposed

2002 GENERAL

David E. Price (D)	132,185	61.2%
Tuan A. Nguyen (R)	78,095	36.2%
Ken Nelson (LIBERT)	5,766	2.7%

PREVIOUS WINNING PERCENTAGES
2000 (62%); 1998 (57%); 1996 (54%); 1992 (65%); 1990 (58%); 1988 (58%); 1986 (56%)

is on their side," he said. Although Price joined the overwhelming majority of House Democrats in opposing 2002 legislation to grant the president fast-track trade negotiating authority, in the 108th he voted in favor of free-trade agreements with Australia, Singapore and Chile. Still, he worries about the outsourcing of white-collar jobs. "The first thing to make clear is that protectionism is not an option," he said in a 2004 speech on the subject. Instead, he said, the United States should invest more heavily in research, education, and worker training, particularly in high-tech fields.

Democratic leaders called on Price's political science background in 2001, naming him to an ad hoc committee to recommend improvements in election procedures. He also claims credit for helping to shape the truth-in-advertising provisions of the 2002 campaign finance law. In the 108th, he led an effort to increase cooperation between Congress and legislative bodies in developing nations, including such areas as staff training, information and technology access, and general promotion of "legislative transparency and accountability."

On a more partisan level, national Democratic Party leaders in December 2004 tapped Price and former Labor Secretary Alexis Herman to lead a review of the party's nominating system, including its reliance on initial Iowa and New Hampshire contests dominated by rural, white voters.

Born in East Tennessee, Price got his undergraduate degree at the University of North Carolina and then went to Yale for graduate study, earning political science and divinity degrees. While teaching political science at Duke University in the 1970s, he became heavily involved in state Democratic politics. He served as chairman of the state party in 1983 and 1984, and in 1985 became a founding member of the national Democratic Leadership Council, which sought to expand the influence of party moderates.

The contacts Price made in his party work helped him raise money and attract supporters for a successful House race in 1986. After beating out three opponents for the Democratic nomination, he ousted freshman GOP Rep. Bill Cobey by 12 percentage points. He won re-election three times by comfortable margins but lost to former Raleigh Police Chief Fred Heineman by 1,215 votes in the GOP takeover landslide of 1994.

Price avenged that defeat in the next election, waging an aggressive campaign that emphasized door-to-door canvassing and plenty of personal contact with voters. He won by almost 11 percentage points in 1996 and has prevailed easily in subsequent elections. In a district made more comfortably Democratic after reapportionment, Price won in 2002 with 61 percent, then boosted his vote share to 64 percent in 2004.

KEY VOTES

2004

Yes	Extend federal unemployment benefits by 13 weeks
Yes	Pass $283.2 billion, six-year federal highway and mass transit bill
Yes	Approve $146 billion multi-year extension of previously enacted middle-class tax breaks
No	Amend the Constitution to prohibit same-sex marriage
Yes	Cut corporate taxes $137 billion over 10 years
Yes	Reorganize U.S. intelligence agencies as proposed by Sept. 11 commission

2003

No	Cut taxes by $330 billion through fiscal 2013
Yes	Block Bush rule scaling back overtime pay for some white-collar federal workers
Yes	Do not allow use of search warrants without first notifying subjects
No	Allow importation of prescription drugs
No	Create private school voucher program in Washington, D.C.
No	Ban "partial birth" abortion except to save a woman's life
Yes	Split $18.6 billion in Iraq aid into half-grant, half-loan
No	Overhaul Medicare and create prescription drug benefit

CQ VOTE STUDIES

	PARTY UNITY		PRESIDENTIAL SUPPORT	
	Support	Oppose	Support	Oppose
2004	90%	10%	41%	59%
2003	92%	8%	25%	75%
2002	92%	8%	38%	62%
2001	88%	12%	35%	65%
2000	90%	10%	80%	20%

INTEREST GROUPS

	AFL-CIO	ADA	CCUS	ACU
2004	87%	95%	52%	12%
2003	80%	90%	43%	24%
2002	78%	95%	55%	0%
2001	100%	95%	43%	4%
2000	80%	85%	61%	4%

NORTH CAROLINA 4

Central — Durham, Chapel Hill, part of Raleigh

With more than three-fourths of the district's population living in Durham and Wake counties, to understand Research Triangle Park is to understand the 4th. The medical and technological research park was created in the 1950s by a group of academics, politicians and businessmen who saw a need to diversify the state's economy beyond the traditional tobacco and textile industries. In order to tap the brainpower of the three surrounding universities — Duke University in Durham, the University of North Carolina in Chapel Hill, and North Carolina State University in Raleigh — the park was located in the center of the triangle the schools create.

As the park grew, especially in the 1980s, the Durham of James B. Duke's Lucky Strike cigarettes largely disappeared. And as developers began converting tobacco warehouses into apartment buildings, concerns arose over quality-of-life issues. While the district leans to the left, its highly educated voters — one in five holds a post-graduate or professional degree — can be independent-minded. Democrats are boosted by the large black population in the city of Durham. Redistricting following the 2000 census made the 4th slightly more Democratic by cutting out some GOP areas in Wake County. Residents of the 4th voted narrowly for Al Gore in the 2000 presidential election, but more solidly backed John Kerry in 2004.

The new map also slimmed the shape of the 4th, which sits halfway between the ocean and the Blue Ridge Mountains. While based primarily in the Triangle, the district still passes through rolling hills of evergreen forests. But some rural territory was excised in redistricting, and the 4th has a smaller rural element than all but two North Carolina districts (the 9th and the 12th).

MAJOR INDUSTRY
Technology research, higher education

CITIES
Durham, 187,035; Cary (pt.), 83,478; Chapel Hill, 48,715; Raleigh (pt.), 38,149

NOTABLE
Home to the Durham Bulls baseball team; The 1988 movie, "Bull Durham," starring Kevin Costner, was filmed here; The nation's first state university, The University of North Carolina at Chapel Hill, was chartered in 1789 and opened to students in 1795.

Rep. Virginia Foxx (R)

Elected 2004; 1st term

Foxx brings the sensibility of a veteran state lawmaker to Congress. "Having been in the legislature for 10 years, I have some sense of decorum and process," she said. And, she notes, "I'm the eldest child of a very poor family, and I take everything I do seriously."

She also is informed by a lifetime of experience outside politics, as an educator and owner of a nursery and landscaping company. Prior to her 1994 election, at age 51, to the North Carolina Senate, Foxx's only political experience had been a dozen years on her local school board. Her House election at age 61 made her one of the elders of the Class of 2004.

Foxx received a committee assignment, Education and Workforce, that hews closely to her personal background, and another, to Agriculture, that positions her to look out for the state's tobacco industry — a key component of the economy in her 5th District, which includes part of the city of Winston-Salem. She also is on the Government Reform panel.

She is likely to follow in the ideological footsteps of her conservative Republican predecessor, five-term lawmaker Richard M. Burr, who left the seat open for a successful Senate bid. Foxx compiled a conservative voting record in the state Senate and will mainly side with her party leadership on most social and fiscal issues.

Her path to Washington was difficult: After finishing a close second in a crowded GOP primary field to qualify for the runoff, Foxx found herself pitted against Winston-Salem City Councilman Vernon L. Robinson, a black Republican whose campaign featured furious rhetoric and lacerating ads in which he accused opponents of apostasies against conservatism. Foxx nonetheless prevailed by a margin of 9 percentage points, setting up a routine general election win in the Republican stronghold.

Drawing on her campaign experience, Foxx will push for legislation that would add automated political telephone calls to the federal "do not call" list that Congress established in 2003 to restrict most telemarketers, though she would continue to permit calls made directly by campaign workers.

CAPITOL OFFICE
225-2071
www.house.gov/foxx
503 Cannon 20515-3305; fax 225-2995

COMMITTEES
Agriculture
Education & Workforce
Government Reform

HOMETOWN
Banner Elk

BORN
June 29, 1943, Bronx, N.Y.

RELIGION
Roman Catholic

FAMILY
Husband, Tom Foxx; one child

EDUCATION
Lees-McRae College, attended 1961; Appalachian State Teachers' College, attended 1962-63; U. of North Carolina, B.A. 1968 (English), M.A.C.T. 1972 (sociology); U. of North Carolina, Greensboro, Ed.D. 1985 (curriculum and teaching/higher education)

CAREER
Community college president; nursery and landscaping company owner; state government official; professor; secretary

POLITICAL HIGHLIGHTS
Candidate for Watauga County Board of Education, 1974; Watauga County Board of Education, 1977-89; N.C. Senate, 1995-2004

ELECTION RESULTS

2004 GENERAL

Virginia Foxx (R)	167,546	58.8%
Jim A. Harrell Jr. (D)	117,271	41.2%

2004 PRIMARY RUNOFF

Virginia Foxx (R)	23,092	54.6%
Vernon L. Robinson (R)	19,201	45.4%

2004 PRIMARY

Vernon L. Robinson (R)	13,824	23.6%
Virginia Foxx (R)	13,119	22.4%
Ed Broyhill (R)	12,608	21.5%
Jay Helvey (R)	8,517	14.5%
Nathan Tabor (R)	7,660	13.1%
others	2,899	4.9%

NORTH CAROLINA 5

Northwest – part of Winston-Salem

In this northern Piedmont district, Mayberry meets R.J. Reynolds. The 5th's northern counties are filled with small rural towns such as Mount Airy, the childhood home of Andy Griffith and the inspiration for the fictional setting of his 1960s television series.

The district's major population center is Winston-Salem and surrounding Forsyth County, home to R.J. Reynolds Tobacco Co. The company's headquarters is in the 12th District (which has most of Winston-Salem), but its largest plant is in the 5th, in the appropriately named town of Tobaccoville.

The economy of Forsyth County has changed, veering away from its one-time mainstays, textiles and tobacco. Tobacco production still employs many people, but it now ranks second to health care, in part because of Wake Forest University's medical center. Banking also is on the rise, and Dell plans to open a computer-manufacturing plant on the edge of Winston-Salem in 2005. Textile and blue-collar manufacturing still prevail in the other counties, and grazing cattle roam over Surry County's rolling hills.

Redistricting following the 2000 census moved the 5th's lines to the west and south to make room for the state's new 13th District, but the new map kept the 5th's strong GOP bent intact. Republicans dominate in Davie and Yadkin counties, west of Winston-Salem, with Yadkin serving as the best county in the state for both George W. Bush and Richard M. Burr in the 2004 presidential and Senate races respectively. Even the 5th's share of Forsyth leans Republican, with most of Winston-Salem's sizable black population drawn into the 12th.

MAJOR INDUSTRY
Health care, tobacco, textiles, agriculture

CITIES
Winston-Salem (pt.), 69,790; Statesville (pt.), 23,280; Kernersville, 17,126; Clemmons, 13,827

NOTABLE
New River, roughly 300 million years old, is regarded as one of the nation's oldest rivers.

Rep. Howard Coble (R)

Elected 1984; 11th term

CAPITOL OFFICE
225-3065
howard.coble@mail.house.gov
coble.house.gov
2468 Rayburn 20515-3306; fax 225-8611

COMMITTEES
Judiciary
(Crime, Terrorism & Homeland Security -
chairman)
Transportation & Infrastructure

HOMETOWN
Greensboro

BORN
March 18, 1931, Greensboro, N.C.

RELIGION
Presbyterian

FAMILY
Single

EDUCATION
Appalachian State Teachers' College, attended
1949-50 (history); Guilford College, A.B. 1958
(history); U. of North Carolina, J.D. 1962

MILITARY SERVICE
Coast Guard, 1952-56; Coast Guard Reserve, 1960-
82; Coast Guard, 1977-78

CAREER
Lawyer; insurance claims supervisor

POLITICAL HIGHLIGHTS
N.C. House, 1969; assistant U.S. attorney, 1969-73;
N.C. Department of Revenue secretary, 1973-77;
Republican nominee for N.C. treasurer, 1976; N.C.
House, 1979-83

ELECTION RESULTS

2004 GENERAL

Howard Coble (R)	207,470	73.2%
William W. Jordan (D)	76,153	26.9%

2004 PRIMARY

Howard Coble (R)	unopposed

2002 GENERAL

Howard Coble (R)	151,430	90.4%
Tara Grubb (LIBERT)	16,067	9.6%

PREVIOUS WINNING PERCENTAGES
2000 (91%); 1998 (89%); 1996 (73%); 1994 (100%);
1992 (71%); 1990 (67%); 1988 (62%); 1986 (50%);
1984 (51%)

Coble describes himself as an "AM guy in an FM world," seldom using a computer and preferring to write his speeches in longhand. A cigar-smoking, tough-talking former prosecutor, he is positioning himself to seek the chairmanship of the Judiciary Committee in the 110th Congress, if Republicans maintain control of the House.

Currently, he ranks No. 3 among Judiciary Republicans. But Chairman F. James Sensenbrenner Jr. of Wisconsin will complete the six years permitted under GOP term limits when this Congress ends. And the No. 2 Republican, Henry J. Hyde of Illinois, earlier served six years as chairman.

Coble started a political action committee — the "Sharp Pencil" PAC — to raise campaign money for other Republicans and to improve his chances of claiming the gavel in 2007.

He may also need to watch his words a bit more carefully. His outspoken ways got him in trouble briefly in 2003, soon after he took the gavel of Judiciary's newly constituted Crime, Terrorism and Homeland Security Subcommittee. Coble told a radio interviewer that he agreed with the U.S. government's internment of Japanese-Americans during World War II. Democrats, outraged, demanded that he resign his chairmanship. Coble said he was "taken aback" by the controversy. Although he refused to give up the gavel, he offered that the internment was "the wrong decision and an action that should never be repeated." Two years later, however, Coble found no fault with the Bush administration's policy of indefinite detention, without trial, of suspected terrorists at the U.S. naval base in Guantánamo Bay, Cuba. Coble pronounced himself satisfied with the policy, even as federal courts began ruling against it.

Not that Coble is an unquestioning fan of President Bush's Iraq policy. In January 2005, Coble became one of the first House Republicans to openly question the continued U.S. military deployment in Iraq. "I am not convinced that maintaining a presence there is going to serve our national interest measurably," he said in an interview. "For that matter, I'm not convinced it's going to serve the Iraqis' national interest, for this reason: If we're still there, this gives the terrorists . . . an excuse to continue shooting people."

Before Coble took over Judiciary's Crime, Terrorism and Homeland Security Subcommittee, he served six years as chairman of the Courts, the Internet and Intellectual Property Subcommittee.

His current chairmanship puts him squarely in the middle of fights in the 109th Congress over whether to reauthorize parts of the sweeping 2001 anti-terrorism law known as the Patriot Act, and whether to respond to a Supreme Court ruling in 2005 that rendered federal criminal sentencing guidelines advisory, rather than mandatory, for judges.

At a 2003 Justice Department oversight hearing, Coble made a point of praising Attorney General John Ashcroft — a lightning rod for civil libertarians — and downplaying criticism of a controversial provision in the 2001 law that expanded law enforcement authority to seek and execute search warrants without notifying the targets.

Also that year, Coble led an ongoing congressional inquiry into the sentencing practices of a Minnesota federal judge, James M. Rosenbaum. Coble accused Rosenbaum — who had testified before the Crime Subcommittee in 2002 in favor of a U.S. Sentencing Commission proposal to reduce sentences for accomplices in drug trafficking crimes — of illegal sentencing practices and providing false and misleading information to the committee.

Coble threatened to subpoena Rosenbaum for more data. Ultimately, Coble and other Republicans compromised on an arrangement to get the data.

Coble began focusing on homeland security issues before he switched subcommittee gavels, emphasizing his background as a prosecutor and a Coast Guard veteran. He was one of only nine lawmakers to oppose the aviation security law enacted after the Sept. 11, 2001, terrorist attacks that made aviation security workers federal employees. Coble argued that the measure would cost too much and had been "driven by hysteria." He has pushed hard for putting more federal money into port security. "I have a deep feeling the messengers of evil will come next time through a port or harbor," Coble said.

Coble is a solid conservative on social and fiscal issues, and a staunch protector of the dwindling tobacco, textile and furniture industries — all important to North Carolina. A leader in the House Textile Caucus, Coble in 2003 formed the Congressional Furnishings Caucus along with North Carolina Democrat Melvin Watt to promote the U.S. furniture industry.

He regularly attacks what he sees as wasteful spending. He has called for extending the service requirement for graduates of military academies to eight years from five years, saying the current payback for their government-financed education is inadequate. Closer to home, he is one of the few lawmakers who declines to participate in the congressional pension program, calling it "a taxpayer ripoff." Every year, he returns thousands of dollars that had been allocated for running his congressional offices.

But Coble's penuriousness does not extend to his constituents. In 2004, for example, he secured $2 million to build two new shuttle passenger terminals to service a biannual furniture industry trade show in his district.

Coble was a federal prosecutor and then the state's chief tax collector in the mid-1970s. After four years as a state representative, he contemplated a run for governor in 1984, but instead sought the GOP nomination against freshman Democratic Rep. Robin Britt. He won the primary by just 164 votes. In the fall, Coble stressed his fiscal conservatism while painting Britt as an extravagant liberal who had voted against President Reagan on two of every three votes in 1983. Tapping into the flow of conservative Democrats who were crossing party lines in Reagan's re-election landslide that year, Coble won by 2,662 votes.

Britt quickly plotted a comeback, and on Election Day 1986 only 79 votes separated the winner and the loser. Britt challenged the election results, but he was unsuccessful. Coble has had little to worry about since; in 2004, William W. Jordan — his first Democratic challenger since 1996 — garnered just under 27 percent of the vote.

KEY VOTES

2004

No   Extend federal unemployment benefits by 13 weeks

Yes   Pass $283.2 billion, six-year federal highway and mass transit bill

Yes   Approve $146 billion multi-year extension of previously enacted middle-class tax breaks

Yes   Amend the Constitution to prohibit same-sex marriage

Yes   Cut corporate taxes $137 billion over 10 years

No   Reorganize U.S. intelligence agencies as proposed by Sept. 11 commission

2003

Yes   Cut taxes by $330 billion through fiscal 2013

No   Block Bush rule scaling back overtime pay for some white-collar federal workers

No   Do not allow use of search warrants without first notifying subjects

No   Allow importation of prescription drugs

Yes   Create private school voucher program in Washington, D.C.

Yes   Ban "partial birth" abortion except to save a woman's life

Yes   Split $18.6 billion in Iraq aid into half-grant, half-loan

Yes   Overhaul Medicare and create prescription drug benefit

CQ VOTE STUDIES

	PARTY UNITY		PRESIDENTIAL SUPPORT	
	Support	Oppose	Support	Oppose
2004	94%	6%	71%	29%
2003	96%	4%	87%	13%
2002	95%	5%	82%	18%
2001	95%	5%	86%	14%
2000	96%	4%	21%	79%

INTEREST GROUPS

	AFL-CIO	ADA	CCUS	ACU
2004	13%	5%	95%	88%
2003	13%	50%	86%	80%
2002	11%	10%	75%	92%
2001	17%	10%	87%	92%
2000	10%	15%	76%	86%

NORTH CAROLINA 6
Central — parts of Greensboro and High Point

Located in the heart of the state, the 6th takes in part of the city of Greensboro and surrounding Guilford County, then spreads south to Moore County to pick up the upscale golf and retirement centers of Southern Pines and Pinehurst near Fort Bragg. Already solid GOP turf, the 6th became even more Republican after redistricting following the 2000 census, and the district gave George W. Bush his best showing in the state, 69 percent, in the 2004 presidential race.

The new map shed about 100,000 people in Guilford, mainly to facilitate the creation of the state's new 13th District, and added territory in Alamance County to the east. As redrawn, the 6th takes in two large chunks of Guilford that are connected at a single point, on the Reedy Fork Creek in the northeastern part of the county.

Greensboro, the third most-populous city in the state, is home to a blend of manufacturing and service companies. Textiles, furniture and tobacco processing long have been the economic backbone of both the city and the district, including Lorillard Tobacco Company, the manufacturer of

Kent and Newport cigarettes. However, the influence of tobacco on the economy has somewhat decreased. Insurance companies, an American Express regional credit card service center and six colleges and universities have helped to diversify Greensboro's economy. Nearby High Point is a furniture manufacturing hub.

As in much of the state, trade issues loom large in the 6th, particularly in textiles and furniture manufacturing. An increase in U.S. furniture imports at the expense of Greensboro's industry has become a major concern.

The 6th includes all of Randolph County, a heavily Republican area located south of Greensboro, and most of Alamance, which votes Republican in part because of the union-resistant textile industry. The rest of the district is mostly rural, tobacco country.

MAJOR INDUSTRY
Tobacco, textiles, furniture manufacturing

CITIES
Greensboro (pt.), 59,010; High Point (pt.), 33,404; Asheboro, 21,672

NOTABLE
The Richard Petty Museum in Level Cross honors the NASCAR legend, who was the Republican nominee for secretary of state in 1996.

Rep. Mike McIntyre (D)

Elected 1996; 5th term

McIntyre is one of the most conservative Democrats in the House, even by the standards of the "Blue Dogs," the group of Democrats who occupy their party's right flank. But his politics fit nicely with his constituency, which wants a congressman who will look out for the interests of tobacco farmers, boost the military, reduce taxes, oppose abortion, defend gun owners, and advocate for school prayer and protection of the flag.

Republicans sounded him out about switching parties when he first arrived on Capitol Hill. But McIntyre demurred, pointing to his deep Democratic roots. Instead of leaving the party, he has worked, particularly through the Blue Dogs and the slightly less conservative New Democrat Coalition, to move his party toward the center.

McIntyre often tells people they should follow their dreams. "When I was a student at Carolina, both in college and law school," he recalls, "I had a poster up on the wall of my room I kept there those seven years that said, 'The secret of success is constancy of purpose.' " He points to Bill McArthur, another native of southeast North Carolina, who became an astronaut despite being rejected by NASA six times. McIntyre, too, set a goal at an early age and reached it through single-minded pursuit.

His father was a Lumberton city councilman involved in Democratic politics. When his dad took him to a November 1972 victory party for newly elected Democratic Rep. Charlie Rose, McIntyre recalls telling his father that he wanted to be the congressman from the 7th District when he grew up. When Rose retired 24 years later, McIntyre replaced him.

Organized, earnest and conservative on most issues, McIntyre now appears to have a lock on his seat. While he splits with his party on social issues and the occasional fiscal policy vote, McIntyre joins with labor unions and most House Democrats in opposing legislation to liberalize international commerce. "Free trade has been anything but free," McIntyre says. "It's been very costly" to North Carolina's textile and apparel industries.

Rural economic development tops his legislative priorities. In 2001, he sought to expand the federal Trade Adjustment Assistance programs designed to retrain and relocate workers who lost jobs as a result of trade actions. One of the first bills he introduced in the 109th Congress was to provide tax breaks and other aid to communities hard-hit by job losses stemming from the North American Free Trade Agreement. And he developed legislation, introduced in the last three Congresses, to create a seven-state Southeast Crescent Authority, modeled after the Appalachian Regional Council, to assist economically distressed counties in the Southeast United States.

He also works to boost tourism in his area and pushes for substantial federal funding to help restore storm-damaged beaches along the North Carolina coast. Six hurricanes hit the 7th District in McIntyre's first four years in office, harming tourism in the coastal areas. In the 108th and again early in the 109th, he also sponsored a bill to federally recognize the Lumbee Indians, which could lead to a casino in his part of the state.

McIntyre has seats on the Agriculture and Armed Services panels, useful assignments for representing a district where farming is big business and the military is a major influence. Fort Bragg is just west of the district, while Camp Lejeune is just over the 3rd District line to the east.

For years, McIntyre was a stout defender of the federal tobacco program, which he said was essential to preserving small family farms that grow the

CAPITOL OFFICE
225-2731
congmcintyre@mail.house.gov
www.house.gov/mcintyre
2437 Rayburn 20515-3307; fax 225-5773

COMMITTEES
Agriculture
Armed Services

HOMETOWN
Lumberton

BORN
Aug. 6, 1956, Lumberton, N.C.

RELIGION
Presbyterian

FAMILY
Wife, Dee McIntyre; two children

EDUCATION
U. of North Carolina, B.A. 1978 (political science),
J.D. 1981

CAREER
Lawyer

POLITICAL HIGHLIGHTS
No previous office

ELECTION RESULTS

2004 GENERAL

Mike McIntyre (D)	180,382	73.2%
Ken Plonk (R)	66,084	26.8%

2004 PRIMARY

Mike McIntyre (D)	unopposed

2002 GENERAL

Mike McIntyre (D)	118,543	71.1%
James Adams (R)	45,537	27.3%
David Michael Brooks (LIBERT)	2,574	1.6%

PREVIOUS WINNING PERCENTAGES
2000 (70%); 1998 (91%); 1996 (53%)

leaf. But in the 107th, declaring "it is time for a new approach," he developed a controversial plan to buy out tobacco growers and give the Food and Drug Administration authority over the manufacture, sale and distribution of tobacco products. In the 108th, he was the top-ranking Democrat on the Agriculture subcommittee with jurisdiction over tobacco programs, and Congress finally passed a buyout in 2004 as part of a corporate tax bill.

McIntyre is a staunch defender of NASA. He remembers being fascinated by space when he was young, and that interest was rekindled by one of his sons, who aspires to be an astronaut and has attended the Space Camp in Huntsville, Ala.

McIntyre has spent his life as a model Southern Democrat. He was chairman of the Teen Democrats in high school, vice president of the College Democrats in college and law school, and an organizer of the Robeson County Young Democrats after that. He was a student government officer in both high school and college.

He spent the summer after his junior year in high school in Washington, D.C., at a congressional seminar program, and it was then that his ambition to be in Congress was cemented. He was standing at the back of the room the day White House lawyer John Dean testified before the Senate Watergate Committee, chaired by Sam J. Ervin Jr. of North Carolina. McIntyre followed Watergate closely and, instead of being turned off of politics by the scandal, he decided more people should involve themselves in the political process. The next summer, he returned to Capitol Hill as an intern in Rose's office.

He majored in political science at the University of North Carolina. After law school, McIntyre continued to involve himself in dozens of community, church, civic and professional activities as he built a law practice in his hometown of Lumberton.

When Rose announced his retirement in 1996, McIntyre was one of seven Democratic primary entrants. He took 23 percent of the vote, 7 percentage points behind Rose Marie Lowry-Townsend, a well-known American Indian and teachers union president. Shortly before the runoff, McIntyre won the backing of several influential leaders in the district's black community, and their support helped him win the nomination with 52 percent.

McIntyre's Republican opponent was Bill Caster, a New Hanover County commissioner and retired Coast Guard officer. McIntyre's conservative stance on most issues helped blunt the GOP attacks, and he won with 53 percent. That was his last contest of any note. The political makeup of his district was altered only slightly by the latest redistricting, and he won with more than 70 percent of the vote in both 2002 and 2004.

KEY VOTES

2004

Yes Extend federal unemployment benefits by 13 weeks

Yes Pass $283.2 billion, six-year federal highway and mass transit bill

Yes Approve $146 billion multi-year extension of previously enacted middle-class tax breaks

Yes Amend the Constitution to prohibit same-sex marriage

Yes Cut corporate taxes $137 billion over 10 years

Yes Reorganize U.S. intelligence agencies as proposed by Sept. 11 commission

2003

No Cut taxes by $330 billion through fiscal 2013

Yes Block Bush rule scaling back overtime pay for some white-collar federal workers

Yes Do not allow use of search warrants without first notifying subjects

No Allow importation of prescription drugs

No Create private school voucher program in Washington, D.C.

Yes Ban "partial birth" abortion except to save a woman's life

Yes Split $18.6 billion in Iraq aid into half-grant, half-loan

No Overhaul Medicare and create prescription drug benefit

CQ VOTE STUDIES

	PARTY UNITY		PRESIDENTIAL SUPPORT	
	Support	Oppose	Support	Oppose
2004	74%	26%	59%	41%
2003	78%	22%	48%	52%
2002	72%	28%	54%	46%
2001	70%	30%	52%	48%
2000	61%	39%	40%	60%

INTEREST GROUPS

	AFL-CIO	ADA	CCUS	ACU
2004	80%	60%	60%	60%
2003	93%	70%	52%	48%
2002	67%	55%	53%	48%
2001	82%	60%	57%	64%
2000	60%	35%	66%	48%

NORTH CAROLINA 7
Southeast – Wilmington, part of Fayetteville

The 7th stretches from the well-off historic port city of Wilmington in the southeast to the military-based commercial hub of Fayetteville in the north. In between lie tobacco fields, hog farms and manufacturing plants.

Fort Bragg is just outside the 7th (it is shared by the 2nd and 8th districts), but the huge military base is integral to the Fayetteville area. Tobacco, agriculture, and textiles also drive the district's economy, although textile declines have given some counties high unemployment. Free-trade agreements are viewed with suspicion here.

Like Fayetteville (shared with the 2nd and 8th), Wilmington grew significantly in the 1990s, its growth reflected in its expanding medical center and emerging biotechnology industry.

Wealthy condo-dwellers in Wilmington and surrounding New Hanover County exert a rightward influence. But the region's poor farmers, Lumbee Indians (mainly in Robeson County), and cohesive black community in Fayetteville and rural Bladen and Columbus counties give

the district a slight Democratic lean. The 7th voted for George W. Bush in the 2000 and 2004 presidential elections, but both times also supported Democrat Michael F. Easley in the governor's race.

Redistricting following the 2000 census resulted in minimal changes to the 7th, but did give the district all of Robeson County. As a result, the new 7th has the fifth-largest percentage of American Indians of any district in the nation, and the largest percentage of any district east of the Mississippi River. The Hispanic population is rising. Duplin County (shared with the 3rd), in the northeast, was profiled in a 2002 New York Times story about how rural school districts have few qualified people to teach English to immigrants.

MAJOR INDUSTRY
Agriculture, military, manufacturing, tourism

CITIES
Wilmington, 75,838; Lumberton, 20,795; Fayetteville (pt.), 19,418

NOTABLE
Wilmington has a strong film and television production industry, with such movies as "Sleeping with the Enemy," "Blue Velvet" and "Divine Secrets of the Ya-Ya Sisterhood" and the TV series "One Tree Hill" filmed there; Basketball legend Michael Jordan grew up in Wilmington.

Rep. Robin Hayes (R)

Elected 1998; 4th term

CAPITOL OFFICE
225-3715
www.hayes.house.gov
130 Cannon 20515-3308; fax 225-4036

COMMITTEES
Agriculture
    (Livestock & Horticulture - chairman)
Armed Services
Transportation & Infrastructure

HOMETOWN
Concord

BORN
Aug. 14, 1945, Concord, N.C.

RELIGION
Presbyterian

FAMILY
Wife, Barbara Hayes; two children

EDUCATION
Duke U., B.A. 1967 (history)

CAREER
Hosiery mill owner; air transport company owner
and pilot; highway construction company owner

POLITICAL HIGHLIGHTS
Concord Board of Aldermen, 1975-78 (served as a
Democrat); N.C. House, 1993-97; Republican
nominee for governor, 1996

ELECTION RESULTS

2004 GENERAL

Robin Hayes (R)	125,070	55.5%
Beth Troutman (D)	100,101	44.5%

2004 PRIMARY

Robin Hayes (R)	unopposed

2002 GENERAL

Robin Hayes (R)	80,298	53.6%
Chris Kouri (D)	66,819	44.6%
Mark Andrew Johnson (LIBERT)	2,619	1.8%

PREVIOUS WINNING PERCENTAGES
2000 (55%); 1998 (51%)

North Carolina's textile industry has been central to both Hayes' family and the district he now represents. His great-grandfather J.W. Cannon founded the mill town of Kannapolis, in the district's northwest corner, and his grandfather Charles Cannon made his fortune there in textiles. Now as the industry declines, with thousands of jobs already moved overseas, protecting the livelihood of the workers who remain is central to Hayes' agenda in Congress. It is also a political imperative.

Hayes has been haunted by his decision, in 2001, to cast one of the deciding votes in favor of fast-track legislation giving President Bush the authority to negotiate trade agreements that Congress must approve or reject without alteration. Labor unions and textile workers accused Hayes of treachery, saying that fast-track authority just makes it easier to send their jobs overseas.

Hayes, who was in tears as he voted for initial passage of the fast-track measure, said he had used his vote to secure valuable protections for textile dyeing and finishing operations. But the vote has forced him to spend a great deal of time reassuring constituents that he could be trusted to defend the interests of textile workers — even after he switched sides and voted against the final version of the fast-track bill enacted in 2002. Hayes said he objected to the addition of a trade agreement with Andean nations that in his view would hurt U.S. textile and apparel makers. But it also was true that GOP leaders were able to pass the bill without his vote and let him off the hook in advance.

Hayes has earned a reputation at home and on Capitol Hill as one of Congress' staunchest defenders of tobacco, another industry that has been important to his state's economy for generations. He has lobbied the Bush administration to include tobacco companies and farmers in trade deals, despite pressure to keep the industry away from the table.

His committee assignments in the 109th Congress should ensure that he can tend to the needs of his politically competitive district, which had elected a Democrat, W. G. "Bill" Hefner, for a dozen terms until his retirement in 1998. Hayes continues on the Armed Services Committee, a post important to the 8th District's Fort Bragg and Pope Air Force Base (nearby in the 2nd), and the Agriculture Committee, where tobacco tends to get a sympathetic hearing. He is chairman of the panel's Livestock and Horticulture Subcommittee.

On Armed Services, Hayes pursues better equipment along with better pay and housing for military personnel. He also says he would like to see the Pentagon streamline its bidding process and adopt cost-saving innovations developed in the business world. With an eye toward parochial industries, he won a provision in the 2002 defense authorization law requiring that the Department of Defense look first to U.S. producers and suppliers when buying textiles, specialty metals or agriculture products. He has been working since then to ensure that businesses hear about such opportunities and get a chance to compete.

Hayes also has a seat on the Transportation Committee, enabling him to look out for his district's infrastructure needs. He has worked hard, for example, to secure money for expansions and improvements at smaller airports in his district, in hopes that better airports will help spur economic development.

Unpretentious and affable, Hayes is a reliably conservative Republican.

His passion for hunting and fishing is well-known to his friends and colleagues. In the 108th Congress, he was co-chairman of the Congressional Sportsmen's Caucus, composed of about 300 fellow outdoors enthusiasts on Capitol Hill. Not surprisingly, he is a strong supporter of the rights of gun owners. A devout NASCAR fan, he once was part-owner of a racing team, and in 2001 he helped arrange an Air Force flyover honoring the late NASCAR driver Dale Earnhardt before a race at North Carolina Speedway. He has rewarded campaign donors by taking them to a racing school for training to drive a Winston Cup car.

He is also a licensed pilot, and for a time he ran a business in Alaska flying freight and passengers in and out of the bush. He now owns a small air charter business in his hometown.

Growing up in Concord, Hayes says he was "a typical Southern conservative Democrat, raised in a family with a strong work ethic and family beliefs." After college, he began a business career that included jobs in the textile, trucking and highway contracting businesses. He inherited a share of his family's textile fortune and eventually bought his own hosiery mill.

His first taste of politics was serving for three years as a town alderman in the 1970s. By the time he ran for a seat in the state House in 1992, he had been a Republican for two years. In 1994, just as the Republican Party was winning control of Congress, Hayes played a key role in North Carolina's version of the "Republican revolution." He helped organize a GOP takeover of the state House, and his colleagues rewarded him by electing him whip.

Hayes made a statewide name for himself with a 1996 bid for governor. He trounced the establishment's choice for the GOP nomination, former Charlotte Mayor Richard Vinroot, but he took only 43 percent of the vote in the general election against Democratic incumbent James B. Hunt.

In his initial bid for Congress two years later, Hayes outspent Democratic lawyer Mike Taylor by a 3-to-1 margin and won with 51 percent of the vote. He took 55 percent in a rematch with Taylor in 2000. But remapping for this decade added Democrats to the 8th District, and the new demographics, combined with his trade vote, made Hayes look more vulnerable than ever in 2002. With fundraising help from Bush and other leading Republicans, however, he won with 54 percent against Democratic unknown Chris Kouri, a young Charlotte lawyer.

In 2004, Hayes' Democratic opponent was another political newcomer, 27-year-old Beth Troutman, who had worked for a time on the production staff of NBC's "The West Wing." Hayes won with 55 percent.

KEY VOTES

2004

Yes Extend federal unemployment benefits by 13 weeks
Yes Pass $283.2 billion, six-year federal highway and mass transit bill
Yes Approve $146 billion multi-year extension of previously enacted middle-class tax breaks
Yes Amend the Constitution to prohibit same-sex marriage
Yes Cut corporate taxes $137 billion over 10 years
Yes Reorganize U.S. intelligence agencies as proposed by Sept. 11 commission

2003

Yes Cut taxes by $330 billion through fiscal 2013
No Block Bush rule scaling back overtime pay for some white-collar federal workers
No Do not allow use of search warrants without first notifying subjects
No Allow importation of prescription drugs
Yes Create private school voucher program in Washington, D.C.
Yes Ban "partial birth" abortion except to save a woman's life
No Split $18.6 billion in Iraq aid into half-grant, half-loan
Yes Overhaul Medicare and create prescription drug benefit

CQ VOTE STUDIES

	PARTY UNITY		PRESIDENTIAL SUPPORT	
	Support	Oppose	Support	Oppose
2004	94%	6%	76%	24%
2003	99%	1%	91%	9%
2002	97%	3%	82%	18%
2001	98%	2%	91%	9%
2000	89%	11%	19%	81%

INTEREST GROUPS

	AFL-CIO	ADA	CCUS	ACU
2004	21%	5%	95%	88%
2003	20%	5%	93%	84%
2002	22%	5%	75%	96%
2001	8%	5%	87%	96%
2000	10%	5%	76%	76%

NORTH CAROLINA 8

South central – parts of Charlotte, Fayetteville, Concord and Kannapolis

The 8th connects the worlds of eastern and western North Carolina, spanning from Charlotte in the west to military-dominated Fayetteville in the east. This is a district split along geographic, economic and political lines. Redistricting following the 2000 census extended the 8th west to take in a large portion of Charlotte, giving the previously suburban and rural district an urban component.

Cabarrus, a fast-growing county north of Charlotte, and Cumberland, which includes the 8th's share of Fayetteville, are the district's most-populous counties. Cabarrus is largely white and heavily Republican. Cumberland is more politically competitive.

In Mecklenburg County, which includes Charlotte and is the 8th's third major population center, the district reaches as far west as Memorial Stadium and Independence Park, nearly reaching downtown Charlotte. The 8th's share of Charlotte is almost 40 percent black, giving the

district's portion of Mecklenburg a decidedly Democratic lean.

Textile-based economies in the cities along Interstate 85, notably Concord and Kannapolis, have suffered major losses over the last few years as manufacturing jobs have headed overseas. In the east, the district becomes poorer and more rural as it reaches into the Sandhills region. This part of the 8th also has a strong military flavor — Fort Bragg (shared with the 2nd) takes up land in Hoke and Cumberland counties.

The 8th is politically competitive. In 2000 and 2004, George W. Bush took 53 percent and 54 percent of the district's presidential vote, respectively, while Democrat Michael F. Easley won the district's gubernatorial vote.

MAJOR INDUSTRY
Military, manufacturing, agriculture, livestock

MILITARY BASES
Fort Bragg (Army), 41,458 military, 4,431 civilian (2004) (shared with the 2nd)

CITIES
Charlotte (pt.), 100,756; Concord (pt.), 55,938; Fayetteville (pt.), 51,698

NOTABLE
North Carolina Speedway and Rockingham Dragway, known collectively as "The Rock," can draw 250,000 NASCAR fans to races.

Rep. Sue Myrick (R)

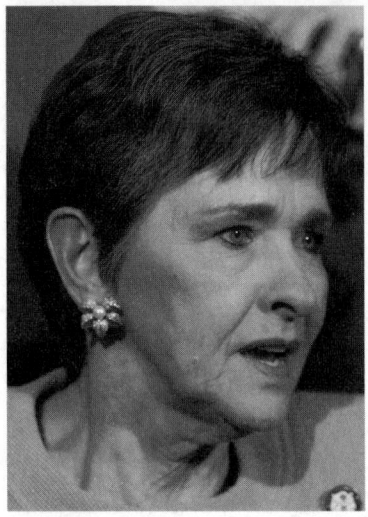

Elected 1994; 6th term

Myrick has shifted her focus for the 109th Congress but not her conservative course. She relinquished her seat on the leadership-controlled Rules Committee for a slot on the Energy and Commerce Committee, where members have more individual power. And she stepped down as head of the Republican Study Committee, a caucus of about 90 of the most conservative House Republicans. But she remains a deputy whip.

A veteran of the GOP Class of 1994 that took control of the House after 40 years of Democratic rule, Myrick tries to maintain that revolutionary spirit, particularly on fiscal issues. She has frequently criticized House appropriators for what she considered their free-spending ways. As a member of the Rules Committee, she sponsored a change in rules for the 108th Congress that curbed the power of House Appropriations subcommittee chairmen. Early in the 109th, the Republican Study Committee threatened to hold up the budget resolution for 2006 spending unless GOP leaders agreed to a new mechanism for enforcing spending caps. While the group cut a deal that appears to have little practical value, the episode demonstrated how bold House GOP conservatives have become.

During the 2004 election campaign, Myrick and the Republican Study Committee produced pocket checklists of "six commandments" for conservatives. Reducing the size and cost of government figured high on the list. "A lot of our base around the country is very disturbed about spending," she told the Washington Times. "We hear about it when we go home."

Despite all her criticism of federal spending, Myrick has worked to secure millions of dollars for projects in her home district. And she has been quick to announce the award of grants for local priorities ranging from homeless aid to parkway improvements.

Some of Myrick's biggest legislative victories have come not from her conservative causes but from a personal battle that turned her into a leading advocate of legislation to expand cancer research and health care coverage of cancer treatment. Myrick, a breast cancer survivor, in 2000 shepherded into law a measure that provides treatment for low-income women diagnosed with breast or cervical cancer.

Myrick underwent surgery for her cancer in December 1999 and received treatments for about six months, cutting back her workload and occasionally showing up for floor votes wearing a pink surgical mask to reduce the risk of infection. She said her experience with cancer had helped her keep things in perspective and persuaded her to work "very hard not to get back in the same rat race." In 2001, she became co-chairwoman of the House Cancer Caucus.

Myrick, whose textile-producing state has suffered significant trade-related job losses, has sharply criticized the Bush administration's free-trade policies, calling the president "out of touch." She has taken particular aim at China, introducing legislation to authorize "appropriate action" if the Asian giant does not revamp its trade practices. "The Bush administration knows we have a problem, and I am going to keep reminding them of it every chance I get," she said in 2003.

Notwithstanding her rhetoric, Myrick in 2000 voted to give China permanent normal trade status. She was one of several Republicans who cast the deciding votes in 2002 granting President Bush fast-track trade negotiating authority. She backed the bill after Bush pledged to help the domestic textile industry. Myrick also voted in the 108th in favor of free-trade pacts

CAPITOL OFFICE
225-1976
myrick@mail.house.gov
myrick.house.gov
230 Cannon 20515-3309; fax 225-3389

COMMITTEES
Energy & Commerce

HOMETOWN
Charlotte

BORN
Aug. 1, 1941, Tiffin, Ohio

RELIGION
Evangelical Methodist

FAMILY
Husband, Ed Myrick; two children, three stepchildren

EDUCATION
Heidelberg College, attended 1959-60 (elementary education)

CAREER
Advertising executive; secretary

POLITICAL HIGHLIGHTS
Candidate for Charlotte City Council, 1981; Charlotte City Council, 1983-85; sought Republican nomination for mayor of Charlotte, 1985; mayor of Charlotte, 1987-91; sought Republican nomination for U.S. Senate, 1992

ELECTION RESULTS

2004 GENERAL

Sue Myrick (R)	210,783	70.2%
Jack Flynn (D)	89,318	29.8%

2004 PRIMARY

Sue Myrick (R)	unopposed

2002 GENERAL

Sue Myrick (R)	140,095	72.4%
Ed McGuire (D)	49,974	25.8%
Christopher S. Cole (LIBERT)	3,374	1.7%

PREVIOUS WINNING PERCENTAGES
2000 (69%); 1998 (69%); 1996 (63%); 1994 (65%)

with Australia and Singapore.

In 2003, she came out against Bush's proposed immigration policy to grant legal status to guest workers, including some already in the country illegally; Myrick said citizens deserved priority. "We need to focus on filling our economic obligation to these American workers and make sure they have jobs before we focus our efforts elsewhere," she said.

Myrick drew criticism from Arab Americans and others in early 2003 for a comment she made during a speech on domestic security threats. As the United States prepared for war in Iraq, the congresswoman said, "Look at who runs all the convenience stores across the country."

Her ardent conservatism and her distinct status as the only Southern Republican woman in the Class of '94 caught the attention of party leaders when she first arrived in Congress. She got a seat on the Budget Committee in her first term and a post on the Rules Committee in her second.

But in 1997, she met with a small group of disgruntled conservatives who, impatient with the pace of the "Republican revolution" and their leaders' willingness to compromise, plotted to depose Newt Gingrich as Speaker. The coup was foiled — coincidentally, about the same time House Republicans met to elect two new leaders. Myrick was a candidate for secretary of the Republican Conference, but she finished second to Deborah Pryce of Ohio.

Born in Tiffin, Ohio, Myrick attended Heidelberg College in her hometown for just a year before her parents decided their limited financial resources should be used for her three brothers' higher education. They figured "I'd just get married," Myrick said. She took a series of jobs in Ohio, beginning with secretarial positions.

Myrick had no political aspirations until the early 1980s, when she and her husband sparred with the Charlotte City Council over the purchase of a property for use as a combination home and business. She ran for the city council in 1981 and lost, but was victorious two years later. In 1985, she lost a bid to become mayor of Charlotte; but in 1987, she won the office, ousting Harvey B. Gantt. She was re-elected in 1989.

After five-term GOP Rep. Alex McMillan announced his retirement in 1994, Myrick's political experience gave her wide name recognition in a five-way Republican primary. Still, she struggled to win the nomination, prevailing only when news broke that her principal opponent, state House Minority Leader David Balmer, had falsified his résumé. That November, she met only modest Democratic resistance. She has easily won re-election since then.

KEY VOTES

2004

No	Extend federal unemployment benefits by 13 weeks
No	Pass $283.2 billion, six-year federal highway and mass transit bill
?	Approve $146 billion multi-year extension of previously enacted middle-class tax breaks
Yes	Amend the Constitution to prohibit same-sex marriage
Yes	Cut corporate taxes $137 billion over 10 years
No	Reorganize U.S. intelligence agencies as proposed by Sept. 11 commission

2003

Yes	Cut taxes by $330 billion through fiscal 2013
No	Block Bush rule scaling back overtime pay for some white-collar federal workers
Yes	Do not allow use of search warrants without first notifying subjects
Yes	Allow importation of prescription drugs
+	Create private school voucher program in Washington, D.C.
Yes	Ban "partial birth" abortion except to save a woman's life
No	Split $18.6 billion in Iraq aid into half-grant, half-loan
Yes	Overhaul Medicare and create prescription drug benefit

CQ VOTE STUDIES

	PARTY UNITY		PRESIDENTIAL SUPPORT	
	Support	Oppose	Support	Oppose
2004	99%	1%	91%	9%
2003	98%	2%	96%	4%
2002	97%	3%	88%	12%
2001	96%	4%	95%	5%
2000	96%	4%	26%	74%

INTEREST GROUPS

	AFL-CIO	ADA	CCUS	ACU
2004	0%	0%	95%	100%
2003	0%	10%	96%	88%
2002	11%	0%	100%	96%
2001	0%	0%	95%	96%
2000	0%	0%	90%	95%

NORTH CAROLINA 9
South central – parts of Charlotte and Gastonia

Redistricting following the 2000 census strengthened the 9th's ties to Charlotte, the largest metropolitan area in the state. Nearly 40 percent of district residents live within its city limits and nearly 60 percent live in Mecklenburg County, which includes Charlotte.

The primarily white suburbs on the southern side of Charlotte feed the city many of its bankers, brokers, accountants, health care professionals and other white-collar workers. Most of Charlotte's black residents are in the 8th and 12th districts. The 9th has the highest median household income in North Carolina, thanks to upper-middle-class areas such as Huntersville, in northern Mecklenburg.

The region's tremendous growth, much of it sparked by 1990s consolidation in the banking industry, has brought the traffic congestion, shopping malls and higher home values that usually accompany suburban sprawl. Charlotte is now known as the nation's biggest banking center after New York.

To the west, Gastonia and its surrounding towns have been hurt by the continuing decline of the textile industry. However, the 9th has decreased its dependence on manufacturing and textiles, and Gastonia's population still grew by 20 percent in the 1990s.

Redistricting kept the 9th's Republican tendencies intact. The district's GOP registration advantage increased with the addition of most of Union County, a suburban bedroom community located southeast of Charlotte, and the excision of Democratic-leaning Cleveland County in the west. Union was Republican gubernatorial nominee Patrick J. Ballantine's fifth-best county in the state in 2004, and the 9th's portion of Union County gave George W. Bush 73 percent of the presidential vote in 2004.

MAJOR INDUSTRY
Finance, service, retail, manufacturing

CITIES
Charlotte (pt.), 243,947; Gastonia (pt.), 60,498; Huntersville, 24,960

NOTABLE
After six years of planning, a Gaston County veterans' group in December 1998 succeeded in hoisting the largest flying American flag in the nation — 114 feet by 65 feet.

Rep. Patrick T. McHenry (R)

Elected 2004; 1st term

CAPITOL OFFICE
225-2576
www.house.gov/mchenry
224 Cannon 20515-3310; fax 225-0316

COMMITTEES
Budget
Financial Services
Government Reform

HOMETOWN
Cherryville

BORN
Oct. 22, 1975, Charlotte, N.C.

RELIGION
Roman Catholic

FAMILY
Single

EDUCATION
North Carolina State U., attended 1994-97;
Belmont Abbey College, B.A. 2000 (history)

CAREER
Real estate broker; U.S. Labor Department special
assistant; campaign aide

POLITICAL HIGHLIGHTS
Republican nominee for N.C. House, 1998; N.C.
House, 2003-05

ELECTION RESULTS

2004 GENERAL

Patrick T. McHenry (R)	157,884	64.2%
Anne N. Fischer (D)	88,233	35.9%

2004 PRIMARY RUNOFF

Patrick T. McHenry (R)	15,015	50.1%
David Huffman (R)	14,930	49.9%

2004 PRIMARY

David Huffman (R)	14,280	35.0%
Patrick T. McHenry (R)	10,760	26.3%
Sandy Lyons (R)	8,000	19.6%
George A. Moretz (R)	7,812	19.1%

Elected to Congress less than two weeks after his 29th birthday, McHenry is the youngest member of the House Class of 2004, which is weighted toward older and more-experienced politicians.

Yet McHenry, a real estate broker, is no political novice: He already had a term in the North Carolina House under his belt when he battled through a crowded primary field, a win that ensured he would succeed retired veteran GOP Rep. Cass Ballenger in the reliably Republican 10th District.

McHenry, whose prematurely graying hair belies his youth, was granted a pair of high-profile committee assignments — on the Budget and Financial Services panels — that provide him with growth potential.

McHenry had already compiled a lengthy résumé when Ballenger announced he would retire from the seat he had held since 1986. He had worked on several campaigns, including fellow North Carolina Republican Rep. Robin Hayes' failed 1996 gubernatorial bid and George W. Bush's successful 2000 presidential race, prior to his own 2002 legislative campaign.

The only congressman in his 20s when the 109th Congress began, McHenry said he planned to push for a sweeping overhaul of the Social Security system. "As the youngest member of Congress, I am going to be quite vocal about allowing younger people, especially, to have more freedom over their own pocketbooks," he said.

Like Ballenger, McHenry styles himself a conservative on most social and fiscal matters. He strongly opposes abortion, supports gun owners' rights, and favors a constitutional amendment to ban same-sex marriage.

But McHenry will break with most in his party by opposing some free-trade measures, which many western North Carolina residents blame for job losses in the state's manufacturing industries.

McHenry was runner-up in a four-way GOP primary, upsetting two wealthy businessmen who outspent him by a wide margin. Four weeks later, he won a bitter runoff campaign against a well-known local sheriff by a scant 85-vote margin. In November, he won by more than 28 percentage points.

NORTH CAROLINA 10
West – Hickory

Set among the small towns of the western part of the state, the 10th has a rustic, small-business and conservative flavor.

While the 10th includes some suburban communities near Charlotte, it is mostly rural — only one town, Hickory, has a population of more than 20,000. The economy of the southern counties is based largely on textile and furniture manufacturing. Redistricting following the 2000 census added some cotton-growing areas. Technology manufacturing is on the upswing, especially involving fiber-optic cable. Tourists visit the mountains near the Tennessee state line and ski in areas like Banner Elk (Avery County).

Suburban sprawl has reached the eastern and southern edges of the 10th, especially in Hickory, where the furniture industry employs a large part of the workforce. Iredell County, most of which is in the 5th District, is mostly rural and agricultural, with some manufacturing.

Redistricting removed a swath of Republican counties to the north and east and added cotton-producing, politically competitive Cleveland County. The changes reduced the GOP registration advantage, but many residents are conservative Democrats who will support Republicans in federal races.

The 10th's political preference is set by Catawba County (Hickory), the district's most populous, which gave George W. Bush 67 percent of its 2004 presidential vote. Democrats run better in Cleveland and Burke counties, but Caldwell and Lincoln counties are heavily Republican. Avery and Mitchell counties, on the Tennessee border, were GOP gubernatorial nominee Patrick J. Ballantine's best counties in 2004.

MAJOR INDUSTRY
Manufacturing, agriculture, livestock

CITIES
Hickory, 37,222; Shelby, 19,477; Mooresville (pt.), 18,782; Morganton, 17,310; Lenoir, 16,793

NOTABLE
The Elliott-Carnegie Public Library in Hickory was the last U.S. public library to receive a grant from the Carnegie Foundation (in 1917).

Rep. Charles H. Taylor (R)

Elected 1990; 8th term

CAPITOL OFFICE
225-6401
www.house.gov/charlestaylor
339 Cannon 20515-3311; fax 226-6422

COMMITTEES
Appropriations
(Interior & Environment - chairman)

HOMETOWN
Brevard

BORN
Jan. 23, 1941, Brevard, N.C.

RELIGION
Baptist

FAMILY
Wife, Elizabeth Taylor; three children

EDUCATION
Wake Forest U., B.A. 1963, J.D. 1966

CAREER
Tree farmer; banker

POLITICAL HIGHLIGHTS
N.C. House, 1967-73 (minority leader, 1969-71);
N.C. Senate, 1973-75 (minority leader, 1973-75);
Republican nominee for U.S. House, 1988

ELECTION RESULTS

2004 GENERAL

Charles H. Taylor (R)	159,709	54.9%
Patsy Keever (D)	131,188	45.1%

2004 PRIMARY

Charles H. Taylor (R)	unopposed

2002 GENERAL

Charles H. Taylor (R)	112,335	55.5%
Sam Neill (D)	86,664	42.9%
Eric Henry (LIBERT)	3,261	1.6%

PREVIOUS WINNING PERCENTAGES
2000 (55%); 1998 (57%); 1996 (58%); 1994 (60%);
1992 (55%); 1990 (51%)

Taylor has skated at the edge of scandal back home but never close enough to be ensnared by it or to threaten his place in the House and its Appropriations Committee hierarchy. Indeed, House Republican leaders appear more concerned about his failure to pony up money for the party than about any of his personal financial dealings.

As House Republican leaders sought to put pro-business lawmakers in charge of environment-related committees in the 108th Congress, Taylor was seen as a good fit. The only registered forester in Congress, he was named chairman of the Interior Appropriations Subcommittee. But he was warned early in the 109th Congress that he was in danger of losing that post because he hadn't anted up his dues of $15,000 to the National Republican Congressional Committee, the campaign unit of House Republicans, or another $15,000 for an incumbent-retention fund. Taylor was the only Appropriations "cardinal," as subcommittee chairmen are known, who had failed to meet the GOP donation test. He had created the Mountain Leadership political action committee early in 2004, but the PAC failed to raise any funds and Taylor did not send any money to GOP campaign units.

That could be because he was immersed in his own contested re-election in 2004. He was dogged by controversy about $48,124 in long-overdue taxes on timberland he owns, which he finally paid in 2003, and fraudulent bank loans at a thrift he controls, although Taylor was not implicated in any wrongdoing there. In addition, a Taylor aide was reported to have negotiated a $60,000 lobbying contract for himself while still on the House payroll. The contract was dropped and the aide left Taylor's office just before the article was published. "I didn't get in the middle of it. . . . Roger France said he was resigning and left the office," Taylor said at the time.

Eyebrows were also raised when Taylor's bank acquired a bank in Russia in September 2003. Taylor's staff said it would further North Carolina banking interests. But there were revelations that Taylor had extensive business ventures in Russia — including stakes in a potato warehouse, an apartment building and a chain of convenience stores — while he was cosponsoring a bill to create a program of U.S. aid for Russian home mortgages.

Environmentalists have criticized Taylor's stewardship of the Interior Subcommittee, noting he owns thousands of acres of timberland and has consistently backed efforts to permit increased logging on public lands. He pushed through a 1995 measure that waived environmental laws for 18 months to allow the removal of dead and dying trees from national forests.

The first Interior spending bill he shepherded provided $177 million for acquiring land for federal parks, forests and other natural preserves, a $136 million reduction from the previous year. Taylor had wanted even less, $100 million, but the figure was raised in negotiations with the Senate.

"Some members will argue that we need to buy a lot more federal land," Taylor said at the time. "What we really need to do is a better job of taking care of the lands we have."

Taylor has not been known for intellectual rigor or legislative acumen. But he has shown a knack for political survival. He has won federal dollars to promote economic growth in his district, including millions of dollars for Internet-related education programs and biotech research, as well as money for an Alzheimer's care unit at the veterans hospital near Asheville.

Initially elected on a "reform Congress" platform, Taylor joined with six other GOP freshmen in his first term to form the "Gang of Seven," which gained national attention for their rabble-rousing campaign against congressional perquisites and for full disclosure during the House bank overdraft scandal in 1992.

Taylor's dim view of the federal government — he once declared on the House floor that "the government will mess up a one-car funeral" — sometimes gives the GOP leadership heartburn. For example, as the chairman of the Legislative Branch Subcommittee, a post he held before taking over the Interior Subcommittee, Taylor stirred things up in 2000 by proposing deep cuts in the budgets of several congressional agencies, including the Capitol Police. (He toyed with the idea of requiring Capitol air conditioners to be turned off after July 1 to encourage adjournment each year by Independence Day.) House leaders added more money to the bill after members objected to Taylor's version.

Taylor wound up with the Legislative Branch gavel in 1999 after being turned down for the Military Construction Subcommittee, partly because of his unhappy stewardship of the panel that funds the District of Columbia's government. In 1997 and 1998, he loaded the D.C. bill with so many policy add-ons reflecting his own conservative views that the legislation met with intense opposition. GOP leaders ultimately took over negotiations on the measure and stripped out most of Taylor's riders.

Taylor has bucked his party leaders on other occasions, too, taking a protectionist stand on trade legislation to try to help an area that has seen many of its textile and furniture-making jobs sent overseas. He has opposed every free-trade bill during his tenure in Congress, from the 1993 North American Free Trade Agreement to the 2002 law granting President Bush fast-track trade negotiating authority.

Taylor first won election to the state House in 1966, fresh out of law school. He later served in the state Senate, and in both chambers served as minority leader. After losing to Democratic Rep. James McClure Clarke in 1988, Taylor won a 1990 rematch for the House seat with 51 percent of the vote. He won his next four re-elections with ease. But in 2000 and in 2002, he had to work hard to hold his seat. Both times, he was opposed by Democrat Sam Neill, a local lawyer, and both times he won with 55 percent.

In 2004, he again faced a strong Democratic candidate, Patsy Keever, a three-term Buncombe County commissioner and retired school teacher who ran a vigorous grass-roots campaign. But, relying heavily on his record of constituent service and success in steering federal funds to the 11th District, Taylor prevailed with just less than 55 percent.

KEY VOTES

2004

Yes Extend federal unemployment benefits by 13 weeks

Yes Pass $283.2 billion, six-year federal highway and mass transit bill

Yes Approve $146 billion multi-year extension of previously enacted middle-class tax breaks

Yes Amend the Constitution to prohibit same-sex marriage

Yes Cut corporate taxes $137 billion over 10 years

No Reorganize U.S. intelligence agencies as proposed by Sept. 11 commission

2003

Yes Cut taxes by $330 billion through fiscal 2013

No Block Bush rule scaling back overtime pay for some white-collar federal workers

Yes Do not allow use of search warrants without first notifying subjects

Yes Allow importation of prescription drugs

Yes Create private school voucher program in Washington, D.C.

Yes Ban "partial birth" abortion except to save a woman's life

No Split $18.6 billion in Iraq aid into half-grant, half-loan

Yes Overhaul Medicare and create prescription drug benefit

CQ VOTE STUDIES

	PARTY UNITY		PRESIDENTIAL SUPPORT	
	Support	Oppose	Support	Oppose
2004	93%	7%	82%	18%
2003	96%	4%	87%	13%
2002	97%	3%	85%	15%
2001	97%	3%	86%	14%
2000	94%	6%	21%	79%

INTEREST GROUPS

	AFL-CIO	ADA	CCUS	ACU
2004	13%	5%	95%	88%
2003	21%	15%	90%	76%
2002	14%	5%	90%	96%
2001	8%	10%	82%	92%
2000	11%	5%	72%	92%

NORTH CAROLINA 11
West – Asheville

Based in the Great Smoky Mountain region, the 11th is a largely rural district dotted with tree farms, wood mills and campgrounds. While agriculture and forestry long have played a key role in the region's economy, retail trade, health care and education are becoming major employers. Tourism also has a large role, with people flocking to the area's ski slopes, as well as to the hiking trails in national parks and on Mount Mitchell (the highest peak east of the Mississippi River). Tourists also enjoy the palatial Biltmore House, once the home of Cornelius Vanderbilt's grandson.

Asheville, which along with surrounding Buncombe County takes in one-third of the district's residents, is the 11th's economic focal point. Residents spruced up the city's downtown, and are trying to attract technology businesses. The decline of the textile industry has led to job loss in the district.

Attractive to retirees, the 11th has the highest median age (41) of any North Carolina district. It also has the smallest black population, as the

only sizable African-American constituency is in Asheville. The Cherokee Indian Reservation in Swain and Jackson counties gives the district a larger than average American Indian population.

The 11th leans Republican, but Democrats have a slight registration edge. Buncombe barely voted for George W. Bush in the 2004 presidential election, awarding him 50 percent of the vote, but every other county in the district gave Bush a higher percentage. Henderson County, the district's second most-populous, votes solidly Republican.

MAJOR INDUSTRY
Retail trade, forest products, tourism, health care

CITIES
Asheville, 68,889; Hendersonville, 10,420; Waynesville, 9,232

NOTABLE
Many of the state's Cherokee Indians are descendants of the estimated 1,000 Cherokees who hid in the mountains of western North Carolina to avoid the forced migration to Oklahoma along the path now known as the Trail of Tears; The Billy Graham Evangelistic Association operates a 1,500-acre training center called "The Cove" in Asheville; Rutherfordton was home to the Bechtler gold mint, which minted more than $2.2 million in gold coins between 1831 and 1840.

Rep. Melvin Watt (D)

Elected 1992; 7th term

A civil rights lawyer for 22 years before being elected to the House, Watt was chosen chairman of the Congressional Black Caucus for the 109th Congress, putting him in charge of one of the most powerful unofficial groups that help shape policy in Washington, particularly for the Democrats.

The selection by his peers is acknowledgement of Watt's considerable political skills. He is a fierce defender of liberal causes and legislation affecting minorities, but he also has friends in the business community and among Republicans. The combination is useful to a group whose influence, while substantial, has been diminished by the conservative tide in American politics.

On the Judiciary Committee, which handles some of the most contentious social legislation, Watt is a partisan and staunch defender of the Constitution. But on Financial Services, his style is more bipartisan, and he frequently pairs with Republican colleagues to broker compromise. "Judiciary is just by its nature a very confrontational and quite often a partisan committee," he says. "It's hard not to have people walk away from those debates with some kind of stereotype of you as uncompromising. So when people see me on the other committee, they think it's Dr. Jekyll and Mr. Hyde."

A Yale-trained lawyer, Watt is the top-ranking Democrat on the Commercial and Administrative Law Subcommittee. He pays meticulous attention to legislative detail. He schools himself in the most arcane corners of the law, then makes his case with both lawyerly precision and passionate oratory.

In the 108th Congress, Watt called a Republican bill to curb the federal court system's authority over constitutional challenges to the Pledge of Allegiance "an assault on the judiciary," and unsuccessfully sought to amend it to preserve the Supreme Court's appellate jurisdiction. During House consideration in 2003 of a proposed constitutional amendment to allow Congress to ban flag-burning, Watt — whose constitutional law teacher at Yale was conservative Robert H. Bork — unsuccessfully offered a substitute amendment that specified that Congress could only do so in a way "not inconsistent" with the First Amendment.

In 2004, Watt authored a provision in the intelligence overhaul measure to create a privacy and civil liberties oversight board. The Judiciary Committee added the provision to the bill but denied the new oversight board subpoena power, as Watt had wanted.

Six weeks after the terrorist attacks of Sept. 11, 2001, Watt was among the 66 House members who voted against legislation granting law enforcement agents broad new powers. He said the measure would erode civil liberties and hand police too much power to monitor the activities of the innocent. "Some of us who have a different history in America with delegation of authority to the government and the abuse of that authority proceed a lot differently than others," Watt said. "We cannot just come in, in the middle of a terrorism episode, and forget all the history that has occurred in our country."

Several controversial provisions of the law are set to expire at the end of 2005, creating an opportunity for Watt and other critics to scale it back.

On Financial Services, Watt eagerly looks for Republicans in search of a deal, often scribbling proposed amendments in the margins of the legislation under discussion. In 2002, he joined with Vito J. Fossella, a New York Republican, to win inclusion in the terrorism insurance law of a provision allowing terrorists' frozen assets to be used to pay compensatory damages.

Although Watt sees his role on Financial Services as an advocate for the

CAPITOL OFFICE
225-1510
nc12@mail.house.gov
www.house.gov/watt
2236 Rayburn 20515-3312; fax 225-1512

COMMITTEES
Financial Services
Judiciary

HOMETOWN
Charlotte

BORN
Aug. 26, 1945, Steele Creek, N.C.

RELIGION
Presbyterian

FAMILY
Wife, Eulada Watt; two children

EDUCATION
U. of North Carolina, B.S. 1967 (business administration); Yale U., J.D. 1970

CAREER
Nursing home owner; campaign manager; lawyer

POLITICAL HIGHLIGHTS
N.C. Senate, 1985-86

ELECTION RESULTS

2004 GENERAL

Melvin Watt (D)	154,908	66.8%
Ada M. Fisher (R)	76,898	33.2%

2004 PRIMARY

Melvin Watt (D)	24,374	85.2%
Kimberly "Kim" Holley (D)	4,241	14.8%

2002 GENERAL

Melvin Watt (D)	98,821	65.3%
Jeff Kish (R)	49,588	32.8%
Carey Head (LIBERT)	2,830	1.9%

PREVIOUS WINNING PERCENTAGES
2000 (65%); 1998 (56%); 1996 (71%); 1994 (66%); 1992 (70%)

little guy, he is on cordial terms with the business community and takes its views into account. Charlotte's big financial services companies, including Wachovia and Bank of America, would no doubt prefer to have a more conservative congressman, but Watt at least gives their opinions a hearing. He occasionally agrees with them, opposing, for example, proposals to raise the $100,000 ceiling on federally insured deposits. "Trying to walk the balance between the banker interests and the consumer interests is very difficult," he says.

Watt is actively involved in the panel's work on housing and urban affairs. In the 108th Congress, he cosponsored a bill with Iowa Republican Jim Leach to reauthorize the HOPE VI public housing grant program.

In 2004, Watt clashed with independent presidential candidate Ralph Nader, who accused Watt of hurling an "obscene racist epithet" at him during a closed-door meeting of Nader and the black caucus members. Watt denied that he had done so and said that Nader's "untruthful focus on his candidacy for president is nothing more than an arrogant ego trip."

The underpinning of Watt's success is the determination he developed during a difficult early life. Raised in a fatherless household, he grew up in a tin-roofed shack in rural Mecklenburg County that lacked running water or electricity. After attending a segregated high school, he went on to graduate Phi Beta Kappa from the University of North Carolina at Chapel Hill, and then earned his law degree.

Watt interrupted his law practice for a brief stint to serve as an appointed state senator and to manage the 1990 Senate campaign of Democrat Harvey Gantt, who nearly upset GOP incumbent Jesse Helms that year.

In 1992, when a circuitously shaped black-majority district was created, Watt won it with relative ease and became one of the first African-American North Carolinians in Congress since 1901. But the boundaries of Watt's district were challenged in court throughout the 1990s, and the 12th District's lines were redrawn twice during the decade in response to lawsuits alleging unconstitutional racial gerrymandering.

In 2001, the state's map was redrawn yet again, this time because North Carolina received an additional House seat as a result of population gains. The Democrats in charge of the process made sure to give Watt an electorally safe territory. But the changing shape of his district has proved more of a distraction than a political threat: Only once in seven elections has he been held to less than three-fifths of the vote.

Watt, a good athlete, is the Democrats' pitcher in the annual charity baseball game that pits his party against GOP lawmakers.

KEY VOTES

2004
Yes   Extend federal unemployment benefits by 13 weeks
Yes   Pass $283.2 billion, six-year federal highway and mass transit bill
Yes   Approve $146 billion multi-year extension of previously enacted middle-class tax breaks
No   Amend the Constitution to prohibit same-sex marriage
Yes   Cut corporate taxes $137 billion over 10 years
Yes   Reorganize U.S. intelligence agencies as proposed by Sept. 11 commission

2003
No   Cut taxes by $330 billion through fiscal 2013
Yes   Block Bush rule scaling back overtime pay for some white-collar federal workers
Yes   Do not allow use of search warrants without first notifying subjects
Yes   Allow importation of prescription drugs
No   Create private school voucher program in Washington, D.C.
No   Ban "partial birth" abortion except to save a woman's life
Yes   Split $18.6 billion in Iraq aid into half-grant, half-loan
No   Overhaul Medicare and create prescription drug benefit

CQ VOTE STUDIES

	PARTY UNITY		PRESIDENTIAL SUPPORT	
	Support	Oppose	Support	Oppose
2004	97%	3%	26%	74%
2003	99%	1%	13%	87%
2002	97%	3%	25%	75%
2001	96%	4%	12%	88%
2000	94%	6%	82%	18%

INTEREST GROUPS

	AFL-CIO	ADA	CCUS	ACU
2004	93%	95%	29%	0%
2003	100%	100%	21%	12%
2002	88%	90%	40%	4%
2001	100%	95%	30%	0%
2000	100%	85%	45%	8%

NORTH CAROLINA 12
Central — parts of Charlotte, Winston-Salem and Greensboro

The 12th became known as the mother of all racial gerrymanders when it was originally drawn for the 1992 elections. Struck down by the courts and widely ridiculed for a serpentine shape that aimed to maximize the black population, the 12th was redrawn twice in the 1990s. Redistricting following the 2000 census made only minimal changes to the district that survived challenge. The new 12th is 45 percent black and, among North Carolina districts, is rivaled only by the black-majority 1st in its massive Democratic tilt. In both the 2000 and 2004 presidential contests, the 12th gave the Democratic nominee his best showing in the state.

While not as contorted as its 1990s predecessors, the current 12th forms a zigzag shape that begins in Charlotte, parallels Interstate 85 north and east to take in part of Salisbury, then scoops up large black populations in Winston-Salem, High Point and Greensboro. It includes about one-third of Charlotte's population but two-thirds of its black residents, and 60

percent of Winston-Salem's population but nearly 90 percent of its black residents. Most of the 12th's black residents are lower- to middle-class.

Charlotte, where nearly one-third of the district population lives, has a booming economy. After a decade of consolidation among banks, the city surprised many by becoming the nation's biggest banking center outside of New York — the massive Bank of America is headquartered here. But the city's downtown — known as "uptown" — also has its share of poverty and crime. The Biddleville neighborhood, west of the business district, is a hub of the black community and is home to the predominately black Johnson C. Smith University. Outside of the city, transplants accustomed to New York City real estate prices have built upscale suburban neighborhoods with matching decorative street signs.

MAJOR INDUSTRY
Finance, transportation, health care

CITIES
Charlotte (pt.), 196,125; Winston-Salem (pt.), 115,986; Greensboro (pt.), 62,075; High Point (pt.), 52,429; Salisbury (pt.), 26,399

NOTABLE
A Woolworth's lunch counter in Greensboro was the site of the first major civil rights sit-in in 1960.

Rep. Brad Miller (D)

Elected 2002; 2nd term

Miller is an anomaly among the small group of white Southern Democrats in the House. Though he considers himself a New Democrat centrist, he is more liberal than most of his Dixie colleagues, particularly on a handful of national issues he cares deeply about. He frequently speaks out in favor of increased funding for public education, stepped up environmental protection and a more equal distribution of tax benefits among income groups. In 2003, he said incredulously of President Bush's tax cuts: "What is the rationale for not taxing stock dividends but taxing unemployment benefits? Why are we not doubling the tax credit for child care?"

His Yankee-style liberal streak reflects the political makeup of North Carolina's northern tier. It is more urban than many Southern districts, and the technology and biotechnology firms in the Research Triangle around Raleigh have drawn thousands of well-educated transplants. The district also takes in sizable black neighborhoods, students at the University of North Carolina's Greensboro campus and blue-collar textile workers, all Democratic-leaning constituencies. One day, Miller might be working to secure $4 million in funding for genome research at the Guilford Genomic Medicine Project in Greensboro and the next he could be trying to get more money for job retraining programs at local community colleges.

Another important constituency for Miller are the district's tobacco farmers who live in the rural stretch between the two population centers of Raleigh and Greensboro. He was an avid supporter in 2004 of the $10 billion government buyout of tobacco farmers, whose product was a staple of the state's economy until the market for tobacco collapsed in recent years.

In his first year in office, he earned a perfect 100 percent score from the nation's biggest union organization, the AFL-CIO. Citing the loss of 160,000 manufacturing jobs in North Carolina since 2001, mainly to overseas factories paying lower wages, Miller is opposed to the Bush administration's free-trade proposals.

A cautious and mild-tempered politician, Miller did not push a slew of new ideas or bills in his first term. As a junior member of the minority party without a major committee assignment, he had limited opportunity to do so, anyway. He told The News & Observer in Raleigh: "I have to look for modest ways to make my opinion matter."

Miller quietly focused on a signature initiative, one that let him take advantage of his seat on the Financial Services Committee. He teamed up with fellow North Carolina Democrat Melvin Watt on a bill to curb predatory lending by banks and other financial institutions. It would stop lenders from taking advantage of people with poor credit ratings by charging them exorbitant points and fees, and by penalizing them for paying back their loans ahead of time. Miller helped pass a similar law in North Carolina as a state senator in 1999.

Miller says he got the political bug early in life. He often cites an inspirational visit to the U.S. Capitol building as a 9-year-old child. Yet reaching his goal of working under the great dome wasn't that easy. His father, Nathan, the manager of the local post office in Fayetteville, N.C., died of a heart attack when Miller was just 12. He and his two older brothers were raised by their mother, Margaret, a school cafeteria bookkeeper.

She pushed her children to go to college — something she and her husband had aspired to but never had the financial means to do themselves.

Miller graduated from the University of North Carolina at Chapel Hill and

CAPITOL OFFICE
225-3032
www.house.gov/bradmiller
1722 Longworth 20515-3313; fax 225-0181

COMMITTEES
Financial Services
Science

HOMETOWN
Raleigh

BORN
May 19, 1953, Fayetteville, N.C.

RELIGION
Episcopalian

FAMILY
Wife, Esther Hall

EDUCATION
U. of North Carolina, B.A. 1975 (political science); London School of Economics, M.S.C. 1978 (comparative government); Columbia U., J.D. 1979

CAREER
Lawyer

POLITICAL HIGHLIGHTS
Sought Democratic nomination for N.C. secretary of state, 1988; N.C. House, 1993-95; defeated for re-election to N.C. House, 1994; N.C. Senate, 1997-2002

ELECTION RESULTS

2004 GENERAL

Brad Miller (D)	160,896	58.8%
Virginia Johnson (R)	112,788	41.2%

2004 PRIMARY

Brad Miller (D)	unopposed

2002 GENERAL

Brad Miller (D)	100,287	54.7%
Carolyn W. Grant (R)	77,688	42.4%
Alex MacDonald (LIBERT)	5,295	2.9%

was accepted at Columbia University law school in New York City. He took a short detour in getting there. Having never set foot outside the United States, Miller decided to broaden his experience by going overseas to get a master's degree in comparative government at the London School of Economics. He finished his law degree when he returned. But unlike many of his fellow law students, Miller had no taste for a career at a big corporate law firm in the city. He wanted to go home to get involved in politics.

Miller clerked for a year for now-retired federal appellate Judge J. Dickson Phillips Jr. in Chapel Hill, then moved to Raleigh to work as a litigator at private firms. He became chairman of the Wake County Democratic Party, and waited for an opportunity to run for office.

In 1988, he entered the Democratic primary for secretary of state and lost by only about 300 votes. Encouraged, he was primed to run for the North Carolina legislature in 1992, after redistricting created a new House district that included his neighborhood. He won the seat, but kept it for only two years. He was swept out by the Republican surge in the 1994 election. Miller waited two years, then got even by unseating a GOP incumbent in the state Senate, where he ultimately served three terms.

While in the legislature, Miller wrote North Carolina's safe gun-storage law, one of the first of its kind; cosponsored a law ending the state sales tax on food; and pushed for higher teacher salaries and smaller class sizes.

When reapportionment after the 2000 census gave North Carolina a new U.S. House seat, Miller was well-positioned to run for it. As chairman of the state Senate redistricting committee, he helped draw the new 13th District himself, giving it a distinct Democratic advantage in voter registration and including much of his political base. He prevailed in a six-way primary.

In a fierce general-election race, Miller defeated GOP businesswoman Carolyn W. Grant, a commercial real estate broker and former state transportation official, by 12 percentage points. He outspent Grant 2-to-1, and benefited from endorsements from labor unions, teachers and environmentalists. Grant charged Miller with voting for $1 billion in new taxes and giving state lawmakers a big pay raise. Miller's ads claimed that Grant used her son's college fund to buy a car — an assertion made in a civil lawsuit by Grant's former husband and one she steadfastly denied. Grant sued Miller for defamation, and their court battle continued long past the election.

Republicans thought Miller vulnerable in 2004, and Speaker J. Dennis Hastert and North Carolina Sen. Elizabeth Dole campaigned for his opponent, lawyer Virginia Johnson, formerly an aide to the House ethics and Armed Services committees. He won easily with 59 percent of the vote.

KEY VOTES

2004

Yes Extend federal unemployment benefits by 13 weeks

Yes Pass $283.2 billion, six-year federal highway and mass transit bill

Yes Approve $146 billion multi-year extension of previously enacted middle-class tax breaks

No Amend the Constitution to prohibit same-sex marriage

Yes Cut corporate taxes $137 billion over 10 years

Yes Reorganize U.S. intelligence agencies as proposed by Sept. 11 commission

2003

No Cut taxes by $330 billion through fiscal 2013

Yes Block Bush rule scaling back overtime pay for some white-collar federal workers

No Do not allow use of search warrants without first notifying subjects

Yes Allow importation of prescription drugs

No Create private school voucher program in Washington, D.C.

No Ban "partial birth" abortion except to save a woman's life

Yes Split $18.6 billion in Iraq aid into half-grant, half-loan

No Overhaul Medicare and create prescription drug benefit

CQ VOTE STUDIES

	PARTY UNITY		PRESIDENTIAL SUPPORT	
	Support	Oppose	Support	Oppose
2004	89%	11%	38%	62%
2003	96%	4%	17%	83%

INTEREST GROUPS

	AFL-CIO	ADA	CCUS	ACU
2004	87%	90%	43%	8%
2003	100%	95%	34%	12%

NORTH CAROLINA 13
North central — parts of Raleigh and Greensboro

The 13th, awarded to growing North Carolina in reapportionment following the 2000 census, is defined by its urban anchors of Greensboro and Raleigh, which are connected by several rural counties along the Virginia border. Slightly less than half of the district's population lives in Wake County (Raleigh), including a large number of government employees and recent arrivals from out of state.

The district encompasses northern and central Raleigh, an area that falls into the Research Triangle and is built around an economy of technology, biotechnology and financial services. The 13th takes in about 70 percent of Raleigh, which it shares with the 2nd and 4th districts. The 13th's slice of the city includes most of downtown and the state Capitol.

While Raleigh and Greensboro have grown rapidly and feature diverse economies, the northern, rural areas of Caswell County, on the Virginia border, and Alamance County, south of Caswell and shared with the 6th, still rely heavily on manufacturing and farming, particularly textiles and tobacco.

The 13th has an overall Democratic lean, in part because of a sizable black population and a number of white moderates and liberals in the urban areas. Registered Democrats outnumber Republicans by nearly 2-to-1, but the actual Democratic advantage at the polls is smaller.

The potential for swing voting exists in both the cities and suburbs, and district voters only narrowly supported Al Gore in the 2000 presidential election with 50 percent of the vote, making the district the closest in the state. In 2004, residents made the 13th the state's closest district in presidential voting again, giving John Kerry the win with 53 percent. Kerry won overwhelmingly in the district's portions of Guilford and Alamance counties but lost heavily in Person County and the 13th's part of Rockingham County.

MAJOR INDUSTRY
Biotechnology, financial services, textiles, agriculture

CITIES
Raleigh (pt.), 192,576; Greensboro (pt.), 102,806; Burlington (pt.), 23,836

NOTABLE
Caswell County features one of the largest Amish communities in the South.

NORTH DAKOTA

Gov. John Hoeven (R)

First elected: 2000
Length of term: 4 years
Term expires: 12/08
Salary: $87,216
Phone: (701) 328-2200

Hometown: Bismarck
Born: March 13, 1957; Bismarck, N.D.
Religion: Roman Catholic
Family: Wife, Mical Hoeven; two children
Education: Dartmouth College, B.A. 1979 (history & economics); Northwestern U., M.B.A. 1981
Career: Bank CEO
Political highlights: No previous office

Election results:
2004 GENERAL

John Hoeven (R)	220,803	71.3%
Joseph A. Satrom (D)	84,877	27.4%
Roland Riemers (I)	4,193	1.4%

Lt. Gov. Jack Dalrymple (R)

First elected: 2000
Length of term: 4 years
Term expires: 12/08
Salary: $67,708
Phone: (701) 328-2200

STATE LEGISLATURE

Legislative Assembly: January-April in odd-numbered years

House: 94 members, 4-year terms
2005 breakdown: 67R, 27D; 76 men, 18 women
Salary: $3,000; $125/day in session
Phone: (701) 328-2916

Senate: 47 members, 4-year terms
2005 breakdown: 32R, 15D; 42 men, 5 women
Salary: $3,000; $125/day in session
Phone: (701) 328-2916

STATE TERM LIMITS

Governor: No
House: No
Senate: No

URBAN STATISTICS

CITY	POPULATION
Fargo	90,599
Bismarck	55,532
Grand Forks	49,321
Minot	36,567
Mandan	16,718

REGISTERED VOTERS

Voters do not register by party.

POPULATION

2004 population (est.)	634,366
2000 population	642,200
1990 population	638,800
Percent change (1990-2000)	+0.5%
Rank among states (2004)	48
Median age	36.2
Born in state	72.5%
Foreign born	1.9%
Violent crime rate	81/100,000
Poverty level	11.9%
Federal workers	9,656
Military	12,479

REDISTRICTING

North Dakota retained its one House seat in reapportionment.

MISCELLANEOUS

Web: www.discovernd.com
Capital: Bismarck
STATE ELECTION OFFICIAL
(701) 328-4146
DEMOCRATIC HEADQUARTERS
(701) 255-0460
REPUBLICAN HEADQUARTERS
(701) 255-0030

District Statistics

DIST.	2004 VOTE FOR PRESIDENT BUSH	KERRY	WHITE	BLACK	ASIAN	HISP	MEDIAN INCOME	WHITE COLLAR	BLUE COLLAR	SERVICE INDUSTRY	OVER 64	UNDER 18	COLLEGE EDUCATION	RURAL	SQ. MILES
AL	60%	38%	88%	1%	1%	1%	$35,282	59%	25%	16%	14%	27%	22%	48%	75,885
STATE	60	38	88	1	1	1	$35,282	59	25	16	14	27	22	48	75,885
U.S.	50.7	48.3	69	12	4	13	$41,994	60	25	15	12	26	24	21	3,537,438

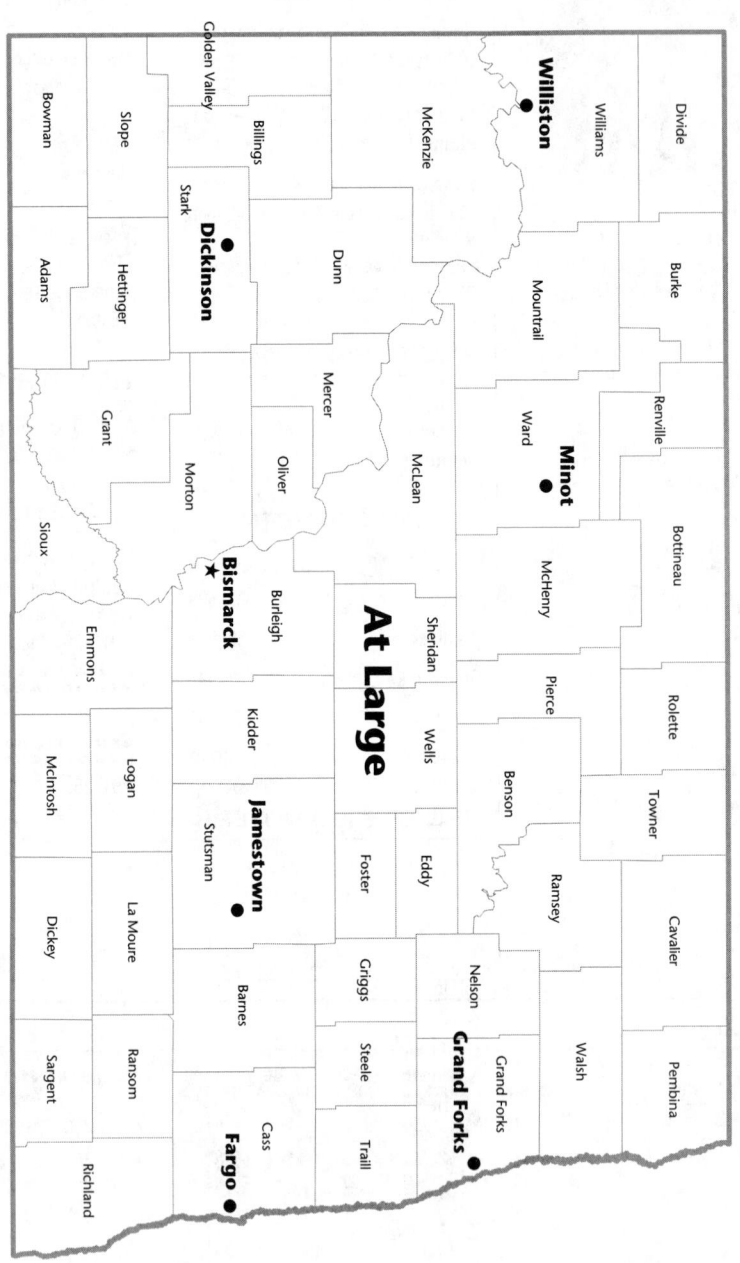

Sen. Kent Conrad (D)

Elected 1986; 3rd full term

Conrad does not fit the stereotype of rugged Westerner; he looks more like a bookish "Jeopardy" contestant. But he is a relentless advocate for farmers, and he strives to make sure the people of North Dakota and other sparsely populated states are not ignored in Washington. As the senior Democrat on the Budget Committee, Conrad is also the leader of the minority opposition on budget policy.

Although he is a member of the moderate, pro-business wing of the party known as the New Democrats, Conrad has always been a leadership loyalist. He was a close ally of Democratic leader Tom Daschle, who lost a re-election bid in 2004. Conrad is up for re-election in 2006, but he has not changed voting patterns in election cycles before, and he's unlikely to start now.

He is a certified budget hawk who for years has been voicing concern about the long-term solvency of Social Security. That gives him the background to weigh in on President Bush's second-term initiative to overhaul the program to include private investment accounts for younger taxpayers.

Indeed, Conrad's early moves in the 109th Congress — penning a newspaper editorial on Social Security with Republican Lindsey Graham of South Carolina and chatting up Bush on Air Force One on the way to a campaign-style presidential forum on Social Security in Fargo — illustrated a desire to get into the legislative sandbox.

But Conrad also has a tendency to talk as though he wants to join the Republicans in solving the big problems, while then setting the price of his cooperation higher than they can accept. So despite an eagerness to work things out, his fundamental opposition to Bush administration policies on Social Security private accounts and further tax cuts would seem to ensure he stays on the outside looking in as major decisions are made.

Conrad's skills were put to the test in the middle of 2001, when the switch of partisan control of the Senate made him the Budget Committee chairman. He had been preparing for the post his entire Senate career. A self-styled budget purist devoted to the ideal of fiscal discipline, Conrad had to write a budget that would please Democrats of all fiscal stripes, from Southern conservatives to traditional Northeastern liberals, who tend to favor preserving government programs.

Conrad managed to get a budget out of his committee on a party-line vote in 2002, but it never came to the floor for lack of votes. That marked the first time since the advent of the modern budget process in 1974 that the Senate did not adopt a budget resolution, a fact Republicans noted with glee.

When the Republicans regained control of the Senate in 2003, Conrad resumed his role as the vocal opposition leader on Budget. With his trademark sheaf of pie charts and bar graphs at the ready, Conrad stepped up his attacks on Bush's fiscal strategy — especially as the budget deficit hit new records — blasting the administration for sending the government "back in the deficit ditch." Conrad seems intent on having the last word in any debate, a trait that sometimes grates on his GOP colleagues.

Conrad concedes that his fiscal sensibilities sometimes conflict with his desire to help out his agrarian constituents. He was a strong supporter of Western lawmakers' efforts throughout Bush's first term to provide emergency aid to farmers and ranchers hit by drought.

A constant critic of the GOP-engineered 1996 farm law, which sought to phase out traditional crop subsidies and replace them with fixed but declining annual payments, Conrad played a central role in writing the 2002

CAPITOL OFFICE
224-2043
senator@conrad.senate.gov
conrad.senate.gov
530 Hart 20510-3403; fax 224-7776

COMMITTEES
Agriculture, Nutrition & Forestry
Budget - ranking member
Finance
Indian Affairs

HOMETOWN
Bismarck

BORN
March 12, 1948, Bismarck, N.D.

RELIGION
Unitarian

FAMILY
Wife, Lucy Calautti; one child

EDUCATION
U. of Missouri, attended 1967; Stanford U., A.B. 1971 (government & political science); George Washington U., M.B.A. 1975

CAREER
Management and personnel director

POLITICAL HIGHLIGHTS
Candidate for N.D. auditor, 1976; N.D. tax commissioner, 1981-87

ELECTION RESULTS

2000 GENERAL
Kent Conrad (D)	176,470	61.5%
Duane Sand (R)	110,420	38.5%

2000 PRIMARY
Kent Conrad (D)	unopposed

PREVIOUS WINNING PERCENTAGES
1994 (58%); 1992 Special Election (63%); 1986 (50%)

reversal of that policy that substantially expanded farm subsidies.

Conrad also has not been bashful about pressing for millions of dollars in improvements to the Air Force bases in Grand Forks and Minot. He is a defender of funding for the state National Guard's 119th Fighter Wing — nicknamed the Happy Hooligans — whose F-16 fighter pilots were the first scrambled to guard the airspace over Washington on Sept. 11, 2001.

His record on international trade tracks his concerns about the farm economy. Conrad voted against the North American Free Trade Agreement in 1993 because he feared that U.S. wheat prices would drop after an influx of Canadian wheat. He supported the 2000 law making permanent the normal U.S.-China trade relationship, predicting it would help grain growers. And he opposed the 2002 law that renewed presidential powers to more easily negotiate trade deals without interference from Congress, arguing that it would put U.S. farmers at a competitive disadvantage. He voted no even though the law provides for federal aid to farmers hurt by imports, a provision he had pursued for years.

Conrad has disappointed conservatives at times by signaling he might support them, then opposing them at the last minute. In the 106th Congress, he decided after much deliberation to oppose a constitutional amendment barring flag desecration. In the 104th, Conrad made a late decision to oppose a constitutional amendment mandating a balanced federal budget, which he said could threaten Social Security.

On most social issues, Conrad's positions reflect the more conservative side of the prairie populist tradition from which he hails. In 2004, he voted to make it a criminal offense to injure or kill a fetus during the commission of a violent crime. Before that, he opposed allowing federal employees' health care plans to cover abortion. But he sides with most Democrats in objecting to a constitutional amendment to ban same-sex marriage.

Conrad's early years were marked by the death of his parents, who were killed by a drunken driver when he was 5. He and his brothers were raised by his grandparents. He went to high school at a U.S. military base in Libya, where he lived with family friends. Upon his return to North Dakota, he headed a successful statewide campaign — while still a teenager — to grant voting rights to 19-year-olds.

He was elected state tax commissioner in 1980, and he gained widespread popularity by vigorously auditing out-of-state corporations. In 1986, he unseated Republican Sen. Mark Andrews by 2,000 votes after linking the incumbent to the Reagan administration's unpopular farm policy.

Conrad moved to Washington, and shortly thereafter married Lucy Calautti, chief of staff to his North Dakota colleague Byron L. Dorgan, who was then serving in the House. An avid baseball fan like Conrad, she became a lobbyist for Major League Baseball in 2000. Conrad has said he'd like to be baseball commissioner someday.

One of Conrad's pledges during his first Senate campaign was that he would not seek re-election unless the trade and budget deficits were significantly reduced during his term in office. In April 1992, Conrad kept his promise by announcing his retirement, even though he joked that he had written the pledge while suffering from a 104-degree fever.

But in September of that year, North Dakota's senior senator, Democrat Quentin N. Burdick, died at age 84. Democrats urged Conrad to run in a special election the following December, and he was unchallenged for the party's nomination. He won the special election with 63 percent of the vote and enjoyed comfortable margins in his 1994 and 2000 elections.

On the wall in Conrad's office in Bismarck hangs a prized gift from the state's Standing Rock Indian Tribe — a framed resolution bearing his honorary Sioux name, "Namni Sni," which means, "Never Turns Back."

KEY VOTES

2004

Yes Pass $318.9 billion, six-year highway and mass transit bill
Yes Extend assault weapons ban for 10 years
Yes Restore pay-as-you-go rules for new tax cuts and entitlement spending
Yes Criminalize harm to a fetus in an attack on the mother
Yes Increase mandatory child care funding to states by $6 billion over five years
No   Amend the Constitution to prohibit same-sex marriage
Yes Approve $146 billion multi-year extension of previously enacted middle-class tax breaks
Yes Reorganize U.S. intelligence agencies as proposed by Sept. 11 commission
Yes Cut corporate taxes $137 billion over 10 years

2003

Yes Delay Bush changes to Clean Air Act
No   Allow confirmation vote on Miguel A. Estrada to the U.S. Court of Appeals for the D.C. Circuit
Yes Block a Bush proposal opening Alaska's Arctic National Wildlife Refuge to oil drilling
Yes Limit size of Bush's proposed tax cut to $350 billion through fiscal 2013
Yes Overhaul Medicare and create prescription drug benefit
Yes Block Bush rule scaling back overtime pay for some white-collar federal workers
Yes Split $20 billion in Iraq aid into half-grant, half-loan
Yes Ban "partial birth" abortion except to save a woman's life
No   Stop proposal allowing travel to Cuba
Yes Allow final vote on energy policy overhaul

CQ VOTE STUDIES

	PARTY UNITY		PRESIDENTIAL SUPPORT	
	Support	Oppose	Support	Oppose
2004	81%	19%	62%	38%
2003	85%	15%	58%	42%
2002	86%	14%	66%	34%
2001	90%	10%	66%	34%
2000	87%	13%	90%	10%
1999	87%	13%	73%	27%
1998	87%	13%	75%	25%
1997	82%	18%	81%	19%
1996	87%	13%	83%	17%
1995	87%	13%	84%	16%

INTEREST GROUPS

	AFL-CIO	ADA	CCUS	ACU
2004	100%	90%	53%	20%
2003	77%	80%	70%	15%
2002	100%	95%	45%	10%
2001	94%	85%	50%	36%
2000	71%	85%	42%	29%
1999	89%	90%	53%	16%
1998	88%	90%	61%	16%
1997	57%	65%	50%	16%
1996	71%	85%	23%	15%
1995	100%	90%	42%	9%

Sen. Byron L. Dorgan (D)

Elected 1992; 3rd term

CAPITOL OFFICE
224-2551
senator@dorgan.senate.gov
dorgan.senate.gov
322 Hart 20510-3405; fax 224-1193

COMMITTEES
Appropriations
Commerce, Science & Transportation
Energy & Natural Resources
Indian Affairs - ranking member

HOMETOWN
Bismarck

BORN
May 14, 1942, Regent, N.D.

RELIGION
Lutheran

FAMILY
Wife, Kimberly Dorgan; four children (one deceased)

EDUCATION
U. of North Dakota, B.S. 1965; U. of Denver, M.B.A. 1966

CAREER
Aerospace company management trainer

POLITICAL HIGHLIGHTS
N.D. tax commissioner, 1969-80; Democratic nominee for U.S. House, 1974; U.S. House, 1981-92

ELECTION RESULTS

2004 GENERAL

Byron L. Dorgan (D)	211,843	68.3%
Mike Liffrig (R)	98,553	31.8%

2004 PRIMARY

Byron L. Dorgan (D)	unopposed

PREVIOUS WINNING PERCENTAGES
1998 (63%); 1992 (59%); 1990 House Election (65%); 1988 House Election (71%); 1986 House Election (76%); 1984 House Election (79%); 1982 House Election (72%); 1980 House Election (57%)

Dorgan is a "true blue" voice in a state where voters, for all their support of Republican presidents, retain a strong streak of the prairie populism that swept the Upper Midwest in the 1910s. A passionate critic of the rich and powerful, he rails against the large and distant forces — multinational corporations, foreign governments, drug companies — that, he says, don't care a whit for hard-working folk such as those on the windswept plains.

Even one-on-one, Dorgan is intense about his beliefs, especially when it comes to helping struggling farmers. His birthplace is the wheat-growing and ranching community of Regent, where, he likes to say, he graduated in the top five in his high school class — of nine. Although he has fought most of President Bush's efforts to scale back the 2002 farm law, he strongly supported Bush's proposal to put a $250,000 limit on federal farm payments, cosponsoring legislation in the 109th Congress to impose such a cap. Dorgan wants federal payments to go to family farms, not agribusiness.

Among Dorgan's causes in the 108th Congress was legislation to allow consumers to buy inexpensive prescription drugs imported from Canada and other nations with price controls as a means of countering what he views as gouging by U.S. pharmaceutical companies. After failing to get such language included in the 2003 Medicare prescription drug law, Dorgan sponsored a bill in 2004 requiring the Food and Drug Administration to implement a system to import drugs from Canada and other countries.

Although his bill had strong support from constituents and many senators in both parties, GOP leaders refused to allow it on the floor. Dorgan in 2004 held up the nomination of Mark McClellan to be head of the Medicare program until he got assurances that the Senate leadership would "begin a process for developing proposals that will allow for the safe importation of FDA-approved prescription drugs." Dorgan took that to mean full consideration of a bill, while the leadership said they had promised only to begin exploring the idea. Believing he had been wronged, Dorgan in 2005 threatened to hold up the nomination of Michael O. Leavitt to be Health and Human Services secretary until he was promised a hearing on his drug bill.

Dorgan has a strong attachment to his home state, but he is also tied into the Washington elite. He and his family have a second home in the tony suburb of McLean, Va., where the senator can be found playing tennis and golfing, sometimes with well-known politicos. His wife Kimberly was Linda Hall's maid of honor when she married Democratic Sen. Tom Daschle of South Dakota in 1984. A year later, Mrs. Daschle was maid of honor when Kimberly Olson became Dorgan's second wife.

Dorgan is similarly tight with his North Dakota partner in the Senate. When he first ran for Congress in 1974, his campaign manager was Kent Conrad, and when Dorgan won a House seat six years later, his successor as state tax commissioner was Conrad. Lucy Calautti, Conrad's wife, was Dorgan's chief of staff for 10 years.

When Daschle, the Senate's Democratic leader, was defeated by Republican John Thune in 2004 and Harry Reid ascended to the minority leader's post, Dorgan briefly considered running for whip, the No. 2 job. He bowed out just days later as Richard J. Durbin of Illinois claimed enough votes to prevail. Instead, Dorgan continued on as chairman of the Democratic Policy Committee, helping chart the party's legislative and political course in the Senate. It is a comfortable post for a master of the sound bite; Dorgan willingly takes to the floor at a moment's notice to explain the party position or to fend off Republican challenges.

Big business is a favorite target for the populist Dorgan. The collapse of the energy giant Enron Corp. in 2001 and numerous accounting misdeeds by other multinational corporations gave him plenty of ammunition. Then chairman of the Commerce Subcommittee on Consumer Affairs, Dorgan called one of the first hearings on the issue and later held a well-publicized session featuring former Enron CEO Jeffrey Skilling. "This is disgusting to me — corporate behavior without a moral base," Dorgan said.

Dorgan led an effort in the 108th Congress to bar the Federal Communications Commission from easing media ownership rules to allow giant media conglomerates to own more radio and television stations in a single market and to own a newspaper and TV station in the same market. He succeeded in attaching a ban on the rules change to a GOP bill strengthening broadcasting indecency laws. Because the White House and Republican leaders strongly opposed Dorgan's media ownership effort, his actions had the effect of sinking the indecency legislation.

Dorgan long has been a leader in the effort to end the embargo on trade with Cuba, which otherwise would be a market for peas and other North Dakota crops. And he backed the 2000 law making permanent the normal trade relationship between the United States and China. But Dorgan opposed the 2002 law granting Bush expedited trade negotiating authority, predicting the consequence would be agreements that harmed U.S. farmers. He voted against three key trade pacts — with Australia, Chile and Singapore — submitted to the 108th Congress.

As one of the few remaining Democrats from "red" states, Dorgan must always take care not to stray too far to the left of his constituents. His voting record puts him toward the conservative end of the Senate Democratic spectrum. He joined Republicans, for example, in supporting the 1996 welfare overhaul. He was in the minority of Democrats who voted in 2002 to authorize the use of force in Iraq. In 2003, he supported a ban on a procedure opponents call "partial birth" abortion. Also that year, he was one of 11 Democrats (including his colleague, Conrad) voting for the final version of the GOP-drafted Medicare overhaul legislation, which included huge payment increases for rural hospitals and doctors.

In the 108th, only 10 Senate Democrats supported Bush more frequently than Dorgan or split with their fellow Democrats more often on votes pitting the parties against each other.

Other than a brief stint with a Denver-based aerospace firm, Dorgan has spent virtually all of his career in government. He was working in the state tax department in 1969 when the governor appointed him commissioner, making Dorgan, at 26, the youngest constitutional officer in North Dakota history. By speaking out on an array of issues and suing out-of-state corporations for unpaid taxes, he made a name for himself with voters.

Dorgan took on GOP Rep. Mark Andrews in 1974, holding him to 56 percent of the vote. When Andrews ran for the Senate in 1980, Dorgan captured the House seat in a campaign in which he tempered his liberal reputation by supporting an anti-abortion constitutional amendment and decrying government waste. He won five re-elections with ease and became a leading opponent on the Ways and Means Committee of the tax cuts proposed by Presidents Ronald Reagan and George Bush.

He won election to the Senate with 59 percent of the vote in 1992, after Conrad announced he was retiring to fulfill a campaign pledge to leave the Senate that year unless the deficit was reduced. (Conrad won a Senate seat that year anyway, after Sen. Quentin N. Burdick died.)

Dorgan was re-elected in 1998 with 63 percent and widened that edge to 68 percent in 2004, despite Bush's victory in the state.

KEY VOTES

2004

Yes Pass $318.9 billion, six-year highway and mass transit bill
Yes Extend assault weapons ban for 10 years
Yes Restore pay-as-you-go rules for new tax cuts and entitlement spending
Yes Criminalize harm to a fetus in an attack on the mother
Yes Increase mandatory child care funding to states by $6 billion over five years
No Amend the Constitution to prohibit same-sex marriage
Yes Approve $146 billion multi-year extension of previously enacted middle-class tax breaks
Yes Reorganize U.S. intelligence agencies as proposed by Sept. 11 commission
? Cut corporate taxes $137 billion over 10 years

2003

Yes Delay Bush changes to Clean Air Act
No Allow confirmation vote on Miguel A. Estrada to the U.S. Court of Appeals for the D.C. Circuit
Yes Block a Bush proposal opening Alaska's Arctic National Wildlife Refuge to oil drilling
Yes Limit size of Bush's proposed tax cut to $350 billion through fiscal 2013
Yes Overhaul Medicare and create prescription drug benefit
Yes Block Bush rule scaling back overtime pay for some white-collar federal workers
Yes Split $20 billion in Iraq aid into half-grant, half-loan
Yes Ban "partial birth" abortion except to save a woman's life
No Stop proposal allowing travel to Cuba
Yes Allow final vote on energy policy overhaul

CQ VOTE STUDIES

	PARTY UNITY		PRESIDENTIAL SUPPORT	
	Support	Oppose	Support	Oppose
2004	84%	16%	62%	38%
2003	90%	10%	55%	45%
2002	88%	12%	70%	30%
2001	91%	9%	68%	32%
2000	90%	10%	90%	10%
1999	88%	12%	73%	27%
1998	87%	13%	76%	24%
1997	87%	13%	81%	19%
1996	84%	16%	80%	20%
1995	89%	11%	86%	14%

INTEREST GROUPS

	AFL-CIO	ADA	CCUS	ACU
2004	100%	95%	50%	20%
2003	92%	80%	61%	10%
2002	100%	90%	50%	20%
2001	94%	85%	50%	36%
2000	75%	90%	46%	16%
1999	100%	95%	35%	12%
1998	88%	90%	61%	12%
1997	86%	80%	50%	16%
1996	71%	85%	38%	20%
1995	100%	90%	47%	13%

Rep. Earl Pomeroy (D)

CAPITOL OFFICE
225-2611
rep.earl.pomeroy@mail.house.gov
www.pomeroy.house.gov
1501 Longworth 20515-3401; fax 226-0893

COMMITTEES
Agriculture
Ways & Means

HOMETOWN
Bismarck

BORN
Sept. 2, 1952, Valley City, N.D.

RELIGION
Presbyterian

FAMILY
Divorced; two children

EDUCATION
Valley City State U., attended 1970-71; U. of North Dakota, B.A. 1974 (political science); U. of Durham (United Kingdom), attended 1975 (legal history); U. of North Dakota, J.D. 1979

CAREER
Lawyer

POLITICAL HIGHLIGHTS
N.D. House, 1981-85; N.D. insurance commissioner, 1985-93

ELECTION RESULTS

2004 GENERAL
Earl Pomeroy (D)	185,130	59.6%
Duane Sand (R)	125,684	40.4%

2004 PRIMARY
Earl Pomeroy (D)	unopposed

2002 GENERAL
Earl Pomeroy (D)	121,073	52.4%
Rick Clayburgh (R)	109,957	47.6%

PREVIOUS WINNING PERCENTAGES
2000 (53%); 1998 (56%); 1996 (55%); 1994 (52%); 1992 (57%)

Elected 1992; 7th term

As a Democrat in a GOP-leaning state, Pomeroy has relied on his likability and plum committee assignments to fend off attempts to end his 12-year run in Congress.

Blessed with a schoolboy grin and natural friendliness, Pomeroy comes across as a throwback to an earlier era. "He's the kind of guy you sit down with and talk about anything. . . . He's just the kind of person that people in this state like," says Terry Devine, a political columnist for the Fargo Forum, the state's largest newspaper.

In Washington, Pomeroy has developed an expertise in technical financial issues, particularly in insurance and pension law. In 2001, he bested about 20 Democrats to win appointment to the party's one open seat on the Ways and Means Committee, which oversees taxes, trade, Medicare and Social Security. Even though Ways and Means is supposed to be an exclusive assignment, Pomeroy in the 108th Congress was also given a seat on the Agriculture Committee, where he had served for eight years before moving to Ways and Means.

He has used those positions to fight against administration attempts to reopen the border to Canadian live beef cattle imports and pass a free-trade agreement with Australia that he says could harm wheat growers. But his legislative passion is shoring up the retirement system, both Social Security and private pension plans.

His interest was sparked at a young age. Pomeroy grew up in a small town where his father ran a feed-and-fertilizer store and where he and his brother raised chickens on the family's small farm to make a few extra dollars. His family relied on Social Security survivor benefits to put him through college after his father died. He has sharply criticized President Bush's proposal to allow diversion of payroll taxes into private investment accounts.

Members of both parties often seek out Pomeroy's views on private pension issues. He worked with Republican Rob Portman of Ohio and Democrat Benjamin L. Cardin of Maryland on a bipartisan pension overhaul bill that included Pomeroy's proposal to make it easier for workers to transfer their retirement savings to a new job.

Pomeroy has sided with Bush on several high-profile issues, including use of military force against Iraq and passage of the Medicare prescription drug bill in 2003, which included significant benefits for rural health care. He also voted to outlaw a procedure that critics call "partial birth" abortion. He supports gun ownership rights and has been a main proponent, with Texas Republican Lamar Smith, of legislation to ban child pornography and obscenity on the Internet.

Pomeroy teamed up with Republican Tom Osborne of Nebraska to press a portion of Bush's education bill that allows more flexibility for rural school districts. But in 2004, he endorsed school boards suing the Education Department if officials do not reverse a ruling that thousands of North Dakota elementary school teachers do not meet new qualification standards under the No Child Left Behind Act.

On most economic issues, Pomeroy sides with Democrats. He was an unabashed proponent of the $410 billion farm bill that attempted to restore a "safety net" for agricultural producers. And he opposed all three of the big tax cut bills of Bush's first term as fiscally imprudent for a government trying to ensure funding for Social Security and other costly programs. The National Taxpayers Union annually gives him an "F" grade for his votes on spending, although the group in 2005 applauded budget recommendations made by the House Democrats' Blue Dog Coalition, of which Pomeroy has been a member since 2003.

He backed a plan to postpone the base-closing process until 2007 in a bid to protect North Dakota's Grand Forks Air Force Base. Grand Forks' designation as one of three key aerial refueling bases gives Pomeroy a keen interest in a scandal-plagued tanker-plane deal with Boeing Co.

Pomeroy honed his knowledge of pension law during eight years as North Dakota's insurance commissioner. He also served as president of the National Association of Insurance Commissioners. He receives more campaign money from the insurance industry than most other House candidates.

His younger brother, Glenn, succeeded him in both insurance posts and has since moved into an insurance-related job for General Electric Corp. The Pomeroy brothers' ties to the industry raised conflict of interest questions in the 107th, when Pomeroy strongly supported Republican-led plans to make permanent a tax break that allowed U.S. financial services companies and manufacturers to defer taxes on the income they earn overseas. Insurance companies, including General Electric, stood to reap a windfall from the bill. Glenn Pomeroy had lobbied for its passage.

Pomeroy has been close to North Dakota's two Democratic senators, Kent Conrad and Byron L. Dorgan, since the 1970s. When he was just a year out of college, Pomeroy drove Dorgan around as the latter ran unsuccessfully for the House in 1974. Conrad was Dorgan's campaign manager.

Having lived abroad as a student and worked in the South with the Methodist church, Pomeroy decided in the early 1990s to set politics aside and return to social outreach. As he neared the end of his second term as insurance commissioner, Pomeroy and his then wife announced plans to move to Russia to work in the Peace Corps.

Instead, he answered entreaties from the state Democratic Party to run for the House after a series of unexpected events leading up to the 1992 election. Conrad announced he would retire from the Senate rather than break a 1986 campaign promise not to seek re-election unless the deficit was reduced. Dorgan, the state's six-term House member, jumped into the Senate contest, leaving the House seat open. Hours before the nominations were to begin, Pomeroy agreed to run for Dorgan's seat. (Conrad later ran for the other Senate seat after Democrat Quentin N. Burdick died.)

Pomeroy and his ex-wife have two adopted children from Korea. In 1999, he helped reunite a family that had been torn apart by the war in Kosovo, and, in thanks, the family named a newborn baby Dakota.

KEY VOTES

2004

Yes Extend federal unemployment benefits by 13 weeks

Yes Pass $283.2 billion, six-year federal highway and mass transit bill

Yes Approve $146 billion multi-year extension of previously enacted middle-class tax breaks

No Amend the Constitution to prohibit same-sex marriage

Yes Cut corporate taxes $137 billion over 10 years

Yes Reorganize U.S. intelligence agencies as proposed by Sept. 11 commission

2003

No Cut taxes by $330 billion through fiscal 2013

Yes Block Bush rule scaling back overtime pay for some white-collar federal workers

Yes Do not allow use of search warrants without first notifying subjects

Yes Allow importation of prescription drugs

No Create private school voucher program in Washington, D.C.

Yes Ban "partial birth" abortion except to save a woman's life

Yes Split $18.6 billion in Iraq aid into half-grant, half-loan

Yes Overhaul Medicare and create prescription drug benefit

CQ VOTE STUDIES

	PARTY UNITY		PRESIDENTIAL SUPPORT	
	Support	Oppose	Support	Oppose
2004	82%	18%	47%	53%
2003	76%	24%	51%	49%
2002	78%	22%	58%	42%
2001	78%	22%	35%	65%
2000	88%	12%	85%	15%

INTEREST GROUPS

	AFL-CIO	ADA	CCUS	ACU
2004	93%	85%	67%	28%
2003	73%	65%	57%	36%
2002	78%	70%	60%	32%
2001	92%	85%	39%	28%
2000	90%	85%	57%	8%

NORTH DAKOTA

At large

North Dakota includes fertile eastern Red River farmlands, wheat-covered plains, arid grasslands farther west and Teddy Roosevelt's beloved ranches near the western border.

The state's agriculture-based economy was shaken in the 1990s by floods, blizzards, foreign competition and the reduction of federal support systems. Agricultural income dropped drastically in the wake of devastating Red River floods and steep declines in the price of wheat. Economic trends intensified a migration of the state's young people away from rural farming communities and into the cities of Fargo and Grand Forks, where a diversified economy and several universities provide greater job choice.

Democrats have represented North Dakota in the House since 1981, and the state's congressional delegation has been entirely Democratic since 1987. Before then, the state had elected only three Democratic representatives (for a total of only six years) since statehood and had supported only five Democratic presidential nominees in the 20th

century. Republicans are more numerous and unwavering in the western part of the state, while eastern communities and American Indian reservations are more supportive of Democrats. But Republican roots are strong throughout the state — the state legislature and governorship are GOP-controlled and George W. Bush handily carried the state in 2004.

MAJOR INDUSTRY
Agriculture, health care, higher education

MILITARY
Minot Air Force Base, 4,940 military, 1,142 civilian; Grand Forks Air Force Base, 2,842 military, 1,152 civilian (2004)

CITIES
Fargo, 90,599; Bismarck, 55,532; Grand Forks, 49,321; Minot, 36,567

NOTABLE
Lewis and Clark met Sacagawea, the Shoshone Indian woman who guided them to the Pacific Ocean, near the Mandan Indian village; Sitting Bull surrendered at Fort Buford in 1881; Gen. George Custer was stationed at Fort Lincoln, near Bismarck, in 1876 when his unit headed west to ultimate defeat at Little Big Horn; The National Buffalo Museum is in Jamestown.

OHIO

Gov. Bob Taft (R)

First elected: 1998
Length of term: 4 years
Term expires: 1/07
Salary: $130,292
Phone: (614) 466-3555

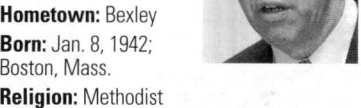

Hometown: Bexley
Born: Jan. 8, 1942; Boston, Mass.
Religion: Methodist
Family: Wife, Hope Taft; one child
Education: Yale U., B.A. 1963; Princeton U., M.A. 1967 (government); U. of Cincinnati, J.D. 1976
Career: State budget officer; U.S. State Department employee; Peace Corps volunteer
Political highlights: Ohio House, 1976-80; Hamilton County Commission, 1981-90; Ohio secretary of state, 1991-99

Election results:

2002 GENERAL

Bob Taft (R)	1,865,007	57.8%
Tim Hagan (D)	1,236,924	38.3%
John A. Eastman (I)	126,686	3.9%

Lt. Gov. Bruce Johnson (R)

Assumed office: 2005
Length of term: 4 years
Term expires: 1/07
Salary: Does not receive salary as lieutenant governor; earns $125,000 as the director of the Department of Development
Phone: (614) 466-0990

STATE LEGISLATURE

General Assembly: January-June in odd-numbered years; January-July in even-numbered years

House: 99 members, 2-year terms
2005 breakdown: 60R, 39D; 78 men, 21 women
Salary: $56,261
Phone: (614) 466-3357

Senate: 33 members, 4-year terms
2005 breakdown: 22R, 11D; 28 men, 5 women
Salary: $56,261
Phone: (614) 466-4900

STATE TERM LIMITS

Governor: 2 terms
House: 4 consecutive terms
Senate: 2 consecutive terms

URBAN STATISTICS

CITY	POPULATION
Columbus	711,470
Cleveland	478,403
Cincinnati	331,285
Toledo	313,619
Akron	217,074

REGISTERED VOTERS

Voters do not register by party.

POPULATION

2004 population (est.)	11,459,011
2000 population	11,353,140
1990 population	10,847,115
Percent change (1990-2000)	+4.7%
Rank among states (2004)	7

Median age	36.2
Born in state	74.7%
Foreign born	3%
Violent crime rate	334/100,000
Poverty level	10.6%
Federal workers	80,445
Military	36,713

REDISTRICTING

Ohio lost one House seat in reapportionment. The state legislature drew a new, 18-district map, which the governor signed on Jan. 24, 2002.

MISCELLANEOUS

Web: www.ohio.gov
Capital: Columbus
STATE ELECTION OFFICIAL
(614) 466-2585
DEMOCRATIC HEADQUARTERS
(614) 221-6563
REPUBLICAN HEADQUARTERS
(614) 228-2481

District Statistics

DIST.	2004 VOTE FOR PRESIDENT BUSH	KERRY	WHITE	BLACK	ASIAN	HISP	MEDIAN INCOME	WHITE COLLAR	BLUE COLLAR	SERVICE INDUSTRY	OVER 64	UNDER 18	COLLEGE EDUCATION	RURAL	SQ. MILES
1	50%	49%	69%	27%	1%	1%	$37,414	60%	23%	16%	13%	26%	22%	5%	416
2	64	36	92	5	1	1	$46,813	64	23	13	12	26	29	27	2,612
3	54	45	79	17	1	1	$41,591	60	26	14	14	25	23	15	1,595
4	65	34	92	5	1	1	$40,100	47	38	15	14	26	13	41	4,620
5	61	38	94	1	0	4	$41,701	46	40	14	13	26	15	51	6,128
6	50	49	95	2	0	1	$32,888	52	32	16	15	23	14	50	5,198
7	57	42	89	7	1	1	$43,248	57	28	14	12	25	19	29	2,848
8	64	35	92	4	1	1	$43,753	56	30	14	12	26	19	22	2,014
9	42	58	80	14	1	4	$40,265	55	29	16	14	26	20	14	1,102
10	41	58	87	4	2	5	$41,841	63	23	14	16	23	23	1	195
11	18	81	39	56	2	2	$31,998	61	21	17	15	26	23	0	135
12	51	49	72	22	2	2	$47,289	68	18	13	10	27	32	12	1,016
13	44	56	82	12	1	4	$44,524	59	27	14	14	26	22	7	531
14	52	47	94	2	1	1	$51,304	62	25	12	13	26	27	26	1,797
15	50	49	85	7	3	2	$43,885	66	20	14	10	23	32	9	1,178

District Statistics

DIST.	2004 VOTE FOR PRESIDENT BUSH	KERRY	WHITE	BLACK	ASIAN	HISP	MEDIAN INCOME	WHITE COLLAR	BLUE COLLAR	SERVICE INDUSTRY	OVER 64	UNDER 18	COLLEGE EDUCATION	RURAL	SQ. MILES
16	54%	46%	92%	5%	1%	1%	$41,801	55%	31%	14%	14%	26%	19%	26%	1,732
17	37	63	85	12	1	2	$36,705	52	32	16	15	24	16	16	1,006
18	57	42	96	2	0	1	$34,462	46	38	16	14	26	11	57	6,826
STATE	51	49	84	11	1	2	$40,956	57	28	15	13	25	21	23	40,948
U.S.	50.7	48.3	69	12	4	13	$41,994	60	25	15	12	26	24	21	3,537,438

Sen. Mike DeWine (R)

Elected 1994; 2nd term

CAPITOL OFFICE
224-2315
dewine.senate.gov
140 Russell 20510-3503; fax 224-6519

COMMITTEES
Appropriations
Health, Education, Labor & Pensions
  (Retirement Security & Aging - chairman)
Judiciary
  (Antitrust, Competition Policy & Consumer
  Rights - chairman)
Select Intelligence

HOMETOWN
Cedarville

BORN
Jan. 5, 1947, Springfield, Ohio

RELIGION
Roman Catholic

FAMILY
Wife, Fran DeWine; eight children (one deceased)

EDUCATION
Miami U. (Ohio), B.S. 1969; Ohio Northern U.,
J.D. 1972

CAREER
Lawyer

POLITICAL HIGHLIGHTS
Greene County prosecuting attorney, 1977-81;
Ohio Senate, 1981-82; U.S. House, 1983-91;
lieutenant governor, 1991-95; Republican nominee
for U.S. Senate, 1992

ELECTION RESULTS

2000 GENERAL

Mike DeWine (R)	2,665,512	59.9%
Ted Celeste (D)	1,595,066	35.9%
John R. McAlister (LIBERT)	116,724	2.6%
John A. Eastman (NL)	70,713	1.6%

2000 PRIMARY

Mike DeWine (R)	1,029,860	79.5%
Ronald R. Dickson (R)	161,185	12.4%
Frank A. Cremeans (R)	104,219	8.1%

PREVIOUS WINNING PERCENTAGES
1994 (53%); 1988 House Election (74%); 1986 House
Election (100%); 1984 House Election (77%); 1982
House Election (56%)

DeWine is a methodical, deliberate legislator who reads detailed Government Accountability Office reports, and keeps a calculator handy so he can test the mathematical assertions of a report or a bill. He is remembered for diligently attending every class in law school.

It is precisely his rush to the drafting desk and bargaining table — while many colleagues tumble over each other to get to the Capitol television studios — that has made DeWine an effective legislative force on issues close to his heart. He wants to enhance the government's role in helping children and families and in providing humanitarian support overseas. His wire-rim glasses and lopsided grin help him look every bit the policy wonk he is, and his basic conservatism is often overshadowed by a distinctly nonpartisan approach to legislating that has won him credibility in both parties.

DeWine most frequently crosses the aisle on legislation involving the welfare of children, often drawing on his own experience as the father of eight and the child-related cases he handled as a prosecutor.

DeWine's third child, Becky, was killed in 1993 in a car accident when she was 22 years old. The event devastated DeWine and his wife, Fran; he says he still probably doesn't know all the ways that Becky's death has affected him. He counts among his biggest personal achievements a postage stamp encouraging organ and tissue donation. Becky's corneas were donated to two people after her death.

DeWine has a knack for navigating legislative labyrinths. In the 108th Congress, when New Hampshire Republican Judd Gregg, then chairman of the Senate's Health, Education, Labor and Pensions Committee, backed away from bipartisan negotiations on legislation allowing the Food and Drug Administration to regulate tobacco, DeWine quietly but persistently kept the issue alive. He worked on a deal with two liberal Democrats, Edward M. Kennedy of Massachusetts and Richard J. Durbin of Illinois. Over time, his role in driving the legislation toward Senate passage became clear and he found himself in the spotlight.

"The FDA requires printed ingredients for chewing gum, lipstick, bottled water, ice cream, and macaroni and cheese, but not for cigarettes, a product that causes 20 percent of all heart disease deaths and is the leading cause of preventable death in the United States," DeWine said.

But he ultimately was disappointed. The buyout was coupled with a corporate tax cut in the House and the tobacco regulation provisions were not included in the final bill. DeWine was one of three Republicans who voted against the corporate tax cut.

His deviations from party doctrine mark him as a player to watch in the major debates of the 109th Congress, particularly on the president's plan to retool Social Security with personal investment accounts.

DeWine, who is chairman of the HELP Subcommittee on Retirement Security and Aging, was among a handful of congressional Republicans who kept their seats when President Bush said in his 2005 State of the Union address that personal accounts were the best way to improve Social Security for younger workers. DeWine's spokeswoman later said he had yet to make up his mind on Bush's plan.

In 2005, DeWine joined a bipartisan coalition calling for reinstatement of the ban on assault weapons, which expired the previous year after pressure from the powerful, Republican-friendly gun lobby. DeWine shares the point of view of the law enforcement community, which maintains that the ban has been effective in curbing violent crime. "As a former prosecutor, I understand the challenges Ohio's mayors and law enforcement officials face, and we owe it to them to reestablish this law," DeWine said.

Those deviations don't make him a full-blooded moderate, but they leave him voting less often with his leaders than other rank-and-file Republicans — about 85 percent of the time. The fact that DeWine is noted for his cooperation with Democrats is probably more a sign of the heightened partisanship of the times than a reflection of his values.

He is solidly conservative on many cultural issues that divide the parties, most notably abortion, the appointment of conservative judges to the federal judiciary and same-sex marriage, though he has supported including gender and sexual orientation in hate crimes legislation. He also has supported Bush's tax cuts and limiting eligibility for overtime pay. As chairman of Judiciary's Antitrust, Competition Policy and Consumer Rights Subcommittee, he sided with the administration on regulations involving the consolidation of media ownership.

In the highly partisan 108th Congress, DeWine backed the Republican leadership's position on all but two of 49 votes to cut off debate and end delaying tactics by Democrats. The exceptions were corporate tax cut legislation and an effort by the National Rifle Association to limit liability for gun manufacturers whose products are used in crimes.

Despite having campaigned for Sen. John McCain of Arizona during the 2000 Republican presidential primary, DeWine turned out to be a loyal ally for Bush on the Judiciary Committee, championing the president's controversial nominees. During the 107th, he gave an exhaustive defense of Charles W. Pickering Sr., countering nearly every claim against the judge from his liberal critics in a lengthy point-by-point presentation. When the committee in the 108th considered two appeals court nominees from Ohio, DeWine was able to persuade Durbin to vote for one. Durbin said he trusted DeWine's judgment because of his moderation on other issues.

DeWine frequently joins Democrats in bipartisan efforts to force delinquent parents to pay child support, to help poorly paid child care workers retire their college loans, and to curb drunken driving. DeWine teamed up with West Virginia Democrat John D. Rockefeller IV in sponsoring legislation that changed the government's emphasis in custody cases from preserving family structure to protecting the best interests of children. When he was chairman of the Appropriations Subcommittee on the District of Columbia, DeWine's pet project was securing millions of dollars to revamp the capital city's foster care system.

In the foreign policy arena, Latin America is of particular interest to DeWine. The United States "ignore[s] our own hemisphere at our peril," he says, noting that Latin America plays important roles in drug trafficking, illegal immigration and international trade. He favors tough anti-drug laws, and has visited Colombia to investigate a major source of the U.S. drug trade.

Although low-key in temperament, DeWine has never lacked ambition. After law school, he worked as an assistant county prosecutor before running against his boss and beating him in 1976. In 1980, he won a seat in the Ohio Senate. Just two years later, he won election to the U.S. House, where he served eight years. He left to become lieutenant governor under George V. Voinovich, now his colleague in the Senate.

In 1992, DeWine challenged Democratic Sen. John Glenn, but lost. Two years later, he ran for the seat of retiring Democrat Howard M. Metzenbaum. DeWine faced Metzenbaum's son-in-law Joel Hyatt, a political novice who founded the Hyatt Legal Services chain. Stressing his government experience, DeWine won with 53 percent of the vote. In 2000, he easily defeated Ted Celeste, younger brother of former Gov. Richard Celeste.

KEY VOTES

2004
Yes Pass $318.9 billion, six-year highway and mass transit bill
Yes Extend assault weapons ban for 10 years
No Restore pay-as-you-go rules for new tax cuts and entitlement spending
Yes Criminalize harm to a fetus in an attack on the mother
Yes Increase mandatory child care funding to states by $6 billion over five years
Yes Amend the Constitution to prohibit same-sex marriage
Yes Approve $146 billion multi-year extension of previously enacted middle-class tax breaks
Yes Reorganize U.S. intelligence agencies as proposed by Sept. 11 commission
No Cut corporate taxes $137 billion over 10 years

2003
No Delay Bush changes to Clean Air Act
Yes Allow confirmation vote on Miguel A. Estrada to the U.S. Court of Appeals for the D.C. Circuit
Yes Block a Bush proposal opening Alaska's Arctic National Wildlife Refuge to oil drilling
No Limit size of Bush's proposed tax cut to $350 billion through fiscal 2013
Yes Overhaul Medicare and create prescription drug benefit
No Block Bush rule scaling back overtime pay for some white-collar federal workers
No Split $20 billion in Iraq aid into half-grant, half-loan
Yes Ban "partial birth" abortion except to save a woman's life
No Stop proposal allowing travel to Cuba
Yes Allow final vote on energy policy overhaul

CQ VOTE STUDIES

	PARTY UNITY		PRESIDENTIAL SUPPORT	
	Support	Oppose	Support	Oppose
2004	79%	21%	94%	6%
2003	92%	8%	97%	3%
2002	89%	11%	98%	2%
2001	83%	17%	95%	5%
2000	86%	14%	52%	48%
1999	84%	16%	38%	62%
1998	82%	18%	51%	49%
1997	81%	19%	62%	38%
1996	88%	12%	41%	59%
1995	87%	13%	30%	70%

INTEREST GROUPS

	AFL-CIO	ADA	CCUS	ACU
2004	33%	35%	88%	68%
2003	0%	15%	96%	85%
2002	23%	15%	95%	95%
2001	25%	25%	79%	72%
2000	0%	10%	93%	80%
1999	22%	10%	82%	84%
1998	0%	10%	89%	64%
1997	0%	15%	80%	68%
1996	29%	15%	85%	85%
1995	8%	0%	89%	70%

Sen. George V. Voinovich (R)

Elected 1998; 2nd term

CAPITOL OFFICE
224-3353
voinovich.senate.gov
524 Hart 20510-3504; fax 228-1382

COMMITTEES
Environment & Public Works
(Clean Air, Climate Change & Nuclear Safety -
chairman)
Foreign Relations
Homeland Security & Governmental Affairs
(Government Management, Federal Workforce
& the District of Columbia - chairman)
Select Ethics - chairman

HOMETOWN
Cleveland

BORN
July 15, 1936, Cleveland, Ohio

RELIGION
Roman Catholic

FAMILY
Wife, Janet Voinovich; four children (one
deceased)

EDUCATION
Ohio U., B.A. 1958 (government); Ohio State U.,
J.D. 1961

CAREER
Lawyer; state prosecutor

POLITICAL HIGHLIGHTS
Ohio House, 1967-71; Cuyahoga County auditor,
1971-76; Cuyahoga County Commission, 1977-78;
lieutenant governor, 1979; mayor of Cleveland,
1979-89; Republican nominee for U.S. Senate, 1988;
governor, 1991-99

ELECTION RESULTS

2004 GENERAL

George V. Voinovich (R)	3,464,356	63.9%
Eric D. Fingerhut (D)	1,961,171	36.2%

2004 PRIMARY

George V. Voinovich (R)	640,082	76.6%
John R. Mitchel (R)	195,476	23.4%

PREVIOUS WINNING PERCENTAGES
1998 (56%)

Unassuming and understated, Voinovich is a Senate workhorse, not a headline-grabbing show horse. He is adamant about deficit reduction and sometimes sympathetic to labor's concerns, putting him at odds with conservatives in the party. He also chairs the Ethics Committee, where he sits in judgment of his colleagues' ethical behavior, a thankless but institutionally important task.

After voting for President Bush's massive tax cuts from 2001 to 2004, Voinovich at the start of the 109th Congress was one of the few Republicans exhibiting buyer's remorse. As the deficit spiraled, he expressed reservations about further tax cuts. Democrat Richard J. Durbin of Illinois has called Voinovich's views a "breath of fresh air," according to The Columbus Dispatch. But the compliment, coming from one of Congress' most prominent liberals, could not have pleased the conservatives who dominate the party.

"I think at this stage of the game, because of all the uncertainties we have, it would be fiscally irresponsible for us to make these tax reductions permanent," he said.

Voinovich often casts lonely votes against GOP spending bills. Excessive spending is one of the few things that can get him riled, and he has railed from the floor about his colleagues spending money "like drunken sailors."

He voted against Republican-sponsored tax cuts in 1999 and 2000, when President Clinton was in the White House. But he supported Bush's aggressive tax cut drive beginning in 2001. He also backed a major expansion of spending for Medicare, voting for the president's proposal to create a prescription drug benefit for senior citizens. The 10-year cost of that program has ballooned from its original estimate of $400 billion.

The treatment of the government worker unions also sets Voinovich apart from conservatives. He insisted that the views of employee unions be considered in creating the Department of Homeland Security, while Bush and many Republicans wanted to curb the unions' power. He is chairman of the Homeland Security panel's Subcommittee on Government Management, Federal Workforce and the District of Columbia, where he often deals with federal workforce issues.

A member of the Senate's Centrist Coalition, Voinovich voted with the GOP 92 percent of the time in the 108th Congress when the two parties were in disagreement. That was a higher mark than he has tallied in the past, but still ranked him as the 10th-least-loyal Senate Republican.

His positions appear to sit well back home. Voinovich was re-elected to a second term in 2004 with 64 percent of the vote, when Bush, at the top of the ticket, was just squeaking by in Ohio. Voinovich is well-known in the state. He was Cleveland's mayor for 10 years and governor for eight years. He held top leadership posts in both the National League of Cities and the National Governors Association.

Voinovich was first elected in 1998 on a platform that included criticism of Republican plans to cut taxes by tapping into projected budget surpluses, which he said should be used first to pay down the national debt and shore up Social Security. During his first two and a half years in the Senate, he crusaded to hold the line on government spending. He was one of just two GOP senators to vote against a $792 billion tax cut in 1999.

But he said his view on spending changed dramatically after the terrorist attacks of Sept. 11, 2001. His priorities, he said, "shifted from saving for our future to fighting for our future."

He still considers himself a "debt hawk," but he says budget deficits are warranted during a war on terrorism. And in keeping with his campaign against pet project spending, he has voted against a number of spending bills since Sept. 11, complaining that some senators were "wrapping every pork project in the flag and calling it a national security priority."

During the Senate's work on legislation to create the Department of Homeland Security, Voinovich's colleagues often called on his knowledge of government personnel issues. As mayor of Cleveland, he had enlisted the help of the public employee unions to rescue the city from insolvency. But although he was actively engaged in the congressional debate, which centered on personnel policies, Voinovich was not included in the inner circle of GOP negotiators. His historically good working relations with government employee unions gave other Republicans pause.

As a former mayor and governor, Voinovich frequently argues for more local control in deciding how to spend federal funds. He applauded the 1999 "Ed-Flex" law that gave states the flexibility to spend federal education money with fewer strings attached. But in 2001, he cast one of only three Republican no votes in the Senate against Bush's No Child Left Behind law, a major rewrite of education policy that tied federal aid to performance on student achievement tests. Voinovich called it an "all-out assault on local control."

Of Serbian and Slovenian ancestry, Voinovich in his first year as a senator took a politically risky stance as a vocal opponent of the NATO military action in Kosovo, which involved U.S. forces. He advocated continued diplomatic negotiations with Serb leader Slobodan Milosevic, but he also refused to go to Serbia as long as Milosevic was in control.

To his dismay, he got the most public attention in his first term for boycotting a Capitol Hill hearing on coal mining regulations at which a member of the teen idol band Backstreet Boys was to testify. Voinovich, who had worked to bring the Rock and Roll Hall of Fame to Cleveland, said he objected to the growing trend of using celebrities to get media attention on issues where they have no expertise. "This isn't about music, it's about substance," he said. "Even if this guy was a polka musician, I would still object to him."

As Ethics chairman in the 108th Congress, he had to review the case against fellow Republican Richard C. Shelby of Alabama, who was alleged to have passed classified national security information to the media. The committee declined to discuss the case publicly or divulge its conclusions.

A white Republican from a working-class neighborhood in Cleveland's largely black and ethnic East Side, where he still lives, Voinovich's climb up the government ladder began with a brief stint in the early 1960s as a state assistant attorney general. After serving in the state House and as an auditor for Cuyahoga County, he was elected lieutenant governor in 1978. The next year, he unseated Cleveland Mayor Dennis J. Kucinich, now an Ohio congressman, after the city's financial default. With the help of a financial control board, Voinovich reversed some of the city's problems.

His initial Senate bid failed miserably. He lost a 1988 race to unseat Democratic incumbent Howard M. Metzenbaum, by 14 percentage points.

But Voinovich rebounded two years later and won the governorship. During his two terms, he won acclaim for putting the state on solid financial footing. In 1998, the timing seemed right for a second Senate run when Democrat John Glenn retired after four terms. Voinovich immediately became the presumptive successor. He was not seriously challenged for the GOP nomination and won the general election easily over Democrat Mary O. Boyle, a former Cuyahoga County commissioner. His 2004 re-election was effortless; he won by almost 28 percentage points.

KEY VOTES

2004

Yes Pass $318.9 billion, six-year highway and mass transit bill

Yes Extend assault weapons ban for 10 years

No Restore pay-as-you-go rules for new tax cuts and entitlement spending

Yes Criminalize harm to a fetus in an attack on the mother

Yes Increase mandatory child care funding to states by $6 billion over five years

Yes Amend the Constitution to prohibit same-sex marriage

Yes Approve $146 billion multi-year extension of previously enacted middle-class tax breaks

Yes Reorganize U.S. intelligence agencies as proposed by Sept. 11 commission

Yes Cut corporate taxes $137 billion over 10 years

2003

No Delay Bush changes to Clean Air Act

Yes Allow confirmation vote on Miguel A. Estrada to the U.S. Court of Appeals for the D.C. Circuit

No Block a Bush proposal opening Alaska's Arctic National Wildlife Refuge to oil drilling

Yes Limit size of Bush's proposed tax cut to $350 billion through fiscal 2013

Yes Overhaul Medicare and create prescription drug benefit

No Block Bush rule scaling back overtime pay for some white-collar federal workers

No Split $20 billion in Iraq aid into half-grant, half-loan

Yes Ban "partial birth" abortion except to save a woman's life

No Stop proposal allowing travel to Cuba

Yes Allow final vote on energy policy overhaul

CQ VOTE STUDIES

	PARTY UNITY		PRESIDENTIAL SUPPORT	
	Support	Oppose	Support	Oppose
2004	88%	12%	90%	10%
2003	93%	7%	95%	5%
2002	88%	12%	96%	4%
2001	92%	8%	95%	5%
2000	78%	22%	59%	41%
1999	87%	13%	45%	55%

INTEREST GROUPS

	AFL-CIO	ADA	CCUS	ACU
2004	42%	30%	94%	76%
2003	15%	15%	100%	83%
2002	33%	5%	95%	90%
2001	13%	15%	93%	83%
2000	13%	10%	80%	64%
1999	33%	20%	82%	88%

www.cqpress.com

Rep. Steve Chabot (R)

Elected 1994; 6th term

CAPITOL OFFICE
225-2216
www.house.gov/chabot
129 Cannon 20515-3501; fax 225-3012

COMMITTEES
International Relations
Judiciary
  (Constitution - chairman)
Small Business

HOMETOWN
Cincinnati

BORN
Jan. 22, 1953, Cincinnati, Ohio

RELIGION
Roman Catholic

FAMILY
Wife, Donna Chabot; two children

EDUCATION
College of William & Mary, B.A. 1975 (history);
Northern Kentucky U., J.D. 1978

CAREER
Lawyer; teacher

POLITICAL HIGHLIGHTS
Independent candidate for Cincinnati City Council,
1979; Republican candidate for Cincinnati City
Council, 1983; Cincinnati City Council, 1985-90;
Republican nominee for U.S. House, 1988;
Hamilton County Board of Commissioners, 1990-95

ELECTION RESULTS

2004 GENERAL

Steve Chabot (R)	173,430	59.8%
Greg Harris (D)	116,235	40.1%

2004 PRIMARY

Steve Chabot (R)	unopposed

2002 GENERAL

Steve Chabot (R)	110,760	64.8%
Greg Harris (D)	60,168	35.2%

PREVIOUS WINNING PERCENTAGES
2000 (53%); 1998 (53%); 1996 (54%); 1994 (56%)

A hard-core conservative from the Republican Class of 1994, Chabot has chaired the Judiciary Subcommittee on the Constitution since 2001. And while the nation's fundamental document has been altered only infrequently in more than two centuries, Chabot is among those seeking to change it according to his view of the social contract.

In the 108th Congress alone, he either sponsored, cosponsored or voted for proposed amendments to the Constitution that seek to ban flag desecration, outlaw gay marriage, require a balanced budget, protect crime victims' rights and give people the right to pray and to recognize their religious beliefs, heritage and traditions on public property, including schools.

Chabot (SHAB-it) contends that a wide array of constitutional amendments are becoming necessary because "rogue" federal judges are destroying the social fabric of the nation. "One way or another, we know the Constitution will be amended," he said during debate on the gay marriage ban, which the House approved in 2004. "The question is: Is it done the appropriate way, or is it done by unelected, activist judges?"

Among the jurists who have displeased him are those on the Supreme Court who in 2000 struck down a Nebraska law seeking to ban a procedure opponents call "partial birth" abortion. In 2003, Chabot sponsored a bill outlawing the procedure and incorporating "findings" designed to get around the high court's ruling. The measure was signed into law by President Bush but in 2004 was struck down by three different federal courts. The Supreme Court ultimately will decide the matter.

During his first term as chairman of the Constitution Subcommittee, Chabot sponsored legislation, enacted in 2002, designed to guarantee legal protection to babies "born alive" at any stage of development.

Though not shy about voicing his conservative beliefs, Chabot often does so with a soft-spoken demeanor that stands out on Judiciary, where passionate and combative oratory is generally the order of the day. He cast off his normally low-key persona when the spotlight fell on him in 1999 as one of the 13 "managers" who presented the House's case for removing President Clinton from office in the Senate impeachment trial. During his presentation to the Senate summarizing perjury law, Chabot said of Clinton: "He raised his right hand and swore to tell the truth, the whole truth and nothing but the truth. Then he lied."

Chabot remembers feeling deep disappointment in the Watergate scandal and the subsequent pardoning of President Nixon, whom he had voted for in 1972. The Watergate revelations spurred his move toward a political career, he said, because he felt the public deserved to have leaders they could trust. During the Clinton impeachment trial, Chabot surprised colleagues by acknowledging that he had voted for Democrat Jimmy Carter in the 1976 presidential election instead of President Ford, who had pardoned Nixon.

From his seat on Judiciary, Chabot generally backs efforts to toughen enforcement of crime and immigration laws, but he keeps a wary eye on measures that could lead to invasion of privacy. After the Sept. 11, 2001, terrorist attacks, he backed enactment of the law known as the USA Patriot Act that beefed up law enforcement authority to combat terrorism. "People want the full power of the United States to be used against the cowards who carried out these attacks," he said. But he warned, "We must not cave in to their demands by suspending or weakening our constitutional rights."

In the 108th Congress, Chabot won Judiciary Committee approval of a bill he sponsored with New York Democrat Jerrold Nadler to require all federal agencies to issue a "privacy impact analysis" considering the effects of new regulations on individual privacy. In 1999, he teamed up with Democrat Patrick J. Kennedy of Rhode Island on legislation to limit the government's ability to collect DNA samples for a national database, warning that the practice could infringe on Americans' privacy.

Chabot is among the influential bloc of conservatives who have stuck by their initial "Contract With America" campaign pledges to reduce federal spending — even, at times, when it means fewer dollars for his Cincinnati district. He has been recognized by conservative groups for his consistent anti-tax voting record, and at times he shows more zeal than House GOP leaders for reducing the federal budget. His frequent no votes on Republican-written spending bills usually put him in the company of perhaps only two or three dozen others in his caucus.

Chabot was born and raised in Cincinnati. His father worked as an optician, and Chabot — who lived in a trailer for the first few years of his life — remembers working part-time jobs to help pay the tuition at his parochial high school. He majored in history and earned a teaching certificate at William and Mary College, returning to Cincinnati after graduation. He taught elementary school by day and worked his way through law school at night, taking classes across the river at Northern Kentucky University. A few years after getting his law degree, he opened his own neighborhood law practice, with his father serving as his assistant.

Chabot's political career began on the Cincinnati City Council. After two failed bids for a seat on the council, the first at 26 as an independent, Chabot ran as a Republican and won in 1985. He fell short in a congressional bid against Democrat Thomas A. Luken in 1988, then won an election in 1990 to the Hamilton County Board of Commissioners.

Chabot launched his second congressional campaign in 1994 against first-term Democrat David Mann. Emphasizing his blue-collar beginnings and Catholic roots, Chabot campaigned on a platform of lower taxes, less government and change in Washington. With national trends strongly favoring the GOP, he won with 56 percent of the vote.

In the next three elections, he had to fend off charges of being too far to the right for his constituents, who voted for Bill Clinton twice and for Al Gore in 2000. He never earned more than 54 percent. But redistricting after the 2000 census made the 1st more Republican, and in 2002 Chabot cruised to a fifth term with 65 percent against volunteerism advocate Greg Harris. During their 2004 rematch, Chabot prevailed with 60 percent.

KEY VOTES

2004
No Extend federal unemployment benefits by 13 weeks
Yes Pass $283.2 billion, six-year federal highway and mass transit bill
Yes Approve $146 billion multi-year extension of previously enacted middle-class tax breaks
Yes Amend the Constitution to prohibit same-sex marriage
Yes Cut corporate taxes $137 billion over 10 years
No Reorganize U.S. intelligence agencies as proposed by Sept. 11 commission

2003
Yes Cut taxes by $330 billion through fiscal 2013
No Block Bush rule scaling back overtime pay for some white-collar federal workers
No Do not allow use of search warrants without first notifying subjects
No Allow importation of prescription drugs
Yes Create private school voucher program in Washington, D.C.
Yes Ban "partial birth" abortion except to save a woman's life
Yes Split $18.6 billion in Iraq aid into half-grant, half-loan
No Overhaul Medicare and create prescription drug benefit

CQ VOTE STUDIES

	PARTY UNITY		PRESIDENTIAL SUPPORT	
	Support	Oppose	Support	Oppose
2004	95%	5%	79%	21%
2003	95%	5%	91%	9%
2002	96%	4%	85%	15%
2001	94%	6%	81%	19%
2000	94%	6%	21%	79%

INTEREST GROUPS

	AFL-CIO	ADA	CCUS	ACU
2004	20%	10%	95%	96%
2003	7%	10%	90%	96%
2002	11%	0%	90%	96%
2001	8%	5%	87%	96%
2000	0%	5%	76%	100%

OHIO 1
Western Cincinnati and suburbs

Nestled in Ohio's southwest corner, the 1st contains about three-fourths of Cincinnati's residents. The city's 43 percent black population is critical to Democrats, as Cincinnati's traditional German Catholic conservatives, a growing suburban base and a GOP-friendly redistricting plan have made the Hamilton County-based 1st politically competitive.

The 1st's southern border is the Ohio River, which serves as a major thoroughfare for barges laden with cargo, helping Cincinnati earn its reputation as a regional center of commerce.

The city's diverse economy prevented it from suffering the degree of hardship that hit other industrial cities in the 1980s, although the region has not been immune to defense cutbacks. Aircraft engine manufacturing and machine toolmaking account for a large portion of blue-collar jobs. The city also houses the headquarters of major U.S. companies (including Procter & Gamble) and is a magnet for research and development firms.

The district takes in Cincinnati's heavily black neighborhoods, including West End and Over-the-Rhine, where in April 2001 a white police officer shot an unarmed black man, leading to several days of riots. The black population is decreasing in this area of the city but is increasing in neighborhoods west of Interstate 75, including Westwood, Mount Airy, Northside and College Hill.

Redistricting following the 2000 census drew the 1st to closely resemble its 1980s configuration, when the district also included most of Cincinnati and points north and west. Added to the 1st were GOP-friendly suburbs such as Reading and upper-income Evendale and Springdale (which had been in the 2nd District). In 2004, George W. Bush narrowly lost the 1st's share of Hamilton, but his margin in southwestern Butler County — also added in redistricting — enabled him to eke out a win districtwide.

MAJOR INDUSTRY
Consumer products development and manufacturing, service

CITIES
Cincinnati (pt.), 257,122; Norwood (pt.), 21,675; Forest Park, 19,463

NOTABLE
Talk show host Jerry Springer is a former Cincinnati mayor; The National Underground Railroad Freedom Center opened in Cincinnati in 2004.

Vacant Seat

Rep. Rob Portman (R)
Resigned April 29, 2005

The 2nd District seat was left open at the start of the 109th Congress when Rob Portman was confirmed as the new United States trade representative. Portman, who represented the district for more than a decade, resigned in April 2005. President Bush picked him for the key trade policy post and he was confirmed by the Senate.

Ohio Gov. Bob Taft, a Republican, called an Aug. 2 special election to fill the vacancy. A primary election was scheduled for June.

The Republican Party was in a good position to retain the seat. The Cincinnati-based district is a GOP stronghold. Portman routinely won re-election by ratios of about 3-to-1, and Bush carried the district in 2004 with 64 percent of the vote. The district takes in some of the wealthiest enclaves in the Cincinnati metropolitan area.

After Bush nominated Portman for the executive branch posting in early 2005, a number of well-known Republicans entered the fray. Among the promising candidates out of the chute were Pat DeWine, a commissioner in Hamilton County, the most-populous jurisdiction in the 2nd District. DeWine is the eldest child of the state's senior senator, Republican Mike DeWine.

Other Republicans in the running included state Rep. Tom Brinkman, who emphasized his anti-tax philosophy; former state Rep. Jean Schmidt, who heads a local anti-abortion organization; and former Rep. Bob McEwen, a lobbyist who served in the House from 1981 to 1993. McEwen was making a comeback effort a dozen years after losing a special GOP primary to Portman.

The Democratic race was taking shape more slowly. The half-dozen candidates who expressed interest had little name recognition or history of political success. Among them was Democrat Charles W. Sanders, who ran against Portman four times, never reaching 30 percent of the vote.

The eventual successor to Portman will have big shoes to fill. He had been a key player in the House GOP conference, the group of all House Republicans. Portman had an unofficial seat at the leadership table as the designated liaison to Bush — the president's "eyes and ears" in the House. Speaker J. Dennis Hastert also gave Portman the job of leading the GOP leadership meetings, giving him a role in shaping the party's message.

In addition to his considerable leadership credentials, Portman held seats on the Ways and Means and Budget committees. He also was a member of the House Republican Policy Committee and the National Republican Congressional Committee, the campaign arm of the House GOP.

In choosing Portman, Bush put a stalwart free-trader at the top echelon of trade policy in the United States. Portman helped persuade fellow Republicans to support the 2002 law giving the president greater powers to negotiate trade deals that cannot be amended by Congress. In 2000, he was a leading advocate of making permanent the normalized U.S.-China trade relationship.

Portman's first major task as trade representative was to press for congressional approval of the Central American Free Trade Agreement. Early in his career, after graduating from law school, Portman was an international trade lawyer for Patton, Boggs and Blow in Washington, D.C., where the Cincinnati-based Chiquita Brands International Inc. was a client.

OHIO 2
Eastern Cincinnati and suburbs; Portsmouth

The 2nd stretches from some of Ohio's wealthiest communities in eastern Cincinnati and Hamilton County in southwestern Ohio to some economically struggling areas in rural southern Ohio. It is one of the state's most solidly GOP districts and has a distinct split between its suburban and rural elements. While Cincinnati's wealthy Republican establishment — including the Taft family — has had significant political influence over the years, the district's rural counties have considerably less political pull.

The area economy revolves around light manufacturing and the retail and service industries, and the district's economic health has been boosted by construction around Cincinnati's downtown. The district takes in less than one-fourth of the city's residents, including the upscale neighborhoods of Hyde Park and Mount Lookout. Almost 40 percent of the population lives in Hamilton County, including the well-to-do areas of Madeira, Mariemont, Blue Ash and the Village of Indian Hill.

To the east, fast-growing Clermont County has become more Republican as it has edged closer to Cincinnati's metropolitan orbit. Once undeveloped farmland is bursting with development. To the north, Warren County is filling up with Dayton-area commuters. George W. Bush took more than 70 percent of the vote in Clermont and Warren in the 2004 presidential election.

Economically, rural Adams County has one of the state's highest unemployment rates, and Pike and Scioto counties also are struggling. Pike County includes a uranium enrichment facility that ceased enriching operations in 2001, but the plant is scheduled to resume operations by 2007 with more-modern technology.

MAJOR INDUSTRY
Manufacturing, service, retail

CITIES
Cincinnati (pt.), 74,163; Portsmouth, 20,909

NOTABLE
Ulysses S. Grant was born in Point Pleasant.

RECENT ELECTION RESULTS

2004 GENERAL		
Rob Portman (R)	227,102	71.7%
Charles W. Sanders (D)	89,598	28.3%
2002 GENERAL		
Rob Portman (R)	139,218	74.1%
Charles W. Sanders (D)	48,785	26.0%
2000 GENERAL		
Rob Portman (R)	204,184	73.6%
Charles W. Sanders (D)	64,091	23.1%
Robert E. Bidwell (LIBERT)	9,266	3.3%
1998 GENERAL		
Rob Portman (R)	154,344	75.8%
Charles W. Sanders (D)	49,293	24.2%
1996 GENERAL		
Rob Portman (R)	186,853	72.0%
Thomas R. Chandler (D)	58,715	22.6%
Kathleen M. McKnight (NL)	13,905	5.4%
1994 GENERAL		
Rob Portman (R)	150,128	77.4%
Les Mann (D)	43,730	22.6%

Rep. Michael R. Turner (R)

Elected 2002; 2nd term

CAPITOL OFFICE
225-6465
oh03.wyr@mail.house.gov
www.house.gov/miketurner
1740 Longworth 20515-3503; fax 225-6754

COMMITTEES
Armed Services
Government Reform
  (Federalism & the Census - chairman)
Veterans' Affairs

HOMETOWN
Centerville

BORN
Jan. 11, 1960, Dayton, Ohio

RELIGION
Protestant

FAMILY
Wife, Lori Turner; two children

EDUCATION
Ohio Northern U., B.A. 1982 (political science);
Case Western Reserve U., J.D. 1985; U. of Dayton,
M.B.A. 1992

CAREER
Real estate developer; lawyer

POLITICAL HIGHLIGHTS
Mayor of Dayton, 1994-2002; defeated for
re-election as mayor of Dayton, 2001

ELECTION RESULTS

2004 GENERAL

Michael R. Turner (R)	197,290	62.3%
Jane Mitakides (D)	119,448	37.7%

2004 PRIMARY

Michael R. Turner (R)	unopposed

2002 GENERAL

Michael R. Turner (R)	111,630	58.8%
Rick Carne (D)	78,307	41.2%

Turner considers himself one of the "traditional values" conservatives who are having a big impact on the Republican Party, but a part of him also belongs to the Rust Belt and its blue-collar politics. He is outspoken in his opposition to abortion and same-sex marriage, but this son of a union-card-holding autoworker from Dayton is just as apt to cross his party to vote for extended unemployment checks for workers.

In his first term, he focused on a problem common for old industrial cities like Dayton, where manufacturing was once king — how the federal government can invest in so-called brownfields, abandoned industrial sites that are prime for redevelopment except for their huge cleanup costs. Turner introduced a bill creating tax credits for cleaning up brownfields, continuing a commitment to the issue he established as mayor of Dayton.

As a freshman, he didn't move much legislation. Turner sponsored no major bills and had little involvement in the issues that dominated the 108th Congress, such as tax cuts and the Medicare prescription drug benefit. Also, he was often overshadowed in the 108th by powerhouse Ohio Republicans, like John A. Boehner, chairman of the Education and Workforce Committee, and Rob Portman, an influential GOP leader with close ties to the Bush White House.

But his background as an accomplished, two-term city mayor suggests he will eventually carve out a niche. In the early part of the 109th, Government Reform Committee Chairman Thomas M. Davis III gave Turner the chairmanship of the new Federalism and the Census Subcommittee to handle oversight of federal mandates on states and localities — a post that fits his background in local government.

When he ran the 166,000-population city, Turner reversed the slide of its downtown core, orchestrating the building of a new arts center, a minor league baseball stadium and a restored riverfront. A project he dubbed "Rehabarama" produced a public and private partnership to restore historic houses and was recognized by the National Trust for Historic Preservation. He also was involved in a state task force that came up with ways to develop brownfields areas. "From being a Republican mayor for a 10 percent Republican city, I have a great deal of experience working in a nonpartisan way, working together to pull together a broad coalition," he says.

One of his major parochial preoccupations is looking out for Wright-Patterson Air Force Base from his seat on the Armed Services Committee. Turner got the seat in his first term, as promised by Speaker J. Dennis Hastert. Military spending is critical to the district's economy, especially as Wright-Patterson draws more and more private aerospace and high-technology firms to the area. Turner was involved in efforts to secure nearly $700 million in federal money for research and development programs at the base in 2005, though he received help from veteran Ohio Republican David L. Hobson, a senior member of the Defense Appropriations Subcommittee. Turner also gained a seat on the Veterans' Affairs Committee in the 109th.

Dayton and the surrounding area take no small measure of pride in flying and the modern aerospace industry. It was there that two brothers named Wright ran a bicycle shop, from which they did some of their early pioneering experiments in flight. The brothers eventually relocated to Kitty Hawk, N.C., where their famous early flying tests were conducted on vast open stretches of beach.

In his first term, Turner found a number of ways to promote his social beliefs. In 2003, he voted for a bill to make illegal a procedure its critics call "partial birth" abortion. He also was a vocal supporter of the Republicans' Unborn Victims of Violence Act, which recognizes a fetus as a legal victim if it is injured or killed in the course of an attack on the mother.

Turner is a booster of Bush administration proposals to provide federal incentives for charitable and religious groups to treat social ills, such as homelessness and drug addiction. He cosponsored a bill making it easier for people to deduct charitable contributions from their income taxes. Turner also favors government-paid vouchers for private or parochial school tuition, which critics say will undermine the public school system.

In general, he built a strong voting record in support of President Bush, sticking with the president more than 90 percent of the time on key votes during the 108th. But on issues affecting workers, Turner returned to his blue-collar roots. He was one of only 39 Republicans to vote for a Democratic amendment to give workers who had exhausted their state unemployment an additional 13 weeks of benefits.

A local boy, Turner was raised in Dayton and attended public schools there. His father, Ray, worked for more than 40 years at a General Motors plant and was a member of the electrical workers union. Turner's mother, Vivian, was a high school teacher. He went far with his college studies, but did so without leaving Ohio. He earned a law degree from Case Western University in Cleveland and a master's degree in business administration from the University of Dayton.

Turner practiced law before winning his first term as mayor in 1994. He lost a bid for a third term in 2001 to a popular Democratic state senator, but Turner's bipartisan appeal was not lost on GOP recruiters scouring the country for House candidates.

When Bush tapped 12-term Democratic incumbent Tony P. Hall to serve in the administration as ambassador to a trio of world hunger-relief organizations, Turner was a GOP favorite to run for the seat. The Republican-dominated Ohio General Assembly, forced to give up one House seat after the 2000 reapportionment, had redrawn the 3rd District to make it more amenable to a Republican.

Turner first beat back a big-spending primary challenge from newspaper publisher Roy Brown, whose father and grandfather had served in the House, and then took 59 percent of the vote to defeat Democrat Rick Carne, Hall's former chief of staff, in November. He was easily re-elected in 2004 with 62 percent.

KEY VOTES

2004
Yes Extend federal unemployment benefits by 13 weeks
Yes Pass $283.2 billion, six-year federal highway and mass transit bill
Yes Approve $146 billion multi-year extension of previously enacted middle-class tax breaks
Yes Amend the Constitution to prohibit same-sex marriage
Yes Cut corporate taxes $137 billion over 10 years
Yes Reorganize U.S. intelligence agencies as proposed by Sept. 11 commission

2003
Yes Cut taxes by $330 billion through fiscal 2013
No   Block Bush rule scaling back overtime pay for some white-collar federal workers
No   Do not allow use of search warrants without first notifying subjects
No   Allow importation of prescription drugs
Yes Create private school voucher program in Washington, D.C.
Yes Ban "partial birth" abortion except to save a woman's life
No   Split $18.6 billion in Iraq aid into half-grant, half-loan
Yes Overhaul Medicare and create prescription drug benefit

CQ VOTE STUDIES

	PARTY UNITY		PRESIDENTIAL SUPPORT	
	Support	Oppose	Support	Oppose
2004	92%	8%	88%	12%
2003	98%	2%	96%	4%

INTEREST GROUPS

	AFL-CIO	ADA	CCUS	ACU
2004	33%	5%	100%	88%
2003	7%	5%	100%	88%

OHIO 3
Southwest — most of Dayton, Kettering

Dayton, once one of the state's most successful manufacturing centers, has suffered economic setbacks in recent years. A torrent of departures has displaced its manufacturing base, and the city has struggled to diversify what has become an increasingly service-oriented economy. Montgomery County, which surrounds Dayton, had minuscule population growth in the 1980s, and actually lost residents in the 1990s after decades of robust population growth. Still, the area's defense industry, revolving around Wright-Patterson Air Force Base, has had some success in attracting aerospace and technology research companies.

Local officials envision a "Tech Town" district in eastern Dayton (shared with the 8th) that would serve as a robust technology corridor and complement Wright-Patterson as an economic engine for the region. The 30-acre site formerly housed a General Motors manufacturing plant.

Montgomery County is the dominant jurisdiction in the 3rd, comprising nearly three-fourths of the district vote. Most of Dayton is included in the 3rd, although some of the northeastern part of the city was appended to the 8th District in the redistricting following the 2000 census. The urban vote — driven by Dayton's ample black population and large blue-collar workforce — makes Montgomery slightly Democratic. Dayton's southern suburbs include GOP-inclined, white-collar areas such as Kettering and Centerville.

The counties outside of Montgomery give the 3rd its GOP lean. Warren County, a fast-growing area between Cincinnati and Dayton that is shared with the 2nd, gave George W. Bush 72 percent of its 2004 presidential vote, and Bush nearly reached that mark in Clinton and Highland counties, which are more-rural areas southeast of Dayton.

MAJOR INDUSTRY
Auto manufacturing, defense, service

MILITARY BASES
Wright-Patterson Air Force Base, 8,002 military, 11,343 civilian (2004) (shared with the 7th District)

CITIES
Dayton (pt.), 137,180; Kettering, 57,502; Trotwood, 27,420

NOTABLE
The Dayton Peace Agreement to end fighting in the former Yugoslavia was signed in 1995 at Wright-Patterson.

Rep. Michael G. Oxley (R)

Elected June 1981; 12th full term

CAPITOL OFFICE
225-2676
oxley.house.gov
2308 Rayburn 20515-3504; fax 226-0577

COMMITTEES
Financial Services - chairman

HOMETOWN
Findlay

BORN
Feb. 11, 1944, Findlay, Ohio

RELIGION
Lutheran

FAMILY
Wife, Patricia Oxley; one child

EDUCATION
Miami U. (Ohio), B.A. 1966 (government); Ohio
State U., J.D. 1969

CAREER
FBI agent; lawyer

POLITICAL HIGHLIGHTS
Ohio House, 1973-81

ELECTION RESULTS

2004 GENERAL

Michael G. Oxley (R)	167,807	58.6%
Ben Konop (D)	118,538	41.4%

2004 PRIMARY

Michael G. Oxley (R)	unopposed

2002 GENERAL

Michael G. Oxley (R)	120,001	67.5%
Jim Clark (D)	57,726	32.5%

PREVIOUS WINNING PERCENTAGES
2000 (67%); 1998 (64%); 1996 (65%); 1994 (100%);
1992 (61%); 1990 (62%); 1988 (100%); 1986 (75%);
1984 (78%); 1982 (65%); 1981 Special Election (50%)

Oxley's name is forever tied to the law that is the bane of the accounting and business world — the Sarbanes-Oxley bill that slapped new regulations on business in the wake of the Enron Corp. scandal. Often lost in the brouhaha is the fact that Oxley, left to his own devices, would have opted for much less sweeping governmental regulation.

At heart, Oxley is a free-market conservative well appreciated by the banking industry during his tenure as chairman of the Financial Services Committee. He was one of the lobbying community's most feted members of Congress at the Republican convention in 2004 in New York City, the cradle of the financial industry. Wall Street was pleased that he did not follow up on the Sarbanes-Oxley law with rules restricting the way companies raise capital prior to issuing public stock, as some had expected. Neither did he push for tighter regulation of the mutual fund industry as some had feared.

In the wake of a spate of corporate financial scandals in the early 2000s, Oxley penned a bill panned by critics as too vague to be effective. It was quickly subsumed by a more assertive Senate measure as subsequent corporate scandals quickened political momentum for government action. Oxley fought unsuccessfully to limit the scope of the final bill. Still, the law that Congress finally enacted in 2002 was the most sweeping new regulation of publicly traded companies since the Depression and it carried Oxley's name, along with that of the Senate sponsor, Democrat Paul S. Sarbanes of Maryland.

As the chairman of a committee with enormous sway over American business, Oxley has no trouble attracting campaign contributions, many of which he redistributes to other Republicans through his political action committee. At the convention, financial barons held parties for him at the storied Rainbow Room and other swank locations, which prompted scrutiny from New York's aggressive attorney general, Eliot Spitzer, who questioned whether one of the host organizations was truly a charity.

In the 108th Congress, Oxley backed legislation to make it a federal crime to surreptitiously photograph or videotape people who are unclothed or undressing on federal property. The legislation targeted "video voyeurism," a practice that Oxley and others said was becoming more prevalent because of the availability of low-cost, high-resolution cameras, such as those installed in cell phones.

In Oxley's first year as chairman, his main achievement was a law cutting the fees that the Securities and Exchange Commission charges on securities sales, a top priority of Wall Street. He also won passage in 2001 of legislation to combat money laundering as a means of reducing terrorists' access to cash, a plan that was incorporated into a major counterterrorism law that year.

On Capitol Hill, Oxley's wisecracking, backslapping style belies a strong competitive streak and a drive to do things his way. His approach regularly leaves Democrats on the Financial Services panel annoyed that they have little say in crafting legislation. While independent-minded, he is deferential to his party's leadership. He accepted the addition of stringent legal provisions to the 2002 terrorism insurance bill, for example, and then acquiesced in a deal that President Bush cut with Senate Democrats without him.

Before taking over at Financial Services, Oxley was chairman of a powerful Energy and Commerce subcommittee, where he played a significant role in writing the 1999 law repealing Depression-era regulatory barriers separating banks, insurance companies and securities firms. He also helped shepherd to passage a 1995 bill — one of just two enacted over a veto by President Clinton — insulating companies from securities fraud lawsuits when they distribute erroneous but good-faith profit projections.

Though tough in political combat, Oxley has a reputation as one of the more jovial members of Congress, known for his quick laugh and megawatt smile. He surprised constituents accustomed to seeing him on cable news channels talking politics and finance when in 2005 he appeared on a show to give romantic advice on Valentine's Day. He discussed his 30 years with wife Patricia and said the secret to a successful marriage if you're in Congress is mutual trust and a spouse's patience with late-night votes.

Oxley was a jock in high school, and many of his colleagues know him through golf. He is good enough to have once merited a feature in a golf magazine, and he also plays basketball, tennis and baseball. For years, he started for the GOP in the annual congressional charity baseball game. But his playing days ended after he broke his wrist in the 1994 game in a collision at first base with Democrat Sherrod Brown of Ohio. He had to have steel pins inserted in his arm.

Oxley traces his conservatism to his upbringing in rural Findlay, Ohio, where his father was a county prosecutor. He sported a flat-top haircut in high school. He recalls jousting with liberal professors in college, where Barry Goldwater's "The Conscience of a Conservative" and free-market economist Milton Friedman were important influences. While many of his generation protested the Vietnam War and participated in the social revolution, Oxley went to law school and signed on with the FBI. He received a commendation for his role in the arrest of two suspected bank robbers who belonged to the Black Panthers.

In 1972, at age 28, he won a seat in the Ohio House. He got an opening to run for Congress in April 1981, when Republican Rep. Tennyson Guyer died. Oxley was an early favorite in the special election, but he had stiff primary competition and won narrowly. Oxley struggled to a 341-vote victory in the general election. He handily won a rematch in 1982.

In the 2002 election, Oxley had a war chest that topped $1 million, compared with his rival's approximately $10,000, and he won with 68 percent of the vote. In 2004, he faced a tougher challenge from Democratic lawyer Ben Konop, who was vastly outspent but who campaigned energetically. Oxley won with 59 percent. After the election, a Toledo Blade editorial said, "We believe the numbers suggest that Mr. Oxley no longer has the luxury of feeling comfortable."

KEY VOTES

2004

No	Extend federal unemployment benefits by 13 weeks
Yes	Pass $283.2 billion, six-year federal highway and mass transit bill
Yes	Approve $146 billion multi-year extension of previously enacted middle-class tax breaks
Yes	Amend the Constitution to prohibit same-sex marriage
Yes	Cut corporate taxes $137 billion over 10 years
Yes	Reorganize U.S. intelligence agencies as proposed by Sept. 11 commission

2003

Yes	Cut taxes by $330 billion through fiscal 2013
No	Block Bush rule scaling back overtime pay for some white-collar federal workers
No	Do not allow use of search warrants without first notifying subjects
No	Allow importation of prescription drugs
Yes	Create private school voucher program in Washington, D.C.
Yes	Ban "partial birth" abortion except to save a woman's life
No	Split $18.6 billion in Iraq aid into half-grant, half-loan
Yes	Overhaul Medicare and create prescription drug benefit

CQ VOTE STUDIES

	PARTY UNITY		PRESIDENTIAL SUPPORT	
	Support	Oppose	Support	Oppose
2004	94%	6%	97%	3%
2003	97%	3%	98%	2%
2002	96%	4%	95%	5%
2001	99%	1%	98%	2%
2000	96%	4%	30%	70%

INTEREST GROUPS

	AFL-CIO	ADA	CCUS	ACU
2004	13%	0%	100%	96%
2003	7%	0%	97%	80%
2002	13%	0%	100%	96%
2001	10%	0%	100%	92%
2000	0%	0%	95%	81%

OHIO 4
West central — Mansfield, Lima, Findlay

The 4th is a solid block of Ohio Corn Belt counties. The land supports soybeans, corn, livestock and Republicans. Not one of the 11 counties in the 4th has backed a Democratic presidential candidate since 1964, and George W. Bush swept the counties again in 2004 with between 59 percent and 74 percent of the vote. Two of the three most populous, Allen and Hancock counties, last voted Democratic in the Roosevelt-Landon contest of 1936.

Democrats have few pockets of support. They can normally count on votes in Mansfield, the district's largest city, which has a 20 percent black population. While those votes help Democrats locally, they barely dent the district's underlying Republican lean. Bush took 65 percent of the 4th's vote in 2004, his best showing in Ohio.

Along with corn and soybeans, manufacturing is important to the 4th. Declines in the automobile industry in the 1980s and defense cutbacks in the 1990s caused economic hardships in parts of the district, but small industrial companies and large auto manufacturing plants — including a

Ford engine plant in Lima, a General Motors plant in Mansfield and Honda facilities in East Liberty (Logan County) and Anna (Shelby County) — continue to spur the economy. Ada is home to a Wilson Sporting Goods facility, and Findlay, where Cooper Tire & Rubber Co. and the joint venture Marathon Ashland Petroleum are based, is the 4th's most prosperous city.

Redistricting following the 2000 census did not make significant changes to the 4th. It picked up some territory in the southwest, adding the rest of Auglaize and Logan counties and all of Champaign and Shelby counties.

MAJOR INDUSTRY
Agriculture, auto manufacturing, oil

CITIES
Mansfield, 49,346; Lima, 40,081; Findlay, 38,967; Marion, 35,318

NOTABLE
Lima was one of the original refinery centers for John D. Rockefeller's Standard Oil; Richland Carrousel Park in downtown Mansfield boasts one of the world's largest carousels; Astronaut Neil Armstrong's hometown of Wapakoneta has a museum in his honor; Warren G. Harding's home and tomb are in Marion, which also hosts an annual Popcorn Festival.

Rep. Paul E. Gillmor (R)

Elected 1988; 9th term

In a Congress full of self-promoters, Gillmor is so self-effacing that he rarely draws notice in the national media and does not even get much coverage in Ohio. In 2003, his low profile earned him a spot as one of 10 lawmakers on a Capitol Hill newspaper's "obscure caucus."

The lack of attention suits him just fine. "Gillmor has learned that being steady and cautious can be an asset in a Capitol stuffed with attitude and ego," the Gannett News Service concluded in a 2000 profile.

His seniority and diligence have brought him rewards. In the 107th Congress, he was one of four members of the Energy and Commerce Committee — usually an exclusive assignment for Republicans — to also win a seat on the newly constituted Financial Services Committee at the behest of that panel's chairman, fellow Ohioan Michael G. Oxley.

Also in the 107th, Gillmor took the gavel of the Energy panel's Environment and Hazardous Materials Subcommittee. By the end of his first year as chairman, he had shepherded to enactment a law to help clean up and develop contaminated industrial sites known as "brownfields," mainly by giving states more control over the process and shielding some small businesses from liability to clean up superfund toxic waste sites. A picture of the presidential bill-signing ceremony adorned the "accomplishments" section of his 2004 re-election Web site; no other legislative successes were listed.

But after 22 years in the state Senate — the last 10 of them as either minority leader or Senate president — Gillmor knows a legislative body cannot have effective leaders unless it also has loyal followers. And loyal he has been, voting with the majority of his fellow Republicans more than 90 percent of the time in the 107th and 108th Congresses. His reliability has been put to use in enforcing party unity: The 109th is his sixth term as a deputy whip, helping to round up votes for the GOP leadership.

Gillmor is a solid conservative on fiscal and social issues, but not so ideological that he balks at compromising when party leaders say it is time to do so. He also associates with the moderate Republican Main Street Partnership. "I'll leave it to others to say whether I am moderate or conservative or some shade in between," he offered in the Gannett profile.

Gillmor sometimes breaks ranks with party leaders. In the 108th, he parted company with Oxley and voted against a bill that sought to block implementation of a new accounting rule requiring companies to treat stock options as an expense in calculating their bottom line. "American workers may invest . . . in unprofitable companies because they will continue to be given misleading financial statements," Gillmor said.

He also worked with liberal Democrat Barney Frank of Massachusetts to resolve concerns over regulation that might have allowed commercial entities, such as discount giant Wal-Mart, to set up their own nationwide banks. Gillmor, whose wealth was estimated by Roll Call newspaper to be near $6 million, is director of his family's financial services company.

In 2003, Gillmor split with House GOP leaders and Republican Billy Tauzin of Louisiana, chairman of the Energy and Commerce Committee, in backing efforts to overturn a ruling by the Federal Communications Commission allowing greater media ownership consolidation.

In the 106th Congress, Gillmor played a role in the sweeping rewrite of financial services laws. He worked with Democrat Edward J. Markey of Massachusetts on legislation that restricted sales of a customer's financial and medical information. He has pushed for a measure that would require

CAPITOL OFFICE
225-6405
www.house.gov/gillmor
1203 Longworth 20515-3505; fax 225-1985

COMMITTEES
Energy & Commerce
(Environment & Hazardous Materials - chairman)
Financial Services

HOMETOWN
Old Fort

BORN
Feb. 1, 1939, Tiffin, Ohio

RELIGION
Methodist

FAMILY
Wife, Karen L. Gillmor; five children

EDUCATION
Ohio Wesleyan U., B.A. 1961; U. of Michigan, J.D. 1964

MILITARY SERVICE
Air Force, 1965-66

CAREER
Lawyer

POLITICAL HIGHLIGHTS
Ohio Senate, 1967-89 (minority leader, 1978-80, 1983-84; president, 1981-82, 1985-88); sought Republican nomination for governor, 1986

ELECTION RESULTS

2004 GENERAL

Paul E. Gillmor (R)	196,649	67.1%
Robin Weirauch (D)	96,656	33.0%

2004 PRIMARY

Paul E. Gillmor (R)	unopposed

2002 GENERAL

Paul E. Gillmor (R)	126,286	67.1%
Roger Anderson (D)	51,872	27.6%
John F. Green (LIBERT)	10,096	5.4%

PREVIOUS WINNING PERCENTAGES
2000 (70%); 1998 (67%); 1996 (61%); 1994 (73%); 1992 (100%); 1990 (68%); 1988 (61%)

mutual funds to show the impact of taxes on performance results, contending investors need such information to identify the funds best for them. He also remains committed to an effort to require corporations to disclose charitable donations. Business leaders worry that the measure could discourage donations, but Gillmor argues that shareholders should be informed of such donations since it is their money.

In 2004, he pushed a bill through his Energy and Commerce Subcommittee that would let states regulate shipments of trash coming from other states. "Ohio is one of the states most adversely affected," he said. "My bill places control in the hands of local communities, allowing them to make the decision to import interstate waste."

His concern for states' rights goes beyond garbage. Gillmor and his legislative assistant co-authored an article published in the Spring 1993 installment of the Harvard Journal on Legislation. The piece advocated a constitutional amendment prohibiting unfunded mandates — laws requiring state and local governments to implement specific programs but providing no funds to carry out the directives. Unfunded mandates are "repugnant to our constitutional scheme," Gillmor wrote, giving Congress "unchecked power to burden state and local governments with mandated costs."

In recent years, Gillmor has pressed for legislation to provide greater Federal Deposit Insurance Corp. protection for municipalities' deposits in their local banks and to create a national sex offender database.

After graduating from law school, Gillmor served in the Air Force as a judge advocate in 1965-66. Returning to civilian life, he won a seat in the state Senate. Thirteen years later, after the GOP took over the chamber with a one-vote majority, Gillmor won the Senate presidency over a fiery conservative by stressing the need for negotiation within the GOP as well as with the Democrats, who still controlled the House and governorship.

After losing a 1986 bid for the gubernatorial nomination, Gillmor in 1988 sought the seat of fellow Republican Delbert L. Latta, who was retiring after 30 years in the House. Gillmor's principal primary opponent turned out to be Latta's son, Robert, a 32-year-old lawyer. In a bitter contest, Gillmor towered over the newcomer in personal recognition, stressing his fiscal conservatism and successes in Columbus. But Latta campaigned aggressively, aided by his father's ready-made organization.

Gillmor won the primary by just 27 votes — the smallest margin in any 1988 House contest. But he topped 60 percent of the vote in November, as he has done in every re-election bid since, despite criticism from opponents and editorial writers that he does not live in the district.

OHIO 5
Northwest — Bowling Green, Tiffin, Fremont

A mixture of flat farmland, limestone plains and small towns, the 5th runs from Ohio's northwest corner to the north-central portion of the state.

At the district's center is the university town of Bowling Green, located in Wood County, the largest and most-populous jurisdiction in the 5th. The Maumee River divides Wood from Toledo-dominated Lucas County (most of which is in the 9th), and more people are finding northern Wood an attractive place to live. Perrysburg increased its population 35 percent in the 1990s. Still, most of Wood's land area is devoted to farming. The county produces wheat, tomatoes, soybeans and corn.

The remaining constituents are almost evenly divided between counties west and east of Wood. Many of the counties are devoted almost exclusively to agriculture and food packaging. This area is the heart of Ohio's wheat-growing country: Some of the top-producing counties are Henry, Paulding, Putnam and Wood. Migrant workers who live in farm camps during the harvesting months help boost the district's Hispanic population to 4 percent, double the state's average of about 2 percent.

Manufacturing is important here as well, with Heinz Ketchup and Arm & Hammer Baking Soda among the products made in the 5th's facilities. Whirlpool Corp. has a large facility in Clyde that builds washing machines.

Redistricting following the 2000 census made some adjustments to the lines in the district's east. The 5th no longer borders Lake Erie; the district boundaries were moved south to give the 5th all of Crawford County and parts of Wyandot and Ashland counties.

The 5th is strong GOP territory. Fifteen of the 16 counties that lie wholly or partly within the 5th voted for George W. Bush in the 2004 presidential election — the lone exception was Lucas County, although the 5th's small share of that county also backed Bush. Putnam County, located southwest of Wood, gave Bush his best showing in Ohio, 76 percent.

MAJOR INDUSTRY
Agriculture, manufacturing

CITIES
Bowling Green, 29,636; Tiffin, 18,135; Fremont, 17,345; Perrysburg, 16,945

NOTABLE
The Rutherford B. Hayes Presidential Center is located in Fremont.

KEY VOTES

2004
No Extend federal unemployment benefits by 13 weeks
Yes Pass $283.2 billion, six-year federal highway and mass transit bill
Yes Approve $146 billion multi-year extension of previously enacted middle-class tax breaks
Yes Amend the Constitution to prohibit same-sex marriage
Yes Cut corporate taxes $137 billion over 10 years
Yes Reorganize U.S. intelligence agencies as proposed by Sept. 11 commission

2003
Yes Cut taxes by $330 billion through fiscal 2013
No Block Bush rule scaling back overtime pay for some white-collar federal workers
No Do not allow use of search warrants without first notifying subjects
No Allow importation of prescription drugs
Yes Create private school voucher program in Washington, D.C.
Yes Ban "partial birth" abortion except to save a woman's life
No Split $18.6 billion in Iraq aid into half-grant, half-loan
Yes Overhaul Medicare and create prescription drug benefit

CQ VOTE STUDIES

	PARTY UNITY		PRESIDENTIAL SUPPORT	
	Support	Oppose	Support	Oppose
2004	93%	7%	91%	9%
2003	94%	6%	94%	6%
2002	93%	7%	92%	8%
2001	95%	5%	90%	10%
2000	91%	9%	32%	68%

INTEREST GROUPS

	AFL-CIO	ADA	CCUS	ACU
2004	27%	5%	100%	84%
2003	20%	5%	93%	72%
2002	13%	5%	100%	88%
2001	18%	15%	96%	79%
2000	0%	10%	80%	76%

Rep. Ted Strickland (D)

Elected 1992; 6th term
Did not serve 1995-97

Strickland no longer has to struggle to hold onto his seat in what had been a swing district until the boundaries were realigned in 2002. His constituency's voting patterns are now more predictably Democratic.

Long a reliable vote for the Democratic leadership on issues such as education, taxes and health care, Strickland in 2004 faced no Republican challenger for his House seat, and in early 2005 was seriously weighing a run for Ohio governor. That gives him greater incentive than he has had in the past to jump into partisan skirmishes with the GOP.

A staunch ally of labor, Strickland voted against giving the president power to negotiate trade deals that cannot be amended by Congress. And he opposed making permanent the normalized U.S.-China trade relationship. Steelmaking figures prominently in his redrawn district and Strickland strongly endorsed the Bush administration's 2002 move to impose tariffs as high as 30 percent on certain steel imports.

He has also taken on the Bush administration, in particular during the 108th Congress, acting from his position as a new member of the Veterans' Affairs Committee. Strickland repeatedly wrote to Defense Secretary Donald H. Rumsfeld complaining that U.S. troops operating in Iraq had been issued inadequate body and vehicle armor, and were returning from the war zone with more serious wounds than were necessary given the state of modern military equipment.

He has also pressed for court-ordered payments to former prisoners of war captured during the 1991 Persian Gulf War, who were tortured by the regime of Saddam Hussein. And in early 2005, the Department of Veterans Affairs responded to pressure from Strickland and began contacting about 4,500 World War II veterans who were never told they might qualify for medical benefits because of chemical warfare experiments. In the 109th Congress, he is the top-ranking Democrat on the Veterans' Affairs panel's Oversight and Investigations Subcommittee.

Strickland will break with his party, however, in deference to the views of his economically struggling and culturally conservative constituents. He opposed tougher clean air standards proposed by the Clinton administration, and in the 2002 energy debate he opposed Democratic proposals to curb emissions of carbon dioxide, a "greenhouse gas" that most scientists say contributes to global warming. It is formed by burning fossil fuels such as coal in power plants. "If I didn't have responsibilities to the people who hire me, I might have a very different attitude," Strickland said. "I want clean air, too, but I've got power plants and coal mines in my district. That has tempered my point of view, because I have to fight for my people and their livelihoods."

Even before the 6th District was remade for this decade, Strickland had succeeded in bolstering his job security by luring federal dollars to the impoverished areas of his rural district and seeking a middle ground on what he calls "socially divisive issues." He has supported funds for family planning but voted to ban a procedure its critics call "partial birth" abortion. Strickland also will side with conservatives in opposing gun control initiatives, and he was one of 52 Democrats who voted in 2004 to repeal a ban on gun ownership in the District of Columbia.

Strickland's seat on the Energy and Commerce Committee, with its broad legislative jurisdiction, has helped him take a high profile on many of the bread-and-butter economic issues for his constituents. "Someone

CAPITOL OFFICE
225-5705
www.house.gov/strickland
336 Cannon 20515-3506; fax 225-5907

COMMITTEES
Energy & Commerce
Veterans' Affairs

HOMETOWN
Lisbon

BORN
Aug. 4, 1941, Lucasville, Ohio

RELIGION
Methodist

FAMILY
Wife, Frances Smith Strickland

EDUCATION
Asbury College, B.A. 1963 (history); U. of Kentucky, M.A. 1966 (guidance counseling); Asbury Theological Seminary, M.A. 1967 (divinity); U. of Kentucky, Ph.D. 1980 (counseling psychology)

CAREER
Professor; psychologist; minister

POLITICAL HIGHLIGHTS
Democratic nominee for U.S. House, 1976, 1978, 1980; U.S. House, 1993-95; defeated for re-election to U.S. House, 1994

ELECTION RESULTS

2004 GENERAL

Ted Strickland (D)		unopposed

2004 PRIMARY

Ted Strickland (D)	73,405	83.0%
Diane DiCarlo Murphy (D)	15,054	17.0%

2002 GENERAL

Ted Strickland (D)	113,972	59.5%
Mike Halleck (R)	77,643	40.5%

PREVIOUS WINNING PERCENTAGES
2000 (58%); 1998 (57%); 1996 (51%); 1992 (51%)

once described me as their congressional commissioner," he says. "I take that as a compliment. I represent a part of Appalachia that has lots of poverty, an older population, people with health care problems. People struggle day by day. They need a strong advocate."

The son of a steelworker and one of nine siblings, Strickland has an eclectic professional background. He holds a divinity degree and a doctorate in counseling psychology, and he has worked as a minister, a college professor and director of a Methodist children's home. Drawing on his experience as a psychologist in a maximum security prison, Strickland has routinely opposed the privatization of prisons, warning that such institutions would focus on profits rather than safety.

Strickland's prison work led to his teaming with Ohio GOP Sen. Mike DeWine to sponsor a bill to finance grants to states for cooperative ventures between corrections and mental health agencies that would provide services to mentally ill prisoners upon their release. The measure, enacted in 2004, also sought funds for state grants to train law enforcement personnel to handle mentally ill offenders. In the 106th Congress (1999-2000), Strickland and DeWine both sponsored legislation that was enacted to provide grants to create specialized local courts to handle mental illness cases.

Strickland has now won more races for Congress than he has lost, but until very recently that was not the case. He was an unsuccessful nominee for Congress in 1976, 1978 and 1980 before winning in a narrow upset in 1992. He benefited that year from the previous redistricting of Ohio, which resulted in two veteran GOP incumbents vying for the same seat. Strickland narrowly defeated the eventual GOP nominee, Bob McEwen, who had gone through a tough primary against colleague Clarence E. Miller and was damaged by publicity about his 166 overdrafts at the private bank for House members.

Two years later, Strickland was swept out of office in that year's GOP landslide, losing narrowly to conservative Republican businessman Frank A. Cremeans. Strickland had hurt himself with voters by supporting abortion rights, voting for President Clinton's tax-raising deficit reduction package and suggesting that taxes might have to be raised again to create a universal health care benefit, an idea he supported.

But he won the seat back in 1996, besting Cremeans in a rematch that was viewed as something of a referendum on Republican stewardship of the 104th Congress. In the following three elections, Strickland recorded ever wider victory margins before the Republicans took a pass on challenging him in 2004.

KEY VOTES

2004
Yes	Extend federal unemployment benefits by 13 weeks
Yes	Pass $283.2 billion, six-year federal highway and mass transit bill
Yes	Approve $146 billion multi-year extension of previously enacted middle-class tax breaks
No	Amend the Constitution to prohibit same-sex marriage
No	Cut corporate taxes $137 billion over 10 years
Yes	Reorganize U.S. intelligence agencies as proposed by Sept. 11 commission

2003
No	Cut taxes by $330 billion through fiscal 2013
Yes	Block Bush rule scaling back overtime pay for some white-collar federal workers
Yes	Do not allow use of search warrants without first notifying subjects
Yes	Allow importation of prescription drugs
No	Create private school voucher program in Washington, D.C.
Yes	Ban "partial birth" abortion except to save a woman's life
Yes	Split $18.6 billion in Iraq aid into half-grant, half-loan
No	Overhaul Medicare and create prescription drug benefit

CQ VOTE STUDIES

	PARTY UNITY		PRESIDENTIAL SUPPORT	
	Support	Oppose	Support	Oppose
2004	94%	6%	30%	70%
2003	92%	8%	22%	78%
2002	90%	10%	32%	68%
2001	89%	11%	26%	74%
2000	85%	15%	67%	33%

INTEREST GROUPS

	AFL-CIO	ADA	CCUS	ACU
2004	100%	95%	38%	8%
2003	100%	95%	33%	28%
2002	89%	90%	40%	12%
2001	100%	90%	35%	16%
2000	100%	90%	31%	12%

OHIO 6
South and east – Boardman, Athens, Steubenville

The 6th parallels the Ohio River for more than 300 miles, bordering three states and enveloping the hardscrabble areas from southern Ohio's Appalachia to the Mahoning Valley near Youngstown.

Many of the district's counties, especially those along the Ohio River in old coal mining territory, suffer high unemployment and have difficulty retaining younger people. Meigs County has Ohio's lowest median household income, and Scioto (shared with the 2nd) and Lawrence counties, which form the southwest border of the 6th, also struggle.

Athens County (shared with the 18th) is home to Ohio University and has a liberal slant. Green Party presidential candidate Ralph Nader had a better showing in Athens than in any other Ohio county in 2000, and in 2004, John Kerry did better only in Cuyahoga County (Cleveland) than in Athens. East of Athens lies Washington County, which takes in Marietta and is one of the few solidly Republican areas in the district.

North of Washington, the district tilts Democratic. Belmont (shared with the 18th) and Monroe counties, along with Jefferson County, which includes Steubenville, vote dependably Democratic. Jefferson has lost population in each of the past four censuses and has the highest proportion of elderly residents of any Ohio county. About one-third of residents live in Mahoning and Columbiana counties in the district's northern extreme. The 6th's share of Mahoning takes in Boardman and Poland, south of Youngstown, and is more politically competitive than the areas of the county that lie in the 17th District.

The 6th has a Democratic orientation, and redistricting following the 2000 census moved the district's boundaries east and north to scoop up voters who support Democrats. Still, the 6th has a conservative bent on social issues and is highly competitive in presidential elections. George W. Bush won seven of the 12 counties wholly or partly in the 6th en route to narrowly winning the district in both 2000 and 2004.

MAJOR INDUSTRY
Service, manufacturing

CITIES
Boardman (unincorporated), 37,215; Athens, 21,342; Steubenville, 19,015

NOTABLE
Marietta was the first European settlement in the Northwest Territories.

Rep. David L. Hobson (R)

Elected 1990; 8th term

CAPITOL OFFICE
225-4324
www.house.gov/hobson
2346 Rayburn 20515-3507; fax 225-1984

COMMITTEES
Appropriations
(Energy & Water - chairman)

HOMETOWN
Springfield

BORN
Oct. 17, 1936, Cincinnati, Ohio

RELIGION
Methodist

FAMILY
Wife, Carolyn Hobson; three children

EDUCATION
Ohio Wesleyan U., B.A. 1958; Ohio State U.,
J.D. 1963

MILITARY SERVICE
Ohio Air National Guard, 1958-63

CAREER
Financial executive

POLITICAL HIGHLIGHTS
Candidate for Ohio House, 1982; Ohio Senate,
1982-90 (majority whip, 1986-88; president pro
tempore, 1988-90)

ELECTION RESULTS

2004 GENERAL
| David L. Hobson (R) | 186,534 | 65.0% |
| Kara Anastasio (D) | 100,617 | 35.0% |

2004 PRIMARY
| David L. Hobson (R) | | unopposed |

2002 GENERAL
David L. Hobson (R)	113,252	67.6%
Kara Anastasio (D)	45,568	27.2%
Frank A. Doden (I)	8,812	5.3%

PREVIOUS WINNING PERCENTAGES
2000 (68%); 1998 (67%); 1996 (68%); 1994 (100%);
1992 (71%); 1990 (62%)

An easygoing legislator who prefers to work behind the scenes, Hobson enjoys the trust and respect not only of the Republican leadership but also of members from both sides of the aisle. He has long been known around Capitol Hill as "Uncle Dave" for his calm and effective style as a mediator.

He is not one to toot his own horn. Most lawmakers maintain Web sites filled with flattering photos, tributes from admirers, promotional material about the member's latest triumphs, and the like. In early April 2005, the most recent press release on Hobson's site was dated Dec. 14, 2003, hailing the capture of Saddam Hussein. A "Hot Issues" button produced a link to "Dave Hobson's 2002 Annual Report" and a warning that the anthrax attacks of 2001 had resulted in delays in the delivery of mail to the Capitol complex.

Hobson needs no advertising. His congressional résumé shows how much the GOP leadership has relied on him since his arrival in 1991. He was appointed to the Rules Committee as a freshman, a rare honor. He was named to the Appropriations Committee as a sophomore. And he was Speaker Newt Gingrich's personal appointee to the Budget Committee in the 104th and 105th Congresses. (In that role, he served as a conduit between the Speaker and John R. Kasich, his fellow Ohio Republican who chaired Budget at the height of the fiscal policy showdowns with the Clinton administration.)

Hobson arrived on Capitol Hill with years of experience in politics and business. Not only had he risen to a leadership position in the Ohio state Senate, but he had also served as chairman of a financial services company and on the boards of a bank, an oil company and a restaurant concern. In his 50s when he was first elected to Congress, he had a broader perspective than younger, more ambitious and less patient colleagues.

Although his voting record is pretty typical for a House Republican, in 2004 he voted against a constitutional amendment to ban same-sex marriage. And he has consistently shown a willingness to compromise as part of the lawmaking process, an approach that has come in handy in the horse-trading world of the Appropriations Committee.

Despite his avuncular manner, Hobson has caused a feud or two in the Republican family, mostly over nuclear issues. As chairman of the Energy and Water Subcommittee since January 2003, he has tried to block funding for a Bush administration plan to convert certain existing nuclear warheads into "bunker buster" models that have less yield and more ability to penetrate hardened, underground facilities. At times during the debate, Hobson sounded almost like an anti-nuclear activist. "With all the proliferation threats we now face with countries like Iran, Pakistan and North Korea, are we really sending the right signal to those countries and the rest of the world when we embark on nuclear weapons initiatives?" Hobson asked Defense Secretary Donald H. Rumsfeld at a 2004 hearing.

"I can't believe this country would ever drop a [nuclear] weapon again," he said on another occasion.

Hobson's stance drew some flak from conservatives such as commentator Frank J. Gaffney Jr., who wrote in the Washington Times in early 2005 that Hobson's view "is utterly inimical to U.S. security."

Hobson also clashed with Senate appropriators in the 108th Congress over his support for a nuclear waste repository at Yucca Mountain in Nevada and his proposals to cut spending on nuclear weapons labs in the home state of his Senate Appropriations counterpart, Republican Pete V.

www.cqpress.com

Domenici of New Mexico.

Before taking the helm of the Energy and Water Subcommittee, Hobson chaired the Military Construction Subcommittee for four years. That post allowed him to safeguard key local interests, including Wright-Patterson Air Force Base — one of the largest employers in the state — as well as the Springfield Air National Guard Base, which he has worked to save from elimination. While Hobson's switch in chairmanships may mean less construction money for Wright-Patterson, he will still be able to look out for base concerns from his seat on the Defense Appropriations panel.

Building on interests he developed as chairman of the Ohio state Senate Health Committee, Hobson in 1996 helped win passage of legislation to protect the health insurance of families that lose or change jobs. In the 105th Congress, he was part of the Speaker's Health Care Working Group, which drafted a GOP version of patients' rights legislation that ultimately died in a standoff with the more sweeping Senate version.

Hobson has broken with GOP hard-liners on issues other than nuclear weapons. In 1996, for example, he expressed a willingness to negotiate with President Clinton on a balanced-budget plan, rather than risk a government shutdown. The next year, when Congress and the White House struck a balanced-budget deal, he fought to keep lawmakers on that course. He voted against a massive highway bill that authorized more spending than the agreement called for, and he counseled against tax cuts that might endanger the deficit-reduction plan.

He was one of the last Republicans to make known how he would vote on Clinton's impeachment in 1998, and his votes finally mirrored the action of the House. He voted for the two articles that were adopted and against the two articles that were rejected.

In 1982, a month after losing respectably in a state House race, Hobson was appointed to the state Senate seat that Republican Mike DeWine gave up in a successful bid for the U.S. House. After four years in Columbus, he was chosen by his GOP colleagues to be majority whip.

Hobson was elected to Congress with 62 percent of the vote in 1990, when DeWine (now Ohio's senior senator) gave up his House seat to run for lieutenant governor. He has won with 65 percent or better ever since — including in 2002, when the district was reconfigured for this decade and 125,000 voters were people he had not represented before. In fact, his 65 percent total in 2004 was his lowest since his initial campaign, a reflection, in all likelihood, of the huge turnout engendered by Ohio's role as the pivotal battleground in the presidential election.

KEY VOTES

2004

No   Extend federal unemployment benefits by 13 weeks

Yes   Pass $283.2 billion, six-year federal highway and mass transit bill

Yes   Approve $146 billion multi-year extension of previously enacted middle-class tax breaks

No   Amend the Constitution to prohibit same-sex marriage

Yes   Cut corporate taxes $137 billion over 10 years

Yes   Reorganize U.S. intelligence agencies as proposed by Sept. 11 commission

2003

Yes   Cut taxes by $330 billion through fiscal 2013

No   Block Bush rule scaling back overtime pay for some white-collar federal workers

Yes   Do not allow use of search warrants without first notifying subjects

No   Allow importation of prescription drugs

Yes   Create private school voucher program in Washington, D.C.

Yes   Ban "partial birth" abortion except to save a woman's life

No   Split $18.6 billion in Iraq aid into half-grant, half-loan

Yes   Overhaul Medicare and create prescription drug benefit

CQ VOTE STUDIES

	PARTY UNITY		PRESIDENTIAL SUPPORT	
	Support	Oppose	Support	Oppose
2004	92%	8%	82%	18%
2003	95%	5%	96%	4%
2002	94%	6%	90%	10%
2001	95%	5%	88%	12%
2000	90%	10%	33%	67%

INTEREST GROUPS

	AFL-CIO	ADA	CCUS	ACU
2004	20%	5%	100%	88%
2003	7%	5%	100%	88%
2002	11%	0%	100%	88%
2001	17%	15%	96%	80%
2000	0%	0%	90%	72%

OHIO 7
Central — Springfield, Lancaster, part of Columbus

Taking in a roughly U-shaped swath of land across south central Ohio, the 7th is a Republican-leaning and diverse district that includes urban, suburban and rural areas.

The district's two most-populous counties — Greene and Clark — form the western portion of the 7th. Wright-Patterson Air Force Base, most of which is in Greene, is the largest single-site employer in Ohio. Greene also has several colleges and universities.

Clark and its county seat, Springfield, suffered economically in the early 1980s but have seen a dramatic turnaround. New companies, including trucking and auto manufacturing plants and distribution firms, now call the area home. Clark voted Democratic for president in 2000 — a rare western Ohio county to do so — but George W. Bush narrowly won there in 2004.

Residential growth around Columbus, a small part of which was added to the 7th in redistricting following the 2000 census, has especially affected

Clark and Fairfield counties, which serve as bedroom communities and are filling up with white-collar commuters. Fairfield is solidly Republican, as are Fayette and Pickaway counties to its west. Fayette, the least-populous county wholly within the 7th, is a major horse-breeding area. Perry, the easternmost county in the 7th, has above-average unemployment and is more competitive politically. Bush captured 57 percent of the district's overall presidential vote in 2004, but he won only 52 percent of the Perry County vote.

MAJOR INDUSTRY
Auto manufacturing, military, technology research, agriculture

MILITARY BASES
Wright-Patterson Air Force Base, 8,002 military, 11,343 civilian (2004) (shared with the 3rd District)

CITIES
Springfield, 65,358; Columbus (pt.), 51,097; Beavercreek, 37,984; Lancaster, 35,335; Fairborn, 32,052; Xenia, 24,164

NOTABLE
Gen. William Tecumseh Sherman was born in Lancaster; The modern combine, invented in Springfield, helped revolutionize harvesting and the agriculture industry.

Rep. John A. Boehner (R)

Elected 1990; 8th term

Once a fierce partisan who helped lead the Republicans to the majority in the House, Boehner is now more regarded as a serious legislator credited with steering President Bush's landmark education bill to passage. As chairman of the Education and Workforce Committee, he won respect from GOP colleagues by overcoming the sting of the 1998 loss of his leadership post, when he was voted out as Republican Conference chairman.

Talk of Boehner's eventual return to the leadership no longer seems like idle chatter. His name has been floated as a possible candidate for House majority leader — he is no fan of Tom DeLay, who has held the job since 2003 — or even as a future Speaker if J. Dennis Hastert retires in 2008 as expected. Until then, Boehner (BAY-ner) has plenty of projects to keep his hands full: a reauthorization of the federal college aid system, a rewrite of the Head Start early childhood development program and an overhaul of the pension system.

Boehner is one of the most distinctive personalities in the House. Always tanned, usually chain-smoking Barclay cigarettes, he delivers his statements in a booming baritone voice that resonates throughout a hearing room. But he is not always a talker. He is known for responding to difficult questions with a motion called the "Boehner shrug," a stiff, unquotable raising of the shoulders that encourages the questioner to drop the subject.

And while he has had his share of partisan tensions with committee Democrats, it was his flair for bipartisan negotiations on the 2001 education bill, called the No Child Left Behind Act, that set the tone for his transformation from leadership has-been to committee chairman. When he met with President-elect Bush in Austin in late 2000 to discuss the bill, Boehner insisted that transition team officials also invite George Miller of California, who was about to become the top-ranking Democrat on the panel. The unlikely partnership forged that day helped get Bush's initiative past the many obstacles engineered by opponents in both parties.

Since then, Boehner and Miller have clashed over funding for the law and other subjects, such as the Bush administration's attempt to rewrite the rules on overtime pay, which Boehner supported and Miller opposed. But those tensions have not stopped the panel from building a track record of success on other issues. In 2004, Boehner's committee was the starting point for legislation reauthorizing the child nutrition and school lunch program and for renewing the federal law that governs education for disabled students. Boehner also helped advance a longtime Republican education priority that year by co-authoring legislation creating a private school voucher program in the District of Columbia.

In the 109th Congress, Boehner has turned his sights to financial mismanagement in the Head Start program, saying the law needs to be rewritten to crack down on abuses. He will also try again to reauthorize the Higher Education Act, an effort that bogged down in 2004 over changes he wanted to make to interest rates for student loans. And he hopes to persuade Congress to overhaul the pension system to avoid a taxpayer bailout of the Pension Benefit Guaranty Corporation, the public agency that is responsible for pension payments when companies default on them. (In 2004, he helped push through Congress a temporary fix that allows companies to reduce their pension plan contributions by about $80 billion in 2004 and 2005.)

When he entered Congress in 1991, Boehner was one of the rabble-rousing Gang of Seven, a group of minority party freshmen eager to rein in, or

CAPITOL OFFICE
225-6205
john.boehner@mail.house.gov
johnboehner.house.gov
1011 Longworth 20515-3508; fax 225-0704

COMMITTEES
Agriculture
Education & Workforce - chairman

HOMETOWN
West Chester

BORN
Nov. 17, 1949, Cincinnati, Ohio

RELIGION
Roman Catholic

FAMILY
Wife, Debbie Boehner; two children

EDUCATION
Xavier U., B.S. 1977

MILITARY SERVICE
Navy, 1968

CAREER
Plastics and packaging executive

POLITICAL HIGHLIGHTS
Ohio House, 1985-91

ELECTION RESULTS

2004 GENERAL

John A. Boehner (R)	201,675	69.0%
Jeff Hardenbrook (D)	90,574	31.0%

2004 PRIMARY

John A. Boehner (R)	unopposed

2002 GENERAL

John A. Boehner (R)	119,947	70.8%
Jeff Hardenbrook (D)	49,444	29.2%

PREVIOUS WINNING PERCENTAGES
2000 (71%); 1998 (71%); 1996 (70%); 1994 (100%); 1992 (74%); 1990 (61%)

at least rail against, what they saw as the incumbent excesses that culminated in the House bank scandal. In that episode, lawmakers were discovered to have written checks on the chamber's internal bank without the funds to back them up. Boehner's zeal for a partisan fight made him a favorite of the new breed of confrontational Republicans led by Newt Gingrich of Georgia. After Republicans gained the majority in 1995, Boehner became chairman of the House Republican Conference, the fourth-ranking leadership post that handled message and communications for the new GOP leadership.

But when the party suffered setbacks in the 1998 election, Boehner was labeled by his colleagues as an ineffectual messenger. And he was embarrassed by revelations that he had participated in a secret and ultimately unsuccessful effort to oust Gingrich from power. He was defeated for reelection as conference chairman. He swallowed the loss and began his transformation into a legislative workhorse, and two years later he was named chairman of the Education panel. He also kept up his record as a prolific fundraiser for his party.

The second of 12 children and the son of tavern owners, Boehner worked his way through school. Soon after his graduation from college, he and a partner took control of a small plastics and packaging firm, Nucite Sales Inc., and built it into a multimillion-dollar business.

After six years in the state House, Boehner joined the 1990 GOP primary field against incumbent Donald E. "Buz" Lukens, who had been convicted of a misdemeanor charge stemming from a sexual liaison with a 16-year-old girl. Boehner heavily outspent the front-runner, former Rep. Thomas N. Kindness, and won the primary with 49 percent of the vote.

In the general election, he won a 3-to-2 victory over former Democratic Mayor Gregory V. Jolivette of Hamilton. He has won every election since, with about 70 percent or better. In 2004, he handily beat Democrat Jeff Hardenbrook for the second election in a row.

One of Boehner's frequent trips to Florida to golf resulted in an unusual legal dispute between two lawmakers. In 1996, a Florida couple intercepted a conference phone call in which Boehner and other leaders discussed Gingrich's ethical troubles. They gave a copy of the tape to Rep. Jim McDermott of Washington, then the senior Democrat on the House ethics committee. When newspapers ran excerpts, Boehner sued, alleging a violation of his privacy. McDermott said he was within his First Amendment rights. In 2004, a federal judge ordered him to pay $60,000 in damages, plus attorney's fees, to Boehner. McDermott appealed.

KEY VOTES

2004

No — Extend federal unemployment benefits by 13 weeks

No — Pass $283.2 billion, six-year federal highway and mass transit bill

Yes — Approve $146 billion multi-year extension of previously enacted middle-class tax breaks

Yes — Amend the Constitution to prohibit same-sex marriage

Yes — Cut corporate taxes $137 billion over 10 years

Yes — Reorganize U.S. intelligence agencies as proposed by Sept. 11 commission

2003

? — Cut taxes by $330 billion through fiscal 2013

No — Block Bush rule scaling back overtime pay for some white-collar federal workers

Yes — Do not allow use of search warrants without first notifying subjects

No — Allow importation of prescription drugs

Yes — Create private school voucher program in Washington, D.C.

Yes — Ban "partial birth" abortion except to save a woman's life

No — Split $18.6 billion in Iraq aid into half-grant, half-loan

Yes — Overhaul Medicare and create prescription drug benefit

CQ VOTE STUDIES

	PARTY UNITY		PRESIDENTIAL SUPPORT	
	Support	Oppose	Support	Oppose
2004	97%	3%	100%	0%
2003	97%	3%	100%	0%
2002	97%	3%	92%	8%
2001	99%	1%	98%	2%
2000	95%	5%	30%	70%

INTEREST GROUPS

	AFL-CIO	ADA	CCUS	ACU
2004	7%	0%	100%	100%
2003	7%	5%	100%	84%
2002	11%	0%	100%	88%
2001	8%	0%	100%	96%
2000	0%	5%	85%	87%

OHIO 8

Southwest — Hamilton, most of Middletown

Hugging the state's western border, the 8th is fertile GOP ground that is anchored by Butler County, home to the district's two largest cities, Hamilton and Middletown.

Butler has long voted solidly Republican, but its expanding suburbs have escalated the rightward trend. The county is known for electing some of Ohio's more conservative state and congressional legislators. George W. Bush defeated John Kerry in Butler by more than 30 percentage points in the 2004 presidential election. One exception to the GOP dominance is Oxford, which includes Miami University and backed Kerry in 2004.

Butler and Miami counties have propelled the district's rapid growth. Union Township, in Butler County, is one of the state's fastest-growing suburbs, and many residents there commute to Cincinnati or Dayton. While bad weather and low pork prices hurt the 8th's dominant agriculture industry in the late 1990s, the district's strong manufacturing base, along with new construction and commercial development, helped prevent economic hardship.

About half of the 8th's residents live outside Butler County in a string of fertile Corn Belt counties. Corn and soybeans are the major cash crops here, and poultry and livestock also are moneymakers. Mercer (shared with the 5th) and Darke also yield plenty of Republican votes, backing Bush with 75 percent and 70 percent, respectively, in 2004. Miami County, the district's second-most-populous, gave Bush 66 percent in 2004.

Redistricting following the 2000 census gave the 8th a bigger chunk of Montgomery County, including parts of northeast Dayton near Wright-Patterson Air Force Base, which is in the 3rd and 7th districts. The new map ceded a small part of southwestern Butler County to the 1st District and moved the 8th's northeastern border farther south.

MAJOR INDUSTRY
Agriculture, manufacturing, higher education

CITIES
Hamilton, 60,675; Middletown (pt.), 49,574; Fairfield, 42,097; Huber Heights, 38,212; Dayton (pt.), 28,999

NOTABLE
Hamilton once was known as the "Safe Capital of the World" for the burglar-resistant safes made there; Darke County hosts an Annie Oakley festival each year in honor of their homegrown sharpshooter.

Rep. Marcy Kaptur (D)

Elected 1982; 12th term

The senior Democratic woman in the House, Kaptur in 2004 savored what may be the crowning achievement of her career when she helped preside over the grand opening of the World War II Memorial on the National Mall, capping a 17-year political and legislative effort to create it.

The project was sparked by a constituent, now-deceased veteran Roger Durbin, who asked Kaptur at a 1987 fish fry why there was no memorial for those who served in World War II. She first introduced a bill to create the memorial in December of that year, reintroducing the legislation each Congress until it finally won enactment in 1993. But this was only the prelude to a long and complex fight over the memorial's location and design.

Despite the difficulties, the memorial project gave Kaptur the opportunity "to be a real representative," she said, "which is the way that our government should work — to take this idea from the people, to bring it here and to make it happen, and to give it to the future."

This achievement aside, Kaptur's long tenure has not brought notable influence. Late in 2002, as House Democrats prepared to choose a new leader, Kaptur entered the race just the day before the vote. She said she was under no illusion that she could defeat Californian Nancy Pelosi, but wanted a forum to express her view that the party's emphasis on fundraising had caused it to lose its historical focus on the needs of the working class. Kaptur gave her speech and then withdrew her name.

The GOP takeover of the House in 1995 has stopped her from claiming a subcommittee gavel on the Appropriations Committee, where she was the top-ranking Democrat on the Agriculture panel from 1997 to 2005. With no other committee base — Appropriations is an exclusive assignment — she has had to settle for snagging funds for her Toledo-based District. (She gave up the senior post on Agriculture in the 109th Congress so she could also sit on the Defense Appropriations Subcommittee.)

Agriculture is Ohio's biggest industry and, as a reminder of that, Kaptur sometimes gives her colleagues samples of items — Hirzel spaghetti sauce, Heritage seeds — produced in the state. She also looks out for the interests of the sugar beet growers who are her principal farming constituency; Kaptur has been a leading player in campaigns to save federal sugar subsidies. It is only fair, in her view, to help U.S. industries survive when they have to comply with labor, environmental and health standards that are higher than in other nations.

Kaptur has been a leader in fighting all the major trade expansion initiatives of Presidents Clinton and Bush: the 1993 law to implement the North American Free Trade Agreement, the 1994 law creating the World Trade Organization, the permanent normalization of trade relations with China in 2000, and the revival in 2002 of fast-track authority to negotiate trade agreements that Congress cannot amend. In the 108th Congress, she voted against free-trade agreements with Australia, Chile and Singapore.

Discussing the anti-globalization protests at the 2003 Free Trade Area of the Americas conference in Miami, the 1999 WTO meetings in Seattle and the 2001 Group of Eight trade talks in Genoa, Kaptur compared the struggle to the abolition and civil rights movements. "It is as great as the battle to throw off slavery," she said. "We lose soldiers but we are winning the war."

Unlike most of her Democratic colleagues in the House — especially the women — Kaptur is not an abortion rights advocate and opposes using federal funds to pay for abortions. Her stance reflects that of many of her eth-

CAPITOL OFFICE
225-4146
rep.kaptur@mail.house.gov
www.house.gov/kaptur
2366 Rayburn 20515-3509; fax 225-7711

COMMITTEES
Appropriations

HOMETOWN
Toledo

BORN
June 17, 1946, Toledo, Ohio

RELIGION
Roman Catholic

FAMILY
Single

EDUCATION
U. of Wisconsin, B.A. 1968 (history); U. of Michigan, M.U.P. 1974 (urban planning); Massachusetts Institute of Technology, attended 1981 (urban planning)

CAREER
White House aide; urban planner

POLITICAL HIGHLIGHTS
No previous office

ELECTION RESULTS

2004 GENERAL

Marcy Kaptur (D)	205,149	68.1%
Larry A. Kaczala (R)	95,983	31.9%

2004 PRIMARY

Marcy Kaptur (D)	unopposed

2002 GENERAL

Marcy Kaptur (D)	132,236	74.0%
Edward Emery (R)	46,481	26.0%

PREVIOUS WINNING PERCENTAGES
2000 (75%); 1998 (81%); 1996 (77%); 1994 (75%); 1992 (74%); 1990 (78%); 1988 (81%); 1986 (78%); 1984 (55%); 1982 (58%)

nic blue-collar constituents — Germans, Irish, Poles and Hungarians — who share the Roman Catholic Church's opposition to abortion.

After the 1997 death of her mother, Anastasia, Kaptur and her brother founded the nonprofit Anastasia Fund to promote liberty, community development and free religious expression in the face of political and economic pressures. The fund has helped support groups in Ukraine, China and Mexico. Kaptur also has established the Kaptur Community Fund, which makes charitable donations in Toledo; she regularly contributes her congressional pay raise to the fund.

Kaptur remains emblematic of her Main Street roots. She lives with her brother, Stephen, in the same small house where they were reared, and she attends Mass at the same church where she was baptized. Her parents ran grocery stores in Toledo and nearby Rossford and worked in local auto plants. Kaptur also was an autoworker to help pay for college. Although she was born during the start of the baby boom, some of her domestic pursuits hark back to a bygone era. She maintains the family garden and cans some of the produce; she bakes Polish coffee cakes and makes Polish sausages at the holidays; she paints watercolors; she sews her own curtains.

Kaptur was the first member of her family to attend college. She then worked as a city planner, helping to create community development corporations to revitalize low-income areas of Toledo. That led to a job in the Carter administration as an adviser on urban policy.

Kaptur was working on her doctorate in urban planning at the Massachusetts Institute of Technology when she was recruited to challenge first-term GOP Rep. Ed Weber in 1982. With northwest Ohio in a deep recession, Weber's support for President Reagan's economic agenda proved politically fatal; Kaptur won by 19 percentage points.

She was held to 55 percent of the vote in 1984 but has won by overwhelming margins since. Redistricting by the GOP-controlled legislature in 2002 added territory to the 9th District that maintained its strong Democratic tilt. Kaptur won with almost three-quarters of the vote.

In the 2004 cycle, however, she annoyed her 12 Republican colleagues in the Ohio delegation by helping to recruit Democratic candidates to run against all of them, in a breach of longstanding political protocol. That move was part of a Democratic effort to rebuild from the ground up after years of dwindling electoral success. The GOP members retaliated by helping raise significant funds for her opponent, Lucas County Auditor Larry A. Kaczala, who held her to a mere 68 percent, her lowest vote share since 1984.

KEY VOTES

2004
Yes   Extend federal unemployment benefits by 13 weeks
Yes   Pass $283.2 billion, six-year federal highway and mass transit bill
Yes   Approve $146 billion multi-year extension of previously enacted middle-class tax breaks
No   Amend the Constitution to prohibit same-sex marriage
Yes   Cut corporate taxes $137 billion over 10 years
Yes   Reorganize U.S. intelligence agencies as proposed by Sept. 11 commission

2003
No   Cut taxes by $330 billion through fiscal 2013
Yes   Block Bush rule scaling back overtime pay for some white-collar federal workers
Yes   Do not allow use of search warrants without first notifying subjects
Yes   Allow importation of prescription drugs
No   Create private school voucher program in Washington, D.C.
Yes   Ban "partial birth" abortion except to save a woman's life
Yes   Split $18.6 billion in Iraq aid into half-grant, half-loan
No   Overhaul Medicare and create prescription drug benefit

CQ VOTE STUDIES

	PARTY UNITY		PRESIDENTIAL SUPPORT	
	Support	Oppose	Support	Oppose
2004	97%	3%	33%	67%
2003	95%	5%	25%	75%
2002	96%	4%	24%	76%
2001	89%	11%	23%	77%
2000	91%	9%	73%	27%

INTEREST GROUPS

	AFL-CIO	ADA	CCUS	ACU
2004	100%	95%	33%	8%
2003	100%	95%	24%	28%
2002	100%	95%	30%	18%
2001	100%	85%	30%	30%
2000	100%	75%	30%	18%

OHIO 9
North — Toledo, Sandusky

Toledo sits at the mouth of the Maumee River, the largest river flowing into the Great Lakes, and is the dominant population center in the strongly Democratic 9th, which stretches for 100 miles from the Michigan border eastward to Lorain County in the orbit of Cleveland. More than two-thirds of the 9th's residents live in Lucas County, which envelops Toledo, and the city itself comprises about half of the district's population.

Toledo's economy has long depended on the auto industry, which closed several area factories in the 1980s. But the industry is back, albeit in smaller form, with DaimlerChrysler and General Motors among the area's top employers. Growth in the city's petroleum and manufacturing industries, including glass and machinery, also has spurred some economic recovery.

Toledo's large concentrations of ethnic blue-collar workers — Germans, Irish, Poles and Hungarians — make it a lonely Democratic outpost in rural, Republican northwestern Ohio. John Kerry took 61 percent of the 2004 presidential vote in the 9th's share of Lucas and 58 percent overall in the district. Republicans are concentrated in the more affluent suburbs on Toledo's west side, such as Ottawa Hills.

East of Lucas is Ottawa County, which backed George W. Bush in the 2004 presidential election and includes Port Clinton and some islands near Canada's Pelee Island, and Erie County, which includes Sandusky and has a blue-collar feel and a Democratic lean. The district's easternmost county is Lorain, which is shared with the 13th District and also leans Democratic. The 9th's share of Lorain includes the strongly liberal area around Oberlin College.

MAJOR INDUSTRY
Auto manufacturing, agriculture, health care

CITIES
Toledo, 313,619; Sandusky, 27,844; Oregon, 19,355; Sylvania, 18,670

NOTABLE
Toledo's historic "Old West End" is known for its Victorian homes and claims to have been the nation's largest residential neighborhood at the turn of the century; Oberlin College, founded in 1833, was the first coeducational institution of higher learning in the United States.

Rep. Dennis J. Kucinich (D)

Elected 1996; 5th term

CAPITOL OFFICE
225-5871
www.house.gov/kucinich
1730 Longworth 20515-3510; fax 225-5745

COMMITTEES
Education & Workforce
Government Reform

HOMETOWN
Cleveland

BORN
Oct. 8, 1946, Cleveland, Ohio

RELIGION
Roman Catholic

FAMILY
Divorced; one child

EDUCATION
Case Western Reserve U., B.A., M.A. 1973 (speech communications)

CAREER
Video producer; public power consultant; sportswriter

POLITICAL HIGHLIGHTS
Cleveland City Council, 1969-75; Democratic nominee for U.S. House, 1972; independent candidate for U.S. House, 1974; mayor of Cleveland, 1977-79; defeated for re-election as mayor of Cleveland, 1979; Cleveland City Council, 1983-85; sought Democratic nomination for U.S. House, 1988, 1992; Ohio Senate, 1995-97; sought Democratic nomination for president, 2004

ELECTION RESULTS

2004 GENERAL

Dennis J. Kucinich (D)	172,406	60.0%
Edward Fitzpatrick Herman (R)	96,463	33.6%
Barbara Ann Ferris (I)	18,343	6.4%

2004 PRIMARY

Dennis J. Kucinich (D)	74,692	85.5%
George Pulling (D)	12,639	14.5%

2002 GENERAL

Dennis J. Kucinich (D)	129,997	74.1%
Jon A. Heben (R)	41,778	23.8%
Judy Locy (I)	3,761	2.1%

PREVIOUS WINNING PERCENTAGES
2000 (75%); 1998 (67%); 1996 (49%)

Back in Congress after a quixotic quest for the presidency, Kucinich has settled into his old role as an anti-war anchor for his party in the House. Kucinich failed spectacularly in his 2004 bid for the Democratic presidential nomination, but he managed to burnish his image as a clever liberal who uses self-deprecation and unusual parliamentary moves to attract attention to his causes.

For example, Kucinich (ku-SIN-itch) was among several Ohioans who backed a symbolic challenge to the certification of President Bush as the winner of the 2004 election. Kucinich had no illusions about the effectiveness of the challenge, but, characteristically, he used it to make a larger point. "The outcome of the election will remain unchanged," he said. "But what we must change is a system which denied citizens of a great state their opportunity to change the outcome. Election reform is our solemn duty."

Kucinich fought the 2002 law authorizing Bush to launch a pre-emptive military strike on Iraq. While his attempt to build support for a longer course of diplomacy came up short, Kucinich managed to force a floor vote on the issue. His proposal for a delay received 101 votes.

He and five other Democrats then sued to bar Bush from attacking without a specific congressional declaration of war. A federal appeals court tossed out the suit in March 2003. Similarly, in 1999 he joined two dozen other lawmakers in an unsuccessful suit maintaining that President Clinton had illegally committed U.S. troops to a NATO bombing campaign for too long without congressional approval.

Kucinich opposed the 2001 anti-terrorism law known as the Patriot Act, calling it an unconscionable erosion of constitutionally guaranteed civil liberties. In a February 2002 speech that generated thousands of mostly supportive e-mail responses, Kucinich railed against Bush's conduct of the campaign against terrorism as a "war without end."

Kucinich was a co-chairman of the Congressional Progressive Caucus, the group of the most liberal House Democrats, in both the 107th and 108th Congresses. A self-described pacifist, he regularly presses a bill to establish a Cabinet-level Department of Peace.

As a presidential contender, Kucinich described himself as "pro-choice." But as a House member, he compiled a consistent anti-abortion record until 2002, when he voted "present" on both a bill to ban a procedure opponents call "partial birth" abortion and on a measure to allow doctors, hospitals and insurance companies to refuse to provide or pay for abortions. Kucinich says his views on abortion have "evolved," but he voted no on the partial-birth bill in 2003.

Where Kucinich distinguishes himself is in his perseverance, rhetorical flourishes and self-deprecating wit. When he arrived in Congress, he handed out trading cards featuring himself as a 4-foot-9-inch, 97-pound backup high school quarterback in 1960. Speaking at a journalists' black-tie awards dinner a few months later, he brought down the house by promising to civilize Washington through the introduction of three Cleveland staples: kielbasa, polka and bowling.

In his campaign for president, a highly publicized contest by a political Web site to get him a dinner date brought more recognition than any of his political stances. He did go on a date with the eventual winner of the Web contest, but nothing more came of it. After the campaign, in an effort to pay off his debts, he put autographed campaign memorabilia up for sale on eBay, including Democratic National Convention hall passes and a donkey-shaped Beanie Baby stuffed toy.

In the 108th Congress, when he wasn't off running for president, Kucinich engaged in his usual pursuit of the impossible. For example, he tried in an Education and Workforce Committee meeting to increase funding for Head Start, the preschool program for low-income children, from $6.9 billion to $22.9 billion. Even Democrats said that was completely out of line.

The son of a truck driver, Kucinich earned a master's degree in communications and has worked as a copy editor, sportswriter and political commentator, a background that has helped make him a master at reducing complicated public policy disagreements to easily understood terms. But both the substance and style of his arguments can work to his detriment. As he began his fifth term in the House, he had won enactment of only one law, a 1998 measure to make a television program, "Window on America," available to the Ukrainian Museum and Archives in Cleveland through the U.S. Information Agency.

One of Kucinich's passions is warning Americans about genetically modified food, which would carry government labels under legislation he has proposed since the 106th Congress. "If we are what we eat, shouldn't we know what is in our food, so we know what we will become?" he asked.

Practicing what he preaches, Kucinich made a radical change in his own diet in 1995, becoming a vegetarian after almost five decades eating kielbasa and other rich Eastern European fare. Now his meals include rice, tofu and green tea. "Once I was able to make the transition, I've had enormous amounts of energy, I sleep better, and I don't get tired as much," he said.

Energy is a Kucinich trademark. Elected Cleveland mayor at age 30, he served a single controversial term. The city fell into financial default, and Kucinich's popularity sank so low he wore a bulletproof vest when he threw out the first pitch of the Cleveland Indians' 1978 season. Later that year, he barely survived a recall vote, and the next year he was defeated by Republican George V. Voinovich, now Ohio's junior senator.

But then both Cleveland and its former mayor rebounded. Bucking the GOP tide, Kucinich seized a state Senate seat from a Republican incumbent in 1994. Two years later, he toppled two-term Republican Rep. Martin R. Hoke on his fifth try for Congress, a quest he began as an anti-Vietnam War candidate in 1972. Kucinich put together a strong grass-roots effort in a Democratic-leaning district and won by 3 percentage points after linking Hoke to Speaker Newt Gingrich of Georgia, a polarizing figure in 1996. His subsequent elections have been cakewalks.

KEY VOTES

2004

?	Extend federal unemployment benefits by 13 weeks
Yes	Pass $283.2 billion, six-year federal highway and mass transit bill
Yes	Approve $146 billion multi-year extension of previously enacted middle-class tax breaks
No	Amend the Constitution to prohibit same-sex marriage
No	Cut corporate taxes $137 billion over 10 years
No	Reorganize U.S. intelligence agencies as proposed by Sept. 11 commission

2003

No	Cut taxes by $330 billion through fiscal 2013
Yes	Block Bush rule scaling back overtime pay for some white-collar federal workers
Yes	Do not allow use of search warrants without first notifying subjects
Yes	Allow importation of prescription drugs
?	Create private school voucher program in Washington, D.C.
No	Ban "partial birth" abortion except to save a woman's life
No	Split $18.6 billion in Iraq aid into half-grant, half-loan
No	Overhaul Medicare and create prescription drug benefit

CQ VOTE STUDIES

	PARTY UNITY		PRESIDENTIAL SUPPORT	
	Support	Oppose	Support	Oppose
2004	96%	4%	22%	78%
2003	96%	4%	22%	78%
2002	96%	4%	26%	74%
2001	89%	11%	23%	77%
2000	89%	11%	76%	24%

INTEREST GROUPS

	AFL-CIO	ADA	CCUS	ACU
2004	100%	90%	6%	0%
2003	100%	90%	15%	24%
2002	100%	80%	20%	0%
2001	100%	85%	17%	20%
2000	90%	80%	28%	16%

OHIO 10
Cleveland — West Side and suburbs

The 10th includes the western portion of Cleveland and follows the migration of its ethnic residents into the western and southern suburbs. The district, composed mainly of Reagan Democrats, has successfully navigated the transition from an industrial to a service economy.

The line between the 10th and 11th districts generally divides Cleveland's white and black neighborhoods. The 10th contains the state's largest concentration of ethnic voters, mostly Poles, Czechs, Italians, Irish and Germans. Although industry still provides the backbone of the city's economy, the 10th has attracted smaller technology companies and undergone a downtown restoration, helping the district maintain its steady employment base.

The immediate suburbs have a strong union presence and a Democratic lean. The communities of Brooklyn and Lakewood, which abut western Cleveland, are middle-income and lean Democratic. Farther west the incomes rise, as does the level of Republicanism: Bay Village, Westlake and Rocky River residents have above-average incomes and voted

solidly for George W. Bush in the 2004 presidential election.

Redistricting following the 2000 census gave the 10th parts of central Cuyahoga County — including Brook Park, Middleburg Heights and Parma Heights — that had been in the old 19th District. Brook Park is a blue-collar autoworkers' community that is decidedly Democratic.

The strong Democratic tendencies of Cleveland — the 10th's share of the city gave John Kerry 70 percent of its 2004 presidential vote — coupled with the GOP lean of some of the city's western and southern suburbs, give the 10th a decided but not overwhelming Democratic tilt. Overall, Kerry took 58 percent of the district's presidential vote in 2004.

MAJOR INDUSTRY
Manufacturing, banking, technology, auto parts

CITIES
Cleveland (pt.), 190,224; Parma, 85,655; Lakewood, 56,646; North Olmsted, 34,113; Westlake, 31,719

NOTABLE
A publisher dropped an "a" from city founder Moses Cleaveland's name so that it would fit neatly on his page, giving the city's name its current spelling; The city is home to NASA's John H. Glenn Research Center.

Rep. Stephanie Tubbs Jones (D)

Elected 1998; 4th term

CAPITOL OFFICE
225-7032
www.house.gov/tubbsjones
1009 Longworth 20515-3511; fax 225-1339

COMMITTEES
Standards of Official Conduct
Ways & Means

HOMETOWN
Cleveland

BORN
Sept. 10, 1949, Cleveland, Ohio

RELIGION
Baptist

FAMILY
Widowed; one child

EDUCATION
Case Western Reserve U., B.A. 1971 (sociology),
J.D. 1974

CAREER
Lawyer; municipal judge

POLITICAL HIGHLIGHTS
Cleveland Municipal Court judge, 1982-83;
Cuyahoga County Common Pleas Court judge,
1983-91; Cuyahoga County prosecutor, 1991-99

ELECTION RESULTS

2004 GENERAL

Stephanie Tubbs Jones (D)		unopposed

2004 PRIMARY

Stephanie Tubbs Jones (D)		unopposed

2002 GENERAL

Stephanie Tubbs Jones (D)	116,590	76.3%
Patrick A. Pappano (R)	36,146	23.7%

PREVIOUS WINNING PERCENTAGES
2000 (85%); 1998 (80%)

As a liberal in the minority party, Jones makes up for her relative powerlessness by using her House seat as a megaphone for people she believes are under-represented in the policy decisions in Washington.

She grabbed the spotlight in the 109th Congress by launching a protest of George W. Bush's electoral victory in her home state, throwing a monkey wrench into the normally pro forma approval by Congress of the Electoral College results. In January 2005, she rose in a half-empty chamber to register the protest and was joined by the requisite one senator, Democrat Barbara Boxer of California. That met the legal threshold for forcing debate.

The actual outcome was never in doubt; Bush was certified as the winner. Jones said the point was to call attention to problems with voting machines and voter registration in the state, where Bush beat Democratic Sen. John Kerry of Massachusetts by 119,000 votes. "I respect the presidency and I respect that George Bush was elected. All I was trying to do is to ensure that everyone who has the right to vote is able to do so," she said.

The move put Jones in the history books. The tally of electoral votes was last challenged in 1969, when the vote of one elector for Gov. George Wallace was contested. Congress certified Richard M. Nixon as the winner.

Jones was co-chairwoman of Kerry's campaign in 2004 and traveled the country tirelessly in his behalf. The year before, both her husband and mother died, within 97 days of each other, an experience that Jones said compelled her to dive into her work on the campaign.

Her most important posting in the House is her seat on the coveted Ways and Means Committee, which writes tax, trade, health care and social welfare legislation. She got the seat in the 108th Congress by publicly protesting that the panel had no African-American woman member. Republicans at the time were trying to shrink the committee, which would have shut out Jones. To avoid embarrassment, they left the number of seats the same, and Democratic leaders appointed Jones.

She has a slim legislative record if you count bills with her name on them. On the Ways and Means panel, she tends to work on issues that, while not resulting in legislation, are advanced through her efforts. For example, she promoted a bill to increase spending on research of uterine fibroids, which are benign tumors that sometimes result in unnecessary hysterectomies. Black women are at higher risk for fibroids. Although Jones' bill went nowhere in the House, it attracted the attention of the National Institutes of Health, which greatly increased its budget for research in the area.

Although her political leanings are decidedly liberal — she voted with House Democrats 97 percent of the time on votes pitting the two parties against each other in the 108th Congress — Jones has shown a willingness to work across party lines in the pursuit of her legislative goals.

Before getting on Ways and Means, she used her seats on the Financial Services and Small Business committees to boost economic development in her district, attack predatory lending practices and champion laid-off workers who lose severance pay or pensions when their employers go bankrupt. As chairwoman of the Congressional Black Caucus' Housing Task Force, Jones held hearings on alleged abuses by some lenders who make sub-prime, or high-risk, loans with high interest rates and fees.

Jones also holds a seat on the ethics committee, which faced a shake-up among Republicans in early 2005 after it admonished Majority Leader Tom DeLay for ethical lapses. Jones pledged to work in a nonpartisan way with the Republicans on the panel.

She enjoys increasing popularity at home, despite a financial snafu that required her to reimburse her campaign in 2004 for thousands of dollars that a Federal Election Commission audit said may have been for personal use. She was unopposed in the 2004 election, and in 2002 won with 76 percent of the vote against token GOP opposition.

Jones is a player in local politics. She considered a run for the 2002 Democratic nomination for governor, and she briefly entertained entreaties that she make a bid in 2001 for mayor of Cleveland. She has not ruled out a run for that job in the future.

In her early years in Congress, Jones was criticized back home for being slow on the uptake on local issues; some people grumbled that she failed to speak out strongly when Mt. Sinai Hospital in Cleveland closed. So when the Cleveland Clinic threatened to close the trauma unit at Huron Hospital, Jones organized a protest and threatened to withhold her support for $60 million in federal dollars for the clinic. The clinic relented.

Jones got active in politics as a college student, when she was among a group of Vietnam War demonstrators who forced Case Western Reserve University to shut down in the spring of 1970.

After planning for a career in social work, Jones changed her mind and went to law school. Her first job as an attorney was litigating for the Equal Employment Opportunity Commission. Seven years later, in 1981, she was elected to a Cleveland municipal judgeship. Two years after that, she was appointed by the governor to a judgeship handling felony cases. Jones was elected in 1991 as the Cuyahoga County prosecutor, overseeing a staff of about 300.

In 1998, she ran for the House seat held by retiring Rep. Louis Stokes, a 15-term Democrat who was Ohio's first black member of Congress. Jones called Stokes a "mentor and close friend." He called her his chosen successor. Jones' convincing victory in the Democratic primary — her two closest rivals were Rev. Marvin A. McMickle and state Sen. Jeffrey Johnson — sealed her succession to Stokes in the overwhelmingly Democratic district.

She also had received nationwide attention that same year for refusing to reopen the case of the late Dr. Sam Sheppard, the basis for "The Fugitive" television series and movie. He was convicted in 1954 of murdering his wife and served 10 years in prison before being acquitted in a retrial.

KEY VOTES

2004
Yes Extend federal unemployment benefits by 13 weeks
Yes Pass $283.2 billion, six-year federal highway and mass transit bill
Yes Approve $146 billion multi-year extension of previously enacted middle-class tax breaks
No Amend the Constitution to prohibit same-sex marriage
No Cut corporate taxes $137 billion over 10 years
? Reorganize U.S. intelligence agencies as proposed by Sept. 11 commission

2003
No Cut taxes by $330 billion through fiscal 2013
Yes Block Bush rule scaling back overtime pay for some white-collar federal workers
Yes Do not allow use of search warrants without first notifying subjects
Yes Allow importation of prescription drugs
No Create private school voucher program in Washington, D.C.
No Ban "partial birth" abortion except to save a woman's life
? Split $18.6 billion in Iraq aid into half-grant, half-loan
No Overhaul Medicare and create prescription drug benefit

CQ VOTE STUDIES

	PARTY UNITY		PRESIDENTIAL SUPPORT	
	Support	Oppose	Support	Oppose
2004	97%	3%	29%	71%
2003	98%	2%	16%	84%
2002	98%	2%	24%	76%
2001	97%	3%	20%	80%
2000	98%	2%	89%	11%

INTEREST GROUPS

	AFL-CIO	ADA	CCUS	ACU
2004	100%	85%	38%	5%
2003	100%	90%	22%	16%
2002	100%	85%	39%	0%
2001	100%	100%	35%	4%
2000	100%	100%	47%	0%

OHIO 11
Cleveland — East Side and suburbs

The 11th consists of the poor, inner-city areas of Cleveland's East Side and fans out to the east to include upper-middle-class suburbs. The district's black majority and liberal suburbanites combine to make it very Democratic, and John Kerry received 81 percent of the 2004 presidential vote here, making the 11th easily Kerry's best district in the state.

Propelling the district's staunch Democratic bent is its 60 percent share of Cleveland, which gave Kerry 92 percent of the vote in 2004. Although suburban growth has lured many businesses and residents outside the city, a smattering of commercial and residential development has occurred in the downtown area. Redistricting following the 2000 census moved the district line west to take in the Rock and Roll Hall of Fame and the sports stadiums for baseball's Indians, football's Browns and basketball's Cavaliers.

Much of the 11th's black majority lives in inner-city neighborhoods, often below the poverty line. There are some middle-class neighborhoods toward Lake Erie, inhabited mostly by Italians and Eastern Europeans.

The upper-middle-class suburbs of Cleveland Heights, Shaker Heights and University Heights to the east are home to large communities of Jews and young professionals, forming some of Ohio's most liberal and racially integrated areas. Redistricting pushed the 11th farther east to take in communities such as Mayfield Heights, Richmond Heights, Lyndhurst and Pepper Pike, which has one of the highest incomes in the state. Case Western Reserve University is located in University Circle, Cleveland's cultural center.

From the circle area, commuters drive along historic Euclid Avenue to their jobs downtown. While the avenue now bears the marks of poverty, it was known as "Millionaire's Row" at the beginning of the 20th century. Few of the old mansions remain. The one belonging to John D. Rockefeller, founder of Standard Oil, was razed after his death in 1937.

MAJOR INDUSTRY
Health care, manufacturing, utilities

CITIES
Cleveland (pt.), 288,179; Euclid, 52,717; Cleveland Heights, 49,958; Shaker Heights, 29,405; East Cleveland, 27,217; Maple Heights, 26,156

NOTABLE
The Shaker Historical Museum is in Shaker Heights.

Rep. Pat Tiberi (R)

CAPITOL OFFICE
225-5355
www.house.gov/tiberi
113 Cannon 20515-3512; fax 226-4523

COMMITTEES
Education & Workforce
  (Select Education - chairman)
Financial Services

HOMETOWN
Columbus

BORN
Oct. 21, 1962, Columbus, Ohio

RELIGION
Roman Catholic

FAMILY
Wife, Denice Tiberi; one child

EDUCATION
Ohio State U., B.A. 1985 (journalism)

CAREER
Realtor; congressional district aide

POLITICAL HIGHLIGHTS
Ohio House, 1993-2001 (majority leader, 1999-2001)

ELECTION RESULTS

2004 GENERAL

Pat Tiberi (R)	198,912	62.0%
Edward S. Brown (D)	122,109	38.0%

2004 PRIMARY

Pat Tiberi (R)	unopposed

2002 GENERAL

Pat Tiberi (R)	116,982	64.4%
Edward S. Brown (D)	64,707	35.6%

PREVIOUS WINNING PERCENTAGES
2000 (53%)

Elected 2000; 3rd term

An able and diligent lawmaker, Tiberi's name is in play for promotion to a major committee when an opening arises. He has the enthusiastic backing of Deborah Pryce of Ohio, who as the Republican Conference chairwoman is a member of the House leadership.

Pryce put Tiberi (TEA-berry) in line for a seat on the Appropriations Committee. At the start of the 109th Congress, he was named to the panel on a provisional basis, making him eligible to claim a seat when either of the two Ohioans on the committee leaves.

"We just want to protect Ohio for the future," Pryce told the Columbus Dispatch, calling Tiberi "Ohio's future on the Appropriations Committee."

Tiberi narrowly missed out on an appointment to the Ways and Means Committee at the start of the Congress. When President Bush nominated Ohio Republican Rob Portman to be the U.S. trade representative, creating a vacancy on the tax-writing panel, the 12 Republicans in the Ohio delegation promoted Tiberi for the seat.

But there was a hitch. Within hours of Portman's selection, Republican Devin Nunes of California also staked a claim to the seat. Tiberi and Nunes tussled behind the scenes over whose claim was more legitimate. Nunes said he was entitled to occupy the first Republican seat available, and the Ohioans argued that Nunes was supposed to wait until a Californian left — or until the 110th Congress. Ultimately, Nunes was appointed to the seat by Speaker J. Dennis Hastert.

Tiberi was no stranger to Capitol Hill when he won his seat in the 2000 election. He had spent eight years handling constituent casework for Republican Rep. John R. Kasich and another eight as a member of the state House. When Kasich decided to step out of public life, Tiberi leapt at the chance to run for the seat, and Kasich quickly endorsed his former staff member.

Some of Kasich's other aides, who had been Tiberi's supervisors and co-workers in the 1980s, now work for the congressman — an unusual display of both staff longevity and loyalty. Like Kasich, Tiberi has fostered a collegial atmosphere in his office. Tiberi's time as a congressional aide was spent at Kasich's district office in Columbus, not on Capitol Hill, and during the initial years of his new career Tiberi has made diligent constituent service a high priority. He holds "office hours" in his district, and makes a point of having evening hours to accommodate working constituents.

He is still most comfortable, he says, in the Columbus neighborhood where he grew up and has spent most of his life. He lives within walking distance of his 12th District field office, and his polling place is in the same elementary school that he attended in the 1960s. As one local newspaper columnist said, "Every groundbreaking, every parade, every ribbon-cutting with a pair of scissors to spare . . . is likely to find Pat Tiberi." And, the columnist continued, "that's bad news for the Democrats, who now stand about 4,000 chicken lunches behind Tiberi."

In the 108th Congress, he championed programs to expand homeownership. He introduced a bill to eliminate down payment requirements for first-time homebuyers seeking mortgages insured by the Federal Housing Administration. He touted his proposal as a way to boost minority homebuying, and said the Department of Housing and Urban Development estimated 150,000 families could benefit from the program in its first year.

In his first two terms, Tiberi was a dependable supporter of the president and the GOP leadership. In the 109th, however, he expressed some skepticism about Bush's proposal to allow workers to divert some Social Security payroll taxes into private accounts. He said his constituents were cool to the idea.

Tiberi is the eldest of three children of Italian immigrants who arrived in the United States three years before he was born. His father worked as a machinist, while his mother was a seamstress. In describing the formation of his first political allegiances, Tiberi told the Columbus Dispatch that, given their working-class background, he and some school friends "looked at each other and said, 'I guess we're Democrats.' "

Although he served as his high school's senior class president, Tiberi says he had no interest in politics as a career until a political science class at Ohio State University led to an internship in Kasich's office — and a change of ideological heart. Working for his predecessor, he says, made him reassess his political philosophy.

Tiberi was working in Kasich's district office and involved in a variety of civic activities when the 1992 remapping of state legislative districts created an open seat in his neighborhood. Tiberi's wife, Denice, told the Columbus newspaper that she didn't think her husband had ever really considered running for office before the seat opened. He met his wife at a Northlands High School marching band alumni gathering — he played trumpet; she played flute.

During his four terms in the General Assembly, Tiberi, who rose to become state House majority leader in the 1999-2001 session, developed a reputation as a conservative Republican who was willing and able to work with Democrats. He established a DNA database to track violent criminals and was a prime mover behind a state law that for a time limited large jury awards. The measure later was ruled unconstitutional. Tiberi also wrote legislation requiring performance audits for schools.

Barred by an Ohio term limit law from seeking re-election to the state House in 2000, Tiberi was considering a career change when Kasich announced he was leaving the U.S. House. Kasich's support helped Tiberi cruise to an easy primary victory over three rivals. Democrats put up a formidable opponent, Columbus City Councilwoman Maryellen O'Shaughnessy. Tiberi lost Franklin County (Columbus) but racked up big margins in the suburban GOP strongholds of Delaware and Licking counties. He won by 9 percentage points.

In 2002 and 2004, he won re-election comfortably, with around 65 percent of the vote each time.

KEY VOTES

2004

No   Extend federal unemployment benefits by 13 weeks

Yes   Pass $283.2 billion, six-year federal highway and mass transit bill

Yes   Approve $146 billion multi-year extension of previously enacted middle-class tax breaks

Yes   Amend the Constitution to prohibit same-sex marriage

Yes   Cut corporate taxes $137 billion over 10 years

Yes   Reorganize U.S. intelligence agencies as proposed by Sept. 11 commission

2003

Yes   Cut taxes by $330 billion through fiscal 2013

No   Block Bush rule scaling back overtime pay for some white-collar federal workers

Yes   Do not allow use of search warrants without first notifying subjects

No   Allow importation of prescription drugs

Yes   Create private school voucher program in Washington, D.C.

Yes   Ban "partial birth" abortion except to save a woman's life

Yes   Split $18.6 billion in Iraq aid into half-grant, half-loan

Yes   Overhaul Medicare and create prescription drug benefit

CQ VOTE STUDIES

	PARTY UNITY		PRESIDENTIAL SUPPORT	
	Support	Oppose	Support	Oppose
2004	92%	8%	82%	18%
2003	95%	5%	91%	9%
2002	95%	5%	88%	12%
2001	97%	3%	95%	5%

INTEREST GROUPS

	AFL-CIO	ADA	CCUS	ACU
2004	13%	10%	100%	96%
2003	7%	5%	100%	84%
2002	11%	0%	100%	96%
2001	0%	0%	100%	92%

OHIO 12

Central — Eastern Columbus and suburbs

The 12th includes the eastern half of Columbus and the suburban counties to the north and east of the city. Columbus has become primarily white-collar, and its thriving service economy has led to significant growth in both the city and its adjacent areas. The district has a slight Republican lean, with the strong GOP influence in the Columbus suburbs overcoming the Democratic tilt of the city.

Democrats thrive in the urban portion of the district, which is heavily black and poorer than the surrounding areas. The 12th includes the bulk of Columbus' black population, which is concentrated east of High Street, near Bexley. Farther east along Broad Street and into the suburbs, black Democratic support diminishes and Republican support goes up. Blacks make up 22 percent of district residents.

Within Franklin County, but outside Columbus, the 12th includes the comfortable suburb of Dublin, an upscale, solidly Republican area in northwest Franklin that is known to many as the headquarters of Wendy's. In eastern Franklin, the 12th also takes in Westerville, Gahanna

and Reynoldsburg, which also vote dependably Republican. Still, Columbus' underlying Democratic tilt allowed John Kerry to carry the 12th's share of Franklin County by a double-digit margin in the 2004 presidential election.

Offsetting the Democrats in Franklin County are Republicans in Delaware County and western Licking County, which are north and east of Franklin, respectively. Delaware has experienced enormous growth (64 percent in the 1990s) and startlingly low unemployment, and its well-educated workforce helps make it one of Ohio's top counties in household income. George W. Bush took 66 percent of the vote in Delaware County and 63 percent in Licking (shared with the 18th District) in 2004, a margin large enough to give him 51 percent of the vote and a narrow win over Kerry districtwide.

MAJOR INDUSTRY
Financial services, manufacturing, service

CITIES
Columbus (pt.), 275,882; Westerville, 35,318; Gahanna, 32,636; Reynoldsburg, 32,069; Dublin (pt.), 31,370; Delaware, 25,243

NOTABLE
Columbus is home to the Ohio Expo Center and State Fair.

Rep. Sherrod Brown (D)

CAPITOL OFFICE
225-3401
sherrod@mail.house.gov
www.house.gov/sherrodbrown
2332 Rayburn 20515-3513; fax 225-2266

COMMITTEES
Energy & Commerce
International Relations

HOMETOWN
Lorain

BORN
Nov. 9, 1952, Mansfield, Ohio

RELIGION
Lutheran

FAMILY
Wife, Connie Schultz; two children

EDUCATION
Yale U., B.A. 1974 (Russian & East European studies); Ohio State U., M.A. 1979 (education), M.A. 1981 (public administration)

CAREER
Teacher

POLITICAL HIGHLIGHTS
Ohio House, 1975-83; Ohio secretary of state, 1983-91; defeated for re-election as Ohio secretary of state, 1990

ELECTION RESULTS

2004 GENERAL

Sherrod Brown (D)	201,004	67.4%
Robert Lucas (R)	97,090	32.6%

2004 PRIMARY

Sherrod Brown (D)	unopposed

2002 GENERAL

Sherrod Brown (D)	123,025	69.0%
Ed Oliveros (R)	55,357	31.0%

PREVIOUS WINNING PERCENTAGES
2000 (65%); 1998 (62%); 1996 (60%); 1994 (49%); 1992 (53%)

Elected 1992; 7th term

Brown has carved out a solid niche for himself by taking on health care issues with down-to-earth, no-nonsense populist fervor. He has an astute political ear for the issues of the moment — issues such as prescription drug benefits under Medicare, tighter regulation of health maintenance organizations and health coverage for the uninsured.

As the top-ranking Democrat on Energy and Commerce's Health Subcommittee, Brown was one of the party's leading voices against a 2003 Republican proposal to add prescription drug coverage to Medicare. He deemed the measure a payoff to insurers and pharmaceutical manufacturers that would do little for the elderly and would be the first step toward dismantling Medicare's traditional fee-for-service program.

Other health care issues Brown focused on include detecting and treating breast and prostate cancer, phasing out the use of human antibiotics in animal feed and speeding the availability of low-cost generic drugs. He voted in 2004 against a free-trade agreement with Australia, insisting it was a giveaway to large drug companies because it would prohibit drug importation from foreign countries, where prescription drugs are often sold for less than in the United States.

But Brown represents a labor-dominated industrial district, and he is not too keen on trade pacts in general. As a freshman in 1993, Brown worked tirelessly to defeat the North American Free Trade Agreement — lobbying fellow freshmen, repeatedly taking the House floor to detail the pact's flaws, and publishing a newsletter that kept track of anti-NAFTA activities. He has continued to argue about NAFTA's defects, complaining in 2001 about unsafe Mexican trucks operating in the United States. He also argues that NAFTA has dislocated American workers. He is fond of saying that in his district "trade is a four-letter word: J-O-B-S."

Brown also has been a steadfast opponent of giving President Bush fast-track authority to negotiate trade agreements that Congress cannot amend. During the 108th Congress, Brown wrote "Myths of Free Trade," a book that argued that unregulated free trade hurts more people than it helps, not only in the United States but throughout the world.

Brown also has a seat on the International Relations Committee. As co-chairman of the Congressional Taiwan Caucus, Brown wrote legislation endorsing Taiwan's participation in the World Health Organization. When Taiwan wasn't allowed to participate at the group's 2003 meeting in Geneva, Brown blamed it on Bush. "If the president would use his diplomatic muscle, we could change this," Brown said at the time.

Brown sticks with his party on most issues, siding with Democrats in the 108th Congress 98 percent of the time on votes that pitted one party against the other. He voted in agreement with Bush 17 percent of the time. Yet he has strayed from the majority of Democrats by supporting constitutional amendments to balance the budget and limit congressional terms.

Earlier in his career, Brown wrote a book about his experiences entitled, "Congress from the Inside." In a 1999 television interview in which he discussed the book, he listed four important steps for freshmen. Leading the list was getting on the right committee, which Brown did by landing a coveted seat on Energy and Commerce in his first term. He recalls in his book that he even parted with a favorite baseball card — that of 1950s Boston Red Sox outfielder Jimmy Piersall, who suffered from mental illness. Brown gave the card to influential California Democrat Vic Fazio with the note, "Don't be crazy. Vote for Sherrod Brown for Energy and Commerce."

Brown has spent his adult life in politics, first elected to the Ohio House in 1974 when he was turning 22. Since winning the 13th District seat in 1992, he has usually been re-elected with ease. But with the GOP in control of the redistricting process after the 2000 census, Brown's safe perch appeared to be in some jeopardy. But he "bluff[ed] his way to job security," said the Cleveland Plain Dealer, by threatening to run for governor against Republican Bob Taft if the new district lines were unfavorable. At Taft's direction, the lines were drawn to the congressman's liking.

Aspiring to the governor's mansion may not, however, be out of the picture for Brown. According to the Plain Dealer, he has called the Republicans who rule the state "corrupt and arrogant and incompetent." He was particularly unhappy with how the 2004 presidential election was conducted in his state. Brown and other Democrats charged that there were widespread irregularities at the Ohio polls. "Ohio voters should never again be forced to wait three, five, sometimes even 10 hours to cast a vote," Brown said. "Ohioans should never again, as too many people did this November, lose their right to vote."

Brown's first taste of elective office came as student council president in high school, where he also made time to become an Eagle Scout. He spent summers working on the family dairy farm. His interest in politics was sparked by the Vietnam War, the civil rights movement and the 1968 presidential candidacy of Robert F. Kennedy. He earned a degree in Russian studies from Yale.

After serving four terms in the Ohio House, Brown was elected secretary of state in 1982. He was re-elected to the post in 1986 but lost a re-election bid in 1990 to Bob Taft, the latest in a long line of politically successful Ohio Tafts. Taft was elected governor in 1998.

In 1992, Brown made a bid for the House, joining seven other Democrats in the race for the open 13th District. He was his party's front-runner, though he had moved into the 13th to run, and he easily won the Democratic nomination. In the November election, he handily defeated Republican Margaret R. Mueller, a millionaire social worker who had lost three times to Democrat Dennis E. Eckart in the old 11th.

Brown prevailed with just a plurality of the vote in 1994 — a bad year for Ohio Democrats — but has won with ease since. In 2002, with a district that tilts Democratic, Brown won easily with 69 percent of the vote. He earned 67 percent in 2004. In April of that year, he married Plain Dealer columnist Connie Schultz, who won a Pulitzer Prize for commentary in 2005.

KEY VOTES

2004

Yes Extend federal unemployment benefits by 13 weeks
Yes Pass $283.2 billion, six-year federal highway and mass transit bill
Yes Approve $146 billion multi-year extension of previously enacted middle-class tax breaks
No Amend the Constitution to prohibit same-sex marriage
No Cut corporate taxes $137 billion over 10 years
Yes Reorganize U.S. intelligence agencies as proposed by Sept. 11 commission

2003

No Cut taxes by $330 billion through fiscal 2013
Yes Block Bush rule scaling back overtime pay for some white-collar federal workers
Yes Do not allow use of search warrants without first notifying subjects
Yes Allow importation of prescription drugs
No Create private school voucher program in Washington, D.C.
No Ban "partial birth" abortion except to save a woman's life
Yes Split $18.6 billion in Iraq aid into half-grant, half-loan
No Overhaul Medicare and create prescription drug benefit

CQ VOTE STUDIES

	PARTY UNITY		PRESIDENTIAL SUPPORT	
	Support	Oppose	Support	Oppose
2004	98%	2%	26%	74%
2003	99%	1%	11%	89%
2002	98%	2%	22%	78%
2001	98%	2%	12%	88%
2000	97%	3%	81%	19%

INTEREST GROUPS

	AFL-CIO	ADA	CCUS	ACU
2004	100%	95%	24%	4%
2003	100%	100%	25%	16%
2002	100%	95%	25%	4%
2001	100%	95%	22%	4%
2000	100%	90%	25%	4%

OHIO 13

Northeast — parts of Akron and suburbs, Cleveland suburbs

The lightning bolt-shaped 13th runs from the shores of Lake Erie west of Cleveland, southeast through the city's mostly middle-class suburbs to Akron. Redistricting following the 2000 census increased the district's Democratic heft by adding western Summit County, including part of Akron (shared with the 17th). Summit is the most populous county in the 13th, making up 44 percent of the population. The district includes 60 percent of Akron's residents, including much of its black population.

Akron had a long history as a blue-collar factory town and was known as the world's rubber capital. Although the tire companies have moved many of their factories, many of their corporate headquarters and research facilities remain, keeping the city alive through tough years.

The city also has been renovating its downtown and recreational areas along the Ohio & Erie Canal. Blue-collar descendants combine with blacks, ethnic whites and the University of Akron's academic community to help the city retain its Democratic character from its blue-collar past.

Bordering Lake Erie at the district's other end is Lorain County, which includes one-third of the 13th's residents and has an industrial, blue-collar heritage. The 13th's portions of Lorain include staunchly Democratic Lorain and Sheffield Lake and Democratic-leaning Elyria. Farther northeast, the Avon and Avon Lake communities are upper-middle-class and dependably Republican. Lorain and Avon Lake are home to some of the district's automotive plants.

In the district's middle are some Republican-leaning communities in southern Cuyahoga County and northern Medina County. But Summit and Lorain's dominance gives the 13th a Democratic tilt.

MAJOR INDUSTRY
Auto and auto parts manufacturing, steel, polymer research

CITIES
Akron (pt.), 129,298; Lorain, 68,652; Elyria, 55,953; Cuyahoga Falls (pt.), 39,051; Brunswick, 33,388; Strongsville (pt.), 29,715; North Royalton, 28,648

NOTABLE
The National Inventors Hall of Fame is in Akron; The All-American Soap Box Derby race has been held in Akron since 1935.

Rep. Steven C. LaTourette (R)

Elected 1994; 6th term

CAPITOL OFFICE
225-5731
www.house.gov/latourette
2453 Rayburn 20515-3514; fax 225-3307

COMMITTEES
Financial Services
Government Reform
Transportation & Infrastructure
(Railroads - chairman)

HOMETOWN
Concord

BORN
July 22, 1954, Cleveland, Ohio

RELIGION
Methodist

FAMILY
Wife, Jennifer LaTourette; four children

EDUCATION
U. of Michigan, B.A. 1976 (history); Cleveland
State U., J.D. 1979

CAREER
Lawyer

POLITICAL HIGHLIGHTS
Candidate for Lake County prosecutor, 1984;
Lake County prosecutor, 1989-94

ELECTION RESULTS

2004 GENERAL

Steven C. LaTourette (R)	201,652	62.8%
Capri S. Cafaro (D)	119,714	37.3%

2004 PRIMARY

Steven C. LaTourette (R)	unopposed

2002 GENERAL

Steven C. LaTourette (R)	134,413	72.1%
Dale Virgil Blanchard (D)	51,846	27.8%

PREVIOUS WINNING PERCENTAGES
2000 (65%); 1998 (66%); 1996 (55%); 1994 (48%)

Usually an easygoing and reasonably loyal Republican, LaTourette endured a bruising re-election battle in 2004 that focused public attention on his private life. The experience left him somewhat battered but unbowed.

Now in his sixth term, he brings some seniority to the Ohio delegation even though he twice broke a term-limit pledge to get it. When LaTourette was first elected, he hoped to win a seat on the Judiciary Committee, given his background as a private attorney, public defender and prosecutor. (He still says his long-range aspiration is to be a judge.) But Ralph Regula, dean of the Ohio GOP delegation, told him he would be more useful to the state on the Transportation and Infrastructure Committee. The assignment has allowed him to funnel highway funds to his district and state.

LaTourette succeeded in attaching a "buy American" provision to the massive six-year highway bill passed by the House in 2004. And at his insistence, the Defense Department in 2003 reconsidered its non-competitive award to a German company of a $1 million construction contract to apply sealant to the exterior of the Pentagon; instead, it gave the work to ChemMasters Specialty Construction Co. of Madison, Ohio — in LaTourette's district.

As chairman of the Economic Development, Public Buildings and Emergency Management Subcommittee in the 108th Congress, LaTourette (la-tuh-RETT) rewrote a homeland security bill to maintain the status quo under which all states are guaranteed a minimum amount in federal grants to pass on to local police, fire and emergency medical agencies. The alternative, pressed by lawmakers representing the biggest metropolitan areas, would base grants on a federal assessment of each area's risk of attack. For the 109th, LaTourette chairs the Railroads Subcommittee.

LaTourette is a conservative on social policy: He votes with anti-abortion forces, supported repeal of the ban on assault-style weapons and backed the proposed constitutional amendment to ban gay marriage.

However, reflecting his district's interests, he sometimes breaks ranks with GOP leaders on trade and other issues important to organized labor. In the 107th, LaTourette opposed revival of fast-track trade negotiating authority, and in the 108th, he voted for a Democratic amendment to offer supplemental unemployment insurance benefits to jobless workers. In 2001, he teamed with Ohio Democrat Dennis J. Kucinich in an unsuccessful attempt to make it easier for ailing steel companies to qualify for federal loan guarantees, a futile bid to save Cleveland-based LTV Steel.

Despite his best efforts to highlight the federal monies he has directed home, LaTourette received the most press in 2004 for his nasty re-election battle. The Akron Beacon Journal summed up the congressman's status in an October story by saying he had "reneged on a pledge not to seek a sixth term; cheated on and left his wife for a woman who now lobbies one of his committees; taken money from the tainted campaign war chest of House Majority Leader Tom DeLay, R-Texas, then refused to recuse himself from the ethics committee hearings that eventually rebuked DeLay."

LaTourette's ex-wife posted lawn signs supporting his opponent, Democratic shopping mall heiress Capri S. Cafaro. The state Democratic Party asked the Justice Department to investigate LaTourette's relationship with the lobbyist, Jennifer Laptook, his former chief of staff. The congressman fought back, telling the Cleveland Plain Dealer he had broken no laws or ethics rules. "I am a divorced person who has stayed overnight at her home," he said of his former aide. "I am involved in a serious personal relationship." (LaTourette and Laptook married in February 2005.)

The whole brouhaha was only part of what wound up as the most expensive House race in Ohio. Cafaro spent $2 million on the race, most of it her own money. LaTourette countered with a huge bankroll of his own. Their total spending reached $4.3 million, according to campaign finance reports. LaTourette won the race handily with 63 percent of the vote.

The race indirectly kept before the public LaTourette's links to former Democratic Rep. James A. Traficant Jr., whom the House expelled in 2002 following his conviction on corruption charges. Cafaro's father, J.J. Cafaro, was sentenced to probation for bribing Traficant to help his company. Traficant was a friend of LaTourette's, so the ethics case was especially painful for him, though he ultimately voted to expel Traficant.

In early 2005, LaTourette was removed from his seat on the House ethics committee by GOP leaders who felt he and other Republican members had been too quick to vote to admonish DeLay for ethical lapses.

LaTourette is less confrontational than many of his colleagues in the "revolutionary" Class of 1994. Perhaps it was growing up in the progressive suburb of Cleveland Heights — which declared itself a "nuclear free" zone — that taught him to be inclusive. Or perhaps it is the political character of his constituency. The portion of northeastern Ohio he represented until redistricting for this decade, known as the 19th District, voted Democratic for president in 1992, 1996 and 2000. (His new territory, renamed the 14th, has a more Republican tilt.)

LaTourette was raised in a politically active home. His mother and grandmother were volunteers for the Cleveland area's longtime Republican congresswoman, Frances Payne Bolton. His grandmother has been the inspiration for several legislative efforts, including a bill to require sweepstakes mailers to disclose the slim odds of winning. He cites the example of his grandmother, in her mid-80s, who subscribed to Field and Stream magazine thinking it would boost her chances of winning a mail-order sweepstakes.

Even as a youth, LaTourette was not afraid to rock the boat a bit. In high school, he led a petition drive to permit students to wear jeans and grow facial hair. He has sported a beard since he was 18 "because I've always thought my face looked better that way."

LaTourette says working as a public defender taught him how it felt to have "nobody like you." He was in his second term as Lake County prosecutor when he decided to run for Congress. Dubbing Democratic freshman Eric Fingerhut an out-of-touch liberal, LaTourette won by 5 percentage points. He has been re-elected by comfortable margins since then.

KEY VOTES

2004
Yes Extend federal unemployment benefits by 13 weeks
Yes Pass $283.2 billion, six-year federal highway and mass transit bill
Yes Approve $146 billion multi-year extension of previously enacted middle-class tax breaks
Yes Amend the Constitution to prohibit same-sex marriage
Yes Cut corporate taxes $137 billion over 10 years
Yes Reorganize U.S. intelligence agencies as proposed by Sept. 11 commission

2003
Yes Cut taxes by $330 billion through fiscal 2013
Yes Block Bush rule scaling back overtime pay for some white-collar federal workers
Yes Do not allow use of search warrants without first notifying subjects
Yes Allow importation of prescription drugs
Yes Create private school voucher program in Washington, D.C.
Yes Ban "partial birth" abortion except to save a woman's life
No Split $18.6 billion in Iraq aid into half-grant, half-loan
Yes Overhaul Medicare and create prescription drug benefit

CQ VOTE STUDIES

	PARTY UNITY		PRESIDENTIAL SUPPORT	
	Support	Oppose	Support	Oppose
2004	86%	14%	82%	18%
2003	88%	12%	85%	15%
2002	89%	11%	82%	18%
2001	88%	12%	86%	14%
2000	84%	16%	35%	65%

INTEREST GROUPS

	AFL-CIO	ADA	CCUS	ACU
2004	47%	15%	86%	71%
2003	33%	25%	87%	72%
2002	22%	15%	85%	76%
2001	36%	20%	77%	72%
2000	30%	25%	80%	68%

OHIO 14
Northeast — Cleveland and Akron suburbs

The Republican-leaning 14th moves along the Lake Erie shoreline eastward from just outside Cleveland to the Pennsylvania border in the state's northeast corner. The depressed far northeastern communities remain reliant on the ailing steel, chemical and auto manufacturing industries but have seen some new life from migrants from Cleveland. Plants along Lake Erie have been hurt by foreign competition.

Lake County is the district's most-populous area (more than one-third of its residents live there), despite being Ohio's smallest county in land area. Mentor, traditionally an industrial swing area, has seen an influx of GOP residents with its recent growth. Republicans generally perform better in areas south of Mentor, such as in upper-income Kirtland. Democrats do well in Painesville, where more than half of Lake's blacks and Hispanics live, and in western Lake, including Wickliffe and Willowick. Lake overall narrowly backed George W. Bush in the 2004 presidential election.

South of Lake are Geauga County, a Republican-leaning, affluent, well-educated area, and northern Portage County. The 14th also includes northeastern Summit County, taking in Stow and Twinsburg. The 14th's share of Summit gave Bush 52 percent of the vote in 2004, matching the districtwide result. Ashtabula County, a mostly agricultural region that borders Pennsylvania and is known for its covered bridges, is the state's largest county in land area and backed John Kerry in the 2004 presidential election.

The 14th is descended from the 1990s-era 19th District that included many of Cuyahoga County's eastern Cleveland suburbs. Redistricting following the 2000 census left the 14th with only a small portion of the county, including the upscale communities of Bentleyville and Moreland Hills in eastern Cuyahoga.

MAJOR INDUSTRY
Auto manufacturing, health care, chemicals

CITIES
Mentor, 50,278; Stow, 32,139; Willoughby, 22,621; Hudson, 22,439; Solon, 21,802; Ashtabula, 20,962; Eastlake, 20,255

NOTABLE
Holden Arboretum, the nation's largest, is in Kirtland; Twinsburg hosts a gathering of twins each August that it calls the largest in the world; There is a President James A. Garfield Historic Site in Mentor.

Rep. Deborah Pryce (R)

Elected 1992; 7th term

CAPITOL OFFICE
225-2015
www.house.gov/pryce
204 Cannon 20515-3515; fax 225-3529

COMMITTEES
Financial Services
    (Domestic & International Monetary Policy,
    Trade & Technology - chairwoman)

HOMETOWN
Upper Arlington

BORN
July 29, 1951, Warren, Ohio

RELIGION
Presbyterian

FAMILY
Divorced; two children (one deceased)

EDUCATION
Ohio State U., B.A. 1973; Capital U., J.D. 1976

CAREER
City prosecutor

POLITICAL HIGHLIGHTS
Franklin County Municipal Court judge, 1985-92

ELECTION RESULTS

2004 GENERAL

Deborah Pryce (R)	166,520	60.0%
Mark P. Brown (D)	110,915	40.0%

2004 PRIMARY

Deborah Pryce (R)	36,860	83.6%
Charles Morrison (R)	7,254	16.4%

2002 GENERAL

Deborah Pryce (R)	108,193	66.6%
Mark P. Brown (D)	54,286	33.4%

PREVIOUS WINNING PERCENTAGES
2000 (68%); 1998 (66%); 1996 (71%); 1994 (71%);
1992 (44%)

As chairwoman of the Republican Conference, Pryce is the House's highest-ranking Republican woman ever. The only other GOP woman to attain an equivalent post was Margaret Chase Smith of Maine, who headed the Senate Republican Conference for the six years before her retirement in 1972.

Pryce is more moderate than the rest of the GOP leadership, and seems unlikely to move further up in the hierarchy. She does not make the short-list of possible successors to Speaker J. Dennis Hastert. But she is positioning herself for a new leadership role on one of the standing committees.

In the 109th Congress, Pryce gave up a coveted post — her spot on the Speaker-appointed Rules Committee — for a seat on the Financial Services Committee, where she immediately took the helm of the Subcommittee on Domestic and International Monetary Policy, Trade and Technology. As a top GOP fundraiser, she could be the next full committee chairman when fellow Ohioan Michael G. Oxley is forced by GOP term limits to step down at the end of the Congress. Her PRYCE (Promoting Republicans You Can Elect) political action committee doled out about a half-million dollars to GOP candidates for the House and Senate in the 2004 election cycle.

Under GOP rules, Pryce would have to give up her chairmanship of the Republican Conference to take a committee gavel. The Columbus Dispatch said in 2005: "The move would represent a recognition that she has advanced as far as anyone who believes in abortion rights can in the Republican leadership."

Pryce's moderation, even more apparent in her tone and temperament than in her voting record, may be a hindrance to her leadership aspirations, but it has made her invaluable in the role of the party's chief communicator in the House. At times in the past decade, House Republicans were hurt by the public personas of their more bellicose leaders, and Pryce seemed reasonable by comparison.

Pryce has long been a member of Hastert's inner circle, where he relies on her to provide unvarnished assessments of what the rank and file are thinking. Top House Republicans tacitly supported her bid for conference chairwoman in 2002, when she beat out conservatives J.D. Hayworth of Arizona and Jim Ryun of Kansas and gave moderates a voice at the leadership table. Her election also allowed the conservative leaders to show that they wanted to reach out to all factions. They also appreciated her penchant for keeping disagreements private as well as her background as a consensus-seeking judge.

As one of only three GOP women elected to the House in the Class of 1992, Pryce was a star from the start. Her first-term colleagues named her their "interim leader" for the early weeks of the 103rd Congress, and when Republicans became the House majority in 1995, she was assigned to the Rules Committee. In 1997, Pryce won election as Republican Conference secretary, an entry-level rung on the leadership ladder.

As she has risen in the ranks, Pryce has increasingly hewed close to the GOP line on votes that split the parties. Her votes on fiscal policy are reliably Republican and she is viewed with less suspicion by conservatives than most of the party's social policy moderates.

Her big-ticket legislative item in the 109th Congress, as in the previous two Congresses, is a reauthorization of welfare laws. Her bill, backed by the White House and other GOP leaders, would build on the 1996 overhaul of welfare by requiring adults to work 40 hours a week, an increase of 10 hours over current law. Her bill also increases mandatory child care funding by $1 billion over five years.

Her political success has been clouded by personal tragedy. She became a champion of legislation to improve cancer care, particularly for children, after her 9-year-old daughter, Caroline, died in 1999 from cancer. Two years later, she and her husband, Randy Walker, began divorce proceedings, ending a 21-year marriage. Even as their marriage foundered, Pryce and Walker formed Hope Street Kids, a program to support cancer research.

In 2002, Pryce adopted an infant daughter, Mia, after realizing, she said, that she missed being a mother. It has helped her see the challenges that single parents face. "Being a single mom is tough, no matter what your occupation," she said.

Pryce reintroduced legislation early in the 109th Congress, cosponsored by moderate Pennsylvania Democrat John P. Murtha, that would provide grants to promote pain management and end-of-life care for children with life-threatening conditions such as cancer. She sponsored the 2000 law to boost funding to prevent child abuse and to investigate such crimes. She also has worked to make adoption easier for qualified applicants, and cosponsored the 1996 law that streamlined adoption procedures for children in foster care.

Pryce has indicated that she may try to build on the Family and Medical Leave Act, which requires businesses to give employees time off to care for relatives. She voted against the original legislation in 1993, saying it would put a costly burden on employers. But during her daughter's illness, Pryce took a leave from the House, and she says she supports family leave proposals that would help families but "are compatible with good, conservative principles."

While she generally votes the party line, there have been notable exceptions. In 1999, Pryce opposed two impeachment articles brought against President Clinton, and was the only elected GOP leader who did not vote yes on all four charges. She has voted in some instances with gun control proponents and abortion rights advocates.

Having studied, worked and lived in the Columbus area for three decades, Pryce is well-versed in the nuances of her district. After getting her law degree from Capital University, she was a city prosecutor. In 1985, she was elected judge on the Franklin County Municipal Court.

She resigned in 1992 to enter the crowded GOP field for the House seat of retiring Republican Chalmers P. Wylie. She won the party's endorsement and prevailed in a tight, three-way general-election race by just 6 percentage points. Since then, she has been re-elected by large margins.

KEY VOTES

2004
No Extend federal unemployment benefits by 13 weeks
Yes Pass $283.2 billion, six-year federal highway and mass transit bill
Yes Approve $146 billion multi-year extension of previously enacted middle-class tax breaks
No Amend the Constitution to prohibit same-sex marriage
Yes Cut corporate taxes $137 billion over 10 years
Yes Reorganize U.S. intelligence agencies as proposed by Sept. 11 commission

2003
Yes Cut taxes by $330 billion through fiscal 2013
No Block Bush rule scaling back overtime pay for some white-collar federal workers
Yes Do not allow use of search warrants without first notifying subjects
No Allow importation of prescription drugs
Yes Create private school voucher program in Washington, D.C.
Yes Ban "partial birth" abortion except to save a woman's life
No Split $18.6 billion in Iraq aid into half-grant, half-loan
Yes Overhaul Medicare and create prescription drug benefit

CQ VOTE STUDIES

	PARTY UNITY		PRESIDENTIAL SUPPORT	
	Support	Oppose	Support	Oppose
2004	91%	9%	85%	15%
2003	94%	6%	93%	7%
2002	95%	5%	92%	8%
2001	93%	7%	86%	14%
2000	90%	10%	35%	65%

INTEREST GROUPS

	AFL-CIO	ADA	CCUS	ACU
2004	14%	15%	100%	83%
2003	7%	0%	100%	72%
2002	13%	5%	100%	88%
2001	17%	15%	100%	68%
2000	0%	15%	90%	80%

OHIO 15
Western Columbus and suburbs

The 15th is centered on Columbus, the state's centrally located capital. The district includes most of the city, taking in all of Columbus that lies west of High Street, a major north-south thoroughfare. The 15th has some city attractions, including the State Capitol, City Hall, Ohio State University and the Columbus Museum of Art. It also includes the stadium of professional soccer's Crew and the arena of hockey's Blue Jackets.

Columbus is not known to draw large numbers of tourists except on Saturdays in autumn, when Ohio State plays football at home. But the region is generally regarded as a good place to raise a family. Covering much of Franklin County's expanding service sector, which includes several large technology research centers, the district has a steady employment base. Nationwide Mutual Insurance Co., Bob Evans Farms and American Electric Power also are based in the 15th.

Columbus has continued to grow since surpassing Cleveland in the early 1980s to become Ohio's most populous city. The 15th traditionally has been the more Republican of the two districts that divide the capital —

the neighboring 12th includes most of the heavily black East Side. Ohio State's academic community and neighborhoods in the nearby West Side of Columbus support Democrats, but they are offset by Republican suburbs west of the Olentangy and Scioto rivers. GOP candidates are strong in comfortable suburbs such as Upper Arlington and Worthington.

Still, John Kerry in 2004 carried the 15th's share of Franklin County, where about 90 percent of district residents live. George W. Bush achieved a razor-thin victory districtwide by dominating the vote in Madison County, a major corn-producing area to the west, and in Union County, which is northwest of Columbus and last voted Democratic for president in 1932. Marysville, in Union County, is home to a major Honda auto plant and a Honda motorcycle plant.

MAJOR INDUSTRY
Retail trade, health care, research, higher education

CITIES
Columbus (pt.), 384,491; Upper Arlington, 33,686; Grove City, 27,075; Hilliard (pt.), 23,853; Marysville, 15,942

NOTABLE
A full-scale replica of Christopher Columbus' ship, the Santa Maria, is in Columbus.

Rep. Ralph Regula (R)

Elected 1972; 17th term

At the start of the 109th Congress, Regula was denied what would have been the penultimate prize of his career — the chairmanship of the powerful Appropriations Committee. The third-most-senior Republican in the House, Regula remains an influential "cardinal," as chairman of the Labor, Health and Human Services and Education Subcommittee for two more years. But the octogenarian pragmatist appears to be entering the twilight of a career on Capitol Hill that has spanned more than three decades.

Regula's low-key approach and calm shrewdness in seeking the middle ground on controversial matters has in the main allowed him to maneuver deftly among GOP factions and across party lines. The top-ranking Democrat on Appropriations, David R. Obey of Wisconsin, describes Regula (REG-you-luh) as "one of the most laid-back members" of the House.

Partly because of that political facility, the Republican leadership's decision to pass over Regula, the candidate with the most seniority, in replacing term-limited Chairman C.W. Bill Young of Florida in the 109th was not entirely unexpected. In the modern House, leaders have made it clear that seniority does not rule in handing out powerful committee gavels. Regula's longtime aversion to fundraising and his moderation on some spending and policy issues made him a long shot from the start.

But to the surprise of many, Regula transformed himself from an afterthought into a top contender for the job by currying favor with his more conservative leaders during the 108th Congress. Regula turned into a party fundraising machine almost overnight, reversing his longstanding policy of not accepting contributions from the political action committees of businesses, trade associations or ideological groups.

Moreover, the easygoing Regula started playing hardball with Democratic colleagues, denying valuable funding earmarks on the 2003 Labor-HHS-Education spending bill to members who opposed it on the floor — a sharp reversal of his well-earned reputation as a bipartisan operator. And he made sure that the Labor-HHS spending bill, the focal point of a running battle among appropriators from both parties and a Republican White House intent on restraining the growth of domestic spending, stayed within budget limits despite his perennial support for higher levels of medical research and education funding.

But in the end, the GOP leadership bypassed Regula in favor of California Republican Jerry Lewis, a prolific fundraiser viewed as more of a team player by conservatives intent on tightening the federal purse strings in President Bush's second term.

Regula's politics have at times provoked suspicion among some Republicans and conservative groups who have pegged Regula, who lives on a farm in Ohio and calls himself a "tree hugger," as too liberal. He has handled the charges — hurled most violently by Western private property rights advocates after he took over the Interior Subcommittee chairmanship in 1995 — with disarming candor. He met with his detractors to listen to their criticism, traveled to the West to witness the roots of their concerns and attended meetings of the Western Caucus. Regula served as Interior Appropriations chairman until 2003, when he took the reins of the Labor-HHS Subcommittee.

Some conservative lawmakers raised concerns not only about Regula's willingness to compromise on environmental issues, but also about a few other moderate streaks in his record: He has supported a minimum wage increase and family planning programs and resisted proposals for taxpay-

CAPITOL OFFICE
225-3876
www.house.gov/regula
2306 Rayburn 20515-3516; fax 225-3059

COMMITTEES
Appropriations
(Labor, Health & Human Services & Education - chairman)

HOMETOWN
Navarre

BORN
Dec. 3, 1924, Beach City, Ohio

RELIGION
Episcopalian

FAMILY
Wife, Mary Regula; three children

EDUCATION
Mount Union College, B.A. 1948 (business administration); William McKinley School of Law, LL.B. 1952

MILITARY SERVICE
Navy, 1944-46

CAREER
Lawyer; teacher; principal

POLITICAL HIGHLIGHTS
Ohio Board of Education, 1960-64; Ohio House, 1965-67; Ohio Senate, 1967-73

ELECTION RESULTS

2004 GENERAL

Ralph Regula (R)	202,544	66.6%
Jeff Seemann (D)	101,817	33.5%

2004 PRIMARY

Ralph Regula (R)	unopposed

2002 GENERAL

Ralph Regula (R)	129,734	68.9%
Jim Rice (D)	58,644	31.1%

PREVIOUS WINNING PERCENTAGES
2000 (69%); 1998 (64%); 1996 (69%); 1994 (75%); 1992 (64%); 1990 (59%); 1988 (79%); 1986 (76%); 1984 (72%); 1982 (66%); 1980 (79%); 1978 (78%); 1976 (67%); 1974 (66%); 1972 (57%)

er-financed private school vouchers. He also voted in 2002 against a measure granting the president expanded fast-track negotiating authority for certain trade agreements — a vote that some powerful Republicans recalled as they decided whether to make Regula the Appropriations chairman.

But overall, in the 108th Congress he voted in agreement with Bush 92 percent of the time and stood with other Republicans 94 percent of the time on votes that set the two parties against each other.

Regula is dean of the Ohio Republican delegation, and his popularity among House colleagues has proved useful in bipartisan efforts by Ohio lawmakers to stand united on parochial issues. He defends federal support of clean-coal technology research, a program of particular interest in his area, where most electricity is produced by coal-fired plants. He also has been a champion of aggressive moves to support the domestic steel industry, which remains a potent economic force in northeastern Ohio. He has been a champion of Bush's imposition of tariffs on steel imports.

His hometown causes also include preserving the memory of President McKinley, Canton's most famous son. Regula — who graduated from a now-defunct law school named after the 25th president — helped engineer the purchase of a house where McKinley lived when he was a congressman, and since 1998 the building has been home to the National First Ladies' Library, which was founded by Regula's wife, Mary. Regula has directed more than $1 million in spending to the library.

And at the beginning of each Congress, Regula introduces a bill that has the effect of preventing Alaskans from changing the name of Mount McKinley — the nation's tallest peak — to Denali, its Indian name.

Regula is the son of an Ohio farmer, and he returns every weekend to his family's cattle farm in Navarre. He also was a schoolteacher and principal and served on the Ohio Board of Education for four years before his election to the General Assembly, where he represented a large swath of Stark County — the heart of the 16th District.

When Republican Frank Bow retired in 1972 after 22 years in the House, Regula was viewed as the logical successor. He won with 57 percent of the vote and has had a solid hold on the seat since. He has been held to less than three-fifths of the vote only once — in 1990, when college professor Warner D. Mendenhall won a surprising 41 percent.

Redistricting following the 2000 census did not alter the Republican lean of the 16th District. Regula won re-election in 2004 with almost 67 percent of the vote. His son, Richard, is commissioner of Stark County and is viewed as a potential successor whenever his father retires.

KEY VOTES

2004

No Extend federal unemployment benefits by 13 weeks

Yes Pass $283.2 billion, six-year federal highway and mass transit bill

Yes Approve $146 billion multi-year extension of previously enacted middle-class tax breaks

Yes Amend the Constitution to prohibit same-sex marriage

Yes Cut corporate taxes $137 billion over 10 years

Yes Reorganize U.S. intelligence agencies as proposed by Sept. 11 commission

2003

Yes Cut taxes by $330 billion through fiscal 2013

No Block Bush rule scaling back overtime pay for some white-collar federal workers

No Do not allow use of search warrants without first notifying subjects

No Allow importation of prescription drugs

Yes Create private school voucher program in Washington, D.C.

Yes Ban "partial birth" abortion except to save a woman's life

No Split $18.6 billion in Iraq aid into half-grant, half-loan

Yes Overhaul Medicare and create prescription drug benefit

CQ VOTE STUDIES

	PARTY UNITY		PRESIDENTIAL SUPPORT	
	Support	Oppose	Support	Oppose
2004	93%	7%	85%	15%
2003	95%	5%	96%	4%
2002	94%	6%	90%	10%
2001	95%	5%	88%	12%
2000	88%	12%	36%	64%

INTEREST GROUPS

	AFL-CIO	ADA	CCUS	ACU
2004	20%	0%	100%	88%
2003	7%	5%	97%	88%
2002	22%	5%	95%	88%
2001	25%	20%	91%	76%
2000	10%	10%	80%	76%

OHIO 16

Northeast – Canton

Canton, the most-populous city in northeastern Ohio's 16th District, is known in historical circles as the home base of William McKinley, who represented the city in the U.S. House and who ran much of his 1896 presidential campaign from a front porch on North Market Street.

Canton also has a rich manufacturing and steel-producing history, and high-skill manufacturing remains at the core of the region's economy. Recent times have brought some economic hardships: Timken Co., which manufactures bearings, and Hoover, a vacuum cleaner maker, struggle to retain jobs. But local officials are hopeful that the economy, including the steel industry, can rebound after recent lean times.

With a median income more than $10,000 below the state average, Canton is a working-class city that votes solidly Democratic. In 2004, John Kerry defeated George W. Bush by a better than 2-to-1 ratio in the city, which also has a black population that exceeds 20 percent.

But as Canton's population has declined since the 1950s, the city has become less important to the 16th's political outlook. The city now accounts for just one-fifth of Stark County's population. Massillon and Alliance, the county's next-most-populous cities, grew only marginally in the 1990s and also lean Democratic. Northern Stark County is upper-middle-class and GOP-leaning. Stark overall backed Bush in 2000, but opted for Kerry in 2004.

As a whole, the 16th leans Republican because of the rural conservative areas west of Stark. Wayne County is a top state producer of oats, hay and dairy products. The 16th also takes in most of Ashland County, which is even more solidly conservative than Wayne. Redistricting following the 2000 census added most of Medina County, another dependably Republican area that is northwest of Canton and west of Akron.

MAJOR INDUSTRY
Steel, manufacturing, health care

CITIES
Canton, 80,806; Massillon, 31,325; Medina, 25,139; Wooster, 24,811

NOTABLE
The Professional Football Hall of Fame and William McKinley's burial site are in Canton; Jacob Coxey, whose "army" of unemployed men marched to Washington, D.C., after the Panic of 1893, was from Massillon.

Rep. Tim Ryan (D)

CAPITOL OFFICE
225-5261
timryan.house.gov
222 Cannon 20515-3517; fax 225-3719

COMMITTEES
Armed Services
Education & Workforce

HOMETOWN
Niles

BORN
July 16, 1973, Niles, Ohio

RELIGION
Roman Catholic

FAMILY
Wife, Julie Ryan

EDUCATION
Bowling Green State U., B.A. 1995 (political science); Franklin Pierce Law Center, J.D. 2000

CAREER
Congressional aide

POLITICAL HIGHLIGHTS
Ohio Senate, 2001-02

ELECTION RESULTS

2004 GENERAL

Tim Ryan (D)	212,800	77.2%
Frank V. Cusimano (R)	62,871	22.8%

2004 PRIMARY

Tim Ryan (D)	unopposed

2002 GENERAL

Tim Ryan (D)	94,441	51.1%
Ann Womer Benjamin (R)	62,188	33.7%
James A. Traficant Jr. (I)	28,045	15.2%

Elected 2002; 2nd term

Representing one of the most depressed industrial regions in the country, Ryan is singularly dedicated to bringing jobs and federal resources to his ailing district. The second-youngest Democrat in the House, he is becoming a party messenger on the economic double whammy of cheap imports and outsourcing of jobs overseas.

Ryan beat a veteran Democrat in a 2002 primary by attacking his record of supporting free trade. He opposes current U.S. trade policies, and he is trying to work with majority Republicans, many of whom are free-trade advocates, to build a bipartisan effort to address trade disparities.

He is the co-chairman of the Manufacturing Caucus, which he founded in his first term with Republican Donald Manzullo of Illinois. Manzullo represents Rockford, a one-time manufacturing giant whose reversal of fortune and decline mirrors that of Ryan's district, which is dominated by blue-collar Youngstown and parts of Akron.

Like a growing number of lawmakers from both parties, Ryan is critical of the trade and monetary practices of China. He is at the forefront of House efforts to punish the Asian giant if it does not take steps to improve its balance of trade with the United States. In the 109th Congress, Ryan joined with California Republican Duncan Hunter, chairman of the Armed Services Committee, in sponsoring a bill to force the administration to take action against China unless it moves to increase the value of its currency. Artificially devaluing currency, as China is accused of doing, creates an unfair advantage by making goods cheaper to produce and sell.

"When dealing with China, I think it is immensely important to state the obvious — while the United States might be playing by the rules, China is playing to win," Ryan told the federal U.S.-China Economic and Security Review Commission in 2005. "The rest of the world does not have the same sense of fair play and ethics as we do in America, and we should always be very cognizant of that fact."

Ryan is a reliably liberal vote on most issues, but he is far from being a doctrinaire Democrat. Like many of his colleagues from socially conservative, working-class districts, Ryan opposes abortion and supports gun ownership rights. But in what he regards as the toughest vote of his freshman term, he bucked strong sentiment in his district and voted against a constitutional amendment to ban flag burning because he said he feared civil liberties were under assault.

After Democratic losses in the 2004 election, Ryan argued that the party's strong voice on economic and labor issues was weakened by what appears to voters to be unreasonable stances on social issues. "The Democratic Party has to be a little more inclusive on issues like abortion, not that we want to all of a sudden go out and overturn *Roe v. Wade*. . . . [On] issues like partial-birth abortion or the Unborn Victims Bill, it's hard to argue to a woman or a man in Ohio that a pregnant woman getting murdered is not a double homicide. That's a tough sell in Ohio, and until we begin to realize that, we're going to have a difficult time," Ryan said in 2004 on The NewsHour with Jim Lehrer, a television program.

Ryan is passionate about finding creative ways to bring jobs and new businesses to his district. In 2004, he secured $300,000 in federal money to study the potential gains of building the first indoor motor speedway near Youngstown as a tourist attraction. He also got $16 million for projects in a transportation bill, including $3 million to expand the National Packard

www.cqpress.com

Museum in Warren, Ohio, where the first Packard car was built. When that project was singled out by budget watchdog groups as an example of pork-barrel spending, Ryan said, "I make no apologies for getting federal money for one of the most economically depressed areas of the country. Sixty years ago, no one complained when the citizens of my district were funding the war effort and the interstate highway system and the GI bill."

Ryan is working closely with Ohio's Republican governor and other lawmakers to prevent what would be another severe blow to the region's economy — the shuttering of Youngstown Air Reserve Station. Already a member of the Armed Services Committee, Ryan snared a seat on the Readiness Subcommittee at the start of the 109th Congress. The panel oversees the round of base closures that began in 2005.

Unlike many small cities of the Rust Belt, Youngstown's three colleges and a medical school mean it has retained a concentration of young people, whom Ryan sees as key to an economic turnaround. He uses his seat on the Education and Workforce Committee to look out for the interests of those institutions. The cost of higher education is a barrier to upward mobility in his view, and he is pushing legislation to make textbooks tax deductible and to simplify the paperwork to apply for federal financial aid.

Ryan got his first taste of Capitol Hill in the mid-1990s as an aide to the man who long represented the area in the House, the quirky and ultimately disgraced James A. Traficant Jr. Only the second House lawmaker to be expelled since the Civil War, Traficant was convicted in 2002 of bribery and racketeering.

At the time, Ryan was serving in the Ohio Senate, a post he won in 2000, the same year he completed law school.

Entering a highly competitive congressional primary in 2002, Ryan faced eight-term Rep. Tom Sawyer, who was thrown into the district by reapportionment. Sawyer outspent him 10-to-1, but he had lost much of his old political base in redistricting and had alienated labor by supporting free-trade bills. Ryan, too, had some problems. He helped finance his campaign with a $50,000 loan co-signed by his high school basketball coach, and was later fined $6,000 by the Federal Election Commission for a campaign finance law violation. The coach also was fined, $4,000, but Ryan's campaign paid it.

Ryan went on to defeat Republican state Sen. Ann Womer Benjamin by 17 percentage points. Traficant, who ran for re-election from federal prison as an independent, still took 15 percent of the vote in a district where many still consider him a working-class hero. In 2004, Ryan was unchallenged in the primary and brushed off a political novice in the general election.

KEY VOTES

2004

Yes Extend federal unemployment benefits by 13 weeks

Yes Pass $283.2 billion, six-year federal highway and mass transit bill

Yes Approve $146 billion multi-year extension of previously enacted middle-class tax breaks

No Amend the Constitution to prohibit same-sex marriage

No Cut corporate taxes $137 billion over 10 years

Yes Reorganize U.S. intelligence agencies as proposed by Sept. 11 commission

2003

No Cut taxes by $330 billion through fiscal 2013

Yes Block Bush rule scaling back overtime pay for some white-collar federal workers

Yes Do not allow use of search warrants without first notifying subjects

Yes Allow importation of prescription drugs

No Create private school voucher program in Washington, D.C.

Yes Ban "partial birth" abortion except to save a woman's life

Yes Split $18.6 billion in Iraq aid into half-grant, half-loan

No Overhaul Medicare and create prescription drug benefit

CQ VOTE STUDIES

	PARTY UNITY		PRESIDENTIAL SUPPORT	
	Support	Oppose	Support	Oppose
2004	95%	5%	30%	70%
2003	95%	5%	29%	71%

INTEREST GROUPS

	AFL-CIO	ADA	CCUS	ACU
2004	100%	80%	35%	17%
2003	100%	95%	30%	32%

OHIO 17

Northeast — Youngstown, Warren, part of Akron

Bordering Pennsylvania in the northeastern part of the state, the 17th is a Democratic bastion that takes in part of the Mahoning Valley, including Youngstown. Once a leading steel-producing area, the valley now symbolizes industrial decline; the remaining steel mills are predominately silent and abandoned.

Despite some economic diversification, young people searching for jobs often look elsewhere (the district's median age — 37 — is above the national median), and the population of most cities has declined. Youngstown's population hovered around 170,000 from the 1930s to the 1960s; the 2000 census found just 82,000 people living in the city.

Officials hope the manufacturing industry is starting to turn around. Several auto plants are in the area, and the regional airport, which houses a large Air Force Reserve base, is undergoing an expansion that local officials hope will turn it into an air cargo hub.

Trumbull County (shared with the 14th) is home to a plurality of district residents. Some of the cities that propel Trumbull's staunch Democratic lean are Warren, the county's most populous city, and Niles and Girard. The 17th's share of Mahoning County, which includes Youngstown, gave 71 percent of its votes to John Kerry in the 2004 presidential election, and the county overall last voted for a GOP presidential candidate in 1972.

Redistricting following the 2000 census added parts of Summit and Portage counties, which are west of Youngstown and are less solidly Democratic. The Summit portion includes the eastern half of Akron, a city that once produced 90 percent of the nation's tires. The Portage portion includes Kent, where Kent State University is located, and Ravenna. While Summit and Portage are not as staunchly Democratic as Trumbull and Mahoning, they still supported Kerry by a double-digit margin in 2004. Kerry took 63 percent of the vote districtwide, which made the 17th his second-best district in Ohio.

MAJOR INDUSTRY
Automobile assembly, manufacturing

CITIES
Akron (pt.), 87,776; Youngstown, 82,026; Warren, 46,832

NOTABLE
Mill Creek Park in Youngstown covers 2,530 acres.

Rep. Bob Ney (R)

CAPITOL OFFICE
225-6265
bobney@mail.house.gov
ney.house.gov
2438 Rayburn 20515-3518; fax 225-3394

COMMITTEES
Financial Services
(Housing & Community Opportunity - chairman)
House Administration - chairman
Transportation & Infrastructure
Joint Library - chairman
Joint Printing

HOMETOWN
St. Clairsville

BORN
July 5, 1954, Wheeling, W.Va.

RELIGION
Roman Catholic

FAMILY
Wife, Elizabeth Ney; two children

EDUCATION
Ohio U., attended 1972-74; Ohio State U., B.S. 1976
(history)

CAREER
State health and education program manager;
local safety director; educator

POLITICAL HIGHLIGHTS
Ohio House, 1981-83; defeated for re-election to
Ohio House, 1982; Ohio Senate, 1984-95

ELECTION RESULTS

2004 GENERAL

Bob Ney (R)	177,600	66.2%
Brian R. Thomas (D)	90,820	33.8%

2004 PRIMARY

Bob Ney (R)	unopposed

2002 GENERAL

Bob Ney (R)	unopposed

PREVIOUS WINNING PERCENTAGES
2000 (64%); 1998 (60%); 1996 (50%); 1994 (54%)

Elected 1994; 6th term

Try telling Ney that being chairman of the House Administration Committee is a dull job. Ney and the committee, normally charged with the mundane task of keeping the internal machinery of the House humming, had a hand in certifying the results of the acrimonious 2004 presidential election and in efforts to secure the Capitol building and its occupants against a terrorist attack.

Not all of the attention has been welcome. At the start of the 109th Congress, Ney (NAY) was defending himself against ethics allegations involving the same lobbyist named in the widely publicized ethics probe of Majority Leader Tom DeLay.

The Administration Committee chairman is sometimes referred to as the mayor of the House, and Ney, a former Ohio state legislator, fits the role.

When Democratic Sen. Barbara Boxer of California challenged the normally routine certification of presidential electors in December 2004, Ney led the defense of the election results, saying the challenge was driven by people embittered by President Bush's re-election and Democratic Sen. John Kerry's defeat. "It used to be a given," he lamented on the House floor, "That once a campaign was over, the winner claimed victory, the loser accepted defeat, everyone else went on with their lives and the country moved forward."

Ney also held hearings into charges that election officials in Ohio and Florida purposely depressed the Democratic vote to Bush's benefit. Ney took strong exception to the charges. But in a field hearing in Columbus, he allowed Democratic Rep. Stephanie Tubbs Jones of Ohio to question witnesses though she was not a committee member.

The rise of well-financed so-called 527 groups in the 2004 presidential campaign convinced Ney his opposition to the campaign finance overhaul of 2002 was justified. (The 527s are named for the section of the tax code that governs their operations.) He called a hearing in 2004 to investigate the groups, and in the process frayed the committee's typically bipartisan cordiality — which Ney usually gets credit for fostering — as panel Democrats accused him of singling out groups that backed them for a "fishing expedition."

The disputed 2000 presidential election also put Ney's committee in the spotlight. He championed, with the top-ranking Democrat on his panel — Steny H. Hoyer of Maryland — a landmark law that set the first federal standards for the conduct of federal elections and gave states funds to help local election boards modernize.

Ney had other worries as the 109th Congress got under way. The House ethics committee was looking into his ties to Jack Abramoff, a lobbyist for Indian gaming interests who was alleged to have funneled money through a conservative think tank to pay for a 2002 trip Ney took to Scotland. Abramoff was also reported to have paid for travel for DeLay. Abramoff was seeking to get Ney to insert a provision into an appropriations bill to allow a shuttered Indian gaming casino to reopen. The provision never made it into the bill, and Ney said he was misled by Abramoff. But Democratic Party officials say they see an opening to mount an aggressive challenge against him in 2006.

Ney's district may be the only one in the nation that considers the House Administration Committee a power center. One of its own, Democrat Wayne L. Hays, chaired the panel for five years and was able to leverage its authority over funding for other committees to win projects for eastern Ohio. "Down home, this committee is known as the most important in the House," Ney recalled in 2001, so he made it his top priority as a freshman to win a seat on the panel.

The Sept. 11, 2001, terrorist attacks raised the committee's profile considerably. Ney successfully pushed for all House member offices to have hand-held e-mail devices and laptops for use in the event of a major disruption of official business. After anthrax-tainted letters were sent anonymously to lawmakers, he started a program to scan congressional mail. In 2005, the House approved the committee's plan for quickly holding elections to replace members of Congress lost as a result of a catastrophe.

Although he chairs the ultimate insider's committee, Ney says he has spent not more than a couple of weekends in Washington since he was first elected in 1994, nearly always driving the seven hours to his eastern Ohio district. He has connections to the world outside the 18th District. Fluent in Farsi, Ney taught English in Iran in 1978; he left before the country's revolution, but continues to meet with prominent exiles in Washington.

Reliably conservative on most issues, Ney is nonetheless vocal in his support for labor unions, which have a sizable constituency in his district, home to most of Ohio's remaining coal and steel producers. He assiduously looks out for those industries and their workers, whether by blocking tougher Clean Air Act regulations, opposing trade deals or trying to stop more visas for high-technology workers — all of which he believes can threaten jobs. His attention to those issues is one reason he has won election six times in a district that previously had not elected a Republican in 48 years. He sided with unions and against a majority of Republicans in the 108th Congress by voting to extend unemployment benefits by an additional 13 weeks.

Raised in a middle-class family — his father was a camera operator for a television station and his mother worked in a liquor store — Ney worked his way through college and got his start in elective politics at age 26, winning a seat in the state House in 1980 by defeating Hays, who was attempting a political comeback. In 1984, Ney was appointed to the state Senate, where he eventually rose to be chairman of its Finance Committee.

After nine-term Democrat Douglas Applegate retired in 1994, the well-funded Ney easily dispatched five rivals in the GOP primary and then defeated conservative Democratic state Rep. Greg L. DiDonato. After a close call two years later, Ney has won handily. He drew no opponent in 2002 after his district had been redrawn for the decade to enhance his electability, and in 2004 he easily defeated labor activist Brian R. Thomas.

KEY VOTES

2004
Yes Extend federal unemployment benefits by 13 weeks
Yes Pass $283.2 billion, six-year federal highway and mass transit bill
Yes Approve $146 billion multi-year extension of previously enacted middle-class tax breaks
Yes Amend the Constitution to prohibit same-sex marriage
Yes Cut corporate taxes $137 billion over 10 years
Yes Reorganize U.S. intelligence agencies as proposed by Sept. 11 commission

2003
Yes Cut taxes by $330 billion through fiscal 2013
No   Block Bush rule scaling back overtime pay for some white-collar federal workers
Yes Do not allow use of search warrants without first notifying subjects
No   Allow importation of prescription drugs
No   Create private school voucher program in Washington, D.C.
Yes Ban "partial birth" abortion except to save a woman's life
No   Split $18.6 billion in Iraq aid into half-grant, half-loan
Yes Overhaul Medicare and create prescription drug benefit

CQ VOTE STUDIES

	PARTY UNITY		PRESIDENTIAL SUPPORT	
	Support	Oppose	Support	Oppose
2004	92%	8%	82%	18%
2003	93%	7%	93%	7%
2002	95%	5%	90%	10%
2001	91%	9%	79%	21%
2000	88%	12%	29%	71%

INTEREST GROUPS

	AFL-CIO	ADA	CCUS	ACU
2004	27%	10%	100%	92%
2003	20%	10%	100%	80%
2002	11%	0%	100%	92%
2001	25%	10%	96%	88%
2000	40%	20%	61%	83%

OHIO 18

East — Zanesville, Chillicothe

Ohio's most geographically vast district, the 18th envelops 12 whole counties and parts of four others in southern and eastern Ohio. Beginning in the north, the 18th takes in the rolling hills south of Canton and runs southwest to the rugged areas in Appalachia. The district, which roughly parallels but does not touch the Ohio River, depends on the steel and coal industries and includes a large Catholic population of Eastern European and Greek immigrants.

The 18th's most-populous county is Tuscarawas, whose name is derived from an Indian word meaning "open mouth." Located in the northern area of the district, Tuscarawas is abutted by several solidly Republican counties, including Holmes County, where George W. Bush took 75 percent of the 2004 presidential vote.

Newark (shared with the 12th), in Licking County, survived the closure of an Air Force base in the 1990s and has become a growing research and manufacturing center. Carroll, Harrison and Guernsey counties on the district's eastern border are ancestrally Democratic areas that tend to be populist on economics but strongly conservative on cultural issues. Southeast of Harrison, the district takes in a northern sliver of Belmont County that includes Rep. Ney's hometown of St. Clairsville. Republicans who controlled the post-census redistricting process drew the bulk of Democratic-leaning Belmont County into the 6th.

The 18th narrows south of Muskingum County (Zanesville) to reach Morgan County and northwestern Athens County, although not the portion that includes Ohio University. Moving westward, the 18th remains rural as it crosses forests to take in most of Ross County, including Chillicothe. Bush took 57 percent of the 18th's 2004 vote and won 15 of the 16 counties fully or partially in the district (he lost only Athens).

MAJOR INDUSTRY
Steel, manufacturing, agriculture, coal

CITIES
Zanesville, 25,586; Chillicothe, 21,796; Newark (pt.), 21,118

NOTABLE
Astronaut and former Sen. John Glenn was born in New Concord; A memorial to baseball pitcher Cy Young is in his hometown of Newcomerstown; A basket-shaped building serves as headquarters for the Longaberger basket company in Newark.

Gov. Brad Henry (D)

First elected: 2002
Length of term: 4 years
Term expires: 1/07
Salary: $110,299
Phone: (405) 521-2342

Hometown: Shawnee
Born: July 10, 1963; Shawnee, Okla.
Religion: Baptist
Family: Wife, Kim Henry; three children
Education: U. of Oklahoma, B.A. 1985 (economics), J.D. 1988
Career: Lawyer
Political highlights: Okla. Senate, 1993-2002

Election results:
2002 GENERAL
Brad Henry (D)	448,143	43.3%
Steve Largent (R)	441,277	42.6%
Gary L. Richardson (I)	146,200	14.1%

Lt. Gov. Mary Fallin (R)

First elected: 1994
Length of term: 4 years
Term expires: 1/07
Salary: $85,500
Phone: (405) 521-2161

STATE LEGISLATURE

Legislature: February-May

House: 101 members, 2-year terms
2005 breakdown: 57R, 44D; 87 men, 14 women
Salary: $38,400
Phone: (405) 521-2711

Senate: 48 members, 4-year terms
2005 breakdown: 26D, 22R; 40 men, 8 women
Salary: $38,400
Phone: (405) 524-0126

STATE TERM LIMITS

Governor: 2 terms
House: No more than 12 years combined
Senate: No more than 12 years combined

URBAN STATISTICS

CITY	POPULATION
Oklahoma City	506,132
Tulsa	393,049
Norman	95,694
Lawton	92,757
Broken Arrow	74,859

REGISTERED VOTERS

Democrat	51%
Republican	38%
Unaffiliated	11%

POPULATION

2004 population (est.)	3,523,553
2000 population	3,450,654
1990 population	3,145,585
Percent change (1990-2000)	+9.7%
Rank among states (2004)	28

Median age	35.5
Born in state	62.6%
Foreign born	3.8%
Violent crime rate	498/100,000
Poverty level	14.7%
Federal workers	44,984
Military	41,575

REDISTRICTING

Oklahoma lost one House seat in reapportionment. The state legislature failed to agree on a plan and a county judge implemented a new, five-district map on May 31, 2002.

MISCELLANEOUS

Web: www.ok.gov
Capital: Oklahoma City
STATE ELECTION OFFICIAL
(405) 521-2391
DEMOCRATIC HEADQUARTERS
(405) 427-3366
REPUBLICAN HEADQUARTERS
(405) 528-3501

District Statistics

DIST.	2004 VOTE FOR PRESIDENT BUSH	KERRY	WHITE	BLACK	ASIAN	HISP	MEDIAN INCOME	WHITE COLLAR	BLUE COLLAR	SERVICE INDUSTRY	OVER 64	UNDER 18	COLLEGE EDUCATION	RURAL	SQ. MILES
1	65%	35%	74%	9%	1%	5%	$38,610	63%	23%	14%	12%	26%	26%	10%	1,737
2	59	41	70	4	0	2	$27,885	48	35	17	15	26	13	64	20,563
3	72	28	81	4	1	5	$32,098	54	30	16	14	26	18	49	34,089
4	67	33	78	7	2	5	$35,510	57	27	16	12	26	20	37	10,212
5	64	36	68	14	3	8	$33,893	61	24	15	13	26	25	12	2,067
STATE	66	34	74	7	1	5	$33,400	57	28	16	13	26	20	35	68,667
U.S.	50.7	48.3	69	12	4	13	$41,994	60	25	15	12	26	24	21	3,537,438

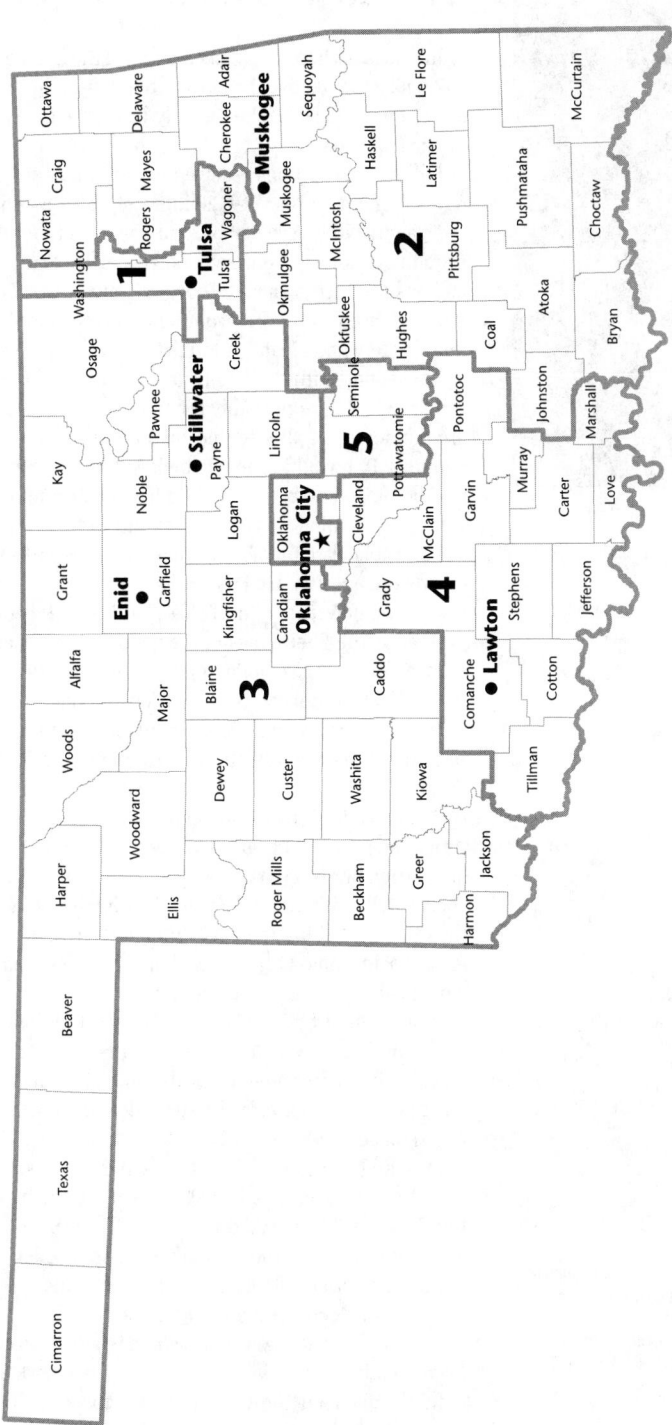

Sen. James M. Inhofe (R)

Elected 1994; 2nd full term

CAPITOL OFFICE
224-4721
inhofe.senate.gov
453 Russell 20510-3603; fax 228-0380

COMMITTEES
Armed Services
Environment & Public Works - chairman

HOMETOWN
Tulsa

BORN
Nov. 17, 1934, Des Moines, Iowa

RELIGION
Presbyterian

FAMILY
Wife, Kay Inhofe; four children

EDUCATION
U. of Tulsa, B.A. 1973

MILITARY SERVICE
Army, 1956-58

CAREER
Real estate developer; insurance executive

POLITICAL HIGHLIGHTS
Okla. House, 1967-69; Okla. Senate, 1969-77;
Republican nominee for governor, 1974;
Republican nominee for U.S. House, 1976; mayor
of Tulsa, 1978-84; defeated for re-election as
mayor of Tulsa, 1984; U.S. House, 1987-94

ELECTION RESULTS

2002 GENERAL

James M. Inhofe (R)	583,579	57.3%
David L. Walters (D)	369,789	36.3%
James Germalic (I)	65,056	6.4%

2002 PRIMARY

James M. Inhofe (R)	unopposed

PREVIOUS WINNING PERCENTAGES
1996 (57%); 1994 Special Election (55%); 1992 House
Election (53%); 1990 House Election (56%); 1988
House Election (53%); 1986 House Election (55%)

Inhofe is perhaps the best example of the Senate's evolution in tone from collegial to combative. Brash and blunt, he pushes hard for a conservative agenda in a place that historically has prided itself on its ability to bridge political divides.

Inhofe (IN-hoff) has received numerous awards from the National Taxpayers' Union for his tax-slashing votes. He has a lifetime "A+" grade from the National Rifle Association, and a zero score for the past four congresses from the League of Conservation Voters. He consistently has sided with oil and gas producers against "burdensome" environmental regulations, and once referred to the Environmental Protection Agency and the Occupational Safety and Health Administration as "Gestapo bureaucracies."

In clashing with the late Democratic Sen. Paul Wellstone, Inhofe once remarked, "There probably are not two members of the U.S. Senate who are further apart philosophically than the senior senator from Minnesota and myself. I would probably believe him to be an extreme left-wing radical liberal, and he believes me to be an extreme right-wing radical conservative. And I think maybe we are both right."

For a politician, Inhofe can come across as stiff and even awkward in one-on-one encounters. He has feuded for years with the editorial page of his hometown newspaper, the Tulsa World, and he remains suspicious of what he sees as the liberal bias of the national news media. "Don't look for any fair treatment. We're not going to get it," he told the Oklahoma delegation to the 2000 Republican National Convention.

Inhofe drew some national media interest in 2003, a few months after becoming chairman of the Environment and Public Works Committee. "With all of the hysteria, all of the fear, all of the phony science, could it be that man-made global warming is the greatest hoax ever perpetrated on the American people?" he asked in a two-hour Senate floor speech. Six months later, when he visited Italy for an international conference on the topic, environmentalists distributed posters bearing his photo and a caption based on the quotation. "I think Senator Inhofe is a general without an army on this issue," said Philip Clapp, president of the National Environmental Trust, which came up with the poster.

Inhofe stood by his remarks. On the Environment and Public Works panel, he has vowed to make sure that "sound science" underpins any changes in environmental regulation. "The political agenda of extremists must not dictate our efforts to provide common-sense protections that are based on science," he said.

Despite his conservatism, Inhofe has not hesitated to tangle with President Bush on occasion. In 2003, he warned Bush's chief political strategist, Karl Rove, that he would drop Bush's "Clear Skies" legislation if the administration did not do more to lobby for it. The legislation was intended to reduce industrial pollution from sulfur dioxide, nitrogen oxides and, for the first time, mercury emissions. In early 2005, his panel remained deadlocked, 9-9, on the legislation, which would replace the current structure for regulating industrial air pollution with a market-driven system.

Inhofe focused the committee's efforts in the 108th Congress on a sweeping, multi-year bill that would authorize funding for highways, public transportation systems and road safety programs. However, lawmakers were unable to complete work on the bill because of disagreements, both among Republicans and between Congress and the Bush administration, over the generosity of new funding and the way it should apportioned to the states. The bill's failure was a disappointment for Inhofe, who had made the issue a top priority. His plan was to provide a major boost in road spending nationally and additional equity to Oklahoma and other so-called "donor" states that generate more road revenue than they receive back for building and maintenance projects.

A staunchly pro-defense lawmaker whose state has several military installations, Inhofe also sits on the Armed Services Committee, where he has strongly supported a national missile defense system and increased spending to improve the military's readiness for combat. He fought a losing battle in the 107th Congress against the Pentagon's cancellation of the Crusader howitzer system, which was to be manufactured in Oklahoma.

An Army veteran and experienced pilot, Inhofe has had his brushes with danger. While traveling to Oklahoma City in 1999, his private plane lost its propeller, forcing him to glide about seven miles to make an emergency high-speed landing. He said it was his third forced landing in 41 years of flying.

Inhofe's frequently fiery rhetoric from the right has made him a hero to Tulsa's hard-core conservatives, including religious fundamentalists. He predicted in a 1999 speech that President Clinton's affair with White House intern Monica Lewinsky would trigger a moral revolution and end the "age of perversion." He described protesters outside the 2004 Republican National Convention in New York as "perverted people."

Sometimes his intemperate words land him in hot water. In 2001, he told the Senate that Israel had a right to take harsh measures with the Palestinians because God had promised that land to the Jews. He also likened Palestinian terrorist attacks to "satanic evil," prompting an outcry from American Muslim groups. In 1972, he said Democratic presidential nominee George McGovern should "be hanged with Jane Fonda" for implying that American soldiers were guilty of atrocities in Vietnam.

His conservative base of support helped him through 10 years in the state legislature, a mayoral career and four close House election victories, but it did not look sufficient to sustain a statewide campaign until 1994.

While a state senator, Inhofe lost a 1974 campaign for governor to Democrat David L. Boren and a 1976 race for Congress. Elected mayor of Tulsa in 1978, he was defeated for re-election in 1984. He bounced back two years later and picked up a House seat for the GOP, taking 55 percent of the vote to succeed Democrat James R. Jones, who ran for the Senate. He never did better than 56 percent in four elections in the state's most Republican district. In 1988, his campaign was complicated when he sued his brother over a stock sale involving the family insurance business.

In 1994, a Senate seat came open when Boren, who had gone on to serve as a senator, decided to leave midterm. Inhofe's competition was Rep. Dave McCurdy, a conservative and pro-business Democrat favored to win. But McCurdy made one error that proved fatal in Oklahoma. He became associated with Clinton, whom he introduced at the 1992 Democratic National Convention. The GOP transformed the race into a referendum on Clinton. No matter what McCurdy said about having differences with the president, Inhofe could top it; he had opposed virtually every move Clinton had made. Inhofe won by 15 percentage points.

When he stood for election to a full term in 1996, Democrats were deterred by Inhofe's lopsided victory of two years earlier and did not mount a significant challenge. Inhofe defeated Jim Boren, a cousin of the former senator, by 17 points. In 2002, Inhofe won by 21 points against former Democratic Gov. David L. Walters, who was hobbled by past campaign finance improprieties.

KEY VOTES

2004
Yes Pass $318.9 billion, six-year highway and mass transit bill
No Extend assault weapons ban for 10 years
No Restore pay-as-you-go rules for new tax cuts and entitlement spending
Yes Criminalize harm to a fetus in an attack on the mother
No Increase mandatory child care funding to states by $6 billion over five years
Yes Amend the Constitution to prohibit same-sex marriage
Yes Approve $146 billion multi-year extension of previously enacted middle-class tax breaks
Yes Reorganize U.S. intelligence agencies as proposed by Sept. 11 commission
Yes Cut corporate taxes $137 billion over 10 years

2003
No Delay Bush changes to Clean Air Act
Yes Allow confirmation vote on Miguel A. Estrada to the U.S. Court of Appeals for the D.C. Circuit
No Block a Bush proposal opening Alaska's Arctic National Wildlife Refuge to oil drilling
No Limit size of Bush's proposed tax cut to $350 billion through fiscal 2013
? Overhaul Medicare and create prescription drug benefit
No Block Bush rule scaling back overtime pay for some white-collar federal workers
No Split $20 billion in Iraq aid into half-grant, half-loan
Yes Ban "partial birth" abortion except to save a woman's life
No Stop proposal allowing travel to Cuba
Yes Allow final vote on energy policy overhaul

CQ VOTE STUDIES

	PARTY UNITY		PRESIDENTIAL SUPPORT	
	Support	Oppose	Support	Oppose
2004	98%	2%	92%	8%
2003	98%	2%	97%	3%
2002	96%	4%	96%	4%
2001	96%	4%	95%	5%
2000	100%	0%	30%	70%
1999	95%	5%	23%	77%
1998	97%	3%	14%	86%
1997	99%	1%	49%	51%
1996	100%	0%	28%	72%
1995	98%	2%	24%	76%

INTEREST GROUPS

	AFL-CIO	ADA	CCUS	ACU
2004	17%	10%	100%	100%
2003	0%	5%	100%	84%
2002	17%	10%	100%	100%
2001	25%	10%	93%	96%
2000	13%	5%	85%	100%
1999	11%	0%	94%	100%
1998	0%	5%	76%	100%
1997	14%	5%	50%	100%
1996	0%	0%	100%	100%
1995	0%	0%	100%	100%

Sen. Tom Coburn (R)

Elected 2004; 1st term

With Coburn's election, Oklahomans managed to elect a senator more conservative than their senior senator, James M. Inhofe, which wasn't easy. Coburn is among the most zealous of the fist-thumping Republicans who came to power in 1995. Together, they make for one of the Senate's most conservative duos.

A practicing obstetrician, the self-styled "citizen legislator" rails against an incumbency mindset in Congress. He laments that for too many Republicans, pushing conservative principles becomes secondary to staying in power. While he was in the House, Coburn was among the group that plotted in 1997 to oust then-Speaker Newt Gingrich of Georgia for abandoning conservative principles. "We have a deficit of moral courage in the United States Congress," Coburn likes to say.

Unlike other lawmakers elected in the GOP takeover of Congress, Coburn stuck to his term-limits pledge, serving three terms in the House and then leaving. He promises to serve no more than two Senate terms. "Washington tends to change people," Coburn said. "What makes me valuable to my district is [that] there's nothing in Washington that I want."

Coburn hopes to continue practicing medicine on the weekends and during congressional breaks, in defiance of Senate rules. Senators are permitted outside income from investments and property, but cannot make money from professional jobs. The Senate Ethics Committee instructed Coburn to stop practicing medicine in 2005, but he launched a campaign to persuade fellow senators to change the rules.

Under House rules, he was able to work as a doctor. Coburn says it kept him in touch with his constituents in a way no amount of politicking could. "I got to hear straight from the horse's mouth things I never would have heard just as a congressman," he told the Associated Press.

Coburn will find the Senate different in other ways. Old-school Republicans occupy many senior posts and a go-along-get-along ethos dominates. Compromise is often necessary to achieve the comfortable majorities needed to pass most legislation. And even some of the Senate's devout fiscal conservatives focus on delivering federal dollars to their states, a practice Coburn singles out for criticism in his book, "Breach of Trust: How Washington Resists Reform and Makes Outsiders Insiders."

Coburn also might have to smooth over relations with the House and Senate leadership. House Speaker J. Dennis Hastert publicly predicted before Coburn's November 2004 election that the Oklahoman would lose. Hastert may have been smarting over Coburn's portrayal of him in his book as needing a "spinal transplant" to do a better job curbing government spending.

In his first few months in the Senate, Coburn won assignment to the Judiciary Committee, which would be at the center of a confirmation battle should there be a Supreme Court vacancy in President Bush's second term. Coburn was one of the most outspoken anti-abortion rights advocates in the House and no doubt takes those ideals onto the Judiciary panel. He said during his Senate campaign that he has advocated the death penalty for doctors who perform abortions because it is murder.

One of his first acts was to cosponsor the Unborn Child Pain Awareness Act of 2005, which would require physicians to tell women seeking an abortion 20 weeks or more into a pregnancy that "evidence suggests" the procedure causes the fetus to feel pain. The bill would require women to

CAPITOL OFFICE
224-5754
www.coburn.senate.gov
172 Russell 20510-3602; fax 224-6008

COMMITTEES
Homeland Security & Governmental Affairs
 (Federal Financial Management, Government
 Information & International Security - chairman)
Indian Affairs
Judiciary
 (Corrections & Rehabilitation - chairman)

HOMETOWN
Muskogee

BORN
March 14, 1948, Casper, Wyo.

RELIGION
Baptist

FAMILY
Wife, Carolyn Coburn; three children

EDUCATION
Oklahoma State U., B.S. 1970 (accounting); U. of Oklahoma, M.D. 1983

CAREER
Physician; optical firm manager

POLITICAL HIGHLIGHTS
U.S. House, 1995-2001

ELECTION RESULTS

2004 GENERAL

Tom Coburn (R)	763,433	52.8%
Brad Carson (D)	596,750	41.3%
Sheila Bilyeu (I)	86,663	6.0%

2004 PRIMARY

Tom Coburn (R)	145,974	61.2%
Kirk Humphreys (R)	59,877	25.1%
Bob Anthony (R)	29,596	12.4%
Jay Richard Hunt (R)	2,944	1.2%

PREVIOUS WINNING PERCENTAGES
1998 House Election (58%); 1996 House Election (55%); 1994 House Election (52%)

accept or reject anesthesia for the fetus. "This bill is a good step toward recognizing what the medical community has known for years — all unborn children feel excruciating pain during an abortion procedure," Coburn told the Gannett News Service. Coburn also is a cosponsor of legislation that would make it a crime to transport minors across state lines to obtain an abortion in order to avoid parental notification laws.

Coburn says he will use his medical background to focus on health care issues, as he did in the House. And despite his sharp political leanings, he said he will work to forge bipartisan coalitions, as he did in 2000 as the chief House sponsor of the reauthorization of the Ryan White AIDS law, which passed unanimously. Coburn's proposals for health savings accounts and overhauling medical liability laws come straight out of the Republican playbook. Still, Coburn has said he would not have supported Bush's Medicare bill that added a prescription drug benefit to the health care entitlement for senior citizens.

On the issue of spending, Coburn can be expected to take a hard line. He favors a freeze in non-defense discretionary appropriations, and he promises to assume an active role in search of wasteful programs. And although he advocates keeping pet projects for congressmen out of spending bills, he is not above using the bills to further a conservative agenda. During the 104th Congress (1995-1996), in his first term in the House, Coburn helped lead the charge when members of the GOP's right wing sought to tack conservative social policies onto must-pass spending bills.

Coburn sits on the Indian Affairs Committee, where he may have to mend fences with tribal leaders in the state. During his Senate campaign, Coburn drew opposition from his state's large American Indian population by describing treaties between Indians and the federal government as "primitive agreements" that could undermine Oklahoma's future. He also suggested some members of the Cherokee Nation were not really Indians.

Blunt talk is not new to Coburn, who during his campaign said that he thought lesbianism was running rampant in some southeastern Oklahoma schools and called state legislators "a bunch of crapheads" — statements that Democrats sought to use against him.

He also got himself into hot water while in the House with remarks about NBC's 1997 broadcast of a widely acclaimed dramatic film about the Holocaust called "Schindler's List." Coburn said that the broadcast took network television "to an all-time low with full frontal nudity, violence and profanity being shown in our homes." His comments sparked criticism from some prominent Republicans, who castigated him for failing to recognize the historical accuracy of the film. Coburn took to the House floor and said, "I feel terrible that my criticism of NBC has been misinterpreted as a criticism of 'Schindler's List' or the millions of Jews who died senselessly during the Holocaust."

Coburn was a first-time candidate for public office when he ran for a House seat in 1994. Before becoming a doctor, he ran a small business manufacturing optical supplies. After establishing a medical practice in 1986 in Muskogee, he made a favorable impression in the community with his dedication, delivering by his count more than 3,000 babies.

In 2004, when he sought a Senate seat, Coburn faced the political fight of his life. Democratic opponent Rep. Brad Carson's moderate record in the House seemed to put him in line with the historically Democratic yet conservative state. But despite his many gaffes and Carson's well-run campaign, Coburn defeated Carson by more than 11 percentage points. Carson might have been hurt by sharing the ballot with a successful measure to add a same-sex marriage ban to the Oklahoma Constitution. The initiative increased turnout among Coburn's most solid base — the Christian right.

CQ VOTE STUDIES

House Service:

	PARTY UNITY		PRESIDENTIAL SUPPORT	
	Support	Oppose	Support	Oppose
2000	91%	9%	23%	77%
1999	90%	10%	14%	86%
1998	94%	6%	16%	84%
1997	93%	7%	24%	76%
1996	91%	9%	29%	71%
1995	93%	7%	18%	82%

INTEREST GROUPS

House Service:

	AFL-CIO	ADA	CCUS	ACU
2000	20%	15%	63%	95%
1999	38%	10%	67%	100%
1998	22%	5%	71%	100%
1997	0%	5%	78%	95%
1996	9%	10%	80%	89%
1995	0%	0%	96%	100%

Rep. John Sullivan (R)

Elected January 2002; 2nd full term

Though he's been a loyal Republican during his short time in Congress, Sullivan is among a group of conservatives in the House who are increasingly unhappy with some of President Bush's fiscal and social policies.

Sullivan is emerging as a leading critic of the White House on immigration, particularly the Bush administration's plan to allow some illegal immigrants to remain in the country as guest workers. He also opposed Bush on a bill overhauling the nation's intelligence agencies that passed in late 2004.

And while Sullivan loves to trumpet his successes in bringing pork barrel spending to his district — his biggest catches were $21 million for the Oklahoma National Guard and over $13 million in defense contracts — he is a fierce critic of Washington's spending habits. He joined the Republican Study Committee, a group of the most conservative Republicans that aggressively challenge Bush when he strays from the conservative path on government spending issues.

Sullivan's main focus in the 109th Congress is what he regards as the shortchanging of Oklahoma by the federal office of Immigration and Customs Enforcement, whose sole office in the state is hundreds of miles away from Tulsa, his political base. In two incidents, one in 2002 and another in 2004, a total of 35 likely illegal immigrants were found but then released by immigration officers. Sullivan has written a bill requiring the government to place a second office in Tulsa.

His star turn in the 108th Congress came in July 2003 when he defied a doctor's orders to stay in bed, and arrived on the House floor in a wheelchair to cast the deciding vote on a bill, being pushed by the administration and GOP leaders, making significant changes in the Head Start early education program. Sullivan had been injured two days before when a security barrier at a Capitol parking lot malfunctioned and hit the car in which he was riding, setting off the air bag. "The people of the 1st District of Oklahoma trust me to do my job," Sullivan said. "That's exactly what I'm going to do in Washington, no matter how hard it may be at times." The bill ultimately died in the Senate.

He suffered some bruising of the political sort during a surprisingly rough primary contest and general-election campaign in 2004. His integrity was questioned, mostly over youthful drinking-related arrests that have been public for years.

In the 108th Congress, Sullivan had a solid voting record of loyalty to both the party and the president, agreeing with his leaders on major votes 98 percent of the time and with Bush 94 percent of the time.

Republican leaders rewarded him with a hard-to-get seat on the Energy and Commerce Committee, a huge plum for a lawmaker from energy-producing Tulsa. And he was added to the Republican whip team. Sullivan also enjoys a close enough personal relationship with Bush that he once asked the president to give his then 10-year-old son Tommy some pointers before the fourth-grader delivered a speech.

Sullivan had his first taste of politics as a boy when he accompanied his father around the neighborhood doing campaign work. He says his father was a Republican and his mother a Democrat.

In college, Sullivan initially was a political science major, but after his father died he switched to business administration. He worked his way through college and graduated when he was 27. Though Sullivan worked as a real estate broker and a petroleum marketing executive, he continued

CAPITOL OFFICE
225-2211
sullivan.house.gov
114 Cannon 20515-3601; fax 225-9187

COMMITTEES
Energy & Commerce

HOMETOWN
Tulsa

BORN
Jan. 1, 1965, Tulsa, Okla.

RELIGION
Roman Catholic

FAMILY
Wife, Judy Sullivan; five children (one deceased)

EDUCATION
Northeastern State U., B.B.A 1992 (marketing)

CAREER
Real estate broker; petroleum marketing executive

POLITICAL HIGHLIGHTS
Okla. House, 1995-2002

ELECTION RESULTS

2004 GENERAL

John Sullivan (R)	187,145	60.2%
Doug Dodd (D)	116,731	37.5%
John Krymski (I)	7,058	2.3%

2004 PRIMARY

John Sullivan (R)	44,082	70.4%
Bill Wortman (R)	15,778	25.2%
Evelyn L. Rogers (R)	2,779	4.4%

2002 GENERAL

John Sullivan (R)	119,566	55.6%
Doug Dodd (D)	90,649	42.2%
Joseph V. Cristiano (LIBERT)	4,740	2.2%

PREVIOUS WINNING PERCENTAGES
2002 Special Election (54%)

to be fascinated by politics and ran a political memorabilia business. He also worked on several Republican campaigns.

Sullivan decided to seek office himself in 1994 when the local state House member ran for Congress. He won election to the state legislature at age 29, and hasn't lost an election since. During his seven years there, he waged a long battle to reduce the sales tax on groceries, backed reductions in the estate tax and championed an annual one-day sales tax "holiday" on school-related purchases.

In 2001, GOP Rep. Steve Largent, a football Hall of Famer, decided to leave his House seat to run for governor. Cathy Keating, wife of GOP Gov. Frank Keating, was viewed as the front-runner in the five-way Republican primary. But Sullivan bested her by 15 percentage points in that December race. While his 46 percent vote share was not enough to avoid a runoff with Keating, she dropped out to avoid an intraparty fight.

In the special election, Sullivan faced former Tulsa School Board member Doug Dodd, a Democrat. Sullivan's 9-point margin of victory was narrower than had been expected in the solidly Republican district, which had gone for Bush by 25 points in 2000. But by the time Sullivan ran for his first full term in the fall of 2002, the district had been redrawn to make it even more safely Republican. He beat Dodd in a rematch by 13 points.

While Sullivan's re-election two years later, in 2004, never seemed in doubt, the campaign was harsh. Past supporters, including an earlier political consultant to Sullivan who accused his former boss of cheating him out of nearly $20,000 in fees, got behind GOP businessman Bill Wortman in the primary. Sullivan's office later was forced to acknowledge that his aides used phony names to telephone call-in radio shows and pose easy questions to their boss. Several listeners of one show recognized the voice of aide George Wiland, who identified himself only as "Charlie." Wortman seized on that incident and two cases in which he said Sullivan lied about his past arrest record.

Sullivan has long acknowledged a rocky youth where, he said, careless drinking led to several arrests, including one for assault. He has often spoken about the dangers that alcohol consumption poses in high schools. But Wortman insisted that even though Sullivan's arrests were more than 15 years old, "the lies are still going on today."

Sullivan prevailed easily in the primary, but then questions about his integrity were picked up by Democrat Dodd, who challenged him in the fall. Voters evidently were untroubled by his past and gave Sullivan a nearly 23-point victory over Dodd.

KEY VOTES

2004

No   Extend federal unemployment benefits by 13 weeks

No   Pass $283.2 billion, six-year federal highway and mass transit bill

Yes   Approve $146 billion multi-year extension of previously enacted middle-class tax breaks

Yes   Amend the Constitution to prohibit same-sex marriage

Yes   Cut corporate taxes $137 billion over 10 years

No   Reorganize U.S. intelligence agencies as proposed by Sept. 11 commission

2003

Yes   Cut taxes by $330 billion through fiscal 2013

No   Block Bush rule scaling back overtime pay for some white-collar federal workers

Yes   Do not allow use of search warrants without first notifying subjects

No   Allow importation of prescription drugs

?   Create private school voucher program in Washington, D.C.

Yes   Ban "partial birth" abortion except to save a woman's life

No   Split $18.6 billion in Iraq aid into half-grant, half-loan

Yes   Overhaul Medicare and create prescription drug benefit

CQ VOTE STUDIES

	PARTY UNITY		PRESIDENTIAL SUPPORT	
	Support	Oppose	Support	Oppose
2004	97%	3%	85%	15%
2003	98%	2%	100%	0%
2002	99%	1%	88%	12%

INTEREST GROUPS

	AFL-CIO	ADA	CCUS	ACU
2004	7%	0%	100%	100%
2003	0%	0%	100%	88%
2002	13%	0%	89%	—

OKLAHOMA 1
Tulsa; Wagoner and Washington counties

Wooden homes on small plots of land in the city's outskirts contrast with the skyscrapers of downtown Tulsa, the heart of the 1st and one of the most solidly Republican enclaves in Oklahoma. More insular and tied to old money than Oklahoma City and the rest of the state, Tulsans like to distinguish themselves from the "dust-on-their-boots" stereotype of the rest of Oklahoma.

Once the "oil capital of the world," Tulsa thrived on drilling for "black gold" until the market dried up in the 1980s. It is now a city seeking an economic identity to fit with its historical self-image. In the late 1980s, an effort to attract a diverse range of businesses through tax breaks and other incentives started to pay off. Tulsa has become a manufacturing hub of flight simulators. While aviation and aerospace manufacturing have remained productive, the telecommunications and financial services industries have helped prolong growth.

With the economy on the mend, real estate prices are beginning to rise as Tulsa expands to the east and south. Young professionals are moving into the more established sections of the city's center. South Tulsa is sprinkled with executive homes, and new subdivisions are springing up in the bedroom communities of Broken Arrow, Owasso and Jenks. Redistricting after the 2000 census added Bartlesville in Washington County to the north and fast-growing suburbs in Wagoner County to the east.

Democrats split the votes in the 1st's local elections, but Republicans dominate at the federal level. The region has voted for a Democratic presidential candidate only twice since 1920. Socially conservative issues play well here, the home of Oral Roberts University.

MAJOR INDUSTRY
Aerospace, defense manufacturing, oil, agriculture

CITIES
Tulsa (pt.), 387,419; Broken Arrow, 74,859; Bartlesville, 34,746; Owasso, 18,502; Sand Springs (pt.), 17,172; Bixby, 13,336

NOTABLE
One of the deadliest race riots in American history took place in the Tulsa neighborhood of Greenwood in June 1921 — nearly 300 people died; Oral Roberts University is known for its 200-foot prayer tower and "Praying Hands" sculpture.

Rep. Dan Boren (D)

CAPITOL OFFICE
225-2701
www.house.gov/boren
216 Cannon 20515-3602; fax 225-3038

COMMITTEES
Armed Services
Resources

HOMETOWN
Paden

BORN
Aug. 2, 1973, Shawnee, Okla.

RELIGION
Methodist

FAMILY
Engaged to Andrea Heupel

EDUCATION
Texas Christian U., B.A. 1997 (economics); U. of
Oklahoma, M.B.A. 2001

CAREER
College fundraiser; congressional district aide;
bank teller; state utility regulation commission
aide

POLITICAL HIGHLIGHTS
Okla. House, 2002-04

ELECTION RESULTS

2004 GENERAL		
Dan Boren (D)	179,579	65.9%
Wayland Smalley (R)	92,963	34.1%
2004 PRIMARY		
Dan Boren (D)	73,421	57.7%
Kalyn Free (D)	46,061	36.2%
Bryan J. Bigby (D)	5,328	4.2%
Vern L. Cassity (D)	2,497	2.0%

Elected 2004; 1st term

Boren first got an insider's view of the Capitol at 5 years old — in 1979, when his father, Democrat David L. Boren, began his career in the Senate.

When the younger Boren returned in 2005, at age 31, he took his place as the third generation of his family to serve as a Democratic member of Congress from Oklahoma: His father was a senator until 1994, when he resigned to become president of the University of Oklahoma; his grandfather, Lyle Boren, was a House member from 1937 to 1947.

The youngest Boren's preparation for Congress was one term in the Oklahoma House, where he compiled a center-right record as a proponent of tax cuts and backer of efforts to make it more difficult for trial lawyers to press what he termed frivolous lawsuits. He calls himself a fiscally conservative "pro-business, pro-gun Democrat."

Hailing from a state where resources development is a mainstay, Boren said he hoped for a seat on the Energy and Commerce Committee but would settle for a seat on the Resources panel. He got the latter, along with an Armed Services post that should help him burnish his pro-military credentials — which could benefit him down the line in a state that includes such major military facilities as Tinker Air Force Base and the Army's Fort Sill.

Boren's famous name and status as the delegation's only Democrat give him automatic potential as a future statewide candidate. And he says his Democratic stripes should not hinder him from working with his colleagues on issues of parochial importance. His No. 1 concern, he says, is the need to create jobs in his district, where incomes run well below the state's average.

He got the chance to step up from the legislature when two-term Democratic Rep. Brad Carson left for a Senate bid that ultimately failed. Though the electorate in the largely rural 2nd District supports conservatives, it has been more loyal to its Democratic traditions than the rest of the GOP-trending state. So Boren was a shoo-in after a handy primary win over former local district attorney Kalyn Free, a member of the Cherokee Nation. Boren then sprinted past Republican Wayland Smalley, a horse breeder.

OKLAHOMA 2
East — Muskogee, 'Little Dixie'

The 2nd has a Democratic lean, but partisanship does not disguise a cultural split between the district's regions. Running from Kansas to Texas in eastern Oklahoma, the 2nd takes in outlying areas of Tulsa to the north and the "Little Dixie" region in the south. Southeastern Oklahoma relies on farming and has "Yellow Dog" Democrats, while residents in the northeastern part of the state are more liberal, at least by Oklahoma's standards. Both areas support Republicans in presidential races.

In Little Dixie, a 1998 drought was as severe as any in the 1930s Dust Bowl era, but conservation techniques prevented similar sandstorms. The economy does suffer from these droughts, however, as farmers are forced to use feed for grazing animals several months earlier than normal. In addition to beef and poultry, farmers cultivate peanuts and wheat, and in rocky southeastern McCurtain County, the timber industry thrives. Marginal oil and natural gas wells compose the energy businesses that survived the 1980s industry depression.

Up north, the forested section in the foothills of the Ozark Mountains is a poor rural area with Democratic sympathies. The lakes and waterways, the state's most extensive, attract tourists and the elderly. Delaware County, which contains most of Grand Lake O' the Cherokees, was the state's fastest-growing county in the 1990s (32 percent). The 2nd also has the third-largest percentage of American Indians in the nation (17 percent), and includes Tahlequah, the capital of the Cherokee Nation.

MAJOR INDUSTRY
Timber, ranching, oil and gas, agriculture

MILITARY BASES
McAlester Army Ammunition Plant, 3 military, 1,400 civilian (2005)

CITIES
Muskogee, 38,310; McAlester, 17,783; Claremore, 15,873; Tahlequah, 14,458

NOTABLE
The American Indian "Trail of Tears" of 1838-39 ended in Tahlequah — nearly 20 percent of the Cherokee Nation died en route.

Rep. Frank D. Lucas (R)

Elected May 1994; 6th full term

CAPITOL OFFICE
225-5565
www.house.gov/lucas
2342 Rayburn 20515-3603; fax 225-8698

COMMITTEES
Agriculture
(Conservation, Credit, Rural Development &
Research - chairman)
Financial Services
Science

HOMETOWN
Cheyenne

BORN
Jan. 6, 1960, Cheyenne, Okla.

RELIGION
Baptist

FAMILY
Wife, Lynda Lucas; three children

EDUCATION
Oklahoma State U., B.S. 1982 (agricultural
economics)

CAREER
Farmer; rancher

POLITICAL HIGHLIGHTS
Republican nominee for Okla. House, 1984, 1986;
Okla. House, 1989-94

ELECTION RESULTS

2004 GENERAL

Frank D. Lucas (R)	215,510	82.2%
Gregory M. Wilson (I)	46,621	17.8%

2004 PRIMARY

Frank D. Lucas (R)	unopposed

2002 GENERAL

Frank D. Lucas (R)	148,206	75.6%
Robert T. Murphy (LIBERT)	47,884	24.4%

PREVIOUS WINNING PERCENTAGES
2000 (59%); 1998 (65%); 1996 (64%); 1994 (70%);
1994 Special Election (54%)

A fifth-generation farmer and rancher from sparsely populated western Oklahoma, Lucas has held on to the family spread while many of his neighbors have moved to towns and cities. The population of Roger Mills County, where he farms, dropped 28 percent since 1980 and was one of a dozen counties in that part of the state to lose population during the 1990s.

The steady emptying of rural Oklahoma is an underlying factor in much of Lucas' conservative legislative agenda and his close attention to constituent service. He wants to develop concrete reasons — jobs, health care, education — for people to stay in places such as his hometown of Cheyenne, the county seat, population 778. The population drain led to the Sooner State losing one of its House seats in reapportionment after the 2000 census, leaving it with five.

Lucas' district encompasses almost half the geographic area of the state, stretching nearly 400 miles from the New Mexico border in the Oklahoma panhandle to the outskirts of Oklahoma City and Tulsa. While many of his constituents are suburbanites attached to those cities, Lucas' main focus is rural life. Although he has been an elected official for more than a decade and a half, Lucas likes to say he "still tries to earn an honest living" on his farm, where his great-great-grandfather was a homesteader in 1900. When Lucas is in Washington, his wife runs their beef cattle and wheat operation on land that has been in the family since 1912.

As chairman of the Agriculture Committee's Conservation Subcommittee, Lucas played a major role in developing the farm bill that Congress enacted in 2002. That bill reversed many of the fundamental changes made to farm policy by Republicans just after their takeover of Congress. Although he supported the GOP's "Freedom to Farm" law in 1996, which was supposed to wean farmers from government support, Lucas told the Tulsa World in 2002, "That was never real to start with. . . . It is obvious that we must support legislation which helps provide a reliable safety net for Oklahoma producers."

Lucas was a member of the negotiating team that resolved differences between the House and Senate versions of the 2002 farm bill. The resulting measure included conservation provisions written by his subcommittee as well as substantial federal support for farmers growing wheat and peanuts, both of which are important crops in his district. As he urged colleagues to vote for the bill, Lucas said, "The only people who should be concerned about agriculture policy are people who eat."

He has continued to fight to improve the lives of farmers, too, taking on even members of his own party in battles over agriculture spending levels and pressing for aid to farmers hurt financially by drought and low prices. In early 2005, he expressed concern over provisions in President Bush's proposed budget resolution that would cut programs to aid farmers. In the 108th Congress, he criticized the administration's plan to reopen U.S. borders to Canadian cattle and requested a delay based on widespread concern about foreign beef and the spread of mad cow disease.

He also opposed the White House when administration officials sought to change a provision in the farm bill and designate "technical assistance" funding — training and other conservation-related tasks, such as limiting air pollution or building dams — as discretionary, rather than mandatory. The change would have made the programs vulnerable to congressional whim in the future. Late in 2001, when the White House was expressing reticence about moving on the farm bill because it involved "large new financial commitments," Lucas pressed for speedy action in Congress, saying, "I just don't think the folks at the administration have a clear idea of where they're going on agriculture policy."

On most other issues, Lucas is a party loyalist and reliable supporter of the president's agenda. In the 108th Congress, he supported Republican positions more than 95 percent of the time on major votes and sided with Bush more than 90 percent of the time. The president, who makes up nicknames for people he likes, refers to the 6-foot-4 Lucas as "Big Frank."

Lucas has parochial concerns that do not involve agriculture. He sponsored a bill in the 108th Congress that would let the Osage Nation of Oklahoma set its own rules for tribal membership. He also has secured federal money to help local law enforcement authorities track down and clean up labs for methamphetamines, a serious problem in rural areas because of the explosive gases and hazardous wastes created.

Lucas spent a lot of time working on legislation stemming from the April 1995 bombing in downtown Oklahoma City that destroyed the Alfred P. Murrah Federal Building and killed 168 people. The federal building used to be in Lucas' old district, the 6th. In the years after the bombing, Lucas helped secure more than $100 million in federal funds for the relief, recovery and rebuilding of the area affected by the blast. He also won passage of a measure to establish a national memorial on the bombing site.

Lucas became interested in politics while at Oklahoma State University. He was president of the College Republicans while working on a degree in agricultural economics. After graduating, he returned home to Cheyenne and made two unsuccessful bids for a state House seat in what was then a mostly Democratic area. He then captured a state House seat in a sprawling rural district in 1988.

When 10-term Democratic Rep. Glenn English resigned the 6th District seat in early 1994 to head a rural electric lobbying association, Lucas made his run for the House. He outpolled four other Republicans to win the nomination. Stressing his work in agriculture and his lifelong residency in the district, he won 54 percent of the vote in the special election against Democrat Dan Webber Jr., who had spent years in Washington as an aide to Oklahoma Democratic Sen. David L. Boren.

That was Lucas' closest election. In 2002, after introducing himself to his new constituents in the Tulsa, Stillwater and Enid areas, Lucas racked up a big victory in the new 3rd District, drawn to be favorable to the GOP. He won a fifth full term two years later with 82 percent of the vote.

KEY VOTES

2004

? Extend federal unemployment benefits by 13 weeks
No Pass $283.2 billion, six-year federal highway and mass transit bill
Yes Approve $146 billion multi-year extension of previously enacted middle-class tax breaks
Yes Amend the Constitution to prohibit same-sex marriage
Yes Cut corporate taxes $137 billion over 10 years
No Reorganize U.S. intelligence agencies as proposed by Sept. 11 commission

2003

Yes Cut taxes by $330 billion through fiscal 2013
No Block Bush rule scaling back overtime pay for some white-collar federal workers
Yes Do not allow use of search warrants without first notifying subjects
No Allow importation of prescription drugs
Yes Create private school voucher program in Washington, D.C.
Yes Ban "partial birth" abortion except to save a woman's life
No Split $18.6 billion in Iraq aid into half-grant, half-loan
Yes Overhaul Medicare and create prescription drug benefit

CQ VOTE STUDIES

	PARTY UNITY		PRESIDENTIAL SUPPORT	
	Support	Oppose	Support	Oppose
2004	94%	6%	87%	13%
2003	97%	3%	94%	6%
2002	98%	2%	88%	12%
2001	98%	2%	88%	12%
2000	97%	3%	22%	78%

INTEREST GROUPS

	AFL-CIO	ADA	CCUS	ACU
2004	17%	0%	95%	96%
2003	7%	10%	97%	92%
2002	0%	0%	100%	96%
2001	25%	5%	96%	96%
2000	0%	0%	85%	91%

OKLAHOMA 3
Panhandle, west and north-central Oklahoma

With nothing to stop it on the flat plains, the wind blows with constant force in the 3rd, an area devastated by the Dust Bowl of the 1930s. Few areas felt the boom or the bust of the 1980s oil market more than the 3rd, as those who had made fortunes on oil had their rigs and property auctioned and their Mercedes and Lincolns repossessed. Western Oklahoma had never fully recovered from the Dust Bowl, and the oil bust was another reason to leave the area.

The 3rd contains most of the old 6th District that existed before redistricting following the 2000 census, covering huge swaths of Oklahoma's land in the western and north-central parts of the state, including much of its border with Kansas. In the western areas, more than half of the district's counties lost population in the first half of the 1990s because of the oil market downturn. Locals are striving to diversify beyond agriculture and oil. Midwestern plains become more evident in the eastern portions of the 3rd — north of Oklahoma City — which is characterized by Bible Belt conservatism.

The three panhandle counties — Cimarron, Texas and Beaver — are perhaps the most heavily Republican-voting in the state. George W. Bush topped 80 percent in each of these counties in the 2004 presidential election, and 2002 GOP gubernatorial nominee Steve Largent surpassed 65 percent in each county. The southern part of the district is home to conservative Democrats whose families relocated from Texas. Overall, the 3rd was Bush's best Oklahoma district in 2004, and he took 72 percent of the vote here.

MAJOR INDUSTRY
Agriculture, oil

MILITARY BASES
Altus Air Force Base, 2,409 military, 2,353 civilian; Vance Air Force Base, 1,300 military, 140 civilian (2004)

CITIES
Enid, 47,045; Stillwater, 39,065; Ponca City, 25,919; Altus, 21,447; Yukon, 21,043; Sapulpa (pt.), 19,044

NOTABLE
Roger Mills County on the western border was named in 1892 through a referendum for U.S. Rep. and later Sen. Roger Q. Mills, who represented neighboring Texas in Congress from 1873 until 1899.

Rep. Tom Cole (R)

CAPITOL OFFICE
225-6165
www.house.gov/cole
236 Cannon 20515-3604; fax 225-3512

COMMITTEES
Rules
Standards of Official Conduct

HOMETOWN
Moore

BORN
April 28, 1949, Shreveport, La.

RELIGION
Methodist

FAMILY
Wife, Ellen Cole; one child

EDUCATION
Grinnell College, B.A. 1971 (history); Yale U., M.A. 1974 (British history); U. of Oklahoma, Ph.D. 1984 (19th Century British history)

CAREER
Political consultant; party official; congressional aide; professor

POLITICAL HIGHLIGHTS
Okla. Republican Party chairman, 1985-89; Okla. Senate, 1989-91; Okla. secretary of state, 1995-99

ELECTION RESULTS

2004 GENERAL		
Tom Cole (R)	198,985	77.8%
Charlene K. Bradshaw (I)	56,869	22.2%
2004 PRIMARY		
Tom Cole (R)		unopposed
2002 GENERAL		
Tom Cole (R)	106,452	53.8%
Darryl Roberts (D)	91,322	46.2%

Elected 2002; 2nd term

Cole is an admitted party loyalist, so much so that, after just two years in the House, he has been placed on the ethics and Rules committees and promoted to deputy whip. His rise through the ranks is not surprising, given his background. He's headed the staffs of the National Republican Congressional Committee and the Republican National Committee, and he's also been a state party chairman, state senator and Oklahoma's secretary of state.

An affable, chatty man with a wry sense of humor, Cole claims to have mixed feelings about his loyalist reputation. He knows he was named to the ethics committee in the 109th Congress because he is expected to be a good soldier. Few lawmakers like the assignment because it requires them to sit in judgment of their colleagues. Also, the circumstances were awkward: Speaker J. Dennis Hastert, whom Cole considers "an old friend," had just booted Chairman Joel Hefley and two other Republicans off the committee after the previous members of the panel had scolded Majority Leader Tom DeLay for his ethical conduct.

Cole's independence on the panel will be under severe scrutiny, particularly since he gave $5,000 to DeLay's legal defense fund in 2004. Between the ethics issue and his post on Rules, which is often criticized for setting strict terms for House debate on bills, Cole jokes that his top priority for the 109th Congress is "survival." He insists that "these were not my chosen two [committees]. I did them because I was requested to." In exchange, he was taken off the Resources and the Education and Workforce committees, two of his assignments in his first term, and is taking a leave of absence from a third panel, Armed Services.

Cole doesn't try to hide his commitment to his party's success. "Keeping our majority is very important, because everything else flows from that," he says. And while he doesn't agree with President Bush on everything — he thinks the president has stretched the military too thin, for example — "he's gotten the big things right." Still, Cole doesn't want his party to take his support for granted, particularly on important legislation. "Legislatively, you need to be reliable, but never predictable," he says.

One issue he insists he will always put above his party is American Indian priorities. The only American Indian currently serving in Congress, Cole is a member of the Chickasaw Nation, a tribe of 40,000 members. One of his first legislative accomplishments was a 2004 law that allowed the city of Sulphur to swap land with the federal government so the Chickasaws could build a cultural center at the edge of a federally protected area. "I'm not going to sell my constituents down the river," Cole says. "If they're going to do something to Native Americans, I'm not going to be with them."

Indeed, Cole criticized the Interior Department's handling of the land swap bill, saying it tried to insist late in the process on adding language to prohibit gaming on the land. "It was pretty insulting to the Chickasaws," he says. "To spring something on us like that at the last minute — what a microcosm of Indian history." Still, Cole does have ties to the American Indian gambling industry; the Chickasaws own 12 casinos in Oklahoma, and Cole's campaign committee accepted more than $36,000 in 2003 and 2004 from donors linked to the industry. That could become an issue if the ethics panel explores whether GOP lawmakers, including DeLay, had improper dealings with American Indian gambling lobbyist Jack Abramoff.

So far, Cole's voting record doesn't show many examples of straying from the party line. He voted for the controversial March 2005 legislation that allowed federal courts to intervene in the case of Terri Schiavo, the severely brain-damaged Florida woman whose husband and parents were feuding over her fate. He also supported all three tax cut bills Congress considered in his first term. But he opposed the White House by voting in 2003 to block a provision of the anti-terrorism law known as the Patriot Act that allows search warrants to be used without warning the subjects in advance.

He says he looks at every bill in terms of how it would affect small-business owners, an experience he shared as the founding partner of Cole, Hargrave, Snodgrass & Associates, his old political consulting firm. "That taught me a lot of things. There's nothing like being the last guy to get paid," Cole says. Starting a business, he says, "really is the social mobility ladder in America. . . . Government needs to make this easier, not harder."

Cole plans to keep close watch on the next round of base closings to make sure two installations in his district, Tinker Air Force Base and the Army's Fort Sill, do not become targets. And he asked some of the toughest questions of Defense Secretary Donald H. Rumsfeld when Armed Services held its 2004 hearing into the abuses of Iraqi inmates at the Abu Ghraib prison. He told Rumsfeld the Defense Department was "extraordinarily slow in understanding the implications of what was going on," adding, "When were you planning to let us know?"

Cole says he was motivated partly by his memories of an uncle who was abused as a prisoner of war in Japan during World War II. "He weighed 92 pounds when he got out," he recalls. "It scarred him for his whole life." Cole doesn't think top military officers planned the abuses of the Iraqi prisoners, but he says he worried that the incident would undermine the United States' moral authority and put other U.S. troops in danger of retaliation.

Cole has a historian's view of the world. He has a master's degree from Yale University and a doctorate from the University of Oklahoma, both in British history, and has taught courses at the George Washington University School of Political Management in Washington, D.C. He compares Bush to Harry S Truman, saying both were underestimated in their time, and compares the restructuring of the Iraqi government to the rebuilding of the German and Japanese societies after World War II.

Cole ran the campaign of his friend J.C. Watts Jr. for the 4th District seat in 1994, so it was not a big stretch for him to get into the race to replace Watts when he retired in 2002. Cole withstood a tough contest from Democratic former state Sen. Darryl Roberts to win with 54 percent of the vote. In 2004, he faced no Democratic opposition and cruised to re-election with 78 percent.

KEY VOTES

2004

No Extend federal unemployment benefits by 13 weeks

No Pass $283.2 billion, six-year federal highway and mass transit bill

Yes Approve $146 billion multi-year extension of previously enacted middle-class tax breaks

Yes Amend the Constitution to prohibit same-sex marriage

Yes Cut corporate taxes $137 billion over 10 years

Yes Reorganize U.S. intelligence agencies as proposed by Sept. 11 commission

2003

Yes Cut taxes by $330 billion through fiscal 2013

No Block Bush rule scaling back overtime pay for some white-collar federal workers

Yes Do not allow use of search warrants without first notifying subjects

No Allow importation of prescription drugs

Yes Create private school voucher program in Washington, D.C.

Yes Ban "partial birth" abortion except to save a woman's life

No Split $18.6 billion in Iraq aid into half-grant, half-loan

Yes Overhaul Medicare and create prescription drug benefit

CQ VOTE STUDIES

	PARTY UNITY		PRESIDENTIAL SUPPORT	
	Support	Oppose	Support	Oppose
2004	97%	3%	91%	9%
2003	96%	4%	98%	2%

INTEREST GROUPS

	AFL-CIO	ADA	CCUS	ACU
2004	20%	0%	100%	96%
2003	7%	5%	100%	84%

OKLAHOMA 4
South central — Norman, Lawton, part of Oklahoma City

Home to the state's largest university and two military bases, the 4th contains part of Oklahoma City, its southern suburbs and the western edges of "Little Dixie," a part of the state named for its southern influence.

The 4th's once-booming oil economy suffered from the low prices of the 1990s, and a concurrent drought helped decimate the southwest. Still, agriculture remains an essential economic cog. Soybeans, cotton, wheat and peanuts fill many of the district's family farms. Overall, the district's population increased by the end of the 1990s, as the military maintained its ubiquitous presence. The cancellation of the Crusader artillery system was a blow to Fort Sill and the city of Lawton, however, and many worry that Lawton's economy will collapse completely if Fort Sill does not survive the next round of base closures, which is scheduled for 2005.

The district has epitomized the Oklahoman trend toward voting

Republican in national elections. Although once confined in the 4th to presidential elections, this GOP swing now extends to congressional candidates and trickles down to some state legislators. But Democrats remain competitive, especially in the rural, southern parts of the district and around the University of Oklahoma in Norman, though Republicans have strength in other parts of Norman. Overall, George W. Bush received 67 percent of the 4th District vote in the 2004 presidential election.

MAJOR INDUSTRY
Military, higher education, oil, agriculture

MILITARY BASES
Tinker Air Force Base, 7,010 military, 15,027 civilian (2005); Fort Sill (Army), 9,746 military, 2,087 civilian (2004)

CITIES
Norman, 95,694; Lawton, 92,757; Oklahoma City (pt.), 70,896; Midwest City (pt.), 45,044; Moore, 41,138

NOTABLE
The National Oceanic and Atmospheric Administration's National Weather Service Storm Prediction Center is located in Norman; Apache warrior Geronimo was imprisoned at the Fort Sill Military Reservation.

Rep. Ernest Istook (R)

Elected 1992; 7th term

CAPITOL OFFICE
225-2132
istook@mail.house.gov
www.house.gov/istook
2404 Rayburn 20515-3605; fax 226-1463

COMMITTEES
Appropriations

HOMETOWN
Warr Acres

BORN
Feb. 11, 1950, Fort Worth, Texas

RELIGION
Mormon

FAMILY
Wife, Judy Lee Istook; five children

EDUCATION
Baylor U., B.A. 1971 (journalism); Oklahoma City U., J.D. 1976

CAREER
Lawyer; gubernatorial aide; journalist

POLITICAL HIGHLIGHTS
Warr Acres City Council, 1983-87; Okla. House, 1987-93

ELECTION RESULTS

2004 GENERAL

Ernest Istook (R)	180,430	66.1%
Bert Smith (D)	92,719	33.9%

2004 PRIMARY

Ernest Istook (R)	unopposed

2002 GENERAL

Ernest Istook (R)	121,374	62.2%
Lou Barlow (D)	63,208	32.4%
Donna Davis (I)	10,469	5.4%

PREVIOUS WINNING PERCENTAGES
2000 (68%); 1998 (68%); 1996 (70%); 1994 (78%); 1992 (53%)

Istook is a bare-knuckles conservative and a darling of the Christian Right whose contrary ways cost him dearly at the start of the 109th Congress. GOP House leaders took away his appropriations subcommittee chairmanship after Istook defied them one too many times.

There had long been grumbling among Republicans about Istook's overall effectiveness. But because he is such a conservative stalwart — he helped found the Conservative Action Team that became the influential Republican Study Committee — Republican leaders had long tolerated his independence and even made him one of the 13 appropriations "cardinals," as the spending panel chairmen are known. He was put in charge of the transportation spending panel.

But as the 108th Congress wound down, their patience wore thin. Istook ignored the much-prized requests for transportation projects from 21 Republicans who had bucked him by supporting continued federal subsidies for the Amtrak train service. When they protested to leaders, Istook apologized at a meeting of GOP lawmakers and in a letter pledged to help his colleagues with the projects in the next Congress. But any chance he had of keeping his chairmanship was dashed when the leadership decided to trim the number of subcommittees from 13 to 10. Istook was weakened and he lost his gavel.

Even before that, Istook had ruffled feathers by persistently displaying little interest in the political niceties, trade-offs and routines that other lawmakers accept as part of day-to-day legislative life. During a breakfast with small-business owners, Istook said lawmakers should practice straightforward dialogue with their constituents rather than parroting the ideas in the leadership's "message of the day," distributed to the rank-and-file. "My office receives them, too, but I just don't pay as much attention to them as some people do," Istook was quoted saying in Oklahoma City's Journal Record newspaper in 2003.

Like many House conservatives, he has a strong but not perfect record of party loyalty on major floor votes. In the 108th Congress, he voted with the GOP 96 percent of the time on votes on which the two parties squared off.

Along with many members of the Republican Study Committee, Istook is disgruntled with growth in federal spending during the watch of a conservative Republican president. He opposed the 2003 Medicare prescription drug bill, a major Bush initiative, because of a price tag in the hundreds of billions. He wound up voting for it only under intense pressure from leaders during an extraordinary all-night vote in the House. Istook adamantly opposes one of the president's top priorities for the 109th Congress — giving temporary legal status to some illegal immigrants.

He is a warrior on cultural issues, especially efforts to allow greater religious expression in public schools and other public places. He is the author of a proposed constitutional amendment that would allow prayer in public schools.

Perhaps his greatest victory in the 108th Congress was not on the floor of the House but in the courts. The Supreme Court upheld his legislation requiring public libraries that use federal funds to install filters on computers to prevent children from accessing pornographic Web sites.

With President Bush's backing, Istook in the 107th Congress pushed to enactment a ban on the financing of abortions through federal employees' health care plans. But his efforts to restrict the coverage of contraception came up short.

As chairman of the District of Columbia Appropriations Subcommittee in the 106th, Istook angered many city residents by blocking ordinances he did not like, including publicly funded abortions and needle-exchange programs. He later made amends by leaving the city's budget largely intact and softening some of his social positions. "Here is an example of a right-wing ideologue maturing to the point where he should rightfully be considered a serious legislator," James P. Moran of Virginia, the top-ranking Democrat on the subcommittee, told The Washington Post.

While social issues are his passion, Istook's seat on the spending committee has thrust him more and more into fiscal issues. He is a leading champion of an effort to end a link in pay for military and civilian government employees, arguing that it was both fair and practical to give soldiers higher pay raises during a time of war. He also sponsored a bill authorizing states to band together to establish a uniform tax system for Internet sales. While many Republicans in Washington found the idea anathema to their low-tax ideals, Istook said the federal government should not dictate how states tax commerce.

While Istook is aggressive about seeking highway projects for his district, he is more willing than others to oppose excesses in pork barrel spending. In 1996, he nixed financing for a proposed trolley system for Oklahoma City, despite strong support for it by city fathers and others in the state's congressional delegation.

Istook began his career as radio reporter covering the Oklahoma capitol after graduating from Baylor University. He went to law school at night, ultimately getting his degree. He worked as an aide to Democratic Gov. David L. Boren and then went into private practice. He won a city council seat in the Oklahoma City suburb of Warr Acres in 1982, and four years later a seat in the state House, where he rose to assistant minority leader.

To get to Congress in 1992, Istook had to get by two better-known Republicans — eight-term Rep. Mickey Edwards and former U.S. Attorney Bill Price. Edwards was tarred in the scandal surrounding a private bank then maintained for lawmakers and didn't make the primary runoff. Istook won by 12 percentage points, then won the general election with 53 percent.

Istook's stands have limited his popularity in some parts of Oklahoma, and for a time it looked as though he might be in danger of losing his reliably Republican base of support when the state legislature redrew congressional lines for the 2000s. While the 5th District did gain some Democratic areas, Istook won in 2002 with 62 percent of the vote and in 2004 with 66 percent.

KEY VOTES

2004

No Extend federal unemployment benefits by 13 weeks

No Pass $283.2 billion, six-year federal highway and mass transit bill

+ Approve $146 billion multi-year extension of previously enacted middle-class tax breaks

Yes Amend the Constitution to prohibit same-sex marriage

Yes Cut corporate taxes $137 billion over 10 years

No Reorganize U.S. intelligence agencies as proposed by Sept. 11 commission

2003

Yes Cut taxes by $330 billion through fiscal 2013

No Block Bush rule scaling back overtime pay for some white-collar federal workers

Yes Do not allow use of search warrants without first notifying subjects

Yes Allow importation of prescription drugs

Yes Create private school voucher program in Washington, D.C.

Yes Ban "partial birth" abortion except to save a woman's life

Yes Split $18.6 billion in Iraq aid into half-grant, half-loan

Yes Overhaul Medicare and create prescription drug benefit

CQ VOTE STUDIES

	PARTY UNITY		PRESIDENTIAL SUPPORT	
	Support	Oppose	Support	Oppose
2004	96%	4%	87%	13%
2003	97%	3%	90%	10%
2002	94%	6%	85%	15%
2001	95%	5%	95%	5%
2000	93%	7%	25%	75%

INTEREST GROUPS

	AFL-CIO	ADA	CCUS	ACU
2004	0%	0%	94%	92%
2003	0%	10%	90%	84%
2002	11%	5%	90%	92%
2001	8%	0%	91%	100%
2000	10%	5%	73%	90%

OKLAHOMA 5
Most of Oklahoma City; Pottawatomie and Seminole counties

The 5th contains all of downtown Oklahoma City, where an early-1980s boom swelled the population, but the economic stagnation that gripped the area at decade's end caused residents to leave and forced the city's economy to diversify in the 1990s.

Oil and gas, along with some agriculture, still compose a large chunk of the economy, but energy companies have been forced to expand their businesses into plastics and other industries. Telecommunications firms took hold in the district, although an economic downturn has forced layoffs. Lucent Technologies was once Oklahoma City's largest employer, but the ailing company sold its plant to an electronics company in 2001.

Oklahoma City is indelibly linked to the 1995 bombing of the Alfred P. Murrah Federal Building that killed 168 people. A memorial and the Institute for the Prevention of Terrorism commemorate the site. But just north of the site, a new federal campus opened in 2003, and downtown

Oklahoma City has undergone a revitalization, with a new arena, restaurants and apartments. Once filled with abandoned warehouses, "Bricktown" is now a staple in the city's nightlife.

The 5th contains the towns of Shawnee and Seminole, both home to large American Indian populations. Although Tinker Air Force Base is in the 4th, many who work there live in the 5th. The district is also home to several colleges and universities in Oklahoma City.

Republicans dominate in the 5th. The addition of Seminole County, Shawnee and the largely black northeastern portion of Oklahoma City in redistricting following the 2000 census made the district more Democratic, but not enough to threaten the GOP hold. George W. Bush took 64 percent of the vote here in the 2004 presidential election.

MAJOR INDUSTRY
Oil, computer hardware, state government, higher education

CITIES
Oklahoma City (pt.), 420,387; Edmond, 68,315; Shawnee, 28,692

NOTABLE
Seminole County is the historic Seminole Nation territory, accepted by the tribes in exchange for their departure from the Florida Territory.

OREGON

Gov. Theodore R. Kulongoski (D)

First elected: 2002
Length of term: 4 years
Term expires: 1/07
Salary: $88,920
Phone: (503) 378-3111

Hometown: Portland
Born: Nov. 5, 1940; Missouri
Religion: Roman Catholic
Family: Wife, Mary Oberst; three children
Education: U. of Missouri, B.A. 1967 (political science & public administration), J.D. 1970
Military Service: Marine Corps, 1960-63
Career: Lawyer
Political highlights: Ore. House, 1975-79; Ore. Senate, 1979-81; Democratic nominee for U.S. Senate, 1980; Democratic nominee for governor, 1982; Ore. insurance commissioner, 1987-91; Ore. attorney general, 1993-97; Ore. Supreme Court, 1997-2001

Election results:
2002 GENERAL

Theodore R. Kulongoski (D)	618,004	49.0%
Kevin L. Mannix (R)	581,785	46.2%
Tom Cox (LIBERT)	57,760	4.6%

Secretary of State Bill Bradbury (D)

(no lieutenant governor)
First elected: 2000 (appointed 1999)
Length of term: 4 years
Term expires: 12/09
Salary: $72,000
Phone: (503) 986-1523

STATE LEGISLATURE

Legislative Assembly: January-June in odd-numbered years

House: 60 members, 2-year terms
2005 breakdown: 33R, 27D; 44 men, 16 women
Salary: $1,283/month; $91/day in session
Phone: (503) 986-1187

Senate: 30 members, 4-year terms
2005 breakdown: 18D, 12R; 21 men, 9 women
Salary: $1,283/month; $91/day in session
Phone: (503) 986-1187

STATE TERM LIMITS

Governor: 2 terms
House: No
Senate: No

URBAN STATISTICS

CITY	POPULATION
Portland	529,121
Eugene	137,893
Salem	136,924
Gresham	90,205

REGISTERED VOTERS

Democrat	39%
Republican	36%
Unaffiliated	22%

POPULATION

2004 population (est.)	3,594,586
2000 population	3,421,399
1990 population	2,842,321
Percent change (1990-2000)	+20.4
Rank among states (2004)	27

Median age	36.3
Born in state	45.3%
Foreign born	8.5%
Violent crime rate	351/100,000
Poverty level	11.6%
Federal workers	29,090
Military	12,984

REDISTRICTING

Oregon retained its five House seats in reapportionment. Democratic Gov. John Kitzhaber vetoed the state legislature's plan and a county judge implemented a new map on Oct. 19, 2001.

MISCELLANEOUS

Web: www.oregon.gov
Capital: Salem
STATE ELECTION OFFICIAL
(503) 986-1518
DEMOCRATIC HEADQUARTERS
(503) 224-8200
REPUBLICAN HEADQUARTERS
(503) 587-9233

District Statistics

DIST.	2004 VOTE FOR PRESIDENT BUSH	KERRY	WHITE	BLACK	ASIAN	HISP	MEDIAN INCOME	WHITE COLLAR	BLUE COLLAR	SERVICE INDUSTRY	OVER 64	UNDER 18	COLLEGE EDUCATION	RURAL	SQ. MILES
1	44%	55%	81%	1%	5%	9%	$48,464	65%	22%	13%	10%	25%	33%	13%	2,941
2	61	38	86	0	1	9	$35,600	54	29	17	15	26	19	36	69,491
3	32	66	77	5	5	8	$42,063	59	25	16	11	24	25	7	1,021
4	49.0	49.3	90	1	2	4	$35,796	55	28	17	15	23	21	31	17,181
5	50	49	84	1	2	10	$44,409	61	25	15	13	26	27	20	5,362
STATE	47	51	84	2	3	8	$40,916	59	26	15	13	25	25	21	95,997
U.S.	50.7	48.3	69	12	4	13	$41,994	60	25	15	12	26	24	21	3,537,438

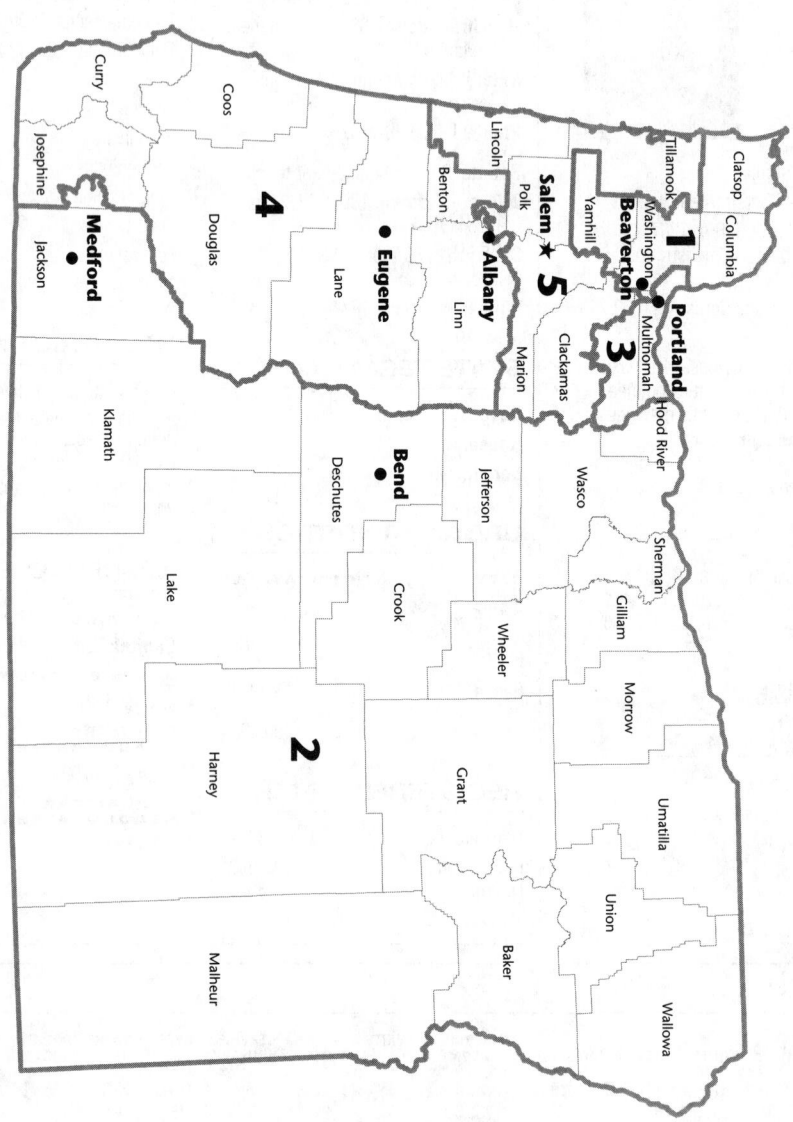

Sen. Ron Wyden (D)

CAPITOL OFFICE
224-5244
wyden.senate.gov
230 Dirksen 20510-3703; fax 228-2717

COMMITTEES
Budget
Energy & Natural Resources
Finance
Select Intelligence
Special Aging

HOMETOWN
Portland

BORN
May 3, 1949, Wichita, Kan.

RELIGION
Jewish

FAMILY
Divorced; two children

EDUCATION
U. of California, Santa Barbara, attended 1967-69; Stanford U., A.B. 1971 (political science); U. of Oregon, J.D. 1974

CAREER
Senior citizen advocacy group state director; lawyer; professor

POLITICAL HIGHLIGHTS
U.S. House, 1981-96

ELECTION RESULTS

2004 GENERAL

Ron Wyden (D)	1,128,728	63.4%
Al King (R)	565,254	31.8%
Teresa Keane (I)	43,053	2.4%
Dan Fitzgerald (LIBERT)	29,582	1.7%

2004 PRIMARY

Ron Wyden (D)	unopposed

PREVIOUS WINNING PERCENTAGES
1998 (61%); 1996 Special Election (48%); 1994 House Election (73%); 1992 House Election (77%); 1990 House Election (81%); 1988 House Election (99%); 1986 House Election (86%); 1984 House Election (72%); 1982 House Election (78%); 1980 House Election (72%)

Elected January 1996; 2nd full term

Wyden has developed a reputation as a skillful dealmaker and a leading voice on technology issues. His new seat on the Finance Committee gives him a chance to help shape health care policy, a major focus of his congressional career.

Although the prestigious committee assignment speaks to his rising status in the chamber, Wyden professes no interest in a leadership post or advancement on the national stage. "I'm not running for president," Wyden said. "I'll be the Senate's designated driver, so that if everybody's out running and folks get a little intoxicated, I can take them home."

The son of a librarian and a prolific author, Wyden approaches issues as a workhorse and a student, which allows him to tackle some of the most technical matters that have come before Congress during his tenure. While in the House, Wyden was a senior member of the Energy and Commerce Committee, where he developed significant expertise on health care.

He was an outspoken advocate of expanding Medicare to cover prescription drug costs for seniors well before that issue caught fire in the 107th and 108th Congresses, and he is a longtime critic of managed care. In the 109th, he fought Republican proposals to make deep cuts in Medicaid, the joint federal-state health program for the poor, and championed both the importation of cheaper prescription drugs from abroad and legislation to allow Medicare officials to negotiate lower drug prices for seniors.

He is a foe of the tobacco industry, garnering wide television coverage in 1994 when he asked a panel of tobacco executive witnesses whether they considered tobacco addictive. Under oath, they all denied any such thing. He repeated the question in 1998 during Senate Commerce hearings, and four of the five CEOs recanted.

There is one health-related issue unique to Oregon: The state is the only one in the country with a law permitting physician-assisted suicide. Wyden considers his vigorous defense of that law his finest hour. He faced an uphill fight in the 106th Congress (1999-2000) after House conservatives easily passed a bill prohibiting doctors from prescribing drugs designed to cause a patient's death, and many senators signaled their support for the measure. But Wyden waged a furious battle to run out the legislative clock in 2000, threatening to filibuster the bill, enlisting the support of influential groups such as the American Cancer Society, and combing through other bills to ensure that no one slipped the House plan into them.

In the 109th Congress, Wyden was again front and center on a right-to-die issue. As a grueling court battle over a severely brain-damaged Florida woman named Terri Schiavo was ending, House GOP conservatives rushed through a bill designed to restore a feeding tube that had been removed at her husband's request. The measure authorized the removal to federal courts — after all state remedies were exhausted — of cases, such as Schiavo's, that involve incapacitated people who had not executed an advance directive authorizing the withholding of sustenance. Wyden twice blocked Senate consideration of that measure, relenting only when a compromise was crafted allowing federal courts to intervene only in the Schiavo case. They did not, and the 41-year-old woman died shortly thereafter.

Oregon is the only state in the nation to conduct all its elections by mail. Wyden successfully protected Oregon's unique mail-ballot system from changes under a law overhauling voting procedures that was enacted at the end of 2002.

Accustomed to pursuing alliances with Republicans even on politically charged issues such as health care, Wyden found it easy to build coalitions across the aisle when he shifted his focus to technology concerns. "If ever there were issues that are truly bipartisan," he says, "technology really illustrates the point." Wyden acknowledges that his own computer skills are mostly limited to reading newspapers on the Internet and keeping in touch by e-mail. Nevertheless, he is widely viewed as one of the most tech-savvy members of Congress, in large part because of his work on the Commerce Committee, a seat he gave up in the 109th for the Finance slot.

In the 108th Congress, Wyden worked with Republican George Allen of Virginia to extend the ban on state taxation of Internet access. He was a central figure in the Senate's overwhelming rejection, early in 2003, of a plan sought by the Pentagon to permit domestic collection — through the monitoring of computer activity — of a wide array of personal data on individuals, with the aim of finding terrorists. And in 2004, he joined with Republican Conrad Burns of Montana to promote a crackdown on "spyware," software programs that track what Internet pages Web surfers are viewing. They reintroduced the measure in the 109th.

Wyden has waged war against secret "holds," which senators can impose to hold up action on a nominee or bill. Early in 1999, he won a change in the practice but new procedures adopted by Senate leaders proved ineffective. Within two years, Wyden and his ally, Republican Charles E. Grassley of Iowa, were urging that those imposing such holds be required to enter their objections in the Congressional Record.

During his 15 years in the House, Wyden developed a reputation as something of a media hound. His style has since mellowed, however. "He gets his share of publicity, but he does more than his share of work," said Republican Sen. Gordon H. Smith, Oregon's junior senator.

Wyden has forged an unusually close working relationship with Smith, whom he edged in a bitter 1996 Senate special-election contest. (Smith won the state's other Senate seat later that year.) "We just decided that out of this crucible we had learned a lot about each other," Wyden said. "If anything, we respected each other more for what we had been through." The two have a standing lunch date on Thursdays, and now they will be serving together on the Finance Committee, making Oregon the only state with two senators on that powerful panel.

Their friendship put Wyden in a difficult position in the 2002 election, when Democrats mounted a strong challenge to Smith. Wyden made clear he was happy to campaign for the Democratic candidate, Bill Bradbury, but would not say anything negative about Smith.

Wyden was Oregon executive director for the Gray Panthers, an organization promoting senior citizens' interests, when he first ran for the House in 1980. He ousted Democratic Rep. Robert Duncan in the primary and won with 72 percent in November in a Democratic Portland-based district.

When GOP Sen. Bob Packwood resigned in 1995 rather than face expulsion for personal misconduct, Wyden jumped into the special-election race. Despite some stumbles — most notably on a televised quiz show in which he failed to quote the price of common grocery items — he edged fellow Democratic Rep. Peter A. DeFazio in the primary.

In the general election, the gangly, rumpled Wyden refused to trade in his wrinkled sweaters for natty suits on the campaign trail, despite the urging of his staff. But he narrowly defeated Smith by portraying himself as a reasonable-minded alternative to the conservative state Senate president on such issues as education, the environment, revamping Medicare and balancing the budget. He won re-election in 1998 with 61 percent of the vote and in 2004 with 63 percent.

KEY VOTES

2004
Yes Pass $318.9 billion, six-year highway and mass transit bill
Yes Extend assault weapons ban for 10 years
Yes Restore pay-as-you-go rules for new tax cuts and entitlement spending
No Criminalize harm to a fetus in an attack on the mother
Yes Increase mandatory child care funding to states by $6 billion over five years
No Amend the Constitution to prohibit same-sex marriage
Yes Approve $146 billion multi-year extension of previously enacted middle-class tax breaks
Yes Reorganize U.S. intelligence agencies as proposed by Sept. 11 commission
Yes Cut corporate taxes $137 billion over 10 years

2003
Yes Delay Bush changes to Clean Air Act
No Allow confirmation vote on Miguel A. Estrada to the U.S. Court of Appeals for the D.C. Circuit
Yes Block a Bush proposal opening Alaska's Arctic National Wildlife Refuge to oil drilling
Yes Limit size of Bush's proposed tax cut to $350 billion through fiscal 2013
Yes Overhaul Medicare and create prescription drug benefit
Yes Block Bush rule scaling back overtime pay for some white-collar federal workers
Yes Split $20 billion in Iraq aid into half-grant, half-loan
No Ban "partial birth" abortion except to save a woman's life
No Stop proposal allowing travel to Cuba
No Allow final vote on energy policy overhaul

CQ VOTE STUDIES

	PARTY UNITY		PRESIDENTIAL SUPPORT	
	Support	Oppose	Support	Oppose
2004	93%	7%	62%	38%
2003	93%	7%	47%	53%
2002	87%	13%	74%	26%
2001	90%	10%	64%	36%
2000	97%	3%	95%	5%
1999	91%	9%	91%	9%
1998	88%	12%	85%	15%
1997	83%	17%	86%	14%
1996	92%	8%	95%	5%
House Service:				
1995	90%	10%	83%	17%

INTEREST GROUPS

	AFL-CIO	ADA	CCUS	ACU
2004	100%	100%	59%	4%
2003	92%	90%	43%	15%
2002	85%	85%	60%	15%
2001	100%	95%	43%	8%
2000	63%	90%	60%	8%
1999	78%	100%	59%	4%
1998	75%	100%	56%	4%
1997	71%	80%	70%	8%
1996	86%	95%	38%	15%
House Service:				
1995	100%	90%	29%	12%

Sen. Gordon H. Smith (R)

Elected 1996; 2nd term

CAPITOL OFFICE
224-3753
gsmith.senate.gov
404 Russell 20510-3704; fax 228-3997

COMMITTEES
Commerce, Science & Transportation
(Trade, Tourism & Economic Development -
chairman)
Energy & Natural Resources
Finance
(Long-Term Growth & Debt Reduction -
chairman)
Indian Affairs
Special Aging - chairman

HOMETOWN
Pendleton

BORN
May 25, 1952, Pendleton, Ore.

RELIGION
Mormon

FAMILY
Wife, Sharon Smith; three children (one deceased)

EDUCATION
Brigham Young U., B.A. 1976 (history);
Southwestern U., J.D. 1979

CAREER
Frozen food company owner; lawyer

POLITICAL HIGHLIGHTS
Ore. Senate, 1993-97 (president, 1995-97);
Republican nominee for U.S. Senate, 1996
(special election)

ELECTION RESULTS

2002 GENERAL

Gordon H. Smith (R)	712,287	56.2%
Bill Bradbury (D)	501,898	39.6%
Dan Fitzgerald (LIBERT)	29,979	2.4%
Lon Mabon (CNSTP)	21,703	1.7%

2002 PRIMARY

Gordon H. Smith (R)	306,504	98.9%
write-ins	3,439	1.1%

PREVIOUS WINNING PERCENTAGES
1996 (50%)

A former Mormon bishop with deep moral convictions, Smith has made his mark on the Senate as a thoughtful moderate who works to ensure that the poor can obtain health care, that homosexuals are treated with respect and that promising medical research is not stifled by anti-abortion strictures. He has dealt with life-and-death issues throughout his Senate career, but in the 108th Congress, it was on a heartbreaking personal level.

On Sept. 8, 2003, Smith's son Garrett, who suffered from depression, committed suicide one day before his 22nd birthday. On July 8, 2004, Smith took the Senate floor seeking support for a suicide prevention bill. "He was a beautiful child, a handsome baby boy," Smith said, choking back sobs. "His exuberance for life, however, began to dim in his elementary years. . . . There are simply no parental preparations adequate to this crisis in one's child's life, no owner's manual to help you bury a child, especially when the cause is suicide. So I've committed myself to trying to find meaning in Garrett's life." Senators streamed to the floor, rallying around their anguished colleague. Two of them, Democrat Harry Reid of Nevada and the now-retired Don Nickles, an Oklahoma Republican, quietly spoke about the suicides of their fathers. The bill passed unanimously that night and President Bush signed the $82 billion, three-year Garrett Lee Smith Memorial Act in October 2004.

In 2005, when the Senate Budget Committee proposed a fiscal 2006 budget resolution cutting Medicaid by $15 billion, Smith led a revolt on the floor that struck that section from the measure. "I'm afraid of the consequences for the disabled if we do Medicaid reform in a hurry," Smith said. "I'm specifically also concerned about how Medicaid cuts are first made against mental health coverage," he added. "I have a personal interest in making sure we don't shortchange mental health." While he later said he would not torpedo a final budget resolution over the issue, Smith repeatedly made clear that he would use his Senate Finance seat as best he could to protect the joint federal-state health care program for the poor.

Smith is personally opposed to abortion and homosexuality. But he weighs carefully when and how his personal values should shape his policy decisions. "If you want to talk to me about sin, go with me to church," he told the Portland Oregonian. "If you want to talk about public policy, then go with me to the U.S. Senate."

In fact, Smith sometimes seems to go out of his way to promote positions social conservatives find objectionable. He frequently supports gay rights and co-authored legislation with Massachusetts Democrat Edward M. Kennedy to make attacks perpetrated against homosexuals because of their sexual orientation a federal crime. He broke with the anti-abortion movement to support federal funding of stem cell research using embryos discarded by fertility clinics. Smith pointed to the potential for treating deadly genetic diseases, including one that runs in his family, Parkinson's disease. "Everyone will pass away — I know that," he said. "But there are some ways that are just beyond hideousness, and this is one."

However, when Democrats castigated Bush in the 2004 campaign for limiting federal funding for stem cell research to a narrow line of cells many researchers considered flawed, Smith accused Bush's detractors of unfairly denying him credit for allowing at least some research with federal money. And Smith angered usually friendly gay rights groups the same year by voting to allow the Senate to consider a proposed constitutional amendment to ban same-sex marriage. Smith himself supported a less restrictive measure that would allow states to approve gay unions.

Personable, telegenic and noted for eye-catching double-breasted suits that stand out from the more drab traditional Senate garb, Smith is a self-made millionaire who transformed his family's unprofitable frozen vegetable processing company into one of the largest in the country. He's a proud member of the Frozen Food Industry Hall of Fame.

His business background has helped him master often obscure but essential details of tax and business policy. During the writing of a corporate tax bill that passed in late 2004, Smith was the chief champion of giving U.S.-based multinationals like Oregon's own Nike a huge one-time tax break if they invest foreign profits back home. While skeptics feared the incentive to "repatriate" foreign profits amounts to a corporate giveaway, Smith argued the move would create thousands of new American jobs.

Smith became chairman of the Committee on Aging in the 109th Congress, giving him a bigger stage to push a favorite cause opposed by the administration, the reimportation of prescription drugs. Smith is a member of the health insurance task force set up by Majority Leader Bill Frist and is committed to passing legislation to help the uninsured, even though the issue was missing from Bush's list of priorities after the election. Smith also formed an anti-hunger caucus in the Senate in mid-2004.

Smith's bouts of independence continue a political tradition in liberal-leaning Oregon. Voters there sent moderate Republican Sens. Mark Hatfield and Bob Packwood to Washington to give party leaders fits for decades. While Smith can do the same, he does not always bow to the views of his constituents. Torn between representing the will of Oregon voters, who passed a referendum legalizing physician-assisted suicide, and his own belief that human life should not be cut short, Smith announced in 2000 that he would back a bill forbidding doctors to prescribe drugs designed to cause a patient's death.

He earns top marks from business groups and casts frugal votes on fiscal matters. But he has sided with Democrats on gun control and protecting Alaska's Arctic National Wildlife Refuge from oil and gas drilling. On votes pitting one party against the other in the 108th Congress, Smith bucked his party more often than all but seven other Republicans.

Smith entered politics in 1992, winning a state Senate seat and then becoming Senate president in just two years. In a bid to move to the U.S. Senate, he battled veteran Democratic Rep. Ron Wyden in a January 1996 special election to replace Republican Bob Packwood, who had to resign because of personal and financial transgressions. Wyden won after attacking Smith for receiving support from groups opposed to abortion and gay rights, for environmental violations at his food processing plant, and for his lavish personal spending. When Hatfield announced his retirement later that year, Smith initially said he would not run again. But national Republicans urged him into the fray. Easily winning the GOP nod, he managed a 4 percentage point win over Democratic businessman Tom Bruggere. In 2002, Smith beat Oregon Secretary of State Bill Bradbury by more than 16 points.

The bitterness of their 1996 contest faded relatively quickly, and Smith and Wyden now enjoy an especially good working relationship. The two crisscrossed Oregon together after the 1999 impeachment trial of President Clinton — Wyden voted to acquit, Smith to convict — to give their constituents a real-life demonstration of bipartisanship. They make similar trips at the start of each new Congress, and they are bound to team up often in the 109th as the only same-state senators on the Senate Finance Committee. "Our natures are to find solutions, not just confrontations," Smith said. "He simply starts from the left. I start from the right."

KEY VOTES

2004
Yes Pass $318.9 billion, six-year highway and mass transit bill
Yes Extend assault weapons ban for 10 years
No Restore pay-as-you-go rules for new tax cuts and entitlement spending
Yes Criminalize harm to a fetus in an attack on the mother
Yes Increase mandatory child care funding to states by $6 billion over five years
Yes Amend the Constitution to prohibit same-sex marriage
Yes Approve $146 billion multi-year extension of previously enacted middle-class tax breaks
Yes Reorganize U.S. intelligence agencies as proposed by Sept. 11 commission
Yes Cut corporate taxes $137 billion over 10 years

2003
No Delay Bush changes to Clean Air Act
Yes Allow confirmation vote on Miguel A. Estrada to the U.S. Court of Appeals for the D.C. Circuit
Yes Block a Bush proposal opening Alaska's Arctic National Wildlife Refuge to oil drilling
No Limit size of Bush's proposed tax cut to $350 billion through fiscal 2013
Yes Overhaul Medicare and create prescription drug benefit
? Block Bush rule scaling back overtime pay for some white-collar federal workers
No Split $20 billion in Iraq aid into half-grant, half-loan
Yes Ban "partial birth" abortion except to save a woman's life
Yes Stop proposal allowing travel to Cuba
Yes Allow final vote on energy policy overhaul

CQ VOTE STUDIES

	PARTY UNITY		PRESIDENTIAL SUPPORT	
	Support	Oppose	Support	Oppose
2004	89%	11%	94%	6%
2003	92%	8%	97%	3%
2002	66%	34%	91%	9%
2001	82%	18%	93%	7%
2000	89%	11%	62%	38%
1999	86%	14%	43%	57%
1998	85%	15%	55%	45%
1997	83%	17%	65%	35%

INTEREST GROUPS

	AFL-CIO	ADA	CCUS	ACU
2004	33%	40%	100%	76%
2003	0%	20%	86%	78%
2002	38%	35%	85%	75%
2001	44%	25%	79%	80%
2000	0%	10%	100%	84%
1999	11%	15%	94%	76%
1998	0%	5%	94%	72%
1997	0%	25%	100%	72%

Rep. David Wu (D)

CAPITOL OFFICE
225-0855
www.house.gov/wu
1023 Longworth 20515-3701; fax 225-9497

COMMITTEES
Education & Workforce
Science

HOMETOWN
Portland

BORN
April 8, 1955, Hsinchu, Taiwan

RELIGION
Presbyterian

FAMILY
Wife, Michelle Wu; two children

EDUCATION
Stanford U., B.S. 1977; Harvard Medical School, attended 1978; Yale U., J.D. 1982

CAREER
Lawyer

POLITICAL HIGHLIGHTS
No previous office

ELECTION RESULTS

2004 GENERAL

David Wu (D)	203,771	57.5%
Goli Ameri (R)	135,164	38.2%
Dean Wolf (I)	13,882	3.9%

2004 PRIMARY

David Wu (D)	unopposed

2002 GENERAL

David Wu (D)	149,215	62.7%
Jim Greenfield (R)	80,917	34.0%
Beth King (LIBERT)	7,639	3.2%

PREVIOUS WINNING PERCENTAGES
2000 (58%); 1998 (50%)

Elected 1998; 4th term

After the most tumultuous two years of his political career on Capitol Hill and back home, Wu is hoping to return to his accustomed role as a solid lawmaker who operates largely out of the spotlight.

Not usually an attention-getter, Wu had something of a career-defining moment in the House in 2003, when he cast the last vote during the nearly three-hour roll call by which the House passed the final version of the GOP-drafted bill to add a prescription drug benefit to Medicare. Only after Republican leaders had engineered a victory by switching four GOP votes did Wu cast his ballot in favor of the measure. He was one of just 16 Democrats (8 percent of the caucus) who did so, and his vote surprised and angered many of his colleagues and constituents.

It was not the first time — or the last — that Wu crossed party lines. A member of the pro-business centrists known as the New Democrat Coalition, he supported a repeal of the tax code's "marriage penalty" in 2000, and he backed a GOP welfare bill in 2002. In the 108th Congress, he joined fellow moderate Democrat Ron Kind of Wisconsin on the Education and Workforce Committee to support a GOP-backed measure to rewrite rules governing employer-provided retirement plans.

But the Medicare vote was in a class of its own, and House Democratic leaders are not likely to forget it. All the other Democrats who voted for the final bill were from the most conservative edge of the Democratic Caucus; two of them, in fact, subsequently switched affiliation to the GOP. Wu normally sides with the majority of his party, so his defection stung. He had tried for several years to win an assignment to the Appropriations or Energy and Commerce committees, but the 109th found him right where he has always been — on the Education and Workforce and the Science panels.

Wu's troubles back home hit late in the 2004 election campaign, as he was battling his strongest Republican challenger in years. On Oct. 12, three weeks before the Nov. 2 election, the Portland Oregonian published a story saying that as a Stanford University student in 1976, Wu "was brought to the campus police annex after his ex-girlfriend said he tried to force her to have sex." The woman declined criminal prosecution and did not file a formal disciplinary complaint, the newspaper said, quoting school officials. She also declined to talk to the newspaper, citing privacy reasons.

Wu issued an apology the same day. "Twenty-eight years ago, I had a two-year relationship with a fellow college student that ended with inexcusable behavior on my part. As a 21-year-old, I hurt someone I cared very much about. I take full responsibility for my actions, and I am very sorry."

He also said he was "disappointed" that the Portland newspaper "chose to bring up a 28-year-old incident three weeks before an election." The Oregonian had endorsed his opponent four days before it published the story.

Portland area voters apparently viewed the story as a low blow. Wu won re-election comfortably, albeit by a smaller margin than his 2002 victory.

Before the Medicare fight of 2003, the most difficult policy decision Wu had faced occurred in his first term. Born in Taiwan and the first person of full Chinese ancestry to serve in the House, Wu had said during his 1998 campaign that unless human rights abuses abated in China, he would vote against permanently granting that nation the same low tariff rates as most other nations. When the issue came to a vote in 2000, many doubted Wu would stick to that position. After all, he had been elected by just 7,000 votes to represent part of Oregon's "Silicon Forest," which is heavily dependent on the success of Pacific Rim trade, and he had been a partner in a law firm that represented high-technology businesses on issues including trade. In addition, many of the ethnic Chinese who hailed his victory as a great advance for Asian-Americans wanted to see their homeland become a full member of the world trading system.

Though Wu was pushed hard, he stuck by his campaign promise. Not only did he vote against the legislation, but he also helped opponents round up votes for an ultimately unsuccessful effort to defeat it. Wu's decision so angered the computer-chip behemoth Intel Corp. and the athletic shoe giant Nike Inc. that both gave money to his 2000 opponent.

Although Wu served as chairman of the Congressional Asian Pacific Caucus in the 107th and 108th Congresses, he wants to be known for more than his ethnic heritage. In 2001, however, he drew sympathy over his treatment by a security guard at the Department of Energy. Wu was detained for 15 minutes along with an Asian-American colleague, even after he displayed his congressional identification.

Wu arrived in the United States with his mother and sisters in 1961, when he was 7 years old. The family joined Wu's father, who had come to this country to study when Wu was four months old.

Addressing the 2000 Democratic National Convention, Wu said he had become involved in public life because of the difference that government decisions had made to his family. He said his family had been able to move to the United States because President John F. Kennedy had expanded quotas that had been used to limit Chinese immigrants. "Public decisions make a difference," he said. "Elections change the course of nations."

In homage to his adopted homeland, Wu has made a habit of naming those in his household after famous Americans. His son, born on the Fourth of July 1997, is Matthew Jefferson Adams Wu. (He also has a daughter named Sarah.) Family pets have included dogs Sam Rayburn and Teddy Roosevelt and a cat, Lyndon Johnson.

Wu had never held public office when Democrat Elizabeth Furse's retirement opened up a House seat in 1998. He was well-known in the Portland legal and business community and was able to edge past Washington County Commission Chairman Linda Peters in the Democratic primary. In the general election, the district's Democratic leanings lifted Wu to a 3 percentage point victory over public relations consultant Molly Bordonaro. His 2004 opponent, Iranian immigrant and local businesswoman Goli Ameri, put up a tough fight, but he pulled through, winning with 57 percent of the vote.

KEY VOTES

2004
Yes Extend federal unemployment benefits by 13 weeks

Yes Pass $283.2 billion, six-year federal highway and mass transit bill

Yes Approve $146 billion multi-year extension of previously enacted middle-class tax breaks

No Amend the Constitution to prohibit same-sex marriage

Yes Cut corporate taxes $137 billion over 10 years

Yes Reorganize U.S. intelligence agencies as proposed by Sept. 11 commission

2003
No Cut taxes by $330 billion through fiscal 2013

Yes Block Bush rule scaling back overtime pay for some white-collar federal workers

Yes Do not allow use of search warrants without first notifying subjects

Yes Allow importation of prescription drugs

No Create private school voucher program in Washington, D.C.

No Ban "partial birth" abortion except to save a woman's life

Yes Split $18.6 billion in Iraq aid into half-grant, half-loan

Yes Overhaul Medicare and create prescription drug benefit

CQ VOTE STUDIES

	PARTY UNITY		PRESIDENTIAL SUPPORT	
	Support	Oppose	Support	Oppose
2004	90%	10%	38%	62%
2003	90%	10%	33%	67%
2002	88%	12%	42%	58%
2001	81%	19%	30%	70%
2000	83%	17%	67%	33%

INTEREST GROUPS

	AFL-CIO	ADA	CCUS	ACU
2004	87%	90%	55%	12%
2003	80%	90%	37%	16%
2002	89%	95%	45%	16%
2001	92%	100%	30%	8%
2000	90%	90%	52%	20%

OREGON 1
Western Portland and suburbs; Beaverton

Nestled on the western bank of the Willamette River, Portland's "Silicon Forest" hums with new companies assembling computer chips. Californians and other migrants have come to Portland in droves, looking for an urban economy with a leisurely lifestyle.

Many of the most affluent transplants have settled in the city, while others are filling up fast-growing suburbs in Washington and Yamhill counties. Aided by a western light rail that stretches to Hillsboro, towns that were once bedroom communities have turned into satellite cities with their own streams of commuters. The populations of Hillsboro, Beaverton and suburbs farther west exploded in the 1990s.

Outside the Portland metro area, the 1st is struggling to keep its traditional industries intact. A highly public battle between loggers and environmentalists over the fate of the spotted owl dampened forestry. Salmon stocks are dwindling because of excessive harvests and hydroelectric dams. State officials are working to transition workers in both fields to emerging industries in the area.

Electronics, vineyards and nurseries now lead the 1st's economy, and tourism and the remnants of the timber industry round out much of the job market. With a number of large businesses in the district, international trade is a hot issue.

Redistricting following the 2000 census removed the 1st's share of Clackamas County and reduced its share of Multnomah County (Portland). Washington County, which accounts for 65 percent of the population, epitomizes the 1st's competitiveness — John Kerry won the county with 52 percent of the vote in the 2004 presidential election. Democrats do well in Multnomah and in the far northern counties of Clatsop and Columbia, while the GOP has the edge in Yamhill.

MAJOR INDUSTRY
Electronics, computer manufacturing, wine production, nurseries

CITIES
Beaverton, 76,129; Portland (pt.), 74,097; Hillsboro, 70,186; Aloha (unincorporated), 41,741; Tigard, 41,223

NOTABLE
Nike Inc. is headquartered in Beaverton; The Lewis and Clark expedition set up a winter camp in 1805-06 in what is now the Fort Clatsop National Memorial, near Astoria.

Rep. Greg Walden (R)

Elected 1998; 4th term

Walden has developed a knack for building bipartisan support on issues vital to his rural and forest-rich district, and he used those skills in the 108th Congress to score the biggest victory of his House career: enactment of the 2003 "healthy forests" law, which reversed decades of environmental policy and authorized logging and other steps to thin forests on public lands to reduce wild fires, an enormous concern throughout the West.

The measure had been stymied for three years by opposition from environmentalists, but Walden and Republican Scott McInnis of Colorado worked with others on the Resources Committee to draw in Democrats from timber states in the East by addressing bug infestations and other concerns. Then Walden teamed with Ron Wyden of Oregon, his Democratic colleague in the Senate, to push the bill to enactment.

"In recent years, the effort to improve the management of America's forests has become a truly national movement," Walden said after passage of the bill. "From Southern forests infested with ravenous insects and Midwestern tree stands sickened by disease to the overstocked Western forests that go up in smoke every year, there are few parts of the country unaffected by the mismanagement of our forests."

Walden will monitor the new law and pursue follow-up measures as the chairman of the Resources Subcommittee on Forests and Forest Health, a post he was awarded less than four months after passage of the forest bill. One objective, which he is working on with Wyden, is creation of a forest research center in Prineville, Ore., in the Ochoco National Forest.

Walden and many of his constituents have long bridled at tight federal regulation; the government owns more than half of the land in the 2nd District, which includes at least part of 10 national forests. Walden has called the area he represents "a district under siege by federal policies."

Walden has repeatedly pushed legislation to require reviews by outside scientists before the government makes decisions about endangered animals and plants, and to encourage federal agencies to consider input from affected landowners before adding new species to those protected by the Endangered Species Act. He has high hopes that the more conservative 109th will finally provide the backing he needs at act on these concerns.

During the 108th, Walden aggressively attacked one relatively new scourge threatening small towns in Oregon and elsewhere around the nation — methamphetamine. He said that in 2004 his district had 20 percent of Oregon's population but 35 percent of meth lab seizures. He won $250,000 to tackle the manufacturing, sale and use of meth in the state in fiscal 2005. Just two months into the 109th, he had cosponsored three meth-related bills and held more than a half-dozen town hall meetings on the issue across the 2nd District. He also is pushing the Food and Drug Administration to urge drug companies to find substitutes for cold remedies that currently contain ingredients for methamphetamine.

On Energy and Commerce, Walden has been a strong defender of the Bonneville Power Administration, which manages hydroelectric power in the Northwest. He is helping lead a bipartisan push by the Washington and Oregon delegations to reject proposals by President Bush to charge market rates for its electricity instead of just breaking even. That would mean extra cash for the Treasury but higher rates for customers.

Walden is also suspicious of GOP-driven efforts to require broadcasters to give up their analog spectrum and switch to digital television by a fixed

CAPITOL OFFICE
225-6730
www.walden.house.gov
1210 Longworth 20515-3702; fax 225-5774

COMMITTEES
Energy & Commerce
Resources
 (Forests & Forest Health - chairman)

HOMETOWN
Hood River

BORN
Jan. 10, 1957, The Dalles, Ore.

RELIGION
Episcopalian

FAMILY
Wife, Mylene Walden; two children (one deceased)

EDUCATION
U. of Alaska, Fairbanks, attended 1974-75; U. of Oregon, B.S. 1981 (journalism)

CAREER
Radio station owner; congressional aide

POLITICAL HIGHLIGHTS
Ore. House, 1989-95 (majority leader, 1991-93); Ore. Senate, 1995-97 (assistant majority leader, 1995-97)

ELECTION RESULTS

2004 GENERAL

Greg Walden (R)	248,461	71.6%
John C. McColgan (D)	88,914	25.6%
Jim Lindsay (LIBERT)	4,792	1.4%
Jack Alan Brown (I)	4,060	1.2%

2004 PRIMARY

Greg Walden (R)	unopposed

2002 GENERAL

Greg Walden (R)	181,295	71.9%
Peter Buckley (D)	64,991	25.8%
Mike Wood (LIBERT)	5,681	2.3%

PREVIOUS WINNING PERCENTAGES
2000 (74%); 1998 (61%)

date, largely because many consumers would be forced to buy new television sets to receive digital signals. "If we drop the hammer on consumers, the sledgehammer is going to come back and hit us," Walden warned.

Although agriculture dominates the economy of the 2nd, the area also is becoming a magnet for windsurfing and snowboarding tourists. Walden himself enjoys downhill skiing at Mount Hood and sailing on the Columbia River. He co-chairs the House's Renewable Energy Caucus, which advocates use of wind, solar and geothermal power.

Like most House Republicans, Walden is a steadfast opponent of new gun controls, but he has adopted a middle-ground position on abortion. He opposes federal funding for abortions and voted to outlaw a procedure its opponents call "partial birth" abortion. But he does not support a repeal of the Supreme Court's *Roe v. Wade* decision establishing the right to abortion, saying the decision to have an abortion should be left to individuals. He says his views on that question were shaped after 1993, when he and his wife, Mylene, considered but rejected aborting a fetus diagnosed with a congenital heart defect. The baby boy was born prematurely and died.

Reared on a cherry orchard, Walden as a youth earned the rank of Eagle Scout and worked at his father's radio station in Hood River. He developed his own broadcast voice as a disc jockey and talk-show host, and later bought the business with his wife. Their company, Columbia Gorge Broadcasters Inc., now operates five popular music and news radio stations. He also worked in television while going to school in Alaska.

Walden got his introduction to politics in the early 1980s as an aide to former GOP Rep. Denny Smith of Oregon, a political maverick. But his own low-key, consensus-seeking style was honed during eight years in the state legislature, including three years as House majority leader and two as assistant Senate majority leader. In temperament, he more closely resembles another Republican from Oregon named Smith: his predecessor, Bob Smith.

Walden threatened to run for the House as an independent in 1996 against Republican Rep. Wes Cooley, who had been accused of lying about his military record in a voter pamphlet after winning the GOP primary two years before. But Bob Smith was lured out of retirement with the promise of the Agriculture Committee chairmanship. When he agreed to run, both Walden and Cooley bowed out.

Smith decided to retire once again in 1998, and Walden became the frontrunner. He breezed to victory in the GOP primary and easily defeated Democrat Kevin M. Campbell, a former county judge, in the heavily Republican district. He has romped to re-election since then.

KEY VOTES

2004

Yes Extend federal unemployment benefits by 13 weeks

Yes Pass $283.2 billion, six-year federal highway and mass transit bill

Yes Approve $146 billion multi-year extension of previously enacted middle-class tax breaks

Yes Amend the Constitution to prohibit same-sex marriage

Yes Cut corporate taxes $137 billion over 10 years

Yes Reorganize U.S. intelligence agencies as proposed by Sept. 11 commission

2003

Yes Cut taxes by $330 billion through fiscal 2013

No Block Bush rule scaling back overtime pay for some white-collar federal workers

Yes Do not allow use of search warrants without first notifying subjects

No Allow importation of prescription drugs

Yes Create private school voucher program in Washington, D.C.

Yes Ban "partial birth" abortion except to save a woman's life

No Split $18.6 billion in Iraq aid into half-grant, half-loan

Yes Overhaul Medicare and create prescription drug benefit

CQ VOTE STUDIES

	PARTY UNITY		PRESIDENTIAL SUPPORT	
	Support	Oppose	Support	Oppose
2004	93%	7%	82%	18%
2003	92%	8%	94%	6%
2002	95%	5%	90%	10%
2001	97%	3%	91%	9%
2000	96%	4%	25%	75%

INTEREST GROUPS

	AFL-CIO	ADA	CCUS	ACU
2004	27%	15%	100%	80%
2003	13%	15%	96%	76%
2002	11%	5%	100%	96%
2001	17%	10%	100%	84%
2000	20%	5%	90%	88%

OREGON 2

East and Southwest — Medford, Bend

The 2nd covers the eastern two-thirds of Oregon, bordering Washington, Idaho, Nevada and California. Most of the land is owned by the federal government, causing considerable strife with the district's residents, who depend on fishing, farming and logging to make a living.

The 2nd lost timber jobs when the spotted owl was deemed an endangered species and its Oregon forest habitat was protected from clear-cutting. Those jobs have been difficult to replace in a district with few urban areas. Farmers produce fruit, wheat and hay in the plateaus and river valleys, but cattle farmers have seen their access to public grazing lands limited. At the same time, the Columbia River's fishing industry has faced restrictions on salmon under the Endangered Species Act. Fishers, farmers and environmentalists have staged high-profile battles over how federal regulators should allocate the Klamath River's water. Shortages led to the loss of crops and thousands of salmon.

During the 1980s, economic difficulties drove enough people from the district that it declined in population, but numbers rebounded in the 1990s as retired couples moved to the area.

Medford, in Jackson County, is the largest city in the 2nd. It is surrounded by pear, cherry and apple orchards in the Rogue River Valley. Less than 20 miles southeast of Medford is Ashland, which has played host to the Oregon Shakespeare Festival since 1935.

Hostility toward the federal government makes the 2nd Oregon's most reliably Republican district. In the 2004 presidential election, George W. Bush won 19 of the 20 counties wholly or partly within the 2nd — Hood River County was the exception. Democrats are scattered through parts of Ashland and Bend, but they are too few to swing the district. Overall, Bush took 61 percent of the district's vote in 2004.

MAJOR INDUSTRY
Agriculture, forestry, tourism

CITIES
Medford, 63,154; Bend, 52,029; Grants Pass, 23,003; Altamont (unincorporated), 19,603; Ashland, 19,522; Klamath Falls, 19,462

NOTABLE
Crater Lake National Park, designated in 1902, is in Klamath County; The Warm Springs Indian Reservation is in the northwest part of the district.

Rep. Earl Blumenauer (D)

Elected May 1996; 5th full term

With concerns over urban sprawl taking a more prominent spot on the national agenda, Blumenauer has sought out bipartisan opportunities to advance his progressive agenda emphasizing community livability and "smart growth."

A native of Portland, a city known for its carefully planned land-use policies, Blumenauer (BLUE-men-hour) pursues his goals in a variety of ways: by retooling federal flood insurance regulations to affect housing patterns, urging the Postal Service to keep open older facilities that have become downtown gathering spots, proposing expanded transit benefits for federal employees and new benefits for bicycle commuters, and by lobbying from his Transportation Committee seat to spend billions on bicycle trails, historic preservation, community enhancement and mass transit systems.

Visiting Honolulu in 2004 when a multimillion-dollar light-rail system was under consideration, Blumenauer advised a balanced approach. "You can't just declare war on the auto and expect to offer a new transportation project in its place and to be successful," he told the Honolulu Advertiser. "Everything's got to be done in coordination with land-use planning."

Using federal money that Blumenauer secured for the project, Portland in 2004 opened its 5.8-mile Interstate Max light-rail line extension, which runs between downtown and the Columbia River. "We have been proud to be leaders in understanding the connection between land use and transportation," Blumenauer said. "Our light-rail system has not only provided additional choices to our residents, it has also helped with environmental problems."

An avid runner and cyclist, Blumenauer has won admiring profiles in USA Today and other publications for his refusal to own a car in Washington. He bikes to his Capitol Hill office from his nearby apartment and cycles to meetings at the White House. A bow tie is his sartorial signature.

While his agenda has not always been well-received by Republicans wary of proposals that may resemble 1960s-style "social engineering," Blumenauer says those proposals can place more power in the hands of state and local governments — an argument that dovetails with the GOP intermittent desire to shift more decision-making away from Washington. He also casts his ideas in a nonpartisan light. "Local officials dealing with police and parks and people's back yards can't afford to be gratuitously partisan," he says.

In the 108th Congress, Blumenauer saw years of bipartisan persistence pay off as President Bush signed his "Two Floods and You're Out" legislation into law. The measure aims to discourage homeowners from rebuilding in flood-ravaged areas, which can result in repeated claims on the government flood insurance program. Since the 106th Congress, Blumenauer had worked with Nebraska Republican Doug Bereuter, now retired, to move the legislation. "This is one issue where the fiscal conservatives can join with the environmental protection folks," Blumenauer said.

Also in the 108th Congress, when the Transportation and Infrastructure Committee wrote legislation to reauthorize the nation's surface transportation programs, Blumenauer sought to ensure that all of the legislation's inevitably competing interests were satisfied. "I have been in Congress for two authorizations," he said, "and some of the strongest support has been from groups and organizations . . . that are in sympathy with the environmental community. This is a lesson that everybody has learned, that they don't want to take on the gardening club, the bicyclists and the historic preservationists. This should not be a zero-sum game."

CAPITOL OFFICE
225-4811
blumenauer.house.gov
2446 Rayburn 20515-3703; fax 225-8941

COMMITTEES
International Relations
Transportation & Infrastructure

HOMETOWN
Portland

BORN
Aug. 16, 1948, Portland, Ore.

RELIGION
Unspecified

FAMILY
Wife, Margaret Kirkpatrick; two children

EDUCATION
Lewis and Clark College, B.A. 1970 (political science), J.D. 1976

CAREER
Public official

POLITICAL HIGHLIGHTS
Ore. House, 1973-77; Multnomah County Commission, 1978-86; candidate for Portland City Council, 1980; Portland City Council, 1986-96; candidate for mayor of Portland, 1992

ELECTION RESULTS

2004 GENERAL

Earl Blumenauer (D)	245,559	70.9%
Tami Mars (R)	82,045	23.7%
Walter F. "Walt" Brown (S)	10,678	3.1%
Dale Winegarden (I)	7,119	2.1%

2004 PRIMARY

Earl Blumenauer (D)	76,811	89.0%
John Sweeney (D)	9,207	10.7%

2002 GENERAL

Earl Blumenauer (D)	156,851	66.8%
Sarah Seale (R)	62,821	26.7%
Walter F. "Walt" Brown (S)	6,588	2.8%
Kevin Jones (LIBERT)	4,704	2.0%
David Brownlow (CNSTP)	3,495	1.5%

PREVIOUS WINNING PERCENTAGES
2000 (67%); 1998 (84%); 1996 (67%); 1996 Special Election (70%)

In keeping with the sentiment of his constituents, Blumenauer consistently votes to protect the environment, boost federal funding for the arts and support abortion rights.

He also voted against the Iraq war, and in remarks at the World Affairs Council in Portland, Ore., just weeks after the 2002 vote, he proved painfully prescient. "It is important to realize that there could be something worse than Saddam Hussein," he warned. "Outbreaks of violence, recrimination and revenge within Iraq could unleash a chain of events which would make Iraq's neighbors and the United States long for the relative stability of the last 15 years." Now, he says, "I have never felt so bad about being right about something."

The Oregonian broke with many in his party, as well as organized labor, to support enactment of the 2000 law making permanent normal U.S. trade relations with China. He noted at the time that one in five jobs in his district was tied to trade with the Pacific Rim. But on the next marquee trade vote, in 2002, he opposed the revival of fast-track trade negotiating authority for the president. The 108th Congress saw him back on the other side, helping to round up House votes for a free-trade agreement with Chile, and eventually coming to support reduced tariffs with Singapore, despite initial fears over the erosion of labor protections.

An activist since his teens, Blumenauer was just one year out of college in 1971 when he testified before Congress in support of a constitutional amendment to lower the voting age to 18. Elected to the state House at 24, in four years he rose to chair the Revenue Committee. He then spent eight years on the Multnomah County Commission, followed by a decade on the Portland City Council. In those jobs, he was instrumental in establishing the ambitious and much-praised land-use planning procedures Portland uses to control metropolitan sprawl.

Despite some political stumbles — he failed in a 1980 city council bid and ran unsuccessfully for mayor of Portland in 1992 — his widespread name recognition and appeal put him in a good position to win election to the House in a 1996 special election. The 3rd District seat was vacant after Democrat Ron Wyden won a special Senate election that January to replace Republican Bob Packwood, who had resigned the previous fall rather than face expulsion for sexual harassment and personal misconduct. Blumenauer swamped two opponents in the Democratic primary and — bolstered by the endorsement of Republican Sen. Mark O. Hatfield — cruised past the GOP nominee as well. He has won re-election with ease ever since, carrying 71 percent of the vote in 2004.

KEY VOTES

2004

Yes Extend federal unemployment benefits by 13 weeks

Yes Pass $283.2 billion, six-year federal highway and mass transit bill

No Approve $146 billion multi-year extension of previously enacted middle-class tax breaks

No Amend the Constitution to prohibit same-sex marriage

No Cut corporate taxes $137 billion over 10 years

Yes Reorganize U.S. intelligence agencies as proposed by Sept. 11 commission

2003

No Cut taxes by $330 billion through fiscal 2013

Yes Block Bush rule scaling back overtime pay for some white-collar federal workers

Yes Do not allow use of search warrants without first notifying subjects

Yes Allow importation of prescription drugs

No Create private school voucher program in Washington, D.C.

No Ban "partial birth" abortion except to save a woman's life

Yes Split $18.6 billion in Iraq aid into half-grant, half-loan

No Overhaul Medicare and create prescription drug benefit

CQ VOTE STUDIES

| | PARTY UNITY | | PRESIDENTIAL SUPPORT | |
	Support	Oppose	Support	Oppose
2004	93%	7%	23%	77%
2003	95%	5%	20%	80%
2002	96%	4%	25%	75%
2001	89%	11%	19%	81%
2000	93%	7%	88%	12%

INTEREST GROUPS

	AFL-CIO	ADA	CCUS	ACU
2004	93%	95%	26%	9%
2003	87%	100%	27%	16%
2002	100%	100%	35%	4%
2001	91%	90%	30%	0%
2000	90%	90%	42%	0%

OREGON 3

North and east Portland; eastern suburbs

Split by the Willamette River, the city of Portland has two personalities. The eastern portion, covered by the 3rd, still depends on the blue-collar economy that made the city a thriving international port for lumber and fruit. The Port of Portland and Portland International Airport make the city a leading center of trade and distribution. Computer chips and cappuccino drive the city's western side (in the 1st and 5th districts).

Compared with the rest of Portland, the 3rd is a multicultural haven. There is a large African-American population in precincts just east of the Willamette River, near Interstate 5 and Martin Luther King Jr. Blvd., where Democrats regularly win more than 80 percent of the vote in competitive statewide elections. A sizable Hispanic population resides in northeastern Portland and in Gresham and Wood Village east of the city. Asians are numerous in east-central Portland, near 82nd Avenue and Interstate 205.

The 3rd's second-largest city, Gresham, was once a thriving farm community. It is now the easternmost stop on Portland's light-rail system

and is growing rapidly. Beyond the Portland metropolitan area, the district quickly turns rural. Mount Hood National Forest covers the far eastern part of the district.

Portland's liberal leanings make the 3rd Oregon's most staunchly Democratic district. John Kerry won 71 percent of the 3rd's share of Multnomah County in the 2004 presidential election, while he took only 51 percent of the vote statewide. Redistricting following the 2000 census gave the 3rd a larger share of Clackamas County, which is more rural and politically competitive. George W. Bush narrowly won the district's portion of Clackamas with 50 percent of the 2004 presidential vote. But any Republican strength there is not large enough to weaken Portland's strong Democratic slant.

MAJOR INDUSTRY
Wholesale trade and distribution, health care, education

CITIES
Portland (pt.), 432,388; Gresham, 90,205; Milwaukie, 20,490

NOTABLE
Forest Park is the nation's largest natural forested park within a city's limits; Mount Hood, on the district's eastern border, is Oregon's highest peak at 11,239 feet.

Rep. Peter A. DeFazio (D)

Elected 1986; 10th term

CAPITOL OFFICE
225-6416
www.house.gov/defazio
2134 Rayburn 20515-3704; fax 225-0032

COMMITTEES
Homeland Security
Resources
Transportation & Infrastrucure

HOMETOWN
Springfield

BORN
May 27, 1947, Needham, Mass.

RELIGION
Roman Catholic

FAMILY
Wife, Myrnie L. Daut

EDUCATION
Tufts U., B.A. 1969 (economics & political science);
U. of Oregon, attended 1969-71 (international
studies), M.S. 1977 (public administration &
gerontology)

MILITARY SERVICE
Air Force, 1967-71

CAREER
Congressional aide

POLITICAL HIGHLIGHTS
Lane County Commission, 1982-86; sought
Democratic nomination for U.S. Senate (special
election), 1996

ELECTION RESULTS

2004 GENERAL

Peter A. DeFazio (D)	228,611	61.0%
Jim Feldkamp (R)	140,882	37.6%

2004 PRIMARY

Peter A. DeFazio (D)	unopposed

2002 GENERAL

Peter A. DeFazio (D)	168,150	63.8%
Liz VanLeeuwen (R)	90,523	34.4%
Chris Bigelow (LIBERT)	4,602	1.8%

PREVIOUS WINNING PERCENTAGES
2000 (68%); 1998 (70%); 1996 (66%); 1994 (67%);
1992 (71%); 1990 (86%); 1988 (72%); 1986 (54%)

In this polarized, partisan era, DeFazio is a bit of an oddity. One of the most liberal Democrats in Congress, he is easily re-elected year after year from a district that twice this decade split its presidential vote evenly between the two parties. He loves to taunt Republicans in Congress and to spotlight the political makeup of his rural district as he argues that President Bush and the GOP are out of step with voters.

Early in the 109th Congress, when the president was promoting his plan to allow private investment accounts within Social Security, DeFazio held eight town hall meetings on the subject. After noting the strong vote Bush had drawn in his district in 2000 and 2004, he said, "I've had a handful of people come in and say 'I'm with the president on this proposal, I think its great.' I can count them on one hand. I've seen 1,500 people in a couple of weeks."

DeFazio (da-FAH-zee-o) has pushed a liberal, populist agenda since the day he arrived in Congress in 1987. He is loud, persistent and viewed by his critics as a smart aleck — characteristics that earned him a reputation as "long on straight talk and short on political rhetoric," according to an editorial in The World newspaper of Coos Bay.

A leader in the Progressive Caucus, a group of about 55 of the most liberal House members, DeFazio enhances his image by driving a 1964 Dodge Dart around Oregon and wearing jeans and khakis as he meets with constituents. He seems to connect not only with the liberals in the urban part of his district but also with more-conservative voters in the 4th's rural reaches. He hasn't polled under 60 percent since his first race.

DeFazio often faces a tough juggling act on forest and resource management questions. His constituency includes two groups with strongly conflicting interests on those issues — loggers, who oppose curbs on timber cutting, and environmentalists who want restrictions. The competing pressures were evident in 2003, when DeFazio first opposed a sweeping forest-thinning bill championed by Republican Greg Walden of Oregon, and then voted to enact the final version after it had been significantly altered in the Senate at the insistence of Oregon Democrat Ron Wyden, among others.

DeFazio is a senior Democrat on the Transportation and Infrastructure Committee, which moved a six-year highway and transit reauthorization bill through the House in both the 108th and 109th Congresses. He gave up his top-ranking spot on the Aviation Subcommittee to be the top Democrat on the Highways and Transit Subcommittee in the 109th. He helped write the latest version of the highway bill, which he calls "perhaps the most important piece of legislation in this Congress."

After the Sept. 11, 2001, terrorist attacks, he led the House Democrats' campaign against GOP efforts to retain private contract workers as airport screeners. The aviation security law ultimately enacted not only federalized the baggage screeners but also made a number of other security changes that DeFazio had been urging for years. In 2004, DeFazio forced the Transportation Security Administration to further tighten security by forcing all airline workers and contractors to go through security checkpoints.

With a district that depends heavily on timber and fishing, DeFazio sought a seat on the Resources Committee in the 109th. He also managed to keep a spot on the newly enhanced Homeland Security Committee, which is an additional platform for him to oversee aviation security. DeFazio teams up with Walden, a subcommittee chairman on Resources, to protect Oregon interests on public lands issues. They represent most of the state outside of the populated northwest corner and, even though Walden is the sole Republican in the House delegation, they work well together. DeFazio and Walden teamed up with the rest of the delegation in the 109th to combat efforts by the Bush administration to force the federally owned BonnevillePower Administration, headquartered in Portland, to charge higher rates for its electricity as a deficit-trimming step. Walden did not campaign against DeFazio in 2004, although he did, at the behest of his leadership, help raise money for the GOP candidate.

DeFazio is an ardent advocate for Oregon National Guard troops called up to serve in Iraq. After hearing disturbing stories about the housing conditions and shortages of supplies at Fort Hood in Texas, where many Oregon units trained before going to Iraq, DeFazio and Democrat Darlene Hooley of the 5th District visited the base. They found health-threatening molds in barracks, unreliable food service and supply shortages so severe troops were using their own money to buy radios, computers and cleaning supplies.

"The attitude that the National Guard is inferior to the regular Army and can make do with second-rate equipment has to change. . . . They serve in the same hostile environments and must have the training, equipment, and support they need to accomplish their mission and return home safe and sound," DeFazio and Hooley wrote in a December 2003 letter to Defense Secretary Donald H. Rumsfeld. DeFazio said most of the problems were remedied quickly after their trip.

DeFazio grew up in Massachusetts and his first taste of politics came as a youth at the knee of his great-uncle, a classic Boston pol who followed the word Republican with the Boston-accented epithet "bastuhd" so often that it sounded like one word to the young DeFazio.

DeFazio first moved to Oregon to attend the University of Oregon, where, as a student, he established a seniors employment program that is still in existence today. After earning a graduate degree in gerontology, he went to work for Democratic Rep. James Weaver, a hot-tempered populist. He then struck out on his own, winning election to the Lane County Commission in 1982 and earning a reputation for aggressiveness by suing to nullify contracts between Oregon utilities and the Washington Public Power Supply System, whose failed nuclear projects had resulted in utility rate increases.

When Weaver announced he would not seek re-election in 1986, DeFazio stepped in. Portraying himself as heir to Weaver's populist mantle, he narrowly prevailed in the primary, won the seat with 54 percent of the vote and has held it safely since. He made a special-election primary bid for the Senate in 1995 but lost out to Wyden.

KEY VOTES

2004

Yes	Extend federal unemployment benefits by 13 weeks
Yes	Pass $283.2 billion, six-year federal highway and mass transit bill
Yes	Approve $146 billion multi-year extension of previously enacted middle-class tax breaks
No	Amend the Constitution to prohibit same-sex marriage
No	Cut corporate taxes $137 billion over 10 years
Yes	Reorganize U.S. intelligence agencies as proposed by Sept. 11 commission

2003

No	Cut taxes by $330 billion through fiscal 2013
Yes	Block Bush rule scaling back overtime pay for some white-collar federal workers
Yes	Do not allow use of search warrants without first notifying subjects
Yes	Allow importation of prescription drugs
No	Create private school voucher program in Washington, D.C.
No	Ban "partial birth" abortion except to save a woman's life
Yes	Split $18.6 billion in Iraq aid into half-grant, half-loan
No	Overhaul Medicare and create prescription drug benefit

CQ VOTE STUDIES

	PARTY UNITY		PRESIDENTIAL SUPPORT	
	Support	Oppose	Support	Oppose
2004	90%	10%	27%	73%
2003	94%	6%	17%	83%
2002	94%	6%	24%	76%
2001	96%	4%	19%	81%
2000	86%	14%	67%	33%

INTEREST GROUPS

	AFL-CIO	ADA	CCUS	ACU
2004	100%	95%	43%	16%
2003	100%	100%	14%	25%
2002	100%	95%	30%	12%
2001	100%	100%	25%	16%
2000	100%	90%	25%	8%

OREGON 4

Southwest — Eugene, Springfield, part of Corvallis

Loggers, fishermen and environmentalists combine to give the 4th a potentially combustible political mix. In the early 1990s, the district was a prime battleground in the fight between lumber mills and environmental groups over the fate of the spotted owl. But after the courts and the Clinton administration turned against the lumber industry, the furor quieted down. Possible forest policy revisions in the Bush administration's second term may reignite the controversy.

Fishing, another economic mainstay here, also has dwindled. Many commercial fishermen, in towns such as Charleston, Bandon and Port Orford, are looking for a way out, having been harmed by frequent run closings, short seasons and low prices. While this rural region's unemployment has decreased, it is still higher than average, which may explain why the 4th experienced the slowest population growth of any Oregon district in the 1990s. The district increasingly has looked to tourists and expanding retirement communities to aid its economy.

Eugene and Springfield, the district's most populous cities, have fared

better. Research at the University of Oregon in Eugene, still a hotbed of environmentalism, has lured technology companies. Computer manufacturers, software developers, retailers and the service industry now drive this area's economy.

The electoral success of liberal Rep. DeFazio belies the 4th's political competitiveness. Eugene and Springfield make Lane County reliably Democratic. Linn and Douglas counties vote solidly Republican, and Coos and Curry counties, which once had a strong union tradition, now lean Republican as a result of upper-middle-class retirees flocking from outside the state. Twenty-seven percent of Curry's residents are 65 or older, the highest percentage in the state. Redistricting following the 2000 census made minimal changes to the 4th, adding more of Benton County in the north and more of Josephine County in the south.

MAJOR INDUSTRY
Forestry, agriculture, fishing, technology, tourism

CITIES
Eugene, 137,893; Springfield, 52,864; Albany (pt.), 36,950; Corvallis (pt.), 32,076; Roseburg, 20,017; Coos Bay, 15,374

NOTABLE
Much of the movie "Stand by Me" was filmed in Lane County.

Rep. Darlene Hooley (D)

Elected 1996; 5th term

CAPITOL OFFICE
225-5711
www.house.gov/hooley
2430 Rayburn 20515-3705; fax 225-5699

COMMITTEES
Financial Services
Science
Veterans' Affairs

HOMETOWN
West Linn

BORN
April 4, 1939, Williston, N.D.

RELIGION
Lutheran

FAMILY
Divorced; two children

EDUCATION
Pasadena Nazarene College, attended 1957-59
(psychology); Oregon State U., B.S. 1961
(education)

CAREER
Teacher

POLITICAL HIGHLIGHTS
West Linn City Council, 1977-81; Ore. House,
1981-87; Clackamas County Commission, 1987-97

ELECTION RESULTS

2004 GENERAL

Darlene Hooley (D)	184,833	52.9%
Jim Zupancic (R)	154,993	44.3%
Jerry Defoe (LIBERT)	6,463	1.9%

2004 PRIMARY

Darlene Hooley (D)	59,407	85.1%
Andrew Kaza (D)	10,027	14.4%

2002 GENERAL

Darlene Hooley (D)	137,713	54.8%
Brian Boquist (R)	113,441	45.1%

PREVIOUS WINNING PERCENTAGES
2000 (57%); 1998 (55%); 1996 (51%)

Hooley isn't the kind of lawmaker who seeks out the spotlight for herself. She doesn't work on the high-profile issues, and to the extent that she draws attention at the Capitol, it's because of her habit of running around in business suits and sneakers — a fashion choice some of her colleagues wish they could emulate. But she has earned a reputation as a pragmatic, conciliatory lawmaker who is more skilled than many Democrats at working with the majority Republicans to get bills passed.

A member of the Financial Services Committee, Hooley got several identity theft provisions signed into law in 2003 by working with Republican Spencer Bachus of Alabama. He added her proposals to a bill he sponsored that prevents states from regulating the way financial services companies use consumers' information. Hooley said her identify theft measures — which include federal medical privacy protections and a right for all consumers to see free copies of their credit reports once a year — were needed not just to protect consumers, but also to prevent terrorists from getting fake identifications by stealing Americans' identities.

Liberal-to-moderate on most issues, she is more interested in getting bills passed than in ideological purity. She attributes her narrow 1996 election to the House to her bipartisan style. "I think that's what people are looking for," she said. In the 108th Congress, she sided with her party on 89 percent of the votes that pitted a majority of Republicans against a majority of Democrats — a score that may sound high, but was actually in the lowest third of House Democrats.

Hooley is a member of the centrist New Democrat Coalition and has a fairly strong record of voting for tax reduction and free-trade initiatives. She supported President Bush's $1.35 trillion tax cut in 2001 and voted for corporate tax cuts and extensions of existing tax breaks in 2004. But she opposed Bush's $330 billion tax cut in 2003, saying it would not benefit a broad segment of the population.

The same year, though, Hooley was one of 41 Democrats who voted to repeal the estate tax permanently, and in 2004 she supported a measure to get rid of the "marriage penalty," which forced some married couples to pay higher taxes than they would if they were single. Both taxes were repealed during Bush's first term, but only through 2010. The marriage penalty repeal split Democrats about evenly, but Hooley called it "common-sense tax relief." Her very first bill as a House member was a joint effort with Republican John Cooksey of Louisiana that reduced estate taxes on family-owned small businesses and farms.

She takes more-liberal stands on other domestic issues. Like most Democrats, Hooley voted against the 2003 Medicare prescription drug bill, which was written mostly by Republicans. She opposed a constitutional amendment to ban same-sex marriage, a ban on a procedure opponents call "partial birth" abortion, and Republican measures to revamp the Head Start program and to create a school voucher program in the District of Columbia.

Her interests in Congress include many of the issues she worked on during two decades in state and local government, most notably education. Hooley has proposed increasing funding for the No Child Left Behind education law and wants to boost special education spending so the federal government picks up 40 percent of the costs. With many other Democrats, she opposes vouchers for private school tuition, contending that the government instead should focus on improving public schools.

Hooley also takes a close interest in the treatment of military personnel and their families, a necessity in a district where a high percentage of National Guard soldiers are serving in Iraq. In March 2005, House Republicans rejected her efforts to add $1.3 billion in veterans' health care funding to a supplemental spending bill, and the House voted down her measure that would have added $100 million for military health care and $50 million for job training assistance.

On the environment, Hooley opposes GOP-led attempts to reduce clean air and clean water regulations. But she also has to be politically attuned to her district's economic reliance on logging, agriculture and fishing. Hooley contends that the federal government should set standards but not dictate the ways in which local governments and industry comply.

During debate on the farm bill in 2002, Hooley helped win a significant victory for Oregon fruit and produce farmers. Along with Republican Mary Bono of California, she added a provision to the final legislation that requires fruit, vegetables, fish and meat to include a label noting the country of origin. The provision had long been opposed by grocery stores, which said it would increase their costs. But U.S. producers said they would benefit because consumers would be more likely to select U.S.-grown produce.

A former reading, music and physical education teacher, Hooley decided to run for a seat on the West Linn City Council in 1977 because she was unhappy with the response she got when she complained that her son had been injured in a fall on a public playground. Told by council members that safety improvements to the playground would be too expensive, she decided to run for the city council herself and won.

After four years on the city council, Hooley went on to serve in the Oregon House and on the Clackamas County Commission, focusing on issues ranging from recycling to welfare.

In her 1996 House race, she easily outpaced two lesser-known Democrats to claim the party's nomination and the right to take on conservative GOP freshman Rep. Jim Bunn, who had won narrowly in 1994. Hooley quickly gained the support of national Democrats, who helped with a barrage of negative ads portraying Bunn as too conservative for the district. Bunn, who depended on support from religious conservatives, was also hurt by his divorce and subsequent marriage to his 31-year-old chief of staff.

Hooley prevailed with 51 percent of the vote. Her re-election contests have been competitive. In 2004, she defeated Republican attorney Jim Zupancic with 53 percent.

KEY VOTES

2004

Yes   Extend federal unemployment benefits by 13 weeks

Yes   Pass $283.2 billion, six-year federal highway and mass transit bill

Yes   Approve $146 billion multi-year extension of previously enacted middle-class tax breaks

No   Amend the Constitution to prohibit same-sex marriage

Yes   Cut corporate taxes $137 billion over 10 years

Yes   Reorganize U.S. intelligence agencies as proposed by Sept. 11 commission

2003

No   Cut taxes by $330 billion through fiscal 2013

Yes   Block Bush rule scaling back overtime pay for some white-collar federal workers

Yes   Do not allow use of search warrants without first notifying subjects

Yes   Allow importation of prescription drugs

No   Create private school voucher program in Washington, D.C.

No   Ban "partial birth" abortion except to save a woman's life

Yes   Split $18.6 billion in Iraq aid into half-grant, half-loan

No   Overhaul Medicare and create prescription drug benefit

CQ VOTE STUDIES

	PARTY UNITY		PRESIDENTIAL SUPPORT	
	Support	Oppose	Support	Oppose
2004	87%	13%	35%	65%
2003	91%	9%	24%	76%
2002	87%	13%	37%	63%
2001	89%	11%	36%	64%
2000	85%	15%	67%	33%

INTEREST GROUPS

	AFL-CIO	ADA	CCUS	ACU
2004	87%	95%	60%	16%
2003	87%	95%	38%	25%
2002	88%	90%	50%	12%
2001	83%	90%	43%	4%
2000	80%	70%	61%	16%

OREGON 5

Willamette Valley – Salem, part of Portland

Oregon City, the western terminus of the 2,000-mile Oregon Trail, in 1844 became the first incorporated city west of the Mississippi River. For settlers who made the five-month journey from Independence, Mo., the area marked the end of an arduous trek to Oregon's fertile Willamette Valley. The 5th takes in the northern part of that valley and the state capital of Salem, then spills over the Coast Range to cover two Pacific counties, Tillamook and Lincoln. It also includes a small part of Portland (shared with the 1st and 3rd districts).

Clackamas, Marion and Polk counties are at the heart of the Willamette Valley, Oregon's most fertile farmland. The valley is the center of the state's profitable trade in greenhouse crops, seeds and berries. Hops from Marion and Clackamas counties go into some of the nation's finest beers. Polk County grows cherries and wine grapes; wineries dot Polk and Marion counties.

Once exclusively dependent on agriculture and timber, the district's economy has diversified and now supports environmental research,

technology manufacturing and tourism. Portland's residential suburbs have begun expanding south into Clackamas County.

The 5th is highly competitive, thanks largely to independent voters in Marion (Salem) and Clackamas counties. Marion, the district's most populous jurisdiction, tends to vote narrowly Republican in competitive statewide races: George W. Bush in 2004 took 54 percent of the county's presidential vote. Bush also narrowly carried the 5th's share of Clackamas. Strong Democratic areas include Corvallis (shared with the 4th District), which is home to Oregon State University, and southwestern Multnomah County, an area added in redistricting following the 2000 census that hosts some affluent Portland-area liberals around Lewis & Clark College. Overall, Bush carried the district in 2004 with 50 percent of the vote.

MAJOR INDUSTRY

Agriculture, timber, paper, food processing, state government

CITIES

Salem, 136,924; Lake Oswego (pt.), 35,263; Keizer, 32,203

NOTABLE

The Oregon Coast Aquarium is in Newport; Salem's Willamette University, established in 1842, was the first university in the west.

PENNSYLVANIA

Gov. Edward G. Rendell (D)

First elected: 2002
Length of term: 4 years
Term expires: 1/07
Salary: $155,572
Phone: (717) 787-2500

Hometown:
Philadelphia
Born: Jan. 5, 1944;
New York, N.Y.
Religion: Jewish
Family: Wife, Marjorie O. Rendell; one child
Education: U. of Pennsylvania, B.A. 1965
(political science); Villanova U., J.D. 1968
Military Service: Army Reserve, 1968-74
Career: Lawyer; city prosecutor
Political highlights: Philadelphia district
attorney, 1978-86; sought Democratic
nomination for governor, 1986; sought
Democratic nomination for mayor of
Philadelphia, 1987; mayor of Philadelphia,
1992-2000; Democratic National Committee
chairman, 1999-2001

Election results:

2002 GENERAL

Edward G. Rendell (D)	1,899,518	53.6%
Mike Fisher (R)	1,566,567	44.2%
Ken V. Krawchuk (LIBERT)	40,923	1.2%
Michael Morrill (GREEN)	38,423	1.1%

Lt. Gov. Catherine B. Knoll (D)

First elected: 2002
Length of term: 4 years
Term expires: 1/07
Salary: $130,679
Phone: (717) 787-3300

STATE LEGISLATURE

General Assembly: Year-round with
recess

House: 203 members, 2-year terms
2005 breakdown: 110R, 93D; 178
men, 24 women
Salary: $69,648
Phone: (717) 787-2372

Senate: 50 members, 4-year terms
2005 breakdown: 29R, 18D,
3 vacancies; 39 men, 8 women
Salary: $69,648
Phone: (717) 787-5920

STATE TERM LIMITS

Governor: 2 consecutive terms
House: No
Senate: No

URBAN STATISTICS

CITY	POPULATION
Philadelphia	1,517,550
Pittsburgh	334,563
Allentown	106,632
Erie	103,717
Upper Darby	81,821

REGISTERED VOTERS

Democrat	48%
Republican	41%
Others	11%

POPULATION

2004 population (est.)	12,406,292
2000 population	12,281,054
1990 population	11,881,643
Percent change (1990-2000)	+3.4%
Rank among states (2004)	6

Median age	38
Born in state	77.7%
Foreign born	4.1%
Violent crime rate	420/100,000
Poverty level	11%
Federal workers	105,903
Military	43,271

REDISTRICTING

Pennsylvania lost two House seats in
reapportionment. The legislature drew
a 19-district map, which the governor
signed on Jan. 7, 2002. A three-judge
panel struck down the map but
permitted the 2002 elections to be
held under it. The legislature drew a
new map, effective for 2004, which
the governor signed on April 18, 2002.

MISCELLANEOUS

Web: www.state.pa.us
Capital: Harrisburg
STATE ELECTION OFFICIAL
(717) 787-5280
**DEMOCRATIC
HEADQUARTERS**
(717) 238-9381
**REPUBLICAN
HEADQUARTERS**
(717) 234-4901

District Statistics

DIST.	2004 VOTE FOR PRESIDENT BUSH	KERRY	WHITE	BLACK	ASIAN	HISP	MEDIAN INCOME	WHITE COLLAR	BLUE COLLAR	SERVICE INDUSTRY	OVER 64	UNDER 18	COLLEGE EDUCATION	RURAL	SQ. MILES
1	15%	84%	33%	45%	5%	15%	$28,261	57%	21%	22%	12%	28%	14%	0%	59
2	12	87	30	61	4	3	$30,646	66	15	19	14	24	24	0	59
3	53	46	94	3	0	1	$35,884	52	31	16	15	24	18	42	3,969
4	54	45	94	3	1	1	$43,547	64	23	14	17	24	27	22	1,302
5	61	39	96	1	1	1	$33,254	51	33	15	15	22	17	54	11,042
6	48	51	86	7	2	4	$55,611	68	20	12	14	25	34	14	813
7	47	53	88	5	4	1	$56,126	73	16	11	15	24	36	1	290
8	48	51	91	3	2	2	$59,207	68	21	11	13	26	31	9	619
9	67	33	96	2	0	1	$34,910	49	36	16	16	24	13	59	7,160
10	60	40	95	2	0	1	$35,996	53	32	15	17	23	17	55	6,558
11	47	52	93	2	1	3	$34,979	54	30	16	18	22	16	27	2,218
12	48	51	95	3	0	1	$30,612	51	31	18	19	21	14	38	2,752
13	43	56	86	6	4	3	$49,319	68	19	12	17	23	29	2	255
14	30	69	73	23	2	1	$30,139	62	19	20	18	21	21	0	162
15	49	50	86	3	2	8	$45,330	59	27	14	16	24	22	13	845

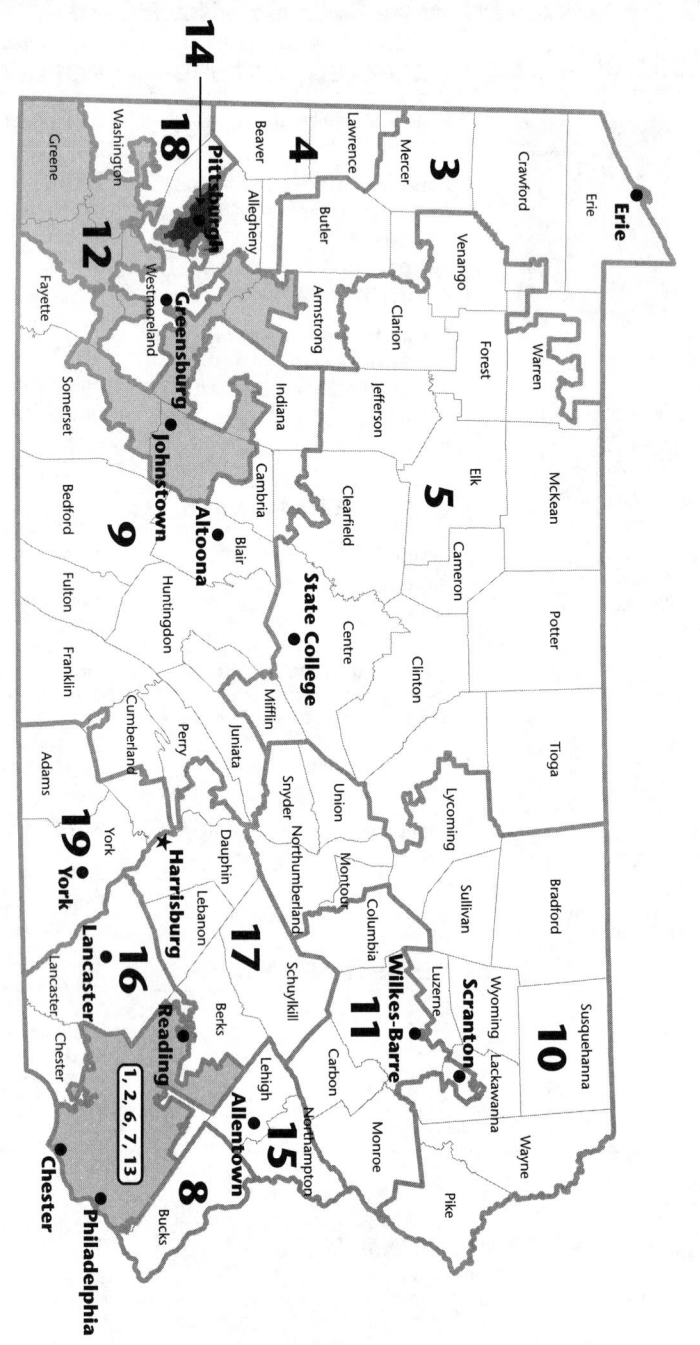

District Statistics

DIST.	2004 VOTE FOR PRESIDENT BUSH	KERRY	WHITE	BLACK	ASIAN	HISP	MEDIAN INCOME	WHITE COLLAR	BLUE COLLAR	SERVICE INDUSTRY	OVER 64	UNDER 18	COLLEGE EDUCATION	RURAL	SQ. MILES
16	61%	38%	85%	4%	1%	9%	$45,934	54%	31%	14%	13%	27%	23%	24%	1,290
17	58	42	87	7	1	3	$40,473	55	31	14	16	23	17	31	2,335
18	54	45	95	2	1	1	$44,938	66	20	14	18	22	29	16	1,432
19	64	36	92	3	1	3	$45,345	57	30	13	14	24	21	29	1,658
STATE	48	51	84	10	2	3	$40,106	60	26	15	16	24	22	23	44,817
U.S.	50.7	48.3	69	12	4	13	$41,994	60	25	15	12	26	24	21	3,537,438

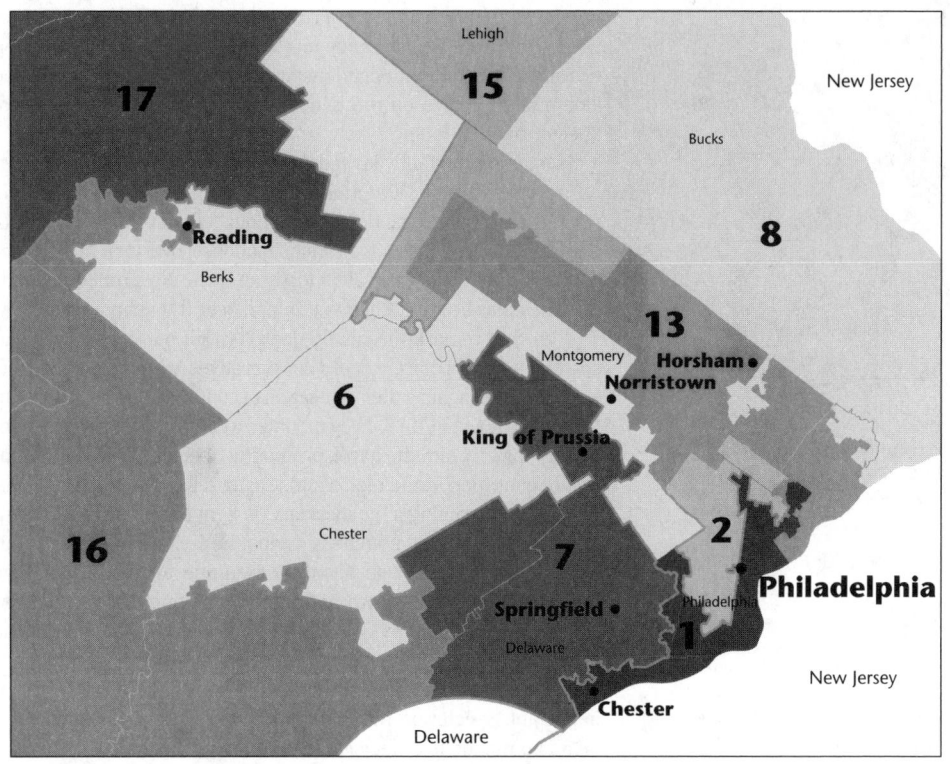

Sen. Arlen Specter (R)

Elected 1980; 5th term

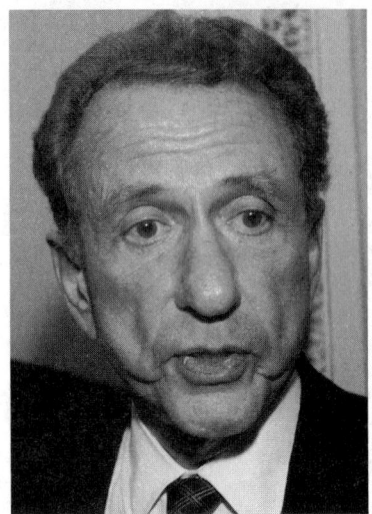

CAPITOL OFFICE
224-4254
arlen_specter@specter.senate.gov
specter.senate.gov
711 Hart 20510-3802; fax 228-1229

COMMITTEES
Appropriations
(Labor, Health & Human Services & Education -
chairman)
Judiciary - chairman
Veterans' Affairs

HOMETOWN
Philadelphia

BORN
Feb. 12, 1930, Wichita, Kan.

RELIGION
Jewish

FAMILY
Wife, Joan Specter; two children

EDUCATION
U. of Pennsylvania, B.A. 1951 (international
relations); Yale U., LL.B. 1956

MILITARY SERVICE
Air Force, 1951-53

CAREER
Lawyer; professor

POLITICAL HIGHLIGHTS
Philadelphia district attorney, 1966-74; Republican
nominee for mayor of Philadelphia, 1967; defeated
for re-election as Philadelphia district attorney,
1973; sought Republican nomination for U.S.
Senate, 1976; sought Republican nomination for
governor, 1978

ELECTION RESULTS

2004 GENERAL

Arlen Specter (R)	2,925,080	52.6%
Joseph M. Hoeffel (D)	2,334,126	42.0%
James N. Clymer (CNSTP)	220,056	4.0%
Betsy Summers (LIBERT)	79,263	1.4%

2004 PRIMARY

Arlen Specter (R)	530,839	50.8%
Patrick J. Toomey (R)	513,693	49.2%

PREVIOUS WINNING PERCENTAGES
1998 (61%); 1992 (49%); 1986 (56%); 1980 (50%)

As the chairman of the Judiciary Committee in the 109th Congress, Specter is at the center of the partisan food fight over President Bush's nominees to federal courts, a role that could include a confirmation battle should there be a vacancy on the Supreme Court. His moderate politics and trademark independence worry conservatives determined to put like-minded judges on the bench. They extracted an early pledge from Specter to fall into line.

Specter inadvertently invited the intense scrutiny by conservatives when he declared in late 2004 that he would oppose judicial nominees who favored ending the legal right to abortion. "When you talk about judges who would change the right of a woman to choose, overturn *Roe v. Wade*, I think that is unlikely," Specter said shortly after the November election, when it became clear he would be next to take over the helm at Judiciary.

With that remark, he nearly dealt himself out of the chairmanship. It sparked a firestorm from social conservatives, who have distrusted Specter since he voted against the nomination of conservative Judge Robert H. Bork to the high court in 1987. They mounted a campaign to convince Senate GOP leaders to deny him the gavel, prompting Specter to launch a counteroffensive of contrition in the media and among fellow Republicans. Specter said he was simply stating a "political fact" in light of Democratic filibusters of 10 of Bush's lower court nominees during the 108th Congress.

Ultimately, Specter survived by pledging to move Bush's nominees through the committee promptly, and by hinting that he might support a controversial gambit by conservatives to force a change in Senate procedure so that only a simple majority of senators, rather than the current 60, would be required to end filibusters of judicial nominees. Perhaps more important, Specter promised not to use the Judiciary chairmanship to bottle up nominations or legislation that he opposed.

That stance runs counter to Specter's track record. Like other states in the region, Pennsylvania tilts Democratic, and Specter has one of the most liberal voting records among Senate Republicans. He joined with his party on major votes in the 108th Congress just 81 percent of the time, less frequently than all but three other senators. "I represent a very diverse state, and every time I cast a vote, I run the risk of having 50 percent of the people disagree with me. I'm used to that," Specter told The Philadelphia Inquirer in 2003.

Specter joins with Democrats on closely watched issues such as increasing education spending and extending the unemployment benefits of jobless workers. In the 108th Congress, he unsuccessfully tried to weaken a House bill aimed at preventing human cloning. Specter argued that it could be construed to apply to patents on stem cell and genetic research.

He held up passage of a major fiscal 2004 spending bill because it left out a provision he favored to stop the Bush administration from curtailing overtime pay for some federal workers. Specter offered a compromise that would have created a commission to study the issue, but GOP leaders rejected it and he ultimately relented.

Specter was one of only three Senate Republicans to insist that Bush scale back his tax cut in 2001 from $1.6 trillion to $1.35 trillion over 10 years to make room in the budget for more education spending. And, since 1999, he has been one of the few Republicans to join liberal Democrat Edward M. Kennedy of Massachusetts to endorse "hate crime" protections for homosexuals.

Specter possesses one of the quickest minds on Capitol Hill and is not shy about promoting his ideas. As chairman of the Appropriations subcommittee that funds the departments of Labor, Health and Human Services, and Education, Specter has sided with liberal Democrats in demanding that the administration spend more money to meet the goals of Bush's 2001 education bill, which ties federal aid to improvements on test scores.

During the historic impeachment of President Clinton in 1999, Specter invoked Scottish law by voting "Not proven, therefore not guilty." The other senators voted "guilty" or "not guilty," but Specter said he wanted to make the point that the trial had been too superficial in his view. Clinton ultimately was acquitted.

Specter is known for a tart tongue and blunt manner, especially with employees whom he suspects of not doing their homework. But he can get away with a lot because even senators who do not like dealing with him personally do not want to get on the wrong side of the Labor-HHS Subcommittee chairman. There is too much money at stake for critical health care and job training programs.

But as was evident in the furor over judicial nominations, Specter sometimes sets his moderate beliefs aside if party leaders are determined to assert a more conservative position. In 2002, he voted for repeal of the federal ergonomics rule though he had long sided with organized labor on the issue of protecting office workers from repetitive stress injuries. The Bush White House had pressed hard for repeal of the Clinton-era rule.

Specter, who has a law degree from Yale University, first made a name for himself in the 1960s as a top aide to the Warren Commission. He helped devise the "single bullet" theory that a lone gunman was responsible for the assassination of President Kennedy in 1963.

Specter was elected district attorney in Philadelphia twice, in 1965 and 1969, but then suffered several political setbacks, including losing a race for mayor. He decided to make one more attempt when GOP Sen. Richard S. Schweiker announced he would retire in 1980. Luckily for Specter, his Democratic opponent, Pittsburgh Mayor Pete Flaherty, was a two-time statewide loser. Carrying Philadelphia and its suburbs helped Specter overcome Flaherty's strength in the western part of the state.

In his second Senate term, Specter attracted national attention in 1991 by aggressively grilling law professor Anita Hill during the confirmation of Supreme Court nominee Clarence Thomas. Back then, Specter struck many women voters as insensitive. He accused Hill of "flat-out perjury" in her allegations of sexual harassment by Thomas.

Specter had to fight to keep his seat the following year. Democratic challenger Lynn Yeakel, head of a Philadelphia-based women's fundraising organization, said his treatment of Hill demonstrated the need for more women in Congress. Specter prevailed by just 3 percentage points.

In 1998, Specter won 61 percent of the vote over state Rep. Bill Lloyd. But he only narrowly survived a 2004 GOP primary challenge from Rep. Patrick. J. Toomey, who argued that Specter's views were out of step with the majority of Keystone State Republicans. The White House, which had tried to discourage Toomey from an intraparty battle, quickly endorsed Specter, who won the primary with 51 percent. He was re-elected with 53 percent over Democratic Rep. Joseph M. Hoeffel.

Specter has suffered health problems over the years. In early 2005, he was diagnosed with Hodgkin's disease and had to undergo chemotherapy. His doctor said he stood a good chance of being cured, and Specter kept working while in treatment. In the 1990s, he survived a brain tumor as well as heart problems that led to bypass surgery.

KEY VOTES

2004
No Pass $318.9 billion, six-year highway and mass transit bill
No Extend assault weapons ban for 10 years
No Restore pay-as-you-go rules for new tax cuts and entitlement spending
Yes Criminalize harm to a fetus in an attack on the mother
Yes Increase mandatory child care funding to states by $6 billion over five years
Yes Amend the Constitution to prohibit same-sex marriage
Yes Approve $146 billion multi-year extension of previously enacted middle-class tax breaks
Yes Reorganize U.S. intelligence agencies as proposed by Sept. 11 commission
? Cut corporate taxes $137 billion over 10 years

2003
No Delay Bush changes to Clean Air Act
Yes Allow confirmation vote on Miguel A. Estrada to the U.S. Court of Appeals for the D.C. Circuit
No Block a Bush proposal opening Alaska's Arctic National Wildlife Refuge to oil drilling
No Limit size of Bush's proposed tax cut to $350 billion through fiscal 2013
Yes Overhaul Medicare and create prescription drug benefit
Yes Block Bush rule scaling back overtime pay for some white-collar federal workers
No Split $20 billion in Iraq aid into half-grant, half-loan
Yes Ban "partial birth" abortion except to save a woman's life
No Stop proposal allowing travel to Cuba
Yes Allow final vote on energy policy overhaul

CQ VOTE STUDIES

	PARTY UNITY		PRESIDENTIAL SUPPORT	
	Support	Oppose	Support	Oppose
2004	70%	30%	88%	12%
2003	84%	16%	89%	11%
2002	60%	40%	89%	11%
2001	60%	40%	87%	13%
2000	67%	33%	59%	41%
1999	64%	36%	53%	47%
1998	49%	51%	60%	40%
1997	50%	50%	71%	29%
1996	64%	36%	59%	41%
1995	65%	35%	49%	51%

INTEREST GROUPS

	AFL-CIO	ADA	CCUS	ACU
2004	64%	45%	87%	75%
2003	16%	25%	87%	65%
2002	46%	35%	85%	50%
2001	63%	40%	79%	56%
2000	50%	40%	53%	62%
1999	44%	40%	47%	48%
1998	83%	45%	60%	33%
1997	57%	70%	50%	32%
1996	57%	50%	77%	50%
1995	33%	55%	79%	36%

Sen. Rick Santorum (R)

Elected 1994; 2nd term

CAPITOL OFFICE
224-6324
santorum.senate.gov
511 Dirksen 20510-3804; fax 228-0604

COMMITTEES
Agriculture, Nutrition & Forestry
(Research, Nutrition & General Legislation - chairman)
Banking, Housing & Urban Affairs
Finance
(Social Security & Family Policy - chairman)
Rules & Administration
Special Aging

HOMETOWN
Penn Hills

BORN
May 10, 1958, Winchester, Va.

RELIGION
Roman Catholic

FAMILY
Wife, Karen Garver Santorum; seven children (one deceased)

EDUCATION
Pennsylvania State U., B.A. 1980 (political science); U. of Pittsburgh, M.B.A. 1981; Dickinson School of Law, J.D. 1986

CAREER
Lawyer; state legislative aide

POLITICAL HIGHLIGHTS
U.S. House, 1991-95

ELECTION RESULTS

2000 GENERAL
Rick Santorum (R)	2,481,962	52.4%
Ron Klink (D)	2,154,908	45.5%

2000 PRIMARY
Rick Santorum (R)	unopposed

PREVIOUS WINNING PERCENTAGES
1994 (49%); 1992 House Election (61%); 1990 House Election (51%)

One of Congress' leading social conservatives, Santorum is chairman of the Senate Republican Conference, the third-ranking leadership post. His job is to shape the Senate majority's political message, and in his hands, the message usually has a partisan edge.

Santorum is positioned to succeed Majority Whip Mitch McConnell of Kentucky, if McConnell moves up to majority leader in 2007. (The current majority leader, Bill Frist, has said he plans to retire in 2007.) Santorum was returned to the post of conference chairman at the start of the 109th Congress, after serving in the job the previous four years. He chairs the meetings of the conference, which is the group of all Senate Republicans.

The bump up in the number of fire-breathing conservatives in the Senate as a result of the 2004 election strengthened Santorum's standing. As a House member in the early 1990s, he was part of the group of junior Republicans who called themselves the "Gang of Seven" and adhered to the confrontational politics of Newt Gingrich of Georgia, instead of the pragmatic deal-making approach of the Republican minority leader at that time, Robert H. Michel of Illinois. When he switched to the other side of the Capitol in 1995, Santorum brought his grenade-tossing style with him.

In addition to promoting the GOP agenda, Santorum leads the charge against the Democrats. He was among the first Republican leaders to focus on one person — former Senate Minority Leader Tom Daschle — to illustrate the point that Democrats were "obstructing" President Bush's agenda. Santorum asserted that Bush offered his hand in compromise and Daschle was "biting it and chewing it like a rabid dog." Daschle was defeated for re-election in 2004 after a concerted and well-financed effort by the Republican Party. Santorum also holds regular meetings with K Street lobbyists to discuss policy and to urge them to hire more Republicans.

Santorum got into the leadership at a relatively young age. He was 42 and beginning his second Senate term when he defeated Missouri's Christopher S. Bond for the conference chairmanship. He began with such energy that some GOP colleagues lamented that Santorum was overdoing it, presenting senators with long lists of assignments. Since then, they say, he has calmed down and done a better job of coordinating with House Republicans and the White House.

Santorum has made no secret of his wish to move up in the leadership. When Mississippi's Trent Lott was forced to resign as majority leader late in 2002 after praising the 1948 segregationist presidential campaign of Strom Thurmond, Santorum briefly considered going for the top job. But he decided against it when Frist quickly locked up the votes he needed to win.

Since then, Santorum has earned points for loyalty by raising money for Republicans and working closely with Frist. And, to ease Lott's fall, Santorum gave up the chairmanship of the Rules Committee so that Lott could take the gavel.

Santorum's style does not lend itself to the routine give-and-take of passing legislation. He spent much of the 107th and the 108th Congresses working with Connecticut Democrat Joseph I. Lieberman to pass Bush's faith-based initiative making it easier for religious groups to win federal social services grants. Despite their efforts at whittling down the measure to overcome Democratic opposition, the bill stalled over the Democrats' main issue — that federal aid to faith-based groups should come with conditions against discriminating against people outside the group. Santorum sometimes expressed annoyance at deals he had to make with Democrats. But he planned to revive the measure in the 109th with Lieberman, an occasional ally who worked with him in 2000 to pass anti-poverty legislation.

Santorum is usually on the front lines of the culture wars. He took the lead in the 108th Congress in promoting a constitutional amendment to ban same-sex marriage, calling it a defense of the "right for children to have moms and dads." He is especially committed to the anti-abortion movement, helping win passage in 2003 of a law banning a procedure opponents call "partial birth" abortion and he describes as "barbaric."

On his desk, Santorum keeps a photograph of an underdeveloped baby — his own late son, Gabriel Michael. The baby was born after only five months of gestation when complications forced an early delivery, and he died two hours later. The experience fuels Santorum's view that abortion is tantamount to murder. His strong feelings on the subject prompted one of his few public disagreements with Bush, over the president's decision in 2001 to fund research on stem cells extracted from human embryos.

In 2004, Santorum lost a fight with a Pennsylvania public school district that stopped paying tuition for five of his children to take private online courses, on grounds that they were living in Virginia. Santorum, who divides his time between a home in Virginia and one in a Pittsburgh suburb, announced he and his wife would home-school their children.

He may be an ideologue, but Santorum is also a politician when he needs to be, and one from a swing state that supported the Democratic presidential candidate, Sen. John Kerry of Massachusetts, in 2004. He supports home-state priorities, such as farm programs, and some labor-backed causes, such as increasing the minimum wage. In early 2005, he took a seat on the Agriculture Committee to watch out for Pennsylvania's farm and forestry interests. To stay visible, Santorum visits all of Pennsylvania's 67 counties every year.

Drawing on his own experience of having a full-time job while attending law school, Santorum stresses individual responsibility and self-reliance, not government aid. But he supports some social services popular at home, voting in 2003 for the final version of a major expansion of Medicare that created a new prescription drug benefit for the elderly.

He also has been helpful to the state's far more liberal senior senator, Arlen Specter. Santorum backed Specter in a 2004 primary race against conservative Rep. Patrick J. Toomey, and also helped him secure the Judiciary Committee chairmanship after conservatives sought to block Specter for saying judicial nominees opposed to legal abortion would not get through the committee.

The son of an Italian immigrant, the boyish-faced Santorum was the state chairman of the College Republicans while he was a student at Penn State University. After working as an aide in the state legislature, he ran for the House in 1990 to unseat Democratic Rep. Doug Walgren, organizing a grassroots campaign and winning by 2 percentage points.

In 1994, he took on Democratic Sen. Harris Wofford, who had won a special election in 1991. Santorum painted Wofford as an out-of-date liberal and assailed his support for gun control laws. Santorum took a narrow two-point victory.

Democrats targeted Santorum as a vulnerable incumbent in 2000, contending he was too conservative for Pennsylvania. But a divisive Democratic primary weakened their cause, and the eventual nominee, Rep. Ron Klink, struggled to raise money. By moderating his image and emphasizing his work on a range of issues, including welfare and Social Security, Santorum won re-election by 7 percentage points.

KEY VOTES

2004

No   Pass $318.9 billion, six-year highway and mass transit bill

No   Extend assault weapons ban for 10 years

No   Restore pay-as-you-go rules for new tax cuts and entitlement spending

Yes   Criminalize harm to a fetus in an attack on the mother

No   Increase mandatory child care funding to states by $6 billion over five years

Yes   Amend the Constitution to prohibit same-sex marriage

Yes   Approve $146 billion multi-year extension of previously enacted middle-class tax breaks

Yes   Reorganize U.S. intelligence agencies as proposed by Sept. 11 commission

Yes   Cut corporate taxes $137 billion over 10 years

2003

No   Delay Bush changes to Clean Air Act

Yes   Allow confirmation vote on Miguel A. Estrada to the U.S. Court of Appeals for the D.C. Circuit

No   Block a Bush proposal opening Alaska's Arctic National Wildlife Refuge to oil drilling

No   Limit size of Bush's proposed tax cut to $350 billion through fiscal 2013

No   Overhaul Medicare and create prescription drug benefit

No   Block Bush rule scaling back overtime pay for some white-collar federal workers

No   Split $20 billion in Iraq aid into half-grant, half-loan

Yes   Ban "partial birth" abortion except to save a woman's life

Yes   Stop proposal allowing travel to Cuba

Yes   Allow final vote on energy policy overhaul

CQ VOTE STUDIES

	PARTY UNITY		PRESIDENTIAL SUPPORT	
	Support	Oppose	Support	Oppose
2004	96%	4%	100%	0%
2003	98%	2%	99%	1%
2002	96%	4%	96%	4%
2001	95%	5%	97%	3%
2000	96%	4%	49%	51%
1999	91%	9%	30%	70%
1998	91%	9%	40%	60%
1997	91%	9%	61%	39%
1996	93%	7%	40%	60%
1995	96%	4%	24%	76%

INTEREST GROUPS

	AFL-CIO	ADA	CCUS	ACU
2004	10%	15%	94%	96%
2003	0%	10%	100%	90%
2002	15%	5%	95%	95%
2001	13%	10%	86%	100%
2000	0%	0%	93%	100%
1999	25%	5%	81%	88%
1998	0%	0%	89%	84%
1997	14%	15%	90%	84%
1996	43%	15%	77%	95%
1995	8%	5%	100%	83%

Rep. Robert A. Brady (D)

Elected May 1998; 4th full term

CAPITOL OFFICE
225-4731
www.house.gov/robertbrady
206 Cannon 20515-3801; fax 225-0088

COMMITTEES
Armed Services
House Administration
Joint Printing

HOMETOWN
Philadelphia

BORN
April 7, 1945, Philadelphia, Pa.

RELIGION
Roman Catholic

FAMILY
Wife, Debra Brady; two children

EDUCATION
St. Thomas More H.S., graduated 1963

CAREER
Union lobbyist; local government official;
carpenter

POLITICAL HIGHLIGHTS
34th Ward Democratic Executive Committee,
1967-present (leader, 1980-present); candidate
for Philadelphia City Council, 1983; Philadelphia
Democratic Party chairman, 1986-present

ELECTION RESULTS

2004 GENERAL

Robert A. Brady (D)	214,462	86.3%
Deborah L. Williams (R)	33,266	13.4%

2004 PRIMARY

Robert A. Brady (D)	unopposed

2002 GENERAL

Robert A. Brady (D)	121,076	86.4%
Marie G. Delany (R)	17,444	12.5%
Michael J. "Mike" Ewall (GREEN)	1,570	1.1%

PREVIOUS WINNING PERCENTAGES
2000 (88%); 1998 (81%); 1998 Special Election (74%)

It's not easy working two jobs, but Brady pulls it off. In addition to his "day job" as a congressman, he also serves as chairman of Philadelphia's Democratic organization, one of the last political machines in the country worthy of the name. Brady is effective enough in the House that he has a commanding grip on the 1st District, which has the largest black population of any district in the nation represented by a white.

But it is Brady's role as local party boss that gives him real clout, as Al Gore confirmed early in his 2000 presidential campaign. As the Philadelphia Inquirer recounted the story, Gore came into the House and walked over to John P. Murtha, the Pennsylvania Democrat who is an acknowledged master of appropriations politics — and Brady's mentor. Not unreasonably, Murtha assumed Gore wanted to talk to him until the vice president asked, "Where's Brady?"

Gore's attentiveness was vindicated on Election Day, when a Brady turn-out-the-vote drive gave him a 350,000-vote margin in Philadelphia — more than offsetting George W. Bush's strength in other parts of the state. In 2004, Brady attended Philadelphia rallies with both Democratic nominee John Kerry and his running mate, John Edwards, but skipped the Democratic National Convention in Boston to spend time with his grandchildren. Philadelphia and several suburban counties voted overwhelmingly for Kerry.

Brady is as loyal a spear-carrier as the House Democratic leadership is likely to find, and fittingly for someone of his background, he was named in the 108th Congress to one of three Democratic slots on the House Administration Committee, the ultimate insider's panel, which writes election laws and oversees a wide range of accounts, Capitol Hill agency employment and perks for House members.

His loyalty to organized labor is unassailable, reflecting his working-class roots. Brady was an athlete in his younger days, teaming up once with Wilt Chamberlain in a neighborhood pickup game. But he had to forgo scholarship offers and go to work as a carpenter to help support his family. After 12 years in the trade, he moved into a full-time post with the carpenter's union. Brady still carries a union card and has a lifetime score of 100 percent in the AFL-CIO's rating of members' voting records.

In 2001, he infuriated some longtime environmentalist allies by backing President Bush's proposal to allow oil drilling in Alaska's Arctic National Wildlife Refuge — an idea backed by the Teamsters Union and the AFL-CIO's building trades division.

During the 107th, while a member of the Small Business Committee, Brady pushed a bill through the House that would establish a pilot program to help vocational schools teach students how to start a small business. The measure never cleared the Senate, however, and it did not make it out of committee in the 108th. (Brady had left the panel by then to join House Administration.) In the 109th, Brady introduced it once again.

Brady also does the routine work of bringing the bacon home to his district. In 2001, for example, he used his seat on the Armed Services Committee to pump an additional $15 million into the scaled-down Navy facility at the former Philadelphia Naval Shipyard.

In the 108th Congress, the city relied more heavily on Brady following the retirement of Robert Borski, who had represented Philadelphia's northeast side and was a senior Democrat on the Transportation Committee. Redistricting left Philadelphia with only two and a half members of Congress (one splits his district with the suburbs). Brady works through his close friend and patron, appropriations kingpin Murtha. "I'm Murtha's guy. I say to him, 'What do you need me to do,'" Brady declared in 2003. Brady honored his mentor by having one of the nation's biggest cranes at the Philadelphia Naval Shipyard named in his honor.

But Brady spends much of his time operating outside congressional — or even federal — channels to meet his constituents' needs. His tools are his keen negotiating skills, the dense web of contacts he has built up over four decades in union work and politics and the large pile of markers he holds from people who owe him.

According to Brady's congressional Web site, he was "widely praised as key to the settlement of a labor impasse that threatened to shut down public schools" in his city in 2001. Building on his years of union negotiating experience, Brady also hosted a fence-mending session after the bitter 1999 Philadelphia Democratic mayoral primary and brokered the end to a transit strike in 1998. In 2003, he focused much of his attention on re-electing Philadelphia Mayor John F. Street.

Brady's approach to the job embodies a lesson he learned years ago. He decided to become involved politically when his mother concluded that the local party boss was being insufficiently attentive to her request for a new bulb in a street lamp. (In 2002, it was Brady who put $600,000 for "security lighting" for a Philadelphia bridge into the annual defense budget bill.)

Just 22 when he was elected to the 34th Ward Democratic Executive Committee, Brady has been in the local party organization ever since. He held a variety of posts at City Hall, the city's redevelopment agency and the Pennsylvania Turnpike Authority. Many of those positions enabled him to find jobs for people; the Philadelphia Inquirer reported that Brady once dubbed himself "the largest employment agency in Pennsylvania." He remains the go-to guy for Philadelphians seeking a judgeship in the city.

Before he ran for the House, Brady had sought elective office just once, losing his bid for a seat on the City Council in 1983. But his grasp of city politics — as well as nominating rules that favored the candidate with the backing of the party machinery — made him a formidable candidate in the 1998 special election when Democratic Rep. Thomas M. Foglietta resigned to become ambassador to Italy. He easily received the Democratic nomination, which practically ensured his victory in the overwhelmingly Democratic district. He won the special election with 74 percent of the vote, and has rolled up even bigger tallies ever since.

KEY VOTES

2004

Yes Extend federal unemployment benefits by 13 weeks

Yes Pass $283.2 billion, six-year federal highway and mass transit bill

No Approve $146 billion multi-year extension of previously enacted middle-class tax breaks

No Amend the Constitution to prohibit same-sex marriage

No Cut corporate taxes $137 billion over 10 years

Yes Reorganize U.S. intelligence agencies as proposed by Sept. 11 commission

2003

No Cut taxes by $330 billion through fiscal 2013

Yes Block Bush rule scaling back overtime pay for some white-collar federal workers

Yes Do not allow use of search warrants without first notifying subjects

Yes Allow importation of prescription drugs

No Create private school voucher program in Washington, D.C.

No Ban "partial birth" abortion except to save a woman's life

Yes Split $18.6 billion in Iraq aid into half-grant, half-loan

No Overhaul Medicare and create prescription drug benefit

CQ VOTE STUDIES

	PARTY UNITY		PRESIDENTIAL SUPPORT	
	Support	Oppose	Support	Oppose
2004	96%	4%	18%	82%
2003	91%	9%	21%	79%
2002	94%	6%	31%	69%
2001	92%	8%	33%	67%
2000	95%	5%	86%	14%

INTEREST GROUPS

	AFL-CIO	ADA	CCUS	ACU
2004	100%	95%	19%	4%
2003	100%	100%	31%	21%
2002	100%	95%	45%	4%
2001	100%	95%	43%	16%
2000	100%	90%	42%	12%

PENNSYLVANIA 1
South and central Philadelphia; Chester

Home of the Philly cheesesteak, the 1st is known for its patriotic attractions, including the Liberty Bell and Independence Hall, the birthplace of the Constitution. Its Italian population supports a famous food market, and many Catholic churches still hold Mass in Italian.

The W-shaped 1st is the state's most racially and ethnically diverse district. Already home to Philadelphia's Chinatown, an influx of Vietnamese and Chinese residents and businesses has boosted the Asian presence. Nearly three-fourths of Philadelphia's Hispanic population resides in the 1st, with the highest concentration in the northern part of the district. But African-Americans represent the largest population block in the district (45 percent).

Once home to factory workers and a large ethnic, blue-collar workforce, factory closings have left swaths of the 1st with a bleak economic landscape. While Philadelphia overall won notice for substantial economic recovery in the 1990s and is seeing a surge of construction jobs, major sections have yet to recover from a long period of industrial decay. The 1st has the lowest median income in the state, although several neighborhoods are beginning to see an influx of upwardly mobile residents. New stadiums for football's Eagles (2003) and baseball's Phillies (2004), along with the Wachovia Center, are located in the 1st.

The booming Kvaerner Philadelphia and Metro Machine shipyards have picked up where the closed Philadelphia Naval Shipyard left off. The region is working to become an important shipbuilding, refurbishing and decommissioning center. Philadelphia International Airport also has grown rapidly.

Philadelphia is home to almost 90 percent of the 1st's residents, with the rest living just outside the city in working-class areas of Delaware County. The district's strong union presence and substantial minority population make it a slam-dunk for Democratic candidates.

MAJOR INDUSTRY
Government, service, health care, shipbuilding, airport

CITIES
Philadelphia (pt.), 571,130; Chester, 36,854

NOTABLE
Eastern State Penitentiary, the most expensive upon its opening in 1829, held gangster Al Capone.

Rep. Chaka Fattah (D)

Elected 1994; 6th term

CAPITOL OFFICE
225-4001
www.house.gov/fattah
2301 Rayburn 20515-3802; fax 225-5392

COMMITTEES
Appropriations

HOMETOWN
Philadelphia

BORN
Nov. 21, 1956, Philadelphia, Pa.

RELIGION
Baptist

FAMILY
Wife, Renee Chenault-Fattah; four children

EDUCATION
Community College of Philadelphia, attended 1976
(political science); U. of Pennsylvania, M.A. 1986
(government administration)

CAREER
Public official

POLITICAL HIGHLIGHTS
Democratic candidate for Philadelphia City
Commission, 1978; Pa. House, 1983-89; Pa. Senate,
1989-95; Consumer Party nominee for U.S. House
(special election), 1991

ELECTION RESULTS

2004 GENERAL

Chaka Fattah (D)	253,226	88.0%
Stewart Bolno (R)	34,411	12.0%

2004 PRIMARY

Chaka Fattah (D)	unopposed

2002 GENERAL

Chaka Fattah (D)	150,623	87.8%
Thomas G. Dougherty (R)	20,988	12.2%

PREVIOUS WINNING PERCENTAGES
2000 (98%); 1998 (87%); 1996 (88%); 1994 (86%)

Fattah spent his first four terms in Congress winning power and influence on two important House committees and the next two losing all the ground he had gained. In one case, he was the victim of a Republican leadership decision. In the other, he was hurt by his own party's leader.

Fattah (full name: SHOCK-ah fa-TAH) was rising fast in the 107th Congress, when he won a coveted seat on the Appropriations Committee, and immediately became the top-ranking Democrat on its District of Columbia Subcommittee. But at the start of the 109th, three Appropriations subcommittees — including the District of Columbia panel — were eliminated at the dictate of Majority Leader Tom DeLay. Fattah not only lost his ranking post on the D.C. panel, his other subcommittee — for veterans' affairs and housing — was dismantled as well. He is now the most junior Democrat on two different appropriations subcommittees.

Two years earlier, at the start of the 108th Congress, Minority Leader Nancy Pelosi forced Fattah to choose between his seat on Appropriations and his ranking member slot on the House Administration Committee. He picked Appropriations. He also had to give up a seat on the Education and Workforce Committee to claim the Appropriations seat.

Fattah says he's less interested in climbing the minority leadership ranks than in helping the Democrats craft an agenda to reassume the majority. "I can help shape a set of ideas that can empower Democrats over the next generation because I don't have the ambitions to take on some particular title," he says. He concedes there is little chance for success while Democrats are in the minority but says, "You have to put your ideas out there, so that people know where you're coming from and so, when you're in the majority, folks will have an idea of where you want to go."

Where Fattah goes next is not entirely clear. A well-known political figure in Philadelphia, in 2007 he may refocus his ambitions and run for mayor of the city.

Since his days in Pennsylvania's state legislature, Fattah has championed educational equality. In the 109th Congress, Fattah, who describes himself as a "practical idealist," plans to push again for his "Student Bill of Rights," legislation to require states to ensure that students in urban areas have the same access to quality education as do their suburban counterparts.

He is also seeking to reauthorize and expand Gear Up, a program to encourage low-income youths to set their sights on college. The education program became law in 1998 after Fattah joined with conservative Republican Mark Souder of Indiana and won key support from the Clinton administration. It provides tutoring, mentoring and counseling as early as sixth or seventh grade, and gives schools incentives to offer classes that prepare students for college.

Fattah also wants the federal government to allow a 24-month grace period for homeowners who default on their mortgage because of unforeseen circumstances. He contends the ultimate cost would be less than the costs associated with taking and reselling the properties. When Fattah was in the state Senate, he helped enact such a program in Pennsylvania.

On the Appropriations Committee, Fattah worked well with Republican Rodney Frelinghuysen of New Jersey, chairman of the D.C. Subcommittee. He sought to keep the annual spending bill free of social policy add-ons and the restrictions on municipal spending often pushed by the GOP. But he was unable to block creation of a $14 million program giving vouchers to city students to pay for private schools.

Fattah arrived in Congress in 1995, just as Republicans assumed control. He became whip for the Congressional Black Caucus and wasted no time denouncing the new majority's ideas. During a debate early in the 104th on a GOP proposal to overhaul the welfare system, he said: "We have some tough cowboys here on the floor of the House. This is a new, interesting kind of wagon train in which the cowboys have decided to throw the women and infants and the children and the senior citizens out of the wagon train so they can get where they are going faster. It is cruel."

Named Arthur Davenport at birth, one of six boys in an inner-city household headed by his widowed mother, his name changed when his mother married community activist David Fattah. According to a Philadelphia Inquirer profile displayed on his office wall, Fattah's mother named him "Chaka" in honor of a Zulu warrior. Fattah's parents produced a magazine for the black community and established the House of Umoja, a neighborhood gathering place and haven for youths trying to work their way out of gang life.

Fattah remembers political discussions and his family's efforts to improve housing in the area. He met Democratic Rep. William H. Gray III and worked on one of his campaigns, and then, at age 22, finished fourth in a run for a municipal office. Four years later, he successfully challenged a Democratic Party-backed incumbent for a state House seat and, at 25, became the youngest person ever elected to the state legislature.

After six years in the state House and two in the state Senate, Fattah entered the 1991 special-election race to succeed Gray, who had resigned to become president of the United Negro College Fund. The Democratic Party backed longtime City Councilman Lucien E. Blackwell, and Fattah temporarily quit the party to run on the Consumer Party ticket. Blackwell won with 39 percent to Fattah's 28 percent.

Redistricting for the 1990s — in which Fattah had a hand as a member of the state Senate — reduced the percentage of African-Americans in the 2nd District from 80 percent to 62 percent. That put Blackwell at risk because his appeal was strongest among West Philly's poor and working-class blacks, and in 1994 Fattah challenged Blackwell's renomination. The incumbent had the backing of then-Mayor Ed Rendell and then-City Council President John F. Street. But Fattah outworked Blackwell and claimed the primary victory with an impressive 58 percent of the vote. In the overwhelmingly Democratic 2nd, which was changed only marginally in the most recent redistricting following the 2000 census, Fattah has not been seriously challenged in any of his re-election bids.

KEY VOTES

2004

Yes	Extend federal unemployment benefits by 13 weeks
Yes	Pass $283.2 billion, six-year federal highway and mass transit bill
?	Approve $146 billion multi-year extension of previously enacted middle-class tax breaks
No	Amend the Constitution to prohibit same-sex marriage
No	Cut corporate taxes $137 billion over 10 years
?	Reorganize U.S. intelligence agencies as proposed by Sept. 11 commission

2003

No	Cut taxes by $330 billion through fiscal 2013
Yes	Block Bush rule scaling back overtime pay for some white-collar federal workers
Yes	Do not allow use of search warrants without first notifying subjects
Yes	Allow importation of prescription drugs
No	Create private school voucher program in Washington, D.C.
No	Ban "partial birth" abortion except to save a woman's life
Yes	Split $18.6 billion in Iraq aid into half-grant, half-loan
No	Overhaul Medicare and create prescription drug benefit

CQ VOTE STUDIES

	PARTY UNITY		PRESIDENTIAL SUPPORT	
	Support	Oppose	Support	Oppose
2004	99%	1%	20%	80%
2003	95%	5%	17%	83%
2002	97%	3%	28%	72%
2001	95%	5%	22%	78%
2000	97%	3%	94%	6%

INTEREST GROUPS

	AFL-CIO	ADA	CCUS	ACU
2004	100%	85%	22%	0%
2003	100%	95%	21%	20%
2002	100%	95%	37%	0%
2001	100%	100%	27%	0%
2000	100%	95%	40%	0%

PENNSYLVANIA 2
West Philadelphia; Chestnut Hill; Cheltenham

From the vantage point of the William Penn statue atop City Hall, one can see the 2nd stretching west and north over some of Philadelphia's long-established neighborhoods. The district encompasses Center City skyscrapers, then moves west across the Schuylkill River past the University of Pennsylvania. West Philadelphia, once Irish, Greek and Jewish, is now nearly all black and features pockets of middle-class and poor communities. Overall, African-Americans represent more than three-fifths of the 2nd's residents.

Except for the Montgomery County township of Cheltenham, the 2nd is wholly within Philadelphia. The district takes in the affluent city neighborhoods of Rittenhouse Square, one of five squares Penn included in his original design of the city, and Chestnut Hill, in the city's northwest corner. It also includes Fairmount Park, which houses the city's art museum, zoo and "Boathouse Row." The park, which flanks the Schuylkill River, runs north along diverse, middle-class neighborhoods, some of which have seen some recent gentrification, and ends in

Chestnut Hill. Some of the homes in Center City Philadelphia are among the oldest in the United States.

Economic struggles continue to grip many areas of the district; some of the city's lowest family incomes are found in neighborhoods just north of downtown. The University of Pennsylvania has invested in West Philadelphia, creating incentives for school staff members to live in the neighborhood. This includes financial help for home buyers and the creation of a University of Pennsylvania-assisted public school.

The 2nd's blue-collar workforce and large minority population give it an overwhelming Democratic majority. In the 2004 presidential election, John Kerry had his best showing in the state here, taking 87 percent of the district's vote.

MAJOR INDUSTRY
Education, health care, tourism

CITIES
Philadelphia (pt.), 609,480; Glenside (unincorporated) (pt.), 3,093

NOTABLE
The Philadelphia Zoo is home to the first surviving giant river otter born in a North American zoo; The 30th Street Station is in West Philadelphia.

Rep. Phil English (R)

Elected 1994; 6th term

CAPITOL OFFICE
225-5406
www.house.gov/english
1410 Longworth 20515-3803; fax 225-3103

COMMITTEES
Ways & Means
Joint Economic

HOMETOWN
Erie

BORN
June 20, 1956, Erie, Pa.

RELIGION
Roman Catholic

FAMILY
Wife, Christiane English

EDUCATION
U. of Pennsylvania, B.A. 1979 (political science)

CAREER
State legislative aide

POLITICAL HIGHLIGHTS
Erie City controller, 1986-89; Republican nominee
for Pa. treasurer, 1988

ELECTION RESULTS

2004 GENERAL

Phil English (R)	166,580	60.1%
Steven Porter (D)	110,684	39.9%

2004 PRIMARY

Phil English (R)	unopposed

2002 GENERAL

Phil English (R)	116,763	77.7%
AnnDrea M. Benson (GREEN)	33,554	22.3%

PREVIOUS WINNING PERCENTAGES
2000 (61%); 1998 (63%); 1996 (51%); 1994 (49%)

English is a rare commodity in the House these days — a Republican moderate and a political pragmatist. His centrist tendencies come from his former career as a state legislative aide and from the nature of his district.

While somewhat more Republican since redistricting, the 3rd District still lies within a partisan battleground. Bill Clinton won northwestern Pennsylvania comfortably; George W. Bush carried it narrowly. Organized labor has substantial clout in the region, and English won his first two races with little to spare. His evolving ideology helped him crack 60 percent of the vote in his third and fourth elections, however. In 2002, the Democrats did not field a candidate. In 2004, English won easily with 60 percent.

A trusted GOP strategist, English helped Ohio Republican Bob Ney lead a 2004 incumbent retention campaign by the National Republican Congressional Committee. He also is part of the Republican Policy Committee. And English's expertise on tax issues helped persuade GOP leaders to make him the first Republican freshman member of the Ways and Means panel in decades. "I am a social conservative, who is also an economic populist, who is also pro-business," English said.

When GOP leaders in the 109th Congress began discussing proposals to replace the income tax, English pushed hard for a less ambitious strategy of modifying the income tax by providing incentives for savings and investment. English wants to promote tax breaks to help people increase their rate of saving, a plan with broad bipartisan support, while seeking to persuade his own party to pull back from the idea of replacing the entire income tax. English has called the current tax system "a Frankenstein's monster that haunts individual taxpayers while casting a cold shadow" over businesses.

In 2004, English helped win a "homeland investment" provision in the corporate tax law that provided a reduced tax rate for one year on foreign profits brought home by multinational companies. He often works with business groups to promote tax proposals such as faster write-offs on equipment purchases. He wants to repeal the alternative minimum tax, which was created in 1969 to ensure that the wealthiest Americans could not avoid paying income tax. Now, the AMT effectively has become a flat 26 percent income tax hitting more than 3 million Americans because it is not indexed for inflation. "The AMT is terrible tax policy," English said, adding that it will "probably take fundamental tax reform to get rid of it."

He once tried to saw through the 5,000-page U.S. tax code in his hometown of Erie. But the chainsaw knocked the book off the table twice. Even after putting the code on the sidewalk, he was just able to nick it with the chainsaw. English finally joked about how difficult it was to enact tax reform.

English was also out front in 2002 when he set aside his traditional support of free trade to advocate steel tariffs. He sided with steel workers by leading an effort to persuade President Bush to impose tariffs on imported steel to help domestic steel companies, at the expense of manufacturers that wanted low-cost steel imports. The tariffs were repealed in 2003.

He has also sided with unions by backing trade adjustment assistance programs, which help workers who lose their jobs to foreign competition. In 2004, he was one of 22 Republicans who voted to prevent the Labor Department from taking away eligibility of workers for overtime pay. (He had backed his party on a similar vote in 2003.) Also in 2004, he was one of 39 Republicans to vote in favor of providing an additional 13 weeks of unemployment benefits for people who had exhausted their state benefits, an important vote for his blue-collar district.

But he does not always side with labor. He voted in 2001 to grant the president fast-track authority to negotiate trade deals that Congress cannot amend and to give the administration more flexibility in dealing with government workers at the new Homeland Security Department.

With his experience in writing legislation on the state level, English masters the details of his bills and keeps close track of the legislative action on them. He often builds support for his proposals on trade and taxes by developing caucuses and coalitions on Capitol Hill and K Street.

A reliable conservative on most social issues, he was one of 14 Republicans in 2003 to oppose an amendment creating a school voucher program in the District of Columbia. Under the plan, students would be eligible for up to $7,500 in funds to attend a private elementary or high school in the city.

On Ways and Means, English sits on the Health, Human Resources and Trade subcommittees. In the 109th, English plans to use his Health Subcommittee assignment to push a proposal that had 244 House cosponsors in the 108th — the repeal of Medicare payment caps for outpatient rehabilitation services. The caps were contained in the 1997 balanced budget law, but their implementation has been delayed since then.

English's interest in politics began at an early age. The son of an Erie lawyer who was active in community affairs, English was a political science major in college and an alternate delegate, at age 20, to the 1976 Republican National Convention.

After college, English specialized in tax and social welfare issues for eight years as a legislative aide in a closely divided Pennsylvania state legislature. His career in public office began in 1985 when he was elected city controller of Erie, on a pledge to be a watchdog over the Democratic-dominated government. In 1988, at the midpoint of his four-year term, he ran for state treasurer. He lost by nearly 500,000 votes.

When his term as controller was over, he moved from candidate to strategist. He helped a little-known underdog, Rick Santorum, organize his 1990 upset of Democratic Rep. Doug Walgren. English then returned to Harrisburg as a legislative staffer, including a stint as chief of staff to a state senator, Melissa A. Hart, who is now a House colleague. He appeared content with his behind-the-scenes career as a top legislative staff member but jumped at the chance to run for an open congressional seat in 1994, when GOP Rep. Tom Ridge ran, successfully, for governor.

KEY VOTES

2004

Yes Extend federal unemployment benefits by 13 weeks

Yes Pass $283.2 billion, six-year federal highway and mass transit bill

Yes Approve $146 billion multi-year extension of previously enacted middle-class tax breaks

Yes Amend the Constitution to prohibit same-sex marriage

Yes Cut corporate taxes $137 billion over 10 years

Yes Reorganize U.S. intelligence agencies as proposed by Sept. 11 commission

2003

Yes Cut taxes by $330 billion through fiscal 2013

No Block Bush rule scaling back overtime pay for some white-collar federal workers

Yes Do not allow use of search warrants without first notifying subjects

No Allow importation of prescription drugs

No Create private school voucher program in Washington, D.C.

Yes Ban "partial birth" abortion except to save a woman's life

No Split $18.6 billion in Iraq aid into half-grant, half-loan

Yes Overhaul Medicare and create prescription drug benefit

CQ VOTE STUDIES

	PARTY UNITY		PRESIDENTIAL SUPPORT	
	Support	Oppose	Support	Oppose
2004	88%	12%	76%	24%
2003	93%	7%	91%	9%
2002	93%	7%	87%	13%
2001	89%	11%	81%	19%
2000	83%	17%	38%	62%

INTEREST GROUPS

	AFL-CIO	ADA	CCUS	ACU
2004	40%	25%	90%	68%
2003	21%	20%	93%	68%
2002	11%	0%	95%	92%
2001	25%	10%	95%	68%
2000	30%	25%	76%	56%

PENNSYLVANIA 3

Northwest – Erie

Located in the northwestern corner of the state, the 3rd takes in all of Erie County and portions of six others. This historically blue-collar center includes Erie, the state's fourth-most-populous city. A port on Lake Erie, the city has been an industrial center for more than a century.

Although hard-hit by economic restructuring in the 1980s, the 3rd remained an industrial area. The number of jobs in the service sector in Erie has increased by more than 20 percent since 1990. Fewer steel mills line Mercer County (a small portion of which is in the 4th District), and those remaining now operate with a smaller employment base.

Despite those changes, Mercer boasts the largest concentration of pipe and tube production firms in the nation. In Crawford County, scores of tooling and machine shops dominate the landscape. Industrial expansion in Erie also is on the rise with the addition of several new manufacturing facilities by companies such as Sunburst Electronics.

The city of Erie's median household income is well below the state

median, with townships west and east of the city above the median. Overall, Erie County's household income is slightly below the median, and the county, like the district overall, is largely white. Pockets of black residents in northern and central Erie help give the county a Democratic lean. Mercer County, home to about one in six district residents, also has a Democratic lean, although George W. Bush won the county in the 2004 presidential election after losing it narrowly in 2000.

Democratic tendencies in Erie and Mercer are offset by the Republican leanings in Butler and Crawford counties. Overall, the district (numbered the 21st prior to redistricting following the 2000 census) gave Bush 53 percent of the vote in 2004.

MAJOR INDUSTRY
Manufacturing, law enforcement, service

CITIES
Erie, 103,717; Sharon, 16,328; Butler, 15,121; Meadville, 13,685

NOTABLE
Former Homeland Security Secretary Tom Ridge represented Erie in the U.S. House from 1983 to 1995; The reconstructed *U.S. Brig Niagara*, a fighting ship from the War of 1812, is docked in Erie; Erie's Presque Isle State Park includes a Coast Guard station and Perry Monument.

Rep. Melissa A. Hart (R)

Elected 2000; 3rd term

CAPITOL OFFICE
225-2565
www.hart.house.gov
1024 Longworth 20515-3804; fax 226-2274

COMMITTEES
Standards of Official Conduct
Ways & Means

HOMETOWN
Bradford Woods

BORN
April 4, 1962, Pittsburgh, Pa.

RELIGION
Roman Catholic

FAMILY
Single

EDUCATION
Washington & Jefferson College, B.A. 1984
(business & German); U. of Pittsburgh, J.D. 1987

CAREER
Lawyer

POLITICAL HIGHLIGHTS
Pa. Senate, 1991-2001

ELECTION RESULTS

2004 GENERAL

Melissa A. Hart (R)	204,329	63.1%
Stevan Drobac Jr. (D)	116,303	35.9%
Steven B. Larchuck (X)	3,285	1.0%

2004 PRIMARY

Melissa A. Hart (R)	unopposed

2002 GENERAL

Melissa A. Hart (R)	130,534	64.6%
Stevan Drobac Jr. (D)	71,674	35.5%

PREVIOUS WINNING PERCENTAGES
2000 (59%)

Hart entered the 109th Congress with two new committee assignments — one that she wanted and one in which party leaders wanted her. She gained a seat on Ways and Means after making a somewhat convoluted argument that the proximity of Pittsburgh to the Ohio River, a main artery of the Midwest, gave her familiarity with the concerns of workers in the heartland. "Arguably, I represent both the Northeast and the Midwest," Hart said. "I'm from a place in the East that is as far west as you can be."

Assignment to the powerful tax and trade committee is based on political need, expertise and regional representation, and seldom does a state get more than one seat. Pennsylvania Republican Phil English has been on the committee since 1995. But Hart pointed out other states with two GOP tax writers: California with Chairman Bill Thomas and Wally Herger, and Florida with E. Clay Shaw Jr. and Mark Foley. She also emphasized her expertise on taxes as former chairwoman of the Finance Committee in the Pennsylvania Senate.

Hart also sits on the Standards of Official Conduct Committee, the House's ethics panel, a favor to Speaker J. Dennis Hastert, who wanted to fill the committee with conservative party loyalists. The ethics panel may need to take up allegations connecting Majority Leader Tom DeLay with overseas junkets, American Indian casino money and powerful lobbyists. DeLay was admonished three times last year by the ethics committee.

In winning a historically Democratic district, Hart has gained extra attention from the GOP congressional leadership and the White House. Vice President Dick Cheney visited the 4th District in early 2005 to discuss the administration's plan to create private accounts as part of the Social Security system. Hart said she agreed that Social Security needs to be looked at as it "is facing looming demographic threats and must be updated to fit the realities of today's American public or otherwise face insolvency."

Ambitious and assertive, Hart is both fiscally and socially conservative and her opposition to abortion and support of gun owners' rights are in sync with the district she represents. In the 108th, she sponsored legislation creating a separate class of federal crimes against pregnant women in which the fetuses they carry also are harmed. The bill became law and was a big win for social conservatives. The House had passed versions of it in 1999 and 2001, but those measures stalled in the Senate. The legislation then gained fresh momentum with the discoveries in April 2003 of the bodies of Laci Peterson, a Modesto, Calif., woman, and her unborn son.

The law for the first time gave federal legal status to a fetus. Abortion rights advocates opposed the measure, saying it would essentially give a fetus the same legal standing as the woman carrying it. Yet Hart successfully argued that crimes against women should carry stiffer penalties if they involve pregnant victims. She also offered a bill to withhold federal funds to schools that give students access to a "morning after" birth control pill.

The 4th District may be socially conservative, but it has a long history of union support that in the past has kept it in the Democratic column. Hart has joined with other lawmakers from steel-producing areas in urging the administration to impose quotas on imported steel.

She does not always take the side of labor, however. Hart voted in 2004 against an amendment to provide an additional 13 weeks of unemployment benefits for people who have lost their state benefits, and in 2002 against a measure to give federal employees of the Homeland Security

Department the right to join a union. She backed a bailout of the airline industry that did not include assistance for laid-off workers, including employees of U.S. Airways, which has a hub in Pittsburgh. She then sponsored legislation to help airline workers, but it went nowhere.

Hart is committed to fostering economic development for her district. Her specific proposals have included providing business tax breaks for hiring new workers and funding Army Corps of Engineers water and sewer projects in the Pittsburgh area.

Proving her ambition, Hart ran for the vice chairmanship of the Republican Conference at the start of her second term in 2003. She lost, 159-56, to Jack Kingston of Georgia, a six-term member.

Hart grew up in the Pittsburgh suburbs, where her father was a research chemist for PPG Industries. She told the Pittsburgh Post-Gazette that she recalls writing an eighth grade paper entitled, "Why Ronald Reagan is a patriot." After her father died suddenly, Hart and her two siblings had to work their way through school to help out with the family finances.

She majored in business and German in college and joined the Young Republicans. After law school and a few years with a Pittsburgh law firm, Hart, then 28, decided to run for the state Senate. She wasn't expected to win in the traditionally Democratic district, but her aggressive door-to-door campaign surprised even GOP strategists, allowing Republicans to keep slim control of the state Senate.

Hart made a name for herself during her 10 years in the chamber. As chairwoman of the Finance Committee, she sponsored a measure to eliminate Pennsylvania's tax on computer company services, such as software design, and offered a bill to facilitate electronic commerce in the state. She mentored Phil English, who was her chief of staff and also worked for the Finance Committee before he was elected to the House in 1994.

In 2000, when four-term Democratic Rep. Ron Klink left the seat open to run for the Senate, party leaders cleared the way for Hart's candidacy. As in 1990, Hart faced a tough battle in a Democratic-leaning district, with the GOP's hopes for control of the House at stake. With help from the national Republican Party and the conservative, business-oriented Club for Growth, Hart won impressively with 59 percent of the vote over state Rep. Terry Van Horne, becoming the first Republican elected in the district since 1976. Remapping in 2002 gave her a slightly more Republican constituency. The Pittsburgh Post-Gazette grudgingly backed her over the untested Democratic candidate, Stevan Drobac Jr. Hart won easily with 65 percent. In 2004, she faced Drobac again and took 63 percent.

KEY VOTES

2004

No Extend federal unemployment benefits by 13 weeks

Yes Pass $283.2 billion, six-year federal highway and mass transit bill

Yes Approve $146 billion multi-year extension of previously enacted middle-class tax breaks

Yes Amend the Constitution to prohibit same-sex marriage

Yes Cut corporate taxes $137 billion over 10 years

Yes Reorganize U.S. intelligence agencies as proposed by Sept. 11 commission

2003

Yes Cut taxes by $330 billion through fiscal 2013

No Block Bush rule scaling back overtime pay for some white-collar federal workers

No Do not allow use of search warrants without first notifying subjects

No Allow importation of prescription drugs

Yes Create private school voucher program in Washington, D.C.

Yes Ban "partial birth" abortion except to save a woman's life

No Split $18.6 billion in Iraq aid into half-grant, half-loan

Yes Overhaul Medicare and create prescription drug benefit

CQ VOTE STUDIES

	PARTY UNITY		PRESIDENTIAL SUPPORT	
	Support	Oppose	Support	Oppose
2004	96%	4%	94%	6%
2003	97%	3%	100%	0%
2002	97%	3%	92%	8%
2001	93%	7%	88%	12%

INTEREST GROUPS

	AFL-CIO	ADA	CCUS	ACU
2004	14%	10%	100%	92%
2003	13%	5%	100%	80%
2002	11%	0%	95%	96%
2001	17%	5%	96%	88%

PENNSYLVANIA 4
West — Pittsburgh suburbs, exurbs

The 4th starts at the western Pennsylvania border in Beaver and Lawrence counties and wraps around the northern and eastern sides of Pittsburgh. Once a top producer of iron and steel, this traditionally blue-collar district is struggling to bounce back from hard economic times.

The area's major highways and proximity to Pittsburgh make the 4th attractive to commuters and expanding companies. Although abandoned steel mills still line the rivers, other sectors are beginning to prosper, bringing some much-needed diversity to the economy. Along with the health care industry, which is a major employer, the 4th has a growing number of computer firms. The district also is dabbling in the biotech industry as surrounding universities expand research grants in the field.

Larger companies, such as Respironics in Murrysville, TRACO in Cranberry Township and USG in Aliquippa bring jobs to the area. The district has yet to regain the population of its booming steel days, but some areas, including parts of southern Butler County, are experiencing rapid residential growth.

Although union tradition has generally kept the district's area Democratic from the township level to the presidency, socially conservative Republicans can break the Democratic grip. That happened in 2000, when George W. Bush captured the 4th and Rep. Hart easily won the Democratic-held open seat. Much of the district's GOP base can be found in small farming communities, wealthy Pittsburgh suburbs such as Franklin Park, Fox Chapel and Marshall Township, and the southern tier of Butler County. Redistricting following the 2000 census made the 4th slightly more Republican by moving the boundary farther into Allegheny County, where the GOP's strength has increased in recent years. In 2004, Bush took 54 percent of the district's presidential vote.

MAJOR INDUSTRY
Health care, steel, manufacturing

CITIES
Ross Township (unincorporated), 32,551; Shaler Township (unincorporated), 29,757; McCandless Township (unincorporated), 29,022

NOTABLE
Oliver B. Shallenberger invented the electric meter, which indicated the amount of electrical energy dispensed or applied, in Rochester; New Castle calls itself the fireworks capital of America.

Rep. John E. Peterson (R)

Elected 1996; 5th term

CAPITOL OFFICE
225-5121
www.house.gov/johnpeterson
123 Cannon 20515-3805; fax 225-5796

COMMITTEES
Appropriations
Resources

HOMETOWN
Pleasantville

BORN
Dec. 25, 1938, Titusville, Pa.

RELIGION
Methodist

FAMILY
Wife, Saundra Peterson; one child

EDUCATION
Titusville H.S., graduated 1956

MILITARY SERVICE
Army Reserve, 1957-63

CAREER
Supermarket owner

POLITICAL HIGHLIGHTS
Pleasantville Borough Council, 1969-77; Pa. House,
1977-85; Pa. Senate, 1985-97

ELECTION RESULTS

2004 GENERAL

John E. Peterson (R)	192,852	88.0%
Thomas A. Martin (LIBERT)	26,239	12.0%

2004 PRIMARY

John E. Peterson (R)	47,216	77.8%
Bob Perry (R)	13,501	22.2%

2002 GENERAL

John E. Peterson (R)	124,942	87.4%
Thomas A. Martin (LIBERT)	18,078	12.6%

PREVIOUS WINNING PERCENTAGES
2000 (83%); 1998 (85%); 1996 (60%)

Peterson arrived in the nation's capital determined to enhance the lives of his rural constituents. He represents a district that covers almost one-quarter of the state's land, sprawling across more than 10,000 square miles of mountains, valleys, hamlets and a sizable national forest. It is the birthplace of America's oil industry and the home of Punxsutawney Phil, the famous groundhog who every February determines whether spring is on its way. The largest urban area is a college town — State College, home of Pennsylvania State University.

Peterson has tailored his legislative portfolio to fit rural needs. He has focused on rural health care, economic development, the multiple use of the Allegheny National Forest and development of the 5th's remaining fossil energy reserves. From his seat on the Appropriations Committee, he also secures funding for Pennsylvania's medical schools.

Peterson is the co-chairman, along with Florida Democrat Allen Boyd, of the 100-plus member Congressional Rural Caucus, which he also looks after legislatively. When the House passed the huge surface transportation authorization measure early in the 109th Congress, Peterson noted that it included $590 million for a new rural road safety program for two-lane roads. He said the program was a priority for caucus members. Peterson is also one of the few Northeastern lawmakers who have joined the Western Caucus.

Peterson often pleads for federal help to boost the economy of his district, which has pockets of rural Appalachian poverty. He was publicly unhappy with President Bush's proposed 2005 budget that aimed to cut farm subsidies and other programs that aid rural Americans. Peterson issued a stern rebuke that drew national attention. "Those who are currently advocating these draconian cuts would not be in office today if it weren't for rural America," he said. "These cuts disproportionately target essential programs in rural communities while turning a blind eye to the wasteful spending that is rampant in many big cities across the country."

It was a rare break from party loyalty for Peterson. On a broad range of issues, Peterson is as conservative as they come. He opposes abortion, supports gun owners' right and wants to give parents taxpayer-financed vouchers to pay tuition at private schools. Yet he can also stray from a majority of his party when trying to protect his district's workers. In 2004, he was one of only 39 Republicans to vote to extend unemployment benefits for an additional 13 weeks. In the 108th, he voted with his party 94 percent of the time, but he agreed with Bush's position only 86 percent of the time.

Peterson also takes an active role advising Pennsylvania universities on federal funding priorities for medical research. As a member of the Appropriations subcommittee with jurisdiction over the National Institutes of Health budget, Peterson has helped Penn State and Pennsylvania's five other medical schools win a hefty share of federal research money. And when Congress in late 2004 passed the catchall appropriations measure, Peterson said rural health care programs were increased by more than $3 million, to nearly $146 million, because of his efforts. He was also able to gain funding for Pennsylvania's Office of Rural Health, located at Penn State University, he said.

Peterson has a seat on the Resources Committee, where he has warned that environmental extremism tramples the rights of private property owners. He has badgered the Forest Service to ensure the Allegheny National Forest is kept open for logging and other uses, and that local communities are helped in providing fire and emergency services. He also has said he would support expanding the forest's wilderness area to include old-growth forest that has never been logged.

Peterson was born and raised in the small town of Titusville near the spot where Edwin Drake drilled the country's first oil well. He grew up in a household headed by a steelworker father who never went to high school and who was a recovering alcoholic. The four children went to work to help with family expenses, and college was never an option for Peterson.

From this childhood, Peterson emerged with a strong work ethic, as well as an aversion to alcohol that has led to his work combating substance abuse among rural youths. Peterson is among the most vocal advocates of legislation mandating random drug testing for all high school students, saying it could reduce overall drug use and school violence. In the 108th, he introduced a bill that would establish a new program to randomly test high school students for drug use. The proposal drew plaudits from Bush, who made a brief reference to it in his 2004 State of the Union address. "Schools that use random drug testing not only provide young people with a good reason to say 'no' to drugs, but also give parents a report card that may help save their child's life," Peterson said.

A year after completing high school, Peterson joined the Army Reserve and then opened a small grocery store in nearby Pleasantville with his brother and a family friend, who put up the money. Peterson eventually bought out his partners and expanded the store, which he sold in 1984.

He entered politics in 1969, at the urging of other local businessmen in Pleasantville, winning a seat on the borough council. After eight years, he was elected to the state House in a special election; eight years after that he moved to the state Senate, where he chaired the Public Health and Welfare Committee and the Republican Policy Committee.

When Republican William F. Clinger did not seek re-election in 1996, Peterson was well-situated to succeed him in Congress: His state Senate district covered roughly the western half of the big 5th. Peterson's winning vote share in November was 60 percent, but his victory did not come easily. In the spring, he had had to fight off three opponents in the Republican primary, including Bob Shuster, a son of Bud Shuster, then the veteran congressman from a neighboring district.

His GOP base secure, Peterson has had no re-election difficulty. The Democrats have not fielded a candidate since 1996. In 2004, Peterson defeated Libertarian Thomas A. Martin, rolling up 88 percent.

KEY VOTES

2004
Yes Extend federal unemployment benefits by 13 weeks
Yes Pass $283.2 billion, six-year federal highway and mass transit bill
Yes Approve $146 billion multi-year extension of previously enacted middle-class tax breaks
Yes Amend the Constitution to prohibit same-sex marriage
Yes Cut corporate taxes $137 billion over 10 years
Yes Reorganize U.S. intelligence agencies as proposed by Sept. 11 commission

2003
Yes Cut taxes by $330 billion through fiscal 2013
No Block Bush rule scaling back overtime pay for some white-collar federal workers
Yes Do not allow use of search warrants without first notifying subjects
Yes Allow importation of prescription drugs
Yes Create private school voucher program in Washington, D.C.
Yes Ban "partial birth" abortion except to save a woman's life
No Split $18.6 billion in Iraq aid into half-grant, half-loan
Yes Overhaul Medicare and create prescription drug benefit

CQ VOTE STUDIES

	PARTY UNITY		PRESIDENTIAL SUPPORT	
	Support	Oppose	Support	Oppose
2004	92%	8%	79%	21%
2003	96%	4%	91%	9%
2002	94%	6%	84%	16%
2001	96%	4%	93%	7%
2000	94%	6%	27%	73%

INTEREST GROUPS

	AFL-CIO	ADA	CCUS	ACU
2004	33%	15%	100%	83%
2003	13%	10%	90%	83%
2002	13%	0%	100%	100%
2001	8%	0%	100%	88%
2000	0%	0%	90%	96%

PENNSYLVANIA 5
North central — State College

The giant, sprawling 5th takes in all or part of 17 counties, totaling one-fourth of Pennsylvania's land area, as well as the state's largest university, Pennsylvania State University. The district's upper counties border New York State, and its westernmost point is only about 30 miles from the Ohio border. In land framed by the Appalachian Mountains sit struggling towns and pockets of poverty.

State College (Centre County), the district's largest city and home of Penn State, has brought in manufacturing firms that specialize in electronics and computer products. The area's technology-driven development mimics the tide that brought the Silicon Valley to prominence, although on a much smaller scale. The district also boasts a contingent of more than 200 meteorologists.

While State College's workforce is technologically advanced, the 5th's other counties remain tied to timber production, manufacturing and oil refining. The district's population is overwhelmingly white. At 96 percent, it has the second-highest percentage in the state.

Much of the 5th — particularly the northern counties — votes Republican, and George W. Bush won all of its counties in 2004. Some exceptions exist: Penn State keeps Centre County competitive for Democrats. Neighboring Clinton County and Elk County, which is farther west, lean toward Democrats in local elections, although they generally support Republicans in statewide and federal elections. Jefferson, Tioga, McKean, Clarion and Potter counties are staunchly Republican. Bush received more than twice as many votes as John Kerry in seven of the counties either wholly or partially within the 5th.

MAJOR INDUSTRY
Manufacturing, higher education, timber

CITIES
State College, 38,420; St. Marys, 14,502; Oil City, 11,504

NOTABLE
The town of Punxsutawney (Jefferson County) holds a yearly celebration for groundhog Punxsutawney Phil, who becomes a national media star on Groundhog Day; Situated amid about 160,000 acres of the Tioga State Forest lies the Grand Canyon of Pennsylvania; Drake's Well, the so-called birthplace of the petroleum industry, is located along the banks of Oil Creek near Titusville.

Rep. Jim Gerlach (R)

CAPITOL OFFICE
225-4315
www.house.gov/gerlach
308 Cannon 20515-3806; fax 225-8440

COMMITTEES
Financial Services
Transportation & Infrastructure

HOMETOWN
West Pikeland Township

BORN
Feb. 25, 1955, Ellwood City, Pa.

RELIGION
Protestant

FAMILY
Wife, Karen Gerlach; three children, three
stepchildren

EDUCATION
Dickinson College, B.A. 1977 (political science);
Dickinson School of Law, J.D. 1980

CAREER
Lawyer

POLITICAL HIGHLIGHTS
Republican nominee for Pa. House, 1986;
Pa. House, 1991-95; Pa. Senate, 1995-2003

ELECTION RESULTS

2004 GENERAL

Jim Gerlach (R)	160,348	51.0%
Lois Murphy (D)	153,977	49.0%

2004 PRIMARY

Jim Gerlach (R)	unopposed

2002 GENERAL

Jim Gerlach (R)	103,648	51.4%
Dan Wofford (D)	98,128	48.6%

Elected 2002; 2nd term

Gerlach represents a classic swing district that was redrawn after the 2000 census with a slight Republican edge. He has won both of his past two elections by less than 3 percentage points. The GOP leadership is understanding, therefore, if Gerlach drifts away occasionally from the party's point of view. And the leadership has also done what it can to help him keep the 6th District in GOP hands.

For example, Gerlach (GUR-lock) was given a coveted slot on the Transportation and Infrastructure Committee to funnel highway money to his district. Then he was tapped as the lead sponsor of high-profile legislation eliminating the "marriage penalty" in the income tax code, even though he played hardly any role in the legislative deal-making. The measure represented the first of four leadership measures aimed at extending President Bush's tax cut legacy.

"No, I've not worked that much on tax bills since I'm not on the Ways and Means Committee," Gerlach acknowledged in April 2004. "But this is a bill I'm proud to sponsor." Near the end of the 108th Congress, Gerlach was given a seat on the Financial Services Committee.

Within three months of arriving in Washington, Gerlach was named by Speaker J. Dennis Hastert to a 49-member "Prescription Drug Action Team." The group was stacked with other members who narrowly won in 2002 and who it was believed could accrue political benefits from associating with an effort to lower prescription drug prices.

Gerlach generally supports GOP initiatives, though he does stray from the party at times. He was one of 27 Republicans to vote against amending the Constitution to prohibit same-sex marriage, and he first voted against an amendment to allow drilling in Alaska's Arctic National Wildlife Refuge before voting for a full energy bill that included the drilling.

His presidential support score for the 108th Congress was 85 percent — lower than anyone in Pennsylvania's GOP delegation except for moderate James C. Greenwood. He voted with a majority of Republicans 88 percent of the time on votes pitting one party against the other.

Six weeks before the 2004 election, the House approved a Gerlach-sponsored bill to reauthorize the National Estuary Program, an initiative within the Environmental Protection Agency that restores coastal habitat and protects public water supplies.

"Nowhere has the National Estuary Program been more successful than in Pennsylvania," Gerlach said in announcing the bill's passage. Earlier, he sponsored legislation that became law to establish a national veterans' cemetery in southeastern Pennsylvania.

Gerlach had to deal with the realities of the war in Iraq in May 2004 when a videotape posted on an Islamic militant Web site showed al Qaeda's leader in Iraq beheading a man identified as Nicholas Berg. Berg's family lived in Gerlach's suburban Philadelphia district. Gerlach met with family members and told reporters the family had been frustrated by a lack of information from the U.S. government when Berg was detained without charge by Iraqi police for nearly two weeks before his capture.

Before coming to Congress, Gerlach spent 12 years as a state legislator. He was well-regarded in Republican circles for his ability to understand complex issues, and his official House Web site contains a lengthy list of his accomplishments in Harrisburg. But his image as a policy wonk is a bit leavened: He is known for his rendition of "Get Me to the Church on

Time," from the musical "My Fair Lady," which he says provided him with his only acting credit in local theater.

While serving in Harrisburg, Gerlach was the prime sponsor of Pennsylvania's high-profile 1996 welfare law overhaul. He also championed legislation to combat suburban sprawl, and he used his state Senate seat to mediate some development disputes between local authorities.

Though Pennsylvania lost two seats in reapportionment after the 2000 census, Gerlach's colleagues in the Republican-dominated General Assembly redrew the congressional map for this decade with him in mind. No House incumbent chose to run in the redrawn 6th District — which had a close partisan split, but overlapped with much of Gerlach's state Senate constituency — and he was unopposed for the GOP nomination.

In November 2002, he won by 5,520 votes over Democratic lawyer Dan Wofford, the son of former Sen. Harris Wofford, whose Washington connections and behind-the-scenes political experience helped him raise money for an effective campaign.

His 2004 opponent, Lower Merion lawyer Lois Murphy, proved to be an even more difficult adversary. Calling herself a "fiscally disciplined Democrat," Murphy said she would work to reduce the deficit and government waste. She released a 26-page economic plan that discussed expanding industries in the sprawling district to promote job growth, and she criticized Gerlach for voting against legislation that would have prohibited government contracts to U.S. businesses whose headquarters are overseas.

Murphy collected endorsements from the Sierra Club and national issue groups, such as MoveOn.org and Emily's List, a group that supports women candidates. She also was able to keep pace with Gerlach in fundraising, thanks in no small measure to recruiting Pennsylvania Democratic Gov. Edward G. Rendell as one of her campaign co-chairmen.

But Gerlach questioned whether Murphy was too inexperienced to serve in Congress. He was helped by national Republican attack ads, one of which showed a picture of Murphy next to the phrase, "Negotiating with Taliban." In the next image, Murphy shared the screen with the description, "Opposes Using Military to Fight Terrorism."

Murphy called the ads "an outrageous smear," but Gerlach defended the attack, saying it simply listed the position of groups that supported his opponent. The charge that she associated with groups who would negotiate with the Taliban was based on an opinion piece by one board member from a group called the Council for a Livable World, which had endorsed Murphy.

Gerlach won the contest with 51 percent of the vote.

KEY VOTES

2004

No Extend federal unemployment benefits by 13 weeks
Yes Pass $283.2 billion, six-year federal highway and mass transit bill
Yes Approve $146 billion multi-year extension of previously enacted middle-class tax breaks
No Amend the Constitution to prohibit same-sex marriage
Yes Cut corporate taxes $137 billion over 10 years
Yes Reorganize U.S. intelligence agencies as proposed by Sept. 11 commission

2003

Yes Cut taxes by $330 billion through fiscal 2013
No Block Bush rule scaling back overtime pay for some white-collar federal workers
No Do not allow use of search warrants without first notifying subjects
No Allow importation of prescription drugs
Yes Create private school voucher program in Washington, D.C.
Yes Ban "partial birth" abortion except to save a woman's life
No Split $18.6 billion in Iraq aid into half-grant, half-loan
Yes Overhaul Medicare and create prescription drug benefit

CQ VOTE STUDIES

	PARTY UNITY		PRESIDENTIAL SUPPORT	
	Support	Oppose	Support	Oppose
2004	84%	16%	76%	24%
2003	91%	9%	91%	9%

INTEREST GROUPS

	AFL-CIO	ADA	CCUS	ACU
2004	14%	20%	100%	68%
2003	7%	5%	97%	72%

PENNSYLVANIA 6

Southeast — part of Berks and Chester counties, Philadelphia suburbs

The 6th takes in urban, suburban and rural communities stretching from a slice of Montgomery County in the Philadelphia area through northern Chester County and southern and eastern portions of Berks County, including part of Reading and all of Kutztown. Most of the district's land is spread through sparsely populated towns.

Once known for its railroads and industrial prowess, the economy of Berks County has branched out in recent years to include service and retail jobs. With its share of historical sites and untouched land, the 6th enjoys a modest tourism industry. Reading is home to a minor league baseball team, and, in the neighboring 16th District, a performing arts center and minor league hockey team.

Growth and water-use issues dominate much of the political discussion in the region, which is mostly situated in the area triangulated by Philadelphia, Reading and Lancaster.

Remnants of an earlier time are evident, as the 6th is home to numerous covered bridges, old mill towns and Pennsylvania Dutch communities, as well as the Hopewell Furnace National Historic Site, a preserved iron plantation in Elverson that dates back to the 18th century.

The GOP-controlled legislature vastly altered the district during redistricting following the 2000 census, redrawing it to give a Republican candidate a small but significant edge. The new 6th is now much closer to Philadelphia and takes in Norristown, the Montgomery County seat, where more than one-third of residents are black.

The revised 6th certainly makes the nation's dwindling list of competitive districts. John Kerry defeated George W. Bush in the 2004 presidential election by 3 percentage points here, while GOP Rep. Gerlach defeated his opponent by 2 percentage points.

MAJOR INDUSTRY
Manufacturing, tourism, retail

CITIES
Reading (pt.), 36,911; Norristown, 31,282; Pottstown, 21,859

NOTABLE
Daniel Boone was born in Exeter Township.

Rep. Curt Weldon (R)

Elected 1986; 10th term

CAPITOL OFFICE
225-2011
curtpa07@mail.house.gov
www.house.gov/curtweldon
2466 Rayburn 20515-3807; fax 225-8137

COMMITTEES
Armed Services
(Tactical Air & Land Forces - chairman)
Homeland Security
Science

HOMETOWN
Glen Mills

BORN
July 22, 1947, Marcus Hook, Pa.

RELIGION
Protestant

FAMILY
Wife, Mary Gallagher Weldon; five children

EDUCATION
West Chester State College, B.A. 1969 (humanities)

CAREER
Teacher; consultant

POLITICAL HIGHLIGHTS
Mayor of Marcus Hook, 1977-82; Delaware County Council, 1981-86 (chairman, 1982-86); Republican nominee for U.S. House, 1984

ELECTION RESULTS

2004 GENERAL

Curt Weldon (R)	196,556	58.8%
Paul Scoles (D)	134,932	40.3%

2004 PRIMARY

Curt Weldon (R)	unopposed

2002 GENERAL

Curt Weldon (R)	146,296	66.1%
Peter A. Lennon (D)	75,055	33.9%

PREVIOUS WINNING PERCENTAGES
2000 (65%); 1998 (72%); 1996 (67%); 1994 (70%); 1992 (66%); 1990 (65%); 1988 (68%); 1986 (61%)

National security issues are Weldon's passion. He has taught a course on international security at three different Pennsylvania universities, Widener, Drexel and Eastern. As one of the most pro-military members of the House, Weldon has used his seat on Armed Services through four administrations to argue for ever-larger Pentagon budgets.

The second-ranking Republican on the Armed Services Committee and chairman of its Tactical Air and Land Forces Subcommittee, Weldon was disappointed in being passed over twice as full committee chairman. But his disappointment has not stopped him from being fully engaged in committee affairs. And despite his long commitment to robust military budgets, he is not reluctant to criticize Pentagon officials, particularly when their policies affect the troops in the field.

In early 2005, he expressed frustration that the Army has deployed only a quarter of the countermeasures military officials say are needed to detect and disrupt roadside explosives, which are one of the leading killers of U.S. troops in Iraq. Army leaders said they are developing countermeasures, such as jammers, which suppress remote-controlled bomb-detonating signals. Weldon complained the jammers were not being produced quickly enough. "We should be building what we have available today and building it at mass production rates to get maximum availability in the field," Weldon said.

He also has long assailed as unrealistic Pentagon plans to buy three different types of multibillion-dollar fighter jets at about the same time. In 2003, Weldon said it was "disgusting" that one of the planes, the F/A-22 Raptor, was subject to cockpit computer crashes an average of once an hour. And, in 2005, he was particularly unhappy to learn that a Pentagon plan to terminate production of the C-130J Hercules transport plane could cost nearly $2 billion in termination payments to the contractor. Killing the C-130 and cutting back the F/A-22 "could exceed $2 billion" in termination and other costs, said Weldon. "That's unacceptable; it's outrageous," he said.

On the other hand, Weldon has long been Capitol Hill's most ardent advocate of a U.S. anti-missile program. During the Clinton years, he was one of the first in Congress to raise concerns about the missile capacity of North Korea, Iran and Iraq or the possibility of an accidental launch of a Russian ICBM. In 1999, Congress approved his bill declaring it a national policy to deploy the missile shield "as soon as technologically possible."

Weldon's interests fit well with those of his district, which is heavily blue-collar, mostly Republican and in part dependent on the defense industry. Boeing employs more than 4,500 people at a helicopter plant in Ridley Park, Pa. Weldon has been one of the main reasons that Boeing's V-22 Osprey helicopter project remains alive, despite repeated setbacks including two crashes that killed 23 Marines in 2000.

Weldon tried in the 107th Congress to gain the Armed Services chair. He raised campaign funds for fellow Republicans and even spent $17,000 on a glossy booklet touting his vision. But the leadership instead elevated Arizona Republican Bob Stump, who ranked first in seniority on the panel. When Stump gave up the gavel in 2002 for health reasons, Weldon again had to step aside for the more senior Duncan Hunter of California.

After the creation of the Homeland Security Committee in the 108th, GOP leaders skipped over Weldon and instead chose Christopher Cox of California, an ally of Speaker J. Dennis Hastert, to chair the new panel. Weldon sits on the committee, which gained permanent status in the 109th.

Weldon, who speaks Russian, is a friend of top Russian politicians, including several members of the Duma, Russia's parliament. He has visited the country and its former republics more than 40 times. During a meeting he set up in 1999 in Vienna between members of Congress and the Duma, the parties laid out the principles of a peace settlement in Kosovo, which became the blueprint for negotiations between NATO and Yugoslavian strongman Slobodan Milosevic.

Weldon has also taken the lead in trying to persuade North Korean officials to resume talks on their nuclear weapons program. When Pyongyang announced early in 2005 that it has nuclear weapons, Weldon, who has traveled twice to North Korea, said the announcement came as no surprise and appeared to be an attempt to win concessions before returning to the negotiating table. "That is not going to happen," Weldon said. "Their allies need to pressure them to come back to the table. But we're not going to provide a reward for bad behavior."

Weldon's blue-collar roots often put him on the side of organized labor in key trade votes. He opposed the 1993 North American Free Trade Agreement, and in 2002, he voted against granting the president fast-track authority to negotiate trade agreements that Congress cannot amend. He supported bills to ban the permanent replacement of striking workers and to raise the minimum wage.

The youngest of nine children, Weldon grew up in the small, working-class town of Marcus Hook, south of Philadelphia. His father was a machinist. Weldon graduated from West Chester State College, went into teaching and joined the volunteer fire department. He attracted the attention of Delaware County's powerful Republican Party organization after he became mayor of Marcus Hook and helped rescue it from a spiral of factory shutdowns, economic decline and gang warfare. In 1981, he won a seat on the Delaware County Council.

Local Republicans saw Weldon as a good fit for the district's conservative mix of blue- and white-collar workers, and in 1984 he got the GOP nod for a run against Democratic Rep. Bob Edgar. His near-win (he lost by only 412 votes) made him the favorite two years later when Edgar ran for the Senate, leaving the House seat open. Weldon prevailed with 61 percent of the vote and has usually won re-election easily. In 2004, he won with 59 percent, his lowest percentage since gaining the seat in 1986.

He never forgot his beginnings in Marcus Hook, though. As a House member, Weldon founded the Congressional Fire Services Caucus, which now has several hundred members.

KEY VOTES

2004
Yes Extend federal unemployment benefits by 13 weeks
Yes Pass $283.2 billion, six-year federal highway and mass transit bill
Yes Approve $146 billion multi-year extension of previously enacted middle-class tax breaks
Yes Amend the Constitution to prohibit same-sex marriage
Yes Cut corporate taxes $137 billion over 10 years
Yes Reorganize U.S. intelligence agencies as proposed by Sept. 11 commission

2003
Yes Cut taxes by $330 billion through fiscal 2013
No Block Bush rule scaling back overtime pay for some white-collar federal workers
Yes Do not allow use of search warrants without first notifying subjects
? Allow importation of prescription drugs
Yes Create private school voucher program in Washington, D.C.
Yes Ban "partial birth" abortion except to save a woman's life
No Split $18.6 billion in Iraq aid into half-grant, half-loan
Yes Overhaul Medicare and create prescription drug benefit

CQ VOTE STUDIES

	PARTY UNITY		PRESIDENTIAL SUPPORT	
	Support	Oppose	Support	Oppose
2004	85%	15%	85%	15%
2003	89%	11%	90%	10%
2002	86%	14%	71%	29%
2001	88%	12%	80%	20%
2000	85%	15%	33%	67%

INTEREST GROUPS

	AFL-CIO	ADA	CCUS	ACU
2004	33%	15%	100%	79%
2003	13%	5%	96%	88%
2002	25%	15%	79%	79%
2001	42%	15%	82%	70%
2000	20%	5%	80%	76%

PENNSYLVANIA 7
Suburban Philadelphia – most of Delaware County

Anchored in the suburbs south and west of Philadelphia, the politically competitive 7th takes in vast tracts of middle-class suburbia, including most of Delaware County, the district's population center, as well as southwestern Montgomery and eastern Chester counties.

The 7th attracted significant economic growth in the 1990s. Its defense industry, driven by Lockheed Martin and Boeing, is a large employer, as are the pharmaceutical and technology sectors. New developments, many of which are springing up in the less-populated areas of Chester County, are attracting Philadelphia residents.

Upper Merion Township in Montgomery County has been expanding rapidly since the 1990s opening of the Blue Route (Interstate 476), which links Interstate 95 along the Delaware River with the Schuylkill Expressway near King of Prussia. Farther south, older suburbs such as Norwood, Ridley Park, Media and Upper Darby are mostly white and working class. So is Marcus Hook, an old refinery town along the Delaware River. The 7th has the state's highest percentage of residents with Irish (31 percent) or Italian (20 percent) ancestry.

As recently as 1988, Delaware County voted Republican for president by 21 percentage points. But the county now supports Democrats in presidential elections. The county's hefty GOP registration advantage is shrinking, and John Kerry won Delaware in 2004 with 57 percent, the highest total for a Democratic presidential candidate since 1964. The county's strongest Democratic areas, including the mostly black city of Chester, are in the 1st District.

The GOP still does well in the expanding, upper-income areas of Delaware County, including Edgmont Township in the west and fast-growing Concord and Bethel townships in the southwest.

MAJOR INDUSTRY
Pharmaceuticals, defense

CITIES
Radnor Township (unincorporated), 30,878; Drexel Hill (unincorporated), 29,364; Springfield (unincorporated), 23,677

NOTABLE
The King of Prussia Mall claims to be the East Coast's largest shopping center.

Rep. Michael G. Fitzpatrick (R)

Elected 2004; 1st term

CAPITOL OFFICE
225-4276
michael.fitzpatrick@mail.house.gov
www.house.gov/fitzpatrick
1516 Longworth 20515-3808; fax 225-9511

COMMITTEES
Financial Services
Small Business

HOMETOWN
Levittown

BORN
June 28, 1963, Philadelphia, Pa.

RELIGION
Roman Catholic

FAMILY
Wife, Kathy Fitzpatrick; six children

EDUCATION
St. Thomas U. (Fla.), B.A. 1985 (political science);
Dickinson School of Law, J.D. 1988

CAREER
Lawyer

POLITICAL HIGHLIGHTS
Republican nominee for Pa. House, 1990, 1994;
Bucks County Board of Commissioners, 1995-2005

ELECTION RESULTS

2004 GENERAL

Michael G. Fitzpatrick (R)	183,229	55.3%
Virginia Waters Schrader (D)	143,427	43.3%
Arthur L. Farnsworth (LIBERT)	3,710	1.1%

As late as mid-2004, Fitzpatrick had no designs on a seat in the 109th Congress. But the surprise retirement decision by six-term Republican James C. Greenwood opened up an opportunity in suburban Philadelphia's 8th District. Fitzpatrick — the favorite of the GOP leaders in Bucks County, the district's dominant jurisdiction, where he had served for a decade as a commissioner — grabbed the chance and won a relatively easy victory.

Fitzpatrick is more conservative on social issues than his predecessor, but he does not emphasize this aspect of his political persona, instead focusing on pragmatic, locally related issues. His freshman committee assignments, to Financial Services and Small Business, could help him in the largely affluent and business-oriented 8th.

Fitzpatrick believes that government services work best at the local level and that Washington should allow more local flexibility in spending federal aid. His years as county official might give him insight on how to improve the relationship between Washington and localities. When Hurricane Floyd ravaged the area in 1999, Fitzpatrick aggressively pursued the county's "fair share" of federal disaster funds and helped institute an innovative program that included elevating houses above the flood plain.

He advocates basing homeland security grants more on risk and less on population so first-responders in his county could receive more aid. He also plans to meet with health care providers on malpractice liability costs that he said are causing doctors to flee the state.

Greenwood had already been nominated for another term in the April primary when he decided to retire to take a lobbying job. Though Greenwood favored a Republican with more-centrist views on social issues, local GOP leaders rallied around Fitzpatrick and nominated him at a party meeting.

But his 12 percentage point win over little-known Democrat Virginia Waters Schrader was less impressive than Greenwood's usual margins, leaving Fitzpatrick vulnerable in 2006, perhaps even in the primary, in a district where voters tend to be fiscally conservative but more-liberal on social issues.

PENNSYLVANIA 8

Northern Philadelphia suburbs — Bucks County

Nestled north of Philadelphia, the 8th takes in all of Bucks County, a small portion of Montgomery County and a sliver of Northeast Philadelphia. Established in 1682 as one of the state's three original counties, Bucks features stately mansions. The scenery and charm continue to attract wealthy new residents.

Bucks County grew about 10 percent in the 1990s, and the area's healthy, white-collar economy claims to support more than 20,000 small businesses. But during the decade, blue-collar workers faced cutbacks in the steel industry, once a major employer in Bucks. A new deep-water port has helped, making the 8th something of a distribution and warehouse center. The district also is home to several hospitals. Voters in the 8th tend to be fiscally conservative but support environmentalism and hold moderate stances on some social issues.

Upper Bucks leans Republican. Bedminster Township in north-central Bucks was a rare Philadelphia suburb that did not vote for the former Philadelphia mayor, Democrat Edward G. Rendell, in the 2002 gubernatorial election. The GOP also does well in wealthy Upper and Lower Makefield townships. Democrats are strong in southeastern Bucks, near the Philadelphia line, and in the Pennsylvania suburbs of Trenton, N.J.

Although Republicans dominate local elections in the 8th, Democrats can compete in statewide and federal elections here. Rendell won 63 percent of the Bucks County vote in 2002, and the 8th gave John Kerry a 3 percentage point cushion in the 2004 presidential election.

MAJOR INDUSTRY
Health care, wholesale and retail trade

CITIES
Levittown (unincorporated), 53,966; Philadelphia (pt.), 31,549

NOTABLE
George Washington's Delaware River crossing is re-enacted in Washington Crossing each Christmas Day.

Rep. Bill Shuster (R)

Elected May 2001; 2nd full term

Shuster has diligently followed in his father's footsteps by directing federal funds home for roads and other public works improvements in the rural 9th District. Known as the "king of asphalt," veteran GOP Rep. Bud Shuster paved the way for his son Bill to follow him into the House.

Bud Shuster, who had been chairman of the Transportation and Infrastructure Committee for six years, resigned in January 2001 citing health concerns, a move that allowed his son to make a successful bid for his seat after an abbreviated special election.

Bill Shuster not only followed his father by gaining assignment to the Transportation Committee, he also got the gavel of the Economic Development, Public Buildings and Emergency Management Subcommittee at the start of the 109th Congress. The panel has jurisdiction over economic development for distressed urban and rural areas, including programs administered by the Appalachian Regional Commission and the Federal Emergency Management Agency.

"I believe every son wants to make their parents proud, and since my father knows the value of the Transportation Committee to central and western Pennsylvanians, it was nice to get a pat on the back from him," Shuster said when his chairmanship was announced.

Shuster has big shoes to fill. As full committee chairman, his father rose to national prominence as the reigning wheeler-dealer on roads and bridges. He had numerous Pennsylvania roadways named after him as a thank-you from grateful constituents — including a "Bud Shuster Highway" and a separate "Bud Shuster Byway."

Now in his second full term, Bill Shuster has kept a low media profile. He talks to reporters from newspapers and broadcast stations in his district, but declines interviews with national journalists unless they want to discuss issues related to Pennsylvania. And he has been forthcoming about his ability to send money home. By the end of his freshman year, he boasted of winning funding for 18 district projects, including $700,000 for water service improvements in one town and $40,000 for two new girls' softball fields.

Shuster will have another shot at gaining highway and public works largess in the 109th Congress. The Transportation Committee tried to move an update of the 1998 surface transportation law in the 108th, but was stymied by disagreements among GOP members and between lawmakers and the Bush administration. President Bush wanted a less expensive measure as an example of fiscal discipline in an election year. The measure was reintroduced at the start of the 109th.

A loyal Republican and devout conservative, Shuster rarely opposes his party's leaders. During his 2001 bid to succeed his father, he emphasized his opposition to abortion and support for gun owners' rights. Shuster also campaigned on his support for Bush's tax cut plan.

His loyalty was rewarded when he was named one of several dozen assistant whips in Majority Whip Roy Blunt's operation. Shuster was also given a seat on the Armed Services Committee in the 109th. The posting will help in his efforts to keep open Letterkenny Army Depot, a target of earlier base-closing rounds. Shuster says keeping the district facility from being closed or downsized in the next round of base evaluations in 2005 will be "a tough battle."

Shuster has shown an interest in defense and foreign affairs, joining in 2002 congressional delegations to Moscow, Afghanistan and Uzbekistan to

CAPITOL OFFICE
225-2431
www.house.gov/shuster
1108 Longworth 20515-3809; fax 225-2486

COMMITTEES
Armed Services
Small Business
Transportation & Infrastructure
(Economic Development, Public Buildings &
Emergency Management - chairman)

HOMETOWN
Hollidaysburg

BORN
Jan. 10, 1961, McKeesport, Pa.

RELIGION
Lutheran

FAMILY
Wife, Rebecca Shuster; two children

EDUCATION
Dickinson College, B.A. 1983 (political science & history); American U., M.B.A. 1987

CAREER
Car dealer; tire company manager

POLITICAL HIGHLIGHTS
No previous office

ELECTION RESULTS

2004 GENERAL
Bill Shuster (R)	184,320	69.5%
Paul I. Politis (D)	80,787	30.5%

2004 PRIMARY
Bill Shuster (R)	43,097	51.3%
Michael DelGrosso (R)	40,845	48.7%

2002 GENERAL
Bill Shuster (R)	124,184	71.1%
John R. Henry (D)	50,558	28.9%

PREVIOUS WINNING PERCENTAGES
2001 Special Election (52%)

meet with foreign leaders and U.S. troops stationed there. Two months later, he went to Guantánamo Bay, Cuba, where imprisoned al Qaeda and Taliban prisoners were kept, to assess the need for improvements.

Shuster had to deal with an ethical issue during his first full House term. As his hard-fought 2004 primary campaign was under way, one of his congressional aides was accused of spying on his political opponent at his home and at fundraising events. Shuster said the aide was acting independently, but the aide said Shuster ordered the spying.

Members of the ethics committee determined that Shuster did not violate House ethics rules that prohibit the use of paid staff members to carry out campaign work. Shuster overcame the accusations and narrowly won the primary, thanks in part to the political value of his family name.

Bill Shuster was not the first of Bud Shuster's sons to seek a House seat. Bill's brother, Bob, ran in 1996 to succeed retiring nine-term Republican Rep. William F. Clinger in the 5th District, which borders the 9th. He lost the Republican primary to John E. Peterson, who went on to win and hold the seat. Bob Shuster was mentioned as a possible 9th District candidate after his father's resignation, but Bill emerged as the Shuster of choice.

An automobile dealer, Bill Shuster had no prior experience in elective office. "This is about Bill Shuster, and Bill Shuster standing on his own two feet," Shuster told the Chambersburg (Pa.) Public Opinion. "I run my own show." But he acknowledged his father would be a tough act to follow, saying, "He set very high standards that I have to live up to."

Despite his family ties, Shuster's initial election victory in 2001 was closer than expected. He defeated Democrat Scott Conklin, a Centre County commissioner, with 52 percent of the vote to Conklin's 44 percent.

Although seriously outspent by Shuster, conservative Democrat Conklin ran a tireless campaign, driving throughout the expansive district in his own car. Shuster appeared to be hindered by hard feelings from some fellow Republicans who might have run themselves if they had had the same kind of name recognition.

After an easy bid for re-election in 2002, Shuster had another tough campaign in 2004. But this time the challenge came during the primary, not in the general election. Republican Michael DelGrosso, a financial consultant who also enjoyed a high degree of name recognition as his family name is found on pasta sauces, went after him in the primary. DelGrosso came within 2 percentage points of ousting Shuster. Shuster then went on to win in November with almost 70 percent of the vote.

KEY VOTES

2004
No Extend federal unemployment benefits by 13 weeks
Yes Pass $283.2 billion, six-year federal highway and mass transit bill
Yes Approve $146 billion multi-year extension of previously enacted middle-class tax breaks
Yes Amend the Constitution to prohibit same-sex marriage
Yes Cut corporate taxes $137 billion over 10 years
Yes Reorganize U.S. intelligence agencies as proposed by Sept. 11 commission

2003
Yes Cut taxes by $330 billion through fiscal 2013
No Block Bush rule scaling back overtime pay for some white-collar federal workers
Yes Do not allow use of search warrants without first notifying subjects
Yes Allow importation of prescription drugs
Yes Create private school voucher program in Washington, D.C.
Yes Ban "partial birth" abortion except to save a woman's life
No Split $18.6 billion in Iraq aid into half-grant, half-loan
Yes Overhaul Medicare and create prescription drug benefit

CQ VOTE STUDIES

	PARTY UNITY		PRESIDENTIAL SUPPORT	
	Support	Oppose	Support	Oppose
2004	96%	4%	82%	18%
2003	97%	3%	91%	9%
2002	98%	2%	88%	12%
2001	95%	5%	89%	11%

INTEREST GROUPS

	AFL-CIO	ADA	CCUS	ACU
2004	15%	5%	100%	96%
2003	20%	10%	93%	88%
2002	11%	0%	95%	96%
2001	30%	5%	94%	94%

PENNSYLVANIA 9
South central — Altoona

Situated in the south-central part of Pennsylvania, the 9th contains no booming metropolis — Altoona, the largest city, is tucked into the Allegheny Mountains and maintains a small-town feel. Most of the 9th's towns have populations under 5,000, making this one of the most rural districts in the nation. The district borders western Maryland and West Virginia to the south and expanded to the west as a result of redistricting following the 2000 census.

After decades of decline brought about by the waning of the railroad and mining industries, the area has begun to rebound, and once again residents can thank transportation-related industry for the growth. Bedford County saw its job creation rate shoot up as improvements began on the aging Pennsylvania Turnpike, which opened as the nation's first superhighway in 1940. And the city of Breezewood continues to draw in travelers with its garish display of signs adorning hotels and fast-food restaurants at the turnpike interchange.

Still, the bulk of the district's land is rural and dependent on agriculture.

The 9th has a religious population, one of the most conservative in the state. Voters oppose most gun control and "big government" policies. Its small-business owners and farmers tend also to be fiscally conservative.

Voters solidly back Republicans for all offices, from the local level to the presidency. The 9th includes George W. Bush's top three counties in the state in the 2004 election, Fulton (76 percent), Bedford (73 percent) and the district's part of Perry County (72 percent). Overall, the 9th gave Bush 67 percent of the vote — his best showing in the state.

MAJOR INDUSTRY
Agriculture, manufacturing, service

MILITARY BASES
Letterkenny Army Depot, 3 military, 1,196 civilian (2005)

CITIES
Altoona, 49,523; Chambersburg, 17,862; Waynesboro, 9,614

NOTABLE
A memorial to United Airlines Flight 93 is in Shanksville, where the hijacked airplane crashed in a field Sept. 11, 2001; James Buchanan, a native of Mercersburg, vacationed at the Bedford Springs Hotel; Architect Frank Lloyd Wright's Fallingwater house is in Fayette County.

Rep. Don Sherwood (R)

CAPITOL OFFICE
225-3731
www.house.gov/sherwood
1131 Longworth 20515-3810; fax 225-9594

COMMITTEES
Appropriations

HOMETOWN
Tunkhannock

BORN
March 5, 1941, Nicholson, Pa.

RELIGION
Methodist

FAMILY
Wife, Carol Sherwood; three children

EDUCATION
Dartmouth College, B.A. 1963 (economics)

MILITARY SERVICE
Army, 1964-66

CAREER
Car dealer; bank executive; horse farm owner;
forestry equipment company owner

POLITICAL HIGHLIGHTS
Tunkhannock Area School Board, 1975-99
(president, 1992-98)

ELECTION RESULTS

2004 GENERAL

Don Sherwood (R)	191,967	92.8%
Veronica A. Hannevig (CNSTP)	14,805	7.2%

2004 PRIMARY

Don Sherwood (R)	unopposed

2002 GENERAL

Don Sherwood (R)	152,017	92.9%
Kurt J. Shotko (GREEN)	11,613	7.1%

PREVIOUS WINNING PERCENTAGES
2000 (53%); 1998 (49%)

Elected 1998; 4th term

Money and the right friends are a potent combination, as Sherwood well knows. His first two House races were at times too close to call, and so in 2001 the Republican leadership gave him a seat on the Appropriations Committee. Then the Republicans who ran Pennsylvania's redistricting process for this decade chipped in by placing more Republicans in the 10th District. They did a good job, as the Democrats did not even bother to field a candidate against Sherwood in the last two elections.

Sherwood now seems free to focus on promoting economic development in northeastern Pennsylvania and helping the state's struggling dairy farmers. He used his Appropriations seat to bring home $15.6 million for local projects in 2004 as part of the catchall appropriations package.

He led an unsuccessful effort to authorize the expansion and extension of the Northeast Dairy Compact and the creation of three other regional dairy compacts across the nation during debate on the 2002 farm bill. But he and other dairy state lawmakers did succeed that year in winning a program to help dairy farmers when milk prices are low.

One of his top priorities for the 109th Congress is extending for at least two years the Milk Income Loss Contract, which expires in September 2005. He praised the 2005 budget plan put forth by President Bush because it included a two-year extension of the milk income loss program. He is also working to tighten restrictions on some European dairy products used in making processed foods and cheese.

Sherwood and other members of the Pennsylvania delegation have also taken up the cause of an ugly fruit. Sherwood introduced legislation early in 2005 to force Florida to allow the export of the UglyRipe, a tomato said to be far sweeter than most of those available in winter. But it is so wrinkled and deeply grooved that Florida farmers regard it as an embarrassment and refuse to let it be shipped out of state. "We can't deny that UglyRipes are ugly — but consumers should not be denied the opportunity to purchase a good tomato just because of its appearance," Sherwood said.

To help their rural constituents, Sherwood and Democrat Paul E. Kanjorski, who represents the neighboring 11th District, won House passage in 2002 of an increase in Medicare funding for a select list of rural hospitals. That bid ultimately failed, but Sherwood came back early in 2003 and was successful. More important, the Republicans' Medicare prescription drug bill that passed late in 2003 also included significantly higher payments for rural hospitals. Area hospitals were expected to receive $15 million to $17 million more a year under that bill.

Sherwood has a mixed record on his support for organized labor. Before his district was redrawn after the 2000 census, it included the blue-collar city of Scranton, where labor unions are strong. Sherwood cast several pro-labor votes in his first two terms, including backing a raise in the minimum wage in 2000. But in 2002, he opposed labor to vote for reviving fast-track procedures for trade agreements that Congress cannot amend, and in 2004 he voted against an amendment to provide an additional 13 weeks of unemployment benefits for people who had exhausted their state benefits.

Before Sherwood gained his Appropriations post, he sat on the Armed Services Committee, where he kept close tabs on issues affecting military bases — as the largest employer in his district at the time was the sprawling Tobyhanna Army Depot. The Army uses the depot to repair and maintain communications and electronic equipment. Tobyhanna is now in the neighboring 11th District; Sherwood and Kanjorski mounted a major lobbying effort in the 109th Congress to keep Tobyhanna off the 2005 list of military bases to be closed.

Sherwood told the Allentown Morning Call that he is letting the base-closing commission know about the highly specialized work of the depot's 4,300 employees. "They are known for doing the right kind of work, and we are convincing people of that," Sherwood said.

Sherwood grew up in the hamlet of Nicholson, where his father operated a car dealership and the neighbor kid three doors down was H. James Saxton Jr., now a New Jersey House colleague. They went to the same school, were in the same Boy Scout troop and recall building a log cabin together on Saxton's property.

After getting his degree in economics from Dartmouth and putting in a stint in the Army, Sherwood settled in Tunkhannock, a dozen miles southwest of Nicholson. At age 26, he opened a car dealership, becoming the youngest Chevrolet dealer on the East Coast.

He also became active in local civic affairs. Appointed to the local school board in 1975, he was re-elected six times, serving more than 20 years, including six years as its president. He said that watching many young people move out of the area in search of economic opportunity sparked his interest in national politics.

In 1998, when veteran Republican Joseph M. McDade decided to retire after 36 years in the House, Sherwood jumped into the fray, along with seven other Republicans. He easily outdistanced the GOP field, winning almost half the votes cast.

With McDade's departure, Democrats saw an opportunity that November. They tapped attorney Patrick Casey, a son of former Democratic Gov. Robert P. Casey, hoping the younger Casey's mix of social conservatism and economic populism would dovetail with the district. Sherwood stressed his varied business experience, spent more than $770,000 of his own money on his campaign — and won by 515 votes out of 173,000 cast.

Casey was back for a rematch in 2000, criticizing Sherwood's stances on health care and Social Security and referring to him in advertisements as "millionaire Don Sherwood." But Sherwood emphasized his experience and legislative accomplishments during his first term. In the close race, Sherwood prevailed by 12,000 votes.

Sherwood's hobby for more than a quarter-century has been raising Belgian horses. In partnership with another man, Sherwood has won dozens of first-place ribbons in local horse shows.

KEY VOTES

2004

No Extend federal unemployment benefits by 13 weeks
Yes Pass $283.2 billion, six-year federal highway and mass transit bill
Yes Approve $146 billion multi-year extension of previously enacted middle-class tax breaks
Yes Amend the Constitution to prohibit same-sex marriage
Yes Cut corporate taxes $137 billion over 10 years
Yes Reorganize U.S. intelligence agencies as proposed by Sept. 11 commission

2003

Yes Cut taxes by $330 billion through fiscal 2013
No Block Bush rule scaling back overtime pay for some white-collar federal workers
No Do not allow use of search warrants without first notifying subjects
Yes Allow importation of prescription drugs
Yes Create private school voucher program in Washington, D.C.
Yes Ban "partial birth" abortion except to save a woman's life
No Split $18.6 billion in Iraq aid into half-grant, half-loan
Yes Overhaul Medicare and create prescription drug benefit

CQ VOTE STUDIES

	PARTY UNITY		PRESIDENTIAL SUPPORT	
	Support	Oppose	Support	Oppose
2004	92%	8%	84%	16%
2003	97%	3%	93%	7%
2002	96%	4%	89%	11%
2001	94%	6%	93%	7%
2000	86%	14%	38%	62%

INTEREST GROUPS

	AFL-CIO	ADA	CCUS	ACU
2004	20%	0%	100%	88%
2003	7%	10%	93%	84%
2002	11%	5%	100%	96%
2001	17%	0%	100%	88%
2000	20%	10%	85%	75%

PENNSYLVANIA 10
Northeast — Central Susquehanna Valley

Situated in the upper northeast corner of Pennsylvania, the 10th is home to a portion of the Pocono Mountains region, a popular honeymoon retreat known for its skiing, fishing and golfing.

Redistricting following the 2000 census significantly expanded the 10th, which ceded Scranton to the neighboring 11th but stretched farther into central Pennsylvania to pick up four Central Susquehanna Valley counties — Montour, Northumberland, Union and Snyder. While Scranton was once the 10th's major hub, the four new counties account for about 30 percent of the population. The district retained Williamsport, now its largest city, and Sunbury.

This region includes some of the state's best areas for lumber and agriculture. The latter is particularly prominent in Bradford County, which is among the state and national leaders in dairy production, and in Northumberland and Snyder counties, known for their poultry. Tourism remains strong, especially during the summer months, when visitors come for the scenery and sporting in the eastern part of the district and

for the Little League World Series held annually in Williamsport, in the western reaches. Pike County, which increased its population by almost two-thirds in the 1990s, is rapidly filling up with early-rising commuters to New Jersey and New York City who prefer Pike's small-town setting, affordable land and access to interstate highways.

The 10th has large swaths of rural, socially conservative heartland. With Scranton and its strong union ties no longer in the district, the 10th is more rural and Republican. Democrats still have a presence in areas like Carbondale and Archbald in Lackawanna County and in parts of Northumberland County. But most voters are heavily inclined to support the GOP for federal and state offices. George W. Bush won the 10th by 20 percentage points in the 2004 presidential election.

MAJOR INDUSTRY
Agriculture, manufacturing, tourism, timber

CITIES
Williamsport, 30,706; Back Mountain (unincorporated) (pt.), 22,237

NOTABLE
The Starrucca Viaduct, which is 1,200 feet long and 110 feet high and has 18 stone arches spanning 50 feet each, has carried trains across Starrucca Creek in Lanesboro since 1848.

Rep. Paul E. Kanjorski (D)

Elected 1984; 11th term

CAPITOL OFFICE
225-6511
www.kanjorski.house.gov
2188 Rayburn 20515-3811; fax 225-0764

COMMITTEES
Financial Services
Government Reform

HOMETOWN
Nanticoke

BORN
April 2, 1937, Nanticoke, Pa.

RELIGION
Roman Catholic

FAMILY
Wife, Nancy Kanjorski; one child

EDUCATION
Temple U., attended 1957-62; Dickinson School of
Law, attended 1962-65

MILITARY SERVICE
Army, 1960-61

CAREER
Lawyer

POLITICAL HIGHLIGHTS
Sought Democratic nomination for U.S. House
(special election), 1980; sought Democratic
nomination for U.S. House, 1980

ELECTION RESULTS

2004 GENERAL

Paul E. Kanjorski (D)	171,147	94.4%
Kenneth C. Brenneman (CNSTP)	10,105	5.6%

2004 PRIMARY

Paul E. Kanjorski (D)	unopposed

2002 GENERAL

Paul E. Kanjorski (D)	93,758	55.6%
Louis J. Barletta (R)	71,543	42.4%
Thomas J. McLaughlin (REF)	3,304	2.0%

PREVIOUS WINNING PERCENTAGES
2000 (66%); 1998 (67%); 1996 (68%); 1994 (67%);
1992 (67%); 1990 (100%); 1988 (100%); 1986 (71%);
1984 (59%)

Kanjorski has seen many partisan battles in his two decades of House service, but he is probably able to put the sharp words into perspective. As a House page in 1954, he narrowly missed becoming a casualty when Puerto Rican terrorists sprayed gunfire on the House chamber from the visitor's gallery. In the aftermath, he helped carry three wounded congressmen from the floor.

Actually, Kanjorski appears more interested in his responsibility to his 11th District constituents than to his broader role as a longtime Washington legislator. The economy of the 11th continues to struggle as it moves beyond its historical dependence on the coal industry.

He was happy to announce in late 2004 that he obtained $1.4 million for the city of Wilkes-Barre in the catchall spending bill that passed at the end of the 108th Congress. Of the funds, $1.25 million is to be used to enhance downtown transportation infrastructure, including new streetlights, he said. Kanjorski also touts the work he has done to resurrect the Wyoming Valley Levee Raising Project, a roughly $200 million flood control project on the Susquehanna River that had languished for years after its authorization. To spur economic development, he won $29 million for renovations of the Wilkes-Barre/Scranton International Airport, and he wants to construct a new cargo airport, and restore passenger and freight rail service between New York City and Northeastern Pennsylvania.

He blasted President Bush's 2005 budget proposal for slashing $2 billion from the Community Development Block Grant program. Kanjorski called the administration's cuts morally and fiscally irresponsible, saying "communities in Northeastern Pennsylvania count on this funding for vital economic and community development initiatives."

Kanjorski is the second-ranking Democrat on the Financial Services Committee and the top-ranking Democrat on the Capital Markets, Insurance and Government-Sponsored Enterprises Subcommittee. He helped negotiate legislation in 2003 to modernize the nation's credit reporting system and combat identity theft. Although an ardent supporter of Freddie Mac and Fannie Mae, he urged Congress during the 108th to move "judiciously and objectively" toward closer oversight of the mortgage financiers following reports of erroneous accounting practices.

Kanjorski is not happy with Bush's second-term effort to overhaul the Social Security system. "While there is no question that Social Security faces increased challenges in the years to come, these challenges are manageable and should not be used as an excuse by some to attempt to fundamentally alter or 'reform' this trusted system," he wrote in 2004 in an op-ed story for the Scranton Times. "Proposals that seek to allow individuals to invest some or all of their Social Security funds in the stock market are, in my view, ill-conceived and potentially harmful."

A Polish American Catholic, Kanjorski reflects the concerns of the white, ethnic, working-class people who still dominate politics in his part of Pennsylvania. He holds a conservative social view, opposing abortion and gun control and supporting school prayer. But in 2004, he voted against a constitutional amendment to ban same-sex marriage. A staunch supporter of organized labor and a loyal Democrat on fiscal matters, he has repeatedly weighed in against Bush's proposed tax cuts.

In 2002, Kanjorski sided with most of his colleagues in authorizing military action against Iraq. The following year, however, he voted against appropriating $87.5 billion for the Iraqi war effort, saying he supported the troops but worried that the administration lacked a "clear objective and well-reasoned plan" in Iraq. Subsequently, he turned more decisively against the war, criticizing the misleading intelligence reports that had persuaded him to vote to authorize military force, and voting against a 2004 resolution declaring the world was made safer by Saddam Hussein's removal.

In 2002, Kanjorski was the subject of news reports that the FBI was looking into allegations that he had steered federal grants to businesses connected to his family, and some House Republicans considered filing an ethics complaint against him. The FBI never confirmed or denied the reports. The GOP effort was squelched after Democratic leaders reportedly threatened to file a retaliatory complaint against a GOP lawmaker.

Kanjorski was born and grew up in Nanticoke, just southwest of Wilkes-Barre. He attended Temple University and the Dickinson College School of Law, but did not graduate from either. He became a lawyer and worked as an attorney in Northeast Pennsylvania for almost 20 years. He was an administrative law judge for workers' compensation cases, and served as the unpaid assistant city solicitor for Nanticoke for more than a decade.

After two unsuccessful House campaigns in 1980 (one in a special election), Kanjorski owed his 1984 House victory to an intestinal parasite and a sunny beach. The outcome of his primary challenge to Democratic Rep. Frank Harrison might have been different if not for the discovery that water supplies in parts of the 11th District were contaminated with the Giardia parasite. As people boiled their water to make it drinkable, Kanjorski noted that his opponent had flown off on a congressional excursion to Costa Rica, and ran an ad that included a shot of Harrison on the beach.

Harrison tried to ignore Kanjorski and stressed his experience in Washington, but Kanjorski leaped from long shot to victor. In November, he defeated Republican Robert P. Hudock with 59 percent of the vote.

That was his closest election — he has been unopposed twice — until 2002. That year, the national GOP, taking note of the unfavorable publicity stemming from the FBI investigation, invested heavily in the race. Their candidate, Hazleton Mayor Louis J. Barletta, pursued the ethics attack aggressively, saying in one televised debate that while Kanjorski may have brought home the bacon, "he put it in his own refrigerator."

But Kanjorski prevailed by 13 percentage points, thanks to a big margin in the Lackawanna County portion of the district, which had been added to the 11th in decennial redistricting earlier in the year. He did not face a Republican opponent in 2004.

KEY VOTES

2004

Yes Extend federal unemployment benefits by 13 weeks

Yes Pass $283.2 billion, six-year federal highway and mass transit bill

No Approve $146 billion multi-year extension of previously enacted middle-class tax breaks

No Amend the Constitution to prohibit same-sex marriage

No Cut corporate taxes $137 billion over 10 years

Yes Reorganize U.S. intelligence agencies as proposed by Sept. 11 commission

2003

No Cut taxes by $330 billion through fiscal 2013

Yes Block Bush rule scaling back overtime pay for some white-collar federal workers

Yes Do not allow use of search warrants without first notifying subjects

Yes Allow importation of prescription drugs

No Create private school voucher program in Washington, D.C.

Yes Ban "partial birth" abortion except to save a woman's life

Yes Split $18.6 billion in Iraq aid into half-grant, half-loan

No Overhaul Medicare and create prescription drug benefit

CQ VOTE STUDIES

	PARTY UNITY		PRESIDENTIAL SUPPORT	
	Support	Oppose	Support	Oppose
2004	88%	12%	27%	73%
2003	84%	16%	31%	69%
2002	79%	21%	42%	58%
2001	75%	25%	47%	53%
2000	82%	18%	80%	20%

INTEREST GROUPS

	AFL-CIO	ADA	CCUS	ACU
2004	100%	80%	30%	21%
2003	100%	85%	27%	36%
2002	100%	75%	50%	24%
2001	100%	65%	43%	36%
2000	100%	65%	42%	16%

PENNSYLVANIA 11
Northeast — Scranton, Wilkes-Barre

Since the beginning of the 20th century, the health of the 11th District has been inextricably linked to the production, manufacturing and sale of coal. Demand for the district's anthracite coal peaked in the 1910s. Since then, a few cities in this district have disappeared with the long decline of the coal industry and the rise of oil and natural gas. Centralia, site of a burning underground mine, turned into a ghost town after a federally ordered evacuation.

Other towns, such as Jim Thorpe and Wilkes-Barre, have been more prosperous. Jim Thorpe, given that name in 1954 for the decathlon Olympic gold medalist who is buried in town, was a haven for millionaires and has maintained its historic charm as a preservation project of the Department of the Interior. Economic development needs along with an elderly population help drive the push for federal dollars.

The 11th has a decided but not monolithic Democratic lean, the result of a large Irish population and a strong union tradition. Redistricting following the 2000 census moved Scranton (Lackawanna County) from

the neighboring 10th into the 11th, making it more Democratic. Democrats also do well in Luzerne County, with strong showings in Wilkes-Barre and in smaller cities to the north and east, but not at a level commensurate with their wide registration advantage in the county. Overall, John Kerry won the 11th by 5 percentage points in the 2004 presidential election.

The decline of coal and an investment in technology-driven businesses have helped Republicans, who do well in Columbia County. George W. Bush won both Carbon and Monroe counties, fast-growing areas in the Poconos where many newcomers commute via Interstate 80 to their jobs in New Jersey and New York.

MAJOR INDUSTRY
Manufacturing, retail trade, tourism

MILITARY BASES
Tobyhanna Army Depot, 30 military, 4,300 civilian (2005)

CITIES
Scranton, 76,415; Wilkes-Barre, 43,123; Hazleton, 23,329

NOTABLE
Berwick prides itself on its high school football team, a perennial power in Pennsylvania that has produced several NFL players.

Rep. John P. Murtha (D)

Elected February 1974; 16th full term

CAPITOL OFFICE
225-2065
www.house.gov/murtha
2423 Rayburn 20515-3812; fax 225-5709

COMMITTEES
Appropriations

HOMETOWN
Johnstown

BORN
June 17, 1932, New Martinsville, W.Va.

RELIGION
Roman Catholic

FAMILY
Wife, Joyce Murtha; three children

EDUCATION
U. of Pittsburgh, B.A. 1962 (economics)

MILITARY SERVICE
Marine Corps, 1952-55, 1966-67; Marine Corps
Reserve, 1967-90

CAREER
Car wash owner and operator

POLITICAL HIGHLIGHTS
Democratic nominee for U.S. House, 1968;
Pa. House, 1969-74

ELECTION RESULTS

2004 GENERAL

John P. Murtha (D)		unopposed

2004 PRIMARY

John P. Murtha (D)		unopposed

2002 GENERAL

John P. Murtha (D)	124,201	73.5%
Bill Choby (R)	44,818	26.5%

PREVIOUS WINNING PERCENTAGES
2000 (71%); 1998 (68%); 1996 (70%); 1994 (69%);
1992 (100%); 1990 (62%); 1988 (100%); 1986 (67%);
1984 (69%); 1982 (61%); 1980 (59%); 1978 (69%);
1976 (68%); 1974 (58%); 1974 Special Election (50%)

On any given day the House is in session, the most reliable way for any lawmaker to find Murtha is to make a beeline to the last row of the chamber to the immediate right of the center aisle. That's where Murtha — powerful and profane — holds court.

Now in his 16th full term, Murtha has been either chairman or the top-ranking minority member of the Defense Appropriations Subcommittee since 1989. He sees himself as indispensable in keeping the wheels of government turning through compromise and judicious applications of legislative lubricant, such as added funds for hometown projects of great importance to individual members.

In the 108th Congress, while President Bush's veto threats dampened increases in spending for domestic programs, the Pentagon budget continued to grow, giving Murtha, who enjoys extensive control over the Democrats' share of home-state largess, even more power. Murtha's effectiveness hinges on finding out what his colleagues want, touching base with interested parties to determine what he realistically can get, and delivering on his commitments. This requires personal attention, which Murtha gives generously. During roll call votes, members who need a sympathetic hearing for some hometown priority simply head to the Pennsylvania Corner.

Murtha does not merely grease the legislative wheels. He tries to use his mastery of the process to shape defense policy. His views on the subject have credibility because he works the military establishment the way he works the House — face to face, so he can look his interlocutor in the eye. Impatient with the PowerPoint presentations beloved by Pentagon briefers, Murtha travels without fanfare to deployments in far-off regions to assess the situation.

He also speaks on military affairs with the moral authority of a decorated veteran of Vietnam ground combat, one of the few in the House. While some congressional veterans use their military experience to rhetorically bludgeon their opponents, Murtha rarely mentions his Vietnam record in public, but his colleagues are well aware of it. So his words carried extra weight in 2004, when, standing next to Minority Leader Nancy Pelosi, he said the Pentagon had to devote more troops and resources to the Iraq war or else it was "unwinnable." Pelosi and Murtha are friends and confidants — he chaired her campaign for the leadership — despite having very different views on defense policy.

Republicans fired back in terms that questioned Murtha's patriotism. "In a calculated, craven political stunt, the national Democratic Party has declared surrender in the war on terrorism," said Majority Leader Tom DeLay. DeLay and Murtha, in fact, usually have a good working relationship. When the Texas Republican shops for a dozen or two Democratic votes to pass appropriations bills, Murtha routinely helps to supply them.

Murtha's response was to find DeLay, a former exterminator, on the House floor and upbraid him. "After all the goddamn deals we've done," he scolded. "When I was in Vietnam, you were killing bugs." DeLay turned crimson, Murtha recalled later.

Murtha has decried Bush's defense budget requests as inadequate, particularly after the Sept. 11, 2001, terrorist attacks. But like other defense hawks of both parties, he ran into a wall of White House opposition when he proposed significant increases in the requests. In 2004, the administration responded to pressure from Murtha and other pro-defense lawmakers for additional Iraq funding with a request, quickly approved, for $25 billion to ensure a stream of funding to finance the war after Congress adjourned.

Murtha also has defended congressional prerogatives, taking the administration to task in 2004 for failing to inform lawmakers when it used some of the money provided for the war on terrorism to prepare for the Iraq invasion. While acknowledging that Congress granted Bush great flexibility in the use of funds appropriated to fight terrorism, the Democrats said the White House should have provided more information about how the money was spent. "The thing that concerns me is the consultation," Murtha said.

In 2002, Murtha's strong defense credentials made him a key figure in shaping the Democrats' response to Bush's push for congressional authorization for military action against Iraq. But he disagreed with the president's desire to reshape the nation's intelligence gathering agencies as a result of the Sept. 11 attacks. He was one of only eight Democrats to vote against the final version of the reorganization measure that also created a new director of intelligence to oversee all national intelligence activities.

Probably because of his own military experience, Murtha is attentive to the troops' quality of life. He was a leader in the successful drive by military brass in the late 1990s to increase pay, liberalize military pensions and expand retirees' health benefits.

The 12th remains a working-class Democratic stronghold, and Murtha is a reliable ally of organized labor, regularly pressing to raise the minimum wage and protect workers against adverse impacts of trade agreements. He voted with most of his party in 2004 to provide an additional 13 weeks of unemployment benefits for people who had exhausted their state benefits.

Once a car-wash operator, Murtha supports small-business priorities, such as a larger health insurance tax deduction for the self-employed. Reflecting his district's social conservatism, Murtha, a Catholic, opposes abortion rights. He also backs gun owners' rights.

When longtime GOP Rep. John P. Saylor died in 1973, Murtha, then a state legislator, won narrowly over Harry M. Fox, a former Saylor aide, in a special election that focused on the Republicans' Watergate problems.

After Pennsylvania lost two House seats as a result of the 2000 census, the GOP-dominated legislature drew a map that threw Murtha into a primary duel with fellow Democratic Rep. Frank R. Mascara. Four-term veteran Mascara's old district accounted for about half the registered Democrats. But he was swamped by Murtha's fundraising, in which defense contractors and labor unions played a large role. Murtha won the primary by nearly 2-to-1 and coasted to re-election by nearly 3-to-1. He was unopposed in 2004.

KEY VOTES

2004

Yes   Extend federal unemployment benefits by 13 weeks

Yes   Pass $283.2 billion, six-year federal highway and mass transit bill

No   Approve $146 billion multi-year extension of previously enacted middle-class tax breaks

?   Amend the Constitution to prohibit same-sex marriage

No   Cut corporate taxes $137 billion over 10 years

No   Reorganize U.S. intelligence agencies as proposed by Sept. 11 commission

2003

No   Cut taxes by $330 billion through fiscal 2013

Yes   Block Bush rule scaling back overtime pay for some white-collar federal workers

Yes   Do not allow use of search warrants without first notifying subjects

Yes   Allow importation of prescription drugs

?   Create private school voucher program in Washington, D.C.

Yes   Ban "partial birth" abortion except to save a woman's life

No   Split $18.6 billion in Iraq aid into half-grant, half-loan

No   Overhaul Medicare and create prescription drug benefit

CQ VOTE STUDIES

	PARTY UNITY		PRESIDENTIAL SUPPORT	
	Support	Oppose	Support	Oppose
2004	80%	20%	34%	66%
2003	73%	27%	51%	49%
2002	75%	25%	55%	45%
2001	66%	34%	47%	53%
2000	70%	30%	74%	26%

INTEREST GROUPS

	AFL-CIO	ADA	CCUS	ACU
2004	93%	50%	48%	30%
2003	100%	85%	43%	56%
2002	100%	55%	61%	32%
2001	100%	65%	52%	48%
2000	100%	55%	45%	24%

PENNSYLVANIA 12
Southwest — Johnstown

Described by an aide to Rep. Murtha as "an upside-down Chinese dragon," the strangely contorted 12th hopscotches in southwestern Pennsylvania across nine counties, eight of which are shared with other districts. A once-booming center of coal, steel and iron production, this area is diversifying to escape economic distress and industrial loss.

The 12th has been the unfortunate victim of floods that devastated Johnstown (Cambria County), the district's largest city, three times in history. The Great Flood of 1889, the most severe, destroyed the town and killed more than 2,200 people. Again in 1936 and 1977, floods took lives and caused significant damage. The area celebrated its 25th anniversary of being flood-free with a "The Flood's Over! Come on Back" advertising campaign. The 1980s recession had a devastating effect on the economy as well. The coal and steel industries declined and the unemployment rate skyrocketed to more than 27 percent.

More recently, the district has bounced back, in part by attracting some technology business, including a Sony plant in Westmoreland and a

number of defense and research firms. Capitalizing on past hardships, the Johnstown Flood Museum also draws tourists to the area, and the city's large health care base has remained stable. The unemployment rate in Johnstown has been in the single digits since early 1994, although it generally exceeds the national rate.

This district has been a Democratic stronghold since the New Deal, and Republican mapmakers in redistricting following the 2000 census packed Democrats into the 12th to give the GOP an edge in adjacent districts. Like other towns in the state with an industrial past and an aging population, Johnstown wants federal help, but many voters are more socially conservative than the national Democratic Party. George W. Bush won both Cambria and Greene counties in 2004. He narrowly lost Washington County, but received the highest vote share of any GOP presidential candidate there since Richard M. Nixon in 1972.

MAJOR INDUSTRY
Manufacturing, service, health care, tourism

CITIES
Johnstown, 23,906; Washington, 15,268; New Kensington, 14,701

NOTABLE
The National Drug Intelligence Center in Johnstown tracks illegal drugs.

Rep. Allyson Y. Schwartz (D)

Elected 2004; 1st term

Schwartz, a Democrat of experience and activist temperament, will doubtless have much to say on a wide range of issues before her in Congress. But she used her first House speech to make a personal statement.

Schwartz, who is Jewish, spoke during a commemoration of the 60th anniversary of the liberation of the Nazis' Auschwitz death camp in Poland, describing her mother's escape from Austria to America as a teenager in the early days of World War II. "Those who survived the Holocaust could not hide their gratitude and love for this country, relishing the opportunity and freedom granted to them as new Americans," Schwartz said. "My own love and respect for our country and my belief in our responsibility to each other stems in great part from this strong sense of patriotism."

Schwartz had already built a nearly 14-year career in the Pennsylvania Senate — and waged a competitive but unsuccessful primary bid for the U.S. Senate in 2000 — before her election to Congress in 2004 in one of the most expensive House races in the country.

Schwartz, who calls her state's Children's Health Insurance Program "one of my proudest accomplishments," wants to expand child health care coverage for working families. She says she also wants to make it easier for small businesses to band together to reduce their health care costs.

She first entered the public eye in 1975 as the co-founder and first director of a women's health clinic. She also managed Philadelphia's Department of Human Services before her election to the state Senate. Her focus on health should continue in Congress, but her freshman assignments will take her in broader directions: She is on the Budget and the Transportation and Infrastructure committees.

A long-shot bid by 13th District Democrat Joseph M. Hoeffel to unseat Republican Sen. Arlen Specter in 2004 gave Schwartz a chance to make a second try at Congress. She defeated former Philadelphia official Joe Torsella in a hard-fought primary; then, calling on her solid political base and campaign bankroll, she trounced Republican Melissa Brown by 13 percentage points.

CAPITOL OFFICE
225-6111
www.house.gov/schwartz
423 Cannon 20515-3813; fax 226-0611

COMMITTEES
Budget
Transportation & Infrastructure

HOMETOWN
Jenkintown

BORN
Oct. 3, 1948, Queens, N.Y.

RELIGION
Jewish

FAMILY
Husband, David Schwartz; two children

EDUCATION
Simmons College, B.A. 1970 (sociology); Bryn Mawr College, M.S.W. 1972

CAREER
Municipal child and elderly welfare official; women's health center founder; nonprofit health plan assistant director

POLITICAL HIGHLIGHTS
Pa. Senate, 1991-2004; sought Democratic nomination for U.S. Senate, 2000

ELECTION RESULTS

2004 GENERAL

Allyson Y. Schwartz (D)	171,763	55.8%
Melissa Brown (R)	127,205	41.3%
John P. McDermott (CNSTP)	5,291	1.7%
Chuck Moulton (LIBERT)	3,865	1.3%

2004 PRIMARY

Allyson Y. Schwartz (D)	24,309	52.2%
Joe Torsella (D)	22,232	47.8%

PENNSYLVANIA 13

East – Northeast Philadelphia, part of Montgomery County

With its residents nearly evenly divided between Montgomery County and Northeast Philadelphia, the 13th combines white-collar suburbia with a portion of the city known for its blue-collar grit. Registration is roughly even between the two major parties, but Democrats have enjoyed an advantage in recent statewide and federal races.

Prescription drugs and health care are prevalent issues in the district, thanks to a large senior citizen population in Northeast Philadelphia. Education is drawing more attention, as Philadelphia public schools are in worse shape than Montgomery County schools. Public housing also has been a subject of debate, as many residents are concerned about how federal housing assistance is being administered.

Many shopping centers, strip malls, health care facilities and small businesses are in

Northeast Philadelphia, where a riverfront redevelopment project has sparked hopes of aiding the 13th's dragging economy.

Although the GOP still runs well at the local level in Montgomery County, Democrats have made major inroads here in state and federal races. Since 1988, Montgomery has gone from voting Republican for president by 22 percentage points to backing John Kerry by 12 points (in 2004). Close-in Abington and Upper Dublin (both shared with the 8th) now support Democratic presidential nominees, while Republicans run well in northwestern Montgomery, in areas like Upper and Lower Salford, Upper and Lower Frederick and New Hanover Township.

MAJOR INDUSTRY
Health and business services, chemicals

MILITARY BASES
Naval Air Station Willow Grove, 2,500 military, 350 civilian (2004)

CITIES
Philadelphia (pt.), 305,391; Lansdale, 16,071

NOTABLE
Pennypack Park is known as the green heart of Northeast Philadelphia.

Rep. Mike Doyle (D)

CAPITOL OFFICE
225-2135
rep.doyle@mail.house.gov
www.house.gov/doyle
401 Cannon 20515-3814; fax 225-3084

COMMITTEES
Energy & Commerce
Standards of Official Conduct

HOMETOWN
Swissvale

BORN
Aug. 5, 1953, Pittsburgh, Pa.

RELIGION
Roman Catholic

FAMILY
Wife, Susan Doyle; four children

EDUCATION
Pennsylvania State U., B.S. 1975 (community development)

CAREER
Insurance company executive; state legislative aide

POLITICAL HIGHLIGHTS
Swissvale Borough Council, 1977-81 (served as a Republican)

ELECTION RESULTS

2004 GENERAL
Mike Doyle (D)   unopposed
2004 PRIMARY
Mike Doyle (D)   unopposed
2002 GENERAL
Mike Doyle (D)   unopposed
PREVIOUS WINNING PERCENTAGES
2000 (69%); 1998 (68%); 1996 (56%); 1994 (55%)

Elected 1994; 6th term

The son and grandson of steelworkers, Doyle worked in the mills during summers while in college — just enough, he says, to know he wanted to do something else. That something else was business and eventually politics, an arena where he has fought above all else to help revitalize western Pennsylvania's troubled steel towns.

In his six terms in office, Doyle has pursued an agenda aimed at transforming the area's industry into a more broadly based modern-day economy that includes high-technology manufacturing processes. From his seat on the Energy and Commerce Committee, he has focused on funneling federal money into local enterprises that develop alternative energy sources and more efficient uses of energy. He also has pressed for the cleanup of polluted industrial sites, known as "brownfields," to permit their use again.

At the same time, Doyle continues to look out for the interests of the steel industry. He urges the federal government to take steps to protect domestic firms from what he regards as unfair foreign competition, and he watches out for retired steelworkers whose benefits are in jeopardy. He has also pressed for legislation creating a national historic park outside Pittsburgh that would highlight the historic role of the steel industry. "I'm the first Mike Doyle in the family to not work in the mills, but that's the benefit of their hard work," he told the Greensburg Tribune-Review.

Doyle's voting record is similar to those of his Democratic colleagues who affiliate with the conservative Blue Dog Coalition, but he says he has never considered joining. He voted against President Bush's tax cut proposals and the 2003 Republican Medicare measure providing prescription drug coverage for seniors.

He has become more of a party loyalist over time. In the 108th Congress, he sided with his party 90 percent of the time on votes that pitted a majority of Democrats against Republicans. That was his all-time high party unity score, up from 70 percent in his first term. He agreed with Bush's position 34 percent of the time in the 108th. He also showed party loyalty in the 108th by agreeing to sit on the ethics committee, generally regarded as a thankless assignment.

Early in the 109th, Doyle joined his party's criticism of Bush's budget plan, which would cut federal spending on social programs, and of the president's effort to allow workers to place a portion of their Social Security payroll taxes into individual investment accounts. He has been a reliable ally of organized labor and generally has toed the party line on issues such as access to health care, background checks for gun purchases and opposing amendment of the Constitution to ban same-sex marriage.

But Doyle differs from many Democrats as a particularly vocal critic on environmental issues. He opposes stricter clean air standards because they would place a high burden on the auto, steel and coal industries.

Doyle may be more comfortable with some GOP positions than most of his colleagues because he once was a member of the other party. For 16 years, he was chief of staff to a Pennsylvania Senate Republican. He was a GOP member for many of those years, switching parties in 1992.

Doyle had to give up a seat on the Veterans' Affairs Committee when he won the Energy and Commerce spot, but he has remained active on veterans' issues. In the 107th, he sponsored legislation, which became law, requiring the Department of Veterans Affairs to fully inform the more than half-million surviving spouses and dependents of veterans of their eligibility for veterans' benefits and health care services.

After Doyle earned a community development degree from Pennsylvania State, he returned in the mid-1970s to his hometown of Swissvale, just east of Pittsburgh. He entered the insurance business, became involved in community affairs as executive director of the Turtle Creek Valley Citizens Union, and was elected to the Swissvale Borough Council, serving as finance and recreation chairman.

For many years, he worked for Republican state Sen. Frank A. Pecora, and it was out of deference to his boss that Doyle switched his party registration to the GOP. But in 1992, Pecora switched his affiliation to the Democrats and fought through a crowded House primary to win the right to challenge Republican Rick Santorum, then seeking election to a second House term. Pecora lost decisively. Doyle jumped back to the Democratic Party that same year.

In 1994, when Santorum first ran for the Senate, Doyle took up where his old boss had left off and ran in the open 18th District, surviving a seven-person primary and winning the Democratic nomination with 20 percent of the vote. In the general election, Doyle was not well-known across the district, but neither was GOP nominee John McCarty. Using some of the "time for a change" rhetoric popularized by GOP conservatives, Doyle capitalized on the district's Democratic leanings to win by 10 percentage points. He was one of just four Democrats who swam against the national GOP tide that year to capture a House seat that had been in Republican hands.

Doyle won re-election by 16 points in 1996, even though the Pittsburgh Post-Gazette endorsed the GOP candidate, lawyer David B. Fawcett. Doyle won by 35 points in 1998 and by 39 points in 2000.

Heading into post-census redistricting, Doyle was regarded as one of the more vulnerable incumbents in the nation, given Pennsylvania's loss of two House seats and the GOP's control of the redistricting process. But Doyle caught a series of breaks.

Redistricting at first seemed to have dealt him a tough hand, shoving him into the 14th District of fellow Democrat William J. Coyne. But Coyne decided to retire after 11 terms, and none of a number of potentially tough Democratic challengers decided to make a run in 2002. State Republicans, who had made the new 14th heavily Democratic in order to put more Republicans in surrounding districts, declined to field a candidate against Doyle in November. He also was unopposed in 2004.

KEY VOTES

2004
Yes Extend federal unemployment benefits by 13 weeks
Yes Pass $283.2 billion, six-year federal highway and mass transit bill
No Approve $146 billion multi-year extension of previously enacted middle-class tax breaks
No Amend the Constitution to prohibit same-sex marriage
No Cut corporate taxes $137 billion over 10 years
Yes Reorganize U.S. intelligence agencies as proposed by Sept. 11 commission

2003
No Cut taxes by $330 billion through fiscal 2013
Yes Block Bush rule scaling back overtime pay for some white-collar federal workers
Yes Do not allow use of search warrants without first notifying subjects
Yes Allow importation of prescription drugs
No Create private school voucher program in Washington, D.C.
Yes Ban "partial birth" abortion except to save a woman's life
Yes Split $18.6 billion in Iraq aid into half-grant, half-loan
No Overhaul Medicare and create prescription drug benefit

CQ VOTE STUDIES

	PARTY UNITY		PRESIDENTIAL SUPPORT	
	Support	Oppose	Support	Oppose
2004	93%	7%	29%	71%
2003	88%	12%	37%	63%
2002	90%	10%	38%	62%
2001	78%	22%	40%	60%
2000	79%	21%	70%	30%

INTEREST GROUPS

	AFL-CIO	ADA	CCUS	ACU
2004	100%	80%	48%	12%
2003	100%	85%	34%	42%
2002	100%	80%	45%	8%
2001	100%	85%	43%	32%
2000	100%	65%	47%	20%

PENNSYLVANIA 14
Pittsburgh and some close-in suburbs

The 14th, which includes all of Pittsburgh and some of its close-in suburbs, has undergone an economic transformation while maintaining its Democratic tradition and ethnic character.

Medical centers and universities, parks, skyscrapers and technology firms have replaced the smoke stacks from the steel industry once nestled between and along the Allegheny, Monongahela and Ohio rivers. A thriving, corporate downtown has grown up in the "Golden Triangle," where the Allegheny and Monongahela rivers meet. Major League Baseball's Pittsburgh Pirates, at PNC Park, and the National Football League's Pittsburgh Steelers, at Heinz Field, both play in stadiums that opened in 2001.

Areas such as Monroeville and Penn Hills, only parts of which are in the district, have seen commercial development and some technology jobs move in, while others have languished. Many of Pittsburgh's neighborhoods, such as Bloomfield and Lawrenceville, retain their ethnic roots — mainly German, Italian, Irish and Polish. Squirrel Hill long has

been the center of the city's Jewish population.

Even with the diversification of the 14th's economy, the district retains strong Democratic roots. Union strength translates into lopsided Democratic margins, and Democrats far outnumber Republicans, whose outposts in the region are found mostly in the neighboring 4th and 18th districts. Pittsburgh is staunchly Democratic, and the party's candidates also rack up big margins in Wilkinsburg, a heavily black area that abuts Pittsburgh to the east, and McKeesport, West Mifflin and Duquesne, south of the city. John Kerry took 75 percent of the Pittsburgh vote and 69 percent of the 14th's vote in the 2004 presidential election. Democrat Joseph M. Hoeffel took 64 percent in Pittsburgh in the 2004 senatorial election.

MAJOR INDUSTRY
Banking, government, health care

CITIES
Pittsburgh, 334,563; Penn Hills (unincorporated) (pt.), 35,864; McKeesport, 24,040; West Mifflin, 22,464; Wilkinsburg, 19,196

NOTABLE
The Andy Warhol Museum, named for the city's native son, opened in Pittsburgh in 1994; Playwright August Wilson also was born in Pittsburgh.

Rep. Charlie Dent (R)

CAPITOL OFFICE
225-6411
www.house.gov/dent
502 Cannon 20515-3815; fax 226-0778

COMMITTEES
Government Reform
Homeland Security
Transportation & Infrastructure

HOMETOWN
Allentown

BORN
May 24, 1960, Allentown, Pa.

RELIGION
Presbyterian

FAMILY
Wife, Pamela Dent; three children

EDUCATION
Penn State U., B.A. 1982 (foreign service & international politics); Lehigh U., M.P.A. 1993

CAREER
College fundraiser; electronics salesman; hotel clerk; congressional aide

POLITICAL HIGHLIGHTS
Pa. House, 1991-99; Pa. Senate, 1999-2005

ELECTION RESULTS

2004 GENERAL

Charlie Dent (R)	170,634	58.6%
Joe Driscoll (D)	114,646	39.4%
Richard J. Piotrowski (LIBERT)	3,660	1.3%

2004 PRIMARY

Charlie Dent (R)	25,376	51.5%
Joe Pascuzzo (R)	16,152	32.8%
Brian O'Neill (R)	7,749	15.7%

Elected 2004; 1st term

A veteran state lawmaker whose views are considerably closer to the center of the political spectrum than the conservative three-term Rep. Patrick J. Toomey, whom he succeeded in Lehigh Valley's 15th District, Dent hopes to focus on local issues in his freshman term.

While Dent's record will largely echo Toomey on economic issues, the two part ways on some social issues. Unlike Toomey, Dent supports some abortion rights and expansion of embryonic stem cell research.

But such broad national issues are not among Dent's top priorities. Instead, he said he hopes to spend his first term steering federal assistance to his home base — something avoided by fiscal hawk Toomey.

Dent's efforts should be aided by his assignment to the Transportation and Infrastructure Committee, along with posts on the Homeland Security and Government Reform panels.

His list of concerns includes preventing other states from shipping waste to Pennsylvania and providing funds to build a new bridge across the Lehigh River in his hometown of Allentown. "Some of them may not be great campaign issues, but they're important issues nonetheless," said Dent. "We have continuing infrastructure needs in the city of Bethlehem. We need to make improvements along the Route 412 corridor."

He signaled early in his tenure on Capitol Hill that he should not be counted on as an automatic vote for President Bush's policies, citing disagreements on immigration and Social Security overhaul.

Dent, who had represented parts of the 15th District in the state legislature since 1991, built support for a House run after Toomey announced in early 2003 that he would challenge Specter. Though he had to overcome two more-conservative primary opponents, Democrats had even bigger problems: After failing to persuade any well-known local figures to enter the contest, Democratic officials settled on Joe Driscoll, a wealthy former consultant who had to move into the district to run — a point Dent brought up as often as possible on his way to an easy 19 percentage point victory.

PENNSYLVANIA 15
East — Allentown, Bethlehem

Centered in the Lehigh Valley about 60 miles north of Philadelphia and abutting the Delaware River, the 15th takes in the cities of Allentown, Bethlehem and Easton — longtime strongholds of heavy industry.

The region once suffered from "Rust Belt" blues that singer Billy Joel enshrined in his 1982 song "Allentown." But the area began to reinvent its economy in the 1990s after unsuccessful attempts to revive the economic might of Bethlehem Steel and Mack Trucks.

Technology office parks and highway freight centers now cover a landscape where factories and small farms once were mainstays. Major employers include Air Products and Chemicals, the Lehigh Valley Hospital complex, electric utility PPL Corp. and technology company Agere Systems.

Many of the district's towns date to colonial times, some with well-established Pennsylvania Dutch heritages. But the 250-year-old German influence has been diluted by a century of immigration and recent migration from New Jersey and New York. Allentown was the only city among the state's top four not to lose residents in the 1990s.

Blue-collar, ethnic workers provide a dwindling yet still powerful base for Democrats. But the increasing white-collar constituency and a socially conservative streak among blue-collar Democrats have helped Republicans win House contests here. Al Gore captured the 15th's presidential vote by 1 percentage point in 2000 — a feat duplicated by John Kerry in 2004.

MAJOR INDUSTRY
Manufacturing, technology, health care

CITIES
Allentown, 106,632; Bethlehem, 71,329; Easton, 26,263

NOTABLE
Easton is home to the Crayola crayon factory; Just Born, based in Bethlehem, makes more than 600 million Peeps (marshmallow candies) around Easter.

Rep. Joe Pitts (R)

CAPITOL OFFICE
225-2411
www.house.gov/pitts
221 Cannon 20515-3816; fax 225-2013

COMMITTEES
Energy & Commerce

HOMETOWN
Kennett Square

BORN
Oct. 10, 1939, Lexington, Ky.

RELIGION
Protestant

FAMILY
Wife, Virginia M. "Ginny" Pitts; three children

EDUCATION
Asbury College, A.B. 1961 (philosophy & religion);
West Chester State College, M.Ed. 1972
(comprehensive sciences)

MILITARY SERVICE
Air Force, 1963-69

CAREER
Nursery and landscaping business owner; teacher

POLITICAL HIGHLIGHTS
Pa. House, 1973-97

ELECTION RESULTS

2004 GENERAL

Joe Pitts (R)	183,620	64.4%
Lois K. Herr (D)	98,410	34.5%
William R. Hagen (GREEN)	3,269	1.2%

2004 PRIMARY

Joe Pitts (R)	unopposed

2002 GENERAL

Joe Pitts (R)	119,046	88.5%
Will Todd (GREEN)	8,720	6.5%
Kenneth C. Brenneman (CNSTP)	6,766	5.0%

PREVIOUS WINNING PERCENTAGES
2000 (67%); 1998 (71%); 1996 (59%)

Elected 1996; 5th term

The son of missionaries who worked for many years in the Philippines, Pitts glides easily from fostering ties with Asian nations, championing conservative religious values, and protecting the unique ways of Amish life.

In Congress, he follows the same road that he traveled during 24 years in the Pennsylvania legislature — one with few left turns. He is a strong proponent of cutting taxes and limiting the scope of the federal government, and a fervent opponent of abortion.

Pitts also has a far stronger interest in and understanding of foreign policy issues than many House members. In the aftermath of the Sept. 11, 2001, terrorist attacks, Pitts and a handful of other lawmakers formed the Silk Road Caucus, which promotes greater contact between the United States and the nations of Central Asia. He has organized equipment drives for hospitals in Pakistan and cultural and governmental exchange programs to his Pennsylvania district for officials from the region. He is also active in a number of human rights organizations, including the Helsinki Commission. But unlike many lawmakers with strong human rights agendas, he favored the 2000 law normalizing trade with China, arguing that increased engagement would spur China to improve its human rights record.

Pitts sits on the Energy and Commerce Committee, where he is an advocate of tougher broadcast standards and increased prosecutions for violations of obscenity and child exploitation laws. When the House approved a measure in early 2005 to increase to $500,000 the amount that the Federal Communications Commission can fine broadcasters who air obscene or indecent material, Pitts was a strong supporter. The bill "sends a clear message to the entertainment industry we are no longer going to idly stand by and force our parents to put up with this filth," Pitts said on the floor. He also wants to ensure that customers can keep their cell phone numbers out of information directories, for no fee.

As the House member representing Lancaster County, the best-known Amish community in the nation, Pitts has become the chief defender of their simple, rural lifestyle. He has fought to win the Amish an exemption from child labor laws to ensure Amish teenagers could enter apprenticeships once their formal education is complete. The proposal was included in a catchall spending bill President Bush signed in early 2004. Pitts also led an unsuccessful effort to get the UPN television network to scrap its reality series "Amish in the City," or to have experts preview the show and offer criticism.

Pitts is right at the center of most battles on social issues. His stance on abortion put him in a leading role in negotiations over a bill to revamp federal bankruptcy law. Although supportive of the bill's goal, Pitts and other conservatives objected to an amendment aimed at preventing demonstrators — particularly protesters at abortion clinics — from filing for bankruptcy to avoid paying court-ordered fines. When Congress considered the bill early in 2005, Pitts was pleased the Senate rejected the amendment aimed at stopping demonstrators from filing for bankruptcy. "I commend the Senate for opposing this effort to subvert the constitutional rights of peaceful protesters," Pitts said. "This is a victory for free speech."

Pitts forges alliances with groups that advocate a larger role in civic life for families, businesses and religious groups. These organizations include the Republican Study Committee, the Renewal Alliance, the Fatherhood Promotion Task Force, the Pro-Life Caucus, and the Values Action Team, a group of about 60 social conservatives co-founded in 1998 by Majority Leader Tom DeLay, which Pitts leads. Pitts and other social conservatives showed their muscle in 2005 when the House voted to clear Senate-passed legislation bringing the federal courts into the Florida dispute over whether to reconnect a feeding tube that had been sustaining the life of Teresa Schiavo, a severely brain-damaged woman. "We played a role in that, in urging the leadership to act," Pitts said after the vote.

Many of Pitts' goals derive from his experiences as a child of missionaries and as a young father. He spent most of his youth in the back country of the Philippines, where his parents were engaged in missionary work. He says he witnessed poverty and devastation close up, as well as the personal satisfaction that a life in public service can bring.

After returning to his native Kentucky, marrying and earning a college degree in philosophy and religion, Pitts embarked on a teaching career along with his wife. When his wife became pregnant, he discovered that the family could not live on just one teaching salary. So he joined the Air Force, where he spent five and a half years, including three tours of duty in Southeast Asia in which he flew 116 combat missions as the navigator and electronic warfare officer of a B-52. He considered an Air Force career, but discarded the idea when his 3-year-old son did not recognize him when he returned home from an active duty tour.

After the Air Force stint, the family moved to Pennsylvania and Pitts returned to teaching high school math and science. He eventually joined his wife's family's landscape and nursery business and then started his own landscaping firm. Though he was active on local campaigns, Pitts did not think of running for office himself until colleagues convinced him to make a bid for an open state House seat in 1972. He upset the party-endorsed candidate and served in the House for 24 years, including eight years as chairman of the Appropriations Committee.

When Robert S. Walker, a leading figure in the GOP takeover of the House, decided to retire after 10 terms in 1996, Pitts won a hard-fought five-way primary race and, given the GOP's more than 2-to-1 edge in registered voters, prevailed in the general election by 22 percentage points. He has not been challenged seriously in his re-election bids. His territory was made even more Republican in redistricting for this decade, and in 2002 the Democrats did not bother to field a candidate. He won easily in 2004 with 64 percent of the vote. Pitts pledged when he first ran in 1996 to serve no more than 10 years, but he announced before the 2002 election that he had changed his mind. Term limits diminish a "lame duck" lawmaker's effectiveness, he said.

KEY VOTES

2004

No   Extend federal unemployment benefits by 13 weeks

Yes   Pass $283.2 billion, six-year federal highway and mass transit bill

Yes   Approve $146 billion multi-year extension of previously enacted middle-class tax breaks

Yes   Amend the Constitution to prohibit same-sex marriage

Yes   Cut corporate taxes $137 billion over 10 years

No   Reorganize U.S. intelligence agencies as proposed by Sept. 11 commission

2003

Yes   Cut taxes by $330 billion through fiscal 2013

No   Block Bush rule scaling back overtime pay for some white-collar federal workers

No   Do not allow use of search warrants without first notifying subjects

No   Allow importation of prescription drugs

Yes   Create private school voucher program in Washington, D.C.

Yes   Ban "partial birth" abortion except to save a woman's life

No   Split $18.6 billion in Iraq aid into half-grant, half-loan

Yes   Overhaul Medicare and create prescription drug benefit

CQ VOTE STUDIES

	PARTY UNITY		PRESIDENTIAL SUPPORT	
	Support	Oppose	Support	Oppose
2004	97%	3%	91%	9%
2003	98%	2%	98%	2%
2002	97%	3%	88%	12%
2001	96%	4%	91%	9%
2000	98%	2%	19%	81%

INTEREST GROUPS

	AFL-CIO	ADA	CCUS	ACU
2004	13%	5%	95%	100%
2003	7%	5%	100%	88%
2002	0%	0%	94%	100%
2001	0%	0%	91%	100%
2000	0%	0%	85%	100%

PENNSYLVANIA 16
Southeast – Lancaster, part of Reading

Located in southeastern Pennsylvania and bordering Delaware and Maryland to the south, the 16th includes all of Lancaster County, the southern half of Chester County and a slice of Berks County, including part of Reading. Containing much of the so-called "Pennsylvania Dutch Country," the 16th is a Republican bastion.

The strong work ethic of the local labor force and the district's proximity to major roadways attract companies to the area, which is central to the mid-Atlantic's major markets. Economic expansion has attracted new residents, and some of the area's farmland has been built over with tract housing. Rolling and pastoral Chester County was the seventh-fastest-growing county in the state in the 1990s.

Although the 16th welcomes the development, farm preservation remains a major concern, especially in Lancaster, a national leader in agricultural product sales. Tourism also enhances the 16th's robust economy. More than 8 million visitors annually flock to Dutch Country to gaze at Amish horse-drawn carriages, browse at quilt shops and dine in family-style restaurants.

Since the dawn of the Civil War, the areas in the 16th have favored the GOP at all levels. Lancaster County, which accounts for more than 70 percent of the district population, sets the district's conservative political tone with its Amish heritage. George W. Bush won 66 percent of the county's vote in the 2004 presidential election. Chester County is more socially moderate, but Bush still won the 16th's share of the county by 4 percentage points in 2004. The only real Democratic strength is in Reading (shared with the 6th District), which is heavily Democratic as a result of its large Hispanic and black populations. Overall, Bush won the 16th with 61 percent of the vote in 2004.

MAJOR INDUSTRY
Agriculture, tourism, manufacturing

CITIES
Lancaster, 56,348; Reading (pt.), 44,296; West Chester, 17,861

NOTABLE
Frank Woolworth's original five-and-ten-cent store opened in Lancaster in 1879; One of the architects of the U.S. Capitol designed the Chester County Courthouse.

Rep. Tim Holden (D)

Elected 1992; 7th term

In his last two re-election races, Holden proved to be far more resilient than the state Republicans who tried to map him out of his district had expected. Holden, who built his political popularity as a local sheriff, survived when pitted against 20-year-veteran Republican Rep. George W. Gekas in a tight 2002 race. And in 2004, he had to fend off an aggressive challenge by the son of a near-deity, legendary Penn State football coach Joe Paterno, in a district that voted for President Bush.

Holden understands his working-class constituency who are concerned with holding on to their jobs and their guns. And his willingness to break with Democrats on certain social issues, such as abortion and same-sex marriage, has convinced his constituents he is the right man to represent them.

His centrist views are reflected in his voting record. In the 108th Congress, Holden agreed with Bush's position 49 percent of the time; only 17 Democrats voted with Bush more frequently. Holden voted with Democrats on only 77 percent of votes that split the parties.

Holden is a member of the "Blue Dogs," a coalition of conservative Democrats. On welfare, the budget and other issues, the group has staked out positions to the right of most Democrats but to the left of the majority of Republicans. Holden said he opposed the GOP's $1.35 trillion, 10-year tax cut enacted in 2001 in the belief that the surplus at the time should be devoted to paying down the national debt while leaving room for an increase in defense spending.

Holden at the start of the 109th had hoped he would be named the top-ranking Democrat on the Agriculture Committee, where he is second in seniority. But the job went to one of the few Democrats who votes with the GOP more often than Holden, Collin C. Peterson of Minnesota. Peterson's lack of partisan zeal led to talk of passing him over in favor of Holden. But Peterson quelled his leadership's concerns. Both Holden and Peterson are outspoken advocates of dairy farmers. Reauthorizing a crucial milk income support program adopted in 2002 is one of their chief priorities in the 109th. Holden is the top-ranking Democrat on the Conservation, Credit, Rural Development and Research Subcommittee.

Holden also sits on the Transportation and Infrastructure Committee, where he aims to secure funding for local highway and transit projects. He is active in the Congressional Mining Caucus, where he works to make the 17th District's large reserves of coal more marketable by spurring researchers to develop technology to burn the fuel more cleanly.

While he offers remarks on the House floor only a handful of times each year, Holden will speak out when he feels Pennsylvania's interests are threatened. In 2002, he argued for an extension of bankruptcy protections for family farmers when a broader bankruptcy measure bogged down.

Holden is most often in sync with his party on issues important to organized labor. He sides with unions in their disputes with the more pro-business GOP leadership by supporting a higher minimum wage and extension of unemployment benefits, and by blocking Bush administration efforts to scale back overtime pay for certain white-collar federal workers.

Trade issues for Holden are complicated by the fact that his district includes not only union workers, who worry about the loss of jobs to foreign companies, but also export-minded businesses in such industries as communications and steel, as well as a number of firms that must import

CAPITOL OFFICE
225-5546
www.holden.house.gov
2417 Rayburn 20515-3817; fax 226-0996

COMMITTEES
Agriculture
Transportation & Infrastructure

HOMETOWN
St. Clair

BORN
March 5, 1957, St. Clair, Pa.

RELIGION
Roman Catholic

FAMILY
Wife, Gwen Holden

EDUCATION
U. of Richmond, attended 1976-77; Bloomsburg U., B.A. 1980 (sociology)

CAREER
Probation officer; insurance broker; realtor

POLITICAL HIGHLIGHTS
Schuylkill County sheriff, 1985-93

ELECTION RESULTS

2004 GENERAL

Tim Holden (D)	172,412	59.1%
Scott Paterno (R)	113,592	38.9%
Russ Diamond (LIBERT)	5,782	2.0%

2004 PRIMARY

Tim Holden (D)	unopposed

2002 GENERAL

Tim Holden (D)	103,483	51.4%
George W. Gekas (R)	97,802	48.6%

PREVIOUS WINNING PERCENTAGES
2000 (66%); 1998 (61%); 1996 (59%); 1994 (57%); 1992 (52%)

chemicals for use in their manufacturing processes. Still, he voted against all the landmark trade laws enacted in his first five terms. And he has signed onto efforts in the 109th to strip China of its normal trade relations with the United States.

When reapportionment after the 2000 census took a pair of House seats from Pennsylvania, the Republicans who redid the state map figured Gekas could defeat Holden in the newly drawn 17th. But they were wrong. In one debate, Gekas tried to use trade against Holden. When Holden claimed that the 1993 North American Free Trade Agreement had resulted in 36,000 lost manufacturing jobs in the 17th, Gekas replied that the number of statewide jobs had increased. Holden pounced. "Maybe because of McDonald's and maybe because of Arby's, there were more jobs created. . . . But the good manufacturing jobs that were the heart and soul of Berks County are gone." Holden kept his seat by less than 3 percentage points.

In 2004, Scott Paterno, with the help of some GOP heavyweights who again thought Holden was vulnerable, tried to tie Holden to Democratic liberals, including Democratic presidential candidate John Kerry.

When Speaker J. Dennis Hastert came to the 17th, he said, "Quite frankly, Tim Holden's a nice guy . . . but how he votes in Washington and how he talks back home are two different things." Holden again turned the remark back on his GOP opponent. "I have the utmost respect for Speaker Hastert, but that's exactly what's wrong with Washington. There's too much bickering, too much divide." He clobbered Paterno by 20 points.

Holden's family has a tradition of public service. His father, Joseph "Sox" Holden, was a Schuylkill County commissioner for almost two decades. His great-grandfather, John Siney, founded the Miner's Benevolent Association, the forerunner of the United Mine Workers. Holden is an easygoing and affable man whose constituents often call him Timmy.

A star linebacker, Holden started college in Virginia on a football scholarship but returned home after a year to recuperate from a bout of tuberculosis and then stayed close by to finish school.

After working in the insurance and real estate businesses, Holden was a probation officer and sergeant-at-arms in the Pennsylvania House. At 28, he won the first of two terms as Schuylkill County sheriff. When 12-term Democratic Rep. Gus Yatron retired in 1992, Holden won by 4 percentage points in what was then the 6th District, waging a "man of the people" campaign against John E. Jones, a Republican lawyer and judge. Though the district generally votes reliably Republican, Holden won four more times by increasing margins until his 2002 race with Gekas.

KEY VOTES

2004

Yes Extend federal unemployment benefits by 13 weeks
Yes Pass $283.2 billion, six-year federal highway and mass transit bill
Yes Approve $146 billion multi-year extension of previously enacted middle-class tax breaks
Yes Amend the Constitution to prohibit same-sex marriage
No Cut corporate taxes $137 billion over 10 years
Yes Reorganize U.S. intelligence agencies as proposed by Sept. 11 commission

2003

No Cut taxes by $330 billion through fiscal 2013
Yes Block Bush rule scaling back overtime pay for some white-collar federal workers
Yes Do not allow use of search warrants without first notifying subjects
Yes Allow importation of prescription drugs
No Create private school voucher program in Washington, D.C.
Yes Ban "partial birth" abortion except to save a woman's life
Yes Split $18.6 billion in Iraq aid into half-grant, half-loan
No Overhaul Medicare and create prescription drug benefit

CQ VOTE STUDIES

	PARTY UNITY		PRESIDENTIAL SUPPORT	
	Support	Oppose	Support	Oppose
2004	76%	24%	48%	52%
2003	78%	22%	49%	51%
2002	67%	33%	60%	40%
2001	71%	29%	40%	60%
2000	75%	25%	68%	32%

INTEREST GROUPS

	AFL-CIO	ADA	CCUS	ACU
2004	93%	70%	67%	48%
2003	93%	70%	40%	60%
2002	89%	65%	60%	40%
2001	100%	80%	41%	48%
2000	90%	55%	50%	32%

PENNSYLVANIA 17
East central — Harrisburg, Lebanon, Pottsville

Anchored in the eastern part of south-central Pennsylvania, the 17th is home to Harrisburg, the state capital, which sits 100 miles west of Philadelphia and 200 miles east of Pittsburgh. Here, in GOP-minded central Pennsylvania, state government and manufacturing remain key sources of employment. The district contains all of Dauphin, Lebanon and Schuylkill counties along with parts of Berks and Perry counties.

Harrisburg's skyline is dominated by the Capitol, with a dome inspired by St. Peter's Basilica in Rome. With many state government employees and an African-American majority, the city typically votes Democratic, although the rest of Dauphin County favors Republicans. Those wanting a real taste of Dauphin County skip Harrisburg and go to Hershey, also known as "Chocolatetown, U.S.A." The chocolate factory stands at Hershey's center, emitting the most pleasant of industrial odors.

Computer and electrical components manufacturing drive the economy in Dauphin and Lebanon counties. EDS, Giant Food, Blue Cross/Blue Shield, Bayer Corp. and area hospitals are major employers in the region.

The proliferation of service jobs has helped mitigate the impact of other losses. Officials look to balance the needs of agricultural producers with those of industrial workers, making trade a potent issue in the 17th.

The district has a distinct Republican lean, but Rep. Holden demonstrated in 2002 that moderate Democrats can play here. The GOP runs strongly in Lebanon County and in the areas of Dauphin outside Harrisburg. Democrats are competitive in Schuylkill County, long a coal mining powerhouse, with comfortable margins in Pottsville, Mahanoy and Shenandoah. Holden won Dauphin and Schuylkill counties and the 17th's share of Berks County in 2004, but lost Lebanon County and the district's part of Perry County. George W. Bush took 58 percent of the district's vote in the 2004 presidential election.

MAJOR INDUSTRY
Government, service, manufacturing, agriculture

CITIES
Harrisburg, 48,950; Lebanon, 24,461; Pottsville, 15,549; Colonial Park (unincorporated), 13,259; Hershey (unincorporated), 12,771

NOTABLE
Streetlights in the town of Hershey are shaped like Hershey Kisses; Pottsville is home to Yuengling, America's oldest active brewery.

Rep. Tim Murphy (R)

CAPITOL OFFICE
225-2301
murphy.house.gov
322 Cannon 20515-3818; fax 225-1844

COMMITTEES
Energy & Commerce

HOMETOWN
Upper St. Clair

BORN
Sept. 11, 1952, Cleveland, Ohio

RELIGION
Roman Catholic

FAMILY
Wife, Nan Murphy; one child

EDUCATION
Wheeling College, B.S. 1974 (psychology);
Cleveland State U., M.A. 1976 (psychology);
U. of Pittsburgh, Ph.D. 1979 (psychology)

CAREER
Psychologist; professor

POLITICAL HIGHLIGHTS
Pa. Senate, 1997-2003

ELECTION RESULTS

2004 GENERAL

Tim Murphy (R)	197,894	62.8%
Mark G. Boles (D)	117,420	37.2%

2004 PRIMARY

Tim Murphy (R)	unopposed

2002 GENERAL

Tim Murphy (R)	119,885	60.1%
Jack M. Machek (D)	79,451	39.9%

Elected 2002; 2nd term

A well-spoken child psychologist who was once known on Pittsburgh television and radio as "Dr. Tim," Murphy brings a firsthand perspective to the complex field of health care policy. In the 109th Congress, he will tackle the issue as a member of the Energy and Commerce Committee.

Murphy also co-chairs the Republican Conference's Healthcare Access and Affordability Team, one of eight new working groups designed to increase grass-roots communications on specific issues. In endorsing Murphy for re-election in 2004, the Pittsburgh Post-Gazette said Murphy "is sincerely interested in health care issues, and often puts a more eloquent and articulate spin on the administration's positions than it does itself."

As the 109th Congress began, Murphy gave a weekly series of speeches on the House floor in which he beseeched colleagues not to neglect health care as they focused on overhauling Social Security and the war in Iraq. "It is the key issue," he told the Post-Gazette. "During campaign time, people kept saying: 'It's terrorism; it's Iraq.' I said, 'It's health care.' We have to set a major shift and a long-term plan for what we're doing here, and not just say, 'OK, what Band-Aid can we put on it this year?' "

Murphy wants to create incentives for hospitals and doctors to use electronic systems for maintaining health records. He also hopes to encourage health care providers to use more electronic systems to track every aspect of a patient's care, from their first physical onward. He wants to win tax incentives and grants for hospitals that agree to adopt such systems. "Electronic medical records can save hours and provide essential, up-to-the-minute patient history that improves safety and facilitates accurate diagnosis and treatment," he said in early 2005. "Similarly, electronic prescribing could eliminate many of the 14 million medication errors that occur each year."

Murphy also said Congress should set a national goal of zero medical errors, citing a National Academy of Sciences 1999 report that found as many as 98,000 people die annually from health care workers' mistakes. And he said he would like to provide incentives to doctors and nurses who volunteer at federally approved health centers in poverty-stricken areas.

When Murphy entered public life by winning a state Senate seat in 1996, he did not set his professional interests aside. Motivated to run by a desire to address problems in managed care, Murphy wrote Pennsylvania's Patients' Bill of Rights. In 2001, he co-wrote a book titled "The Angry Child: Regaining Control When Your Child Is Out of Control." The book explored the various sources of anger in children and recommended how parents could respond by choosing their battles carefully, using distractions and knowing a child's limitations.

Murphy grew up as one of 11 children, cleaning out horse stalls and digging graves to pay his way through school. He wants to help low-income children, who he believes are not served well by the public education system. He supports vouchers and other programs that could allow low-income families to send their children to private or parochial schools.

Like most freshmen, Murphy closely followed his party's line. But in a nod to the working-class constituents in his district, he did depart from the GOP on some economic matters. In 2004, he joined 21 Republicans in voting with all the Democrats to overturn the Bush administration's new rules on overtime pay. Seven months earlier, he backed a Democratic amendment to offer federal supplemental unemployment insurance benefits for 13 weeks to jobless workers. He said he thought the latter vote was symbolic, but that it was "important to signal that we're trying to help."

In 2003, he and several other freshmen joined labor groups in expressing concerns over a bill that would have allowed companies to offer employees compensatory time off in lieu of overtime pay. Republican leaders responded by pulling the bill from consideration.

Murphy has backed President Bush on the Iraq war, saying that progress has been made. But he has also made clear he sees room for improvement in the overall war on terrorism. At a Government Reform Committee hearing in 2003, he joined other GOP lawmakers in questioning an intricate organizational chart created by the Government Accountability Office to show how the administration's anti-terrorism strategies are linked. "I'm sure it makes sense to someone," said Murphy after commenting that the analysis reminded him of Civil War Gen. Stonewall Jackson's strategic mantra, to "mystify, mislead and surprise."

In addition to the Government Reform panel, Murphy served on the Veterans' Affairs and Financial Services committees in the 108th Congress. He exchanged those assignments to take the seat on Energy and Commerce in the 109th.

Pennsylvania lost a pair of House seats in reapportionment after the 2000 census. The Republican-controlled General Assembly was nonetheless able to draw a congressional map for this decade with an 18th District south of Pittsburgh configured to favor a Republican — Murphy in particular. He was unopposed for the GOP nod. He had become the heir presumptive to the seat when the incumbent House member living in the new 18th, four-term Democrat Frank R. Mascara, decided instead to mount what proved to be an unsuccessful primary challenge to Rep. John P. Murtha.

Murphy took 60 percent of the vote against Democrat Jack M. Machek, a school tax administrator. Two years later, he won with 63 percent over political newcomer Mark G. Boles, a physician, after having raised almost 10 times more money than his opponent.

In addition to his psychology background, Murphy is also an accomplished singer-songwriter. As the Post-Gazette said in publicizing his appearance as headliner at a local celebrity night, "Even die-hard Democrats admit [he] sings folk songs with liberal passion."

Murphy taught himself to play guitar and performed in acoustic bands in high school, college and graduate school. The bands played coffeehouses where, he said, he would earn enough to buy an expensive hamburger, though he also once opened in Cleveland for banjo legend Earl Scruggs.

KEY VOTES

2004
Yes Extend federal unemployment benefits by 13 weeks
Yes Pass $283.2 billion, six-year federal highway and mass transit bill
Yes Approve $146 billion multi-year extension of previously enacted middle-class tax breaks
Yes Amend the Constitution to prohibit same-sex marriage
Yes Cut corporate taxes $137 billion over 10 years
Yes Reorganize U.S. intelligence agencies as proposed by Sept. 11 commission

2003
Yes Cut taxes by $330 billion through fiscal 2013
No Block Bush rule scaling back overtime pay for some white-collar federal workers
No Do not allow use of search warrants without first notifying subjects
No Allow importation of prescription drugs
Yes Create private school voucher program in Washington, D.C.
Yes Ban "partial birth" abortion except to save a woman's life
No Split $18.6 billion in Iraq aid into half-grant, half-loan
Yes Overhaul Medicare and create prescription drug benefit

CQ VOTE STUDIES

	PARTY UNITY		PRESIDENTIAL SUPPORT	
	Support	Oppose	Support	Oppose
2004	92%	8%	84%	16%
2003	97%	3%	98%	2%

INTEREST GROUPS

	AFL-CIO	ADA	CCUS	ACU
2004	36%	20%	95%	92%
2003	27%	10%	97%	88%

PENNSYLVANIA 18

West — Pittsburgh suburbs, part of Washington and Westmoreland counties

The 18th is a socially conservative, ancestrally Democratic area that takes in parts of Allegheny, Washington and Westmoreland counties in the orbit of Pittsburgh. The area's access to major waterways made the first half of the 20th century prosperous for parts of the 18th, which was once a prodigious producer of steel. Now, many areas are struggling to make an economic comeback.

The presence of universities and hospitals in the district has led some technology companies to relocate to the area. However, an economic downturn early in the 21st century and the troubles of several technology firms have left the region grasping for a way to deal with unemployment. High property taxes also are a volatile issue here.

About 55 percent of the 18th's residents live in Allegheny County, which is dominated by Pittsburgh. The Democratic-leaning city is in the 14th District, and most of Allegheny's wealthy Republican suburbs are in the

4th. The 18th's share includes well-off areas in southwestern Allegheny like Upper St. Clair and Mount Lebanon, as well as middle- and working-class Democratic enclaves like Carnegie and Dormont, which are just southwest of Pittsburgh.

The 18th also includes most of Westmoreland County, a former Democratic bastion east of Allegheny County that voted for Walter F. Mondale for president in 1984 and Michael S. Dukakis in 1988. The county has since moved to the right, supporting George W. Bush by 12 percentage points in the 2004 presidential election. Overall, Bush captured 54 percent of the 18th's presidential vote in 2004.

MAJOR INDUSTRY
Health care, technology, manufacturing, air cargo, steel

CITIES
Bethel Park, 33,556; Mount Lebanon (unincorporated), 33,017; Monroeville (pt.), 24,294

NOTABLE
Singer Perry Como was born in Canonsburg (shared with the 12th); Andy Warhol is buried in Bethel Park; Meadowcroft Museum of Rural Life, near Avella in Washington County, preserves the history of 19th century rural life in western Pennsylvania.

Rep. Todd R. Platts (R)

Elected 2000; 3rd term

CAPITOL OFFICE
225-5836
www.house.gov/platts
1032 Longworth 20515-3819; fax 226-1000

COMMITTEES
Education & Workforce
Government Reform
(Government Management, Finance &
Accountability - chairman)
Transportation & Infrastructure

HOMETOWN
York

BORN
March 5, 1962, York, Pa.

RELIGION
Episcopalian

FAMILY
Wife, Leslie Platts; two children

EDUCATION
Shippensburg U., B.S. 1984 (public administration);
Pepperdine U., J.D. 1991

CAREER
Lawyer; gubernatorial and state legislative aide

POLITICAL HIGHLIGHTS
Pa. House, 1993-2000; sought Republican
nomination for York County Commission, 1995

ELECTION RESULTS

2004 GENERAL

Todd R. Platts (R)	224,274	91.5%
Charles J. Steel (GREEN)	8,890	3.6%
Michael L. Paoletta (LIBERT)	8,456	3.5%
Lester B. Searer (CNSTP)	3,474	1.4%

2004 PRIMARY

Todd R. Platts (R)	unopposed

2002 GENERAL

Todd R. Platts (R)	143,097	91.1%
Ben G. Price (GREEN)	7,900	5.0%
Michael L. Paoletta (LIBERT)	6,008	3.8%

PREVIOUS WINNING PERCENTAGES
2000 (73%)

Platts positions himself as a "good government legislator" — right down to having a "Mr. Smith Goes to Washington" poster in his congressional office.

He takes no political action committee money, supports campaign finance reform, writes dry-sounding bills on government management practices, and wonders why the government's books are not as tidy as his own finances. "If my checkbook is off by 10 cents, I'll stay up all night until I find that 10 cents. Your checkbook is off by $2 billion," Platts lectured a NASA official, who was appearing before his Government Reform subcommittee.

And like Jimmy Stewart's Mr. Smith, Platts has even gotten crosswise with his own party for some of his positions. His biggest act of apostasy came in his first term, when he was one of 20 Republicans who signed a discharge petition that forced the GOP leadership to bring campaign finance legislation to a vote. And then he was one of the 41 Republicans to vote for the measure that became law in 2002. One leader still doesn't speak to Platts.

"The voters of the 19th District sent me here to use my judgment," he told the Philadelphia Inquirer in 2004. "They didn't say they were electing me to be a yes man for the White House or the House leadership."

Platts plays down any repercussions, and, in fact, he was given the chairmanship of a Government Reform subcommittee less than a year after the campaign finance reform vote. In the 109th Congress, he is chairman of the Government Management, Finance and Accountability Subcommittee. Platts has used that subcommittee post to pursue an agenda aimed at making the government run better and cheaper.

His biggest accomplishment in the 108th was applying the same accounting and management rules that other departments have to live under to the new Department of Homeland Security. Pursuing these rules meant going against the wishes of the Bush administration, however. Bush had promised to live within the rules voluntarily, but Platts successfully pushed his bill into law to bind future presidents.

Platts' reputation for playing square and trying to keep government on the straight and narrow dates back to his days as a member of the state House. He aggravated colleagues there by being unbending and by going after their perquisites of office. The York Daily Record once dubbed him the "King of Clean," referring to Platts' upright image.

Platts says he is not unwilling to compromise, but that there comes a time when a politician has to take a stand. He may have picked up his stubborn tendencies from his father, who bucked the local Little League establishment with his belief that every child who showed up at practice should play.

With a seat on the Education and Workforce Committee, Platts follows in the footsteps of his predecessor, Republican Bill Goodling, who was committee chairman during the last three of his 13 terms in the House. Platts brings his own education expertise to the panel, as he was chairman of the state House Education Committee's Subcommittee on Basic Education. He argues that the federal government should keep its longstanding promise to pay its full share of the costs of educating disabled students under the Individuals with Disabilities Education Act, to free up local education dollars.

Unlike many Republicans, Platts opposes vouchers for private schools, and found himself voicing this opinion to newly elected President Bush less than a week after they both began their first terms in 2001.

Education is one area where Platts has tried to work across the aisle. He wrote an early childhood education bill with liberal Democratic Rep. George Miller of California that tries to bolster the pay and improve the training of qualified child care workers.

Platts' other legislative priorities include funding for his district's transportation needs. From his seat on the Transportation and Infrastructure Committee, he will have a chance in the 109th to push for local funding when the House considers an update of a six-year highway and mass transit law.

Even though he has a maverick streak, Platts is still a party loyalist. In the 108th, he sided with his party 90 percent of the time on votes in which the two parties faced off. He supported Bush's position 88 percent of the time.

Even though they are no longer in political fashion, Platts is a supporter of congressional term limits. He has not taken a term limits pledge himself, however, because, he says, such a unilateral decision would hurt his constituents by keeping their representative from building valuable seniority. Platts says working his way through college as a Teamster proved to him the advantages of longevity in a job.

For the same reason, Platts endorsed the re-election of Republican Pennsylvania Sen. Arlen Specter in 2004 when many other conservative Republicans lined up behind the primary challenge of Rep. Patrick J. Toomey. "Seniority mattered on the warehouse floor, and it matters here in Washington," Platts told the Centre Daily Times of State College.

Platts says being a member of Congress has been his ambition since he was a teenager. He won election to the state legislature at the age of 30 after paying his dues in local and state politics and civic organizations.

After working for Republican Gov. Dick Thornburgh and then serving as a legislative committee staff member and assistant finance director for the state Republican Party, Platts in 1992 made his first bid for elective office, a seat in the state House. He campaigned on a "reform" platform, assembled a large band of volunteers and won comfortably.

He made an unsuccessful run for the York County Commission in 1995, but then went on to win two more state House terms. In early 1999, when Goodling announced he would not seek re-election in 2000, Platts was the first candidate to jump into the race. Though greatly outspent in the GOP primary, and still eschewing PAC contributions, Platts won with 33 percent of the vote. The district's Republican leanings ensured his victory against a nominal Democrat. He has not had a Democratic opponent since.

Platts has two young children, and he commutes almost 200 miles daily from his home in York to Capitol Hill and back. He says a hands-free cell phone and books on tape help make the commute possible.

KEY VOTES

2004

No Extend federal unemployment benefits by 13 weeks
Yes Pass $283.2 billion, six-year federal highway and mass transit bill
Yes Approve $146 billion multi-year extension of previously enacted middle-class tax breaks
Yes Amend the Constitution to prohibit same-sex marriage
No Cut corporate taxes $137 billion over 10 years
Yes Reorganize U.S. intelligence agencies as proposed by Sept. 11 commission

2003

Yes Cut taxes by $330 billion through fiscal 2013
No Block Bush rule scaling back overtime pay for some white-collar federal workers
No Do not allow use of search warrants without first notifying subjects
Yes Allow importation of prescription drugs
No Create private school voucher program in Washington, D.C.
Yes Ban "partial birth" abortion except to save a woman's life
No Split $18.6 billion in Iraq aid into half-grant, half-loan
Yes Overhaul Medicare and create prescription drug benefit

CQ VOTE STUDIES

	PARTY UNITY		PRESIDENTIAL SUPPORT	
	Support	Oppose	Support	Oppose
2004	88%	12%	85%	15%
2003	91%	9%	89%	11%
2002	85%	15%	82%	18%
2001	91%	9%	86%	14%

INTEREST GROUPS

	AFL-CIO	ADA	CCUS	ACU
2004	33%	20%	95%	84%
2003	27%	20%	90%	76%
2002	11%	5%	85%	88%
2001	18%	5%	83%	80%

PENNSYLVANIA 19

South central — York, Gettysburg

Situated west of the Susquehanna River, mostly east of the South Mountains and mostly south of Harrisburg, the 19th's historic landscape has a reliably Republican constituency and flourishing agricultural and manufacturing industries.

Located along several major highways, the district is a prime location for manufacturing and distribution centers, including depots and logistical support facilities for the Department of Defense. York County, where 60 percent of residents live, serves as the 19th's industrial hub. Residential growth, a more recent trend, also can be attributed to the district's location — Marylanders have moved here for the lower taxes and affordable real estate. But many residents, or their forefathers, traveled much farther than from a neighboring state — the 19th has the highest percentage of residents with German ancestry (38 percent) in the state.

Tourism also plays a major role. Nearly 2 million visitors a year come to see the site of the 1863 Battle of Gettysburg in Adams County, a largely agricultural area. Many come for the annual re-enactment of one of the

Civil War's most significant battles.

George W. Bush won 64 percent of the 19th's vote in the 2004 presidential election. Cumberland County, which is shared with the 9th, is strongly Republican, with Bush winning 63 percent of the district's portion of the county. York and Adams also have strong GOP leans, with Democrats only finding strength in the city of York, where blacks and Hispanics together make up more than 40 percent of the population, and Gettysburg, which has a large college-age population.

MAJOR INDUSTRY
Agriculture, manufacturing, distribution, defense, tourism

MILITARY BASES
Defense Distribution Depot Susquehanna, 296 military, 1,047 civilian (2004); Carlisle Barracks, 325 military, 500 civilian (2005)

CITIES
York, 40,862; Carlisle, 17,970; Hanover, 14,535

NOTABLE
Birthplace of the Articles of Confederation; York served as the first U.S. Capital from 1777-78 while the British occupied Philadelphia; Harley Davidson's largest manufacturing facility is in York; President Abraham Lincoln gave his famed Gettysburg Address in Adams County.

RHODE ISLAND

Gov. Donald L. Carcieri (R)

First elected: 2002
Length of term: 4 years
Term expires: 1/07
Salary: $105,194
Phone: (401) 222-2080

Hometown: East Greenwich
Born: Dec. 16, 1942; East Greenwich, R.I.
Religion: Roman Catholic
Family: Wife, Sue Carcieri; four children
Education: Brown U., A.B. 1965 (international relations)
Career: Manufacturing company executive; aid relief worker; bank executive; teacher
Political highlights: No previous office

Election results:
2002 GENERAL
Donald L. Carcieri (R)	181,687	54.8%
Myrth York (D)	150,147	45.3%

Lt. Gov. Charles J. Fogarty (D)

First elected: 1998
Length of term: 4 years
Term expires: 1/07
Salary: $88,584
Phone: (401) 222-2371

STATE LEGISLATURE

General Assembly: January-June

House: 75 members, 2-year terms
2005 breakdown: 60D, 15R; 64 men, 11 women
Salary: $12,285
Phone: (401) 222-2466

Senate: 38 members, 2-year terms
2005 breakdown: 33D, 5R; 30 men, 8 women
Salary: $12,285
Phone: (401) 222-6655

STATE TERM LIMITS

Governor: 2 terms
House: No
Senate: No

URBAN STATISTICS

CITY	POPULATION
Providence	173,618
Warwick	85,808
Cranston	79,269
Pawtucket	72,958
East Providence	48,688

REGISTERED VOTERS

Voters do not register by party.

POPULATION

2004 population (est.)	1,080,632
2000 population	1,048,319
1990 population	1,003,464
Percent change (1990-2000)	+4.5%
Rank among states (2004)	43

Median age	36.7
Born in state	61.4%
Foreign born	11.4%
Violent crime rate	298/100,000
Poverty level	11.9%
Federal workers	10,207
Military	9,161

REDISTRICTING

Rhode Island retained its two House seats in reapportionment. The state legislature drew a new map, which the governor allowed to become law without his signature on Feb. 20, 2002.

MISCELLANEOUS

Web: www.ri.gov
Capital: Providence
STATE ELECTION OFFICIAL
(401) 222-2345
DEMOCRATIC HEADQUARTERS
(401) 721-9900
REPUBLICAN HEADQUARTERS
(401) 732-8282

District Statistics

DIST.	2004 VOTE FOR PRESIDENT BUSH	KERRY	WHITE	BLACK	ASIAN	HISP	MEDIAN INCOME	WHITE COLLAR	BLUE COLLAR	SERVICE INDUSTRY	OVER 64	UNDER 18	COLLEGE EDUCATION	RURAL	SQ. MILES
1	36%	62%	83%	4%	2%	7%	$40,616	61%	23%	15%	15%	23%	26%	4%	325
2	41	57	81	4	3	10	$44,129	61	23	16	14	25	25	14	720
STATE	39	59	82	4	2	9	$42,090	61	23	16	15	24	26	9	1,045
U.S.	50.7	48.3	69	12	4	13	$41,994	60	25	15	12	26	24	21	3,537,438

R H O D E   I S L A N D

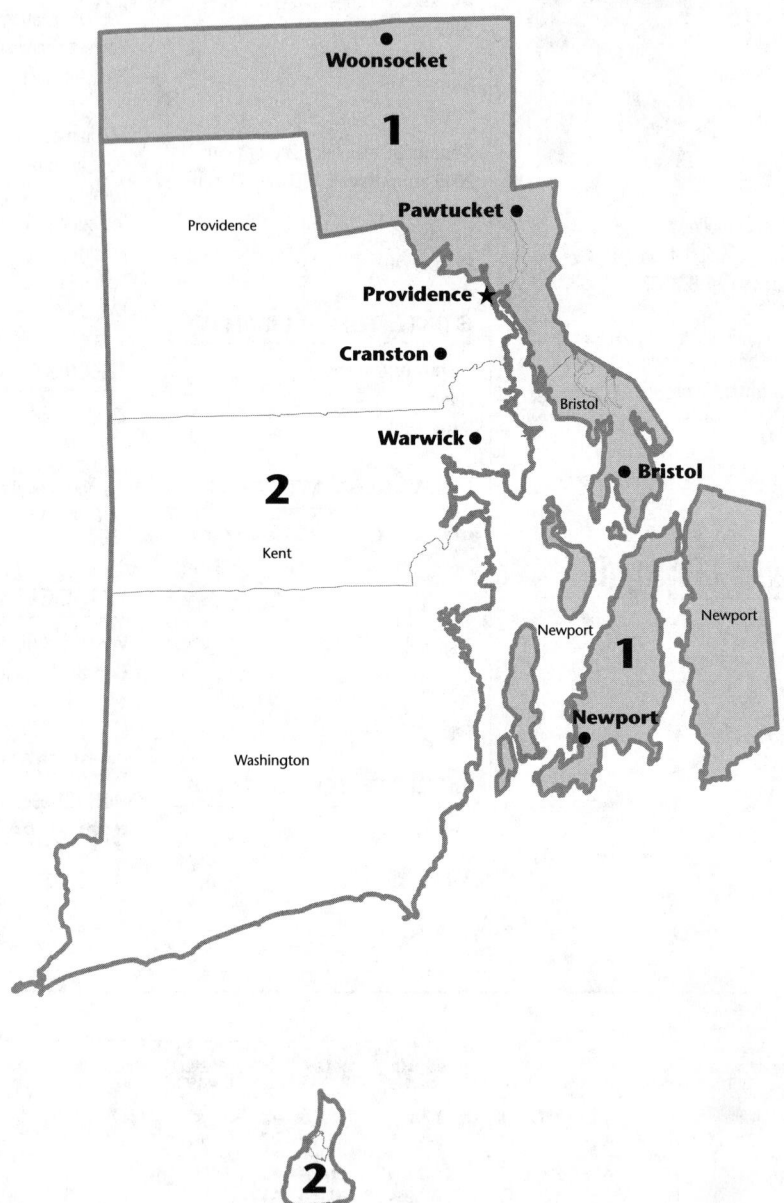

906

www.cqpress.com

Sen. Jack Reed (D)

CAPITOL OFFICE
224-4642
jack@reed.senate.gov
reed.senate.gov
728 Hart 20510-3903; fax 224-4680

COMMITTEES
Armed Services
Banking, Housing & Urban Affairs
Health, Education, Labor & Pensions
Joint Economic - ranking member

HOMETOWN
Cranston

BORN
Nov. 12, 1949, Providence, R.I.

RELIGION
Roman Catholic

FAMILY
Wife, Julia Reed

EDUCATION
U.S. Military Academy, B.S. 1971 (engineering);
Harvard U., M.P.P. 1973, J.D. 1982

MILITARY SERVICE
Army, 1971-79; Army Reserve, 1979-91

CAREER
Lawyer

POLITICAL HIGHLIGHTS
R.I. Senate, 1985-91; U.S. House, 1991-97

ELECTION RESULTS

2002 GENERAL

Jack Reed (D)	253,774	78.4%
Robert G. Tingle (R)	69,808	21.6%

2002 PRIMARY

Jack Reed (D)	unopposed

PREVIOUS WINNING PERCENTAGES
1996 (63%); 1994 House Election (68%); 1992 House
Election (71%); 1990 House Election (59%)

Elected 1996; 2nd term

As a West Point graduate and Army paratrooper, Reed is a leading Democratic voice on matters military, especially the timely topic of how best to prepare for and fight wars.

Reed was one of 21 Democrats to vote against authorizing the war in Iraq in 2002 (fellow Rhode Island Sen. Lincoln Chafee was the sole Republican opponent). But once the invasion began, Reed supported extra funding for the war and turned his attentions to how to secure victory because he felt failure would be catastrophic. He has visited Iraq and Afghanistan numerous times and on at least one occasion brought Dunkin' Donuts coffee, a New England staple, to the Rhode Island troops.

In 2003, Reed and Nebraska Republican Chuck Hagel, who supported the war but has sharply questioned how it has been carried out, fought to increase the size of the Army to relieve the soldiers and reservists whose tours have been extended in Iraq. Over the objections of the Pentagon, Congress ultimately agreed in late 2004 to add 20,000 soldiers and take the Army's active duty roster over 500,000. The reserves, which by mid-2004 accounted for 40 percent of U.S. forces in Iraq, "are stretched to the limit and beyond," Reed said. "We can't sustain the reserve force if they're being called up every other year."

From his seat on the Armed Services Committee, Reed's concerns about the Army Reserve are a top priority in the 109th Congress. When a December 2004 memo by the head of the Army Reserve warned that the reserves were nearly a "broken force," Reed said, "By consistently underestimating the number of troops necessary for the successful occupation of Iraq, the administration . . . created this crisis." In the 109th, he is the top-ranking Democrat on the committee's Emerging Threats and Capabilities Subcommittee.

Reed had a number of questions after President Bush asserted in his 2005 State of the Union address that the U.S. mission in Iraq had changed to one of preparing Iraqi forces to take over responsibility for their own security. As the president offered no timetable for a withdrawal of U.S. forces from Iraq, Reed said a major issue was how rapidly Iraqi forces can replace the 17 U.S. brigades estimated to be in Iraq next year. "How long will it take?" asked Reed. "If we don't know that, then we don't have an idea of how long the mission is or how much it will cost."

Reed has long been a critic of the administration's unproven national missile defense system — a battle certain to grow more fierce as the system is actually deployed.

His Armed Services seat also allows Reed to push for continued support for the Rhode Island-based Naval Undersea Warfare Center and the Naval Education Training Center and to protect federal contracts for the building of attack submarines at the General Dynamics Electric Boat Corp., which employs more than 11,000 workers in its Rhode Island and nearby Groton, Conn., facilities.

Reed has developed a reputation for a serious-minded approach to legislating. As a columnist for the Providence Journal put it, the lawmaker's critique of the Bush missile defense plan "was vintage Reed: exhaustive, respectful, heavy on the factual findings, light on the polemics."

Reed increased his focus on Armed Services after losing a cherished spot on the Appropriations Committee in the 108th, where he served only 18 months. When the GOP captured control of the Senate in 2002, Democrats had to reduce by one their numbers on the committee.

Reed kept his post as the top-ranking Democrat on the Joint Economic Committee, and was named to the Democratic whip organization. In the 109th, he is taking on a larger political role. Senate Democratic leader Harry Reid restructured the Democratic Senatorial Campaign Committee by creating regional chairs, and gave Reed the Northeast slot.

Reed is a dependable liberal on most social issues. In 2004, he voted to extend the assault weapons ban for another 10 years; and he has taken the lead among Senate Democrats in efforts to more closely regulate gun shows, by promoting legislation requiring background checks for people who buy guns from private dealers. He has voted against banning a procedure critics call "partial birth" abortion, and he opposed amending the Constitution to prohibit same-sex marriage.

He took to the Senate floor in early 2005 to rail against Bush's plan to create private investment accounts within Social Security. "The president's private accounts would cut Social Security's funding, weaken the program, and make its financial problems worse, not better," Reed said. "In short, private accounts pose a serious threat to the future economic security of all Americans, particularly the most vulnerable members of our society."

And when the Bush administration and congressional Republicans look for places to cut in the domestic side of the budget, Reed can be counted on to use his post as the top-ranking Democrat on the Banking panel's Housing and Transportation Subcommittee to protect vulnerable federal housing programs. In the preface to a 2001 report by the National Low Income Housing Coalition, Reed wrote, "Nowhere in the country does the minimum wage work of one person come close to paying the rent."

Each year, Reed comes to the aid of the estimated several thousand Liberian refugees who have settled in Rhode Island, part of the more than 10,000 refugees from that country who fled to the United States to escape a long-running civil war. The refugees have not been granted permanent residency, and until they are, Reed annually asks the White House to permit them to stay another year.

Reed grew up in a working-class family in Cranston, where his father was a school custodian and his mother a factory worker. He announced his candidacy for the Senate at the Cranston school administration building, in a room named after his father. His parents placed great importance on education, a value that carries over into Reed's legislative agenda.

He finished second in his class at his Catholic prep school, where he was an overachieving, 124-pound defensive back who won admission to West Point. He barely met the minimum height requirement. After graduation, the Army put him through a master's program at the John F. Kennedy School of Government at Harvard University. Reed then commanded a company of the Army's 82nd Airborne Division and taught at West Point.

After attaining the rank of captain, he left the Army at age 29 to attend Harvard Law School. He returned home to a job in Rhode Island's biggest corporate law firm. In 1984, he won a seat in the state Senate.

Six years later, Reed took 59 percent of the vote to win the 2nd District House seat, which Republican Claudine Schneider gave up to make an unsuccessful challenge to Democratic Sen. Claiborne Pell. Before long, Reed was regarded as heir apparent to Pell, whose health was failing.

When Pell announced that he would retire in 1996, after 36 years in office, Reed was well-prepared to run. He overcame a vigorous negative advertising campaign paid for by the National Republican Senatorial Committee, which sought to convince voters that Reed was a tax-and-spend liberal. He won with 63 percent of the vote against Republican state Treasurer Nancy J. Mayer. In 2002, he won handily with 78 percent.

KEY VOTES

2004

Yes Pass $318.9 billion, six-year highway and mass transit bill

Yes Extend assault weapons ban for 10 years

Yes Restore pay-as-you-go rules for new tax cuts and entitlement spending

No Criminalize harm to a fetus in an attack on the mother

Yes Increase mandatory child care funding to states by $6 billion over five years

No Amend the Constitution to prohibit same-sex marriage

Yes Approve $146 billion multi-year extension of previously enacted middle-class tax breaks

Yes Reorganize U.S. intelligence agencies as proposed by Sept. 11 commission

No Cut corporate taxes $137 billion over 10 years

2003

Yes Delay Bush changes to Clean Air Act

No Allow confirmation vote on Miguel A. Estrada to the U.S. Court of Appeals for the D.C. Circuit

Yes Block a Bush proposal opening Alaska's Arctic National Wildlife Refuge to oil drilling

Yes Limit size of Bush's proposed tax cut to $350 billion through fiscal 2013

No Overhaul Medicare and create prescription drug benefit

Yes Block Bush rule scaling back overtime pay for some white-collar federal workers

Yes Split $20 billion in Iraq aid into half-grant, half-loan

No Ban "partial birth" abortion except to save a woman's life

No Stop proposal allowing travel to Cuba

No Allow final vote on energy policy overhaul

CQ VOTE STUDIES

	PARTY UNITY		PRESIDENTIAL SUPPORT	
	Support	Oppose	Support	Oppose
2004	98%	2%	60%	40%
2003	98%	2%	45%	55%
2002	98%	2%	66%	34%
2001	99%	1%	64%	36%
2000	97%	3%	95%	5%
1999	96%	4%	89%	11%
1998	98%	2%	90%	10%
1997	99%	1%	86%	14%
House Service:				
1996	88%	12%	81%	19%
1995	92%	8%	82%	18%

INTEREST GROUPS

	AFL-CIO	ADA	CCUS	ACU
2004	100%	100%	35%	0%
2003	100%	100%	26%	20%
2002	100%	100%	40%	0%
2001	100%	100%	36%	4%
2000	75%	95%	46%	12%
1999	100%	100%	47%	4%
1998	88%	95%	56%	0%
1997	100%	100%	44%	0%
House Service:				
1996	82%	80%	31%	5%
1995	100%	90%	25%	12%

Sen. Lincoln Chafee (R)

Elected 2000; 1st full term
Appointed November 1999

CAPITOL OFFICE
224-2921
chafee.senate.gov
141-A Russell 20510-3904; fax 228-2853

COMMITTEES
Environment & Public Works
  (Fisheries, Wildlife & Water - chairman)
Foreign Relations
  (Near Eastern & South Asian Affairs - chairman)
Homeland Security & Governmental Affairs

HOMETOWN
Warwick

BORN
March 26, 1953, Warwick, R.I.

RELIGION
Episcopalian

FAMILY
Wife, Stephanie Chafee; three children

EDUCATION
Brown U., A.B. 1975 (classics)

CAREER
Defense company machine shop planner;
blacksmith

POLITICAL HIGHLIGHTS
Warwick City Council, 1986-91; Republican
nominee for mayor of Warwick, 1990; mayor of
Warwick, 1992-99

ELECTION RESULTS

2000 GENERAL

Lincoln Chafee (R)	222,588	56.9%
Bob Weygand (D)	161,023	41.2%
Christopher Young (REF)	4,107	1.1%

2000 PRIMARY

Lincoln Chafee (R)	unopposed

Among the last in the dying breed of the Rockefeller Republicans, Chafee is the senator most likely to vote against his party and against his president on any given day Congress is in session. Chafee's apostasy does not go unnoticed but it does go largely unpunished: He has made it clear that excessive pressure from conservative GOP leaders could lead him to bolt the party, reducing Republican strength by one at a time President Bush needs every last vote in the Senate for his second-term agenda.

Still, Chafee was increasingly isolated after the 2004 election brought an unexpectedly strong wave of conservative freshmen to the Senate and witnessed the retirement of several prominent moderates. Chafee has very few people left to turn to in order to build the kind of moderate-centrist coalitions that had a significant impact on outcomes in the 108th Congress. And, with a more comfortable majority numerically, conservative Senate leaders are in a better position to try to push the stubborn centrist to the right.

In person, Chafee is the most unlikely of rebels. Shy to the point of seeming timorous, he comes and goes from the Senate floor almost unnoticed in the crush of well-known faces, lobbyists and reporters outside the chamber doors during votes. Politically, the former professional horse-shoer who once worked the harness-racing circuit and to this day looks uncomfortable in a business suit, is as brazen as they come.

In the fall of 2004, he announced he would not vote to re-elect Bush, whom he supported in 2000 over Arizona Republican Sen. John McCain. Instead, he said he would vote for Bush's father, former President George H.W. Bush, as a write-in candidate. Critics dismissed the move as a publicity stunt, but Chafee said it was a "symbolic act" of protest against Bush's failure to honor his 2000 campaign promises to usher in an era of bipartisanship and to pursue humble domestic and foreign policies after the divisive election.

Bush, the elder, "had a good record on the issues I care about: deficit reduction, the environment and the conduct of foreign relations," he told the Providence Journal. "It's very different than his son, the president."

The comments capped a gradual but steady break from his party, which began in 1999 when he was appointed to fill the seat of his late father, Republican Sen. John H. Chafee. Since then, the younger Chafee, named after Abraham Lincoln, has been nicknamed "Missing Linc" by GOP aides for his seeming lack of interest in deal-cutting and his frequent departures from the party line. The most notable of these came in 2002, when he was the only Republican in the Senate to vote against the law that authorized the war against Iraq.

Since the war began, in March 2003, Chafee has been a constant critic of the administration's policy in Iraq in his role as chairman of the Foreign Relations Subcommittee on Near Eastern and South Asian Affairs. He has questioned both the military campaign and the subsequent occupation. In the fall of 2003, he was among the first lawmakers to link the conflict in Iraq with the U.S. involvement in the Vietnam quagmire.

But it is on tax policy that Chafee's independence has had the most impact on policy. In 2004, he was among a handful of moderates who derailed the GOP-drafted budget with their demands for a pay-as-you-go rule to curb deficit spending. In 2003, citing concerns about the impact of tax cuts on the rising deficit, he teamed with fellow moderates to halve Bush's proposed $726 billion tax cut. Two years earlier, he and other moderates joined forces to shave $440 billion from the president's $1.6 trillion tax cut bill.

A pet issue of Chafee's is the environment. A member of the Environment and Public Works Committee, which his father once chaired, Chafee and other Northeastern Republicans supported a Democratic filibuster that scuttled major energy legislation for 2003 because it would have waived liability for producers of methyl tertiary butyl ether, MTBE, a fuel additive that has been found to contaminate groundwater. And he worked with Democratic Sen. Thomas R. Carper of Delaware and two other Republicans to propose an alternative to the administration's 2002 "Clear Skies" initiative that would limit carbon dioxide emissions.

When other Republicans bided their time after Senate Majority Leader Trent Lott of Mississippi, in 2002, made controversial remarks in apparent support of segregation, Chafee was the first Republican senator to call publicly for him to step down, which Lott ultimately did.

Chafee scored lowest among Republicans in the Senate for the frequency with which he supported his party and president on major votes in the 108th Congress. His record has given Democrats what so far has been false hope that he will follow in the footsteps of James M. Jeffords of Vermont and leave the GOP. He publicly pondered such a move after the 2004 elections, but abandoned it after Majority Leader Bill Frist and top White House adviser Karl Rove called to reassure him that they appreciated his loyalty to the GOP and understood the political pressures on Northeastern Republicans. Chafee had little to gain from life as a Democrat in the minority — and an apparent license to oppose his party without consequence.

In some areas, Chafee can be quite loyal to his party. He has not voted against a single of Bush's judicial nominees, though some have been highly contested. He votes with the president on free-trade initiatives, and he espouses a fiscal policy that eschews big tax cuts as fiscally irresponsible, a position not uncommon among some budget conservatives.

Rhode Island's Democratic tendencies help explain Chafee's iconoclastic political behavior. His vote to confirm John Ashcroft, the conservative former senator from Missouri, as Bush's attorney general in 2001 created waves in the Ocean State. "I'm getting hammered back home," Chafee lamented at the time.

With roots in Rhode Island that go back to the earliest settlers, Chafee has an eclectic background. A prep school peer of Florida GOP Gov. Jeb Bush, Chafee later studied the classics at Brown University, spending summers sweeping up at construction sites. After graduating, he set off for a horseshoeing program at Montana State University, apprenticed in Kentucky and Florida and then headed to the harness tracks of Edmonton and Calgary, in Alberta. He is quite likely the most prominent politician ever mentioned in Hoofcare & Lameness: The Journal of Equine Foot Science. Its August 1999 issue quoted Chafee saying, "I wanted to see something of life. And I enjoyed working at a trade."

Chafee returned to Rhode Island in 1983 and worked as a machine shop planner for General Dynamics Corp. He followed his father into elective office in 1986 by winning a seat on the Warwick City Council. He lost his first bid for Warwick mayor in 1990 but won the job two years later, becoming the first GOP mayor in 32 years in the state's second-biggest city, where Democrats outnumber Republicans by more than 10-to-1.

Chafee began campaigning in March 1999 to succeed his father, who had announced he would not seek a fifth term. When the senator died that fall, Chafee was appointed to the seat. Meanwhile, the Democrats were having a bruising primary between Rep. Bob Weygand and former Lt. Gov. Richard A. Licht. Weygand won the primary, but his opposition to abortion cost him support among abortion rights Democrats in the general election. Chafee won the backing of about half of Rhode Island's Democrats.

KEY VOTES

2004

Yes Pass $318.9 billion, six-year highway and mass transit bill
Yes Extend assault weapons ban for 10 years
Yes Restore pay-as-you-go rules for new tax cuts and entitlement spending
No Criminalize harm to a fetus in an attack on the mother
Yes Increase mandatory child care funding to states by $6 billion over five years
No Amend the Constitution to prohibit same-sex marriage
No Approve $146 billion multi-year extension of previously enacted middle-class tax breaks
Yes Reorganize U.S. intelligence agencies as proposed by Sept. 11 commission
Yes Cut corporate taxes $137 billion over 10 years

2003

Yes Delay Bush changes to Clean Air Act
Yes Allow confirmation vote on Miguel A. Estrada to the U.S. Court of Appeals for the D.C. Circuit
Yes Block a Bush proposal opening Alaska's Arctic National Wildlife Refuge to oil drilling
Yes Limit size of Bush's proposed tax cut to $350 billion through fiscal 2013
Yes Overhaul Medicare and create prescription drug benefit
Yes Block Bush rule scaling back overtime pay for some white-collar federal workers
No Split $20 billion in Iraq aid into half-grant, half-loan
No Ban "partial birth" abortion except to save a woman's life
No Stop proposal allowing travel to Cuba
No Allow final vote on energy policy overhaul

CQ VOTE STUDIES

	PARTY UNITY		PRESIDENTIAL SUPPORT	
	Support	Oppose	Support	Oppose
2004	65%	35%	76%	24%
2003	71%	29%	77%	23%
2002	54%	46%	93%	7%
2001	50%	50%	84%	16%
2000	37%	63%	88%	12%
1999	56%	44%	100%	0%

INTEREST GROUPS

	AFL-CIO	ADA	CCUS	ACU
2004	58%	55%	82%	40%
2003	31%	65%	57%	35%
2002	46%	45%	63%	53%
2001	63%	65%	64%	44%
2000	50%	70%	66%	44%

Rep. Patrick J. Kennedy (D)

Elected 1994; 6th term

CAPITOL OFFICE
225-4911
patrick.kennedy@mail.house.gov
www.house.gov/patrickkennedy
407 Cannon 20515-3901; fax 225-3290

COMMITTEES
Appropriations

HOMETOWN
Portsmouth

BORN
July 14, 1967, Brighton, Mass.

RELIGION
Roman Catholic

FAMILY
Single

EDUCATION
Providence College, B.A. 1991 (social science)

CAREER
Public official

POLITICAL HIGHLIGHTS
R.I. House, 1989-95

ELECTION RESULTS

2004 GENERAL

Patrick J. Kennedy (D)	124,923	64.1%
David W. Rogers (R)	69,819	35.8%

2004 PRIMARY

Patrick J. Kennedy (D)	22,681	75.5%
Mark Binder (D)	7,359	24.5%

2002 GENERAL

Patrick J. Kennedy (D)	95,233	60.0%
David W. Rogers (R)	59,316	37.3%
Frank A. Carter (I)	4,314	2.7%

PREVIOUS WINNING PERCENTAGES
2000 (67%); 1998 (67%); 1996 (69%); 1994 (54%)

After a spate of embarrassing personal episodes in recent years, Kennedy has buckled down to business, tending to his district as diligently as any freshman would and working to rebuild his reputation at home. His seat on the Appropriations Committee is a big help in targeting federal dollars to his district, always a good way of repairing political bridges.

Although his seat remains relatively safe, Kennedy has encountered more-aggressive challenges by Republicans and smaller election margins in his last few races. "I've gotten the message. People have been disappointed in me," Kennedy told The Providence Journal-Bulletin in 2002.

His famous family name gives him a natural entree to seeking higher office, but he is biding his time. Kennedy has been talked about as a possible challenger to Sen. Lincoln Chafee of Rhode Island, regarded as one of the vulnerable GOP senators in 2006. But he declined to take preparatory steps in 2005, and instead focused on local issues, saying he wanted to build his influence in the House. Kennedy's Web site is dominated by announcements of grants for local programs and by updates on local causes, such as fighting a proposed liquid natural gas plant in Providence.

On national issues, he is outspoken on parity for victims of mental illness, advocating insurance coverage for those illnesses equal to that available for other kinds of medical conditions. Kennedy himself has suffered from depression. He also has pressed for legislation to enhance childhood development.

While Kennedy still sometimes snaps at colleagues, there have been no repeats of the temper that made him fodder for the news tabloids and encouraged Republicans to try to unhorse him. In 2000, he shoved a Los Angeles International Airport security guard who told him his carry-on bag was too big. She filed a battery suit, but the Los Angeles district attorney's office declined to bring charges. Later that year, the Coast Guard was called to take his distraught date off a chartered yacht following an argument with Kennedy.

The only similar flash of anger in recent years came in a June 2004 exchange with Rep. Randy "Duke" Cunningham, a conservative California Republican with his own reputation for outbursts. During a committee debate over whether gun owners' files ought to be made public under some circumstances, the pro-gun rights Cunningham suggested files also should be opened dealing with the 1969 car accident in which Kennedy's father, Sen. Edward M. Kennedy of Massachusetts, drove off a Chappaquiddick Island bridge, killing companion Mary Jo Kopechne. Patrick Kennedy snapped at Cunningham: "You're an idiot!" Moments later, the men apologized to one another.

Kennedy is more conservative than his father. In the biggest political split with the liberal senator, the younger Kennedy voted in 2002 to authorize President Bush to wage war in Iraq. His father was one of the sharpest opponents of the war. Patrick Kennedy also was the only member of the Rhode Island delegation to favor the war, a vote he says he has never doubted.

Unlike his father, Kennedy backed a ban on a procedure opponents call "partial birth" abortion that became law in 2003, though he otherwise supports abortion rights. In 2000, Kennedy was one of only a dozen Democratic House members who opposed taking away the Boy Scouts of America's federal charter as punishment for banning homosexuals as troop leaders.

The most memorable moment of Kennedy's legislative career may have been a 1996 floor speech in which he urged Congress to retain a ban on certain semiautomatic assault-style weapons. "Families like mine know all too well what the damage of weapons can do," said a choked-up Kennedy, who lost two famous uncles to assassinations with guns. "You will never know what it's like because you don't have someone in your family killed. It's not the person who's killed, it's the whole family that's affected."

No one else in Congress can boast of such a legendary political lineage, which still counts for something in New England. His late uncles were President John F. Kennedy and Sen. Robert F. Kennedy of New York. A grandfather, Joseph P. Kennedy, was the first Securities and Exchange Commission chairman and ambassador to Great Britain. A great-grandfather, John Francis Fitzgerald, represented Boston in the House at the end of the 19th century. A cousin, Joseph P. Kennedy II, represented Boston in the House a century later, from 1987 to 1999.

Patrick Kennedy's political ascent began early, like most Kennedys' do. As a 21-year-old student at Providence College, he won election to the state House in 1988. Six years later, he was sent to Washington, one of just 13 Democrats elected to the House during the 1994 Republican tide that year. Kennedy was the youngest person in the 104th Congress.

At the start of his third term, Kennedy was appointed chairman of the Democratic Congressional Campaign Committee, a leadership role that put him in charge of raising money for Democratic House candidates. He pulled in almost $100 million for the 2000 campaigns, a record that was more than double what had been raised by the committee in 1998.

Kennedy was unabashed about the value of the Kennedy name, saying, "When we're going around the country, it helps get your calls returned." He rewarded major donors with visits to the family's fabled compound in Hyannis Port, Massachusetts. "He's crowding me," Sen. Kennedy grumbled in jest after his son's successful fund drive.

Nevertheless, Republicans had a hunch Kennedy might be vulnerable because of the earlier bad press. In 2002, they criticized him for spending too little time in his district, calculating he'd spent only 40 nights in Rhode Island during his stint as the Democratic fundraising chairman.

But the GOP could not get a serious challenge off the ground. The party's preferred candidate lost the Republican primary to political neophyte David W. Rogers, whose conservatism was ill-matched to the 1st District. Rogers spent almost $2 million to criticize Kennedy's behavior, and Kennedy spent almost $3 million to respond. He won with 60 percent of the vote. Rogers came back for a rematch in 2004, and Kennedy beat him 64 percent to 36 percent.

KEY VOTES

2004

Yes Extend federal unemployment benefits by 13 weeks

Yes Pass $283.2 billion, six-year federal highway and mass transit bill

Yes Approve $146 billion multi-year extension of previously enacted middle-class tax breaks

No Amend the Constitution to prohibit same-sex marriage

No Cut corporate taxes $137 billion over 10 years

Yes Reorganize U.S. intelligence agencies as proposed by Sept. 11 commission

2003

No Cut taxes by $330 billion through fiscal 2013

Yes Block Bush rule scaling back overtime pay for some white-collar federal workers

Yes Do not allow use of search warrants without first notifying subjects

Yes Allow importation of prescription drugs

No Create private school voucher program in Washington, D.C.

Yes Ban "partial birth" abortion except to save a woman's life

Yes Split $18.6 billion in Iraq aid into half-grant, half-loan

No Overhaul Medicare and create prescription drug benefit

CQ VOTE STUDIES

	PARTY UNITY		PRESIDENTIAL SUPPORT	
	Support	Oppose	Support	Oppose
2004	95%	5%	35%	65%
2003	96%	4%	27%	73%
2002	89%	11%	40%	60%
2001	93%	7%	29%	71%
2000	97%	3%	81%	19%

INTEREST GROUPS

	AFL-CIO	ADA	CCUS	ACU
2004	93%	95%	40%	8%
2003	100%	95%	27%	25%
2002	100%	90%	40%	8%
2001	100%	95%	32%	4%
2000	100%	90%	15%	16%

RHODE ISLAND 1
East – Pawtucket, part of Providence, Newport

The Democratic 1st occupies the top of Rhode Island, along the Massachusetts border, then moves south to take in Pawtucket and the northeastern part of Providence, the capital, before running along Narragansett Bay to pick up Newport and the island communities in the southeast.

The 1st's industry is mostly centered in northern Rhode Island's Blackstone Valley. Woonsocket, a manufacturing city, is home to the headquarters of CVS, the largest drugstore in the nation.

The district's portion of Providence takes in several colleges, such as Brown University and Providence College, and includes the state capitol. Students and government workers push the 1st's political lean to the left.

The coastal economy south of Providence relies largely on maritime defense. Companies such as Raytheon, which makes components for Navy submarines in Portsmouth, as well as a large naval base and training center in Newport, fuel the industry. Visitors to Newport, as well

as Providence, make tourism an important economic component.

Democrats dominate the district, getting support from ethnic minorities as well as the area's large Catholic majority. Some small, wealthy coastal towns support the GOP, but larger towns lean Democratic. In statewide elections, however, the district will support Republicans for governor, such as Donald L. Carcieri in 2002, and for U.S. senator, such as Lincoln Chafee in 2000.

MAJOR INDUSTRY
Defense, higher education, manufacturing, tourism, government

MILITARY BASES
Naval Station Newport, 3,521 military, 3,955 civilian (2004)

CITIES
Pawtucket, 72,958; Providence (pt.), 72,102; East Providence, 48,688; Woonsocket, 43,224; North Providence (unincorporated), 32,411; Newport, 26,475; Bristol (unincorporated), 22,469

NOTABLE
One of the nation's oldest taverns, the White Horse Tavern, opened in Newport before 1673; The International Tennis Hall of Fame is in Newport; Touro Synagogue in Newport, designed by colonial architect Peter Harrison and dedicated in 1762, is the oldest U.S. synagogue.

2nd DISTRICT/**RHODE ISLAND**

Rep. Jim Langevin (D)

Elected 2000; 3rd term

CAPITOL OFFICE
225-2735
james.langevin@mail.house.gov
www.house.gov/langevin
109 Cannon 20515-3902; fax 225-5976

COMMITTEES
Armed Services
Homeland Security

HOMETOWN
Warwick

BORN
April 22, 1964, Warwick, R.I.

RELIGION
Roman Catholic

FAMILY
Single

EDUCATION
Rhode Island College, B.A. 1990 (political science & public administration); Harvard U., M.P.A. 1994

CAREER
Public official

POLITICAL HIGHLIGHTS
R.I. House, 1989-95; R.I. secretary of state, 1995-2001

ELECTION RESULTS

2004 GENERAL

Jim Langevin (D)	154,392	74.5%
Arthur "Chuck" Barton III (R)	43,139	20.8%
Edward M. Morabito (I)	6,196	3.0%
Dorman J. Hayes Jr. (I)	3,303	1.6%

2004 PRIMARY

Jim Langevin (D)	19,242	85.6%
John Hamilton (D)	3,230	14.4%

2002 GENERAL

Jim Langevin (D)	129,312	76.4%
John O. Matson (R)	37,740	22.3%
Dorman J. Hayes Jr. (I)	2,323	1.4%

PREVIOUS WINNING PERCENTAGES
2000 (62%)

Langevin takes a center-of-the-road view on what he calls "life issues," which means he makes those on both sides of these issues mad.

He is opposed to abortion except in cases of rape, incest or to save a woman's life, and so abortion rights advocates have demonstrated outside his fundraisers. But he supports embryonic stem cell research, which angers anti-abortion advocates who believe that destroying an embryo for any reason is wrong. Langevin (LAN-juh-vin) acknowledges that he has struggled with this issue, but he has concluded that it is more "life affirming" to use aborted embryos to help people. He believes stem cell research holds great promise for millions of people who have diseases such as ,Parkinson's, Alzheimer's and diabetes, as well as those who have spinal cord injuries such as his own.

Langevin is the first quadriplegic to serve in the House. He says his views on life issues have been formed largely by his own experience. He was accidentally shot while serving in a police cadet program as a teenager. He says he is convinced he will walk again one day.

Understandably, he has introduced a number of bills on gun safety, including requirements for trigger locks. Although as a Roman Catholic he opposes abortion, he takes a liberal view on most other social issues. He voted in 2004 against amending the Constitution to prohibit same-sex marriage, and he also opposed an effort in 2003 to create a private school voucher program in Washington, D.C.

Like many of his New England Democratic colleagues, Langevin is a dedicated ally of organized labor. He agreed with the unions in 2002 and voted against giving President Bush fast-track negotiating authority on trade agreements that Congress cannot amend. He also voted in 2003 to block a Bush rule scaling back overtime pay for white-collar federal workers.

Much of Langevin's energy and rhetoric is devoted to health care, a policy area in which his interest ranges far beyond issues that primarily affect disabled people. Late in 2004, Langevin introduced legislation that would create a government-subsidized comprehensive health coverage system for Americans not already covered by government health care programs. He hopes to use the leverage of the federal government's purchasing power to drive down the price of health care. But Langevin's plan, which aims to provide the kind of coverage enjoyed by federal employees, would be underpinned by the imposition of a tax on all employers, making it an unlikely candidate for consideration in the Republican-controlled House.

As a member of the Armed Services Committee, Langevin is well-situated to keep a watchful eye on the needs of Electric Boat's facility at Quonset Point, which makes and assembles large sections of nuclear submarines. He also serves on Homeland Security, where in the 109th he is the top-ranking Democrat on the Prevention of Nuclear and Biological Attack panel.

When Armed Services took up a measure reauthorizing defense programs in 2004, Langevin attached language that would have required the Pentagon to hold a competition comparing costs and quality standards before hiring a private contractor to do any job that would otherwise be performed by 10 or more Defense Department civilians. The amendment was adopted. But it was later dropped because a similar provision was included in the 2004 defense appropriations bill.

Like most lawmakers, Langevin pays particular attention to protecting the business back home. He introduced several measures in the 108th to suspend duties temporarily on various pigments, used in paints and inks. His district includes a Clariant Corp. factory that makes and dries pigments for use in a wide variety of goods.

Langevin originally hoped to enforce laws, not write them. As a boy, he dreamt of being a police officer or an FBI agent. He enrolled in a police department cadet program in his hometown of Warwick, riding along with police officers and getting to know the daily police routine.

On Aug. 22, 1980, when he was 16 years old, his life and ambitions changed forever. He was in the police locker room with two members of the SWAT team, when one of them inadvertently pulled the trigger of a loaded gun. The bullet ricocheted off a locker and hit Langevin in the neck, severing his spinal cord and leaving him paralyzed. He has no use of his legs and only minimal use of his hands and arms. Langevin has an aide to help him with domestic chores, and he uses a motorized wheelchair. Congressional leaders gave him a ground-floor office and renovated access to the House chamber so it is easier for him to vote and speak during debates.

After Langevin's injury, he and his family were amazed at the hundreds of strangers who pitched in to help. He resolved to somehow repay them, and soon realized that public service and politics was the way he could do that. He volunteered in Frank Flaherty's 1984 campaign for mayor of Warwick, and Flaherty recalls being amazed at how tenacious Langevin was, making phone calls and stuffing envelopes even with limited use of his hands. Later, when Flaherty was still mayor and Langevin was in the legislature, "he'd come in looking for something for his area of the city and he'd drive me crazy, chase me around. I used to threaten to unplug the battery on his wheelchair so I wouldn't have to listen," Flaherty told the Providence Journal.

At age 21, while still a college student, Langevin was elected as a delegate to the Rhode Island Constitutional Convention. In 1988, he was elected to the first of three terms in the Rhode Island House, where he played a key role in drafting a ballot issue that resulted in a reduction in the size of the state legislature. In 1994, he successfully ran for secretary of state, vowing to make the state government more accessible to its citizens by upgrading voting machines and modernizing the office to improve access to government information by businesses and citizens.

In 2000, when 2nd District Democratic Rep. Bob Weygand decided to run for the Senate, Langevin was ready to make a bid for the House. In the solidly Democratic district, Langevin's 62 percent of the vote easily outpaced the Republican and a third-party candidate, who actually placed second. In both 2002 and 2004, Langevin won easily with three-quarters of the vote.

KEY VOTES

2004

?	Extend federal unemployment benefits by 13 weeks
Yes	Pass $283.2 billion, six-year federal highway and mass transit bill
Yes	Approve $146 billion multi-year extension of previously enacted middle-class tax breaks
No	Amend the Constitution to prohibit same-sex marriage
No	Cut corporate taxes $137 billion over 10 years
Yes	Reorganize U.S. intelligence agencies as proposed by Sept. 11 commission

2003

No	Cut taxes by $330 billion through fiscal 2013
Yes	Block Bush rule scaling back overtime pay for some white-collar federal workers
Yes	Do not allow use of search warrants without first notifying subjects
Yes	Allow importation of prescription drugs
No	Create private school voucher program in Washington, D.C.
Yes	Ban "partial birth" abortion except to save a woman's life
Yes	Split $18.6 billion in Iraq aid into half-grant, half-loan
No	Overhaul Medicare and create prescription drug benefit

CQ VOTE STUDIES

	PARTY UNITY		PRESIDENTIAL SUPPORT	
	Support	Oppose	Support	Oppose
2004	91%	9%	42%	58%
2003	95%	5%	28%	72%
2002	91%	9%	35%	65%
2001	90%	10%	35%	65%

INTEREST GROUPS

	AFL-CIO	ADA	CCUS	ACU
2004	93%	85%	45%	25%
2003	100%	85%	27%	24%
2002	100%	85%	45%	8%
2001	100%	85%	35%	28%

RHODE ISLAND 2
West — part of Providence, Warwick, Cranston

Bordering Connecticut on one side and the Narragansett Bay on the other, the 2nd occupies the western two-thirds of Rhode Island, covering the upstate rolling hills and most of the metropolitan area around Providence. Washington County, the southernmost part of the district, has beaches and lakes that attract tourists and residents alike. Twelve miles off the southern coast lies Block Island, a scenic vacation spot with more than 365 ponds.

The 2nd's economy is shifting from manufacturing to service. The change has caused a population shift, with people leaving Providence (shared with the 1st District) for Washington County, attracted by the growing businesses centered in the county's idyllic landscape. As white residents have departed the Providence area, more blacks and Hispanics have moved in, increasing the city's already Democratic tendency. The 2nd's portion of Providence includes a few schools, including Johnson & Wales University and Rhode Island College.

General Dynamics' Electric Boat has a submarine facility at Quonset

Point in Washington County, and some county residents commute to the company's Groton, Conn., plant as well. Most of the district experienced modest growth during the 1990s, although the median age of the population is getting younger.

The 2nd is home to many working- and middle-class towns, with a substantial union presence that votes Democratic. No Republican presidential candidate has carried the district since Ronald Reagan in 1984. Despite the Democratic dominance, the district's large Catholic population makes abortion a key issue. Redistricting following the 2000 census shifted a few Providence neighborhoods into the 1st District, but the change did not affect the 2nd's political makeup.

MAJOR INDUSTRY
Defense, banking, service, tourism, higher education

CITIES
Providence (pt.), 101,516; Warwick, 85,808; Cranston, 79,269; West Warwick (unincorporated), 29,581; Westerly (unincorporated), 17,682

NOTABLE
The first armed conflict of the American Revolution took place near Warwick in 1772, when patriots in eight longboats captured and burned two British revenue ships.

SOUTH CAROLINA

Gov. Mark Sanford (R)

First elected: 2002
Length of term: 4 years
Term expires: 1/07
Salary: $106,078
Phone: (803) 734-2100

Hometown: Sullivan's Island
Born: May 28, 1960; Fort Lauderdale, Fla.
Religion: Episcopalian
Family: Wife, Jenny Sanford; four children
Education: Furman U., B.A. 1983 (business administration); U. of Virginia, M.B.A. 1988
Military Service: Air Force Reserve, 2002-present
Career: Real estate investor; investment banker
Political highlights: U.S. House, 1995-2001

Election results:
2002 GENERAL

Mark Sanford (R)	580,459	52.8%
Jim Hodges (D)	518,288	47.1%

Lt. Gov. André Bauer (R)

First elected: 2002
Length of term: 4 years
Term expires: 1/07
Salary: $46,545
Phone: (803) 734-2080

STATE LEGISLATURE

General Assembly: January-June

House: 124 members, 2-year terms
2005 breakdown: 74R, 50D; 110 men, 14 women
Salary: $10,400; $95/day in session; $1,000/month expenses
Phone: (803) 734-2010

Senate: 46 members, 4-year terms
2005 breakdown: 26R, 20D; 45 men, 1 woman
Salary: $10,400; $95/day in session; $1,000/month expenses
Phone: (803) 212-6200

STATE TERM LIMITS

Governor: 2 consecutive terms
House: No
Senate: No

URBAN STATISTICS

CITY	POPULATION
Columbia	116,278
Charleston	96,650
North Charleston	79,641
Greenville	56,002
Rock Hill	49,765

REGISTERED VOTERS

Voters do not register by party.

POPULATION

2004 population (est.)	4,198,068
2000 population	4,012,012
1990 population	3,486,703
Percent change (1990-2000)	+15.1%
Rank among states (2004)	25

Median age	35.4
Born in state	64%
Foreign born	2.9%
Violent crime rate	805/100,000
Poverty level	14.1%
Federal workers	27,923
Military	57,585

REDISTRICTING

South Carolina retained its six House seats in reapportionment. Democratic Gov. Jim Hodges vetoed the state legislature's plan and a three-judge federal panel implemented a new map on March 20, 2002.

MISCELLANEOUS

Web: www.mysc.gov
Capital: Columbia
STATE ELECTION OFFICIAL
(803) 734-9060
DEMOCRATIC HEADQUARTERS
(803) 799-7798
REPUBLICAN HEADQUARTERS
(803) 988-8440

District Statistics

DIST.	2004 VOTE FOR PRESIDENT BUSH	KERRY	WHITE	BLACK	ASIAN	HISP	MEDIAN INCOME	WHITE COLLAR	BLUE COLLAR	SERVICE INDUSTRY	OVER 64	UNDER 18	COLLEGE EDUCATION	RURAL	SQ. MILES
1	61%	38%	74%	21%	1%	3%	$40,713	60%	23%	17%	12%	24%	25%	22%	2,645
2	60	40	68	26	1	3	$42,915	63	23	14	11	25	29	34	4,767
3	65	34	76	21	1	2	$36,092	49	37	14	13	24	17	50	5,392
4	65	34	75	20	1	3	$39,417	56	31	13	12	25	22	26	2,151
5	57	42	64	32	1	2	$35,416	48	38	13	12	26	15	53	7,035
6	39	61	40	57	1	1	$28,967	48	34	18	12	26	14	52	8,120
STATE	58	41	66	29	1	2	$37,082	54	31	15	12	25	20	40	30,109
U.S.	50.7	48.3	69	12	4	13	$41,994	60	25	15	12	26	24	21	3,537,438

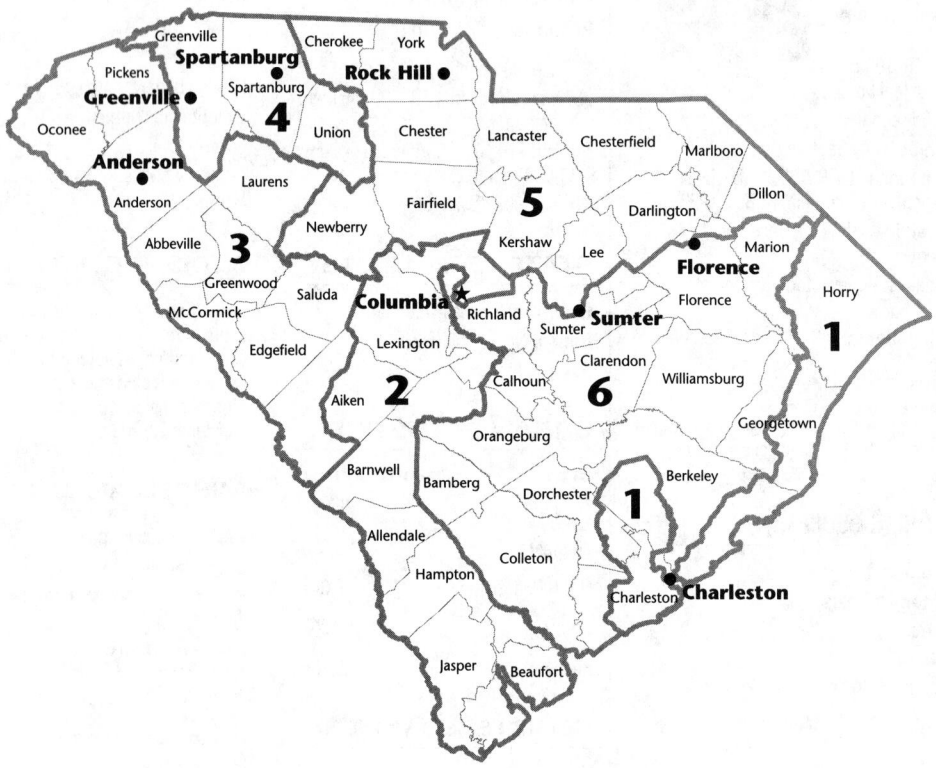

Sen. Lindsey Graham (R)

Elected 2002; 1st term

CAPITOL OFFICE
224-5972
lgraham.senate.gov
290 Russell 20510-4001; fax 224-3808

COMMITTEES
Armed Services
  (Personnel - chairman)
Budget
Judiciary
  (Crime & Drugs - chairman)
Veterans' Affairs

HOMETOWN
Seneca

BORN
July 9, 1955, Seneca, S.C.

RELIGION
Southern Baptist

FAMILY
Single

EDUCATION
U. of South Carolina, B.A. 1977 (psychology),
attended 1977-78 (public administration), J.D. 1981

MILITARY SERVICE
Air Force, 1982-88, 90; S.C. Air National Guard,
1989-94; Air Force Reserve, 1995-present

CAREER
Lawyer

POLITICAL HIGHLIGHTS
S.C. House, 1993-95; U.S. House, 1995-2003

ELECTION RESULTS

2002 GENERAL

Lindsey Graham (R)	595,218	54.4%
Alex Sanders (D)	484,422	44.2%

2002 PRIMARY

Lindsey Graham (R)	unopposed

PREVIOUS WINNING PERCENTAGES
2000 House Election (68%); 1998 House Election
(100%); 1996 House Election (60%); 1994 House
Election (60%)

When Graham starts one of his softly drawling, sharply pointed sentences with the words "Long story short," you know the conservative South Carolinian is about to raise some eyebrows. The boyish-looking, fast-talking former military lawyer has a maverick streak, along with a gift for a snappy sound bite. Whether it is scrutinizing the Bush administration's role in the abuse of Iraqi detainees or looking for ways to shore up Social Security, Graham is not inclined to quietly toe the party line or play it safe.

Forging his own role in the Senate has been vital to Graham, who faced the daunting challenge in 2002 of replacing Strom Thurmond, a political legend and the Senate's sole centenarian. But Graham, who came to Congress as part of the Republican takeover Class of '94, stands in stark contrast to Thurmond. A product of the "New South," Graham is closer to the model sought by the 21st century Republican Party than was Thurmond, who made his reputation as a champion of the old Southern ways of segregation and states' rights.

Graham is perhaps best-known for his role as one of the 13 House managers in the impeachment case against President Clinton, although he bristles at the distinction. "I don't want to be remembered as the impeachment boy. That shortchanges who I am," he told The New York Times in 2000. Still, it was Graham's personal touch that put him in the impeachment spotlight. Just before delving into the case, which involved Clinton's sexual affair with a White House intern, Graham sounded a note of caution, giving voice to the private musings of many Americans, as he asked, "Is this Watergate or Peyton Place?"

That talent for cutting to the heart of politically sensitive issues often distinguishes Graham from more-timid colleagues. Asked how he came up with his plan to overhaul Social Security — which includes creating personal retirement accounts for younger workers — Graham said, "A bunch of smart people told me that's what you needed to do." In late 2004, he teamed with Democratic Sen. Kent Conrad of North Dakota in an op-ed piece that rejected the idea of not counting the cost of Social Security as part of the regular federal budget, the approach said to be favored by the Bush administration. And he discussed the idea of raising taxes and cutting benefits as the price of fixing the system. "The politically smart people told me to keep my mouth shut about Social Security," he said, "But we're way beyond that."

The same might have been said of his decision during the 2000 GOP presidential primary to back Sen. John McCain of Arizona over then-Texas Gov. George W. Bush. During the turning-point days in the battle for the Republican nomination, Graham was an ardent, oft-quoted supporter of McCain, even though Bush had the backing of South Carolina's GOP establishment. Bush's win in the state's primary effectively doomed the McCain campaign. Two years later, Graham was among only 41 House Republicans who voted for the campaign finance overhaul that was at the core of McCain's candidacy. President Bush later signed the bill into law.

Graham portrays himself as a traditional Republican from one of the nation's most conservative and GOP-leaning states, and yet he mixes a large dollop of independence with his party loyalties. As he ran for the Senate in the 107th Congress, he voted the way Bush wanted him to on only seven out of eight votes; three-quarters of his GOP colleagues in the House supported the president more often than he did. Once elected to the Senate, Graham supported the president 94 percent of the time and his party 95 percent of the time. But he continued his contrarian ways, and broke with most Republicans to oppose the president's Medicare overhaul creating a prescription drug benefit, which he called costly and ineffective. He joined Democrats in 2003 in pushing to make half of the $20 billion Bush requested for the reconstruction of Iraq a loan instead of a grant.

While he has been a strong backer of the war in Iraq, Graham has sometimes been a thorn in the Bush administration's side when it comes to the details of the conflict. His questions were perhaps most pointed in 2004, when Graham, the only senator who serves in the National Guard or reserves, harshly questioned Defense Secretary Donald H. Rumsfeld about his role in the Iraqi prisoner abuse scandal. During a packed hearing, Graham asked Rumsfeld: "Do you believe, based on all the things that have happened and will happen, that you're able to carry out your duties in a bipartisan manner? And what do you say to those people who are calling for your resignation?" Later, Graham indirectly chided Vice President Dick Cheney for issuing a statement saying of Rumsfeld that people should "get off his case" and let him do his job. Graham told NBC, "Nobody is on his back. We have an independent duty to look at this."

Graham later said the scandal reminded him of the case that first won him national attention. As a military lawyer, he defended a demoted Air Force pilot on a drug charge, which exposed flaws in the Air Force's drug-testing system and led to an overhaul of the program. The case landed the young Graham on the popular television news show "60 Minutes."

For all his headline-grabbing defections from the Republican fold, Graham mainly exhibits a strict conservatism. He once joined an effort to shut down the National Endowment for the Arts, he is a staunch opponent of gun control, and he favors amending the Constitution to outlaw flag desecration. He backed legislation making it a federal crime to harm a fetus while committing any of 68 federal offenses or a crime under military law.

Graham typically seeks to limit the scope of the federal government, although he is a proponent of robust defense spending, which plays well in a state with six major military bases.

Born in July 1955, six months after Thurmond was first sworn in to the Senate, Graham was the son of a tavern owner and grew up racking billiards in the bar where both his parents worked. But he was forced into a parental role before he had graduated from college, when the death of both parents left him to care for his 13-year-old sister Darlene, whom he later legally adopted so that she could receive military survivor benefits in the event of his death. After earning his law degree, he joined the Air Force and later transferred to Germany to be a prosecutor. As a major in the Air National Guard, he was called to active duty and served as a military lawyer in South Carolina during the 1991 Persian Gulf War. He still periodically reports for duty as a judge.

Graham won a state House seat in 1992, but his stay was brief. He saw an opportunity for advancement early in 1994, when 10-term Democratic Rep. Butler Derrick decided to retire. With the 3rd District, like South Carolina as a whole, trending Republican, Graham won easily that fall, beating Democratic state Sen. James Bryan with 60 percent of the vote. He won three more terms with relative ease and began planning for a Senate run after Thurmond made it clear that his seventh full term would be his last.

By 2002, Graham had become the senior Republican in the state's congressional delegation, and he was unopposed for his party's nomination. The Democrats put up Alex Sanders, a quick-witted former president of the College of Charleston who stressed his conservative credentials. But Graham repeatedly portrayed him as a party loyalist who would vote with "Washington liberals" and won by 10 percentage points.

KEY VOTES

2004

No Pass $318.9 billion, six-year highway and mass transit bill

No Extend assault weapons ban for 10 years

No Restore pay-as-you-go rules for new tax cuts and entitlement spending

Yes Criminalize harm to a fetus in an attack on the mother

Yes Increase mandatory child care funding to states by $6 billion over five years

Yes Amend the Constitution to prohibit same-sex marriage

Yes Approve $146 billion multi-year extension of previously enacted middle-class tax breaks

Yes Reorganize U.S. intelligence agencies as proposed by Sept. 11 commission

Yes Cut corporate taxes $137 billion over 10 years

2003

No Delay Bush changes to Clean Air Act

Yes Allow confirmation vote on Miguel A. Estrada to the U.S. Court of Appeals for the D.C. Circuit

No Block a Bush proposal opening Alaska's Arctic National Wildlife Refuge to oil drilling

No Limit size of Bush's proposed tax cut to $350 billion through fiscal 2013

No Overhaul Medicare and create prescription drug benefit

No Block Bush rule scaling back overtime pay for some white-collar federal workers

Yes Split $20 billion in Iraq aid into half-grant, half-loan

Yes Ban "partial birth" abortion except to save a woman's life

Yes Stop proposal allowing travel to Cuba

Yes Allow final vote on energy policy overhaul

CQ VOTE STUDIES

	PARTY UNITY		PRESIDENTIAL SUPPORT	
	Support	Oppose	Support	Oppose
2004	92%	8%	92%	8%
2003	96%	4%	95%	5%
House Service:				
2002	89%	11%	82%	18%
2001	93%	7%	84%	16%
2000	98%	2%	17%	83%
1999	89%	11%	18%	82%
1998	92%	8%	22%	78%
1997	95%	5%	25%	75%
1996	96%	4%	35%	65%
1995	95%	5%	20%	80%

INTEREST GROUPS

	AFL-CIO	ADA	CCUS	ACU
2004	8%	25%	88%	92%
2003	17%	15%	83%	90%
House Service:				
2002	22%	15%	70%	83%
2001	17%	15%	78%	88%
2000	10%	5%	70%	100%
1999	56%	20%	50%	88%
1998	10%	15%	76%	88%
1997	0%	5%	90%	92%
1996	0%	0%	100%	100%
1995	0%	5%	96%	96%

Sen. Jim DeMint (R)

CAPITOL OFFICE
224-6121
demint.senate.gov
340 Russell 20510-4002; fax 224-4293

COMMITTEES
Commerce, Science & Transportation
(Disaster Prevention & Prediction - chairman)
Environment & Public Works
Special Aging
Joint Economic

HOMETOWN
Greenville

BORN
Sept. 2, 1951, Greenville, S.C.

RELIGION
Presbyterian

FAMILY
Wife, Debbie DeMint; four children

EDUCATION
U. of Tennessee, B.S. 1973 (communications);
Clemson U., M.B.A. 1981

CAREER
Market research company owner; advertising and
sales representative

POLITICAL HIGHLIGHTS
U.S. House, 1999-2005

ELECTION RESULTS

2004 GENERAL

Jim DeMint (R)	857,167	53.7%
Inez Tenenbaum (D)	704,384	44.1%

2004 PRIMARY RUNOFF

Jim DeMint (R)	154,644	59.2%
David Beasley (R)	106,480	40.8%

2004 PRIMARY

David Beasley (R)	107,847	36.6%
Jim DeMint (R)	77,567	26.3%
Thomas Ravenel (R)	73,167	24.8%
Charlie Condon (R)	27,694	9.4%
Mark McBride (R)	6,479	2.2%

PREVIOUS WINNING PERCENTAGES
2002 House Election (69%); 2000 House Election
(80%); 1998 House Election (58%)

Elected 2004; 1st term

A market researcher by profession, DeMint likes making bold proposals that spark lively debate on sensitive issues, such as his call to scrap the tax code, which he once illustrated by dropping the 17,000-page Internal Revenue Code from a hot air balloon over his hometown of Greenville. He distinguished himself as a leader among ultra-conservative Republicans while he was in the House, and is poised to play a prominent role in the Senate on overhauling Social Security and the tax code, both of which rank high on President Bush's agenda.

While DeMint has been a loyal Bush ally on most issues, he sometimes finds himself standing stubbornly to the president's right, as the last conservative line of defense. He was one of a faction of Republicans who fiercely opposed Bush's Medicare prescription drug bill in 2003 because of its price tag in the hundreds of billions of dollars. DeMint also joined with a band of fellow anti-abortion rights members in 2002 to block a GOP-written bankruptcy measure because it contained a provision that blocked abortion protesters from filing for bankruptcy to avoid paying court-ordered fines.

Still, like the advertising expert he was trained to be, DeMint prefers to emphasize his work on bipartisan legislation that creates more jobs back home and addresses pocketbook issues, such as the tax burden on working families. The GOP needs spokesmen, DeMint says, who "can take the Republican message and communicate it persuasively to swing voters, someone who can say Republicans have a heart and soul, as well as good logic."

Though a political neophyte when he was first elected to the House in 1998, DeMint was elected president of his freshman class. He quickly put his marketing skills to work, developing a communications plan for Republican ideas and producing a laminated card of GOP themes to "secure the future" that his colleagues could keep handy.

While running a market research firm in Greenville, DeMint became an expert at positioning a product in a crowded marketplace, be it Homelite chainsaws or St. Pauli Girl beer. He uses that background in Washington to tout his ideas.

His marketing savvy helped him gather more than 280 cosponsorships in 2001 on legislation to double the adoption tax credit to $10,000. "When I present something to the chairman of Ways and Means, I need to show there is overwhelming support, because I am not a member of the committee," DeMint said. His work led to the credit being included in the $1.35 trillion, 10-year tax cut enacted that year. In the 109th Congress, DeMint is working to make the adoption credit permanent.

Like other staunch conservatives, DeMint is no fan of the current federal income tax system, and would like to see it replaced by a consumption tax, which is a levy on the consumption of goods and services. Opponents, many of them Democrats, oppose the move because a consumption tax is regressive, and so affects the poor disproportionately to the rich.

In the 107th Congress, when he was in the House, DeMint teamed up with Republican Dick Armey of Texas to push a proposal to address long-term financing problems in the Social Security system. Their bill would have offered investors a chance to increase their benefits by investing some of their payroll taxes in stocks and bonds, but it also would have guaranteed that benefits did not fall below current levels. After a series of corporate scandals in 2001 and 2002, and a stock market swoon, there was little support for the private accounts. But the idea has gained currency once again as Bush has vowed to make adding private accounts to Social Security a top priority of his second term.

DeMint knows that some of his positions make him a punching bag for the opposition. "That's the painful part. You make yourself very vulnerable in a campaign," he says. "But the only way to get something done is to stake out an idea and stand outside the box. To come up with a better solution, you have to understand what your choices are and get a debate going."

DeMint teamed in the 107th Congress with Democrat John Kerry of Massachusetts on a proposal to help small businesses by allowing them to retain as much as $250,000 in federal income taxes over two years, as long as they paid what they had deferred, with interest, in the next four years.

His loyalty to a pro-business agenda has gotten DeMint into trouble at home, especially for his pro-trade stances. In the House, he was derided for joining the razor-thin majority that helped enact the law reviving fast-track trade authority, which allows the president to negotiate treaties that Congress must approve or reject, but may not amend.

That infuriated the state's powerful textile interests, which see themselves as losers if trade is liberalized. The businesses were not mollified when DeMint and North Carolina Republican Rep. Robin Hayes secured in a separate law a provision to enhance the domestic textile industry's position in its competition with African and Caribbean clothing manufacturers.

The trade vote became the key issue when DeMint sought re-election to the House in 2002, but he won with a solid 62 percent of the vote in the primary and 69 percent in the general election.

DeMint's political positioning has meshed well with the changes in South Carolina. Social conservatism runs deep there, in an area squarely in the Bible Belt and home to Bob Jones University, a bastion of evangelicalism. The textile industry is still prevalent, though not as dominant as it once was, and other industries have moved in, such as automobile manufacturing. That makes DeMint's support for trade liberalization more palatable.

In Congress, DeMint meets weekly in a small interdenominational Bible study group, a practice he's followed for more than 20 years. He says the meetings keep him focused on spiritual matters.

Raised by a single mother who operated a dance school out of the home, DeMint and his three siblings grew up quickly, vacuuming the house and handling adult household chores at a young age. Yet DeMint sparked controversy during his Senate campaign when he asserted during a debate that unwed mothers should not teach in public schools. He also said that a "practicing homosexual" should be similarly barred from teaching in the schools. He later apologized for both remarks, saying it was up to states to decide who is fit to teach.

DeMint entered politics in 1992 as an unpaid adviser to his predecessor in the House, Republican Bob Inglis. Six years later, when Inglis gave up the seat for a Senate bid, DeMint won the GOP nomination against state Sen. Mike Fair, who had the backing of the Christian Coalition. DeMint won by 18 percentage points in the fall.

When Democratic Sen. Ernest "Fritz" Hollings announced his retirement in 2004, DeMint, who was facing a self-imposed six-year term limit in the House, jumped at the chance to run. After easily defeating former Gov. David Beasley in the GOP primary, he entered the race against Democrat Inez Tenenbaum, the popular state education superintendent, with the hefty advantage of being a Republican in a state trending strongly toward his party. He prevailed by 10 percentage points. With DeMint's victory, South Carolina has two Republican senators for the first time since Reconstruction.

KEY VOTES

House Service:
2004
No Extend federal unemployment benefits by 13 weeks
?   Pass $283.2 billion, six-year federal highway and mass transit bill
Yes Approve $146 billion multi-year extension of previously enacted middle-class tax breaks
Yes Amend the Constitution to prohibit same-sex marriage
Yes Cut corporate taxes $137 billion over 10 years
Yes Reorganize U.S. intelligence agencies as proposed by Sept. 11 commission

2003
Yes Cut taxes by $330 billion through fiscal 2013
No Block Bush rule scaling back overtime pay for some white-collar federal workers
No Do not allow use of search warrants without first notifying subjects
Yes Allow importation of prescription drugs
Yes Create private school voucher program in Washington, D.C.
Yes Ban "partial birth" abortion except to save a woman's life
No Split $18.6 billion in Iraq aid into half-grant, half-loan
No Overhaul Medicare and create prescription drug benefit

CQ VOTE STUDIES

House Service:

	PARTY UNITY		PRESIDENTIAL SUPPORT	
	Support	Oppose	Support	Oppose
2004	98%	2%	92%	8%
2003	98%	2%	89%	11%
2002	97%	3%	85%	15%
2001	98%	2%	95%	5%
2000	98%	2%	22%	78%
1999	97%	3%	11%	89%

INTEREST GROUPS

House Service:

	AFL-CIO	ADA	CCUS	ACU
2004	0%	0%	92%	100%
2003	7%	20%	93%	96%
2002	11%	0%	90%	100%
2001	0%	0%	96%	100%
2000	0%	0%	90%	100%
1999	11%	0%	92%	91%

Rep. Henry E. Brown Jr. (R)

CAPITOL OFFICE
225-3176
www.house.gov/henrybrown
1124 Longworth 20515-4001; fax 225-3407

COMMITTEES
Resources
Transportation & Infrastructure
Veterans' Affairs
 (Health - chairman)

HOMETOWN
Hanahan

BORN
Dec. 20, 1935, Bishopville, S.C.

RELIGION
Baptist

FAMILY
Wife, Billye Brown; three children

EDUCATION
Berkeley H.S., graduated 1953

MILITARY SERVICE
S.C. National Guard, 1953-62

CAREER
Grocery chain executive; grocery store data
processor; shipyard worker

POLITICAL HIGHLIGHTS
Hanahan City Council, 1981-85; S.C. House, 1985-
2000

ELECTION RESULTS

2004 GENERAL

Henry E. Brown Jr. (R)	186,448	87.8%
James E. Dunn (GREEN)	25,674	12.1%

2004 PRIMARY

Henry E. Brown Jr. (R)	47,066	83.5%
Bob Batchelder (R)	9,326	16.5%

2002 GENERAL

Henry E. Brown Jr. (R)	122,518	89.5%
James E. Dunn (UC)	9,560	7.0%
Joseph F. Innella (NL)	4,775	3.5%

PREVIOUS WINNING PERCENTAGES
2000 (60%)

Elected 2000; 3rd term

Brown makes no apology for his conservative conduct. He says, "I represent a conservative district and vote accordingly."

Brown showed his conservative mettle in his first term when his resolution backing public schools that display the words "God Bless America" won unanimous House approval. He was angry when the American Civil Liberties Union objected to a "God Bless America" display mounted at a California public school in response to the Sept. 11, 2001, terrorist attacks.

Not surprisingly, Brown is a reliable supporter of President Bush's tax cuts and takes a conservative view on most social issues, opposing abortion and same-sex marriage. He voted in agreement with Bush 94 percent of the time in the 108th Congress, and supported his party 97 percent of the time on votes that pitted the two parties against each other.

Brown was the oldest freshman elected to the House in 2000 — he was 65 at the time — and he soon positioned himself as an interesting contrast to his predecessor, Republican Mark Sanford, who was elected governor in 2002. Both Brown and Sanford are fiscal conservatives. But while Sanford had fought against some transportation earmarks for the district, Brown has pressed readily for federal dollars to help pay for deepening Charleston harbor, replacing the aging bridge across the Cooper River and pumping additional sand onto South Carolina's tourist-attracting beaches.

When Brown was given a seat on the Transportation and Infrastructure Committee, he made funding for the 1st District a priority. One of his top goals is to win federal support to extend Interstate 73 to Myrtle Beach.

He has found other ways to direct money back home. He worked to secure a $500,000 earmark in the 2004 catchall spending bill to finish work on the Freewoods Farm living farm museum near Myrtle Beach, which is run like a Civil War-era farm. And he has used the annual Defense appropriations bill to help Charleston-area military facilities and contractors.

From his seat on the Veterans' Affairs Committee, Brown worked to repeal the so-called widow's tax. He was concerned that widows of military retirees received 55 percent of their deceased husband's pay until reaching the age of 62, when the benefit dropped to 35 percent because the widow then became eligible for Social Security. "This offset is patently unfair and hits our seniors hard," Brown said.

Brown has focused on increasing benefits for veterans in other ways, such as permitting retired members of the military who have a service-connected disability to receive concurrently both their military retirement pay and disability compensation. He also has backed efforts to require military hospitals and VA facilities that are close to each other to share facilities, staff and patients; to increase the funding that a veteran can receive for on-the-job training; and to permit spouses of deceased veterans to remarry without losing benefits. At the start of the 109th, he moved from the chair of the panel's Benefits Subcommittee to head the Health Subcommittee.

He also joined the Resources Committee, which will allow him to weigh in on such issues as private property rights and the management of national forests, as well as to watch over South Carolina's coastal resources.

In 2004, Brown ended up in a squabble with the U.S. Forest Service. A fire he set on his property in March burned out of control on a windy day and scorched 20 acres of the Francis Marion National Forest. The matter became controversial after a pair of Forest Service whistleblowers claimed the agency delayed ticketing Brown because he threatened a congressional review of the agency. Even after issuing a $250 ticket in September, agency officials held off charging Brown an additional $4,000 or more for the cost of fighting the fire while they reviewed their policy of charging those responsible for accidental fires.

Brown, who denied any wrongdoing, paid the $250 fine reluctantly and contended the fire had not been his fault. "It's an arrogance in the government, and not just because it's Henry Brown, but everybody," he told The Post and Courier in Charleston. "There is no consideration for no-fault accidents in the code. I just felt like the fire was out of my control."

Brown grew up on a farm about 25 miles north of Charleston. In high school, he worked part-time in a small general store. He told the South Carolina Business Journal it was that job that taught him the importance of being smart with his money.

After high school, he entered the National Guard and took a job in North Charleston with the local electric company, where he was among the early workers in the budding computer field. Later, Brown took a job at the Charleston Naval Shipyard, where his father had worked. He then began a long career with Piggly Wiggly Carolina Co., the South Carolina franchisee of the Southern grocery chain. Brown took a few classes at The Citadel and continued to move up in the grocery business, eventually becoming a vice president of the firm's computer operations.

Brown was active in civic affairs in the town of Hanahan, north of Charleston; he served first on the planning board and then, in 1981, won a seat on the nonpartisan city council in a special election. Four years later, he won another special election to the state legislature. During his nearly 16 years in the South Carolina House, Brown developed a reputation as a pragmatic and dependable legislator, and in 1995 he became the first Republican in more than 100 years to chair the Ways and Means Committee.

Sanford had announced at the start of his tenure in Congress that he would serve only six years. So in 1998, just a few days after Brown won re-election to the state House and Sanford won the last of his three terms, Brown filed documents stating his intent to run for Congress in two years.

Running against five other Republicans, Brown drew attention to his first name by mailing 20,000 Oh Henry! candy bars to voters. He finished first in the primary and took 55 percent of the vote in a runoff election to defeat former state transportation official Buck Limehouse. Although Democrats nominated a credible candidate in Internet entrepreneur Andy Brack — a longtime aide to Democratic Sen. Ernest F. Hollings — Brown coasted to victory with 60 percent. He has not faced a Democratic opponent since.

KEY VOTES

2004
No	Extend federal unemployment benefits by 13 weeks
Yes	Pass $283.2 billion, six-year federal highway and mass transit bill
Yes	Approve $146 billion multi-year extension of previously enacted middle-class tax breaks
Yes	Amend the Constitution to prohibit same-sex marriage
Yes	Cut corporate taxes $137 billion over 10 years
Yes	Reorganize U.S. intelligence agencies as proposed by Sept. 11 commission

2003
Yes	Cut taxes by $330 billion through fiscal 2013
No	Block Bush rule scaling back overtime pay for some white-collar federal workers
No	Do not allow use of search warrants without first notifying subjects
Yes	Allow importation of prescription drugs
Yes	Create private school voucher program in Washington, D.C.
Yes	Ban "partial birth" abortion except to save a woman's life
No	Split $18.6 billion in Iraq aid into half-grant, half-loan
Yes	Overhaul Medicare and create prescription drug benefit

CQ VOTE STUDIES

	PARTY UNITY		PRESIDENTIAL SUPPORT	
	Support	Oppose	Support	Oppose
2004	97%	3%	91%	9%
2003	97%	3%	96%	4%
2002	95%	5%	82%	18%
2001	97%	3%	88%	12%

INTEREST GROUPS

	AFL-CIO	ADA	CCUS	ACU
2004	20%	0%	100%	96%
2003	7%	10%	97%	88%
2002	11%	0%	95%	96%
2001	8%	0%	96%	92%

SOUTH CAROLINA 1
East — part of Charleston, Myrtle Beach

Taking in the northeastern half of the state's coastline, the 1st is marked by two of South Carolina's landmark tourism cities, Charleston and Myrtle Beach. Horry County, which includes Myrtle Beach, still has plenty of farmland but is one of the state's fastest-growing areas. The 1st is the least rural of South Carolina's six congressional districts.

Hurricane Hugo wrought devastation all along the state's coastline in 1989, and defense downsizing further hurt Charleston in the early 1990s. But these events also heralded a wave of redevelopment, as the city shifted its economy to manufacturing, shipping, health care and technology. Charleston (80 percent of whose residents live in the 1st) is an icon of the New South but retains its traditional culture. Surrounded by reminders of antebellum history, it is nicknamed the "Holy City" because of the church steeples marking its skyline.

Moving north, tourism and agriculture dominate the 1st. Myrtle Beach's tourist-resort economy welcomes 13 million visitors a year, and Horry is often the state's top tobacco-producing county.

The district's demographics — mostly white, suburban and comfortably middle-class — make it reliable Republican territory. One exception is the strong environmental and anti-development sentiment shared by many coastal residents in response to rapid population growth, rising pollution and beach erosion.

Horry County gave George W. Bush 62 percent of the vote in the 2004 presidential election, while Bush took 61 percent of the 1st's overall vote.

MAJOR INDUSTRY
Tourism, agriculture, shipping, health care, tobacco

MILITARY BASES
Charleston Air Force Base, 3,700 military, 1,300 civilian (2004); Charleston Naval Weapons Station, 237 military, 236 civilian (2005)

CITIES
Charleston (pt.), 77,434; Mount Pleasant, 47,609; North Charleston (pt.), 45,530; Goose Creek, 29,208; Summerville, 27,752; Myrtle Beach, 22,759

NOTABLE
Charleston Harbor is home to Fort Sumter, where the Civil War began in April 1861; Fort Moultrie on Sullivan's Island nearby marks the first decisive victory in the War for Independence; 18-year-old Edgar Allan Poe arrived in Charleston in 1827 to enlist at Fort Moultrie.

Rep. Joe Wilson (R)

CAPITOL OFFICE
225-2452
joe.wilson@mail.house.gov
www.joewilson.house.gov
212 Cannon 20515-4002; fax 225-2455

COMMITTEES
Armed Services
Education & Workforce
International Relations

HOMETOWN
Springdale

BORN
July 31, 1947, Charleston, S.C.

RELIGION
Presbyterian

FAMILY
Wife, Roxanne Wilson; four children

EDUCATION
Washington and Lee U., B.A. 1969 (political science); U. of South Carolina, J.D. 1972

MILITARY SERVICE
Army Reserve, 1972-75; S.C. National Guard, 1975-2003

CAREER
Lawyer; campaign manager; U.S. Energy Department official

POLITICAL HIGHLIGHTS
Pine Ridge town judge, 1974-76; Republican nominee for S.C. Senate, 1976; Springdale town judge, 1977-80; S.C. Senate, 1985-2001

ELECTION RESULTS

2004 GENERAL

Joe Wilson (R)	181,862	65.0%
Michael Ray Ellisor (D)	93,249	33.3%
Steve Lefemine (CNSTP)	4,447	1.6%

2004 PRIMARY

Joe Wilson (R)	unopposed

2002 GENERAL

Joe Wilson (R)	144,149	84.1%
Mark Whittington (UC)	17,189	10.0%
James R. "Jim" Legg (LIBERT)	9,650	5.6%

PREVIOUS WINNING PERCENTAGES
2001 Special Election (73%)

Elected December 2001; 2nd full term

A thorough and vocal conservative, Wilson is a fierce advocate for military reservists, which is not surprising given that he was in the Army Reserves for three years and a colonel in the South Carolina National Guard until he retired in the summer of 2003. Wilson's son Alan served in Iraq as an intelligence officer for the National Guard, providing Wilson with frontline reports on his wireless BlackBerry that usually buzzes with mundane reminders about floor votes and committee hearings.

From his seat on the Armed Services Committee, Wilson was angry when the Pentagon planned to scrap a rule that limits active duty deployment of reserve forces to two years. Wilson promised to try in the 109th Congress to tighten the limit to six months. Long before a 2005 commission was formed to begin a new round of base closings, Wilson was working to protect the installations in his district and the rest of the Palmetto state.

Wilson took the Armed Services seat of his mentor, Floyd Spence, upon winning a 2001 special election after Spence's death. Spence had chaired the committee for six years.

Wilson is known for his sharp tongue and his unwavering support for the war on Iraq and President Bush's overall campaign to combat terrorism. When former South Carolina Democratic Sen. Ernest F. Hollings protested the Bush administration's refusal to spell out how it planned to finance the Iraq war by being the sole no vote on a non-binding resolution supporting the troops in 2003, Wilson was livid. "He voted against commending our men and women who have sweated, bled and died to protect our children from future terrorist attacks," Wilson said.

He also was a dogged critic of Democrat John Kerry during the 2004 presidential campaign, and caught some flack for demanding that Kerry apologize for remarks he made more than 30 years ago about supposed atrocities in Vietnam. Former Democratic Sen. Max Cleland of Georgia, a Kerry supporter who lost an arm and both legs in Vietnam, denounced Wilson and similar critics as "a bunch of chickenhawks who never went to war, never felt a wound, but are so quick to criticize a man who went to war and got wounded doing it." Wilson had a student deferment during Vietnam.

It's not an accident that Wilson often finds himself out front for the GOP. He is a member of the Republican "theme team," which helps the party make its points in forums such as C-SPAN interviews and House one-minute floor speeches. He also is a part of the GOP whip operation.

Wilson's greatest legislative success came when his bill to expand a loan forgiveness program for teachers in poverty-stricken public schools was made part of a bill signed by Bush at the end of 2004. All qualifying teachers in poor public schools can be forgiven up to $5,000, but Wilson's provision raises the amount to $17,500 for math, science and special education teachers. He sits on the Education and Workforce Committee.

Wilson also is interested in promoting the long-delayed renewal of the landmark 1996 welfare law, an interest dating back to when he was part of a key state Senate committee that drafted state welfare legislation.

Wilson gained a seat on the International Relations Committee in the 109th. He has long been outspoken in promoting closer ties with India, supporting Israel and backing NATO membership for Bulgaria and Romania. Wilson's father was stationed in India with the Flying Tigers during World War II, and his stories sparked the congressman's interest in India.

Wilson's sharp and careless remarks sometimes land him in hot water.

A few months after the June 2003 death of South Carolina GOP Sen. Strom Thurmond, a South Carolina icon and former segregationist, a black woman named Essie Mae Washington-Williams acknowledged that she was Thurmond's illegitimate daughter. She said she had long enjoyed his financial support and occasional visits. Despite compelling evidence and quick acceptance by Thurmond's family, Wilson told The State newspaper of Columbia: "It's a smear on the image that [Thurmond] has as a person of high integrity who has been so loyal to the people of South Carolina." Wilson, his wife and three of his sons had all interned in Thurmond's office. He apologized for his remark a few days later.

Wilson said his first recollection of politics was when he was a "pop runner" — fetching soft drinks for poll workers. His mother was a Democrat, but Wilson, recalling his great admiration for President Eisenhower, always thought he might be a Republican. He made the transition from working on Democratic races to Republican ones in 1960. In 1963, he rode a bus to Washington, D.C., to attend a Draft Goldwater rally.

In addition to working for Thurmond while in college, Wilson joined Spence's office while in law school — the start of a relationship that would last until Spence's death. He managed five of Spence's re-election campaigns, as well as being involved in numerous statewide GOP campaigns in the 1980s and 1990s while working as a real estate lawyer in Columbia.

Wilson was just short in a contest for the state Senate in 1976, losing after a recount. After a two-year stint with the Department of Energy in Washington, Wilson successfully challenged a GOP incumbent in 1984 for the first of five trips to the state Senate. Wilson's tenure in the legislature was marked by proposals to eliminate property taxes and to cap state spending. He also sought to increase penalties for gun-related felonies, make it easier to impose the death penalty, and require school children to recite portions of the Declaration of Independence.

After Spence died in 2001, Wilson said he had his deathbed endorsement. While Wilson's claim rankled some of his rivals, it was backed up by Spence's widow. He won the five-way GOP primary with 76 percent of the vote and cruised to a 48 percentage point win in the heavily GOP district.

Democrats did not even come up with a challenger in 2002, freeing Wilson to devote his time to GOP Rep. Lindsey Graham's successful run for Thurmond's Senate seat. He and Graham have worked together for years. Wilson was the staff judge advocate for the Army National Guard while Graham held the same post for the Air National Guard. Wilson won with 65 percent of the vote in 2004.

KEY VOTES

2004
No Extend federal unemployment benefits by 13 weeks
Yes Pass $283.2 billion, six-year federal highway and mass transit bill
Yes Approve $146 billion multi-year extension of previously enacted middle-class tax breaks
Yes Amend the Constitution to prohibit same-sex marriage
Yes Cut corporate taxes $137 billion over 10 years
Yes Reorganize U.S. intelligence agencies as proposed by Sept. 11 commission

2003
Yes Cut taxes by $330 billion through fiscal 2013
No Block Bush rule scaling back overtime pay for some white-collar federal workers
Yes Do not allow use of search warrants without first notifying subjects
No Allow importation of prescription drugs
Yes Create private school voucher program in Washington, D.C.
Yes Ban "partial birth" abortion except to save a woman's life
No Split $18.6 billion in Iraq aid into half-grant, half-loan
Yes Overhaul Medicare and create prescription drug benefit

CQ VOTE STUDIES

	PARTY UNITY		PRESIDENTIAL SUPPORT	
	Support	Oppose	Support	Oppose
2004	99%	1%	91%	9%
2003	98%	2%	94%	6%
2002	97%	3%	82%	18%
2001	100%	0%	100%	0%

INTEREST GROUPS

	AFL-CIO	ADA	CCUS	ACU
2004	13%	0%	100%	96%
2003	13%	5%	93%	84%
2002	22%	10%	80%	92%
2001	—	—	100%	—

SOUTH CAROLINA 2
Central and south — part of Columbia and suburbs, Hilton Head Island

The oddly shaped 2nd winds from the state capital of Columbia down through the middle of the state to a sandy stretch along the coast. The two ends of the district encapsulate some of the state's wealthiest communities — the suburbs of Columbia, in Richland and Lexington counties, and Beaufort and Hilton Head Island on the southern tip.

Columbia's suburbs have grown steadily. While state and local government are still the city's largest employers, its private sector is becoming more of a force. At the southern end of the 2nd, retirees and tourists are drawn to Hilton Head Island, making surrounding Beaufort the state's fastest-growing county in population in the 1990s.

Military issues are important here. Just up the shore from the swank resorts, recruits sweat at the Parris Island Marine Corps camp. Fort Jackson in Richland County at the district's northern end and another Marine installation also contribute to the military presence.

Smaller towns and rural areas that are considerably poorer dot the land between Columbia and Hilton Head. Many families in the black-majority counties of Allendale, Hampton and Jasper live below the poverty line, relying on tenant farming and sharecropping. Barnwell and Allendale counties produce peanuts, corn and cotton, among other crops.

Heavy Democratic support in the poor areas is offset by wealthy white-collar professionals in the north and south, who push the district firmly into the GOP column. Lexington County, the 2nd's most-populous, gave George W. Bush 72 percent of its 2004 presidential vote.

MAJOR INDUSTRY
Tourism, government, military, agriculture

MILITARY BASES
Fort Jackson (Army), 3,600 military, 4,400 civilian (2003); Beaufort Marine Corps Air Station, 4,190 military, 578 civilian (2005); Marine Corps Recruitment Depot (Parris Island), 1,883 military, 399 civilian (2004)

CITIES
Columbia (pt.), 59,771; Hilton Head Island, 33,862

NOTABLE
The first federally authorized black unit to fight for the Union, the First South Carolina Volunteers, camped in Beaufort.

Rep. J. Gresham Barrett (R)

Elected 2002; 2nd term

CAPITOL OFFICE
225-5301
www.house.gov/barrett
1523 Longworth 20515-4003; fax 225-3216

COMMITTEES
Budget
Financial Services
International Relations

HOMETOWN
Westminster

BORN
Feb. 14, 1961, Westminster, S.C.

RELIGION
Baptist

FAMILY
Wife, Natalie Barrett; three children

EDUCATION
The Citadel, B.S. 1983 (business administration)

MILITARY SERVICE
Army, 1983-87

CAREER
Furniture store owner

POLITICAL HIGHLIGHTS
S.C. House, 1997-2002

ELECTION RESULTS

2004 GENERAL

J. Gresham Barrett (R)		unopposed

2004 PRIMARY

J. Gresham Barrett (R)		unopposed

2002 GENERAL

J. Gresham Barrett (R)	119,644	67.1%
George Brightharp (D)	55,743	31.3%
Mike Boerste (LIBERT)	2,785	1.6%

Barrett is one of the youthful, confident and maximally conservative lawmakers that give the House its rightward bent. He is typically a reliable vote for GOP leaders, and is among the handful of Republicans who align with the party on major votes almost all of the time. But as President Bush is finding out, Barrett will side with hard-line conservatives on fiscal issues even when the stakes are high.

Barrett in November 2003 voted against the GOP bill to add a prescription drug benefit to Medicare, though Bush lobbied hard for it and Republican leaders held an all-night session to round up sufficient votes. Barrett said the bill would do more harm than good, telling the State newspaper of Columbia, S.C., "What we did today was take a 30-year loan out on an old broken-down boat, slapped some patches on it and stuck it back in the water."

With snappy analogies like that, Barrett is a chip off the block of his predecessor in the House, Sen. Lindsey Graham, a conservative maverick who is his political mentor. Describing his beliefs to the State in 2003, Barrett said, "I have a lot of traditional values. . . . I'll say Southern values."

A member of the Budget Committee, he frequently calls for more fiscal discipline. In 2004, he was one of nine House members to receive a 95 percent score from Citizens Against Government Waste, a citizens' group that fights pork-barrel spending. The ranking came four months after he introduced his bill seeking to rein in government spending, which he says resembles "a teenager on a shopping spree and not a responsible parent paying the bills."

In his first term during the 108th Congress, he was among just 15 House Republicans who voted with the majority of their party 99 percent of the time on votes that split the two parties. He introduced bills to ban immigrants from terrorist-designated states from entering the United States and to limit the growth of domestic spending.

Nine months before Election Day 2004, Barrett publicly declared his intention to vote for Bush's re-election, saying the president "has shown true leadership during one of the most trying times in American history."

In criticizing judges in Massachusetts who had authorized same-sex marriages, Barrett said, "The decision we are now left with is not whether the Constitution will be amended, but who will amend it — activist judges or the American people?"

Barrett is strongly pro-defense. He went to The Citadel military academy and graduated from the Army's Airborne School, and now carries himself with a soldier's straight-backed assurance. He eventually resigned his commission to join the family furniture business, which closed in 2004.

In November 2004, his leadership abilities were recognized by his fellow Class of 2002 colleagues, who unanimously elected him vice president of their class for the 109th Congress. He was also named along with a handful of his freshman colleagues as an assistant GOP whip.

Barrett has formed a friendship with another ambitious young conservative, Indiana's Mike Pence, who chairs the Republican Study Committee. The two men met at a prayer breakfast, and Barrett says that on the topics of religion, politics and family, the two think alike.

Barrett devotes much of his time to looking out for the Energy Department's Savannah River Site, a sprawling nuclear weapons complex located mostly in his district that has been seeking new missions since the end of the Cold War to stabilize its shrinking workforce. A staunch advocate of nuclear power, he has championed the idea of building a new reactor at the site. In 2003, he added a provision to the energy bill calling for the energy secretary to study developing commercial nuclear energy production facilities at existing department sites.

Barrett is undeterred by criticism from environmentalists and others who say nuclear power is unsafe and not economical when factoring in the start-up costs of a plant. After visiting France, a country that derives more than three-quarters of its energy from such plants, he said he believes that it's the only way to keep up with demand in the United States.

Like other South Carolina delegation members, Barrett tries to help the state's beleaguered textile industry. He has opposed granting the president fast-track authority to negotiate trade agreements that Congress cannot amend, even though many business-oriented Republicans support fast track. To salvage the remaining plants in the state, he says that Congress has to act on taxation, regulatory and litigation overhaul measures to make domestic manufacturers more competitive.

Barrett also has seats on the Financial Services and International Relations committees. The former seat helped him attract donations from the banking, finance and real estate industries, which have made up the biggest chunk of his campaign contributors.

Barrett's conservative credentials were forged in the state House, where he served three terms. He led the fight there to ban late-term abortion. He also sponsored a 1998 education measure that established statewide standards for all subjects and grades.

Barrett's involvement in George W. Bush's 2000 South Carolina presidential primary campaign helped him build a strong organization for his first House bid, which arose after 3rd District Rep. Graham decided to run for the Senate. In 2002, Barrett easily won the Republican nod over five rivals, then claimed the general-election win by better than 2-to-1 over George Brightharp, a high school guidance counselor.

Barrett's and Graham's homes are about 10 miles apart, and Barrett often was compared to Graham during the campaign. Upon his election, Barrett told the Greenville News that he considered his predecessor "a wonderful mentor and a wonderful friend."

In 2004, bowing to the district's strong conservative leanings, Democrats did not even try to field a candidate against Barrett, and he ran unopposed in both the primary and general elections.

KEY VOTES

2004
No Extend federal unemployment benefits by 13 weeks
No Pass $283.2 billion, six-year federal highway and mass transit bill
Yes Approve $146 billion multi-year extension of previously enacted middle-class tax breaks
Yes Amend the Constitution to prohibit same-sex marriage
Yes Cut corporate taxes $137 billion over 10 years
No Reorganize U.S. intelligence agencies as proposed by Sept. 11 commission

2003
Yes Cut taxes by $330 billion through fiscal 2013
No Block Bush rule scaling back overtime pay for some white-collar federal workers
Yes Do not allow use of search warrants without first notifying subjects
No Allow importation of prescription drugs
Yes Create private school voucher program in Washington, D.C.
Yes Ban "partial birth" abortion except to save a woman's life
No Split $18.6 billion in Iraq aid into half-grant, half-loan
No Overhaul Medicare and create prescription drug benefit

CQ VOTE STUDIES

	PARTY UNITY		PRESIDENTIAL SUPPORT	
	Support	Oppose	Support	Oppose
2004	99%	1%	85%	15%
2003	98%	2%	91%	9%

INTEREST GROUPS

	AFL-CIO	ADA	CCUS	ACU
2004	0%	0%	100%	100%
2003	20%	10%	87%	92%

SOUTH CAROLINA 3
West – Anderson, Aiken

Encompassing the northwestern corner of the state, the 3rd is a predominately rural district. Many voters here are converts to the Republican Party, having shifted over from "Yellow Dog" Democrat status. When former Rep. (and now senator) Lindsey Graham won this seat in 1994, he was the first Republican to do so since Reconstruction.

The brimming economy has further boosted GOP opportunities. The base of engineers surrounding the Savannah River nuclear complex (shared with the 2nd) — the district's largest employer — has helped attract Fortune 500 firms to the area, as well as several U.S. divisions of foreign companies. An example is Fujifilm in Greenwood, which employs 1,500 South Carolinians and has invested more than $1.3 billion in the state. Fujifilm's medical products plant is the first built outside of Japan.

To the northwest, Anderson has built a more industrial economy, moving away from its rural roots. Many area textile mills have successfully shifted to high-tech fiber manufacturing. Clemson University provides the economic and social nexus for Pickens County at the 3rd's northern tip.

Agriculture is important here, as Edgefield and Saluda counties are two of the top peach-producing counties in the state. Aiken County, which is shared with the 2nd District, also ranks high in peach production and has some cotton production as well.

The district votes solidly Republican in federal and statewide races. The 3rd's most populous voting jurisdictions — Anderson, Aiken and Pickens counties — are heavily Republican. Pickens County gave 73 percent of its vote to George W. Bush in the 2004 presidential election. The counties in the 3rd's midsection are more rural, less prosperous and less Republican-leaning. This area includes McCormick County, where the majority of the population is black.

MAJOR INDUSTRY
Manufacturing, textiles, agriculture

CITIES
Anderson, 25,514; Aiken (pt.), 22,810; Greenwood, 22,071; Easley, 17,754

NOTABLE
The 70,000-acre Lake Thurmond, previously known as Clarks Hill Lake, was renamed for former GOP Sen. Strom Thurmond, the oldest person ever to serve in the Senate; Aiken is known as the polo center of the South.

Rep. Bob Inglis (R)

Elected 2004; 1st term
Also served 1993-99

Inglis returns to the House after a six-year hiatus. He had a rather short first tenure: Standing by a pledge he had taken to serve no more than three terms in the House, he ran for the Senate in 1998 but lost to veteran Democratic incumbent Ernest F. Hollings.

Inglis, though, got a chance to return in 2004, after six years in private life, when his successor in the 4th District seat — Republican Jim DeMint — left it open for a successful bid to succeed the retiring Hollings.

By then, Inglis had changed his mind about several of the things that propelled him to Washington the first time around. Like many Republican candidates then, he campaigned vigorously against bloated federal spending and vowed to stay no more than three terms.

But Inglis now says that individual term-limit pledges amount to "unilateral disarmament" in the seniority-driven world of Capitol Hill. In fact, the returning Inglis did not have to start from square one despite his hiatus: Republican leaders gave him partial credit for past service and placed him in the seat he had held on the Judiciary Committee during his first tour. He also is a member of the Science Committee — on which he chairs the Research Subcommittee — and the Education and Workforce panel.

And he has softened his original vehement opposition to federal "pork" spending, saying that he will try to bring money back to his district as long as it is spent on projects that would have broader national implications.

Yet Inglis plans to use his second turn in Congress to prod his GOP colleagues back toward ideals that he believes are fading after more than a decade in the House majority, notably, fiscal responsibility. We are quick to criticize Democrats for being tax-and-spend liberals," he said. "But that may be more honest than being no-tax and spend Republicans."

His still-familiar name and the district's overwhelming GOP leanings enabled Inglis to cruise through his comeback campaign in 2004. He won by landslide margins both in the three-candidate Republican primary and in his general-election contest against little-known Democrat Brandon P. Brown.

CAPITOL OFFICE
225-6030
www.house.gov/inglis
330 Cannon 20515-4004; fax 226-1177

COMMITTEES
Education & Workforce
Judiciary
Science
   (Research - chairman)

HOMETOWN
Travelers Rest

BORN
Oct. 11, 1959, Savannah, Ga.

RELIGION
Presbyterian

FAMILY
Wife, Mary Anne Inglis; five children

EDUCATION
Duke U., B.A. 1981 (political science); U. of Virginia, J.D. 1984

CAREER
Lawyer

POLITICAL HIGHLIGHTS
U.S. House, 1993-99; Republican nominee for U.S. Senate, 1998

ELECTION RESULTS

2004 GENERAL

Bob Inglis (R)	188,795	69.8%
Brandon P. Brown (D)	78,376	29.0%
C. Faye Walters (NL)	3,273	1.2%

2004 PRIMARY

Bob Inglis (R)	52,125	84.2%
Carole Wells (R)	7,140	11.5%
Jack Adams (R)	2,628	4.3%

PREVIOUS WINNING PERCENTAGES
1996 (71%); 1994 (73%); 1992 (50%)

SOUTH CAROLINA 4
Northwest — Greenville, Spartanburg

The 4th is South Carolina's most compact district and is centered on Greenville County, the state's most-populous. Greenville and Spartanburg counties together account for 95 percent of the district population. The 4th also takes in Union County, a heavily forested and lightly populated area, and a tiny part of Laurens County.

Successful manufacturing and warehousing ventures have transformed the area from its textile past. The cities of Greenville and Spartanburg are leaders in per capita investment by foreign companies. Michelin's North American base is in Greenville, and BMW is a major presence in Spartanburg.

While no longer the textile capital of the world, the 4th retains a strong textile presence. Industry giant Milliken & Co. is headquartered in Spartanburg. Trade issues are important here, although textile companies have less political influence than they once did. Agriculture also plays a role in the Spartanburg area, as the county's orchards yield one of the biggest peach crops in the South.

Expanding wealth has helped keep the 4th solidly Republican. But the local GOP has two distinct camps: mainstream, business-oriented conservatives and social conservatives focused around Greenville-based Bob Jones University. In recent years, an influx of professionals has diluted the influence of hard-line social conservatives.

With its rank-and-file textile workers and farm laborers, Spartanburg is less heavily Republican than Greenville. Nonetheless, in key 2004 races both counties voted for GOP candidates by landslide margins.

MAJOR INDUSTRY
Manufacturing, textiles, agriculture

CITIES
Greenville, 56,002; Spartanburg, 39,673

NOTABLE
Vietnam War Gen. William C. Westmoreland was born in Spartanburg County.

Rep. John M. Spratt Jr. (D)

Elected 1982; 12th term

CAPITOL OFFICE
225-5501
www.house.gov/spratt
1401 Longworth 20515-4005; fax 225-0464

COMMITTEES
Armed Services
Budget - ranking member

HOMETOWN
York

BORN
Nov. 1, 1942, Charlotte, N.C.

RELIGION
Presbyterian

FAMILY
Wife, Jane Spratt; three children

EDUCATION
Davidson College, A.B. 1964 (history); Oxford U.,
M.A. 1966 (philosophy, politics & economics;
Marshall scholar); Yale U., LL.B. 1969

MILITARY SERVICE
Army, 1969-71

CAREER
Lawyer; insurance agency owner

POLITICAL HIGHLIGHTS
No previous office

ELECTION RESULTS

2004 GENERAL

John M. Spratt Jr. (D)	152,867	63.0%
Albert F. Spencer (R)	89,568	36.9%

2004 PRIMARY

John M. Spratt Jr. (D)	unopposed

2002 GENERAL

John M. Spratt Jr. (D)	121,912	85.9%
Doug Kendall (LIBERT)	11,013	7.8%
Steve Lefemine (CNSTP)	8,930	6.3%

PREVIOUS WINNING PERCENTAGES
2000 (59%); 1998 (58%); 1996 (54%); 1994 (52%);
1992 (61%); 1990 (100%); 1988 (70%); 1986 (100%);
1984 (92%); 1982 (68%)

Spratt serves as Nancy Pelosi's hand-picked demographic counterweight in the Democratic leadership — a politically moderate and courtly Southern man to complement the House minority leader's West Coast liberalism, feminism and high-wattage style.

His job in the Democratic leadership is assistant to the minority leader, an appointive post that Pelosi gave him at the start of the 108th Congress. It is not as powerful as an elected leader's job — Pelosi and other leaders are chosen by a secret ballot cast by all House Democrats — but it gives Spratt a seat at the table where party decisions are made.

Spratt is respected for his credentials on the budget and national defense, two issues on which many Democrats feel they need improvement. A deficit hawk, Spratt is the top-ranking Democrat on the Budget Committee at a time of record federal deficits. Also a defense hawk, he is the No. 2 Democrat on the Armed Services Committee, when the country is fighting wars in Iraq and against a cagey terrorist network around the globe.

Now in his third decade in the House, Spratt has a long memory for many of its big debates, a rarity in a chamber where most members have served less than a decade. His centrist leanings have made him an ideal envoy to negotiate with Republicans, though that role has diminished since he joined the minority leadership, an inherently partisan group.

Spratt has been a member of Armed Services since 1983, when he first arrived on Capitol Hill. He tends to side with Republicans in support of most missile defense programs, though in 2004 he proposed shifting $414 million from anti-missile defense to cover some pay raises, troop security and $250,000 in life insurance for every soldier in a combat zone. After the Sept. 11, 2001, terrorist attacks, Spratt led Democrats to abandon plans to press for cuts in missile defense spending, a tacit acknowledgement that the timing was bad for a fight with President Bush over national security.

Spratt is pro-defense but with an eye toward fiscal consequences. In 2003, when Bush asked Congress for the authority to invade Iraq, Spratt backed him, but also commissioned the Congressional Budget Office to study the costs. As the costs of the war escalated, Spratt in 2004 called on the administration to request additional money to cover them before the November election that year. Bush waited until after he won his second term to send Congress an $82 billion supplemental spending request to finance military operations in Iraq and Afghanistan, and provide aid to the victims of the 2004 Asian tsunami.

Spratt became the top-ranking Democrat on the Budget panel in 1997, and since then has been the leading Democratic advocate for reversing budget deficits. He supported a Republican proposal to amend the Constitution to require balanced federal budgets and backed the 1996 law that gave the president line-item veto power. The Supreme Court later struck the law down as unconstitutional.

Spratt has repeatedly called on Bush to convene a budget summit like the one in 1997 that led to the balanced-budget deal between President Clinton and the GOP-run Congress. Spratt was a lead negotiator in that legislation, which he calls "the biggest achievement that I can lay any claim to."

Despite his pro-defense record, he has been insistent that Congress not give the Bush administration a blank check for its increased defense and homeland security spending. Early in 2003, he pressed his party colleagues to unite behind a budget that would eventually generate a small surplus.

During the 2005 debate over the president's $726 billion tax cut, Spratt proposed an alternative, calling for a $136 billion "stimulus" tax cut, a balanced budget by 2010 and $528 billion for a prescription drug benefit under Medicare. The effort was symbolic — a Democratically written budget had little chance of passing in a GOP-controlled House — but it helped show how the Democrats would prioritize if they were in control. In November 2004, Spratt voted against raising the federal debt ceiling, saying, "We must take action to prevent passing this burden on to our children and grandchildren."

His conservative tilt also has been evident on other issues. He cosponsored a 1996 law requiring that most new TV sets come with a "v-chip" to allow parents to block violent or otherwise objectionable programming.

Spratt has been a leading advocate for the textile industry, which helps fuel the 5th District's economy. He voted for the North American Free Trade Agreement in 1993 after Clinton got the Philippines and some other developing countries to accept a longer phaseout of U.S. quotas limiting textile imports. He voted against the 2002 law giving the president authority to negotiate fast-track trade deals that would be subject to a vote by Congress, but not open to amendment.

Besides textiles, the 5th district depends heavily on tobacco farming, especially in the eastern counties, which tend to vote narrowly Republican. Spratt's fiscal discipline took a back seat to supporting tobacco farmers in 2004, when he voted for a $137 billion corporate tax bill that included a $10 billion buyout of tobacco farmers.

Spratt has generally had to work to convince his conservative-leaning constituents that he understands and defends their interests. With his lofty academic credentials — Spratt holds degrees from Davidson, Oxford and Yale — and his background as a lawyer and insurance agency owner, Spratt is not the obvious choice to represent voters from poor textile towns. But he has been their choice for a long time.

Spratt won his first House race in 1982 by arguing that his work with small-town law clients and bank depositors gave him an understanding of their circumstances. He trounced a longtime friend and legal client, Republican John Wilkerson, by 36 percentage points, and he won re-election with ease throughout the 1980s.

But in the 1990s, he was targeted by the national GOP. He survived the Republican sweep of 1994 by just 4 points and did not get above 60 percent of the vote in the next three elections. The GOP did not field a candidate against Spratt in 2002. In 2004, Spratt won with 63 percent.

KEY VOTES

2004

Yes Extend federal unemployment benefits by 13 weeks

Yes Pass $283.2 billion, six-year federal highway and mass transit bill

Yes Approve $146 billion multi-year extension of previously enacted middle-class tax breaks

Yes Amend the Constitution to prohibit same-sex marriage

Yes Cut corporate taxes $137 billion over 10 years

Yes Reorganize U.S. intelligence agencies as proposed by Sept. 11 commission

2003

No Cut taxes by $330 billion through fiscal 2013

Yes Block Bush rule scaling back overtime pay for some white-collar federal workers

Yes Do not allow use of search warrants without first notifying subjects

Yes Allow importation of prescription drugs

No Create private school voucher program in Washington, D.C.

Yes Ban "partial birth" abortion except to save a woman's life

Yes Split $18.6 billion in Iraq aid into half-grant, half-loan

No Overhaul Medicare and create prescription drug benefit

CQ VOTE STUDIES

	PARTY UNITY		PRESIDENTIAL SUPPORT	
	Support	Oppose	Support	Oppose
2004	86%	14%	41%	59%
2003	90%	10%	25%	75%
2002	88%	12%	42%	58%
2001	82%	18%	33%	67%
2000	82%	18%	59%	41%

INTEREST GROUPS

	AFL-CIO	ADA	CCUS	ACU
2004	93%	80%	48%	20%
2003	100%	95%	32%	33%
2002	100%	80%	55%	16%
2001	92%	85%	45%	36%
2000	78%	70%	52%	20%

SOUTH CAROLINA 5
North central – Rock Hill

The 5th spans all or part of 14 mostly rural counties in the north-central part of the state, stretching from near Charlotte, N.C., to the Columbia suburbs, with considerable territory spreading east and west. Redistricting following the 2000 census added even more rural sections to the district. The combination of tobacco farmers, white-collar Charlotte commuters and textile workers makes this a conservative district, although it still clings to its traditional Southern Democrat roots.

In the midsection and east, Lee, Darlington, Marlboro and Dillon counties produce wheat, as well as cotton for the textile mills that historically have dominated the region's economy. The two largest cities, Rock Hill and Sumter (shared with the 6th), add immigrants from the North. Rock Hill, once dependent on the textile industry, now serves as a home for white-collar commuters and Winthrop University.

Many residents of Fairfield County — an area that already had a double-digit unemployment rate — have lost their jobs because of businesses downsizing or moving overseas.

The city of Sumter, once the center of a large agricultural area, is shifting toward industry. Seven miles west of Sumter, Shaw Air Force Base makes up one-third of the area's economy. In the east, Darlington and Dillon counties depend heavily on tobacco farming.

Politically, the 5th tends to vote narrowly Republican in federal races, but conservative Democrats who appeal to the district's numerous poor and rural residents can win here. Democrats also are helped by the district's 32 percent black population, the largest of any South Carolina district except the black-majority 6th.

MAJOR INDUSTRY
Cotton, textiles, tobacco, agriculture

MILITARY BASES
Shaw Air Force Base, 6,000 military, 700 civilian (2004)

CITIES
Rock Hill, 49,765; Sumter (pt.), 20,518; Gaffney, 12,968

NOTABLE
The Lee County Cotton Festival, held every October, celebrates the agricultural history of "King Cotton"; Home to the Darlington 500 NASCAR race track, where two major races are held; Televangelist Jim Bakker's PTL ministries were located in Fort Mill.

Rep. James E. Clyburn (D)

Elected 1992; 7th term

CAPITOL OFFICE
225-3315
jclyburn@mail.house.gov
www.house.gov/clyburn
2135 Rayburn 20515-4006; fax 225-2313

COMMITTEES
Appropriations

HOMETOWN
Columbia

BORN
July 21, 1940, Sumter, S.C.

RELIGION
African Methodist Episcopal

FAMILY
Wife, Emily Clyburn; three children

EDUCATION
South Carolina State College, B.S. 1962 (social studies)

CAREER
State official; teacher

POLITICAL HIGHLIGHTS
S.C. human affairs commissioner, 1974-92; sought Democratic nomination for S.C. secretary of state, 1978, 1986

ELECTION RESULTS

2004 GENERAL

James E. Clyburn (D)	161,987	67.0%
Gary McLeod (R, C)	79,600	32.9%

2004 PRIMARY

James E. Clyburn (D)	unopposed

2002 GENERAL

James E. Clyburn (D)	115,855	67.0%
Gary McLeod (R)	55,490	32.1%

PREVIOUS WINNING PERCENTAGES
2000 (72%); 1998 (73%); 1996 (69%); 1994 (64%); 1992 (65%)

Clyburn was not a young man when he first came to Congress; elected at 52, he seemed unworried about cutting a dynamic public figure in Washington. But he was a skilled inside operator, and his political savvy and leadership abilities were recognized early on by his colleagues, who chose him as co-president of the House freshman Class of 1992.

Quietly and methodically, he has kept advancing, taking a seat on the Appropriations Committee and serving as Congressional Black Caucus chairman in the 106th Congress, and winning election in the 108th as vice chairman of the Democratic Caucus, the No. 4 position in the House Democratic leadership. In early 2005, Clyburn said he planned to run for caucus chairman when Democrats organize for the 110th.

Clyburn was called on by his party after Democrats failed to gain ground on the House GOP majority in the 2004 elections. Analysts said the Democratic disappointment stemmed from their party's weakness among "values voters." Exit polling on Election Day had shown that a substantial number of voters believed moral values were a significant factor in their voting decision. House Democratic leaders put Clyburn, a minister's son, in charge of a party task force charged with reaching out to religious leaders and helping the party frame issues in faith-based terms.

"The Democrats have a clear and convincing record of walking the walk when it comes to moral values," Clyburn said. "Democrats gave the country Social Security, Medicare. That was our way of taking care of the widows and orphans, taking care of the 'least of these.' We've walked the walk. . . . The problem is we haven't done a good job at talking the talk . . . and talking the talk is what makes headlines."

He urged Democrats not to shy away from using religious references when debating issues involving Medicare, a higher minimum wage, universal health care and additional federal funding for education. "If we ground our advocacy in biblical terms, let our opponents fight against feeding the hungry and clothing the naked," he said.

In early 2003, Clyburn was asked to give the Democratic response to President Bush's weekly radio address, where he focused on the president's economic agenda. "African-Americans and Latinos stand to suffer disproportionately from this administration's economic policies that, by all accounts, favor the wealthy," Clyburn said.

When Bush in the 109th Congress proposed overhauling Social Security, Clyburn said he had heard from hundreds of constituents urging him "not to fiddle" with the program.

Clyburn sides with his party on most issues, voting 94 percent of the time with a majority of Democrats against a majority of Republicans in the 108th Congress. He opposed Bush's 2001 and 2003 tax cuts, and he is a strong supporter of organized labor. Yet in 2003, he was one of 63 Democrats who voted in favor of banning a procedure that opponents call "partial birth" abortion. The next year, he opposed a GOP effort to amend the Constitution to ban same-sex marriage.

As he has taken on a larger role in Democratic Party politics, Clyburn has continued to make it a priority to advocate for his district — the poorest in South Carolina and among the poorest in the nation. From his seat on the Appropriations Committee, and particularly its Transportation Subcommittee, he seeks federal funds to help the 6th District pay for new bridges, roads, water systems, housing, and economic development.

www.cqpress.com

Even before his assignment to Appropriations, Clyburn managed to bring home federal aid as his state's only member of the Transportation and Infrastructure Committee when Congress passed a sweeping surface transportation bill in the 105th (1997-1998). He proudly reported the measure authorized a huge spending increase for the Palmetto State.

As part of that process, Clyburn was able to establish a Transportation Center at South Carolina State University and greatly increase his state's return from the Highway Trust Fund. He also was instrumental in continuing a program that seeks to give 10 percent of construction contracts to disadvantaged businesses.

The 6th is home to a number of historically black colleges, including Clyburn's alma mater, South Carolina State, and Clyburn has been at the forefront of efforts to obtain federal funding to help maintain the schools. He has a strong commitment to higher education. He told The State newspaper that his father loved school so much that he attended the 7th grade three times because blacks in Kershaw County at the time were not allowed to go to high school.

When Democratic Gov. John West named him a special assistant for human resources in 1971, Clyburn, who had taught school and headed the state's Commission for Farm Workers, was the first black in more than 70 years to serve as a gubernatorial appointee in the state. Three years later, he became the state's Human Affairs commissioner, where he earned a reputation as an able conciliator.

A member of one of the most prominent black families in South Carolina politics, Clyburn always had his eye on moving up. In 1978 and 1986, he unsuccessfully sought the Democratic nomination for secretary of state. During his political career in South Carolina, Clyburn saw "the system" become more open to blacks, an evolution confirmed when 1992 redistricting created the black-majority 6th.

White Democratic incumbent Robin Tallon at first said he would seek re-election. But he backed out, citing his unwillingness to provoke a racially divisive campaign. Clyburn and four other black Democrats ran in the primary. While all had some political experience, none could match Clyburn's name recognition in the black community or his high-level contacts in the white Democratic Party establishment.

Clyburn took 56 percent of the primary vote and won with 65 percent in November, becoming the first black representative elected from South Carolina since 1896 (when his great-uncle, George Washington Murray, served). He has always won re-election with ease.

KEY VOTES

2004
Yes Extend federal unemployment benefits by 13 weeks
Yes Pass $283.2 billion, six-year federal highway and mass transit bill
Yes Approve $146 billion multi-year extension of previously enacted middle-class tax breaks
No Amend the Constitution to prohibit same-sex marriage
Yes Cut corporate taxes $137 billion over 10 years
Yes Reorganize U.S. intelligence agencies as proposed by Sept. 11 commission

2003
No Cut taxes by $330 billion through fiscal 2013
Yes Block Bush rule scaling back overtime pay for some white-collar federal workers
Yes Do not allow use of search warrants without first notifying subjects
No Allow importation of prescription drugs
No Create private school voucher program in Washington, D.C.
Yes Ban "partial birth" abortion except to save a woman's life
Yes Split $18.6 billion in Iraq aid into half-grant, half-loan
No Overhaul Medicare and create prescription drug benefit

CQ VOTE STUDIES

	PARTY UNITY		PRESIDENTIAL SUPPORT	
	Support	Oppose	Support	Oppose
2004	93%	7%	30%	70%
2003	95%	5%	25%	75%
2002	97%	3%	31%	69%
2001	84%	16%	33%	67%
2000	91%	9%	75%	25%

INTEREST GROUPS

	AFL-CIO	ADA	CCUS	ACU
2004	86%	90%	45%	13%
2003	100%	90%	39%	25%
2002	100%	95%	50%	0%
2001	92%	70%	61%	20%
2000	100%	85%	57%	8%

SOUTH CAROLINA 6

Central and east — parts of Columbia, Florence and Charleston

A black-majority district designed to take in African-American areas in Columbia, Charleston and elsewhere in the state, the 6th comprises all or part of 15 counties in the eastern half of the state, starting near the North Carolina border and reaching the southeastern coast. With five of South Carolina's six poorest counties, the 6th District has the state's lowest median household income.

In the rural portions of the district, many families depend on tobacco and tobacco-related agribusiness for their incomes. In the 1980s, Bamberg, Marion and Williamsburg counties lost population as residents left farms and jobs in the textile industry disappeared. For those who remain, agriculture continues to be the economic mainstay, with important corn and cotton production here to go along with tobacco. Many other residents who live in the district find work in Charleston (shared with the 1st) or Columbia (shared with the 2nd).

Other sectors of the district's economy have fared better. Plastics, pharmaceuticals, textiles and paperboard manufacturing sustain many in the city of Florence (shared with the 5th), which is more middle-class than most of the rest of the 6th. In the coastal parts of the district, maritime industries and tourism provide the economic base. Government services, higher education and manufacturing create jobs in the 6th's midsection.

The 6th gives solid and consistent support to Democrats at all levels. The district's black-majority areas — including the 6th's shares of Columbia and North Charleston, which are more than two-thirds African-American — make this seat a Democratic lock.

MAJOR INDUSTRY
Agriculture, government, textiles, tourism, tobacco, cotton

CITIES
Columbia (pt.), 56,507; North Charleston (pt.), 34,111; Florence (pt.), 26,623; Charleston (pt.), 19,216; Sumter (pt.), 19,125

NOTABLE
All of the state's four historically black colleges and universities are in the district; Clarendon County (pop. 32,502) can claim five South Carolina governors — all related to one another.

SOUTH DAKOTA

Gov. Michael Rounds (R)

First elected: 2002
Length of term: 4 years
Term expires: 1/07
Salary: $103,222
Phone: (605) 773-3212

Hometown: Pierre
Born: Oct. 24, 1954; Pierre, S.D.
Religion: Roman Catholic
Family: Wife, Jean Rounds; four children
Education: South Dakota State U., B.S. 1977 (political science)
Career: Insurance and real estate executive; insurance agent; campaign aide
Political highlights: S.D. Senate, 1991-2000 (majority leader, 1995-2000)

Election results:
2002 GENERAL

Michael Rounds (R)	189,920	56.8%
Jim Abbott (D)	140,263	41.9%

Lt. Gov. Dennis Daugaard (R)

First elected: 2002
Length of term: 4 years
Term expires: 1/07
Salary: $13,404
Phone: (605) 773-3661

STATE LEGISLATURE

Legislature: 40 days in odd-numbered years starting in January; 35 days in even-numbered years, starting in January

House: 70 members, 2-year terms
2005 breakdown: 51R, 19D; 56 men, 14 women
Salary: $12,000/2-year-term; $110/day in session
Phone: (605) 773-3851

Senate: 35 members, 2-year terms
2005 breakdown: 25R, 10D; 32 men, 3 women
Salary: $12,000/2-year-term; $110/day in session
Phone: (605) 773-3821

STATE TERM LIMITS

Governor: 2 consecutive terms
House: 4 consecutive terms
Senate: 2 consecutive terms

URBAN STATISTICS

CITY	POPULATION
Sioux Falls	123,975
Rapid City	59,607
Aberdeen	24,658

REGISTERED VOTERS

Republican	48%
Democrat	39%
Others	13%

POPULATION

2004 population (est.)	770,883
2000 population	754,844
1990 population	696,004
Percent change (1990-2000)	+8.5%
Rank among states (2004)	46

Median age	35.6
Born in state	68.1%
Foreign born	1.8%
Violent crime rate	167/100,000
Poverty level	13.2%
Federal workers	10,803
Military	8,489

REDISTRICTING

South Dakota retained its one House seat in reapportionment.

MISCELLANEOUS

Web: www.state.sd.us
Capital: Pierre
STATE ELECTION OFFICIAL
(605) 773-3537
DEMOCRATIC HEADQUARTERS
(605) 224-1750
REPUBLICAN HEADQUARTERS
(605) 224-7347

District Statistics

DIST.	2004 VOTE FOR PRESIDENT BUSH	KERRY	WHITE	BLACK	ASIAN	HISP	MEDIAN INCOME	WHITE COLLAR	BLUE COLLAR	SERVICE INDUSTRY	OVER 64	UNDER 18	COLLEGE EDUCATION	RURAL	SQ. MILES
AL	60%	38%	88%	1%	1%	1%	$35,282	59%	25%	16%	14%	27%	22%	48%	75,885
STATE	60	38	88	1	1	1	$35,282	59	25	16	14	27	22	48	75,885
U.S.	50.7	48.3	69	12	4	13	$41,994	60	25	15	12	26	24	21	3,537,438

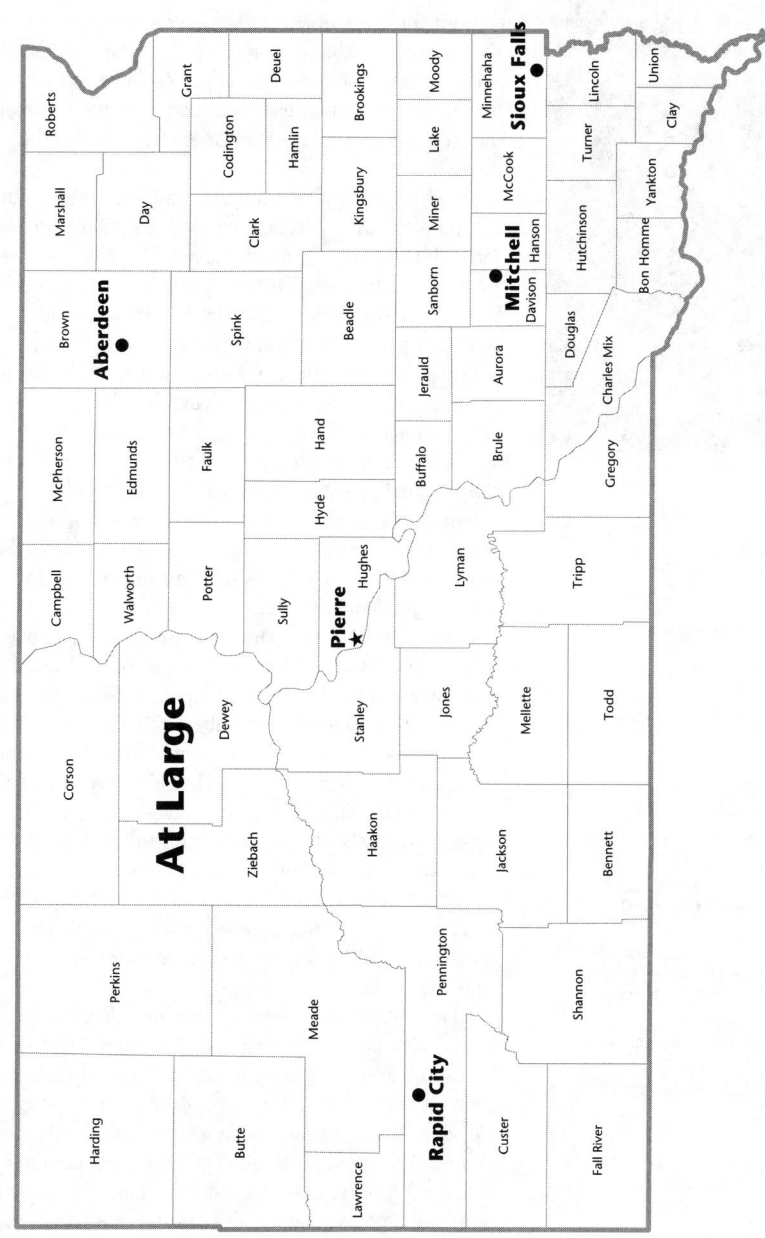

Sen. Tim Johnson (D)

Elected 1996; 2nd term

CAPITOL OFFICE
224-5842
tim@johnson.senate.gov
johnson.senate.gov
136 Hart 20510-4104; fax 228-5765

COMMITTEES
Appropriations
Banking, Housing & Urban Affairs
Budget
Energy & Natural Resources
Indian Affairs
Select Ethics - vice chairman

HOMETOWN
Vermillion

BORN
Dec. 28, 1946, Canton, S.D.

RELIGION
Lutheran

FAMILY
Wife, Barbara Johnson; three children

EDUCATION
U. of South Dakota, B.A. 1969 (political science),
M.A. 1970 (political science), J.D. 1975; Michigan
State U., attended 1970-71 (political science)

CAREER
Lawyer; county prosecutor; state legislative aide

POLITICAL HIGHLIGHTS
S.D. House, 1979-83; S.D. Senate, 1983-87; U.S.
House, 1987-97

ELECTION RESULTS

2002 GENERAL

Tim Johnson (D)	167,481	49.6%
John Thune (R)	166,957	49.5%

2002 PRIMARY

Tim Johnson (D)	65,438	94.8%
Herman Eilers (D)	3,558	5.2%

PREVIOUS WINNING PERCENTAGES
1996 (51%); 1994 House Election (60%); 1992 House
Election (69%); 1990 House Election (68%); 1988
House Election (72%); 1986 House Election (59%)

With the 2004 defeat of Democratic Leader Tom Daschle, in whose shadow he had labored for years, Johnson suddenly finds himself South Dakota's senior senator. But there's no sign the bookish lawyer will change his quiet style or his steady focus on veterans' issues and matters close to the interests of ranchers, Native Americans and other constituencies back home.

Daschle's narrow defeat was a double blow for Johnson — Daschle is a longtime friend and colleague, and the man who beat him, Republican John Thune, had very nearly unseated Johnson himself two years earlier. Johnson, in fact, might have lost his 2002 race if it had not been for Daschle's hard work in his behalf. National Republicans had managed to turn the race into a referendum on Daschle.

While most senators covet media attention, Johnson shuns it. Instead of staging news conferences or delivering floor speeches, he retires to his office and spends hours poring over dense background materials on subjects such as revamping ground rules for the Federal Deposit Insurance Corp. "Good policy is good politics" is his mantra.

Not long after the 2004 election, Johnson without fanfare joined forces with his old nemesis Thune on two issues crucial to the state's agriculture sector — stricter country-of-origin labeling of beef products and greater support for the fledgling ethanol fuel industry.

It was Johnson's son who drew some rare national attention to the senator, in 2003. Staff Sgt. Brooks Johnson of the U.S. Army's 101st Airborne Division was an active participant in the war against Iraq, making his father one of only a handful of members of Congress with children who have fought in the war. Johnson had voted for the resolution giving President Bush authority to go to war, and he said he would do so again. But with his son's life on the line, Johnson was, at least for a time, a powerful voice speaking out against Bush's failure to rally international support to the effort.

He was reluctant, however, to get too personal in talking about his son. Of his fellow lawmakers, Johnson said, "While their sons and daughters may not be at risk, their constituents are. . . . I would be the last one to hold myself out as having any deeper or more profound appreciation of the risks than anyone else."

His private life is no flashier than his political style. He and his wife, Barbara, maintain a modest second home in the Virginia suburbs. Although Johnson has served as an usher at the local Lutheran church for years, many in the congregation do not know he is a senator. "I've seen him introduce himself as someone who works with the government," the Rev. Thomas Prinz told the Argus Leader newspaper in Sioux Falls.

Instead of focusing on making a name for himself, Johnson has concentrated on providing for his constituents and maintaining a normal family life. One of his priorities was making it home in time for supper each night as his kids grew up. He introduced legislation in the 108th Congress to bar telemarketers from calling between 5:30 p.m. and 7:30 p.m. as a way of keeping family dinner hours "sacred."

When Johnson was elected to the House in 1986, his wife gave up her tenured position as a University of South Dakota social work professor to move the family to Washington. She later became a social worker in the Northern Virginia public schools. All three Johnson children went to school in Virginia but returned to South Dakota for college.

Family issues almost stopped Johnson from running for the Senate in the first place. With five terms as a House member under his belt, he had a good shot at unseating 18-year GOP incumbent Larry Pressler in 1996. In the middle of the campaign, however, Johnson's wife learned she had breast cancer. He offered to drop out, but she encouraged him to stay in the race. He won by 8,600 votes, the only person to defeat a sitting senator that year.

As a freshman, Johnson landed seats on three Senate committees important to his state — Agriculture, Banking and Energy and Natural Resources. In 2001, he added the Indian Affairs Committee, and gave up Agriculture for an assignment to one of the most powerful panels, Appropriations. From there, he has directed federal funds to South Dakota projects, particularly those aimed at helping American Indians and veterans. As the 109th began, Democratic leader Harry Reid chose Johnson to succeed him as the top-ranking Democrat on the Ethics Committee.

Johnson has spent his time in Congress tenaciously advocating for his state's farmers and seeking federal funds for local water projects, bridges and roads. Early in 2005, he sponsored a bill to foster wind energy production, a potential alternative income stream for rural landowners.

He was a strong proponent of the 2002 farm bill that gave producers, particularly those in the Midwest, a sturdier federal safety net. He inserted a provision into that bill to require mandatory labels on meat, fruit and vegetables indicating their country of origin, and he has fought ever since to implement it. The labeling is, in part, a marketing tool for U.S. meat producers, important to South Dakota's economy. Meatpackers and food retailers oppose it. But the discovery of imported cattle infected with so-called mad cow disease has given it new life as a health issue.

Although generally content to tend to state concerns, on occasion Johnson has taken a leading role on broader national issues. With FDIC reserves steadily declining and a number of banks failing, he has been pushing legislation to increase insurance coverage for depositors.

Improving veterans' programs is a major goal. Johnson has sponsored legislation to make most Department of Veterans Affairs funding mandatory and to extend more health care benefits to veterans. He also has focused on issues affecting senior citizens, an important constituency in a state with a rapidly aging population. He sponsored legislation in the House that would have penalized companies found to be charging excessive prices for prescription drugs.

A fourth-generation South Dakotan, Johnson became familiar with the legislative process by working as a budget analyst in the Michigan state Senate. After returning to his home state to start a law practice, he ran for the legislature in 1978, serving a total of eight years. He made a bid for Congress in 1986 when Daschle gave up the state's single House seat for a Senate run. After a narrow primary win over a folksy state senator with longstanding farm credentials, Johnson easily took the general election and did not face significant opposition until taking on Pressler in the Senate race.

Republicans from Bush on down went to enormous lengths to try to prevent Johnson from winning a second term in 2002, and Daschle battled to save his friend's career. The state's 760,000 residents were bombarded with millions of dollars in advertising. Total spending in the election came to about $24 million — $70 per vote. In the end, Johnson survived by 524 votes. Thune declined to seek a recount.

Throughout the campaign, Johnson's quiet style was compared to that of the more gregarious, and handsome, Thune. Johnson's son Brendan told the Argus Leader that the race was "a little humbling. . . . No one's ever asked my father to pose shirtless for a calendar." In the end, Johnson's camp believed their candidate's down-home style had been a key to his victory.

KEY VOTES

2004

Yes Pass $318.9 billion, six-year highway and mass transit bill
? Extend assault weapons ban for 10 years
? Restore pay-as-you-go rules for new tax cuts and entitlement spending
No Criminalize harm to a fetus in an attack on the mother
Yes Increase mandatory child care funding to states by $6 billion over five years
No Amend the Constitution to prohibit same-sex marriage
Yes Approve $146 billion multi-year extension of previously enacted middle-class tax breaks
Yes Reorganize U.S. intelligence agencies as proposed by Sept. 11 commission
Yes Cut corporate taxes $137 billion over 10 years

2003

Yes Delay Bush changes to Clean Air Act
No Allow confirmation vote on Miguel A. Estrada to the U.S. Court of Appeals for the D.C. Circuit
Yes Block a Bush proposal opening Alaska's Arctic National Wildlife Refuge to oil drilling
Yes Limit size of Bush's proposed tax cut to $350 billion through fiscal 2013
Yes Overhaul Medicare and create prescription drug benefit
Yes Block Bush rule scaling back overtime pay for some white-collar federal workers
Yes Split $20 billion in Iraq aid into half-grant, half-loan
Yes Ban "partial birth" abortion except to save a woman's life
No Stop proposal allowing travel to Cuba
Yes Allow final vote on energy policy overhaul

CQ VOTE STUDIES

	PARTY UNITY		PRESIDENTIAL SUPPORT	
	Support	Oppose	Support	Oppose
2004	90%	10%	60%	40%
2003	93%	7%	50%	50%
2002	85%	15%	68%	32%
2001	87%	13%	71%	29%
2000	91%	9%	98%	2%
1999	93%	7%	78%	22%
1998	93%	7%	89%	11%
1997	86%	14%	87%	13%
House Service:				
1996	80%	20%	69%	31%
1995	82%	18%	77%	23%

INTEREST GROUPS

	AFL-CIO	ADA	CCUS	ACU
2004	100%	85%	59%	11%
2003	100%	80%	39%	15%
2002	100%	90%	53%	15%
2001	94%	85%	64%	32%
2000	75%	80%	60%	16%
1999	89%	95%	47%	8%
1998	88%	90%	56%	4%
1997	71%	80%	70%	12%
House Service:				
1996	73%	55%	33%	37%
1995	75%	85%	50%	28%

Sen. John Thune (R)

Elected 2004; 1st term

Thune is the clean-cut conservative dragonslayer who ousted Senate Democratic leader Tom Daschle, a feat that earned him the respect of Republican leaders. Having taken Daschle's seat by accusing him of "going Washington," Thune can be expected to spend his first term defending South Dakota's priorities.

A mounted pheasant and native American quilts decorate his Capitol Hill office, constant reminders of what sets his state apart and shapes his portfolio in Congress. The former House member is a passionate advocate for South Dakota's agricultural interests, fighting for free-trade deals that open foreign markets to the state's crops and for energy legislation that encourages the use of farm-based renewable fuels, like ethanol from corn.

Thune (THOON) had hoped for a seat on the Agriculture Committee in his first term, but lost out to more-senior Republicans, including Rick Santorum of Pennsylvania, the influential GOP Conference chairman who is up for re-election in 2006 and has an important agriculture sector in his state.

As compensation, Thune says, the leaders told him he would get on to the committee by the time the next major farm bill is due to be drafted in 2007. And for the present, they gave Thune a coveted seat on the Armed Services Committee, putting him in a prominent role in Congress' oversight of the war in Iraq and other high-profile national security issues. It will also give him influence to defend Ellsworth Air Force Base near Rapid City, which he protected during his House career. Thune has vowed to oppose any efforts by the Pentagon to close Ellsworth, home of the B-1 bomber.

GOP leaders also gave him a spot on the Environment and Public Works Committee, where Thune has a chance to be a player in enacting energy legislation that has long been a priority of President Bush. Spotted by Republican leaders early on for his sharp political instincts, Thune has the potential to be a fresh-faced messenger for his party's agenda. Among his national priorities are revamping the tax code and overhauling Social Security, an issue also atop the president's agenda for the 109th Congress.

Thune considers himself a "right-of-center conservative," and says South Dakota's populist traditions keep leaders there from drifting to the hard right of the political spectrum. But his strong religious faith, which he says guides his actions in Congress, keeps Thune rooted on the right. He favors a constitutional amendment to ban same-sex marriage and opposes embryonic stem cell research, which uses human embryos.

Normally a loyal GOP soldier in favor of cutting taxes, limiting spending, restricting abortion and banning desecration of the flag, Thune is nonetheless willing to buck his party when an issue is important to South Dakota. Tall, lanky, and usually ready with a wide grin, Thune's low-key style masks a determination to protect his state's interests.

In the House, he broke with GOP leaders to support legislation to allow the importation of prescription drugs from Canada, something that enjoys wide support in his state. Thune renewed the push for the legislation soon after he became a senator in 2005.

He put aside his fiscally conservative orthodoxy several times to back spending on programs that benefited South Dakota. Shortly after arriving in the House in 1996, he did battle with his party leaders over a drought-aid package that the state's farmers said they desperately needed. Top Republicans wanted instead to use the measure as a bargaining chip to wrest concessions on other issues from President Clinton.

CAPITOL OFFICE
224-2321
www.thune.senate.gov
383 Russell 20510-4103; fax 224-6603

COMMITTEES
Armed Services
Environment & Public Works
 (Superfund & Waste Management - chairman)
Small Business & Entrepreneurship
Veterans' Affairs

HOMETOWN
Sioux Falls

BORN
Jan. 7, 1961, Pierre, S.D.

RELIGION
Protestant

FAMILY
Wife, Kimberley Thune; two children

EDUCATION
Biola U., B.S. 1983 (business administration); U. of South Dakota, M.B.A. 1984

CAREER
Lobbyist; local governments association executive; U. S. Small Business Administration official; congressional aide

POLITICAL HIGHLIGHTS
S.D. Republican Party executive director, 1989-91; S.D. railroad director, 1991-93; U.S. House, 1997-2003; Republican nominee for U.S. Senate, 2002

ELECTION RESULTS

2004 GENERAL

John Thune (R)	197,848	50.6%
Tom Daschle (D)	193,340	49.4%

2004 PRIMARY

John Thune (R)	unopposed

PREVIOUS WINNING PERCENTAGES
2000 House Election (73%); 1998 House Election (75%); 1996 House Election (58%)

"It was hot," Thune later said of his confrontation with the leadership. "You learn a lot about when to fight, and that you have to pick and choose your battles. I try to be selective and do that when it's something important. You have to try to, not detach, but at least put aside sometimes the emotion and focus on the solution."

A longtime participant in congressional and charity basketball games, Thune cultivates allies after hours in the gym. "It really gets you outside the partisan, highly charged environment of politics," he says. Among his Democratic workout buddies are Rep. Harold E. Ford Jr. of Tennessee, and Rep. Ron Kind of Wisconsin, a fellow early riser with whom Thune shares a love of the Green Bay Packers.

Thune also is an avid pheasant hunter. "There's no place I'm happier than out in a CRP," he says, referring to the federal Conservation Reserve Program, which pays farmers to set aside acreage for wildlife habitat.

The son of a high school teacher and a librarian, Thune stresses support for the small towns and small businesses that dot South Dakota.

He supports federal funding to help sell U.S. farm products overseas and efforts to quickly implement a mandate for country-of-origin labeling for meat, an idea promoted by ranchers who compete with beef imported from Canada. In 2000, Thune voted in the House for permanent normal trade relations with China. But on the campaign trail in 2004, he took a stand against a free-trade deal Congress approved with Australia, citing concerns about tariff reductions on imported beef and wheat.

He sees trade deals opening overseas markets for South Dakota's agricultural producers as a solution to the problem of the shaky farm economy, one that is preferable to increasing federal farm supports. Among the trade-liberalizing measures he favors is ending the policy of withholding food exports to selected nations as part of punitive sanctions.

Thune grew up in the small town of Murdo, about 40 miles south of the capital city of Pierre. He was a star athlete in both high school and college, and his basketball prowess set him on his course to the Senate.

Impressed with Thune's performance in a basketball game during his freshman year in high school, South Dakota Rep. James Abdnor struck up a conversation with the young man, and they stayed in touch over the years. After Thune completed graduate school, he moved to Washington to work for then-Sen. Abdnor, specializing in tax and small-business issues. After Abdnor was defeated for re-election in 1986, Thune followed him to the Small Business Administration, where Abdnor served as administrator.

Later, Thune was deputy staff director of the Senate Small Business Committee. In 1989, he returned to South Dakota, where he served as executive director of the state GOP and then as state railroad director. In 1993, Thune was named executive director of the South Dakota Municipal League, an association of local governments.

Thune considered passing up the run that landed him in the Senate, after a painful, and very close, loss in 2002 to Democratic Sen. Tim Johnson.

"It hurt for a while," Thune told the Argus Leader in Sioux Falls, of his 524-vote defeat. "But then I got up and got going again."

Ironically, it was Johnson who first gave Thune the opportunity to run for Congress, when he left South Dakota's lone House seat open in 1996 to mount a successful challenge to Republican Sen. Larry Pressler.

Thune made a bid for the House seat, convincingly winning the primary over Lt. Gov. Carole Hillard to get the GOP nod. In November, Thune handily defeated Rick Weiland, a longtime Daschle aide, by 21 percentage points and was re-elected by impressive margins in 1998 and 2000. Eight years after trouncing his aide, Thune eked out a victory over Daschle, by just over 1 percentage point, in the most closely watched Senate race of 2004.

CQ VOTE STUDIES

House Service:

	PARTY UNITY		PRESIDENTIAL SUPPORT	
	Support	Oppose	Support	Oppose
2002	83%	17%	82%	18%
2001	92%	8%	81%	19%
2000	91%	9%	29%	71%
1999	91%	9%	22%	78%
1998	95%	5%	23%	77%
1997	95%	5%	27%	73%

INTEREST GROUPS

House Service:

	AFL-CIO	ADA	CCUS	ACU
2002	13%	10%	90%	88%
2001	33%	10%	91%	80%
2000	10%	5%	85%	76%
1999	11%	10%	92%	80%
1998	0%	5%	100%	92%
1997	13%	5%	90%	88%

Rep. Stephanie Herseth (D)

Elected June 2004; 1st full term

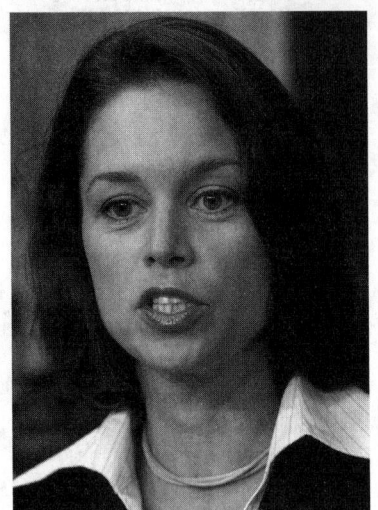

CAPITOL OFFICE
225-2801
stephanie.herseth@mail.house.gov
www.house.gov/herseth
331 Cannon 20515-4101; fax 225-5823

COMMITTEES
Agriculture
Resources
Veterans' Affairs

HOMETOWN
Brookings

BORN
Dec. 3, 1970, Aberdeen, S.D.

RELIGION
Lutheran

FAMILY
Single

EDUCATION
Georgetown U., B.A. 1993 (government), M.A. 1996
(government), J.D. 1996

CAREER
Farm union official; lawyer; professor

POLITICAL HIGHLIGHTS
Democratic nominee for U.S. House, 2002

ELECTION RESULTS

2004 GENERAL

Stephanie Herseth (D)	207,837	53.4%
Larry Diedrich (R)	178,823	45.9%

2004 SPECIAL

Stephanie Herseth (D)	132,420	50.6%
Larry Diedrich (R)	129,415	49.4%

2004 PRIMARY

Stephanie Herseth (D)	unopposed

From a distinguished family of state political figures, Herseth's dual election victories in 2004 were lonely bright moments for the state's Democrats, who suffered the defeat of Senate Minority Leader Tom Daschle in the biggest upset of the year.

Young and single, with telegenic looks, Herseth is an altogether different breed than the typical member of Congress from the region — a middle-aged or older man. She is one of the few women in Congress to represent a sparsely populated, non-urban district. Herseth has pledged to return to the state as frequently as possible, commuting to Washington when the House is in session and keeping her primary residence in Brookings.

"Still being single without children gives me the luxury of doing this commute without too much impact on anybody else," she says. "It's good for me. It makes me a more effective member of Congress. And it's good for me psychologically. It's just good being back home."

One of only 10 House members born in the 1970s, Herseth was 33 when she won her first full term in 2004. She had already served five months in the House, after winning a special election called to fill the seat of GOP Rep. Bill Janklow, who resigned early in 2004 after his conviction for manslaughter arising from a fatal automobile accident.

She became the first woman from South Dakota to win a House seat, though two Republican women briefly served in the Senate — Gladys Pyle, who was appointed (but was never sworn in) after the death of an incumbent in 1938, and Vera C. Bushfield, who was appointed in 1948 to serve out the term of her husband when he died in office.

Herseth's election to a full term in November was one of the Democrats' few accomplishments in an otherwise demoralizing election. Daschle was toppled by Republican John Thune from one of the most powerful jobs in Congress. National Republican organizations and GOP-leaning independent groups had targeted Daschle for defeat. That enabled Democrat Herseth to operate under the radar. She relied on her warm personality, moderate voting record and roots in the state to beat back Republican Larry Diedrich, a former state senator, who came back for a rematch after she beat him in the June special election.

Herseth's political roots in the state run deep. Her grandfather, Ralph E. Herseth, was the Democratic governor from 1959 to 1961. And her grandmother, Lorna B. Herseth, was South Dakota secretary of state from 1973 to 1979. Herseth's father, Lars Herseth, spent 20 years in the legislature and was the unsuccessful gubernatorial nominee in 1986.

Democratic leaders welcomed Herseth in the House with some key committee assignments. Minority Leader Nancy Pelosi of California arranged for Mike Thompson, a fellow Californian, to resign from the Agriculture Committee to open a seat for Herseth. That posting, along with a slot on the Resources Committee, were crucial for a representative of one of the nation's biggest producers of wheat and corn. Her Veterans' Affairs Committee assignment plays to the state's older population.

Like many rural Democrats, Herseth frequently aligns with conservatives on "values" issues. She supports a proposed constitutional amendment to ban same-sex marriage. She is a member of the Blue Dog Coalition, a group of moderate-to-conservative House Democrats. Herseth supported President Bush's decision to wage war in Iraq. But she supports abortion rights and argued for repeal of Bush administration tax cuts that Democrats contend were aimed at the wealthy.

Herseth said that growing up on a South Dakota farm gives her a unique perspective to promote the idea that rural means more than just agriculture — it includes energy policy, housing policy, health care policy and economic development.

Herseth has made meat labeling a primary issue and believes that the border with Canada should remain closed to cattle imports from the north until the United States implements a mandatory country-of-origin labeling system for beef. "The evidence keeps mounting that opening the border presents a real and serious risk to our food supply and cattle producers, and the [USDA] has no reasonable rationale remaining for maintaining its timeline for opening the border," she told the Aberdeen American News.

One of her initial moves in the 109th Congress was to introduce legislation to increase payments to two American Indian trust funds by a combined $226 million. The Tribal Parity Act would add money to the trust funds established nearly 10 years ago for the Crow Creek and Lower Brule Sioux tribes in South Dakota. Interest earned by the funds is paid to the tribes to compensate for land lost to reservoirs created by the Missouri River dams. Americans Indians make up about 8 percent of the state's total population, and their concerns are a high priority for Herseth.

Herseth grew up on her family's farm and ranch near Houghton, in the northeast part of the state. She graduated summa cum laude from Georgetown University in Washington, D.C., with a bachelor's degree in government. She went on to get her law degree from Georgetown, as well.

After law school, Herseth worked on energy and telecommunications issues for the South Dakota Public Utilities Commission in Pierre, organizing meetings with tribal leaders on utility regulation. She was also executive director of the South Dakota Farmers Union Foundation.

Herseth first ran for the House in 2002, but lost. In that contest — for the open seat vacated by Republican John Thune in his unsuccessful Senate bid — she took 46 percent of the vote against Janklow. But the freshman lawmaker's career effectively ended when he killed a motorcyclist in August 2003 by running a stop sign at high speed. Convicted of second-degree manslaughter, Janklow resigned in January 2004.

In a June 1 special election, Herseth won with 51 percent of the vote, a victory of just 3,005 votes out of some 262,000 cast. She made note of the unusual circumstances of her arrival to Congress in a speech on the House floor two days after her victory. "My standing here was born from tragedy," she said, "but from great sorrows come new beginnings."

KEY VOTES

2004

? Approve $146 billion multi-year extension of previously enacted middle-class tax breaks

Yes Amend the Constitution to prohibit same-sex marriage

Yes Cut corporate taxes $137 billion over 10 years

Yes Reorganize U.S. intelligence agencies as proposed by Sept. 11 commission

CQ VOTE STUDIES

	PARTY UNITY		PRESIDENTIAL SUPPORT	
	Support	Oppose	Support	Oppose
2004	76%	24%	45%	55%

INTEREST GROUPS

	AFL-CIO	ADA	CCUS	ACU
2004	63%	55%	50%	31%

SOUTH DAKOTA
At large

Low crop prices wounded eastern South Dakota's agriculture-based economy in the 1990s, adding to a steady migration into cities, where finance, computers and health care gradually have overtaken meatpacking as the primary industries. Citibank, Gateway and others moved into the state during the 1990s to take advantage of low taxes and wages. In the west, away from the more populated areas, the arid, hilly portion of the state relies on ranching, mining and tourism — Mount Rushmore, the Black Hills and the Badlands are located here.

South Dakota has one of the nation's highest percentages of American Indians, at just more than 8 percent of the population. The traditionally poor Indian communities found a bright spot in casinos in the 1990s; all nine of the state's Indian reservations grew in population over the decade. But poverty is still a major problem. Shannon County, home of the Pine Ridge Indian Reservation, is one of the poorest counties in the nation.

South Dakotans often vote Republican on the local level, while

Democrats can be more popular in federal races. But with only three exceptions — 1932, 1936 and 1964 — GOP presidential candidates won the state during the 20th century. The state also has an independent streak, giving Ross Perot 22 percent in 1992 and 10 percent in 1996.

The Missouri River, which splits the state, sometimes is considered a political divide as well — western, ranching Republicans outnumber eastern urban and agricultural Democrats. American Indians, found predominately in the west, traditionally support Democrats, but overall, Republicans have about a 10 percentage point voter registration edge.

MAJOR INDUSTRY
Agriculture, finance, tourism

MILITARY
Ellsworth Air Force Base, 3,550 military, 1,050 civilian (2004)

CITIES
Sioux Falls, 123,975; Rapid City, 59,607; Aberdeen, 24,658; Watertown, 20,237; Brookings, 18,504

NOTABLE
More than 200 Sioux were massacred in one day at Wounded Knee in 1890; The Crazy Horse Memorial, near Custer, is a massive mountain carving begun in 1948 that will not be completed for many years.

Gov. Phil Bredesen (D)

First elected: 2002
Length of term: 4 years
Term expires: 1/07
Salary: $85,000
Phone: (615) 741-2001

Hometown: Nashville
Born: Nov. 21, 1943; Oceanport, N.J.
Religion: Presbyterian
Family: Wife, Andrea Conte; one child
Education: Harvard U., S.B. 1967 (physics)
Career: Health insurance company founder; health care executive; computer programmer
Political highlights: Candidate for Mass. Senate, 1970; candidate for mayor of Nashville, 1987; sought Democratic nomination for U.S. House, 1987; mayor of Nashville, 1991-99

Election results:
2002 GENERAL

Phil Bredesen (D)	837,284	50.6%
Van Hilleary (R)	786,803	47.6%

Lt. Gov. John S. Wilder (D)

First elected: 1971*
Length of term: 2 years
Term expires: 1/07
Salary: $49,500
Phone: (615) 741-2368
*Elected by the Senate

STATE LEGISLATURE

General Assembly: 90 days over 2 years starting in January

House: 99 members, 2-year terms
2005 breakdown: 53D, 46R; 82 men, 17 women
Salary: $16,500; $141/day in session
Phone: (615) 741-2901

Senate: 33 members, 4-year terms
2005 breakdown: 17R, 16D; 27 men, 6 women
Salary: $16,500; $141/day in session
Phone: (615) 741-2730

STATE TERM LIMITS

Governor: 2 terms
House: No
Senate: No

URBAN STATISTICS

CITY	POPULATION
Memphis	650,100
Nashville-Davidson	569,891
Knoxville	173,890
Chattanooga	155,554
Clarksville	103,455

REGISTERED VOTERS

Voters do not register by party.

POPULATION

2004 population (est.)	5,900,962
2000 population	5,689,283
1990 population	4,877,185
Percent change (1990-2000)	+16.7%
Rank among states (2004)	16

Median age	35.9
Born in state	64.7%
Foreign born	2.8%
Violent crime rate	707/100,000
Poverty level	13.5%
Federal workers	50,140
Military	25,585

REDISTRICTING

Tennessee retained its nine House seats in reapportionment. The state legislature drew a new map, which the governor signed on Jan. 17, 2002.

MISCELLANEOUS

Web: www.state.tn.us
Capital: Nashville
STATE ELECTION OFFICIAL
(615) 741-7956
DEMOCRATIC HEADQUARTERS
(615) 327-9779
REPUBLICAN HEADQUARTERS
(615) 269-4260

District Statistics

DIST.	2004 VOTE FOR PRESIDENT BUSH	KERRY	WHITE	BLACK	ASIAN	HISP	MEDIAN INCOME	WHITE COLLAR	BLUE COLLAR	SERVICE INDUSTRY	OVER 64	UNDER 18	COLLEGE EDUCATION	RURAL	SQ. MILES
1	68%	32%	95%	2%	0%	1%	$31,228	50%	35%	15%	15%	22%	15%	45%	4,093
2	65	35	90	6	1	1	$36,796	60	26	14	13	23	23	29	2,427
3	61	38	85	11	1	2	$35,434	54	32	14	14	23	19	36	3,411
4	58	41	93	4	0	2	$31,645	45	42	13	14	24	11	68	10,038
5	47	52	68	23	2	4	$40,419	64	22	14	11	23	28	11	894
6	60	40	89	6	1	3	$39,721	53	35	12	11	25	16	47	5,480
7	68	32	83	11	1	2	$50,090	64	24	12	10	27	29	39	6,292
8	53	46	74	22	0	2	$33,001	48	38	15	13	26	13	53	8,262
9	29	70	35	59	2	3	$33,806	60	24	15	11	27	22	0	321
STATE	57	43	79	16	1	2	$36,360	56	31	14	12	25	20	36	41,217
U.S.	50.7	48.3	69	12	4	13	$41,994	60	25	15	12	26	24	21	3,537,438

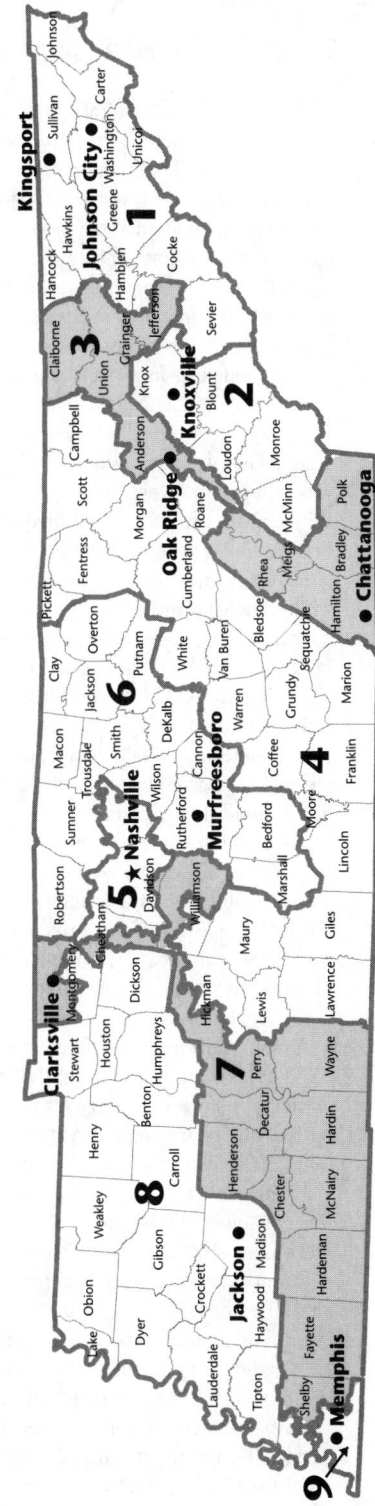

Sen. Bill Frist (R)

Elected 1994; 2nd term

CAPITOL OFFICE
224-3344
frist.senate.gov
509 Hart 20510-4205; fax 228-1264

COMMITTEES
Finance
Health, Education, Labor & Pensions
Rules & Administration

HOMETOWN
Nashville

BORN
Feb. 22, 1952, Nashville, Tenn.

RELIGION
Presbyterian

FAMILY
Wife, Karyn Frist; three children

EDUCATION
Princeton U., A.B. 1974; Harvard U., M.D. 1978

CAREER
Surgeon

POLITICAL HIGHLIGHTS
No previous office

ELECTION RESULTS

2000 GENERAL

Bill Frist (R)	1,255,444	65.1%
Jeff Clark (D)	621,152	32.2%
Tom Burrell (GREEN)	25,815	1.3%

2000 PRIMARY

Bill Frist (R)	unopposed

PREVIOUS WINNING PERCENTAGES
1994 (56%)

With presidential aspirations, Frist has a great deal left to do — and to prove — as a leader. Elevated to majority leader without the usual apprenticeship, he got a lesson in frustration from the closely divided and fractious Senate in his first two years in the job. Time and again, he was foiled by a determined Democratic minority or bedeviled by divisions within his own party between conservatives and a small band of moderates.

His time for turning things around is limited. Frist plans to leave the Senate when his current term runs out at the end of this Congress, keeping a promise he made to Tennessee voters that he would serve just two terms.

The good news for Frist is that he has more votes he can count on in the 109th Congress. The 2004 election increased the number of Republicans in the Senate from 51 to 55. And in early 2005, the balance of opinion among GOP senators and around Washington's conservative think tanks was still in his favor. He also had retained the confidence of the Bush White House, which had lobbied hard to make him leader and to which Frist will be looking for support if he seeks the presidency in 2008.

His challenge is keeping the Senate from devolving into partisan gridlock while satisfying the demands of the party's assertive social and religious conservatives. Those groups would be key to a presidential primary race, but the Senate by nature resists extreme positions by either party.

During the 108th Congress, Democrats employed the filibuster to block a number of controversial judicial appointments. Urged on by conservatives, Frist countered in 2005 by pushing for an unprecedented change in Senate rules that would prevent the use of the filibuster to hold up confirmation of judicial nominees.

Frist won praise from conservative groups in 2005 for getting involved in the case of Terri Schiavo, a severely brain-damaged Florida woman, whose feeding tube was removed. After reading court affidavits and viewing a videotape of Schiavo, Frist questioned the opinion of doctors who had said the woman's case was hopeless, a move that earned him the derision of some physicians. Schiavo ultimately died despite Congress' intervention in the legal process.

A transplant surgeon before turning to politics, Frist has a well-deserved reputation as an overachiever. He was the Senate GOP's chief campaign strategist before becoming majority leader, winning the gratitude of his party by helping Republicans retake the Senate in the 2002 midterm elections. He is also an author, a licensed pilot and a marathon runner.

Brainy and likable, with a doctor's calm, confident air, he quickly became the consensus choice to replace Mississippi's Trent Lott as leader in December 2002 after Lott kicked off a firestorm by praising the pro-segregation 1948 presidential campaign of Sen. Strom Thurmond. Frist was viewed as the kind of leader unlikely to make such a mistake. His laid-back charm and medical expertise were a bonus for a party trying to win the public's confidence on health care, an issue dominated by the Democrats.

But the relatively junior senator from Tennessee also was perhaps the least experienced majority leader in history, and he stumbled at first. In April 2003, he announced a deal with two Republican senators to cap President Bush's tax cut after apparently promising to work with House GOP leaders for a larger tax cut. House Republicans were furious with him, and the misstep nearly killed the legislation. Some of them grumbled that a more adept leader would have closed the deal.

Frist patched up his relations with House Republicans and cultivated a close working relationship with Speaker J. Dennis Hastert. He also won over many conservatives, who had worried that he would be too moderate and too willing to compromise with Democrats. They soon said they trusted him to be a forceful advocate for their positions on judicial nominees, taxes and social policy.

Frist's style as leader is more open and looser-reined than that of many of his predecessors. He calls himself a "leader-manager," and he views himself as a facilitator, aiming to forge consensus among Senate Republicans and to avoid mandates. He prefers arguing from facts, not politics. He wants to persuade, not strong-arm. That style wins praise from many of his colleagues, particularly committee chairmen, to whom he gives wide latitude.

He also has had notable successes, particularly on his signature issue — the Medicare drug benefit signed into law at the end of 2003. The new benefit has generated anxiety among senior citizens, and its acceptance by the public has yet to be judged, but Frist played a central role in overcoming divisions within his party and institutional resistance to get it enacted.

Republicans play up Frist's credential as a doctor — with Tom Coburn of Oklahoma, he's one of two physicians in the Senate — and Frist doesn't shy from the role. He frequently uses stories from his career as a surgeon to illustrate points, and he relishes recounting the details of transplant surgeries. In the 108th Congress, Frist loaded the Senate agenda with health care priorities, including an initiative to fight AIDS in Africa and the Caribbean. He had a special interest in that legislation. For years, he has done volunteer medical work in Africa, where he has witnessed the horrors of AIDS.

In 2003, he led the Senate to passage of a ban on a procedure opponents call "partial birth" abortion. He also was a central player in enacting a law designed to improve defenses against bioterrorism. For all of his expertise, however, he rarely deviates from the GOP line on health care issues, even if his arguments are more detailed and sophisticated than others.

He has put his medical skills to practical use numerous times. After a gun battle in 1998 left two Capitol Police officers dead, he rushed to the scene and helped save the life of the assailant, Russell Eugene Weston Jr. He tended to Thurmond when the South Carolina senator, then 98, collapsed on the Senate floor in 2001. And in 1995, he gave constituent service new meaning by administering cardiopulmonary resuscitation to a heart attack victim from Tennessee.

Some Democrats have suggested Frist stay out of health care policy deliberations because his father founded the hospital chain formerly known as Columbia HCA Corp., now called HCA. Frist has put his stock holdings in a blind trust and says recusal on health issues would be a waste of his knowledge and experience.

Before entering politics, Frist founded and ran Vanderbilt University's transplant center and performed the first successful heart-lung transplant in the South. An interest in public policy, which he studied in college, and in public service, which he practiced as a physician, enticed him to seek public office though he did not register to vote until he was 36 years old.

In 1972, while a Princeton undergraduate, he interned for Democratic Rep. Joe Evins of Tennessee. When Frist told Evins that he might want to serve in Congress someday, Evins urged him to do something else for about 20 years before going to Washington. So he went into medicine.

Then in 1994, Frist spent $9.5 million, most of it his own money, to defeat three-term Democratic Sen. Jim Sasser. Portraying himself as a political outsider running against a career politician, Frist won by 14 percentage points. In 2000, he was handily re-elected.

KEY VOTES

2004

Yes Pass $318.9 billion, six-year highway and mass transit bill
No Extend assault weapons ban for 10 years
No Restore pay-as-you-go rules for new tax cuts and entitlement spending
Yes Criminalize harm to a fetus in an attack on the mother
Yes Increase mandatory child care funding to states by $6 billion over five years
Yes Amend the Constitution to prohibit same-sex marriage
Yes Approve $146 billion multi-year extension of previously enacted middle-class tax breaks
Yes Reorganize U.S. intelligence agencies as proposed by Sept. 11 commission
Yes Cut corporate taxes $137 billion over 10 years

2003

No Delay Bush changes to Clean Air Act
Yes Allow confirmation vote on Miguel A. Estrada to the U.S. Court of Appeals for the D.C. Circuit
No Block a Bush proposal opening Alaska's Arctic National Wildlife Refuge to oil drilling
No Limit size of Bush's proposed tax cut to $350 billion through fiscal 2013
Yes Overhaul Medicare and create prescription drug benefit
No Block Bush rule scaling back overtime pay for some white-collar federal workers
No Split $20 billion in Iraq aid into half-grant, half-loan
Yes Ban "partial birth" abortion except to save a woman's life
Yes Stop proposal allowing travel to Cuba
No Allow final vote on energy policy overhaul

CQ VOTE STUDIES

	PARTY UNITY		PRESIDENTIAL SUPPORT	
	Support	Oppose	Support	Oppose
2004	96%	4%	92%	8%
2003	98%	2%	98%	2%
2002	97%	3%	100%	0%
2001	97%	3%	99%	1%
2000	95%	5%	50%	50%
1999	96%	4%	33%	67%
1998	94%	6%	45%	55%
1997	89%	11%	59%	41%
1996	96%	4%	40%	60%
1995	96%	4%	25%	75%

INTEREST GROUPS

	AFL-CIO	ADA	CCUS	ACU
2004	17%	20%	100%	92%
2003	8%	10%	96%	90%
2002	15%	0%	100%	100%
2001	13%	10%	100%	100%
2000	0%	0%	86%	92%
1999	0%	0%	100%	92%
1998	0%	5%	94%	80%
1997	0%	10%	100%	72%
1996	0%	0%	100%	95%
1995	0%	0%	100%	83%

Sen. Lamar Alexander (R)

Elected 2002; 1st term

CAPITOL OFFICE
224-4944
alexander.senate.gov
302 Hart 20510-4204; fax 228-3398

COMMITTEES
Budget
Energy & Natural Resources
 (Energy - chairman)
Foreign Relations
Health, Education, Labor & Pensions
 (Education & Early Childhood Development -
 chairman)
Special Aging

HOMETOWN
Walland

BORN
July 3, 1940, Maryville, Tenn.

RELIGION
Presbyterian

FAMILY
Wife, Honey Alexander; four children

EDUCATION
Vanderbilt U., B.A. 1962 (Latin American history);
New York U., J.D. 1965

CAREER
Education consulting firm chairman; lobbyist;
university president; White House aide; lawyer

POLITICAL HIGHLIGHTS
Republican nominee for governor, 1974; governor,
1979-87; Education secretary, 1991-93; sought
Republican nomination for president, 1996, 2000

ELECTION RESULTS

2002 GENERAL

Lamar Alexander (R)	891,420	54.3%
Bob Clement (D)	728,295	44.3%

2002 PRIMARY

Lamar Alexander (R)	295,052	53.8%
Ed Bryant (R)	233,678	42.6%
Mary Taylor Shelby (R)	5,589	1.0%

It took Alexander little time to apply the depth of experience and knowledge he had accumulated as governor of Tennessee and as a former secretary of education to the policy-making arena of Capitol Hill. The two-time presidential candidate has drawn from his background in both those jobs in distinguishing himself while displaying an independent streak not usually seen among freshmen.

When Senate Republicans made a concerted push in 2003 to keep the Internet free of taxation, Alexander diverged from the party line, angering some of the anti-tax party faithful who thought an Internet tax moratorium would be a slam-dunk issue. Instead, Alexander fell back on his experience as governor in examining whether states and localities should be allowed to tax utilities.

Alexander also expressed concern about whether President Bush's "Clear Skies" clean-air initiative would go far enough in dealing with pollutants, citing his unhappiness with smog in Great Smoky Mountains National Park. And he criticized Bush's decision to impose tariffs on foreign-made steel, saying they made the cost of steel imports higher for companies making auto parts in Tennessee. Bush eventually lifted the tariffs after threats of trade retaliation from Europe and Asia.

"When I announced for the Senate, I said that I'm running to support President Bush and I'm running with an independent attitude," Alexander told the Associated Press in late 2003. "I think I've displayed both in my first year."

To be sure, Alexander has remained in sync with much of Bush's agenda. He joined the president in strongly backing the construction of new nuclear power plants, something that has not been done since before the 1979 mishap at Pennsylvania's Three Mile Island plant. "If we're really serious about clean air, I think we're going to have to build more nuclear plants," he told the Nashville Tennesseean in 2004.

Alexander works on nuclear issues as a member of the Energy and Natural Resources Committee, where he chairs the Energy Subcommittee. He has looked out for the interests of the Tennessee Valley Authority, a power wholesaler, and his state's Oak Ridge National Laboratory, while pushing an agenda that would double the amount of money spent on physical sciences over the next five to six years. He has tried to build support for advanced computing initiatives at Oak Ridge, which has been involved in developing high-end supercomputers.

Having nurtured an interest in international affairs since his time as governor, when he traveled often to Japan, Alexander asked for and received a seat on the Foreign Relations Committee. He also serves on the Budget and Special Aging committees.

But education remains Alexander's main area of expertise. It is unusual for two senators from the same state and the same party to serve on the same committee, but Alexander received special permission upon arriving in Congress to join his home-state Republican colleague and friend Bill Frist on the Health, Education, Labor and Pensions Committee. Alexander chairs the Education and Early Childhood Development Subcommittee.

Alexander — whose education credentials also include a stint as president of the University of Tennessee — wants to improve the teaching of history and civics in schools. In the 108th Congress, he pushed into law a measure to create summer academies for outstanding teachers and students to teach and learn about those subjects. "Here we are, a nation at war," he said. "Our principles are being attacked, and we're not teaching our children what those principles are."

Alexander also has focused on strengthening Head Start, an education and nutrition program that provides services to almost 1 million children annually. He has called for the creation of 200 centers of excellence and governors' councils to identify good teaching practices.

He is likely to play an influential role in the 109th as Congress takes up reauthorization of the Higher Education Act, the primary law regulating federal aid to postsecondary students and schools. He has made it clear that colleges and universities should not be burdened by federal regulations designed to cap tuition increases, something lawmakers worried about escalating college costs have suggested. "It's a bad idea, because what made our system of higher education superior is autonomy and choice," he said in a 2005 speech.

Alexander is also a realist. After the House passed legislation in March 2005 to enable states to turn driver's licenses into national identification cards, he endorsed the concept in a Washington Post op-ed column. "I still detest the idea of a government ID card. . . . But I'm afraid this is one of the ways Sept. 11 has changed our lives," Alexander wrote.

A seventh-generation Tennessean, Alexander was born and raised in the state's mountainous east. He worked his way through Vanderbilt University, where, as a student newspaper editor, he led a campaign to desegregate the school. After graduating with a degree in Latin American history, he earned a law degree at New York University.

His first run for office, at age 34, was an unsuccessful 1974 bid for governor against Democrat Roy Blanton. Four years later, with the help and advice of his mentor and friend, Senate GOP leader Howard H. Baker Jr. of Tennessee, Alexander ran again. This time, he gained national attention by traversing the state on foot — he is a lifelong hiker — in what would become his trademark red-and-black plaid shirt. The voters loved it, electing him with 56 percent of the vote over financier Jake Butcher, whom the Democrats nominated when the scandal-scarred Blanton stepped aside.

During eight years in the governor's mansion, Alexander built a reputation as a pragmatist who lured businesses to Tennessee and pushed a major education package — including a 1-cent sales tax increase — through a Democratic-controlled General Assembly. After a brief break, he spent more than three years as the chief executive of Tennessee's state university system. He joined President George Bush's Cabinet in 1991 after Bush's first education secretary, Lauro F. Cavazos, was dismissed as ineffectual.

Alexander started running for president soon after his Cabinet service ended. But his campaign foundered when — fundraising zeal and plaid shirt aside — he had a hard time coming up with memorable campaign themes. He won only slightly more than 3 percent of the total GOP primary vote in 1996, though he dropped out soon after finishing third behind Bob Dole and Patrick J. Buchanan in the New Hampshire primary. He set his sights on the 2000 nomination but stopped campaigning in the summer of 1999, when George W. Bush had become the clear front-runner.

Two years later, when Fred Thompson announced he was retiring after eight years in the Senate, Republicans immediately looked to Alexander to take his place, viewing him as their best chance of maintaining their political pre-eminence in the state. The Democrats nominated Bob Clement, who had been Nashville's congressman since 1988. With both national parties pumping money into the race, it turned ugly; the candidates dredged up decades-old allegations about each other's business dealings and political history. But Alexander won by 10 percentage points.

KEY VOTES

2004

No	Pass $318.9 billion, six-year highway and mass transit bill
No	Extend assault weapons ban for 10 years
No	Restore pay-as-you-go rules for new tax cuts and entitlement spending
Yes	Criminalize harm to a fetus in an attack on the mother
Yes	Increase mandatory child care funding to states by $6 billion over five years
Yes	Amend the Constitution to prohibit same-sex marriage
Yes	Approve $146 billion multi-year extension of previously enacted middle-class tax breaks
Yes	Reorganize U.S. intelligence agencies as proposed by Sept. 11 commission
Yes	Cut corporate taxes $137 billion over 10 years

2003

No	Delay Bush changes to Clean Air Act
Yes	Allow confirmation vote on Miguel A. Estrada to the U.S. Court of Appeals for the D.C. Circuit
No	Block a Bush proposal opening Alaska's Arctic National Wildlife Refuge to oil drilling
No	Limit size of Bush's proposed tax cut to $350 billion through fiscal 2013
Yes	Overhaul Medicare and create prescription drug benefit
No	Block Bush rule scaling back overtime pay for some white-collar federal workers
No	Split $20 billion in Iraq aid into half-grant, half-loan
Yes	Ban "partial birth" abortion except to save a woman's life
Yes	Stop proposal allowing travel to Cuba
Yes	Allow final vote on energy policy overhaul

CQ VOTE STUDIES

	PARTY UNITY		PRESIDENTIAL SUPPORT	
	Support	Oppose	Support	Oppose
2004	95%	5%	98%	2%
2003	98%	2%	98%	2%

INTEREST GROUPS

	AFL-CIO	ADA	CCUS	ACU
2004	0%	15%	94%	92%
2003	0%	10%	100%	85%

Rep. Bill Jenkins (R)

Elected 1996; 5th term

Watching how quietly Jenkins serves in Congress, it's hard to imagine that he was once a fast-rising young whippersnapper in Tennessee politics — Speaker of the state House at age 32, the first and only Republican elected to that position in the 20th century.

From that perch, he quickly sought to move up, running in 1970 for governor. But he lost in the primary. More than a quarter-century passed before Jenkins, in 1997, came to Congress as a 60-year-old freshman.

To say that Jenkins' style in the House is "low key" would be an understatement. He rarely speaks on the House floor, and a combination of reticence and frugality leads him to refrain from sending his constituents taxpayer-funded newsletters.

He holds one of the nation's most safely Republican district seats, and he knows he can keep it as long as he wants if he votes the GOP line and closely watches out for his constituents' concerns. That he does, assiduously tending the high-quality constituent service operation he inherited from his predecessor, Republican James H. Quillen, who held the seat for 34 years.

But if Jenkins does not seem consumed with pushing himself to center stage, sometimes the legislative action finds him. In the 108th Congress, he moved into the chairmanship of the Agriculture Committee's Specialty Crops and Foreign Agriculture Subcommittee, and there he had a hand in congressional passage of a landmark $10 billion buyout of tobacco farmers.

Jenkins is a tobacco farmer himself, and from his earliest days on Agriculture he worked to guard the interests of the many small-scale farmers in his district for whom tobacco has traditionally been a reliable cash crop. But recent years brought growing dissatisfaction among farmers with the Depression-era federal tobacco program, whose strict growing allotments made it hard for domestic growers to compete with foreign tobacco farmers. In the 108th, Jenkins and a bipartisan group of lawmakers from tobacco districts pushed legislation to abolish the federal quota system and reimburse farmers for their losses.

They said the measure would aid farmers' transition to other crops, or, if they kept raising tobacco, it would unfetter them from a federal support price and thus help them compete with cheaper imports. "It would help prevent an economic train wreck in those areas that have depended on this crop as a mainstay of their economy," Jenkins said.

Some senators insisted the buyout be paired with giving the Food and Drug Administration regulatory authority over tobacco products, a proposal the House GOP leadership strongly opposed. In the final days of the 108th, the tobacco buyout without the FDA provision was attached to a corporate tax overhaul bill by Ways and Means Committee Chairman Bill Thomas of California. In a conference committee with the Senate, House Majority Leader Tom DeLay successfully held out against FDA regulation, and the buyout was approved as part of the corporate tax measure.

Jenkins regularly returns to the U.S. Treasury at least $150,000 of his office's yearly expense allowance, and he explained his vote for the 2001 tax cut by saying the Treasury was generating too much revenue that would have tempted too much spending.

But Jenkins walks a fine line philosophically when it comes to government spending. He told the Knoxville News-Sentinel in 1996, "There are things that every congressional district is entitled to . . . water projects, sewer projects, highway projects that will be needed. I certainly think it is

CAPITOL OFFICE
225-6356
www.house.gov/jenkins
1207 Longworth 20515-4201; fax 225-5714

COMMITTEES
Agriculture
    (Specialty Crops & Foreign Agriculture -
    chairman)
Judiciary

HOMETOWN
Rogersville

BORN
Nov. 29, 1936, Detroit, Mich.

RELIGION
Baptist

FAMILY
Wife, Kathryn Jenkins; four children

EDUCATION
Tennessee Technological U., B.B.A. 1958; U. of
Tennessee, J.D. 1961

MILITARY SERVICE
Army, 1959-60; Army Reserve, 1960-69

CAREER
Lawyer; farmer

POLITICAL HIGHLIGHTS
Tenn. House, 1963-71 (Speaker, 1969-71); sought
Republican nomination for governor, 1970; Tenn.
Environment and Conservation Department
commissioner, 1971; Tennessee Valley Authority
Board of Directors, 1971-78; circuit court judge,
1990-96

ELECTION RESULTS

2004 GENERAL

Bill Jenkins (R)	172,543	73.9%
Graham Leonard (D)	56,361	24.1%
Ralph J. Ball (X)	3,061	1.3%

2004 PRIMARY

Bill Jenkins (R)	32,726	89.7%
David R. Smith II (R)	3,747	10.3%

2002 GENERAL

Bill Jenkins (R)	127,300	98.8%
write-ins	1,586	1.2%

PREVIOUS WINNING PERCENTAGES
2000 (100%); 1998 (69%); 1996 (65%)

legitimate to try to obtain those." When Quillen held the seat, he ambitiously sought federal investment in the 1st — a medical school, veterans hospital, courthouse and local highway bear Quillen's name. And Jenkins' office, in regular, albeit brief, press releases, can point to federal grants secured for highways and other public works projects, cultural programs and tourism promotion in the district. Jonesborough, for instance, got $100,000 to advance its annual National Storytelling Festival.

One Jenkins project in the 108th was signing up more than 300 cosponsors to a bill requiring the U.S. Mint to produce coins celebrating the recovery and restoration of the American bald eagle. Proceeds from sales of the coin would go to the American Eagle Foundation, which maintains a large aviary at the Dollywood amusement park in Pigeon Forge, and is involved in eagle recovery and other conservation efforts. The bill became law.

Four decades ago, Jenkins was a boy wonder in Tennessee politics. Out of law school just one year, he won election to the state House in 1962. Before the decade was out, with the House split 49-49 and at odds over whom to elect as Speaker, Jenkins persuaded an African-American Democrat to switch sides and vote for him in the leadership race, and Jenkins was elected to the top spot.

His tenure in the job was brief. In his 1970 attempt to win the Republican gubernatorial nomination, he ran third in the primary. The man who defeated him in that race and went on to become governor, Winfield Dunn, named Jenkins to head the state Environment and Conservation Department, and President Nixon appointed him in 1971 to the three-member Tennessee Valley Authority board, where he served until 1978.

For the next dozen years, Jenkins focused on the law and his beef cattle and burley tobacco farm in Rogersville. But he stayed involved in GOP circles, and in 1990 he entered the judicial arena with an appointment as a circuit court judge. (He serves on the Judiciary Committee in the House.)

In 1996, Quillen's retirement after 17 terms unleashed pent-up political ambition in northeastern Tennessee. Jenkins noted he was the only farmer among the leading candidates in the 11-person Republican field, and he claimed to be the only "dyed-in-the-wool, card-carrying bona fide hillbilly" in the race. Thanks to his many years of political involvement, Jenkins proved to have friends all across the district. He took 18 percent of the vote, besting conservative state Sen. Jim Holcomb by 331 votes to win the nomination.

That November, Jenkins won the general-election contest with 65 percent, starting a string of easy victories. He had no Democratic opponent in 2000 or 2002 and collected 74 percent to win in 2004.

KEY VOTES

2004

No Extend federal unemployment benefits by 13 weeks
Yes Pass $283.2 billion, six-year federal highway and mass transit bill
Yes Approve $146 billion multi-year extension of previously enacted middle-class tax breaks
Yes Amend the Constitution to prohibit same-sex marriage
Yes Cut corporate taxes $137 billion over 10 years
No Reorganize U.S. intelligence agencies as proposed by Sept. 11 commission

2003

Yes Cut taxes by $330 billion through fiscal 2013
No Block Bush rule scaling back overtime pay for some white-collar federal workers
Yes Do not allow use of search warrants without first notifying subjects
Yes Allow importation of prescription drugs
Yes Create private school voucher program in Washington, D.C.
Yes Ban "partial birth" abortion except to save a woman's life
No Split $18.6 billion in Iraq aid into half-grant, half-loan
Yes Overhaul Medicare and create prescription drug benefit

CQ VOTE STUDIES

	PARTY UNITY		PRESIDENTIAL SUPPORT	
	Support	Oppose	Support	Oppose
2004	95%	5%	81%	19%
2003	96%	4%	89%	11%
2002	97%	3%	86%	14%
2001	96%	4%	91%	9%
2000	94%	6%	22%	78%

INTEREST GROUPS

	AFL-CIO	ADA	CCUS	ACU
2004	14%	0%	95%	91%
2003	7%	10%	89%	84%
2002	0%	0%	95%	100%
2001	8%	5%	87%	96%
2000	0%	0%	80%	91%

TENNESSEE 1
Northeast — Tri-Cities, Morristown

Rolling hills and mountains cover the 1st, which borders Virginia and North Carolina. Thanks to Tennessee Valley Authority power, what were once isolated highland towns and tobacco patches are now scattered small cities with moderate economic growth.

Kingsport, Johnson City and Bristol, known collectively as the Tri-Cities, center their industry on plastics, chemicals and drug manufacturing. East Tennessee State University, a major employer in Johnson City, is a regional medical hub for much of the lower Appalachian region. The Tri-Cities have grown to become the area's economic anchor, while rural areas have lost clout.

Campers, hikers and other visitors seeking the serenity of Great Smoky Mountains National Park must pass through an area jam-packed with large hotels, outlet shopping malls and neon amusement parks. Pigeon Forge and Gatlinburg bring in millions of dollars each year through a booming tourist industry.

In the district's northwest, Hancock and Hawkins counties are severely impoverished. Farmers here raise tobacco, poultry and livestock. There also is zinc and limestone mining, although the coal mining industry's long-ago shutdown has left the area poor.

East Tennessee's strong Republican lean dates to the Civil War, when the region was supportive of the Union. This area has sent a Republican to the House since the 1880 election. Nine of George W. Bush's top 13 Tennessee counties in the 2004 presidential election were wholly or partly in the 1st, and Bush did not take less than 66 percent of the vote in any of the district's dozen counties.

MAJOR INDUSTRY
Manufacturing, tourism, health care

CITIES
Johnson City, 55,469; Kingsport, 44,905; Morristown, 24,965; Bristol, 24,821

NOTABLE
Dollywood, in Pigeon Forge, is country music star Dolly Parton's theme park; Jonesborough is the state's oldest settlement and is home to the National Storytelling Festival; The Star Cars Museum in Gatlinburg has famous cars from movies; Bristol Motor Speedway, which seats 160,000, has become a major attraction, paralleling the rise of NASCAR.

Rep. John J. 'Jimmy' Duncan Jr. (R)

Elected 1988; 9th full term

CAPITOL OFFICE
225-5435
www.house.gov/duncan
2267 Rayburn 20515-4202; fax 225-6440

COMMITTEES
Government Reform
Resources
Transportation & Infrastructure
(Water Resources & Environment - chairman)

HOMETOWN
Knoxville

BORN
July 21, 1947, Lebanon, Tenn.

RELIGION
Presbyterian

FAMILY
Wife, Lynn Duncan; four children

EDUCATION
U. of Tennessee, B.S. 1969 (journalism); George
Washington U., J.D. 1973

MILITARY SERVICE
Tenn. National Guard and Army Reserve, 1970-87

CAREER
Judge; lawyer

POLITICAL HIGHLIGHTS
Knox County Criminal Court judge, 1981-88

ELECTION RESULTS

2004 GENERAL

John J. "Jimmy" Duncan Jr. (R)	215,575	79.1%
John Greene (D)	52,155	19.1%
Charles E. Howard (X)	4,978	1.8%

2004 PRIMARY

John J. "Jimmy" Duncan Jr. (R)	41,362	91.5%
Debbie Jones Howard (R)	3,861	8.5%

2002 GENERAL

John J. "Jimmy" Duncan Jr. (R)	146,887	79.0%
John Greene (D)	37,035	19.9%

PREVIOUS WINNING PERCENTAGES
2000 (89%); 1998 (89%); 1996 (71%); 1994 (90%); 1992 (72%); 1990 (81%); 1988 (56%); 1988 Special Election (56%)

Duncan would be the quintessential rank-and-file Republican — an unassuming, hard-working conservative who likes to concentrate on local issues — except he keeps getting crosswise with President Bush and the House leadership.

Though he takes a quieter approach than some of the GOP firebrands, Duncan was among the first of a group of conservatives to challenge Bush on a range of issues, including Iraq policy, government spending, civil liberties, free-trade agreements and immigration. "As I have said many times, even husbands, wives and best friends cannot agree on everything. But President Bush and I agree on almost everything. Our differences have been very few and generally minor," Duncan told the Chattanooga Times Free Press in 2004.

One of his toughest votes was being one of six House Republicans in October 2002 to vote against giving Bush authority to wage war against Iraq. Duncan said he was not convinced that Iraqi leader Saddam Hussein was an imminent threat. A year later, angry that the administration was not pushing Iraq to pick up a portion of the reconstruction tab, Duncan opposed a funding bill for the war, one of just five House GOP members to do so.

Given votes like those and an overall record of bucking Bush more often than most Republicans — a high of 38 percent of the time in 2002 and a low of 18 percent in 2004 — Duncan was not terribly surprised to be among three senior members of the Resources Committee to be passed over as chairman at the start of the 108th Congress. "I can't just surrender my voting card because it could help me get a chairmanship down the road," Duncan told the Associated Press in December 2003 before casting his vote on the Iraq spending bill.

He is conservative on both fiscal policy and social issues, and he usually votes with the majority of his party. He retains a high regard for the House as an institution, a reflection of the fact that his father, John J. Duncan, held the seat before him. He says he seeks to emulate his father, who was a popular congressman for more than 23 years, by tending to local concerns and eschewing the national spotlight.

Duncan is serious about cutting federal spending. He says the first thing he asks his staff when they discuss a proposal is, "How much does it cost?" He often votes against appropriations bills he regards as bloated. He voted no on the huge catchall spending bill for fiscal 2004, even though it included $10.8 million for projects and programs he sought for his district. And in 1997, he voted to abolish crop insurance subsidies for tobacco, even though it was the largest cash crop grown by East Tennessee farmers.

Despite his fiscal prudence, Duncan is a big booster of federal transportation and infrastructure projects and he is certain to be at the center of efforts to pass a huge highway and mass transit bill in the 109th Congress that is bigger than Bush wants. A similar clash kept the bill bottled up in the 108th Congress. When a report by civil engineers bemoaned the state of the nation's highways, bridges and other public infrastructure in 2003, Duncan said dryly that the federal government ought to spend at least as much on U.S. projects as it does on similar ones in Iraq.

He has carved out an area of influence as chairman of the Transportation Subcommittee on Water Resources and Environment, which has jurisdiction over development of dams, ports, water quality and the locally crucial Tennessee Valley Authority. The Transportation Committee as a whole operates in a bipartisan manner, and Duncan has been known to preside over his subcommittees with the even-handedness of a judge, which he once was.

Duncan previously chaired the Aviation Subcommittee, where he was influential in writing the aviation security law enacted two months after the Sept. 11, 2001, terrorist attacks. Many of its main features were ideas he pushed, including those calling for tighter screening requirements for airports, better equipment to detect explosives and stronger cockpit doors.

Although Duncan voted for the North American Free Trade Agreement in 1993, he says he has become increasingly concerned about domestic job losses to overseas manufacturers. He was one of only 27 Republicans who voted against enacting the 2002 law giving the president fast-track authority to negotiate trade agreements that Congress cannot amend. And Duncan used his clout to persuade the TVA board to end a contract with a company that employed workers from overseas.

From his seat on the Resources panel, Duncan contends that out-of-control preservationists "will absolutely destroy our standard of living. Unfortunately, we cannot turn our entire nation into a giant tourist attraction." But he pays close attention to preserving the wilderness area in his own backyard — the Great Smoky Mountains National Park, the most-visited of the national parks.

Having followed his father into politics, Duncan occasionally wonders what his life would have been like if the senior Duncan had chosen another career. His father was part of a business group that brought minor league baseball to Knoxville in 1956; young Duncan spent five-and-a-half happy seasons as the Smokies bat boy and was the public address announcer during his first year in college. Then his father switched to politics, becoming mayor of Knoxville from 1959 to 1964, and Jimmy Duncan followed in his footsteps.

The younger Duncan took the courtroom route into politics. He served seven years as a criminal court judge in Knox County. The years on the bench helped him build the reputation to be a candidate in his own right when his father, in failing health, announced that the 100th Congress would be his last. (His father died in 1988, shortly after that announcement.)

In his first House campaign, Duncan campaigned primarily as his father's successor, even appearing on the ballot as John J. Duncan though he goes by Jimmy. He won 56 percent of the vote in both the special and general elections that year and has not been seriously challenged since.

KEY VOTES

2004

No Extend federal unemployment benefits by 13 weeks
Yes Pass $283.2 billion, six-year federal highway and mass transit bill
Yes Approve $146 billion multi-year extension of previously enacted middle-class tax breaks
Yes Amend the Constitution to prohibit same-sex marriage
Yes Cut corporate taxes $137 billion over 10 years
No Reorganize U.S. intelligence agencies as proposed by Sept. 11 commission

2003

Yes Cut taxes by $330 billion through fiscal 2013
No Block Bush rule scaling back overtime pay for some white-collar federal workers
Yes Do not allow use of search warrants without first notifying subjects
Yes Allow importation of prescription drugs
Yes Create private school voucher program in Washington, D.C.
Yes Ban "partial birth" abortion except to save a woman's life
Yes Split $18.6 billion in Iraq aid into half-grant, half-loan
Yes Overhaul Medicare and create prescription drug benefit

CQ VOTE STUDIES

	PARTY UNITY		PRESIDENTIAL SUPPORT	
	Support	Oppose	Support	Oppose
2004	92%	8%	82%	18%
2003	89%	11%	76%	24%
2002	91%	9%	62%	38%
2001	91%	9%	76%	24%
2000	89%	11%	12%	88%

INTEREST GROUPS

	AFL-CIO	ADA	CCUS	ACU
2004	20%	5%	90%	88%
2003	13%	15%	83%	80%
2002	11%	5%	75%	92%
2001	25%	10%	70%	92%
2000	10%	15%	71%	84%

TENNESSEE 2

East – Knoxville

Nestled in the valley of the Great Smoky Mountains at the mouth of the Tennessee River, the 2nd envelopes Knoxville and stretches south and west to include several conservative, rural counties.

State and federal jobs in the district are abundant for residents despite their criticisms of big government year after year. The Tennessee Valley Authority is headquartered in Knoxville, and the Pellissippi Parkway enables commuters to quickly travel west of Knoxville to the Oak Ridge National Laboratory, in the 3rd District.

Knoxvillians will tell you their pride and joy is University of Tennessee athletics. Restaurants, hotels and other businesses thrive on the fans that flock to the university's gargantuan football stadium and basketball arenas each year.

Nonetheless, Knoxville has struggled to revitalize its downtown since playing host to the World's Fair in 1982, after which businesses and hotels began to depart. The Women's Basketball Hall of Fame that

opened in 1999 has helped, as have medical facilities that take up the slack from shuttered hospitals outside the city. The rural areas have attracted tourists, while Knoxville itself opened a new convention center in 2002.

Like all of East Tennessee, the mountainous 2nd has a long history of voting Republican, and the district has not sent a Democrat to the House since before the Civil War. The 2nd's only real Democratic pockets are in downtown Knoxville, which includes much of the city's black population. Yet even Knox County, which envelops the city, backed George W. Bush in the 2004 presidential election by 24 percentage points — a margin that Bush exceeded in each of the other five counties in the 2nd.

MAJOR INDUSTRY
Higher education, medical services, tourism, government

CITIES
Knoxville, 173,890; Maryville, 23,120; Farragut, 17,720; Athens, 13,220

NOTABLE
On home football game days, the University of Tennessee's Neyland Stadium becomes the state's fifth-largest city, with more than 104,000 in attendance; A statue in Haley Heritage Square honors "Roots" author Alex Haley, who made his home in Knoxville.

Rep. Zach Wamp (R)

Elected 1994; 6th term

Wamp's sharp edges have softened somewhat since his days as a conservative "Contract With America" rebel. He now accepts political action committee contributions, a practice that was anathema when he entered Congress in the Republican sweep of 1994. He is leaning strongly toward breaking a term limit pledge and running for re-election in 2006. His service on the Appropriations Committee has not erased his zeal for cutting federal spending but has eased it somewhat.

However, Wamp can still muster the old revolutionary spirit. After House Republicans voted in November 2004 to change their ethics rules in a way that could have allowed Majority Leader Tom DeLay to retain his leadership post if indicted in his home state of Texas, Wamp drew the line. He warned that he and a number of other Republicans might break ranks on one of the first votes of the 109th Congress if the leadership brought the proposed change to the floor. DeLay and other GOP leaders backed off. Wamp briefly weighed a challenge to DeLay but decided against it.

Wamp also broke ranks with his party leaders in 2003, when he tried to convert part of President Bush's funding request for Iraq from a grant to a loan. And he turned heads and rankled party leaders in 2002, when he joined Democrats in pushing for an overhaul of campaign finance laws.

More than anything, Wamp views himself as a "spiritual" man. He uses the word often to describe both his personal life and his career. His deep religious beliefs compel him to reach out to and work with all lawmakers regardless of party affiliation and political ideology.

Much of Wamp's energy is devoted to the House Prayer Breakfast, an institution in which several dozen members from both parties meet once a week to sing hymns, discuss their family problems and pray. He co-chaired the group during the 106th Congress and is also a former chairman of the annual National Prayer Breakfast. "It's not about religion. It's about relationships," Wamp says of the House group. "It's the sweet spirit. There's a lot of power in the spiritual realm."

Wamp started down his spiritual path in 1984, when he decided to clean up his life and seek help for drug and alcohol abuse. After that, he immersed himself in community and church activities, drawing inspiration from a comment by the golfer Chi Chi Rodriguez: "Takers eat well, but givers sleep well."

On the other end of the scale — the physical life — Wamp, a self-described "gym rat," is the co-founder, along with Colorado's Mark Udall, of the Congressional Fitness Caucus, which aims to encourage their time-strapped colleagues to make time for fitness activities. He organizes pick-up basketball games in the House gym and off campus.

He also cites his work with the bipartisan Energy Efficiency and Renewable Energy Caucus, which he has co-chaired since 2001, as a highlight of his congressional career.

The friendships and alliances Wamp has fostered will benefit him in the future if he pursues a party leadership position. He cited an interest in winning a leadership post as a reason to bow out of the GOP primary race for the Senate seat Majority Leader Bill Frist of Tennessee will vacate in 2006.

Asked whether his maverick efforts on campaign finance and renewable energy were signs he was wavering in his conservative leanings, Wamp countered that both are "smart things, good investments" and that "neither party has the exclusive on good ideas."

Wamp's interests and voting record generally put him in the heart of the

CAPITOL OFFICE
225-3271
www.house.gov/wamp
1436 Longworth 20515-4203; fax 225-3494

COMMITTEES
Appropriations

HOMETOWN
Chattanooga

BORN
Oct. 28, 1957, Fort Benning, Ga.

RELIGION
Baptist

FAMILY
Wife, Kim Wamp; two children

EDUCATION
U. of North Carolina, attended 1977-78 (industrial relations); U. of Tennessee, attended 1978-79; U. of North Carolina, attended 1979-80 (political science)

CAREER
Real estate broker

POLITICAL HIGHLIGHTS
Republican nominee for U.S. House, 1992

ELECTION RESULTS

2004 GENERAL

Zach Wamp (R)	166,154	64.7%
John Wolfe Jr. (D)	84,295	32.9%
June Griffin (X)	3,018	1.2%

2004 PRIMARY

Zach Wamp (R)	30,183	90.1%
Timothy A. Sevier (R)	3,334	10.0%

2002 GENERAL

Zach Wamp (R)	112,254	64.6%
John Wolfe Jr. (D)	58,824	33.9%

PREVIOUS WINNING PERCENTAGES
2000 (64%); 1998 (66%); 1996 (56%); 1994 (52%)

conservative mainstream. He voted in 2001 to overturn the workplace safety rules instituted by the Clinton administration. He belongs to the House Pro-Life Caucus, which works to thwart abortion rights legislation, and is a reliable vote for tax cuts. He has repeatedly pushed, unsuccessfully, for legislation requiring the labeling of entertainment products, such as video games, that contain violence. He was named vice chairman of a Bipartisan Working Group on Youth Violence in 1999.

Wamp was first elected in 1994, when Republicans gained control of the House for the first time in 40 years. As a signer of the Contract With America, he campaigned on a pledge to cut spending and balance the budget. But in his first term, he continued a Tennessee tradition of fighting GOP efforts to save money by abolishing agencies that are the economic lifeblood of his state — the Tennessee Valley Authority and the Appalachian Regional Commission. At the start of his second term, he became the first Republican from Tennessee since 1910 to sit on the Appropriations Committee.

Wamp describes himself as one of the more fiscally conservative members of Appropriations. But he knows that compromises are needed to advance the annual spending bills. He and others who once styled themselves as GOP "revolutionaries" are "not so dogmatic anymore. Most of us are more pragmatic," Wamp has said. "You can't be a strident ideologue on Appropriations."

Wamp was raised in a Democratic family with deep roots in Southern politics. His great-great-great-grandfather spent 40 years in the Alabama Legislature, and his great-uncle was a leader in the Alabama General Assembly. Both were Democrats. Wamp himself voted for Jimmy Carter in 1976. He entered the GOP fold four years later, concluding that Ronald Reagan offered a "breath of hope and optimism for America" in the depths of the Iran hostage crisis. He was so taken with Reagan's campaign that he drove with several University of North Carolina fraternity brothers from Chapel Hill to Washington, D.C., on election night to celebrate the GOP victory.

Wamp won his first election in high school, as student body president. At 26, he became the youth coordinator for a victorious Chattanooga mayoral candidate. Four years later, he chaired his local GOP organization. Community leaders urged him to run for public office, but he demurred, saying he had "been through too many mud puddles in my life." But when his wife joined in, Wamp, a real estate broker, decided to run. He came within 3,000 votes of unseating Democratic Rep. Marilyn Lloyd in 1992. He tried again in 1994, when Lloyd retired after 10 terms, and won with 52 percent of the vote. He has won his past four re-elections with 64 percent or better.

KEY VOTES

2004

No Extend federal unemployment benefits by 13 weeks

Yes Pass $283.2 billion, six-year federal highway and mass transit bill

Yes Approve $146 billion multi-year extension of previously enacted middle-class tax breaks

Yes Amend the Constitution to prohibit same-sex marriage

Yes Cut corporate taxes $137 billion over 10 years

No Reorganize U.S. intelligence agencies as proposed by Sept. 11 commission

2003

Yes Cut taxes by $330 billion through fiscal 2013

No Block Bush rule scaling back overtime pay for some white-collar federal workers

Yes Do not allow use of search warrants without first notifying subjects

Yes Allow importation of prescription drugs

Yes Create private school voucher program in Washington, D.C.

Yes Ban "partial birth" abortion except to save a woman's life

No Split $18.6 billion in Iraq aid into half-grant, half-loan

No Overhaul Medicare and create prescription drug benefit

CQ VOTE STUDIES

	PARTY UNITY		PRESIDENTIAL SUPPORT	
	Support	Oppose	Support	Oppose
2004	93%	7%	79%	21%
2003	93%	7%	89%	11%
2002	90%	10%	82%	18%
2001	95%	5%	88%	12%
2000	93%	7%	19%	81%

INTEREST GROUPS

	AFL-CIO	ADA	CCUS	ACU
2004	13%	0%	100%	88%
2003	7%	15%	90%	100%
2002	0%	5%	80%	96%
2001	9%	15%	87%	88%
2000	10%	10%	71%	87%

TENNESSEE 3

East — Chattanooga, Oak Ridge

The elongated 3rd spans the height of Tennessee and touches four other states — Kentucky and Virginia in the district's north and Georgia and North Carolina in its south.

The 3rd is dominated by Hamilton County, which is on the Georgia border and is home to the district's largest city, Chattanooga. Once mostly industrial, Chattanooga is attempting to attract high-tech jobs with a "Technology Corridor" similar to Research Triangle Park in North Carolina. The plan encourages collaboration among technology companies in Knoxville (in the neighboring 2nd District), Chattanooga and Oak Ridge, and an extensive highway system makes such commuting practical. A highway linking the Knoxville airport to Oak Ridge — home of nuclear laboratories established during World War II — has boosted growth.

Chattanooga has injected life into its downtown through projects such as the Tennessee Aquarium, the world's largest freshwater aquarium, and new apartments, nightlife and museums. Since the aquarium opened in 1992, the city has attracted hundreds of millions of dollars in investments.

The district's geographic center falls roughly at Oak Ridge, where the national laboratory sprawls over parts of Anderson and Roane Counties. Oak Ridge, once full of scientists and heavily dependent on federal dollars, has diversified as wealth has moved west of Knoxville.

The 3rd was altered in redistricting following the 2000 census to give it a more East Tennessee — and hence Republican — flavor. About half of the district vote comes out of Hamilton County, where George W. Bush took 57 percent of the vote in 2004. The president did even better (65 percent) in the rest of the district, taking 73 percent of the vote in Bradley County, which provides the second-largest supply of votes in the 2nd.

MAJOR INDUSTRY
Nuclear and high-tech research, technology

CITIES
Chattanooga, 155,554; Cleveland, 37,192; Oak Ridge, 27,387

NOTABLE
Popularized by the Glenn Miller song, the Chattanooga Choo-Choo has been restored as a historic landmark; The 1925 Scopes "Monkey" Trial in Dayton (Rhea County) upheld a ruling making it illegal to teach evolution; Bryan College in Dayton was founded to honor William Jennings Bryan, who died in the town five days after winning the Scopes Trial.

Rep. Lincoln Davis (D)

Elected 2002; 2nd term

CAPITOL OFFICE
225-6831
www.house.gov/lincolndavis
410 Cannon 20515-4204; fax 226-5172

COMMITTEES
Agriculture
Science
Transportation & Infrastructure

HOMETOWN
Pall Mall

BORN
Sept. 13, 1943, Pall Mall, Tenn.

RELIGION
Baptist

FAMILY
Wife, Lynda Davis; three children

EDUCATION
Tennessee Technological U., B.S. 1966 (agronomy)

CAREER
Farmer; construction company owner; U.S.
Agriculture Department official

POLITICAL HIGHLIGHTS
Mayor of Byrdstown, 1979-83; Tenn. House, 1981-85; sought Democratic nomination for U.S. House, 1984, 1994; Tenn. Senate, 1997-2003

ELECTION RESULTS

2004 GENERAL

Lincoln Davis (D)	138,459	54.8%
Janice H. Bowling (R)	109,993	43.5%
Ken Martin (X)	4,194	1.7%

2004 PRIMARY

Lincoln Davis (D)	36,462	91.4%
Harvey Howard (D)	3,435	8.6%

2002 GENERAL

Lincoln Davis (D)	95,989	52.1%
Janice H. Bowling (R)	85,680	46.5%

Davis campaigned for Congress in 2002 on the pledge that no candidate would "outgun me, outpray me or outdaddy me." Now in his second term, the blunt, down-to-earth Tennessean has established a socially conservative record that reflects his campaign rhetoric, but also a populist streak that keeps him voting with his Democratic colleagues on economic issues.

One of a shrinking group of white Southern Democrats, Davis says he ran for Congress to give people in his low-income, rural district "a voice of understanding from someone who grew up the same way they did." A farmer who started a construction business before launching his political career, Davis says he dug the water lines for his house himself and identifies with people in his district who still don't have running water. For them, the most immediate needs are economic development — which means federal aid to help build roads to support businesses — and more-personal needs such as health care, he says.

But Davis knows his constituents also hold conservative views on social issues. He was one of 36 Democrats who voted in 2004 for a proposed constitutional amendment to ban same-sex marriage, saying he and most of his constituents "insist that our nation define marriage as a union between a man and a woman." He also voted for the 2003 legislation that banned a procedure opponents call "partial birth" abortion. That was no surprise, since one of the highlights of his career in the state Senate, where he spent six years before being elected to Congress, was his sponsorship of the Tennessee law that banned the procedure at the state level.

Davis is a classic example of the kind of socially conservative, economically progressive Southerner whom the Democrats are trying to win back to their ranks. A devout Baptist who delivered the closing prayer at the National Prayer Breakfast in early 2005, Davis' experiences with the national Democratic Party when he ran for Congress foreshadowed the party's later struggle with "values" issues. "We were told by the [Democratic Congressional Campaign Committee]: 'You're running this election wrong. You're running it on values, and you're going to lose,'" Davis told The New York Times in September 2002. "When I heard that, I just giggled at them." In 2004, he was the only Democratic congressman to win the endorsement of the anti-abortion group Tennessee Right to Life.

Social issues are not the only area where Davis departs from the party line. He is a member of the centrist Blue Dog Coalition because, as he puts it, the group is made up of "deficit hawks and defense hawks." In his first two years in Congress, Davis supported President Bush on 57 percent of the votes where Bush took a stand in advance, the seventh-highest presidential support score among House Democrats. He sided with his party on only 72 percent of the votes that pitted a majority of Democrats against a majority of Republicans — the 12th-lowest party unity score.

Still, Davis votes with Democrats on many high-profile domestic issues. He voted to allow prescription drugs to be imported from Canada, arguing that "it's so unfair for Americans to be paying for research and development" that adds to the costs of the same medications Canadians get for less money. He opposed Republican bills to create a school voucher program in the District of Columbia and give states more control over the Head Start program for poor children.

Davis clearly has no love for the Republican Party, and Democrats have enough confidence in him that they named him a regional whip in 2005. He reserves special scorn for the GOP tax cut and budget policies. He voted against Bush's 2003 tax cut package and called it "political hypocrisy" because the bill kept the cost of the tax cuts down by ending most of them after 2008. "They made a promise to America, but to me, it's a lie," he says. He also accuses Republicans of using the Blue Dogs' 2004 budget proposal against them in the elections, accusing vulnerable Democrats of raising taxes because their budget would not have continued the tax cuts.

But Davis angered some members of his party when he voted for the 2003 Medicare prescription drug benefit bill, written mostly by Republicans. He voted against the original House version, and sponsored a measure instructing the House and Senate negotiators to include a "fallback" provision in the final legislation, which gives seniors a government-run drug plan in case no private plans wanted to serve their area. He struggled with his vote for the final bill.

On balance, though, he decided it contained assistance his constituents could not afford to lose, including drug coverage at reduced rates for 30,000 low-income Medicare beneficiaries in his district and an increase in payments to rural hospitals that "probably kept some of our hospitals open." Davis says he took heat from his Democratic colleagues and some of his own constituents for his vote. But when he explains at town hall meetings what the district gained from the legislation, he says, "they tell me, 'I don't like it, but I understand why you did it.' "

A member of the Transportation and Infrastructure Committee, Davis pushed unsuccessfully to expand the House's $283 billion highway bill to a $375 billion package, purely because of the potential to create jobs. He says every $1 billion of federal transportation spending creates 47,000 jobs, and that his district needs roads to be able to compete for auto manufacturing plants and other businesses. He also sits on the Science and Agriculture committees.

Davis lost Democratic primaries for open House seats in 1984 and 1994 before winning on his third try in 2002. Republican Van Hilleary was leaving the House after four terms to run for governor, and Davis worked with the General Assembly in the redistricting process to increase Democratic strength in the 4th District.

He won the primary with 57 percent of the vote against Fran Marchum, a well-funded opponent running to his left, and then defeated Republican Janice H. Bowling, a former top aide to Hilleary, by 6 percentage points in the general election. In 2004, he won a rematch against Bowling, increasing his margin to 11 percentage points.

KEY VOTES

2004

Yes Extend federal unemployment benefits by 13 weeks

Yes Pass $283.2 billion, six-year federal highway and mass transit bill

Yes Approve $146 billion multi-year extension of previously enacted middle-class tax breaks

Yes Amend the Constitution to prohibit same-sex marriage

Yes Cut corporate taxes $137 billion over 10 years

Yes Reorganize U.S. intelligence agencies as proposed by Sept. 11 commission

2003

No   Cut taxes by $330 billion through fiscal 2013

Yes Block Bush rule scaling back overtime pay for some white-collar federal workers

?   Do not allow use of search warrants without first notifying subjects

Yes Allow importation of prescription drugs

No   Create private school voucher program in Washington, D.C.

Yes Ban "partial birth" abortion except to save a woman's life

Yes Split $18.6 billion in Iraq aid into half-grant, half-loan

Yes Overhaul Medicare and create prescription drug benefit

CQ VOTE STUDIES

	PARTY UNITY		PRESIDENTIAL SUPPORT	
	Support	Oppose	Support	Oppose
2004	68%	32%	59%	41%
2003	74%	26%	56%	44%

INTEREST GROUPS

	AFL-CIO	ADA	CCUS	ACU
2004	67%	60%	86%	56%
2003	79%	75%	70%	61%

TENNESSEE 4
Middle Tennessee — northeast and south

Spanning more than 10,000 square miles and touching Tennessee's borders with Kentucky in the north and Alabama and Georgia in the south, the 4th is the state's most geographically vast district. It is a melting pot of Tennessee's three regions, as plains turn east into rolling hills that merge with the Cumberland Plateau and eventually the Appalachian Mountains.

While the 4th falls in the orbit of Oak Ridge and Chattanooga in the east and Nashville in the west, it is predominately rural. Columbia, with just 33,000 residents, is the 4th's most populous city. The district's median income is well below that of the state, and its constituency has the lowest level of formal education of any Tennessee district.

The 4th includes tobacco farms and light manufacturing in the south. In the west, a major employer is automaker Saturn in Spring Hill (Maury County). The presence of Saturn and the counties' proximity to Nashville are two reasons why residents in Maury and next-door Williamson County (shared with the 7th) have the district's highest median household

incomes. But economic struggles in isolated rural areas such as Morgan County and Grundy County, which has the lowest median income in the district, leave water and electricity service unreliable.

The 4th has an ancestrally Democratic lean and was drawn in post-census redistricting to elect a Democrat, which it did in 2002. But the district's underlying social conservatism — manifested in opposition to abortion and gun control measures — makes the 4th lean Republican in federal contests. George W. Bush won here by 17 percentage points, winning 21 of the 24 counties that are wholly or partly in the district.

MAJOR INDUSTRY
Agriculture, auto parts, manufacturing, tobacco

MILITARY BASES
Arnold Air Force Base, 92 military, 2,621 civilian (2004)

CITIES
Columbia, 33,055; Tullahoma, 17,994

NOTABLE
The Jack Daniel's sour mash whiskey distillery in Lynchburg is located in a dry county (Moore); James K. Polk's home is in Columbia; Cordell Hull Birthplace and Museum in Byrdstown includes memorabilia of the former secretary of state and "Father of the United Nations."

Rep. Jim Cooper (D)

CAPITOL OFFICE
225-4311
cooper.house.gov
1536 Longworth 20515-4205; fax 226-1035

COMMITTEES
Armed Services
Budget

HOMETOWN
Nashville

BORN
June 19, 1954, Nashville, Tenn.

RELIGION
Episcopalian

FAMILY
Wife, Martha Hayes Cooper; three children

EDUCATION
U. of North Carolina, B.A. 1975 (history & economics); Oxford U., B.A., M.A. 1977 (Rhodes scholar); Harvard U., J.D. 1980

CAREER
Investment firm owner; investment bank managing director; lawyer

POLITICAL HIGHLIGHTS
U.S. House, 1983-95; Democratic nominee for U.S. Senate, 1994

ELECTION RESULTS

2004 GENERAL
Jim Cooper (D)	168,970	69.3%
Scott Knapp (R)	74,978	30.7%

2004 PRIMARY
Jim Cooper (D)	unopposed

2002 GENERAL
Jim Cooper (D)	108,903	63.7%
Robert Duvall (R)	56,825	33.3%
John Jay Hooker (I)	3,063	1.8%

PREVIOUS WINNING PERCENTAGES
1992 (66%); 1990 (69%); 1988 (100%); 1986 (100%); 1984 (75%); 1982 (66%)

Elected 2002; 8th term
Also served 1983-95

Returning to Congress in 2003 after an eight-year absence, Cooper found himself in a vastly different world than the one he left. His ability to adapt as a member of the minority speaks to his skill as a savvy, pragmatic moderate.

Cooper developed a reputation as an accomplished dealmaker during his first tour in the House, a dozen years that ended with an unsuccessful Senate campaign in 1994. From his seat on the Energy and Commerce Committee, he was a key player in issues from health care to telecommunications policy to clean air. "I'm not a very ideological person. Practicality is the hallmark," Cooper said upon coming back to Capitol Hill.

But one of the first things he learned upon returning — "older, wiser and balder," he joked — was that ideological polarization was rampant. "Some [Republicans] never met a Democrat they can be nice to," he told The Tennesseean in 2003, recalling a chilly encounter when Budget Committee members took a break during a 14-hour hearing. "A lot of Republicans wouldn't even say hello, and here you are eating pizza right next to them. It really shocked me, because I've never been treated so rudely before."

Another jarring experience for Cooper was finding out his limitations as a Democrat in shaping legislation. With Republican leaders often unwilling to give Democrats a chance to write and amend bills, he lamented in 2004, "We're training a whole generation of congressmen who don't know what it's like to have a real debate, a real discussion, a real hearing, a real vote."

In a 2003 column for The Tennesseean, Cooper recounted his discovery that a GOP bill intended to provide tax relief for National Guard and reserve members in Iraq contained tax breaks for special interests such as bow and arrow manufacturers and foreign gamblers on U.S. horse races. "I did not come to Congress to be blackmailed into supporting bad bills," he wrote. "I quickly stud[ied] up on guerrilla tactics on the floor, using parliamentary procedure." He decided to make a series of adjournment motions — an unpopular tactic on a Thursday afternoon when lawmakers are itching to leave for the weekend — and succeeded in forcing Republicans to pull the bill temporarily. "I didn't make sausage that Thursday," he concluded, "but I stopped some bad sausage from being made."

On the Armed Services Committee, Cooper has regularly joined other Democrats in rebuking the Bush administration for what they consider poor planning to rebuild postwar Iraq. Unhappy with the administration's reluctance to request more money for the effort, he introduced a bill in 2004 that would provide $50 billion in supplemental appropriations to fund military operations in Iraq and Afghanistan. "I'm tired of waiting for the administration," he said. "Why risk a funding interruption? Our troops are in the field, they're at war. . . . It's absurd that the administration will wait to ask for the money until after the election."

Despite his disappointment with the White House on that issue, Cooper does seek to work with Republicans. He has introduced clean-air legislation with Republican Charles Bass of New Hampshire and a measure to reduce decision-making in court-ordered consent decrees with Majority Whip Roy Blunt of Missouri.

In late 2004, Cooper joined Republican Heather A. Wilson of New Mexico in rounding up 128 signatures for a bipartisan letter urging President Bush to "significantly increase" active duty military forces and reduce reliance on the Guard and reserve. The lawmakers asked Bush to add two divisions to the Army, which was downsized from 18 active divisions in 1990 to 10.

Cooper fought Defense Secretary Donald H. Rumsfeld's 2003 proposal to change how the Pentagon's 730,000 civilian employees are hired and earn raises. Calling the secretary's proposals unfair to workers, he tried to roll back the proposed personnel rules in the House version of the defense authorization bill. Cooper told the House in 2003: "Now is your chance, your only chance, to help these people." He added, "65 of them died Sept. 11" when a hijacked plane struck the Pentagon. His amendment was narrowly rejected, 204-224.

In the fall of 2004, Cooper sought to bring the House Armed Services panel's portion of the intelligence overhaul bill in line with the Senate Government Affairs Committee's bipartisan legislation. But his amendment to substitute a slightly modified version of the Senate's legislation failed, 26-33. Cooper irritated some Republicans when he said before the vote that the committee had done "precious little" to respond to the Sept. 11, 2001, terrorist attacks. New Mexico Republican Wilson testily replied: "When this is over, my colleague from Tennessee does owe some of us an apology."

Cooper joined the Blue Dog Coalition of conservative Democrats and in late 2004 was elected its policy co-chairman. On the Budget Committee, he has called for a return to pay-as-you-go rules to rein in the growing budget deficit. The deficit "looks permanent and structural," he said in 2004.

A governor's son educated at Groton, Harvard and Oxford, Cooper previously had no trouble holding a conservative-leaning, mainly rural district that sprawled across Tennessee. He appears just as secure in his new district, which is centered in Nashville and is more reliably Democratic.

During his time away from Washington, Cooper entered the investment banking world and taught business at the Owen Graduate School of Management at Vanderbilt University. He believes every committee in Congress ought to be more knowledgeable on financial issues, noting that even members of Armed Services need to understand the business world in looking at procurement issues.

Despite surgery in June 2002 to remove a tumor from his colon — doctors said the cancer had not spread — Cooper won the August primary with 47 percent of the vote; the runner-up, state Rep. John Arriola, had 24 percent. In the fall, he won with 64 percent against businessman Robert Duvall. Two years later, Cooper had even less trouble, receiving 69 percent against Republican Scott Knapp, a self-employed electrician making his first run for public office.

KEY VOTES

2004

Yes Extend federal unemployment benefits by 13 weeks
Yes Pass $283.2 billion, six-year federal highway and mass transit bill
No Approve $146 billion multi-year extension of previously enacted middle-class tax breaks
Yes Amend the Constitution to prohibit same-sex marriage
Yes Cut corporate taxes $137 billion over 10 years
Yes Reorganize U.S. intelligence agencies as proposed by Sept. 11 commission

2003

No Cut taxes by $330 billion through fiscal 2013
Yes Block Bush rule scaling back overtime pay for some white-collar federal workers
Yes Do not allow use of search warrants without first notifying subjects
Yes Allow importation of prescription drugs
No Create private school voucher program in Washington, D.C.
Yes Ban "partial birth" abortion except to save a woman's life
Yes Split $18.6 billion in Iraq aid into half-grant, half-loan
No Overhaul Medicare and create prescription drug benefit

CQ VOTE STUDIES

	PARTY UNITY		PRESIDENTIAL SUPPORT	
	Support	Oppose	Support	Oppose
2004	82%	18%	35%	65%
2003	85%	15%	33%	67%
1994	50%	40%	69%	28%
1993	69%	26%	76%	19%
1992	75%	22%	42%	56%

INTEREST GROUPS

	AFL-CIO	ADA	CCUS	ACU
2004	79%	85%	57%	13%
2003	87%	80%	53%	36%
1994	33%	40%	92%	67%
1993	73%	55%	50%	38%
1992	67%	70%	63%	32%

TENNESSEE 5

Nashville

Home to state capital Nashville, the 5th is Tennessee's second-smallest district geographically, but it looms large in economic, political and cultural value.

"Music City" is known for the Grand Ole Opry and homes of country music stars. And while country music is unquestionably Nashville's most famous industry, state government is its top employer. Vanderbilt University and several other schools make the district a hub for higher education in the state. And, as a national health care center, the district hosts several insurance companies and research facilities, including the Vanderbilt University Medical Center.

A population boom in Middle Tennessee has kept businesses in downtown Nashville while settlers flock to the Davidson County suburbs. Two large sports stadiums — home to football's Titans and hockey's Predators — opened downtown in the late-1990s. The 5th takes in 95 percent of the county's residents.

Bargain retail stores and other attractions have drawn tourists and locals to suburban Nashville. The Belle Meade suburb long has been one of the state's wealthiest areas, and the hilly district includes parts of more-rural Wilson and Cheatham counties.

The area's economic boom attracted young, Republican-leaning, upper-class couples to neighborhoods such as Bellevue and the Hermitage. But the city core, home to many government employees, academics and labor unions, is so strongly Democratic that control of the seat is not in doubt. No Republican won Nashville's congressional seat during the 20th century. John Kerry took 56 percent of the Davidson County vote and 52 percent of the vote districtwide in the 2004 presidential election.

MAJOR INDUSTRY

Government, music, higher education, religious publishing, auto manufacturing, health care

CITIES

Nashville-Davidson (pt.), 524,339; Lebanon (pt.), 12,718

NOTABLE

"The Hermitage" was the home of Andrew Jackson; Nashville is home to a life-size reproduction of the Parthenon and to the Country Music Hall of Fame.

Rep. Bart Gordon (D)

CAPITOL OFFICE
225-4231
gordon.house.gov
2304 Rayburn 20515-4206; fax 225-6887

COMMITTEES
Energy & Commerce
Science - ranking member

HOMETOWN
Murfreesboro

BORN
Jan. 24, 1949, Murfreesboro, Tenn.

RELIGION
Methodist

FAMILY
Wife, Leslie Gordon; one child

EDUCATION
Middle Tennessee State U., B.S. 1971; U. of
Tennessee, J.D. 1973

MILITARY SERVICE
Army Reserve, 1971-72

CAREER
Lawyer; state party official

POLITICAL HIGHLIGHTS
Tenn. Democratic Party chairman, 1981-83

ELECTION RESULTS

2004 GENERAL

Bart Gordon (D)	167,448	64.2%
Nick Demas (R)	87,523	33.6%
J. Patrick Lyons (X)	3,869	1.5%

2004 PRIMARY

Bart Gordon (D)	28,524	93.3%
Robert C. Hall (D)	2,066	6.8%

2002 GENERAL

Bart Gordon (D)	117,119	65.9%
Robert L. Garrison (R)	57,397	32.3%
J. Patrick Lyons (I)	3,065	1.7%

PREVIOUS WINNING PERCENTAGES
2000 (62%); 1998 (55%); 1996 (54%); 1994 (51%);
1992 (57%); 1990 (67%); 1988 (76%); 1986 (77%);
1984 (63%)

Elected 1984; 11th term

Gordon is well-known in the House for being the fastest man in Congress when it comes to a road race. He also seems to be running quickly away from his party — he was one of the top 10 Democrats in 2004 to side most often with President Bush.

Gordon annually finishes first among lawmakers in the three-mile Capital Challenge road race (his 2004 victory was his 15th straight win), beating out such fellow athletes as GOP Rep. Jim Ryun of Kansas, the first high school miler to break the four-minute mark. Gordon says he runs three to four times a week to keep ahead of his racing foes.

Tennessee has grown more Republican over the years and Gordon, now in his second decade in the House, has grown more conservative along with it. He supports tax cuts and gun owners' rights, and he takes a hard line on immigration and most social issues. In 2001, he was one of only 28 Democrats to vote for Bush's signature tax cut, and in 2004 he sided with social conservatives in supporting a constitutional ban on same-sex marriage.

Gordon voted in agreement with Bush's position 55 percent of the time in 2004, while siding with a majority of Democrats against a majority of Republicans 72 percent of the time.

The one area where he finds common ground with his own party is in protecting the rights of workers. He has sided with organized labor for an increase in the minimum wage, and in the 108th he opposed Bush administration efforts to change overtime rules for some federal workers. He voted in 2002 to extend union protections to employees in the new Homeland Security Department. Gordon also voted against two trade liberalization measures: the 2002 law that granted permanent normalized trade relations with China and the 2002 legislation that gave the president fast-track authority for trade agreements that Congress must vote on without amending.

A member of the Energy and Commerce Committee, Gordon opposed the Bush administration's 2003 plan to overhaul Medicare to provide a prescription drug benefit for seniors, and he has voted to allow the importation of prescription drugs from other industrialized nations.

In his first decade in the House, Gordon would occasionally take a more liberal stance on social issues. He was an architect of compromises in 1990 and 1991 that ultimately led to the Family and Medical Leave Act, requiring businesses to give workers unpaid time off to be with newborn children or ill family members. But after a close call at the polls in 1994, Gordon became more mindful of his constituents' conservative impulses.

Gordon is the top Democrat on the Science Committee, where he sometimes disagrees with the Bush administration's science priorities. Following the *Columbia* shuttle disaster in 2003, Gordon pressed for an independent probe. He introduced a bill authorizing the president to appoint an independent commission to investigate future shuttle or space station accidents.

In 2004, he voiced concern about Bush's ambitious initiative to send astronauts to the Moon and Mars, saying this should not come at the expense of other space exploration programs. "It will not send a good message to NASA's workforce if the new initiative winds up being paid for by cannibalizing other important NASA activities," Gordon said. Siding with many in the scientific community, he called on the administration to support funding to repair the Hubble Space Telescope.

Gordon scored a legislative win on a bipartisan issue in the 108th, when Congress passed legislation to crack down on unscrupulous sports agents who make false promises or provide gifts to get student athletes to sign representation contracts. Gordon has pursued such a law since 1996, working with Republican Tom Osborne, the former Nebraska football coach. "When you have a child being promised the moon, it's not too hard to understand why we have the problems we do in college sports," Gordon says.

Gordon also won congressional passage of a 2004 bill to authorize grants for youth suicide prevention and intervention programs. His motivation came from a resident of Middle Tennessee who lost his 16-year-old son to suicide. These services "are vital to helping those who are contemplating suicide," Gordon said in a news release. "We must not neglect our children by failing to fund programs that fight this silent killer."

He has a mixed record on environmental issues. After initially siding with environmentalists on increasing funding for farm conservation initiatives, Gordon and other Tennessee Democrats in 2001 voted against shifting $19 billion from crop subsidies to conservation programs, saying it would hurt Tennessee farmers. And he has proposed requiring the Tennessee Valley Authority to consider recreation as its primary goal in the operation of its dams and reservoirs. Yet he has voted against opening up Alaska's Arctic National Wildlife Refuge to oil drilling.

Gordon picked up a lasting taste for congressional politics as a college student, when he went to work in the 1968 congressional campaign of Democratic state Rep. John Bragg, who lost the race. Fresh out of law school, Gordon won a seat on the state Democratic Executive Committee, and in 1979, he parlayed his contacts into a position as the party's executive director. Two years later, he won the party chairmanship, attracting notice with his computerized mailing lists and fundraising efforts.

When Al Gore gave up his House seat in 1984 to run for the Senate, Gordon was ready. He won a six-way primary with 28 percent of the vote. Despite facing the potentially explosive issue of a paternity suit that had been brought against him and later was dismissed, he won all but two counties on Election Day. Gordon generally won re-election by comfortable margins until 1994, the year the Republicans took over Congress; he was held to 51 percent by lawyer Steve Gill, who sought to tie Gordon to President Clinton.

His next three re-election victories were also comparatively close. But the Democratic state legislature helped Gordon substantially in redistricting, adding two Democratic-leaning counties and taking away some heavily GOP territory in suburban Nashville. As a result, he trounced Robert L. Garrison, a libertarian GOP gadfly, by 34 percentage points in 2002. He defeated his Republican opponent in 2004 by a nearly 2-to-1 margin.

KEY VOTES

2004
Yes Extend federal unemployment benefits by 13 weeks
Yes Pass $283.2 billion, six-year federal highway and mass transit bill
Yes Approve $146 billion multi-year extension of previously enacted middle-class tax breaks
Yes Amend the Constitution to prohibit same-sex marriage
Yes Cut corporate taxes $137 billion over 10 years
No Reorganize U.S. intelligence agencies as proposed by Sept. 11 commission

2003
No Cut taxes by $330 billion through fiscal 2013
Yes Block Bush rule scaling back overtime pay for some white-collar federal workers
Yes Do not allow use of search warrants without first notifying subjects
Yes Allow importation of prescription drugs
No Create private school voucher program in Washington, D.C.
Yes Ban "partial birth" abortion except to save a woman's life
Yes Split $18.6 billion in Iraq aid into half-grant, half-loan
No Overhaul Medicare and create prescription drug benefit

CQ VOTE STUDIES

	PARTY UNITY		PRESIDENTIAL SUPPORT	
	Support	Oppose	Support	Oppose
2004	72%	28%	55%	45%
2003	81%	19%	37%	63%
2002	74%	26%	54%	46%
2001	66%	34%	54%	46%
2000	71%	29%	50%	50%

INTEREST GROUPS

	AFL-CIO	ADA	CCUS	ACU
2004	87%	75%	75%	42%
2003	100%	75%	53%	52%
2002	75%	70%	68%	40%
2001	83%	65%	65%	42%
2000	80%	60%	71%	44%

TENNESSEE 6
Middle Tennessee — Murfreesboro

Nashville's population boom has spilled over into much of the 6th District, which forms a crescent shape around Tennessee's capital city clockwise from the north to the south.

The hilly countryside includes two college communities: Murfreesboro, which is home to Middle Tennessee State University and has grown rapidly, and Cookeville, where Tennessee Tech University is located. Rutherford County, which includes Murfreesboro, grew by more than 50 percent in the 1990s, and Wilson County grew by almost one-third.

In the Nashville area's orbit, the economy was strong in the 1990s. A well-developed highway system facilitates commuting from Nashville, in the 5th District, to Murfreesboro. Some residents have government jobs, but employment relies more on automobile parts manufacturers spurred by a sprawling Nissan plant in Smyrna and a Saturn plant in the 4th District. Tobacco farming and book distribution also are big businesses.

The 6th has remained fairly loyal to the Democratic Party since the days

of Andrew Jackson, who built his political career in the area. The district's election of Rep. Gordon, and Al Gore before him, to the House signals a predilection for centrist Democrats, but the 6th tends to lean Republican in the presidential voting. Gore, as vice president in 2000, could parlay his previous tenure and favorite-son status into only a narrow victory against George W. Bush in that year's presidential election. Bush then thrashed John Kerry by 20 percentage points in 2004, taking more than 60 percent of the vote in Rutherford and Sumner counties, which cast the most votes in the 6th. Kerry prevailed in five sparsely populated counties — including Gore's home county of Smith — in the 15-county district.

MAJOR INDUSTRY
Auto and textile manufacturing, book and video distribution, tobacco

CITIES
Murfreesboro, 68,816; Hendersonville, 40,620; Smyrna, 25,569; Cookeville, 23,923; Gallatin, 23,230

NOTABLE
Former secretary of state Cordell Hull practiced law in Celina before beginning his political career; Shelbyville is the heart of Tennessee Walking Horse country.

Rep. Marsha Blackburn (R)

Elected 2002; 2nd term

CAPITOL OFFICE
225-2811
www.house.gov/blackburn
509 Cannon 20515-4207; fax 225-3004

COMMITTEES
Energy & Commerce

HOMETOWN
Brentwood

BORN
June 6, 1952, Laurel, Miss.

RELIGION
Presbyterian

FAMILY
Husband, Chuck Blackburn; two children

EDUCATION
Mississippi State U., B.S. 1973 (home economics)

CAREER
Retail marketing company owner; state economic development official; sales manager

POLITICAL HIGHLIGHTS
Williamson County Republican Party chairwoman, 1989-91; Republican nominee for U.S. House, 1992; Tenn. Senate, 1999-2002

ELECTION RESULTS

2004 GENERAL

Marsha Blackburn (R)		unopposed

2004 PRIMARY

Marsha Blackburn (R)		unopposed

2002 GENERAL

Marsha Blackburn (R)	138,314	70.7%
Tim Barron (D)	51,790	26.5%
Rick Patterson (I)	5,423	2.8%

Telegenic, energetic and enthusiastic about her conservative beliefs, Blackburn is regarded as a rising star among House Republicans.

As a freshman, Blackburn quickly developed a reputation as someone who could influence other Republicans. A member of the GOP's whip team, she also became known for speaking her mind in conference meetings and discussions of rounding up votes. In a 2004 Washingtonian magazine survey in which House aides were polled anonymously, she took third place in the "Best Newcomer" category.

Blackburn said her inclination to make her views known mirrored what she tried to do for three years as a Tennessee state senator. "One of the things I learned while I was in the statehouse is that it's very easy to just keep your mouth shut and vote no," she said in 2003. "But that's not fair to everyone who's involved. It's much more honest to get involved in how the legislation is shaped."

Blackburn was known as a firebrand at the Tennessee statehouse, particularly in her relentless crusade against a state income tax. She was so outspoken on the tax issue that a Memphis newspaper headline asked, "Can Rabble-Rouser Become Team Player?" as she arrived on Capitol Hill. She displays a gold-plated ax, with the words "Ax the Tax," in her House office as a reminder of that crusade.

"Marsha has brought the same drive and leadership she had in Nashville to Washington," Senate Majority Leader Bill Frist, her home-state colleague, told the Memphis Commercial Appeal in 2004.

Blackburn continued her zealous campaign against taxes in the House. She cosponsored legislation to allow residents of states without income tax to deduct state sales taxes when calculating their federal tax liability. The amendment, which she estimated would save the average taxpayer around $470 a year, was added to a jobs creation bill and signed into law by President Bush in 2004. She has promised to address several other tax-related concerns. "We need to make the federal income tax codes flatter, fairer and simpler," she told the Jackson Sun. "We need to continue working on lowering the marginal [tax] rates."

From her seat on the Government Reform Committee in the 108th Congress, Blackburn delved into issues ranging from compensatory and overtime pay to seeking to ferret out "waste, fraud and abuse." And she made known her strong opposition to abortion and her staunch support of gun rights, the war in Iraq and an overall smaller federal government.

"I have come to realize that those who favor big government and want to grow government are always going to be looking for new revenue streams and ways to grow that government," she told The Commercial Appeal in 2004.

Her backing of gun rights was so enthusiastic that in one of her 2002 campaign ads, she cited not just her avid support of the right to bear arms, but her perfect score on a marksmanship test with her Smith & Wesson .38.

Republican leaders rewarded Blackburn at the start of the 109th Congress with a coveted assignment to the Energy and Commerce Committee. She had hoped for a seat on that panel when she arrived in Washington, but instead was given posts on the Education and Workforce and Judiciary committees, in addition to Government Reform.

One business-related issue on which Blackburn may continue working as a member of Energy and Commerce is changing a longstanding federal law that prevents airlines from flying between Dallas' Love Field and most states. The move would benefit Southwest Airlines, which flies more than five times more passengers through Nashville than the next-busiest carrier. Blackburn told the Associated Press that she introduced legislation on the issue in 2004 as a way to get more-affordable airfares between cities, such as Dallas and Nashville, with "a lot of business synergy."

Despite her conservatism, some Democrats see Blackburn as someone they can work with. Democrat Harold E. Ford Jr., whose district adjoins Blackburn's, told the Commercial Appeal he had a "great personal and professional relationship" with her, especially on issues affecting Tennessee.

In early 2005, ending months of speculation, Blackburn announced she would not join Ford and other Tennessee lawmakers in running in 2006 for the Senate seat that will be vacated with the expected departure of Frist, who has said he will not seek another term. Blackburn said she wanted to concentrate on her House work.

She made the announcement a week after she filed papers with the Federal Election Commission to start a new political action committee, called WedgePAC, to support conservative candidates for state and national office. The name reflected her maiden name, Wedgeworth, as well as "wedge issues" such as gay marriage and abortion about which she feels strongly.

Blackburn worked in a series of business and government jobs before coming to Congress. She paid her way through college selling books door-to-door for the Nashville-based Southwestern Company, and worked there after college as well. She said the experience helped develop her confidence. "It allows you to work through a process of self-awareness, to recognize your strengths and weaknesses and learn to work in an area where you can excel," she told the Tennesseean in June 2004. In the mid-1990s, she served a stint as executive director of Tennessee's Film, Entertainment, and Music Commission.

In 2002, Blackburn leveraged the tax issue and her base in the Nashville suburbs to prevail in a crowded primary field after four-term Republican Rep. Ed Bryant left his 7th District seat open for what would prove an unsuccessful Senate bid. The nomination ensured her victory in the Republican stronghold.

Two years later, Democrats declined to field a candidate against Blackburn and she ran unopposed, an acknowledgment of her popularity in the district. The situation did not prevent her from raising more than $800,000, much of it from health care, legal and business services groups.

KEY VOTES

2004

No	Extend federal unemployment benefits by 13 weeks
Yes	Pass $283.2 billion, six-year federal highway and mass transit bill
Yes	Approve $146 billion multi-year extension of previously enacted middle-class tax breaks
Yes	Amend the Constitution to prohibit same-sex marriage
Yes	Cut corporate taxes $137 billion over 10 years
No	Reorganize U.S. intelligence agencies as proposed by Sept. 11 commission

2003

Yes	Cut taxes by $330 billion through fiscal 2013
No	Block Bush rule scaling back overtime pay for some white-collar federal workers
No	Do not allow use of search warrants without first notifying subjects
No	Allow importation of prescription drugs
Yes	Create private school voucher program in Washington, D.C.
Yes	Ban "partial birth" abortion except to save a woman's life
No	Split $18.6 billion in Iraq aid into half-grant, half-loan
Yes	Overhaul Medicare and create prescription drug benefit

CQ VOTE STUDIES

	PARTY UNITY		PRESIDENTIAL SUPPORT	
	Support	Oppose	Support	Oppose
2004	99%	1%	91%	9%
2003	98%	2%	96%	4%

INTEREST GROUPS

	AFL-CIO	ADA	CCUS	ACU
2004	7%	0%	100%	100%
2003	0%	5%	97%	88%

TENNESSEE 7

Eastern Memphis suburbs; southern Nashville suburbs; most of Clarksville

Bordering Kentucky to the north and Mississippi and Alabama to the south, the 7th is Tennessee's most prosperous, best-educated district — a Republican bastion that is dominated by conservative suburbanites near Memphis in the southwest and Nashville in the east.

White flight from Memphis, which is mostly in the 9th District, has driven growth in suburban Shelby County, where about one-third of district voters live. The migration has transformed traditionally Democratic West Tennessee into a GOP-leaning area dominated by small churches. This new strain of activism is strongly anti-tax and socially conservative.

The district's other major population center is Williamson County, which matches Shelby in its Republican leanings. George W. Bush took more than 70 percent of the 2004 vote in Williamson's share of the 7th. Prosperous areas around Nashville that are at least partially in the 7th include Brentwood, Oak Hill and Forest Hills.

The area between Shelby and Williamson is primarily rural and agricultural. Chief crops include corn, tobacco, hogs and cattle. Bush earned robust percentages in most of these counties, with John Kerry winning only in Hardeman and Perry counties.

Northwest of Williamson, the district meanders northward to take in most of Clarksville near the Kentucky border. This area has benefited from diverse manufacturing and the expansion of Fort Campbell, which straddles the Tennessee-Kentucky line. The 7th's portion of Montgomery County gave 60 percent of its vote to Bush in 2004.

MAJOR INDUSTRY
Tobacco, cattle, military, agriculture

MILITARY BASES
Fort Campbell, 26,046 military, 4,111 civilian (2004) (shared with Kentucky's 1st District)

CITIES
Clarksville (pt.), 83,680; Bartlett (pt.), 40,409; Germantown (pt.), 34,200; Franklin (pt.), 33,627; Collierville (pt.), 27,779; Memphis (pt.), 25,359

NOTABLE
Shiloh National Military Park memorializes those who died in one of the bloodiest battles of the Civil War.

Rep. John Tanner (D)

Elected 1988; 9th term

CAPITOL OFFICE
225-4714
www.house.gov/tanner
1226 Longworth 20515-4208; fax 225-1765

COMMITTEES
Ways & Means

HOMETOWN
Union City

BORN
Sept. 22, 1944, Halls, Tenn.

RELIGION
Disciples of Christ

FAMILY
Wife, Betty Ann Tanner; two children

EDUCATION
U. of Tennessee, B.S. 1966 (business), J.D. 1968

MILITARY SERVICE
Navy, 1968-72; Tenn. National Guard, 1974-2000

CAREER
Lawyer; insurance company owner

POLITICAL HIGHLIGHTS
Tenn. House, 1977-89

ELECTION RESULTS

2004 GENERAL

John Tanner (D)	173,623	74.3%
James L. Hart (R)	59,853	25.6%

2004 PRIMARY

John Tanner (D)	unopposed

2002 GENERAL

John Tanner (D)	117,811	70.1%
Mat McClain (R)	45,853	27.3%
James L. Hart (I)	4,288	2.6%

PREVIOUS WINNING PERCENTAGES
2000 (72%); 1998 (100%); 1996 (67%); 1994 (64%);
1992 (84%); 1990 (100%); 1988 (62%)

Tanner is a man whose votes place him squarely in the middle — the middle of the conservative Democratic "Blue Dogs," that is. He is a fiscal conservative of the old school, who is deeply disturbed by the return of federal deficits. He opposes tax cuts, even popular ones, unless they are offset. He sees the ballooning national debt as an internal enemy nearly as dangerous as external threats to the country.

He has expressed particular concern that U.S. debts have grown so large that the nation no longer relies primarily on domestic investors to purchase Treasury securities. "Foreigners are financing our deficit spending, and if you do not think that is dangerous, then you have not studied history," Tanner said in 2004 on the House floor.

Tanner voted against President Bush's $1.35 trillion tax cut in 2001, as well as a $350 billion tax package in 2003. And in 2004, he was on the losing side of a lopsided 339-65 vote for a $146 billion package extending expiring tax breaks for individuals and families.

As a founding member of the Blue Dogs, a coalition of the House's most fiscally conservative Democrats, Tanner says he believes he has a responsibility to constantly remind his colleagues that their priorities go beyond fighting terrorism, and to persuade Congress of its moral responsibility to reduce the national debt. "One of the heartbreaking things about this is that people just do not focus on it and do not understand the magnitude of the problem," he said.

Tanner also has a conservative tilt on many social issues, and as a result he is among the Democrats most likely to cross party lines. He supported Bush 39 percent of the time in 2004, and 44 percent of the time in 2003. But his frequent departures from the Democratic pack have not hurt his standing with party leaders. In fact, Minority Whip Steny H. Hoyer of Maryland added Tanner to his whip team at the start of the 109th Congress.

Tanner was one of 52 Democrats who voted in 2004 for a bill that would have repealed the municipal gun control laws of Washington, D.C. That same year, he was one of only 36 House Democrats who voted for a proposed constitutional amendment to ban same-sex marriage.

Tanner has used his seat on the Ways and Means Committee to try to quietly pull the Democratic Party to the political center — the ground preferred by his rural and small-town constituents. His willingness to work across the aisle has made him a player on a host of bills.

A free-trade advocate, Tanner supported the 2000 law granting China permanent normal trade status. He also voted for the fast-track trade law in 2002, which gave the president expanded powers to negotiate international trade pacts. Tanner was a key player in inserting a provision limiting the fees the Customs Service charges to inspect packages arriving in the United States from overseas. The provision was sought by Memphis-based FedEx Corp. and other express delivery companies.

In the 104th (1995-1996), he worked with moderate Delaware Republican Michael N. Castle to introduce a bipartisan bill overhauling the welfare system. President Clinton endorsed the Tanner-Castle measure, and elements of their bill eventually became part of the landmark law enacted in 1996.

Tanner supports eliminating all taxation of estates, which he considers a threat to family farms. Still, he voted against the 2001 tax cut — even though it includes a provision to roll back and briefly repeal the estate tax — because the cost of the package was too steep. And he was among the first

Democrats to openly talk about whether Congress should reconsider the 2001 tax cuts in light of costs related to the Sept. 11, 2001, terrorist attacks.

The Blue Dogs group, which Tanner helped form in 1994, has become a significant force within the liberal-dominated House Democratic Caucus. Tanner has been a leader in drafting the group's alternative budget proposals, which have served as a basis for compromise between Democrats and the GOP. He called the 1997 balanced-budget deal a "constructive middle ground" that included "significant parts of the Blue Dog budget."

Tanner voted in favor of giving Bush the authority to wage war in Iraq, and in the 2004 anti-war screed "Fahrenheit 9/11," filmmaker Michael Moore included a brief clip featuring Tanner. Moore stopped Tanner and several other lawmakers on the street outside the Capitol to ask them whether they would like to enlist their own kids to go to war in Iraq. Tanner gave Moore a friendly greeting, accepted a military recruitment brochure from him and exchanged a few polite words. He said afterward that he was not pleased with Moore's tactics. "You don't have to agree with the man, but there's no need to be ugly either," Tanner said.

Tanner's father was a farmer who also worked in the family's insurance business. His mother taught school. Tanner attended the University of Tennessee, playing guard on the freshman basketball team and earning bachelor's and law degrees. After four years prosecuting courts-martial in the Navy, Tanner joined a private practice in his hometown of Union City. In 1976, he ran for the state House at the urging of colleagues in the American Legion, where he was a state officer. He also was encouraged by state House Speaker Ned Ray McWherter, a distant relative by marriage.

Tanner served in the General Assembly for 12 years. In 1988, when Democrat Ed Jones, a longtime family friend, retired after nearly two decades in the House, Tanner came out of the blocks fast. He assembled an enviable organization and financial base, boosted by his connections to Jones and McWherter. His relaxed, "good ol' boy" style helped him win over rural and small-town voters. He took 62 percent of the vote against Republican Ed Bryant, a Jackson lawyer, and has rolled to re-election ever since. (Bryant was elected to the House from the neighboring 7th District in 1994.)

After Al Gore was elected vice president in 1992, the Tennessee governor — who happened to be McWherter — needed to appoint an interim replacement to fill Gore's seat in the Senate. The job was said to be Tanner's for the asking, but he told McWherter he preferred to stay on in the House. A decade later, Tanner also quickly killed expectations that he might run for the Senate when Republican Fred Thompson decided to retire.

KEY VOTES

2004

Yes	Extend federal unemployment benefits by 13 weeks
?	Pass $283.2 billion, six-year federal highway and mass transit bill
No	Approve $146 billion multi-year extension of previously enacted middle-class tax breaks
Yes	Amend the Constitution to prohibit same-sex marriage
Yes	Cut corporate taxes $137 billion over 10 years
Yes	Reorganize U.S. intelligence agencies as proposed by Sept. 11 commission

2003

No	Cut taxes by $330 billion through fiscal 2013
Yes	Block Bush rule scaling back overtime pay for some white-collar federal workers
Yes	Do not allow use of search warrants without first notifying subjects
No	Allow importation of prescription drugs
No	Create private school voucher program in Washington, D.C.
Yes	Ban "partial birth" abortion except to save a woman's life
Yes	Split $18.6 billion in Iraq aid into half-grant, half-loan
No	Overhaul Medicare and create prescription drug benefit

CQ VOTE STUDIES

	PARTY UNITY		PRESIDENTIAL SUPPORT	
	Support	Oppose	Support	Oppose
2004	74%	26%	39%	61%
2003	77%	23%	44%	56%
2002	70%	30%	56%	44%
2001	64%	36%	48%	52%
2000	71%	29%	56%	44%

INTEREST GROUPS

	AFL-CIO	ADA	CCUS	ACU
2004	69%	60%	56%	43%
2003	80%	90%	70%	48%
2002	67%	70%	80%	39%
2001	64%	60%	70%	50%
2000	60%	45%	85%	36%

TENNESSEE 8
West — Jackson, parts of Memphis and Clarksville

The mighty Mississippi to the west and the Tennessee and Cumberland rivers to the east frame the rolling hills and flat farmland that make up the 8th. Except for Memphis' northern suburbs and Jackson, the district is predominately rural, Democratic-leaning and working-class.

Democrats — usually conservative-leaning ones — have held this northwest Tennessee district since the Reconstruction era. Redistricting following the 2000 census sliced away some growing Republican parts of Shelby County north of Memphis, augmenting a Democratic lean in the district that is belied by George W. Bush's single-digit victory in the 8th in the 2004 presidential election. Bush won by double-digits in Madison County, which includes Jackson, and Tipton County, which is just north of Shelby County. Large black populations in Shelby, Lake, Lauderdale and Haywood counties helped John Kerry to victories there.

The district is poor, but a few manufacturing plants prevent the economy from slipping further. A Pringles potato chip facility employs more than 1,300 in Jackson, and tire, auto and textile plants are scattered around less-populated areas. Mechanization has decreased factory employment but has increased production on small farms. Chicken-processing plants and cotton farmers also are here, and there are much-needed government jobs via two large state prisons and a downsized, but still significant, naval air station in Millington. Redistricting moved the 8th's eastern border into Clarksville and closer to Nashville.

The northern section of the Tennessee River feeds into Kentucky Lake in the northeast. Tennessee Valley Authority dams and power plants are here, and these waterways also draw many avid hunters and fishermen to the district. Thousands of birdwatchers flock to Reelfoot Lake in the northwest each winter to view the migration of hundreds of bald eagles.

MAJOR INDUSTRY
Manufacturing, agriculture, government

MILITARY BASES
Naval Support Activity Mid-South, 1,800 military, 200 civilian (2004)

CITIES
Jackson, 59,643; Memphis (pt.), 53,080; Clarksville (pt.), 19,775

NOTABLE
A 60-foot tall replica of the Eiffel Tower is in Paris, which also is home to the World's Biggest Fish Fry.

Rep. Harold E. Ford Jr. (D)

Elected 1996; 5th term

CAPITOL OFFICE
225-3265
rep.harold.ford.jr@mail.house.gov
www.house.gov/ford
325 Cannon 20515-4209; fax 225-5663

COMMITTEES
Budget
Financial Services

HOMETOWN
Memphis

BORN
May 11, 1970, Memphis, Tenn.

RELIGION
Baptist

FAMILY
Single

EDUCATION
U. of Pennsylvania, B.A. 1992 (American history);
U. of Michigan, J.D. 1996

CAREER
Law clerk; U.S. Commerce Department aide

POLITICAL HIGHLIGHTS
No previous office

ELECTION RESULTS

2004 GENERAL

Harold E. Ford Jr. (D)	190,648	82.0%
Ruben M. Fort (R)	41,578	17.9%

2004 PRIMARY

Harold E. Ford Jr. (D)	unopposed

2002 GENERAL

Harold E. Ford Jr. (D)	120,904	83.8%
Tony Rush (I)	23,208	16.1%

PREVIOUS WINNING PERCENTAGES
2000 (100%); 1998 (79%); 1996 (61%)

By both circumstance and political temperament, Ford is a man in the middle. He is precisely the kind of Democrat that President Bush will need if he is going to have any kind of bipartisan support for his second-term agenda, especially Social Security reform. Ford is also precisely the kind of moderate the Democrats need if they are going to be more competitive in the South, Southwest and Midwest.

Ford himself may end up being a test case of whether inventive, centrist Democrats can still win statewide below the Mason-Dixon line. The son of a former House member, Ford wants to run for the Senate seat that Republican Majority Leader Bill Frist of Tennessee plans to vacate in 2006.

Ford has made clear he intends to make the direction of the party a theme in any Senate campaign and a dominant part of his work in the 109th Congress. "It is not enough anymore to be against everything," he told supporters in 2004, according to the Chattanooga Times Free Press. "To win, it takes ideas. It takes a vision. We have to do a lot more with that vision thing to win nationally and win statewide."

Ford certainly has ideas. As a member of the New Democrat Coalition, the conservative-to-moderate "Blue Dogs," the House Centrist Coalition, the Faith-Based-Initiative Caucus and the National Service Congressional Caucus, Ford is among a group of busy centrist activists pushing novel ideas they think can draw bipartisan support.

He is especially interested in the notion of asset-building — helping the poor save money, own their own homes and build businesses through a variety of tax breaks and incentives. He and Patrick J. Kennedy, a Rhode Island Democrat, joined with two Republicans, Tom Petri of Wisconsin and Phil English of Pennsylvania, on a bill that would guarantee every child born after Dec. 31, 2005, a $500 savings account. Poor children would be eligible for up to an additional $500. There would be a series of incentives to help build that account through adolescence.

In defending the costs of such programs, Ford says it's time to try something new to address poverty. "We spend $350 billion a year to help keep people poor," he is fond of saying. Ford also is a strong advocate of national service programs, such as AmeriCorps.

While many Democrats are keen on the asset-building concept and national service, Ford also backs ideas most Democrats oppose. He supported giving private school vouchers to students in Washington, D.C. public schools, a conservative-backed idea aimed at getting poor children out of failing public schools. He is also a strong voice for making it easier for faith-based charities to get federal grants, a Bush White House initiative. He supports gun control laws, such as background checks and trigger locks, but opposes broader steps, such as registration of gun owners.

Unlike more-liberal Democrats, Ford is open to creating private accounts within the Social Security system, Bush's top domestic proposal for his second term. But he opposes the president's plan to do so by increasing government borrowing.

While Ford clearly tilts to the left, his voting record is not cut and dried. Between 1999 and 2003, the liberal Americans for Democratic Action gave him scores over five years ranging from 60 percent to 100 percent while the American Conservative Union gave him scores that ran from 4 percent to 40 percent. The Chamber of Commerce gave him relatively solid pro-business ratings, at least for a Democrat, with a low score of 40 percent and a high of 70 percent.

While Ford is still regarded as a potential Democratic star, he carries some scars from a premature and poorly executed challenge to Nancy Pelosi of California for the top Democratic leadership post in the 108th Congress, after Minority Leader Dick Gephardt stepped down. At age 32, Ford had completed three terms in the House, delivered the keynote address at the 2000 Democratic National Convention, been profiled in Newsweek and flirted twice with running for the Senate, most recently in 2002 when Republican Fred Thompson retired. He was a prime candidate to move into the leadership someday, just not as soon as he thought.

He was trounced by Pelosi, 177-29, in a vote among House Democrats. Suddenly, the praise he had been getting as a smart, independent-thinking lawmaker was supplanted by grumbling about his perceived arrogance and impatience. Ford had tagged Pelosi as the candidate of the failed old guard, and sent around videos urging his colleagues to give him a chance. But the rest of his campaign was waged on the airwaves rather than by the traditional lobbying of colleagues one-on-one.

His main difference with Pelosi was that he had voted for the law authorizing the president to wage war against Iraq. That stance alienated him from many rank-and-file Democrats, who thought they had suffered at the polls because their supporters wanted them to fight harder against Bush's Iraq policies, not because they had not been supportive enough. He also misjudged the appeal of Pelosi, a personable liberal who had worked her way up through the ranks and been the party whip, the No. 2 job.

Ford followed his father, Harold E. Ford, into the House after the elder Ford served 22 years. He's been politically active since he was 4, when he made a radio ad for his father's first campaign in which he said: "If you want better housing, better jobs and lower cookie prices, go to the polls and vote for my Daddy for Congress."

Over the years, Ford earned a history degree, worked on President Clinton's first transition team, interned at the Senate Budget Committee under Tennessee Democrat James Sasser and served in the Clinton Commerce Department. After working on his father's 1992 and 1994 House campaigns, Ford launched his own 1996 campaign shortly before his graduation from law school at the University of Michigan. With his father serving as campaign coordinator, he distributed campaign buttons and T-shirts that said, simply, "Jr." Ford rolled to victory in the three-way Democratic primary with 60 percent of the vote. He defeated GOP candidate Rod DeBerry in the general election and has easily won re-election since.

KEY VOTES

2004
Yes Extend federal unemployment benefits by 13 weeks
Yes Pass $283.2 billion, six-year federal highway and mass transit bill
Yes Approve $146 billion multi-year extension of previously enacted middle-class tax breaks
Yes Amend the Constitution to prohibit same-sex marriage
Yes Cut corporate taxes $137 billion over 10 years
Yes Reorganize U.S. intelligence agencies as proposed by Sept. 11 commission

2003
No Cut taxes by $330 billion through fiscal 2013
Yes Block Bush rule scaling back overtime pay for some white-collar federal workers
? Do not allow use of search warrants without first notifying subjects
? Allow importation of prescription drugs
Yes Create private school voucher program in Washington, D.C.
Yes Ban "partial birth" abortion except to save a woman's life
Yes Split $18.6 billion in Iraq aid into half-grant, half-loan
No Overhaul Medicare and create prescription drug benefit

CQ VOTE STUDIES

	PARTY UNITY		PRESIDENTIAL SUPPORT	
	Support	Oppose	Support	Oppose
2004	90%	10%	41%	59%
2003	89%	11%	34%	66%
2002	87%	13%	46%	54%
2001	83%	17%	38%	62%
2000	89%	11%	74%	26%

INTEREST GROUPS

	AFL-CIO	ADA	CCUS	ACU
2004	86%	75%	55%	21%
2003	86%	80%	48%	40%
2002	86%	70%	63%	24%
2001	91%	85%	55%	8%
2000	80%	60%	70%	24%

TENNESSEE 9
Memphis

The 9th includes most of Tennessee's largest city, Memphis, which sits atop the bluffs of the Mississippi River. With approximately 400,000 black residents as of the 2000 census, Memphis is three-fifths African-American and counts more black residents than any Southern city outside of Texas. Many white residents have gravitated northward and eastward over time to populate surrounding suburbs of Shelby County.

The huge black population explains why the 9th is easily the most rock-ribbed Democratic area in Tennessee. Democratic presidential candidates frequently take 70 percent of the vote — as John Kerry did in 2004 — or more. The area first sent an African-American to Congress in 1974, initiating the reign of Democratic black political power in Memphis.

Memphis is a key distribution center. Federal Express is based at the Memphis International Airport, making it the world's busiest cargo airport and a magnet for attracting international companies. The economy also depends on St. Jude Children's Research Hospital, one of the nation's top pediatric care centers. Revitalization efforts have paved the way for inner-city economic development and integrated downtown residences such as Harbourtown and South Bluffs. The National Basketball Association's Grizzlies play at the new FedExForum, which opened in late 2004 and also hosts University of Memphis basketball games.

Tourism also is an economic mainstay here. Millions of music-minded Memphis visitors take in Beale Street, and people flock to the city to honor two American icons — Elvis Presley and Martin Luther King, Jr. The Lorraine Motel, where King was assassinated in 1968, is now a civil rights museum.

MAJOR INDUSTRY
Distribution, health care, government, tourism

CITIES
Memphis (pt.), 571,661

NOTABLE
Graceland was the home of Elvis Presley; W.C. Handy developed the blues musical style on Beale Street; Memphis takes its name from the Egyptian city with ports on the banks of another meandering waterway, the Nile; The Peabody hotel in downtown Memphis has ducks that ride the elevator from the rooftop to the ground floor twice each day.

TEXAS

Gov. Rick Perry (R)

First elected: 2002
(assumed office 2000)
Length of term: 4 years
Term expires: 1/07
Salary: $115,345
Phone: (512) 463-2000

Hometown: Austin
Born: March 4, 1950;
Paint Creek, Texas
Religion: Methodist
Family: Wife, Anita Perry; two children
Education: Texas A&M U., B.S. 1972
(animal science)
Military Service: Air Force, 1972-77
Career: Farmer; rancher
Political highlights: Texas House, 1984-90;
Texas department of Agriculture
commissioner, 1990-98; lieutenant governor,
1999-2000

Election results:
2002 GENERAL

Rick Perry (R)	2,632,541	57.8%
Tony Sanchez (D)	1,819,843	40.0%
Jeff Daiell (LIBERT)	66,717	1.5%

Lt. Gov. David Dewhurst (R)

First elected: 2002
Length of term: 4 years
Term expires: 1/07
Salary: $7,200; $128/day in Senate session
Phone: (512) 463-0001

STATE LEGISLATURE

Legislature: January-May in odd-
numbered years
House: 150 members, 2-year terms
2005 breakdown: 87R, 63D;
118 men, 32 women
Salary: $7,200; $125/day in session
Phone: (512) 463-0845
Senate: 31 members, 4-year terms
2005 breakdown: 21R, 10D; 27 men,
4 women
Salary: $7,200; $125/day in session
Phone: (512) 463-0001

STATE TERM LIMITS

Governor: No
House: No
Senate: No

URBAN STATISTICS

CITY	POPULATION
Houston	1,953,631
Dallas	1,188,580
San Antonio	1,144,646
Austin	656,562
El Paso	563,662

REGISTERED VOTERS

Voters do not register by party.

POPULATION

2004 population (est.)	22,490,022
2000 population	20,851,820
1990 population	16,986,510
Percent change (1990-2000)	+22.8%
Rank among states (2004)	2

Median age	32.3
Born in state	62.2%
Foreign born	13.9%
Violent crime rate	545/100,000
Poverty level	15.4%
Federal workers	173,367
Military	170,659

REDISTRICTING

Texas gained two House seats in
reapportionment. The state legislature
failed to agree on a plan and a three-
judge federal panel implemented a
new, 32-district map on Nov. 14, 2001.
The legislature drew a new map that
the governor signed on Oct. 13, 2003.

MISCELLANEOUS

Web: www.state.tx.us
Capital: Austin
STATE ELECTION OFFICIAL
(512) 463-5650
**DEMOCRATIC
HEADQUARTERS**
(512) 478-9800
**REPUBLICAN
HEADQUARTERS**
(512) 477-9821

District Statistics

DIST.	2004 VOTE FOR PRESIDENT BUSH	KERRY	WHITE	BLACK	ASIAN	HISP	MEDIAN INCOME	WHITE COLLAR	BLUE COLLAR	SERVICE INDUSTRY	OVER 64	UNDER 18	COLLEGE EDUCATION	RURAL	SQ. MILES
1	69%	30%	71%	18%	1%	9%	$33,461	53%	31%	15%	14%	26%	18%	49%	8,508
2	63	36	64	19	3	13	$47,029	63	24	13	10	27	23	11	1,937
3	66	33	63	9	8	17	$60,878	75	15	10	5	29	41	1	265
4	70	29	79	10	1	8	$38,276	56	29	14	13	27	18	50	9,534
5	67	33	72	12	2	13	$41,007	60	27	14	12	27	19	32	5,429
6	66	33	66	13	3	16	$45,857	62	24	13	9	28	24	20	6,198
7	64	35	67	6	7	18	$57,846	79	11	9	9	24	50	0	198
8	72	27	80	9	1	9	$40,459	56	30	15	11	27	18	50	8,150
9	30	70	17	37	11	33	$34,870	58	23	19	6	30	24	0	154
10	61	38	66	9	4	19	$52,465	70	19	11	8	28	35	19	3,803
11	78	22	65	4	1	30	$32,711	55	28	17	15	27	17	29	34,995
12	67	33	67	6	2	24	$41,735	58	28	14	10	28	21	17	2,168
13	77	22	74	6	1	18	$33,501	53	29	18	14	26	17	30	40,197
14	67	33	62	10	2	25	$41,335	56	29	15	11	28	19	29	7,095
15	55	45	27	3	0	69	$28,061	51	30	18	12	32	13	25	10,694

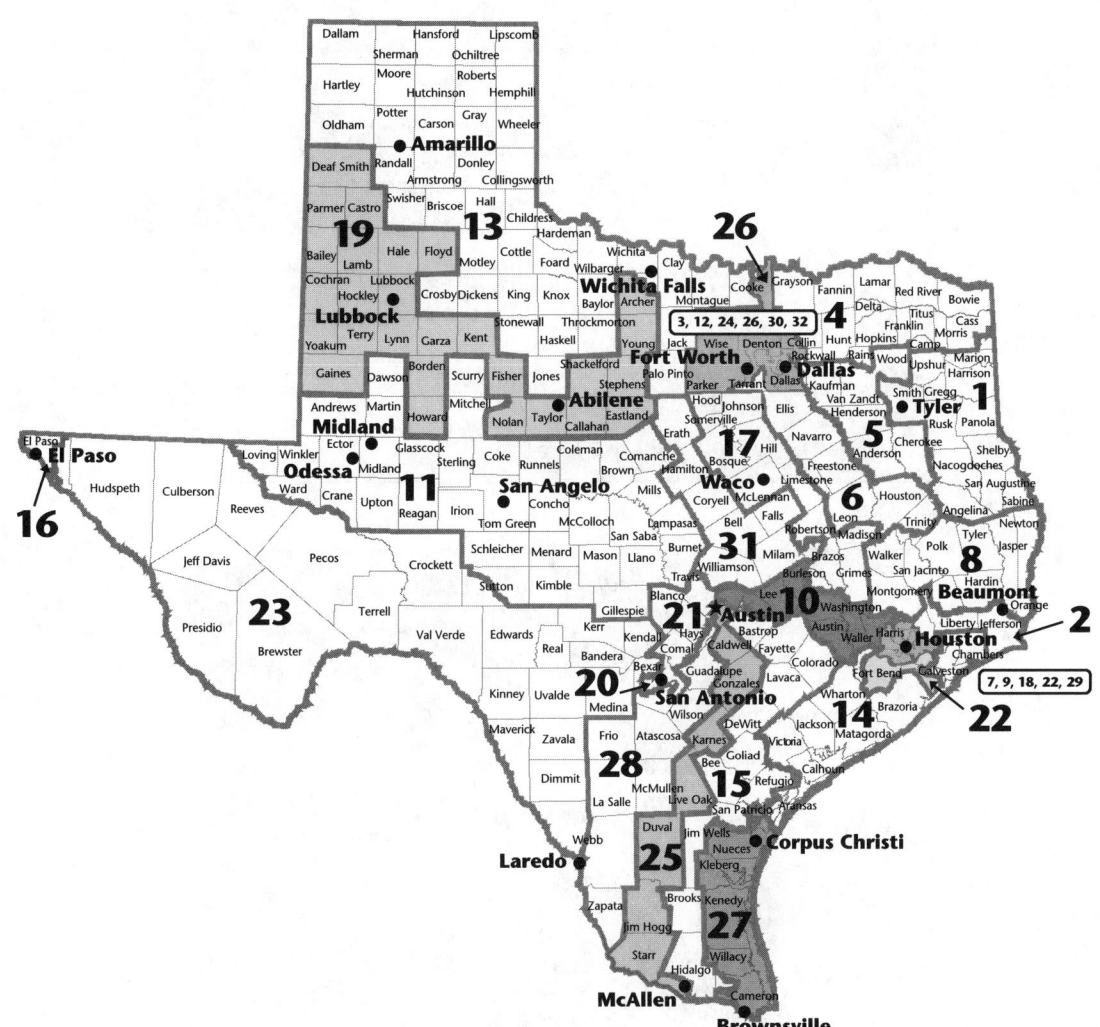

District Statistics

DIST.	2004 VOTE FOR PRESIDENT BUSH	KERRY	WHITE	BLACK	ASIAN	HISP	MEDIAN INCOME	WHITE COLLAR	BLUE COLLAR	SERVICE INDUSTRY	OVER 64	UNDER 18	COLLEGE EDUCATION	RURAL	SQ. MILES
16	43%	56%	17%	3%	1%	78%	$31,245	58%	25%	17%	10%	32%	17%	2%	581
17	69	30	71	10	1	15	$35,253	57	27	16	12	25	20	36	7,691
18	28	72	20	40	3	36	$31,291	52	30	18	8	29	14	0	227
19	77	22	64	5	1	29	$31,575	57	26	17	13	27	19	26	25,268
20	44	55	23	7	1	67	$31,937	57	24	19	10	29	15	0	184
21	60	39	73	4	3	18	$55,609	76	14	11	10	24	43	18	2,582
22	64	35	61	9	8	20	$57,932	69	20	11	7	29	32	5	971
23	64	35	41	2	1	55	$38,081	63	21	15	11	30	26	26	52,621
24	65	35	64	10	6	18	$56,098	73	17	10	6	27	36	1	334
25	37	62	22	7	1	69	$28,348	52	29	19	9	30	15	13	8,015

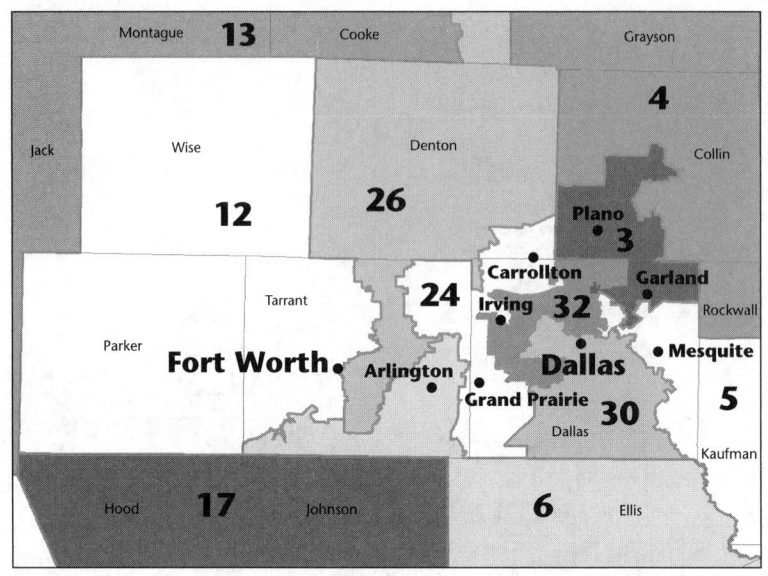

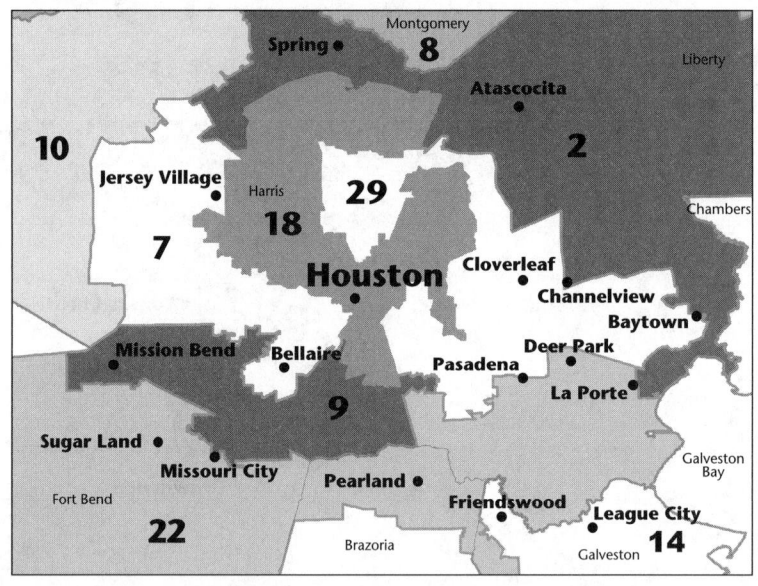

District Statistics

DIST.	2004 VOTE FOR PRESIDENT BUSH	KERRY	WHITE	BLACK	ASIAN	HISP	MEDIAN INCOME	WHITE COLLAR	BLUE COLLAR	SERVICE INDUSTRY	OVER 64	UNDER 18	COLLEGE EDUCATION	RURAL	SQ. MILES
26	64%	35%	66%	15%	2%	14%	$48,714	64%	22%	13%	8%	29%	27%	9%	1,292
27	55	45	28	2	1	68	$31,327	55	26	18	11	31	16	11	4,720
28	52	47	28	6	0	65	$31,355	50	31	19	10	31	11	24	10,139
29	44	55	22	10	1	66	$31,751	40	43	16	7	33	6	1	236
30	25	75	22	41	1	34	$33,505	52	31	17	8	30	16	1	317
31	66	33	66	13	2	16	$43,381	63	23	14	9	29	24	22	7,134
32	59	40	50	8	4	36	$45,725	66	21	13	9	25	36	0	160
STATE	61	38	52	11	3	32	$39,927	61	25	15	10	28	23	17	261,797
U.S.	50.7	48.3	69	12	4	13	$41,994	60	25	15	12	26	24	21	3,537,438

Sen. Kay Bailey Hutchison (R)

Elected June 1993; 2nd full term

CAPITOL OFFICE
224-5922
hutchison.senate.gov
284 Russell 20510-4304; fax 224-0776

COMMITTEES
Appropriations
(Military Construction & Veterans Affairs -
chairwoman)
Commerce, Science & Transportation
(Science & Space - chairwoman)
Rules & Administration
Veterans' Affairs

HOMETOWN
Dallas

BORN
July 22, 1943, Galveston, Texas

RELIGION
Episcopalian

FAMILY
Husband, Ray Hutchison; two children

EDUCATION
U. of Texas, J.D. 1967, B.A. 1992

CAREER
Broadcast journalist; lawyer; banking executive;
candy manufacturer

POLITICAL HIGHLIGHTS
Texas House, 1973-76; National Transportation
Safety Board, 1976-78; sought Republican
nomination for U.S. House, 1982; Texas treasurer,
1991-93

ELECTION RESULTS

2000 GENERAL

Kay Bailey Hutchison (R)	4,082,091	65.0%
Gene Kelly (D)	2,030,315	32.4%
Douglas S. Sandage (GREEN)	91,448	1.5%
Mary Ruwart (LIBERT)	72,798	1.2%

2000 PRIMARY

Kay Bailey Hutchison (R)	unopposed

PREVIOUS WINNING PERCENTAGES
1994 (61%); 1993 Special Runoff Election (67%)

A politician once dismissed by her critics as "The Breck Girl," Hutchison began the 109th Congress at the peak of her power. She is the senior Republican from the president's home state and a member of the Senate majority leadership.

Up for election again in 2006, she is favored to win, provided she does not make a bid for Texas governor — the launching pad of presidents — against incumbent Gov. Rick Perry, a fellow Republican. Perry has suggested Hutchison is too liberal for Texas. She departs with conservatives most notably on abortion-related issues, supporting basic abortion rights and federal funding for stem cell research, which many in her party oppose because it uses embryonic cells.

In her early 60s, the former cheerleader and TV newscaster had a hand in some of the most important legislation considered by the Senate in the 108th Congress, including the corporate tax bill and the intelligence bill. She also chairs the Military Construction and Veterans Affairs Subcommittee on the Appropriations panel, a post that allows Hutchison to watch out for the military's many installations in Texas. The Veterans Affairs jurisdiction was added to the subcommittee's bailiwick at the outset of the 109th.

Hutchison has leveraged her seniority to help her state. When the Senate passed a $137 billion corporate tax bill in 2004, it carried Hutchison's last-minute provision allowing architectural and engineering firms to take advantage of the manufacturers' tax cut. Late in the session, just before Congress adjourned, Hutchison was able to include a proposal in the intelligence bill to tighten security at air cargo facilities.

As the vice chairwoman of the Republican Conference, which is the group of all Republicans in the Senate, she holds the fifth-ranking leadership post in the majority. She views her role as showing that conservatism can have a friendly face, and she has reached out to varied groups with "summits" on issues affecting women and Hispanics.

She first joined the leadership at the end of 2000, breaking into the ranks of what used to be an all-male Senate GOP leadership team following the death of Georgia's Paul Coverdell, a Republican. Her ascension into the leadership quieted the Democratic critics who like to portray her as a superficial former prom queen. When she was the Texas state treasurer, liberal Texas newspaper columnist Molly Ivins got great mileage from dubbing her "The Breck Girl," after an old shampoo commercial featuring a woman tossing her long tresses. Hutchison said she has fought her entire career against being trivialized in spite of her job performance, which in actuality has put her at the top of the political heap.

In 2004, she published a book, "American Heroines," about women pioneers. The volume, which profiles women who have overcome adversity in the arts, business, education and government, got positive reviews and landed Hutchison an appearance on "The Daily Show with Jon Stewart." Aware she is role model for young women, she is fond of telling young audiences to persevere over adversity. "Never give up," she says in her speeches. "If a door closes, open a window."

Her friends on the Democratic side of the Senate aisle include Barbara A. Mikulski of Maryland and Dianne Feinstein of California. It was Mikulski who invited Hutchison to lunch after Republicans took control of Congress in January 1995 to discuss how to maintain civility in the chamber. That same year, Hutchison and Mikulski formed a successful alliance to pass Homemaker IRA legislation, which gave stay-at-home mothers the same standing as women working outside the home in establishing tax-deductible individual retirement accounts. Hutchison teamed with Feinstein in the 108th on legislation to create a nationwide Amber Alert network to help quickly locate abducted children. In 2004, she advocated fitness by wearing a pedometer, with a personal goal of taking 12,000 steps a day.

In her first Senate term, Hutchison was the lead sponsor on a bill to repeal the "marriage penalty," a provision in the tax code that resulted in some two-earner married couples paying higher income taxes than if each person were single. It was incorporated into the president's tax bill of 2001.

As with many women of her generation, Hutchison has had to overcome obstacles on her career path. From an old Texas family, she grew up in La Marque, a town near the state's Gulf Coast. Her great-great grandfather, Charles S. Taylor, was a signer of the Texas Declaration of Independence.

She graduated in 1967 from the University of Texas School of Law, one of only five women in a class of 500. In "Nine and Counting: The Women of the Senate," a book Hutchison and her colleagues wrote in 2000, she recalled that about 30 law firms made clear they would not risk hiring a woman who they assumed would get married and quit or move away. "I had all of the confidence in the world, and suddenly it was meaningless because I couldn't get a job," she wrote.

The rejections led Hutchison to journalism. She worked for a Texas television station until she ran successfully for the state legislature as a representative from Houston in 1972, at the age of 29. At the time, most women in Texas politics were Democrats. While in Austin, Hutchison teamed on legislation with Democrat Sarah Weddington, the lawyer who filed the abortion rights suit that became the landmark *Roe v. Wade* case establishing a woman's right to an abortion. The two sponsored bills protecting victims of sex offenses, including a ban on publishing the names of rape victims. Hutchison herself has been the victim of a stalker.

She came on the Washington scene in 1976, when President Ford appointed her to the National Transportation Safety Board. She later moved to Dallas and unsuccessfully sought the Republican nomination for an open U.S. House seat in 1982.

She married Ray Hutchison, and spent much of the next decade in the business world as a banking executive and candy manufacturer. Returning to elective politics in 1990, she was elected state treasurer. In 1993, she won a special Senate election called after President Clinton chose longtime Democratic incumbent Sen. Lloyd Bentsen to be his Treasury secretary.

Democratic Gov. Ann Richards appointed Bob Krueger, a former House member, to the seat. Hutchison challenged him in the state's open primary in 1993, also competing against Republican Reps. Joe Barton and Jack Fields. Krueger was hurt by Clinton's unpopularity in the state, and he tied Hutchison with 29 percent of the vote. But she dominated the runoff, beating Krueger with 67 percent.

Just over a year later, after finishing Bentsen's term, Hutchison had to run for her first full Senate term. Her biggest threat was Mike Andrews, a telegenic House member from Houston. But Andrews lost in a primary contest that splintered the Democrats. And Hutchison easily defeated Dallas businessman Richard Fisher in the general election, taking 61 percent of the vote. She won re-election in 2000 with 65 percent.

In 2001, Hutchison and her husband, Ray, adopted an infant girl, whom they named Kathryn Bailey Hutchison, and an infant boy, whom they named Houston Taylor Hutchison. "We have, for many years, been trying to add to our wonderful family, and this is truly a dream come true," the Hutchisons said after the adoptions.

KEY VOTES

2004

No Pass $318.9 billion, six-year highway and mass transit bill
No Extend assault weapons ban for 10 years
No Restore pay-as-you-go rules for new tax cuts and entitlement spending
Yes Criminalize harm to a fetus in an attack on the mother
Yes Increase mandatory child care funding to states by $6 billion over five years
Yes Amend the Constitution to prohibit same-sex marriage
Yes Approve $146 billion multi-year extension of previously enacted middle-class tax breaks
Yes Reorganize U.S. intelligence agencies as proposed by Sept. 11 commission
Yes Cut corporate taxes $137 billion over 10 years

2003

No Delay Bush changes to Clean Air Act
Yes Allow confirmation vote on Miguel A. Estrada to the U.S. Court of Appeals for the D.C. Circuit
No Block a Bush proposal opening Alaska's Arctic National Wildlife Refuge to oil drilling
No Limit size of Bush's proposed tax cut to $350 billion through fiscal 2013
Yes Overhaul Medicare and create prescription drug benefit
No Block Bush rule scaling back overtime pay for some white-collar federal workers
No Split $20 billion in Iraq aid into half-grant, half-loan
? Ban "partial birth" abortion except to save a woman's life
No Stop proposal allowing travel to Cuba
Yes Allow final vote on energy policy overhaul

CQ VOTE STUDIES

	PARTY UNITY		PRESIDENTIAL SUPPORT	
	Support	Oppose	Support	Oppose
2004	89%	11%	94%	6%
2003	94%	6%	96%	4%
2002	92%	8%	96%	4%
2001	90%	10%	96%	4%
2000	96%	4%	45%	55%
1999	90%	10%	29%	71%
1998	92%	8%	37%	63%
1997	95%	5%	63%	37%
1996	98%	2%	34%	66%
1995	96%	4%	29%	71%

INTEREST GROUPS

	AFL-CIO	ADA	CCUS	ACU
2004	8%	25%	94%	84%
2003	0%	10%	100%	75%
2002	23%	5%	95%	100%
2001	19%	10%	85%	96%
2000	0%	0%	93%	96%
1999	0%	0%	94%	88%
1998	0%	0%	100%	88%
1997	0%	5%	100%	92%
1996	0%	5%	92%	100%
1995	8%	0%	100%	87%

Sen. John Cornyn (R)

Elected 2002; 1st term

CAPITOL OFFICE
224-2934
cornyn.senate.gov
517 Hart 20510-4302; fax 228-2856

COMMITTEES
Armed Services
   (Emerging Threats & Capabilities - chairman)
Budget
Judiciary
   (Immigration, Border Security & Citizenship -
   chairman)
Small Business & Entrepreneurship
Joint Economic

HOMETOWN
San Antonio

BORN
Feb. 2, 1952, Houston, Texas

RELIGION
Church of Christ

FAMILY
Wife, Sandy Cornyn; two children

EDUCATION
Trinity U., B.A. 1973 (journalism); St. Mary's U.
(Texas), J.D. 1977; U. of Virginia, LL.M. 1995

CAREER
Lawyer

POLITICAL HIGHLIGHTS
Texas District Court judge, 1985-91; Texas Supreme
Court, 1991-97; Texas attorney general, 1999-2002

ELECTION RESULTS

2002 GENERAL

John Cornyn (R)	2,496,243	55.3%
Ron Kirk (D)	1,955,758	43.3%

2002 PRIMARY

John Cornyn (R)	478,825	77.3%
Bruce Rusty Lang (R)	46,907	7.6%
Douglas G. Deffenbaugh (R)	43,611	7.0%
Dudley F. Mooney (R)	32,202	5.2%
Lawrence Cranberg (R)	17,757	2.9%

Although he is a freshman, Cornyn has swiftly become a Republican spokesman for the conservative point of view on several hot-button issues, including gay marriage and judicial nominations.

A former state Supreme Court judge, he was elected to the Senate in 2002 eager to end an acrimonious partisan impasse over judicial confirmations. He led his fellow freshmen in urging Senate leaders to seek a way out of the impasse. But the quagmire over judges proved too difficult to navigate for the newcomers, and, from his seat on the Judiciary Committee, Cornyn (CORE-nin) became a vocal defender of President Bush's nominees against the threat of Democratic filibusters. He had personal experience with one of the nominees; he served on the Texas Supreme Court with Priscilla Owen, whom Bush nominated for the 5th U.S. Circuit Court of Appeals.

As chairman of the Judiciary Subcommittee on the Constitution in the 108th Congress, Cornyn spearheaded efforts to pass proposed constitutional amendments banning gay marriage and flag-burning. He sponsored a constitutional amendment in both the 108th and 109th to allow Congress to pass a law establishing a mechanism for replacing lawmakers in the event that a quarter of the House or Senate are killed or incapacitated.

Cornyn played a prominent role during Senate debate in 2004 on the constitutional amendment that would have banned gay marriage. Like many social conservatives, he fears that a 1996 law barring gay marriage will eventually be struck down as unconstitutional. "We see the ongoing march of litigation as part of a national strategy to undermine the traditional institution of marriage that we know is the most important stabilizing influence in our society and one that functions in the best interests of our children," he said.

A former Texas attorney general and district court judge, Cornyn chafes at judicial rulings in recent years on certain social issues. "If the judiciary gets into the business of making blatantly political decisions, it pretty much does away with the need for a Congress," he said. Early in 2005, he raised some eyebrows with a Senate floor speech in which he suggested that public anger over politically charged decisions might be responsible for several instances of violence against judges, though he added the violence was in no way justified.

Cornyn has close ties to both Bush and Karl Rove, the president's senior political strategist. He rose to Republican prominence in Texas in the 1990s a few years ahead of Bush, the former governor of Texas, but the two became friends during their time together in Austin. Bush, who is fond of giving his friends nicknames, telephoned Cornyn on election night in 2002 to say, "Congratulations, Johnny Boy."

Cornyn is an advocate of permanently extending the tax cuts Bush pushed to enactment in 2001, which will otherwise lapse after 2010. From his seat on the Armed Services Committee, Cornyn also backed without reservation Bush's decision to wage war in Iraq, and he supports the president's effort to deploy a national missile defense system.

Cornyn was among a number of Republicans who urged Armed Services Chairman John W. Warner of Virginia to back off from investigating allegations of prisoner abuse by the U.S. military at Iraq's Abu Ghraib prison. He worried that Warner's inquiry could become "a distraction."

Like Bush, Cornyn advocates the concept of allowing people to invest a part of their Social Security taxes in securities. He touted the proposal in his campaign, though it had fallen out of favor as a campaign issue because of a sharp drop in stock values. But the idea was resurrected in the 109th Congress, when Bush made it a centerpiece of his second term.

A pet cause of Cornyn's puts him at odds with the White House. He is a strong proponent of the government remaining accountable to the public through more openness. True to form, he opposes Bush's plan to exempt the Department of Homeland Security from federal open records rules. And he was critical of the administration's efforts to keep secret the deliberations of its energy policy task force.

Nor was Cornyn a rubber stamp for the Republican viewpoint while in Austin. On the Texas Supreme Court, which handles only civil cases, he wrote the majority opinion upholding the state's so-called Robin Hood school finance law, which requires wealthier school districts to share money with poorer ones. The plan is unpopular with many Republicans.

When he was elected attorney general in 1998, he was the first Republican to hold the post since Reconstruction. He sought to reduce partisanship in the office. And he angered some Republicans by working, unsuccessfully, to scale back a ruling by his Democratic predecessor that had eliminated affirmative action programs in Texas universities.

Like Bush, however, Cornyn's career in state government was characterized by a pro-business, limited-government philosophy. He favored strict restrictions on medical malpractice lawsuits, and while on the state Supreme Court, he joined a ruling allowing cigarette companies to partially escape blame for smoking-related health claims.

The son of a B-17 pilot in World War II, Cornyn and his family eventually settled in San Antonio, where his father became an Air Force pathologist. A wrestler in high school and college, Cornyn majored in journalism at Texas' Trinity University. But he was eventually turned off by reporters' low salaries and waited tables at a Steak and Ale restaurant while earning his real estate license. When that career faltered in a sagging economy, Cornyn went to law school. He later practiced law in San Antonio, specializing in defending doctors against medical malpractice lawsuits.

His break into politics was almost unexpected. In 1984, some Republican friends of his — looking to crack the Democrats' longstanding hold on Texas' judicial elections — approached him at a Super Bowl party and asked him to run for a state district court seat. He did, and he won. Six years later, he was elected to the state Supreme Court. In 1998, he won a bruising attorney general's race against Democrat Jim Mattox, who had held the office for eight years ending in 1991 and had served in the House before that.

Cornyn's opportunity to run for Congress came at the start of the decade, when as attorney general he was chairman of a commission that proposed new political boundaries to the state legislature. He presented a redistricting plan that likely would have resulted in major Republican gains. A less partisan map was eventually imposed by the courts, but Cornyn's efforts raised his standing with Rove. When Texas GOP Sen. Phil Gramm decided to retire, several Republicans expressed interest in running, including Rep. Henry Bonilla. But the field was quickly cleared for Cornyn, and he won a GOP primary against four minimally known opponents with 77 percent of the vote.

Democrats nominated Ron Kirk, who defeated Rep. Ken Bentsen of Houston in a primary contest. Kirk, a charismatic and politically centrist former mayor of Dallas, wanted to become the state's first African-American senator. But Cornyn's conservative credentials outweighed Kirk's personality and history-making appeal. Running on his allegiance to Bush — an overwhelmingly popular figure in the state he served as governor from 1995 to 2000 — Cornyn won with 55 percent.

KEY VOTES

2004

Yes Pass $318.9 billion, six-year highway and mass transit bill
No Extend assault weapons ban for 10 years
No Restore pay-as-you-go rules for new tax cuts and entitlement spending
Yes Criminalize harm to a fetus in an attack on the mother
No Increase mandatory child care funding to states by $6 billion over five years
Yes Amend the Constitution to prohibit same-sex marriage
Yes Approve $146 billion multi-year extension of previously enacted middle-class tax breaks
Yes Reorganize U.S. intelligence agencies as proposed by Sept. 11 commission
Yes Cut corporate taxes $137 billion over 10 years

2003

No Delay Bush changes to Clean Air Act
Yes Allow confirmation vote on Miguel A. Estrada to the U.S. Court of Appeals for the D.C. Circuit
No Block a Bush proposal opening Alaska's Arctic National Wildlife Refuge to oil drilling
No Limit size of Bush's proposed tax cut to $350 billion through fiscal 2013
No Overhaul Medicare and create prescription drug benefit
No Block Bush rule scaling back overtime pay for some white-collar federal workers
No Split $20 billion in Iraq aid into half-grant, half-loan
Yes Ban "partial birth" abortion except to save a woman's life
Yes Stop proposal allowing travel to Cuba
Yes Allow final vote on energy policy overhaul

CQ VOTE STUDIES

	PARTY UNITY		PRESIDENTIAL SUPPORT	
	Support	Oppose	Support	Oppose
2004	97%	3%	96%	4%
2003	99%	1%	98%	2%

INTEREST GROUPS

	AFL-CIO	ADA	CCUS	ACU
2004	8%	5%	100%	100%
2003	0%	10%	100%	85%

Rep. Louie Gohmert (R)

Elected 2004; 1st term

Freshman House members do not always get their top choices for committee assignments, but some requests are too obvious for the leadership to overlook. That was the case with the Judiciary Committee seat awarded to Gohmert, who was a state prosecutor, county judge and chief justice of the state appeals court before entering legislative politics at age 51.

Gohmert, who said he considers national defense to be the federal government's No. 1 priority, said a key component of keeping the United States safe is further securing its borders. A former Army captain, Gohmert said he is reluctant to use the military to protect the borders, but that the critical effort of combating terrorism might require such a deployment until enough border agents are trained to do the job effectively.

On economic issues, Gohmert says Congress needs to further cut income taxes, eliminate the inheritance tax and further reduce the "marriage penalty." Gohmert said the current tax code is broken and needs to be replaced with a simpler system that he said would be fairer: He said he would be willing to consider a flat tax or a national sales tax.

On social issues, Gohmert advocates gun owners' rights, anti-abortion policies and the traditional definition of marriage. As a judge, Gohmert angered AIDS activists in 1996 when he ordered a man with the disease to obtain written consent from future sex partners as part of his probation in a car theft conviction. In 2005, he asserted the Supreme Court ignored the Constitution and its own precedents in discarding federal sentencing guidelines and instead following "the fleeting whims of a daydreaming child."

Gohmert owes thanks for his House seat to fellow Texan Tom DeLay, the House majority leader, who spearheaded the highly partisan mid-decade congressional redistricting plan that produced a net gain of seven seats for Texas Republicans from the beginning of the 108th Congress. Gohmert unseated four-term Democratic Rep. Max Sandlin handily, winning by almost 24 percentage points. Although Sandlin portrayed himself as a Democrat of center-right philosophy, he was no match for Gohmert's fervent conservatism in a greatly overhauled and strongly Republican 1st District.

CAPITOL OFFICE
225-3035
www.house.gov/gohmert
508 Cannon 20515-4301; fax 225-5866

COMMITTEES
Judiciary
Resources
Small Business

HOMETOWN
Tyler

BORN
Aug. 18, 1953, Pittsburg, Texas

RELIGION
Baptist

FAMILY
Wife, Kathy Gohmert; three children

EDUCATION
Texas A&M U., B.A. 1975 (history); Baylor U., J.D. 1977

MILITARY SERVICE
Army, 1978-82

CAREER
Lawyer; state prosecutor

POLITICAL HIGHLIGHTS
Smith County District Court judge, 1993-2002; Texas Court of Appeals chief justice, 2002-03

ELECTION RESULTS

2004 GENERAL

Louie Gohmert (R)	157,068	61.5%
Max Sandlin (D)	96,281	37.7%

2004 PRIMARY RUNOFF

Louie Gohmert (R)	16,841	57.2%
John Graves (R)	12,618	42.8%

2004 PRIMARY

Louie Gohmert (R)	19,421	41.7%
John Graves (R)	13,933	29.9%
Wayne Christian (R)	6,854	14.7%
Lyle Thornstenson (R)	4,604	9.9%
Emily Mathews (R)	1,266	2.7%

TEXAS 1
Northeast – Tyler, Longview

In this lush portion of East Texas, tree-covered hills and cypress swamps share space with what remains of the once-prominent oil centers in Longview and Tyler. But recently the economic dominance of other natural resources — timber and natural gas — has driven the economy following the oil bust of the 1980s and the rise of the manufacturing sector.

Although redistricting prior to the 2004 elections changed the 1st geographically, its industry remained largely the same. The addition of ranching areas offset the loss of rice farming and most of the old 1st's dairy production. Slow population growth and miles of forests and agricultural land remain hallmarks of the district, and the area still faces economic challenges from foreign timber companies and cattle ranchers.

Running about 150 miles along the Louisiana border, the district shares more traits with its traditionally laid-back cajun neighbors than with the fast-paced urban life of nearby Dallas and its suburbs. Residents tend to be conservative, even among Democrats, and the region associates itself with the Bible Belt that stretches through much of the South. The district has one of the largest percentages of elderly residents in the state, making health care an important issue.

Many of the largest and most-populated counties in the district — such as Gregg, Rusk, Smith and Nacogdoches — vote reliably Republican. Conservative Democrats can win pockets in the 1st, especially in Marion County. GOP Gov. Rick Perry and now-Sen. John Cornyn, R, both lost Marion County during their statewide wins in 2002.

MAJOR INDUSTRY
Timber, agriculture, manufacturing, steel, oil

CITIES
Tyler, 83,650; Longview, 73,344; Lufkin, 32,709; Nacogdoches, 29,914

NOTABLE
Tyler hosts an annual weeklong festival and calls itself the "Rose Capital of the World."

Rep. Ted Poe (R)

Elected 2004; 1st term

During his 22 years as a judge in Harris County, which includes most of metropolitan Houston, Poe was known for unusual sentences that came to be labeled as "Poe-etic justice." One famous punishment required an auto thief to serve jail time — and hand over the keys of his Trans Am to his victim, a 75-year-old grandmother, who drove the car until the stolen vehicle was recovered and repaired. Poe also made a burglar stand on a sidewalk wearing a sign that read "I stole from this store," and required convicted killers to keep pictures of their victims in their jail cells.

Poe was one of two judges — Louie Gohmert of the neighboring 1st District was the other — elected in 2004 as Republican House freshmen from Texas. While Gohmert was posted to the Judiciary Committee, Poe got assignments that would take him in new directions.

One assignment was pragmatic. With airport noise an issue in his suburban Houston base and Gulf Coast shipping important in the eastern end of his 2nd District, Poe will keep busy on the Transportation and Infrastructure Committee.

Given new ground to cover with seats on the Small Business and International Relations committees, Poe adjusted quickly: He was an observer during the January 2005 national elections in Iraq.

Poe nonetheless has not abandoned judicial interests that were his focus until he won his seat in Congress. He says one of his priorities will be to create a national registry for convicted pedophiles.

The 2nd District won by Poe had been redrawn prior to the 2004 election in a redistricting plan spearheaded by Texan Tom DeLay, the House majority leader. It included little of the previous 2nd District represented by Democrat Jim Turner — whose district was so subdivided that he chose to retire from Congress — and included almost half of the former 9th District constituent base represented by four-term Democrat Nick Lampson. It also has a strong Republican lean that benefited Poe, who ousted Lampson by a comfortable margin of 13 percentage points.

CAPITOL OFFICE
225-6565
www.house.gov/poe
1605 Longworth 20515-4302; fax 225-5547

COMMITTEES
International Relations
Small Business
Transportation & Infrastructure

HOMETOWN
Humble

BORN
Sept. 10, 1948, Temple, Texas

RELIGION
United Church of Christ

FAMILY
Wife, Carol Poe; four children

EDUCATION
Abilene Christian College, B.A. 1970 (political science); U. of Houston, J.D. 1973

MILITARY SERVICE
Air Force Reserve, 1970-76

CAREER
County prosecutor; college instructor

POLITICAL HIGHLIGHTS
Harris County District Court judge, 1981-2003

ELECTION RESULTS

2004 GENERAL

Ted Poe (R)	139,951	55.5%
Nick Lampson (D)	108,156	42.9%
Sandra Leigh Saulsbury (LIBERT)	3,931	1.6%

2004 PRIMARY

Ted Poe (R)	14,932	61.1%
George Fastuca (R)	3,668	15.0%
Clint Moore (R)	2,868	11.7%
Mark Henry (R)	2,423	9.9%
John Nickell (R)	285	1.2%
Andrew J. Bolton (R)	246	1.0%

TEXAS 2

East — Beaumont, Port Arthur, part of Houston and northern and eastern suburbs

A 100-mile-wide rail of a district that stretches from the Louisiana border into the northern suburbs of Houston, the 2nd takes in the oil city of Beaumont in the east and touches some of Houston's more affluent communities in its western reaches.

A southern branch dips into Houston's east suburbs and takes in the petrochemical city of Baytown. The petrochemical industry dominates as the district moves through the cities of Liberty, Beaumont and Port Arthur in Liberty and Jefferson counties. Ports in Beaumont and Port Arthur provide shipping-industry jobs in the 2nd's eastern portion.

Government jobs and contracts became increasingly important to the region as its industrial and manufacturing economies slipped somewhat during the late 1980s and early 1990s. Slow population growth and a

high percentage of blue-collar workers have made it difficult to attract higher-paying service jobs.

The 2nd remains a mostly rural district with unpopulated areas in Jefferson and Liberty counties. But Liberty County began experiencing population growth in the 1990s, and many Liberty residents make long commutes to work in Houston.

The district tends to vote like Texas overall — mostly conservative and Republican — but not overwhelmingly enough to shut out Democrats. The Harris County (Houston) portion of the district provides candidates with a solid Republican base, while the Beaumont area tends to favor moderate to conservative Democrats.

MAJOR INDUSTRY
Petrochemicals, shipping

CITIES
Beaumont, 113,866; Port Arthur, 57,755; Houston (pt.), 57,580

NOTABLE
A gusher in 1901 at the Spindletop oilfield, located south of Beaumont, marked the birth of the modern petroleum industry.

Rep. Sam Johnson (R)

CAPITOL OFFICE
225-4201
www.samjohnson.house.gov
1211 Longworth 20515-4303; fax 225-1485

COMMITTEES
Education & Workforce
 (Employer-Employee Relations - chairman)
Ways & Means

HOMETOWN
Plano

BORN
Oct. 11, 1930, San Antonio, Texas

RELIGION
Methodist

FAMILY
Wife, Shirley Johnson; three children

EDUCATION
Southern Methodist U., B.B.A. 1951; George
Washington U., M.S.I.A. 1974 (international affairs)

MILITARY SERVICE
Air Force, 1951-79

CAREER
Home builder; Top Gun flight school director;
Air Force pilot

POLITICAL HIGHLIGHTS
Texas House, 1985-91

ELECTION RESULTS

2004 GENERAL

Sam Johnson (R)	180,099	85.6%
Paul Jenkins (I)	16,966	8.1%
James Vessels (LIBERT)	13,287	6.3%

2004 PRIMARY

Sam Johnson (R)	12,429	84.1%
Brian Rubarts (R)	2,357	15.9%

2002 GENERAL

Sam Johnson (R)	113,974	74.0%
Manny Molera (D)	37,503	24.3%
John Davis (LIBERT)	2,656	1.7%

PREVIOUS WINNING PERCENTAGES
2000 (72%); 1998 (91%); 1996 (73%); 1994 (91%);
1992 (86%); 1991 Special Runoff Election (53%)

Elected May 1991; 7th full term

Now in his 70s, Johnson is a dependable anchor for the conservative faction of House Republicans, offering his younger compatriots the lessons of his experience while helping them to remain focused on their goal of limiting federal government. He is one of the four founders of the Republican Study Committee, originally known as the Conservative Action Team, a group that claims more than 100 members in the 109th Congress.

A member of the Ways and Means Committee, he would go well beyond President Bush's proposal for personal accounts within Social Security. Johnson introduced a bill in 2005 to allow workers to divert their entire Social Security payroll tax into private accounts. Bush sought only a partial tax diversion. "It's time to give the American people a say in how their retirement money is invested and an opportunity to do better," Johnson said.

As the political struggle over Social Security intensified in 2005, Johnson joined Ohio Republican John A. Boehner, chairman of the Education and Workforce Committee, in asking Labor Secretary Elaine L. Chao to investigate whether the AFL-CIO's member unions had violated labor law by allegedly threatening to withdraw their assets from financial firms that supported Bush's proposal. Johnson chairs the full committee's Employer-Employee Relations Subcommittee.

A career Air Force pilot who spent nearly seven years as a prisoner of war in Vietnam — more than half of that in solitary confinement — Johnson doesn't have much use for federal programs. But he says he decided to become active in politics while he was being held as a POW after his plane was shot down in 1966. "You can sit there and shoot bullets at the government all day, but unless you get personally involved, you can't get a lot done," he says in a slow Texas drawl.

Since then, he says, he has developed this additional credo: "Sometimes I think you're more effective if you're not in somebody's face. You have to work with everyone in your party and the other party." As a result, everyone seems to like Johnson, even those with whom he disagrees. His friendly and easygoing personality also has resulted in a loyal staff. Many of his top aides have worked with him since he first came to Congress in 1991.

Johnson has worked hard to help the military. He pressed legislation to increase the "death gratuity" paid to the families of military personnel killed while on duty and to make the sum tax-exempt. "It's unconscionable to me that the knock on the door by the military chaplain is followed by a knock on the door from the tax man," he said in 2003 when the House passed a modest increase in the benefit. A far more generous boost was included in the Iraq war supplemental spending bill passed early in 2005.

After the terrorist attacks of Sept. 11, 2001, Johnson's focus on national security and the military became even more intense. During a speech on the House floor the next day, Johnson said the devastation in New York and Virginia was worse than the B-52 bombing raids he lived through while a prisoner in Hanoi. Although he supported authorizing the president to use "all necessary and appropriate force" against those who perpetrated the attacks, Johnson said he would prefer a straight-out declaration of war.

When the military campaign began, Johnson encouraged people to write letters and e-mails to the troops. As an outgrowth of his interest in military morale, he promoted legislation in the 107th Congress to protect the voting rights of overseas military members and their families.

From his Ways and Means seat, long before Bush took office, Johnson was promoting several of the proposals that ended up in the 2001 tax cut package, including elimination of the estate tax and alleviation of the "marriage penalty," which left some couples paying higher taxes than they would if each person were single. Johnson says he would favor repealing the 16th Amendment, which authorized the collection of federal income tax.

Johnson has long pushed legislation to make it easier for small businesses to band together to purchase health insurance. He ushered such a bill through the House in the 108th Congress, and the Education and Workforce Committee sent it forward once again early in the 109th. But the proposal draws fire from Democrats and many other critics, including major insurance companies, because it would allow "association health plans" to bypass state insurance laws mandating benefits and treatment coverage that other insurers must obey.

Johnson did not plan on a military career. He says participation in the ROTC was mandatory when he went to high school. He was aiming at a career in business and law when the Korean War intervened, and his entire ROTC class at Southern Methodist University was called to duty. Accepted into flight training school, he soon fell in love with flying and was sold on a career in the Air Force. In addition to his combat missions over Korea and Vietnam, Johnson was a member of the Thunderbirds precision flying team for two years and served as director of the Air Force's "Top Gun" fighter pilot school.

Johnson persuaded Speaker Newt Gingrich to name him to the Smithsonian Institution board in 1995 when he and other lawmakers objected to an exhibit on the "Enola Gay" — the plane that dropped the first atomic bomb on Japan — because it depicted Japan as a victim. Johnson then helped arrange for a scaled-back exhibit that focused on the mechanics of the plane rather than the morality of its mission.

Johnson does not talk much about his days as a POW, but he did write a book about his experience, "Captive Warriors." After his solitary confinement ended, he roomed with John McCain, now the senator from Arizona, at the prison camp. Upon his release in 1973, he had three operations on his right hand, including a tendon transplant, and resumed flying.

After retiring from the Air Force in 1979 as a colonel, Johnson went into the home building business in Dallas. He got into local Republican Party affairs and, in 1984, won a seat in the Texas House. When GOP Rep. Steve Bartlett resigned in March 1991 to run for mayor of Dallas, Johnson overcame a tough scramble to win his party's nomination. He's had no trouble since then in the wealthy, solidly Republican 3rd District.

KEY VOTES

2004

No Extend federal unemployment benefits by 13 weeks
No Pass $283.2 billion, six-year federal highway and mass transit bill
Yes Approve $146 billion multi-year extension of previously enacted middle-class tax breaks
Yes Amend the Constitution to prohibit same-sex marriage
Yes Cut corporate taxes $137 billion over 10 years
No Reorganize U.S. intelligence agencies as proposed by Sept. 11 commission

2003

Yes Cut taxes by $330 billion through fiscal 2013
No Block Bush rule scaling back overtime pay for some white-collar federal workers
No Do not allow use of search warrants without first notifying subjects
No Allow importation of prescription drugs
Yes Create private school voucher program in Washington, D.C.
Yes Ban "partial birth" abortion except to save a woman's life
No Split $18.6 billion in Iraq aid into half-grant, half-loan
Yes Overhaul Medicare and create prescription drug benefit

CQ VOTE STUDIES

	PARTY UNITY		PRESIDENTIAL SUPPORT	
	Support	Oppose	Support	Oppose
2004	99%	1%	93%	7%
2003	99%	1%	96%	4%
2002	98%	2%	89%	11%
2001	97%	3%	91%	9%
2000	98%	2%	25%	75%

INTEREST GROUPS

	AFL-CIO	ADA	CCUS	ACU
2004	0%	0%	100%	100%
2003	0%	5%	100%	88%
2002	13%	0%	90%	100%
2001	0%	0%	91%	100%
2000	0%	0%	85%	100%

TEXAS 3

Part of Dallas and northeast suburbs – Plano, most of Garland and McKinney

The rapidly expanding Dallas suburbs of Plano, McKinley, Frisco and Allen in Collin County form the heart of the 3rd, which also takes in part of Dallas itself and most of Garland and Rowlett in northeast Dallas County.

The district is economically well-off, white and Republican. Many corporate headquarters have moved into the Plano area, and wealthy executives have built expensive homes in Frisco and surrounding areas. The concentration of electronic and telecommunications firms along U.S. Highway 75 has earned that area the name "Telecom Corridor." Texas Instruments and Electronic Data Systems are a major presence along the corridor. Just north of the Lyndon B. Johnson Freeway along U.S. 75, Richardson (shared with the 32nd) has benefited greatly from technology firms and is growing at a rapid rate. Frisco also is undergoing a population and development boom, and Garland (shared with the 5th) grew at a steady pace in the 1980s and 1990s. Downtown Dallas is in the

30th, but many white-collar workers commute from the 3rd.

Although the 3rd's boundaries were altered in redistricting prior to the 2004 election, the demographics of the district did not change. The new 3rd is more compact, having lost many of the Collin County exurbs and small towns that sat on the edge of the old district. About 40 percent of the new district's residents live in Dallas County. Redistricting removed part of Richardson and added a few Democratic pockets closer to downtown Dallas.

Collin County, the state's fastest-growing county in the 1990s, is filled with upwardly mobile professionals and is strongly Republican. In 2004, George W. Bush won 70 percent of the presidential vote in the 3rd's share of Collin and 57 percent of the district's Dallas County portion.

MAJOR INDUSTRY
Telecommunications, transportation, banking, defense

CITIES
Plano, 219,890; Garland (pt.), 142,379; Dallas (pt.), 128,651

NOTABLE
Southfork Ranch, the fictional home of the Ewing family in the long-running television program "Dallas," is located in Parker.

Rep. Ralph M. Hall (R)

Elected 1980; 13th term

CAPITOL OFFICE
225-6673
www.house.gov/ralphhall
2405 Rayburn 20515-4304; fax 225-3332

COMMITTEES
Energy & Commerce
   (Energy & Air Quality - chairman)
Science

HOMETOWN
Rockwall

BORN
May 3, 1923, Fate, Texas

RELIGION
Methodist

FAMILY
Wife, Mary Ellen Hall; three children

EDUCATION
Texas Christian U., attended 1943 (pre-law); U. of
Texas, attended 1946-47 (pre-law); Southern
Methodist U., LL.B. 1951

MILITARY SERVICE
Navy, 1942-45

CAREER
Lawyer; aluminum company president

POLITICAL HIGHLIGHTS
Rockwall County judge, 1951-63; Texas Senate,
1963-73 (president pro tempore, 1968-69; served as
a Democrat); sought Democratic nomination for
lieutenant governor, 1972

ELECTION RESULTS

2004 GENERAL
Ralph M. Hall (R)	182,866	68.3%
Jim Nickerson (D)	81,585	30.5%

2004 PRIMARY
Ralph M. Hall (R)	22,484	77.2%
Mike Murphy (R)	3,524	12.1%
Mike Mosher (R)	3,122	10.7%

2002 GENERAL
Ralph M. Hall (D)	97,304	57.8%
John Graves (R)	67,939	40.4%

PREVIOUS WINNING PERCENTAGES*
2000 (60%); 1998 (58%); 1996 (64%); 1994 (59%);
1992 (58%); 1990 (100%); 1988 (66%); 1986 (72%);
1984 (58%); 1982 (74%); 1980 (52%)
*Elected as a Democrat 1980-2000

When Hall announced in January 2004 that he was switching to the Republican Party, it hardly stunned the political establishment. For years he had compiled one of the most conservative voting records of any House Democrat, and rumors of a possible party switch had circulated since the Republicans took control of Congress in 1995.

"Everyone knows that my voting record has not aligned with the Democratic Party for many years," Hall said in a statement on his decision. "I don't think this will come as a complete surprise to many."

In addition to his conservative leanings, Hall appeared influenced by two other factors. One was a concern that his affiliation with the minority party was costing his district funding. The other was the controversial Texas GOP redistricting plan, which appeared to place his re-election prospects in jeopardy. The new 4th District, while still Republican-leaning, was no more conservative than before, but Hall kept only about one-third of his former constituents — meaning he faced a tough battle as a Democrat winning over Republicans who were unfamiliar with him.

Hall, who turned 82 in 2005 and is the oldest member of the House, has long seemed more comfortable with the GOP than with the Democrats. An old friend of the Bush family, he was invited to the White House to celebrate his 80th birthday. As a Democrat in 2003, he supported President Bush's position on legislation 85 percent of the time — a far higher percentage than any other Democrat. His support was particularly helpful to the Republicans on a close 2003 floor vote on a GOP tax cut plan. Hall's new party affiliation in 2004 changed little: He supported Bush 82 percent of the time.

Hall's ambivalence with party labels drew attention before the 2002 election, when he told GOP leaders he would consider backing J. Dennis Hastert of Illinois for Speaker if his vote were the deciding one. And when the vote for Speaker came as the 108th Congress convened, Hall voted "present" instead of backing Minority Leader Nancy Pelosi of California. He said his oil-patch district supports the rights of gun owners and is at odds with California on energy policy. It was not the first time Hall had cast such a maverick vote: In 1985, he voted "present" rather than support the re-election of Democrat Thomas P. "Tip" O'Neill Jr. of Massachusetts as Speaker.

In between those votes, Hall compiled a long history of rebuffing Democratic leaders. In 1998, he was one of only five Democrats to support the impeachment of President Clinton on the critical first charge of lying to a federal grand jury. In 2000, he publicly championed the presidential candidacy of Republican Texas Gov. George W. Bush. He strayed from the party line more often than any other House member in both the 106th and 107th Congresses. But rather than switch after the GOP gains of 1994, he helped start the Blue Dog Coalition, a group of about 30 conservative House Democrats that sought to pull the party to the right.

Stylistically, Hall is anything but a firebrand. An infrequent sponsor of legislation, he prefers to look quietly after the interests of his home state's oil and gas industry through his membership on the Energy and Commerce Committee. "I don't have any pride of authorship," he says, "and I'll take somebody else's bill if it gives me what I want."

A fiscal conservative, Hall favors scrapping most of the existing tax code and replacing it with a flat tax or national sales tax. In 2001, he was one of only nine House Democrats to support an indefinite extension of the $1.35 trillion tax cut of 2001, which is set to expire in 2010. Hall stands with the right on social issues as well, opposing abortion and same-sex marriage.

As chairman of the Energy panel's Energy and Air Quality Subcommittee, one of Hall's priorities in the 109th is to help shepherd a comprehensive energy bill through Congress. He authored a provision in the 108th, which he promised to pursue again, to help the industry develop technologies for ultra-deep drilling beneath the Gulf of Mexico, as well as in difficult-to-assess onshore areas. "The fact is that the easy-to-find-and-produce oil and gas have already been consumed — the challenge is getting at the more difficult producing horizons," Hall said when describing the provision.

Hall kept his assignment on the Science Committee after becoming a Republican, and he has tried to enhance the panel's prominence. After the Sept. 11, 2001, terrorist attacks, he lobbied for designating an undersecretary of science and technology in the new Homeland Security Department. Hall believes cutting-edge research should be an integral part of the government's counterterrorism efforts in order to address vulnerabilities and respond quickly to future attacks.

Hall is also a strong advocate for NASA and has championed the space agency's biomedical and basic science programs. After the 2003 loss of the space shuttle *Columbia*, Hall pressed NASA to put a greater focus on safety. He added an amendment to the annual NASA funding bill that directed the space agency to conduct studies on how to improve space shuttle crew survivability.

Hall's folksy humor and encyclopedic supply of rural Texas stories can defuse tension, and his political acumen gives him influence when he decides to weigh in. He generally eschews quick legislative fixes. He says he places more of a premium on "doing it right, rather than doing it now."

Hall got an early start in politics. He was elected the county judge, or chief executive, of tiny Rockwall County in 1950 while still attending law school nearby in Dallas. Twelve years later, he moved up to the state Senate and spent a decade there, rising to become president pro tempore. After finishing fourth in the Democratic primary for lieutenant governor in 1972, he left public life to concentrate on business. But when 4th District Democrat Ray Roberts announced his retirement in 1980 after 18 years, Hall won the seat by defeating Republican John H. Wright, a Tyler business manager, with 52 percent of the vote. He won by comfortable margins as a Democrat through 2002.

In 2004, he easily bested two rivals in the GOP primary after riding with Bush on Air Force One to a Houston fundraiser. He won the general election with more than two-thirds of the vote.

KEY VOTES

2004

No Extend federal unemployment benefits by 13 weeks

Yes Pass $283.2 billion, six-year federal highway and mass transit bill

Yes Approve $146 billion multi-year extension of previously enacted middle-class tax breaks

Yes Amend the Constitution to prohibit same-sex marriage

Yes Cut corporate taxes $137 billion over 10 years

Yes Reorganize U.S. intelligence agencies as proposed by Sept. 11 commission

2003

Yes Cut taxes by $330 billion through fiscal 2013

No Block Bush rule scaling back overtime pay for some white-collar federal workers

Yes Do not allow use of search warrants without first notifying subjects

No Allow importation of prescription drugs

Yes Create private school voucher program in Washington, D.C.

Yes Ban "partial birth" abortion except to save a woman's life

Yes Split $18.6 billion in Iraq aid into half-grant, half-loan

Yes Overhaul Medicare and create prescription drug benefit

CQ VOTE STUDIES

	PARTY UNITY		PRESIDENTIAL SUPPORT	
	Support	Oppose	Support	Oppose
2004	92%	8%	82%	18%
2003	51%	49%	85%	15%
2002	40%	60%	70%	30%
2001	25%	75%	86%	14%
2000	35%	65%	22%	78%

INTEREST GROUPS

	AFL-CIO	ADA	CCUS	ACU
2004	13%	5%	100%	84%
2003	33%	15%	93%	72%
2002	22%	15%	85%	88%
2001	25%	25%	83%	96%
2000	10%	20%	80%	88%

TEXAS 4

Northeast – Sherman, Texarkana, Paris

The 4th begins in Dallas' eastern and northern suburbs before moving east to sparsely populated and rural areas that have a Southern feel that is harder to find in other Texas districts. The district extends along the Oklahoma and Arkansas borders, taking in Texarkana, but its four western counties contain about half of the population. Democrats once ruled the Red River Valley region north and east of Dallas, but the area is now fertile territory for the GOP.

Dallas commuters and other white-collar workers populate the burgeoning western counties. In the east, natural resources — timber, oil and natural gas — remain prominent, but this portion of the 4th faces some economic challenges from foreign timber companies and cattle ranchers who can sell their products at lower prices. The manufacturing sector, including companies such as Pilgrim's Pride chicken, has come to drive economic growth.

The 4th has the second-highest percentage of white residents (79 percent) and the smallest percentage of Hispanics (8 percent) in the state. Residents tend to be conservative, even among Democrats, and the region associates itself with the Bible Belt that stretches through much of the South.

The 4th became slightly less Republican in redistricting before the 2004 election, and it remains a place where Democrats can win local races in the east, but overall GOP candidates generally dominate. In the 2004 presidential election, George W. Bush won every county in the 4th, with his advantage running from slight in Morris County to overwhelming in Rockwall County.

MAJOR INDUSTRY
Manufacturing, agriculture, retail, health care

MILITARY BASES
Red River Army Depot, 3 military, 2,632 civilian (2005)

CITIES
Sherman, 35,082; Texarkana, 34,782; Paris, 25,898; Greenville, 23,960

NOTABLE
Former House Speaker Sam Rayburn hailed from Bonham, which is now home to the Sam Rayburn Library and Museum; Uncle Jesse's Memorial Big Bass Classic, inspired by the TV show "Dukes of Hazzard," is an annual event in Paris; Texarkana is split between Texas and Arkansas.

Rep. Jeb Hensarling (R)

Elected 2002; 2nd term

CAPITOL OFFICE
225-3484
www.house.gov/hensarling
132 Cannon 20515-4305; fax 226-4888

COMMITTEES
Budget
Financial Services

HOMETOWN
Dallas

BORN
May 29, 1957, Stephenville, Texas

RELIGION
Episcopalian

FAMILY
Wife, Melissa Hensarling; two children

EDUCATION
Texas A&M U., B.A. 1979 (economics); U. of Texas, J.D. 1982

CAREER
Child support collection software firm owner; corporate communications executive; senatorial campaign committee executive director; congressional and campaign aide; lawyer

POLITICAL HIGHLIGHTS
No previous office

ELECTION RESULTS

2004 GENERAL

Jeb Hensarling (R)	148,816	64.5%
Bill Bernstein (D)	75,911	32.9%
John Gonzalez (LIBERT)	6,118	2.7%

2004 PRIMARY

Jeb Hensarling (R)	unopposed

2002 GENERAL

Jeb Hensarling (R)	81,439	58.2%
Ron Chapman (D)	56,330	40.3%

Hensarling's mentor is former Sen. Phil Gramm of Texas, a conservative known for his assaults on the growth in the federal budget. Hensarling has picked up where Gramm left off when he retired in 2002 and has made the budget and federal spending his signature issue.

Like Gramm, Hensarling (HENN-sur-ling) is a true believer in tax cuts to stimulate the economy and spending cuts to curb the deficit, and rarely does he find the two in conflict with each other. "I view the deficit as a symptom and spending as the disease," he says.

His immersion in the principles of low taxes and small government goes back to his college days. Hensarling was a student of Gramm's at Texas A & M University, where Gramm taught economics. Hensarling later ran one of the senator's re-election campaigns and his Senate leadership office.

At the outset of the 109th Congress, Hensarling also was a vocal supporter of President Bush's plan to overhaul Social Security by introducing private investment. And he aggressively defended fellow Texan, Majority Leader Tom DeLay, when DeLay came under investigation over the way he raised political contributions. "I support our leader. I support him yesterday, today and tomorrow, and I think he is doing a great job for our caucus," Hensarling told The New York Times.

He is also conservative on social policy. In early 2005, he advocated giving the federal courts jurisdiction in the Terry Schiavo "right to die" case after a state judge in Florida ordered the woman's feeding tube removed. Hensarling also backs a proposed constitutional amendment to ban same-sex marriage and supports government-paid vouchers for private and parochial school tuition.

"I believe that faith and family are the genius of America," says the former Eagle Scout. "The government does a lot in a poor or mediocre fashion."

His prime focus is the federal budget; he sits on the Budget Committee. Hensarling is an outspoken advocate for Bush's economic policies, including the administration's aggressive pursuit of tax cuts. In 2003, Hensarling cosponsored Bush's jobs and growth legislation and has stumped tirelessly for additional tax relief.

But he would go further than Bush and GOP House leaders in forcing the White House and Congress to show more spending restraint. A member of the conservative Republican Study Committee, Hensarling wants to make the annual federal budget approved by Congress mandatory, rather than the guideline for spending that it currently is. He also would outlaw the funding "emergencies" often used by lawmakers to spend more than they originally said they would, and he would require a two-thirds majority vote in the House and Senate to approve any spending over the budget.

After a tense face-off with Republican leaders in 2004, Hensarling and fellow conservatives won a provision to make excess spending subject to a House vote; spending beyond caps set out in the budget resolution could only occur if a majority of the House agreed.

House GOP leaders argued that the change would give Democrats an opening to work mischief on the floor. Opponents, including DeLay, backed down, however, after realizing they did not have enough votes to pass the budget resolution without support from Hensarling's conservative group. His stand angered Republican leaders but it brought him acclaim from influential conservatives, including the American Conservative Union.

Even though he is only in his second term, Hensarling's roots in Congress extend much deeper, reaching back two decades. Three years out of law school, Hensarling was hired in 1985 to oversee Gramm's field offices in Texas. By that time, Gramm had become well-known for the deficit-reduction law that bears his name, Gramm-Rudman-Hollings. It ultimately did not work, though the government finally was able to get to a balanced budget in the 1990s after an economic boom resulted in windfall tax revenues. Deficits crept back with the economic downturn in the early 2000s.

When Gramm was promoted to the leadership as chairman of the National Republican Senatorial Committee in the run-up to the 1992 election, he made Hensarling his executive director. The committee is the main fundraising arm for Senate GOP candidates, and running it helped Hensarling build a network of political friends on Capitol Hill.

He took a break from government to go home to Texas to start his own business, founding a firm that made computer software that helps parents collect child support payments.

Born in Stephenville, Texas, Hensarling grew up working on his father's poultry farm. His grandfather also was a poultry farmer, and Hensarling sometimes makes use in Washington of the wisdom he accrued doing farm work. He once compared his efforts to cut spending and curb waste and fraud in government to the time his father directed him to clean out the chicken coop. "What I discovered was one does not clean up overnight what took many years to accumulate," he told the Dallas Morning News in 2004.

The newspaper, the most influential in his Dallas-based district, endorsed him for re-election that year but chided him for failing to specify how he would cut spending, waste and fraud. "That sounds good, but isn't terribly specific," the News' editorial said. "The only meaningful way to cut the deficit is by cutting spending or hiking taxes. Mr. Hensarling, like most candidates, ducked the hard question."

Hensarling's opening to run for Congress came in 2002, when Texas gained two seats in reapportionment after the 2000 census and the 5th District was reconfigured. Republican Pete Sessions, who had represented the 5th for three terms, decided to run in the new 32nd District.

Hensarling ran in a five-way primary and won. In the general election, he faced Democrat Ron Chapman, a Dallas-area judge for two decades. Hensarling prevailed by 18 percentage points.

In 2004, his Democratic opponent — Bill Bernstein, deputy director of a Dallas family services organization — ran on providing health coverage to the uninsured and repealing Bush's tax cuts. Hensarling trounced him by almost 32 points.

KEY VOTES

2004

No Extend federal unemployment benefits by 13 weeks

No Pass $283.2 billion, six-year federal highway and mass transit bill

Yes Approve $146 billion multi-year extension of previously enacted middle-class tax breaks

Yes Amend the Constitution to prohibit same-sex marriage

Yes Cut corporate taxes $137 billion over 10 years

Yes Reorganize U.S. intelligence agencies as proposed by Sept. 11 commission

2003

Yes Cut taxes by $330 billion through fiscal 2013

No Block Bush rule scaling back overtime pay for some white-collar federal workers

Yes Do not allow use of search warrants without first notifying subjects

Yes Allow importation of prescription drugs

Yes Create private school voucher program in Washington, D.C.

Yes Ban "partial birth" abortion except to save a woman's life

No Split $18.6 billion in Iraq aid into half-grant, half-loan

Yes Overhaul Medicare and create prescription drug benefit

CQ VOTE STUDIES

	PARTY UNITY		PRESIDENTIAL SUPPORT	
	Support	Oppose	Support	Oppose
2004	98%	2%	100%	0%
2003	97%	3%	98%	2%

INTEREST GROUPS

	AFL-CIO	ADA	CCUS	ACU
2004	8%	0%	95%	100%
2003	0%	5%	90%	88%

TEXAS 5

Part of Dallas and east suburbs — Mesquite, part of Garland; Palestine

The 5th begins in Dallas and its eastern suburbs, then winds east and southeast through six other counties. Although only 14 percent of Dallas County's population is included in the 5th, the county is home to almost half of the district's residents.

The district's part of Dallas differs from the glitz and wealth that characterize the portion in the neighboring 32nd. The 5th takes in eastern and northeastern Dallas, which have more of a working-class flavor and are home to many small businesses. Mesquite, a suburb east of the city, also is a major voting base.

Many of the city's suburbs have growing populations and provide easy access to a bustling metropolis while supplying the benefits of small-town life. Prisons are large employers in rural parts of the district. Cattle, natural gas and coal continue to be big industries as well. Many of the smaller towns relied on steel or lumber and were hit hard when those

markets declined, as was most of East Texas.

The 5th generally favors Republicans. GOP areas abound in northeastern Dallas, in neighborhoods on both sides of the Lyndon B. Johnson Freeway and in Anderson and Henderson counties well southeast of the city. Some heavily Hispanic areas in Dallas County's southeastern precincts tend to vote more Democratic, and Mesquite often is politically competitive.

Despite this, George W. Bush carried all seven counties in the 5th in the 2004 presidential election. He garnered 70 percent or more of the vote in the six rural counties, including 76 percent in Wood County, which was added in redistricting prior to the 2004 election.

MAJOR INDUSTRY
Small business, technology, prisons, ranching

CITIES
Mesquite, 124,523; Dallas (pt.), 95,286; Garland (pt.), 73,389; Palestine, 17,598

NOTABLE
The Dallas Arboretum and Botanical Garden; Resistol Arena is home to the Mesquite Championship Rodeo.

Rep. Joe L. Barton (R)

Elected 1984; 11th term

CAPITOL OFFICE
225-2002
joebarton.house.gov
2109 Rayburn 20515-4306; fax 225-3052

COMMITTEES
Energy & Commerce - chairman

HOMETOWN
Ennis

BORN
Sept. 15, 1949, Waco, Texas

RELIGION
Methodist

FAMILY
Wife, Terri Barton; three children

EDUCATION
Texas A&M U., B.S. 1972 (industrial engineering);
Purdue U., M.S. 1973 (industrial administration)

CAREER
Engineering consultant

POLITICAL HIGHLIGHTS
Sought Republican nomination for U.S. Senate
(special election), 1993

ELECTION RESULTS

2004 GENERAL

Joe L. Barton (R)	168,767	66.0%
Morris Meyer (D)	83,609	32.7%
Stephen Schrader (LIBERT)	3,251	1.3%

2004 PRIMARY

Joe L. Barton (R)	unopposed

2002 GENERAL

Joe L. Barton (R)	115,396	70.4%
Felix Alvarado (D)	45,404	27.7%
Frank Brady (LIBERT)	1,992	1.2%

PREVIOUS WINNING PERCENTAGES
2000 (88%); 1998 (73%); 1996 (77%); 1994 (76%);
1992 (72%); 1990 (66%); 1988 (68%); 1986 (56%);
1984 (57%)

Barton has had a slow but steady climb in the House, finally landing one of the most prized committee chairmanships. He heads the Energy and Commerce Committee, with its broad portfolio covering telecommunications, health care and environmental policy.

The 11-term congressman replaced the affable Billy Tauzin as chairman in early 2004, and brought a more dour and partisan tone to committee meetings, in contrast to his joke-cracking predecessor from Louisiana. With a driven nature, Barton set an ambitious agenda for the 109th Congress, signaling his interest in overhauling the Medicaid program, resuming the congressional battle over energy policy and curbing environmental regulations.

Barton has been around long enough to be savvy about the political complexities of passing major bills; nonetheless he hasn't always been able to close the deal. He is a staunch conservative, with an abiding faith in the power of free markets, and he's often reluctant to compromise with his liberal opponents if it means creating more government regulation. He is also a tough partisan whose take-it-or-leave-it approach sometimes stymies the bipartisanship necessary to enact major bills. Barton chaired the Energy and Air Quality Subcommittee before taking the helm of the full committee, and he is a close ally of Majority Leader Tom DeLay.

In the 109th Congress, the Dallas-Fort Worth-area congressman renewed his push for comprehensive energy legislation — which in the 108th had died in a divided Senate. It stalled in part because Barton had insisted on a provision opening up Alaska's Arctic National Wildlife Refuge to oil and gas exploration. Senate Democrats and environmental groups fought the provision, but Barton maintained that a bill without Alaska drilling wasn't worth pursuing. A stronger Senate Republican majority in the 109th Congress could affect the politics of the bill.

As part of any energy overhaul, Barton wants liability protections for companies that produce MTBE, a fuel additive that has been found to contaminate groundwater. Many of the companies that make MTBE are based in Texas. Also of interest are changes to the Clean Air Act that would tighten some federal controls on harmful plant emissions but loosen others.

Barton has been a force, too, behind efforts to build a permanent nuclear waste storage facility at Yucca Mountain in Nevada. In a rare departure from the White House's position, Barton wants to create a special operating fund for the site that would be separate from the government's general revenues. Barton said in 2002, "Nuclear waste is a special commodity. It's in the public good to build this thing and operate it as quickly as possible."

Before the Republicans took control of the House in 1995, the chairmanship of Energy and Commerce was a powerful oversight tool in the hands of Democrat John D. Dingell of Michigan, well-known for his demands for documents from balky government agencies and for his interrogation of witnesses. Barton would like to restore some of the panel's oversight clout. In the 108th Congress, he held hearings into the Food and Drug Administration's having overlooked antidepressants' possible suicidal effects on children, and sought documents from the agency about its examination of Vioxx and other anti-inflammatory drugs linked to increased risks of heart attacks and strokes.

Barton's plans for the 109th Congress included hearings on overhauling Medicaid, the federal-state health insurance program for the poor. Barton would like to curb spending on the federal behemoth as a way of paring the budget deficit, though governors and the Senate are resistant to wholesale changes. "I'd like to see real reform this year," he said as the Congress began.

In the telecommunications arena, Barton would like to increase penalties for broadcast outlets that carry indecent programming and wants to hasten the shift to digital TV programming.

Barton is a balanced-budget crusader whose political mentor is former Texas Republican Sen. Phil Gramm, one of the most well-known budget conservatives of the 1980s and 1990s. In the House, Barton advocates lower taxes and spending restraint, and has pushed for a constitutional amendment requiring a three-fifths majority in Congress to approve an increase in taxes. In 1996, after GOP budget confrontations with the White House led to two government shutdowns, Barton was one of the last GOP holdouts resisting a compromise with the Clinton administration to resolve the impasse.

Also during the Clinton years, Barton led the charge on his subcommittee against Energy Secretary Hazel R. O'Leary's controversial travel budget and demanded more efficiency at national laboratories. In 1997, he and California Democrat Anna G. Eshoo brokered an agreement expediting FDA review of medical devices.

A graduate of Texas A&M University, Barton is a former engineering consultant for Atlantic Richfield Co. Inspired by President Reagan to get into politics, Barton's only policy experience before winning election to the House in 1984 was as a White House fellow for the Department of Energy, an opportunity he learned about in Smithsonian magazine.

Having won Gramm's House seat after he moved to the Senate, Barton too hoped one day to be elected to the Senate. But two opportunities have come and gone, with Barton twice being outflanked by other GOP candidates.

When Texas Democrat Lloyd Bentsen left the Senate in 1993 to be President Clinton's Treasury secretary, Barton jumped into the GOP primary for the special election, but finished a distant third in an all-party primary. Later, upon Gramm's Senate retirement in 2002, Barton mulled a bid for that seat but demurred when the White House backed the ultimately successful candidacy of Texas Republican John Cornyn — the former Texas attorney general who had been appointed to fill out the remainder of Gramm's term.

Barton runs strong in his House re-election races, however. In 1998, American Airlines bankrolled a challenger after Barton supported a bill that brought the airline more competition at its Dallas-Fort Worth International hub. Barton prevailed in the primary with 73 percent and cruised to re-election in the fall. He has enjoyed lopsided victories ever since.

KEY VOTES

2004

No   Extend federal unemployment benefits by 13 weeks

No   Pass $283.2 billion, six-year federal highway and mass transit bill

Yes   Approve $146 billion multi-year extension of previously enacted middle-class tax breaks

Yes   Amend the Constitution to prohibit same-sex marriage

Yes   Cut corporate taxes $137 billion over 10 years

No   Reorganize U.S. intelligence agencies as proposed by Sept. 11 commission

2003

Yes   Cut taxes by $330 billion through fiscal 2013

No   Block Bush rule scaling back overtime pay for some white-collar federal workers

Yes   Do not allow use of search warrants without first notifying subjects

No   Allow importation of prescription drugs

Yes   Create private school voucher program in Washington, D.C.

Yes   Ban "partial birth" abortion except to save a woman's life

No   Split $18.6 billion in Iraq aid into half-grant, half-loan

Yes   Overhaul Medicare and create prescription drug benefit

CQ VOTE STUDIES

	PARTY UNITY		PRESIDENTIAL SUPPORT	
	Support	Oppose	Support	Oppose
2004	97%	3%	94%	6%
2003	98%	2%	96%	4%
2002	98%	2%	90%	10%
2001	98%	2%	86%	14%
2000	93%	7%	23%	77%

INTEREST GROUPS

	AFL-CIO	ADA	CCUS	ACU
2004	7%	0%	100%	96%
2003	7%	5%	97%	88%
2002	13%	0%	100%	96%
2001	0%	5%	91%	96%
2000	11%	10%	83%	100%

TEXAS 6

Suburban Dallas – Arlington; parts of Fort Worth and Mansfield; Corsicana

A serpentine district in its 1990s configuration that hopped between GOP areas in and outside of Fort Worth and Arlington, the 6th, as redrawn in redistricting prior to the 2004 election, now consists of a boot-shaped band of counties extending southeast from the Dallas-Fort Worth Metroplex. The suburban-rural district takes in southern and eastern Tarrant County, including about 5 percent of Fort Worth and all of Arlington, and then moves to the southeast along Interstate 45.

Slightly less than two-thirds of district residents live in Tarrant, while most of the rest live in Ellis and Navarro counties. Ellis, which includes Waxahachie and Ennis, used to be dependent on cotton farming, but the cement industry has taken hold there. Redistricting added more counties in East Texas such as Freestone and Leon, which are rural, less-populated and sustained by oil, ranching and farming. The district also has a fairly large timber industry in Houston and northern Trinity counties.

Fort Worth's and Arlington's economies have diversified and expanded in recent years, while population growth in Arlington has leveled out after a tremendous boom from the 1950s through the 1990s. There are some black, Hispanic and Asian areas in the district, and the overall minority population of the new district has increased. Still, the 6th is nearly two-thirds white and generally financially secure and suburban.

The district also is heavily Republican. Most of the Tarrant precincts are aligned with the GOP, although there is some Democratic strength in southern Fort Worth and eastern Arlington. The overwhelming GOP advantage in Ellis, which George W. Bush won with 75 percent of the vote in 2004, makes the 6th a safe haven for Republican candidates.

MAJOR INDUSTRY
Transportation, home building, technology, agriculture

CITIES
Arlington, 332,968; Mansfield (pt.), 27,409; Fort Worth (pt.), 26,709

NOTABLE
A superconducting supercollider — or atom smasher — was to be located in Waxahachie, but Congress cut all funding for the project in 1993; Crockett is home to the World Championship Fiddler's Festival each summer, something near and dear to the heart of Davy Crockett.

Rep. John Culberson (R)

Elected 2000; 3rd term

CAPITOL OFFICE
225-2571
www.culberson.house.gov
1728 Longworth 20515-4307; fax 225-4381

COMMITTEES
Appropriations

HOMETOWN
Houston

BORN
Aug. 24, 1956, Houston, Texas

RELIGION
Methodist

FAMILY
Wife, Belinda Culberson; one child

EDUCATION
Southern Methodist U., B.A. 1981 (history); South Texas College of Law, J.D. 1988

CAREER
Lawyer; political advertising agency employee; oil rig mud logger

POLITICAL HIGHLIGHTS
Texas House, 1987-2001

ELECTION RESULTS

2004 GENERAL

John Culberson (R)	175,440	64.1%
John Martinez (D)	91,126	33.3%
Paul Staton (I)	3,713	1.4%
Drew Parks (LIBERT)	3,372	1.2%

2004 PRIMARY

John Culberson (R)	26,561	92.2%
Sam Texas (R)	2,245	7.8%

2002 GENERAL

John Culberson (R)	96,795	89.2%
Drew Parks (LIBERT)	11,674	10.8%

PREVIOUS WINNING PERCENTAGES
2000 (74%)

Culberson plays a crucial role in the Republican-led House as one of those little noticed but effective conservative foot soldiers who give GOP leaders key victories and keep the party on a rightward tack.

He is a stalwart conservative who is suspicious of the successful, and expensive, efforts by President Bush and GOP leaders to expand certain government programs during Bush's first term in office. But Culberson is above all a team player.

He voted with a majority of his party 97 percent of the time in the 108th Congress, but even that high number understated Culberson's loyalty. In one of his few splits with Republicans, he voted against a 2003 Medicare prescription drug bill wanted by Bush and GOP leaders — but during a dramatic all-night session, he switched his vote from yes to no when it became clear GOP leaders had secured the votes they needed.

Now in his third term, Culberson has largely remained behind the scenes. He prefers to sign on as a cosponsor of another lawmaker's bill rather than introduce an identical one with his name on it. He says he directs most of his attention to local concerns, including expanding the Interstate 10 freeway and fighting a plan to locate a concrete plant in a small town in west Harris County.

But early in the 109th Congress, Culberson began taking on a slightly higher profile. After Majority Leader Tom DeLay was chastised three times by the ethics committee in 2004 and then came under increased scrutiny and criticism in early 2005, Culberson spoke out repeatedly in his behalf. He and DeLay have worked together for years on local issues. They both represent parts of Houston and its suburbs.

"During the Civil War, Confederate General Stonewall Jackson ordered his troops to target Union commanders telling them to always shoot the brave ones first because it would scare the others," he said in October 2004. "In the same way, the Democrats are targeting Tom DeLay because he is an effective and courageous leader, and they have been unable to defeat him in key votes on the House floor."

Culberson came close to scoring a major victory in the 108th. A longtime critic of U.S. efforts to combat illegal immigration, he is interested in the use of documents provided by the Mexican government to its citizens, known as "matricula consular" cards. The cards are often used by illegal immigrants as identification in the United States, particularly for banking.

Culberson charges that the cards are easily forged and could be used by terrorists to cross the border and gain money. He successfully added language to the 2004 Transportation-Treasury spending bill to prohibit banks from accepting the cards as identification. But, after complaints from Hispanic groups and the banking industry, the White House and key GOP lawmakers opposed the language. It was stripped out on the House floor.

In his first term, Culberson was put on the Republican Steering Committee, which makes panel assignments. He won high marks from other lawmakers because he focused on lobbying for good appointments for other freshmen. That cost him a chance at his top committee choice — Transportation and Infrastructure. But 13 other freshmen got slots on the panel, and he told the Houston Chronicle that all 13 had promised to support funding for Culberson's No. 1 legislative priority — expansion of the Katy Freeway, a 22-mile stretch of Interstate 10 heading west, from Houston to Katy. It is among the most congested highways in the country.

In the 108th, Culberson was rewarded for his unselfish work of two years before, and he gained assignment to the Appropriations Committee, including a seat on the subcommittee that provides transportation funds.

Although he wants funding for Houston's highways, Culberson at first opposed building then expanding a light-rail system in Houston. But despite an expensive campaign by rail opponents, voters overwhelmingly supported expanding the system in 2003. Culberson said he would comply with the voters' wishes.

A visit to Culberson's Capitol Hill office makes it clear he is an ardent fan of the principal author of the Declaration of Independence and the third president of the United States. Several portraits of Thomas Jefferson are on display, including one hung at precisely Jefferson's 6-foot, 2 1/2-inch height. He has collected other items of Jeffersoniana as well as countless books about the statesman.

Culberson had plenty of experience in state governance when he arrived in Washington, having spent 14 years in the Texas House. He proudly pointed out to his House colleagues that he already had a working relationship with the newly elected president. Bush was governor of Texas from 1995 through 2000. Culberson's predecessors in his affluent suburban Houston district included the president's father, George Bush, who held the seat for four years, and Bill Archer, the former Ways and Means Committee chairman, who won the seat after Bush and stayed for 30 years.

His desk in his House office is a refurbished mahogany roll-top that he bought in an antique store when he discovered that it had once belonged to his great-great-uncle Charles Culberson, who was governor of Texas from 1895 to 1899 and a U.S. senator from 1899 to 1923.

Culberson's father owned an advertising agency, where he often produced public relations materials for local candidates. Culberson worked with his father and said he became interested in politics as a result. After high school, he worked on offshore oil rigs before college. He was elected to the Texas House at 30, while in law school.

During his years in the state House, Culberson served as the Republican whip and compiled a staunchly conservative voting record.

When Archer announced his retirement in 2000, a passel of Republicans filed to succeed him, but Culberson finished first in the seven-way GOP primary and survived an expensive runoff. Winning the runoff ensured his election: The 7th is a solidly Republican district and he earned almost three-quarters of the vote. Democrats did not field a challenger in 2002. In 2004, he won with 64 percent of the vote.

KEY VOTES

2004
? Extend federal unemployment benefits by 13 weeks
? Pass $283.2 billion, six-year federal highway and mass transit bill
Yes Approve $146 billion multi-year extension of previously enacted middle-class tax breaks
Yes Amend the Constitution to prohibit same-sex marriage
Yes Cut corporate taxes $137 billion over 10 years
No Reorganize U.S. intelligence agencies as proposed by Sept. 11 commission

2003
Yes Cut taxes by $330 billion through fiscal 2013
No Block Bush rule scaling back overtime pay for some white-collar federal workers
Yes Do not allow use of search warrants without first notifying subjects
Yes Allow importation of prescription drugs
Yes Create private school voucher program in Washington, D.C.
Yes Ban "partial birth" abortion except to save a woman's life
No Split $18.6 billion in Iraq aid into half-grant, half-loan
No Overhaul Medicare and create prescription drug benefit

CQ VOTE STUDIES

	PARTY UNITY		PRESIDENTIAL SUPPORT	
	Support	Oppose	Support	Oppose
2004	97%	3%	90%	10%
2003	97%	3%	91%	9%
2002	99%	1%	85%	15%
2001	99%	1%	95%	5%

INTEREST GROUPS

	AFL-CIO	ADA	CCUS	ACU
2004	0%	0%	100%	96%
2003	7%	15%	93%	96%
2002	11%	0%	90%	100%
2001	0%	0%	96%	100%

TEXAS 7

Western Houston and suburbs — Bellaire, West University Place, Jersey Village

Situated in western Houston, the 7th includes a portion of Houston's oil and gas industry, as well as much of the Texas Medical Center — a vast medical complex shared with the 9th District — and Rice University, both of which were added during redistricting prior to the 2004 election. The 7th also includes The Galleria, a huge shopping and office complex that provides jobs and a major retail presence.

Like other areas around Houston, the district rebounded slowly after the oil industry's troubles in the 1980s. But an increasing emphasis on technology firms and corporate headquarters enabled the 7th to enjoy sustained economic growth during the 1990s.

Redistricting pushed the 7th farther east, deeper inside the Interstate 610 beltway encircling Houston. The district's easternmost point hits Main Street just south of downtown Houston and extends down Main to the southwest. The 7th takes in one-fifth of Harris County's population.

Minorities make up almost one-third of the 7th's population, with Hispanics comprising 18 percent of that total. Three-fifths of district residents live in Houston, and the 7th's share of the city is mostly middle-class. Northwest Houston includes a large Hispanic population, and there are sizable black and Asian populations in southwest Houston.

Much of the district is characterized by white-collar executives, good schools and religious conservatism. The 7th's median income is brought up by wealthy villages such as Piney Point, Bunker Hill and Hunters Creek, which are near Interstate 10 and surrounded on all sides by Houston, and the exclusive neighborhood River Oaks.

Redistricting only slightly increased the 7th's strong Republican trend. In 2002, Republican Gov. Rick Perry took 71 percent of the district's vote, and George W. Bush took 64 percent of the 2004 presidential vote here.

MAJOR INDUSTRY
Energy, health care, education and research, retail

CITIES
Houston (pt.), 390,922; Bellaire, 15,642; West University Place, 14,211

NOTABLE
George Bush, who later served as vice president and president, represented the 7th from 1967 to 1971 and currently resides here.

Rep. Kevin Brady (R)

Elected 1996; 5th term

After four terms in the House, the unassuming Brady has gradually worked his way into the limelight. His membership on the Ways and Means Committee enables him to be a player on trade and tax issues, although his diverse interests range from health care and education to criminal justice and campaign finance law.

Brady's profile began to rise in the 108th Congress, when he added an appointment as one of about 20 Republican deputy whips to his Ways and Means slot, and he began the 109th as an influential voice on Central American trade and tax cuts.

Brady comes across as a regular guy: a dad who sometimes brings his young son to his congressional office, a baseball devotee who relishes the annual charity ballgame against the Democrats. He is a loyal party man, siding 98 percent of the time with the GOP in the 108th and 93 percent of the time with President Bush. But he was born into a family of Democrats. His uncle was a state senator, his father a county party official.

He credits his early experiences with a host of civic groups and his 18 years as a Chamber of Commerce executive with molding his pro-business, staunchly Republican political philosophy. He says he has observed numerous business leaders who are role models for civic involvement and who have shown that private sector solutions to community problems are often more effective than government programs.

As both a tax writer and a Texan, Brady scored a major legislative win in 2004 as he took on a wrinkle in the federal tax code that allowed taxpayers to deduct state and local income taxes, but not sales taxes, from their federal income taxes. He authored legislation, which made its way into an international tax bill, to allow for the deduction of sales taxes as well — an important issue for Texas and a half-dozen other states that do not have an income tax. "The tax code shouldn't be biased in favor of income taxes," Brady said. As signed into law, the provision would allow taxpayers to deduct sales taxes for two years. Brady immediately began pressing to make the deduction permanent.

In the 108th, Republicans tapped Brady to be the point person on Ways and Means in the effort to garner congressional approval for the Central America Free Trade Agreement. In that role, Brady helped keep the administration up to date on the latest vote count, and he counseled trade officials on the timing of sending the controversial legislation to Congress. After the measure stalled in 2004, he expressed guarded optimism about its prospects in the 109th. "We need to find new customers abroad for American and Texas products," he said.

Transforming government has been a theme for Brady almost since the moment he arrived in Congress. He routinely sponsors legislation — similar to a law in Texas that has eliminated 29 agencies — to set expiration dates for each federal agency, department and program. His "sunset" bill, which he first introduced as a freshman, would create a commission of eight members of Congress and four private citizens who would evaluate each agency and recommend streamlining, privatization or abolishment of those that did not justify their existence. At the beginning of the 109th, President Bush included a similar plan in his fiscal 2006 budget.

Brady, whose interest in reining in government includes education, won inclusion in the 2001 education overhaul of a provision to protect teachers from frivolous lawsuits when they discipline children in school.

CAPITOL OFFICE
225-4901
rep.brady@mail.house.gov
www.house.gov/brady
428 Cannon 20515-4308; fax 225-5524

COMMITTEES
Ways & Means
Joint Economic

HOMETOWN
The Woodlands

BORN
April 11, 1955, Vermillion, S.D.

RELIGION
Roman Catholic

FAMILY
Wife, Cathy Brady; two children

EDUCATION
U. of South Dakota, B.S. 1990 (mass communication)

CAREER
Chamber of commerce executive

POLITICAL HIGHLIGHTS
Texas House, 1991-96

ELECTION RESULTS

2004 GENERAL

Kevin Brady (R)	179,599	68.9%
James "Jim" Wright (D)	77,324	29.7%
Paul Hansen (LIBERT)	3,705	1.4%

2004 PRIMARY

Kevin Brady (R)	unopposed

2002 GENERAL

Kevin Brady (R)	140,575	93.1%
Gil Guillory (LIBERT)	10,351	6.9%

PREVIOUS WINNING PERCENTAGES
2000 (92%); 1998 (93%); 1996 General Runoff Election (59%)

Brady sometimes has parted with his party on the issue of gun rights. When Brady was 12 years old, his father, a lawyer, was shot and killed in a South Dakota courtroom by the deranged spouse of a client, and the incident has shaped his policy position in the politically volatile arena of gun control ever since. As a state representative, Brady also refused to vote for a bill to allow Texans to carry concealed weapons, and he says he still opposes such measures today.

Although he generally shuns the spotlight, Brady momentarily became associated with one of the more unseemly partisan disputes in the 108th. When Republicans and Democrats on Ways and Means squared off over the handling of a pension bill in 2003, the situation escalated to the point of Chairman Bill Thomas of California calling the Capitol Police and members exchanging vicious verbal taunts and possibly physical threats. Putting much of the blame on California Democrat Pete Stark, Brady said on the House floor, "I did not know whether this gentleman could control either his emotions or his bodily functions." Following Democratic protests, Brady apologized and agreed to withdraw his comments.

Brady attended the University of South Dakota. He left college in 1978, but he did not graduate until 1990 because he had neglected to complete the paperwork for a work-study class. After an opponent in his first Texas House race unearthed Brady's lack of a degree, Brady dug out the old course work to clear up the incomplete grade.

He spent about six years as a state representative in Austin. When Republican Jack Fields announced he would not seek re-election in the 8th District in 1996, it took Brady an arduous four races to become his successor. Wealthy Republican physician Gene Fontenot emerged on top in the March GOP primary, but did not win a majority of the vote. Brady had much stronger ties to the district and defeated Fontenot in the April runoff.

Later in the year, however, a panel of three federal judges redrew the 8th as well as 12 other Texas congressional districts in response to a Supreme Court ruling that found illegal "racial gerrymandering" at play in the Texas map. The federal court threw out the primary results from those districts and ordered new elections. In November, Fontenot forced Brady into a December runoff. Brady finally prevailed with 59 percent of the vote.

He has been safely ensconced in Congress ever since. His district changed dramatically during the 108th when the Texas Legislature redrew the state's congressional map, stretching the 8th more than 150 miles from Houston to Louisiana. But it remained solidly Republican, and Brady won re-election easily in 2004 with 69 percent.

KEY VOTES

2004

No Extend federal unemployment benefits by 13 weeks
No Pass $283.2 billion, six-year federal highway and mass transit bill
Yes Approve $146 billion multi-year extension of previously enacted middle-class tax breaks
Yes Amend the Constitution to prohibit same-sex marriage
Yes Cut corporate taxes $137 billion over 10 years
Yes Reorganize U.S. intelligence agencies as proposed by Sept. 11 commission

2003

Yes Cut taxes by $330 billion through fiscal 2013
No Block Bush rule scaling back overtime pay for some white-collar federal workers
No Do not allow use of search warrants without first notifying subjects
Yes Allow importation of prescription drugs
Yes Create private school voucher program in Washington, D.C.
+   Ban "partial birth" abortion except to save a woman's life
No Split $18.6 billion in Iraq aid into half-grant, half-loan
Yes Overhaul Medicare and create prescription drug benefit

CQ VOTE STUDIES

| | PARTY UNITY | | PRESIDENTIAL SUPPORT | |
	Support	Oppose	Support	Oppose
2004	98%	2%	94%	6%
2003	98%	2%	92%	8%
2002	97%	3%	85%	15%
2001	98%	2%	90%	10%
2000	97%	3%	24%	76%

INTEREST GROUPS

	AFL-CIO	ADA	CCUS	ACU
2004	7%	0%	100%	100%
2003	0%	10%	97%	84%
2002	13%	0%	100%	100%
2001	8%	0%	100%	96%
2000	0%	0%	80%	100%

TEXAS 8
East central — The Woodlands, Conroe

A Republican stronghold, the 8th begins in Houston's rapidly growing Montgomery County suburbs north of the city and moves east through rural areas to the Louisiana border. Four-fifths of district residents are white, the highest percentage of white residents in any Texas district.

Located about 30 miles north of downtown Houston, The Woodlands — a large planned community that gets its name from its proximity to Sam Houston National Forest — is an exclusive area filled with large houses and good schools. The area has aggressively courted businesses, and several petroleum and biotechnology companies make their homes here.

The timber industry and some cattle ranches populate the northern part of Montgomery County, although these areas are quickly becoming suburbs of Houston as well. Conroe has one of the largest lakes in the area and is home to many wealthy lakefront homeowners. Farther north are Huntsville and Livingston, where a Texas State Penitentiary that houses the state's death row is a major employer.

In the southeastern part of the district, the economy relies on the chemical and shipping industries in Orange County and nearby Beaumont and Port Arthur (in the 2nd District). Slow population growth and a high percentage of blue-collar workers have made it difficult to attract higher-paying service jobs.

Prior to redistricting before the 2004 elections, the 8th routinely gave GOP candidates more than 75 percent of the vote in statewide elections, regularly topping every other Texas congressional district in its support for Republicans. With the addition of a swath of East Texas counties to its Montgomery County base, the 8th remains consistently conservative, but some Democratic areas in the southeast have lowered Republican vote percentages here so they are closer to two-thirds than three-fourths.

MAJOR INDUSTRY
Petrochemicals, shipping, timber, education, prisons

CITIES
The Woodlands (unincorporated), 55,649; Conroe, 36,811; Huntsville, 35,078

NOTABLE
Texas' Lone Star flag was designed in Montgomery County in 1839; Huntsville's Sam Houston was the first president of the Republic of Texas.

Rep. Al Green (D)

Elected 2004; 1st term

Although he challenged an incumbent in the primary election in order to get to Congress, shaking things up in Washington does not appear a high priority for Green: He exhibited a subdued and deliberate manner in his campaign and thereafter.

He sought and received a seat on the Financial Services Committee and obtained assignments to subcommittees with jurisdiction over issues that are relevant to his 9th District constituency — such as consumer credit, housing and community development.

His Science Committee assignment got him on the Space and Aeronautics Subcommittee, which is something of a local plum, given the proximity of NASA's Johnson Space Flight Center in Houston.

Green said a main focus would be fortifying Social Security, the primary income source for many in a district that has a large low-income population. Like most Democrats, he dismissed President Bush's early 2005 proposal to allow diversion of some Social Security taxes into personal savings accounts.

Green took advantage of the GOP-inspired remapping of Texas' congressional districts prior to the 2004 election, which, in order to help Republicans elsewhere, significantly altered the demographics of the district.

Whereas the pre-remap 25th District that elected Democrat Chris Bell in 2002 took in mainly suburban areas of Houston and its environs, the new 9th District has a much more urban cast. More important, the black population was greatly increased — providing a good opportunity for Green, a justice of the peace in Houston for 27 years and a veteran civil rights advocate who was the city's NAACP chapter president for a decade in the late 1980s and early 1990s.

Green scored a crushing 2-to-1 victory over Bell, then won his general election over Republican attorney Arlette Molina with even greater ease in one of Texas' few remaining Democratic strongholds. The win enabled him to join two other black House members from Texas, Democrats Eddie Bernice Johnson of Dallas and Sheila Jackson-Lee of Houston.

CAPITOL OFFICE
225-7508
www.house.gov/algreen
1529 Longworth 20515-4309; fax 225-2947

COMMITTEES
Financial Services
Science

HOMETOWN
Houston

BORN
Sept. 1, 1947, New Orleans, La.

RELIGION
Christian

FAMILY
Divorced

EDUCATION
Florida A&M U., attended 1966-71; Tuskegee Institute of Technology, attended; Texas Southern U., J.D. 1973

CAREER
Lawyer; NAACP chapter president

POLITICAL HIGHLIGHTS
Harris County Justice of the Peace Court judge, 1977-2004; candidate for mayor of Houston, 1981

ELECTION RESULTS

2004 GENERAL

Al Green (D)	114,462	72.2%
Arlette Molina (R)	42,132	26.6%
Stacey Lynn Bourland (LIBERT)	1,972	1.2%

2004 PRIMARY

Al Green (D)	18,034	66.5%
Chris Bell (D)	8,492	31.3%
Beverly A. Spencer (D)	607	2.2%

TEXAS 9
Southern Houston and suburbs — Mission Bend

The 9th, which takes in southern Houston, is one of the country's most diverse districts. Thirty-seven percent black, one-third Hispanic and 11 percent Asian, its large minority presence makes the district solidly Democratic. Its residents gave John Kerry 70 percent of the 2004 presidential vote.

The east side of the district takes in largely black communities such as Sunnyside, then stretches west to take in the new football park, Reliant Stadium, and the old Astrodome where the Astros and the Oilers used to play. Although the Astrodome sits vacant, officials have discussed turning the building into either an amusement park or a convention hotel, which would bring new jobs and revenue to the district. In the area around Reliant Stadium, the hotel and entertainment industry prevails.

The west portion of the 9th takes in much of Houston's Asian community, with Chinese, Korean and Japanese enclaves in addition to several South Asian immigrant communities. In this growing area, retail dominates as businesses spring up with signs in both English and Asian languages. The Chinatown area boasts one of the nation's largest Asian-themed malls, the Hong Kong City Mall. Almost one-third of district residents are foreign-born, the highest percentage in the state.

Part of the Texas Medical Center (shared with the 7th) also lands in the 9th, bringing health care issues to the forefront here. Job creation also is a high priority among the area's many poor residents.

MAJOR INDUSTRY
Retail, health care, entertainment

CITIES
Houston (pt.), 551,793; Mission Bend (unincorporated), 30,831; Missouri City (pt.), 20,058

NOTABLE
The Astrodome was once dubbed the eighth wonder of the world when it first opened in 1965 and led to the development of Astroturf.

Rep. Michael McCaul (R)

Elected 2004; 1st term

McCaul says his career path "stems from my religious beliefs that say you have to do something worthwhile with your life in the service of others." He describes himself as a "conservative Republican" and he clearly has strong partisan instincts. But he says he is willing to work with Democratic members to get more accomplished for his district.

A former prosecutor and counterterrorism official in the U.S. Justice Department, McCaul didn't get his first choice for a committee assignment, a seat on the Judiciary Committee. But he did get a sought-after seat on the Homeland Security panel, along with a post on the International Relations Committee and its Subcommittee on International Terrorism.

McCaul's assignment to the Science Committee and its Subcommittee on Space and Aeronautics is relevant to Houston's Johnson Space Flight Center, not that far from the southeastern reaches of his 10th District.

He says his top legislative priority is to make permanent the tax cuts that President Bush pushed to enactment in 2001 and 2003.

The 2004 Republican primary that marked McCaul's political debut was an eight-candidate free-for-all. McCaul, who amassed key support from Republican insiders, made the runoff but trailed front-running businessman Ben Streusand by 4 percentage points. Nonetheless, McCaul surged in the runoff and won comfortably with 63 percent of the vote.

Democrats did not even field a candidate in the general election, and with opposition only from a Libertarian nominee and a write-in candidate, McCaul coasted home in the general election with 79 percent, thanks to new district lines that split his home town of Austin and brought in many more GOP-leaning voters to counter Austin's Democratic bent.

The almost free ride he received after winning a tough primary had a big benefit for McCaul. It gave him time to cultivate ties with other would-be Republican House newcomers, which paid off with his selection by members of the Class of 2004 to be their representative to the Republican leadership.

CAPITOL OFFICE
225-2401
www.house.gov/mccaul
415 Cannon 20515-4310; fax 225-5955

COMMITTEES
Homeland Security
International Relations
Science

HOMETOWN
Austin

BORN
Jan. 14, 1962, Dallas, Texas

RELIGION
Roman Catholic

FAMILY
Wife, Linda McCaul; five children

EDUCATION
Trinity U., B.A. 1984 (business & history); St. Mary's U. (Texas), J.D. 1987

CAREER
U.S. Justice Department official; state and federal prosecutor; lawyer

POLITICAL HIGHLIGHTS
No previous office

ELECTION RESULTS

2004 GENERAL

Michael McCaul (R)	182,113	78.6%
Robert Fritsche (LIBERT)	35,569	15.4%
Lorenzo Sadun (I) - write-in	13,961	6.0%

2004 PRIMARY RUNOFF

Michael McCaul (R)	15,084	63.2%
Ben Streusand (R)	8,803	36.9%

2004 PRIMARY

Ben Streusand (R)	9,364	28.2%
Michael McCaul (R)	7,953	23.9%
John Devine (R)	7,096	21.4%
Dave Phillips (R)	4,460	13.4%
Teresa Doggett Taylor (R)	1,494	4.5%
Pat Elliott (R)	1,245	3.7%
John Kelley (R)	952	2.9%
Brad Tashenberg (R)	695	2.1%

TEXAS 10

East central — eastern Austin and western Houston suburbs

The 10th mimics a drive that many University of Texas students from the Houston area know well as they travel back and forth to school in Austin. Spanning about 150 miles, the district stretches west from the northern Houston suburbs and follows U.S. Highway 290 to Austin, where it hugs downtown as it wraps around the city's northwestern edge.

Narrowly missing the Democratic stronghold of Hyde Park and the University of Texas in Austin, the 10th instead takes in the more upscale areas of the Arboretum, Far West and the neighborhood of West Lake, part of Austin's hill country. The district also reaches up to Pflugerville and the northern suburbs, where many of Austin's technology companies are located. IBM has a lab in Austin, and Dell is based in Round Rock, just across the district line in the 31st.

As the district moves east from Austin, it becomes increasingly rural, taking in the towns of Elgin and Giddings and cities such as Brenham, Hempstead and Prairie View, where agriculture dominates.

The district then dips back into more-urban areas as it takes in the affluent suburbs in northwest Harris County, including Tomball and part of Spring, which have experienced high growth as people move farther from downtown Houston. Most residents here have lengthy commutes, which makes transportation policy an important issue.

Although the 10th includes vastly different urban, suburban and rural areas, it is reliably Republican. George W. Bush captured 61 percent of the area's vote in 2004, and no Democrat ran for the open seat in 2004 following mid-decade redistricting.

MAJOR INDUSTRY
Software, technology, agriculture

CITIES
Austin (pt.), 209,200; Pflugerville, 16,335

NOTABLE
The Presidential Corridor runs from the Johnson Library in Austin to the Bush Library in College Station (in the neighboring 17th).

Rep. K. Michael Conaway (R)

CAPITOL OFFICE
225-3605
conaway.house.gov
511 Cannon 20515-4311; fax 225-1783

COMMITTEES
Agriculture
Armed Services
Budget

HOMETOWN
Midland

BORN
June 11, 1948, Borger, Texas

RELIGION
Baptist

FAMILY
Wife, Suzanne Conaway; four children

EDUCATION
East Texas State U., B.B.A. 1970 (accounting)

MILITARY SERVICE
Army, 1970-72

CAREER
Accountant; bank chief financial officer; oil and gas exploration company chief financial officer

POLITICAL HIGHLIGHTS
Midland school board, 1985-88; candidate for U.S. House (special election), 2003

ELECTION RESULTS

2004 GENERAL

K. Michael Conaway (R)	177,291	76.8%
Wayne Raasch (D)	50,339	21.8%
Jeffrey C. Blunt (LIBERT)	3,347	1.5%

2004 PRIMARY

K. Michael Conaway (R)	38,792	74.5%
Bill Lester (R)	13,255	25.5%

Elected 2004; 1st term

As a former business partner of President Bush and someone who Bush — as governor of Texas — named to a state board, Conaway can boast some of the best connections of any incoming freshman.

Conaway and Bush are nearly the same age and knew each other socially in Midland, the hub of the 11th District. From 1981 until 1986, Conaway was chief financial officer of Arbusto Energy Inc. (later Bush Exploration), which Bush owned. In 1995, his first year as Texas governor, Bush appointed Conaway to the state Board of Public Accountancy; Conaway served on that panel for seven years, including five as chairman.

Conaway's assignment to the Budget Committee reflects his background as a certified public accountant and his ties to Bush. He also got a seat on the Armed Services panel. His support of the military is bolstered by his personal experience as a military police officer at Fort Hood in central Texas, where he served from 1970 to 1972.

The importance of oil and gas to his district's economy has made increasing domestic energy production one of Conaway's top priorities. But the 11th also includes expanses of farm country — cotton is the principal crop — which explains why Conaway sought and obtained a seat on the Agriculture Committee.

A self-described fiscal and social conservative, Conaway says his voting record will reflect a commitment to lower taxes, smaller government and a stronger military.

Conaway, whose only previous experience in elective office had been on the Midland school board, won the 2004 race just 17 months after losing a close special-election race, by just 587 votes, to fellow Republican Randy Neugebauer in the 19th District.

But the GOP-inspired mid-decade congressional redistricting for the 2004 elections deliberately put Neugebauer and Conaway in different districts, and Conaway breezed to victory in the new Midland-based 11th. He won both his primary and general-election contests by ratios of roughly 3-to-1.

TEXAS 11
West central — Midland, Odessa, San Angelo

Starting west of Austin in Burnet County, the 11th moves across the state through San Angelo to Midland, Odessa and the border with New Mexico. Although there are stark contrasts in the topography, the 11th's residents remain mostly the same — white, rural and Republican.

In the west lies oil country and the Permian Basin, home to Midland and Odessa. The 11th's economy, with its dependence on oil and agriculture, was nearly devastated during the worldwide oil glut of the 1980s and bad weather in the 1990s. Famine and drought have harmed cattle and cotton, and the oil industry has declined.

While the western portion of the district is mostly high desert plains, the southeast section moves into the highland lakes region, taking in part of the state's hill country. Here, agriculture dominates, with cotton being the

key crop, followed by row crops, cattle, sheep, goats and small grains. This region also has grown in popularity with hunters, and tourism has become a major industry.

The immense 11th gave George W. Bush 78 percent of the 2004 presidential vote, the highest percentage Bush received in any Texas congressional district.

Despite solidly Republican and socially conservative leanings, economic hardships have forced district residents to turn to government agriculture assistance. The 11th also has the state's highest percentage of residents over age 65 (15 percent).

MAJOR INDUSTRY
Oil and gas, agriculture, cattle, tourism

MILITARY BASES
Goodfellow Air Force Base, 1,548 military, 624 civilian (2004)

CITIES
Midland, 94,996; Odessa, 90,943; San Angelo, 88,439; Brownwood, 18,813

NOTABLE
Loving County (population 67) has the fewest residents of any U.S. county.

Rep. Kay Granger (R)

CAPITOL OFFICE
225-5071
texas.granger@mail.house.gov
kaygranger.house.gov
440 Cannon 20515-4312; fax 225-5683

COMMITTEES
Appropriations

HOMETOWN
Fort Worth

BORN
Jan. 18, 1943, Greenville, Texas

RELIGION
Methodist

FAMILY
Divorced; three children

EDUCATION
Texas Wesleyan U., B.S. 1965

CAREER
Insurance agency owner; teacher

POLITICAL HIGHLIGHTS
Fort Worth Zoning Commission, 1981-89; Fort
Worth City Council, 1989-91; mayor of Fort Worth,
1991-95

ELECTION RESULTS

2004 GENERAL

Kay Granger (R)	173,222	72.3%
Felix Alvarado (D)	66,316	27.7%

2004 PRIMARY

Kay Granger (R)	unopposed

2002 GENERAL

Kay Granger (R)	121,208	91.9%
Edward A. Hanson (LIBERT)	10,723	8.1%

PREVIOUS WINNING PERCENTAGES
2000 (63%); 1998 (62%); 1996 (58%)

Elected 1996; 5th term

Smart and ambitious, Granger is the kind of politician GOP leaders need to help translate their legislative agenda into terms that will resonate with voters, particularly women.

A divorced mother of three, Granger can speak with authority from the perspective of a teacher, a businesswoman, a working parent and a local elected official on topics ranging from crime, drugs and military needs, to such "Democratic" issues as education and health care. A solid vote for the leadership on most issues, she is often tapped to explain the party's views.

The Bush campaign put her to use in the 2004 elections, when she helped lead a "W Stands for Women" campaign to attract women voters. After the elections, Granger reached out to women outside of the United States, heading up the Iraqi Women's Caucus, a bipartisan group of lawmakers who traveled to Iraq prior to the country's January 2005 elections to meet with women candidates seeking a role in the new Iraqi government. "I learned more probably than they learned from me," she said of that experience. "I learned what real courage is."

GOP leaders made her an assistant whip in her freshman term, a post she still holds. She weighed a bid in the 107th Congress for a low-level position in the leadership but dropped out at the last moment. In the 108th, she was mentioned as a potential chief deputy whip, but the newly elected majority whip, Roy Blunt of Missouri, selected Eric Cantor of Virginia.

Even if her leadership aspirations have been stymied thus far, she has won plum assignments during her tenure. Named to the Appropriations Committee in her second term, she was assigned to its Defense Subcommittee in the 109th Congress, a major plus for someone whose district's employers include defense manufacturers Lockheed Martin Corp. and Bell Helicopter Textron. In the 108th, she chaired a House-Senate working group on aerospace and defense policy. She also sits on a 15-member board that has oversight over the U.S. Air Force Academy. In the 107th Congress, she served on the Budget Committee but left in the 108th for a post on the Homeland Security panel. She left that committee when it was downsized in the 109th Congress.

Early in 2000, her district office in a Fort Worth office building was destroyed by a tornado, presaging another uncomfortably close brush with disaster: Granger had just left a meeting at the Pentagon on Sept. 11, 2001, when hijacked American Airlines Flight 77 slammed into the building. She reunited with those present at the meeting on the third anniversary of the terrorist attacks to discuss progress on the war against terrorism. Defense Secretary Donald H. Rumsfeld presented all in attendance with the first honorary Global War on Terrorism coins.

Granger's legislative priorities are shaped by her background. Her interest in championing tax-free education savings accounts for college can be traced to her own experience working her way through school and to the difficulties a favorite niece had in saving enough money to pay for her daughter's education. A former public school teacher, Granger has promoted the creation of a National Commission on Youth Crime and School Violence. As a single parent, she wrote legislation in the 107th to provide a $1,000 tax credit to help uninsured people get health coverage.

Though she supports abortion rights in certain, limited circumstances, Granger says changing the Republican Party's official line against abortion is not a priority. "To some, I think it's the most important issue, but that's not really where I'm coming from," she has said.

Granger works to keep federal dollars flowing to her district's defense manufacturers and other businesses. She supports continued funding of the F-35 Joint Strike Fighter, the F-22 and the V-22 Osprey aircraft. And late in the 107th Congress, as a year-end deadline loomed for airports to install expensive new explosive detection machines, Granger successfully pushed to extend the deadline, noting it would cost the Dallas-Fort Worth Airport $40 million to comply. In the 108th, she backed a $3.5 billion airline bailout package. American Airlines is headquartered in Dallas.

Granger was born in Greenville, Texas, to two public school teachers who divorced when she was 13. Granger told the Fort Worth Star-Telegram that her mother, a teacher for 45 years, never told her she could be anything she wanted — rather, she was told she had to be whatever she wanted. "I was not self-made," Granger says. "I was made by my mother."

Granger became a teacher in the same Birdville school district that named an elementary school after her mother. She taught literature and journalism for 10 years. Then, in 1978, she went into the insurance business, eventually founding her own agency. In 1981, she was appointed to the Fort Worth Zoning Commission, where she served until she won a seat on the city council in 1989. Two years later, she won a nonpartisan election to become mayor.

During her mayoral tenure, citizen patrol initiatives and other anti-gang efforts helped cut city crime by 50 percent. She lured new businesses to the city, and she was able to reduce property taxes for the first time in 11 years. Her pro-business stands endeared her to the Fort Worth business community, which in 1999 made her the first woman chosen as outstanding business executive of the year. Both parties courted her when Democratic Rep. Pete Geren decided not to seek re-election in 1996.

After choosing to run under the Republican banner and resigning as mayor, Granger heard grumbling from some on the GOP right. She was attacked by two primary opponents as a liberal and was opposed by the Tarrant County Republican chairman. But she won nomination with a whopping 69 percent of the GOP primary vote. That November, she defeated another former Fort Worth mayor, Hugh Parmer, by 17 percentage points, becoming the first Republican woman elected to the House from Texas.

Granger has not faced a serious contest since then, although she narrowly escaped a redistricting-inspired faceoff against Democratic Rep. Martin Frost in 2004. Instead, he ran against Pete Sessions, and Granger coasted against Democrat Felix Alvarado.

KEY VOTES

2004
? Extend federal unemployment benefits by 13 weeks
Yes Pass $283.2 billion, six-year federal highway and mass transit bill
Yes Approve $146 billion multi-year extension of previously enacted middle-class tax breaks
Yes Amend the Constitution to prohibit same-sex marriage
Yes Cut corporate taxes $137 billion over 10 years
Yes Reorganize U.S. intelligence agencies as proposed by Sept. 11 commission

2003
Yes Cut taxes by $330 billion through fiscal 2013
No Block Bush rule scaling back overtime pay for some white-collar federal workers
No Do not allow use of search warrants without first notifying subjects
No Allow importation of prescription drugs
Yes Create private school voucher program in Washington, D.C.
Yes Ban "partial birth" abortion except to save a woman's life
No Split $18.6 billion in Iraq aid into half-grant, half-loan
Yes Overhaul Medicare and create prescription drug benefit

CQ VOTE STUDIES

	PARTY UNITY		PRESIDENTIAL SUPPORT	
	Support	Oppose	Support	Oppose
2004	96%	4%	94%	6%
2003	96%	4%	96%	4%
2002	96%	4%	85%	15%
2001	97%	3%	88%	12%
2000	93%	7%	25%	75%

INTEREST GROUPS

	AFL-CIO	ADA	CCUS	ACU
2004	15%	0%	100%	91%
2003	13%	5%	100%	80%
2002	0%	0%	95%	96%
2001	0%	0%	100%	80%
2000	0%	5%	84%	84%

TEXAS 12
Part of Fort Worth and suburbs; Parker and Wise counties

The Republican-leaning 12th takes in most of western Tarrant County, including two-thirds of Fort Worth and all of rural Wise and Parker counties. The mostly white, middle-class district contains downtown Fort Worth but also takes in a mix of suburban and rural areas.

The 12th's solid economy is built around transportation. A major airport, a Naval air base, several main railroad lines and interstate highways are in or adjacent to the district, supporting a myriad of businesses. While the Union Pacific and Burlington Northern Santa Fe (BNSF) railroads both are active in the district — and BNSF's headquarters are in the 12th — the air industry has surpassed rail here. Large government defense contractors, including Lockheed Martin, which bases its aeronautics division in the district, have helped create jobs and fuel economic growth. Radio Shack also makes its headquarters in the 12th.

Parker County includes Weatherford, which is becoming more

Republican as it undergoes a transition from rural town into part of the Fort Worth suburbs. Although Parker and Wise counties cover the vast majority of the district's land area, even combined they comprise only 21 percent of the 12th's population.

Redistricting following the 2000 census changed the 12th from a politically competitive district to one dominated by Republicans. Prior to the 2004 election, the mid-decade Texas remap added all of Wise County and removed southwest Tarrant County and neighboring areas, but did not diminish the district's GOP strength. The 12th still includes some Democratic areas in downtown Fort Worth, but areas outside the city are overwhelmingly Republican, as are Parker and Wise counties.

MAJOR INDUSTRY
Defense technology, transportation, medicine

MILITARY BASES
Naval Air Station Fort Worth, 2,100 military, 2,251 civilian (2005)

CITIES
Fort Worth (pt.), 349,997; Haltom City, 39,018; Watauga, 21,908

NOTABLE
The National Cowgirl Museum in Fort Worth showcases women rodeo riders and contributors to Western heritage.

Rep. William M. 'Mac' Thornberry (R)

Elected 1994; 6th term

CAPITOL OFFICE
225-3706
www.house.gov/thornberry
2457 Rayburn 20515-4313; fax 225-3486

COMMITTEES
Armed Services
Select Intelligence
  (Oversight - chairman)

HOMETOWN
Clarendon

BORN
July 15, 1958, Clarendon, Texas

RELIGION
Presbyterian

FAMILY
Wife, Sally Thornberry; two children

EDUCATION
Texas Tech U., B.A. 1980 (history); U. of Texas, J.D. 1983

CAREER
Lawyer; cattleman; U.S. State Department official; congressional aide

POLITICAL HIGHLIGHTS
No previous office

ELECTION RESULTS

2004 GENERAL

William M. Thornberry (R)	189,448	92.3%
M.J. "Smitty" Smith (LIBERT)	15,793	7.7%

2004 PRIMARY

William M. Thornberry (R)	unopposed

2002 GENERAL

William M. Thornberry (R)	119,401	79.3%
Zane Reese (D)	31,218	20.7%

PREVIOUS WINNING PERCENTAGES
2000 (68%); 1998 (68%); 1996 (67%); 1994 (55%)

Thornberry has established himself as a leading Republican expert on the things that preoccupy a wartime Congress: intelligence, homeland security and overall military policy.

He has always had an intense interest in national security. Thornberry drafted a bill to create a new department to oversee homeland security — almost six months before Sept. 11, 2001. After the terrorist attacks on the World Trade Center and the Pentagon, creating such a department suddenly topped everyone's to-do list, and Thornberry's bill became the foundation for the legislation that passed the House in 2002.

As the Department of Homeland Security was conceived, Thornberry was overshadowed by President Bush and GOP congressional leaders, but his understanding of the government's multifaceted jurisdiction over domestic security made him a valuable adviser to bill drafters. He was rewarded by Republican leaders in 2003 with a seat on the new Homeland Security Committee, giving him oversight of the new department as it was built from the ground up.

But, in September 2004, Thornberry was moved from that committee to one dealing with an even more sensitive aspect of national security: gathering and evaluating intelligence. He was given a seat on the Intelligence Committee after its chairman, Porter J. Goss, left to assume control of the struggling and demoralized CIA. The agency had come under criticism after repeatedly assuring Congress and the Bush administration that Iraqi leader Saddam Hussein possessed weapons of mass destruction. The House and Senate Intelligence committees will spend much of the 109th Congress reviewing the recommendations of an independent commission named to investigate how U.S. intelligence on Iraq went so badly astray.

Months after his appointment to Intelligence, Thornberry was made chairman of the panel's new Oversight Subcommittee, which was established to help Congress keep track of how the 2004 law uniting U.S. intelligence functions under one director is working. When he was named chairman of the new panel, Thornberry said the intelligence measure "offers us a great opportunity to strengthen the various elements of our intelligence community. But that bill will be beneficial only if it is implemented in as quick and effective a manner as possible."

While he is no longer on the Homeland Security panel, Thornberry will pursue what he regards as some unfinished business there. He and California Democrat Zoe Lofgren are renewing efforts to create an assistant secretary of cybersecurity in the department, an idea that has strong backing from the technology industry. "Creating an assistant secretary is far more than just an organizational change. It is an essential move to assure that cybersecurity is not buried among the many homeland security challenges we face," Thornberry said.

A longtime member of the Armed Services Committee, Thornberry is a player on other defense and security issues as well — and, importantly, a good provider for his district.

He is a major booster of Bush's plan to develop a controversial U.S. anti-missile defense system, which critics say is technologically infeasible. And Thornberry has taken a lead role in nuclear weapons security, in part because the giant Pantex weapons assembly complex is in his district. He is a strong administration ally of efforts to develop a nuclear-enabled "bunker buster" bomb capable of destroying well-constructed military installations burrowed deep in the earth. He has vowed to restore research funds for the weapon that were deleted in the 108th Congress.

Thornberry also watches out for the interests of Sheppard Air Force Base, near Wichita Falls. He is a defender of the troubled V-22 Osprey tilt-rotor aircraft, which is made by Bell Helicopter in Amarillo. The Bell facility also was chosen to make the latest version of Marine One, the presidential helicopter.

The Texas lawmaker, who backed his party 98 percent of the time in the 108th Congress, traces his conservatism to his upbringing on the ranch that has been in his family for more than 70 years. He grew up in a modest house built by his grandfather in the 1930s.

A business-suit-and-boots-wearing member of Capitol Hill's unofficial Boot Caucus, Thornberry is a frequent advocate for ranchers' concerns. He is a staunch proponent of property owners' rights and says federal laws and regulations impinge unduly on farmers' land-use decisions. He regularly supports bills to overhaul the Endangered Species Act, which allows the government to block development on private land.

Agriculture is important to Thornberry's district, which is among the nation's leading producers of cotton, wheat and peanuts. So Thornberry has a keen interest in federal subsidies for those crops, despite the ideological leanings that prompted him to support the Republican Party's 1996 Freedom to Farm law, which sought to replace New Deal-era crop subsidies with a system based on the free market.

Thornberry worked for five years as an aide on Capitol Hill after graduating from the University of Texas law school in 1983. He first was a legislative aide to Texas GOP Rep. Tom Loeffler, and then was chief of staff for Rep. Larry Combest, another Texas Republican. In 1988, Thornberry was deputy assistant secretary of state for legislative affairs in the Reagan administration. He got to know the inner workings of the House and was unflappable in dealing with crises. Now, he is often tapped by Republican leaders to preside over contentious legislative debates.

Thornberry took a break from politics in 1989 and went to work in an Amarillo law firm while helping run his family's cattle ranch. Then in 1994, he challenged Democratic incumbent Bill Sarpalius, who had become vulnerable in the conservative district because of his support for raising taxes as part of President Clinton's 1993 budget plan. Thornberry played up his family's close ties to the land and beat Sarpalius with 55 percent of the vote. He has had no trouble winning re-election since and faced no Democratic opposition in 2004.

KEY VOTES

2004

No Extend federal unemployment benefits by 13 weeks

No Pass $283.2 billion, six-year federal highway and mass transit bill

Yes Approve $146 billion multi-year extension of previously enacted middle-class tax breaks

Yes Amend the Constitution to prohibit same-sex marriage

Yes Cut corporate taxes $137 billion over 10 years

Yes Reorganize U.S. intelligence agencies as proposed by Sept. 11 commission

2003

Yes Cut taxes by $330 billion through fiscal 2013

No Block Bush rule scaling back overtime pay for some white-collar federal workers

No Do not allow use of search warrants without first notifying subjects

Yes Allow importation of prescription drugs

Yes Create private school voucher program in Washington, D.C.

Yes Ban "partial birth" abortion except to save a woman's life

No Split $18.6 billion in Iraq aid into half-grant, half-loan

Yes Overhaul Medicare and create prescription drug benefit

CQ VOTE STUDIES

	PARTY UNITY		PRESIDENTIAL SUPPORT	
	Support	Oppose	Support	Oppose
2004	98%	2%	97%	3%
2003	98%	2%	96%	4%
2002	94%	6%	92%	8%
2001	99%	1%	95%	5%
2000	97%	3%	25%	75%

INTEREST GROUPS

	AFL-CIO	ADA	CCUS	ACU
2004	7%	0%	100%	100%
2003	0%	10%	97%	88%
2002	0%	0%	95%	92%
2001	8%	0%	100%	96%
2000	0%	0%	76%	88%

TEXAS 13
Panhandle – Amarillo; Wichita Falls

The conservative 13th encompasses much of the Texas Panhandle, including the city of Amarillo, then extends east along the Oklahoma border to take in the South Plains and much of the Red River Valley. It juts south twice to add more agricultural territory as well as pick up Jones County's small portion of Abilene. The district takes in Wichita Falls and reaches east to haul in the western half of Cooke County, about 50 miles north of Fort Worth. Monstrous and mainly rural, the 13th includes all or part of 44 counties, 40 of which have a population of under 25,000.

Oil and cotton dominate the district's economy, and both industries suffered during the 1980s and early 1990s as oil prices dropped and droughts parched the land. Other industries allowed the main cities to weather the difficulties. In Amarillo, Pantex is the nation's only nuclear weapons assembly and disassembly plant. The city also contributes to the military's V-22 Osprey, which takes off like a helicopter but flies like a plane. After several crashes, the aircraft's future is uncertain.

In Wichita Falls, factories are numerous, but the jewel of the economy is

Sheppard Air Force Base, which so far has escaped downsizing. Many of the district's rural counties depend on the Ogallala Aquifer to grow wheat, sorghum, sugar beets, corn and hay.

The 13th is one of the most Republican districts in Texas. The GOP excels in many of the rural small towns that dot the district, particularly around Amarillo. Ochiltree County, in the Panhandle, gave 92 percent of the vote to George W. Bush in the 2004 presidential election. Closer to blue-collar Wichita Falls, voters have traditionally favored Democrats at the local level, but even this area votes solidly Republican in state and national elections. Overall, Bush captured 77 percent of the district's 2004 vote.

MAJOR INDUSTRY
Agriculture, oil, defense

MILITARY BASES
Sheppard Air Force Base, 5,211 military, 2,544 civilian (2004)

CITIES
Amarillo, 173,627; Wichita Falls, 104,197; Pampa, 17,887

NOTABLE
Mineral Wells was a popular destination for people seeking to drink the water and soak in specially constructed bathhouses — the water was seen as a cure-all and was bottled and shipped around the country.

Rep. Ron Paul (R)

Elected 1996; 8th full term
Also served 1976-77, 1979-85

In modern-day electoral politics, marching to the beat of your own drummer usually means you're destined for a fairly short parade. But Ron Paul is the exception that proves the rule: Now five terms into his third stint in Congress, the incorrigible libertarian loner has cultivated a safe seat and a nationwide following.

Known on Capitol Hill as "Dr. No" (he was a practicing obstetrician), Paul is unafraid to stand alone. Whenever there is a lone no vote on a House roll call, it is usually safe to bet that Paul has cast it. In the 108th Congress, he cast the lone dissenting vote against legislation to combat computer spyware, federal funding for regional poison control centers, a Coast Guard authorization bill, a resolution commending Afghan women for their participation in their country's emerging society and a "sense of the Congress" measure expressing support for a peaceful resolution of a conflict in Uganda. In the 106th Congress, Paul was the only House member to vote against giving a congressional gold medal to "Peanuts" comic strip creator Charles M. Schulz.

On other occasions, Paul finds himself in a tiny minority. In 2002, he was among just six Republicans who voted against giving President Bush authority to wage war on Iraq, saying the move amounted to an unconstitutional transfer of the power to declare war from Congress to the executive branch. And in the 108th Congress, he sometimes paired up with a junior iconoclast, Arizona Republican Jeff Flake, who similarly opposes most government spending, regardless of the situation. Paul and Flake cast the only votes against appropriations for the Homeland Security Department, emergency funding for military operations in Iraq and increased spending on security at sewage treatment facilities across the United States.

In 2004, Paul's yes vote in favor of prescription drug importation led him to comment on the House floor about his distinctive record. Paul hailed the measure's sponsors for offering a bill "that I can vote for enthusiastically."

"I finally found one," he said, praising the legislation for increasing consumers' freedom of choice.

The 1988 Libertarian nominee for president — he won 432,179 votes — Paul argues that the government has no right to take any action not specifically authorized by the Constitution. He would like to require lawmakers to document the constitutional authority for every bill they introduce.

Paul's absolutist views, and the refusal to compromise that comes with them, mean his effectiveness at the Capitol is limited. But he has nonetheless gained a small but loyal national following that brings him campaign contributions from all corners of the country; the majority of his campaign donations regularly come from outside of Texas.

After starting to frame his political theories in medical school and working as an obstetrician, Paul served two stints in the House in the late 1970s and early 1980s, when there were just a few Republicans in Texas' overwhelmingly Democratic delegation. As the Libertarian presidential candidate, he renounced the GOP, spoke out against "corporate welfare" — certain tax breaks and subsidies for big business — and advocated drug legalization.

His Libertarian beliefs make Paul an erratic ally of GOP causes. He opposes legislation that would prohibit same-sex marriage, saying "everyone is an individual and ought to be treated equally." He also opposes a constitutional amendment to ban flag burning. But he parts company with his former Libertarian brethren in adopting an anti-abortion stand.

CAPITOL OFFICE
225-2831
rep.paul@mail.house.gov
www.house.gov/paul
203 Cannon 20515-4314; fax 225-1655

COMMITTEES
Financial Services
International Relations
Joint Economic

HOMETOWN
Lake Jackson

BORN
Aug. 20, 1935, Pittsburgh, Pa.

RELIGION
Protestant

FAMILY
Wife, Carol Wells Paul; five children

EDUCATION
Gettysburg College, B.S. 1957 (pre-med); Duke U., M.D. 1961

MILITARY SERVICE
Air Force, 1963-65; Pa. Air National Guard, 1965-68

CAREER
Physician

POLITICAL HIGHLIGHTS
Republican nominee for U.S. House, 1974; U.S. House, 1976-77; defeated for re-election to U.S. House, 1976; U.S. House, 1979-85; sought Republican nomination for U.S. Senate, 1984; Libertarian nominee for president, 1988

ELECTION RESULTS

2004 GENERAL
Ron Paul (R)		unopposed

2004 PRIMARY
Ron Paul (R)		unopposed

2002 GENERAL
Ron Paul (R)	102,905	68.1%
Corby Windham (D)	48,224	31.9%

PREVIOUS WINNING PERCENTAGES
2000 (60%); 1998 (55%); 1996 (51%); 1982 (99%); 1980 (51%); 1978 (51%); 1976 Special Runoff Election (56%)

When he returned to the House in 1996 (defeating the preferred GOP candidate in a hard-fought primary), Paul received a lukewarm reception from his party. In the 108th, he crossed party lines to vote with Democrats more often than all but two other House Republicans. And Paul opposed Bush on 57 percent of votes on which the president took a stand — far more often than any other Republican in Congress.

At times, Paul has shown a bit of flexibility with the GOP leadership. When his party was struggling in 1997 to pass a District of Columbia spending bill, he changed his vote from no to "present," allowing the measure to pass by one vote.

As a member of the International Relations Committee, he has decried American foreign policy as "worldwide imperialism" that spurred the Sept. 11, 2001, terrorist attacks. "A growing number of Americans are concluding that the threat we now face comes more as a consequence of our foreign policy than because the bad guys envy our freedoms and prosperity," Paul said nine months afterward.

Taking a dim view of U.S. aid to foreign countries, Paul opposes U.S. support for the International Monetary Fund and the World Trade Organization. He also opposes "so-called peacekeeping missions" and has sponsored legislation requiring the United States to withdraw from the United Nations and the World Trade Organization.

Although he had in the past voted for trade liberalization, Paul opposed granting China permanent normal trade status in 2000, and voted against the 2002 bill renewing presidential fast-track trade negotiating authority. In 2004, together with avowed socialist Bernard Sanders of Vermont, Paul introduced a bill to block federal assistance to companies that outsource American jobs to foreign countries.

Paul first was elected to Congress in an April 1976 special election to replace Democrat Bob Casey, defeating former Democratic state Rep. Bob Gammage. In the general election seven months later, though, Gammage felled Paul by 268 votes. In 1978, Paul won back the seat by 1,200 votes.

In 1984, Paul left his House seat to run for the Senate but lost the primary to Phil Gramm. Twelve years later, Paul won election in the 14th, which included areas he represented in his earlier House career. In the GOP primary, he ousted Greg Laughlin, who had held the seat since 1989 but had switched to the GOP from the Democrats in 1995. Paul prevailed by pressing his anti-tax and anti-government message; he won the general election by just 3 percentage points, despite criticism that he supported the legalization of drugs. He has since won re-election by comfortable margins.

KEY VOTES

2004

No Extend federal unemployment benefits by 13 weeks

No Pass $283.2 billion, six-year federal highway and mass transit bill

Yes Approve $146 billion multi-year extension of previously enacted middle-class tax breaks

No Amend the Constitution to prohibit same-sex marriage

? Cut corporate taxes $137 billion over 10 years

No Reorganize U.S. intelligence agencies as proposed by Sept. 11 commission

2003

Yes Cut taxes by $330 billion through fiscal 2013

No Block Bush rule scaling back overtime pay for some white-collar federal workers

Yes Do not allow use of search warrants without first notifying subjects

Yes Allow importation of prescription drugs

No Create private school voucher program in Washington, D.C.

Yes Ban "partial birth" abortion except to save a woman's life

Yes Split $18.6 billion in Iraq aid into half-grant, half-loan

No Overhaul Medicare and create prescription drug benefit

CQ VOTE STUDIES

	PARTY UNITY		PRESIDENTIAL SUPPORT	
	Support	Oppose	Support	Oppose
2004	82%	18%	44%	56%
2003	74%	26%	43%	57%
2002	76%	24%	51%	49%
2001	79%	21%	49%	51%
2000	80%	20%	27%	73%

INTEREST GROUPS

	AFL-CIO	ADA	CCUS	ACU
2004	20%	50%	56%	78%
2003	47%	60%	46%	75%
2002	29%	30%	50%	76%
2001	27%	20%	62%	70%
2000	44%	30%	45%	76%

TEXAS 14
Northern Gulf Coast — Victoria, Galveston

The 14th takes in a roughly 200-mile stretch of coastal land, extending from north of Galveston to Rockport just north of Corpus Christi.

Despite some suburban areas, the district is overwhelmingly coastal and agricultural. Although the 14th was mostly rural with very few populated cities before redistricting prior to the 2004 elections, the new lines include five cities with populations of over 25,000 people.

Although the 1980s oil bust hurt the 14th's economy, the rapid growth of the petrochemical industry in the 1990s helped the district. Chemical companies, such as Dow, have facilities near the Gulf Coast, where they rode the oil glut to success by making antifreeze and other products. Victoria is a leading oil and chemical center. Mingled with the chemical producers on the coast are commercial shrimpers.

A growing service sector near Galveston has helped diversify the economy. And with its nearby beaches, Galveston also has emerged as a tourist destination. Farmers in the 14th's interior grow rice, grain, and

sorghum and raise cattle. The district also draws nature lovers, who can visit Goose Island State Park, the Aransas National Wildlife Refuge and several bird sanctuaries.

Dominated by farms and petrochemical plants, the 14th leans Republican but has Democratic roots and a sizable minority population (38 percent). One-fourth of residents are Hispanic. The 14th elects Republicans, but generally not by the overwhelming margins the more solidly Republican suburban Houston districts rack up. Locally, Republicans tend to do very well in the rural counties of the 14th, but the large number of factory jobs in the Galveston area allows unions to wield some political power. Residents also tend to be socially conservative.

MAJOR INDUSTRY
Petrochemicals, agriculture, shrimping

CITIES
Victoria, 60,603; Galveston, 57,247; League City, 45,279; Texas City (pt.), 31,979; Lake Jackson, 26,386

NOTABLE
Galveston, known for a devastating storm and flood in 1900, claims to be the site of many Texas firsts, including the first telephone (1878), first medical college (1886) and first golf course (1898).

Rep. Rubén Hinojosa (D)

Elected 1996; 5th term

CAPITOL OFFICE
225-2531
rep.hinojosa@mail.house.gov
hinojosa.house.gov
2463 Rayburn 20515-4315; fax 225-5688

COMMITTEES
Education & Workforce
Financial Services

HOMETOWN
Mercedes

BORN
Aug. 20, 1940, Edcouch, Texas

RELIGION
Roman Catholic

FAMILY
Wife, Martha Hinojosa; five children

EDUCATION
U. of Texas, B.B.A. 1962; U. of Texas, Pan American, M.B.A. 1980

CAREER
Food processing executive

POLITICAL HIGHLIGHTS
Texas State Board of Education, 1974-84 (chairman of special populations)

ELECTION RESULTS

2004 GENERAL

Rubén Hinojosa (D)	96,089	57.8%
Michael D. Thamm (R)	67,917	40.8%
William R. Cady (LIBERT)	2,352	1.4%

2004 PRIMARY

Rubén Hinojosa (D)	unopposed

2002 GENERAL

Rubén Hinojosa (D)	unopposed

PREVIOUS WINNING PERCENTAGES
2000 (88%); 1998 (58%); 1996 (62%)

Now a wealthy business owner, Hinojosa rose from modest beginnings in a South Texas farm community. At the elementary school he attended, Mexican-American children were segregated from white students and he spoke only Spanish, as he did at home. Those life experiences have shaped the priorities he brings to Congress, and they inform his positions on issues as far-flung as free trade, education and border control.

Hinojosa (full name: ru-BEN ee-na-HO-suh) was one of four Texas Democrats who broke ranks with their party in 2002 and voted to enhance President Bush's trade negotiating power by resurrecting fast-track procedures for congressional consideration of trade agreements. The idea is anathema to labor unions, a bedrock Democratic constituency. But to the congressman representing some of Texas' poorest border towns, trade offers the hope of the highways, commerce and jobs that could help his constituents.

In the 108th Congress, he continued to press for a resolution to a water dispute — Mexico owes Texas a considerable amount of water that is badly needed by South Texas irrigators, and Hinojosa says the Bush administration "literally sold South Texas down the river" in a 2002 agreement. In 2004, he offered his support to a group of irrigators and farmers who have used a North American Free Trade Agreement (NAFTA) provision to file a $500 million claim against Mexico for previous failures to release water to the United States.

Water conservation remains an important issue in his district, and he takes pride in winning funding for water conservation projects — he has secured grants for more than 15 such projects since arriving in Congress. But at the start of the 109th Congress, because he is on two other major committees, Hinojosa lost his seat on the Resources panel after a single term.

Those two major panels are the Financial Services and Education and Workforce committees, and he has used those posts to pursue legislation that he believes will help promote educational opportunities and small-business development for the people of his heavily Hispanic district.

He became chairman of the Congressional Hispanic Caucus education task force soon after arriving in Washington. He has helped to direct millions of federal dollars to Hispanic colleges and universities and to put more money into efforts to connect schools and libraries to the Internet. In the 108th, he inserted language into a teacher training bill that would include English as a second language (ESL) teachers in a program that offers merit pay to outstanding teachers.

In recognition of his lifelong support of education, two Texas school districts in 2002 announced they were naming schools after him.

In 1997, Hinojosa promoted legislation seeking to redirect existing Higher Education Act programs to target resources to the neediest schoolchildren, including Hispanics and American Indians. The following year, he won a substantial increase in federal aid to colleges that serve large numbers of Hispanic students. Funding also was increased for bilingual and migrant education and for Head Start — all Hinojosa priorities.

Hinojosa has broken with the liberal majority of his fellow Democrats on occasion. He supported a ban on a procedure that opponents call "partial birth" abortion. He supported congressional term limits and voted for a constitutional amendment to prohibit flag desecration. And in the 108th, he backed Bush on 37 percent of the House votes on which the president had taken a position, a score about 10 points higher than that of the average House Democrat.

An advocate of strict privacy protections for individuals, Hinojosa in the 108th helped sink a bill in the House that would have extended a pilot program allowing employers to search federal databases and screen potential employees to verify that they have legal work status. He said it was a precursor to a national identification program and "comes dangerously close to threatening the privacy of U.S. citizens and non-citizens alike."

His concern for small businesses and affordable housing led him to spearhead a campaign against a Bush administration proposal aimed at making home buying simpler and more transparent. He said the plan could cause too large a regulatory burden on smaller lenders, forcing them out of business and raising prices for consumers. The effort held up Alphonso R. Jackson's confirmation to be secretary of the Department of Housing and Urban Development, and the White House finally backed down.

Hinojosa has lobbied for a new interstate highway in the 15th District to serve as a trade route from Mexico and to relieve local traffic bottlenecks occurring from increased cross-border commercial traffic, a result of NAFTA. The massive 1998 transportation measure included money to upgrade U.S. 281 from the Mexican border as far north as its intersection with Interstate 37.

The eighth of 11 children born to parents who had immigrated to the United States from Mexico, Hinojosa eventually became president of a food-processing company with more than 400 employees.

He served for a decade on the Texas State Board of Education and was instrumental in creating the South Texas Community College system in the upper Rio Grande Valley.

The Hinojosa family's prominence and his own community involvement helped Hinojosa win the open 15th District seat in 1996. He succeeded Democrat E. "Kika" de la Garza, who retired after 32 years in the House. Given the 15th's strong one-party voting tradition — it is a Democratic bulwark in the Lone Star State — Hinojosa's biggest challenge in taking the seat was winning his party's nomination. In a hotly contested five-way battle for the Democratic nod, he edged out lawyer Jim Selman.

Against Republican minister Tom Haughey, Hinojosa won by 26 percentage points in 1996 and by 17 points in a 1998 rematch. His 2000 victory with 88 percent of the vote discouraged the GOP. With his district only marginally altered by redistricting, Republicans declined to field a candidate against him in 2002. In 2004, after a second round of redistricting, he defeated Republican Michael D. Thamm with 58 percent of the vote.

KEY VOTES

2004
Yes Extend federal unemployment benefits by 13 weeks
Yes Pass $283.2 billion, six-year federal highway and mass transit bill
Yes Approve $146 billion multi-year extension of previously enacted middle-class tax breaks
No Amend the Constitution to prohibit same-sex marriage
Yes Cut corporate taxes $137 billion over 10 years
Yes Reorganize U.S. intelligence agencies as proposed by Sept. 11 commission

2003
No Cut taxes by $330 billion through fiscal 2013
Yes Block Bush rule scaling back overtime pay for some white-collar federal workers
Yes Do not allow use of search warrants without first notifying subjects
Yes Allow importation of prescription drugs
No Create private school voucher program in Washington, D.C.
Yes Ban "partial birth" abortion except to save a woman's life
Yes Split $18.6 billion in Iraq aid into half-grant, half-loan
No Overhaul Medicare and create prescription drug benefit

CQ VOTE STUDIES

	PARTY UNITY		PRESIDENTIAL SUPPORT	
	Support	Oppose	Support	Oppose
2004	90%	10%	36%	64%
2003	85%	15%	38%	62%
2002	89%	11%	41%	59%
2001	85%	15%	33%	67%
2000	92%	8%	88%	12%

INTEREST GROUPS

	AFL-CIO	ADA	CCUS	ACU
2004	93%	90%	63%	13%
2003	87%	80%	53%	36%
2002	71%	80%	61%	20%
2001	75%	85%	52%	13%
2000	90%	80%	50%	8%

TEXAS 15

South central — Harlingen, Edinburg, part of McAllen, Bastrop

Focused in southern Texas, the convoluted boundaries of the 15th take in agricultural and cattle areas southeast of Austin in Central Texas and then dip down to the Texas-Mexico border. The district had its Hispanic population cut during redistricting prior to the 2004 election, from a nationwide high of 78 percent under the old lines to 69 percent. The large minority presence contributes to the district's overall Democratic lean.

The southern portion of the 15th is one of the nation's poorest areas. Community leaders struggle to establish jobs and provide job training. Hidalgo County, an agricultural area, is by far the most populous and fastest-growing in the district, but its unemployment rate only dipped below 10 percent in late 2004. Along the Mexican border, *maquiladoras* — assembly or manufacturing plants that use low-cost labor and import many parts from the United States — are the mainstay. NAFTA has helped the economy, and trade with Mexican border cities adds jobs.

Transportation is an issue — the region claims to be the largest populated area without easy access to an interstate highway. Plans are in the works to upgrade existing roads and create a new interstate called Interstate 69 that would connect South Texas to Indianapolis.

The 15th's congressional seat has never been held by a Republican, although the GOP became more competitive in the 1990s. Redistricting may bring them even closer, as the new map added several heavily GOP counties to the northern part of the district, including DeWitt and Fayette. George W. Bush took 76 percent in DeWitt County in 2004, compared with the 32 percent he received closer to the Mexican border in Brooks County. Overall, Bush captured 55 percent of the 15th's presidential vote.

MAJOR INDUSTRY
Trade, manufacturing, agriculture, health care

CITIES
Harlingen, 57,564; Edinburg, 48,465; McAllen (pt.), 28,002; Weslaco, 26,935

NOTABLE
James W. Fannin of the Texas independence movement was executed in 1836 with members of his troop in what became known as the Goliad Massacre; Caro Brown, the first woman to win a Pulitzer Prize for journalism, worked at the Alice Daily News during the 1940s and 1950s.

Rep. Silvestre Reyes (D)

Elected 1996; 5th term

CAPITOL OFFICE
225-4831
talk2silver@mail.house.gov
www.house.gov/reyes
2433 Rayburn 20515-4316; fax 225-2016

COMMITTEES
Armed Services
Veterans' Affairs
Select Intelligence

HOMETOWN
El Paso

BORN
Nov. 10, 1944, Canutillo, Texas

RELIGION
Roman Catholic

FAMILY
Wife, Carolina Reyes; three children

EDUCATION
U. of Texas, attended 1964-65; Texas Western
College, attended 1965-66 (criminal justice);
El Paso Community College, A.A. 1977 (criminal
justice)

MILITARY SERVICE
Army, 1966-68

CAREER
U.S. Border Patrol assistant regional official and
agent

POLITICAL HIGHLIGHTS
Canutillo School Board, 1968-70

ELECTION RESULTS

2004 GENERAL

Silvestre Reyes (D)	108,577	67.5%
David Brigham (R)	49,972	31.1%
Brad Clardy (LIBERT)	2,224	1.4%

2004 PRIMARY

Silvestre Reyes (D)	unopposed

2002 GENERAL

Silvestre Reyes (D)	unopposed

PREVIOUS WINNING PERCENTAGES
2000 (68%); 1998 (88%); 1996 (71%)

A representative of the border town of El Paso, and the former chairman of the Congressional Hispanic Caucus, Reyes is uniquely positioned in the 109th Congress to play a role in the ongoing debate over the nation's immigration laws. And with more than a quarter-century of service with the U.S. Border Patrol before moving to Washington, he brings a broad and deep base of knowledge to the issue.

Reyes (full name: sil-VES-treh RAY-ess, with rolled r's) has called for broad legalization for many undocumented immigrants since he was first elected in 1996. He saw an opportunity in August 2001, when President Bush signaled support for legalizing 3 million Mexican immigrants. As co-chairman of a Democratic immigration task force, Reyes issued a set of principles that called for legal status for "longtime, hard-working residents of good moral character," speedier approval of legal status for immigrants' family members, an enhanced temporary worker program and Border Patrol funding.

The Sept. 11, 2001, terrorist attacks took the wind out of his sails one month later. Bush and Congress shifted their focus to tightening border security, not easing legalization. But in the 108th Congress, Bush proposed an initiative that would give millions of undocumented workers in the United States a chance to legalize their status temporarily with guest worker visas.

In January 2005, amid growing public concern about illegal immigration, Reyes joined California Republican David Dreier in offering a bill to stiffen penalties for employers who hire illegal aliens or do not attempt to verify workers' immigration status before hiring them. Their bill also called for new Social Security cards with digital pictures and encrypted identification codes that could be checked against an electronic data base. At the same time, Reyes reaffirmed his support for a legal guest worker program.

A member of the Intelligence Committee, Reyes saw many of his border enforcement proposals enacted as part of 2004 legislation that overhauled the intelligence community. Among other things, those provisions sought to boost the number of Border Patrol agents and Immigration and Customs Enforcement personnel, improve infrastructure at ports of entry, improve monitoring technology along the border and fight human smuggling rings.

But in 2005, Reyes assailed the administration for failing to seek funding for most of the new Border Patrol positions created by the act and for seeking to slash spending on programs that assist border communities in dealing with the impact of illegal immigration. "I have heard a lot about how we need to crack down on illegal immigration in this country, but have seen very little action when it comes to providing adequate funding for the kinds of programs that work in dealing with the problem of illegal immigration," Reyes said.

Although he no longer chairs the Hispanic Caucus, Reyes still speaks out on what Congress can do to show more sensitivity to the concerns of this fast-growing demographic group — particularly when he sees old insensitivities returning. That happened in the 107th Congress during the debate on revamping the campaign finance system, when Mississippi Democrat Roger Wicker offered an amendment to bar legal permanent residents from contributing to campaigns. To counter what he saw as an immigrant-bashing amendment, Reyes noted that Alfred V. Rascon, the director of the U.S. Selective Service System, had fought in Vietnam and earned the Congressional Medal of Honor while he was a legal permanent resident.

The amendment was soundly defeated.

Called "Silver" by his friends, Reyes is the first Hispanic to represent the 16th District; when the boundaries were drawn for this decade in 2001, Hispanics made up 78 percent of the population. To help what he terms "one of the poorest districts in the country," Reyes seeks federal funding not only for better roads and bridges to handle increased commercial traffic, but also for retraining for those unemployed since many of El Paso's garment industry jobs have shifted to lower-wage Mexico.

Reyes is vice chairman of the Democratic Task Force on Homeland Security and a member of the U.S.-Mexico Interparliamentary Group. He chaired the Congressional Hispanic Caucus in the 107th Congress.

Reyes usually sides with the majority in his party, but he has backed a few measures pushed by conservatives, including a bill in the 108th to repeal local gun control laws in Washington, D.C. He also backed a ban on a procedure opponents call "partial birth" abortion and supported constitutional amendments limiting congressional terms and outlawing flag desecration.

On the Armed Services Committee, Reyes has parted with many of his colleagues to support Bush's requests for research into a nuclear weapon encased in a hardened shell that could burrow into the earth to destroy deeply buried targets. Reyes said studying such "bunker buster" weapons is a good idea because it serves as an "attention getter" to rogue nations such as North Korea. "It's better to have the capability and not use it," Reyes said in early 2005.

In 1969, after returning from Vietnam, Reyes went to work for the Immigration and Naturalization Service. Rising to assistant regional commissioner, he oversaw the Border Patrol in McAllen and El Paso. He instituted "Operation Hold the Line" in El Paso, stationing more officers at the border to prevent unauthorized crossings of the Rio Grande — a shift from the previous emphasis on rounding up people already in the country illegally.

When Democrat Ronald D. Coleman announced that he would not seek an eighth term, Reyes retired from the Border Patrol in the fall of 1995 to launch a bid for the House seat. In the primary and subsequent runoff, he narrowly defeated a former Coleman aide, Jose Luis Sanchez, before easily dispatching a Republican insurance agent in the general election.

Untouched by the 2003 redistricting plan engineered by Majority Leader Tom DeLay that led to the ouster of several Texas Democrats, Reyes has had no difficulty in his re-election bids — before or since. Nonetheless, he was outraged by DeLay's maneuver, calling it "the first great heist of the 21st century."

KEY VOTES

2004

Yes	Extend federal unemployment benefits by 13 weeks
?	Pass $283.2 billion, six-year federal highway and mass transit bill
Yes	Approve $146 billion multi-year extension of previously enacted middle-class tax breaks
?	Amend the Constitution to prohibit same-sex marriage
Yes	Cut corporate taxes $137 billion over 10 years
Yes	Reorganize U.S. intelligence agencies as proposed by Sept. 11 commission

2003

No	Cut taxes by $330 billion through fiscal 2013
Yes	Block Bush rule scaling back overtime pay for some white-collar federal workers
Yes	Do not allow use of search warrants without first notifying subjects
Yes	Allow importation of prescription drugs
No	Create private school voucher program in Washington, D.C.
Yes	Ban "partial birth" abortion except to save a woman's life
Yes	Split $18.6 billion in Iraq aid into half-grant, half-loan
No	Overhaul Medicare and create prescription drug benefit

CQ VOTE STUDIES

	PARTY UNITY		PRESIDENTIAL SUPPORT	
	Support	Oppose	Support	Oppose
2004	86%	14%	38%	62%
2003	82%	18%	38%	62%
2002	85%	15%	41%	59%
2001	81%	19%	37%	63%
2000	88%	12%	88%	12%

INTEREST GROUPS

	AFL-CIO	ADA	CCUS	ACU
2004	92%	70%	62%	26%
2003	87%	80%	50%	36%
2002	100%	75%	39%	19%
2001	83%	90%	43%	30%
2000	90%	80%	42%	16%

TEXAS 16
West — El Paso and suburbs

Looking more toward Mexico than Texas, the solidly Democratic 16th includes El Paso and some suburbs. Joined to Mexico by the Bridge of the Americas, the 16th has a 77.7 percent Hispanic population, more than any other district in the nation.

Redistricting following the 2000 census pushed the district north, removing some of the 16th's border with Mexico and taking out a few small towns. Remapping also gave the 16th all of Fort Bliss, removing it entirely from the 23rd. The base, a major employer, gives the area a military flavor. Redistricting prior to the 2004 election kept the lines the same — the only district in the state to remain unchanged.

Mexico has had a long and deep effect on the 16th's economy. El Paso's growth was credited to trade with Mexico long before free-trade zones and global markets flourished. Companies on the U.S. side of the border provide supplies and services to manufacturing plants in Mexico, and residents from El Paso's sister city, Ciudad Juarez, regularly cross the border to spend money in El Paso's stores. In recent years, leaders have been concerned with the effects of NAFTA, which they blame for displacing American workers. The trade agreement has been partially responsible for an explosion of *maquiladoras,* twin plants in which Mexican workers do the bulk of the manufacturing labor and Americans complete the products with final details.

Democrats held the 16th's congressional seat for all but two years in the 20th century, often unchallenged by Republicans since the 1960s. In 2004, John Kerry won 56 percent of the presidential vote in the 16th, his fifth-best showing in the state.

MAJOR INDUSTRY
Manufacturing, apparel, defense

MILITARY BASES
Fort Bliss (Army), 23,000 military, 7,500 civilian (2005)

CITIES
El Paso, 563,662; Socorro, 27,152

NOTABLE
The Border Patrol Museum displays aircraft and vehicles used by the patrol as well as surveillance equipment and confiscated items; Fort Bliss, the largest air defense artillery training center in the world, occupies an area larger than Rhode Island.

Rep. Chet Edwards (D)

Elected 1990; 8th term

CAPITOL OFFICE
225-6105
www.house.gov/edwards
2264 Rayburn 20515-4317; fax 225-0350

COMMITTEES
Appropriations
Budget

HOMETOWN
Waco

BORN
Nov. 24, 1951, Corpus Christi, Texas

RELIGION
Methodist

FAMILY
Wife, Lea Ann Edwards; two children

EDUCATION
Texas A&M U., B.A. 1974 (economics); Harvard U., M.B.A. 1981

CAREER
Radio station executive; congressional aide

POLITICAL HIGHLIGHTS
Sought Democratic nomination for U.S. House, 1978; Texas Senate, 1983-91

ELECTION RESULTS

2004 GENERAL

Chet Edwards (D)	125,309	51.2%
Arlene Wohlgemuth (R)	116,049	47.4%
Clyde Garland (LIBERT)	3,390	1.4%

2004 PRIMARY

Chet Edwards (D)	unopposed

2002 GENERAL

Chet Edwards (D)	74,678	51.6%
Ramsey W. Farley (R)	68,236	47.1%
Andrew Paul Farris (LIBERT)	1,943	1.3%

PREVIOUS WINNING PERCENTAGES
2000 (55%); 1998 (82%); 1996 (57%); 1994 (59%); 1992 (67%); 1990 (53%)

Edwards entered the 109th Congress as the lone "star" among fellow Democrats who were endangered by the controversial GOP-engineered Texas remap. Six lost and one retired, but Edwards won, though just barely, beating back his heavily financed opponent's attempts to label him as a liberal obstructionist standing in the way of the Bush agenda. Edwards had been re-elected by Republican-leaning constituencies before, albeit by shrinking margins in 2000 and 2002. He is a moderate-to-conservative Democrat, appreciated for his work in behalf of veterans and military families, and respected for an independent-minded, bipartisan approach to lawmaking.

His campaign skills draw praise from the opposition. "He was very good one-on-one," David Kent, a Republican county chairman told the Waco Tribune-Herald. "His personality helped him win the race."

Edwards stakes out a pro-military position for himself and fellow Democrats, chiding Republicans for neglecting veterans' concerns even as they lead troops to war. He promotes increased funding for veterans' health services and expanded benefits for military retirees.

In 2003, Edwards gave up his Democratic leadership post, allowing him to focus on his tough re-election fight in 2004. For four terms, Edwards had been chief deputy whip for the House Democrats, making him a vital link between the liberal-leaning leadership and the party's conservatives. He gave up the job to devote himself to his work as the senior Democrat on the Budget Committee and on the Military Construction Appropriations Subcommittee, where he could concentrate on the military and business issues important to a district that is not naturally friendly to Democrats.

The newly drawn 17th District is a place that not only voted heavily for President Bush in 2004 but is home to the president's Crawford ranch. It includes Edwards' alma mater, Texas A&M, and the city of Waco, home to Baylor University, the largest Baptist-affiliated university in the world.

Overall, Edwards' support of Bush is greater than most Democrats'. He voted for the president's positions 50 percent of the time in 2004. But on certain key votes, Edwards follows his leadership, opposing the Medicare prescription drug bill, supporting affirmative action policies in college admissions, and voting against the ban on a procedure opponents call "partial birth" abortion. He believes that when a pregnant woman's health is in danger, the decision is up to her and her doctors, not lawmakers. But he offered bills in both the 107th and 108th Congresses to ban most third-trimester abortions.

Those abortion bills are among the measures Edwards has sponsored. Many of the 16 bills he introduced from 1997 through 2004 would benefit veterans and military personnel. "The reality is, in most cases, bills that become law will be sponsored by the majority party or committee chairmen," he says. "I don't feel a great need to have my name on dozens of bills."

Edwards prides himself on his work to preserve the separation of church and state, opposing Bush's "charitable choice" initiative because it would allow religious organizations to discriminate in hiring. Nor does he support government-funded vouchers for private-school education. Finessing the potential conflict between his views and those of the many religious conservatives in his district, Edwards argues that religion is too important to be entangled in the corporeal world of politics.

Edwards' record on gun control has been a reason for the GOP to target him at election time. In 1994, he voted for a ban on 19 types of assault-style weapons in the wake of two mass killings in his district. In 1991, a man with an automatic pistol killed 22 people and wounded 20 in a Killeen cafeteria. Two years later, guns were responsible for some of the deaths in a violent confrontation between federal agents and members of the Branch Davidian religious sect in Waco. In 2004, however, Edwards reversed his earlier position on the assault weapons ban, saying he had become convinced that banning the weapons had not reduced crime.

Edwards, who is Appropriations' only Texas Democrat, is the go-to guy for his home-state colleagues. Before the Texas redistricting in 2003, he represented the massive Army base at Fort Hood and he continues to look out for defense interests though he no longer represents the base's 48,000 occupants.

Edwards was a high schooler during the civil rights movement and says that two books — "Black Like Me"and "To Kill a Mockingbird"— influenced him strongly and persuaded him that government should play a vital role in righting social wrongs.

At Texas A&M University, he was a leader in the Student Conference on National Affairs, where he got to know the local congressman, Olin E. Teague. As he was finishing college, Edwards accepted a job on Teague's congressional staff, intending to stay a year and then attend Harvard Business School. One year stretched into two, and then "Tiger" Teague told Edwards he planned to retire and that Edwards should run for his seat. The crowded Democratic primary in 1978 included a young Texas A&M economics professor, Phil Gramm. He edged out Edwards by fewer than 200 votes and went on to win the House seat and, later, a Senate seat.

Edwards earned a master's degree at Harvard, then returned to Texas. He jumped at a chance to run for the state Senate in 1982 and, at 31, became the youngest senator in the state Legislature. When Democratic Rep. Marvin Leath announced he would step down in 1990, Edwards moved to the 11th District to run for the House.

The GOP nominee, state Rep. Hugh D. Shine, outspent Edwards, but Edwards secured a pledge from Speaker Thomas S. Foley to give him Leath's Armed Services seat. Edwards won with 53 percent of the vote.

He had little re-election difficulty until his last three campaigns, when Republican Ramsey W. Farley held him to 55 percent in 2000 and less than 52 percent in 2002. In 2004, he squeaked out a 4 percentage point victory against state Rep. Arlene Wohlgemuth, who had difficulty defending her role in shrinking the state human services budget so severely that it cut into a popular children's health insurance program.

KEY VOTES

2004

Yes Extend federal unemployment benefits by 13 weeks

Yes Pass $283.2 billion, six-year federal highway and mass transit bill

Yes Approve $146 billion multi-year extension of previously enacted middle-class tax breaks

Yes Amend the Constitution to prohibit same-sex marriage

Yes Cut corporate taxes $137 billion over 10 years

Yes Reorganize U.S. intelligence agencies as proposed by Sept. 11 commission

2003

No Cut taxes by $330 billion through fiscal 2013

Yes Block Bush rule scaling back overtime pay for some white-collar federal workers

Yes Do not allow use of search warrants without first notifying subjects

Yes Allow importation of prescription drugs

No Create private school voucher program in Washington, D.C.

No Ban "partial birth" abortion except to save a woman's life

Yes Split $18.6 billion in Iraq aid into half-grant, half-loan

No Overhaul Medicare and create prescription drug benefit

CQ VOTE STUDIES

	PARTY UNITY		PRESIDENTIAL SUPPORT	
	Support	Oppose	Support	Oppose
2004	73%	27%	50%	50%
2003	76%	24%	46%	54%
2002	76%	24%	47%	53%
2001	72%	28%	47%	53%
2000	84%	16%	78%	22%

INTEREST GROUPS

	AFL-CIO	ADA	CCUS	ACU
2004	73%	65%	81%	48%
2003	80%	80%	64%	40%
2002	89%	75%	65%	36%
2001	100%	80%	57%	40%
2000	70%	80%	52%	8%

TEXAS 17

East central – Waco, College Station, Bryan

The 17th is home to George W. Bush's "Western White House." Located in Crawford, the ranch has given the area a new level of recognition and has contributed to small boosts in the economy when Bush — and his many media followers — travel here.

The district's southern portion is centered in Brazos County, which includes Bryan and College Station, home of Texas A&M University. Texas A&M — including the George Bush Presidential Library and Museum — is a major employer here. Unlike the more liberal University of Texas at Austin, Texas A&M has a conservative agricultural and military tradition that boosts GOP candidates.

Moving northwest from Brazos, the 17th includes several sparsely populated counties and McLennan County (Waco), before reaching north to Johnson County. Rapidly growing Johnson has become a bedroom community for Fort Worth and is home to many of the city's southern suburbs. Waco, home to Baylor University, is the 17th's largest city and is the largest marketing center between Austin and Dallas. One-

third of district residents live in McLennan County.

Bush's connection to the area and revisions made during redistricting prior to the 2004 election give the district a distinct Republican lean, and Bush captured 69 percent of the 17th's 2004 presidential vote. But Rep. Edwards' 2004 re-election showed that conservative "Yellow Dog" Democrats and ticket splitters can still provide a winning margin for Democrats, at least for the time being.

Voters in the Waco-area continue to embrace longevity in their House members — in 68 years, the city has had just three congressmen: Democrats Edwards (1991-present), Marvin Leath (1979-91) and William Poage (1937-78).

MAJOR INDUSTRY
Agriculture, higher education, light manufacturing

CITIES
Waco, 113,726; College Station, 67,890; Bryan, 65,660; Cleburne, 26,005

NOTABLE
The Texas Ranger Hall of Fame and Museum is in Waco; A complex outside Waco was the scene of a deadly standoff in 1993 between federal agents and members of the Branch Davidian religious group.

Rep. Sheila Jackson-Lee (D)

Elected 1994; 6th term

CAPITOL OFFICE
225-3816
www.jacksonlee.house.gov
2435 Rayburn 20515-4318; fax 225-3317

COMMITTEES
Homeland Security
Judiciary
Science

HOMETOWN
Houston

BORN
Jan. 12, 1950, Queens, N.Y.

RELIGION
Seventh-day Adventist

FAMILY
Husband, Elwyn Lee; two children

EDUCATION
Yale U., B.A. 1972 (political science); U. of Virginia,
J.D. 1975

CAREER
Lawyer; congressional aide

POLITICAL HIGHLIGHTS
Democratic nominee for Texas District Court
judge, 1984; Democratic nominee for Harris
County Probate Court judge, 1986; Houston
municipal judge, 1987-89; Democratic nominee
for Texas District Court judge, 1988; Houston City
Council, 1990-95

ELECTION RESULTS

2004 GENERAL

Sheila Jackson-Lee (D)	136,018	88.9%
Tom Bazan (I)	9,787	6.4%
Brent Sullivan (LIBERT)	7,183	4.7%

2004 PRIMARY

Sheila Jackson-Lee (D)	unopposed

2002 GENERAL

Sheila Jackson-Lee (D)	99,161	76.9%
Phillip J. Abbott (R)	27,980	21.7%
Brent Sullivan (LIBERT)	1,785	1.4%

PREVIOUS WINNING PERCENTAGES
2000 (76%); 1998 (90%); 1996 (77%); 1994 (73%)

On topics ranging from Saddam Hussein to space travel, Jackson-Lee is never at a loss for words. Lots of words.

Her loquacity on the House floor and in front of television cameras prompts some in Congress to dismiss her as a publicity hound, but Jackson-Lee's outspokenness guarantees that C-SPAN audiences will hear at least one set of liberal views in the conservative-run House.

Labeling the GOP's proposals "shameless" or "outrageous," Jackson-Lee wages a ceaseless rhetorical battle with the majority. Her supporters have counseled her to be more selective about her issues, but she shuns the advice, enjoying the chance to reach a national television audience. She also is adept at securing a center aisle seat in the chamber, where the TV cameras focus on her at least briefly, whenever the president enters or leaves the House for his State of the Union address or other speeches.

Like Democratic Rep. Barbara Jordan, a famed black liberal from Houston who served from 1973 to 1979, Jackson-Lee uses her seat on the Judiciary Committee to focus on civil rights, abortion rights and other liberal causes. In the 108th, she fiercely opposed a measure outlawing a procedure critics label "partial birth" abortion, calling the legislation "a travesty to women's reproductive progress." In a typically flamboyant move, she unsuccessfully offered an amendment to rename the legislation the "Safe Abortion Procedures Ban Act of 2003."

As the top-ranking Democrat on Judiciary's Immigration Subcommittee, she is quick to defend the rights of immigrants. After President Bush outlined a guest worker plan in 2004 that would have given thousands more immigrant workers temporary legal status in the United States, Jackson-Lee introduced her own, far more generous reform legislation.

A fierce critic of Bush's foreign policy, Jackson-Lee was among a small group of Democrats who called for Defense Secretary Donald H. Rumsfeld's resignation upon revelations of Iraqi prisoner abuse at the Abu Ghraib prison facility. In late March 2003, with the war under way, Jackson-Lee pressed the Democratic Caucus to adopt an official stance against it. Concerned about the potential embarrassment that would come from trying to retract congressional authorization for a war that already had started, other Democrats used a procedural motion to cancel the meeting.

Jackson-Lee's opposition to Republican foreign policy extends to the mundane. In 2003, she circulated a "Dear Colleague" letter urging that House cafeterias revert to serving french fries rather than "freedom fries" — the name adopted courtesy of GOP leaders irked at French opposition to the Iraq war.

Although Jackson-Lee has sometimes joined her ideological nemesis but fellow Texan, Majority Leader Tom DeLay, on parochial Houston-area problems or bipartisan issues such as strengthening child protective services, she went after him ferociously in the 108th Congress. Working with the Republican Texas governor, DeLay helped engineer a congressional redistricting plan that tilted Texas toward the GOP. "Washington Republicans are controlling Texas," Jackson-Lee said. "Gov. Perry continues to fritter away millions of dollars on Tom DeLay's redistricting dreams. It is nothing less than shameful."

Usually a reliable vote for her party, Jackson-Lee occasionally strays on trade issues. In 2000, she voted to grant China permanent normal trade status, arguing that an improved economic picture would aid human rights conditions in that country while also helping Houston's economy.

Jackson-Lee is attentive to parochial needs. From her seat on the Science Committee, she is a stout defender of NASA, whose Houston facility is in an adjoining district. In a rare show of support for Bush, Jackson-Lee in 2004 praised his ambitious vision for the space agency, including a manned mission to Mars. "I wholeheartedly support his vision for going back to the moon," she said, "and from there to worlds beyond."

Her constant presence on the House floor to speak on a wide array of topics has raised the bar on political long-windedness. Some colleagues defend their own talkativeness by declaring, "but I'm no Sheila Jackson-Lee."

Two topics leave Jackson-Lee with little to say: Her political ties to criminally indicted Enron Corp. Chairman Kenneth L. Lay and the high turnover rate of her congressional staff.

Enron's financial collapse in 2001 had a major economic impact on Jackson-Lee's district, but she let other Democrats rail against alleged corporate abuses. Lay was one of her chief fundraisers and backers in 1994 when she won a hotly contested Democratic primary. She also was one of the biggest recipients of campaign donations from Enron.

Regarding her staff, The Weekly Standard magazine reported in February 2002 that Jackson-Lee had overseen 85 full-time staffers since taking office in 1995. The article said Jackson-Lee insists on being chauffeured between her congressional office and nearby apartment and berates staff for minor failures. The same year, Texas Monthly dubbed her "a royal pain" for breaching protocol by arriving 50 minutes late and in business attire at a formal dinner hosted by Queen Sirikit of Thailand.

Born in Queens, N.Y., and educated at Yale and the University of Virginia law school, Jackson-Lee moved to Texas when her husband took a job with the University of Houston. She made two unsuccessful bids for local judgeships before winning appointment as a municipal judge in 1987. In 1990, after another unsuccessful election campaign for a judgeship, she won an at-large seat on the city council, where her initiatives included a gun safety law imposing penalties on parents who failed to keep guns locked up and away from children. She also pushed for expanded summer hours at city parks and recreation centers as a way to reduce gang activity.

In 1994, she challenged incumbent Democrat Craig Washington, who had lost the support of the Houston business establishment and several other important constituencies. She won with 63 percent of the vote, and in the heavily Democratic district, her primary victory was tantamount to election. She has never faced a serious re-election challenge.

KEY VOTES

2004

Yes Extend federal unemployment benefits by 13 weeks

Yes Pass $283.2 billion, six-year federal highway and mass transit bill

Yes Approve $146 billion multi-year extension of previously enacted middle-class tax breaks

No Amend the Constitution to prohibit same-sex marriage

Yes Cut corporate taxes $137 billion over 10 years

Yes Reorganize U.S. intelligence agencies as proposed by Sept. 11 commission

2003

No Cut taxes by $330 billion through fiscal 2013

Yes Block Bush rule scaling back overtime pay for some white-collar federal workers

Yes Do not allow use of search warrants without first notifying subjects

Yes Allow importation of prescription drugs

No Create private school voucher program in Washington, D.C.

No Ban "partial birth" abortion except to save a woman's life

Yes Split $18.6 billion in Iraq aid into half-grant, half-loan

No Overhaul Medicare and create prescription drug benefit

CQ VOTE STUDIES

	PARTY UNITY		PRESIDENTIAL SUPPORT	
	Support	Oppose	Support	Oppose
2004	96%	4%	21%	79%
2003	96%	4%	17%	83%
2002	97%	3%	21%	79%
2001	93%	7%	16%	84%
2000	92%	8%	88%	12%

INTEREST GROUPS

	AFL-CIO	ADA	CCUS	ACU
2004	93%	95%	53%	4%
2003	100%	95%	31%	12%
2002	100%	100%	26%	4%
2001	100%	100%	35%	8%
2000	90%	80%	50%	4%

TEXAS 18

Downtown Houston

Downtown Houston's older black neighborhoods and more-progressive residents make up the 18th, which includes one of the city's poorest areas. Though economically struggling, the district has seen revitalization as downtown experiences a resurgence in construction, aided by the opening of a new baseball stadium here in 2000 and a new basketball arena here in 2003.

The 18th is diverse: 40 percent of residents are black and 36 percent are Hispanic, and a large portion of the city's gay and lesbian residents live in the district. Some of the district's most heavily black areas are just south of downtown, and heavily Hispanic neighborhoods can be found just north of downtown, between Interstate 45 and the Eastex Freeway. Texas Southern University and the University of Houston add to the area's liberal tendencies.

Although the district is overwhelmingly inner-city urban, it does include some areas around downtown, as well as the Heights, a trendier neighborhood populated with some young professionals.

Downtown office buildings are filled with oil and gas employees and other white-collar businesses and service workers, but most commute from outside the district. Downtown also houses some corporate giants, such as Halliburton, and was home to the once-powerful Enron Corp. This area includes the city's Theater District, where the Hobby Center for the Performing Arts opened in 2002. The northern portion of the district, added in redistricting prior to the 2004 elections, takes in George Bush Intercontinental Airport.

The large black and Hispanic populations make the 18th one of the most strongly Democratic districts in Texas. In 2004, George W. Bush took 28 percent of the vote here, his second-worst showing in Texas.

MAJOR INDUSTRY
Energy, government, business services, entertainment

CITIES
Houston (pt.), 507,631

NOTABLE
Downtown Houston was once represented by Rep. Barbara Jordan, D-Texas (1973-79); Minute Maid Park, home of the Houston Astros baseball team, was originally named Enron Field but was renamed in 2002 after the collapse of the energy giant.

Rep. Randy Neugebauer (R)

Elected June 2003; 1st full term

CAPITOL OFFICE
225-4005
www.randy.house.gov
429 Cannon 20515-4319; fax 225-9615

COMMITTEES
Agriculture
Financial Services

HOMETOWN
Lubbock

BORN
Dec. 24, 1949, St. Louis, Mo.

RELIGION
Baptist

FAMILY
Wife, Dana Neugebauer; two children

EDUCATION
Texas Tech U., B.B.A. 1972 (accounting)

CAREER
Land developer; homebuilding company executive; bank executive

POLITICAL HIGHLIGHTS
Lubbock City Council, 1992-98

ELECTION RESULTS

2004 GENERAL

Randy Neugebauer (R)	136,459	58.4%
Charles W. Stenholm (D)	93,531	40.1%
Richard Peterson (LIBERT)	3,524	1.5%

2004 PRIMARY

Randy Neugebauer (R)	unopposed

2003 SPECIAL RUNOFF

Randy Neugebauer (R)	28,546	50.5%
K. Michael Conaway (R)	27,959	49.5%

Neugebauer was a major beneficiary of the Texas remap engineered by Majority Leader Tom DeLay and the state Republican Party. He owes his victory in 2004 to redrawn boundaries that carved a strongly GOP district out of political turf that had belonged to Democrat Charles W. Stenholm for a quarter-century.

Neugebauer (NAW-geh-bow-er) beat the popular 26-year veteran after Republicans in 2003 sliced up Stenholm's old district six ways and added areas that voted 3-to-1 for George W. Bush in 2000 to the portion Stenholm still had. The new district, based in Neugebauer's Lubbock stronghold, threw the two incumbents together. The 2004 election was one of the most hotly contested and expensive races of the year, with Neugebauer alone spending $3 million.

A self-described "less government, less taxes kind of person," Neugebauer by trade is a land developer and home builder who built several subdivisions in Lubbock. His success in business made it possible for him to contribute $150,000 to his campaign war chest.

His entrepreneurial perspective fits his new Financial Services Committee assignment in the 109th Congress. He sits on subcommittees overseeing financial institutions, housing, and domestic and international monetary policy.

Neugebauer supports reducing taxes beyond the $330 billion in cuts enacted by Congress in 2003, and in particular, he wants to abolish the estate tax. Socially conservative, he opposes abortion rights. And he supports opening the Arctic National Wildlife Refuge to oil drilling.

"He's a very conservative Republican who is very much in the mold of Larry Combest and other Texas Republicans," said Dan Isett, chairman of the Lubbock County GOP, referring to the retired congressman from West Texas, who represented many of the areas Neugebauer looks after now.

Neugebauer arrived in the House in June 2003 after winning a special election to replace Combest, who resigned his 19th District seat early in the 108th Congress for personal reasons.

A deacon in his Baptist church and a fly fisherman, Neugebauer says his political style is to be "a consensus-builder and a coalition-builder."

Boosting trade is a priority for him. While on the Lubbock City Council for six years, he headed the Ports-to-Plains Coalition, which pushed to widen local highways to bring more commercial traffic from Canada and Mexico through West Texas.

His seat on the Agriculture Committee is perhaps his most important assignment. Neugebauer's district takes in cotton, peanut and wheat farms and a number of cattle ranches. Combest had chaired the Agriculture Committee in the 106th and 107th Congresses. Stenholm had been the senior Democrat on the committee, and with Combest shepherded the 2002 farm subsidy bill through the Congress, reversing a six-year trend of declining crop supports. Neugebauer opposes tinkering with that law, calling it a "six-year pact" with the agriculture industry.

Born in St. Louis, Mo., and raised in Lubbock, Neugebauer graduated from Texas Tech University with a degree in accounting. He was elected to the Lubbock City Council in 1992 and served until 1998.

Saying he was inspired to run for Congress "in the spirit of Ronald Reagan," Neugebauer had to take on 13 Republicans and two Democrats in the 2003 special election. In an initial round of balloting, he and accountant K.

Michael Conaway finished first and second, respectively. Conaway had close ties to the president. He was a partner in the oil business with Bush in the 1980s and hailed from Midland, the district's second-largest city and Bush's former home.

Neugebauer's home and political base was in Lubbock, the district's largest city, which helped him considerably in the runoff. He won in June 2003 by just 587 votes — 1 percent of the ballots cast — over Conaway. Turnout was only 14 percent, and geography factored heavily in the outcome. Neugebauer dominated the northern, heavily agricultural counties near Lubbock while Conaway won in the southern counties, home to the oil-rich Permian Basin. (In the 2003 remapping, that southern edge was put in another, newly carved 11th District centered around Midland, which favored Conaway. Given a second chance in the new district, Conaway triumphed and joined Neugebauer in Congress at the start of the 109th.)

After a year in office, Neugebauer had to stand for re-election in 2004. By that time, GOP map-makers had carved out a modified district for him, keeping Lubbock and some heavily Republican areas, while throwing in Stenholm's hometown and political base of Abilene. The incumbent-versus-incumbent contest forced Stenholm to run in places where people didn't know him well, and where his party label was a liability, even though he was among the most conservative of congressional Democrats.

Neugebauer campaigned vigorously, greeting voters anywhere he could find them and pumping hands at Friday night high school football games. After his long tenure in Congress, Stenholm was forced to court new constituents because only 31 percent of the redrawn 19th District was his old turf. By nature a reserved man, Stenholm was not used to doing the hard sell.

Then, just a month before the election, the Republican Party helped Neugebauer a little more. Stenholm had offered a drought relief bill popular with farmers in West Texas. But the GOP leadership-controlled Rules Committee refused to allow his amendment to go to the floor. Instead, Agriculture Committee Chairman Robert W. Goodlatte of Virginia wrote a version that added offsetting limits on farm conservation spending. And Neugebauer was allowed to sponsor the bill, which passed as part of a hurricane relief measure. Neugebauer thus could take credit for securing $2.9 billion in drought relief for farmers and ranchers.

Neugebauer had no competition in the 2004 primary. In the general election, the heavily Republican district favored the relative newcomer, Neugebauer, over Stenholm by 18 percentage points.

KEY VOTES

2004

No   Extend federal unemployment benefits by 13 weeks

Yes   Pass $283.2 billion, six-year federal highway and mass transit bill

Yes   Approve $146 billion multi-year extension of previously enacted middle-class tax breaks

Yes   Amend the Constitution to prohibit same-sex marriage

Yes   Cut corporate taxes $137 billion over 10 years

No   Reorganize U.S. intelligence agencies as proposed by Sept. 11 commission

2003

No   Block Bush rule scaling back overtime pay for some white-collar federal workers

Yes   Do not allow use of search warrants without first notifying subjects

Yes   Allow importation of prescription drugs

Yes   Create private school voucher program in Washington, D.C.

Yes   Ban "partial birth" abortion except to save a woman's life

No   Split $18.6 billion in Iraq aid into half-grant, half-loan

Yes   Overhaul Medicare and create prescription drug benefit

CQ VOTE STUDIES

	PARTY UNITY		PRESIDENTIAL SUPPORT	
	Support	Oppose	Support	Oppose
2004	98%	2%	85%	15%
2003	98%	2%	97%	3%

INTEREST GROUPS

	AFL-CIO	ADA	CCUS	ACU
2004	20%	5%	100%	96%
2003	0%	10%	95%	83%

TEXAS 19
West central — Lubbock, Abilene, Big Spring

The conservative 19th starts in the Panhandle and extends south through cattle and cotton country around Lubbock, then heads south and east, meandering through West Texas to Abilene before heading north almost to Wichita Falls. With ranches, cattle and remnants of the cowboy lifestyle, the 19th offers a taste of the Wild West and feels little like the "Old South," which never reached this far west.

The western part of the district, which includes Lubbock, is heavily agricultural, and that industry extends east through most of the district. In redistricting prior to the 2004 election, the southern part of the old 19th — home to Midland and Odessa —was moved into the new 11th. This removed the problem of Lubbock's farmers and ranchers needing to compete for influence with Midland's energy producers.

The district's largest city, Lubbock, thrives on the surrounding acres of cotton. The city calls itself the world's largest cottonseed-processing center and is home to Texas Tech University. But famine and drought have hurt cattle and cotton over the past decade, and continued low prices have dampened the oil industry. Reese Air Force Base, once a major employer, was shut down under the 1995 military restructuring.

Abilene, the district's second-largest city, has made an effort to revitalize its downtown. An Air Force base near the city has added a measure of stability to the economy. The prison industry also has done well, with several state and contract facilities around the district.

Conservative Democrats used to dominate the area: As recently as 1978, George W. Bush lost a race for the Lubbock-area House seat to Democrat Kent Hance. More recently, Republicans have done well at all levels. George W. Bush received more than 70 percent of the 2004 vote in 24 of the 25 counties wholly included in the 19th.

MAJOR INDUSTRY
Cattle, agriculture, oil and gas, defense

MILITARY BASES
Dyess Air Force Base, 5,900 military, 800 civilian (2005)

CITIES
Lubbock, 199,564; Abilene (pt.), 110,442; Big Spring, 25,233

NOTABLE
Singer Buddy Holly was born and raised in Lubbock.

Rep. Charlie Gonzalez (D)

Elected 1998; 4th term

CAPITOL OFFICE
225-3236
www.house.gov/gonzalez
327 Cannon 20515-4320; fax 225-1915

COMMITTEES
Energy & Commerce

HOMETOWN
San Antonio

BORN
May 5, 1945, San Antonio, Texas

RELIGION
Roman Catholic

FAMILY
Divorced; one child

EDUCATION
U. of Texas, B.A. 1969 (government); St. Mary's U. (Texas), J.D. 1972

MILITARY SERVICE
Texas Air National Guard, 1969-75

CAREER
Lawyer; teacher

POLITICAL HIGHLIGHTS
Bexar County judge, 1982-87; Texas District Court judge, 1988-97

ELECTION RESULTS

2004 GENERAL

Charlie Gonzalez (D)	112,480	65.5%
Roger Scott (R)	54,976	32.0%
Jessie Bouley (LIBERT)	2,377	1.4%
Michael Idrogo (I)	1,971	1.2%

2004 PRIMARY

Charlie Gonzalez (D)	unopposed

2002 GENERAL

Charlie Gonzalez (D)	unopposed

PREVIOUS WINNING PERCENTAGES
2000 (88%); 1998 (63%)

The son of the first Hispanic Texan in Congress — who served 37 years — Charlie Gonzalez has an equally secure seat in his fourth term in the House. His San Antonio-based district was spared in the ruthless Republican-engineered remap in 2003 that threw most Democrats into unfriendly GOP territory.

The wealth of affection in the 20th District for the Gonzalez name, coupled with its two-thirds Hispanic population, may have made even remap mastermind Tom DeLay, the House majority leader from Texas, think twice about gerrymandering the lines. Gonzalez's father was the famously feisty Henry B. Gonzalez, known in the region as simply "Henry B."

The son's pragmatic, New Democrat brand of politics contrasts with his father's passionate and stubborn populism. Gonzalez, a self-described moderate, voted the party line 89 percent of the time on major votes in the 108th Congress.

Gonzalez got a coveted seat on the Energy and Commerce Committee in 2004 after being passed over once before. The Congressional Hispanic Caucus had promoted him for a seat on the panel that went to California Democrat Hilda L. Solis, who is close to House Democratic leader Nancy Pelosi of California. But a year later, Gonzalez was given the seat vacated when Ralph M. Hall of Texas defected to the Republican Party.

As a member of the Telecommunications Subcommittee, Gonzalez speaks out in behalf of the interests of Spanish-speaking consumers. He advocated a bill to force satellite television companies to put all shows on one satellite dish, rather than relegating some lesser-watched shows to a second dish. Gonzalez testified at a hearing that the change would be "incredibly beneficial to the Spanish-speaking audiences."

In the 109th Congress, he is in a position to watch over the hometown interests of SBC Communications, the San Antonio-based telecommunications giant, as the committee considers an overhaul of the 1996 telecommunications act. The law has been ripe for an update because of the magnitude of changes in the marketplace since its passage. Phone and cable companies have been pressing for further deregulation.

As the chairman of the civil rights task force for the Congressional Hispanic Caucus, Gonzalez has been outspoken on President Bush's controversial Hispanic nominees. He voiced strong but futile opposition in 2005 to the appointment of Alberto R. Gonzales as attorney general, after Gonzales declined to seek the caucus' endorsement. "While much has been said about the historic nature of his nomination, Mr. Gonzales' nomination is rendered meaningless for the Hispanic community when he declines to meet with the group of Hispanic Members of Congress who have worked for so many years to open the doors of opportunity for all Hispanics," he said.

He led the caucus' successful campaign in 2002 and 2003 against the confirmation of Miguel A. Estrada as the first Latino on the Court of Appeals for the District of Columbia Circuit, considered the most influential federal bench after the Supreme Court. Gonzalez said the Bush nominee failed the caucus' minimum standards for having an appreciation of the legal rights of minorities and victims of discrimination. Estrada met fierce opposition from other Democrats as well and withdrew from consideration.

A strong supporter of trade liberalization, Gonzalez enthusiastically touted the benefits of the 1993 North American Free Trade Agreement, which his father virulently opposed. In his first term, he voted to make permanent normal trade relations with China. But, siding with labor unions, which had promoted his initial congressional bid, he reversed course to vote against the 2002 law giving the president authority to negotiate trade deals that cannot be amended by Congress. In the 108th, he voted in favor of trade agreements with Chile, Singapore, Morocco and Australia.

Gonzalez regards himself as a team player, and has been active in fundraising for the Democratic Congressional Campaign Committee, the House Democrats' political arm. He was vice president of his freshman class in 1999, and co-chaired a Democratic task force on the census, which pushed for the use of statistical sampling to augment the 2000 head count.

Gonzalez's role on the civil rights group for the Hispanic Caucus also involved him in census issues. He was a member of the election task force that Democrats formed in the aftermath of the contested 2000 presidential results in Florida.

Gonzalez is the third of eight children and the only one who followed his father into public life. He was a teenager when his father was first elected to Congress. He taught fifth grade for a year in San Antonio and then worked as a lawyer in private practice. He was elected to the county bench in 1982. During 15 years as a local and state trial judge, his proudest accomplishments were speeding the resolution of domestic violence cases and promoting mediation as an alternative to litigation.

Gonzalez moved up to a state district court judgeship in 1988, but he resigned in 1997 when his father announced plans to retire. A San Antonio Democratic official, Gabe Quintanilla, told the San Antonio Express-News, "Charlie is not in anybody's shadow. Certainly his father is a legend, but he is his own person."

In his first campaign, he survived a seven-way Democratic primary, winning the nomination with 62 percent of the vote in a runoff against former San Antonio council member Maria A. Berriozabal. In the general election, he won with 63 percent. In both 2000 and 2002, Gonzalez had no major-party opposition, in either the primary or the general election. In 2004, he had no primary opposition; and in the general election, the Republican was a political novice, Roger Scott. Gonzalez garnered 66 percent of the vote.

Gonzalez escaped the fate of six other Texas Democratic incumbents who lost seats after the 2003 remap of the state's congressional districts. He also was spared the embarrassment of running against his ex-wife, Becky Whetstone, in the 2004 general election. She had threatened to run against him as an independent, but was unable to get the required 500 petition signatures to get on the ballot.

KEY VOTES

2004
Yes Extend federal unemployment benefits by 13 weeks
Yes Pass $283.2 billion, six-year federal highway and mass transit bill
Yes Approve $146 billion multi-year extension of previously enacted middle-class tax breaks
No Amend the Constitution to prohibit same-sex marriage
Yes Cut corporate taxes $137 billion over 10 years
Yes Reorganize U.S. intelligence agencies as proposed by Sept. 11 commission

2003
No Cut taxes by $330 billion through fiscal 2013
Yes Block Bush rule scaling back overtime pay for some white-collar federal workers
Yes Do not allow use of search warrants without first notifying subjects
Yes Allow importation of prescription drugs
No Create private school voucher program in Washington, D.C.
No Ban "partial birth" abortion except to save a woman's life
Yes Split $18.6 billion in Iraq aid into half-grant, half-loan
No Overhaul Medicare and create prescription drug benefit

CQ VOTE STUDIES

	PARTY UNITY		PRESIDENTIAL SUPPORT	
	Support	Oppose	Support	Oppose
2004	88%	12%	35%	65%
2003	90%	10%	27%	73%
2002	94%	6%	28%	72%
2001	86%	14%	32%	68%
2000	93%	7%	88%	12%

INTEREST GROUPS

	AFL-CIO	ADA	CCUS	ACU
2004	87%	95%	62%	20%
2003	80%	95%	50%	20%
2002	100%	100%	45%	0%
2001	78%	95%	43%	4%
2000	90%	80%	50%	8%

TEXAS 20
Downtown San Antonio

A city rich in history, San Antonio witnessed the death of Davy Crockett and the famed fall of the Alamo. Since those rugged days in the early 1800s, San Antonio has grown into one of the nation's largest cities (9th, according to the 2000 census). The strongly Democratic 20th takes in much of the city, including the heavily Hispanic West Side, downtown San Antonio and some close-in communities.

A huge military presence in San Antonio once fueled the economy, but mid-1990s downsizing diminished its importance. Kelly Air Force Base, one of the city's largest employers, closed in 2001. Local leaders have redeveloped it as a business park, bringing some jobs back to the area. Two other bases are still significant employers, although redistricting prior to the 2004 election moved one of them, Fort Sam Houston, out of the 20th and into the neighboring 21st. Redistricting also shifted another major employer, the San Antonio International Airport, into the 21st.

Tourism and convention business have boosted the city's economy and contributed to a revitalization of the urban center. The Alamo, site of the 1836 battle with Mexico, is in the heart of downtown. The city's scenic Paseo del Rio, or Riverwalk, also draws visitors with its shops, hotels and restaurants that wind along the San Antonio River. Beyond tourism, health care and telecommunications are fast-growing industries.

The mid-decade redistricting added several predominately black neighborhoods to the 20th along its southeastern edge near downtown, increasing Democratic strength in this Hispanic-majority district that Democrats have long dominated. The only significant Republican presence in the district is in the largely white, higher-income areas northwest and northeast of downtown San Antonio.

MAJOR INDUSTRY
Health care, tourism, military, telecommunications, trade

MILITARY BASES
Lackland Air Force Base, 27,123 military, 6,726 civilian (2005)

CITIES
San Antonio (pt.), 590,575

NOTABLE
Future President Theodore Roosevelt recruited for the "Rough Riders," the first volunteer cavalry in the Spanish-American War, at the bar in the Menger Hotel (built 1859), which is adjacent to the Alamo and still open.

Rep. Lamar Smith (R)

Elected 1986; 10th term

CAPITOL OFFICE
225-4236
lamarsmith.house.gov
2184 Rayburn 20515-4321; fax 225-8628

COMMITTEES
Homeland Security
Judiciary
   (Courts, the Internet & Intellectual Property -
   chairman)
Science
Standards of Official Conduct

HOMETOWN
San Antonio

BORN
Nov. 19, 1947, San Antonio, Texas

RELIGION
Christian Scientist

FAMILY
Wife, Beth Smith; two children

EDUCATION
Yale U., B.A. 1969 (American studies); Southern
Methodist U., J.D. 1975

CAREER
Lawyer; rancher; reporter

POLITICAL HIGHLIGHTS
Texas House, 1981-82; Bexar County
Commissioners Court, 1983-85

ELECTION RESULTS

2004 GENERAL

Lamar Smith (R)	209,774	61.5%
Rhett R. Smith (D)	121,129	35.5%
Jason Pratt (LIBERT)	10,216	3.0%

2004 PRIMARY

Lamar Smith (R)	unopposed

2002 GENERAL

Lamar Smith (R)	161,836	72.9%
John Courage (D)	56,206	25.3%
DG Roberts (LIBERT)	4,051	1.8%

PREVIOUS WINNING PERCENTAGES
2000 (76%); 1998 (91%); 1996 (76%); 1994 (90%);
1992 (72%); 1990 (75%); 1988 (93%); 1986 (61%)

An ardent conservative and party loyalist, Smith is a crusader against illegal immigration and a zealous defender of law enforcement powers. His other distinction is as Majority Leader Tom DeLay's handpicked appointee to the ethics committee, certain to be a hot seat if DeLay's ethical troubles escalate in the 109th Congress.

Smith cherishes his seat on the Judiciary Committee, where the war between the parties on social issues often plays out. Known for his conservative approach to immigration matters, he also has been one of the foremost Republican critics of the federal judiciary and "activist" judges. He currently chairs the panel's Courts, the Internet and Intellectual Property Subcommittee, and has aspirations of one day ascending to the full committee chairmanship.

That may explain in part why Smith agreed to go back on the ethics panel — formally the Committee on Standards of Official Conduct — though he already had done a tour on the panel and chaired it in 1999 and 2000. Service on the ethics panel is universally thought of as a thankless duty, and Smith arguably had done his share, including being involved in the bitterly partisan ethics case of former Speaker Newt Gingrich of Georgia.

At the outset of the 109th Congress, DeLay and Speaker J. Dennis Hastert, in a raw exercise of power, purged some committee members after DeLay was admonished by the panel for ethical lapses in the previous Congress. The leaders replaced them with loyalists like Smith, and no doubt Smith's favor will be remembered when it comes time for GOP leaders to select a new Judiciary chairman for the 110th Congress.

Outside of the Judiciary Committee, Smith is co-chairman of the House Working Group on Judicial Accountability, a group of conservatives who believe federal judges have overstepped their bounds. In 2002, Smith spearheaded a congressional inquiry into the sentencing practices of James M. Rosenbaum, chief judge for the U.S. District Court for the District of Minnesota, who had advocated allowing judges discretion in giving low-level drug offenders shorter jail terms than major traffickers.

Smith also is heavily involved in Republican efforts to revamp the civil justice system. Early in 2005, he backed a successful measure to overhaul the rules for class action lawsuits. And in the 108th Congress, he sponsored a bill aimed at reducing "frivolous" lawsuits with mandatory sanctions on attorneys who file them. That bill passed the House.

Right after the Sept. 11, 2001, terrorist attacks, Smith, who was chairing Judiciary's Crime Subcommittee, introduced legislation to greatly expand law enforcement's wiretapping authority by applying the federal eavesdropping law to electronic communications, such as e-mail and instant messaging. The measure became part of the anti-terrorism law enacted later in 2001.

Civil libertarians and privacy advocates criticized Smith for giving police agencies too much power. The criticism did not faze Smith, who responded that the country's desire to combat terrorism required law enforcement to have more tools "to confront the daunting tasks ahead."

Smith later promoted legislation to curb computer hacking by boosting the maximum penalty to life in prison for hackers who plot or cause someone's death. The measure, enacted in the 2002 law establishing the Homeland Security Department, also gave the government new powers to seek information — including financial transactions and e-mails — from Internet service providers. Under Smith's measure, police can conduct emergency surveillance of computers without first obtaining court approval.

His hard-line stances are not limited to criminal law. Smith's passion for tighter immigration policies is well-known on Capitol Hill. He believes lax enforcement of immigration laws contributed to the terrorist attacks on New York and Washington.

His signature legislative accomplishment was the 1996 law that cracked down on illegal immigration by increasing penalties for document fraud and the smuggling of aliens. It also made it easier for illegal immigrants to be detained at the border or deported. In 2004, he butted heads with GOP leaders and the high-tech industry when he at first refused to move a bill making more visas available to foreign high-tech workers. Smith demanded that the businesses first demonstrate they had tried without success to hire U.S. workers, but the leaders overruled him and the visa expansion passed.

Smith is also active on intellectual property issues. In 2004, he won enactment of legislation to protect intellectual property from counterfeiters and to crack down on Internet domain name fraud. The same year, the House passed Smith's bill to make it easier for federal prosecutors to prove criminal copyright infringement. It stalled in the Senate, but the Intellectual Property Owners Association named Smith "Legislator of the Year".

On the Science Committee, Smith, an occasional stargazer, joined with Democrat Nick Lampson of Texas in 2002 to press legislation to lay out clear goals for NASA's human space flight program after completion of the International Space Station. Among the goals is developing, by 2022, a reusable vehicle that can travel to Mars and back.

Smith's genial personality blunts his conservative edge and he enjoys warm relations with many Democrats. He sometimes works across party lines, once collaborating with Democratic Sen. Joseph I. Lieberman of Connecticut to increase family-friendly programming on television.

A fifth-generation Texan, Smith went to Yale for college and was a business reporter for the Christian Science Monitor in Boston. After earning a law degree in Dallas, he returned home to San Antonio, where he was a Bexar County commissioner and served in the state legislature.

He won his seat in Congress in 1986 when Republican Tom Loeffler left to run, unsuccessfully, for governor. When George W. Bush — then a Midland oilman with one losing congressional race under his belt — did not seek the seat, Smith won a six-way contest for the GOP nod. With Karl Rove as his consultant, Smith won that fall with 61 percent of the vote over former Democratic state Sen. Pete Snelson. He garnered at least 70 percent of the vote in subsequent elections until 2004, when he won with 61 percent.

KEY VOTES

2004
No Extend federal unemployment benefits by 13 weeks
Yes Pass $283.2 billion, six-year federal highway and mass transit bill
Yes Approve $146 billion multi-year extension of previously enacted middle-class tax breaks
Yes Amend the Constitution to prohibit same-sex marriage
Yes Cut corporate taxes $137 billion over 10 years
No Reorganize U.S. intelligence agencies as proposed by Sept. 11 commission

2003
Yes Cut taxes by $330 billion through fiscal 2013
No Block Bush rule scaling back overtime pay for some white-collar federal workers
No Do not allow use of search warrants without first notifying subjects
No Allow importation of prescription drugs
Yes Create private school voucher program in Washington, D.C.
Yes Ban "partial birth" abortion except to save a woman's life
No Split $18.6 billion in Iraq aid into half-grant, half-loan
Yes Overhaul Medicare and create prescription drug benefit

CQ VOTE STUDIES

	PARTY UNITY		PRESIDENTIAL SUPPORT	
	Support	Oppose	Support	Oppose
2004	97%	3%	88%	12%
2003	99%	1%	100%	0%
2002	97%	3%	89%	11%
2001	99%	1%	95%	5%
2000	99%	1%	25%	75%

INTEREST GROUPS

	AFL-CIO	ADA	CCUS	ACU
2004	7%	0%	100%	92%
2003	0%	5%	100%	88%
2002	13%	0%	100%	96%
2001	8%	0%	100%	96%
2000	0%	5%	85%	96%

TEXAS 21
Central — west Austin and suburbs, northeast San Antonio and suburbs

The 21st is a heavily Republican, mostly urban and suburban district that connects the cities of Austin and San Antonio by moving southwest parallel to Interstate 35.

A slight plurality of district residents live in Austin's Travis County. The 21st takes in most of the wealthy western suburbs that are populated with technology industry employees. It also includes Austin's core downtown, including the Capitol and governor's mansion, and the nearby University of Texas at Austin, which were added in redistricting prior to the 2004 election. UT's presence adds to the city's liberal political bent, but the 21st takes in predominately the main campus, leaving much of the area to the north and east — where many students live — in the 10th and 25th districts.

San Antonio's Bexar (pronounced BEAR) County is home to two-fifths of district residents. The district includes the mostly comfortable north and

northeast parts of San Antonio and its suburbs, and takes in San Antonio International Airport, Fort Sam Houston and Randolph Air Force Base, all of which are employment anchors in the district.

Comal County, located northeast of San Antonio, makes up only 10 percent of the district's population, but its strong Republican tilt helps balance out Austin's Democratic-leaning areas. The addition of downtown Austin, coupled with the removal of GOP counties in Texas' Hill Country, reduced Republican strength in the 21st, but George W. Bush still captured 60 percent of the 2004 presidential vote here.

MAJOR INDUSTRY
Technology, government, education, defense

MILITARY BASES
Fort Sam Houston (Army), 16,221 military, 9,878 civilian; Randolph Air Force Base, 4,499 military, 3,773 civilian (2004)

CITIES
Austin (pt.), 200,191; San Antonio (pt.), 172,502; New Braunfels (pt.), 21,321

NOTABLE
Lyndon B. Johnson was born in Blanco County; South by Southwest, a pop and rock music festival in Austin, is held each spring; Austin is home to North America's largest urban colony of Mexican free tailed-bats.

Rep. Tom DeLay (R)

Elected 1984; 11th term

The shrewd and pugnacious DeLay has played politics close to the edge in the service of the House Republican majority, efforts that have earned him the gratitude of the rank and file. But in the first year of the 109th Congress, DeLay faced a career crisis as questions about his ethics and his campaign fundraising were investigated by a Texas grand jury, a Senate committee and by the media.

Usually the dispenser of favors and perks, the second-ranking House leader found himself in the unfamiliar position of needing the goodwill of his GOP colleagues. During a private meeting of Senate Republicans, he even made a plea for patience while he dealt with the barrage of criticism and negative news stories. DeLay's public defense was characteristically confrontational. "Bring it on," he told Fox News. "It's nothing but a bunch of leftist organizations that have a public strategy to demonize me, and usually they overreach."

Events began to spiral out of DeLay's control in 2004. In the fall, the House ethics committee admonished him for improperly offering to help the political campaign of a Republican congressman's son in exchange for the House member's vote on the 2003 GOP prescription drug bill.

In early 2005, newspapers reported overseas trips he took with lobbyist Jack Abramoff, who was being investigated by the Senate Indian Affairs Committee for allegedly trading on his ties with DeLay to get fees from Indian tribes that own casinos. And a Texas grand jury indicted three of DeLay's political associates for allegedly raising money from corporations to influence the outcome of the 2002 Texas House election.

That election, which resulted in the state House changing from a Democratic to a Republican majority, was a significant first step toward DeLay's goal of defeating U.S. House Democratic incumbents in 2004. A sign that his political problems were serious was the assessment of him on the usually admiring editorial page of The Wall Street Journal, which said in March 2005 that he'd gone from anti-Beltway crusader to "the living exemplar of some of its worst habits."

Though some Republicans began to distance themselves, DeLay retained the support of most of the House Republican Conference in 2005, as well as the backing of conservative organizations outside Congress.

DeLay gets most of the credit for the growth in the Republican majority since 2002. That year, he organized a massive get-out-the-vote drive aimed at offsetting a well-financed push by labor unions for Democrats. Republicans defied the usual historical trend by gaining, not losing, seats in a midterm election in which they also held the White House.

Two years later, Republicans gained three seats overall, mainly because a DeLay-backed remapping of Texas congressional districts resulted in five Democrats losing their seats to Republicans. Later, the ethics panel rebuked DeLay for using his power to direct the Federal Aviation Administration to help find a group of Texas Democrats who had left the state in a vain attempt to block adoption of the new map.

DeLay has flourished in part because of his unique, mutually beholden relationship with the only man who outranks him, Speaker J. Dennis Hastert. When Republicans took power in 1995, Hastert was instrumental in helping DeLay become GOP whip over the objections of then-Speaker Newt Gingrich, who preferred one of his close allies for the job. Four years later, after Gingrich left office, DeLay helped Hastert become Speaker by quickly

CAPITOL OFFICE
225-5951
tomdelay.house.gov
242 Cannon 20515-4322; fax 225-5241

COMMITTEES
Majority leader — no committee assignments

HOMETOWN
Sugar Land

BORN
April 8, 1947, Laredo, Texas

RELIGION
Baptist

FAMILY
Wife, Christine DeLay; one child

EDUCATION
Baylor U., attended 1965-67; U. of Houston, B.S. 1970 (biology)

CAREER
Pest control business owner

POLITICAL HIGHLIGHTS
Texas House, 1979-85

ELECTION RESULTS

2004 GENERAL

Tom DeLay (R)	150,386	55.2%
Richard R. Morrison (D)	112,034	41.1%
Michael "Fjet" Fjetland (I)	5,314	2.0%
Tom Morrison (LIBERT)	4,886	1.8%

2004 PRIMARY

Tom DeLay (R)	unopposed

2002 GENERAL

Tom DeLay (R)	100,499	63.2%
Tim Riley (D)	55,716	35.0%
Gerald W. "Jerry" LaFleur (LIBERT)	1,612	1.0%

PREVIOUS WINNING PERCENTAGES
2000 (60%); 1998 (65%); 1996 (68%); 1994 (74%); 1992 (69%); 1990 (71%); 1988 (67%); 1986 (72%); 1984 (65%)

throwing his weight behind his candidacy. The even-tempered Illinoisan and DeLay have worked together since in a "good cop-bad cop" way, as one aide described it. In his 2004 book titled "Speaker," Hastert described DeLay as a "street-smart politician" and wrote, "I rely on his instincts."

DeLay's style is a mixture of high-handedness and persuasiveness, partisan fervor and political practicality. Although he can be intense in his pursuit of victory on even minor bills, he lets fellow Republicans know that he has their interests at heart. He makes sure they get their share of pet projects in spending bills. His office caters meals during late-night House sessions. He knows individual members down to the kind of beverage they prefer.

DeLay's relationship with President Bush is not a warm one, and at times he has stood in the way of Bush's agenda. In the 108th Congress, he blocked a major energy bill by insisting it include a provision protecting the makers of a gasoline additive known as MTBE from product liability lawsuits. MTBE producers — many based in Texas and other Gulf Coast states — are being sued by local governments for cleanup costs of contaminated water supplies.

DeLay sees himself as a guardian of conservative ideology. In 2005, he was applauded by religious conservatives for leading the drive in Congress to intervene in several judges' decision to let a severely brain-damaged Florida woman named Terri Schiavo die. A born-again Christian, DeLay's religious views influence his political thinking. He is one of Israel's strongest allies in Congress, believing that Jewish control over the West Bank is a fulfillment of biblical prophecy.

He is also staunchly against government regulation. His frustration with what he said was too much red tape when he ran a pest exterminating business led him into politics. "I was struggling to build a company, and the government was getting in my way every time I turned around," he says.

DeLay spent much of his childhood in Venezuela with his father, an oil drilling contractor. After six years in the Texas House, he won a GOP-leaning seat in Congress in 1984 with 65 percent of the vote. He was re-elected with 60 percent or more each time until 2004, when an underfunded Democratic opponent, lawyer Richard R. Morrison, held him to 55 percent.

Before becoming majority leader, DeLay was the Republican whip for eight years. He quietly encouraged a reputation for ruthlessness. When he was nicknamed "The Hammer" for pressuring lobbyists for political donations, DeLay not only didn't object, he said that it helped him do his job.

At the end of 2002, when Majority Leader Dick Armey of Texas retired from Congress, House Republicans elevated DeLay by acclamation.

KEY VOTES

2004

No Extend federal unemployment benefits by 13 weeks
Yes Pass $283.2 billion, six-year federal highway and mass transit bill
Yes Approve $146 billion multi-year extension of previously enacted middle-class tax breaks
Yes Amend the Constitution to prohibit same-sex marriage
Yes Cut corporate taxes $137 billion over 10 years
Yes Reorganize U.S. intelligence agencies as proposed by Sept. 11 commission

2003

Yes Cut taxes by $330 billion through fiscal 2013
No Block Bush rule scaling back overtime pay for some white-collar federal workers
No Do not allow use of search warrants without first notifying subjects
No Allow importation of prescription drugs
Yes Create private school voucher program in Washington, D.C.
Yes Ban "partial birth" abortion except to save a woman's life
No Split $18.6 billion in Iraq aid into half-grant, half-loan
Yes Overhaul Medicare and create prescription drug benefit

CQ VOTE STUDIES

	PARTY UNITY		PRESIDENTIAL SUPPORT	
	Support	Oppose	Support	Oppose
2004	98%	2%	91%	9%
2003	99%	1%	100%	0%
2002	99%	1%	92%	8%
2001	99%	1%	98%	2%
2000	99%	1%	23%	77%

INTEREST GROUPS

	AFL-CIO	ADA	CCUS	ACU
2004	13%	0%	100%	100%
2003	0%	5%	100%	88%
2002	0%	0%	95%	92%
2001	0%	0%	100%	100%
2000	0%	0%	84%	88%

TEXAS 22
Southeast Houston and southern suburbs — Sugar Land, Pearland, part of Pasadena

The solidly Republican 22nd includes a majority of Fort Bend County, a chunk of northern Brazoria County and a piece of Galveston County south of Houston, plus a small southeastern slice of the city itself. Most residents live in the fast-growing Houston suburbs in or just outside of Harris County.

The district contains booming communities such as Sugar Land and Pearland, as well as upscale homes surrounding the Lyndon B. Johnson Space Center — which was moved into the 22nd during redistricting prior to the 2004 election — where many NASA scientists and astronauts live in a wealthy area known as Clear Lake.

Slightly less than two-fifths of the population resides in Fort Bend County, which includes Rep. DeLay's hometown of Sugar Land. Since the 1960s, the area has changed from a sugar-growing center into suburbia. Sugar refiner Imperial Holly still maintains its presence in Sugar Land, but the

city has welcomed new planned developments and a range of corporations. It is not uncommon to find six-figure earners living here.

On its eastern edge, the 22nd takes in part of southeastern Harris County, where 45 percent of district residents live. This area tends toward the upscale: Some of the wealthiest areas in the county are in southeastern Houston, near Ellington Field, a former Air Force base that now houses the space center's aircraft operations and offers support for military reserve and guard units. The district also dips down to take in Houston Hobby Airport, making transportation a key issue as well.

MAJOR INDUSTRY
Aerospace, transportation, agriculture, retail

CITIES
Houston (pt.), 109,880; Sugar Land, 63,328; Pasadena (pt.), 57,020; Pearland, 37,628; Missouri City (pt.), 32,855; Deer Park, 28,493

NOTABLE
The annual "Texian Market Days" in Fort Bend County include re-enactments of 1830s pioneer life, when the area was settled by some of the "Old 300" families led by Stephen F. Austin; George Observatory in Brazos Bend State Park includes a memorial to the seven astronauts who died aboard the space shuttle Challenger in 1986.

Rep. Henry Bonilla (R)

CAPITOL OFFICE
225-4511
www.house.gov/bonilla
2458 Rayburn 20515-4323; fax 225-2237

COMMITTEES
Appropriations
(Agriculture, Rural Development & FDA -
chairman)

HOMETOWN
San Antonio

BORN
Jan. 2, 1954, San Antonio, Texas

RELIGION
Baptist

FAMILY
Divorced; two children

EDUCATION
U. of Texas, B.A. 1976 (journalism)

CAREER
Television reporter, producer and executive;
gubernatorial aide

POLITICAL HIGHLIGHTS
No previous office

ELECTION RESULTS

2004 GENERAL

Henry Bonilla (R)	170,716	69.3%
Joseph P. "Joe" Sullivan (D)	72,480	29.4%
Nazirite "Comrade" Perez (LIBERT)	3,307	1.3%

2004 PRIMARY

Henry Bonilla (R)	unopposed

2002 GENERAL

Henry Bonilla (R)	77,573	51.5%
Henry Cuellar (D)	71,067	47.2%

PREVIOUS WINNING PERCENTAGES
2000 (59%); 1998 (64%); 1996 (62%); 1994 (63%);
1992 (59%)

Elected 1992; 7th term

A favorite of Republican leaders, Bonilla is at the center of the party's effort to broaden its appeal among Hispanics. His life story is often retold, from his childhood in a San Antonio housing project to his political career as a congressman and a potential candidate for statewide office.

Now in his seventh term, Bonilla (bo-NEE-uh) has ambitions to become the first Mexican-American to occupy a Senate seat. He already has passed up one opportunity to run, in 2002, when Sen. Phil Gramm retired and Texas Attorney General John Cornyn bested him for the Republican nomination. Bonilla has said he would run in 2006 if GOP Sen. Kay Bailey Hutchison of Texas leaves to make a bid for Texas governor.

Bonilla is a close ally of Majority Leader Tom DeLay, and also has his own locus of power as one of the 10 "cardinals," as the Appropriations subcommittee chairmen are known. Representing a rural southwest Texas district, he heads the agriculture spending subcommittee.

His relationship with DeLay hasn't always been a plus for him politically. In 2004, he led the ill-fated charge in DeLay's behalf for a proposed change in GOP rules that would have permitted the powerful No. 2 Republican leader to stay in his post if indicted. DeLay was under scrutiny by Texas investigators for allegedly funneling corporate contributions to GOP state legislative candidates in 2002, which is against state law. Bonilla's proposal — he insisted he was not working in concert with DeLay — prompted a backlash from Republicans who said it showed a tin ear on ethics and wouldn't play well with voters. The plan was quickly shelved.

On Appropriations, Bonilla has proved to be a loyal soldier of the Republican leadership, sometimes using tough tactics to serve their goals. But he also sticks up for his prerogatives as an appropriator.

In 2004, Bonilla tried to amend the farm spending bill to weaken country-of-origin labeling requirements for meats and other foods after food producers in the Southwest complained that compliance was too costly. He was out-muscled by then-Minority Leader Tom Daschle of South Dakota, who represented ranchers who liked the labeling mandate because it gave them a competitive edge against foreign beef suppliers at a time consumers were worried about spongiform encephalopathy, known as mad cow disease.

With the administration's backing, however, Bonilla succeeded in removing provisons to ease the importation of prescription drugs from Canada and to boost the sale of medical supplies and farm goods in Cuba.

Bonilla, who got his Appropriations seat in his first term, played hardball for the party in 2002, when some lawmakers tried to reopen contentious issues that had been settled in the rewrite of federal farm policy earlier in the year. Marcy Kaptur of Ohio, the top Democrat on Bonilla's subcommittee, prepared an amendment to cut farmer subsidies, so Bonilla readied an amendment to eliminate 18 projects benefiting Ohio. Kaptur backed off, saying she would not risk the retaliation.

Bonilla was one of three co-chairmen of the Republican National Convention that nominated George W. Bush for president in 2000. He was frequently mentioned as a Bush Cabinet prospect.

To Bonilla, Hispanics should be natural Republican allies because they speak the same political language, favoring small businesses and a strong military, opposing high taxes and intrusive government. But, he says, the GOP has not done a good job getting that message to Hispanic voters.

Until his rise to a subcommittee chairmanship, Bonilla was best-known on Appropriations for fighting often-futile battles against President Clinton's efforts to impose new regulations on business. For years, Bonilla helped hold up the annual funding bill for the Department of Labor in a bid to block the implementation of workplace standards for repetitive-motion injuries. (After Clinton issued new ergonomics rules in the final days of his administration, GOP lawmakers repealed them in 2001.)

On environmental issues, Bonilla is usually friendly to business interests and private property owners. When a 2000 drought forced water rationing in Texas, he said, "The plain fact is that the source of all the pain inflicted on this region is the Endangered Species Act." He was the only member of the Hispanic Caucus to vote for the 1996 law creating work requirements for welfare recipients. He has sought to bar the children of illegal immigrants from attending public schools. And he has criticized the Department of Education's bilingual education requirements, arguing that schools should be able to adopt a more English-centered approach.

A former television newsman, Bonilla worked at several TV stations and was press secretary to GOP Gov. Richard Thornburgh of Pennsylvania before returning to San Antonio in 1986 to work as a public affairs executive at the local CBS affiliate. Six years later, he took on four-term Democratic Rep. Albert G. Bustamante, whose increasingly luxurious lifestyle made him seem out of touch with a district that has some of the poorest neighborhoods in the country. Bonilla chatted with voters in Spanish and campaigned beside his wife (they have since divorced), who was the anchor of the region's highest-rated TV newscast. Bonilla won by 21 percentage points.

After Bonilla won four relatively easy re-elections, Democrats turned the tables on him in 2002. Henry Cuellar, a former Texas secretary of state, cast himself as a moderate and characterized Bonilla as having lost touch with the district. But the coattails of Tony Sanchez — the unsuccessful Democratic gubernatorial candidate, who like Cuellar was from Laredo — proved insufficient and Bonilla hung on to win by 4 points.

After mid-decade remapping in 2004 made the district more reliably Republican by removing some Hispanic voters, Bonilla defeated a little-known challenger by 40 points.

Bonilla seriously considered running for the Senate when Gramm announced his retirement in 2002. But Cornyn was named by Gov. Rick Perry to fill out the remainder of the term, giving Cornyn a big advantage in the fall. A poll Bonilla commissioned also showed that Cornyn had most of the GOP support locked up.

KEY VOTES

2004
No   Extend federal unemployment benefits by 13 weeks
Yes   Pass $283.2 billion, six-year federal highway and mass transit bill
Yes   Approve $146 billion multi-year extension of previously enacted middle-class tax breaks
Yes   Amend the Constitution to prohibit same-sex marriage
Yes   Cut corporate taxes $137 billion over 10 years
Yes   Reorganize U.S. intelligence agencies as proposed by Sept. 11 commission

2003
?   Cut taxes by $330 billion through fiscal 2013
No   Block Bush rule scaling back overtime pay for some white-collar federal workers
No   Do not allow use of search warrants without first notifying subjects
No   Allow importation of prescription drugs
Yes   Create private school voucher program in Washington, D.C.
Yes   Ban "partial birth" abortion except to save a woman's life
No   Split $18.6 billion in Iraq aid into half-grant, half-loan
Yes   Overhaul Medicare and create prescription drug benefit

CQ VOTE STUDIES

	PARTY UNITY		PRESIDENTIAL SUPPORT	
	Support	Oppose	Support	Oppose
2004	94%	6%	88%	12%
2003	97%	3%	98%	2%
2002	97%	3%	88%	12%
2001	99%	1%	95%	5%
2000	92%	8%	30%	70%

INTEREST GROUPS

	AFL-CIO	ADA	CCUS	ACU
2004	13%	0%	100%	92%
2003	7%	5%	100%	88%
2002	11%	0%	95%	92%
2001	8%	0%	96%	92%
2000	0%	0%	90%	82%

TEXAS 23

Southwest — northwest San Antonio and suburbs, part of Laredo, Del Rio

The 23rd is larger than most states east of the Mississippi River — residents like to say the area has two time zones and three climates. Taking in 800 miles of the border with Mexico along the Rio Grande River, it skims El Paso in the west and heads over to San Antonio in the east.

The district was one of the focal points of the disputed GOP-led, mid-decade remap prior to the 2004 election. Many Democrats argued unsuccessfully that by taking heavily Hispanic Laredo from wholly within the old 23rd and splitting it between the new 23rd and 28th districts, the map diluted the Hispanic vote and disenfranchised minority voters.

With Laredo's Webb County split, the percentage of Hispanics in the 23rd decreased from 67 percent to 55 percent. The district also picked up some rural, strongly Republican and heavily white counties in Texas' Hill Country, including Kerr, Kendall and Bandera counties — which each gave George W. Bush more than 78 percent of the vote in 2004. Overall,

the new 23rd is less politically competitive, with Republicans holding a huge advantage in the northern, San Antonio region and Democrats holding a lesser edge in what remains of Webb County and in some heavily Hispanic counties in the west. Bush handily won the 23rd in the 2004 presidential election with 64 percent of the vote.

The 23rd includes some of the nation's poorest counties along its southern border. Seasonal employment, the influx of immigrants and an abundance of cheaper Mexican labor contribute to high unemployment. Manufacturing operations along the border known as *maquiladoras* are an integral part of the economy. An increase in trade and manufacturing in the 1990s has benefited the area.

MAJOR INDUSTRY
Agriculture, trade, tourism, defense

MILITARY BASES
Laughlin Air Force Base, 1,456 military, 944 civilian (2003)

CITIES
San Antonio (pt.), 154,516; Laredo (pt.), 92,102; Del Rio, 33,867

NOTABLE
Texas' largest county, Brewster, is roughly 6,200 square miles, about the size of Connecticut and Rhode Island combined.

Rep. Kenny Marchant (R)

Elected 2004; 1st term

Marchant took advantage of his key post in the Texas Legislature to get to Washington, and his ties with Majority Leader Tom DeLay to get his Capitol Hill career off to a good start.

The freshman congressman spent 18 years in the Texas House and was a member of that body's Redistricting Committee when it began — with DeLay's enthusiastic backing — the mid-decade redrawing of congressional district maps. The resulting map created a revised, heavily Republican 24th District that had no incumbent and encompassed Marchant's base. He cruised to Congress over token primary competition and a little-known Democratic opponent.

His long legislative experience and alliance with DeLay appeared to help Marchant (MARCH-unt) in obtaining committee assignments. Representing a district that includes part of Dallas-Fort Worth International Airport and which has serious commuter traffic problems, Marchant got a seat on the Transportation and Infrastructure Committee. He also got seats on the Government Reform and the Education and Workforce panels.

Marchant is a familiar face to President Bush, who was governor of Texas for six of the years that Marchant was in the state House. The conservative Marchant says the two agree on social and fiscal policy "99 percent of the time." But he said his top congressional goal is pushing down the deficit, because "the No. 1 priority in my district is getting spending under control."

Marchant, who says he is a deeply religious man, has had to deal with hardship. In 1998, his wife and two youngest children were in a car accident while on a church trip to Mexico. Though his wife and daughter have recovered, Marchant's son remains paralyzed from the waist down.

Marchant had planned to run for Congress in 2002, when post-2000 census remapping put a new district in Marchant's suburban Dallas territory. But he was shunted aside when Pete Sessions, the Republican incumbent, decided he would rather run in the new district than in the redrawn version of his old one.

CAPITOL OFFICE
225-6605
www.marchant.house.gov
501 Cannon 20515-4324; fax 225-0074

COMMITTEES
Education & Workforce
Government Reform
Transportation & Infrastructure

HOMETOWN
Coppell

BORN
Feb. 23, 1951, Bonham, Texas

RELIGION
Nazarene

FAMILY
Wife, Donna Marchant; four children

EDUCATION
Southern Nazarene U., B.A. 1974 (religion);
Nazarene Theological Seminary, attended 1975-76

CAREER
Real estate developer; homebuilding company owner

POLITICAL HIGHLIGHTS
Carrollton City Council, 1980-84 (mayor pro tempore, 1983-84); mayor of Carrollton, 1984-86; Texas House, 1987-2005

ELECTION RESULTS

2004 GENERAL

Kenny Marchant (R)	154,435	64.0%
Gary R. Page (D)	82,599	34.2%
James H. Lawrence (LIBERT)	4,340	1.8%

2004 PRIMARY

Kenny Marchant (R)	9,073	73.5%
Cynthia Newman (R)	1,103	8.9%
Bill Dunn (R)	1,096	8.9%
Terry Waldrum (R)	1,074	8.7%

TEXAS 24

Part of Dallas and western suburbs – Grand Prairie

Redistricting prior to the 2004 election made the 24th into a Republican stronghold by carving out a Dallas-Fort Worth district designed to guarantee a GOP win. Taking in most of the more affluent suburbs sandwiched between the two cities, the district is heavily white (64 percent) and Republican — its constituents gave George W. Bush 65 percent of the vote in 2004.

The district's industry revolves largely around Dallas-Fort Worth International Airport, most of which is in the 24th. The airport is one of the largest in the country, but also is the largest employer in the district. Additionally, American Airlines makes its headquarters in the 24th.

In the wake of the Sept. 11, 2001, terrorist attacks, the airline industry suffered huge losses. This downturn hurt the 24th by forcing airlines to lay off area workers as air traffic decreased. American Airlines was considering filing for bankruptcy until a deal was reached with its unions in 2003.

A corporate hub in Irving's Las Colinas financial district, which is shared with the 32nd District, also fuels the district's economy. Several corporate headquarters are here, and other large businesses, such as Citigroup and Comcast, provide the district with revenue and jobs.

The 24th takes in several wealthy suburbs, with many residents commuting into either Fort Worth or Dallas, making transportation policy a major issue in the district.

MAJOR INDUSTRY
Transportation, manufacturing, corporate headquarters

CITIES
Grand Prairie (pt.), 122,502; Carrollton, 109,576; Irving (pt.), 59,755; Bedford; 47,152; Euless, 46,005; Grapevine, 42,057; Dallas (pt.), 37,512

NOTABLE
The Mustangs of Las Colinas, a statue located in the district, is the world's largest equestrian sculpture.

Rep. Lloyd Doggett (D)

Elected 1994; 6th term

CAPITOL OFFICE
225-4865
lloyd.doggett@mail.house.gov
www.house.gov/doggett
201 Cannon 20515-4325; fax 225-3073

COMMITTEES
Ways & Means

HOMETOWN
Austin

BORN
Oct. 6, 1946, Austin, Texas

RELIGION
Methodist

FAMILY
Wife, Libby Belk Doggett; two children

EDUCATION
U. of Texas, B.B.A. 1967, J.D. 1970

CAREER
Lawyer

POLITICAL HIGHLIGHTS
Texas Senate, 1973-85; Democratic nominee for
U.S. Senate, 1984; Texas Supreme Court, 1989-94

ELECTION RESULTS

2004 GENERAL

Lloyd Doggett (D)	108,309	67.6%
Rebecca Armendariz Klein (R)	49,252	30.7%
James Warner (LIBERT)	2,656	1.7%

2004 PRIMARY

Lloyd Doggett (D)	40,306	64.4%
Leticia Hinojosa (D)	22,305	35.6%

2002 GENERAL

Lloyd Doggett (D)	114,428	84.4%
Michele Messina (LIBERT)	21,196	15.6%

PREVIOUS WINNING PERCENTAGES
2000 (85%); 1998 (85%); 1996 (56%); 1994 (56%)

Doggett seldom misses an opportunity to upbraid, outmaneuver or otherwise confound Republican conservatives, particularly fellow Texan Tom DeLay, the House majority leader.

The liberal former Texas Supreme Court justice once told his hometown newspaper, the Austin American-Statesman: "When the rules of the game are changed, when the voice of the minority is restricted so severely that we can't be heard, then we consider parliamentary tactics." In the 109th Congress, he continues to co-chair a parliamentary group that uses various delaying devices to hold up the GOP agenda.

Despite his effective tongue wagging at the opposition, Doggett's failure to contribute to the Democratic Congressional Campaign Committee — the House Democrats' campaign arm — hasn't endeared him to the Democratic leadership. But his massive war chest came in handy during a messier-than-expected re-election bid in 2004.

Doggett, whose scathing words about DeLay often turn up in the Texas media, was a top target when DeLay led a drive to redraw Texas' congressional districts in 2003 in a successful bid to enlarge the Republican majority in the House. Democrats in the state legislature attempted to block the redistricting by fleeing the state to prevent a quorum — borrowing a legislative tactic Doggett and his friends once used in the legislature. When he was a state senator, he was one of the "Killer Bees," a dozen liberal lawmakers who in 1979 hid in an Austin garage apartment to stop work on a bill championed by conservative Democrats.

With a seat on the Ways and Means Committee, Doggett focuses on doing away with corporate tax shelters and looking for political vulnerabilities in Republican tax cut proposals. He has been on the committee since 1999, when he beat out several competitors for a post on the influential tax-writing panel. In a sense, he took the place of his predecessor, Democratic Rep. J.J. Pickle, who was on Ways and Means until he retired in 1994. The posting puts Doggett in prime position in the 109th Congress to fight President Bush's plan to allow workers to divert a portion of their Social Security taxes into personal investment accounts.

In 2004, Doggett and Democrat Rosa DeLauro of Connecticut tried to prevent Accenture Ltd., which has its headquarters in Bermuda, from getting a $10 billion Homeland Security contract to track foreign visitors as they enter and leave the United States. They argued that tax-dodging companies shouldn't be rewarded. In the end, Accenture got the contract, but a provision was added to the 2005 Homeland Security appropriations bill to prevent expatriate companies from securing future contracts.

In March 2003, Doggett helped block temporarily a bill to prevent Texas teachers from maximizing their benefits from Social Security and a state pension program. His phone calls to Texas teachers resulted in a flood of letters to Congress from national teacher unions. When the bill first came to the floor, it failed to garner the two-thirds majority required under the procedure in force then. But it was enacted nearly a year later.

Doggett's liberal philosophy extends to foreign policy and defense issues. During House consideration in late 2002 of a resolution authorizing the president to take military action against Iraq, he led an ad hoc whip organization to round up votes in opposition.

Doggett has a passion for protecting the environment that is showcased in his congressional office, where he is obsessive about recycling. During his House tenure, he has repeatedly complained that his Republican colleagues have been sub par in their recycling efforts on Capitol Hill.

A workaholic — he's often the last person out of the office each evening — Doggett frequently can be found on the floor during the period set aside each day for one-minute speeches. During major floor debates, his punchy quotes sometimes make the network news.

Born and reared in Austin, Doggett went to the University of Texas, where he was elected student body president. Within two years of earning his law degree in 1970, he won election to the state Senate. He served until 1985, compiling a record of support for consumers and civil rights while backing the death penalty and tough criminal sanctions against drug traffickers and violent criminals. Fellow state senators knew he was ready to filibuster when he donned white leather tennis shoes, which kept him comfortable during long stints on his feet. (The shoes now hang in his congressional office.)

In 1984, he ran for the U.S. Senate, beating two veteran House members, Bob Krueger and Kent Hance, in the Democratic primary. But in November, he was crushed by GOP Rep. Phil Gramm. Four years later, Doggett won a seat on the Texas Supreme Court, which handles only civil cases. He was on the bench when 81-year-old Democratic Rep. Pickle announced his retirement in 1994.

Doggett was the first Democrat to announce his candidacy, and his quick start spared him primary competition. Raising $1.2 million, he bucked that year's GOP takeover tide and won with 16 percent of the vote over real estate consultant A. Jo Baylor, who had hoped to become the first black Republican woman elected to Congress.

As the 2004 elections approached, the DeLay-inspired redistricting dismantled the 10th District, which had encompassed Austin, splintering it into three districts. Doggett quickly decided to run in the new, nine-county 25th District, which stretches 350 miles from Austin to the Texas-Mexico border and was drawn to elect a Hispanic candidate.

He gave up his hillside West Austin home and moved to the heavily Hispanic east side, the portion of the city he retains. He faced state Judge Leticia Hinojosa in the primary. Many district residents saw the choice as between a local candidate and a big-city candidate. But Doggett collected campaign cash and touted his influence as a member of Ways and Means. He beat Hinojosa by a wide margin and went on to solidly defeat Republican Becky Armendariz Klein, who worked for both Bush and his father, the former president.

KEY VOTES

2004

Yes Extend federal unemployment benefits by 13 weeks

Yes Pass $283.2 billion, six-year federal highway and mass transit bill

? Approve $146 billion multi-year extension of previously enacted middle-class tax breaks

No Amend the Constitution to prohibit same-sex marriage

No Cut corporate taxes $137 billion over 10 years

Yes Reorganize U.S. intelligence agencies as proposed by Sept. 11 commission

2003

No Cut taxes by $330 billion through fiscal 2013

Yes Block Bush rule scaling back overtime pay for some white-collar federal workers

Yes Do not allow use of search warrants without first notifying subjects

Yes Allow importation of prescription drugs

No Create private school voucher program in Washington, D.C.

No Ban "partial birth" abortion except to save a woman's life

Yes Split $18.6 billion in Iraq aid into half-grant, half-loan

No Overhaul Medicare and create prescription drug benefit

CQ VOTE STUDIES

	PARTY UNITY		PRESIDENTIAL SUPPORT	
	Support	Oppose	Support	Oppose
2004	95%	5%	27%	73%
2003	97%	3%	18%	82%
2002	95%	5%	22%	78%
2001	92%	8%	29%	71%
2000	90%	10%	86%	14%

INTEREST GROUPS

	AFL-CIO	ADA	CCUS	ACU
2004	93%	95%	39%	4%
2003	93%	90%	30%	12%
2002	100%	100%	30%	4%
2001	100%	85%	35%	4%
2000	80%	85%	33%	12%

TEXAS 25

South central — southeast Austin, most of McAllen, Mission

The 25th stretches south in a narrow band from Austin to the Rio Grande River on the Mexican border. Its population centers are on the extreme ends, in Austin to the north and in McAllen and Mission to the south.

The district takes in the eastern and southern portions of Austin, including Austin-Bergstrom International Airport. This area has a higher Hispanic population and is comparatively poorer than rest of the city. Like Austin overall, the economy here revolves around the University of Texas, state government and the technology industry, and residents elect Democrats to office.

The district's geographic middle belongs to Republicans. Farming and ranching is abundant in the four lightly populated counties south of Travis County (Austin), all of which voted for George W. Bush in 2004. The three southernmost counties wholly within the district, as well as Hidalgo County, of which the 25th has the populous southwestern portion, all

voted for John Kerry in 2004, although the large Catholic influence gives the area a socially conservative bent.

The district is heavily Hispanic (69 percent), and the southern portion's population is booming. Starr County is the nation's most heavily Hispanic county (97.5 percent), and Hidalgo County is one of the fastest-growing areas in the state. Hidalgo and Starr also are among the most economically depressed counties in the nation. In Starr County, nearly half of all families live below the poverty line. But the economy is starting to show improvement as the number of small businesses rise. In South Texas' Valley region, citrus growing, textiles and manufacturing are dominant, with many of the area factory sites located in Mexico.

MAJOR INDUSTRY
Technology, ranching, agriculture

CITIES
Austin (pt.), 235,361; McAllen (pt.), 78,412; Mission, 45,408

NOTABLE
The Texas Legislature deemed Lockhart the barbecue capital of Texas in 1999; When Three Rivers' only funeral home refused to bury World War II veteran Felix Longoria because of his race, then-Sen. Lyndon B. Johnson had him buried at Arlington National Cemetery in 1949.

Rep. Michael C. Burgess (R)

Elected 2002; 2nd term

CAPITOL OFFICE
225-7772
burgess.house.gov
1721 Longworth 20515-4326; fax 225-2919

COMMITTEES
Energy & Commerce

HOMETOWN
Flower Mound

BORN
Dec. 23, 1950, Rochester, Minn.

RELIGION
Episcopalian

FAMILY
Wife, Laura Lee Burgess; three children

EDUCATION
North Texas State U., B.S. 1972 (biology), M.S. 1976
(physiology); U. of Texas, Houston, M.D. 1977; U. of
Texas, Dallas, M.S. 2000 (medical management)

CAREER
Physician

POLITICAL HIGHLIGHTS
No previous office

ELECTION RESULTS

2004 GENERAL

Michael C. Burgess (R)	180,519	65.8%
Lico Reyes (D)	89,809	32.7%
James Gholston (LIBERT)	4,211	1.5%

2004 PRIMARY

Michael C. Burgess (R)	unopposed

2002 GENERAL

Michael C. Burgess (R)	123,195	74.8%
Paul William Lebon (D)	37,485	22.8%
David Wallace Croft (LIBERT)	2,367	1.4%

An obstetrician-gynecologist who says he delivered more than 3,000 babies in his 21 years of practice, Burgess hasn't had time to make a mark on health care policy yet. But he hopes that is about to change in the 109th Congress with his new posting to the Energy and Commerce Committee, one of the two main House panels that address health care issues.

Burgess, who sits on the Health Subcommittee, wants to take a leading role in advancing Republican health care priorities, such as cutting down on malpractice lawsuits. Burgess has personal experience with the issue. In the late 1980s, he says he was sued by a family who lost a baby during a difficult C-section. He was not in charge of the delivery, he says, but was called in to assist another obstetrician. What struck Burgess about the lawsuit, he says, was the wide swath of physicians it targeted — including his father and his brother, who had nothing to do with the case except that they also practice medicine and share the name "Burgess." "They didn't even do their homework enough to pick the right Dr. Burgess," he recalls. "They just blanketed the hospital with lawsuits."

Eventually, Burgess and his father and brother were dropped from the lawsuit, but that incident helped convince him that the medical liability system needed to be overhauled. He says that even though Texas and other states are taking steps such as caps on damage awards, "we need more than just a piece-by-piece, state-by-state solution." Frivolous lawsuits and the costs of defensive medicine are a national problem, he says.

Burgess adds that he has seen other growing problems with the health care system firsthand: red tape from health maintenance organizations, low reimbursements from Medicaid to health care providers, the financial drain of uncompensated care for illegal immigrants. He wants to work on issues such as how to encourage people to buy private insurance to cover long-term care costs, possibly through tax credits or vouchers, so that Medicaid doesn't become "the middle-class entitlement to long-term care." In his first two years in Congress, he served as chairman of the health subcommittee of the House Republican Policy Committee.

As a supporter of the Medicare prescription drug legislation in 2003, Burgess takes issue with conservatives in his party who worry that the bill saddled the country with trillions of dollars of debt it cannot afford. He is a big supporter of Bush administration officials and others who say Medicare's future costs will be reduced by the new law's measures to encourage wellness and preventive care, rather than simply treating diseases. "These are big ideas that are really transformational," he says, adding that the cost estimates of the legislation are probably too high because analysts don't know how to predict those kinds of savings.

Burgess is one of the many lawmakers who have had to decide how to fill the shoes of a celebrity. He was the man who replaced Dick Armey, who held the 26th District seat for 18 years, including eight as House majority leader. Armey still casts a big shadow, but Burgess is carving out an identity for himself — not as a high-profile ideological warrior, as Armey was, but as a dependable rank-and-file conservative. He has also taken up the cause of the flat tax, the issue Armey championed for many years. Burgess has introduced a bill to let people choose to be taxed at a flat rate as an alternative to the current income tax, and he hopes it will become part of the discussions in Congress now that President Bush has called for a tax code overhaul to simplify the system.

In his first two years, Burgess racked up a record as a fairly reliable supporter of the party line, siding with the GOP on 97 percent of the votes that pitted a majority of Republicans against a majority of Democrats. He has won praise from business and anti-tax groups. In the 108th Congress, he won a 100 percent voting score from the U.S. Chamber of Commerce, and he received the "Hero of the Taxpayer" award from Americans for Tax Reform two years in a row.

But there have been exceptions to his support for leadership priorities. In 2004, he voted against the intelligence overhaul legislation that had been recommended by the independent, bipartisan commission that investigated the Sept. 11, 2001, terrorist attacks. Burgess sided with Judiciary Committee Chairman F. James Sensenbrenner Jr., who argued that the final bill did not do enough to improve border security. Burgess also opposed a Bush administration rule requiring banks to accept Mexican identification cards; he said such measures show too little respect for the importance of earning U.S. citizenship.

And he shares the concerns of some Republicans who want to keep the war on terrorism from weakening civil liberties at home. In 2003, he voted for a measure to block a provision of the Patriot Act, the 2001 anti-terrorism law, that allows search warrants to be served without advance notice. The measure did not become law, but Burgess says he will support the bill again if it comes up when Congress debates renewing the Patriot Act.

To take Armey's place in Congress, Burgess had to defeat the nine-term lawmaker's son, Scott Armey, in the 2002 primary to fill the retiring majority leader's seat. The 26th District had just been redrawn to make Scott Armey the front-runner, and he finished first in the six-way primary. But he only won 45 percent of the vote, not enough to prevent a runoff, and Burgess campaigned against him by handing out literature declaring, "My dad is not Dick Armey." Burgess prevailed in the runoff with 55 percent of the vote. He won easily in November in the solidly Republican district.

Since then, Burgess insists he gets along with the elder Armey, who calls his son's bitter primary battle "water under the bridge." Armey has been working to promote Burgess' flat-tax proposal, and Burgess paid tribute to his predecessor in a March 2003 speech on the House floor.

In 2004, Burgess cruised to a second-term victory with 66 percent of the vote against Democrat Lico Reyes, a local political activist and owner of a disc jockey business.

KEY VOTES

2004

No   Extend federal unemployment benefits by 13 weeks

Yes Pass $283.2 billion, six-year federal highway and mass transit bill

Yes Approve $146 billion multi-year extension of previously enacted middle-class tax breaks

Yes Amend the Constitution to prohibit same-sex marriage

Yes Cut corporate taxes $137 billion over 10 years

No   Reorganize U.S. intelligence agencies as proposed by Sept. 11 commission

2003

Yes Cut taxes by $330 billion through fiscal 2013

No   Block Bush rule scaling back overtime pay for some white-collar federal workers

Yes Do not allow use of search warrants without first notifying subjects

No   Allow importation of prescription drugs

Yes Create private school voucher program in Washington, D.C.

Yes Ban "partial birth" abortion except to save a woman's life

No   Split $18.6 billion in Iraq aid into half-grant, half-loan

Yes Overhaul Medicare and create prescription drug benefit

CQ VOTE STUDIES

	PARTY UNITY		PRESIDENTIAL SUPPORT	
	Support	Oppose	Support	Oppose
2004	96%	4%	88%	12%
2003	98%	2%	93%	7%

INTEREST GROUPS

	AFL-CIO	ADA	CCUS	ACU
2004	20%	5%	100%	96%
2003	7%	5%	100%	88%

TEXAS 26

Eastern Fort Worth and suburbs; most of Denton County

The 26th stretches north from southeastern Fort Worth to take in almost all of Denton County and the eastern part of Cooke County. The district grew larger in redistricting prior to the 2004 election, expanding from its base in suburban Denton County farther south into urban and suburban Fort Worth, as well as farther north into rural areas in Cooke County.

The district's heart is still Denton County, the southern part of which is filled with burgeoning upper-middle-class Dallas-Fort Worth suburbs that have steadily grown in population since the 1970s. But Tarrant County residents now make up 45 percent of the 26th, making it more diverse and slightly more Democratic. These residents live mostly in Fort Worth and its middle-class suburbs of North Richland Hills, Keller and Richland Hills. The 26th also reaches down into Forest Hill and Everman, areas south of downtown Fort Worth that have large black populations.

Much of Cooke County is agricultural, with most of the economy dependent on cattle and dairy farms, and with wheat and oat farms also in the area. Voters here are predominately white and Republican.

In the suburban areas closer to Dallas and Fort Worth, transportation is a major economic force. A small part of Dallas-Fort Worth International Airport lies in the 26th, and the airport — one of the largest in the nation — is a major employer. Fort Worth Alliance Airport (shared with the 12th) was the first airport in the nation to be built specifically to serve the needs of business, and Bell Helicopter Textron's main plant is in Hurst.

The 26th supports Republicans. Voters in the district's portion of Denton County gave George W. Bush 71 percent of the vote in 2004, while the district's part of Tarrant County gave Bush 53 percent of the vote.

MAJOR INDUSTRY
Transportation, telecommunications

CITIES
Fort Worth (pt.), 153,549; Denton, 80,537; Lewisville (pt.), 58,106; North Richland Hills, 55,445; Flower Mound, 50,702; Hurst (pt.), 30,832

NOTABLE
Texas Motor Speedway, the nation's second-largest sports facility, is in Denton County.

Rep. Solomon P. Ortiz (D)

Elected 1982; 12th term

CAPITOL OFFICE
225-7742
www.house.gov/ortiz
2470 Rayburn 20515-4327; fax 226-1134

COMMITTEES
Armed Services
Resources

HOMETOWN
Corpus Christi

BORN
June 3, 1937, Robstown, Texas

RELIGION
Methodist

FAMILY
Divorced; two children

EDUCATION
Institute of Applied Science, attended 1962;
Del Mar College, attended 1965-67

MILITARY SERVICE
Army, 1960-62

CAREER
Law enforcement official

POLITICAL HIGHLIGHTS
Nueces County constable, 1965-69; Nueces
County Commission, 1969-77; Nueces County
sheriff, 1977-83

ELECTION RESULTS

2004 GENERAL

Solomon P. Ortiz (D)	112,081	63.1%
William "Willie" Vaden (R)	61,955	34.9%
Christopher J. Claytor (LIBERT)	3,500	2.0%

2004 PRIMARY

Solomon P. Ortiz (D)	unopposed

2002 GENERAL

Solomon P. Ortiz (D)	68,559	61.1%
Pat Ahumada (R)	41,004	36.5%
Christopher J. Claytor (LIBERT)	2,646	2.4%

PREVIOUS WINNING PERCENTAGES
2000 (63%); 1998 (63%); 1996 (65%); 1994 (59%);
1992 (55%); 1990 (100%); 1988 (100%); 1986 (100%);
1984 (64%); 1982 (64%)

When Ortiz first tried his hand at politics, running for county constable in 1964, Hispanics wanting to vote in South Texas still had to contend with poll taxes and literacy tests. But Ortiz, no stranger to adversity, won that race, drawing on the grit and determination he had learned when working in his youth to help his migrant family make ends meet.

Now, beginning his fifth decade in elective office, Ortiz stands as the most-senior Democrat in the Texas House delegation, holding his party's No. 3 seat on the Armed Services Committee, whose work is vital to the 27th District's military facilities, and the No. 5 Democratic seat on the Resources Committee, which deals with U.S.-Mexico water issues, fisheries policy and other matters important to his border-and-coastal constituency.

Ortiz's overall voting record is less liberal than those of other Hispanic Democrats in the House; he voted with President Bush 45 percent of the time in the 108th Congress. He calls himself conservative on social issues, opposing same-sex marriage, for instance, and progressive on economic ones. This mirrors attitudes in his district, which is two-thirds Hispanic and has many people in need of better educational and employment opportunities and health care services.

Because he sometimes votes with the GOP and always tries to stay on good terms with his Republican colleagues, Ortiz was better situated than many Democrats to deal with the shock of the GOP takeover of the House in 1995. His personal relationships with many Republicans help him gain an ear for his proposals. "He worms his way into their hearts," says one longtime aide.

Four major military installations in the 27th account for 20 percent of local economic activity, and Ortiz is an ever-vigilant watchdog for those facilities from his seat on Armed Services. He particularly opposes Pentagon proposals to privatize repair work done at large military maintenance depots, such as the one in Corpus Christi where more than 2,500 civilian federal employees service Army helicopters.

Ortiz argues that it is dangerous to rely for critical repair work on private companies that might have labor problems or use their monopoly as leverage to boost the cost of the work. Taking note in early 2005 of the continued fighting in Iraq, Ortiz said, "One only needs to watch the evening news to know how much wear and tear we are putting on our helicopters and how much rapid, reliable maintenance we need on those birds."

On Armed Services' Readiness Subcommittee, Ortiz has taken a dim view of efforts by the Pentagon to close military bases as part of force-and-facilities restructuring. The bases in Ortiz's district survived the base-closing rounds of the 1990s, and Ortiz vigorously opposed a new round of base closings in 2005, which Congress enacted in 2001 under threat of a presidential veto. With the latest base realignment and closure process getting under way in early 2005, Ortiz voiced concern about any proposal to abandon bases while the U.S. military is "in the midst of a global shadowy war on terrorism" and fighting in Iraq.

As a young man, Ortiz served in the Army's military police, gaining experience that helped put him on his path to a career in law enforcement and government. He shows a special interest in troop quality of life and in seeing that military personnel are given a chance at upward mobility. When Bush proposed his budget in 2005, Ortiz said it did not include enough money for pay raises for the troops, for veterans' drug benefits, and for payments for families of those killed in service.

On the Resources Committee, water is a major Ortiz concern — specifically, the lack of water that plagues farmers and municipalities in the Rio Grande Valley. He has been a leader among Texas politicians demanding that Washington pressure Mexico to deliver billions of gallons of water it owes the United States under a 1944 treaty.

As one would expect from a lawmaker whose district borders Mexico, Ortiz has been active in such issues as cross-border trade and tourism, immigration and drug smuggling. He is co-chairman of the bipartisan Border Caucus, with GOP Rep. Henry Bonilla of Texas' 23rd District.

In dealing with the panoply of homeland defense issues facing Congress since the Sept. 11, 2001, terrorist attacks, Ortiz has had to balance three priorities: his conservative instinct on questions of national security; the economic dependence of many of his constituents on easy access for day-trippers crossing the Rio Grande; and his determination to protect Hispanics against discrimination.

In the 108th, he supported a measure to increase the number of Border Patrol agents by 10,000 over five years. When Bush's budget in 2005 asked for far fewer agents, Ortiz scowled. "The border is in near chaos," he said, citing increased narco-trafficking violence and an influx of Central American illegals that has led to gang problems in U.S. cities.

Ortiz has long been concerned about the treatment of Hispanics in the United States. As chairman of the Congressional Hispanic Caucus in the 102nd Congress (1991-1992), he helped push through legislation increasing access to voting materials in languages other than English.

The child of a migrant family, Ortiz grew up poor near Corpus Christi, working a variety of odd jobs to help his family. When he was 16, his father died. He dropped out of high school and later joined the Army. "It was the one place that would give me free room and board and let me send my check back home to my mother," he recalls.

He left the Army in 1962 and two years later waged his first political campaign, defeating the incumbent Nueces County constable. In 1968, he became the first Hispanic elected to the county commission; then in 1976, he was the first Hispanic to win election as county sheriff, his springboard to the House in 1982. That year, the three-judge federal panel in charge of redistricting created the 27th with a 60 percent Hispanic majority. He won the seat with 64 percent of the vote. His district's boundaries have not changed much since, and in his recent re-elections he has consistently topped 60 percent.

KEY VOTES

2004

?	Extend federal unemployment benefits by 13 weeks
Yes	Pass $283.2 billion, six-year federal highway and mass transit bill
Yes	Approve $146 billion multi-year extension of previously enacted middle-class tax breaks
Yes	Amend the Constitution to prohibit same-sex marriage
?	Cut corporate taxes $137 billion over 10 years
Yes	Reorganize U.S. intelligence agencies as proposed by Sept. 11 commission

2003

No	Cut taxes by $330 billion through fiscal 2013
Yes	Block Bush rule scaling back overtime pay for some white-collar federal workers
Yes	Do not allow use of search warrants without first notifying subjects
Yes	Allow importation of prescription drugs
No	Create private school voucher program in Washington, D.C.
Yes	Ban "partial birth" abortion except to save a woman's life
Yes	Split $18.6 billion in Iraq aid into half-grant, half-loan
No	Overhaul Medicare and create prescription drug benefit

CQ VOTE STUDIES

	PARTY UNITY		PRESIDENTIAL SUPPORT	
	Support	Oppose	Support	Oppose
2004	83%	17%	47%	53%
2003	79%	21%	44%	56%
2002	82%	18%	42%	58%
2001	66%	34%	58%	42%
2000	76%	24%	71%	29%

INTEREST GROUPS

	AFL-CIO	ADA	CCUS	ACU
2004	93%	55%	47%	28%
2003	87%	80%	54%	56%
2002	78%	85%	42%	25%
2001	75%	70%	65%	60%
2000	90%	65%	45%	24%

TEXAS 27
Southern Gulf Coast – Corpus Christi, Brownsville

Anchored by Corpus Christi in the north, the 27th runs south to the Rio Grande River, with the Gulf of Mexico on its eastern coast. Ranches are the mainstay between the two largest cities, Corpus Christi and Brownsville, which together contain more than half of the 27th's population. But much of the district is coastal, and its two deep-water ports are major economic generators.

Corpus Christi's economy relies on the tourism industry and a growing military presence. Oil and gas remain among the biggest industries in the city, and petrochemical refining, also found up and down the coast, is becoming more common. Farther south, the port city of Brownsville struggles with an influx of illegal immigrants and high poverty, but new manufacturing plants and *maquiladoras* — plants that use low-cost labor and import many parts from the United States — have brightened the area and lowered unemployment rates. Visitors coming from Mexico boost Brownsville's retail industry, and "ecotourism" also adds to the economy by drawing bird and turtle watchers to the area's wetlands.

Willacy County is competing to be the location of a new spaceport that would launch satellites and planes into space.

The Hispanic-majority district (68 percent) supports Democrats, and the same Democrat has represented the 27th since its creation prior to the 1982 election. But the Democratic lean is not overwhelming, and George W. Bush took 55 percent of the district's 2004 presidential vote. Redistricting prior to the 2004 election added more than half of San Patricio County's population — a change that increased the number of white residents but left the district's overall political lean unchanged.

MAJOR INDUSTRY
Manufacturing, trade, tourism

MILITARY BASES
Corpus Christi Naval Air Station, 1,800 military, 2,700 civilian; Corpus Christi Army Depot, 12 military, 3,315 civilian (2004); Naval Station Ingleside, 2,390 military, 310 civilian (2005); Naval Air Station Kingsville, 754 military, 1,210 civilian (2004)

CITIES
Corpus Christi, 277,454; Brownsville, 139,722; Kingsville, 25,575

NOTABLE
South Padre Island is a popular college spring break location.

Rep. Henry Cuellar (D)

CAPITOL OFFICE
225-1640
www.house.gov/cuellar
1404 Longworth 20515-4328; fax 225-1641

COMMITTEES
Agriculture
Budget

HOMETOWN
Laredo

BORN
Sept. 19, 1955, Laredo, Texas

RELIGION
Roman Catholic

FAMILY
Wife, Imelda Cuellar; two children

EDUCATION
Laredo Community College, A.A. 1976 (political science); Georgetown U., B.S.F.S. 1978; U. of Texas, J.D. 1981; Laredo State U., M.B.A. 1982 (international trade); U. of Texas, Ph.D. 1998 (government)

CAREER
Lawyer; international trade firm owner

POLITICAL HIGHLIGHTS
Texas House, 1987-2001; Texas secretary of state, 2001; Democratic nominee for U.S. House, 2002

ELECTION RESULTS

2004 GENERAL

Henry Cuellar (D)	106,323	59.0%
James F. "Jim" Hopson (R)	69,538	38.6%
Ken Ashby (LIBERT)	4,305	2.4%

2004 PRIMARY

Henry Cuellar (D)	24,651	50.2%
Ciro D. Rodriguez (D)	24,448	49.8%

Elected 2004; 1st term

No member of the Class of 2004 came to the House under a bigger cloud of controversy, nor a greater likelihood of a serious 2006 primary challenge, than Cuellar. He won the seat in south Texas' strongly Democratic, Hispanic-majority 28th District by defeating Democratic incumbent Ciro D. Rodriguez in the March 2004 primary — but by a margin of just 203 votes that was certified after a series of recounts, lawsuits and accusations of voting fraud lodged by Rodriguez and his supporters.

Reluctantly conceding the election more than four months after the primary, Rodriguez said he would be back to challenge Cuellar in 2006.

While attempting to mend fences with Rodriguez backers in the 28th District, Cuellar (QUAY-are) also has to do some damage control within the Congressional Hispanic Caucus, which Rodriguez had been chairing at the time of his defeat. And he may have to assuage concerns among some Democrats about his loyalty: Cuellar endorsed Republican George W. Bush, then governor of Texas, for president in 2000 and the next year took a plum job as secretary of state under Bush's successor, Republican Gov. Rick Perry. Early in the 109th Congress, Cuellar joined the GOP in voting for tough new immigration standards and clamping down on class action lawsuits.

Describing himself as a "moderate conservative," Cuellar promises to reach across the aisle to cut deals. But he says he will not join the GOP.

Cuellar, who says his long-term goal is a seat on the Appropriations Committee, had hoped for a seat on Transportation and Infrastructure, to help repave and widen many roads in south Texas, and Armed Services, to look out for San Antonio's multiple military bases in and around the 28th District. He got neither. But he did get a relatively high-profile slot on the Budget Committee and was placed on Agriculture, which should help back home: The 28th is mostly rural between its San Antonio anchor in the north and Cuellar's Laredo base in the south.

Cuellar's victory in the 28th came after he ran an unexpectedly close challenge to 23rd District Republican Henry Bonilla in 2002.

TEXAS 28
South central – south San Antonio, part of Laredo

The 28th starts in Hays County near Austin and runs south along Interstate 35 through San Marcos and San Antonio all the way to Mexico at the border city of Laredo. The district's population center is in its northern half, in the low- and middle-class areas of San Antonio and the counties running north toward Austin. With the exception of Laredo, the southern part of the district is mostly sparsely populated agricultural land.

The 28th was one of the most carefully drawn districts in the GOP-led, mid-decade remap prior to the 2004 election. The new map moved nearly half of Laredo's residents from the 23rd to the 28th, bolstering GOP efforts to hold the 23rd. Democrats argued that dividing the heavily Hispanic and typically Democratic city disenfranchised minority voters, but the courts did not agree.

International trade is crucial here, as Laredo

serves as the nation's largest land port. Agriculture also is important, with peanuts, cotton, sorghum, carrots and beef dominating the market.

Toyota's decision to build an $800 million Tundra pickup plant in the 28th should aid the economy. The plant, scheduled to open in 2006, will employ 2,000 people. San Antonio's four military bases help the district's northern part, but Brooks Air Force base, the only one in the 28th, has been scaled back.

Democrats do well in the Hispanic-majority 28th, although a large Catholic influence gives the district a socially conservative bent. George W. Bush received 52 percent of the 2004 presidential vote here.

MAJOR INDUSTRY
Agriculture, international trade, defense

MILITARY BASES
Brooks City-Base (Air Force), 1,300 military, 1,300 civilian (2004)

CITIES
San Antonio (pt.), 227,053; Laredo (pt.), 84,474

NOTABLE
Laredo has flown seven flags in its history.

Rep. Gene Green (D)

Elected 1992; 7th term

CAPITOL OFFICE
225-1688
www.house.gov/green
2335 Rayburn 20515-4329; fax 225-9903

COMMITTEES
Energy & Commerce
Standards of Official Conduct

HOMETOWN
Houston

BORN
Oct. 17, 1947, Houston, Texas

RELIGION
Methodist

FAMILY
Wife, Helen Albers Green; two children

EDUCATION
U. of Houston, B.B.A. 1971; Bates College of Law,
attended 1971-77

CAREER
Lawyer

POLITICAL HIGHLIGHTS
Texas House, 1973-85; Texas Senate, 1985-92

ELECTION RESULTS

2004 GENERAL

Gene Green (D)	78,256	94.1%
Clifford Lee Messina (LIBERT)	4,868	5.9%

2004 PRIMARY

Gene Green (D)	unopposed

2002 GENERAL

Gene Green (D)	55,760	95.2%
Paul Hansen (LIBERT)	2,833	4.8%

PREVIOUS WINNING PERCENTAGES
2000 (73%); 1998 (93%); 1996 (68%); 1994 (73%);
1992 (65%)

Times have changed for this Houston native, who grew up in a part of the 29th District then known as "redneck alley." The majority of the district's population is now Hispanic, one good reason for Green's 2001 decision to organize a group of House Democrats to enroll in Spanish classes.

The new demographic reality means Green must focus his attention on constituent services and core Democratic issues such as support for public education, expanded health care, federal programs for minorities and pocketbook concerns of the working class. But although he regularly fights those battles, particularly for broader health coverage, one of his most notable recent accomplishments involved high-tech regulation.

Green says his constituents had urged him for years to do something about unsolicited e-mail, or spam, and he worked closely with members of both parties to craft legislation in the 108th Congress addressing the problem. His House partner in the effort was Republican Heather A. Wilson of New Mexico, who bucked the GOP chairmen of two powerful committees to help win enactment of the initiative. The Green-Wilson version of the bill found so much support among House members, including a majority on Energy and Commerce, that then-Chairman Billy Tauzin of Louisiana and Judiciary Chairman F. James Sensenbrenner Jr. of Wisconsin were forced to produce legislation stricter than they originally proposed.

Although the folksy Green strays from his party on the environment, gun control, juvenile crime and selected other issues important to his constituents, he enjoys good relations with Democratic leaders, in part because he doesn't trumpet his disagreements. Since August 2001, he has served on the ethics committee, a generally thankless post, but one that enables members to build up chits with the leadership.

Part of the reason party leaders value Green is that he is one of a rapidly dwindling breed on Capitol Hill — the non-Hispanic white Southern Democrat. Their numbers in the House have dropped from 64 in the 103rd Congress to just 28 as the 109th began. And six of those losses involved fellow Texas Democrats who retired or were defeated after a 2003 Texas redistricting coup engineered by Green's fellow Texan, Majority Leader Tom DeLay. Although the redistricting barely nicked Green's territory, it did put his residence in the neighboring 10th District. He rented an apartment inside the 29th and bought a home there after the election.

Green and DeLay don't agree on much, but at a May 2004 town hall meeting they hosted jointly to quell fears of police raids aimed at finding illegal immigrants, they discovered a common bond: They are the only House members who graduated from the University of Houston. "So we got to talking about UH football; we've been able to joke with each other," Green told the Pasadena Citizen.

Given the demographics of his district, Green has been careful to showcase his efforts to increase funding for bilingual education and education for disadvantaged children. He served on the Education and Workforce Committee his first two terms, and remains attentive to education issues. Each year, Green also seeks to assist minority groups by sponsoring events such as Immunization Day, which provides free vaccinations to children, and Citizenship Day, which helps residents obtain citizenship.

The congressman uses his seat on the Energy and Commerce Committee, which he joined in 1997, to push for expanded health coverage. In the 108th, he sought to broaden coverage under the GOP-backed Medicare prescription drug legislation. But he eventually voted against the bill, which passed the House by just one vote. Signing on to a measure in the 106th to provide Medicaid and other benefits to pregnant women and children who are legal immigrants, he said, "Investing in the preventive services Medicaid provides saves taxpayers money in the long run."

Unlike some conservative Democrats, Green has opposed most GOP tax-cutting efforts. He voted against a popular bill in the 106th to cut taxes on married couples, saying it "only benefits the wealthiest of Americans and does nothing to help the working folks in my district." In 2001 and 2003, he opposed President Bush's signature tax cuts for much the same reason, although he did support the 2004 corporate tax cut package.

Green has opposed most recent trade bills, reflecting the views of workers in his blue-collar district. In the 108th, he voted against free-trade agreements with Chile, Singapore and Morocco, and in the 107th Congress he voted against giving the president fast-track trade negotiating authority. He also voted against the North American Free Trade Agreement in 1993, despite support for it from Houston's business community.

Although he votes with his party more often than most white Southern Democrats, party leaders cannot take Green for granted. He voted for Republican-sponsored legislation to toughen criminal penalties for violent juvenile offenders and to overhaul public housing policies. On environmental matters, Green joins with Republicans in opposing new Environmental Protection Agency clean air standards that would affect Houston. He generally favors gun owners' rights, and he has sided with social conservatives in support of a measure to allow the display of the Ten Commandments in public schools and government buildings.

On abortion, Green's current view differs from his earlier position. In February 1992, a month before his first House primary, he dropped his opposition to abortion when he came under attack for having sponsored anti-abortion bills in the state legislature. Green said he had gradually changed his views on abortion, but critics said he changed his mind to enhance his prospects of winning the congressional seat. In 2002 and 2003, he voted against banning a procedure critics call "partial birth" abortion.

Green won a hard-fought five-way primary in 1992, besting Houston City Council member Ben Reyes in two runoffs — the first was voided after election officials found some Republicans had illegally crossed over and cast ballots. Green won the general election with 65 percent of the vote in the largely Democratic 29th District. He continued to strengthen his hold over the district and won easily in 2004, even after the GOP redistricting.

KEY VOTES

2004
Yes	Extend federal unemployment benefits by 13 weeks
Yes	Pass $283.2 billion, six-year federal highway and mass transit bill
?	Approve $146 billion multi-year extension of previously enacted middle-class tax breaks
No	Amend the Constitution to prohibit same-sex marriage
Yes	Cut corporate taxes $137 billion over 10 years
Yes	Reorganize U.S. intelligence agencies as proposed by Sept. 11 commission

2003
No	Cut taxes by $330 billion through fiscal 2013
Yes	Block Bush rule scaling back overtime pay for some white-collar federal workers
No	Do not allow use of search warrants without first notifying subjects
Yes	Allow importation of prescription drugs
No	Create private school voucher program in Washington, D.C.
No	Ban "partial birth" abortion except to save a woman's life
Yes	Split $18.6 billion in Iraq aid into half-grant, half-loan
No	Overhaul Medicare and create prescription drug benefit

CQ VOTE STUDIES

	PARTY UNITY		PRESIDENTIAL SUPPORT	
	Support	Oppose	Support	Oppose
2004	87%	13%	27%	73%
2003	85%	15%	28%	72%
2002	86%	14%	31%	69%
2001	80%	20%	33%	67%
2000	81%	19%	69%	31%

INTEREST GROUPS

	AFL-CIO	ADA	CCUS	ACU
2004	93%	85%	45%	20%
2003	93%	85%	43%	36%
2002	100%	90%	35%	16%
2001	100%	90%	43%	36%
2000	100%	90%	33%	20%

TEXAS 29

Part of Houston and eastern suburbs — most of Pasadena and Baytown

Located on the eastern side of Houston's downtown, the 29th is a blue-collar, working-class, Hispanic-majority district near refineries and factories that employ many union members.

The district arcs from northern to southeastern Houston, and slightly more than half of district residents live in the city. The 29th includes one-fifth of Harris County's population and most of the Houston Ship Channel, a major shipping route that has seen increased business since the NAFTA and GATT trade agreements. It also takes in most of middle-class Channelview, which is located east of Houston.

The 29th includes working-class areas outside of the Interstate 610 loop such as Jacinto City, Galena Park, South Houston and much of Pasadena. The district's eastern edge stretches to Baytown.

The Hispanic majority increased here in redistricting prior to the 2004

election; Hispanics now comprise two-thirds of the district's population. The heaviest concentrations of Hispanics are in South Houston, Jacinto City, Houston and Pasadena. According to 2000 census data, one-quarter of district residents are not U.S. citizens, the highest percentage in the state, and 60 percent of residents speak a language other than English at home.

The 29th has the largest blue-collar workforce and the smallest percentage of high school graduates (50 percent of the over-25 population) in Texas. One-third of district residents are age 17 or under, also the highest percentage in the state.

The district is solidly Democratic, even with the traditionally poor voter turnout in the Hispanic community.

MAJOR INDUSTRY
Chemicals, energy, construction, shipping

CITIES
Houston (pt.), 334,766; Pasadena (pt.), 84,654; Baytown (pt.) 35,003

NOTABLE
The district houses much of Houston's $15 billion petrochemical complex, the second-largest in the world behind Rotterdam in the Netherlands.

Rep. Eddie Bernice Johnson (D)

Elected 1992; 7th term

CAPITOL OFFICE
225-8885
rep.e.b.johnson@mail.house.gov
www.house.gov/ebjohnson
1511 Longworth 20515-4330; fax 226-1477

COMMITTEES
Science
Transportation & Infrastructure

HOMETOWN
Dallas

BORN
Dec. 3, 1935, Waco, Texas

RELIGION
Baptist

FAMILY
Divorced; one child

EDUCATION
Texas Christian U., B.S. 1967 (nursing); Southern Methodist U., M.P.A. 1976

CAREER
Business relocation company owner; nurse; U.S. Health, Education & Welfare Department official

POLITICAL HIGHLIGHTS
Texas House, 1973-77; Texas Senate, 1987-93

ELECTION RESULTS

2004 GENERAL

Eddie Bernice Johnson (D)	144,513	93.0%
John Davis (LIBERT)	10,821	7.0%

2004 PRIMARY

Eddie Bernice Johnson (D)	unopposed

2002 GENERAL

Eddie Bernice Johnson (D)	88,980	74.3%
Ron Bush (R)	28,981	24.2%
Lance Flores (LIBERT)	1,856	1.6%

PREVIOUS WINNING PERCENTAGES
2000 (92%); 1998 (72%); 1996 (55%); 1994 (73%); 1992 (72%)

In a manner both gracious and shrewd, Johnson has long been a trailblazer for women and blacks. She is the first African-American elected official to represent Dallas in Congress. Johnson has a strong commitment to liberal social causes, but she also will compromise across the aisle and reach out to business interests to advance her policy goals.

A former small-business owner, Johnson hopes part of her legacy in Congress will be to have steered the liberal Congressional Black Caucus to build effective coalitions with business groups rather than relying exclusively on its traditional allies in labor, the clergy and civil rights organizations. Johnson chaired the caucus in the 107th Congress.

It was her idea for the Black Caucus to hold its first technology and energy summits. Those summits speak directly to Johnson's longstanding vision that bridging the digital divide in poor communities and encouraging minority students to study the hard sciences are two important ways to help black Americans achieve true equality.

Johnson also has cast some pro-business votes in recent years. Breaking ranks with organized labor, she supported legislation in 2000 granting China permanent normal trade status. She said, "Trade with China means jobs for North Texas, growth for Dallas-Fort Worth and the export of American values to the world's most populous nation." Yet in the 108th, she went against the oil industry, which was a powerful presence in her district, by opposing the GOP's energy plan. She was one of just five Texas lawmakers to vote against the plan, which she said would undermine environmental protections.

Johnson uses her seat on the Science Committee to emphasize the importance of federal investment in scientific research. She has lobbied for a federal grant program to encourage children to study math and science. She was particularly critical of Bush's 2003 budget proposal for the National Science Foundation, which funds nearly 2,000 educational and research institutions nationwide. She said the administration's NSF budget trailed its congressional authorization by about $3 billion. "This marks a fundamental breach of trust with our institutions of higher education and with our children, who depend on NSF to fund the best and brightest to pursue the most promising scientific insights," she said.

A former nurse, Johnson has an unswerving commitment to the Clean Air Act, which she views as a health issue. She issued an unusually sharp statement assailing Texas Republican Joe L. Barton, after he added a provision to the 2003 energy bill that would have given certain urban areas, including Dallas-Fort Worth, two additional years to comply with air quality requirements. "We now know what it cost Congressman Barton to sell his soul to the devils of dirty air," she said in a biting 2003 news release. "For a little over $700,000 in campaign contributions from companies that will benefit from his dirty air rider, Congressman Barton will condemn the children of Dallas and Forth Worth to breathe dirty air until 2012."

Johnson has yet to make it to a top House committee, though she has made known her interest in serving on Ways and Means. She uses her assignments on Science and the Transportation and Infrastructure committees to fight for projects important to her district. At the beginning of the 109th, Johnson gained the top Democratic slot on Transportation's Water Resources and Environment Subcommittee.

Johnson has been instrumental in bringing federal dollars to the Dallas-Fort Worth International Airport. To promote jobs at an area Northrop

Grumman plant, she supported production of additional B-2 stealth bombers, a stand that put her at odds with fellow liberals in the Black Caucus. Despite that vote, she is leery of overseas military invention. She voted against the 2002 resolution authorizing the war in Iraq.

During the 108th, Johnson generated some controversy after a former aide accused her of discrimination. After failing to get the federal lawsuit dismissed on technical grounds, Johnson turned to an unusual legal strategy, invoking constitutional language that protected members of Congress from being questioned about "Speech or Debate in either House . . . in any other place." It appeared to be the first time that a House member had used such a defense since lawmakers in 1995 passed a bill that applied anti-discrimination laws to Congress.

Johnson grew up attending a segregated school in Waco. Her father insisted that she go to college, where she earned a nursing degree. She went on to get a master's in public administration from Southern Methodist University. Johnson rose to be chief psychiatric nurse at the Veterans Administration Hospital in Dallas.

She won her first state House election in 1972, serving as a legislator until she resigned in 1977 to work as regional director for the Department of Health, Education and Welfare in the Carter administration. She then turned to private business, setting up Eddie Bernice Johnson and Associates, which helped businesses expand or relocate in the Dallas-Fort Worth area. She still operated the business after her 1986 election to the state Senate, and she expanded it in 1988 to include airport concessions management. She was so adept at wielding power in the state legislature that she ran for the U.S. House in 1992 by drawing a district preordained to elect her.

Johnson generally has won re-election with ease. Initially, her electoral fate was caught up in the judicial and legislative wrangling over minority-majority House districts, including the 30th. After the U.S. Supreme Court threw out certain House districts in Texas as "racial gerrymanders" in 1996, Johnson landed in a substantially redrawn district that was 42 percent new to her. But she captured a 55 percent majority in an eight-person contest, and has won by wide margins since. She had no GOP opponent in 2004.

Johnson sharply criticized Texas Republicans for their redistricting plan during the 108th. Her own district became even more secure as it absorbed additional minorities from a neighboring district. But she lamented that the redistricting turned two minority-controlled districts into just one. "I've never needed that many minorities," Johnson told the Dallas Morning News. "It would definitely diminish minority impact."

KEY VOTES

2004

Yes Extend federal unemployment benefits by 13 weeks

Yes Pass $283.2 billion, six-year federal highway and mass transit bill

Yes Approve $146 billion multi-year extension of previously enacted middle-class tax breaks

No Amend the Constitution to prohibit same-sex marriage

Yes Cut corporate taxes $137 billion over 10 years

Yes Reorganize U.S. intelligence agencies as proposed by Sept. 11 commission

2003

No Cut taxes by $330 billion through fiscal 2013

Yes Block Bush rule scaling back overtime pay for some white-collar federal workers

Yes Do not allow use of search warrants without first notifying subjects

No Allow importation of prescription drugs

No Create private school voucher program in Washington, D.C.

No Ban "partial birth" abortion except to save a woman's life

Yes Split $18.6 billion in Iraq aid into half-grant, half-loan

No Overhaul Medicare and create prescription drug benefit

CQ VOTE STUDIES

	PARTY UNITY		PRESIDENTIAL SUPPORT	
	Support	Oppose	Support	Oppose
2004	93%	7%	34%	66%
2003	96%	4%	20%	80%
2002	95%	5%	22%	78%
2001	88%	12%	26%	74%
2000	95%	5%	88%	12%

INTEREST GROUPS

	AFL-CIO	ADA	CCUS	ACU
2004	87%	100%	63%	17%
2003	100%	95%	34%	20%
2002	89%	95%	45%	0%
2001	100%	95%	48%	4%
2000	88%	75%	57%	9%

TEXAS 30

Downtown Dallas and southern suburbs

Confined to Dallas County, the 30th stretches from Dallas Love Field southeast into downtown Dallas. It then dips south and farther east to take in some suburbs, such as Lancaster, where many African-American families have relocated after leaving the city.

When the district was drawn after the 1990 census, blacks made up 50 percent of the 30th's constituency. After three subsequent redrawings, blacks now account for just 41 percent of the population. That is still the highest percentage in any Texas district, and when combined with the 34 percent of residents who are Hispanic, minorities make up more than three-fourths of residents. There has been a rise in Asian and Indian populations because of corporate expansions. As the population grows, road congestion and air pollution have become concerns. Leaders hope the ongoing expansion of the Dallas light-rail system into the suburbs will alleviate some of the problems.

Redistricting prior to the 2004 election carved the more conservative, suburban Irving out of the 30th and placed it in the 32nd and 24th

districts. The 30th also lost its portion of Dallas-Fort Worth International Airport, but it still includes Love Field, a smaller airport closer to downtown that by law is limited to serving flights to and from Texas and nearby states. Despite these limits, the presence of low-cost Southwest Airlines, which is headquartered in the district, has made the airport a popular hub and an alternative to DFW.

Although redistricting added some suburban areas such as Balch Springs, southeast of downtown, it generally reinforced the district's overwhelming Democratic advantage. The 30th was John Kerry's best Texas district, as he took 75 percent of the 2004 presidential vote here. Democrats run strongly in the heavily black precincts just south of Illinois Avenue, and in largely Hispanic precincts near Love Field.

MAJOR INDUSTRY

Banking, technology, transportation

CITIES

Dallas (pt.), 533,878; DeSoto, 37,646; Lancaster, 25,894

NOTABLE

Dealey Plaza and the Texas School Book Depository, where John F. Kennedy was assassinated in 1963; The Texas State Fair attracts 3 million people and features Big Tex — a 52-foot-tall talking cowboy.

Rep. John Carter (R)

Elected 2002; 2nd term

CAPITOL OFFICE
225-3864
www.house.gov/carter
408 Cannon 20515-4331; fax 225-5886

COMMITTEES
Appropriations

HOMETOWN
Round Rock

BORN
Nov. 6, 1941, Houston, Texas

RELIGION
Lutheran

FAMILY
Wife, Erika Carter; four children

EDUCATION
Texas Technological College, B.A. 1964 (history);
U. of Texas, J.D. 1969

CAREER
Lawyer; state legislative aide

POLITICAL HIGHLIGHTS
Candidate for Texas House, 1980; Texas District
Court judge, 1981-2001

ELECTION RESULTS

2004 GENERAL

John Carter (R)	160,247	64.8%
Jon Porter (D)	80,292	32.5%
Celeste Adams (LIBERT)	6,888	2.8%

2004 PRIMARY

John Carter (R)	25,293	69.5%
Wes Riddle (R)	8,215	22.6%
Dick Armbrust (R)	2,868	7.9%

2002 GENERAL

John Carter (R)	111,556	69.1%
David Bagley (D)	44,183	27.4%
Clark Simmons (LIBERT)	2,037	1.3%
John S. Petersen (GREEN)	1,992	1.2%
R.C. Crawford (I)	1,716	1.1%

Carter got to Congress with the help of GOP leaders and with their help, he'll stay. In his second term, they gave Carter in 2005 a choice seat on the Appropriations Committee, a posting some lawmakers wait years to get and one that all but entitles him to a piece of the large federal spending pie for his district — no doubt a plus for future re-election campaigns.

Carter holds one of two new seats that Texas got as a result of population gains in the 1990s. An ally of Tom DeLay, Carter is from the same part of the state as the powerful House majority leader, the Houston metro area. Carter's district is heavily Republican and conservative-leaning, and includes Texas A & M University, the epicenter of the state's conservative, free-market-loving Republicanism and the school where former Sen. Phil Gramm once taught economics.

In addition to the Appropriations seat, Carter's ties to the leadership resulted in assignments to two groups of GOP insiders — the Republican Policy Committee, which develops legislative positions, and the Steering Committee, which assigns committee seats. As the Class of 2002 representative to that panel, Carter earned political chits with his colleagues by helping them obtain their preferred assignments.

On Appropriations, he is assigned to three subcommittees that hold the purse strings for homeland security, military housing and quality of life issues, veterans affairs and foreign operations. To get the slot on the spending panel, he gave up seats on the Education and Workforce Committee and the Government Reform Committee.

Carter spent his first term like many freshmen, learning the ways of the House and taking care of constituents. But Carter, who first arrived on Capitol Hill at age 61, is older than many newcomers and more politically seasoned. He was an elected state judge for two decades before running for the House in 2002.

He was one of the few newcomers to get a major bill passed in his first term. In 2004, President Bush signed into law legislation Carter sponsored that stiffens criminal penalties for identity theft, a problem of growing concern with the public. The new law created a felony crime of "aggravated identity theft" for bank, wire or mail fraud involving identity theft.

GOP Conference Chairwoman Deborah Pryce of Ohio named Carter early in the 109th Congress to handle the GOP message on the Republican's proposed overhaul of tort laws. Carter and other Republicans say they want to curb "lawsuit abuse," which they define as the proliferation of frivolous civil litigation.

Carter is a reliable vote for his party, supporting the party leaders' positions 99 percent of the time on votes that split the parties in the 108th Congress. But he bucked Bush on a handful of issues, taking a different position on immigration policy, and urging the White House to preserve a particular tax cut important to Texans.

Carter opposed the Bush plan to extend amnesty to some illegal aliens. "It's absolutely objectionable," he told the Dallas Morning News. "We tried amnesty under Reagan, and illegal immigration tripled over the next decade. . . . If we do it again, the wave is just going to be unbelievable."

He also wants to convince the White House to extend a new law that allows taxpayers to deduct state sales taxes from their federal returns. The change was signed into law in 2004, but for only two years. The White House has been ambivalent about whether it should continue.

Texas does not collect a state income tax, relying instead for revenue on a sales tax. People who live in states with a state income tax can deduct those payments from their federal income tax. But people in the seven states, including Texas, without an income tax have no comparable deduction unless they can deduct what they pay in sales taxes. Texas officials estimate that the sales tax deduction saves the average taxpayer about $400. Keeping the deduction is only fair, Carter says, because "not having an income tax is as sacred to Texans as the Alamo."

Still another issue that could put Carter at odds with White House plans is the Pentagon's effort to close military bases. Carter and other Texas lawmakers in early 2005 were working aggressively to protect the state's 17 bases.

Despite a promising start, Carter encountered some bumps in the House. He was one of eight lawmakers and 15 House aides who accepted trips to South Korea from a registered foreign agent, despite House ethics rules prohibiting the practice. The lawmakers said they were unaware that the Korea-United States Exchange Council had registered as an agent of the South Korean government.

The incident drew Carter into the controversy around DeLay, who also accepted the trip and was the subject of several unflattering news stories about his ethics and also was under investigation by Ronnie Earle, a Democratic district attorney looking into whether DeLay helped raise contributions for state legislature candidates that are illegal under Texas law.

Carter was interviewed for a segment on DeLay on the CBS television program "60 Minutes." He defended DeLay and said Earle was politically motivated. "A good district attorney can indict a ham sandwich if he wants to, and Mr. Earle understands that," Carter said. "The accusations harm, as much as the convictions."

While he was a trial court judge north of Austin, Carter helped found the Williamson County Juvenile Academy, which he calls a "quasi-military boot camp and alternative education program." He also established the Central Texas Treatment Center for substance abusers.

In his first House race in 2002, after redistricting, Carter competed in an eight-person field in the Republican primary, which was where the real contest was fought. He finished second behind Houston oil executive Peter Wareing, and then prevailed in the runoff election with 57 percent of the vote. In the general election that year, Carter easily defeated Democratic computer consultant David Bagley with 69 percent. In 2004, Carter won a second term easily, beating Democrat Jon Porter by a better than 2-to-1 ratio.

KEY VOTES

2004
No Extend federal unemployment benefits by 13 weeks
Yes Pass $283.2 billion, six-year federal highway and mass transit bill
Yes Approve $146 billion multi-year extension of previously enacted middle-class tax breaks
Yes Amend the Constitution to prohibit same-sex marriage
Yes Cut corporate taxes $137 billion over 10 years
Yes Reorganize U.S. intelligence agencies as proposed by Sept. 11 commission

2003
Yes Cut taxes by $330 billion through fiscal 2013
No Block Bush rule scaling back overtime pay for some white-collar federal workers
No Do not allow use of search warrants without first notifying subjects
No Allow importation of prescription drugs
Yes Create private school voucher program in Washington, D.C.
Yes Ban "partial birth" abortion except to save a woman's life
No Split $18.6 billion in Iraq aid into half-grant, half-loan
Yes Overhaul Medicare and create prescription drug benefit

CQ VOTE STUDIES

	PARTY UNITY		PRESIDENTIAL SUPPORT	
	Support	Oppose	Support	Oppose
2004	98%	2%	94%	6%
2003	99%	1%	94%	6%

INTEREST GROUPS

	AFL-CIO	ADA	CCUS	ACU
2004	7%	0%	100%	96%
2003	0%	5%	100%	88%

TEXAS 31
East central — north Austin suburbs, Killeen

The solidly Republican 31st is made up of suburbs and rural areas extending from the northern Austin suburbs through fertile agricultural land in central Texas to Erath County, about 60 miles southwest of Fort Worth.

In the south, the district takes in Williamson County, its largest population base and one of the fastest-growing areas of the state. A bedroom enclave north of Austin, the county is home to many who left the city for a more suburban lifestyle. Dell Computer is headquartered here in Round Rock, giving the district a chunk of the technology industry that has blossomed in the Austin area in recent years.

The district's other main population center is just north in Bell County. Killeen is the 31st's largest city, and Fort Hood, the massive military base split with Coryell County, is an economic mainstay that has yet to be substantially affected by defense cutbacks. Scott and White Memorial Hospital is an important health care entity located in the city of Temple in Bell County.

In the 31st's eastern end are Milam and Falls counties, where agriculture, including cotton, corn, cattle and pecans, is the main staple. The discovery of a large deposit of lignite in southern Milam County resulted in Aluminum Company of America (ALCOA) locating its largest U.S. smelter near Rockdale. Roughly 1,000 employees work at the plant.

Dairy farms dominate the northern part of the district, which strongly favors Republicans. Erath County, for example, gave George W. Bush 77 percent of the presidential vote in 2004.

MAJOR INDUSTRY
Technology, agriculture, military

MILITARY BASES
Fort Hood (Army), 49,000 military, 3,600 civilian (2005)

CITIES
Killeen, 86,911; Round Rock (pt.), 60,060; Temple, 54,514

NOTABLE
Former baseball pitcher Nolan Ryan owns the Round Rock Express, a minor-league team of the Houston Astros; Outside the Erath County Courthouse in Stephenville is Moo-La, a fiberglass Holstein cow, which stands on a platform and notes that the county is the "No.1 Dairy County in Texas."

Rep. Pete Sessions (R)

Elected 1996; 5th term

CAPITOL OFFICE
225-2231
petes@mail.house.gov
sessions.house.gov
1514 Longworth 20515-4332; fax 225-5878

COMMITTEES
Budget
Rules

HOMETOWN
Dallas

BORN
March 22, 1955, Waco, Texas

RELIGION
United Methodist

FAMILY
Wife, Nete Sessions; two children

EDUCATION
Southwest Texas State U., attended 1973-74;
Southwestern U., B.S. 1978 (political science)

CAREER
Public policy analyst; telephone company
executive

POLITICAL HIGHLIGHTS
Sought Republican nomination for U.S. House
(special election), 1991; Republican nominee for
U.S. House, 1994

ELECTION RESULTS

2004 GENERAL

Pete Sessions (R)	109,859	54.3%
Martin Frost (D)	89,030	44.0%
Michael D. Needleman (LIBERT)	3,347	1.7%

2004 PRIMARY

Pete Sessions (R)	unopposed

2002 GENERAL

Pete Sessions (R)	100,226	67.8%
Pauline K. Dixon (D)	44,886	30.4%
Steve Martin (LIBERT)	1,582	1.1%

PREVIOUS WINNING PERCENTAGES
2000 (54%); 1998 (56%); 1996 (53%)

The costliest House campaign of 2004 did the job Republican leaders wanted: It kept Sessions, a stalwart conservative, in the House and ended the 13-term career of Democrat Martin Frost, who ran in the 32nd District after his old district was dismantled by the mid-decade redistricting engineered by Majority Leader Tom DeLay.

The Sessions vs. Frost matchup provoked a weird and wild media campaign. Funds for both candidates' campaigns flowed in from partisans around the country. Expenditures reached the $9 million mark, according to the Federal Election Commission, with Frost's campaign spending $4.6 million and Sessions' campaign spending $4.4 million.

During the campaign, voters were inundated by ugly images of terrorist attacks and accusations back and forth of cavorting with child molesters or streakers. But the message also came through that Frost and Sessions were separated by the same philosophical and cultural fault line that distinguished the Democratic and Republican candidates for the White House.

Sessions' campaign ads extolled his conservative views: "I believe our federal government should do a few important things and do them well," such as "defend our borders and our security. It should help children and the truly needy." His ads slammed "the Martin Frost tax-and-spend vision for America." And he aligned himself closely with President Bush, who made Dallas his last campaign stop the night before the election. "It is really important that you send Pete Sessions back to the United States Congress," Bush proclaimed.

Sessions plays a prominent role in the House Results Caucus, a group whose motto is, "Give the government the money it needs, but not a penny more." The caucus aims to make the federal government more efficient. Sessions favors "outsourcing" some government functions to take advantage of possibly lower costs and private sector innovation.

His speech is pure Texas drawl. He sometimes greets visitors to his office wearing a cowboy hat, and his photographer asks to snap a photo for his growing collection. Sessions is just putting a face to the names of all the people he meets, to help him build relationships into the future.

Although he is a fierce partisan on most matters, there is one issue on which Sessions regularly reaches across the aisle. As the father of a son with Down syndrome, Sessions since 2000 has joined with liberal Democratic Rep. Henry A. Waxman of California in an effort to help families with incomes above the poverty line buy into Medicaid coverage for children with special needs. "I know firsthand why families with disabled children are turning down jobs, turning down overtime and are unable to earn enough money to adequately provide for their family — just so their child can qualify for Medicaid," Sessions said.

In the 108th Congress, the bill came close to passing, only to hit a snag when House GOP leaders decided the $900 million price tag was too hefty unless other social services were cut by an equivalent amount. Reducing ongoing programs for other disabled patients or foster care was an unacceptable choice to many cosponsors, so the bill died. Sessions introduced the measure again in the 109th Congress.

Sessions' wife, Nete Sessions, and their two sons live in Dallas. He pulls out a photo of his wife, who is Mexican, when asked how he can appeal to the 36 percent of his constituents who are Hispanic. "I am very aware of Hispanic needs and am in tune with their needs as parents on the issues of jobs, health care, and education," he said.

Sessions' loyalty to the GOP leadership won him an assignment to the Rules Committee in his second term and a post on the Homeland Security Committee in his fourth. He gave up that slot at the start of the 109th Congress for a seat on the Budget Committee.

He belongs to the Immigration Reform Caucus, a group of about six dozen lawmakers who want to get tough on illegal immigration and impose a temporary moratorium on legal immigration. He generally backs a free-trade approach, supporting fast-track authority for the president to negotiate trade agreements that Congress cannot amend. In 2000, he supported permanent normal trade status for China. But Sessions says that his support of expanded trade does not extend to situations in which the United States is at an unfair disadvantage. He has expressed concern that the 1993 North American Free Trade Agreement and the 1994 General Agreement on Tariffs and Trade created an "uneven playing field" for Americans. He has said, however, that "people who are anti-NAFTA are many times isolationists. I am not an isolationist."

Born in Waco, the son of William F. Sessions, a former federal judge and FBI director, Sessions was educated at Southwestern University in Georgetown, Texas. After college, he went to work at Southwestern Bell Telephone Co. and Bell Communications Research.

It took him three tries to get to Congress. In 1991, he was sixth in a special-election contest to succeed 3rd District GOP Rep. Steve Bartlett, who left to run for mayor of Dallas. In 1994, after leaving his job at Bell, Sessions lost with 47 percent of the vote to incumbent Democrat John Bryant. After his defeat, he became vice president for public policy at the National Center for Policy Analysis, a Dallas-based conservative think tank.

Federal court-ordered redistricting gave the 5th a slightly more Republican tilt by 1996. With Bryant running for the Senate, Sessions won the seat with 53 percent against John Pouland, a former Dallas County Democratic chairman.

After Texas districts were initially redrawn following the 2000 census, Sessions upset GOP colleagues by abandoning his 5th District seat to seek election in 2002 in the new, solidly Republican 32nd District. He said the more-compact 32nd would require less campaign travel, important to his family life. As it turned out, Jeb Hensarling held onto the 5th for the GOP, and Sessions cruised to victory in the 32nd. Then came the 2003 Republican-dictated redistricting engineered by DeLay and Sessions' epic battle with Frost. He won that 2004 face-off by 10 percentage points.

KEY VOTES

2004

No Extend federal unemployment benefits by 13 weeks

Yes Pass $283.2 billion, six-year federal highway and mass transit bill

Yes Approve $146 billion multi-year extension of previously enacted middle-class tax breaks

Yes Amend the Constitution to prohibit same-sex marriage

Yes Cut corporate taxes $137 billion over 10 years

Yes Reorganize U.S. intelligence agencies as proposed by Sept. 11 commission

2003

Yes Cut taxes by $330 billion through fiscal 2013

No Block Bush rule scaling back overtime pay for some white-collar federal workers

No Do not allow use of search warrants without first notifying subjects

No Allow importation of prescription drugs

Yes Create private school voucher program in Washington, D.C.

Yes Ban "partial birth" abortion except to save a woman's life

No Split $18.6 billion in Iraq aid into half-grant, half-loan

Yes Overhaul Medicare and create prescription drug benefit

CQ VOTE STUDIES

	PARTY UNITY		PRESIDENTIAL SUPPORT	
	Support	Oppose	Support	Oppose
2004	99%	1%	94%	6%
2003	99%	1%	98%	2%
2002	99%	1%	87%	13%
2001	99%	1%	91%	9%
2000	98%	2%	26%	74%

INTEREST GROUPS

	AFL-CIO	ADA	CCUS	ACU
2004	13%	0%	100%	100%
2003	0%	5%	100%	88%
2002	13%	0%	100%	100%
2001	9%	0%	96%	100%
2000	0%	0%	76%	96%

TEXAS 32
Northern Dallas; most of Irving and Richardson

The hook-shaped 32nd is located in northern and western Dallas County and essentially encircles downtown Dallas. It includes a chunk of the city and part of Dallas' north and west suburbs. Although it does not include downtown, the 32nd is home to much of the Dallas business community. Many who work downtown live here, and several Fortune 500 companies are located off the Lyndon B. Johnson Freeway, which encircles the city and runs as the northwestern border of the district.

Beginning just southwest of downtown, in the Hispanic area of Oak Cliff, the district moves west through heavily Hispanic Cockrell Hill and a Hispanic section of Grand Prairie into the southern part of Irving before turning north. Southern Irving has a vibrant Hispanic population, while central Irving is becoming increasing white with a blue-collar middle class, and northern Irving is taking in many upper-income, tech-heavy professionals. ExxonMobil is based in the 32nd's part of Irving.

The district then curves east to re-enter Dallas and take in the exclusive "Park Cities," made up of Highland Park and University Park. This area, almost entirely white, has its own school system and local government. The 32nd continues north to the county line, through less exclusive but equally wealthy neighborhoods. The city's "telecom corridor" also is in northern Dallas, with Texas Instruments, the standard-bearer, based just outside the district in the 3rd. Many TI employees reside in the 32nd, and the company is building a new plant in Richardson. Many residents work at Dallas-Forth Worth airport or Dallas Love Field airport, both of which border the 32nd. There are some middle-class areas north of the L.B.J. Freeway, including Addison and Richardson.

The 32nd is solidly Republican. George W. Bush took 59 percent of the presidential vote here in 2004. The GOP is particularly strong in precincts around University Park and Southern Methodist University, while Democrats do well in the far southern reaches of the district near downtown Dallas.

MAJOR INDUSTRY
Telecommunications, oil, retail, real estate

CITIES
Dallas (pt.), 393,211; Irving (pt.), 131,860; Richardson (pt.), 70,890

NOTABLE
Texas Stadium, the Dallas Cowboys' home, is in the 32nd's part of Irving.

Gov. Jon Huntsman Jr. (R)

First elected: 2004
Length of term: 4 years
Term expires: 1/09
Salary: $101,600
Phone: (801) 538-1000

Hometown: Salt Lake City
Born: March 26, 1960; Palo Alto, Calif.
Religion: Mormon
Family: Wife, Mary Kaye Huntsman; six children
Education: U. of Utah, attended 1981-84; U. of Pennsylvania, B.A. 1987 (international politics)
Career: Chemical company CEO; U.S. Commerce Department official
Political highlights: U.S. ambassador to Singapore, 1992-93; deputy U.S. trade representative, 2001-03

Election results:
2004 GENERAL
Jon Huntsman Jr. (R)	531,190	57.7%
Scott M. Matheson Jr. (D)	380,359	41.3%

Lt. Gov. Gary R. Herbert (R)

First elected: 2004
Length of term: 4 years
Term expires: 1/09
Salary: $79,000
Phone: (801) 538-1000

STATE LEGISLATURE

Legislature: 45 days yearly January-March

House: 75 members, 2-year terms
2005 breakdown: 56R, 19D; 59 men, 16 women
Salary: $120/day in session
Phone: (801) 538-1029

Senate: 29 members, 4-year terms
2005 breakdown: 21R, 8R; 25 men, 4 women
Salary: $120/day in session
Phone: (801) 538-1035

STATE TERM LIMITS

Governor: 3 consecutive terms
House: No
Senate: No

URBAN STATISTICS

CITY	POPULATION
Salt Lake City	181,743
West Valley City	108,896
Provo	105,166
Sandy	88,418
Orem	84,324

REGISTERED VOTERS

Registration by party began in May 1999, however, not all voters have declared an affiliation and the numbers are kept on a county basis.

POPULATION

2004 population (est.)	2,389,039
2000 population	2,233,169
1990 population	1,722,850
Percent change (1990-2000)	+29.6%
Rank among states (2004)	34

Median age	27.1
Born in state	62.9%
Foreign born	7.1%
Violent crime rate	256/100,000
Poverty level	9.4%
Federal workers	32,961
Military	16,621

REDISTRICTING

Utah retained its three House seats in reapportionment. The state legislature drew a new map, which the governor signed on Oct. 11, 2001.

MISCELLANEOUS

Web: www.utah.gov
Capital: Salt Lake City
STATE ELECTION OFFICIAL
(801) 538-1041
DEMOCRATIC HEADQUARTERS
(801) 328-1212
REPUBLICAN HEADQUARTERS
(801) 533-9777

District Statistics

DIST.	2004 VOTE FOR PRESIDENT BUSH	KERRY	WHITE	BLACK	ASIAN	HISP	MEDIAN INCOME	WHITE COLLAR	BLUE COLLAR	SERVICE INDUSTRY	OVER 64	UNDER 18	COLLEGE EDUCATION	RURAL	SQ. MILES
1	73%	25%	83%	1%	2%	11%	$45,058	59%	27%	14%	9%	32%	25%	11%	20,768
2	66	31	88	1	2	6	$45,583	66	21	14	11	30	31	15	45,624
3	77	20	85	0	2	10	$46,568	60	27	14	6	35	22	9	15,751
STATE	72	26	85	1	2	9	$45,726	61	25	14	9	32	26	12	82,144
U.S.	50.7	48.3	69	12	4	13	$41,994	60	25	15	12	26	24	21	3,537,438

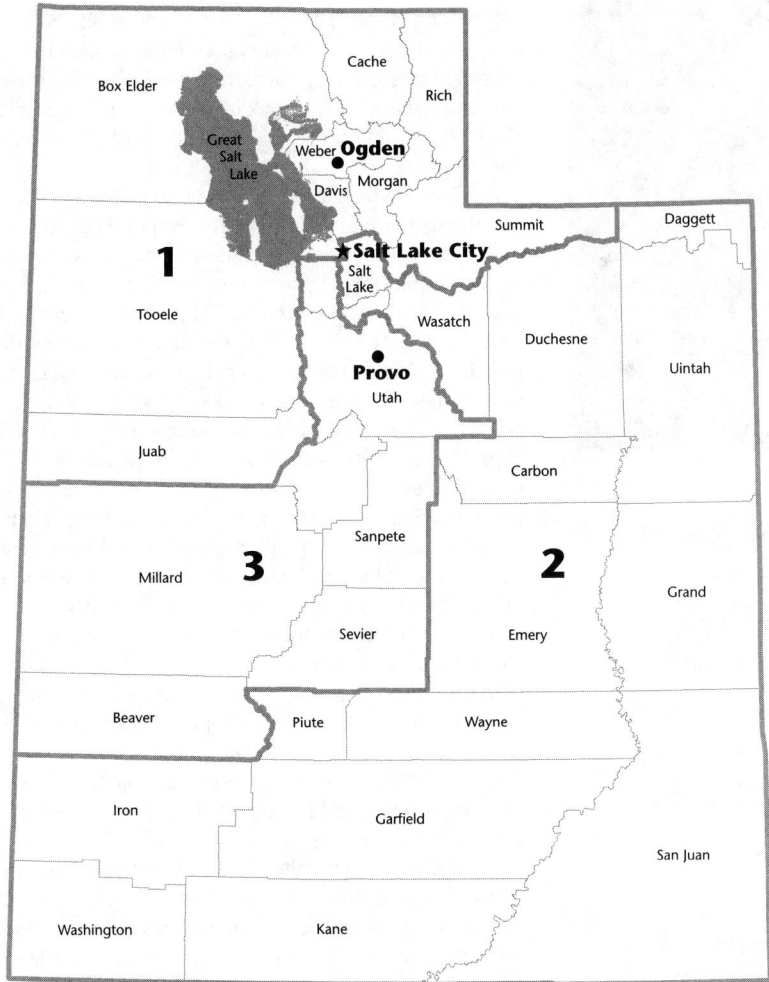

Sen. Orrin G. Hatch (R)

Elected 1976; 5th term

CAPITOL OFFICE
224-5251
hatch.senate.gov
104 Hart 20510-4402; fax 224-6331

COMMITTEES
Finance
   (Health Care - chairman)
Health, Education, Labor & Pensions
Judiciary
   (Intellectual Property - chairman)
Select Intelligence
Joint Taxation

HOMETOWN
Salt Lake City

BORN
March 22, 1934, Pittsburgh, Pa.

RELIGION
Mormon

FAMILY
Wife, Elaine Hatch; six children

EDUCATION
Brigham Young U., B.S. 1959 (history); U. of
Pittsburgh, J.D. 1962

CAREER
Lawyer

POLITICAL HIGHLIGHTS
Sought Republican nomination for president, 2000

ELECTION RESULTS

2000 GENERAL

Orrin G. Hatch (R)	504,803	65.6%
Scott N. Howell (D)	242,569	31.5%
Carlton Edward Bowen (AMI)	11,938	1.6%
Jim Dexter (LIBERT)	10,394	1.4%

2000 PRIMARY

Orrin G. Hatch (R)	unopposed

PREVIOUS WINNING PERCENTAGES
1994 (69%); 1988 (67%); 1982 (58%); 1976 (54%)

Hatch has been called plenty of names in his 28 years in Washington. During debates over conservative judicial nominees, Democrats have labeled him a right-wing partisan. Republicans have occasionally criticized him as a turncoat. And New York Times critic Frank Rich, writing in 2003 about Hatch's appearance on the HBO show "K Street," described him as "an inveterate ham."

Hatch has led a lengthy life of political non-conformity, one that inspired him to title his autobiography "The Square Peg." He is now the Senate's fourth-longest-serving Republican, albeit one without a full committee chairmanship. Term limits forced him to relinquish the helm of the Judiciary Committee, where he had been the top-ranking Republican since 1995. He was the only one of the four Republicans losing their gavels because of term limits who did not have another chairmanship waiting for him. If Hatch is re-elected in 2006, he would likely succeed Charles E. Grassley of Iowa as chairman of the powerful Finance Committee.

As Judiciary chairman, Hatch was in the middle of some of Congress' hottest issues, including tort reform, the expansion of law enforcement's powers to fight terrorism and the human cloning debate. He also pushed for confirmation of some of President Bush's most controversial judicial picks, just as in the past he supported conservatives Clarence Thomas and Robert Bork for Supreme Court appointments in the face of a torrent of criticism from the left. Hatch himself sometimes is mentioned as a possible candidate for a future opening on the nation's highest court.

In the 109th Congress, Hatch took charge of a newly created Judiciary Subcommittee on Intellectual Property. In January 2005, he introduced a bipartisan package of legislation similar to a set of bills that stalled at the end of the 108th. The provisions sought to outlaw the use of camcorders in movie theaters and punish the distribution of pirated movies or songs before they are released.

Hatch devoted much attention to intellectual property issues as full committee chairman. In 2004, he tried to write legislation to make it illegal for companies to intentionally induce customers to infringe copyrights through digital file sharing. Opponents, including software makers and Internet service providers, have said they could be harmed by such a law. "Like the mythical free lunch, there's no such thing as a free CD or movie," Hatch said. "Allowing your children to illegally download a CD is actually worse than shoplifting a record from a record store."

Much of his interest in the issue stems from his own hobby as a songwriter whose work has been performed by the Osmonds and Gladys Knight, the pop singer who belongs to the Mormon church, as does Hatch. He has produced several discs of religious, romantic and patriotic songs. He dedicated a love song to Sen. Edward M. Kennedy and his second wife, Victoria, on their fifth wedding anniversary and is often spotted scribbling song lyrics between Senate votes. Singer Bono of the rock group U2 called his work "actually beautiful" and jokingly suggested the straight-laced senator could boost his chances of getting airplay by changing his name to something catchier, like "Johnny Trapdoor."

Hatch is confounding to many conservatives, who do not understand his relationship with Kennedy. The two senators, who often take opposing positions on the Judiciary Committee, regularly exchange heated words on the floor. During a debate in 2003, Kennedy told his friend, "You may bully some, but you're not going to bully me." But the senators also team up on bills, such as one that provided health care to poor children. Kennedy once crossed the Senate aisle to give Hatch a hug.

The party's right wing also finds fault with Hatch's tendency to join with Democrats on issues of intense personal importance to him. After the Sept. 11, 2001, terrorist attacks, the Judiciary Committee came under heavy pressure from the administration to rapidly approve a major expansion of law enforcement's investigative powers, raising concerns about possible encroachments on civil liberties. While the White House negotiated with Chairman Patrick J. Leahy, a liberal Democrat from Vermont, Hatch quietly courted support from other Democrats, including Dianne Feinstein of California and Charles E. Schumer of New York.

Hatch is more willing than many GOP conservatives to support government programs for the poor, an outlook rooted in his childhood and in his religious faith, which encourages helping the disadvantaged.

He was born in Pittsburgh, the son of a metal lather. The family lost their home during the Depression, so Hatch's father built another one of lumber salvaged from a fire. Hatch remembers that a dairy sign constituted one wall of the house. He worked his way through school, variously toiling as a janitor, an all-night desk clerk in a girls' dormitory and a metal lather like his father. As a lather, he joined the AFL-CIO union.

Hatch has supported federal programs to immunize children, offer job training and give workers time off for family and medical reasons. A 1997 partnership with Kennedy produced a bill to provide insurance to children whose low-income parents do not qualify for Medicaid. It was financed with a 43-cents-a-pack cigarette tax increase.

Conservatives question whether Hatch is too quick to strike deals on their cherished issues. In response, the generally gracious Hatch told the National Review in 1997 that he does not harbor ill will toward people on the opposing side of issues. He said, "One of my biggest failings is that . . . I can't hold a grudge. I can't stay mad."

Hatch's political philosophy is influenced by his membership in the Church of Jesus Christ of Latter-day Saints, the Mormon religion that dominates in Utah and prohibits the consumption of alcohol, tobacco and caffeine. It also encourages large families. Hatch is the father of six.

He is a staunch opponent of abortion, though in 2002 he supported a bill allowing human cloning for medical research. Most anti-abortion groups oppose cloning even for research, and Hatch was assailed by leading groups, such as the Family Research Council.

In 1999, Hatch launched a quixotic bid for president. Lacking money and broad political support, he finished last in Iowa's GOP caucuses. He dropped out of the race the next week and endorsed Bush, later mending bridges with the new administration by guiding Bush nominee and fellow Sen. John Ashcroft, of Missouri, through a difficult confirmation as attorney general.

Hatch's first Senate campaign, in 1976, was a textbook example of anti-Washington politics. His total lack of government experience was an asset. In his legal practice, he had represented clients fighting federal regulations, and he made Washington's burdensome rulemaking a campaign theme. He won the GOP nomination over Jack W. Carlson, a former assistant secretary of interior, and then defeated incumbent Democrat Frank E. Moss with 54 percent of the vote.

He was re-elected in 1982 with 58 percent in spite of a serious challenge from two-term Salt Lake City Mayor Ted Wilson. In 1988, he defeated Brian Moss, the son of the senator he had ousted, by a 2-to-1 ratio, and his last two re-elections have been by similarly impressive margins.

KEY VOTES

2004

Yes	Pass $318.9 billion, six-year highway and mass transit bill
No	Extend assault weapons ban for 10 years
No	Restore pay-as-you-go rules for new tax cuts and entitlement spending
Yes	Criminalize harm to a fetus in an attack on the mother
Yes	Increase mandatory child care funding to states by $6 billion over five years
Yes	Amend the Constitution to prohibit same-sex marriage
Yes	Approve $146 billion multi-year extension of previously enacted middle-class tax breaks
Yes	Reorganize U.S. intelligence agencies as proposed by Sept. 11 commission
Yes	Cut corporate taxes $137 billion over 10 years

2003

No	Delay Bush changes to Clean Air Act
Yes	Allow confirmation vote on Miguel A. Estrada to the U.S. Court of Appeals for the D.C. Circuit
No	Block a Bush proposal opening Alaska's Arctic National Wildlife Refuge to oil drilling
No	Limit size of Bush's proposed tax cut to $350 billion through fiscal 2013
Yes	Overhaul Medicare and create prescription drug benefit
No	Block Bush rule scaling back overtime pay for some white-collar federal workers
No	Split $20 billion in Iraq aid into half-grant, half-loan
Yes	Ban "partial birth" abortion except to save a woman's life
Yes	Stop proposal allowing travel to Cuba
Yes	Allow final vote on energy policy overhaul

CQ VOTE STUDIES

	PARTY UNITY		PRESIDENTIAL SUPPORT	
	Support	Oppose	Support	Oppose
2004	98%	2%	94%	6%
2003	98%	2%	99%	1%
2002	93%	7%	98%	2%
2001	95%	5%	97%	3%
2000	94%	6%	55%	45%
1999	92%	8%	30%	70%
1998	87%	13%	48%	52%
1997	87%	13%	63%	37%
1996	94%	6%	32%	68%
1995	95%	5%	27%	73%

INTEREST GROUPS

	AFL-CIO	ADA	CCUS	ACU
2004	8%	10%	100%	96%
2003	0%	10%	100%	80%
2002	23%	5%	100%	95%
2001	6%	5%	86%	96%
2000	0%	0%	100%	95%
1999	11%	0%	88%	84%
1998	0%	5%	94%	80%
1997	0%	15%	100%	68%
1996	0%	5%	92%	100%
1995	0%	0%	100%	83%

Sen. Robert F. Bennett (R)

Elected 1992; 3rd term

As chief deputy whip for the Republicans in the Senate, Bennett has a mostly behind-the-scenes role in the leadership, one usually given to a trusted party loyalist. It's a good fit. Steady and thoughtful, with more substance than flash, he measures his words carefully, doesn't get publicly ruffled and generally leaves the television podium to others. His description of how he works with Majority Whip Mitch McConnell of Kentucky is as understated as he is. "He will assign me this one, or that situation. And I'll go talk to somebody," Bennett says.

For the 109th Congress, McConnell appointed Bennett to a second stint as his top assistant. McConnell is the second-ranking Republican in the Senate GOP leadership, after Majority Leader Bill Frist.

Though Bennett owes much to his old mentor, Bob Dole, who left the Senate to run unsuccessfully for president in 1996, Bennett won the trust of two subsequent leaders. Trent Lott of Mississippi, the former minority and majority leader, named Bennett the founding chairman of the Senate GOP's High Tech Task Force in 1999. When Frist took over from Lott in the 108th Congress, Bennett won the Agriculture Appropriations Subcommittee chairmanship, beating out Larry Craig of Idaho.

In the 109th, Bennett serves as vice chairman of the Joint Economic Committee, a position he uses to promote his own proposals, such as tax breaks to help individuals buy health care insurance. "We need to highlight issues," he said in late 2004. "There's a great ignorance about economics in the country and in Congress as well." He also plans to use the post to highlight proposals overhauling Social Security. He said he is inclined to back President Bush's proposal, which includes moving some Social Security funds to personal savings accounts, "but just in case it won't go through I am working on an alternative."

Also the No. 2 Republican on the Banking, Housing and Urban Affairs Committee, Bennett is a plain-spoken consensus builder. He learned how to achieve bipartisan compromise from his father, Wallace F. Bennett, who preceded him as a senator from Utah. The senior Bennett served from 1951 to 1974, and people who knew both say the son is taller, but is otherwise the image of his dad in looks and mannerisms.

Bennett disagrees at times with Banking Chairman Richard C. Shelby of Alabama, but often works with him. In the 108th, he worked out a deal with Shelby on a bill to block regulators from putting mortgage financiers Fannie Mae and Freddie Mac into receivership. The Bush White House fought it and it ultimately died. Bennett took the lead on another issue: his plan to extend a federal guarantee for companies that provide insurance against terrorist acts. And he opposed Shelby's efforts to repeal restrictions on securities litigation enacted in 1995. "We agree on lots of things. But he has more of a trial lawyer's perspective than I do," Bennett said. Bennett and Shelby cut a deal on a 2003 law that allowed consumers to keep credit rating companies from getting information about problems caused by identity theft.

On the Agriculture Appropriations Subcommittee, Bennett keeps an eye on pet programs. In the 108th, he increased funding for a child nutrition program to cover higher milk prices, which is important to Utah, a big producer of fresh and canned milk. Bennett also looks out for Hill Air Force Base and the Dugway Proving Ground in Utah.

His expertise in computer and privacy issues has helped make Bennett

CAPITOL OFFICE
224-5444
bennett.senate.gov
431 Dirksen 20510-4403; fax 228-1168

COMMITTEES
Appropriations
  (Agriculture & Rural Development - chairman)
Banking, Housing & Urban Affairs
  (Financial Institutions - chairman)
Homeland Security & Governmental Affairs
Rules & Administration
Joint Economic - vice chairman

HOMETOWN
Salt Lake City

BORN
Sept. 18, 1933, Salt Lake City, Utah

RELIGION
Mormon

FAMILY
Wife, Joyce Bennett; six children

EDUCATION
U. of Utah, B.S. 1957 (political science)

MILITARY SERVICE
Utah National Guard, 1957-60

CAREER
Time management company CEO; management consultant; public relations and marketing executive; U.S. Transportation Department official; congressional aide

POLITICAL HIGHLIGHTS
No previous office

ELECTION RESULTS

2004 GENERAL

Robert F. Bennett (R)	626,640	68.7%
R. Paul Van Dam (D)	258,955	28.4%
Gary R. Van Horn (C)	17,289	1.9%

2004 PRIMARY

Robert F. Bennett (R)	unopposed

PREVIOUS WINNING PERCENTAGES
1998 (64%); 1992 (55%)

a leader on homeland security. In 2002, he worked with Democrats on computer security issues. They wanted to allow companies with computer security problems to keep those reports confidential if they affected homeland security, but otherwise make them accessible to the public through the Freedom of Information Act. GOP leaders insisted that businesses be allowed to keep secret all reports made to the government about computer security problems.

That's just the kind of issue that appeals to the fastidious, Felix-not-Oscar side of Bennett. Before he came to Congress, he was a time management company executive. He has a strong interest in technology and a penchant for gadgets. In 2000, he was the first senator to drive a high-mileage, low-emissions gasoline-electric hybrid car. (He's now on his second model, a Ford Escape SUV.) And he can actually conjure enthusiasm for administrative issues. As a member of the Governmental Affairs Committee in 1993, he proposed legislation to reorganize congressional committees, adopt a two-year budget cycle and establish congressional task forces to set priorities for floor action.

Bennett's rangy physique is hard to miss around the Capitol. The 6-foot-6-inch Utahan often bypasses the elevators to get his exercise on the stairs. And his homespun sense of humor can be endearing. In 2004, his campaign billboards carried the slogan: "Big Heart. Big Ideas. Big Ears."

Usually amiable, Bennett has had some pointed exchanges with Arizona Republican John McCain. When McCain in 1999 alleged that campaign contributions corrupted the political system, Bennett took it personally and chastised McCain on the floor in a rare moment of ire.

Although a solid conservative on regulatory and fiscal issues, Bennett breaks party ranks on occasion. He backs efforts to curb tobacco sales to youths and opposes a constitutional amendment to ban desecration of the U.S. flag. He also supports funding for the National Endowment for the Arts, citing his passion for preserving American culture.

Bennett has joined other Western Republicans who oppose environmental restraints on public lands. He was outraged when President Clinton used his executive authority to create national monuments in Utah and other states in the West after 1999, blocking mining and ranching on the lands.

Originally a businessman, Bennett made a fortune with the Franklin Day Planner, a popular schedule organizer. His successful 1992 bid for the Senate at age 59 was his first campaign, but he was no stranger to Washington even then. He had worked for his father as an aide, and in the 1970s was an adviser to President Nixon. Bennett also owned a public relations firm that employed E. Howard Hunt, who was indicted in the Watergate burglary that ultimately led to Nixon's resignation.

Leonard Garment, the former White House counsel under Nixon, named Bennett in a 2000 book as one of the people who could have been "Deep Throat," the anonymous source for the Washington Post in its coverage of the scandal. But Garment concluded that Bennett was not the most likely suspect, and Bennett has denied he was Deep Throat.

In his first Senate bid, Bennett faced primary competition but edged past steel company executive Joe Cannon, the brother of Rep. Christopher B. Cannon, who now represents the 3rd District. He went on to beat Democratic Rep. Wayne Owens in the general election. Bennett raised $4.5 million and outspent Owens more than 2-to-1 en route to a 15 percentage point victory.

In 1996, Bennett paid a $55,000 fine to the Federal Election Commission for what he called "unintentional violations" during the 1992 campaign. That seemed to have little effect on his re-election campaign 1998, when he handily defeated Democratic surgeon Scott Leckman. In 2004, he easily beat former Utah Attorney General R. Paul Van Dam with 69 percent of the vote.

KEY VOTES

2004

Yes   Pass $318.9 billion, six-year highway and mass transit bill

No   Extend assault weapons ban for 10 years

No   Restore pay-as-you-go rules for new tax cuts and entitlement spending

Yes   Criminalize harm to a fetus in an attack on the mother

Yes   Increase mandatory child care funding to states by $6 billion over five years

Yes   Amend the Constitution to prohibit same-sex marriage

Yes   Approve $146 billion multi-year extension of previously enacted middle-class tax breaks

Yes   Reorganize U.S. intelligence agencies as proposed by Sept. 11 commission

Yes   Cut corporate taxes $137 billion over 10 years

2003

No   Delay Bush changes to Clean Air Act

Yes   Allow confirmation vote on Miguel A. Estrada to the U.S. Court of Appeals for the D.C. Circuit

No   Block a Bush proposal opening Alaska's Arctic National Wildlife Refuge to oil drilling

No   Limit size of Bush's proposed tax cut to $350 billion through fiscal 2013

Yes   Overhaul Medicare and create prescription drug benefit

No   Block Bush rule scaling back overtime pay for some white-collar federal workers

No   Split $20 billion in Iraq aid into half-grant, half-loan

Yes   Ban "partial birth" abortion except to save a woman's life

No   Stop proposal allowing travel to Cuba

Yes   Allow final vote on energy policy overhaul

CQ VOTE STUDIES

| | PARTY UNITY | | PRESIDENTIAL SUPPORT | |
	Support	Oppose	Support	Oppose
2004	97%	3%	94%	6%
2003	97%	3%	97%	3%
2002	94%	6%	98%	2%
2001	96%	4%	96%	4%
2000	92%	8%	52%	48%
1999	93%	7%	31%	69%
1998	84%	16%	53%	47%
1997	87%	13%	62%	38%
1996	92%	8%	36%	64%
1995	96%	4%	27%	73%

INTEREST GROUPS

	AFL-CIO	ADA	CCUS	ACU
2004	8%	20%	100%	88%
2003	0%	10%	100%	80%
2002	23%	5%	100%	100%
2001	13%	5%	100%	100%
2000	0%	5%	100%	95%
1999	11%	0%	94%	84%
1998	0%	10%	89%	64%
1997	0%	10%	100%	68%
1996	0%	5%	92%	95%
1995	0%	0%	100%	81%

Rep. Rob Bishop (R)

CAPITOL OFFICE
225-0453
www.house.gov/robbishop
124 Cannon 20515-4401; fax 225-5857

COMMITTEES
Rules

HOMETOWN
Kaysville

BORN
July 13, 1951, Salt Lake City, Utah

RELIGION
Mormon

FAMILY
Wife, Jeralynn Bishop; five children

EDUCATION
U. of Utah, B.A. 1974 (political science)

CAREER
Teacher; lobbyist

POLITICAL HIGHLIGHTS
Utah House, 1979-95 (Speaker, 1993-95); Utah
Republican Party chairman, 1997-2001

ELECTION RESULTS

2004 GENERAL

Rob Bishop (R)	199,615	67.9%
Steve Thompson (D)	85,630	29.1%
Charles Johnston (C)	4,510	1.5%
Richard W. Soderberg (PC)	4,206	1.4%

2004 PRIMARY

Rob Bishop (R)	unopposed

2002 GENERAL

Rob Bishop (R)	109,265	60.9%
Dave Thomas (D)	66,104	36.9%
Craig Axford (GREEN)	4,027	2.3%

Elected 2002; 2nd term

A former high school history instructor, Bishop still loves to teach. He has returned to his old classroom to lecture during Christmas recess, tutored teenagers visiting Washington under a nonprofit program exposing them to government and taken over some Capitol tours to provide humorous and irreverent commentaries on Congress.

"Since people don't know the history, you can make it up," he joked to the Salt Lake Tribune in December 2003. "I don't know what I am as a congressman yet, but I am a darn good tour guide."

Bishop describes himself as a "classic conservative," who fits the mold of other Western Republicans as a "fierce" proponent of states' rights and an "ardent" defender of gun owners' rights. One of his priorities is to press the federal government to reimburse his state for taxes lost on federally owned land.

He is a strong supporter of the Bush administration's war against Iraq, and he publicly defended Defense Secretary Donald H. Rumsfeld after he came under fire in 2004 from some GOP lawmakers for the Pentagon's failure to provide appropriate protective equipment for the troops. "I'm still comfortable with his leadership," Bishop told the Tribune in early 2005. "No one ever has ultimate authority to snap their fingers and make something happen, outside of a 'Bewitched' episode."

In the 108th Congress, Bishop voted with a majority of his party 97 percent of the time, and he is a loyal foot soldier for the GOP leadership. During House debate in 2004 on provisions in the Patriot Act, Bishop originally voted in favor of an amendment by Vermont independent Bernard Sanders to prevent the Justice Department from reviewing records of library and bookstore patrons thought to be terrorist suspects. But as the vote dragged on, he joined a handful of other Republicans in switching their votes, sparing the Bush administration an embarrassing defeat.

He explained his vote switch by saying he considered the vote "more symbolic than real" because the amendment would never survive in the Senate. "What I'm really looking for are some fixes to some real excesses in the Patriot Act," he told the Tribune.

In the 109th, Bishop has a seat on the Rules Committee, a choice assignment, particularly for a second-termer. During his service as a state legislator, Bishop had served on the Utah House Rules Committee.

His appointment to Rules required Bishop to relinquish his seats on the Science, Armed Services and Resources committees. From his Resources seat, Bishop sponsored a bill in 2004 establishing a wilderness area to protect the Air Force's Utah Test and Training Range and block disposal of high-level nuclear waste on the Goshute Indian Reservation. Though the measure was defeated, Bishop was able to bring some environmentalists on board — a feat that had eluded his House predecessor, Republican James V. Hansen, who had chaired Resources.

Bishop is keen to add a congressional seat to his state's delegation. Utah barely missed gaining a fourth seat during reapportionment that followed the 2000 census. Virginia Republican Thomas M. Davis III and Bishop devised a solution: temporarily increase the size of the House to 437 members, giving one seat to Republican Utah and the other to Democratic Washington, D.C., which has limited representation in Congress.

The measure failed to move in the 108th Congress, so Davis and Bishop reintroduced it in the 109th. They would leave the drawing of the new

www.cqpress.com

Utah district to the state legislature, but Bishop admitted that his district would probably not be affected. The Republican-dominated state legislature would probably seek to carve up the district of his Utah colleague, Democrat Jim Matheson.

Bishop in 2004 went to bat for his district's Perry City community in its battle with the Army Corps of Engineers over the city's plan to replace a portion of seasonal wetlands near the Great Salt Lake with a sewage lagoon. The Salt Lake Tribune called the city's proposal "indefensible." The newspaper also wrote that Bishop's "boorish" criticism of a Corps official led to the employee's transfer.

The Tribune also criticized Bishop in his first term for seeking favors for a local company. In July 2003, he wrote a letter to the authors of a measure on national energy policy asking them to reclassify waste at the Energy Department's defunct Fernald nuclear bomb plant in Ohio so that a Utah company, Envirocare, could compete for a federal contract to dispose of the waste. After two months of widespread and intense public opposition, Envirocare withdrew its application. Bishop, who had done lobbying work for the company before coming to Congress, was criticized by the Utah media. He declined any interview requests from the Salt Lake Tribune for more than a month to demonstrate his displeasure with its coverage.

"I'm still the only person involved in the issue that didn't make any money out of anything," he told the newspaper after breaking his silence. "I still have no vested interest in Envirocare."

Bishop's 2002 bid to succeed Hansen was founded on his 16 years of experience in the state House, including a stint as Speaker during his last two years. He later served as chairman of the Utah Republican Party.

After easily defeating state House Majority Leader Kevin Garn for the GOP nomination, Bishop faced wealthy advertising executive Dave Thomas in the general election. Bishop had the advantage in the strongly Republican 1st District and won with 61 percent of the vote.

His path to re-election in 2004 was easier. His chief opponent was Democrat Steve Thompson, a Logan City council member, who attacked Bishop on the Envirocare issue but had trouble raising enough money to pose a serious threat. Bishop cruised to victory with 68 percent.

Bishop plans to use his time in Washington to indulge in another of his passions besides teaching — playing softball. Though most congressional offices have teams, Bishop told the Deseret Morning News that he is among the few congressmen who actually plays on his office's squad. "I really get frustrated when they have votes on softball night," he said.

KEY VOTES

2004

No	Extend federal unemployment benefits by 13 weeks
Yes	Pass $283.2 billion, six-year federal highway and mass transit bill
Yes	Approve $146 billion multi-year extension of previously enacted middle-class tax breaks
Yes	Amend the Constitution to prohibit same-sex marriage
Yes	Cut corporate taxes $137 billion over 10 years
No	Reorganize U.S. intelligence agencies as proposed by Sept. 11 commission

2003

Yes	Cut taxes by $330 billion through fiscal 2013
No	Block Bush rule scaling back overtime pay for some white-collar federal workers
Yes	Do not allow use of search warrants without first notifying subjects
No	Allow importation of prescription drugs
Yes	Create private school voucher program in Washington, D.C.
Yes	Ban "partial birth" abortion except to save a woman's life
No	Split $18.6 billion in Iraq aid into half-grant, half-loan
Yes	Overhaul Medicare and create prescription drug benefit

CQ VOTE STUDIES

	PARTY UNITY		PRESIDENTIAL SUPPORT	
	Support	Oppose	Support	Oppose
2004	97%	3%	85%	15%
2003	97%	3%	92%	8%

INTEREST GROUPS

	AFL-CIO	ADA	CCUS	ACU
2004	14%	5%	95%	100%
2003	0%	0%	100%	88%

UTAH 1
North — part of Salt Lake City, Ogden

In the 1840s, Mormon pioneers journeyed into the mountainous terrain of northern Utah. Today, the 1st — covering the northernmost part of the state — retains that Mormon influence. Redistricting following the 2000 census added more than half of Salt Lake City, bringing in most of downtown and Temple Square, which includes the Tabernacle and the headquarters of the Church of Jesus Christ of Latter-day Saints.

Ogden, the 1st's second-largest city, was once a lively railroad town but today looks more toward defense. Hill Air Force Base is one of the state's largest employers. The 1st also contains much of Utah's ski country in the north-central part of the state, including Park City, a wealthy resort town.

In rural parts of the district, agriculture is king. The aerospace industry also employs many residents. The 2002 Winter Olympics provided an influx of tourism dollars.

Despite the district's overall GOP tilt, many of the added areas in Salt Lake City lean Democratic. The new 1st combines some of Utah's poorest urban areas with some of its most wealthy, including the heavily populated Davis County, a solidly Republican suburb. Most of the rural areas favor Republicans, although Democrats pick up some votes in Park City and in Weber County — once a center of railroad-related work. Overall, George W. Bush took 73 percent of the district's 2004 presidential vote.

MAJOR INDUSTRY
Manufacturing, defense, technology, tourism, agriculture

MILITARY BASES
Hill Air Force Base, 3,500 military, 12,500 civilian; Deseret Chemical Depot, 2 military, 514 civilian; Dugway Proving Ground, 16 military, 500 civilian; Tooele Army Depot, 2 military, 495 civilian (2004)

CITIES
Salt Lake City (pt.), 94,049; Ogden, 77,226; Layton, 58,474; Logan, 42,670; Bountiful, 41,301; Roy, 32,885; Clearfield, 25,974; Tooele, 22,502

NOTABLE
Great Salt Lake is the world's second-largest saltwater lake; Park City has been the home of the U.S. Ski and Snowboard Team since 1974 and home of the U.S. Ski Association since 1988.

Rep. Jim Matheson (D)

Elected 2000; 3rd term

CAPITOL OFFICE
225-3011
www.house.gov/matheson
1222 Longworth 20515-4402; fax 225-5638

COMMITTEES
Financial Services
Science
Transportation & Infrastructure

HOMETOWN
Salt Lake City

BORN
March 21, 1960, Salt Lake City, Utah

RELIGION
Mormon

FAMILY
Wife, Amy Matheson; one child

EDUCATION
Harvard U., A.B. 1982 (government); U. of
California, Los Angeles, M.B.A. 1987

CAREER
Energy consulting firm owner; energy company
project manager; environmental group advocate

POLITICAL HIGHLIGHTS
No previous office

ELECTION RESULTS

2004 GENERAL

Jim Matheson (D)	187,250	54.8%
John Swallow (R)	147,778	43.2%
Jeremy Paul Petersen (C)	3,541	1.0%

2004 PRIMARY

Jim Matheson (D)	unopposed

2002 GENERAL

Jim Matheson (D)	110,764	49.4%
John Swallow (R)	109,123	48.7%
Patrick S. Diehl (GREEN)	2,589	1.2%

PREVIOUS WINNING PERCENTAGES
2000 (56%)

Matheson wakes up every morning with the knowledge that he ranks near the top of the Republican Party's political target lists. He is the only Democrat in the congressional delegation of one of the most conservative states in the country.

Matheson was regarded as his party's most vulnerable incumbent in the 2004 congressional elections, yet he managed to defeat his conservative opponent by 12 percentage points — a veritable landslide in a district that in the same year backed George W. Bush by 35 points. Matheson's victory was a bright spot for his party in an otherwise discouraging election year. But his win does not mean he will be ignored by the Republicans. Utah legislators want an all-GOP congressional delegation, which was their goal when they redrew the 2nd District after the 2000 census.

Matheson says he tries not to dwell on the small number of Democrats in his district, saying instead that he believes his centrist politics and hard work can win over his Republican constituents. During his campaigns, he downplays his party affiliation and instead calls attention to his independence. The strategy seems to be working: He enjoyed high approval ratings in 2004 and built up a fat war chest. Those advantages, as well as his name recognition (his late father, Scott Matheson, was a well-liked two-term governor) have helped him keep his seat.

In the House, Matheson affiliates with the "Blue Dogs," a group of fiscally conservative Democrats. Shortly after the 2004 elections, the three-dozen Blue Dogs elected Matheson to serve as a co-chairman of the group in the 109th Congress. Matheson consistently ranks as one of the 25 least-loyal Democrats. In the 108th, he sided with a majority of his party just 70 percent of the time on votes in which the two parties were in opposition.

Matheson keeps his seat by responding to the conservative social and fiscal views of his constituents. In 2004, he voted with a majority of Republicans to amend the Constitution to prohibit same-sex marriage and on a measure to repeal municipal gun control laws in Washington, D.C. In 2001, he was one of just 28 Democrats who voted for President Bush's $1.35 trillion tax cut, and in 2003, he was one of only 16 Democrats who supported the final version of a GOP bill to provide prescription drug coverage for Medicare recipients.

Matheson is most likely to join with other Democrats on votes affecting union workers. In 2004, he voted to extend federal unemployment benefits by 13 weeks for workers whose state benefits had run out, and in 2003, he voted with his party to block Bush administration rules to scale back overtime pay for some white-collar federal workers.

Democratic leaders understand that Matheson's voting record is a reflection of his narrow hold on his district. He has seats on the Financial Services, Science and Transportation committees, all of which are good fits for his district. On Transportation, he has taken the lead in the authorization of a number of pilot projects at airports around the country to test new security technologies that use biometric identifiers, such as retinal scans, photographs, fingerprints, palm prints and voice prints. He has also worked to gain highway and transit funding, including a massive overhaul of Interstate 15 and a new light-rail commuter line in Salt Lake County.

Matheson joined with Utah Republicans in an effort to win resumption of federal compensation to people who had become ill as a result of exposure to radiation from Cold War-era atomic bomb testing in Nevada, including 185 Utahans. Compensation for those who were called "downwinders" was authorized in 1990, but funding had halted in 2000.

The issue resonates with Matheson, whose father died in 1990 of bone marrow cancer, a disease linked to radiation exposure. Scott Matheson was living in an area of southern Utah affected by the nuclear tests, but he never sought compensation. Matheson remembered his father when legislation to further the construction of a nuclear waste dump site at Nevada's Yucca Mountain came before the 107th Congress. He voted no, saying that Westerners had been exposed to enough nuclear dangers.

Although his father was the governor, Matheson says that his mother, Norma, who involved herself in all sorts of civic projects, was actually more responsible for his own interest in public service. During his college days as a government major at Harvard, Matheson served a summer internship in the office of Speaker Thomas P. O'Neill Jr. After college, he worked at an environmental policy think tank in Washington for three years. He earned a graduate degree from the University of California at Los Angeles, returned to Utah and worked in a number of private sector energy jobs. He also started his own energy consulting firm.

Matheson decided to run for Congress in 2000 because of the turmoil surrounding Merrill Cook, the mercurial two-term GOP incumbent in the 2nd District. Cook had received reams of bad publicity over his temperamental outbursts and lost the GOP primary to Internet executive Derek W. Smith. Smith then received his own dose of bad press over his past business practices, and Matheson sailed to victory by 15 percentage points.

In post-2000 census redistricting, the 2nd District may have undergone the most radical transformation of any district in the country. Utah's GOP mapmakers turned the compact, urban 458-square-mile Salt Lake County district into an almost 46,000-square-mile behemoth that stretches from the eastern, and mostly Republican, portion of Salt Lake City far south into rural areas.

Matheson complained mightily about the reconfiguration of the Salt Lake County district, but to no avail. He then set out to introduce himself to his new southern Utah electorate, reminding them of his family's southern Utah roots. His father was an Iron County deputy attorney and is buried in the southern Utah town of Parowan.

Matheson lost 11 of the 16 counties, but a large margin in the Salt Lake County portion of the district enabled him to edge past Republican state Rep. John Swallow in the fourth-closest House race of 2002. Swallow had tried to boost his chances with a last-minute blitz of negative advertisements and a visit from Vice President Dick Cheney. Swallow tried again in 2004, but Matheson defeated him soundly.

KEY VOTES

2004
Yes Extend federal unemployment benefits by 13 weeks
Yes Pass $283.2 billion, six-year federal highway and mass transit bill
Yes Approve $146 billion multi-year extension of previously enacted middle-class tax breaks
Yes Amend the Constitution to prohibit same-sex marriage
Yes Cut corporate taxes $137 billion over 10 years
Yes Reorganize U.S. intelligence agencies as proposed by Sept. 11 commission

2003
Yes Cut taxes by $330 billion through fiscal 2013
Yes Block Bush rule scaling back overtime pay for some white-collar federal workers
Yes Do not allow use of search warrants without first notifying subjects
No   Allow importation of prescription drugs
No   Create private school voucher program in Washington, D.C.
Yes Ban "partial birth" abortion except to save a woman's life
Yes Split $18.6 billion in Iraq aid into half-grant, half-loan
Yes Overhaul Medicare and create prescription drug benefit

CQ VOTE STUDIES

	PARTY UNITY		PRESIDENTIAL SUPPORT	
	Support	Oppose	Support	Oppose
2004	64%	36%	50%	50%
2003	75%	25%	56%	44%
2002	76%	24%	48%	52%
2001	67%	33%	51%	49%

INTEREST GROUPS

	AFL-CIO	ADA	CCUS	ACU
2004	60%	70%	86%	48%
2003	73%	70%	70%	36%
2002	56%	80%	65%	40%
2001	75%	70%	65%	32%

UTAH 2
South and east — part of Salt Lake City, rural Utah

The 2nd was a compact Salt Lake County district for 20 years before redistricting following the 2000 census dramatically altered it to be much more rural. The 2nd now forms a reverse "L" shape, moving south from Salt Lake City to take in the eastern half of the state and moving westward to take in the state's southwest corner, a ranching center and growing retirement hub.

While some of the 2nd's rural eastern communities saw sharp population declines during the 1980s, these areas have begun to rebound. Grand County, once devastated by the collapse of the uranium mining industry, has seen new life since telecommuter and artist communities have sprung up in the town of Moab. However, the area has not yet fully recovered — it is still losing some of its population and unemployment is high.

Democratic areas of Salt Lake City used to make the 2nd a swing district, but the part of Salt Lake County that remains in the redrawn district — and totals about 60 percent of the 2nd's voters — is now more

Republican. In the old 2nd, George W. Bush took 56 percent of the vote in the 2000 presidential election, but Bush took 66 percent of the vote in 2004 under the new 2nd District lines. The eastern portion of Salt Lake County provides some Democratic votes, as does Carbon County, a mining center in the middle of the state. Washington and Iron counties, in the southwest, are the district's most Republican.

Land-use issues are important in the district, which includes all five of the state's national parks — Arches, Bryce Canyon, Canyonlands, Capitol Reef and Zion. Much of the district is federal land. President Clinton's designation of the 1.7 million-acre Grand Staircase-Escalante as a national monument in 1996 angered many in the state.

MAJOR INDUSTRY
Financial services, manufacturing, tourism, ranching

CITIES
Sandy, 88,418; Salt Lake City (pt.), 87,694; St. George, 49,663; Murray, 34,024; Millcreek (unincorporated), 30,377

NOTABLE
Moab, located just south of Arches National Park, hosts the Fat Tire Festival for mountain-biking enthusiasts every October.

Rep. Chris Cannon (R)

Elected 1996; 5th term

CAPITOL OFFICE
225-7751
cannon.ut03@mail.house.gov
www.house.gov/cannon
2436 Rayburn 20515-4403; fax 225-5629

COMMITTEES
Government Reform
Judiciary
 (Commercial & Administrative Law - chairman)
Resources

HOMETOWN
Mapleton

BORN
Oct. 20, 1950, Salt Lake City, Utah

RELIGION
Mormon

FAMILY
Wife, Claudia Fox Cannon; eight children (one deceased)

EDUCATION
Brigham Young U., B.S. 1974 (economics); Harvard Business School, attended 1975-76; Brigham Young U., J.D. 1980

CAREER
Venture capital executive; steel company executive; Cabinet department lawyer

POLITICAL HIGHLIGHTS
Utah Republican Party finance chairman, 1992-94

ELECTION RESULTS

2004 GENERAL

Chris Cannon (R)	173,010	63.4%
Beau Babka (D)	88,748	32.5%
Ronald Winfield (C)	5,089	1.9%
Jim Dexter (LIBERT)	3,691	1.4%

2004 PRIMARY

Chris Cannon (R)	27,663	58.4%
Matt Throckmorton (R)	19,672	41.6%

2002 GENERAL

Chris Cannon (R)	103,598	67.4%
Nancy Jane Woodside (D)	44,533	29.0%
Kitty K. Burton (LIBERT)	5,511	3.6%

PREVIOUS WINNING PERCENTAGES
2000 (59%); 1998 (77%); 1996 (51%)

Cannon has become a consensus-seeking, pragmatic legislator whose ability to work across party lines belies his early partisan intensity. When he first arrived in the House, he didn't stand out much from his like-minded conservative colleagues, except in his persistent pursuit of President Clinton's impeachment. For four years, Cannon was best-known for his focus on Clinton's removal from office. It was an obsession that continued beyond the president's acquittal by the Senate in 1999.

Actually, Cannon first gained his House seat because of Clinton. He ousted the incumbent Democrat by riding his state's wave of anger over Clinton's 1996 unilateral designation of a 1.7 million-acre national monument, called Grand Staircase-Escalante, which largely precluded the development of the area's rich mineral reserves. Cannon joined Utah Republican James V. Hansen, chairman of the Resources Committee, in trying several times to remove the president's authority to create such monuments.

A Salt Lake Tribune profile once said: "There is no lukewarm setting" on Cannon, whose "rhetoric conveys a sort of Armageddon style of politics: The ultimate showdown between good and evil looms behind every vote." But from his seat on the Judiciary Committee, historically one of the most partisan House panels, Cannon now willingly teams with committee Democrats to work on a wide range of topics, including immigration, high-technology concerns and anti-terrorism legislation.

By the close of the 108th Congress, The Tribune had titled another short profile of Cannon "Amnesty International," because of his emergence as a leading moderate on immigration policy. He backed measures to provide amnesty to more than 250,000 Central Americans living in the United States, to offer green cards to undocumented immigrant children who plan to complete higher education or serve in the military and to give immigrant farmworkers temporary work visas and possibly green cards.

The measures stalled in Congress over concerns that liberalized immigration policies would hurt the U.S. economy and threaten national security. Cannon says he first formed his views on immigration as a Mormon missionary in Guatemala, and insists he will continue to fight for new policies. "It's the right thing to do," he told the Tribune. "America has the responsibility to bring freedom to people around the world."

Cannon's actions raised the ire of some conservatives, including Matt Throckmorton, who challenged the incumbent in Utah's 2004 GOP primary. Throckmorton lost, but he held Cannon to 58 percent and forced the incumbent to spend almost a half-million dollars to defend his seat.

Immigration is not the only subject on which Cannon has worked with Democrats. During Judiciary's consideration of the anti-terrorism package that became law six weeks after the terrorist attacks of Sept. 11, 2001, Cannon was among a coalition of conservative and liberal lawmakers who insisted that some of the sweeping law enforcement powers granted by the measure be phased out after four years. In the 109th Congress, he is likely to be in the thick of the debate over reauthorizing those elements of what has become known as the Patriot Act.

Cannon also helped form bipartisan coalitions on high-technology matters — a topic of considerable importance to his district, which is the birthplace of WordPerfect and home to a significant computer software industry, including Novell and hundreds of other firms. He played a key role in the enactment in the 108th of a three-year moratorium on taxing all forms of consumer Internet access and service providers. It was a last-ditch compromise measure that fell short of a permanent ban, a goal he plans to continue pursuing in the 109th. He also helped shepherd through a law allowing businesses to store a common employment form, called an I-9, electronically, freeing them from keeping reams of paperwork.

Land-use issues are important to Cannon, who served as a lawyer in the Interior Department during the Reagan administration. He has sponsored a number of measures to set limited land protections, while permitting multiple other uses as well. He supports opening up Alaska's Arctic National Wildlife Refuge to oil drilling. Cannon served as chairman of the Western Caucus in the 108th Congress, and keeps the position for the 109th.

On the Government Reform panel, he continues his call to require the Census Bureau to design a plan to count Americans living abroad in the 2010 census. The state's population would have warranted a fourth seat in the House, if Mormon missionaries and all other Utahans abroad were counted in 2000, instead of just military personnel.

At the start of his second term, Cannon was one of the 13 Republican "managers" from the Judiciary Committee who presented the House's case for removing Clinton from office in the Senate trial. After the Senate rejected the articles of impeachment, Cannon continued to call for Clinton's resignation and to defend the actions of the managers. He established an Internet-based political action committee — the House Managers PAC — to help ensure his re-election and that of his fellow House prosecutors.

Cannon earned a degree from Brigham Young University in 1974, after taking time out to serve on his church mission to Guatemala. He flunked out of Harvard Business School in 1976, then returned to BYU for a law degree. After three years as an associate solicitor in the Interior Department and a stint as a Commerce Department lawyer, he returned to Utah to gain success in the business world.

He teamed up with his brother, Joe, to buy and reopen Geneva Steel Co. in 1987. After a falling out with his sibling, Cannon started his own venture capital company, Cannon Industries. Active in state party politics, he headed up Lamar Alexander's 1996 presidential campaign in Utah.

Cannon's financial statements put his worth at more than $10 million — and he made liberal use of his own money to help fund his 8,000-vote 1996 victory over Democrat Bill Orton. His re-elections since have been comparatively easy. The solid GOP nature of his constituency was not altered in redistricting after the 2000 census. In 2002, he won by 38 percentage points, and in 2004 by 31 points.

KEY VOTES

2004

No Extend federal unemployment benefits by 13 weeks
Yes Pass $283.2 billion, six-year federal highway and mass transit bill
? Approve $146 billion multi-year extension of previously enacted middle-class tax breaks
? Amend the Constitution to prohibit same-sex marriage
Yes Cut corporate taxes $137 billion over 10 years
? Reorganize U.S. intelligence agencies as proposed by Sept. 11 commission

2003

Yes Cut taxes by $330 billion through fiscal 2013
No Block Bush rule scaling back overtime pay for some white-collar federal workers
No Do not allow use of search warrants without first notifying subjects
No Allow importation of prescription drugs
Yes Create private school voucher program in Washington, D.C.
Yes Ban "partial birth" abortion except to save a woman's life
No Split $18.6 billion in Iraq aid into half-grant, half-loan
Yes Overhaul Medicare and create prescription drug benefit

CQ VOTE STUDIES

	PARTY UNITY		PRESIDENTIAL SUPPORT	
	Support	Oppose	Support	Oppose
2004	98%	2%	87%	13%
2003	98%	2%	98%	2%
2002	96%	4%	87%	13%
2001	99%	1%	95%	5%
2000	99%	1%	24%	76%

INTEREST GROUPS

	AFL-CIO	ADA	CCUS	ACU
2004	18%	0%	100%	100%
2003	0%	5%	97%	88%
2002	0%	0%	94%	95%
2001	8%	0%	100%	100%
2000	0%	0%	95%	100%

UTAH 3

Central — part of Salt Lake County, Provo

Utah's conservative 3rd is located in the central part of the state, taking in some Salt Lake City suburbs and heading south on Interstate 15 to Provo and Orem, the district's economic centers. It also stretches west to pick up rural Millard and Beaver counties on the state's western border. A heavily Mormon-influenced district, the 3rd has one of the highest concentrations of married couples and has the lowest median age (24.5) of any district in the nation.

The Provo-Orem area has a flourishing computer industry. Newly minted graduates from the 3rd's colleges have helped make the area attractive to some of the industry's big-name companies. Brigham Young University, located in Provo, is one of the largest employers in the state. Outside Utah County, cattle ranching, mining and tourism sustain small-town life.

The 3rd included the state's eastern half for 20 years, but redistricting after the 2000 census made the district smaller. The boundary change did not affect the 3rd's GOP tilt — George W. Bush received 77 percent of the 3rd's vote in the 2004 presidential election.

Salt Lake County's residents make up slightly less than half of the 3rd's population. These western suburbs grew rapidly in the 1990s. Many are lower income, socially conservative areas that tend to vote Republican. Most of the state's Asian population is located in this part of the district. The 3rd also takes in some of the city's southern suburbs, which recently have attracted younger married couples.

Ranchers in Millard County and hog farmers in Beaver County also tend to vote Republican. Small Democratic pockets exist in the mining community of Magna, the Salt Lake City suburb of West Valley City and the railroad town of Milford.

MAJOR INDUSTRY
Technology, mining, higher education, ranching

CITIES
West Valley City, 108,896; Provo, 105,166; Orem, 84,324; West Jordan, 68,336; Taylorsville, 57,439

NOTABLE
Philo T. Farnsworth, credited with inventing TV, lived in Provo; Brigham Young University was founded on an acre of land on Oct. 16, 1875.

VERMONT

Gov. Jim Douglas (R)

First elected: 2002
Length of term: 2 years
Term expires: 1/07
Salary: $133,166
Phone: (802) 828-3333

Hometown: Middlebury
Born: June 21, 1951; East Longmeadow, Mass.
Religion: United Church of Christ
Family: Wife, Dorothy Douglas; two children
Education: Middlebury College, A.B. 1972 (Russian)
Career: Gubernatorial aide
Political highlights: Vt. House, 1973-79 (majority leader, 1977-79); Vt. secretary of state, 1981-93; Republican nominee for U.S. Senate, 1992; Vt. treasurer, 1995-2003

Election results:
2004 GENERAL
Jim Douglas (R)	181,540	58.7%
Peter Clavelle (D)	117,327	37.9%
others	6,197	2.0%
Cris Ericson (M)	4,221	1.4%

Lt. Gov. Brian Dubie (R)

First elected: 2002
Length of term: 2 years
Term expires: 1/07
Salary: $56,513
Phone: (802) 828-2226

STATE LEGISLATURE

General Assembly: January-April

House: 150 members, 2-year terms
2005 breakdown: 83D, 60R, 6 Progressive, 1I; 100 men, 50 women
Salary: $589/week
Phone: (802) 828-2247

Senate: 30 members, 2-year terms
2005 breakdown: 21D, 9R; 20 men, 10 women
Salary: $589/week
Phone: (802) 828-2241

STATE TERM LIMITS

Governor: No
House: No
Senate: No

URBAN STATISTICS

CITY	POPULATION
Burlington	38,889
Essex	18,626
Rutland	17,292
Colchester	16,986
South Burlington	15,814

REGISTERED VOTERS

Voters do not register by party.

POPULATION

2004 population (est.)	621,394
2000 population	608,827
1990 population	562,758
Percent change (1990-2000)	+8.2%
Rank among states (2004)	49
Median age	37.7
Born in state	54.3%
Foreign born	3.8%
Violent crime rate	114/100,000
Poverty level	9.4%
Federal workers	5,630
Military	4,605

REDISTRICTING

Vermont retained its one House seat in reapportionment.

MISCELLANEOUS

Web: www.vermont.gov
Capital: Montpelier
STATE ELECTION OFFICIAL
(802) 828-2304
DEMOCRATIC HEADQUARTERS
(802) 229-1783
REPUBLICAN HEADQUARTERS
(802) 223-3411

District Statistics

DIST.	2004 VOTE FOR PRESIDENT BUSH	KERRY	WHITE	BLACK	ASIAN	HISP	MEDIAN INCOME	WHITE COLLAR	BLUE COLLAR	SERVICE INDUSTRY	OVER 64	UNDER 18	COLLEGE EDUCATION	RURAL	SQ. MILES
AL	39%	59%	96%	0%	1%	1%	$40,856	61%	25%	15%	13%	24%	29%	62%	9,250
STATE	39	59	96	0	1	1	$40,856	61	25	15	13	24	29	62	9,250
U.S.	50.7	48.3	69	12	4	13	$41,994	60	25	15	12	26	24	21	3,537,438

www.cqpress.com

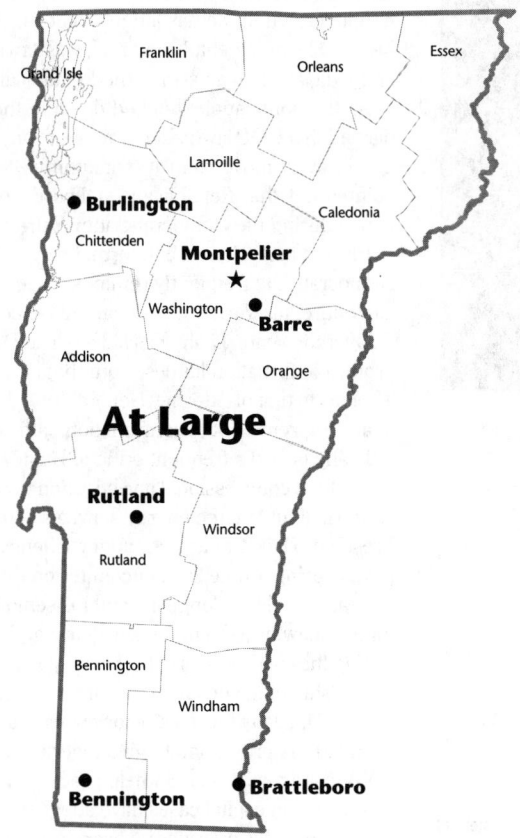

Sen. Patrick J. Leahy (D)

Elected 1974; 6th term

CAPITOL OFFICE
224-4242
senator_leahy@leahy.senate.gov
leahy.senate.gov
433 Russell 20510-4502; fax 224-3479

COMMITTEES
Agriculture, Nutrition & Forestry
Appropriations
Judiciary - ranking member

HOMETOWN
Middlesex

BORN
March 31, 1940, Montpelier, Vt.

RELIGION
Roman Catholic

FAMILY
Wife, Marcelle Leahy; three children

EDUCATION
St. Michael's College, B.A. 1961 (political science);
Georgetown U., J.D. 1964

CAREER
Lawyer

POLITICAL HIGHLIGHTS
Chittenden County state's attorney, 1966-75

ELECTION RESULTS

2004 GENERAL

Patrick J. Leahy (D)	216,972	70.6%
John "Jack" McMullen (R)	75,398	24.5%
Cris Ericson (M)	6,486	2.1%
Craig Hill (GREEN)	3,999	1.3%
Keith Stern (I)	3,300	1.1%

2004 PRIMARY

Patrick J. Leahy (D)	27,459	94.3%
Craig Hill (D)	1,573	5.4%

PREVIOUS WINNING PERCENTAGES
1998 (72%); 1992 (54%); 1986 (63%); 1980 (50%);
1974 (50%)

As the top Democrat on the Judiciary Committee, Leahy has been the main antagonist during a series of filibusters of President Bush's judicial nominees, whom he has judged to be far too conservative for the federal bench. The president, Leahy said, was "trying to turn the independent federal judiciary into an arm of the Republican Party."

As the nominations bogged down in the 108th Congress, Leahy complained that GOP lawmakers trampled longstanding traditions by trying to aggressively move controversial nominees through the Senate. He often pointed out that Republicans stalled dozens of nominees to the federal bench during the Democratic administration of President Clinton.

Elected in 2004 to a sixth term, Leahy is fifth in seniority among Senate Democrats. He frequently reminds his fellow senators of his lengthy Senate tenure, his Vermont roots and his experience as a state prosecutor.

Over the years, Leahy has helped lead Democrats through several high-profile confirmation battles, from that of Supreme Court Justice Clarence Thomas to that of Attorney General John Ashcroft. He will reprise that role in any Supreme Court confirmation battle during Bush's second term.

Leahy is also a frequent critic of Bush's conduct of the war in Iraq. He called for a congressional investigation of reconstruction contracts awarded to Halliburton, the energy services company formerly headed by Vice President Dick Cheney. An angry Cheney lashed out at Leahy in vulgar terms during a June 2004 encounter on the Senate floor.

Leahy's political longevity and his seniority on the busy Judiciary Committee allow him to pursue a wide range of legislative interests, from protecting the civil liberties of people suspected of crimes, to revising copyright law, to shielding consumers from privacy invasions over the Internet.

In 2004, Leahy scored a victory when Bush signed a major crime law that included his provisions to give federal inmates access to post-conviction DNA testing, which could help prove their innocence, and to ensure that defendants in capital cases have adequate legal representation.

Another of his priorities is a worldwide ban on land mines, including U.S. exports. Land mines, easy to plant but difficult to remove after war ends, often maim and kill civilians. Leahy clashed frequently on this issue with the Clinton administration, which opposed a total ban. He criticized the Bush administration's decision to skip an international summit on the issue in 2004 as "aloof and ill-considered." As the top-ranking Democrat on the Appropriations Foreign Operations Subcommittee, Leahy has pushed through funding for medical help for land mine victims. He will continue efforts to pressure the United Nations for a ban as one of two congressional representatives in the U.S. delegation to the 59th session of the U.N. General Assembly.

Leahy was the chairman of the Judiciary panel at the time of the Sept. 11, 2001, terrorist attacks. The first major legislation to result was an administration bill greatly expanding law enforcement powers to investigate terrorists. Leahy was the leading voice for concerns that the law overreached, infringing on basic civil liberties. He huddled daily to make revisions with Utah Sen. Orrin G. Hatch, the panel's senior Republican, and Attorney General Ashcroft, whom he previously opposed for appointment. He said later that he at least managed to rid the bill of bolder encroachments on civil liberties. "As draconian as it was, the terrorism bill was far more constitutional than it would have been had I not been chairman," he said.

Since then, Leahy has often voiced frustration with the Justice Department for failing to respond quickly to his requests for information about the war on terrorism. He is very skeptical of arguments for renewing parts of the Patriot Act in the 109th Congress or of granting law enforcement more powers.

Leahy was unsuccessful in pressing for a congressional subpoena to investigate the Justice Department's role in the alleged mistreatment of prisoners by the U.S. military in Iraq, Cuba and Afghanistan. But the Senate adopted Leahy's amendment to the defense authorization bill in 2004 to require the Pentagon to report to Congress on the status of detainees.

A month after the 2001 anti-terrorism bill became law, Leahy's office received an anonymous letter addressed to him and laced with deadly anthrax spores, putting him at the center of a weeks-long bioterrorism scare in Congress. Now, Leahy is often trailed by a security guard when moving around Capitol Hill.

During the 1991 confirmation hearings of Thomas to the highest court, the senator pressed the conservative judge to reveal his position on several issues, including abortion rights. Leahy elicited Thomas' claim that he had never discussed the landmark *Roe v. Wade* decision legalizing abortion, which Thomas' critics seized on as proof of evasiveness.

Leahy is relatively plugged into pop culture and new technology. He is a fan of both the comic book character Batman and The Grateful Dead band. In 1996, he was one of the first lawmakers to launch a Web site, and he often checks his Blackberry during committee meetings.

He dives into technology-related issues on Judiciary. In light of the now widespread use of the Internet, Leahy wants to update copyright law to include, for example, more privacy protections for medical and financial records. In 2000, he pushed to enactment a law that establishes ways to make electronic signatures legally binding, while also protecting consumers.

Like most other liberals, Leahy supports abortion rights. As the senior Democrat on the Appropriations subcommittee on foreign aid, he's been particularly active in supporting international family planning groups that perform abortions. But in a rare union with conservatives, Leahy voted in the 108th Congress for a ban on a procedure that opponents call "partial birth" abortion.

Tiny Vermont has just three representatives in Congress, and Leahy is quick to protect the interests of his rural state. A senior member of the Agriculture Committee, he is a defender of Northeastern dairy farmers during the perennial conflicts among dairy-producing regions of the country.

Leahy was just 34 when he was first elected to the Senate in 1974. The Watergate-inspired backlash helped him beat a favored Republican to become Vermont's first Democratic senator since the Republican Party was founded in 1854.

He overcame the GOP landslide of 1980 to win his first re-election by just 2,500 votes. Emphasizing his Vermont roots, he beat New York native Stewart Ledbetter, a former state banking commissioner. That close call lured former GOP Gov. Richard A. Snelling out of retirement to challenge him six years later. But by then Leahy was well-financed and won with 63 percent of the vote.

In 1998, Leahy faced one of the year's most talked-about opponents, 79-year-old dairy farmer Fred Tuttle. The star of a 1996 mock documentary about an unlikely congressional candidate, Tuttle turned fiction into fact by winning the GOP nomination. Spending just $251 — one dollar for each town in Vermont — Tuttle got national media attention but just 22 percent of the vote. In 2004, Leahy was easily re-elected with 71 percent against Republican John "Jack" McMullen.

KEY VOTES

2004
Yes Pass $318.9 billion, six-year highway and mass transit bill
Yes Extend assault weapons ban for 10 years
Yes Restore pay-as-you-go rules for new tax cuts and entitlement spending
No   Criminalize harm to a fetus in an attack on the mother
Yes Increase mandatory child care funding to states by $6 billion over five years
No   Amend the Constitution to prohibit same-sex marriage
Yes Approve $146 billion multi-year extension of previously enacted middle-class tax breaks
Yes Reorganize U.S. intelligence agencies as proposed by Sept. 11 commission
?   Cut corporate taxes $137 billion over 10 years

2003
Yes Delay Bush changes to Clean Air Act
No   Allow confirmation vote on Miguel A. Estrada to the U.S. Court of Appeals for the D.C. Circuit
Yes Block a Bush proposal opening Alaska's Arctic National Wildlife Refuge to oil drilling
Yes Limit size of Bush's proposed tax cut to $350 billion through fiscal 2013
Yes Overhaul Medicare and create prescription drug benefit
Yes Block Bush rule scaling back overtime pay for some white-collar federal workers
Yes Split $20 billion in Iraq aid into half-grant, half-loan
Yes Ban "partial birth" abortion except to save a woman's life
No   Stop proposal allowing travel to Cuba
No   Allow final vote on energy policy overhaul

CQ VOTE STUDIES

	PARTY UNITY		PRESIDENTIAL SUPPORT	
	Support	Oppose	Support	Oppose
2004	94%	6%	58%	42%
2003	97%	3%	51%	49%
2002	98%	2%	67%	33%
2001	98%	2%	62%	38%
2000	94%	6%	89%	11%
1999	94%	6%	82%	18%
1998	87%	13%	83%	17%
1997	89%	11%	87%	13%
1996	88%	12%	75%	25%
1995	96%	4%	89%	11%

INTEREST GROUPS

	AFL-CIO	ADA	CCUS	ACU
2004	100%	100%	50%	8%
2003	85%	85%	35%	16%
2002	100%	95%	55%	0%
2001	100%	100%	38%	8%
2000	75%	85%	58%	8%
1999	100%	95%	41%	4%
1998	88%	90%	56%	12%
1997	67%	80%	60%	13%
1996	100%	90%	23%	5%
1995	100%	100%	16%	0%

Sen. James M. Jeffords (I)

Elected 1988; 3rd term

CAPITOL OFFICE
224-5141
jeffords.senate.gov
413 Dirksen 20510-4503; fax 228-0776

COMMITTEES
Environment & Public Works - ranking member
Finance
Health, Education, Labor & Pensions
Veterans' Affairs
Special Aging

HOMETOWN
Shrewsbury

BORN
May 11, 1934, Rutland, Vt.

RELIGION
Congregationalist

FAMILY
Wife, Elizabeth Daley Jeffords; two children

EDUCATION
Yale U., B.S.I.A. 1956; Harvard U., LL.B. 1962

MILITARY SERVICE
Navy, 1956-59; Naval Reserve, 1959-90

CAREER
Lawyer

POLITICAL HIGHLIGHTS
Vt. Senate, 1967-69 (served as a Republican); Vt. attorney general, 1969-73 (served as a Republican); sought Republican nomination for governor, 1972; U.S. House, 1975-89 (served as a Republican)

ELECTION RESULTS

2000 GENERAL

James M. Jeffords (R)	189,133	65.6%
Ed Flanagan (D)	73,352	25.4%
Charles W. Russell (CNSTP)	10,079	3.5%
Rick Hubbard (I)	5,366	1.9%

2000 PRIMARY

James M. Jeffords (R)	60,234	77.8%
Rick Hubbard (R)	15,991	20.7%

PREVIOUS WINNING PERCENTAGES *
1994 (50%); 1988 (68%); 1986 House Election (89%); 1984 House Election (65%); 1982 House Election (69%); 1980 House Election (79%); 1978 House Election (75%); 1976 House Election (67%); 1974 House Election (53%)
* Elected as a Republican 1974-2000

Known for single-handedly rearranging the balance of power in the Senate in 2001, Jeffords is still a force on certain issues, but his influence has diminished since Republicans took the majority back. He is not the dominant leader in education policy that he once aspired to be, instead carving out a role as a leading critic of President Bush's environmental policies.

Jeffords in 2005 announced plans to leave Congress when his term ends in 2006, saying he wanted to spend time with his wife, Elizabeth, who was battling cancer, and a new grandchild.

He is officially an independent although he votes with the Democratic caucus, campaigns for Democrats and is the senior minority member of the Senate Environment and Public Works Committee. He even chaired the panel for 18 months before the Republicans won back control of the Senate in the 2002 election.

His centrist views and pragmatic approach to legislating may give him some added influence with Democrats as they try to find their way after the disastrous 2004 elections, when they lost seats in the Senate. Jeffords certainly has the ear of new Democratic leader Harry Reid, who was influential in wooing Jeffords away from the GOP. He also remains close to Republican moderate pals from the Northeast, especially Sens. Lincoln Chafee of Rhode Island and Olympia J. Snowe of Maine. He works with them and other moderates in the newly revived Centrist Coalition.

Jeffords' voting record is somewhere in the middle of the political pack. He is typically a reliable liberal vote for abortion rights, gay rights, civil liberty issues and environmental causes. But he is closer to the GOP on fiscal matters, health care policy and business-related issues. In the 108th Congress, he sided with Democrats more frequently than he did Republicans, voting with Democrats 88 percent of the time on votes pitting the two parties against each other.

Jeffords is a strong environmentalist, and occupies the top Democratic slot on the Environmental and Public Works Committee. He is the polar opposite of Chairman James M. Inhofe of Oklahoma, an anti-regulation conservative. In the 109th Congress, the two were set to square off on Bush's "Clear Skies" initiative, which Republicans say will reduce emissions of three major pollutants but Democrats and environmentalists claim will weaken current air pollution laws.

At a 2005 confirmation hearing for Stephen L. Johnson, Bush's pick to head the Environmental Protection Agency, Jeffords said, "Our once-prominent leadership on environmental matters has become a joke around the world. Mr. Johnson, you have quite a job ahead to restore the agency's credibility here and abroad — if it can be done."

Jeffords and Inhofe worked fairly well together on a massive and politically delicate transportation bill in 2004. By crafting a $319 billion bill that was large enough to avoid the traditional battles between large and small states and between those favoring mass transit projects over highways, they were rewarded with a veto-proof 76-21 vote in the Senate. Despite its popularity, the bill died because of objections to the cost from the White House. Efforts to enact a six-year bill were to resume in the 109th Congress.

The "I" for independent that always follows Jeffords' name allows coalition builders who win his support to claim "tripartisan" backing for a bill. Jeffords backed a carefully crafted Medicare prescription drug bill in 2003, though the final legislation from the Senate and House negotiations was ultimately rejected by all but 11 Senate Democrats.

Jeffords' true policy passion has been and remains education. He tutors at a public school on Capitol Hill each week as part of a literacy program he created that gets Washington-area companies involved in supporting public schools. He has long felt the federal government falls short in helping to finance public schools, which is the issue that ultimately drove him from the Republican Party.

Even before Bush became the party's nominee for president in 2000, Jeffords backed most of the president's education reform proposals, which were the foundation of the No Child Left Behind Act that passed during his first year in office. Also from the beginning, Jeffords warned that the federal effort to improve the quality of public schools would fail if its new testing regimens were not backed up by money to help schools pay for them.

The first battle over school funding came, not on the education bill, but on Bush's other top priority for the year, a proposed $1.6 trillion tax cut. Jeffords allied with Democrats to force the Senate to accept a provision that would have added $448 billion over 10 years for special education and to pay down the federal debt. Jeffords is one of Congress' strongest advocates of boosting federal spending for special education because he believes it would free up other money for schools at the local level. The proposal ultimately was rebuffed by Republican leaders in final negotiations.

Within a month, Jeffords began informing colleagues that he had decided to leave the party. Two days later, he flew home to explain his decision to his constituents, who less than a year before had re-elected him to the Senate as a Republican. While the refusal to fully fund special education was the last straw, Jeffords' defection was about much more — his utter disaffection with his party and a president he felt was governing from the far right.

"It was a unique time in history," Jeffords recalled. "It was the first time you had a situation of a 50-50 Senate. That opened up an opportunity for one individual, myself or any other Republicans that wanted to, within the rules, to change the whole thing. And then I got to thinking. . . . I said, 'If you don't do it, you're going to be to blame for everything that happens from now on — Supreme Court appointments — all of that. Because you had the power to make that change, to stop the abuse of power.' So that's when I decided I had to do it."

Jeffords has deep roots in his state. His family tree dates to 1792, and his father was the chief justice of the Vermont Supreme Court. After serving a term in the state Senate and four years as attorney general, Jeffords lost a GOP gubernatorial primary in 1972, his sole career defeat. In a preview of his future, the party hierarchy viewed him as too liberal.

He bounced back in 1974, winning a three-way primary for Vermont's lone House seat. He went on to win the general election with 53 percent of the vote over a former Burlington mayor and held the seat for 14 years. In 1988, he was the heir apparent to the Senate seat of retiring Republican Robert T. Stafford, another liberal advocate of public education. Jeffords entered the election a heavy favorite, and won with 68 percent.

In 1994, he faced a tough challenge for a second term from Democratic opponent Jan Backus, an underfunded liberal who had scored an upset victory in the primary. Jeffords eventually won by 10 percentage points.

By 2000, Jeffords faced a new challenge — a politically sensitive run against Democrat Ed Flanagan, the first openly gay Senate candidate to be nominated by a major party. Neither candidate made an issue of Flanagan's sexual orientation, and Jeffords retained the backing of gay rights groups. He won re-election with 66 percent of the vote.

KEY VOTES

2004

Yes	Pass $318.9 billion, six-year highway and mass transit bill
Yes	Extend assault weapons ban for 10 years
Yes	Restore pay-as-you-go rules for new tax cuts and entitlement spending
No	Criminalize harm to a fetus in an attack on the mother
Yes	Increase mandatory child care funding to states by $6 billion over five years
No	Amend the Constitution to prohibit same-sex marriage
Yes	Approve $146 billion multi-year extension of previously enacted middle-class tax breaks
Yes	Reorganize U.S. intelligence agencies as proposed by Sept. 11 commission
Yes	Cut corporate taxes $137 billion over 10 years

2003

Yes	Delay Bush changes to Clean Air Act
No	Allow confirmation vote on Miguel A. Estrada to the U.S. Court of Appeals for the D.C. Circuit
Yes	Block a Bush proposal opening Alaska's Arctic National Wildlife Refuge to oil drilling
Yes	Limit size of Bush's proposed tax cut to $350 billion through fiscal 2013
Yes	Overhaul Medicare and create prescription drug benefit
Yes	Block Bush rule scaling back overtime pay for some white-collar federal workers
Yes	Split $20 billion in Iraq aid into half-grant, half-loan
No	Ban "partial birth" abortion except to save a woman's life
No	Stop proposal allowing travel to Cuba
No	Allow final vote on energy policy overhaul

CQ VOTE STUDIES

	PARTY UNITY		PRESIDENTIAL SUPPORT	
	Support	Oppose	Support	Oppose
2004	92%	8%	60%	40%
2003	86%	14%	51%	49%
2002	88%	12%	71%	29%
2001	85%	15%	80%	20%
2000	55%	45%	75%	25%
1999	67%	33%	56%	44%
1998	49%	51%	69%	31%
1997	53%	47%	78%	22%
1996	58%	42%	53%	47%
1995	59%	41%	51%	49%

INTEREST GROUPS

	AFL-CIO	ADA	CCUS	ACU
2004	83%	85%	59%	4%
2003	92%	85%	36%	10%
2002	92%	95%	53%	6%
2001	56%	40%	64%	29%
2000	38%	55%	73%	36%
1999	22%	45%	76%	40%
1998	38%	55%	89%	24%
1997	0%	45%	100%	21%
1996	43%	50%	62%	45%
1995	36%	55%	76%	23%

Rep. Bernard Sanders (I)

Elected 1990; 8th term

CAPITOL OFFICE
225-4115
bernie.house.gov
2233 Rayburn 20515-4501; fax 225-6790

COMMITTEES
Financial Services
Government Reform

HOMETOWN
Burlington

BORN
Sept. 8, 1941, Brooklyn, N.Y.

RELIGION
Jewish

FAMILY
Wife, Jane O'Meara Sanders; one child, three stepchildren

EDUCATION
U. of Chicago, B.A. 1964 (political science)

CAREER
Professor; freelance writer; documentary filmmaker; Head Start assistant teacher

POLITICAL HIGHLIGHTS
Liberty Union candidate for U.S. Senate, 1972; Liberty Union candidate for governor, 1972; Liberty Union candidate for U.S. Senate, 1974; Liberty Union candidate for governor, 1976; mayor of Burlington, 1981-89; independent candidate for governor, 1986; independent candidate for U.S. House, 1988

ELECTION RESULTS

2004 GENERAL

Bernard Sanders (I, PRO)	205,774	67.5%
Greg Parke (R)	74,271	24.4%
Larry Drown (D)	21,684	7.1%
Jane Newton (LU)	3,018	1.0%

2002 GENERAL

Bernard Sanders (I)	144,880	64.3%
William Meub (R)	72,813	32.3%
Jane Newton (PRO)	3,185	1.4%
Fawn Skinner (VG)	2,344	1.0%
others	2,254	1.0%

PREVIOUS WINNING PERCENTAGES
2000 (69%); 1998 (63%); 1996 (55%); 1994 (50%); 1992 (58%); 1990 (56%)

A rumpled appearance and informal manner — he calls himself "Bernie" and encourages others to do the same — might give the impression that Sanders is a lightweight. But his low-key demeanor belies a passionate activism and willingness to make himself heard for a cause he feels is just. One of these days, he may yet seek a bigger megaphone.

A self-styled "Democratic socialist," Sanders and Vermont's junior senator, James M. Jeffords, are the only independents serving in Congress. Both caucus with the Democrats, but Jeffords is a former Republican while Sanders is the founder of the Progressive Caucus, a group of the most liberal members of the House.

Sanders has said that he will run for Jeffords' seat in the Senate in 2006. Jeffords plans to retire at the end of his term.

These days, Sanders pays homage to his progressive roots with a plaque on the wall of his Capitol Hill office honoring Eugene V. Debs, founder of the American Socialist Party. He is the chamber's first identifiable socialist since Victor L. Berger of Wisconsin, who served four terms in the 1910s and 1920s. Sanders has harsh words for both the Republican and Democratic parties. He once told a Washington Post online chat audience, "I am not a Republican or a Democrat, and the reason I am not is because both parties are heavily influenced by big money."

Though he voted with the majority of House Democrats 98 percent of the time in 2004, his relations with party leaders have not always been warm. Sanders was initially blocked from joining the party caucus by colleagues who thought the presence of a declared socialist would be politically risky. In a compromise, he stayed out of the caucus for several years and was given committee assignments by the Democrats, rising to the top minority spot on a Banking (now Financial Services) subcommittee in 1998.

Sanders regularly assails "corporate greed," argues the case for workers' rights, and demands protection of civil liberties. In 2003, he battled political and procedural pitfalls to promote legislative language limiting the ability of federal prosecutors to obtain information about the reading habits of library and bookstore patrons. "The American people have the right to take books out of the library without the FBI and the American government knowing what they are reading," Sanders said.

In 2005, he was one of 38 House members to vote against increased fines for broadcast indecency, declaring, "As someone who last year voted in favor of similar legislation, I am increasingly alarmed by the culture of censorship that seems to be developing in this country. . . . This censorship is being conducted by the corporate owners of our increasingly consolidated, less-diverse media. And it is being done by the government. This result is an insidious chill on free expression on our airwaves."

Sanders opposes foreign trade agreements that he says put U.S. workers at a disadvantage, and favors a sizable increase in the minimum wage. In the 108th Congress, he introduced legislation to end normalized trade relations with China, arguing that the massive U.S. trade deficit with that nation is hurting American workers and propping up a regime notorious for human rights violations. Along with libertarian Republican Ron Paul of Texas, Sanders also introduced legislation to block federal financial assistance to companies that outsource U.S. jobs to overseas labor markets. He and Paul also teamed up on a measure in the 109th to withdraw the United States from the World Trade Organization.

www.cqpress.com

Sanders says a national health care system would solve the problem of rising health care costs. He was one of the first lawmakers to organize bus trips for senior citizens to go to Canada to fill their prescriptions at a fraction of the U.S. cost and a strong advocate of allowing drug imports from Canada and other nations.

Sanders hoped to get a seat on Appropriations in the 108th Congress, having been promised one by Democratic leader Richard A. Gephardt back in 1999. Sanders declined to run for the Senate in 2000 and for governor in 2002 based, in part, on that promise. But, with the GOP increasing its majority in the 108th, there were few vacancies, and Sanders retained the same two committees — Financial Services and Government Reform — he has had since he arrived on Capitol Hill.

Sanders was born and raised in Brooklyn, where his father, an immigrant from Poland, was a paint salesman. His political philosophy was largely influenced by his older brother and then by his experiences as a student at the University of Chicago. After taking some graduate courses and working for Head Start, he left New York in 1968, part of a wave of liberals abandoning urban life for Vermont's green acres.

While many of his fellow transplants flocked to the Democratic Party, Sanders helped found Vermont's anti-capitalist, anti-Vietnam War Liberty Union Party, from which he ran for statewide office four times in the early 1970s. He never captured more than 6 percent of the vote, but the strong grass-roots base he built paid off in 1981 when he unseated the Democratic incumbent by 10 votes to become Burlington's first socialist mayor. He won three more two-year terms by increasing margins, pursuing populist goals while presiding over the revitalization of the city's downtown.

Sanders was seen as a spoiler when he ran in 1988 for Vermont's lone House seat, vacated when Republican Jeffords, who later became an independent himself, left to run for the Senate. Still, Sanders lost to Republican Peter Smith by only 4 percentage points. When the two squared off in 1990, Smith's efforts to paint Sanders as an admirer of Communist Cuban dictator Fidel Castro backfired, and Sanders won with 56 percent of the vote.

In 1992, he won re-election comfortably against Tim Philbin, a favorite of the state GOP's conservative wing, but he barely held on in 1994, a banner year for Republicans nationwide. In 1996, he prevailed over two major-party opponents with 55 percent. His vote share rose above 60 percent in 1998 and stayed there. In 2004, he carried more than two-thirds of the vote against a Republican, a Democrat and a Liberty Union Party candidate.

KEY VOTES

2004

Yes	Extend federal unemployment benefits by 13 weeks
Yes	Pass $283.2 billion, six-year federal highway and mass transit bill
Yes	Approve $146 billion multi-year extension of previously enacted middle-class tax breaks
No	Amend the Constitution to prohibit same-sex marriage
No	Cut corporate taxes $137 billion over 10 years
Yes	Reorganize U.S. intelligence agencies as proposed by Sept. 11 commission

2003

No	Cut taxes by $330 billion through fiscal 2013
Yes	Block Bush rule scaling back overtime pay for some white-collar federal workers
Yes	Do not allow use of search warrants without first notifying subjects
Yes	Allow importation of prescription drugs
No	Create private school voucher program in Washington, D.C.
No	Ban "partial birth" abortion except to save a woman's life
Yes	Split $18.6 billion in Iraq aid into half-grant, half-loan
No	Overhaul Medicare and create prescription drug benefit

CQ VOTE STUDIES

	PARTY UNITY		PRESIDENTIAL SUPPORT	
	Support	Oppose	Support	Oppose
2004	98%	2%	29%	71%
2003	95%	5%	15%	85%
2002	98%	2%	18%	82%
2001	97%	3%	16%	84%
2000	96%	4%	78%	22%

INTEREST GROUPS

	AFL-CIO	ADA	CCUS	ACU
2004	100%	95%	30%	4%
2003	100%	100%	14%	20%
2002	100%	95%	16%	0%
2001	100%	100%	22%	8%
2000	100%	95%	23%	4%

VERMONT
At large

Resting on the shores of Lake Champlain and rolling through the rustic Green Mountains, the second-least-populous state in the nation feels like a good, small-town neighbor.

Small businesses mix with dairy farms and manufacturing plants, as well as with the electronics companies that arrived in the 1980s. While the technology boom died down in the early 1990s, the state has continued to try to reignite it. Officials also are hoping to convince tourists to visit the state year-round, so prevalent on the ski slopes in winter, to visit the state year-round, although none of Vermont's attractions are advertised on roadside billboards — state law prohibits them.

A growth spurt that began in the early 1960s, when people outnumbered cows for the first time, has altered the state's political profile. Once a bastion of Yankee Republicanism, the state moved solidly to the left with the 1980s and 1990s influx of young liberal urbanites, who joined the remnants of the late-1960s counterculture settlers. In state and federal elections, the strong progressive contingency based in Burlington and

surrounding Chittenden County usually outvotes the numerous Yankee libertarian conservatives, based mostly in East Montpelier and some of the Burlington suburbs. Rural areas of the state, especially the Northeast Kingdom, also hold a few Republican votes. Democrats dominate the central swath of land along Interstates 89 and 91, as well as the southeast corner. Many small urban centers, such as Montpelier and Rutland, once reliably Republican, now have more Democrats.

Vermont's decision in 2000 to become the first state to recognize same-gender civil unions briefly energized a wave of social conservatism, but the quiet state tired of the controversy and the anticipated backlash quickly fizzled.

MAJOR INDUSTRY
Manufacturing, tourism, dairy farming

CITIES
Burlington, 38,889; Essex, 18,626; Rutland, 17,292; Colchester, 16,986

NOTABLE
In Bristol, the Lord's Prayer Rock stands beside a road — Dr. Joseph Greene had the prayer carved in the rock in 1891, hoping wagon drivers would stop cursing their horses during the muddy season; Ben & Jerry's ice cream was started in Burlington in an old gas station.

Gov. Mark Warner (D)

First elected: 2001
Length of term: 4 years
Term expires: 1/06
Salary: $124,855
Phone: (804) 786-2211

Hometown: Alexandria
Born: Dec. 15, 1954; Indianapolis, Ind.
Religion: Presbyterian
Family: Wife, Lisa Collis; three children
Education: George Washington U., B.A. 1977 (political science); Harvard U., J.D. 1980
Career: Technology venture capitalist; campaign manager
Political highlights: Va. Democratic Party chairman, 1993-95; Democratic nominee for U.S. Senate, 1996

Election results:

2001 GENERAL

Mark Warner (D)	984,177	52.2%
Mark Earley (R)	887,234	47.0%

Lt. Gov. Tim Kaine (D)

First elected: 2001
Length of term: 4 years
Term expires: 1/06
Salary: $36,321
Phone: (804) 786-2078

STATE LEGISLATURE

General Assembly: 60 days January-March in even-numbered years; 40 days January-February in odd-numbered years

House: 100 members, 2-year terms
2005 breakdown: 60R, 38D, 2I; 87 men, 13 women
Salary: $17,640; $117/day in session
Phone: (804) 698-1500

Senate: 40 members, 4-year terms
2005 breakdown: 24R, 16D; 32 men, 8 women
Salary: $18,000; $117/day in session
Phone: (804) 698-7410

STATE TERM LIMITS

Governor: Cannot serve consecutive terms
House: No
Senate: No

URBAN STATISTICS

CITY	POPULATION
Virginia Beach	425,257
Norfolk	234,403
Chesapeake	199,184
Richmond	197,790
Newport News	180,150

REGISTERED VOTERS

Voters do not register by party.

POPULATION

2004 population (est.)	7,459,827
2000 population	7,078,515
1990 population	6,187,358
Percent change (1990-2000)	+14.4%
Rank among states (2004)	12

Median age	35.7
Born in state	51.9%
Foreign born	8.1%
Violent crime rate	282/100,000
Poverty level	9.6%
Federal workers	156,871
Military	170,046

REDISTRICTING

Virginia retained its 11 House seats in reapportionment. The state legislature drew a new map, which the governor signed on July 19, 2001.

MISCELLANEOUS

Web: www.virginia.gov
Capital: Richmond
STATE ELECTION OFFICIAL
(804) 864-8901
DEMOCRATIC HEADQUARTERS
(804) 644-1966
REPUBLICAN HEADQUARTERS
(804) 780-0111

District Statistics

DIST.	2004 VOTE FOR PRESIDENT BUSH	KERRY	WHITE	BLACK	ASIAN	HISP	MEDIAN INCOME	WHITE COLLAR	BLUE COLLAR	SERVICE INDUSTRY	OVER 64	UNDER 18	COLLEGE EDUCATION	RURAL	SQ. MILES
1	60%	39%	75%	18%	2%	3%	$50,257	63%	23%	14%	11%	26%	27%	36%	3,773
2	58	42	67	21	4	4	$44,193	63	22	15	9	26	26	8	961
3	33	66	38	56	1	3	$32,238	55	26	19	12	26	17	8	1,118
4	57	43	62	33	1	2	$45,249	58	28	14	11	27	20	29	4,489
5	56	43	72	24	1	2	$35,739	53	33	14	15	23	19	64	8,922
6	63	36	85	11	1	2	$37,773	56	29	15	15	22	21	35	5,647
7	61	38	78	16	2	2	$50,990	68	20	12	12	25	33	30	3,514
8	35	64	57	13	9	16	$63,430	77	11	12	9	20	54	0	123
9	59	39	93	4	1	1	$29,783	49	36	15	15	21	14	66	8,803
10	55	44	77	7	7	7	$71,560	72	16	11	7	28	43	17	1,856
11	50	49	67	10	11	9	$80,397	77	12	12	8	27	49	4	388
STATE	54	45	70	19	4	5	$46,677	64	23	14	11	25	30	27	39,594
U.S.	50.7	48.3	69	12	4	13	$41,994	60	25	15	12	26	24	21	3,537,438

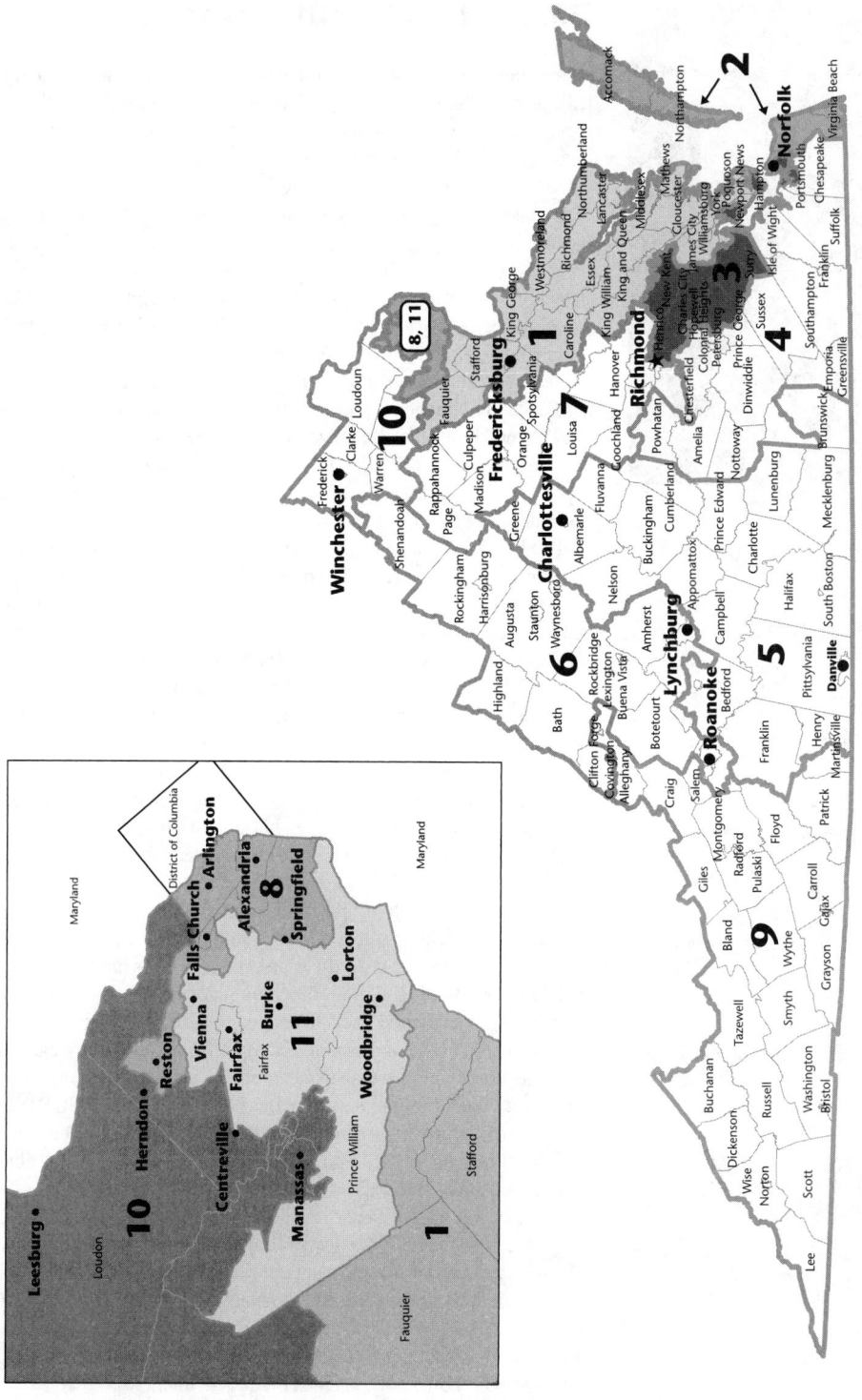

Sen. John W. Warner (R)

Elected 1978; 5th term

Warner wields a unique brand of gentlemanly clout in the national security debates that have occupied Congress since Sept. 11, 2001. He has been at the center of events as the Senate has acted out in microcosm the country's conflicts over the Iraq war, the struggle against al Qaeda and the merits of higher defense spending.

To all of those arguments, Warner has brought his personal zest for the issues, his instinct for developing consensus solutions and his aptitude for Senate politics. And while many members seem obsessed with writing finely calibrated messages to foster a politically appealing image, Warner pursues his high-profile policy agenda with the insouciance of an elder statesman who is comfortable in his skin.

Warner had chaired the Armed Services Committee from 1999 until 2001, when Republican James M. Jeffords of Vermont turned independent and aligned himself with the Democrats to give them control of the Senate. In the 2002 elections, Republicans regained the majority and Warner resumed his chairmanship of Armed Services. He is scheduled to keep the job until the 110th Congress begins in 2007.

But that is not his only platform of influence on national security issues. Under the 2004 reorganization of Senate intelligence oversight, the Armed Services chairman serves as an ex officio member of the Intelligence Committee. And at the start of the 109th, Warner also joined a beefed-up Homeland Security and Governmental Affairs Committee, relinquishing his seat on Health, Education, Labor and Pensions to do so. Carl Levin of Michigan, top-ranking Democrat on Armed Services, is the only other senator to serve on all three panels. He and Warner work together like an old married couple, even though they are not always on the same page politically.

Warner still displays a grandiloquent speaking style that almost defies parody. Early in his Senate career, his stentorian voice, combined with his rugged good looks and marriage to actress Elizabeth Taylor, led some to dismiss him as a wealthy dilettante. But those days are long gone. Today, Warner has no need to establish his bona fides.

Warner's palpable self-confidence may reflect his dominance of Virginia's electoral arena. Over the years, conservatives have railed against his independent streak and moderation on many issues, such as gun control. But Warner has turned back all challenges, from the right and left.

The most recent and visible example of his autonomy came in May 2004, as horrifying photos surfaced of U.S. soldiers abusing Iraqi prisoners at the Abu Ghraib prison near Baghdad. While some GOP lawmakers sought to minimize the matter, Warner bucked the White House and many of his colleagues by summoning the military brass to high-profile public hearings. Although he did not institute an independent Armed Services probe, Warner in all other ways shone a harsh light on the abuses.

"Most significant," Warner said at the time, "the replaying of these images day after day throughout the Middle East, and indeed the world, has the potential to undermine the substantial gains — emphasize the substantial gains — toward the goal of peace and freedom in various operation areas of the world, most particularly Iraq, and the substantial sacrifice by our forces and those of our allies in the war on terror."

In another display of independence, Warner's committee held numerous hearings in 2004 on the Iraq war, at which Republicans and Democrats alike criticized what they termed the administration's lack of preparedness for

CAPITOL OFFICE
224-2023
warner.senate.gov
225 Russell 20510-4601; fax 224-6295

COMMITTEES
Armed Services - chairman
Environment & Public Works
Homeland Security & Governmental Affairs

HOMETOWN
Alexandria

BORN
Feb. 18, 1927, Washington, D.C.

RELIGION
Episcopalian

FAMILY
Wife, Jeanne Warner; three children

EDUCATION
Washington and Lee U., B.S. 1949 (engineering);
U. of Virginia, LL.B. 1953

MILITARY SERVICE
Navy, 1944-46; Marine Corps, 1950-52; Marine Corps Reserve, 1952-64

CAREER
Lawyer; farmer

POLITICAL HIGHLIGHTS
Assistant U.S. attorney, 1956-60; under secretary of the Navy, 1969-72; secretary of the Navy, 1972-74

ELECTION RESULTS

2002 GENERAL

John W. Warner (R)	1,229,894	82.6%
Nancy Spannaus (I)	145,102	9.7%
Jacob G. Hornberger Jr. (I)	106,055	7.1%

2002 PRIMARY

John W. Warner (R)	unopposed

PREVIOUS WINNING PERCENTAGES
1996 (52%); 1990 (81%); 1984 (70%); 1978 (50%)

what would follow the fall of Baghdad. Warner also joined Levin and Republican John McCain of Arizona in demanding that the Pentagon turn over internal e-mails revealing Defense Department officials' sometimes bare-knuckled advocacy of a controversial $23.5 billion proposal to obtain midair refueling tankers from the Boeing Co.

In the closing controversy of the 108th Congress — the reorganization of U.S. intelligence agencies — Warner joined his sometime rival and fellow Republican, House Armed Services Chairman Duncan Hunter of California, in opposing a conference report, which had the support of the president, until it was altered to assuage their concerns that it could imperil the flow of intelligence to U.S. troops in the field.

While Warner has cut his own path when necessary, he has acted in concert with others when possible, with much work done out of public view. When Senate Majority Leader Trent Lott in December 2002 seemed to laud the segregationist platform on which retiring Sen. Strom Thurmond had run for president in 1948, Warner was one of the first Senate heavyweights to quietly begin engineering Lott's replacement by Tennessee's Bill Frist.

Warner has shown attention to detail and legislative savvy. He informs himself and influences his colleagues through personal observation and face-to-face conversation, rather than through think-tank seminars and academic analyses. He makes trips to see U.S. troops in gritty backwaters, as when in October 2001, he and Levin were the first elected officials to visit U.S. troops in Pakistan.

Warner has been a loyal Republican on most defense issues that divide the two parties. In 2002, for instance, he led an unprecedented party-line revolt by Armed Services Republicans against the Democratic majority's effort to rein in Bush's anti-missile defense program — an initiative the Democrats dropped in the face of a veto threat.

During the 1980s, however, Warner angered some party colleagues by favoring compromise when fellow Republicans wanted a showdown, on such issues, for example, as the deployment of anti-satellite weapons and U.S. ships in the Persian Gulf. And many Republicans complained that he did not do enough to salvage the 1989 nomination of a former Armed Services chairman, John Tower of Texas, to be secretary of defense in the first Bush administration.

In a move widely regarded as payback for that, Thurmond, who had yielded the senior Republican slot on Armed Services to Warner, reasserted his seniority in 1993. Warner assiduously began shoring up his party standing. When Thurmond became Armed Services chairman in 1995 at the age of 92, Warner took on the delicate task of quietly keeping the panel on course. When Thurmond stepped down as chairman four years later, there was no challenge to Warner's succession.

Warner has never been the choice of conservatives among Virginia's Republicans. Some saw him as a socialite and fortune hunter. Before his marriage to Taylor, he was married to heiress Catherine Mellon and received a reported $7 million from her in their divorce settlement.

He became the party's Senate nominee in 1978 only after their pick, Richard Obenshain, died in a plane crash two months after defeating Warner at the state GOP convention. On the campaign trail, Taylor's celebrity guaranteed large crowds, and Warner held on to win by fewer than 5,000 votes in the closest Senate election in Virginia history.

He won re-election handily in 1984 and 1990, but in 1996, after fending off an intraparty challenge, he was held to 52 percent of the vote by Democrat Mark Warner, a cellular telephone entrepreneur (and now governor) who spent more than $10 million of his own money to challenge the incumbent. In 2002, however, Warner drew no Democratic opponent.

KEY VOTES

2004
Yes Pass $318.9 billion, six-year highway and mass transit bill
Yes Extend assault weapons ban for 10 years
No Restore pay-as-you-go rules for new tax cuts and entitlement spending
Yes Criminalize harm to a fetus in an attack on the mother
Yes Increase mandatory child care funding to states by $6 billion over five years
Yes Amend the Constitution to prohibit same-sex marriage
Yes Approve $146 billion multi-year extension of previously enacted middle-class tax breaks
Yes Reorganize U.S. intelligence agencies as proposed by Sept. 11 commission
Yes Cut corporate taxes $137 billion over 10 years

2003
No Delay Bush changes to Clean Air Act
Yes Allow confirmation vote on Miguel A. Estrada to the U.S. Court of Appeals for the D.C. Circuit
No Block a Bush proposal opening Alaska's Arctic National Wildlife Refuge to oil drilling
No Limit size of Bush's proposed tax cut to $350 billion through fiscal 2013
Yes Overhaul Medicare and create prescription drug benefit
No Block Bush rule scaling back overtime pay for some white-collar federal workers
No Split $20 billion in Iraq aid into half-grant, half-loan
Yes Ban "partial birth" abortion except to save a woman's life
No Stop proposal allowing travel to Cuba
Yes Allow final vote on energy policy overhaul

CQ VOTE STUDIES

	PARTY UNITY		PRESIDENTIAL SUPPORT	
	Support	Oppose	Support	Oppose
2004	88%	12%	90%	10%
2003	95%	5%	97%	3%
2002	82%	18%	91%	9%
2001	85%	15%	96%	4%
2000	92%	8%	52%	48%
1999	87%	13%	39%	61%
1998	85%	15%	39%	61%
1997	89%	11%	67%	33%
1996	93%	7%	42%	58%
1995	94%	6%	26%	74%

INTEREST GROUPS

	AFL-CIO	ADA	CCUS	ACU
2004	17%	25%	100%	72%
2003	0%	10%	100%	80%
2002	31%	15%	95%	79%
2001	25%	20%	86%	96%
2000	0%	0%	100%	92%
1999	0%	10%	100%	84%
1998	13%	20%	100%	79%
1997	0%	10%	100%	80%
1996	0%	5%	85%	95%
1995	0%	5%	100%	91%

Sen. George Allen (R)

Elected 2000; 1st term

CAPITOL OFFICE
224-4024
allen.senate.gov
204 Russell 20510-4604; fax 224-5432

COMMITTEES
Commerce, Science & Transportation
(Consumer Affairs, Product Safety & Insurance
- chairman)
Energy & Natural Resources
Foreign Relations
(European Affairs - chairman)
Small Business & Entrepreneurship

HOMETOWN
Mount Vernon

BORN
March 8, 1952, Whittier, Calif.

RELIGION
Presbyterian

FAMILY
Wife, Susan Allen; three children

EDUCATION
U. of Virginia, B.A. 1974 (history), J.D. 1977

CAREER
Lawyer

POLITICAL HIGHLIGHTS
Republican nominee for Va. House, 1979; Va.
House, 1982-91; U.S. House, 1991-93; governor,
1994-98

ELECTION RESULTS

2000 GENERAL

George Allen (R)	1,420,460	52.3%
Charles S. Robb (D)	1,296,093	47.7%

2000 PRIMARY

George Allen (R)	unopposed

PREVIOUS WINNING PERCENTAGES
1991 House Special Election (62%)

After a successful stint as quarterback of the Senate Republicans' 2004 campaign team, Allen, a former college football star who likes to carry pigskins to press events, kicked off the 109th Congress with no current leadership role but plenty of ambition. The only question was how far he hoped to advance the ball.

The son of a Hall of Fame football coach for the National Football League's Washington Redskins and Los Angeles Rams, Allen likens primaries to "intrasquad scrimmages," his staff to the "A-team," freshman colleagues to "rookies" and the between-sessions Senate recess to "halftime." Although no longer chairman of the National Republican Senatorial Committee, Allen remains one of Senate Majority Leader Bill Frist's closest confidants and could become one of his toughest rivals if both seek the GOP's presidential nomination in 2008.

Speculation about Allen's future arose in early 2005 after he hired highly regarded political strategist Dick Wadhams as his chief of staff. He made what the news media portrayed as a candidate-like appearance in February at the Conservative Political Action Conference, where he declared that "the state of our conservative union is vibrant, energized, innovating and moving forward," according to the Newport News Daily Press. In a straw poll of more than 600 conference participants, Allen drew 11 percent of the vote — enough to tie fellow GOP senators Bill Frist of Tennessee and John McCain of Arizona for third place.

Allen shares some traits with President Bush. Both are former governors and sons of famous men. Both have President Reagan's knack for projecting an amiable, regular-guy persona. (Allen co-chaired Young Virginians for Reagan during Reagan's 1976 challenge to President Ford.) Allen's fondness for chewing tobacco is well-known, and he seems equally at ease in a business suit or jeans and cowboy boots. Detractors also say neither Bush nor Allen can be considered particularly intellectual.

Allen has brushed off talk of a possible White House bid by emphasizing his commitment to winning re-election in 2006. He is likely to face difficulty only if popular Democratic Virginia Gov. Mark Warner — who also was seen to be eyeing a presidential bid — decides to challenge him.

Allen first gained entry to Frist's inner circle in December 2002, when he approached Frist and urged him to challenge Trent Lott of Mississippi for the top Senate GOP job, just days after Lott ignited a political furor with his praise for Strom Thurmond's 1948 segregationist presidential campaign. Allen had concluded that sticking with Lott as leader would imperil the GOP majority in 2004. When Frist did not dismiss Allen's suggestion, the Virginian, with home-state colleague John W. Warner and a few other senators, began testing support for Frist among other senators. After those checks, it was Allen who telephoned Mississippi to deliver the news to Lott that his claim to the job was eroding fast. Lott stepped aside as leader two days later, by which point Frist had locked up the race to replace him.

Frist had served as chairman of the Republican campaign committee in the 107th Congress, and with his tacit blessing, Allen was elected chairman for the 108th without opposition. He then earned his own political capital by helping his party pick up a net four seats and expand its majority from 51 to 55 seats — a big gain that will help Bush and Republican leaders muscle their agenda through the famously obstinate chamber.

Despite his conservatism and his partisan activities, Allen has worked successfully with Democrats on high-tech issues and other matters dear to him. He joined forces with Democrat Ron Wyden of Oregon in the 108th Congress to reinstate a ban on state taxation of Internet access, a top priority of the technology industry. In the 107th, he helped devise the compromise that led to enactment of a law aimed at creating a child-friendly zone on the Internet.

Allen also has teamed with liberal Democrat Barbara Boxer of California on a plan to sell part of the federally controlled broadcast spectrum to Internet providers that want to supply customers with wireless access. And with Louisiana Democrat Mary L. Landrieu, he introduced legislation in 2004 to have the Senate apologize for failing to pass legislation years ago that would have banned the lynching of blacks and others — an oversight Allen described as "just flat wrong and downright shameful."

Allen is attentive to Virginia's parochial interests, pressing for a reopening of Ronald Reagan Washington National Airport to private plane traffic that has been banned there since the Sept. 11, 2001, terrorist attacks. He champions the concerns of the high-tech industry, which has a huge presence in Northern Virginia; his seat on the Commerce, Science and Transportation Committee and his chairmanship of the Senate GOP High Tech Task Force give him considerable clout on technology policy.

Allen also serves on the Foreign Relations Committee, where he chairs the European Affairs Subcommittee. It is another good match for Virginia, which has a substantial military presence and thus an acute concern about world affairs. Allen's senior colleague, Warner, covers the other half of U.S. global policy as chairman of the Armed Services Committee. Allen is a stalwart defender of the administration's actions in Iraq and elsewhere overseas, saying he prefers not to go public with all of his concerns. "I don't see that as being beneficial — publicly criticizing our own team and our own leaders who are trying to do the best they can," he said in January 2005.

Allen is broadening his legislative portfolio in the 109th, claiming a seat on the Energy and Natural Resources Committee. His assignment prompted ethics questions from the Virginia media — Allen's wife, Susan, held a seat on the board of directors of Virginia-based energy company Dominion Resources Inc. She resigned from the board in January 2005, saying she did not want her husband to feel limited on what he could do on the panel.

Allen has a gold-plated political résumé. In 1982, he won a seat in the state House, beating the Democratic incumbent who had defeated him in his initial foray three years earlier. After serving nine years in the General Assembly, Allen easily won a special House election in 1991 to replace Republican D. French Slaughter Jr., who resigned in the face of declining health.

Allen did not seek a full term, however, after a Democratic-drawn redistricting plan put his home in the same district as veteran Republican Thomas J. Bliley Jr. Instead, Allen launched a long campaign for governor, which ended with his easy 1993 victory over Democratic state Attorney General Mary Sue Terry. As governor, he focused on abolishing parole and attracting high-tech industry to Virginia. His popularity helped spark a surge that carried the GOP to its current dominance in Virginia politics.

Barred by state law from succeeding himself, Allen left office in 1998. But he quickly geared up for another long campaign to unseat two-term Democratic Sen. Charles S. Robb. The son-in-law of President Lyndon B. Johnson and once a towering political figure in Virginia, Robb never recovered from a spate of questions about his personal life, and his cold demeanor contrasted poorly with Allen's backslapping fellowship. Allen gained an early advantage in campaign fundraising and moved quickly to secure support in populous Northern Virginia, Robb's home base. He won by 5 percentage points.

KEY VOTES

2004

Yes Pass $318.9 billion, six-year highway and mass transit bill

No Extend assault weapons ban for 10 years

No Restore pay-as-you-go rules for new tax cuts and entitlement spending

Yes Criminalize harm to a fetus in an attack on the mother

No Increase mandatory child care funding to states by $6 billion over five years

Yes Amend the Constitution to prohibit same-sex marriage

Yes Approve $146 billion multi-year extension of previously enacted middle-class tax breaks

Yes Reorganize U.S. intelligence agencies as proposed by Sept. 11 commission

Yes Cut corporate taxes $137 billion over 10 years

2003

No Delay Bush changes to Clean Air Act

Yes Allow confirmation vote on Miguel A. Estrada to the U.S. Court of Appeals for the D.C. Circuit

No Block a Bush proposal opening Alaska's Arctic National Wildlife Refuge to oil drilling

No Limit size of Bush's proposed tax cut to $350 billion through fiscal 2013

Yes Overhaul Medicare and create prescription drug benefit

No Block Bush rule scaling back overtime pay for some white-collar federal workers

No Split $20 billion in Iraq aid into half-grant, half-loan

Yes Ban "partial birth" abortion except to save a woman's life

Yes Stop proposal allowing travel to Cuba

Yes Allow final vote on energy policy overhaul

CQ VOTE STUDIES

	PARTY UNITY		PRESIDENTIAL SUPPORT	
	Support	Oppose	Support	Oppose
2004	94%	6%	96%	4%
2003	98%	2%	98%	2%
2002	90%	10%	93%	7%
2001	93%	7%	97%	3%
House Service:				
1992	95%	5%	78%	22%
1991	86%	14%	69%	31%

INTEREST GROUPS

	AFL-CIO	ADA	CCUS	ACU
2004	17%	15%	100%	92%
2003	0%	5%	100%	85%
2002	23%	10%	95%	84%
2001	13%	15%	100%	96%
House Service:				
1992	25%	15%	75%	88%
1991	33%	—	—	100%

Rep. Jo Ann Davis (R)

Elected 2000; 3rd term

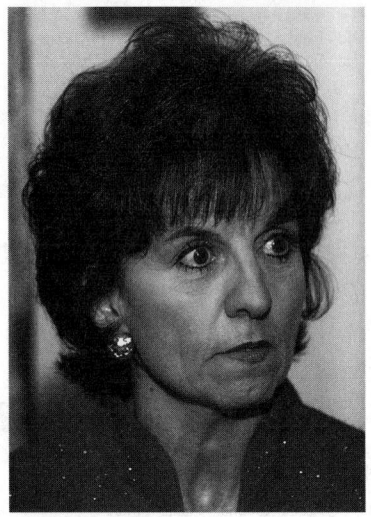

CAPITOL OFFICE
225-4261
www.house.gov/joanndavis
1123 Longworth 20515-4601; fax 225-4382

COMMITTEES
Armed Services
International Relations
Select Intelligence
(Intelligence Policy - chairwoman)

HOMETOWN
Gloucester

BORN
June 29, 1950, Rowan, N.C.

RELIGION
Assemblies of God

FAMILY
Husband, Chuck Davis; two children

EDUCATION
Kecoughtan H.S., graduated 1968

CAREER
Realtor; administrative assistant

POLITICAL HIGHLIGHTS
Va. House, 1998-2001

ELECTION RESULTS

2004 GENERAL

Jo Ann Davis (R)	225,071	78.6%
William A. Lee (I)	57,434	20.0%
write-ins	4,029	1.4%

2004 PRIMARY

Jo Ann Davis (R)	unopposed

2002 GENERAL

Jo Ann Davis (R)	113,168	95.9%
write-ins	4,829	4.1%

PREVIOUS WINNING PERCENTAGES
2000 (58%)

Davis is a classic American success story — a woman who has risen from humble beginnings to wield influence on one of the most important issues of our time: national intelligence policy. Davis, who quit college after one day because she was homesick, now chairs the Intelligence Committee's Subcommittee on Intelligence Policy. Its job is to identify and analyze emerging threats to U.S. national security and recommend what the intelligence community should do to respond.

She is one of Congress' most determined and vocal advocates for the Defense Department, which employs many of her constituents, and she is a staunch conservative on social policy issues.

Davis is one of three junior GOP lawmakers from the Tidewater area — Thelma Drake and J. Randy Forbes are the others — who serve on the House Armed Services Committee. Their predecessors, Republicans Herbert H. Bateman and Owen B. Pickett and Democrat Norman Sisisky, had a combined service record of almost a half-century on the committee and gave the Tidewater extraordinary clout. The region's lawmakers, however, can argue that their clout is not disproportionate, because the area is home to the shipbuilding cities of Newport News and Hampton as well as numerous military installations, including Norfolk Naval Base, which is the world's largest.

Davis often takes to the House floor to pay tribute to the military, occasionally giving speeches in recognition of servicemen, firefighters or other "fallen heroes" killed in the line of duty. (Her husband is a retired firefighter.) Over the course of eight days in late 2001 and early 2002, she stood in the well of the House to lead a reading of the names of every known victim of the Sept. 11, 2001, terrorist attacks.

One of Davis' first legislative victories came after only a few months in office, when she won approval of legislation to expand the Servicemembers' Group Life Insurance program to include spouses and children of veterans. The changes were retroactive, to cover service members killed in the terrorist attack on the *USS Cole* in Yemen in October 2000, as well as national guardsmen (including 18 from Virginia) who were killed in an airplane crash in March 2001.

On Armed Services, Davis led an effort in 2001 to increase funding for a major overhaul of the aircraft carrier *Dwight D. Eisenhower* at the Newport News shipyard. In 2005, she and Democrat Gene Taylor of Mississippi formed the Congressional Shipbuilding Caucus, issuing a call for the Navy to build more ships. "Navy shipbuilding is facing some of its deepest cuts in years," Davis warned. "This is detrimental to our national security as we protect America in the global war on terror."

Davis affiliates with the Republican Study Committee, a group of the most conservative members of the House GOP. She opposes abortion, including in cases of rape or incest, and she boasts a grade of "A" from the National Rifle Association.

She is a firm opponent of same-sex marriage and has introduced legislation to define marriage in the District of Columbia as "the union of one man and one woman." In the 108th Congress, she was talked out of attaching her proposal to the annual spending bill that funds the District of Columbia, a measure that is often used to test the effects of a policy on a local level before trying to implement it nationwide. She reintroduced the bill early in the 109th.

Sometimes, though, Davis will stray from the conservative Republican line. Early in the 109th, she joined an ideologically mixed group of 43 House Republicans in protesting proposed Medicaid funding cuts in the annual congressional budget resolution. Leaders in her party were pushing for the cuts in an effort to rein in spending.

Davis also has opposed her party on other issues, voting against drilling for oil in national monument areas, against cutting sugar subsidies and against mandatory testing for third- and eighth-graders. In 2002, she was one of only 27 House Republicans who voted against enacting the law that gave President Bush fast-track authority to negotiate trade deals that Congress cannot amend.

A North Carolina native, Davis moved with her family to the Tidewater area when she was 9. Her father worked at a number of blue-collar jobs, and both he and her mother played in a bluegrass band. She says she lived in trailers for much of her childhood. Religion plays a large role in her life. She told the Richmond Times-Dispatch that her model in seeking to overcome her youthful shyness was her father, an outgoing person who made friends easily.

After briefly attending business college, Davis became a secretary for a real estate company and stayed for more than a decade. She later earned a real estate license at the suggestion of her former boss and opened her own firm. She went on to start two businesses — a management company and a real estate company. She was one of the founding partners of a worldwide network of real estate firms that specialize in helping military families relocate from one base to another.

Active in professional and civic organizations, Davis did not consider politics until a friend suggested it. She won a close election to the Virginia House in 1997, capitalizing on grass-roots support from conservatives.

Early in 2000, Davis was the first Republican to announce her candidacy when Rep. Bateman said his ninth term would be his last. (He died that September.) She was outspent by almost $1 million in the Republican primary by Paul Jost, a candidate who had the endorsement of GOP Gov. James S. Gilmore III. But Davis' strong support from district conservatives propelled her to a narrow victory in the five-way race.

The 1st District's solidly conservative character made it easy for Davis in November. She won by more than 20 percentage points, becoming the first Republican woman ever to represent Virginia in Congress. Redistricting did not alter the partisan tilt of the 1st, and she drew no Democratic opponent in 2002 or 2004.

KEY VOTES

2004

No	Extend federal unemployment benefits by 13 weeks
Yes	Pass $283.2 billion, six-year federal highway and mass transit bill
Yes	Approve $146 billion multi-year extension of previously enacted middle-class tax breaks
Yes	Amend the Constitution to prohibit same-sex marriage
Yes	Cut corporate taxes $137 billion over 10 years
No	Reorganize U.S. intelligence agencies as proposed by Sept. 11 commission

2003

Yes	Cut taxes by $330 billion through fiscal 2013
No	Block Bush rule scaling back overtime pay for some white-collar federal workers
Yes	Do not allow use of search warrants without first notifying subjects
Yes	Allow importation of prescription drugs
Yes	Create private school voucher program in Washington, D.C.
Yes	Ban "partial birth" abortion except to save a woman's life
No	Split $18.6 billion in Iraq aid into half-grant, half-loan
Yes	Overhaul Medicare and create prescription drug benefit

CQ VOTE STUDIES

	PARTY UNITY		PRESIDENTIAL SUPPORT	
	Support	Oppose	Support	Oppose
2004	91%	9%	76%	24%
2003	93%	7%	82%	18%
2002	96%	4%	82%	18%
2001	92%	8%	86%	14%

INTEREST GROUPS

	AFL-CIO	ADA	CCUS	ACU
2004	33%	10%	90%	88%
2003	27%	15%	80%	80%
2002	25%	5%	75%	96%
2001	17%	5%	83%	100%

VIRGINIA 1

East — parts of Newport News and Hampton, Fredericksburg

The Republican-friendly 1st lies along the Potomac River and Chesapeake Bay, stretching from outer Northern Virginia suburbs and exurbs of Washington, D.C., all the way south to the shipbuilding cities of Hampton and Newport News.

Industry in the 1st revolves around its military installations and NASA sites, which have attracted a growing technology private sector. Colleges and universities also contribute to the district's economic base, as do shipbuilding and tourism. The most popular tourist destinations — Williamsburg, Jamestown and Yorktown — recall Virginia's colonial past. Inland, agriculture and chickens help drive the economy.

Virginia's population expansion is not confined to the Washington suburbs. Spotsylvania County (one-fifth of which is in the 7th District) has experienced rapid growth as a result of its proximity to both Richmond and Washington and its location on the Interstate 95 corridor.

Spotsylvania's 58 percent growth in the 1990s was the third-fastest clip in the state. Stafford County, located just north of Fredericksburg, grew by nearly 50 percent in the 1990s, and is now the most populous county in the 1st.

Redistricting following the 2000 census shifted the 1st slightly north toward Washington. The new map removed parts of Newport News and Hampton and added parts of Prince William and Fauquier counties. The changes kept the 1st's solidly GOP orientation intact: George W. Bush took 60 percent in the 2004 presidential election, third-best in the state.

MAJOR INDUSTRY
Defense, technology, agriculture, tourism, higher education

MILITARY BASES
Marine Corps Base Quantico, 6,846 military, 3,300 civilian (2004); Naval Surface Warfare Center, Dahlgren Division, 500 military, 4,600 civilian; Yorktown Naval Weapons Station, 117 military, 1,229 civilian (2005); Fort A.P. Hill (Army), 153 military, 404 civilian (2004)

CITIES
Newport News (pt.), 71,800; Hampton (pt.), 31,755; Fredericksburg, 19,279

NOTABLE
Jamestown was the first English settlement in North America.

Rep. Thelma Drake (R)

Elected 2004; 1st term

Drake's socially conservative and anti-tax stances and her experience gained during almost a decade in the state general assembly eased her way to Congress and prepped her to step into multiple roles as her congressional tenure began in 2005.

She landed a seat on the Armed Services Committee, which Speaker J. Dennis Hastert had promised her during the campaign. The post has become expected for lawmakers from Virginia's Tidewater area since it is home to a number of key military installations.

The big issue, she says, is making sure "that our military has the most modern weapons systems, that they've got the armaments and the tools that they need to be on the front line." Shipyards employ thousands of district residents, and Drake supports the Navy's next-generation aircraft carrier, CVN-21. "I think that people here are concerned about the number of ships in our military." Drake sees the military as an instrument of job creation through partnerships with local colleges and universities.

She also was chosen by her freshman peers as their representative on the Republican leadership's Policy Committee and got assignments on the Education and Workforce Committee and the Resources panel.

Until late August 2004, Drake fully expected to return to Richmond in 2005 for her 10th year in the state House. But she quickly switched gears when she was hand-picked by local party officials as an emergency replacement nominee for the 2nd District seat after two-term GOP incumbent Ed Schrock unexpectedly decided to retire.

Though she had to jump-start her campaign, Drake never lost a grip on the Republicans' advantage in the conservative-leaning and military-oriented Tidewater district: She benefited from name recognition she had developed in her legislative career, the strong district showing by President Bush and aid from the state and national Republican parties. Although Democrat David Ashe, a Marine Corps veteran who served in Iraq, ran aggressively, Drake won by a comfortable 10 percentage point margin.

CAPITOL OFFICE
225-4215
drake.house.gov
1208 Rayburn 20515-4602; fax 225-4218

COMMITTEES
Armed Services
Education & Workforce
Resources

HOMETOWN
Norfolk

BORN
Nov. 20, 1949, Elyria, Ohio

RELIGION
United Church of Christ

FAMILY
Husband, Thomas E. "Ted" Drake; two children

EDUCATION
Elyria H.S., graduated 1967

CAREER
Realtor; siding company owner

POLITICAL HIGHLIGHTS
Republican nominee for Va. House, 1993; Va. House, 1996-2004

ELECTION RESULTS

2004 GENERAL

Thelma Drake (R)	132,946	55.1%
David Ashe (D)	108,180	44.8%

VIRGINIA 2

Southeast – Virginia Beach, parts of Norfolk and Hampton

The 2nd is dominated by Virginia Beach, a center for white-collar, suburban military families and retirees. It also extends north to include parts of Norfolk and Hampton and crosses the Chesapeake Bay inlet to reach Virginia's portion of the Eastern Shore.

Virginia Beach's tourism-driven population boom of the 1980s is over, but the area has held its ground in the face of military base closings. The Norfolk Naval Base continues to dominate the economy, which also is bolstered by shipbuilding and shipping companies. About two-thirds of the district's population lives in Virginia Beach.

The 2nd includes half of the city of Norfolk (shared with the 3rd), a largely blue-collar and Democratic-leaning area that was surpassed by Virginia Beach in the early 1980s as Virginia's most-populous city. Norfolk has lost population at about the same rate Virginia Beach has gained it.

The district is home to Pat Robertson's religious broadcast network. But the 2nd's conservatism derives more from military and economic issues than social questions. Voters here typically side with the GOP: Republicans hold most state legislative seats in Virginia Beach and have made major inroads in Norfolk.

MAJOR INDUSTRY
Military, tourism, shipbuilding

MILITARY BASES
Naval Station Norfolk, 64,000 military, 29,000 civilian (2004); Naval Air Station Oceana, 9,247 military, 2,545 civilian; Langley Air Force Base, 8,800 military, 2,000 civilian; Naval Amphibious Base Little Creek, 7,700 military, 1,815 civilian; Naval Air Station Oceana Dam Neck Annex, 3,600 military, 1,300 civilian (2005); Fort Monroe (Army), 912 military, 1,490 civilian (2004); Fort Story (Army), 1,146 military, 84 civilian (2003)

CITIES
Virginia Beach, 425,257; Norfolk (pt.), 112,102; Hampton (pt.), 54,753

NOTABLE
Cape Henry Lighthouse in Virginia Beach.

Rep. Robert C. Scott (D)

Elected 1992; 7th term

For more than a decade, Scott has been an unwavering liberal voice in the House, battling often against amendments to the Constitution, anti-crime provisions that he regards as overreaching and calls by President Bush to give faith-based organizations exemptions from federal laws intended to erect barriers to discrimination.

The first black person to represent Virginia in Congress since 1891, Scott is a supporter of abortion rights, an opponent of the death penalty and a critic of Republicans for spending generously to punish criminals while shortchanging social programs that he says are key to crime prevention.

Scott's unambiguous place on the political spectrum, with his strong civil libertarian strain, occasionally puts him in the awkward position of challenging his own party. In 2002, for example, he was one of only 12 House Democrats who voted against enacting the revamp of campaign finance law. He viewed one of its core provisions — prohibiting advocacy groups from mentioning specific candidates in their broadcast advertisements close to an election — as an unconstitutional restriction on free speech.

But mostly Scott is a stalwart on the Judiciary Committee, where in the 109th Congress he held onto the top Democratic spot on the Crime Subcommittee for a fourth term. From that position, he has been a persistent opponent of proposals to expand law enforcement authority, which he views as a violation of the rights of defendants, consumers and the poor. He often points out that federal wiretap rules were created as "a tool of last resort" for investigations of organized crime, but that there is now persistent pressure from Republicans — inappropriately so, in his view — to allow wiretapping in probes of a broad array of alleged crimes.

As a consequence, Scott was a vocal opponent of the 2001 law, enacted with overwhelming support by Congress six weeks after the terrorist attacks of Sept. 11, that gave federal law enforcement officers new tools to combat terrorism. Scott said new intelligence-gathering provisions in the statute trample on individual liberties. In late 2001, Scott opposed a border security measure containing provisions that, he said, "reduce the rights of victims of unconstitutional, unreasonable searches by government officials."

Scott has long argued that the GOP's "tough on crime" approach does not work. He says education and jobs are the answer. "It makes no sense, waiting for the children to mess up and then lock them up, when it is cheaper to invest in crime prevention programs and prevent them from getting in trouble in the first place," he said.

Scott is also a leading critic of Bush administration faith-based initiatives, such as a House-passed bill in 2001 that would have funneled federal dollars to groups that would be allowed to use religion as a basis for hiring — which Scott and many Democrats view as discriminatory. Early in the 109th, Scott failed on a party-line floor vote to preserve a ban on religious discrimination in federal job training programs.

When Republicans try to pass constitutional amendments to protect the flag, promote school prayer, limit taxation or extend rights to crime victims, Scott admonishes members that they took an oath to "support and defend" the Constitution, not "support and amend" it. In 2004, Scott helped lead Democratic opposition to a balanced-budget constitutional amendment, with criticism that Republicans were being hypocritical to embrace the amendment and vote for tax cuts that were helping create record deficits.

From his seat on the Education and Workforce Committee, Scott argues

CAPITOL OFFICE
225-8351
bobby.scott@mail.house.gov
www.house.gov/scott
1201 Longworth 20515-4603; fax 225-8354

COMMITTEES
Education & Workforce
Judiciary

HOMETOWN
Newport News

BORN
April 30, 1947, Washington, D.C.

RELIGION
Episcopalian

FAMILY
Divorced

EDUCATION
Harvard U., A.B. 1969; Boston College, J.D. 1973

MILITARY SERVICE
Army Reserve, 1970-74; Mass. National Guard, 1974-76

CAREER
Lawyer

POLITICAL HIGHLIGHTS
Va. House, 1979-83; Va. Senate, 1983-93; Democratic nominee for U.S. House, 1986

ELECTION RESULTS

2004 GENERAL
Robert C. Scott (D)	159,373	69.3%
Winsome Sears (R)	70,194	30.5%

2004 PRIMARY
Robert C. Scott (D)	unopposed

2002 GENERAL
Robert C. Scott (D)	87,521	96.1%
write-ins	3,552	3.9%

PREVIOUS WINNING PERCENTAGES
2000 (98%); 1998 (76%); 1996 (82%); 1994 (79%); 1992 (79%)

that standardized test scores place low-income school districts and their students at a disadvantage. He is in his sixth term on that panel after taking a one-term leave of absence in the 108th to serve on the Budget Committee.

Scott leaves behind his liberal mantle when it comes to looking out for southeast Virginia's military and tobacco interests. A former member of the Army Reserve and the National Guard, Scott is one of the stronger pro-Pentagon voices in the Congressional Black Caucus. He seeks to advance the interests of the military bases and shipbuilders of the 3rd District, where Northrup Grumman Newport News and the Army's Fort Eustis are major employers. The district is also home to one of the nation's largest cigarette plants, a south Richmond facility operated by Philip Morris USA.

Scott was a leading critic of the Republican drive to impeach President Clinton in 1998. He even opposed censuring Clinton for his relationship with Monica Lewinsky, a former White House intern, arguing that the branches of the federal government should not censure one another.

Scott is the son of a surgeon and a teacher. When local white officials resisted court-ordered integration of the public schools, the Scotts, along with other well-to-do black families, sent their son to Groton, the prestigious Massachusetts prep school. He graduated from Harvard University and earned his law degree from Boston College. He returned home to Newport News after law school and became active in local civic groups and political organizations.

Scott won a seat in the state House in 1978 and moved up to the state Senate five years later. In his first run for Congress, in 1986, he failed to unseat Republican Herbert H. Bateman, but he nevertheless captured 44 percent of the vote and broadened his name recognition. Six years later, when redistricting at the start of the 1990s resulted in a 3rd District that was 64 percent black, Scott tried again. With no incumbent running, he took two-thirds of the vote in a three-way Democratic primary and four-fifths of the vote in November. He became the second black Virginian in the House after John Mercer Langston, a Republican elected to the 51st Congress.

Scott won by similarly lopsided margins in 1994 and 1996. When a three-judge federal panel struck down the 3rd's boundaries in 1997, Scott's political future seemed in jeopardy, but the new lines drawn by the General Assembly kept the black population at 54 percent, and he won handily. The GOP did not field a candidate from 1998 to 2002. But in 2004, even though redistricting after the 2000 census kept his district majority African-American, Scott won election to a seventh term with 69 percent the vote, his lowest percentage yet.

KEY VOTES

2004
Yes Extend federal unemployment benefits by 13 weeks
Yes Pass $283.2 billion, six-year federal highway and mass transit bill
No Approve $146 billion multi-year extension of previously enacted middle-class tax breaks
No Amend the Constitution to prohibit same-sex marriage
No Cut corporate taxes $137 billion over 10 years
Yes Reorganize U.S. intelligence agencies as proposed by Sept. 11 commission

2003
No Cut taxes by $330 billion through fiscal 2013
Yes Block Bush rule scaling back overtime pay for some white-collar federal workers
Yes Do not allow use of search warrants without first notifying subjects
Yes Allow importation of prescription drugs
No Create private school voucher program in Washington, D.C.
No Ban "partial birth" abortion except to save a woman's life
Yes Split $18.6 billion in Iraq aid into half-grant, half-loan
No Overhaul Medicare and create prescription drug benefit

CQ VOTE STUDIES

	PARTY UNITY		PRESIDENTIAL SUPPORT	
	Support	Oppose	Support	Oppose
2004	98%	2%	12%	88%
2003	97%	3%	9%	91%
2002	96%	4%	23%	77%
2001	94%	6%	14%	86%
2000	93%	7%	81%	19%

INTEREST GROUPS

	AFL-CIO	ADA	CCUS	ACU
2004	100%	100%	29%	4%
2003	100%	100%	23%	12%
2002	100%	95%	42%	4%
2001	100%	100%	35%	4%
2000	100%	95%	42%	4%

VIRGINIA 3
Southeast — parts of Richmond, Norfolk and Newport News, Portsmouth

The black-majority 3rd begins in Richmond and reaches southeast into military and shipbuilding territory, including parts of Newport News, Hampton and Norfolk. Redistricting following the 2000 census added the city of Portsmouth, which had been in the 4th District. The 3rd is the strongest Democratic district in the state.

Originally drawn as a 64 percent black district, the 3rd has been the focal point of Virginia redistricting since 1991. It saw its black population reduced under a court-ordered remap for the 1998 elections, then slightly increased in redistricting following the 2000 census. Richmond, Portsmouth and Norfolk, which have substantial black populations, all gave John Kerry more than 60 percent of their vote in the 2004 presidential election. Overall, Kerry took 66 percent of the 3rd's vote, his best showing in any Virginia congressional district.

The 3rd long has benefited from one of the nation's largest ports at

Hampton Roads and from growing financial firms in Richmond. State government also drives the economy of Richmond and its environs, as does manufacturing. Richmond boasts one of the largest cigarette plants in the nation (Philip Morris USA).

The Hampton Roads area has a heavy concentration of naval installations as well as shipbuilding and ship repair companies. Among these is the nation's largest privately owned shipyard — Northrop Grumman Newport News — which builds Naval aircraft carriers and submarines.

MAJOR INDUSTRY
Defense, shipbuilding and repair, shipping, tobacco

MILITARY BASES
Norfolk Naval Shipyard at Portsmouth, 750 military, 8,100 civilian; Fort Eustis (Army), 4,516 military, 2,407 civilian (2004); Naval Medical Center Portsmouth, 2,644 military, 1,211 civilian (2005)

CITIES
Richmond (pt.), 144,520; Norfolk (pt.), 122,301; Newport News (pt.), 108,350; Portsmouth, 100,565; Hampton (pt.), 59,929

NOTABLE
The Edgar Allan Poe Museum is in Richmond, where the author lived.

Rep. J. Randy Forbes (R)

Elected June 2001; 2nd full term

CAPITOL OFFICE
225-6365
www.house.gov/forbes
307 Cannon 20515-4604; fax 226-1170

COMMITTEES
Armed Services
Judiciary
Science

HOMETOWN
Chesapeake

BORN
Feb. 17, 1952, Chesapeake, Va.

RELIGION
Baptist

FAMILY
Wife, Shirley Forbes; four children

EDUCATION
Randolph-Macon College, B.A. 1974 (political science); U. of Virginia, J.D. 1977

CAREER
Lawyer; state legislative aide

POLITICAL HIGHLIGHTS
Va. House, 1990-97 (Republican floor leader, 1994-97); Va. Republican Party chairman, 1996-2000; Va. Senate, 1997-2001 (Republican floor leader, 1998-2000)

ELECTION RESULTS

2004 GENERAL

J. Randy Forbes (R)	182,444	64.5%
Jonathan Menefee (D)	100,413	35.5%

2004 PRIMARY

J. Randy Forbes (R)	unopposed

2002 GENERAL

J. Randy Forbes (R)	108,733	97.9%
write-ins	2,308	2.1%

PREVIOUS WINNING PERCENTAGES
2001 Special Election (52%)

Forbes may not have a high-wattage personality — The Economist magazine once described him as "dour and lugubrious; seemingly incapable of smiling, let alone flirting" — yet his conservative view of the world and his long experience in Virginia politics won him high initial standing with his party leadership. His 2001 special-election victory was a "takeaway" from Democrats that solidified the GOP's grip on the House.

So it was somewhat out of character when Forbes joined his chairman on the Judiciary Committee, F. James Sensenbrenner Jr., in voting against the intelligence overhaul bill in 2004 against the wishes of GOP leaders and the White House. The final bill omitted House-passed immigration provisions Forbes favored, including stricter regulations of driver's licenses.

He expects to pay a price for his no vote. "That was made clear to me," he told the Virginian-Pilot. The price, however, may not be very steep. Forbes usually follows the leadership's wishes, and he maintains a party unity score comfortably above the average for House Republicans — 97 percent in the 108th Congress vs. 90 percent for the average House Republican.

As state GOP chairman from 1996 to 2000, the soft-spoken but intensely competitive Forbes helped boost the political fortunes of former Virginia Gov. James S. Gilmore III, who later served as Republican National Committee chairman, and GOP Sen. George Allen. Both were classmates of Forbes at the University of Virginia law school.

Forbes served in the Virginia General Assembly while Allen was governor (1994-98) and helped shepherd into law Allen's proposal to abolish parole. A Sunday school teacher at his Baptist church, Forbes opposes abortion and gun control. Those conservative credentials, combined with Forbes' background in business law, led House leaders to appoint Forbes to a seat on the Judiciary Committee.

Forbes pursues a tough law-and-order agenda, backing a bill that increased prison terms and fines for corporate wrongdoing and another to arm airline pilots with handguns in cockpits for a two-year trial period. In 2004, he strongly supported a bill to exempt off-duty and retired law enforcement officers from concealed weapons laws. He also pressed for a ban on a procedure critics call "partial birth" abortion. And he assailed Janet Jackson's much-publicized "wardrobe malfunction" at the Super Bowl in January 2004, rounding up about 50 signatures on a letter to CBS President Leslie Moonves urging that the individuals responsible be punished.

Forbes also serves on the Armed Services Committee, with two other Tidewater Virginia Republicans, Jo Ann Davis and Thelma Drake. He looks out for such facilities as the Army's Fort Lee and the nearby Norfolk Naval Shipyard. All three Virginians will be battling in the 109th Congress to protect their military facilities during a new round of base closures.

Another big federal facility in the 4th that Forbes will try to protect is NASA's Langley Research Center in Hampton, a center for aeronautics research that periodically has been mentioned as a potential target if the space agency decides to close one or more of its regional centers.

Forbes also tends to the concerns of his rural constituents. He went to bat for peanut farmers, voting against the conference report to the 2002 farm bill because it scrapped the Depression-era peanut quota system — a program in which farmers owned licenses to produce only a certain amount in order to maintain high market prices. The bill provided fixed and counter-cyclical payments and marketing loans and compensated quota holders at 11 cents per pound per year for five years to transition out of the old program. Forbes and other members from peanut-growing areas successfully pressed the Internal Revenue Service to treat any gain from peanut quotas as capital assets instead of regular income, which is taxed at a higher rate.

Forbes remains a political force in his hometown of Chesapeake, where the Virginian-Pilot reported local Republicans grumbling about his micro-managing of politics and remaining a kingmaker for other local candidates.

A former legislative aide and state representative, Forbes in 1997 won a state Senate seat that Republican Mark Earley had left open to run successfully for state attorney general. He considered running for the House in 2000, but demurred. He began 2001 as a candidate for lieutenant governor. But when 4th District Rep. Norman Sisisky, a conservative Democrat, died March 29, 2001, shortly after lung cancer surgery, Forbes switched to the special election to succeed him with encouragement from the Bush administration and the House GOP leadership. Forbes won the nomination in April at a contentious convention and went on to face Democratic state Sen. Louise Lucas, who was bidding to become the first black woman elected to Congress from Virginia.

The race captured national attention, quickly turning into the first referendum on the Bush presidency and Republican efforts to boost their slim majority in the House. The candidates and national parties spent more than $7 million during the 32-day campaign — about $52 for every vote cast.

The contest also was a reminder of the GOP's sometimes tense relationship with African-American voters. Forbes won in balloting that broke heavily along racial lines. His hold on the competitive swing district improved dramatically following the controversial redistricting for 2002 that moved a number of African-American, Democratic-leaning neighborhoods into the neighboring 3rd District, where blacks already constituted the majority of registered voters. Democrats complained the move "packed" minority votes into a single district. The redistricting boosted the population of white voters in the 4th from 57 percent to more than 60 percent. A federal appeals court upheld the plan in September 2004.

Forbes and Lucas were headed for a rematch in 2002, but Lucas withdrew less than three months before the election, citing weak financial support from the Democratic Party and a desire to protect jobs in her district at a time when the state was facing a $1.5 billion revenue shortfall. With no Democratic opponent, Forbes cruised to his first full term, capturing 98 percent of the vote. In 2004, he easily beat 26-year-old Democratic challenger Jonathan Menefee by almost 2-to-1.

KEY VOTES

2004
No Extend federal unemployment benefits by 13 weeks
Yes Pass $283.2 billion, six-year federal highway and mass transit bill
Yes Approve $146 billion multi-year extension of previously enacted middle-class tax breaks
Yes Amend the Constitution to prohibit same-sex marriage
Yes Cut corporate taxes $137 billion over 10 years
No Reorganize U.S. intelligence agencies as proposed by Sept. 11 commission

2003
Yes Cut taxes by $330 billion through fiscal 2013
No Block Bush rule scaling back overtime pay for some white-collar federal workers
Yes Do not allow use of search warrants without first notifying subjects
Yes Allow importation of prescription drugs
Yes Create private school voucher program in Washington, D.C.
Yes Ban "partial birth" abortion except to save a woman's life
No Split $18.6 billion in Iraq aid into half-grant, half-loan
Yes Overhaul Medicare and create prescription drug benefit

CQ VOTE STUDIES

	PARTY UNITY		PRESIDENTIAL SUPPORT	
	Support	Oppose	Support	Oppose
2004	96%	4%	82%	18%
2003	97%	3%	93%	7%
2002	98%	2%	85%	15%
2001	97%	3%	93%	7%

INTEREST GROUPS

	AFL-CIO	ADA	CCUS	ACU
2004	14%	5%	100%	100%
2003	7%	10%	97%	88%
2002	11%	0%	85%	100%
2001	13%	0%	94%	100%

VIRGINIA 4
Southeast – Chesapeake

Located in southeastern and south-central Virginia, the 4th includes burgeoning Chesapeake, as well as rural tobacco-growing areas to the west.

Redistricting following the 2000 census transformed the 4th from highly competitive territory to a Republican-leaning district that comfortably backed George W. Bush for president in 2004 with 57 percent of the vote. Mapmakers removed the heavily black, strongly Democratic city of Portsmouth, and reduced the district's black population from 39 percent to 33 percent.

Chesapeake, the 4th's most-populous city, grew by nearly one-third in the 1990s. The city votes dependably Republican, as do the portions of Chesterfield County south of Richmond that are included in the northern part of the district.

Democrats fare better in areas with sizable black voting blocs. Petersburg, which is four-fifths black, gave John Kerry his best vote

percentage (81 percent) in the state in the 2004 presidential election. Across the Appomattox River from Petersburg is Colonial Heights, which is largely white and gave 74 percent of the vote to Bush in 2004.

Although the 4th's military installations lost civilian employees in the 1990s wave of downsizing, the overall effect on the district was negligible, as Chesapeake compensated by attracting new manufacturing businesses. Outside of the 4th's population centers, tobacco and peanut farming play a central role in the economy.

MAJOR INDUSTRY
Military, agriculture, tobacco, health care, manufacturing

MILITARY BASES
Fort Lee (Army), 3,165 military, 2,428 civilian; U.S. Joint Forces Command Joint Warfighting Center, 1,487 military, 1,129 civilian; Defense Supply Center, Richmond, 44 military, 2,430 civilian; Naval Support Activity Norfolk, Northwest Annex, 1,500 military, 700 civilian (2004)

CITIES
Chesapeake, 199,184; Suffolk, 63,677; Petersburg, 33,740; Hopewell, 22,354

NOTABLE
Suffolk, considered the peanut capital of the world, has a small museum dedicated to Planters' Mr. Peanut and hosts an annual "peanut fest."

Rep. Virgil H. Goode Jr. (R)

Elected 1996; 5th term

CAPITOL OFFICE
225-4711
www.house.gov/goode
1520 Longworth 20515-4605; fax 225-5681

COMMITTEES
Appropriations

HOMETOWN
Rocky Mount

BORN
Oct. 17, 1946, Richmond, Va.

RELIGION
Baptist

FAMILY
Wife, Lucy D. Goode; one child

EDUCATION
U. of Richmond, B.A. 1969; U. of Virginia, J.D. 1973

MILITARY SERVICE
Va. National Guard, 1969-75

CAREER
Lawyer

POLITICAL HIGHLIGHTS
Va. Senate, 1973-97 (served as a Democrat);
sought Democratic nomination for U.S. Senate,
1982, 1994

ELECTION RESULTS

2004 GENERAL

Virgil H. Goode Jr. (R)	172,431	63.7%
Al Weed (D)	98,237	36.3%

2004 PRIMARY

Virgil H. Goode Jr. (R)	unopposed

2002 GENERAL

Virgil H. Goode Jr. (R)	95,360	63.5%
Meredith Richards (D)	54,805	36.5%

PREVIOUS WINNING PERCENTAGES *
2000 (67%); 1998 (99%); 1996 (60%)
*Elected as a Democrat 1996-98; elected as an
independent 2000

Although first elected to Congress as a Democrat in 1996, Goode was never comfortable with the policies espoused by the liberal-leaning majority of his colleagues. By 1999, his last year as a Democrat, he sided with his party less than a quarter of the time. He is much more at home ideologically as a Republican.

That is not to say that Goode (GUDE — rhymes with food) always walks in lockstep with GOP leaders and the White House; especially on immigration and trade, he does not.

He is among the conservatives who have denounced President Bush's proposal to grant millions of illegal immigrants temporary legal work status in the United States. "I'm not for allowing illegals to stay in this country," Goode told the Associated Press. "I think they should have to go back to their home countries . . . and get in line with Jack, Suzy and John and apply for a guest worker position."

In the 108th Congress, Goode proposed to amend the Constitution to establish English as the official language of the United States. He also won adoption of a floor amendment to authorize Pentagon troop deployments along U.S. borders. These forces "could be of significant assistance to prevent the infiltration of terrorists, drug traffickers and illegal aliens," he said. Goode also led a drive to block a 2004 agreement with Mexico to end double payroll taxation of workers who hold jobs in each other's country. Workers could pay into just one system but obtain credit for all years worked, whether in Mexico or the United States. "Those who today want to protect the Social Security trust fund need to exclaim a resounding 'no' to the proposed totalization agreement with Mexico," Goode declared early in 2005.

Goode also parts company with the White House on trade deals, arguing that the loss of textile plants in his district is a prime example of the downside of trade liberalization. In the 108th, he voted against free-trade agreements with Australia, Morocco, Singapore and Chile. Referring to the North American Free Trade Agreement and fast-track trade negotiation authority that Congress approved in 2002, Goode declared on his campaign Web site that he does "not favor international trade agreements such as these that result in a loss of American sovereignty and jobs." Goode had voted against the fast-track bill.

Goode declared himself an independent in early 2000, resigning from the House Democratic Caucus. The GOP leadership rewarded him with a prized seat on the Appropriations Committee, from which he can steer federal dollars to projects in his district.

In 2002, he announced he would seek re-election as a Republican, and in April he filed papers seeking the GOP nomination. He was not challenged and became the nominee in June. But on Capitol Hill, he remained an independent in the eyes of the Clerk of the House, who said Goode needed to provide written notice before he officially would be considered a Republican. Eventually, Goode dotted the i's and crossed the necessary t's, and his House party affiliation was officially changed.

His languid approach to the matter is a reflection of Goode's go-slow style. His soft, syrupy accent reflects his Southern roots, and his district, which borders North Carolina, is known locally as Southside.

During the many years Goode resisted entreaties to switch to the GOP, he would tell people that "Daddy was a Democrat" who had instilled in his son an appreciation for New Deal programs that aided rural areas. Virgil

Sr. was in the state legislature and also served as a state prosecutor; a stretch of highway in Rocky Mount is named after him. Virgil Jr. recalls tagging along as his father attended gatherings around the wood stoves at the general stores that were the prime small-town meeting places. "If you could get the country store vote, you had it made," Goode recalls.

Goode's opposition to abortion, gay marriage and desecration of the flag is typical of GOP conservatives. He also opposes gun control, and in 2004 helped found the Second Amendment Caucus, a forum for lawmakers devoted to protecting the right to bear arms.

Tobacco farming, a major industry in Goode's district, is very much a threatened vocation. In the 107th, Goode joined with Democrat Rick Boucher of the neighboring 9th District on a proposal to end the quota system — providing lump sum payments to farmers who grow a certain quota of tobacco — and replace it with federal licenses. Under their plan, no one would be permitted to raise tobacco without having a license, which, unlike the quotas, could not be sold. In the 108th, Goode was among a number of lawmakers from tobacco states who signed on to a corporate tax bill only after a $10 billion tobacco buyout provision was included.

After graduation from law school, Goode quickly jumped into politics when an opening developed in the state Senate. He made no secret about his ambitions for higher office, and in 1982 and 1994 he unsuccessfully pursued the Democratic nomination for the U.S. Senate.

His reputation as a political maverick intensified after the 1995 election yielded a state Senate in partisan deadlock. Democrats retained effective control because the Democratic lieutenant governor held a tie-breaking vote. But Goode insisted on an "equitable division" of power in the committee system, and he forced a power-sharing arrangement in which the GOP gained control of four committees. Goode himself surrendered a gavel to a Republican to help grease the deal.

In 1996, the day after Democrat L. F. Payne Jr. announced he would not seek another term, Goode launched his bid for Congress. He campaigned in a down-home style reminiscent of his father's, driving to small-town events where he spoke off the cuff and handed out emery boards and pencils embossed with his name. (His father used to give out small kitchen implements.) He won by 24 percentage points. In 1998, he drew no GOP foe.

Democratic party officials were conflicted by Goode's Republican tilt. While he was likely the only Democrat who could win the seat, his votes in the House rankled. If Goode had not left the party in 2000, he probably would not have gained Democratic backing anyway.

KEY VOTES

2004
Yes Extend federal unemployment benefits by 13 weeks
Yes Pass $283.2 billion, six-year federal highway and mass transit bill
Yes Approve $146 billion multi-year extension of previously enacted middle-class tax breaks
Yes Amend the Constitution to prohibit same-sex marriage
Yes Cut corporate taxes $137 billion over 10 years
No Reorganize U.S. intelligence agencies as proposed by Sept. 11 commission

2003
Yes Cut taxes by $330 billion through fiscal 2013
No Block Bush rule scaling back overtime pay for some white-collar federal workers
No Do not allow use of search warrants without first notifying subjects
Yes Allow importation of prescription drugs
Yes Create private school voucher program in Washington, D.C.
Yes Ban "partial birth" abortion except to save a woman's life
No Split $18.6 billion in Iraq aid into half-grant, half-loan
Yes Overhaul Medicare and create prescription drug benefit

CQ VOTE STUDIES

	PARTY UNITY		PRESIDENTIAL SUPPORT	
	Support	Oppose	Support	Oppose
2004	91%	9%	76%	24%
2003	93%	7%	87%	13%
2002	93%	7%	74%	26%
2001	92%	8%	79%	21%
2000	94%	6%	14%	86%

INTEREST GROUPS

	AFL-CIO	ADA	CCUS	ACU
2004	33%	10%	90%	96%
2003	20%	10%	87%	84%
2002	11%	5%	75%	96%
2001	25%	10%	83%	96%
2000	10%	10%	66%	100%

VIRGINIA 5
South central — Danville, Charlottesville

Rich in Civil War landmarks, the 5th extends from just north of Charlottesville, in the central part of the state, to the south-central tier bordering North Carolina, an area known as Southside.

The mostly rural 5th is relatively poor, and the district relies heavily on agriculture and textiles. Known as the heart of tobacco country, the 5th still supports a vast tobacco industry, but in recent years manufacturing has taken a more prominent role. Danville, the district's largest city, is a tobacco and textile center on the North Carolina border. To the west is Martinsville, a textile and furniture town.

The seasonal nature of the economy led to above-average unemployment during some of the 1990s in the district's southwest corner. But the 5th's economy also saw some strong performances during that decade. Bedford County, between Roanoke and Lynchburg (both of which are in the 6th), and Fluvanna County, in the orbit of Charlottesville, grew by attracting commuters as well as many small businesses. Fluvanna County grew by 61 percent in the 1990s, and

Greene County, located north of Charlottesville, grew by 48 percent.

Redistricting following the 2000 census made minor changes to the reliably conservative district, which typically gives GOP candidates vote percentages hovering in the mid-50s. One notable exception is the city of Charlottesville, which is home to the University of Virginia and almost always backs Democrats. The city gave John Kerry 72 percent of its vote in the 2004 presidential election — his second-best showing in the state.

But the conservative rural areas also can support Democratic candidates, provided they express right-of-center views on issues such as gun owners' rights. Democrat Mark Warner employed such a strategy with success in the 5th District during his 2001 gubernatorial bid.

MAJOR INDUSTRY
Agriculture, manufacturing, textiles, tobacco, service

CITIES
Danville, 48,411; Charlottesville, 45,049; Martinsville, 15,416

NOTABLE
Appomattox Court House; Thomas Jefferson's estate, Monticello, and James Monroe's estate, Ash Lawn-Highland, are south of Charlottesville.

Rep. Robert W. Goodlatte (R)

Elected 1992; 7th term

CAPITOL OFFICE
225-5431
talk2bob@mail.house.gov
www.house.gov/goodlatte
2240 Rayburn 20515-4606; fax 225-9681

COMMITTEES
Agriculture - chairman
Judiciary

HOMETOWN
Roanoke

BORN
Sept. 22, 1952, Holyoke, Mass.

RELIGION
Christian Scientist

FAMILY
Wife, Maryellen Goodlatte; two children

EDUCATION
Bates College, B.A. 1974 (government);
Washington and Lee U., J.D. 1977

CAREER
Lawyer; congressional aide

POLITICAL HIGHLIGHTS
Roanoke City Republican Committee chairman,
1980-83; 6th Congressional District Republican
Party chairman, 1983-88

ELECTION RESULTS

2004 GENERAL

Robert W. Goodlatte (R)	206,560	96.7%
write-ins	7,088	3.3%

2004 PRIMARY

Robert W. Goodlatte (R)	unopposed

2002 GENERAL

Robert W. Goodlatte (R)	105,530	97.1%
write-ins	3,202	3.0%

PREVIOUS WINNING PERCENTAGES
2000 (99%); 1998 (69%); 1996 (67%); 1994 (100%);
1992 (60%)

Goodlatte's legislative interests are broad, encompassing agriculture and trade policy, technology issues such as cyber-security, and class action lawsuits. As chairman of the Agriculture Committee, he tries to remain faithful to his conservative fiscal beliefs while also responding to farmers who worry about a GOP administration that is targeting crop subsidies as it tries to reduce the federal budget deficit.

A member of the Agriculture Committee since 1993, Goodlatte (GOOD-lat) represents a district with many dairy and poultry farms. The committee also has jurisdiction over national forests, which account for about a third of the land area in Goodlatte's Shenandoah Valley district.

Goodlatte had some successes as Agriculture chairman in the 108th Congress, his first two years at the helm. He had a hand in passing President Bush's "healthy forests" initiative, and a long-sought buyout program for tobacco farmers passed on his watch as well.

The 2004 election cost Goodlatte his top Democratic partner on Agriculture, Charles W. Stenholm of Texas, a moderate with a reputation for working well with Republicans. Stenholm lost re-election after his district was substantially altered in redistricting. For the 109th, the new top-ranking Democrat on Agriculture is Collin C. Peterson of Minnesota, whose record also shows a willingness to cross party lines.

The two will be seeing a lot of each other, as Congress turns to rewriting the massive, multi-year farm bill, due for renewal in 2007. A hint of the hard road ahead came in the president's agriculture budget proposal in early 2005: Bush called for a 5 percent cut in crop subsidies and lowering the maximum individual payment cap.

"One of the purposes of the farm bill is to give predictability to farmers over a six-year cycle, so anything like this can be disruptive of that and we want to do it in such a way that's the least disruptive possible," Goodlatte said early in the 109th. But he warned that all programs under the panel's jurisdiction would get close scrutiny, including crop subsidies, nutrition programs, food stamps and conservation programs.

After Republicans took control of the House in 1995, Goodlatte helped engineer changes that reduced food stamp spending by more than $10 billion annually. The changes included a requirement that able-bodied recipients work, a ban on convicted food stamp traffickers and on prison inmates receiving food stamps, and improved record-keeping to ensure that dead people are not on the rolls.

Goodlatte's other major area of endeavor is technology policy, particularly as it affects rural areas. He says rural America will be economically competitive in the future only if it keeps pace in the computer age. He sees communications technology today as comparable to the railroad in the 19th century. "If the railroad came through your town and connected you with the rest of the country, you'd boom. If it didn't, you'd go bust," he says.

New technologies actually can give bucolic areas such as the 6th District an advantage over big cities, Goodlatte says. The region's natural beauty, low cost of living, low crime and unclogged roads are a powerful draw, as long as information technology is available to enable people to hold 21st century jobs. As a lawyer in Roanoke, Goodlatte took advantage of the latest communications and information technology to build a competitive practice that included a specialty in immigration law. "Using technology, I was able to compete with lawyers from Washington and New York," he recalls.

During his dozen years in the House, Goodlatte has been a player on almost every major computer-related bill before Congress, including those aimed at protecting users' privacy, preserving intellectual copyright protections for artists and creators of software, shielding children from indecent material, and safeguarding consumers from fraud. Late in the 108th, the House overwhelmingly passed his measure setting criminal penalties for using privacy-invading "spyware" to tap into personal computers to steal information or damage hardware. That bill died at the end of the Congress, but Goodlatte reintroduced it in the 109th.

He was instrumental in drafting the "eContract," a House Republican high-tech legislative manifesto aimed at promoting the Internet economy while reducing taxation, regulation and lawsuits. He also sponsored legislation providing loan guarantees to help rural satellite and cable television systems deliver local broadcast stations to viewers who would otherwise have no reception.

His positions on technology are driven by the philosophy that government generally should stay out of the way of innovators and entrepreneurs. That is a conservative's perspective, but Goodlatte notes that many Internet-related issues lend themselves to bipartisanship. A frequent Goodlatte partner on technology matters is Democrat Rick Boucher, who represents the neighboring Virginia 9th and sits on the Judiciary Committee with Goodlatte.

Boucher and Goodlatte also paired up to promote a bill making it easier for parties involved in some class action lawsuits to transfer cases from state to federal court. Proponents of the legislation said it would prevent "venue shopping" by trial lawyers who deliberately bring cases in jurisdictions friendly to plaintiffs. The measure was signed into law by Bush in 2005.

Goodlatte had a middle-class upbringing in western Massachusetts. His father managed a Friendly's ice cream store, and his mother worked part-time in a department store. Though his parents were not politically active, Goodlatte remembers being fascinated early on by current affairs and politics. He was president of the College Republicans at Bates College in Maine. After getting a law degree at Washington & Lee in Lexington, Va., Goodlatte entered private practice and also worked for the area's Republican congressman, M. Caldwell Butler.

Goodlatte considered running for Congress in 1986, but the arrival of his second child at the start of the campaign season kept him out of the race. In 1992, however, when Democratic Rep. Jim Olin retired after five terms, Goodlatte decided the time was right. He won easily and has not had a formidable opponent since.

KEY VOTES

2004
No Extend federal unemployment benefits by 13 weeks
Yes Pass $283.2 billion, six-year federal highway and mass transit bill
Yes Approve $146 billion multi-year extension of previously enacted middle-class tax breaks
Yes Amend the Constitution to prohibit same-sex marriage
Yes Cut corporate taxes $137 billion over 10 years
Yes Reorganize U.S. intelligence agencies as proposed by Sept. 11 commission

2003
Yes Cut taxes by $330 billion through fiscal 2013
No Block Bush rule scaling back overtime pay for some white-collar federal workers
No Do not allow use of search warrants without first notifying subjects
Yes Allow importation of prescription drugs
Yes Create private school voucher program in Washington, D.C.
Yes Ban "partial birth" abortion except to save a woman's life
No Split $18.6 billion in Iraq aid into half-grant, half-loan
Yes Overhaul Medicare and create prescription drug benefit

CQ VOTE STUDIES

	PARTY UNITY		PRESIDENTIAL SUPPORT	
	Support	Oppose	Support	Oppose
2004	98%	2%	88%	12%
2003	96%	4%	95%	5%
2002	99%	1%	88%	12%
2001	97%	3%	91%	9%
2000	97%	3%	22%	78%

INTEREST GROUPS

	AFL-CIO	ADA	CCUS	ACU
2004	13%	0%	100%	100%
2003	7%	10%	97%	84%
2002	0%	0%	95%	100%
2001	17%	0%	91%	96%
2000	0%	0%	85%	100%

VIRGINIA 6

Northwest — Roanoke, Lynchburg

Running along the Shenandoah Valley, the conservative 6th is a collage of mountainous terrain, small towns, medium-size cities and natural beauty. Beginning in Roanoke, the district's most populous city, one can drive 160 miles northeast along Interstate 81 to Interstate 66, without leaving the 6th District.

Roanoke has a variety of industries, including furniture and electrical products manufacturing. Both Roanoke and Lynchburg saw their populations shrink slightly in the 1990s, but the manufacturing economy was generally solid. Several colleges are in the district as well.

Outside the Roanoke and Lynchburg metropolitan areas, the 6th depends mainly on dairy farming, livestock and poultry. In the north, Rockingham County leads the state in livestock and hay production. Tourists traveling to the district's national parks and caverns also help boost the economy. There are some chemical plants and pulpwood and paper mills in the area north of Roanoke.

The 6th has one of the largest populations of senior citizens in the state, a mostly white-collar workforce and a generous dose of Republicans, although the rural valley's brand of Republicanism traditionally has been a moderate one. The 1992 election of GOP Rep. Goodlatte ended the Democrats' decade-long domination of the 6th seat, but Democrats still won in local elections in the 1990s. Roanoke has a strong Democratic base with union ties. But Republicans have done well in Roanoke's suburbs, in Lynchburg and in most rural areas.

Overall, George W. Bush captured 63 percent of the vote here in the 2004 presidential election, making the 6th Bush's best Virginia district. The president won all 11 counties, with Augusta, Rockingham and Bedford each giving him more than 70 percent of the vote.

MAJOR INDUSTRY
Agriculture, livestock, manufacturing, tourism

CITIES
Roanoke, 94,911; Lynchburg, 65,269; Harrisonburg, 40,468; Cave Spring (unincorporated), 24,941; Salem, 24,747; Staunton, 23,853

NOTABLE
Lynchburg is the home of evangelist Jerry Falwell's Liberty University; Woodrow Wilson was born in Staunton (pronounced "Stanton").

Rep. Eric Cantor (R)

Elected 2000; 3rd term

A comer in the GOP hierarchy, Cantor is the able assistant to Whip Roy Blunt and has been involved in political campaigns since he was a teen. As the sole Jewish Republican in the House, he also is the congressional point man in efforts to expand the party's franchise within that traditionally Democratic constituency.

A talented protégé of former Commerce Chairman Thomas J. Bliley of Virginia, Cantor was named chief deputy majority whip in late 2002, after just one term in the House. It is an appointive, not elective post, so it is less powerful than other leadership jobs, but it has been a steppingstone for GOP leaders in the past. J. Dennis Hastert once had the job, and it helped him on his way to becoming Speaker.

Cantor's inclusion in leadership circles paid dividends for the party at the end of the 108th Congress, when he worked to ensure House passage of a corporate tax cut by helping affix tobacco buyout legislation to the package. He advanced the bill even though it was at odds with the interests of a campaign contributor, Philip Morris USA. A top Richmond-area employer, the company had lobbied for provisions related to the regulation of tobacco that were left out of the legislation.

Though he is becoming recognizable on political talk shows and on the Republican fundraising circuit, particularly among pro-Israel donors, Cantor is in just his third term in the House. His position in the leadership, like his prized seat on the Ways and Means panel, is still owed more to well-placed benefactors than a formidable base of his own among the rank and file.

When Majority Leader Tom DeLay turned over the whip operation to his deputy, Blunt of Missouri, at the close of the 107th Congress, Blunt bypassed several senior members of DeLay's operation to make Cantor his chief lieutenant. Since then, tension has developed between the hard-boiled DeLay and the soft-edged Blunt, but Cantor has managed to keep himself out of the conflict. Instead, he has been supportive of both, rushing to DeLay's defense in 2004 and 2005 when the majority leader came under fire for questionable ethics but not wavering in his support of Blunt and the goals of the whip's office.

Acting as a party spokesman helped him increase his constituency among colleagues, some of whom were displeased with Blunt's decision to tap so junior a lawmaker to fill the role of deputy vote-counter.

Labeled by the chairman of the Virginia Democratic Party as a "Bush attack dog," Cantor truly found his voice in the 108th Congress, excoriating everyone from 2004 Democratic presidential nominee John Kerry to the members of the bipartisan commission that investigated the Sept. 11, 2001, terrorist attacks.

"With the latest commission finding coming out that there were allegedly no ties between [Saddam] Hussein and al Qaeda, I think they are totally off their mission and I think that's indicative of the political partisanship," he told the Washington Post in June 2004, when the House Republican leaders were working to discredit the commissioners.

Cantor has fashioned a particularly high profile on national security, terrorism and the ongoing conflicts in the Middle East. He is chairman of the Congressional Task Force on Terrorism and Unconventional Warfare, an unofficial caucus that briefs Republicans on issues and makes legislative recommendations.

He has urged a tougher U.S. stance against Syria, Iran and Iraq. When

CAPITOL OFFICE
225-2815
cantor.house.gov
329 Cannon 20515-4607; fax 225-0011

COMMITTEES
Ways & Means

HOMETOWN
Glen Allen

BORN
June 6, 1963, Richmond, Va.

RELIGION
Jewish

FAMILY
Wife, Diana Cantor; three children

EDUCATION
George Washington U., B.A. 1985 (political science); College of William & Mary, J.D. 1988; Columbia U., M.S. 1989 (real estate development)

CAREER
Lawyer; real estate developer; campaign aide

POLITICAL HIGHLIGHTS
Va. House, 1992-2001

ELECTION RESULTS

2004 GENERAL
Eric Cantor (R)	230,765	75.5%
W. Brad Blanton (I)	74,325	24.3%

2004 PRIMARY
Eric Cantor (R)	unopposed

2002 GENERAL
Eric Cantor (R)	113,658	69.5%
Ben L. "Cooter" Jones (D)	49,854	30.5%

PREVIOUS WINNING PERCENTAGES
2000 (67%)

longtime Palestinian leader Yasser Arafat died in 2004, Cantor called him "the father of the modern terrorist state" and said his death ended "an era of failed leadership and absolute corruption."

Cantor is a natural nexus between Christian conservatives in the leadership and the Jewish donors and voters they court with their hawkish support for Israel. Despite his short congressional tenure, he ranks among the top beneficiaries of pro-Israel campaign donors and is a spokesman for the party on Israel and other issues of concern to Jews.

But Cantor recognizes there is much work to be done on that front. The GOP has not yet made many inroads in the Jewish community. "Republicans are not as good at talking about some of the issues that Jewish communities may care about," he said in 2004. "I don't think that Jews in this country necessarily in the mainstream support bloated government programs and entitlements."

That is certainly true of Cantor. Like most Republicans, he advocates limited government, lower taxes and a stronger military.

Cantor grew up in a well-to-do, politically active Richmond family and, while still a teenager, helped out Bliley in 1982 by driving his campaign car. He also worked as an aide to Virginia lawmaker Walter A. Stosch during a legislative session.

When his old boss, Stosch, a member of the Virginia House of Delegates, decided to run for the state Senate in 1991, Cantor was well-positioned to make a bid for the open seat. He out-organized and outspent two more-experienced rivals, becoming, at age 28, the youngest member of the state House. When he was in the state legislature, he was described in the local press as a "calm voice" who, despite a voting record lauded by the National Rifle Association, the Christian Coalition and the Family Foundation, "does not come across as a firebrand."

Bliley's campaign machinery stood behind Cantor when needed, and Cantor returned the favor by serving as Bliley's campaign chairman in several of the elder lawmaker's re-election bids. When Bliley announced his retirement, Cantor jumped into the Republican primary to replace him. But despite the backing from Bliley's organization and help with fundraising, Cantor won by a scant 263 votes over state Sen. Stephen H. Martin. But the primary win in the heavily Republican district ensured his success in November, and he swept the general election with two-thirds of the vote.

Cantor has twice coasted to re-election, including a 2002 pasting of Ben L. "Cooter" Jones, who served in the Georgia House a decade ago but is best-known as Cooter from the "The Dukes of Hazzard" television series.

KEY VOTES

2004
No   Extend federal unemployment benefits by 13 weeks
No   Pass $283.2 billion, six-year federal highway and mass transit bill
Yes   Approve $146 billion multi-year extension of previously enacted middle-class tax breaks
Yes   Amend the Constitution to prohibit same-sex marriage
Yes   Cut corporate taxes $137 billion over 10 years
Yes   Reorganize U.S. intelligence agencies as proposed by Sept. 11 commission

2003
Yes   Cut taxes by $330 billion through fiscal 2013
No   Block Bush rule scaling back overtime pay for some white-collar federal workers
No   Do not allow use of search warrants without first notifying subjects
No   Allow importation of prescription drugs
Yes   Create private school voucher program in Washington, D.C.
Yes   Ban "partial birth" abortion except to save a woman's life
No   Split $18.6 billion in Iraq aid into half-grant, half-loan
Yes   Overhaul Medicare and create prescription drug benefit

CQ VOTE STUDIES

	PARTY UNITY		PRESIDENTIAL SUPPORT	
	Support	Oppose	Support	Oppose
2004	98%	2%	97%	3%
2003	99%	1%	100%	0%
2002	99%	1%	90%	10%
2001	98%	2%	95%	5%

INTEREST GROUPS

	AFL-CIO	ADA	CCUS	ACU
2004	7%	0%	100%	100%
2003	0%	50%	100%	88%
2002	11%	0%	100%	100%
2001	8%	0%	100%	100%

VIRGINIA 7
Central – part of Richmond and suburbs

The solidly Republican 7th contains parts of Richmond and its affluent old-money suburbs, and then reaches northwest into farmlands.

Many of the 7th's residents work in Richmond, which grew steadily in the 1990s on the strength of banking and manufacturing. The longtime center of state government and commerce, Richmond also was one of the South's early manufacturing centers, concentrating on tobacco processing. Richmond-based Philip Morris USA continues to employ thousands of district residents.

A plurality of district residents live in Henrico County (shared with the 3rd), which cups Richmond in a backward C-shape. Henrico generally leans Republican, although it backed Democrat Mark Warner in the 2001 gubernatorial election. Chesterfield County, which is shared with the 4th, borders Richmond to the south and west and has a stronger GOP lean. The 7th's portion of Richmond includes some strong Republican voters who live in the city's western end.

The northern stretch of the 7th is home to traditional farming communities that gradually are being taken over by people who take long commutes to jobs in metropolitan Washington, D.C.

Redistricting following the 2000 census made the 7th slightly less Republican by adding some Democratic precincts in Richmond and Henrico County. But as a whole the district is still reliably Republican, and it is difficult for any Democratic candidate to stitch together a victory here. In the 2004 presidential race, John Kerry carried only the district's portions of Caroline County and the city of Richmond from within the 7th's territory. George W. Bush took 61 percent of the district's overall vote.

MAJOR INDUSTRY
Agriculture, government, manufacturing

CITIES
Richmond (pt.), 53,270; Tuckahoe (unincorporated), 43,242; Mechanicsville (unincorporated), 30,464

NOTABLE
Luray Caverns is in Page County; The late tennis star Arthur Ashe was born in Richmond in 1943; During a 1960 presidential campaign stop in Culpeper, Lyndon B. Johnson famously asked, "What has Richard Nixon ever done for Culpeper?"

Rep. James P. Moran (D)

CAPITOL OFFICE
225-4376
www.moran.house.gov
2239 Rayburn 20515-4608; fax 225-0017

COMMITTEES
Appropriations

HOMETOWN
Arlington

BORN
May 16, 1945, Buffalo, N.Y.

RELIGION
Roman Catholic

FAMILY
Wife LuAnn Bennett; four children

EDUCATION
College of the Holy Cross, B.A. 1967 (economics);
City U. of New York, Bernard M. Baruch School of
Finance, attended 1967-68; U. of Pittsburgh, M.P.A.
1970

CAREER
Investment broker; congressional aide

POLITICAL HIGHLIGHTS
Alexandria City Council, 1979-84 (vice mayor, 1982-
84); mayor of Alexandria, 1985-90 (served as an
independent 1985-88)

ELECTION RESULTS

2004 GENERAL

James P. Moran (D)	171,986	59.7%
Lisa Marie Cheney (R)	106,231	36.9%
James T. Hurysz (I)	9,004	3.1%

2004 PRIMARY

James P. Moran (D)	24,121	58.6%
Andrew M. Rosenberg (D)	17,067	41.4%

2002 GENERAL

James P. Moran (D)	102,759	59.8%
Scott C. Tate (R)	64,121	37.3%
Ron Crickenberger (I)	4,558	2.7%

PREVIOUS WINNING PERCENTAGES
2000 (63%); 1998 (67%); 1996 (66%); 1994 (59%);
1992 (56%); 1990 (52%)

Elected 1990; 8th term

Moran has been that rare House member who has struggled for re-election, despite the political advantages that convey with incumbency, including ready access to campaign cash and usually favorable visibility in the media. But the eight-term congressman has a penchant for saying and doing things that generate negative media attention and spawn aggressive campaign challenges, including, in 2004, serious primary opposition.

And yet, Moran has endured, fending off the 2004 primary challenge with 59 percent of the vote and winning in November with 60 percent.

Several factors contribute to Moran's success. One is that he is a staunch advocate for more pay and better health, transit and retirement benefits for federal workers, a significant presence in his Northern Virginia district, across the river from Washington, D.C. From his seat on the Appropriations Committee, Moran has cut deals across party lines and behind the scenes to bring in millions of dollars for local roads, education programs, law enforcement, low-income housing and social services.

Redistricting has also helped him: When Virginia's House district lines were redrawn after the 2000 census, Moran benefited from a bipartisan, pro-incumbent gerrymander that made his 8th District more Democratic and the neighboring 10th and 11th Districts securely Republican.

And third, while "mellow" is an adjective that will never be used to describe Moran — the son of a professional boxer and Washington Redskins football player — he cut a steady, even-tempered figure in the 2004 campaign, refraining from the kind of fiery rhetoric that had in the past made him so highly quotable. Once, in a committee dispute, Moran told Indiana Republican Dan Burton, "You pull that again and I'll break your nose."

The shift in Moran's pugilistic style that was evident in the 2004 campaign came after he brought down a hailstorm of criticism on himself with a remark he made in early 2003. At a meeting with constituents in Reston, Va., Moran suggested that Jewish influence was a major factor in the Bush administration's push to wage war in Iraq. Moran was immediately and roundly repudiated by his Democratic colleagues, many of whom characterized his comments as offensive. He apologized, but House Democratic leader Nancy Pelosi stripped Moran of his post in the party's whip organization. Moran's blunder helped propel the campaign of his 2004 primary challenger, Andrew M. Rosenberg.

Returning to the House in 2005, Moran saw his top-ranking seat on Appropriations' Legislative Branch Subcommittee evaporate when the GOP leadership abolished that panel, folding its work into the full committee. Moran holds his party's No. 2 slot on Appropriations' Interior and Environment Subcommittee, and he sits on the Defense Subcommittee.

On Appropriations, Moran has earned a reputation as an able if sometimes confrontational negotiator. He has shown a capacity for forging coalitions across party lines. He often works in tandem on parochial issues with Virginia's two GOP senators, John W. Warner and George Allen. And he collaborates frequently with Republican Thomas M. Davis III from the neighboring 11th District. Their alliance was instrumental in getting the District of Columbia to close its prison in the Virginia suburb of Lorton and in securing federal funds to replace the Woodrow Wilson Bridge.

Moran joined with two House colleagues in 1997 to found the New Democrat Coalition, which seeks "mainstream, bipartisan solutions." While he normally votes with the majority of his party, he sometimes goes against the partisan grain. For example, he has voted for trade liberalization measures, and he supported a bill backed by President Bush to rein in class action lawsuits that became law in 2005.

Through a quarter-century political career, Moran has always portrayed himself as putting his fighting spirit to work for his constituents. He takes pride in his prowess as an amateur heavyweight, including college bouts at Holy Cross and an exhibition match with former heavyweight champion Joe Frazier.

First elected to the Alexandria City Council in 1979, Moran saw his career derailed briefly in 1984 when, after pleading no contest to a misdemeanor conflict-of-interest charge, he resigned as vice mayor as part of a plea agreement. Running as an independent the next year, he unseated the incumbent mayor. He was serving as mayor in 1990 when he ran for Congress, unseating six-term Republican Stan Parris. The policy difference Moran focused on was his support for abortion rights and the incumbent's anti-abortion views. Moran won with 52 percent of the vote.

Though the 8th gained Democrats in redistricting for the 1990s, Republicans tested Moran in 1992 and 1994 with a quality challenger in Kyle E. McSlarrow. Moran won by solid margins. Despite another friendly remap, Moran slipped to 60 percent in 2002, the first real sign that voters were becoming uneasy about reports of his family troubles and financial dealings.

Moran's wife of 11 years, Mary, filed for divorce in 1999, one day after placing an emergency call to police during a domestic argument. Moran soon brought his own divorce complaint. Court filings outlined the couple's financial losses: He blamed her for profligate spending; she blamed him for losing $120,000 in stock trading. Moran has since remarried.

Also, Moran drew negative attention for his support of legislation that helped a credit card company which in 1998 gave him an unusually low interest rate for a loan of nearly $450,000.

In 2004, Moran took a one-two-three series of punches — in the primary from Rosenberg, in the general election from Republican Lisa Marie Cheney, and on the editorial page of The Washington Post, which said it hoped "that next time [Moran's] party will show the self-respect to nominate someone of greater stature."

Moran did not rise to the bait. Instead of duking it out with his critics, he emphasized his advocacy for district concerns and how his Appropriations seat helps funnel money into the 8th. As the district went Democratic for president, Moran's liberal stands on social and environmental issues helped carry him to victory.

KEY VOTES

2004

Yes	Extend federal unemployment benefits by 13 weeks
Yes	Pass $283.2 billion, six-year federal highway and mass transit bill
Yes	Approve $146 billion multi-year extension of previously enacted middle-class tax breaks
No	Amend the Constitution to prohibit same-sex marriage
No	Cut corporate taxes $137 billion over 10 years
Yes	Reorganize U.S. intelligence agencies as proposed by Sept. 11 commission

2003

No	Cut taxes by $330 billion through fiscal 2013
Yes	Block Bush rule scaling back overtime pay for some white-collar federal workers
Yes	Do not allow use of search warrants without first notifying subjects
Yes	Allow importation of prescription drugs
No	Create private school voucher program in Washington, D.C.
No	Ban "partial birth" abortion except to save a woman's life
+	Split $18.6 billion in Iraq aid into half-grant, half-loan
No	Overhaul Medicare and create prescription drug benefit

CQ VOTE STUDIES

	PARTY UNITY		PRESIDENTIAL SUPPORT	
	Support	Oppose	Support	Oppose
2004	89%	11%	41%	59%
2003	89%	11%	26%	74%
2002	84%	16%	42%	58%
2001	79%	21%	40%	60%
2000	83%	17%	77%	23%

INTEREST GROUPS

	AFL-CIO	ADA	CCUS	ACU
2004	87%	95%	67%	24%
2003	86%	95%	54%	88%
2002	67%	70%	68%	21%
2001	83%	85%	57%	8%
2000	60%	70%	66%	12%

VIRGINIA 8

Washington suburbs – Arlington, Alexandria, part of Fairfax County

Taking in the close-in Northern Virginia suburbs of Washington, D.C., the 8th is primarily upper-income and strongly Democratic — in no small part because of a racially and ethnically diverse population of blacks, Asians and Hispanics, who together total about 40 percent of residents.

The 8th bustles with technology businesses and defense contractors, drawn to the district's substantial military presence, including the Pentagon. While government and defense-related jobs are important to the economy, technology took off as the hot industry of the 1990s.

Roughly half of the 8th's residents live in an elongated swath of Fairfax County that reaches from the Potomac River, near Mount Vernon (shared with the 11th), past Falls Church and Tysons Corner to Democratic-leaning Reston. Redistricting following the 2000 census revised the 8th's portion of Fairfax to boost the district's overall Democratic lean. The new Fairfax portion gave John Kerry 60 percent of the 2004 presidential vote.

Yet Fairfax is not the 8th's main source of Democratic strength. Closer to the D.C. line, Alexandria and Arlington typically give Democratic statewide candidates their highest vote percentages in Republican-leaning Virginia. A GOP presidential candidate has not won a majority in either jurisdiction since 1972. Kerry captured 68 percent of the vote in Arlington and 67 percent in Alexandria, where one-in-four residents is black. Overall, the 8th was Kerry's second-best Virginia district.

MAJOR INDUSTRY
Government, technology, defense, service

MILITARY BASES
Pentagon, 11,000 military, 13,000 civilian (2005); Fort Belvoir (Army), 4,601 military, 6,500 civilian; Fort Myer (Army), 2,843 military, 1,330 civilian (2004); Naval Sea Systems Command, 379 military, 2,364 civilian; Henderson Hall, 2,156 military, 441 civilian (2005)

CITIES
Arlington (unincorporated), 189,453; Alexandria, 128,283; Reston (unincorporated) (pt.), 56,275; Franconia (unincorporated), 31,907

NOTABLE
Despite the Pentagon's 17.5 miles of corridors, it takes only seven minutes to walk between any two points.

Rep. Rick Boucher (D)

Elected 1982; 12th term

CAPITOL OFFICE
225-3861
ninthnet@mail.house.gov
www.house.gov/boucher
2187 Rayburn 20515-4609; fax 225-0442

COMMITTEES
Energy & Commerce
Judiciary

HOMETOWN
Abingdon

BORN
Aug. 1, 1946, Abingdon, Va.

RELIGION
Methodist

FAMILY
Single

EDUCATION
Roanoke College, B.A. 1968 (political science);
U. of Virginia, J.D. 1971

CAREER
Lawyer

POLITICAL HIGHLIGHTS
Va. Senate, 1976-82

ELECTION RESULTS

2004 GENERAL

Rick Boucher (D)	150,039	59.3%
Kevin Triplett (R)	98,499	38.9%
Seth Davis (I)	4,341	1.7%

2004 PRIMARY

Rick Boucher (D)	unopposed

2002 GENERAL

Rick Boucher (D)	100,075	65.8%
Jay Katzen (R)	52,076	34.2%

PREVIOUS WINNING PERCENTAGES
2000 (70%); 1998 (61%); 1996 (65%); 1994 (59%);
1992 (63%); 1990 (97%); 1988 (63%); 1986 (99%);
1984 (52%); 1982 (50%)

It annoys Republican partisans in Washington that the wonkish Boucher has been able to lock up the 9th District, a land of farms and small towns that looks like it ought to be trending "red," like so much else of the rural South. In 2004, the GOP made a serious run at Boucher, opposing him with Kevin Triplett, a former NASCAR executive.

But when Speaker J. Dennis Hastert came to Roanoke in late October to campaign for Triplett, just about the worst he could say about Boucher was this: "He doesn't do a bad job. He's a nice guy." Voters agreed, electing Boucher to his 12th House term with a solid 59 percent of the vote.

There are several secrets to Boucher's success. First, he does not take a strongly partisan approach to his work. This has something to do with his bipartisan family background: His father was a Republican commonwealth's attorney in Washington County, and both his grandfather and great-grandfather were Democratic state delegates.

Second, on the hot-button issues of guns and gays, Boucher (BOW — rhymes with NOW — cher) parts ways with the majority of Democrats to side with the overwhelming sentiment in his district, where gun owners' rights are sacred and same-sex marriage is considered an alien concept.

Third, and most important, Boucher has been able to convince voters that his abiding passion for working on high-technology issues in Congress can help improve economic conditions in the 9th. By bringing high-speed Internet connections and other trappings of the digital age into the district, he hopes to expand local job opportunities beyond the traditional pillars of coal mining, livestock raising and tobacco farming.

Boucher says that his interest in technology issues stems in part from the fact that they do not break along traditional party lines. One of Boucher's partners on high-tech legislation is Republican Robert W. Goodlatte, a colleague on the Judiciary Committee and his neighbor in Virginia's 6th District. Technology matters have engrossed Boucher since he tried to improve satellite TV service for his constituents in the 1980s. He is a co-founder of the Congressional Internet Caucus.

Holding seats on both Judiciary and Energy and Commerce, whose jurisdictions include satellite, digital copyright and intellectual property issues, Boucher is well-positioned to influence the fast-evolving field of telecommunications policy.

At the start of the 109th Congress, he was expecting to be busy working on an overhaul of telecom policy affecting the wireless, cable and Internet industries. As new technologies have taken off — wireless, broadband and Internet-based voice services — each has put strains on the web of regulations established by the 1996 Telecommunications Act. "It clearly is time to look at what significant changes need to be made," Boucher said.

With the music and motion picture industries lobbying to tighten piracy laws, Boucher has worked to protect the right of consumers to copy films and music at home for personal use. Support for Boucher's position has grown as lawmakers hear from constituents who are frustrated that they cannot do with DVDs what they can do with home videos — copy them. "What we have is a coalition of business and consumer groups saying the law is too broad," Boucher says.

In his own House office, Boucher has decreed that all staff communication be done by e-mail or telephone. He has a grand vision of the future, one in which members carry wireless "personal digital assistants" with

Internet access and e-mail onto the House floor. When legislation is debated, a stream of information literally would be at lawmakers' fingertips.

On Judiciary, Boucher often is the rare Democrat siding with Republicans. With Republican Goodlatte, Boucher has sponsored legislation to make it easier to transfer class action lawsuits from state to federal court. Opponents say the measure is an attempt to cut down on generous sums awarded by state juries, while supporters say the bill is needed to correct abuses in the current system. The bill passed the House by a wide margin in the 108th, but was not taken up by the Senate.

Always mindful of his district's coal-mining industry, Boucher in the 108th expressed support for tax incentives that would encourage utilities to adopt clean-coal technologies and build new coal plants. Boucher said that promoting coal for electric generation would take some of the pressure off the market for natural gas, where prices were escalating — and, of course, it would be good business for coal mining.

Tobacco farmers are another important Boucher constituency; he voted in the 108th for legislation to abolish the federal quota system for tobacco and reimburse farmers for their losses. The buyout was approved as part of the corporate tax overhaul approved at the end of the 108th. Boucher said it would help 10,000 quota-holders in his district.

Boucher has said that, by the time he was 12, he had decided to become a lawyer and be a part of public life. After graduating from the University of Virginia Law School, he joined a Wall Street firm, worked as an advance man for George McGovern's 1972 presidential campaign, and joined the family law firm in 1978.

He won a seat in the state Senate, then took on GOP Rep. William C. Wampler in 1982. With high unemployment plaguing the district's coal fields, Boucher won the hard-fought contest by just 1,123 votes out of more than 150,000 cast. Two years later, he edged to a 4 percentage point victory over state Rep. Jefferson Stafford.

Solid re-election victories then became the Boucher norm, but 2004 looked like it might be different when Republicans came forward with former NASCAR executive Triplett. He preached a conservative message and said too many local jobs had been lost on Boucher's watch.

Boucher said he had "an agenda for progress" that was offsetting job losses in textiles and manufacturing and helping the district's economy grow. For the first time ever, he served as the grand marshal for NASCAR's Food City 500 at the Bristol Motor Speedway, in the southern part of the 9th. On Election Day, he crossed the finish line far ahead of Triplett.

KEY VOTES

2004

Yes Extend federal unemployment benefits by 13 weeks

Yes Pass $283.2 billion, six-year federal highway and mass transit bill

Yes Approve $146 billion multi-year extension of previously enacted middle-class tax breaks

Yes Amend the Constitution to prohibit same-sex marriage

Yes Cut corporate taxes $137 billion over 10 years

Yes Reorganize U.S. intelligence agencies as proposed by Sept. 11 commission

2003

No Cut taxes by $330 billion through fiscal 2013

Yes Block Bush rule scaling back overtime pay for some white-collar federal workers

Yes Do not allow use of search warrants without first notifying subjects

Yes Allow importation of prescription drugs

No Create private school voucher program in Washington, D.C.

No Ban "partial birth" abortion except to save a woman's life

Yes Split $18.6 billion in Iraq aid into half-grant, half-loan

Yes Overhaul Medicare and create prescription drug benefit

CQ VOTE STUDIES

	PARTY UNITY		PRESIDENTIAL SUPPORT	
	Support	Oppose	Support	Oppose
2004	81%	19%	38%	62%
2003	83%	17%	31%	69%
2002	81%	19%	49%	51%
2001	82%	18%	33%	67%
2000	80%	20%	61%	39%

INTEREST GROUPS

	AFL-CIO	ADA	CCUS	ACU
2004	73%	75%	67%	32%
2003	93%	90%	53%	28%
2002	89%	80%	70%	21%
2001	100%	90%	57%	16%
2000	80%	75%	55%	29%

VIRGINIA 9
Southwest — Blacksburg, Bristol

Covered with forests, mountainous terrain and a slew of small factory and coal towns, the 9th is rich in beauty but also is Virginia's poorest district. Located in the southwestern part of the state, the 9th has struggled with high poverty rates and a weak economic base. The median income here is less than $30,000.

Coal mining provides jobs in counties at the western tip of the 9th, which also is the most economically depressed part of the district. Elsewhere, manufacturing is the major industry.

Major priorities for the district include diversifying the economy and ensuring clean drinking water for the thousands of residents who lack it. Local officials view the Internet as a way to get community exposure and offer residents new learning opportunities. Although the district's population stagnated in the 1990s, Craig County, with its commuters to Salem and Roanoke (in the 6th) grew in population. Blacksburg remains the largest city and is home to the state's largest university, Virginia Tech. Surrounding Montgomery County is economically atypical of the 9th.

The district is known as the Fighting 9th, a name that reflects the area's fiercely competitive politics and its ornery isolation from the political establishment in Richmond. In the post-World War II era, when Democrats routinely dominated Virginia politics, the 9th was one of the only areas in which Republicans were consistently strong. Now Republicans dominate most Virginia offices, but Rep. Boucher easily has kept the 9th in Democratic hands for two decades, and Democrats perform well in local races.

The 9th has swung to the GOP in recent presidential elections, however, and voted strongly for George W. Bush in 2000 and 2004. Four years after carrying the 9th by a dozen percentage points, Bush dominated John Kerry by 20 percentage points in 2004, marking the president's biggest four-year improvement in any Virginia district.

MAJOR INDUSTRY
Manufacturing, coal mining, agriculture

CITIES
Blacksburg, 39,573; Bristol, 17,367; Christiansburg, 16,947; Radford, 15,859

NOTABLE
Brass markers placed through the city of Bristol mark the Virginia-Tennessee state line.

Rep. Frank R. Wolf (R)

CAPITOL OFFICE
225-5136
www.house.gov/wolf
241 Cannon 20515-4610; fax 225-0437

COMMITTEES
Appropriations
(Science, State, Justice & Commerce -
chairman)

HOMETOWN
Vienna

BORN
Jan. 30, 1939, Philadelphia, Pa.

RELIGION
Presbyterian

FAMILY
Wife, Carolyn Wolf; five children

EDUCATION
Pennsylvania State U., B.A. 1961 (political
science); Georgetown U., LL.B. 1965

MILITARY SERVICE
Army Reserve, 1962-63

CAREER
Lawyer; U.S. Interior Department official;
congressional aide; lobbyist

POLITICAL HIGHLIGHTS
Sought Republican nomination for U.S. House,
1976; Republican nominee for U.S. House, 1978

ELECTION RESULTS

2004 GENERAL
Frank R. Wolf (R)	205,982	63.8%
James Socas (D)	116,654	36.1%

2004 PRIMARY
Frank R. Wolf (R)	unopposed

2002 GENERAL
Frank R. Wolf (R)	115,917	71.7%
John B. Stevens Jr. (D)	45,464	28.1%

PREVIOUS WINNING PERCENTAGES
2000 (84%); 1998 (72%); 1996 (72%); 1994 (87%);
1992 (64%); 1990 (61%); 1988 (68%); 1986 (60%);
1984 (63%); 1982 (53%); 1980 (51%)

Elected 1980; 13th term

A veteran lawmaker from a district with a sizable population of federal workers, Wolf stands apart from some of his conservative colleagues who have a more doctrinaire attitude about shrinking the federal government.

Wolf, now in his 13th term, is in a position to bring home the federal dollars. He is an Appropriations subcommittee chairman, and his press releases regularly tout the millions of dollars he helps direct to his Northern Virginia district.

Wolf is also one of Congress' foremost spokesmen on human rights issues and often can be found in such far-flung trouble spots as Sudan, Ethiopia, Iraq and Tibet. Wolf's religious faith is a driving force in his work. After a January 2003 trip to famine-stricken Ethiopia, Wolf said, "Every member of the world community bears responsibility to ensure that this crisis receives the attention it deserves. . . . Luke 12:48 says, 'From everyone who has been given much, much will be demanded; and from the one who has been entrusted with much, much more will be asked.' "

Over the years, he has strongly criticized countries he regards as guilty of human rights violations and religious persecution, including China, Sudan and Saddam Hussein's Iraq. In an emergency spending bill passed in 2002, Wolf included millions for overseas media campaigns aimed at fostering religious tolerance and democracy. To try to make sure that U.S. foreign aid is spent wisely, in 2004 he won creation of a commission to study the effectiveness of aid and development programs.

In a realignment of House Appropriations subcommittees early in the 109th Congress, Wolf's clout emerged intact. He holds the gavel of the Science, State, Justice and Commerce Subcommittee, whose jurisdiction includes NASA as well as the departments of State, Justice and Commerce. He also serves on the Appropriations subcommittee that funds transportation and housing programs and the federal judiciary.

One display of how Wolf cashes in on his Appropriations assignment came in the 2003 transportation spending bill, which included almost $50 million for several Northern Virginia transportation improvements and another $5 million to establish a national first-responder training center in his district, to prepare firefighters, paramedics and law enforcement officers to handle major emergencies, including acts of terrorism.

In the 108th, Wolf sought federal help to combat two problems tormenting parts of Northern Virginia: gangs and traffic. The 2005 catchall spending bill gave the FBI $10 million to set up a clearinghouse for information on gang activity across the country. It also sent $2 million to the Northern Virginia Regional Gang Task Force.

Frustrated by the slow pace of government efforts to implement "telecommuting," which would at least slightly ease traffic congestion, Wolf authored a measure to withhold $5 million from the budgets of a number of federal departments until each ensured that workers could do their jobs by computer from home.

Wolf generally votes with his party and is regarded as a team player, but he has been willing to buck President Bush and the GOP on some issues. Wolf joined other Washington, D.C.-area lawmakers in 2002 to push for a larger pay raise for civilian federal workers than Bush wanted.

Wolf was one of 25 House Republicans who went against their party to support creation of an independent probe of the Sept. 11, 2001, terrorist attacks. He also was one of eight House Republicans to oppose his party's leaders on an aviation security bill because it would have allowed private security companies to continue manning airport screening checkpoints. Wolf voted for a Democratic amendment to make all airport security workers federal employees.

However, on another key homeland security issue affecting federal workers in his district, Wolf sided with party leaders. He voted against an amendment to affirm federal employees' rights to union representation unless their jobs were materially changed after transfer to the new Department of Homeland Security.

Wolf presided over a reorganization of the FBI's resources in the wake of the Sept. 11 attacks. The FBI was blamed for shortcomings that may have made the terrorists' job easier. Sept. 11 also showed Wolf the need for better emergency communications in the D.C. metropolitan area. With the help of other area representatives, he has garnered millions of dollars to improve communications among emergency responders in Northern Virginia.

Wolf is a staunch opponent of legalized gambling and was the chief author of a law to create a national gambling commission to study the impact of gambling on society. He says gambling has led to "human misery" that the industry has ignored.

Wolf was instrumental in 2002 in forcing NBC to reconsider plans to end a decades-long ban on TV commercials for hard liquor. Wolf, who oversees the Federal Communications Commission's budget, worked with fellow appropriator Lucille Roybal-Allard, a Democrat from California, to pressure NBC. Mothers Against Drunk Driving gave Wolf a 2004 Congressional Excellence Award, largely for his role in helping enact a national .08 blood alcohol concentration standard.

Wolf first began his quest for a congressional seat barely a year after Democrat Joseph L. Fisher won election to the House in 1974. Wolf's 1976 effort had the backing of the most conservative activists in the local GOP, but he lost the primary. In 1978, with higher name recognition and better financing, Wolf won the Republican nomination but lost to Fisher in November. In 1980, Wolf benefited from a national Republican surge that elected Ronald Reagan president and, capping a five-year effort, he won a narrow victory over Fisher. After a tough re-election race in 1982, he has enjoyed smooth rides to victory every two years.

Before his election, Wolf was an aide to Pennsylvania Republican Rep. Edward G. Biester, a deputy assistant secretary of interior, and a lobbyist for baby food and farm implement manufacturers.

KEY VOTES

2004
No   Extend federal unemployment benefits by 13 weeks

Yes   Pass $283.2 billion, six-year federal highway and mass transit bill

Yes   Approve $146 billion multi-year extension of previously enacted middle-class tax breaks

Yes   Amend the Constitution to prohibit same-sex marriage

No   Cut corporate taxes $137 billion over 10 years

Yes   Reorganize U.S. intelligence agencies as proposed by Sept. 11 commission

2003
Yes   Cut taxes by $330 billion through fiscal 2013

No   Block Bush rule scaling back overtime pay for some white-collar federal workers

No   Do not allow use of search warrants without first notifying subjects

Yes   Allow importation of prescription drugs

Yes   Create private school voucher program in Washington, D.C.

Yes   Ban "partial birth" abortion except to save a woman's life

No   Split $18.6 billion in Iraq aid into half-grant, half-loan

Yes   Overhaul Medicare and create prescription drug benefit

CQ VOTE STUDIES

	PARTY UNITY		PRESIDENTIAL SUPPORT	
	Support	Oppose	Support	Oppose
2004	85%	15%	85%	15%
2003	93%	7%	93%	7%
2002	89%	11%	82%	18%
2001	95%	5%	86%	14%
2000	85%	15%	30%	70%

INTEREST GROUPS

	AFL-CIO	ADA	CCUS	ACU
2004	40%	25%	90%	76%
2003	27%	15%	83%	80%
2002	11%	5%	80%	92%
2001	17%	10%	91%	79%
2000	20%	10%	71%	72%

VIRGINIA 10

North — part of Fairfax County, Loudoun County

Located in the northern part of Virginia, the Republican-friendly 10th bridges a dizzying range of economies and lifestyles, with mountains and farmland at one end and congested Washington, D.C., suburbs at the other. A hotbed of economic activity in the 1990s, the 10th is a mostly white-collar area that includes some of the state's wealthiest counties — Loudoun and parts of Fauquier and Fairfax.

Most of the district's population resides in suburban Northern Virginia, and many residents commute to jobs in Washington or the inner suburbs just outside the nation's capital. Nearly all of the 10th's counties grew substantially in the 1990s. Technology-magnet Loudoun County, which includes Leesburg and Washington Dulles International Airport, nearly doubled in population during the 1990s, and Census Bureau projections show its population swelled by another one-third in the first three years of the 2000s. The area is grappling with its expansion, and slow-growth advocates have fared well in recent local elections. In presidential races, Loudoun continues to vote decidedly Republican, although not as

overwhelmingly as in past elections.

About one-third of residents live in Fairfax County (shared with the 8th and 11th), which includes Chantilly. This area is more politically competitive, with John Kerry narrowly carrying the 10th's share of Fairfax County in the 2004 presidential election.

Agriculture and manufacturing fuel the economy in the balance of the district, which is solidly Republican and less densely populated. Clarke and Frederick counties produce about half of Virginia's apples and peaches. Winchester (Frederick County), the center of the state's apple-growing industry, is the home base of the Byrd family, which dominated Democratic politics in Virginia for decades. But the district has long since abandoned its Democratic roots.

MAJOR INDUSTRY
Federal government, technology, manufacturing, agriculture

CITIES
Chantilly (unincorporated), 41,041; McLean (unincorporated) (pt.), 37,427; Manassas, 35,135; Centreville (unincorporated) (pt.), 33,053

NOTABLE
The CIA headquarters are in Langley.

Rep. Thomas M. Davis III (R)

Elected 1994; 6th term

CAPITOL OFFICE
225-1492
tomdavis.house.gov
2348 Rayburn 20515-4611; fax 225-3071

COMMITTEES
Government Reform - chairman
Homeland Security

HOMETOWN
Vienna

BORN
Jan. 5, 1949, Minot, N.D.

RELIGION
Christian Scientist

FAMILY
Wife, Jeannemarie A. Devolites-Davis; three children

EDUCATION
Amherst College, B.A. 1971 (political science); U. of Virginia, J.D. 1975

MILITARY SERVICE
Army, 1971-72; Va. National Guard, 1972-79; Army Reserve, 1972-79

CAREER
Lawyer; professional services firm executive; state legislative aide

POLITICAL HIGHLIGHTS
Fairfax County Board of Supervisors, 1980-94 (chairman, 1991-94)

ELECTION RESULTS

2004 GENERAL

Thomas M. Davis III (R)	186,299	60.3%
Ken Longmyer (D)	118,305	38.3%
Joseph Oddo (I)	4,338	1.4%

2004 PRIMARY

Thomas M. Davis III (R)	unopposed

2002 GENERAL

Thomas M. Davis III (R)	135,379	82.9%
Frank W. Creel (CNSTP)	26,892	16.5%

PREVIOUS WINNING PERCENTAGES
2000 (62%); 1998 (82%); 1996 (64%); 1994 (53%)

One of the most savvy politicians in the House, Davis uses his perch as chairman of the Government Reform Committee to put himself in the thick of high-profile debates. He was responsible for the spectacle in 2005 of beloved figures in Major League Baseball publicly answering questions about the use of steroids to improve their game.

Davis already has been on the lower rung of the leadership ladder, as chairman of the House Republicans' campaign committee in two successful elections, and he is sure to be a contender in any new lineup at the top if Speaker J. Dennis Hastert retires in the next few years. Davis is also weighing a bid for the Senate in 2008.

A political junkie since childhood, Davis cemented his reputation as one of the party's most adept operatives — and built himself a constituency among colleagues — by guiding House Republicans to a larger majority in the 2002 election. As chairman of the National Republican Congressional Committee, he helped defend incumbents, raised money for them and recruited candidates for open seats.

The conservative GOP leadership showed him its appreciation by giving him the Government Reform gavel at the start of the 108th Congress. Speaker Hastert passed over more-senior committee Republicans to give the job to Davis, including moderate Christopher Shays of Connecticut.

In early 2005, Davis became familiar to viewers of the ESPN cable sports network with his hearings on steroid use in baseball. Some of the sport's biggest stars testified, a few under subpoena. The witnesses included sluggers Sammy Sosa and Rafael Palmeiro and former players Jose Canseco and Mark McGwire. "We can help kids understand that steroids aren't cool," Davis said. The subject matter was dear to Davis. As a kid, he used to memorize Washington Senators box scores and now recites district-by-district political data with the same extraordinary recall. Davis is a season ticket holder of the Nationals, Washington, D.C.'s new baseball team.

He won the cooperation of Government Reform's senior Democrat, Henry A. Waxman of California, who has fought bitterly with past chairmen whom he considered too partisan. Davis said he planned to expand the probe to several more sports during the 109th Congress.

As he has cultivated his base of support among Republicans, Davis has tried to improve his standing with conservatives, who are key to his future ambitions. He toed the party line 89 percent of the time on votes that divided the parties in the 108th Congress, compared with scores in the high 90s for the most conservative and most loyal Republicans.

Shortly after the baseball hearing, Davis issued a subpoena to Terri Schiavo, a severely brain-damaged Florida woman, in a legal maneuver to prevent her feeding tube from being removed. Schiavo's case became a cause célèbre for conservatives, including House and Senate leaders. The subpoena was brushed aside by a state judge and Schiavo later died.

Davis applies to the legislative process the same considerable strategic and tactical skills that made him a star at the NRCC. He has pushed efforts to prevent illegal aliens from obtaining driver's licenses, an idea President Bush endorsed in 2005, and to implement tougher rules for people claiming political asylum.

He has been an indefatigable ally for Bush in reshaping the federal bureaucracy, focusing the Government Reform panel on "legislating, not investigating." Former GOP Chairman Dan Burton's vigorous pursuit of the

Clinton administration went too far even for some Republicans. Davis, by contrast, has delved into federal employment and purchasing practices, which are important issues for the government workers and contractors in Northern Virginia and the suburbs just outside of D.C.

After becoming actively involved in the 2002 debate over creating the Department of Homeland Security — his proposals on procurement and contracting policies were included in the law — Davis has tried to implement the president's management agenda, which includes efforts to boost competition between the government and private companies to provide public services.

In the 108th Congress, Davis also played a prominent role in advancing the first federally funded school voucher program in the nation, a favorite initiative of many conservatives and of the president as well.

In 2005, Davis renewed efforts to overhaul the U.S. Postal Service. Despite a unanimous bipartisan majority in committee, the measure died in the 108th Congress because of a disagreement between lawmakers and the White House over how to handle retirement benefits for postal workers.

He is frequently mentioned as a contender to succeed GOP Sen. John W. Warner should Warner decide not to seek re-election in 2008. He is also on the shortlist of future candidates for elected leadership in the House.

Davis' often rumpled appearance and intemperance with Diet Coke belie the sharp organizational skills he possesses, including a mental Rolodex of district-level political data and a keen sense of legislative playing fields. A Senate page in the mid-1960s, he wrote a college paper titled "The Political Realignment of the Outer South."

When he splits with the Republican leadership, it is often on issues affecting the government workers in his district. He called federal employees "hostages" to the government shutdowns of 1995 and 1996 as he pressured GOP leaders to end the standoff with President Clinton.

Conservatives complain that he is too friendly toward labor unions, and sometimes toward Democrats. In 2002, he declined to campaign against Democratic Rep. James P. Moran, who's in a neighboring district, and he reportedly influenced the state's redistricting after the 2000 census to strengthen Moran's hold on his seat.

Davis built his career in government. He had been on the board of supervisors in Fairfax County, Washington's fastest-growing suburb, for about 15 years when he took on one-term Democratic Rep. Leslie L. Byrne, a member of her party's leadership and an aggressive partisan. He won by 8 percentage points and has been easily re-elected ever since. The 60 percent share of the vote he won in 2004 was his lowest in five re-election bids.

KEY VOTES

2004

No Extend federal unemployment benefits by 13 weeks

Yes Pass $283.2 billion, six-year federal highway and mass transit bill

Yes Approve $146 billion multi-year extension of previously enacted middle-class tax breaks

Yes Amend the Constitution to prohibit same-sex marriage

Yes Cut corporate taxes $137 billion over 10 years

Yes Reorganize U.S. intelligence agencies as proposed by Sept. 11 commission

2003

Yes Cut taxes by $330 billion through fiscal 2013

No Block Bush rule scaling back overtime pay for some white-collar federal workers

Yes Do not allow use of search warrants without first notifying subjects

No Allow importation of prescription drugs

Yes Create private school voucher program in Washington, D.C.

Yes Ban "partial birth" abortion except to save a woman's life

No Split $18.6 billion in Iraq aid into half-grant, half-loan

Yes Overhaul Medicare and create prescription drug benefit

CQ VOTE STUDIES

	PARTY UNITY		PRESIDENTIAL SUPPORT	
	Support	Oppose	Support	Oppose
2004	88%	12%	91%	9%
2003	90%	10%	96%	4%
2002	90%	10%	82%	18%
2001	90%	10%	88%	12%
2000	87%	13%	36%	64%

INTEREST GROUPS

	AFL-CIO	ADA	CCUS	ACU
2004	20%	10%	100%	80%
2003	15%	5%	93%	68%
2002	11%	10%	84%	88%
2001	17%	15%	90%	60%
2000	0%	5%	80%	70%

VIRGINIA 11

Washington suburbs — parts of Fairfax and Prince William counties

Anchored in the suburbs of Washington, D.C., the 11th is home to a well-educated, professional and upper-income workforce that has the highest median income in the nation (more than $80,000). As in surrounding suburban areas, the 11th has become more racially and ethnically diverse, with robust populations of Asians and Hispanics.

Tailor-made for a centrist Republican, the 11th leans to the right on fiscal questions. But traffic congestion is so rampant that many residents are willing to accept tax increases to pay for transportation improvements. In the 2001 gubernatorial election, Democrat Mark Warner emphasized transportation policy en route to winning in the 11th and statewide.

Two-thirds of the population lives in Fairfax County, which the 11th shares with the 8th and 10th districts. The balance lives in Prince William County, a burgeoning area south and west of Fairfax, or in Fairfax city, a separate jurisdiction that is geographically within Fairfax County.

Many residents work in Washington, either for the federal government or for companies whose business is linked to the government. Despite the public sector influence, technology is the area's fastest-growing industry, and dozens of firms have put down roots in office-park developments in Fairfax County. Technological advances — and traffic woes — have made telecommuting an increasingly attractive option for area workers.

A quintessential swing district in the 1990s, the 11th was revised in GOP-controlled redistricting following the 2000 census to have a Republican lean, mainly by revising the district's boundaries in Fairfax County. Still, George W. Bush's razor-thin victory here in the 2004 presidential election — he won the district's share of Prince William County but lost its share of Fairfax County — indicates that the 11th remains highly competitive.

MAJOR INDUSTRY

Government, technology, service

CITIES

Burke (unincorporated), 57,737; Dale City (unincorporated), 55,971; Annandale (unincorporated) (pt.), 51,350

NOTABLE

Fairfax Court House is where George and Martha Washington's wills were recorded and still are kept.

Gov. Christine Gregoire (D)

First elected: 2004
Length of term: 4 years
Term expires: 1/09
Salary: $145,132
Phone: (360) 902-4111

Hometown: Olympia
Born: March 24, 1947; Adrian, Mich.
Religion: Roman Catholic
Family: Husband, Mike Gregoire; two children
Education: U. of Washington, B.A. 1969 (speech & sociology); Gonzaga U., J.D. 1977
Career: Lawyer; state social services department caseworker; clerk typist
Political highlights: Wash. Department of Ecology director, 1988-92; Wash. attorney general, 1993-2004

Election results:

2004 GENERAL

Christine Gregoire (D)	1,373,361	48.87%
Dino Rossi (R)	1,373,232	48.86%
Ruth Bennett (LIBERT)	63,465	2.3%

Lt. Gov. Brad Owen (D)

First elected: 1996
Length of term: 4 years
Term expires: 1/09
Salary: $75,865
Phone: (360) 786-7700

STATE LEGISLATURE

Legislature: 105 days January-May in odd-numbered years; 60 days January-March in even-numbered years

House: 98 members, 2-year terms
2005 breakdown: 55D, 43R; 69 men, 29 women
Salary: $34,227; $90/day in session
Phone: (360) 786-7750

Senate: 49 members, 4-year terms
2005 breakdown: 26D, 23R; 29 men, 20 women
Salary: $34,227; $90/day in session
Phone: (360) 786-7550

STATE TERM LIMITS

Governor: 2 terms
House: No
Senate: No

URBAN STATISTICS

CITY	POPULATION
Seattle	563,374
Spokane	195,629
Tacoma	193,556
Vancouver	143,560
Bellevue	109,569

REGISTERED VOTERS

Voters do not register by party.

POPULATION

2004 population (est.)	6,203,788
2000 population	5,894,121
1990 population	4,866,692
Percent change (1990-2000)	+21.1%
Rank among states (2004)	15

Median age	35.3
Born in state	47.2%
Foreign born	10.4%
Violent crime rate	370/100,000
Poverty level	10.6%
Federal workers	66,061
Military	74,250

REDISTRICTING

Washington retained its nine House seats in reapportionment. The Washington State Redistricting Commission adopted a new map on Jan. 1, 2002.

MISCELLANEOUS

Web: www.access.wa.gov
Capital: Olympia
STATE ELECTION OFFICIAL
(360) 902-4151
DEMOCRATIC HEADQUARTERS
(206) 583-0664
REPUBLICAN HEADQUARTERS
(206) 575-2900

District Statistics

DIST.	2004 VOTE FOR PRESIDENT BUSH	KERRY	WHITE	BLACK	ASIAN	HISP	MEDIAN INCOME	WHITE COLLAR	BLUE COLLAR	SERVICE INDUSTRY	OVER 64	UNDER 18	COLLEGE EDUCATION	RURAL	SQ. MILES
1	42%	56%	82%	2%	8%	4%	$58,565	69%	18%	12%	10%	26%	36%	5%	439
2	47	51	86	1	3	6	$45,441	55	29	16	12	26	22	31	6,564
3	50	48	88	1	3	5	$44,426	57	28	15	11	27	21	29	7,515
4	63	35	68	1	1	26	$37,764	53	31	16	11	30	19	29	19,051
5	57	41	88	1	2	5	$35,720	60	23	17	13	25	24	28	22,864
6	45	53	78	6	4	5	$39,205	55	27	18	14	25	20	21	6,781
7	19	79	67	8	13	6	$45,864	71	15	14	12	17	44	2	141
8	48	51	82	2	8	4	$63,854	69	20	11	9	28	37	12	2,579
9	46	53	73	6	7	7	$46,495	59	25	15	10	26	22	5	608
STATE	46	53	79	3	5	7	$45,776	61	24	15	11	26	28	18	66,544
U.S.	50.7	48.3	69	12	4	13	$41,994	60	25	15	12	26	24	21	3,537,438

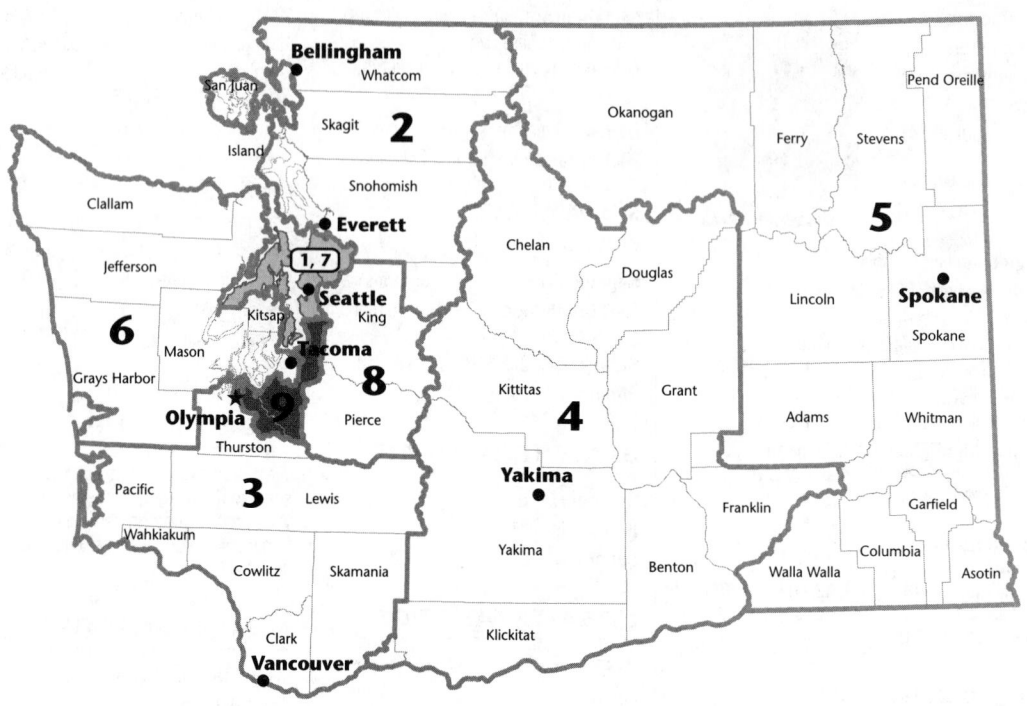

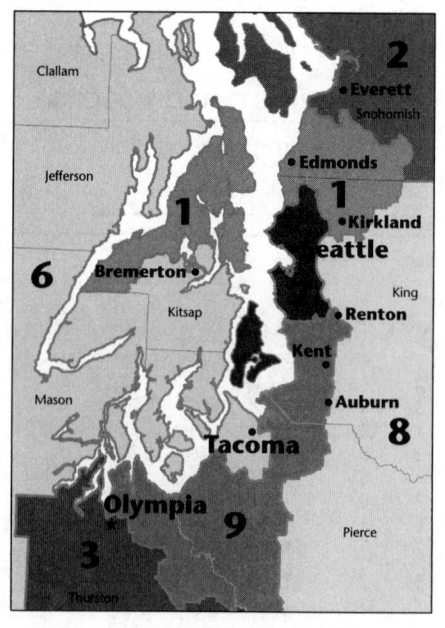

Sen. Patty Murray (D)

Elected 1992; 3rd term

CAPITOL OFFICE
224-2621
murray.senate.gov
173 Russell 20510-4704; fax 224-0238

COMMITTEES
Appropriations
Budget
Health, Education, Labor & Pensions
Veterans' Affairs

HOMETOWN
Seattle

BORN
Oct. 11, 1950, Bothell, Wash.

RELIGION
Roman Catholic

FAMILY
Husband, Rob Murray; two children

EDUCATION
Washington State U., B.A. 1972

CAREER
Parenting class instructor

POLITICAL HIGHLIGHTS
Candidate for Shoreline School Board, 1983;
Shoreline School Board, 1983-89; Wash. Senate,
1989-93

ELECTION RESULTS

2004 GENERAL

Patty Murray (D)	1,549,708	55.0%
George Nethercutt (R)	1,204,584	42.7%
J. Mills (LIBERT)	34,055	1.2%
Mark B. Wilson (GREEN)	30,304	1.1%

2004 PRIMARY

Patty Murray (D)	709,497	92.2%
Warren E. Hanson (D)	46,490	6.0%
Mohammad H. Said (D)	13,527	1.8%

PREVIOUS WINNING PERCENTAGES
1998 (58%); 1992 (54%)

Murray has made a career of being underestimated. Despite a stubborn caricature as a lightweight, she has become a dominant political figure in Washington state and increasingly on Capitol Hill.

In 1992, launching a long-shot Senate campaign as "a mom in tennis shoes," she beat two sitting House members in the primary and general elections. In 2004, when she was up for re-election the last time, the head of the Republican Senate campaign committee suggested Murray would be no match for "giant killer" George Nethercutt, who had knocked off Democratic Speaker Tom Foley in 1994. She beat him by 12 percentage points.

Murray is a senior member of the Appropriations Committee and the top-ranking Democrat on its Transportation Subcommittee. She is the No. 3 Democrat on the Budget Committee. At the start of the 109th Congress in 2005, new Minority Leader Harry Reid made her assistant floor leader, responsible for helping him coordinate activity during floor debates. In the run-up to the 2002 elections, she headed the Democratic Senatorial Campaign Committee, bringing in $143 million for party candidates.

It is no accident that Murray has arrived at this point. Her career is the result of an endless series of small steps, carefully planned and executed. Her success "is a combination of careful, calculated evolution, political smarts and a state that is often sympathetic to Democrats," said the Seattle Post-Intelligencer. She is also willing to take chances. Murray personally intervened in late 2000 to end a strike affecting the state's two largest newspapers, the Post-Intelligencer and The Seattle Times. Political analysts said her involvement carried many political risks and few benefits, but it was later seen as instrumental in ending the strike.

Mindful of the price Foley paid for being painted as a national political figure who had neglected folks back home, Murray takes care of her state's needs. Her Appropriations post gives her a say over the allocation of $90 billion in transportation spending each year, and she makes sure Washington gets a healthy share. Endorsing her over Nethercutt in 2004, the Vancouver Columbian said, "Murray is a hard-working, visible, hands-on senator who never takes her eye off the people back home. Her place on the Senate Appropriations Committee gives her important clout when deciding where federal dollars will be spent." Her prowess in that area has prompted some to call her "Patty Magnuson," a reference to Washington's legendary Democratic Sen. Warren Magnuson, who was famed for securing billions of federal dollars for the state.

Murray's penchant for directing tax dollars back home has not gone unnoticed. When she attached $3 million for a maritime museum to the transportation spending bill in 2001, she incurred the wrath of Arizona Republican John McCain, a frequent critic of lawmakers' earmarks. As Murray sat stone-faced in the chamber, McCain blasted her project as an example of "pork barrel spending."

She is a fierce defender and promoter of Washington's biggest employers, including Microsoft and Boeing. She repeatedly denounced the long-running federal antitrust case against Microsoft even though it was triggered by Democratic President Clinton. And she was one of the prime movers behind a $23 billion deal to buy and lease 100 Boeing 767s for the Air Force to use as aerial tankers. Criticized by McCain, the deal fell apart amid corruption allegations. Murray has fought to salvage some part of the arrangement. "It's unfortunate that Sen. McCain is once again trying to slow up a deal . . . that will benefit our troops and keep them safe," she said in 2004.

She has also pressed the Bush administration to take action against Boeing's chief nemesis, Airbus, a French conglomerate that has supplanted Boeing as the world's biggest maker of commercial jetliners.

Murray has won some fights with the administration, including funding for her Operation Safe Commerce, a pilot project that tracks U.S.-bound cargo containers in foreign ports to prevent them from being used to smuggle terrorists or weapons into the United States. She also blocked Senate confirmation of a sub-Cabinet appointee until the administration backed down on its plan to redirect money away from security projects at the nation's three largest ports, including Seattle-Tacoma.

In 2005, she joined a bipartisan group of lawmakers from Washington and Oregon fighting a Bush effort to require the Bonneville Power Administration to raise its rates, forcing consumers to pay more for electricity. She took on another fight from her seat on the Health, Education, Labor and Pensions Committee, vowing to hold up the nomination of the head of the Food and Drug Administration until the agency made a decision on approving over-the-counter sales of morning-after birth control pills. Murray argued that the FDA "continues to drag its feet . . . for ideological reasons."

Murray has emerged as a leading Democratic voice on education issues. She has sought to reduce class sizes for first-, second-, and third-graders by providing federal dollars to hire 100,000 teachers. That goal remains unrealized. She also serves on the Veterans' Affairs Committee, and has tried to boost funding for veterans' health care, citing the needs of returning Iraq war veterans. In 2004, she fought, and eventually defeated, a Bush administration plan to close three VA hospitals in her state.

Murray's strong support of most government programs stems from her childhood. She and her six siblings just got by on her father's salary as a dime-store manager. They often fended off childhood ailments without health care because her parents could not afford it. While she was a teenager, Murray's father was diagnosed with multiple sclerosis, and her family briefly went on welfare until her mother could complete a government-funded training program that enabled her to get a job as a bookkeeper. Without that aid, Murray has said, "my family wouldn't have made it."

Her fire for politics was stoked in the early 1980s when she packed her two young children in the car and drove to the state Capitol in Olympia to complain about the legislature's plan to discontinue a preschool program. While there, Murray recalls, one of the legislators dismissed her by saying: "You can't make a difference. You're just a mom in tennis shoes."

In the 2001 book "Nine and Counting: The Women of the Senate," Murray said that offhand comment propelled her into political life: "I figured that I could sit at home and say, 'Oh, well, that's too bad,' or I could get involved and be a part of the decision-making process." The cancellation of the preschool program prompted her to organize a statewide parents' effort to revive it. That led to six years on her local school board, followed by four years in the state Senate.

Then came her 1992 Senate quest. Democratic incumbent Brock Adams dropped out after allegations of sexual impropriety, and popular Democratic Gov. Booth Gardner decided against seeking the seat. Still, to win the primary and the general election, Murray had to get past two better-known, popular moderates with years of congressional experience. She did just that, besting former Democratic Rep. Don Bonker in the primary and winning the general election with 54 percent of the vote against GOP Rep. Rod Chandler.

Through it all, Murray has used her trademark tennis shoes to remind voters of her humble roots. She passes out "Golden Tennis Shoe" awards to constituents who, like her, have been community activists.

KEY VOTES

2004

Yes	Pass $318.9 billion, six-year highway and mass transit bill
Yes	Extend assault weapons ban for 10 years
Yes	Restore pay-as-you-go rules for new tax cuts and entitlement spending
No	Criminalize harm to a fetus in an attack on the mother
Yes	Increase mandatory child care funding to states by $6 billion over five years
No	Amend the Constitution to prohibit same-sex marriage
Yes	Approve $146 billion multi-year extension of previously enacted middle-class tax breaks
Yes	Reorganize U.S. intelligence agencies as proposed by Sept. 11 commission
Yes	Cut corporate taxes $137 billion over 10 years

2003

Yes	Delay Bush changes to Clean Air Act
No	Allow confirmation vote on Miguel A. Estrada to the U.S. Court of Appeals for the D.C. Circuit
Yes	Block a Bush proposal opening Alaska's Arctic National Wildlife Refuge to oil drilling
Yes	Limit size of Bush's proposed tax cut to $350 billion through fiscal 2013
Yes	Overhaul Medicare and create prescription drug benefit
Yes	Block Bush rule scaling back overtime pay for some white-collar federal workers
Yes	Split $20 billion in Iraq aid into half-grant, half-loan
No	Ban "partial birth" abortion except to save a woman's life
No	Stop proposal allowing travel to Cuba
No	Allow final vote on energy policy overhaul

CQ VOTE STUDIES

	PARTY UNITY		PRESIDENTIAL SUPPORT	
	Support	Oppose	Support	Oppose
2004	91%	9%	63%	37%
2003	97%	3%	49%	51%
2002	86%	14%	75%	25%
2001	96%	4%	65%	35%
2000	94%	6%	87%	13%
1999	93%	7%	88%	12%
1998	91%	9%	82%	18%
1997	93%	7%	87%	13%
1996	95%	5%	89%	11%
1995	93%	7%	91%	9%

INTEREST GROUPS

	AFL-CIO	ADA	CCUS	ACU
2004	92%	90%	75%	8%
2003	85%	90%	43%	10%
2002	92%	90%	55%	10%
2001	100%	85%	64%	4%
2000	63%	90%	64%	8%
1999	88%	100%	59%	4%
1998	88%	90%	56%	4%
1997	71%	90%	70%	0%
1996	100%	90%	17%	0%
1995	100%	95%	33%	0%

Sen. Maria Cantwell (D)

Elected 2000; 1st term

CAPITOL OFFICE
224-3441
cantwell.senate.gov
717 Hart 20510-4705; fax 228-0514

COMMITTEES
Commerce, Science & Transportation
Energy & Natural Resources
Indian Affairs
Small Business & Entrepreneurship

HOMETOWN
Edmonds

BORN
Oct. 13, 1958, Indianapolis, Ind.

RELIGION
Roman Catholic

FAMILY
Single

EDUCATION
Miami U. (Ohio), B.A. 1980 (public policy)

CAREER
Internet audio company executive; public relations
consultant

POLITICAL HIGHLIGHTS
Wash. House, 1987-92; U.S. House, 1993-95;
defeated for re-election to U.S. House, 1994

ELECTION RESULTS

2000 GENERAL

Maria Cantwell (D)	1,199,437	48.7%
Slade Gorton (R)	1,197,208	48.6%
Jeff Jared (LIBERT)	64,734	2.6%

2000 PRIMARY (OPEN)

Slade Gorton (R)	560,787	43.6%
Maria Cantwell (D)	472,609	36.7%
Deborah Senn (D)	168,110	13.1%
Warren E. Hanson (R)	17,782	1.4%
Jeff Jared (LIBERT)	16,247	1.3%
Barbara Lampert (D)	15,150	1.2%
Robert Tilden Medley (D)	14,009	1.1%

PREVIOUS WINNING PERCENTAGES
1992 House Election (55%)

Cantwell rode the high-tech bubble to Washington, cashing in stock options she got in the go-go 1990s to finance her campaign and arriving on Capitol Hill with the cool composure of a senior executive used to getting her way. She since has softened the straight-ahead approach that unnerved some of her colleagues in the clubby Senate, and has had some success making the transition from the boardroom to the cloakroom.

When Majority Leader Tom Daschle worked out a critical agreement for sharing power with Republicans in early 2001, Cantwell sent him a bottle of champagne to acknowledge his work. She says she sometimes sends hand-written notes to people on her committees thanking them for their help.

"She's very product-driven, very strategic in her approach. She's not a back-slapping pol. She's like a chess player thinking 20 moves ahead," said Michael Meehan, a political consultant who was Cantwell's chief of staff during her first months in Washington. "Some people mistake that for aloofness. If anybody gets a chance to be in a room with Maria Cantwell, they quickly find out she's very smart, is willing to take risks, and she's very focused."

As a senior executive in Seattle's high-tech boom, Cantwell could not afford to go slow. Time was money; to wait was to lose. That is not a recipe for success in the staid, tradition-bound Senate. But Cantwell was not a stranger to politics, having served in the House for a single term after nearly six years in the Washington state legislature. In her 40s and among the Senate's youngest members, she quickly figured out the value of slowly building a case, of moving in increments with small but relentless steps. In the four years since she upset incumbent Republican Slade Gorton by 2,229 votes, Cantwell has focused on issues that are important to her state but seldom get much national attention.

In 2004, she cosponsored legislation to allow state sales taxes to be deducted from federal tax returns, a popular policy that will allow taxpayers in Washington to save $500 on average on their federal taxes this year. In 2003, she was able to secure $500,000 in federal funding for a Federal Aviation Administration Center of Excellence at the University of Washington. The center will find ways to use new composite materials in airplanes, helping the Boeing Co.'s efforts to build the 7E7 jetliner.

She has worked to gain federal benefits for former workers at the Hanford Nuclear Reservation in Washington, some of whom became ill when they worked with plutonium for nuclear weapons. She also fought efforts to slow cleanup at the highly contaminated Hanford plant.

Cantwell went to Cuba in 2002 to try to open that country to agriculture imports from the United States, including lentils from Washington. She also traveled to Mexico to push Washington state potatoes.

On one issue that got national attention, Cantwell was a Senate leader in efforts to hold Enron Corp. accountable for creating an energy crisis in the West that cost Washington state utility customers more than $1 billion in unnecessary charges. In 2004, she also was a leader in a Democratic push to extend unemployment benefits for laid-off workers.

Cantwell combines a pro-business stance with support for traditional Democratic views on core social issues such as abortion rights. Her voting record is more liberal than some had expected it to be. She voted with fellow Democrats 95 percent of the time on major votes that broke along party lines in the 108th Congress. However, she voted in favor of giving President

Bush the authority to invade Iraq in October 2003, a position that many liberals opposed.

Usually when she breaks with her party, it is on matters important to her constituents. She won accolades from major companies when she voted to grant the president fast-track authority to negotiate trade agreements that Congress may not amend.

In the 108th Congress, Cantwell got a seat on the influential Commerce, Science and Transportation Committee, which she calls "the key committee for Washington state's economy," dealing as it does with telecommunication, aviation, fishing and Commerce Department export promotion efforts. The assignment also plays to her technology background.

Cantwell is the second of five children and the first person in her family to graduate from college. Her father, Paul Cantwell, started his career as a construction worker, then went on to serve as a county commissioner, a city councilman and a state legislator in Indiana. He also served as chief of staff for Democratic Rep. Andrew Jacobs of Indiana.

A native of Indiana, Cantwell got involved in politics in 1977 as a volunteer for television host Jerry Springer's successful campaign for mayor of Cincinnati. She was a paid staffer for Springer for a time, but then moved to the Seattle area in the early 1980s to be a political organizer for Democratic presidential candidate Alan Cranston.

She stayed in Washington, doing public relations consulting, and was elected to the state legislature at the age of 28. In the state House, she was noted for balancing environmental concerns and economic growth. Cantwell won a seat in the U.S. House in 1992 but then lost it in the Republican sweep in the 1994 election, which gave majority control of Congress to the GOP.

She put politics aside and jumped into business, joining the Internet start-up RealNetworks, a Seattle-based software company that invented RealPlayer and other products designed to deliver audio and video over the Internet. She rose to be senior vice president of consumer products, becoming a multimillionaire in the process.

Cantwell used most of those earnings to fund her 2000 campaign to unseat Gorton, selling off nearly $10 million in RealNetworks stock options to finance her Senate campaign. That allowed her to blow past the favored Democratic opponent, state Insurance Commissioner Deborah Senn, in Washington's open primary.

She leveraged her popularity with left-leaning voters in the western part of Washington to prevail over Gorton in the general election. But the tally was so close that her victory was not declared official until nearly a month after the election. Cantwell won big in the Seattle area, but Gorton's portrayal of her as the city's candidate hurt her in the state's far more conservative rural areas. She carried only five of the state's 39 counties.

When all of the state's absentee ballots were counted, Cantwell's hard-fought win by little more than 2,000 votes brought the Senate membership at the start of the 107th Congress to a 50-50 partisan split.

She was at first overshadowed by her Democratic colleague, Patty Murray, the state's senior senator who in the 107th chaired the Democratic Senatorial Campaign Committee, the main fundraising arm for Democratic candidates for the Senate. But the junior senator began honing her image as a protector of her constituents, citing former Democratic Sen. Henry M. "Scoop" Jackson of Washington as her inspiration.

During Energy and Natural Resources Committee hearings in 2002, for example, Cantwell grilled the chairman of the Federal Energy Regulatory Commission, Patrick Wood III, about his panel's oversight of electricity markets. She called on Wood to allow her state to cancel long-term electricity contracts that had been signed during the electricity crisis.

KEY VOTES

2004

Yes Pass $318.9 billion, six-year highway and mass transit bill

Yes Extend assault weapons ban for 10 years

Yes Restore pay-as-you-go rules for new tax cuts and entitlement spending

No Criminalize harm to a fetus in an attack on the mother

Yes Increase mandatory child care funding to states by $6 billion over five years

No Amend the Constitution to prohibit same-sex marriage

Yes Approve $146 billion multi-year extension of previously enacted middle-class tax breaks

Yes Reorganize U.S. intelligence agencies as proposed by Sept. 11 commission

Yes Cut corporate taxes $137 billion over 10 years

2003

Yes Delay Bush changes to Clean Air Act

No Allow confirmation vote on Miguel A. Estrada to the U.S. Court of Appeals for the D.C. Circuit

Yes Block a Bush proposal opening Alaska's Arctic National Wildlife Refuge to oil drilling

Yes Limit size of Bush's proposed tax cut to $350 billion through fiscal 2013

Yes Overhaul Medicare and create prescription drug benefit

Yes Block Bush rule scaling back overtime pay for some white-collar federal workers

No Split $20 billion in Iraq aid into half-grant, half-loan

No Ban "partial birth" abortion except to save a woman's life

No Stop proposal allowing travel to Cuba

No Allow final vote on energy policy overhaul

CQ VOTE STUDIES

	PARTY UNITY		PRESIDENTIAL SUPPORT	
	Support	Oppose	Support	Oppose
2004	90%	10%	66%	34%
2003	96%	4%	52%	48%
2002	82%	18%	81%	19%
2001	98%	2%	64%	36%
House Service:				
1994	92%	8%	86%	14%
1993	92%	8%	80%	20%

INTEREST GROUPS

	AFL-CIO	ADA	CCUS	ACU
2004	83%	95%	65%	8%
2003	85%	90%	39%	15%
2002	85%	80%	55%	25%
2001	100%	100%	50%	12%
House Service:				
1994	67%	70%	83%	14%
1993	83%	80%	36%	17%

Rep. Jay Inslee (D)

CAPITOL OFFICE
225-6311
jay.inslee@mail.house.gov
www.house.gov/inslee
403 Cannon 20515-4701; fax 226-1606

COMMITTEES
Energy & Commerce
Resources

HOMETOWN
Bainbridge Island

BORN
Feb. 9, 1951, Seattle, Wash.

RELIGION
Protestant

FAMILY
Wife, Trudi Inslee; three children

EDUCATION
Stanford U., attended 1969-70; U. of Washington,
B.A. 1973 (economics); Willamette U., J.D. 1976

CAREER
Lawyer

POLITICAL HIGHLIGHTS
Wash. House, 1989-93; U.S. House, 1993-95;
defeated for re-election to U.S. House, 1994;
sought Democratic nomination for governor, 1996

ELECTION RESULTS

2004 GENERAL

Jay Inslee (D)	204,121	62.3%
Randy Eastwood (R)	117,850	36.0%
Charles Moore (LIBERT)	5,798	1.8%

2004 PRIMARY

Jay Inslee (D)	unopposed

2002 GENERAL

Jay Inslee (D)	114,087	55.6%
Joe Marine (R)	84,696	41.3%
Mark B. Wilson (LIBERT)	6,251	3.1%

PREVIOUS WINNING PERCENTAGES
2000 (55%); 1998 (50%); 1992 (51%)

Elected 1998; 5th term
Also served 1993-95

After years of battling Republicans over logging and other public lands controversies, Inslee is shifting his focus somewhat to the broad array of issues addressed by the Energy and Commerce Committee. He was one of three Democrats to win a coveted seat on the panel at the start of the 109th Congress, a particularly plum assignment given the importance of the technology industry to his Seattle-area district.

Inslee's legislative efforts already were influenced by his district's economic superpowers, Boeing Co. and Microsoft Corp., which employ many of his constituents. Seven of the 11 bills he introduced in the 108th Congress addressed issues in the purview of Energy and Commerce.

Inslee gave up his perch on the Financial Services Committee to take the Energy and Commerce assignment. But he retained his seat on the Resources Committee, where he is a vocal critic of GOP efforts to loosen restrictions on commercial uses of public lands.

In the 108th Congress, he battled Resources Chairman Richard W. Pombo of California for more than a year in an unsuccessful effort to derail enactment of a law permitting the thinning of millions of acres of national forests in order to prevent forest fires. Inslee charged that the bill's main goal was to give timber companies unprecedented access to federal trees. He introduced his own legislation to preserve roadless forest areas.

Inslee's record on environmental protection has won him kudos from groups such as the Sierra Club and the League of Conservation Voters, but it also led Republican Don Young of Alaska, the previous chairman of Resources, to tell Inslee he was "just mimicking the words fed into your ears from the so-called environmental community."

Still, Inslee has worked across the aisle on issues of regional interest. In 2004, he joined the Forest Subcommittee chairman, Republican Greg Walden of Oregon, to seek a way to get 33 grounded tanker planes, used to fight forest fires, airborne once again.

Inslee says he has steadily increased his victory margins in the 1st District — from 6 percentage points in 1998 to 26 points in 2004 — because of his determination to "sharpen those bipartisan skills." He seeks out GOP cosponsors for bills he introduces and casts himself as a moderate. He is part of the New Democrat Coalition, a group of pro-business Democrats.

That positioning may help, but it is also clear that Inslee is considerably more comfortable representing the Democratic-leaning Seattle suburbs than he was in his first House term, a 1993-95 stint representing a rural and much more conservative stretch across the center of the state.

Inslee generally favors increased foreign trade, but in the 107th he voted against the 2002 law giving the president fast-track authority to negotiate trade agreements that Congress may not amend. "It takes a lot of political incompetence to get me to vote no on a trade deal," Inslee said.

Inslee has worked on legislation to deal with the large increases in electricity prices, particularly on the West Coast. In 2004, he cosponsored legislation requiring full public disclosure of all evidence uncovered in the government's investigation of alleged energy market manipulation by Enron Corp. in the power crisis that affected Western states during 2000-2001.

An advocate of consumer privacy, Inslee cosponsored legislation in the 106th to protect personal banking records. In the 108th, he introduced a bill to regulate "spyware," software that monitors the behavior of computer users and collects sensitive information about them. He doesn't worry so much about his own privacy, however; his home phone is publicly listed. But now that he has a teenager at home, his staff tells constituents they are more likely to reach the congressman if they call the office.

Inslee grew up in Seattle, where his father was a high school biology teacher and coach. A star football and basketball player, Inslee told the Seattle Post-Intelligencer that he learned valuable lessons of leadership and teamwork through sports that have proved important in politics. He is still athletically active, playing in the annual congressional baseball and basketball games and back home with a group he cofounded called the Hoopaholics. The group of middle-aged men play basketball games to raise money for children's charities.

After marrying his high school sweetheart and earning a law degree, Inslee moved to the Yakima area in south central Washington, joined a law firm and became involved in civic affairs. His experiences during a debate over a school bond measure inspired him to run for the legislature in 1988. There, he served as vice chairman of the Appropriations Committee and on a panel that helped negotiate a budget deal to reduce the state's deficit.

When 4th District Republican Rep. Sid Morrison announced he was giving up his seat to run for governor in 1992, Inslee wavered on whether to run, first saying that he was considering a bid, then that he wasn't interested. In April 1992, he finally decided to try for the seat. Inslee's folksy style and tireless campaigning lifted him to a narrow primary victory and to an equally narrow win in November over Republican Doc Hastings.

As a member of the 103rd, Inslee bucked his party on some high-visibility votes: He voted against President Clinton's deficit-reduction package that raised taxes and opposed a five-day waiting period for handgun purchases. But he also voted to ban some types of assault-style weapons. With the National Rifle Association targeting him for defeat, Inslee lost by almost 7 percentage points in a 1994 rematch with Hastings.

After the loss, Inslee moved back to the Seattle area, settling on Bainbridge Island and returning to legal work. He waged an unsuccessful primary bid for governor in 1996, but in 1998 he unseated two-term Republican Rep. Rick White in the suburban Seattle 1st District. His victory was aided by the third-party candidacy of Bruce Craswell, whose 6 percent tally was regarded as coming largely from White's GOP base.

In 2003, Inslee considered a run for governor to replace retiring Democrat Gary Locke. He decided against it, however, an won re-election in 2004 with 62 percent of the vote.

KEY VOTES

2004

Yes Extend federal unemployment benefits by 13 weeks

Yes Pass $283.2 billion, six-year federal highway and mass transit bill

No Approve $146 billion multi-year extension of previously enacted middle-class tax breaks

No Amend the Constitution to prohibit same-sex marriage

Yes Cut corporate taxes $137 billion over 10 years

Yes Reorganize U.S. intelligence agencies as proposed by Sept. 11 commission

2003

No Cut taxes by $330 billion through fiscal 2013

Yes Block Bush rule scaling back overtime pay for some white-collar federal workers

Yes Do not allow use of search warrants without first notifying subjects

Yes Allow importation of prescription drugs

No Create private school voucher program in Washington, D.C.

No Ban "partial birth" abortion except to save a woman's life

Yes Split $18.6 billion in Iraq aid into half-grant, half-loan

No Overhaul Medicare and create prescription drug benefit

CQ VOTE STUDIES

	PARTY UNITY		PRESIDENTIAL SUPPORT	
	Support	Oppose	Support	Oppose
2004	94%	6%	26%	74%
2003	96%	4%	22%	78%
2002	96%	4%	28%	72%
2001	91%	9%	33%	67%
2000	80%	20%	67%	33%

INTEREST GROUPS

	AFL-CIO	ADA	CCUS	ACU
2004	93%	100%	43%	4%
2003	87%	100%	37%	20%
2002	89%	95%	45%	4%
2001	92%	90%	41%	4%
2000	70%	70%	71%	28%

WASHINGTON 1

Puget Sound (west and east) – north Seattle suburbs

The technology boom, though dulled in recent years, continues to drive growth in the suburban 1st. Microsoft's main Redmond campus, which is just over the district line in the 8th, is the best-known of many technology and biotechnology companies in the region. Suburban areas around Lake Washington and Puget Sound have continued to expand, with many of the "Microsoft Millionaires" moving into the crescent north of Seattle.

Military bases spur the economy on the west side of Puget Sound, but technology companies — especially along Interstate 405 on the eastern side of the Sound — and home buyers in Seattle's first ring of suburbs have led to growth here. More than 80 percent of the district's population lives on the eastern side, in King and Snohomish counties. Redistricting following the 2000 census gave the 1st a greater share of Snohomish, including a small part of Everett and most of Monroe, and a smaller

share of King. The 1st, which had only a small piece of Seattle before redistricting, received an even smaller share of the city after the remap.

Democrats have the edge in the district, with its well-educated, socially liberal professionals. The Snohomish portion is probably the most politically competitive of the three counties; the King and Kitsap County portions are slightly more Democratic.

MAJOR INDUSTRY
Software, military, aviation

MILITARY BASES
Naval Base Kitsap - Bangor, 5,743 military, 2,779 civilian (2004); Naval Undersea Warfare Center Keyport, 33 military, 1,417 civilian (2005)

CITIES
Kirkland (pt.), 44,406; Edmonds, 39,515; Shoreline (pt.), 35,694; Seattle Hill-Silver Firs (unincorporated), 35,311; Redmond (pt.), 34,759

NOTABLE
Bainbridge Island is a 35-minute ferry ride from downtown Seattle; The city of Lynnwood hosts an annual Trolley Days Festival; Mill Creek is a master-planned community, complete with a new high school, middle school and 18-hole golf course; Poulsbo is home to the annual Scandinavian celebration Viking Fest.

Rep. Rick Larsen (D)

Elected 2000; 3rd term

A moderate Democrat in a politically competitive district, Larsen maintains a pragmatic and bipartisan approach to his work — good traits to have in his part of northwestern Washington, where the winner in five of the last eight elections received no more than 52 percent of the vote.

Larsen's modesty in a profession known for its outsize egos has won him praise. The father of young children who rides the subway to work every day, Larsen willingly acknowledges that, as a relative newcomer to a Congress controlled by the other party, he is no mover and shaker. "I'm in no position to change the world," he told his home-state paper, the Seattle Times. "I am in a position to help the people I represent."

Larsen affiliates with the moderate New Democrat Coalition and has posted a middle-of-the-road voting record. He backed President Bush about a third of the time in the 108th Congress, more often than the average Democrat. He was among the minority of House Democrats who supported a bankruptcy overhaul making it harder for consumers to erase their debts, as well as legislation designed to curb class action lawsuits. In 2002, he was one of only 25 Democrats who voted for legislation that gave the president fast-track authority to negotiate trade agreements that Congress may not amend, and in the 108th he voted for bilateral trade accords with Australia, Chile and Singapore. He has repeatedly backed a permanent repeal of the estate tax. And he voted for Bush's big 2001 tax cut package, although not the 2003 follow-on or the 2004 extension of the earlier cuts.

Still, Larsen has opposed other Bush priorities, including the 2003 overhaul of the Medicare system, the invasion of Iraq, medical malpractice damage limits and a proposed energy policy bill.

Larsen tends to put greater focus on local issues than national ones. One of his first legislative successes came in his freshman term, when he helped pass a law to improve pipeline safety after a 1999 explosion in Bellingham killed three people. Previous efforts had been thwarted, and it looked as if Larsen's legislation, introduced soon after he arrived on Capitol Hill, also would founder. But he joined with two members of his state's delegation — Republican Jennifer Dunn in the House and Democrat Patty Murray in the Senate — to offer a revised version. Although not as tough as the original bill, it attracted enough support to become law.

Larsen has had less success on legislation that he and Murray pressed in the 108th to designate more than 100,000 acres about 60 miles northeast of Seattle as a protected wilderness area. Even though their bill had bipartisan support in the state's congressional delegation and passed the Senate, House Resources Chairman Richard W. Pombo of California refused to accept it. Pombo's offer of an alternative protecting fewer acres was unacceptable to Larsen and Murray. Early in the 109th, both sides renewed their battle lines on the reintroduced Murray-Larsen legislation.

In the aftermath of the Sept. 11, 2001, terrorist attacks, when the airlines won federal aid to compensate for a plunge in commercial air traffic, Larsen pointed out that aerospace companies and their workers were just as adversely affected. The Boeing Co. and B.F. Goodrich Aerospace are major employers in the 2nd District, and Larsen said Boeing laid off 25,000 workers in the Puget Sound area in the year after the terrorist attacks. During the 107th, Larsen sought federal help, including extended unemployment benefits, for displaced workers in the aviation, aerospace and other industries hobbled because of the attacks.

CAPITOL OFFICE
225-2605
rick.larsen@mail.house.gov
www.house.gov/larsen
107 Cannon 20515-4702; fax 225-4420

COMMITTEES
Agriculture
Armed Services
Transportation & Infrastructure

HOMETOWN
Everett

BORN
June 15, 1965, Arlington, Wash.

RELIGION
Methodist

FAMILY
Wife, Tiia Karlen; two children

EDUCATION
Pacific Lutheran U., B.A. 1987 (political science);
U. of Minnesota, M.P.A. 1990 (public affairs)

CAREER
Dental association lobbyist; port economic development official

POLITICAL HIGHLIGHTS
Snohomish County Council, 1998-2000 (chairman, 1999)

ELECTION RESULTS

2004 GENERAL

Rick Larsen (D)	202,383	63.9%
Suzanne Sinclair (R)	106,333	33.6%
Bruce Guthrie (LIBERT)	7,966	2.5%

2004 PRIMARY

Rick Larsen (D)	unopposed

2002 GENERAL

Rick Larsen (D)	101,219	50.1%
Norma Smith (R)	92,528	45.8%
Bruce Guthrie (LIBERT)	4,326	2.1%
Bernard Patrick Haggerty (GREEN)	4,077	2.0%

PREVIOUS WINNING PERCENTAGES
2000 (50%)

The post-Sept. 11 effort to tighten border security in order to stop terrorists from entering the United States also drew Larsen's attention. The crackdown dampened the economies of areas near the Canadian border as routine commerce between the two nations was stalled. Larsen successfully nudged the administration to provide more customs and immigration agents at border crossings.

Larsen was born and raised in Snohomish County, just north of Seattle. One of eight children of a utility company power line worker, he says he was influenced to enter public service by his family. His parents were involved in community activities, and his father served as a city councilman.

In college, Larsen said his career goal was to become a city manager. But after earning a bachelor's degree in political science and a master's in public affairs, Larsen worked for the Port of Everett helping businesses comply with clean water requirements. He then became the director of public affairs for the Washington Dental Association.

His first foray into elective office came in 1997, when he waged a successful door-to-door campaign for the Snohomish County Council. He chaired the council in 1999.

When three-term Republican Rep. Jack Metcalf retired in 2000, local Democratic Party strategists saw enough promise in Larsen to persuade a potential rival, state Rep. Jeff Morris, to stay out of the open-seat 2nd District contest and avoid a divisive primary. Running as the moderate, Larsen scored something of a coup by returning the politically split district to Democratic hands.

Although he supports expanded international trade, which the AFL-CIO has fought, Larsen received campaign help from organized labor, as well as other traditional Democratic backers, such as abortion rights advocates and environmental groups. All mounted ground or mail campaigns in Larsen's behalf in the final weeks of the race. The result was a Democratic takeover, with Larsen prevailing by 12,000 votes against Republican state Rep. John Koster, who had run on a strongly conservative platform.

Redistricting following the 2000 census did little to change the competitive nature of the 2nd District, and the 2002 race between Larsen and Norma Smith, a former aide of Metcalf's, was hard fought. Larsen was vigorous in bringing in campaign donations throughout his freshman term and so was able to spend $1.8 million, triple what Smith spent. Larsen again won with just 50 percent of the vote, with a victory margin of less than 9,000 votes. He had a much easier time in 2004 in his bid for a third term, defeating Republican Suzanne Sinclair with 64 percent.

KEY VOTES

2004
Yes   Extend federal unemployment benefits by 13 weeks
Yes   Pass $283.2 billion, six-year federal highway and mass transit bill
No   Approve $146 billion multi-year extension of previously enacted middle-class tax breaks
No   Amend the Constitution to prohibit same-sex marriage
Yes   Cut corporate taxes $137 billion over 10 years
Yes   Reorganize U.S. intelligence agencies as proposed by Sept. 11 commission

2003
No   Cut taxes by $330 billion through fiscal 2013
Yes   Block Bush rule scaling back overtime pay for some white-collar federal workers
Yes   Do not allow use of search warrants without first notifying subjects
Yes   Allow importation of prescription drugs
No   Create private school voucher program in Washington, D.C.
No   Ban "partial birth" abortion except to save a woman's life
No   Split $18.6 billion in Iraq aid into half-grant, half-loan
No   Overhaul Medicare and create prescription drug benefit

CQ VOTE STUDIES

	PARTY UNITY		PRESIDENTIAL SUPPORT	
	Support	Oppose	Support	Oppose
2004	92%	8%	29%	71%
2003	90%	10%	36%	64%
2002	88%	12%	38%	62%
2001	80%	20%	42%	58%

INTEREST GROUPS

	AFL-CIO	ADA	CCUS	ACU
2004	93%	90%	48%	8%
2003	87%	95%	50%	32%
2002	67%	85%	60%	24%
2001	83%	85%	48%	12%

WASHINGTON 2
Puget Sound – Bellingham, most of Everett

West of the Cascade Mountains, in the northwest corner of the state, the 2nd covers an area that is mostly rural in its topography and moderate in its politics. Most of the district's population lives along Interstate 5, a technology corridor that runs up the state's coast, while the rural areas just west of the mountains provide residents with open expanses of land, much of it national forest. Between lies a fertile agricultural plain.

Aspects of the district's economy that were dependent on natural resources — logging, farming and paper production — have continued to decline. But the technology explosion in the 1980s and 1990s helped grow the economy and population. Thousands of Boeing employees work at the company's plant in Everett, but to the east, the district has struggled to find well-paying jobs for those formerly employed in farming and logging. The area seeks to diversify, although technology companies have made inroads as far north as Bellingham.

Traffic congestion in the Seattle area has become such a problem that it is often faster to drive from northern parts of the 2nd into Everett than

from Everett south to Seattle. These northwestern areas are home to many retirees who leave Seattle, and San Juan County, a collection of islands southwest of Bellingham, has the highest median age in the state (47 years). At the northern border, beefed-up security has slowed trade to Canada.

The 2nd is highly competitive. The western urban centers of Everett in the south and Bellingham in the north are liberal, while the eastern rural sections lean conservative. The San Juan Islands, known for their liberal residents, made San Juan County John Kerry's best Washington county in the 2004 presidential election. Kerry took 51 percent of the 2nd's vote.

MAJOR INDUSTRY
Aviation, computer software, shipping

MILITARY BASES
Naval Air Station Whidbey Island, 7,914 military, 1,286 civilian (2001); Naval Station Everett, 5,657 military, 653 civilian (2004)

CITIES
Everett (pt.), 87,329; Bellingham, 67,171; Mount Vernon, 26,232

NOTABLE
Skagit County, home to the world's largest tulip fields, hosts a tulip festival every April.

Rep. Brian Baird (D)

CAPITOL OFFICE
225-3536
www.house.gov/baird
1421 Longworth 20515-4703; fax 225-3478

COMMITTEES
Budget
Science
Transportation & Infrastructure

HOMETOWN
Vancouver

BORN
March 7, 1956, Chama, N.M.

RELIGION
Protestant

FAMILY
Wife, Rachel Nugent; two children

EDUCATION
U. of Utah, B.S. 1977 (psychology); U. of Wyoming, M.S. 1980 (clinical psychology), Ph.D. 1984 (clinical psychology)

CAREER
Professor; psychologist

POLITICAL HIGHLIGHTS
Democratic nominee for U.S. House, 1996

ELECTION RESULTS

2004 GENERAL

Brian Baird (D)	193,626	61.9%
Thomas Crowson (R)	119,027	38.1%

2004 PRIMARY

Brian Baird (D)	61,110	85.3%
Cheryl A. Crist (D)	10,518	14.7%

2002 GENERAL

Brian Baird (D)	119,264	61.7%
Joseph Zarelli (R)	74,065	38.3%

PREVIOUS WINNING PERCENTAGES
2000 (56%); 1998 (55%)

Elected 1998; 4th term

Like most House members, Baird assiduously attends to the needs of his district, whether by securing $2 million to fight methamphetamine abuse or sponsoring legislation to designate the White Salmon River a "wild and scenic" river. He has cultivated a reputation as a town hall warrior for the frequent meetings with constituents that keep him rooted in their needs. He has met the locals in schools, community centers, railroad stations and even held a "Ski with Your Congressman Day."

Baird won a major victory in the 108th Congress when President Bush signed into law legislation to allow residents of seven states without an income tax to instead deduct state sales taxes when calculating their federal tax liability for 2004 and 2005. Washington is one of the seven states, and Baird had fought for four years to pass what he called a matter of tax fairness. He is now working to make the provision permanent.

Baird has emerged as one of Congress' most determined advocates for good government, a crusade that prompts him to invoke the Founding Fathers on many occasions. In the wake of the Sept. 11, 2001, attacks, while most members were preoccupied with pursuing terrorists, Baird and a select few colleagues concentrated on the vulnerability of Congress itself. A clinical psychologist and psychology professor before coming to Congress, Baird organized a series of seminars immediately after the attacks to allow members and their staffs to talk about their fears and to find ways to handle them. Then he turned to the institutional threat.

What would happen, Baird asked, if a terrorist succeeded in killing a majority of lawmakers? "We must acknowledge the possibility that a single terrorist act could virtually eliminate most of the members of Congress," he said in March 2002. "And, given that possibility, we must ask ourselves, what would happen if that were to occur? What would happen if the very institutions and individuals entrusted with national decision-making were eliminated simultaneously?"

His answer was a proposed constitutional amendment to allow each House member to choose two potential successors who could be appointed by the state's governor to serve temporarily in the event that a majority of House members were killed or incapacitated. The appointed members would serve until a special election was held. Baird's proposal drew only 63 votes in 2004. Instead, the House passed legislation requiring special elections to be held to fill vacant House seats within 45 days of a catastrophe killing 100 or more members. In 2005, a similar bill allowing 49 days for a special election passed by an even wider margin.

The continuity question is not the only government reform issue absorbing Baird. He also has pressed unsuccessfully for a constitutional amendment to abolish the Electoral College so that the winner of the popular vote would automatically become president. "Most people's common-sense idea of how a democratic republic should work is based on a basic concept of one person, one vote," he said in October 2004.

For the 109th Congress, Baird sought unsuccessfully to change House rules so members would have more time to read legislation before voting. He wanted a two-thirds vote, rather than a simple majority, to be needed to waive a House rule requiring a three-day layover before a bill can be considered on the floor — a rule that is routinely waived in the chaotic last days of the session. Baird said that making it harder to waive the layover rule would not only help members understand what they were voting on but would result in a healthier democracy.

"Each member of Congress bears a profound responsibility to their constituents and to the constitutional principles of representative democracy," Baird wrote in a "Dear Colleague" letter. "If we are to fulfill those responsibilities, we must insist on the opportunity to read, study and debate legislation before we vote on it."

Baird co-wrote a proposal for a House rule that would forbid members from dating interns who work for them. Ask the congressman about campaign financing, and he will tell you that his colleagues are "literally killing" themselves raising money. Like many would-be reformers, he believes ordinary people are losing out because of the scramble for campaign cash. "People they elected to represent them are spending so much time chasing money, they can't work together on the issues," he says.

In 2001, Baird teamed with Republican Darryl Issa of California on legislation allowing gas-electric hybrid vehicles, such as the Toyota Prius, to travel in high-occupancy-vehicle lanes with a single occupant. Baird, like Issa, owned a Prius. The bill failed, but Baird's enthusiasm was so apparent the Seattle Post-Intelligencer likened him to an honest Joe Isuzu. But "unlike Joe — 'He's lying' — Isuzu, Baird had a higher purpose than unloading a jalopy from the used car lot," the newspaper said.

Although Baird's earnestness can be a bit overwhelming, he has a distinctive sense of humor and a surprisingly refined knack for comedic timing. Baird was one of the featured performers at the Hotline Post-Inaugural Comedy Show, honoring the 55th presidential inaugural and the 125th birthday of Will Rogers. According to an account in The Washington Post, Baird brought the house down with an imitation of Bush describing a series of world-changing initiatives. Among them, Baird-as-Bush announced Operation Solar Landing: "It's gonna put a man on the sun. Now, I know, I know, you pointy-headed academics and you liberal judges, you don't think we can do that. [Pause.] Heh. We're going at night!"

Baird gained his sense of community activism from his parents. His father was a school principal, owned a small business, belonged to a Lion's Club and served on the city council. When no other Democrat opted to run against GOP Rep. Linda Smith in 1996, Baird put together an underfunded, grass-roots campaign that came up 887 votes shy of an upset.

Two years later, when Smith decided to give up her House seat for an ultimately unsuccessful Senate bid, Baird triumphed, winning by 10 percentage points over GOP state Sen. Don Benton. He has won with increasing ease ever since.

KEY VOTES

2004
Yes Extend federal unemployment benefits by 13 weeks
Yes Pass $283.2 billion, six-year federal highway and mass transit bill
Yes Approve $146 billion multi-year extension of previously enacted middle-class tax breaks
No   Amend the Constitution to prohibit same-sex marriage
Yes Cut corporate taxes $137 billion over 10 years
Yes Reorganize U.S. intelligence agencies as proposed by Sept. 11 commission

2003
No   Cut taxes by $330 billion through fiscal 2013
Yes Block Bush rule scaling back overtime pay for some white-collar federal workers
Yes Do not allow use of search warrants without first notifying subjects
Yes Allow importation of prescription drugs
No   Create private school voucher program in Washington, D.C.
No   Ban "partial birth" abortion except to save a woman's life
Yes Split $18.6 billion in Iraq aid into half-grant, half-loan
No   Overhaul Medicare and create prescription drug benefit

CQ VOTE STUDIES

	PARTY UNITY		PRESIDENTIAL SUPPORT	
	Support	Oppose	Support	Oppose
2004	89%	11%	37%	63%
2003	94%	6%	24%	76%
2002	92%	8%	32%	68%
2001	87%	13%	30%	70%
2000	89%	11%	75%	25%

INTEREST GROUPS

	AFL-CIO	ADA	CCUS	ACU
2004	92%	90%	53%	17%
2003	93%	95%	33%	16%
2002	100%	90%	58%	12%
2001	83%	85%	41%	12%
2000	80%	70%	75%	12%

WASHINGTON 3
Southwest — Vancouver, most of Olympia

The 3rd is an eclectic, politically competitive district in southwest Washington that scoops up liberals in the state capital of Olympia and suburbanites in Vancouver, which is just across the Columbia River from Portland, Ore. Joining the two cities and bifurcating the district is Interstate 5, west and east of which lies considerable rural territory.

The district's population center is Clark County (Vancouver), where slightly more than half of the 3rd's residents live. Clark's population grew 45 percent in the 1990s, as Portland residents flocked across the river to buy cheaper land. Trees and farmland are being cleared to make way for suburban developments, and voters have demanded infrastructure improvements to relieve traffic congestion and school overcrowding.

The 3rd still has vast stretches of woodlands, including the scenic Coastal Range and much of the Cascade Mountains, with Mount Rainier just outside the district's borders in the 8th. Although the timber trade has declined in the Cascade Mountains in the east, the western part of the district still sustains hearty logging. Many former timber workers have

transferred to the technology sector.

Clark, like the district at large, is politically competitive. The Democratic vote in Vancouver is offset by Republican strength outside the city, in areas like Battle Ground, Yacolt and La Center. George W. Bush narrowly won Clark in the 2004 presidential election, even as he lost statewide.

Thurston County, which includes Olympia, is more favorable to Democrats. Redistricting following the 2000 census moved about one-sixth of the capital city into the 9th District. Lewis County is strongly Republican, while Cowlitz and Pacific counties vote Democratic, although Bush substantially narrowed the big vote margins Bill Clinton enjoyed. Overall, Bush took 50 percent of the 3rd's vote in 2004.

MAJOR INDUSTRY
Timber, mining, computer hardware

CITIES
Vancouver, 143,560; Olympia (pt.), 35,230; Longview 34,660

NOTABLE
Mount St. Helens erupted May 18, 1980, killing 57 people and destroying enough lumber for 300,000 two-bedroom homes; Lewis and Clark used the Columbia River to reach the Pacific Ocean in 1805.

Rep. Doc Hastings (R)

Elected 1994; 6th term

Hastings is the über party loyalist often called on by Speaker J. Dennis Hastert for difficult, thankless tasks few others will take. During a controversial shakeup of the ethics committee in 2005, in which Republicans seen as disloyal were ousted by the Speaker, Hastings was tapped to chair the panel.

He also is remembered as the member who presided over the House during the historic vote on President Bush's prescription drug bill in November 2003. At the leaders' direction, Hastings held open the vote for an extraordinary three hours while the Speaker and the GOP whip team worked the floor and the phones to furiously round up the final votes they needed to push the legislation to passage in a squeaker.

Hastings had an even tougher role in the ethics imbroglio that unfolded at the start of the 109th Congress. When Hastert put him in charge of the Committee on Standards of Official Conduct, as the ethics panel is officially known, the committee was in disarray after some heavy-handed intervention by Hastert and Majority Leader Tom DeLay, the highly influential and ambitious No. 2 man in the GOP leadership.

Hastert had summarily ousted three fellow Republicans from the panel, including Chairman Joel Hefley of Colorado, after it took the rare step in late 2004 of admonishing DeLay for breaches of the rules, including use of undue pressure in securing votes for the Medicare bill. The leaders also pushed through changes in the ethics rules that favored DeLay.

Hastert put Hastings in Hefley's place. Hastings then stirred a boiling pot of criticism from Democrats and the news media by firing the committee's director and putting in place his own chief of staff, who was not an attorney. The panel's top staff, usually lawyers who conduct investigations of ethics complaints, had traditionally been chosen by the chairman and the senior Democrat. Changes in the rules, too, had usually been bipartisan.

Hastings encountered immediate problems getting the committee to function. Democrats on the panel refused to allow it to organize or conduct even routine business. Hastings and GOP leaders were forced to back down and the rules changes were revoked.

Subdued and quiet by nature, Hastings tried to ride out the storm. Though he had served on the committee since 2001 — all through the DeLay investigation — Hastings said he did not seek the job as chairman and offered few public comments other than promising to do "my best to carry out my duties fairly, with utmost respect for this institution, and without regard to friendship, favor or political party."

Hastings has done his share of hard work on the ethics panel, widely viewed as unsavory duty though necessary for enforcing ethics rules. As a member of the committee in the 107th Congress, he chaired the subcommittee that investigated James A. Traficant, an Ohio Democrat who was eventually expelled from the House and went to prison for accepting bribes and evading taxes.

His efforts have not gone unrewarded. Hastings has a seat on the Rules Committee, which is at the center of most legislative battles. And he served two terms (2001-2005) on the Budget Committee, which writes the annual federal spending blueprint. He is not among the party's rhetorical stars, but he is a solid conservative who usually votes with his party.

His involvement with the unpleasant business of ethics probes has done nothing to diminish Hastings' popularity back home. In the 2004 election,

CAPITOL OFFICE
225-5816
www.house.gov/hastings
1323 Longworth 20515-4704; fax 225-3251

COMMITTEES
Rules
(Rules & the Organization of the House - chairman)
Standards of Official Conduct - chairman

HOMETOWN
Pasco

BORN
Feb. 7, 1941, Spokane, Wash.

RELIGION
Protestant

FAMILY
Wife, Claire Hastings; three children

EDUCATION
Columbia Basin College, attended 1959-61;
Central Washington U., attended 1964

MILITARY SERVICE
Army Reserve, 1964-69

CAREER
Paper supply business owner

POLITICAL HIGHLIGHTS
Wash. House, 1979-87; Republican nominee for U.S. House, 1992

ELECTION RESULTS

2004 GENERAL

Doc Hastings (R)	154,627	62.6%
Sandy Matheson (D)	92,486	37.4%

2004 PRIMARY

Doc Hastings (R)	unopposed

2002 GENERAL

Doc Hastings (R)	108,257	66.9%
Craig Mason (D)	53,572	33.1%

PREVIOUS WINNING PERCENTAGES
2000 (61%); 1998 (69%); 1996 (53%); 1994 (53%)

he easily won a sixth term, claiming 63 percent of the vote from his district in central Washington. First elected in the GOP sweep of 1994, Hastings is from a heavily Republican district and has a safe seat, which is one of the reasons he is often chosen for the tough jobs.

He is known as "Doc," a family nickname he's had since childhood, and he mindfully tends to business at home. As founder and chairman of the House Nuclear Cleanup Caucus, he has led congressional efforts to speed up environmental restoration of radioactive waste sites. In his district is the Hanford Nuclear Reservation, once a major district employer. It now stands idle as the nation's most toxic relic of the Cold War, and Hastings has secured hundreds of millions of dollars to clean it up.

In 2004, he supported a bill, eventually signed by Bush, to get the federal government to study the potential for adding historic Manhattan Project sites, including the Hanford reactor, to the national park system. For years, former nuclear workers and residents have been trying to preserve Hanford's B Reactor as a museum. It was the world's first full-scale plutonium production reactor and was built as part of the top-secret Manhattan Project to produce the atomic bomb.

Hastings aggressively watches over his district's agriculture interests, funneling federal dollars to support farmers and protesting what he sees as unfair foreign competition to Washington's lucrative apple industry. His efforts in the 108th Congress included $1 million to upgrade and refurbish refrigerated rail cars used to transport apples and other perishable crops from farm to market.

Before coming to Washington, Hastings ran his family's paper supply business in Pasco and was active in civic affairs and local Republican politics. He was chairman of the Franklin County GOP central committee and a delegate to two national Republican conventions. He served eight years in the Washington House, winning leadership posts as assistant majority leader and chairman of the GOP caucus.

In 1992, Hastings drew solid backing from GOP religious activists and was considered the most conservative of the four Republicans running to succeed GOP Rep. Sid Morrison, a moderate who ran unsuccessfully for governor that year. Though Hastings won his party's nomination handily, he narrowly lost to Democrat Jay Inslee.

In a 1994 rematch, Hastings cast the campaign as a referendum on Inslee's support for President Clinton, unpopular in the GOP-leaning district. Hastings ousted Inslee, and he has held on to the seat easily since then, capturing more than 60 percent of the vote in the last four elections.

KEY VOTES

2004
No Extend federal unemployment benefits by 13 weeks
Yes Pass $283.2 billion, six-year federal highway and mass transit bill
Yes Approve $146 billion multi-year extension of previously enacted middle-class tax breaks
Yes Amend the Constitution to prohibit same-sex marriage
Yes Cut corporate taxes $137 billion over 10 years
Yes Reorganize U.S. intelligence agencies as proposed by Sept. 11 commission

2003
Yes Cut taxes by $330 billion through fiscal 2013
No Block Bush rule scaling back overtime pay for some white-collar federal workers
Yes Do not allow use of search warrants without first notifying subjects
Yes Allow importation of prescription drugs
Yes Create private school voucher program in Washington, D.C.
Yes Ban "partial birth" abortion except to save a woman's life
No Split $18.6 billion in Iraq aid into half-grant, half-loan
Yes Overhaul Medicare and create prescription drug benefit

CQ VOTE STUDIES

	PARTY UNITY		PRESIDENTIAL SUPPORT	
	Support	Oppose	Support	Oppose
2004	96%	4%	97%	3%
2003	97%	3%	96%	4%
2002	98%	2%	92%	8%
2001	98%	2%	93%	7%
2000	98%	2%	23%	77%

INTEREST GROUPS

	AFL-CIO	ADA	CCUS	ACU
2004	13%	0%	100%	100%
2003	0%	10%	97%	88%
2002	11%	0%	100%	92%
2001	8%	0%	96%	96%
2000	0%	0%	94%	92%

WASHINGTON 4
Central — Yakima and Tri-Cities

Lying just east of the Cascade Mountains, the 4th comprises a huge swath of central Washington that includes the Yakima Valley, known as the fruit bowl of the Northwest, and the Tri-Cities area, which is home to the Hanford Nuclear Reservation.

Yakima County is the district's largest, both in land area and population. To the east is Benton County, which takes in the district's other population center, the Tri-Cities of Pasco, Kennewick and Richland on the Columbia River.

Heavily irrigated agriculture drives the district, which contains an older irrigation area in the Yakima Valley, full of apple orchards and the world's largest producer of hops. It also includes the Columbia Basin project, fed by the Grand Coulee Dam, which has bred hundreds of wineries and potato, corn and fruit farms.

Many of these agricultural areas have attracted large Hispanic populations. Mattawa and Royal City (Grant County) and Mabton,

Granger and Toppenish (Yakima) are more than 75 percent Hispanic.

The Hanford reservation and the Pacific Northwest National Laboratory, the district's largest employer, take up a 570-square-mile tract on the Columbia. Hanford's jobs drove the region during the Cold War, but in 1988 the plutonium plant was shut down. Hanford is now the nation's most contaminated nuclear site, with 54 million gallons of deadly material stored in aging underground tanks.

The 4th is the state's most conservative district. George W. Bush won every county in the district in the 2004 presidential election, most by overwhelming margins.

MAJOR INDUSTRY
Scientific research, timber, fruit orchards

CITIES
Yakima, 71,845; Kennewick, 54,693; Richland, 38,708; Pasco, 32,066; Wenatchee, 27,856

NOTABLE
The oldest skeleton ever found in North America was discovered along the banks of the Columbia River in Richland in 1996; Dubbed the "Kennewick Man," he is believed to be more than 9,300 years old.

Rep. Cathy McMorris (R)

Elected 2004; 1st term

CAPITOL OFFICE
225-2006
cathy.mcmorris@mail.house.gov
www.mcmorris.house.gov
1708 Longworth 20515-4705; fax 225-3392

COMMITTEES
Armed Services
Education & Workforce
Resources

HOMETOWN
Loon Lake

BORN
May 22, 1969, Salem, Ore.

RELIGION
Christian non-denominational

FAMILY
Single

EDUCATION
Pensacola Christian College, B.A. 1990 (pre-law);
U. of Washington, M.B.A. 2002

CAREER
Fruit orchard worker; state legislative aide

POLITICAL HIGHLIGHTS
Wash. House, 1994-2004 (minority leader, 2002-03)

ELECTION RESULTS

2004 GENERAL

Cathy McMorris (R)	179,600	59.7%
Don Barbieri (D)	121,333	40.3%

2004 PRIMARY

Cathy McMorris (R)	42,948	49.7%
Larry Sheahan (R)	23,593	27.3%
Shaun Cross (R)	19,878	23.0%

In terms of personal legislative clout, McMorris' transition from former state House minority leader to Republican House freshman may be a bit of a step down. But McMorris' congressional debut, at the age of 35, did not diminish a reputation as a rising star in her home state of Washington that she developed over more than a decade in Olympia.

McMorris was chosen by her freshman peers as their class representative to the House Republican Steering Committee, the group that determines committee assignments for GOP members. Though such positions are not necessarily harbingers of things to come, John Carter of Texas, who held the same freshman post in the 108th Congress, has since landed a coveted spot on the Appropriations Committee.

McMorris, a former fruit orchard worker, was assigned as well to committees well-suited to her mostly rural, eastern Washington constituency. She sits on the Resources panel, which oversees timber, mining and water rights — all important issues in the 5th District. And she also landed a seat on the Armed Services panel, which McMorris says she will use to expand the role of Fairchild Air Force Base in her district.

McMorris said she plans to continue the focus on health care issues she cultivated in the state legislature. She supports measures that would limit medical malpractice lawsuits and cap jury awards for pain and suffering. Reflecting the needs of her mostly rural constituency, she also wants to increase Medicaid reimbursement rates to rural hospitals.

After her House predecessor, GOP Rep. George Nethercutt, decided to pursue an ultimately unsuccessful challenge to Democratic Sen. Patty Murray, McMorris used the recognition she had received as state House minority leader from 2002 to 2003 to launch her congressional bid. She won a three-way primary with unexpected ease, then faced off in the general election against one of the Democrats' most highly touted recruits, Spokane businessman Don Barbieri. Yet Barbieri ran a lackluster campaign, and a well-organized McMorris won by 19 percentage points.

WASHINGTON 5

East – Spokane

The fertile soil of eastern Washington makes the 5th's protein-rich wheat some of the most desired in the world. Conservative politically, this large district has suffered the decline of some of its traditional industries and enjoyed the emergence of others.

Spokane is a trade hub for the inland Northwest. Largely dependent on manufacturing, the area has suffered intermittent layoffs, although increases in electronics manufacturing and the health care industry have offered opportunities for workers to retrain. Slightly less than two-thirds of district residents live in Spokane or surrounding Spokane County.

Okanogan County, in the northwestern corner of the district, has been particularly hard-hit as the logging and mining industries have slowed and a looming water shortage keeps farmers on edge. But the district remains a top apple producer. Unlike the neighboring Yakima and Columbia irrigation

systems, the 5th's agriculture, based in the southern part of the district, is centered mostly on staple crops such as wheat, which receive federal subsidies.

The 5th's politics more closely resemble neighboring Idaho's than western Washington's. Rural communities and the natural resource-dependent economy make for voters who eschew federal interference and support private property rights. Spokane County can be politically competitive, but the rural areas are heavily Republican. George W. Bush won all 12 of the 5th's counties in 2004, and the district included Bush's four best Washington counties.

MAJOR INDUSTRY
Agriculture, manufacturing, health care

MILITARY BASES
Fairchild Air Force Base, 4,534 military, 1,267 civilian (2004)

CITIES
Spokane, 195,629; Walla Walla, 29,686; Opportunity (unincorporated), 25,065

NOTABLE
Spokane hosts Bloomsday, the largest timed foot race in North America.

Rep. Norm Dicks (D)

Elected 1976; 15th term

CAPITOL OFFICE
225-5916
www.house.gov/dicks
2467 Rayburn 20515-4706; fax 226-1176

COMMITTEES
Appropriations
Homeland Security

HOMETOWN
Belfair

BORN
Dec. 16, 1940, Bremerton, Wash.

RELIGION
Lutheran

FAMILY
Wife, Suzanne Dicks; two children

EDUCATION
U. of Washington, B.A. 1963 (political science),
J.D. 1968

CAREER
Congressional aide

POLITICAL HIGHLIGHTS
No previous office

ELECTION RESULTS

2004 GENERAL

Norm Dicks (D)	202,919	69.0%
Doug Cloud (R)	91,228	31.0%

2004 PRIMARY

Norm Dicks (D)	unopposed

2002 GENERAL

Norm Dicks (D)	126,116	64.2%
Bob Lawrence (R)	61,584	31.4%
John Bennett (LIBERT)	8,744	4.5%

PREVIOUS WINNING PERCENTAGES
2000 (65%); 1998 (68%); 1996 (66%); 1994 (58%);
1992 (64%); 1990 (61%); 1988 (68%); 1986 (71%);
1984 (66%); 1982 (63%); 1980 (54%); 1978 (61%);
1976 (74%)

Many in Washington state consider Dicks, the consummate lawmaker and master of Capitol Hill's inside game, as much a fixture in the state's landscape as Mount Rainier.

Now in his third decade in the House, Dicks rarely fails to deliver for his state. As the No. 3 Democrat on the Appropriations Committee, he has a hand in shaping annual spending decisions, and he seldom misses a chance to bring money home. The garrulous, shrewd Dicks is such a familiar presence in both the state and the nation's capital he's commonly known as "the third senator from Washington."

A former linebacker for the University of Washington, Dicks is not one to be pushed around — even by his own party. Dicks has a well-used independent streak. He is among a small group of pro-defense Democrats who have argued that President Bush's defense budgets are too anemic to pay for modernized weapons and to boost quality of life programs for the troops. He also will pay attention to the president's anti-terrorism proposals from his seat on the Homeland Security Committee.

Yet Dicks remains open-minded about some of Bush's other efforts. After the 2005 State of the Union address when Bush outlined his controversial plan to restructure Social Security, most Democrats rejected Bush's desire to allow private accounts within the government retirement program. Dicks was more open. "He did a good job explaining Social Security's problems, warts and all," Dicks said after the speech. "I'm not saying I'll buy into privatization, but I'm willing to take a look at his ideas."

Dicks' Appropriations seat, which he gained in his freshman year, has allowed him to secure billions of dollars for the Pacific Northwest, including $100 million for salmon protection. But he is best-known for his activities in behalf of his state's defense interests. Washington is home to numerous military bases and defense contractors, including aerospace giant Boeing Co. Fort Lewis in the 9th District is the largest Army base on the West Coast. The Navy has a major nuclear submarine base in Bremerton, located in Dicks' district.

Dicks is a proponent of large military budgets not only because they benefit his state but also because he believes they benefit the country. He is an internationalist who wants to assert U.S. leadership around the world.

He has spent the past four years trying to ensure that Boeing is first in line to gain a contract from the Air Force for more midair refueling tankers. Dicks first proposed that the Air Force lease 100 of Boeing's 767 jetliners to be modified and used as tankers. His proposal was included in the 2001 defense spending bill. But the initiative was then placed on hold amid questions about the need for the planes, the likely costs and a scandal involving a former Air Force official who was hired by Boeing after overseeing the tanker acquisition program for the Pentagon.

In 2004, the defense authorization bill barred the Air Force from leasing the aircraft and appeared to require competitive bids for any new tanker deal, although Dicks and other Boeing allies disputed that a competition was required. The main competitor to Boeing is EADS, a European consortium that owns Airbus, Boeing's rival in the airliner business.

Yet Dicks believes that Boeing came out all right under the defense bill and that the tankers will be made in America. "I believe it is the intention of this Congress that this is going to be built by an American company," Dicks said about the tankers.

In the late 1980s, Dicks was the leading congressional proponent of the B-2 stealth bomber — Boeing served as a major subcontractor in building those planes. He was frustrated in the 107th Congress by the Bush administration's refusal to buy additional B-2's.

Dicks also tries to protect the natural resources of the Evergreen State, with its significant fishing, timber and tourism interests. He is the top-ranking Democrat on Appropriations' Interior and Environment Subcommittee, where he has been outspoken in his support for the country's national parks.

During committee consideration of the 2004 interior spending bill, Dicks made a spirited, but unsuccessful, plea to increase funding for the national parks. He offered an amendment to require the National Park Service to shift $45 million from other programs into operations at 388 park locations. He said personnel and services have declined at many parks, with visitors centers closed and restrooms not being cleaned. "These are the icons of America, our crown jewels," said Dicks. "And we are letting them deteriorate."

Dicks falls in line with his party's liberal wing on most social policy issues. He opposes Republican efforts to offer school vouchers, repeal a ban on certain semiautomatic assault-style weapons and prohibit late-term abortions. On the other hand, he supported the bill giving Bush fast-track authority to negotiate foreign trade agreements, reflecting the importance of export sales to such Washington companies as Boeing and Microsoft Corp.

Dicks' legislative achievements come from a blend of boisterous bonhomie, irrepressible humor, bullheaded tenacity and years of training. He learned from a past master, Washington Democrat Warren G. Magnuson, the influential Senate appropriator for whom Dicks worked from 1968, when he finished law school, to 1976, when he began the first of his unbroken string of successful campaigns for his House seat.

Dicks decided to run in 1976 when the 6th District seat came open. He tapped into the resources of labor and other interest groups to win the primary and had no trouble against a weak Republican that fall.

In 1980, Republican James Beaver held him to 54 percent of the vote. His challenger in 1982, GOP state Sen. Ted Haley, painted Dicks as a profligate spender too friendly with military contractors. But that charge gave Dicks an excuse to talk about projects he had brought home. Dicks' 63 percent indicated he was gaining a comfortable margin of political success.

Since then, he has dropped below 60 percent only once — in the GOP banner year of 1994. In 2004, Dicks walked to an easy victory over little-known Republican Doug Cloud, winning by 38 percentage points.

KEY VOTES

2004
- ? Extend federal unemployment benefits by 13 weeks
- Yes Pass $283.2 billion, six-year federal highway and mass transit bill
- No Approve $146 billion multi-year extension of previously enacted middle-class tax breaks
- No Amend the Constitution to prohibit same-sex marriage
- Yes Cut corporate taxes $137 billion over 10 years
- Yes Reorganize U.S. intelligence agencies as proposed by Sept. 11 commission

2003
- No Cut taxes by $330 billion through fiscal 2013
- Yes Block Bush rule scaling back overtime pay for some white-collar federal workers
- Yes Do not allow use of search warrants without first notifying subjects
- Yes Allow importation of prescription drugs
- No Create private school voucher program in Washington, D.C.
- No Ban "partial birth" abortion except to save a woman's life
- No Split $18.6 billion in Iraq aid into half-grant, half-loan
- No Overhaul Medicare and create prescription drug benefit

CQ VOTE STUDIES

	PARTY UNITY		PRESIDENTIAL SUPPORT	
	Support	Oppose	Support	Oppose
2004	90%	10%	31%	69%
2003	89%	11%	31%	69%
2002	85%	15%	36%	64%
2001	82%	18%	36%	64%
2000	89%	11%	88%	12%

INTEREST GROUPS

	AFL-CIO	ADA	CCUS	ACU
2004	93%	85%	48%	13%
2003	87%	90%	38%	20%
2002	88%	80%	60%	13%
2001	82%	90%	50%	8%
2000	80%	80%	45%	8%

WASHINGTON 6
West — Bremerton, Tacoma, Olympic Peninsula

The green, lush vegetation of the 6th is part of what gives Washington its nickname, the "Evergreen State." Olympic National Park and Olympic National Forest constitute more than half of the district's land, about 2 million protected acres. Along the coast, the mountains drop to the Pacific Ocean.

Logging and fishing remain major industries in the west, but fights over protection for the spotted owl and other endangered species have forced some companies to cut back their workforce.

Communities are trying to diversify their economies and have had some success in attracting technology companies. Trade has increased in the port towns of Grays Harbor County. Bremerton, with the Puget Sound Naval Shipyard and Bremerton Navy base, depends heavily on the military. The 6th also has a substantial Coast Guard presence. The district's representative must balance environmental concerns with labor and defense spending needs.

The 6th includes most of Tacoma and its suburbs. The industrial city's blue-collar, heavily unionized electorate generally gives Democrats the edge in Pierce County, where half of the district population lives. Bremerton, in Kitsap County (nearly one-fifth of the 6th's population), leans Democratic, as do Grays Harbor and Jefferson counties on the coast. John Kerry took 53 percent of the 6th's presidential vote in 2004.

MAJOR INDUSTRY
Lumber, fishing, shipping, health care

MILITARY BASES
Puget Sound Naval Shipyard and Intermediate Maintenance Facility, 927 military, 9,386 civilian (2005); Naval Base Kitsap – Bremerton, 320 military (5,740 military on home-ported ships), 16 civilian (2002)

CITIES
Tacoma (pt.), 176,853; Bremerton, 37,259; University Place, 29,933; Lakewood (pt.), 26,878; Port Angeles, 18,397

NOTABLE
The Olympic Peninsula is home to 15 kinds of animals and eight kinds of plants that are not found elsewhere in the wild; Port Angeles, across the Strait of Juan de Fuca from Victoria, Canada, credits its establishment partly to an 1862 Abraham Lincoln executive order.

Rep. Jim McDermott (D)

Elected 1988; 9th term

R. McDERMOTT

CAPITOL OFFICE
225-3106
www.house.gov/mcdermott
1035 Longworth 20515-4707; fax 225-6197

COMMITTEES
Ways & Means

HOMETOWN
Seattle

BORN
Dec. 28, 1936, Chicago, Ill.

RELIGION
Episcopalian

FAMILY
Wife, Therese Hansen; two children

EDUCATION
Wheaton College (Ill.), B.S. 1958; U. of Illinois, M.D. 1963

MILITARY SERVICE
Navy Medical Corps, 1968-70

CAREER
Psychiatrist

POLITICAL HIGHLIGHTS
Wash. House, 1971-73; sought Democratic nomination for governor, 1972; Wash. Senate, 1975-87; Democratic nominee for governor, 1980; sought Democratic nomination for governor, 1984

ELECTION RESULTS

2004 GENERAL

Jim McDermott (D)	272,302	80.7%
Carol Thorne Cassady (R)	65,226	19.3%

2004 PRIMARY

Jim McDermott (D)	unopposed

2002 GENERAL

Jim McDermott (D)	156,300	74.1%
Carol Thorne Cassady (R)	46,256	21.9%
Stan Lippmann (LIBERT)	8,447	4.0%

PREVIOUS WINNING PERCENTAGES
2000 (73%); 1998 (88%); 1996 (81%); 1994 (75%); 1992 (78%); 1990 (72%); 1988 (76%)

An outgoing man with an instantly recognizable shock of white hair, McDermott can be confrontational in his promotion of Democratic causes, and as others have moved to the political center, he has remained devoted to the liberal wing of the party.

In recent years, McDermott has returned to his roots in the 1960s anti-war movement by taking a strong stand against the war in Iraq. He had a prominent role in filmmaker Michael Moore's documentary "Fahrenheit 9/11," a highly critical look at the Bush White House that became a rallying point for Democrats in the 2004 elections.

During the Vietnam War, McDermott was stationed in Long Beach, Calif., where, as a Navy psychiatrist, his job was to decide whether to return sailors and Marines to battle. McDermott says that one of his heroes from that period is Ernest Gruening, an Alaska Democrat who cast one of only two no votes in the Senate for the 1964 Gulf of Tonkin resolution, which led to U.S. involvement in Vietnam.

A third of a century later, McDermott urged a go-slow approach in attacking Afghanistan to root out terrorists and counseled against the war with Iraq. "The president can flatten Iraq," he told an anti-war rally in 2003. "There's no question what our power is. But this war is unjust and unjustifiable."

McDermott has served as president of the liberal Americans for Democratic Action since 2002. "I got into politics because I was mad about the Vietnam War, and you and I and people like us were the ones who stopped the war," he told the group's annual convention. "I came out of the military in 1970 during the Vietnam era and said to myself, 'You've got to get involved in politics or the world's course is all going to be decided in Washington, D.C., and we're not going to like what that means.' "

Also on the foreign policy front, McDermott has a special interest in Africa and once lived in the Congo. He visited Sudan in 2005 to investigate allegations of genocide. And he joined with Republican Bill Thomas of California in the 108th Congress to enact a U.S.-Africa trade bill making trade partnerships with the United States conditional on improvements in human rights and the rule of law.

McDermott often provides the liberal counterpoint to hot-button social issues raised by the Republican majority. He was one of seven lawmakers to vote in 2003 against a House resolution condemning the 9th U.S. Circuit Court of Appeals after it ruled that the words "under God" in the Pledge of Allegiance were an unconstitutional endorsement of religion. To illustrate his position, McDermott led the House in a recitation of the Pledge that omitted the phrase "under God" — a move that earned him rebukes from all sides, including the Democratic leadership.

McDermott is the only psychiatrist in Congress, and fellow Democrats have looked to him when developing strategy on health care, which remains a top priority for him. He has never moderated the independent streak he exercises on the Ways and Means Committee and as the top-ranking Democrat on the panel's Human Resources Subcommittee. He is often to the left of most Democrats on health care, favoring, for instance, a universal government-run system.

During the big debate on changing the country's employer-based health care system in 1993, McDermott proposed, and pushed vigorously for, a single-payer health care plan under which all Americans would be guaranteed insurance through a taxpayer-financed system. He ignored his own leadership's requests that lawmakers delay introducing health care bills in deference to Democratic President Clinton, who was drafting a White House proposal as one of his first undertakings. The Clinton plan failed to attract sufficient public support, but McDermott helped hasten its death by rallying support among House liberals for his own bill. Since then, he has worked on a number of less-ambitious health care bills, including one to establish federal privacy standards for individuals' medical records.

In the 108th Congress, McDermott remained embroiled in a long-running lawsuit filed against him by Ohio Republican Rep. John A. Boehner over the release of an illegally taped cellular telephone call in late 1996. A conference call among GOP leaders was recorded by a couple in Florida, who heard them discussing the ethical questions being raised about Republican Speaker Newt Gingrich. The tape wound up in McDermott's hands and excerpts appeared in newspaper stories.

McDermott, then a member of the ethics committee, resigned from the panel amid allegations that he had leaked the tape. Boehner, one of the participants in the call, sued in 1998, alleging his privacy had been violated. In October 2004, a federal judge ordered McDermott to pay Boehner $60,000 in damages and eight years' accumulation of attorneys' fees. Boehner's staff estimated the total could reach $550,000, and McDermott appealed the award. Late in 2004, David L. Hobson, another Ohio Republican, filed an ethics complaint against McDermott on the same matter.

Born and raised in Illinois, McDermott was the first member of his family to go to college. After medical school at the University of Illinois, his residency training to become a psychiatrist took him to Seattle. After a two-year stint in the Navy medical corps, he returned to Seattle to launch a career in medicine.

He quickly was attracted to local politics, winning a seat in the state House in 1970 and starting a lengthy legislative career punctuated by three losing bids for governor — in 1972, 1980 and 1984. He served in the state House for two years and, after a two-year break, won four state Senate elections.

McDermott left the state Senate in 1987 to take a three-year job in the Congo, then known as Zaire, as a Foreign Service medical officer. Less than a year later, when Democratic Rep. Mike Lowry announced his plans to run for the U.S. Senate, McDermott arranged to be released from his Foreign Service commitment to return to Washington to run for Lowry's seat.

Since then, his re-election races have been runaways, and McDermott's seat is considered one of the state's safest for the Democratic Party.

KEY VOTES

2004

Yes   Extend federal unemployment benefits by 13 weeks

Yes   Pass $283.2 billion, six-year federal highway and mass transit bill

No   Approve $146 billion multi-year extension of previously enacted middle-class tax breaks

No   Amend the Constitution to prohibit same-sex marriage

No   Cut corporate taxes $137 billion over 10 years

No   Reorganize U.S. intelligence agencies as proposed by Sept. 11 commission

2003

No   Cut taxes by $330 billion through fiscal 2013

Yes   Block Bush rule scaling back overtime pay for some white-collar federal workers

Yes   Do not allow use of search warrants without first notifying subjects

Yes   Allow importation of prescription drugs

No   Create private school voucher program in Washington, D.C.

No   Ban "partial birth" abortion except to save a woman's life

No   Split $18.6 billion in Iraq aid into half-grant, half-loan

No   Overhaul Medicare and create prescription drug benefit

CQ VOTE STUDIES

	PARTY UNITY		PRESIDENTIAL SUPPORT	
	Support	Oppose	Support	Oppose
2004	99%	1%	21%	79%
2003	98%	2%	13%	87%
2002	97%	3%	14%	86%
2001	94%	6%	21%	79%
2000	97%	3%	94%	6%

INTEREST GROUPS

	AFL-CIO	ADA	CCUS	ACU
2004	100%	95%	15%	0%
2003	100%	100%	21%	13%
2002	100%	95%	28%	0%
2001	100%	95%	29%	0%
2000	90%	80%	42%	0%

WASHINGTON 7
Seattle and suburbs

Framed by mountains, lakes and Puget Sound, the 7th provides a serene atmosphere for Seattle. Although more rain falls here than almost any other part of the nation, it is considered one of the most desirable places to live. Despite economic downturns that have killed off parts of Seattle's technology boom, the area remains wealthy, diverse, liberal and cosmopolitan.

The district is still home to high-tech startups and industry leaders, including retailer Amazon.com and software manufacturer Adobe. Microsoft's headquarters is in the neighboring 8th. The aviation and biotechnology industries also are big employers.

Economic downturns doomed many technology startups, and Boeing's decision in 2001 to move its corporate headquarters out of the state, along with subsequent layoffs, also hurt. The cost of housing remains high, forcing most low-income residents out of the city. But top-end restaurants and nightlife abound, catering to young singles and empty nesters. In Seattle, one is almost as likely to live alone as with a family.

The 2000 census measured Seattle's population at just more than its 1960 peak. Asians, at 13 percent of the city's population, are roughly equal to Seattle's combined black and Hispanic populations. The percentage of Seattle residents who describe themselves as members of two races is nearly twice the national average. But the city's population growth has not kept pace with the suburbs, especially in the north.

The Port of Seattle is one of the nation's major gateways to Asian markets and makes the 7th's economy dependent on trade.

The 7th's urban setting and large populations of minorities and singles make it a liberal bastion. Democratic candidates regularly dominate the district, and in 2000 the Green Party's Ralph Nader outpolled George W. Bush in some Seattle precincts. In 2004, John Kerry captured 79 percent of the 7th's presidential vote — easily Kerry's best showing in the state.

MAJOR INDUSTRY
Aviation, computer software, trade, health care

CITIES
Seattle (pt.), 552,834; White Center (unincorporated), 20,975

NOTABLE
In 1971, the first Starbucks Coffee opened at Pike's Place Market.

Rep. Dave Reichert (R)

Elected 2004; 1st term

The popularity that boosted Reichert to his seat in Congress was based on a long career as a law enforcement officer rather than as a lawmaker. The Washington freshman's best-known achievement as King County sheriff was his role in the apprehension of Green River serial killer Gary Ridgway.

In Congress, Reichert (RIKE-ert) got his top choice for a committee assignment — Homeland Security, where House GOP leaders say his law enforcement background will be helpful. Reichert is aware that the leaders may see him as a public voice on crime and emergency preparedness issues. "There will be, I think, some attempt to draw upon my experience as a local leader in law enforcement," he said.

Yet Reichert said he hopes to broaden his profile in Congress by playing an active role on the numerous issues facing suburban Seattle's 8th District. He said his time spent patrolling streets, combating crime and running the sheriff's office also showed him a great deal about the social and economic problems that create a fertile environment for crime. Being sheriff taught him a lot about fiscal management and oversight, he said.

Reichert also got a sought-after seat on the Transportation and Infrastructure Committee, and to its subcommittees on Coast Guard and Maritime Transportation and Highways, Transit and Pipelines. One concern Reichert will address is traffic. His district is rapidly gaining population, and many residents commute to and from Seattle.

Reichert had briefly considered a run for governor in 2004 before deciding to see the Green River case through to its conclusion. It was little surprise, then, that Reichert's name was one of the first mentioned after six-term GOP Rep. Jennifer Dunn decided not to run for re-election in 2004.

Reichert's name recognition gave him a huge advantage in the GOP primary, but he faced another local celebrity — radio commentator Dave Ross — in the general election. The national parties' campaign committees spent more on the contest than any other House race in 2004, and it turned out to be one of the closest, with Reichert nabbing a 5 percentage point win.

CAPITOL OFFICE
225-7761
representative.reichert@mail.house.gov
www.house.gov/reichert
1223 Longworth 20515-4708; fax 225-8673

COMMITTEES
Homeland Security
Science
Transportation & Infrastructure

HOMETOWN
Auburn

BORN
Aug. 29, 1950, Detroit Lakes, Minn.

RELIGION
Lutheran - Missouri Synod

FAMILY
Wife, Julie Reichert; three children

EDUCATION
Concordia College (Ore.), A.A. 1970

MILITARY SERVICE
Air Force Reserve, 1971-76; Air Force, 1976

CAREER
Police officer; grocery warehouse worker

POLITICAL HIGHLIGHTS
King County sheriff, 1997-2005

ELECTION RESULTS

2004 GENERAL

Dave Reichert (R)	173,298	51.5%
Dave Ross (D)	157,148	46.7%
Spencer Garrett (LIBERT)	6,053	1.8%

2004 PRIMARY

Dave Reichert (R)	31,088	43.1%
Diane Tebelius (R)	16,468	22.8%
Luke Esser (R)	16,309	22.6%
Conrad Lee (R)	8,350	11.6%

WASHINGTON 8

Eastside Seattle suburbs — Bellevue

Home to some of suburban Seattle's most prosperous areas, the 8th takes in King County's Eastside suburbs east of Lake Washington, where million-dollar homes dot the lakeshore in wealthy hamlets like Hunts Point, Clyde Hill, Yarrow Point and Medina, where Microsoft founder Bill Gates lives. Commuters continue to fill out the exurban land as they are priced out of more-central neighborhoods. The expansion has caused huge traffic problems and ignited debates on smart growth and preservation.

The Eastside suburbs once were farmland but have become fertile ground for the Northwest's technology businesses. While attracting residents who work for companies such as Microsoft (whose main campus is within the district's boundaries), the 8th also has higher-paid, blue-collar workers. Indian and Russian communities also are growing as they take on the area's technology jobs.

Boeing remains a dominant employer, but its influence on the district waned after the 2001 decision to move its headquarters out of state. Subsequent rounds of layoffs caused some workers to leave the district.

In addition to its near-in Seattle suburbs, the 8th continues east to the border of King County and heads south to take in a mostly rural part of Pierce County, which includes Mt. Rainier National Park.

The 8th's once strongly Republican politics are changing as the first-ring suburbs begin to resemble the urban core. Mainly fiscally conservative and socially moderate, the 8th is politically competitive, backing John Kerry narrowly in 2004. Southeast Asian and Middle Eastern immigrants are diversifying the area and will influence future elections.

MAJOR INDUSTRY
Logging, aviation manufacturing, software

CITIES
Bellevue, 109,569; Kent (pt.), 35,620; Sammamish, 34,104

NOTABLE
Pontoon bridges span Lake Washington to connect Seattle with the Eastside suburbs.

Rep. Adam **Smith** (D)

CAPITOL OFFICE
225-8901
www.house.gov/adamsmith
227 Cannon 20515-4709; fax 225-5893

COMMITTEES
Armed Services
International Relations
Judiciary

HOMETOWN
Tacoma

BORN
June 15, 1965, Washington, D.C.

RELIGION
Christian

FAMILY
Wife, Sara Smith; two children

EDUCATION
Fordham U., B.A. 1987 (political science); U. of
Washington, J.D. 1990

CAREER
City prosecutor; lawyer

POLITICAL HIGHLIGHTS
Wash. Senate, 1991-97

ELECTION RESULTS

2004 GENERAL

Adam Smith (D)	162,433	63.3%
Paul J. Lord (R)	88,304	34.4%
Robert F. Losey (GREEN)	5,934	2.3%

2004 PRIMARY

Adam Smith (D)	unopposed

2002 GENERAL

Adam Smith (D)	95,805	58.5%
Sarah Casada (R)	63,146	38.6%
J. Mills (LIBERT)	4,759	2.9%

PREVIOUS WINNING PERCENTAGES
2000 (62%); 1998 (65%); 1996 (50%)

Elected 1996; 5th term

Smith considers himself a man of the middle. As a leader of the pro-business New Democrat Coalition, he has repeatedly sought to nudge his more liberal colleagues closer toward the ideological center. And as a lawmaker from a politically competitive, largely suburban district, he has found that embracing positions near the middle has paid off at election time.

Even so, it is hard work, especially as Congress and his own party become more polarized. Howard Dean, the liberal presidential candidate who urged Democrats to "take back the Democratic wing of the Democratic Party," has been named chairman of the Democratic National Committee. Smith backed the moderate Simon Rosenberg, head of the centrist New Democrat Network. Formerly a co-chairman of the New Democrat Coalition, Smith in 2005 was tapped to lead its political action committee. But, though he was pleased with his new leadership role, the army around him was shrinking. Membership for the 109th Congress was about half what it was in the 108th, when the coalition included about 70 lawmakers.

Smith sides with his fellow Democrats on social issues, but he sometimes bucks his party's liberal majority on fiscal policy, crime and national security. For example, in 2004 Smith was one of only four Democrats who voted against an amendment that would have changed the 2001 Patriot Act to prohibit federal agents from searching library records and book store customer lists to aid terrorism investigations. The amendment died on a tie vote, and Washington state liberals excoriated Smith. He later told civil libertarians that he should have voted the other way. "It is quite possible that I looked at it incorrectly," he said. Asked if he would vote differently in the future, Smith replied, "Yes, in all likelihood."

Although timber giant Weyerhaeuser Co. is headquartered in the 9th District, Smith generally sides with urban Democrats against more logging on public lands. In 2003, however, he voted for the final version of the "healthy forests" act, which allows thinning of many forest areas for wildfire prevention. He had opposed a more sweeping version of the bill earlier in the year.

He criticizes not only President Bush but also his own party for driving up the federal deficit. "The time to come up with a real plan to pay down the debt and get our budget back on track is now. Otherwise, the costs will be enormous not only to our children and grandchildren, but they will also wreak havoc on our economy and plunge this country into a worse financial crisis for decades to come," he said when the administration reported that the deficit in 2005 would soar to $427 billion.

One of the first bills Smith introduced in the 109th Congress sought to establish an independent commission to comb the federal government for "unnecessary" programs and propose a list for termination.

Smith is a member of the Armed Services Committee, which allows him to look out for the interests of defense contractor Boeing and his district's two military installations — Fort Lewis, the Army's largest training base on the West Coast, and McChord Air Force Base. He has tried to persuade older Cold War veterans to relax export controls on "dual use" technologies — computers, software and other products that could be used for both military and commercial purposes. He argues that such exports should be allowed if similar foreign-made items are readily available to purchasers.

Smith also sits on the International Relations Committee, which gives him another perspective on world affairs. And after losing out in the 108th Congress, he won a seat in the 109th on the Judiciary Committee, which handles intellectual property issues vital to the software and other tech companies in his district. Microsoft Corp. is one of the area's biggest employers.

Smith is a free-trade advocate. After voting against similar bills in 1998 and 2001, Smith in 2002 resisted entreaties from his party leaders and backed legislation giving the president fast-track authority to negotiate trade agreements that Congress cannot amend. In the 108th, he voted for trade accords with Australia, Chile, Morocco and Singapore.

On tax cuts, Smith in 2001 voted for Republican bills to reduce taxes for married couples, phase out the estate tax and boost incentives for retirement savings that became components of the $1.35 trillion, 10-year tax cut enacted later that year. He voted against the overall package, however. In 2005, Smith voted for a GOP bill to permanently repeal estate taxes.

Smith's success in positioning himself as a pragmatic centrist has helped him to cement his political standing among his mainly white-collar constituents. He is the only person ever re-elected to Congress from Washington's 9th District, which was created in 1992 when the state gained an additional seat in that decade's reapportionment. His two predecessors — one a Democrat, the other a Republican — each lost after one term.

His trade votes put him at odds with labor unions, whose backing was pivotal to his initial election. But Smith otherwise usually takes labor's side. His father worked as a baggage handler at the Seattle-Tacoma International Airport, and Smith was a member of the Teamsters union while working for the United Parcel Service during college.

Smith likes to say he is a lifelong resident of the area he represents in Congress. Technically, though, he is an "inside-the-Beltway" native, having been born in the District of Columbia one week before the Smiths adopted him and took him to the "other Washington." Smith's adoptive father died shortly before Smith headed east for college.

The fall after he earned his law degree in 1990, he won a state Senate seat in an upset and, at 25, became the youngest state senator in the country. Four years later, when many Democratic officeholders in the state were swept away by the 1994 Republican tide, he won a second term.

By 1996, at age 31, Smith was well-known as a tireless campaigner who had made repeat visits to many of the 40,000 homes in his legislative district. He challenged GOP Rep. Randy Tate, a favorite of social conservatives, who had ridden into office on the big GOP wave of 1994. Smith triumphed by 3 percentage points and has won fairly comfortably since then. The makeup of the 9th was altered only slightly by the latest redistricting.

KEY VOTES

2004

? Extend federal unemployment benefits by 13 weeks

Yes Pass $283.2 billion, six-year federal highway and mass transit bill

? Approve $146 billion multi-year extension of previously enacted middle-class tax breaks

No Amend the Constitution to prohibit same-sex marriage

Yes Cut corporate taxes $137 billion over 10 years

Yes Reorganize U.S. intelligence agencies as proposed by Sept. 11 commission

2003

No Cut taxes by $330 billion through fiscal 2013

Yes Block Bush rule scaling back overtime pay for some white-collar federal workers

Yes Do not allow use of search warrants without first notifying subjects

No Allow importation of prescription drugs

No Create private school voucher program in Washington, D.C.

No Ban "partial birth" abortion except to save a woman's life

No Split $18.6 billion in Iraq aid into half-grant, half-loan

No Overhaul Medicare and create prescription drug benefit

CQ VOTE STUDIES

	PARTY UNITY		PRESIDENTIAL SUPPORT	
	Support	Oppose	Support	Oppose
2004	84%	16%	38%	62%
2003	85%	15%	40%	60%
2002	81%	19%	38%	62%
2001	80%	20%	43%	57%
2000	80%	20%	78%	22%

INTEREST GROUPS

	AFL-CIO	ADA	CCUS	ACU
2004	86%	90%	55%	17%
2003	80%	85%	50%	24%
2002	63%	85%	63%	23%
2001	83%	80%	48%	20%
2000	67%	45%	80%	21%

WASHINGTON 9
South Seattle suburbs; small part of Tacoma

The 9th is a politically competitive, mostly suburban district south of Seattle that runs along Interstate 5, picking up small parts of Tacoma and the capital of Olympia en route to rural areas that afford great views of the 14,410-foot Mount Rainier (in the 8th), the state's highest point.

The district's northern area, just south of the Seattle line, takes in predominately middle-class King County suburbs, including most of Burien, SeaTac and Tukwila (shared with the 7th) and Renton (shared with the 8th). SeaTac (a partial concatenation of the names of the area's major cities) includes the region's major airport. Boeing has a commercial airplane production facility in Renton. Farther south are slightly more prosperous areas like Kent (shared with the 8th) and Des Moines. Federal Way, in southwest King, includes the headquarters of timber giant Weyerhaeuser Co.

King County accounts for about half of the 9th's population. The rest live in Pierce County, south of King, or in Thurston County, including northeastern Olympia. In Pierce, the 9th takes in the deep-water Port of

Tacoma, which has diversified an economy once dominated by Boeing. The corridor along Interstate 5 has become a magnet for technology companies that provide high-paying jobs for well-educated residents.

Redistricting following the 2000 census made small changes to the 9th, which during the 1990s was a quintessential swing district that elected a Democratic representative in 1992, a Republican in 1994 and a Democrat in 1996. Democrats fare better in the King and Thurston portions of the district than in Pierce.

MAJOR INDUSTRY
Aviation manufacturing, computer software, hardware

MILITARY BASES
Fort Lewis (Army), 20,484 military, 4,500 civilian (2001); McChord Air Force Base, 6,524 military, 2,086 civilian (2004)

CITIES
Federal Way, 83,259; Kent (pt.), 43,904; Puyallup, 33,011; Lakewood (pt.), 31,333; Des Moines, 29,267; Lacey (pt.), 28,829; Auburn (pt.), 23,271

NOTABLE
Before becoming commander of the U.S. forces in the Persian Gulf, Gen. Norman Schwarzkopf was commander of Fort Lewis; Puyallup Valley claims to be the nation's top producer of rhubarb.

Gov. Joe Manchin III (D)

First elected: 2004
Length of term: 4 years
Term expires: 1/09
Salary: $95,000
Phone: (304) 558-2000

Hometown: Fairmont
Born: August 24, 1947; Fairmont, W.Va.
Religion: Roman Catholic
Family: Wife, Gayle Manchin; three children
Education: West Virginia U., B.A. 1970 (business administration)
Career: Coal brokerage company owner; carpet store owner
Political highlights: W.Va. House, 1983-85; W.Va. Senate, 1987-97; sought Democratic nomination for governor, 1996; W.Va. secretary of state, 2001-05

Election results:

2004 GENERAL
Joe Manchin III (D)	472,758	63.5%
Monty Warner (R)	253,131	34.0%
Jesse Johnson (MOUNT)	18,430	2.5%

Senate President Earl Ray Tomblin (D)

(no lieutenant governor)
Phone: (304) 855-7270

STATE LEGISLATURE

General Assembly: January-March, limit of 60 days

House: 100 members, 2-year terms
2005 breakdown: 68D, 32R; 82 men, 18 women
Salary: $15,000
Phone: (304) 340-3200

Senate: 34 members, 4-year terms
2005 breakdown: 21D, 13R; 31 men, 3 women
Salary: $15,000
Phone: (304) 357-7800

STATE TERM LIMITS

Governor: 2 consecutive terms
House: No
Senate: No

URBAN STATISTICS

CITY	POPULATION
Charleston	53,421
Huntington	51,475
Parkersburg	33,099
Wheeling	31,419

REGISTERED VOTERS

Democrat	58%
Republican	30%
Nonpartisan	11%
Others	1%

POPULATION

2004 population (est.)	1,815,354
2000 population	1,808,344
1990 population	1,793,477
Percent change (1990-2000)	+0.8%
Rank among states (2004)	37
Median age	38.9
Born in state	74.2%
Foreign born	1.1%
Violent crime rate	317/100,000
Poverty level	17.9%
Federal workers	21,235
Military	10,203

REDISTRICTING

West Virginia retained its three House seats in reapportionment. The state legislature drew a new map, which the governor signed on Oct. 4, 2001.

MISCELLANEOUS

Web: www.wv.gov
Capital: Charleston
STATE ELECTION OFFICIAL
(304) 558-6000
DEMOCRATIC HEADQUARTERS
(304) 342-8121
REPUBLICAN HEADQUARTERS
(304) 768-0493

District Statistics

DIST.	2004 VOTE FOR PRESIDENT BUSH	KERRY	WHITE	BLACK	ASIAN	HISP	MEDIAN INCOME	WHITE COLLAR	BLUE COLLAR	SERVICE INDUSTRY	OVER 64	UNDER 18	COLLEGE EDUCATION	RURAL	SQ. MILES
1	58%	41%	96%	2%	1%	1%	$30,303	54%	29%	17%	16%	22%	16%	46%	6,286
2	57	42	94	4	1	1	$33,198	55	30	15	15	23	16	54	8,459
3	53	46	94	4	0	1	$25,630	53	30	18	16	22	12	62	9,332
STATE	56	43	95	3	1	1	$29,696	54	29	17	15	22	15	54	24,078
U.S.	50.7	48.3	69	12	4	13	$41,994	60	25	15	12	26	24	21	3,537,438

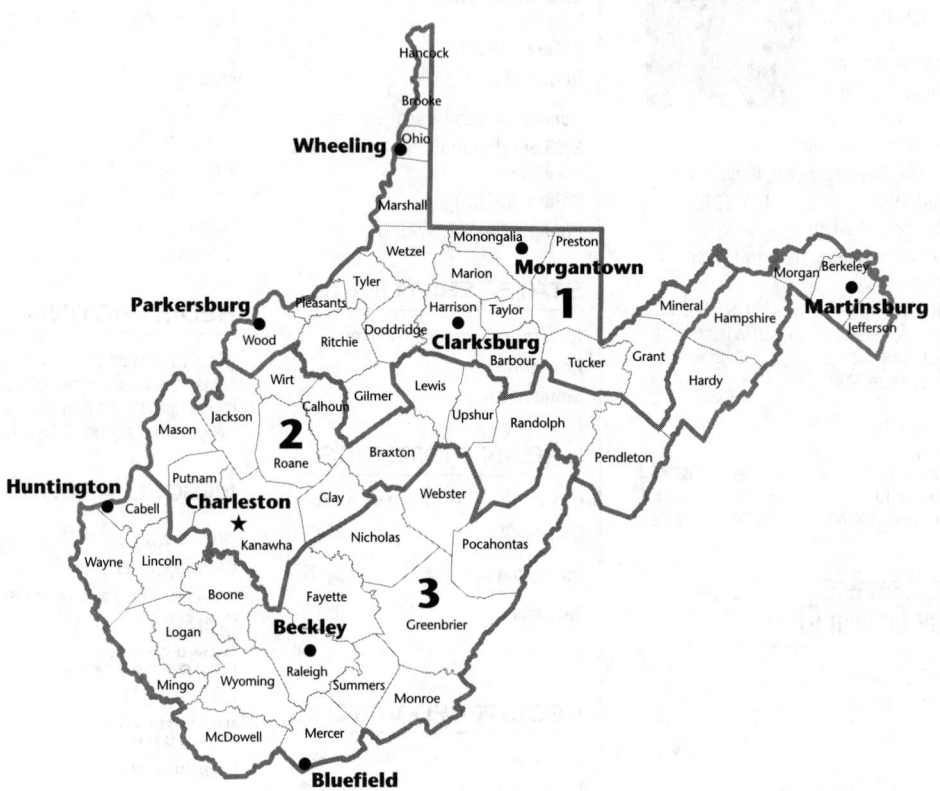

Sen. Robert C. Byrd (D)

Elected 1958; 8th term

Byrd is the longest-serving member of the current Senate. Deeply respected and keenly feared, he solidified his place years ago as the master of the chamber's rules and procedures and as a fierce protector of its prerogatives. Now, as his hands and voice tremble with age, Byrd personifies Senate traditions. He asserts the importance of Senate deliberation on pressing issues. And he is one of President Bush's harshest critics in Congress, deriding the president as an arrogant and insensitive leader.

At the outset of the 109th Congress, Byrd was beginning his 47th year as a senator and ranked as the second-longest-serving senator in history. He was closing in on the record of the late Strom Thurmond of South Carolina, the longest-serving senator — 47 years and five months. Byrd, in his late 80s, intends to run for re-election in 2006.

More important than his longevity is Byrd's vigorous pursuit of his self-appointed roles as guardian of the Senate's prerogatives and precedents, its reverential historian, and grand master of its rules and procedures. He can be prickly and imperious, and he is something of a loner in the institution he so loves. But he literally wrote the book on the Senate — an authoritative four-volume history that began as a series of characteristically flowery speeches.

In 2004, he published a very different book that articulated his sorrow and anger at the emergence of a political culture of deep polarization and expanding executive power. In the thick of the presidential contest between Bush and Democratic Sen. John Kerry of Massachusetts, Byrd went on tour to promote "Losing America," a book in which he asserts that the Sept. 11, 2001, terrorist attacks transformed "a lackluster, inarticulate, visionless president into a national and international leader, nearly unquestioned by the media or by members of either party." He reserves his harshest criticism not for Bush, but for lawmakers who he says shirked their duty by failing to question his policies. "For a long while, I have viewed with dismay each and every assault on the separation of powers and the continual grasping and groping for more power by presidents of both political parties, but never with such alarm as now," he wrote.

As Republicans plotted in 2005 to use parliamentary tactics to prevent Democrats from using the filibuster to block Bush's conservative judicial nominees, Byrd was among his party's strongest voices inveighing against the effort. In his dozen years as majority leader in the 1970s and 1980s, Byrd used his photographic knowledge of Senate rules to get around legislative roadblocks.

Byrd is also scholarly in his understanding of and devotion to the Constitution. "This is my contract with America," he said, holding up a copy of the document when Republicans in the 1990s trumpeted a legislative manifesto of that name.

Among Byrd's favorite passages in the Constitution is Article 1, Section 9, clause 7 — "No money shall be drawn from the Treasury, but in consequence of appropriations made by law." As either the chairman or the top-ranking Democrat on the Appropriations Committee since 1989, Byrd has zealously exercised the power of the purse in behalf of West Virginia, securing money for traditional fare like highways, dams and colleges, but also for relocating federal agencies to his home state. That has made him a ready symbol for critics of Congress' spending culture. When he first took the Appropriations gavel in the 101st Congress (1989-1990), he

CAPITOL OFFICE
224-3954
byrd.senate.gov
311 Hart 20510-4801; fax 228-0002

COMMITTEES
Appropriations - ranking member
Armed Services
Budget
Rules & Administration

HOMETOWN
Sophia

BORN
Nov. 20, 1917, North Wilkesboro, N.C.

RELIGION
Baptist

FAMILY
Wife, Erma Ora Byrd; two children

EDUCATION
American U., J.D. 1963; Marshall U., B.A. 1994 (political science)

CAREER
Butcher

POLITICAL HIGHLIGHTS
W.Va. House, 1947-51; W.Va. Senate, 1951-53; U.S. House, 1953-59

ELECTION RESULTS

2000 GENERAL
Robert C. Byrd (D)	469,215	77.8%
David T. Gallaher (R)	121,635	20.2%
Joe Whelan (LIBERT)	12,627	2.1%

2000 PRIMARY
Robert C. Byrd (D)	unopposed

PREVIOUS WINNING PERCENTAGES
1994 (69%); 1988 (65%); 1982 (69%); 1976 (100%); 1970 (78%); 1964 (68%); 1958 (59%); 1956 House Election (57%); 1954 House Election (63%); 1952 House Election (56%)

promised to steer $1 billion for public works back home, a goal that he met in less than three years. The stream of federal dollars to West Virginia has continued unabated.

The Charleston Gazette, which has called Byrd a "one-man economic development program," has compiled a list of more than 30 existing or pending federal projects named for the senator. Byrd, who has hung a life-size portrait of himself in one of his Capitol offices, makes no pretense of shunning such gestures of gratitude.

He was born Cornelius Calvin Sale Jr. When he was 1, his mother died and his father gave him to an aunt and uncle, Vlurma and Titus Byrd. The couple reared him in the hardscrabble coal country of southern West Virginia. Byrd graduated first in his high school class and married his high school sweetheart, Erma Ora, about whom he still rhapsodizes in Senate speeches. It took him 12 years to save enough money to start college.

He worked as a gas station attendant, grocery store clerk, shipyard welder and butcher before his talents as a fiddle player helped him win a seat in the state legislature in 1946. Friends drove Byrd around the hills and hollows, where he brought the voters out by playing "Cripple Creek" and "Rye Whiskey."

Since that first bid for office, Byrd has never lost an election. "There are four things people believe in in West Virginia," he has often said. "God Almighty; Sears, Roebuck; Carter's Little Liver Pills; and Robert C. Byrd."

In the legislative arena, Byrd has often emerged victorious over more-celebrated lawmakers. And he has bested most of the 11 presidents he has served beside, at least once.

In the early 2000s, he had a rare losing streak on a wide range of issues. He was unable to get his way in the debate over creating the Department of Homeland Security, which he tried to block for fear that it ceded too much authority to the president. He could not persuade even a majority of Senate Democrats to vote against the war in Iraq. He led the opposition to Bush's bid for the power to negotiate trade deals that Congress may not amend, and he lost overwhelmingly.

Most cutting of all, in 2001 Byrd was unable to prevent the Senate from using the budget law he wrote in 1974 — designed to ease procedural impediments to Congress' trimming of the deficit — to instead give parliamentary protections to the deepest tax cut in two decades.

There are signs that age is beginning to take its toll on Byrd. But he often reminds his colleagues, including Democratic leaders, that he will not be silenced. In the Senate, where no deal is ever truly done until everyone signs off on it, word often spreads of an eleventh-hour "Byrd problem," which usually entails time-consuming parliamentary obstacles.

Byrd's political career has featured its share of mistakes, some quite spectacular. As a young man, he joined the Ku Klux Klan because, he said, of his alarm over communism — a decision he came to publicly regret. In 1964, he filibustered the landmark Civil Rights Act, at one point holding the floor with a 14-hour speech that is among the longest on record. He also has lamented that chapter of his career.

Ever the student of history, Byrd has understood its imperatives and changed with the times. But he is becoming increasingly isolated in a Senate of younger, more impatient members whose focus is on the next TV interview or election.

Byrd is proud of his individuality. On his Senate Web site, he proudly cites a tribute from former Democratic Sen. Sam Nunn of Georgia: "Great men are like eagles. They do not flock together. You find them one at a time, soaring alone, using their skill and their strengths to reach new heights and to seek new horizons. Such a man and such an eagle is Robert Byrd."

KEY VOTES

2004
Yes Pass $318.9 billion, six-year highway and mass transit bill
Yes Extend assault weapons ban for 10 years
Yes Restore pay-as-you-go rules for new tax cuts and entitlement spending
No Criminalize harm to a fetus in an attack on the mother
Yes Increase mandatory child care funding to states by $6 billion over five years
Yes Amend the Constitution to prohibit same-sex marriage
Yes Approve $146 billion multi-year extension of previously enacted middle-class tax breaks
No Reorganize U.S. intelligence agencies as proposed by Sept. 11 commission
No Cut corporate taxes $137 billion over 10 years

2003
Yes Delay Bush changes to Clean Air Act
No Allow confirmation vote on Miguel A. Estrada to the U.S. Court of Appeals for the D.C. Circuit
Yes Block a Bush proposal opening Alaska's Arctic National Wildlife Refuge to oil drilling
Yes Limit size of Bush's proposed tax cut to $350 billion through fiscal 2013
No Overhaul Medicare and create prescription drug benefit
Yes Block Bush rule scaling back overtime pay for some white-collar federal workers
? Split $20 billion in Iraq aid into half-grant, half-loan
Yes Ban "partial birth" abortion except to save a woman's life
No Stop proposal allowing travel to Cuba
No Allow final vote on energy policy overhaul

CQ VOTE STUDIES

	PARTY UNITY		PRESIDENTIAL SUPPORT	
	Support	Oppose	Support	Oppose
2004	90%	10%	63%	37%
2003	93%	7%	54%	46%
2002	82%	18%	70%	30%
2001	86%	14%	71%	29%
2000	72%	28%	75%	25%
1999	80%	20%	70%	30%
1998	72%	28%	74%	26%
1997	81%	19%	81%	19%
1996	82%	18%	81%	19%
1995	82%	18%	82%	18%

INTEREST GROUPS

	AFL-CIO	ADA	CCUS	ACU
2004	100%	90%	38%	8%
2003	100%	95%	29%	30%
2002	85%	75%	40%	15%
2001	75%	85%	21%	40%
2000	63%	75%	40%	28%
1999	100%	80%	47%	20%
1998	88%	80%	44%	16%
1997	100%	70%	40%	16%
1996	86%	70%	23%	15%
1995	92%	85%	26%	26%

Sen. John D. Rockefeller IV (D)

Elected 1984; 4th term

CAPITOL OFFICE
224-6472
senator@rockefeller.senate.gov
rockefeller.senate.gov
531 Hart 20510-4802; fax 224-7665

COMMITTEES
Commerce, Science & Transportation
Finance
Veterans' Affairs
Select Intelligence - vice chairman
Joint Taxation

HOMETOWN
Charleston

BORN
June 18, 1937, Manhattan, N.Y.

RELIGION
Presbyterian

FAMILY
Wife, Sharon Percy; four children

EDUCATION
International Christian U. (Tokyo), attended 1957-60; Harvard U., A.B. 1961 (Asian languages & history)

CAREER
College president; VISTA volunteer

POLITICAL HIGHLIGHTS
W.Va. House, 1967-69; W.Va. secretary of state, 1969-73; Democratic nominee for governor, 1972; governor, 1977-85

ELECTION RESULTS

2002 GENERAL

John D. Rockefeller IV (D)	275,281	63.1%
Jay Wolfe (R)	160,902	36.9%

2002 PRIMARY

John D. Rockefeller IV (D)	198,327	89.9%
Bruce Barilla (D)	11,178	5.1%
William "Bill" Galloway (D)	11,173	5.1%

PREVIOUS WINNING PERCENTAGES
1996 (77%); 1990 (68%); 1984 (52%)

The great-grandson and namesake of the founder of Standard Oil Co., Rockefeller went to West Virginia as a young anti-poverty volunteer in the 1960s and never left. His surname may be a symbol of American wealth, but Rockefeller represents a state with one of the nation's lowest per capita personal incomes. He can be the most partisan of Democrats, arguing that Republicans are out to hurt the little guy.

Rockefeller relies on self-deprecating humor to get his constituents to see him as just plain "Jay". And he takes on causes affecting working-class and underclass Americans. In 2003, he refused to vote for President Bush's prescription drug benefit for the elderly because he felt the bill gave private insurers too much power in administering Medicare benefits. And he has fought the administration over a plan to take money away from a federal health insurance program for poor children.

Towering and bookish, Rockefeller cannot hope to match the influence of his senior colleague, Robert C. Byrd, who has used his position as the top-ranking Democrat on the Appropriations Committee to funnel billions of dollars to the state. But Rockefeller is a fierce defender of the struggling steel industry, doing all he can as a member of the minority party to stop cheaper foreign imports of steel. In West Virginia, they call him the "man of steel."

On a national scale, Rockefeller is active in intelligence issues and is the vice chairman of the Intelligence Committee. In the 108th Congress, he was one of just 17 senators who voted against the confirmation of former GOP Rep. Porter J. Goss of Florida to be CIA director. Rockefeller said Goss, the former chairman of the House Intelligence Committee, was too partisan for the job.

After 20 years in the Senate, Rockefeller can play the role of pragmatist, willing to do what it takes to strike a deal. In 2004, he partnered with Intelligence Committee Chairman Pat Roberts, a Kansas Republican, to issue a scathing report on the CIA's information-gathering prior to the invasion of Iraq. The détente did not last long, though. The two split over the best way to overhaul the intelligence community, with Rockefeller favoring recommendations of the independent Sept. 11 commission.

His unhappiness with the cost of a classified Defense Department program caused Rockefeller to discuss it on the Senate floor, a move that angered GOP leaders. Rockefeller described the program — later identified in news reports as a $9.5 billion initiative to develop "stealth" satellites that cannot be detected in orbit — as "totally unjustified and very wasteful and dangerous to national security."

Rockefeller has worked hard to gain the confidence of West Virginians from the day he arrived in 1964 as a 27-year-old with VISTA's Action for Appalachia Youth program. He had been reared on Manhattan's Upper East Side, schooled at Exeter prep and Harvard University, and had just come from three years abroad studying Japanese. Rockefeller got involved in West Virginia politics by running for the state legislature, and has lived there ever since.

In one way, his family wealth insulates him from suspicion back home. With no need to curry favor or solicit campaign cash from special interests, Rockefeller can devote all of his energies to his work in the Senate.

He says that the steel industry's problems are a "life or death" issue in his state, and has waged knock-down fights with administrations of both parties to protect the industry, which he believes is on the verge of collapse as a result of a flood of low-cost imports. After Bush carried West Virginia in 2000 on a promise to consider imposing steel tariffs, Rockefeller pushed for them. In 2002, the Bush administration announced a 30 percent duty on imported tin mill steel, which is produced by Weirton Steel, one of the state's largest employers. Rockefeller hailed the move, but later expressed outrage that Bush had exempted nearly one-fourth of foreign imports.

He also was disillusioned with Bush over health benefits for retired steelworkers. Unfunded benefits are an obstacle to consolidation in the industry, which is considered integral to its survival. Rockefeller proposed using up to $10 billion from steel import tariffs to pay the "legacy costs," but the White House rejected the idea.

In the 108th Congress, Rockefeller was named to the House and Senate negotiating team responsible for drafting the final version of the Medicare prescription drug bill. But he and several other Democratic conferees were shut out of the talks by House Ways and Means Chairman Bill Thomas, a California Republican, who said their partisan behavior was preventing a compromise. Democratic senators Max Baucus of Montana and John B. Breaux of Louisiana were allowed in. Rockefeller had served with Breaux in the 1990s on a blue-ribbon panel studying the long-term solvency of the Medicare program.

The measure passed both chambers, but Rockefeller refused to support it. He said, "The bill's fine print matters and it will have very dangerous consequences for how much seniors have to pay for their Medicare benefit, whether this drug benefit really serves seniors. . . . It is a tragedy and our seniors are going to pay a heavy price."

Rockefeller also clashed with Republicans over the administration's plan to redistribute $1.1 billion in unspent money in the State Children's Health Insurance Program, which gives states grants to cover low-income children whose families are not poor enough to qualify for Medicaid, the federal-state health insurance program for the poor. Rockefeller sponsored legislation that would have allowed states to tap into the money beyond the deadline, which Bush rejected.

During debate on an overhaul of welfare programs in the 107th Congress, Rockefeller and other Democrats called for an additional $8 billion for child care services over five years. As chairman of the Aviation Subcommittee during that period, Rockefeller had a hand in writing the airline industry bailout and aviation security laws enacted soon after the Sept. 11, 2001, terrorist attacks. He opposed Bush's $1.35 trillion tax cut in 2001.

His ascent in West Virginia politics had some bumps. After serving in the state House and as secretary of state, he lost a race for governor in 1972. He strengthened his ties to the state by taking the job as president of West Virginia Wesleyan College. Rockefeller went on to win the governorship on his second try, in 1976, and served two terms.

In the early 1980s, his popularity slid as the state's economy resisted his attempts to fulfill a campaign promise to fix it. He ran for the Senate in 1984 for the seat of retiring Democrat Jennings Randolph. He won with just 52 percent of the vote despite spending $12 million against political neophyte John Raese. He has won more easily since, and was elected to a fourth term in 2002 with 63 percent against former GOP state Sen. Jay Wolfe.

Given his name recognition, wealth and political experience, Rockefeller is sometimes mentioned as a potential presidential candidate, and he considered and declined a race in 1992. Asked about his interest in the 2004 campaign, Rockefeller told The Charleston Daily Mail in 2001, "I am sufficiently private to not want to do this. There's a point where I've decided to say, 'You can't have all of me.' "

KEY VOTES

2004
Yes Pass $318.9 billion, six-year highway and mass transit bill
Yes Extend assault weapons ban for 10 years
Yes Restore pay-as-you-go rules for new tax cuts and entitlement spending
Yes Criminalize harm to a fetus in an attack on the mother
Yes Increase mandatory child care funding to states by $6 billion over five years
No Amend the Constitution to prohibit same-sex marriage
Yes Approve $146 billion multi-year extension of previously enacted middle-class tax breaks
Yes Reorganize U.S. intelligence agencies as proposed by Sept. 11 commission
No Cut corporate taxes $137 billion over 10 years

2003
Yes Delay Bush changes to Clean Air Act
No Allow confirmation vote on Miguel A. Estrada to the U.S. Court of Appeals for the D.C. Circuit
Yes Block a Bush proposal opening Alaska's Arctic National Wildlife Refuge to oil drilling
Yes Limit size of Bush's proposed tax cut to $350 billion through fiscal 2013
No Overhaul Medicare and create prescription drug benefit
Yes Block Bush rule scaling back overtime pay for some white-collar federal workers
Yes Split $20 billion in Iraq aid into half-grant, half-loan
No Ban "partial birth" abortion except to save a woman's life
No Stop proposal allowing travel to Cuba
No Allow final vote on energy policy overhaul

CQ VOTE STUDIES

	PARTY UNITY		PRESIDENTIAL SUPPORT	
	Support	Oppose	Support	Oppose
2004	88%	12%	64%	36%
2003	96%	4%	50%	50%
2002	90%	10%	71%	29%
2001	97%	3%	66%	34%
2000	96%	4%	97%	3%
1999	94%	6%	89%	11%
1998	93%	7%	94%	6%
1997	88%	12%	86%	14%
1996	93%	7%	93%	7%
1995	88%	12%	88%	12%

INTEREST GROUPS

	AFL-CIO	ADA	CCUS	ACU
2004	100%	90%	41%	12%
2003	92%	100%	30%	15%
2002	100%	90%	45%	15%
2001	100%	100%	43%	12%
2000	75%	85%	60%	4%
1999	89%	100%	41%	4%
1998	100%	90%	56%	0%
1997	71%	70%	67%	8%
1996	86%	85%	46%	16%
1995	100%	90%	42%	9%

Rep. Alan B. Mollohan (D)

CAPITOL OFFICE
225-4172
www.house.gov/mollohan
2302 Rayburn 20515-4801; fax 225-7564

COMMITTEES
Appropriations
Standards of Official Conduct - ranking member

HOMETOWN
Fairmont

BORN
May 14, 1943, Fairmont, W.Va.

RELIGION
Baptist

FAMILY
Wife, Barbara Mollohan; five children

EDUCATION
College of William & Mary, A.B. 1966 (political
science); West Virginia U., J.D. 1970

MILITARY SERVICE
Army Reserve, 1970-83

CAREER
Lawyer

POLITICAL HIGHLIGHTS
No previous office

ELECTION RESULTS

2004 GENERAL

Alan B. Mollohan (D)	166,583	67.8%
Alan Lee Parks (R)	79,196	32.2%

2004 PRIMARY

Alan B. Mollohan (D)	unopposed

2002 GENERAL

Alan B. Mollohan (D)	unopposed

PREVIOUS WINNING PERCENTAGES
2000 (88%); 1998 (85%); 1996 (100%); 1994 (70%);
1992 (100%); 1990 (67%); 1988 (75%); 1986 (100%);
1984 (54%); 1982 (53%)

Elected 1982; 12th term

As a senior Democrat on the Appropriations Committee, Mollohan has long been known as a team player, happy to work with Republicans to write spending bills that steer federal funding to his economically depressed state. But in the 109th Congress, his duties as top-ranking Democrat on the Committee on Standards of Official Conduct — better known as the ethics committee — have forced him to become a partisan brawler.

Minority Leader Nancy Pelosi had made him the top Democrat on the evenly divided 10-member committee in the 108th Congress, and the assignment proved all-consuming in 2004, as the panel investigated two ethics complaints lodged against Majority Leader Tom DeLay. The committee voted unanimously to admonish DeLay for three separate instances of inappropriate conduct but did not seek further punishment.

Republican leaders, angered by the committee's action against DeLay, retaliated. At the beginning of the 109th, Speaker J. Dennis Hastert removed the committee's Republican chairman, Joel Hefley of Colorado, and two other GOP members. He replaced them with party loyalists, including new Chairman Doc Hastings of Washington, who promptly fired veteran committee staff members. Republicans pushed new ethics rules through the House that Democrats said gutted the committee's powers.

Backed by party leaders, Mollohan refused to allow the committee to organize or to function. Other Democrats used procedural maneuvers to tie up activity on the floor. Hastert and the Republicans relented, and the rules changes were rescinded.

Mollohan was not accustomed to such a high-profile role in a partisan dispute. The son of a congressman, he worked as a lawyer in Washington before succeeding his father in the House. He gained a seat on the coveted Appropriations Committee in mid-1986 and has devoted his career to winning federal dollars for new prisons, health clinics, research centers, industrial parks and roads, and water projects for his mostly rural district. He regularly combines forces with his state's most revered politician, Robert C. Byrd, the top-ranking Democrat on the Senate Appropriations Committee, to funnel federal dollars to West Virginia.

In Mollohan's hometown of Fairmont, just south of Morgantown, is the Alan B. Mollohan Innovation Center, the headquarters of the West Virginia High Technology Consortium, a nonprofit group founded by Mollohan to nurture the area's fledgling high-technology sector. Also in Fairmont is the National White Collar Crime Center, created to lead the nation's fight against Internet fraud.

From the 106th Congress through the 108th, Mollohan was the top Democrat on the subcommittee that funded the Veterans Affairs and Housing and Urban Development departments. A cozy relationship with the subcommittee's chairman, Republican James T. Walsh of New York — and their shared appreciation of congressional earmarking — put Mollohan in a position to steer even more money to projects in his district.

That all changed in the 109th Congress, when Republicans, at DeLay's insistence, eliminated the VA-HUD panel. The subcommittee had incurred the majority leader's wrath in 2004 by cutting funds for NASA, a major employer in DeLay's district, in order to fund veterans' health care. (The conflict was eventually resolved, with more money for NASA.)

Mollohan is now the top-ranking Democrat on the new Science, State, Justice and Commerce Subcommittee, and he is also assigned to the Interior and Environment Subcommittee.

Mollohan largely reflects the values of his state's residents, who voted to re-elect President Bush in 2004. Like most House Democrats, he opposes free-trade agreements that he believes threaten his constituents' jobs. He voted against the Bush tax cuts and against the war in Iraq. But he maintains a more conservative stance on social issues. Mollohan strongly opposes abortion; he chaired the House Pro-Life Caucus for many years, and he voted to ban a procedure opponents call "partial birth" abortion. An outdoorsman and hunter, he consistently supports gun owners' rights.

Mollohan also has sided with conservatives on some issues of environmental regulation, a stance that grows from his state's dependence on coal mining, steelmaking and other heavy industries. In 1990, his opposition to what he called "unsound" acid rain legislation that penalized coal-burning factories made him one of only 21 House members to vote against a rewrite of the Clean Air Act.

With steel mills in his district struggling for profitability, Mollohan has backed foreign "anti-dumping" measures. He applauded Bush's decision in 2002 to impose stiff tariffs on imported steel, though they were not as steep as Mollohan and other steel allies had sought.

Mollohan was 9 years old when his father, Robert H. Mollohan, was elected to Congress. He was on the House floor when his father was sworn into office and, as he told The Charleston Daily Mail, "I remember it like yesterday. I think it was kind of a biological imprinting on my brain. I said, 'This is what I want to do.' That's when I knew."

The younger Mollohan struggled to claim his father's House seat. Some voters questioned his career as a D.C.-based corporate attorney whose clients included Pittsburgh-based Consolidation Coal Co. But the elder Mollohan had close connections with party officials, as well as business and labor leaders; their support was crucial to the son's narrow primary win in 1982. Mollohan won with just 53 percent of the vote that fall; in 1984, he was held to 54 percent. His general elections since have been easy.

Redistricting after the 1990 census threw him into a primary against colleague Harley O. Staggers Jr. Both men had followed their fathers to Congress, but Staggers portrayed himself as the "outsider," criticizing Mollohan for writing overdrafts at the private bank for House members. Mollohan highlighted the importance of his seat on Appropriations. He won the primary by 24 percentage points and was unopposed in the general election.

In 2004, Mollohan faced GOP competition for the first time since 1994, defeating Republican Alan Lee Parks with 68 percent.

KEY VOTES

2004

Yes Extend federal unemployment benefits by 13 weeks

Yes Pass $283.2 billion, six-year federal highway and mass transit bill

No Approve $146 billion multi-year extension of previously enacted middle-class tax breaks

No Amend the Constitution to prohibit same-sex marriage

No Cut corporate taxes $137 billion over 10 years

No Reorganize U.S. intelligence agencies as proposed by Sept. 11 commission

2003

No Cut taxes by $330 billion through fiscal 2013

Yes Block Bush rule scaling back overtime pay for some white-collar federal workers

Yes Do not allow use of search warrants without first notifying subjects

Yes Allow importation of prescription drugs

? Create private school voucher program in Washington, D.C.

Yes Ban "partial birth" abortion except to save a woman's life

No Split $18.6 billion in Iraq aid into half-grant, half-loan

No Overhaul Medicare and create prescription drug benefit

CQ VOTE STUDIES

	PARTY UNITY		PRESIDENTIAL SUPPORT	
	Support	Oppose	Support	Oppose
2004	81%	19%	29%	71%
2003	77%	23%	42%	58%
2002	78%	22%	34%	66%
2001	65%	35%	45%	55%
2000	70%	30%	69%	31%

INTEREST GROUPS

	AFL-CIO	ADA	CCUS	ACU
2004	92%	65%	37%	24%
2003	100%	80%	41%	50%
2002	89%	75%	40%	24%
2001	92%	65%	48%	48%
2000	90%	60%	52%	28%

WEST VIRGINIA 1

North – Parkersburg, Wheeling, Morgantown

Located in the northernmost part of the state, the Democratic-leaning 1st has a large rural component but is the most urban of West Virginia's three districts. It contains six of the state's 10 largest cities and West Virginia University, the state's largest school. Wheeling, an industrial town and commercial center in the north, and Parkersburg, a regional trade center in the west, are two of the main urban areas.

The district was hit hard by economic depression in the 1980s, losing population as factories shut down and coal mines mechanized. Unemployment remained high in the early 1990s — topping 10 percent in some counties — and 12 of the district's 20 counties lost population during the decade.

Coal and steel are still the district's biggest employers, but a budding technology sector has brightened economic prospects. The FBI, Energy Department and NASA have opened facilities in the district. Located amid the coal fields of Monongalia County (one of the state's leading coal-producing counties), Morgantown, home to West Virginia

University, is attracting technology firms.

The 1st long has elected Democrats to Congress and has more registered Democrats than Republicans, but Parkersburg and Wheeling have some Republican-leaning state House districts. The 1st gave George W. Bush 54 percent of the vote in the 2000 presidential election, and Bush expanded his percentage in 2004, garnering 58 percent of the vote in winning the district a second time.

MAJOR INDUSTRY
Coal, steel, technology, chemicals

CITIES
Parkersburg, 33,099; Wheeling, 31,419; Morgantown, 26,809; Weirton, 20,411; Fairmont, 19,097; Clarksburg, 16,743

NOTABLE
Prabhupada's Palace of Gold was built in Moundsville by the International Society for Krishna Consciousness; The Capitol Music Hall in Wheeling hosts Jamboree USA, a country music program that has aired on radio station WWVA since 1933; 1984 Olympic gold medalist Mary Lou Retton is from Marion County.

Rep. Shelley Moore Capito (R)

Elected 2000; 3rd term

CAPITOL OFFICE
225-2711
capito.house.gov
1431 Longworth 20515-4802; fax 225-7856

COMMITTEES
Rules

HOMETOWN
Charleston

BORN
Nov. 26, 1953, Glen Dale, W.Va.

RELIGION
Presbyterian

FAMILY
Husband, Charles L. Capito Jr.; three children

EDUCATION
Duke U., B.S. 1975 (zoology); U. of Virginia, M.Ed. 1976 (counselor education)

CAREER
University system information center director; college career counselor

POLITICAL HIGHLIGHTS
W.Va. House, 1997-2001

ELECTION RESULTS

2004 GENERAL

Shelley Moore Capito (R)	147,676	57.5%
Erik Wells (D)	106,131	41.3%
Julian Martin (I)	3,218	1.3%

2004 PRIMARY

Shelley Moore Capito (R)	unopposed

2002 GENERAL

Shelley Moore Capito (R)	98,276	60.0%
Jim Humphreys (D)	65,400	40.0%

PREVIOUS WINNING PERCENTAGES
2000 (48%)

Now in her third term, Capito has grown out of her reputation as a vulnerable newcomer and into the role of an increasingly influential centrist legislator. The only Republican in the West Virginia congressional delegation — and the first one from the Mountain State in two decades — Capito is clearly on a roll. The big question is where she wants to go.

Delighted to see a once-Democratic seat nailed down, House Republican leaders rewarded Capito (CAP-ih-toe) at the start of the 109th Congress with a slot on the exclusive Rules Committee. But it was not clear how long she would occupy it. National and state GOP leaders, viewing her as a rising star, were hoping she would run in 2006 against revered but aging Democratic Sen. Robert C. Byrd, who has brought billions of dollars to West Virginia from his post as top Democrat on the Appropriations Committee.

The daughter of former Gov. Arch A. Moore Jr., Capito relied on her moderate views and comfortable campaign style to survive two of the most expensive House election campaigns of the decade. She narrowly won in 2000 against wealthy class action attorney Jim Humphreys, who plowed almost $7 million into the race. In their 2002 rematch, the most expensive House campaign that year, Capito racked up a 20 percentage point win. She prevailed again in 2004 by nearly as big a margin against a new opponent.

An affable and energetic mother of three, Capito is only the second woman to represent the Mountain State in Congress. She was the Republican co-chairwoman of the Congressional Caucus for Women's Issues in the 108th Congress and affiliates with the Republican Main Street Partnership, which includes about 60 moderate congressional Republicans.

Although she votes with a majority of Republicans on most fiscal and regulatory matters, Capito has gone against the party line on a whole array of high-profile issues such as campaign finance, trade, prescription drug imports, family planning and labor concerns. At the start of the 109th, as President Bush was stumping for his proposal to allow diversion of payroll taxes into private investment accounts within Social Security, Capito was signaling discomfort with the idea. Pressed at town hall meetings to say whether she supported the Bush plan, she replied, "Not at this moment."

In 2004, she was one of 39 Republicans who backed a failed Democratic bid to give jobless workers an additional 13 weeks of unemployment insurance. Also in the 108th, she was in the small minority of Republicans who joined Democrats in their unsuccessful fights to provide bigger child care payments to low-income parents under the child tax credit and to block the administration's changes to the rules governing overtime pay.

Capito also favors an increase in the minimum wage, backs the steel industry against low-cost foreign imports and criticizes the Bush administration's narrow interpretation of protections for whistleblowers who disclose corporate wrongdoing. In 2002, she voted for the campaign finance overhaul bill, which included her amendment to increase fundraising limits and to permit extra help from political parties for candidates who face wealthy, self-funded opponents (like Humphreys).

Like her Democratic predecessor, Rep. Bob Wise, Capito backs gun owners' and abortion rights. But she has supported numerous limits to abortion, voting to ban a procedure opponents call "partial birth" abortion and to require that parents be notified before a minor can obtain an abortion. In the 107th Congress, she came under fire from both sides of the abortion debate when she was one of 33 House Republicans who voted to back international family planning programs but also voted to ban cloning for stem cell research and to provide legal protections for a fetus.

Capito took a leading role in the GOP's overhaul of the Medicare system and creation of a prescription drug benefit for seniors. Appointed vice chairman of a GOP prescription drug task force, Capito worked hard to sell the plan before its enactment in 2003 and continued to play up the benefits of the measure's drug discount card after it became law.

In the 107th, GOP leaders named Capito to an energy task force, giving her the chance to fight for federal dollars to study clean uses for coal, a staple resource of the West Virginia economy.

Capito grew up in a political household. She was not quite 3 years old when her father won his first election to the House. He was governor when she went to college, serving 12 years before his career ended when he pled guilty to a five-count federal indictment that included taking illegal campaign contributions for his gubernatorial campaign. He served three years in prison and paid $750,000 to settle a lawsuit brought against him.

Capito says that many people in West Virginia and on Capitol Hill still tell her how her father helped them. "There's no problem too big or too small that he would not get involved in. . . . Every decision we make in Congress touches people's everyday lives, and I always remember that," she told The Associated Press.

She started college with the thought of becoming a doctor. But as Capito told the AP, "I realized I didn't have the absolute commitment and hunger you need to be a female doctor." She said the 24-hour demands of medicine convinced her "it would be harder to be a female doctor mother than it would be to be a female legislator mother."

She did not enter politics until her youngest child was 11, a deliberate decision on her part. She worked as a college career counselor and for the state Board of Regents, and then won a seat in the West Virginia House of Delegates in 1996, earning notice for her work on children's health issues. After four years in the state House, Capito emerged in 2000 as a highly touted Republican recruit in the race for the 2nd District seat, which opened up when nine-term Democratic Rep. Wise ran successfully for governor.

Bolstered by a blizzard of ads paid for by the National Republican Congressional Committee, Capito spent $1.3 million in her race against Humphreys, beating him by 2.5 percentage points despite his heavy personal investment. She won their costly 2002 rematch with 60 percent of the vote. In 2004, she was the one with plenty of money, and she bested a former TV anchorman, Erik Wells, with 58 percent.

KEY VOTES

2004

Yes Extend federal unemployment benefits by 13 weeks

Yes Pass $283.2 billion, six-year federal highway and mass transit bill

Yes Approve $146 billion multi-year extension of previously enacted middle-class tax breaks

Yes Amend the Constitution to prohibit same-sex marriage

Yes Cut corporate taxes $137 billion over 10 years

Yes Reorganize U.S. intelligence agencies as proposed by Sept. 11 commission

2003

Yes Cut taxes by $330 billion through fiscal 2013

No Block Bush rule scaling back overtime pay for some white-collar federal workers

No Do not allow use of search warrants without first notifying subjects

Yes Allow importation of prescription drugs

Yes Create private school voucher program in Washington, D.C.

Yes Ban "partial birth" abortion except to save a woman's life

No Split $18.6 billion in Iraq aid into half-grant, half-loan

Yes Overhaul Medicare and create prescription drug benefit

CQ VOTE STUDIES

	PARTY UNITY		PRESIDENTIAL SUPPORT	
	Support	Oppose	Support	Oppose
2004	89%	11%	79%	21%
2003	90%	10%	85%	15%
2002	89%	11%	80%	20%
2001	89%	11%	79%	21%

INTEREST GROUPS

	AFL-CIO	ADA	CCUS	ACU
2004	47%	30%	90%	72%
2003	33%	15%	87%	68%
2002	22%	15%	85%	76%
2001	33%	20%	87%	76%

WEST VIRGINIA 2

Center — Charleston, Eastern Panhandle

The economically diverse 2nd stretches across the mountainous state from the Ohio border to the Eastern Panhandle at Harpers Ferry. The 2nd is home to poor coal mining areas and isolated towns, as well as the more prosperous capital city of Charleston and commuters in the Eastern Panhandle.

Charleston, the district's dominant city, is a center for chemical plants, state employees and retail shopping. But chemical plants cut back in the late 1990s and a tough economy hit manufacturing companies hard. Much of the recent job growth has come from a boom in telemarketing companies moving to the state and from the expansion of retail around Charleston. The mainly Democratic mountain regions north and east of Kanawha County remain heavily dependent on coal. Putnam County, west of Kanawha County, is the site of a Toyota plant in Buffalo.

Economic depression in the 1980s drove residents from the 2nd. But in the 1990s, eastern counties within commuting distance of Washington, D.C., grew rapidly. That growth forced the 2nd to shed two counties —

Nicholas and Gilmer — in redistricting following the 2000 census.

The 2nd was loyal to Democrats in congressional elections for 18 years before electing a Republican in 2000. Expanding pockets of Republicans dot the district, particularly in the Panhandle, where GOP voters register in strong numbers and where they can be reached through Washington's media market. Berkeley County, which includes Martinsburg, voted a straight GOP ticket in 2004, from the presidential and gubernatorial races down to state legislative contests. Overall, George W. Bush carried the district with 57 percent of the vote in the 2004 presidential election, after winning 54 percent here in 2000.

MAJOR INDUSTRY
Chemicals, lumber, manufacturing, retail, coal

CITIES
Charleston, 53,421; Martinsburg, 14,972; South Charleston, 13,390; Teays Valley (unincorporated), 12,704; St. Albans, 11,567

NOTABLE
Abolitionist John Brown was hanged after attempting to incite a slave revolt in Harpers Ferry in 1859; As of 2005, there were no stoplights in Calhoun County; The U.S. Geological Survey's Leetown Science Center, located near Kearneysville, is the oldest federal fishery research facility.

Rep. Nick J. Rahall II (D)

CAPITOL OFFICE
225-3452
nrahall@mail.house.gov
www.rahall.house.gov
2307 Rayburn 20515-4803; fax 225-9061

COMMITTEES
Resources - ranking member
Transportation & Infrastructure

HOMETOWN
Beckley

BORN
May 20, 1949, Beckley, W.Va.

RELIGION
Presbyterian

FAMILY
Wife, Melinda Rahall; three children

EDUCATION
Duke U., B.A. 1971 (political science); George
Washington U., attended 1972 (graduate studies)

CAREER
Broadcasting executive; travel agent;
congressional aide

POLITICAL HIGHLIGHTS
No previous office

ELECTION RESULTS

2004 GENERAL

Nick J. Rahall II (D)	142,682	65.2%
Rick Snuffer (R)	76,170	34.8%

2004 PRIMARY

Nick J. Rahall II (D)	unopposed

2002 GENERAL

Nick J. Rahall II (D)	87,783	70.2%
Paul E. Chapman (R)	37,229	29.8%

PREVIOUS WINNING PERCENTAGES
2000 (91%); 1998 (87%); 1996 (100%); 1994 (64%);
1992 (66%); 1990 (52%); 1988 (61%); 1986 (71%);
1984 (67%); 1982 (81%); 1980 (77%); 1978 (100%);
1976 (46%)

Elected 1976; 15th term

Rahall has spent just over half his life in Congress, and he has done it on his own terms. He now holds senior positions on two committees, but he has advanced because of his tenure, not because he was pushed ahead by his party's leadership. His voting record in the House reflects his coal-country, rural West Virginia constituency — culturally conservative but pro-labor and welcoming of federal social services and economic development.

That puts Rahall (RAY-haul) out of step with the Democratic mainstream on issues such as abortion, gun control and gay marriage — all of which he opposes. The grandson of Lebanese immigrants, Rahall also stakes out his own territory on a major foreign policy issue: He is a frequent critic of Israel and advocates closer U.S. ties with Arab countries.

Thanks to his years of service in the House, Rahall is the top-ranking Democrat on the Resources Committee, and the No. 2 Democrat on the Transportation and Infrastructure Committee. That puts him in a position to pursue two key concerns: protecting the coal-mining industry and bringing public works and jobs to his economically hard-pressed district.

On the Resources panel, his staunch defense of mining means his record on the environment is ambiguous for a Democrat. In the 108th Congress, however, he increasingly took up the environmentalist standard, lashing out at Republicans. In 2004, he strongly opposed a GOP bill to allow regions with fuel shortages to get waivers from some Clean Air Act requirements. "There's no doubt there was overreaching and arrogance and greediness involved," Rahall said. "We always suspected there was a hidden agenda: destroying environmental laws that have worked and not hindered energy."

Also in the 108th, he opposed President Bush's "Healthy Forests" forest-thinning legislation — not on the more common grounds that the policy shift provided a boon to logging companies, but because it expedited judicial review of environmentalists' challenges to logging. "This bill tells the court that litigation involving thinning trees is more important than prosecuting suspected al Qaeda terrorists," he declared. He cosponsored legislation to decrease snowmobile traffic in national parks, and he opposed efforts by the Pentagon to relax its obligations under the Endangered Species Act and the 1918 Migratory Bird Treaty Act.

At the same time, he supported a bill offered by GOP Rep. Barbara Cubin of Wyoming, another coal mining state, to revamp federal funding for cleanup at mine sites. Rahall had sponsored a similar bill in 2002.

Transportation is an area where Rahall wields substantial influence, especially during the periodic drafting of the huge surface transportation bill. In the 2004 reauthorization, he secured $2.2 billion in transportation infrastructure funding for West Virginia. Responding to White House opposition to the bill's cost, Rahall pulled no punches, saying Bush "is taunting the Congress in order to regain his right-wing wacko base who would rather build roads in Iraq than in this country."

As a member of the Arab-American Caucus, Rahall in 2002 spoke out when the Justice Department began detaining people of Arab descent. "There should not be a wholesale roundup of people, or a denial of services based on the way one looks," he said. "No one should be apprehended just because they wear a turban."

Rahall's pro-Arab stance also led him to oppose the 2002 resolution giving Bush broad authority to use military force against Iraq, and in the 108th he continued to be critical of the administration's overall Middle

East strategy. In 2003, with administration officials issuing ominous warnings to Syria and as Congress moved forward on a sanctions bill aimed at Iraq's Ba'athist neighbor, Rahall and Republican Darryl Issa of California, who shares his Lebanese heritage, traveled to Damascus to meet with President Bashar al-Assad. "Here is a country that has been an ally of America against the real terrorists — al Qaeda," Rahall argued in Syria's defense. "Here is a country that has, by our own secretary of state's admission, helped save American lives. And we want to punch them in the stomach like this? It's absolutely absurd."

Sometimes Rahall's pro-Arab tilt has raised eyebrows. He departed on a "fact finding" trip to Iraq on Sept. 11, 2002, one year after the terrorist attacks. With war looming, Rahall met with Saddam Hussein's foreign minister and with Iraqi citizens. Back in Washington, he pressed for a peaceful resolution that would spare the repressed Iraqis further hardship. He got the cold shoulder from the White House and an upbraiding by his local press, with one newspaper editorial saying, "Nothing substantive can come from Rahall's visit — except from Iraq's perspective."

In 2004, The Los Angeles Times disclosed that Rahall's sister Tanya was paid $15,000 a month to lobby Congress for the tiny Arab country of Qatar, including helping her brother "craft a resolution praising the country for 'years of Democratic reform,' even though it remained a monarchy without organized political opposition." Rahall denied any impropriety.

Rahall comes from an affluent West Virginia family that owns broadcasting properties. His first job on Capitol Hill was a summer stint delivering mail when he was 20. After graduating from Duke University, he was an aide to Democratic Sen. Robert C. Byrd of West Virginia before going home to work in the family businesses.

His chance to run for office came in 1976, when Democratic Rep. Ken Hechler decided to run for governor. Rahall, then 27, spent family money on a media campaign none of his foes could match, and won the nomination with 37 percent of the vote. After the primary, Hechler, who lost for governor, mounted an unsuccessful write-in drive to keep his House seat.

Rahall's only re-election difficulties have come at times his personal behavior was an issue. He racked up gambling debts in the mid-1980s, got divorced (he remarried in 2005), took many trips financed by taxpayers or lobbyists and pleaded guilty to alcohol-related reckless driving charges. The closest call of his entire congressional career came in 1990, when he won by just 4 percentage points against a state representative he had trounced two years earlier. In 2004, he won by 30 points.

KEY VOTES

2004

? Extend federal unemployment benefits by 13 weeks

Yes Pass $283.2 billion, six-year federal highway and mass transit bill

Yes Approve $146 billion multi-year extension of previously enacted middle-class tax breaks

Yes Amend the Constitution to prohibit same-sex marriage

No Cut corporate taxes $137 billion over 10 years

? Reorganize U.S. intelligence agencies as proposed by Sept. 11 commission

2003

No Cut taxes by $330 billion through fiscal 2013

Yes Block Bush rule scaling back overtime pay for some white-collar federal workers

Yes Do not allow use of search warrants without first notifying subjects

Yes Allow importation of prescription drugs

No Create private school voucher program in Washington, D.C.

Yes Ban "partial birth" abortion except to save a woman's life

Yes Split $18.6 billion in Iraq aid into half-grant, half-loan

No Overhaul Medicare and create prescription drug benefit

CQ VOTE STUDIES

	PARTY UNITY		PRESIDENTIAL SUPPORT	
	Support	Oppose	Support	Oppose
2004	87%	13%	45%	55%
2003	89%	11%	35%	65%
2002	88%	12%	28%	72%
2001	77%	23%	33%	67%
2000	79%	21%	71%	29%

INTEREST GROUPS

	AFL-CIO	ADA	CCUS	ACU
2004	86%	75%	52%	28%
2003	100%	85%	30%	44%
2002	100%	80%	40%	24%
2001	100%	80%	39%	36%
2000	90%	70%	42%	28%

WEST VIRGINIA 3
South – Huntington, Beckley

The 3rd is a largely rural region taking in the state's southern counties. Known as the "coal district," it is home to five of the state's 10 leading coal-producing counties, including the top producer, Boone County.

In the 1980s, technological advances in coal mining sharply reduced the need for manpower, and the 3rd struggled to create new jobs. The decline, which also decreased the 3rd's population, added misery to a region that always has had pockets of Appalachian poverty. The situation improved in the 1990s and some counties grew slightly, while other counties continued to see residents leave as unemployment rates remained high. In 1999, the district had the third-lowest median income of any congressional district in the nation, at slightly more than $25,600.

The 3rd contributes to the state's tourism industry with its ski resorts, whitewater rafting and The Greenbrier, a luxury resort hotel in White Sulphur Springs that plays host to congressional party retreats. Huntington, the district's largest city, is cushioned by its location on the Ohio River and a diversified economy that includes tobacco growers as well as oil and steel companies.

While Huntington's white-collar sector and tobacco growers help make Cabell County the most Republican part of the 3rd, overall Democrats have had a lock on the district and continue to lead in party registration. In 2000, George W. Bush made major inroads in the 3rd, losing the district by just 4 percentage points, but he was able to win the 3rd in 2004 with 53 percent of the vote.

MAJOR INDUSTRY
Coal, wood products, tourism

CITIES
Huntington, 51,475; Beckley, 17,254; Bluefield, 11,451

NOTABLE
There is a now-closed nuclear bomb shelter for Congress under The Greenbrier; Sunshine Farm & Gardens, in Renick, houses one of the nation's most extensive plant collections; Mingo County, site of the West Virginia Mine Wars of the 1920s, is depicted in the movie "Matewan"; "Bloody Mingo" also was the site of part of the feuding between the Hatfields and McCoys.

Gov. James E. Doyle (D)

First elected: 2002
Length of term: 4 years
Term expires: 1/07
Salary: $131,768
Phone: (608) 266-1212

Hometown: Madison
Born: Nov. 23, 1945; Washington, D.C.
Religion: Roman Catholic
Family: Wife, Jessica Laird Doyle; two children
Education: Stanford U., attended 1963-66; U. of Wisconsin, B.A. 1967 (history); Harvard U., J.D. 1972
Career: Lawyer; Peace Corps volunteer
Political highlights: Dane County district attorney, 1977-82; Wis. attorney general, 1991-2003

Election results:

2002 GENERAL

James E. Doyle (D)	800,515	45.1%
Scott McCallum (R)	734,779	41.4%
Ed Thompson (LIBERT)	185,455	10.5%
Jim Young (WG)	44,111	2.5%

Lt. Gov. Barbara Lawton (D)

First elected: 2002
Length of term: 4 years
Term expires: 1/07
Salary: $69,579
Phone: (608) 266-3516

STATE LEGISLATURE

General Assembly: 10 floor periods of varying lengths over a 2-year session

Assembly: 99 members, 2-year terms
2005 breakdown: 60R, 39D; 72 men, 27 women
Salary: $45,569; $88/day in session
Phone: (608) 266-1501

Senate: 33 members, 4-year terms
2005 breakdown: 19R, 14D; 26 men, 7 women
Salary: $45,569; $88/day in session
Phone: (608) 266-2517

STATE TERM LIMITS

Governor: No
Assembly: No
Senate: No

URBAN STATISTICS

CITY	POPULATION
Milwaukee	596,974
Madison	208,054
Green Bay	102,313
Kenosha	90,352
Racine	81,855

REGISTERED VOTERS

Voters do not register by party.

POPULATION

2004 population (est.)	5,509,026
2000 population	5,363,675
1990 population	4,891,769
Percent change (1990-2000)	+9.6%
Rank among states (2004)	20

Median age	36
Born in state	73.4%
Foreign born	3.6%
Violent crime rate	237/100,000
Poverty level	8.7%
Federal workers	29,286
Military	18,937

REDISTRICTING

Wisconsin lost one House seat in reapportionment. The state legislature drew a new, eight-district map, which the governor signed on March 27, 2002.

MISCELLANEOUS

Web: www.wisconsin.gov
Capital: Madison
STATE ELECTION OFFICIAL
(608) 266-8005
DEMOCRATIC HEADQUARTERS
(608) 255-5172
REPUBLICAN HEADQUARTERS
(608) 257-4765

District Statistics

DIST.	2004 VOTE FOR PRESIDENT BUSH	KERRY	WHITE	BLACK	ASIAN	HISP	MEDIAN INCOME	WHITE COLLAR	BLUE COLLAR	SERVICE INDUSTRY	OVER 64	UNDER 18	COLLEGE EDUCATION	RURAL	SQ. MILES
1	53%	46%	87%	5%	1%	6%	$50,372	57%	30%	13%	12%	26%	22%	16%	1,680
2	37	62	89	4	2	3	$46,979	64	23	14	11	23	32	24	3,511
3	48	51	96	0	1	1	$40,006	53	31	16	13	25	20	57	13,565
4	30	69	50	33	3	11	$33,121	54	28	18	11	28	18	0	112
5	63	36	94	1	2	2	$58,594	68	22	10	14	25	35	15	1,273
6	56	42	94	1	1	2	$44,242	49	37	14	14	25	17	39	5,641
7	49	50	95	0	1	1	$39,026	52	34	15	15	25	17	58	18,787
8	55	44	92	1	1	2	$43,274	54	33	14	13	26	19	44	9,740
STATE	49	50	87	6	2	4	$43,791	57	29	14	13	26	22	32	54,310
U.S.	50.7	48.3	69	12	4	13	$41,994	60	25	15	12	26	24	21	3,537,438

Sen. Herb Kohl (D)

Elected 1988; 3rd term

His reputation as an independent-minded moderate who is fiercely loyal to Wisconsin's needs has made Kohl a formidable figure in his state and the Senate. A self-made millionaire, Kohl is free to chart his own course. Yet he is also an effective, although quiet, appropriator who steadily looks after his state's interests.

Kohl displayed his independence in early 2005 by supporting a Republican bill making it easier for large businesses to insulate themselves from class action lawsuits. The Democratic leadership opposed the bill, as did many liberal groups. Kohl ignored those concerns and turned back worries that the legislation would shut courthouse doors on deserving plaintiffs. He insisted it would make only modest procedural changes in the legal system.

And in the fall of 2004, he voted "present" on a sweeping corporate tax bill that began as a narrowly written measure to address illegal tariffs but ballooned into a package of $137 billion in tax breaks for manufacturers and other business interests. Kohl was the only member of the Senate to vote "present" when the final bill was passed, 69-17.

Yet he will vote in favor of reducing taxes. In 2001, he was one of only a dozen Democrats to vote for President Bush's $1.35 trillion tax cut, and one of 15 Democrats to back the initial version of the GOP's spending blueprint for the year. But in 2003, he voted with the rest of his party to limit Bush's proposed tax cuts to $350 billion through fiscal 2013. Kohl affiliates with the Senate's moderate New Democrat Coalition.

He has won high marks from budget watchdog groups such as the Concord Coalition and Taxpayers for Common Sense. Kohl has been a solid vote for a constitutional amendment to require a balanced federal budget, and he supported the short-lived presidential line-item veto law. Even when the Treasury had a surplus, he pressed for fiscal restraint, warning against actions that could plunge the government's books back into the red.

Despite his wealth, Kohl is able to come across as an Everyman. He prefers to drive an old Chevy and eat at small diners near his home in Milwaukee. He has routinely rejected pay raises since he entered the Senate in 1989. His net worth is estimated to be $111 million, much of which came from the sale in 1979 of his family-owned chain of Kohl's department and food stores.

Kohl is willing to spend, however, when necessary. In 1985, he bought the Milwaukee Bucks NBA franchise in order to keep the team in Milwaukee. ("I thought it was a stupid investment," he later admitted.) Kohl also gave the University of Wisconsin, his alma mater, $25 million to build a sports arena.

As a member of six appropriations subcommittees, Kohl's fingerprints can be found on the annual bills that determine how two-thirds of the nation's domestic discretionary spending is allocated. His largest imprint is on agriculture spending, a testament to his position as the top-ranking Democrat on the Agriculture Subcommittee. Kohl has learned to leverage this position well for a state whose dairy farmers are both influential politically and dependent on federal spending decisions.

One of the first bills Kohl introduced in the 109th Congress was a measure to renew the Milk Income Loss Contract. The program, which Kohl helped to create in 2002 to replace an even more controversial payment system, expires on Sept. 30, 2005. The program pays dairy farmers cash to smooth out price fluctuations. Since it was created, the program has won

CAPITOL OFFICE
224-5653
senator_kohl@kohl.senate.gov
kohl.senate.gov
330 Hart 20510-4903; fax 224-9787

COMMITTEES
Appropriations
Judiciary
Special Aging - ranking member

HOMETOWN
Milwaukee

BORN
Feb. 7, 1935, Milwaukee, Wis.

RELIGION
Jewish

FAMILY
Single

EDUCATION
U. of Wisconsin, B.A. 1956; Harvard U., M.B.A. 1958

MILITARY SERVICE
Army Reserve, 1958-64

CAREER
Professional basketball team owner; department and grocery store owner

POLITICAL HIGHLIGHTS
Wis. Democratic Party chairman, 1975-77

ELECTION RESULTS

2000 GENERAL

Herb Kohl (D)	1,563,238	61.5%
John Gillespie (R)	940,744	37.0%

2000 PRIMARY

Herb Kohl (D)	184,920	89.8%
Jim Sigl (D)	20,858	10.1%

PREVIOUS WINNING PERCENTAGES
1994 (58%); 1988 (52%)

praise from dairy farmers but complaints from fiscal conservatives, who say it has cost taxpayers about $2 billion.

Kohl also sits on the Judiciary Committee, where he is a strong supporter of gun control. The sniper shootings in the Washington, D.C. area in the fall of 2002 inspired him to renew his campaign for a bill to establish a nationwide ballistics database to trace ammunition used in a crime back to the owner of the firearm. In 2004, he voted to extend the ban on assault weapons for another 10 years. After the Sept. 11, 2001, terrorist attacks, Kohl took a lead role in insisting on tougher security standards for charter aircraft and tighter controls on the sale, transport or possession of explosives.

Like many Democrats, Kohl opposes one of Bush's signature issues: adding private investment accounts to Social Security. "The minute you start talking about privatization, you're talking about costs and risks," he said. In the 109th Congress, he is the top-ranking Democrat on the Special Aging Committee.

Kohl is in line with traditional Democrats on issues such as health care and child nutrition. He supports efforts to lower the cost of prescription drugs by legalizing the reimportation of drugs from Canada. He is a believer in higher education. Every year, his Herb Kohl Educational Foundation awards several hundred scholarships of $1,000 to high school graduates, provides fellowships to teachers and gives grants to schools.

Kohl says his wealth gives him great freedom in Congress. "I'm the luckiest guy here because I don't have to ask anybody for money," he told a Harvard Business School newsletter. "That allows me to do what I think is right on every vote."

Kohl's parents immigrated to the United States in the 1920s — his mother from Russia, his father from Poland. They opened a small food store in Milwaukee, where Kohl worked after school and on weekends. He says that experience taught him the value of hard work. One of his childhood friends (and later his college roommate) was Bud Selig, who went on to become a wealthy car dealer, and then owner of the Milwaukee Brewers baseball team and the commissioner of Major League Baseball.

After earning a master's degree in business from Harvard, Kohl returned home and along with his two brothers set about building a department store chain. There were more than 100 Kohl's when the chain was sold in 1979.

Kohl was involved in the financial side of some political campaigns, but his first public involvement in politics came in 1975 when Democratic Gov. Patrick Lucey asked him to chair the state Democratic Party. He did the job for two years, despite his discomfort with some of its public aspects.

In 1988, when Democrat William Proxmire stepped down after 31 years in the Senate, some Democrats pressed an initially ambivalent Kohl to run. Through retail and basketball he had plenty of name recognition — not that it mattered much, as he spent nearly $7.5 million (most of it his own money) on the campaign. Kohl used his status as one of the state's richest men to stress his independence, based on his ability to self-finance his campaigns. His "nobody's senator but yours" tag line, which he still uses, reminded voters that he was beholden to no special interest group.

It was a campaign on a scale unlike any the state had seen. Kohl's total outlay was double the previous state record. He won a three-way Democratic primary with 47 percent of the vote and defeated GOP state Sen. Susan Engeleiter by 4 percentage points in the fall.

In subsequent re-election campaigns in 1994 and 2000, Kohl spent $6 million and $4.8 million, respectively, of his own money. He won by 17 points in 1994 and 25 points in 2000.

KEY VOTES

2004
No   Pass $318.9 billion, six-year highway and mass transit bill
Yes Extend assault weapons ban for 10 years
Yes Restore pay-as-you-go rules for new tax cuts and entitlement spending
No   Criminalize harm to a fetus in an attack on the mother
Yes Increase mandatory child care funding to states by $6 billion over five years
No   Amend the Constitution to prohibit same-sex marriage
Yes Approve $146 billion multi-year extension of previously enacted middle-class tax breaks
Yes Reorganize U.S. intelligence agencies as proposed by Sept. 11 commission
P   Cut corporate taxes $137 billion over 10 years

2003
Yes Delay Bush changes to Clean Air Act
No   Allow confirmation vote on Miguel A. Estrada to the U.S. Court of Appeals for the D.C. Circuit
Yes Block a Bush proposal opening Alaska's Arctic National Wildlife Refuge to oil drilling
Yes Limit size of Bush's proposed tax cut to $350 billion through fiscal 2013
No   Overhaul Medicare and create prescription drug benefit
Yes Block Bush rule scaling back overtime pay for some white-collar federal workers
Yes Split $20 billion in Iraq aid into half-grant, half-loan
No   Ban "partial birth" abortion except to save a woman's life
No   Stop proposal allowing travel to Cuba
No   Allow final vote on energy policy overhaul

CQ VOTE STUDIES

	PARTY UNITY		PRESIDENTIAL SUPPORT	
	Support	Oppose	Support	Oppose
2004	95%	5%	66%	34%
2003	94%	6%	50%	50%
2002	84%	16%	79%	21%
2001	89%	11%	69%	31%
2000	87%	13%	79%	21%
1999	90%	10%	91%	9%
1998	87%	13%	86%	14%
1997	74%	26%	90%	10%
1996	84%	16%	88%	12%
1995	84%	16%	84%	16%

INTEREST GROUPS

	AFL-CIO	ADA	CCUS	ACU
2004	92%	100%	44%	4%
2003	100%	95%	35%	25%
2002	92%	85%	60%	15%
2001	88%	90%	54%	16%
2000	63%	85%	60%	20%
1999	78%	100%	41%	4%
1998	88%	85%	44%	4%
1997	29%	70%	80%	20%
1996	86%	75%	69%	20%
1995	92%	95%	47%	17%

Sen. Russell D. Feingold (D)

Elected 1992; 3rd term

CAPITOL OFFICE
224-5323
russ_feingold@feingold.senate.gov
feingold.senate.gov
506 Hart 20510-4904; fax 224-2725

COMMITTEES
Budget
Foreign Relations
Judiciary
Special Aging

HOMETOWN
Middleton

BORN
March 2, 1953, Janesville, Wis.

RELIGION
Jewish

FAMILY
Separated; two children

EDUCATION
U. of Wisconsin, B.A. 1975 (history & political science); Oxford U., B.A. 1977 (Rhodes scholar); Harvard U., J.D. 1979

CAREER
Lawyer

POLITICAL HIGHLIGHTS
Wis. Senate, 1983-93

ELECTION RESULTS

2004 GENERAL

Russell D. Feingold (D)	1,632,697	55.4%
Tim Michels (R)	1,301,183	44.1%

2004 PRIMARY

Russell D. Feingold (D)	unopposed

PREVIOUS WINNING PERCENTAGES
1998 (51%); 1992 (53%)

Some senators are known for breaking ranks with their party on critical votes. Feingold breaks ranks with the entire Senate. When the issue is important to him, he doesn't mind voting one way while the rest of his colleagues vote the other. In his third term, Feingold is finally making the maverick approach to politics work for him, with a major overhaul of the campaign finance laws under his belt and a strong win in 2004 that solidified his once shaky hold on his Senate seat.

Together with Republican John McCain of Arizona, Feingold (FINE-gold) is the co-author of the watershed McCain-Feingold law, the first major revision of campaign finance laws in nearly three decades, enacted by Congress in 2002 over the strenuous objections of leaders of both parties. The legislation bans unregulated "soft money," which goes to political parties rather than candidates and was being used in novel ways to influence individual campaigns.

Party leaders opposed McCain-Feingold because it cramped fundraising, but the two senators were able to successfully revive it after the bankruptcy of Enron Corp., which led to revelations about the energy giant's political donations and influence. Feingold's next project is legislation he and McCain have introduced to crack down on so-called 527 issue advocacy groups, which they say have become a channel for the kind of soft money contributions political parties can no longer accept.

His iconoclasm often puts Feingold in a minority of one. Six weeks after the Sept. 11, 2001, terrorist attacks, most senators felt compelled to support a proposal giving the Bush administration broad powers to detain and question possible terrorists. Many Democrats felt, as Feingold did, that the USA Patriot Act raised significant concerns about government encroachments on civil liberties. But they voted for it for the sake of national unity and out of a desire to move aggressively to stop terrorists. Majority Leader Tom Daschle urged Democrats to support what became a bipartisan bill. The final tally was 98-1, with Feingold dissenting. Parts of the bill, he said, were "a grab for powers by the Justice Department," a view shared by many of his colleagues who supported it anyway.

Although he is mostly liberal on issues, Feingold is not always predictable. When many fellow Democrats in 2001 staunchly opposed the nomination of Missouri Sen. John Ashcroft for attorney general because of his ultra-conservative views, Feingold cast the lone Democratic vote in the Judiciary Committee to confirm Ashcroft.

His unwillingness to be part of the crowd can tie up the Senate, a source of aggravation to his colleagues. In the final hours before Congress adjourned in 1999, Feingold and a handful of other Midwesterners refused to let their colleagues go home because they opposed provisions in the sole remaining bill, a session-ending catchall spending deal, that they claimed were unfair to home-state dairy interests. Feingold stalked the Senate floor with books of cheese recipes, among other potential filibuster reading materials, threatening a several-day delay. He gave up only after overwhelmingly losing a test vote.

Neither does Feingold win popularity contests in the Senate with his crusades to raise Congress' ethical standards. He advocates increasing the waiting period from one year to two before former members can begin earning large sums as lobbyists for private interests. He wants to repeal automatic pay raises for members of Congress, he opposes free trips for lawmakers paid for by lobbyists, and he favors a total ban on gifts. When he tried to block an automatic pay raise for lawmakers in 2003, his amendment was soundly voted down in the Senate. The headline of a story in the satirical on-line newspaper The Onion later that year captured his reputation: "Senate Carpool 'Forgets' to Pick Up Feingold Again."

Besides making a show of his political independence, Feingold likes to champion good-government measures. His amendment to a supplemental spending bill in 2003 created an inspector general for Iraq's Coalition Provisional Authority, the U.S.-led body that ran the country immediately after Saddam Hussein's government fell. That year, Feingold also added a provision to the Senate Medicare prescription drug bill that would have created an official advocate for Medicare beneficiaries. A similar provision became law, but Feingold voted against the final Medicare legislation because the bill did not allow the government to use its purchasing power to negotiate lower prices with drug companies.

Feingold is among the socially liberal senators. He favors abolishing the death penalty and supports abortion rights. But unlike other liberals, Feingold has had a long-running interest in balancing the budget. A member of the Budget Committee, he has called for reducing the national debt since his first days in office. Feingold supported the ill-fated line-item veto, and in 1998 he voted to sustain President Clinton's veto of a list of military construction projects even though a $4 million training facility in Milwaukee was on the list.

His most famous break with his party was in 1999, when Feingold was the only Democratic senator to vote against a proposal to dismiss the impeachment charges against Clinton. His decision sparked an avalanche of media attention, but Feingold largely shunned the notoriety. In the end, he joined every other Democratic senator in voting to acquit Clinton of perjury and obstruction of justice, saying the charges were insufficient to warrant the president's removal.

Feingold is attentive to home-state concerns, especially those of dairy farmers. He appears to have a genuine affection for campaigning and constituent service. He has kept a pledge from his first Senate campaign to visit all 72 counties in the state every year he is in office. He spends most of his time in Wisconsin and his children attend school there.

In 1992, he burst on the national political scene as a little-known state senator without much campaign money who scored a long-shot primary victory and then knocked off GOP incumbent Sen. Bob Kasten. In the course of the campaign, he ran a series of humorous, offbeat television ads. One showed him using the back of his left hand as a map of his travels across Wisconsin, boasting he knew the state like the back of his hand. Another showed him opening an empty closet, assuring viewers, "No skeletons."

Six years later, Feingold's tendency to buck the system nearly cost him his seat. He began his 1998 re-election campaign favored to beat GOP Rep. Mark W. Neumann, who had been in the House for three years. At the time, the McCain-Feingold restrictions were not yet law, but Feingold decided to play by his bill's rules anyway. He declined most forms of outside money, and asked national Democrats not to run ads in his behalf paid for with the kind of fundraising that his bill would limit. Feingold barely held on, beating the well-financed Neumann by just 2 percentage points.

In 2004, however, Feingold faced a weaker opponent, Republican construction executive Tim Michels, and had none of the fundraising troubles of his first two campaigns. He built up a $3 million war chest, while Michels had to spend most of his money against two primary opponents and had just seven weeks left to run against Feingold. This time, Feingold won easily, defeating Michels by 11 points.

KEY VOTES

2004

No   Pass $318.9 billion, six-year highway and mass transit bill

No   Extend assault weapons ban for 10 years

Yes Restore pay-as-you-go rules for new tax cuts and entitlement spending

No   Criminalize harm to a fetus in an attack on the mother

Yes Increase mandatory child care funding to states by $6 billion over five years

No   Amend the Constitution to prohibit same-sex marriage

Yes Approve $146 billion multi-year extension of previously enacted middle-class tax breaks

Yes Reorganize U.S. intelligence agencies as proposed by Sept. 11 commission

Yes Cut corporate taxes $137 billion over 10 years

2003

Yes Delay Bush changes to Clean Air Act

No   Allow confirmation vote on Miguel A. Estrada to the U.S. Court of Appeals for the D.C. Circuit

Yes Block a Bush proposal opening Alaska's Arctic National Wildlife Refuge to oil drilling

Yes Limit size of Bush's proposed tax cut to $350 billion through fiscal 2013

Yes Overhaul Medicare and create prescription drug benefit

Yes Block Bush rule scaling back overtime pay for some white-collar federal workers

Yes Split $20 billion in Iraq aid into half-grant, half-loan

No   Ban "partial birth" abortion except to save a woman's life

No   Stop proposal allowing travel to Cuba

No   Allow final vote on energy policy overhaul

CQ VOTE STUDIES

	PARTY UNITY		PRESIDENTIAL SUPPORT	
	Support	Oppose	Support	Oppose
2004	95%	5%	66%	34%
2003	93%	7%	53%	47%
2002	84%	16%	67%	33%
2001	89%	11%	61%	39%
2000	92%	8%	90%	10%
1999	88%	12%	82%	18%
1998	86%	14%	83%	17%
1997	86%	14%	86%	14%
1996	87%	13%	86%	14%
1995	90%	10%	79%	21%

INTEREST GROUPS

	AFL-CIO	ADA	CCUS	ACU
2004	92%	100%	35%	8%
2003	100%	95%	26%	25%
2002	92%	90%	20%	5%
2001	94%	95%	29%	20%
2000	88%	100%	20%	8%
1999	100%	100%	24%	8%
1998	100%	90%	28%	12%
1997	86%	95%	20%	8%
1996	86%	95%	31%	10%
1995	100%	100%	42%	13%

Rep. Paul D. Ryan (R)

Elected 1998; 4th term

CAPITOL OFFICE
225-3031
www.house.gov/ryan
1113 Longworth 20515-4901; fax 225-3393

COMMITTEES
Budget
Ways & Means
Joint Economic

HOMETOWN
Janesville

BORN
Jan. 29, 1970, Janesville, Wis.

RELIGION
Roman Catholic

FAMILY
Wife, Janna Ryan; three children

EDUCATION
Miami U. (Ohio), B.A. 1992 (political science & economics)

CAREER
Congressional aide; economic policy analyst

POLITICAL HIGHLIGHTS
No previous office

ELECTION RESULTS

2004 GENERAL

Paul D. Ryan (R)	233,372	65.4%
Jeffrey Chapman Thomas (D)	116,250	32.6%
Norman Aulabaugh (I)	4,252	1.2%

2004 PRIMARY

Paul D. Ryan (R)	unopposed

2002 GENERAL

Paul D. Ryan (R)	140,176	67.2%
Jeffrey Chapman Thomas (D)	63,895	30.6%
George Meyers (LIBERT)	4,406	2.1%

PREVIOUS WINNING PERCENTAGES
2000 (67%); 1998 (57%)

An influential tax and budget writer, Ryan helps to formulate and promote the GOP's economic message. He stresses the need for tax cuts to stimulate the economy with less reliance on government entitlements. Ryan uses his seat on the Ways and Means Committee to advocate for supply-side economics, the theory which assumes that if taxes and spending are cut faster economic growth will follow.

Ryan is a leader of an emerging group of GOP lawmakers known as "growth hawks," and he worries that members who continue to press for deficit reduction are an obstacle to the tax cuts needed to boost the economy. In the 108th Congress, Ryan remained neutral on GOP tax overhaul proposals such as a flat tax or a national sales tax, saying he wanted to "keep my powder dry" for the tax reform debate expected to occur in the 109th.

Ryan is both articulate and partisan. A former legislative aide, he has a direct speaking style that resembles his two mentors, Jack F. Kemp and William J. Bennett, former Republican Cabinet secretaries and co-founders of the conservative think tank, Empower America.

Ryan gained a seat on the Budget Committee in the 109th. He wanted to change the budget rules in 2004 when the House considered legislation to require Congress to stick to its budget or risk across-the-board spending cuts. The measure would have revived statutory "caps" on appropriations and a pay-as-you-go law that would require offsets in any legislation that would increase mandatory spending. "Right now, the budget process is broken," Ryan said. Yet the House soundly rejected an amendment offered by Ryan and Texas Democrat Charles W. Stenholm to allow the president to force Congress to vote on his recommendations to eliminate earmarked projects from appropriations bills.

Criticizing the number of earmarked projects, Ryan voted in 2004 against a $283.2 billion, six-year measure reauthorizing highway and mass transit programs. Yet Ryan has used his seat on Ways and Means to take care of some home-state interests, such as protecting Wisconsin's groundbreaking welfare system. An avid bow hunter, he helped cut excise taxes on youth bows and razor-like devices used on arrows in the 2004 corporate tax law.

Ryan also sits on the Joint Economic Committee, where he is the second-ranking Republican. In the fall of 2004, he decided to make a run for the chairmanship of the committee even though New Jersey Republican H. James Saxton was still in line for the job. Chairmanship of the panel rotates between the House and Senate, and Saxton was chairman in the 105th and 107th Congresses. House GOP rules permit committee chairmen to serve up to three terms. Ryan said he wanted to make the Joint Economic Committee more of a showcase for the GOP's economic agenda, particularly President Bush's proposal to allow workers to divert some of their payroll taxes into tax-free savings accounts.

Ryan is a vocal proponent of Bush's plan to overhaul the Social Security system by allowing the creation of private investment accounts. "If we stick to the status quo, down the road we will face the awful choice between cutting benefits, raising taxes or boundless borrowing," he said. Ryan sits on Ways and Means' Social Security Subcommittee.

Ryan received Social Security survivor's benefits as a child, and he says that Bush's proposals for Social Security are not intended to change benefits paid to the disabled and children whose parents have died. But congressional Democrats contend that there has to be an impact on those other elements of the Social Security program, because the money needed to transition into the private accounts system would drain the pool of available funds to pay the other benefits. "I have a deep personal affection for this program," Ryan said. "I think people are trying to demagogue Republican reforms by saying somehow they don't care about this program."

Ryan is a staunch social conservative who belongs to the Republican Study Committee. But he has gone against the GOP grain on some votes important to Wisconsin. He was one of 87 Republicans backing a bill to allow the importation of drugs from other industrialized nations, particularly Canada.

Ryan passed on a possible run against Wisconsin Democratic Sen. Russell D. Feingold in 2004, but he continues to be viewed as a possible candidate for statewide office. Ryan and Feingold grew up in the same hometown, Janesville.

When he first arrived in the House, Ryan bragged about his 120-hour, seven-days-a-week work schedule, saying that he was young and vigorous enough to burn the candle at both ends. Now, Ryan says he tries to take most Sundays off to be with his family.

The son of a small-town lawyer who died when he was 16, Ryan once intended to become an economist or work in his family's earth-moving and construction business. After finishing college, he was an aide to Wisconsin GOP Sen. Bob Kasten, both in his personal office and on the Small Business Committee. Then, after a stint at Empower America, Ryan was a top aide for Kansas Republican Sam Brownback in the House and Senate.

After spending five years in Washington, he returned home to Wisconsin to work in the family business. When the 1st District's GOP Rep. Mark W. Neumann decided in late 1997 to run for the Senate, Ryan was persuaded to run for the open seat.

His opponent in the general election was Democrat Lydia Spottswood, a former Kenosha City Council president who nearly beat Neumann in 1996. Ryan proved to have much stronger campaign skills — he earned the nickname "robocandidate" — and he won by more than 27,000 votes, a surprisingly large margin given that the previous three races in the district had been won by margins of 4,000 votes or less.

In 2000, backed by substantial contributions from the Club for Growth, a group of fiscally conservative Republicans, Ryan breezed to a 33 percentage point victory. Redistricting after the 2000 census gave Ryan a GOP-leaning district. He won with more than 65 percent of the vote in both 2002 and 2004. All three re-elections were against the same Democratic opponent.

KEY VOTES

2004

No Extend federal unemployment benefits by 13 weeks

No Pass $283.2 billion, six-year federal highway and mass transit bill

Yes Approve $146 billion multi-year extension of previously enacted middle-class tax breaks

Yes Amend the Constitution to prohibit same-sex marriage

Yes Cut corporate taxes $137 billion over 10 years

Yes Reorganize U.S. intelligence agencies as proposed by Sept. 11 commission

2003

Yes Cut taxes by $330 billion through fiscal 2013

No Block Bush rule scaling back overtime pay for some white-collar federal workers

No Do not allow use of search warrants without first notifying subjects

Yes Allow importation of prescription drugs

Yes Create private school voucher program in Washington, D.C.

Yes Ban "partial birth" abortion except to save a woman's life

No Split $18.6 billion in Iraq aid into half-grant, half-loan

Yes Overhaul Medicare and create prescription drug benefit

CQ VOTE STUDIES

	PARTY UNITY		PRESIDENTIAL SUPPORT	
	Support	Oppose	Support	Oppose
2004	94%	6%	79%	21%
2003	94%	6%	90%	10%
2002	92%	8%	82%	18%
2001	92%	8%	86%	14%
2000	95%	5%	22%	78%

INTEREST GROUPS

	AFL-CIO	ADA	CCUS	ACU
2004	20%	20%	90%	92%
2003	7%	20%	93%	84%
2002	13%	0%	100%	96%
2001	17%	0%	96%	88%
2000	0%	5%	90%	88%

WISCONSIN 1
Southeast — Kenosha, Racine

From the wealthy Milwaukee suburbs on the coast of Lake Michigan to the center of Rock County, the 1st blends rural communities with some of the state's largest industrial areas. The district's two largest cities are sandwiched between Milwaukee and Chicago along the lake: Racine, originally settled by Danish immigrants, and Kenosha, with a large Italian community.

A major manufacturing producer of heavy equipment and other goods, the economy fares best when a weak dollar attracts international buyers. A strengthening dollar in the 1990s — compounded by the shutdown of several manufacturing plants — weakened the economy and depressed real estate prices. This attracted commuters, forming large bedroom communities for Milwaukee and Chicago — both less than an hour's drive away. The influx helped the counties along the Illinois border grow almost twice as fast as the state average in the 1990s. On the other side of the district, Janesville has struggled in recent years as demand has softened for trucks from its General Motors plant.

Resorts catering to wealthy vacationers from nearby cities ring Lake Geneva and Lake Delavan (Walworth County), while Kenosha lures gamblers with Dairyland Greyhound Park, a dog-racing track.

Wisconsin lost one seat in reapportionment after the 2000 census, and redistricting revised the 1st's boundaries to exclude blue-collar, heavily Democratic Beloit (Rock County) and to add more of GOP-leaning Waukesha County and part of Milwaukee County.

The district is about evenly split between the two parties: Of the six counties wholly or partly in the 1st, two are strongly Democratic (Kenosha and Rock), two are strongly Republican (Walworth and Waukesha) and two are highly competitive (Racine and Milwaukee). In the 2004 presidential race, George W. Bush captured 53 percent of the 1st's vote.

MAJOR INDUSTRY
Automotive manufacturing, heavy machine manufacturing, agriculture

CITIES
Kenosha, 90,352; Racine, 81,855; Janesville (pt.), 59,474; Greenfield, 35,476

NOTABLE
Racine hosts the Salmon-A-Rama annual fishing contest.

Rep. Tammy Baldwin (D)

Elected 1998; 4th term

CAPITOL OFFICE
225-2906
tammybaldwin.house.gov
1022 Longworth 20515-4902; fax 225-6942

COMMITTEES
Energy & Commerce

HOMETOWN
Madison

BORN
Feb. 11, 1962, Madison, Wis.

RELIGION
Unspecified

FAMILY
Partner, Lauren Azar

EDUCATION
Smith College, A.B. 1984 (math & government);
U. of Wisconsin, J.D. 1989

CAREER
Lawyer; public policy analyst

POLITICAL HIGHLIGHTS
Madison City Council, 1986; Dane County Board
of Supervisors, 1986-94; Wis. Assembly, 1993-99

ELECTION RESULTS

2004 GENERAL

Tammy Baldwin (D)	251,637	63.3%
David Magnum (R)	145,810	36.7%

2004 PRIMARY

Tammy Baldwin (D)	unopposed

2002 GENERAL

Tammy Baldwin (D)	163,313	66.0%
Ron Greer (R)	83,694	33.8%

PREVIOUS WINNING PERCENTAGES
2000 (51%); 1998 (52%)

Baldwin keeps a framed favorite quote in her office from anthropologist Margaret Mead: "Never doubt that a small group of thoughtful, committed citizens can change the world. Indeed, it is the only thing that ever has."

As she builds her career on Capitol Hill, Baldwin's challenge is to change a legislative world dominated by conservative Republicans who are hostile to her view of government's obligations. It is a frustrating battle, but Baldwin does not give up easily. In her official biography, under the heading, "If at First You Don't Succeed," she recalls: "In 1975, I ran for Student Council President at my middle school . . . AND LOST. In 1980, I competed for a chance to be my high school graduation speaker . . . AND LOST. And in 1983, I ran for class president at my college . . . AND LOST!"

She is politically savvy, personally likeable and ambitious. She is close to Minority Leader Nancy Pelosi, with whom she shares a lot philosophically. And Pelosi rewarded her fealty at the start of the 109th Congress with a coveted assignment to the Energy and Commerce Committee, which Baldwin had sought since she first arrived in the House. In exchange, Baldwin had to give up seats on the Judiciary and Budget committees.

It was a trade she gladly made. She told the Wisconsin State Journal, "I come to work and have meetings now that have to do with health care reform. We'll be working on the energy bill and doing a complete rewrite of the telecommunications laws, which haven't been changed since 1996. Being in the minority is always hard, but I'm really energized."

She hopes to increase her clout on health issues, her primary legislative interest, from a seat on Commerce's Health Subcommittee. Baldwin detailed Massachusetts Sen. John Kerry's health care plan during a prime-time address at the 2004 Democratic National Convention in Boston, although his proposals did not go as far as the single-payer approach she has long advocated. On Medicaid and Medicare, she will fight cuts in coverage.

Despite her liberal politics, Baldwin is pragmatic about making deals with lawmakers on the other side of the aisle. She says simply, "I can't get legislation passed without Republicans."

During work on the Violence Against Women Act in 2000, most Democratic amendments failed. But Baldwin worked with Florida Republican Bill McCollum, Judiciary's Crime Subcommittee chairman, to win approval of a $10 million grant to help disabled victims of violence. In the 107th Congress, she teamed with Pennsylvania Republican Melissa A. Hart on legislation prohibiting hate messages in cereal boxes and other processed food packaging. And in the 108th, she and Republican Nick Smith of Michigan helped win enactment of an extension of the Chapter 12 farm bankruptcy law.

Baldwin is a political trailblazer. She was still in law school when she won her first county board election at age 24. She is the first woman elected to Congress from Wisconsin, and she is the first openly gay woman to be elected to Congress.

Baldwin's self-deprecating humor helps her connect on a personal level, especially with conservatives who frown on her lifestyle. She exchanged marriage vows in 1998 with Lauren Azar, a lawyer, though same-gender unions are not legal in Wisconsin. Baldwin was a hit with her speech in 1999 at the annual Congressional Dinner of the Washington Press Club. "You invited me because I'm one of the first elected officials who represents a group historically discriminated against," she said. "A group that has been kept out of jobs, harassed at the workplace. A group that's been unfairly stereotyped and made the object of rude and base humor. Of course, I'm talking about blondes . . . especially blondes named Tammy."

In 2004, she strongly criticized Republican efforts to pass a Constitutional amendment banning gay marriage or to strip federal courts of jurisdiction over the issue. But as voters in a number of states adopted bans on gay marriage, Baldwin also urged a more gradual approach to fighting for benefits for same-sex couples.

A member of the Progressive Caucus, the most liberal faction in the House, Baldwin supports a minimum wage increase, expansion of Head Start and the Family and Medical Leave Act, and more social service spending. She opposed President Bush's tax cuts.

Baldwin typically sides with her party in foreign policy disputes with the White House. She was one of the first House Democrats to publicly oppose Bush's march toward war against Iraq, nearly 10 months before Congress began consideration of a resolution sanctioning the use of military force. The administration, she said, was preparing to invade Iraq without having shown a clear link between that Arab nation and the Sept. 11, 2001, terrorist attacks on the World Trade Center and Pentagon.

She tends to parochial concerns carefully, pressing for more federal funding to fight the chronic wasting disease that has ravaged the deer population in her hunting-happy state. She opposed a 2004 free-trade agreement with Australia that could have hurt Wisconsin's dairy farmers. And when asked in 2004 what her toughest vote was, she quipped, "Any telecommunications bill (satellite or cable) that might deny my constituents access to Packer games."

While studying law at the University of Wisconsin, Baldwin in 1986 was appointed to the Madison City Council to fill a vacancy. Later that year, she won the first of four terms as a Dane County supervisor. In 1992, she was elected to the Wisconsin Assembly, where she served six years.

Baldwin's impressive fundraising, with help from EMILY's List, helped her win the 1998 primary over two well-known opponents, Dane County Executive Rick Phelps and state Sen. Joe Wineke. Her GOP opponent in the general election, former state Insurance Commissioner Josephine Musser, had won a six-way primary with just 21 percent of the vote and antagonized conservatives with her support of abortion rights. Baldwin beat her by 6 percentage points. The district was a battleground again in 2000, with Baldwin eking out a 3-point victory over moderate Republican John Sharpless, a University of Wisconsin history professor. But in 2002 and 2004, the GOP had trouble mounting a serious challenge and she cruised to victory both years.

KEY VOTES

2004

Yes   Extend federal unemployment benefits by 13 weeks

Yes   Pass $283.2 billion, six-year federal highway and mass transit bill

Yes   Approve $146 billion multi-year extension of previously enacted middle-class tax breaks

No   Amend the Constitution to prohibit same-sex marriage

No   Cut corporate taxes $137 billion over 10 years

Yes   Reorganize U.S. intelligence agencies as proposed by Sept. 11 commission

2003

No   Cut taxes by $330 billion through fiscal 2013

Yes   Block Bush rule scaling back overtime pay for some white-collar federal workers

Yes   Do not allow use of search warrants without first notifying subjects

Yes   Allow importation of prescription drugs

No   Create private school voucher program in Washington, D.C.

No   Ban "partial birth" abortion except to save a woman's life

Yes   Split $18.6 billion in Iraq aid into half-grant, half-loan

No   Overhaul Medicare and create prescription drug benefit

CQ VOTE STUDIES

	PARTY UNITY		PRESIDENTIAL SUPPORT	
	Support	Oppose	Support	Oppose
2004	98%	2%	32%	68%
2003	99%	1%	18%	82%
2002	99%	1%	23%	77%
2001	97%	3%	22%	78%
2000	96%	4%	78%	22%

INTEREST GROUPS

	AFL-CIO	ADA	CCUS	ACU
2004	100%	100%	29%	4%
2003	100%	100%	23%	12%
2002	100%	100%	25%	0%
2001	100%	100%	30%	0%
2000	100%	90%	23%	4%

WISCONSIN 2
South – Madison

Once described by former GOP Gov. Lee Dreyfus as "23 square miles surrounded by reality," Madison long has been Wisconsin's liberal centerpiece. But in the suburbs around Wisconsin's university- and government-dominated capital, growing numbers of socially liberal, fiscally conservative young professionals keep Democrats on their toes.

Many magazines have named Madison as one of the nation's most livable cities, citing the bitter winters as the only negative. The state university system's main campus is a major influence on the city. The stable economy is fueled by an educated, white-collar population, while university-associated industries such as biotechnology have been boosted by school resources and expertise. Other large employers include state government, insurance companies and some light-manufacturing firms.

Outside of Madison, the 2nd resembles most of the rest of the state. Dane County's dairy and beef farms have declined, but it is still the second-largest farming region in the state. Tourists are attracted to the

district by New Glarus, known as America's "Little Switzerland," in Green County, while the Wisconsin Dells — ancient natural limestone formations along the Wisconsin River — attract visitors to the north. Redistricting following the 2000 census gave the 2nd Beloit, a struggling blue-collar manufacturing city near the Illinois border.

In Wisconsin, only the Milwaukee-based 4th District exceeds the 2nd in its Democratic proclivities. In 2002, Republican Gov. Scott McCallum took just 19 percent of the vote in Madison, where he finished behind the Democratic, Green and Libertarian candidates in some precincts. John Kerry took 66 percent of the vote in surrounding Dane County in 2004 while carrying the district with 62 percent of the vote.

MAJOR INDUSTRY
Higher education, agriculture, insurance, government

CITIES
Madison, 208,054; Beloit, 35,755; Fitchburg, 20,501; Sun Prairie, 20,369

NOTABLE
The Ringling brothers were from Baraboo, where the Circus World Museum is now located; In the 1970s, Dane County produced more pounds of tobacco for chewing tobacco than any other county in the United States.

Rep. Ron Kind (D)

Elected 1996; 5th term

Personifying a heartland work ethic and the Wisconsin good-government tradition, Kind is a union leader's son who paid his way through Harvard by scrubbing bathrooms. He donates his congressional pay raises to charity, and he returns about 10 percent of his office allotment to the federal treasury each year.

Kind's political inspiration comes from Wisconsin Democratic Sen. William O. Proxmire, who was famous for showcasing wasteful government spending. As a summer intern for Proxmire in 1984, Kind did research for the senator's annual "Golden Fleece" awards. He says he strives to carry on Proxmire's legacy, and he regularly gets kudos from the budget watchdog group Concord Coalition for his votes on fiscal issues. He was named to the Budget Committee at the outset of the 108th Congress.

Kind was appointed by Minority Leader Nancy Pelosi at the start of the 108th Congress as one of seven chief deputy whips. He also is a co-chairman of the moderate New Democrats group. He is generally more cooperative than combative in his dealings with Republicans, and in the 108th he supported President Bush's positions somewhat more often than the average House Democrat. Only the third Democrat to represent his western Wisconsin district in the past 90 years, Kind believes that bipartisanship is essential to legislative success.

He had hoped to win a seat on the Ways and Means Committee in the 109th Congress, but the prize went to others. On the Education and Workforce Committee, where he focuses much of his legislative energy, Kind presses hard to increase federal funding for education. His amendments to boost professional development for teachers and to help recruit teachers and principals were included in the 2001 No Child Left Behind Act. Kind also supports higher spending on special education, and in the 108th he joined with committee Republicans to craft a reauthorization of the 1975 Individuals with Disabilities Education Act, which guarantees disabled students a free public education in the "least restrictive environment." Even though he didn't get all he hoped for, he was one of three panel Democrats to vote for the bill that was reported out of committee.

Like other New Democrats, Kind was the focus of heavy lobbying pressure when the House voted in 2002 to grant the president expedited trade negotiating authority, known as fast-track. Unions strongly opposed the measure, and Kind already was on the outs with labor for voting in 2000 to normalize trade relations with China. At appearances in his district, Kind was met by placard-wielding constituents. In the end, Kind, the son of a union leader who lost his phone company job after a strike, voted with labor and against the bill. He said it did not adequately address environmental concerns or the needs of displaced U.S. workers.

In the 108th, Kind joined with more-liberal Democrats and union leaders in opposing the Bush administration's proposed changes to overtime pay rules. Still, he was the only Wisconsin Democrat to vote for Republican-backed free-trade agreements with Singapore and Chile — both opposed by major labor unions. Responding to local concerns about the outsourcing of American jobs to foreign labor markets, Kind said there was a "disconnect" between the public's opinion and behavior. "Everyone decries the lack of jobs and jobs going overseas, but they don't think twice about walking into a Wal-Mart and buying this stuff," he told The Twin Cities Pioneer Press. Kind's Republican challenger in 2004, state Sen. Dale W.

CAPITOL OFFICE
225-5506
ron.kind@mail.house.gov
www.house.gov/kind
1406 Longworth 20515-4903; fax 225-5739

COMMITTEES
Budget
Education & Workforce
Resources

HOMETOWN
La Crosse

BORN
March 16, 1963, La Crosse, Wis.

RELIGION
Lutheran

FAMILY
Wife, Tawni Kind; two children

EDUCATION
Harvard U., A.B. 1985; London School of Economics, M.A. 1986; U. of Minnesota, J.D. 1990

CAREER
County prosecutor; lawyer

POLITICAL HIGHLIGHTS
No previous office

ELECTION RESULTS

2004 GENERAL

Ron Kind (D)	204,856	56.4%
Dale W. Schultz (R)	157,866	43.5%

2004 PRIMARY

Ron Kind (D)	unopposed

2002 GENERAL

Ron Kind (D)	131,038	62.8%
Bill Arndt (R)	69,955	33.5%
Jeff Zastrow (LIBERT)	6,674	3.2%

PREVIOUS WINNING PERCENTAGES
2000 (64%); 1998 (71%); 1996 (52%)

Schultz, emphasized his opposition to free-trade policies.

Kind has taken a measured approach to some social issues, such as abortion. He voted in 1997, 1998 and 2000 to ban a procedure that opponents call "partial birth" abortion. But in 2002 and 2003, he did not support the ban, saying that the Supreme Court's rejection of a similar Nebraska law caused him to question the ban's constitutionality.

In 2002, Kind voted to authorize use of military force against Iraq. Back home, a group called the La Crosse Coalition for Peace and Justice launched a write-in campaign against him, putting up as their candidate Mark Twain, the American folk humorist and writer who once called war "a wanton waste of projectiles." The long-deceased Twain got 500 votes, surprising even members of the peace group.

In 2003, Kind proposed halving emergency supplemental funding for Iraq and Afghanistan. Kind told his colleagues that he and his allies were not offering the measure "because we do not believe in the mission, but because we believe the administration should come before Congress to justify in a detailed fashion what current funds are being used for and what future funds are being requested."

Federal protection for the dairy industry is the top parochial issue for Kind. His district includes Eau Claire, the historic center of the U.S. dairy industry. In a political advertisement in 2000, Kind and his family sported milk mustaches and the industry's "Got Milk?" message. In the 108th, Kind successfully proposed several provisions aimed at encouraging increased milk consumption in public schools.

Kind is an up-by-the-bootstraps success story. Reared in a blue-collar neighborhood, he was a high school football and basketball star, and won a scholarship to Harvard University, paying his expenses with a campus janitorial job. He quarterbacked on the football team before suffering a career-ending shoulder injury.

After earning a law degree and working two years for a Milwaukee law firm, Kind returned home to La Crosse to become a county prosecutor.

Part of his inspiration for entering politics was a backpacking trip through Eastern Europe just as communism was crumbling. Kind joined the thousands of people who dismantled the Berlin Wall with sledgehammers, and shook hands with new Czechoslovakian President Vaclav Havel.

When GOP Rep. Steve Gunderson announced his retirement, Kind entered the 1996 race. With little money, he waged a grass-roots campaign, beating Jim Harsdorf with 52 percent of the vote. He has won easily since, topping 63 percent, until 2004, when Schultz held him to 56 percent.

KEY VOTES

2004

Yes   Extend federal unemployment benefits by 13 weeks

Yes   Pass $283.2 billion, six-year federal highway and mass transit bill

Yes   Approve $146 billion multi-year extension of previously enacted middle-class tax breaks

No   Amend the Constitution to prohibit same-sex marriage

No   Cut corporate taxes $137 billion over 10 years

Yes   Reorganize U.S. intelligence agencies as proposed by Sept. 11 commission

2003

No   Cut taxes by $330 billion through fiscal 2013

Yes   Block Bush rule scaling back overtime pay for some white-collar federal workers

Yes   Do not allow use of search warrants without first notifying subjects

Yes   Allow importation of prescription drugs

No   Create private school voucher program in Washington, D.C.

No   Ban "partial birth" abortion except to save a woman's life

Yes   Split $18.6 billion in Iraq aid into half-grant, half-loan

No   Overhaul Medicare and create prescription drug benefit

CQ VOTE STUDIES

	PARTY UNITY		PRESIDENTIAL SUPPORT	
	Support	Oppose	Support	Oppose
2004	87%	13%	41%	59%
2003	89%	11%	26%	74%
2002	86%	14%	29%	71%
2001	87%	13%	28%	72%
2000	86%	14%	81%	19%

INTEREST GROUPS

	AFL-CIO	ADA	CCUS	ACU
2004	93%	90%	47%	24%
2003	80%	95%	38%	20%
2002	78%	90%	47%	8%
2001	92%	90%	39%	12%
2000	80%	80%	50%	8%

WISCONSIN 3
West – Eau Claire, La Crosse

In the 1930s, President Franklin D. Roosevelt declared Eau Claire the heart of the nation's milk industry, establishing a system that pays dairy producers more for their milk the farther they are from the 3rd's biggest city. Today, the district still has more cows than people, but the Roosevelt system is outdated and has contributed to the shutdown of family farms, forcing the 3rd to look elsewhere to boost its economy.

Despite the flat prairie land and nutrient-rich soil, the rural southwestern part of the district has been hardest hit by the lagging dairy industry. In the north, Eau Claire and La Crosse have seen declines in their manufacturing industries as well. But the five branches of Wisconsin's state university system in the 3rd have placed an emphasis on computer and technology education, and both cities have experienced recent growth in their technology sectors. Meanwhile, bedroom communities in St. Croix County — inhabited by commuters to Minneapolis-St. Paul, just across the Minnesota state line — grew rapidly during the 1990s.

Recreational tourism also contributes to the 3rd's economy. The more than 250 miles of Mississippi River that the district takes in along the western border with Minnesota and Iowa provide birdwatchers an opportunity to spot bald eagles perched on bluffs. Lakes in the north attract sportsmen and retirees.

The 3rd has a slight Democratic lean and voted narrowly for Democrat James E. Doyle in the 2002 gubernatorial election and narrowly for John Kerry in the 2004 presidential election. Most of the 19 counties wholly or partly in the district are politically competitive, and in the 2004 presidential contest, all but three gave the winner a margin of victory of less than 10 percentage points.

MAJOR INDUSTRY
Dairy farming, manufacturing, tourism, technology

MILITARY BASES
Fort McCoy (Army), 1,002 military, 2,281 civilian (2003)

CITIES
Eau Claire (pt.), 59,794; La Crosse, 51,818; Menomonie, 14,937

NOTABLE
Laura Ingalls Wilder, author of the "Little House" books, was born in Pepin; Taliesin, Frank Lloyd Wright's estate, is in Spring Green.

www.cqpress.com

Rep. Gwen Moore (D)

Elected 2004; 1st term

CAPITOL OFFICE
225-4572
www.house.gov/gwenmoore
1408 Longworth 20515-4904; fax 225-8135

COMMITTEES
Financial Services
Small Business

HOMETOWN
Milwaukee

BORN
April 18, 1951, Racine, Wis.

RELIGION
Baptist

FAMILY
Single; three children

EDUCATION
Marquette U., B.A. 1978 (political science)

CAREER
State agency legislative analyst; city development specialist; VISTA volunteer

POLITICAL HIGHLIGHTS
Wis. Assembly, 1989-92; Wis. Senate, 1993-2004 (president pro tempore, 1997-98)

ELECTION RESULTS

2004 GENERAL

Gwen Moore (D)	212,382	69.6%
Gerald H. Boyle (R)	85,928	28.2%
Tim Johnson (I)	3,733	1.2%

2004 PRIMARY

Gwen Moore (D)	48,858	64.2%
Matt Flynn (D)	19,377	25.5%
Tim Carpenter (D)	7,801	10.3%

As one of four African-Americans — all Democrats — in the Class of 2004, and as the first black to represent Wisconsin in Congress, veteran lawmaker Moore should be able to find a place on the national stage. But she says she plans to keep her focus local, advocating programs and policies that will benefit her largely working-class Milwaukee constituency.

Moore says her early career in Wisconsin's housing and health departments and her own experiences as a single mother gave her a familiarity with welfare programs. That has led her to advocate expanding the federal definition of poverty to consider not only income levels but also heating, prescription drug and child care costs.

Moore's voting patterns likely will not differ from the liberal, party-loyalist record of her predecessor, Democrat Gerald D. Kleczka. But while Kleczka was best known for his pro-union agenda, Moore has said she will be more business-friendly in working on issues affecting the urban poor and working class — the focus of much of her work during her nearly 16 years as a state legislator.

"I do get it as a Democrat that businesses create jobs, and we've got to create incentives for businesses to remain in our community," she said. "We've got to help them with health care and provide tax credits for job creation." Still, Moore also holds to the idea that the federal government should play a significant role in alleviating local problems, and hopes to win more appropriations for Milwaukee than it has received recently.

Her committee assignments reflect both aspects of Moore's economic philosophy. She is on the Financial Services Committee, which deals with housing, among other issues, and serves on its Consumer Credit Subcommittee, which handles issues pertinent to lower-income constituents who have difficulty obtaining credit. She also is on the Small Business panel.

Unfortunately for Moore, her first brush with the congressional spotlight was a bit glaring: Her son, Sowande Omokunde, was charged in January 2005 for slashing tires on the cars of Republican campaign workers on Election Day 2004. Moore herself was not implicated in the case.

WISCONSIN 4
Milwaukee

As civil rights protesters crossed Milwaukee's 16th Street viaduct over the Menomonee Valley in the 1960s, observers called it the "longest bridge in the world" — quipping that it stretched from Poland to Africa. Redistricting following the 2000 census put the city in a single district for the first time, forcing the 4th to confront the stark racial, cultural and economic differences that divide its northern and southern parts.

Polish immigrants flocked to the valley's southern side in the early 20th century. A large number of blacks migrated to the city after World War II, but regulations forced them to the north side. As the city's population declined since the 1960s, the prominent social and economic differences between the two communities remained.

Milwaukee today is minority-majority, with blacks (37 percent) and Hispanics (12 percent) together outnumbering whites. City officials say Milwaukee is becoming more integrated, but it is not uncommon to find almost completely black areas in north-central Milwaukee and almost exclusively white areas in the southern part of the city.

As the growing Hispanic population displaces wealthier white-collar workers, the city's manufacturing industries — especially some of the breweries and tanneries that defined the economy — continue to decline, leaving the city struggling to find a new identity. Still, bank data processing and other such industries have made an impact in recent years. Milwaukee's large minority population and strong union presence make the 4th the most Democratic district in the state.

MAJOR INDUSTRY
Machinery manufacturing, service

CITIES
Milwaukee, 596,974; South Milwaukee, 21,256; West Allis (pt.), 20,936

NOTABLE
The world's largest four-sided clock is on the Allen-Bradley building.

Rep. F. James **Sensenbrenner** Jr. (R)

Elected 1978; 14th term

CAPITOL OFFICE
225-5101
sensenbrenner@mail.house.gov
www.house.gov/sensenbrenner
2449 Rayburn 20515-4905; fax 225-3190

COMMITTEES
Judiciary - chairman

HOMETOWN
Menomonee Falls

BORN
June 14, 1943, Chicago, Ill.

RELIGION
Episcopalian

FAMILY
Wife, Cheryl Sensenbrenner; two children

EDUCATION
Stanford U., A.B. 1965 (political science); U. of
Wisconsin, J.D. 1968

CAREER
Lawyer

POLITICAL HIGHLIGHTS
Wis. Assembly, 1969-75; Wis. Senate, 1975-79

ELECTION RESULTS

2004 GENERAL

F. James Sensenbrenner Jr. (R)	271,153	66.6%
Bryan Kennedy (D)	129,384	31.8%
Tim Peterson (LIBERT)	6,549	1.6%

2004 PRIMARY

F. James Sensenbrenner Jr. (R)	unopposed

2002 GENERAL

F. James Sensenbrenner Jr. (R)	191,224	86.1%
Robert R. Raymond (I)	29,567	13.3%

PREVIOUS WINNING PERCENTAGES
2000 (74%); 1998 (91%); 1996 (74%); 1994 (100%);
1992 (70%); 1990 (100%); 1988 (75%); 1986 (78%);
1984 (73%); 1982 (100%); 1980 (78%); 1978 (61%)

As chairman of the House Judiciary Committee, Sensenbrenner wields significant clout in the debate over renewing the 2001 Patriot Act, a controversial law giving police agencies broader powers to combat terrorism. Sensenbrenner has questioned the Bush administration's assertion that it needs more authority to thwart terrorists.

The blunt, sometimes abrasive lawmaker frequently clashes with the conservative Republican leadership in the House as well. More than once, House GOP leaders have overruled him, either by substituting their own version of a bill or by bypassing the panel outright.

In 2004, Republican leaders took proposed constitutional amendments on same-sex marriage to the House floor despite Sensenbrenner's opposition to altering the Constitution. In 2002, the Bush White House struck a deal with Democratic Sen. Christopher J. Dodd of Connecticut and Republican Rep. Michael G. Oxley of Ohio on a bill to provide a federal safety net for commercial property and casualty insurers for terrorism-related losses, leaving Sensenbrenner and other GOP conservatives in the cold. The chairman was incensed that the deal did not include their ban on punitive damage awards in lawsuits.

Perhaps the leaders should not have been surprised then when Sensenbrenner in late 2004 helped lead Republican opposition to a sweeping intelligence overhaul measure because it did not include his provision to prohibit states from issuing driver's licenses to illegal immigrants. He ultimately lost the battle and refused to sign the final version of the bill. President Bush and GOP leaders promised to make his immigration legislation a priority the following year. As promised, Bush announced in 2005 that he would support Sensenbrenner's driver's license proposal.

Sensenbrenner is opinionated and direct to a fault and seems ill-suited to play the role of legislative deal-maker. He is sometimes impatient with the long-winded rhetoric that is a staple of Judiciary Committee meetings, where philosophical battles between Republicans and Democrats often play out. But Sensenbrenner spent his first 16 years in the House in the minority, and swore that once he wielded power he would not subject Democrats to the same indignities he endured before the 1995 Republican takeover of Congress. He is more inclined than other conservative chairmen to try to get Democratic support for the major bills that come out of committee. And he protects the panel's jurisdiction and prerogatives.

Sensenbrenner steered the panel to a unanimous vote on anti-terrorism legislation just three weeks after the Sept. 11, 2001, terrorist attacks. He described the moment as a triumph of the committee system over the desires of the Bush administration, which had proposed much greater powers for law enforcement agents to search, eavesdrop on, arrest and detain suspects.

His victory was short-lived. With the public in shock after Sept. 11, the administration was in a position to press Congress for a tougher bill. Attorney General John Ashcroft persuaded Speaker J. Dennis Hastert to have the House vote instead on a bill closer to what Ashcroft wanted, and that version by and large became law. But Sensenbrenner won a key concession, supported by committee Democrats, to allow several of the surveillance and investigatory powers to expire at the end of 2005 unless Congress extended them.

Since the Patriot Act was adopted, Sensenbrenner has had to struggle to get the Justice Department to tell him how it is using its new investigative powers, and has on occasion threatened to subpoena information when Justice officials refused to turn it over. He bluntly told Ashcroft at a June 2003 oversight hearing that his support for the anti-terrorism legislation "is neither perpetual nor unconditional."

The chairman of Judiciary since 2001, Sensenbrenner has proved to be an able tactician. In 2005, Congress passed a major revision of federal bankruptcy law that came out of his committee and had been eight years in the making. The legislation made it more difficult for consumers to avoid repaying debts by filing for bankruptcy protection. It also raised filing fees and required potential filers to receive credit counseling in the six months before seeking such protection.

During the closely watched case of Utah teenager Elizabeth Smart, who was kidnapped from her bedroom and held prisoner for nine months, Smart's father at first criticized Sensenbrenner for not moving quickly on a bill to improve the nationwide missing-child alert system known as AMBER. When the House finally passed the bill, it was amended with a contentious overhaul of federal sentencing guidelines, which made it dicey in the Senate. So Sensenbrenner hitched his bill to a measure by Republican Senate Judiciary Chairman Orrin G. Hatch of Utah aimed at cracking down on computer-generated child pornography. The legislation was enacted, and the Smart family sang Sensenbrenner's praises, calling his strategy "an excellent example of government at its best."

Sensenbrenner is among Congress' wealthiest lawmakers, heir to a paper and cellulose manufacturing fortune that began with his great-grandfather's invention of the sanitary napkin shortly after World War I. Marketing it under the brand name Kotex, Sensenbrenner's ancestor went on to become the chairman of Kimberly-Clark.

He earned a political science degree from Stanford University and was elected to the Wisconsin legislature in 1968, the year he graduated from law school at the University of Wisconsin at Madison. He served a decade in the legislature, part of that time as assistant senate minority leader.

When Republican Bob Kasten left the 9th District seat to run for governor in 1978, Sensenbrenner was seen as the obvious successor because of his experience in state government and because he had a solid political base in the district's older, more affluent suburbs bordering Lake Michigan. Still, he had to dip into family wealth to overcome a strong GOP primary challenge from Susan Engeleiter. Sensenbrenner won with 61 percent of the vote in the general election, and subsequently has been re-elected by wider margins.

KEY VOTES

2004

No	Extend federal unemployment benefits by 13 weeks
No	Pass $283.2 billion, six-year federal highway and mass transit bill
Yes	Approve $146 billion multi-year extension of previously enacted middle-class tax breaks
Yes	Amend the Constitution to prohibit same-sex marriage
No	Cut corporate taxes $137 billion over 10 years
No	Reorganize U.S. intelligence agencies as proposed by Sept. 11 commission

2003

Yes	Cut taxes by $330 billion through fiscal 2013
No	Block Bush rule scaling back overtime pay for some white-collar federal workers
No	Do not allow use of search warrants without first notifying subjects
Yes	Allow importation of prescription drugs
Yes	Create private school voucher program in Washington, D.C.
Yes	Ban "partial birth" abortion except to save a woman's life
Yes	Split $18.6 billion in Iraq aid into half-grant, half-loan
Yes	Overhaul Medicare and create prescription drug benefit

CQ VOTE STUDIES

	PARTY UNITY		PRESIDENTIAL SUPPORT	
	Support	Oppose	Support	Oppose
2004	94%	6%	79%	21%
2003	91%	9%	82%	18%
2002	94%	6%	85%	15%
2001	91%	9%	77%	23%
2000	91%	9%	20%	80%

INTEREST GROUPS

	AFL-CIO	ADA	CCUS	ACU
2004	27%	20%	86%	92%
2003	0%	25%	80%	80%
2002	13%	0%	95%	92%
2001	8%	10%	74%	96%
2000	22%	20%	70%	88%

WISCONSIN 5
Southeast – Milwaukee suburbs

Residents of Waukesha and Ozaukee counties joke that more people commute from Milwaukee to the suburbs that make up the 5th District than the other way around. Indeed, the affluent counties to the west and north of the city have continued to experience rapid growth as Milwaukee middle managers leave downtown and newly transferred white-collar workers settle in the city's outskirts.

As the suburbs expand, they are becoming increasingly self-sufficient, providing employment in all sectors. Most of the manufacturing jobs outside of the city are located in Waukesha County, west of Milwaukee. Quad Graphics, a major printing company, is headquartered in Sussex, while engine manufacturer Briggs and Stratton is located in Wauwatosa. Most residents in Ozaukee County, to the north of the city, hold service and legal-related jobs. Waukesha County's population grew by 18 percent in the 1990s, while Washington County, to Waukesha's north, grew by 23 percent — the fourth-fastest growth rate in the state.

While the northern and western outskirts of the 5th are still mostly rural and populated with dairy farms and cattle ranches, urban sprawl has started to encroach upon them as well. Most residents of the 5th still proudly celebrate their diverse European heritages — German, Belgian, Dutch and Eastern European folk festivals attract tourists almost every weekend of the summer. Vacationers also travel here for the recreational fishing and boating opportunities along Lake Michigan.

The present-day 5th is descended from the 9th District that existed in the 1990s. The renumbering was required after redistricting following the 2000 census dismantled a Milwaukee-based district (the old 5th). The strong GOP lean in Ozaukee, Washington and Waukesha makes the new 5th the state's most heavily Republican district. It gave 63 percent of the vote to George W. Bush in the 2004 presidential election. Democrats are competitive only in Milwaukee County.

MAJOR INDUSTRY
Service, manufacturing, retail

CITIES
Waukesha, 64,825; Wauwatosa, 47,271; West Allis (pt.), 40,318; Brookfield, 38,649; Menomonee Falls, 32,647; New Berlin (pt.), 31,636

NOTABLE
Harley-Davidson offers tours of its manufacturing facility in Wauwatosa.

Rep. Tom Petri (R)

Elected April 1979; 13th full term

In his understated and quiet way, Petri continues to walk his own independent legislative path. He sides with fiscal conservatives on spending issues but moves away from the majority of his party on the issues of campaign finance law and education. He is a leading advocate of generous federal spending on transportation and infrastructure projects.

His independent streak sometimes puts him at odds with the GOP leadership. Though he was next in line in seniority in the 107th Congress for the chairmanship of the Education and Workforce Committee, Republican leaders passed over him and gave the post to John A. Boehner of Ohio, who usually votes with the leadership and is a prolific fundraiser. Later, Petri joined a bipartisan band of rebels who pushed the campaign finance bill to the floor over the objections of the GOP leadership.

Losing the chairmanship of the Education panel was a tough break for Petri (PEA-try), who has a longstanding interest in education policy and will cross party lines to get bipartisan legislation. In early 2005, he stood with Massachusetts Democratic Sen. Edward M. Kennedy and other Democrats during a news conference touting his bill to give colleges an incentive to use a student loan program that draws funds from the U.S. Treasury rather than a guaranteed private lender program favored by many Republicans. Under his bill, colleges could use the savings in bank fees to issue more student loans or Pell grants. He has also supported providing parents with taxpayer-financed vouchers to pay for private school tuition.

As a consolation prize for not receiving the Education gavel, he was made chairman of the Transportation and Infrastructure panel's Highways, Transit and Pipelines Subcommittee. The old Ground Transportation Subcommittee was split in two, with Petri getting the newly constituted highway panel. That allowed him to avoid the term limit on chairmanships and still hold sway over road policy; he already had spent six years as chairman of the Ground Transportation panel.

Petri was on the Transportation Committee in 1998 when it wrote what was then the most expensive transportation funding bill in U.S. history — a six-year, $218 billion measure. When work on reauthorizing the 1998 measure began in 2003, Petri supported a $375 billion bill sponsored by Chairman Don Young of Alaska. They both advocated for the measure, despite the Bush administration's opposition to its dollar amount and its increase in the federal gasoline tax, but Petri's smooth and diplomatic demeanor contrasted markedly with Young's more fiery, unpolished style. And while Young defiantly protested efforts by the White House and GOP leaders to trim his proposal, the soft-spoken Petri was more muted.

He squares his fiscal conservatism with his support for highway spending by arguing that the projects, enormously popular with lawmakers and their constituents, are paid for out of the Highway Trust Fund, which is financed by gasoline and transportation-related excise taxes, not by general revenues. He argues that highway funding should be viewed as an economy-boosting investment. "If we don't spend the money on the infrastructure, it won't save us money; we will spend it in less productive ways, with delays and all the rest of it," he said in 2004.

Petri has been a key supporter of efforts to keep gasoline taxes walled off from other uses. He also has been sympathetic to the arguments of lawmakers from states that contribute more highway taxes to the trust fund than they get back in road projects, touting his own success in getting a

CAPITOL OFFICE
225-2476
www.house.gov/petri
2462 Rayburn 20515-4906; fax 225-2356

COMMITTEES
Education & Workforce
Transportation & Infrastructure
(Highways, Transit & Pipelines - chairman)

HOMETOWN
Fond du Lac

BORN
May 28, 1940, Marinette, Wis.

RELIGION
Lutheran

FAMILY
Wife, Anne Neal Petri; one child

EDUCATION
Harvard U., A.B. 1962 (government), J.D. 1965

CAREER
Lawyer; White House aide; Peace Corps volunteer

POLITICAL HIGHLIGHTS
Wis. Senate, 1973-79; Republican nominee for U.S. Senate, 1974

ELECTION RESULTS

2004 GENERAL

Tom Petri (R)	238,620	67.0%
Jef Hall (D)	107,209	30.1%
Carol Ann Rittenhouse (WG)	10,081	2.8%

2004 PRIMARY

Tom Petri (R)	unopposed

2002 GENERAL

Tom Petri (R)	unopposed

PREVIOUS WINNING PERCENTAGES
2000 (65%); 1998 (93%); 1996 (73%); 1994 (100%); 1992 (53%); 1990 (100%); 1988 (74%); 1986 (97%); 1984 (76%); 1982 (65%); 1980 (59%); 1979 Special Election (50%)

greater share of funds for Wisconsin.

Changes to campaign finance law also continue to occupy a prominent place on Petri's agenda. He introduced legislation in both the 108th and 109th Congresses aimed at encouraging more participation in election campaigns by low-income constituents. His measure allows a 100 percent tax credit for donations of up to $200 per year to federal candidates, or a 100 percent tax deduction for contributions of up to $600 per year.

And he has sponsored a bill to curb what campaign directors sometimes call push polls and what Petri calls "smear polls," in which campaign workers ask prospective voters leading questions intended to cast negative information about a candidate in the form of an ostensibly objective survey.

In 2002, Petri received a "Hero of the Taxpayer Award" for his 90 percent rating from the Americans for Tax Reform. In 2004, he earned an 85 percent rating. But even on the GOP's signature issues, Petri sometimes goes his own way. In one early 2004 vote, he joined 10 other Republicans who supported an unsuccessful Democratic motion intended to put the House on record in favor of making both tax cuts and mandatory spending subject to pay-as-you-go rules — resisting fierce arm-twisting from Republican leaders who saw the motion as an impediment to the administration's tax-cutting agenda. In the end, though, he joined the Republican majority position against any pay-as-you-go rules.

He also has been a leading Republican advocate of expanding the earned-income tax credit, a tax break that helps the working poor. Most efforts to increase the credit come from House Democrats.

Petri, who was born in northern Wisconsin, earned a law degree from Harvard and later joined the Peace Corps, doing work in Somalia. Once home, he started a law practice in Fond du Lac. He won a state Senate seat in 1972 at age 32.

Petri was chosen to be the GOP Senate nominee against Democrat Gaylord Nelson in 1974, but he lost in the aftermath of the Watergate scandal and what turned out to be a terrible year for Republicans. The exposure and increased name recognition from that race, however, helped him win a close contest for the House in a 1979 special election. He replaced Republican Rep. William A. Steiger, who had died in office.

In his 1992 re-election campaign, Petri was hampered by negative publicity about 77 overdrafts at the private bank for House members. He returned to Washington, but with only 53 percent of the vote, his worst re-election total ever. Since then, he has been re-elected easily. He won with 67 percent in 2004.

KEY VOTES

2004

No Extend federal unemployment benefits by 13 weeks

Yes Pass $283.2 billion, six-year federal highway and mass transit bill

Yes Approve $146 billion multi-year extension of previously enacted middle-class tax breaks

Yes Amend the Constitution to prohibit same-sex marriage

Yes Cut corporate taxes $137 billion over 10 years

Yes Reorganize U.S. intelligence agencies as proposed by Sept. 11 commission

2003

Yes Cut taxes by $330 billion through fiscal 2013

No Block Bush rule scaling back overtime pay for some white-collar federal workers

Yes Do not allow use of search warrants without first notifying subjects

Yes Allow importation of prescription drugs

Yes Create private school voucher program in Washington, D.C.

Yes Ban "partial birth" abortion except to save a woman's life

Yes Split $18.6 billion in Iraq aid into half-grant, half-loan

Yes Overhaul Medicare and create prescription drug benefit

CQ VOTE STUDIES

	PARTY UNITY		PRESIDENTIAL SUPPORT	
	Support	Oppose	Support	Oppose
2004	89%	11%	85%	15%
2003	87%	13%	84%	16%
2002	86%	14%	82%	18%
2001	90%	10%	83%	17%
2000	89%	11%	32%	68%

INTEREST GROUPS

	AFL-CIO	ADA	CCUS	ACU
2004	33%	20%	95%	80%
2003	0%	20%	77%	80%
2002	0%	10%	85%	80%
2001	17%	25%	65%	72%
2000	0%	10%	76%	84%

WISCONSIN 6
East central — Oshkosh, Sheboygan, Fond du Lac

In 1854, a group of dissatisfied Whigs, Free Soilers and Democrats met in a Ripon schoolhouse in central Fond du Lac County and created the Republican Party. Today, the rural areas west of Ripon still carry on the GOP tradition of their forefathers, but the blue-collar communities along Lake Michigan's shores, characterized by manufacturing and processing plants, vote Democratic.

On Lake Michigan, Manitowoc County has a longstanding reputation as a shipbuilding center. Sheboygan County is famed for its meat processing — it considers itself the "bratwurst capital of the world" — and also for its manufacturing, including the plumbing company Kohler. Around Lake Winnebago, Oshkosh produces heavy trucks while Neenah and Menasha are major paper-product manufacturers.

The west is farming territory, although family dairy farms have struggled. Some have been assimilated by large corporate farms and others have turned to crops such as beans, peas and corn. Marquette County, located in the southwest, is the least-populous county in the 6th but the fastest-growing in the state (28.5 percent in the 1990s). It is popular among retirees from the Milwaukee and Chicago areas.

Many of the 6th's residents are descendants of German immigrants who settled the area in the 1850s, and the district claims more people of German ancestry (54 percent) than any other in the nation. Although these socially conservative Lutherans combine with a Catholic community to dominate much of the district, some of the state's traditional progressivism remains. The Hmong population — immigrants from East Asia — nearly doubled in the 1990s.

The 6th leans Republican, but not overwhelmingly so. In 2004, George W. Bush won every county here except for Adams, located in the far west. Republican Scott McCallum won the 6th in the 2002 gubernatorial election, narrowly winning Sheboygan and Winnebago.

MAJOR INDUSTRY
Paper, agriculture, tourism, manufacturing

CITIES
Oshkosh, 62,916; Sheboygan, 50,972; Fond du Lac, 42,203

NOTABLE
The Wisconsin Maritime Museum is in Manitowoc.

Rep. David R. Obey (D)

Elected April 1969; 18th full term

CAPITOL OFFICE
225-3365
www.house.gov/obey
2314 Rayburn 20515-4907; fax 225-3240

COMMITTEES
Appropriations - ranking member

HOMETOWN
Wausau

BORN
Oct. 3, 1938, Okmulgee, Okla.

RELIGION
Roman Catholic

FAMILY
Wife, Joan Obey; two children

EDUCATION
U. of Wisconsin, B.S. 1960 (political science), M.A. 1962 (political science)

CAREER
Real estate broker

POLITICAL HIGHLIGHTS
Wis. Assembly, 1963-69

ELECTION RESULTS

2004 GENERAL

David R. Obey (D)	241,306	85.7%
Mike Miles (WG)	26,518	9.4%
Larry Oftedahl (CNSTP)	12,841	4.6%

2004 PRIMARY

David R. Obey (D)	unopposed

2002 GENERAL

David R. Obey (D)	146,364	64.2%
Joe Rothbauer (R)	81,518	35.8%

PREVIOUS WINNING PERCENTAGES
2000 (63%); 1998 (61%); 1996 (57%); 1994 (54%); 1992 (64%); 1990 (62%); 1988 (62%); 1986 (62%); 1984 (61%); 1982 (68%); 1980 (65%); 1978 (62%); 1976 (73%); 1974 (71%); 1972 (63%); 1970 (68%); 1969 Special Election (52%)

These are frustrating times for Obey, the top-ranking Democrat on the Appropriations Committee. The entire budget apparatus is in GOP hands, and outgunned senior Democrats are on the outside looking in for the foreseeable future. Unlike many younger Democrats elected over the past decade, Obey remembers what it was like to have real power.

Through countless battles for liberal causes over more than three decades in Congress, Obey (OH-bee) has gained a reputation as a complex man of indisputable intelligence, occasionally irascible disposition and formidable legislative skill. His combustible manner and brutal honesty on the House floor are matched by his deep understanding of the policy preferences, procedures and politics at work behind the scenes.

For several years after the 1995 Republican takeover of Congress, Obey had either President Clinton or majority Senate Democrats to ensure that his ideas did not get trampled on. But starting in 2003, he was on his own. In a pattern that would become too familiar to him, Republicans early that year pushed through a behemoth package that wrapped together all the unfinished spending bills left over from the end of the 107th Congress.

GOP leaders have stymied Democrats at every turn, not simply because they control both Congress and the White House, but because they have used such catchall spending bills, rather than individual bills, to keep the government running. That maximizes the leverage of GOP leaders and President Bush — and leaves Obey playing at the margins. "It is one thing for Congress to wind up putting numerous appropriation bills into a broad-based omnibus bill because legitimate controversies have delayed the compromises necessary to pass those bills," Obey said in 2004. "It is quite another thing to produce this kind of end-of-session chaos by design."

Divisions among Democrats compound his sense of powerlessness. Obey has long believed that the annual appropriations process gives Democrats an opportunity to define their political differences with Republicans. But Obey's position has led to clashes with Democrats who've adopted a go-along-get-along attitude as their party lingers in minority status.

Obey led the charge in 2003 against the biggest domestic spending bill, saying it badly underfunded education and other programs. After every Democrat voted against the bill, however, subcommittee Chairman Ralph Regula, an Ohio Republican, decreed that not a single hometown project requested by Democrats would get funded. After that, many rank-and-file Democrats signaled they would vote for spending bills even if they didn't like them, to preserve the spending items for their districts.

In 2004, Obey prevailed upon House leaders to schedule a vote on a measure that would have added $14 billion to the $821.4 billion spending cap for appropriations, financed by a repeal of tax cuts for upper-income taxpayers. In exchange for getting that vote (which failed), Obey promised to work to prevent procedural snags and help Republicans advance the spending bills.

Obey considers himself an institutionalist, who respects the ideals of civilized debate and collegiality. He directed a rewrite of the House ethics code after a series of scandals in the 1970s. After the Sept. 11, 2001, terrorist attacks, Obey was a lonely voice insisting that Congress not give Bush unfettered control over $40 billion in emergency spending to respond to the crisis. "When you give any White House $20 billion with not a single string attached, you have abdicated Congress' responsibility under the Constitution," he said. Ultimately, his view prevailed.

His pugnacity and partisanship are legendary. Sometimes, he seems close to boiling over, the array of long pencils in his shirt pocket threatening to topple out as he wags his finger in disgust at GOP leaders. However, Obey generally has good relationships with top Republican appropriators.

He enjoyed a quarter-century in the House majority, and for the final nine months of 1994 he was Appropriations chairman. For all his liberal passion, he understood that lawmaking involves compromise, and his main objective was to resolve problems with the GOP before they could delay the spending bills. As a result, all 13 measures became law by the start of the fiscal year. It has not happened since.

He has a hands-on approach to managing the bills. During the Clinton administration, he used the annual spending wars to sharpen his party's message to the public, all the while maneuvering to ensure the bills received Clinton's approval. Under Bush, he takes a lead role in opposing the White House's spending priorities.

Like all appropriators, Obey uses his perch to take care of his district. He typically shows restraint in that regard, but Republicans singled out one item dear to him in 2003 as an example of wasteful spending — an $80,000 motorized sled for a Wisconsin sheriff for rescues on Lake Superior.

Although he lists his occupation as real estate broker, Obey has been a legislator almost all his adult life. He was elected to the state House when he was 24 and won election to Congress at age 30, in a 1969 special election to succeed Melvin R. Laird, President Nixon's first defense secretary. Obey was the first Democrat ever to represent the 7th District, and he has won three-fifths of the vote in 16 of 18 re-election races.

His reputation as a liberal stalwart stems from Obey's tussles with Republicans over fiscal policy. Mindful of sentiment in his largely rural and small-town district, he supports gun owners' rights and votes for some restrictions on abortion.

Obey grew up in a staunchly Republican family; he once hitched a wagon to his bicycle and campaigned door-to-door for GOP Sen. Joseph R. McCarthy and presidential candidate Dwight D. Eisenhower. He says he changed his mind about McCarthy after followers on the local school board tried to have his high school history teacher fired for teaching that the political platform of the Chamber of Commerce and the Constitution were not the same thing. "When I saw what McCarthyism did to the best teacher I ever had, it showed me that if you had any dedication to individual liberty and freedom of speech, that at that time in that county, there was no room for you in the local Republican Party," he said.

KEY VOTES

2004

Yes	Extend federal unemployment benefits by 13 weeks
Yes	Pass $283.2 billion, six-year federal highway and mass transit bill
No	Approve $146 billion multi-year extension of previously enacted middle-class tax breaks
No	Amend the Constitution to prohibit same-sex marriage
No	Cut corporate taxes $137 billion over 10 years
No	Reorganize U.S. intelligence agencies as proposed by Sept. 11 commission

2003

No	Cut taxes by $330 billion through fiscal 2013
Yes	Block Bush rule scaling back overtime pay for some white-collar federal workers
Yes	Do not allow use of search warrants without first notifying subjects
Yes	Allow importation of prescription drugs
No	Create private school voucher program in Washington, D.C.
Yes	Ban "partial birth" abortion except to save a woman's life
Yes	Split $18.6 billion in Iraq aid into half-grant, half-loan
No	Overhaul Medicare and create prescription drug benefit

CQ VOTE STUDIES

	PARTY UNITY		PRESIDENTIAL SUPPORT	
	Support	Oppose	Support	Oppose
2004	93%	7%	26%	74%
2003	93%	7%	20%	80%
2002	94%	6%	32%	68%
2001	94%	6%	29%	71%
2000	94%	6%	82%	18%

INTEREST GROUPS

	AFL-CIO	ADA	CCUS	ACU
2004	100%	90%	25%	4%
2003	100%	100%	13%	24%
2002	100%	90%	26%	8%
2001	100%	95%	30%	13%
2000	100%	95%	15%	4%

WISCONSIN 7
Northwest — Wausau, Superior, Stevens Point

Wisconsin's most rural district, the 7th stretches north and west from the state's central counties to the Apostle Islands along the southern coast of Lake Superior. Small towns and family farms checker the district, carrying a populist flavor and still retaining some threads of mid-century LaFollette progressivism.

Farming sustains the district's economy, although cold weather in the north shaves a full month off the growing season. The dairy industry has declined since the 1980s, but small, 60-cow farms still populate the northern half of the 7th. The more nutrient-rich soil in the Central Sands country in the state's midsection produces seed potatoes, cranberries, beans and ginseng. Some small metalworking and paper factories — the industries that attracted immigrants to the 7th in the 19th century — still produce their goods. The insurance industry has waned in recent years.

The tranquil lifestyle in small towns and along hundreds of lakes in the north attracts a particularly large number of senior citizens to the 7th. Young people migrate south to cities, such as Milwaukee and Madison,

to find jobs or to take advantage of the University of Wisconsin's main branch, while Hmong immigrants from Asia's eastern coast have settled in the region. One fast-growing area is Polk County, on the St. Croix River northeast of the Minneapolis-St. Paul metro area.

Blue-collar regions around Stevens Point and Wausau and along Lake Superior in the north consistently vote Democratic, but the rest of the area is more politically competitive. Descendants of Scandinavian immigrants in north-central Wisconsin and an emerging Christian Right contingent keep the region competitive. Redistricting following the 2000 census did not significantly alter the 7th's political leanings.

MAJOR INDUSTRY
Agriculture, paper, manufacturing

CITIES
Wausau, 38,426; Superior, 27,368; Stevens Point, 24,551

NOTABLE
Marathon County is the nation's largest producer of ginseng; The American Birkebeiner, from Cable to Hayward, is North America's largest cross-country ski marathon; Poniatowski is the center of the northern half of the western hemisphere; Colby cheese is named after a district town; Hayward is home to the National Fresh Water Fishing Hall of Fame.

Rep. Mark Green (R)

CAPITOL OFFICE
225-5665
mark.green@mail.house.gov
www.house.gov/markgreen
1314 Longworth 20515-4908; fax 225-5729

COMMITTEES
International Relations
Judiciary

HOMETOWN
Green Bay

BORN
June 1, 1960, Boston, Mass.

RELIGION
Roman Catholic

FAMILY
Wife, Susan Green; three children

EDUCATION
U. of Wisconsin, Eau Claire, B.A. 1983; U. of Wisconsin, J.D. 1987

CAREER
Lawyer; teacher

POLITICAL HIGHLIGHTS
Wis. Assembly, 1993-99

ELECTION RESULTS

2004 GENERAL

Mark Green (R)	248,070	70.1%
Dottie Le Clair (D)	105,513	29.8%

2004 PRIMARY

Mark Green (R)	unopposed

2002 GENERAL

Mark Green (R)	152,745	72.6%
Andrew M. Becker (D)	50,284	23.9%
Dick Kaiser (WG)	7,338	3.5%

PREVIOUS WINNING PERCENTAGES
2000 (75%); 1998 (55%)

Elected 1998; 4th term

Green began the 109th Congress with one foot out the door. In May 2005, he formally announced he would run for governor of Wisconsin, challenging the Democratic incumbent. He also transferred $1.3 million from his federal campaign fund to his new state account, which he can use in the gubernatorial contest in 2006.

Green has a lock on his Green Bay-based district and would pose a serious GOP challenge to first-term Democratic Gov. James E. Doyle. But he would face serious primary competition first. That increases the likelihood the campaign will be a distraction to him during his fourth term in the House.

Terming himself a "bleeding-heart conservative," Green does not subscribe to the anti-government rhetoric of many of his Republican colleagues. A teaching stint in a remote Kenyan village after he graduated from law school helped shape Green's views and got him thinking about a career in politics — a pursuit that started before his immigrant parents had become citizens eligible to vote for their son. The Kenyan experience "sensitized me to the problems of the human condition," he says, but he also came away with the belief that government policies can stifle economic opportunity.

He is usually a reliable vote for the GOP leadership; in the 108th Congress, he sided with Republicans on 92 percent of the votes pitting the two parties against each other. Nonetheless, he has broken ranks on some high-profile issues. In 2005, he was one of just a dozen House Republicans to vote against the initial fiscal 2006 budget resolution. In 2004, he was one of 39 voting to provide additional benefits for unemployed workers. The year before, Green was one of a handful of Republicans who signed a letter to Speaker J. Dennis Hastert calling for a vote on a measure to nullify a Federal Communications Commission rule allowing greater media ownership consolidation.

When he arrived in Washington as a freshman in the 106th Congress, Green announced that he intended to focus on taxes, and he did push for the Republican tax agenda from his seat on the Budget Committee. But Green no longer sits on that panel. Instead, he serves on the Judiciary and International Relations committees.

He had to relinquish a seat on the Financial Services Committee at the start of the 109th. He had used that post to push for more affordable housing. "I believe that affordable housing is the great untapped issue for conservatives," he said. In 2004, Green was a founding member of the bipartisan Faith-based Community Solutions Caucus, which worked to improve a federal grant program, frequently used by Habitat for Humanity, to help low-income families buy homes. He also has pushed one bill to give financial assistance to law enforcement officers who purchase homes in high-crime areas and another to help the disabled buy homes.

Green has used his Judiciary seat to push a "two strikes — they're out" bill, which would require mandatory life sentencing of repeat sex offenders in cases involving children. The measure is similar to legislation he wrote in the Wisconsin legislature. Passed by the House in 2000 and again in 2002, the bill was predicated on studies indicating that sex offenders usually repeat their crime. "This bill is not . . . about deterrence. It is about removing bad people from society," he said.

As the only Republican to unseat an incumbent House Democrat in 1998, Green was treated well by party leaders when he arrived in Washington. He received a spot in the GOP whip organization and a place on the Republican Policy Committee. In 2005, when illness prevented Speaker Hastert from attending the Rome funeral of Pope John Paul II, Green was given a coveted slot in the small House delegation attending the rites.

Green carefully tends to the home fires. It is politically imperative for lawmakers from Wisconsin to involve themselves in dairy policy, and Green was a member of the conference committee that wrote the final version of the farm bill enacted in 2002, which included a three-and-a-half year, $1.3 billion dairy price-support program. However, Green and other Badger State lawmakers have been less successful in their push for a sweeping rewrite of the Depression-era milk-pricing policy that has given milk producers in other regions a better deal in order to help them compete with producers in the Upper Midwest. Lawmakers from those other parts of the country have repeatedly blocked the efforts, leading Green to declare: "This place is locked in a time warp. This place is using a milk-pricing mechanism that was created in the era of the manual typewriter."

Green also sought to help Wisconsin farmers by pushing to liberalize the income-averaging provisions of the tax code and by supporting better tax treatment for the sale of a family farm to another member of the same family. And he has backed federal funding to fight chronic wasting disease — the deer equivalent of mad cow disease — which has threatened the whitetail herd in Wisconsin and some other states.

Green's family moved to Green Bay when he was 5 years old, ending a long journey for both his parents. His father, a physician, was born in South Africa and grew up in Kenya. His mother, who trained as a nurse, is from England. They became U.S. citizens in 1995.

Green was a champion swimmer in college. After graduation, he went to law school and worked in the office of the state's attorney general. When he finished law school, Green and his wife, Susan, took teaching assignments in Kenya, as Green wanted to visit his father's former home. When they returned, he joined a law firm and became active in Green Bay GOP politics.

In 1992, he won the first of three two-year terms in the Assembly, where he chaired the Judiciary Committee and the Republican Caucus. He declined to run for Congress when GOP Rep. Toby Roth retired in 1996, but was fast out of the blocks two years later, when Republicans sought to prove that Democrat Jay Johnson's 1996 victory was a fluke in a district that had sent a Democrat to Washington just four times in the 20th century. Portraying Johnson as too liberal for the district, Green won by 9 percentage points. He has breezed to re-election, with at least 70 percent of the vote.

KEY VOTES

2004

Yes Extend federal unemployment benefits by 13 weeks
No Pass $283.2 billion, six-year federal highway and mass transit bill
Yes Approve $146 billion multi-year extension of previously enacted middle-class tax breaks
Yes Amend the Constitution to prohibit same-sex marriage
Yes Cut corporate taxes $137 billion over 10 years
No Reorganize U.S. intelligence agencies as proposed by Sept. 11 commission

2003

Yes Cut taxes by $330 billion through fiscal 2013
No Block Bush rule scaling back overtime pay for some white-collar federal workers
No Do not allow use of search warrants without first notifying subjects
No Allow importation of prescription drugs
Yes Create private school voucher program in Washington, D.C.
Yes Ban "partial birth" abortion except to save a woman's life
No Split $18.6 billion in Iraq aid into half-grant, half-loan
Yes Overhaul Medicare and create prescription drug benefit

CQ VOTE STUDIES

	PARTY UNITY		PRESIDENTIAL SUPPORT	
	Support	Oppose	Support	Oppose
2004	91%	9%	88%	12%
2003	92%	8%	93%	7%
2002	94%	6%	82%	18%
2001	94%	6%	91%	9%
2000	93%	7%	22%	78%

INTEREST GROUPS

	AFL-CIO	ADA	CCUS	ACU
2004	27%	20%	86%	88%
2003	13%	10%	87%	84%
2002	11%	0%	95%	88%
2001	17%	0%	96%	88%
2000	10%	5%	85%	84%

WISCONSIN 8
Northeast – Green Bay, Appleton

Each autumn Sunday, all eyes in Wisconsin turn to the 8th's center to watch football's Green Bay Packers. Regardless of the team's fortunes, the Packers represent the emotional heart of the state — and they draw international attention and pull in millions of dollars. But the district's blue-collar feel stems from the paper industry that stretches southwest from Green Bay along the Fox River Valley, an area with more paper mills than anywhere else in the world.

Much of the economy is stable and dependent on natural resources. The sparsely populated north contains the state's largest tracts of forests, supplying the local paper industry. Fertile land in the southern part of the district supports grain and dairy farming, with some high-skill manufacturing in Green Bay and Appleton. The district also is home to six federally recognized American Indian tribes — each of which boasts a reservation-based casino.

The area is famed for its natural beauty and draws large numbers of tourists from Milwaukee and Chicago during the more temperate

seasons. Forests and lakes in Vilas County, near the Michigan border, lure outdoorsmen and nature lovers, while Door County, the peninsula jutting into Lake Michigan, attracts wealthier vacationers with upscale second homes, scenic apple orchards and a bustling art community.

The 8th leans slightly Republican. Although blue-collar throughout, the district is largely Catholic and socially conservative. It has been home to some far-right icons such as Joseph R. McCarthy and the John Birch Society in Appleton. Brown County, which includes Green Bay, tends to be politically competitive. Waupaca and Shawano counties, in the district's southwestern corner, vote Republican. The GOP runs well in the less-populated northern counties of Vilas and Florence, while Democrats dominate in Menominee County, which is conterminous with an American Indian reservation. Overall, George W. Bush took 55 percent of the 8th's vote in the 2004 presidential election.

MAJOR INDUSTRY
Paper products, casinos, agriculture, tourism

CITIES
Green Bay, 102,313; Appleton (pt.) 69,270; De Pere, 20,559

NOTABLE
About 68,000 people are on the waiting list for Packers season tickets.

WYOMING

Gov. Dave Freudenthal (D)

First elected: 2002
Length of term: 4 years
Term expires: 1/07
Salary: $105,000
Phone: (307) 777-7434

Hometown: Cheyenne
Born: Oct. 12, 1950; Thermopolis, Wyo.
Religion: Episcopalian
Family: Wife, Nancy Freudenthal; four children
Education: Amherst College, B.A. 1973 (economics); U. of Wyoming, J.D. 1980
Career: Lawyer; gubernatorial aide; state economic development official
Political highlights: Wyo. State Planning Coordinator, 1975-77; U.S. attorney, 1994-2001

Election results:

2002 GENERAL
Dave Freudenthal (D)	92,662	50.0%
Eli Bebout (R)	88,873	47.9%
Dave Dawson (LIBERT)	3,924	2.1%

Secretary of State
Joe Meyer (R)

(no lieutenant governor)
First elected: 1998
Length of term: 4 years
Term expires: 1/07
Salary: $92,000
Phone: (307) 777-5333

STATE LEGISLATURE

General Assembly: 40 days January-March in odd-numbered years; 20 days February-March in even-numbered years

House: 60 members, 2-year terms
2005 breakdown: 46R, 14D; 51 men, 9 women
Salary: $150/day in session
Phone: (307) 777-7852

Senate: 30 members, 4-year terms
2005 breakdown: 23R, 7D; 27 men, 3 women
Salary: $150/day in session
Phone: (307) 777-7711

STATE TERM LIMITS

Governor: 2 terms
House: 6 terms
Senate: 3 terms

URBAN STATISTICS

CITY	POPULATION
Cheyenne	53,011
Casper	49,644
Laramie	27,204
Gillette	19,646

REGISTERED VOTERS

Republican	63%
Democrat	27%
Others/unaffiliated	10%

POPULATION

2004 population (est.)	506,529
2000 population	493,782
1990 population	453,588
Percent change (1990-2000)	+8.9%
Rank among states (2004)	50

Median age	36.2
Born in state	42.5%
Foreign born	2.3%
Violent crime rate	267/100,000
Poverty level	11.4%
Federal workers	7,186
Military	6,224

REDISTRICTING

Wyoming retained its one House seat in reapportionment.

MISCELLANEOUS

Web: www.wyoming.gov
Capital: Cheyenne
STATE ELECTION OFFICIAL
(307) 777-7186
DEMOCRATIC HEADQUARTERS
(307) 473-1457
REPUBLICAN HEADQUARTERS
(307) 234-9166

District Statistics

DIST.	2004 VOTE FOR PRESIDENT BUSH	KERRY	WHITE	BLACK	ASIAN	HISP	MEDIAN INCOME	WHITE COLLAR	BLUE COLLAR	SERVICE INDUSTRY	OVER 64	UNDER 18	COLLEGE EDUCATION	RURAL	SQ. MILES
AL	69%	29%	89%	1%	1%	6%	$37,892	54%	29%	17%	12%	26%	22%	35%	97,100
STATE	69	29	89	1	1	6	$37,892	54	29	17	12	26	22	35	97,100
U.S.	50.7	48.3	69	12	4	13	$41,994	60	25	15	12	26	24	21	3,537,438

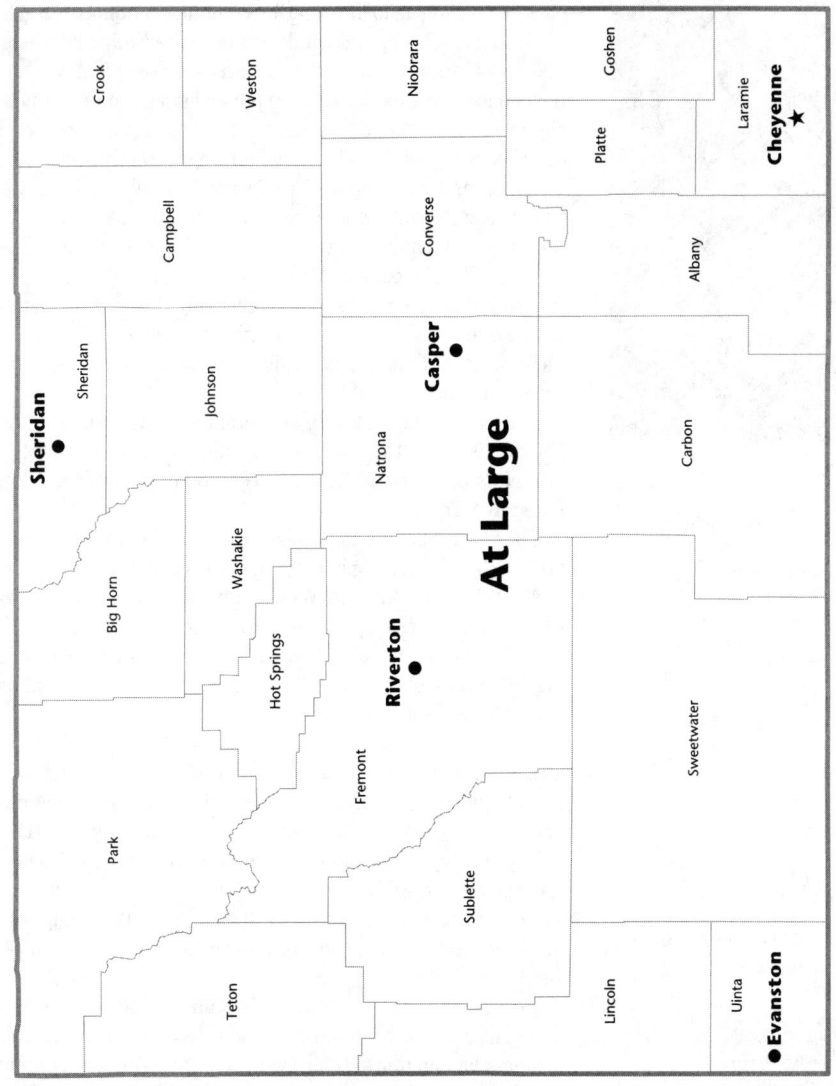

Sen. Craig Thomas (R)

Elected 1994; 2nd term

CAPITOL OFFICE
224-6441
thomas.senate.gov
307 Dirksen 20510-5003; fax 224-1724

COMMITTEES
Agriculture, Nutrition & Forestry
Energy & Natural Resources
  (National Parks - chairman)
Finance
  (International Trade - chairman)
Indian Affairs
Select Ethics

HOMETOWN
Casper

BORN
Feb. 17, 1933, Cody, Wyo.

RELIGION
Methodist

FAMILY
Wife, Susan Thomas; four children

EDUCATION
U. of Wyoming, B.A. 1955; La Salle U., LL.B. 1963

MILITARY SERVICE
Marine Corps, 1955-59

CAREER
Power company trade association executive;
agricultural association executive

POLITICAL HIGHLIGHTS
Sought Republican nomination for Wyo. treasurer,
1978, 1982; Wyo. House, 1985-89; U.S. House,
1989-95

ELECTION RESULTS

2000 GENERAL

Craig Thomas (R)	157,622	73.8%
Mel Logan (D)	47,087	22.0%
Margaret Dawson (LIBERT)	8,950	4.2%

2000 PRIMARY

Craig Thomas (R)	unopposed

PREVIOUS WINNING PERCENTAGES
1994 (59%); 1992 House Election (58%); 1990 House
Election (55%); 1989 Special House Election (52%)

Sure as snow falls in winter in Wyoming, Thomas is a reliable vote for President Bush's agenda and for the conservative interests of his state. Like most Western lawmakers, he is a fiscal conservative who strongly supports oil and gas exploration on public lands, protecting private property rights and making sure farmers in his state get a square deal.

Thomas is positioned to have an impact on those issues in the 109th Congress with a seat on the Energy and Natural Resources Committee and a new appointment to the Agriculture panel. He also has an assignment on the Finance Committee, which handles budget and tax issues.

While Thomas pursues his state's interests, he does it in a quiet, methodical way that has made him remarkably few enemies after nearly two decades in Congress. Known for his courtesy and diplomacy even on bitterly contested issues, he is no pushover. Thomas is a former Marine Corps captain.

As chairman of the Energy Committee's National Parks Subcommittee, Thomas is perfectly positioned to continue his push for expanded oil and gas exploration on public lands. Half the geographic area of Wyoming is federally owned.

Thomas is also the Republican chairman of the Congressional Oil and Gas Forum. He is a big booster of Bush's plan to allow energy exploration in Alaska's Arctic National Wildlife Refuge. And he has proposed revisions to the Endangered Species Act to make it more difficult to get species added to the list. In 2004, Thomas pushed a provision to a catchall spending bill allowing snowmobiles access to Yellowstone National Park and Grand Teton National Park.

"We needed to provide certainty for visitors and those providing services in our parks," Thomas said. "My efforts brought about that certainty and stopped the flow of lawsuits this year, which deny the visitors any confidence about whether they can access our national parks this winter."

Thomas says there should be multiple uses for federal lands, including preservation of wilderness. His views on snowmobiles notwithstanding, Thomas is more likely to side with environmental groups when the issue involves the state's twin jewels in the national park system — Yellowstone and Grand Teton.

He has criticized Bush administration proposals to trim spending on national parks. In 2001 and 2002, he sided with environmentalists by proposing a ban on tours by air over the parks. Thomas' contention that helicopter tours would cause too much disruption won support from the same "green" groups that typically fight him tooth and nail. "It's kind of scary," Thomas mused. "I bet they are asking themselves, 'What the hell are we doing?'"

Thomas had a notable tiff with environmental groups in the 104th Congress (1995-1996), when he took the lead on a bill allowing 12 Western states to take control of 270 million acres of federal land, including wilderness areas that were among the nation's few remaining pristine ecosystems. Thomas said the states could do a better job overseeing the lands than the federal Bureau of Land Management. The proposal got a lot of press attention at a time Republicans were under pressure to prove they cared about the environment. Thomas reluctantly delayed his bill.

Most times, Thomas lines up almost perfectly with Republican priorities. As a member of the Finance panel and chairman of the International

Trade Subcommittee, Thomas has backed Bush's push to cut taxes and trim spending. He generally liked the president's plan to remake Social Security by allowing younger participants to invest their money in private accounts, but he worried in early 2005 that the plan went too far. He withheld an endorsement of it as the White House geared up a national lobbying campaign.

On most topics, Thomas sides with the conservatives in his party, and he and the state's junior senator, Republican Michael B. Enzi, see eye to eye much of the time.

His party loyalty, along with his seniority, won Thomas a seat on the Finance Committee in 2001 after Sen. James M. Jeffords of Vermont abandoned the GOP to become an independent. That freed up a seat for Thomas, and gave him a hand in tax and trade legislation and also in writing health care policy.

Like many senators from rural states, Thomas is acutely aware that many of his constituents lack even basic medical services. He shares the chairmanship of the Senate Rural Health Caucus with Iowa Democrat Tom Harkin, and the two have pressed for legislation to increase physician recruitment incentives, equalize Medicare payments between rural and urban programs and help fund "telemedicine" programs.

Before he came to Congress, Thomas was vice president of the Wyoming Farm Bureau and once headed the rural electric trade association in Wyoming. Raised on a ranch, he is a defender of the state's cattle industry. Thomas and 10 other senators urged the White House to push Japan to reopen its border to U.S. beef after the country banned American beef in 2003, when a cow infected with mad cow disease was found at a slaughterhouse in Washington state.

Thomas grew up on a ranch near Wapiti, just outside Yellowstone Park. Affable and laid-back, he enjoys nothing more than a horseback ride through the wilderness, and he goes to great lengths to preserve hunting and fishing grounds.

He fits well with the attitudes, and voting patterns, of Wyoming, the home state of Vice President Dick Cheney. According to the 2004 election results, Wyoming is the second-most-Republican state in the nation, after Utah. It gave Bush 69 percent of the vote, compared with Utah's 72 percent.

When he decided to run for Congress, Thomas had big shoes to fill. Cheney had been the state's lone House member, and Wyoming's Senate seats had been occupied by forceful, colorful characters such as Malcolm Wallop and Alan K. Simpson.

Thomas had difficulty breaking into that stratosphere. He twice sought the GOP nomination for state treasurer, losing both times. Then in 1984, at 51, he was elected to the Wyoming House. In 1989, when Cheney was nominated by President George Bush to be secretary of defense, Thomas got the nod from the party's state central committee. He won the special election to succeed Cheney in the House with 52 percent of the vote.

Five years later, Wallop retired and Thomas ran for his seat with history weighing heavily on his side. Democrats had not won a U.S. Senate election in Wyoming since 1970. Thomas in 1994 banked on the idea that Wyoming voters would want another senator just as willing to fight the Clinton administration as Wallop, and he was right.

The Democrats nominated popular Gov. Mike Sullivan, who, though hardly a liberal, had ties to Clinton dating to their service together in the National Governors Association. He also was the first sitting governor to endorse Clinton for president. Thomas won handily by almost 20 percentage points. In 2000, he did even better, swamping his Democratic foe, coal miner Mel Logan, by a better than 3-to-1 ratio.

KEY VOTES

2004

Yes Pass $318.9 billion, six-year highway and mass transit bill

No Extend assault weapons ban for 10 years

No Restore pay-as-you-go rules for new tax cuts and entitlement spending

Yes Criminalize harm to a fetus in an attack on the mother

No Increase mandatory child care funding to states by $6 billion over five years

Yes Amend the Constitution to prohibit same-sex marriage

Yes Approve $146 billion multi-year extension of previously enacted middle-class tax breaks

Yes Reorganize U.S. intelligence agencies as proposed by Sept. 11 commission

Yes Cut corporate taxes $137 billion over 10 years

2003

No Delay Bush changes to Clean Air Act

Yes Allow confirmation vote on Miguel A. Estrada to the U.S. Court of Appeals for the D.C. Circuit

No Block a Bush proposal opening Alaska's Arctic National Wildlife Refuge to oil drilling

No Limit size of Bush's proposed tax cut to $350 billion through fiscal 2013

Yes Overhaul Medicare and create prescription drug benefit

No Block Bush rule scaling back overtime pay for some white-collar federal workers

No Split $20 billion in Iraq aid into half-grant, half-loan

Yes Ban "partial birth" abortion except to save a woman's life

Yes Stop proposal allowing travel to Cuba

Yes Allow final vote on energy policy overhaul

CQ VOTE STUDIES

	PARTY UNITY		PRESIDENTIAL SUPPORT	
	Support	Oppose	Support	Oppose
2004	99%	1%	96%	4%
2003	99%	1%	98%	2%
2002	96%	4%	94%	6%
2001	97%	3%	97%	3%
2000	97%	3%	40%	60%
1999	96%	4%	31%	69%
1998	95%	5%	39%	61%
1997	98%	2%	57%	43%
1996	98%	2%	29%	71%
1995	96%	4%	22%	78%

INTEREST GROUPS

	AFL-CIO	ADA	CCUS	ACU
2004	8%	5%	100%	100%
2003	0%	0%	100%	85%
2002	15%	10%	90%	100%
2001	13%	5%	100%	96%
2000	0%	0%	92%	92%
1999	0%	0%	100%	87%
1998	13%	5%	89%	84%
1997	0%	10%	90%	84%
1996	0%	5%	92%	100%
1995	0%	5%	100%	83%

Sen. Michael B. Enzi (R)

Elected 1996; 2nd term

With a knack for numbers and technology, Enzi is a combination of computer nerd and cowboy. A Western conservative who looks out for ranchers on the open range, he also has waged a lonely campaign to open the Senate floor to laptop computers, only to be rebuffed by the tradition-bound Rules Committee.

In the 109th Congress, the former accountant and computer programmer took over the chairmanship of the Health, Education, Labor and Pensions Committee. His Democratic counterpart is liberal icon Edward M. Kennedy of Massachusetts. Though the two are polar opposites politically, they have enjoyed a working relationship on the committee.

At the top of Enzi's agenda is legislation to prevent bioterrorism and to renew the Higher Education Act. He also wants to address the reauthorization of Head Start, the early childhood education program that many conservatives like Enzi (EN-zee) feel should be run by the states and not by the federal government. Enzi quickly laid claim to bioterrorism defense efforts by setting up a new subcommittee called the Bioterrorism Preparedness and Public Health Subcommittee, chaired by freshman Richard M. Burr, a North Carolina Republican.

Early in the 109th Congress, Enzi got legislation through the Senate to reauthorize the 1998 Carl D. Perkins Vocational and Technical Education Act, despite White House efforts to kill the program, which provides federal grants to states for classes in subjects like emerging technologies.

In taking the HELP gavel, Enzi had to give up the chairmanship of the Banking Committee's Securities and Investment Subcommittee, which he held in the 107th and 108th Congresses. From that perch, he was a leading Republican critic of a 2004 Financial Accounting Standards Board rule requiring companies to place values on employee stock options and deduct the amount from their annual income when they report their financial results.

Enzi's major Senate achievement to date is his work with Maryland Democrat Paul Sarbanes, then the chairman of the Banking Committee, to pass the new federal standards for accounting and corporate governance of companies that sell stock. The legislation is known throughout the corporate world by the shorthand, Sarbanes-Oxley.

At a point when the legislation was stuck at a partisan impasse, Enzi led several of his fellow Republicans on the Banking panel away from Republican Phil Gramm of Texas, an influential senator on business and economic issues, to the Sarbanes side. The key concession he obtained then — limiting the new accounting regulations to firms that audit publicly traded companies — remained in the bill even as pressure built for tougher regulation in light of a wave of corporate accounting scandals.

In helping to fashion the rules, and to win support from fellow conservatives, Enzi leveraged a credential that rarely accrues to his benefit as a politician: He is the Senate's only accountant.

Enzi is known as a deliberate legislator and self-effacing colleague who opposes expansion of the federal government's reach in just about every instance. Whether it be workplace rules for businesses or government limits on the export of high-technology items, Enzi's opposition to government regulation is in keeping with the views of many Westerners, who think Washington is intrusive.

His fundamental discomfort with federal regulation has not stopped

CAPITOL OFFICE
224-3424
enzi.senate.gov
379A Russell 20510-5004; fax 228-0359

COMMITTEES
Banking, Housing & Urban Affairs
Budget
Health, Education, Labor & Pensions - chairman
Small Business & Entrepreneurship

HOMETOWN
Gillette

BORN
Feb. 1, 1944, Bremerton, Wash.

RELIGION
Presbyterian

FAMILY
Wife, Diana Enzi; three children

EDUCATION
George Washington U., B.A. 1966 (accounting);
U. of Denver, M.S. 1968 (retail marketing)

MILITARY SERVICE
Wyo. Air National Guard, 1967-73

CAREER
Accountant; computer programmer; shoe store owner

POLITICAL HIGHLIGHTS
Mayor of Gillette, 1975-83; Wyo. House, 1987-91;
Wyo. Senate, 1991-96

ELECTION RESULTS

2002 GENERAL
Michael B. Enzi (R)	133,710	73.0%
Joyce Jansa Corcoran (D)	49,570	27.1%

2002 PRIMARY
Michael B. Enzi (R)	78,612	85.9%
Crosby "Cros" Allen (R)	12,931	14.1%

PREVIOUS WINNING PERCENTAGES
1996 (54%)

Enzi from watching out for parochial concerns, though. He has been a supporter of mandatory "Made in the USA" labels on American food products, an issue of particular concern to upper-Midwest ranchers looking to gain an edge on their Canadian counterparts.

And while Enzi particularly opposes regulations that affect public lands, water supply, resource development and Wyoming's miners and ranchers, he argued in 2002 that ranchers needed generous government help in the form of drought aid.

Enzi generally favors liberalized foreign trade, including agricultural trade with Cuba and expanded ties with China, which could help the farmers and ranchers in his state. In the 107th Congress, he urged the decidedly low-tech export of live sheep to Afghanistan, touting the benefit to the people of the economically struggling country and to Western ranchers.

Enzi often goes to bat for small businesses. He opposed the ergonomics regulations imposed in the final days of the Clinton administration and helped to orchestrate the congressional move to repeal them at the outset of the Bush administration. He applauded moves by the Bush White House to develop voluntary guidelines for businesses.

Enzi says that lawmakers often have no notion of the problems faced by a small business. While some in Congress refer to companies with 100 to 500 workers as small businesses, he says, "To me, a small business is when the person who writes the checks, also sweeps the front walk, cleans the toilets and waits on the customers." Once, faced with a proposal by the Clinton administration to protect mine workers from noise, Enzi commented, "I seriously question whether those who wrote this rule have ever actually been to a mine."

A former computer programmer, Enzi created a stir in his first year in office by announcing his intention to bring his laptop computer onto the Senate floor, where there is a ban on mechanical devices that might be distracting. The Rules Committee voted to keep computers out of the chamber. Enzi continues to push to have the Senate fully embrace the use of computers. "My laptop carries more data than could be packed in dozens of brief cases or notebooks," Enzi says. "My job requires me to tap into material on a moment's notice."

Another of his pet projects is a bill he has twice introduced that would extend Daylight Savings Time for a week to give more daylight to trick-or-treaters on Halloween — at the request of a second-grade teacher and her class in Sheridan. Enzi, whose daughter is a teacher, is following in the footsteps of his predecessor, Republican Sen. Alan K. Simpson, who also tried several times to pass the bill.

After earning a master's degree in retail marketing from the University of Denver, Enzi returned to Wyoming. He and his wife ran the family shoe store business, NZ Shoes.

Enzi began his political career in 1974 at age 30, winning the mayoralty of Gillette. During two terms, he was credited with guiding the city through a population explosion. In 1986, he won a seat in the state House, and in 1991, moved up to the state Senate.

When he launched his 1996 Senate campaign to replace Simpson, who retired after 18 years, Enzi appeared to face long odds against several well-known Republican opponents. By building a network of supporters drawn in part from the Wyoming Christian Coalition and stressing his opposition to abortion rights, he narrowly won the GOP primary. He took the general election by 12 percentage points over Kathy Karpan, a former two-term Wyoming secretary of state.

In 2002, he won re-election with 73 percent of the vote over Democrat Joyce Jansa Corcoran, the former mayor of Lander.

KEY VOTES

2004

Yes	Pass $318.9 billion, six-year highway and mass transit bill
No	Extend assault weapons ban for 10 years
No	Restore pay-as-you-go rules for new tax cuts and entitlement spending
Yes	Criminalize harm to a fetus in an attack on the mother
No	Increase mandatory child care funding to states by $6 billion over five years
Yes	Amend the Constitution to prohibit same-sex marriage
Yes	Approve $146 billion multi-year extension of previously enacted middle-class tax breaks
Yes	Reorganize U.S. intelligence agencies as proposed by Sept. 11 commission
Yes	Cut corporate taxes $137 billion over 10 years

2003

No	Delay Bush changes to Clean Air Act
Yes	Allow confirmation vote on Miguel A. Estrada to the U.S. Court of Appeals for the D.C. Circuit
No	Block a Bush proposal opening Alaska's Arctic National Wildlife Refuge to oil drilling
No	Limit size of Bush's proposed tax cut to $350 billion through fiscal 2013
Yes	Overhaul Medicare and create prescription drug benefit
No	Block Bush rule scaling back overtime pay for some white-collar federal workers
No	Split $20 billion in Iraq aid into half-grant, half-loan
Yes	Ban "partial birth" abortion except to save a woman's life
No	Stop proposal allowing travel to Cuba
Yes	Allow final vote on energy policy overhaul

CQ VOTE STUDIES

	PARTY UNITY		PRESIDENTIAL SUPPORT	
	Support	Oppose	Support	Oppose
2004	97%	3%	98%	2%
2003	99%	1%	97%	3%
2002	95%	5%	93%	7%
2001	95%	5%	99%	1%
2000	97%	3%	35%	65%
1999	95%	5%	24%	76%
1998	96%	4%	31%	69%
1997	98%	2%	51%	49%

INTEREST GROUPS

	AFL-CIO	ADA	CCUS	ACU
2004	9%	5%	100%	96%
2003	0%	5%	100%	80%
2002	17%	10%	89%	100%
2001	20%	10%	100%	92%
2000	0%	0%	100%	92%
1999	0%	0%	94%	92%
1998	0%	0%	94%	92%
1997	14%	10%	70%	88%

Rep. Barbara Cubin (R)

Elected 1994; 6th term

CAPITOL OFFICE
225-2311
www.house.gov/cubin
1114 Longworth 20515-5001; fax 225-3057

COMMITTEES
Energy & Commerce
Resources

HOMETOWN
Casper

BORN
Nov. 30, 1946, Salinas, Calif.

RELIGION
Episcopalian

FAMILY
Husband, Frederick William Cubin; two children

EDUCATION
Creighton U., B.S. 1969 (chemistry); Casper College, attended 1993 (business administration)

CAREER
Medical office manager; realtor; chemist

POLITICAL HIGHLIGHTS
Wyo. House, 1987-93; Wyo. Senate, 1993-95

ELECTION RESULTS

2004 GENERAL

Barbara Cubin (R)	132,107	55.3%
Ted Ladd (D)	99,989	41.8%
Lewis Stock (LIBERT)	6,581	2.8%

2004 PRIMARY

Barbara Cubin (R)	45,433	55.0%
Bruce S. Asay (R)	20,332	24.6%
Cale Case (R)	13,104	15.9%
Marvin "Trip" Applequist (R)	2,352	2.9%
James "Jim" Altebaumer (R)	1,374	1.7%

2002 GENERAL

Barbara Cubin (R)	110,229	60.5%
Ron Akin (D)	65,961	36.2%
Lewis Stock (LIBERT)	5,962	3.3%

PREVIOUS WINNING PERCENTAGES
2000 (67%); 1998 (58%); 1996 (55%); 1994 (53%)

Cubin is a vocal defender of private property rights, including the right of her constituents to mine, drill, log, graze and otherwise develop the bountiful natural resources of the nation's least populous state.

Nearly half of Wyoming's 97,100 square miles are under the federal government's jurisdiction, an important factor in a state whose economy — though tilting more each year toward tourism — still relies heavily on extractive industries and ranching. Cubin (CUE-bin), a descendant of 19th century homesteaders, is convinced that many Easterners do not understand the problems of those who live in the Cowboy State.

A founder of the Congressional Mining Caucus, she has made it a priority to promote two of her state's resource-based industries — the mining of coal and trona, a type of soda ash used in glassware, detergent and baking soda. In the 108th Congress, Cubin, whose state is the nation's leading coal producer, introduced a bill to reauthorize a portion of the 1977 Surface Mining Control and Reclamation Act, which finances mine cleanups nationwide from a fund that mining companies pay into, based on the amount of coal they mine. Western states, such as Wyoming, have accumulated substantial balances in the fund because they have few waste sites to clean up. Eastern states with declining amounts of coal, such as Pennsylvania, have large reclamation projects and less revenue to fund them. Cubin's legislation sought to cut coal company fees by 20 percent and allow states and Indian tribes without cleanup projects to draw their accrued shares from the fund. "Wyoming money is being used to clean up Eastern problems," Cubin complained.

Cubin regularly battles conservation groups bent on shielding land from development. She sees such efforts as a potential threat to the livelihood of her constituents, and to property rights in general. "Our lands are currently being locked away from public use . . . at an alarming pace," she said in 2000, challenging a bill that would have provided billions of dollars for land purchases. "The last thing we need in Wyoming is more federal land when the government can't adequately manage the property it has now."

The League of Conservation Voters gave Cubin a 3 percent rating on environmental issues for the 108th Congress; by contrast, she scored 100 in the most recent ratings from The League of Private Property Voters.

In the 108th, Cubin led opposition to a rule promulgated by the Clinton administration that would have phased out the use of snowmobiles in Wyoming's Yellowstone and Grand Teton National Parks. Cubin argued that the rule, designed to end noise and air pollution caused by hundreds of the machines each winter, would cost Wyoming jobs and was "more about getting President Clinton in the extreme environmental hall of fame than establishing good public policy." The Bush administration rewrote the regulation, permitting continued snowmobile use in the two parks.

Cubin was sufficiently concerned about how the West is treated in Congress that she launched a long-shot bid for the chairmanship of the Resources Committee at the start of the 108th Congress. Richard W. Pombo of California, a like-minded conservative, won the gavel, but Cubin did secure a waiver from GOP leaders to remain chairwoman of the Subcommittee on Energy and Mineral Resources beyond the normal six-year limit. She had to relinquish that gavel at the start of the 109th, but was designated vice chairwoman of the full committee as a consolation prize.

Though she is a reliable conservative on most issues, Cubin — like other

Westerners — sometimes splits from anti-spending Republicans when the interests of her water-starved, rural state are involved. In 2002, she introduced legislation to provide billions of dollars in emergency drought relief to farmers and ranchers. Congress approved a less generous package.

Cubin works with her state's senators, fellow Republicans Craig Thomas and Michael B. Enzi, to increase Wyoming's access to amenities that many Americans take for granted. In the 108th Congress, for example, she helped secure $4.4 million in federal funding to support airport infrastructure. She has also introduced bills to ease regulations on wireless telecommunications companies operating in rural areas and to increase Medicare compensation for rural doctors.

An ardent advocate of gun owners' rights who served three years on the board of the National Rifle Association, Cubin found herself in hot water in the 108th Congress for her rhetoric. During debate on a gun bill, she said one amendment would have barred the sale of guns "to anybody that was on drugs or had drug treatment or something like that. Well, so does that mean if you go into a black community, you can't sell any gun to any black person?" That remark, perceived by some of her colleagues as racist, sparked outrage — but not an official reprimand. Cubin quickly apologized.

Reared in Casper, Cubin earned a degree in chemistry and had a variety of jobs, including work as a chemist and real estate agent. She also served as manager of her husband's medical practice. She was active in local party politics and various civic groups, including the Wyoming State Choir, the PTA, a suicide prevention organization and a homeless shelter.

Over the years, her community activities led her to enter elective politics. Cubin served six years in the Wyoming House and two years in the state Senate, specializing in energy-related matters.

Her opening to Congress came in 1994, when Thomas left the state's lone House seat to run for the Senate. Drawing on her base in Casper and benefiting from the fact that she was the only woman in the race, Cubin prevailed in a five-way primary and went on to defeat Democratic lawyer Bob Schuster by 12 percentage points.

She has won re-election by comfortable margins since then. But in the 2004 primary, she faced multiple challengers after 12 percent of all House roll call votes in the 108th Congress and 27 percent in the 107th to care for her husband, Frederick, who has been hospitalized several times for non-malignant tumors, pancreatic problems and surgical complications. Cubin prevailed again, but her 55 percent share of the vote in both the primary and the general election was below her recent norms.

KEY VOTES

2004

No   Extend federal unemployment benefits by 13 weeks

Yes Pass $283.2 billion, six-year federal highway and mass transit bill

Yes Approve $146 billion multi-year extension of previously enacted middle-class tax breaks

Yes Amend the Constitution to prohibit same-sex marriage

Yes Cut corporate taxes $137 billion over 10 years

No   Reorganize U.S. intelligence agencies as proposed by Sept. 11 commission

2003

Yes Cut taxes by $330 billion through fiscal 2013

No   Block Bush rule scaling back overtime pay for some white-collar federal workers

Yes Do not allow use of search warrants without first notifying subjects

No   Allow importation of prescription drugs

Yes Create private school voucher program in Washington, D.C.

Yes Ban "partial birth" abortion except to save a woman's life

No   Split $18.6 billion in Iraq aid into half-grant, half-loan

Yes Overhaul Medicare and create prescription drug benefit

CQ VOTE STUDIES

| | PARTY UNITY | | PRESIDENTIAL SUPPORT | |
	Support	Oppose	Support	Oppose
2004	97%	3%	82%	18%
2003	97%	3%	94%	6%
2002	97%	3%	85%	15%
2001	98%	2%	89%	11%
2000	97%	3%	24%	76%

INTEREST GROUPS

	AFL-CIO	ADA	CCUS	ACU
2004	13%	0%	100%	100%
2003	0%	5%	96%	91%
2002	0%	0%	88%	100%
2001	0%	5%	93%	100%
2000	10%	5%	80%	100%

WYOMING

At large

Wyoming, the least populated state, basks in its wide open spaces, which define its libertarian politics and natural resource-based economy. Yellowstone National Park is one of the most visited parks in the nation, and tourism is an essential part of Wyoming's economy. The jagged peaks of the Grand Tetons rise more than 5,000 feet from the Jackson Hole Valley floor to their 13,000-foot apex, less than 10 miles from the nation's steepest ski slopes at Jackson Hole Mountain.

The state also relies on mining and commodities sales, so booms and busts coincide with market prices for those goods. After several years of budget shortfalls, the state has experienced surpluses due to rising oil and natural gas prices, and increased coal bed methane mining. Still, the increased income from natural resources did not equal the income from sales and use taxes and investing activities.

Many of the state's oil and gas jobs are temporary, which contributed to the state's fluctuating population in the 1980s and 1990s — a decline in the 1980s was followed by 9 percent growth in the next decade. Many skilled workers have left the state for better-paying jobs, and college graduates often leave for lack of employment.

Wyoming has not elected a Democrat to Congress since 1976. Residents savor their land and resources and abhor government intrusion of any kind, especially in dictating how land may be used. In most regions, residents are happy with the state's relative seclusion and tranquil lifestyle and are not particularly warm to population growth. The state's lawmakers are loath to raise taxes and dare not entertain a dreaded income tax. Wyoming has no corporate or personal income taxes and has a statewide 4 percent sales tax.

MAJOR INDUSTRY
Mining, tourism, agriculture

MILITARY BASES
Francis E. Warren Air Force Base, 3,764 military, 956 civilian (2004)

CITIES
Cheyenne, 53,011; Casper, 49,644; Laramie, 27,204; Gillette, 19,646

NOTABLE
Yellowstone became the first national park in 1872; Jackson was the first U.S. town ever to elect an all-female slate — mayor, council and marshal — in 1920.

Del. Eni F.H. Faleomavaega (D)

Elected 1988; 9th term

The longest-serving of the delegates, Faleomavaega is the fourth-most-senior Democrat on the International Relations Committee (and top-ranking Democrat on its Asia and the Pacific Subcommittee) and third-most-senior on the Resources panel — useful assignments for the nine-term delegate.

On Capitol Hill, he focuses on improving American Samoa's economy, which is dominated by tuna fishing and processing. The territory worries about competition from South American tuna fleets, and Faleomavaega (full name: EN-ee FOL-ee-oh-mav-ah-ENG-uh) has fought to exempt tuna from Andean trade pacts. In the aftermath of the deadly tsunami in Southeast Asia in December 2004, Faleomavaega backs the creation of a tsunami monitoring and early warning system for island territories.

Noting the reliance of many Samoans on public health programs, he introduced legislation in both the 108th and 109th Congresses to remove the limit on federal Medicaid dollars that territories can receive. Faleomavaega also has called on the International Atomic Energy Agency to investigate environmental and health effects of French nuclear testing in the South Pacific. In 1995, Faleomavaega was arrested as he protested the tests.

Faleomavaega went to high school in Hawaii when his father was stationed there in the Navy. Though his parents had little formal schooling — neither graduated from high school — they encouraged their children to pursue an education. He earned a bachelor's from Brigham Young University, joined the Army and served in Vietnam, then returned to the mainland for law school.

He worked for eight years in Washington, first as an executive assistant to American Samoa's first elected representative to the Capitol, A.U. Fuimaono, then for California Democratic Rep. Phillip Burton, the Interior Committee chairman, whom he credits for much of his success. Faleomavaega returned to Pago Pago in 1981, first as a deputy attorney general and then as lieutenant governor.

Faleomavaega is a "matai" — a Samoan chief — a title he has held since 1988. Faleomavaega is actually his title; his family name is Hunkin. Since his initial election in 1988, he has had a series of tough re-election battles.

CAPITOL OFFICE
225-8577
faleomavaega@mail.house.gov
www.house.gov/faleomavaega
2422 Rayburn 20515-5201; fax 225-8757

COMMITTEES
International Relations
Resources
Small Business

HOMETOWN
Pago Pago

BORN
Aug. 15, 1943, Vailoatai, Am. Samoa

RELIGION
Mormon

FAMILY
Wife, Hinanui Bambridge Hunkin; five children

EDUCATION
Brigham Young U., A.A. 1964, B.A. 1966 (political science); Texas Southern U., attended 1969 (law); U. of Houston, J.D. 1972; U. of California, Berkeley, LL.M. 1973

MILITARY SERVICE
Army, 1966-69; Army Reserve, 1983-2001

CAREER
Lawyer; territorial prosecutor; congressional aide

POLITICAL HIGHLIGHTS
Democratic candidate for U.S. House, 1984; lieutenant governor, 1985-89

ELECTION RESULTS

2004 GENERAL

Eni F.H. Faleomavaega (D)	12,108	64.6%
Aumua Amata Coleman (R)	6,646	35.4%

2002 GENERAL RUNOFF

Eni F.H. Faleomavaega (D)	4,959	54.8%
Fagafaga D. Langkilde (I)	4,083	45.2%

2002 GENERAL

Eni F.H. Faleomavaega (D)	4,294	41.3%
Fagafaga D. Langkilde (I)	3,332	32.1%
Aumua Amata Coleman (R)	2,767	26.6%

PREVIOUS WINNING PERCENTAGES
2000 General Runoff Election (61%); 1998 (86%); 1996 General Runoff Election (56%); 1994 (64%); 1992 (65%); 1990 (55%); 1988 (51%)

AMERICAN SAMOA

The least populated entity represented in the House, and the only one south of the equator, American Samoa is composed of five volcanic islands and two outlying coral atolls (total land area, 76 square miles, slightly more than the District of Columbia) in the south Pacific, about 2,300 miles southwest of Hawaii.

An 1899 treaty gave the United States control over the islands, in the eastern portion of the Samoan archipelago. During World War II, the deep-water harbor at Pago Pago attracted the U.S. Marine Corps, which made the island an advanced training and staging center.

American Samoa is an unincorporated territory of the United States, administered by the Interior Department. Residents are U.S. nationals, not citizens. The territory has had a non-voting delegate since 1981.

Most of the land is communally owned. Per capita income in 2000 was $4,357, and federal aid, including welfare and food stamps, is vital. Economic development, including tourism, a promising sector, is hindered by American Samoa's remote location, limited transportation and susceptibility to hurricanes.

Tuna fishing and processing plants are the key elements of the private sector economy, but the islands' tuna processing now is threatened by lower-wage competition from South America and Southeast Asia. In recent years, there has been a concerted government effort to cope with the islands' limited resources of fresh water.

MAJOR INDUSTRY
Tuna processing, government, handicrafts, tourism

VILLAGES
Tafuna, 8,409; Nu'uuli, 5,154; Pago Pago, 4,278

NOTABLE
Anthropologist Margaret Mead studied on Ta'u and wrote "Coming of Age in Samoa."

Del. Eleanor Holmes Norton (D)

Elected 1990; 8th term

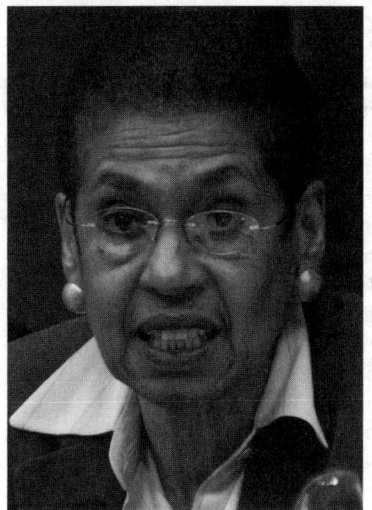

CAPITOL OFFICE
225-8050
dc00.wyr@housemail.house.gov
www.norton.house.gov
2136 Rayburn 20515-5101; fax 225-3002

COMMITTEES
Government Reform
Homeland Security
Transportation & Infrastructure

HOMETOWN
Washington

BORN
June 13, 1937, Washington, D.C.

RELIGION
Episcopalian

FAMILY
Divorced; two children

EDUCATION
Antioch College, B.A. 1960 (history); Yale U., M.A. 1963 (American studies), LL.B. 1964

CAREER
Professor; lawyer

POLITICAL HIGHLIGHTS
New York City Human Rights Commission, 1971-77; Equal Employment Opportunity Commission chairwoman, 1977-81

ELECTION RESULTS

2004 GENERAL

Eleanor Holmes Norton (D)	202,027	91.3%
Michael Monroe (R)	18,296	8.3%

2004 PRIMARY

Eleanor Holmes Norton (D)	58,363	98.4%
write-in (D)	979	1.7%

2002 GENERAL

Eleanor Holmes Norton (D)	119,268	93.0%
Pat Kidd (I)	7,733	6.0%

PREVIOUS WINNING PERCENTAGES
2000 (90%); 1998 (90%); 1996 (90%); 1994 (89%); 1992 (85%); 1990 (62%)

At a time when other elected positions in the District of Columbia are seeing significant turnover, Norton appears to have secured a lock on her job. Her negotiating skills and tenacity have not only helped shield the overwhelmingly Democratic city from assault by a Republican Congress but also have helped her win some victories from it. She is well-regarded by many key Republicans, and she has softened some Capitol Hill attitudes toward the city, which has suffered a series of financial and managerial crises.

She serves on the Government Reform panel, which has jurisdiction over matters involving the District, and has developed a strong working relationship with Chairman Thomas M. Davis III of Virginia, who represents a suburban district. She has fought to restrain congressional meddling in the city's affairs, which often takes the form of mandates or prohibitions added to the annual D.C. appropriations bill. Norton wants to give the District authority to spend locally raised money and to pass city ordinances without congressional review — a losing battle, but one she still wages.

She won enactment of a law that provides tuition grants enabling D.C. residents to pay in-state tuition at public colleges elsewhere in the country.

As security around the capital city has tightened and streets have been closed, Norton has pleaded with federal officials to consider the effect of such actions on traffic and tourism. And she has warned that the numerous street closures do not necessarily promote security. "What does it do to security if you bottle up the city?" she asked in 2005.

A native Washingtonian, Norton graduated in the last segregated class at Dunbar High School. Norton's father was a city employee, and her mother was a teacher. After earning a law degree at Yale and working in Mississippi with civil rights groups, she took a job with the American Civil Liberties Union. She ran New York City's Human Rights Commission in the early 1970s and chaired the Equal Employment Opportunity Commission in the Carter administration. She was teaching law at Georgetown University in 1990 when D.C. Delegate Walter E. Fauntroy stepped down to run for mayor. She has been unassailable ever since.

DISTRICT OF COLUMBIA

Residents of the capital city of the world's leading democracy like to point out, often angrily, that they cannot fully participate in democracy themselves: They have no vote in Congress, and the city's budget and laws are subject to review and veto by Congress.

The slogan on the District's license plates sums this up succinctly: "Taxation Without Representation." Efforts to gain full participation in the U.S. government, including bids for statehood, have never come close to success. The 23rd Amendment gave residents a vote for president starting in 1964, and the city elected its first non-voting delegate to the House in 1971 and chose its first elected mayor in 1974.

As the nation's capital, it is no surprise that government is the city's main business. Hundreds of thousands work for the federal and local governments, and thousands of private sector workers — lobbyists, lawyers, trade association employees, and journalists — have jobs related to government work.

The District has one of the wealthier and most-educated populations in the nation. Per capita income in 1999 was about 33 percent higher than the national average. But the income-earners are not spread evenly throughout the city, and the wealthiest areas are in the northwest quadrant.

The city's population peaked in 1950 at more than 800,000 and has been dropping since then, although the decline slowed in the late 1990s. The 2000 census pegged the population at less than 600,000.

MAJOR INDUSTRY
Government, professional services

MILITARY BASES
Walter Reed Army Medical Center, 1,679 military, 2,206 civilian; Bolling Air Force Base, 1,961 military, 1,007 civilian; Fort McNair (Army), 1,017 military, 1,033 civilian (2004)

NOTABLE
Since residents began casting votes for president in 1964, the Republican candidate's share has ranged from a high of 22 percent in 1972 to a low of 9 percent in 2000 and 2004.

Del. Madeleine Z. Bordallo (D)

Elected 2002; 2nd term

With 40 years in public life, Bordallo returns to her second term in the House with a renewed focus on ensuring that Guam is not overlooked by federal and congressional policy makers. Bordallo (bore-DAA-yo) must balance the roles of ambassador, tourism director and House delegate.

As a member of the Armed Services Committee, Bordallo is particularly interested in Guam's military bases, which are in a strategically significant location near Asia, and in bringing home adequate defense and homeland security funds. She has traveled to Iraq with congressional delegations three times since military operations began there.

Bordallo also is a member of the Resources and Small Business committees. In the 109th Congress, she is the top-ranking Democrat on the latter panel's Subcommittee on Regulatory Reform and Oversight.

She says her goals are to promote Guam's economic development, make adjustments in the tax code to benefit the territories, regain land no longer used by the Defense Department, and prod the government to provide restitution for islanders who spent 32 months under Japanese occupation during World War II. She sponsored legislation enacted in 2004 that creates an independent judiciary branch of Guam's government for all cases in which U.S. laws do not have exclusive jurisdiction.

Bordallo's political experience includes five terms in the island legislature, two terms as lieutenant governor, an unsuccessful run for governor and eight years as Guam's first lady. A Minnesota native, she moved to Guam in 1948 when her father took a job there as a high school principal. She went to college in Indiana and Minnesota, earning an associate's degree in music. She then returned to Guam, where she married Ricardo J. Bordallo, a local businessman and aspiring politician. She says her husband, who served two terms as governor and died in 1990, kindled her interest in politics.

In 2002, when five-term Democratic Del. Robert A. Underwood made what proved to be an unsuccessful run for governor of Guam, Bordallo sought the delegate post. She cruised to victory with 65 percent of the vote. She was unopposed for her second term.

CAPITOL OFFICE
225-1188
madeleine.bordallo@mail.house.gov
www.house.gov/bordallo
427 Cannon 20515-5301; fax 226-0341

COMMITTEES
Armed Services
Resources
Small Business

HOMETOWN
Tumuning

BORN
May 31, 1933, Graceville, Minn.

RELIGION
Roman Catholic

FAMILY
Widowed; one child

EDUCATION
St. Mary's College (Ind.), attended 1952-53; The College of St. Catherine, A.A. 1953 (music & voice)

CAREER
Guam first lady; shoe company founder; radio show host

POLITICAL HIGHLIGHTS
Guam Senate, 1981-83, 1987-95; Democratic nominee for governor, 1990; lieutenant governor, 1995-2003

ELECTION RESULTS

2004 GENERAL

Madeleine Z. Bordallo (D)	31,051	97.4%
write-ins	837	2.6%

2002 GENERAL

Madeleine Z. Bordallo (D)	27,081	64.6%
Joseph F. Ada (R)	14,836	35.4%

2002 PRIMARY

Madeleine Z. Bordallo (D)	17,678	59.1%
Judi Won Pat (D)	12,227	40.9%

GUAM

"Where America's Day starts," Guam is the largest and most southerly island in the Marianas archipelago. More than 3,500 miles west of Hawaii, it is closer to Tokyo than Honolulu. Guam is only 212 square miles — about three times the size of the District of Columbia. The population was 154,805 in 2000, a 16 percent increase during the 1990s.

The indigenous people, the Chamorros, first came into contact with Europeans with the visit of Ferdinand Magellan in 1521. Guam was ceded to the United States by Spain in 1898.

The U.S. Navy administered Guam until 1950, when U.S. citizenship was granted and Guamanians elected a local government. Although residents are citizens, they may not vote in presidential elections. Guam has had a non-voting delegate in the House since 1973.

Guam's economy is heavily dependent on U.S. military spending and tourism. The vast majority of visitors are from Japan and the tourism business is subject to the vagaries of the Asian economy. Per capita income in 1999 was $12,722.

Most food and other consumer goods are imported. In recent years, Guam has had to cope with large influxes of illegal immigrants, mostly from China and Burma, who pay smugglers to sneak them onto the island, where they seek asylum in the United States.

Guam has a competitive two-party system: A Republican took the governor's mansion from a Democrat in 2002, while Democrats recaptured control of the Guam Legislature.

MAJOR INDUSTRY
Military, tourism, construction, shipping

MILITARY BASES
Naval Station Guam, 4,050 military, 1,806 civilian; Andersen Air Force Base, 2,170 military, 400 civilian (2004)

DISTRICTS
Dededo, 42,980; Yigo, 19,474; Tamuning, 18,012

NOTABLE
The U.S. mainland is on the opposite side of the International Date Line from Guam.

Res. Cmmsr. Luis Fortuño (R)

Elected 2004; 1st term

The only House member with a four-year term, Fortuño is the first resident commonwealth commissioner to affiliate with the GOP on Capitol Hill. Fortuño (full name: loo-EES four-TOON-yo) plans to work on parochial issues while serving as a conservative Hispanic voice for the GOP.

GOP leaders "from the Speaker on down" have worked to get his voice heard by lining up television and radio access to Hispanic communities across the country, Fortuño says. He is also vice chairman of the conservative Congressional Hispanic Caucus. But Puerto Rico's territorial status remains a hot-button issue, and Fortuño — a statehood advocate — plans to push for a congressionally mandated plebiscite so that Puerto Rican voters can decide among status options, including statehood.

As a non-voting delegate, Fortuño hopes to promote a mix of island interests and national priorities. As a member of the Transportation and Resources committees, Fortuño will support infrastructure development in the commonwealth and increased funding for the Coast Guard. His first bill was to create a wilderness area within the Caribbean National Forest.

His broader political platform embraces tax cuts, a balanced budget, strong defense and a continued embargo of Cuba. He is a strong opponent of abortion and a supporter of faith- and community-based organizations.

But Fortuño may not fit snugly in a single political ideology. While concerned by the budget deficit, he says government funding can help provide a safety net to prevent some people from slipping through the cracks.

Fortuño, an attorney with a law degree from the University of Virginia, was a Georgetown University student when he volunteered on Ronald Reagan's 1980 presidential campaign. Guidance from former Puerto Rican Gov. Luis A. Ferré, a statehood advocate and influential Republican leader, cemented Fortuño's GOP ideals. In 2004, he eked out a razor-thin victory, with the mainland GOP providing Fortuño a rare endorsement. The commonwealth has long been a Democratic stronghold, and Fortuño's campaign marked the first serious GOP challenge in decades.

CAPITOL OFFICE
225-2615
www.house.gov/fortuno
126 Cannon 20515-5401; fax 225-2154

COMMITTEES
Education & Workforce
Resources
Transportation & Infrastructure

HOMETOWN
Guaynabo

BORN
Oct. 31, 1960, San Juan, P.R.

RELIGION
Roman Catholic

FAMILY
Wife, Luce Fortuño; three children

EDUCATION
Georgetown U., B.S.F.S. 1982; U. of Virginia, J.D. 1985

CAREER
Lawyer

POLITICAL HIGHLIGHTS
P.R. Tourism Company executive director, 1993-96; P.R. Economic Development and Commerce secretary, 1994-96

ELECTION RESULTS

2004 GENERAL

Luis Fortuño (NP)	947,098	48.5%
Roberto Prats-Palerm (POPDEM)	937,572	48.0%
Edwin Irizarry (PRI)	55,503	2.8%

2003 PRIMARY

Luis Fortuño (NP)	363,217	61.4%
Carlos A. Romero-Barceló (NP)	151,898	25.7%
Charlie Rodriquez (NP)	37,828	6.4%
Miriam Ramirez (NP)	25,075	4.2%
write-ins	13,931	2.4%

PUERTO RICO

The largest and most populated (3.8 million) of the territories, Puerto Rico has been a self-governing commonwealth of the United States since 1952. The estimated 3.4 million Puerto Ricans living on the U.S. mainland strengthen the island's ties to the United States. Per capita income here is about $8,000 — high by Caribbean standards, but only about half that of the poorest state.

Christopher Columbus arrived in Puerto Rico in 1493. The Spanish arrived 15 years later and soon brought slaves to work in the sugar cane fields. Slavery was abolished in 1873. Spain ceded Puerto Rico to the United States after the Spanish-American War. Its residents became U.S. citizens in 1917, but they cannot vote for president. Since 1901, Puerto Ricans have been represented in the House by a resident commissioner.

The island's political status has been a longstanding issue, with various factions favoring continued commonwealth status, statehood or independence. In 2004, Puerto Ricans made it clear that public opinion is still closely split between statehood and commonwealth status, as voters sent Res. Cmmsr. Fortuño, who favors statehood, to Congress while Anibal Acevedo-Vilá, a strong proponent of commonwealth status, was elected governor.

Puerto Rico's economy is one of the most stable in the Caribbean, thriving off of its tourism industry and industrial sector. Over 4 million tourists visit Puerto Rico per year. U.S. firms also invest heavily here, encouraged by duty-free access to the United States and by tax incentives. But Roosevelt Roads Naval Station's closure in March 2004 cost 6,000 jobs and $300 million a year in revenue.

MAJOR INDUSTRY
Manufacturing, service, tourism

MILITARY BASES
Fort Buchanan, 190 military, 699 civilian (2004)

CITIES
San Juan (unincorporated), 421,958; Bayamón (unincorporated), 203,499

NOTABLE
El Yunque, southeast of San Juan, is the only U.S. tropical forest.

Del. Donna M.C. Christensen (D)

Elected 1996; 5th term

The daughter of a St. Croix judge, Christensen is a physician by training, and tends to focus on the health and economic well-being of her constituents, and to a lesser extent, issues before the Resources Committee, where she is the top-ranking Democrat on the National Parks Subcommittee.

Christensen's medical degree made her a natural to head the Congressional Black Caucus' Health Brain Trust, which focuses on health issues of particular importance to minorities, including the worldwide AIDS epidemic and the reluctance of health maintenance organizations to do business in medically underserved areas. She wants to ensure that her constituents get their share of dollars from federal programs, such as Supplemental Security Income, and has sponsored legislation to lift the cap on the amount of funding the territory can receive for Medicaid.

On Resources, Christensen devotes much of her effort to obtaining incrementally greater autonomy for the Virgin Islands. A member of the Homeland Security panel, she has won funds for local port defense despite criticism that St. Croix is not large enough to merit significant federal spending.

To promote economic development, Christensen has worked for favorable tax and tariff laws to help the V.I., as it is known locally, attract business and industry, including tax incentives for businesses and a continuation of the rum tax rebate.

Inspired by a booklet encouraging African-American students to consider careers in medicine — a pamphlet she had picked up to deliver to someone else — Christensen went to medical school at George Washington University. After postgraduate training in San Francisco and Washington, D.C., she returned to the Virgin Islands, where, during the course of a 20-year medical career, she worked in clinics and hospitals on St. Croix. She eventually moved into administrative posts, including acting commissioner of health.

She unsuccessfully sought the Democratic nomination for the delegate post in 1994 but came back in 1996 to edge Del. Victor O. Frazer, running as an independent, and Republican Kenneth Mapp, in a three-way battle. In 2004, she got about two-thirds of the vote in a three-way battle.

CAPITOL OFFICE
225-1790
donna.christensen@mail.house.gov
www.house.gov/christian-christensen
1510 Longworth 20515-5501; fax 225-5517

COMMITTEES
Resources
Homeland Security
Small Business

HOMETOWN
St. Croix

BORN
Sept. 19, 1945, Teaneck, N.J.

RELIGION
Moravian

FAMILY
Husband, Chris Christensen; two children, four stepchildren

EDUCATION
Saint Mary's College (Ind.), B.S. 1966 (biology); George Washington U., M.D. 1970

CAREER
Physician; health official

POLITICAL HIGHLIGHTS
Virgin Is. Democratic Territorial Committee, 1980-97 (chairwoman, 1980-82); Virgin Is. Board of Education, 1984-86; Virgin Is. acting commissioner of health, 1993-94; sought Democratic nomination for U.S. House, 1994

ELECTION RESULTS

2004 GENERAL

Donna M.C. Christensen (D)	17,379	65.8%
Warren B. Mosler (I)	7,522	28.5%
Krim M. Ballentine (R)	1,512	5.7%

2002 GENERAL

Donna M.C. Christensen (D)	20,414	67.7%
Virdin C. Brown (ICM)	4,456	14.8%
Lilliana Belardo de O'Neal (R)	4,286	14.2%
Garry A. Sprauve (I)	996	3.3%

PREVIOUS WINNING PERCENTAGES
2000 (78%); 1998 (80%); 1996 General Runoff Election (52%)

VIRGIN ISLANDS

The Virgin Islands, just east of Puerto Rico, are known for their subtropical climate, beautiful beaches, duty-free shopping and — far too often — for being in the path of tropical storms. The first three attributes have helped build a thriving tourism industry, while the latter has made economic development an uneven and difficult process.

Spain asserted its authority over the islands after Christopher Columbus arrived in 1493, and over the next century Spanish settlers killed or drove out the native Indians. Spain showed no real interest in establishing a colony on the Virgin Islands, however.

Denmark established a colony on St. Thomas in the latter half of the 17th century. Sugar plantations drove the islands' economy during the 18th and early 19th centuries, until slavery was abolished in 1848. The U.S. government bought the islands from Denmark for $25 million in 1917.

The Virgin Islands is an unincorporated territory, under the jurisdiction of the Interior Department. Residents are U.S. citizens but may not vote for president. The Virgin Islands has had a non-voting House delegate since 1973.

The U.S. Virgin Islands is actually composed of 68 islands and cays — but only four are inhabited. The territory had a population in 2000 of 108,612, a 7 percent increase over 1990.

Cruise ships make regular stops at the islands, principally at the capital of Charlotte Amalie on St. Thomas, and passengers stream ashore to take advantage of duty-free shopping. Most of the Virgin Islands' tourists arrive on cruise ships and leave without spending a night.

MAJOR INDUSTRY
Tourism, petroleum refining, rum distilling, watch assembly

CITIES
Charlotte Amalie, 11,004; Christiansted, 2,637

NOTABLE
Buck Island Reef National Monument in St. Croix is mainly underwater.

Did You Know?

Knowing a lawmaker's political party or state can be helpful in understanding a member of Congress.

But there are many other factors that contribute to members' priorities and interests and to their standing in the congressional universe. Seniority or committee assignments, for example, can provide some insight into a member's clout and areas of expertise. Which informal congressional groups they belong to, how they vote with respect to the wishes of their party or the president, or how various interest groups view their voting records can also be useful in getting a handle on a particular member.

Each member's background contains unique experiences and interests that often provide some insight into his or her behavior as a member of Congress. And sometimes these personal tidbits can offer a fascinating humanizing touch. For example, did you know that:

Neil Abercrombie, D-Hawaii, wrote a novel in which 125 members of the House were killed.

Gary L. Ackerman, D-N.Y., used to live on a houseboat named "Unsinkable." It sank.

The **Arkansas** delegation is well-versed in the medical field: **Marion Berry**, D, is a pharmacist; **John Boozman**, R, is an optometrist; **Mike Ross**, D, owns a pharmacy; **Vic Snyder**, D, is an M.D. — and **Blanche Lincoln**, D, is married to a physician.

Roscoe G. Bartlett, R-Md., holds 20 patents.

One of **Evan Bayh**'s, D-Ind., babysitters was Lynda Bird Johnson, the president's daughter.

Jeb Bradley, R-N.H., is a member of the Appalachian Mountain Club's Four Thousand Footer Club, signifying that he has climbed all 48 of New Hampshire's peaks of 4,000 feet or more.

Jim Bunning, R-Ky., is a member of the Baseball Hall of Fame.

Thomas R. Carper, D-Del., campaigned for Barry Goldwater in 1964 and Eugene McCarthy in 1968.

To pay for his education at the University of Maryland, **William Lacy Clay**, D-Mo., was a House doorman for seven years.

James E. Clyburn, D-S.C., is the first black elected to Congress from South Carolina since 1896. The last was his great-uncle, George Washington Murray.

Minnesota GOP Sen. **Norm Coleman** and New York Democratic Sen. **Charles E. Schumer** were high school classmates in Brooklyn.

Elijah E. Cummings, D-Md., was thousands of dollars in debt when he arrived in the House. He spent two winters without heat because he couldn't afford to fix his furnace.

Randy "Duke" Cunningham, R-Calif., was the first air ace of the Vietnam War. Later, he was a "top gun" flight instructor.

An aunt of Florida GOP brothers **Lincoln Diaz-Balart** and **Mario Diaz-Balart** was once married to Fidel Castro.

John D. Dingell, D-Mich., succeeded his father. A Dingell has represented Michigan since 1933.

In high school, **Rahm Emanuel**, D-Ill., took a ballet class to improve his soccer agility and liked it so much that he continued to study dance while working on his college degree.

When **Anna G. Eshoo**, D-Calif., was a schoolgirl in Connecticut, President Truman gave her a ride home from school.

American Samoa Democratic Del. **Eni F.H. Faleomavaega**'s last name is Hunkin. Faleomavaega is a Samoan title.

Chaka Fattah, D-Pa., was born Arthur Davenport. Fattah's mother changed his name when she married community activist David Fattah. She called him "Chaka" in honor of a Zulu warrior.

Tom Feeney, R-Fla., has an early edition of economist Adam Smith's seminal 1776 book "Wealth of Nations."

Rodney Frelinghuysen, R-N.J., is the sixth member of his family to serve in Congress.

Republican **Luis Fortuño**, the resident commissioner from Puerto Rico, is the only member of Congress with a four-year term.

Bill Frist, R-Tenn., didn't register to vote until he was 36.

Charles E. Grassley, R-Iowa, returns to Iowa to work the family corn and soybean fields on weekends and has been known to drive his tractor with a cell phone tucked inside his cap so he can feel the vibrations of an incoming call.

Gil Gutknecht, R-Minn., has a culinary passion for Spam and persuaded the Library of Congress to hold an exhibit on the lunchmeat.

As a young Hill aide, **Tom Harkin**, D-Iowa, discovered the "tiger cages," squalid underground cells where the South Vietnamese government secretly kept prisoners of war. Harkin's revelation of abuses by America's ally got worldwide attention.

A former federal judge, **Alcee L. Hastings**, D-Fla., was impeached and removed from office.

Orrin G. Hatch, R-Utah, is a songwriter, with a repertoire ranging from bossa nova to rock and rap. His songs have been on movie soundtracks.

Joel Hefley, R-Colo., won a coin flip with a colleague in the state legislature to determine which of them would run for Congress.

Rush D. Holt, D-N.J., a physicist, is a former champion on the TV quiz show "Jeopardy."

Both **Darlene Hooley**, D-Ore., and **Patty Murray**, D-Wash., got involved in politics because of faulty playground equipment.

Jesse L. Jackson Jr., D-Ill., vacuums his office carpet for relaxation.

Sam Johnson, R-Texas, spent almost seven years in a North Vietnamese prison camp. For a brief stretch, he roomed with **John McCain**, R-Ariz.

Paul E. Kanjorski, D-Pa., a licensed attorney since 1966, never graduated from law school. (He didn't graduate from college, either.)

During his service in the Marine Corps, Minnesota Republican **John Kline** carried the "football" — the briefcase with nuclear war codes — for Presidents Carter and Reagan and flew the presidential helicopter, Marine One.

Dennis J. Kucinich, D-Ohio, was so unpopular as mayor of Cleveland that he wore a bulletproof vest to throw out the first pitch at an Indians game.

Tom Lantos, D-Calif., fought with the Hungarian resistance against the Nazis. He escaped from a Nazi work camp.

Jim Leach, R-Iowa, quit the Foreign Service to protest the 1973 "Saturday Night Massacre."

John Lewis, D-Ga., was a leader of the famous civil rights march in Selma, Ala., in 1965.

A 24-year-old Yale law student named Bill Clinton campaigned for **Joseph I. Lieberman**, D-Conn., in 1970, as Lieberman ran for the state Senate.

Trent Lott, R-Miss., was an aide to a Democratic member of the House.

Stephen F. Lynch, D-Mass., donated more than half of his liver to his brother.

Thaddeus McCotter, R-Mich., once played in a band named Sir Funk-a-Lot and the Knights of the Terrestrial Jam.

At the beginning of the 109th Congress, **Barbara A. Mikulski**, D-Md., was the fourth-most-senior woman in congressional history.

Candice S. Miller, R-Mich., earned the title "Old Goat," in 2001 when she competed in her 25th Port Huron to Mackinac Island sailboat race.

Lisa Murkowski, R-Alaska, is the first woman to represent Alaska. She is also the first person ever appointed to the Senate by her father.

Jim Nussle, R-Iowa, once spoke on the House floor with a paper bag over his head.

As a youth, **David R. Obey**, D-Wis., campaigned for Sen. Joseph R. McCarthy.

Major R. Owens, D-N.Y., writes rap lyrics and poetry.

Of the 43 House votes in the 108th Congress on which there was a solitary nay, **Ron Paul**, R-Texas, cast that vote 29 times.

As a girl, **Nancy Pelosi**, D-Calif., slept above stacks of issues of the Congressional Record. Her father, Thomas D'Alesandro Jr., was a Maryland congressman and

stored them under her bed.

Collin C. Peterson, D-Minn., plays guitar in a country rock band.

Todd R. Platts, R-Pa., commutes to Capitol Hill every day from his home in York, Pa. — 200 miles round trip.

David E. Price, D-N.C., helped judge Illinois Democrat **Daniel Lipinski**'s doctoral thesis at Duke University.

Adam H. Putnam, R-Fla., chaired the Agriculture Committee in the Florida House when he was 24. From 2001-2005, he was the youngest member of Congress.

Ralph Regula, R-Ohio, works to preserve the memory of William McKinley.

Dave Reichert, R-Wash., was the original lead detective in the Green River serial killer task force. Almost 20 years later, as the King County sheriff, he announced the arrest of Gary Ridgway in 2001.

Harry Reid, D-Nev., took on organized crime as chairman of the Nevada Gaming Commission. A bomb was once found under the hood of his car.

John D. Rockefeller IV, D-W.Va., says his favorite food is lima beans.

Dana Rohrabacher, R-Calif., says John Wayne taught him how to drink tequila.

Ileana Ros-Lehtinen, R-Fla., is the first Hispanic woman elected to Congress.

New Jersey Democratic Rep. **Steven R. Rothman** in 2004 took out a personal ad with an online Jewish dating service. The ad identified him only as Steve3366 and a Libra, but under profession he wrote: "U.S. Congress."

Bobby L. Rush, D-Ill., is a former Black Panther. He served six months in prison on a weapons charge.

Jim Ryun, R-Kan., made the cover of Sports Illustrated when he was still in high school.

Colorado Democratic Sen. **Ken Salazar**'s favorite place to eat is a Dairy Queen. (He and his wife own the place.)

H. James Saxton, R-N.J., and **Don Sherwood**, R-Pa., were childhood buddies; they grew up three doors apart in the hamlet of Nicholson, Pa.

F. James Sensenbrenner Jr., R-Wis., was one of the wealthiest members of Congress even before he won $250,000 in the D.C. lottery.

José E. Serrano, D-N.Y., learned to speak English by listening to Frank Sinatra records.

John M. Spratt Jr., D-S.C., broke his arm when he slipped on some Senate bean soup.

A former teacher, **Tom Tancredo**, R-Colo., first ran for office on a dare from his students.

John Thune, R-S.D., was involved in one of the five closest congressional races in both 2002 and 2004 — first losing the second-closest race in 2002 and then winning the fourth-closest in 2004.

Lynn Woolsey, D-Calif., went on welfare after a divorce left her on her own with three young children and no job skills.

Peace Corps Volunteers

Members of Congress who have served in the Peace Corps:

Member	Country	Years
Sen. Christopher J. Dodd, D-Conn.	Dominican Republic	1966-68
Rep. Sam Farr, D-Calif.	Colombia	1964-66
Rep. Michael M. Honda, D-Calif.	El Salvador	1965-67
Rep. Tom Petri, R-Wis.	Somalia	1966-67
Rep. Christopher Shays, R-Conn.	Fiji	1968-70
Rep. James T. Walsh, R-N.Y.	Nepal	1970-72

Rhodes Scholars

Members of Congress who have been Rhodes scholars:

Rep. Tom Allen, D-Maine
Rep. Jim Cooper, D-Tenn.
Sen. Russell D. Feingold, D-Wis.
Rep. Bobby Jindal, R-La.
Sen. Richard G. Lugar, R-Ind.
Sen. Paul S. Sarbanes, D-Md.
Sen. David Vitter, R-La.
Rep. Heather A. Wilson, R-N.M.

Former Pages

Members of Congress who once served as congressional pages:

Member	Years
Rep. Dan Boren, D-Okla.	1989
Rep. Jim Cooper, D-Tenn.	1970
Rep. Ander Crenshaw, R-Fla.	1961
Rep. Thomas M. Davis III, R-Va.	1963-67
Rep. John D. Dingell, D-Mich.	1938-42
Sen. Christopher J. Dodd, D-Conn.	c. 1960
Rep. Rush D. Holt, D-N.J.	1963-64
Rep. Paul E. Kanjorski, D-Pa.	1953-54
Rep. Jim Kolbe, R-Ariz.	1958-60
Sen. Mark Pryor, D-Ark.	1982
Rep. Roger Wicker, R-Miss.	1967

Born Abroad

Members of Congress who were born outside of the 50 states and the District of Columbia:

Member	Country
Rep. Geoff Davis, R-Ky.	Canada
Rep. Diana DeGette, D-Colo.	Japan
Rep. Lincoln Diaz-Balart, R-Fla.	Cuba
Rep. Peter Hoekstra, R-Mich.	Netherlands
Rep. Tom Lantos, D-Calif.	Hungary
Sen. Mel Martinez, R-Fla.	Cuba
Sen. John McCain, R-Ariz.	Panama Canal Zone
Rep. Ileana Ros-Lehtinen, R-Fla.	Cuba
Rep. José E. Serrano, D-N.Y.	Puerto Rico
Rep. Chris Van Hollen, D-Md.	Pakistan
Rep. Nydia M. Velázquez, D-N.Y.	Puerto Rico
Rep. David Wu, D-Ore.	Taiwan

Fastest Members of Congress

Each year a number of members of Congress participate in a three-mile footrace in Washington, D.C. Here are the best times posted by current members of Congress in the 2004 race:

Member	Time	Member	Time
Rep. Bart Gordon, D-Tenn.	18:22	Sen. Jack Reed, D-R.I.	24:13
Sen. John E. Sununu, R-N.H.	19:47	Rep. Kenny Hulshof, R-Mo.	24:54
Rep. Earl Pomeroy, D-N.D.	20:38	Rep. Jay Inslee, D-Wash.	25:22
Rep. Tom Feeney, R-Fla.	20:40	Rep. Brian Baird, D-Wash.	25:41
Sen. John Ensign, R-Nev.	20:41	Rep. C. L. "Butch" Otter, R-Idaho	27:42
Rep. Jim Ryun, R-Kan.	20:59	Sen. Jeff Bingaman, D-N.M.	26:37
Rep. Zack Wamp, R-Tenn.	21:03	Sen. Charles E. Grassley, R-Iowa	29:07
Sen. Lincoln Chafee, R-R.I.	21:25	Rep. James P. Moran, D-Va.	30:30
Rep. Jim Marshall, D-Ga.	21:29	Sen. John Cornyn, R-Texas	30:41
Rep. Tim Ryan, D-Ohio	23:18	Rep. Ray LaHood, R-Ill.	31:58
Rep. Jack Kingston, R-Ga.	23:49	Sen. Kay Bailey Hutchison, R-Texas	33:59
Rep. Mark Udall, D-Colo.	24:02	Sen. Richard G. Lugar, R-Ind.	34:40
Rep. Earl Blumenauer, D-Ore.	24:10	Sen. Craig Thomas, R-Wyo.	38:30
Rep. Peter A. DeFazio, D-Ore.	24:12		

Former Congressional Staffers

Members who were paid, full-time congressional aides. Internships and campaign work are not included.

Member	Congressional Office	Years
Sen. Lamar Alexander, R-Tenn.	Sen. Howard H. Baker Jr., R-Tenn.	1967-68
Rep. Tom Allen, D-Maine	Sen. Edmund S. Muskie, D-Maine	1970-71
Rep. Charles Bass, R-N.H.	Rep. William S. Cohen, R-Maine	1974
	Rep. David F. Emery, R-Maine	1976-79
Sen. Robert F. Bennett, R-Utah	Rep. Sherman P. Lloyd, R-Utah	1963
	Sen. Wallace Bennett, R-Utah	1963-64
Rep. Sherwood Boehlert, R-N.Y.	Rep. Alexander Pirnie, R-N.Y.	1964-72
	Rep. Donald J. Mitchell, R-N.Y.	1973-79
Rep. Jo Bonner, R-Ala.	Rep. Sonny Callahan, R-Ala.	1985-2002
Rep. Dan Boren, D-Okla.	Rep. Wes Watkins, R-Okla.	2000-01
Sen. Barbara Boxer, D-Calif.	Rep. John L. Burton, D-Calif.	1974-76
Rep. Dave Camp, R-Mich.	Rep. Bill Schuette, R-Mich.	1984-87
Rep. Dennis Cardoza, D-Calif.	Rep. Gary A. Condit, D-Calif.	1989
Rep. Julia M. Carson, D-Ind.	Rep. Andrew Jacobs Jr., D-Ind.	1965-72
Rep. Ed Case, D-Hawaii	Rep./Sen. Spark M. Matsunaga, D-Hawaii	1975-78
Rep. William Lacy Clay, D-Mo.	House Clerk	1977-83
Rep. Tom Cole, R-Okla.	Rep. Mickey Edwards, R-Okla.	1982-84
Sen. Susan Collins, R-Maine	Rep./Sen. William S. Cohen, R-Maine	1975-87
Rep. John Conyers Jr., D-Mich.	Rep. John D. Dingell, D-Mich.	1958-61
Rep. Jim Costa, D-Calif.	Rep. John Krebs, D-Calif.	1975-76
Sen. Mark Dayton, D-Minn.	Sen. Walter F. Mondale, D-Minn.	1975-76
Rep. Peter A. DeFazio, D-Ore.	Rep. James Weaver, D-Ore.	1977-82
Rep. Rosa DeLauro, D-Conn.	Sen. Christopher J. Dodd, D-Conn.	1981-87
Rep. Charlie Dent, R-Pa.	Rep. Don Ritter, R-Pa.	1982
Rep. Norm Dicks, D-Wash.	Sen. Warren G. Magnuson, D-Wash.	1968-76
Rep. Chet Edwards, D-Texas	Rep. Olin E. Teague, D-Texas	1974-77
Del. Eni F.H. Faleomavaega, D-Am. Samoa	Del. A.U. Fuimaono, D-Am. Samoa	1973-75
	House Interior and Insular Affairs Committee	1975-81
Rep. Bob Filner, D-Calif.	Sen. Hubert H. Humphrey, D-Minn.	1975
	Rep. Donald M. Fraser, D-Minn.	1976
	Rep. Jim Bates, D-Calif.	1984
Rep. Jeff Fortenberry, R-Neb.	Senate Governmental Affairs subcommittee	1985-86
Rep. Barney Frank, D-Mass.	Rep. Michael Harrington, D-Mass.	1971-72
Rep. Robert W. Goodlatte, R-Va.	Rep. M. Caldwell Butler, R-Va.	1977-79
Sen. Chuck Hagel, R-Neb.	Rep. John Y. McCollister, R-Neb.	1971-77
Sen. Tom Harkin, D-Iowa	Rep. Neal Smith, D-Iowa	1969-70
Rep. Jane Harman, D-Calif.	Sen. John V. Tunney, D-Calif.	1972-73
	Senate Judiciary Committee	1975-77
Rep. Jeb Hensarling, R-Texas	Sen. Phil Gramm, R-Texas	1985-89
Rep. Steve Israel, D-N.Y.	Rep. Richard L. Ottinger, D-N.Y.	1980-83
Rep. Sheila Jackson-Lee, D-Texas	House Select Committee on Assassinations	1977-78
Rep. William J. Jefferson, D-La.	Sen. J. Bennett Johnston Jr., D-La.	1973-75
Rep. Mark Steven Kirk, R-Ill.	Rep. John Edward Porter, R-Ill.	1984-89
	House International Relations Committee	1995-2000
Rep. Ray LaHood, R-Ill.	Rep. Tom Railsback, R-Ill.	1977-82
	Rep. Robert H. Michel, R-Ill.	1983-94
Rep. Tom Lantos, D-Calif.	Sen. Joseph R. Biden Jr., D-Del.	1980
Rep. Jim Leach, R-Iowa	Rep. Donald H. Rumsfeld, R-Ill.	1965-66
Rep. Barbara Lee, D-Calif.	Rep. Ronald V. Dellums, D-Calif.	1975-86
Rep. Jerry Lewis, R-Calif.	Rep. Jerry L. Pettis, R-Calif.	1967
Sen. Blanche Lincoln, D-Ark.	Rep. Bill Alexander, D-Ark.	1982-84

Rep. Daniel Lipinski, D-Ill.	Rep. Rod R. Blagojevich, D-Ill.	1999-2000
Rep. Zoe Lofgren, D-Calif.	Rep. Don Edwards, D-Calif.	1970-79
Sen. Trent Lott, R-Miss.	Rep. William M. Colmer, D-Miss.	1968-72
Sen. Mitch McConnell, R-Ky.	Sen. Marlow W. Cook, R-Ky.	1969-70
Rep. Jim McCrery, R-La.	Rep. Buddy Roemer, D-La.	1981-84
Rep. Jim McGovern, D-Mass.	Rep. Joe Moakley, D-Mass.	1981-93
Rep. Martin T. Meehan, D-Mass.	Rep. James M. Shannon, D-Mass.	1979-81
Rep. John L. Mica, R-Fla.	Sen. Paula Hawkins, R-Fla.	1981-85
Rep. James P. Moran, D-Va.	Senate Appropriations Committee	1976-79
Rep. James L. Oberstar, D-Minn.	Rep. John A. Blatnik, D-Minn.	1964-74
Rep. Charles W. "Chip" Pickering Jr., R-Miss.	Sen. Trent Lott, R-Miss.	1991-95
Rep. Nick J. Rahall II, D-W.Va.	Sen. Robert C. Byrd, D-W.Va.	1971-74
Rep. Jim Ramstad, R-Minn.	Rep. Tom Kleppe, R-N.D.	1970
Rep. Denny Rehberg, R-Mont.	Rep. Ron Marlenee, R-Mont.	1979-82
	Sen. Conrad Burns, R-Mont.	1989-91
Sen. Pat Roberts, R-Kan.	Sen. Frank Carlson, R-Kan.	1967-68
	Rep. Keith G. Sebelius, R-Kan.	1968-80
Rep. Paul D. Ryan, R-Wis.	Sen. Bob Kasten, R-Wis.	1992
	Rep./Sen. Sam Brownback, R-Kan.	1995-97
Rep. Tim Ryan, D-Ohio	Rep. James A. Traficant Jr., D-Ohio	1995-97
Rep. Rob Simmons, R-Conn.	Sen. John H. Chafee, R-R.I.	1979-81
	Senate Intelligence Committee	1981-85
Sen. Olympia J. Snowe, R-Maine	Rep. William S. Cohen, R-Maine	1973
Rep. Mark Souder, R-Ind.	Rep./Sen. Daniel R. Coats, R-Ind.	1983-85, 89-93
	House Select Committee on Children, Youth & Families	1985-89
Rep. William M. "Mac" Thornberry, R-Texas	Rep. Tom Loeffler, R-Texas	1983-85
	Rep. Larry Combest, R-Texas	1985-88
Sen. John Thune, R-S.D.	Sen. James Abdnor, R-S.D.	1985-86
Rep. Pat Tiberi, R-Ohio	Rep. John R. Kasich, R-Ohio	1983-91
Rep. Fred Upton, R-Mich.	Rep. David A. Stockman, R-Mich.	1977-81
Rep. Chris Van Hollen, D-Md.	Sen. Charles McC. Mathias Jr., R-Md.	1985-87
	Senate Foreign Relations Committee	1987-89
Rep. Nydia N. Velázquez, D-N.Y.	Rep. Edolphus Towns, D-N.Y.	1983
Rep. Peter J. Visclosky, D-Ind.	Rep. Adam Benjamin Jr., D-Ind.	1977-82
Rep. Greg Walden, R-Ore.	Rep. Denny Smith, R-Ore.	1981-86
Rep. Anthony Weiner, D-N.Y.	Rep. Charles E. Schumer, D-N.Y.	1985-91
Rep. Jerry Weller, R-Ill.	Rep. Tom Corcoran, R-Ill.	1980-81
Rep. Roger Wicker, R-Miss.	Rep. Trent Lott, R-Miss.	1980-82
Rep. Frank R. Wolf, R-Va.	Rep. Edward G. Biester, R-Pa.	1968-71

Members With Parents Who Served in Congress

There are 30 members of Congress whose mother or father also served in Congress. Twelve of the people on the list — Chafee, Clay, Dingell, Duncan, Ford, Gonzalez, Lipinski, Meek, Mollohan, Murkowski, Roybal-Allard and Shuster — directly succeeded their parent. Jones is the only member on the list who belongs to a different political party than his parent.

Member	Parent	Years Parent Served
Rep. Charles Bass, R-N.H.	Rep. Perkins Bass, R-N.H.	1955-63
Sen. Evan Bayh, D-Ind.	Sen. Birch Bayh, D-Ind.	1963-81
Sen. Robert F. Bennett, R-Utah	Sen. Wallace F. Bennett, R-Utah	1951-74
Rep. Dan Boren, D-Okla.	Sen. David L. Boren, D-Okla.	1979-94
Rep. Shelley Moore Capito, R-W.Va.	Rep. Arch A. Moore Jr., R-W.Va.	1957-69
Rep. Russ Carnahan, D-Mo.	Sen. Jean Carnahan, D-Mo.	2001-02
Sen. Lincoln Chafee, R-R.I.	Sen. John H. Chafee, R-R.I.	1976-99
Rep. William Lacy Clay, D-Mo.	Rep. William L. Clay, D-Mo.	1969-2001
Rep. John D. Dingell, D-Mich.	Rep. John D. Dingell Sr., D-Mich.	1933-55
Sen. Christopher J. Dodd, D-Conn.	Rep./Sen. Thomas J. Dodd, D-Conn.	1953-57, 1959-71
Rep. John J. "Jimmy" Duncan Jr., R-Tenn.	Rep. John J. Duncan, R-Tenn.	1965-88
Rep. Harold E. Ford Jr., D-Tenn.	Rep. Harold E. Ford, D-Tenn.	1975-97
Rep. Rodney Frelinghuysen, R-N.J.	Rep. Peter H. Frelinguysen, R-N.J.	1953-75
Rep. Charlie Gonzalez, D-Texas	Rep. Henry B. Gonzalez, D-Texas	1961-99
Rep. Rush D. Holt, D-N.J.	Sen. Rush Dew Holt, D-W.Va.	1935-41
Rep. Walter B. Jones, R-N.C.	Rep. Walter B. Jones Sr., D-N.C.	1966-92
Rep. Patrick J. Kennedy, D-R.I.	Sen. Edward M. Kennedy, D-Mass.	1962-present
Sen. Jon Kyl, R-Ariz.	Rep. John H. Kyl, R-Iowa	1959-65, 1967-73
Rep. Dan Lipinski, D-Ill.	Rep. William O. Lipinski, D-Ill.	1983-2005
Rep. Connie Mack, R-Fla.	Rep./Sen. Connie Mack, R-Fla.	1983-2001
Rep. Kendrick B. Meek, D-Fla.	Rep. Carrie P. Meek, D-Fla.	1993-2003
Rep. Alan B. Mollohan, D-W.Va.	Rep. Robert H. Mollohan, D-W.Va.	1953-57, 1969-83
Sen. Lisa Murkowski, R-Alaska	Sen. Frank H. Murkowski, R-Alaska	1981-2002
Rep. Nancy Pelosi, D-Calif.	Rep. Thomas D'Alesandro Jr., D-Md.	1939-47
Sen. Mark Pryor, D-Ark.	Rep./Sen. David Pryor, D-Ark.	1966-73, 1979-97
Rep. Lucille Roybal-Allard, D-Calif.	Rep. Edward R. Roybal, D-Calif.	1963-93
Rep. Bill Shuster, R-Pa.	Rep. Bud Shuster, R-Pa.	1973-2001
Rep. Mark Udall, D-Colo.	Rep. Morris K. Udall, D-Ariz.	1961-91
Rep. Tom Udall, D-N.M.	Rep. Stewart L. Udall, D-Ariz.	1955-61
Rep. James T. Walsh, R-N.Y.	Rep. William F. Walsh, R-N.Y.	1973-79

Members Whose Spouses Served in Congress

Member	Spouse	Spouse's Service
Rep. Mary Bono, R-Calif.	Rep. Sonny Bono, R-Calif.	1995-98
Rep. Lois Capps, D-Calif.	Rep. Walter Capps, D-Calif.	1997
Sen. Elizabeth Dole, R-N.C.	Rep./Sen. Bob Dole, R-Kan.	1961-96
Rep. Jo Ann Emerson, R-Mo.	Rep. Bill Emerson, R-Mo.	1981-96
Rep. Doris Matsui, D-Calif.	Rep. Robert T. Matsui, D-Calif.	1979-2005
Sen. Olympia J. Snowe, R-Maine	Rep. John R. McKernan Jr., R-Maine	1983-87

Party Switchers

Members who changed their party affiliations after their election to Congress. A number of other members switched parties before coming to Congress.

Member	Old Party	New Party	Date Switched
Rep. Rodney Alexander, La.	D	R	Sept. 7, 2004
Rep. Nathan Deal, Ga.	D	R	April 10, 1995
Rep. Virgil H. Goode Jr., Va.	D	I	Jan. 24, 2000
Rep. Virgil H. Goode Jr., Va.	I	R	Jan. 24, 2000
Rep. Ralph M. Hall, Texas	D	R	Jan. 5, 2004
Sen. James M. Jeffords, Vt.	R	I	June 5, 2001
Sen. Richard C. Shelby, Ala.	D	R	Nov. 9, 1994

Congressional Half-Life

Members who have served more than half of their lives in Congress. Length of service is as of Jan. 4, 2005.

Member	Age at Swearing-in	Length of Service	Percent of Life in Congress
Rep. John D. Dingell, D-Mich.	29 years, 158 days	49 years, 22 days	63%
Sen. Robert C. Byrd, D-W.Va.	35 years, 44 days	52 years	60
Sen. Edward M. Kennedy, D-Mass.	30 years, 258 days	42 years, 58 days	58
Sen. Daniel K. Inouye, D-Hawaii	34 years, 348 days	45 years, 136 days	56
Rep. David R. Obey, D-Wis.	30 years, 180 days	35 years, 278 days	54
Rep. John Conyers Jr., D-Mich.	35 years, 233 days	40 years	53
Sen. Joseph R. Biden Jr., D-Del.	30 years, 44 days	32 years	52
Sen. Trent Lott, R-Miss.	31 years, 86 days	32 years	51
Rep. Nick J. Rahall II, D-W.Va.	27 years, 229 days	28 years	50
Rep. George Miller, D-Calif.	29 years, 303 days	30 years	50

Note: Sen. Christopher J. Dodd, D-Conn., who began serving in the House of Representatives in 1975, is due to join the list Sept. 3, 2005, when he will have served 30 years, 232 days.

10 Oldest Members of Congress

Member	Birthdate
Sen. Robert C. Byrd, D-W.Va.	Nov. 20, 1917
Rep. Ralph M. Hall, R-Texas	May 3, 1923
Sen. Ted Stevens, R-Alaska	Nov. 18, 1923
Sen. Frank R. Lautenberg, D-N.J.	Jan. 23, 1924
Rep. Henry J. Hyde, R-Ill.	April 18, 1924
Sen. Daniel K. Inouye, D-Hawaii	Sept. 7, 1924
Sen. Daniel K. Akaka, D-Hawaii	Sept. 11, 1924
Rep. Ralph Regula, R-Ohio	Dec. 3, 1924
Rep. Roscoe G. Bartlett, R-Md.	June 3, 1926
Rep. John D. Dingell, D-Mich.	July 8, 1926

10 Youngest Members of Congress

Member	Birthdate
Rep. Patrick T. McHenry, R-N.C.	Oct. 22, 1975
Rep. Adam H. Putnam, R-Fla.	July 31, 1974
Rep. Devin Nunes, R-Calif.	Oct. 1, 1973
Ran. Dan Boren, D-Okla.	Aug. 2, 1973
Rep. Tim Ryan, D-Ohio	July 16, 1973
Rep. Bobby Jindal, R-La.	June 10, 1971
Rep. Stephanie Herseth, D-S.D.	Dec. 3, 1970
Rep. Mike Ferguson, R-N.J.	July 22, 1970
Rep. Harold E. Ford Jr., D-Tenn.	May 11, 1970
Rep. Paul D. Ryan, R-Wis.	Jan. 29, 1970

Members Who Served in the Military

The list includes 109 members of the House and 31 senators. Included is service in the National Guard and reserves. The years of service includes both active and inactive duty. An asterisk denotes a combat veteran.

Senate	Years
Daniel K. Akaka, D-Hawaii *	1945-47
Robert F. Bennett, R-Utah	1957-60
Jeff Bingaman, D-N.M.	1968-74
Conrad Burns, R-Mont.	1955-57
Thomas R. Carper, D-Del. *	1968-92
Thad Cochran, R-Miss.	1959-61
Jon Corzine, D-N.J.	1969-75
Larry E. Craig, R-Idaho	1970-72
Christopher J. Dodd, D-Conn.	1969-75
Michael B. Enzi, R-Wyo.	1967-73
Lindsey Graham, R-S.C.	1982-present
Chuck Hagel, R-Neb. *	1967-68
Tom Harkin, D-Iowa	1962-74
James M. Inhofe, R-Okla.	1956-58
Daniel K. Inouye, D-Hawaii *	1943-47
Johnny Isakson, R-Ga.	1966-72
James M. Jeffords, I-Vt.	1956-90
Edward M. Kennedy, D-Mass.	1951-53
John Kerry, D-Mass. *	1966-70
Herb Kohl, D-Wis.	1958-64
Frank R. Lautenberg, D-N.J.	1942-46
Richard G. Lugar, R-Ind.	1957-60
John McCain, R-Ariz. *	1958-81
Bill Nelson, D-Fla.	1968-71
Jack Reed, D-R.I.	1971-91
Pat Roberts, R-Kan.	1958-62
Jeff Sessions, R-Ala.	1973-86
Arlen Specter, R-Pa.	1951-53
Ted Stevens, R-Alaska *	1943-46
Craig Thomas, R-Wyo.	1955-59
John W. Warner, R-Va. *	1944-46, 1950-64

House	Years
Todd Akin, R-Mo.	1972-80
Rodney Alexander, R-La.	1965-71
Joe Baca, D-Calif.	1966-68
Spencer Bachus, R-Ala.	1969-71
J. Gresham Barrett, R-S.C.	1983-87
Michael Bilirakis, R-Fla.	1951-55
Sanford D. Bishop Jr., D-Ga.	1971
Sherwood Boehlert, R-N.Y.	1956-58
John A. Boehner, R-Ohio	1968
Leonard L. Boswell, D-Iowa *	195-76
Allen Boyd, D-Fla. *	1969-71
Henry E. Brown Jr., R-S.C.	1953-62
Dan Burton, R-Ind.	1956-62
G.K. Butterfield, D-N.C.	1968-70
Steve Buyer, R-Ind. *	1980-present
Howard Coble, R-N.C. *	1952-56, 60-82
K. Michael Conaway, R-Texas	1970-72

	Years
John Conyers Jr., D-Mich. *	1948-57
Robert E. "Bud" Cramer, D-Ala.	1972, 76-78
Randy "Duke" Cunningham, R-Calif. *	1966-87
Thomas M. Davis III, R-Va.	1971-79
Geoff Davis, R-Ky.	1976-87
Nathan Deal, R-Ga.	1966-68
Peter A. DeFazio, D-Ore.	1967-71
Bill Delahunt, D-Mass.	1963-71
John D. Dingell, D-Mich. *	1944-46
John J. "Jimmy" Duncan Jr., R-Tenn.	1970-87
Bob Etheridge, D-N.C.	1965-67
Lane Evans, D-Ill.	1969-71
Terry Everett, R-Ala.	1955-59
Eni F.H. Faleomavaega, D-Am. Samoa	1966-69, 83-2001
Rodney Frelinghuysen, R-N.J. *	1969-71
Jim Gibbons, R-Nev.*	1967-71, 75-95
Wayne T. Gilchrest, R-Md. *	1964-68
Paul E. Gillmor, R-Ohio	1965-66
Louie Gohmert, R-Texas	1978-82
Charlie Gonzalez, D-Texas	1969-75
Virgil H. Goode Jr., R-Va.	1969-75
Bart Gordon, D-Tenn.	1971-72
Ralph M. Hall, R-Texas *	1942-45
Doc Hastings, R-Wash.	1964-69
Maurice D. Hinchey, D-N.Y.	1956-59
David L. Hobson, R-Ohio	1958-63
Duncan Hunter, R-Calif. *	1969-71
Henry J. Hyde, R-Ill. *	1944-68
Darrell Issa, R-Calif.	1970-72, 76-88
William J. Jefferson, D-La.	1969-75
Bill Jenkins, R-Tenn.	1959-69
Sam Johnson, R-Texas *	1951-79
Walter B. Jones, R-N.C.	1967-71
Paul E. Kanjorski, D-Pa.	1960-61
Peter T. King, R-N.Y.	1968-73
Mark Steven Kirk, R-Ill. *	1989
John Kline, R-Minn.*	1969-94
Joe Knollenberg, R-Mich.	1955-57
Jim Kolbe, R-Ariz. *	1965-77
Ron Lewis, R-Ky.	1972
John Linder, R-Ga.	1967-69
Edward J. Markey, D-Mass.	1968-73
Jim Marshall, D-Ga. *	1968-70
Jim McDermott, D-Wash.	1968-70
Gary G. Miller, R-Calif.	1967-68
Alan B. Mollohan, D-W.Va.	1970-83
Dennis Moore, D-Kan.	1970-73
John P. Murtha, D-Pa. *	1952-55, 66-90
Charlie Norwood, R-Ga. *	1967-69
Solomon P. Ortiz, D-Texas	1960-62

Tom Osborne, R-Neb.	1960-66	John Shadegg, R-Ariz.	1969-75
C. L. "Butch" Otter, R-Idaho	1967-73	Don Sherwood, R-Pa.	1964-66
Bill Pascrell Jr., D-N.J.	1961-67	John Shimkus, R-Ill.	1980-86
Ron Paul, R-Texas	1963-68	Rob Simmons, R-Conn. *	1965-68, 70-2000
Steve Pearce, R-N.M. *	1971-76	Vic Snyder, D-Ark.	1967-69
John E. Peterson, R-Pa.	1957-63	Mike Sodrel, R-Ind.	1966-73
Collin C. Peterson, D-Minn.	1963-69	John M. Spratt Jr., D-S.C.	1969-71
Joe Pitts, R-Pa. *	1963-69	Pete Stark, D-Calif.	1955-57
Ted Poe, R-Texas	1970-76	Cliff Stearns, R-Fla.	1963-67
Jim Ramstad, R-Minn.	1968-74	John Tanner, D-Tenn.	1968-72, 74-2000
Charles B. Rangel, D-N.Y. *	1948-52	Gene Taylor, D-Miss.	1971-84
Ralph Regula, R-Ohio	1944-46	Mike Thompson, D-Calif. *	1969-73
Dave Reichert, R-Wash.	1971-76	Edolphus Towns, D-N.Y.	1956-58
Silvestre Reyes, D-Texas *	1966-68	Dave Weldon, R-Fla.	1981-92
Thomas M. Reynolds, R-N.Y.	1970-76	Edward Whitfield, R-Ky.	1967-73
Harold Rogers, R-Ky.	1956-63	Roger Wicker, R-Miss.	1976-2004
Mike Rogers, R-Mich.	1985-88	Joe Wilson, R-S.C.	1972-2003
Bobby L. Rush, D-Ill.	1963-68	Heather A. Wilson, R-N.M.	1978-89
John Salazar, D-Colo.	1973-76	Frank R. Wolf, R-Va.	1962-63
Joe Schwarz, R-Mich. *	1965-67	C.W. Bill Young, R-Fla.	1948-57
Robert C. Scott, D-Va.	1970-76	Don Young, R-Alaska	1955-57
José E. Serrano, D-N.Y.	1964-66		

Members' Children Who Served in Iraq War

Member	Child's Name	Relationship	Branch
Rep. Todd Akin, R-Mo.	Perry Akin	son	Marine Corps
Sen. Christopher S. Bond, R-Mo.	Sam Bond	son	Marine Corps
Rep. Jo Ann Emerson, R-Mo.	Jessica Gladney	stepchild	Army
Rep. Duncan Hunter, R-Calif.	Duncan Duane Hunter	son	Marine Corps
Sen. Tim Johnson, D-S.D.	Brooks Johnson	son	Army
Rep. John Kline, R-Minn.	John Daniel Kline *	son	Army
Rep. Joe Wilson, R-S.C.	Alan Wilson	son	S.C. National Guard

* Expected to be deployed to Iraq in the summer of 2005

Member Occupations

	House			Senate			Congress
	Democrat	Republican	Total	Democrat	Republican	Total	Total
Actor/ Entertainment	1	2	3				3
Aeronautics		3	3				3
Agriculture	9	20	29	1	4	5	34
Artistic/Creative	1*	1	2*				2*
Business	69	142	211	14	28	42	253
Clergy	2	1	3				3
Education	52*	39	91*	6	7	13	104*
Engineering	1	3	4		1	1	5
Health Care	4	2	6				6
Homemaker/Domestic	3	2	5				5
Journalism	3*	7	10*	2	5	7	17*
Labor/Blue Collar	5	4	9	1	3	4	13
Law	91	87	178	30†	34	64†	242†
Law Enforcement	6	4	10				10
Medicine/Doctor	4	12	16		4	4	20
Military		4	4		1	1	5
Professional Sports		2	2		1	1	3
Public Service/Politics	123	99	222	23	23	46	268
Real Estate	3	36	39	1	2	3	42
Science	2	4	6				6
Secretarial/Clerical	4	5	9				9
Technical/Skilled Labor	2	2	4				4
Miscellaneous	1	2	3				3

Some members have had more than one occupation.

* Total includes Independent Bernard Sanders of Vermont

† Total includes Independent James M. Jeffords of Vermont.

Member Religious Affiliations

	House			Senate			Congress
	Democrat	Republican	Total	Democrat	Republican	Total	Total
African Methodist Episcopal	3		3				3
Baptist	29	36	65	1	6	7	72
Christian Church	1		1				1
Christian Reformed Church		2	2				2
Christian Scientist		5	5				5
Community of Christ	1		1				1
Disciples of Christ	1		1				1
Eastern Orthodox	1	2	3	1	1	2	5
Episcopalian	9	23	32	3	7	10	42
Jewish	25*	1	26*	9	2	11	37*
Lutheran	10	8	18	2	1	3	21
Methodist	19	31	50	5	7	12	62
Mormon	2	9	11	1	4	5	16
Pentecostal		4	4				4
Presbyterian	11	25	36	3	11	14	50
Protestant - Unspecified	10	23	33	2	3	5	38
Quaker	1		1				1
Roman Catholic	72	57	129	13	11	24	153
Seventh-day Adventist	1	1	2				2
Unitarian	1	1	2	1		1	3
United Church of Christ/ Congregationalist		3	3	4†	2	6†	9†
Unspecified	6		6				6

* Total includes Independent Bernard Sanders of Vermont
† Total includes Independent James M. Jeffords of Vermont.

Senators Up for Election in 2006

15 Republicans, 17 Democrats, 1 Independent

Daniel K. Akaka	D-Hawaii	James M. Jeffords *	I-Vt.
George F. Allen	R-Va.	Edward M. Kennedy	D-Mass.
Jeff Bingaman	D-N.M.	Herb Kohl	D-Wis.
Conrad Burns	R-Mont.	Jon Kyl	R-Ariz.
Robert C. Byrd	D-W.Va.	Joseph I. Lieberman	D-Conn.
Maria Cantwell	D-Wash.	Trent Lott	R-Miss.
Thomas R. Carper	D-Del.	Richard G. Lugar	R-Ind.
Lincoln Chafee	R-R.I.	Ben Nelson	D-Neb.
Hillary Rodham Clinton	D-N.Y.	Bill Nelson	D-Fla.
Kent Conrad	D-N.D.	Rick Santorum	R-Pa.
Jon Corzine †	D-N.J.	Paul S. Sarbanes *	D-Md.
Mark Dayton *	D-Minn.	Olympia J. Snowe	R-Maine
Mike DeWine	R-Ohio	Debbie Stabenow	D-Mich.
John Ensign	R-Nev.	Jim Talent	R-Mo.
Dianne Feinstein	D-Calif.	Craig Thomas	R-Wyo.
Bill Frist *	R-Tenn.		
Orrin G. Hatch	R-Utah	* Not running for re-election	
Kay Bailey Hutchison	R-Texas	† Running for govenor doesn't preclude running for re-election	

Former Representatives in Senate

30 Republicans, 21 Democrats, 1 Independent

Member	Party, State	Served in House	Member	Party, State	Served in House
Daniel K. Akaka	D-Hawaii	1977-90	James M. Inhofe	R-Okla.	1987-94
Wayne Allard	R-Colo.	1991-97	Daniel K. Inouye	D-Hawaii	1959-63
George Allen	R-Va.	1991-93	Johnny Isakson	R-Ga.	1999-2005
Max Baucus	D-Mont.	1975-78	James M. Jeffords	I-Vt.	1975-89
Barbara Boxer	D-Calif.	1983-93	Tim Johnson	D-S.D.	1987-97
Sam Brownback	R-Kan.	1995-96	Jon Kyl	R-Ariz.	1987-95
Jim Bunning	R-Ky.	1987-99	Blanche Lincoln	D-Ark.	1993-97
Richard M. Burr	R-N.C.	1995-2005	Trent Lott	R-Miss.	1973-89
Robert C. Byrd	D-W.Va.	1953-59	John McCain	R-Ariz.	1983-87
Maria Cantwell	D-Wash.	1993-95	Barbara A. Mikulski	D-Md.	1977-87
Thomas R. Carper	D-Del.	1983-93	Bill Nelson	D-Fla.	1979-91
Saxby Chambliss	R-Ga.	1995-2003	Jack Reed	D-R.I.	1991-97
Tom Coburn	R-Okla.	1995-2001	Harry Reid	D-Nev.	1983-87
Thad Cochran	R-Miss.	1973-78	Pat Roberts	R-Kan.	1981-97
Larry E. Craig	R-Idaho	1981-91	Rick Santorum	R-Pa.	1991-95
Michael D. Crapo	R-Idaho	1993-99	Paul S. Sarbanes	D-Md.	1971-77
Jim DeMint	R-S.C.	1999-2005	Charles E. Schumer	D-N.Y.	1981-99
Mike DeWine	R-Ohio	1983-91	Richard C. Shelby	R-Ala.	1979-87
Christopher J. Dodd	D-Conn.	1975-81	Olympia J. Snowe	R-Maine	1979-95
Byron L. Dorgan	D-N.D.	1981-92	Debbie Stabenow	D-Mich.	1997-2001
Richard J. Durbin	D-Ill.	1983-97	John E. Sununu	R-N.H.	1997-2003
John Ensign	R-Nev.	1995-99	Jim Talent	R-Mo.	1993-2001
Lindsey Graham	R-S.C.	1995-2003	Craig Thomas	R-Wyo.	1989-95
Charles E. Grassley	R-Iowa	1975-81	John Thune	R-S.D.	1997-2003
Judd Gregg	R-N.H.	1981-89	David Vitter	R-La.	1999-2005
Tom Harkin	D-Iowa	1975-85	Ron Wyden	D-Ore.	1981-96

Most Bills — Senate

Current members of the Senate who introduced the most bills and resolutions in the 108th Congress:

Member	Bills, Resolutions
Bill Frist, R-Tenn.	103
Orrin G. Hatch, R-Utah *	91
Olympia J. Snowe, R-Maine *	91
Jeff Bingaman, D-N.M. *	89
Charles E. Grassley, R-Iowa	80
John McCain, R-Ariz.	77
Barbara Boxer, D-Calif.	72
Hillary Rodham Clinton, D-N.Y. *	71
Dianne Feinstein, D-Calif. *	69
Jon Corzine, D-N.J.	66
Charles E. Schumer, D-N.Y.	66

* Also in the top 10 in the 107th Congress

Fewest Bills — Senate

Current members of the Senate who introduced the fewest bills and resolutions in the 108th Congress:

Member	Bills, Resolutions
Thomas R. Carper, D-Del.	4
Mark Pryor, D-Ark.	6
Elizabeth Dole, R-N.C.	7
Robert C. Byrd, D-W.Va. *	10
Lincoln Chafee, R-R.I. *	10
John E. Sununu, R-N.H.	10
Herb Kohl, D-Wis.	12
Robert F. Bennett, R-Utah *	13
Jim Talent, R-Mo.	13
Pat Roberts, R-Kan.	15

* Also in the bottom 10 in the 107th Congress

Fewest Bills — House

Current members of the House who introduced the fewest bills and resolutions in the 108th Congress:

Member	Bills, Resolutions
Lincoln Davis, D-Tenn.	1
Jim Marshall, D-Ga.	1
Alan B. Mollohan, D-W.Va. *	1
Anne M. Northup, R-Ky.	1
Mario Diaz-Balart, R-Fla.	2
Mike Doyle, D-Pa.	2
Gil Gutknecht, R-Minn.	2
Tim Holden, D-Pa.	2
John Tanner, D-Tenn.	2
Eleven members tied at:	3

* Also in the bottom 10 in the 107th Congress

Most Bills — House

Current members of the House who introduced the most bills and resolutions in the 108th Congress:

Member	Bills, Resolutions
Robert E. Andrews, D-N.J. *	117
Charles B. Rangel, D-N.Y*	73
Ron Paul, R-Texas *	68
Phil English, R-Pa. *	61
Don Young, R-Alaska *	59
Carolyn B. Maloney, D-N.Y. *	57
Sue Myrick, R-N.C. *	55
Pete Sessions, R-Texas	53
Christopher H. Smith, R-N.J. *	50
Joe Wilson, R-S.C.	46

* Also in the top 10 in the 107th Congress

Senate Presidential Support and Opposition

Support scores represent how often a senator sided with President Bush on roll call votes on which the president took a clear position beforehand. During the 108th Congress, there were 169 such votes. Opposition scores represent how often a senator voted against the president's position in 2003 and 2004. Scores are expressed as percentages. Only members of the 109th Congress are listed.

108th Congress: Top Scorers

Support — Republicans

Jon Kyl, Ariz.	99.4%
Rick Santorum, Pa.	99.4
Mitch McConnell, Ky.	99.4
John Ensign, Nev.	98.8
Saxby Chambliss, Ga.	98.2
Jeff Sessions, Ala.	98.2
Lamar Alexander, Tenn.	98.2
Jim Bunning, Ky.	98.2
Wayne Allard, Colo.	97.6
Charles E. Grassley, Iowa	97.6
Conrad Burns, Mont.	97.6
John Cornyn, Texas	97.6
George Allen, Va.	97.6
Sam Brownback, Kan.	97.6
Orrin G. Hatch, Utah	97.6
Craig Thomas, Wyo.	97.6
Larry E. Craig, Idaho	97.0
Michael B. Enzi, Wyo.	97.0
Chuck Hagel, Neb.	97.0
Richard G. Lugar, Ind.	97.0
Jim Talent, Mo.	97.0

Support — Democrats

Ben Nelson, Neb.	80.4%
Blanche Lincoln, Ark.	64.0
Mark Pryor, Ark.	62.1
Mary L. Landrieu, La.	61.0
Kent Conrad, N.D.	59.0
Bill Nelson, Fla.	58.0
Evan Bayh, Ind.	57.7
Thomas R. Carper, Del.	57.2
Byron L. Dorgan, N.D.	56.9
Russell D. Feingold, Wis.	56.8
Robert C. Byrd, W.Va.	56.6
Maria Cantwell, Wash.	56.0
Harry Reid, Nev.	55.1
Herb Kohl, Wis.	55.1
Max Baucus, Mont.	54.6
Jeff Bingaman, N.M.	53.9
John D. Rockefeller IV, W.Va.	53.8
James M. Jeffords, Vt. *	53.8
Joseph R. Biden Jr., Del.	53.5
Tim Johnson, S.D.	53.3
Carl Levin, Mich.	53.3

Opposition — Republicans

Lincoln Chafee, R.I.	23.4%
Olympia J. Snowe, Maine	20.7
Susan Collins, Maine	14.8
Arlen Specter, Pa.	11.1
John McCain, Ariz.	8.9
Lisa Murkowski, Alaska	8.7
Richard C. Shelby, Ala.	7.8
George V. Voinovich, Ohio	6.6
Lindsey Graham, S.C.	6.0
Judd Gregg, N.H.	5.6
John W. Warner, Va.	5.5
Ted Stevens, Alaska	5.4
John E. Sununu, N.H.	4.8
Michael D. Crapo, Idaho	4.8
Christopher S. Bond, Mo.	4.3
James M. Inhofe, Okla.	4.3
Kay Bailey Hutchison, Texas	4.3

Opposition — Democrats

John Kerry, Mass. †	67.6%
Joseph I. Lieberman, Conn.	53.5
Jon Corzine, N.J.	52.5
Tom Harkin, Iowa	52.2
Frank R. Lautenberg, N.J.	52.2
Richard J. Durbin, Ill.	51.9
Barbara A. Mikulski, Md.	50.6
Jack Reed, R.I.	50.6
Paul S. Sarbanes, Md.	50.0
Barbara Boxer, Calif.	49.7
Edward M. Kennedy, Mass.	49.4
Hillary Rodham Clinton, N.Y.	49.4
Christopher J. Dodd, Conn.	48.8
Ron Wyden, Ore.	48.8
Daniel K. Inouye, Hawaii	48.7

* An independent, Jeffords caucuses with the Democrats

† Kerry voted on only 22 percent of the votes in the study

Senate Party Unity and Opposition

Support scores represent how often a senator voted with his or her party's majority against a majority of the other party In the 108th Congress there were 419 such party unity votes in the Senate. Opposition scores represent how often a senator voted against his or her party's majority in 2003 and 2004. Scores are expressed as percentages. Only members of the 109th Congress are listed.

108th Congress: Top Scorers

Support — Republicans

Craig Thomas, Wyo.	99.5%
Jon Kyl, Ariz.	98.8
Mitch McConnell, Ky.	98.8
Jim Bunning, Ky.	98.8
John Cornyn, Texas	98.6
Michael B. Enzi, Wyo.	98.3
Larry E. Craig, Idaho	98.3
James M. Inhofe, Okla.	98.3
Wayne Allard, Colo.	98.1
Jeff Sessions, Ala.	98.1
Thad Cochran, Miss.	97.9
Orrin G. Hatch, Utah	97.9
Saxby Chambliss, Ga.	97.8
Rick Santorum, Pa.	97.6
Conrad Burns, Mont.	97.6
Michael D. Crapo, Idaho	97.6
Lamar Alexander, Tenn.	97.3
Robert F. Bennett, Utah	97.3
Bill Frist, Tenn.	97.1
George Allen, Va.	96.9

Support — Democrats

John Kerry, Mass.[†]	100.0%
Paul S. Sarbanes, Md.	99.0
Jack Reed, R.I.	98.3
Barbara Boxer, Calif.	98.3
Carl Levin, Mich.	97.6
Hillary Rodham Clinton, N.Y.	97.3
Edward M. Kennedy, Mass.	97.3
Debbie Stabenow, Mich.	97.1
Richard J. Durbin, Ill.	97.1
Barbara A. Mikulski, Md.	96.9
Tom Harkin, Iowa	96.8
Daniel K. Akaka, Hawaii	96.7
Frank R. Lautenberg, N.J.	96.6
Jon Corzine, N.J.	96.4
Patrick J. Leahy, Vt.	96.1
Christopher J. Dodd, Conn.	95.4
Patty Murray, Wash.	95.2
Maria Cantwell, Wash.	94.7
Charles E. Schumer, N.Y.	94.5
John D. Rockefeller IV, W.Va.	94.0
Herb Kohl, Wis.	94.0

Opposition — Republicans

Lincoln Chafee, R.I.	30.5%
Olympia J. Snowe, Maine	26.0
Susan Collins, Maine	22.0
Arlen Specter, Pa.	19.3
John McCain, Ariz.	15.7
Mike DeWine, Ohio	11.5
Gordon H. Smith, Ore.	8.5
Norm Coleman, Minn.	8.1
George V. Voinovich, Ohio	8.0
Judd Gregg, N.H.	7.7
Kay Bailey Hutchison, Texas	7.5
John W. Warner, Va.	6.7
Lisa Murkowski, Alaska	6.7
John Ensign, Nev.	6.5
Lindsey Graham, S.C.	5.3

Opposition — Democrats

Ben Nelson, Neb.	44.0%
Max Baucus, Mont.	26.7
Mary L. Landrieu, La.	21.2
Blanche Lincoln, Ark.	19.9
Evan Bayh, Ind.	18.7
Thomas R. Carper, Del.	17.7
Mark Pryor, Ark.	16.5
Kent Conrad, N.D.	16.5
James M. Jeffords, Vt. *	12.1
Byron L. Dorgan, N.D.	11.3
Bill Nelson, Fla.	9.2
Jeff Bingaman, N.M.	8.9
Joseph R. Biden Jr., Del.	8.2
Harry Reid, Nev.	7.8
Dianne Feinstein, Calif.	7.7

* An independent, Jeffords caucuses with the Democrats

† Kerry voted on only 33 percent of the votes in the study

House Presidential Support and Opposition

Support scores represent how often a House member sided with President Bush on roll call votes on which the president took a clear position beforehand. During the 108th Congress, there were 89 such votes in the House. Opposition scores represent how often a member voted against the president's position. Scores are expressed as percentages. Only members of the 109th Congress who voted more than half the time in 2003 and 2004 are listed.

108th Congress: Top Scorers

Support — Republicans

Roy Blunt, Mo.	100.0%
John A. Boehner, Ohio	100.0
Eric Cantor, Va.	98.9
Jeb Hensarling, Texas	98.8
Jim McCrery, La.	98.8
Katherine Harris, Fla.	97.8
Mark Kennedy, Minn.	97.8
John Linder, Ga.	97.7
Melissa A. Hart, Pa.	97.7
David Dreier, Calif.	97.7
Michael G. Oxley, Ohio	97.6
Chris Chocola, Ind.	96.6
John Kline, Minn.	96.6
William M. "Mac" Thornberry, Texas	96.6
Pete Sessions, Texas.	96.6
Christopher Cox, Calif.	96.6
Mario Diaz-Balart, Fla.	96.6
Mike Rogers, Mich.	96.6
Tom DeLay, Texas	96.6
Doc Hastings, Wash.	96.6

Support — Democrats

Robert E. "Bud" Cramer, Ala.	69.4%
Ike Skelton, Mo.	64.0
Lincoln Davis, Tenn.	57.0
Collin C. Peterson, Minn.	55.2
Allen Boyd, Fla.	54.2
Jim Matheson, Utah	53.9
Jim Marshall, Ga.	52.9
Mike McIntyre, N.C.	52.3
Gene Taylor, Miss.	50.0
Earl Pomeroy, N.D.	49.4
Tim Holden, Pa.	48.9
Sanford D. Bishop Jr., Ga.	48.2
Chet Edwards, Texas	47.7
Mike Ross, Ark.	47.2
Solomon P. Ortiz, Texas	45.2
John P. Murtha, Pa.	44.8
Bart Gordon, Tenn.	43.5
Marion Berry, Ark.	42.0
John Tanner, Tenn.	42.0
Dennis Cardoza, Calif.	41.9

Opposition — Republicans

Ron Paul, Texas	57.0%
Jim Leach, Iowa	46.5
Rob Simmons, Conn.	36.4
Christopher Shays, Conn.	36.0
Nancy L. Johnson, Conn.	31.8
Timothy V. Johnson, Ill.	30.7
Sherwood Boehlert, N.Y.	30.6
Michael N. Castle, Del.	29.2
John Hostettler, Ind.	29.2
Jeff Flake, Ariz.	28.4
Frank A. LoBiondo, N.J.	27.0
Christopher H. Smith, N.J.	26.4
Walter B. Jones, N.C.	26.4
Charles Bass, N.H.	25.8
Sue W. Kelly, N.Y.	25.8
Mark Steven Kirk, Ill.	25.3
Jim Ramstad, Minn.	24.7
Jerry Moran, Kan.	23.6
Mary Bono, Calif.	22.7
Wayne T. Gilchrest, Md.	22.7
John E. Sweeney, N.Y.	22.7

Opposition — Democrats

John Conyers Jr., Mich.	90.9%
Robert C. Scott, Va.	89.8
Jesse L. Jackson Jr., Ill.	88.8
Maxine Waters, Calif.	88.0
Barbara Lee, Calif.	87.6
Pete Stark, Calif.	87.0
Bill Delahunt, Mass.	86.9
Jan Schakowsky, Ill.	86.5
Edward J. Markey, Mass.	86.5
John F. Tierney, Mass.	86.4
Danny K. Davis, Ill.	85.7
Major R. Owens, N.Y.	85.7
Lynn Woolsey, Calif.	85.5
Raúl M. Grijalva, Ariz.	85.4
Linda T. Sánchez, Calif.	85.2
Henry A. Waxman, Calif.	85.1
Jerrold Nadler, N.Y.	85.1
George Miller, Calif.	84.9
John Lewis, Ga.	84.9
Bob Filner, Calif.	84.7

Ralph Hall, R-Texas, and Rodney Alexander, R-La., are not included, as they changed parties in the 108th Congress.

House Party Unity and Opposition

Support scores represent how often a House member voted with his or her party's majority against a majority of the other party. In the 108th Congress there were 604 such "party unity" votes in the House. Opposition scores represent how often a member voted against his or her party's majority on such party unity tests. Scores are expressed as percentages. Only members of the 109th Congress who voted more than half the time in 2003 and 2004 are listed.

108th Congress: Top Scorers

Support — Republicans

Nathan Deal, Ga.	99.5%
Pete Sessions, Texas	99.2
Sam Johnson, Texas	99.1
Phil Gingrey, Ga.	98.7
Mike Pence, Ind.	98.6
Tom DeLay, Texas	98.6
Wally Herger, Calif.	98.6
Tom Feeney, Fla.	98.6
Sue Myrick, N.C.	98.6
John Carter, Texas	98.6
Chris Chocola, Ind.	98.5
J. Gresham Barrett, S.C.	98.5
Steve King, Iowa	98.5
Marsha Blackburn, Tenn.	98.5
John Kline, Minn.	98.3
Eric Cantor, Va.	98.3
Ric Keller, Fla.	98.3
Gary G. Miller, Calif.	98.2
William M. "Mac" Thornberry, Texas	98.2
Randy Neugebauer, Texas	98.1

Support — Democrats

Linda T. Sánchez, Calif.	99.3%
Jerrold Nadler, N.Y.	99.3
Raúl M. Grijalva, Ariz.	99.2
Hilda L. Solis, Calif.	99.0
Edward J. Markey, Mass.	99.0
John F. Tierney, Mass.	98.8
Xavier Becerra, Calif.	98.8
Lucille Roybal-Allard, Calif.	98.8
Pete Stark, Calif.	98.8
Jan Schakowsky, Ill.	98.7
Grace F. Napolitano, Calif.	98.6
Barbara Lee, Calif.	98.6
John Lewis, Ga.	98.6
Tammy Baldwin, Wis.	98.5
Rosa DeLauro, Conn.	98.5
John W. Olver, Mass.	98.5
Jim McGovern, Mass.	98.5
George Miller, Calif.	98.4
Danny K. Davis, Ill.	98.4
Jim McDermott, Wash.	98.4

Opposition — Republicans

Jim Leach, Iowa	34.9%
Christopher Shays, Conn.	25.3
Ron Paul, Texas	22.5
Michael N. Castle, Del.	22.1
Rob Simmons, Conn.	21.4
Timothy V. Johnson, Ill.	20.1
Sherwood Boehlert, N.Y.	19.2
Christopher H. Smith, N.J.	18.5
Nancy L. Johnson, Conn.	17.5
Frank A. LoBiondo, N.J.	16.7
Jim Ramstad, Minn.	15.6
Vernon J. Ehlers, Mich.	15.1
Sue W. Kelly, N.Y.	15.1
Mark Steven Kirk, Ill.	14.5
Heather A. Wilson, N.M.	14.1
H. James Saxton, N.J.	13.7
Walter B. Jones, N.C.	13.6
Steven C. LaTourette, Ohio	13.2
Wayne T. Gilchrest, Md.	13.0
John M. McHugh, N.Y.	12.8

Opposition — Democrats

Robert E. "Bud" Cramer, Ala.	38.6%
Collin C. Peterson, Minn.	36.1
Gene Taylor, Miss.	30.6
Jim Matheson, Utah	29.8
Jim Marshall, Ga.	28.8
Allen Boyd, Fla.	28.8
Lincoln Davis, Tenn.	28.4
Chet Edwards, Texas	25.0
John Tanner, Tenn.	24.1
John P. Murtha, Pa.	24.0
Mike McIntyre, N.C.	23.9
Ike Skelton, Mo.	23.1
Tim Holden, Pa.	23.1
Bart Gordon, Tenn.	22.9
David Scott, Ga.	22.5
Alan B. Mollohan, W.Va.	21.5
Earl Pomeroy, N.D.	21.4
Sanford D. Bishop Jr., Ga.	21.0
Marion Berry, Ark.	19.8
Solomon P. Ortiz, Texas	19.7

Ralph Hall, R-Texas, and Rodney Alexander, R-La., are not included, as they changed parties in the 108th Congress.

House Blue Dog Coalition

All members are Democrats.

Co-Chairmen: Dennis Cardoza, Calif., Jim Cooper, Tenn., Jim Matheson, Utah

Joe Baca, Calif.	Lincoln Davis, Tenn.	Earl Pomeroy, N.D.
John Barrow, Ga.	Harold E. Ford Jr., Tenn.	Mike Ross, Ark.
Marion Berry, Ark.	Jane Harman, Calif.	John Salazar, Colo.
Sanford D. Bishop Jr., Ga.	Stephanie Herseth, S.D.	Loretta Sanchez, Calif.
Dan Boren, Okla.	Tim Holden, Pa.	Adam B. Schiff, Calif.
Leonard L. Boswell, Iowa	Steve Israel, N.Y.	David Scott, Ga.
Allen Boyd, Fla.	Mike McIntyre, N.C.	John Tanner, Tenn.
Ed Case, Hawaii	Charlie Melancon, La.	Ellen O. Tauscher, Calif.
Ben Chandler, Ky.	Michael H. Michaud, Maine	Gene Taylor, Miss.
Jim Costa, Calif.	Dennis Moore, Kan.	Mike Thompson, Calif.
Robert E. "Bud" Cramer, Ala.	Collin C. Peterson, Minn.	

Progressive Caucus

All members except Sanders are Democrats.

Officers

Rep. Barbara Lee, Calif., co-chairwoman
Rep. Lynn Woolsey, Calif., co-chairwoman
Rep. Peter A. DeFazio, Ore.
Rep. Jesse L. Jackson Jr., Ill.
Rep. Major R. Owens, N.Y.
Rep. Bernard Sanders, Vt.

Members

Rep. Neil Abercrombie, Hawaii
Rep. Tammy Baldwin, Wis.
Rep. Xavier Becerra, Calif.
Rep. Corrine Brown, Fla.
Rep. Sherrod Brown, Ohio
Rep. Michael E. Capuano, Mass.
Rep. Julia Carson, Ind.
Rep. William Lacy Clay, Mo.
Rep. John Conyers Jr., Mich.
Rep. Danny K. Davis, Ill.
Rep. Rosa DeLauro, Conn.
Rep. Lane Evans, Ill.
Rep. Sam Farr, Calif.
Rep. Chaka Fattah, Pa.
Rep. Bob Filner, Calif.
Rep. Barney Frank, Mass.
Rep. Raul M. Grijalva, Ariz.
Rep. Luis V. Gutierrez, Ill.
Rep. Maurice D. Hinchey, N.Y.
Rep. Sheila Jackson-Lee, Texas

Rep. Stephanie Tubbs Jones, Ohio
Rep. Marcy Kaptur, Ohio
Rep. Dennis J. Kucinich, Ohio
Rep. Tom Lantos, Calif.
Rep. John Lewis, Ga.
Rep. Edward J. Markey, Mass.
Rep. Jim McDermott, Wash.
Rep. Jim McGovern, Mass.
Rep. George Miller, Calif.
Rep. Gwen Moore, Wis.
Rep. Jerrold Nadler, N.Y.
Del. Eleanor Holmes Norton, D.C.
Rep. John W. Olver, Mass.
Rep. Ed Pastor, Ariz.
Rep. Donald M. Payne, N.J.
Rep. Nancy Pelosi, Calif.
Rep. Bobby L. Rush, Ill.
Rep. Jan Schakowsky, Ill.
Rep. José E. Serrano, N.Y.
Rep. Hilda L. Solis, Calif.
Rep. Pete Stark, Calif.
Rep. Bennie Thompson, Miss.
Rep. John F. Tierney, Mass.
Rep. Tom Udall, N.M.
Rep. Nydia M. Velázquez, N.Y.
Rep. Maxine Waters, Calif.
Rep. Diane Watson, Calif.
Rep. Melvin Watt, N.C.
Rep. Henry A. Waxman, Calif.

House New Democrat Coalition

All members are Democrats.

Chairwoman: Ellen O. Tauscher, Calif.

Co-Chairmen: Artur Davis, Ala., Ron Kind, Wis., Adam Smith, Wash.

Brian Baird, Wash.	Harold E. Ford Jr., Tenn.	Gregory W. Meeks, N.Y.
Shelley Berkley, Nev.	Jane Harman, Calif.	Juanita Millender-McDonald, Calif.
Lois Capps, Calif.	Stephanie Herseth, S.D.	Dennis Moore, Kan.
Russ Carnahan, Mo.	Brian Higgins, N.Y.	James P. Moran, Va.
Ed Case, Hawaii	Rush D. Holt, N.J.	David E. Price, N.C.
Ben Chandler, Ky.	Darlene Hooley, Ore.	Loretta Sanchez, Calif.
Joseph Crowley, N.Y.	Jay Inslee, Wash.	Adam B. Schiff, Calif.
Jim Davis, Fla.	Steve Israel, N.Y.	Allyson Y. Schwartz, Pa.
Susan A. Davis, Calif.	Rick Larsen, Wash.	David Scott, Ga.
Rahm Emanuel, Ill.	John B. Larson, Conn.	Vic Snyder, Ark.
Eliot L. Engel, N.Y.	Carolyn McCarthy, N.Y.	Tom Udall, N.M.
Bob Etheridge, N.C.	Mike McIntyre, N.C.	David Wu, Ore.

Senate New Democrat Coalition

All members are Democrats.

Co-Chairmen: Evan Bayh, Ind., Thomas R. Carper, Del., Blanche Lincoln, Ark.

Maria Cantwell, Wash.	John Kerry, Mass.	Bill Nelson, Fla.
Kent Conrad, N.D.	Herb Kohl, Wis.	Ben Nelson, Neb.
Dianne Feinstein, Calif.	Mary L. Landrieu, La.	Mark Pryor, Ark.
Tim Johnson, S.D.	Joseph I. Lieberman, Conn.	Debbie Stabenow, Mich.

Republican Main Street Partnership

The partnership also includes several governors and former elected officials. All members are Republicans.

Rep. Charles Bass, N.H.
Rep. Judy Biggert, Ill.
Rep. Sherwood Boehlert, N.Y.
Rep. Mary Bono, Calif.
Rep. Jeb Bradley, N.H.
Rep. Ginny Brown-Waite, Fla.
Rep. Ken Calvert, Calif.
Rep. Dave Camp, Mich.
Rep. Shelley Moore Capito, W.Va.
Rep. Michael N. Castle, Del., president
Sen. Lincoln Chafee, R.I.
Sen. Norm Coleman, Minn.
Sen. Susan Collins, Maine, board member
Rep. Thomas M. Davis III, Va., board member
Rep. Charlie Dent, Pa.
Rep. David Dreier, Calif.
Rep. Vernon J. Ehlers, Mich.
Rep. Phil English, Pa.
Rep. Mike Ferguson, N.J.
Rep. Mark Foley, Fla.
Rep. Rodney Frelinghuysen, N.J.
Rep. Jim Gerlach, Pa.
Rep. Wayne T. Gilchrest, Md.
Rep. Paul E. Gillmor, Ohio
Rep. Kay Granger, Texas
Sen. Chuck Hagel, Neb.
Rep. David L. Hobson, Ohio
Sen. Johnny Isakson, Ga.
Rep. Nancy L. Johnson, Conn.
Rep. Timothy V. Johnson, Ill.
Rep. Sue W. Kelly, N.Y.
Rep. Mark Steven Kirk, Ill.

Rep. Jim Kolbe, Ariz.
Rep. John R. "Randy" Kuhl Jr., N.Y.
Rep. Ray LaHood, Ill.
Rep. Steven C. LaTourette, Ohio
Rep. Jim Leach, Iowa
Rep. Jerry Lewis, Calif.
Rep. Frank A. LoBiondo, N.J.
Sen. John McCain, Ariz.
Rep. Jim McCrery, La.
Sen. Lisa Murkowski, Alaska
Rep. Tom Osborne, Neb.
Rep. Tom Petri, Wis.
Rep. Todd R. Platts, Pa.
Rep. Jon Porter, Nev.
Rep. Deborah Pryce, Ohio
Rep. Jim Ramstad, Minn.
Rep. Ralph Regula, Ohio
Sen. Pat Roberts, Kan.
Rep. Joe Schwarz, Mich.
Rep. E. Clay Shaw Jr., Fla.
Rep. Christopher Shays, Conn.
Rep. Rob Simmons, Conn.
Sen. Gordon H. Smith, Ore.
Sen. Olympia J. Snowe, Maine, board member
Sen. Arlen Specter, Pa.
Sen. Ted Stevens, Alaska
Rep. Michael R. Turner, Ohio
Rep. Fred Upton, Mich., board member
Rep. Greg Walden, Ore.
Rep. James T. Walsh, N.Y.
Rep. Curt Weldon, Pa.
Rep. Jerry Weller, Ill.

Republican Study Committee

The group was formerly known as the Conservative Action Team, or CATs. The list is not comprehensive. The committee permits individual members to decide whether to publicize their membership. All members are Republicans.

Chairman and Founders
Mike Pence, Ind., chairman
Dan Burton, Ind., founder
John T. Doolittle, Calif., founder
Ernest Istook, Okla., founder
Sam Johnson, Texas, founder

Members
Robert B. Aderholt, Ala.
Todd Akin, Mo.
Spencer Bachus, Ala.
J. Gresham Barrett, S.C.
Roscoe G. Bartlett, Md.
Joe L. Barton, Texas
Bob Beauprez, Colo.
Rob Bishop, Utah
Marsha Blackburn, Tenn.
John Boozman, Ark.
Kevin Brady, Texas
Henry E. Brown Jr., S.C.
Michael C. Burgess, Texas
Dave Camp, Mich.
Chris Cannon, Utah
Eric Cantor, Va.
John Carter, Texas
Steve Chabot, Ohio
Chris Chocola, Ind.
Tom Cole, Okla.
K. Michael Conaway, Texas
Christopher Cox, Calif.
Barbara Cubin, Wyo.
John Culberson, Texas
Jo Ann Davis, Va.

Mario Diaz-Balart, Fla.
Thelma Drake, Va.
Tom Feeney, Fla.
Jeff Flake, Ariz.
J. Randy Forbes, Va.
Trent Franks, Ariz.
Scott Garrett, N.J.
Phil Gingrey, Ga.
Louie Gohmert, Texas
Virgil H. Goode Jr., Va.
Robert W. Goodlatte, Va.
Mark Green, Wis.
Gil Gutknecht, Minn.
Melissa A. Hart, Pa.
Robin Hayes, N.C.
J.D. Hayworth, Ariz.
Jeb Hensarling, Texas
Wally Herger, Calif.
Peter Hoekstra, Mich.
John Hostettler, Ind.
Duncan Hunter, Calif.
Bobby Jindal, La.
Walter B. Jones, N.C.
Steve King, Iowa
John Kline, Minn.
Ron Lewis, Ky.
Donald Manzullo, Ill.
Michael McCaul, Texas
Patrick T. McHenry, N.C.
Howard P. "Buck" McKeon, Calif.
Cathy McMorris, Wash.
Gary G. Miller, Calif.
Jeff Miller, Fla.

Jerry Moran, Kan.
Tim Murphy, Pa.
Marilyn Musgrave, Colo.
Sue Myrick, N.C.
Randy Neugebauer, Texas
Anne M. Northup, Ky.
Charlie Norwood, Ga.
Joe Pitts, Pa.
Ted Poe, Texas
Richard W. Pombo, Calif.
Tom Price, Ga.
George P. Radanovich, Calif.
Denny Rehberg, Mont.
Rick Renzi, Ariz.
Thomas M. Reynolds, N.Y.
Paul D. Ryan, Wis.
Jim Ryun, Kan.
Pete Sessions, Texas
John Shadegg, Ariz.
Mark Souder, Ind.
Cliff Stearns, Fla.
John Sullivan, Okla.
Tom Tancredo, Colo.
Charles H. Taylor, N.C.
Lee Terry, Neb.
William M. "Mac" Thornberry, Texas
Todd Tiahrt, Kan.
Pat Tiberi, Ohio
Dave Weldon, Fla.
Lynn Westmoreland, Ga.
Joe Wilson, S.C.

Hispanic Districts

Congressional districts with the largest percentage of Hispanics: (Hispanics may be of any race)

District	Hispanic	Member
Texas 16	77.7%	Reyes, D
California 34	77.2%	Roybal-Allard, D
Illinois 4	74.5%	Gutierrez, D
California 38	70.6%	Napolitano, D
California 31	71.6%	Becerra, D
Florida 21	70.2%	L. Diaz-Balart, R
Texas 15	69.0%	Hinojosa, D
Texas 25	68.6%	Doggett, D
Texas 27	68.1%	Ortiz, D
Texas 20	67.1%	Gonzalez, D

Black Districts

Congressional districts with the largest percentage of African-Americans:

District	Black	Member
Illinois 1	65.2%	Rush, D
Louisiana 2	63.7%	Jefferson, D
Mississippi 2	63.2%	Thompson, D
Illinois 2	62.0%	Jackson, D
Alabama 7	61.7%	Davis, D
Illinois 7	61.6%	Davis, D
Michigan 14	61.1%	Conyers, D
Pennsylvania 2	60.7%	Fattah, D
Michigan 13	60.5%	Kilpatrick, D
New York 10	60.2%	Towns, D

Asian Districts

Congressional districts with the largest percentage of Asians:

District	Asian	Member
Hawaii 1	53.6%	Abercrombie, D
California 15	29.2%	Honda, D
California 8	28.7%	Pelosi, D
California 12	28.5%	Lantos, D
California 13	28.2%	Stark, D
Hawaii 2	28.0%	Case, D
New York 5	24.5%	Ackerman, D
California 29	23.7%	Schiff, D
California 16	23.4%	Lofgren, D
California 32	18.4%	Solis, D

American Indian Districts

Congressional districts with the largest percentage of American Indians:

District	Indian	Member
Arizona 1	22.1%	Renzi, R
New Mexico 3	18.9%	Udall, D
Oklahoma 2	16.8%	Carson, D
Alaska AL	15.4%	Young, R
North Carolina 7	8.5%	McIntyre, D
South Dakota AL	8.1%	Herseth, D
Montana AL	6.0%	Rehberg, R
Oklahoma 3	6.0%	Lucas, R
Oklahoma 1	5.8%	Sullivan, R
Oklahoma 4	5.5%	Cole, R

Oldest Districts

Congressional districts with the highest median age:

District	Median Age	Member
Florida 13	47.4	Harris, R
Florida 14	47.4	Goss, R
Florida 5	45.5	Brown-Waite, R
Florida 19	45.1	Wexler, D
Florida 16	44.5	Foley, R
Florida 10	43.9	Young, R
Florida 22	43.0	Shaw, R
Florida 9	41.1	Bilirakis, R
Florida 15	41.0	Weldon, R
Pennsylvania 18	41.0	Murphy, R

Youngest Districts

Congressional districts with the lowest median age:

District	Median Age	Member
Utah 3	24.5	Cannon, R
California 43	26.7	Baca, D
California 20	26.9	Dooley, D
Arizona 4	27.1	Pastor, D
Illinois 4	27.2	Gutierrez, D
Texas 29	27.4	Green, D
New York 16	27.5	Serrano, D
California 47	27.6	Loretta Sanchez, D
Utah 1	27.6	Bishop, R
California 34	27.9	Roybal-Allard, D

Richest Districts

Congressional districts with the highest median household income in 1999:

District	Income	Member
Virginia 11	$80,397	Davis, R
New Jersey 11	$79,009	Frelinghuysen, R
California 14	$77,985	Eshoo, D
Georgia 6	$75,611	Isakson, R
California 15	$74,947	Honda, D
New Jersey 7	$74,823	Ferguson, R
Colorado 6	$73,393	Tancredo, R
New Jersey 5	$72,781	Garrett, R
Illinois 13	$71,686	Biggert, R
Illinois 10	$71,663	Kirk, R

Poorest Districts

Congressional districts with the lowest median household income in 1999:

District	Income	Member
New York 16	$19,311	Serrano, D
Kentucky 5	$21,915	Rogers, R
West Virgina 3	$25,630	Rahall, D
California 31	$26,093	Becerra, D
Alabama 7	$26,672	Davis, D
California 20	$26,800	Dooley, D
Mississippi 2	$26,894	Thompson, D
Louisiana 5	$27,453	Alexander, D
Louisiana 2	$27,514	Jefferson, D
Missouri 8	$27,865	Emerson, R

Districts With Most Government Workers

Congressional districts with the largest percentage of workers employed by local, state, federal or international government organizations:

District	Workers	Member
Maryland 4	29.0%	Wynn, D
Maryland 5	28.8%	Hoyer, D
Florida 2	28.5%	Boyd, D
Alaska AL	26.8%	Young, R
New Mexico 3	25.8%	Udall, D
California 5	24.8%	Matsui, D
New York 10	24.6%	Towns, D
Arizona 1	24.4%	Renzi, R
Maryland 7	24.3%	Cummings, D
Virginia 11	24.2%	Davis, R

Most Educated Districts

Congressional districts with the largest percentage of people, aged 25 and older, with at least a bachelor's degree:

District	Degree	Member
New York 14	56.9%	Maloney, D
Virginia 8	53.8%	Moran, D
Maryland 8	53.7%	Van Hollen, D
California 30	53.5%	Waxman, D
California 14	52.2%	Eshoo, D
Georgia 6	50.7%	Isakson, R
Texas 7	50.0%	Culberson, R
Virginia 11	48.9%	Davis, R
North Carolina 4	48.0%	Price, D
New York 8	47.8%	Nadler, D

Least Educated Districts

Congressional districts with the largest percentage of people, 25 and older, without a high school diploma:

District	No Diploma	Member
California 34	53.7%	Roybal-Allard, D
California 31	52.5%	Becerra, D
California 20	49.8%	Dooley, D
Texas 29	49.8%	Green, D
California 47	49.6%	Loretta Sanchez, D
New York 16	49.5%	Serrano, D
Illinois 4	48.3%	Gutierrez, D
New York 12	43.6%	Velázquez, D
Texas 25	42.1%	Doggett, D
California 38	41.6%	Napolitano, D

Districts With Most Foreign Born

Congressional districts with the largest percentage of residents born outside the United States (Americans born abroad are not included):

District	Foreign Born	Member
Florida 21	56.6%	L. Diaz-Balart, R
California 31	56.2%	Becerra, D
Florida 18	54.0%	Ros-Lehtinen, R
California 47	50.7%	Loretta Sanchez, D
California 34	47.2%	Roybal-Allard, D
Florida 25	46.6%	M. Diaz-Balart, R
New York 5	45.6%	Ackerman, D
California 28	44.0%	Berman, D
California 29	43.8%	Schiff, D
California 32	41.7%	Solis, D

Closest Elections of 2004

Race	Winner	Votes	Loser	Votes	Margin	Pecent
Louisiana 3	Charlie Melancon, D	57,611	Billy Tauzin III, R	57,042	569	0.4963%
Indiana 9	Mike Sodrel, R	142,197	Baron P. Hill, D	140,772	1,425	0.4956
New York 27	Brian Higgins, D	143,332	Nancy Naples, R	139,558	3,774	1.3
South Dakota Senate *	John Thune, R	197,848	Tom Daschle, D	193,340	4,508	1.2
Pennsylvania 6 *	Jim Gerlach, R	160,348	Lois Murphy, D	153,977	6,371	2.0
California 20	Jim Costa, D	61,005	Roy Ashburn, R	53,231	7,774	6.8
Georgia 12	John Barrow, D	113,036	Max Burns, R	105,132	7,904	3.6
Illinois 8	Melissa Bean, D	139,792	Philip M. Crane, R	130,601	9,191	3.4
Texas 17	Chet Edwards, D	125,309	Arlene Wohlgemuth, R	116,049	9,260	3.8
Alaska Senate	Lisa Murkowski, R	149,773	Tony Knowles, D	140,424	9,349	3.0

* Also finished in the top 10 in the 2002 election

Fewest Votes Received

House members who won with the fewest votes in 2004:

Member	Votes Received
Charlie Melancon, D-La. (3) *	57,611
Jim Costa, D-Calif. (20)	61,005
Loretta Sanchez, D-Calif. (47)	65,684
Charles Boustany Jr., R-La. (7) *	75,039
Ed Pastor, D-Ariz. (4)	77,150
Gene Green, D-Texas (29)	78,256
Lucille Roybal-Allard, D-Calif. (34)	82,282
Joe Baca, D-Calif. (43)	86,830
Xavier Becerra, D-Calif. (31)	89,363
Rubén Hinojosa, D-Texas (15)	96,089

* runoff

Most Votes Received

House candidates who received the most votes in 2004:

Member	Votes Received
Denny Rehberg, R-Mont (AL)	286,076
Michael Bilirakis, R-Fla. (9)	284,035
Jim McDermott, D-Wash. (7)	272,302
F. James Sensenbrenner Jr., R-Wis. (5)	271,153
Tom Price, R-Ga. (6)	267,542
Spencer Bachus, R-Ala. (6)	264,819
John Linder, R-Ga. (7)	258,982
Ander Crenshaw, R-Fla. (4)	256,157
Chaka Fattah, D-Pa. (2)	253,226
Tammy Baldwin, D-Wis. (2)	251,637

Most Votes Cast

The 10 congressional districts in which the most votes were cast in 2004:

District	Votes Cast
Montana AL	444,230
Wisconsin 5	407,291
Wisconsin 2	397,724
South Dakota AL	389,468
Minnesota 6	377,224
Oregon 4	374,909
Maine 1	366,740
Minnesota 2	365,945
Florida 5	364,488
Wisconsin 3	363,008

Fewest Votes Cast

The 10 congressional districts in which the fewest votes were cast in 2004:

District	Votes Cast
Texas 29	83,124
California 47	108,783
Arizona 4	110,027
California 34	110,457
California 31	111,411
California 20	114,236
Louisiana 3 *	114,653
New York 16	117,248
New York 12	124,962
Illinois 4	125,142

* runoff

Under 50 Percent

Winners of 2004 elections who received less than half the votes cast:

Member	Percent
Lisa Murkowski, R-Alaska	48.6
Mel Martinez, R-Fla.	49.5
Mike Sodrel, R-Ind. (9)	49.5

CAMPAIGN FINANCE

Winners Outspent by Opponents

Winners in 2004 who spent less than their opponents. Totals cover the period Jan. 1, 2003, through Dec. 31, 2004.

(in order of spending margin)

Senate

Name, Party, State	Expenditures	Opponent	Expenditures
John Thune, R-S.D.	$14,666,225	Tom Daschle, D	$19,975,170
Tom Coburn, R-Okla.	$5,078,647	Brad Carson, D	$6,256,444
Richard M. Burr, R-N.C.	$12,853,110	Erskine Bowles, D	$13,357,851
Lisa Murkowski, R-Alaska	$5,429,904	Tony Knowles, D	$5,767,707

House

Name, Party, State (Dist.)	Expenditures	Opponent	Expenditures
Emanuel Cleaver II, D-Mo. (5)	$1,521,741	Jeanne Patterson, R	$3,207,825
John Hostettler, R-Ind. (8)	$494,781	Jon Jennings, D	$1,504,920
John Barrow, D-Ga. (11)	$1,857,839	Max Burns, R	$2,798,725
Ted Poe, R-Tex. (2)	$1,522,863	Nick Lampson, D	$2,405,430
Charlie Dent, R-Pa. (15)	$1,971,131	Joe Driscoll, D	$2,295,656
Pete Sessions, R-Tex. (32)	$4,512,464	Martin Frost, D	$4,761,288
Brian Higgins, D-N.Y. (27)	$1,372,162	Nancy Naples, R	$1,581,433
Patrick J. Kennedy, D-R.I. (1)	$1,958,492	David Rogers, R	$2,133,062
Charlie Melancon, D-La. (3)	$1,765,052	Billy Tauzin III, R	$1,924,780
Cathy McMorris, R-Wash. (5)	$1,537,540	Don Barbieri, D	$1,628,666
Mike Sodrel, R-Ind. (3)	$1,546,877	Baron P. Hill, D	$1,634,699
Melissa Bean, D-Ill. (8)	$1,597,053	Philip M. Crane, R	$1,618,074
Linda T. Sánchez, D-Calif. (39)	$782,521	Tim Escobar, R	$790,869

CAMPAIGN FINANCE

10 Least-Expensive Winning House Campaigns

The chart is based on expenditures from Jan. 1, 2003, through Dec. 31, 2004.

Name, Party, State (Dist.)	Expenditures	Name, Party, State (Dist.)	Expenditures
Daniel Lipinski, D-Ill. (3)	$49,004	Henry E. Brown Jr., R-S.C. (1)	$205,460
Tom Osborne, R-Neb. (3)	$63,654	Ted Strickland, D-Ohio (6)	$215,879
Joel Hefley, R-Colo. (5)	$93,332	Luis V. Gutierrez, D-Ill. (4)	$233,086
Bill Jenkins, R-Tenn. (1)	$160,643	Mark Souder, R-Ind. (3)	$238,176
Todd Platts, R-Pa. (19)	$171,605	John L. Mica, R-Fla. (7)	$256,103

CAMPAIGN FINANCE

Top 10 Senate Spenders in 2004

The chart is based on Federal Election Commission reports of expenditures from Jan. 1, 2001, through Dec. 31, 2004. The first column lists the top spenders who were elected or re-elected in the 2004 election.

Name, Party, State	Expenditures	Opponent	Expenditures
Arlen Specter, R-Pa.	$20,307,099	Joseph M. Hoeffel, D	$4,540,209
Charles E. Schumer, D-N.Y.	$15,467,530	Howard Mills, R	$629,170
Barbara Boxer, D-Calif.	$14,886,426	Bill Jones, R	$7,774,352
John Thune, R-S.D.	$14,666,225	Tom Daschle, D	$19,975,170
Barack Obama, D-Ill.	$14,532,493	Alan L. Keyes, R	$2,545,325
Richard M. Burr, R-N.C.	$12,853,110	Erskine Bowles, D	$13,357,851
Mel Martinez, R-Fla.	$12,837,220	Betty Castor, D	$11,472,071
Patty Murray, D-Wash.	$11,556,148	George Nethercutt, R	$7,726,296
Ken Salazar, D-Colo.	$9,886,551	Pete Coors, R	$7,858,598
Russell D. Feingold, D-Wis.	$9,239,908	Tim Michels, R	$5,542,087

CAMPAIGN FINANCE

Top 10 House Spenders in 2004

The chart is based on Federal Election Commission reports of expenditures from Jan. 1, 2003, through Dec. 31, 2004. The first column lists the top spenders who were elected or re-elected in the 2004 election.

Name, Party, State (District)	Expenditures	Opponent	Expenditures
J. Dennis Hastert, R-Ill. (14)	$5,013,947	Rubén Zamora, D	$18,028
Allyson Y. Schwartz, D-Pa. (13)	$4,572,417	Melissa Brown, R	$1,927,499
Pete Sessions, R-Tex. (32)	$4,512,464	Martin Frost, D	$4,761,288
Stephanie Herseth, D-S.D. (AL) *	$4,026,661	Larry Diedrich, R	$2,526,515
Robert Menendez, D-N.J. (13)	$3,941,956	Richard W. Piatowski, R	no data available
Katherine Harris, R-Fla. (13)	$3,556,976	Jan Schneider, D	$655,790
Roy Blunt, R-Mo. (7)	$3,527,363	James Newberry, D	$214,240
Heather Wilson, R-N.M. (1)	$3,401,887	Richard Romero, D	$2,101,102
Anne M. Northup, R-Ky. (3)	$3,339,760	Tony Miller, D	$1,221,092
Marilyn Musgrave, R-Colo. (4)	$3,314,507	Stan Matsunaka, D	$868,439

* Includes spending from a special election

Campaign Finance

Figures are given for all members of Congress and their general election opponents as reported by the Federal Election Commission. If only one candidate is listed, either that candidate was unopposed or the second-leading vote-getter did not raise at least $5,000.

For House members, figures are for the 2004 elections. For senators, figures are for their most recent election.

The campaign finance data covers the receipts and expenditures of each candidate during the two-year election cycle. Data for 2004 covers the period Jan. 1, 2003, to Dec. 31, 2004. Data for 2002 covers the period Jan. 1, 2001, to Nov. 6, 2002, although spending on runoffs or special elections later in 2002 for a few candidates is also included. Data for 2000 covers Jan. 1, 1999, to Dec. 31, 2000.

The figures for political action committee receipts are based on the FEC summary report for each candidate. Amounts listed include contributions from both PACs and candidate committees, but not party committees.

Candidates who ran in special elections in the two-year cycle are marked with †. In these cases, campaign finance figures include money spent on the special elections.

The FEC is constantly receiving amended reports. The figures listed were the latest available, as of April 2005.

Alabama

	RECEIPTS	FROM PACS	EXPENDITURES
SENIOR SENATOR - 2004			
Shelby (R)	$6,610,117	$1,480,707 (22%)	$1,922,646
Sowell (D)	$4,941	$0 (0%)	$4,869
JUNIOR SENATOR - 2002			
Sessions (R)	$4,635,963	$1,018,184 (22%)	$5,070,766
Parker (D)	$1,191,848	$178,820 (15%)	$1,185,718
DISTRICT 1			
Bonner (R)	$1,180,892	$394,354 (33%)	$1,015,702
Belk (D)	$442,450	$72,850 (16%)	$442,141
DISTRICT 2			
Everett (R)	$2,001,443	$336,616 (17%)	$1,937,038
James (D)	$1,320	$0 (0%)	$1,320
DISTRICT 3			
Rogers (R)	$2,120,515	$818,566 (39%)	$1,892,267
Fuller (D)	$280,237	$115,700 (41%)	$240,774
DISTRICT 4			
Aderholt (R)	$748,910	$255,700 (34%)	$735,352
Cole (D)	$25,553	$1,500 (6%)	$25,496
DISTRICT 5			
Cramer (D)	$820,378	$403,466 (49%)	$588,838
Wallace (R)	$12,644	$1,000 (8%)	$12,610
DISTRICT 6			
Bachus (R)	$1,647,636	$867,989 (53%)	$1,376,103
DISTRICT 7			
Davis (D)	$1,086,622	$512,015 (47%)	$1,061,606

Alaska

	RECEIPTS	FROM PACS	EXPENDITURES
SENIOR SENATOR - 2002			
Stevens (R)	$2,718,907	$967,202 (36%)	$2,093,021
Vondersaar (D)	$1,050	$0 (0%)	$1,049
JUNIOR SENATOR - 2004			
Murkowski (R)	$5,702,709	$1,991,677 (35%)	$5,429,904
Knowles (D)	$5,834,694	$784,870 (13%)	$5,767,707
Millican (NON)	$187,850	$0 (0%)	$190,379
Sykes (GREEN)	$15,247	$0 (0%)	$8,771
AT LARGE			
Young (R)	$2,482,929	$928,657 (37%)	$1,747,897

Arizona

	RECEIPTS	FROM PACS	EXPENDITURES
SENIOR SENATOR - 2004			
McCain (R)	$3,419,717	$658,093 (19%)	$2,140,807
Starky (D)	$12,956	$7,000 (54%)	$12,716
JUNIOR SENATOR - 2000			
Kyl (R)	$2,985,612	$880,280 (29%)	$2,503,674
Toel (I)	$21,542	$0 (0%)	$21,541
DISTRICT 1			
Renzi (R)	$2,358,748	$1,205,645 (51%)	$2,207,249
Babbitt (D)	$1,298,530	$409,984 (32%)	$1,274,852
DISTRICT 2			
Franks (R)	$804,990	$381,495 (47%)	$738,525
Camacho (D)	$93,253	$45,000 (48%)	$101,998
DISTRICT 3			
Shadegg (R)	$810,996	$457,769 (56%)	$792,700
DISTRICT 4			
Pastor (D)	$845,637	$469,444 (56%)	$624,271
DISTRICT 5			
Hayworth (R)	$1,370,627	$527,015 (38%)	$1,356,723
Rogers (D)	$5,091	$0 (0%)	$4,898
DISTRICT 6			
Flake (R)	$644,789	$115,000 (18%)	$675,055
DISTRICT 7			
Grijalva (D)	$667,936	$302,610 (45%)	$618,854
DISTRICT 8			
Kolbe (R)	$1,159,245	$446,393 (39%)	$1,146,714
Bacal (D)	$102,191	$5,500 (5%)	$99,691

Arkansas

	RECEIPTS	FROM PACS	EXPENDITURES
SENIOR SENATOR - 2004			
Lincoln (D)	$5,489,103	$2,427,554 (44%)	$5,816,913
Holt (R)	$153,628	$7,000 (5%)	$148,682
JUNIOR SENATOR - 2002			
Pryor (D)	$4,442,708	$843,572 (19%)	$4,365,349
Hutchinson (R)	$4,858,117	$1,693,422 (35%)	$4,942,828
DISTRICT 1			
Berry (D)	$1,099,239	$577,350 (53%)	$947,839
Humphrey (R)	$25,092	$0 (0%)	$23,836

DISTRICT 2
Snyder (D)	$891,220	$251,530 (28%)	$880,496
Parks (R)	$576,854	$76,275 (13%)	$574,023

DISTRICT 3
Boozman (R)	$697,084	$271,450 (39%)	$543,281
Judy (D)	$353,823	$51,750 (15%)	$353,822

DISTRICT 4
Ross (D)	$1,218,961	$704,030 (58%)	$756,922

California

	RECEIPTS	FROM PACS	EXPENDITURES
SENIOR SENATOR - 2000			
Feinstein (D)	$10,464,194	$1,245,727 (12%)	$10,346,170
Campbell (R)	$4,733,507	$11,600 (0%)	$4,378,283
Benjamin (GREEN)	$269,287	$1,100 (0%)	$241,361
Lightfoot (LIBERT)	$20,803	$0 (0%)	$21,085
JUNIOR SENATOR - 2004			
Boxer (D)	$14,301,289	$1,290,551 (9%)	$14,886,426
Jones (R)	$7,766,693	$559,414 (7%)	$7,774,352
Gray (LIBERT)	$251,832	$9,500 (4%)	$250,244
DISTRICT 1			
Thompson (D)	$1,256,758	$449,934 (36%)	$1,272,329
Wiesner (R)	$29,624	$5,000 (17%)	$28,993
DISTRICT 2			
Herger (R)	$673,903	$385,999 (57%)	$580,670
Johnson (D)	$11,235	$0 (0%)	$6,297
DISTRICT 3			
Lungren (R)	$1,424,407	$399,850 (28%)	$1,407,970
Castillo (D)	$98,347	$28,550 (29%)	$98,284
Tuma (LIBERT)	$322	$0 (0%)	$368
DISTRICT 4			
Doolittle (R)	$935,907	$271,597 (29%)	$912,648
Winters (D)	$2,300	$100 (4%)	$2,061
DISTRICT 5 †			
Matsui, D. (D)	$1,113,890	$488,600 (44%)	$941,224
Padilla (D)	$37,401	$0 (0%)	$37,401
Flynn (R)	$46,532	$1,000 (2%)	$46,542
Chernay (R)	$25,451	$0 (0%)	$18,767
Driscoll (GREEN)	$0	$0 (0%)	$5,719
DISTRICT 6			
Woolsey (D)	$554,861	$237,070 (43%)	$562,533
Erickson (R)	$5,063	$0 (0%)	$6,309
DISTRICT 7			
Miller (D)	$573,259	$408,459 (71%)	$571,957
DISTRICT 8			
Pelosi (D)	$1,552,921	$759,000 (49%)	$1,240,543
Depalma (R)	$6,982	$0 (0%)	$5,704
DISTRICT 9			
Lee (D)	$871,025	$234,060 (27%)	$783,143
Bermudez (R)	$474,451	$1,000 (0%)	$478,502
DISTRICT 10			
Tauscher (D)	$817,961	$443,804 (54%)	$780,196
Ketelson (R)	$159,220	$0 (0%)	$159,219
DISTRICT 11			
Pombo (R)	$1,101,279	$604,775 (55%)	$1,018,433
McNerney (D)	$156,726	$15,100 (10%)	$154,677
DISTRICT 12			
Lantos (D)	$2,128,474	$198,122 (9%)	$1,190,646

Gray (GREEN)	$47,955	$0 (0%)	$44,685

DISTRICT 13
Stark (D)	$370,608	$287,935 (78%)	$455,735
Bruno (R)	$31,464	$5,000 (16%)	$31,883

DISTRICT 14
Eshoo (D)	$955,915	$518,700 (54%)	$939,389
Haugen (R)	$52,841	$100 (0%)	$52,623

DISTRICT 15
Honda (D)	$524,602	$266,951 (51%)	$539,475
Chukwu (R)	$76,053	$0 (0%)	$84,998

DISTRICT 16
Lofgren (D)	$533,196	$280,752 (53%)	$598,739
McNea (R)	$145	$0 (0%)	$244

DISTRICT 17
Farr (D)	$612,021	$316,625 (52%)	$616,323
Risley (R)	$145,684	$0 (0%)	$144,619

DISTRICT 18
Cardoza (D)	$883,668	$454,138 (51%)	$809,014
Pringle (R)	$12,130	$0 (0%)	$11,095

DISTRICT 19
Radanovich (R)	$845,103	$382,650 (45%)	$919,414

DISTRICT 20
Costa (D)	$1,963,507	$634,575 (32%)	$1,937,317
Ashburn (R)	$1,123,782	$330,647 (29%)	$1,093,429

DISTRICT 21
Nunes (R)	$795,304	$278,800 (35%)	$667,520

DISTRICT 22
Thomas (R)	$1,675,469	$1,226,562 (73%)	$1,493,678

DISTRICT 23
Capps (D)	$1,110,383	$376,025 (34%)	$1,009,290
Regan (R)	$148,649	$2,000 (1%)	$148,631

DISTRICT 24
Gallegly (R)	$656,534	$145,849 (22%)	$551,059
Wagner (D)	$208,256	$17,847 (9%)	$207,432

DISTRICT 25
McKeon (R)	$961,848	$337,850 (35%)	$954,938
Willoughby (D)	$49,685	$0 (0%)	$47,171

DISTRICT 26
Dreier (R)	$1,185,967	$409,500 (35%)	$1,338,730
Matthews (D)	$55,305	$0 (0%)	$25,535

DISTRICT 27
Sherman (D)	$818,151	$346,350 (42%)	$871,672

DISTRICT 28
Berman (D)	$735,041	$235,975 (32%)	$902,390
Hernandez (R)	$33,128	$0 (0%)	$32,611

DISTRICT 29
Schiff (D)	$1,488,304	$472,900 (32%)	$955,782
Scolinos (R)	$620,423	$6,000 (1%)	$605,280

DISTRICT 30
Waxman (D)	$564,007	$428,113 (76%)	$453,715
Elizalde (R)	$263,523	$8,500 (3%)	$262,130

DISTRICT 31
Becerra (D)	$785,737	$496,021 (63%)	$623,023

DISTRICT 32
Solis (D)	$576,810	$330,665 (57%)	$527,054

DISTRICT 33
Watson (D)	$261,192	$157,475 (60%)	$259,663

DISTRICT 34

Roybal-Allard (D)	$573,212	$263,274 (46%)	$572,055

DISTRICT 35

Waters (D)	$390,923	$111,525 (29%)	$330,980
Moen (R)	$3,550	$0 (0%)	$3,540

DISTRICT 36

Harman (D)	$1,046,238	$330,526 (32%)	$765,112
Whitehead (R)	$68,688	$500 (1%)	$68,635

DISTRICT 37

Millender- McDonald (D)	$321,862	$249,765 (78%)	$307,056

DISTRICT 38

Napolitano (D)	$350,930	$210,725 (60%)	$273,757

DISTRICT 39

Sánchez (D)	$786,141	$349,985 (45%)	$782,521
Escobar (R)	$780,680	$140,410 (18%)	$790,869

DISTRICT 40

Royce (R)	$1,215,928	$374,526 (31%)	$736,717

DISTRICT 41

Lewis (R)	$1,562,561	$683,667 (44%)	$1,450,053

DISTRICT 42

Miller (R)	$640,776	$308,850 (48%)	$421,841

DISTRICT 43

Baca (D)	$492,473	$313,123 (64%)	$450,287
Laning (R)	$55,131	$5,231 (9%)	$40,391

DISTRICT 44

Calvert (R)	$704,410	$294,613 (42%)	$687,467
Vandenberg (D)	$10,473	$3,321 (32%)	$6,196

DISTRICT 45

Bono (R)	$608,781	$267,342 (44%)	$501,088
Meyer (D)	$259,353	$1,410 (1%)	$262,288

DISTRICT 46

Rohrabacher (R)	$748,974	$153,087 (20%)	$517,315
Brandt (D)	$88,424	$9,538 (11%)	$85,456

DISTRICT 47

Sanchez (D)	$1,310,010	$416,919 (32%)	$1,837,079
Coronado (R)	$358,258	$73,799 (21%)	$356,372

DISTRICT 48

Cox (R)	$1,120,427	$465,789 (42%)	$1,038,914
Graham (D)	$40	$0 (0%)	$1,994

DISTRICT 49

Issa (R)	$869,534	$394,228 (45%)	$881,452
Byron (D)	$66,914	$3,500 (5%)	$69,035

DISTRICT 50

Cunningham (R)	$832,173	$402,885 (48%)	$939,542
Busby (D)	$235,925	$2,900 (1%)	$212,154

DISTRICT 51

Filner (D)	$748,440	$325,575 (44%)	$657,867
Giorgino (R)	$114,048	$15,250 (13%)	$111,778

DISTRICT 52

Hunter (R)	$1,064,206	$453,345 (43%)	$1,058,126
Keliher (D)	$15,915	$0 (0%)	$14,828

DISTRICT 53

Davis (D)	$476,368	$193,828 (41%)	$387,177
Hunzeker (R)	$68,083	$2,547 (4%)	$68,081
Rockwood (GREEN)	$14,785	$0 (0%)	$6,015

Colorado

	RECEIPTS	FROM PACS	EXPENDITURES
SENIOR SENATOR - 2002			
Allard (R)	$5,163,810	$1,940,956 (38%)	$5,077,481
Strickland (D)	$5,164,823	$784,890 (15%)	$5,048,097
Stanley (LIBERT)	$14,504	$0 (0%)	$14,283
JUNIOR SENATOR - 2004			
Salazar (D)	$9,925,778	$1,018,212 (10%)	$9,886,551
Coors (R)	$7,879,182	$1,301,667 (17%)	$7,858,598
DISTRICT 1			
DeGette (D)	$632,594	$345,937 (55%)	$620,599
Chicas (R)	$17,034	$3,000 (18%)	$16,968
DISTRICT 2			
Udall (D)	$1,122,459	$309,550 (28%)	$885,440
Hackman (R)	$8,374	$100 (1%)	$10,262
Olsen (LIBERT)	$2,000	$0 (0%)	$181
DISTRICT 3			
Salazar (D)	$1,652,986	$623,036 (38%)	$1,623,509
Walcher (R)	$1,638,304	$472,378 (29%)	$1,562,081
DISTRICT 4			
Musgrave (R)	$3,422,482	$468,903 (14%)	$3,314,507
Kinsey (GREEN)	$6,947	$0 (0%)	$6,946
Matsunaka (D)	$869,007	$89,674 (10%)	$868,439
DISTRICT 5			
Hefley (R)	$100,276	$63,880 (64%)	$93,332
Hardee (D)	$11,130	$2,500 (22%)	$8,949
DISTRICT 6			
Tancredo (R)	$982,522	$92,256 (9%)	$1,178,724
Conti (D)	$827,697	$69,760 (8%)	$827,526
DISTRICT 7			
Beauprez (R)	$2,967,373	$1,228,900 (41%)	$2,970,799
Thomas (D)	$1,158,593	$391,593 (34%)	$1,125,677

Connecticut

	RECEIPTS	FROM PACS	EXPENDITURES
SENIOR SENATOR - 2004			
Dodd (D)	$4,676,379	$1,368,210 (29%)	$3,938,132
Orchulli (R)	$1,476,876	$800 (0%)	$1,462,401
JUNIOR SENATOR - 2000			
Lieberman (D)	$3,666,873	$975,344 (27%)	$3,786,665
Giordano (R)	$1,278,539	$0 (0%)	$1,276,376
DISTRICT 1			
Larson (D)	$643,746	$231,799 (36%)	$604,516
DISTRICT 2			
Simmons (R)	$2,560,043	$1,181,513 (46%)	$2,516,937
Sullivan (D)	$1,052,238	$361,880 (34%)	$1,056,756
DISTRICT 3			
DeLauro (D)	$735,034	$336,377 (46%)	$714,890
Elser (R)	$20,798	$750 (4%)	$21,416
DISTRICT 4			
Shays (R)	$2,233,286	$523,380 (23%)	$2,255,210
Farrell (D)	$1,545,052	$217,919 (14%)	$1,542,410
DISTRICT 5			
Johnson (R)	$2,282,416	$1,288,755 (56%)	$1,241,036
Gerratana (D)	$126,192	$18,756 (15%)	$127,791

Delaware

	RECEIPTS	FROM PACS	EXPENDITURES
SENIOR SENATOR - 2002			
Biden (D)	$2,726,583	$0 (0%)	$2,991,862
Clatworthy (R)	$1,871,163	$13,100 (1%)	$1,804,123
JUNIOR SENATOR - 2000			
Carper (D)	$2,629,812	$599,245 (23%)	$2,608,942
Roth (R)	$4,256,984	$1,727,178 (41%)	$4,366,884
AT LARGE			
Castle (R)	$992,240	$383,263 (39%)	$902,706
Donnelly (D)	$4,429	$2,600 (59%)	$4,429

Florida

	RECEIPTS	FROM PACS	EXPENDITURES
SENIOR SENATOR - 2000			
Nelson (D)	$6,639,259	$1,195,617 (18%)	$6,635,832
McCollum (R)	$7,936,639	$1,391,571 (18%)	$8,664,112
Logan (I)	$361,990	$14,700 (4%)	$361,660
Simonetta (NL)	$22,733	$0 (0%)	$23,600
Deckard (REF)	$16,565	$0 (0%)	$16,563
McCormick (I)	$10,220	$0 (0%)	$10,209
JUNIOR SENATOR - 2004			
Martinez (R)	$12,856,384	$2,245,433 (17%)	$12,837,220
Castor (D)	$11,645,379	$880,326 (8%)	$11,472,071
Bradley (VET)	$15,793	$1,552 (10%)	$15,794
DISTRICT 1			
Miller (R)	$377,378	$139,150 (37%)	$279,318
Coutu (D)	$25,060	$0 (0%)	$33,000
DISTRICT 2			
Boyd (D)	$1,896,811	$870,915 (46%)	$2,064,646
Kilmer (R)	$1,133,100	$216,173 (19%)	$1,132,998
DISTRICT 3			
Brown (D)	$453,938	$266,379 (59%)	$450,589
DISTRICT 4			
Crenshaw (R)	$581,117	$146,878 (25%)	$279,540
DISTRICT 5			
Brown-Waite (R)	$923,134	$599,408 (65%)	$787,436
Whittel (D)	$140,747	$20,019 (14%)	$140,742
DISTRICT 6			
Stearns (R)	$716,968	$474,121 (66%)	$283,334
Bruderly (D)	$121,762	$9,600 (8%)	$118,904
DISTRICT 7			
Mica (R)	$476,005	$303,899 (64%)	$256,103
DISTRICT 8			
Keller (R)	$617,533	$369,862 (60%)	$292,257
Murray (D)	$63,243	$3,000 (5%)	$62,420
DISTRICT 9			
Bilirakis (R)	$772,272	$501,043 (65%)	$596,389
DISTRICT 10			
Young (R)	$556,179	$371,750 (67%)	$681,749
Derry (D)	$91,185	$8,000 (9%)	$85,865
DISTRICT 11			
Davis (D)	$648,911	$437,035 (67%)	$630,804
Johnson (LIBERT)	$33,882	$0 (0%)	$32,700
DISTRICT 12			
Putnam (R)	$837,221	$333,983 (40%)	$700,625
Hagenmaier (D)	$53,500	$2,200 (4%)	$54,002
DISTRICT 13			
Harris (R)	$3,582,920	$724,356 (20%)	$3,556,976
Schneider (D)	$627,279	$64,200 (10%)	$655,790
DISTRICT 14			
Mack (R)	$1,892,757	$459,004 (24%)	$1,854,028
Neeld (D)	$25,276	$0 (0%)	$25,275
DISTRICT 15			
Weldon (R)	$1,058,969	$250,522 (24%)	$733,711
Pristoop (D)	$58,925	$0 (0%)	$54,355
DISTRICT 16			
Foley (R)	$2,240,001	$809,590 (36%)	$1,839,746
DISTRICT 17			
Meek (D)	$556,640	$111,504 (20%)	$488,407
DISTRICT 18			
Ros-Lehtinen (R)	$876,886	$234,608 (27%)	$859,083
Sheldon (D)	$11,883	$0 (0%)	$11,882
DISTRICT 19			
Wexler (D)	$743,428	$217,750 (29%)	$939,363
DISTRICT 20			
Wasserman-Schultz	$1,523,601	$486,183 (32%)	$1,468,898
Hostetter (R)	$35,315	$0 (0%)	$35,045
DISTRICT 21			
Diaz-Balart (R)	$524,622	$237,176 (45%)	$451,555
Gonzalez (LIBERT)	$7,208	$0 (0%)	$12,719
DISTRICT 22			
Shaw (R)	$1,585,007	$721,928 (46%)	$1,237,966
Rorapaugh (D)	$15,845	$9,000 (57%)	$9,800
McLain (CNSTP)	$20,346	$0 (0%)	$20,344
DISTRICT 23			
Hastings (D)	$955,197	$272,300 (29%)	$947,430
DISTRICT 24			
Feeney (R)	$932,254	$505,708 (54%)	$705,578
DISTRICT 25			
Diaz-Balart (R)	$544,127	$208,488 (38%)	$322,024

Georgia

	RECEIPTS	FROM PACS	EXPENDITURES
SENIOR SENATOR - 2002			
Chambliss (R)	$7,422,836	$1,282,955 (17%)	$7,475,943
Cleland (D)	$8,146,827	$1,827,709 (22%)	$9,055,254
Thomas (LIBERT)	$11,109	$0 (0%)	$11,108
JUNIOR SENATOR - 2004			
Isakson (R)	$8,577,130	$1,713,570 (20%)	$8,038,200
Majette (D)	$2,084,294	$602,604 (29%)	$2,470,272
Buckley (LIBERT)	$42,377	$0 (0%)	$42,376
DISTRICT 1			
Kingston (R)	$845,652	$356,140 (42%)	$783,347
DISTRICT 2			
Bishop (D)	$671,352	$324,550 (48%)	$761,275
Eversman (R)	$30,376	$1,000 (3%)	$25,277
DISTRICT 3			
Marshall (D)	$1,328,261	$499,250 (38%)	$1,307,926
Clay (R)	$1,052,684	$293,503 (28%)	$1,054,493

DISTRICT 4
McKinney (D) | $536,473 | $39,155 (7%) | $569,680
Davis (R) | $47,802 | $8,620 (18%) | $39,874

DISTRICT 5
Lewis (D) | $421,030 | $348,775 (83%) | $547,098

DISTRICT 6
Price (R) | $2,545,518 | $544,647 (21%) | $2,283,545

DISTRICT 7
Linder (R) | $796,208 | $283,300 (36%) | $746,763

DISTRICT 8
Westmoreland (R) | $2,140,448 | $525,180 (25%) | $1,943,512
Delamar (D) | $28,590 | $12,980 (45%) | $28,846

DISTRICT 9
Norwood (R) | $1,151,883 | $415,333 (36%) | $890,622
Ellis (D) | $113,774 | $34,000 (30%) | $113,330

DISTRICT 10
Deal (R) | $388,152 | $266,337 (69%) | $372,286

DISTRICT 11
Gingrey (R) | $2,288,758 | $717,542 (31%) | $2,254,633
Crawford (D) | $275,663 | $87,986 (32%) | $283,358

DISTRICT 12
Barrow (D) | $1,878,067 | $493,764 (26%) | $1,857,839
Burns (R) | $2,799,984 | $1,336,297 (48%) | $2,798,725

DISTRICT 13
Scott (D) | $1,102,033 | $683,649 (62%) | $980,333

Hawaii

	RECEIPTS	FROM PACS	EXPENDITURES
SENIOR SENATOR - 2004			
Inouye (D)	$2,788,703	$957,571 (34%)	$1,768,886
Cavasso (R)	$57,514	$8,500 (15%)	$57,122
JUNIOR SENATOR - 2000			
Akaka (D)	$601,881	$316,415 (53%)	$428,516
Carroll (R)	$107,253	$300 (0%)	$97,407
DISTRICT 1			
Abercrombie (D)	$1,089,528	$536,350 (49%)	$1,055,643
Tanonaka (R)	$213,681	$9,500 (4%)	$213,639
DISTRICT 2			
Case (D)	$755,345	$159,602 (21%)	$786,182
Gabbard (R)	$485,134	$25,525 (5%)	$484,160

Idaho

	RECEIPTS	FROM PACS	EXPENDITURES
SENIOR SENATOR - 2002			
Craig (R)	$3,012,333	$1,065,581 (35%)	$2,933,495
Blinken (D)	$2,173,286	$97,000 (4%)	$2,149,333
JUNIOR SENATOR - 2004			
Crapo (R)	$1,948,398	$1,241,988 (64%)	$1,031,912
DISTRICT 1			
Otter (R)	$724,712	$377,730 (52%)	$512,498
Preston (D)	$15,055	$1,000 (7%)	$15,152
DISTRICT 2			
Simpson (R)	$556,129	$422,806 (76%)	$498,082
Whitworth (D)	$72,019	$17,690 (25%)	$68,209

Illinois

	RECEIPTS	FROM PACS	EXPENDITURES
SENIOR SENATOR - 2002			
Durbin (D)	$5,174,051	$1,228,196 (24%)	$4,870,737
Durkin (R)	$795,941	$102,478 (13%)	$770,458
JUNIOR SENATOR - 2004			
Obama (D)	$15,096,157	$1,205,724 (8%)	$14,532,493
Keyes (R)	$2,687,483	$50,608 (2%)	$2,545,325
DISTRICT 1			
Rush (D)	$469,975	$276,700 (59%)	$361,032
DISTRICT 2			
Jackson (D)	$886,995	$292,825 (33%)	$527,367
DISTRICT 3			
Lipinski (D)	$195,065	$89,000 (46%)	$49,004
DISTRICT 4			
Gutierrez (D)	$303,631	$184,875 (61%)	$233,086
DISTRICT 5			
Emanuel (D)	$1,597,260	$431,708 (27%)	$689,463
DISTRICT 6			
Hyde (R)	$643,057	$200,854 (31%)	$804,197
Cegelis (D)	$196,988	$6,500 (3%)	$193,947
DISTRICT 7			
Davis (D)	$483,851	$255,786 (53%)	$438,680
Davis-Fairman (R)	$45,087	$1,250 (3%)	$43,718
DISTRICT 8			
Bean (D)	$1,603,229	$491,391 (31%)	$1,597,053
Crane (R)	$1,594,634	$1,164,087 (73%)	$1,618,074
DISTRICT 9			
Schakowsky (D)	$1,098,204	$295,500 (27%)	$1,068,961
Eckhardt (R)	$9,470	$1,650 (17%)	$2,624
DISTRICT 10			
Kirk (R)	$1,747,924	$367,626 (21%)	$1,653,529
Goodman (D)	$95,992	$4,104 (4%)	$88,520
DISTRICT 11			
Weller (R)	$1,551,284	$811,870 (52%)	$1,792,779
Renner (D)	$318,056	$70,805 (22%)	$315,600
DISTRICT 12			
Costello (D)	$924,936	$374,477 (40%)	$637,567
Zweigart (R)	$16,231	$0 (0%)	$15,983
DISTRICT 13			
Biggert (R)	$632,733	$343,738 (54%)	$542,733
Andersen (D)	$42,318	$9,220 (22%)	$42,129
DISTRICT 14			
Hastert (R)	$4,862,029	$1,911,381 (39%)	$5,013,947
Zamora (D)	$18,674	$0 (0%)	$18,028
DISTRICT 15			
Johnson (R)	$533,478	$306,575 (57%)	$428,750
Gill (D)	$102,352	$9,290 (9%)	$100,106
DISTRICT 16			
Manzullo (R)	$1,253,731	$627,495 (50%)	$1,078,353
Kutsch (D)	$3,650	$300 (8%)	$2,911
DISTRICT 17			
Evans (D)	$780,972	$358,410 (46%)	$752,444
Zinga (R)	$270,494	$25,695 (9%)	$270,256

DISTRICT 18

LaHood (R)	$1,326,583	$464,651 (35%)	$955,764
Waterworth (D)	$4,520	$0 (0%)	$4,519

DISTRICT 19

Shimkus (R)	$1,071,896	$526,899 (49%)	$544,784
Bagwell (D)	$38,734	$7,400 (19%)	$38,229

Indiana

	RECEIPTS	FROM PACS	EXPENDITURES
SENIOR SENATOR - 2000			
Lugar (R)	$3,593,294	$863,899 (24%)	$4,251,603
Johnson (D)	$1,451,828	$138,900 (10%)	$1,451,786
JUNIOR SENATOR - 2004			
Bayh (D)	$4,820,160	$1,583,913 (33%)	$2,250,428
Scott (R)	$2,265,166	$6,450 (0%)	$2,242,526
DISTRICT 1			
Visclosky (D)	$1,237,315	$448,947 (36%)	$1,072,002
Leyva (R)	$21,569	$1,230 (6%)	$20,755
DISTRICT 2			
Chocola (R)	$1,662,745	$699,426 (42%)	$1,480,546
Donnelly (D)	$706,125	$185,610 (26%)	$700,728
DISTRICT 3			
Souder (R)	$256,325	$91,950 (36%)	$238,176
Parra (D)	$18,692	$4,720 (25%)	$18,761
DISTRICT 4			
Buyer (R)	$661,525	$464,297 (70%)	$509,517
Sanders (D)	$21,392	$0 (0%)	$15,480
DISTRICT 5			
Burton (R)	$761,443	$241,085 (32%)	$777,535
Carr (D)	$9,439	$1,500 (16%)	$10,229
DISTRICT 6			
Pence (R)	$1,189,141	$363,322 (31%)	$1,010,228
Fox (D)	$48,626	$29,500 (61%)	$50,071
DISTRICT 7			
Carson (D)	$586,641	$251,835 (43%)	$419,603
Horning (R)	$25,601	$7,350 (29%)	$25,303
Campbell (LIBERT)	$558	$0 (0%)	$431
DISTRICT 8			
Hostettler (R)	$480,210	$14,600 (3%)	$494,781
Jennings (D)	$1,512,445	$390,812 (26%)	$1,504,920
DISTRICT 9			
Sodrel (R)	$1,582,017	$315,795 (20%)	$1,546,877
Hill (D)	$1,625,332	$870,639 (54%)	$1,634,699

Iowa

	RECEIPTS	FROM PACS	EXPENDITURES
SENIOR SENATOR - 2004			
Grassley (R)	$5,655,068	$2,146,135 (38%)	$6,403,445
Small (D)	$140,204	$1,200 (1%)	$135,503
JUNIOR SENATOR - 2002			
Harkin (D)	$7,016,840	$1,441,247 (21%)	$6,727,132
Ganske (R)	$5,426,297	$779,685 (14%)	$5,334,084
DISTRICT 1			
Nussle (R)	$1,881,881	$1,014,029 (54%)	$1,622,743
Gluba (D)	$526,239	$125,800 (24%)	$524,168
Heath (I)	$5,731	$0 (0%)	$5,731

DISTRICT 2

Leach (R)	$529,453	$0 (0%)	$477,879
Franker (D)	$122,376	$17,100 (14%)	$122,489

DISTRICT 3

Boswell (D)	$1,556,335	$834,510 (54%)	$1,545,133
Thompson (R)	$856,740	$300,962 (35%)	$862,304

DISTRICT 4

Latham (R)	$1,074,673	$714,814 (67%)	$988,369
Johnson (D)	$291,237	$17,400 (6%)	$287,843

DISTRICT 5

King (R)	$539,970	$283,389 (52%)	$553,171
Schulte (D)	$60,055	$6,200 (10%)	$59,976

Kansas

	RECEIPTS	FROM PACS	EXPENDITURES
SENIOR SENATOR - 2004			
Brownback (R)	$2,730,682	$893,588 (33%)	$2,476,585
Jones (D)	$71,102	$32,000 (45%)	$31,147
JUNIOR SENATOR - 2002			
Roberts (R)	$1,408,528	$787,087 (56%)	$1,012,747
Cook (REF)	$3,450	$0 (0%)	$3,473
DISTRICT 1			
Moran (R)	$724,488	$438,351 (61%)	$349,807
DISTRICT 2			
Ryun (R)	$976,505	$546,747 (56%)	$1,136,464
Boyda (D)	$1,106,351	$195,679 (18%)	$1,105,838
DISTRICT 3			
Moore (D)	$2,312,590	$1,062,968 (46%)	$2,362,887
Kobach (R)	$1,285,591	$226,025 (18%)	$1,191,231
DISTRICT 4			
Tiahrt (R)	$1,030,804	$513,271 (50%)	$491,456
Kinard (D)	$14,797	$0 (0%)	$15,083

Kentucky

	RECEIPTS	FROM PACS	EXPENDITURES
SENIOR SENATOR - 2002			
McConnell (R)	$4,735,540	$1,192,388 (25%)	$5,241,832
Weinberg (D)	$2,239,125	$198,101 (9%)	$2,189,846
JUNIOR SENATOR - 2004			
Bunning (R)	$5,120,291	$1,903,137 (37%)	$6,075,399
Mongiardo (D)	$3,127,490	$484,365 (15%)	$3,104,981
DISTRICT 1			
Whitfield (R)	$848,124	$499,581 (59%)	$557,233
DISTRICT 2			
Lewis (R)	$768,504	$364,873 (47%)	$688,898
Smith (D)	$3,895	$0 (0%)	$4,172
DISTRICT 3			
Northup (R)	$3,339,733	$1,115,393 (33%)	$3,339,760
Miller (D)	$1,221,093	$398,198 (33%)	$1,221,092
DISTRICT 4			
Davis (R)	$3,076,557	$818,359 (27%)	$2,959,526
Clooney (D)	$1,452,947	$507,165 (35%)	$1,448,282
DISTRICT 5			
Rogers (R)	$643,981	$298,300 (46%)	$737,589

DISTRICT 6

Chandler (D)	$1,801,703	$820,251 (46%)	$1,623,086
Buford (R)	$138,924	$18,750 (13%)	$137,072

Louisiana

	RECEIPTS	FROM PACS	EXPENDITURES
SENIOR SENATOR - 2002			
Landrieu (D)	$6,770,029	$2,614,362 (39%)	$7,326,155
Cooksey (R)	$1,899,166	$65,225 (3%)	$1,835,326
Terrell (R)	$3,387,167	$820,277 (24%)	$2,760,276
Perkins (R)	$639,258	$39,681 (6%)	$634,270
JUNIOR SENATOR - 2004			
Vitter (R)	$7,743,804	$1,182,643 (15%)	$7,206,714
John (D)	$4,893,113	$1,065,880 (22%)	$4,868,165
Kennedy (D)	$1,919,879	$122,570 (6%)	$1,919,774
Morrell (D)	$68,653	$12,050 (18%)	$67,214
DISTRICT 1			
Jindal (R)	$2,323,414	$414,023 (18%)	$1,656,964
Rogers (R)	$26,780	$0 (0%)	$26,465
DISTRICT 2			
Jefferson (D)	$1,034,165	$715,943 (69%)	$960,790
Schwertz (R)	$15,182	$0 (0%)	$15,139
DISTRICT 3			
Melancon (D)	$1,806,028	$610,238 (34%)	$1,765,057
Tauzin (R)	$2,037,349	$842,835 (41%)	$1,924,780
Romero (R)	$1,034,945	$0 (0%)	$1,033,107
Baldone (D)	$362,510	$2,776 (1%)	$359,449
Caccioppi (D)	$256,812	$14,500 (6%)	$247,253
Chiasson (R)	$11,472	$5,000 (44%)	$12,110
DISTRICT 4			
McCrery (R)	$1,179,279	$658,663 (56%)	$939,484
DISTRICT 5			
Alexander (R)	$1,355,844	$743,798 (55%)	$1,344,520
Blakes (D)	$29,059	$0 (0%)	$20,303
Scott (R)	$150,069	$3,000 (2%)	$148,035
DISTRICT 6			
Baker (R)	$1,157,497	$822,121 (71%)	$1,090,347
Craig (D)	$21,801	$0 (0%)	$17,346
DISTRICT 7			
Boustany (R)	$2,846,661	$936,415 (33%)	$2,785,524
Mount (D)	$1,480,940	$341,796 (23%)	$1,340,886
Cravins (D)	$212,316	$18,000 (8%)	$212,315
Thibodaux (R)	$118,305	$100 (0%)	$118,238

Maine

	RECEIPTS	FROM PACS	EXPENDITURES
SENIOR SENATOR - 2000			
Snowe (R)	$2,236,146	$817,009 (37%)	$1,981,504
Lawrence (D)	$739,637	$145,703 (20%)	$727,655
JUNIOR SENATOR - 2002			
Collins (R)	$4,007,560	$1,511,332 (38%)	$3,945,683
Pingree (D)	$3,865,577	$340,306 (9%)	$3,741,905
DISTRICT 1			
Allen (D)	$807,351	$239,231 (30%)	$727,772
Summers (R)	$506,752	$68,900 (14%)	$505,698

DISTRICT 2

Michaud (D)	$1,331,468	$760,027 (57%)	$1,308,237
Hamel (R)	$667,602	$140,650 (21%)	$667,464

Maryland

	RECEIPTS	FROM PACS	EXPENDITURES
SENIOR SENATOR - 2000			
Sarbanes (D)	$1,851,731	$748,964 (40%)	$1,837,286
Rappaport (R)	$147,024	$2,510 (2%)	$146,866
JUNIOR SENATOR - 2004			
Mikulski (D)	$5,911,959	$1,133,700 (19%)	$5,997,093
Pipkin (R)	$2,313,360	$16,310 (1%)	$2,298,709
DISTRICT 1			
Gilchrest (R)	$527,450	$4,100 (1%)	$391,272
Alexakis (D)	$114,071	$5,750 (5%)	$113,435
DISTRICT 2			
Ruppersberger (D)	$746,971	$279,295 (37%)	$648,488
Brooks (R)	$89,478	$75 (0%)	$75,812
DISTRICT 3			
Cardin (D)	$940,148	$588,795 (63%)	$1,011,838
Duckworth (R)	$142,711	$6,032 (4%)	$140,972
DISTRICT 4			
Wynn (D)	$749,441	$374,732 (50%)	$722,207
McKinnis (R)	$94,948	$1,600 (2%)	$91,985
Dudley (GREEN)	$5,627	$0 (0%)	$6,084
DISTRICT 5			
Hoyer (D)	$1,896,026	$1,173,105 (62%)	$1,779,289
Jewitt (R)	$145,576	$10,250 (7%)	$145,559
Krukar (CNSTP)	$7,225	$0 (0%)	$7,198
DISTRICT 6			
Bartlett (R)	$574,294	$209,044 (36%)	$436,891
DISTRICT 7			
Cummings (D)	$814,295	$426,275 (52%)	$877,808
Salazar (R)	$110,447	$4,300 (4%)	$109,426
DISTRICT 8			
Van Hollen (D)	$1,702,772	$496,529 (29%)	$1,235,488
Floyd (R)	$353,801	$9,075 (3%)	$352,644

Massachusetts

	RECEIPTS	FROM PACS	EXPENDITURES
SENIOR SENATOR - 2000			
Kennedy (D)	$6,623,179	$864,078 (13%)	$3,662,652
Robinson (R)	$163,929	$0 (0%)	$163,927
Howell (LIBERT)	$1,027,364	$0 (0%)	$1,057,186
Lawler (CNSTP)	$80,836	$0 (0%)	$87,092
JUNIOR SENATOR - 2002			
Kerry (D)	$8,605,482	$16,200 (0%)	$5,971,092
Cloud (LIBERT)	$199,740	$50 (0%)	$199,476
DISTRICT 1			
Olver (D)	$568,024	$235,201 (41%)	$460,462
DISTRICT 2			
Neal (D)	$572,781	$326,297 (57%)	$427,864
DISTRICT 3			
McGovern (D)	$924,147	$241,499 (26%)	$1,184,239
Crews (R)	$156,655	$8,510 (5%)	$152,853

DISTRICT 4

Frank (D)	$1,319,498	$566,407 (43%)	$1,290,341
Morse (I)	$31,162	$0 (0%)	$21,985

DISTRICT 5

Meehan (D)	$3,170,733	$0 (0%)	$459,977
Tierney (R)	$30,943	$0 (0%)	$30,406

DISTRICT 6

Tierney (D)	$743,793	$228,831 (31%)	$415,107
O'Malley (R)	$48,636	$225 (0%)	$48,633

DISTRICT 7

Markey (D)	$2,840,650	$651,800 (23%)	$1,181,782
Chase (R)	$66,545	$0 (0%)	$62,022

DISTRICT 8

Capuano (D)	$839,302	$300,500 (36%)	$953,342

DISTRICT 9

Lynch (D)	$1,161,368	$310,090 (27%)	$591,797

DISTRICT 10

Delahunt (D)	$1,348,882	$338,525 (25%)	$843,755
Jones (R)	$263,474	$8,325 (3%)	$262,798

Michigan

	RECEIPTS	FROM PACS	EXPENDITURES
SENIOR SENATOR - 2002			
Levin (D)	$5,090,498	$838,109 (16%)	$4,099,215
Raczkowski (R)	$1,096,368	$0 (0%)	$819,356
JUNIOR SENATOR - 2000			
Stabenow (D)	$8,297,375	$955,856 (12%)	$8,194,394
Abraham (R)	$11,838,542	$2,485,419 (21%)	$13,028,636
Forton (REF)	$51,547	$6,300 (12%)	$49,461
Corliss (LIBERT)	$16,685	$0 (0%)	$16,684
Abel (GREEN)	$5,556	$0 (0%)	$4,898
DISTRICT 1			
Stupak (D)	$760,958	$425,593 (56%)	$771,354
Hooper (R)	$10,497	$0 (0%)	$11,070
DISTRICT 2			
Hoekstra (R)	$561,305	$248,166 (44%)	$498,230
Kotos (D)	$7,767	$2,500 (32%)	$14,779
DISTRICT 3			
Ehlers (R)	$404,278	$158,350 (39%)	$308,785
Hickey (D)	$2,850	$1,500 (53%)	$1,054
DISTRICT 4			
Camp (R)	$853,405	$536,460 (63%)	$521,658
Huckleberry (D)	$82,184	$30,672 (37%)	$83,217
DISTRICT 5			
Kildee (D)	$531,697	$309,860 (58%)	$608,283
Kirkwood (R)	$287,755	$21,600 (8%)	$281,615
DISTRICT 6			
Upton (R)	$1,100,825	$627,914 (57%)	$678,684
Elliott (D)	$49,997	$2,000 (4%)	$46,185
DISTRICT 7			
Schwarz (R)	$885,845	$370,898 (42%)	$750,290
Renier (D)	$8,742	$2,750 (31%)	$8,742
Seagraves (GREEN)	$10,275	$0 (0%)	$10,276
Horn (USTAX)	$9,838	$0 (0%)	$9,838
DISTRICT 8			
Rogers (R)	$1,473,630	$689,533 (47%)	$797,146
Alexander (D)	$79,679	$4,510 (6%)	$79,392

DISTRICT 9

Knollenberg (R)	$1,827,581	$451,586 (25%)	$1,412,320
Reifman (D)	$120,313	$13,000 (11%)	$120,386

DISTRICT 10

Miller (R)	$952,739	$377,621 (40%)	$442,297
Casey (D)	$16,684	$0 (0%)	$16,585

DISTRICT 11

McCotter (R)	$830,068	$297,452 (36%)	$735,845
Truran (D)	$43,253	$14,225 (33%)	$43,255

DISTRICT 12

Levin (D)	$978,772	$529,194 (54%)	$826,056

DISTRICT 13

Kilpatrick (D)	$690,156	$283,467 (41%)	$591,551

DISTRICT 14

Conyers (D)	$533,909	$383,651 (72%)	$534,363

DISTRICT 15

Dingell (D)	$1,524,991	$992,555 (65%)	$1,127,151

Minnesota

	RECEIPTS	FROM PACS	EXPENDITURES
SENIOR SENATOR - 2000			
Dayton (D)	$12,040,466	$0 (0%)	$11,957,114
Grams (R)	$5,902,543	$1,623,289 (28%)	$6,024,866
Gibson (INDC)	$261,357	$0 (0%)	$255,415
JUNIOR SENATOR - 2002			
Coleman (R)	$9,912,726	$1,735,858 (18%)	$9,648,999
Mondale (D)	$2,728,910	$380,004 (14%)	$1,731,176
Moore (INDC)	$49,503	$200 (0%)	$45,611
DISTRICT 1			
Gutknecht (R)	$839,764	$286,282 (34%)	$666,410
Pomeroy (D)	$59,327	$3,000 (5%)	$58,826
Mikkelson (INDC)	$7,196	$0 (0%)	$7,472
DISTRICT 2			
Kline (R)	$1,585,892	$689,413 (43%)	$1,610,055
Daly (D)	$1,193,784	$305,401 (26%)	$1,182,465
DISTRICT 3			
Ramstad (R)	$1,011,873	$518,123 (51%)	$921,476
Watts (D)	$38,511	$8,750 (23%)	$36,064
DISTRICT 4			
McCollum (D)	$687,907	$287,505 (42%)	$707,384
Bataglia (R)	$201,403	$11,775 (6%)	$194,717
DISTRICT 5			
Sabo (D)	$556,935	$249,600 (45%)	$497,073
Mathias (R)	$13,193	$1,000 (8%)	$11,504
DISTRICT 6			
Kennedy (R)	$2,691,038	$1,186,150 (44%)	$2,649,747
Wetterling (D)	$1,972,867	$415,806 (21%)	$1,935,813
DISTRICT 7			
Peterson (D)	$425,456	$311,105 (73%)	$523,484
Sturrock (R)	$127,022	$4,650 (4%)	$127,271
DISTRICT 8			
Oberstar (D)	$1,121,919	$724,704 (65%)	$972,916
Groettum (R)	$42,714	$5,000 (12%)	$41,187
Presley (GREEN)	$6,657	$0 (0%)	$5,728

Mississippi

	RECEIPTS	FROM PACS	EXPENDITURES
SENIOR SENATOR - 2002			
Cochran (R)	$1,688,273	$824,510 (49%)	$1,432,856
JUNIOR SENATOR - 2000			
Lott (R)	$4,241,819	$791,025 (19%)	$3,663,052
Brown (D)	$51,716	$7,500 (15%)	$40,349
DISTRICT 1			
Wicker (R)	$547,547	$290,000 (53%)	$426,024
DISTRICT 2			
Thompson (D)	$756,391	$443,292 (59%)	$724,653
LeSueur (R)	$331,443	$29,650 (9%)	$331,464
DISTRICT 3			
Pickering (R)	$873,579	$638,992 (73%)	$832,981
Giles (I)	$300	$0 (0%)	$300
DISTRICT 4			
Taylor (D)	$398,406	$196,190 (49%)	$426,134
Lott (R)	$90,651	$15,750 (17%)	$89,085

Missouri

	RECEIPTS	FROM PACS	EXPENDITURES
SENIOR SENATOR - 2004			
Bond (R)	$8,093,952	$2,098,125 (26%)	$7,848,506
Farmer (D)	$3,600,882	$512,409 (14%)	$3,548,116
JUNIOR SENATOR - 2002			
Talent (R)	$8,547,315	$1,774,818 (21%)	$7,939,585
Carnahan (D)	$12,289,529	$1,618,045 (13%)	$12,164,113
DISTRICT 1			
Clay (D)	$369,305	$196,325 (53%)	$262,648
DISTRICT 2			
Akin (R)	$847,249	$228,661 (27%)	$702,232
DISTRICT 3			
Carnahan (D)	$1,399,940	$447,700 (32%)	$1,392,248
Federer (R)	$1,380,208	$17,050 (1%)	$1,367,643
DISTRICT 4			
Skelton (D)	$696,308	$401,125 (58%)	$703,768
DISTRICT 5			
Cleaver (D)	$1,579,723	$502,927 (32%)	$1,521,741
Patterson (R)	$3,221,807	$65,200 (2%)	$3,207,825
DISTRICT 6			
Graves (R)	$1,691,981	$861,101 (51%)	$1,741,133
Broomfield (D)	$885,981	$165,950 (19%)	$887,833
DISTRICT 7			
Blunt (R)	$2,681,746	$1,483,503 (55%)	$3,527,363
Newberry (D)	$219,487	$15,500 (7%)	$214,240
DISTRICT 8			
Emerson (R)	$996,961	$586,858 (59%)	$1,163,588
Henderson (D)	$17,801	$0 (0%)	$17,801
DISTRICT 9			
Hulshof (R)	$1,157,497	$578,984 (50%)	$1,017,285
Jacobsen (D)	$120,590	$19,407 (16%)	$130,908

Montana

	RECEIPTS	FROM PACS	EXPENDITURES
SENIOR SENATOR - 2002			
Baucus (D)	$5,945,541	$2,620,108 (44%)	$6,106,052
Taylor (R)	$1,798,533	$77,237 (4%)	$1,793,389
JUNIOR SENATOR - 2000			
Burns (R)	$3,931,267	$1,683,501 (43%)	$4,337,961
Schweitzer (D)	$2,103,712	$354,574 (17%)	$2,033,530
AT LARGE			
Rehberg (R)	$668,207	$287,850 (43%)	$608,199
Velazquez (D)	$128,825	$3,447 (3%)	$127,716

Nebraska

	RECEIPTS	FROM PACS	EXPENDITURES
SENIOR SENATOR - 2002			
Hagel (R)	$1,609,967	$883,266 (55%)	$1,350,307
Chase (I)	$24,321	$0 (0%)	$24,293
JUNIOR SENATOR - 2000			
Nelson (D)	$2,782,642	$1,298,059 (47%)	$2,794,887
Stenberg (R)	$1,871,463	$456,076 (24%)	$1,859,252
DISTRICT 1			
Fortenberry (R)	$1,239,879	$500,064 (40%)	$1,224,431
Connealy (D)	$1,020,957	$342,852 (34%)	$990,782
DISTRICT 2			
Terry (R)	$1,335,016	$644,915 (48%)	$1,454,559
Thompson (D)	$898,658	$190,243 (21%)	$899,399
Salvatierra (GREEN)	$1,628	$0 (0%)	$1,212
DISTRICT 3			
Osborne (R)	$119,560	$0 (0%)	$63,654
Anderson (D)	$10,868	$0 (0%)	$10,867

Nevada

	RECEIPTS	FROM PACS	EXPENDITURES
SENIOR SENATOR - 2004			
Reid (D)	$7,015,254	$2,103,980 (30%)	$7,040,588
Ziser (R)	$648,792	$9,343 (1%)	$647,500
JUNIOR SENATOR - 2000			
Ensign (R)	$4,878,526	$1,715,992 (35%)	$4,872,176
Bernstein (D)	$2,483,512	$333,766 (13%)	$2,449,093
DISTRICT 1			
Berkley (D)	$1,653,330	$574,360 (35%)	$1,248,297
Mickelson (R)	$17,982	$0 (0%)	$17,662
DISTRICT 2			
Gibbons (R)	$1,139,202	$352,878 (31%)	$1,171,994
DISTRICT 3			
Porter (R)	$2,762,871	$1,145,916 (41%)	$2,653,136
Gallagher (D)	$2,381,750	$392,845 (16%)	$2,372,518

New Hampshire

	RECEIPTS	FROM PACS	EXPENDITURES
SENIOR SENATOR - 2004			
Gregg (R)	$2,982,530	$1,654,297 (55%)	$1,897,466
Haddock (D)	$177,594	$0 (0%)	$177,199
JUNIOR SENATOR - 2002			
Sununu (R)	$3,622,980	$1,232,534 (34%)	$3,507,470
Shaheen (D)	$5,823,007	$999,209 (17%)	$5,791,661
DISTRICT 1			
Bradley (R)	$1,049,832	$478,997 (46%)	$1,055,083
Nadeau (D)	$529,667	$75,033 (14%)	$530,364
DISTRICT 2			
Bass (R)	$740,299	$363,551 (49%)	$717,749
Hodes (D)	$627,164	$59,700 (10%)	$625,062

New Jersey

	RECEIPTS	FROM PACS	EXPENDITURES
SENIOR SENATOR - 2000			
Corzine (D)	$63,253,520	$235,909 (0%)	$63,209,506
Franks (R)	$6,428,214	$1,221,491 (19%)	$6,394,936
DiNizio (I)	$70,310	$0 (0%)	$34,075
Ellett (I)	$21,470	$1,374 (6%)	$21,469
Pason (I)	$2,110	$0 (0%)	$2,045
JUNIOR SENATOR - 2002			
Lautenberg (D)	$3,109,237	$413,075 (13%)	$2,844,020
Forrester (R)	$10,604,219	$484,793 (5%)	$10,540,687
Glick (GREEN)	$39,421	$0 (0%)	$28,318
DISTRICT 1			
Andrews (D)	$1,039,835	$450,155 (43%)	$848,616
Hutchison (R)	$176,794	$0 (0%)	$176,791
DISTRICT 2			
LoBiondo (R)	$1,293,191	$444,247 (34%)	$872,444
Robb (D)	$8,120	$0 (0%)	$6,325
DISTRICT 3			
Saxton (R)	$1,203,034	$442,270 (37%)	$919,338
Conaway (D)	$54,485	$29,500 (54%)	$42,334
DISTRICT 4			
Smith (R)	$629,395	$230,617 (37%)	$533,725
Vasquez (D)	$32,542	$8,913 (27%)	$33,860
DISTRICT 5			
Garrett (R)	$1,315,574	$386,567 (29%)	$1,268,289
Wolfe (D)	$482,855	$46,000 (10%)	$475,715
DISTRICT 6			
Pallone (D)	$1,595,950	$572,902 (36%)	$1,038,217
Fernandez (R)	$32,500	$0 (0%)	$66,473
DISTRICT 7			
Ferguson (R)	$2,954,861	$1,019,929 (35%)	$2,847,822
Brozak (D)	$804,221	$131,475 (16%)	$792,575
DISTRICT 8			
Pascrell (D)	$1,111,380	$368,600 (33%)	$948,047
Ajjan (R)	$133,324	$50 (0%)	$133,225
Fortunato (GREEN)	$24,395	$0 (0%)	$22,694
DISTRICT 9			
Rothman (D)	$1,299,627	$467,525 (36%)	$630,160
Trawinski (R)	$21,555	$1,000 (5%)	$17,532

DISTRICT 10			
Payne (D)	$649,744	$346,980 (53%)	$474,041
DISTRICT 11			
Frelinghuysen (R)	$942,790	$354,625 (38%)	$801,784
Buell (D)	$3,407	$0 (0%)	$3,406
DISTRICT 12			
Holt (D)	$1,502,832	$280,974 (19%)	$1,651,175
Spadea (R)	$348,062	$26,733 (8%)	$341,354
DISTRICT 13			
Menendez (D)	$3,624,587	$806,071 (22%)	$3,941,956

New Mexico

	RECEIPTS	FROM PACS	EXPENDITURES
SENIOR SENATOR - 2002			
Domenici (R)	$4,195,731	$939,490 (22%)	$4,115,919
Tristani (D)	$732,304	$140,478 (19%)	$834,607
JUNIOR SENATOR - 2000			
Bingaman (D)	$2,730,680	$1,192,335 (44%)	$2,568,649
Redmond (R)	$718,772	$75,409 (10%)	$706,424
DISTRICT 1			
Wilson (R)	$3,415,781	$1,285,215 (38%)	$3,401,887
Romero (D)	$2,090,138	$421,663 (20%)	$2,101,102
DISTRICT 2			
Pearce (R)	$1,980,833	$820,038 (41%)	$1,997,549
King (D)	$1,142,713	$172,275 (15%)	$1,143,705
DISTRICT 3			
Udall (D)	$493,951	$157,100 (32%)	$452,489
Tucker (R)	$63,545	$1,925 (3%)	$56,051

New York

	RECEIPTS	FROM PACS	EXPENDITURES
SENIOR SENATOR - 2004			
Schumer (D)	$11,921,568	$928,698 (8%)	$15,467,530
Mills (R)	$632,319	$51,350 (8%)	$629,170
Hirschfeld (BLD)	$702,000	$0 (0%)	$87,293
O'Grady (C)	$47,143	$0 (0%)	$15,628
McReynolds (GREEN)	$14,275	$0 (0%)	$7,209
Silberger (LIBERT)	$9,999	$0 (0%)	$9,594
JUNIOR SENATOR - 2000			
Clinton (D)	$41,752,247	$930,192 (2%)	$41,469,898
Lazio (R)	$39,020,511	$2,346,311 (6%)	$40,576,273
Graham (INDC)	$25,572	$0 (0%)	$24,570
Dunau (GREEN)	$16,139	$0 (0%)	$8,638
Clifton (LIBERT)	$13,883	$50 (0%)	$13,861
DISTRICT 1			
Bishop (D)	$1,990,911	$795,720 (40%)	$1,908,440
Manger (R)	$1,417,055	$223,266 (16%)	$1,385,362
DISTRICT 2			
Israel (D)	$1,621,141	$503,217 (31%)	$1,077,719
Hoffmann (R)	$12,875	$0 (0%)	$11,679
DISTRICT 3			
King (R)	$610,412	$216,476 (35%)	$536,345
Mathies (D)	$219,347	$3,850 (2%)	$212,580
DISTRICT 4			
McCarthy (D)	$1,769,151	$531,365 (30%)	$1,688,005
Garner (R)	$373,847	$125 (0%)	$304,521

DISTRICT 5
Ackerman (D) | $728,409 | $248,325 (34%) | $675,631

DISTRICT 6
Meeks (D) | $560,071 | $278,826 (50%) | $537,089

DISTRICT 7
Crowley (D) | $1,274,991 | $651,753 (51%) | $1,160,526

DISTRICT 8
Nadler (D) | $899,398 | $241,960 (27%) | $867,427
Hort (R) | $153,612 | $2,881 (2%) | $142,401

DISTRICT 9
Weiner (D) | $806,989 | $220,325 (27%) | $1,329,530
Cronin (R) | $14,086 | $0 (0%) | $8,093

DISTRICT 10
Towns (D) | $769,827 | $450,867 (59%) | $757,121

DISTRICT 11
Owens (D) | $462,212 | $270,830 (59%) | $474,168

DISTRICT 12
Velázquez (D) | $709,017 | $393,964 (56%) | $551,994

DISTRICT 13
Fossella (R) | $1,122,642 | $488,665 (44%) | $1,134,213
Barbaro (D) | $425,228 | $243,377 (57%) | $423,793

DISTRICT 14
Maloney (D) | $943,608 | $375,555 (40%) | $918,162
Srdanovic (R) | $23,108 | $1,000 (4%) | $23,217

DISTRICT 15
Rangel (D) | $1,996,022 | $879,554 (44%) | $1,728,867

DISTRICT 16
Serrano (D) | $244,716 | $169,356 (69%) | $351,845

DISTRICT 17
Engel (D) | $976,712 | $479,468 (49%) | $961,863

DISTRICT 18
Lowey (D) | $1,636,465 | $316,596 (19%) | $1,742,423
Hoffman (R) | $60,550 | $0 (0%) | $53,331

DISTRICT 19
Kelly (R) | $1,270,930 | $622,612 (49%) | $1,250,053
Jaliman (D) | $64,345 | $0 (0%) | $123,608

DISTRICT 20
Sweeney (R) | $1,398,266 | $486,775 (35%) | $1,392,817
Kelly (D) | $32,698 | $0 (0%) | $22,823

DISTRICT 21
McNulty (D) | $315,918 | $191,075 (60%) | $442,149
Redlich (R) | $36,058 | $1,000 (3%) | $41,497

DISTRICT 22
Hinchey (D) | $715,337 | $214,015 (30%) | $631,944
Brenner (R) | $6,506 | $0 (0%) | $6,497

DISTRICT 23
McHugh (R) | $498,029 | $349,438 (70%) | $469,828
Johnson (D) | $21,268 | $0 (0%) | $21,141

DISTRICT 24
Boehlert (R) | $1,450,844 | $710,566 (49%) | $1,524,703
Miller (D) | $39,446 | $8,099 (21%) | $32,965
Walrath (C) | $234,639 | $14,600 (6%) | $234,640

DISTRICT 25
Walsh (R) | $971,887 | $469,129 (48%) | $656,874

DISTRICT 26
Reynolds (R) | $2,361,692 | $812,078 (34%) | $2,522,713
Davis (D) | $1,356,777 | $100 (0%) | $1,356,713

DISTRICT 27
Higgins (D) | $1,397,911 | $559,641 (40%) | $1,372,162
Naples (R) | $1,627,410 | $598,245 (37%) | $1,581,433

DISTRICT 28
Slaughter (D) | $584,409 | $276,347 (47%) | $363,874
Laba (R) | $15,595 | $0 (0%) | $14,725
Cartonia (INDC) | $14,984 | $0 (0%) | $14,984

DISTRICT 29
Kuhl (R) | $998,927 | $427,780 (43%) | $937,340
Barend (D) | $627,952 | $167,115 (27%) | $612,443
Assini (C) | $267,015 | $26,077 (10%) | $267,016

North Carolina

	RECEIPTS	FROM PACS	EXPENDITURES
SENIOR SENATOR - 2002			
Dole (R)	$13,681,111	$1,432,111 (10%)	$13,555,960
Bowles (D)	$13,304,804	$523,128 (4%)	$13,273,188
JUNIOR SENATOR - 2004			
Burr (R)	$12,951,226	$2,796,484 (22%)	$12,853,110
Bowles (D)	$13,405,743	$822,974 (6%)	$13,357,851
DISTRICT 1			
Butterfield (D)	$495,466	$306,800 (62%)	$403,957
Dority (R)	$39,130	$22,200 (57%)	$39,130
DISTRICT 2			
Etheridge (D)	$935,538	$408,720 (44%)	$989,599
Creech (R)	$138,709	$0 (0%)	$137,820
DISTRICT 3			
Jones (R)	$639,986	$296,053 (46%)	$586,012
Eaton (D)	$12,569	$150 (1%)	$15,265
DISTRICT 4			
Price (D)	$954,160	$375,924 (39%)	$1,192,561
Batchelor (R)	$49,475	$5,250 (11%)	$49,474
DISTRICT 5			
Foxx (R)	$1,255,845	$392,464 (31%)	$1,182,132
Harrell (D)	$376,843	$58,247 (15%)	$383,579
DISTRICT 6			
Coble (R)	$419,783	$322,299 (77%)	$400,493
Jordan (D)	$12,223	$0 (0%)	$12,223
DISTRICT 7			
McIntyre (D)	$849,112	$372,375 (44%)	$758,418
DISTRICT 8			
Hayes (R)	$1,693,680	$836,055 (49%)	$1,611,679
Troutman (D)	$231,263	$60,350 (26%)	$225,675
DISTRICT 9			
Myrick (R)	$1,030,424	$408,202 (40%)	$991,241
Flynn (D)	$38,149	$11,773 (31%)	$36,080
DISTRICT 10			
McHenry (R)	$944,795	$363,310 (38%)	$936,071
Fischer (D)	$10,711	$518 (5%)	$10,710
DISTRICT 11			
Taylor (R)	$2,071,478	$340,680 (16%)	$2,083,029
Keever (D)	$1,262,690	$315,066 (25%)	$1,224,306
DISTRICT 12			
Watt (D)	$579,199	$285,294 (49%)	$519,881
Fisher (R)	$108,188	$0 (0%)	$104,667
DISTRICT 13			
Miller (D)	$1,170,367	$547,331 (47%)	$1,181,327
Johnson (R)	$356,403	$124,476 (35%)	$350,395

North Dakota

	RECEIPTS	FROM PACS	EXPENDITURES
SENIOR SENATOR - 2000			
Conrad (D)	$2,256,475	$1,443,306 (64%)	$2,312,543
Sand (R)	$399,590	$49,500 (12%)	$399,584
JUNIOR SENATOR - 2004			
Dorgan (D)	$2,941,662	$1,410,617 (48%)	$2,676,756
Liffrig (R)	$380,351	$12,299 (3%)	$381,125
AT LARGE			
Pomeroy (D)	$1,938,349	$1,352,690 (70%)	$1,809,046
Sand (R)	$1,029,862	$120,691 (12%)	$1,007,576

Ohio

	RECEIPTS	FROM PACS	EXPENDITURES
SENIOR SENATOR - 2000			
DeWine (R)	$5,583,868	$1,218,826 (22%)	$5,699,889
Celeste (D)	$477,784	$91,402 (19%)	$477,176
Eastman (NL)	$14,995	$0 (0%)	$14,726
McAlister (LIBERT)	$6,133	$300 (5%)	$8,996
JUNIOR SENATOR - 2004			
Voinovich (R)	$7,326,196	$1,670,976 (23%)	$8,956,380
Fingerhut (D)	$1,171,554	$97,837 (8%)	$1,166,538
DISTRICT 1			
Chabot (R)	$610,087	$219,900 (36%)	$479,225
Harris (D)	$90,170	$32,768 (36%)	$86,663
DISTRICT 2			
Portman (R)	$1,513,132	$5,755 (0%)	$559,338
Sanders (D)	$20,651	$2,250 (11%)	$20,152
DISTRICT 3			
Turner (R)	$1,090,580	$451,831 (41%)	$1,019,127
Mitakides (D)	$573,885	$107,103 (19%)	$565,435
DISTRICT 4			
Oxley (R)	$1,788,687	$1,100,917 (62%)	$1,909,844
Konop (D)	$184,210	$64,100 (35%)	$178,197
DISTRICT 5			
Gillmor (R)	$440,210	$302,813 (69%)	$440,891
Weirauch (D)	$78,798	$16,320 (21%)	$77,145
DISTRICT 6			
Strickland (D)	$512,410	$369,846 (72%)	$215,879
DISTRICT 7			
Hobson (R)	$1,751,075	$685,133 (39%)	$1,049,259
Anastasio (D)	$25,966	$1,000 (4%)	$25,807
DISTRICT 8			
Boehner (R)	$1,544,255	$749,218 (49%)	$1,407,907
Hardenbrook (D)	$41,478	$12,600 (30%)	$41,184
DISTRICT 9			
Kaptur (D)	$660,254	$336,785 (51%)	$615,506
Kaczala (R)	$257,907	$146,135 (57%)	$255,894
DISTRICT 10			
Kucinich (D)	$415,373	$157,561 (38%)	$406,033
Herman (R)	$300,718	$14,300 (5%)	$298,082
Ferris (I)	$56,470	$0 (0%)	$56,461
DISTRICT 11			
Jones (D)	$602,038	$340,737 (57%)	$501,711

DISTRICT 12			
Tiberi (R)	$1,315,012	$420,050 (32%)	$853,384
Brown (D)	$29,525	$0 (0%)	$29,540
DISTRICT 13			
Brown (D)	$1,047,890	$456,365 (44%)	$601,425
Lucas (R)	$7,885	$500 (6%)	$7,518
DISTRICT 14			
LaTourette (R)	$2,047,534	$897,277 (44%)	$2,430,424
Cafaro (D)	$1,992,169	$70,791 (4%)	$1,989,926
DISTRICT 15			
Pryce (R)	$1,015,362	$621,134 (61%)	$1,008,306
DISTRICT 16			
Regula (R)	$547,638	$214,359 (39%)	$606,430
Seemann (D)	$76,205	$5,800 (8%)	$59,667
DISTRICT 17			
Ryan (D)	$595,600	$413,094 (69%)	$495,122
Cusimano (R)	$10,840	$0 (0%)	$9,700
DISTRICT 18			
Ney (R)	$1,443,027	$800,143 (55%)	$1,483,143
Thomas (D)	$18,549	$12,500 (67%)	$18,417

Oklahoma

	RECEIPTS	FROM PACS	EXPENDITURES
SENIOR SENATOR - 2002			
Inhofe (R)	$2,992,267	$1,069,350 (36%)	$2,955,965
Walters (D)	$2,085,102	$389,927 (19%)	$2,042,689
JUNIOR SENATOR - 2004			
Coburn (R)	$5,106,058	$895,428 (18%)	$5,078,647
Carson (D)	$6,345,497	$1,016,490 (16%)	$6,256,444
DISTRICT 1			
Sullivan (R)	$1,002,859	$501,301 (50%)	$1,019,758
Dodd (D)	$318,018	$31,500 (10%)	$325,976
DISTRICT 2			
Boren (D)	$2,012,080	$539,765 (27%)	$2,018,285
Smalley (R)	$46,844	$200 (0%)	$46,832
DISTRICT 3			
Lucas (R)	$508,883	$315,950 (62%)	$371,139
DISTRICT 4			
Cole (R)	$1,115,699	$469,399 (42%)	$750,550
DISTRICT 5			
Istook (R)	$1,677,044	$763,368 (46%)	$1,268,043
Smith (D)	$12,432	$1,500 (12%)	$11,292

Oregon

	RECEIPTS	FROM PACS	EXPENDITURES
SENIOR SENATOR - 2004			
Wyden (D)	$3,802,681	$1,111,758 (29%)	$2,817,706
King (R)	$33,012	$5,250 (16%)	$32,930
Keane (I)	$9,940	$0 (0%)	$8,511
JUNIOR SENATOR - 2002			
Smith (R)	$5,250,893	$1,543,784 (29%)	$5,530,479
Bradbury (D)	$2,127,941	$326,694 (15%)	$2,104,194
Mabon (CNSTP)	$30,899	$0 (0%)	$30,853
DISTRICT 1			
Wu (D)	$2,216,813	$594,749 (27%)	$2,752,272
Ameri (R)	$2,332,328	$284,493 (12%)	$2,327,527

DISTRICT 2

Walden (R)	$1,226,113	$547,922 (45%)	$1,009,266
McColgan (D)	$30,874	$0 (0%)	$30,874

DISTRICT 3

Blumenauer (D)	$620,058	$304,506 (49%)	$701,713

DISTRICT 4

DeFazio (D)	$664,808	$305,735 (46%)	$909,241
Feldkamp (R)	$600,376	$70,732 (12%)	$586,608

DISTRICT 5

Hooley (D)	$1,934,156	$898,534 (46%)	$2,054,417
Zupancic (R)	$1,291,252	$165,250 (13%)	$1,291,211

Pennsylvania

	RECEIPTS	FROM PACS	EXPENDITURES
SENIOR SENATOR - 2004			
Specter (R)	$14,952,496	$2,605,116 (17%)	$20,307,099
Hoeffel (D)	$4,556,417	$405,686 (9%)	$4,540,209
Clymer (CNSTP)	$218,996	$4,500 (2%)	$212,896
JUNIOR SENATOR - 2000			
Santorum (R)	$9,126,046	$1,878,625 (21%)	$10,616,262
Klink (D)	$3,960,955	$923,833 (23%)	$3,941,166
Domske (REF)	$35,763	$138 (0%)	$35,751
Featherman (LIBERT)	$7,494	$0 (0%)	$7,493
Searer (CNSTP)	$6,400	$0 (0%)	$6,389
DISTRICT 1			
Brady (D)	$654,746	$243,450 (37%)	$361,532
DISTRICT 2			
Fattah (D)	$357,718	$190,650 (53%)	$384,313
Bolno (R)	$14,710	$0 (0%)	$16,973
DISTRICT 3			
English (R)	$1,338,016	$870,459 (65%)	$1,587,945
Porter (D)	$235,126	$3,535 (2%)	$224,002
DISTRICT 4			
Hart (R)	$1,445,691	$570,622 (39%)	$1,368,946
Drobac (D)	$11,279	$6,500 (58%)	$14,082
DISTRICT 5			
Peterson (R)	$507,793	$230,342 (45%)	$511,015
DISTRICT 6			
Gerlach (R)	$2,357,299	$1,129,212 (48%)	$2,231,309
Murphy (D)	$1,947,140	$408,244 (21%)	$1,910,539
DISTRICT 7			
Weldon (R)	$894,581	$400,400 (45%)	$678,444
Scoles (D)	$23,957	$500 (2%)	$23,763
DISTRICT 8			
Fitzpatrick (R)	$1,271,864	$560,975 (44%)	$1,046,153
Schrader (D)	$619,605	$199,376 (32%)	$613,850
DISTRICT 9			
Shuster (R)	$1,269,369	$608,700 (48%)	$1,217,650
Politis (D)	$16,382	$0 (0%)	$15,810
DISTRICT 10			
Sherwood (R)	$1,062,772	$325,255 (31%)	$904,949
DISTRICT 11			
Kanjorski (D)	$863,432	$547,437 (63%)	$378,979
DISTRICT 12			
Murtha (D)	$2,271,169	$707,650 (31%)	$1,559,185
DISTRICT 13			
Schwartz (D)	$4,597,032	$687,224 (15%)	$4,572,417
Brown (R)	$1,956,061	$648,106 (33%)	$1,927,499

DISTRICT 14

Doyle (D)	$670,111	$398,523 (59%)	$745,788

DISTRICT 15

Dent (R)	$2,046,238	$735,949 (36%)	$1,971,131
Driscoll (D)	$2,296,255	$358,039 (16%)	$2,295,656

DISTRICT 16

Pitts (R)	$542,444	$192,225 (35%)	$429,653
Herr (D)	$87,646	$5,989 (7%)	$83,737

DISTRICT 17

Holden (D)	$1,712,136	$965,778 (56%)	$1,608,093
Paterno (R)	$1,075,045	$169,200 (16%)	$1,057,940

DISTRICT 18

Murphy (R)	$1,226,950	$595,085 (49%)	$1,100,937
Boles (D)	$160,003	$1,885 (1%)	$149,356

DISTRICT 19

Platts (R)	$208,208	$0 (0%)	$171,605
Searer (CNSTP)	$14,370	$0 (0%)	$14,369

Rhode Island

	RECEIPTS	FROM PACS	EXPENDITURES
SENIOR SENATOR - 2002			
Reed (D)	$2,322,852	$863,064 (37%)	$1,707,655
JUNIOR SENATOR - 2000			
Chafee (R)	$2,531,413	$699,056 (28%)	$2,265,221
Weygand (D)	$2,420,479	$836,823 (35%)	$2,297,885
DISTRICT 1			
Kennedy (D)	$2,225,879	$461,405 (21%)	$1,958,492
Rogers (R)	$2,174,687	$1,000 (0%)	$2,133,062
DISTRICT 2			
Langevin (D)	$758,683	$329,750 (43%)	$727,295
Barton (R)	$51,926	$1,731 (3%)	$49,633

South Carolina

	RECEIPTS	FROM PACS	EXPENDITURES
SENIOR SENATOR - 2002			
Graham (R)	$6,207,367	$1,639,451 (26%)	$6,147,640
Sanders (D)	$4,284,388	$564,259 (13%)	$4,183,141
JUNIOR SENATOR - 2004			
DeMint (R)	$9,040,100	$2,347,943 (26%)	$9,036,086
Tenenbaum (D)	$6,275,269	$644,938 (10%)	$6,156,183
Tyndall (CNSTP)	$13,319	$0 (0%)	$13,318
DISTRICT 1			
Brown (R)	$488,256	$182,040 (37%)	$205,460
DISTRICT 2			
Wilson (R)	$891,295	$314,632 (35%)	$944,659
Ellisor (D)	$12,980	$0 (0%)	$12,990
DISTRICT 3			
Barrett (R)	$722,483	$310,768 (43%)	$646,938
DISTRICT 4			
Inglis (R)	$504,492	$8,550 (2%)	$511,913
Brown (D)	$15,842	$0 (0%)	$13,666
DISTRICT 5			
Spratt (D)	$830,981	$519,182 (62%)	$757,151
DISTRICT 6			
Clyburn (D)	$692,448	$471,430 (68%)	$725,832
McLeod (R)	$8,067	$0 (0%)	$3,927

South Dakota

	RECEIPTS	FROM PACS	EXPENDITURES
SENIOR SENATOR - 2002			
Johnson (D)	$5,524,580	$2,065,663 (37%)	$6,092,770
Thune (R)	$5,487,625	$1,312,130 (24%)	$5,918,310
JUNIOR SENATOR - 2004			
Thune (R)	$16,103,023	$1,183,602 (7%)	$14,666,225
Daschle (D)	$19,333,685	$2,807,562 (15%)	$19,975,170
AT LARGE			
Herseth (D)	$4,028,861	$1,299,247 (32%)	$4,026,661
Diedrich (R)	$2,555,183	$996,491 (39%)	$2,526,515

Tennessee

	RECEIPTS	FROM PACS	EXPENDITURES
SENIOR SENATOR - 2000			
Frist (R)	$5,825,454	$1,022,063 (18%)	$6,105,303
Clark (D)	$286,469	$85,000 (30%)	$273,406
JUNIOR SENATOR - 2002			
Alexander (R)	$5,841,364	$900,059 (15%)	$3,440,187
Clement (D)	$2,790,653	$660,672 (24%)	$2,791,905
DISTRICT 1			
Jenkins (R)	$214,250	$181,500 (85%)	$160,643
Leonard (D)	$39,663	$2,450 (6%)	$27,775
DISTRICT 2			
Duncan (R)	$568,331	$366,187 (64%)	$418,308
DISTRICT 3			
Wamp (R)	$1,258,296	$297,569 (24%)	$1,003,532
Wolfe (D)	$103,414	$500 (0%)	$92,074
DISTRICT 4			
Davis (D)	$1,149,371	$680,362 (59%)	$1,145,419
Bowling (R)	$306,365	$9,500 (3%)	$322,825
DISTRICT 5			
Cooper (D)	$1,118,924	$349,732 (31%)	$1,169,268
DISTRICT 6			
Gordon (D)	$616,736	$379,435 (62%)	$852,690
Demas (R)	$37,403	$3,000 (8%)	$37,399
DISTRICT 7			
Blackburn (R)	$817,560	$173,586 (21%)	$512,741
DISTRICT 8			
Tanner (D)	$670,330	$531,871 (79%)	$614,785
Hart (R)	$49,218	$0 (0%)	$47,892
DISTRICT 9			
Ford (D)	$1,919,993	$605,849 (32%)	$1,225,931

Texas

	RECEIPTS	FROM PACS	EXPENDITURES
SENIOR SENATOR - 2000			
Hutchison (R)	$3,410,444	$642,467 (19%)	$3,518,862
Kelly (D)	$4,654	$0 (0%)	$4,602
Sandage (GREEN)	$5,819	$0 (0%)	$6,041
JUNIOR SENATOR - 2002			
Cornyn (R)	$9,615,872	$1,627,531 (17%)	$9,513,548
Kirk (D)	$9,517,001	$931,555 (10%)	$9,315,171

DISTRICT 1			
Gohmert (R)	$1,870,800	$360,530 (19%)	$1,829,275
Sandlin (D)	$1,702,223	$916,567 (54%)	$1,690,816
DISTRICT 2			
Poe (R)	$1,671,523	$420,970 (25%)	$1,522,863
Lampson (D)	$2,381,206	$876,234 (37%)	$2,405,430
DISTRICT 3			
Johnson (R)	$959,576	$481,690 (50%)	$771,636
Jenkins (I)	$9,321	$0 (0%)	$9,017
DISTRICT 4			
Hall (R)	$1,178,472	$692,835 (59%)	$1,152,827
Nickerson (D)	$200,065	$0 (0%)	$199,803
DISTRICT 5			
Hensarling (R)	$1,595,840	$663,682 (42%)	$1,043,478
Bernstein (D)	$18,539	$250 (1%)	$18,538
DISTRICT 6			
Barton (R)	$2,517,071	$1,474,272 (59%)	$1,883,891
Meyer (D)	$59,861	$1,274 (2%)	$57,987
DISTRICT 7			
Culberson (R)	$628,783	$210,467 (33%)	$617,860
Martinez (D)	$29,106	$150 (1%)	$26,993
Staton (I)	$7,470	$0 (0%)	$7,469
DISTRICT 8			
Brady (R)	$732,619	$503,978 (69%)	$670,875
DISTRICT 9			
Green (D)	$920,183	$180,908 (20%)	$838,834
Molina (R)	$133,798	$4,600 (3%)	$133,372
DISTRICT 10			
McCaul (R)	$2,990,850	$297,728 (10%)	$2,986,391
DISTRICT 11			
Conaway (R)	$1,589,566	$342,678 (22%)	$1,573,274
DISTRICT 12			
Granger (R)	$1,040,904	$390,019 (37%)	$895,146
Alvarado (D)	$12,358	$3,000 (24%)	$15,948
DISTRICT 13			
Thornberry (R)	$351,862	$129,868 (37%)	$383,724
DISTRICT 14			
Paul (R)	$525,793	$30,400 (6%)	$744,969
DISTRICT 15			
Hinojosa (D)	$603,046	$279,300 (46%)	$818,216
Thamm (R)	$49,997	$1,500 (3%)	$49,898
DISTRICT 16			
Reyes (D)	$589,378	$305,900 (52%)	$618,643
Brigham (R)	$33,965	$0 (0%)	$27,985
DISTRICT 17			
Edwards (D)	$2,628,643	$1,141,103 (43%)	$2,664,661
Wohlgemuth (R)	$2,586,253	$603,332 (23%)	$2,562,877
DISTRICT 18			
Jackson-Lee (D)	$381,325	$198,475 (52%)	$370,856
Bazan (I)	$10,738	$130 (1%)	$10,666
DISTRICT 19			
Neugebauer (R)	$2,994,489	$940,783 (31%)	$3,245,173
Stenholm (D)	$2,432,634	$1,189,208 (49%)	$2,479,274
DISTRICT 20			
Gonzalez (D)	$715,919	$410,510 (57%)	$757,300
Scott (R)	$12,775	$0 (0%)	$13,447
DISTRICT 21			
Smith (R)	$973,780	$326,794 (34%)	$606,121

DISTRICT 22

DeLay (R)	$2,909,844	$1,420,263 (49%)	$3,143,559
Morrison (D)	$642,808	$29,689 (5%)	$685,935
Fjetland (I)	$11,980	$4,000 (33%)	$11,978

DISTRICT 23

Bonilla (R)	$2,204,344	$1,029,951 (47%)	$1,211,717
Sullivan (D)	$9,019	$450 (5%)	$9,335

DISTRICT 24

Marchant (R)	$898,286	$327,600 (36%)	$781,923
Page (D)	$14,491	$0 (0%)	$15,255

DISTRICT 25

Doggett (D)	$1,569,646	$306,035 (19%)	$1,992,987
Klein (R)	$808,469	$197,257 (24%)	$804,160

DISTRICT 26

Burgess (R)	$925,153	$477,696 (52%)	$817,015
Reyes (D)	$7,453	$0 (0%)	$9,564

DISTRICT 27

Ortiz (D)	$607,271	$193,054 (32%)	$666,410
Vaden (R)	$48,980	$0 (0%)	$51,228

DISTRICT 28

Cuellar (D)	$1,407,409	$166,078 (12%)	$1,372,833
Hopson (R)	$43,963	$1,000 (2%)	$43,581

DISTRICT 29

Green (D)	$662,698	$495,605 (75%)	$684,970

DISTRICT 30

Johnson (D)	$379,015	$205,865 (54%)	$405,453

DISTRICT 31

Carter (R)	$1,086,204	$598,540 (55%)	$899,885
Porter (D)	$37,061	$8,043 (22%)	$15,618

DISTRICT 32

Sessions (R)	$4,520,880	$1,692,242 (37%)	$4,512,464
Frost (D)	$4,623,104	$1,302,207 (28%)	$4,761,288

Utah

	RECEIPTS	FROM PACS	EXPENDITURES
SENIOR SENATOR - 2000			
Hatch (R)	$3,082,208	$1,220,662 (40%)	$3,130,550
Howell (D)	$299,747	$14,000 (5%)	$299,239
JUNIOR SENATOR - 2004			
Bennett (R)	$2,755,838	$1,093,642 (40%)	$2,649,234
Van Dam (D)	$118,226	$18,750 (16%)	$116,959
DISTRICT 1			
Bishop (R)	$437,648	$225,155 (51%)	$435,494
Thompson (D)	$73,375	$10,350 (14%)	$72,540
DISTRICT 2			
Matheson (D)	$1,966,015	$1,084,775 (55%)	$2,021,524
Swallow (R)	$1,477,450	$244,640 (17%)	$1,471,198
DISTRICT 3			
Cannon (R)	$640,259	$197,750 (31%)	$634,195
Babka (D)	$35,337	$225 (1%)	$35,111

Vermont

	RECEIPTS	FROM PACS	EXPENDITURES
SENIOR SENATOR - 2004			
Leahy (D)	$2,292,393	$1,500 (0%)	$1,531,833
McMullen (R)	$731,028	$2,100 (0%)	$736,126

JUNIOR SENATOR - 2000

Jeffords (R)	$2,087,965	$1,112,558 (53%)	$1,889,243
Flanagan (D)	$1,093,161	$67,434 (6%)	$1,054,977
Hubbard (I)	$21,651	$0 (0%)	$21,610

AT LARGE

Sanders (I)	$836,307	$125,150 (15%)	$810,050
Parke (R)	$671,903	$1,050 (0%)	$670,350

Virginia

	RECEIPTS	FROM PACS	EXPENDITURES
SENIOR SENATOR - 2002			
Warner (R)	$2,617,764	$887,268 (34%)	$1,674,292
Spannaus (I)	$65,529	$500 (1%)	$65,550
Hornberger (I)	$62,406	$0 (0%)	$61,838
JUNIOR SENATOR - 2000			
Allen (R)	$10,073,255	$1,581,172 (16%)	$9,995,980
Robb (D)	$6,737,158	$1,622,753 (24%)	$6,810,252
DISTRICT 1			
Davis (R)	$450,731	$253,507 (56%)	$375,339
DISTRICT 2			
Drake (R)	$828,326	$441,922 (53%)	$828,185
Ashe (D)	$469,759	$174,875 (37%)	$436,620
DISTRICT 3			
Scott (D)	$499,654	$191,650 (38%)	$525,173
Sears (R)	$207,314	$57,482 (28%)	$205,812
DISTRICT 4			
Forbes (R)	$884,368	$353,445 (40%)	$858,666
Menefee (D)	$29,517	$1,000 (3%)	$30,415
DISTRICT 5			
Goode (R)	$818,460	$282,211 (34%)	$753,167
Weed (D)	$483,890	$12,600 (3%)	$481,071
DISTRICT 6			
Goodlatte (R)	$1,022,701	$666,863 (65%)	$797,676
DISTRICT 7			
Cantor (R)	$2,472,066	$1,167,034 (47%)	$2,193,388
DISTRICT 8			
Moran (D)	$1,761,473	$445,892 (25%)	$1,677,506
Cheney (R)	$343,469	$28,697 (8%)	$337,580
Hurysz (I)	$25,780	$0 (0%)	$24,916
DISTRICT 9			
Boucher (D)	$1,560,930	$882,857 (57%)	$1,628,026
Triplett (R)	$651,079	$159,100 (24%)	$646,669
DISTRICT 10			
Wolf (R)	$1,460,719	$419,598 (29%)	$1,611,149
Socas (D)	$911,198	$14,350 (2%)	$921,094
DISTRICT 11			
Davis (R)	$2,164,488	$758,938 (35%)	$1,835,379
Longmyer (D)	$74,902	$5,379 (7%)	$71,661

Washington

	RECEIPTS	FROM PACS	EXPENDITURES
SENIOR SENATOR - 2004			
Murray (D)	$11,081,050	$1,691,587 (15%)	$11,556,148
Nethercutt (R)	$8,011,311	$1,326,952 (17%)	$7,726,296
JUNIOR SENATOR - 2000			
Cantwell (D)	$11,538,665	$0 (0%)	$11,533,295
Gorton (R)	$6,384,256	$1,770,339 (28%)	$6,402,488
DISTRICT 1			
Inslee (D)	$933,222	$273,515 (29%)	$882,639
Eastwood (R)	$59,074	$2,300 (4%)	$64,780
DISTRICT 2			
Larsen (D)	$1,567,289	$631,063 (40%)	$1,412,604
Sinclair (R)	$38,741	$0 (0%)	$38,740
DISTRICT 3			
Baird (D)	$965,399	$311,549 (32%)	$850,014
Crowson (R)	$60,962	$0 (0%)	$55,727
DISTRICT 4			
Hastings (R)	$691,592	$260,100 (38%)	$557,536
Matheson (D)	$427,536	$74,201 (17%)	$404,802
DISTRICT 5			
McMorris (R)	$1,655,761	$530,612 (32%)	$1,537,540
Barbieri (D)	$1,630,053	$454,412 (28%)	$1,628,666
DISTRICT 6			
Dicks (D)	$956,738	$399,525 (42%)	$871,608
DISTRICT 7			
McDermott (D)	$379,513	$115,594 (30%)	$437,147
Cassady (R)	$25,138	$0 (0%)	$23,632
DISTRICT 8			
Reichert (R)	$1,578,632	$476,800 (30%)	$1,569,196
Ross (D)	$1,453,019	$314,737 (22%)	$1,446,406
DISTRICT 9			
Smith (D)	$763,390	$375,542 (49%)	$527,669
Lord (R)	$7,660	$0 (0%)	$7,660

West Virginia

	RECEIPTS	FROM PACS	EXPENDITURES
SENIOR SENATOR - 2000			
Byrd (D)	$1,127,278	$509,530 (45%)	$1,045,993
Whelan (LIBERT)	$48,666	$1,140 (2%)	$48,514
JUNIOR SENATOR - 2002			
Rockefeller (D)	$2,466,775	$1,010,101 (41%)	$2,158,227
Wolfe (R)	$136,410	$3,742 (3%)	$136,373
DISTRICT 1			
Mollohan (D)	$562,552	$159,050 (28%)	$524,011
DISTRICT 2			
Capito (R)	$1,604,880	$844,084 (53%)	$1,654,898
Wells (D)	$79,175	$20,900 (26%)	$77,410
DISTRICT 3			
Rahall (D)	$539,122	$249,644 (46%)	$930,079
Snuffer (R)	$71,903	$12,550 (17%)	$89,312

Wisconsin

	RECEIPTS	FROM PACS	EXPENDITURES
SENIOR SENATOR - 2000			
Kohl (D)	$4,986,165	$0 (0%)	$4,991,364
Gillespie (R)	$584,877	$13,500 (2%)	$582,221
Peterson (LIBERT)	$43,893	$0 (0%)	$43,604
JUNIOR SENATOR - 2004			
Feingold (D)	$8,377,885	$684,717 (8%)	$9,239,908
Michels (R)	$5,547,838	$397,532 (7%)	$5,542,087
DISTRICT 1			
Ryan (R)	$1,374,025	$620,587 (45%)	$849,365
Thomas (D)	$17,649	$0 (0%)	$43,811
Aulabaugh (I)	$29,075	$0 (0%)	$27,604
DISTRICT 2			
Baldwin (D)	$1,709,070	$281,227 (16%)	$1,448,889
Magnum (R)	$668,944	$7,570 (1%)	$658,153
DISTRICT 3			
Kind (D)	$1,028,469	$473,875 (46%)	$1,186,471
Schultz (R)	$552,215	$134,530 (24%)	$531,538
DISTRICT 4			
Moore (D)	$1,086,301	$330,777 (30%)	$933,653
Boyle (R)	$91,048	$2,400 (3%)	$81,298
DISTRICT 5			
Sensenbrenner (R)	$806,716	$510,789 (63%)	$655,901
Kennedy (D)	$281,226	$89,485 (32%)	$267,814
DISTRICT 6			
Petri (R)	$698,042	$422,641 (61%)	$478,540
Hall (D)	$9,753	$400 (4%)	$4,333
DISTRICT 7			
Obey (D)	$1,205,555	$704,571 (58%)	$764,767
DISTRICT 8			
Green (R)	$1,040,373	$386,266 (37%)	$433,513
Le Clair (D)	$13,191	$0 (0%)	$11,160

Wyoming

	RECEIPTS	FROM PACS	EXPENDITURES
SENIOR SENATOR - 2000			
Thomas (R)	$958,656	$483,343 (50%)	$762,833
Logan (D)	$7,979	$5,700 (71%)	$4,187
JUNIOR SENATOR - 2002			
Enzi (R)	$1,175,276	$791,568 (67%)	$850,095
Corcoran (D)	$8,488	$1,275 (15%)	$8,467
AT LARGE			
Cubin (R)	$959,028	$584,549 (61%)	$944,908
Ladd (D)	$373,436	$30,500 (8%)	$373,436

House Committees

House standing and select committees are listed alphabetically. Membership is in order of seniority on the panel. If a non-voting delegate or resident commissioner is a member, the party ratio reflects that membership. Non-voting members, while they cannot vote on the House floor, enjoy status equal to that of their voting colleagues on committees. Subcommittee membership is listed in order of seniority. Partisan committees are on page 1197.

On full committee rosters, members of the majority party, Republicans, are shown in roman type; members of the minority party, Democrats, are shown in *italic* type.

Independents are labeled. A vacancy indicates that a committee or subcommittee seat had not been filled at press time, April 2005. Subcommittee vacancies do not necessarily indicate vacancies on full committees or vice versa.

The telephone area code for Washington, D.C., is 202. House office buildings are abbreviated as CHOB – Cannon House Office Building, LHOB–Longworth House Office Building, RHOB – Rayburn House Office Building, OHOB – O'Neill House Office Building, FHOB – Ford House Office Building. The ZIP code is 20515; Adams is a Library of Congress building and its zip code is 20540.

AGRICULTURE
225-2171 1301 LHOB
Party Ratio: R 25-D 21
Robert W. Goodlatte, R-Va., chairman

John A. Boehner, Ohio, vice chairman	*Collin C. Peterson, Minn.*
Richard W. Pombo, Calif.	*Tim Holden, Pa.*
Terry Everett, Ala.	*Mike McIntyre, N.C.*
Frank D. Lucas, Okla.	*Bob Etheridge, N.C.*
Jerry Moran, Kan.	*Joe Baca, Calif.*
Bill Jenkins, Tenn.	*Ed Case, Hawaii*
Gil Gutknecht, Minn.	*Dennis Cardoza, Calif.*
Robin Hayes, N.C.	*David Scott, Ga.*
Timothy V. Johnson, Ill.	*Jim Marshall, Ga.*
Tom Osborne, Neb.	*Stephanie Herseth, S.D.*
Mike Pence, Ind.	*G.K. Butterfield, N.C.*
Sam Graves, Mo.	*Henry Cuellar, Texas*
Jo Bonner, Ala.	*Charlie Melancon, La.*
Mike D. Rogers, Ala.	*Jim Costa, Calif.*
Steve King, Iowa	*John Salazar, Colo.*
Marilyn Musgrave, Colo.	*John Barrow, Ga.*
Randy Neugebauer, Texas	*Earl Pomeroy, N.D.*
Charles Boustany Jr., La.	*Leonard L. Boswell, Iowa*
Joe Schwarz, Mich.	*Rick Larsen, Wash.*
John R. "Randy" Kuhl Jr., N.Y.	*Lincoln Davis, Tenn.*
Virginia Foxx, N.C.	*Ben Chandler, Ky.*
K. Michael Conaway, Texas	
Jeff Fortenberry, Neb.	
Vacancy	

CONSERVATION, CREDIT, RURAL DEVELOPMENT & RESEARCH
225-2171 1741P LHOB
Lucas, chairman

Republicans: Moran (Kan.), Osborne, vice chairman, Graves, Rogers (Ala.), King (Iowa), Boustany, Schwarz, Fortenberry
Democrats: Holden, Cuellar, McIntyre, Etheridge, Case, Davis (Tenn.), Herseth, Butterfield

DEPARTMENT OPERATIONS, OVERSIGHT, NUTRITION & FORESTRY
225-2171 1407 LHOB
Gutknecht, chairman

Republicans: Pombo, Moran (Kan.), Bonner, vice chairman, Foxx, Fortenberry, Vacancy
Democrats: Baca, Cardoza, Butterfield, Holden, Cuellar, Costa

GENERAL FARM COMMODITIES & RISK MANAGEMENT
225-2171 1301 LHOB
Moran (Kan.), chairman

Republicans: Boehner, Everett, Lucas, Jenkins, Johnson (Ill.), vice chairman, Pence, Graves, Bonner, King (Iowa), Musgrave, Neugebauer, Boustany, Conaway, Fortenberry
Democrats: Etheridge, Salazar, Marshall, Herseth, Butterfield, Melancon, Barrow, Pomeroy, Boswell, Larsen, Chandler, Scott (Ga.), Costa

LIVESTOCK & HORTICULTURE
225-2171 1336 LHOB
Hayes, chairman

Republicans: Boehner, Pombo, Osborne, Pence, vice chairman, Rogers (Ala.), King (Iowa), Neugebauer, Kuhl, Foxx, Conaway, Vacancy
Democrats: Case, Scott (Ga.), Herseth, Costa, Cardoza, Salazar, Boswell, Larsen, Pomeroy, Barrow

SPECIALTY CROPS & FOREIGN AGRICULTURE
225-2171 1336 LHOB
Jenkins, chairman

Republicans: Everett, vice chairman, Gutknecht, Hayes, Rogers (Ala.), Neugebauer, Schwarz, Foxx
Democrats: McIntyre, Marshall, Melancon, Barrow, Scott (Ga.), Chandler, Cuellar

APPROPRIATIONS

225-2771 H-218 Capitol
Party Ratio: R 37-D 29
Jerry Lewis, R-Calif., chairman

C.W. Bill Young, Fla.	David R. Obey, Wis.
Ralph Regula, Ohio	John P. Murtha, Pa.
Harold Rogers, Ky.	Norm Dicks, Wash.
Frank R. Wolf, Va.	Martin Olav Sabo, Minn.
Jim Kolbe, Ariz.	Steny H. Hoyer, Md.
James T. Walsh, N.Y.	Alan B. Mollohan, W.Va.
Charles H. Taylor, N.C.	Marcy Kaptur, Ohio
David L. Hobson, Ohio	Peter J. Visclosky, Ind.
Ernest Istook, Okla.	Nita M. Lowey, N.Y.
Henry Bonilla, Texas	José E. Serrano, N.Y.
Joe Knollenberg, Mich.	Rosa DeLauro, Conn.
Jack Kingston, Ga.	James P. Moran, Va.
Rodney Frelinghuysen, N.J.	John W. Olver, Mass.
Roger Wicker, Miss.	Ed Pastor, Ariz.
Randy "Duke"	David E. Price, N.C.
Cunningham, Calif.	Chet Edwards, Texas
Todd Tiahrt, Kan.	Robert E. "Bud"
Zach Wamp, Tenn.	Cramer, Ala.
Tom Latham, Iowa	Patrick J. Kennedy, R.I.
Anne M. Northup, Ky.	James E. Clyburn, S.C.
Robert B. Aderholt, Ala.	Maurice D. Hinchey, N.Y.
Jo Ann Emerson, Mo.	Lucille Roybal-Allard, Calif.
Kay Granger, Texas	Sam Farr, Calif.
John E. Peterson, Pa.	Jesse L. Jackson Jr., Ill.
Virgil H. Goode Jr., Va.	Carolyn Cheeks Kilpatrick,
John T. Doolittle, Calif.	Mich.
Ray LaHood, Ill.	Allen Boyd, Fla.
John E. Sweeney, N.Y	Chaka Fattah, Pa.
Don Sherwood, Pa.	Steven R. Rothman, N.J.
Dave Weldon, Fla.	Sanford D. Bishop Jr., Ga.
Mike Simpson, Idaho	Marion Berry, Ark.
John Culberson, Texas	
Mark Steven Kirk, Ill.	
Ander Crenshaw, Fla.	
Denny Rehberg, Mont.	
John Carter, Texas	
Rodney Alexander, La.	

AGRICULTURE, RURAL DEVELOPMENT & FDA
225-2638 2362-A RHOB
Bonilla, chairman

Republicans: Kingston, Latham, Emerson, Goode, LaHood, vice chairman, Doolittle, Alexander
Democrats: DeLauro, Hinchey, Farr, Boyd, Kaptur

DEFENSE
225-2847 H-149 Capitol
Young (Fla.), chairman

Republicans: Hobson, Bonilla, Cunningham, Frelinghuysen, vice chairman, Tiahrt, Wicker, Kingston, Granger
Democrats: Murtha, Dicks, Sabo, Visclosky, Moran (Va.), Kaptur

ENERGY & WATER
225-3421 2362 RHOB
Hobson, chairman

Republicans: Frelinghuysen, Latham, Wamp, Emerson, Doolittle, vice chairman, Simpson, Rehberg
Democrats: Visclosky, Edwards, Pastor, Clyburn, Berry

FOREIGN OPERATIONS & EXPORT FINANCING
225-2041 H-B28 Capitol
Kolbe, chairman

Republicans: Knollenberg, Kirk, Crenshaw, Sherwood, vice chairman, Sweeney, Rehberg, Carter
Democrats: Lowey, Jackson, Kilpatrick, Rothman, Fattah

HOMELAND SECURITY
225-5834 B307 RHOB
Rogers (Ky.), chairman

Republicans: Wamp, Latham, Emerson, Sweeney, Kolbe, Istook, vice chairman, LaHood, Crenshaw, Carter
Democrats: Sabo, Price (N.C.), Serrano, Roybal-Allard, Bishop (Ga.), Berry, Edwards

INTERIOR & ENVIRONMENT
225-3081 B-308 RHOB
Taylor (N.C.), chairman

Republicans: Wamp, Peterson (Pa.), Sherwood, Istook, Aderholt, Doolittle, Simpson, vice chairman
Democrats: Dicks, Moran (Va.), Hinchey, Olver, Mollohan

LABOR, HEALTH & HUMAN SERVICES & EDUCATION
225-3508 2358 RHOB
Regula, chairman

Republicans: Istook, Wicker, Northup, vice chairwoman, Cunningham, Granger, Peterson (Pa.), Sherwood, Weldon (Fla.), Walsh
Democrats: Obey, Hoyer, Lowey, DeLauro, Jackson, Kennedy (R.I.), Roybal-Allard

MILITARY QUALITY OF LIFE & VETERANS AFFAIRS
225-3047 B-300 RHOB
Walsh, chairman

Republicans: Aderholt, vice chairman, Northup, Simpson, Crenshaw, Young (Fla.), Kirk, Rehberg, Carter
Democrats: Edwards, Farr, Boyd, Bishop (Ga.), Price (N.C.), Cramer

SCIENCE, STATE, JUSTICE & COMMERCE
225-3351 H-309 Capitol
Wolf, chairman

Republicans: Taylor (N.C.), Kirk, Weldon (Fla.), vice chairman, Goode, LaHood, Culberson, Alexander
Democrats: Mollohan, Serrano, Cramer, Kennedy (R.I.), Fattah

TRANSPORTATION, TREASURY, HUD, THE JUDICIARY & DISTRICT OF COLUMBIA
225-2141 2358 RHOB
Knollenberg, chairman

Republicans: Wolf, Rogers (Ky.), Tiahrt, Northup, Aderholt, Sweeney, vice chairman, Culberson, Regula
Democrats: Olver, Hoyer, Pastor, Kilpatrick, Clyburn, Rothman

ARMED SERVICES

225-4151 2120 RHOB
Party Ratio: R 34-D 28
Duncan Hunter, R-Calif., chairman

Curt Weldon, Pa.	Ike Skelton, Mo.
Joel Hefley, Colo.	John M. Spratt Jr., S.C.
H. James Saxton, N.J.	Solomon P. Ortiz, Texas
John M. McHugh, N.Y.	Lane Evans, Ill.
Terry Everett, Ala.	Gene Taylor, Miss.
Roscoe G. Bartlett, Md.	Neil Abercrombie, Hawaii
Howard P. "Buck"	Martin T. Meehan, Mass.
McKeon, Calif.	Silvestre Reyes, Texas
William M. "Mac"	Vic Snyder, Ark.
Thornberry, Texas	Adam Smith, Wash.
John Hostettler, Ind.	Loretta Sanchez, Calif.
Walter B. Jones, N.C.	Mike McIntyre, N.C.
Jim Ryun, Kan.	Ellen O. Tauscher, Calif.
Jim Gibbons, Nev.	Robert A. Brady, Pa.
Robin Hayes, N.C.	Robert E. Andrews, N.J.
Ken Calvert, Calif.	Susan A. Davis, Calif.
Rob Simmons, Conn.	Jim Langevin, R.I.
Jo Ann Davis, Va.	Steve Israel, N.Y.
Todd Akin, Mo.	Rick Larsen, Wash.
J. Randy Forbes, Va.	Jim Cooper, Tenn.
Jeff Miller, Fla.	Jim Marshall, Ga.
Joe Wilson, S.C.	Kendrick B. Meek, Fla.
Frank A. LoBiondo, N.J.	Madeleine Z. Bordallo, Guam
Jeb Bradley, N.H.	Tim Ryan, Ohio
Michael R. Turner, Ohio	Mark Udall, Colo.
John Kline, Minn.	G.K. Butterfield, N.C.
Candice S. Miller, Mich.	Cynthia A. McKinney, Ga.
Mike D. Rogers, Ala.	Dan Boren, Okla.
Trent Franks, Ariz.	
Bill Shuster, Pa.	
Thelma Drake, Va.	
Joe Schwarz, Mich.	
Cathy McMorris, Wash.	
K. Michael Conaway, Texas	
Geoff Davis, Ky.	

MILITARY PERSONNEL

225-7560 2340 RHOB
McHugh, chairman

Republicans: Davis (Va.), Kline, Drake, Conaway, Saxton, Jones (N.C.), Ryun, Hayes
Democrats: Snyder, Meehan, Sanchez (Calif.), Andrews, Davis (Calif.), Udall (Colo.), McKinney

PROJECTION FORCES

225-1967 2340 RHOB
Bartlett, chairman

Republicans: Simmons, Davis (Va.), Miller (Mich.), Drake, Weldon (Pa.), Saxton, Hostettler, Calvert
Democrats: Taylor (Miss.), Tauscher, Langevin, Israel, Marshall, Bordallo, Boren

READINESS

226-8979 2117 RHOB
Hefley, chairman

Republicans: Hostettler, Jones (N.C.), Ryun, Forbes, Miller (Fla.), Rogers (Ala.), Schwarz, McMorris, McHugh, McKeon, Hayes, Simmons, Bradley, Miller (Mich.), Franks
Democrats: Ortiz, Evans, Taylor (Miss.), Abercrombie, Reyes, Snyder, Brady (Pa.), Davis (Calif.), Marshall, Meek, Bordallo, Ryan (Ohio), Udall (Colo.), Butterfield

STRATEGIC FORCES

226-7173 2340 RHOB
Everett, chairman

Republicans: Thornberry, Franks, Turner, Rogers (Ala.), Schwarz, McMorris, Davis (Ky.)
Democrats: Reyes, Spratt, Sanchez (Calif.), Tauscher, Larsen, Cooper

TACTICAL AIR & LAND FORCES

225-4440 2340 RHOB
Weldon (Pa.), chairman

Republicans: McKeon, Gibbons, Calvert, LoBiondo, Bradley, Turner, Conaway, Everett, Bartlett, Jones (N.C.), Ryun, Akin, Forbes, Wilson (S.C.), Shuster
Democrats: Abercrombie, Skelton, Spratt, Ortiz, Evans, Smith (Wash.), McIntyre, Brady (Pa.), Israel, Cooper, Meek, Ryan (Ohio), Butterfield, Boren

TERRORISM, UNCONVENTIONAL THREATS & CAPABILITIES

226-2843 2340 RHOB
Saxton, chairman

Republicans: Hayes, Akin, Wilson (S.C.), Kline, Shuster, Davis (Ky.), Hefley, Thornberry, Gibbons, Miller (Fla.) LoBiondo
Democrats: Meehan, Smith (Wash.), McIntyre, Tauscher, Andrews, Langevin, Larsen, Cooper, Marshall, McKinney

BUDGET

226-7270 309 CHOB
Party Ratio: R 22-D 17
Jim Nussle, R-Iowa, chairman

Jim Ryun, Kan.	John M. Spratt Jr., S.C.
Ander Crenshaw, Fla.	Dennis Moore, Kan.
Adam H. Putnam, Fla.	Richard E. Neal, Mass.
Roger Wicker, Miss.	Rosa DeLauro, Conn.
Kenny Hulshof, Mo.	Chet Edwards, Texas
Jo Bonner, Ala.	Harold E. Ford Jr., Tenn.
Scott Garrett, N.J.	Lois Capps, Calif.
J. Gresham Barrett, S.C.	Brian Baird, Wash.
Thaddeus McCotter, Mich.	Jim Cooper, Tenn.
Mario Diaz-Balart, Fla.	Artur Davis, Ala.
Jeb Hensarling, Texas	William J. Jefferson, La.
Ileana Ros-Lehtinen, Fla.	Tom Allen, Maine
Dan Lungren, Calif.	Ed Case, Hawaii
Pete Sessions, Texas	Cynthia A. McKinney, Ga.
Paul D. Ryan, Wis.	Henry Cuellar, Texas
Mike Simpson, Idaho	Allyson Y. Schwartz, Pa.
Jeb Bradley, N.H.	Ron Kind, Wis.
Patrick T. McHenry, N.C.	
Connie Mack, Fla.	
K. Michael Conaway, Texas	
Vacancy	

EDUCATION & WORKFORCE

225-4527 2181 RHOB
Party Ratio: R 27-D 22
John A. Boehner, R-Ohio, chairman

Tom Petri, Wis., vice chairman	George Miller, Calif.
Howard P. "Buck" McKeon, Calif.	Dale E. Kildee, Mich.
	Major R. Owens, N.Y.
Michael N. Castle, Del.	Donald M. Payne, N.J.
Sam Johnson, Texas	Robert E. Andrews, N.J.
Mark Souder, Ind.	Robert C. Scott, Va.
Charlie Norwood, Ga.	Lynn Woolsey, Calif.
Vernon J. Ehlers, Mich.	Rubén Hinojosa, Texas
Judy Biggert, Ill.	Carolyn McCarthy, N.Y.
Todd R. Platts, Pa.	John F. Tierney, Mass.
Pat Tiberi, Ohio	Ron Kind, Wis.
Ric Keller, Fla.	Dennis J. Kucinich, Ohio
Tom Osborne, Neb.	David Wu, Ore.
Joe Wilson, S.C.	Rush D. Holt, N.J.
Jon Porter, Nev.	Susan A. Davis, Calif.
John Kline, Minn.	Betty McCollum, Minn.
Marilyn Musgrave, Colo.	Danny K. Davis, Ill.
Bob Inglis, S.C.	Raúl M. Grijalva, Ariz.
Cathy McMorris, Wash.	Chris Van Hollen, Md.
Kenny Marchant, Texas	Tim Ryan, Ohio
Tom Price, Ga.	Timothy H. Bishop, N.Y.
Luis Fortuño, P.R.	John Barrow, Ga.
Bobby Jindal, La.	
Charles Boustany Jr., La.	
Virginia Foxx, N.C.	
Thelma Drake, Va.	
John R. "Randy" Kuhl Jr., N.Y.	

21ST CENTURY COMPETITIVENESS
225-6658 2181 RHOB
McKeon, chairman

Republicans: Porter, vice chairman, Boehner, Petri, Castle, Johnson (Texas), Ehlers, Tiberi, Keller, Osborne, Inglis, McMorris, Price (Ga.), Fortuño, Boustany, Foxx, Drake, Kuhl
Democrats: Kildee, Payne, McCarthy, Tierney, Kind, Wu, Holt, McCollum, Van Hollen, Ryan (Ohio), Scott (Va.), Davis (Calif.), Bishop (N.Y.), Barrow, Owens

EDUCATION REFORM
225-6558 2181 RHOB
Castle, chairman

Republicans: Osborne, vice chairman, Souder, Ehlers, Biggert, Platts, Keller, Wilson (S.C.), Musgrave, Jindal, Kuhl
Democrats: Woolsey, Davis (Ill.), Grijalva, Andrews, Scott (Va.), Hinojosa, Kind, Kucinich, Davis (Calif.)

EMPLOYER-EMPLOYEE RELATIONS
225-7101 2181 RHOB
Johnson (Texas), chairman

Republicans: Kline, vice chairman, Boehner, McKeon, Platts, Tiberi, Wilson (S.C.), Musgrave, Marchant, Jindal, Boustany, Foxx
Democrats: Andrews, Kildee, Payne, McCarthy, Tierney, Wu, Holt, McCollum, Grijalva

SELECT EDUCATION
225-6558 2181 RHOB
Tiberi, chairman

Republicans: McMorris, vice chairwoman, Souder, Porter, Inglis, Fortuño
Democrats: Hinojosa, Davis (Ill.), Van Hollen, Ryan (Ohio)

WORKFORCE PROTECTIONS
225-7101 2181 RHOB
Norwood, chairman

Republicans: Biggert, vice chairwoman, Keller, Kline, Marchant, Price (Ga.), Drake
Democrats: Owens, Kucinich, Woolsey, Bishop (N.Y.), Barrow

ENERGY & COMMERCE

225-2927 2125 RHOB
Party Ratio: R 31-D 26
Joe L. Barton, R-Texas, chairman

Ralph M. Hall, Texas	John D. Dingell, Mich.
Michael Bilirakis, Fla.	Henry A. Waxman, Calif.
Fred Upton, Mich.	Edward J. Markey, Mass.
Cliff Stearns, Fla.	Rick Boucher, Va.
Paul E. Gillmor, Ohio	Edolphus Towns, N.Y.
Nathan Deal, Ga.	Frank Pallone Jr., N.J.
Edward Whitfield, Ky.	Sherrod Brown, Ohio
Charlie Norwood, Ga.	Bart Gordon, Tenn.
Barbara Cubin, Wyo.	Bobby L. Rush, Ill.
John Shimkus, Ill.	Anna G. Eshoo, Calif.
Heather A. Wilson, N.M.	Bart Stupak, Mich.
John Shadegg, Ariz.	Eliot L. Engel, N.Y.
Charles W. "Chip" Pickering Jr., Miss., vice chairman	Albert R. Wynn, Md.
	Gene Green, Texas
	Ted Strickland, Ohio
Vito J. Fossella, N.Y.	Diana DeGette, Colo.
Roy Blunt, Mo.	Lois Capps, Calif.
Steve Buyer, Ind.	Mike Doyle, Pa.
George P. Radanovich, Calif.	Tom Allen, Maine
Charles Bass, N.H.	Jim Davis, Fla.
Joe Pitts, Pa.	Jan Schakowsky, Ill.
Mary Bono, Calif.	Hilda L. Solis, Calif.
Greg Walden, Ore.	Charlie Gonzalez, Texas
Lee Terry, Neb.	Jay Inslee, Wash.
Mike Ferguson, N.J.	Tammy Baldwin, Wis.
Mike Rogers, Mich.	Mike Ross, Ark.
C. L. "Butch" Otter, Idaho	
Sue Myrick, N.C.	
John Sullivan, Okla.	
Tim Murphy, Pa.	
Michael C. Burgess, Texas	
Marsha Blackburn, Tenn.	

COMMERCE, TRADE & CONSUMER PROTECTION
225-2927 2125 RHOB
Stearns, chairman

Republicans: Upton, Deal, Cubin, Radanovich, Bass, Pitts, Bono, Terry, Ferguson, Rogers (Mich.), Otter, Myrick, Murphy, Blackburn
Democrats: Schakowsky, Ross, Markey, Towns, Brown (Ohio), Rush, Green (Texas), Strickland, DeGette, Davis (Fla.), Gonzalez, Baldwin

ENERGY & AIR QUALITY
225-2927 2125 RHOB
Hall (Texas), chairman

Republicans: Bilirakis, Whitfield, Norwood, Shimkus, Wilson (N.M.), Shadegg, Pickering, Fossella, Radanovich, Bono, Walden, Rogers (Mich.), Otter, Sullivan, Murphy, Burgess
Democrats: Boucher, Ross, Waxman, Markey, Engel, Wynn, Green (Texas), Strickland, Capps, Doyle, Allen, Davis (Fla.), Solis, Gonzalez

ENVIRONMENT & HAZARDOUS MATERIALS
225-2927 2125 RHOB
Gillmor, chairman

Republicans: Hall (Texas), Deal, Wilson (N.M.), Shadegg, Fossella, Bass, Pitts, Bono, Terry, Rogers (Mich.), Otter, Myrick, Sullivan, Murphy
Democrats: Solis, Pallone, Stupak, Wynn, Capps, Doyle, Allen, Schakowsky, Inslee, Green (Texas), Gonzalez, Baldwin

HEALTH
225-2927 2125 RHOB
Deal, chairman

Republicans: Hall (Texas), Bilirakis, Upton, Gillmor, Norwood, Cubin, Shimkus, Shadegg, Pickering, Buyer, Pitts, Bono, Ferguson, vice chairman, Rogers (Mich.), Myrick, Burgess
Democrats: Brown (Ohio), Waxman, Towns, Pallone, Gordon, Rush, Eshoo, Green (Texas), Strickland, DeGette, Capps, Allen, Davis (Fla.), Baldwin

OVERSIGHT & INVESTIGATIONS
225-2927 2125 RHOB
Whitfield, chairman

Republicans: Stearns, Pickering, Bass, Walden, Ferguson, Burgess, Blackburn
Democrats: Stupak, DeGette, Schakowsky, Inslee, Baldwin, Waxman

TELECOMMUNICATIONS AND THE INTERNET
225-2927 2125 RHOB
Upton, chairman

Republicans: Bilirakis, Stearns, Gillmor, Whitfield, Cubin, Shimkus, Wilson (N.M.), Pickering, Fossella, Radanovich, Bass, Walden, Terry, Ferguson, Sullivan, Blackburn
Democrats: Markey, Engel, Wynn, Doyle, Gonzalez, Inslee, Boucher, Towns, Pallone, Brown (Ohio), Gordon, Rush, Eshoo, Stupak

FINANCIAL SERVICES
225-7502 2129 RHOB
Party Ratio: R 37-D 33
Michael G. Oxley, R-Ohio, chairman

Jim Leach, Iowa	*Barney Frank, Mass.*
Richard H. Baker, La.	*Paul E. Kanjorski, Pa.*
Deborah Pryce, Ohio	*Maxine Waters, Calif.*
Spencer Bachus, Ala.	*Bernard Sanders, I-Vt.*
Michael N. Castle, Del.	*Carolyn B. Maloney, N.Y.*
Peter T. King, N.Y.	*Luis V. Gutierrez, Ill.*
Ed Royce, Calif.	*Nydia M. Velázquez, N.Y.*
Frank D. Lucas, Okla.	*Melvin Watt, N.C.*
Bob Ney, Ohio	*Gary L. Ackerman, N.Y.*
Sue W. Kelly, N.Y.	*Darlene Hooley, Ore.*

vice chairwoman	*Julia Carson, Ind.*
Ron Paul, Texas	*Brad Sherman, Calif.*
Paul E. Gillmor, Ohio	*Gregory W. Meeks, N.Y.*
Jim Ryun, Kan.	*Barbara Lee, Calif.*
Steven C. LaTourette, Ohio	*Dennis Moore, Kan.*
Donald Manzullo, Ill.	*Michael E. Capuano, Mass.*
Walter B. Jones, N.C.	*Harold E. Ford Jr., Tenn.*
Judy Biggert, Ill.	*Rubén Hinojosa, Texas*
Christopher Shays, Conn.	*Joseph Crowley, N.Y.*
Vito J. Fossella, N.Y.	*William Lacy Clay, Mo.*
Gary G. Miller, Calif.	*Steve Israel, N.Y.*
Pat Tiberi, Ohio	*Carolyn McCarthy, N.Y.*
Mark Kennedy, Minn.	*Joe Baca, Calif.*
Tom Feeney, Fla.	*Jim Matheson, Utah*
Jeb Hensarling, Texas	*Stephen F. Lynch, Mass.*
Scott Garrett, N.J.	*Brad Miller, N.C.*
Ginny Brown-Waite, Fla.	*David Scott, Ga.*
J. Gresham Barrett, S.C.	*Artur Davis, Ala.*
Katherine Harris, Fla.	*Al Green, Texas*
Rick Renzi, Ariz.	*Emanuel Cleaver II, Mo.*
Jim Gerlach, Pa.	*Melissa Bean, Ill.*
Steve Pearce, N.M.	*Debbie*
Randy Neugebauer, Texas	* Wasserman-Schultz, Fla.*
Tom Price, Ga.	*Gwen Moore, Wis.*
Michael G. Fitzpatrick, Pa.	
Geoff Davis, Ky.	
Patrick T. McHenry, N.C.	

CAPITAL MARKETS, INSURANCE & GSES
225-7502 2129 RHOB
Baker, chairman

Republicans: Ryun, vice chairman, Shays, Gillmor, Bachus, Castle, King (N.Y.), Lucas, Manzullo, Royce, Kelly, Ney, Fossella, Biggert, Miller (Calif.), Kennedy (Minn.), Tiberi, Barrett, Brown-Waite, Feeney, Gerlach, Harris, Hensarling, Renzi, Davis (Ky.), Fitzpatrick
Democrats: Kanjorski, Ackerman, Hooley, Sherman, Meeks, Moore (Kan.), Capuano, Ford, Hinojosa, Crowley, Israel, Clay, McCarthy, Baca, Matheson, Lynch, Miller (N.C.), Scott (Ga.), Velázquez, Watt, Davis (Ala.), Bean, Wasserman-Schultz

DOMESTIC & INTERNATIONAL MONETARY POLICY, TRADE & TECHNOLOGY
225-7502 B-304 RHOB
Pryce, chairwoman

Republicans: Biggert, vice chairwoman, Leach, Castle, Lucas, Paul, LaTourette, Manzullo, Kennedy (Minn.), Harris, Gerlach, Neugebauer, Price (Ga.), McHenry
Democrats: Maloney, Sanders (I), Watt, Waters, Lee, Kanjorski, Sherman, Gutierrez, Bean, Wasserman-Schultz, Moore (Wis.), Crowley

FINANCIAL INSTITUTIONS & CONSUMER CREDIT
225-7502 2129 RHOB
Bachus, chairman

Republicans: Jones (N.C.), vice chairman, Baker, Castle, Royce, Lucas, Kelly, Paul, Gillmor, Ryun, LaTourette, Biggert, Fossella, Miller (Calif.), Tiberi, Feeney, Hensarling, Garrett, Brown-Waite, Barrett, Renzi, Pearce, Neugebauer, Price (Ga.), McHenry
Democrats: Sanders (I), Maloney, Watt, Ackerman, Sherman, Meeks, Gutierrez, Moore (Kan.), Kanjorski, Waters, Hooley, Carson (Ind.), Ford, Hinojosa, Crowley, Israel, McCarthy, Baca, Green (Texas), Moore (Wis.), Clay, Matheson

HOUSING & COMMUNITY OPPORTUNITY
225-6634 B-303 RHOB
Ney, chairman

Republicans: Miller (Calif.), vice chairman, Baker, King (N.Y.), Jones (N.C.), Shays, Tiberi, Brown-Waite, Harris, Renzi, Pearce, Neugebauer, Fitzpatrick, Davis (Ky.)
Democrats: Waters, Velázquez, Carson (Ind.), Lee, Capuano, Sanders (I), Lynch, Miller (N.C.), Scott (Ga.), Davis (Ala.), Cleaver, Green (Texas)

OVERSIGHT & INVESTIGATIONS
225-7502 139 FHOB
Kelly, chairwoman

Republicans: Paul, vice chairman, Royce, LaTourette, Kennedy (Minn.), Garrett, Barrett, Price (Ga.), Fitzpatrick, Davis (Ky.), McHenry
Democrats: Gutierrez, Moore (Kan.), Maloney, Lynch, Davis (Ala.), Cleaver, Scott (Ga.), Wasserman-Schultz, Moore (Wis.)

GOVERNMENT REFORM
225-5074 2157 RHOB
Party Ratio: R 23-D 18
Thomas M. Davis III, R-Va., chairman

Christopher Shays, Conn., vice chairman	Henry A. Waxman, Calif.
Dan Burton, Ind.	Tom Lantos, Calif.
Ileana Ros-Lehtinen, Fla.	Major R. Owens, N.Y.
John M. McHugh, N.Y.	Edolphus Towns, N.Y.
John L. Mica, Fla.	Paul E. Kanjorski, Pa.
Gil Gutknecht, Minn.	Bernard Sanders, I-Vt.
Mark Souder, Ind.	Carolyn B. Maloney, N.Y.
Steven C. LaTourette, Ohio	Elijah E. Cummings, Md.
Todd R. Platts, Pa.	Dennis J. Kucinich, Ohio
Chris Cannon, Utah	Danny K. Davis, Ill.
John J. "Jimmy" Duncan Jr., Tenn.	William Lacy Clay, Mo.
Candice S. Miller, Mich.	Diane Watson, Calif.
Michael R. Turner, Ohio	Stephen F. Lynch, Mass.
Darrell Issa, Calif.	Chris Van Hollen, Md.
Ginny Brown-Waite, Fla.	Linda T. Sánchez, Calif.
Jon Porter, Nev.	C.A. Dutch Ruppersberger, Md.
Kenny Marchant, Texas	Brian Higgins, N.Y.
Lynn Westmoreland, Ga.	Eleanor Holmes Norton, D.C.
Patrick T. McHenry, N.C.	
Charlie Dent, Pa.	
Virginia Foxx, N.C.	
Vacancy	

CRIMINAL JUSTICE, DRUG POLICY & HUMAN RESOURCES
225-2577 B-377 RHOB
Souder, chairman

Republicans: McHenry, vice chairman, Burton, Mica, Gutknecht, LaTourette, Cannon, Miller (Mich.), Brown-Waite, Foxx
Democrats: Cummings, Sanders (I), Davis (Ill.), Watson, Sánchez (Calif.), Ruppersberger, Owens, Vacancy

ENERGY & RESOURCES
225-6427 B-349C RHOB
Issa, chairman

Republicans: Westmoreland, vice chairman, Ros-Lehtinen, McHugh, McHenry, Marchant
Democrats: Watson, Higgins, Lantos, Kucinich

FEDERAL WORKFORCE & AGENCY ORGANIZATION
225-5147 B-373A RHOB
Porter, chairman

Republicans: Mica, vice chairman, Davis (Va.), Issa, Marchant, McHenry, Vacancy
Democrats: Davis (Ill.), Owens, Norton, Cummings, Van Hollen

FEDERALISM & THE CENSUS
225-6751 B-349A RHOB
Turner, chairman

Republicans: Dent, vice chairman, Shays, Foxx, Vacancy
Democrats: Clay, Kanjorski, Maloney

GOVERNMENT MANAGEMENT, FINANCE & ACCOUNTABILITY
225-3741 B-371C RHOB
Platts, chairman

Republicans: Foxx, vice chairwoman, Davis (Va.), Gutknecht, Souder, Duncan
Democrats: Towns, Owens, Kanjorski, Maloney

NATIONAL SECURITY, EMERGING THREATS & INTERNATIONAL RELATIONS
225-2548 B-372 RHOB
Shays, chairman

Republicans: Marchant, vice chairman, Burton, Ros-Lehtinen, McHugh, LaTourette, Platts, Duncan, Turner, Porter, Dent
Democrats: Kucinich, Lantos, Sanders (I), Maloney, Van Hollen, Sánchez (Calif.), Ruppersberger, Lynch, Higgins

REGULATORY AFFAIRS
225-4407 B-373 RHOB
Miller (Mich.), chairwoman

Republicans: Brown-Waite, vice chairwoman, Souder, Cannon, Turner, Westmoreland
Democrats: Lynch, Clay, Norton, Van Hollen

HOMELAND SECURITY
226-8417 202 ADAMS
Party Ratio: R 19-D 15
Christopher Cox, R-Calif., chairman

Don Young, Alaska	Bennie Thompson, Miss.
Lamar Smith, Texas	Loretta Sanchez, Calif.
Curt Weldon, Pa., vice chairman	Edward J. Markey, Mass.
Christopher Shays, Conn.	Norm Dicks, Wash.
	Jane Harman, Calif.
Peter T. King, N.Y.	Peter A. DeFazio, Ore.
John Linder, Ga.	Nita M. Lowey, N.Y.
Mark Souder, Ind.	Eleanor Holmes Norton, D.C.
Thomas M. Davis III, Va.	Zoe Lofgren, Calif.
Dan Lungren, Calif.	Sheila Jackson-Lee, Texas
Jim Gibbons, Nev.	Bill Pascrell Jr., N.J.
Rob Simmons, Conn.	Donna M.C. Christensen, Virgin Is.
Mike D. Rogers, Ala.	

Steve Pearce, N.M.
Katherine Harris, Fla.
Bobby Jindal, La.
Dave Reichert, Wash.
Michael McCaul, Texas
Charlie Dent, Pa.

Bob Etheridge, N.C.
Jim Langevin, R.I.
Kendrick B. Meek, Fla.

ECONOMIC SECURITY, INFRASTRUCTURE PROTECTION & CYBERSECURITY
226-8417   202 ADAMS
Lungren, chairman

Republicans: Young (Alaska), Smith (Texas), Linder, Souder, Davis (Va.), Rogers (Ala.), Pearce, Harris, Jindal
Democrats: Sanchez (Calif.), Markey, Dicks, DeFazio, Lofgren, Jackson-Lee, Pascrell, Langevin

EMERGENCY PREPAREDNESS, SCIENCE & TECHNOLOGY
226-8417   202 ADAMS
King (N.Y.), chairman

Republicans: Smith (Texas), Weldon (Pa.), Simmons, Rogers (Ala.), Pearce, Harris, Reichert, McCaul, Dent
Democrats: Pascrell, Sanchez (Calif.), Dicks, Harman, Lowey, Norton, Christensen, Etheridge

INTELLIGENCE, INFORMATION SHARING & TERRORISM RISK ASSESSMENT
226-8417   202 ADAMS
Simmons, chairman

Republicans: Weldon (Pa.), King (N.Y.), Souder, Lungren, Gibbons, Pearce, Jindal, Reichert, Dent
Democrats: Lofgren, Sanchez (Calif.), Harman, Lowey, Jackson-Lee, Etheridge, Langevin, Meek

MANAGEMENT, INTEGRATION & OVERSIGHT
226-8417   202 ADAMS
Rogers (Ala.), chairman

Republicans: Shays, Linder, Davis (Va.), Harris, Reichert, McCaul, Dent
Democrats: Meek, Markey, Lofgren, Jackson-Lee, Pascrell, Christensen

PREVENTION OF NUCLEAR & BIOLOGICAL ATTACK
226-8417   ADAMS
Linder, chairman

Republicans: Young (Alaska), Shays, Lungren, Gibbons, Simmons, Jindal, vice chairman, McCaul
Democrats: Langevin, Markey, Dicks, Harman, Norton, Christensen

HOUSE ADMINISTRATION
225-8281   1309 LHOB
Party Ratio: R 6-D 3
Bob Ney, R-Ohio, chairman

Vernon J. Ehlers, Mich.
John L. Mica, Fla.
John T. Doolittle, Calif.
Thomas M. Reynolds, N.Y.
Candice S. Miller, Mich.

Juanita Millender-McDonald, Calif.
Robert A. Brady, Pa.
Zoe Lofgren, Calif.

INTERNATIONAL RELATIONS
225-5021   2170 RHOB
Party Ratio: R 27-D 23
Henry J. Hyde, R-Ill., chairman

Jim Leach, Iowa
Christopher H. Smith, N.J.
Dan Burton, Ind.
Elton Gallegly, Calif.
Ileana Ros-Lehtinen, Fla.
Dana Rohrabacher, Calif.
Ed Royce, Calif.
Peter T. King, N.Y.
Steve Chabot, Ohio
Tom Tancredo, Colo.
Ron Paul, Texas
Darrell Issa, Calif.
Jeff Flake, Ariz.
Jo Ann Davis, Va.
Mark Green, Wis.
Jerry Weller, Ill.
Mike Pence, Ind.
Thaddeus McCotter, Mich.
Katherine Harris, Fla.
Joe Wilson, S.C.
John Boozman, Ark.
J. Gresham Barrett, S.C.
Connie Mack, Fla.
Jeff Fortenberry, Neb.
Michael McCaul, Texas
Ted Poe, Texas

Tom Lantos, Calif.
Howard L. Berman, Calif.
Gary L. Ackerman, N.Y.
Eni F.H. Faleomavaega, Am. Samoa
Donald M. Payne, N.J.
Robert Menendez, N.J.
Sherrod Brown, Ohio
Brad Sherman, Calif.
Robert Wexler, Fla.
Eliot L. Engel, N.Y.
Bill Delahunt, Mass.
Gregory W. Meeks, N.Y.
Barbara Lee, Calif.
Joseph Crowley, N.Y.
Earl Blumenauer, Ore.
Shelley Berkley, Nev.
Grace F. Napolitano, Calif.
Adam B. Schiff, Calif.
Diane Watson, Calif.
Adam Smith, Wash.
Betty McCollum, Minn.
Ben Chandler, Ky.
Dennis Cardoza, Calif.

AFRICA, GLOBAL HUMAN RIGHTS & INTERNATIONAL OPERATIONS
226-7812   255 FHOB
Smith (N.J.), chairman

Republicans: Tancredo, Flake, Green (Wis.), Boozman, Fortenberry, Royce, vice chairman
Democrats: Payne, Lee, McCollum, Sherman, Meeks, Watson

ASIA & THE PACIFIC
226-7825   B-358 RHOB
Leach, chairman

Republicans: Burton, vice chairman, Gallegly, Rohrabacher, Chabot, Paul, Wilson (S.C.)
Democrats: Faleomavaega, Brown (Ohio), Blumenauer, Watson, Smith (Wash.), Ackerman

EUROPE & EMERGING THREATS
226-7820   2401-A RHOB
Gallegly, chairman

Republicans: Davis (Va.), King (N.Y.), vice chairman, McCotter, Issa, Poe, Barrett
Democrats: Wexler, Engel, Berkley, Napolitano, Smith (Wash.), Chandler

INTERNATIONAL TERRORISM & NONPROLIFERATION
226-1500   253 FHOB
Royce, chairman

Republicans: King (N.Y.), Tancredo, Issa, vice chairman, McCaul, Poe, Weller, Barrett
Democrats: Sherman, Menendez, Wexler, Crowley, McCollum, Cardoza, Watson

MIDDLE EAST & CENTRAL ASIA
225-3345 257 FHOB
Ros-Lehtinen, chairwoman

Republicans: Chabot, vice chairman, McCotter, Boozman, Mack, Fortenberry, Davis (Va.), Pence, Harris, Issa
Democrats: Ackerman, Berman, Engel, Crowley, Berkley, Schiff, Chandler, Cardoza

OVERSIGHT & INVESTIGATIONS
226-4948 253 FHOB
Rohrabacher, chairman

Republicans: Royce, Flake, vice chairman, Green (Wis.), Pence, Wilson (S.C.)
Democrats: Delahunt, Berman, Blumenauer, Schiff

WESTERN HEMISPHERE
226-9980 259A FHOB
Burton, chairman

Republicans: Paul, Weller, vice chairman, Harris, Leach, Smith (N.J.), Ros-Lehtinen, Mack, McCaul
Democrats: Menendez, Napolitano, Meeks, Faleomavaega, Payne, Delahunt, Lee

JUDICIARY
225-3951 2138 RHOB
Party Ratio: R 23-D 17
F. James Sensenbrenner Jr., R-Wis., chairman

Henry J. Hyde, Ill.	John Conyers Jr., Mich.
Howard Coble, N.C.	Howard L. Berman, Calif.
Lamar Smith, Texas	Rick Boucher, Va.
Elton Gallegly, Calif.	Jerrold Nadler, N.Y.
Robert W. Goodlatte, Va.	Robert C. Scott, Va.
Steve Chabot, Ohio	Melvin Watt, N.C.
Dan Lungren, Calif.	Zoe Lofgren, Calif.
Bill Jenkins, Tenn.	Sheila Jackson-Lee, Texas
Chris Cannon, Utah	Maxine Waters, Calif.
Spencer Bachus, Ala.	Martin T. Meehan, Mass.
Bob Inglis, S.C.	Bill Delahunt, Mass.
John Hostettler, Ind.	Robert Wexler, Fla.
Mark Green, Wis.	Anthony Weiner, N.Y.
Ric Keller, Fla.	Adam B. Schiff, Calif.
Darrell Issa, Calif.	Linda T. Sánchez, Calif.
Jeff Flake, Ariz.	Adam Smith, Wash.
Mike Pence, Ind.	Chris Van Hollen, Md.
J. Randy Forbes, Va.	
Steve King, Iowa	
Tom Feeney, Fla.	
Trent Franks, Ariz.	
Louie Gohmert, Texas	

COMMERCIAL & ADMINISTRATIVE LAW
225-2825 B-353 RHOB
Cannon, chairman

Republicans: Coble, Franks, Chabot, Green (Wis.), Forbes, Gohmert
Democrats: Watt, Delahunt, Smith (Wash.), Van Hollen, Nadler

CONSTITUTION
226-7680 H2-362 FHOB
Chabot, chairman

Republicans: Franks, Jenkins, Bachus, Hostettler, Green Wis.), King (Iowa), Feeney
Democrats: Nadler, Conyers, Scott (Va.), Watt, Van Hollen

COURTS, THE INTERNET & INTELLECTUAL PROPERTY
225-5741 B-352 RHOB
Smith (Texas), chairman

Republicans: Hyde, Gallegly, Goodlatte, Jenkins, Bachus, Inglis, Keller, Issa, Cannon, Pence, Forbes
Democrats: Berman, Conyers, Boucher, Lofgren, Waters, Meehan, Wexler, Weiner, Schiff, Sánchez (Calif.)

CRIME, TERRORISM & HOMELAND SECURITY
225-3926 207 CHOB
Coble, chairman

Republicans: Lungren, Green (Wis.), Feeney, Chabot, Keller, Flake, Pence, Forbes, Gohmert
Democrats: Scott (Va.), Jackson-Lee, Waters, Meehan, Delahunt, Weiner

IMMIGRATION, BORDER SECURITY & CLAIMS
225-5727 B-370B RHOB
Hostettler, chairman

Republicans: King (Iowa), Gohmert, Smith (Texas), Gallegly, Goodlatte, Lungren, Flake, Inglis, Issa
Democrats: Jackson-Lee, Berman, Lofgren, Sánchez (Calif.), Waters, Meehan

RESOURCES
225-2761 1324 LHOB
Party Ratio: R 27-D 22
Richard W. Pombo, R-Calif., chairman

Don Young, Alaska	Nick J. Rahall II, W.Va.
H. James Saxton, N.J.	Dale E. Kildee, Mich.
Elton Gallegly, Calif.	Eni F.H. Faleomavaega,
John J. "Jimmy"	Am. Samoa
Duncan Jr., Tenn.	Neil Abercrombie, Hawaii
Wayne T. Gilchrest, Md.	Solomon P. Ortiz, Texas
Ken Calvert, Calif.	Frank Pallone Jr., N.J.
Barbara Cubin, Wyo.,	Donna M.C. Christensen,
vice chairwoman	Virgin Is.
George P. Radanovich, Calif.	Ron Kind, Wis.
Walter B. Jones, N.C.	Grace F. Napolitano, Calif.
Chris Cannon, Utah	Tom Udall, N.M.
John E. Peterson, Pa.	Raúl M. Grijalva, Ariz.
Jim Gibbons, Nev.	Madeleine Z. Bordallo, Guam
Greg Walden, Ore.	Jim Costa, Calif.
Tom Tancredo, Colo.	Charlie Melancon, La.
J.D. Hayworth, Ariz.	Dan Boren, Okla.
Jeff Flake, Ariz.	George Miller, Calif.
Rick Renzi, Ariz.	Edward J. Markey, Mass.
Steve Pearce, N.M.	Peter A. DeFazio, Ore.
Henry E. Brown Jr., S.C.	Jay Inslee, Wash.
Thelma Drake, Va.	Mark Udall, Colo.
Luis Fortuño, P.R.	Dennis Cardoza, Calif.
Cathy McMorris, Wash.	Stephanie Herseth, S.D.
Bobby Jindal, La.	
Louie Gohmert, Texas	
Marilyn Musgrave, Colo.	
Vacancy	

ENERGY & MINERAL RESOURCES
225-9297 1626 LHOB
Gibbons, chairman

Republicans: Young (Alaska), Cubin, Cannon, Peterson (Pa.), Pearce, Drake, Jindal, Gohmert
Democrats: Grijalva, Faleomavaega, Ortiz, Costa, Melancon, Boren, Markey

FISHERIES & OCEANS
226-0200 H2-188 FHOB
Gilchrest, chairman

Republicans: Young (Alaska), Saxton, Jones (N.C.), Drake, Fortuño, Jindal, Musgrave
Democrats: Pallone, Faleomavaega, Abercrombie, Ortiz, Kind, Bordallo

FORESTS & FOREST HEALTH
225-0691 1337 LHOB
Walden, chairman

Republicans: Duncan, Gilchrest, Cannon, Peterson (Pa.), Tancredo, Hayworth, Flake, Renzi, Brown (S.C.), McMorris
Democrats: Udall (N.M.), Kildee, Abercrombie, Boren, DeFazio, Inslee, Udall (Colo.), Cardoza, Herseth

NATIONAL PARKS
226-7736 H2-187 FHOB
Vacancy, chairman

Republicans: Saxton, Gallegly, Duncan, Radanovich, Jones (N.C.), Brown (S.C.), Fortuño, Musgrave
Democrats: Christensen, Kildee, Abercrombie, Kind, Udall (N.M.), Bordallo, Melancon

WATER & POWER
225-8331 1522 LHOB
Radanovich, chairman

Republicans: Calvert, Cubin, Walden, Tancredo, Hayworth, Pearce, McMorris, Gohmert, Vacancy
Democrats: Napolitano, Grijalva, Costa, Miller (Calif.), Udall (Colo.), Cardoza, Vacancy, Vacancy

RULES
225-9191 H-312 Capitol
Party Ratio: R 9-D 4
David Dreier, R-Calif., chairman

Lincoln Diaz-Balart, Fla.	*Louise M. Slaughter, N.Y.*
Doc Hastings, Wash.	*Jim McGovern, Mass.*
Pete Sessions, Texas	*Alcee L. Hastings, Fla.*
Adam H. Putnam, Fla.	*Doris Matsui, Calif.*
Shelley Moore Capito, W.Va.	
Tom Cole, Okla.	
Rob Bishop, Utah	
Phil Gingrey, Ga.	

LEGISLATIVE & BUDGET PROCESS
225-4211 421 CHOB
Diaz-Balart (Fla.), chairman

Republicans: Sessions, vice chairman, Bishop (Utah), Gingrey, Dreier
Democrats: Hastings (Fla.), Slaughter

RULES & THE ORGANIZATION OF THE HOUSE
225-5816 421 CHOB
Hastings (Wash.), chairman

Republicans: Putnam, Capito, Cole, Dreier
Democrats: McGovern, Matsui (Calif.)

SCIENCE
225-6371 2320 RHOB
Party Ratio: R 24-D 20
Sherwood Boehlert, R-N.Y., chairman

Ralph M. Hall, Texas	*Bart Gordon, Tenn.*
Lamar Smith, Texas	*Jerry F. Costello, Ill.*
Curt Weldon, Pa.	*Eddie Bernice Johnson, Texas*
Dana Rohrabacher, Calif.	
Ken Calvert, Calif.	*Lynn Woolsey, Calif.*
Roscoe G. Bartlett, Md.	*Darlene Hooley, Ore.*
Vernon J. Ehlers, Mich.	*Mark Udall, Colo.*
Gil Gutknecht, Minn.	*David Wu, Ore.*
Frank D. Lucas, Okla.	*Michael M. Honda, Calif.*
Judy Biggert, Ill.	*Brad Miller, N.C.*
Wayne T. Gilchrest, Md.	*Lincoln Davis, Tenn.*
Todd Akin, Mo.	*Russ Carnahan, Mo.*
Timothy V. Johnson, Ill.	*Daniel Lipinski, Ill.*
J. Randy Forbes, Va.	*Sheila Jackson-Lee, Texas*
Jo Bonner, Ala.	*Brad Sherman, Calif.*
Tom Feeney, Fla.	*Brian Baird, Wash.*
Bob Inglis, S.C.	*Jim Matheson, Utah*
Dave Reichert, Wash.	*Jim Costa, Calif.*
Mike Sodrel, Ind.	*Al Green, Texas*
Joe Schwarz, Mich.	*Charlie Melancon, La.*
Michael McCaul, Texas	*Vacancy*
Vacancy	
Vacancy	

ENERGY
225-9662 390 FHOB
Biggert, chairwoman

Republicans: Hall (Texas), Weldon (Pa.), Bartlett, Ehlers, Akin, Bonner, Inglis, Reichert, Sodrel, Schwarz, Vacancy
Democrats: Honda, Woolsey, Davis (Tenn.), Costello, Johnson (Texas), Lipinski, Matheson, Jackson-Lee, Sherman, Green (Texas)

ENVIRONMENT, TECHNOLOGY & STANDARDS
225-8844 2319 RHOB
Ehlers, chairman

Republicans: Gutknecht, Biggert, Gilchrest, Johnson (Ill.), Reichert, Schwarz, Vacancy
Democrats: Wu, Miller (N.C.), Udall (Colo.), Davis (Tenn.), Baird, Matheson

RESEARCH
225-7858 B-374 RHOB
Inglis, chairman

Republicans: Smith (Texas), Weldon (Pa.), Rohrabacher, Gutknecht, Lucas, Akin, Johnson (Ill.), Reichert, Sodrel, McCaul, Vacancy
Democrats: Hooley, Carnahan, Lipinski, Baird, Melancon, Johnson (Texas), Vacancy, Vacancy, Vacancy, Vacancy

SPACE & AERONAUTICS
225-7858 B-374 RHOB
Calvert, chairman

Republicans: Hall (Texas), Smith (Texas), Rohrabacher, Bartlett, Lucas, Forbes, Bonner, Feeney, McCaul, Vacancy
Democrats: Udall (Colo.), Wu, Honda, Miller (N.C.), Jackson-Lee, Sherman, Costa, Green (Texas), Melancon

SELECT INTELLIGENCE
225-4121 H-405 Capitol
Party Ratio: R 12-D 9
Peter Hoekstra, R-Mich., chairman

Ray LaHood, Ill.	Jane Harman, Calif.
Randy "Duke" Cunningham, Calif.	Alcee L. Hastings, Fla.
Terry Everett, Ala.	Silvestre Reyes, Texas
Elton Gallegly, Calif.	Leonard L. Boswell, Iowa
Heather A. Wilson, N.M.	Robert E. "Bud" Cramer, Ala.
Jo Ann Davis, Va.	Anna G. Eshoo, Calif.
William M. "Mac" Thornberry, Texas	Rush D. Holt, N.J.
John M. McHugh, N.Y.	C.A. Dutch Ruppersberger, Md.
Todd Tiahrt, Kan.	John F. Tierney, Mass.
Mike Rogers, Mich.	
Rick Renzi, Ariz.	

INTELLIGENCE POLICY
225-4121 H-405 Capitol
Davis (Va.), chairwoman

Republicans: Wilson (N.M.), vice chairwoman, McHugh, Rogers (Mich.), Renzi
Democrats: Holt, Eshoo, Tierney

OVERSIGHT
225-4121 H-405 Capitol
Thornberry, chairman

Republicans: LaHood, vice chairman, Everett, Wilson (N.M.), Tiahrt, Rogers (Mich.), Renzi
Democrats: Cramer, Hastings (Fla.), Reyes, Ruppersberger, Tierney

TECHNICAL & TACTICAL INTELLIGENCE
225-4121 H-405 Capitol
Wilson (N.M.), chairwoman

Republicans: Everett, vice chairman, Cunningham, Gallegly, Thornberry, McHugh
Democrats: Eshoo, Cramer, Holt, Ruppersberger

TERRORISM/HUMAN INTELLIGENCE, ANALYSIS & COUNTERINTELLIGENCE
225-4121 H-405 Capitol
Cunningham, chairman

Republicans: LaHood, vice chairman, Gallegly, Davis (Va.), McHugh, Tiahrt, Renzi
Democrats: Boswell, Hastings (Fla.), Reyes, Ruppersberger

SMALL BUSINESS
225-5821 2361 RHOB
Party Ratio: R 18-D 15
Donald Manzullo, R-Ill., chairman

Roscoe G. Bartlett, Md.	Nydia M. Velázquez, N.Y.
Sue W. Kelly, N.Y.	Juanita Millender-McDonald, Calif.
Steve Chabot, Ohio	
Sam Graves, Mo.	Tom Udall, N.M.
Todd Akin, Mo.	Daniel Lipinski, Ill.
Bill Shuster, Pa.	Eni F.H. Faleomavaega, Am. Samoa
Marilyn Musgrave, Colo.	
Jeb Bradley, N.H.	Danny K. Davis, Ill.
Steve King, Iowa	Donna M.C. Christensen, Virgin Is.
Thaddeus McCotter, Mich.	
Ric Keller, Fla.	Ed Case, Hawaii
Ted Poe, Texas	Madeleine Z. Bordallo, Guam
Mike Sodrel, Ind.	Raúl M. Grijalva, Ariz.
Jeff Fortenberry, Neb.	Michael H. Michaud, Maine
Michael G. Fitzpatrick, Pa.	Linda T. Sánchez, Calif.
Lynn Westmoreland, Ga.	John Barrow, Ga.
Louie Gohmert, Texas	Melissa Bean, Ill.
	Gwen Moore, Wis.

REGULATORY REFORM & OVERSIGHT
226-2630 B-363 RHOB
Akin, chairman

Republicans: Sodrel, Westmoreland, Gohmert, Kelly, King (Iowa), Poe
Democrats: Bordallo, Faleomavaega, Christensen, Case, Vacancy, Vacancy

RURAL ENTERPRISES, AGRICULTURE & TECHNOLOGY
226-2630 B-363 RHOB
Graves, chairman

Republicans: King (Iowa), Bartlett, Sodrel, Fortenberry, Musgrave
Democrats: Barrow, Udall (N.M.), Case, Michaud, Vacancy

TAX, FINANCE & EXPORTS
226-2630 B-363 RHOB
Bradley, chairman

Republicans: Kelly, Chabot, McCotter, Keller, Poe, Fortenberry, Fitzpatrick
Democrats: Millender-McDonald, Lipinski, Faleomavaega, Davis (Ill.), Case, Michaud, Bean

WORKFORCE, EMPOWERMENT & GOVERNMENT PROGRAMS
226-2630 B-363 RHOB
Musgrave, chairwoman

Republicans: Bartlett, Shuster, Fitzpatrick, Westmoreland, McCotter, Bradley
Democrats: Lipinski, Udall (N.M.), Davis (Ill.), Grijalva, Barrow, Bean

STANDARDS OF OFFICIAL CONDUCT

225-7103 HT-2 Capitol
Party Ratio: R 5-D 5
Doc Hastings, R-Wash., chairman

Judy Biggert, Ill.
Lamar Smith, Texas
Melissa A. Hart, Pa.
Tom Cole, Okla.

Alan B. Mollohan, W.Va.
Stephanie Tubbs Jones, Ohio
Gene Green, Texas
Lucille Roybal-Allard, Calif.
Mike Doyle, Pa.

TRANSPORTATION & INFRASTRUCTURE

225-9446 2165 RHOB
Party Ratio: R 41-D 34
Don Young, R-Alaska, chairman

Tom Petri, Wis.,
  vice chairman
Sherwood Boehlert, N.Y.
Howard Coble, N.C.
John J. "Jimmy"
  Duncan Jr., Tenn.
Wayne T. Gilchrest, Md.
John L. Mica, Fla.
Peter Hoekstra, Mich.
Vernon J. Ehlers, Mich.
Spencer Bachus, Ala.
Steven C. LaTourette, Ohio
Sue W. Kelly, N.Y.
Richard H. Baker, La.
Bob Ney, Ohio
Frank A. LoBiondo, N.J.
Jerry Moran, Kan.
Gary G. Miller, Calif.
Robin Hayes, N.C.
Rob Simmons, Conn.
Henry E. Brown Jr., S.C.
Timothy V. Johnson, Ill.
Todd R. Platts, Pa.
Sam Graves, Mo.
Mark Kennedy, Minn.
Bill Shuster, Pa.
John Boozman, Ark.
Jim Gerlach, Pa.
Mario Diaz-Balart, Fla.
Jon Porter, Nev.
Tom Osborne, Neb.
Kenny Marchant, Texas
Mike Sodrel, Ind.
Charlie Dent, Pa.
Ted Poe, Texas
Dave Reichert, Wash.
Connie Mack, Fla.
John R. "Randy" Kuhl Jr., N.Y.
Luis Fortuño, P.R.
Lynn Westmoreland, Ga.
Charles Boustany Jr., La.
Vacancy

James L. Oberstar, Minn.
Nick J. Rahall II, W.Va.
Peter A. DeFazio, Ore.
Jerry F. Costello, Ill.
Eleanor Holmes Norton, D.C.
Jerrold Nadler, N.Y.
Robert Menendez, N.J.
Corrine Brown, Fla.
Bob Filner, Calif.
Eddie Bernice Johnson,
  Texas
Gene Taylor, Miss.
Juanita Millender-McDonald,
  Calif.
Elijah E. Cummings, Md.
Earl Blumenauer, Ore.
Ellen O. Tauscher, Calif.
Bill Pascrell Jr., N.J.
Leonard L. Boswell, Iowa
Tim Holden, Pa.
Brian Baird, Wash.
Shelley Berkley, Nev.
Jim Matheson, Utah
Michael M. Honda, Calif.
Rick Larsen, Wash.
Michael E. Capuano, Mass.
Anthony Weiner, N.Y.
Julia Carson, Ind.
Timothy H. Bishop, N.Y.
Michael H. Michaud, Maine
Lincoln Davis, Tenn.
Ben Chandler, Ky.
Brian Higgins, N.Y.
Russ Carnahan, Mo.
Allyson Y. Schwartz, Pa.
John Salazar, Colo.

AVIATION

226-3220 2251 RHOB
Mica, chairman

Republicans: Petri, Coble, Duncan, Ehlers, Bachus, Kelly, Baker, Ney, LoBiondo, Moran (Kan.), Hayes, Brown (S.C.), Johnson (Ill.), Graves, Kennedy (Minn.), Boozman, Gerlach, Diaz-Balart (Fla.), Porter, Dent, Poe, Kuhl, vice chairman, Westmoreland, Vacancy
Democrats: Costello, Boswell, DeFazio, Norton, Brown (Fla.), Johnson (Texas), Millender-McDonald, Tauscher, Pascrell, Holden, Berkley, Matheson, Honda, Larsen, Capuano, Weiner, Chandler, Carnahan, Salazar, Rahall, Filner

COAST GUARD & MARITIME TRANSPORTATION

226-3552 507 FHOB
LoBiondo, chairman

Republicans: Coble, Gilchrest, Hoekstra, Simmons, Diaz-Balart (Fla.), Reichert, vice chairman, Mack, Fortuño, Boustany
Democrats: Filner, Brown (Fla.), Taylor (Miss.), Millender-McDonald, Honda, Weiner, Higgins, Baird

ECONOMIC DEVELOPMENT, PUBLIC BUILDINGS & EMERGENCY MGMT.

225-3014 591 FHOB
Shuster, chairman

Republicans: Gerlach, Marchant, vice chairman, Dent, Kuhl
Democrats: Norton, Michaud, Davis (Tenn.), Carson (Ind.)

HIGHWAYS, TRANSIT & PIPELINES

225-6715 B-370A RHOB
Petri, chairman

Republicans: Boehlert, Coble, Duncan, Mica, Hoekstra, Bachus, LaTourette, Kelly, Baker, Ney, LoBiondo, Moran (Kan.), Miller (Calif.), vice chairman, Hayes, Simmons, Brown (S.C.), Johnson (Ill.), Platts, Graves, Kennedy (Minn.), Shuster, Boozman, Diaz-Balart (Fla.), Porter, Osborne, Marchant, Sodrel, Reichert, Vacancy
Democrats: DeFazio, Rahall, Nadler, Taylor (Miss.), Millender-McDonald, Cummings, Blumenauer, Tauscher, Pascrell, Holden, Baird, Berkley, Matheson, Honda, Larsen, Capuano, Weiner, Carson (Ind.), Bishop (N.Y.), Michaud, Davis (Tenn.), Chandler, Higgins, Carnahan, Schwartz

RAILROADS

226-0727 589 FHOB
LaTourette, chairman

Republicans: Petri, Boehlert, Mica, Bachus, Moran (Kan.), Miller (Calif.), Simmons, Platts, Graves, Porter, Osborne, Sodrel, Westmoreland, vice chairman
Democrats: Brown (Fla.), Rahall, Nadler, Menendez, Filner, Cummings, Blumenauer, Boswell, Carson (Ind.), DeFazio, Costello, Johnson (Texas)

WATER RESOURCES & ENVIRONMENT

225-4360 B-376 RHOB
Duncan, chairman

Republicans: Boehlert, Gilchrest, Ehlers, LaTourette, Kelly, Baker, Ney, Miller (Calif.), Brown (S.C.), Shuster, Boozman, Gerlach, Osborne, Poe, Mack, Fortuño, Boustany, vice chairman, Vacancy
Democrats: Johnson (Texas), Menendez, Salazar, Costello, Taylor (Miss.), Baird, Bishop (N.Y.), Higgins, Schwartz, Blumenauer, Tauscher, Pascrell, Carnahan, Rahall, Norton

VETERANS' AFFAIRS

225-3527 335 CHOB
Party Ratio: R 16-D 12
Steve Buyer, R-Ind., chairman

Michael Bilirakis, Fla., vice chairman	*Lane Evans, Ill.*
Terry Everett, Ala.	*Bob Filner, Calif.*
Cliff Stearns, Fla.	*Luis V. Gutierrez, Ill.*
Dan Burton, Ind.	*Corrine Brown, Fla.*
Jerry Moran, Kan.	*Vic Snyder, Ark.*
Richard H. Baker, La.	*Michael H. Michaud, Maine*
Henry E. Brown Jr., S.C.	*Stephanie Herseth, S.D.*
Jeff Miller, Fla.	*Ted Strickland, Ohio*
John Boozman, Ark.	*Darlene Hooley, Ore.*
Jeb Bradley, N.H.	*Silvestre Reyes, Texas*
Ginny Brown-Waite, Fla.	*Shelley Berkley, Nev.*
Michael R. Turner, Ohio	*Tom Udall, N.M.*
Vacancy	
Vacancy	
Vacancy	

DISABILITY ASSISTANCE & MEMORIAL AFFAIRS
225-9164 337 CHOB
Miller (Fla.), chairman

Republicans: Moran (Kan.), Bradley, vice chairman , Brown-Waite
Democrats: Berkley, Udall (N.M.), Evans

ECONOMIC OPPORTUNITY
225-9164 337 CHOB
Boozman, chairman

Republicans: Baker, Brown-Waite, vice chairwoman, Vacancy
Democrats: Herseth, Hooley, Evans

HEALTH
225-9154 338 CHOB
Brown (S.C.), chairman

Republicans: Stearns, vice chairman, Baker, Moran (Kan.), Miller (Fla.), Turner, Vacancy
Democrats: Michaud, Filner, Gutierrez, Brown (Fla.), Snyder

OVERSIGHT & INVESTIGATIONS
225-3569 337A CHOB
Bilirakis, chairman

Republicans: Everett, vice chairman, Boozman, Bradley
Democrats: Strickland, Reyes, Vacancy

WAYS & MEANS

225-3625 1102 LHOB
Party Ratio: R 24-D 17
Bill Thomas, R-Calif., chairman

E. Clay Shaw Jr., Fla.	*Charles B. Rangel, N.Y.*
Nancy L. Johnson, Conn.	*Pete Stark, Calif.*
Wally Herger, Calif.	*Sander M. Levin, Mich.*
Jim McCrery, La.	*Benjamin L. Cardin, Md.*
Dave Camp, Mich.	*Jim McDermott, Wash.*
Jim Ramstad, Minn.	*John Lewis, Ga.*
Jim Nussle, Iowa	*Richard E. Neal, Mass.*
Sam Johnson, Texas	*Michael R. McNulty, N.Y.*
Phil English, Pa.	*William J. Jefferson, La.*
J.D. Hayworth, Ariz.	*John Tanner, Tenn.*

Jerry Weller, Ill.	*Xavier Becerra, Calif.*
Kenny Hulshof, Mo.	*Lloyd Doggett, Texas*
Ron Lewis, Ky.	*Earl Pomeroy, N.D.*
Mark Foley, Fla.	*Stephanie Tubbs Jones, Ohio*
Kevin Brady, Texas	*Mike Thompson, Calif.*
Thomas M. Reynolds, N.Y.	*John B. Larson, Conn.*
Paul D. Ryan, Wis.	*Rahm Emanuel, Ill.*
Eric Cantor, Va.	
John Linder, Ga.	
Bob Beauprez, Colo.	
Melissa A. Hart, Pa.	
Chris Chocola, Ind.	
Devin Nunes, Calif.	

HEALTH
225-3943 1136 LHOB
Johnson (Conn.), chairwoman

Republicans: McCrery, Johnson (Texas), Camp, Ramstad, English, Hayworth, Hulshof
Democrats: Stark, Lewis (Ga.), Doggett, Thompson (Calif.), Emanuel

HUMAN RESOURCES
225-1025 B-317 RHOB
Herger, chairman

Republicans: Johnson (Conn.), Beauprez, Hart, Chocola, McCrery, Camp, English
Democrats: McDermott, Cardin, Stark, Becerra, Emanuel

OVERSIGHT
225-7601 1136 LHOB
Ramstad, chairman

Republicans: Cantor, Beauprez, Reynolds, Linder, Shaw, Johnson (Texas), Vacancy
Democrats: Lewis (Ga.), Pomeroy, McNulty, Tanner, Rangel

SELECT REVENUE MEASURES
226-5911 1135 LHOB
Camp, chairman

Republicans: Weller, Foley, Reynolds, Cantor, Linder, Hart, Chocola
Democrats: McNulty, Doggett, Jones (Ohio), Thompson (Calif.), Larson

SOCIAL SECURITY
225-9263 B-316 RHOB
McCrery, chairman

Republicans: Shaw, Johnson (Texas), Hayworth, Hulshof, Lewis (Ky.), Brady (Texas), Ryan (Wis.)
Democrats: Levin, Pomeroy, Becerra, Jones (Ohio), Neal

TRADE
225-6649 1104 LHOB
Shaw, chairman

Republicans: Herger, English, Nussle, Weller, Lewis (Ky.), Foley, Brady (Texas), Vacancy
Democrats: Cardin, Levin, Jefferson, Tanner, Larson, McDermott

Partisan House Committees

REPUBLICAN LEADERS

Speaker . . . . J. Dennis Hastert
Majority Leader . . . . Tom DeLay
Majority Whip. . . . . Roy Blunt
Conference Chairwoman. . . . . Deborah Pryce
Conference Vice Chairman . . . . Jack Kingston
Conference Secretary. . . . . John T. Doolittle
Chief Deputy Whip. . . . . Eric Cantor

NATIONAL REPUBLICAN CONGRESIONAL COMMITTEE
479-7070 320 First St. S.E. 20003

Chairman . . . . Thomas M. Reynolds
Executive Committee Chairwoman. . . . . Sue Myrick
Audit Chairman . . . . Greg Walden
Candidate Recruitment Chairwoman . . . . . Candice S. Miller
Communications Chairman . . . . Patrick T. McHenry
Community Partnership Chairman . . . . Jerry Weller
Finance Chairwoman . . . . Kay Granger
Incumbent Development Chairman . . . . Don Sherwood
Incumbent Fund Co-Chairman & Get Out the Vote. . . . . Howard P. "Buck" McKeon
Incumbent Fund Co-Chairwoman . . . . Anne M. Northup
Incumbent Retention Chairman . . . . Pete Sessions
Community Partnership Co-Chairmen: Eric Cantor, Tom Cole, Mario Diaz-Balart, Luis Fortuño, Sue W. Kelly, Jack Kingston, Ed Royce
Members: Marsha Blackburn, John A. Boehner, K. Michael Conaway, Ander Crenshaw, John Culberson, Geoff Davis, David Dreier, Phil English, Tom Feeney, Mike Ferguson, Sam Graves, Jeb Hensarling, Mark Steven Kirk, Jim McCrery, Cathy McMorris, Jerry Moran, Bob Ney, Tom Price, Adam H. Putnam, Mike D. Rogers, Mike Rogers, Todd Tiahrt, Pat Tiberi, Fred Upton, Zach Wamp, Roger Wicker
Ex-Officio Members: J. Dennis Hastert, Tom DeLay, Deborah Pryce, John Shadegg

POLICY COMMITTEE
225-6168 2471 RHOB

Chairman. . . . . John Shadegg
Members: Joe L. Barton, Bob Beauprez, Roy Blunt, John Boozman, Charles Boustany Jr., Kevin Brady, Michael C. Burgess, Eric Cantor, Shelley Moore Capito, John Carter, Ander Crenshaw, John Culberson, Tom DeLay, Lincoln Diaz-Balart, John T. Doolittle, Thelma Drake, David Dreier, Phil English, Virginia Foxx, Wayne T. Gilchrest, Phil Gingrey, Louie Gohmert, Robert W. Goodlatte, Mark Green, Katherine Harris, Melissa A. Hart, J. Dennis Hastert, Kenny Hulshof, Darrell Issa, Jack Kingston, Joe Knollenberg, Tom Latham, Jerry Lewis, Ron Lewis, Bob Ney, Jim Nussle, Jon Porter, Deborah Pryce, Thomas M. Reynolds, Bill Thomas, Zach Wamp, Jerry Weller, Roger Wicker, Heather A. Wilson, Joe Wilson

HOUSE REPUBLICAN STEERING COMMITTEE
225-2204 H-232 Capitol

Chairman . . . . J. Dennis Hastert
Members: Spencer Bachus, Joe L. Barton, Roy Blunt, Dave Camp, Eric Cantor, Ken Calvert, John Carter, Tom DeLay, John T. Doolittle, David Dreier, Doc Hastings, Jack Kingston, Tom Latham, Jerry Lewis, John M. McHugh, Cathy McMorris, Marilyn Musgrave, Deborah Pryce, Adam H. Putnam, Ralph Regula, Thomas M. Reynolds, Harold Rogers, John Shadegg, Lamar Smith, Bill Thomas, Curt Weldon, Don Young

DEMOCRATIC LEADERS

Minority Leader. . . . . Nancy Pelosi
Minority Whip . . . . Steny H. Hoyer
Caucus Chairman . . . . Robert Menendez
Caucus Vice Chairman. . . . . James E. Clyburn
Assistant to the Leader. . . . . John M. Spratt Jr.
Chief Deputy Whips: John Lewis (senior), Joseph Crowley, Diana DeGette, Ron Kind, Ed Pastor, Jan Schakowsky, John Tanner, Maxine Waters
Regional Whips: Shelley Berkley, Lincoln Davis, Charlie Gonzalez, Gene Green, Maurice D. Hinchey, Michael M. Honda, Ron Kind, Jim Langevin, Rick Larsen, Stephen F. Lynch, Betty McCollum, Brad Miller, Dennis Moore, Bill Pascrell Jr., Bobby L. Rush, Tim Ryan, David Scott, Vic Snyder, Hilda L. Solis, Diane Watson, Anthony Weiner, Lynn Woolsey, Albert R. Wynn

DEMOCRATIC CONGRESSIONAL CAMPAIGN COMMITTEE
863-1500 430 S. Capitol St. S.E. 20003

Chairman. . . . . Rahm Emanuel
Chairman's Council Chairman . . . . John D. Dingell
Executive Board Chairman . . . . Charles B. Rangel
Vice Chairmen . . . . Zoe Lofgren
. . . . Nita M. Lowey
. . . . Edward J. Markey
. . . . Kendrick B. Meek
. . . . Lucille Roybal-Allard
Business Council Chairman . . . . Joseph Crowley
Frontline Democrats Chairman . . . . Mike Thompson
Recruitment Chairman . . . . Chris Van Hollen
Women Lead Chairwoman . . . . Jan Schakowsky
National Jewish Outreach Chairman . . . . Steve Israel
Regional Recruitment Chairmen: Michael E. Capuano, Artur Davis, Betty McCollum, John P. Murtha, Mike Ross, Tim Ryan, Adam B. Schiff, Hilda L. Solis, Mark Udall, Debbie Wasserman-Schultz
Ex-Officio Members: Patrick J. Kennedy, Nancy Pelosi

HOUSE DEMOCRATIC STEERING COMMITTEE
225-0100 H-204 Capitol

Chairwoman . . . . Nancy Pelosi
Co-Chairwoman . . . . Rosa DeLauro
Co-Chairman . . . . George Miller
Vice Chairmen . . . . José E. Serrano
Vice Chairman . . . . John Tanner
Vice Chairwoman . . . . Maxine Waters
Members: Brian Baird, Robert A. Brady, Earl Blumenauer, G.K. Butterfield, Michael E. Capuano, Benjamin L. Cardin, Dennis Cardoza, James E. Clyburn, Jim Cooper, Jerry F. Costello, Joseph Crowley, Diana DeGette, John D. Dingell, Rahm Emanuel, Barney Frank, Steny H. Hoyer, Sheila Jackson-Lee, Eddie Bernice Johnson, Carolyn Cheeks Kilpatrick, Ron Kind, John B. Larson, John Lewis, Zoe Lofgren, Nita M. Lowey, Carolyn McCarthy, Betty McCollum, Gregory W. Meeks, Robert Menendez, Alan B. Mollohan, John P. Murtha, David R. Obey, Ed Pastor, Donald M. Payne, Charles B. Rangel, Mike Ross, C.A. Dutch Ruppersberger, Loretta Sanchez, Jan Schakowsky, Brad Sherman, Louise M. Slaughter, Hilda L. Solis, John M. Spratt Jr., Mike Thompson, John F. Tierney, Debbie Wasserman-Schultz

Senate Committees

The standing and select committees of the U.S. Senate are listed below in alphabetical order. The listings include a telephone number, room number and party ratio for each full committee. Membership is given in order of seniority on the committee. Subcommittee membership is listed in order of seniority.

On full committee rosters, members of the majority party, Republicans, are shown in roman type; members of the minority party, Democrats, are shown in *italic* type.

The word "vacancy" indicates that a committee or subcommittee seat had not been filled at press time, April 2005. Subcommittee vacancies do not necessarily indicate vacancies on full committees or vice versa.

Partisan committees are listed on page 1205.

The telephone area code for Washington, D.C., is 202. Abbreviations for Senate office buildings are: SD – Dirksen Building, SH – Hart Building, SR – Russell Building. The ZIP code for all Senate offices is 20510.

AGRICULTURE, NUTRITION & FORESTRY
224-2035 328A SR
Party Ratio: R 11-D 9
Saxby Chambliss, R-Ga., chairman

Richard G. Lugar, Ind.	*Tom Harkin, Iowa*
Thad Cochran, Miss.	*Patrick J. Leahy, Vt.*
Mitch McConnell, Ky.	*Kent Conrad, N.D.*
Pat Roberts, Kan.	*Max Baucus, Mont.*
Jim Talent, Mo.	*Blanche Lincoln, Ark.*
Craig Thomas, Wyo.	*Debbie Stabenow, Mich.*
Rick Santorum, Pa.	*Ben Nelson, Neb.*
Norm Coleman, Minn.	*Mark Dayton, Minn.*
Michael D. Crapo, Idaho	*Ken Salazar, Colo.*
Charles E. Grassley, Iowa	

FORESTRY, CONSERVATION & RURAL REVITALIZATION
224-2035 328A SR
Crapo, chairman

Republicans: Lugar, Cochran, Talent, Thomas, Coleman
Democrats: Lincoln, Leahy, Nelson (Neb.), Dayton, Salazar

MARKETING, INSPECTION & PRODUCT PROMOTION
224-2035 328A SR
Talent, chairman

Republicans: McConnell, Thomas, Roberts, Grassley, Lugar
Democrats: Baucus, Nelson (Neb.), Salazar, Conrad, Stabenow

PRODUCTION & PRICE COMPETITIVENESS
224-2035 328A SR
McConnell, chairman

Republicans: Cochran, Roberts, Santorum, Coleman, Grassley
Democrats: Conrad, Dayton, Baucus, Leahy, Lincoln

RESEARCH, NUTRITION & GENERAL LEGISLATION
224-2035 328A SR
Santorum, chairman

Republicans: Lugar, Crapo, Cochran, McConnell, Roberts
Democrats: Leahy, Stabenow, Lincoln, Baucus, Nelson (Neb.)

APPROPRIATIONS
224-7363 S-128 Capitol
Party Ratio: R 15-D 13
Thad Cochran, R-Miss., chairman

Ted Stevens, Alaska	*Robert C. Byrd, W.Va.*
Arlen Specter, Pa.	*Daniel K. Inouye, Hawaii*
Pete V. Domenici, N.M.	*Patrick J. Leahy, Vt.*
Christopher S. Bond, Mo.	*Tom Harkin, Iowa*
Mitch McConnell, Ky.	*Barbara A. Mikulski, Md.*
Conrad Burns, Mont.	*Harry Reid, Nev.*
Richard C. Shelby, Ala.	*Herb Kohl, Wis.*
Judd Gregg, N.H.	*Patty Murray, Wash.*
Robert F. Bennett, Utah	*Byron L. Dorgan, N.D.*
Larry E. Craig, Idaho	*Dianne Feinstein, Calif.*
Kay Bailey Hutchison, Texas	*Richard J. Durbin, Ill.*
Mike DeWine, Ohio	*Tim Johnson, S.D.*
Sam Brownback, Kan.	*Mary L. Landrieu, La.*
Wayne Allard, Colo.	

AGRICULTURE & RURAL DEVELOPMENT
224-5270 188 SD
Bennett, chairman

Republicans: Cochran, Specter, Bond, McConnell, Burns, Craig, Brownback
Democrats: Kohl, Harkin, Dorgan, Feinstein, Durbin, Johnson, Landrieu

COMMERCE, JUSTICE & SCIENCE
224-7277 S-146A Capitol
Shelby, chairman

Republicans: Gregg, Stevens, Domenici, McConnell, Hutchison, Brownback, Bond
Democrats: Mikulski, Inouye, Leahy, Kohl, Murray, Harkin, Dorgan

DEFENSE
224-7255 119 SD
Stevens, chairman

Republicans: Cochran, Specter, Domenici, Bond, McConnell, Shelby, Gregg, Hutchison, Burns
Democrats: Inouye, Byrd, Leahy, Harkin, Dorgan, Durbin, Reid, Feinstein, Mikulski

DISTRICT OF COLUMBIA
224-7643 127 SD
Brownback, chairman

Republicans: DeWine, Allard
Democrats: Landrieu, Durbin

ENERGY & WATER
224-8119 129 SD
Domenici, chairman

Republicans: Cochran, McConnell, Bennett, Burns, Craig, Bond, Hutchison, Allard
Democrats: Reid, Byrd, Murray, Dorgan, Feinstein, Johnson, Landrieu, Inouye

HOMELAND SECURITY
224-4319 135 SD
Gregg, chairman

Republicans: Cochran, Stevens, Specter, Domenici, Shelby, Craig, Bennett, Allard
Democrats: Byrd, Inouye, Leahy, Mikulski, Kohl, Murray, Reid, Feinstein

INTERIOR
224-7233 132 SD
Burns, chairman

Republicans: Stevens, Cochran, Domenici, Bennett, Gregg, Craig, Allard
Democrats: Dorgan, Byrd, Leahy, Reid, Feinstein, Mikulski, Kohl

LABOR, HEALTH & HUMAN SERVICES & EDUCATION
224-8221 184 SD
Specter, chairman

Republicans: Cochran, Gregg, Craig, Hutchison, Stevens, DeWine, Shelby
Democrats: Harkin, Inouye, Reid, Kohl, Murray, Landrieu, Durbin

LEGISLATIVE BRANCH
224-7363 S-128 Capitol
Allard, chairman

Republicans: Cochran, DeWine
Democrats: Durbin, Johnson

MILITARY CONSTRUCTION & VETERANS AFFAIRS
224-8224 127 SD
Hutchison, chairwoman

Republicans: Burns, Craig, DeWine, Brownback, Allard, McConnell
Democrats: Feinstein, Inouye, Johnson, Landrieu, Byrd, Murray

STATE & FOREIGN OPERATIONS
224-8202 142 SD
McConnell, chairman

Republicans: Specter, Gregg, Shelby, Bennett, Bond, DeWine, Brownback
Democrats: Leahy, Inouye, Harkin, Mikulski, Durbin, Johnson, Landrieu

TRANSPORTATION, TREASURY, THE JUDICIARY & HUD
224-4869 130 SD
Bond, chairman

Republicans: Shelby, Specter, Bennett, Hutchison, DeWine, Brownback, Stevens, Domenici, Burns
Democrats: Murray, Byrd, Mikulski, Reid, Kohl, Durbin, Dorgan, Leahy, Harkin

ARMED SERVICES
224-3871 228 SR
Party Ratio: R 13-D 11
John W. Warner, R-Va., chairman

John McCain, Ariz.	Carl Levin, Mich.
James M. Inhofe, Okla.	Edward M. Kennedy, Mass.
Pat Roberts, Kan.	Robert C. Byrd, W.Va.
Jeff Sessions, Ala.	Joseph I. Lieberman, Conn.
Susan Collins, Maine	Jack Reed, R.I.
John Ensign, Nev.	Daniel K. Akaka, Hawaii
Jim Talent, Mo.	Bill Nelson, Fla.
Saxby Chambliss, Ga.	Ben Nelson, Neb.
Lindsey Graham, S.C.	Mark Dayton, Minn.
Elizabeth Dole, N.C.	Evan Bayh, Ind.
John Cornyn, Texas	Hillary Rodham Clinton, N.Y.
John Thune, S.D.	

AIRLAND
224-3871 228 SR
McCain, chairman

Republicans: Inhofe, Sessions, Ensign, Talent, Chambliss, Graham, Dole
Democrats: Lieberman, Reed, Akaka, Nelson (Fla.), Dayton, Bayh, Clinton

EMERGING THREATS & CAPABILITIES
224-3871 228 SR
Cornyn, chairman

Republicans: Roberts, Collins, Ensign, Talent, Graham, Dole, Thune
Democrats: Reed, Kennedy, Byrd, Nelson (Fla.), Nelson (Neb.), Bayh, Clinton

PERSONNEL
224-3871 228 SR
Graham, chairman

Republicans: McCain, Collins, Chambliss, Dole
Democrats: Nelson (Neb.), Kennedy, Lieberman, Akaka

READINESS & MANAGEMENT SUPPORT
224-3871 228 SR
Ensign, chairman

Republicans: McCain, Inhofe, Roberts, Sessions, Chambliss, Cornyn, Thune
Democrats: Akaka, Byrd, Nelson (Fla.), Nelson (Neb.), Dayton, Bayh, Clinton

SEAPOWER
224-3871 228 SR
Talent, chairman

Republicans: McCain, Collins, Chambliss
Democrats: Kennedy, Lieberman, Reed

STRATEGIC FORCES
224-3871 228 SR
Sessions, chairman

Republicans: Inhofe, Roberts, Graham, Cornyn, Thune
Democrats: Nelson (Fla.), Byrd, Reed, Nelson (Neb.), Dayton

BANKING, HOUSING & URBAN AFFAIRS

224-7391 534 SD
Party Ratio: R 11-D 9
Richard C. Shelby, R-Ala., chairman

Robert F. Bennett, Utah	*Paul S. Sarbanes, Md.*
Wayne Allard, Colo.	*Christopher J. Dodd, Conn.*
Michael B. Enzi, Wyo.	*Tim Johnson, S.D.*
Chuck Hagel, Neb.	*Jack Reed, R.I.*
Rick Santorum, Pa.	*Charles E. Schumer, N.Y.*
Jim Bunning, Ky.	*Evan Bayh, Ind.*
Michael D. Crapo, Idaho	*Thomas R. Carper, Del.*
John E. Sununu, N.H.	*Debbie Stabenow, Mich.*
Elizabeth Dole, N.C.	*Jon Corzine, N.J.*
Mel Martinez, Fla.	

ECONOMIC POLICY
224-7391 534 SD
Bunning, chairman

Republican: Shelby
Democrat: Schumer

FINANCIAL INSTITUTIONS
224-7391 534 SD
Bennett, chairman

Republicans: Allard, Santorum, Sununu, Martinez, Hagel, Bunning, Crapo
Democrats: Johnson, Carper, Dodd, Reed, Stabenow, Bayh

HOUSING & TRANSPORTATION
224-7391 534 SD
Allard, chairman

Republicans: Santorum, Dole, Enzi, Bennett, Martinez, Shelby
Democrats: Reed, Stabenow, Corzine, Dodd, Carper, Schumer

INTERNATIONAL TRADE & FINANCE
224-7391 534 SD
Crapo, chairman

Republicans: Hagel, Enzi, Sununu, Dole
Democrats: Bayh, Johnson, Corzine

SECURITIES & INVESTMENT
224-7391 534 SD
Hagel, chairman

Republicans: Enzi, Sununu, Martinez, Bennett, Bunning, Crapo, Dole, Allard, Santorum
Democrats: Dodd, Johnson, Reed, Schumer, Bayh, Stabenow, Corzine, Carper

BUDGET

224-0642 624 SD
Party Ratio: R 12-D 10
Judd Gregg, R-N.H., chairman

Pete V. Domenici, N.M.	*Kent Conrad, N.D.*
Charles E. Grassley, Iowa	*Paul S. Sarbanes, Md.*
Wayne Allard, Colo.	*Patty Murray, Wash.*
Michael B. Enzi, Wyo.	*Ron Wyden, Ore.*
Jeff Sessions, Ala.	*Russell D. Feingold, Wis.*
Jim Bunning, Ky.	*Tim Johnson, S.D.*
Michael D. Crapo, Idaho	*Robert C. Byrd, W.Va.*
John Ensign, Nev.	*Bill Nelson, Fla.*
John Cornyn, Texas	*Debbie Stabenow, Mich.*
Lamar Alexander, Tenn.	*Jon Corzine, N.J.*
Lindsey Graham, S.C.	

COMMERCE, SCIENCE & TRANSPORTATION

224-1251 508 SD
Party Ratio: R 12-D 10
Ted Stevens, R-Alaska, chairman

John McCain, Ariz.	*Daniel K. Inouye, Hawaii*
Conrad Burns, Mont.	*John D. Rockefeller IV, W.Va.*
Trent Lott, Miss.	*John Kerry, Mass.*
Kay Bailey Hutchison, Texas	*Byron L. Dorgan, N.D.*
Olympia J. Snowe, Maine	*Barbara Boxer, Calif.*
Gordon H. Smith, Ore.	*Bill Nelson, Fla.*
John Ensign, Nev.	*Maria Cantwell, Wash.*
George Allen, Va.	*Frank R. Lautenberg, N.J.*
John E. Sununu, N.H.	*Ben Nelson, Neb.*
Jim DeMint, S.C.	*Mark Pryor, Ark.*
David Vitter, La.	

AVIATION
224-4852 427 SH
Burns, chairman

Republicans: Stevens, McCain, Lott, Hutchison, Snowe, Smith, Ensign, Allen, Sununu, DeMint
Democrats: Rockefeller, Inouye, Dorgan, Boxer, Cantwell, Lautenberg, Nelson (Fla.), Nelson (Neb.), Pryor

CONSUMER AFFAIRS, PRODUCT SAFETY & INSURANCE
224-5183 428 SH
Allen, chairman

Republicans: Stevens, Burns, DeMint, Vitter
Democrats: Pryor, Inouye, *ex officio*, Boxer

DISASTER PREVENTION & PREDICTION
DeMint, chairman

Republicans: Stevens, Smith, Vitter
Democrats: Nelson (Neb.), Cantwell, Nelson (Fla.)

FISHERIES & THE COAST GUARD
224-8172 227 SH
Snowe, chairwoman

Republicans: Stevens, Lott, Smith, Sununu, Vitter
Democrats: Cantwell, Inouye, Kerry, Lautenberg

GLOBAL CLIMATE CHANGE & IMPACTS
Vitter, chairman

Republicans: Stevens, McCain, Snowe
Democrats: Lautenberg, Kerry

OCEAN POLICY STUDY
Sununu, chairman

Republicans: Stevens, Lott, Hutchison, Snowe, Smith, DeMint, Vitter
Democrats: Boxer, Inouye, Kerry, Cantwell, Lautenberg

SCIENCE & SPACE
224-8972 227 SH
Hutchison, chairwoman

Republicans: Stevens, Burns, Lott, Ensign, Allen, Sununu
Democrats: Nelson (Fla.), Rockefeller, Dorgan, Nelson (Neb.), Pryor

SURFACE TRANSPORTATION & MERCHANT MARINE
224-4852 427 SH
Lott, chairman

Republicans: Stevens, McCain, Burns, Hutchison, Snowe, Smith, Allen, Sununu, Vitter
Democrats: Inouye, Rockefeller, Dorgan, Boxer, Cantwell, Lautenberg, Nelson (Neb.), Pryor

TECHNOLOGY, INNOVATION & COMPETITIVENESS
Ensign, chairman

Republicans: Stevens, Burns, Lott, Hutchison, Allen, Sununu, DeMint
Democrats: Kerry, Inouye, ex officio, Rockefeller, Dorgan, Nelson (Neb.), Pryor

TRADE, TOURISM & ECONOMIC DEVELOPMENT
Smith, chairman

Republicans: Stevens, McCain, Burns, Ensign, Allen, Sununu, DeMint, Vitter
Democrats: Dorgan, Inouye, ex officio, Rockefeller, Kerry, Cantwell, Lautenberg, Nelson (Fla.), Nelson (Neb.), Pryor

ENERGY & NATURAL RESOURCES
224-4971 364 SD
Party Ratio: R 12-D 10
Pete V. Domenici, R-N.M., chairman

Larry E. Craig, Idaho	Jeff Bingaman, N.M.
Craig Thomas, Wyo.	Daniel K. Akaka, Hawaii
Lamar Alexander, Tenn.	Byron L. Dorgan, N.D.
Lisa Murkowski, Alaska	Ron Wyden, Ore.
Richard M. Burr, N.C.	Tim Johnson, S.D.
Mel Martinez, Fla.	Mary L. Landrieu, La.
Jim Talent, Mo.	Dianne Feinstein, Calif.
Conrad Burns, Mont.	Maria Cantwell, Wash.
George Allen, Va.	Jon Corzine, N.J.
Gordon H. Smith, Ore.	Ken Salazar, Colo.
Jim Bunning, Ky.	

ENERGY
224-4971 364 SD
Alexander, chairman

Republicans: Burr, vice chairman, Martinez, Talent, Allen, Bunning, Murkowski, Craig, Thomas, Burns
Democrats: Dorgan, Akaka, Johnson, Landrieu, Feinstein, Cantwell, Corzine, Salazar

NATIONAL PARKS
224-4971 364 SD
Thomas, chairman

Republicans: Alexander, vice chairman, Allen, Burr, Martinez, Smith
Democrats: Akaka, Wyden, Landrieu, Corzine, Salazar

PUBLIC LANDS & FORESTS
224-4971 364 SD
Craig, chairman

Republicans: Burns, vice chairman, Thomas, Talent, Smith, Alexander, Murkowski, Allen
Democrats: Wyden, Akaka, Dorgan, Johnson, Landrieu, Feinstein, Cantwell

WATER & POWER
224-4971 364 SD
Murkowski, chairwoman

Republicans: Smith, vice chairman, Craig, Burr, Martinez, Burns, Bunning, Talent
Democrats: Johnson, Dorgan, Wyden, Feinstein, Cantwell, Corzine, Salazar

ENVIRONMENT & PUBLIC WORKS
224-6176 410 SD
Party Ratio: R 10-D 8
James M. Inhofe, R-Okla., chairman

John W. Warner, Va.	James M. Jeffords, I-Vt.
Christopher S. Bond, Mo.	Max Baucus, Mont.
George V. Voinovich, Ohio	Joseph I. Lieberman, Conn.
Lincoln Chafee, R.I.	Barbara Boxer, Calif.
Lisa Murkowski, Alaska	Thomas R. Carper, Del.
John Thune, S.D.	Hillary Rodham Clinton, N.Y.
Jim DeMint, S.C.	Frank R. Lautenberg, N.J.
Johnny Isakson, Ga.	Barack Obama, Ill.
David Vitter, La.	

CLEAN AIR, CLIMATE CHANGE & NUCLEAR SAFETY
224-6176 410 SD
Voinovich, chairman

Republicans: Bond, DeMint, Isakson, Vitter
Democrats: Carper, Lieberman, Lautenberg, Obama

FISHERIES, WILDLIFE & WATER
224-6176 410 SD
Chafee, chairman

Republicans: Warner, Murkowski, DeMint, Vitter
Democrats: Clinton, Lieberman, Lautenberg, Obama

SUPERFUND & WASTE MANAGEMENT
224-6176 410 SD
Thune, chairman

Republicans: Warner, Bond, Isakson
Democrats: Boxer, Baucus, Lautenberg

TRANSPORTATION & INFRASTRUCTURE
224-6176 410 SD
Bond, chairman

Republicans: Warner, Voinovich, Chafee, Murkowski, Thune
Democrats: Baucus, Lieberman, Boxer, Carper, Clinton

FINANCE

224-4515   219 SD
Party Ratio: R 11-D 9
Charles E. Grassley, R-Iowa, chairman

Orrin G. Hatch, Utah	Max Baucus, Mont.
Trent Lott, Miss.	John D. Rockefeller IV, W.Va.
Olympia J. Snowe, Maine	Kent Conrad, N.D.
Jon Kyl, Ariz.	James M. Jeffords, I-Vt.
Craig Thomas, Wyo.	Jeff Bingaman, N.M.
Rick Santorum, Pa.	John Kerry, Mass.
Bill Frist, Tenn.	Blanche Lincoln, Ark.
Gordon H. Smith, Ore.	Ron Wyden, Ore.
Jim Bunning, Ky.	Charles E. Schumer, N.Y.
Michael D. Crapo, Idaho	

HEALTH CARE
224-4515   219 SD
Hatch, chairman

Republicans: Snowe, Frist, Kyl, Thomas, Santorum, Bunning
Democrats: Rockefeller, Jeffords (I), Bingaman, Kerry, Wyden

INTERNATIONAL TRADE
224-4515   219 SD
Thomas, chairman

Republicans: Crapo, Lott, Smith, Bunning, Hatch, Snowe, Frist
Democrats: Bingaman, Baucus, Rockefeller, Conrad, Wyden, Schumer

LONG-TERM GROWTH & DEBT REDUCTION
224-4515   219 SD
Smith, chairman

Republican: Grassley
Democrat: Kerry

SOCIAL SECURITY & FAMILY POLICY
224-4515   219 SD
Santorum, chairman

Republicans: Grassley, Bunning, Frist, Lott, Kyl, Smith, Crapo
Democrats: Conrad, Rockefeller, Jeffords (I), Bingaman, Kerry, Lincoln

TAXATION & IRS OVERSIGHT
224-4515   219 SD
Kyl, chairman

Republicans: Lott, Hatch, Snowe, Crapo, Thomas, Santorum
Democrats: Jeffords (I), Baucus, Conrad, Lincoln, Schumer

FOREIGN RELATIONS

224-4651   450 SD
Party Ratio: R 10-D 8
Richard G. Lugar, R-Ind., chairman

Chuck Hagel, Neb.	Joseph R. Biden Jr., Del.
Lincoln Chafee, R.I.	Paul S. Sarbanes, Md.
George Allen, Va.	Christopher J. Dodd, Conn.
Norm Coleman, Minn.	John Kerry, Mass.
George V. Voinovich, Ohio	Russell D. Feingold, Wis.
Lamar Alexander, Tenn.	Barbara Boxer, Calif.
John E. Sununu, N.H.	Bill Nelson, Fla.
Lisa Murkowski, Alaska	Barack Obama, Ill.
Mel Martinez, Fla.	

AFRICAN AFFAIRS
224-4651   450 SD
Martinez, chairman

Republicans: Alexander, Coleman, Sununu, Murkowski
Democrats: Feingold, Sarbanes, Dodd, Obama

EAST ASIAN & PACIFIC AFFAIRS
224-4651   450 SD
Murkowski, chairwoman

Republicans: Alexander, Hagel, Chafee, Allen
Democrats: Kerry, Biden, Feingold, Obama

EUROPEAN AFFAIRS
224-4651   450 SD
Allen, chairman

Republicans: Voinovich, Murkowski, Hagel, Chafee
Democrats: Biden, Sarbanes, Dodd, Feingold

INTERNATIONAL ECONOMIC POLICY, EXPORT & TRADE PROMOTION
224-4651   450 SD
Hagel, chairman

Republicans: Alexander, Murkowski, Martinez, Voinovich
Democrats: Sarbanes, Dodd, Kerry, Obama

INTERNATIONAL OPERATIONS & TERRORISM
224-4651   450 SD
Sununu, chairman

Republicans: Voinovich, Allen, Coleman, Alexander
Democrats: Nelson (Fla.), Biden, Kerry, Boxer

NEAR EASTERN & SOUTH ASIAN AFFAIRS
224-4651   446 SD
Chafee, chairman

Republicans: Hagel, Coleman, Voinovich, Sununu
Democrats: Boxer, Sarbanes, Nelson (Fla.), Obama

WESTERN HEMISPHERE, PEACE CORPS & NARCOTICS AFFAIRS
224-4651   450 SD
Coleman, chairman

Republicans: Chafee, Allen, Martinez, Sununu
Democrats: Dodd, Kerry, Boxer, Nelson (Fla.)

HEALTH, EDUCATION, LABOR & PENSIONS

224-5375   428 SD
Party Ratio: R 11-D 9
Michael B. Enzi, R-Wyo., chairman

Judd Gregg, N.H.	Edward M. Kennedy, Mass.
Bill Frist, Tenn.	Christopher J. Dodd, Conn.
Lamar Alexander, Tenn.	Tom Harkin, Iowa
Richard M. Burr, N.C.	Barbara A. Mikulski, Md.
Johnny Isakson, Ga.	James M. Jeffords, I-Vt.
Mike DeWine, Ohio	Jeff Bingaman, N.M.
John Ensign, Nev.	Patty Murray, Wash.
Orrin G. Hatch, Utah	Jack Reed, R.I.
Jeff Sessions, Ala.	Hillary Rodham Clinton, N.Y.
Pat Roberts, Kan.	

BIOTERRORISM & PUBLIC HEALTH PREPAREDNESS
224-7900 608 SH
Burr, chairman

Republicans: Gregg, Frist, Alexander, DeWine, Ensign, Hatch, Roberts
Democrats: Kennedy, Dodd, Harkin, Mikulski, Bingaman, Murray, Reed

EDUCATION & EARLY CHILDHOOD DEVELOPMENT
224-5800 632 SH
Alexander, chairman

Republicans: Gregg, Burr, Isakson, DeWine, Ensign, Hatch, Sessions
Democrats: Dodd, Harkin, Jeffords (I), Bingaman, Murray, Reed, Clinton

EMPLOYMENT & WORKPLACE SAFETY
224-7229 615 SH
Isakson, chairman

Republicans: Alexander, Burr, Ensign, Sessions, Roberts
Democrats: Murray, Dodd, Harkin, Mikulski, Jeffords (I)

RETIREMENT SECURITY & AGING
228-4838 132 SH
DeWine, chairman

Republicans: Isakson, Hatch, Sessions, Roberts
Democrats: Mikulski, Jeffords (I), Bingaman, Clinton

HOMELAND SECURITY & GOVERNMENTAL AFFAIRS
224-4751 340 SD
Party Ratio: R 9-D 7
Susan Collins, R-Maine, chairwoman

Ted Stevens, Alaska	Joseph I. Lieberman, Conn.
George V. Voinovich, Ohio	Carl Levin, Mich.
Norm Coleman, Minn.	Daniel K. Akaka, Hawaii
Tom Coburn, Okla.	Thomas R. Carper, Del.
Lincoln Chafee, R.I.	Mark Dayton, Minn.
Robert F. Bennett, Utah	Frank R. Lautenberg, N.J.
Pete V. Domenici, N.M.	Mark Pryor, Ark.
John W. Warner, Va.	

FEDERAL FINANCIAL MANAGEMENT, GOVERNMENT INFORMATION & INTERNATIONAL SECURITY
224-2254 439 SH
Coburn, chairman

Republicans: Stevens, Voinovich, Chafee, Bennett, Domenici, Warner
Democrats: Carper, Levin, Akaka, Dayton, Lautenberg

GOVERNMENT MANAGEMENT, FEDERAL WORKFORCE & THE DISTRICT OF COLUMBIA
224-3682 442 SH
Voinovich, chairman

Republicans: Stevens, Coleman, Coburn, Chafee, Bennett, Domenici, Warner
Democrats: Akaka, Levin, Carper, Dayton, Lautenberg, Pryor

PERMANENT INVESTIGATIONS
224-3721 199 SR
Coleman, chairman

Republicans: Stevens, Coburn, Chafee, Bennett, Domenici, Warner
Democrats: Levin, Akaka, Carper, Dayton, Lautenberg, Pryor

INDIAN AFFAIRS
224-2251 836 SH
Party Ratio: R 8-D 6
John McCain, R-Ariz., chairman

Craig Thomas, Wyo.	Byron L. Dorgan, N.D.
Lisa Murkowski, Alaska	Daniel K. Inouye, Hawaii
Tom Coburn, Okla.	Kent Conrad, N.D.
Pete V. Domenici, N.M.	Daniel K. Akaka, Hawaii
Gordon H. Smith, Ore.	Tim Johnson, S.D.
Michael D. Crapo, Idaho	Maria Cantwell, Wash.
Richard M. Burr, N.C.	

JUDICIARY
224-5225 224 SD
Party Ratio: R 10-D 8
Arlen Specter, R-Pa., chairman

Orrin G. Hatch, Utah	Patrick J. Leahy, Vt.
Charles E. Grassley, Iowa	Edward M. Kennedy, Mass.
Jon Kyl, Ariz.	Joseph R. Biden Jr., Del.
Mike DeWine, Ohio	Herb Kohl, Wis.
Jeff Sessions, Ala.	Dianne Feinstein, Calif.
Lindsey Graham, S.C.	Russell D. Feingold, Wis.
John Cornyn, Texas	Charles E. Schumer, N.Y.
Sam Brownback, Kan.	Richard J. Durbin, Ill.
Tom Coburn, Okla.	

ADMINISTRATIVE OVERSIGHT & THE COURTS
224-7572 G-66 SD
Sessions, chairman

Republicans: Specter, Grassley, Kyl
Democrats: Schumer, Feinstein, Feingold

ANTITRUST, COMPETITION POLICY & CONSUMER RIGHTS
224-9494 161 SD
DeWine, chairman

Republicans: Specter, Hatch, Grassley, Graham, Brownback
Democrats: Kohl, Leahy, Biden, Feingold, Schumer

CONSTITUTION, CIVIL RIGHTS & PROPERTY RIGHTS
224-7840 524 SD
Brownback, chairman

Republicans: Specter, Graham, Cornyn, Coburn
Democrats: Feingold, Kennedy, Feinstein, Durbin

CORRECTIONS & REHABILITATION
224-5754 SD-B40 SD
Coburn, chairman

Republicans: Specter, Sessions, Cornyn, Brownback
Democrats: Durbin, Leahy, Biden, Feingold

CRIME & DRUGS
224-5972 147 SD
Graham, chairman

Republicans: Grassley, Kyl, DeWine, Sessions, Coburn
Democrats: Biden, Kohl, Feinstein, Feingold, Schumer

IMMIGRATION, BORDER SECURITY & CITIZENSHIP
224-3521 416 SR
Cornyn, chairman

Republicans: Grassley, Kyl, DeWine, Sessions, Brownback, Coburn
Democrats: Kennedy, Biden, Feinstein, Feingold, Schumer, Durbin

INTELLECTUAL PROPERTY
224-7703 152 SD
Hatch, chairman

Republicans: Kyl, DeWine, Graham, Cornyn, Brownback, Coburn
Democrats: Leahy, Kennedy, Biden, Feinstein, Kohl, Durbin

TERRORISM, TECHNOLOGY & HOMELAND SECURITY
224-4933 325 SH
Kyl, chairman

Republicans: Hatch, Grassley, Cornyn, DeWine, Sessions, Graham
Democrats: Feinstein, Kennedy, Biden, Kohl, Feingold, Durbin

RULES & ADMINISTRATION

224-6352 305 SR
Party Ratio: R 10-D 8
Trent Lott, R-Miss., chairman

Ted Stevens, Alaska	Christopher J. Dodd, Conn.
Mitch McConnell, Ky.	Robert C. Byrd, W.Va.
Thad Cochran, Miss.	Daniel K. Inouye, Hawaii
Rick Santorum, Pa.	Dianne Feinstein, Calif.
Kay Bailey Hutchison, Texas	Charles E. Schumer, N.Y.
Bill Frist, Tenn.	Mark Dayton, Minn.
Saxby Chambliss, Ga.	Richard J. Durbin, Ill.
Robert F. Bennett, Utah	Ben Nelson, Neb.
Chuck Hagel, Neb.	

SELECT ETHICS

224-2981 220 SH
Party Ratio: R 3-D 3
George V. Voinovich, R-Ohio, chairman

Pat Roberts, Kan.	Tim Johnson, S.D.
Craig Thomas, Wyo.	Daniel K. Akaka, Hawaii
	Mark Pryor, Ark.

SELECT INTELLIGENCE

224-1700 211 SH
Party Ratio: R 8-D 7
Pat Roberts, R-Kan., chairman

Orrin G. Hatch, Utah	John D. Rockefeller IV, W.Va.
Mike DeWine, Ohio	vice chairman
Christopher S. Bond, Mo.	Carl Levin, Mich.
Trent Lott, Miss.	Dianne Feinstein, Calif.
Olympia J. Snowe, Maine	Ron Wyden, Ore.
Chuck Hagel, Neb.	Evan Bayh, Ind.
Saxby Chambliss, Ga.	Barbara A. Mikulski, Md.
	Jon Corzine, N.J.

SMALL BUSINESS & ENTREPRENEURSHIP

224-5175 428A SR
Party Ratio: R 10-D 8
Olympia J. Snowe, R-Maine, chairwoman

Christopher S. Bond, Mo.	John Kerry, Mass.
Conrad Burns, Mont.	Carl Levin, Mich.
George Allen, Va.	Tom Harkin, Iowa
Norm Coleman, Minn.	Joseph I. Lieberman, Conn.
John Thune, S.D.	Mary L. Landrieu, La.
Johnny Isakson, Ga.	Maria Cantwell, Wash.
David Vitter, La.	Evan Bayh, Ind.
Michael B. Enzi, Wyo.	Mark Pryor, Ark.
John Cornyn, Texas	

SPECIAL AGING

224-5364 G31 SD
Party Ratio: R 11-D 9
Gordon H. Smith, R-Ore., chairman

Richard C. Shelby, Ala.	Herb Kohl, Wis.
Susan Collins, Maine	James M. Jeffords, I-Vt.
Jim Talent, Mo.	Russell D. Feingold, Wis.
Elizabeth Dole, N.C.	Ron Wyden, Ore.
Mel Martinez, Fla.	Blanche Lincoln, Ark.
Larry E. Craig, Idaho	Evan Bayh, Ind.
Rick Santorum, Pa.	Thomas R. Carper, Del.
Conrad Burns, Mont.	Bill Nelson, Fla.
Lamar Alexander, Tenn.	Hillary Rodham Clinton, N.Y.
Jim DeMint, S.C.	

VETERANS' AFFAIRS

224-9126 412 SR
Party Ratio: R 8-D 6
Larry E. Craig, R-Idaho, chairman

Arlen Specter, Pa.	Daniel K. Akaka, Hawaii
Kay Bailey Hutchison, Texas	John D. Rockefeller IV, W.Va.
Lindsey Graham, S.C.	James M. Jeffords, I-Vt.
Richard M. Burr, N.C.	Patty Murray, Wash.
John Ensign, Nev.	Barack Obama, Ill.
John Thune, S.D.	Ken Salazar, Colo.
Johnny Isakson, Ga.	

Partisan Senate Committees

REPUBLICAN LEADERS

President . . . . Vice President Dick Cheney
President Pro Tempore . . . . Ted Stevens
Majority Leader . . . . Bill Frist
Majority Whip . . . . Mitch McConnell
Conference Chairman . . . . Rick Santorum
Conference Vice Chairwoman . . . . Kay Bailey Hutchison
Chief Deputy Whip . . . . Robert F. Bennett
Deputy Whips: Lamar Alexander, Wayne Allard, Jon Cornyn, Conrad Burns, Michael D. Crapo, Jim DeMint, Johnny Isakson, Lisa Murkowski, Gordon H. Smith, John E. Sununu, Jim Talent, Craig Thomas, John Thune

NATIONAL REPUBLICAN SENATORIAL COMMITTEE
675-6000   425 Second St. N.E. 20002

Chairwoman . . . . Elizabeth Dole
Regional Chairmen: Christopher S. Bond, John Cornyn, Orrin G. Hatch, Trent Lott, Richard C. Shelby, Ted Stevens, John E. Sununu

POLICY COMMITTEE
224-2946   347 SR

Chairman . . . . Jon Kyl

COMMITTEE ON COMMITTEES
224-6142   239 SD

Chairman . . . . Michael D. Crapo

DEMOCRATIC LEADERS

Minority Leader . . . . Harry Reid
Minority Whip . . . . Richard J. Durbin
Conference Secretary . . . . Debbie Stabenow
Chief Deputy Whip . . . . Barbara Boxer
Assistant Floor Leader . . . . Patty Murray
Ranking Member Outreach Chairman . . . . Paul S. Sarbanes
Ranking Member Outreach Vice Chairman . . Jeff Bingaman
Rural Outreach Chairwoman . . . . Blanche Lincoln
Deputy Whips: Thomas R. Carper, Russell D. Feingold, Bill Nelson

DEMOCRATIC SENATORIAL CAMPAIGN COMMITTEE
224-2447   120 Maryland Ave. N.E. 20002

Chairman . . . . Charles E. Schumer
Regional Vice Chairmen: Barbara Boxer, Barack Obama, Mark Pryor, Jack Reed, Ron Wyden

POLICY COMMITTEE
224-3232   419 SH

Chairman . . . . Byron L. Dorgan
Regional Chairmen: Evan Bayh, Mary L. Landrieu, Patty Murray, Jack Reed
Members: Daniel K. Akaka, Thomas R. Carper, Jon Corzine, Mark Dayton, Russell D. Feingold, Dianne Feinstein, Tim Johnson, Joseph I. Lieberman, Blanche Lincoln, Bill Nelson, Harry Reid, John D. Rockefeller IV, Charles E. Schumer, Ron Wyden
Ex-Officio Members: Richard J. Durbin, Debbie Stabenow

STEERING AND OUTREACH COMMITTEE
224-9048   712 SH

Chairwoman . . . . Hillary Rodham Clinton

Joint Committees

JOINT ECONOMIC
224-5171 G-01 SD
H. James Saxton, N.J., chairman

Senate Members
Republicans: Robert F. Bennett, Utah, vice chairman, Sam Brownback, Kan., John E. Sununu, N.H., Jim DeMint, S.C., Jeff Sessions, Ala., John Cornyn, Texas
Democrats: Jack Reed, R.I., Edward M. Kennedy, Mass., Paul S. Sarbanes, Md., Jeff Bingaman, N.M.

House Members
Republicans: Paul D. Ryan, Wis., Phil English, Pa., Ron Paul, Texas, Kevin Brady, Texas, Thaddeus McCotter, Mich.
Democrats: Carolyn B. Maloney, N.Y., Maurice D. Hinchey, N.Y., Loretta Sanchez, Calif., Elijah E. Cummings, Md.

JOINT LIBRARY
224-3004 S-237 Capitol
Bob Ney, Ohio, chairman

Senate Members
Republicans: Ted Stevens, Alaska, vice chairman, Trent Lott, Miss., Thad Cochran, Miss.
Democrats: Christopher J. Dodd, Conn., Charles E. Schumer, N.Y.

House Members
Republicans: Vernon J. Ehlers, Mich., Candice S. Miller, Mich.
Democrats: Juanita Millender-McDonald, Calif., Zoe Lofgren, Calif.

JOINT PRINTING
225-8281 1309 LHOB
Trent Lott, R-Miss., chairman

Senate Members
Republicans: Thad Cochran, Miss., Saxby Chambliss, Ga.
Democrats: Daniel K. Inouye, Hawaii, Mark Dayton, Minn.

House Members
Republicans: Bob Ney, Ohio, vice chairman, John T. Doolittle, Calif., Thomas M. Reynolds, N.Y.
Democrats: Juanita Millender-McDonald, Calif., Robert A. Brady, Pa.

JOINT TAXATION
225-3621 1015 LHOB
Bill Thomas, R-Calif., chairman

Senate Members
Republicans: Charles E. Grassley, Iowa, vice chairman, Orrin G. Hatch, Utah, Trent Lott, Miss.
Democrats: Max Baucus, Mont., John D. Rockefeller IV, W.Va.

House Members
Republicans: E. Clay Shaw Jr., Fla., Nancy L. Johnson, Conn.
Democrats: Charles B. Rangel, N.Y., Pete Stark, Calif.

Senate Seniority

Senate rank is first determined by the length of consecutive service in the Senate.

For senators who entered the Senate on the same day, several tie-breaking procedures determine seniority.

In order of precedence, these factors are: previous Senate service, service as the vice president, previous House service, service in the Cabinet, service as a state governor. If a tie still exists, senators are ranked according to their state's population at the time of swearing in.

Note: Sen. Richard C. Shelby began his service as a Democrat and the Republican Conference credited his service as a Democrat towards his seniority ranking.

REPUBLICANS

1	Ted Stevens, Alaska	Dec. 24, 1968
2.	Pete V. Domenici, N.M.	Jan. 3, 1973
3.	Richard G. Lugar, Ind.	Jan. 4, 1977
4.	Orrin G. Hatch, Utah	Jan. 4, 1977
5.	Thad Cochran, Miss.	Dec. 27, 1978
6.	John W. Warner, Va.	Jan. 2, 1979
7.	Charles E. Grassley, Iowa	Jan. 5, 1981
8.	Arlen Specter, Pa.	Jan. 5, 1981
9.	Mitch McConnell, Ky.	Jan. 3, 1985
10.	Richard C. Shelby, Ala.	Jan. 6, 1987
11.	John McCain, Ariz.	Jan. 6, 1987
12.	Christopher S. Bond, Mo.	Jan. 6, 1987
13.	Trent Lott, Miss.	Jan. 3, 1989
14.	Conrad Burns, Mont.	Jan. 3, 1989
15.	Larry E. Craig, Idaho	Jan. 3, 1991
16.	Judd Gregg, N.H.	Jan. 5, 1993
17.	Robert F. Bennett, Utah	Jan. 5, 1993
18.	Kay Bailey Hutchison, Texas	June 14, 1993
19.	James M. Inhofe, Okla.	Nov. 30, 1994
20.	Olympia J. Snowe, Maine	Jan. 4, 1995
21.	Mike DeWine, Ohio	Jan. 4, 1995
22.	Jon Kyl, Ariz.	Jan. 4, 1995
23.	Craig Thomas, Wyo.	Jan. 4, 1995
24.	Rick Santorum, Pa.	Jan. 4, 1995
25.	Bill Frist, Tenn.	Jan. 4, 1995
26.	Sam Brownback, Kan.	Nov. 27, 1996
27.	Pat Roberts, Kan.	Jan. 7, 1997
28.	Wayne Allard, Colo.	Jan. 7, 1997
29.	Jeff Sessions, Ala.	Jan. 7, 1997
30.	Gordon H. Smith, Ore.	Jan. 7, 1997
31.	Chuck Hagel, Neb.	Jan. 7, 1997
32.	Susan Collins, Maine	Jan. 7, 1997
33.	Michael B. Enzi, Wyo.	Jan. 7, 1997
34.	Jim Bunning, Ky.	Jan. 6, 1999
35.	Michael D. Crapo, Idaho	Jan. 6, 1999
36.	George V. Voinovich, Ohio	Jan. 6, 1999
37.	Lincoln Chafee, R.I.	Nov. 4, 1999
38.	John Ensign, Nev.	Jan. 3, 2001
39.	George Allen, Va.	Jan. 3, 2001
40.	Jim Talent, Mo.	Nov. 25, 2002
41.	Lisa Murkowski, Alaska	Dec. 20, 2002
42.	Saxby Chambliss, Ga.	Jan. 7, 2003
43.	Lindsey Graham, S.C.	Jan. 7, 2003
44.	John E. Sununu, N.H.	Jan. 7, 2003
45.	Elizabeth Dole, N.C.	Jan. 7, 2003
46.	Lamar Alexander, Tenn.	Jan. 7, 2003
47.	John Cornyn, Texas	Jan. 7, 2003
48.	Norm Coleman, Minn.	Jan. 7, 2003
49.	Richard M. Burr, N.C.	Jan. 3, 2005
50.	Jim DeMint, S.C.	Jan. 3, 2005
51.	Tom Coburn, R-Okla.	Jan. 3, 2005
52.	John Thune, R-S.D.	Jan. 3, 2005
53.	Johnny Isakson, R-Ga.	Jan. 3, 2005
54.	David Vitter, R-La.	Jan. 3, 2005
55.	Mel Martinez, R-Fla.	Jan. 3, 2005

DEMOCRATS

1.	Robert C. Byrd, W.Va.	Jan. 7, 1959
2.	Edward M. Kennedy, Mass.	Nov. 7, 1962
3.	Daniel K. Inouye, Hawaii	Jan. 9, 1963
4.	Joseph R. Biden Jr., Del.	Jan. 3, 1973
5.	Patrick J. Leahy, Vt.	Jan. 14, 1975
6.	Paul S. Sarbanes, Md.	Jan. 4, 1977
7.	Max Baucus, Mont.	Dec. 15, 1978
8.	Carl Levin, Mich.	Jan. 15, 1979
9.	Christopher J. Dodd, Conn.	Jan. 5, 1981
10.	Jeff Bingaman, N.M.	Jan. 3, 1983
11.	John Kerry, Mass.	Jan. 2, 1985
12.	Tom Harkin, Iowa	Jan. 3, 1985
13.	John D. Rockefeller IV, W.Va.	Jan. 15, 1985
14.	Barbara A. Mikulski, Md.	Jan. 6, 1987
15.	Harry Reid, Nev.	Jan. 6, 1987
16.	Kent Conrad, N.D.	Jan. 6, 1987
17.	Herb Kohl, Wis.	Jan. 3, 1989
18.	Joseph I. Lieberman, Conn.	Jan. 3, 1989
19.	Daniel K. Akaka, Hawaii	April 28, 1990
20.	Dianne Feinstein, Calif.	Nov. 4, 1992
21.	Byron L. Dorgan, N.D.	Dec. 15, 1992
22.	Barbara Boxer, Calif.	Jan. 5, 1993
23.	Russell D. Feingold, Wis.	Jan. 5, 1993
24.	Patty Murray, Wash.	Jan. 5, 1993
25.	Ron Wyden, Ore.	Feb. 6, 1996
26.	Richard J. Durbin, Ill.	Jan. 7, 1997
27.	Tim Johnson, S.D.	Jan. 7, 1997
28.	Jack Reed, R.I.	Jan. 7, 1997
29.	Mary L. Landrieu, La.	Jan. 7, 1997
30.	Charles E. Schumer, N.Y.	Jan. 6, 1999
31.	Blanche Lincoln, Ark.	Jan. 6, 1999
32.	Evan Bayh, Ind.	Jan. 6, 1999
33.	Bill Nelson, Fla.	Jan. 3, 2001
34.	Thomas R. Carper, Del.	Jan. 3, 2001
35.	Debbie Stabenow, Mich.	Jan. 3, 2001
36.	Maria Cantwell, Wash.	Jan. 3, 2001
37.	Ben Nelson, Neb.	Jan. 3, 2001
38.	Hillary Rodham Clinton, N.Y.	Jan. 3, 2001
39.	Jon Corzine, N.J.	Jan. 3, 2001
40.	Mark Dayton, Minn.	Jan. 3, 2001
41.	Frank R. Lautenberg, N.J.	Jan. 7, 2003
	Also served 1983-2001	
42.	Mark Pryor, Ark.	Jan. 7, 2003
43.	Barack Obama, Ill.	Jan. 3, 2005
44.	Ken Salazar, Colo.	Jan. 3, 2005

INDEPENDENT

| 1. | James M. Jeffords, Vt. | Jan. 3, 1989 |

House Seniority

REPUBLICANS

House Republicans determine seniority by length of service. Members who previously served in the House are usually given credit for most of that service.

For members who joined at the beginning of a Congress, service is credited from the first day of the session. Seniority for members who won special elections is credited from the date of the election.

Note: Reps. Rodney Alexander, Nathan Deal, Virgil H. Goode Jr., and Ralph M. Hall began their service as Democrats. The GOP Conference has credited their service as Democrats toward their seniority. No credit is given for other public service, such as a governor.

1.	C.W. Bill Young, Fla.	Jan. 21, 1971
2.	Ralph Regula, Ohio	Jan. 3, 1973
3.	Don Young, Alaska	March 6, 1973
4.	Henry J. Hyde, Ill.	Jan. 14, 1975
5.	Jim Leach, Iowa	Jan. 4, 1977
6.	Jerry Lewis, Calif.	Jan. 15, 1979
7.	F. James Sensenbrenner Jr., Wis.	Jan. 15, 1979
8.	Bill Thomas, Calif.	Jan. 15, 1979
9.	Tom Petri, Wis.	April 3, 1979
10.	David Dreier, Calif.	Jan. 5, 1981
11.	Ralph M. Hall, Texas	Jan. 5, 1981
12.	Duncan Hunter, Calif.	Jan. 5, 1981
13.	Harold Rogers, Ky.	Jan. 5, 1981
14.	E. Clay Shaw Jr., Fla.	Jan. 5, 1981
15.	Christopher H. Smith, N.J.	Jan. 5, 1981
16.	Frank R. Wolf, Va.	Jan. 5, 1981
17.	Michael G. Oxley, Ohio	June 25, 1981
18.	Michael Bilirakis, Fla.	Jan. 3, 1983
19.	Sherwood Boehlert, N.Y.	Jan. 3, 1983
20.	Dan Burton, Ind.	Jan. 3, 1983
21.	Nancy L. Johnson, Conn.	Jan. 3, 1983
22.	H. James Saxton, N.J.	Nov. 6, 1984
23.	Joe L. Barton, Texas	Jan. 3, 1985
24.	Howard Coble, N.C.	Jan. 3, 1985
25.	Tom DeLay, Texas	Jan. 3, 1985
26.	Jim Kolbe, Ariz.	Jan. 3, 1985
27.	Richard H. Baker, La.	Jan. 6, 1987
28.	Elton Gallegly, Calif.	Jan. 6, 1987
29.	J. Dennis Hastert, Ill.	Jan. 6, 1987
30.	Joel Hefley, Colo.	Jan. 6, 1987
31.	Wally Herger, Calif.	Jan. 6, 1987
32.	Lamar Smith, Texas	Jan. 6, 1987
33.	Fred Upton, Mich.	Jan. 6, 1987
34.	Curt Weldon, Pa.	Jan. 6, 1987
35.	Christopher Shays, Conn.	Aug. 18, 1987
36.	Jim McCrery, La.	April 16, 1988
37.	John J. "Jimmy" Duncan Jr., Tenn.	Nov. 8, 1988
38.	Christopher Cox, Calif.	Jan. 3, 1989
39.	Paul E. Gillmor, Ohio	Jan. 3, 1989
40.	Dana Rohrabacher, Calif.	Jan. 3, 1989
41.	Cliff Stearns, Fla.	Jan. 3, 1989
42.	James T. Walsh, N.Y.	Jan. 3, 1989
43.	Ileana Ros-Lehtinen, Fla.	Aug. 29, 1989
44.	Ron Paul, Texas	Jan. 6, 1997
	Also served 1976-77, 1979-85	
45.	John A. Boehner, Ohio	Jan. 3, 1991
46.	Dave Camp, Mich.	Jan. 3, 1991
47.	Randy "Duke" Cunningham, Calif.	Jan. 3, 1991
48.	John T. Doolittle, Calif.	Jan. 3, 1991
49.	Wayne T. Gilchrest, Md.	Jan. 3, 1991
50.	David L. Hobson, Ohio	Jan. 3, 1991
51.	Jim Nussle, Iowa	Jan. 3, 1991
52.	Jim Ramstad, Minn.	Jan. 3, 1991
53.	Charles H. Taylor, N.C.	Jan. 3, 1991

54.	Sam Johnson, Texas	May 18, 1991
55.	Spencer Bachus, Ala.	Jan. 5, 1993
56.	Roscoe G. Bartlett, Md.	Jan. 5, 1993
57.	Henry Bonilla, Texas	Jan. 5, 1993
58.	Steve Buyer, Ind.	Jan. 5, 1993
59.	Ken Calvert, Calif.	Jan. 5, 1993
60.	Michael N. Castle, Del.	Jan. 5, 1993
61.	Nathan Deal, Ga.	Jan. 5, 1993
62.	Lincoln Diaz-Balart, Fla.	Jan. 5, 1993
63.	Terry Everett, Ala.	Jan. 5, 1993
64.	Robert W. Goodlatte, Va.	Jan. 5, 1993
65.	Peter Hoekstra, Mich.	Jan. 5, 1993
66.	Ernest Istook, Okla.	Jan. 5, 1993
67.	Peter T. King, N.Y.	Jan. 5, 1993
68.	Jack Kingston, Ga.	Jan. 5, 1993
69.	Joe Knollenberg, Mich.	Jan. 5, 1993
70.	John Linder, Ga.	Jan. 5, 1993
71.	Donald Manzullo, Ill.	Jan. 5, 1993
72.	John M. McHugh, N.Y.	Jan. 5, 1993
73.	Howard P. "Buck" McKeon, Calif.	Jan. 5, 1993
74.	John L. Mica, Fla.	Jan. 5, 1993
75.	Richard W. Pombo, Calif.	Jan. 5, 1993
76.	Deborah Pryce, Ohio	Jan. 5, 1993
77.	Ed Royce, Calif.	Jan. 5, 1993
78.	Vernon J. Ehlers, Mich.	Dec. 7, 1993
79.	Frank D. Lucas, Okla.	May 10, 1994
80.	Ron Lewis, Ky.	May 24, 1994
81.	Charles Bass, N.H.	Jan. 4, 1995
82.	Steve Chabot, Ohio	Jan. 4, 1995
83.	Barbara Cubin, Wyo.	Jan. 4, 1995
84.	Thomas M. Davis III, Va.	Jan. 4, 1995
85.	Phil English, Pa.	Jan. 4, 1995
86.	Mark Foley, Fla.	Jan. 4, 1995
87.	Rodney Frelinghuysen, N.J.	Jan. 4, 1995
88.	Gil Gutknecht, Minn.	Jan. 4, 1995
89.	Doc Hastings, Wash.	Jan. 4, 1995
90.	J.D. Hayworth, Ariz.	Jan. 4, 1995
91.	John Hostettler, Ind.	Jan. 4, 1995
92.	Walter B. Jones, N.C.	Jan. 4, 1995
93.	Sue W. Kelly, N.Y.	Jan. 4, 1995
94.	Ray LaHood, Ill.	Jan. 4, 1995
95.	Tom Latham, Iowa	Jan. 4, 1995
96.	Steven C. LaTourette, Ohio	Jan. 4, 1995
97.	Frank A. LoBiondo, N.J.	Jan. 4, 1995
98.	Dan Lungren, Calif.	Jan. 3, 1979
	Also served 1979-89	
99.	Sue Myrick, N.C.	Jan. 4, 1995
100.	Bob Ney, Ohio	Jan. 4, 1995
101.	Charlie Norwood, Ga.	Jan. 4, 1995
102.	George P. Radanovich, Calif.	Jan. 4, 1995
103.	John Shadegg, Ariz.	Jan. 4, 1995
104.	Mark Souder, Ind.	Jan. 4, 1995
105.	William M. "Mac" Thornberry, Texas	Jan. 4, 1995
106.	Todd Tiahrt, Kan.	Jan. 4, 1995

107. Zach Wamp, Tenn.	Jan. 4, 1995	
108. Dave Weldon, Fla.	Jan. 4, 1995	
109. Jerry Weller, Ill.	Jan. 4, 1995	
110. Edward Whitfield, Ky.	Jan. 4, 1995	
111. Roger Wicker, Miss.	Jan. 4, 1995	
112. Jo Ann Emerson, Mo.	Nov. 5, 1996	
113. Jim Ryun, Kan.	Nov. 27, 1996	
114. Robert B. Aderholt, Ala.	Jan. 6, 1997	
115. Roy Blunt, Mo.	Jan. 6, 1997	
116. Kevin Brady, Texas	Jan. 6, 1997	
117. Chris Cannon, Utah	Jan. 6, 1997	
118. Jim Gibbons, Nev.	Jan. 6, 1997	
119. Virgil H. Goode Jr., Va.	Jan. 6, 1997	
120. Kay Granger, Texas	Jan. 6, 1997	
121. Kenny Hulshof, Mo.	Jan. 6, 1997	
122. Bill Jenkins, Tenn.	Jan. 6, 1997	
123. Jerry Moran, Kan.	Jan. 6, 1997	
124. Anne M. Northup, Ky.	Jan. 6, 1997	
125. John E. Peterson, Pa.	Jan. 6, 1997	
126. Charles W. "Chip" Pickering Jr., Miss.	Jan. 6, 1997	
127. Joe Pitts, Pa.	Jan. 6, 1997	
128. Pete Sessions, Texas	Jan. 6, 1997	
129. John Shimkus, Ill.	Jan. 6, 1997	
130. Vito J. Fossella, N.Y.	Nov. 4, 1997	
131. Mary Bono, Calif.	April 7, 1998	
132. Heather A. Wilson, N.M.	June 23, 1998	
133. Judy Biggert, Ill.	Jan. 6, 1999	
134. Mark Green, Wis.	Jan. 6, 1999	
135. Robin Hayes, N.C.	Jan. 6, 1999	
136. Bob Inglis, S.C.	Jan. 5, 1993	
Also served 1993-99		
137. Gary G. Miller, Calif.	Jan. 6, 1999	
138. Thomas M. Reynolds, N.Y.	Jan. 6, 1999	
139. Paul D. Ryan, Wis.	Jan. 6, 1999	
140. Don Sherwood, Pa.	Jan. 6, 1999	
141. Mike Simpson, Idaho	Jan. 6, 1999	
142. John E. Sweeey, N.Y.	Jan. 6, 1999	
143. Tom Tancredo, Colo.	Jan. 6, 1999	
144. Lee Terry, Neb.	Jan. 6, 1999	
145. Greg Walden, Ore.	Jan. 6, 1999	
146. Todd Akin, Mo.	Jan. 3, 2001	
147. Henry E. Brown Jr., S.C.	Jan. 3, 2001	
148. Eric Cantor, Va.	Jan. 3, 2001	
149. Shelley Moonre Capito, W.Va.	Jan. 3, 2001	
150. Ander Crenshaw, Fla.	Jan. 3, 2001	
151. John Culberson, Texas	Jan. 3, 2001	
152. Jo Ann Davis, Va.	Jan. 3, 2001	
153. Mike Ferguson, N.J.	Jan. 3, 2001	
154. Jeff Flake, Ariz.	Jan. 3, 2001	
155. Sam Graves, Mo.	Jan. 3, 2001	
156. Melissa A. Hart, Pa.	Jan. 3, 2001	
157. Darrell Issa, Calif.	Jan. 3, 2001	
158. Timothy V. Johnson, Ill.	Jan. 3, 2001	
159. Ric Keller, Fla.	Jan. 3, 2001	
160. Mark Kennedy, Minn.	Jan. 3, 2001	
161. Mark Steven Kirk, Ill.	Jan. 3, 2001	
162. Tom Osborne, Neb.	Jan. 3, 2001	
163. C. L. "Butch" Otter, Idaho	Jan. 3, 2001	
164. Mike Pence, Ind.	Jan. 3, 2001	
165. Todd R. Platts, Pa.	Jan. 3, 2001	
166. Adam H. Putnam, Fla.	Jan. 3, 2001	
167. Denny Rehberg, Mont.	Jan. 3, 2001	
168. Mike Rogers, Mich.	Jan. 3, 2001	
169. Rob Simmons, Conn.	Jan. 3, 2001	
170. Pat Tiberi, Ohio	Jan. 3, 2001	
171. Bill Shuster, Pa.	May 15, 2001	
178. J. Randy Forbes, Va.	June 19, 2001	
173. Jeff Miller, Fla.	Oct. 16, 2001	
174. John Boozman, Ark.	Nov. 20, 2001	
175. Joe Wilson, S.C.	Dec. 18, 2001	
176. John Sullivan, Okla.	Feb. 15, 2002	
177. Rodney Alexander, La.	Jan. 7, 2003	
178. J. Gresham Barrett, S.C.	Jan. 7, 2003	
179. Bob Beauprez, Colo.	Jan. 7, 2003	
180. Rob Bishop, Utah	Jan. 7, 2003	
181. Marsha Blackburn, Tenn.	Jan. 7, 2003	
182. Jo Bonner, Ala.	Jan. 7, 2003	
183. Jeb Bradley, N.H.	Jan. 7, 2003	
184. Ginny Brown-Waite, Fla.	Jan. 7, 2003	
185. Michael C. Burgess, Texas	Jan. 7, 2003	
186. John Carter, Texas	Jan. 7, 2003	
187. Chris Chocola, Ind.	Jan. 7, 2003	
188. Tom Cole, Okla.	Jan. 7, 2003	
189. Mario Diaz-Balart, Fla.	Jan. 7, 2003	
190. Tom Feeney, Fla.	Jan. 7, 2003	
191. Trent Franks, Ariz.	Jan. 7, 2003	
192. Scott Garrett, N.J.	Jan. 7, 2003	
193. Jim Gerlach, Pa.	Jan. 7, 2003	
194. Phil Gingrey, Ga.	Jan. 7, 2003	
195. Katherine Harris, Fla.	Jan. 7, 2003	
196. Jeb Hensarling, Texas	Jan. 7, 2003	
197. Steve King, Iowa	Jan. 7, 2003	
198. John Kline, Minn.	Jan. 7, 2003	
199. Thaddeus McCotter, Mich.	Jan. 7, 2003	
200. Candice S. Miller, Mich.	Jan. 7, 2003	
201. Tim Murphy, Pa.	Jan. 7, 2003	
202. Marilyn Musgrave, Colo.	Jan. 7, 2003	
203. Devin Nunes, Calif.	Jan. 7, 2003	
204. Steve Pearce, N.M.	Jan. 7, 2003	
205. Jon Porter, Nev.	Jan. 7, 2003	
206. Rick Renzi, Ariz.	Jan. 7, 2003	
207. Mike D. Rogers, Ala.	Jan. 7, 2003	
208. Michael R. Turner, Ohio	Jan. 7, 2003	
209. Randy Neugebauer, Texas	June 3, 2003	
210. Charles Boustany Jr., La.	Jan. 4, 2005	
211. K. Michael Conaway, Texas	Jan. 4, 2005	
212. Geoff Davis, Ky.	Jan. 4, 2005	
213. Charlie Dent, Pa.	Jan. 4, 2005	
214. Thelma Drake, Va.	Jan. 4, 2005	
215. Michael G. Fitzpatrick, Pa.	Jan. 4, 2005	
216. Jeff Fortenberry, Neb.	Jan. 4, 2005	
217. Virginia Foxx, N.C.	Jan. 4, 2005	
218. Louis Gohmert, Texas	Jan. 4, 2005	
219. Bobby Jindal, La.	Jan. 4, 2005	
220. John R. "Randy" Kuhl Jr., N.Y.	Jan. 4, 2005	
221. Connie Mack, Fla.	Jan. 4, 2005	
222. Kenny Marchant, Texas	Jan. 4, 2005	
223. Michael McCaul, Texas	Jan. 4, 2005	
224. Patrick T. McHenry, N.C.	Jan. 4, 2005	
225. Cathy McMorris, Wash.	Jan. 4, 2005	
226. Ted Poe, Texas	Jan. 4, 2005	
227. Tom Price, Ga.	Jan. 4, 2005	
228. Dave Reichert, Wash.	Jan. 4, 2005	
229. Joe Schwarz, Mich.	Jan. 4, 2005	
230. Mike Sodrel, Ind.	Jan. 4, 2005	
231. Lynn Westmoreland, Ga.	Jan. 4, 2005	

DEMOCRATS

House Democrats determine seniority by length of service. Members who previously served in the House are given some credit for that service — when they return they are ranked above other members of that entering class.

For members who joined at the beginning of a Congress, service is credited from the first day of the session. Seniority for members who won special elections is credited from the date of the election. No credit is given for other previous service, such as a senator or governor.

1.	John D. Dingell, Mich.	Dec. 13, 1955
2.	John Conyers Jr., Mich.	Jan. 4, 1965
3.	David R. Obey, Wis.	April 1, 1969
4.	Charles B. Rangel, N.Y.	Jan. 21, 1971
5.	Pete Stark, Calif.	Jan. 3, 1973
6.	John P. Murtha, Pa.	Feb. 5, 1974
7.	George Miller, Calif.	Jan. 14, 1975
8.	James L. Oberstar, Minn.	Jan. 14, 1975
9.	Henry A. Waxman, Calif.	Jan. 14, 1975
10.	Edward J. Markey, Mass.	Nov. 2, 1976
11.	Norm Dicks, Wash.	Jan. 4, 1977
12.	Dale E. Kildee, Mich.	Jan. 4, 1977
13.	Nick J. Rahall II, W.Va.	Jan. 4, 1977
14.	Ike Skelton, Mo.	Jan. 4, 1977
15.	Martin Olav Sabo, Minn.	Jan. 15, 1979
16.	Barney Frank, Mass.	Jan. 5, 1981
17.	Tom Lantos, Calif.	Jan. 5, 1981
18.	Steny H. Hoyer, Md.	May 19, 1981
19.	Howard L. Berman, Calif.	Jan. 3, 1983
20.	Rick Boucher, Va.	Jan. 3, 1983
21.	Lane Evans, Ill.	Jan. 3, 1983
22.	Marcy Kaptur, Ohio	Jan. 3, 1983
23.	Sander M. Levin, Mich.	Jan. 3, 1983
24.	Alan B. Mollohan, W.Va.	Jan. 3, 1983
25.	Solomon P. Ortiz, Texas	Jan. 3, 1983
26.	Major R. Owens, N.Y.	Jan. 3, 1983
27.	John M. Spratt Jr., S.C.	Jan. 3, 1983
28.	Edolphus Towns, N.Y.	Jan. 3, 1983
29.	Gary L. Ackerman, N.Y.	March 1, 1983
30.	Bart Gordon, Tenn.	Jan. 3, 1985
31.	Paul E. Kanjorski, Pa.	Jan. 3, 1985
32.	Peter J. Visclosky, Ind.	Jan. 3, 1985
33.	Benjamin L. Cardin, Md.	Jan. 6, 1987
34.	Peter A. DeFazio, Ore.	Jan. 6, 1987
35.	John Lewis, Ga.	Jan. 6, 1987
36.	Louise M. Slaughter, N.Y.	Jan. 6, 1987
37.	Nancy Pelosi, Calif.	June 2, 1987
38.	Jerry F. Costello, Ill.	Aug. 9, 1988
39.	Frank Pallone Jr., N.J.	Nov. 8, 1988
40.	Eliot L. Engel, N.Y.	Jan. 3, 1989
41.	Nita M. Lowey, N.Y.	Jan. 3, 1989
42.	Jim McDermott, Wash.	Jan. 3, 1989
43.	Michael R. McNulty, N.Y.	Jan. 3, 1989
44.	Richard E. Neal, Mass.	Jan. 3, 1989
45.	Donald M. Payne, N.J.	Jan. 3, 1989
46.	John Tanner, Tenn.	Jan. 3, 1989
47.	Gene Taylor, Miss.	Oct. 17, 1989
48.	José E. Serrano, N.Y.	March 20, 1990
49.	Robert E. Andrews, N.J.	Nov. 6, 1990
50.	Neil Abercrombie, Hawaii *Also served Sept. 1986-Jan. 1987*	Jan. 3, 1991
51.	Robert E. "Bud" Cramer, Ala.	Jan. 3, 1991
52.	Rosa DeLauro, Conn.	Jan. 3, 1991
53.	Chet Edwards, Texas	Jan. 3, 1991
54.	William J. Jefferson, La.	Jan. 3, 1991
55.	James P. Moran, Va.	Jan. 3, 1991
56.	Collin C. Peterson, Minn.	Jan. 3, 1991
57.	Maxine Waters, Calif.	Jan. 3, 1991
58.	John W. Olver, Mass.	June 4, 1991
59.	Ed Pastor, Ariz.	Sept. 24, 1991
60.	Jerrold Nadler, N.Y.	Nov. 3, 1992
61.	Xavier Becerra, Calif.	Jan. 5, 1993
62.	Sanford D. Bishop Jr., Ga.	Jan. 5, 1993
63.	Corrine Brown, Fla.	Jan. 5, 1993
64.	Sherrod Brown, Ohio	Jan. 5, 1993
65.	James E. Clyburn, S.C.	Jan. 5, 1993
66.	Anna G. Eshoo, Calif.	Jan. 5, 1993
67.	Bob Filner, Calif.	Jan. 5, 1993
68.	Gene Green, Texas	Jan. 5, 1993
69.	Luis V. Gutierrez, Ill.	Jan. 5, 1993
70.	Alcee L. Hastings, Fla.	Jan. 5, 1993
71.	Maurice D. Hinchey, N.Y.	Jan. 5, 1993
72.	Tim Holden, Pa.	Jan. 5, 1993
73.	Eddie Bernice Johnson, Texas	Jan. 5, 1993
74.	Carolyn B. Maloney, N.Y.	Jan. 5, 1993
75.	Martin T. Meehan, Mass.	Jan. 5, 1993
76.	Robert Menendez, N.J.	Jan. 5, 1993
77.	Earl Pomeroy, N.D.	Jan. 5, 1993
78.	Lucille Roybal-Allard, Calif.	Jan. 5, 1993
79.	Bobby L. Rush, Ill.	Jan. 5, 1993
80.	Robert C. Scott, Va.	Jan. 5, 1993
81.	Bart Stupak, Mich.	Jan. 5, 1993
82.	Nydia M. Velázquez, N.Y.	Jan. 5, 1993
83.	Melvin Watt, N.C.	Jan. 5, 1993
84.	Lynn Woolsey, Calif.	Jan. 5, 1993
85.	Albert R. Wynn, Md.	Jan. 5, 1993
86.	Bennie Thompson, Miss.	April 13, 1993
87.	Sam Farr, Calif.	June 8, 1993
88.	Lloyd Doggett, Texas	Jan. 4, 1995
89.	Mike Doyle, Pa.	Jan. 4, 1995
90.	Chaka Fattah, Pa.	Jan. 4, 1995
91.	Sheila Jackson-Lee, Texas	Jan. 4, 1995
92.	Patrick J. Kennedy, R.I.	Jan. 4, 1995
93.	Zoe Lofgren, Calif.	Jan. 4, 1995
94.	Jesse L. Jackson Jr., Ill.	Dec. 12, 1995
95.	Juanita Millender-McDonald, Calif.	March 26, 1996
96.	Elijah E. Cummings, Md.	April 16, 1996
97.	Earl Blumenauer, Ore.	May 21, 1996
98.	David E. Price, N.C. *Also served 1987-95*	Jan. 6, 1997
99.	Ted Strickland, Ohio *Also served 1993-95*	Jan. 6, 1997
100.	Tom Allen, Maine	Jan. 6, 1997
101.	Marion Berry, Ark.	Jan. 6, 1997
102.	Leonard L. Boswell, Iowa	Jan. 6, 1997
103.	Allen Boyd, Fla.	Jan. 6, 1997
104.	Julia Carson, Ind.	Jan. 6, 1997
105.	Danny K. Davis, Ill.	Jan. 6, 1997

106. Jim Davis, Fla.	Jan. 6, 1997	
107. Diana DeGette, Colo.	Jan. 6, 1997	
108. Bill Delahunt, Mass.	Jan. 6, 1997	
109. Bob Etheridge, N.C.	Jan. 6, 1997	
110. Harold E. Ford Jr., Tenn.	Jan. 6, 1997	
111. Rubén Hinojosa, Texas	Jan. 6, 1997	
112. Darlene Hooley, Ore.	Jan. 6, 1997	
113. Carolyn Cheeks Kilpatrick, Mich.	Jan. 6, 1997	
114. Ron Kind, Wis.	Jan. 6, 1997	
115. Dennis J. Kucinich, Ohio	Jan. 6, 1997	
116. Carolyn McCarthy, N.Y.	Jan. 6, 1997	
117. Jim McGovern, Mass.	Jan. 6, 1997	
118. Mike McIntyre, N.C.	Jan. 6, 1997	
119. Bill Pascrell Jr., N.J.	Jan. 6, 1997	
120. Silvestre Reyes, Texas	Jan. 6, 1997	
121. Steven R. Rothman, N.J.	Jan. 6, 1997	
122. Loretta Sanchez, Calif.	Jan. 6, 1997	
123. Brad Sherman, Calif.	Jan. 6, 1997	
124. Adam Smith, Wash.	Jan. 6, 1997	
125. Vic Snyder, Ark.	Jan. 6, 1997	
126. Ellen O. Tauscher, Calif.	Jan. 6, 1997	
127. John F. Tierney, Mass.	Jan. 6, 1997	
128. Robert Wexler, Fla.	Jan. 6, 1997	
129. Gregory W. Meeks, N.Y.	Feb. 3, 1998	
130. Lois Capps, Calif.	March 10, 1998	
131. Barbara Lee, Calif.	April 7, 1998	
132. Robert A. Brady, Pa.	May 19, 1998	
133. Jay Inslee, Wash.	Jan. 6, 1999	
Also served 1993-95		
134. Brian Baird, Wash.	Jan. 6, 1999	
135. Tammy Baldwin, Wis.	Jan. 6, 1999	
136. Shelley Berkley, Nev.	Jan. 6, 1999	
137. Michael E. Capuano, Mass.	Jan. 6, 1999	
138. Joseph Crowley, N.Y.	Jan. 6, 1999	
139. Charlie Gonzalez, Texas	Jan. 6, 1999	
140. Rush D. Holt, N.J.	Jan. 6, 1999	
141. Stephanie Tubbs Jones, Ohio	Jan. 6, 1999	
142. John B. Larson, Conn.	Jan. 6, 1999	
143. Dennis Moore, Kan.	Jan. 6, 1999	
144. Grace F. Napolitano, Calif.	Jan. 6, 1999	
145. Jan Schakowsky, Ill.	Jan. 6, 1999	
146. Mike Thompson, Calif.	Jan. 6, 1999	
147. Mark Udall, Colo.	Jan. 6, 1999	
148. Tom Udall, N.M.	Jan. 6, 1999	
149. Anthony Weiner, N.Y.	Jan. 6, 1999	
150. David Wu, Ore.	Jan. 6, 1999	
151. Joe Baca, Calif.	Nov. 16, 1999	
152. Jane Harman, Calif.	Jan. 3, 2001	
Also served 1993-99		
153. William Lacy Clay, Mo.	Jan. 3, 2001	
154. Susan A. Davis, Calif.	Jan. 3, 2001	
155. Michael M. Honda, Calif.	Jan. 3, 2001	
156. Steve Israel, N.Y.	Jan. 3, 2001	
157. Jim Langevin, R.I.	Jan. 3, 2001	
158. Rick Larsen, Wash.	Jan. 3, 2001	
159. Jim Matheson, Utah	Jan. 3, 2001	
160. Betty McCollum, Minn.	Jan. 3, 2001	
161. Mike Ross, Ark.	Jan. 3, 2001	
162. Adam B. Schiff, Calif.	Jan. 3, 2001	
163. Hilda L. Solis, Calif.	Jan. 3, 2001	
164. Diane Watson, Calif.	June 5, 2001	
165. Stephen F. Lynch, Mass.	Oct. 16, 2001	
166. Ed Case, Hawaii	Nov. 30, 2002	

167. Jim Cooper, Tenn.	Jan. 7, 2003
Also served 1983-95	
168. Timothy H. Bishop, N.Y.	Jan. 7, 2003
169. Dennis Cardoza, Calif.	Jan. 7, 2003
170. Artur Davis, Ala.	Jan. 7, 2003
171. Lincoln Davis, Tenn.	Jan. 7, 2003
172. Rahm Emanuel, Ill.	Jan. 7, 2003
173. Raúl M. Grijalva, Ariz.	Jan. 7, 2003
174. Jim Marshall, Ga.	Jan. 7, 2003
175. Kendrick B. Meek, Fla.	Jan. 7, 2003
176. Michael H. Michaud, Maine	Jan. 7, 2003
177. Brad Miller, N.C.	Jan. 7, 2003
178. C.A. Dutch Ruppersberger, Md.	Jan. 7, 2003
179. Tim Ryan, Ohio	Jan. 7, 2003
180. Linda T. Sánchez, Calif.	Jan. 7, 2003
181. David Scott, Ga.	Jan. 7, 2003
182. Chris Van Hollen, Md.	Jan. 7, 2003
183. Ben Chandler, Ky.	Feb. 17, 2004
184. Stephanie Herseth, S.D.	June 1, 2004
185. G.K. Butterfield, N.C.	July 20, 2004
186. Cynthia A. McKinney, Ga.	Jan. 4, 2005
Also served 1993-2003	
187. John Barrow, Ga.	Jan. 4, 2005
188. Melissa Bean, Ill.	Jan. 4, 2005
189. Dan Boren, Okla.	Jan. 4, 2005
190. Russ Carnahan, Mo.	Jan. 4, 2005
191. Emanuel Cleaver II, Mo.	Jan. 4, 2005
192. Jim Costa, Calif.	Jan. 4, 2005
193. Henry Cuellar, Texas 28	Jan. 4, 2005
194. Al Green, Texas	Jan. 4, 2005
195. Brian Higgins, N.Y.	Jan. 4, 2005
196. Daniel Lipinski, Ill.	Jan. 4, 2005
197. Charlie Melancon, La.	Jan. 4, 2005
198. Gwen Moore, Wis.	Jan. 4, 2005
199. John Salazar, Colo.	Jan. 4, 2005
200. Allyson Y. Schwartz, Pa.	Jan. 4, 2005
201. Debbie Wasserman-Schultz, Fla.	Jan. 4, 2005
201. Doris Matsui, Calif.	March 10, 2005

INDEPENDENT

1. Bernard Sanders, Vt.	Jan. 3, 1991

Index

A

Abercrombie, Neil, D-Hawaii (1), **310**
Ackerman, Gary L., D-N.Y. (5), 170, **705**
Aderholt, Robert B., R-Ala. (4), **13**
Akaka, Daniel K., D-Hawaii, **308**, 458
Akin, Todd, R-Mo. (2), **591**
Alexander, Lamar, R-Tenn., 575, **944**, 1039
Alexander, Rodney, R-La. (5), 445, **449**
Allard, Wayne, R-Colo., **179**
Allen, George, R-Va., 850, **1052**, 1059, 1067
Allen, Tom, D-Maine (1), **460**
Andrews, Robert E., D-N.J. (1), **652**, 662

B

Baca, Joe, D-Calif. (43), **155**
Bachus, Spencer, R-Ala. (6), **17**, 861
Baird, Brian, D-Wash. (3), **1085**
Baker, Richard H., R-La. (6), **451**
Baldwin, Tammy, D-Wis. (2), **1117**
Barrett, J. Gresham, R-S.C. (3), **925**
Barrow, John, D-Ga. (12), **301**
Bartlett, Roscoe G., R-Md. (6), **480**
Barton, Joe L., R-Texas (6), 684, **979**, 1022
Bass, Charles, R-N.H. (2), **644**, 954
Baucus, Max, D-Mont., 392, **607**, 612, 693, 1102
Bayh, Evan, D-Ind., 53, **371**, 372
Bean, Melissa, D-Ill. (8), **344**
Beauprez, Bob, R-Colo. (7), **194**, 676
Becerra, Xavier, D-Calif. (31), **131**
Bennett, Robert F., R-Utah, **1032**
Berkley, Shelley, D-Nev. (1), **630**, 635
Berman, Howard L., D-Calif. (28), **125**, 130
Berry, Marion, D-Ark. (1), **57**, 63, 284
Biden, Joseph R. Jr., D-Del., 6, **214**, 217, 491, 616
Biggert, Judy, R-Ill. (13), **353**
Bilirakis, Michael, R-Fla. (9), **243**
Bingaman, Jeff, D-N.M., **682**, 689
Bishop, Rob, R-Utah (1), **1034**
Bishop, Sanford D. Jr., D-Ga. (2), **284**
Bishop, Timothy H., D-N.Y. (1), **697**
Blackburn, Marsha, R-Tenn. (7), **958**
Blumenauer, Earl, D-Ore. (3), **857**
Blunt, Roy, R-Mo. (7), 106, 251, 331, 347, 363, 478, 531, **599**, 601, 705, 885, 954, 988, 1065
Boehlert, Sherwood, R-N.Y. (24), 98, 522, 713, 735, 742, **743**
Boehner, John A., R-Ohio (8), 174, 218, 800, **810**, 973, 1093, 1124
Bond, Christopher S., R-Mo., 199, **585**, 591, 600, 604, 868
Bonilla, Henry, R-Texas (23), 231, 970, **1010**, 1018, 1019
Bonner, Jo, R-Ala. (1), **7**
Bono, Mary, R-Calif. (45), **159**, 167, 862
Boozman, John, R-Ark. (3), **61**
Bordallo, Madeleine Z., D-Guam (AL), **1140**
Boren, Dan, D-Okla. (2), **840**
Boswell, Leonard L., D-Iowa (3), **400**
Boucher, Rick, D-Va. (9), 80, 1062, 1064, **1069**
Boustany, Charles Jr., R-La. (7), **453**
Boxer, Barbara, D-Calif., 70, **72**, 74, 83, 121, 134, 168, 333, 516, 816, 830, 1053
Boyd, Allen, D-Fla. (2), 49, **229**, 878
Bradley, Jeb, R-N.H. (1), **642**

Brady, Kevin, R-Texas (8), **983**
Brady, Robert A., D-Pa. (1), **870**
Brown, Corrine, D-Fla. (3), **231**
Brown, Henry E. Jr., R-S.C. (1), **921**
Brown, Sherrod, D-Ohio (13), 244, 297, 803, **820**, 821
Brown-Waite, Ginny, R-Fla. (5), **235**
Brownback, Sam, R-Kan., **408**, 414, 417, 440, 1116
Bunning, Jim, R-Ky., **424**
Burgess, Michael C., R-Texas (26), **1015**
Burns, Conrad, R-Mont., **609**, 612, 850
Burr, Richard M., R-N.C., **757**, 767, 1134
Burton, Dan, R-Ind. (5), 135, 208, **381**, 504, 1067, 1073
Butterfield, G.K., D-N.C. (1), **759**
Buyer, Steve, R-Ind. (4), 171, 231, 361, **379**, 658
Byrd, Robert C., D-W.Va., 23, 214, 306, 550, **1099**, 1100, 1101, 1103, 1105, 1108

C

Calvert, Ken, R-Calif. (44), **157**
Camp, Dave, R-Mich. (4), **524**
Cannon, Chris, R-Utah (3), **1038**
Cantor, Eric, R-Va. (7), 531, 988, **1065**
Cantwell, Maria, D-Wash., **1079**
Capito, Shelley Moore, R-W.Va. (2), **1105**
Capps, Lois, D-Calif. (23), **115**, 116, 426
Capuano, Michael E., D-Mass. (8), **506**, 508
Cardin, Benjamin L., D-Md. (3), **474**, 789
Cardoza, Dennis, D-Calif. (18), **106**
Carnahan, Russ, D-Mo. (3), **593**
Carper, Thomas R., D-Del., 53, **216**, 910
Carson, Julia, D-Ind. (7), **385**
Carter, John, R-Texas (31), 499, **1024**, 1089
Case, Ed, D-Hawaii (2), **312**
Castle, Michael N., R-Del. (AL), 183, **218**, 960
Chabot, Steve, R-Ohio (1), **797**
Chafee, Lincoln, R-R.I., 457, 907, **909**, 911, 912, 1044
Chambliss, Saxby, R-Ga., **278**, 281, 283, 287
Chandler, Ben, D-Ky. (6), 420, **435**
Chocola, Chris, R-Ind. (2), **375**
Christensen, Donna M.C., D-Virgin Is. (AL), **1142**
Clay, William Lacy, D-Mo. (1), **589**
Cleaver, Emanuel II, D-Mo. (5), **596**
Clinton, Hillary Rodham, D-N.Y., 223, 329, 693, **695**, 700, 701, 710, 718, 721, 723, 731, 732, 734, 747
Clyburn, James E., D-S.C. (6), 707, **930**
Coble, Howard, R-N.C. (6), 98, **768**
Coburn, Tom, R-Okla., 706, **836**, 943
Cochran, Thad, R-Miss., 5, 278, **571**, 574, 576, 579
Cole, Tom, R-Okla. (4), **843**
Coleman, Norm, R-Minn., **551**, 755
Collins, Susan, R-Maine, 200, 410, 457, **458**, 520
Conaway, K. Michael, R-Texas (11), **987**, 1002
Conrad, Kent, D-N.D., 683, **785**, 787, 790, 917
Conyers, John Jr., D-Mich. (14), 333, 541, **543**
Cooper, Jim, D-Tenn. (5), 684, **954**
Cornyn, John, R-Texas, **969**, 971, 980, 1010
Corzine, Jon, D-N.J., **648**, 651, 652, 662, 667, 669, 676
Costa, Jim, D-Calif. (20), **110**
Costello, Jerry F., D-Ill. (12), **351**
Cox, Christopher, R-Calif. (48), **165**, 577, 882
Craig, Larry E., R-Idaho, 71, **316**
Cramer, Robert E. "Bud", D-Ala. (5), **15**, 16, 246

R

S

T

U

V

W, Y

Pronunciation Guide for Congress

Some members of Congress whose names are frequently mispronounced:

SENATE

Daniel K. Akaka, D-Hawaii – uh-KAH-kuh
Evan Bayh, D-Ind. – BY
Lincoln Chafee, R-R.I. – CHAY-fee
Saxby Chambliss, R-Ga. – SAX-bee CHAM-bliss
John Cornyn, R-Texas – CORE-nin
Jon Corzine, D-N.J. – COR-zyne
Michael D. Crapo, R-Idaho – CRAY-poe
Pete V. Domenici, R-N.M. – doe-MEN-ih-chee
Michael B. Enzi, R-Wyo. – EN-zee
Russell D. Feingold, D-Wis. – FINE-gold
Dianne Feinstein, D-Calif. – FINE-stine
James M. Inhofe, R-Okla. – IN-hoff
Daniel K. Inouye, D-Hawaii – in-NO-ay
Mary L. Landrieu, D-La. – LAN-drew
Barack Obama, D-Ill. – buh-ROCK oh-BAH-mah
Rick Santorum, R-Pa. – san-TORE-um
Debbie Stabenow, D-Mich. – STAB-uh-now
John E. Sununu, R-N.H. – suh-NU-nu
John Thune, R-S.D. – THOON
George V. Voinovich, R-Ohio – VOY-no-vitch

HOUSE

Robert B. Aderholt, R-Ala. – ADD-er-holt
Spencer Bachus, R-Ala. – BACK-us
John Barrow, D-Ga. – BEAR-oh
Bob Beauprez, R-Colo. – bo-PRAY
Xavier Becerra, D-Calif. – HAH-vee-air beh-SEH-ra
Michael Bilirakis, R-Fla. – bil-uh-RACK-iss
Earl Blumenauer, D-Ore. – BLUE-men-hour
Sherwood Boehlert, R-N.Y. – BO-lert
John A. Boehner, R-Ohio – BAY-ner
Henry Bonilla, R-Texas – bo-NEE-uh
John Boozman, R-Ark. – BOZE-man
Madeleine Z. Bordallo, D-Guam – bore-DAA-yo
Rick Boucher, D-Va. – BOW (rhymes with "now")-chur
Charles Boustany Jr., R-La. – boo-STAN-knee
Steve Buyer, R-Ind. – BOO-yer
Shelley Moore Capito, R-W.Va. – CAP-ih-toe
Michael E. Capuano, D-Mass. – KAP-you-AH-no
Steve Chabot, R-Ohio – SHAB-it
Chris Chocola, R-Ind. – cha-KO-luh
Joseph Crowley, D-N.Y. – KRAU-lee
Barbara Cubin, R-Wyo. – CUE-bin
Henry Cuellar, D-Texas – QUAY-are
Artur Davis, D-Ala. – ar-TOUR
Peter A. DeFazio, D-Ore. – da-FAH-zee-o
Diana DeGette, D-Colo. – de-GET
Bill Delahunt, D-Mass. – DELL-a-hunt
Rosa DeLauro, D-Conn. – da-LAUR-o
Lincoln Diaz-Balart, R-Fla. – DEE-az ba-LART
Mario Diaz-Balart, R-Fla. – DEE-az ba-LART
Vernon J. Ehlers, R-Mich. – AY-lurz
Anna G. Eshoo, D-Calif. – EH-shoo
Eni F.H. Faleomavaega, D-Am. Samoa –
    EN-ee FOL-ee-oh-mav-ah-ENG-uh
Chaka Fattah, D-Pa. – SHOCK-ah fa-TAH
Luis Fortuño, R-P.R. – loo-EES four-TOON-yo
Vito J. Fossella, R-N.Y. – VEE-toe Fuh-SELL-ah
Rodney Frelinghuysen, R-N.J. – FREE-ling-high-zen
Elton Gallegly, R-Calif. – GAL-uh-glee
Jim Gerlach, R-Pa. – GUR-lock
Virgil H. Goode Jr., R-Va. – GUDE (rhymes with "food")

Robert W. Goodlatte, R-Va. – GOOD-lat
Raúl M. Grijalva, D-Ariz. – gree-HAHL-va
Luis V. Gutierrez, D-Ill. – loo-EES goo-tee-AIR-ez
Gil Gutknecht, R-Minn. – GOOT-neck
Jeb Hensarling, R-Texas – HENN-sur-ling
Rubén Hinojosa, D-Texas – ru-BEN ee-na-HO-suh
Peter Hoekstra, R-Mich. – HOOK-struh
John Hostettler, R-Ind. – HO-stet-lur
Kenny Hulshof, R-Mo. – HULLZ-hoff
Bob Inglis, R-S.C. – ING-lis
Darrell Issa, R-Calif. – EYE-sah
Ernest Istook, R-Okla. – IZ-took
Bobby Jindal, R-La. – JIN-dle
Jim Kolbe, R-Ariz. – COLE-bee
Dennis J. Kucinich, D-Ohio – ku-SIN-itch
John R. "Randy" Kuhl Jr., R-N.Y. – COOL
Jim Langevin, D-R.I. – LAN-juh-vin
Steven C. LaTourette, R-Ohio – la-tuh-RETT
Frank A. LoBiondo, R-N.J. – lo-bee-ON-dough
Zoe Lofgren, D-Calif. – ZO
Nita M. Lowey, D-N.Y. – LOW-ee
Donald Manzullo, R-Ill. – man-ZOO-low
Kenny Marchant, R-Texas – MARCH-unt
Charlie Melancon, D-La. – meh-LAW-sawn
Michael H. Michaud, D-Maine – ME-shoo
Jerrold Nadler, D-N.Y. – NAD-ler
Randy Neugebauer, R-Texas – NAW-geh-bow-er
Bob Ney, R-Ohio – NAY
David R. Obey, D-Wis. – OH-bee
Frank Pallone Jr., D-N.J. – puh-LOAN
Bill Pascrell Jr., D-N.J. – pass-KRELL
Ed Pastor, D-Ariz. – pas-TORE
Nancy Pelosi, D-Calif. – pa-LO-see
Tom Petri, R-Wis. – PEA-try
Richard W. Pombo, R-Calif. – POM-bo
George P. Radanovich, R-Calif. – ruh-DON-o-vitch
Nick J. Rahall II, D-W.Va. – RAY-haul
Ralph Regula, R-Ohio – REG-you-luh
Denny Rehberg, R-Mont. – REE-berg
Dave Reichert, R-Wash. – RIKE-ert
Silvestre Reyes, D-Texas – sil-VES-treh RAY-ess (rolled 'R')
Dana Rohrabacher, R-Calif. – ROAR-ah-BAH-ker
Ileana Ros-Lehtinen, R-Fla. – il-ee-AH-na ross-LAY-tin-nen
Jan Schakowsky, D-Ill. – shuh-KOW-ski
Joe Schwarz, R-Mich. – SCHWARTZ
José E. Serrano, D-N.Y. – ho-ZAY sa-RAH-no (rolled 'R')
John Shadegg, R-Ariz. – SHAD-egg
John Shimkus, R-Ill. – SHIM-kus
Mike Sodrel, R-Ind. – SOD-drell
Hilda L. Solis, D-Calif. – soh-LEEZ
Mark Souder, R-Ind. – SOW (rhymes with "now")-dur
Bart Stupak, D-Mich. – STU-pack
Tom Tancredo, R-Colo. – tan-CRAY-doe
Ellen O. Tauscher, D-Calif. – TAU (rhymes with "now")-sher
Todd Tiahrt, R-Kan. – TEE-hart
Pat Tiberi, R-Ohio – TEA-berry
Nydia M. Velázquez, D-N.Y. – NID-ee-uh veh-LASS-kez
Peter J. Visclosky, D-Ind. – vis-KLOSS-key
Anthony Weiner, D-N.Y. – WEE-ner
Lynn Woolsey, D-Calif. – WOOL-zee

www.cqpress.com